Top 40 Music
on Compact Disc
1955-1997

Pat Downey

pat downey
enterprises
pd

ISBN 0-9633718-6-X

Printed in the United States of America and published independently by Pat Downey Enterprises, 5692 Aurora Place, Boulder, CO 80303.

Contents

Introduction

When I published the first edition of TOP 40 MUSIC ON COMPACT DISC back in 1992, there were a significant number of Top 40 hits which were not available on compact disc. Today there are relatively few Top 40 hits which you cannot find on compact disc but just as in 1992, the quality of the transfer from analog tape (or vinyl for that matter) to the digital medium remains a major concern. For instance, in this edition you will notice a first time appearance on compact disc of the hit song "Alley Oop" by Dante & The Evergreens but, as you will see noted in this book, the song was mastered from a fairly scratchy vinyl record. Since there are about 1,200 new compact discs released each year that include Top 40 hits, I realize that you need to be aware not only of these individual titles but the quality of these new compact discs as well. All of this information is included, so now I just need to explain to you how to navigate through the rest of the book.

The first section of this book, "Top 40 Music By Artist," is an alphabetical listing of all artists who scored a concensus Top 40 hit single on national trade publications' charts. Listed below each artist you will find a chronological listing of each song that artist placed in the national Top 40. The Year of peak popularity (not the year the song was released) is included for each Top 40 song title, followed by the label, catalog number and title of each CD that includes that song. This information is then followed by any pertinent comments peculiar to that CD appearance.

If you recognize a song by its title and not the artist, then the second section, the "Song Title Index" will refer you to all the artists that charted in the national Top 40 with a specific song. The "Song Title Index" also offers a flag to indicate which songs have actually been released on CD (rerecordings and live versions excluded).

In preparing this book I have elected not to include the following genres of compact discs:

1. Import compact discs

2. Compact discs that contain obviously "live" versions of original studio recordings, such as "The Beatles At The Hollywood Bowl"

3. Compact discs that are not readily available for retail stores to order, such as "special products" divisions of certain major record labels

4. Special promotional samplers that were never available for retail sale

5. CD singles

The decision as to which domestic compact discs to include in this book was made entirely at the author's discretion. Due to the burgeoning popularity of used compact disc stores, I am continuing to list compact discs that have long been out of print as well as the currently available titles. Your local CD store or reputable mail order dealer, such as "Discollector" (303-841-3000), should be able to advise you if a compact disc listed is currently in print or whether you should look to a used compact disc store to find titles that are out of print.

Compact discs available by mail order from "Time-Life" and "Collectors' Choice Music" are also included in this edition. To order "Time-Life" cd's, call (800-621-7026); to order "Collectors' Choice" cd's call (800-923-1122).

Every reasonable effort has been made to assure accuracy of the data included in this book, but due to the size of the publication, some errors will unfortunately occur. Please pass along any comments or corrections to Pat Downey Enterprises, 5692 Aurora Place, Boulder, CO 80303 or by e-mail to patdowney@uswest.net.

I also wish to thank Mike Hawkinson and Bill Cahill whose insight and encouragement helped guide me through the completion of this laborious project.

As I have always done, I have included every domestic compact disc that I could get my hands on since the introduction of the compact disc in 1982. This means that a good number of these compact discs are now out of print and if you are to find them, you will have to look in a used compact disc store.

Here is where I need your input: should future editions of this book include cd's from the first 10 years of the compact disc era most of which are now out of print? The inclusion of these older cd's greatly increases the size of this book and will inevitably require a price increase. Your response will help me in the preparation of future editions.

Explanation of Symbols and Terminology

Symbols:

(M)	MONOPHONIC, with no separation in sound from left to right channel.
(S)	STEREOPHONIC, with a separation in sound from left to right channel.
(E)	ELECTRONIC, indicating some form of processing used to make a mono recording sound like it has separation from left to right channel. An example would be taking a mono recording and adding a slight time delay to one channel in an attempt to trick the ear into believing a song is really stereo. Another example of electronic processing would be emphasizing the high frequencies on one channel while emphasizing the low frequencies on the other. Processing of this nature must be done after the session tape has been recorded so that you may be assured of not getting a first generation transfer from analog tape to digital when you see the (E) symbol. Electronic "doctoring" almost always results in a degradation of sound quality.
O.S.T.	ORIGINAL SOUND TRACK.
cd	COMPACT DISC.
LP	LONG PLAY, which is the nomenclature originally used for the record album.
45	45 RPM 7" RECORD, also known as a "single."
(X:XX)	TIME in minutes and seconds. This is the exact playing time of the song, not necessarily the time printed on the cd jacket, the cd itself, or the cd packaging. Even the time encoded on the cd and displayed on your cd player can be inaccurate if there is some "dead air" placed at the beginning or end of a selection.
dj	DISC JOCKEY.
◆	This symbol is used exclusively in the "Song Title Index" to designate that a title is available on compact disc.

Terminology:

alternate take	Not the version used for the original hit recording but another very similar sounding take probably recorded at the same recording session as the hit version.
cold	No fadeout.
countoff	Brief counting of numbers such as "one, two, three" that musicians use to synchronize all members of the recording session to the start of a song.
dropout	A temporary loss of signal.
fadeout	Slow drop in volume to the inaudible level at the end of a song.
intro	Introduction
label	Company issuing the cd or vinyl record; also the printed paper identifier on a vinyl record.

length (45 or LP)	An indication that the time differs from the 45 to the LP format and that the difference in time is not due to new lyrics or instrumentation but simply an extension of the song before it fades out.
medley	Two or more songs strung together.
noncharting	Never entered the best seller charts.
number	Catalog identifier for ordering the cd or vinyl record.
outro	The final few audible seconds of a song.
overdub	A vocal, instrumental, or sound effect addition to what was on the original recording session tape. This is always done as an afterthought to try and strengthen the sound of a song. Because these overdubs are added on, they do not exist on the session master tape and are often overlooked when master tapes are resurrected for release on compact disc.
remixed	Either the instrumentation or vocals have been tampered with resulting in a sound that differs slightly from the original version.
rerecording	Not the original hit recording but a version recorded at a completely different recording session, usually a long period of time after the hit recording session.
segue/track	To continue without break into the next selection.
truncated fade	An abrupt end to a song that is in the process of fading out.
version (45 or LP)	An indication that the song in question had more than one form. This term is used to denote a difference in lyrics, vocal take, instrumentation, sound effects, or editing involving more than the length of fade at the end of a song.

Key to Top 40 Listings

For descriptions of the symbols and terminology, see pages ix-x.

Artist name   *Song title*   *Label & Number*   *CD title*   *Comments on the recording*

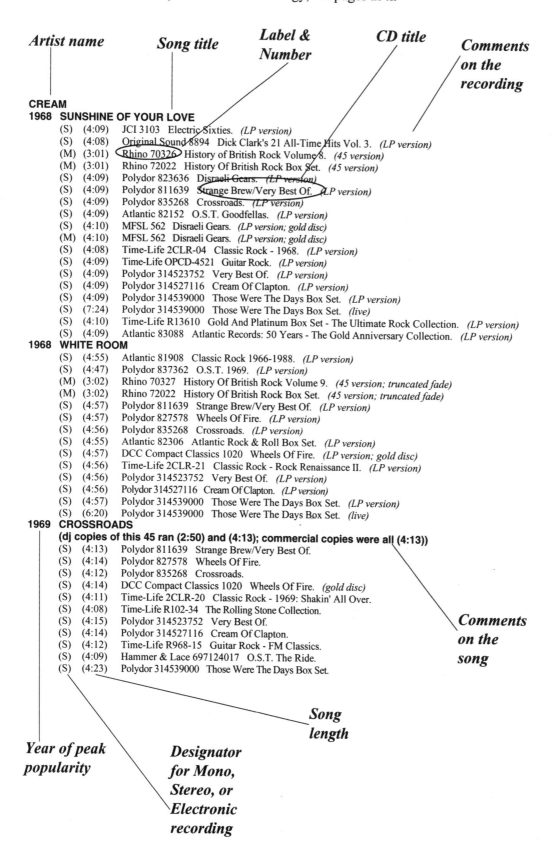

CREAM
1968 SUNSHINE OF YOUR LOVE
    (S) (4:09)   JCI 3103 Electric Sixties. *(LP version)*
    (S) (4:08)   Original Sound 8894 Dick Clark's 21 All-Time Hits Vol. 3. *(LP version)*
    (M) (3:01)   Rhino 70326 History of British Rock Volume 8. *(45 version)*
    (M) (3:01)   Rhino 72022 History Of British Rock Box Set. *(45 version)*
    (S) (4:09)   Polydor 823636 Disraeli Gears. *(LP version)*
    (S) (4:09)   Polydor 811639 Strange Brew/Very Best Of. *(LP version)*
    (S) (4:09)   Polydor 835268 Crossroads. *(LP version)*
    (S) (4:09)   Atlantic 82152 O.S.T. Goodfellas. *(LP version)*
    (S) (4:10)   MFSL 562 Disraeli Gears. *(LP version; gold disc)*
    (M) (4:10)   MFSL 562 Disraeli Gears. *(LP version; gold disc)*
    (S) (4:08)   Time-Life 2CLR-04 Classic Rock - 1968. *(LP version)*
    (S) (4:09)   Time-Life OPCD-4521 Guitar Rock. *(LP version)*
    (S) (4:09)   Polydor 314523752 Very Best Of. *(LP version)*
    (S) (4:09)   Polydor 314527116 Cream Of Clapton. *(LP version)*
    (S) (4:09)   Polydor 314539000 Those Were The Days Box Set. *(LP version)*
    (S) (7:24)   Polydor 314539000 Those Were The Days Box Set. *(live)*
    (S) (4:10)   Time-Life R13610 Gold And Platinum Box Set - The Ultimate Rock Collection. *(LP version)*
    (S) (4:09)   Atlantic 83088 Atlantic Records: 50 Years - The Gold Anniversary Collection. *(LP version)*
1968 WHITE ROOM
    (S) (4:55)   Atlantic 81908 Classic Rock 1966-1988. *(LP version)*
    (S) (4:47)   Polydor 837362 O.S.T. 1969. *(LP version)*
    (M) (3:02)   Rhino 70327 History Of British Rock Volume 9. *(45 version; truncated fade)*
    (M) (3:02)   Rhino 72022 History Of British Rock Box Set. *(45 version; truncated fade)*
    (S) (4:57)   Polydor 811639 Strange Brew/Very Best Of. *(LP version)*
    (S) (4:57)   Polydor 827578 Wheels Of Fire. *(LP version)*
    (S) (4:56)   Polydor 835268 Crossroads. *(LP version)*
    (S) (4:55)   Atlantic 82306 Atlantic Rock & Roll Box Set. *(LP version)*
    (S) (4:57)   DCC Compact Classics 1020 Wheels Of Fire. *(LP version; gold disc)*
    (S) (4:56)   Time-Life 2CLR-21 Classic Rock - Rock Renaissance II. *(LP version)*
    (S) (4:56)   Polydor 314523752 Very Best Of. *(LP version)*
    (S) (4:56)   Polydor 314527116 Cream Of Clapton. *(LP version)*
    (S) (4:57)   Polydor 314539000 Those Were The Days Box Set. *(LP version)*
    (S) (6:20)   Polydor 314539000 Those Were The Days Box Set. *(live)*
1969 CROSSROADS
    (dj copies of this 45 ran (2:50) and (4:13); commercial copies were all (4:13))
    (S) (4:13)   Polydor 811639 Strange Brew/Very Best Of.
    (S) (4:14)   Polydor 827578 Wheels Of Fire.
    (S) (4:12)   Polydor 835268 Crossroads.
    (S) (4:14)   DCC Compact Classics 1020 Wheels Of Fire. *(gold disc)*
    (S) (4:11)   Time-Life 2CLR-20 Classic Rock - 1969: Shakin' All Over.
    (S) (4:08)   Time-Life R102-34 The Rolling Stone Collection.
    (S) (4:15)   Polydor 314523752 Very Best Of.
    (S) (4:14)   Polydor 314527116 Cream Of Clapton.
    (S) (4:12)   Time-Life R968-15 Guitar Rock - FM Classics.
    (S) (4:09)   Hammer & Lace 697124017 O.S.T. The Ride.
    (S) (4:23)   Polydor 314539000 Those Were The Days Box Set.

Comments on the song

Song length

Year of peak popularity

Designator for Mono, Stereo, or Electronic recording

AALIYAH
1994 BACK & FORTH
    (S)   (3:49)   Jive 41533 Age Ain't Nothing But A Number.
    (S)   (3:48)   Rhino 72159 Black Entertainment Television -
                          15th Anniversary.
    (S)   (3:49)   K-Tel 3850 90s Now Volume 3.
1994 AT YOUR BEST (YOU ARE LOVE)
    (S)   (4:50)   Jive 41533 Age Ain't Nothing But A Number.
    (S)   (4:49)   EMI-Capitol Music Group 54548 Smooth Luv.
    (S)   (4:49)   Beast 53012 Smooth Love Of The 90's Vol. 1.
1996 IF YOUR GIRL ONLY KNEW
    (S)   (4:50)   Blackground/Atlantic 92715 One In A Million.
    (S)   (4:44)   Tommy Boy 1234 MTV Party To Go '98. *(all
                          songs on this cd are segued together)*
1997 THE ONE I GAVE MY HEART TO
    (S)   (4:29)   Blackground/Atlantic 92715 One In A Million.

ABBA
1974 WATERLOO
    (S)   (2:40)   Atlantic 19114 Greatest Hits.
    (S)   (2:41)   Polydor 314517007 Greatest Hits.
    (S)   (2:41)   Polydor 314523472 Thank You For The Music.
    (S)   (2:42)   Polydor 422843643 Waterloo.
    (S)   (2:41)   Polydor 314527493 O.S.T. Muriel's Wedding.
1974 HONEY, HONEY
    (S)   (2:53)   Atlantic 19114 Greatest Hits. *(truncated fade)*
    (S)   (2:54)   Polydor 314523472 Thank You For The Music.
    (S)   (2:53)   Polydor 422843643 Waterloo.
    (S)   (2:54)   Polydor 314519353 More Abba Gold.
1975 SOS
    (S)   (3:19)   Atlantic 19114 Greatest Hits.
    (S)   (3:20)   Polydor 314517007 Greatest Hits.
    (S)   (3:19)   Time-Life SOD-16 Sounds Of The Seventies -
                          1975: Take Two.
    (S)   (3:20)   Polydor 314523472 Thank You For The Music.
    (S)   (3:20)   Polydor 422835832 Abba.
1976 I DO, I DO, I DO, I DO, I DO
    (S)   (3:14)   Atlantic 19114 Greatest Hits.
    (S)   (3:15)   Polydor 314523472 Thank You For The Music.
    (S)   (3:14)   Polydor 422835832 Abba.
    (S)   (3:15)   Polydor 314527493 O.S.T. Muriel's Wedding.
    (S)   (3:14)   Polydor 314519353 More Abba Gold.
1976 MAMMA MIA
    (S)   (3:29)   Atlantic 19114 Greatest Hits.
    (S)   (3:31)   Polydor 314517007 Greatest Hits.
    (S)   (3:31)   Polydor 314523472 Thank You For The Music.
    (S)   (3:31)   Mother 314516937 O.S.T. The Adventures Of
                          Priscilla - Queen Of The Desert.
    (S)   (3:31)   Polydor 422835832 Abba.
1976 FERNANDO
    (S)   (4:09)   Atlantic 19114 Greatest Hits.
    (S)   (4:11)   Polydor 314517007 Greatest Hits.
    (S)   (4:10)   Polydor 314523472 Thank You For The Music.
    (S)   (4:11)   Rebound 314520372 The Roots Of Rock: Soft Rock.
    (S)   (4:10)   Polygram TV 314555610 The One And Only
                          Love Album.
1977 DANCING QUEEN
    (S)   (3:49)   Atlantic 16009 Greatest Hits Volume 2.
    (S)   (3:49)   Polydor 314517007 Greatest Hits.
    (S)   (3:48)   Polydor 314523472 Thank You For The Music.
    (S)   (3:50)   Polydor 422821319 Arrival.
    (S)   (3:48)   Polydor 314527493 O.S.T. Muriel's Wedding.
    (S)   (3:46)   Polydor 314535877 Pure Disco.
1977 KNOWING ME, KNOWING YOU
    (S)   (4:01)   Atlantic 16009 Greatest Hits Volume 2.
    (S)   (3:59)   Polydor 314517007 Greatest Hits.

    (S)   (4:00)   Polydor 314523472 Thank You For The Music.
    (S)   (4:00)   Polydor 422821319 Arrival.
1978 THE NAME OF THE GAME
    (dj copies of this 45 ran (3:52); commercial copies
    were all (4:53))
    (S)   (4:50)   Atlantic 16009 Greatest Hits Volume 2.
    (S)   (3:57)   Polydor 314517007 Greatest Hits.
    (S)   (3:57)   Polydor 314523472 Thank You For The Music.
    (S)   (4:51)   Polydor 422821217 The Album.
1978 TAKE A CHANCE ON ME
    (dj copies of this 45 ran (3:30); commercial copies
    were all (4:05))
    (S)   (3:57)   Rhino 70673 Billboard Top Hits - 1978.
    (S)   (3:58)   Atlantic 16009 Greatest Hits Volume 2.
    (S)   (4:02)   Polydor 314517007 Greatest Hits.
    (S)   (4:03)   Polydor 314523472 Thank You For The Music.
    (S)   (4:01)   Polydor 422821217 The Album.
1979 DOES YOUR MOTHER KNOW
    (S)   (3:12)   Atlantic 16009 Greatest Hits Volume 2.
    (S)   (3:13)   Polydor 314517007 Greatest Hits.
    (S)   (3:13)   Polydor 314523472 Thank You For The Music.
    (S)   (3:13)   Polydor 422821320 Voulez-Vous.
1980 CHIQUITITA
    (dj copies of this 45 ran (5:26) and (4:38);
    commercial copies were all (5:26))
    (S)   (5:22)   Atlantic 16009 Greatest Hits Volume 2.
    (S)   (5:25)   Polydor 314517007 Greatest Hits.
    (S)   (5:24)   Polydor 314523472 Thank You For The Music.
    (S)   (5:23)   Polydor 422821320 Voulez-Vous.
1981 THE WINNER TAKES IT ALL
    (dj copies of this 45 ran (4:20); commercial copies
    were all (4:56))
    (S)   (4:52)   Polydor 314517007 Greatest Hits.
    (S)   (4:53)   Polydor 314523472 Thank You For The Music.
    (S)   (4:54)   Polydor 422800023 Super Trouper.
1982 WHEN ALL IS SAID AND DONE
    (S)   (3:14)   Polydor 314523472 Thank You For The Music.
    (S)   (3:17)   Polydor 422800011 The Visitors.
    (S)   (3:13)   Polydor 314519353 More Abba Gold.

GREGORY ABBOTT
1987 SHAKE YOU DOWN
    (S)   (4:02)   Columbia 44382 Heart Of Soul.
    (S)   (4:04)   Sony Music Distribution 57854 For Your Love.
    (S)   (4:04)   Thump 4710 Old School Love Songs.
    (S)   (3:42)   Original Sound 9308 Dedicated To You Vol. 8.
                          (faded :22 sooner than the 45 or LP)
    (S)   (4:04)   Columbia 40437 Shake You Down.
    (S)   (4:04)   Priority 53700 80's Greatest Rock Hits Volume 13 -
                          Soft Sounds.
    (S)   (3:28)   Time-Life R138-18 Body Talk. *(faded :36
                          sooner than the 45 or LP)*
    (S)   (4:03)   Scotti Bros. 75481 Quiet Storm Memories.
    (S)   (4:04)   Rhino 72141 Billboard Hot R&B Hits 1986.
    (S)   (3:22)   JCI 3177 1985 - Only Soul - 1989. *(faded :42
                          sooner than the 45 or LP)*
    (S)   (4:04)   Hip-O 40031 The Glory Of Love - '80s Sweet &
                          Soulful Love Songs.
    (S)   (4:03)   Time-Life R988-20 Sounds Of The Eighties: The
                          Late '80s Take Two.
    (S)   (4:04)   Time-Life R834-01 Body Talk - Forever Yours.

ABC
1983 THE LOOK OF LOVE (PART 1)
    (S)   (3:28)   Priority 53705 Rock Of The 80's Volume 2.
    (S)   (3:29)   Rhino 71699 New Wave Hits Of The 80's Vol. 6.

ABC *(Continued)*

- (S) (3:28) Sandstone 33046 and 5012 Rock The First Volume Six.
- (S) (3:28) Mercury 810003 Lexicon Of Love.
- (S) (3:28) Mercury 842967 Absolutely.
- (S) (3:29) Time-Life R988-26 Sounds Of The Eighties: The Rolling Stone Collection 1982-1983.
- (S) (4:35) Rebound 314520354 World Of Dance: New Wave - The 80's. *(remix)*
- (S) (3:28) JCI 3159 18 Modern Rock Classics From The 80's.
- (S) (3:28) Rebound 314520438 No. 1 Hits Of The 80's.
- (S) (4:35) Rebound 314520442 The Roots Of Rock: 80's New Wave. *(remix)*
- (S) (3:29) Rhino 72894 Hard Rock Cafe: New Wave.
- (S) (3:26) Arista 18985 Ultimate New Wave Party 1998. *(all selections on this cd are segued together)*

1983 POISON ARROW

- (S) (3:22) EMI 27674 Living In Oblivion: The 80's Greatest Hits Volume Three.
- (S) (3:24) Rhino 71702 New Wave Hits Of The 80's Vol. 9.
- (S) (3:21) Right Stuff 27754 Sedated In The Eighties.
- (S) (3:21) Mercury 810003 Lexicon Of Love.
- (S) (3:22) Mercury 842967 Absolutely.
- (S) (3:24) Risky Business 66396 Oldies But 80's: Best Of The 80's.
- (S) (3:22) Rebound 314520493 Class Reunion '83.
- (S) (3:22) Polygram Special Markets 314520457 #1 Radio Hits Of The 80's.

1985 BE NEAR ME

- (S) (3:36) Rebound 314520324 Alterno-Daze: Survival Of 80's The Fittest.
- (S) (3:37) Mercury 824904 How To Be A Zillionaire.
- (S) (3:37) Mercury 842967 Absolutely.
- (S) (4:46) Cold Front 6284 More Of! Club Mix's Biggest Jams. *(all selections on this cd are segued together; remix)*
- (S) (3:36) Time-Life R988-23 Sounds Of The Eighties 1984-1985.

1986 (HOW TO BE A) MILLIONAIRE

- (S) (3:34) Mercury 824904 How To Be A Zillionaire.
- (S) (3:34) Mercury 842967 Absolutely.

1987 WHEN SMOKEY SINGS

- (S) (4:21) Priority 53732 80's Greatest Rock Hits Volume 8 - Dance Party.
- (S) (4:21) JCI 3128 1985 - Only Rock 'N Roll - 1989.
- (S) (4:18) Mercury 832391 Alphabet City.
- (S) (7:03) Mercury 832391 Alphabet City. *(remixed)*
- (S) (4:21) Mercury 842967 Absolutely.
- (S) (4:21) Time-Life R988-19 Sounds Of The Eighties: The Late '80s.
- (S) (4:07) Cold Front 6330 Club Mix: The 80s. *(all selections on this cd are segued together)*

PAULA ABDUL

1989 STRAIGHT UP
(dj copies of this 45 ran (3:50); commercial copies were (4:11) and (4:57))

- (S) (4:08) JCI 2702 Hot Moves.
- (S) (4:09) Virgin 90943 and 86067 Forever Your Girl.
- (S) (6:54) Virgin 91362 and 86163 Shut Up And Dance (The Dance Mixes). *(remixed)*
- (S) (4:09) Rhino 72838 Disco Queens: The 80's.
- (S) (4:09) K-Tel 3868 Hot Ladies Of Pop.
- (S) (4:10) Hip-O 40080 Essential '80s: 1985-1989.

1989 FOREVER YOUR GIRL

- (S) (4:56) K-Tel 842 Hot Ladies Of The 80's. *(LP version)*
- (S) (4:56) Virgin 90943 and 86067 Forever Your Girl. *(LP version)*
- (S) (6:06) Virgin 91362 and 86163 Shut Up And Dance (The Dance Mixes). *(remixed)*

1989 COLDHEARTED
(this song originally appeared as the flip side of "STRAIGHT UP" and at that time was issued as a straight reissue of the LP version; when released as the "A" side several months later, it was released in a different 45 version)

- (S) (3:50) Virgin 90943 and 86067 Forever Your Girl. *(LP version)*

- (S) (5:12) Virgin 91362 and 86163 Shut Up And Dance (The Dance Mixes). *(remixed)*
- (S) (3:50) Priority 53731 80's Greatest Rock Hits Volume 10 - Dance All Night. *(LP version)*

1989 (IT'S JUST) THE WAY THAT YOU LOVE ME

- (S) (5:20) Virgin 90943 and 86067 Forever Your Girl. *(LP version)*
- (S) (4:42) Virgin 91362 and 86163 Shut Up And Dance (The Dance Mixes). *(remixed)*

1990 OPPOSITES ATTRACT

- (S) (6:47) Foundation/Capitol 96427 Hearts Of Gold: The Pop Collection. *(remixed)*
- (S) (4:23) Sandstone 33043 and 5009 Rock The First Volume Three. *(LP version)*
- (S) (4:23) Virgin 90943 and 86067 Forever Your Girl. *(LP version)*
- (S) (6:47) Virgin 91362 and 86163 Shut Up And Dance (The Dance Mixes). *(remixed)*
- (S) (4:15) Priority 50946 100% Party Hits Of The 90's Volume One. *(LP version faded :08 early)*
- (S) (4:22) Time-Life R988-21 Sounds Of The Eighties: 1986-1989. *(LP version)*

1991 RUSH RUSH

- (S) (4:52) Virgin 91611 and 86210 Spellbound.
- (S) (4:52) K-Tel 3850 90s Now Volume 3.

1991 THE PROMISE OF A NEW DAY

- (S) (4:31) Virgin 91611 and 86210 Spellbound. *(LP version)*

1991 BLOWING KISSES IN THE WIND

- (S) (4:41) Virgin 91611 and 86210 Spellbound.
- (S) (4:41) Cold Front 3865 Club Mix - Women Of Dance Vol. 2.

1992 VIBEOLOGY

- (S) (5:14) Virgin 91611 and 86210 Spellbound. *(LP version)*
- (S) (7:04) Rhino 75234 Rupaul's Go-Go Box Classics. *(remix)*

1992 WILL YOU MARRY ME?

- (S) (4:23) Virgin 91611 and 86210 Spellbound.

1995 MY LOVE IS FOR REAL

- (S) (5:19) Virgin 40525 Head Over Heels.

AC/DC

1980 YOU SHOOK ME ALL NIGHT LONG

- (S) (3:29) Atco 92418 Back In Black. *(remastered edition)*
- (S) (3:29) Atlantic 16018 Back In Black.
- (S) (3:29) Atlantic 81650 Who Made Who.
- (S) (3:52) Warner Brothers 46477 Howard Stern Private Parts: The Album. *(live)*
- (S) (3:30) EastWest 62119 Bonfire.

1981 BACK IN BLACK
(dj copies of this 45 ran (3:53) and (4:17); commercial copies were all (4:17))

- (S) (4:14) Atlantic 81908 Classic Rock 1966-1988.
- (S) (4:14) Atlantic 82306 Atlantic Rock & Roll Box Set.
- (S) (4:14) Atlantic 16018 Back In Black.
- (S) (4:15) Atco 92418 Back In Black. *(remastered edition)*
- (S) (4:15) EastWest 62119 Bonfire.

1991 MONEY TALKS

- (S) (3:44) Atco 91413 Razor's Edge.

ACE

1975 HOW LONG

- (S) (3:17) Priority 8667 FM Hits/70's Greatest Rock Hits Volume 6. *(LP version)*
- (S) (3:21) Rhino 70761 Super Hits Of The 70's Volume 14. *(LP version)*
- (S) (3:19) Razor & Tie 22047 Sweet 70's Soul. *(LP version)*
- (S) (3:21) Time-Life SOD-08 Sounds Of The Seventies - 1975. *(LP version)*
- (S) (3:21) Chrysalis 41663 The Carrack Collection. *(LP version)*
- (S) (3:21) Chrysalis 27221 Twenty-One Good Reasons/The Paul Carrack Collection. *(LP version)*
- (S) (3:20) Madacy Entertainment 1975 Rock On 1975. *(LP version)*
- (S) (3:20) Hip-O 40096 '70s Hit(s) Back Again. *(LP version)*

JOHNNY ACE
1955 PLEDGING MY LOVE
(M) (2:29) Rhino 70641 Billboard's Top R&B Hits Of 1955.
(major dropout at 1:25)
(M) (2:25) Original Sound 8860 Oldies But Goodies Vol. 10.
(this compact disc uses the "Waring - fds" noise reduction process)
(M) (2:25) Original Sound 2221 Oldies But Goodies Volumes 1,4,6,8 and 10 Box Set. *(this box set uses the "Waring - fds" noise reduction process)*
(M) (2:25) Original Sound 2500 Oldies But Goodies Volumes 1-15 Box Set. *(this box set uses the "Waring - fds" noise reduction process)*
(M) (2:25) Original Sound CDGO-1 Golden Oldies Volume. 1.
(M) (2:25) Original Sound 9602 Best Of Oldies But Goodies Vol. 2.
(M) (2:25) Original Sound 9307 Dedicated To You Vol. 7.
(M) (2:28) MCA 31200 Vintage Music Volume 3. *(major dropout at 1:24)*
(M) (2:28) MCA 5778 Vintage Music Volumes 3 & 4. *(major dropout at 1:24)*
(M) (2:26) Sire 26617 Music From The Film A Rage In Harlem. *(major dropout at 1:23)*
(M) (2:27) MCA 31183 Johnny Ace Memorial Album. *(major dropout at 1:24)*
(M) (2:27) MCA 10666 Duke-Peacock's Greatest Hits. *(major dropout at 1:24)*
(M) (2:27) Time-Life 2RNR-08 Rock 'N' Roll Era - 1954-1955. *(major dropout at 1:24)*
(M) (2:27) Time-Life RHD-17 Rhythm & Blues - 1955. *(major dropout at 1:24)*
(M) (2:28) MCA Special Products 20751 Rock Around The Oldies #2. *(major dropout at 1:24)*
(M) (2:26) Rhino 71806 The R&B Box: Thirty Years Of Rhythm & Blues. *(major dropout at 1:23)*
(M) (2:26) Hip-O 40028 The Glory Of Love - '50s Sweet & Soulful Love Songs. *(major dropout at 1:24)*
(M) (2:26) Rhino 72580 Soul Serenade - Intimate R&B. *(major dropout at 1:24)*
(M) (2:27) Time-Life R857-15 The Heart Of Rock 'n' Roll 1953-1955. *(major dropout at 1:24)*
(M) (2:25) Collectables 1514 and 2514 The Anniversary Album - The 50's.

ACE OF BASE
1993 ALL THAT SHE WANTS
(S) (4:15) Tommy Boy 1109 MTV Party To Go Volume 6. *(remix; all tracks on this cd are segued together)*
(S) (3:31) Arista 18740 The Sign.
1994 THE SIGN
(S) (3:08) Arista 18740 The Sign.
(S) (3:08) EMI-Capitol Music Group 54547 Hot Luv.
1994 DON'T TURN AROUND
(S) (3:48) Arista 18740 The Sign.
1994 LIVING IN DANGER
(S) (3:41) Arista 18740 The Sign.
1995 BEAUTIFUL LIFE
(S) (3:38) Arista 18806 The Bridge.
(S) (5:25) Tommy Boy 1164 MTV Party To Go Volume 9. *(remix; all selections on this cd are segued together)*
(S) (3:34) Arista 18943 Ultimate Dance Party 1997. *(all selections on this cd are segued together)*
1996 LUCKY LOVE
(S) (2:51) Arista 18806 The Bridge.

BARBARA ACKLIN
1968 LOVE MAKES A WOMAN
(S) (2:56) Rhino 75770 Soul Shots Volume 2.
(S) (2:55) Time-Life RHD-04 Rhythm & Blues - 1968.
(S) (2:55) Time-Life 2CLR-28 Classic Rock - On The Soul Side II.
(S) (2:54) Brunswick 81003 Greatest Hits.
(S) (2:54) K-Tel 3518 Sweet Soul Music.
(S) (2:54) Brunswick 81009 The Brunswick Years Volume One.

(S) (2:55) MCA Special Products 20941 R&B Crossover Oldies Vol. 1.
(S) (2:54) Rebound 314520369 Soul Classics - Quiet Storm/The 60's.
(S) (2:55) Time-Life R838-03 Solid Gold Soul - 1968.
(M) (2:54) Rhino 72815 Beg, Scream & Shout! The Big Ol' Box Of '60s Soul.

released as by GENE CHANDLER and BARBARA ACKLIN:
1968 FROM THE TEACHER TO THE PREACHER
(M) (2:24) Brunswick 81003 Barbara Acklin - Greatest Hits.
(M) (2:21) MCA Special Products 20869 Gene Chandler - Soul Master.
(M) (2:24) Brunswick 81009 The Brunswick Years Volume One.
(M) (2:24) Brunswick 81017 Gene Chandler - The Soul Of.

BRYAN ADAMS
1983 STRAIGHT FROM THE HEART
(S) (3:30) A&M 3288 Cuts Like A Knife.
(S) (3:29) A&M 314540157 So Far So Good.
1983 CUTS LIKE A KNIFE
(dj copies of this 45 ran (3:59); commercial copies were all (5:16))
(S) (5:16) A&M 3288 Cuts Like A Knife.
(S) (5:12) A&M 314540157 So Far So Good.
1983 THIS TIME
(S) (3:18) A&M 3288 Cuts Like A Knife.
(S) (3:18) A&M 314540157 So Far So Good.
1985 RUN TO YOU
(S) (3:49) T.J. Martell Foundation/Columbia 40315 Music For The Miracle.
(S) (3:53) A&M 5013 Reckless.
(S) (3:53) MFSL 544 Reckless. *(gold disc)*
(S) (3:53) A&M 314540157 So Far So Good.
1985 SOMEBODY
(S) (4:41) Geffen 24236 Greenpeace - Rainbow Warriors.
(S) (4:42) A&M 5013 Reckless.
(S) (4:42) MFSL 544 Reckless. *(gold disc)*
(S) (4:42) A&M 314540157 So Far So Good.
1985 HEAVEN
(S) (4:03) A&M 5013 Reckless.
(S) (4:03) MFSL 544 Reckless. *(gold disc)*
(S) (4:03) A&M 314540157 So Far So Good.
1985 SUMMER OF '69
(S) (3:34) Polydor 314515913 Classic Rock Box.
(S) (3:36) A&M 5013 Reckless.
(S) (3:36) MFSL 544 Reckless. *(gold disc)*
(S) (3:33) A&M 314540157 So Far So Good.
(S) (3:33) Time-Life R13610 Gold And Platinum Box Set - The Ultimate Rock Collection.
1985 ONE NIGHT LOVE AFFAIR
(S) (4:32) A&M 5013 Reckless.
(S) (4:32) MFSL 544 Reckless. *(gold disc)*
released as by BRYAN ADAMS/TINA TURNER:
1986 IT'S ONLY LOVE
(S) (3:15) Capitol 29724 Tina Turner - Collected Recordings Sixties To Nineties.
(S) (3:14) A&M 5013 Bryan Adams - Reckless.
(S) (3:14) MFSL 544 Bryan Adams - Reckless. *(gold disc)*
(S) (3:14) A&M 314540157 Bryan Adams - So Far So Good.
released as by BRYAN ADAMS:
1987 HEAT OF THE NIGHT
(S) (5:06) A&M 3313 Into The Fire.
(S) (5:05) A&M 314540157 So Far So Good.
1987 HEARTS ON FIRE
(S) (3:29) A&M 3313 Into The Fire.
1987 VICTIM OF LOVE
(S) (4:06) A&M 3313 Into The Fire.
1991 (EVERYTHING I DO) I DO IT FOR YOU
(S) (6:36) Morgan Creek 20004 O.S.T. Robin Hood Prince Of Thieves. *(LP version)*
(S) (6:33) A&M 314540157 So Far So Good. *(LP version)*
1991 CAN'T STOP THIS THING WE STARTED
(S) (4:29) A&M 5367 Waking Up The Neighbours. *(LP version)*
(S) (4:27) A&M 314540157 So Far So Good. *(LP version)*

3

BRYAN ADAMS (Continued)
1992 THERE WILL NEVER BE ANOTHER TONIGHT
  (S) (4:39) A&M 5367 Waking Up The Neighbours.
1992 THOUGHT I'D DIED AND GONE TO HEAVEN
  (S) (5:48) A&M 5367 Waking Up The Neighbours.
1992 DO I HAVE TO SAY THE WORDS
  (S) (6:11) A&M 5367 Waking Up The Neighbours. *(LP version)*
  (S) (6:10) A&M 314540157 So Far So Good. *(LP version)*
1993 PLEASE FORGIVE ME
  (S) (5:54) A&M 314540157 So Far So Good.
released as by BRYAN ADAMS/ROD STEWART/STING:
1994 ALL FOR LOVE
  (S) (4:43) Hollywood 61581 O.S.T. The Three Musketeers.
  (S) (4:40) Warner Brothers 46452 Rod Stewart - If We Fall In Love Tonight.
released as by BRYAN ADAMS:
1995 HAVE YOU EVER REALLY LOVED A WOMAN?
  (S) (4:50) A&M 314540357 O.S.T. Don Juan DeMarco.
  (S) (4:50) A&M 314540551 18 Til I Die.
1996 LET'S MAKE A NIGHT TO REMEMBER
  (S) (6:18) A&M 314540551 18 Til I Die.
released as by BARBRA STREISAND and BRYAN ADAMS:
1997 I FINALLY FOUND SOMEONE
  (S) (3:41) Columbia 67887 O.S.T. The Mirror Has Two Faces.

JOHNNY ADAMS
1969 RECONSIDER ME
  (S) (3:47) Time-Life RHD-13 Rhythm & Blues - 1969.
  (S) (3:44) Time-Life 2CLR-25 Classic Rock - On The Soul Side.
  (S) (3:47) Time-Life R838-04 Solid Gold Soul - 1969.
  (S) (3:55) Repeat/Relativity 1610 Tighten Up: #1 Soul Hits Of The 60's Volume 2.
  (S) (3:56) Collectables 5741 Reconsider Me - A Golden Classics Edition.

OLETA ADAMS
1991 GET HERE
  (dj copies of this 45 ran (3:27); commercial copies were all (4:32))
  (S) (4:33) Mercury 314525354 Women For Women.
  (S) (4:34) Fontana 846346 Circle Of One.
  (S) (4:33) Rebound 314520439 Soul Classics - Best Of The 90's.
  (S) (4:32) Simitar 55562 The Number One's: Smooth Love.
  (S) (4:34) Polygram TV 314555610 The One And Only Love Album.

CANNONBALL ADDERLEY
1967 MERCY, MERCY, MERCY
  (S) (5:09) Curb 77399 Best Of. *(LP version)*
  (S) (5:07) Capitol 95482 Best Of - The Capitol Years. *(LP version)*
  (S) (5:06) Verve 314521007 Playboy's 40th Anniversary: Four Decades Of Jazz (1953-1993). *(LP version)*
  (S) (3:07) Rhino 71604 Rock Instrumental Classics Vol. 4: Soul. *(45 version)*
  (S) (3:07) Rhino 72035 Rock Instrumental Classics Vols. 1-5 Box Set. *(45 version)*
  (S) (3:05) Time-Life RHD-10 Rhythm & Blues - 1967. *(45 version)*
  (S) (5:10) Capitol 29915 Mercy, Mercy, Mercy. *(LP version)*
  (S) (3:07) Hip-O 40007 Soulful Grooves - R&B Instrumental Classics Volume 1. *(45 version)*
  (S) (3:07) Rhino 72474 Masters Of Jazz, Vol. 7: Jazz Hit Singles. *(45 version)*
  (S) (3:05) Time-Life R838-02 Solid Gold Soul - 1967. *(45 version)*

ADDRISI BROTHERS
1972 WE'VE GOT TO GET IT ON AGAIN
  (S) (2:46) Rhino 70928 Super Hits Of The 70's Volume 8.
  (S) (2:44) Columbia/Legacy 46763 Rock Artifacts Volume 2.

  (S) (2:44) Eclipse Music Group 64892 Rock 'n Roll Relix 1970-1971.
  (S) (2:44) Eclipse Music Group 64897 Rock 'n Roll Relix 1970-1979.
  (S) (2:44) Collectables 5831 We've Got To Get It On Again.
1977 SLOW DANCIN' DON'T TURN ME ON
  (S) (3:10) Essex 7060 The Buddah Box.

AD LIBS
1965 BOY FROM NEW YORK CITY
  (M) (2:59) Rhino 75891 Wonder Women.
  (M) (2:58) Rhino 70988 Best Of The Girl Groups Volume 1.
  (M) (3:03) Original Sound 8856 Oldies But Goodies Vol. 6. *(this compact disc uses the "Waring - fds" noise reduction process)*
  (M) (3:03) Original Sound 2221 Oldies But Goodies Volumes 1,4,6,8 and 10 Box Set. *(this box set uses the "Waring - fds" noise reduction process)*
  (M) (3:03) Original Sound 2500 Oldies But Goodies Volumes 1-15 Box Set. *(this box set uses the "Waring - fds" noise reduction process)*
  (M) (3:02) Original Sound CDGO-14 Golden Oldies Volume. 14.
  (M) (2:58) Garland 011 Footstompin' Oldies.
  (M) (2:58) Era 5025 The Brill Building Sound.
  (S) (3:01) Ripete 0001 Coolin' Out/24 Carolina Classics Volume 1.
  (M) (2:58) Time-Life 2CLR-08 Classic Rock - 1965: The Beat Goes On.
  (M) (2:59) Collectables 2510 WCBS-FM History Of Rock - The Rockin' 60's.
  (M) (2:59) Collectables 4510 History Of Rock/The Rockin' 60s.
  (M) (3:02) Collectables 2501 WCBS-FM History Of Rock - The 60's Part 2.
  (M) (3:02) Collectables 4501 History Of Rock/The 60s Part Two.
  (M) (2:58) Rhino 71935 Billboard Top Pop Hits, 1965.
  (M) (2:59) Columbia 67650 O.S.T. Stonewall.
  (M) (2:58) Columbia 67916 O.S.T. One Fine Day.
  (M) (2:59) Eclipse Music Group 64869 Rock 'n Roll Relix 1964-1965.
  (M) (2:59) Eclipse Music Group 64872 Rock 'n Roll Relix 1960-1969.
  (S) (3:02) Collectables 5742 Ad Libs & Friends.
  (S) (3:03) Collectables 5740 Jelly Beans And Friends.
  (M) (2:59) K-Tel 3888 Great R&B Female Groups Hits Of The 60's.
  (S) (3:06) Taragon 1029 Very Best Of Red Bird/Blue Cat Records.

ADVENTURES OF STEVIE V
1990 DIRTY CASH (MONEY TALKS)
  (S) (7:31) Mercury 848010 Adventures Of Stevie V. *(LP version)*
  (S) (3:46) Mercury 848010 Adventures Of Stevie V. *(remix)*
  (S) (4:00) Priority 53770 Techno Dance Classics Volume 1 - Pump Up The Jam. *(remix)*
  (S) (3:54) Mercury 314532494 100% Pure Dance. *(remix; all songs on this cd are segued together)*
  (S) (3:53) Robbins 75002 Strip Jointz - Hot Songs For Sexy Dancers. *(remix)*

AEROSMITH
1975 SWEET EMOTION
  (S) (4:34) Columbia 33479 and 57362 and 52857 Toys In The Attic. *(LP version)*
  (S) (3:12) Columbia 36865 and 57367 Greatest Hits. *(45 version)*
  (S) (4:34) Columbia 46209 and 67995 Pandora's Box. *(LP version; remixed)*
  (S) (4:34) Columbia 66687 Box Of Fire. *(LP version)*
  (S) (4:34) Columbia/Legacy 64401 Toys In The Attic. *(gold disc; LP version)*

4

1976 DREAM ON
(when this commercial 45 was originally released in
1973, the length was edited to (3:25) and remixed but
it was rereleased in 1976 with the full length time of
(4:26); the 1976 dj copies ran (3:25) and (4:28))
- (S) (4:24)   Columbia 32005 and 57360   Aerosmith.
- (S) (4:25)   Columbia 36865 and 57367   Greatest Hits.
- (S) (4:25)   Columbia 46209 and 67995   Pandora's Box.
- (S) (4:24)   Columbia 66687   Box Of Fire.
- (S) (5:42)   Columbia 57127   O.S.T. Last Action Hero.   *(live)*

1976 LAST CHILD
- (S) (3:25)   Columbia 34165 and 57363   Rocks.   *(tracks into the next selection)*
- (S) (3:26)   Columbia 36865 and 57367   Greatest Hits.
- (S) (3:51)   Columbia 46209 and 67995   Pandora's Box. *(slightly remixed; previously unreleased extended version)*
- (S) (3:25)   Columbia 66687   Box Of Fire.   *(tracks into the next selection)*

1977 WALK THIS WAY
- (S) (3:39)   Columbia 33479 and 57362 and 52857   Toys In The Attic.   *(LP version)*
- (S) (3:29)   Columbia 36865 and 57367   Greatest Hits.   *(45 version)*
- (S) (3:39)   Columbia 46209 and 67995   Pandora's Box.   *(LP version)*
- (S) (3:39)   Columbia 66687   Box Of Fire.   *(LP version)*
- (S) (3:39)   Columbia/Legacy 64401   Toys In The Attic. *(gold disc; LP version)*
- (S) (3:30)   Time-Life R13610   Gold And Platinum Box Set - The Ultimate Rock Collection.   *(45 version)*

1977 DRAW THE LINE
- (S) (3:21)   Columbia 36865 and 57367   Greatest Hits.
- (S) (3:42)   Columbia 46209 and 67995   Pandora's Box. *(previously unreleased version)*
- (S) (3:21)   Columbia 37389 and 57364   Draw The Line. *(very poor stereo separation)*
- (S) (3:21)   Columbia 66687   Box Of Fire.

1978 COME TOGETHER
- (S) (3:43)   Columbia 36865 and 57367   Greatest Hits.
- (S) (3:43)   Columbia 46209 and 67995   Pandora's Box.
- (S) (3:43)   Columbia 66687   Box Of Fire.
- (S) (3:45)   Polydor 314557076   O.S.T. Sgt. Pepper's Lonely Hearts Club Band.

1987 DUDE (LOOKS LIKE A LADY)
- (S) (5:04)   Reprise 45485   O.S.T. Wayne's World 2.   *(live)*
- (S) (4:22)   Geffen 24162   Permanent Vacation.   *(LP version)*
- (S) (4:23)   Geffen 24716   Big Ones.   *(LP version)*

1988 ANGEL
(dj copies of this 45 ran (3:58) and (4:03);
commercial copies were all (3:58))
- (S) (5:06)   Geffen 24162   Permanent Vacation.   *(LP version)*
- (S) (5:06)   Geffen 24716   Big Ones.   *(LP version)*

1988 RAG DOLL
(dj copies of this 45 ran (2:50) and (3:05);
commercial copies were all (4:21))
- (S) (4:22)   Geffen 24162   Permanent Vacation.
- (S) (4:23)   Geffen 24716   Big Ones.

1989 LOVE IN AN ELEVATOR
- (S) (5:38)   Geffen 24254   Pump.   *(LP version with introduction)*
- (S) (5:20)   Geffen 24716   Big Ones.   *(LP version)*

1990 JANIE'S GOT A GUN
- (S) (5:33)   Geffen 24254   Pump.   *(LP version with introduction)*
- (S) (5:29)   Geffen 24716   Big Ones.   *(LP version)*

1990 WHAT IT TAKES
- (S) (6:28)   Geffen 24254   Pump.   *(LP version)*
- (S) (5:10)   Geffen 24716   Big Ones.   *(neither the 45 or LP version)*

1990 THE OTHER SIDE
- (S) (4:56)   Geffen 24254   Pump.   *(LP version with introduction)*
- (S) (4:03)   Geffen 24716   Big Ones.

1993 LIVIN' ON THE EDGE
- (S) (6:06)   Geffen 24455   Get A Grip.
- (S) (6:18)   Geffen 24716   Big Ones.

1993 CRYIN'
- (S) (5:07)   Geffen 24455   Get A Grip.
- (S) (5:07)   Geffen 24716   Big Ones.

1994 AMAZING
- (S) (5:55)   Geffen 24455   Get A Grip.
- (S) (5:55)   Geffen 24716   Big Ones.

1994 CRAZY
- (S) (5:15)   Geffen 24716   Big Ones.
- (S) (5:16)   Geffen 24455   Get A Grip.

1997 FALLING IN LOVE (IS HARD ON THE KNEES)
- (S) (3:24)   Columbia 67547   Nine Lives.

AFTERNOON DELIGHTS
1981 GENERAL HOSPI-TALE

AFTER 7
1990 READY OR NOT
- (S) (4:32)   Virgin 91061 and 86104   After 7.
- (S) (4:32)   Virgin 42756   Very Best Of.
- (S) (4:31)   Rhino 72978   Smooth Grooves - New Jack Ballads Volume 2.

1990 CAN'T STOP
- (S) (4:05)   Virgin 91061 and 86104   After 7.   *(LP version)*
- (S) (4:55)   Virgin 42756   Very Best Of.   *(remix)*

1991 HEAT OF THE MOMENT
- (S) (4:25)   Virgin 91061 and 86104   After 7.
- (S) (4:17)   Virgin 42756   Very Best Of.   *(remix)*

1991 NIGHTS LIKE THIS
- (S) (4:03)   Virgin 91609 and 86208   O.S.T. Five Heartbeats.
- (S) (4:01)   Virgin 42756   Very Best Of.

1995 'TIL YOU DO ME RIGHT
- (S) (4:53)   Virgin 40547   Reflections.

AFTER THE FIRE
1983 DER KOMMISSAR
- (S) (5:44)   Priority 53684   Rock Of The 80's Volume 4.   *(LP version)*
- (S) (5:41)   Risky Business 57468   This Ain't No Disco/New Wave Dance Hits.   *(LP version)*
- (S) (4:05)   Rhino 71977   New Wave Hits Of The 80's Vol. 14. *(45 version)*
- (S) (5:40)   Epic 67534   Club Epic Volume 5.   *(LP version)*
- (S) (4:06)   Hip-O 40023   Smash Alternatives - 14 Classic New Wave Hits.   *(45 version)*
- (S) (4:07)   Time-Life R988-16   Sounds Of The Eighties: The Early '80s.   *(45 version)*
- (S) (4:05)   Rhino 72820   VH1 - More Of The Big 80's.   *(45 version)*

A-HA
1985 TAKE ON ME
- (S) (3:45)   K-Tel 3342   The 80's Pop Explosion.
- (S) (3:46)   Reprise 25300   Hunting High And Low.
- (S) (3:46)   Priority 53773   80's Greatest Rock Hits Volume II - Teen Idols.
- (S) (3:47)   Time-Life R988-02   Sounds Of The Eighties: 1985.
- (S) (3:47)   Madacy Entertainment 1985   Rock On 1985.
- (S) (3:46)   Rhino 72771   The Big 80's.
- (S) (3:47)   JCI 3150   1985 - Only Dance - 1989.
- (S) (3:45)   London 422828944   More Music From O.S.T. Grosse Pointe Blank.

1986 THE SUN ALWAYS SHINES ON TV
- (S) (5:06)   Reprise 25300   Hunting High And Low.   *(LP version)*

AHMAD
1994 BACK IN THE DAY
- (S) (5:17)   Giant 24548   Ahmad.

AIR SUPPLY
1980 LOST IN LOVE
(actual 45 time is (3:53) not (3:44) as stated on
the record label)
- (S) (3:53)   Arista 8216   Lost In Love.
- (S) (3:53)   Arista 8024   Greatest Hits.

AIR SUPPLY (Continued)

- (S) (3:50) Madacy Entertainment 1980 Rock On 1980.
- (S) (3:52) JCI 3170 #1 Radio Hits 1980 - Only Rock 'n Roll - 1984.
- (S) (3:52) Time-Life R988-16 Sounds Of The Eighties: The Early '80s.
- (S) (3:52) Time-Life R834-05 Body Talk - Sealed With A Kiss.
- (S) (3:52) Milan 35788 O.S.T. Hotel De Love.
- (S) (3:51) K-Tel 3906 Starflight Vol. 1.

1980 ALL OUT OF LOVE
(actual 45 time is (3:51) not (3:41) as stated on the record label)

- (S) (4:01) Arista 8216 Lost In Love. *(LP version which has a :10 longer introduction than the 45)*
- (S) (4:01) Arista 8024 Greatest Hits. *(LP version which has a :10 longer introduction than the 45)*
- (S) (4:00) RCA 66812 Do You Love Me? (All-Time Best Love Songs). *(LP version which has a :10 longer introduction than the 45)*
- (S) (3:52) JCI 3147 1980 - Only Love - 1984. *(45 version)*
- (S) (4:00) Time-Life R988-14 Sounds Of The Eighties: 1980-1982. *(LP version which has a :10 longer introduction than the 45)*
- (S) (3:53) Razor & Tie 4543 The '70s Preservation Society Presents: Easy '70s. *(45 version)*
- (S) (4:00) Polygram TV 314555610 The One And Only Love Album. *(LP version which has a :10 longer introduction than the 45)*
- (S) (4:00) Time-Life R834-15 Body Talk - Once In Lifetime. *(LP version which has a :10 longer introduction than the 45)*

1981 EVERY WOMAN IN THE WORLD

- (S) (3:29) Arista 8216 Lost In Love. *(LP version)*
- (S) (3:29) Arista 8024 Greatest Hits. *(LP version)*
- (S) (3:28) Time-Life R834-17 Body Talk - Heart To Heart. *(LP version)*

1981 THE ONE THAT YOU LOVE
(actual 45 time is (4:15) not (4:07) as stated on the record label)

- (S) (4:16) Arista 8217 The One That You Love.
- (S) (4:16) Arista 8024 Greatest Hits.
- (S) (4:11) Rhino 70676 Billboard Top Hits - 1981.
- (S) (4:15) Original Sound 8909 Best Love Songs Vol. 4.
- (S) (4:15) Original Sound 9327 Best Love Songs Vol. 3 & 4.
- (S) (4:15) Original Sound 1236 Best Love Songs Box Set.
- (S) (4:16) Priority 53699 80's Greatest Rock Hits Volume 7 - Light & Easy.
- (S) (4:11) Time-Life R988-08 Sounds Of The Eighties: 1981.
- (S) (4:11) Time-Life R138-18 Body Talk.
- (S) (4:16) Rebound 314520361 Class Reunion '81.
- (S) (4:15) Time-Life R834-02 Body Talk - Just For You.
- (S) (4:15) Time-Life R814-05 Love Songs.

1981 HERE I AM (JUST WHEN I THOUGHT I WAS OVER YOU)

- (S) (3:48) Arista 8217 The One That You Love.
- (S) (3:47) Arista 8024 Greatest Hits.
- (S) (3:46) Time-Life R834-11 Body Talk - After Dark.

1982 SWEET DREAMS

- (S) (5:20) Arista 8217 The One That You Love. *(LP version)*
- (S) (5:17) Arista 8024 Greatest Hits. *(LP version)*
- (S) (5:17) Time-Life R834-10 Body Talk - From The Heart. *(LP version)*

1982 EVEN THE NIGHTS ARE BETTER

- (S) (3:56) Arista 8292 Now And Forever.
- (S) (3:57) Arista 8024 Greatest Hits.
- (S) (3:56) Time-Life R834-10 Body Talk - From The Heart.

1983 TWO LESS LONELY PEOPLE IN THE WORLD

- (S) (4:00) Arista 8292 Now And Forever.

1983 MAKING LOVE OUT OF NOTHING AT ALL
(actual 45 time is (4:54) not (4:29) as stated on the record label)

- (S) (5:18) Arista 8268 Arista's Perfect 10. *(45 version but :24 longer fade)*
- (S) (4:58) Rhino 70678 Billboard Top Hits - 1983. *(45 version)*
- (S) (5:41) Arista 8024 Greatest Hits. *(LP version)*

- (S) (5:40) Madacy Entertainment 1983 Rock On 1983. *(LP version)*
- (S) (4:58) Time-Life R988-18 Sounds Of The Eighties: The Early '80s Take Two. *(45 version)*
- (S) (4:59) Time-Life R834-07 Body Talk - Hearts In Motion. *(45 version)*

1983 JUST AS I AM
(actual 45 time is (4:43) not (4:31) as stated on the record label)

- (S) (4:43) K-Tel 898 Romantic Hits Of The 80's.
- (S) (4:43) Arista 8283 Air Supply.
- (S) (4:43) JCI 3186 1985 - Only Love - 1989.

JEWEL AKENS
1965 THE BIRDS AND THE BEES

- (M) (2:07) Collectables 5064 History Of Rock Volume 4.
- (M) (2:06) Time-Life 2CLR-23 Classic Rock - 1965: Blowin' Your Mind.
- (S) (2:09) Original Sound 8859 Oldies But Goodies Vol. 9. *(this compact disc uses the "Waring - fds" noise reduction process)*
- (S) (2:08) Collectables 2504 WCBS-FM History Of Rock - The 60's Part 4.
- (S) (2:08) Collectables 4504 History Of Rock/The 60s Part Four.
- (M) (2:08) Collectables 2604 WCBS-FM Jukebox Giants Vol. 2.
- (S) (2:09) Era 5020 The Birds And The Bees: Best Of.
- (S) (2:09) Rhino 71935 Billboard Top Pop Hits, 1965.
- (S) (2:08) Collectables 2554 CBS-FM History Of Rock Volume 2.
- (E) (2:05) LaserLight 12314 and 15936 The Wonder Years - Party Time.

ALABAMA
1981 FEELS SO RIGHT

- (S) (3:34) RCA 7170 Greatest Hits. *(LP length)*
- (S) (3:36) RCA 3930 Feels So Right. *(LP length)*
- (S) (3:20) K-Tel 3047 Country Music Classics Volume VI. *(45 length)*
- (S) (3:34) RCA 66848 Super Hits. *(LP length)*
- (S) (3:23) Time-Life R990-19 Alabama - Legendary Country Singers. *(45 length)*
- (S) (3:35) Hip-O 40042 The Class Of Country 1980-1984. *(LP length)*

1982 LOVE IN THE FIRST DEGREE

- (S) (3:02) RCA 9970 Nipper's Greatest Hits - The 80's. *(live)*
- (S) (3:10) Time-Life CCD-03 Contemporary Country - The Early 80's.
- (S) (3:18) RCA 3930 Feels So Right.
- (S) (3:17) RCA 7170 Greatest Hits.
- (S) (3:17) RCA 66848 Super Hits.
- (S) (3:17) RCA 66945 Super Hits Sampler.
- (S) (3:18) Time-Life R990-19 Alabama - Legendary Country Singers.

1982 TAKE ME DOWN

- (S) (4:53) RCA 4229 Mountain Music. *(LP version)*
- (S) (4:52) RCA 61040 Greatest Hits II. *(LP version)*
- (S) (3:43) Time-Life R990-19 Alabama - Legendary Country Singers. *(45 version)*

1983 THE CLOSER YOU GET
(dj copies of this 45 ran (4:32) and (3:35); commercial copies were all (3:35))

- (S) (3:36) RCA 66241 RCA Award Winners.
- (S) (3:34) Time-Life CCD-09 Contemporary Country - The Early 80's Pure Gold.
- (S) (4:29) Pair 1329 Country Side Of Life.
- (S) (4:31) RCA 4663 The Closer You Get.
- (S) (3:35) RCA 61040 Greatest Hits II.
- (S) (3:36) RCA 66848 Super Hits.
- (S) (3:35) RCA 66945 Super Hits Sampler.

MORRIS ALBERT
1975 FEELINGS

- (S) (3:43) RCA 8476 Nipper's Greatest Hits - The 70's.
- (S) (3:41) Rhino 71197 Super Hits Of The 70's Volume 17. *(bad dropout at :04; hissy)*

(S) (3:40) Original Sound 8853 Oldies But Goodies Vol. 3. *(this compact disc uses the "Waring - fds" noise reduction process)*

(S) (3:40) Original Sound 2222 Oldies But Goodies Volumes 3,5,11,14 and 15 Box Set. *(this box set uses the "Waring - fds" noise reduction process)*

(S) (3:40) Original Sound 2500 Oldies But Goodies Volumes 1-15 Box Set. *(this box set uses the "Waring - fds" noise reduction process)*

(S) (3:39) Original Sound 8907 Best Love Songs Vol. 2.

(S) (3:39) Original Sound 9326 Best Love Songs Vol. 1 & 2.

(S) (3:39) Original Sound 1236 Best Love Songs Box Set.

(S) (3:41) Rhino 75233 '70s Party (Killers) Classics.

(S) (3:43) Time-Life R814-02 Love Songs.

WILLY ALBERTI
1959 MARINA

AL B. SURE!
1988 NITE AND DAY

(S) (3:56) JCI 2701 Slow Grooves. *(LP version)*

(S) (3:58) Warner Brothers 25662 In Effect Mode. *(LP version)*

(S) (3:59) Rhino 72159 Black Entertainment Television - 15th Anniversary. *(LP version)*

(S) (3:42) Rhino 72140 Billboard Hot R&B Hits 1985. *(45 version)*

(S) (3:30) JCI 3177 1985 - Only Soul - 1989. *(neither the 45, LP or 12" single version)*

(S) (3:42) Time-Life R834-03 Body Talk - Moonlit Nights. *(45 version)*

(S) (3:59) Rhino 72978 Smooth Grooves - New Jack Ballads Volume 2. *(LP version)*

released as by QUINCY JONES featuring AL B.SURE!/ JAMES INGRAM/EL DeBARGE/BARRY WHITE:
1990 THE SECRET GARDEN

(S) (6:39) Qwest/Warner Brothers 26020 Quincy Jones - Back On The Block.

(S) (6:45) Mercury 314514143 Barry White - Just For You. *(includes a :06 previously unreleased introduction by Barry White)*

ARTHUR ALEXANDER
1962 YOU BETTER MOVE ON

(S) (2:42) MCA 31202 Vintage Music Volume 5. *(45 version but missing a guitar overdub)*

(S) (2:42) MCA 5804 Vintage Music Volumes 5 & 6. *(45 version but missing a guitar overdub)*

(M) (2:42) Rhino 71517 The Muscle Shoals Sound.

(M) (2:42) Razor & Tie 2014 Ultimate.

(S) (2:41) Time-Life 2RNR-16 Rock 'N' Roll Era - 1962 Still Rockin'. *(45 version but missing a guitar overdub)*

(M) (2:42) Chess 9347 Stone Rock Blues.

(M) (2:36) Time-Life R102-17 Lost Treasures Of Rock 'N' Roll.

(M) (2:43) Time-Life R857-18 The Heart Of Rock 'n' Roll 1962-1963 Take Two.

ALIAS
1990 MORE THAN WORDS CAN SAY

(S) (3:51) Priority 7049 Metal Heat.

(S) (3:52) Priority 7077 80's Greatest Rock Hits Volume 5 - From The Heart.

(S) (3:52) EMI 93908 Alias.

(S) (3:51) SBK 31181 Moments In Love.

(S) (3:51) K-Tel 3847 90s Now Volume 1.

(S) (3:51) Time-Life R834-15 Body Talk - Once In Lifetime.

1991 WAITING FOR LOVE

(S) (4:33) EMI 93908 Alias. *(LP version)*

ALIVE AND KICKING
1970 TIGHTER, TIGHTER

(S) (2:42) Rhino 70923 Super Hits Of The 70's Volume 3.

(S) (2:42) Rhino 72009 Super Hits Of The 70's Volumes 1-4 Box Set.

(S) (2:42) Rhino 71207 70's Smash Hits Volume 3.

(S) (2:41) Time-Life SOD-31 Sounds Of The Seventies - AM Top Twenty.

(S) (2:41) JCI 3191 1970 - Only Dance - 1974.

(S) (2:42) Flashback 72683 '70s Radio Hits Volume 3.

(S) (2:42) Flashback 72090 '70s Radio Hits Box Set.

DAVIE ALLAN and THE ARROWS
1967 BLUES THEME

(M) (2:09) K-Tel 713 Battle Of The Bands.

(M) (2:09) Curb 77402 All-Time Great Instrumental Hits Volume 2.

(E) (2:09) K-Tel 3133 Biker Rock.

(M) (2:08) Time-Life R968-09 Guitar Rock 1966-1967.

(E) (2:09) Curb 77607 and 77866 O.S.T. The Wild Angels.

(E) (2:09) Simitar 55362 Garage Band Classics.

DEBORAH ALLEN
1984 BABY I LIED

DONNA ALLEN
1987 SERIOUS

(S) (4:05) 21 Records 90548 Perfect Timing.

REX ALLEN
1962 DON'T GO NEAR THE INDIANS

(S) (3:02) Rhino 70683 Billboard's Top Country Hits Of 1962.

(S) (3:04) Rhino 71263 and 71451 Songs Of The West.

(S) (3:04) Rhino 71682 Songs Of The West Vol. Two: Silver Screen Cowboys.

(S) (3:03) Risky Business 57475 Silver Screen Cowboys.

(S) (3:03) Mercury 314526691 Fifty Years Of Country Music From Mercury.

ALL-4-ONE
1994 SO MUCH IN LOVE

(S) (3:29) Blitz/Atlantic 82588 All-4-One.

(S) (3:29) MCA 11329 Soul Train 25th Anniversary Box Set.

1994 I SWEAR

(S) (4:18) Blitz/Atlantic 82588 All-4-One.

1995 I CAN LOVE YOU LIKE THAT

(S) (4:21) Blitzz/Atlantic 82746 And The Music Speaks.

(S) (4:21) Grammy Recordings/Sony 67565 1996 Grammy Nominees.

1996 SOMEDAY

(S) (4:17) Walt Disney 60893 O.S.T. The Hunchback Of Notre Dame.

GENE ALLISON
1958 YOU CAN MAKE IT IF YOU TRY

(M) (2:07) Vee-Jay 710 A Taste Of Soul Volume One.

(M) (2:06) Stax 8559 Super Blues - All-Time Classic Blues Hits Vol. 2.

(M) (2:05) Time-Life RHD-16 Rhythm & Blues - 1958.

(M) (2:05) Time-Life 2RNR-49 The Rock 'N' Roll Era - Lost Treasures II.

(M) (2:07) Vee-Jay 400 Celebrating 40 Years Of Classic Hits 1953-1993.

(M) (2:05) Ripete 2223 Soul Patrol Vol. 5.

GREGG ALLMAN
1974 MIDNIGHT RIDER
(dj copies of this 45 ran (3:22); commercial copies were all (4:26))

(S) (2:56) Priority 8663 The South Rules/70's Greatest Rock Hits Volume 2. *(this is the ALLMAN BROTHERS version mistakenly credited to GREG ALLMAN)*

(S) (4:24) Sandstone 33003 Reelin' In The Years Volume 4.

(S) (4:24) Polydor 831941 Laid Back.

(S) (4:23) Polydor 839426 Allman Brothers Dreams.

(S) (4:24) DCC Compact Classics 065 Rock Of The 70's Volume 4.

GREGG ALLMAN *(Continued)*

- (S) (4:25) Time-Life SOD-07 Sounds Of The Seventies - 1974.
- (S) (4:27) K-Tel 6045 Southern Fried Rock.
- (S) (2:54) Special Music 5025 Rebel Rousers! Best Of Southern Rock. *(this is the ALLMAN BROTHERS version mistakenly credited to GREG ALLMAN)*
- (S) (4:24) Time-Life R968-08 Guitar Rock - The Mid '70s.
- (S) (4:28) Capricorn 314529725 One More Try: An Anthology.
- (S) (4:24) Simitar 55152 Blue Eyed Soul.

ALLMAN BROTHERS BAND
1973 RAMBLIN' MAN
(dj copies of this 45 ran (3:36) and (4:58);
commercial copies were all (4:58))

- (S) (4:54) Rhino 70634 Billboard's Top Rock & Roll Hits Of 1973. *(45 speed)*
- (S) (4:46) Polydor 839426 Dreams. *(LP speed)*
- (S) (4:45) Priority 7995 Country's Greatest Hits: Southern Country Rock Volume 2. *(LP speed)*
- (S) (4:46) Sandstone 33002 Reelin' In The Years Volume 3. *(LP speed)*
- (S) (4:42) Polydor 511156 A Decade Of Hits 1969 - 1979. *(LP speed)*
- (S) (4:46) Polydor 825092 Brothers And Sisters. *(LP speed)*
- (S) (4:51) JCI 3304 Mellow Seventies. *(45 speed)*
- (S) (4:46) Foundation/Capitol 96647 Hearts Of Gold - The Classic Rock Collection. *(LP speed)*
- (S) (4:46) Special Music 843771 Ramblin' Man. *(LP speed)*
- (S) (4:46) DCC Compact Classics 064 Rock Of The 70's Volume Three. *(LP speed)*
- (S) (4:44) Compose 9923 James Dean/Tribute To A Rebel. *(LP speed)*
- (S) (4:54) Razor & Tie 22502 Those Rocking 70's. *(45 speed)*
- (S) (4:40) Time-Life R102-34 The Rolling Stone Collection. *(LP speed)*
- (S) (4:54) Time-Life R968-05 Guitar Rock 1972-1973. *(45 speed)*
- (S) (4:54) Time-Life SOD-06 Sounds Of The Seventies - 1973. *(45 speed)*
- (S) (4:44) Time-Life OPCD-4521 Guitar Rock. *(LP speed)*
- (S) (4:46) K-Tel 621 Rock Classics. *(LP speed)*
- (S) (4:41) Rebound 314520256 Best Of Southern Rock. *(LP speed)*
- (S) (4:42) Rebound 314520247 Class Reunion 1974. *(LP speed)*
- (S) (4:42) K-Tel 6083 Southern Fried Rock - Second Helping. *(LP speed)*
- (S) (4:42) Special Music/Essex 5036 Prom Night - The 70's. *(LP speed)*
- (S) (4:46) Rhino 72132 Frat Rock: More Of The 70's. *(LP speed)*
- (S) (4:46) MFSL 617 Brothers And Sisters. *(gold disc; LP speed))*
- (S) (4:41) Cabin Fever Music 973 Harley Davidson: The American Motorcycle Soundtrack. *(LP speed)*
- (S) (4:46) Varese 5635 and 5654 and 5655 and 5657 Arrow: All Rock & Roll Oldies Volume Two. *(LP speed)*
- (S) (4:42) Rebound 314520290 Allman Brothers/Wet Willie Back To Back. *(LP speed)*
- (S) (4:46) Varese Sarabande 5708 All Rock & Roll Hits Vol. One. *(LP speed)*
- (S) (4:54) K-Tel 3972 Southern Rockin' Rebels: The South's Gone And Done It. *(45 speed)*
- (S) (4:46) Capricorn 314531262 Brothers And Sisters. *(LP speed; remastered edition)*
- (S) (4:46) Critique 15467 Fast Cars And Southern Stars. *(LP speed)*
- (S) (4:40) K-Tel 3996 Rockin' Down The Highway. *(LP speed)*
- (S) (4:42) Thump 6020 Easyriders Volume 2. *(LP speed)*

1974 JESSICA

- (S) (7:28) Polydor 825092 Brothers And Sisters. *(LP version)*
- (S) (7:27) Polydor 511156 A Decade Of Hits (1969-1979). *(LP version)*
- (S) (7:27) Polydor 839426 Dreams. *(LP version)*
- (S) (7:27) MFSL 617 Brothers And Sisters. *(gold disc; LP version)*
- (S) (4:02) JCI 3139 18 Free And Easy Hits From The 70's. *(45 version)*
- (S) (7:27) Capricorn 314531262 Brothers And Sisters. *(LP version; remastered edition)*
- (S) (4:02) JCI 3192 18 Rock Classics Volume 2. *(45 version)*
- (S) (7:27) Rebound 314520507 Class Reunion '73. *(LP version)*

1979 CRAZY LOVE

- (S) (3:42) Polydor 831589 Enlightened Rogues.
- (S) (3:42) Polydor 511156 A Decade Of Hits (1969-1979).
- (S) (3:42) Polydor 839426 Dreams.
- (S) (3:43) Capricorn 314531265 Enlightened Rogues. *(remastered edition)*

1981 STRAIGHT FROM THE HEART

- (S) (3:45) Arista 18724 Hell & High Water/Best Of Arista Years.
- (S) (3:46) Razor & Tie 2132 Brothers Of The Road.

ALLURE
1997 HEAD OVER HEELS
released as by ALLURE featuring NAS:

- (S) (4:11) Crave/Track Masters 67848 Allure. *(tracks into next selection)*

released as by ALLURE featuring 112:
1997 ALL CRIED OUT

- (S) (4:35) Crave/Track Masters 67848 Allure. *(tracks into the next selection)*
- (S) (4:36) Beast 54112 Boom! *(remix)*

HERB ALPERT & THE TIJUANA BRASS
1962 THE LONELY BULL

- (S) (2:14) A&M 3101 The Lonely Bull.
- (S) (2:14) A&M 6011 Foursider.
- (S) (2:14) A&M 3267 Greatest Hits.
- (S) (2:14) A&M 2501 Classics Volume 1.

1965 A TASTE OF HONEY

- (S) (2:42) A&M 3157 Whipped Cream & Other Delights.
- (S) (2:42) A&M 6011 Foursider.
- (S) (2:42) A&M 3267 Greatest Hits.
- (S) (2:42) A&M 2501 Classics Volume 1.
- (S) (2:42) Time-Life R986-22 Instrumental Classics - Pop Classics.

1966 ZORBA THE GREEK

- (S) (4:22) A&M 6011 Foursider. *(LP version)*
- (S) (4:23) A&M 3267 Greatest Hits. *(LP version)*
- (S) (4:22) A&M 2501 Classics Volume 1. *(LP version)*
- (S) (4:23) A&M 3264 Going Places. *(LP version)*

1966 WHAT NOW MY LOVE

- (S) (2:14) A&M 6011 Foursider.
- (S) (2:14) A&M 3269 Greatest Hits Volume 2.
- (S) (2:14) A&M 2501 Classics Volume 1.
- (S) (2:14) A&M 3268 Solid Brass.
- (S) (2:14) A&M 3265 What Now My Love.

1966 SPANISH FLEA

- (S) (2:06) A&M 3267 Greatest Hits.
- (S) (2:05) A&M 2501 Classics Volume 1.
- (S) (2:06) A&M 3264 Going Places.

1966 WORK SONG

- (S) (2:09) A&M 3269 Greatest Hits Volume 2.
- (S) (2:06) A&M 2501 Classics Volume 1.
- (S) (2:10) A&M 3268 Solid Brass.

1966 FLAMINGO

- (S) (2:24) A&M 3269 Greatest Hits Volume 2.
- (S) (2:24) A&M 3268 Solid Brass.

1966 MAME

- (S) (2:07) A&M 6011 Foursider.
- (S) (2:07) A&M 2501 Classics Volume 1.

1967 CASINO ROYALE
(S) (2:35) A&M 6011 Foursider.
(S) (2:34) A&M 2501 Classics Volume 1.
(S) (2:35) A&M 3268 Solid Brass. ✓
(S) (2:35) Varese 5265 O.S.T. Casino Royale.
1967 THE HAPPENING
1967 A BANDA
(S) (2:09) A&M 3269 Greatest Hits Volume 2.
(S) (2:10) A&M 2501 Classics Volume 1.
(S) (2:10) A&M 3268 Solid Brass.
released as by HERB ALPERT:
1968 THIS GUY'S IN LOVE WITH YOU
(S) (3:57) A&M 2501 Classics Volume 1.
(S) (3:57) A&M 3269 Greatest Hits Volume 2.
(S) (3:58) A&M 6011 Foursider.
(S) (3:58) A&M 3268 Solid Brass.
(S) (3:57) A&M 3266 Beat Of The Brass.
released as by HERB ALPERT & THE TIJUANA BRASS:
1969 MY FAVORITE THINGS
(S) (3:02) A&M 3113 Christmas Album.
released as by HERB ALPERT:
1979 RISE
(S) (7:34) A&M 2518 Classics Volume 20. *(LP version)*
(S) (7:36) A&M 3274 Rise. *(LP version)*
1980 ROTATION
(S) (5:11) A&M 3274 Rise. *(LP version)*
(S) (5:07) A&M 2518 Classics Volume 20. *(LP version)*
1982 ROUTE 101
(S) (3:18) A&M 2518 Classics Volume 20.
1987 DIAMONDS
(S) (4:52) A&M 5125 Keep Your Eye On Me.
1987 MAKING LOVE IN THE RAIN
(S) (5:54) A&M 5125 Keep Your Eye On Me.

AMAZING RHYTHM ACES
1975 THIRD RATE ROMANCE

AMBER
1996 THIS IS YOUR NIGHT
(S) (5:24) Tommy Boy 1168 MTV Party To Go Volume 10.
(all songs on this cd are segued together; remix)
(S) (3:44) Arista 18943 Ultimate Dance Party 1997. *(all selections on this cd are segued together)*
(S) (3:58) Tommy Boy 1170 This Is Your Night.
(S) (3:45) Strictly Rhythm 6313 Strictly Rhythm Superjams.
(all selections on this cd are segued together)
(S) (3:50) Polygram TV 314553847 Pure Dance 1998. *(all songs on this cd are segued together)*
(S) (4:02) Interhit/Priority 51088 DMA Dance Vol. 4: Eurodance.

AMBOY DUKES
1968 JOURNEY TO THE CENTER OF THE MIND
(S) (3:32) Rhino 75892 Nuggets. *(bad dropout from 2:25 - 2:28)*
(S) (3:33) Original Sound 8894 Dick Clark's 21 All-Time Hits Vol. 3. *(bad dropout from 2:26 -2:34; two drum stick taps before the song begins)*
(S) (3:33) Epic/Legacy 47039 Ted Nugent: Out Of Control. *(bad dropout from 2:26 - 2:33)*
(S) (3:32) Time-Life 2CLR-19 Classic Rock - 1968: Shakin' All Over. *(bad dropout from 2:25 - 2:28)*
(S) (3:33) Mainstream 911 Journey To The Center Of The Mind. *(bad dropout from 2:26 - 2:29; tracks into next selection)*
(S) (3:33) Time-Life R968-07 Guitar Rock 1968-1969. *(bad dropout from 2:26 - 2:29)*
(S) (3:33) K-Tel 3183 Psychedelic Mind Trip. *(bad dropout from 2:26 - 2:29)*

AMBROSIA
1975 HOLDIN' ON TO YESTERDAY
(S) (4:19) Priority 8666 Kickin' Back/70's Greatest Rock Hits Volume 5. *(includes a :04 countoff; LP version)*
(S) (3:22) Time-Life SOD-33 Sounds Of The Seventies - AM Pop Classics II. *(45 version)*

(S) (4:14) Warner Brothers 45163 Anthology. *(LP version)*
(S) (3:21) JCI 3192 18 Rock Classics Volume 2. *(45 version; truncated fade)*
(S) (3:21) Time-Life R834-19 Body Talk - Always And Forever. *(45 version)*
1978 HOW MUCH I FEEL
(S) (4:46) JCI 3307 Easy Seventies.
(S) (4:46) Razor & Tie 4543 The '70s Preservation Society Presents: Easy '70s.
(S) (4:45) Time-Life R138-18 Body Talk.
(S) (4:44) Rhino 72299 Superhits Of The 70's Volume 25.
(S) (4:45) JCI 3146 1975 - Only Love - 1979.
(S) (4:45) K-Tel 3639 Dim The Lights - Soft Rock Hits Of The 70's.
(S) (4:44) Rhino 72518 Mellow Rock Hits Of The 70's - Summer Breeze.
(S) (4:46) Time-Life R834-03 Body Talk - Moonlit Nights.
(S) (4:46) Time-Life R840-01 Sounds Of The Seventies - Pop Nuggets: Late '70s.
(S) (4:42) Warner Brothers 45163 Anthology.
(S) (4:45) K-Tel 4017 70s Heavy Hitters: Summer Love.
(S) (4:45) Madacy Entertainment 6806 Best Of Love.
(S) (4:41) Polygram TV 314555610 The One And Only Love Album.
(S) (4:46) K-Tel 6257 The Greatest Love Songs - 16 Soft Rock Hits.
(S) (4:46) Time-Life AM1-25 AM Gold - 1978.
1980 THE BIGGEST PART OF ME
(dj copies of this 45 state times of (3:59) and (5:26) but the actual running times are (4:07) and (5:26); commercial copies were all (5:26))
(S) (5:24) Rhino 71891 Radio Daze: Pop Hits Of The 80's Volume Two.
(S) (4:08) Madacy Entertainment 1980 Rock On 1980.
(S) (4:07) JCI 3147 1980 - Only Love - 1984.
(S) (5:24) Time-Life R834-02 Body Talk - Just For You.
(S) (5:24) Warner Brothers 45163 Anthology.
1980 YOU'RE THE ONLY WOMAN (YOU & I)
(dj copies of this 45 ran (4:05) and (4:20); commercial copies were all (4:20))
(S) (4:17) Rhino 71892 Radio Daze: Pop Hits Of The 80's Volume Three.
(S) (4:17) Time-Life R834-06 Body Talk - Only You.
(S) (4:18) Warner Brothers 45163 Anthology.

AMERICA
1972 HORSE WITH NO NAME
(S) (4:10) Rhino 70633 Billboard's Top Rock & Roll Hits Of 1972.
(S) (4:10) Rhino 72005 Billboard's Top Rock & Roll Hits 1968-1972 Box Set.
(S) (4:07) Warner Brothers 3110 History/America's Greatest Hits. *(tracks into next selection)*
(S) (4:10) Warner Brothers 2576 America.
(S) (4:06) Razor & Tie 4543 The '70s Preservation Society Presents: Easy '70s.
(S) (4:06) Priority 7066 #1 Groups/70's Greatest Rock Hits Volume 12.
(S) (4:06) Time-Life SUD-11 Superhits - 1972.
(S) (4:10) Time-Life SOD-03 Sounds Of The Seventies - 1972.
(S) (4:08) Time-Life R103-33 Singers & Songwriters.
(S) (4:05) JCI 3130 1970 - Only Rock 'N Roll - 1974.
(S) (4:07) K-Tel 3454 70s Folk Rock Hits.
(S) (4:09) Madacy Entertainment 1972 Rock On 1972.
(S) (4:09) Rhino 72518 Mellow Rock Hits Of The 70's - Summer Breeze.
(S) (4:06) Time-Life AM1-07 AM Gold - 1972.
1972 I NEED YOU
(S) (3:05) Warner Brothers 3110 History/America's Greatest Hits. *(previous selection tracks over intro; tracks into next selection; "Greatest Hits" vinyl LP version)*
(S) (3:04) Warner Brothers 2576 America. *(45 and "America" vinyl LP version)*

AMERICA *(Continued)*

- (S) (2:58) JCI 3303 Love Seventies. *(45 and "America" vinyl LP version)*
- (S) (2:32) CEMA Special Markets 35959 Ventura Highway & Other Favorites. *(live)*
- (S) (3:03) JCI 3145 1970 - Only Love - 1974. *(45 and "America" vinyl LP version)*
- (S) (3:03) Time-Life R834-10 Body Talk - From The Heart. *(45 and "America" vinyl LP version)*

1972 VENTURA HIGHWAY

- (S) (3:22) Warner Brothers 3110 History/America's Greatest Hits. *(previous selection tracks over intro; tracks into next selection; "Greatest Hits" vinyl LP version)*
- (S) (3:21) Priority 8667 FM Hits/70's Greatest Rock Hits Volume 6. *("Greatest Hits" vinyl LP version)*
- (S) (3:27) JCI 3307 Easy Seventies. *(45 and "Homecoming" LP version)*
- (S) (3:29) Time-Life SUD-16 Superhits - The Early 70's. *(45 and "Homecoming" vinyl LP version)*
- (S) (3:31) Time-Life SOD-13 Sounds Of The Seventies - 1972: Take Two. *(45 and "Homecoming" vinyl LP version)*
- (S) (3:28) Time-Life R105-26 Our Songs: Singers & Songwriters Encore. *(45 and "Homecoming" vinyl LP version)*
- (S) (3:30) Warner Brothers 2655 Homecoming. *(45 and "Homecoming" vinyl LP version)*
- (S) (3:46) CEMA Special Markets 35959 Ventura Highway & Other Favorites. *(live)*
- (S) (3:27) JCI 3168 #1 Radio Hits 1970 - Only Rock 'n Roll - 1974. *(45 and "Homecoming" vinyl LP version)*
- (S) (3:30) Rhino 72517 Mellow Rock Hits Of The 70's - Ventura Highway. *(45 and "Homecoming" vinyl LP version)*
- (S) (3:29) Time-Life AM1-13 AM Gold - The Early '70s. *(45 and "Homecoming" vinyl LP version)*

1973 DON'T CROSS THE RIVER

- (S) (2:30) Warner Brothers 3110 History/America's Greatest Hits. *(previous selection tracks over the introduction)*
- (S) (2:29) Warner Brothers 2655 Homecoming.

1974 TIN MAN

- (S) (3:26) Warner Brothers 3110 History/America's Greatest Hits.
- (S) (3:24) Time-Life SOD-15 Sounds Of The Seventies - 1974: Take Two.
- (S) (3:24) Time-Life AM1-21 AM Gold - 1974.
- (S) (3:25) Rhino 72740 Billboard Top Soft Rock Hits - 1974.

1975 LONELY PEOPLE

- (S) (2:28) Warner Brothers 3110 History/America's Greatest Hits.
- (S) (2:27) Time-Life R834-17 Body Talk - Heart To Heart.

1975 SISTER GOLDEN HAIR

- (S) (3:11) JCI 3304 Mellow Seventies. *(much faster than the 45 or LP)*
- (S) (3:17) Rhino 70670 Billboard Top Hits - 1975.
- (S) (3:18) Warner Brothers 3110 History/America's Greatest Hits.
- (S) (3:18) Time-Life SOD-08 Sounds Of The Seventies - 1975.
- (S) (3:17) Rebound 314520317 Class Reunion 1975.
- (S) (3:15) JCI 3146 1975 - Only Love - 1979.
- (S) (3:16) Time-Life AM1-22 AM Gold - 1975.
- (S) (3:18) Priority 50991 The Best Of The 70's - Rock Chart Toppers.
- (S) (3:17) Madacy Entertainment 6805 The Power Of Rock.
- (S) (3:18) Simitar 55502 The Number One's: Classic Rock.

1975 DAISY JANE

- (S) (3:08) Warner Brothers 3110 History/America's Greatest Hits. *(tracks into next selection)*
- (S) (3:07) Time-Life R834-19 Body Talk - Always And Forever.

1976 TODAY'S THE DAY

- (S) (3:14) Rhino 70529 Encore: More Greatest Hits.

1982 YOU CAN DO MAGIC

- (S) (3:52) Rhino 70529 Encore: More Greatest Hits.

- (S) (3:58) CEMA Special Markets 35959 Ventura Highway & Other Favorites. *(live)*
- (S) (3:54) One Way 18497 View From The Ground.

1983 THE BORDER

- (S) (3:56) Rhino 70529 Encore: More Greatest Hits.
- (S) (4:04) CEMA Special Markets 35959 Ventura Highway & Other Favorites. *(live)*

AMERICAN BREED
1967 STEP OUT OF YOUR MIND

- (S) (2:27) Varese Sarabande 5493 Bend Me, Shape Me: Best Of.

1968 BEND ME SHAPE ME

- (S) (2:12) K-Tel 686 Battle Of The Bands Volume 4. *(45 length)*
- (S) (2:14) MCA 31204 Vintage Music Volume 7. *(45 length)*
- (S) (2:14) MCA 5805 Vintage Music Volumes 7 & 8. *(45 length)*
- (S) (2:09) Time-Life 2CLR-11 Classic Rock - 1968: The Beat Goes On. *(45 length)*
- (S) (2:12) Collectables 2504 WCBS-FM History Of Rock - The 60's Part 4. *(45 length)*
- (S) (2:12) Collectables 4504 History Of Rock/The 60s Part Four. *(45 length)*
- (S) (2:23) Varese Sarabande 5493 Bend Me, Shape Me: Best Of. *(LP length)*
- (S) (2:14) MCA Special Products 22135 Vintage Collectibles Volume 6. *(45 length)*
- (S) (2:13) Time-Life 2CLR-31 Classic Rock - Totally Fantastic '60s. *(45 length)*
- (S) (2:13) MCA Special Products 21017 The Rockin' Sixties. *(45 length)*

1968 GREEN LIGHT

- (S) (2:14) Varese Sarabande 5493 Bend Me, Shape Me: Best Of.

ED AMES
1967 MY CUP RUNNETH OVER

- (S) (2:45) RCA 8475 Nipper's Greatest Hits Of The 60's Volume 2.
- (S) (2:44) Time-Life R138/05 Look Of Love.
- (S) (2:44) RCA 53774 My Cup Runneth Over.
- (S) (2:44) Time-Life R974-04 Many Moods Of Romance - As Time Goes By.
- (S) (2:43) K-Tel 3630 Lounge Legends.
- (S) (2:44) Hammer & Lace 697124114 Leading Men: Masters Of Style Volume Two.
- (S) (2:44) Collectables 2704 Who Will Answer?/My Cup Runneth Over.
- (S) (2:43) Simitar 55382 The Crooners.
- (S) (2:44) Time-Life R814-04 Love Songs.

1968 WHO WILL ANSWER?

- (S) (3:40) Collectables 2704 Who Will Answer?/My Cup Runneth Over.

AMES BROTHERS
1955 THE NAUGHTY LADY OF SHADY LANE

- (M) (2:48) Pair 1215 Best Of.
- (M) (2:48) RCA 8467 Nipper's Greatest Hits Of The 50's Volume 2.
- (M) (2:49) Time-Life HPD-09 Your Hit Parade 1955.
- (M) (2:49) Time-Life R132-14 Golden Groups Of Your Hit Parade.

1955 MY BONNIE LASSIE

- (M) (2:26) Pair 1215 Best Of.

1956 IT ONLY HURTS FOR A LITTLE WHILE

- (M) (2:40) Pair 1215 Best Of.
- (M) (2:41) Time-Life HPD-27 Your Hit Parade - The Unforgettable 50's.

1957 TAMMY

- (M) (2:22) Pair 1215 Best Of.

1957 MELODIE D'AMOUR

- (M) (2:36) Pair 1215 Best Of.
- (M) (2:37) RCA 8466 Nipper's Greatest Hits Of The 50's Volume 1.
- (S) (2:38) Time-Life HPD-17 Your Hit Parade - 1957.

1958 A VERY PRECIOUS LOVE
   (M) (2:41)   Pair 1215 Best Of.
1958 PUSSY CAT
1958 NO ONE BUT YOU
1959 RED RIVER ROSE

BILL ANDERSON
1963 STILL
   (S) (2:46)   Rhino 70684 Billboard's Top Country Hits Of 1963.
   (M) (2:46)   Curb 77436 Best Of.
   (S) (2:46)   Time-Life CTD-11 Country USA - 1963.
   (S) (2:46)   MCA 11069 From The Vaults - Decca Country Classics 1934-1973.
   (S) (2:46)   MCA Special Products 20435 Country's Greatest Hits Of The 60's Vol. 1.
   (S) (2:45)   K-Tel 320 Country Music Classics Volume II.
   (S) (2:47)   Varese Sarabande 5643 Greatest Hits.
   (S) (2:46)   JCI 3153 1960 - Only Country - 1964.
   (S) (2:48)   Curb 77871 Greatest Songs. *(rerecording)*
   (S) (2:45)   K-Tel 3358 101 Greatest Country Hits Vol. Four: Mellow Country.
   (S) (2:46)   Time-Life R808-01 Classic Country 1960-1964.

JOHN ANDERSON
1983 SWINGIN'
   (S) (3:00)   Warner Brothers 25169 Greatest Hits.
   (S) (3:01)   Warner Brothers 45664 Greatest Country Hits Of The '80s Volume 1.
   (S) (3:00)   Warner Brothers 45356 Country Jukebox Greatest Hits Volume One.
   (S) (3:01)   Warner Brothers 25966 Swingin' Country Favorites.
   (S) (3:01)   Time-Life CCD-09 Contemporary Country - Early 80's.
   (S) (3:00)   Priority 7928 Wild Wild Country.
   (S) (3:02)   Priority 9703 Hot Country Rock.
   (S) (3:00)   K-Tel 3047 Country Music Classics Volume VI.
   (S) (2:58)   JCI 3157 1980 - Only Country - 1984.
   (S) (2:58)   BNA 66982 Greatest Hits. *(rerecording)*
   (S) (3:00)   K-Tel 3945 The 80's: Country's Number One Men.
   (S) (3:01)   Simitar 55092 80's Country 1982-94.
   (S) (2:58)   BNA 67629 Super Hits. *(rerecording)*

LYNN ANDERSON
1971 ROSE GARDEN
   (S) (2:47)   Rhino 70924 Super Hits Of The 70's Volume 4.
   (S) (2:47)   Rhino 72009 Super Hits Of The 70's Volumes 1-4 Box Set.
   (S) (2:47)   Columbia 45047 Pop Classics Of The 70's.
   (S) (2:52)   Columbia 46032 Columbia Country Classics Volume 4.
   (S) (2:47)   Time-Life CTD-04 Country USA - 1970.
   (S) (2:47)   Time-Life CCD-06 Contemporary Country - The Early 70's.
   (S) (2:54)   K-Tel 3085 Great Ladies Of Country.
   (S) (2:53)   Columbia/Legacy 53817 All-Time Legends Of Country Music.
   (S) (2:54)   K-Tel 567 Country Music Classics Volume IV.
   (S) (2:45)   JCI 3155 1970 - Only Country - 1974.
   (S) (2:54)   Epic 67942 Super Hits Of The '70s.
   (S) (2:55)   K-Tel 3357 101 Greatest Country Hits Vol. Three: Easy Country. *(rerecording)*
   (S) (2:54)   Collectables 5848 Rose Garden/You're My Man. *(noisy fadeout)*
   (S) (2:54)   Hip-O 40085 The Class Of Country 1970-1974.
   (S) (2:53)   Columbia 69083 Ladies Choice Super Hits.
   (S) (2:46)   Time-Life R808-04 Classic Country 1970-1974.

LEE ANDREWS and THE HEARTS
1957 LONG LONELY NIGHTS
   (M) (2:52)   MCA 31200 Vintage Music Volume 3.
   (M) (2:52)   MCA 5778 Vintage Music Volumes 3 & 4.
   (M) (2:52)   Chess 9282 Best Of Chess Vocal Groups Volume 1.
   (S) (2:52)   Garland 012 Remember When. *(rerecording)*

   (M) (2:50)   Collectables 2508 History Of Rock - The Doo Wop Era Part 2.
   (M) (2:50)   Collectables 4508 History Of Rock/The Doo Wop Era Part Two.
   (M) (2:52)   Collectables 5028 Biggest Hits.
   (M) (2:48)   Collectables 5003 Gotham Recording Sessions. *(alternate take)*
   (M) (2:51)   Collectables 5068 History Of Rock Volume 8.
   (M) (2:50)   Rhino 71463 Doo Wop Box.
   (M) (2:52)   Time-Life 2RNR-28 Rock 'N' Roll Era - The 50's Rave On.
   (M) (2:51)   Collectables 2606 WCBS-FM For Lovers Only Vol. 2.
   (M) (2:52)   Collectables 8827 For Collectors Only.
   (M) (2:50)   Collectables 8827 For Collectors Only. *(demo version)*
   (M) (2:51)   Collectables 8827 For Collectors Only. *(demo version)*
   (M) (2:49)   Time-Life R857-13 The Heart Of Rock 'n' Roll 1956-1957.
1957 TEAR DROPS
   (M) (2:21)   Rhino 75763 Best Of Doo Wop Ballads.
   (M) (2:20)   Chess 31320 Best Of Chess Rock & Roll Volume 2.
   (M) (2:19)   Collectables 5028 Biggest Hits.
   (M) (2:20)   Original Sound 9329 Oldies But Goodies Doo Wop Classics.
   (M) (2:20)   Rhino 71463 Doo Wop Box.
   (M) (2:20)   Time-Life 2RNR-24 Rock 'N' Roll Era - The 50's Keep On Rockin'.
   (M) (2:20)   Collectables 2509 WCBS-FM For Lovers Only Part 1.
   (M) (2:21)   Collectables 2552 WOGL History Of Rock Vol. 2.
   (M) (2:20)   Chess 9352 Chess Rhythm & Roll.
   (M) (2:20)   Collectables 8827 For Collectors Only.
   (M) (2:20)   Time-Life R857-05 The Heart Of Rock 'n' Roll 1957.
1958 TRY THE IMPOSSIBLE
   (M) (3:02)   Collectables 5028 Biggest Hits. *(mastered from vinyl)*
   (M) (3:04)   Collectables 5003 Gotham Recording Sessions. *(alternate version)*
   (M) (3:02)   Collectables 5175 Memories Of Times Square Record Shop Vol. 4.
   (M) (3:08)   Collectables 8827 For Collectors Only. *(demo version)*
   (M) (3:02)   Collectables 8827 For Collectors Only.

ANGELICA
1992 ANGEL BABY
   (S) (4:34)   Quality 15183 Angel Baby.

ANGELS
1961 'TIL
   (M) (2:27)   K-Tel 3051 Lesley Gore/Angels.
   (S) (2:24)   Collectables 5061 History Of Rock Volume 1.
   (S) (2:25)   Collectables 5085 My Boyfriend's Back.
   (S) (2:25)   Time-Life 2RNR-35 Rock 'N' Roll Era - The 60's Last Dance.
   (S) (2:25)   Time-Life SUD-06 Superhits - 1962.
   (S) (2:25)   Collectables 2504 WCBS-FM History Of Rock - The 60's Part 4.
   (S) (2:25)   Collectables 4504 History Of Rock/The 60s Part Four.
   (S) (2:26)   Collectables 2509 WCBS-FM For Lovers Only Part 1.
   (S) (2:25)   Time-Life R102-17 Lost Treasures Of Rock 'N' Roll.
   (S) (2:27)   LaserLight 12320 Love Songs.
   (E) (2:28)   Mercury 314532484 Best Of.
   (S) (2:25)   Time-Life R857-06 The Heart Of Rock 'n' Roll 1962.
   (S) (2:25)   Time-Life AM1-18 AM Gold - 1962.
1962 CRY BABY CRY
   (S) (2:46)   Collectables 5070 History Of Rock Volume 10.
   (S) (2:47)   Collectables 5085 My Boyfriend's Back.

ANGELS *(Continued)*

- (M) (2:47) Time-Life 2RNR-40 Rock 'N' Roll Era - The 60's Teen Time.
- (S) (2:47) Collectables 2505 History Of Rock - The 60's Part 5.
- (S) (2:47) Collectables 4505 History Of Rock/The 60s Part Five.
- (E) (2:49) Mercury 314532484 Best Of.
- (S) (2:47) Time-Life R857-18 The Heart Of Rock 'n' Roll 1962-1963 Take Two.

1963 MY BOYFRIEND'S BACK

- (S) (2:35) Rhino 70624 Billboard's Top Rock & Roll Hits Of 1963. *(stereo LP version)*
- (S) (2:35) Rhino 72007 Billboard's Top Rock & Roll Hits 1962-1966 Box Set. *(stereo LP version)*
- (M) (2:13) Mercury 826448 Oldies Golden Million Sellers. *(45 and mono LP version)*
- (S) (2:35) Mercury 816555 45's On CD Volume 2. *(stereo LP version)*
- (S) (2:35) Rhino 70989 Best Of The Girl Groups Volume 2. *(stereo LP version)*
- (S) (2:37) JCI 3110 Sock Hoppin' Sixties. *(stereo LP version)*
- (S) (2:37) Original Sound 8861 Oldies But Goodies Vol. 11. *(this compact disc uses the "Waring - fds" noise reduction process; stereo LP version)*
- (S) (2:37) Original Sound 2222 Oldies But Goodies Volumes 3,5,11,14 and 15 Box Set. *(this box set uses the "Waring - fds" noise reduction process; stereo LP version)*
- (S) (2:37) Original Sound 2500 Oldies But Goodies Volumes 1-15 Box Set. *(this box set uses the "Waring - fds" noise reduction process; stereo LP version)*
- (S) (2:35) Warner Brothers 3359 O.S.T. The Wanderers. *(stereo LP version)*
- (S) (2:35) Motown 5322 and 9087 Girl Groups: The Story Of A Sound. *(stereo LP version)*
- (S) (2:35) K-Tel 3051 Lesley Gore/Angels. *(stereo LP version)*
- (S) (2:34) Collectables 5085 My Boyfriend's Back. *(stereo LP version)*
- (S) (2:35) Time-Life 2RNR-25 Rock 'N' Roll Era - The 60's Keep On Rockin'. *(stereo LP version)*
- (S) (2:37) Collectables 2505 History Of Rock - The 60's Part 5. *(stereo LP version)*
- (S) (2:37) Collectables 4505 History Of Rock/The 60s Part Five. *(stereo LP version)*
- (S) (2:35) Polygram Special Markets 314520260 Number One Hits Of The Sixties. *(stereo LP version)*
- (S) (2:36) DCC Compact Classics 077 Too Cute! *(stereo LP version)*
- (M) (2:14) Mercury 314528171 Growin' Up Too Fast - The Girl Group Anthology. *(45 and mono LP version)*
- (S) (2:36) Mercury 314532484 Best Of. *(stereo LP version)*
- (M) (2:13) Mercury 314532484 Best Of. *(45 and mono LP version)*
- (S) (2:35) Nick At Nite/550 Music/Epic 67689 Stand By Your Man. *(stereo LP version)*
- (S) (2:35) JCI 3166 #1 Radio Hits 1960 - Only Rock 'n Roll - 1964. *(stereo LP version)*
- (S) (2:35) Eclipse Music Group 64868 Rock 'n Roll Relix 1962-1963. *(stereo LP version)*
- (S) (2:35) Eclipse Music Group 64872 Rock 'n Roll Relix 1960-1969. *(stereo LP version)*
- (M) (2:13) Polygram Special Markets 314520500 My Boyfriend's Back. *(45 and mono LP version)*
- (S) (2:35) Polygram Special Markets 314520516 45's On CD Volume 1. *(stereo LP version)*

1963 I ADORE HIM

- (S) (2:47) K-Tel 3051 Lesley Gore/Angels.
- (M) (2:45) Mercury 314528171 Growin' Up Too Fast - The Girl Group Anthology.
- (S) (2:47) Mercury 314532484 Best Of.
- (M) (2:44) Polygram Special Markets 314520500 My Boyfriend's Back.

1964 WOW WOW WEE (HE'S THE BOY FOR ME)

- (S) (1:58) K-Tel 3051 Lesley Gore/Angels.
- (M) (1:59) Mercury 314528171 Growin' Up Too Fast - The Girl Group Anthology.
- (S) (1:57) Mercury 314532484 Best Of.
- (S) (1:59) Eclipse Music Group 64869 Rock 'n Roll Relix 1964-1965.
- (S) (1:59) Eclipse Music Group 64872 Rock 'n Roll Relix 1960-1969.
- (M) (1:59) Polygram Special Markets 314520500 My Boyfriend's Back.

ANIMALS (also ERIC BURDON & THE ANIMALS)

1964 THE HOUSE OF THE RISING SUN (the original U.S. LP and 45 version both ran (2:58); the (4:26) version first appeared on the Animals "Greatest Hits" vinyl LP)

- (M) (4:26) Abkco 4324 Best Of.
- (M) (4:33) JCI 3107 British Sixties.
- (M) (4:43) Avenue/Rhino 71708 Eric Burdon Sings The Animals Greatest Hits. *(all selections on this cd are rerecordings)*
- (M) (4:43) Pair 1209 Eric Burdon Sings The Animals Greatest Hits. *(all selections on this cd are rerecordings)*
- (M) (4:43) Special Music 4919 Animals' Greatest Hits Sung By Eric Burdon. *(all selections on this cd are rerecordings)*
- (S) (4:36) MCA 11389 O.S.T. Casino. *(rerecording)*

1964 I'M CRYING

- (M) (2:43) Abkco 4324 Best Of.

1965 BOOM BOOM

- (M) (3:00) Abkco 4324 Best Of.

1965 DON'T LET ME BE MISUNDERSTOOD

- (M) (2:25) Abkco 4324 Best Of.
- (S) (4:38) Avenue/Rhino 71708 Eric Burdon Sings The Animals Greatest Hits. *(all selections on this cd are rerecordings)*
- (S) (4:38) Pair 1209 Eric Burdon Sings The Animals Greatest Hits. *(all selections on this cd are rerecordings)*
- (S) (4:38) Special Music 4919 Animals' Greatest Hits Sung By Eric Burdon. *(all selections on this cd are rerecordings)*

1965 BRING IT ON HOME TO ME

- (M) (2:34) Abkco 4324 Best Of.

1965 WE GOTTA GET OUT OF THIS PLACE

- (M) (3:12) Abkco 4324 Best Of. *(alternate take)*
- (E) (4:06) Avenue/Rhino 71708 Eric Burdon Sings The Animals Greatest Hits. *(all selections on this cd are rerecordings)*
- (E) (4:06) Pair 1209 Eric Burdon Sings The Animals Greatest Hits. *(all selections on this cd are rerecordings)*
- (E) (4:06) Special Music 4919 Animals' Greatest Hits Sung By Eric Burdon. *(all selections on this cd are rerecordings)*

1966 IT'S MY LIFE

- (M) (3:10) Abkco 4324 Best Of.
- (S) (3:34) Avenue/Rhino 71708 Eric Burdon Sings The Animals Greatest Hits. *(all selections on this cd are rerecordings)*
- (S) (3:34) Pair 1209 Eric Burdon Sings The Animals Greatest Hits. *(all selections on this cd are rerecordings)*
- (S) (3:34) Special Music 4919 Animals' Greatest Hits Sung By Eric Burdon. *(all selections on this cd are rerecordings)*

1966 INSIDE-LOOKING OUT

- (M) (3:44) Polydor 849388 Best Of Eric Burdon & The Animals.

1966 DON'T BRING ME DOWN

- (S) (3:13) Polydor 849388 Best Of Eric Burdon & The Animals.
- (M) (3:11) Mercury 816555 45's On CD Volume 2.
- (S) (3:13) Time-Life R962-07 History Of Rock 'N' Roll: The British Invasion 1964-1966.

(S) (3:13) Rebound 314520277 Hard Rock Essentials - The 60's.

(M) (3:14) Special Music/Essex 5027 Animal Tracks (Heavy Hits).

(S) (3:13) Time-Life R968-09 Guitar Rock 1966-1967.

(S) (3:13) Special Music 5039 Great Britons! Volume One.

released as by ERIC BURDON & THE ANIMALS:

1966 SEE SEE RIDER

(S) (3:59) Polydor 849388 Best Of. *(LP version)*

(M) (2:47) Rhino 70325 History Of British Rock Volume 7. *(45 version)*

(M) (2:47) Rhino 72022 History Of British Rock Box Set. *(45 version)*

(E) (3:57) Special Music/Essex 5027 Animal Tracks (Heavy Hits). *(LP version; distorted)*

1967 HELP ME GIRL

(S) (2:37) Polydor 849388 Best Of.

(M) (2:37) Special Music/Essex 5027 Animal Tracks (Heavy Hits).

(S) (2:39) One Way 31376 Eric Is Here.

(S) (2:39) Special Music 5040 Great Britons! Volume Two.

1967 WHEN I WAS YOUNG

(M) (2:59) Polydor 849388 Best Of.

(M) (3:00) Polydor 837362 O.S.T. 1969.

(M) (2:59) Rhino 70326 History Of British Rock Volume 8.

(M) (2:59) Rhino 72022 History Of British Rock Box Set.

(M) (2:58) Time-Life 2CLR-30 Classic Rock - Rock Renaissance IV.

(S) (3:55) Avenue/Rhino 71708 Eric Burdon Sings The Animals Greatest Hits. *(all selections on this cd are rerecordings)*

(S) (3:55) Pair 1209 Eric Burdon Sings The Animals Greatest Hits. *(all selections on this cd are rerecordings)*

(M) (2:59) Time-Life R968-12 Guitar Rock - The Late '60s.

1967 SAN FRANCISCAN NIGHTS

(S) (3:19) Polydor 849388 Best Of.

(S) (3:18) Mercury 834216 45's On CD Volume 3.

(S) (3:19) Rhino 70326 History Of British Rock Volume 8.

(S) (3:19) Rhino 72022 History Of British Rock Box Set.

(M) (3:22) Rhino 71065 Summer Of Love Volume 1.

(S) (3:18) Special Music/Essex 5027 Animal Tracks (Heavy Hits).

(S) (3:18) Polygram Special Markets 314520271 Hits Of The 70's.

(S) (3:19) One Way 30335 Winds Of Change.

(S) (3:19) Polygram Special Markets 314520401 Best Of Eric Burdon And The Animals.

(S) (3:18) Polygram Special Markets 314520464 60's Rock Hits.

1968 MONTEREY
(dj copies of this song ran (3:29) and (4:14); commercial copies were all (4:14))

(S) (4:14) Polydor 849388 Best Of. *(45 version)*

(S) (4:16) Buddah 49507 Psychedelic Pop. *(45 version)*

(S) (4:14) Rebound 314520435 Classic Rock - 60's. *(45 version)*

(S) (4:14) Polygram Special Markets 314520401 Best Of Eric Burdon And The Animals. *(45 version)*

1968 SKY PILOT
(the LP version tracked Parts 1 & 2 together; the 45 version had Part 1 on side 1 and Part 2 on side 2)

(S) (7:29) Polydor 849388 Best Of. *(LP version)*

(S) (7:24) Rhino 70734 Songs Of Protest. *(LP version)*

(M) (2:57) Rhino 70327 History Of British Rock Volume 9. *(45 version of Part 1)*

(M) (2:57) Rhino 72022 History Of British Rock Box Set. *(45 version of Part 1)*

(S) (7:26) Special Music/Essex 5027 Animal Tracks (Heavy Hits). *(LP version)*

(S) (2:59) LaserLight 12314 and 15936 The Wonder Years - Party Time. *(edit of the LP version in an unsuccessful attempt at recreating the 45 version)*

(M) (4:29) K-Tel 3610 Psychedelic Mind Trip Vol. 2: Another Flashback. *(Part 2)*

(M) (4:32) Polygram Special Markets 314520401 Best Of Eric Burdon And The Animals. *(Part 2; hum noticeable on the fadeout)*

(S) (2:58) Varese Sarabande 5846 On The Radio Volume One. *(45 version of Part 1)*

ANIMOTION
1985 OBSESSION

(S) (4:00) K-Tel 3262 The 80's Video Stars. *(45 version)*

(S) (3:54) JCI 3128 1985 - Only Rock 'N Roll - 1989. *(45 version)*

(S) (5:33) Mercury 822580 Animotion. *(LP version)*

(S) (4:02) Rhino 71978 New Wave Hits Of The 80's Vol. 15. *(45 version)*

(S) (4:00) Priority 53797 Best Of 80's Rock Volume 4. *(45 version)*

(S) (3:54) Time-Life R988-12 Sounds Of The 80's: 1985-1986. *(45 version)*

(S) (5:33) Rebound 314520354 World Of Dance: New Wave - The 80's. *(LP version)*

(S) (5:34) Mercury 314532319 Obsession - Best Of. *(LP version)*

(S) (5:34) Rebound 314520442 The Roots Of Rock: 80's New Wave. *(LP version)*

(S) (4:01) Rhino 72820 VH1 - More Of The Big 80's. *(45 version)*

(S) (4:02) Rhino 72856 Just Can't Get Enough: New Wave Women. *(45 version)*

(S) (3:40) Cold Front 6330 Club Mix: The 80s. *(all selections on this cd are segued together)*

(S) (5:35) Rebound 314520501 Obsession. *(LP version)*

1985 LET HIM GO

(S) (4:15) Mercury 822580 Animotion.

(S) (4:25) Mercury 314532319 Obsession - Best Of.

1989 ROOM TO MOVE

(S) (4:13) Polydor 837798 O.S.T. My Stepmother Is An Alien. *(:09 longer fade than the 45 version)*

(S) (4:34) Polydor 837314 Animotion. *(LP version)*

(S) (4:34) Mercury 314532319 Obsession - Best Of. *(LP version)*

(S) (4:34) Rebound 314520501 Obsession. *(LP version)*

PAUL ANKA
1957 DIANA

(M) (2:25) Rhino 71489 30th Anniversary Collection.

(E) (2:25) Rhino 70618 Billboard's Top Rock & Roll Hits Of 1957.

(E) (2:25) Rhino 72004 Billboard's Top Rock & Roll Hits 1957-1961 Box Set.

(E) (2:22) Original Sound 8852 Oldies But Goodies Vol. 2. *(this compact disc uses the "Waring - fds" noise reduction process)*

(E) (2:22) Original Sound 2223 Oldies But Goodies Volumes 2,7,9,12 and 13 Box Set. *(this box set uses the "Waring - fds" noise reduction process)*

(E) (2:22) Original Sound 2500 Oldies But Goodies Volumes 1-15 Box Set. *(this box set uses the "Waring - fds" noise reduction process)*

(E) (2:21) Original Sound 8891 Dick Clark's 21 All-Time Hits Vol. 1.

(M) (2:25) Curb 77467 Five Decades Greatest Hits.

(M) (2:23) Curb 77525 Greatest Hits Of Rock 'N' Roll Volume 2.

(S) (2:18) RCA 3808 21 Golden Hits. *(rerecorded)*

(M) (2:25) Curb 77557 Sings His Big 10 Volume 1.

(M) (2:25) Curb 77558 Sings His Big 10 Volume 2.

(S) (2:17) Special Music 2713 Remember Diana. *(rerecorded)*

(E) (2:23) Time-Life 2RNR-17 Rock 'N' Roll Era - 1957 Still Rockin'.

(E) (2:22) Original Sound 8883 21 Legendary Superstars.

1958 YOU ARE MY DESTINY

(M) (2:44) Rhino 71489 30th Anniversary Collection.

(M) (2:45) Curb 77467 Five Decades Greatest Hits.

(S) (2:26) RCA 3808 21 Golden Hits. *(rerecorded)*

(M) (2:45) Curb 77557 Sings His Big 10 Volume 1.

(S) (2:25) Special Music 2713 Remember Diana. *(rerecorded)*

PAUL ANKA *(Continued)*

(M) (2:44) Time-Life 2RNR-28 Rock 'N' Roll Era - The 50's Rave On.

1958 CRAZY LOVE
(S) (2:26) Rhino 71489 30th Anniversary Collection.
(S) (2:25) RCA 3808 21 Golden Hits. *(rerecorded)*
(M) (2:24) Curb 77557 Sings His Big 10 Volume 1.

1958 LET THE BELLS KEEP RINGING
(M) (1:57) Rhino 71489 30th Anniversary Collection.
(M) (1:59) Rhino 70588 Rockin' & Rollin' Wedding Songs Volume 1.
(M) (2:02) Curb 77557 Sings His Big 10 Volume 1.

released as by PAUL ANKA-GEORGE HAMILTON IV-JOHNNY NASH:

1959 THE TEEN COMMANDMENTS
(M) (1:41) Rhino 71489 Paul Anka - 30th Anniversary Collection.

released as by PAUL ANKA:

1959 (ALL OF A SUDDEN) MY HEART SINGS
(S) (3:01) Rhino 71489 30th Anniversary Collection.
(M) (3:01) Curb 77467 Five Decades Greatest Hits.
(S) (3:01) Curb 77558 Sings His Big 10 Volume 2.

1959 I MISS YOU SO
(M) (2:20) Curb 77558 Sings His Big 10 Volume 2.

1959 LONELY BOY
(M) (2:34) Rhino 71489 30th Anniversary Collection.
(E) (2:32) Rhino 70620 Billboard's Top Rock & Roll Hits Of 1959.
(E) (2:32) Rhino 72004 Billboard's Top Rock & Roll Hits 1957-1961 Box Set.
(E) (2:31) Original Sound 8862 Oldies But Goodies Vol. 12. *(this compact disc uses the "Waring - fds" noise reduction process)*
(E) (2:31) Original Sound 2223 Oldies But Goodies Volumes 2,7,9,12 and 13 Box Set. *(this box set uses the "Waring - fds" noise reduction process)*
(E) (2:31) Original Sound 2500 Oldies But Goodies Volumes 1-15 Box Set. *(this box set uses the "Waring - fds" noise reduction process)*
(M) (2:32) Curb 77467 Five Decades Greatest Hits.
(S) (2:22) RCA 3808 21 Golden Hits. *(rerecorded)*
(M) (2:32) Curb 77558 Sings His Big 10 Volume 2.
(M) (2:32) Curb 77637 All Time Greatest Hits Of Rock 'N' Roll Volume 3.
(M) (2:29) Time-Life 2RNR-20 Rock 'N' Roll Era - 1959 Still Rockin'.

1959 PUT YOUR HEAD ON MY SHOULDER
(S) (2:37) Rhino 71489 30th Anniversary Collection.
(S) (2:36) Curb 77467 Five Decades Greatest Hits.
(E) (2:37) Original Sound 8850 Oldies But Goodies Vol. 1. *(this compact disc uses the "Waring - fds" noise reduction process)*
(E) (2:37) Original Sound 2221 Oldies But Goodies Volumes 1,4,6,8 and 10 Box Set. *(this box set uses the "Waring - fds" noise reduction process)*
(E) (2:37) Original Sound 2500 Oldies But Goodies Volumes 1-15 Box Set. *(this box set uses the "Waring - fds" noise reduction process)*
(S) (2:33) RCA 3808 21 Golden Hits. *(rerecorded)*
(E) (2:37) Curb 77557 Sings His Big 10 Volume 1.
(S) (2:32) Special Music 2713 Remember Diana. *(rerecorded)*
(S) (2:36) Time-Life 2RNR-27 Rock 'N' Roll Era - Teen Idols.
(S) (2:36) JCI 3183 1955 - Only Love - 1959.

1960 IT'S TIME TO CRY
(M) (2:24) Rhino 71489 30th Anniversary Collection.
(E) (2:22) Curb 77467 Five Decades Greatest Hits.
(S) (2:28) RCA 3808 21 Golden Hits. *(rerecorded)*
(E) (2:22) Curb 77557 Sings His Big 10 Volume 1.

1960 PUPPY LOVE
(S) (2:39) Rhino 71489 30th Anniversary Collection.
(M) (2:39) Curb 77467 Five Decades Greatest Hits.
(M) (2:37) Original Sound 8858 Oldies But Goodies Vol. 8. *(this compact disc uses the "Waring - fds" noise reduction process)*

(M) (2:37) Original Sound 2221 Oldies But Goodies Volumes 1,4,6,8 and 10 Box Set. *(this box set uses the "Waring - fds" noise reduction process)*
(M) (2:37) Original Sound 2500 Oldies But Goodies Volumes 1-15 Box Set. *(this box set uses the "Waring - fds" noise reduction process)*
(S) (2:43) RCA 3808 21 Golden Hits. *(rerecorded)*
(M) (2:39) Curb 77558 Sings His Big 10 Volume 2.
(S) (2:43) Special Music 2713 Remember Diana. *(rerecorded)*
(S) (2:39) Time-Life 2RNR-27 Rock 'N' Roll Era - Teen Idols.
(S) (2:39) Time-Life SUD-19 Superhits - Early 60's Classics.
(S) (2:39) Time-Life AM1-20 AM Gold - Early '60s Classics.
(S) (2:43) Walt Disney 60870 Dog Songs.

1960 MY HOME TOWN
(S) (2:28) Rhino 71489 30th Anniversary Collection.
(S) (2:04) RCA 3808 21 Golden Hits. *(rerecorded)*
(S) (2:27) Curb 77558 Sings His Big 10 Volume 2.
(S) (2:24) Time-Life 2RNR-40 Rock 'N' Roll Era - The 60's Teen Time.

1960 HELLO YOUNG LOVERS
1960 SUMMER'S GONE
(S) (2:41) Rhino 71489 30th Anniversary Collection.
(S) (2:22) RCA 3808 21 Golden Hits. *(rerecorded)*
(S) (2:41) Curb 77558 Sings His Big 10 Volume 2.

1961 THE STORY OF MY LOVE
1961 TONIGHT MY LOVE, TONIGHT
(S) (2:06) Rhino 71489 30th Anniversary Collection.
(S) (2:04) RCA 3808 21 Golden Hits. *(rerecorded)*

1961 DANCE ON LITTLE GIRL
(S) (2:17) Rhino 71489 30th Anniversary Collection.
(S) (1:50) RCA 3808 21 Golden Hits. *(rerecorded)*
(S) (2:17) Curb 77558 Sings His Big 10 Volume 2.

1961 KISSIN' ON THE PHONE
1962 LOVE ME WARM AND TENDER
(S) (2:16) Rhino 71489 30th Anniversary Collection.
(S) (2:17) RCA 8474 Nipper's Greatest Hits Of The 60's Volume 1.
(E) (2:13) Special Music 2713 Remember Diana.
(S) (2:16) Time-Life SUD-06 Superhits - 1962.
(S) (2:16) Time-Life AM1-18 AM Gold - 1962.

1962 A STEEL GUITAR AND A GLASS OF WINE
(S) (2:09) RCA 8475 Nipper's Greatest Hits Of The 60's Volume 2.
(S) (3:10) Curb 77566 Classic Hits. *(rerecording)*
(E) (2:09) Special Music 2713 Remember Diana.

1962 ESO BESO (THAT KISS!)
(S) (2:24) Rhino 71489 30th Anniversary Collection. *(:10 longer introduction than the 45 or LP)*
(E) (2:11) Special Music 2713 Remember Diana.

1963 LOVE (MAKES THE WORLD GO 'ROUND)
(S) (2:24) Special Music 2713 Remember Diana.

1963 REMEMBER DIANA
(E) (1:55) Special Music 2713 Remember Diana. *(truncated fade)*

1969 GOODNIGHT MY LOVE
(S) (3:13) Rhino 71489 30th Anniversary Collection.

1974 (YOU'RE) HAVING MY BABY
(S) (2:30) Curb 77467 Five Decades Greatest Hits.
(S) (2:34) EMI 46739 His Best.
(S) (2:31) Rhino 71489 30th Anniversary Collection.
(S) (2:33) Curb 77566 Classic Hits.
(S) (2:32) Razor & Tie 21640 Those Fabulous 70's.
(S) (2:29) EMI 36993 Best Of The United Artists Years.
(S) (2:32) K-Tel 3627 Out Of Sight.
(S) (2:32) K-Tel 3630 Lounge Legends.
(S) (2:31) Rhino 72516 Behind Closed Doors - '70s Swingers.
(S) (2:31) Rhino 75233 '70s Party (Killers) Classics.

released as by PAUL ANKA with ODIA COATES:

1975 ONE MAN WOMAN/ONE WOMAN MAN
(S) (3:03) EMI 46739 His Best.
(S) (3:01) Rhino 71489 30th Anniversary Collection.
(S) (3:03) Curb 77566 Classic Hits.
(S) (3:00) EMI 36993 Best Of The United Artists Years.

released as by PAUL ANKA:
1975 **I DON'T LIKE TO SLEEP ALONE**
    (S) (3:15) EMI 46739 His Best.
    (S) (3:15) Rhino 71489 30th Anniversary Collection.
    (S) (3:15) Curb 77566 Classic Hits.
    (S) (3:14) EMI 36993 Best Of The United Artists Years.

released as by PAUL ANKA with ODIA COATES:
1975 **(I BELIEVE) THERE'S NOTHING STRONGER THAN OUR LOVE**
    (S) (2:50) EMI 46739 His Best.
    (S) (2:58) Rhino 71489 30th Anniversary Collection.
    (S) (2:49) Curb 77566 Classic Hits.
    (S) (2:48) EMI 36993 Best Of The United Artists Years.

released as by PAUL ANKA:
1976 **TIMES OF YOUR LIFE**
    (S) (3:13) Curb 77467 Five Decades Greatest Hits.
    (S) (3:14) EMI 46739 His Best.
    (S) (3:14) Rhino 71489 30th Anniversary Collection.
    (S) (3:11) Curb 77566 Classic Hits.
    (S) (3:09) EMI 36993 Best Of The United Artists Years.

1976 **ANYTIME (I'LL BE THERE)**
    (S) (3:16) Curb 77566 Classic Hits.
    (S) (3:14) EMI 36993 Best Of The United Artists Years.

1978 **THIS IS LOVE**
    (S) (3:42) RCA 66203 In The 70s.

1983 **HOLD ME 'TIL THE MORNIN' COMES**
    (S) (4:37) Curb 77467 Five Decades Greatest Hits.

ANNETTE (Annette Funnicello)
1959 **TALL PAUL**
    (M) (1:51) Walt Disney 60010 A Musical Reunion With America's Girl Next Door. *(includes :18 of studio talk and countoff)*
    (M) (1:33) DCC Compact Classics 077 Too Cute!
    (M) (1:32) Nick At Nite/550 Music/Epic 67689 Stand By Your Man.

1960 **FIRST NAME INITIAL**
    (M) (2:19) Walt Disney 60010 A Musical Reunion With America's Girl Next Door.

1960 **O DIO MIO**
    (M) (2:48) Walt Disney 60010 A Musical Reunion With America's Girl Next Door. *(Italian version)*

1960 **TRAIN OF LOVE**
    (M) (2:41) Walt Disney 60010 A Musical Reunion With America's Girl Next Door.

1960 **PINEAPPLE PRINCESS**
    (S) (2:28) Walt Disney 60010 A Musical Reunion With America's Girl Next Door. *(includes :04 of studio talk)*

ANN-MARGRET
1961 **I JUST DON'T UNDERSTAND**
    (S) (2:35) RCA 8474 Nipper's Greatest Hits Of The 60's Volume 1.
    (S) (2:36) RCA 66882 Let Me Entertain You.
    (S) (2:35) Time-Life R857-17 The Heart Of Rock 'n' Roll: The Early '60s.

ANOTHER BAD CREATION
1991 **IESHA**
    (S) (4:21) Motown 6318 Coolin' At The Playground Ya' Know!
    (S) (4:19) Rhino 71916 Whats Up? Rap Hits Of The 90's.
    (S) (4:19) Motown 6358 Hitsville USA Volume Two.

1991 **PLAYGROUND**
    (S) (5:16) Motown 3746366352 East Coast Family Volume One. *(remixed)*
    (S) (4:46) Tommy Boy 1053 MTV Party To Go Volume 2. *(remix; all tracks on this cd are segued together)*
    (S) (4:09) Motown 6318 Coolin' At The Playground Ya' Know!
    (S) (4:16) Rhino 75217 Heartthrob Hits.

ADAM ANT
1983 **GOODY TWO SHOES**
    (S) (3:28) CBS Special Products 44363 Rock Of The 80's.

    (S) (3:28) Priority 53721 Rock Of The 80's Volume 5.
    (S) (3:28) Risky Business 57468 This Ain't No Disco/New Wave Dance Hits.
    (S) (3:26) Risky Business 57833 Read The Hits/Best Of The 80's.
    (S) (3:28) Epic 38370 Friend Or Foe.
    (S) (3:29) Rhino 72133 Frat Rock: The 80's.
    (S) (3:28) Epic 67534 Club Epic Volume 5.
    (S) (3:28) Hip-O 40023 Smash Alternatives - 14 Classic New Wave Hits.
    (S) (3:28) Time-Life R988-16 Sounds Of The Eighties: The Early '80s.
    (S) (3:29) Epic/Legacy 65254 Fizz Pop Modern Rock Volume 1.
    (S) (3:28) Epic/Legacy 65443 Super Hits.

1990 **ROOM AT THE TOP**
    (S) (4:41) MCA 6315 Manners & Physique. *(LP version)*
    (S) (4:09) Hip-O 40023 Smash Alternatives - 14 Classic New Wave Hits. *(45 version)*

1995 **WONDERFUL**
    (S) (4:21) Capitol 30335 Wonderful.

RAY ANTHONY
1959 **PETER GUNN**
    (S) (1:51) Curb 77403 All-Time Great Instrumental Hits Volume 1. *(rerecorded)*
    (S) (1:51) Curb 77402 All-Time Great Instrumental Hits Volume 2. *(rerecorded)*
    (M) (1:48) Capitol 94079 Capitol Collector's Series.
    (M) (1:49) Capitol 98670 Memories Are Made Of This.
    (M) (1:48) K-Tel 3472 Those Wonderful Instrumentals Volume 2.
    (S) (1:51) Capitol 38376 Ultra Lounge Sampler. *(rerecorded)*

APOLLO 100
1972 **JOY**
(actual 45 time is (2:45) not (3:10) as stated on the record label)
    (S) (2:44) Rhino 70927 Super Hits Of The 70's Volume 7.
    (S) (2:44) Rhino 71603 Rock Instrumental Classics Volume 3: The Seventies.
    (S) (2:44) Rhino 72035 Rock Instrumental Classics Vols. 1-5 Box Set.
    (S) (2:43) Time-Life R840-04 Sounds Of The Seventies: A Loss For Words.
    (S) (2:43) K-Tel 3913 Superstars Greatest Hits Volume 2.
    (S) (2:43) Capitol 93076 More Music From O.S.T. Boogie Nights.

FIONA APPLE
1997 **CRIMINAL**
    (S) (5:41) Clean Slate/Work 67439 Tidal.
    (S) (5:41) MCA 11752 1998 Grammy Nominees.

APPLEJACKS
1958 **MEXICAN HAT ROCK**
1959 **ROCKA-CONGA**

APRIL WINE
1972 **YOU COULD HAVE BEEN A LADY**
    (S) (3:20) Varese Sarabande 5706 Dick Bartley Presents Collector's Essentials: The 70's. *(LP version)*

1979 **ROLLER**
(dj copies of this 45 ran (3:34); commercial copies were all (4:16))
    (S) (4:16) JCI 4520 Masters Of Metal: Wrecking Havoc 1975-1985 Volume 1.
    (S) (4:16) Priority 7963 First Degree Metal.
    (S) (4:16) Capitol 48416 First Glance.
    (S) (4:16) Time-Life R968-17 Guitar Rock - The Late '70s: Take Two.

1981 **JUST BETWEEN YOU AND ME**
    (S) (3:55) Capitol 46067 The Nature Of The Beast.
    (S) (3:53) Priority 7965 Heavy Metal Love.

APRIL WINE (Continued)

- (S) (3:53) Rhino 71894 Radio Daze: Pop Hits Of The 80's Volume Five.
- (S) (3:53) Madacy Entertainment 1981 Rock On 1981.
- (S) (3:54) Time-Life R988-18 Sounds Of The Eighties: The Early '80s Take Two.
- (S) (3:53) Simitar 55582 The Number One's: Rock It Up.
- (S) (3:53) JCI 3193 18 Rock Classics Volume 3.
- (S) (3:54) Time-Life R834-18 Body Talk - Romantic Moments.

AQUA
1997 BARBIE GIRL
- (S) (3:14) MCA 11705 Aquarium.
1998 LOLLIPOP (CANDYMAN)
- (S) (3:34) MCA 11705 Aquarium.

AQUATONES
1958 YOU
- (M) (1:56) Relic 7051 Sing For "You".
- (M) (1:56) Time-Life R857-11 The Heart Of Rock 'n' Roll 1958-1959.

ARBORS
1969 THE LETTER
- (S) (3:30) Columbia/Legacy 46763 Rock Artifacts Volume 2. (the last :45 of this song are (M))

ARCADIA
1985 ELECTION DAY
- (S) (4:29) EMI 27674 Living In Oblivion: The 80's Greatest Hits Volume Three. (45 version)
- (S) (4:28) Priority 53715 80's Greatest Rock Hits Volume 3 - Arena Rock. (45 version)
- (S) (5:26) Right Stuff 27754 Sedated In The Eighties. (LP version)
- (S) (5:26) Sandstone 33045 and 5011 Rock The First Volume Five. (LP version)
- (S) (5:26) Capitol 96358 So Red The Rose. (LP version)
- (S) (4:30) Rhino 71978 New Wave Hits Of The 80's Vol. 15. (45 version)
1986 GOODBYE IS FOREVER
- (S) (3:44) Capitol 96358 So Red The Rose.

TASMIN ARCHER
1993 SLEEPING SATELLITE
- (S) (3:19) EMI 32393 Loaded Volume 1. (acoustic version)
- (S) (4:39) SBK 80134 Great Expectations.
- (S) (4:35) SBK 31181 Moments In Love.

ARCHIES
1968 BANG-SHANG-A-LANG
1969 SUGAR SUGAR
- (S) (2:45) Rhino 70630 Billboard's Top Rock & Roll Hits Of 1969.
- (S) (2:45) Rhino 72005 Billboard's Top Rock & Roll Hits 1968-1972 Box Set.
- (S) (2:45) Time-Life 2CLR-12 Classic Rock - 1969: The Beat Goes On.
- (S) (2:46) Collectables 2510 WCBS-FM History Of Rock - The Rockin' 60's.
- (S) (2:46) Collectables 4510 History Of Rock/The Rockin' 60s.
- (S) (2:46) Collectables 2501 WCBS-FM History Of Rock - The 60's Part 2.
- (S) (2:46) Collectables 4501 History Of Rock/The 60s Part Two.
- (S) (2:46) LaserLight 12318 Chart Busters.
- (S) (2:46) Ripete 2187-RE Preppy Deluxe.
- (S) (2:44) Varese Sarabande 5719 Bubblegum Classics Volume Three.
- (S) (2:44) Columbia 67380 O.S.T. Now And Then.
- (S) (2:44) Play-Tone/Epic 69179 Music From The HBO Miniseries "From The Earth To The Moon". (hum noticeable on the ending of every song on this cd)

1970 JINGLE JANGLE
1970 WHO'S YOUR BABY?

JANN ARDEN
1996 INSENSITIVE
- (S) (4:15) A&M 314540248 and 314540336 Living Under June.
- (S) (4:14) Mercury 314535671 Women For Women 2.

TONI ARDEN
1958 PADRE
- (S) (3:01) Time-Life HPD-23 Your Hit Parade - The Late 50's.
- (S) (3:01) Varese Sarabande 5783 The '50s Remembered: Arden, Kallen, Morgan & Syms.

TINA ARENA
1996 CHAINS
- (S) (4:21) Epic 67533 Don't Ask.

ARGENT
1972 HOLD YOUR HEAD UP
(dj copies of this 45 ran (2:52); commercial copies were all (3:15))
- (S) (3:31) Rhino 70928 Super Hits Of The 70's Volume 8. (neither the LP or 45 version)
- (S) (3:16) JCI 3301 Rockin' Seventies. (45 version)
- (S) (2:53) Epic 46490 O.S.T. Queens Logic. (this is a fade of the LP version apparently intended to be a replica of the dj 45 but it is not)
- (S) (3:14) Priority 7942 Hard Rockin' 70's. (45 version)
- (S) (6:15) Columbia/Legacy 46160 Rock Artifacts Volume 1. (LP version)
- (S) (6:15) Epic 33955 Greatest Hits. (LP version)
- (S) (3:15) Razor & Tie 22502 Those Rocking 70's. (45 version)
- (S) (3:16) Time-Life R968-05 Guitar Rock 1972-1973. (45 version)
- (S) (3:35) Time-Life SOD-03 Sounds Of The Seventies - 1972. (45 version but :20 longer)
- (S) (6:15) Varese Sarabande 5503 and 5504 and 5505 and 5506 and 5507 and 5508 and 5509 and 5513 and 5571 Arrow: All Rock & Roll Oldies Volume One. (LP version)
- (S) (3:16) Risky Business 66871 Polyester Dreams/Greatest Hits Of The 70's. (45 version)
- (S) (6:15) Epic/Legacy 65020 Ultimate Rock 'n' Roll Collection. (LP version)
- (S) (3:16) JCI 3168 #1 Radio Hits 1970 - Only Rock 'n Roll - 1974. (45 version)
- (S) (6:15) Eclipse Music Group 64893 Rock 'n Roll Relix 1972-1973. (LP version)
- (S) (6:15) Eclipse Music Group 64897 Rock 'n Roll Relix 1970-1979. (LP version)
- (S) (6:15) Koch 7941 All Together Now. (LP version)
- (S) (3:16) Madacy Entertainment 6805 The Power Of Rock. (45 version)
- (S) (3:16) Hip-O 40095 '70s Hit(s) Back. (45 version)

RUSSELL ARMS
1957 CINCO ROBLES (FIVE OAKS)
- (M) (2:13) Curb 77775 Hard To Find Original Recordings - Classic Hits. (glitch at 1:05; mastered from vinyl)

LOUIS ARMSTRONG
1964 HELLO DOLLY
- (S) (2:23) MCA 5938 Vintage Music Volumes 15 & 16.
- (S) (2:23) MCA 31213 Vintage Music Volume 16.
- (S) (2:23) Curb 77339 Greatest Hits.
- (S) (2:24) MCA 538 Hello Dolly!
- (S) (2:24) Time-Life HPD-33 Your Hit Parade - The Early 60's.
- (S) (2:24) MCA 11032 All Time Greatest Hits.
- (S) (2:23) MCA 11120 Stardust/The Classic Decca Hits & Standards Collection.
- (S) (2:23) Rhino 71585 Billboard Top Pop Hits, 1964.

(S) (2:23) MCA Special Products 22173 Vintage Collectibles Volume 11.
(S) (2:24) Time-Life R135-04 Broadway Hit Parade.
(S) (2:24) JCI 7022 Those Wonderful Years - It Must Be Him.
(S) (2:23) MCA Special Products 21046 Top Singles Of The Sixties.

released as by LOUIS ARMSTRONG and THE ALL STARS:
1964 I STILL GET JEALOUS
(S) (2:10) MCA 538 Hello Dolly!
(S) (2:10) Curb 77339 Greatest Hits.
(S) (2:10) MCA 11032 All Time Greatest Hits.

released as by LOUIS ARMSTRONG:
1988 WHAT A WONDERFUL WORLD
(S) (2:15) MCA 6330 Soundtrack Smashes - The 80's.
(S) (2:15) A&M 3913 and 3340 O.S.T. Good Morning Vietnam.
(S) (2:16) Curb 77339 Greatest Hits.
(S) (2:16) MCA 11032 All Time Greatest Hits.
(S) (2:16) MCA 25204 and 11168 What A Wonderful World.
(S) (2:16) K-Tel 3471 High Hopes - Songs To Lift Your Spirits.
(S) (2:15) MCA 11392 O.S.T. 12 Monkeys.
(S) (2:16) Decca Jazz/GRP 656 What A Wonderful World.
(S) (2:15) MCA Special Products 20765 Best Of Dixieland.
(S) (2:16) MCA Special Products 20958 Mellow Classics.
(S) (3:18) Bluebird/RCA 66072 Jazz Masters/The Vocalists. *(rerecording; time includes a 1:10 introduction)*
(S) (2:16) Time-Life R988-31 Sounds Of The Eighties: Cinemax Movie Hits Of The '80s.
(S) (2:17) MCA 11168 What A Wonderful World. *(gold disc)*
(S) (2:16) Time-Life R814-01 Love Songs.

EDDY ARNOLD
1966 MAKE THE WORLD GO AWAY
(S) (2:38) RCA 3675 Best Of.
(S) (2:37) RCA 8474 Nipper's Greatest Hits Of The 60's Volume 1.
(S) (2:36) Curb 77416 Best Of.
(S) (2:38) RCA 58398 Pure Gold.
(S) (2:38) RCA 66046 Then & Now.
(S) (2:36) Time-Life CTD-10 Country USA - 1965. *(timing index is off by :01 on all tracks of this cd)*
(S) (2:37) Time-Life R138/05 Look Of Love.
(S) (2:37) K-Tel 3109 Country Music Classics Volume XVII.
(S) (2:38) RCA 66854 Essential.
(S) (2:37) JCI 7022 Those Wonderful Years - It Must Be Him.
(S) (2:38) RCA 66948 The Essential Series Sampler Volume II.
(S) (2:37) K-Tel 3355 101 Greatest Country Hits Vol. One: Forever Country.
(S) (2:37) Time-Life R990-16 Eddy Arnold - Legendary Country Singers.
(S) (2:30) Mercury 314558083 The Hits. *(rerecording)*
(S) (2:37) Time-Life R814-02 Love Songs.
(S) (2:37) Time-Life R808-02 Classic Country 1965-1969.

1966 I WANT TO GO WITH YOU
(S) (2:35) RCA 3675 Best Of.
(S) (2:39) RCA 66046 Then & Now.
(S) (2:39) RCA 66854 Essential.
(S) (2:28) Mercury 314558083 The Hits. *(rerecording)*

1966 THE LAST WORD IN LONESOME IS ME
(S) (2:12) RCA 3675 Best Of.
(S) (2:11) Time-Life CTD-21 Country USA - 1966.
(S) (2:11) Time-Life R990-16 Eddy Arnold - Legendary Country Singers.

1966 THE TIP OF MY FINGERS
(S) (2:57) RCA 66046 Then & Now.
(S) (2:57) RCA 66854 Essential.

ARRESTED DEVELOPMENT
1992 TENNESSEE
(S) (4:32) Foundation/RCA 66563 Number 1 Hit Mix.

(S) (4:32) Chrysalis 21929 3 Years, 5 Months & 2 Days In The Life Of.
(S) (4:19) Priority 50934 Shut Up And Dance! The 90's Volume One. *(all selections on this cd are segued together)*
(S) (4:32) K-Tel 3847 90s Now Volume 1.

1992 PEOPLE EVERYDAY
(S) (3:26) Chrysalis 21929 3 Years, 5 Months & 2 Days In The Life Of.
(S) (3:27) JCI 3132 1990 - Only Rock 'n Roll - 1994.
(S) (3:20) Priority 50935 100% Party Hits Of The 90's Volume Two. *(all selections on this cd are segued together)*

1993 MR. WENDALL
(S) (4:06) Chrysalis 21929 3 Years, 5 Months & 2 Days In The Life Of.

ARTISTS UNITED AGAINST APARTHEID
1985 SUN CITY
(S) (7:09) Razor & Tie 2007 Sun City. *(LP version)*

ART OF NOISE
released as by THE ART OF NOISE with MAX HEADROOM:
1986 PARANOIMIA
(S) (6:40) China/Polydor 835806 In Visible Silence. *(LP version)*
(S) (6:40) China/Polydor 837367 Best Of. *(LP version)*
(S) (3:17) Discovery 74108 Best Of. *(45 version)*

released as by THE ART OF NOISE featuring TOM JONES:
1988 KISS
(S) (3:29) Priority 53721 Rock Of The 80's Volume 5.
(S) (8:09) China/Polydor 837367 Art Of Noise - Best Of. *(remixed)*
(S) (3:29) Discovery 74108 Art Of Noise - Best Of.

ASHFORD & SIMPSON
1979 FOUND A CURE
(S) (7:02) Capitol 80515 Capitol Gold: The Best Of. *(LP version)*
(S) (3:41) Time-Life SOD-19 Sounds Of The Seventies - 1979: Take Two. *(45 version)*
(S) (7:01) Rhino 71971 Video Soul - Best Soul Of The 80's Vol. 1. *(LP version)*
(S) (3:43) Rhino 72123 Disco Years, Vol. 7. *(45 version)*
(S) (3:43) Rhino 72130 Soul Hits Of The 70's Vol. 20. *(45 version)*
(S) (7:00) Warner Brothers 3357 Stay Free. *(LP version)*
(S) (3:43) Time-Life R838-15 Solid Gold Soul 1979. *(45 version)*
(S) (3:42) Simitar 55542 The Number One's: Soul On Fire. *(45 version)*

1985 SOLID
(S) (5:06) Capitol 80515 Capitol Gold: The Best Of. *(LP version)*
(S) (5:07) Capitol 46466 Solid Plus Seven. *(LP version)*
(S) (5:06) Rebound 314520357 World Of Dance - The 80's. *(LP version)*
(S) (3:43) Rhino 72139 Billboard Hot R&B Hits 1984. *(45 version)*
(S) (5:06) Madacy Entertainment 1984 Rock On 1984. *(LP version)*
(S) (5:07) K-Tel 3673 The 80's - Funky Love. *(LP version)*
(S) (3:44) Hip-O 40031 The Glory Of Love - '80s Sweet & Soulful Love Songs. *(45 version)*
(S) (5:06) EMI 53908 The Gospel According To Ashford & Simpson: Count Your Blessings. *(LP version)*
(S) (5:06) Angel 56580 Men Are From Mars, Women Are From Venus - Songs For Loving Couples. *(LP version)*

ASHTON, GARDNER & DYKE
1971 RESURRECTION SHUFFLE
(S) (3:17) Time-Life SOD-33 Sounds Of The Seventies - AM Pop Classics II.

ASIA
1982 HEAT OF THE MOMENT
(dj copies of this 45 ran (3:25) and (3:50);
commercial copies were all (3:50))
- (S) (3:46) Priority 53768 Rock Of The 80's Volume 14.
- (S) (3:49) Time-Life R105-40 Rock Dreams.
- (S) (3:50) Geffen 24298 Then & Now.
- (S) (3:49) Geffen 2008 Asia.
- (S) (3:47) Time-Life R988-05 Sounds Of The Eighties: 1982.
- (S) (3:47) Time-Life R968-13 Guitar Rock - The Early '80s.
- (S) (3:47) Madacy Entertainment 1982 Rock On 1982.
- (S) (3:47) K-Tel 3742 The 80's: Hot Rock.
- (S) (3:50) Hip-O 40040 Power Chords Volume 3.
- (S) (3:50) Rhino 72595 Billboard Top Album Rock Hits, 1982.
- (S) (3:48) Geffen 25151 Geffen Vintage 80s Vol. II.
- (S) (3:47) Madacy Entertainment 6805 The Power Of Rock.
- (S) (3:47) Simitar 55752 Stud Rock - Heart Breakers.

1982 ONLY TIME WILL TELL
(dj copies of this 45 ran (3:23) and (4:05);
commercial copies were all (4:05))
- (S) (4:44) Geffen 24298 Then & Now. *(LP version)*
- (S) (4:44) Geffen 2008 Asia. *(LP version)*

1983 DON'T CRY
- (S) (3:35) JCI 3119 18 Rock Classics.
- (S) (3:36) Geffen 24298 Then & Now.
- (S) (3:32) Geffen 4008 Alpha.
- (S) (3:36) Time-Life R968-24 Guitar Rock - The '80s Take Two.
- (S) (3:34) Rhino 72596 Billboard Top Album Rock Hits, 1983.
- (S) (3:31) MCA Special Products 21028 The Best Of Hard Rock.

1983 THE SMILE HAS LEFT YOUR EYES
- (S) (3:12) Geffen 24298 Then & Now.
- (S) (3:12) Geffen 4008 Alpha.

ASSEMBLED MULTITUDE
1970 OVERTURE FROM TOMMY (A ROCK OPERA)
- (S) (2:28) Rhino 71196 Super Hits Of The 70's Vol. 16.
- (S) (2:28) Time-Life R840-04 Sounds Of The Seventies: A Loss For Words.

ASSOCIATION
1966 ALONG COMES MARY
- (S) (2:47) Rhino 70906 American Bandstand Greatest Hits Collection.
- (S) (2:48) Warner Brothers 1767 Greatest Hits.
- (S) (2:47) Pair 2701 Songs That Made Them Famous.
- (S) (2:47) JCI 3114 Easy Sixties.
- (S) (2:48) Time-Life 2CLR-07 Classic Rock - 1966: The Beat Goes On.
- (S) (2:47) Time-Life SUD-12 Superhits - The Mid 60's.
- (S) (2:47) Time-Life R962-04 History Of Rock 'N' Roll: California Pop 1963-1967.
- (S) (2:47) JCI 3160 18 Free & Easy Hits From The 60's.
- (S) (2:46) Time-Life AM1-05 AM Gold - The Mid '60s.

1966 CHERISH
- (S) (3:25) Warner Brothers 1767 Greatest Hits. *(LP version)*
- (S) (3:24) Pair 2701 Songs That Made Them Famous. *(LP version)*
- (S) (3:23) Time-Life SUD-01 Superhits - 1966. *(LP version)*
- (S) (3:21) Rhino 71936 Billboard Top Pop Hits, 1966. *(LP version)*
- (S) (3:23) JCI 3167 #1 Radio Hits 1965 - Only Rock 'n Roll - 1969. *(LP version)*
- (S) (3:23) Time-Life AM1-09 AM Gold - 1966. *(LP version)*
- (S) (3:24) Time-Life R857-20 The Heart Of Rock 'n' Roll 1965-1966. *(LP version)*
- (S) (3:23) Time-Life R814-03 Love Songs. *(LP version)*

1966 PANDORA'S GOLDEN HEEBIE JEEBIES
- (S) (2:48) Risky Business 53923 Guilty Pleasures.

1967 WINDY
- (S) (2:54) Warner Brothers 1767 Greatest Hits. *(truncated fade)*

- (S) (2:52) Rhino 70628 Billboard's Top Rock & Roll Hits Of 1967.
- (S) (2:53) Pair 2701 Songs That Made Them Famous.
- (M) (2:54) Rhino 71065 Summer Of Love Volume 1.
- (S) (2:51) Time-Life 2CLR-15 Classic Rock - 1967: Shakin' All Over.
- (S) (2:49) Time-Life SUD-05 Superhits - 1967.
- (S) (2:50) JCI 3126 1965 - Only Rock 'N Roll - 1969.
- (S) (2:54) Buddah 49506 Feelin' Groovy.
- (S) (2:49) Time-Life AM1-08 AM Gold - 1967.

1967 NEVER MY LOVE
- (S) (3:08) Warner Brothers 1767 Greatest Hits. *(LP version; truncated fade)*
- (S) (3:08) JCI 3104 Mellow Sixties. *(LP version; truncated fade)*
- (S) (3:07) Pair 2701 Songs That Made Them Famous. *(LP version; truncated fade)*
- (S) (3:07) Scotti Brothers 75405 There Is Still Love (The Anniversary Songs). *(LP version)*
- (S) (3:05) Time-Life SUD-14 Superhits - The Late 60's. *(LP version)*
- (M) (2:52) Rhino 71937 Billboard Top Pop Hits, 1967. *(45 version)*
- (S) (3:05) JCI 3185 1965 - Only Love - 1969. *(LP version)*
- (S) (3:05) Time-Life AM1-14 AM Gold - The Late '60s. *(LP version)*
- (S) (3:08) Polygram TV 314555610 The One And Only Love Album. *(LP version)*
- (S) (3:05) Time-Life R857-22 The Heart Of Rock 'n' Roll 1967-1969. *(LP version)*
- (S) (3:05) Time-Life R814-01 Love Songs. *(LP version)*

1968 EVERYTHING THAT TOUCHES YOU
- (S) (3:17) Warner Brothers 1767 Greatest Hits. *(truncated fade)*
- (S) (3:16) Time-Life SUD-18 Superhits - Late 60's Classics.
- (S) (3:16) Time-Life AM1-12 AM Gold - Late '60s Classics.

1968 TIME FOR LIVIN'
- (S) (2:44) Warner Brothers 1767 Greatest Hits. *(truncated fade)*

1968 SIX MAN BAND
- (S) (2:12) Warner Special Products 27607 Highs Of The 60's.
- (S) (2:12) Warner Brothers 1767 Greatest Hits.

RICK ASTLEY
1988 NEVER GONNA GIVE YOU UP
- (S) (3:31) RCA 6822 Whenever You Need Somebody.
- (S) (3:28) JCI 3186 1985 - Only Love - 1989.
- (S) (3:18) Priority 50941 Shut Up And Dance! Volume Two - The 80's. *(all songs on this cd are segued together)*
- (S) (3:31) Time-Life R988-19 Sounds Of The Eighties: The Late '80s.
- (S) (3:30) Rhino 75217 Heartthrob Hits.
- (S) (3:36) Cold Front 6330 Club Mix: The 80s. *(all selections on this cd are segued together)*

1988 TOGETHER FOREVER
- (S) (3:24) RCA 6822 Whenever You Need Somebody. *(LP version)*
- (S) (3:23) Time-Life R988-21 Sounds Of The Eighties: 1986-1989. *(LP version)*
- (S) (3:24) Time-Life R988-20 Sounds Of The Eighties: The Late '80s Take Two. *(LP version)*
- (S) (3:24) Hollywood 62123 More Music From The Motion Picture "Romy And Michele's High School Reunion". *(LP version)*

1988 IT WOULD TAKE A STRONG STRONG MAN
- (S) (3:38) RCA 6822 Whenever You Need Somebody.

1989 SHE WANTS TO DANCE WITH ME
- (S) (3:14) RCA 8589 Hold Me In Your Arms.

1989 GIVING UP ON LOVE
- (S) (4:01) RCA 8589 Hold Me In Your Arms.

1991 CRY FOR HELP
- (S) (4:49) RCA 3004 Free. *(LP version)*

1993 HOPELESSLY
- (S) (3:34) RCA 66295 Body & Soul.

ATLANTA RHYTHM SECTION
1974 DORAVILLE
- (S) (3:26) Polydor 849375 Best Of.

1977 SO INTO YOU
- (S) (4:20) Priority 8665 Southern Comfort/70's Greatest Rock Hits Volume 4. *(LP length)*
- (S) (4:21) Polydor 849375 Best Of. *(LP length)*
- (S) (3:12) Time-Life R968-03 Guitar Rock 1976-1977. *(45 length)*
- (S) (3:16) Time-Life SOD-05 Sounds Of The Seventies - 1977. *(45 length)*
- (S) (4:20) K-Tel 6045 Southern Fried Rock. *(LP length)*
- (S) (3:12) Time-Life R138-18 Body Talk. *(45 length)*
- (S) (4:20) Varese 5635 and 5654 and 5655 and 5657 Arrow: All Rock & Roll Oldies Volume Two. *(LP length)*
- (S) (4:20) Rebound 314520372 The Roots Of Rock: Soft Rock. *(LP length)*
- (S) (4:20) Varese Sarabande 5708 All Rock & Roll Hits Vol. One. *(LP length)*
- (S) (4:19) K-Tel 3639 Dim The Lights - Soft Rock Hits Of The 70's. *(LP length)*
- (S) (4:20) Polygram Special Markets 314520382 Best Of. *(LP length)*
- (S) (4:20) Rebound 314520406 The Roots Of Rock: Southern Rock. *(LP length)*
- (S) (3:15) Time-Life AM1-24 AM Gold - 1977. *(45 length)*
- (S) (4:20) Time-Life R834-08 Body Talk - On My Mind. *(LP length)*
- (S) (4:20) K-Tel 3972 Southern Rockin' Rebels: The South's Gone And Done It. *(LP length)*
- (S) (4:20) Critique 15467 Fast Cars And Southern Stars. *(LP length)*
- (S) (4:20) Rebound 314520475 The Roots Of Rock: Southern Rock. *(LP length)*

1978 IMAGINARY LOVER
- (S) (5:05) Priority 8668 Rough And Rowdy/70's Greatest Rock Hits Volume 7. *(truncated fade; LP length)*
- (S) (5:03) Polydor 849375 Best Of. *(LP length)*
- (S) (4:06) Time-Life SOD-20 Sounds Of The Seventies - 1978: Take Two. *(45 length)*
- (S) (5:03) K-Tel 6083 Southern Fried Rock - Second Helping. *(LP length)*
- (S) (4:06) Time-Life R834-15 Body Talk - Once In Lifetime. *(45 length)*
- (S) (5:05) Rebound 314520492 Class Reunion '78. *(LP length)*

1978 I'M NOT GONNA LET IT BOTHER ME TONIGHT
- (S) (4:05) Polydor 849375 Best Of. *(LP version)*
- (S) (4:05) Polygram Special Markets 314520382 Best Of. *(LP version)*

1979 DO IT OR DIE
- (S) (3:23) Polydor 849375 Best Of.
- (S) (3:23) K-Tel 3906 Starflight Vol. 1.

1979 SPOOKY
- (S) (4:57) Polydor 849375 Best Of. *(LP version)*
- (S) (4:56) Special Music/Essex 5036 Prom Night - The 70's. *(LP version)*
- (S) (4:56) K-Tel 3510 Platinum Rock Volume 2. *(LP version)*

1981 ALIEN
- (S) (4:52) Columbia 37550 Quinella. *(LP version)*
- (S) (3:29) Nick At Nite/550 Music 63437 Nick At Nite Goes To Outer Space. *(45 version)*

ATLANTIC STARR
1982 CIRCLES
- (S) (4:51) A&M 2508 Classics Volume 10. *(LP version)*
- (S) (4:52) A&M 3320 Secret Lovers....Best Of. *(LP version)*
- (S) (4:02) Rhino 72137 Billboard Hot R&B Hits 1982. *(45 version)*
- (S) (4:51) Rebound 314520431 Soul Classics - Best Of The 80's. *(LP version)*
- (S) (4:02) JCI 3176 1980 - Only Soul - 1984. *(45 version)*

1986 SECRET LOVERS
- (S) (5:28) A&M 3320 Secret Lovers....Best Of. *(LP version)*
- (S) (5:28) A&M 2508 Classics Volume 10. *(LP version)*
- (S) (5:31) A&M 5019 As The Band Turns. *(LP version)*
- (S) (4:03) Time-Life R988-15 Sounds Of The Eighties: The Mid 80's. *(45 version)*
- (S) (4:03) Time-Life R834-07 Body Talk - Hearts In Motion. *(45 version)*

1987 ALWAYS
- (S) (3:59) JCI 2701 Slow Grooves. *(45 version)*
- (S) (4:46) Warner Brothers 25560 All In The Name Of Love. *(LP version)*
- (S) (3:59) Time-Life R988-20 Sounds Of The Eighties: The Late '80s Take Two. *(45 version)*
- (S) (3:59) Time-Life R834-05 Body Talk - Sealed With A Kiss. *(45 version)*
- (S) (4:46) K-Tel 6257 The Greatest Love Songs - 16 Soft Rock Hits. *(LP version)*

1992 MASTERPIECE
- (S) (4:17) JCI 3124 Rhythm Of The Night. *(45 length)*
- (S) (4:53) Reprise 26545 Love Crazy. *(LP length)*

PATTI AUSTIN with JAMES INGRAM
1983 BABY, COME TO ME
- (S) (3:35) Original Sound 8909 Best Love Songs Vol. 4.
- (S) (3:35) Original Sound 9322 Best Love Songs Vol. 3 & 4.
- (S) (3:35) Original Sound 1236 Best Love Songs Box Set.
- (S) (3:35) Scotti Brothers 75434 Romantic Duets.
- (S) (3:35) Qwest 3591 Patti Austin - Every Home Should Have One.
- (S) (3:35) K-Tel 3263 The 80's Love Jams.
- (S) (3:34) Rhino 71972 Video Soul - Best Soul Of The 80's Vol. 2.
- (S) (3:35) Priority 53700 80's Greatest Rock Hits Volume 13 - Soft Sounds.
- (S) (3:34) Warner Brothers 26700 James Ingram - Greatest Hits.
- (S) (3:36) Time-Life R138-18 Body Talk.
- (S) (3:34) MCA 11431 Quiet Storms 2.
- (S) (3:34) JCI 3147 1980 - Only Love - 1984.
- (S) (3:32) Madacy Entertainment 6803 Power Of Love.
- (S) (3:33) Rhino 72580 Soul Serenade - Intimate R&B.
- (S) (3:35) Time-Life R988-18 Sounds Of The Eighties: The Early '80s Take Two.
- (S) (3:34) Time-Life R834-03 Body Talk - Moonlit Nights.

SIL AUSTIN
1956 SLOW WALK
- (M) (2:38) Mercury 832041 45's On CD Volume 1.
- (M) (2:38) Time-Life 2RNR-23 Rock 'N' Roll Era - 1956 Still Rockin'.
- (M) (2:37) Time-Life RHD-05 Rhythm & Blues - 1956.
- (M) (2:38) K-Tel 3059 Saxy Rock.
- (M) (2:37) Polygram Special Markets 314520273 Great Instrumental Hits.
- (M) (2:38) Time-Life R857-07 The Heart Of Rock 'n' Roll 1956.
- (E) (2:39) Polygram Special Markets 314520462 50's Soul.
- (M) (2:37) Time-Life R838-24 Solid Gold Soul 1956.

AUTOGRAPH
1985 TURN UP THE RADIO
(dj copies of this 45 ran (3:46) and (4:28);
commercial copies were all (4:28))
- (S) (4:34) RCA 5423 Sign In Please.
- (S) (4:35) RCA 66862 Hi Octane Hard Drivin' Hits.
- (S) (4:34) JCI 3144 18 Headbangers From The 80's.
- (S) (4:32) K-Tel 3883 The 80's: Glam Rock.
- (S) (4:32) Razor & Tie 89004 Monsters Of Rock.

FRANKIE AVALON
1958 DEDE DINAH
- (M) (2:10) LaserLight 12319 Frankie Avalon/Fabian/Ritchie Valens - Their Greatest Hits.
- (M) (2:10) Varese Sarabande 5594 Best Of.

19

FRANKIE AVALON (Continued)

    (M) (2:10) Curb 77757 Greatest Hits.
    (M) (2:10) JCI 3188 1955 - Only Dance - 1959.
    (M) (2:10) Taragon 1019 Chancellor Records Story, Volume 2.
    (M) (2:11) Music Club 50030 The Teen Idols: Very Best Of Frankie Avalon & Fabian.

1958 GINGER BREAD

    (M) (2:02) Varese Sarabande 5594 Best Of.
    (E) (2:02) K-Tel 3409 Funniest Food Songs.
    (M) (2:01) Curb 77757 Greatest Hits.
    (M) (2:03) Taragon 1018 Chancellor Records Story, Volume 1.
    (M) (2:01) Music Club 50030 The Teen Idols: Very Best Of Frankie Avalon & Fabian.

1958 I'LL WAIT FOR YOU

    (M) (2:52) Varese Sarabande 5594 Best Of.
    (M) (2:52) Curb 77757 Greatest Hits.
    (M) (2:52) Music Club 50030 The Teen Idols: Very Best Of Frankie Avalon & Fabian.

1959 VENUS

    (S) (2:19) Rhino 75893 Jukebox Classics Volume 1.
    (S) (2:18) Original Sound 8860 Oldies But Goodies Vol. 10. *(this compact disc uses the "Waring - fds" noise reduction process)*
    (S) (2:18) Original Sound 2221 Oldies But Goodies Volumes 1,4,6,8 and 10 Box Set. *(this box set uses the "Waring - fds" noise reduction process)*
    (S) (2:18) Original Sound 2500 Oldies But Goodies Volumes 1-15 Box Set. *(this box set uses the "Waring - fds" noise reduction process)*
    (S) (2:19) Rhino 70620 Billboard's Top Rock & Roll Hits Of 1959.
    (S) (2:19) Rhino 72004 Billboard's Top Rock & Roll Hits 1957-1961 Box Set.
    (S) (2:20) JCI 3203 Lovin' Fifties.
    (S) (2:18) Original Sound 8881 Twenty-One #1 Hits. *(this compact disc uses the "Waring - fds" noise reduction process; song slowly fades out rather than ending cold)*
    (S) (2:18) Garland 012 Remember When.
    (S) (2:20) MCA 6340 O.S.T. Born On The Fourth Of July.
    (S) (2:19) Collectables 5061 History Of Rock Volume 1.
    (S) (2:18) Collectables 2503 WCBS-FM History Of Rock - The 50's Part 2.
    (S) (2:18) Collectables 4503 History Of Rock/The 50s Part Two.
    (S) (2:19) Collectables 2603 WCBS-FM Jukebox Giants Vol. 1.
    (S) (2:19) Time-Life 2RNR-27 Rock 'N' Roll Era - Teen Idols.
    (S) (2:19) LaserLight 12319 Frankie Avalon/Fabian/Ritchie Valens - Their Greatest Hits.
    (S) (2:19) K-Tel 478 More 50's Jukebox Favorites.
    (S) (2:19) K-Tel 3007 50's Sock Hop.
    (S) (2:21) Varese Sarabande 5594 Best Of.
    (S) (2:19) K-Tel 3125 Solid Gold Rock N' Roll.
    (S) (2:20) Curb 77757 Greatest Hits.
    (S) (2:18) Collectables 2554 CBS-FM History Of Rock Volume 2.
    (S) (2:19) JCI 3183 1955 - Only Love - 1959.
    (S) (2:19) Music Club 50015 Love Me Forever - 18 Rock'N' Roll Love Songs.
    (S) (2:21) Priority 50950 I Love Rock & Roll Volume 1: Hits Of The 50's.
    (S) (2:19) Time-Life R857-11 The Heart Of Rock 'n' Roll 1958-1959.
    (S) (2:25) Taragon 1018 Chancellor Records Story, Volume 1. *(with countoff)*
    (S) (2:19) Priority 50974 Premiere The Movie Magazine Presents The Greatest Soundtrack Love Songs.
    (S) (2:20) Music Club 50030 The Teen Idols: Very Best Of Frankie Avalon & Fabian.

1959 BOBBY SOX TO STOCKINGS

    (S) (2:36) Collectables 5063 History Of Rock Volume 3. *(sounds like it was mastered from vinyl)*
    (S) (2:36) Time-Life 2RNR-47 Rock 'N' Roll Era - Teen Idols II. *(sounds like it was mastered from vinyl)*

    (S) (2:38) LaserLight 12319 Frankie Avalon/Fabian/Ritchie Valens - Their Greatest Hits.
    (S) (2:38) Varese Sarabande 5594 Best Of.
    (S) (2:37) Curb 77757 Greatest Hits.
    (S) (2:38) Taragon 1019 Chancellor Records Story, Volume 2.
    (S) (2:37) Music Club 50030 The Teen Idols: Very Best Of Frankie Avalon & Fabian.

1959 A BOY WITHOUT A GIRL

    (M) (1:57) Varese Sarabande 5594 Best Of.
    (M) (1:57) Curb 77757 Greatest Hits.
    (S) (1:57) Taragon 1019 Chancellor Records Story, Volume 2.
    (M) (1:57) Music Club 50030 The Teen Idols: Very Best Of Frankie Avalon & Fabian.

1959 JUST ASK YOUR HEART

    (E) (2:27) LaserLight 12323 American Dreams.
    (S) (2:27) Varese Sarabande 5594 Best Of.
    (S) (2:27) Curb 77757 Greatest Hits.
    (S) (2:24) Taragon 1019 Chancellor Records Story, Volume 1.
    (S) (2:26) Music Club 50030 The Teen Idols: Very Best Of Frankie Avalon & Fabian.

1960 WHY

    (S) (2:35) Time-Life 2RNR-27 Rock 'N' Roll Era - Teen Idols.
    (S) (2:36) LaserLight 12319 Frankie Avalon/Fabian/Ritchie Valens - Their Greatest Hits.
    (S) (2:35) Varese Sarabande 5594 Best Of.
    (S) (2:35) Curb 77757 Greatest Hits.
    (S) (2:36) Music Club 50015 Love Me Forever - 18 Rock'N' Roll Love Songs.
    (S) (2:35) Taragon 1019 Chancellor Records Story, Volume 2.
    (S) (2:35) Music Club 50030 The Teen Idols: Very Best Of Frankie Avalon & Fabian.
    (S) (2:35) Time-Life R857-16 The Heart Of Rock 'n' Roll The Late '50s.

1960 DON'T THROW AWAY ALL THOSE TEARDROPS

    (S) (2:28) Varese Sarabande 5594 Best Of.
    (S) (2:28) Curb 77757 Greatest Hits.
    (S) (2:28) Music Club 50030 The Teen Idols: Very Best Of Frankie Avalon & Fabian.

1960 WHERE ARE YOU

    (M) (2:39) Varese Sarabande 5594 Best Of.

1960 TOGETHERNESS

    (S) (2:31) Varese Sarabande 5594 Best Of.
    (S) (2:29) Music Club 50030 The Teen Idols: Very Best Of Frankie Avalon & Fabian.

1962 YOU ARE MINE

    (S) (3:02) Varese Sarabande 5594 Best Of.
    (S) (3:02) Curb 77757 Greatest Hits.

AVANT-GARDE

1968 NATURALLY STONED

    (M) (2:11) Columbia/Legacy 46983 Rock Artifacts Volume 3.

AVERAGE WHITE BAND

1975 PICK UP THE PIECES

    (S) (3:58) Atlantic 81909 Hit Singles 1958-1977. *(LP version)*
    (S) (3:02) Rhino 70554 Soul Hits Of The 70's Volume 14. *(45 version)*
    (S) (3:58) Atlantic 19116 Average White Band. *(LP version)*
    (S) (3:58) Rhino 71054 Best Of. *(LP version)*
    (S) (18:21) Rhino 71270 Person To Person. *(live)*
    (S) (3:58) Rhino 71432 In Yo Face! History Of Funk Volume 2. *(LP version)*
    (S) (3:02) Rhino 71603 Rock Instrumental Classics Volume 3: The Seventies. *(45 version)*
    (S) (3:02) Rhino 72035 Rock Instrumental Classics Vols. 1-5 Box Set. *(45 version)*
    (S) (3:01) JCI 3306 Dance Seventies. *(45 version)*
    (S) (3:55) Razor & Tie 22045 Those Funky 70's. *(LP version)*
    (S) (3:55) Time-Life SOD-08 Sounds Of The Seventies - 1975. *(LP version)*
    (S) (3:58) Rhino 71588 Average White Band. *(LP version)*
    (S) (7:08) Rhino 71588 Average White Band. *(live)*
    (S) (3:01) Rhino 72213 Stadium Rock. *(45 version)*

(S)	(3:01)	Rhino 72248 O.S.T. Fox Hunt. *(45 version)*
(S)	(3:00)	Madacy Entertainment 1975 Rock On 1975. *(45 version)*
(S)	(3:57)	Rhino 72489 Street Jams - Back 2 The Old Skool, Part 3. *(LP version)*
(S)	(3:00)	JCI 3169 #1 Radio Hits 1975 - Only Rock 'n Roll - 1979. *(45 version)*
(S)	(3:59)	Rhino 72478 Beverly Hills 90210: Songs From The Peach Pit. *(LP version)*
(S)	(3:00)	Eclipse Music Group 64894 Rock 'n Roll Relix 1974-1975. *(45 version)*
(S)	(3:00)	Eclipse Music Group 64897 Rock 'n Roll Relix 1970-1979. *(45 version)*
(S)	(3:01)	Time-Life R840-04 Sounds Of The Seventies: A Loss For Words. *(45 version)*
(S)	(3:01)	Flashback 72711 Sports Rock. *(45 version)*
(S)	(3:58)	Miramax/Hollywood 206162091 O.S.T. Swingers. *(LP version)*
(S)	(3:58)	Flashback 72805 Pick Up The Pieces And Other Hits. *(LP version)*
(S)	(3:02)	Rhino 75200 Basketball's Greatest Hits. *(45 version)*
(S)	(3:02)	Rhino 72964 Ultimate '70s R&B Smashes! *(45 version)*
(S)	(3:01)	Time-Life R840-05 Sounds Of The Seventies: '70s Dance Party 1972-1974. *(45 version)*

1975 CUT THE CAKE

(S)	(3:36)	Rhino 70555 Soul Hits Of The 70's Volume 15. *(45 version)*
(S)	(4:04)	Rhino 71054 Best Of. *(LP version)*
(S)	(4:04)	Rhino 71271 Cut The Cake. *(LP version)*
(S)	(5:04)	Rhino 71270 Person To Person. *(live)*
(S)	(3:36)	Rhino 71433 In Yo Face! History Of Funk Volume 3. *(45 version)*

(S)	(3:36)	Razor & Tie 22047 Sweet 70's Soul. *(45 version)*
(S)	(3:36)	Time-Life SOD-16 Sounds Of The Seventies - 1975: Take Two. *(45 version)*
(S)	(3:36)	MCA 11329 Soul Train 25th Anniversary Box Set. *(45 version)*
(S)	(4:04)	Chronicles 314555139 Funk Jazz. *(LP version)*

1975 IF I EVER LOSE THIS HEAVEN
(dj copies of this 45 ran (3:41); commercial copies were all (4:57))

(S)	(4:59)	Rhino 71054 Best Of.
(S)	(4:59)	Rhino 71271 Cut The Cake.
(S)	(4:59)	Flashback 72805 Pick Up The Pieces And Other Hits.

1976 SCHOOL BOY CRUSH

(S)	(4:55)	Rhino 71054 Best Of.
(S)	(4:58)	Rhino 71271 Cut The Cake.
(S)	(7:37)	Rhino 71270 Person To Person. *(live)*
(S)	(4:56)	Rhino 71434 In Yo Face! History Of Funk Volume 4.
(S)	(4:57)	Priority 53074 Da Funk.
(S)	(4:55)	Flashback 72805 Pick Up The Pieces And Other Hits.

AZ
1995 SUGAR HILL

(S)	(4:07)	EMI 32631 Doe Or Die.

AZ YET
1996 LAST NIGHT

(S)	(4:28)	LaFace 26034 Az Yet.

released as by AZ YET featuring PETER CETERA:
1997 HARD TO SAY I'M SORRY

(S)	(3:14)	LaFace 26034 Az Yet.

BABYFACE
1989 IT'S NO CRIME
 (S) (4:01) Solar/Epic 45288 Tender Lover.
 (S) (6:56) Solar/Epic 75329 A Closer Look. *(remixed)*
1990 TENDER LOVER
 (S) (4:15) Solar/Epic 45288 Tender Lover.
1990 WHIP APPEAL
 (S) (5:45) K-Tel 6006 Lite Rock. *(LP version)*
 (S) (5:45) Solar/Epic 45288 Tender Lover. *(LP version)*
 (S) (5:33) Solar/Epic 75329 A Closer Look. *(remixed)*
 (S) (4:30) MCA 11329 Soul Train 25th Anniversary Box Set. *(45 version)*
1990 MY KINDA GIRL
 (S) (4:38) Solar/Epic 45288 Tender Lover.
 (S) (7:33) Solar/Epic 75329 A Closer Look. *(remixed)*
released as by BABYFACE featuring TONI BRAXTON:
1992 GIVE U MY HEART
 (S) (5:01) LaFace 26006 O.S.T. Boomerang.
released as by BABYFACE:
1994 NEVER KEEPING SECRETS
 (S) (4:52) Epic 53558 For The Cool In You.
1994 AND OUR FEELINGS
 (S) (5:39) Epic 53558 For The Cool In You.
1994 WHEN CAN I SEE YOU
 (S) (3:48) Epic 53558 For The Cool In You.
released as by JON B featuring BABYFACE:
1995 SOMEONE TO LOVE
 (S) (4:32) Yab Yum/550 Music 66436 Bonafide.
 (S) (4:30) Work 67009 O.S.T. Bad Boys.
released as by BABYFACE:
1996 THIS IS FOR THE LOVER IN YOU
 (S) (3:59) Epic 67293 The Day.
1997 EVERYTIME I CLOSE MY EYES
 (S) (4:56) Epic 67293 The Day.

BABYS
1977 ISN'T IT TIME
 (S) (4:03) Chrysalis 21150 and 41150 Broken Heart. *(LP length)*
 (S) (4:01) Chrysalis 21351 and 41351 Anthology. *(LP length)*
 (S) (3:22) Time-Life SOD-17 Sounds Of The Seventies - 1977: Take Two. *(45 length)*
 (S) (4:01) EMI 54241 The Complete John Waite, Volume One: Falling Backwards. *(LP length)*
 (S) (3:59) K-Tel 3904 The Rock Album Volume 2. *(LP length)*
1979 EVERY TIME I THINK OF YOU
 (S) (3:59) Priority 7961 Three Decades Of Rock. *(LP length)*
 (S) (4:01) Chrysalis 21195 and 41195 Head First. *(LP length)*
 (S) (3:59) Chrysalis 21351 and 41351 Anthology. *(LP length)*
 (S) (3:48) Time-Life SOD-19 Sounds Of The Seventies - 1979: Take Two. *(45 length)*
 (S) (3:56) Time-Life R105-40 Rock Dreams. *(LP length)*
 (S) (3:56) Madacy Entertainment 1979 Rock On 1979. *(LP length)*
 (S) (3:59) Time-Life R834-15 Body Talk - Once In Lifetime. *(LP length)*
 (S) (3:48) Time-Life AM1-26 AM Gold - 1979. *(45 length)*
1980 BACK ON MY FEET AGAIN
 (S) (3:18) Chrysalis 21267 and 41267 Union Jacks.
 (S) (3:16) Chrysalis 21351 and 41351 Anthology.

 (S) (3:16) EMI 54241 The Complete John Waite, Volume One: Falling Backwards.
 (S) (3:13) JCI 3193 18 Rock Classics Volume 3.

BACHELORS
1964 DIANE
 (M) (2:29) Rhino 70323 History Of British Rock Volume 5.
 (M) (2:29) Rhino 72022 History Of British Rock Box Set.
 (M) (2:29) Time-Life HPD-37 Your Hit Parade - The 60's.
 (S) (2:29) Eric 11503 Hard To Find 45's On CD (Volume II) 1961-64.
1964 I BELIEVE
 (E) (2:03) Polygram Special Markets 314520459 Vocal Treasures.
1965 NO ARMS CAN EVER HOLD YOU
 (S) (3:02) Special Music 5039 Great Britons! Volume One.
 (S) (3:02) Polygram Special Markets 314520459 Vocal Treasures.
1965 MARIE
 (S) (2:17) Rhino 70324 History Of British Rock Volume 6.
 (S) (2:17) Rhino 72022 History Of British Rock Box Set.
1965 CHAPEL IN THE MOONLIGHT

BACHMAN-TURNER OVERDRIVE
1974 LET IT RIDE
(dj copies of this 45 ran (3:33) and (4:21);
commercial copies were all (3:33))
 (S) (4:26) Sandstone 33001 Reelin' In The Years Volume 2. *(LP version)*
 (S) (4:26) Mercury 830039 BTO's Greatest. *(LP version)*
 (S) (4:24) Mercury 822504 Bachman Turner Overdrive II. *(LP version)*
 (S) (4:26) DCC Compact Classics 063 Rock Of The 70's Volume 2. *(LP version)*
 (S) (4:23) Mercury 314514902 Anthology. *(LP version)*
 (S) (4:24) Time-Life SOD-23 Sounds Of The Seventies - Guitar Power. *(LP version)*
 (S) (4:26) Time-Life R968-16 Guitar Rock - The Mid '70s: Take Two. *(LP version)*
 (S) (3:30) Epic/Legacy 65020 Ultimate Rock 'n' Roll Collection. *(45 version)*
 (S) (4:24) JCI 3140 18 Screamers From The 70's. *(LP version)*
 (S) (4:26) Hip-O 40039 Power Chords Volume 2. *(LP version)*
 (S) (4:23) Rebound 314520440 No. 1 Hits Of The 70's. *(LP version)*
 (S) (4:22) Polygram Special Markets 314520479 70's Rock Hits. *(LP version)*
1974 TAKIN' CARE OF BUSINESS
(dj copies of this 45 ran (3:13) and (4:51);
commercial copies were all (4:51))
 (S) (4:50) Priority 8668 Rough And Rowdy/70's Greatest Rock Hits Volume 7.
 (S) (5:17) Rhino 70799 O.S.T. Spirit Of '76. *(live)*
 (S) (4:50) Original Sound 8894 Dick Clark's 21 All-Time Hits Vol. 3.
 (S) (4:48) Warner Special Products 27614 Highs Of The Seventies.
 (S) (4:50) Sandstone 33000 Reelin' In The Years Volume 1.
 (S) (4:50) Mercury 830039 BTO's Greatest.
 (S) (4:49) Mercury 822504 Bachman Turner Overdrive II.
 (S) (4:49) Special Music 838165 You Ain't Seen Nothing Yet.
 (S) (4:50) DCC Compact Classics 062 Rock Of The 70's Volume 1.

(S) (4:49) Mercury 314514902 Anthology.
(S) (4:48) Razor & Tie 22502 Those Rocking 70's.
(S) (4:50) Time-Life R968-01 Guitar Rock 1974-1975.
(S) (4:50) Time-Life SOD-15 Sounds Of The Seventies - 1974: Take Two.
(S) (4:50) Time-Life OPCD-4521 Guitar Rock.
(S) (4:47) Tommy Boy 1100 ESPN Presents Jock Rock. *(sound effects added to the ending)*
(S) (4:49) Rhino 72131 Frat Rock: The 70's.
(S) (4:50) Cabin Fever Music 973 Harley Davidson: The American Motorcycle Soundtrack.
(S) (4:49) Rhino 72275 More Stadium Rock.
(S) (4:50) K-Tel 3510 Platinum Rock Volume 2.
(S) (4:50) LaserLight 12314 and 15936 The Wonder Years - Party Time.
(S) (4:49) Flashback 72712 Arena Rock.
(S) (4:49) Polygram Special Markets 314520499 Takin' Care Of Business.

1974 YOU AIN'T SEEN NOTHING YET
(S) (3:54) Priority 7055 Heavy Hitters/70's Greatest Rock Hits Volume 11. *(LP length)*
(S) (3:53) JCI 3301 Rockin' Seventies. *(LP length)*
(S) (3:53) Rhino 70272 Metal Age: The Roots Of Metal. *(LP length)*
(S) (3:36) Mercury 830039 BTO's Greatest. *(:06 longer than the 45 length)*
(S) (3:54) Mercury 830178 Not Fragile. *(LP length)*
(S) (3:54) Special Music 838165 You Ain't Seen Nothing Yet. *(LP length)*
(S) (3:52) Mercury 314514902 Anthology. *(LP length)*
(S) (3:53) Time-Life R968-01 Guitar Rock 1974-1975. *(LP length)*
(S) (3:36) Time-Life SOD-15 Sounds Of The Seventies - 1974: Take Two. *(45 length)*
(S) (3:35) Time-Life OPCD-4521 Guitar Rock. *(45 length)*
(S) (3:52) Varese Sarabande 5503 and 5504 and 5505 and 5506 and 5507 and 5508 and 5509 and 5513 and 5571 Arrow: All Rock & Roll Oldies Volume One. *(LP length)*
(S) (3:50) JCI 3130 1970 - Only Rock 'N Roll - 1974. *(LP length)*
(S) (3:54) Polygram Special Markets 314520271 Hits Of The 70's. *(LP length)*
(S) (3:52) Rebound 314520247 Class Reunion 1974. *(LP length)*
(S) (3:52) Special Music/Essex 5036 Prom Night - The 70's. *(LP length)*
(S) (3:53) Risky Business 67310 We Came To Play. *(LP length)*
(S) (3:52) K-Tel 3463 Platinum Rock. *(LP length)*
(S) (3:51) K-Tel 3627 Out Of Sight. *(LP length)*
(S) (3:54) Hollywood 62077 Official Party Album - ABC's Monday Night Football. *(LP length)*
(S) (3:34) Eclipse Music Group 64894 Rock 'n Roll Relix 1974-1975. *(45 length)*
(S) (3:34) Eclipse Music Group 64897 Rock 'n Roll Relix 1970-1979. *(45 length)*
(S) (3:36) Rebound 314520437 Classic Rock - 70's. *(45 length)*
(S) (3:50) K-Tel 3911 Fantastic Volume 2. *(LP length)*
(S) (3:50) Cold Front 6255 Greatest Sports Rock And Jams Volume 2. *(LP length; all selections on this cd are segued together)*
(S) (3:51) K-Tel 3986 70's Heavy Hitters: Arena Rockers 1975-79. *(LP length)*
(S) (3:52) Simitar 55582 The Number One's: Rock It Up. *(LP length)*
(S) (3:52) Hip-O 40095 '70s Hit(s) Back. *(LP length)*
(S) (3:35) Thump 6020 Easyriders Volume 2. *(45 length)*
(S) (3:52) Rebound 314520522 Rockin' Sports Jams. *(LP length)*

1975 ROLL ON DOWN THE HIGHWAY
(S) (3:54) Sandstone 33004 Reelin' In The Years Volume 5.
(S) (3:54) Mercury 830039 BTO's Greatest.
(S) (3:57) Mercury 830178 Not Fragile.
(S) (3:57) Special Music 838165 You Ain't Seen Nothing Yet.

(S) (3:54) DCC Compact Classics 066 Rock Of The 70's Volume Five.
(S) (3:56) Mercury 314514902 Anthology.
(S) (3:54) Time-Life SOD-16 Sounds Of The Seventies - 1975: Take Two.
(S) (3:54) Time-Life R105-24 Guitar Rock Monsters.
(S) (3:57) Priority 53713 Classic Rock Volume 1 - Highway Rockers.
(S) (3:57) Risky Business 57471 Godfathers Of Grunge.
(S) (3:56) Rebound 314520317 Class Reunion 1975.
(S) (3:54) Time-Life R968-15 Guitar Rock - FM Classics.
(S) (3:57) MCA Special Products 20903 The 70's Come Alive Again.
(S) (3:53) K-Tel 3996 Rockin' Down The Highway.
(S) (3:57) K-Tel 4030 Rock Anthems.
(S) (3:56) Rebound 314520521 Highway Rockin'.
(S) (3:56) Polygram Special Markets 314520456 #1 Radio Hits Of The 70's.

1975 HEY YOU
(S) (3:33) Mercury 830039 BTO's Greatest.
(S) (3:33) Mercury 830970 Four Wheel Drive.
(S) (3:33) Special Music 838165 You Ain't Seen Nothing Yet.
(S) (3:33) Mercury 314514902 Anthology.
(S) (3:33) Polygram Special Markets 314520499 Takin' Care Of Business.

1976 DOWN TO THE LINE
(S) (4:00) Mercury 314514902 Anthology.

1976 TAKE IT LIKE A MAN
(S) (3:40) Mercury 314514902 Anthology.
(S) (3:40) Time-Life R968-17 Guitar Rock - The Late '70s: Take Two.
(S) (3:39) Polygram Special Markets 314520499 Takin' Care Of Business.

JIM BACKUS and FRIEND
1958 DELICIOUS!
(M) (3:05) Rhino 70743 Dr. Demento 20th Anniversary Collection.

BACKSTREET BOYS
1997 QUIT PLAYING GAMES (WITH MY HEART)
(S) (3:52) Jive 41589 Backstreet Boys.
(S) (3:28) Cold Front 6254 Club Mix '98. *(all selections on this cd are segued together)*
(S) (4:05) Tommy Boy 1234 MTV Party To Go '98. *(all songs on this cd are segued together)*

BAD COMPANY
1974 CAN'T GET ENOUGH
(S) (4:13) Atlantic 81908 Classic Rock 1966-1988. *(LP version)*
(S) (4:13) Atlantic 82306 Atlantic Rock & Roll Box Set. *(LP version)*
(S) (4:13) Warner Special Products 27614 Highs Of The Seventies. *(LP version)*
(S) (4:13) Foundation/Capitol 96647 Hearts Of Gold - The Classic Rock Collection. *(LP version)*
(S) (4:13) Swan Song 8501 Bad Company. *(LP version)*
(S) (4:13) Atlantic 81625 10 From 6. *(LP version)*
(S) (4:13) Reprise 45485 O.S.T. Wayne's World 2. *(LP version)*
(S) (4:13) Time-Life R968-01 Guitar Rock 1974-1975. *(LP version)*
(S) (3:30) Time-Life SOD-07 Sounds Of The Seventies - 1974. *(45 version)*
(S) (4:13) Time-Life R105-24 Guitar Rock Monsters. *(LP version)*
(S) (4:13) Swan Song 92441 Bad Company. *(remastered edition; LP version)*
(S) (4:13) Rhino 72132 Frat Rock: More Of The 70's. *(LP version)*
(S) (4:13) K-Tel 3463 Platinum Rock. *(LP version)*
(S) (3:40) EastWest 61976 Stories Told & Untold. *(rerecording)*
(S) (4:13) Madacy Entertainment 6805 The Power Of Rock. *(LP version)*

BAD COMPANY *(Continued)*
- (S) (4:13) Simitar 55762 Stud Rock - Wild Ride. *(LP version)*

1975 MOVIN' ON
- (S) (3:20) Swan Song 8501 Bad Company.
- (S) (3:20) Atlantic 81625 10 From 6.
- (S) (3:20) Time-Life SOD-16 Sounds Of The Seventies - 1975: Take Two.
- (S) (3:20) Priority 53713 Classic Rock Volume 1 - Highway Rockers.
- (S) (3:19) Swan Song 92441 Bad Company. *(remastered edition)*
- (S) (3:20) Time-Life R968-08 Guitar Rock - The Mid '70s.

1975 GOOD LOVIN' GONE BAD
- (S) (3:34) Swan Song 8502 Straight Shooter.
- (S) (3:34) Time-Life SOD-37 Sounds Of The Seventies - AM Heavy Hits.
- (S) (3:34) Time-Life R105-40 Rock Dreams.
- (S) (3:35) Swan Song 92436 Straight Shooter. *(remastered edition)*
- (S) (3:34) Time-Life R968-16 Guitar Rock - The Mid '70s: Take Two.
- (S) (3:35) Hip-O 40039 Power Chords Volume 2.

1975 FEEL LIKE MAKIN' LOVE
(dj copies of this 45 ran (3:30); commercial copies were all (5:12))
- (S) (5:11) Swan Song 8502 Straight Shooter.
- (S) (5:11) Atlantic 81625 10 From 6.
- (S) (5:09) Time-Life SOD-08 Sounds Of The Seventies - 1975.
- (S) (5:07) Time-Life R105-40 Rock Dreams.
- (S) (5:06) Time-Life OPCD-4521 Guitar Rock.
- (S) (5:12) Swan Song 92436 Straight Shooter. *(remastered edition)*
- (S) (4:07) JCI 3119 18 Rock Classics. *(edited)*
- (S) (5:10) Time-Life R968-10 Guitar Rock Classics.
- (S) (5:10) Epic/Legacy 65020 Ultimate Rock 'n' Roll Collection.
- (S) (4:06) JCI 3169 #1 Radio Hits 1975 - Only Rock 'n Roll - 1979. *(edited)*
- (S) (5:10) Rhino 72579 Feel Like Makin' Love - Romantic Power Ballads.
- (S) (5:10) Rhino 72893 Hard Rock Cafe: Classic Rock.
- (S) (5:12) Hollywood 62109 O.S.T. G.I. Jane.
- (S) (4:08) Simitar 55502 The Number One's: Classic Rock. *(edited)*
- (S) (5:11) Hip-O 40095 '70s Hit(s) Back.
- (S) (5:06) Simitar 55752 Stud Rock - Heart Breakers.
- (S) (5:06) Thump 6010 Easyriders Volume 1.

1976 YOUNG BLOOD
- (S) (2:37) Swan Song 8503 Run With The Pack.
- (S) (2:37) Time-Life SOD-18 Sounds Of The Seventies - 1976: Take Two.
- (S) (2:37) Swan Song 92435 Run With The Pack. *(remastered edition)*
- (S) (2:37) Simitar 55772 Stud Rock - Rock Me.

1979 ROCK 'N' ROLL FANTASY
- (S) (3:16) Swan Song 8506 Desolation Angels.
- (S) (3:16) Atlantic 81625 10 From 6.
- (S) (3:18) Foundation/RCA 66109 Ultimate Rock Album.
- (S) (3:16) Time-Life SOD-09 Sounds Of The Seventies - 1979.
- (S) (3:16) Time-Life R105-24 Guitar Rock Monsters.
- (S) (3:16) Swan Song 92451 Desolation Angels. *(remastered edition)*
- (S) (3:16) Time-Life R968-17 Guitar Rock - The Late '70s: Take Two.
- (S) (3:15) JCI 3140 18 Screamers From The 70's.
- (S) (3:16) K-Tel 3904 The Rock Album Volume 2.
- (S) (3:16) JCI 3192 18 Rock Classics Volume 2.
- (S) (3:16) Time-Life R840-10 Sounds Of The Seventies: '70s Dance Party 1979.

1991 IF YOU NEEDED SOMEBODY
- (S) (4:19) JCI 3135 14 Original Metal Ballads.
- (S) (4:20) Atco 91371 Holy Water.

1991 WALK THROUGH FIRE
- (S) (4:47) Atco 91371 Holy Water.

1992 HOW ABOUT THAT
- (S) (5:25) Atco 91759 Here Comes Trouble. *(LP version)*

BAD ENGLISH
1989 WHEN I SEE YOU SMILE
- (S) (4:17) Priority 7077 80's Greatest Rock Hits Volume 5 - From The Heart.
- (S) (4:17) Rhino 71644 Billboard Top Hits - 1989.
- (S) (4:17) Sony Music Distribution 57854 For Your Love.
- (S) (4:17) Risky Business 57833 Read The Hits/Best Of The 80's.
- (S) (4:17) K-Tel 6006 Lite Rock.
- (S) (4:17) Epic 45083 Bad English.
- (S) (4:15) EMI 54241 The Complete John Waite, Volume One: Falling Backwards.
- (S) (4:16) Rhino 72579 Feel Like Makin' Love - Romantic Power Ballads.
- (S) (4:17) Time-Life R988-13 Sounds Of The Eighties: 1989.
- (S) (4:17) Time-Life R834-10 Body Talk - From The Heart.

1990 PRICE OF LOVE
- (S) (4:41) Foundation/Capitol 96427 Hearts Of Gold: The Pop Collection.
- (S) (4:46) Epic 45083 Bad English.
- (S) (4:42) EMI 54241 The Complete John Waite, Volume One: Falling Backwards.

1990 POSSESSION
- (S) (5:07) Priority 7049 Metal Heat. *(LP version)*
- (S) (5:07) Epic 45083 Bad English. *(LP version)*

1991 STRAIGHT TO YOUR HEART
- (S) (4:08) Epic 46935 Backlash.
- (S) (4:05) EMI 54241 The Complete John Waite, Volume One: Falling Backwards.

BADFINGER
1970 COME AND GET IT
- (S) (2:20) Capitol 97579 Magic Christian Music.
- (S) (2:20) Capitol 30129 Best Of.

1970 NO MATTER WHAT
- (S) (2:58) Capitol 98698 No Dice.
- (S) (2:58) Capitol 30129 Best Of.
- (S) (2:58) Columbia 67380 O.S.T. Now And Then.

1972 DAY AFTER DAY
- (S) (3:08) Capitol 81403 Straight Up.
- (S) (3:08) Capitol 30129 Best Of.
- (S) (3:10) DCC Compact Classics 1088 Straight Up. *(gold disc)*

1972 BABY BLUE
- (S) (3:34) Capitol 81403 Straight Up. *(LP version)*
- (S) (3:33) Capitol 81403 Straight Up. *(45 version)*
- (S) (3:33) Capitol 30129 Best Of. *(45 version)*
- (S) (3:36) DCC Compact Classics 1088 Straight Up. *(LP version; gold disc)*
- (S) (3:34) DCC Compact Classics 1088 Straight Up. *(45 version; gold disc)*

ERYKAH BADU
1997 ON & ON
- (S) (3:45) Universal 53027 Baduizm.
- (S) (3:41) Tommy Boy 1234 MTV Party To Go '98. *(all songs on this cd are segued together)*
- (S) (3:45) MCA 11752 1998 Grammy Nominees.

JOAN BAEZ
1965 THERE BUT FOR FORTUNE
- (S) (3:13) Vanguard 79332 Hits/Greatest & Others.
- (S) (3:12) Vanguard 6560/1 The First Ten Years.
- (S) (3:12) Vanguard 79160 Joan Baez 5.
- (S) (3:12) Vanguard 125/27 Rare, Live & Classic.
- (S) (3:12) JCI 3109 Folk Sixties.
- (S) (3:11) Rebound 314450371 The Roots Of Rock: 60's Folk.

1971 THE NIGHT THEY DROVE OLD DIXIE DOWN
- (S) (3:23) Vanguard 79332 Hits/Greatest & Others.
- (S) (3:21) Vanguard 125/27 Rare, Live & Classic.
- (S) (3:19) Time-Life SUD-10 Superhits - 1971.

(S)	(3:20)	Time-Life SOD-12 Sounds Of The Seventies - 1971: Take Two.	

(S) (3:20) Time-Life SOD-12 Sounds Of The Seventies - 1971: Take Two.
(S) (3:21) Time-Life R103-33 Singers & Songwriters.
(S) (3:39) A&M 314540510 Greatest Hits. *(live)*
(S) (3:19) Time-Life AM1-06 AM Gold - 1971.
(S) (3:19) Vanguard 163/66 Vanguard Collector's Edition Box Set.

1975 DIAMONDS AND RUST
(S) (4:41) Rhino 71843 Troubadours Of The Folk Era Vol. 4. *(LP version)*
(S) (4:34) A&M 3234 Best Of. *(LP version)*
(S) (4:44) A&M 3233 Diamonds & Rust. *(LP version)*
(S) (4:43) A&M 2506 Classics Volume 8. *(LP version)*
(S) (4:43) MFSL 646 Diamonds & Rust. *(LP version; gold disc)*
(S) (4:34) K-Tel 3454 70s Folk Rock Hits. *(LP version)*
(S) (4:41) Rhino 72447 Listen To The Music: 70's Female Singer/Songwriters. *(LP version)*
(S) (4:45) A&M 314540510 Greatest Hits. *(LP version)*

PHILIP BAILEY with PHIL COLLINS
1985 EASY LOVER
(actual 45 time is (4:47) not (4:40) as stated on the record label)
(S) (5:04) Columbia 39542 Philip Bailey - Chinese Wall. *(LP length)*
(S) (4:40) Time-Life R988-17 Sounds Of The Eighties: The Mid '80s Take Two. *(:07 shorter than the 45 length)*

MERRIL BAINBRIDGE
1996 MOUTH
(S) (3:23) Universal 53019 The Garden.

DAN BAIRD
1993 I LOVE YOU PERIOD
(S) (4:23) Def American 26999 Love Songs For The Hearing Impaired.

ANITA BAKER
1986 SWEET LOVE
(S) (4:26) Elektra 60444 Rapture.
1987 CAUGHT UP IN THE RAPTURE
(S) (5:16) Elektra 60444 Rapture.
1988 GIVING YOU THE BEST THAT I GOT
(S) (4:17) Elektra 60827 Giving You The Best That I Got.
1989 JUST BECAUSE
(S) (5:09) Elektra 60827 Giving You The Best That I Got.
1994 BODY AND SOUL
(S) (5:41) Elektra 61555 Rhythm Of Love.

GEORGE BAKER SELECTION
1970 LITTLE GREEN BAG
(S) (3:15) Rhino 70922 Super Hits Of The 70's Volume 2. *(neither the LP or 45 version)*
(S) (3:15) Rhino 72009 Super Hits Of The 70's Volumes 1-4 Box Set. *(neither the LP or 45 version)*
(S) (3:15) JCI 3115 Groovin' Sixties. *(neither the LP or 45 version)*
(S) (3:15) Original Sound 8865 Oldies But Goodies Vol. 15. *(this compact disc uses the "Waring - fds" noise reduction process; neither the 45 or LP version)*
(S) (3:15) Original Sound 2222 Oldies But Goodies Volumes 3,5,11,14 and 15 Box Set. *(this box set uses the "Waring - fds" noise reduction process; neither the 45 or LP version)*
(S) (3:15) Original Sound 2500 Oldies But Goodies Volumes 1-15 Box Set. *(this box set uses the "Waring - fds" noise reduction process; neither the 45 or LP version)*
(S) (3:14) Original Sound CDGO-7 Golden Oldies Volume. 7. *(neither the 45 or LP version)*
(S) (3:15) Rhino 71206 70's Smash Hits Volume 2. *(neither the LP or 45 version)*

(S) (3:14) Time-Life SOD-32 Sounds Of The Seventies - AM Pop Classics. *(neither the 45 or LP version)*
(E) (4:24) Collectables 0560 Little Green Bag. *(LP version)*
(S) (3:14) MCA 10541 and 11188 O.S.T. Reservoir Dogs. *(neither the 45 or LP version)*
(S) (3:15) Flashback 72682 '70s Radio Hits Volume 2. *(neither the 45 or LP version)*
(S) (3:15) Flashback 72090 '70s Radio Hits Box Set. *(neither the 45 or LP version)*

1976 PALOMA BLANCA
(S) (3:36) Popular/Critique 12009 Dutch Treats. *(rerecording)*

LAVERN BAKER
1955 TWEEDLEE DEE
(M) (3:07) Rhino 70598 Billboard's Top Rock & Roll Hits Of 1955.
(M) (3:07) Atlantic 81294 Atlantic Rhythm & Blues Volume 2.
(M) (3:08) Atlantic 82311 Soul On Fire.
(M) (3:02) JCI 3552 Best Of.
(M) (3:08) Atlantic 82305 Atlantic Rhythm And Blues 1947-1974 Box Set.
(M) (3:06) Time-Life 2RNR-08 Rock 'N' Roll Era - 1954-1955.
(M) (3:05) Time-Life RHD-17 Rhythm & Blues - 1955.
(M) (3:07) Time-Life R962-03 History Of Rock 'N' Roll: Rock 'N' Roll Classics 1954-1956.
(M) (3:06) Rhino 71806 The R&B Box: Thirty Years Of Rhythm & Blues.
(M) (3:05) JCI 3165 #1 Radio Hits 1955 - Only Rock 'n Roll - 1959.

1956 I CAN'T LOVE YOU ENOUGH
(M) (2:36) Atlantic 82311 Soul On Fire.

1957 JIM DANDY
(M) (2:10) JCI 3204 Heart & Soul Fifties.
(M) (2:11) Atlantic 81295 Atlantic Rhythm & Blues Volume 3.
(M) (2:11) Atlantic 81769 O.S.T. Big Town.
(M) (2:11) Atlantic 82311 Soul On Fire.
(M) (2:11) JCI 3552 Best Of.
(M) (2:11) Atlantic 82305 Atlantic Rhythm And Blues 1947-1974 Box Set.
(M) (2:10) Time-Life 2RNR-01 Rock 'N' Roll Era - 1957.
(M) (2:10) Time-Life RHD-08 Rhythm & Blues - 1957.
(M) (2:11) Hip-O 40058 O.S.T. Pink Flamingos.
(M) (2:10) Rhino 72961 Ultimate '50s R&B Smashes!
(M) (2:10) Time-Life R838-23 Solid Gold Soul 1957.

1959 I CRIED A TEAR
(S) (2:34) Rhino 70645 Billboard's Top R&B Hits Of 1959.
(S) (2:35) Atlantic 81296 Atlantic Rhythm & Blues Volume 4.
(M) (2:33) Atlantic 82311 Soul On Fire.
(M) (2:33) JCI 3552 Best Of.
(M) (2:33) Atlantic 82305 Atlantic Rhythm And Blues 1947-1974 Box Set.
(S) (2:34) Time-Life 2RNR-13 Rock 'N' Roll Era - 1959.
(S) (2:32) Time-Life RHD-03 Rhythm & Blues - 1959.
(S) (2:33) Time-Life R857-01 The Heart Of Rock 'n' Roll - 1959.
(S) (2:32) Time-Life R838-21 Solid Gold Soul 1959.

1959 I WAITED TOO LONG
(M) (2:31) Atlantic 82311 Soul On Fire.
(M) (2:30) JCI 3552 Best Of.

1961 BUMBLE BEE
(S) (2:26) Time-Life 2RNR-44 Rock 'N' Roll Era - Lost Treasures.

1963 SEE SEE RIDER
(M) (2:30) Atlantic 81297 Atlantic Rhythm & Blues Volume 5.
(S) (2:27) Atlantic 82311 Soul On Fire.
(M) (2:29) JCI 3552 Best Of.
(S) (2:27) Atlantic 82305 Atlantic Rhythm And Blues 1947-1974 Box Set.

BALANCE
1981 BREAKING AWAY
    (S) (3:10)   Renaissance 0104 Balance/In For The Count.

MARTY BALIN
1981 HEARTS
    (actual 45 time is (4:15) not (3:54) as stated on the record label)
    (S) (4:16)   Rhino 70968 Balance. *(45 version)*
    (S) (4:15)   Madacy Entertainment 1981 Rock On 1981. *(45 version)*
    (S) (4:15)   Time-Life R988-14 Sounds Of The Eighties: 1980-1982. *(45 version)*
    (S) (4:14)   Time-Life R834-11 Body Talk - After Dark. *(45 version)*
1981 ATLANTA LADY (SOMETHING ABOUT YOUR LOVE)
    (S) (3:26)   Rhino 70968 Balance.

DAVID BALL
1994 THINKIN' PROBLEM
    (S) (3:00)   Atlantic 45562 Thinkin' Problem.

KENNY BALL
1962 MIDNIGHT IN MOSCOW
    (S) (2:58)   Time-Life HPD-34 Your Hit Parade - 60's Instrumentals.
    (S) (2:58)   Rhino 71583 Billboard Top Pop Hits, 1962.
    (S) (2:57)   K-Tel 3472 Those Wonderful Instrumentals Volume 2.
    (S) (2:58)   Time-Life R986-17 Instrumental Favorites - Around The World.

HANK BALLARD and THE MIDNIGHTERS
1960 FINGER POPPIN' TIME
    (M) (1:49)   Capitol 91184 O.S.T. Everybody's All American. *(edited)*
    (M) (1:49)   Rhino 71512 Sexy Ways: Best Of. *(edited)*
    (S) (2:33)   Time-Life 2RNR-11 Rock 'N' Roll Era - 1960.
    (M) (2:33)   Time-Life R10513 40 Lovin' Oldies.
    (M) (1:48)   RCA 66443 O.S.T. Corrina, Corrina. *(edited)*
    (M) (1:48)   King 7002 King R&B Box Set. *(edited)*
    (M) (2:24)   King 498 Greatest Hits.
    (M) (1:48)   King 5003 All 20 Of Their Chart Hits. *(edited)*
    (M) (1:48)   King 700 Mr. Rhythm & Blues. *(edited)*
    (M) (1:47)   King 950 Hank Ballard And His Midnighters. *(edited)*
1960 THE TWIST
    (M) (2:35)   Rhino 71512 Sexy Ways: Best Of.
    (M) (2:34)   Time-Life 2RNR-22 1960: Still Rockin'.
    (M) (2:33)   Time-Life RHD-03 Rhythm & Blues - 1959.
    (M) (2:10)   Vee-Jay 709 A Taste Of Doo Wop - Volume One. *(first demo recording)*
    (M) (2:33)   King 7002 King R&B Box Set.
    (M) (2:35)   King 1421 Party Time Rock & Roll.
    (M) (2:34)   King 498 Greatest Hits.
    (M) (2:33)   King 5003 All 20 Of Their Chart Hits.
    (M) (2:34)   King 618 Singin' And Swingin'.
    (M) (1:59)   King 950 Hank Ballard And His Midnighters. *(alternate take)*
    (M) (2:33)   Time-Life R838-21 Solid Gold Soul 1959.
1960 LET'S GO, LET'S GO, LET'S GO
    (M) (2:25)   Rhino 71512 Sexy Ways: Best Of.
    (S) (2:21)   Time-Life 2RNR-11 Rock 'N' Roll Era - 1960.
    (S) (2:21)   Time-Life RHD-15 Rhythm & Blues - 1960.
    (S) (2:26)   King 740 Spotlight On. *(high frequency tone throughout this cd)*
    (M) (2:23)   King 7002 King R&B Box Set.
    (M) (2:24)   King 498 Greatest Hits.
    (M) (2:23)   King 5003 All 20 Of Their Chart Hits.
    (S) (2:21)   Time-Life R838-20 Solid Gold Soul 1960.
1961 THE HOOCHI COOCHI COO
    (S) (2:35)   King 740 Spotlight On. *(high frequency tone throughout this cd)*
    (M) (2:32)   King 498 Greatest Hits.
    (M) (2:30)   King 5003 All 20 Of Their Chart Hits.

1961 THE CONTINENTAL WALK
    (M) (3:39)   Rhino 71512 Sexy Ways: Best Of.
    (M) (3:38)   King 5003 All 20 Of Their Chart Hits.
1961 THE SWITCH-A-ROO
    (M) (2:45)   Rhino 71512 Sexy Ways: Best Of.
    (M) (2:44)   King 5003 All 20 Of Their Chart Hits.

BALLOON FARM
1968 A QUESTION OF TEMPERATURE
    (M) (2:38)   K-Tel 713 Battle Of The Bands.
    (M) (2:36)   Time-Life 2CLR-21 Rock Renaissance II.
    (M) (2:36)   Time-Life R968-22 Guitar Rock - The Late '60s Take Two.

BALTIMORA
1986 TARZAN BOY
    (S) (3:43)   SBK 89016 O.S.T. Teenage Mutant Ninja Turtles III.
    (S) (3:44)   SBK 89016 O.S.T. Teenage Mutant Ninja Turtles III. *(remix)*
    (S) (3:50)   EMI 55204 O.S.T. Beverly Hills Ninja.
    (S) (5:27)   Beast 53032 Club Hitz Of The 90's Vol. 2. *(all songs on this cd are segued together)*

BANANARAMA
1984 CRUEL SUMMER
    (S) (3:28)   EMI 27674 Living In Oblivion: The 80's Greatest Hits Volume Three.
    (S) (3:33)   London 820036 Bananarama.
    (S) (3:28)   London 828158 Greatest Hits Collection.
    (S) (3:34)   Rhino 71976 New Wave Hits Of The 80's Vol. 13.
    (S) (3:28)   Priority 53797 Best Of 80's Rock Volume 4.
    (S) (3:28)   Time-Life R988-11 Sounds Of The 80's: 1983-1984.
    (S) (3:34)   Hip-O 40004 The '80s Hit(s) Back!
    (S) (3:27)   Rebound 314520438 No. 1 Hits Of The 80's.
    (S) (3:28)   Hollywood 62123 More Music From The Motion Picture "Romy And Michele's High School Reunion".
    (S) (3:27)   Simitar 55552 The Number One's: Eighties Rock.
    (S) (3:28)   Rebound 314520493 Class Reunion '83.
1986 VENUS
    (S) (3:38)   Priority 53684 Rock Of The 80's Volume 4. *(:10 shorter than the 45 or LP)*
    (S) (3:35)   K-Tel 3343 The 80's Hot Dance Trax. *(:13 shorter than the 45 or LP)*
    (S) (3:48)   Rhino 71641 Billboard Top Hits - 1986.
    (S) (3:38)   Sandstone 33041 and 5007 Rock The First Volume 1. *(:10 shorter than the 45 or LP)*
    (S) (3:48)   Razor & Tie 2063 True Confessions.
    (S) (3:48)   London 828013 True Confessions.
    (S) (3:38)   London 828158 Greatest Hits Collection. *(:10 shorter than the 45 or LP)*
    (S) (3:48)   Time-Life R988-04 Sounds Of The Eighties: 1986.
    (S) (4:22)   Rebound 314520354 World Of Dance: New Wave - The 80's. *(neither the 45, LP or 12" single version)*
    (S) (7:25)   DCC Compact Classics 131 HI-NRG Dance Classics Volume 1. *(remix)*
    (S) (3:48)   Rhino 72500 Modern Rock 1986 - Hang The DJ.
    (S) (3:47)   JCI 3150 1985 - Only Dance - 1989.
    (S) (3:37)   Hollywood 62098 O.S.T. Romy And Michele's High School Reunion. *(:11 shorter than the 45 or LP)*
    (S) (3:48)   Hip-O 40075 Rock She Said: On The Pop Side.
    (S) (3:37)   Simitar 55522 The Number One's: Party Time. *(:11 shorter than the 45 or LP)*
1987 I HEARD A RUMOUR
    (S) (3:23)   Rhino 71642 Billboard Top Hits - 1987.
    (S) (3:23)   London 828061 Wow!
    (S) (3:23)   London 828158 Greatest Hits Collection.
    (S) (3:23)   Time-Life R988-09 Sounds Of The Eighties: 1987.
    (S) (3:24)   Rhino 72501 Modern Rock 1987 - Hang The DJ.
    (S) (3:23)   Polygram Special Markets 314520457 #1 Radio Hits Of The 80's.

BAND
1969 UP ON CRIPPLE CREEK
- (S) (4:27) Capitol 46070 Best Of. *(LP version)*
- (S) (4:29) Capitol 46493 The Band. *(LP version)*
- (S) (4:29) Capitol 48419 Anthology Volume 1. *(LP version)*
- (S) (4:31) Capitol 92170 To Kingdom Come. *(LP version)*
- (S) (3:31) Rhino 71548 Let There Be Drums Volume 2: The 60's. *(45 version)*
- (S) (3:31) Time-Life SOD-11 Sounds Of The Seventies - 1970: Take Two. *(45 version)*
- (S) (4:29) Capitol 89565 Across The Great Divide. *(LP version)*
- (S) (4:29) Priority 50952 I Love Rock & Roll Volume 3: Hits Of The 70's. *(LP version)*

1972 DON'T DO IT
- (S) (4:33) Capitol 46070 Best Of. *(LP version but with the (1:38) introduction removed)*
- (S) (4:40) Capitol 92170 To Kingdom Come. *(LP version but with the (1:38) introduction removed)*
- (S) (6:05) Capitol 93595 Rock Of Ages. *(LP version)*
- (S) (4:42) Capitol 89565 Across The Great Divide. *(LP version but with a shorter introduction and different audience background noise preceding the start of the song)*

BAND AID
1985 DO THEY KNOW IT'S CHRISTMAS

BANGLES
1986 MANIC MONDAY
- (S) (3:03) Sandstone 33051 and 5019 Cosmopolitan Volume 5.
- (S) (3:02) Time-Life R102-34 The Rolling Stone Collection.
- (S) (3:03) DCC Compact Classics 083 Night Moves Volume 3.
- (S) (3:03) Columbia 46125 Greatest Hits.
- (S) (3:03) Columbia 40039 Different Light.
- (S) (3:02) Time-Life R988-01 Sounds Of The Eighties: The Rockin' Eighties.
- (S) (3:03) Columbia 65366 All Over The Place/Different Light/Everything.
- (S) (3:03) Epic/Legacy 65255 Fizz Pop Modern Rock Volume 2.
- (S) (3:03) Hip-O 40075 Rock She Said: On The Pop Side.

1986 IF SHE KNEW WHAT SHE WANTS
- (S) (3:47) Columbia 46125 Greatest Hits.
- (S) (3:47) Columbia 40039 Different Light.
- (S) (3:47) Columbia 65366 All Over The Place/Different Light/Everything.

1986 WALK LIKE AN EGYPTIAN
- (S) (3:21) Priority 7076 80's Greatest Rock Hits Volume 2 - Leather And Lace.
- (S) (3:22) Rhino 71641 Billboard Top Hits - 1986.
- (S) (3:22) Risky Business 57833 Read The Hits/Best Of The 80's.
- (S) (3:22) JCI 3128 1985 - Only Rock 'N Roll - 1989.
- (S) (3:21) Columbia 46125 Greatest Hits.
- (S) (3:22) Columbia 40039 Different Light.
- (S) (3:22) Time-Life R988-28 Sounds Of The Eighties: The Rolling Stone Collection 1986-1987.
- (S) (3:21) Big Ear Music 4003 Only In The 80's Volume Three.
- (S) (3:21) Rhino 72500 Modern Rock 1986 - Hang The DJ.
- (S) (3:23) Rhino 72894 Hard Rock Cafe: New Wave.
- (S) (3:22) Rhino 72856 Just Can't Get Enough: New Wave Women.
- (S) (3:22) Columbia 65366 All Over The Place/Different Light/Everything.

1987 WALKING DOWN YOUR STREET
- (S) (3:15) Columbia 46125 Greatest Hits. *(45 version)*
- (S) (3:02) Columbia 40039 Different Light. *(LP version)*
- (S) (3:01) JCI 3150 1985 - Only Dance - 1989. *(LP version)*
- (S) (3:02) Columbia 65366 All Over The Place/Different Light/Everything. *(LP version)*

1988 HAZY SHADE OF WINTER
- (S) (2:45) Columbia/Def Jam 44042 O.S.T. Less Than Zero.
- (S) (2:45) Def Jam 314527360 O.S.T. Less Than Zero.
- (S) (2:44) Sandstone 33046 and 5012 Rock The First Volume Six.
- (S) (2:45) Columbia 46125 Greatest Hits.
- (S) (2:44) Time-Life R988-10 Sounds Of The 80's: 1988.
- (S) (2:47) Rhino 72501 Modern Rock 1987 - Hang The DJ.

1988 IN YOUR ROOM
- (S) (3:26) Foundation/WEA 26096 Super Sessions Volume One.
- (S) (3:27) Columbia 46125 Greatest Hits.
- (S) (3:27) Columbia 44056 Everything.
- (S) (3:26) Time-Life R988-19 Sounds Of The Eighties: The Late '80s.
- (S) (3:27) Columbia 65366 All Over The Place/Different Light/Everything.

1989 ETERNAL FLAME
- (S) (3:55) Foundation/Capitol 96427 Hearts Of Gold: The Pop Collection.
- (S) (3:55) Rhino 71644 Billboard Top Hits - 1989.
- (S) (3:55) Sony Music Distribution 57854 For Your Love.
- (S) (3:55) K-Tel 6006 Lite Rock.
- (S) (3:55) Columbia 46125 Greatest Hits.
- (S) (3:55) Columbia 44056 Everything.
- (S) (3:54) Hip-O 40000 Thinking About You - A Collection Of Modern Love Songs.
- (S) (3:54) Time-Life R988-20 Sounds Of The Eighties: The Late '80s Take Two.
- (S) (3:55) Time-Life R834-09 Body Talk - Magic Moments.
- (S) (3:55) K-Tel 3868 Hot Ladies Of Pop.
- (S) (3:55) Columbia 65366 All Over The Place/Different Light/Everything.

1989 BE WITH YOU
- (S) (3:00) Columbia 46125 Greatest Hits.
- (S) (3:00) Columbia 44056 Everything.
- (S) (3:00) Columbia 65366 All Over The Place/Different Light/Everything.

DARRELL BANKS
1966 OPEN THE DOOR TO YOUR HEART
- (M) (2:34) Ripete 0002 Coolin' Out/24 Carolina Classics Vol. 2.
- (M) (2:34) Time-Life RHD-01 Rhythm & Blues - 1966.
- (M) (2:34) Time-Life R838-01 Solid Gold Soul - 1966.
- (M) (2:28) Rhino 72815 Beg, Scream & Shout! The Big Ol' Box Of '60s Soul.

CHRIS BARBER'S JAZZ BAND
1959 PETITE FLEUR (LITTLE FLOWER)
- (M) (2:42) Time-Life HPD-13 Your Hit Parade - 1959.
- (M) (2:42) JCI 7010 Those Wonderful Years - Melodies Of Love.

KEITH BARBOUR
1969 ECHO PARK
- (S) (3:42) Columbia/Legacy 46160 Rock Artifacts Volume 1.

BARDEUX
1988 WHEN WE KISS
- (S) (4:51) Synthicide 73312 Bold As Love.

BOBBY BARE
released as by BILL PARSONS:
1959 THE ALL AMERICAN BOY
- (M) (2:55) Collectables 5070 History Of Rock Volume 10.
- (M) (2:56) Time-Life 2RNR-13 Rock 'N' Roll Era - 1959.
- (E) (2:52) Original Sound CDGO-14 Golden Oldies Volume 14. *(mastered from a fairly scratchy record)*
- (M) (2:58) Razor & Tie 2043 Best Of.
- (M) (2:52) Curb 77773 Hard To Find Hits Of Rock 'N' Roll Volume One.
- (M) (2:57) K-Tel 3411 Tacky Tunes. *(credited on the cd as by BOBBY BARE)*

BOBBY BARE (Continued)

(E)　(2:58)　RCA 67405　The Essential. *(no mention of BILL PARSONS is made on the cd jacket)*

released as by BOBBY BARE:

1962　SHAME ON ME

(S)　(2:44)　RCA 67405　The Essential.

1963　DETROIT CITY

(S)　(2:46)　RCA 8475　Nipper's Greatest Hits Of The 60's Volume 2.

(S)　(2:44)　Time-Life CTD-11　Country USA - 1963.

(S)　(2:46)　K-Tel 3109　Country Music Classics Volume XVII.

(S)　(2:46)　Razor & Tie 2043　Best Of.

(S)　(2:46)　K-Tel 3369　101 Greatest Country Hits Vol. Ten: Country Roads.

(S)　(2:48)　RCA 67405　The Essential.

(S)　(2:44)　Time-Life R808-01　Classic Country 1960-1964.

1963　500 MILES AWAY FROM HOME

(S)　(2:40)　RCA 8474　Nipper's Greatest Hits Of The 60'S Volume 1.

(S)　(2:40)　Time-Life CTD-11　Country USA - 1963.

(S)　(2:41)　Razor & Tie 2043　Best Of.

(S)　(2:42)　RCA 67405　The Essential.

1964　MILLER'S CAVE

(S)　(2:53)　Razor & Tie 2043　Best Of.

(S)　(2:51)　RCA 67405　The Essential.

BAR-KAYS

1967　SOUL FINGER

(M)　(2:18)　Atlantic Group 88218　Complete Stax/Volt Singles.

(M)　(2:18)　Warner Special Products 27609　Memphis Soul Classics.

(M)　(2:18)　JCI 3105　Soul Sixties.

(M)　(2:18)　Stax 88008　Top Of The Stax Volume 2.

(S)　(2:19)　Atlantic 82305　Atlantic Rhythm And Blues 1947-1974 Box Set. *(truncated fade)*

(S)　(2:19)　Rhino 70298　Soul Finger. *(truncated fade)*

(S)　(2:18)　Rhino 71460　Soul Hits, Volume 2.

(M)　(2:18)　Rhino 71604　Rock Instrumental Classics Vol. 4: Soul.

(M)　(2:18)　Rhino 72035　Rock Instrumental Classics Vols. 1-5 Box Set.

(S)　(2:16)　Time-Life RHD-10　Rhythm & Blues - 1967.

(S)　(2:17)　Time-Life 2CLR-15　Classic Rock - 1967: Shakin' All Over.

(M)　(2:18)　Milan 35683　O.S.T. Mystery Train.

(S)　(2:16)　JCI 3161　18 Soul Hits From The 60's.

(S)　(2:16)　Time-Life R838-02　Solid Gold Soul - 1967.

(M)　(2:18)　Flashback 72658　'60s Soul: Baby I Love You.

(M)　(2:18)　Flashback 72091　'60s Soul Hits Box Set.

(M)　(2:19)　Rhino 72815　Beg, Scream & Shout! The Big Ol' Box Of '60s Soul.

(M)　(2:19)　Flashback 72897　25 Years Of R&B - 1967.

(M)　(2:19)　Rhino 72962　Ultimate '60s Soul Sensations.

(S)　(4:42)　Curb 77826　Best Of. *(1996 rerecording)*

1977　SHAKE YOUR RUMP TO THE FUNK

(S)　(3:28)　Mercury 314514823　Best Of. *(45 length)*

(S)　(3:30)　Rhino 71434　In Yo Face! History Of Funk Vol. 4. *(45 length)*

(S)　(3:30)　Rhino 72129　Soul Hits Of The 70's Vol. 19. *(45 length)*

(S)　(3:48)　Rebound 314520333　Too Hot To Stop. *(LP length)*

(S)　(3:27)　Chronicles 314555137　Funk Of The 70's. *(45 length)*

(S)　(4:02)　Curb 77826　Best Of. *(1996 rerecording)*

RAY BARRETTO

1963　EL WATUSI

(S)　(2:37)　Epic 57620　O.S.T. Carlito's Way.

(S)　(2:40)　Rhino 71604　Rock Instrumental Classics Vol. 4: Soul.

(S)　(2:40)　Rhino 72035　Rock Instrumental Classics Vols. 1-5 Box Set.

(M)　(2:40)　Elektra 61293　O.S.T. JFK. *(mastered from vinyl)*

JOE BARRY

1961　I'M A FOOL TO CARE

(M)　(2:19)　Time-Life 2RNR-39　Rock 'N' Roll Era - The New Orleans Sound.

LEN BARRY

1965　1-2-3

(S)　(2:21)　Rhino 70626　Billboard's Top Rock & Roll Hits Of 1965.

(S)　(2:21)　Rhino 72007　Billboard's Top Rock & Roll Hits 1962-1966 Box Set.

(S)　(2:25)　MCA 31204　Vintage Music Volume 7. *(with countoff)*

(S)　(2:25)　MCA 5805　Vintage Music Volumes 7 & 8. *(with countoff)*

(S)　(2:20)　Time-Life 2CLR-08　Classic Rock - 1965: The Beat Goes On.

(S)　(2:25)　Collectables 2504　WCBS-FM History Of Rock - The 60's Part 4. *(with countoff)*

(S)　(2:25)　Collectables 4504　History Of Rock/The 60s Part Four. *(with countoff)*

(S)　(2:25)　MCA Special Products 22135　Vintage Collectibles Volume 6. *(with countoff)*

(S)　(2:21)　Taragon 1004　Very Best Of.

(S)　(2:24)　Polydor 314529508　O.S.T. Mr. Holland's Opus. *(with countoff)*

(S)　(2:21)　MCA Special Products 20997　Mellow Rock.

(S)　(2:25)　MCA Special Products 21017　The Rockin' Sixties. *(with countoff)*

(S)　(2:21)　MCA Special Products 21046　Top Singles Of The Sixties.

1966　LIKE A BABY

(S)　(2:54)　MCA Special Products 20783　Rock Around The Oldies #1.

(S)　(2:54)　Taragon 1004　Very Best Of.

1966　SOMEWHERE

(S)　(2:24)　Taragon 1004　Very Best Of.

BARRY and THE TAMERLANES

1963　I WONDER WHAT SHE'S DOING TONIGHT

(M)　(1:50)　Rhino 70995　One Hit Wonders Of The 60's Volume 1.

(M)　(1:49)　Time-Life 2RNR-46　Rock 'N' Roll Era - 60's Juke Box Memories.

CHRIS BARTLEY

1967　THE SWEETEST THING THIS SIDE OF HEAVEN

(S)　(2:52)　Ripete 2148-RE　Beach Beat Classics Volume III.

(E)　(3:01)　Collectables 5590　The Sweetest Thing This Side Of Heaven.

(M)　(2:53)　Rhino 72619　Smooth Grooves: The '60s Volume 2 Mid '60s.

BASIA

1988　TIME AND TIDE

(S)　(4:01)　Foundation/WEA 26097　Super Sessions Volume Two.

(S)　(4:02)　Epic 40767　Time And Tide.

(S)　(4:02)　Epic/Legacy 53791　Time And Tide. *(gold disc)*

1990　CRUISING FOR BRUISING

(S)　(4:08)　Sandstone 33053 and 5021　Cosmopolitan Volume 7.

(S)　(4:08)　DCC Compact Classics 081　Night Moves Volume 1.

(S)　(4:08)　Epic 45472　London Warsaw New York.

TONI BASIL

1982　MICKEY

(S)　(3:36)　EMI 89605　Living In Oblivion: The 80's Greatest Hits Volume Two. *(45 version)*

(S)　(3:25)　Rhino 71698　New Wave Hits Of The 80's Vol. 5. *(45 version faded :11 early)*

(S)　(3:25)　Rhino 71879　More Music From O.S.T. Valley Girl. *(45 version faded :11 early)*

(S)　(4:12)　Razor & Tie 2057　Best Of. *(LP version)*

(S) (3:25) Time-Life R988-05 Sounds Of The Eighties: 1982. *(45 version faded :11 early)*
(S) (4:12) Big Ear Music 4001 Only In The 80's Volume One. *(LP version)*
(S) (4:08) K-Tel 3473 The 80s: New Wave. *(LP version)*
(S) (3:25) JCI 3149 1980 - Only Dance - 1984. *(45 version faded :11 early)*
(S) (3:35) Madacy Entertainment 1982 Rock On 1982. *(45 version)*
(S) (3:25) Rhino 72491 New Wave Hits, Vol. 2. *(45 version faded :11 early)*
(S) (3:25) JCI 3170 #1 Radio Hits 1980 - Only Rock 'n Roll - 1984. *(45 version faded :11 early)*
(S) (4:06) Scotti Bros. 75504 Club Ladies Night. *(LP version)*
(S) (4:12) Priority 53126 Best Of 80's Rock Volume 6. *(LP version)*
(S) (3:26) Flashback 72714 Ultimate New Wave Hits. *(45 version faded :10 early)*
(S) (3:26) Flashback 72092 New Wave Hits Box Set. *(45 version faded :10 early)*
(S) (3:25) Rhino 72820 VH1 - More Of The Big 80's. *(45 version faded :11 early)*
(S) (4:12) Hip-O 40075 Rock She Said: On The Pop Side. *(LP version)*
(S) (4:12) Hip-O 40079 Essential '80s: 1980-1984. *(LP version)*
(S) (4:11) Simitar 55612 The Number One's: The '80s. *(LP version)*

FONTELLA BASS
released as by FONTELLA BASS & BOBBY McCLURE:
1965 DON'T MESS UP A GOOD THING
(M) (2:51) Chess 9335 Rescued: The Best Of.
(S) (2:59) Chess 9352 Chess Rhythm & Roll.
(M) (2:51) Ichiban 2512 Soulful Love - Duets Vol. 1.
(S) (2:59) Chess 9388 Chess Soul - A Decade Of Chicago's Finest.

released as by FONTELLA BASS:
1965 RESCUE ME
(S) (2:54) Rhino 75774 Soul Shots.
(S) (2:50) Rhino 70651 Billboard's Top R&B Hits Of 1965.
(S) (2:50) Rhino 72006 Billboard's Top R&B Hits 1965-1969 Box Set.
(S) (2:54) Original Sound 8862 Oldies But Goodies Vol. 12. *(this compact disc uses the "Waring - fds" noise reduction process)*
(S) (2:54) Original Sound 2223 Oldies But Goodies Volumes 2,7,9,12 and 13 Box Set. *(this box set uses the "Waring - fds" noise reduction process)*
(S) (2:54) Original Sound 2500 Oldies But Goodies Volumes 1-15 Box Set. *(this box set uses the "Waring - fds" noise reduction process)*
(S) (2:54) MCA 31206 Vintage Music Volume 9.
(S) (2:54) MCA 5806 Vintage Music Volumes 9 & 10.
(S) (2:50) JCI 3100 Dance Sixties.
(S) (2:53) Chess 31318 Best Of Chess Rhythm & Blues Volume 2.
(S) (2:53) MCA 6467 O.S.T. Air America.
(S) (2:52) Chess 9335 Rescued: The Best Of.
(S) (2:54) Ripete 2392192 Beach Music Anthology Box Set.
(S) (2:53) Hollywood 61334 O.S.T. Sister Act.
(S) (2:53) Hollywood 62080 O.S.T. Sister Act & Sister Act 2: Back In The Habit.
(S) (2:54) Rhino 71460 Soul Hits, Volume 2.
(S) (2:48) Time-Life RHD-07 Rhythm & Blues - 1965.
(S) (2:53) Time-Life 2CLR-08 Classic Rock - 1965: The Beat Goes On.
(S) (2:53) MCA Special Products 20753 Classic R&B Oldies From The 60's.
(S) (2:50) JCI/Telstar 3516 Sweet Soul Sisters.
(S) (2:54) Collectables 2505 History Of Rock - The 60's Part 5.
(S) (2:54) Collectables 4505 History Of Rock/The 60s Part Five.

(S) (2:54) MCA Special Products 22131 Vintage Collectibles Volume 2.
(S) (2:50) Collectables 2554 CBS-FM History Of Rock Volume 2.
(S) (2:54) Right Stuff 52660 Flick Hits - Old School Tracks.
(S) (2:48) JCI 3161 18 Soul Hits From The 60's.
(S) (2:48) JCI 3190 1965 - Only Dance - 1969.
(S) (2:51) Priority 50951 I Love Rock & Roll Volume 2: Hits Of The 60's.
(S) (2:48) Time-Life R838-12 Solid Gold Soul - 1965.
(S) (2:54) Flashback 72658 '60s Soul: Baby I Love You.
(S) (2:54) Flashback 72091 '60s Soul Hits Box Set.
(S) (2:51) Compose 131 Unforgettable - Gold For The Road.
(S) (2:53) MCA Special Products 21030 Beach Music Hits.
(S) (2:51) MCA Special Products 21010 R&B Crossover Hits Volume 2.
(S) (2:51) Rhino 72815 Beg, Scream & Shout! The Big Ol' Box Of '60s Soul.
(S) (2:51) Chess 9388 Chess Soul - A Decade Of Chicago's Finest.
(S) (2:51) TVT 4010 Rhythm Revue.
(S) (2:52) MCA Special Products 21032 Soul Legends.
(S) (2:53) Simitar 55572 The Number One's: Hot In The '60s.
(S) (2:54) Play-Tone/Epic 69179 Music From The HBO Miniseries "From The Earth To The Moon". *(hum noticeable at the end of every song on this cd)*

1966 RECOVERY
(S) (2:28) Chess 9335 Rescued: The Best Of.

SHIRLEY BASSEY
1965 GOLDFINGER
(S) (2:48) EMI 46079 James Bond 13 Original Themes. *(LP version)*
(S) (2:47) EMI 95345 O.S.T. Goldfinger. *(LP version)*
(S) (3:19) Pair 1057 Sassy Bassey. *(live)*
(S) (2:47) EMI 98560 Best Of James Bond 30th Anniversary. *(LP version)*
(S) (2:46) EMI 81128 Rock Is Dead But It Won't Lie Down. *(LP version)*
(S) (2:47) EMI 98413 Best Of James Bond 30th Anniversary Collection. *(LP version)*
(S) (2:47) Time-Life SUD-03 Superhits - 1965. *(LP version)*
(S) (2:47) Rhino 71749 Spy Magazine Presents: Spy Music. *(LP version)*
(S) (2:46) EMI 35880 Goldsinger/Best Of. *(LP version)*
(M) (2:48) EMI 35880 Goldsinger/Best Of. *(45 version)*
(S) (2:47) Time-Life AM1-10 AM Gold - 1965. *(LP version)*

LES BAXTER
1955 UNCHAINED MELODY
(M) (2:31) Curb 77403 All Time Great Instrumental Hits Volume 1.
(M) (2:31) Capitol 91218 and 37028 Baxter's Best.
(M) (2:31) Capitol 98670 Memories Are Made Of This.
(M) (2:30) Rhino 71580 Billboard Pop Memories 1955-1959.
(M) (2:31) JCI 7010 Those Wonderful Years - Melodies Of Love.
(M) (2:31) Rhino 72422 Billboard Top Movie Hits 1955-1959.
1955 WAKE THE TOWN AND TELL THE PEOPLE
(M) (2:31) Capitol 91218 and 37028 Baxter's Best.
(M) (2:32) Time-Life HPD-09 Your Hit Parade 1955.
1956 THE POOR PEOPLE OF PARIS
(M) (2:23) Capitol 91218 and 37028 Baxter's Best.
(E) (2:23) Capitol 90592 Memories Are Made Of This.
(M) (2:23) Curb 77403 All-Time Great Instrumental Hits Volume 1.
(M) (2:23) Capitol 98670 Memories Are Made Of This.
(M) (2:23) Time-Life HPD-15 Your Hit Parade - 1956.
(E) (2:23) K-Tel 3091 Those Wonderful Instrumentals.
(E) (2:23) JCI 7010 Those Wonderful Years - Melodies Of Love.
(M) (2:23) Time-Life R986-17 Instrumental Favorites - Around The World.

BAY CITY ROLLERS
1975 SATURDAY NIGHT
- (S) (2:53) Rhino 70671 Billboard Top Hits - 1976.
- (S) (2:53) Rhino 70762 Super Hits Of The 70's Volume 15.
- (S) (2:54) Rhino 70799 O.S.T. Spirit Of '76.
- (S) (2:53) Arista 8694 Greatest Hits.
- (S) (2:53) Rhino 71228 Yesterday's Heroes: 70's Teen Idols.
- (S) (2:52) Razor & Tie 21640 Those Fabulous 70's.
- (S) (2:53) Time-Life SOD-25 Sounds Of The Seventies - Seventies Generation.
- (S) (2:53) JCI 3131 1975 - Only Rock 'N Roll - 1979.
- (S) (2:53) Madacy Entertainment 1976 Rock On 1976.
- (S) (2:51) Eclipse Music Group 64894 Rock 'n Roll Relix 1974-1975.
- (S) (2:51) Eclipse Music Group 64897 Rock 'n Roll Relix 1970-1979.
- (S) (2:53) Time-Life AM1-23 AM Gold - 1976.
- (S) (2:53) Time-Life R840-01 Sounds Of The Seventies - Pop Nuggets: Late '70s.
- (S) (2:53) Rhino 72819 16 Magazine - Who's Your Fave Rave.

1976 MONEY HONEY
- (S) (3:15) Arista 8694 Greatest Hits.
- (S) (3:15) Rhino 72297 Superhits Of The 70's Volume 23.

1976 ROCK AND ROLL LOVE LETTER
- (S) (2:54) Arista 8694 Greatest Hits.

1976 I ONLY WANT TO BE WITH YOU
- (S) (3:35) Arista 8694 Greatest Hits.

1977 YOU MADE ME BELIEVE IN MAGIC
- (S) (2:41) Arista 8694 Greatest Hits.
- (S) (2:39) Time-Life SOD-35 Sounds Of The Seventies - AM Nuggets.

1978 THE WAY I FEEL TONIGHT
- (S) (3:52) Arista 8694 Greatest Hits. *(LP length)*

BAZUKA
1975 DYNOMITE (PART 1)
- (S) (5:09) K-Tel 3624 Music Express. *(LP version)*

B. BUMBLE & THE STINGERS
1961 BUMBLE BOOGIE
- (M) (2:09) Rhino 71602 Rock Instrumental Classics Volume 2: The Sixties.
- (M) (2:09) Rhino 72035 Rock Instrumental Classics Vols. 1-5 Box Set.
- (E) (2:10) Original Sound 8857 Oldies But Goodies Vol. 7. *(this compact disc uses the "Waring - fds" noise reduction process)*
- (E) (2:10) Original Sound 2223 Oldies But Goodies Volumes 2,7,9,12 and 13 Box Set. *(this box set uses the "Waring - fds" noise reduction process)*
- (E) (2:10) Original Sound 2500 Oldies But Goodies Volumes 1-15 Box Set. *(this box set uses the "Waring - fds" noise reduction process)*
- (M) (2:10) LaserLight 12316 Rebel Rousers.
- (M) (2:10) K-Tel 3453 Rockin' Instrumentals.
- (M) (2:10) Collectables 5578 A Golden Classics Edition.
- (M) (2:10) JCI 3189 1960 - Only Dance - 1964.

1962 NUT ROCKER
- (M) (1:58) Rhino 71602 Rock Instrumental Classics Volume 2: The Sixties.
- (M) (1:58) Rhino 72035 Rock Instrumental Classics Vols. 1-5 Box Set.
- (M) (1:58) Time-Life 2RNR-29 Rock 'N' Roll Era - The 60's Rave On.
- (M) (1:58) LaserLight 12316 Rebel Rousers.
- (M) (1:58) Collectables 5578 A Golden Classics Edition.

BC-52's (see B-52's)

BEACH BOYS
1962 SURFIN' SAFARI
- (M) (2:04) Capitol 46467 Endless Summer.
- (M) (1:59) Original Sound CDGO-3 Golden Oldies Volume. 3. *(original Candix label recording)*
- (M) (1:59) Original Sound 2222 Oldies But Goodies Volumes 3,5,11,14 and 15 Box Set. *(this box set uses the "Waring - fds" noise reduction process; original Candix label recording)*
- (M) (1:59) Original Sound 2500 Oldies But Goodies Volumes 1-15 Box Set. *(this box set uses the "Waring - fds" noise reduction process; original Candix label recording)*
- (M) (1:59) Original Sound 8853 Oldies But Goodies Vol. 3. *(this compact disc uses the "Waring - fds" noise reduction process; original Candix label recording)*
- (M) (2:30) Original Sound 9601 Best Of Oldies But Goodies Vol. 1. *(original Candix label recording)*
- (M) (2:04) Capitol 46324 Made In U.S.A.
- (M) (2:04) Capitol 93691 Surfin' Safari/Surfin' U.S.A.
- (M) (2:03) Rhino 70089 Surfin' Hits.
- (M) (2:04) Capitol 96861 Monster Summer Hits - Wild Surf.
- (M) (2:04) Capitol 96795 Absolute Best Volume 1.
- (M) (2:15) Capitol 81294 Thirty Years Of. *(:11 longer fade than either the 45 or LP)*
- (M) (2:03) MCA 8001 O.S.T. American Graffiti.
- (M) (2:03) Rhino 71229 Summer Hits.
- (M) (2:03) Time-Life 2RNR-02 Rock 'N' Roll Era - 1962.
- (M) (2:04) Capitol 29661 Surfin' Safari.
- (M) (2:04) Capitol 29418 20 Good Vibrations - Greatest Hits.
- (M) (2:12) DCC Compact Classics 1076 Endless Summer. *(gold disc; :08 longer fade than either the 45 or LP)*
- (M) (2:03) Flashback 72710 Golden Summer.
- (E) (1:59) K-Tel 6256 Kahuna Classics. *(original Candix label recording; no fidelity)*
- (E) (2:05) I.D. 90072 Jenny McCarthy's Surfin' Safari.

1963 SURFIN' U.S.A.
- (M) (2:26) Capitol 91318 Best Of.
- (M) (2:26) Capitol 46467 Endless Summer.
- (M) (2:26) Capitol 46324 Made In U.S.A.
- (S) (2:27) Capitol 93691 Surfin' Safari/Surfin' U.S.A.
- (S) (2:27) Rhino 70089 Surfin' Hits.
- (S) (2:27) Rhino 70624 Billboard's Top Rock & Roll Hits Of 1963.
- (S) (2:27) Rhino 72007 Billboard's Top Rock & Roll Hits 1962-1966 Box Set.
- (S) (2:27) Capitol 96861 Monster Summer Hits - Wild Surf.
- (S) (2:27) Capitol 96795 Absolute Best Volume 1.
- (S) (2:28) EMI 90604 Beach Party Blasts.
- (S) (2:28) MFSL 521 Surfin' U.S.A./Surfer Girl. *(timing index on this song only is off by :03; gold disc)*
- (M) (1:48) Capitol 81294 Thirty Years Of. *(demo version)*
- (M) (2:26) Capitol 81294 Thirty Years Of.
- (S) (2:26) Time-Life 2RNR-07 Rock 'N' Roll Era - 1963.
- (S) (2:26) Time-Life R962-04 History Of Rock 'N' Roll: California Pop 1963-1967.
- (S) (2:27) Capitol 48422 Surfin' U.S.A.
- (S) (2:26) JCI 3125 1960 - Only Rock 'N Roll - 1964.
- (S) (2:27) Capitol 29418 20 Good Vibrations - Greatest Hits.
- (S) (2:28) DCC Compact Classics 1076 Endless Summer. *(gold disc)*
- (S) (2:26) Rhino 72418 Cowabunga! The Surf Box.
- (S) (2:27) Pointblank 42088 Fender 50th Anniversary Guitar Legends.
- (M) (2:27) Capitol 55900 Greatest Surfing Songs.
- (S) (2:28) I.D. 90072 Jenny McCarthy's Surfin' Safari.

1963 SHUT DOWN
- (M) (1:48) Capitol 46467 Endless Summer.
- (S) (1:49) Capitol 93691 Surfin' Safari/Surfin' U.S.A.
- (M) (1:50) Capitol 96862 Monster Summer Hits - Drag City.
- (S) (1:48) Capitol 93693 Little Deuce Coupe/All Summer Long.
- (S) (1:49) Capitol 96795 Absolute Best Volume 1.
- (S) (1:49) MFSL 521 Surfin' U.S.A./Surfer Girl. *(gold disc)*
- (M) (1:48) Capitol 81294 Thirty Years Of.
- (S) (1:49) Compose 9923 James Dean/Tribute To A Rebel.
- (S) (1:49) Compose 9927 Car And Driver/Greatest Car Songs.
- (S) (1:48) Time-Life 2RNR-03 Rock 'N' Roll Era - The Beach Boys 1962-1967.

(S) (1:49) Capitol 48422 Surfin' U.S.A.
(S) (1:48) Capitol 29418 20 Good Vibrations - Greatest Hits.
(S) (1:50) DCC Compact Classics 1076 Endless Summer. *(gold disc)*

1963 SURFER GIRL
(M) (2:24) Capitol 91318 Best Of.
(S) (2:24) Capitol 46467 Endless Summer.
(M) (2:22) Capitol 46324 Made In U.S.A.
(S) (2:25) Capitol 93692 Surfer Girl/Shut Down Volume 2.
(S) (2:25) Capitol 96861 Monster Summer Hits - Wild Surf.
(S) (2:25) Capitol 96795 Absolute Best Volume 1.
(S) (2:25) MFSL 521 Surfin' U.S.A./Surfer Girl. *(gold disc)*
(M) (2:23) Capitol 81294 Thirty Years Of.
(S) (2:25) Time-Life 2RNR-03 Rock 'N' Roll Era - The Beach Boys 1962-1967.
(S) (2:24) Time-Life SUD-08 Superhits - 1963.
(S) (2:25) Capitol 29628 Surfer Girl.
(S) (2:25) Capitol 29418 20 Good Vibrations - Greatest Hits.
(S) (2:26) DCC Compact Classics 1076 Endless Summer. *(gold disc)*
(S) (2:25) Rhino 72418 Cowabunga! The Surf Box.
(S) (2:25) Time-Life R857-12 The Heart Of Rock 'n' Roll 1962-1963.
(S) (2:24) Time-Life AM1-17 AM Gold - 1963.
(E) (2:12) K-Tel 6256 Kahuna Classics. *(rerecording; no fidelity)*
(M) (2:23) Capitol 21277 Essential Beach Boys - Perfect Harmony.
(S) (2:25) Time-Life R857-21 The Heart Of Rock 'n' Roll Slow Dancing Classics.
(S) (2:25) Collectables 1515 and 2515 The Anniversary Album - The 60's.

1963 LITTLE DEUCE COUPE
(M) (1:49) Capitol 91318 Best Of. *(mono LP length)*
(S) (1:38) Capitol 46467 Endless Summer.
(S) (1:38) Capitol 93692 Surfer Girl/Shut Down Volume 2.
(S) (1:37) Capitol 96862 Monster Summer Hits - Drag City.
(S) (1:37) Capitol 93693 Little Deuce Coupe/All Summer Long.
(S) (1:37) Capitol 96795 Absolute Best Volume 1.
(S) (1:38) MFSL 521 Surfin' U.S.A./Surfer Girl. *(gold disc)*
(M) (1:46) Capitol 81294 Thirty Years Of. *(mono LP length)*
(S) (1:38) Compose 9927 Car And Driver/Greatest Car Songs.
(S) (1:38) Time-Life 2RNR-03 Rock 'N' Roll Era - The Beach Boys 1962-1967.
(S) (1:38) Capitol 29628 Surfer Girl.
(S) (1:37) Capitol 29418 20 Good Vibrations - Greatest Hits.
(S) (1:39) DCC Compact Classics 1076 Endless Summer. *(gold disc)*
(M) (1:49) Capitol 55900 Greatest Surfing Songs. *(mono LP length)*
(S) (1:38) Right Stuff 53316 Hot Rod Rock Volume 1: Rev It Up.

1963 BE TRUE TO YOUR SCHOOL
(S) (2:05) Capitol 46467 Endless Summer. *(LP version)*
(M) (2:06) Capitol 46324 Made In U.S.A. *(45 version)*
(S) (2:04) Capitol 93693 Little Deuce Coupe/All Summer Long. *(LP version)*
(M) (2:06) Capitol 93693 Little Deuce Coupe/All Summer Long. *(45 version)*
(S) (2:04) Capitol 96795 Absolute Best Volume 1. *(LP version)*
(M) (2:05) Capitol 81294 Thirty Years Of. *(45 version)*
(M) (2:06) Time-Life 2RNR-03 Rock 'N' Roll Era - The Beach Boys 1962-1967. *(45 version)*
(S) (2:04) Capitol 29630 Little Deuce Coupe. *(LP version)*
(S) (2:04) Capitol 29418 20 Good Vibrations - Greatest Hits. *(LP version)*
(M) (2:07) DCC Compact Classics 1076 Endless Summer. *(gold disc; 45 version)*

1963 IN MY ROOM
(M) (2:12) Capitol 91318 Best Of.
(S) (2:11) Capitol 46467 Endless Summer.
(S) (2:11) Capitol 93692 Surfer Girl/Shut Down Volume 2.
(S) (2:11) Capitol 96795 Absolute Best Volume 1.
(S) (2:12) MFSL 521 Surfin' U.S.A./Surfer Girl. *(gold disc)*
(S) (2:11) Time-Life 2RNR-03 Rock 'N' Roll Era - The Beach Boys 1962-1967.
(S) (2:11) Time-Life R962-05 History Of Rock 'N' Roll: The Teenage Years 1957-1964.
(S) (2:11) Capitol 29628 Surfer Girl.
(S) (2:12) DCC Compact Classics 1076 Endless Summer. *(gold disc)*
(M) (2:31) Capitol 21277 Essential Beach Boys - Perfect Harmony. *(demo version)*

1964 FUN FUN FUN
(M) (2:17) Capitol 91318 Best Of. *(mono LP mix)*
(S) (2:02) Capitol 46467 Endless Summer. *(stereo LP mix)*
(S) (2:02) Capitol 93692 Surfer Girl/Shut Down Volume 2. *(stereo LP mix)*
(M) (2:18) Capitol 93692 Surfer Girl/Shut Down Volume 2. *(45 version)*
(M) (2:15) Capitol 46324 Made In U.S.A. *(mono LP mix)*
(S) (2:02) Capitol 96862 Monster Summer Hits - Drag City. *(stereo LP mix)*
(M) (2:18) Capitol 96795 Absolute Best Volume 1. *(45 version)*
(M) (2:18) Capitol 98139 Spring Break Volume 2. *(45 version)*
(M) (2:18) Capitol 81294 Thirty Years Of. *(45 version)*
(S) (2:02) Time-Life 2RNR-03 Rock 'N' Roll Era - The Beach Boys 1962-1967. *(stereo LP mix)*
(S) (2:01) Time-Life 2CLR-03 Classic Rock - 1964. *(stereo LP mix)*
(S) (2:02) Capitol 29629 Shut Down Volume 2. *(stereo LP mix)*
(M) (2:17) Rhino 71585 Billboard Top Pop Hits, 1964. *(45 version)*
(S) (2:02) Capitol 29418 20 Good Vibrations - Greatest Hits. *(stereo LP mix)*
(S) (2:03) DCC Compact Classics 1076 Endless Summer. *(gold disc; stereo LP mix)*

1964 I GET AROUND
(M) (2:10) Capitol 92639 Still Crusin'.
(M) (2:11) Capitol 46467 Endless Summer.
(M) (2:10) Capitol 46324 Made In U.S.A.
(M) (2:12) Rhino 70625 Billboard's Top Rock & Roll Hits Of 1964.
(M) (2:12) Rhino 72007 Billboard's Top Rock & Roll Hits 1962-1966 Box Set.
(E) (2:13) EMI 90604 Beach Party Blasts.
(M) (2:09) Capitol 48993 Spuds Mackenzie's Party Faves.
(M) (2:08) A&M 3913 and 3340 O.S.T. Good Morning Vietnam.
(M) (2:12) Rhino 70794 KFOG Presents M. Dung's Idiot Show.
(M) (2:12) Capitol 93693 Little Deuce Coupe/All Summer Long.
(M) (2:11) Capitol 96795 Absolute Best Volume 1.
(M) (2:11) Capitol 98138 Spring Break Volume 1.
(M) (2:10) Capitol 98665 When AM Was King.
(M) (2:12) Capitol 81294 Thirty Years Of.
(M) (2:09) Time-Life 2RNR-03 Rock 'N' Roll Era - The Beach Boys 1962-1967.
(M) (2:06) Time-Life 2CLR-03 Classic Rock - 1964.
(M) (2:09) Time-Life R962-04 History Of Rock 'N' Roll: California Pop 1963-1967.
(M) (2:11) MCA Special Products 20751 Rock Around The Oldies #2.
(M) (2:12) Capitol 29631 All Summer Long.
(M) (2:12) Capitol 29418 20 Good Vibrations - Greatest Hits.

BEACH BOYS (Continued)

(M) (2:12) DCC Compact Classics 1076 Endless Summer. *(gold disc)*
(M) (2:13) Mercury 314553774 Bean - The Album. *(includes :08 of movie dialog overlapping the end of the song)*

1964 DON'T WORRY BABY

(S) (2:46) Capitol 46467 Endless Summer.
(M) (2:40) Capitol 46324 Made In U.S.A.
(S) (2:46) Capitol 93692 Surfer Girl/Shut Down Volume 2.
(S) (2:47) EMI 90604 Beach Party Blasts.
(S) (2:46) Capitol 96795 Absolute Best Volume 1.
(M) (2:46) Capitol 81294 Thirty Years Of.
(S) (2:41) Time-Life 2RNR-03 Rock 'N' Roll Era - The Beach Boys 1962-1967.
(S) (2:46) Time-Life 2CLR-16 Classic Rock - 1964: Shakin' All Over.
(S) (2:43) Time-Life SUD-17 Superhits - Mid 60's Classics.
(S) (2:46) Capitol 29629 Shut Down Volume 2.
(S) (2:46) Epic 57871 O.S.T. My Girl 2.
(S) (2:47) DCC Compact Classics 1076 Endless Summer. *(gold disc)*
(S) (2:45) Capitol 55900 Greatest Surfing Songs.
(S) (2:43) Time-Life AM1-16 AM Gold - Mid '60s Classics.
(M) (2:46) Capitol 21277 Essential Beach Boys - Perfect Harmony.
(S) (2:46) Time-Life R857-17 The Heart Of Rock 'n' Roll: The Early '60s.

1964 WHEN I GROW UP TO BE A MAN

(M) (1:58) Capitol 46618 Spirit of America.
(M) (1:59) Capitol 46324 Made In U.S.A.
(M) (1:59) Capitol 96795 Absolute Best Volume 1.
(M) (1:59) Capitol 81294 Thirty Years Of.
(S) (2:17) Capitol 81294 Thirty Years Of. *(includes :11 of studio talk and a :06 longer fade than either the 45 or LP)*
(M) (2:00) Capitol 93694 Today/Summer Days And Summer Nights.
(M) (1:59) Time-Life 2RNR-03 Rock 'N' Roll Era - The Beach Boys 1962-1967.
(M) (1:59) Time-Life 2CLR-09 Classic Rock - 1964: The Beat Goes On.
(M) (1:56) Time-Life SUD-09 Superhits - 1964.
(M) (2:00) Capitol 29632 Today.
(M) (2:01) DCC Compact Classics 1089 Spirit Of America. *(gold disc)*
(M) (1:55) Time-Life AM1-11 AM Gold - 1964.
(M) (2:04) Capitol 21277 Essential Beach Boys - Perfect Harmony.

1964 DANCE DANCE DANCE

(M) (1:58) Capitol 46618 Spirit of America.
(M) (1:58) Capitol 46324 Made In U.S.A.
(M) (1:58) Capitol 93694 Today/Summer Days And Summer Nights.
(S) (1:58) Capitol 93694 Today/Summer Days And Summer Nights. *(alternate take)*
(M) (1:58) Capitol 96795 Absolute Best Volume 1.
(M) (1:58) Capitol 81294 Thirty Years Of.
(M) (1:57) Time-Life 2RNR-03 Rock 'N' Roll Era - The Beach Boys 1962-1967.
(M) (1:58) Capitol 29632 Today.
(M) (1:58) Capitol 29418 20 Good Vibrations - Greatest Hits.
(M) (1:59) DCC Compact Classics 1089 Spirit Of America. *(gold disc)*
(M) (1:58) JCI 3189 1960 - Only Dance - 1964.

1965 DO YOU WANNA DANCE?

(M) (2:16) Capitol 46618 Spirit of America.
(M) (2:17) Capitol 93694 Today/Summer Days And Summer Nights.
(M) (2:16) Capitol 96795 Absolute Best Volume 1.
(M) (2:15) Capitol 81294 Thirty Years Of.
(M) (2:16) Time-Life 2RNR-03 Rock 'N' Roll Era - The Beach Boys 1962-1967.
(M) (2:17) Capitol 29632 Today.
(M) (2:16) Capitol 29418 20 Good Vibrations - Greatest Hits.
(M) (2:17) DCC Compact Classics 1089 Spirit Of America. *(gold disc)*

(M) (2:16) Capitol 55900 Greatest Surfing Songs.

1965 HELP ME RHONDA
(the 45 spelling of this song was "RHONDA"; the LP spelling was "RONDA")

(M) (3:06) Capitol 46467 Endless Summer. *(LP version)*
(M) (2:44) Capitol 46324 Made In U.S.A. *(45 version)*
(M) (2:45) Capitol 93694 Today/Summer Days And Summer Nights. *(45 version)*
(M) (3:07) Capitol 93694 Today/Summer Days And Summer Nights. *(LP version)*
(M) (2:45) Rhino 70626 Billboard's Top Rock & Roll Hits Of 1965. *(45 version)*
(M) (2:45) Rhino 72007 Billboard's Top Rock & Roll Hits 1962-1966 Box Set. *(45 version)*
(M) (2:45) Curb 77355 60's Hits Volume 1. *(45 version)*
(M) (2:44) Capitol 48046 California Girls. *(45 version)*
(M) (3:07) Capitol 96795 Absolute Best Volume 1. *(LP version)*
(M) (2:45) Capitol 81294 Thirty Years Of. *(45 version)*
(M) (2:45) Time-Life 2RNR-03 Rock 'N' Roll Era - The Beach Boys 1962-1967. *(45 version)*
(M) (2:44) Time-Life 2CLR-01 Classic Rock - 1965. *(45 version)*
(M) (3:07) Capitol 29632 Today. *(LP version)*
(M) (2:43) Original Sound 8883 21 Legendary Superstars. *(45 version)*
(M) (3:07) Capitol 29418 20 Good Vibrations - Greatest Hits. *(LP version)*
(M) (2:46) DCC Compact Classics 1076 Endless Summer. *(gold disc; 45 version)*
(M) (3:07) Capitol 55900 Greatest Surfing Songs. *(LP version)*

1965 CALIFORNIA GIRLS

(M) (2:36) Capitol 92639 Still Crusin'.
(E) (2:36) Capitol 46467 Endless Summer.
(M) (2:36) Capitol 46324 Made In U.S.A.
(M) (2:36) Capitol 93694 Today/Summer Days And Summer Nights.
(M) (2:36) Capitol 48046 California Girls.
(M) (2:35) Capitol 96796 Absolute Best Volume 2.
(M) (2:36) Capitol 81294 Thirty Years Of.
(M) (2:35) Time-Life 2RNR-03 Rock 'N' Roll Era - The Beach Boys 1962-1967.
(M) (2:35) Time-Life 2CLR-08 Classic Rock - 1965: The Beat Goes On.
(M) (2:31) Time-Life SUD-03 Superhits - 1965.
(M) (2:36) Capitol 29633 Summer Days And Summer Nights.
(M) (2:35) Capitol 29418 20 Good Vibrations - Greatest Hits.
(M) (2:37) Rhino 71935 Billboard Top Pop Hits, 1965.
(M) (2:38) DCC Compact Classics 1076 Endless Summer. *(gold disc)*
(M) (2:31) JCI 3185 1965 - Only Love - 1969.
(M) (2:31) Time-Life AM1-10 AM Gold - 1965.
(M) (2:31) Capitol 21277 Essential Beach Boys - Perfect Harmony.

1965 THE LITTLE GIRL I ONCE KNEW

(M) (2:35) Capitol 46618 Spirit Of America.
(M) (2:34) Capitol 96796 Absolute Best Volume 2.
(M) (2:35) Capitol 93694 Today/Summer Days & Summer Nights.
(M) (2:35) Capitol 81294 Thirty Years Of.
(M) (2:35) Time-Life 2RNR-03 Rock 'N' Roll Era - The Beach Boys 1962-1967.
(M) (2:35) DCC Compact Classics 1089 Spirit Of America. *(gold disc)*

1966 BARBARA ANN

(M) (2:05) Capitol 46618 Spirit of America. *(45 version)*
(M) (2:04) Capitol 46324 Made In U.S.A. *(45 version)*
(M) (2:01) Original Sound 8852 Oldies But Goodies Vol. 2. *(this compact disc uses the "Waring - fds" noise reduction process; 45 version)*
(M) (2:01) Original Sound 2223 Oldies But Goodies Volumes 2,7,9,12 and 13 Box Set. *(this box set uses the "Waring - fds" noise reduction process; 45 version)*
(M) (2:01) Original Sound 2500 Oldies But Goodies Volumes 1-15 Box Set. *(this box set uses the "Waring - fds" noise reduction process; 45 version)*

(M) (3:05) Capitol 93698 Party/Stack-O-Tracks. *(LP version)*

(M) (2:05) Rhino 75778 Frat Rock. *(45 version)*

(M) (2:02) Capitol 96796 Absolute Best Volume 2. *(45 version)*

(M) (2:03) Capitol 81294 Thirty Years Of. *(45 version)*

(M) (2:04) Time-Life 2RNR-03 Rock 'N' Roll Era - The Beach Boys 1962-1967. *(45 version)*

(M) (2:03) Time-Life 2CLR-02 Classic Rock - 1966. *(45 version)*

(M) (3:05) Capitol 29640 Party. *(LP version)*

(M) (2:16) Capitol 29418 20 Good Vibrations - Greatest Hits. *(edit of LP version)*

(M) (3:07) DCC Compact Classics 1089 Spirit Of America. *(gold disc; LP version)*

(M) (2:05) Capitol 55900 Greatest Surfing Songs. *(45 version)*

1966 SLOOP JOHN B

(M) (2:56) Capitol 48421 Pet Sounds.

(M) (2:54) Capitol 46324 Made In U.S.A.

(M) (2:55) Capitol 96796 Absolute Best Volume 2.

(M) (2:55) Capitol 81294 Thirty Years Of.

(M) (2:56) DCC Compact Classics 1035 Pet Sounds. *(gold disc)*

(M) (2:54) Time-Life 2RNR-03 Rock 'N' Roll Era - The Beach Boys 1962-1967.

(M) (2:51) Time-Life 2CLR-22 Classic Rock - 1966: Blowin' Your Mind.

(M) (2:55) Time-Life R962-02 History Of Rock 'N' Roll: Folk Rock 1964-1967.

(M) (2:54) Epic 66329 O.S.T. Forrest Gump.

(M) (2:55) Capitol 29418 20 Good Vibrations - Greatest Hits.

(M) (2:55) Rhino 71936 Billboard Top Pop Hits, 1966.

(M) (2:54) Capitol 21277 Essential Beach Boys - Perfect Harmony.

(S) (2:56) Capitol 37662 The Pet Sounds Sessions.

(S) (3:15) Capitol 37662 The Pet Sounds Sessions. *(instrumental track)*

(S) (3:05) Capitol 37662 The Pet Sounds Sessions. *(vocals only)*

(S) (3:15) Capitol 37662 The Pet Sounds Sessions. *(several alternate takes strung together)*

(M) (2:55) Capitol 37662 The Pet Sounds Sessions. *(found on the bonus disc titled "Pet Sounds" included with this box set)*

1966 WOULDN'T IT BE NICE

(M) (2:21) Capitol 92639 Still Crusin'. *(alternate Mike Love single tracked vocal from 1:06 to 1:19)*

(M) (2:23) Capitol 48421 Pet Sounds.

(M) (2:21) Capitol 46324 Made In U.S.A. *(alternate Mike Love single tracked vocal from 1:06 to 1:19)*

(M) (2:21) Capitol 96796 Absolute Best Volume 2. *(alternate Mike Love single tracked vocal from 1:06 to 1:19)*

(M) (2:22) Rhino 70588 Rockin' & Rollin' Wedding Songs Volume 1.

(M) (2:21) Motown 6094 More Songs From The Original Soundtrack Of The "Big Chill".

(M) (2:22) Capitol 81294 Thirty Years Of.

(M) (2:23) DCC Compact Classics 1035 Pet Sounds. *(gold disc)*

(M) (2:21) Time-Life 2RNR-03 Rock 'N' Roll Era - The Beach Boys 1962-1967. *(alternate Mike Love single tracked vocal from 1:06 to 1:19)*

(M) (2:21) Time-Life 2CLR-07 Classic Rock - 1966: The Beat Goes On. *(alternate Mike Love single tracked vocal from 1:06 to 1:19)*

(M) (2:21) Capitol 29418 20 Good Vibrations - Greatest Hits.

(S) (2:32) Capitol 21277 Essential Beach Boys - Perfect Harmony. *(vocals only)*

(S) (2:32) Capitol 37662 The Pet Sounds Sessions.

(S) (2:32) Capitol 37662 The Pet Sounds Sessions. *(instrumental track)*

(S) (2:34) Capitol 37662 The Pet Sounds Sessions. *(vocals only)*

(S) (2:32) Capitol 37662 The Pet Sounds Sessions. *(with backing vocals)*

(S) (7:19) Capitol 37662 The Pet Sounds Sessions. *(several alternate takes strung together)*

(M) (2:21) Capitol 37662 The Pet Sounds Sessions. *(found on the bonus disc titled "Pet Sounds" included with this box set)*

1966 GOD ONLY KNOWS

(M) (2:49) Capitol 48421 Pet Sounds.

(M) (2:47) Capitol 46324 Made In U.S.A.

(M) (2:49) Capitol 96796 Absolute Best Volume 2.

(M) (2:47) Capitol 81294 Thirty Years Of.

(M) (2:49) DCC Compact Classics 1035 Pet Sounds. *(gold disc)*

(M) (2:47) Time-Life 2RNR-03 Rock 'N' Roll Era - The Beach Boys 1962-1967.

(M) (2:49) Capitol 29418 20 Good Vibrations - Greatest Hits.

(M) (2:47) Capitol 21277 Essential Beach Boys - Perfect Harmony.

(S) (2:53) Capitol 37662 The Pet Sounds Sessions.

(S) (3:04) Capitol 37662 The Pet Sounds Sessions. *(instrumental track)*

(S) (2:45) Capitol 37662 The Pet Sounds Sessions. *(vocals only)*

(S) (9:25) Capitol 37662 The Pet Sounds Sessions. *(several alternate takes strung together)*

(M) (2:48) Capitol 37662 The Pet Sounds Sessions. *(found on the bonus disc titled "Pet Sounds" included with this box set)*

(M) (2:47) Capitol 56312 O.S.T. Boogie Nights.

1966 GOOD VIBRATIONS

(M) (3:35) Capitol 46467 Endless Summer.

(M) (3:34) Capitol 46324 Made In U.S.A.

(M) (3:35) Rhino 70627 Billboard's Top Rock & Roll Hits Of 1966.

(M) (3:35) Rhino 72007 Billboard's Top Rock & Roll Hits 1962-1966 Box Set.

(E) (3:34) Original Sound 8858 Oldies But Goodies Vol. 8. *(this compact disc uses the "Waring - fds" noise reduction process)*

(E) (3:34) Original Sound 2221 Oldies But Goodies Volumes 1,4,6,8 and 10 Box Set. *(this box set uses the "Waring - fds" noise reduction process)*

(E) (3:34) Original Sound 2500 Oldies But Goodies Volumes 1-15 Box Set. *(this box set uses the "Waring - fds" noise reduction process)*

(M) (3:34) Capitol 93696 Smiley Smile/Wild Honey.

(M) (6:52) Capitol 93696 Smiley Smile/Wild Honey. *(several alternate takes strung together)*

(M) (2:59) Capitol 93696 Smiley Smile/Wild Honey. *(alternate take)*

(M) (3:35) Capitol 96796 Absolute Best Volume 2.

(M) (3:35) Capitol 81294 Thirty Years Of.

(M) (3:34) Time-Life 2RNR-03 Rock 'N' Roll Era - The Beach Boys 1962-1967.

(M) (3:35) Time-Life 2CLR-02 Classic Rock - 1966.

(M) (3:34) Time-Life SUD-01 Superhits - 1966.

(M) (3:36) Time-Life R962-04 History Of Rock 'N' Roll: California Pop 1963-1967.

(M) (3:35) Time-Life R921-38 Get Together.

(M) (3:34) MCA Special Products 22105 Greatest Classic Rock Hits.

(M) (3:34) Capitol 29635 Smiley Smile.

(M) (3:34) Capitol 29418 20 Good Vibrations - Greatest Hits.

(M) (3:43) DCC Compact Classics 1076 Endless Summer. *(gold disc; 08 longer fade than either the 45 or LP)*

(M) (3:34) Time-Life AM1-09 AM Gold - 1966.

(M) (3:35) Madacy Entertainment 6804 More Sun Splashin'.

(M) (3:34) Capitol 21277 Essential Beach Boys - Perfect Harmony.

BEACH BOYS *(Continued)*

- (S) (3:11) Capitol 37662 The Pet Sounds Sessions. *(alternate instrumental track)*
- (S) (2:41) Capitol 37662 The Pet Sounds Sessions. *(several alternate takes strung together)*
- (M) (3:35) Time-Life R13610 Gold And Platinum Box Set - The Ultimate Rock Collection.
- (M) (3:34) Simitar 55532 The Number One's: The '60s.

1967 HEROES AND VILLAINS
- (M) (3:35) Capitol 46324 Made In U.S.A.
- (M) (3:37) Capitol 93696 Smiley Smile/Wild Honey.
- (M) (2:56) Capitol 93696 Smiley Smile/Wild Honey. *(alternate take)*
- (M) (3:35) Capitol 96796 Absolute Best Volume 2.
- (M) (2:55) Capitol 81294 Thirty Years Of. *(alternate take)*
- (M) (6:39) Capitol 81294 Thirty Years Of. *(alternate take)*
- (M) (0:35) Capitol 81294 Thirty Years Of. *(alternate take)*
- (M) (3:35) Capitol 81294 Thirty Years Of.
- (M) (3:35) Time-Life 2RNR-03 Rock 'N' Roll Era - The Beach Boys 1962-1967.
- (M) (3:32) Time-Life 2CLR-24 Classic Rock - 1967: Blowin' Your Mind.
- (M) (3:37) Capitol 29635 Smiley Smile.

1967 WILD HONEY
- (M) (2:36) Capitol 93696 Smiley Smile/Wild Honey.
- (M) (2:36) Capitol 96796 Absolute Best Volume 2.
- (M) (2:35) Capitol 81294 Thirty Years Of.
- (M) (2:36) Capitol 29636 Wild Honey.

1968 DARLIN'
- (M) (2:10) Capitol 93696 Smiley Smile/Wild Honey.
- (M) (2:11) Capitol 96796 Absolute Best Volume 2.
- (M) (2:11) Capitol 81294 Thirty Years Of.
- (M) (2:10) Time-Life 2CLR-27 Classic Rock - 1968: Blowin' Your Mind.
- (M) (2:10) Capitol 29636 Wild Honey.
- (M) (2:11) DCC Compact Classics 1089 Spirit Of America. *(gold disc)*

1968 FRIENDS
- (S) (2:29) Capitol 93697 Friends/20-20.
- (S) (2:30) Capitol 81294 Thirty Years Of.
- (S) (2:29) Capitol 29637 Friends.

1968 DO IT AGAIN
- (M) (2:17) Capitol 46324 Made In U.S.A. *(45 version)*
- (E) (2:24) Capitol 93697 Friends/20-20. *(LP version)*
- (E) (2:24) Capitol 96796 Absolute Best Volume 2. *(LP version)*
- (E) (2:24) Capitol 81294 Thirty Years Of. *(LP version)*
- (E) (2:24) Capitol 29638 20-20. *(LP version)*
- (M) (2:24) Track Factory 11445 O.S.T. Flipper. *(LP version)*
- (M) (2:23) Capitol 21277 Essential Beach Boys - Perfect Harmony. *(LP version)*

1969 I CAN HEAR MUSIC
- (S) (2:37) Capitol 93697 Friends/20-20.
- (S) (2:37) Capitol 81294 Thirty Years Of.
- (E) (2:24) Capitol 29638 20-20.
- (S) (2:36) DCC Compact Classics 1089 Spirit Of America. *(gold disc)*
- (S) (2:37) Capitol 21277 Essential Beach Boys - Perfect Harmony.

1974 SURFIN' U.S.A.
(this song was a hit in 1963 and 1974; see 1963 listings)

1976 ROCK AND ROLL MUSIC
- (S) (2:26) Caribou/Epic 37445 Ten Years Of Harmony. *(some pressings of this cd feature the 45 version, others the LP version)*
- (S) (2:27) Caribou/Epic 46955 15 Big Ones. *(LP version)*
- (S) (2:27) Capitol 46324 Made In U.S.A. *(LP version)*
- (S) (2:26) Capitol 81294 Thirty Years Of. *(LP version)*
- (S) (2:27) Hip-O 40076 Chuck B. Covered: A Tribute To Chuck Berry. *(LP version)*

1976 IT'S O.K.
- (S) (2:09) Caribou/Epic 37445 Ten Years Of Harmony.
- (S) (2:09) Caribou/Epic 46955 15 Big Ones.
- (S) (2:09) Capitol 81294 Thirty Years Of.

1979 GOOD TIMIN'
- (S) (2:10) Caribou/Epic 37445 Ten Years Of Harmony.

- (S) (2:11) Caribou/Epic 35752 L.A. (Light Album).
- (S) (2:09) Capitol 81294 Thirty Years Of.

1981 THE BEACH BOYS MEDLEY
1982 COME GO WITH ME
- (S) (2:04) Capitol 46324 Made In U.S.A.
- (S) (2:08) Caribou/Epic 46957 M.I.U. Album. *(alternate take - not the version found on the vinyl album "M.I.U.")*
- (S) (2:08) Caribou/Epic 37445 Ten Years Of Harmony. *(alternate take - not the version found on the vinyl album "Ten Years Of Harmony")*
- (S) (2:03) Capitol 81294 Thirty Years Of.

1985 GETCHA BACK
- (S) (3:00) Capitol 46324 Made In U.S.A.
- (S) (3:02) Caribou/Epic 39946 The Beach Boys.
- (S) (3:00) Capitol 81294 Thirty Years Of.

released as by THE FAT BOYS and THE BEACH BOYS:
1987 WIPEOUT
(actual 45 time is (3:57) not (3:50) as stated on the record label)
- (S) (4:27) Tin Pan Apple/Polydor 831948 Fat Boys - Crushin'. *(LP version)*
- (S) (3:59) Capitol 92639 Beach Boys - Still Cruisin'. *(45 version)*
- (S) (3:59) Capitol 21277 Essential Beach Boys - Perfect Harmony. *(45 version)*
- (S) (3:59) Rhino 72632 Fat Boys - Best Of. *(45 version)*
- (S) (4:27) Polygram Special Markets 314520445 Soul Hits Of The 80's. *(LP version)*

released as by THE BEACH BOYS:
1988 KOKOMO
- (S) (3:34) Elektra 60806 O.S.T. Cocktail.
- (S) (3:35) Foundation/WEA 26097 Super Sessions Volume Two.
- (S) (3:35) Capitol 92639 Still Cruisin'.
- (S) (3:35) Capitol 29418 20 Good Vibrations - Greatest Hits.
- (S) (3:34) Capitol 81294 Thirty Years Of.
- (S) (3:34) Time-Life R988-10 Sounds Of The 80's: 1988.
- (S) (3:33) Madacy Entertainment 26927 Sun Splashin'.

BEASTIE BOYS
1987 (YOU GOTTA) FIGHT FOR YOUR RIGHT (TO PARTY!)
- (S) (3:27) Def Jam/Columbia 45035 Def Jam Classics Vol. 1.
- (S) (3:27) Columbia 44382 Heart Of Soul.
- (S) (3:25) JCI 4540 Masters Of Metal: Strikeforce Volume 1.
- (S) (3:26) Priority 9753 Rap The Beat.
- (S) (3:29) K-Tel 315 Rap's Biggest Hits.
- (S) (3:28) Risky Business 57833 Read The Hits/Best Of The 80's.
- (S) (3:28) Def Jam 314527362 Def Jam Classics Vol. 1.
- (S) (3:27) Def Jam/Columbia 40238 Licensed To Ill.
- (S) (3:27) Def Jam 314527351 Licensed To Ill.
- (S) (3:27) Time-Life R988-28 Sounds Of The Eighties: The Rolling Stone Collection 1986-1987.
- (S) (3:27) Time-Life R968-18 Guitar Rock - The Heavy '80s.
- (S) (3:27) Def Jam 314523848 Def Jam Music Group 10th Year Anniversary.
- (S) (3:26) Tommy Boy 1173 ESPN Presents X Games Vol. 1.

1989 HEY LADIES
- (S) (3:47) Capitol 91743 Paul's Boutique.

BEATLES
1964 I WANT TO HOLD YOUR HAND
- (S) (2:24) Parlophone 90043 Past Masters Volume 1.
- (S) (2:24) Parlophone 91302 Box Set.
- (M) (2:23) Parlophone 15852 Compact Disc EP Collection.
- (M) (2:23) Parlophone 15901 CD Singles Collection.
- (S) (2:24) Capitol 97036 Beatles 1962-1966.
- (M) (2:36) Apple 34445 Anthology 1. *(live)*
- (S) (2:24) Time-Life R13610 Gold And Platinum Box Set - The Ultimate Rock Collection.

1964 I SAW HER STANDING THERE
- (M) (2:51) Parlophone 46435 Please Please Me.
- (M) (2:51) Parlophone 15852 Compact Disc EP Collection.

(M) (2:51) Parlophone 91302 Box Set.
(M) (2:48) Apple 34445 Anthology 1. *(live)*

1964 SHE LOVES YOU

(M) (2:19) Parlophone 90043 Past Masters Volume 1.
(M) (2:19) Parlophone 91302 Box Set.
(M) (2:19) Parlophone 15852 Compact Disc EP Collection.
(M) (2:19) Parlophone 15901 CD Singles Collection.
(M) (2:18) Capitol 97036 Beatles 1962-1966.
(M) (2:49) Apple 34445 Anthology 1. *(live)*

1964 PLEASE PLEASE ME

(M) (1:59) Parlophone 46435 Please Please Me. *(45 version)*
(M) (1:59) Parlophone 91302 Box Set. *(45 version)*
(M) (1:59) Parlophone 15852 Compact Disc EP Collection. *(45 version)*
(M) (1:59) Parlophone 15901 CD Singles Collection. *(45 version)*
(M) (1:59) Capitol 97036 Beatles 1962-1966. *(45 version)*
(M) (1:57) Apple 34445 Anthology 1. *(first known recording of this song featuring Andy White on drums)*

1964 MY BONNIE
(first released as by TONY SHERIDAN and THE BEAT BROTHERS and then after THE BEATLES scored big in the U.S., it was rereleased with credit given to THE BEATLES with TONY SHERIDAN)

(S) (2:41) Polydor 823701 Early Tapes Of The Beatles.
(M) (2:04) Rhino 70323 History Of British Rock Volume 5. *(this was the U.S. 45 version)*
(M) (2:04) Rhino 72022 History Of British Rock Box Set. *(this was the U.S. 45 version)*
(S) (2:40) Apple 34445 Anthology 1. *(Paul McCartney talks over the introduction)*

1964 TWIST AND SHOUT

(M) (2:32) Parlophone 46435 Please Please Me.
(M) (2:32) Parlophone 91302 Box Set.
(M) (2:32) Capitol 90803 Music From The Original Motion Picture Imagine.
(M) (2:32) Parlophone 15852 Compact Disc EP Collection.
(M) (3:05) Apple 34445 Anthology 1. *(live)*

1964 ROLL OVER BEETHOVEN

(M) (2:43) Parlophone 46436 With The Beatles.
(M) (2:43) Parlophone 91302 Box Set.
(M) (2:20) Apple 34445 Anthology 1. *(live)*

1964 ALL MY LOVING

(M) (2:05) Parlophone 46436 With The Beatles.
(M) (2:05) Parlophone 91302 Box Set.
(M) (2:05) Parlophone 15852 Compact Disc EP Collection.
(S) (2:05) Capitol 97036 Beatles 1962-1966.
(M) (2:18) Apple 34445 Anthology 1. *(live)*

1964 CAN'T BUY ME LOVE

(M) (2:10) Parlophone 46437 A Hard Day's Night.
(M) (2:10) Parlophone 91302 Box Set.
(M) (2:11) Parlophone 15852 Compact Disc EP Collection.
(M) (2:11) Parlophone 15901 CD Singles Collection.
(S) (2:09) Capitol 97036 Beatles 1962-1966.
(M) (2:08) Apple 34445 Anthology 1. *(alternate take)*

1964 DO YOU WANT TO KNOW A SECRET

(M) (1:55) Parlophone 46435 Please Please Me.
(M) (1:55) Parlophone 91302 Box Set.
(M) (1:54) Parlophone 15852 Compact Disc EP Collection.

1964 THANK YOU GIRL

(M) (2:01) Parlophone 90043 Past Masters Volume 1. *(45 version)*
(M) (2:01) Parlophone 91302 Box Set. *(45 version)*
(M) (2:01) Parlophone 15852 Compact Disc EP Collection. *(45 version)*
(M) (2:01) Parlophone 15901 CD Singles Collection. *(45 version)*

1964 LOVE ME DO

(M) (2:18) Parlophone 46435 Please Please Me. *(U.S. 45 and LP version with Andy White on drums)*
(M) (2:18) Parlophone 91302 Box Set. *(U.S. 45 and LP version with Andy White on drums)*
(M) (2:21) Parlophone 90043 Past Masters Volume 1. *(Ringo Starr on drums but this was not the U.S. hit version)*

(M) (2:21) Parlophone 91302 Box Set. *(Ringo Starr on drums but this was not the U.S. hit version)*
(M) (2:18) Parlophone 15852 Compact Disc EP Collection. *(U.S. 45 and LP version with Andy White on drums)*
(M) (2:18) Parlophone 15901 CD Singles Collection. *(U.S. 45 and LP version with Andy White on drums)*
(M) (2:18) Capitol 97036 Beatles 1962-1966. *(U.S. 45 and LP version with Andy White on drums)*
(M) (2:30) Apple 34445 Anthology 1. *(first known recording of this song featuring Pete Best on drums)*

1964 P.S. I LOVE YOU

(M) (2:01) Parlophone 46435 Please Please Me.
(M) (2:01) Parlophone 91302 Box Set.
(M) (2:01) Parlophone 15852 Compact Disc EP Collection.
(M) (2:01) Parlophone 15901 CD Singles Collection.

1964 A HARD DAY'S NIGHT

(M) (2:28) Parlophone 46437 A Hard Day's Night.
(M) (2:28) Parlophone 91302 Box Set.
(M) (2:28) Parlophone 15901 CD Singles Collection.
(S) (2:30) Capitol 97036 Beatles 1962-1966.
(M) (1:24) Apple 34445 Anthology 1. *(alternate take)*

1964 AIN'T SHE SWEET

(M) (2:12) Polydor 823701 Early Tapes Of The Beatles. *(U.S. 45 version)*
(M) (2:10) Rhino 70323 History Of British Rock Volume 5. *(U.S. 45 version)*
(M) (2:10) Rhino 72022 History Of British Rock Box Set. *(U.S. 45 version)*
(M) (2:11) Apple 34445 Anthology 1. *(U.S. 45 version)*
(S) (2:05) Apple 34451 Anthology 3. *(1969 rerecording)*
(M) (2:11) Polygram Special Markets 314520495 45's On CD Volume 2. *(U.S. 45 version)*

1964 AND I LOVE HER

(M) (2:27) Parlophone 46437 A Hard Day's Night. *(this was not the U.S. 45 or LP version as Paul's voice is double tracked on this version)*
(M) (2:27) Parlophone 91302 Box Set. *(same comments as for Parlophone 46437)*
(M) (2:27) Parlophone 15852 Compact Disc EP Collection. *(same comments as for Parlophone 46437)*
(S) (2:27) Capitol 97036 Beatles 1962-1966. *(same comments as for Parlophone 46437)*
(M) (1:50) Apple 34445 Anthology 1. *(alternate take)*

1964 I'LL CRY INSTEAD
(the actual "Something New" LP time is (1:44) not (2:04) as stated on the record label)

(M) (1:43) Parlophone 46437 A Hard Day's Night. *(this is the "Something New" LP version)*
(M) (1:43) Parlophone 91302 Box Set. *(this is the "Something New" LP version)*
(M) (1:43) Parlophone 15852 Compact Disc EP Collection. *(this is the "Something New" LP version)*

1964 MATCHBOX

(S) (1:56) Parlophone 90043 Past Masters Volume 1.
(S) (1:56) Parlophone 91302 Box Set.
(M) (1:56) Parlophone 15852 Compact Disc EP Collection.

1964 SLOW DOWN

(S) (2:54) Parlophone 90043 Past Masters Volume 1. *(LP version)*
(S) (2:54) Parlophone 91302 Box Set. *(LP version)*
(M) (2:54) Parlophone 15852 Compact Disc EP Collection. *(45 version)*

1964 I FEEL FINE

(S) (2:17) Parlophone 90043 Past Masters Volume 1. *(British mix)*
(S) (2:17) Parlophone 91302 Box Set. *(British mix)*
(M) (2:21) Parlophone 15852 Compact Disc EP Collection. *(British mix)*
(M) (2:20) Parlophone 15901 CD Singles Collection. *(British mix)*
(S) (2:16) Capitol 97036 Beatles 1962-1966. *(British mix)*
(M) (2:15) Apple 34448 Anthology 2. *(live)*

1964 SHE'S A WOMAN

(S) (3:00) Parlophone 90043 Past Masters Volume 1. *(British mix)*
(S) (3:00) Parlophone 91302 Box Set. *(British mix)*

BEATLES *(Continued)*

(S) (3:01) Parlophone 15852 Compact Disc EP Collection. *(with countoff; British mix)*

(M) (3:00) Parlophone 15901 CD Singles Collection. *(British mix)*

(M) (2:53) Apple 34448 Anthology 2. *(live)*

1965 EIGHT DAYS A WEEK
(M) (2:41) Parlophone 46438 Beatles For Sale.
(M) (2:41) Parlophone 91302 Box Set.
(M) (2:42) Parlophone 15852 Compact Disc EP Collection.
(S) (2:42) Capitol 97036 Beatles 1962-1966.
(M) (2:46) Apple 34445 Anthology 1. *(alternate take)*

1965 TICKET TO RIDE
(S) (3:08) Parlophone 46439 Help!
(S) (3:08) Parlophone 91302 Box Set.
(M) (3:01) Parlophone 15901 CD Singles Collection.
(S) (3:08) Capitol 97036 Beatles 1962-1966.
(M) (2:44) Apple 34448 Anthology 2. *(live)*

1965 HELP
(S) (2:17) Parlophone 46439 Help! *(LP version but missing the James Bond introduction)*
(S) (2:17) Parlophone 91302 Box Set. *(LP version but missing the James Bond introduction)*
(S) (2:16) Capitol 90803 Music From The Original Motion Picture Imagine. *(LP version but missing the James Bond introduction)*
(M) (2:16) Parlophone 15901 CD Singles Collection. *(45 version)*
(S) (2:16) Capitol 97036 Beatles 1962-1966. *(LP version but missing the James Bond introduction)*
(M) (2:53) Apple 34448 Anthology 2. *(live)*

1965 YESTERDAY
(S) (2:03) Parlophone 46439 Help!
(S) (2:03) Parlophone 91302 Box Set.
(M) (2:03) Parlophone 15852 Compact Disc EP Collection.
(S) (2:03) Capitol 97036 Beatles 1962-1966.
(S) (2:32) Apple 34448 Anthology 2. *(alternate take with studio talk)*
(M) (2:42) Apple 34448 Anthology 2. *(live)*

1965 ACT NATURALLY
(S) (2:28) Parlophone 46439 Help!
(S) (2:28) Parlophone 91302 Box Set.
(M) (2:27) Parlophone 15852 Compact Disc EP Collection.

1966 WE CAN WORK IT OUT
(S) (2:13) Parlophone 90044 Past Masters Volume 2. *(British mix)*
(S) (2:13) Parlophone 91302 Box Set. *(British mix)*
(M) (2:12) Parlophone 15901 CD Singles Collection.
(S) (2:13) Capitol 97036 Beatles 1962-1966. *(British mix)*

1966 DAY TRIPPER
(S) (2:47) Parlophone 90044 Past Masters Volume 2. *(truncated fade; British mix)*
(S) (2:47) Parlophone 91302 Box Set. *(truncated fade; British mix)*
(M) (2:49) Parlophone 15901 CD Singles Collection.
(S) (2:46) Capitol 97036 Beatles 1962-1966. *(British mix)*

1966 NOWHERE MAN
(S) (2:41) Parlophone 46440 Rubber Soul.
(S) (2:41) Parlophone 91302 Box Set.
(M) (2:40) Parlophone 15852 Compact Disc EP Collection.
(S) (2:41) Capitol 97036 Beatles 1962-1966.

1966 PAPERBACK WRITER
(S) (2:16) Parlophone 90044 Past Masters Volume 2. *(stereo length)*
(S) (2:16) Parlophone 91302 Box Set. *(stereo length)*
(M) (2:23) Parlophone 15901 CD Singles Collection. *(mono length)*
(S) (2:16) Capitol 97036 Beatles 1962-1966. *(stereo length)*

1966 RAIN
(S) (2:59) Parlophone 90044 Past Masters Volume 2.
(S) (2:59) Parlophone 91302 Box Set.
(M) (2:59) Parlophone 15901 CD Singles Collection.

1966 YELLOW SUBMARINE
(S) (2:36) Parlophone 46441 Revolver. *(LP version)*
(S) (2:37) Parlophone 46445 Yellow Submarine. *(LP version)*
(S) (2:36) Parlophone 91302 Box Set. *(LP version)*
(M) (2:36) Parlophone 15901 CD Singles Collection. *(45 version)*
(S) (2:36) Capitol 97036 Beatles 1962-1966. *(LP version)*

1966 ELEANOR RIGBY
(S) (2:03) Parlophone 46441 Revolver.
(S) (2:03) Parlophone 91302 Box Set.
(M) (2:04) Parlophone 15901 CD Singles Collection.
(S) (2:03) Capitol 97036 Beatles 1962-1966.
(S) (2:05) Apple 34448 Anthology 2. *(string portion only)*

1967 PENNY LANE
(radio stations were serviced with a special 45 version of this song which featured trumpets on the ending)
(S) (2:58) Parlophone 48062 Magical Mystery Tour.
(S) (2:58) Parlophone 91302 Box Set.
(M) (2:57) Parlophone 15901 CD Singles Collection.
(S) (2:58) Capitol 97039 Beatles 1967-1970.
(S) (3:11) Apple 34448 Anthology 2. *(alternate take)*

1967 STRAWBERRY FIELDS FOREVER
(S) (4:05) Parlophone 48062 Magical Mystery Tour. *(German mix)*
(S) (4:05) Parlophone 91302 Box Set. *(German mix)*
(S) (4:05) Capitol 90803 Music From The Original Motion Picture Imagine. *(German mix)*
(M) (4:05) Parlophone 15901 CD Singles Collection.
(S) (4:04) Capitol 97039 Beatles 1967-1970. *(German mix)*
(M) (1:41) Apple 34448 Anthology 2. *(demo)*
(S) (2:33) Apple 34448 Anthology 2. *(alternate take)*
(M) (4:12) Apple 34448 Anthology 2. *(alternate take)*

1967 ALL YOU NEED IS LOVE
(S) (3:46) Parlophone 48062 Magical Mystery Tour. *(LP length)*
(S) (3:46) Parlophone 46445 Yellow Submarine. *(LP length)*
(S) (3:46) Parlophone 91302 Box Set. *(LP length)*
(M) (3:57) Parlophone 15901 CD Singles Collection. *(45 length)*
(S) (3:46) Capitol 97039 Beatles 1967-1970. *(LP length)*

1967 BABY YOU'RE A RICH MAN
(S) (2:59) Parlophone 48062 Magical Mystery Tour. *(missing some reverb effect)*
(S) (2:59) Parlophone 91302 Box Set. *(missing some reverb effect)*
(M) (3:03) Parlophone 15901 CD Singles Collection.
(S) (2:57) Parlophone 15852 Compact Disc EP Collection. *(missing some reverb effect)*

1967 HELLO GOODBYE
(S) (3:27) Parlophone 48062 Magical Mystery Tour.
(S) (3:27) Parlophone 91302 Box Set.
(M) (3:23) Parlophone 15901 CD Singles Collection.
(S) (3:26) Capitol 97039 Beatles 1967-1970.
(S) (3:17) Apple 34448 Anthology 2. *(alternate take)*

1968 LADY MADONNA
(S) (2:15) Parlophone 90044 Past Masters Volume 2. *(truncated fade)*
(S) (2:15) Parlophone 91302 Box Set. *(truncated fade)*
(M) (2:14) Parlophone 15901 CD Singles Collection.
(S) (2:14) Capitol 97039 Beatles 1967-1970.
(S) (2:20) Apple 34448 Anthology 2. *(alternate take)*

1968 HEY JUDE
(S) (7:06) Parlophone 90044 Past Masters Volume 2.
(S) (7:06) Parlophone 91302 Box Set.
(M) (7:14) Parlophone 15901 CD Singles Collection.
(S) (7:06) Capitol 97039 Beatles 1967-1970.
(S) (4:18) Apple 34451 Anthology 3. *(alternate take)*

1968 REVOLUTION
(S) (4:13) Parlophone 46444 The Beatles. *(LP version which is technically titled "REVOLUTION 1")*
(S) (4:13) Parlophone 91302 Box Set. *(LP version which is technically titled "REVOLUTION 1")*
(S) (3:22) Parlophone 90044 Past Masters Volume 2. *(45 version)*
(S) (3:22) Parlophone 91302 Box Set. *(45 version)*
(S) (3:22) Capitol 90803 Music From The Original Motion Picture Imagine. *(45 version)*
(M) (3:21) Parlophone 15901 CD Singles Collection. *(45 version)*

(S) (3:22) Capitol 97039 Beatles 1967-1970. *(45 version)*

1969 GET BACK
- (S) (3:05) Parlophone 46447 Let It Be. *(LP version)*
- (S) (3:05) Parlophone 91302 Box Set. *(LP version)*
- (S) (3:11) Parlophone 90044 Past Masters Volume 2. *(45 version)*
- (S) (3:11) Parlophone 91302 Box Set. *(45 version)*
- (M) (3:09) Parlophone 15901 CD Singles Collection. *(45 version)*
- (S) (3:09) Capitol 97039 Beatles 1967-1970. *(45 version)*
- (S) (3:05) Apple 34451 Anthology 3. *(alternate take)*

1969 DON'T LET ME DOWN
- (M) (3:29) Parlophone 15901 CD Singles Collection.
- (S) (3:33) Parlophone 90044 Past Masters Volume Two.
- (S) (3:33) Parlophone 91302 Box Set.
- (S) (3:33) Capitol 90803 Music From The Original Motion Picture Imagine.

1969 BALLAD OF JOHN AND YOKO
- (S) (2:57) Parlophone 90044 Past Masters Volume 2.
- (S) (2:57) Parlophone 91302 Box Set.
- (S) (2:57) Capitol 90803 Music From The Original Motion Picture Imagine.
- (S) (2:57) Parlophone 15901 CD Singles Collection.
- (S) (2:56) Capitol 97039 Beatles 1967-1970.

1969 COME TOGETHER
- (S) (4:16) Parlophone 46446 Abbey Road.
- (S) (4:16) Parlophone 91302 Box Set.
- (S) (4:15) Parlophone 15901 CD Singles Collection.
- (S) (4:15) Capitol 97039 Beatles 1967-1970.
- (S) (3:37) Apple 34451 Anthology 3. *(alternate take)*

1969 SOMETHING
- (S) (2:59) Parlophone 46446 Abbey Road.
- (S) (2:59) Parlophone 91302 Box Set.
- (S) (2:59) Capitol 46682 Best Of George Harrison.
- (S) (2:59) Parlophone 15901 CD Singles Collection.
- (S) (2:59) Capitol 97039 Beatles 1967-1970.
- (M) (3:16) Apple 34451 Anthology 3. *(demo)*

1970 LET IT BE
- (S) (4:01) Parlophone 46447 Let It Be. *(LP version)*
- (S) (4:01) Parlophone 91302 Box Set. *(LP version)*
- (S) (3:48) Parlophone 90044 Past Masters Volume 2. *(45 version)*
- (S) (3:48) Parlophone 91302 Box Set. *(45 version)*
- (S) (3:48) Parlophone 15901 CD Singles Collection. *(45 version)*
- (S) (3:48) Capitol 97039 Beatles 1967-1970. *(45 version)*
- (S) (4:01) Apple 34451 Anthology 3. *(alternate take)*

1970 THE LONG AND WINDING ROAD
- (S) (3:36) Parlophone 46447 Let It Be.
- (S) (3:36) Parlophone 91302 Box Set.
- (S) (3:35) Capitol 97039 Beatles 1967-1970.
- (S) (3:38) Apple 34451 Anthology 3. *(alternate take)*

1976 GOT TO GET YOU INTO MY LIFE
- (S) (2:26) Parlophone 46441 Revolver.
- (S) (2:52) Apple 34448 Anthology 2. *(alternate take; poor stereo separation)*

1982 THE BEATLES' MOVIE MEDLEY
1986 TWIST AND SHOUT
(this song was a hit in 1964 and 1986; see 1964 listing)
1996 FREE AS A BIRD
- (S) (4:23) Apple 34445 Anthology 1.

1996 REAL LOVE
- (S) (3:51) Apple 34448 Anthology 2.

BEAU BRUMMELS
1965 LAUGH LAUGH
(original 45 and LP versions of this song faded out)
- (S) (3:01) K-Tel 686 Battle Of The Bands Volume 4. *(ends cold)*
- (S) (3:02) Rhino 75892 Nuggets. *(ends cold)*
- (S) (3:01) Rhino 70906 American Bandstand Greatest Hits Collection. *(ends cold)*
- (S) (2:51) Garland 012 Remember When. *(ending fades)*
- (M) (2:52) Rhino 70536 San Francisco Nights. *(ending fades)*
- (S) (3:01) Warner Special Products 27607 Highs Of The 60's. *(ends cold)*
- (S) (3:01) Rhino 75779 Best Of. *(ends cold)*

- (S) (2:56) Collectables 5063 History Of Rock Volume 3. *(ending fades)*
- (S) (3:01) Time-Life 2CLR-08 Classic Rock - 1965: The Beat Goes On. *(ends cold)*
- (S) (3:01) Time-Life R962-02 History Of Rock 'N' Roll: Folk Rock 1964-1967. *(ends cold)*
- (S) (3:01) Collectables 2501 WCBS-FM History Of Rock - The 60's Part 2. *(ends cold)*
- (S) (3:01) Collectables 4501 History Of Rock/The 60s Part Two. *(ends cold)*
- (S) (3:01) Rhino 71729 '60s Rock Classics, Vol. 2. *(ends cold)*
- (M) (2:51) Rhino 71648 The Flintstones: Original Songs From The Classic TV Show Soundtrack. *(ending fades)*
- (S) (2:52) Sundazed 6039 Introducing. *(ending fades)*
- (S) (3:01) Collectables 2554 CBS-FM History Of Rock Volume 2. *(ends cold)*
- (S) (3:01) Flashback 72702 '60s Rock: The Beat Goes On. *(ends cold)*
- (S) (3:01) Flashback 72088 '60s Rock Hits Box Set. *(ends cold)*

1965 JUST A LITTLE
- (S) (2:23) Rhino 75892 Nuggets.
- (S) (2:23) Garland 012 Remember When.
- (M) (2:22) Rhino 70536 San Francisco Nights.
- (S) (2:23) Rhino 75779 Best Of. *("JUST A LITTLE" is listed on the cd jacket as track 3 when in reality it is track 4)*
- (S) (2:23) Time-Life 2CLR-01 Classic Rock - 1965.
- (*) (*:**) Rhino 71728 '60s Rock Classics, Vol. 1. *(this is not the song "JUST A LITTLE" as stated on the cd jacket but "THEY'LL MAKE YOU CRY" instead)*
- (S) (2:21) Sundazed 6039 Introducing.
- (M) (2:21) Sundazed 6039 Introducing. *(demo version)*
- (S) (2:21) Rhino 71935 Billboard Top Pop Hits, 1965.
- (S) (2:23) Flashback 72701 '60s Rock: Mony Mony.
- (S) (2:23) Flashback 72088 '60s Rock Hits Box Set.

1965 YOU TELL ME WHY
- (S) (3:03) Rhino 75779 Best Of.
- (S) (3:02) Time-Life 2CLR-23 Classic Rock - 1965: Blowin' Your Mind.
- (S) (3:03) Sundazed 6040 Volume 2.

BECK
1994 LOSER
- (S) (3:54) DGC 24634 Mellow Gold.

BOB BECKHAM
1959 JUST AS MUCH AS EVER
1960 CRAZY ARMS

BEE GEES
1967 NEW YORK MINING DISASTER 1941 (HAVE YOU SEEN MY WIFE, MR. JONES)
- (S) (2:08) Polydor 843911 Tales From The Brothers Gibb. *(LP version)*
- (S) (2:08) Polydor 831594 Best Of. *(LP version)*
- (S) (2:08) Polydor 825220 Bee Gees' 1st. *(LP version)*
- (M) (2:08) Rhino 70326 History Of British Rock Volume 8. *(45 version)*
- (M) (2:08) Rhino 72022 History Of British Rock Box Set. *(45 version)*
- (S) (2:08) Time-Life 2CLR-24 Classic Rock - 1967: Blowin' Your Mind. *(LP version)*
- (S) (2:08) Rebound 314520279 Bee Gee's First. *(LP version)*

1967 TO LOVE SOMEBODY
- (S) (2:59) Polydor 843911 Tales From The Brothers Gibb.
- (S) (2:59) Polydor 825220 Bee Gees' 1st.
- (S) (2:59) Polydor 831594 Best Of.
- (S) (2:59) Rhino 70325 History Of British Rock Volume 7.
- (S) (2:59) Rhino 72022 History Of British Rock Box Set.
- (S) (2:55) Time-Life SUD-05 Superhits - 1967.
- (S) (2:59) Rebound 314520279 Bee Gee's First.
- (S) (2:55) Time-Life AM1-08 AM Gold - 1967.

BEE GEES (Continued)

1967 HOLIDAY
- (S) (2:52) Polydor 843911 Tales From The Brothers Gibb.
- (S) (2:52) Polydor 825220 Bee Gees' 1st.
- (S) (2:52) Polydor 831594 Best Of.
- (S) (2:52) Time-Life SUD-18 Superhits - Late 60's Classics.
- (S) (2:52) Rebound 314520279 Bee Gee's First.
- (S) (2:52) Time-Life AM1-12 AM Gold - Late '60s Classics.

1967 (THE LIGHTS WENT OUT IN) MASSACHUSETTS
- (S) (2:21) Polydor 843911 Tales From The Brothers Gibb.
- (S) (2:23) Polydor 833659 Horizontal.
- (S) (2:22) Polydor 831594 Best Of.
- (S) (2:19) Time-Life SUD-05 Superhits - 1967.
- (S) (2:19) Time-Life AM1-08 AM Gold - 1967.

1968 WORDS
- (S) (3:13) Polydor 843911 Tales From The Brothers Gibb.
- (S) (3:14) Polydor 831594 Best Of.
- (M) (3:16) Rhino 70327 History Of British Rock Volume 9.
- (M) (3:16) Rhino 72022 History Of British Rock Box Set.
- (S) (3:13) Time-Life 2CLR-27 Classic Rock - 1968: Blowin' Your Mind.

1968 I'VE GOTTA GET A MESSAGE TO YOU
- (S) (3:05) Polydor 843911 Tales From The Brothers Gibb. *(45 version)*
- (S) (2:55) Polydor 831594 Best Of. *(LP version)*
- (S) (2:55) Polydor 833660 Idea. *(LP version)*
- (S) (3:04) Rhino 70327 History Of British Rock Volume 9. *(45 version)*
- (S) (3:04) Rhino 72022 History Of British Rock Box Set. *(45 version)*

1969 I STARTED A JOKE
- (S) (3:05) Polydor 843911 Tales From The Brothers Gibb.
- (S) (3:06) Polydor 831594 Best Of.
- (S) (3:07) Polydor 833660 Idea.
- (S) (3:05) Time-Life 2CLR-20 Classic Rock - 1969: Shakin' All Over.

1969 FIRST OF MAY
- (S) (2:46) Polydor 843911 Tales From The Brothers Gibb.
- (S) (2:46) Polydor 825451 Odessa.
- (S) (2:46) Polydor 831594 Best Of.

1971 LONELY DAYS
- (S) (3:44) Polydor 843911 Tales From The Brothers Gibb.
- (S) (3:44) Polydor 833785 2 Years On.
- (S) (3:44) Polydor 831960 Best Of Volume 2.
- (S) (3:44) Time-Life SOD-01 Sounds Of The Seventies - 1970.

1971 HOW CAN YOU MEND A BROKEN HEART
- (S) (3:55) Polydor 843911 Tales From The Brothers Gibb.
- (S) (3:55) Polydor 831960 Best Of Volume 2.
- (S) (3:56) Polydor 833786 Trafalgar.
- (S) (3:55) Time-Life SUD-10 Superhits - 1971.
- (S) (3:56) Time-Life SOD-02 Sounds Of The Seventies - 1971.
- (S) (3:56) MFSL 680 Trafalgar. *(gold disc)*
- (S) (3:55) Polygram TV 314555610 The One And Only Love Album.

1972 MY WORLD
- (S) (4:18) Polydor 843911 Tales From The Brothers Gibb.
- (S) (4:19) Polydor 831960 Best Of Volume 2.

1972 RUN TO ME
- (S) (3:04) Polydor 843911 Tales From The Brothers Gibb.
- (S) (3:07) Polydor 831960 Best Of Volume 2.
- (S) (3:10) Polydor 833787 To Whom It May Concern.

1972 ALIVE
- (S) (4:01) Polydor 843911 Tales From The Brothers Gibb.
- (S) (3:58) Polydor 831960 Best Of Volume 2.
- (S) (4:02) Polydor 833787 To Whom It May Concern.

1975 JIVE TALKIN'
- (S) (3:42) Polydor 800068 O.S.T. Saturday Night Fever. *(LP version)*
- (S) (3:41) Polydor 833790 Main Course. *(LP version)*
- (S) (3:42) Polydor 800071 Greatest. *(LP version)*
- (S) (3:41) Polydor 422825389 O.S.T. Saturday Night Fever. *(LP version; remastered edition)*
- (S) (3:41) Time-Life R13610 Gold And Platinum Box Set - The Ultimate Rock Collection. *(LP version)*
- (S) (3:42) Mobile Fidelity 716 O.S.T. Saturday Night Fever. *(gold disc; LP version)*

1975 NIGHTS ON BROADWAY
(dj copies of this 45 ran (2:52); commercial copies were all (4:26))
- (S) (4:30) Polydor 833790 Main Course. *(LP length)*
- (S) (4:31) Polydor 800071 Greatest. *(LP length)*

1976 FANNY (BE TENDER WITH MY LOVE)
- (S) (4:02) Polydor 833790 Main Course. *(LP length)*
- (S) (4:01) Polydor 800071 Greatest. *(LP length)*

1976 YOU SHOULD BE DANCING
(dj copies of this 45 ran (3:31); commercial copies were all (4:15))
- (S) (4:13) Polydor 800068 O.S.T. Saturday Night Fever.
- (S) (4:14) Priority 7059 Mega-Hits Dance Classics Volume 10.
- (S) (4:15) Rhino 70490 Billboard Top Dance Hits - 1976.
- (S) (4:15) Polydor 823658 Children Of The World.
- (S) (4:14) Polydor 800071 Greatest.
- (S) (4:14) Time-Life SOD-04 Sounds Of The Seventies - 1976.
- (S) (4:12) Polydor 422825389 O.S.T. Saturday Night Fever. *(remastered edition)*
- (S) (4:14) Mobile Fidelity 716 O.S.T. Saturday Night Fever. *(gold disc)*

1976 LOVE SO RIGHT
- (S) (3:34) Polydor 823658 Children Of The World. *(LP length)*
- (S) (3:32) Polydor 800071 Greatest. *(LP length)*

1977 BOOGIE CHILD
- (S) (4:11) Polydor 823658 Children Of The World. *(LP version)*

1977 EDGE OF THE UNIVERSE
- (S) (5:15) Polydor 833791 Here At Last...Live. *(LP version)*

1977 HOW DEEP IS YOUR LOVE
- (S) (4:01) Polydor 800068 O.S.T. Saturday Night Fever. *(LP length)*
- (S) (4:01) Polydor 800071 Greatest. *(LP length)*
- (S) (3:36) Time-Life SOD-05 Sounds Of The Seventies - 1977. *(45 length)*
- (S) (4:02) Polydor 422825389 O.S.T. Saturday Night Fever. *(LP length; remastered edition)*
- (S) (4:04) Mobile Fidelity 716 O.S.T. Saturday Night Fever. *(gold disc; LP length)*

1978 STAYIN' ALIVE
(actual 45 time is (3:41) not (3:29) as stated on the record label)
- (S) (4:41) Polydor 800068 O.S.T. Saturday Night Fever. *(LP version)*
- (S) (1:30) Polydor 813269 O.S.T. Staying Alive. *(highly edited)*
- (S) (4:44) Polydor 800071 Greatest. *(LP version)*
- (S) (3:40) Time-Life SOD-05 Sounds Of The Seventies - 1977. *(45 version)*
- (S) (4:41) TVT 6810 O.S.T. Grumpier Old Men. *(LP version)*
- (S) (4:41) Polydor 422825389 O.S.T. Saturday Night Fever. *(LP version; remastered edition)*
- (S) (4:45) Mobile Fidelity 716 O.S.T. Saturday Night Fever. *(gold disc; LP version)*

1978 NIGHT FEVER
- (S) (3:31) Polydor 800068 O.S.T. Saturday Night Fever.
- (S) (3:28) Polydor 800071 Greatest. *(truncated fade)*
- (S) (3:31) Razor & Tie 22496 Disco Fever.
- (S) (3:31) Time-Life SOD-10 Sounds Of The Seventies - 1978.
- (S) (3:30) Polydor 422825389 O.S.T. Saturday Night Fever. *(remastered edition)*
- (S) (3:29) Mobile Fidelity 716 O.S.T. Saturday Night Fever. *(gold disc)*

1978 TOO MUCH HEAVEN
(dj copies of this 45 ran (3:52); commercial copies were all (4:54))
- (S) (4:55) Polydor 827335 Spirits Having Flown.
- (S) (4:53) Polydor 800071 Greatest.
- (S) (4:54) Time-Life SOD-09 Sounds Of The Seventies - 1979.

38

(S) (4:54) Time-Life R840-10 Sounds Of The Seventies: '70s Dance Party 1979.

1979 TRAGEDY
(dj copies of this 45 ran (5:01) and (4:10);
commercial copies were all (5:01))
(S) (4:59) Priority 7057 Mega-Hits Dance Classics Volume 8.
(S) (5:02) Polydor 827335 Spirits Having Flown.
(S) (5:00) Polydor 800071 Greatest.
(S) (5:01) Time-Life SOD-09 Sounds Of The Seventies - 1979.
(S) (5:01) Time-Life R840-10 Sounds Of The Seventies: '70s Dance Party 1979.

1979 LOVE YOU INSIDE OUT
(dj copies of this 45 ran (3:47) not (3:27) as
stated on the record label)
(S) (4:10) Polydor 827335 Spirits Having Flown. *(LP length)*
(S) (4:08) Polydor 800071 Greatest. *(LP length)*

1981 HE'S A LIAR
1983 THE WOMAN IN YOU
(S) (4:01) Polydor 813269 O.S.T. Staying Alive.

1989 ONE
(S) (4:53) Warner Brothers 25887 One. *(LP version)*

1997 ALONE
(S) (4:49) Polydor 314537302 Still Waters.

BEGINNING OF THE END
1971 FUNKY NASSAU (PART 1)
(S) (3:11) Atlantic 81299 Atlantic Rhythm & Blues Volume 7.
(S) (3:09) Rhino 70785 Soul Hits Of The 70's Volume 5.
(S) (3:09) Rhino 72028 Soul Hits Of The 70's Volumes 1-5 Box Set.
(S) (5:10) Atlantic 82305 Atlantic Rhythm And Blues 1947-1974 Box Set. *(Parts 1 & 2)*
(S) (3:09) Time-Life SOD-36 Sounds Of The Seventies - More AM Nuggets.
(S) (4:57) TK/Hot Productions 33 Best Of T.K. Soul Singles. *(Parts 1 & 2)*

HARRY BELAFONTE
1957 JAMAICA FAREWELL
(M) (3:03) RCA 6877 All Time Greatest Hits Volume 1. *(LP version)*
(M) (3:02) RCA 53860 Pure Gold. *(LP version)*
(M) (3:04) Pair 1060 The Belafonte Songbook. *(LP version)*
(M) (3:02) RCA 53801 Calypso. *(LP version)*
(M) (3:02) RCA 52469 A Legendary Performer. *(LP version)*
(M) (2:48) Time-Life HPD-17 Your Hit Parade - 1957. *(45 version)*
(M) (2:47) Time-Life R132-22 Treasury Of Folk Music Volume Two. *(45 version)*

1957 MARY'S BOY CHILD
(M) (2:56) RCA 6877 All Time Greatest Hits Volume 1. *(45 version)*
(M) (2:59) Rhino 70636 Billboard's Greatest Christmas Hits (1955-Present). *(45 version)*
(E) (4:21) RCA 9859 Nipper's Greatest Christmas Hits. *(LP version)*
(E) (4:22) RCA 2626 To Wish You A Merry Christmas. *(LP version)*
(E) (4:21) RCA 66301 Christmas Classics Volume 1. *(LP version)*
(E) (4:22) Time-Life TCD-107 A Time-Life Treasury Of Christmas. *(LP version)*
(M) (2:59) Time-Life R135-12 The Spirit Of Christmas. *(45 versioin)*

1957 BANANA BOAT (DAY-O)
(M) (3:02) RCA 6877 All Time Greatest Hits Volume 1.
(M) (3:02) RCA 8466 Nipper's Greatest Hits Of The 50's Volume 1.
(M) (3:01) RCA 53860 Pure Gold.
(M) (3:01) RCA 52082 Day-O & Other Hits.

(E) (3:01) RCA 61144 The RCA Records Label: The First Note In Black Music.
(M) (3:01) RCA 53801 Calypso.
(M) (3:01) RCA 52469 A Legendary Performer.
(M) (3:03) Time-Life HPD-17 Your Hit Parade - 1957.
(M) (3:02) K-Tel 3575 Hot, Hot Vacation Jams - Week One.
(M) (3:02) JCI 7021 Those Wonderful Years - April Love.
(M) (3:02) Time-Life R132-22 Treasury Of Folk Music Volume One.
(M) (3:02) Hammer & Lace 697124114 Leading Men: Masters Of Style Volume Three.

1957 MAMA LOOK AT BUBU
(M) (2:53) RCA 6877 All Time Greatest Hits Volume 1.
(S) (3:05) RCA 8467 Nipper's Greates Hits Of The 50's Volume 2.
(S) (5:10) RCA 52469 A Legendary Performer. *(live)*
(S) (2:56) Time-Life HPD-36 Your Hit Parade - The 50's Pop Revival.
(M) (3:00) Pair 1295 Island In The Sun.

1957 ISLAND IN THE SUN
(M) (3:06) RCA 6877 All Time Greatest Hits Volume 1.
(M) (3:06) RCA 52082 Day-O & Other Hits.
(M) (3:06) RCA 66099 Hooray For Hollywood.
(M) (3:21) Time-Life HPD-27 Your Hit Parade - The Unforgettable 50's.
(E) (3:25) Pair 1295 Island In The Sun. *(slightly slower than the 45)*

1957 COCOANUT WOMAN
(M) (2:57) RCA 6877 All Time Greatest Hits Volume 1.
(E) (3:19) Pair 1295 Island In The Sun.

ARCHIE BELL & THE DRELLS
1968 TIGHTEN UP
(S) (3:10) Warner Special Products 27601 Atlantic Soul Classics. *(LP version)*
(S) (3:10) JCI 3100 Dance Sixties. *(LP version)*
(S) (3:09) Atlantic 81298 Atlantic Rhythm & Blues Volume 6. *(LP version)*
(S) (3:10) Atlantic 82305 Atlantic Rhythm And Blues 1947-1974 Box Set. *(LP version)*
(S) (3:11) Rhino 71459 Soul Hits, Volume 1. *(LP version)*
(S) (3:07) Time-Life RHD-04 Rhythm & Blues - 1968. *(LP version)*
(S) (3:09) Time-Life 2CLR-04 Classic Rock - 1968. *(LP version)*
(M) (2:37) Rhino 71615 In Yo Face! The Roots Of Funk Vol. 1/2. *(45 version)*
(M) (2:37) Rhino 71725 Tightening It Up - Best Of. *(45 version)*
(S) (3:10) JCI 3161 18 Soul Hits From The 60's. *(LP version)*
(S) (3:09) JCI 3190 1965 - Only Dance - 1969. *(LP version)*
(S) (3:07) Time-Life R838-03 Solid Gold Soul - 1968. *(LP version)*
(S) (3:11) Flashback 72657 '60s Soul: Try A Little Tenderness. *(LP version)*
(S) (3:11) Flashback 72091 '60s Soul Hits Box Set. *(LP version)*
(S) (3:07) Nick At Nite/550 Music 63407 Dancing At The Nick At Niteclub. *(LP version)*
(M) (2:38) Rhino 72815 Beg, Scream & Shout! The Big Ol' Box Of '60s Soul. *(45 version)*
(M) (2:49) TVT 4010 Rhythm Revue. *(segues into the next track - "TIGHTEN UP PART 2")*
(S) (3:09) Repeat/Relativity 1610 Tighten Up: #1 Soul Hits Of The 60's Volume 2. *(LP version)*
(M) (2:37) Flashback 72898 25 Years Of R&B - 1968. *(45 version)*
(M) (2:38) Rhino 72962 Ultimate '60s Soul Sensations. *(45 version)*
(M) (2:36) Thump 7070 Lowrider Oldies Volume 7. *(45 version)*

1968 I CAN'T STOP DANCING
(S) (2:19) Time-Life 2CLR-27 Classic Rock - 1968: Blowin' Your Mind.
(M) (2:19) Rhino 71725 Tightening It Up - Best Of.
(M) (2:18) Epic/Legacy 64647 The Philly Sound Box Set.

ARCHIE BELL & THE DRELLS *(Continued)*
1969 THERE'S GONNA BE A SHOWDOWN
- (S) (2:41) Rhino 70277 Rare Soul: Beach Music Classics Volume 1. *(LP length)*
- (S) (2:36) Time-Life 2CLR-25 Classic Rock - On The Soul Side. *(45 length)*
- (M) (2:34) Rhino 71725 Tightening It Up - Best Of. *(45 length)*
- (M) (2:34) Flashback 72899 25 Years Of Soul - 1969. *(45 length)*
- (S) (2:41) K-Tel 3886 Great R&B Male Groups: Hits Of The 60's. *(LP length)*

BENNY BELL
1975 SHAVING CREAM
- (M) (2:43) Rhino 72124 Dr. Demento 25th Anniversary Collection. *(mastered from vinyl)*
- (M) (2:43) Time-Life R830-01 The Dr. Demento Collection - The Mid 70's. *(mastered from vinyl)*

MADELINE BELL
1968 I'M GONNA MAKE YOU LOVE ME
- (M) (2:31) Ripete 392165 Ebb Tide Volume II.

VINCENT BELL
1970 AIRPORT LOVE THEME (GWEN AND VERN)
- (S) (3:01) Time-Life R986-07 Instrumental Favorites - Movie Magic.
- (S) (3:01) Rhino 72736 Billboard Top Soft Rock Hits - 1970.

WILLIAM BELL
1969 I FORGOT TO BE YOUR LOVER
- (S) (2:39) Stax 88005 Top Of The Stax. *(LP length)*
- (S) (2:18) Stax 8541 Best Of. *(45 length)*
- (M) (2:18) Stax 4411 Complete Stax/Volt Soul Singles 1968 - 1971. *(45 length)*
- (S) (3:52) Wilbe 4196 Greatest Hits Volume One. *(rerecording)*
- (S) (2:18) Rhino 72620 Smooth Grooves: The '60s Volume 3 Late '60s. *(45 length)*

1977 TRYIN' TO LOVE TWO
(dj copies of this 45 ran (3:10); commercial copies were all (3:28))
- (S) (3:25) Wilbe 4196 Greatest Hits Volume One. *(rerecording)*
- (S) (3:25) Ichiban 2508 Cheatin': From A Man's Point Of View. *(rerecording)*
- (S) (3:26) Razor & Tie 2066 Coming Back For More.
- (S) (3:28) Rhino 72128 Hot Soul Hits Of The 70's Vol. 18.
- (S) (3:28) Ripete 5151 Ocean Drive 4.
- (S) (3:26) Time-Life R838-16 Solid Gold Soul 1977.
- (S) (3:26) JCI 3175 1975 - Only Soul - 1979.

BELLAMY BROTHERS
1976 LET YOUR LOVE FLOW
- (S) (3:14) Curb 77317 70's Hits Volume 1.
- (S) (3:15) Rhino 70671 Billboard Top Hits - 1976.
- (S) (3:14) Curb 77532 Your Favorite Songs.
- (S) (3:14) MCA 10078 16 Top Country Hits Volume 4. *(truncated fade)*
- (S) (3:15) MCA 31012 Greatest Hits.
- (S) (3:15) Rhino 71198 Super Hits Of The 70's Volume 18.
- (S) (3:15) Curb 77554 Best Of.
- (S) (6:25) Curb 77651 Retro Rock Dance Hits. *(all selections on this cd are remixed with extra instrumentation added)*
- (S) (2:48) Intersound 1105 20 Years Of Hits. *(rerecording)*
- (S) (3:14) Curb 77803 Greatest Hits - Vol. 1.
- (S) (2:45) Rebound 314520368 Class Reunion '76. *(rerecording)*
- (S) (2:48) Madacy Entertainment 1976 Rock On 1976. *(rerecording)*
- (S) (3:13) JCI 3169 #1 Radio Hits 1975 - Only Rock 'n Roll - 1979.

- (S) (3:14) Simitar 55512 The Number One's: Lovin' Feelings.
- (S) (3:15) Priority 50962 70's Greatest Rock Hits Volume 7: Southern Rock.

BELL & JAMES
1979 LIVIN' IT UP (FRIDAY NIGHT)
- (S) (3:19) Time-Life SOD-19 Sounds Of The Seventies - 1979: Take Two.
- (S) (7:01) Rebound 314520309 Disco Nights Vol. VII - D.J. Pix. *(neither the 45 or LP version)*
- (S) (3:20) Rhino 72123 Disco Years, Vol. 7.
- (S) (3:20) Rhino 72130 Soul Hits Of The 70's Vol. 20.
- (S) (3:20) Time-Life R838-15 Solid Gold Soul 1979.
- (S) (3:20) K-Tel 3906 Starflight Vol. 1.

BELL BIV DeVOE
1990 POISON
- (S) (6:25) Tommy Boy 1037 MTV Party To Go Volume 1. *(remix; all tracks on this cd are segued together)*
- (S) (4:21) MCA 6387 Poison.
- (S) (6:14) MCA 10345 WBBD Boot City! The Remix Album. *(remixed)*
- (S) (4:21) Rhino 72409 New Jack Hits.
- (S) (4:21) MCA 11570 New Edition Solo Hits.

1990 DO ME!
- (S) (4:32) MCA 6387 Poison.
- (S) (5:25) MCA 10345 WBBD Boot City! The Remix Album. *(remixed)*
- (S) (5:30) Rhino 72409 New Jack Hits. *(remixed)*
- (S) (4:32) MCA 11570 New Edition Solo Hits.

1990 B.B.D. (I THOUGHT IT WAS ME)?
- (S) (4:34) MCA 6387 Poison.
- (S) (6:14) MCA 10345 WBBD Boot City! The Remix Album. *(remixed)*
- (S) (4:34) MCA 11570 New Edition Solo Hits.

released as by LUTHER VANDROSS and JANET JACKSON with BBD and RALPH TRESVANT:
1992 THE BEST THINGS IN LIFE ARE FREE
- (S) (4:35) Perspective 1004 O.S.T. Mo' Money.
- (S) (4:01) LV Records/Epic 68220 Luther Vandross - One Night With You: The Best Of Love Volume 2.

released as by BELL BIV DeVOE:
1993 GANGSTA
1993 SOMETHING IN YOUR EYES
- (S) (4:51) MCA 10682 Hootie Mack. *(LP version)*
- (S) (4:02) MCA 11570 New Edition Solo Hits. *(45 version)*

BELLE STARS
1989 IKO IKO
- (S) (2:51) Capitol 91866 O.S.T. Rain Man.

BELL NOTES
1959 I'VE HAD IT
- (M) (2:37) Time-Life 2RNR-13 Rock 'N' Roll Era - 1959.
- (M) (2:36) Time-Life R102-17 Lost Treasures Of Rock 'N' Roll.
- (M) (2:36) Original Sound CDGO-14 Golden Oldies Volume. 14.

BELLS
1971 STAY AWHILE
- (S) (3:21) Rhino 70924 Super Hits Of The 70's Volume 4.
- (S) (3:21) Rhino 72009 Super Hits Of The 70's Volumes 1-4 Box Set.
- (S) (3:20) Rhino 71208 70's Smash Hits Volume 4.
- (S) (3:21) Time-Life SOD-33 Sounds Of The Seventies - AM Pop Classics II.
- (S) (3:20) Flashback 72684 '70s Radio Hits Volume 4.
- (S) (3:20) Flashback 72090 '70s Radio Hits Box Set.
- (S) (3:21) K-Tel 3911 Fantastic Volume 2.
- (S) (3:20) Time-Life R834-18 Body Talk - Romantic Moments.

TONY BELLUS
1959 ROBBIN' THE CRADLE
- (M) (2:33) Vee-Jay 708 The Unavailable 16 & The Original Nitty Gritty.
- (M) (2:32) Collectables 5069 The History Of Rock Volume Nine.

BELMONTS
1961 TELL ME WHY
- (M) (2:34) Arista 8206 Dion: 24 Original Classics 1958-1978.
- (M) (2:33) Collectables 2508 History Of Rock - The Doo Wop Era Part 2.
- (M) (2:33) Collectables 4508 History Of Rock/The Doo Wop Era Part Two.
- (M) (2:32) Time-Life 2RNR-40 Rock 'N' Roll Era - The 60's Teen Time.
- (S) (2:41) Relic 7085 Best Of.
- (S) (2:41) Relic 7089 Lost Treasures. *(alternate take; truncated fade)*
- (M) (2:32) Music Club 50015 Love Me Forever - 18 Rock'N' Roll Love Songs.

1962 COME ON LITTLE ANGEL
- (M) (2:58) Time-Life 2RNR-42 Rock 'N' Roll Era - The 60's Sock Hop.
- (S) (2:59) Relic 7085 Best Of. *(alternate take)*
- (M) (3:05) Relic 7089 Lost Treasures. *(alternate take)*

JESSE BELVIN
1957 GOODNIGHT MY LOVE
- (M) (3:04) Atlantic 81769 O.S.T. Big Town.
- (M) (3:04) Virgin 86301 Goodnight My Love.
- (M) (3:10) Virgin 86301 Goodnight My Love. *(includes :07 of studio talk on the introduction and :01 at the end; alternate take)*
- (M) (3:06) Original Sound 8852 Oldies But Goodies Vol. 2. *(this compact disc uses the "Waring - fds" noise reduction process)*
- (M) (3:06) Original Sound 2223 Oldies But Goodies Volumes 2,7,9,12 and 13 Box Set. *(this box set uses the "Waring - fds" noise reduction process)*
- (M) (3:06) Original Sound 2500 Oldies But Goodies Volumes 1-15 Box Set. *(this box set uses the "Waring - fds" noise reduction process)*
- (M) (3:05) Time-Life 2RNR-23 Rock 'N' Roll Era - 1956 Still Rockin'.
- (M) (3:05) Time-Life RHD-05 Rhythm & Blues - 1956.
- (M) (3:06) Time-Life R103-27 Love Me Tender.
- (M) (3:05) Hip-O 40028 The Glory Of Love - '50s Sweet & Soulful Love Songs.
- (M) (3:04) Time-Life R857-07 The Heart Of Rock 'n' Roll 1956.
- (M) (3:05) Collectables 2701 Golden Classics.
- (M) (3:05) Time-Life R838-24 Solid Gold Soul 1956.

1959 GUESS WHO
- (S) (2:51) RCA 8466 Nipper's Greatest Hits Of The 50's Volume 1.
- (S) (2:51) RCA 66881 RCA's Greatest One-Hit Wonders.
- (S) (2:52) RCA 66859 To Mom With Love.
- (S) (2:51) Time-Life R857-11 The Heart Of Rock 'n' Roll 1958-1959.
- (M) (2:53) Collectables 2701 Golden Classics.

PAT BENATAR
1980 HEARTBREAKER
- (S) (3:26) Chrysalis 21715 Best Shots.
- (S) (3:27) Chrysalis 21236 and 41236 In The Heat Of The Night.
- (S) (3:26) Chrysalis 31094 All Fired Up: Best Of.
- (S) (3:27) JCI 3127 1980 - Only Rock 'N Roll - 1984.
- (S) (3:27) DCC Compact Classics 1056 In The Heat Of The Night. *(gold disc)*
- (S) (3:26) Chrysalis 52256 Heartbreaker - 16 Classic Performances.
- (S) (3:27) Eclipse Music Group 64896 Rock 'n Roll Relix 1978-1979.
- (S) (3:27) Eclipse Music Group 64897 Rock 'n Roll Relix 1970-1979.
- (S) (3:27) Time-Life R988-18 Sounds Of The Eighties: The Early '80s Take Two.
- (S) (3:27) Time-Life R968-24 Guitar Rock - The '80s Take Two.
- (S) (3:25) Hip-O 40077 Rock She Said: Guitars + Attitudes.

1980 WE LIVE FOR LOVE
- (S) (3:52) Chrysalis 21715 Best Shots. *(LP length)*
- (S) (3:53) Chrysalis 21236 and 41236 In The Heat Of The Night. *(LP length)*
- (S) (3:33) Chrysalis 31094 All Fired Up: Best Of. *(45 length)*
- (S) (3:53) DCC Compact Classics 1056 In The Heat Of The Night. *(gold disc; LP length)*
- (S) (3:34) Chrysalis 52256 Heartbreaker - 16 Classic Performances. *(45 length)*

1980 HIT ME WITH YOUR BEST SHOT
- (S) (2:50) Chrysalis 21715 Best Shots. *(LP version)*
- (S) (2:50) Chrysalis 21275 and 41275 Crimes Of Passion. *(LP version)*
- (S) (2:50) JCI 2720 Rockin' Ladies Of The 80's. *(LP version)*
- (S) (2:49) Chrysalis 31094 All Fired Up: Best Of. *(LP version)*
- (S) (2:50) Time-Life R988-07 Sounds Of The Eighties: 1980. *(LP version)*
- (S) (2:49) K-Tel 3742 The 80's: Hot Rock. *(LP version)*
- (S) (3:57) Chrysalis 52256 Heartbreaker - 16 Classic Performances. *(live)*
- (S) (2:50) Priority 50953 I Love Rock & Roll Volume 4: Hits Of The 80's. *(LP version)*
- (S) (2:50) Time-Life R968-20 Guitar Rock - The '80s. *(LP version)*
- (S) (2:48) Cold Front 6255 Greatest Sports Rock And Jams Volume 2. *(LP version; all selections on this cd are segued together)*
- (S) (2:49) K-Tel 3997 Arena Rock - The 80's. *(LP version)*
- (S) (2:50) Simitar 55582 The Number One's: Rock It Up. *(LP version)*

1981 TREAT ME RIGHT
- (S) (3:14) Island 90017 and 422842715 O.S.T. An Officer And A Gentleman. *(45 length)*
- (S) (3:25) Chrysalis 21275 and 41275 Crimes Of Passion. *(LP length)*
- (S) (3:12) Chrysalis 31094 All Fired Up: Best Of. *(45 length)*

1981 FIRE AND ICE
- (S) (3:18) Chrysalis 21715 Best Shots.
- (S) (3:20) Chrysalis 21346 and 41346 Precious Time.
- (S) (3:18) Chrysalis 31094 All Fired Up: Best Of.
- (S) (3:17) Madacy Entertainment 1981 Rock On 1981.
- (S) (3:18) Rhino 72594 Billboard Top Album Rock Hits, 1981.
- (S) (3:15) Time-Life R988-22 Sounds Of The Eighties 1980-1983.

1981 PROMISES IN THE DARK
(dj copies of this 45 ran (4:07) and (4:48); commercial copies were all (4:48))
- (S) (4:47) Chrysalis 21715 Best Shots.
- (S) (4:47) Chrysalis 21346 and 41346 Precious Time.
- (S) (4:46) Chrysalis 31094 All Fired Up: Best Of.
- (S) (4:47) Time-Life R968-13 Guitar Rock - The Early '80s.
- (S) (4:46) Chrysalis 52256 Heartbreaker - 16 Classic Performances.

1982 SHADOWS OF THE NIGHT
- (S) (4:21) Chrysalis 21396 and 41396 Get Nervous. *(LP version)*
- (S) (3:40) Chrysalis 31094 All Fired Up: Best Of. *(45 version)*
- (S) (4:18) Chrysalis 21715 Best Shots. *(LP version)*

1983 LITTLE TOO LATE
- (S) (3:23) Chrysalis 31094 All Fired Up: Best Of. *(45 version)*
- (S) (4:07) Chrysalis 21396 and 41396 Get Nervous. *(LP version)*

1983 LOVE IS A BATTLEFIELD
- (S) (4:08) Time-Life R105-40 Rock Dreams. *(45 version)*

41

PAT BENATAR *(Continued)*

- (S) (5:21) Chrysalis 21444 and 41444 Live From Earth. *(LP version)*
- (S) (4:08) Chrysalis 31094 All Fired Up: Best Of. *(45 version)*
- (S) (5:20) Chrysalis 21715 Best Shots. *(LP version)*
- (S) (4:08) Time-Life R988-11 Sounds Of The 80's: 1983-1984. *(45 version)*
- (S) (5:18) Big Ear Music 4002 Only In The 80's Volume Two. *(LP version)*
- (S) (5:20) Madacy Entertainment 1983 Rock On 1983. *(LP version)*
- (S) (5:17) Nick At Nite/550 Music 67690 I Am Woman. *(LP version)*
- (S) (4:08) Chrysalis 52256 Heartbreaker - 16 Classic Performances. *(45 version)*
- (S) (5:20) Rhino 72596 Billboard Top Album Rock Hits, 1983. *(LP version)*
- (S) (5:19) K-Tel 3867 The 80's: Hot Ladies. *(LP version)*

1984 WE BELONG

- (S) (3:39) Priority 7076 80's Greatest Rock Hits Volume 2 - Leather And Lace.
- (S) (3:40) Chrysalis 21471 and 41471 Tropico.
- (S) (3:37) Chrysalis 31094 All Fired Up: Best Of.
- (S) (3:39) Chrysalis 21715 Best Shots.
- (S) (3:39) Madacy Entertainment 1984 Rock On 1984.
- (S) (3:37) Chrysalis 52256 Heartbreaker - 16 Classic Performances.
- (S) (3:40) Hip-O 40047 The '80s Hit(s) Back 3.
- (S) (3:37) Rhino 72597 Billboard Top Album Rock Hits, 1984.
- (S) (3:39) Time-Life R834-15 Body Talk - Once In Lifetime.

1985 OOH OOH SONG

- (S) (4:07) Chrysalis 21471 and 41471 Tropico.
- (S) (4:07) Chrysalis 31094 All Fired Up: Best Of.

1985 INVINCIBLE (THEME FROM THE LEGEND OF BILLIE JEAN)

- (S) (4:28) Chrysalis 21507 and 41507 Seven The Hard Way. *(LP version)*
- (S) (4:02) Chrysalis 31094 All Fired Up: Best Of. *(45 version)*
- (S) (4:26) Chrysalis 21715 Best Shots. *(LP version)*
- (S) (4:26) Time-Life R988-23 Sounds Of The Eighties 1984-1985. *(LP version)*

1986 SEX AS A WEAPON

- (S) (4:19) Chrysalis 21507 and 41507 Seven The Hard Way.
- (S) (4:17) Chrysalis 31094 All Fired Up: Best Of.
- (S) (4:18) Big Ear Music 4003 Only In The 80's Volume Three.
- (S) (4:18) Chrysalis 52256 Heartbreaker - 16 Classic Performances.

1988 ALL FIRED UP

- (S) (4:28) Chrysalis 21628 and 41628 Wide Awake In Dreamland. *(LP version)*
- (S) (4:08) Chrysalis 31094 All Fired Up: Best Of. *(45 version)*
- (S) (4:28) Chrysalis 21715 Best Shots. *(LP version)*
- (S) (4:08) Chrysalis 52256 Heartbreaker - 16 Classic Performances. *(45 version)*

BOYD BENNETT & HIS ROCKETS

1955 SEVENTEEN

- (M) (2:06) Time-Life 2RNR-49 Rock 'N' Roll Era - Lost Treasures II.

JOE BENNETT and THE SPARKLETONES

1957 BLACK SLACKS

- (M) (2:03) MCA 5938 Vintage Music Volumes 15 & 16.
- (M) (2:03) MCA 31213 Vintage Music Volume 16.
- (M) (2:00) Time-Life 2RNR-17 Rock 'N' Roll Era - 1957 Still Rockin'.
- (M) (2:03) Time-Life R102-17 Lost Treasures Of Rock 'N' Roll.
- (M) (2:03) MCA Special Products 22173 Vintage Collectibles Volume 11.

TONY BENNETT

1956 CAN YOU FIND IT IN YOUR HEART

- (M) (2:39) Time-Life HPD-23 Your Hit Parade - The Late 50's.

1956 FROM THE CANDY STORE ON THE CORNER TO THE CHAPEL ON THE HILL

1956 HAPPINESS STREET (CORNER SUNSHINE SQUARE)

1956 THE AUTUMN WALTZ

1956 JUST IN TIME

- (M) (2:33) Columbia 40215 16 Most Requested Songs.
- (M) (2:33) Columbia/Legacy 46884 and 65412 Forty Years:The Artistry Of.
- (M) (2:32) Rhino 71252 Sentimental Journey: Pop Vocal Classics Volume 4 (1954-1959).
- (M) (2:32) Rhino 72034 Sentimental Journey Pop Vocal Classics Volumes 1-4 Box Set.
- (M) (2:33) Epic 57682 More Songs For Sleepless Nights.
- (M) (2:32) Columbia 65316 All-Time Greatest Hits.

1957 IN THE MIDDLE OF AN ISLAND

- (M) (2:06) Time-Life HPD-17 Your Hit Parade - 1957.

1958 YOUNG AND WARM AND WONDERFUL

1958 FIREFLY

- (S) (1:36) Columbia/Legacy 46843and 65412 Forty Years: The Artistry Of.
- (S) (1:36) Columbia 65316 All-Time Greatest Hits.

1962 I LEFT MY HEART IN SAN FRANCISCO

- (S) (2:50) Columbia 45019 Pop Classics Of The 60's.
- (S) (2:50) Columbia/Legacy 46843 and 65412 Forty Years: The Artistry Of.
- (S) (2:51) Columbia 8669 I Left My Heart In San Francisco.
- (S) (2:50) Columbia 40215 16 Most Requested Songs.
- (S) (2:50) Hollywood 60974 O.S.T. Arachnophobia.
- (S) (2:50) Columbia/Legacy 53571 The Essence Of.
- (S) (2:50) Time-Life HPD-32 Your Hit Parade - Into The 60's.
- (S) (2:50) Time-Life R974-05 Many Moods Of Romance - You Belong To Me.
- (S) (2:51) Columbia 65367 I Left My Heart In San Francisco/The Art Of Excellence/Astoria.
- (S) (2:49) Columbia 65316 All-Time Greatest Hits.
- (S) (2:49) Columbia 65405 Sings His All-Time Hall Of Fame Hits.

1963 I WANNA BE AROUND

- (S) (2:09) Columbia/Legacy 46843 and 65412 Forty Years: The Artistry Of.
- (S) (2:09) Columbia 40215 16 Most Requested Songs.
- (S) (2:09) Rhino 71504 Great American Songwriters Volume 2: Johnny Mercer.
- (S) (2:09) Rhino 72033 Great American Songwriters Vol. 1-5 Box Set.
- (S) (2:09) Time-Life HPD-33 Your Hit Parade - The Early 60's.
- (S) (2:09) Columbia 66504 I Wanna Be Around.
- (S) (2:09) Malpaso/Warner Brothers 46829 O.S.T. Midnight In The Garden Of Good And Evil.
- (S) (2:09) Columbia 65316 All-Time Greatest Hits.
- (S) (2:09) Columbia 65405 Sings His All-Time Hall Of Fame Hits.

1963 THE GOOD LIFE

- (S) (2:13) Columbia/Legacy 46843 and 65412 Forty Years: The Artistry Of.
- (S) (2:14) Columbia 40215 16 Most Requested Songs.
- (S) (2:13) Time-Life R138/05 Look Of Love.
- (S) (2:14) Columbia 66504 I Wanna Be Around.
- (S) (2:24) Columbia 65405 Sings His All-Time Hall Of Fame Hits. *(rerecording)*

1964 WHO CAN I TURN TO (WHEN NOBODY NEEDS ME)

- (S) (2:55) Columbia/Legacy 46843 and 65412 Forty Years: The Artistry Of.
- (S) (2:55) Columbia 40215 16 Most Requested Songs.
- (S) (2:54) MCA 11389 O.S.T. Casino.
- (S) (2:54) Columbia 65316 All-Time Greatest Hits.
- (S) (2:54) Columbia 65405 Sings His All-Time Hall Of Fame Hits.

GEORGE BENSON

1976 THIS MASQUERADE

- (S) (8:02) Warner Brothers 3111 Breezin'. *(LP version)*
- (S) (3:16) Warner Brothers 3577 Collection. *(45 version)*
- (S) (3:16) Warner Brothers 46050 Best Of. *(45 version)*

1977 THE GREATEST LOVE OF ALL

- (S) (5:32) Warner Brothers 3577 Collection. *(LP version)*
- (S) (5:33) Razor & Tie 2139 O.S.T. The Greatest. *(LP version)*

(S) (4:24)   Hip-O 40107 Super Bad On Celluloid: Music From '70s Black Cinema. *(dj 45 version)*

1978 ON BROADWAY
(S) (10:06) Warner Brothers 3139 Weekend In L.A. *(LP version)*
(S) (5:15)   Warner Brothers 3577 Collection. *(45 version)*
(S) (5:11)   Warner Brothers 46050 Best Of. *(45 version)*

1979 LOVE BALLAD
(S) (5:14)   Warner Brothers 3277 Livin' Inside Your Love. *(LP version)*
(S) (4:15)   Warner Brothers 3577 Collection. *(45 version)*
(S) (4:16)   Warner Brothers 46050 Best Of. *(45 version)*

1980 GIVE ME THE NIGHT
(dj copies of this 45 ran (3:41); commercial copies were all (3:52))
(S) (4:59)   Warner Brothers 3453 Give Me The Night. *(LP length)*
(S) (3:41)   Warner Brothers 3577 Collection. *(dj 45 length)*
(S) (3:42)   Warner Brothers 46050 Best Of. *(dj 45 length)*

1982 TURN YOUR LOVE AROUND
(S) (3:49)   Warner Brothers 3577 Collection.
(S) (3:48)   Warner Brothers 46050 Best Of.

1983 INSIDE LOVE (SO PERSONAL)
(S) (5:14)   Warner Brothers 23744 In Your Eyes. *(LP version)*
(S) (5:14)   Warner Brothers 46050 Best Of. *(LP version)*

1983 LADY LOVE ME (ONE MORE TIME)
(S) (4:00)   Warner Brothers 23744 In Your Eyes.
(S) (3:55)   Warner Brothers 46050 Best Of.

BROOK BENTON
1959 IT'S JUST A MATTER OF TIME
(M) (2:25)   Mercury 832041 45's On CD Volume 1.
(M) (2:25)   Rhino 70645 Billboard's Top R&B Hits Of 1959.
(M) (2:25)   Mercury 830772 Best Of.
(M) (2:25)   Mercury 836755 Forty Greatest Hits.
(M) (2:25)   Time-Life RHD-03 Rhythm & Blues - 1959.
(M) (2:25)   Time-Life HPD-13 Your Hit Parade - 1959.
(M) (2:26)   Time-Life R138/05 Look Of Love.
(S) (2:28)   Curb 77741 Greatest Songs. *(rerecording)*
(M) (2:25)   Time-Life R857-01 The Heart Of Rock 'n' Roll - 1959.
(M) (2:25)   Time-Life R974-16 Many Moods Of Romance - The Look Of Love.
(M) (2:25)   JCI 3183 1955 - Only Love - 1959.
(M) (2:26)   Hip-O 40028 The Glory Of Love - '50s Sweet & Soulful Love Songs.
(M) (2:26)   Hammer & Lace 697124113 Leading Men: Masters Of Style Volume One.
(M) (2:25)   Time-Life R838-21 Solid Gold Soul 1959.
(M) (2:26)   Polygram Special Markets 314520462 50's Soul.
(M) (2:26)   Time-Life R814-04 Love Songs.

1959 ENDLESSLY
(S) (2:19)   Mercury 830772 Best Of.
(S) (2:19)   Mercury 836755 Forty Greatest Hits.
(S) (2:18)   Curb 77445 Best Of.
(M) (2:21)   Time-Life HPD-28 Your Hit Parade - The Fabulous 50's.
(S) (2:25)   Curb 77741 Greatest Songs. *(rerecording)*

1959 THANK YOU PRETTY BABY
(S) (2:29)   Mercury 830772 Best Of.
(S) (2:28)   Mercury 836755 Forty Greatest Hits.
(M) (2:30)   Time-Life HPD-31 Your Hit Parade - The 50's Forever.
(S) (2:31)   Curb 77741 Greatest Songs. *(rerecording)*

1959 SO MANY WAYS
(S) (2:29)   Mercury 830772 Best Of.
(S) (2:29)   Mercury 836755 Forty Greatest Hits.
(S) (2:29)   Curb 77445 Best Of.
(M) (2:31)   Time-Life HPD-23 Your Hit Parade - The Late 50's.
(S) (2:30)   Curb 77741 Greatest Songs. *(rerecording)*

released as by DINAH WASHINGTON & BROOK BENTON:
1960 BABY (YOU'VE GOT WHAT IT TAKES)
(S) (2:44)   Mercury 816555 45's On CD Volume 2.
(S) (2:44)   Mercury 836755 Brook Benton: Forty Greatest Hits.
(S) (2:43)   Rhino 70646 Billboard's Top R&B Hits Of 1960.

(S) (2:44)   Mercury 838956 Complete Dinah Washington On Mercury Volume 6.
(S) (2:44)   Verve 314512905 Essential Dinah Washington: The Great Songs.
(S) (2:44)   Mercury 314514841 First Issue: The Dinah Washington Story.
(S) (2:41)   Time-Life RHD-15 Rhythm & Blues - 1960.
(S) (2:42)   Time-Life SUD-15 Superhits - The Early 60's.
(S) (2:42)   Verve/Mercury 314526467 The Two Of Us.
(S) (2:53)   Curb 77741 Brook Benton - Greatest Songs. *(rerecording)*
(S) (2:43)   Ripete 5151 Ocean Drive 4.
(S) (2:44)   Ichiban 2512 Soulful Love - Duets Vol. 1.
(S) (2:44)   Polygram Special Markets 314520405 Brook Benton - Greatest Hits.
(S) (2:42)   Time-Life AM1-19 AM Gold - The Early '60s.
(S) (2:43)   Rebound 314520420 Soul Classics - Best Of The 60's.
(S) (2:41)   Time-Life R838-20 Solid Gold Soul 1960.
(S) (2:44)   Polygram Special Markets 314520454 Soul Hits Of The 60's.

released as by BROOK BENTON:
1960 THE TIES THAT BIND
(S) (2:49)   Mercury 836755 Forty Greatest Hits.

released as by DINAH WASHINGTON & BROOK BENTON:
1960 A ROCKIN' GOOD WAY (TO MESS AROUND AND FALL IN LOVE)
(S) (2:25)   Rhino 70646 Billboard's Top R&B Hits Of 1960.
(S) (2:25)   Mercury 836755 Brook Benton: Forty Greatest Hits.
(S) (2:25)   Curb 77445 Best Of Brook Benton.
(S) (2:25)   Mercury 838956 Complete Dinah Washington On Mercury Volume 6.
(S) (2:25)   Mercury 314514841 First Issue: The Dinah Washington Story.
(S) (2:25)   Polygram Special Markets 314520264 Soul Hits Of The 60's.
(S) (2:24)   Verve/Mercury 314526467 The Two Of Us.
(S) (2:25)   Curb 77741 Brook Benton - Greatest Songs. *(rerecording)*
(S) (2:25)   Ripete 5151 Ocean Drive 4.

released as by BROOK BENTON:
1960 KIDDIO
(S) (2:37)   Rhino 70646 Billboard's Top R&B Hits Of 1960.
(S) (2:36)   Mercury 830772 Best Of.
(S) (2:37)   Mercury 836755 Forty Greatest Hits.
(S) (2:36)   Time-Life RHD-15 Rhythm & Blues - 1960.
(S) (2:37)   Time-Life HPD-33 Your Hit Parade - The Early 60's.
(S) (2:39)   Curb 77741 Greatest Songs. *(rerecording)*
(S) (2:36)   Time-Life R838-20 Solid Gold Soul 1960.

1960 THE SAME ONE
(S) (2:29)   Mercury 830772 Best Of.
(S) (2:28)   Mercury 836755 Forty Greatest Hits.

1960 FOOLS RUSH IN
(M) (2:26)   Mercury 830772 Best Of.
(M) (2:25)   Mercury 836755 Forty Greatest Hits.
(M) (2:26)   Capitol 81475 Rites Of Rhythm & Blues.
(M) (2:25)   Special Music/Essex 5035 Prom Night - The 60's.
(S) (2:25)   Eric 11502 Hard To Find 45's On CD (Volume I) 1955-60.

1961 THINK TWICE
(S) (2:32)   Mercury 830772 Best Of.
(S) (2:31)   Mercury 836755 Forty Greatest Hits.

1961 FOR MY BABY
(M) (2:39)   Mercury 836755 Forty Greatest Hits.

1961 THE BOLL WEEVIL SONG
(S) (2:37)   Mercury 830772 Best Of.
(S) (2:36)   Mercury 836755 Forty Greatest Hits.
(S) (2:36)   Curb 77445 Best Of.
(S) (2:35)   Time-Life SUD-19 Superhits - Early 60's Classics.
(S) (2:35)   Time-Life HPD-35 Your Hit Parade - The Fun-Times 50's & 60's.
(S) (2:37)   Rhino 71582 Billboard Top Pop Hits, 1961.
(S) (2:47)   Curb 77741 Greatest Songs. *(rerecording)*
(S) (2:47)   K-Tel 3629 Madcap Melodies. *(rerecording)*

BROOK BENTON *(Continued)*

- (S) (2:36) Polygram Special Markets 314520405 Greatest Hits.
- (S) (2:34) Time-Life AM1-20 AM Gold - Early '60s Classics.

1961 FRANKIE AND JOHNNY
- (S) (2:26) Mercury 830772 Best Of.
- (S) (2:27) Mercury 836755 Forty Greatest Hits.
- (S) (2:27) Polygram Special Markets 314520405 Greatest Hits.

1962 REVENGE
- (S) (2:35) Mercury 836755 Forty Greatest Hits.

1962 SHADRACK
- (S) (2:21) Mercury 836755 Forty Greatest Hits.

1962 HIT RECORD
- (S) (2:35) Mercury 836755 Forty Greatest Hits.

1962 LIE TO ME
- (S) (2:15) Mercury 830772 Best Of.
- (M) (2:13) Mercury 836755 Forty Greatest Hits.
- (M) (2:13) Polygram Special Markets 314520405 Greatest Hits.

1963 HOTEL HAPPINESS
- (S) (2:40) Mercury 830772 Best Of.
- (S) (2:40) Mercury 836755 Forty Greatest Hits.
- (S) (2:40) Time-Life HPD-32 Your Hit Parade - Into The 60's.
- (S) (2:34) Curb 77741 Greatest Songs. *(rerecording)*
- (S) (2:40) Time-Life R857-08 The Heart Of Rock 'n' Roll 1963.

1963 I GOT WHAT I WANTED
- (M) (2:34) Mercury 836755 Forty Greatest Hits.
- (M) (2:34) Polygram Special Markets 314520405 Greatest Hits.

1963 MY TRUE CONFESSION
- (S) (2:20) Mercury 836755 Forty Greatest Hits.
- (S) (2:20) Polygram Special Markets 314520264 Soul Hits Of The 60's.

1963 TWO TICKETS TO PARADISE
- (S) (2:36) Mercury 836755 Forty Greatest Hits.

1964 GOING GOING GONE
- (S) (2:47) Mercury 836755 Forty Greatest Hits.

1970 RAINY NIGHT IN GEORGIA
- (S) (3:49) Mercury 836755 Forty Greatest Hits. *(LP version)*
- (S) (3:49) Rhino 70658 Billboard's Top R&B Hits Of 1970. *(LP version)*
- (S) (3:49) Rhino 70781 Soul Hits Of The 70's Volume 1. *(LP version)*
- (S) (3:49) Rhino 72028 Soul Hits Of The 70's Volumes 1-5 Box Set. *(LP version)*
- (S) (3:49) Atlantic 81911 Golden Age Of Black Music (1960-1970). *(LP version)*
- (S) (3:49) Atlantic 81298 Atlantic Rhythm & Blues Volume 6. *(LP version)*
- (S) (3:49) Curb 77445 Best Of. *(LP version)*
- (S) (3:47) JCI 3303 Love Seventies. *(LP version)*
- (S) (3:49) Atlantic 82305 Atlantic Rhythm And Blues 1947-1974 Box Set. *(LP version)*
- (S) (3:49) Rhino 71205 70's Smash Hits Volume 1. *(LP version)*
- (S) (3:46) Time-Life RHD-18 Rhythm & Blues - 1970. *(LP version)*
- (S) (3:48) Time-Life SUD-04 Superhits - 1970. *(LP version)*
- (M) (3:36) Time-Life SOD-11 Sounds Of The Seventies - 1970: Take Two. *(45 version)*
- (S) (3:48) Varese Sarabande 5534 Rhythm Of The Rain. *(LP version)*
- (S) (3:49) Rhino 71806 The R&B Box: Thirty Years Of Rhythm & Blues. *(LP version)*
- (S) (3:46) Curb 77741 Greatest Songs. *(rerecording)*
- (S) (3:49) Rhino 72112 Billboard Hot Soul Hits - 1970. *(LP version)*
- (S) (3:48) Polygram Special Markets 314520405 Greatest Hits. *(LP version)*
- (S) (3:48) Time-Life AM1-02 AM Gold - 1970. *(LP version)*

- (S) (3:46) Time-Life R838-05 Solid Gold Soul - 1970. *(LP version)*
- (S) (3:48) Time-Life R834-10 Body Talk - From The Heart. *(LP version)*
- (S) (3:49) Flashback 72681 '70s Radio Hits Volume 1. *(LP version)*
- (S) (3:49) Flashback 72090 '70s Radio Hits Box Set. *(LP version)*
- (S) (3:49) Flashback 72900 25 Years Of Soul - 1970. *(LP version)*
- (S) (3:48) Time-Life R814-03 Love Songs. *(LP version)*

BERLIN
1984 NO MORE WORDS
- (S) (3:51) Geffen 24187 Best Of.
- (S) (3:54) Geffen 4025 Love Life.
- (S) (3:51) Geffen 24805 Geffen Vintage 80's Volume 1.
- (S) (5:43) Right Stuff 34661 Sedated In The Eighties No. 4. *(remix)*
- (S) (3:51) Hip-O 40077 Rock She Said: Guitars + Attitudes.

1986 TAKE MY BREATH AWAY
- (S) (4:11) Columbia 40323 O.S.T. Top Gun.
- (S) (4:10) Sandstone 33045 and 5011 Rock The First Volume Five.
- (S) (4:10) Geffen 24187 Best Of.
- (S) (4:10) Geffen 24121 Count Three And Pray.
- (S) (4:10) EMI-Capitol Music Group 54555 Movie Luv.
- (S) (3:40) Arista 18985 Ultimate New Wave Party 1998. *(remix; all selections on this cd are segued together)*
- (S) (4:10) Geffen 25151 Geffen Vintage 80s Vol. II.

ROD BERNARD
1959 THIS SHOULD GO ON FOREVER
- (M) (2:42) Time-Life 2RNR-20 Rock 'N' Roll Era - 1959 Still Rockin'. *(mastered from vinyl)*
- (M) (2:43) Chess 9352 Chess Rhythm & Roll.
- (M) (2:43) Chess 9355 Chess New Orleans.
- (M) (2:43) Time-Life R857-11 The Heart Of Rock 'n' Roll 1958-1959.

CHUCK BERRY
1955 MAYBELLENE
- (M) (2:19) Rhino 70598 Billboard's Top Rock & Roll Hits Of 1955.
- (M) (2:18) MCA 31198 Vintage Music Volume 1.
- (M) (2:18) MCA 5777 Vintage Music Volumes 1 & 2.
- (M) (2:20) JCI 3202 Rockin' Fifties.
- (M) (2:17) Original Sound 8850 Oldies But Goodies Vol. 1. *(this compact disc uses the "Waring - fds" noise reduction process)*
- (M) (2:17) Original Sound 2221 Oldies But Goodies Volumes 1,4,6,8 and 10 Box Set. *(this box set uses the "Waring - fds" noise reduction process)*
- (M) (2:17) Original Sound 2500 Oldies But Goodies Volumes 1-15 Box Set. *(this box set uses the "Waring - fds" noise reduction process)*
- (M) (2:18) Chess 31319 Best Of Chess Rock 'n' Roll Volume 1.
- (M) (2:16) RCA 5463 Rock & Roll - The Early Days.
- (M) (2:19) Rhino 70719 Legends Of Guitar - Rock: The 50's.
- (M) (2:18) Chess 31260 Berry Is On Top.
- (M) (2:20) Chess 92500 The Great Twenty Eight.
- (M) (2:19) Chess 80001 The Chess Box.
- (M) (2:19) Chess 31270 From The Motion Picture "Rock, Rock, Rock".
- (M) (2:19) Telstar 1002 Duckwalkin' Volume 1.
- (S) (2:37) MCA 6217 O.S.T. Hail! Hail! Rock 'N' Roll. *(live)*
- (S) (2:33) Mercury 826256 Golden Hits. *(all selections on this cd are rerecorded)*
- (M) (2:19) JCI/Telstar 3508 Best Of.
- (M) (2:18) Curb 77637 All Time Greatest Hits Of Rock 'N' Roll Volume 3.
- (M) (2:18) Time-Life 2RNR-08 Rock 'N' Roll Era - 1954-1955.

(M) (2:19) Chess 9352 Chess Rhythm & Roll.
(M) (2:17) JCI 3129 1955 - Only Rock 'N Roll - 1959.
(M) (2:19) Chess 9371 His Best, Volume 1.
(M) (2:20) Right Stuff 53319 Hot Rod Rock Volume 4: Hot Rod Rebels.
(M) (2:17) K-Tel 4018 Forefathers Of Rock.
(S) (2:34) Rebound 314520521 Highway Rockin'. *(live)*

1956 ROLL OVER BEETHOVEN
(M) (2:21) Chess 92500 The Great Twenty Eight.
(S) (2:00) Mercury 826256 Golden Hits. *(all selections on this cd are rerecorded)*
(M) (2:21) Chess 31260 Berry Is On Top.
(M) (2:21) Original Sound 8860 Oldies But Goodies Vol. 10. *(this compact disc uses the "Waring - fds" noise reduction process)*
(M) (2:21) Original Sound 2221 Oldies But Goodies Volumes 1,4,6,8 and 10 Box Set. *(this box set uses the "Waring - fds" noise reduction process)*
(M) (2:21) Original Sound 2500 Oldies But Goodies Volumes 1-15 Box Set. *(this box set uses the "Waring - fds" noise reduction process)*
(M) (2:22) Telstar 1002 Duckwalkin' Volume 1.
(M) (2:22) JCI/Telstar 3508 Best Of.
(M) (2:21) Chess 80001 The Chess Box.
(M) (2:21) Garland 011 Footstompin' Oldies.
(M) (2:21) Time-Life 2RNR-14 Rock 'N' Roll Era - 1956.
(M) (2:21) MCA 31199 Vintage Music Volume 2.
(M) (2:21) MCA 5777 Vintage Music Volumes 1 & 2.
(M) (2:21) Chess 31270 From The Motion Picture "Rock, Rock, Rock".
(S) (3:14) MCA 6217 O.S.T. Hail! Hail! Rock 'N' Roll. *(live)*
(M) (2:22) MCA Special Products 20974 Chuck Berry & Bo Diddley - Guitar Legends.
(M) (2:22) Chess 9371 His Best, Volume 1.
(M) (2:22) Chess 9389 The Chess Blues-Rock Songbook.

1957 SCHOOL DAY
(M) (2:40) Rhino 70618 Billboard's Top Rock & Roll Hits Of 1957.
(M) (2:40) Rhino 72004 Billboard's Top Rock & Roll Hits 1957-1961 Box Set.
(M) (2:41) MCA 31200 Vintage Music Volume 3.
(M) (2:41) MCA 5778 Vintage Music Volumes 3 & 4.
(M) (2:39) Chess 92500 The Great Twenty Eight.
(M) (2:39) Chess 80001 The Chess Box.
(M) (2:39) Chess 9284 After School Session.
(M) (2:42) Sire 6070 Rock 'N' Roll High School.
(M) (2:39) Atlantic 82155 O.S.T. Book Of Love.
(S) (2:34) Mercury 826256 Golden Hits. *(all selections on this cd are rerecorded)*
(M) (2:40) JCI/Telstar 3508 Best Of.
(M) (2:39) Time-Life 2RNR-01 Rock 'N' Roll Era - 1957.
(M) (2:40) Chess 9352 Chess Rhythm & Roll.
(M) (2:40) MCA Special Products 20873 After School Session.
(M) (2:40) Chess 9371 His Best, Volume 1.
(M) (2:40) Hollywood 62138 O.S.T. Home Alone 3.

1957 ROCK & ROLL MUSIC
(M) (2:31) MCA 31203 Vintage Music Volume 6.
(M) (2:31) MCA 5804 Vintage Music Volumes 5 & 6.
(M) (2:30) Chess 92500 The Great Twenty Eight.
(M) (2:30) Chess 80001 The Chess Box.
(M) (2:24) Chess 92521 Rock N Roll Rarities. *(alternate take)*
(M) (2:30) Telstar 1002 Duckwalkin' Volume 1.
(S) (2:31) Mercury 826256 Golden Hits. *(all selections on this cd are rerecorded)*
(M) (2:30) JCI/Telstar 3508 Best Of.
(M) (2:37) Chess 9190 More Rock 'N' Roll Rarities. *(alternate take)*
(M) (2:31) Rhino 71547 Let There Be Drums Volume 1: The 50's.
(M) (2:30) Time-Life 2RNR-17 Rock 'N' Roll Era - 1957 Still Rockin'.
(M) (2:30) Time-Life R962-01 History Of Rock 'N' Roll: Rock 'N' Roll Classics 1957-1959.
(M) (2:29) Original Sound 8883 21 Legendary Superstars.
(M) (2:31) K-Tel 3062 Rockin' Rebels.

(M) (2:31) MCA Special Products 22172 Vintage Collectibles Volume 10.
(M) (2:31) Chess 9371 His Best, Volume 1.
(M) (2:30) Chess 9389 The Chess Blues-Rock Songbook.

1958 SWEET LITTLE SIXTEEN
(M) (3:10) MCA 31202 Vintage Music Volume 5. *(original recording speed)*
(M) (3:10) MCA 5804 Vintage Music Volumes 5 & 6. *(original recording speed)*
(M) (2:59) Chess 92500 The Great Twenty Eight. *(speed of the 45 and LP, both of which were sped up considerably over the original recording speed)*
(M) (2:59) Original Sound 8862 Oldies But Goodies Vol. 12. *(this compact disc uses the "Waring - fds" noise reduction process; speed of the 45 and LP, both of which were sped up considerably over the original recording speed)*
(M) (2:59) Original Sound 2223 Oldies But Goodies Volumes 2,7,9,12 and 13 Box Set. *(this box set uses the "Waring - fds" noise reduction process; speed of the 45 and LP, both of which were sped up considerably over the original recording speed)*
(M) (2:59) Original Sound 2500 Oldies But Goodies Volumes 1-15 Box Set. *(this box set uses the "Waring - fds" noise reduction process; speed of the 45 and LP, both of which were sped up considerably over the original recording speed)*
(M) (3:09) Chess 80001 The Chess Box. *(original recording speed)*
(M) (2:59) Curb 77323 All Time Greatest Hits Of Rock 'N' Roll. *(speed of the 45 and LP, both of which were sped up considerably over the original recording speed)*
(M) (3:10) Chess 92521 Rock N Roll Rarities. *(alternate take with false start)*
(S) (2:38) MCA 6217 O.S.T. Hail! Hail! Rock 'N' Roll. *(live)*
(S) (2:12) Mercury 826256 Golden Hits. *(all selections on this cd are rerecorded)*
(M) (2:59) JCI/Telstar 3508 Best Of. *(speed of the 45 and LP, both of which were sped up considerably over the original recording speed)*
(M) (3:12) Chess 9190 More Rock 'N' Roll Rarities. *(alternate take with :04 false start)*
(M) (2:59) Time-Life 2RNR-05 Rock 'N' Roll Era - 1958. *(speed of the 45 and LP, both of which were sped up considerably over the original recording speed)*
(M) (3:10) MCA Special Products 22179 Vintage Collectibles Volume 9. *(original recording speed)*
(M) (2:59) Chess 9371 His Best, Volume 1. *(speed of the 45 and LP, both of which were sped up considerably over the original recording speed)*

1958 JOHNNY B. GOODE
(M) (2:37) MCA 31201 Vintage Music Volume 4.
(M) (2:37) MCA 5778 Vintage Music Volumes 3 & 4.
(M) (2:38) JCI 3201 Party Time Fifties.
(M) (2:37) MCA 31274 Classic Rock Volume 2.
(M) (2:37) Rhino 70732 Grandson Of Frat Rock.
(M) (2:37) Chess 31319 Best Of Chess Rock 'n' Roll Volume 1.
(M) (2:38) Capitol 48993 Spuds Mackenzie's Party Faves.
(M) (2:37) Chess 31260 Berry Is On Top.
(M) (2:37) Chess 92500 The Great Twenty Eight.
(M) (2:37) Chess 80001 The Chess Box.
(M) (3:08) Chess 92521 Rock N Roll Rarities. *(alternate take with false start)*
(S) (2:42) Mercury 826256 Golden Hits. *(all selections on this cd are rerecorded)*
(M) (2:38) JCI/Telstar 3508 Best Of.
(M) (2:38) MCA 8001 O.S.T. American Graffiti.
(M) (2:37) Time-Life 2RNR-05 Rock 'N' Roll Era - 1958.
(M) (2:38) Chess 9352 Chess Rhythm & Roll.
(M) (2:37) MCA Special Products 22166 Vintage Collectibles Volume 8.
(M) (2:37) MCA 11329 Soul Train 25th Anniversary Box Set.
(S) (2:42) LaserLight 12312 and 15936 The Wonder Years - Good Times, Good Friends. *(rerecording)*

CHUCK BERRY (Continued)

- (S) (4:23) MCA Special Products 20956 Rockin' Guitars. *(live)*
- (M) (2:34) Priority 50950 I Love Rock & Roll Volume 1: Hits Of The 50's. *(alternate take)*
- (M) (2:38) Chess 9371 His Best, Volume 1.
- (M) (2:38) Chess 9389 The Chess Blues-Rock Songbook.
- (M) (2:34) Collectables 1514 and 2514 The Anniversary Album - The 50's.

1958 CAROL

- (M) (2:45) MCA 5936 Vintage Music Volumes 11 & 12.
- (M) (2:45) MCA 31208 Vintage Music Volume 11.
- (M) (2:44) Rhino 70561 Legends Of Guitar - Rock: The 50's Volume 2.
- (M) (2:44) Chess 31260 Berry Is On Top.
- (M) (2:45) Chess 92500 The Great Twenty Eight.
- (M) (2:46) Chess 80001 The Chess Box.
- (M) (2:46) Telstar 1002 Duckwalkin' Volume 1.
- (S) (2:23) Mercury 826256 Golden Hits. *(all selections on this cd are rerecorded)*
- (M) (2:46) JCI/Telstar 3508 Best Of.
- (M) (2:45) Time-Life 2RNR-21 Rock 'N' Roll Era - 1958 Still Rockin'.
- (M) (2:46) Chess 9347 Stone Rock Blues.
- (M) (2:45) MCA Special Products 21742 Vintage Collectibles Volume 12.
- (M) (2:46) MCA Special Products 20974 Chuck Berry & Bo Diddley - Guitar Legends.
- (M) (2:46) Chess 9371 His Best, Volume 1.

1959 ALMOST GROWN

- (M) (2:18) Chess 31260 Berry Is On Top.
- (M) (2:18) Chess 92500 The Great Twenty Eight.
- (M) (2:18) Chess 80001 The Chess Box.
- (M) (2:18) Telstar 1002 Duckwalkin' Volume 1.
- (M) (2:19) JCI/Telstar 3508 Best Of.
- (M) (2:18) MCA 8001 O.S.T. American Graffiti.
- (M) (2:18) Time-Life 2RNR-28 Rock 'N' Roll Era - The 50's Rave On.
- (M) (2:18) MCA Special Products 20931 Let It Rock.
- (M) (2:18) MCA Special Products 20974 Chuck Berry & Bo Diddley - Guitar Legends.
- (M) (2:19) Chess 9381 His Best, Volume 2.
- (M) (2:18) Hollywood 62138 O.S.T. Home Alone 3.

1959 BACK IN THE U.S.A.

- (M) (2:24) Chess 92500 The Great Twenty Eight.
- (S) (2:27) Mercury 826256 Golden Hits. *(all selections on this cd are rerecorded)*
- (M) (2:25) JCI/Telstar 3508 Best Of.
- (M) (2:26) Chess 80001 The Chess Box.
- (M) (2:26) MCA 5936 Vintage Music Volumes 11 & 12.
- (M) (2:26) MCA 31208 Vintage Music Volume 11.
- (M) (2:23) Time-Life 2RNR-33 Rock 'N' Roll Era - The 50's Last Dance.
- (S) (3:28) MCA 6217 O.S.T. Hail! Hail! Rock 'N' Roll. *(live)*
- (M) (2:26) MCA Special Products 20931 Let It Rock.
- (M) (2:26) MCA 11239 You Can Still Rock In America.
- (M) (2:26) Chess 9381 His Best, Volume 2.
- (M) (2:26) Chess 9389 The Chess Blues-Rock Songbook.

1964 NADINE (IS IT YOU?)

- (M) (2:33) MCA 5939 Vintage Music Volumes 17 & 18.
- (M) (2:33) MCA 31215 Vintage Music Volume 18.
- (S) (2:46) Chess 92521 Rock N Roll Rarities. *(:13 longer fade than the 45 or LP)*
- (M) (2:32) Chess 92500 The Great Twenty Eight.
- (S) (2:34) Chess 80001 The Chess Box.
- (M) (2:32) Telstar 1002 Duckwalkin' Volume 1.
- (M) (2:32) JCI/Telstar 3508 Best Of.
- (M) (2:34) Time-Life 2RNR-25 Rock 'N' Roll Era - The 60's Keep On Rockin'.
- (S) (2:32) Time-Life RHD-12 Rhythm & Blues - 1964.
- (M) (2:30) Time-Life 2CLR-16 Classic Rock - 1964: Shakin' All Over.
- (M) (2:33) MCA Special Products 22132 Vintage Collectibles Volume 3.
- (S) (2:32) Time-Life R838-13 Solid Gold Soul - 1964.
- (S) (2:33) Chess 9381 His Best, Volume 2.

1964 NO PARTICULAR PLACE TO GO

- (S) (2:41) Chess 31320 Best Of Chess Rock 'n' Roll Volume 2.
- (S) (2:41) MCA 31204 Vintage Music Volume 7.
- (S) (2:41) MCA 5805 Vintage Music Volumes 7 & 8.
- (S) (2:41) Chess 92521 Rock N Roll Rarities.
- (M) (2:40) Chess 92500 The Great Twenty Eight.
- (S) (2:41) Chess 80001 The Chess Box.
- (S) (2:41) Chess 31261 St. Louis To Liverpool.
- (M) (2:40) Telstar 1002 Duckwalkin' Volume 1.
- (M) (2:40) JCI/Telstar 3508 Best Of.
- (S) (2:41) Compose 9923 James Dean/Tribute To A Rebel.
- (M) (2:40) Compose 9927 Car And Driver/Greatest Car Songs.
- (S) (2:41) Time-Life 2RNR-10 Rock 'N' Roll Era - 1964.
- (S) (2:41) MCA Special Products 22135 Vintage Collectibles Volume 6.
- (S) (2:41) Chess 9352 Chess Rhythm & Roll.
- (S) (2:41) Collectables 2505 History Of Rock - The 60's Part 5.
- (S) (2:41) Collectables 4505 History Of Rock/The 60s Part Five.
- (M) (2:40) Right Stuff 53316 Hot Rod Rock Volume 1: Rev It Up.
- (S) (2:41) Chess 9381 His Best, Volume 2.

1964 YOU NEVER CAN TELL

- (S) (2:40) MCA 31205 Vintage Music Volume 8.
- (S) (2:40) MCA 5805 Vintage Music Volumes 7 & 8.
- (S) (2:42) Chess 92521 Rock N Roll Rarities.
- (S) (2:41) Chess 80001 The Chess Box.
- (S) (2:41) Chess 31261 St. Louis To Liverpool.
- (S) (2:40) Time-Life 2CLR-03 Classic Rock - 1964.
- (S) (3:12) MCA 11103 and 11188 O.S.T. Pulp Fiction. *(time includes :32 of dialogue preceding song)*
- (S) (2:40) MCA Special Products 20931 Let It Rock.
- (S) (2:41) Chess 9381 His Best, Volume 2.

1965 PROMISED LAND

- (S) (2:21) Chess 80001 The Chess Box.
- (S) (2:21) Chess 31261 St. Louis To Liverpool.
- (S) (2:28) Chess 92521 Rock N Roll Rarities. *(remixed)*
- (S) (2:21) Chess 9381 His Best, Volume 2.
- (S) (2:21) Hip-O 40083 The King's Record Collection Vol. 2.

1972 MY DING-A-LING

- (M) (4:20) Rhino 70633 Billboard's Top Rock & Roll Hits Of 1972. *(a very close approximation to the 45 version but an extra line appears in the introduction)*
- (M) (4:20) Rhino 72005 Billboard's Top Rock & Roll Hits 1968-1972 Box Set. *(same comments as for Rhino 70633)*
- (S) (4:21) Chess 80001 The Chess Box. *(same comments as for Rhino 70633)*
- (S) (11:32) Chess 9295 London Chuck Berry Sessions. *(LP version; very poor stereo separation)*
- (E) (4:13) Telstar 1002 Duckwalkin' Volume 1. *(45 version)*
- (E) (4:14) JCI/Telstar 3508 Best Of. *(45 version)*
- (M) (4:21) Time-Life SOD-36 Sounds Of The Seventies - More AM Nuggets. *(same comments as for Rhino 70633)*
- (S) (4:21) Priority 53747 Wild & Crazy Tunes. *(same comments as for Rhino 70633)*
- (E) (4:16) Madacy Entertainment 1972 Rock On 1972. *(45 version)*
- (M) (4:21) K-Tel 3629 Madcap Melodies. *(a very close approximation to the 45 version but an extra line appears in the introduction)*
- (S) (11:33) MCA Special Products 20974 Chuck Berry & Bo Diddley - Guitar Legends. *(LP version; very poor stereo separation)*
- (E) (4:16) Chess 9381 His Best, Volume 2. *(45 version)*
- (M) (4:15) Time-Life R830-03 The Dr. Demento Collection: The Early '70s. *(45 version)*

1973 REELIN' & ROCKIN'

- (S) (6:58) Rhino 75778 Frat Rock. *(live 1973 LP version)*
- (S) (7:06) Chess 9295 London Chuck Berry Sessions. *(live 1973 LP version)*

(S) (7:06) Chess 80001 The Chess Box. *(live 1973 LP version)*
(M) (3:14) MCA 5940 Vintage Music Volumes 19 & 20. *(1958 studio version)*
(M) (3:14) MCA 31217 Vintage Music Volume 20. *(1958 studio version)*
(M) (3:14) Chess 80001 The Chess Box. *(1958 studio version)*
(M) (3:36) Chess 92521 Rock N Roll Rarities. *(1958 studio version; alternate take)*
(M) (3:13) Chess 92500 The Great Twenty Eight. *(1958 studio version)*
(S) (4:14) Mercury 826256 Golden Hits. *(all selections on this cd are rerecorded; 1958 lyrics)*
(M) (3:14) JCI/Telstar 3508 Best Of. *(1958 studio version)*
(M) (3:14) MCA Special Products 22134 Vintage Collectibles Volume 5. *(1958 studio version)*
(M) (3:13) Era 511 Ultimate 50's Party. *(1958 studio version)*
(M) (3:13) Risky Business 66387 Rock Around The Clock. *(1958 studio version)*
(M) (3:13) Madacy Entertainment 1973 Rock On 1973. *(1958 studio version)*
(M) (3:14) Chess 9371 His Best, Volume 1. *(1958 studio version)*
(S) (7:06) Chess 9381 His Best, Volume 2. *(live 1973 LP version)*

BETTER THAN EZRA
1995 GOOD
(S) (3:04) Elektra 61784 Deluxe.

BEVERLY SISTERS
1957 GREENSLEEVES

B-52's
1989 LOVE SHACK
(S) (5:20) Time-Life R102-34 The Rolling Stone Collection. *(LP version)*
(S) (5:21) Reprise 25854 Cosmic Thing. *(LP version)*
(S) (5:20) Time-Life R988-01 Sounds Of The Eighties: The Rockin' Eighties. *(LP version)*
1990 ROAM
(S) (8:16) JCI 3117 Lost Mixes - Extended Ecstasy. *(remix)*
(S) (4:54) Reprise 25854 Cosmic Thing. *(LP version)*
(S) (4:03) Time-Life R988-21 Sounds Of The Eighties: 1986-1989. *(45 version)*
(S) (4:04) Time-Life R13610 Gold And Platinum Box Set - The Ultimate Rock Collection. *(45 version)*
1990 DEAD BEAT CLUB
(S) (4:45) Reprise 25854 Cosmic Thing.
1992 GOOD STUFF
(S) (5:57) Reprise 26943 Good Stuff. *(LP version)*
released as by the BC-52's:
1994 (MEET) THE FLINTSTONES
(S) (2:22) MCA 11045 The Flintstones: Music From Bedrock.

BIG AUDIO DYNAMITE II
1991 RUSH
(S) (3:54) Chaos/Columbia 57303 O.S.T. So I Married An Axe Murderer. *(rerecorded)*
(S) (4:17) Columbia 46147 The Globe. *(LP version)*
(S) (3:08) Columbia 67350 Greatest Hits. *(45 version)*
(S) (7:09) DCC Compact Classics 140 Rock The First Volume 10. *(live)*
(S) (4:17) Rhino 72651 Billboard Top Modern Rock Tracks, 1991. *(LP version)*

BIG BOPPER
1958 CHANTILLY LACE
(M) (2:20) Rhino 70164 Hellooo Baby! The Best Of.
(M) (2:21) Mercury 832041 45's On CD Volume 1.
(M) (2:22) Mercury 826448 Oldies Golden Million Sellers.

(M) (2:20) Original Sound 8854 Oldies But Goodies Vol. 4. *(this compact disc uses the "Waring - fds" noise reduction process)*
(M) (2:20) Original Sound 2221 Oldies But Goodies Volumes 1,4,6,8 and 10 Box Set. *(this box set uses the "Waring - fds" noise reduction process)*
(M) (2:20) Original Sound 2500 Oldies But Goodies Volumes 1-15 Box Set. *(this box set uses the "Waring - fds" noise reduction process)*
(M) (2:21) JCI 3202 Rockin' Fifties.
(M) (2:19) MCA 8001 O.S.T. American Graffiti.
(M) (2:20) Time-Life 2RNR-05 Rock 'N' Roll Era - 1958.
(M) (2:21) Mercury 832902 Chantilly Lace.
(M) (2:21) K-Tel 3007 50's Sock Hop.
(M) (2:21) JCI 3129 1955 - Only Rock 'N Roll - 1959.
(M) (2:21) K-Tel 3035 Goofy Greats.
(M) (2:21) DCC Compact Classics 077 Too Cute!
(M) (2:20) Special Music/Essex 5034 Prom Night - The 50's.
(M) (2:20) Nick At Nite/550 Music/Epic 67770 Happy Days Jukebox.
(M) (2:20) Priority 50950 I Love Rock & Roll Volume 1: Hits Of The 50's.
(M) (2:21) Polygram Special Markets 314520478 50's Jukebox Hits.
(M) (2:19) Collectables 1514 and 2514 The Anniversary Album - The 50's.

1958 BIG BOPPER'S WEDDING
(M) (2:07) Rhino 70164 Hellooo Baby! The Best Of.
(M) (2:07) Rhino 70794 KFOG Presents M. Dung's Idiot Show.
(M) (2:07) Rhino 70589 Rockin' & Rollin' Wedding Songs Volume 2.
(M) (2:08) Mercury 832902 Chantilly Lace.
(M) (2:07) Eric 11502 Hard To Find 45's On CD (Volume I) 1955-60.

BIG BROTHER and THE HOLDING COMPANY (see also JANIS JOPLIN)
1968 PIECE OF MY HEART
(S) (4:13) Columbia 32168 Janis Joplin's Greatest Hits. *(LP version)*
(S) (4:12) Columbia 45018 Rock Classics Of The 60's. *(LP version)*
(S) (4:13) SBK 93744 China Beach - Music & Memories. *(LP version)*
(S) (4:13) Columbia 9700 Cheap Thrills. *(LP version)*
(S) (4:26) Columbia/Legacy 48845 Janis. *(:13 longer than the LP version)*
(S) (4:11) Time-Life 2CLR-19 Classic Rock - 1968: Shakin' All Over. *(LP version)*
(S) (4:10) Time-Life R102-34 The Rolling Stone Collection. *(LP version)*
(S) (4:13) Legacy/Epic 67005 Janis Joplin: 18 Essential Songs. *(LP version)*
(S) (4:13) Mercury 314528871 O.S.T. Home For The Holidays. *(LP version)*
(S) (4:26) Time-Life R13610 Gold And Platinum Box Set - The Ultimate Rock Collection. *(:13 longer than the LP version)*

BIG COUNTRY
1983 IN A BIG COUNTRY
(S) (3:52) Priority 53754 Rock Of The 80's Volume 15. *(45 version)*
(S) (3:51) Rhino 71834 Classic MTV: Class Of 1983. *(45 version)*
(S) (4:43) Mercury 812870 The Crossing. *(LP version)*
(S) (3:52) Mercury 314518716 Best Of. *(45 version)*
(S) (3:53) Rhino 71974 New Wave Hits Of The 80's Vol. 11. *(45 version)*
(S) (4:43) Time-Life R988-26 Sounds Of The Eighties: The Rolling Stone Collection 1982-1983. *(LP version)*
(S) (4:43) Special Music 5040 Great Britons! Volume Two. *(LP version)*
(S) (4:43) Rebound 314520434 Classic Rock - 80's. *(LP version)*

BIG COUNTRY *(Continued)*
- (S) (4:43) Time-Life R968-20 Guitar Rock - The '80s. *(LP version)*
- (S) (4:43) Rebound 314520442 The Roots Of Rock: 80's New Wave. *(LP version)*
- (S) (4:44) Hip-O 40047 The '80s Hit(s) Back 3. *(LP version)*
- (S) (3:52) Rebound 314520493 Class Reunion '83. *(45 version)*

BIG MOUNTAIN
1994 BABY I LOVE YOUR WAY
- (S) (4:21) RCA 66364 O.S.T. Reality Bites.
- (S) (4:21) Giant 24563 Unity.
- (S) (4:21) Hip-O 40000 Thinking About You - A Collection Of Modern Love Songs.
- (S) (4:21) Razor & Tie 4569 '90s Style.
- (S) (4:21) K-Tel 3850 90s Now Volume 3.
- (S) (4:21) Priority 50974 Premiere The Movie Magazine Presents The Greatest Soundtrack Hits.

MR. ACKER BILK
1962 STRANGER ON THE SHORE
- (M) (2:54) Collectables 5068 History Of Rock Volume 8.
- (S) (2:53) Time-Life HPD-34 Your Hit Parade - 60's Instrumentals.
- (S) (3:16) GNP Crescendo 2116 Best Of. *(rerecording)*
- (S) (2:54) Polygram Special Markets 314520273 Great Instrumental Hits.
- (S) (3:17) K-Tel 3583 Those Wonderful Instrumentals Volume 3. *(rerecording)*
- (S) (2:53) Time-Life R857-06 The Heart Of Rock 'n' Roll 1962.
- (S) (2:53) Collectors' Choice 5190 More Instrumental Gems Of The 60's.
- (S) (2:55) Taragon 1035 Very Best Of.
- (S) (2:44) Taragon 1035 Very Best Of. *(rerecording)*
- (S) (2:53) Time-Life R814-02 Love Songs.
- (S) (2:53) Time-Life R986-22 Instrumental Classics - Pop Classics.

BILLY & LILLIE
1958 LA DEE DAH
1959 LUCKY LADYBUG
- (M) (2:36) Forevermore 5008 Oldies I Forgot To Buy.

BILLY & THE BEATERS (see BILLY VERA)

BILLY JOE & THE CHECKMATES
1962 PERCOLATOR (TWIST)
- (M) (2:09) Time-Life 2RNR-36 Rock 'N' Roll Era - Axes & Saxes/The Great Instrumentals.
- (M) (2:09) MCA Special Products 21035 Classic Rock & Roll Instrumental Hits, Volume 2.

BINGOBOYS
1991 HOW TO DANCE
- (S) (3:46) Atlantic 82240 Best Of.

ELVIN BISHOP
1976 FOOLED AROUND AND FELL IN LOVE
- (S) (2:54) Priority 7995 Country's Greatest Hits: Southern Country Rock Volume 2. *(45 version)*
- (S) (2:56) Rhino 70671 Billboard Top Hits - 1976. *(45 version)*
- (S) (2:56) Rhino 70586 Rebel Rousers: Southern Rock Classics. *(45 version)*
- (S) (4:34) K-Tel 30522 Elvin Bishop/Wet Willie. *(LP version)*
- (S) (4:33) Polydor 314513307 Sure Feels Good: Best Of. *(LP version)*
- (S) (2:56) Time-Life R968-03 Guitar Rock 1976-1977. *(45 version)*
- (S) (2:56) Time-Life SOD-04 Sounds Of The Seventies - 1976. *(45 version)*
- (S) (4:34) K-Tel 6045 Southern Fried Rock. *(LP version)*
- (S) (4:33) Rebound 314520256 Best Of Southern Rock. *(LP version)*

- (S) (4:33) Special Music 5025 Rebel Rousers! Best Of Southern Rock. *(LP version)*
- (S) (4:33) Special Music/Essex 5036 Prom Night - The 70's. *(LP version)*
- (S) (4:33) Rebound 314520368 Class Reunion '76. *(LP version)*
- (S) (2:56) Polygram Special Markets 314520387 Best Of. *(45 version)*
- (S) (2:55) Time-Life AM1-23 AM Gold - 1976. *(45 version)*
- (S) (2:56) Time-Life R834-04 Body Talk - Together Forever. *(45 version)*
- (S) (4:34) K-Tel 3972 Southern Rockin' Rebels: The South's Gone And Done It. *(LP version)*
- (S) (4:34) Capricorn 314536135 Struttin' My Stuff. *(LP version)*
- (S) (4:33) Critique 15467 Fast Cars And Southern Stars. *(LP version)*
- (S) (4:33) Capitol 93076 More Music From O.S.T. Boogie Nights. *(LP version)*
- (S) (4:33) Hip-O 40095 '70s Hit(s) Back. *(LP version)*

STEPHEN BISHOP
1977 SAVE IT FOR A RAINY DAY
- (S) (3:14) Rhino 70833 Best Of Bish.
- (S) (3:14) Varese Sarabande 5534 Rhythm Of The Rain.
- (S) (3:13) MCA 11035 On And On/The Hits Of.
- (S) (3:09) Rhino 72446 Listen To The Music: 70's Male Singer/Songwriters.

1977 ON AND ON
- (S) (2:58) Priority 53706 Singers/Songwriters/70's Greatest Rock Hits Volume 15.
- (S) (3:06) Rhino 70833 Best Of Bish.
- (S) (2:59) Time-Life SOD-35 Sounds Of The Seventies - AM Nuggets.
- (S) (3:01) MCA 11035 On And On/The Hits Of.
- (S) (3:01) MCA Special Products 20910 Rockin' 70's.
- (S) (3:01) Hip-O 40096 '70s Hit(s) Back Again.
- (S) (2:58) Time-Life R834-12 Body Talk - By Candlelight.

1978 EVERYBODY NEEDS LOVE
- (S) (3:41) MCA 11035 On And On/The Hits Of.

1983 IT MIGHT BE YOU
- (S) (4:13) Rhino 70833 Best Of Bish.
- (S) (4:12) MCA 11035 On And On/The Hits Of.
- (S) (4:12) Time-Life R834-14 Body Talk - Love And Tenderness.
- (S) (4:11) Rebound 314520519 Love At The Movies.

BIZ MARKIE
1990 JUST A FRIEND
- (S) (3:59) Luke/Atlantic 91598 Bass Waves Volume Three.
- (S) (4:00) Cold Chillin'/Reprise 26003 Biz Never Sleeps.
- (S) (4:01) Rhino 72853 Kurtis Blow Presents The History Of Rap Vol. 3.

BILL BLACK'S COMBO
1960 SMOKIE (PART 2)
- (M) (2:06) MCA 25226 History Of Hi Records Rhythm & Blues Volume 1.
- (M) (2:05) Time-Life 2RNR-36 Rock 'N' Roll Era - Axes & Saxes/The Great Instrumentals.
- (M) (2:06) K-Tel 3059 Saxy Rock.
- (M) (2:06) Right Stuff 30584 Hi Times - The Hi Records R&B Years.

1960 WHITE SILVER SANDS
- (M) (2:29) Collectors' Choice 003/4 Instrumental Gems Of The 60's.

1960 JOSEPHINE
1960 DON'T BE CRUEL
- (M) (1:55) MCA 25226 History Of Hi Records Rhythm & Blues Volume 1.

1960 BLUE TANGO
1961 HEARTS OF STONE
1961 OLE BUTTERMILK SKY
1961 MOVIN'
- (M) (2:01) Right Stuff 53318 Hot Rod Rock Volume 3: Big Boss Instrumentals.

1962 TWIST-HER

CILLA BLACK
1964 YOU'RE MY WORLD
- (S) (2:57) Rhino 70320 History Of British Rock Volume 2.
- (S) (2:57) Rhino 72022 History Of British Rock Box Set.
- (S) (2:57) Rhino 72008 History Of British Rock Volumes 1-4 Box Set.
- (S) (2:56) Time-Life R138/05 Look Of Love.

JEANNE BLACK
1960 HE'LL HAVE TO STAY
- (S) (2:39) Rhino 70681 Billboard's Top Country Hits Of 1960.

BLACK BOX
1990 EVERYBODY EVERYBODY
- (S) (5:20) JCI 2717 Shake It Up. *(remixed)*
- (S) (4:06) Sandstone 33055 and 5014 Rock The First Volume Eight.
- (S) (4:06) Sandstone 5022 Cosmopolitan Volume 8.
- (S) (4:06) Rebound 314520246 Disco Nights Vol. 5 - Best Of Housemusic.
- (S) (4:06) DCC Compact Classics 082 Night Moves Volume 2.
- (S) (4:06) RCA 2221 Dreamland.
- (S) (5:20) RCA 61051 Mixed Up! *(remixed)*
- (S) (4:05) Priority 53770 Techno Dance Classics Volume 1 - Pump Up The Jam.
- (S) (4:04) Tommy Boy 1163 Jock Jams Volume 2. *(all selections on this cd are segued together)*
- (S) (3:47) Priority 50934 Shut Up And Dance! The 90's Volume One. *(all selections on this cd are segued together)*
- (S) (4:04) Cold Front 6245 Greatest Sports Rock And Jams. *(all selections on this cd are segued together)*
- (S) (5:12) Boxtunes 162531071 Big Ones Of Dance Volume 1. *(remixed; all selections on this cd are segued together)*

1991 I DON'T KNOW ANYBODY ELSE
- (M) (4:33) RCA 2221 Dreamland.
- (S) (3:57) RCA 61051 Mixed Up! *(remixed)*
- (M) (4:33) DCC Compact Classics 121 Divas Of Dance Volume 1.

1991 STRIKE IT UP
- (S) (5:15) RCA 2221 Dreamland.
- (S) (4:28) RCA 61051 Mixed Up! *(remixed)*
- (S) (3:34) Tommy Boy 1137 ESPN Presents Jock Jams. *(all songs on this cd are segued together with crowd sound effects added)*
- (S) (5:14) Rebound 314520359 World Of Dance - The 90's.
- (S) (5:14) DCC Compact Classics 123 Divas Of Dance Volume 3.
- (S) (5:15) Rhino 72839 Disco Queens: The 90's.
- (S) (5:00) Logic 46895 Martha Wash Collection. *(alternate take)*
- (S) (4:25) Beast 53232 Club Hitz Of The 90's Vol. 3. *(all songs on this cd are segued together)*

BLACKBYRDS
1975 WALKING IN RHYTHM
- (S) (4:11) Priority 8666 Kickin' Back/70's Greatest Rock Hits Volume 5. *(LP version)*
- (S) (2:53) Rhino 70555 Soul Hits Of The 70's Volume 15. *(45 version)*
- (S) (4:11) Fantasy 7707 Greatest Hits. *(LP version)*
- (S) (4:09) Razor & Tie 22047 Sweet 70's Soul. *(LP version)*
- (S) (2:51) Time-Life SOD-32 Sounds Of The Seventies - AM Pop Classics. *(45 version)*
- (S) (2:53) Time-Life R838-10 Solid Gold Soul - 1975. *(45 version)*

1976 HAPPY MUSIC
- (S) (4:55) Fantasy 7707 Greatest Hits. *(LP version)*
- (S) (3:04) Rhino 72127 Soul Hits Of The 70's Vol. 17. *(45 version)*

BLACK CROWES
1991 HARD TO HANDLE
- (S) (3:07) Time-Life R102-34 The Rolling Stone Collection.
- (S) (3:08) Def American 24278 Shake Your Money Maker.

1991 SHE TALKS TO ANGELS
- (S) (5:30) Def American 24278 Shake Your Money Maker. *(LP version)*

BLACKFOOT
1979 HIGHWAY SONG
- (S) (4:24) Priority 7995 Country's Greatest Hits: Southern Country Rock Volume 2. *(neither the 45 or LP version)*
- (S) (7:00) Atco 38112 Strikes. *(LP version)*
- (S) (7:00) Time-Life R968-02 Guitar Rock 1978-1979. *(LP version)*
- (S) (7:00) Time-Life SOD-22 Sounds Of The Seventies - Seventies Top Forty. *(LP version)*
- (S) (6:59) Priority 53713 Classic Rock Volume 1 - Highway Rockers. *(LP version)*
- (S) (7:30) Rhino 71614 Best Of. *(:30 longer than the LP version)*
- (S) (7:28) DCC Compact Classics 139 Rock The First Volume 9. *(:28 longer than the LP version)*
- (S) (7:00) Hip-O 40062 Under My Wheels: 12 Road Trippin' Tracks. *(LP version)*
- (S) (4:24) K-Tel 3996 Rockin' Down The Highway. *(neither the 45 or LP version)*

1979 TRAIN, TRAIN
- (S) (3:33) Priority 8663 The South Rules/70's Greatest Rock Hits Volume 2.
- (S) (3:34) Rhino 70721 Legends Of Guitar: The 70's Volume 1.
- (S) (3:33) Atco 38112 Strikes.
- (S) (3:33) Time-Life SOD-23 Sounds Of The Seventies - Guitar Power.
- (S) (3:34) Rhino 71614 Best Of.
- (S) (2:57) K-Tel 6083 Southern Fried Rock - Second Helping. *(missing the :36 prelude)*
- (S) (3:33) Time-Life R968-14 Guitar Rock - The Late '70s.
- (S) (3:33) JCI 3140 18 Screamers From The 70's.
- (S) (3:34) Simitar 55762 Stud Rock - Wild Ride.

BLACK OAK ARKANSAS
1974 JIM DANDY
- (S) (2:39) Rhino 70759 Super Hits Of The 70's Volume 12.
- (S) (2:39) Rhino 70586 Rebel Rousers: Southern Rock Classics.
- (S) (2:39) Rhino 71146 Hot & Nasty: Best Of.
- (S) (2:39) Medicine Label 24533 O.S.T. Dazed And Confused.
- (S) (2:39) Time-Life R968-08 Guitar Rock - The Mid '70s.
- (S) (2:39) Rhino 72222 High On The Hog.
- (S) (2:39) Rhino 72419 Jim Dandy.
- (S) (2:39) Rebound 314520406 The Roots Of Rock: Southern Rock.
- (S) (2:39) Flashback 72680 Hot And Nasty And Other Hits.
- (S) (2:39) Flashback 72089 '70s Rock Legends Box Set.
- (S) (2:39) Rebound 314520475 The Roots Of Rock: Southern Rock.

BLACKOUT ALLSTARS
1997 I LIKE IT
- (S) (3:46) Columbia 57761 O.S.T. I Like It Like That Vol. 1.
- (M) (4:17) Robbins Entertainment 75008 Dance Party (Like It's 1998). *(remix; all songs on this cd are segued together)*
- (M) (4:18) Beast 54112 Boom! *(remix)*
- (S) (4:51) Columbia 68602 Total Dance Explosion. *(remix; all songs on this cd are segued together)*

BLACKSTREET ∞

1994 BOOTI CALL
    (S) (4:25)   Interscope 92351 Blackstreet.

1995 BEFORE I LET YOU GO
    (S) (4:59)   Interscope 92351 Blackstreet.
    (S) (4:59)   EMI-Capitol Music Group 54548 Smooth Luv.

released as by BLACKSTREET featuring DR. DRE:
1996 NO DIGGITY
    (S) (5:04)   Interscope 90071 Blackstreet - Another Level.
    (S) (3:41)   Tommy Boy 1214 Jock Jams Volume 3. *(all selections on this cd are segued together)*
    (S) (5:00)   Tommy Boy 1234 MTV Party To Go '98. *(all songs on this cd are segued together)*
    (M) (4:54)   Elektra 62088 Party Over Here '98. *(all tracks on this cd are segued together)*
    (S) (5:05)   Priority 51021 Hip Hop Coast 2 Coast.

JACK BLANCHARD & MISTY MORGAN
1970 TENNESSEE BIRD WALK
    (S) (2:41)   K-Tel 3243 Kooky Kountry. *(rerecording)*
    (S) (2:40)   K-Tel 3368 101 Greatest Country Hits Vol. Nine: Country Classics. *(rerecording)*
    (S) (2:50)   Time-Life R830-03 The Dr. Demento Collection: The Early '70s.

BILLY BLAND
1960 LET THE LITTLE GIRL DANCE
    (M) (2:18)   Time-Life 2RNR-11 Rock 'N' Roll Era - 1960.

BOBBY BLAND
1962 TURN ON YOUR LOVE LIGHT
    (M) (2:28)   MCA 31219 Best Of.
    (S) (2:36)   Rhino 70647 Billboard's Top R&B Hits Of 1961.
    (S) (2:34)   MCA 31202 Vintage Music Volume 5. *(alternate take)*
    (S) (2:34)   MCA 5804 Vintage Music Volumes 5 & 6. *(alternate take)*
    (E) (2:33)   JCI 3204 Heart & Soul Fifties. *(alternate take)*
    (E) (2:28)   Original Sound 8859 Oldies But Goodies Vol. 9. *(this compact disc uses the "Waring - fds" noise reduction process)*
    (S) (2:36)   MCA 10667 Best Of Duke-Peacock Blues.
    (M) (2:36)   Time-Life 2RNR-16 Rock 'N' Roll Era - 1962 Still Rockin'.
    (S) (2:30)   Time-Life RHD-11 Rhythm & Blues - 1962.
    (S) (2:37)   MCA 10957 Turn On Your Love Light.
    (M) (2:29)   MCA Special Products 22020 Best Of The Blues.
    (M) (2:34)   MCA Special Products 22179 Vintage Collectibles Volume 9.
    (S) (2:34)   K-Tel 3345 Got The Blues.
    (S) (2:36)   Time-Life R859-02 Living The Blues - Blues Masters.
    (S) (2:35)   MCA 11441 Blues Classics Box Set.
    (S) (2:35)   Platinum Entertainment 514161183 Essential Blues 2.
    (S) (2:30)   Time-Life R838-18 Solid Gold Soul 1962.
    (S) (2:34)   MCA 11670 Eve's Bayou - The Collection.
    (S) (2:36)   MCA 11783 Greatest Hits Vol. One: The Duke Recordings.

1963 CALL ON ME
    (M) (2:36)   MCA 31219 Best Of. *(45 version)*
    (S) (2:32)   MCA 10957 Turn On Your Love Light. *(45 version)*
    (S) (3:47)   MCA Special Products 22008 You've Got Me Loving You. *(LP version)*
    (S) (2:30)   Hip-O 40009 ABC's Of Soul Volume 1. *(45 version)*
    (S) (2:31)   MCA Special Products 20973 Soul Legend. *(45 version)*
    (S) (2:30)   MCA 11783 Greatest Hits Vol. One: The Duke Recordings. *(45 version)*

1963 THAT'S THE WAY LOVE IS
    (M) (2:29)   Time-Life RHD-02 Rhythm & Blues - 1963.
    (M) (2:36)   MCA 10957 Turn On Your Love Light.
    (M) (2:36)   MCA Special Products 20973 Soul Legend.
    (M) (2:29)   Time-Life R838-14 Solid Gold Soul - 1963.

    (M) (2:34)   MCA Special Products 21030 Beach Music Hits.
    (M) (2:35)   MCA 11783 Greatest Hits Vol. One: The Duke Recordings.

1964 AIN'T NOTHING YOU CAN DO
    (M) (2:37)   MCA 31219 Best Of.
    (S) (2:28)   Time-Life RHD-12 Rhythm & Blues - 1964.
    (S) (2:27)   Time-Life 2CLR-16 Classic Rock - 1964: Shakin' All Over.
    (M) (2:37)   MCA 10957 Turn On Your Love Light.
    (M) (2:37)   MCA Special Products 20941 R&B Crossover Oldies Vol. 1.
    (M) (2:37)   MCA Special Products 20973 Soul Legend.
    (S) (2:28)   Time-Life R838-13 Solid Gold Soul - 1964.

1964 AIN'T DOING TOO BAD (PART 1)
    (M) (2:40)   MCA 10957 Turn On Your Love Light. *(tracks into Part 2)*

MARCIE BLANE
1962 BOBBY'S GIRL
    (S) (2:15)   Collectables 5065 History Of Rock Volume 5.
    (S) (2:14)   Time-Life 2RNR-35 Rock 'N' Roll Era - The 60's Last Dance.
    (E) (2:15)   Collectables 2505 History Of Rock - The 60's Part 5.
    (E) (2:15)   Collectables 4505 History Of Rock/The 60s Part Five.
    (S) (2:15)   DCC Compact Classics 077 Too Cute!
    (S) (2:23)   Eric 11503 Hard To Find 45's On CD (Volume II) 1961-64. *(:09 longer fade than the 45)*

BLESSID UNION OF SOULS ∞
1995 I BELIEVE
    (S) (4:26)   EMI 31836 Home.

1995 LET ME BE THE ONE
    (S) (4:36)   EMI 31836 Home.

1997 I WANNA BE THERE
    (S) (4:27)   EMI 56716 Blessid Union Of Souls.

MARY J. BLIGE
1992 YOU REMIND ME
    (S) (4:16)   MCA/Uptown 10681 What's The 411?.

1992 REAL LOVE
    (S) (4:57)   Tommy Boy 1074 MTV Party To Go Volume 3. *(remix; all tracks on this cd are segued together)*
    (S) (4:29)   MCA/Uptown 10681 What's The 411?.
    (S) (4:29)   Uptown 53022 Uptown's Block Party Volume 1.

1993 SWEET THING
    (S) (3:44)   MCA/Uptown 10681 What's The 411?.

1994 BE HAPPY
    (S) (5:48)   Uptown/MCA 11156 My Life.

1995 I'M GOIN' DOWN
    (S) (3:41)   Uptown/MCA 11156 My Life.

released as by METHOD MAN/MARY J. BLIGE:
1995 I'LL BE THERE FOR YOU/YOU'RE ALL I NEED TO GET BY
    (S) (5:06)   Def Jam 314523848 Def Jam Music Group Ten Year Anniversary.
    (S) (4:48)   Tommy Boy 1139 MTV Party To Go Volume 8. *(all selections on this cd are segued together; remix)*
    (S) (3:56)   Rebound 314520449 Hip Hop With R&B Flava.

released as by MARY J. BLIGE:
1996 NOT GON' CRY
    (S) (4:55)   Arista 18796 O.S.T. Waiting To Exhale.

1997 I CAN LOVE YOU
    (S) (4:46)   MCA 11606 Share My World. *(tracks into the next selection)*

1997 EVERYTHING
    (S) (4:58)   MCA 11606 Share My World. *(tracks into the next selection)*

BLIND MELON ∞
1993 NO RAIN
    (S) (3:35)   Capitol 96585 Blind Melon.
    (S) (3:34)   Mammoth 92672 and 354980125 MTV Buzz Bin Volume 1.
    (S) (3:34)   Priority 50947 A Bunch O' Hits: The Best Rock Of The 90's Volume 1.
    (S) (3:34)   Razor & Tie 4569 '90s Style.

BLONDIE
1979 HEART OF GLASS
(actual LP time is (3:44) not (3:54) as stated on the record label)

(S)	(3:22)	Priority 7971 Mega-Hits Dance Classics Volume 1. *(45 version)*
(S)	(3:23)	Rhino 70985 The Disco Years Volume 2. *(45 version)*
(S)	(3:22)	Rhino 70674 Billboard Top Hits - 1979. *(45 version)*
(S)	(4:33)	Sandstone 33002 Reelin' In The Years Volume 3. *(this extended version first appeared on the "Best Of Blondie" vinyl LP)*
(S)	(3:44)	Chrysalis 21192 and 41192 Parallel Lines. *(LP version)*
(S)	(4:33)	Chrysalis 21337 and 41337 Best Of. *(this extended version first appeared on the "Best Of Blondie" vinyl LP)*
(S)	(4:33)	DCC Compact Classics 064 Rock Of The 70's Volume Three. *(this extended version first appeared on the "Best Of Blondie" vinyl LP)*
(S)	(5:47)	Chrysalis 21990 Blonde And Beyond. *(12" single version)*
(S)	(4:32)	Razor & Tie 22496 Disco Fever. *(this extended version first appeared on the "Best Of Blondie" vinyl LP)*
(S)	(3:22)	Time-Life SOD-09 Sounds Of The Seventies - 1979. *(45 version)*
(S)	(4:09)	Chrysalis 31100 Platinum Collection. *(previously unreleased version)*
(S)	(8:42)	Chrysalis 32748 Remixed Remade Remodeled. *(remix)*
(S)	(7:14)	Chrysalis 32748 Remixed Remade Remodeled. *(remix)*
(S)	(3:45)	DCC Compact Classics 1062 Parallel Lines. *(gold disc; LP version)*
(S)	(5:50)	DCC Compact Classics 1062 Parallel Lines. *(gold disc; 12" single version)*
(S)	(3:23)	Madacy Entertainment 1979 Rock On 1979. *(45 version)*
(S)	(3:23)	JCI 3148 1975 - Only Dance - 1979. *(45 version)*
(S)	(8:41)	EMI 54099 Retro Dance Club Volume Two. *(remix)*
(S)	(3:45)	Priority 50956 Mega Hits - Disco Heat. *(LP version)*
(S)	(4:32)	Eclipse Music Group 64896 Rock 'n Roll Relix 1978-1979. *(this extended version first appeared on the "Best Of Blondie" vinyl LP)*
(S)	(4:32)	Eclipse Music Group 64897 Rock 'n Roll Relix 1970-1979. *(this extended version first appeared on the "Best Of Blondie" vinyl LP)*
(S)	(4:20)	Arista 18985 Ultimate New Wave Party 1998. *(this extended version first appeared on the "Best Of Blondie" vinyl LP; all selections on this cd are segued together)*
(S)	(3:23)	K-Tel 3909 High Energy Volume 2. *(45 version)*
(S)	(3:22)	Time-Life R840-10 Sounds Of The Seventies: '70s Dance Party 1979. *(45 version)*
(S)	(3:22)	Time-Life AM1-26 AM Gold - 1979. *(45 version)*

1979 ONE WAY OR ANOTHER

(S)	(3:33)	Priority 7997 Super Songs/70's Greatest Rock Hits Volume 8.
(S)	(3:30)	Chrysalis 21192 and 41192 Parallel Lines.
(S)	(3:34)	Chrysalis 21337 and 41337 Best Of.
(S)	(3:25)	Time-Life R968-02 Guitar Rock 1978-1979.
(S)	(3:26)	Time-Life SOD-19 Sounds Of The Seventies - 1979: Take Two.
(S)	(3:26)	Rhino 71694 New Wave Hits Of The 80's Vol. 1.
(S)	(3:26)	Chrysalis 31100 Platinum Collection.
(S)	(8:22)	Chrysalis 32748 Remixed Remade Remodeled. *(remix)*
(S)	(3:31)	DCC Compact Classics 1062 Parallel Lines. *(gold disc)*
(S)	(3:33)	EMI 55204 O.S.T. Beverly Hills Ninja.
(S)	(3:25)	Simitar 55582 The Number One's: Rock It Up.

1979 DREAMING

(S)	(3:04)	Chrysalis 21225 and 41225 Eat To The Beat.
(S)	(3:06)	Chrysalis 21337 and 41337 Best Of.
(S)	(3:00)	Time-Life SOD-34 Sounds Of The Seventies - The Late 70's.
(S)	(3:03)	Chrysalis 31100 Platinum Collection.
(S)	(7:38)	Chrysalis 32748 Remixed Remade Remodeled. *(remix)*
(S)	(6:20)	Chrysalis 32748 Remixed Remade Remodeled. *(remix)*

1980 CALL ME

(S)	(3:30)	Rhino 70494 Billboard Top Dance Hits - 1980.
(S)	(3:32)	Chrysalis 21337 and 41337 Best Of.
(S)	(3:29)	Rhino 70675 Billboard Top Hits - 1980.
(S)	(3:32)	Priority 7994 Rock Of The 80's.
(S)	(3:28)	Time-Life R968-04 Guitar Rock 1980-1981.
(S)	(3:31)	Priority 53730 Mega Hits Dance Classics Vol. 13.
(S)	(3:30)	Chrysalis 31100 Platinum Collection.
(S)	(3:28)	JCI 3127 1980 - Only Rock 'N Roll - 1984.
(S)	(7:01)	Chrysalis 32748 Remixed Remade Remodeled. *(remix)*
(S)	(3:29)	Time-Life R988-07 Sounds Of The Eighties: 1980.
(S)	(3:30)	Time-Life R988-25 Sounds Of The Eighties: The Rolling Stone Collection 1980-1981.
(S)	(3:29)	Time-Life R138-38 Celebration.
(S)	(3:30)	Rebound 314520366 Disco Nights Vol. 10 - Disco's Greatest Movie Hits.
(S)	(3:28)	Madacy Entertainment 1980 Rock On 1980.
(S)	(3:28)	JCI 3163 18 Disco Superhits.
(S)	(7:00)	EMI 54101 Retro Dance Club Volume Four. *(remix)*
(S)	(3:31)	Rebound 314520434 Classic Rock - 80's.
(S)	(3:30)	Rhino 72894 Hard Rock Cafe: New Wave.
(S)	(3:30)	Simitar 55552 The Number One's: Eighties Rock.

1981 THE TIDE IS HIGH

(S)	(4:39)	Chrysalis 21290 and 41290 Autoamerican. *(LP version)*
(S)	(4:42)	Chrysalis 21337 and 41337 Best Of. *(LP version)*
(S)	(3:50)	Rhino 70676 Billboard Top Hits - 1981. *(45 version)*
(S)	(3:50)	Chrysalis 31100 Platinum Collection. *(45 version)*
(S)	(3:50)	Rhino 71818 Ranking & Skanking - Best Of Punky Reggae. *(45 version)*
(S)	(4:40)	Rebound 314520313 Caribbean Nights I. *(LP version)*
(S)	(7:04)	Chrysalis 32748 Remixed Remade Remodeled. *(remix)*
(S)	(3:50)	Time-Life R988-01 Sounds Of The Eighties: The Rockin' Eighties. *(45 version)*
(S)	(4:40)	Rebound 314520373 Rock 'n' Reggae. *(LP version)*
(S)	(4:40)	EMI 52498 O.S.T. Striptease. *(LP version)*
(S)	(4:32)	Polydor 314527493 O.S.T. Muriel's Wedding. *(LP version)*
(S)	(4:41)	JCI 3170 #1 Radio Hits 1980 - Only Rock 'n Roll - 1984. *(LP version)*
(S)	(4:40)	Madacy Entertainment 6804 More Sun Splashin'. *(LP version)*
(S)	(3:50)	Hip-O 40075 Rock She Said: On The Pop Side. *(45 version)*
(S)	(4:40)	Rebound 314520313 Reggae Dance Party I. *(LP version)*

1981 RAPTURE
(dj copies of this 45 ran (4:55) and (6:33); commercial copies were all (6:33))

(S)	(6:28)	Chrysalis 21290 and 41290 Autoamerican.
(S)	(5:35)	Chrysalis 21337 and 41337 Best Of. *(this version first appeared on the "Best Of Blondie" vinyl LP)*
(S)	(5:35)	Sandstone 33044 and 5010 Rock The First Volume 4. *(this version first appeared on the "Best Of Blondie" vinyl LP)*
(S)	(5:34)	Priority 53729 Mega Hits Dance Classics Vol 11. *(this version first appeared on the "Best Of Blondie" vinyl LP)*

BLONDIE (Continued)

- (S) (4:56) Chrysalis 31100 Platinum Collection.
- (S) (7:05) SBK 31179 Brilliant! Volume 5. *(remix)*
- (S) (7:06) Chrysalis 32748 Remixed Remade Remodeled. *(remix)*
- (S) (5:35) JCI 3149 1980 - Only Dance - 1984. *(this version first appeared on the "Best Of Blondie" vinyl LP)*
- (S) (5:35) Madacy Entertainment 1981 Rock On 1981. *(this version first appeared on the "Best Of Blondie" vinyl LP)*
- (S) (6:29) Rhino 72771 The Big 80's.
- (S) (7:06) EMI 54100 Retro Dance Club Volume Three. *(remix)*
- (S) (5:34) Time-Life R988-14 Sounds Of The Eighties: 1980-1982. *(this version first appeared on the "Best Of Blondie" vinyl LP)*
- (S) (9:59) Rhino 72586 Just Can't Get Enough: New Wave Dance Hits Of The 80's. *(remix)*
- (S) (5:34) K-Tel 3867 The 80's: Hot Ladies. *(this version first appeared on the "Best Of Blondie" vinyl LP)*
- (S) (5:35) Nick At Nite/550 Music 63437 Nick At Nite Goes To Outer Space. *(this version first appeared on the "Best Of Blondie" vinyl LP)*
- (S) (5:34) Time-Life R13610 Gold And Platinum Box Set - The Ultimate Rock Collection. *(this version first appeared on the "Best Of Blondie" vinyl LP)*

BLOODROCK
1971 D.O.A.
- (S) (8:26) Capitol 91622 Bloodrock 'N' Roll. *(LP version)*
- (S) (4:33) Rhino 70986 Heavy Metal Memories. *(45 version)*
- (S) (4:33) Time-Life SOD-28 Sounds Of The Seventies - FM Rock III. *(45 version)*
- (S) (8:25) Risky Business 57471 Godfathers Of Grunge. *(LP version)*
- (S) (8:27) One Way 18405 Bloodrock 2. *(LP version)*
- (S) (4:32) Time-Life R968-06 Guitar Rock 1970-1971. *(45 version)*
- (S) (8:27) EMI-Capitol Music Special Markets 19545 Lost Hits Of The '70s. *(LP version)*
- (S) (4:33) K-Tel 3985 70s Heavy Hitters: Arena Rockers 1970-74. *(45 version)*
- (S) (8:25) K-Tel 4030 Rock Anthems. *(LP version)*

BLOODSTONE
1973 NATURAL HIGH
(dj copies of this 45 ran (3:06) and (4:02); commercial copies were all (4:02))
- (S) (4:07) Rhino 70551 Soul Hits Of The 70's Volume 11. *(45 version)*
- (S) (4:04) Time-Life SOD-33 Sounds Of The Seventies - AM Pop Classics II. *(45 version)*
- (S) (4:03) Original Sound 4001 Art Laboe's 60 Killer Oldies. *(45 version)*
- (S) (4:03) Original Sound 8911 Art Laboe's Dedicated To You Vol. 2. *(45 version)*
- (S) (4:51) Right Stuff 30576 Slow Jams: The 70's Volume 4. *(LP version)*
- (S) (4:51) Thump 4720 Old School Love Songs Volume 2. *(LP version)*
- (S) (4:52) Rebound 314520367 Soul Classics - Quiet Storm/The 70's. *(LP version)*
- (S) (4:07) Hip-O 40001 The Glory Of Love - Sweet & Soulful Love Songs. *(45 version)*
- (S) (4:52) Rhino 72460 Natural High. *(LP version)*
- (S) (4:07) Time-Life R838-08 Solid Gold Soul - 1973. *(45 version)*
- (S) (4:08) Rhino 72753 Very Best Of. *(45 version)*
- (S) (4:08) Rhino 72870 Brown Eyed Soul Vol. 3. *(45 version)*
- (S) (4:52) Maverick 46841 O.S.T. Jackie Brown. *(LP version)*
- (S) (4:07) Time-Life R834-14 Body Talk - Love And Tenderness. *(45 version)*

1973 NEVER LET YOU GO
- (S) (5:27) Rhino 72460 Natural High. *(LP version)*
- (S) (3:33) Rhino 72753 Very Best Of. *(45 version)*
1974 OUTSIDE WOMAN
- (S) (4:47) Priority 53131 Deep Soul Volume Two. *(LP version)*
- (S) (4:51) Rhino 72460 Natural High. *(LP version)*
- (S) (3:37) Rhino 72753 Very Best Of. *(45 version)*

BLOOD, SWEAT & TEARS
1969 YOU'VE MADE ME SO VERY HAPPY
- (S) (4:15) Columbia 31170 Blood, Sweat & Tears Greatest Hits. *(LP version)*
- (S) (4:13) Columbia 45019 Pop Classics Of The 60's. *(LP version)*
- (S) (4:15) Columbia 9720 Blood, Sweat And Tears. *(LP version; truncated fade)*
- (S) (4:15) MFSL 559 Blood, Sweat And Tears. *(LP version; gold disc)*
- (S) (4:14) Time-Life SUD-18 Superhits - Late 60's Classics. *(LP version)*
- (M) (3:28) CBS Special Products 16641 Found Treasures. *(45 version)*
- (S) (4:11) Sony Music Distribution 57854 For Your Love. *(LP version)*
- (S) (4:15) K-Tel 3585 Horn Rock Bands. *(LP version)*
- (S) (4:15) Legacy/Columbia 64166 Best Of: What Goes Up! *(LP version)*
- (S) (4:14) Time-Life AM1-12 AM Gold - Late '60s Classics. *(LP version)*
1969 SPINNING WHEEL
- (S) (4:05) JCI 3101 Rockin' Sixties. *(LP version)*
- (S) (4:03) Columbia 45018 Rock Classics Of The 60's. *(LP version)*
- (S) (4:04) Columbia 31170 Blood, Sweat & Tears Greatest Hits. *(LP version)*
- (S) (4:04) Columbia 9720 Blood, Sweat And Tears. *(LP version)*
- (S) (4:05) MFSL 559 Blood, Sweat And Tears. *(LP version; gold disc)*
- (S) (4:04) Time-Life 2CLR-12 Classic Rock - 1969: The Beat Goes On. *(LP version)*
- (S) (3:27) CBS Special Products 16641 Found Treasures. *(edit of the LP version)*
- (S) (2:38) Rhino 71939 Billboard Top Pop Hits, 1969. *(45 version)*
- (S) (4:05) Legacy/Columbia 64166 Best Of: What Goes Up! *(LP version)*
- (S) (2:38) Varese Sarabande 5847 On The Radio Volume Two. *(45 version)*
1969 AND WHEN I DIE
- (S) (4:01) Columbia 31170 Blood, Sweat & Tears Greatest Hits. *(LP version)*
- (S) (4:00) Priority 8670 Hitchin A Ride/70's Greatest Rock Hits Volume 10. *(LP version)*
- (S) (4:01) Columbia 9720 Blood, Sweat And Tears. *(LP version)*
- (S) (4:02) MFSL 559 Blood, Sweat And Tears. *(LP version; gold disc)*
- (M) (3:25) CBS Special Products 16641 Found Treasures. *(45 version)*
- (S) (4:01) JCI 3126 1965 - Only Rock 'N Roll - 1969. *(LP version)*
- (S) (4:02) Legacy/Columbia 64166 Best Of: What Goes Up! *(LP version)*
1970 HI-DE-HO
- (S) (4:23) Columbia 31170 Blood, Sweat & Tears Greatest Hits. *(LP version)*
- (S) (4:23) Columbia 30090 Blood, Sweat & Tears 3. *(LP version)*
- (S) (4:24) Legacy/Columbia 64166 Best Of: What Goes Up! *(LP version)*
- (S) (4:23) JCI 3160 18 Free & Easy Hits From The 60's. *(LP version)*
- (S) (4:23) Priority 50989 70's Greatest Rock Hits Volume 2: Rock & Soul. *(LP version)*

1970 LUCRETIA MAC EVIL
- (S) (5:27) Columbia 31170 Blood, Sweat & Tears Greatest Hits. *(:16 shorter than the original vinyl LP version of "LUCRETIA MAC EVIL" and "LUCRETIA'S REPRISE" which run together as one track.)*
- (S) (3:03) Columbia 30090 Blood, Sweat & Tears 3. *(as with the original vinyl LP, "LUCRETIA MAC EVIL" is ever so slightly separated from "LUCRETIA'S REPRISE")*
- (S) (5:56) Legacy/Columbia 64166 Best Of: What Goes Up! *(:13 longer than the original vinyl LP version of "LUCRETIA MAC EVIL" and "LUCRETIA'S REPRISE")*
- (S) (5:27) Eclipse Music Group 64892 Rock 'n Roll Relix 1970-1971. *(:16 shorter than the original vinyl LP version of "LUCRETIA MAC EVIL" and "LUCRETIA'S REPRISE" which run together as one track)*
- (S) (5:27) Eclipse Music Group 64897 Rock 'n Roll Relix 1970-1979. *(:16 shorter than the original vinyl LP version of "LUCRETIA MAC EVIL" and "LUCRETIA'S REPRISE" which run together as one track)*

1971 GO DOWN GAMBLIN'
- (S) (4:12) Columbia 31170 Blood, Sweat & Tears Greatest Hits. *(LP version)*
- (S) (4:11) CBS Special Products 16641 Found Treasures. *(LP version)*
- (S) (4:14) Columbia/Legacy 66422 Blood, Sweat & Tears 4. *(LP version)*
- (S) (4:13) Legacy/Columbia 64166 Best Of: What Goes Up! *(LP version)*

BOBBY BLOOM
1970 MONTEGO BAY
(actual 45 time is (2:24) not (2:53) as stated on the record label)
- (S) (2:55) Rhino 70923 Super Hits Of The 70's Volume 3. *(LP version)*
- (S) (2:55) Rhino 72009 Super Hits Of The 70's Volumes 1-4 Box Set. *(LP version)*
- (S) (2:55) Time-Life SUD-20 Superhits - Early 70's Classics. *(LP version)*
- (S) (2:54) Time-Life SOD-32 Sounds Of The Seventies - AM Pop Classics. *(LP version)*
- (S) (2:31) Varese Sarabande 5575 Bubblegum Classics Volume Two. *(neither the 45 or LP version)*
- (S) (2:54) Rebound 314520313 Caribbean Nights I. *(LP version)*
- (S) (2:54) Polygram Special Markets 314520272 One Hit Wonders. *(LP version)*
- (S) (2:54) Special Music/Essex 5036 Prom Night - The 70's. *(LP version)*
- (S) (2:55) Time-Life AM1-15 AM Gold - Early '70s Classics. *(LP version)*
- (S) (2:55) Velvel/Reel Sounds 79713 O.S.T. The Ice Storm. *(LP version)*
- (S) (2:54) Rebound 314520313 Reggae Dance Party I. *(LP version)*

BLOW MONKEYS
1986 DIGGING YOUR SCENE
- (S) (4:14) RCA 8065 Animal Magic. *(LP version)*
- (S) (4:41) EMI 28339 Living In Oblivion: The 80's Greatest Hits - Volume Four. *(45 version)*
- (S) (4:04) Rhino 72500 Modern Rock 1986 - Hang The DJ. *(LP version faded :10 early)*
- (S) (4:35) Cold Front 6330 Club Mix: The 80s. *(all selections on this cd are segued together)*

BLUE-BELLES
1962 I SOLD MY HEART TO THE JUNKMAN
- (M) (2:25) Collectables 5090 Patti Labelle And The Bluebelles Golden Classics.
- (M) (2:25) Relic 7044 Patti Labelle And The Bluebelles - Down The Aisle.
- (S) (2:41) Relic 7044 Patti Labelle And The Bluebelles - Down The Aisle. *(alternate take)*
- (M) (2:25) Rhino 72815 Beg, Scream & Shout! The Big Ol' Box Of '60s Soul.

BLUE CHEER
1968 SUMMERTIME BLUES
- (S) (3:44) Mercury 834030 Good Times Are So Hard To Find.
- (S) (3:44) Original Sound 8894 Dick Clark's 21 All-Time Hits Vol. 3.
- (S) (3:44) Warner Special Products 27607 Highs Of The 60's.
- (S) (3:44) Mercury 834216 45's On CD Volume 3.
- (S) (3:45) Rhino 70536 San Francisco Nights.
- (S) (3:45) Mercury 314514685 Vincebus Eruptum.
- (S) (3:44) Time-Life 2CLR-19 Classic Rock - 1968: Shakin' All Over.
- (S) (3:44) K-Tel 6090 Hit Parader Salutes 20 Years Of Metal.
- (S) (3:45) K-Tel 3133 Biker Rock.
- (S) (3:44) Rebound 314520277 Hard Rock Essentials - The 60's.
- (S) (3:44) Time-Life R968-07 Guitar Rock 1968-1969.
- (S) (3:44) LaserLight 12313 and 15936 The Wonder Years - Summer Time.
- (S) (3:45) Special Music 5038 Guitar Heroes.
- (S) (3:44) Eclipse Music Group 64871 Rock 'n Roll Relix 1968-1969.
- (S) (3:44) Eclipse Music Group 64872 Rock 'n Roll Relix 1960-1969.
- (S) (3:45) Simitar 55362 Garage Band Classics.
- (S) (3:45) Rebound 314520521 Highway Rockin'.

BLUE HAZE
1973 SMOKE GETS IN YOUR EYES
- (S) (3:16) A&M 6015 Reggae Spectacular.

BLUE JAYS
1961 LOVER'S ISLAND
- (M) (2:17) Rhino 75763 Best Of Doo Wop Ballads.
- (M) (2:16) Collectables 5069 History Of Rock Volume 9.
- (M) (2:16) Time-Life 2RNR-25 Rock 'N' Roll Era - The 60's Keep On Rockin'.
- (E) (2:12) Original Sound CDGO-12 Golden Oldies Volume. 12.
- (M) (2:16) Collectables 2501 WCBS-FM History Of Rock - The 60's Part 2.
- (M) (2:16) Collectables 4501 History Of Rock/The 60s Part Two.
- (M) (2:15) Collectables 2604 WCBS-FM Jukebox Giants Vol. 2.
- (M) (2:16) Rhino 72507 Doo Wop Box II.
- (M) (2:16) Time-Life R857-19 The Heart Of Rock 'n' Roll 1960-1961 Take Three.

BLUE MAGIC
1974 SIDESHOW
(dj copies of this 45 ran (3:25); commercial copies were all (4:06))
- (S) (4:08) Atlantic 82305 Atlantic Rhythm And Blues (1947-1974) Box Set.
- (S) (4:08) Atlantic 81912 Golden Age Of Black Music (1970-1975).
- (S) (4:11) Rhino 70553 Soul Hits Of The 70's Volume 13.
- (S) (4:08) Omni 90527 Greatest Hits.
- (S) (4:08) Collectables 5031 Magic Of The Blue: Greatest Hits.
- (S) (4:06) Original Sound 9307 Dedicated To You Vol. 7.
- (S) (4:10) Razor & Tie 22047 Sweet 70's Soul.
- (S) (4:07) Time-Life SOD-15 Sounds Of The Seventies - 1974: Take Two.
- (S) (4:08) Right Stuff 28372 Slow Jams: The 70's Volume Two.
- (S) (4:12) Thump 4710 Old School Love Songs.
- (S) (4:10) Rhino 72116 Billboard Hot Soul Hits - 1974.

53

BLUE MAGIC *(Continued)*

- (S) (4:10) Rhino 72207 Best Of.
- (S) (4:10) DCC Compact Classics 142 Groove On! Volume 2.
- (S) (4:11) Time-Life R838-09 Solid Gold Soul - 1974.
- (S) (4:10) Rhino 72964 Ultimate '70s R&B Smashes!
- (S) (4:11) K-Tel 3900 Great R&B Male Groups: Hits Of The 70's.

1974 THREE RING CIRCUS
(dj copies of this 45 ran (3:20); commercial copies were all (4:51))

- (S) (3:41) Rhino 72127 Soul Hits Of The 70's Vol. 17. *(this is the dj edit with a :20 longer fade)*
- (S) (5:16) Collectables 5031 Magic Of The Blue: Greatest Hits. *(LP version)*
- (S) (5:16) Omni 90527 Greatest Hits. *(LP version)*
- (S) (4:48) Rhino 72207 Best Of. *(45 version)*

BLUE OYSTER CULT
1976 (DON'T FEAR) THE REAPER

- (S) (5:02) Priority 8668 Rough And Rowdy/70's Greatest Rock Hits Volume 7. *(LP version)*
- (S) (5:02) Priority 7961 Three Decades Of Rock. *(LP version)*
- (S) (5:08) Sandstone 33000 Reelin' In The Years Volume 1. *(LP version; truncated fade)*
- (S) (5:08) Columbia 34164 Agents Of Fortune. *(LP version)*
- (S) (5:08) DCC Compact Classics 062 Rock Of The 70's Volume 1. *(LP version)*
- (S) (5:02) Razor & Tie 22502 Those Rocking 70's. *(LP version)*
- (S) (5:02) Time-Life R968-03 Guitar Rock 1976-1977. *(LP version)*
- (S) (3:49) Time-Life SOD-18 Sounds Of The Seventies - 1976: Take Two. *(45 version)*
- (S) (5:02) Time-Life R105-24 Guitar Rock Monsters. *(LP version)*
- (S) (5:07) Risky Business 66871 Polyester Dreams/Greatest Hits Of The 70's. *(LP version)*
- (S) (5:08) Legacy/Columbia 64163 Workshop Of The Telescopes. *(LP version)*
- (S) (5:08) Epic/Legacy 65020 Ultimate Rock 'n' Roll Collection. *(LP version)*
- (S) (3:48) JCI 3169 #1 Radio Hits 1975 - Only Rock 'n Roll - 1979. *(45 version)*
- (S) (5:05) Eclipse Music Group 64895 Rock 'n Roll Relix 1976-1977. *(LP version)*
- (S) (5:05) Eclipse Music Group 64897 Rock 'n Roll Relix 1970-1979. *(LP version)*
- (S) (5:07) Hip-O 40070 Rock For The Ages. *(LP version)*
- (S) (5:04) K-Tel 3904 The Rock Album Volume 1. *(LP version)*
- (S) (5:08) MFSL 697 Agents Of Fortune. *(gold disc; LP version)*

1981 BURNIN' FOR YOU
(dj copies of this 45 ran (3:38) and (4:29); commercial 45's were all (3:38))

- (S) (4:30) Columbia 37389 Fire Of Unknown Origin. *(LP version)*
- (S) (4:30) Risky Business 57833 Read The Hits/Best Of The 80's. *(LP version)*
- (S) (4:28) JCI 3119 18 Rock Classics. *(LP version)*
- (S) (4:29) Rebound 314520257 Hard Rock Essentials - The 80's. *(LP version)*
- (S) (4:29) Legacy/Columbia 64163 Workshop Of The Telescopes. *(LP version)*
- (S) (4:29) Time-Life R968-24 Guitar Rock - The '80s Take Two. *(LP version)*
- (S) (4:30) Rhino 72594 Billboard Top Album Rock Hits, 1981. *(LP version)*
- (S) (4:27) K-Tel 3997 Arena Rock - The 80's. *(LP version)*

BLUE RIDGE RANGERS
1973 JAMBALAYA (ON THE BAYOU)

- (S) (3:14) Fantasy 4502 John Fogerty/The Blue Ridge Rangers.

1973 HEARTS OF STONE

- (S) (2:10) Fantasy 4502 John Fogerty/The Blue Ridge Rangers.

BLUES BROTHERS
1979 SOUL MAN

- (S) (3:02) Atlantic 19217 Briefcase Full Of Blues.
- (S) (3:01) Atlantic 19331 Best Of.
- (S) (3:28) Atlantic 82788 Briefcase Full Of Blues. *(remastered edition; last :25 of this song on this cd were previously the introduction to the following track)*
- (S) (3:01) Atlantic 82790 Best Of. *(remastered edition)*
- (S) (3:21) Atlantic 82428 The Definitive Collection. *(the last :19 were previously the introduction to the following track, "B MOVIE BOX CAR BLUES" on the "Briefcase Full Of Blues" cd)*

1980 GIMME SOME LOVIN'

- (S) (3:05) Atlantic 16017 Original Soundtrack Recording.
- (S) (3:06) Atlantic 19331 Best Of.
- (S) (3:05) Atlantic 82790 Best Of. *(remastered edition)*
- (S) (3:05) Atlantic 82787 Original Soundtrack Recording. *(remastered edition)*
- (S) (3:04) Time-Life R988-31 Sounds Of The Eighties: Cinemax Movie Hits Of The '80s.
- (S) (3:03) Atlantic 82428 The Definitive Collection.

BLUES IMAGE
1970 RIDE CAPTAIN RIDE

- (S) (3:41) JCI 3301 Rockin' Seventies. *(LP length)*
- (S) (3:41) Atlantic 81909 Hit Singles 1958-1977. *(LP length)*
- (S) (3:40) Rhino 71206 70's Smash Hits Volume 2. *(LP length)*
- (S) (3:40) Rhino 71196 Super Hits Of The 70's Volume 16. *(LP length)*
- (S) (3:40) Time-Life SOD-01 Sounds Of The Seventies - 1970. *(LP length)*
- (S) (3:39) JCI 3168 #1 Radio Hits 1970 - Only Rock 'n Roll - 1974. *(LP length)*
- (S) (3:40) Eclipse Music Group 64892 Rock 'n Roll Relix 1970-1971. *(LP length)*
- (S) (3:40) Eclipse Music Group 64897 Rock 'n Roll Relix 1970-1979. *(LP length)*
- (S) (3:40) Flashback 72682 '70s Radio Hits Volume 2. *(LP length)*
- (S) (3:40) Flashback 72090 '70s Radio Hits Box Set. *(LP length)*
- (S) (3:40) Simitar 55502 The Number One's: Classic Rock. *(LP length)*
- (S) (3:40) JCI 3192 18 Rock Classics Volume 2. *(LP length)*
- (S) (3:40) Thump 6010 Easyriders Volume 1. *(LP length)*

BLUES MAGOOS
1967 (WE AIN'T GOT) NOTHIN' YET

- (S) (2:14) K-Tel 713 Battle Of The Bands.
- (S) (2:14) Rhino 75777 More Nuggets.
- (S) (2:14) Mercury 834216 45's On CD Volume 3.
- (S) (2:15) Mercury 314512313 Kaleidoscopic Compendium: The Best Of.
- (S) (2:14) Time-Life 2CLR-10 Classic Rock - 1967: The Beat Goes On.
- (S) (2:15) Rhino 71937 Billboard Top Pop Hits, 1967.
- (S) (2:14) Time-Life R968-09 Guitar Rock 1966-1967.
- (S) (2:15) Buddah 49507 Psychedelic Pop.
- (S) (2:14) Eclipse Music Group 64870 Rock 'n Roll Relix 1966-1967.
- (S) (2:14) Eclipse Music Group 64872 Rock 'n Roll Relix 1960-1969.
- (S) (2:15) Rebound 314520435 Classic Rock - 60's.

BLUES TRAVELER
1995 RUN-AROUND

- (S) (4:38) A&M 31454265 Four.
- (S) (4:37) A&M 314540507 O.S.T. The Truth About Cats & Dogs.
- (S) (4:01) Atlantic 82895 VH1 Crossroads. *(live)*

1996 HOOK

- (S) (4:48) A&M 31454265 Four.

BLUE SWEDE
1974 HOOKED ON A FEELING
    (S) (2:52)   Rhino 70759 Super Hits Of The 70's Volume 12.
    (S) (2:48)   Curb 77356 70's Hits Volume 2.
    (S) (2:51)   Razor & Tie 22505 More Fabulous 70's Volume 2.
    (S) (2:51)   Time-Life SOD-31 Sounds Of The Seventies - AM Top Twenty.
    (S) (2:52)   MCA 10541 and 11188 O.S.T. Reservoir Dogs.
    (S) (2:52)   Capitol 98665 When AM Was King.
    (S) (2:50)   Madacy Entertainment 1974 Rock On 1974.
    (S) (2:52)   Collectables 5863 Golden Classics.

1974 NEVER MY LOVE
    (S) (2:25)   Rhino 72297 Superhits Of The 70's Volume 23.
    (S) (2:27)   Collectables 5863 Golden Classics.

B.M.U. (BLACK MEN UNITED)
1994 U WILL KNOW
    (S) (4:00)   Mercury 314522915 and 314526211 O.S.T. Jason's Lyric.

BOB & EARL
1964 HARLEM SHUFFLE
(actual 45 time is (2:50) not (2:30) as stated on the record label)
    (M) (2:51)   Rhino 70992 Groove 'N' Grind.
    (E) (2:50)   Original Sound 8855 Oldies But Goodies Vol. 5. *(this compact disc uses the "Waring - fds" noise reduction process; ambient background noise throughout the disc; mastered from vinyl)*
    (E) (2:50)   Original Sound 2222 Oldies But Goodies Volumes 3,5,11,14 and 15 Box Set. *(this box set uses the "Waring - fds" noise reduction process; ambient background noise throughout the song; mastered from vinyl)*
    (E) (2:50)   Original Sound 2500 Oldies But Goodies Volumes 1-15 Box Set. *(this box set uses the "Waring - fds" noise reduction process; ambient background noise throughout the song; mastered from vinyl)*
    (E) (2:49)   Original Sound CDGO-5 Golden Oldies Volume. 5.
    (E) (2:49)   Original Sound 8892 Dick Clark's 21 All-Time Hits Vol. 2.
    (S) (2:28)   Motown 6215 and 9067 Hits From The Legendary Vee-Jay Records. *(rerecording)*
    (M) (2:51)   Ripete 2392192 Beach Music Anthology Box Set.
    (M) (2:51)   Ripete 0002 Coolin' Out/24 Carolina Classics Vol. 2.
    (M) (2:44)   Time-Life 2RNR-35 Rock 'N' Roll Era - The 60's Last Dance.
    (M) (2:47)   Island 314524394 Island Records 40th Anniversary Volume 2 1964-1969: Rhythm & Blues.
    (M) (2:51)   Rhino 72815 Beg, Scream & Shout! The Big Ol' Box Of '60s Soul.

BOBBETTES
1957 MR. LEE
    (M) (2:13)   Rhino 70643 Billboard's Top R&B Hits Of 1957.
    (M) (2:13)   Atlantic 81677 O.S.T. Stand By Me.
    (M) (2:12)   Atlantic 81295 Atlantic Rhythm & Blues Volume 3.
    (M) (2:13)   Warner Special Products 27602 20 Party Classics.
    (M) (2:12)   Atlantic 82305 Atlantic Rhythm And Blues 1947-1974 Box Set.
    (M) (2:13)   Time-Life 2RNR-01 Rock 'N' Roll Era - 1957.
    (M) (2:11)   Time-Life RHD-08 Rhythm & Blues - 1957.
    (M) (2:13)   Rhino 72507 Doo Wop Box II.
    (M) (2:13)   Flashback 72717 Doo Wop - Blue Moon.
    (M) (2:11)   Time-Life R838-23 Solid Gold Soul 1957.

BOB B. SOXX and THE BLUE JEANS
1963 ZIP-A-DEE-DOO-DAH
    (M) (2:48)   Abkco 7118 Phil Spector/Back To Mono (1958-1969).
    (M) (2:48)   Abkco 7213 Best Of Darlene Love.

1963 WHY DO LOVERS BREAK EACH OTHER'S HEART?
    (M) (2:47)   Abkco 7213 Best Of Darlene Love.
    (M) (2:47)   Abkco 7118 Phil Spector/Back To Mono (1958-1969).

BODEANS
1996 CLOSER TO FREE
    (S) (3:08)   Slash Reprise 45455 Go Slow Down.

MICHAEL BOLTON
1987 THAT'S WHAT LOVE IS ALL ABOUT
    (S) (3:56)   Columbia 40473 The Hunger.
    (S) (3:55)   Columbia 67300 Greatest Hits 1985-1995.

1988 (SITTIN' ON) THE DOCK OF THE BAY
    (S) (3:51)   Columbia 40473 The Hunger.
    (S) (3:50)   Columbia 67300 Greatest Hits 1985-1995.

1989 SOUL PROVIDER
    (S) (4:27)   Columbia 45012 Soul Provider.
    (S) (4:24)   Columbia 67300 Greatest Hits 1985-1995.

1990 HOW AM I SUPPOSED TO LIVE WITHOUT YOU
    (S) (4:14)   Foundation/Capitol 96427 Hearts Of Gold: The Pop Collection. *(45 version)*
    (S) (4:47)   Columbia 45012 Soul Provider. *(LP version)*
    (S) (4:13)   Columbia 67300 Greatest Hits 1985-1995. *(45 version)*

1990 HOW CAN WE BE LOVERS
    (S) (3:54)   Columbia 45012 Soul Provider.
    (S) (3:54)   Columbia 67300 Greatest Hits 1985-1995.

1990 WHEN I'M BACK ON MY FEET AGAIN
    (S) (3:46)   Columbia 45012 Soul Provider.
    (S) (3:46)   Columbia 67300 Greatest Hits 1985-1995.

1990 GEORGIA ON MY MIND
    (S) (4:57)   Columbia 45012 Soul Provider.
    (S) (4:55)   Columbia 67300 Greatest Hits 1985-1995.

1991 LOVE IS A WONDERFUL THING
    (S) (4:43)   Columbia 46771 Time, Love & Tenderness. *(LP version)*

1991 TIME, LOVE AND TENDERNESS
    (S) (5:29)   Columbia 46771 Time, Love & Tenderness. *(LP version)*
    (S) (4:16)   Columbia 67300 Greatest Hits 1985-1995. *(45 version)*

1991 WHEN A MAN LOVES A WOMAN
    (S) (3:49)   Foundation/RCA 66104 Hot #1 Hits.
    (S) (3:50)   Columbia 46771 Time, Love & Tenderness.
    (S) (3:50)   Columbia 67300 Greatest Hits 1985-1995.

1992 MISSING YOU NOW
    (S) (4:33)   Columbia 46771 Time, Love & Tenderness.
    (S) (4:24)   Columbia 67300 Greatest Hits 1985-1995.

1993 TO LOVE SOMEBODY
    (S) (4:07)   Columbia 52783 Timeless (The Classics).

1994 SAID I LOVED YOU....BUT I LIED
    (S) (5:04)   Columbia 53567 The One Thing.
    (S) (5:04)   Grammy Recordings/Sony Music 67043 1995 Grammy Nominees.
    (S) (4:59)   Columbia 67300 Greatest Hits 1985-1995.

1994 COMPLETELY
    (S) (4:24)   Columbia 53567 The One Thing.

1995 CAN I TOUCH YOU.....THERE?
    (S) (5:15)   Columbia 67300 Greatest Hits 1985-1995.

1997 GO THE DISTANCE
    (S) (4:40)   Walt Disney 60864 O.S.T. Hercules.

JOHNNY BOND
1960 HOT ROD LINCOLN
    (E) (2:44)   Right Stuff 53317 Hot Rod Rock Volume 2: Hot Rod Cowboys. *(rerecording; truncated fade)*

1965 10 LITTLE BOTTLES
    (M) (3:30)   Time-Life CTD-10 Country USA - 1965. *(timing index is off by :01 on all tracks of this cd; opening word truncated; rerecording)*
    (M) (2:56)   Risky Business 66395 Jokers & Wildcards. *(rerecording)*
    (M) (3:33)   King 1424 Truckstop Comedy.

GARY U.S. BONDS
1960 NEW ORLEANS
   (M) (2:49) Legrand 17001 Greatest Hits.
   (M) (2:49) Rhino 70971 Best Of.
   (S) (5:52) Special Music 4913 Rock & Roll Revival. *(live)*
   (M) (2:48) Time-Life 2RNR-11 Rock 'N' Roll Era - 1960.
   (M) (2:48) Time-Life RHD-15 Rhythm & Blues - 1960.
   (M) (2:49) Risky Business 66914 Party On.
   (M) (2:48) Time-Life R838-20 Solid Gold Soul 1960.

1961 QUARTER TO THREE
   (M) (2:27) Rhino 70971 Best Of.
   (E) (2:31) Original Sound 1081 All #1 Hits.
   (M) (2:28) Rhino 75772 Son Of Frat Rock.
   (M) (2:27) Rhino 70622 Billboard's Top Rock & Roll Hits Of 1961.
   (M) (2:27) Rhino 72004 Billboard's Top Rock & Roll Hits 1957-1961 Box Set.
   (M) (2:32) Legrand 17001 Greatest Hits.
   (S) (4:56) Special Music 4913 Rock & Roll Revival. *(live)*
   (M) (2:27) Time-Life 2RNR-04 Rock 'N' Roll Era - 1961.
   (M) (2:27) Risky Business 66387 Rock Around The Clock.
   (M) (2:27) JCI 3125 1960 - Only Rock 'N Roll - 1964.
   (M) (2:32) Eclipse Music Group 64867 Rock 'n Roll Relix 1960-1961.
   (M) (2:32) Eclipse Music Group 64872 Rock 'n Roll Relix 1960-1969.

1961 SCHOOL IS OUT
   (S) (2:26) Rhino 70971 Best Of.
   (S) (2:27) Legrand 17001 Greatest Hits.
   (S) (2:28) Time-Life 2RNR-18 Rock 'N' Roll Era - 1961 Still Rockin'. *(no fidelity)*
   (S) (2:27) JCI 3166 #1 Radio Hits 1960 - Only Rock 'n Roll - 1964.

1961 SCHOOL IS IN
   (M) (2:05) Legrand 17001 Greatest Hits.
   (M) (2:05) Rhino 70971 Best Of.

1962 DEAR LADY TWIST
   (S) (2:29) Rhino 70971 Best Of. *(:04 longer than the 45 or LP)*
   (S) (2:38) Legrand 17001 Greatest Hits. *(:13 longer than the 45 or LP)*
   (S) (2:37) Time-Life 2RNR-25 Rock 'N' Roll Era - The 60's Keep On Rockin'. *(:12 longer than the 45 or LP)*

1962 TWIST, TWIST SENORA
   (M) (2:38) Legrand 17001 Greatest Hits.
   (M) (2:34) Rhino 70971 Best Of.
   (M) (2:37) Time-Life 2RNR-35 Rock 'N' Roll Era - The 60's Last Dance.
   (M) (2:34) K-Tel 3241 Let's Twist.
   (M) (2:39) JCI 3189 1960 - Only Dance - 1964.

1962 SEVEN DAY WEEKEND
   (S) (2:30) Rhino 70971 Best Of.

1981 THIS LITTLE GIRL
   (S) (3:41) Razor Edge 1986 Dedication.
   (S) (3:40) Ripete 2200 Ocean Drive Volume 3.
   (S) (3:41) Risky Business 53920 Blood, Sweat And Beers/Best Of Bar Bands.
   (S) (3:41) Time-Life R988-08 Sounds Of The Eighties: 1981.
   (S) (3:41) EMI 37812 Best Of.
   (S) (3:41) Rhino 72594 Billboard Top Album Rock Hits, 1981.

1982 OUT OF WORK
   (S) (2:53) Razor Edge 1988 On The Line.
   (S) (2:52) EMI 37812 Best Of.

BONE THUGS-n-HARMONY
1994 THUGGISH RUGGISH BONE
   (S) (4:41) Ruthless 5526 Creepin On Ah Come Up.
   (S) (4:25) Tommy Boy 1138 MTV Party To Go Volume 7. *(all selections on this cd are segued together)*
   (S) (4:40) Priority 50927 Da Underground Sound: West Side Volume 2. *(all selections on this cd are segued together)*

1995 1st OF THA MONTH
   (S) (5:14) Ruthless 5539 "E. 1999 Eternal". *(all selections on this cd are segued together)*

   (S) (5:28) Tommy Boy 1139 MTV Party To Go Volume 8. *(all selections on this cd are segued together)*
   (S) (5:12) Priority 53107 Hip Hop's Most Wanted.

1996 THA CROSSROADS
   (S) (3:43) Ruthless 5539 "E 1999 Eternal". *(all selections on this cd are segued together)*
   (S) (4:01) Tommy Boy 1168 MTV Party To Go Volume 10. *(all songs on this cd are segued together; remix)*
   (S) (4:23) Cold Front 6242 Club Mix '97. *(all selections on this cd are segued together; remix)*
   (S) (3:50) Def Jam 314534746 Yo! MTV Raps Compilation.
   (S) (3:44) Boxtunes 314524387 Big Phat Ones Of Hip-Hop Volume 2. *(all songs on this cd are segued together)*
   (S) (3:43) Priority 50978 Hip Hop's Most Wanted 2.

1997 LOOK INTO MY EYES
   (S) (4:26) Warner Sunset/Warner Brothers 46620 O.S.T. Batman & Robin.
   (S) (4:19) Polygram TV 314536204 The Source Presents Hip Hop Hits Volume 1.

1997 IF I COULD TEACH THE WORLD
   (S) (4:24) Ruthless 6340 The Art Of War. *(tracks into the next selection)*

BONEY M
1978 RIVERS OF BABYLON

BON JOVI
1984 RUNAWAY
   (S) (3:50) Mercury 314526013 Cross Road.
   (S) (3:49) Mercury 814982 Bon Jovi.

1986 YOU GIVE LOVE A BAD NAME
   (S) (3:42) Sandstone 33042 and 5008 Rock The First Volume 2.
   (S) (3:43) Mercury 830264 Slippery When Wet.
   (S) (3:42) Mercury 314526013 Cross Road.

1987 LIVIN' ON A PRAYER
   (S) (4:09) Mercury 830264 Slippery When Wet.
   (S) (4:09) Mercury 314526013 Cross Road.
   (S) (4:08) Time-Life R13610 Gold And Platinum Box Set - The Ultimate Rock Collection.

1987 WANTED DEAD OR ALIVE
   (S) (5:06) Polydor 314515913 Classic Rock Box.
   (S) (5:07) Mercury 830264 Slippery When Wet.
   (S) (5:06) Mercury 314526013 Cross Road.

1988 BAD MEDICINE
   (S) (5:14) Mercury 836345 New Jersey. *(LP version)*
   (S) (5:15) Mercury 314526013 Cross Road. *(LP version)*

1989 BORN TO BE MY BABY
   (S) (4:37) Mercury 836345 New Jersey.

1989 I'LL BE THERE FOR YOU
   (S) (5:45) Mercury 836345 New Jersey.
   (S) (5:40) Mercury 314526013 Cross Road.

1989 LAY YOUR HANDS ON ME
   (S) (5:58) Mercury 836345 New Jersey. *(LP version)*
   (S) (5:58) Mercury 314526013 Cross Road. *(LP version)*

1989 LIVING IN SIN
   (S) (4:38) Mercury 836345 New Jersey.

1992 KEEP THE FAITH
   (S) (5:44) Mercury 314514045 Keep The Faith. *(LP version)*
   (S) (5:43) Mercury 314526013 Cross Road. *(LP version)*

1993 BED OF ROSES
   (S) (6:32) Mercury 314514045 Keep The Faith.
   (S) (6:32) Mercury 314526013 Cross Road.

1993 IN THESE ARMS
   (S) (5:18) Mercury 314514045 Keep The Faith.

1994 ALWAYS
   (S) (5:51) Mercury 314526013 Cross Road.

1995 THIS AIN'T A LOVE SONG
   (S) (5:04) Mercury 314528181 These Days.

JON BON JOVI
1990 BLAZE OF GLORY
   (S) (5:33) Foundation/RCA 66104 Hot #1 Hits. *(LP version)*
   (S) (5:38) Mercury 314522367 Soccer Rocks The Globe. *(LP version)*

(S) (5:39) Sandstone 33042 and 5008 Rock The First Volume 2. *(LP version)*
(S) (5:38) Mercury 314526013 Cross Road. *(LP version)*
(S) (5:33) Mercury 846473 Blaze Of Glory. *(LP version)*
1990 MIRACLE
(S) (5:06) Mercury 846473 Blaze Of Glory. *(LP version)*

BONNIE LOU
1956 DADDY-O

KARLA BONOFF
1982 PERSONALLY
(S) (3:35) Columbia 37444 Wild Heart Of The Young.
(S) (3:33) JCI 3147 1980 - Only Love - 1984.

JAMES BOOKER
1960 GONZO
(M) (2:23) MCA 10666 Duke-Peacock's Greatest Hits.
(M) (2:25) Hip-O 40008 Soulful Grooves - R&B Instrumental Classics Volume 2.
(M) (2:23) MCA Special Products 21035 Classic Rock & Roll Instrumental Hits, Volume 2.

BOOKER T & THE MG'S
1962 GREEN ONIONS
(M) (2:51) Atlantic 81281 Best Of.
(M) (2:51) Atlantic Group 88218 Complete Stax/Volt Singles 1959 - 1968. *(truncated fade)*
(E) (2:48) Stax 88005 Top Of The Stax. *(intro fades in)*
(M) (2:51) Rhino 70648 Billboard's Top R&B Hits Of 1962.
(E) (2:50) Warner Special Products 27601 Atlantic Soul Classics. *(intro fades in)*
(M) (2:50) Atlantic 81296 Atlantic Rhythm & Blues Volume 4.
(M) (2:51) Atlantic 82305 Atlantic Rhythm And Blues 1947-1974 Box Set.
(M) (2:28) MCA 8001 O.S.T. American Graffiti. *(edited; Wolfman Jack talks over fadeout)*
(M) (2:51) Rhino 71459 Soul Hits, Volume 1.
(M) (2:51) Rhino 71548 Let There Be Drums Volume 2: The 60's.
(M) (2:51) Rhino 71604 Rock Instrumental Classics Vol. 4: Soul.
(M) (2:51) Rhino 72035 Rock Instrumental Classics Vols. 1-5 Box Set.
(M) (2:51) Time-Life 2RNR-02 Rock 'N' Roll Era - 1962.
(M) (2:48) Time-Life RHD-11 Rhythm & Blues - 1962.
(M) (2:51) Rhino 71234 Groovin'.
(M) (2:51) Rhino 71738 Very Best Of.
(M) (2:52) Rhino 71806 The R&B Box: Thirty Years Of Rhythm & Blues.
(M) (2:51) Rhino 72213 Stadium Rock.
(M) (2:51) Rhino 71802 O.S.T. Andre.
(M) (2:50) EMI 52498 O.S.T. Striptease.
(M) (2:51) Antilles 314529310 O.S.T. Get Shorty.
(M) (2:52) Flashback 72711 Sports Rock.
(M) (2:51) Flashback 72657 '60s Soul: Try A Little Tenderness.
(M) (2:51) Flashback 72091 '60s Soul Hits Box Set.
(M) (2:51) Right Stuff 53318 Hot Rod Rock Volume 3: Big Boss Instrumentals.
(M) (2:48) Time-Life R838-18 Solid Gold Soul 1962.
(M) (2:52) Rhino 72962 Ultimate '60s Soul Sensations.
1967 HIP HUG-HER
(S) (2:24) Atlantic 81281 Best Of.
(M) (2:22) Atlantic Group 88218 Complete Stax/Volt Singles 1959 - 1968.
(M) (2:26) Warner Special Products 27602 20 Party Classics.
(M) (2:22) Atlantic 82305 Atlantic Rhythm And Blues 1947-1974 Box Set.
(S) (2:24) Rhino 71013 Hip Hug-Her.
(M) (2:23) Rhino 71604 Rock Instrumental Classics Vol. 4: Soul.
(M) (2:23) Rhino 72035 Rock Instrumental Classics Vols. 1-5 Box Set.

(M) (2:23) Rhino 71738 Very Best Of.
(M) (2:23) Flashback 72897 25 Years Of R&B - 1967.
1967 GROOVIN'
(S) (2:40) Atlantic 81281 Best Of.
(M) (2:41) Atlantic Group 88218 Complete Stax/Volt Singles 1959 - 1968.
(S) (2:41) Rhino 71013 Hip Hug-Her.
(M) (2:41) Rhino 71234 Groovin'.
(M) (2:41) Rhino 71738 Very Best Of.
1968 SOUL LIMBO
(S) (2:21) Stax 60-004 Best Of.
(S) (2:20) Stax 88008 Top Of The Stax Volume 2.
(S) (2:21) Stax 4113 Soul Limbo.
(S) (2:21) Stax 4411 Complete Stax/Volt Soul Singles 1968 - 1971.
(M) (2:22) Rhino 71738 Very Best Of.
1969 HANG 'EM HIGH
(S) (3:55) Stax 60-004 Best Of.
(S) (3:54) CBS Special Products 46808 Rock Goes To The Movies Volume 5.
(S) (3:55) Stax 4113 Soul Limbo.
(M) (3:51) Stax 4411 Complete Stax/Volt Soul Singles 1968 - 1971.
(M) (3:52) Rhino 71604 Rock Instrumental Classics Vol. 4: Soul.
(M) (3:52) Rhino 72035 Rock Instrumental Classics Vols. 1-5 Box Set.
(S) (3:53) Time-Life 2CLR-20 Classic Rock - 1969: Shakin' All Over.
(M) (3:52) Rhino 71738 Very Best Of.
(S) (3:54) Hip-O 40008 Soulful Grooves - R&B Instrumental Classics Volume 2.
1969 TIME IS TIGHT
(S) (4:55) Stax 60-004 Best Of. *(LP version)*
(S) (3:15) Warner Special Products 27609 Memphis Soul Classics. *(45 version)*
(S) (3:16) Rhino 75770 Soul Shots Volume 2. *(45 version)*
(S) (4:55) Stax 8562 O.S.T. Uptight. *(LP version)*
(S) (3:14) Stax 4411 Complete Stax/Volt Soul Singles 1968 - 1971. *(45 version)*
(M) (3:13) Rhino 71604 Rock Instrumental Classics Vol. 4: Soul. *(45 version)*
(M) (3:13) Rhino 72035 Rock Instrumental Classics Vols. 1-5 Box Set. *(45 version)*
(S) (3:15) Time-Life RHD-13 Rhythm & Blues - 1969. *(45 version)*
(S) (3:15) Time-Life 2CLR-12 Classic Rock - 1969: The Beat Goes On. *(45 version)*
(M) (3:13) Rhino 71738 Very Best Of. *(45 version)*
(M) (3:12) Risky Business 66387 Rock Around The Clock. *(45 version)*
(S) (3:15) Time-Life R838-04 Solid Gold Soul - 1969. *(45 version)*
(M) (3:14) Rhino 72815 Beg, Scream & Shout! The Big Ol' Box Of '60s Soul. *(45 version)*
(M) (3:13) Flashback 72899 25 Years Of Soul - 1969. *(45 version)*
(S) (3:29) Geffen 25218 O.S.T. Fear And Loathing In Las Vegas. *(time includes :16 of movie dialogue; all songs and the movie dialogue are segued together)*
1969 MRS. ROBINSON
(S) (3:41) Stax 60004 Best Of.
(S) (3:41) Stax 8531 The Booker T Set.
(S) (3:38) Stax 4411 Complete Stax/Volt Soul Singles 1968 - 1971.
(S) (3:39) Rhino 71738 Very Best Of.

DANIEL BOONE
1972 BEAUTIFUL SUNDAY
(S) (3:01) Rhino 70929 Super Hits Of The 70's Volume 9.
(S) (2:59) Time-Life SOD-31 Sounds Of The Seventies - AM Top Twenty.
(S) (3:02) Special Music 5041 Great Britons! Volume Three.
(S) (3:02) Special Music 5039 Great Britons! Volume One.

DEBBY BOONE

1977 YOU LIGHT UP MY LIFE
- (S) (3:35) Curb 77317 70's Hits Volume 1.
- (S) (3:35) Curb 77532 Your Favorite Songs.
- (S) (3:35) Curb 77258 Best Of.
- (S) (3:35) Scotti Brothers 75262 There Is Love (The Wedding Songs).
- (S) (3:35) Rhino 71868 Academy Award Winning Songs.
- (S) (3:35) Rhino 72279 Academy Award Winning Songs Volume 4.
- (S) (3:34) Rhino 72424 Billboard Top Movie Hits - 1970s.
- (S) (3:35) Razor & Tie 4543 The '70s Preservation Society Presents: Easy '70s.
- (S) (3:35) Priority 50974 Premiere The Movie Magazine Presents The Greatest Soundtrack Love Songs.
- (S) (3:37) Time-Life R814-01 Love Songs.

PAT BOONE

1955 TWO HEARTS
- (M) (2:35) MCA 10885 Greatest Hits.
- (M) (2:34) Varese Sarabande 5687 History Of Dot Records Volume Two.

1955 AIN'T THAT A SHAME
- (M) (2:23) MCA 10885 Greatest Hits.
- (S) (2:22) LaserLight 12121 Best Of. *(all songs on this cd were recorded in 1974)*

1955 AT MY FRONT DOOR (CRAZY LITTLE MAMA)
- (M) (2:00) Pair 1311 A Date With. *(mastered from vinyl)*

1956 I'LL BE HOME
- (M) (2:58) Curb 77298 Greatest Hits.
- (M) (2:58) MCA 10885 Greatest Hits.
- (M) (2:59) Time-Life HPD-21 Your Hit Parade - The Mid 50's.
- (M) (2:58) Curb 77655 Pat's Greatest Hits.

1956 TUTTI FRUTTI
- (M) (2:26) Pair 1311 A Date With.

1956 LONG TALL SALLY
- (M) (2:11) Rhino 71751 Spy Magazine Presents, Vol. 3: Soft, Safe & Sanitized.
- (M) (2:10) Pair 1311 A Date With.

1956 I ALMOST LOST MY MIND
- (S) (2:30) Curb 77298 Greatest Hits. *(rerecorded)*
- (M) (2:36) MCA 10885 Greatest Hits.
- (M) (2:37) Time-Life HPD-15 Your Hit Parade - 1956.
- (M) (2:36) Curb 77655 Pat's Greatest Hits.
- (S) (2:31) LaserLight 12121 Best Of. *(all songs on this cd were recorded in 1974)*

1956 FRIENDLY PERSUASION (THEE I LOVE)
- (S) (3:01) Curb 77298 Greatest Hits. *(rerecorded)*
- (M) (2:55) Pair 1311 A Date With.
- (M) (2:54) MCA 10885 Greatest Hits.
- (M) (2:55) Time-Life HPD-25 Your Hit Parade - The 50's.
- (M) (2:54) JCI 7011 Those Wonderful Years - That's Hollywood.
- (S) (3:04) LaserLight 12121 Best Of. *(all songs on this cd were recorded in 1974)*

1956 CHAINS OF LOVE
- (M) (2:54) MCA 10885 Greatest Hits.

1956 ANASTASIA
- (M) (2:57) Varese Sarabande 5686 History Of Dot Records Volume One.

1957 DON'T FORBID ME
- (S) (2:12) Curb 77298 Greatest Hits. *(rerecorded)*
- (M) (2:17) MCA 10885 Greatest Hits.
- (M) (2:14) Time-Life 2RNR-47 Rock 'N' Roll Era - Teen Idols II.
- (M) (2:15) Time-Life HPD-31 Your Hit Parade - The 50's Forever.
- (M) (2:18) Curb 77655 Pat's Greatest Hits.
- (M) (2:15) Time-Life R857-07 The Heart Of Rock 'n' Roll 1956.
- (S) (2:13) LaserLight 12121 Best Of. *(all songs on this cd were recorded in 1974)*

1957 WHY BABY WHY
- (M) (1:56) MCA 10885 Greatest Hits.
- (E) (1:56) Curb 77655 Pat's Greatest Hits.

1957 I'M WAITING JUST FOR YOU

1957 LOVE LETTERS IN THE SAND
- (M) (2:22) MCA 31199 Vintage Music Volume 2. *(whistling in the introduction that was not on the original 45)*
- (M) (2:22) MCA 5777 Vintage Music Volumes 1 & 2. *(whistling in the introduction that was not on the original 45)*
- (S) (2:13) Curb 77298 Greatest Hits. *(rerecording)*
- (S) (2:13) Curb 77354 50's Hits Volume 1. *(rerecording)*
- (S) (2:13) Curb 77525 Greatest Hits Of Rock 'N' Roll Volume 2. *(rerecording)*
- (M) (2:11) MCA 10885 Greatest Hits.
- (M) (2:21) Time-Life 2RNR-27 Rock 'N' Roll Era - Teen Idols. *(whistling in the introduction that was not on the original 45)*
- (M) (2:21) Time-Life HPD-17 Your Hit Parade - 1957. *(whistling in the introduction that was not on the original 45)*
- (S) (2:13) Curb 77655 Pat's Greatest Hits. *(rerecording)*
- (M) (2:21) Time-Life R103-27 Love Me Tender. *(whistling in the introduction that was not on the original 45)*
- (M) (2:21) Rhino 71580 Billboard Pop Memories 1955-1959. *(whistling in the introduction that was not on the original 45)*
- (M) (2:22) MCA Special Products 22165 Vintage Collectibles Volume 7. *(whistling in the introduction that was not on the original 45)*
- (M) (2:21) JCI 3183 1955 - Only Love - 1959. *(whistling in the introduction that was not on the original 45)*
- (M) (2:21) Time-Life R857-05 The Heart Of Rock 'n' Roll 1957. *(whistling in the introduction that was not on the original 45)*
- (M) (2:21) Time-Life R132-12 Your Hit Parade - #1 Hits Of The '50s. *(whistling in the introduction that was not on the original 45)*
- (M) (2:21) Time-Life R132-10 Love Songs Of Your Hit Parade. *(whistling in the introduction that was not on the original 45)*

1957 BERNADINE
- (M) (2:08) MCA 10885 Greatest Hits.
- (S) (2:07) LaserLight 12121 Best Of. *(all songs on this cd were recorded in 1974)*

1957 REMEMBER YOU'RE MINE
- (S) (2:15) Curb 77298 Greatest Hits. *(rerecording)*
- (M) (2:13) MCA 10885 Greatest Hits.
- (M) (2:14) Time-Life HPD-27 Your Hit Parade - The Unforgettable 50's.
- (S) (2:15) Curb 77655 Pat's Greatest Hits. *(rerecording)*
- (S) (2:13) LaserLight 12121 Best Of. *(all songs on this cd were recorded in 1974)*
- (M) (2:13) Time-Life R857-16 The Heart Of Rock 'n' Roll The Late '50s.

1957 THERE'S A GOLDMINE IN THE SKY
- (M) (2:15) Varese Sarabande 5522 More Greatest Hits.

1957 APRIL LOVE
- (S) (2:40) Curb 77298 Greatest Hits. *(rerecording)*
- (M) (2:38) MCA 10885 Greatest Hits.
- (M) (2:39) Time-Life 2RNR-47 Rock 'N' Roll Era - Teen Idols II.
- (M) (2:39) Time-Life HPD-17 Your Hit Parade - 1957.
- (S) (2:40) Curb 77655 Pat's Greatest Hits. *(rerecording)*
- (S) (2:40) MCA Special Products 20580 Teen Idols. *(rerecording)*
- (M) (2:39) Rhino 72422 Billboard Top Movie Hits 1955-1959.
- (M) (2:38) JCI 7021 Those Wonderful Years - April Love.
- (M) (2:38) Time-Life R857-13 The Heart Of Rock 'n' Roll 1956-1957.
- (S) (2:28) LaserLight 12121 Best Of. *(all songs on this cd were recorded in 1974)*

1958 A WONDERFUL TIME UP THERE
- (S) (2:00) Curb 77298 Greatest Hits. *(rerecording)*
- (M) (2:05) MCA 10885 Greatest Hits.
- (M) (2:06) Time-Life HPD-11 Your Hit Parade 1958.

1958 IT'S TOO SOON TO KNOW
- (M) (2:32) MCA 10885 Greatest Hits.

1958 SUGAR MOON
(M) (1:52) MCA 10885 Greatest Hits.
(S) (1:53) Time-Life HPD-23 Your Hit Parade - The Late 50's.
(S) (1:53) Time-Life R857-04 The Heart Of Rock 'n' Roll - 1958.

1958 IF DREAMS CAME TRUE
(M) (2:40) MCA 10885 Greatest Hits.
(M) (2:40) Time-Life HPD-25 Your Hit Parade - The 50's.

1958 GEE, BUT IT'S LONELY
(S) (2:09) Varese Sarabande 5522 More Greatest Hits.

1958 FOR MY GOOD FORTUNE
(S) (2:07) Varese Sarabande 5522 More Greatest Hits. *(alternate take)*

1958 I'LL REMEMBER TONIGHT
(S) (2:27) Varese Sarabande 5522 More Greatest Hits. *(alternate take)*

1959 WITH THE WIND AND RAIN IN YOUR HAIR
(S) (2:31) Varese Sarabande 5522 More Greatest Hits. *(not the same saxophone as found on the 45)*

1959 FOR A PENNY
(S) (2:16) Varese Sarabande 5522 More Greatest Hits.

1959 TWIXT TWELVE AND TWENTY
(S) (2:14) Varese Sarabande 5522 More Greatest Hits.

1959 FOOLS HALL OF FAME
(S) (2:42) Varese Sarabande 5522 More Greatest Hits.

1960 (WELCOME) NEW LOVERS
(S) (2:29) Varese Sarabande 5522 More Greatest Hits.

1960 WALKING THE FLOOR OVER YOU
(S) (2:21) Varese Sarabande 5522 More Greatest Hits.

1961 MOODY RIVER
(S) (2:35) MCA 31205 Vintage Music Volume 8.
(S) (2:35) MCA 5805 Vintage Music Volumes 7 & 8.
(S) (2:35) Curb 77298 Greatest Hits.
(S) (2:35) MCA 10885 Greatest Hits.
(S) (2:34) Time-Life 2RNR-46 Rock 'N' Roll Era - 60's Juke Box Memories.
(S) (2:35) Curb 77655 Pat's Greatest Hits.
(S) (2:35) Time-Life HPD-32 Your Hit Parade - Into The 60's.
(S) (2:36) Rhino 71582 Billboard Top Pop Hits, 1961.
(S) (2:35) MCA Special Products 20957 Solid Gold Rock & Roll.
(S) (2:35) MCA Special Products 21046 Top Singles Of The Sixties.
(S) (2:30) LaserLight 12121 Best Of. *(all songs on this cd were recorded in 1974)*

1961 BIG COLD WIND
(S) (2:09) Varese Sarabande 5522 More Greatest Hits.

1961 JOHNNY WILL
(S) (2:24) Varese Sarabande 5522 More Greatest Hits.

1962 I'LL SEE YOU IN MY DREAMS
(S) (2:43) Varese Sarabande 5522 More Greatest Hits.

1962 SPEEDY GONZALES
(S) (2:32) MCA 5937 Vintage Music Volumes 13 & 14.
(S) (2:32) MCA 31211 Vintage Music Volume 14.
(S) (2:30) Curb 77298 Greatest Hits. *(rerecorded)*
(S) (2:32) MCA 10885 Greatest Hits.
(S) (2:33) K-Tel 3150 Dumb Ditties. *(rerecording)*
(S) (2:30) Time-Life HPD-35 Your Hit Parade - The Fun-Times 50's & 60's.
(S) (2:30) MCA Special Products 22028 Cra-a-zy Hits.
(S) (2:32) LaserLight 12121 Best Of. *(all songs on this cd were recorded in 1974)*

BOSTON
1976 MORE THAN A FEELING
(S) (4:45) Epic 34188 and 52856 Boston. *(LP version)*
(S) (4:44) Razor & Tie 22502 Those Rocking 70's. *(LP version)*
(S) (3:23) Time-Life SOD-34 Sounds Of The Seventies - The Late 70's. *(45 version)*
(S) (4:43) MCA Special Products 22105 Greatest Classic Rock Hits. *(LP version)*
(S) (4:43) Risky Business 66662 Swingin' Singles/Greatest Hits Of The 70's. *(LP version)*
(S) (4:44) Rhino 72131 Frat Rock: The 70's. *(LP version)*

(S) (3:23) Time-Life R968-10 Guitar Rock Classics. *(45 version)*
(S) (4:45) Epic/Legacy 65020 Ultimate Rock 'n' Roll Collection. *(LP version)*
(S) (4:39) Eclipse Music Group 64895 Rock 'n Roll Relix 1976-1977. *(LP version)*
(S) (4:39) Eclipse Music Group 64897 Rock 'n Roll Relix 1970-1979. *(LP version)*
(S) (4:42) Hip-O 40070 Rock For The Ages. *(LP version)*
(S) (4:45) Epic/Legacy 64402 Boston. *(gold disc; LP version)*
(S) (4:44) Epic 67622 Greatest Hits. *(LP version)*
(S) (3:22) Time-Life R13610 Gold And Platinum Box Set - The Ultimate Rock Collection. *(45 version)*
(S) (4:44) K-Tel 3904 The Rock Album Volume 1. *(LP version)*

1977 LONG TIME
(S) (7:46) Epic 34188 and 52856 Boston. *(LP version which is a medley of "FOREPLAY"/"LONG TIME")*
(S) (3:01) Time-Life R968-03 Guitar Rock 1976-1977. *(45 version)*
(S) (3:01) Time-Life SOD-37 Sounds Of The Seventies - AM Heavy Hits. *(45 version)*
(S) (7:46) Epic/Legacy 64402 Boston. *(gold disc; LP version which is a medley of "FOREPLAY"/"LONG TIME")*
(S) (7:47) Epic 67622 Greatest Hits. *(LP version which is a medley of "FOREPLAY"/"LONG TIME")*

1977 PEACE OF MIND
(S) (5:00) Epic 34188 and 52856 Boston. *(LP version)*
(S) (4:58) Time-Life R968-17 Guitar Rock - The Late '70s: Take Two. *(LP version)*
(S) (5:00) Epic/Legacy 64402 Boston. *(gold disc; LP version)*
(S) (5:02) Epic 67622 Greatest Hits. *(LP version)*

1978 DON'T LOOK BACK
(S) (5:58) Epic 35050 Don't Look Back. *(LP version)*
(S) (6:08) Time-Life R968-02 Guitar Rock 1978-1979. *(LP version)*
(S) (6:08) Time-Life SOD-35 Sounds Of The Seventies - AM Nuggets. *(LP version)*
(S) (6:02) Eclipse Music Group 64896 Rock 'n Roll Relix 1978-1979. *(LP version)*
(S) (6:02) Eclipse Music Group 64897 Rock 'n Roll Relix 1970-1979. *(LP version)*
(S) (5:58) Epic/Legacy 66404 Don't Look Back. *(gold disc; LP version)*
(S) (5:57) Epic 67622 Greatest Hits. *(LP version)*
(S) (6:08) Time-Life AM1-25 AM Gold - 1978. *(LP version)*

1979 A MAN I'LL NEVER BE
(S) (6:35) Epic 35050 Don't Look Back. *(LP version)*
(S) (3:55) Time-Life R968-14 Guitar Rock - The Late '70s. *(45 version)*
(S) (6:35) Epic/Legacy 66404 Don't Look Back. *(gold disc; LP version)*
(S) (6:32) Epic 67622 Greatest Hits. *(LP version)*
(S) (6:35) Sony Music Special Products 26069 Rock Hits Of The 70's. *(LP version)*

1986 AMANDA
(S) (4:14) Priority 53715 80's Greatest Rock Hits Volume 3 - Arena Rock.
(S) (4:16) MCA 6188 Third Stage.
(S) (4:16) MFSL 582 Third Stage. *(gold disc)*
(S) (4:14) Time-Life R988-12 Sounds Of The 80's: 1985-1986.
(S) (4:16) Hip-O 40005 The '80s Hit(s) Back....Again!
(S) (4:13) Rhino 72579 Feel Like Makin' Love - Romantic Power Ballads.
(S) (4:14) Epic 67622 Greatest Hits.
(S) (4:16) Hip-O 40080 Essential '80s: 1985-1989.
(S) (4:16) Time-Life R834-12 Body Talk - By Candlelight.

1987 WE'RE READY
(S) (3:58) MCA 6188 Third Stage.
(S) (3:58) MFSL 582 Third Stage. *(gold disc)*

BOSTON (Continued)

    (S) (3:56)   Time-Life R988-09 Sounds Of The Eighties: 1987.

1987 CAN'TCHA SAY (YOU BELIEVE IN ME)/STILL IN LOVE

    (S) (5:13)   MCA 6188 Third Stage. *(LP version)*

    (S) (5:13)   MFSL 582 Third Stage. *(LP version; gold disc)*

PERRY BOTKIN JR.

1976 NADIA'S THEME

BRENT BOURGEOIS ∞

1990 DARE TO FALL IN LOVE

    (S) (4:05)   Charisma 91364 and 86346 Brent Bourgeois.

JIMMY BOWEN

1957 I'M STICKIN' WITH YOU

    (M) (2:06)   Collectables 5416 Murray The K - Sing Along With The Golden Gassers. *(truncated fade)*

    (M) (2:06)   Collectables 5406 Best Of. *(truncated fade)*

    (M) (2:02)   Time-Life 2RNR-17 Rock 'N' Roll Era - 1957 Still Rockin'. *(no fidelity)*

DAVID BOWIE

1973 SPACE ODDITY

(dj copies of this 45 state times of (3:49) and (5:05) while the actual times are (3:58) and (5:12); commercial copies stated a time of (5:05) but had an actual time of (5:12))

    (S) (5:15)   RCA 1732 Changesonebowie.

    (S) (5:13)   Rykodisc 20171 Changesbowie.

    (S) (5:13)   Rykodisc 80171 Changesbowie. *(gold disc)*

    (S) (5:13)   Rykodisc 10131 Space Oddity.

    (M) (5:07)   Rykodisc 90120 Sound + Vision. *(demo version with :14 of studio talk)*

    (S) (5:13)   RCA 4813 Space Oddity.

    (S) (5:13)   RCA 4919 Fame And Fashion.

    (S) (3:31)   Rykodisc 10218/19 The Singles 1969-1993. *(this is the 1969 noncharting version recorded for Mercury records)*

    (S) (5:12)   EMI-Capitol Entertainment Properties 21320 Essential - Best Of 1969-1974.

1975 CHANGES

(actual 45 time is (3:32) not (2:32) as stated on both the commercial and dj copies)

    (S) (3:33)   Rykodisc 90120 Sound + Vision.

    (S) (3:34)   RCA 1732 Changesonebowie.

    (S) (3:33)   Rykodisc 20171 Changesbowie.

    (S) (3:33)   Rykodisc 80171 Changesbowie. *(gold disc)*

    (S) (3:34)   RCA 4919 Fame And Fashion.

    (S) (3:33)   Rykodisc 10133 Hunky Dory.

    (S) (3:33)   Rykodisc 10218/19 The Singles 1969-1993.

1975 YOUNG AMERICANS

(dj copies of this 45 ran (3:11) and (5:06); commercial copies were all (3:11))

    (S) (5:10)   Rykodisc 90120 Sound + Vision. *(LP version)*

    (S) (5:09)   RCA 1732 Changesonebowie. *(LP version)*

    (S) (5:09)   Rykodisc 20171 Changesbowie. *(LP version)*

    (S) (5:09)   Rykodisc 80171 Changesbowie. *(gold disc)*

    (S) (5:09)   RCA 4919 Fame And Fashion. *(LP version)*

    (S) (5:10)   Rykodisc 10140 Young Americans. *(LP version)*

    (S) (5:09)   RCA 0998 Young Americans. *(LP version)*

    (S) (5:10)   Rykodisc 10218/19 The Singles 1969-1993. *(LP version)*

    (S) (5:10)   EMI-Capitol Entertainment Properties 96436 Young Americans. *(LP version)*

1975 FAME

(dj copies of this 45 ran (4:12) and (3:30); commercial copies were all (3:30))

    (S) (4:13)   RCA 1732 Changesonebowie. *(LP version)*

    (S) (4:14)   RCA 4919 Fame And Fashion. *(LP version)*

    (S) (4:15)   Rykodisc 10140 Young Americans. *(LP version)*

    (S) (4:15)   Rykodisc 10218/19 The Singles 1969-1993. *(LP version)*

    (S) (4:15)   RCA 0998 Young Americans. *(LP version)*

    (S) (4:14)   Time-Life R968-10 Guitar Rock Classics. *(LP version)*

    (S) (4:14)   MCA 11329 Soul Train 25th Anniversary Box Set. *(LP version)*

    (S) (4:14)   Time-Life R13610 Gold And Platinum Box Set - The Ultimate Rock Collection. *(LP version)*

    (S) (4:15)   Emi-Capitol Entertainment Properties 96436 Young Americans. *(LP version)*

1976 GOLDEN YEARS

    (S) (4:00)   RCA 1327 Station To Station. *(LP length)*

    (S) (3:58)   RCA 4792 Golden Years. *(LP length)*

    (S) (3:57)   RCA 1732 Changesonebowie. *(LP length)*

    (S) (3:58)   Rykodisc 20171 Changesbowie. *(LP length)*

    (S) (3:58)   Rykodisc 80171 Changesbowie. *(gold disc; LP length)*

    (S) (3:58)   RCA 4919 Fame And Fashion. *(LP length)*

    (S) (3:59)   Rykodisc 10141 Station To Station. *(LP length)*

    (S) (3:58)   Rykodisc 10218/19 The Singles 1969-1993. *(LP length)*

released as by QUEEN & DAVID BOWIE:

1982 UNDER PRESSURE

    (S) (4:01)   Hollywood 61407 Queen Collection.

    (S) (4:01)   Hollywood 61311 Classic Queen.

    (S) (4:02)   Elektra 564 Queen - Greatest Hits.

    (S) (4:03)   Hollywood 61038 Queen - Hot Space.

    (S) (4:01)   Rykodisc 10218/19 David Bowie - The Singles 1969-1993.

    (S) (4:03)   Virgin 40982 David Bowie - Let's Dance.

    (S) (3:55)   Hollywood 62042 Queen - Greatest Hits I & II.

    (S) (4:01)   London 422828867 O.S.T. Grosse Pointe Blank.

released as by DAVID BOWIE:

1983 LET'S DANCE

    (S) (4:07)   Rykodisc 10218/19 The Singles 1969-1993. *(45 version)*

    (S) (4:07)   Rykodisc 20171 Changesbowie. *(45 version)*

    (S) (4:07)   Rykodisc 80171 Changesbowie. *(gold disc; 45 version)*

    (S) (7:36)   EMI America 46002 Let's Dance. *(LP version)*

    (S) (4:07)   Time-Life R988-26 Sounds Of The Eighties: The Rolling Stone Collection 1982-1983. *(45 version)*

    (S) (7:37)   Virgin 40982 Let's Dance. *(LP version)*

    (S) (4:07)   Madacy Entertainment 1983 Rock On 1983. *(45 version)*

    (S) (4:45)   Arista 18985 Ultimate New Wave Party 1998. *(all selections on this cd are segued together)*

1983 CHINA GIRL

    (S) (5:30)   Rhino 71834 Classic MTV: Class Of 1983. *(LP version)*

    (S) (4:14)   Rykodisc 10218/19 The Singles 1969-1993. *(45 version)*

    (S) (4:14)   Rykodisc 20171 Changesbowie. *(45 version)*

    (S) (4:14)   Rykodisc 80171 Changesbowie. *(gold disc; 45 version)*

    (S) (5:31)   EMI America 46002 Let's Dance. *(LP version)*

    (S) (4:14)   Time-Life R988-03 Sounds Of The Eighties: 1983. *(45 version)*

    (S) (5:31)   Virgin 40982 Let's Dance. *(LP version)*

    (S) (5:28)   Maverick/Warner Brothers 46840 O.S.T. The Wedding Singer. *(LP version)*

1983 MODERN LOVE

    (S) (3:56)   Rykodisc 10218/19 The Singles 1969-1993. *(45 version)*

    (S) (3:56)   Rykodisc 20171 Changesbowie. *(45 version)*

    (S) (3:56)   Rykodisc 80171 Changesbowie. *(gold disc; 45 version)*

    (S) (4:46)   EMI America 46002 Let's Dance. *(LP version)*

    (S) (3:56)   Time-Life R988-01 Sounds Of The Eighties: The Rockin' Eighties. *(45 version)*

    (S) (4:46)   Virgin 40982 Let's Dance. *(LP version)*

1984 BLUE JEAN

    (S) (3:09)   Rykodisc 10218/19 The Singles 1969-1993.

    (S) (3:09)   Rykodisc 20171 Changesbowie.

    (S) (3:09)   Rykodisc 80171 Changesbowie. *(gold disc)*

    (S) (3:09)   EMI America 46047 Tonight.

(S) (3:09) Time-Life R988-06 Sounds Of The Eighties: 1984.
(S) (3:09) Virgin 40983 Tonight.

released as by DAVID BOWIE/PAT METHENY GROUP:
1985 THIS IS NOT AMERICA
(S) (3:52) EMI Manhattan 48411 O.S.T. Falcon And The Snowman.
(S) (3:49) Virgin 40983 Tonight.

released as by MICK JAGGER/DAVID BOWIE:
1985 DANCING IN THE STREET
(S) (3:14) Rykodisc 10218/19 David Bowie - The Singles 1969-1993.

released as by DAVID BOWIE:
1987 DAY-IN-DAY-OUT
(S) (4:14) Rykodisc 10218/19 The Singles 1969-1993. *(45 version)*
(S) (5:35) EMI America 46677 Never Let Me Down. *(LP version)*
(S) (5:34) Virgin 40986 Never Let Me Down. *(LP version)*

1987 NEVER LET ME DOWN
(S) (4:03) Rykodisc 10218/19 The Singles 1969-1993.
(S) (4:03) EMI America 46677 Never Let Me Down.
(S) (4:03) Virgin 40986 Never Let Me Down.

BOX TOPS
1967 THE LETTER
(actual LP time is (1:52) not (1:58) as stated on record labels; actual 45 time is (1:56) not (1:58) as stated on the record label)
(S) (1:50) K-Tel 686 Battle Of The Bands Volume 4.
(S) (1:52) Rhino 70628 Billboard's Top Rock & Roll Hits of 1967.
(S) (1:50) Warner Special Products 27611 Ultimate.
(S) (1:50) Collectables 5061 History Of Rock Volume 1.
(M) (1:54) Original Sound CDGO-14 Golden Oldies Volume. 14.
(M) (1:55) Original Sound 8862 Oldies But Goodies Vol. 12. *(this compact disc uses the "Waring - fds" noise reduction process)*
(M) (1:55) Original Sound 2223 Oldies But Goodies Volumes 2,7,9,12 and 13 Box Set. *(this box set uses the "Waring - fds" noise reduction process)*
(M) (1:55) Original Sound 2500 Oldies But Goodies Volumes 1-15 Box Set. *(this box set uses the "Waring - fds" noise reduction process)*
(E) (1:59) JCI 3111 Good Time Sixties. *(:03 longer than any previously released version)*
(S) (1:50) Time-Life 2CLR-05 Classic Rock - 1967.
(S) (1:50) Collectables 2504 WCBS-FM History Of Rock - The 60's Part 4.
(S) (1:50) Collectables 4504 History Of Rock/The 60s Part Four.
(M) (1:54) Collectables 2510 WCBS-FM History Of Rock - The Rockin' 60's. *(mastered from vinyl; distorted)*
(M) (1:54) Collectables 4510 History Of Rock/The Rockin' 60s. *(mastered from vinyl; distorted)*
(S) (1:50) Collectables 2605 WCBS-FM Jukebox Giants Vol. 3.
(S) (1:52) Varese Sarabande 5503 and 5504 and 5505 and 5506 and 5507 and 5508 and 5509 and 5513 and 5571 Arrow: All Rock & Roll Oldies Volume One.
(S) (1:50) JCI 3126 1965 - Only Rock 'N Roll - 1969.
(S) (1:52) K-Tel 3130 60's Sound Explosion.
(S) (1:52) Arista 18937 Best Of.
(S) (1:52) Eclipse Music Group 64870 Rock 'n Roll Relix 1966-1967.
(S) (1:52) Eclipse Music Group 64872 Rock 'n Roll Relix 1960-1969.
(M) (1:56) Varese Sarabande 5846 On The Radio Volume One.
(S) (1:52) Simitar 55532 The Number One's: The '60s.
(S) (1:52) Simitar 55152 Blue Eyed Soul.

1967 NEON RAINBOW
(S) (2:58) Warner Special Products 27611 Ultimate. *(LP version)*
(M) (2:53) Rhino 71065 Summer Of Love Volume 1. *(45 version)*

(S) (2:57) Time-Life 2CLR-24 Classic Rock - 1967: Blowin' Your Mind. *(LP version)*
(S) (3:01) Arista 18937 Best Of. *(LP version)*

1968 CRY LIKE A BABY
(S) (2:31) Rhino 70629 Billboard's Top Rock & Roll Hits of 1968.
(S) (2:31) Rhino 72005 Billboard's Top Rock & Roll Hits 1968-1972 Box Set.
(S) (2:31) Warner Special Products 27610 More Party Classics.
(S) (2:31) Warner Special Products 27611 Ultimate.
(S) (2:30) Collectables 5063 History Of Rock Volume 3.
(S) (2:31) Time-Life 2CLR-04 Classic Rock - 1968.
(S) (2:31) Collectables 2504 WCBS-FM History Of Rock - The 60's Part 4.
(S) (2:31) Collectables 4504 History Of Rock/The 60s Part Four.
(M) (2:32) Collectables 2510 WCBS-FM History Of Rock - The Rockin' 60's. *(mastered from vinyl; distorted; no fidelity)*
(M) (2:32) Collectables 4510 History Of Rock/The Rockin' 60s. *(mastered from vinyl; distorted; no fidelity)*
(S) (2:31) Collectables 2554 CBS-FM History Of Rock Volume 2.
(S) (2:31) Arista 18937 Best Of.
(S) (2:31) Eclipse Music Group 64871 Rock 'n Roll Relix 1968-1969.
(S) (2:31) Eclipse Music Group 64872 Rock 'n Roll Relix 1960-1969.

1968 CHOO CHOO TRAIN
(S) (2:50) Warner Special Products 27611 Ultimate.
(S) (2:49) Arista 18937 Best Of.

1969 SWEET CREAM LADIES, FORWARD MARCH
(S) (2:12) Warner Special Products 27611 Ultimate.
(S) (2:12) Collectables 5065 History Of Rock Volume 5.
(S) (2:13) Arista 18937 Best Of.

1969 SOUL DEEP
(S) (2:26) Warner Special Products 27609 Memphis Soul Classics.
(S) (2:26) Warner Special Products 27611 Ultimate.
(S) (2:25) Collectables 5067 History Of Rock Volume 7.
(S) (2:26) Time-Life 2CLR-06 Classic Rock - 1969.
(S) (2:26) Arista 18937 Best Of.

TOMMY BOYCE & BOBBY HART
1967 OUT & ABOUT
(S) (2:27) Varese Sarabande 5670 Songs Of Tommy Boyce And Bobby Hart.

1968 I WONDER WHAT SHE'S DOING TONIGHT
(S) (2:42) Rhino 75777 More Nuggets.
(S) (2:42) Time-Life 2CLR-27 Classic Rock - 1968: Blowin' Your Mind.
(S) (2:42) Varese Sarabande 5670 Songs Of Tommy Boyce And Bobby Hart.
(S) (2:41) LaserLight 12311 and 15936 The Wonder Years - First Love.
(S) (2:42) Time-Life 2CLR-31 Classic Rock - Totally Fantastic '60s.

1968 ALICE LONG (YOU'RE STILL MY FAVORITE GIRLFRIEND)
(M) (2:49) Varese Sarabande 5535 Bubblegum Classics Volume One.
(M) (2:48) Varese Sarabande 5670 Songs Of Tommy Boyce And Bobby Hart.
(M) (2:48) K-Tel 3386 Best Of Bubblegum Music.

BOY GEORGE
1993 THE CRYING GAME
(S) (7:00) SBK 28559 Brilliant! The Global Dance Music Experience Volume 2. *(remix)*
(S) (3:20) SBK 89024 O.S.T. The Crying Game.
(S) (3:21) SBK 39014 At Worst...Best Of Boy George And Culture Club.
(S) (6:59) EMI 54099 Retro Dance Club Volume Two. *(remix)*
(S) (3:20) Time-Life R834-11 Body Talk - After Dark.

BOY KRAZY
1993 THAT'S WHAT LOVE CAN DO
- (S) (3:21) Next Plateau 828403 Boy Krazy.
- (S) (3:21) Right Stuff 52286 Free To Be Volume 2.
- (S) (3:20) K-Tel 3850 90s Now Volume 3.
- (S) (3:20) Cold Front 3832 Club Mix - Women Of Dance Vol. 1.

BOY MEETS GIRL
1985 OH GIRL
- (S) (4:17) A&M 5176 Boy Meets Girl.
1988 WAITING FOR A STAR TO FALL
- (S) (4:28) Priority 53769 Rock Of The 80's Volume 10.
- (S) (4:26) RCA 9970 Nipper's Greatest Hits - The 80's.
- (S) (4:26) Scotti Brothers 75434 Romantic Duets.
- (S) (4:30) RCA 8414 Reel Life.
- (S) (4:31) RCA 66812 Do You Love Me? (All-Time Best Love Songs).
- (S) (4:30) Time-Life R988-19 Sounds Of The Eighties: The Late '80s.
- (S) (4:31) Time-Life R834-19 Body Talk - Always And Forever.

BOYS
1989 DIAL MY HEART
- (S) (4:22) Motown 6260 Messages From The Boys.
- (S) (4:22) Motown 6358 Hitsville USA Volume Two.
- (S) (4:22) Rhino 72140 Billboard Hot R&B Hits 1985.
1990 CRAZY
- (S) (5:05) Motown 6302 The Boys.
- (S) (5:10) Rhino 72409 New Jack Hits.

BOYS CLUB
1989 I REMEMBER HOLDING YOU
- (S) (4:51) K-Tel 898 Romantic Hits Of The 80's.
- (S) (4:52) MCA 42242 Boys Club.
- (S) (4:52) Priority 53773 80's Greatest Rock Hits Volume II - Teen Idols.

BOYS DON'T CRY
1986 I WANNA BE A COWBOY
- (S) (3:41) Priority 53767 Rock Of The 80's Volume 11. *(45 version)*
- (S) (3:40) EMI 32694 Living In Oblivion - The 80's Greatest Hits Volume Five. *(45 version)*
- (S) (6:02) Cold Front 6247 Classic Club Mix - Dance Jams. *(all selections on this cd are segued together; LP version)*
- (S) (3:40) Intersound 9521 Retro Lunch Box - Squeeze The Cheese. *(45 version)*
- (S) (4:44) Cold Front 6330 Club Mix: The 80s. *(all selections on this cd are segued together)*

BOYZ II MEN
1991 MOTOWNPHILLY
- (S) (4:05) Motown 3746366352 East Coast Family Volume One. *(remixed)*
- (S) (3:52) Tommy Boy 1053 MTV Party To Go Volume 2. *(all tracks on this cd are segued together)*
- (S) (3:54) Motown 6320 and 314530231 Cooleyhighharmony.
- (S) (3:51) Motown 6358 Hitsville USA Volume Two.
- (S) (4:03) Motown 314530584 The Remix Collection. *(all tracks on this cd are segued together; remixed)*
- (S) (3:50) Motown 314530231 Cooleyhighharmony. *(remixed radio edit)*
1991 IT'S SO HARD TO SAY GOODBYE TO YESTERDAY
- (S) (2:47) Foundation/RCA 66104 Hot #1 Hits.
- (S) (3:49) Motown 3746366352 East Coast Family Volume One. *(remixed)*
- (S) (3:07) Motown 314530436 A Tribute To Berry Gordy. *(radio version)*
- (S) (2:47) Motown 6320 and 314530231 Cooleyhighharmony.
- (S) (3:06) Motown 314530231 Cooleyhighharmony. *(radio version)*

1992 UHH AHH
- (S) (4:48) Motown 3746366352 East Coast Family Volume One. *(sequel version)*
- (S) (3:48) Motown 6320 and 314530231 Cooleyhighharmony.
- (S) (4:30) Motown 314530584 The Remix Collection. *(all tracks on this cd are segued together; remixed)*
- (S) (4:13) Motown 314530231 Cooleyhighharmony. *(sequel version)*
1992 END OF THE ROAD
- (S) (5:48) Motown 3746366352 East Coast Family Volume One.
- (S) (5:47) Tommy Boy 1074 MTV Party To Go Volume 3. *(all tracks on this cd are segued together)*
- (S) (5:47) Foundation/RCA 66563 Number 1 Hit Mix.
- (S) (5:47) LaFace 26006 O.S.T. Boomerang.
- (S) (5:49) Motown 6358 Hitsville USA Volume Two.
- (S) (5:48) Motown 314530231 Cooleyhighharmony.
- (S) (5:49) Motown 314530231 Cooleyhighharmony. *(Spanish version)*
- (S) (5:48) Time-Life R13610 Gold And Platinum Box Set - The Ultimate Rock Collection.
1993 IN THE STILL OF THE NIGHT
- (S) (2:50) Motown 374636356 Album Inspired By "The Jacksons: An American Dream" Mini Series.
- (S) (2:48) Motown 314530231 Cooleyhighharmony.
1994 I'LL MAKE LOVE TO YOU
- (S) (3:56) Motown 314530323 II.
- (S) (3:57) Grammy Recordings/Sony Music 67043 1995 Grammy Nominees.
- (S) (4:56) Motown 314530584 The Remix Collection. *(all tracks on this cd are segued together; remixed)*
- (S) (3:58) Tommy Boy 1138 MTV Party To Go Volume 7. *(all selections on this cd are segued together)*
- (S) (3:56) MCA 11329 Soul Train 25th Anniversary Box Set.
- (S) (3:54) Rhino 72159 Black Entertainment Television - 15th Anniversary.
- (S) (3:55) Motown 314530849 Motown 40 Forever.
1995 ON BENDED KNEE
- (S) (5:29) Motown 314530323 II.
- (S) (4:15) Motown 314530584 The Remix Collection. *(all tracks on this cd are segued together; remixed)*
1995 THANK YOU
- (S) (4:35) Motown 314530323 II.
1995 WATER RUNS DRY
- (S) (3:20) Motown 314530323 II.
released as by MARIAH CAREY & BOYZ II MEN:
1996 ONE SWEET DAY
- (S) (4:40) Columbia 66700 Mariah Carey - Daydream.
- (S) (4:40) Grammy Recordings/Sony 67565 1996 Grammy Nominees.
released as by BOYZ II MEN:
1997 4 SEASONS OF LONELINESS
- (S) (4:52) Motown 314530819 Evolution.
1998 A SONG FOR MAMA
- (S) (5:03) Motown 314530819 Evolution. *(tracks into the next selection)*

JAN BRADLEY
1963 MAMA DIDN'T LIE
- (M) (2:01) MCA 5937 Vintage Music Volumes 13 & 14.
- (M) (2:01) MCA 31210 Vintage Music Volume 13.
- (M) (2:00) MCA 6228 O.S.T. Hairspray.
- (M) (2:00) Chess 31317 Best Of Chess Rhythm & Blues Volume 1.
- (M) (2:01) Time-Life 2RNR-19 Rock 'N' Roll Era - 1963 Still Rockin'.
- (M) (2:00) Time-Life RHD-02 Rhythm & Blues - 1963.
- (M) (2:00) JCI/Telstar 3516 Sweet Soul Sisters.
- (M) (2:00) Chess 9352 Chess Rhythm & Roll.
- (M) (2:00) Time-Life R838-14 Solid Gold Soul - 1963.
- (M) (2:01) Chess 9388 Chess Soul - A Decade Of Chicago's Finest.
- (M) (1:59) TVT 4010 Rhythm Revue.
- (M) (2:01) Time-Life R857-18 The Heart Of Rock 'n' Roll 1962-1963 Take Two.

OWEN BRADLEY QUINTET
1957 WHITE SILVER SANDS
1958 BIG GUITAR

BRAM TCHAIKOVSKY
1979 GIRL OF MY DREAMS
  (dj copies of this 45 ran (3:13) and (4:06);
  commercial copies were all (4:06))
  (S) (4:07) Time-Life SOD-37 Sounds Of The Seventies -
             AM Heavy Hits.
  (S) (4:07) Rhino 71174 DIY: Starry Eyes - UK Pop II.

BRANDY
1994 I WANNA BE DOWN
  (S) (4:51) Atlantic 82610 Brandy.
  (S) (4:02) Tommy Boy 1138 MTV Party To Go Volume 7.
             *(all selections on this cd are segued together;
             remixed)*
  (S) (4:51) EMI-Capitol Music Group 54548 Smooth Luv.
  (S) (4:14) Elektra 62089 Maximum R&B.
1995 BABY
  (S) (5:12) Atlantic 82610 Brandy.
  (S) (4:19) Tommy Boy 1164 MTV Party To Go Volume 9.
             (all selections on this cd are segued together)
  (S) (5:13) Grammy Recordings/Sony 67565 1996 Grammy
             Nominees.
  (S) (5:12) Loud/RCA 67423 All That - The Album.
  (S) (5:13) Atlantic 83088 Atlantic Records: 50 Years - The
             Gold Anniversary Collection.
1995 BEST FRIEND
  (S) (4:48) Atlantic 82610 Brandy.
1995 BROKENHEARTED
  (S) (5:51) Atlantic 82610 Brandy.
1996 SITTIN' UP IN MY ROOM
  (S) (4:50) Arista 18796 O.S.T. Waiting To Exhale.
  (S) (3:45) Arista 18977 Ultimate Hip Hop Party 1998. *(remix;
             all selections on this cd are segued together)*
**released as by BRANDY, TAMIA, GLADYS KNIGHT and
CHAKA KHAN:**
1996 MISSING YOU
  (S) (4:22) EastWest 61951 O.S.T. Set It Off.

LAURA BRANIGAN
1982 GLORIA
  **(dj copies of this 45 ran (3:49) and (4:50) even
  though times of (3:41) and (4:50) were stated on
  the record label; commercial copies were all (4:50))**
  (S) (4:49) Priority 53728 Mega-Hits Dance Classics
             (Volume 12).
  (S) (3:50) Rhino 70677 Billboard Top Hits - 1982.
  (S) (4:49) Sandstone 33043 and 5009 Rock The First
             Volume Three.
  (S) (3:49) JCI 3127 1980 - Only Rock 'N Roll - 1984.
  (S) (4:49) Atlantic 19289 Branigan.
  (S) (4:49) Atlantic 82757 Best Of.
  (S) (3:50) Time-Life R988-05 Sounds Of The Eighties: 1982.
  (S) (3:49) Time-Life R138-38 Celebration.
  (S) (3:50) Rhino 72838 Disco Queens: The 80's.
  (S) (3:49) K-Tel 3867 The 80's: Hot Ladies.
1983 SOLITAIRE
  (S) (4:04) Priority 7076 80's Greatest Rock Hits Volume 2 -
             Leather And Lace.
  (S) (4:04) Atlantic 80052 Branigan 2.
  (S) (4:05) Atlantic 82757 Best Of.
1983 HOW AM I SUPPOSED TO LIVE WITHOUT YOU
  (S) (4:26) Atlantic 80052 Branigan 2.
  (S) (4:29) Atlantic 82757 Best Of.
  (S) (4:28) Time-Life R834-06 Body Talk - Only You.
1984 SELF CONTROL
  (S) (4:05) Atlantic 81910 Hit Singles 1980-1988.
  (S) (4:06) Atlantic 80147 Self Control.
  (S) (4:05) Atlantic 82757 Best Of.
  (S) (4:06) JCI 3149 1980 - Only Dance - 1984.
  (S) (4:00) Time-Life R988-15 Sounds Of The Eighties: The
             Mid 80's.

1984 THE LUCKY ONE
  (S) (4:09) Atlantic 80147 Self Control.
  (S) (4:09) Atlantic 82757 Best Of.
1985 SPANISH EDDIE
  (S) (4:12) Atlantic 82757 Best Of.
  (S) (4:06) Atlantic 81265 Hold Me.
1988 POWER OF LOVE
  (S) (5:24) Atlantic 81747 Touch. *(LP version)*
  (S) (5:23) Atlantic 82757 Best Of. *(LP version)*
  (S) (5:23) Madacy Entertainment 1988 Rock On 1988. *(LP
             version)*

BRASS CONSTRUCTION
1976 MOVIN'
  (S) (3:49) Rhino 71603 Rock Instrumental Classics Volume
             3: The Seventies. *(45 version)*
  (S) (3:49) Rhino 72035 Rock Instrumental Classics Vols. 1-
             5 Box Set. *(45 version)*
  (S) (8:38) Collectables 5239 Golden Classics. *(LP version)*
  (S) (8:38) EMI 27591 Best Of. *(LP version)*
  (S) (3:56) Rhino 72127 Soul Hits Of The 70's Vol. 17. *(45
             version)*
  (S) (5:28) Collectables 5878 Roadshow Classics. *(live)*

BRASS RING
1966 PHOENIX LOVE THEME
  (S) (2:20) Collectors' Choice 003/4 Instrumental Gems Of
             The 60's.
1967 THE DIS-ADVANTAGES OF YOU
  (S) (2:22) Time-Life R986-20 Instrumental Favorites -
             Whimsical Interludes.
  (S) (2:22) Varese Sarabande 5802 Sunshine Days - Pop
             Classics Of The '60s Volume 2.

BOB BRAUN
1962 TILL DEATH DO US PART

TONI BRAXTON
released as by BABYFACE featuring TONI BRAXTON:
1992 GIVE U MY HEART
  (S) (5:01) LaFace 26006 O.S.T. Boomerang.
released as by TONI BRAXTON:
1993 LOVE SHOULDA BROUGHT YOU HOME
  (S) (4:56) LaFace 26006 O.S.T. Boomerang.
  (S) (4:57) LaFace 26007 Toni Braxton.
1993 ANOTHER SAD LOVE SONG
  (S) (5:01) LaFace 26007 Toni Braxton.
1994 BREATHE AGAIN
  (S) (4:28) LaFace 26007 Toni Braxton.
1994 YOU MEAN THE WORLD TO ME
  (S) (4:54) LaFace 26007 Toni Braxton.
1995 HOW MANY WAYS
  (S) (4:47) LaFace 26007 Toni Braxton.
1995 I BELONG TO YOU
  (S) (3:54) LaFace 26007 Toni Braxton.
1996 YOU'RE MAKIN' ME HIGH
  (S) (4:26) LaFace 26020 Secrets.
1996 LET IT FLOW
  (S) (4:22) LaFace 26020 Secrets.
1996 UN-BREAK MY HEART
  (S) (4:29) LaFace 26020 Secrets.
  (S) (4:29) Grammy Recordings/Chronicles 314553292 1997
             Grammy Nominees.
  (S) (4:36) Arista 18988 Ultimate Dance Party 1998. *(all
             selections on this cd are segued together)*
1997 I DON'T WANT TO
  (S) (4:15) LaFace 26020 Secrets.
1997 I LOVE ME SOME HIM
  (S) (5:06) LaFace 26020 Secrets.

BREAD
1970 MAKE IT WITH YOU
  (S) (3:09) Elektra 60414 Anthology.
  (S) (3:09) Original Sound 8909 Best Love Songs Vol 4.

BREAD (Continued)

- (S) (3:09) Original Sound 9327 Best Love Songs Vol. 3 & 4.
- (S) (3:09) Original Sound 1236 Best Love Songs Box Set.
- (S) (3:09) Time-Life SUD-04 Superhits - 1970.
- (S) (3:14) Rhino 73503 On The Waters.
- (S) (3:13) Rhino 73509 Retrospective.
- (S) (3:11) JCI 3145 1970 - Only Love - 1974.
- (S) (3:09) Eclipse Music Group 64892 Rock 'n Roll Relix 1970-1971.
- (S) (3:09) Eclipse Music Group 64897 Rock 'n Roll Relix 1970-1979.
- (S) (3:08) Time-Life AM1-02 AM Gold - 1970.
- (S) (3:09) Time-Life R834-06 Body Talk - Only You.
- (S) (3:09) Time-Life R840-03 Sounds Of The Seventies - Pop Nuggets: Early '70s.
- (S) (3:11) Razor & Tie 4543 The '70s Preservation Society Presents: Easy '70s.
- (S) (3:13) Polygram TV 314555610 The One And Only Love Album.

1970 IT DON'T MATTER TO ME

- (S) (2:46) Elektra 60414 Anthology. *(45 version)*
- (S) (2:41) Rhino 73502 Bread. *(LP version)*
- (S) (2:47) Rhino 73509 Retrospective. *(45 version)*
- (S) (2:47) Rhino 72736 Billboard Top Soft Rock Hits - 1970. *(45 version)*
- (S) (2:47) Time-Life R834-19 Body Talk - Always And Forever. *(45 version)*

1971 LET YOUR LOVE GO

- (S) (2:18) Elektra 60414 Anthology.
- (S) (2:24) Rhino 73504 Manna.
- (S) (2:22) Rhino 73509 Retrospective.

1971 IF

- (S) (2:31) Elektra 60414 Anthology.
- (S) (2:32) Time-Life SUD-16 Superhits - The Early 70's.
- (S) (2:32) Scotti Brothers 75262 There Is Love (The Wedding Songs).
- (S) (2:33) Rhino 73504 Manna.
- (S) (2:33) Rhino 73509 Retrospective.
- (S) (2:33) Rhino 72517 Mellow Rock Hits Of The 70's - Ventura Highway.
- (S) (2:32) Time-Life AM1-13 AM Gold - The Early '70s.
- (S) (2:33) Rhino 72737 Billboard Top Soft Rock Hits - 1971.

1971 BABY I'M A WANT YOU

- (S) (2:23) Elektra 60414 Anthology.
- (S) (2:29) Elektra 75015 Baby I'm A Want You.
- (S) (2:25) JCI 3307 Easy Seventies.
- (S) (2:19) Time-Life SUD-10 Superhits - 1971.
- (S) (2:27) Rhino 73509 Retrospective.
- (S) (2:19) Time-Life AM1-06 AM Gold - 1971.
- (S) (2:24) Time-Life R834-05 Body Talk - Sealed With A Kiss.

1972 EVERYTHING I OWN

- (S) (3:04) Elektra 60414 Anthology.
- (S) (3:05) Elektra 75015 Baby I'm A Want You.
- (S) (3:05) Rhino 73509 Retrospective.
- (S) (3:06) JCI 3168 #1 Radio Hits 1970 - Only Rock 'n Roll - 1974.
- (S) (3:04) Time-Life R834-14 Body Talk - Love And Tenderness.

1972 DIARY

- (S) (3:04) Elektra 60414 Anthology.
- (S) (3:05) Elektra 75015 Baby I'm A Want You.
- (S) (3:05) Rhino 73509 Retrospective.

1972 THE GUITAR MAN

- (S) (3:41) Elektra 60414 Anthology.
- (S) (3:45) Elektra 60918 Guitar Man.
- (S) (3:42) Time-Life SUD-20 Superhits - Early 70's Classics.
- (S) (3:42) Time-Life SOD-33 Sounds Of The Seventies - AM Pop Classics II.
- (S) (3:44) Rhino 73509 Retrospective.
- (S) (3:42) Time-Life AM1-15 AM Gold - Early '70s Classics.
- (S) (3:44) Rhino 72738 Billboard Top Soft Rock Hits - 1972.
- (S) (3:42) Time-Life R834-18 Body Talk - Romantic Moments.

1972 SWEET SURRENDER

- (S) (2:33) Elektra 60414 Anthology.
- (S) (2:35) Elektra 60918 Guitar Man.
- (S) (2:34) Rhino 73509 Retrospective.

1973 AUBREY

- (S) (3:34) Elektra 60414 Anthology.
- (S) (3:38) Elektra 60918 Guitar Man.
- (S) (3:37) Rhino 73509 Retrospective.

1977 LOST WITHOUT YOUR LOVE

- (S) (2:52) Elektra 60414 Anthology.
- (S) (2:54) Rhino 73509 Retrospective.
- (S) (2:52) JCI 3146 1975 - Only Love - 1979.

BREAKFAST CLUB

1987 RIGHT ON TRACK

- (S) (4:15) MCA 5821 Breakfast Club.
- (S) (4:15) MCA Special Products 20897 Greatest Rock Hits Of The 80's.
- (S) (4:16) Risky Business 66390 Hazy Shade Of 80's.
- (S) (4:15) Hip-O 40047 The '80s Hit(s) Back 3.
- (S) (4:16) MCA Special Products 21034 Club Disco Dance Hits.

BREATHE

1988 HANDS TO HEAVEN

- (S) (4:17) A&M 5163 All That Jazz.

1988 HOW CAN I FALL?

- (S) (4:41) A&M 5163 All That Jazz. *(LP length)*

1989 DON'T TELL ME LIES

- (S) (3:39) A&M 5163 All That Jazz.

1990 SAY A PRAYER

- (S) (3:49) A&M 5320 Peace Of Mind.

1991 DOES SHE LOVE THAT MAN?

- (S) (4:45) A&M 5320 Peace Of Mind.

BEVERLY BREMERS

1972 DON'T SAY YOU DON'T REMEMBER

- (S) (3:23) Rhino 70927 Super Hits Of The 70's Volume 7.
- (S) (3:23) Varese Sarabande 5803 Sunshine Days - Pop Classics Of The '60s Volume 3.
- (S) (3:22) Collectables 5907 Very Best Of.

BRENDA & THE TABULATIONS

1967 DRY YOUR EYES

- (M) (2:34) Time-Life 2CLR-15 Classic Rock - 1967: Shakin' All Over.
- (E) (2:35) Thump 7010 Low Rider Oldies Volume 1. *(mastered from vinyl)*
- (S) (2:48) Rhino 72619 Smooth Grooves: The '60s Volume 2 Mid '60s.
- (M) (2:41) Rhino 72815 Beg, Scream & Shout! The Big Ol' Box Of '60s Soul.
- (E) (2:34) K-Tel 3901 Soul Brothers & Sisters Of The 60's. *(sounds like it was mastered from vinyl)*
- (M) (2:41) TVT 4010 Rhythm Revue.
- (M) (2:40) Jamie/Guyden 4001 Dry Your Eyes.

1971 RIGHT ON THE TIP OF MY TONGUE

- (M) (3:15) Rhino 70784 Soul Hits Of The 70's Volume 4. *(mastered from vinyl)*
- (M) (3:15) Rhino 72028 Soul Hits Of The 70's Volumes 1-5 Box Set. *(mastered from vinyl)*
- (M) (3:15) Thump 7020 Low Rider Oldies Volume II. *(mastered from vinyl)*
- (M) (3:15) Priority 53129 Deep Soul Volume One. *(mastered from vinyl)*
- (M) (3:19) Jamie/Guyden 4003 Philly Original Soul Classics Volume One: Storm Warning.

WALTER BRENNAN

1960 DUTCHMAN'S GOLD

1962 OLD RIVERS

- (S) (2:44) Rhino 70683 Billboard's Top Country Hits Of 1962.
- (S) (2:45) Rhino 71263 and 71451 Songs Of The West.
- (S) (2:43) Time-Life SUD-19 Superhits - Early 60's Classics.

(S) (2:45) Rhino 71682 Songs Of The West Vol. Two: Silver Screen Cowboys.
(M) (2:46) Collectors' Choice 027 Old Rivers/'Twas The Night Before Christmas...Back Home.
(S) (2:43) Time-Life AM1-20 AM Gold - Early '60s Classics.

1962 MAMA SANG A SONG

TERESA BREWER
released as by TERESA BREWER with THE LANCERS:
1955 LET ME GO, LOVER!
(M) (2:29) Varese Sarabande 5616 Music! Music! Music! - Best Of.
(S) (2:28) Special Music 2711 Best Of. *(rerecording)*
released as by TERESA BREWER:
1955 PLEDGING MY LOVE
(M) (2:41) MCA 1545 Best Of.
(M) (2:42) Varese Sarabande 5616 Music! Music! Music! - Best Of.
1956 A TEAR FELL
(M) (2:33) MCA 1545 Best Of.
(S) (2:53) Special Music 2711 Best Of. *(rerecording)*
(M) (2:34) Time-Life HPD-23 Your Hit Parade - The Late 50's.
(M) (2:34) Varese Sarabande 5616 Music! Music! Music! - Best Of.
(M) (2:33) Time-Life R132-10 Love Songs Of Your Hit Parade.
1956 BO WEEVIL
(M) (2:20) Varese Sarabande 5616 Music! Music! Music! - Best Of.
(S) (2:02) Special Music 2711 Best Of. *(rerecording)*
1956 A SWEET OLD FASHIONED GIRL
(S) (2:55) Special Music 2711 Best Of. *(rerecording)*
(M) (2:55) Time-Life HPD-21 Your Hit Parade - The Mid 50's.
(M) (2:54) Varese Sarabande 5616 Music! Music! Music! - Best Of.
1956 MUTUAL ADMIRATION SOCIETY
(M) (2:16) Time-Life HPD-38 Your Hit Parade - The 50's Generation.
(M) (2:15) Varese Sarabande 5616 Music! Music! Music! - Best Of.
1957 EMPTY ARMS
(M) (2:47) MCA 1545 Best Of.
(S) (2:32) Special Music 2711 Best Of. *(rerecording)*
(M) (2:48) Varese Sarabande 5616 Music! Music! Music! - Best Of.
1957 YOU SEND ME
(M) (2:58) Varese Sarabande 5616 Music! Music! Music! - Best Of.
1958 THE HULA HOOP SONG
(S) (2:48) Nick At Nite/550 Music 63435 Beach Blanket Bash.

1960 ANYMORE

BREWER & SHIPLEY
1971 ONE TOKE OVER THE LINE
(S) (3:18) Rhino 70924 Super Hits Of The 70's Volume 4.
(S) (3:18) Rhino 72009 Super Hits Of The 70's Volumes 1-4 Box Set.
(S) (3:19) Pair 1202 Best Of Buddah.
(S) (3:18) Priority 8670 Hitchin A Ride/70's Greatest Rock Hits Volume 10.
(S) (3:20) Pair 1231 Greatest Hits.
(S) (3:20) Special Music 4920 Best Of.
(S) (3:18) Rhino 71208 70's Smash Hits Volume 4.
(S) (3:18) Essex 7060 The Buddah Box.
(S) (3:18) Time-Life SUD-10 Superhits - 1971.
(S) (3:19) Buddah 49510 Tarkio.
(S) (3:18) Madacy Entertainment 1971 Rock On 1971.
(S) (3:18) Time-Life AM1-06 AM Gold - 1971.
(S) (3:18) Flashback 72684 '70s Radio Hits Volume 4.
(S) (3:18) Flashback 72090 '70s Radio Hits Box Set.
(S) (3:18) K-Tel 3911 Fantastic Volume 2.
(S) (3:18) BMG Special Products 44643 The Best Of Buddah.

(S) (3:43) Geffen 25218 O.S.T. Fear And Loathing In Las Vegas. *(time includes :27 of movie dialogue; all songs and the movie dialogue are segued together)*

BRICK
1977 DAZZ
(dj copies of this 45 ran (3:25) and (5:35); commercial copies were all (5:35))
(S) (3:22) Priority 7975 Mega-Hits Dance Classics Volume 5.
(S) (5:36) Rhino 71434 In Yo Face! History Of Funk Volume 4.
(S) (3:21) Razor & Tie 22045 Those Funky 70's.
(S) (5:36) Rhino 71752 and 72829 Phat Trax: The Best Of Old School Volume 1.
(S) (3:21) Thump 4020 Old School Vol. 2.
(S) (3:22) Original Sound 9305 Art Laboe's Dedicated To You Volume 5.
(S) (3:24) Priority 53766 All Star Funk Vol. 2.
(S) (5:36) Rhino 72128 Hot Soul Hits Of The 70's Vol. 18.
(S) (3:23) K-Tel 3470 Get Up And Disco.
(S) (3:23) Epic/Bang 66870 Best Of.
(S) (5:35) Epic 67506 Club Epic Volume 4.
(S) (5:35) Rhino 72487 Street Jams - Back 2 The Old Skool, Part 1.
(S) (3:23) Coldfront 3638 Funk Nation - Free Your Mind And Your @#s Will Follow.
(S) (5:36) Time-Life R838-11 Solid Gold Soul - 1976.
(S) (5:35) Epic/Legacy 65504 Disco Super Hits.
(S) (5:36) Time-Life R840-07 Sounds Of The Seventies: '70s Dance Party 1976-1977.

1977 DUSIC
(S) (5:40) Priority 53730 Mega Hits Dance Classics Vol. 13. *(LP version; mastered from a scratchy record)*
(S) (5:42) Rhino 71753 and 72830 Phat Trax: The Best Of Old School Volume 2. *(LP version)*
(S) (5:37) Thump 4030 Old School Vol. 3. *(LP version; tracks into next selection; mastered from a scratchy record)*
(S) (5:42) Epic/Bang 66870 Best Of. *(LP version)*
(S) (5:42) Rhino 72488 Street Jams - Back 2 The Old Skool, Part 2. *(LP version)*

EDIE BRICKELL & THE NEW BOHEMIANS
1989 WHAT I AM
(S) (4:55) Sandstone 33047 and 5015 Cosmopolitan Volume 1. *(LP version)*
(S) (4:55) Geffen 24192 Shooting Rubberbands At The Stars. *(LP version)*
(S) (4:55) Madacy Entertainment 1989 Rock On 1989. *(LP version)*
(S) (4:54) Time-Life R988-19 Sounds Of The Eighties: The Late '80s. *(LP version)*
(S) (4:54) Geffen 25151 Geffen Vintage 80s Vol. II. *(LP version)*

ALICIA BRIDGES
1978 I LOVE THE NIGHTLIFE (DISCO 'ROUND)
(S) (3:08) Priority 7971 Mega-Hits Dance Classics Volume 1.
(S) (5:35) Original Sound 8864 Oldies But Goodies Vol. 14. *(this compact disc uses the "Waring - fds" noise reduction process; 12" single version)*
(S) (5:35) Original Sound 2222 Oldies But Goodies Volumes 3,5,11,14 and 15 Box Set. *(this box set uses the "Waring - fds" noise reduction process; 12" single version)*
(S) (5:35) Original Sound 2500 Oldies But Goodies Volumes 1-15 Box Set. *(this box set uses the "Waring - fds" noise reduction process; 12" single version)*
(S) (2:58) Rhino 70274 The Disco Years Volume 3. *(:10 shorter than the 45 and LP length)*
(S) (3:07) Razor & Tie 22496 Disco Fever.
(S) (3:07) Time-Life SOD-10 Sounds Of The Seventies - 1978.
(S) (5:35) Rebound 314520217 Disco Nights Vol. 1 - Divas Of Dance. *(12" single version)*
(S) (3:07) Rebound 314520265 Dance Fever.

ALICIA BRIDGES *(Continued)*
- (S) (3:25) Mother 314516937 O.S.T. The Adventures Of Priscilla - Queen Of The Desert. *(liner notes claim that this is the original version, which it might be, but it is not the hit version)*
- (S) (3:29) Mother 314516937 O.S.T. The Adventures Of Priscilla - Queen Of The Desert. *(remix)*
- (S) (6:21) Mother 314516937 O.S.T. The Adventures Of Priscilla - Queen Of The Desert. *(remix)*
- (S) (3:05) Polydor 314535877 Pure Disco.
- (S) (3:07) JCI 3148 1975 - Only Dance - 1979.
- (S) (2:59) Rhino 72812 VH1 8-Track Flashback: The One Hit Wonders. *(:09 shorter than the 45 and LP length)*
- (S) (3:05) Rebound 314520492 Class Reunion '78.
- (S) (4:45) Rebound 314520520 Body Moves - Non-Stop Disco Workout Vol. 1. *(all selections on this cd are segued together)*

BRIGHTER SIDE OF DARKNESS
1973 LOVE JONES
- (S) (3:18) Rhino 70790 Soul Hits Of The 70's Volume 10. *(45 version)*
- (S) (4:28) Right Stuff 30576 Slow Jams: The 70's Volume 4. *(LP version)*
- (S) (3:17) Rhino 72115 Billboard Hot Soul Hits - 1973. *(45 version)*
- (S) (3:17) Time-Life R838-08 Solid Gold Soul - 1973. *(45 version)*
- (S) (3:19) Polygram Special Markets 314520446 Soul Hits Of The 70's. *(45 version)*

MARTIN BRILEY
1983 THE SALT IN MY TEARS
- (S) (3:13) Priority 53681 80's Greatest Rock Hits - Agony & Ecstasy.

JOHNNY BRISTOL
1974 HANG ON IN THERE BABY
- (S) (3:21) Rhino 70553 Soul Hits Of The 70's Volume 13.
- (S) (5:08) Rebound 314520218 Disco Nights Vol. 2. *(rerecording)*
- (S) (3:20) Rebound 314520265 Dance Fever.
- (S) (3:19) K-Tel 3535 Slow Groove Love Jams Of The 70's.
- (S) (3:20) Ripete 5151 Ocean Drive 4.
- (S) (3:19) Beast 53442 Original Players Of Love.
- (S) (3:20) Polygram Special Markets 314520446 Soul Hits Of The 70's.
- (S) (3:20) Rebound 314520522 Rockin' Sports Jams.

B-ROCK & THE BIZZ
1997 MY BABY DADDY
- (S) (3:34) Tony Mercedes/LaFace 26037 ...And Then There Was Bass.
- (S) (3:32) Polygram TV 314553847 Pure Dance 1998. *(all songs on this cd are segued together)*

HERMAN BROOD
1979 SATURDAYNIGHT

BROOKLYN BRIDGE
1969 WORST THAT COULD HAPPEN
- (M) (3:05) Pair 1202 Best Of Buddah.
- (S) (3:07) Collectables 5015 Greatest Hits Of Johnny Maestro & The Brooklyn Bridge.
- (S) (3:05) Collectables 5064 History Of Rock Volume 4.
- (S) (3:06) Collectables 8808 For Collectors Only.
- (S) (3:05) Essex 7060 The Buddah Box.
- (S) (3:00) Time-Life 2CLR-20 Classic Rock - 1969: Shakin' All Over.
- (S) (3:00) Time-Life SUD-07 Superhits - 1969.
- (S) (3:03) Collectables 2501 WCBS-FM History Of Rock - The 60's Part 2.
- (S) (3:03) Collectables 4501 History Of Rock/The 60s Part Two.

- (S) (3:05) Rhino 71939 Billboard Top Pop Hits, 1969.
- (S) (3:04) Buddah 49517 Complete Buddah Chart Singles Volume Two.
- (S) (2:59) Time-Life AM1-01 AM Gold - 1969.
- (S) (3:07) Varese Sarabande 5803 Sunshine Days - Pop Classics Of The '60s Volume 3.
- (S) (3:05) BMG Special Products 44643 The Best Of Buddah.

1969 BLESSED IS THE RAIN
- (S) (3:17) Collectables 5015 Greatest Hits Of Johnny Maestro & The Brooklyn Bridge.
- (S) (3:17) Collectables 8808 For Collectors Only.
- (M) (3:15) Buddah 49517 Complete Buddah Chart Singles Volume Two.

DONNIE BROOKS
1960 MISSION BELL
- (M) (2:20) Collectables 5068 History Of Rock Volume 8. *(with more echo than the original 45 or LP)*
- (M) (2:21) Time-Life 2RNR-35 Rock 'N' Roll Era - The 60's Last Dance. *(with more echo than the original 45 or LP)*
- (E) (2:21) LaserLight 12322 Greatest Hit Singles Collection. *(with more echo than the original 45 or LP)*
- (E) (2:21) Curb 77773 Hard To Find Hits Of Rock 'N' Roll Volume One. *(with more echo than the original 45 or LP)*
- (M) (2:21) Collectors' Choice 002 Teen Idols....For A Moment. *(with more echo than the original 45 or LP; incorrectly titled "MISSION BELLS" on the cd jacket)*

1961 DOLL HOUSE
(actual 45 time is (2:22) not (2:03) as stated on the record label)
- (S) (2:25) Collectors' Choice 002 Teen Idols....For A Moment. *(slower than the 45 or LP)*

MEREDITH BROOKS
1997 BITCH
- (S) (4:12) Capitol 36919 Blurring The Edges.
- (S) (6:10) Beast 54112 Boom! *(remix)*

BROTHER BEYOND
1990 THE GIRL I USED TO KNOW
- (S) (4:21) EMI 93940 Trust.

BROTHERHOOD OF MAN
1970 UNITED WE STAND
- (S) (2:52) Rhino 70922 Super Hits Of The 70's Volume 2.
- (S) (2:52) Rhino 72009 Super Hits Of The 70's Volumes 1-4 Box Set.
- (S) (2:50) Time-Life SOD-32 Sounds Of The Seventies - AM Pop Classics.
- (S) (2:52) Collectables 0563 Golden Classics. *(truncated fade)*
- (S) (2:52) Time-Life R921-38 Get Together.
- (S) (2:51) Rebound 3145200320 Class Reunion 1970.
- (S) (2:51) LaserLight 12312 and 15936 The Wonder Years - Good Times, Good Friends.
- (S) (2:52) Varese Sarabande 5725 Love Grows (Where My Rosemary Goes) - The Voice Of Tony Burrows. *(truncated fade)*
- (S) (2:51) Special Music 5041 Great Britons! Volume Three.

1976 SAVE YOUR KISSES FOR ME
- (S) (3:01) Rhino 72298 Superhits Of The 70's Volume 24.

BROTHERS FOUR
1960 GREENFIELDS
- (S) (2:54) Columbia 44373 Hollywood Magic The 60's.
- (S) (3:01) Columbia 45017 Radio Classics Of The 50's.
- (S) (3:02) Columbia 8603 Greatest Hits.
- (S) (3:02) Rhino 70264 Troubadours Of The Folk Era Volume 3.
- (E) (3:01) JCI 3109 Folk Sixties.
- (S) (3:01) Time-Life SUD-19 Superhits - Early 60's Classics.
- (S) (3:01) Time-Life HPD-32 Your Hit Parade - Into The 60's.

(S) (3:01) Time-Life AM1-20 AM Gold - Early '60s Classics.

(S) (3:01) Time-Life R132-22 Treasury Of Folk Music Volume One.

(S) (3:01) Collectors' Choice 040-2 The Brothers Four/B.M.O.C.

BROTHERS JOHNSON
1976 I'LL BE GOOD TO YOU
(S) (4:44) A&M 2509 Classics Volume 11. *(LP version)*

(S) (3:27) Rhino 71618 Soul Train Hall Of Fame/20th Anniversary. *(45 version)*

(S) (4:39) Razor & Tie 22047 Sweet 70's Soul. *(LP version)*

(S) (3:29) Time-Life SOD-18 Sounds Of The Seventies - 1976: Take Two. *(45 version)*

(S) (3:31) Rhino 72128 Hot Soul Hits Of The 70's Vol. 18. *(45 version)*

(S) (4:42) Rebound 314520368 Class Reunion '76. *(LP version)*

(S) (4:45) A&M 314540552 Greatest Hits. *(LP version)*

(S) (4:45) A&M 750213142 Look Out For #1. *(LP version)*

(S) (3:31) Time-Life R838-11 Solid Gold Soul - 1976. *(45 version)*

(S) (4:43) Time-Life R834-04 Body Talk - Together Forever. *(LP version)*

(S) (4:44) Rebound 314520447 Soul Classics - Best Of The 70's. *(LP version)*

(S) (3:29) JCI 3175 1975 - Only Soul - 1979. *(45 version)*

(S) (4:41) Beast 53442 Original Players Of Love. *(LP version)*

1976 GET THE FUNK OUT MA FACE
(commercial 45's ran (5:59); dj 45's ran (2:27); LP length was (2:27))
(S) (5:59) A&M 2509 Classics Volume 11.

(S) (5:59) Rhino 71433 In Yo Face! History Of Funk Volume 3.

(S) (5:57) Rebound 314520034 Funk Classics Of The 70's.

(S) (2:26) A&M 314540552 Greatest Hits.

(S) (2:26) A&M 750213142 Look Out For #1.

(S) (2:26) Chronicles 314553403 Cosmic Funk.

1977 STRAWBERRY LETTER 23
(actual 45 time is (3:34) not (3:39) as stated on the record label)
(S) (5:04) A&M 2509 Classics Volume 11. *(LP version)*

(S) (3:47) Thump 4020 Old School Vol. 2. *(45 version but :13 longer fade)*

(S) (3:36) Rhino 72129 Soul Hits Of The 70's Vol. 19. *(45 version)*

(S) (4:57) A&M 314540552 Greatest Hits. *(LP version)*

(S) (4:57) A&M 750213147 Right On Time. *(LP version)*

(S) (3:35) Time-Life R838-16 Solid Gold Soul 1977. *(45 version)*

(S) (4:57) Maverick 46841 O.S.T. Jackie Brown. *(LP version)*

(S) (5:04) Time-Life R834-16 Body Talk - Sweet Nothings. *(LP version)*

1980 STOMP!
(actual 45 time is (4:05) not (3:58) as stated on the record label)
(S) (4:07) Priority 7975 Mega-Hits Dance Classics Volume 5. *(45 version)*

(S) (4:06) Rhino 70494 Billboard Top Dance Hits - 1980. *(45 version)*

(S) (5:59) A&M 2509 Classics Volume 11. *(:24 shorter than the LP version)*

(S) (5:59) Rebound 314520218 Disco Nights Vol. 2. *(:24 shorter than the LP version)*

(S) (4:05) Rhino 71891 Radio Daze: Pop Hits Of The 80's Volume Two. *(45 version)*

(S) (4:05) Rebound 314520365 Funk Classics - The 80's. *(45 version)*

(S) (6:18) A&M 314540552 Greatest Hits. *(LP version)*

(S) (6:18) A&M 750213716 Light Up The Night. *(LP version)*

AL BROWN'S TUNETOPPERS
1960 THE MADISON

ARTHUR BROWN (see CRAZY WORLD OF ARTHUR BROWN)

BOBBY BROWN
1988 DON'T BE CRUEL
(S) (6:46) MCA 42185 Don't Be Cruel. *(LP version)*

(S) (6:24) MCA 6342 Dance!...Ya Know It. *(remixed)*

(S) (4:07) Time-Life R988-10 Sounds Of The 80's: 1988. *(45 version)*

(S) (4:07) MCA 11329 Soul Train 25th Anniversary Box Set. *(45 version)*

(S) (4:07) JCI 3150 1985 - Only Dance - 1989. *(45 version)*

1988 MY PREROGATIVE
(actual 45 time is (4:33) not (4:25) as stated on the record label)
(S) (4:49) Sandstone 33041 and 5007 Rock The First Volume 1. *(LP version)*

(S) (3:29) JCI 3128 1985 - Only Rock 'N Roll - 1989. *(highly edited)*

(S) (4:56) MCA 11218 On The Beat - 80's Jams Vol. II. *(LP version)*

(S) (4:49) MCA 42185 Don't Be Cruel. *(LP version)*

(S) (5:25) MCA 6342 Dance!...Ya Know It. *(remixed)*

(S) (4:49) Time-Life R988-30 Sounds Of The Eighties: The Rolling Stone Collection 1988-1989. *(LP version)*

(S) (4:34) Rhino 72159 Black Entertainment Television - 15th Anniversary. *(45 version)*

(S) (4:35) Rhino 72140 Billboard Hot R&B Hits 1985. *(45 version)*

(S) (4:31) MCA 11570 New Edition Solo Hits. *(45 version)*

(S) (4:49) MCA Special Products 21034 Club Disco Dance Hits. *(LP version)*

1989 RONI
(S) (5:56) MCA 42185 Don't Be Cruel. *(LP version)*

(S) (6:18) MCA 6342 Dance!...Ya Know It. *(remixed)*

(S) (4:34) Time-Life R988-20 Sounds Of The Eighties: The Late '80s Take Two. *(45 version)*

(S) (5:55) Time-Life R834-12 Body Talk - By Candlelight. *(LP version)*

1989 EVERY LITTLE STEP
(S) (3:56) Sandstone 33050 and 5018 Cosmopolitan Volume 4.

(S) (3:56) DCC Compact Classics 089 Night Moves Volume 7.

(S) (3:56) MCA 42185 Don't Be Cruel.

(S) (4:41) MCA 6342 Dance!...Ya Know It. *(remixed)*

(S) (3:55) MCA 11570 New Edition Solo Hits.

1989 ON OUR OWN
(S) (4:54) MCA 6306 O.S.T. Ghostbusters II. *(LP version)*

(S) (4:32) MCA 6342 Dance!...Ya Know It. *(remixed)*

(S) (4:51) MCA 11570 New Edition Solo Hits. *(LP version)*

1989 ROCK WIT'CHA
(S) (4:47) MCA 42185 Don't Be Cruel. *(LP version)*

(S) (5:03) MCA 6342 Dance!...Ya Know It. *(remixed)*

released as by GLENN MEDEIROS featuring BOBBY BROWN:
1990 SHE AIN'T WORTH IT
(S) (3:35) MCA 6399 Glenn Medeiros.

(S) (3:25) Priority 50934 Shut Up And Dance! The 90's Volume One. *(all selections on this cd are segued together)*

released as by BOBBY BROWN:
1992 HUMPIN' AROUND
(S) (6:17) MCA 10417 Bobby. *(LP version)*

(S) (8:07) MCA 10974 Remixes N The Key Of B. *(remixed)*

(S) (5:21) MCA 11570 New Edition Solo Hits. *(neither the 45 or LP version)*

1993 GOOD ENOUGH
(S) (5:01) MCA 10417 Bobby. *(LP version)*

(S) (4:48) MCA 10974 Remixes N The Key Of B. *(remixed)*

BOBBY BROWN (Continued)

(S) (3:54) Priority 50946 100% Party Hits Of The 90's Volume One. *(45 version)*

1993 GET AWAY

(S) (5:09) MCA 10417 Bobby.

BOOTS BROWN and HIS BLOCKBUSTERS
1958 CERVEZA

(M) (2:03) RCA 66881 RCA's Greatest One-Hit Wonders.

BUSTER BROWN
1960 FANNIE MAE

(M) (2:52) Rhino 70646 Billboard's Top R&B Hits Of 1960.

(S) (2:56) Relic 7009 Raging Harlem Hit Parade.

(S) (2:56) Ripete 2392192 Beach Music Anthology Box Set.

(S) (2:56) Capricorn 42009 Fire/Fury Records Story.

(S) (2:55) MCA 8001 O.S.T. American Graffiti. *(Wolfman Jack talks over the introduction)*

(S) (2:55) Relic 7064 Raise A Ruckus Tonight.

(S) (2:55) Time-Life RHD-15 Rhythm & Blues - 1960.

(M) (2:53) Collectables 5127 Collectables Blues Collection Volume 1.

(S) (2:56) Collectables 5110 The New King Of The Blues. *(originally issued in 1988; remastered in 1994)*

(S) (2:55) Ripete 2223 Soul Patrol Vol. 5.

(S) (2:55) Time-Life R859-03 Living The Blues: Blues Greats.

(S) (2:55) Time-Life R838-20 Solid Gold Soul 1960.

CHUCK BROWN & THE SOUL SEARCHERS
1979 BUSTIN' LOOSE (PART 1)
(dj copies of this 45 ran (3:03); commercial copies were all (3:52))

(S) (3:49) Rhino 71435 In Yo Face! History Of Funk Volume 5. *(Part 1)*

(S) (3:45) Time-Life SOD-27 Sounds Of The Seventies - Dance Fever. *(Part 1)*

(S) (7:38) Valley Vue 53903 Bustin' Loose. *(Parts 1 & 2)*

(S) (3:48) Coldfront 3638 Funk Nation - Free Your Mind And Your @#s Will Follow. *(Part 1)*

(S) (7:41) Rhino 72587 Phat Trax: The Best Of Old School, Vol. 6. *(Parts 1 & 2)*

JAMES BROWN
1961 LOST SOMEONE

(S) (3:26) Polydor 817304 Roots Of A Revolution. *(LP length)*

(S) (3:26) Polydor 849108 Star Time. *(LP length)*

(M) (3:04) Polydor 314533409 JB 40: 40th Anniversary Collection. *(45 length)*

(S) (3:25) TVT 4010 Rhythm Revue. *(LP length)*

1962 NIGHT TRAIN

(S) (3:31) Rhino 75774 Soul Shots Volume 1. *(original session recording speed; the 45 was sped up considerably)*

(S) (3:31) Polydor 831700 CD Of JB II. *(same comments as for Rhino 75774)*

(M) (3:38) Polydor 849108 Star Time. *(same comments as for Rhino 75774)*

(M) (3:30) Polydor 511326 20 All Time Greatest Hits. *(same comments as for Rhino 75774)*

(M) (3:27) MCA 11241 O.S.T. Apollo 13. *(all selections on this cd are segued together; track selection numbers on the cd jacket are incorrect; this cd is a disaster)*

(M) (3:31) Risky Business 67308 Train Trax. *(same comments as for Rhino 75774)*

(M) (3:30) Hip-O 40008 Soulful Grooves - R&B Instrumental Classics Volume 2. *(same comments as for Rhino 75774)*

(M) (3:29) Polydor 314533409 JB 40: 40th Anniversary Collection. *(same comments as for Rhino 75774)*

1963 PRISONER OF LOVE

(S) (2:25) Polydor 825714 CD Of JB.

(S) (2:24) Polydor 849108 Star Time.

(S) (2:23) Polydor 817304 Roots Of A Revolution.

(M) (2:21) Polydor 314533409 JB 40: 40th Anniversary Collection.

(M) (2:21) Rhino 72618 Smooth Grooves: The '60s Volume 1 Early '60s.

1964 OH BABY DON'T YOU WEEP (PART 1)

(S) (6:30) Polydor 817304 Roots Of A Revolution. *(Parts 1 & 2; Part 1 is the 45 version without overdubbed audience applause)*

1964 OUT OF SIGHT

(E) (2:21) Polydor 825714 CD Of JB.

(M) (2:20) Polydor 849108 Star Time.

(M) (2:21) Polydor 314531165 Foundations Of Funk.

(E) (2:21) Polydor 314533080 Out Of Sight.

(M) (2:21) Polydor 314533409 JB 40: 40th Anniversary Collection.

(M) (2:21) Rhino 72815 Beg, Scream & Shout! The Big Ol' Box Of '60s Soul.

1965 PAPA'S GOT A BRAND NEW BAG (PART 1)

(M) (2:05) Polydor 825714 CD Of JB.

(M) (6:57) Polydor 849108 Star Time. *(original session recording speed; the 45 was sped up considerably; Parts 1, 2 & 3)*

(M) (2:07) Polydor 849108 Star Time.

(M) (2:05) Polydor 511326 20 All Time Greatest Hits.

(M) (2:05) Special Music 847982 Papa's Got A Brand New Bag.

(M) (1:59) Time-Life RHD-07 Rhythm & Blues - 1965.

(M) (2:05) Time-Life 2CLR-14 Classic Rock - 1965: Shakin' All Over.

(M) (2:03) Ripete 2198 Soul Patrol.

(M) (2:01) Original Sound 8883 21 Legendary Superstars.

(M) (2:04) King 7002 King R&B Box Set.

(M) (4:16) Polydor 314531165 Foundations Of Funk. *(Parts 1 & 2)*

(M) (4:16) Polydor 314533409 JB 40: 40th Anniversary Collection. *(Parts 1 & 2)*

(M) (1:59) JCI 3161 18 Soul Hits From The 60's.

(M) (1:59) JCI 3190 1965 - Only Dance - 1969.

(M) (2:05) Polygram Special Markets 314520396 Greatest Hits.

(M) (1:59) Time-Life R838-12 Solid Gold Soul - 1965.

(M) (2:04) Repeat/Relativity 1611 A Brand New Bag: #1 Soul Hits Of The 60's Volume 3.

(M) (2:05) Rebound 314520522 Rockin' Sports Jams.

1965 I GOT YOU (I FEEL GOOD)

(S) (2:44) Rhino 75774 Soul Shots.

(S) (2:44) Rhino 70651 Billboard's Top R&B Hits Of 1965.

(S) (2:44) Rhino 72006 Billboard's Top R&B Hits 1965-1969 Box Set.

(S) (2:44) A&M 3913 and 3340 O.S.T. Good Morning Vietnam.

(S) (2:25) Polydor 825714 CD Of JB. *(this version actually preceded the hit version and was technically titled simply "I GOT YOU")*

(S) (2:27) Polydor 849108 Star Time. *(this version actually preceded the hit version and was technically titled simply "I GOT YOU")*

(M) (2:44) Polydor 849109 Star Time.

(S) (2:42) Priority 7909 Vietnam: Rockin' The Delta.

(M) (2:45) Polydor 511326 20 All Time Greatest Hits.

(S) (2:44) Time-Life RHD-07 Rhythm & Blues - 1965.

(M) (2:45) Thump 4020 Old School Vol. 2.

(M) (2:46) Tommy Boy 1100 ESPN Presents Jock Rock. *(sound effects added to the introduction and ending)*

(M) (2:45) Polydor 314531165 Foundations Of Funk.

(S) (2:26) Polydor 314533080 Out Of Sight. *(this version actually preceded the hit version and was technically titled simply "I GOT YOU")*

(M) (2:45) Polydor 314533409 JB 40: 40th Anniversary Collection.

(S) (2:44) Time-Life R838-12 Solid Gold Soul - 1965.

(M) (2:45) Elektra 62093 O.S.T. A Smile Like Yours.

1966 IT'S A MAN'S MAN'S MAN'S WORLD

(M) (2:43) Rhino 70652 Billboard's Top R&B Hits Of 1966.

(M) (2:43) Rhino 72006 Billboard's Top R&B Hits 1965-1969 Box Set.

(M) (3:13) Polydor 825714 CD Of JB. *(not the hit version; this version actually preceded the hit version and was technically titled "IT'S A MAN'S WORLD")*

(S) (3:17) Polydor 849108 Star Time. *(not the hit version; this version actually preceded the hit version and was technically titled "IT'S A MAN'S WORLD")*
(M) (2:46) Polydor 849108 Star Time.
(M) (2:46) Polydor 511326 20 All Time Greatest Hits.
(M) (2:46) Epic 57560 O.S.T. A Bronx Tale.
(M) (3:14) Right Stuff 28371 Slow Jams: The 60's Volume Two. *(not the hit version; this version actually preceded the hit version and was technically titled "IT'S A MAN'S WORLD")*
(M) (2:46) MCA 10462 The Coach Collection.
(M) (2:46) Polygram Special Markets 314520264 Soul Hits Of The 60's.
(S) (2:46) MCA 11329 Soul Train 25th Anniversary Box Set.
(M) (2:46) Rebound 314520369 Soul Classics - Quiet Storm/The 60's.
(M) (2:46) Polydor 314533409 JB 40: 40th Anniversary Collection.
(M) (2:46) Repeat/Relativity 1610 Tighten Up: #1 Soul Hits Of The 60's Volume 2.

1966 DON'T BE A DROPOUT
(S) (4:31) Polydor 849108 Star Time. *(complete version; the 45 was an edit taken from this version)*
(S) (3:41) Polydor 314533081 Sings Raw Soul.

1967 BRING IT UP
(S) (3:48) Polydor 849108 Star Time. *(complete version; the 45 was an edit taken from this version)*
(S) (2:44) Polydor 314533081 Sings Raw Soul.

1967 COLD SWEAT (PART 1)
(S) (3:00) Rhino 70653 Billboard's Top R&B Hits Of 1967.
(S) (3:00) Rhino 72006 Billboard's Top R&B Hits 1965-1969 Box Set.
(S) (7:26) Polydor 831700 CD Of JB II. *(Parts 1 & 2)*
(S) (7:31) Polydor 849108 Star Time. *(Parts 1 & 2; stereo was remixed for this box set and is much narrower than the vinyl album stereo mix; includes a :04 countoff)*
(M) (2:50) Polydor 511326 20 All Time Greatest Hits.
(M) (2:50) Special Music 847982 Papa's Got A Brand New Bag.
(M) (2:56) Rhino 71618 Soul Train Hall Of Fame/20th Anniversary.
(M) (7:24) Polydor 314531165 Foundations Of Funk. *(mono LP version)*
(M) (0:23) Polydor 314531165 Foundations Of Funk. *(false start with studio talk)*
(M) (6:50) Polydor 314531165 Foundations Of Funk. *(alternate take with studio talk)*
(M) (7:24) Polydor 314533409 JB 40: 40th Anniversary Collection. *(mono LP version)*
(M) (2:50) Polygram Special Markets 314520396 Greatest Hits.
(M) (2:50) Polygram Special Markets 314520454 Soul Hits Of The 60's.

1967 GET IT TOGETHER (PART 1)
(M) (8:57) Polydor 849108 Star Time. *(Parts 1 & 2)*
(M) (8:57) Polydor 314531165 Foundations Of Funk. *(Parts 1 & 2)*

1968 I CAN'T STAND MYSELF (WHEN YOU TOUCH ME)
(S) (3:25) Polydor 831700 CD Of JB II.
(S) (3:29) Polydor 849108 Star Time. *(original recording session speed which was faster than the 45)*
(M) (7:18) Polydor 314531165 Foundations Of Funk. *(Parts 1 & 2)*

1968 THERE WAS A TIME
(S) (4:57) Polydor 849108 Star Time. *(this is a different live performance than the hit version; tracks into next selection)*
(S) (4:18) Polydor 823001 Live At The Apollo.
(S) (7:20) Polydor 314531684 Funk Power - 1970: A Brand New Thang. *(1970 rerecording with the title "THERE WAS A TIME (I GOT TO MOVE)")*
(S) (4:25) Polydor 314531165 Foundations Of Funk.
(S) (4:24) Polydor 314533409 JB 40: 40th Anniversary Collection.

1968 I GOT THE FEELIN'
(M) (2:39) Polydor 825714 CD Of JB. *(ends cold)*
(S) (2:37) Polydor 849108 Star Time.
(M) (2:37) Polydor 511326 20 All Time Greatest Hits.
(S) (2:37) Special Music 837726 Spank.
(M) (3:04) Polydor 314531165 Foundations Of Funk. *(two takes edited together)*
(S) (2:38) Capitol 35818 O.S.T. Dead Presidents Volume II.
(M) (2:36) Polydor 314533409 JB 40: 40th Anniversary Collection.
(S) (2:38) Repeat/Relativity 1609 Tell It Like It Is: #1 Soul Hits Of The 60's Volume 1.

1968 LICKING STICK - LICKING STICK (PART 1)
(S) (2:46) Polydor 825714 CD Of JB. *(45 mix)*
(S) (4:52) Polydor 849108 Star Time. *(Parts 1 & 2)*
(S) (4:15) Polydor 314531165 Foundations Of Funk. *(live)*
(S) (2:51) Polydor 422841992 Say It Loud - I'm Black And I'm Proud. *(LP mix)*
(S) (2:46) Polydor 314533409 JB 40: 40th Anniversary Collection. *(45 mix)*

1968 SAY IT LOUD - I'M BLACK AND I'M PROUD (PART 1)
(S) (2:48) Rhino 70654 Billboard's Top R&B Hits Of 1968.
(S) (2:48) Rhino 72006 Billboard's Top R&B Hits 1965-1969 Box Set.
(S) (4:46) Polydor 831700 CD Of JB II. *(Parts 1 & 2)*
(S) (2:59) Polydor 849108 Star Time. *(:12 longer fade than the 45)*
(S) (2:46) Polydor 511326 20 All Time Greatest Hits.
(S) (4:46) Right Stuff 28373 Movin' On Up. *(Parts 1 & 2)*
(S) (4:50) Polydor 314531165 Foundations Of Funk. *(Parts 1 & 2)*
(S) (4:46) Polydor 422841992 Say It Loud - I'm Black And I'm Proud. *(Parts 1 & 2)*
(S) (4:50) Polydor 314533409 JB 40: 40th Anniversary Collection. *(Parts 1 & 2)*

1968 GOODBYE MY LOVE
(M) (5:36) Polydor 314531165 Foundations Of Funk. *(Parts 1 & 2)*
(S) (5:31) Polydor 422841992 Say It Loud - I'm Black And I'm Proud. *(Parts 1 & 2)*

1969 GIVE IT UP OR TURN IT A LOOSE
(S) (3:16) Polydor 831700 CD Of JB II. *(:31 longer than the 45)*
(S) (3:10) Polydor 849108 Star Time. *(segues together with the preceding selection; :25 longer than the 45)*
(M) (3:10) Polydor 511326 20 All Time Greatest Hits. *(:25 longer than the 45)*
(S) (6:09) Polydor 829624 In The Jungle Groove. *(remixed; 1970 rerecording)*
(S) (6:26) Polydor 314517984 Sex Machine. *(1970 rerecording with overdubbed audience applause)*
(S) (6:24) Polydor 314531684 Funk Power - 1970: A Brand New Thang. *(1970 rerecording without overdubbed audience applause)*
(M) (4:30) Polydor 314531165 Foundations Of Funk. *(45 version but 1:50 longer)*
(S) (2:49) Polydor 314533409 JB 40: 40th Anniversary Collection. *(stereo LP mix)*
(S) (6:09) Rhino 72851 Kurtis Blow Presents The History Of Rap Vol. 1. *(remixed; 1970 rerecording)*

1969 I DON'T WANT NOBODY TO GIVE ME NOTHING (OPEN UP THE DOOR, I'LL GET IT MYSELF) PART 1
(S) (7:01) Polydor 831700 CD Of JB II. *(remix; edit of complete recording session)*
(S) (5:59) Polydor 849108 Star Time. *(Parts 1 & 2; stereo remix)*
(S) (7:01) Right Stuff 28373 Movin' On Up. *(remix; edit of complete recording session)*
(S) (9:42) Polydor 314531165 Foundations Of Funk. *(stereo remix; complete recording session)*
(M) (3:04) Polydor 314533409 JB 40: 40th Anniversary Collection. *(Part 1)*

1969 THE POPCORN
(S) (3:01) Polydor 314517845 Soul Pride - The Instrumentals 1960-1969.

69

JAMES BROWN (Continued)

(S) (4:30) Polydor 314531165 Foundations Of Funk. *(includes :09 of studio talk; complete session recording)*

1969 MOTHER POPCORN (YOU GOT TO HAVE A MOTHER FOR ME) (PART 1)

(S) (3:10) Polydor 825714 CD Of JB.
(S) (3:15) Polydor 511326 20 All Time Greatest Hits.
(S) (6:15) Polydor 849108 Star Time. *(Parts 1 & 2)*
(S) (5:50) Polydor 314517984 Sex Machine. *(live; edited)*
(S) (9:02) Polydor 314531165 Foundations Of Funk. *(live; remixed; unedited)*
(S) (3:15) Polydor 314533409 JB 40: 40th Anniversary Collection.

1969 WORLD (PART 1)

1969 LET A MAN COME IN AND DO THE POPCORN (PART 1)

(S) (7:47) Polydor 314531165 Foundations Of Funk. *(Parts 1 & 2)*

1970 AIN'T IT FUNKY NOW (PART 1)

(S) (7:11) Polydor 314517845 Soul Pride: The Instrumentals 1960-1969. *(slightly longer fade than Parts 1 & 2)*
(S) (7:11) Polygram Special Markets 314520304 70's Funk Classics. *(slightly longer fade than Parts 1 & 2)*
(M) (9:28) Polydor 314531165 Foundations Of Funk. *(LP version at the original recording speed)*
(S) (3:08) Polydor 314533409 JB 40: 40th Anniversary Collection. *(Part 1)*
(M) (3:09) Rebound 314520420 Soul Classics - Best Of The 60's. *(Part 1)*

1970 IT'S A NEW DAY (PART 1)

(S) (3:49) Polydor 849108 Star Time. *(live)*
(S) (6:18) Polydor 829624 In The Jungle Groove. *(Parts 1 & 2)*
(S) (6:25) Polydor 314531165 Foundations Of Funk. *(Parts 1 & 2)*

1970 BROTHER RAPP (PARTS 1 & 2)

(S) (5:09) Polydor 314517984 Sex Machine. *(original studio recording of Parts 1 & 2 overdubbed with audience applause)*
(S) (7:00) Polydor 314531165 Foundations Of Funk. *(remix)*

1970 GET UP (I FEEL LIKE BEING A) SEX MACHINE (PART 1)

(S) (5:03) Polydor 825714 CD Of JB. *(Parts 1 & 2 but missing the :12 introduction)*
(S) (5:16) Polydor 849108 Star Time. *(Parts 1 & 2)*
(M) (5:15) Polydor 511326 20 All Time Greatest Hits. *(Parts 1 & 2)*
(M) (2:52) Rhino 71431 In Yo Face! History Of Funk Volume 1.
(M) (5:15) Time-Life RHD-18 Rhythm & Blues - 1970. *(Parts 1 & 2)*
(S) (5:16) Risky Business 66663 Sex In The Seventies.
(S) (2:48) Rebound 314520034 Funk Classics Of The 70's.
(M) (5:15) Polygram Special Markets 314520304 70's Funk Classics. *(Parts 1 & 2)*
(S) (5:16) Priority 57194 Old School Friday - More Music From The Original Motion Picture. *(Parts 1 & 2)*
(M) (5:15) Hammer & Lace 697124017 O.S.T. The Ride. *(Parts 1 & 2)*
(S) (5:16) Polydor 314531684 Funk Power - 1970: A Brand New Thang. *(Parts 1 & 2)*
(S) (10:30) Polydor 314531684 Funk Power - 1970: A Brand New Thang. *(rerecording with no overdubbed audience applause from the "Sex Machine" LP)*
(S) (5:16) Polydor 314533409 JB 40: 40th Anniversary Collection. *(Parts 1 & 2)*
(M) (5:15) Rebound 314520432 Disco Nights Vol. XI - Disco's Leading Men. *(Parts 1 & 2)*
(M) (5:15) Time-Life R838-05 Solid Gold Soul - 1970. *(Parts 1 & 2)*
(M) (2:52) Rhino 72943 VH1 8-Track Flashback: Classic '70s Soul.

1970 SUPER BAD (PARTS 1 & 2)

(M) (4:11) Rhino 70658 Billboard's Top R&B Hits Of 1970.
(M) (2:57) Polydor 825714 CD Of JB. *(Part 1)*

(M) (4:59) Polydor 511326 20 All Time Greatest Hits. *(Parts 1 & 2 but :50 longer)*
(M) (4:26) Polydor 849108 Star Time. *(Parts 1 & 2 but :17 longer)*
(S) (2:57) Special Music 837726 Spank. *(Part 1)*
(M) (2:57) K-Tel 6011 70's Soul: Super Funky Hits. *(Part 1)*
(M) (2:57) Polygram Special Markets 314520304 70's Funk Classics. *(Part 1)*
(M) (5:01) Rhino 72112 Billboard Hot Soul Hits - 1970. *(Parts 1 & 2 but :52 longer)*
(M) (9:02) Polydor 314531684 Funk Power - 1970: A Brand New Thang. *(LP version without fake audience applause)*
(M) (4:59) Polydor 314533409 JB 40: 40th Anniversary Collection. *(Parts 1 & 2 but :50 longer)*
(M) (2:56) Cold Front 4024 Old School Mega Mix Volume 2. *(Part 1)*

1971 GET UP, GET INTO IT, GET INVOLVED

(S) (7:03) Polydor 849109 Star Time. *(time does not include :28 of "hidden" studio talk and a false start preceding this track)*
(M) (7:05) Polydor 829624 In The Jungle Groove. *(45 mix of Parts 1 & 2)*
(S) (7:04) Polygram Special Markets 314520304 70's Funk Classics.
(S) (7:06) Polydor 314531684 Funk Power - 1970: A Brand New Thang.

1971 SOUL POWER (PART 1)

(M) (3:00) Polydor 825714 CD Of JB. *(:16 shorter than the 45 version)*
(S) (4:24) Polydor 849108 Star Time. *(Parts 1 & 2 with early fade)*
(M) (8:00) Polydor 829624 In The Jungle Groove. *(remixed; edit of Parts 1, 2 & 3)*
(S) (4:23) MCA 11065 O.S.T. Crooklyn Volume II. *(Parts 1 & 2 with early fade)*
(M) (12:04) Polydor 314531684 Funk Power - 1970: A Brand New Thang. *(complete session recording)*
(M) (3:19) Polydor 314533409 JB 40: 40th Anniversary Collection. *(Part 1)*

1971 ESCAPE-ISM (PART 1)

(S) (3:17) Polydor 314517985 Hot Pants.
(S) (19:09) Polydor 314517985 Hot Pants. *(complete recording session; includes :06 of studio talk)*
(S) (3:17) Polygram Special Markets 314520304 70's Funk Classics.
(S) (4:02) Polydor 314533052 Make It Funky - The Big Payback 1971-1975.

1971 HOT PANTS (SHE GOT TO USE WHAT SHE GOT TO GET WHAT SHE WANTS)

(M) (3:06) Polydor 849109 Star Time.
(S) (3:06) Polydor 511326 20 All Time Greatest Hits.
(S) (8:40) Polydor 829624 In The Jungle Groove. *(LP version which is a rerecording of the 45)*
(S) (8:41) Polydor 314517985 Hot Pants. *(LP version which is a rerecording of the 45)*
(M) (3:06) Rebound 314520265 Dance Fever.
(S) (3:08) Rhino 72113 Billboard Hot Soul Hits - 1971.
(S) (6:55) Polydor 314533052 Make It Funky - The Big Payback 1971-1975. *(Parts 1 & 2)*
(S) (3:06) Polydor 314533409 JB 40: 40th Anniversary Collection.

1971 MAKE IT FUNKY (PART 1)

(M) (3:14) Rhino 70659 Billboard's Top R&B Hits Of 1971.
(S) (7:21) Polydor 831700 CD Of JB II. *(remixed and edited version of Parts 1,2,3 &4)*
(M) (3:35) Polydor 849108 Star Time. *(:20 longer fade than the 45)*
(M) (3:15) Polydor 511326 20 All Time Greatest Hits.
(M) (3:16) Rhino 71432 In Yo Face! History Of Funk Volume 2.
(M) (3:15) Polygram Special Markets 314520304 70's Funk Classics.
(M) (3:14) Thump 4040 Old School Volume 4.
(M) (12:45) Polydor 314533052 Make It Funky - The Big Payback 1971-1975. *(Parts 1, 2, 3 & 4)*
(M) (3:14) Polydor 314533409 JB 40: 40th Anniversary Collection.

1971 I'M A GREEDY MAN (PART 1)
- (S) (6:29) Polydor 831700 CD Of JB II. *(remix and edit of Parts 1 & 2)*
- (S) (3:35) Polydor 849108 Star Time.
- (S) (7:03) Polydor 314517986 There It Is. *(Parts 1 & 2)*
- (S) (3:36) Special Music 837726 Spank.
- (S) (7:07) Polydor 314533052 Make It Funky - The Big Payback 1971-1975. *(Parts 1 & 2)*

1972 TALKING LOUD AND SAYING NOTHING (PART 1)
- (S) (7:42) Polydor 829624 In The Jungle Groove. *(remix of Parts 1 & 2)*
- (S) (9:00) Polydor 849108 Star Time. *(extended version of Parts 1 & 2)*
- (S) (7:45) Polydor 314517986 There It Is. *(Parts 1 & 2 of the 45 release)*
- (S) (3:15) Rhino 72114 Billboard Hot Soul Hits - 1972.
- (S) (14:41) Polydor 314531684 Funk Power - 1970: A Brand New Thang. *(complete session recording)*
- (S) (3:22) Polydor 314533409 JB 40: 40th Anniversary Collection.

1972 KING HEROIN
- (S) (3:56) Polydor 849108 Star Time.
- (S) (3:56) Polydor 314517986 There It Is.
- (S) (3:55) Polydor 314533052 Make It Funky - The Big Payback 1971-1975.
- (S) (3:55) Polydor 314533409 JB 40: 40th Anniversary Collection.

1972 THERE IT IS (PART 1)
- (M) (5:47) Polydor 314517986 There It Is. *(Parts 1 & 2)*
- (M) (3:21) Polydor 849108 Star Time. *(Part 1 but :16 longer fade)*
- (M) (5:47) Polydor 314533052 Make It Funky - The Big Payback 1971-1975. *(Parts 1 & 2)*
- (M) (3:05) Polydor 314533409 JB 40: 40th Anniversary Collection. *(Part 1)*
- (M) (2:55) Chronicles 314555140 Dance Funk. *(all selections on this cd are segued together)*

1972 HONKY TONK (PART 1)
- (S) (6:07) Polydor 847258 Messing With The Blues. *(edited version of Parts 1 & 2; ends cold)*

1972 GET ON THE GOOD FOOT (PART 1)
- (M) (3:32) Rhino 70660 Billboard's Top R&B Hits Of 1972.
- (S) (5:16) Polydor 831700 CD Of JB II. *(Parts 1 & 2)*
- (M) (4:08) Polydor 849108 Star Time. *(remixed and extended fade)*
- (M) (3:34) Polydor 511326 20 All Time Greatest Hits.
- (M) (3:34) Time-Life RHD-20 Rhythm & Blues - 1972.
- (M) (5:44) Polydor 314523982 Get On The Good Foot. *(complete session recording)*
- (M) (5:44) Polydor 314533052 Make It Funky - The Big Payback 1971-1975. *(complete session recording)*
- (M) (3:34) Polydor 314533409 JB 40: 40th Anniversary Collection.
- (M) (3:34) Time-Life R838-07 Solid Gold Soul - 1972.
- (M) (3:34) Polygram Special Markets 314520446 Soul Hits Of The 70's.

1972 I GOT A BAG OF MY OWN
- (S) (3:47) Polydor 849108 Star Time. *(remixed LP version with extended fade)*
- (S) (3:30) Polydor 314523982 Get On The Good Foot. *(LP version; tracks into next selection)*
- (S) (3:46) Polydor 314533052 Make It Funky - The Big Payback 1971-1975. *(LP version with extended fade)*

1973 I GOT ANTS IN MY PANTS (AND I WANT TO DANCE) (PART 1)
- (S) (3:01) Polydor 849108 Star Time.
- (S) (7:25) Polydor 314533052 Make It Funky - The Big Payback 1971-1975. *(complete session recording but remixed)*

1974 THE PAYBACK (PART 1)
- (S) (3:29) Rhino 70662 Billboard's Top R&B Hits Of 1974. *(45 version)*
- (S) (7:38) Polydor 511326 20 All-Time Greatest Hits! *(LP version)*
- (S) (7:27) Polydor 849108 Star Time. *(LP version but missing the sound effects at the end)*
- (S) (7:39) Polydor 314517137 The Payback. *(LP version)*
- (S) (7:31) Rhino 71434 In Yo Face! History Of Funk Volume 4. *(LP version but missing the sound effects at the end)*
- (S) (7:26) Thump 7030 Low Rider Oldies Volume III. *(LP version but missing the sound effects at the end)*
- (S) (3:19) Original Sound 9304 Art Laboe's Dedicated To You Vol. 4. *(45 version)*
- (S) (7:39) Polygram Special Markets 314520304 70's Funk Classics. *(LP version)*
- (S) (7:39) Capitol 32438 O.S.T. Dead Presidents. *(LP version)*
- (S) (7:39) Priority 53074 Da Funk. *(LP version)*
- (S) (7:36) Polydor 314533052 Make It Funky - The Big Payback 1971-1975. *(LP version; tracks into next selection)*
- (S) (7:38) Polydor 314533409 JB 40: 40th Anniversary Collection. *(LP version)*
- (S) (3:29) Rebound 314520430 Funk Classics Of The 70's Vol. 2. *(45 version; on original pressings of this cd this track was not "THE PAYBACK" as stated on the cd jacket but a medley of James Brown hits performed live)*
- (S) (7:27) Chronicles 314555137 Funk Of The 70's. *(LP version but missing the sound effects at the end)*

1974 MY THANG
- (S) (4:38) Polydor 849108 Star Time. *(remixed without percussion overdubs)*
- (S) (4:15) Special Music 837726 Spank. *(45 version)*
- (S) (4:19) Polygram Special Markets 314520304 70's Funk Classics. *(LP version)*
- (S) (4:19) Polydor 314523983 Hell. *(LP version)*
- (S) (4:17) Rhino 72116 Billboard Hot Soul Hits - 1974. *(45 version)*
- (S) (4:14) Polydor 314533052 Make It Funky - The Big Payback 1971-1975. *(45 version)*
- (S) (4:14) Polydor 314533409 JB 40: 40th Anniversary Collection. *(45 version)*

1974 PAPA DON'T TAKE NO MESS (PART 1)
- (S) (4:33) Polydor 511326 20 All-Time Greatest Hits! *(LP version with 45 fade)*
- (S) (4:33) Polydor 831700 CD Of JB II. *(LP version with 45 fade)*
- (S) (4:24) Polydor 849108 Star Time. *(LP version faded :09 early)*
- (S) (4:30) Rhino 71433 In Yo Face! History Of Funk Volume 3. *(45 version)*
- (S) (4:29) Special Music 837726 Spank. *(LP version with 45 fade)*
- (S) (13:49) Polydor 314523983 Hell. *(LP version)*
- (S) (13:49) Polydor 314533052 Make It Funky - The Big Payback 1971-1975. *(LP version)*
- (S) (4:29) Polydor 314533409 JB 40: 40th Anniversary Collection. *(45 version)*
- (S) (4:30) Time-Life R838-09 Solid Gold Soul - 1974. *(45 version)*

1986 LIVING IN AMERICA
- (S) (5:57) Capitol 81475 Rites Of Rhythm & Blues. *(remixed)*
- (S) (5:57) Scotti Brothers 5212 and 75212 Gravity. *(remixed)*
- (S) (4:42) Scotti Brothers 40203 and 75420 O.S.T. Rocky IV. *(LP version)*
- (S) (4:41) Scotti Brothers 5201 and 75201 The Rocky Story. *(LP version)*
- (S) (4:07) Scotti Brothers 75467 Living In America. *(45 version)*
- (S) (5:57) Scotti Brothers 75259 Greatest Hits Of The Fourth Decade. *(remixed)*

71

MAXINE BROWN
1961 ALL IN MY MIND
- (M) (2:32) Capricorn 42003 The Scepter Records Story.
- (E) (2:30) Original Sound CDGO-1 Golden Oldies Volume. 1.
- (M) (2:24) Collectables 5116 Golden Classics.
- (M) (2:30) Time-Life 2RNR-25 Rock 'N' Roll Era - The 60's Keep On Rockin'.
- (M) (2:29) Time-Life RHD-14 Rhythm & Blues - 1961.
- (M) (2:29) Tomato 71740 Greatest Hits.
- (M) (2:32) Curb 77829 Greatest Hits.
- (M) (2:29) Ripete 2223 Soul Patrol Vol. 5.
- (M) (2:32) Time-Life R857-14 The Heart Of Rock 'n' Roll 1960-1961 Take Two.
- (M) (2:29) Time-Life R838-19 Solid Gold Soul 1961.

1961 FUNNY
- (S) (2:32) Capricorn 42003 The Scepter Records Story.
- (M) (2:15) Collectables 5116 Golden Classics. (mastered from vinyl)
- (M) (2:28) Tomato 71740 Greatest Hits.
- (S) (2:29) Curb 77829 Greatest Hits.

1964 OH NO NOT MY BABY
- (S) (2:35) Capricorn 42003 The Scepter Records Story.
- (S) (2:34) Collectables 5116 Golden Classics.
- (M) (2:37) Era 5025 The Brill Building Sound. (buzz noticeable on fadeout)
- (S) (2:34) Time-Life RHD-12 Rhythm & Blues - 1964.
- (M) (2:34) Time-Life 2CLR-09 Classic Rock - 1964: The Beat Goes On.
- (S) (2:34) Time-Life R962-08 History Of Rock 'N' Roll: Sound Of The City 1959-1965.
- (S) (2:34) Ripete 2163-RE Ebb Tide.
- (M) (2:33) Tomato 71740 Greatest Hits.
- (S) (2:35) Right Stuff 30578 Slow Jams: The 60's Volume 4.
- (S) (2:34) Curb 77829 Greatest Hits.
- (S) (2:34) Time-Life R838-13 Solid Gold Soul - 1964.
- (M) (2:40) Rhino 72815 Beg, Scream & Shout! The Big Ol' Box Of '60s Soul.
- (S) (2:35) Repeat/Relativity 1610 Tighten Up: #1 Soul Hits Of The 60's Volume 2.

NAPPY BROWN
1955 DON'T BE ANGRY
- (M) (2:24) Time-Life 2RNR-43 Rock 'N' Roll Era - Roots Of Rock II.
- (M) (2:23) Time-Life RHD-17 Rhythm & Blues - 1955.
- (M) (2:23) Savoy Jazz 0259 Don't Be Angry.

PETER BROWN
1977 DO YA WANNA GET FUNKY WITH ME
- (S) (6:38) Hot Productions 11 Best Of The Sound Of Sunshine. (neither the 45, LP or 12" version)
- (S) (2:46) Collectables 5431 Disco Party: Best Of The T.K. Collection. (neither the 45, LP or 12" version)
- (S) (3:41) Rhino 71095 Disco Hits, Vol. 2. (45 version)
- (S) (3:42) Rhino 71003 Get Down tonight: The Best Of T.K. Records. (45 version)
- (S) (3:41) K-Tel 3251 Disco Fever. (45 version)
- (S) (3:41) JCI 3163 18 Disco Superhits. (45 version)
- (S) (9:06) Rhino 72588 Phat Trax: The Best Of Old School, Vol. 7. (neither the 45, LP or 12" version)
- (S) (3:41) Flashback 72689 Disco Hits: Shake Your Booty. (45 version)

1978 DANCE WITH ME
- (S) (5:09) Priority 7976 Mega-Hits Dance Classics Volume 6. (LP version)
- (S) (3:48) Rhino 70984 The Disco Years Volume 1. (45 version)
- (S) (3:48) Rhino 71003 Get Down Tonight: The Best Of T.K. Records. (45 version)
- (S) (3:47) Rhino 71095 Disco Hits Volume 2. (45 version)
- (S) (3:48) Essex 7051 Non-Stop Dance Hits. (45 version)
- (S) (5:18) Hot Productions 11 Best Of The Sound Of Sunshine. (LP version)
- (S) (3:48) Rhino 72130 Soul Hits Of The 70's Vol. 20. (45 version)

- (S) (3:47) Flashback 72689 Disco Hits: Shake Your Booty. (45 version)
- (S) (3:47) Time-Life R840-08 Sounds Of The Seventies: '70s Dance Party 1978-1979. (45 version)

POLLY BROWN
1975 UP IN A PUFF OF SMOKE
- (S) (3:26) Rhino 70761 Super Hits Of The 70's Volume 14.

ROY BROWN
1957 LET THE FOUR WINDS BLOW
- (M) (2:01) Rhino 75765 The Best Of New Orleans Rhythm & Blues, Vol. 1.
- (M) (2:01) EMI 37350 Crescent City Soul: The Sound Of New Orleans 1947-1974.
- (M) (2:01) EMI 37355 Highlights From Crescent City Soul: The Sound Of New Orleans 1947-1974.
- (M) (2:00) EMI 37356 That's Fats! - A Tribute To Fats Domino.

RUTH BROWN
1957 LUCKY LIPS
- (M) (2:07) Atlantic 81295 Atlantic Rhythm & Blues Volume 3.
- (M) (2:05) Atlantic 82061 Miss Rhythm.
- (M) (2:07) Atlantic 82305 Atlantic Rhythm And Blues 1947-1974 Box Set.
- (E) (2:05) Rhino 70279 Rare Soul: Beach Music Classics Volume 3.
- (M) (2:06) Rhino 72450 Best Of.

1958 THIS LITTLE GIRL'S GONE ROCKIN'
- (M) (1:45) Atlantic 82061 Miss Rhythm.
- (M) (1:46) Rhino 72450 Best Of.

SHIRLEY BROWN
1974 WOMAN TO WOMAN
- (S) (3:53) Rhino 70662 Billboard's Top R&B Hits Of 1974.
- (S) (3:53) Rhino 70555 Soul Hits Of The 70's Volume 15.
- (S) (3:53) Stax 88005 Top Of The Stax.
- (S) (3:53) Stax 4135 Woman To Woman.
- (S) (3:53) Original Sound 8911 Art Laboe's Dedicated To You Vol. 2.
- (S) (3:53) Original Sound 4001 Art Laboe's 60 Killer Oldies.
- (S) (3:52) Right Stuff 29140 Slow Jams: The Timeless Collection Volume 2.
- (S) (3:53) Stax 4415 Complete Stax/Volt Soul Singles Volume 3 1972-1975.

JACKSON BROWNE
1972 DOCTOR MY EYES
- (S) (3:14) Asylum 5051 Saturate Before Using. (remixed)
- (S) (3:11) Epic 57871 O.S.T. My Girl 2.
- (S) (3:18) Elektra 62111 The Next Voice You Hear: Best Of. (remixed)
- (S) (3:13) Time-Life R13610 Gold And Platinum Box Set - The Ultimate Rock Collection. (remixed)

1977 HERE COME THOSE TEARS AGAIN
- (S) (3:36) Asylum 107 The Pretender. (LP length)
- (S) (3:36) DCC Compact Classics 1047 The Pretender. (LP length; gold disc)

1978 RUNNING ON EMPTY
- (S) (5:29) Asylum 113 Running On Empty. (LP version)
- (S) (4:54) Elektra 62111 The Next Voice You Hear: Best Of. (45 version)

1978 STAY
- (S) (3:25) Asylum 113 Running On Empty. (LP version which is a medley of "THE LOAD OUT" (5:35)/"STAY" (3:25))

1978 THE LOAD OUT
- (S) (5:35) Asylum 113 Running On Empty. (LP version which is a medley of "THE LOAD OUT" (5:35)/"STAY" (3:25))

1980 BOULEVARD
- (S) (3:19) Asylum 511 Hold Out.

1980 THAT GIRL COULD SING
- (S) (4:34) Asylum 511 Hold Out.

1982 SOMEBODY'S BABY
- (S) (4:02) Full Moon/Elektra 60158 O.S.T. Fast Times At Ridgemont High.

(S) (4:22) Elektra 62111 The Next Voice You Hear: Best Of. *(previously unreleased version)*

1983 LAWYERS IN LOVE
(S) (4:18) Asylum 60268 Lawyers In Love.

1983 TENDER IS THE NIGHT
(S) (4:52) Asylum 60268 Lawyers In Love.
(S) (4:53) Elektra 62111 The Next Voice You Hear: Best Of.

released as by CLARENCE CLEMONS and JACKSON BROWNE:
1986 YOU'RE A FRIEND OF MINE
(S) (4:49) Risky Business 57833 Read The Hits/Best Of The 80's. *(LP version)*
(S) (4:50) Columbia 40010 Clarence Clemons - Hero. *(LP version)*
(S) (4:48) Time-Life R988-17 Sounds Of The Eighties: The Mid '80s Take Two. *(LP version)*

released as by JACKSON BROWNE:
1986 FOR AMERICA
(dj copies of this 45 ran (4:14) and (5:10);
commercial copies were all (5:10))
(S) (5:09) Asylum 60457 Lives In The Balance.

BROWNS
1959 THE THREE BELLS
(M) (2:49) RCA 9902 Nipper's #1 Hits 1956-1986.
(S) (2:49) RCA 8466 Nipper's Greatest Hits Of The 50's Volume 1.
(S) (2:49) Rhino 70680 Billboard's Top Country Hits Of 1959.
(S) (2:49) Time-Life CTD-09 Country USA - 1959.
(S) (2:48) Time-Life HPD-13 Your Hit Parade - 1959.
(M) (2:51) RCA 66783 The Essential.
(S) (2:48) Time-Life R132-14 Golden Groups Of Your Hit Parade.
(S) (2:49) Time-Life R808-03 Classic Country 1950-1959.

1959 SCARLET RIBBONS (FOR HER HAIR)
(S) (2:34) Time-Life HPD-13 Your Hit Parade - 1959.
(M) (2:37) RCA 66783 The Essential. *(part of the first word is clipped off)*

1960 THE OLD LAMPLIGHTER
(S) (2:20) RCA 8475 Nipper's Greatest Hits Of The 60's Volume 2.
(S) (2:20) Time-Life R857-10 The Heart Of Rock 'n' Roll 1960-1961.

BROWNSTONE
1995 IF YOU LOVE ME
(S) (5:03) MJJ Music 57827 From The Bottom Up.
(S) (3:40) Tommy Boy 1139 MTV Party To Go Volume 8. *(all selections on this cd are segued together)*
(S) (7:33) Epic 67505 If You Love Dance. *(remix)*
(S) (5:02) EMI-Capitol Music Group 54548 Smooth Luv.

BROWNSVILLE STATION
1974 SMOKIN' IN THE BOYS ROOM
(S) (2:56) JCI 3302 Electric Seventies.
(S) (2:56) Atlantic 81909 Hit Singles 1958-1977.
(S) (2:56) Rhino 70721 Legends Of Guitar: The 70's Volume 1.
(S) (2:55) Sire 6070 Rock 'N' Roll High School.
(S) (2:55) Rhino 71197 Super Hits Of The 70's Volume 17.
(S) (2:56) Rhino 71456 Smokin' In The Boys Room: Best Of.
(S) (2:55) Razor & Tie 22502 Those Rocking 70's.
(S) (2:55) Time-Life R968-01 Guitar Rock 1974-1975.
(S) (2:55) Time-Life SOD-07 Sounds Of The Seventies - 1974.
(S) (2:56) Time-Life OPCD-4521 Guitar Rock.
(S) (2:56) Rhino 72131 Frat Rock: The 70's.
(S) (2:56) JCI 3140 18 Screamers From The 70's.
(S) (2:55) K-Tel 3913 Superstars Greatest Hits Volume 2.
(S) (2:56) Simitar 55502 The Number One's: Classic Rock.
(S) (2:56) Hip-O 40095 '70s Hit(s) Back.

1974 I'M THE LEADER OF THE GANG
(S) (3:21) Rhino 71456 Smokin' In The Boys Room: Best Of. *(with countoff)*

1974 KINGS OF THE PARTY
(S) (4:14) Rhino 71456 Smokin' In The Boys Room: Best Of. *(LP version)*

DAVE BRUBECK QUARTET
1961 TAKE FIVE
(S) (5:23) Columbia 40585 and 52860 and 65122 Time Out. *(LP version)*
(S) (5:23) Columbia/Legacy 52945 Time Signatures. *(LP version)*
(S) (5:22) Verve 314521007 Playboy's 40th Anniversary: Four Decades Of Jazz (1953-1993). *(LP version)*
(S) (5:23) Columbia/Legacy 47931 The Essence Of. *(LP version)*
(M) (2:52) Time-Life HPD-32 Your Hit Parade - Into The 60's. *(45 version)*
(S) (5:24) Legacy/Columbia 64160 Jazz Collection. *(LP version)*
(S) (5:24) Columbia/Legacy 65417 Greatest Hits. *(LP version)*

ANITA BRYANT
1959 TILL THERE WAS YOU
(S) (2:07) Collectables 5649 A Golden Classics Edition. *(rerecording)*

1960 PAPER ROSES
(S) (2:49) Collectables 5649 A Golden Classics Edition. *(rerecording)*

1960 IN MY LITTLE CORNER OF THE WORLD
(S) (2:36) Collectables 5649 A Golden Classics Edition. *(rerecording)*

1960 WONDERLAND BY NIGHT

RAY BRYANT COMBO
1960 MADISON TIME (PART 1)
(S) (3:05) Rhino 70992 Groove 'n' Grind.
(M) (3:05) MCA 6228 O.S.T. Hairspray.
(M) (3:06) Rhino 71602 Rock Instrumental Classics Volume 2: The Sixties.
(M) (3:06) Rhino 72035 Rock Instrumental Classics Vols. 1-5 Box Set.
(S) (3:05) Time-Life 2RNR-44 Rock 'N' Roll Era - Lost Treasures.
(S) (3:05) Time-Life RHD-15 Rhythm & Blues - 1960.
(S) (3:05) Collectables 5499 The Madison Time With A Hollywood Jazz Beat.
(S) (3:05) Nick At Nite/550 Music 63407 Dancing At The Nick At Niteclub.
(S) (3:05) Time-Life R838-20 Solid Gold Soul 1960.

SHARON BRYANT
1989 LET GO
(S) (4:51) Wing 837313 Here I Am.

PEABO BRYSON
released as by PEABO BRYSON/ROBERTA FLACK:
1983 TONIGHT, I CELEBRATE MY LOVE
(S) (3:29) Priority 7040 Making Love.
(S) (3:29) Scotti Brothers 75434 Romantic Duets.
(S) (3:28) Capitol 46071 Peabo Bryson Collection.
(S) (3:29) Atlantic 82498 Roberta Flack - Softly With These Songs: Best Of.
(S) (3:29) CEMA Special Markets 35966 Tonight I Celebrate My Love.
(S) (3:29) DCC Compact Classics 104 Duets - A Man & A Woman.
(S) (3:29) MCA 11431 Quiet Storms 2.
(S) (3:28) Madacy Entertainment 6803 Power Of Love.
(S) (3:29) Time-Life R834-08 Body Talk - On My Mind.
(S) (3:29) Angel 56580 Men Are From Mars, Women Are From Venus - Songs For Loving Couples.

released as by PEABO BRYSON:
1984 IF EVER YOU'RE IN MY ARMS AGAIN
(S) (3:55) K-Tel 3263 The 80's Love Jams. *(45 speed and length)*

PEABO BRYSON *(Continued)*

    (S)   (4:13)   Elektra 60362 Straight From The Heart. *(LP speed and length)*

    (S)   (4:13)   Priority 53700 80's Greatest Rock Hits Volume 13 - Soft Sounds. *(LP speed and length)*

    (S)   (4:13)   Time-Life R138-18 Body Talk. *(LP speed and length)*

    (S)   (4:12)   Time-Life R988-15 Sounds Of The Eighties: The Mid 80's. *(LP speed and length)*

    (S)   (4:13)   Time-Life R834-02 Body Talk - Just For You. *(LP speed and length)*

    (S)   (4:13)   JCI 3176 1980 - Only Soul - 1984. *(LP speed and length)*

    (S)   (4:14)   K-Tel 6257 The Greatest Love Songs - 16 Soft Rock Hits. *(LP speed and length)*

released as by CELINE DION and PEABO BRYSON:
1992 BEAUTY AND THE BEAST

    (S)   (4:02)   Walt Disney 60618 O.S.T. Beauty And The Beast.

    (S)   (4:03)   Epic 52473 Celine Dion.

released as by PEABO BRYSON and REGINA BELLE:
1993 A WHOLE NEW WORLD (ALADDIN'S THEME)

    (S)   (4:04)   Walt Disney 60846 O.S.T. Aladdin.

    (S)   (4:03)   Columbia 48826 Regina Belle - Passion.

    (S)   (4:04)   EMI-Capitol Music Group 54555 Movie Luv.

released as by KENNY G with PEABO BRYSON:
1993 BY THE TIME THIS NIGHT IS OVER

    (S)   (4:44)   Arista 18646 Kenny G - Breathless.

B.T. EXPRESS
1974 DO IT ('TIL YOU'RE SATISFIED)

    (S)   (5:40)   Priority 7976 Mega-Hits Dance Classics Volume 6. *(introduction is :10 shorter than the LP version)*

    (S)   (3:11)   Rhino 70553 Soul Hits Of The 70's Volume 13. *(first pressings of this cd erroneously inserted "EXPRESS" instead of "DO IT ('TIL YOU'RE SATISFIED)"; 45 version)*

    (S)   (5:51)   Collectables 5190 Golden Classics. *(LP version)*

    (S)   (3:11)   Rhino 71432 In Yo Face! History Of Funk Volume 2. *(45 version)*

    (S)   (5:51)   Pair 1325 Do It!! Non Stop. *(LP version; incorrectly identified on the cd jacket as "EXPRESS")*

    (S)   (5:39)   Time-Life SOD-27 Sounds Of The Seventies - Dance Fever. *(introduction is :11 shorter than the LP version)*

    (S)   (5:51)   K-Tel 6011 70's Soul: Super Funky Hits. *(LP version)*

    (S)   (3:11)   Rhino 72116 Billboard Hot Soul Hits - 1974. *(45 version)*

    (S)   (5:50)   Giant 24571 O.S.T. Inkwell. *(LP version)*

    (S)   (5:50)   Priority 53142 Mega Hits - Disco Express. *(LP version)*

    (S)   (3:11)   Time-Life R838-09 Solid Gold Soul - 1974. *(45 version)*

    (S)   (5:51)   Rebound 314520430 Funk Classics Of The 70's Vol. 2. *(LP version)*

    (S)   (5:50)   Rebound 314520447 Soul Classics - Best Of The 70's. *(LP version)*

    (S)   (5:51)   Rhino 72735 Best Of. *(LP version)*

    (S)   (3:11)   Robbins 75002 Strip Jointz - Hot Songs For Sexy Dancers. *(45 version)*

    (S)   (5:50)   K-Tel 4020 Great R&B Funk Bands Of The 70's. *(LP version)*

    (S)   (5:50)   Chronicles 314555137 Funk Of The 70's. *(LP version)*

    (S)   (5:49)   Cold Front 4024 Old School Mega Mix Volume 2. *(LP version)*

    (S)   (5:48)   Collectables 5878 Roadshow Classics. *(LP version)*

    (S)   (3:11)   Hip-O 40092 Disco 54: Where We Started From. *(45 version)*

    (S)   (3:11)   Time-Life R840-05 Sounds Of The Seventies: '70s Dance Party 1972-1974. *(45 version)*

1975 EXPRESS
(actual 45 time is (3:30) not (3:25) as stated on the record label)

    (S)   (4:49)   Priority 7975 Mega-Hits Dance Classics Volume 5. *(:14 shorter than the LP version)*

    (S)   (3:30)   Rhino 70554 Soul Hits Of The 70's Volume 14. *(45 version)*

    (S)   (5:03)   Collectables 5190 Golden Classics. *(LP version)*

    (S)   (3:31)   Rhino 71603 Rock Instrumental Classics Volume 3: The Seventies. *(45 version)*

    (S)   (3:31)   Rhino 72035 Rock Instrumental Classics Vols. 1-5 Box Set. *(45 version)*

    (S)   (5:04)   Pair 1325 Do It!! Non Stop. *(LP version; incorrectly identified on the cd jacket as "THE HOUSE IS SMOKIN'")*

    (S)   (5:04)   Priority 53789 Disco Attack. *(LP version)*

    (S)   (3:29)   Time-Life R840-04 Sounds Of The Seventies: A Loss For Words. *(45 version)*

    (S)   (3:30)   Time-Life R838-10 Solid Gold Soul - 1975. *(45 version)*

    (S)   (5:04)   Rhino 72735 Best Of. *(LP version)*

    (S)   (4:58)   Collectables 5878 Roadshow Classics. *(LP version)*

1975 PEACE PIPE
(dj copies of this 45 ran (6:04) and (3:36); commercial copies were all (3:36))

    (S)   (6:03)   Collectables 5190 Golden Classics. *(LP version)*

    (S)   (6:03)   Pair 1325 Do It!! Non Stop. *(LP version)*

    (S)   (6:02)   Rhino 72735 Best Of. *(LP version)*

    (S)   (3:31)   Robbins Entertainment 75005 Super Rare Disco. *(45 version)*

1975 GIVE IT WHAT YOU GOT

    (S)   (3:26)   Rhino 72128 Hot Soul Hits Of The 70's Vol. 18. *(faded :18 earlier than the 45)*

    (S)   (4:17)   Collectables 5190 Golden Classics. *(LP length)*

    (S)   (4:08)   Pair 1325 Do It!! Non Stop. *(:10 shorter than LP length)*

    (S)   (3:26)   Rhino 72128 Soul Hits Of The 70's Vol. 18. *(faded :18 earlier than the 45)*

    (S)   (4:16)   Rhino 72735 Best Of. *(LP length)*

BUBBLE PUPPY
1969 HOT SMOKE & SASAFRASS

    (S)   (2:35)   K-Tel 686 Battle Of The Bands Volume 4.

    (S)   (2:30)   Original Sound CDGO-4 Golden Oldies Volume. 4.

    (S)   (2:33)   Collectables 0558 A Gathering Of Promises.

    (S)   (2:37)   Time-Life R968-07 Guitar Rock 1968-1969.

    (S)   (2:38)   Varese Sarabande 5705 Dick Bartley Presents Collector's Essentials: The 60's.

    (S)   (2:35)   K-Tel 3610 Psychedelic Mind Trip Vol. 2: Another Flashback.

BUCHANAN and GOODMAN
1956 THE FLYING SAUCER (PARTS 1 & 2)

    (M)   (4:19)   Rhino 70599 Billboard's Top Rock & Roll Hits Of 1956. *(mastered from vinyl)*

    (M)   (4:18)   Time-Life 2RNR-37 Rock 'N' Roll Era - Weird, Wild & Wacky. *(mastered from vinyl)*

    (M)   (4:18)   K-Tel 3037 Wacky Weirdos. *(mastered from vinyl)*

    (E)   (2:12)   Hot 33205 Greatest Fables. *(Part 1)*

    (E)   (1:44)   Hot 33205 Greatest Fables. *(Part 2)*

    (M)   (4:18)   Varese Sarabande 5882 They Came From Outer Space.

1957 FLYING SAUCER THE 2ND

    (E)   (2:10)   Hot 33205 Greatest Fables.

BUCHANAN BROTHERS
1969 MEDICINE MAN (PART 1)

    (S)   (3:17)   Razor & Tie 2028 Cashman & West: The AM-FM Blues (Their Very Best). *(neither the 45 or LP version; 45 introduction but different ending)*

    (S)   (3:14)   Collectables 0599 Medicine Man. *(LP version; previous selction tracks over the introduction just like the vinyl LP)*

    (S)   (3:17)   Varese Sarabande 5705 Dick Bartley Presents Collector's Essentials: The 60's. *(neither the 45 or LP version; 45 introduction but different ending)*

LINDSEY BUCKINGHAM ✕
1982 TROUBLE
  (S) (3:53) Warner Brothers 561   Law And Order.
1984 GO INSANE
  (S) (3:05) Elektra 60363   Go Insane.
  (S) (3:04) Time-Life R988-27   Sounds Of The Eighties: The Rolling Stone Collection 1983-1985.

BUCKINGHAMS
1967 KIND OF A DRAG
  (S) (2:07) Rhino 70628   Billboard's Top Rock & Roll Hits Of 1967. *(remixed)*
  (S) (2:04) Columbia 45019   Pop Classics Of The 60's. *(remixed)*
  (S) (2:06) Columbia/Legacy 46984   Rock Artifacts Volume 4. *(original mix)*
  (S) (2:07) Columbia 9812   Greatest Hits. *(remixed)*
  (S) (2:06) Columbia/Legacy 47718   Mercy, Mercy, Mercy. *(original mix)*
  (M) (2:08) Time-Life 2CLR-05   Classic Rock - 1967. *(no fidelity)*
1967 LAUDY MISS CLAUDY
  (S) (2:05) Columbia/Legacy 46984   Rock Artifacts Volume 4. *(includes :03 of studio talk and :02 of guitar intro that was spliced off the 45 version)*
  (S) (1:59) Columbia 9812   Greatest Hits.
  (S) (2:04) Columbia/Legacy 47718   Mercy, Mercy, Mercy. *(includes :03 of studio talk and :02 of guitar intro that was spliced off the 45 version)*
1967 DON'T YOU CARE
  (S) (2:25) Columbia 9812   Greatest Hits.
  (S) (2:27) Columbia/Legacy 47718   Mercy, Mercy, Mercy.
  (M) (2:29) Varese Sarabande 5802   Sunshine Days - Pop Classics Of The '60s Volume 2.
1967 MERCY, MERCY, MERCY
  (S) (2:46) Columbia 45018   Rock Classics Of The 60's.
  (S) (2:46) Columbia 9812   Greatest Hits.
  (S) (2:46) Columbia/Legacy 47718   Mercy, Mercy, Mercy.
  (S) (2:46) Time-Life 2CLR-10   Classic Rock - 1967: The Beat Goes On.
1967 HEY BABY (THEY'RE PLAYING OUR SONG)
  (S) (2:48) Columbia/Legacy 46983   Rock Artifacts Volume 3. *(:04 seconds of studio talk prior to the intro and more talk over the first few seconds of the song; slightly longer fade than the single)*
  (S) (2:37) Columbia 9812   Greatest Hits.
  (S) (2:48) Columbia/Legacy 47718   Mercy, Mercy, Mercy. *(same comments as for Columbia/Legacy 46983)*
1968 SUSAN
  (dj copies ran (2:17) and (2:48); commercial copies were all (2:48))
  (S) (2:55) Columbia/Legacy 46983   Rock Artifacts Volume 3. *(:07 longer than the 45 or LP)*
  (S) (2:43) Columbia 9812   Greatest Hits. *(:05 shorter than the 45 or LP)*
  (S) (2:55) Columbia/Legacy 47718   Mercy, Mercy, Mercy. *(:07 longer than the 45 or LP)*
  (S) (2:14) Varese Sarabande 5847   On The Radio Volume Two. *(dj 45 edit)*

BUCKNER & GARCIA ✕
1982 PAC-MAN FEVER
  (S) (3:46) K-Tel 3629   Madcap Melodies.

BUFFALO SPRINGFIELD
1967 FOR WHAT IT'S WORTH (STOP, HEY WHAT'S THAT SOUND)
  (S) (2:36) Atlantic 81909   Hit Singles 1958-1977.
  (S) (2:33) Atlantic 82032   The Wonder Years.
  (S) (2:34) Atco 33200   Buffalo Springfield.
  (S) (2:37) Atco 38105   Best Of.
  (S) (2:34) Time-Life R102-34   The Rolling Stone Collection.
  (S) (2:37) Epic 66329   O.S.T. Forrest Gump.
  (S) (2:38) Elektra 62080   Buffalo Springfield.

JIMMY BUFFETT
1974 COME MONDAY
  (S) (3:08) MCA 5633 and 11169   Songs You Know By Heart/Greatest Hits.
  (S) (3:08) MCA 31059   Living And Dying In 3/4 Time.
  (S) (3:07) MCA 10613   Boats Beaches Bars & Ballads.
  (S) (3:08) MCA 11169   Songs You Know By Heart/Greatest Hits. *(gold disc)*
1977 MARGARITAVILLE
  (S) (4:10) MCA 5633 and 11169   Songs You Know By Heart/Greatest Hits. *(LP version)*
  (S) (4:09) MCA 31070   Changes In Latitudes, Changes In Attitudes. *(LP version)*
  (S) (4:09) MCA 10613   Boats Beaches Bars & Ballads. *(LP version)*
  (S) (4:09) MCA 11169   Songs You Know By Heart/Greatest Hits. *(gold disc; LP version)*
  (S) (4:09) MCA 10951   Changes In Latitudes, Changes In Attitudes. *(gold disc; LP version)*
  (S) (4:09) Time-Life R13610   Gold And Platinum Box Set - The Ultimate Rock Collection. *(LP version)*
1977 CHANGES IN LATITUDES, CHANGES IN ATTITUDES
  (S) (3:14) MCA 5633 and 11169   Songs You Know By Heart/Greatest Hits.
  (S) (3:16) MCA 31070   Changes In Latitudes, Changes In Attitudes.
  (S) (3:14) MCA 10613   Boats Beaches Bars & Ballads.
  (S) (3:16) MCA 11169   Songs You Know By Heart/Greatest Hits. *(gold disc)*
  (S) (3:17) MCA 10951   Changes In Latitudes, Changes In Attitudes. *(gold disc)*
1978 CHEESEBURGER IN PARADISE
  (S) (2:49) MCA 5633 and 11169   Songs You Know By Heart/Greatest Hits.
  (S) (2:50) MCA 31091   Son Of A Son Of A Sailor.
  (S) (2:49) MCA 10613   Boats Beaches Bars & Ballads.
  (S) (2:51) MCA 11169   Songs You Know By Heart/Greatest Hits. *(gold disc)*
  (S) (2:51) MFSL 713   Son Of A Son Of A Sailor. *(gold disc)*
1979 FINS
  (S) (3:24) MCA 5633 and 11169   Songs You Know By Heart/Greatest Hits.
  (S) (3:24) MCA 10613   Boats Beaches Bars & Ballads.
  (S) (3:26) MCA 1657   Volcano.
  (S) (3:25) MCA 11169   Songs You Know By Heart/Greatest Hits. *(gold disc)*

BUGGLES
1979 VIDEO KILLED THE RADIO STAR
  (S) (4:11) Priority 53705   Rock Of The 80's Volume 2. *(LP version)*
  (S) (3:20) Island 90684 and 842901   The Island Story. *(45 version)*
  (S) (4:11) Island 842849   The Age Of Plastic. *(LP version)*
  (S) (3:19) Time-Life SOD-34   Sounds Of The Seventies - The Late 70's. *(45 version)*
  (S) (3:26) Rhino 71694   New Wave Hits Of The 80's Vol. 1. *(45 version)*
  (S) (4:10) Rebound 314520324   Alterno-Daze: Survival Of 80's The Fittest. *(LP version)*
  (S) (3:21) Maverick/Warner Brothers 46840   O.S.T. The Wedding Singer. *(45 version)*

BULLET
1972 WHITE LIES, BLUE EYES
  (S) (2:51) Rhino 70927   Super Hits Of The 70's Volume 7.
  (S) (2:49) Time-Life SOD-32   Sounds Of The Seventies - AM Pop Classics.

BUOYS
1971 TIMOTHY
  (there were three different versions of this song; the uncensored commercial 45 & LP version plus two different dj only censored versions)
  (S) (2:45) Rhino 70926   Super Hits Of The 70's Volume 6. *(uncensored version)*

BUOYS *(Continued)*

- (S) (2:45) Capricorn 42003 The Scepter Records Story. *(uncensored version)*
- (S) (2:44) Time-Life SUD-16 Superhits - The Early 70's. *(uncensored version)*
- (S) (2:44) Collectables 0513 Golden Classics. *(uncensored version)*
- (S) (2:45) Rhino 72124 Dr. Demento 25th Anniversary Collection. *(uncensored version)*
- (S) (2:44) Time-Life AM1-13 AM Gold - The Early '70s. *(uncensored version)*
- (S) (2:46) Varese Sarabande 5847 On The Radio Volume Two. *(uncensored version)*

ERIC BURDON & THE ANIMALS (see ANIMALS)

ERIC BURDON and WAR (see WAR)

SOLOMON BURKE
1961 JUST OUT OF REACH (OF MY TWO OPEN ARMS)
- (M) (2:46) Atlantic 81296 Atlantic Rhythm & Blues Volume 4.
- (S) (2:41) Atlantic 8109 Best Of.
- (S) (2:41) Curb 77422 Best Of.
- (S) (2:46) Atlantic 82305 Atlantic Rhythm And Blues 1947-1974 Box Set.
- (S) (2:41) Rhino 70284 Home In Your Heart.
- (M) (2:47) Rhino 71806 The R&B Box: Thirty Years Of Rhythm & Blues.
- (M) (2:47) Rhino 72618 Smooth Grooves: The '60s Volume 1 Early '60s.
- (M) (2:47) Rhino 72972 Very Best Of.

1962 CRY TO ME
- (E) (2:31) RCA 6965 More Dirty Dancing.
- (M) (2:31) Atlantic 81296 Atlantic Rhythm & Blues Volume 4.
- (S) (2:31) Curb 77422 Best Of.
- (S) (2:31) Atlantic 8109 Best Of.
- (S) (2:34) Atlantic 82305 Atlantic Rhythm And Blues 1947-1974 Box Set.
- (S) (2:30) Rhino 70284 Home In Your Heart.
- (S) (2:29) Time-Life 2RNR-48 Rock 'N' Roll Era - R&B Gems II.
- (S) (2:28) Time-Life RHD-11 Rhythm & Blues - 1962.
- (S) (2:28) Time-Life R838-18 Solid Gold Soul 1962.
- (M) (2:32) Rhino 72972 Very Best Of.

1963 IF YOU NEED ME
- (M) (2:32) Atlantic 81297 Atlantic Rhythm & Blues Volume 5.
- (S) (2:30) Atlantic 8109 Best Of.
- (S) (2:30) Curb 77422 Best Of.
- (S) (2:30) Atlantic 82305 Atlantic Rhythm And Blues 1947-1974 Box Set.
- (S) (2:30) Rhino 70284 Home In Your Heart.
- (M) (2:31) Time-Life 2RNR-29 Rock 'N' Roll Era - The 60's Rave On.
- (S) (2:29) Time-Life RHD-02 Rhythm & Blues - 1963.
- (S) (2:29) Time-Life 2CLR-25 Classic Rock - On The Soul Side.
- (M) (2:33) Right Stuff 30577 Slow Jams: The 60's Volume 3.
- (S) (2:29) Time-Life R838-14 Solid Gold Soul - 1963.
- (M) (2:32) Rhino 72972 Very Best Of.

1964 GOODBYE BABY (BABY GOODBYE)
- (S) (3:21) Atlantic 8109 Best Of.
- (S) (3:20) Rhino 70284 Home In Your Heart.
- (S) (3:19) Time-Life RHD-12 Rhythm & Blues - 1964.
- (S) (3:19) Time-Life R838-13 Solid Gold Soul - 1964.
- (M) (3:12) Rhino 72972 Very Best Of.

1965 GOT TO GET YOU OFF MY MIND
- (S) (1:56) Atlantic 8109 Best Of.
- (S) (1:55) Atlantic 82305 Atlantic Rhythm And Blues 1947-1974 Box Set.
- (S) (1:55) Rhino 70284 Home In Your Heart.
- (S) (1:55) Scotti Brothers 75402 There Was Love (The Divorce Songs).
- (S) (1:55) Capitol 81475 Rites Of Rhythm & Blues.
- (S) (1:56) Time-Life RHD-07 Rhythm & Blues - 1965.
- (S) (1:56) Time-Life R838-12 Solid Gold Soul - 1965.

- (M) (2:32) Rhino 72815 Beg, Scream & Shout! The Big Ol' Box Of '60s Soul.
- (S) (1:55) Repeat/Relativity 1609 Tell It Like It Is: #1 Soul Hits Of The 60's Volume 1.
- (S) (1:56) Flashback 72895 25 Years Of R&B - 1965.
- (M) (2:32) Rhino 72962 Ultimate '60s Soul Sensations.
- (M) (2:33) Rhino 72972 Very Best Of.

1965 TONIGHT'S THE NIGHT
- (S) (2:45) Atlantic 8109 Best Of.
- (S) (2:45) Rhino 70284 Home In Your Heart.
- (M) (2:37) Rhino 72972 Very Best Of.

DORSEY BURNETTE
1960 (THERE WAS A) TALL OAK TREE
- (S) (2:04) Collectables 5065 History Of Rock Volume 5.
- (S) (2:07) LaserLight 12322 Greatest Hit Singles Collection.
- (S) (2:06) Era 5021 Best Of - The Era Years.

1960 HEY LITTLE ONE
- (S) (2:17) Era 5021 Best Of - The Era Years.

JOHNNY BURNETTE
1960 DREAMIN'
- (S) (2:18) Enigma 73531 O.S.T. Scandal.
- (S) (2:54) EMI 99997 Best Of/You're Sixteen. *(time includes two false starts of :34)*
- (S) (2:19) EMI 81128 Rock Is Dead But It Won't Lie Down.
- (S) (2:17) Time-Life 2RNR-27 Rock 'N' Roll Era - Teen Idols.
- (S) (2:17) Time-Life R857-02 The Heart Of Rock 'n' Roll - 1960.
- (S) (2:19) JCI 3184 1960 - Only Love - 1964.

1960 YOU'RE SIXTEEN
- (S) (1:56) EMI 99997 Best Of/You're Sixteen.
- (S) (1:55) MCA 8001 O.S.T. American Graffiti.
- (S) (1:55) Time-Life 2RNR-27 Rock 'N' Roll Era - Teen Idols.
- (S) (1:54) Time-Life SUD-19 Superhits - Early 60's Classics.
- (S) (1:54) Time-Life AM1-20 AM Gold - Early '60s Classics.
- (S) (1:56) Right Stuff 53319 Hot Rod Rock Volume 4: Hot Rod Rebels.

1961 LITTLE BOY SAD
- (S) (2:07) EMI 99997 Best Of/You're Sixteen. *(:06 longer than the 45)*
- (S) (1:54) Time-Life 2RNR-47 Rock 'N' Roll Era - Teen Idols II. *(faded :07 sooner than the 45)*

1961 GOD, COUNTRY AND MY BABY
- (S) (2:10) EMI 99997 Best Of/You're Sixteen.

ROCKY BURNETTE
1980 TIRED OF TOEIN' THE LINE
- (S) (3:36) Time-Life R968-04 Guitar Rock 1980-1981.
- (S) (3:41) Rhino 71892 Radio Daze: Pop Hits Of The 80's Volume Three.
- (S) (3:35) Time-Life R988-07 Sounds Of The Eighties: 1980.

BUSH
1995 COMEDOWN
- (S) (5:24) Trauma 92531 Sixteen Stone.
1996 GLYCERINE
- (S) (4:24) Trauma 92531 Sixteen Stone.

KATE BUSH
1985 RUNNING UP THAT HILL
- (S) (4:55) EMI 89605 Living In Oblivion: The 80's Greatest Hits Volume Two.
- (S) (5:02) EMI Manhattan 46164 Hounds Of Love.

BUSTA RHYMES
1996 WOO-HAH!! GOT YOU ALL IN CHECK
- (S) (4:31) Elektra 61742 The Coming.

BUSTERS
1963 BUST OUT

76

JERRY BUTLER
released as by JERRY BUTLER and THE IMPRESSIONS:
1958 FOR YOUR PRECIOUS LOVE

- (S) (2:43) Rhino 75893 Jukebox Classics Volume 1.
- (E) (2:41) Original Sound 8853 Oldies But Goodies Vol. 3. *(this compact disc uses the "Waring - fds" noise reduction process)*
- (E) (2:41) Original Sound 2222 Oldies But Goodies Volumes 3,5,11,14 and 15 Box Set. *(this box set uses the "Waring - fds" noise reduction process)*
- (E) (2:41) Original Sound 2500 Oldies But Goodies Volumes 1-15 Box Set. *(this box set uses the "Waring - fds" noise reduction process)*
- (S) (2:41) Motown 6215 and 9067 Hits From The Legendary Vee-Jay Records.
- (S) (2:43) Rhino 75881 Jerry Butler: Best Of.
- (E) (2:38) Curb 77419 Jerry Butler: Greatest Hits.
- (S) (2:42) Ripete 2392192 Beach Music Anthology Box Set.
- (S) (2:43) Vee Jay 700 Jerry Butler: The Ice Man.
- (S) (2:41) Collectables 5063 History Of Rock Volume 3.
- (S) (2:42) Vee Jay 719 Impressions: Their Complete Vee-Jay Recordings.
- (S) (2:42) Rhino 71463 Doo Wop Box.
- (S) (2:43) Vee Jay 3-400 Celebrating 40 Years Of Classic Hits (1953-1993).
- (S) (2:43) Epic 57560 O.S.T. A Bronx Tale.
- (S) (2:42) Time-Life 2RNR-21 Rock 'N' Roll Era - 1958 Still Rockin'.
- (S) (2:42) Time-Life RHD-16 Rhythm & Blues - 1958.
- (E) (2:41) Collectables 2506 WCBS-FM History Of Rock - The 50's Part 1. *(sounds like it was mastered from vinyl)*
- (E) (2:41) Collectables 4506 History Of Rock/The 50s Part One. *(sounds like it was mastered from vinyl)*
- (S) (2:43) Collectables 2607 WCBS-FM For Lovers Only Vol. 3.
- (S) (2:43) Motown 6763 Rites Of Rhythm & Blues Volume Two.
- (S) (2:43) Time-Life R103-27 Love Me Tender.
- (S) (5:08) Varese Sarabande 5486 A Celebration Of Soul Vol. 1: The Chi-Sound Records Collection. *(rerecording)*
- (S) (2:41) LaserLight 12321 Soulful Love.
- (S) (2:42) Ripete 2163-RE Ebb Tide.
- (S) (2:42) Rhino 71806 The R&B Box: Thirty Years Of Rhythm & Blues.
- (S) (2:42) SBK 28336 Original Songs From The Daytime Drama "One Life To Live".
- (S) (2:42) Ripete 2220 Soul Patrol Vol. 2.
- (S) (2:43) Time-Life R857-04 The Heart Of Rock 'n' Roll - 1958.
- (S) (2:42) JCI 3164 Eighteen Soulful Ballads.
- (S) (2:43) Hip-O 40028 The Glory Of Love - '50s Sweet & Soulful Love Songs.
- (S) (2:43) Rhino 72580 Soul Serenade - Intimate R&B.
- (S) (2:42) Time-Life R838-22 Solid Gold Soul 1958.

released as by JERRY BUTLER:
1960 HE WILL BREAK YOUR HEART

- (S) (2:46) Rhino 70646 Billboard's Top R&B Hits Of 1960.
- (S) (2:46) Rhino 75894 Jukebox Classics Volume 2.
- (E) (2:46) Original Sound 8857 Oldies But Goodies Vol. 7. *(this compact disc uses the "Waring - fds" noise reduction process)*
- (E) (2:46) Original Sound 2223 Oldies But Goodies Volumes 2,7,9,12 and 13 Box Set. *(this box set uses the "Waring - fds" noise reduction process)*
- (E) (2:46) Original Sound 2500 Oldies But Goodies Volumes 1-15 Box Set. *(this box set uses the "Waring - fds" noise reduction process)*
- (E) (2:44) Original Sound CDGO-11 Golden Oldies Volume. 11.
- (S) (2:44) Original Sound 8881 Twenty-One #1 Hits. *(this compact disc uses the "Waring - fds" noise reduction process)*
- (S) (2:43) Original Sound 9602 Best Of Oldies But Goodies Vol. 2.

- (M) (2:41) Motown 6215 and 9067 Hits From The Legendary Vee-Jay Records.
- (S) (2:46) Rhino 75881 Best Of.
- (E) (2:43) Curb 77419 Greatest Hits.
- (S) (2:46) Ripete 2392192 Beach Music Anthology Box Set.
- (S) (2:47) Vee Jay 700 The Ice Man.
- (S) (2:45) Collectables 5069 History Of Rock Volume 9.
- (S) (2:47) Vee Jay 3-400 Celebrating 40 Years Of Classic Hits (1953-1993).
- (S) (2:45) Ripete 0001 Coolin' Out/24 Carolina Classics Volume 1.
- (S) (2:45) Time-Life 2RNR-11 Rock 'N' Roll Era - 1960.
- (S) (2:45) Time-Life RHD-15 Rhythm & Blues - 1960.
- (M) (2:41) Collectables 2504 WCBS-FM History Of Rock - The 60's Part 4.
- (M) (2:41) Collectables 4504 History Of Rock/The 60s Part Four.
- (S) (2:46) Time-Life R857-14 The Heart Of Rock 'n' Roll 1960-1961 Take Two.
- (S) (2:45) Time-Life R838-20 Solid Gold Soul 1960.

1961 FIND ANOTHER GIRL

- (S) (2:49) Rhino 75881 Best Of.
- (S) (2:46) Vee Jay 700 The Ice Man.

1961 I'M A TELLING YOU

- (S) (2:21) Rhino 75881 Best Of.
- (S) (2:20) Vee Jay 700 The Ice Man.
- (S) (2:17) Time-Life 2RNR-41 Rock 'N' Roll Era - R&B Gems.

1961 MOON RIVER

- (M) (2:34) Motown 6215 and 9067 Hits From The Legendary Vee-Jay Records.
- (S) (2:38) Rhino 75881 Best Of.
- (E) (2:37) Curb 77419 Greatest Hits.
- (S) (2:38) Vee Jay 700 The Ice Man.
- (S) (2:38) Vee Jay 3-400 Celebrating 40 Years Of Classic Hits (1953-1993).
- (S) (2:38) Time-Life OPCD-4517 Tonight's The Night.
- (S) (2:37) Ripete 2163-RE Ebb Tide.
- (S) (2:37) Time-Life R857-03 The Heart Of Rock 'n' Roll - 1961.

1962 MAKE IT EASY ON YOURSELF

- (S) (2:35) DCC Compact Classics 028 Sock Hop.
- (S) (2:42) Rhino 75881 Best Of.
- (E) (2:35) Curb 77419 Greatest Hits.
- (S) (2:42) Vee Jay 700 The Ice Man.
- (M) (2:33) Collectables 5064 History Of Rock Volume 4.
- (S) (2:41) Vee Jay 3-400 Celebrating 40 Years Of Classic Hits (1953-1993).
- (S) (2:36) Time-Life 2RNR-48 Rock 'N' Roll Era - R&B Gems II.
- (M) (2:34) Thump 7030 Low Rider Oldies Volume III.
- (S) (2:41) Ripete 2156-RE Grand Stand Gold Vol. 1.
- (S) (2:42) K-Tel 3518 Sweet Soul Music.
- (S) (2:42) Time-Life R857-17 The Heart Of Rock 'n' Roll: The Early '60s.
- (S) (2:41) Varese Sarabande 5873 The Burt Bacharach Songbook.

1964 NEED TO BELONG

- (S) (2:55) Rhino 75881 Best Of.
- (S) (2:54) Vee Jay 700 The Ice Man.
- (S) (2:55) Rhino 72618 Smooth Grooves: The '60s Volume 1 Early '60s.

released as by BETTY EVERETT & JERRY BUTLER:
1964 LET IT BE ME

- (M) (2:48) DCC Compact Classics 028 Sock Hop.
- (M) (2:47) JCI 3102 Love Sixties.
- (S) (2:39) Original Sound 8860 Oldies But Goodies Vol. 10. *(this compact disc uses the "Waring - fds" noise reduction process; :08 shorter and faster than the 45 or LP)*
- (S) (2:39) Original Sound 2221 Oldies But Goodies Volumes 1,4,6,8 and 10 Box Set. *(this box set uses the "Waring - fds" noise reduction process; :08 shorter and faster than the 45 or LP)*
- (S) (2:39) Original Sound 2500 Oldies But Goodies Volumes 1-15 Box Set. *(this box set uses the "Waring - fds" noise reduction process; :08 shorter and faster than the 45 or LP)*

JERRY BUTLER *(Continued)*

(S) (2:42) Motown 6215 and 9067 Hits From The Legendary Vee-Jay Records. *(much faster than the 45 or LP)*
(M) (2:48) Rhino 75881 Best Of Jerry Butler.
(M) (2:47) Curb 77419 Jerry Butler's Greatest Hits.
(S) (2:37) Vee Jay 700 The Ice Man. *(:10 shorter and faster than the 45 or LP)*
(S) (2:41) Collectables 5061 History Of Rock Volume 1. *(:06 shorter and faster than the 45 or LP)*
(S) (2:37) Vee Jay 3-400 Celebrating 40 Years Of Classic Hits (1953-1993). *(:10 shorter and faster than the 45 or LP)*
(M) (2:47) Time-Life RHD-12 Rhythm & Blues - 1964.
(S) (2:41) Time-Life SUD-09 Superhits - 1964. *(:06 shorter and faster than the 45 or LP)*
(S) (2:40) Collectables 2502 WCBS-FM History Of Rock - The 60's Part 3. *(:07 shorter and faster than the 45 or LP)*
(S) (2:40) Collectables 4502 History Of Rock/The 60s Part Three. *(:07 shorter and faster than the 45 or LP)*
(S) (2:39) Collectables 2509 WCBS-FM For Lovers Only Part 1. *(:08 shorter and faster than the 45 or LP)*
(S) (2:41) Collectables 2603 WCBS-FM Jukebox Giants Vol. 1. *(:06 shorter and faster than the 45 or LP)*
(M) (2:49) Right Stuff 28371 Slow Jams: The 60's Volume Two.
(M) (2:48) Time-Life OPCD-4517 Tonight's The Night.
(S) (2:42) LaserLight 12321 Soulful Love. *(:05 shorter and faster than the 45 or LP)*
(S) (2:38) Ripete 2163-RE Ebb Tide. *(:09 shorter and faster than the 45 or LP)*
(S) (2:37) Ichiban 2512 Soulful Love - Duets Vol. 1. *(:10 shorter and faster than the 45 or LP)*
(S) (2:40) JCI 3164 Eighteen Soulful Ballads. *(:07 shorter and faster than the 45 or LP)*
(S) (2:37) Hip-O 40029 The Glory Of Love - '60s Sweet & Soulful Love Songs. *(:10 shorter and faster than the 45 or LP)*
(M) (2:49) Rhino 72618 Smooth Grooves: The '60s Volume 1 Early '60s.
(M) (2:47) Time-Life R857-09 The Heart Of Rock 'n' Roll 1964.
(S) (2:41) Time-Life AM1-11 AM Gold - 1964. *(:06 shorter and faster than the 45 or LP)*
(M) (2:47) Time-Life R838-13 Solid Gold Soul - 1964.

released as by JERRY BUTLER:
1968 NEVER GIVE YOU UP
(S) (3:04) Rhino 75881 Best Of.
(M) (2:55) Mercury 510967 Very Best Of.
(M) (2:55) Mercury 510968 Iceman/The Mercury Years.
(S) (3:03) Time-Life 2CLR-28 Classic Rock - On The Soul Side II.
(M) (2:55) Original Sound 9304 Art Laboe's Dedicated To You Vol. 4.
(M) (2:55) Capitol 35818 O.S.T. Dead Presidents Volume II.

1968 HEY, WESTERN UNION MAN
(S) (2:42) Rhino 70654 Billboard's Top R&B Hits Of 1968.
(S) (2:42) Rhino 72006 Billboard's Top R&B Hits 1965-1969 Box Set.
(S) (2:39) Rhino 75881 Best Of.
(M) (2:44) Curb 77419 Greatest Hits.
(S) (2:41) Mercury 510967 Very Best Of.
(S) (2:40) Mercury 510968 Iceman/The Mercury Years.
(S) (2:40) Time-Life RHD-04 Rhythm & Blues - 1968.
(S) (2:35) Time-Life 2CLR-27 Classic Rock - 1968: Blowin' Your Mind.
(S) (2:40) Time-Life R838-03 Solid Gold Soul - 1968.
(S) (2:41) Polygram Special Markets 314520395 The Essential Jerry Butler.
(S) (2:40) Repeat/Relativity 1610 Tighten Up: #1 Soul Hits Of The 60's Volume 2.
(S) (2:40) Polygram Special Markets 314520454 Soul Hits Of The 60's.

1969 ARE YOU HAPPY
(S) (2:36) Mercury 510967 Very Best Of.
(S) (2:38) Mercury 510968 Iceman/The Mercury Years.

1969 ONLY THE STRONG SURVIVE
(S) (2:35) Rhino 70655 Billboard's Top R&B Hits Of 1969. *(truncated fade)*
(S) (2:35) Rhino 72006 Billboard's Top R&B Hits 1965-1969 Box Set. *(truncated fade)*
(S) (2:32) Rhino 75881 Best Of.
(M) (2:35) Curb 77419 Greatest Hits.
(S) (2:35) Mercury 510967 Very Best Of.
(S) (2:35) Mercury 510968 Iceman/The Mercury Years.
(S) (3:12) Mercury 510968 Iceman/The Mercury Years. *(previously unreleased version)*
(S) (2:30) Time-Life RHD-13 Rhythm & Blues - 1969.
(S) (2:31) Time-Life 2CLR-06 Classic Rock - 1969.
(S) (2:35) Original Sound 9303 Art Laboe's Dedicated To You Vol. 3.
(S) (2:34) Motown 6763 Rites Of Rhythm & Blues Volume Two.
(S) (2:35) Polygram Special Markets 314520264 Soul Hits Of The 60's.
(S) (2:35) Ripete 5151 Ocean Drive 4.
(S) (2:35) Rebound 314520369 Soul Classics - Quiet Storm/The 60's.
(S) (2:30) Time-Life R838-04 Solid Gold Soul - 1969.
(S) (2:35) Rebound 314520420 Soul Classics - Best Of The 60's.
(S) (2:36) Polygram Special Markets 314520395 The Essential Jerry Butler.
(S) (2:34) Epic/Legacy 64647 The Philly Sound Box Set.
(M) (2:35) Rhino 72815 Beg, Scream & Shout! The Big Ol' Box Of '60s Soul.
(S) (2:35) Repeat/Relativity 1611 A Brand New Bag: #1 Soul Hits Of The 60's Volume 3.

1969 MOODY WOMAN
(S) (2:20) Mercury 510967 Very Best Of.
(S) (2:20) Mercury 510968 Iceman/The Mercury Years.
(S) (2:20) Polygram Special Markets 314520395 The Essential Jerry Butler.

1969 WHAT'S THE USE OF BREAKING UP
(S) (2:35) Curb 77419 Greatest Hits.
(S) (2:35) Mercury 510967 Very Best Of.
(S) (2:35) Mercury 510968 Iceman/The Mercury Years.
(S) (2:35) Special Music/Essex 5035 Prom Night - The 60's.

released as by JERRY BUTLER and BRENDA LEE EAGER:
1972 AIN'T UNDERSTANDING MELLOW
(S) (4:18) Rhino 70787 Soul Hits Of The 70's Volume 7.
(S) (4:20) Ichiban 2513 Soulful Love - Duets Vol. 2.
(S) (4:19) Rebound 314520367 Soul Classics - Quiet Storm/The 70's.
(S) (4:19) Polygram Special Markets 314520446 Soul Hits Of The 70's.

JONATHAN BUTLER
1986 LIES
(S) (5:17) Jive 41521 Best Of. *(neither the 45 or LP version)*
(S) (4:37) Jive 1032 Jonathan Butler. *(LP version)*

BYRDS
1965 MR. TAMBOURINE MAN
(M) (2:17) Rhino 70626 Billboard's Top Rock & Roll Hits Of 1965. *(found only on the first pressings of this cd)*
(M) (2:17) Rhino 72007 Billboard's Top Rock & Roll Hits 1962-1966 Box Set.
(E) (2:17) Columbia 45019 Pop Classics Of The 60's.
(E) (2:17) Columbia 9516 Greatest Hits.
(M) (2:19) Columbia 9172 Mr. Tambourine Man.
(S) (2:16) Columbia/Legacy 46773 The Byrds. *(very poor stereo separation)*
(M) (2:17) Columbia 37335 Original Singles 1965-67.
(S) (2:16) Murray Hill 21143 Never Before. *(very poor stereo separation)*
(S) (2:29) Columbia/Legacy 47884 20 Essential Tracks. *(:10 longer than any previously released vinyl version; nice stereo separation)*
(E) (2:19) JCI 3111 Good Time Sixties.
(S) (2:17) Time-Life 2CLR-01 Classic Rock - 1965. *(very poor stereo separation)*

(M) (2:17) Time-Life R962-02 History Of Rock 'N' Roll: Folk Rock 1964-1967.

(E) (2:17) JCI 3126 1965 - Only Rock 'N Roll - 1969.

(S) (2:29) Columbia/Legacy 64845 Mr. Tambourine Man. *(:10 longer than any previously released vinyl version; nice stereo separation)*

(S) (2:28) Eclipse Music Group 64869 Rock 'n Roll Relix 1964-1965. *(:09 longer than any previously released vinyl version; nice stereo separation)*

(S) (2:28) Eclipse Music Group 64872 Rock 'n Roll Relix 1960-1969. *(:09 longer than any previously released vinyl version; nice stereo separation)*

(E) (2:16) Thump 6010 Easyriders Volume 1.

1965 ALL I REALLY WANT TO DO

(S) (2:00) Columbia 9516 Greatest Hits. *(LP version)*

(S) (2:01) Columbia 9172 Mr. Tambourine Man. *(LP version)*

(S) (2:02) Columbia/Legacy 46773 The Byrds. *(LP version)*

(M) (2:01) Columbia 37335 Original Singles 1965-67. *(45 version)*

(S) (2:02) Columbia/Legacy 47884 20 Essential Tracks. *(LP version)*

(S) (2:01) Time-Life 2CLR-17 Classic Rock - Rock Renaissance. *(LP version)*

(S) (2:03) Columbia/Legacy 64845 Mr. Tambourine Man. *(LP version)*

(M) (2:01) Columbia/Legacy 64845 Mr. Tambourine Man. *(45 version)*

1965 TURN! TURN! TURN! (TO EVERYTHING THERE IS A SEASON)

(M) (3:34) Rhino 70626 Billboard's Top Rock & Roll Hits Of 1965. *(found only on the first presings of this cd)*

(M) (3:34) Rhino 72007 Billboard's Top Rock & Roll Hits 1962-1966 Box Set.

(E) (3:33) Columbia 9516 Greatest Hits.

(M) (3:41) Columbia 9254 Turn! Turn! Turn! *(LP speed)*

(S) (3:53) Columbia/Legacy 46773 The Byrds. *(:12 longer fade than either the LP or 45; LP speed)*

(M) (3:34) Columbia 37335 Original Singles 1965-67.

(S) (3:53) Columbia/Legacy 47884 20 Essential Tracks. *(LP speed; :12 longer than either the LP or 45)*

(S) (3:52) Priority 53701 Best Of The 60's & 70's Rock: Protest Rock. *(LP speed; :11 longer than either the LP or 45)*

(E) (3:41) Time-Life 2CLR-08 Classic Rock - 1965: The Beat Goes On. *(LP speed)*

(S) (3:35) Time-Life SUD-12 Superhits - The Mid 60's.

(M) (3:37) Time-Life R962-02 History Of Rock 'N' Roll: Folk Rock 1964-1967.

(M) (3:37) Time-Life R921-38 Get Together.

(S) (3:53) Epic 66329 O.S.T. Forrest Gump. *(:12 longer fade than either the LP or 45; LP speed)*

(M) (3:41) K-Tel 3438 Best Of Folk Rock. *(LP speed)*

(M) (3:49) Columbia/Legacy 64846 Turn! Turn! Turn! *(LP speed; :09 longer fade than either the 45 or LP)*

(S) (3:52) Priority 50951 I Love Rock & Roll Volume 2: Hits Of The 60's. *(LP speed; :11 longer than either the 45 or LP)*

(S) (3:35) Time-Life AM1-05 AM Gold - The Mid '60s.

(M) (3:34) Time-Life R132-22 Treasury Of Folk Music Volume Two.

1966 EIGHT MILES HIGH (commercial pressings of this 45 had a drum roll at the very end of the song which was missing from the LP and dj 45's)

(S) (3:33) Columbia 9516 Greatest Hits. *(LP version)*

(S) (3:33) Columbia/Legacy 46773 The Byrds. *(LP version)*

(S) (3:33) Columbia 9349 Fifth Dimension. *(LP version)*

(M) (3:33) Columbia 37335 Original Singles 1965-67. *(Early pressings of this cd had the commercial 45 version but the remastered pressings include the LP version)*

(S) (3:18) Murray Hill 21143 Never Before. *(alternate take)*

(S) (3:33) Columbia/Legacy 47884 20 Essential Tracks. *(LP version)*

(S) (3:34) Time-Life 2CLR-07 Classic Rock - 1966: The Beat Goes On. *(LP version)*

(S) (3:34) Time-Life R962-04 History Of Rock 'N' Roll: California Pop 1963-1967. *(LP version)*

(S) (3:33) K-Tel 621 Rock Classics. *(LP version)*

(S) (3:33) Time-Life R968-09 Guitar Rock 1966-1967. *(LP version)*

(S) (3:33) K-Tel 3183 Psychedelic Mind Trip. *(LP version)*

(S) (3:33) Buddah 49507 Psychedelic Pop. *(LP version)*

(S) (3:34) Columbia/Legacy 64847 Fifth Dimension. *(LP version)*

(S) (3:18) Columbia/Legacy 64847 Fifth Dimension. *(alternate take)*

(S) (3:33) Time-Life R13610 Gold And Platinum Box Set - The Ultimate Rock Collection. *(LP version)*

(M) (3:33) Play-Tone/Epic 69179 Music From The HBO Miniseries "From The Earth To The Moon". *(LP version; hum noticeable at the end of every song on this cd)*

1966 MR. SPACEMAN

(S) (2:07) Columbia 9516 Greatest Hits.

(S) (2:09) Columbia/Legacy 46773 The Byrds.

(S) (2:07) Columbia 9349 Fifth Dimension.

(M) (2:07) Columbia 37335 Original Singles 1965-67.

(S) (2:09) Columbia/Legacy 47884 20 Essential Tracks.

(S) (2:08) Columbia/Legacy 64847 Fifth Dimension.

(S) (2:08) Nick At Nite/550 Music 63437 Nick At Nite Goes To Outer Space.

1967 SO YOU WANT TO BE A ROCK 'N' ROLL STAR

(S) (2:02) Columbia 45018 Rock Classics Of The 60's.

(S) (2:01) DCC Compact Classics 045 Golden Age Of Underground Radio.

(S) (2:03) Columbia 9516 Greatest Hits.

(S) (2:04) Columbia/Legacy 46773 The Byrds.

(S) (2:04) Columbia 9442 Younger Than Yesterday.

(M) (2:03) Columbia 37335 Original Singles 1965-67.

(S) (2:04) Columbia/Legacy 47884 20 Essential Tracks.

(S) (2:01) JCI 3116 Psychedelic Sixties.

(S) (2:02) Time-Life 2CLR-24 Classic Rock - 1967: Blowin' Your Mind.

(S) (2:03) Time-Life R968-12 Guitar Rock - The Late '60s.

(S) (2:04) Columbia/Legacy 64848 Younger Than Yesterday.

1967 MY BACK PAGES

(S) (3:06) Columbia 9516 Greatest Hits.

(S) (3:06) Columbia/Legacy 46773 The Byrds.

(S) (3:06) Columbia 9442 Younger Than Yesterday.

(S) (3:06) Sandstone 33001 Reelin' In The Years Volume 2.

(S) (3:06) Columbia/Legacy 47884 20 Essential Tracks.

(S) (3:06) DCC Compact Classics 063 Rock Of The 70's Volume 2.

(S) (3:06) Time-Life 2CLR-21 Classic Rock - Rock Renaissance II.

(S) (3:06) Columbia/Legacy 64848 Younger Than Yesterday.

(S) (2:42) Columbia/Legacy 64848 Younger Than Yesterday. *(alternate take)*

EDWARD BYRNES and CONNIE STEVENS
1959 KOOKIE, KOOKIE (LEND ME YOUR COMB)

(S) (2:03) Time-Life 2RNR-47 Rock 'N' Roll Era - Teen Idols II.

(S) (2:03) K-Tel 3037 Wacky Weirdos.

(S) (2:04) DCC Compact Classics 077 Too Cute!

(S) (2:04) Collectors' Choice 002 Teen Idols....For A Moment.

(S) (2:03) K-Tel 3388 TV Stars Sing.

C + C MUSIC FACTORY
1991 GONNA MAKE YOU SWEAT
- (S) (4:03) Foundation/RCA 66104 Hot #1 Hits.
- (S) (6:47) JCI 2717 Shake It Up. *(12" single version)*
- (S) (4:03) Priority 7053 Best Of Hip Hop.
- (S) (4:03) Sandstone 33055 and 5014 Rock The First Volume Eight.
- (S) (4:03) Columbia 47093 Gonna Make You Sweat.
- (S) (4:01) Tommy Boy 1137 ESPN Presents Jock Jams. *(all songs on this cd are segued together with crowd sound effects added)*
- (S) (6:47) Columbia 67367 Ultimate. *(12" single version)*
- (S) (4:02) Priority 50946 100% Party Hits Of The 90's Volume One.
- (S) (4:03) Madacy Entertainment 6804 More Sun Splashin'.
- (S) (4:03) Logic 46895 Martha Wash Collection.
- (S) (4:03) Beast 53022 Club Hitz Of The 90's Vol. 1. *(all songs on this cd are segued together)*

1991 HERE WE GO
- (S) (5:47) Tommy Boy 1053 MTV Party To Go Volume 2. *(remix; all tracks on this cd are segued together)*
- (S) (5:40) Columbia 47093 Gonna Make You Sweat. *(LP version)*
- (S) (9:30) Columbia 67367 Ultimate. *(remix)*
- (S) (5:37) Beast 53032 Club Hitz Of The 90's Vol. 2. *(all songs on this cd are segued together)*

1991 THINGS THAT MAKE YOU GO HMMMM
- (S) (5:21) Sandstone 5022 Cosmopolitan Volume 8. *(LP version)*
- (S) (5:21) DCC Compact Classics 082 Night Moves Volume 2. *(LP version)*
- (S) (5:22) Columbia 47093 Gonna Make You Sweat. *(LP version)*
- (S) (4:09) JCI 3132 1990 - Only Rock 'n Roll - 1994. *(45 version)*
- (S) (5:14) Columbia 67367 Ultimate. *(remix)*
- (S) (4:46) Priority 50934 Shut Up And Dance! The 90's Volume One. *(all selections on this cd are segued together)*

1994 DO YOU WANNA GET FUNKY
- (S) (4:05) Columbia 66160 Anything Goes!
- (S) (4:29) Columbia 67367 Ultimate. *(remix)*
- (S) (9:32) Right Stuff 57093 Free To Be Volume 10. *(remix)*

CADETS
1956 STRANDED IN THE JUNGLE
- (M) (3:11) Time-Life 2RNR-14 Rock 'N' Roll Era - 1956.
- (M) (3:02) Time-Life RHD-05 Rhythm & Blues - 1956.
- (M) (3:01) Original Sound 8850 Oldies But Goodies Vol. 1. *(this compact disc uses the "Waring - fds" noise reduction process)*
- (M) (3:01) Original Sound 2221 Oldies But Goodies Volumes 1,4,6,8 and 10 Box Set. *(this box set uses the "Waring - fds" noise reduction process)*
- (M) (3:01) Original Sound 2500 Oldies But Goodies Volumes 1-15 Box Set. *(this box set uses the "Waring - fds" noise reduction process)*
- (M) (3:11) JCI 3165 #1 Radio Hits 1955 - Only Rock 'n Roll - 1959.
- (M) (3:02) Time-Life R838-24 Solid Gold Soul 1956.

CADILLACS
1956 SPEEDO
- (M) (2:20) Rhino 71806 The R&B Box: Thirty Years Of Rhythm & Blues.

- (M) (2:18) Rhino 70906 American Bandstand Greatest Hits Collection.
- (M) (2:20) Rhino 75764 Best Of Doo Wop Uptempo.
- (M) (2:20) Rhino 70642 Billboard Top R&B Hits - 1956.
- (M) (2:18) Rhino 71463 Doo Wop Box.
- (M) (2:19) Collectables 5412 The Cadillacs Meet The Orioles.
- (M) (2:18) Collectables 8800 For Collectors Only.
- (M) (2:19) Rhino 70955 Best Of.
- (M) (2:19) Collectables 2600 WCBS-FM History Of Rock - The Group Sounds Vol. 1.
- (M) (2:17) Time-Life 2RNR-08 The Rock 'N' Roll Era - 1954-1955.
- (M) (2:19) Time-Life RHD-05 Rhythm & Blues - 1956.
- (M) (2:20) Atlantic 82152 O.S.T. Goodfellas.
- (M) (2:17) Time-Life R10513 40 Lovin' Oldies.
- (M) (2:19) Time-Life R962-03 Rock 'N' Roll Classics 1954-1956.
- (M) (2:18) Rhino 72156 Doo Wop Memories, Vol. 1.
- (M) (2:17) Collectables 5465 Spotlite On Josie Records Vol. 2.
- (M) (2:17) Cypress 71334 O.S.T. Coupe De Ville.
- (M) (2:19) Time-Life R838-24 Solid Gold Soul 1956.

1959 PEEK-A-BOO
- (S) (2:12) Rhino 70955 Best Of.
- (S) (2:09) Collectables 8800 For Collectors Only.
- (S) (2:10) Time-Life 2RNR-44 Rock 'N' Roll Era - Lost Treasures.

JOHN CAFFERTY and THE BEAVER BROWN BAND
1984 ON THE DARK SIDE
- (S) (2:43) Scotti Bros. 38929 and 5202 O.S.T. Eddie And The Cruisers.
- (S) (2:41) Scotti Bros. 75518 Big Screen Rock.

1985 TENDER YEARS
- (S) (4:43) Scotti Bros. 38929 O.S.T. Eddie And The Cruisers. *(LP version)*

1985 TOUGH ALL OVER
- (S) (4:34) Risky Business 53920 Blood, Sweat And Beers/Best Of Bar Bands. *(LP version)*
- (S) (4:35) Scotti Brothers 39405 and 75410 Tough All Over. *(LP version)*

1985 C-I-T-Y
- (S) (3:34) Scotti Brothers 39405 and 75410 Tough All Over.

TANE CAIN
1982 HOLDIN' ON

AL CAIOLA
1961 THE MAGNIFICENT SEVEN
- (M) (2:02) Curb 77402 All-Time Great Instrumental Hits Volume 2.
- (M) (2:02) Rhino 71263 and 71451 Songs Of The West.
- (S) (2:02) Time-Life HPD-39 Your Hit Parade - 60's Instrumentals: Take Two.
- (M) (2:02) Rhino 71684 Songs Of The West Vol. Four: Movie And Television Themes.
- (S) (2:02) Collectors' Choice 003/4 Instrumental Gems Of The 60's.

1961 BONANZA
- (S) (2:16) Curb 77403 All-Time Great Instrumental Hits Volume 1.
- (S) (2:15) Rhino 71263 and 71451 Songs Of The West.
- (S) (2:15) Time-Life HPD-34 Your Hit Parade - 60's Instrumentals.
- (S) (2:15) Rhino 71684 Songs Of The West Vol. Four: Movie And Television Themes.

(S) (2:16) Collectors' Choice 003/4 Instrumental Gems Of
The 60's.

BOBBY CALDWELL
1979 WHAT YOU WON'T DO FOR LOVE
(S) (4:45) Sin-Drome 8889 Bobby Caldwell. *(LP length)*
(S) (4:45) Sin-Drome 2001 Be My Valentine. *(LP length)*
(S) (4:44) Rhino 71860 Smooth Grooves Volume 2. *(LP length)*
(S) (3:29) Rhino 72130 Soul Hits Of The 70's Vol. 20. *(45 length)*
(S) (4:45) Thump 4730 Old School Love Songs Volume 3. *(LP length)*
(S) (4:45) Rebound 314520367 Soul Classics - Quiet Storm/The 70's. *(LP length)*
(S) (4:45) Madacy Entertainment 1978 Rock On 1978. *(LP length)*
(S) (3:29) Rhino 72478 Beverly Hills 90210: Songs From The Peach Pit. *(45 length)*
(S) (4:46) TK/Hot Productions 33 Best Of T.K. Soul Singles. *(LP length)*
(S) (3:28) Beast 53442 Original Players Of Love. *(45 length)*
(S) (3:29) K-Tel 6257 The Greatest Love Songs - 16 Soft Rock Hits. *(45 length)*

J.J. CALE
1972 CRAZY MAMA
(S) (2:21) Mercury 830042 Naturally.
(S) (2:26) Time-Life SOD-21 Sounds Of The Seventies - Rock 'N' Soul Seventies.
(S) (2:26) Time-Life R968-19 Guitar Rock - The Early '70s: Take Two.

CALLOWAY
1990 I WANNA BE RICH
(S) (5:06) Solar/Epic 75310 All The Way. *(LP version)*
(S) (4:42) Priority 50934 Shut Up And Dance! The 90's Volume One. *(all selections on this cd are segued together)*

CAMEO
1986 WORD UP
(S) (4:18) Mercury 830265 Word Up!
(S) (4:18) Mercury 314514824 Best Of.
(S) (4:18) K-Tel 3500 The 80's - Urban Countdown.
(S) (4:17) Time-Life R988-04 Sounds Of The Eighties: 1986.
(S) (4:19) Thump 4040 Old School Volume 4.
(S) (4:17) Rhino 72159 Black Entertainment Television - 15th Anniversary.
(S) (5:58) Rebound 314520357 World Of Dance - The 80's. *(12" single version)*
(S) (4:09) JCI 3177 1985 - Only Soul - 1989. *(45 version faded :08 early)*
(S) (4:04) Coldfront 3375 Old School Megamix. *(all selections on this cd are segued together)*
(S) (3:13) Thump 4100 Old School Mix. *(all selections on this cd are segued together and remixed)*
1987 CANDY
(S) (5:38) Mercury 830265 Word Up! *(LP version)*
(S) (5:39) Mercury 314514824 Best Of. *(LP version)*
(S) (4:25) Rhino 72142 Billboard Hot R&B Hits 1987. *(45 version)*

GLEN CAMPBELL
1967 GENTLE ON MY MIND
(S) (2:55) Capitol 33829 Essential Volume Two.
(S) (2:56) Capitol 95848 All Time Country Classics Volume One.
(S) (2:56) Capitol 94165 Classics Collection.
(S) (2:56) Capitol 46483 Very Best Of.
(S) (2:56) Pair 1089 All-Time Favorites.
(S) (2:56) Curb 77343 60's Hits...Country Volume 1.
(S) (2:56) Collectables 5645 Classics Collection.
(S) (2:56) Capitol 52040 Gentle On My Mind.
(S) (2:55) Razor & Tie 2129 Glen Campbell Collection (1962-1989).

1967 BY THE TIME I GET TO PHOENIX
(S) (2:42) Capitol 46483 Very Best Of. *(this song appears (M) on the original pressings of this cd but (S) on the remastered version)*
(S) (2:42) Capitol 94165 Classics Collection.
(S) (2:42) Capitol 95848 All Time Country Classics.
(S) (2:41) Pair 1089 All-Time Favorites.
(S) (2:41) Time-Life CTD-17 Country USA - 1967.
(S) (2:41) CBS Special Products 46850 Society Of Singers Presents A Gift Of Music Vol. 2.
(S) (2:42) Varese Sarabande 5606 Through The Years - Country Hits Of The 60's.
(S) (2:41) Capitol 33834 Essential Volume Three.
(S) (2:42) Collectables 5645 Classics Collection.
(S) (2:42) Capitol 52041 By The Time I Get To Phoenix.
(S) (2:41) Razor & Tie 2129 Glen Campbell Collection (1962-1989).
(S) (2:41) Time-Life R814-01 Love Songs.

1968 I WANNA LIVE
(S) (2:42) Capitol 33834 Essential Volume Three.
(S) (2:42) Razor & Tie 2129 Glen Campbell Collection (1962-1989).

1968 DREAMS OF THE EVERYDAY HOUSEWIFE
(S) (2:33) Capitol 46483 Very Best Of.
(S) (2:33) Capitol 94165 Classics Collection.
(S) (2:32) Pair 1089 All-Time Favorites.
(S) (2:33) Capitol 30288 Essential Volume One.
(S) (2:33) Collectables 5645 Classics Collection.
(S) (2:33) Capitol 52039 Wichita Lineman.
(S) (2:33) Razor & Tie 2129 Glen Campbell Collection (1962-1989).

1969 WICHITA LINEMAN
(S) (3:04) Capitol 46483 Very Best Of.
(S) (3:04) Capitol 94165 Classics Collection.
(S) (3:04) Pair 1089 All-Time Favorites.
(S) (3:00) Time-Life CTD-06 Country USA - 1968.
(S) (2:59) Time-Life SUD-02 Superhits - 1968.
(S) (3:03) Time-Life R138/05 Look Of Love.
(S) (3:04) K-Tel 3151 Working Man's Country.
(S) (3:04) K-Tel 413 Country Music Classics Volume III.
(S) (3:03) Rhino 71939 Billboard Top Pop Hits, 1969.
(S) (3:04) Capitol 33834 Essential Volume Three.
(S) (3:04) Collectables 5645 Classics Collection.
(S) (3:04) Capitol 52039 Wichita Lineman.
(S) (3:04) Razor & Tie 2129 Glen Campbell Collection (1962-1989).
(S) (3:03) Priority 50966 I Love Country Volume One: Hits Of The 60's.
(S) (2:59) Time-Life AM1-04 AM Gold - 1968.
(S) (3:05) Time-Life R814-02 Love Songs.
(S) (3:03) Time-Life R808-02 Classic Country 1965-1969.

1969 GALVESTON
(S) (2:39) Curb 77355 60's Hits Volume 1.
(S) (2:39) Capitol 46483 Very Best Of.
(S) (2:39) Capitol 94165 Classics Collection.
(S) (2:39) Pair 1089 All-Time Favorites.
(S) (2:38) Time-Life CTD-08 Country USA - 1969.
(S) (2:37) Time-Life SUD-14 Superhits - The Late 60's.
(S) (2:38) K-Tel 3110 Country Music Classics Volume XVIII.
(S) (2:28) K-Tel 3299 Country 'Round The Country.
(S) (2:39) Capitol 30288 Essential Volume One.
(S) (2:39) Collectables 5645 Classics Collection.
(S) (2:38) JCI 3154 1965 - Only Country - 1969.
(S) (2:38) Razor & Tie 2129 Glen Campbell Collection (1962-1989).
(S) (2:37) Time-Life AM1-14 AM Gold - The Late '60s.
(S) (2:39) Time-Life R808-02 Classic Country 1965-1969.

1969 WHERE'S THE PLAYGROUND SUSIE
(S) (2:54) Capitol 46483 Very Best Of.
(S) (2:54) Pair 1089 All-Time Favorites.
(S) (2:54) Capitol 33834 Essential Volume Three.
(S) (2:53) Razor & Tie 2129 Glen Campbell Collection (1962-1989).

1969 TRUE GRIT
(S) (2:30) Capitol 30288 Essential Volume One.
(S) (2:29) Razor & Tie 2129 Glen Campbell Collection (1962-1989).

GLEN CAMPBELL *(Continued)*
1969 TRY A LITTLE KINDNESS
  (S) (2:24) Capitol 46483 Very Best Of.
  (S) (2:23) Pair 1089 All-Time Favorites.
  (S) (2:23) Capitol 33829 Essential Volume Two.
  (S) (2:23) Razor & Tie 2129 Glen Campbell Collection
          (1962-1989).
1970 HONEY COME BACK
  (S) (2:58) Pair 1089 All-Time Favorites. *(truncated fade)*
  (S) (2:55) Capitol 33834 Essential Volume Three.
  (S) (2:55) Razor & Tie 2129 Glen Campbell Collection
          (1962-1989).

released as by BOBBIE GENTRY & GLEN CAMPBELL:
1970 ALL I HAVE TO DO IS DREAM
  (S) (2:33) Capitol 46483 Very Best Of Glen Campbell.
  (S) (2:32) Priority 8675 Country's Greatest Hits Volume 10:
          Duets Of The 70's.
  (S) (2:32) Capitol 33829 Glen Campbell - Essential Volume
          Two.
  (S) (2:31) Razor & Tie 2129 Glen Campbell Collection
          (1962-1989).
  (S) (2:32) Priority 50967 I Love Country Volume Two: Hits
          Of The 70's.
  (S) (2:32) Collectables 5862 Bobbie Gentry - Golden Classics.

released as by GLEN CAMPBELL:
1970 OH HAPPY DAY
  (S) (3:32) Razor & Tie 2129 Glen Campbell Collection
          (1962-1989).
1970 IT'S ONLY MAKE BELIEVE
  (S) (2:25) Capitol 46483 Very Best Of.
  (S) (2:24) Pair 1089 All-Time Favorites.
  (S) (2:25) Capitol 30288 Essential Volume One.
  (S) (2:23) Razor & Tie 2129 Glen Campbell Collection
          (1962-1989).
  (S) (2:24) Rhino 72736 Billboard Top Soft Rock Hits - 1970.
1971 DREAM BABY (HOW LONG MUST I DREAM)
  (S) (2:30) Capitol 46483 Very Best Of. *(truncated fade)*
  (S) (2:30) Pair 1089 All-Time Favorites. *(truncated fade)*
  (S) (2:29) Razor & Tie 2129 Glen Campbell Collection
          (1962-1989).
  (S) (2:29) Rhino 72737 Billboard Top Soft Rock Hits - 1971.
1975 RHINESTONE COWBOY
  (S) (3:14) Curb 77356 70's Hits Volume 2.
  (S) (3:15) Capitol 95956 All Time Country Classics Volume
          2.
  (S) (3:15) Capitol 46483 Very Best Of.
  (S) (3:14) Capitol 94165 Classics Collection.
  (S) (3:14) Curb 77362 Greatest Country Hits.
  (S) (3:14) Priority 8671 Country's Greatest Hits: Superstars.
  (S) (3:11) Razor & Tie 21640 Those Fabulous 70's.
  (S) (3:10) Time-Life CCD-04 Contemporary Country - The
          Mid 70's.
  (S) (3:12) K-Tel 605 Country Music Classics Volume V.
  (S) (3:13) Capitol 33829 Essential Volume Two.
  (S) (3:14) Collectables 5645 Classics Collection.
  (S) (3:12) K-Tel 3584 Cowboy Country.
  (S) (3:13) Razor & Tie 2129 Glen Campbell Collection
          (1962-1989).
  (S) (3:14) Priority 50967 I Love Country Volume Two: Hits
          Of The 70's.
  (S) (3:12) K-Tel 3369 101 Greatest Country Hits Vol. Ten:
          Country Roads.
  (S) (3:13) Time-Life AM1-22 AM Gold - 1975.
  (S) (3:10) Time-Life R840-01 Sounds Of The Seventies -
          Pop Nuggets: Late '70s.
  (S) (3:14) Hip-O 40086 The Class Of Country 1975-1979.
1976 COUNTRY BOY (YOU GOT YOUR FEET IN L.A.)
  (S) (3:07) Capitol 46483 Very Best Of.
  (S) (3:07) Capitol 94165 Classics Collection.
  (S) (3:07) Curb 77362 Greatest Country Hits.
  (S) (3:06) Capitol 30288 Essential Volume One.
  (S) (3:07) Collectables 5645 Classics Collection.
  (S) (3:06) Razor & Tie 2129 Glen Campbell Collection
          (1962-1989).

**1976 DON'T PULL YOUR LOVE/THEN YOU CAN TELL ME
     GOODBYE**
  (S) (3:19) Capitol 33834 Essential Volume Three.
  (S) (3:19) Razor & Tie 2129 Glen Campbell Collection
          (1962-1989).
1977 SOUTHERN NIGHTS
  (S) (2:57) Curb 77344 70's Hits - Country Volume 1.
  (S) (2:57) Capitol 46483 Very Best Of.
  (S) (2:57) Capitol 94165 Classics Collection.
  (S) (2:57) Curb 77362 Greatest Country Hits.
  (S) (2:57) Time-Life CCD-02 Contemporary Country - The
          Late 70's.
  (S) (2:57) Time-Life SOD-05 Sounds Of The Seventies - 1977.
  (S) (2:56) Priority 53716 Branson USA Vol. 3 - Country
          Legends.
  (S) (2:55) K-Tel 3111 Country Music Classics Vol. XIX.
  (S) (2:56) Capitol 33829 Essential Volume Two.
  (S) (2:57) Collectables 5645 Classics Collection.
  (S) (2:57) Madacy Entertainment 1977 Rock On 1977.
  (S) (2:56) JCI 3156 1975 - Only Country - 1979.
  (S) (2:56) Razor & Tie 2129 Glen Campbell Collection
          (1962-1989).
  (S) (2:57) Time-Life AM1-24 AM Gold - 1977.
1977 SUNFLOWER
  (S) (2:50) Capitol 46483 Very Best Of.
  (S) (2:49) Capitol 30288 Essential Volume One.
  (S) (2:49) Razor & Tie 2129 Glen Campbell Collection
          (1962-1989).
  (S) (2:50) Rhino 72516 Behind Closed Doors - '70s Swingers.
1978 CAN YOU FOOL
  (S) (3:09) Capitol 95956 All Time Country Classics Volume
          Two.
  (S) (3:15) Capitol 33834 Essential Volume Three.
  (S) (3:15) Razor & Tie 2129 Glen Campbell Collection
          (1962-1989).

JO ANN CAMPBELL
1962 (I'M THE GIRL ON) WOLVERTON MOUNTAIN

TEVIN CAMPBELL
1991 ROUND AND ROUND
  (S) (4:52) Qwest/Warner Brothers 26291 T.E.V.I.N.
          Campbell. *(LP version)*
1992 TELL ME WHAT YOU WANT ME TO DO
  (S) (5:00) Qwest/Warner Brothers 26291 T.E.V.I.N.
          Campbell.
1994 CAN WE TALK
  (S) (4:29) Tommy Boy 1109 MTV Party To Go Volume 6.
          (all tracks on this cd are segued together)
  (S) (4:43) Qwest/Warner Brothers 45388 I'm Ready.
  (S) (4:21) MCA 11329 Soul Train 25th Anniversary Box Set.
  (S) (4:42) Rebound 314520439 Soul Classics - Best Of The
          90's.
  (S) (4:42) Beast 53012 Smooth Love Of The 90's Vol. 1.
1994 I'M READY
  (S) (4:44) Qwest/Warner Brothers 45388 I'm Ready.
  (S) (4:44) Rhino 72159 Black Entertainment Television -
          15th Anniversary.
  (S) (4:42) Warner Brothers 46024 Love Jams......Volume
          One.
1994 ALWAYS IN MY HEART
  (S) (5:37) Qwest/Warner Brothers 45388 I'm Ready.

CANDLEBOX
1994 FAR BEHIND
  (S) (4:57) Maverick/Sire/Warner Brothers 45313 Candlebox.

CANDYMAN
1990 KNOCKIN' BOOTS
  (S) (4:42) Tommy Boy 1037 MTV Party To Go Volume 1.
          (remix; all tracks on this cd are segued together)
  (S) (3:52) Epic 46947 Ain't No Shame In My Game.
  (S) (3:57) Thump 9951 Power 106 10th Anniversary Collection.
          (all songs on this cd are segued together)

(S) (4:01) Priority 50946 100% Party Hits Of The 90's Volume One.

(S) (3:52) Rhino 72734 Latin Lingo: Hip-Hop From La Raza, Vol. 2.

(S) (3:52) Cold Front 6246 Classic Club Mix - R&B Grooves. *(all selections on this cd are segued together)*

CANNED HEAT
1968 ON THE ROAD AGAIN
(S) (3:21) DCC Compact Classics 045 Golden Age Of Underground Radio. *(45 version)*

(S) (3:23) EMI 48377 Best Of. *(45 version)*

(S) (3:20) Priority 8670 Hitchin A Ride/70's Greatest Rock Hits Volume 10. *(45 version)*

(S) (4:54) WTG 46042 O.S.T. Flashback. *(LP version)*

(M) (3:22) Rhino 71128 Blues Masters Volume 7: Blues Revival. *(45 version)*

(S) (3:23) Compose 9927 Car And Driver/Greatest Car Songs. *(45 version)*

(S) (3:22) Time-Life 2CLR-04 Classic Rock - 1968. *(45 version)*

(S) (3:22) Time-Life OPCD-4521 Guitar Rock. *(45 version)*

(S) (7:05) EMI 29165 Uncanned!/Best Of. *(alternate take; :19 of studio talk and a countoff)*

(S) (4:59) EMI 29165 Uncanned!/Best Of. *(LP version)*

(S) (3:22) Right Stuff 31324 and 31327 Harley-Davidson Road Songs. *(45 version)*

(S) (3:22) Time-Life R968-11 Guitar Rock - The Early '70s. *(45 version)*

(S) (3:21) K-Tel 3996 Rockin' Down The Highway. *(45 version)*

1969 GOING UP THE COUNTRY
(actual 45 time is (2:50) not (2:30) as stated on the record label)
(S) (2:48) JCI 3101 Rockin' 60's.

(S) (2:49) Original Sound 8894 Dick Clark's 21 All-Time Hits Vol. 3.

(S) (2:49) Polydor 837362 O.S.T. 1969.

(S) (2:49) EMI 48377 Best Of.

(S) (2:48) Time-Life 2CLR-12 Classic Rock - 1969: The Beat Goes On.

(S) (2:50) EMI 29165 Uncanned!/Best Of.

(S) (2:48) Rebound 314520269 Class Reunion 1969.

(S) (2:49) Hip-O 40062 Under My Wheels: 12 Road Trippin' Tracks.

1970 LET'S WORK TOGETHER
(E) (2:46) EMI 48377 Best Of.

(E) (2:46) Essex 7052 All Time Rock Classics.

(M) (2:46) Time-Life SOD-11 Sounds Of The Seventies - 1970: Take Two.

(M) (2:46) Time-Life R921-38 Get Together.

(S) (3:11) EMI 29165 Uncanned!/Best Of. *(remixed; contains previously unreleased verse)*

(M) (2:46) Time-Life R968-12 Guitar Rock - The Late '60s.

CANNIBAL & THE HEADHUNTERS
1965 LAND OF 1000 DANCES
(M) (2:14) Rhino 75772 Son Of Frat Rock.

(M) (2:14) Rhino 70992 Groove 'n' Grind.

(E) (2:15) JCI 3100 Dance Sixties.

(M) (2:15) DCC Compact Classics 029 Toga Rock.

(S) (2:30) Original Sound CDGO-5 Golden Oldies Volume 5. *(:16 longer fade than the single version and with 1 extra line added to intro, "c'mon everybody just clap with me" that appeared on the LP version but not the 45 version)*

(M) (2:14) Collectables 5069 History Of Rock Volume 9.

(M) (2:12) Time-Life 2CLR-14 Classic Rock - 1965: Shakin' All Over.

(M) (2:14) Collectables 2605 WCBS-FM Jukebox Giants Vol. 3.

(M) (2:14) K-Tel 3008 60's Sock Hop.

(M) (2:32) Collectables 5806 A Golden Classics Edition. *(:18 longer fade than the 45 version)*

(M) (2:47) Rhino 72870 Brown Eyed Soul Vol. 3. *(with previously unreleased introduction)*

ACE CANNON
1962 TUFF
(actual 45 time is (2:19) not (2:01) as stated on the record label)
(S) (3:18) MCA 25226 History Of Hi Records Rhythm & Blues Volume 1. *(LP version)*

(S) (2:25) Ranwood 8238 Golden Favorites. *(rerecording)*

(M) (2:19) Time-Life 2RNR-36 Rock 'N' Roll Era - Axes & Saxes/The Great Instrumentals. *(45 version)*

(S) (2:27) K-Tel 3059 Saxy Rock. *(rerecording)*

(S) (2:26) Curb 77878 Best Of. *(rerecording)*

FREDDY CANNON
1959 TALLAHASSEE LASSIE
(actual 45 time is (2:11) not (2:30) as stated on the record label)
(E) (2:31) JCI 3201 Party Time Fifties. *(LP version)*

(E) (2:32) Critique 5402 His Latest & Greatest. *(LP version)*

(E) (2:30) Essex 7053 A Hot Summer Night In '59. *(LP version)*

(M) (2:30) Original Sound 8891 Dick Clark's 21 All-Time Hits Vol. 1. *(LP version)*

(M) (2:29) Time-Life 2RNR-20 Rock 'N' Roll Era - 1959 Still Rockin'. *(LP version)*

(M) (2:10) Rhino 72210 Best Of. *(45 version)*

(M) (2:29) JCI 3188 1955 - Only Dance - 1959. *(LP version)*

1960 WAY DOWN YONDER IN NEW ORLEANS
(E) (2:30) Critique 5402 His Latest & Greatest.

(M) (2:29) Collectables 5063 History Of Rock Volume 3.

(E) (2:29) Original Sound CDGO-14 Golden Oldies Volume. 14.

(M) (2:29) Time-Life 2RNR-22 Rock 'N' Roll Era - 1960 Still Rockin'.

(M) (2:29) Rhino 72210 Best Of.

(M) (2:29) JCI 3166 #1 Radio Hits 1960 - Only Rock 'n Roll - 1964.

1960 CHATTANOOGA SHOE SHINE BOY
(M) (2:18) Critique 5402 His Latest & Greatest.

(M) (2:16) Rhino 72210 Best Of.

1960 JUMP OVER
(E) (2:40) Critique 5402 His Latest & Greatest.

(M) (2:44) Rhino 72210 Best Of.

1961 TRANSISTOR SISTER
(E) (2:22) Critique 5402 His Latest & Greatest.

(M) (2:18) Time-Life 2RNR-40 Rock 'N' Roll Era - The 60's Teen Time.

(M) (2:21) Rhino 72210 Best Of.

1962 PALISADES PARK
(M) (1:52) Rhino 70623 Billboard Top Rock & Roll Hits Of 1962.

(M) (1:52) Rhino 72007 Billboard Top Rock & Roll Hits 1962-1966 Box Set.

(E) (1:53) JCI 3110 Sock Hoppin' Sixties.

(M) (1:50) Original Sound 8861 Oldies But Goodies Vol. 11. *(this compact disc uses the "Waring - fds" noise reduction process)*

(M) (1:50) Original Sound 2222 Oldies But Goodies Volumes 3,5,11,14 and 15 Box Set. *(this box set uses the "Waring - fds" noise reduction process)*

(M) (1:50) Original Sound 2500 Oldies But Goodies Volumes 1-15 Box Set. *(this box set uses the "Waring - fds" noise reduction process)*

(M) (1:50) Original Sound 8892 Dick Clark's 21 All-Time Hits Vol. 2.

(E) (1:52) Critique 5402 His Latest & Greatest.

(M) (1:49) Collectables 5061 History Of Rock Volume 1.

(M) (1:49) Time-Life 2RNR-02 Rock 'N' Roll Era - 1962.

(M) (1:51) Rhino 72210 Best Of.

(M) (1:49) Collectables 1515 and 2515 The Anniversary Album - The 60's.

1964 ABIGAIL BEECHER
(S) (2:24) Critique 5402 His Latest & Greatest.

(S) (2:21) Time-Life 2RNR-46 Rock 'N' Roll Era - 60's Juke Box Memories.

(M) (2:22) Rhino 72210 Best Of.

FREDDY CANNON *(Continued)*
1965 ACTION
- (S) (2:07) Critique 5402 His Latest & Greatest.
- (S) (2:06) Collectables 5069 History Of Rock Volume 9.
- (S) (2:06) Time-Life SUD-17 Superhits - Mid 60's Classics.
- (S) (2:05) Varese Sarabande 5670 Songs Of Tommy Boyce And Bobby Hart.
- (S) (2:06) Rhino 72210 Best Of.
- (S) (2:06) Time-Life AM1-16 AM Gold - Mid '60s Classics.

JIM CAPALDI
1983 THAT'S LOVE

CAPITOLS
1966 COOL JERK
(45 time is (2:32); LP time is (2:41))
- (S) (2:41) Rhino 75757 Soul Shots Volume 3.
- (S) (2:41) Rhino 75772 Son Of Frat Rock.
- (S) (2:41) Rhino 70652 Billboard's Top R&B Hits Of 1966.
- (S) (2:41) Rhino 72006 Billboard's Top R&B Hits 1966-1969 Box Set.
- (S) (2:41) Rhino 70992 Groove 'n' Grind.
- (S) (2:25) Garland 011 Footstompin' Oldies.
- (M) (2:33) Atlantic 81297 Atlantic Rhythm & Blues Volume 5.
- (M) (2:32) Atlantic 82305 Atlantic Rhythm And Blues 1947-1974 Box Set.
- (S) (2:40) Collectables 5065 History Of Rock Volume 5.
- (S) (2:41) Rhino 71460 Soul Hits, Volume 2.
- (S) (2:38) Time-Life RHD-01 Rhythm & Blues - 1966.
- (S) (2:24) Time-Life 2CLR-07 Classic Rock - 1966: The Beat Goes On.
- (S) (2:25) Collectables 2504 WCBS-FM History Of Rock - The 60's Part 4.
- (S) (2:25) Collectables 4504 History Of Rock/The 60s Part Four.
- (S) (2:43) Collectables 5105 Golden Classics.
- (M) (2:32) Columbia 57317 O.S.T. Calendar Girl.
- (E) (2:30) K-Tel 3331 Do You Wanna Dance.
- (S) (2:41) Curb 77774 Hard To Find Hits Of Rock 'N' Roll Volume Two.
- (S) (2:36) Tommy Boy 1136 ESPN Presents Jock Rock Vol. 2. *(all songs on this cd are segued together with crowd sound effects added)*
- (M) (2:32) Nick At Nite/Epic 67149 Dick Van Dyke's Dance Party.
- (S) (2:38) JCI 3161 18 Soul Hits From The 60's.
- (S) (2:38) Time-Life R838-01 Solid Gold Soul - 1966.
- (S) (2:41) Flashback 72658 '60s Soul: Baby I Love You.
- (S) (2:41) Flashback 72091 '60s Soul Hits Box Set.
- (M) (2:33) Rhino 72815 Beg, Scream & Shout! The Big Ol' Box Of '60s Soul.
- (S) (2:41) Flashback 72896 25 Years Of R&B - 1966.
- (M) (2:33) Rhino 72963 Ultimate '60s Soul Smashes.

CAPRIS
1961 THERE'S A MOON OUT TONIGHT
- (M) (2:10) Collectables 2507 History Of Rock - The Doo Wop Era Volume 1.
- (M) (2:10) Collectables 4507 History Of Rock/The Doo Wop Era Part One.
- (M) (2:11) DCC Compact Classics 031 Back Seat Jams.
- (M) (2:11) Collectables 5063 History Of Rock Volume 3.
- (M) (2:11) Collectables 5450 Morse Code Of Love.
- (S) (2:23) Special Music 4913 Rock & Roll Revival. *(live)*
- (M) (2:11) Rhino 71463 Doo Wop Box.
- (M) (2:11) Time-Life 2RNR-04 Rock 'N' Roll Era - 1961. *(original pressings of this song on this cd were (E))*
- (M) (2:11) Time-Life R962-06 History Of Rock 'N' Roll: Doo Wop And Vocal Group Tradition 1955-1962.
- (M) (2:10) Collectables 2500 WCBS-FM History Of Rock - The 60's Part 1.
- (M) (2:10) Collectables 4500 History Of Rock/The 60s Part One.
- (M) (2:10) Collectables 2509 WCBS-FM For Lovers Only Part 1.
- (M) (2:11) Collectables 5173 Memories Of Times Square Record Shop Volume 2.

- (M) (2:11) Collectables 2605 WCBS-FM Jukebox Giants Vol. 3.
- (M) (2:11) Time-Life R103-27 Love Me Tender.
- (M) (2:11) Time-Life R10513 40 Lovin' Oldies.
- (M) (2:11) Time-Life OPCD-4517 Tonight's The Night.
- (M) (2:11) Time-Life R857-03 The Heart Of Rock 'n' Roll - 1961.
- (M) (2:11) Thump 7050 Low Rider Oldies Volume 5.
- (M) (2:12) JCI 3166 #1 Radio Hits 1960 - Only Rock 'n Roll - 1964.
- (M) (2:11) K-Tel 3812 Doo Wop's Greatest Hits.

CAPTAIN & TENNILLE
1975 LOVE WILL KEEP US TOGETHER
- (S) (3:23) Priority 8669 Hits/70's Greatest Rock Hits Volume 9.
- (S) (3:22) Rhino 70670 Billboard Top Hits - 1975.
- (S) (3:23) A&M 3105 Greatest Hits.
- (S) (3:22) Time-Life SOD-36 Sounds Of The Seventies - More AM Nuggets.
- (S) (3:21) Rebound 314520294 Love Will Keep Us Together.
- (S) (3:21) Time-Life AM1-22 AM Gold - 1975.
- (S) (3:21) Time-Life R840-03 Sounds Of The Seventies - Pop Nuggets: Early '70s.
- (S) (3:21) Time-Life R814-02 Love Songs.
- (S) (3:21) Collectables 1516 and 2516 The Anniversary Album - The 70's. *(truncated fade)*
1975 THE WAY I WANT TO TOUCH YOU
- (S) (2:45) A&M 3105 Greatest Hits.
- (S) (2:42) Rebound 314520317 Class Reunion 1975.
- (S) (2:43) Rebound 314520294 Love Will Keep Us Together.
- (S) (2:42) Time-Life R834-07 Body Talk - Hearts In Motion.
1976 LONELY NIGHT (ANGEL FACE)
- (S) (3:15) A&M 3105 Greatest Hits.
- (S) (3:15) Rebound 314520368 Class Reunion '76.
1976 SHOP AROUND
- (S) (3:28) A&M 3105 Greatest Hits.
1976 MUSKRAT LOVE
- (S) (3:46) A&M 3105 Greatest Hits. *(LP length)*
- (S) (3:46) Time-Life AM1-23 AM Gold - 1976. *(LP length)*
- (S) (3:29) Rhino 75233 '70s Party (Killers) Classics. *(45 length)*
- (S) (3:46) Time-Life R834-13 Body Talk - Just The Two Of Us. *(LP length)*
1977 CAN'T STOP DANCIN'
- (S) (3:49) A&M 3105 Greatest Hits.
1978 YOU NEVER DONE IT LIKE THAT
- (S) (3:29) K-Tel 3908 High Energy Volume 1.
1979 YOU NEED A WOMAN TONIGHT
1980 DO THAT TO ME ONE MORE TIME
(actual 45 time is (3:49) not (4:17) as stated on the record label; LP length is (4:13))
- (S) (3:51) Rhino 70675 Billboard Top Hits - 1980.
- (S) (3:49) Priority 53699 80's Greatest Rock Hits Volume 7 - Light & Easy.
- (S) (4:12) Casablanca 314516918 Casablanca Records Story.
- (S) (3:49) Rebound 314520270 Class Reunion 1979.
- (S) (4:14) Polygram Special Markets 314520271 Hits Of The 70's.
- (S) (4:12) Special Music/Essex 5036 Prom Night - The 70's.
- (S) (3:49) Rhino 71890 Radio Daze: Pop Hits Of The 80's Volume One.
- (S) (3:51) Time-Life R138-18 Body Talk.
- (S) (4:12) Casablanca 314526253 Casablanca Records Greatest Hits.
- (S) (4:09) JCI 3147 1980 - Only Love - 1984.
- (S) (3:52) Time-Life R834-04 Body Talk - Together Forever.
- (S) (3:52) Time-Life R840-01 Sounds Of The Seventies - Pop Nuggets: Late '70s.
- (S) (3:48) K-Tel 3906 Starflight Vol. 1.
- (S) (3:50) Hip-O 40079 Essential '80s: 1980-1984.

CAPTAIN HOLLYWOOD PROJECT
1993 MORE AND MORE
    (S) (5:55) Imago 21027 Love Is Not Sex. *(remix)*
    (S) (3:55) Imago 21027 Love Is Not Sex.
    (S) (4:07) Rhino 72839 Disco Queens: The 90's.
    (S) (3:54) K-Tel 3848 90s Now Volume 2.
    (S) (5:07) Beast 53292 Club Hitz Of The 90's Vol. 4. *(all songs on this cd are segued together)*
    (S) (4:08) Interhit/Priority 51080 DMA Dance Vol. 1: Eurodance.

IRENE CARA
1980 FAME
    (S) (3:48) Priority 7971 Mega-Hits Dance Classics Volume 1. *(45 version)*
    (S) (5:13) Polydor 800034 O.S.T. Fame. *(LP version)*
    (S) (3:48) Rhino 70494 Billboard Top Dance Hits - 1980. *(45 version)*
    (S) (3:47) Rhino 70675 Billboard Top Hits - 1980. *(45 version)*
    (S) (5:12) Rebound 314520217 Disco Nights Vol. 1 - Divas Of Dance. *(LP version)*
    (S) (3:45) Rebound 314520318 Class Reunion 1980. *(45 version)*
    (S) (3:47) Time-Life R988-07 Sounds Of The Eighties: 1980. *(45 version)*
    (S) (3:47) Time-Life R138-38 Celebration. *(45 version)*
    (S) (3:48) Time-Life R840-09 Sounds Of The Seventies: '70s Dance Party 1979-1981. *(45 version)*
    (S) (4:52) Rebound 314520520 Body Moves - Non-Stop Disco Workout Vol. 1. *(all selections on this cd are segued together)*
1980 OUT HERE ON MY OWN
    (S) (3:10) Polydor 800034 O.S.T. Fame.
1983 FLASHDANCE......WHAT A FEELING
    (S) (3:52) Casablanca 811492 O.S.T. Flashdance.
    (S) (7:13) Casablanca 314516917 The Casablanca Records Story. *(12" dj single version)*
    (S) (3:54) Geffen 4021 What A Feelin'.
    (S) (3:49) Rebound 314520366 Disco Nights Vol. 10 - Disco's Greatest Movie Hits.
    (S) (3:52) Rebound 314520438 No. 1 Hits Of The 80's.
    (S) (7:26) Chronicles 314553404 Non-Stop Disco Vol. 1. *(all songs on this cd are segued together; megamix medley with Michael Sembello's "MANIAC")*
    (S) (3:49) RCA 68904 O.S.T. The Full Monty.
    (S) (3:54) Polydor 314555120 Pure Disco 2.
    (S) (3:51) Polygram Special Markets 314520457 #1 Radio Hits Of The 80's.
1983 WHY ME?
    (S) (4:36) Geffen 4021 What A Feelin'. *(LP length)*
1984 THE DREAM (HOLD ON TO YOUR DREAM)
    (S) (4:49) Geffen 4021 What A Feelin'.
1984 BREAKDANCE
    (S) (3:25) Geffen 4021 What A Feelin'. *(LP version)*
    (S) (3:01) Madacy Entertainment 1984 Rock On 1984. *(45 version)*
    (S) (2:59) Time-Life R988-23 Sounds Of The Eighties 1984-1985. *(45 version)*

CARAVELLES
1963 YOU DON'T HAVE TO BE A BABY TO CRY
    (M) (1:58) Rhino 70989 Best Of The Girl Groups Volume 2.
    (M) (1:57) Time-Life 2RNR-46 Rock 'N' Roll Era - 60's Juke Box Memories.
    (M) (1:57) Time-Life SUD-08 Superhits - 1963.
    (M) (1:58) Polygram Special Markets 314520272 One Hit Wonders.
    (M) (1:56) Eric 11503 Hard To Find 45's On CD (Volume II) 1961-64.
    (M) (1:58) Eclipse Music Group 64868 Rock 'n Roll Relix 1962-1963.
    (M) (1:58) Eclipse Music Group 64872 Rock 'n Roll Relix 1960-1969.
    (M) (1:57) Time-Life AM1-17 AM Gold - 1963.
    (M) (1:58) Time-Life R857-18 The Heart Of Rock 'n' Roll 1962-1963 Take Two.

    (M) (1:56) Polygram Special Markets 314520516 45's On CD Volume 1.

CAREFREES
1964 WE LOVE YOU BEATLES

MARIAH CAREY
1990 VISION OF LOVE
    (S) (3:29) Columbia 45202 Mariah Carey.
1990 LOVE TAKES TIME
    (S) (3:47) Columbia 45202 Mariah Carey. *(this track is not listed on the cd jacket but it is track 11)*
1991 SOMEDAY
    (S) (4:05) Columbia 45202 Mariah Carey.
1991 I DON'T WANNA CRY
    (S) (4:47) Columbia 45202 Mariah Carey.
1991 EMOTIONS
    (S) (4:08) Columbia 47980 Emotions.
1992 CAN'T LET GO
    (S) (4:25) Columbia 47980 Emotions.
1992 MAKE IT HAPPEN
    (S) (5:06) Columbia 47980 Emotions. *(LP version)*
1992 I'LL BE THERE
    (S) (4:42) Columbia 52758 MTV Unplugged EP.
1993 DREAMLOVER
    (S) (3:52) Columbia 53205 Music Box.
1993 HERO
    (S) (4:17) Columbia 53205 Music Box.
    (S) (4:17) Grammy Recordings/Sony Music 67043 1995 Grammy Nominees.
    (S) (4:35) Columbia 69012 Diana Princess Of Wales Tribute. *(live)*
1994 WITHOUT YOU
    (S) (3:33) Columbia 53205 Music Box.
1994 NEVER FORGET YOU
    (S) (3:44) Columbia 53205 Music Box.
1994 ANYTIME YOU NEED A FRIEND
    (S) (4:25) Columbia 53205 Music Box.
released as by LUTHER VANDROSS & MARIAH CAREY:
1994 ENDLESS LOVE
    (S) (4:18) Epic/LV 57775 Luther Vandross - Songs.
    (S) (4:18) LV Records/Epic 68220 Luther Vandross - One Night With You: The Best Of Love Volume 2.
released as by MARIAH CAREY:
1995 FANTASY
    (S) (4:03) Columbia 66700 Daydream. *(LP version)*
released as by MARIAH CAREY & BOYZ II MEN:
1996 ONE SWEET DAY
    (S) (4:40) Columbia 66700 Mariah Carey - Daydream.
    (S) (4:40) Grammy Recordings/Sony 67565 1996 Grammy Nominees.
released as by MARIAH CAREY:
1996 ALWAYS BE MY BABY
    (S) (4:16) Columbia 66700 Daydream.
1997 HONEY
    (S) (4:59) Columbia 67835 Butterfly.

TONY CAREY
1984 A FINE FINE DAY
    (S) (4:25) Priority 53680 Spring Break.
    (S) (4:24) Rhino 72597 Billboard Top Album Rock Hits, 1984.
1984 THE FIRST DAY OF SUMMER

HENSON CARGILL
1968 SKIP A ROPE
    (S) (2:35) Rhino 70689 Billboard's Top Country Hits Of 1968.
    (S) (2:35) Time-Life CTD-06 Country USA - 1968.
    (S) (2:35) Sony Music Special Products 66106 The Monument Story.
    (S) (2:34) JCI 3154 1965 - Only Country - 1969.
    (S) (2:34) K-Tel 3359 101 Greatest Country Hits Vol. Five: Country Memories. *(rerecording)*
    (S) (2:35) Time-Life R808-02 Classic Country 1965-1969.

BELINDA CARLISLE
1986 MAD ABOUT YOU
- (S) (3:35) IRS 29695 On The Charts: IRS Records 1979-1994.
- (S) (3:35) IRS 5741 Belinda.
- (S) (3:34) MCA 10606 Her Greatest Hits.
- (S) (3:34) Priority 53765 Rock Of The 80's Volume 9.
- (S) (3:35) Time-Life R988-04 Sounds Of The Eighties: 1986.
- (S) (3:35) Big Ear Music 4003 Only In The 80's Volume Three.
- (S) (3:34) JCI 3171 #1 Radio Hits 1985 - Only Rock 'n Roll - 1989.

1987 HEAVEN IS A PLACE ON EARTH
(actual 45 time is (4:04) not (3:49) as stated on the record label)
- (S) (4:03) Geffen 24236 Greenpeace - Rainbow Warriors.
- (S) (4:10) Rhino 71642 Billboard Top Hits - 1987.
- (S) (4:05) Sandstone 33041 and 5007 Rock The First Volume 1.
- (S) (4:05) MCA 42080 Heaven On Earth.
- (S) (4:03) MCA 10606 Her Greatest Hits.
- (S) (4:10) Time-Life R988-09 Sounds Of The Eighties: 1987.
- (S) (4:05) MCA Special Products 20897 Greatest Rock Hits Of The 80's.
- (S) (4:09) Madacy Entertainment 1987 Rock On 1987.
- (S) (4:05) Hip-O 40004 The '80s Hit(s) Back!
- (S) (4:05) Priority 50953 I Love Rock & Roll Volume 4: Hits Of The 80's.
- (S) (4:09) Hollywood 62098 O.S.T. Romy And Michele's High School Reunion.
- (S) (4:09) K-Tel 3867 The 80's: Hot Ladies.
- (S) (4:04) Hip-O 40080 Essential '80s: 1985-1989.

1988 I GET WEAK
(dj copies of this 45 were issued in two lengths - one side ran (4:15) not (3:58) as stated on the record label, and the other ran (4:34) not (4:40) as stated on the record label; commercial copies ran (4:15) not (3:58) as stated on the record label)
- (S) (4:50) MCA 42080 Heaven On Earth. *(LP version)*
- (S) (4:50) MCA 10606 Her Greatest Hits. *(LP version)*
- (S) (4:15) Time-Life R988-10 Sounds Of The 80's: 1988. *(45 version)*
- (S) (4:50) Madacy Entertainment 1988 Rock On 1988. *(LP version)*
- (S) (4:49) Hip-O 40000 Thinking About You - A Collection Of Modern Love Songs. *(LP version)*
- (S) (4:50) Time-Life R834-05 Body Talk - Sealed With A Kiss. *(LP version)*
- (S) (4:15) Hip-O 40075 Rock She Said: On The Pop Side. *(45 version)*

1988 CIRCLE IN THE SAND
- (S) (4:25) Sandstone 33050 and 5018 Cosmopolitan Volume 4. *(LP version)*
- (S) (4:25) DCC Compact Classics 089 Night Moves Volume 7. *(LP version)*
- (S) (4:25) MCA 42080 Heaven On Earth. *(LP version)*
- (S) (4:23) MCA 10606 Her Greatest Hits. *(LP version)*
- (S) (4:23) Hip-O 40005 The '80s Hit(s) Back....Again! *(LP version)*
- (S) (4:24) MCA Special Products 20958 Mellow Classics. *(LP version)*

1989 LEAVE A LIGHT ON
- (S) (4:35) MCA 6639 Runaway Horses.
- (S) (4:31) MCA 10606 Her Greatest Hits.

1990 SUMMER RAIN
- (S) (5:26) MCA 6639 Runaway Horses.
- (S) (5:26) MCA 10606 Her Greatest Hits.

CARL CARLTON
1974 EVERLASTING LOVE
(actual 45 time is (2:33) not (2:20) as stated on the record label)
- (S) (2:34) Rhino 70553 Soul Hits Of The 70's Volume 13.
- (S) (2:34) Priority 7058 Mega-Hits Dance Classics Volume 9.
- (S) (2:33) MCA 10666 Duke-Peacock's Greatest Hits.
- (S) (2:33) Essex 7051 Non-Stop Dance Hits.
- (S) (2:33) Time-Life SOD-15 Sounds Of The Seventies - 1974: Take Two.
- (S) (2:33) MCA Special Products 20752 Classic R&B Oldies From The 70's Vol. 2.
- (S) (2:33) Hip-O 40010 ABC's Of Soul Volume 2.
- (S) (2:33) Hip-O 40030 The Glory Of Love - '70s Sweet & Soulful Love Songs.
- (S) (2:34) Priority 50956 Mega Hits - Disco Heat.
- (S) (2:33) Hip-O 40035 Cigar Classics Volume 2 - Urban Fire.
- (S) (2:33) MCA Special Products 21010 R&B Crossover Hits Volume 2.
- (S) (2:33) MCA Special Products 21032 Soul Legends.
- (S) (2:34) Polydor 314555120 Pure Disco 2.
- (S) (2:34) Time-Life R840-05 Sounds Of The Seventies: '70s Dance Party 1972-1974.

1981 SHE'S A BAD MAMA JAMA (SHE'S BUILT, SHE'S STACKED)
- (S) (5:48) Mercury 314522460 Funk Funk: Best Of Funk Essentials 2. *(LP version)*
- (S) (5:50) Rhino 71755 and 72832 Phat Trax: The Best Of Old School Volume 4. *(LP version)*
- (S) (3:54) Thump 4030 Old School Vol. 3. *(45 version; tracks into next selection)*
- (S) (3:54) Rebound 314520365 Funk Classics - The 80's. *(45 version)*
- (S) (4:02) Thump 4100 Old School Mix. *(all selections on this cd are segued together and remixed)*
- (S) (5:12) Chronicles 314555140 Dance Funk. *(all selections on this cd are segued together)*
- (S) (3:56) Simitar 55542 The Number One's: Soul On Fire. *(45 version)*
- (S) (3:54) JCI 3176 1980 - Only Soul - 1984. *(45 version)*

ERIC CARMEN
1976 ALL BY MYSELF
(actual 45 time is (4:26) not (4:22) as stated on the record label; LP length is (7:10))
- (S) (4:53) Rhino 70671 Billboard Top Hits - 1976. *(:27 longer than the 45 version)*
- (S) (4:53) Sandstone 33003 Reelin' In The Years Volume 4. *(:27 longer than the 45 version)*
- (S) (4:31) Original Sound 8895 Dick Clark's 21 All-Time Hits Vol. 4. *(45 version)*
- (S) (4:04) Razor & Tie 4543 The '70s Preservation Society Presents: Easy '70s. *(:22 shorter than the 45 version)*
- (S) (4:53) Arista 8548 Best Of. *(:27 longer than the 45 version)*
- (S) (7:08) Rhino 71141 Eric Carmen. *(LP version)*
- (S) (4:57) Rhino 71141 Eric Carmen. *(:31 longer than the 45 version)*
- (S) (4:53) DCC Compact Classics 065 Rock Of The 70's Volume 4. *(:27 longer than the 45 version)*
- (S) (4:52) Time-Life SOD-04 Sounds Of The Seventies - 1976. *(:26 longer than the 45 version)*
- (S) (4:51) Rebound 314520368 Class Reunion '76. *(:25 longer than the 45 version)*
- (S) (4:15) Madacy Entertainment 1975 Rock On 1975. *(:11 shorter than the 45 version)*
- (S) (4:03) JCI 3146 1975 - Only Love - 1979. *(:23 shorter than the 45 version)*
- (S) (4:27) Time-Life AM1-23 AM Gold - 1976. *(45 version)*
- (S) (4:52) Time-Life R834-02 Body Talk - Just For You. *(:26 longer than the 45 version)*
- (S) (4:30) Arista 18963 Eric Carmen -- The Definitive Collection. *(45 version)*
- (S) (4:53) K-Tel 4017 70s Heavy Hitters: Summer Love. *(:27 longer than the 45 version)*
- (S) (4:30) Simitar 55512 The Number One's: Lovin' Feelings. *(45 version)*
- (S) (4:31) Simitar 55152 Blue Eyed Soul. *(45 version)*
- (S) (4:53) Time-Life R814-04 Love Songs. *(:27 longer than the 45 version)*

1976 NEVER GONNA FALL IN LOVE AGAIN
- (S) (3:45) Arista 8548 Best Of.
- (S) (3:45) Rhino 71141 Eric Carmen.

(S) (3:43) Arista 18963 Eric Carmen -- The Definitive Collection.

(S) (3:43) Time-Life R834-13 Body Talk - Just The Two Of Us.

1976 SUNRISE

(S) (5:22) Rhino 71141 Eric Carmen. *(LP version)*

(S) (5:20) Arista 18963 Eric Carmen -- The Definitive Collection. *(LP version)*

1977 SHE DID IT

(S) (3:45) Arista 8548 Best Of.

(S) (3:45) Arista 18963 Eric Carmen -- The Definitive Collection.

1978 CHANGE OF HEART

(S) (3:38) Arista 8548 Best Of.

(S) (3:39) Arista 18963 Eric Carmen -- The Definitive Collection.

1985 I WANNA HEAR IT FROM YOUR LIPS

(S) (3:13) Geffen 24042 Eric Carmen.

1988 HUNGRY EYES

(S) (4:07) RCA 6408 O.S.T. Dirty Dancing.

(S) (4:02) Arista 8548 Best Of.

(S) (4:07) Time-Life R988-19 Sounds Of The Eighties: The Late '80s.

(S) (4:00) Arista 18963 Eric Carmen -- The Definitive Collection.

1988 MAKE ME LOSE CONTROL

(S) (4:45) K-Tel 898 Romantic Hits Of The 80's.

(S) (4:45) Priority 53714 80's Greatest Rock Hits Volume 1 - Passion & Power.

(S) (4:45) Arista 8548 Best Of.

(S) (4:46) Priority 53681 80's Greatest Rock Hits - Agony & Ecstasy.

(S) (4:45) Time-Life R988-10 Sounds Of The 80's: 1988.

(S) (4:45) Time-Life R138-18 Body Talk.

(S) (4:42) JCI 3186 1985 - Only Love - 1989.

(S) (4:44) Arista 18963 Eric Carmen -- The Definitive Collection.

(S) (4:45) K-Tel 3864 Slow Dancin'.

(S) (4:45) Time-Life R834-17 Body Talk - Heart To Heart.

KIM CARNES
released as by GENE COTTON with KIM CARNES:
1978 YOU'RE A PART OF ME

(S) (3:43) EMI 98223 Gypsy Honeymoon: Best Of Kim Carnes.

released as by KENNY ROGERS with KIM CARNES:
1980 DON'T FALL IN LOVE WITH A DREAMER

(S) (3:38) EMI 98223 Gypsy Honeymoon: Best Of Kim Carnes.

(S) (3:37) Liberty 46004 Kenny Rogers - Greatest Hits.

(S) (3:38) EMI 46106 Kenny Rogers - Twenty Greatest Hits.

(S) (3:39) EMI 46595 Kenny Rogers - Duets.

(S) (3:38) EMI 46673 Kenny Rogers - 25 Greatest Hits.

(S) (3:42) Reprise 26711 Kenny Rogers - 20 Great Years. *(all selections on this cd are rerecorded)*

(S) (3:38) Razor & Tie 2042 Kenny Rogers - Gideon.

(S) (3:38) Capitol 35779 Kenny Rogers - Best Of.

(S) (3:38) K-Tel 4041 Kim Carnes/Juice Newton Back To Back.

released as by KIM CARNES:
1980 MORE LOVE

(S) (3:36) EMI 98223 Gypsy Honeymoon: Best Of Kim Carnes.

(S) (3:31) K-Tel 4041 Kim Carnes/Juice Newton Back To Back.

1981 BETTE DAVIS EYES

(S) (3:46) EMI 91665 Mistaken Identity.

(S) (3:45) Rhino 70676 Billboard Top Hits - 1981.

(S) (3:45) EMI 98223 Gypsy Honeymoon: Best Of Kim Carnes.

(S) (3:45) Priority 7076 80's Greatest Rock Hits Volume 2: Leather & Lace.

(S) (3:43) JCI 3127 1980 - Only Rock 'N Roll - 1984.

(S) (3:45) Rhino 71894 Radio Daze: Pop Hits Of The 80's Volume Five.

(S) (3:45) Time-Life R988-08 Sounds Of The Eighties: 1981.

(S) (3:43) Hip-O 40079 Essential '80s: 1980-1984.

(S) (3:44) K-Tel 4041 Kim Carnes/Juice Newton Back To Back.

1981 DRAW OF THE CARDS

(S) (4:51) EMI 91665 Mistaken Identity. *(LP length)*

(S) (4:50) K-Tel 4041 Kim Carnes/Juice Newton Back To Back. *(LP length)*

1982 VOYEUR

(S) (3:56) Big Ear Music 4001 Only In The 80's Volume One.

1983 DOES IT MAKE YOU REMEMBER

(S) (3:56) K-Tel 4041 Kim Carnes/Juice Newton Back To Back.

1983 INVISIBLE HANDS
released as by KENNY ROGERS with KIM CARNES and JAMES INGRAM:
1984 WHAT ABOUT ME

(S) (4:22) RCA 5335 Kenny Rogers - What About Me?.

(S) (4:20) Reprise 46571 Kenny Rogers - A Decade Of Hits.

released as by KIM CARNES:
1985 CRAZY IN THE NIGHT (BARKING AT AIRPLANES)

(S) (3:34) EMI 98223 Gypsy Honeymoon: Best Of Kim Carnes.

RENATO CAROSONE
1958 TORERO

(M) (3:01) EMI-Capitol Music Special Markets 19446 Lost Hits Of The '50s.

CARPENTERS
1970 (THEY LONG TO BE) CLOSE TO YOU

(S) (4:33) A&M 3184 Close To You. *(LP version)*

(S) (3:41) A&M 6750 Classics Volume 2. *(45 version)*

(S) (3:40) A&M 3601 The Singles 1969-1973. *(45 version)*

(S) (3:41) A&M 6601 Yesterday Once More. *(45 version)*

(S) (3:41) A&M 6875 and 314540000 From The Top. *(45 version)*

(S) (3:40) A&M 314540312 Interpretations: A 25th Anniversary Celebration. *(45 version; remixed)*

(S) (3:40) A&M 314540838 Love Songs. *(45 version; remixed)*

1970 WE'VE ONLY JUST BEGUN

(S) (3:05) A&M 3184 Close To You. *(tracks into next selection)*

(S) (3:03) A&M 6750 Classics Volume 2.

(S) (3:03) A&M 6601 Yesterday Once More.

(S) (4:09) A&M 3601 The Singles 1969-1973. *(with a (1:05) prelude that tracks over the introduction)*

(S) (3:03) A&M 6875 and 314540000 From The Top.

(S) (3:03) A&M 314540312 Interpretations: A 25th Anniversary Celebration. *(some instrumentation rerecorded; remixed)*

(S) (3:03) Polydor 314527493 O.S.T. Muriel's Wedding.

(S) (3:04) A&M 314540838 Love Songs.

1971 FOR ALL WE KNOW

(S) (2:30) A&M 6750 Classics Volume 2. *(tracks into next selection)*

(S) (2:30) A&M 6601 Yesterday Once More. *(tracks into next selection)*

(S) (2:32) A&M 3601 The Singles 1969-1973.

(S) (2:31) A&M 6875 and 314540000 From The Top. *(remixed; some instrumentation rerecorded)*

(S) (2:33) A&M 3502 Carpenters.

(S) (2:31) A&M 314540838 Love Songs.

1971 RAINY DAYS AND MONDAYS

(S) (3:35) A&M 6750 Classics Volume 2. *(previous selection tracks over introduction)*

(S) (3:35) A&M 6601 Yesterday Once More. *(previous selection tracks over introduction)*

(S) (3:19) A&M 3601 The Singles 1969-1973. *(previous selection tracks over introduction; ending is edited and tracks into next selection)*

(S) (3:35) A&M 6875 and 314540000 From The Top. *(previous song just barely tracks over introduction; some instrumentation rerecorded)*

(S) (3:35) A&M 3502 Carpenters.

CARPENTERS (Continued)

(S) (3:47) A&M 314540312 Interpretations: A 25th Anniversary Celebration. *(remixed; some instrumentation rerecorded)*
(S) (3:35) A&M 314540838 Love Songs.

1971 SUPERSTAR
(S) (3:45) A&M 6750 Classics Volume 2. *(tracks into next selection)*
(S) (3:40) A&M 3601 The Singles 1969-1973. *(tracks into next selection)*
(S) (3:45) A&M 6601 Yesterday Once More. *(tracks into next selection)*
(S) (3:45) A&M 6875 and 314540000 From The Top. *(remixed; tracks into following selection)*
(S) (3:47) A&M 3502 Carpenters.
(S) (3:47) A&M 314540312 Interpretations: A 25th Anniversary Celebration. *(remixed)*
(S) (3:45) Warner Brothers 45904 O.S.T. Tommy Boy (The Movie).
(S) (3:48) A&M 314540838 Love Songs.

1972 HURTING EACH OTHER
(S) (2:45) A&M 6750 Classics Volume 2.
(S) (2:45) A&M 6601 Yesterday Once More.
(S) (2:45) A&M 3601 The Singles 1969-1973.
(S) (2:46) A&M 3511 A Song For You.
(S) (2:45) A&M 6875 and 314540000 From The Top. *(remixed; piano track rerecorded)*
(S) (2:46) MFSL 525 A Song For You. *(gold disc)*
(S) (2:45) A&M 314540838 Love Songs. *(remixed; piano track rerecorded)*

1972 IT'S GOING TO TAKE SOME TIME
(S) (2:55) A&M 6750 Classics Volume 2.
(S) (2:54) A&M 3601 The Singles 1969-1973.
(S) (2:55) A&M 6601 Yesterday Once More.
(S) (2:57) A&M 3511 A Song For You.
(S) (2:57) MFSL 525 A Song For You. *(gold disc)*

1972 GOODBYE TO LOVE
(S) (3:55) A&M 6750 Classics Volume 2. *(piano track rerecorded)*
(S) (3:55) A&M 6601 Yesterday Once More. *(previous selection tracks over introduction; piano track rerecorded)*
(S) (3:50) A&M 3601 The Singles 1969-1973. *(previous selection tracks over introduction; includes :05 introduction first heard on the vinyl LP "The Singles 1969-1973")*
(S) (3:54) A&M 3511 A Song For You. *(piano track rerecorded)*
(S) (3:58) A&M 6875 and 314540000 From The Top. *(remixed; piano track rerecorded; includes countoff)*
(S) (3:55) MFSL 525 A Song For You. *(piano track rerecorded; gold disc)*
(S) (3:55) A&M 314540838 Love Songs. *(piano track rerecorded)*

1973 SING
(S) (3:17) A&M 6750 Classics Volume 2.
(S) (3:16) A&M 3601 The Singles 1969-1973.
(S) (3:17) A&M 6601 Yesterday Once More.
(S) (3:17) A&M 3519 Now & Then.

1973 YESTERDAY ONCE MORE
(S) (3:57) A&M 6750 Classics Volume 2. *(piano track rerecorded)*
(S) (3:56) A&M 3601 The Singles 1969-1973.
(S) (3:57) A&M 6601 Yesterday Once More. *(piano track rerecorded)*
(S) (3:57) A&M 3519 Now & Then. *(tracks into next selection)*
(S) (3:50) A&M 6875 and 314540000 From The Top. *(piano track rerecorded; tracks into next selection)*

1973 TOP OF THE WORLD
(S) (2:56) A&M 6750 Classics Volume 2. *(tracks into next selection; 45 version)*
(S) (2:56) A&M 6601 Yesterday Once More. *(tracks into next selection; 45 version)*
(S) (2:58) A&M 3601 The Singles 1969-1973. *(tracks into next selection; 45 version)*

(S) (2:58) A&M 3511 A Song For You. *(45 version)*
(S) (2:58) A&M 6875 and 314540000 From The Top. *(LP version)*
(S) (2:58) MFSL 525 A Song For You. *(45 version; gold disc)*
(S) (2:59) A&M 314540838 Love Songs. *(45 version)*

1974 I WON'T LAST A DAY WITHOUT YOU
(S) (3:49) A&M 6601 Yesterday Once More.
(S) (3:46) MFSL 525 A Song For You. *(gold disc)*
(S) (3:49) A&M 6750 Classics Volume 2. *(previous selection tracks over introduction)*
(S) (3:47) A&M 3511 A Song For You.
(S) (3:53) A&M 314540838 Love Songs.

1975 PLEASE MR. POSTMAN
(S) (2:50) A&M 6601 Yesterday Once More.
(S) (2:50) A&M 6750 Classics Volume 2.
(S) (2:49) A&M 4530 Horizon.
(S) (2:49) A&M 6875 and 314540000 From The Top.

1975 ONLY YESTERDAY
(S) (3:50) A&M 6601 Yesterday Once More. *(:05 longer than the 45 length)*
(S) (3:50) A&M 6750 Classics Volume 2. *(:05 longer than the 45 length)*
(S) (4:09) A&M 4530 Horizon. *(LP length)*
(S) (3:56) A&M 6875 and 314540000 From The Top. *(:11 longer than the 45 length)*
(S) (3:56) A&M 314540838 Love Songs. *(:11 longer than the 45 length)*

1975 SOLITAIRE
(S) (4:39) A&M 4530 Horizon.
(S) (4:39) A&M 6875 and 314540000 From The Top.
(S) (4:39) A&M 314540312 Interpretations: A 25th Anniversary Celebration.
(S) (4:39) A&M 314540838 Love Songs.

1976 THERE'S A KIND OF HUSH (ALL OVER THE WORLD)
(S) (3:03) A&M 6601 Yesterday Once More.
(S) (3:03) A&M 6750 Classics Volume 2.
(S) (3:02) A&M 3197 A Kind Of Hush.

1976 I NEED TO BE IN LOVE
(S) (3:30) A&M 6601 Yesterday Once More. *(tracks into next selection)*
(S) (3:30) A&M 6750 Classics Volume 2. *(tracks into next selection)*
(S) (3:34) A&M 3197 A Kind Of Hush.
(S) (3:47) A&M 6875 and 314540000 From The Top.
(S) (3:49) A&M 314540838 Love Songs.

1977 CALLING OCCUPANTS OF INTERPLANETARY CRAFT
(S) (7:06) A&M 6601 Yesterday Once More. *(LP version)*
(S) (7:06) A&M 6750 Classics Volume 2. *(LP version)*
(S) (7:06) A&M 3199 Passage. *(LP version)*
(S) (7:07) A&M 6875 and 314540000 From The Top. *(LP version)*
(S) (7:07) A&M 314540312 Interpretations: A 25th Anniversary Celebration. *(LP version; remixed)*

1981 TOUCH ME WHEN WE'RE DANCING
(S) (3:18) A&M 6601 Yesterday Once More.
(S) (3:18) A&M 6750 Classics Volume 2. *(previous selection tracks over introduction)*
(S) (3:19) A&M 3723 Made In America.
(S) (3:19) A&M 6875 and 314540000 From The Top.

CATHY CARR
1956 IVORY TOWER
(M) (2:34) Rhino 75894 Jukebox Classics Volume 2.
(M) (2:33) Time-Life HPD-15 Your Hit Parade - 1956.
(E) (2:34) Curb 77775 Hard To Find Original Recordings - Classic Hits.
(M) (2:33) Time-Life R132-10 Love Songs Of Your Hit Parade.
1959 FIRST ANNIVERSARY

VALERIE CARR
1958 WHEN THE BOYS TALK ABOUT THE GIRLS

VIKKI CARR
1967 IT MUST BE HIM
(S) (2:50) EMI 96268 24 Greatest Hits Of All Time.
(S) (2:51) EMI 92776 Best Of.

(S) (2:48) Capitol 90231 O.S.T. Moonstruck.
(S) (2:56) Pair 1082 From The Heart. *(timing index is off by :05)*
(S) (2:50) EMI 93450 Best Of.
(S) (2:46) Time-Life R138/05 Look Of Love.
(S) (2:51) Curb 77677 Greatest Hits.
(S) (2:48) JCI 7022 Those Wonderful Years - It Must Be Him.
(S) (2:46) Time-Life R814-05 Love Songs.

1968 THE LESSON
(S) (2:30) EMI 92776 Best Of.
(S) (2:29) EMI 93450 Best Of.

PAUL CARRACK
1982 I NEED YOU
(S) (2:45) Rhino 71700 New Wave Hits Of The 80's Vol. 7.
(S) (2:47) Chrysalis 41663 and 21663 Carrack Collection.
(S) (2:47) Chrysalis 27221 The Paul Carrack Collection.
(S) (2:46) Epic 38161 Suburban Voodoo.

1988 DON'T SHED A TEAR
(S) (3:42) Chrysalis 27221 The Paul Carrack Collection. *(45 version)*
(S) (4:53) Chrysalis 21578 One Good Reason. *(LP version)*
(S) (4:54) Priority 53681 80's Greatest Rock Hits - Agony & Ecstasy. *(LP version)*
(S) (3:41) Time-Life R988-10 Sounds Of The 80's: 1988. *(45 version)*
(S) (3:41) Madacy Entertainment 1988 Rock On 1988. *(45 version)*

1988 ONE GOOD REASON
(S) (3:19) Chrysalis 27221 The Paul Carrack Collection.
(S) (3:19) Chrysalis 21578 One Good Reason.

1989 I LIVE BY THE GROOVE
(S) (3:57) Chrysalis 27221 The Paul Carrack Collection.
(S) (4:09) Chrysalis 21709 Groove Approved.

KEITH CARRADINE
1976 I'M EASY
(S) (3:02) Rhino 71868 Academy Award Winning Songs.
(S) (3:02) Rhino 72279 Academy Award Winning Songs Volume 4.
(S) (3:10) JCI 3146 1975 - Only Love - 1979.

DAVID CARROLL
1955 MELODY OF LOVE

CARS
1978 JUST WHAT I NEEDED
(S) (3:42) Elektra 135 The Cars.
(S) (3:43) Elektra 60464 Greatest Hits.
(S) (3:43) Polydor 314515913 Classic Rock Box.
(S) (3:43) DCC Compact Classics 1031 The Cars. *(gold disc)*
(S) (3:42) Time-Life R102-34 The Rolling Stone Collection.
(S) (3:42) Time-Life R968-02 Guitar Rock 1978-1979.
(S) (3:42) Time-Life SOD-20 Sounds Of The Seventies - 1978: Take Two.
(S) (3:43) Rhino 73506 Anthology - Just What I Needed.
(S) (3:43) Epic/Legacy 65020 Ultimate Rock 'n' Roll Collection.
(S) (3:42) JCI 3169 #1 Radio Hits 1975 - Only Rock 'n Roll - 1979.
(S) (3:43) Eclipse Music Group 64896 Rock 'n Roll Relix 1978-1979.
(S) (3:43) Eclipse Music Group 64897 Rock 'n Roll Relix 1970-1979.
(S) (3:38) Arista 18985 Ultimate New Wave Party 1998. *(all selections on this cd are segued together)*
(S) (3:43) Time-Life R13610 Gold And Platinum Box Set - The Ultimate Rock Collection.

1979 LET'S GO
(S) (3:32) Elektra 507 Candy-O.
(S) (3:32) Elektra 60464 Greatest Hits.

(S) (3:32) Time-Life R968-02 Guitar Rock 1978-1979.
(S) (3:32) Time-Life SOD-19 Sounds Of The Seventies - 1979: Take Two.
(S) (3:32) Time-Life R105-24 Guitar Rock Monsters.
(S) (3:33) Rhino 73506 Anthology - Just What I Needed.

1979 IT'S ALL I CAN DO
(S) (3:43) Elektra 507 Candy-O.
(S) (3:44) Rhino 73506 Anthology - Just What I Needed.

1980 TOUCH AND GO
(S) (4:53) Elektra 514 Panorama. *(LP version)*
(S) (4:54) Elektra 60464 Greatest Hits. *(LP version)*
(S) (4:55) Rhino 73506 Anthology - Just What I Needed. *(LP version)*

1982 SHAKE IT UP
(S) (3:31) Time-Life R968-04 Guitar Rock 1980-81.
(S) (3:31) JCI 3127 1980 - Only Rock 'N Roll - 1984.
(S) (3:32) Elektra 60464 Greatest Hits.
(S) (3:32) Elektra 60585 Shake It Up.
(S) (3:31) Time-Life R988-05 Sounds Of The Eighties: 1982.
(S) (3:33) Rhino 73506 Anthology - Just What I Needed.
(S) (3:33) Rhino 72595 Billboard Top Album Rock Hits, 1982.
(S) (3:33) Rhino 72894 Hard Rock Cafe: New Wave.
(S) (3:31) Madacy Entertainment 6805 The Power Of Rock.
(S) (3:31) JCI 3192 18 Rock Classics Volume 2.

1984 YOU MIGHT THINK
(S) (3:03) Elektra 60464 Greatest Hits.
(S) (3:04) Elektra 60296 Heartbeat City.
(S) (3:03) Time-Life R988-06 Sounds Of The Eighties: 1984.
(S) (3:05) Rhino 73506 Anthology - Just What I Needed.
(S) (3:05) Rhino 72771 The Big 80's.
(S) (3:05) Rhino 72597 Billboard Top Album Rock Hits, 1984.

1984 MAGIC
(S) (3:56) Elektra 60464 Greatest Hits.
(S) (3:56) Elektra 60296 Heartbeat City.
(S) (3:57) Rhino 73506 Anthology - Just What I Needed.
(S) (3:56) Madacy Entertainment 1984 Rock On 1984.
(S) (3:57) JCI 3170 #1 Radio Hits 1980 - Only Rock 'n Roll - 1984.
(S) (3:54) Priority 50953 I Love Rock & Roll Volume 4: Hits Of The 80's.
(S) (3:56) Time-Life R988-23 Sounds Of The Eighties 1984-1985.

1984 DRIVE
(S) (3:54) Sandstone 33048 and 5016 Cosmopolitan Volume 2.
(S) (3:53) Time-Life R105-40 Rock Dreams.
(S) (3:53) JCI 3119 18 Rock Classics.
(S) (3:54) DCC Compact Classics 087 Night Moves Volume 5.
(S) (3:53) Elektra 60464 Greatest Hits.
(S) (3:53) Elektra 60296 Heartbeat City.
(S) (3:52) Time-Life R988-27 Sounds Of The Eighties: The Rolling Stone Collection 1983-1985.
(S) (3:53) Time-Life R138-18 Body Talk.
(S) (3:54) Rhino 73506 Anthology - Just What I Needed.
(S) (3:53) JCI 3147 1980 - Only Love - 1984.
(S) (3:53) Time-Life R834-10 Body Talk - From The Heart.
(S) (3:54) K-Tel 6257 The Greatest Love Songs - 16 Soft Rock Hits.

1984 HELLO AGAIN
(S) (5:54) JCI 3122 Lost Mixes. *(remixed)*
(S) (3:45) Elektra 60296 Heartbeat City.
(S) (3:46) Rhino 73506 Anthology - Just What I Needed.

1985 WHY CAN'T I HAVE YOU
(S) (4:03) Elektra 60296 Heartbeat City.
(S) (4:03) Rhino 73506 Anthology - Just What I Needed.

1986 TONIGHT SHE COMES
(S) (3:45) JCI 3128 1985 - Only Rock 'N Roll - 1989.
(S) (3:53) Elektra 60464 Greatest Hits.
(S) (3:54) Rhino 73506 Anthology - Just What I Needed.
(S) (3:50) Time-Life R988-15 Sounds Of The Eighties: The Mid 80's.

1986 I'M NOT THE ONE
(S) (4:10) Elektra 60464 Greatest Hits.
(S) (4:08) Elektra 60585 Shake It Up.
(S) (4:12) Rhino 73506 Anthology - Just What I Needed.

CARS *(Continued)*
1987 YOU ARE THE GIRL
- (S) (3:53)   Elektra 60747   Door To Door.
- (S) (3:53)   Rhino 73506   Anthology - Just What I Needed.

KIT CARSON
1956 BAND OF GOLD
- (M) (2:33)   EMI-Capitol Music Special Markets 19446   Lost Hits Of The '50s.

MINDY CARSON
1955 WAKE THE TOWN AND TELL THE PEOPLE

CLARENCE CARTER
1968 SLIP AWAY
- (S) (2:29)   Atlantic 81911   Golden Age Of Black Music (1960-1970).
- (M) (2:31)   Atlantic 81298   Atlantic Rhythm & Blues Volume 6.
- (S) (2:30)   Atco 91813   Classic Recordings.
- (S) (2:27)   Atlantic 82305   Atlantic Rhythm And Blues 1947-1974 Box Set.
- (S) (2:30)   Rhino 70286   Snatching It Back.
- (S) (2:27)   Rhino 71459   Soul Hits, Volume 1.
- (M) (2:31)   Time-Life RHD-04   Rhythm & Blues - 1968.
- (M) (2:31)   Time-Life 2CLR-11   Classic Rock - 1968: The Beat Goes On.
- (S) (2:29)   Rhino 71517   The Muscle Shoals Sound.
- (S) (2:30)   Motown 6763   Rites Of Rhythm & Blues Volume Two.
- (S) (2:30)   Ripete 2198   Soul Patrol.
- (S) (2:29)   Rhino 71806   The R&B Box: Thirty Years Of Rhythm & Blues.
- (S) (2:37)   Ichiban 2508   Cheatin': From A Man's Point Of View.
- (S) (2:29)   Rhino 71938   Billboard Top Pop Hits, 1968.
- (M) (2:31)   Time-Life R838-03   Solid Gold Soul - 1968.
- (S) (2:28)   Flashback 72657   '60s Soul: Try A Little Tenderness.
- (S) (2:28)   Flashback 72091   '60s Soul Hits Box Set.
- (S) (2:30)   Flashback 72898   25 Years Of R&B - 1968.
- (S) (2:29)   Rhino 72963   Ultimate '60s Soul Smashes.

1969 TOO WEAK TO FIGHT
- (S) (2:15)   Atlantic 81911   Golden Age Of Black Music (1960-1970).
- (S) (2:15)   Atlantic 82305   Atlantic Rhythm And Blues 1947-1974 Box Set.
- (S) (2:15)   Rhino 70286   Snatching It Back.
- (S) (2:15)   Rhino 70277   Rare Soul: Beach Music Classics Volume 1.
- (S) (2:15)   Time-Life 2CLR-28   Classic Rock - On The Soul Side II.
- (S) (2:15)   Flashback 72898   25 Years Of R&B - 1968.

1969 SNATCHING IT BACK
- (S) (2:49)   Rhino 70286   Snatching It Back.
- (M) (2:39)   Rhino 72815   Beg, Scream & Shout! The Big Ol' Box Of '60s Soul.
- (M) (2:39)   Flashback 72899   25 Years Of Soul - 1969.

1970 PATCHES
- (S) (3:09)   Atlantic 82305   Atlantic Rhythm And Blues 1947-1974 Box Set. *(LP version)*
- (S) (3:09)   Atlantic 81299   Atlantic Rhythm & Blues Volume 7. *(LP version)*
- (S) (3:10)   Rhino 70286   Snatching It Back. *(LP version)*
- (S) (3:05)   Time-Life RHD-18   Rhythm & Blues - 1970. *(LP version)*
- (S) (3:06)   Time-Life SUD-04   Superhits - 1970. *(LP version)*
- (S) (3:10)   Ripete 2183-RE   Ocean Drive Volume 1. *(LP version)*
- (S) (2:59)   Rhino 71517   The Muscle Shoals Sound. *(remixed 45 version faded :11 early)*
- (S) (3:10)   Rhino 72126   Soul Hits Of The 70's Vol. 16. *(LP version)*
- (S) (3:10)   Rhino 72112   Billboard Hot Soul Hits - 1970. *(LP version)*
- (S) (3:06)   Time-Life AM1-02   AM Gold - 1970. *(LP version)*

- (S) (3:05)   Time-Life R838-05   Solid Gold Soul - 1970. *(LP version)*
- (S) (2:59)   Flashback 72900   25 Years Of Soul - 1970. *(remixed 45 version faded :11 early)*
- (S) (2:59)   Rhino 72964   Ultimate '70s R&B Smashes! *(remixed 45 version faded :11 early)*

MEL CARTER
1963 WHEN A BOY FALLS IN LOVE
- (M) (2:52)   Abkco 2231   Sam Cooke's Sar Records Story.
1965 HOLD ME, THRILL ME, KISS ME
- (S) (2:29)   JCI 3102   Love Sixties.
- (S) (2:27)   RCA 9819   O.S.T. True Love.
- (S) (2:26)   Time-Life SUD-17   Superhits - Mid 60's Classics.
- (S) (2:27)   Time-Life OPCD-4517   Tonight's The Night.
- (S) (2:26)   Time-Life R138/05   Look Of Love.
- (S) (2:27)   Right Stuff 30578   Slow Jams: The 60's Volume 4.
- (S) (2:26)   Ripete 2219   Beach Fever.
- (M) (2:27)   EMI 37810   Best Of.
- (S) (2:25)   Time-Life AM1-16   AM Gold - Mid '60s Classics.
- (S) (2:27)   Right Stuff 53320   Hot Rod Rock Volume 5: Back Seat Movers.
- (S) (2:25)   Time-Life R857-20   The Heart Of Rock 'n' Roll 1965-1966.
- (S) (2:26)   Time-Life R814-02   Love Songs.
- (S) (2:25)   Collectables 1515 and 2515   The Anniversary Album - The 60's.
1965 (ALL OF A SUDDEN) MY HEART SINGS
- (M) (2:42)   EMI 37810   Best Of.
1966 BAND OF GOLD
- (M) (2:16)   EMI 37810   Best Of.

CASCADES
1963 RHYTHM OF THE RAIN
- (M) (2:30)   Time-Life 2RNR-19   Rock 'N' Roll Era - 1963 Still Rockin'.
- (M) (2:28)   Time-Life SUD-08   Superhits - 1963.
- (M) (2:29)   Time-Life R962-05   History Of Rock 'N' Roll: The Teenage Years 1957-1964.
- (M) (2:30)   Varese Sarabande 5534   Rhythm Of The Rain.
- (M) (2:30)   Rhino 71584   Billboard Top Pop Hits, 1963.
- (E) (2:31)   LaserLight 12322   Greatest Hit Singles Collection.
- (E) (2:31)   Eclipse Music Group 64868   Rock 'n Roll Relix 1962-1963.
- (E) (2:31)   Eclipse Music Group 64872   Rock 'n Roll Relix 1960-1969.
- (M) (2:27)   Time-Life AM1-17   AM Gold - 1963.
- (M) (2:30)   Time-Life R857-18   The Heart Of Rock 'n' Roll 1962-1963 Take Two.

CASE featuring FOXY BROWN
1996 TOUCH ME, TEASE ME
- (S) (3:51)   Def Jam 314531911   O.S.T. The Nutty Professor.

ALVIN CASH & THE CRAWLERS
1965 TWINE TIME
- (M) (2:21)   Rhino 71604   Rock Instrumental Classics Vol. 4: Soul.
- (M) (2:21)   Rhino 72035   Rock Instrumental Classics Vols. 1-5 Box Set.
- (M) (2:21)   Rhino 72815   Beg, Scream & Shout! The Big Ol' Box Of '60s Soul.

JOHNNY CASH
1956 I WALK THE LINE
- (M) (2:41)   Rhino 75884   The Sun Story.
- (M) (2:43)   Rhino 75893   Jukebox Classics Volume 1.
- (M) (2:41)   Rhino 70950   The Sun Years.
- (M) (2:42)   DCC Compact Classics 009   Legends.
- (S) (2:33)   Columbia 9478   Greatest Hits Volume 1. *(rerecording)*
- (M) (2:41)   Columbia 47991   Essential.
- (S) (2:33)   Mercury 834526   Classic Cash. *(all selections on this cd are rerecordings)*
- (M) (2:43)   RCA 66059   Sun's Greatest Hits.

(M) (2:41) Time-Life 2RNR-23 Rock 'N' Roll Era - 1956 Still Rockin'.
(M) (2:40) Time-Life CTD-13 Country USA - 1956.
(M) (2:41) Rhino 71780 Sun Records Collection.
(M) (2:41) Columbia 66773 Super Hits.
(S) (2:54) Risky Business 57473 Country Goes To The Movies. *(rerecording)*
(M) (2:38) K-Tel 225 Country Music Classics Volume I.
(M) (2:42) Curb 77494 Best Of.
(M) (2:41) Time-Life R990-09 Legendary Country Singers.
(M) (2:42) K-Tel 3187 Country's Greatest Singer/Songwriters.
(M) (2:42) K-Tel 3193 Johnny Cash/George Jones.
(M) (2:43) JCI 3152 1955 - Only Country - 1959.
(M) (2:41) Hammer & Lace 697124114 Leading Men: Masters Of Style Volume Two.
(S) (2:32) Mercury 314534665 The Hits. *(all selections on this cd are rerecorded)*
(M) (2:41) Time-Life R808-03 Classic Country 1950-1959.

1958 BALLAD OF A TEENAGE QUEEN
(M) (2:09) Rhino 70950 The Sun Years.
(M) (2:10) DCC Compact Classics 009 Legends.
(M) (2:09) Columbia 47991 Essential.
(M) (2:09) RCA 66059 Sun's Greatest Hits.
(M) (2:09) Time-Life CTD-07 Country USA - 1958.
(M) (2:10) Curb 77494 Best Of.
(M) (2:09) Varese Sarabande 5605 Through The Years - Country Hits Of The 50's.
(M) (2:09) Columbia 69075 Great Balls Of Fire Super Hits.
(S) (2:45) Rebound 314520510 Water From The Wells Of Home.

1958 GUESS THINGS HAPPEN THAT WAY
(M) (1:49) DCC Compact Classics 009 Legends.
(M) (1:47) Rhino 70950 The Sun Years.
(M) (1:48) Columbia 47991 Essential.
(S) (1:43) Mercury 834526 Classic Cash. *(all selections on this cd are rerecordings)*
(M) (1:48) Reprise 45516 O.S.T. A Perfect World.
(M) (1:47) Time-Life CTD-07 Country USA - 1958.
(M) (1:46) Rhino 71780 Sun Records Collection.
(M) (1:48) K-Tel 3108 Country Music Classics Volume XVI.
(M) (1:48) Curb 77494 Best Of.
(M) (1:48) Time-Life R990-09 Legendary Country Singers.
(S) (1:43) Mercury 314534665 The Hits. *(all selections on this cd are rerecorded)*

1958 WAYS OF A WOMAN IN LOVE
(M) (2:22) Rhino 70950 The Sun Years.
(M) (2:13) Columbia 47991 Essential.

1959 DON'T TAKE YOUR GUNS TO TOWN
(S) (3:01) Rhino 70680 Billboard's Top Country Hits Of 1959.
(S) (3:01) Columbia 46031 Columbia Country Classics Volume 3.
(S) (3:01) Columbia 40637 Columbia Records 1958-1986.
(S) (3:01) Columbia 9478 Greatest Hits Volume 1.
(S) (3:00) Columbia 47991 Essential.
(S) (2:55) Mercury 834526 Classic Cash. *(all selections on this cd are rerecordings)*
(S) (3:01) CBS Special Products 8122 The Fabulous.
(S) (3:01) Time-Life CTD-09 Country USA - 1959.
(S) (2:59) Time-Life R990-09 Legendary Country Singers.
(S) (3:00) K-Tel 3323 Gunfighter Ballads.

1963 RING OF FIRE
(S) (2:35) Columbia 46032 Columbia Country Classics Volume 4.
(S) (2:35) Columbia 40637 Columbia Records 1958-1986.
(S) (2:36) Columbia 9478 Greatest Hits Volume 1.
(S) (2:35) Columbia 47991 Essential.
(S) (2:42) Mercury 834526 Classic Cash. *(all selections on this cd are rerecordings)*
(S) (2:32) Time-Life CTD-11 Country USA - 1963.
(S) (2:35) Epic 66632 Music From The Motion Picture "Love & A .45".
(S) (2:35) Columbia 66773 Super Hits.
(S) (2:35) Columbia/Legacy 53817 All-Time Legends Of Country Music.

(S) (2:37) Legacy/Columbia 66890 Ring Of Fire.
(S) (2:36) K-Tel 763 Country Music Classics Volume VIII.
(S) (2:34) Curb 77494 Best Of.
(S) (2:35) Time-Life R990-09 Legendary Country Singers.
(S) (2:37) Columbia 64812 Ring Of Fire/Blood, Sweat & Tears/Ballads Of The American Indian.
(S) (2:35) JCI 3160 1960 - Only Country - 1964.
(S) (2:35) Epic 67941 Super Hits Of The 60's.
(S) (2:36) K-Tel 3365 101 Greatest Country Hits Vol. Six: Timeless Country.
(S) (2:42) Mercury 314534665 The Hits. *(all selections on this cd are rerecorded)*
(S) (2:35) Epic 68778 O.S.T. U Turn.
(S) (2:35) Time-Life R808-01 Classic Country 1960-1964.

1964 UNDERSTAND YOUR MAN
(S) (2:40) Columbia 66773 Super Hits.
(S) (2:41) Time-Life R990-09 Legendary Country Singers.
(S) (2:39) Rhino 70685 Billboard Top Country Hits - 1964.
(S) (2:40) Time-Life CTD-14 Country U.S.A. - 1964.
(S) (2:41) Columbia 9478 Greatest Hits Volume One.

1968 FOLSOM PRISON BLUES
(M) (2:47) Rhino 75894 Jukebox Classics Volume 2. *(Sun Records studio recording - not the hit single version)*
(M) (2:47) Rhino 75884 The Sun Records Story. *(Sun Records studio recording - not the hit single version)*
(M) (2:48) Rhino 70950 The Sun Years. *(Sun Records studio recording - not the hit single version)*
(M) (2:44) Columbia 40637 Columbia Records 1958-1986.
(M) (2:47) DCC Compact Classics 009 Legends. *(Sun Records studio recording - not the hit single version)*
(S) (2:39) Columbia 33639 At Folsom Prison And San Quentin.
(S) (2:41) Columbia 47991 Essential.
(M) (2:47) Columbia 47991 Essential. *(Sun Records studio recording - not the hit single version)*
(S) (2:44) Mercury 834526 Classic Cash. *(all selections on this cd are rerecordings)*
(M) (2:47) RCA 66059 Sun's Greatest Hits. *(Sun Records studio recording - not the hit single version)*
(M) (2:43) Time-Life CTD-06 Country USA - 1968.
(E) (2:46) Time-Life CTD-13 Country USA - 1956. *(Sun Records studio recording - not the hit single version)*
(M) (2:46) Rhino 71780 Sun Records Collection. *(Sun Records studio recording - not the hit single version)*
(M) (2:47) Columbia 66773 Super Hits. *(Sun Records studio recording - not the hit single version)*
(M) (2:47) Risky Business 66393 Jailhouse Rock. *(Sun Records studio version - not the hit single version)*
(S) (2:42) K-Tel 3110 Country Music Classics Volume XVIII.
(S) (2:43) Curb 77494 Best Of.
(M) (2:45) Time-Life R990-09 Legendary Country Singers. *(Sun Records studio version - not the hit single version)*
(M) (2:47) K-Tel 3193 Johnny Cash/George Jones. *(Sun Records studio version - not the hit single version)*
(S) (2:43) A&M 314540424 O.S.T. Things To Do In Denver When You're Dead.
(M) (2:47) K-Tel 3507 Die-Hard Copuntry. *(Sun Records studio version - not the hit single version)*
(S) (2:44) Mercury 314534665 The Hits. *(all selections on this cd are rerecorded)*

1969 A BOY NAMED SUE
(S) (3:44) Columbia 46031 Columbia Country Classics Volume 3.
(S) (3:44) Columbia 40637 Columbia Records 1958-1986.
(S) (3:42) Columbia 38317 Biggest Hits.
(S) (3:36) Columbia 33639 At Folsom Prison And San Quentin.
(S) (3:45) Columbia 47991 Essential.
(S) (3:42) Time-Life CTD-08 Country USA - 1969.
(S) (3:41) K-Tel 3243 Kooky Kountry.

JOHNNY CASH *(Continued)*
- (S) (3:45)   Columbia 66773   Super Hits.
- (S) (3:41)   K-Tel 3095   Country Comedy Classics.
- (S) (3:43)   Curb 77494   Best Of.
- (S) (3:44)   Priority 53717   Branson USA Vol. 2.
- (S) (3:45)   Time-Life R990-09   Legendary Country Singers.

released as by JOHNNY CASH & JUNE CARTER:
1970 IF I WERE A CARPENTER
- (S) (2:58)   Time-Life CTD-04   Country USA - 1970.

released as by JOHNNY CASH:
1970 WHAT IS TRUTH
- (S) (2:36)   Columbia 47991   Essential.
- (S) (2:36)   Eclipse Music Group 64892   Rock 'n Roll Relix 1970-1971.
- (S) (2:36)   Eclipse Music Group 64897   Rock 'n Roll Relix 1970-1979.

1976 ONE PIECE AT A TIME
- (S) (3:59)   Time-Life R990-09   Legendary Country Singers.
- (S) (3:59)   Columbia 66773   Super Hits.
- (S) (4:00)   Columbia 40637   Columbia Records 1958-1986.
- (S) (4:00)   Time-Life R830-01   The Dr. Demento Collection - The Mid 70's.
- (S) (4:02)   Columbia/Legacy 47732   Trucker's Jukebox Volume 2.
- (S) (4:02)   Epic/Legacy 65396   Trucker's Jukebox/Trucker's Jukebox...Top Radio Requests/Trucker's Jukebox Volume 2.

ROSANNE CASH
1981 SEVEN YEAR ACHE
- (S) (3:15)   Columbia 44431   Greatest Country Hits Of The 80's - 1981. *(truncated fade)*
- (S) (3:14)   Columbia 46033   Columbia Country Classics Volume 5. *(truncated fade)*
- (S) (3:15)   Columbia 36965   Seven Year Ache.
- (S) (3:15)   Columbia 53064   30 Years Of Hits Volume 15.
- (S) (3:12)   Time-Life CCD-03   Contemporary Country - The Early 80's.
- (S) (3:14)   Rhino 72447   Listen To The Music: 70's Female Singer/Songwriters.
- (S) (3:16)   Columbia 69070   Super Hits.

CASHMAN & WEST
1972 AMERICAN CITY SUITE
- (S) (7:44)   Rhino 70929   Super Hits Of The 70's Volume 9. *(45 version)*
- (S) (10:47)   Razor & Tie 2028   The AM-FM Blues (Their Very Best). *(LP version)*

CASINOS
1967 THEN YOU CAN TELL ME GOODBYE
- (M) (3:03)   DCC Compact Classics 031   Back Seat Jams.
- (E) (3:03)   Original Sound 8859   Oldies But Goodies Vol. 9. *(this compact disc uses the "Waring - fds" noise reduction process)*
- (M) (3:03)   Original Sound 8859r   Oldies But Goodies Vol. 9. *(remastered edition)*
- (M) (3:03)   Original Sound 2223   Oldies But Goodies Volumes 2,7,9,12 and 13 Box Set. *(Volumes 2, 7 and 12 of this box set use the "Waring - fds" noise reduction process)*
- (M) (3:03)   Original Sound 2500   Oldies But Goodies Volumes 1-15 Box Set. *(most volumes in this box set use the "Waring - fds" noise reduction process)*
- (E) (3:02)   Original Sound CDGO-1   Golden Oldies Volume. 1.
- (E) (3:02)   Original Sound 8892   Dick Clark's 21 All-Time Hits Vol. 2.
- (S) (3:05)   Rhino 70996   One Hit Wonders Of The 60's Volume 2.
- (S) (3:04)   Collectables 5061   History Of Rock Volume 1.
- (M) (3:02)   Time-Life 2CLR-24   Classic Rock - 1967: Blowin' Your Mind.
- (M) (3:00)   Time-Life SUD-05   Superhits - 1967.
- (S) (3:06)   Collectables 2607   WCBS-FM For Lovers Only Vol. 3.

- (E) (3:03)   Collectables 2510   WCBS-FM History Of Rock - The Rockin' 60's.
- (E) (3:03)   Collectables 4510   History Of Rock/The Rockin' 60s.
- (E) (3:02)   Collectables 2501   WCBS-FM History Of Rock - The 60's Part 2.
- (E) (3:02)   Collectables 4501   History Of Rock/The 60s Part Two.
- (S) (3:05)   Collectables 2605   WCBS-FM Jukebox Giants Vol. 3.
- (S) (3:06)   LaserLight 12318   Chart Busters.
- (E) (3:02)   Collectables 2554   CBS-FM History Of Rock Volume 2.
- (E) (3:02)   Music Club 50015   Love Me Forever - 18 Rock'N' Roll Love Songs.
- (M) (3:34)   Varese Sarabande 5786   Best Of. *(complete recording session)*
- (S) (3:06)   Varese Sarabande 5786   Best Of.
- (M) (3:00)   Time-Life AM1-08   AM Gold - 1967.
- (M) (3:01)   Compose 131   Unforgettable - Gold For The Road.
- (S) (3:05)   Time-Life R857-22   The Heart Of Rock 'n' Roll 1967-1969.

DAVID CASSIDY
1972 CHERISH
- (S) (3:46)   Arista 8604   Partridge Family Greatest Hits.

1972 COULD IT BE FOREVER
- (S) (2:18)   Arista 8604   Partridge Family Greatest Hits.

1972 HOW CAN I BE SURE
1972 ROCK ME BABY
1990 LYIN' TO MYSELF
- (S) (3:58)   Enigma 73554   David Cassidy.

SHAUN CASSIDY
1977 DA DOO RON RON
- (S) (2:47)   Curb 77551   Greatest Hits.
- (S) (2:46)   K-Tel 3211   70's Teen Heart-Throbs.

1977 THAT'S ROCK 'N' ROLL
- (S) (2:53)   Curb 77317   70's Hits Volume 1.
- (S) (2:53)   Curb 77551   Greatest Hits.
- (S) (2:51)   Rhino 71228   Yesterday's Heroes: 70's Teen Idols.
- (S) (2:51)   Time-Life AM1-24   AM Gold - 1977.

1978 HEY DEANIE
- (S) (3:36)   Curb 77551   Greatest Hits.
- (S) (3:36)   Time-Life SOD-35   Sounds Of The Seventies - AM Nuggets.
- (S) (3:34)   Rhino 72298   Superhits Of The 70's Volume 24.
- (S) (3:34)   Rhino 72819   16 Magazine - Who's Your Fave Rave.

1978 DO YOU BELIEVE IN MAGIC
- (S) (2:15)   Curb 77551   Greatest Hits.

CASTAWAYS
1965 LIAR LIAR
- (S) (1:50)   K-Tel 205   Battle Of The Bands Volume 3.
- (S) (1:50)   Rhino 75777   More Nuggets.
- (S) (1:51)   A&M 3913 and 3340   O.S.T. Good Morning Vietnam.
- (S) (1:51)   Rhino 70732   Grandson Of Frat Rock.
- (S) (1:50)   Collectables 5068   History Of Rock Volume 8.
- (S) (1:50)   Time-Life 2CLR-01   Classic Rock - 1965.
- (S) (1:50)   LaserLight 12318   Chart Busters.
- (S) (1:50)   Collectables 2505   History Of Rock - The 60's Part 5.
- (S) (1:50)   Collectables 4505   History Of Rock/The 60s Part Five.
- (S) (1:50)   K-Tel 3130   60's Sound Explosion.
- (S) (1:50)   Collectables 2554   CBS-FM History Of Rock Volume 2.
- (S) (1:50)   Eclipse Music Group 64869   Rock 'n Roll Relix 1964-1965.
- (S) (1:50)   Eclipse Music Group 64872   Rock 'n Roll Relix 1960-1969.
- (S) (1:51)   Simitar 55572   The Number One's: Hot In The '60s.

CASTELLS
1961 SACRED
- (S) (2:11) LaserLight 12320 Love Songs.
- (S) (2:11) Era 5019 Best Of.
- (S) (2:10) Curb 77773 Hard To Find Hits Of Rock 'N' Roll Volume One.

1962 SO THIS IS LOVE
- (M) (2:42) Time-Life HPD-37 Your Hit Parade - The 60's.
- (S) (2:42) Era 5019 Best Of.

BOOMER CASTLEMAN
1975 JUDY MAE
- (S) (3:33) Rhino 71200 Super Hits Of The 70's Volume 20.

JIMMY CASTOR
1967 HEY, LEROY, YOUR MAMA'S CALLIN' YOU
- (S) (2:25) Polygram Special Markets 314520264 Soul Hits Of The 60's.
- (S) (2:24) Rhino 72209 Best Of.
- (S) (2:24) Collectables 5620 Hey Leroy, Your Mama's Callin' You.
- (S) (2:24) Hip-O 40007 Soulful Grooves - R&B Instrumental Classics Volume 1.

released as by the JIMMY CASTOR BUNCH:
1972 TROGLODYTE (CAVE MAN)
- (S) (3:33) RCA 8476 and 9684 Nipper's Greatest Hits Of The 70's. *(LP version)*
- (S) (3:23) Rhino 70788 Soul Hits Of The 70's Volume 8. *(45 version)*
- (S) (3:32) RCA 61144 The RCA Records Label: The First Note In Black Music. *(LP version)*
- (S) (3:34) K-Tel 3150 Dumb Ditties. *(rerecording)*
- (S) (3:20) Time-Life SOD-32 Sounds Of The Seventies - AM Pop Classics. *(45 version)*
- (S) (3:36) Rhino 72209 Best Of. *(LP version)*
- (S) (3:21) Time-Life R830-03 The Dr. Demento Collection: The Early '70s. *(45 version)*

1975 BERTHA BUTT BOOGIE
- (S) (3:12) Rhino 70555 Soul Hits Of The 70's Volume 15. *(45 version)*
- (S) (6:09) Rhino 72209 Best Of. *(LP version)*
- (S) (6:09) Thump 4099 Old School Boogie. *(LP version)*
- (S) (3:12) Rhino 72258 Dumb And Dumber: Get Down, Get Dumb. *(45 version)*
- (S) (3:48) K-Tel 3629 Madcap Melodies. *(rerecording)*
- (S) (3:12) Time-Life R830-01 The Dr. Demento Collection - The Mid 70's. *(45 version)*
- (S) (3:13) Rhino 72964 Ultimate '70s R&B Smashes! *(45 version)*

CATE BROTHERS
1976 UNION MAN
- (S) (4:47) Time-Life SOD-21 Sounds Of The Seventies - Rock 'N' Soul Seventies.

GEORGE CATES
1956 MOONGLOW AND THEME FROM "PICNIC"

CATHY JEAN & THE ROOMMATES
1961 PLEASE LOVE ME FOREVER
- (M) (2:53) Time-Life 2RNR-44 Rock 'N' Roll Era - Lost Treasures.
- (E) (2:51) Original Sound 8859 Oldies But Goodies Vol. 9. *(this compact disc uses the "Waring - fds" noise reduction process)*
- (M) (2:52) Original Sound 8859r Oldies But Goodies Vol. 9. *(remastered edition)*
- (M) (2:52) Original Sound 2223 Oldies But Goodies Volumes 2,7,9,12 and 13 Box Set. *(Volumes 2, 7 and 12 of this box set use the "Waring - fds" noise reduction process)*
- (M) (2:52) Original Sound 2500 Oldies But Goodies Volumes 1-15 Box Set. *(most volumes in this box set use the "Waring - fds" noise reduction process)*
- (E) (2:50) Original Sound CDGO-2 Golden Oldies Volume. 2.
- (E) (2:50) Original Sound 9602 Best Of Oldies But Goodies Vol. 2.
- (M) (2:52) Time-Life R857-14 The Heart Of Rock 'n' Roll 1960-1961 Take Two.

CAT MOTHER and THE ALL NIGHT NEWS BOYS
1969 GOOD OLD ROCK 'N ROLL
- (S) (3:10) Rhino 70732 Grandson Of Frat Rock.
- (S) (3:10) Rebound 314520269 Class Reunion 1969.
- (S) (3:11) Polydor 314537616 The Street Giveth...And The Street Taketh Away. *(segues into next selection)*

CAUSE & EFFECT
1992 YOU THINK YOU KNOW HER
- (S) (4:43) SRC/Zoo 11019 and 31019 Another Minute.

FELIX CAVALIERE
1980 ONLY A LONELY HEART SEES
- (S) (3:49) Rhino 71892 Radio Daze: Pop Hits Of The 80's Volume Three.

C COMPANY featuring TERRY NELSON
1971 BATTLE HYMN OF LT. CALLEY

CELEBRATION
1978 ALMOST SUMMER
- (S) (2:28) Risky Business 53923 Guilty Pleasures.

PETER CETERA
1986 GLORY OF LOVE
- (S) (4:20) Warner Brothers 25474 Solitude/Solitaire.
- (S) (4:19) Time-Life R988-04 Sounds Of The Eighties: 1986.
- (S) (4:20) Time-Life R834-03 Body Talk - Moonlit Nights.

released as by PETER CETERA with AMY GRANT:
1986 THE NEXT TIME I FALL
- (S) (3:43) Warner Brothers 25474 Peter Cetera - Solitude/Solitaire.
- (S) (3:43) Time-Life R138-18 Body Talk.
- (S) (3:43) Time-Life R834-06 Body Talk - Only You.
- (S) (3:39) River North 514161250 Peter Cetera - You're The Inspiration - A Collection.

released as by PETER CETERA:
1988 ONE GOOD WOMAN
- (S) (4:34) Warner Brothers 25704 One More Story.

released as by CHER and PETER CETERA:
1989 AFTER ALL
- (S) (4:03) Geffen 24239 Cher - Heart Of Stone.
- (S) (4:03) River North 514161250 Peter Cetera - You're The Inspiration - A Collection.

released as by PETER CETERA:
1992 RESTLESS HEART
- (S) (4:08) Warner Brothers 26894 World Falling Down.

released as by AZ YET featuring PETER CETERA:
1997 HARD TO SAY I'M SORRY
- (S) (3:14) LaFace 26034 Az Yet.

CHAD & JEREMY
1964 YESTERDAY'S GONE
- (M) (2:30) Rhino 70319 History Of British Rock Volume 1.
- (M) (2:30) Rhino 72022 History Of British Rock Box Set.
- (M) (2:30) Rhino 72008 History Of British Rock Volumes 1-4 Box Set.
- (M) (2:28) Collectables 0526 Yesterday's Gone.
- (M) (2:29) One Way 31380 Best Of.
- (M) (2:29) K-Tel 3699 Best Of.

1964 A SUMMER SONG
- (S) (2:36) Rhino 70087 Summer & Sun.
- (S) (2:36) Rhino 70320 History Of British Rock Volume 2.
- (S) (2:36) Rhino 72022 History Of British Rock Box Set.
- (S) (2:36) Rhino 72008 History Of British Rock Volumes 1-4 Box Set.
- (S) (2:35) Rhino 71229 Summer Hits.
- (S) (2:37) JCI 3107 British Sixties. *(alternate take)*

CHAD & JEREMY (Continued)

- (S) (2:35) Time-Life 2CLR-03 Classic Rock - 1964. *(found only on original pressings of this cd)*
- (S) (2:37) Collectables 2505 History Of Rock - The 60's Part 5. *(mastered from vinyl)*
- (S) (2:37) Collectables 4505 History Of Rock/The 60s Part Five. *(mastered from vinyl)*
- (S) (2:36) Collectables 0526 Yesterday's Gone.
- (S) (2:36) K-Tel 3437 Summer Songs.
- (S) (2:36) K-Tel 3465 A Summer Song.
- (S) (2:36) One Way 31380 Best Of.
- (S) (2:36) K-Tel 3699 Best Of.
- (S) (2:36) LaserLight 12317 The British Invasion.
- (S) (2:36) Time-Life R857-09 The Heart Of Rock 'n' Roll 1964.
- (S) (2:35) Time-Life R132-22 Treasury Of Folk Music Volume One.
- (S) (2:36) Flashback 72710 Golden Summer.
- (S) (2:36) Rhino 72819 16 Magazine - Who's Your Fave Rave.
- (S) (2:35) Nick At Nite/550 Music 63436 Patio Pool Party.
- (S) (2:35) Time-Life R814-02 Love Songs.

1965 WILLOW WEEP FOR ME
- (S) (2:31) Rhino 70321 History Of British Rock Volume 3.
- (S) (2:31) Rhino 72022 History Of British Rock Box Set.
- (S) (2:31) Rhino 72008 History Of British Rock Volumes 1-4 Box Set.
- (S) (2:31) Collectables 0526 Yesterday's Gone.
- (S) (2:31) K-Tel 3465 A Summer Song.
- (S) (2:31) One Way 31380 Best Of.
- (S) (2:31) K-Tel 3699 Best Of.

1965 IF I LOVED YOU
- (S) (2:14) Collectables 0526 Yesterday's Gone.
- (S) (2:14) K-Tel 3465 A Summer Song.
- (S) (2:14) One Way 31380 Best Of.
- (S) (2:14) K-Tel 3699 Best Of.

1965 BEFORE AND AFTER
- (S) (2:41) Rhino 70323 History Of British Rock Volume 5.
- (S) (2:41) Rhino 72022 History Of British Rock Box Set.
- (S) (2:41) Columbia/Legacy 47719 Painted Dayglow Smile.

1965 I DON'T WANNA LOSE YOU BABY
- (S) (3:06) Columbia/Legacy 46983 Rock Artifacts Volume 3.
- (S) (3:06) Columbia/Legacy 47719 Painted Dayglow Smile.

1966 DISTANT SHORES
- (S) (2:43) Columbia/Legacy 46984 Rock Artifacts Volume 4.
- (S) (2:43) Columbia/Legacy 47719 Painted Dayglow Smile.
- (M) (2:45) Varese Sarabande 5802 Sunshine Days - Pop Classics Of The '60s Volume 2.

CHAIRMEN OF THE BOARD
1970 GIVE ME JUST A LITTLE MORE TIME
- (S) (2:37) DCC Compact Classics 033 Beachbeat Shaggin'.
- (S) (2:38) Rhino 70781 Soul Hits Of The 70's Volume 1.
- (S) (2:38) Rhino 72028 Soul Hits Of The 70's Volumes 1-5 Box Set.
- (S) (2:39) HDH 3901 Greatest Hits.
- (S) (2:38) Ripete 2392156 Grand Stand Gold.
- (S) (2:38) Ripete 3292146 Beach Beat Classics Volume 1.
- (S) (2:37) Time-Life RHD-18 Rhythm & Blues - 1970.
- (S) (2:38) Time-Life SUD-16 Superhits - The Early 70's.
- (S) (2:36) Time-Life SOD-21 Sounds Of The Seventies - Rock 'N' Soul Seventies.
- (S) (2:38) Ripete 2146-RE Beach Beat Classics Vol. 1.
- (S) (2:38) Ripete 2156-RE Grand Stand Gold Vol. 1.
- (S) (2:38) K-Tel 3269 Carolina Beach Music.
- (S) (2:39) Priority 53130 Deep Soul Volume Three.
- (S) (2:38) Time-Life AM1-13 AM Gold - The Early '70s.
- (S) (2:37) Time-Life R838-05 Solid Gold Soul - 1970.
- (S) (2:39) Flashback 72900 25 Years Of Soul - 1970.

1970 (YOU'VE GOT ME) DANGLING ON A STRING
- (S) (2:57) HDH 3901 Greatest Hits. *(LP length)*
- (M) (2:44) Rhino 70783 Soul Hits Of The 70's Volume 3. *(45 length)*
- (M) (2:44) Rhino 72028 Soul Hits Of The 70's Volumes 1-5 Box Set. *(45 length)*
- (M) (2:44) Varese Sarabande 5718 Soulful Pop. *(45 length)*
- (M) (2:45) Varese Sarabande 5890 Bubblegum Classics Volume Four - Soulful Pop. *(45 length)*

1970 EVERYTHING'S TUESDAY
- (M) (2:46) Rhino 70783 Soul Hits Of The 70's Volume 3.
- (M) (2:46) Rhino 72028 Soul Hits Of The 70's Volumes 1-5 Box Set.
- (S) (2:47) HDH 3901 Greatest Hits.

1971 PAY TO THE PIPER
- (S) (3:05) Rhino 70784 Soul Hits Of The 70's Volume 4.
- (S) (3:05) Rhino 72028 Soul Hits Of The 70's Volumes 1-5 Box Set.
- (S) (3:03) HDH 3901 Greatest Hits.
- (S) (3:01) K-Tel 3900 Great R&B Male Groups: Hits Of The 70's.

1971 CHAIRMAN OF THE BOARD
- (S) (3:07) Rhino 70784 Soul Hits Of The 70's Volume 4. *(neither the LP or 45 version as this is :10 longer than the 45 and :24 shorter than the LP length, yet recorded at the LP speed)*
- (S) (3:07) Rhino 72028 Soul Hits Of The 70's Volumes 1-5 Box Set. *(neither the 45 or LP version as this is :10 longer than the 45 and :24 shorter than the LP length, yet recorded at the LP speed)*
- (S) (3:31) HDH 3901 Greatest Hits. *(LP version)*

CHAKACHAS
1972 JUNGLE FEVER
- (S) (4:20) Rhino 70787 Soul Hits Of The 70's Volume 7.
- (S) (4:21) Rhino 71210 70's Smash Hits Volume 6.
- (S) (4:20) Rhino 71603 Rock Instrumental Classics Volume 3: The Seventies.
- (S) (4:20) Rhino 72035 Rock Instrumental Classics Vols. 1-5 Box Set.
- (S) (4:21) Time-Life SOD-31 Sounds Of The Seventies - AM Top Twenty.
- (M) (4:21) Polygram Special Markets 314520272 One Hit Wonders.
- (S) (4:20) Time-Life R840-04 Sounds Of The Seventies: A Loss For Words.
- (S) (4:21) Flashback 72686 '70s Radio Hits Volume 6.
- (S) (4:20) Capitol 56312 O.S.T. Boogie Nights.

RICHARD CHAMBERLAIN
1962 THEME FROM DR. KILDARE (THREE STARS WILL SHINE TONIGHT)
- (S) (2:38) Collectors' Choice 002 Teen Idols....For A Moment.
- (S) (2:38) K-Tel 3388 TV Stars Sing.
- (S) (2:37) Eric 11503 Hard To Find 45's On CD (Volume II) 1961-64.

1962 LOVE ME TENDER
1963 ALL I HAVE TO DO IS DREAM
- (S) (2:27) Collectors' Choice 002 Teen Idols....For A Moment.

CHAMBERS BROTHERS
1968 TIME HAS COME TODAY
(dj copies of this song ran (4:45); commercial copies ran (3:05) and (4:45))
- (S) (4:54) Rhino 75754 Even More Nuggets. *(45 version)*
- (S) (11:03) DCC Compact Classics 045 Golden Age Of Underground Radio. *(LP version)*
- (S) (11:02) Columbia 30871 Greatest Hits. *(LP version)*
- (S) (11:01) Columbia 9522 The Time Has Come. *(LP version)*
- (M) (4:47) Columbia 45018 Rock Classics Of The 60's. *(45 version)*
- (S) (3:31) Sandstone 33004 Reelin' In The Years Volume 5. *(neither the LP or 45 version)*
- (S) (11:01) DCC Compact Classics 066 Rock Of The 70's Volume Five. *(LP version)*
- (S) (4:55) Time-Life 2CLR-19 Classic Rock - 1968: Shakin' All Over. *(45 version)*
- (S) (4:54) MCA 11036 O.S.T. Crooklyn. *(45 version)*
- (E) (4:49) Risky Business 66387 Rock Around The Clock. *(45 version)*
- (S) (4:53) Time-Life R968-12 Guitar Rock - The Late '70s. *(45 version)*
- (S) (4:51) Columbia/Legacy 65036 Time Has Come: Best Of. *(45 version)*

(S) (2:39) Columbia/Legacy 65036 Time Has Come: Best Of. *(original 45 version but not the hit 45 version)*
(S) (11:01) K-Tel 3610 Psychedelic Mind Trip Vol. 2: Another Flashback. *(LP version)*
(M) (4:47) Thump 6010 Easyriders Volume 1. *(45 version)*

1968 I CAN'T TURN YOU LOOSE
(S) (4:53) Columbia 30871 Greatest Hits.
(S) (4:53) Risky Business 66914 Party On.
(S) (4:54) Columbia/Legacy 65036 Time Has Come: Best Of.

CHAMPAIGN
1981 HOW 'BOUT US
(S) (4:33) Rhino 71859 Smooth Grooves Volume 1. *(LP version)*
(S) (3:20) Rhino 71894 Radio Daze: Pop Hits Of The 80's Volume Five. *(45 version)*
(S) (4:33) Thump 4730 Old School Love Songs Volume 3. *(LP version)*
(S) (4:33) Time-Life R834-08 Body Talk - On My Mind. *(LP version)*
(S) (4:33) JCI 3176 1980 - Only Soul - 1984. *(LP version)*

1983 TRY AGAIN
(S) (3:46) Rhino 71865 Smooth Grooves Volume 7.
(S) (3:46) Rhino 72138 Billboard Hot R&B Hits 1983.
(S) (3:46) Time-Life R834-09 Body Talk - Magic Moments.

CHAMPS
1958 TEQUILA
(M) (2:10) Rhino 70619 Billboard's Top Rock & Roll Hits Of 1958.
(M) (2:10) Rhino 72004 Billboard's Top Rock & Roll Hits 1957-1961 Box Set.
(E) (2:10) DCC Compact Classics 028 Sock Hop.
(M) (2:10) Original Sound 8857 Oldies But Goodies Vol. 7. *(this compact disc uses the "Waring - fds" noise reduction process)*
(M) (2:10) Original Sound 2223 Oldies But Goodies Volumes 2,7,9,12 and 13 Box Set. *(this box set uses the "Waring - fds" noise reduction process)*
(M) (2:10) Original Sound 2500 Oldies But Goodies Volumes 1-15 Box Set. *(this box set uses the "Waring - fds" noise reduction process)*
(M) (2:11) Original Sound 8881 Twenty-One #1 Hits. *(this compact disc uses the "Waring - fds" noise reduction process)*
(M) (2:10) Rhino 70732 Grandson Of Frat Rock.
(M) (2:09) Collectables 5069 History Of Rock Volume 9.
(M) (2:11) Collectables 0530 Tequila: Golden Classics.
(M) (2:10) Rhino 71601 Rock Instrumental Classics Volume 1: The Fifties.
(M) (2:10) Rhino 72035 Rock Instrumental Classics Vols. 1-5 Box Set.
(M) (2:09) Time-Life 2RNR-05 Rock 'N' Roll Era - 1958. *(original pressings of this song on this cd were (S) but an alternate take)*
(M) (2:11) Collectables 2506 WCBS-FM History Of Rock - The 50's Part 1.
(M) (2:11) Collectables 4506 History Of Rock/The 50s Part One.
(M) (2:12) Curb 77670 Greatest Hits.
(E) (2:10) K-Tel 852 100 Proof Hits. *(dropout at :40)*
(E) (2:08) Tommy Boy 1100 ESPN Presents Jock Rock. *(sound effects added to the introduction and ending)*
(M) (2:10) K-Tel 3059 Saxy Rock.
(E) (2:09) Era 511 Ultimate 50's Party.
(M) (2:09) JCI 3129 1955 - Only Rock 'N Roll - 1959.
(M) (2:11) Ripete 2187-RE Preppy Deluxe.
(E) (2:10) K-Tel 3453 Rockin' Instrumentals. *(dropout at :40)*
(M) (2:10) Nick At Nite/Epic 67149 Dick Van Dyke's Dance Party.
(M) (2:10) Rhino 72213 Stadium Rock.
(M) (2:09) K-Tel 3575 Hot, Hot Vacation Jams - Week One.

(E) (2:09) LaserLight 12312 and 15936 The Wonder Years - Good Times, Good Friends. *(dropout at :40)*
(E) (2:10) K-Tel 3795 Music For Your Halloween Party. *(dropout at :40)*
(E) (2:10) K-Tel 3795 Spooktacular Party Songs. *(dropout at :40)*
(M) (2:11) One Way 34488 The Challenge Album Collection.
(M) (2:08) Cold Front 6245 Greatest Sports Rock And Jams. *(all selections on this cd are segued together)*
(M) (2:11) Music Club 50018 Best Of.
(M) (2:11) Thump 7200 Latin Oldies Volume Two.
(M) (2:10) Flashback 72711 Sports Rock.
(M) (2:11) Columbia 69059 Party Super Hits.
(M) (2:11) Simitar 55522 The Number One's: Party Time.
(M) (2:11) I.D. 90072 Jenny McCarthy's Surfin' Safari.
(E) (2:09) K-Tel 4066 K-Tel's Original Party Music Vol. 2.

1958 EL RANCHO ROCK
(M) (2:17) Collectables 0530 Tequila: Golden Classics.
(E) (2:14) Time-Life 2RNR-36 Rock 'N' Roll Era - Axes & Saxes/The Great Instrumentals.
(M) (2:17) Curb 77670 Greatest Hits.
(M) (2:17) One Way 34488 The Challenge Album Collection.
(M) (2:16) Music Club 283 Best Of.

1960 TOO MUCH TEQUILA
(M) (2:11) Collectables 0530 Tequila: Golden Classics.
(M) (2:11) Curb 77670 Greatest Hits.
(M) (2:11) One Way 34488 The Challenge Album Collection.
(M) (2:11) Music Club 50018 Best Of.

1962 LIMBO ROCK
(M) (2:03) Collectables 0530 Tequila: Golden Classics.
(S) (2:02) Curb 77670 Greatest Hits.
(M) (2:04) LaserLight 12316 Rebel Rousers.
(M) (2:03) Risky Business 67311 The Ultimate Party Survival Kit.
(M) (2:03) One Way 34488 The Challenge Album Collection. *(missing some overdubs)*
(M) (2:03) Music Club 50018 Best Of.

GENE CHANDLER
1962 DUKE OF EARL
(M) (2:22) Rhino 70623 Billboard's Top Rock & Roll Hits Of 1962.
(M) (2:22) Rhino 72007 Billboard's Top Rock & Roll Hits 1962-1966 Box Set.
(M) (2:18) Original Sound 8856 Oldies But Goodies Vol. 6. *(this compact disc uses the "Waring - fds" noise reduction process)*
(M) (2:18) Original Sound 2221 Oldies But Goodies Volumes 1,4,6,8 and 10 Box Set. *(this box set uses the "Waring - fds" noise reduction process)*
(M) (2:18) Original Sound 2500 Oldies But Goodies Volumes 1-15 Box Set. *(this box set uses the "Waring - fds" noise reduction process)*
(E) (2:17) Original Sound CDGO-10 Golden Oldies Volume. 10.
(E) (2:18) Original Sound 8881 Twenty-One #1 Hits. *(this compact disc uses the "Waring - fds" noise reduction process)*
(E) (2:18) Original Sound 8892 Dick Clark's 21 All-Time Hits Vol. 2.
(M) (2:18) Original Sound 9602 Best Of Oldies But Goodies Vol. 2.
(M) (2:18) Original Sound 1081 All #1 Hits.
(M) (2:21) Motown 6215 and 9067 Hits From The Legendary Vee-Jay Records.
(M) (2:22) DCC Compact Classics 028 Sock Hop.
(S) (2:23) Ripete 2392192 Beach Music Anthology Box Set. *(mastered from vinyl)*
(S) (2:25) Collectables 5062 History Of Rock Volume 2. *(mastered from vinyl)*
(S) (2:25) Vee Jay 712 Duke Of Earl.
(S) (2:25) Vee Jay 3-400 Celebrating 40 Years Of Classic Hits (1953-1993).
(M) (2:21) JCI 3112 Pop Sixties.

GENE CHANDLER *(Continued)*

- (S) (2:22) Ripete 0001   Coolin' Out/24 Carolina Classics Volume 1.   *(mastered from vinyl)*
- (M) (2:21) Time-Life 2RNR-02   Rock 'N' Roll Era - 1962.
- (M) (2:19) Time-Life RHD-11   Rhythm & Blues - 1962.
- (M) (2:22) Time-Life R962-06   History Of Rock 'N' Roll: Doo Wop And Vocal Group Tradition 1955-1962.
- (M) (2:20) Collectables 2502   WCBS-FM History Of Rock - The 60's Part 3.
- (M) (2:20) Collectables 4502   History Of Rock/The 60s Part Three.
- (S) (2:24) Collectables 2605   WCBS-FM Jukebox Giants Vol. 3.   *(mastered from vinyl)*
- (E) (2:21) Thump 7020   Low Rider Oldies Volume II.
- (S) (2:25) Varese Sarabande 5515   Nothing Can Stop Me/Greatest Hits.
- (S) (2:25) Rhino 71806   The R&B Box: Thirty Years Of Rhythm & Blues.
- (M) (2:22) K-Tel 3008   60's Sock Hop.
- (S) (2:25) Collectables 5518   Greatest Hits.
- (M) (2:21) JCI 3125   1960 - Only Rock 'N' Roll - 1964.
- (M) (2:20) Collectables 2554   CBS-FM History Of Rock Volume 2.
- (S) (2:25) Rhino 72507   Doo Wop Box II.
- (S) (2:25) Eclipse Music Group 64867   Rock 'n Roll Relix 1960-1961.
- (S) (2:25) Eclipse Music Group 64872   Rock 'n Roll Relix 1960-1969.
- (S) (2:24) Repeat/Relativity 1611   A Brand New Bag: #1 Soul Hits Of The 60's Volume 3.
- (M) (2:19) Time-Life R838-18   Solid Gold Soul 1962.

1964 JUST BE TRUE
- (M) (2:33) Varese Sarabande 5515   Nothing Can Stop Me/Greatest Hits.
- (M) (2:29) Collectables 5518   Greatest Hits.
- (M) (2:32) MCA Special Products 20869   Soul Master.
- (M) (2:32) MCA Special Products 20868   Clarence Carter & Gene Chandler Together Again.
- (M) (2:33) Collectables 5735   Just Be True.

1965 NOTHING CAN STOP ME
- (M) (2:53) Ripete 0001   Coolin' Out/24 Carolina Classics Volume 1.
- (M) (2:53) Varese Sarabande 5515   Nothing Can Stop Me/Greatest Hits.
- (M) (2:53) Collectables 5518   Greatest Hits.
- (M) (2:53) MCA Special Products 20869   Soul Master.
- (M) (2:53) MCA Special Products 20868   Clarence Carter & Gene Chandler Together Again.

released as by GENE CHANDLER and BARBARA ACKLIN:
1968 FROM THE TEACHER TO THE PREACHER
- (M) (2:24) Brunswick 81003   Barbara Acklin - Greatest Hits.
- (M) (2:21) MCA Special Products 20869   Gene Chandler - Soul Master.
- (M) (2:24) Brunswick 81009   The Brunswick Years Volume One.
- (M) (2:24) Brunswick 81017   Gene Chandler - The Soul Of.

released as by GENE CHANDLER:
1970 GROOVY SITUATION
- (S) (3:12) Rhino 70783   Soul Hits Of The 70's Volume 3.
- (S) (3:12) Rhino 72028   Soul Hits Of The 70's Volumes 1-5 Box Set.
- (S) (3:12) Rhino 71207   70's Smash Hits Volume 3.
- (S) (3:11) Time-Life SOD-25   Sounds Of The Seventies - Seventies Generation.
- (S) (3:11) Varese Sarabande 5515   Nothing Can Stop Me/Greatest Hits.
- (S) (3:11) MCA Special Products 20869   Soul Master.
- (S) (3:11) Ripete 5151   Ocean Drive 4.
- (S) (3:12) Flashback 72683   '70s Radio Hits Volume 3.
- (S) (3:12) Flashback 72090   '70s Radio Hits Box Set.

CHANGING FACES
1994 STROKE YOU UP
- (S) (5:49) Big Beat/Atlantic 92369   Changing Faces.
1995 FOOLIN' AROUND
- (S) (4:26) Big Beat/Atlantic 92369   Changing Faces.
1997 G.H.E.T.T.O.U.T.
- (S) (4:26) Big Beat/Atlantic 92720   All Day, All Night.

BRUCE CHANNEL
1962 HEY! BABY
- (E) (2:22) RCA 6408   O.S.T. Dirty Dancing.
- (M) (2:18) JCI 3112   Pop Sixties.
- (M) (2:21) Time-Life 2RNR-02   Rock 'N' Roll Era - 1962.
- (M) (2:20) Collectables 2605   WCBS-FM Jukebox Giants Vol. 3.
- (M) (2:22) Ripete 0003   Coolin' Out/24 Carolina Classics Vol. 3.
- (M) (2:23) Rhino 71583   Billboard Top Pop Hits, 1962.
- (M) (2:22) Collectables 5623   Hey! Baby.
- (M) (2:21) JCI 3125   1960 - Only Rock 'N Roll - 1964.
- (M) (2:21) K-Tel 3125   Solid Gold Rock N' Roll.
- (M) (2:22) Special Music/Essex 5035   Prom Night - The 60's.
- (M) (2:22) Mercury 314526691   Fifty Years Of Country Music From Mercury.
- (M) (2:22) Eclipse Music Group 64867   Rock 'n Roll Relix 1960-1961.
- (M) (2:22) Eclipse Music Group 64872   Rock 'n Roll Relix 1960-1969.
- (M) (2:21) Time-Life R857-12   The Heart Of Rock 'n' Roll 1962-1963.

CHANSON
1979 DON'T HOLD BACK

CHANTAYS
1963 PIPELINE
- (S) (2:16) Rhino 70089   Surfin' Hits.
- (S) (2:17) MCA 31204   Vintage Music Volume 7.
- (S) (2:17) MCA 5805   Vintage Music Volumes 7 & 8.
- (S) (2:18) JCI 3106   Surfin' Sixties.
- (S) (2:17) DCC Compact Classics 915   Surf Legends.
- (S) (2:18) Rhino 71605   Rock Instrumental Classics Volume 5: Surf.
- (S) (2:18) Rhino 72035   Rock Instrumental Classics Vols. 1-5 Box Set.
- (S) (2:18) Time-Life 2RNR-07   Rock 'N' Roll Era - 1963.
- (S) (2:17) Collectables 2510   WCBS-FM History Of Rock - The Rockin' 60's.
- (S) (2:17) Collectables 4510   History Of Rock/The Rockin' 60s.
- (S) (2:17) Era 840   Rock N' Roll Guitar Classics.
- (S) (2:18) Varese Sarabande 5491   Pipeline.
- (S) (2:18) Rhino 71584   Billboard Top Pop Hits, 1963.
- (S) (2:17) MCA Special Products 22135   Vintage Collectibles Volume 6.
- (S) (2:18) MCA 11234   Revenge Of The Surf Instrumentals.
- (S) (2:17) MCA Special Products 20899   Rock Around The Oldies #4.
- (S) (2:18) MCA Special Products 20902   Classic Rock & Roll Instrumental Hits, Volume 1.
- (S) (2:16) Rhino 72418   Cowabunga! The Surf Box.
- (S) (2:19) I.D. 90072   Jenny McCarthy's Surfin' Safari.

CHANTELS
1958 MAYBE
(both the 45 and LP length was (2:38))
- (M) (2:51) Rhino 70644   Billboard's Top R&B Hits Of 1958.
- (M) (2:52) Rhino 70954   Best Of.
- (M) (2:48) Collectables 8802   For Collectors Only.
- (M) (2:51) Collectables 8802   For Collectors Only.   *(alternate take; time includes an :11 false start)*
- (M) (2:48) Collectables 5423   The Chantels.
- (M) (2:48) Rhino 71463   Doo Wop Box.
- (M) (2:48) Time-Life 2RNR-05   Rock 'N' Roll Era - 1958.
- (M) (2:49) Time-Life RHD-16   Rhythm & Blues - 1958.
- (M) (2:38) Original Sound 9329   Oldies But Goodies Doo Wop Classics.
- (M) (2:38) Original Sound 9328   13 Of The Best Doo Wop Love Songs Vol. 2.
- (M) (2:45) Collectables 5471   The Spotlight Series - End Records Vol. 2.
- (M) (2:52) Collectables 2601   WCBS-FM History Of Rock - The Group Sounds Vol. 2.
- (M) (2:46) Collectables 2607   WCBS-FM For Lovers Only Vol. 3.   *(truncated fade)*

(M) (2:50) Time-Life R103-27 Love Me Tender.
(M) (2:48) Time-Life R10513 40 Lovin' Oldies.
(M) (2:49) Time-Life R102-17 Lost Treasures Of Rock 'N' Roll.
(M) (2:52) Rhino 71806 The R&B Box: Thirty Years Of Rhythm & Blues.
(M) (2:47) Time-Life R857-04 The Heart Of Rock 'n' Roll - 1958.
(M) (2:52) Thump 7050 Low Rider Oldies Volume 5.
(M) (2:48) Rhino 72157 Doo Wop Memories, Vol. 2.
(M) (2:49) JCI 3183 1955 - Only Love - 1959.
(M) (2:48) Flashback 72717 Doo Wop - Blue Moon.
(M) (2:49) Time-Life R838-22 Solid Gold Soul 1958.

1958 EVERY NIGHT (I PRAY)
(M) (2:03) Rhino 70954 Best Of. *(truncated fade)*
(M) (2:01) Collectables 8802 For Collectors Only. *(alternate take)*
(M) (2:01) Collectables 5423 The Chantels. *(truncated fade)*
(M) (2:01) Time-Life 2RNR-48 Rock 'N' Roll Era - R&B Gems II.

1961 LOOK IN MY EYES
(S) (2:16) Rhino 70954 Best Of.
(M) (2:16) Atlantic 82152 O.S.T. Goodfellas. *(mastered from vinyl)*
(S) (2:15) Collectables 8802 For Collectors Only.
(S) (2:15) Collectables 5066 History Of Rock Volume 6.
(M) (2:15) Time-Life 2RNR-18 Rock 'N' Roll Era - 1961 Still Rockin'.
(M) (2:18) Collectables 2500 WCBS-FM History Of Rock - The 60's Part 1.
(M) (2:18) Collectables 4500 History Of Rock/The 60s Part One.
(S) (2:14) Collectables 2608 WCBS-FM For Lovers Only Vol. 4.
(S) (2:15) Time-Life R857-03 The Heart Of Rock 'n' Roll - 1961.
(S) (2:15) Thump 7050 Low Rider Oldies Volume 5.
(S) (2:16) Rhino 72507 Doo Wop Box II.
(S) (2:16) Flashback 72716 Doo Wop - Sh-Boom.
(S) (2:15) Collectables 5785 Look In My Eyes - Best Of The Carlton & Ludix Years.

1961 WELL, I TOLD YOU
(S) (2:24) Rhino 70954 Best Of.
(S) (2:24) Collectables 5785 Look In My Eyes - Best Of The Carlton & Ludix Years.

HARRY CHAPIN
1972 TAXI
(S) (6:41) Elektra 75023 Heads & Tales.
(S) (6:40) Elektra 60773 Gold Medal Collection.
(S) (6:37) Time-Life R103-33 Singers & Songwriters.
(S) (6:41) Rhino 71843 Troubadours Of The Folk Era Vol. 4.
(S) (6:40) K-Tel 3454 70s Folk Rock Hits.
(S) (6:41) Rhino 72446 Listen To The Music: 70's Male Singer/Songwriters.

1974 WOLD
(S) (4:55) Elektra 60773 Gold Medal Collection. *(live)*
(S) (5:10) Time-Life R105-26 Our Songs: Singers & Songwriters Encore.

1974 CAT'S IN THE CRADLE
(S) (3:44) Elektra 60773 Gold Medal Collection.
(S) (3:45) Elektra 1012 Verities & Balderdash.
(S) (3:44) Razor & Tie 4543 The '70s Preservation Society Presents: Easy '70s.
(S) (3:43) Time-Life R103-33 Singers & Songwriters.
(S) (3:45) K-Tel 3455 Folk Hits Around The Campfire.
(S) (3:43) JCI 3168 #1 Radio Hits 1970 - Only Rock 'n Roll - 1974.

1975 I WANNA LEARN A LOVE SONG
(S) (4:20) Elektra 60773 Gold Medal Collection. *(LP version)*
(S) (4:21) Elektra 1012 Verities & Balderdash. *(LP version)*

1980 SEQUEL
(S) (6:35) Elektra 60773 Gold Medal Collection.

(S) (6:35) Rhino 71893 Radio Daze: Pop Hits Of The 80's Volume Four.
(S) (6:36) DCC Compact Classics 035 Remember When The Music.

TRACY CHAPMAN
1988 FAST CAR
(S) (4:56) Elektra 60774 Tracy Chapman. *(LP version)*
1988 BABY CAN I HOLD YOU
(S) (3:11) Elektra 60774 Tracy Chapman.
1996 GIVE ME ONE REASON
(S) (4:27) Elektra 61850 New Beginning.
(S) (4:26) Grammy Recordings/Chronicles 314553292 1997 Grammy Nominees.

CHARLENE
1982 I'VE NEVER BEEN TO ME
(dj copies of this 45 were issued in two versions; one was the same as the commercial 45 but the other removed the vocals from (2:12) to (2:32))
(S) (3:53) Motown 9082 and 5385 Three Times A Lady - Great Motown Love Songs. *(different ending than the 45 or LP)*
(S) (3:52) Motown 9110 Motown Memories Vol. 4 - Where Were You When. *(different ending than the 45 or LP)*
(S) (3:52) Motown 6177 Endless Love: 15 Of Motown's Greatest Love Songs. *(different ending than the 45 or LP)*
(S) (3:53) Mother 314516937 O.S.T. The Adventures Of Priscilla - Queen Of The Desert. *(different ending than the 45 or LP)*
(S) (3:52) Time-Life R834-10 Body Talk - From The Heart. *(different ending than the 45 or LP)*

JIMMY CHARLES
1960 A MILLION TO ONE
(M) (2:29) Time-Life 2RNR-44 Rock 'N' Roll Era - Lost Treasures.
(M) (2:29) Time-Life SUD-15 Superhits - The Early 60's.
(M) (2:29) Collectables 2502 WCBS-FM History Of Rock - The 60's Part 3.
(M) (2:29) Collectables 4502 History Of Rock/The 60s Part Three.
(M) (2:29) Collectables 2606 WCBS-FM For Lovers Only Vol. 2.
(M) (2:30) Time-Life OPCD-4517 Tonight's The Night.
(M) (2:29) Time-Life R857-02 The Heart Of Rock 'n' Roll - 1960.
(M) (2:29) Time-Life AM1-19 AM Gold - The Early '60s.
(E) (2:28) Compose 131 Unforgettable - Gold For The Road.
(M) (2:29) Time-Life R857-21 The Heart Of Rock 'n' Roll Slow Dancing Classics.

RAY CHARLES
1959 WHAT'D I SAY (PART 1)
(S) (6:25) Warner Special Products 27601 Atlantic Soul Classics. *(LP version of Parts 1 & 2)*
(S) (6:25) JCI 3202 Rockin' Fifties. *(LP version of Parts 1 & 2)*
(S) (6:26) Original Sound 8863 Oldies But Goodies Vol. 13. *(LP version of Parts 1 & 2)*
(S) (6:26) Original Sound 2223 Oldies But Goodies Volumes 2,7,9,12 and 13 Box Set. *(Volumes 2, 7 and 12 of this box set use the "Waring - fds" noise reduction process; LP version of Parts 1 & 2)*
(S) (6:26) Original Sound 2500 Oldies But Goodies Volumes 1-15 Box Set. *(most volumes in this box set use the "Waring - fds" noise reduction process; LP version of Parts 1 & 2)*
(M) (5:05) Atlantic 81296 Atlantic Rhythm & Blues Volume 4. *(45 edit of Parts 1 & 2)*
(M) (3:05) Rhino 70732 Grandson Of Frat Rock. *(45 version of just Part 1)*
(S) (4:31) Rhino 75759 Anthology. *(rerecording)*

97

RAY CHARLES (Continued)

- (M) (5:04) Atlantic 82305 Atlantic Rhythm And Blues 1947-1974 Box Set. *(45 edit of Parts 1 & 2)*
- (S) (6:25) Atlantic 82310 Birth Of Soul Box Set. *(LP version of Parts 1 & 2)*
- (S) (6:27) Sandstone 33079 and 5002 Uh Huh His Greatest Hits. *(LP version of Parts 1 & 2)*
- (M) (5:02) MCA 10919 O.S.T. Heart And Souls. *(45 edit of Parts 1 & 2)*
- (M) (3:08) Rhino 71547 Let There Be Drums Volume 1: The 50's. *(45 version of just Part 1)*
- (M) (5:04) Time-Life 2RNR-13 Rock 'N' Roll Era - 1959. *(45 edit of Parts 1 & 2)*
- (S) (6:27) Time-Life RHD-06 Rhythm & Blues - Ray Charles 1954-1966. *(LP version of Parts 1 & 2)*
- (M) (3:08) Rhino 71722 Best Of The Atlantic Years. *(45 version of just Part 1)*
- (M) (3:08) Flashback 72704 I've Got A Woman And Other Hits. *(45 version of just Part 1)*
- (M) (3:08) Flashback 72085 '50s R&B Golden Archives Box Set. *(45 version of just Part 1)*
- (M) (5:03) Rhino 72859 Genius & Soul - The 50th Anniversary Collection. *(45 edit of Parts 1 & 2)*
- (M) (3:08) Rhino 72961 Ultimate '50s R&B Smashes! *(45 version of just Part 1)*
- (S) (6:25) Atlantic 83088 Atlantic Records: 50 Years - The Gold Anniversary Collection. *(LP version of Parts 1 & 2)*

1960 STICKS AND STONES

- (S) (2:11) Rhino 75759 Anthology.
- (S) (2:11) Sandstone 33079 and 5002 Uh Huh His Greatest Hits.
- (S) (2:10) Time-Life RHD-06 Rhythm & Blues - Ray Charles 1954-1966.
- (S) (2:11) Garland 2121 The World Of.
- (S) (2:12) Rhino 72859 Genius & Soul - The 50th Anniversary Collection.

1960 GEORGIA ON MY MIND

- (S) (3:37) Rhino 75759 Anthology.
- (S) (3:37) DCC Compact Classics 036 His Greatest Volume 1.
- (S) (3:37) Sandstone 33079 and 5002 Uh Huh His Greatest Hits.
- (S) (3:36) Time-Life RHD-06 Rhythm & Blues - Ray Charles 1954-1966.
- (S) (3:37) Garland 2121 The World Of.
- (S) (3:33) Rhino 72813 The Genius Hits The Road.
- (S) (3:37) Rhino 72859 Genius & Soul - The 50th Anniversary Collection.

1960 RUBY

- (S) (3:49) DCC Compact Classics 037 His Greatest Volume 2. *(LP version)*
- (S) (3:50) Sandstone 33079 and 5002 Uh Huh His Greatest Hits. *(LP version)*
- (S) (3:49) Garland 2121 The World Of. *(LP version)*
- (S) (3:50) Rhino 72859 Genius & Soul - The 50th Anniversary Collection. *(LP version)*

1961 ONE MINT JULEP

- (S) (3:05) Rhino 75759 Anthology.
- (S) (3:05) DCC Compact Classics 038 Genius + Soul = Jazz.
- (S) (3:05) DCC Compact Classics 036 His Greatest Volume 1.
- (S) (3:05) Sandstone 33079 and 5002 Uh Huh His Greatest Hits.
- (S) (3:05) Sandstone 33073 and 5003 Genius + Soul = Jazz.
- (S) (3:04) Time-Life RHD-06 Rhythm & Blues - Ray Charles 1954-1966.
- (S) (3:05) Garland 2121 The World Of.
- (S) (3:04) Rhino 72814 Genius + Soul = Jazz/My Kind Of Jazz.
- (S) (3:03) Rhino 72859 Genius & Soul - The 50th Anniversary Collection.

1961 HIT THE ROAD JACK

- (S) (1:57) Rhino 75759 Anthology.
- (S) (1:57) DCC Compact Classics 037 His Greatest Volume 2.
- (S) (1:57) Sandstone 33079 and 5002 Uh Huh His Greatest Hits.

- (S) (1:57) Time-Life RHD-06 Rhythm & Blues - Ray Charles 1954-1966.
- (S) (1:57) Garland 2121 The World Of. *(with countoff)*
- (S) (1:57) Rhino 72813 The Genius Hits The Road.
- (S) (1:56) Rhino 72859 Genius & Soul - The 50th Anniversary Collection.

1962 UNCHAIN MY HEART

- (S) (2:49) Rhino 75759 Anthology.
- (S) (2:49) DCC Compact Classics 036 His Greatest Volume 1.
- (S) (2:49) Sandstone 33079 and 5002 Uh Huh His Greatest Hits.
- (S) (2:47) Time-Life RHD-06 Rhythm & Blues - Ray Charles 1954-1966.
- (S) (2:49) Garland 2121 The World Of.
- (S) (2:49) Rhino 72859 Genius & Soul - The 50th Anniversary Collection.

1962 HIDE 'NOR HAIR

- (S) (3:09) DCC Compact Classics 036 His Greatest Volume 1.
- (S) (3:08) Sandstone 33079 and 5002 Uh Huh His Greatest Hits.
- (S) (3:08) Time-Life RHD-06 Rhythm & Blues - Ray Charles 1954-1966.
- (S) (3:09) Garland 2121 The World Of.
- (S) (3:08) Rhino 72859 Genius & Soul - The 50th Anniversary Collection.

1962 I CAN'T STOP LOVING YOU

- (S) (4:11) Rhino 75759 Anthology. *(LP version)*
- (S) (4:11) Rhino 70099 Modern Sounds In Country & Western Music. *(LP version)*
- (S) (4:11) DCC Compact Classics 040 Greatest Country & Western Hits. *(LP version)*
- (S) (4:10) DCC Compact Classics 037 His Greatest Volume 2. *(LP version)*
- (S) (4:10) Sandstone 33079 and 5002 Uh Huh His Greatest Hits. *(LP version)*
- (S) (4:09) Time-Life RHD-06 Rhythm & Blues - Ray Charles 1954-1966. *(LP version)*
- (S) (4:11) Garland 2121 The World Of. *(LP version)*
- (S) (4:15) Rhino 72859 Genius & Soul - The 50th Anniversary Collection. *(LP version)*

1962 BORN TO LOSE

- (S) (3:13) Rhino 70099 Modern Sounds In Country & Western Music.
- (S) (3:14) DCC Compact Classics 036 His Greatest Hits Volume 1.
- (S) (3:13) Rhino 75759 Anthology.
- (S) (3:12) Sandstone 33079 and 5002 Uh Huh His Greatest Hits.
- (S) (3:14) Garland 2121 The World Of.
- (S) (3:15) Rhino 72859 Genius & Soul - The 50th Anniversary Collection.

1962 YOU DON'T KNOW ME

- (S) (3:13) Rhino 70099 Modern Sounds In Country & Western Music.
- (S) (3:13) DCC Compact Classics 040 Greatest Country & Western Hits.
- (S) (3:14) DCC Compact Classics 036 His Greatest Volume 1.
- (S) (3:12) Sandstone 33079 and 5002 Uh Huh His Greatest Hits.
- (S) (3:14) Time-Life RHD-06 Rhythm & Blues - Ray Charles 1954-1966.
- (S) (3:14) Garland 2121 The World Of.
- (S) (3:13) Rhino 72859 Genius & Soul - The 50th Anniversary Collection.

1962 YOU ARE MY SUNSHINE

- (S) (2:57) Rhino 75759 Anthology.
- (S) (2:57) Rhino 70099 Modern Sounds In Country & Western Music.
- (S) (2:57) DCC Compact Classics 040 Greatest Country & Western Hits.
- (S) (2:57) DCC Compact Classics 037 His Greatest Volume 2.
- (S) (2:57) Sandstone 33079 and 5002 Uh Huh His Greatest Hits.
- (S) (2:57) Time-Life RHD-06 Rhythm & Blues - Ray Charles 1954-1966.

(S) (2:57) Garland 2121 The World Of.
(S) (2:56) Rhino 72859 Genius & Soul - The 50th
Anniversary Collection. *(truncated fade)*

1962 YOUR CHEATING HEART
(S) (3:32) Sandstone 33079 and 5002 Uh Huh His Greatest
Hits.
(S) (3:32) Garland 2121 The World Of.
(S) (3:32) DCC Compact Classics 036 His Greatest Volume 1.
(S) (3:32) DCC Compact Classics 040 Greatest Country &
Western Hits.
(S) (3:32) Rhino 72859 Genius & Soul - The 50th
Anniversary Collection.

1963 DON'T SET ME FREE
(S) (2:35) Rhino 75759 Anthology.
(S) (2:35) DCC Compact Classics 037 His Greatest Volume 2.
(S) (2:35) Sandstone 33079 and 5002 Uh Huh His Greatest
Hits.
(S) (2:35) Garland 2121 The World Of.

1963 TAKE THESE CHAINS FROM MY HEART
(S) (2:54) DCC Compact Classics 040 Greatest Country &
Western Hits.
(S) (2:53) DCC Compact Classics 037 His Greatest Volume 2.
(S) (2:54) Sandstone 33079 and 5002 Uh Huh His Greatest
Hits.
(S) (2:53) Time-Life RHD-06 Rhythm & Blues - Ray
Charles 1954-1966.
(S) (2:53) Garland 2121 The World Of.
(S) (2:54) Rhino 72859 Genius & Soul - The 50th
Anniversary Collection.

1963 NO ONE
(S) (3:07) DCC Compact Classics 037 His Greatest Volume 2.
(S) (3:08) Sandstone 33079 and 5002 Uh Huh His Greatest
Hits.
(S) (3:08) Garland 2121 The World Of.

1963 WITHOUT LOVE (THERE IS NOTHING)
(S) (3:33) DCC Compact Classics 037 His Greatest Volume 2.
(S) (3:34) Sandstone 33079 and 5002 Uh Huh His Greatest
Hits.
(S) (3:34) Garland 2121 The World Of.
(S) (3:32) Rhino 72859 Genius & Soul - The 50th
Anniversary Collection.

1963 BUSTED
(S) (2:05) Rhino 75759 Anthology.
(S) (2:11) DCC Compact Classics 047 Ingredients In A
Recipe For Soul. *(with countoff)*
(S) (2:08) DCC Compact Classics 037 His Greatest Volume
2. *(with countoff)*
(S) (2:08) Sandstone 33079 and 5002 Uh Huh His Greatest
Hits.
(S) (2:11) Sandstone 33074 and 5004 Ingredients In A
Recipe For Soul. *(with countoff)*
(S) (2:05) Time-Life RHD-06 Rhythm & Blues - Ray
Charles 1954-1966.
(S) (2:09) Garland 2121 The World Of. *(with countoff)*
(S) (2:06) Rhino 72843 Ingredients In A Recipe For
Soul/Have A Smile With Me.
(S) (2:08) Rhino 72859 Genius & Soul - The 50th
Anniversary Collection. *(truncated fade)*

1964 THAT LUCKY OLD SUN
(S) (4:20) Rhino 75759 Anthology. *(LP version)*
(S) (4:20) Rhino 70099 Modern Sounds In Country &
Western Music. *(LP version)*
(S) (4:19) DCC Compact Classics 047 Ingredients In A
Recipe For Soul. *(LP version)*
(S) (4:19) DCC Compact Classics 036 His Greatest Volume
1. *(LP version)*
(S) (4:19) Sandstone 33079 and 5002 Uh Huh His Greatest
Hits. *(LP version)*
(S) (4:19) Sandstone 33074 and 5004 Ingredients In A
Recipe For Soul. *(LP version)*
(S) (4:19) DCC Compact Classics 1027 Ingredients In A
Recipe For Soul. *(LP version; gold disc)*
(S) (4:20) Garland 2121 The World Of. *(LP version)*
(S) (4:20) Qwest/Reprise 45130 O.S.T. Malcolm X. *(LP
version)*

(S) (4:22) Rhino 72843 Ingredients In A Recipe For
Soul/Have A Smile With Me. *(LP version)*
(S) (4:22) Rhino 72859 Genius & Soul - The 50th
Anniversary Collection. *(LP version)*

1966 CRYING TIME
(S) (2:55) Rhino 75759 Anthology.
(S) (2:59) DCC Compact Classics 040 Greatest Country &
Western Hits. *(with countoff)*
(S) (2:54) DCC Compact Classics 036 His Greatest Volume 1.
(S) (2:55) Sandstone 33079 and 5002 Uh Huh His Greatest
Hits.
(S) (2:54) Time-Life RHD-06 Rhythm & Blues - Ray
Charles 1954-1966.
(S) (2:55) Garland 2121 The World Of.
(S) (2:55) Rhino 72844 Sweet & Sour Tears.
(S) (2:55) Rhino 72859 Genius & Soul - The 50th
Anniversary Collection.

1966 TOGETHER AGAIN
(S) (2:36) DCC Compact Classics 040 Greatest Country &
Western Hits.
(S) (2:37) Sandstone 33079 and 5002 Uh Huh His Greatest
Hits.
(S) (2:37) Garland 2121 The World Of.
(S) (2:37) Rhino 72859 Genius & Soul - The 50th
Anniversary Collection.

1966 LET'S GO GET STONED
(S) (2:58) Rhino 75759 Anthology. *(truncated fade)*
(S) (2:58) DCC Compact Classics 036 His Greatest Volume 1.
(S) (2:58) Sandstone 33079 and 5002 Uh Huh His Greatest
Hits.
(S) (2:56) Time-Life RHD-06 Rhythm & Blues - Ray
Charles 1954-1966.
(S) (2:58) Garland 2121 The World Of.
(S) (2:59) Rhino 72859 Genius & Soul - The 50th
Anniversary Collection.

1966 I CHOSE TO SING THE BLUES
(S) (2:29) DCC Compact Classics 036 His Greatest Volume 1.
(S) (2:29) Sandstone 33079 and 5002 Uh Huh His Greatest
Hits.
(S) (2:29) Garland 2121 The World Of.
(S) (2:28) Rhino 72859 Genius & Soul - The 50th
Anniversary Collection.

1967 HERE WE GO AGAIN
(S) (3:14) Rhino 75759 Anthology.
(S) (3:14) Rhino 70099 Modern Sounds in Country &
Western Music.
(S) (3:14) DCC Compact Classics 036 His Greatest Volume 1.
(S) (3:16) Sandstone 33079 and 5002 Uh Huh His Greatest
Hits.
(S) (3:14) Garland 2121 The World Of.
(S) (3:14) Rhino 72859 Genius & Soul - The 50th
Anniversary Collection.

1967 IN THE HEAT OF THE NIGHT
(S) (2:33) Garland 2121 The World Of. *(soundtrack
version)*
(S) (2:33) Sandstone 33079 and 5002 Uh Huh His Greatest
Hits. *(soundtrack version)*
(S) (2:33) DCC Compact Classics 037 His Greatest Volume
2. *(soundtrack version)*
(S) (2:35) Rhino 72859 Genius & Soul - The 50th
Anniversary Collection. *(soundtrack version)*
(M) (3:21) Rhino 72815 Beg, Scream & Shout! The Big Ol'
Box Of '60s Soul. *(45 version)*

1967 YESTERDAY
(S) (2:44) DCC Compact Classics 036 His Greatest Volume 1.
(S) (2:45) Sandstone 33079 and 5002 Uh Huh His Greatest Hits.
(S) (2:44) Garland 2121 The World Of.
(S) (2:44) Rhino 72859 Genius & Soul - The 50th
Anniversary Collection.

1968 ELEANOR RIGBY
(S) (2:56) Rhino 75759 Anthology.
(S) (2:55) DCC Compact Classics 037 His Greatest Volume 2.
(S) (2:55) Sandstone 33079 and 5002 Uh Huh His Greatest
Hits.
(S) (2:56) Garland 2121 The World Of.

RAY CHARLES *(Continued)*

    (S)   (2:55)   Rhino 72859 Genius & Soul - The 50th Anniversary Collection.

1971 DON'T CHANGE ON ME

    (S)   (3:02)   DCC Compact Classics 036 His Greatest Volume 1.

    (S)   (3:02)   Sandstone 33079 and 5002 Uh Huh His Greatest Hits.

    (S)   (3:02)   Garland 2121 The World Of.

    (S)   (3:23)   Rhino 72859 Genius & Soul - The 50th Anniversary Collection.

released as by THE RAY CHARLES ORCHESTRA:

1971 BOOTY BUTT

(actual 45 time is (4:11) not (3:30) as stated on the record label)

    (S)   (4:11)   Rhino 72859 Genius & Soul - The 50th Anniversary Collection.

released as by QUINCY JONES featuring RAY CHARLES and CHAKA KHAN:

1990 I'LL BE GOOD TO YOU

    (S)   (4:54)   Qwest/Warner Brothers 26020 Quincy Jones - Back On The Block. *(LP version)*

    (S)   (3:55)   JCI 3177 1985 - Only Soul - 1989. *(45 version faded :22 early)*

    (S)   (4:54)   Rhino 72859 Genius & Soul - The 50th Anniversary Collection. *(LP version)*

RAY CHARLES SINGERS

1964 LOVE ME WITH ALL YOUR HEART

    (S)   (2:18)   Varese Sarabande 5626 Love Me With All Your Heart - The Command Performances.

1964 AL-DI-LA

    (S)   (2:07)   Varese Sarabande 5626 Love Me With All Your Heart - The Command Performances.

1965 ONE MORE TIME

    (S)   (2:54)   Varese Sarabande 5626 Love Me With All Your Heart - The Command Performances.

SONNY CHARLES and THE CHECKMATES, LTD.

1969 BLACK PEARL

    (S)   (3:26)   Rhino 75774 Soul Shots.

    (M)   (3:17)   Abkco 7118 Phil Spector/Back To Mono (1958-1969). *(:09 shorter than the 45 or LP)*

    (S)   (3:25)   Rebound 314520369 Soul Classics - Quiet Storm/The 60's.

CHARLES & EDDIE

1992 WOULD I LIE TO YOU?

    (S)   (4:37)   Capitol 97150 Duophonic.

    (S)   (3:38)   JCI 3132 1990 - Only Rock 'n Roll - 1994. *(edited)*

    (S)   (4:36)   Original Sound 9308 Dedicated To You Vol. 8.

    (S)   (3:33)   Priority 50934 Shut Up And Dance! The 90's Volume One. *(remixed; all selections on this cd are segued together)*

CHARMS

1955 HEARTS OF STONE

    (M)   (2:34)   King 570 All-Time Hits.

    (M)   (2:32)   King 7002 King R&B Box Set.

    (M)   (2:31)   King 513 All Star Rock And Roll.

    (M)   (2:33)   King 1402 Otis Williams & The Charms - Original Blues.

1955 LING, TING, TONG

    (M)   (2:13)   King 570 All-Time Hits.

    (M)   (2:13)   King 1402 Otis Williams & The Charms - Original Blues.

released as by OTIS WILLIAMS and HIS CHARMS:

1956 IVORY TOWER

    (M)   (2:11)   Time-Life 2RNR-23 Rock 'N' Roll Era - 1956 Still Rockin'.

    (M)   (2:14)   King 570 All-Time Hits.

    (M)   (2:14)   King 7002 King R&B Box Set.

    (M)   (2:13)   King 1402 Otis Williams & The Charms - Original Blues.

    (M)   (2:12)   Time-Life R857-07 The Heart Of Rock 'n' Roll 1956.

CHARTBUSTERS

1964 SHE'S THE ONE

CHASE

1971 GET IT ON

    (S)   (2:57)   Rhino 70925 Super Hits Of The 70's Volume 5.

    (S)   (2:57)   Columbia/Legacy 46160 Rock Artifacts Volume 1.

    (S)   (2:56)   K-Tel 3585 Horn Rock Bands.

    (S)   (2:56)   Eclipse Music Group 64892 Rock 'n Roll Relix 1970-1971.

    (S)   (2:56)   Eclipse Music Group 64897 Rock 'n Roll Relix 1970-1979.

    (S)   (2:57)   Sony Music Special Products 26069 Rock Hits Of The 70's.

CHEAP TRICK

1979 I WANT YOU TO WANT ME

    (S)   (3:05)   Epic 46940 O.S.T. Queens Logic. *(studio version from the "In Color" album - not the hit version)*

    (S)   (3:39)   Foundation/Capitol 96647 Hearts Of Gold - The Classic Rock Collection.

    (S)   (3:38)   Epic 48681 Greatest Hits.

    (S)   (3:36)   Epic 35795 At Budokan.

    (S)   (3:08)   Razor & Tie 22502 Those Rocking 70's. *(studio version from the "In Color" album - not the hit version)*

    (S)   (3:37)   Time-Life R968-02 Guitar Rock 1978-1979.

    (S)   (3:37)   Time-Life SOD-09 Sounds Of The Seventies - 1979.

    (S)   (3:07)   MCA Special Products 22105 Greatest Classic Rock Hits. *(studio version from the "In Color" album - not the hit version)*

    (S)   (3:38)   Priority 53745 Back Stage Pass - Live & Rockin' Vol. 1.

    (S)   (3:07)   Epic 34884 In Color. *(studio version from the "In Color" album - not the hit version)*

    (S)   (3:07)   Epic 64805 Cheap Trick/In Color/Heaven Tonight. *(studio version from the "In Color" album - not the hit version)*

    (S)   (3:38)   Epic/Legacy 65020 Ultimate Rock 'n' Roll Collection.

    (S)   (2:59)   Epic/Legacy 64938 Sex, America, Cheap Trick. *(alternate take)*

    (S)   (3:43)   Epic/Legacy 64938 Sex, America, Cheap Trick.

    (S)   (3:37)   Time-Life R968-23 Guitar Rock - Live!

    (S)   (3:37)   Warner Brothers 46477 Howard Stern Private Parts: The Album.

    (S)   (3:38)   Mobile Fidelity 709 At Budokan. *(gold disc)*

    (S)   (3:05)   K-Tel 3907 Starflight Vol. 2. *(studio version from the "In Color" album - not the hit version)*

    (S)   (3:37)   Time-Life R840-10 Sounds Of The Seventies: '70s Dance Party 1979.

1979 AIN'T THAT A SHAME

    (S)   (5:10)   Epic 48681 Greatest Hits. *(LP version)*

    (S)   (5:12)   Epic 35795 At Budokan. *(LP version)*

    (S)   (5:09)   Time-Life R968-17 Guitar Rock - The Late '70s: Take Two. *(LP version)*

    (S)   (5:10)   EMI 37356 That's Fats! - A Tribute To Fats Domino. *(LP version)*

    (S)   (5:12)   Mobile Fidelity 709 At Budokan. *(gold disc; LP version)*

    (S)   (5:09)   Simitar 55762 Stud Rock - Wild Ride. *(LP version)*

1979 DREAM POLICE

(dj copies of this 45 ran (3:14) and (3:49); commercial copies were all (3:49))

    (S)   (3:50)   Epic 48681 Greatest Hits.

    (S)   (3:52)   Epic 35773 Dream Police.

    (S)   (3:49)   Time-Life R968-14 Guitar Rock - The Late '70s.

    (S)   (3:51)   Epic/Legacy 64938 Sex, America, Cheap Trick.

    (S)   (3:52)   K-Tel 3904 The Rock Album Volume 1.

1980 VOICES

    (S)   (4:18)   Epic 48681 Greatest Hits.

    (S)   (4:20)   Epic 35773 Dream Police.

    (S)   (4:21)   Epic/Legacy 64938 Sex, America, Cheap Trick.

1988 THE FLAME
- (S) (4:41) Priority 7077 80's Greatest Rock Hits Volume 5 - From The Heart. *(45 version)*
- (S) (4:45) Rhino 71643 Billboard Top Hits - 1988. *(45 version)*
- (S) (5:36) Risky Business 57833 Read The Hits/Best Of The 80's. *(LP version)*
- (S) (3:41) JCI 3119 18 Rock Classics. *(neither the 45 or LP version)*
- (S) (5:36) Epic 40922 Lap Of Luxury. *(LP version)*
- (S) (5:35) Epic 48681 Greatest Hits. *(LP version)*
- (S) (4:45) Time-Life R988-10 Sounds Of The 80's: 1988. *(45 version)*
- (S) (5:37) Epic/Legacy 64938 Sex, America, Cheap Trick. *(LP version)*
- (S) (5:34) Rhino 72579 Feel Like Makin' Love - Romantic Power Ballads. *(LP version)*
- (S) (4:41) K-Tel 3866 The 80's: Number One Pop Hits. *(45 version)*
- (S) (4:46) Time-Life R834-16 Body Talk - Sweet Nothings. *(45 version)*

1988 DON'T BE CRUEL
- (S) (3:06) Epic 40922 Lap Of Luxury.
- (S) (3:07) Epic 48681 Greatest Hits.
- (S) (3:07) Time-Life R988-20 Sounds Of The Eighties: The Late '80s Take Two.

1988 GHOST TOWN
- (S) (4:10) Epic 40922 Lap Of Luxury.

1990 CAN'T STOP FALLIN' INTO LOVE
- (S) (3:47) Priority 7049 Metal Heat.
- (S) (3:47) Epic 46013 Busted.
- (S) (3:45) Epic 48681 Greatest Hits.
- (S) (3:48) Epic/Legacy 64938 Sex, America, Cheap Trick.
- (S) (3:45) Time-Life R968-25 Guitar Rock - The '90s.

CHUBBY CHECKER
1959 THE CLASS
1960 THE TWIST
- (S) (2:33) Rhino 70621 Billboard's Top Rock & Roll Hits Of 1960. *(rerecording)*
- (S) (2:33) Rhino 72004 Billboard's Top Rock & Roll Hits 1957-1961. *(rerecording)*
- (S) (2:33) Rhino 70992 Groove 'n' Grind. *(rerecording)*
- (S) (2:35) Enigma 73531 O.S.T. Scandal. *(rerecording)*
- (S) (2:36) K-Tel 3241 Let's Twist. *(rerecording)*
- (S) (2:35) K-Tel 3331 Do You Wanna Dance. *(rerecording)*
- (S) (2:33) Risky Business 67311 The Ultimate Party Survival Kit. *(rerecording)*
- (S) (2:34) Cold Front 6245 Greatest Sports Rock And Jams. *(all selections on this cd are segued together; rerecording)*
- (S) (2:35) K-Tel 4046 More Music For Your Party. *(rerecording)*
- (S) (2:36) K-Tel 4066 K-Tel's Original Party Music Vol. 2. *(rerecording)*

1960 THE HUCKLEBUCK
1961 PONY TIME
- (S) (1:30) MCA 6171 Good Time Rock 'N' Roll. *(all selections on this cd are recorded live)*
- (S) (2:22) K-Tel 3331 Do You Wanna Dance. *(rerecording)*
- (S) (2:23) Nick At Nite/550 Music 63407 Dancing At The Nick At Niteclub. *(rerecording)*

1961 (DANCE THE) MESS AROUND
1961 LET'S TWIST AGAIN
- (S) (3:10) MCA 6171 Good Time Rock 'N' Roll. *(all selections on this cd are recorded live)*
- (S) (2:20) K-Tel 3241 Let's Twist. *(rerecording)*
- (S) (2:20) K-Tel 3796 Music For Your Party. *(rerecording)*
- (S) (2:20) K-Tel 4066 K-Tel's Original Party Music Vol. 2. *(rerecording)*

1961 THE FLY

1962 THE TWIST
(this song charted in two different years: 1960 & 1962; see 1960 listings)
released as by BOBBY RYDELL/CHUBBY CHECKER:
1962 JINGLE BELL ROCK
released as by CHUBBY CHECKER:
1962 SLOW TWISTIN'
- (S) (2:41) K-Tel 3241 Let's Twist. *(rerecording)*

1962 DANCIN' PARTY
1962 LIMBO ROCK
- (E) (2:22) MCA 6214 Moonlighting - TV Soundtrack.
- (S) (2:23) Columbia 57317 O.S.T. Calendar Girl. *(rerecording)*
- (S) (2:22) K-Tel 3331 Do You Wanna Dance. *(rerecording)*
- (E) (2:23) K-Tel 3575 Hot, Hot Vacation Jams - Week One. *(rerecording)*
- (S) (2:24) Nick At Nite/550 Music 63407 Dancing At The Nick At Niteclub. *(rerecording)*
- (S) (2:24) K-Tel 4065 K-Tel's Original Party Music Vol. 1. *(rerecording)*

1962 POPEYE (THE HITCHHIKER)
1963 LET'S LIMBO SOME MORE
1963 TWENTY MILES
1963 BIRDLAND
1963 TWIST IT UP
1963 LODDY LO
1964 HOOKA TOOKA
1964 HEY, BOBBA NEEDLE
1964 LAZY ELSIE MOLLY
1965 LET'S DO THE FREDDIE
released as by THE FAT BOYS with CHUBBY CHECKER:
1988 THE TWIST (YO, TWIST!)
- (S) (4:04) Tin Pan Apple/Polydor 835809 Fat Boys - Coming Back Hard Again.
- (S) (4:05) Rhino 72632 Fat Boys - Best Of.

CHEECH & CHONG
1973 BASKETBALL JONES FEATURING TYRONE SHOELACES
- (S) (4:04) Warner Brothers 3252 Los Cochinos.
- (S) (4:01) Warner Brothers 3614 Greatest Hit.
- (S) (4:04) Rhino 75200 Basketball's Greatest Hits.

1974 SISTER MARY ELEPHANT (SHUDD-UP!)
- (S) (3:30) Warner Brothers 3614 Greatest Hit. *(tracks into next selection)*
- (S) (3:33) Warner Brothers 3251 Big Bambu.

1974 EARACHE MY EYE
- (S) (5:18) Rhino 75768 Dr. Demento Presents The Greatest Novelty CD Of All Time.
- (S) (5:18) Rhino 70743 Dr. Demento 20th Anniversary Collection.
- (S) (2:29) Warner Brothers 3614 Greatest Hit. *(edited)*
- (S) (5:16) Warner Brothers 3253 Wedding Album.
- (S) (5:17) Time-Life R830-01 The Dr. Demento Collection - The Mid 70's.

CHER
1965 ALL I REALLY WANT TO DO
- (S) (2:54) EMI 92773 Legendary Masters Series. *(very poor stereo separation)*
- (S) (2:56) EMI 91836 Best Of.
- (S) (2:56) EMI 80241 All I Really Want To Do/The Sonny Side Of Cher.
- (S) (2:54) Time-Life 2CLR-14 Classic Rock - 1965: Shakin' All Over.
- (S) (2:54) Time-Life R962-02 History Of Rock 'N' Roll: Folk Rock 1964-1967.
- (S) (2:55) K-Tel 3438 Best Of Folk Rock.
- (S) (2:55) CEMA Special Markets 56684 Bang Bang & Other Hits.

1965 WHERE DO YOU GO
- (S) (3:16) EMI 92773 Legendary Masters Series.
- (S) (3:12) EMI 91836 Best Of.
- (S) (3:18) EMI 80241 All I Really Want To Do/The Sonny Side Of Cher.

CHER *(Continued)*

- (S) (3:12) CEMA Special Markets 56684 Bang Bang & Other Hits.

1966 BANG BANG (MY BABY SHOT ME DOWN)
- (S) (2:42) EMI 96268 24 Greatest Hits Of All Time.
- (S) (2:46) EMI 92773 Legendary Masters Series. *(with countoff)*
- (S) (2:42) EMI 91836 Best Of.
- (S) (2:41) EMI 80241 All I Really Want To Do/The Sonny Side Of Cher.
- (S) (2:42) Time-Life 2CLR-13 Classic Rock - 1966: Shakin' All Over.
- (S) (2:41) Time-Life SUD-01 Superhits - 1966.
- (S) (3:50) Geffen 24164 Cher. *(1987 rerecording)*
- (S) (2:42) Time-Life AM1-09 AM Gold - 1966.
- (S) (2:42) CEMA Special Markets 56684 Bang Bang & Other Hits.

1966 ALFIE
- (S) (2:57) EMI 92773 Legendary Masters Series. *(:10 longer than the 45 or LP)*
- (S) (2:46) CEMA Special Markets 56684 Bang Bang & Other Hits.

1967 YOU BETTER SIT DOWN KIDS
- (S) (4:17) EMI 92773 Legendary Masters Series. *(LP version; includes :09 of studio talk; :26 longer fade than either the 45 or LP version)*
- (S) (3:41) EMI 91836 Best Of. *(LP version)*
- (S) (3:36) CEMA Special Markets 56684 Bang Bang & Other Hits. *(LP version)*

1971 GYPSYS, TRAMPS & THIEVES
- (S) (2:36) Rhino 70632 Billboard's Top Rock & Roll Hits Of 1971.
- (S) (2:36) Rhino 72005 Billboard's Top Rock & Roll Hits 1968-1972 Box Set.
- (S) (2:35) MCA 31376 Gypsys, Tramps & Thieves.
- (S) (2:34) MCA 922 Greatest Hits.
- (S) (2:36) MCA Special Products 20210 Half Breed.
- (S) (2:35) MCA 11300 All I Ever Need - The Kapp/MCA Anthology.
- (S) (2:35) MCA 11745 Cher And Sonny & Cher - Greatest Hits.

1972 THE WAY OF LOVE
- (S) (2:29) MCA 31376 Gypsys, Tramps & Thieves.
- (S) (2:29) MCA 922 Greatest Hits.
- (S) (2:29) MCA Special Products 20210 Half Breed.
- (S) (2:30) MCA 11300 All I Ever Need - The Kapp/MCA Anthology.
- (S) (2:30) MCA 11745 Cher And Sonny & Cher - Greatest Hits.

1972 LIVING IN A HOUSE DIVIDED
- (S) (2:54) MCA 922 Greatest Hits.
- (S) (2:56) MCA 11300 All I Ever Need - The Kapp/MCA Anthology.
- (S) (2:56) MCA 11745 Cher And Sonny & Cher - Greatest Hits.

1973 HALF-BREED
- (S) (2:42) MCA 922 Greatest Hits.
- (S) (2:44) MCA Special Products 20210 Half Breed.
- (S) (2:43) MCA 11300 All I Ever Need - The Kapp/MCA Anthology.
- (S) (2:43) MCA 11745 Cher And Sonny & Cher - Greatest Hits.

1974 DARK LADY
- (S) (3:25) MCA 922 Greatest Hits.
- (S) (3:26) MCA Special Products 20210 Half Breed.
- (S) (3:25) MCA 11300 All I Ever Need - The Kapp/MCA Anthology.
- (S) (3:26) MCA 11745 Cher And Sonny & Cher - Greatest Hits.

1974 TRAIN OF THOUGHT
- (S) (2:33) MCA 922 Greatest Hits.
- (S) (2:33) MCA Special Products 20210 Half Breed.
- (S) (2:34) MCA 11300 All I Ever Need - The Kapp/MCA Anthology.
- (S) (2:34) MCA 11745 Cher And Sonny & Cher - Greatest Hits.

1974 I SAW A MAN AND HE DANCED WITH HIS WIFE
- (S) (3:12) MCA 922 Greatest Hits.

1979 TAKE ME HOME
- (S) (7:30) Casablanca 838810 Let's Start The Dance (Polygram Dance Classics) Volume 1. *(12" single version)*

- (S) (3:26) Rhino 70493 Billboard Top Dance Hits - 1979. *(45 version)*
- (S) (3:29) Priority 53728 Mega Hits Dance Classics Vol 12. *(45 version)*
- (S) (7:29) Casablanca 314516918 Casablanca Records Story. *(12" single version)*
- (S) (3:26) Rebound 314520307 Disco Nights Volume VIII. *(45 version)*
- (S) (7:22) Rebound 314520270 Class Reunion 1979. *(12" single version)*
- (S) (3:26) Special Music/Essex 5036 Prom Night - The 70's. *(45 version)*
- (S) (3:26) Time-Life R138-38 Celebration. *(45 version)*
- (S) (3:26) Casablanca 314526253 Casablanca Records Greatest Hits. *(45 version)*
- (S) (6:44) Casablanca 314532320 The Casablanca Years. *(LP version)*
- (S) (3:26) Time-Life R840-09 Sounds Of The Seventies: '70s Dance Party 1979-1981. *(45 version)*

1988 I FOUND SOMEONE
- (S) (3:41) Geffen 24164 Cher.

1988 WE ALL SLEEP ALONE
- (S) (3:51) Geffen 24164 Cher.

released as by CHER and PETER CETERA:
1989 AFTER ALL
- (S) (4:03) Geffen 24239 Cher - Heart Of Stone.
- (S) (4:03) River North 514161250 Peter Cetera - You're The Inspiration - A Collection.

released as by CHER:
1989 IF I COULD TURN BACK TIME
- (S) (4:12) Geffen 24239 Heart Of Stone.
- (S) (4:07) Geffen 25151 Geffen Vintage 80s Vol. II.

1989 JUST LIKE JESSE JAMES
- (S) (4:04) Geffen 24239 Heart Of Stone.

1990 HEART OF STONE
- (S) (4:15) Geffen 24239 Heart Of Stone. *(LP version)*

1991 THE SHOOP SHOOP SONG (IT'S IN HIS KISS)
- (S) (2:49) Geffen 24310 O.S.T. Mermaids.
- (S) (6:52) Geffen 25102 Global Grooves - Remixes. *(remixed)*

1991 LOVE AND UNDERSTANDING
- (S) (4:41) Geffen 24369 and 24421 Love Hurts.

1991 SAVE UP ALL YOUR TEARS
- (S) (3:59) Geffen 24369 and 24421 Love Hurts.

CHERI
1982 MURPHY'S LAW

CHERRELLE
released as by CHERRELLE with ALEXANDER O'NEAL:
1986 SATURDAY LOVE
- (S) (8:41) Epic 46087 Club Epic. *(remix)*
- (S) (6:28) Tabu 40094 Cherrelle - High Priority. *(LP version)*
- (S) (4:56) Tabu 314530592 Cherrelle - Best Of. *(LP version but missing the introduction)*

released as by ALEXANDER O'NEAL featuring CHERRELLE:
1988 NEVER KNEW LOVE LIKE THIS
- (S) (5:08) Tabu 40320 Alexander O'Neal - Hearsay. *(LP version)*
- (S) (3:28) Tabu 53833 Alexander O'Neal - Greatest Hits. *(45 version)*
- (S) (5:09) Tabu 314530591 Alexander O'Neal - Best Of. *(LP version)*

DON CHERRY
1956 BAND OF GOLD
- (M) (2:35) Rhino 70588 Rockin' & Rollin' Wedding songs Volume 1.
- (M) (2:35) Time-Life HPD-21 Your Hit Parade - The Mid 50's.
- (M) (2:35) Varese Sarabande 5782 The '50s Remembered: Haymes, Dale, Desmond & Cherry.

1956 GHOST TOWN

NENEH CHERRY
1989 BUFFALO STANCE
- (S) (5:41) K-Tel 3343 The 80's Hot Dance Trax. *(LP version)*
- (S) (5:41) K-Tel 842 Hot Ladies Of The 80's. *(LP version)*
- (S) (5:41) Virgin 91252 and 86116 Raw Like Sushi. *(LP version)*
- (S) (5:41) Priority 53731 80's Greatest Rock Hits Volume 10 - Dance All Night. *(LP version)*
- (S) (4:06) Virgin 91229 O.S.T. Slaves Of New York. *(45 version)*
- (S) (3:47) JCI 3177 1985 - Only Soul - 1989. *(neither the 45, LP or 12" single version)*
- (S) (4:03) Time-Life R988-20 Sounds Of The Eighties: The Late '80s Take Two. *(45 version)*

1989 KISSES ON THE WIND
(dj copies of this 45 ran (3:25) and (3:49); commercial copies were all (3:49))
- (S) (3:56) Virgin 91252 and 86116 Raw Like Sushi.

CHIC
1978 DANCE, DANCE, DANCE (YOWSAH, YOWSAH, YOWSAH)
- (S) (3:42) Atlantic 81913 Golden Age Of Black Music (1977-1988). *(45 version)*
- (S) (8:19) Atlantic 82333 Best Of. *(LP version)*
- (S) (8:19) Atlantic 80407 Chic. *(LP version)*
- (S) (8:19) Rhino 71095 Disco Hits Volume 2. *(LP version)*
- (S) (3:41) Time-Life SOD-27 Sounds Of The Seventies - Dance Fever. *(45 version)*
- (S) (8:19) Rhino 71851 Everybody Dance. *(LP version)*
- (S) (3:41) JCI 3169 #1 Radio Hits 1975 - Only Rock 'n Roll - 1979. *(45 version)*
- (S) (3:41) Hip-O 40041 The Studio Collection Disco 54. *(45 version)*
- (S) (8:19) Flashback 72689 Disco Hits: Shake Your Booty. *(LP version)*
- (S) (8:19) Flashback 72674 Dance, Dance, Dance And Other Hits. *(LP version)*
- (S) (3:41) Time-Life R840-08 Sounds Of The Seventies: '70s Dance Party 1978-1979. *(45 version)*

1978 EVERYBODY DANCE
- (S) (3:31) Rhino 72122 Disco Years, Vol. 6. *(45 version)*
- (S) (6:38) Rhino 71851 Everybody Dance. *(LP version)*
- (S) (6:40) Atlantic 80407 Chic. *(LP version)*
- (S) (8:26) Atlantic 82333 Dance, Dance, Dance. *(12" single version)*
- (S) (6:38) Flashback 72674 Dance, Dance, Dance And Other Hits. *(LP version)*

1978 LE FREAK
- (S) (3:45) Atlantic 81913 Golden Age Of Black Music (1977-1988). *(45 version)*
- (S) (4:17) Rhino 70274 The Disco Years Volume 3. *(edit of the LP version)*
- (S) (3:32) Priority 7059 Mega-Hits Dance Classics Volume 10. *(45 version; truncated fade)*
- (S) (5:28) Atlantic 82333 Best Of. *(LP version)*
- (S) (5:28) Atlantic 81552 C'est Chic. *(LP version)*
- (S) (4:17) Rhino 71096 Disco Hits Volume 3. *(edit of the LP version)*
- (S) (3:32) Time-Life SOD-10 Sounds Of The Seventies - 1978. *(45 version)*
- (S) (5:28) Rhino 71851 Everybody Dance. *(LP version)*
- (S) (4:17) Rhino 72414 Dance Floor Divas: The 70's. *(edit of the LP version)*
- (S) (5:27) Hip-O 40041 The Studio Collection Disco 54. *(LP version)*
- (S) (4:17) Flashback 72691 Disco Hits: Le Freak. *(edit of the LP version)*
- (S) (4:17) Flashback 72086 Disco Hits Box Set. *(edit of the LP version)*
- (S) (5:28) Flashback 72674 Dance, Dance, Dance And Other Hits. *(LP version)*
- (S) (4:16) K-Tel 3887 Soul Brothers & Sisters Of The 70's. *(edit of the LP version)*
- (S) (3:32) Time-Life R838-17 Solid Gold Soul 1978. *(45 version)*

- (S) (4:17) K-Tel 3909 High Energy Volume 2. *(edit of the LP version)*
- (S) (4:16) Cold Front 4025 Old School Mega Mix Volume 3. *(edit of the LP version)*
- (S) (3:32) Atlantic 83088 Atlantic Records: 50 Years - The Gold Anniversary Collection. *(45 version)*
- (S) (5:28) Elektra 62218 Maximum Club Classics Vol. 2. *(LP version)*
- (S) (3:32) Time-Life AM1-25 AM Gold - 1978. *(45 version)*

1979 I WANT YOUR LOVE
- (S) (3:29) Rhino 70985 The Disco Years Volume 2. *(45 version)*
- (S) (6:53) Atlantic 82333 Best Of. *(LP version)*
- (S) (6:53) Atlantic 81552 C'est Chic. *(LP version)*
- (S) (3:29) Time-Life SOD-36 Sounds Of The Seventies - More AM Nuggets. *(45 version)*
- (S) (3:29) Rhino 71667 Disco Hits Vol. 4. *(45 version)*
- (S) (6:53) Rhino 71851 Everybody Dance. *(LP version)*
- (S) (3:29) Madacy Entertainment 1979 Rock On 1979. *(45 version)*
- (S) (3:29) Flashback 72690 Disco Hits: That's The Way I Like It. *(45 version)*
- (S) (6:53) Flashback 72674 Dance, Dance, Dance And Other Hits. *(LP version)*
- (S) (3:28) Simitar 55542 The Number One's: Soul On Fire. *(45 version)*

1979 GOOD TIMES
- (S) (3:43) Atlantic 81913 Golden Age Of Black Music (1977-1988). *(45 version)*
- (S) (3:42) Rhino 70275 The Disco Years Volume 4. *(45 version)*
- (S) (3:43) Original Sound 9308 Dedicated To You Vol. 8. *(45 version)*
- (S) (8:13) Atlantic 82333 Best Of. *(LP version)*
- (S) (8:06) Atlantic 80406 Risque. *(LP version)*
- (S) (3:42) Rhino 71096 Disco Hits Volume 3. *(45 version)*
- (S) (8:00) JCI 3306 Dance Seventies. *(LP version)*
- (S) (3:41) Time-Life SOD-09 Sounds Of The Seventies - 1979. *(45 version)*
- (S) (8:13) Rhino 71851 Everybody Dance. *(LP version)*
- (S) (6:21) Rebound 314520220 Disco Nights Vol. 4 - Greatest Disco Groups. *(neither the 45 or LP version)*
- (S) (3:43) Priority 53786 Planet Funk Volume 3. *(45 version)*
- (S) (8:06) Rhino 72489 Street Jams - Back 2 The Old Skool, Part 3. *(LP version)*
- (S) (3:42) JCI 3148 1975 - Only Dance - 1979. *(45 version)*
- (S) (3:40) JCI 3163 18 Disco Superhits. *(45 version)*
- (S) (3:42) Flashback 72693 Disco Hits: Good Times. *(45 version)*
- (S) (3:42) Flashback 72086 Disco Hits Box Set. *(45 version)*
- (S) (8:13) Flashback 72674 Dance, Dance, Dance And Other Hits. *(LP version)*
- (S) (3:42) Rhino 72837 Disco Queens: The 70's. *(45 version)*
- (S) (3:42) Time-Life R838-15 Solid Gold Soul 1979. *(45 version)*
- (S) (3:39) Cold Front 4024 Old School Mega Mix Volume 2. *(45 version)*
- (S) (3:41) Time-Life R840-10 Sounds Of The Seventies: '70s Dance Party 1979. *(45 version)*
- (S) (3:41) Time-Life AM1-26 AM Gold - 1979. *(45 version)*
- (S) (3:39) K-Tel 4065 K-Tel's Original Party Music Vol. 1. *(45 version)*

CHICAGO
1970 MAKE ME SMILE
- (S) (2:58) Columbia 33900 Greatest Hits. *(45 version)*
- (S) (2:58) Chicago Records 3009 Greatest Hits. *(45 version)*
- (S) (3:15) Columbia 00024 Chicago II. *(LP version; tracks into next selection)*

CHICAGO (Continued)

- (S) (3:15) Chicago Records 3002 Chicago II. *(LP version; tracks into next selection)*
- (S) (3:28) Columbia/Legacy 47416 Group Portrait. *(LP version; tracks into next selection)*
- (S) (3:28) Chicago Records 3018 Group Portrait. *(LP version; tracks into next selection)*
- (S) (2:58) Reprise 46554 The Heart Of Chicago 1967-1997. *(45 version)*

1970 25 OR 6 TO 4

- (S) (4:49) Columbia 33900 Greatest Hits. *(LP version)*
- (S) (4:49) Chicago Records 3009 Greatest Hits. *(LP version)*
- (S) (4:49) Columbia 00024 Chicago II. *(LP version)*
- (S) (4:49) Chicago Records 3002 Chicago II. *(LP version)*
- (S) (4:49) Columbia/Legacy 47416 Group Portrait. *(LP version)*
- (S) (4:49) Chicago Records 3018 Group Portrait. *(LP version)*
- (S) (4:50) Columbia 38590 If You Leave Me Now. *(LP version)*
- (S) (4:50) Chicago Records 3016 If You Leave Me Now. *(LP version)*
- (S) (4:50) Time-Life R13610 Gold And Platinum Box Set - The Ultimate Rock Collection. *(LP version)*
- (S) (4:49) Reprise 46911 The Heart Of Chicago 1967-1998 Volume II. *(LP version)*

1971 DOES ANYBODY REALLY KNOW WHAT TIME IT IS?
(dj copies of this 45 ran (2:53) and (3:17);
commercial copies were all (3:17))

- (S) (3:18) Columbia 33900 Greatest Hits. *(edit of the LP version in an unsuccessful attempt at recreating the 45 version)*
- (S) (3:18) Chicago Records 3009 Greatest Hits. *(edit of the LP versiion in an unsuccessful attempt at recreating the 45 version)*
- (S) (4:33) Columbia 00008 and 57186 Chicago Transit Authority. *(LP version)*
- (S) (4:33) Chicago Records 3001 Chicago Transit Authority. *(LP version)*
- (S) (4:34) Columbia/Legacy 47416 Group Portrait. *(LP version)*
- (S) (4:34) Chicago Records 3018 Group Portrait. *(LP version)*
- (S) (2:52) Columbia 38590 If You Leave Me Now. *(this is the dj 45 edit)*
- (S) (2:52) Chicago Records 3016 If You Leave Me Now. *(this is the dj 45 edit)*
- (S) (3:18) Reprise 46554 The Heart Of Chicago 1967-1997. *(edit of the LP version in an unsuccessful attempt at recreating the 45 version)*

1971 FREE

- (S) (2:15) Columbia 39579 Take Me Back To Chicago.
- (S) (2:15) Columbia 30110 Chicago III. *(previous selection tracks into introduction; tracks into next selection)*
- (S) (2:15) Chicago Records 3003 Chicago III. *(previous selection tracks into introduction; tracks into next selection)*
- oR (S) (2:15) Columbia/Legacy 47416 Group Portrait.
- (S) (2:15) Chicago Records 3018 Group Portrait.

1971 LOWDOWN

- (S) (3:33) Columbia 39579 Take Me Back To Chicago.
- (S) (3:33) Columbia 30110 Chicago III.
- (S) (3:33) Chicago Records 3003 Chicago III.
- oR (S) (3:34) Columbia/Legacy 47416 Group Portrait.
- (S) (3:34) Chicago Records 3018 Group Portrait.

1971 BEGINNINGS

- (S) (7:49) Columbia 33900 Greatest Hits. *(LP version)*
- (S) (7:49) Chicago Records 3009 Greatest Hits. *(LP version)*
- (S) (7:49) Columbia 00008 and 57186 Chicago Transit Authority. *(LP version)*
- (S) (7:49) Chicago Records 3001 Chicago Transit Authority. *(LP version)*
- oR (S) (7:53) Columbia/Legacy 47416 Group Portrait. *(LP version)*
- (S) (7:53) Chicago Records 3018 Group Portrait. *(LP version)*
- (S) (7:53) Reprise 46554 The Heart Of Chicago 1967-1997. *(LP version)*

1971 COLOUR MY WORLD

- (S) (2:59) Columbia/Legacy 47416 Group Portrait.
- (S) (2:59) Chicago Records 3018 Group Portrait.
- (S) (2:58) Columbia 33900 Greatest Hits.
- (S) (2:58) Chicago Records 3009 Greatest Hits.
- (S) (2:59) Columbia 00024 Chicago II.
- (S) (2:59) Chicago Records 3002 Chicago II.
- (S) (2:58) Reprise 46554 The Heart Of Chicago 1967-1997.

1971 QUESTIONS 67 & 68
(when this 45 was originally issued in 1969,
dj copies ran (3:07) and (4:45) and were a
different mix than the 1971 hit version)

- (S) (3:24) Columbia 37682 Greatest Hits Volume 2. *(45 version)*
- (S) (3:24) Chicago Records 3015 Greatest Hits Volume 2. *(45 version)*
- (S) (4:58) Columbia 00008 and 57186 Chicago Transit Authority. *(LP version)*
- (S) (4:58) Chicago Records 3001 Chicago Transit Authority. *(LP version)*
- (S) (5:02) Columbia/Legacy 47416 Group Portrait. *(LP version; tracks into next selection)*
- (S) (5:02) Chicago Records 3018 Group Portrait. *(LP version; tracks into next selection)*

1972 SATURDAY IN THE PARK

- (S) (3:52) Columbia 33900 Greatest Hits.
- (S) (3:52) Chicago Records 3009 Greatest Hits.
- (S) (3:52) Columbia 31102 Chicago V.
- (S) (3:52) Chicago Records 3005 Chicago V.
- (S) (3:54) Columbia/Legacy 47416 Group Portrait.
- (S) (3:54) Chicago Records 3018 Group Portrait.
- (S) (3:52) Epic 48732 O.S.T. My Girl.
- (S) (3:53) Columbia 38590 If You Leave Me Now.
- (S) (3:53) Chicago Records 3016 If You Leave Me Now.
- (S) (3:54) Reprise 46554 The Heart Of Chicago 1967-1997.

1972 DIALOGUE (PART 1 & 2)

- (S) (4:07) Columbia 37682 Greatest Hits Volume 2. *(Part II only; not quite the LP version as this ending fades while the LP version ends cold)*
- (S) (4:07) Chicago Records 3015 Greatest Hits Volume 2. *(Part II only; not quite the LP version as this ending fades while the LP version ends cold)*
- (S) (2:56) Columbia 31102 Chicago V. *(Part I; tracks into Part II just like the vinyl LP version)*
- (S) (2:56) Chicago Records 3005 Chicago V. *(Part I; tracks into Part II just like the vinyl LP version)*
- (S) (4:12) Columbia 31102 Chicago V. *(Part II; Part I tracks right into Part II just like the vinyl LP version)*
- (S) (4:12) Chicago Records 3005 Chicago V. *(Part II; Part I tracks right into Part II just like the vinyl LP version)*
- (S) (2:56) Columbia/Legacy 47416 Group Portrait. *(Part I; tracks into Part II just like the vinyl LP version)*
- (S) (2:56) Chicago Records 3018 Group Portrait. *(Part I; tracks into Part II just like the vinyl LP version)*
- (S) (4:12) Columbia/Legacy 47416 Group Portrait. *(Part II; Part I tracks right into Part II just like the vinyl LP version)*
- (S) (4:12) Chicago Records 3018 Group Portrait. *(Part II; Part I tracks right into Part II just like the vinyl LP version)*
- (S) (7:09) Reprise 46911 The Heart Of Chicago 1967-1998 Volume II. *(LP version)*

1973 FEELIN' STRONGER EVERY DAY

- (S) (4:12) Columbia 33900 Greatest Hits.
- (S) (4:12) Chicago Records 3009 Greatest Hits.
- (S) (4:13) Columbia 32400 Chicago VI.
- (S) (4:13) Chicago Records 3006 Chicago VI.
- (S) (4:13) Columbia/Legacy 47416 Group Portrait.
- (S) (4:13) Chicago Records 3018 Group Portrait.
- (S) (4:11) Columbia 38590 If You Leave Me Now.
- (S) (4:11) Chicago Records 3016 If You Leave Me Now.
- (S) (4:12) Reprise 46911 The Heart Of Chicago 1967-1998 Volume II.

1973 JUST YOU 'N' ME
(S) (3:41) Columbia 33900 Greatest Hits.
(S) (3:41) Chicago Records 3009 Greatest Hits.
(S) (3:41) Columbia 32400 Chicago VI.
(S) (3:41) Chicago Records 3006 Chicago VI.
(S) (3:41) Columbia/Legacy 47416 Group Portrait.
(S) (3:41) Chicago Records 3018 Group Portrait.
(S) (3:41) Reprise 46554 The Heart Of Chicago 1967-1997.

1974 (I'VE BEEN) SEARCHIN' SO LONG
(S) (4:28) Columbia/Legacy 47416 Group Portrait. *(LP version)*
(S) (4:28) Chicago Records 3018 Group Portrait. *(LP version)*
(S) (4:27) Columbia 33900 Greatest Hits. *(LP version)*
(S) (4:27) Chicago Records 3009 Greatest Hits. *(LP version)*
(S) (4:27) Columbia 38590 If You Leave Me Now. *(LP version)*
(S) (4:27) Chicago Records 3016 If You Leave Me Now. *(LP version)*
(S) (4:27) Columbia 32810 Chicago VII. *(LP version; tracks into next selection)*
(S) (4:27) Chicago Records 3007 Chicago VII. *(LP version; tracks into next selection)*
(S) (4:28) Reprise 46911 The Heart Of Chicago 1967-1998 Volume II. *(LP version)*

1974 CALL ON ME
(S) (4:00) Columbia/Legacy 47416 Group Portrait.
(S) (4:00) Chicago Records 3018 Group Portrait.
(S) (3:59) Columbia 33900 Greatest Hits.
(S) (3:59) Chicago Records 3009 Greatest Hits.
(S) (4:00) Columbia 32810 Chicago VII.
(S) (4:00) Chicago Records 3007 Chicago VII.
(S) (4:01) Reprise 46911 The Heart Of Chicago 1967-1998 Volume II.

1974 WISHING YOU WERE HERE
(dj copies of this 45 ran (2:54) and (4:26);
commercial copies were all (4:26))
(S) (4:32) Columbia/Legacy 47416 Group Portrait.
(S) (4:32) Chicago Records 3018 Group Portrait.
(S) (4:33) Columbia 33900 Greatest Hits.
(S) (4:33) Chicago Records 3009 Greatest HIts.
(S) (4:33) Columbia 38590 If You Leave Me Now.
(S) (4:33) Chicago Records 3016 If You Leave Me Now.
(S) (4:32) Columbia 32810 Chicago VII.
(S) (4:32) Chicago Records 3007 Chicago VII.
(S) (4:34) Reprise 46554 The Heart Of Chicago 1967-1997.

1975 HARRY TRUMAN
(S) (3:00) Columbia/Legacy 47416 Group Portrait.
(S) (3:00) Chicago Records 3018 Group Portrait.
(S) (2:59) Columbia 39579 Take Me Back To Chicago.
(S) (2:59) Columbia 33100 Chicago VIII.
(S) (2:59) Chicago Records 3008 Chicago VIII.

1975 OLD DAYS
(S) (3:29) Columbia/Legacy 47416 Group Portrait.
(S) (3:29) Chicago Records 3018 Group Portrait.
(S) (3:28) Columbia 37682 Greatest Hits Volume 2.
(S) (3:28) Chicago Records 3015 Greatest Hits Volume 2.
(S) (3:29) Columbia 33100 Chicago VIII.
(S) (3:29) Chicago Records 3008 Chicago VIII.
(S) (3:28) Reprise 46911 The Heart Of Chicago 1967-1998 Volume II.

1976 ANOTHER RAINY DAY IN NEW YORK CITY
(S) (2:59) Columbia/Legacy 47416 Group Portrait.
(S) (2:59) Chicago Records 3018 Group Portrait.
(S) (3:00) Columbia 38590 If You Leave Me Now.
(S) (3:00) Chicago Records 3016 If You Leave Me Now.
(S) (3:01) Columbia 34200 Chicago X.
(S) (3:01) Chicago Records 3010 Chicago X.

1976 IF YOU LEAVE ME NOW
(S) (3:53) Columbia/Legacy 47416 Group Portrait.
(S) (3:53) Chicago Records 3018 Group Portrait.
(S) (3:53) Columbia 37682 Greatest Hits Volume 2.
(S) (3:53) Chicago Records 3015 Greatest Hits Volume 2.
(S) (3:55) Columbia 38590 If You Leave Me Now.

(S) (3:55) Chicago Records 3016 If You Leave Me Now.
(S) (3:55) Columbia 34200 Chicago X.
(S) (3:55) Chicago Records 3010 Chicago X.
(S) (3:53) Reprise 46554 The Heart Of Chicago 1967-1997.
(S) (4:21) River North 514161250 Peter Cetera: You're The Inspiration - A Collection. *(rerecording)*

1977 BABY, WHAT A BIG SURPRISE
(S) (3:03) Columbia/Legacy 47416 Group Portrait.
(S) (3:03) Chicago Records 3018 Group Portrait.
(S) (3:01) Columbia 37682 Greatest Hits Volume 2.
(S) (3:01) Chicago Records 3015 Greatest Hits Volume 2.
(S) (3:03) Columbia 38590 If You Leave Me Now.
(S) (3:03) Chicago Records 3016 If You Leave Me Now.
(S) (3:03) Columbia 34860 Chicago XI.
(S) (3:03) Chicago Records 3011 Chicago XI.
(S) (3:30) River North 514161250 Peter Cetera: You're The Inspiration - A Collection. *(rerecording)*
(S) (3:04) Reprise 46911 The Heart Of Chicago 1967-1998 Volume II.

1978 ALIVE AGAIN
(S) (4:04) Columbia/Legacy 47416 Group Portrait. *(LP version)*
(S) (4:04) Chicago Records 3018 Group Portrait. *(LP version)*
(S) (3:31) Columbia 37682 Greatest Hits Volume 2. *(45 version)*
(S) (3:31) Chicago Records 3015 Greatest Hits Volume 2. *(45 version)*
(S) (4:06) Columbia 35512 Hot Streets. *(LP version)*

1979 NO TELL LOVER
(S) (4:11) Columbia/Legacy 47416 Group Portrait. *(LP version)*
(S) (4:11) Chicago Records 3018 Group Portrait. *(LP version)*
(S) (3:45) Columbia 37682 Greatest Hits Volume 2. *(45 version)*
(S) (3:45) Chicago Records 3015 Greatest Hits Volume 2. *(45 version)*
(S) (3:50) Columbia 38590 If You Leave Me Now. *(45 version)*
(S) (3:50) Chicago Records 3016 If You Leave Me Now. *(45 version)*
(S) (4:11) Columbia 35512 Hot Streets. *(LP version)*
(S) (3:48) Reprise 46911 The Heart Of Chicago 1967-1998 Volume II. *(45 version)*

1982 HARD TO SAY I'M SORRY
(S) (5:05) Reprise 26080 Greatest Hits 1982-1989. *(LP version which is a medley of "HARD TO SAY I'M SORRY"/"GET AWAY")*
(S) (5:05) Reprise 23689 Chicago 16. *(LP version which is a medley of "HARD TO SAY I'M SORRY"/"GET AWAY")*
(S) (5:04) Reprise 46554 The Heart Of Chicago 1967-1997. *(LP version which is a medley of "HARD TO SAY I'M SORRY"/"GET AWAY")*

1982 LOVE ME TOMORROW
(S) (5:05) Reprise 26080 Greatest Hits 1982-1989. *(LP version)*
(S) (5:05) Reprise 23689 Chicago 16. *(LP version)*
(S) (4:58) Reprise 46911 The Heart Of Chicago 1967-1998 Volume II. *(LP version)*

1984 STAY THE NIGHT
(S) (3:46) Reprise 26080 Greatest Hits 1982-1989.
(S) (3:48) Reprise 25060 Chicago 17.
(S) (3:45) Reprise 46911 The Heart Of Chicago 1967-1998 Volume II.

1984 HARD HABIT TO BREAK
(S) (4:41) Reprise 26080 Greatest Hits 1982-1989. *(LP version)*
(S) (4:43) Reprise 25060 Chicago 17. *(LP version)*
(S) (4:43) Reprise 46554 The Heart Of Chicago 1967-1997. *(LP version)*

1985 YOU'RE THE INSPIRATION
(S) (3:46) Reprise 26080 Greatest Hits 1982-1989.
(S) (3:48) Reprise 25060 Chicago 17.
(S) (3:48) Reprise 46554 The Heart Of Chicago 1967-1997.

CHICAGO (Continued)
    (S) (4:05)   River North 514161250 Peter Cetera: You're The Inspiration - A Collection. *(rerecording)*

1985 ALONG COMES A WOMAN
    (S) (4:12)   Reprise 26080 Greatest Hits 1982-1989. *(LP version)*
    (S) (4:13)   Reprise 25060 Chicago 17. *(LP version)*

1987 WILL YOU STILL LOVE ME?
    (S) (5:41)   Reprise 26080 Greatest Hits 1982-1989. *(LP version)*
    (S) (5:41)   Reprise 25509 Chicago 18. *(LP version)*
    (S) (5:41)   Reprise 46554 The Heart Of Chicago 1967-1997. *(LP version)*

1987 IF SHE WOULD HAVE BEEN FAITHFUL
    (S) (3:50)   Reprise 26080 Greatest Hits 1982-1989.
    (S) (3:50)   Reprise 25509 Chicago 18.

1988 I DON'T WANNA LIVE WITHOUT YOUR LOVE
    (S) (3:51)   Reprise 26080 Greatest Hits 1982-1989.
    (S) (3:53)   Reprise 25714 Chicago 19.
    (S) (3:56)   Reprise 46911 The Heart Of Chicago 1967-1998 Volume II.

1988 LOOK AWAY
    (S) (3:59)   Reprise 26080 Greatest Hits 1982-1989.
    (S) (4:00)   Reprise 25714 Chicago 19.
    (S) (3:59)   Reprise 46554 The Heart Of Chicago 1967-1997.

1989 YOU'RE NOT ALONE
    (S) (3:55)   Reprise 25714 Chicago 19.
    (S) (3:55)   Reprise 46911 The Heart Of Chicago 1967-1998 Volume II.

1990 WHAT KIND OF MAN WOULD I BE
    (S) (4:12)   Reprise 26080 Greatest Hits 1982-1989. *(remix)*
    (S) (4:19)   Reprise 25714 Chicago 19.
    (S) (4:17)   Reprise 46911 The Heart Of Chicago 1967-1998 Volume II.

1991 CHASIN' THE WIND
    (S) (4:15)   Reprise 26391 Chicago 21.

CHIFFONS
1963 HE'S SO FINE
    (M) (1:51)   Rhino 70624 Billboard's Top Rock & Roll Hits Of 1963.
    (M) (1:51)   Rhino 72007 Billboard's Top Rock & Roll Hits 1962-1966 Box Set.
    (M) (1:50)   Original Sound 8864 Oldies But Goodies Vol. 14. *(this compact disc uses the "Waring - fds" noise reduction process)*
    (M) (1:50)   Original Sound 2222 Oldies But Goodies Volumes 3,5,11,14 and 15 Box Set. *(this box set uses the "Waring - fds" noise reduction process)*
    (M) (1:50)   Original Sound 2500 Oldies But Goodies Volumes 1-15 Box Set. *(this box set uses the "Waring - fds" noise reduction process)*
    (E) (1:52)   Original Sound CDGO-6 Golden Oldies Volume. 6.
    (E) (1:53)   Original Sound 8881 Twenty-One #1 Hits. *(this compact disc uses the "Waring - fds" noise reduction process)*
    (M) (1:53)   Original Sound 1081 All #1 Hits.
    (M) (1:51)   Rhino 70988 Best Of The Girl Groups Volume 1.
    (M) (1:54)   JCI 3110 Sock Hoppin' Sixties.
    (M) (1:53)   3C/Laurie 104 Best Of.
    (M) (1:53)   Collectables 5063 History Of Rock Volume 3.
    (M) (1:52)   Time-Life 2RNR-07 Rock 'N' Roll Era - 1963.
    (M) (1:50)   Time-Life RHD-02 Rhythm & Blues - 1963.
    (M) (1:54)   Collectables 2500 WCBS-FM History Of Rock - The 60's Part 1.
    (M) (1:54)   Collectables 4500 History Of Rock/The 60s Part One.
    (M) (1:51)   Right Stuff 36333 Greatest Hits.
    (M) (1:52)   Time-Life R857-12 The Heart Of Rock 'n' Roll 1962-1963.
    (M) (1:50)   Time-Life R838-14 Solid Gold Soul - 1963.
    (M) (1:52)   Right Stuff 53320 Hot Rod Rock Volume 5: Back Seat Movers.

1963 ONE FINE DAY
    (M) (2:07)   Rhino 70988 Best Of The Girl Groups Volume 1.
    (M) (2:08)   Original Sound 8862 Oldies But Goodies Vol. 12. *(this compact disc uses the "Waring - fds" noise reduction process)*

    (M) (2:08)   Original Sound 2223 Oldies But Goodies Volumes 2,7,9,12 and 13 Box Set. *(this box set uses the "Waring - fds" noise reduction process)*
    (M) (2:08)   Original Sound 2500 Oldies But Goodies Volumes 1-15 Box Set. *(this box set uses the "Waring - fds" noise reduction process)*
    (M) (2:08)   3C/Laurie 104 Best Of.
    (M) (2:07)   Collectables 5069 History Of Rock Volume 9.
    (M) (2:06)   Era 5025 The Brill Building Sound.
    (M) (2:07)   Time-Life 2RNR-07 Rock 'N' Roll Era - 1963.
    (M) (2:06)   Time-Life R962-08 History Of Rock 'N' Roll: Sound Of The City 1959-1965.
    (M) (2:08)   Collectables 2504 WCBS-FM History Of Rock - The 60's Part 4.
    (M) (2:08)   Collectables 4504 History Of Rock/The 60s Part Four.
    (M) (2:06)   Right Stuff 36333 Greatest Hits.
    (M) (2:06)   Columbia 67916 O.S.T. One Fine Day.

1963 A LOVE SO FINE
    (M) (1:53)   3C/Laurie 104 Best Of.
    (M) (1:53)   Right Stuff 36333 Greatest Hits.

1964 I HAVE A BOYFRIEND
    (M) (2:02)   Time-Life 2RNR-40 Rock 'N' Roll Era - The 60's Teen Time.
    (M) (2:03)   Right Stuff 36333 Greatest Hits.

1966 SWEET TALKIN' GUY
    (M) (2:26)   Warner Special Products 27602 20 Party Classics.
    (S) (2:25)   Rhino 70989 Best Of The Girl Groups Volume 2.
    (S) (2:23)   Original Sound 8858 Oldies But Goodies Vol. 8. *(this compact disc uses the "Waring - fds" noise reduction process)*
    (S) (2:23)   Original Sound 2221 Oldies But Goodies Volumes 1,4,6,8 and 10 Box Set. *(this box set uses the "Waring - fds" noise reduction process)*
    (S) (2:23)   Original Sound 2500 Oldies But Goodies Volumes 1-15 Box Set. *(this box set uses the "Waring - fds" noise reduction process)*
    (M) (2:24)   3C/Laurie 104 Best Of.
    (S) (2:24)   Collectables 5061 History Of Rock Volume 1.
    (S) (2:24)   Time-Life 2CLR-13 Classic Rock - 1966: Shakin' All Over.
    (S) (2:24)   Time-Life SUD-01 Superhits - 1966.
    (S) (2:24)   Collectables 2501 WCBS-FM History Of Rock - The 60's Part 2.
    (S) (2:24)   Collectables 4501 History Of Rock/The 60s Part Two.
    (S) (2:24)   Right Stuff 36333 Greatest Hits.
    (S) (2:24)   Time-Life AM1-09 AM Gold - 1966.

DESMOND CHILD
1991 LOVE ON A ROOFTOP
    (S) (5:16)   Elektra 61048 Discipline.

JANE CHILD
1990 DON'T WANNA FALL IN LOVE
    (S) (6:11)   Tommy Boy 1037 MTV Party To Go Volume 1. *(remix; all tracks on this cd are segued together)*
    (S) (4:03)   Warner Brothers 25858 Jane Child.

CHI-LITES
1971 (FOR GOD'S SAKE) GIVE MORE POWER TO THE PEOPLE
    (S) (3:05)   Rhino 70784 Soul Hits Of The 70's Volume 4. *(an apparant attempt to reproduce the 45 version but several audience noise overdubs are missing)*
    (S) (3:05)   Rhino 72028 Soul Hits Of The 70's Volumes 1-5 Box Set. *(an apparant attempt to reproduce the 45 version but several audience noise overdubs are missing)*
    (S) (3:45)   Epic 38627 Greatest Hits. *("Greatest Hits" vinyl LP version, which was longer than either the 45 or the original LP version)*
    (S) (2:57)   Rhino 70532 Greatest Hits. *(45 version)*
    (S) (3:51)   Brunswick 81009 The Brunswick Years Volume One. *("Greatest Hits" vinyl LP version, which was longer than either the 45 or the original LP version)*

1971 HAVE YOU SEEN HER
- (S) (5:09) Rhino 70659 Billboard's Top R&B Hits Of 1971. *(contains extra instrumentation not found on the 45 or LP)*
- (S) (5:00) Rhino 70786 Soul Hits Of The 70's Volume 6. *(contains extra instrumentation not found on the 45 or LP)*
- (S) (5:04) Epic 38627 Greatest Hits. *(contains extra instrumentation not found on the 45 or LP)*
- (S) (5:08) Rhino 70532 Greatest Hits.
- (S) (5:08) Rhino 71209 70's Smash Hits Volume 5.
- (S) (5:06) Time-Life RHD-09 Rhythm & Blues - 1971. *(contains extra instrumentation not found on the 45 or LP)*
- (S) (5:08) Time-Life SUD-10 Superhits - 1971. *(contains extra instrumentation not found on the 45 or LP)*
- (S) (5:09) Time-Life SOD-12 Sounds Of The Seventies - 1971: Take Two. *(contains extra instrumentation not found on the 45 or LP)*
- (S) (5:07) Right Stuff 28372 Slow Jams: The 70's Volume Two.
- (S) (5:07) Thump 7030 Low Rider Oldies Volume III.
- (S) (5:37) Varese Sarabande 5486 A Celebration Of Soul Vol. 1: The Chi-Sound Records Collection. *(rerecording)*
- (S) (5:08) Ripete 2163-RE Ebb Tide.
- (S) (5:08) Rhino 72113 Billboard Hot Soul Hits - 1971.
- (S) (5:07) MCA Special Products 20857 Classic Soul Greatest Hits.
- (S) (4:55) Madacy Entertainment 1971 Rock On 1971. *(contains extra instrumentation not found on the 45 or LP)*
- (S) (4:59) JCI 3173 1970 - Only Soul - 1974. *(contains extra instrumentation not found on the 45 or LP)*
- (S) (5:08) Time-Life AM1-06 AM Gold - 1971. *(contains extra instrumentation not found on the 45 or LP)*
- (S) (5:06) Time-Life R838-06 Solid Gold Soul - 1971. *(contains extra instrumentation not found on the 45 or LP)*
- (S) (5:08) Flashback 72685 '70s Radio Hits Volume 5.

1972 OH GIRL
(45 length is (3:12); LP length is (3:47))
- (S) (3:28) Rhino 70660 Billboard's Top R&B Hits Of 1972.
- (S) (3:17) Rhino 70787 Soul Hits Of The 70's Volume 7.
- (S) (3:40) Epic 38627 Greatest Hits.
- (S) (3:47) Rhino 70532 Greatest Hits.
- (S) (3:47) Rhino 71210 70's Smash Hits Volume 6.
- (S) (3:17) Rhino 71618 Soul Train Hall Of Fame/20th Anniversary.
- (S) (3:32) Razor & Tie 22047 Sweet 70's Soul.
- (S) (3:27) Time-Life RHD-20 Rhythm & Blues - 1972.
- (S) (3:27) Time-Life SUD-11 Superhits - 1972.
- (S) (3:27) Time-Life SOD-03 Sounds Of The Seventies - 1972.
- (S) (3:18) Right Stuff 27307 Slow Jams: The 70's Volume One.
- (S) (3:47) MCA 11036 O.S.T. Crooklyn.
- (S) (3:43) Thump 7020 Low Rider Oldies Volume II.
- (S) (4:47) Varese Sarabande 5494 A Celebration Of Soul Vol. 2: The Chi-Sound Records Collection. *(rerecording)*
- (S) (3:47) LaserLight 12321 Soulful Love.
- (S) (3:47) Ripete 2163-RE Ebb Tide.
- (S) (3:46) JCI 3131 1975 - Only Rock 'N Roll - 1979.
- (S) (3:31) K-Tel 6013 70's Soul - Sexy Ballads.
- (S) (3:27) Time-Life R138-18 Body Talk.
- (S) (3:44) K-Tel 3535 Slow Groove Love Jams Of The 70's.
- (S) (3:46) K-Tel 3518 Sweet Soul Music.
- (S) (3:47) Rhino 72114 Billboard Hot Soul Hits - 1972.
- (S) (3:45) Brunswick 81009 The Brunswick Years Volume One.
- (S) (3:46) MCA Special Products 20857 Classic Soul Greatest Hits.
- (S) (3:44) K-Tel 3626 Music Power.
- (S) (3:47) Right Stuff 52660 Flick Hits - Old School Tracks.
- (S) (3:17) Priority 53146 Slow Grind Volume Two.

- (S) (3:27) Time-Life AM1-07 AM Gold - 1972.
- (S) (3:27) Time-Life R838-07 Solid Gold Soul - 1972.
- (S) (3:47) Flashback 72686 '70s Radio Hits Volume 6.

1973 A LETTER TO MYSELF
- (S) (5:29) Epic 38627 Greatest Hits. *(LP version)*
- (S) (5:31) Rhino 70532 Greatest Hits. *(LP version)*

1973 STONED OUT OF MY MIND
- (S) (3:02) Rhino 72115 Billboard Hot Soul Hits - 1973.
- (S) (3:02) Rhino 70552 Soul Hits Of The 70's Vol. 12.
- (S) (3:01) Epic 38627 Greatest Hits.
- (S) (3:02) Rhino 70532 Greatest Hits.

CHILLIWACK
1981 MY GIRL (GONE, GONE, GONE)
1982 I BELIEVE
1982 WHATCHA GONNA DO

CHIMES
1961 ONCE IN AWHILE
- (M) (2:25) Collectables 2507 History Of Rock - The Doo Wop Era Volume 1. *(sounds like it was mastered from vinyl)*
- (M) (2:25) Collectables 4507 History Of Rock/The Doo Wop Era Part One. *(sounds like it was mastered from vinyl)*
- (E) (2:27) Original Sound 8857 Oldies But Goodies Vol. 7. *(this compact disc uses the "Waring - fds" noise reduction process)*
- (E) (2:27) Original Sound 2223 Oldies But Goodies Volumes 2,7,9,12 and 13 Box Set. *(this box set uses the "Waring - fds" noise reduction process)*
- (E) (2:27) Original Sound 2500 Oldies But Goodies Volumes 1-15 Box Set. *(this box set uses the "Waring - fds" noise reduction process)*
- (E) (2:27) Original Sound CDGO-1 Golden Oldies Volume. 1.
- (M) (2:26) Original Sound 9328 13 Of The Best Doo Wop Love Songs Vol. 2.
- (M) (2:26) Time-Life 2RNR-42 Rock 'N' Roll Era - The 60's Sock Hop. *(sounds like it was mastered from vinyl)*
- (M) (2:25) Collectables 2500 WCBS-FM History Of Rock - The 60's Part 1. *(sounds like it was mastered from vinyl)*
- (M) (2:25) Collectables 4500 History Of Rock/The 60s Part One. *(sounds like it was mastered from vinyl)*
- (M) (2:25) Collectables 2509 WCBS-FM For Lovers Only Part 1. *(sounds like it was mastered from vinyl)*
- (M) (2:27) LaserLight 12320 Love Songs.
- (M) (2:26) Collectables 5560 The Chimes Meet The Videls.
- (M) (2:26) Rhino 72507 Doo Wop Box II.
- (M) (2:26) Time-Life R857-19 The Heart Of Rock 'n' Roll 1960-1961 Take Three.

1961 I'M IN THE MOOD FOR LOVE
- (M) (2:26) Collectables 2606 WCBS-FM For Lovers Only Vol. 2.
- (M) (2:26) Collectables 5560 The Chimes Meet The Videls.

CHIPMUNKS (see also DAVID SEVILLE)
released as by THE CHIPMUNKS with DAVID SEVILLE:
1958 THE CHIPMUNK SONG
- (S) (2:20) Rhino 75755 Dr. Demento Presents The Greatest Christmas Novelty CD.
- (S) (2:18) Rhino 70636 Billboard's Greatest Christmas Hits.
- (E) (2:20) EMI 91684 Best Of.
- (E) (2:19) EMI 48378 Christmas With The Chipmunks.
- (S) (2:18) EMI 99987 Legends Of Christmas Past.
- (E) (2:19) Curb 77591 Greatest Hits.
- (S) (2:19) Collectables 1511 and 2511 and 3511 and 4511 and 9611 and 9711 The Ultimate Christmas Album.
- (E) (2:20) Priority 9306 Christmas Comedy Classics.
- (E) (2:19) Rhino 72171 Billboard Presents: Family Christmas Classics.
- (E) (2:20) EMI 35977 Very Best Of.
- (E) (2:21) Time-Life R135-14 Havin' A Fun Christmas.

107

CHIPMUNKS *(Continued)*
released as by DAVID SEVILLE and THE CHIPMUNKS:
1959 ALVIN'S HARMONICA
    (S) (2:41) EMI 91684 Best Of.
    (S) (2:41) Curb 77591 Greatest Hits.
    (M) (2:39) Pair 1124 Chipmunk Songbook.
    (S) (2:40) EMI 35977 Very Best Of.
1959 RAGTIME COWBOY JOE
    (S) (2:06) EMI 91684 Best Of.
    (S) (2:05) Curb 77591 Greatest Hits.
    (S) (2:06) Pair 1124 Chipmunk Songbook.
    (S) (2:06) EMI 35977 Very Best Of.
1960 ALVIN'S ORCHESTRA
    (E) (3:00) EMI 95049 Sing Again With The Chipmunks.
    (E) (3:00) Curb 77591 Greatest Hits.

CHORDETTES
1956 EDDIE MY LOVE
    (M) (2:12) Rhino 70849 Best Of.
    (M) (2:12) Curb 77781 Greatest Hits.
    (M) (2:12) Music Club 50015 Love Me Forever - 18 Rock'N' Roll Love Songs.
    (M) (2:12) Collectables 5250 Golden Classics.
1956 BORN TO BE WITH YOU
    (M) (2:47) Rhino 70849 Best Of.
    (M) (2:47) Time-Life HPD-15 Your Hit Parade - 1956.
    (M) (2:47) Varese Sarabande 5578 History Of Cadence Records Volume 1.
    (M) (2:47) Curb 77781 Greatest Hits.
    (M) (2:47) JCI 3165 #1 Radio Hits 1955 - Only Rock 'n Roll - 1959.
    (M) (2:47) JCI 3183 1955 - Only Love - 1959.
    (M) (2:47) Music Club 50015 Love Me Forever - 18 Rock'N' Roll Love Songs.
    (M) (2:47) Collectables 5250 Golden Classics.
1956 LAY DOWN YOUR ARMS
    (M) (2:27) Rhino 70849 Best Of.
    (M) (2:26) Curb 77781 Greatest Hits.
    (M) (2:27) Collectables 5250 Golden Classics.
1957 JUST BETWEEN YOU AND ME
    (M) (2:07) Rhino 70849 Best Of.
    (M) (2:07) Varese Sarabande 5579 History Of Cadence Records Volume 2.
    (M) (2:06) Curb 77781 Greatest Hits.
    (M) (2:06) Collectables 5250 Golden Classics.
1958 LOLLIPOP
    (M) (2:09) Atlantic 81677 O.S.T. Stand By Me.
    (M) (2:08) Rhino 75894 Jukebox Classics Volume 2.
    (M) (2:08) Rhino 70849 Best Of.
    (M) (2:07) Original Sound 8891 Dick Clark's 21 All-Time Hits Vol. 1.
    (M) (2:07) Time-Life 2RNR-21 Rock 'N' Roll Era - 1958 Still Rockin'.
    (M) (2:08) Time-Life HPD-11 Your Hit Parade 1958.
    (M) (2:08) Time-Life R962-05 History Of Rock 'N' Roll: The Teenage Years 1957-1964.
    (M) (2:08) K-Tel 3409 Funniest Food Songs.
    (M) (2:08) Varese Sarabande 5579 History Of Cadence Records Volume 2.
    (M) (2:07) Music For Little People 42581 A Child's Celebration Of Rock 'N' Roll.
    (M) (2:07) Curb 77781 Greatest Hits.
    (M) (2:07) Collectables 5250 Golden Classics.
1958 ZORRO
    (M) (2:01) Rhino 70849 Best Of.
    (M) (1:59) Time-Life HPD-35 Your Hit Parade - The Fun-Times 50's & 60's.
    (M) (1:59) Risky Business 57474 Small Screen Cowboys.
    (M) (1:58) Curb 77781 Greatest Hits.
    (M) (1:58) Collectables 5250 Golden Classics.
1959 NO OTHER ARMS, NO OTHER LIPS
    (M) (2:32) Rhino 70849 Best Of.
    (M) (2:32) Curb 77781 Greatest Hits.
    (M) (2:31) Collectables 5250 Golden Classics.
1961 NEVER ON SUNDAY
    (S) (2:40) Rhino 70849 Best Of.
    (S) (2:39) Time-Life HPD-33 Your Hit Parade - The Early 60's.

    (S) (2:39) Curb 77781 Greatest Hits.
    (S) (2:39) LaserLight 12313 and 15936 The Wonder Years - Summer Time.
    (S) (2:38) Collectables 5250 Golden Classics.

CHRIS CHRISTIAN
1981 I WANT YOU, I NEED YOU

CHRISTIE
1970 YELLOW RIVER
    (S) (2:46) Rhino 70924 Super Hits Of The 70's Volume 4.
    (S) (2:46) Rhino 72009 Super Hits Of The 70's Volumes 1-4 Box Set.
    (S) (2:45) Columbia/Legacy 46160 Rock Artifacts Volume 1.
    (S) (2:44) Time-Life SOD-22 Sounds Of The Seventies - Seventies Top Forty.
    (S) (2:45) Collectables 5824 Yellow River.
    (M) (2:41) Eclipse Music Group 64892 Rock 'n Roll Relix 1970-1971.
    (M) (2:41) Eclipse Music Group 64897 Rock 'n Roll Relix 1970-1979.

LOU CHRISTIE
1963 THE GYPSY CRIED
    (M) (2:09) Rhino 70246 Enlightenment: The Best Of. *(truncated fade)*
    (M) (2:08) Time-Life 2RNR-40 Rock 'N' Roll Era - The 60's Teen Time.
    (M) (2:08) Collectables 2504 WCBS-FM History Of Rock - The 60's Part 4.
    (M) (2:08) Collectables 4504 History Of Rock/The 60s Part Four.
1963 TWO FACES HAVE I
    (M) (2:43) Rhino 70246 Enlightenment: The Best Of.
    (M) (2:44) Time-Life 2RNR-19 Rock 'N' Roll Era - 1963 Still Rockin'.
    (S) (2:46) Varese Sarabande 5521 Beyond The Blue Horizon: More Of The Best Of. *(alternate take)*
    (M) (2:43) Collectables 2505 History Of Rock - The 60's Part 5.
    (M) (2:43) Collectables 4505 History Of Rock/The 60s Part Five.
1966 LIGHTNIN' STRIKES
    (S) (2:58) Mercury 816555 45's On CD Volume 2.
    (S) (2:58) Rhino 70246 Enlightenment: The Best Of.
    (S) (2:49) MCA 6171 Good Time Rock 'N' Roll. *(all selections on this cd are recorded live)*
    (S) (2:56) JCI 3112 Pop Sixties.
    (S) (2:56) Original Sound 8864 Oldies But Goodies Vol. 14. *(this compact disc uses the "Waring - fds" noise reduction process)*
    (S) (2:56) Original Sound 2222 Oldies But Goodies Volumes 3,5,11,14 and 15 Box Set. *(this box set uses the "Waring - fds" noise reduction process)*
    (S) (2:56) Original Sound 2500 Oldies But Goodies Volumes 1-15 Box Set. *(this box set uses the "Waring - fds" noise reduction process)*
    (S) (2:58) Time-Life 2CLR-07 Classic Rock - 1966: The Beat Goes On.
    (S) (2:58) Capitol 89098 O.S.T. Wild Palms.
    (S) (2:58) Collectables 2505 History Of Rock - The 60's Part 5.
    (S) (2:58) Collectables 4505 History Of Rock/The 60s Part Five.
    (S) (2:58) Polygram Special Markets 314520260 Number One Hits Of The Sixties.
    (S) (2:58) Eclipse Music Group 64870 Rock 'n Roll Relix 1966-1967.
    (S) (2:58) Eclipse Music Group 64872 Rock 'n Roll Relix 1960-1969.
    (S) (2:58) Polygram Special Markets 314520460 #1 Radio Hits Of The 60's.
1966 RHAPSODY IN THE RAIN
    (M) (2:45) Rhino 70246 Enlightenment: The Best Of. *(uncensored version)*
    (E) (2:43) Time-Life 2CLR-22 Classic Rock - 1966: Blowin' Your Mind. *(uncensored version)*

(M) (2:44) Varese Sarabande 5534 Rhythm Of The Rain.
(censored version)
(M) (2:44) Varese Sarabande 5521 Beyond The Blue
Horizon: More Of The Best Of. *(censored version)*
(M) (2:44) Special Music/Essex 5035 Prom Night - The 60's.
(censored version)

1969 I'M GONNA MAKE YOU MINE
(E) (2:39) Pair 1202 Best Of Buddah.
(E) (2:40) Rhino 70246 Enlightenment: The Best Of.
(S) (2:23) MCA 6171 Good Time Rock 'N' Roll. *(all
selections on this cd are recorded live)*
(E) (2:39) Essex 7060 The Buddah Box.
(E) (2:35) Time-Life 2CLR-20 Classic Rock - 1969: Shakin'
All Over.
(M) (2:40) Varese Sarabande 5575 Bubblegum Classics
Volume Two.

GAVIN CHRISTOPHER
1986 ONE STEP CLOSER TO YOU
(S) (5:05) Madacy Entertainment 1986 Rock On 1986. *(LP
version; mistakenly credited on the cd jacket to
"Christopher Gavin")*

CHUMBAWAMBA
1997 TUBTHUMPING
(S) (4:38) Republic/Universal 53099 Tubthumper. *(tracks
into the next selection)*

CHURCH
1988 UNDER THE MILKY WAY
(S) (4:56) Priority 53741 Cutting Edge Vol. 1 - Best Of
Modern Rock Hits. *(LP version)*
(S) (4:56) Rhino 70545 Best Of MTV's 120 Minutes Vol. 1.
(LP version)
(S) (4:56) K-Tel 3342 The 80's Pop Explosion. *(LP
version)*
(S) (4:57) Arista 8521 Starfish. *(LP version)*
(S) (4:55) EMI 28339 Living In Oblivion: The 80's Greatest
Hits - Volume Four. *(LP version)*
(S) (4:56) Time-Life R988-29 Sounds Of The Eighties: The
Rolling Stone Collection 1987-1988. *(LP version)*
(S) (4:56) Risky Business 67307 Wave Goodbye To The
80's. *(LP version)*
(S) (4:56) Rhino 72502 Modern Rock 1988 - Hang The DJ.
(LP version)
(S) (4:56) Hip-O 40022 That Sound From Down Under.
(LP version)

CINDERELLA
1987 NOBODY'S FOOL
(S) (4:46) Rebound 314520257 Hard Rock Essentials - The
80's. *(LP version)*
(S) (4:46) Mercury 830076 Night Songs. *(LP version)*
(S) (4:47) Priority 50937 Best Of 80's Metal Volume Two:
Bang Your Head. *(LP version)*
(S) (4:47) Time-Life R968-24 Guitar Rock - The '80s Take
Two. *(LP version)*
(S) (4:46) Mercury 314534775 Once Upon A..... *(LP
version)*
(S) (4:46) K-Tel 3999 Glam Rock Vol. 2: The 80's And
Beyond. *(LP version)*
(S) (4:46) Razor & Tie 89004 Monsters Of Rock. *(LP
version)*

1988 DON'T KNOW WHAT YOU GOT (TILL IT'S GONE)
(S) (5:54) Mercury 834612 Long Cold Winter. *(LP version)*
(S) (5:48) Rhino 72579 Feel Like Makin' Love - Romantic
Power Ballads. *(LP version)*
(S) (5:53) Priority 50938 Best Of 80's Metal Volume Three:
Bang Your Head. *(LP version)*
(S) (5:54) Mercury 314534775 Once Upon A..... *(LP
version)*

1989 THE LAST MILE
(S) (3:47) Mercury 834612 Long Cold Winter.

(S) (3:46) Mercury 314534775 Once Upon A.....
1989 COMING HOME
(S) (4:51) JCI 4545 Masters Of Metal: Thunder 'N Spice.
(S) (4:53) Mercury 834612 Long Cold Winter.
(S) (4:53) Mercury 314534775 Once Upon A.....
1991 SHELTER ME
(S) (4:46) Mercury 848018 Heartbreak Station.
(S) (4:44) Time-Life R968-25 Guitar Rock - The '90s.
(S) (4:46) Mercury 314534775 Once Upon A.....

CITY BOY
1978 5.7.0.5.
(S) (3:11) Rhino 72299 Superhits Of The 70's Volume 25.
(S) (3:13) Special Music 5040 Great Britons! Volume Two.
(S) (3:12) Renaissance 0217 Young Men Gone West/Book
Early.

JIMMY CLANTON
1958 JUST A DREAM
(M) (2:29) Ace 2039 Very Best Of. *(mastered from vinyl)*
(M) (2:28) Rock N' Roll/Scotti Brothers 75266 Best Of Ace
Records Volume 1. *(mastered from vinyl)*
(M) (2:30) Time-Life 2RNR-05 Rock 'N' Roll Era - 1958.
(mastered from vinyl)
(M) (2:28) Collectables 2503 WCBS-FM History Of Rock -
The 50's Part 2. *(mastered from vinyl)*
(M) (2:30) LaserLight 12323 American Dreams. *(no
fidelity)*
(M) (2:30) Time-Life R857-04 The Heart Of Rock 'n' Roll -
1958.
(M) (2:29) JCI 3183 1955 - Only Love - 1959.
(M) (2:29) Music Club 50047 This Is.
1958 A LETTER TO AN ANGEL
(M) (2:49) Rock N' Roll/Scotti Brothers 75266 Best Of Ace
Records Volume 1.
(M) (2:50) Music Club 50047 This Is.
1959 MY OWN TRUE LOVE
(M) (2:31) Rock N' Roll/Scotti Brothers 75266 Best Of Ace
Records Volume 1.
(M) (2:33) Music Club 50047 This Is.
1960 GO, JIMMY, GO
(M) (2:09) Ace 2039 Very Best Of.
(S) (2:07) Rock N' Roll/Scotti Brothers 75266 Best Of Ace
Records Volume 1.
(M) (2:13) Music Club 50047 This Is.
1960 ANOTHER SLEEPLESS NIGHT
(M) (2:07) Ace 2039 Very Best Of.
(S) (2:08) Rock N' Roll/Scotti Brothers 75266 Best Of Ace
Records Volume 1.
(M) (2:07) Music Club 50047 This Is.
1962 VENUS IN BLUE JEANS
(M) (2:21) Ace 2039 Very Best Of.
(E) (2:19) Original Sound 8892 Dick Clark's 21 All-Time
Hits Vol. 2.
(M) (2:24) Rock N' Roll/Scotti Brothers 75266 Best Of Ace
Records Volume 1.
(M) (2:19) Time-Life 2RNR-27 Rock 'N' Roll Era - Teen
Idols.
(M) (2:19) LaserLight 12323 American Dreams.
(M) (2:20) Time-Life R857-12 The Heart Of Rock 'n' Roll
1962-1963.
(M) (2:23) Music Club 50047 This Is.

ERIC CLAPTON
1970 AFTER MIDNIGHT
**(actual 45 time is (2:51) not (3:15) as stated on
the record label; LP length is (3:11))**
(S) (2:50) Polydor 825093 Eric Clapton.
(S) (3:08) Polydor 800014 Time Pieces.
(S) (3:16) Polydor 835269 Crossroads. *(alternate take)*
(S) (4:06) Polydor 835269 Crossroads. *(1987 rerecording)*
(S) (2:51) Time-Life SOD-01 Sounds Of The Seventies -
1970.
(S) (2:50) Time-Life OPCD-4521 Guitar Rock.

ERIC CLAPTON *(Continued)*
- (S) (2:42) Polydor 314527116 Cream Of Clapton.
- (S) (2:51) Time-Life R968-19 Guitar Rock - The Early '70s: Take Two.
- (S) (2:50) Polydor 314531819 Eric Clapton. *(remastered edition)*
- (S) (2:50) MFSL 639 Eric Clapton. *(gold disc)*

1974 I SHOT THE SHERIFF
- (S) (4:23) JCI 3301 Rockin' Seventies. *(LP version)*
- (S) (4:22) Foundation/Capitol 96647 Hearts Of Gold - The Classic Rock Collection. *(LP version)*
- (S) (7:47) Polydor 835269 Crossroads. *(live)*
- (S) (4:22) Polydor 811697 461 Ocean Boulevard. *(LP version)*
- (S) (4:22) MFSL 594 461 Ocean Boulevard. *(LP version; gold disc)*
- (S) (4:20) Polydor 800014 Time Pieces. *(LP version)*
- (S) (3:30) Time-Life SOD-07 Sounds Of The Seventies - 1974. *(45 version)*
- (S) (4:18) Time-Life OPCD-4521 Guitar Rock. *(LP version)*
- (S) (4:22) Polydor 314527116 Cream Of Clapton. *(LP version)*
- (S) (4:22) Polydor 314531821 461 Ocean Boulevard. *(remastered edition; LP version)*
- (S) (3:29) Time-Life R13610 Gold And Platinum Box Set - The Ultimate Rock Collection. *(45 version)*

1974 WILLIE AND THE HAND JIVE
- (S) (3:27) Polydor 811697 461 Ocean Boulevard. *(LP length)*
- (S) (3:27) MFSL 594 461 Ocean Boulevard. *(LP length; gold disc)*
- (S) (3:26) Polydor 800014 Time Pieces. *(LP length)*
- (S) (3:28) Polydor 314531821 461 Ocean Boulevard. *(remastered edition; LP length)*

1976 HELLO OLD FRIEND
- (S) (3:33) Polydor 835269 Crossroads. *(LP version)*
- (S) (3:33) Polydor 813582 No Reason To Cry. *(LP version)*
- (S) (3:00) Time-Life SOD-04 Sounds Of The Seventies - 1976. *(45 version)*
- (S) (3:34) Polydor 314527116 Cream Of Clapton. *(LP version)*
- (S) (3:33) Polydor 314531824 No Reason To Cry. *(remastered edition; LP version)*

1978 LAY DOWN SALLY
(actual 45 time is (3:30) not (3:20) as stated on the record label; LP length is (3:52))
- (S) (3:30) Rhino 70673 Billboard Top Hits - 1978.
- (S) (3:49) Polydor 835269 Crossroads.
- (S) (3:47) Polydor 800014 Time Pieces.
- (S) (3:53) Polydor 823276 Slowhand.
- (S) (3:53) MFSL 553 Slowhand. *(gold disc)*
- (S) (3:29) Time-Life SOD-10 Sounds Of The Seventies - 1978.
- (S) (3:51) Polydor 314531825 Slowhand. *(remastered edition)*

1978 WONDERFUL TONIGHT
- (S) (3:41) Polydor 835269 Crossroads. *(LP version)*
- (S) (3:38) Polydor 800014 Time Pieces. *(LP version)*
- (S) (3:42) Polydor 823276 Slowhand. *(LP version)*
- (S) (3:42) MFSL 553 Slowhand. *(LP version; gold disc)*
- (S) (3:06) Time-Life SOD-20 Sounds Of The Seventies - 1978: Take Two. *(45 version)*
- (S) (5:24) Warner Brothers 26974 Barcelona Gold. *(live)*
- (S) (3:41) Polydor 314527116 Cream Of Clapton. *(LP version)*
- (S) (3:41) Polydor 314531825 Slowhand. *(remastered edition; LP version)*
- (S) (3:41) Polygram TV 314555610 The One And Only Love Album. *(LP version)*

1979 PROMISES
- (S) (2:59) Polydor 835269 Crossroads.
- (S) (2:58) Polydor 800014 Time Pieces.
- (S) (2:59) Polydor 813581 Backless.
- (S) (2:58) Time-Life SOD-09 Sounds Of The Seventies - 1979.
- (S) (2:59) Polydor 314527116 Cream Of Clapton.
- (S) (2:58) Polydor 314531826 Backless. *(remastered edition)*

- (S) (2:58) MFSL 653 Backless. *(gold disc)*
- (S) (2:57) Time-Life R840-10 Sounds Of The Seventies: '70s Dance Party 1979.

1980 TULSA TIME
- (S) (3:24) Polydor 813581 Backless. *(LP version)*
- (S) (3:26) Polydor 314531826 Backless. *(remastered edition; LP version)*
- (S) (3:26) MFSL 653 Backless. *(gold disc; LP version)*

1981 I CAN'T STAND IT
- (S) (4:08) Polydor 835269 Crossroads.
- (S) (4:07) Polydor 827579 Another Ticket.
- (S) (4:07) Polydor 314527116 Cream Of Clapton.
- (S) (4:07) Polydor 314531830 Another Ticket. *(remastered edition)*

1983 I'VE GOT A ROCK N' ROLL HEART
- (S) (3:14) Warner Brothers 23773 Money And Cigarettes.

1985 FOREVER MAN
- (S) (3:10) Warner Brothers 25166 Behind The Sun.
- (S) (3:09) Time-Life R988-27 Sounds Of The Eighties: The Rolling Stone Collection 1983-1985.

1992 TEARS IN HEAVEN
- (S) (4:31) Reprise 26794 O.S.T. Rush.
- (S) (4:31) Columbia 69012 Diana Princess Of Wales Tribute.

1992 LAYLA
- (S) (4:40) Reprise 45024 Unplugged. *(LP version)*

1996 CHANGE THE WORLD
- (S) (3:53) Reprise 45360 O.S.T. Phenomenon.
- (S) (3:52) Grammy Recordings/Chronicles 314553292 1997 Grammy Nominees.

CLAUDINE CLARK
1962 PARTY LIGHTS
- (M) (2:22) Rhino 75891 Wonder Women.
- (M) (2:21) Rhino 70988 Best Of The Girl Groups Volume 1.
- (M) (2:22) Rhino 70648 Billboard's Top R&B Hits Of 1962.
- (M) (2:21) JCI 3110 Sock Hoppin' Sixties.
- (M) (2:21) Collectables 5064 History Of Rock Volume 4.
- (M) (2:21) Time-Life 2RNR-02 Rock 'N' Roll Era - 1962.
- (M) (2:15) Collectables 2502 WCBS-FM History Of Rock - The 60's Part 3.
- (M) (2:15) Collectables 4502 History Of Rock/The 60s Part Three.
- (M) (2:22) Collectables 2603 WCBS-FM Jukebox Giants Vol. 1.
- (M) (2:21) K-Tel 3008 60's Sock Hop.
- (M) (2:20) Taragon 1019 Chancellor Records Story, Volume 2.
- (M) (2:21) Collectables 5799 Party Lights.
- (M) (2:21) Nick At Nite/550 Music 63436 Patio Pool Party.
- (M) (2:21) JCI 3189 1960 - Only Dance - 1964.

DAVE CLARK FIVE
1964 GLAD ALL OVER
- (M) (2:41) Hollywood 61482 History Of.
1964 BITS AND PIECES
- (M) (1:58) Hollywood 61482 History Of.
1964 DO YOU LOVE ME
- (M) (2:43) Hollywood 61482 History Of.
1964 CAN'T YOU SEE THAT SHE'S MINE
- (M) (2:21) Hollywood 61482 History Of.
1964 BECAUSE
- (M) (2:21) Hollywood 61482 History Of.
1964 EVERYBODY KNOWS (I STILL LOVE YOU)
- (M) (1:40) Hollywood 61482 History Of.
1964 ANY WAY YOU WANT IT
- (M) (2:28) Hollywood 61482 History Of.
1965 COME HOME
- (M) (2:47) Hollywood 61482 History Of.
1965 REELIN' AND ROCKIN'
- (M) (2:45) Hollywood 61482 History Of.
1965 I LIKE IT LIKE THAT
- (M) (1:37) Hollywood 61482 History Of.
1965 CATCH US IF YOU CAN
- (M) (1:53) Hollywood 61482 History Of.
1965 OVER AND OVER
- (M) (1:59) Hollywood 61482 History Of.
1966 AT THE SCENE
- (M) (1:51) Hollywood 61482 History Of.

1966 TRY TOO HARD
    (M) (2:07) Hollywood 61482 History Of.

1966 PLEASE TELL ME WHY
    (M) (1:31) Hollywood 61482 History Of.

1967 YOU GOT WHAT IT TAKES
    (M) (2:57) Hollywood 61482 History Of.

1967 YOU MUST HAVE BEEN A BEAUTIFUL BABY

DEE CLARK
1959 NOBODY BUT YOU
    (M) (2:25) Vee Jay 710 A Taste Of Soul Volume 1.
    (M) (2:25) Vee Jay 703 Raindrops.
    (M) (2:25) Vee Jay 3-400 Celebrating 40 Years Of Classic Hits (1953-1993).
    (S) (2:24) Time-Life 2RNR-41 Rock 'N' Roll Era - R&B Gems.
    (S) (2:25) Time-Life RHD-16 Rhythm & Blues - 1958.
    (S) (2:24) Ripete 0003 Coolin' Out/24 Carolina Classics Vol. 3.
    (S) (2:24) Collectables 5760 Golden Classics.
    (M) (2:25) Time-Life R857-16 The Heart Of Rock 'n' Roll The Late '50s.
    (S) (2:25) Time-Life R838-22 Solid Gold Soul 1958.

1959 JUST KEEP IT UP
(actual 45 time is (2:04) not (2:14) as stated on the record label)
    (S) (2:10) Vee Jay 703 Raindrops.
    (S) (2:09) Vee Jay 3-400 Celebrating 40 Years Of Classic Hits (1953-1993).
    (M) (1:56) Time-Life 2RNR-28 Rock 'N' Roll Era - The 50's Rave On. *(faded :08 early)*

1959 HEY LITTLE GIRL
    (S) (2:18) Rhino 75893 Jukebox Classics Volume 1.
    (S) (2:16) Rhino 70645 Billboard's Top R&B Hits Of 1959.
    (S) (2:12) Motown 6215 and 9067 Hits From The Legendary Vee-Jay Records.
    (S) (2:12) Garland 011 Footstompin' Oldies.
    (M) (2:10) DCC Compact Classics 028 Sock Hop.
    (S) (2:16) Collectables 5062 History Of Rock Volume 2.
    (S) (2:14) Vee Jay 703 Raindrops.
    (S) (2:14) Vee Jay 3-400 Celebrating 40 Years Of Classic Hits (1953-1993).
    (S) (2:16) Time-Life 2RNR-24 Rock 'N' Roll Era - The 50's Keep On Rockin'.
    (S) (2:11) Time-Life RHD-03 Rhythm & Blues - 1959.
    (S) (2:14) Collectables 2604 WCBS-FM Jukebox Giants Vol. 2.
    (S) (2:16) Rhino 71806 The R&B Box: Thirty Years Of Rhythm & Blues.
    (S) (2:14) Collectables 5760 Golden Classics.
    (S) (2:11) Time-Life R838-21 Solid Gold Soul 1959.

1960 HOW ABOUT THAT
    (S) (2:39) Vee Jay 703 Raindrops.

1960 YOU'RE LOOKING GOOD
    (S) (2:02) Vee Jay 703 Raindrops.

1961 YOUR FRIENDS
    (S) (2:08) Vee Jay 703 Raindrops.

1961 RAINDROPS
    (S) (2:52) Rhino 75894 Jukebox Classics Volume 2.
    (S) (2:53) Rhino 70647 Billboard's Top R&B Hits Of 1961.
    (M) (2:49) Motown 6215 and 9067 Hits From The Legendary Vee-Jay Records.
    (E) (2:47) Original Sound 8856 Oldies But Goodies Vol. 6. *(this compact disc uses the "Waring - fds" noise reduction process)*
    (E) (2:47) Original Sound 2221 Oldies But Goodies Volumes 1,4,6,8 and 10 Box Set. *(this box set uses the "Waring - fds" noise reduction process)*
    (E) (2:47) Original Sound 2500 Oldies But Goodies Volumes 1-15 Box Set. *(this box set uses the "Waring - fds" noise reduction process)*
    (E) (2:47) Original Sound CDGO-10 Golden Oldies Volume. 10.
    (S) (2:48) Original Sound 9602 Best Of Oldies But Goodies Vol. 2.
    (M) (2:52) DCC Compact Classics 028 Sock Hop.

    (S) (2:49) Collectables 5067 History Of Rock Volume 7.
    (S) (2:43) Vee Jay 710 A Taste Of Soul Volume 1. *(alternate take)*
    (S) (2:52) Vee Jay 703 Raindrops.
    (S) (2:51) Vee Jay 3-400 Celebrating 40 Years Of Classic Hits (1953-1993).
    (S) (2:52) Time-Life 2RNR-04 Rock 'N' Roll Era - 1961.
    (S) (2:50) Time-Life RHD-14 Rhythm & Blues - 1961.
    (M) (2:48) Collectables 2504 WCBS-FM History Of Rock - The 60's Part 4.
    (M) (2:48) Collectables 4504 History Of Rock/The 60s Part Four.
    (S) (2:51) Collectables 2605 WCBS-FM Jukebox Giants Vol. 3.
    (S) (2:53) Varese Sarabande 5534 Rhythm Of The Rain.
    (S) (2:51) Ripete 2163-RE Ebb Tide.
    (S) (2:52) Time-Life R857-03 The Heart Of Rock 'n' Roll - 1961.
    (S) (2:48) Collectables 5760 Golden Classics.
    (S) (2:50) JCI 3166 #1 Radio Hits 1960 - Only Rock 'n Roll - 1964.
    (S) (2:53) Eclipse Music Group 64867 Rock 'n Roll Relix 1960-1961.
    (S) (2:53) Eclipse Music Group 64872 Rock 'n Roll Relix 1960-1969.
    (M) (2:49) Compose 131 Unforgettable - Gold For The Road.
    (S) (2:50) Time-Life R838-19 Solid Gold Soul 1961.

PETULA CLARK
1965 DOWNTOWN
    (S) (3:04) Rhino 70323 History Of British Rock Volume 5.
    (S) (3:04) Rhino 72022 History Of British Rock Box Set.
    (S) (3:01) Original Sound CDGO-8 Golden Oldies Volume. 8.
    (S) (3:01) Original Sound 8892 Dick Clark's 21 All-Time Hits Vol. 2.
    (S) (3:08) GNP/Crescendo 2170 Greatest Hits Of.
    (S) (3:06) Time-Life 2CLR-14 Classic Rock - 1965: Shakin' All Over.
    (S) (3:01) Time-Life SUD-03 Superhits - 1965.
    (S) (3:07) Collectables 2510 WCBS-FM History Of Rock - The Rockin' 60's.
    (S) (3:07) Collectables 4510 History Of Rock/The Rockin' 60s.
    (S) (3:01) Collectables 2505 History Of Rock - The 60's Part 5.
    (S) (3:01) Collectables 4505 History Of Rock/The 60s Part Five.
    (S) (3:05) LaserLight 12317 The British Invasion.
    (S) (3:01) Time-Life AM1-10 AM Gold - 1965.
    (M) (3:00) Inner-State/London 314540735 O.S.T. Twin Town.
    (S) (3:05) JCI 3189 1960 - Only Dance - 1964.

1965 I KNOW A PLACE
    (S) (2:43) Rhino 70324 History Of British Rock Volume 6. *(truncated fade)*
    (S) (2:43) Rhino 72022 History Of British Rock Box Set. *(truncated fade)*
    (S) (2:45) GNP/Crescendo 2170 Greatest Hits Of.
    (S) (2:44) Scotti Brothers 75260 Treasures Volume 1.
    (S) (2:42) Time-Life SUD-12 Superhits - The Mid 60's.
    (S) (2:42) Time-Life AM1-05 AM Gold - The Mid '60s.

1965 YOU'D BETTER COME HOME
    (S) (2:55) GNP/Crescendo 2170 Greatest Hits Of.

1965 ROUND EVERY CORNER
    (S) (2:39) GNP/Crescendo 2170 Greatest Hits Of. *(truncated fade)*

1966 MY LOVE
    (S) (2:44) Rhino 70325 History Of British Rock Volume 7.
    (S) (2:44) Rhino 72022 History Of British Rock Box Set.
    (S) (2:45) GNP/Crescendo 2170 Greatest Hits Of.
    (S) (2:43) Time-Life SUD-01 Superhits - 1966.
    (S) (2:43) Time-Life AM1-09 AM Gold - 1966.

1966 A SIGN OF THE TIMES
    (S) (2:57) GNP/Crescendo 2170 Greatest Hits Of.

1966 I COULDN'T LIVE WITHOUT YOUR LOVE
    (S) (2:58) GNP/Crescendo 2170 Greatest Hits Of.
    (S) (2:53) Time-Life SUD-17 Superhits - Mid 60's Classics.

PETULA CLARK (Continued)

- (S) (2:53) Time-Life R138/05 Look Of Love.
- (S) (2:52) Time-Life AM1-16 AM Gold - Mid '60s Classics.
- (S) (2:53) Time-Life R814-05 Love Songs.

1966 WHO AM I
- (S) (2:23) GNP/Crescendo 2170 Greatest Hits Of.

1967 COLOR MY WORLD
- (S) (2:54) GNP/Crescendo 2170 Greatest Hits Of.

1967 THIS IS MY SONG
- (S) (3:18) GNP/Crescendo 2170 Greatest Hits Of. *(LP version)*
- (S) (3:13) Time-Life SUD-14 Superhits - The Late 60's. *(LP version)*
- (S) (3:13) Time-Life AM1-14 AM Gold - The Late '60s. *(LP version)*
- (S) (3:13) Time-Life R814-01 Love Songs. *(LP version)*

1967 DON'T SLEEP IN THE SUBWAY
- (S) (2:58) GNP/Crescendo 2170 Greatest Hits Of.
- (S) (2:57) Scotti Brothers 75260 Treasures Volume 1.
- (S) (2:54) Time-Life SUD-05 Superhits - 1967.
- (S) (2:54) Time-Life AM1-08 AM Gold - 1967.
- (S) (2:54) Varese Sarabande 5803 Sunshine Days - Pop Classics Of The '60s Volume 3.

1967 THE CAT IN THE WINDOW (THE BIRD IN THE SKY)
1967 THE OTHER MAN'S GRASS IS ALWAYS GREENER
- (S) (2:56) GNP/Crescendo 2170 Greatest Hits Of.
- (S) (2:58) Inner-State/London 314540735 O.S.T. Twin Town.

1968 KISS ME GOODBYE
- (S) (3:56) GNP/Crescendo 2170 Greatest Hits Of. *(slower in pitch than the 45 or LP)*

1968 DON'T GIVE UP

ROY CLARK
1969 YESTERDAY, WHEN I WAS YOUNG
- (S) (3:17) MCA Special Products 20435 Country's Greatest Hits Of The 60's Vol. 1.
- (S) (3:17) K-Tel 3110 Country Music Classics Volume XVIII.
- (S) (3:18) Varese Sarabande 5608 Greatest Hits.
- (S) (3:17) JCI 3154 1965 - Only Country - 1969.

SANFORD CLARK
1956 THE FOOL
- (M) (2:43) Rhino 70599 Billboard's Top Rock & Roll Hits Of 1956.
- (M) (2:43) MCA 5939 Vintage Music Volumes 17 & 18.
- (M) (2:43) MCA 31214 Vintage Music Volume 17.
- (M) (2:43) Rhino 70741 Rock This Town: Rockabilly Hits Volume 1.
- (M) (2:42) Time-Life 2RNR-14 Rock 'N' Roll Era - 1956.
- (M) (2:42) Varese Sarabande 5687 History Of Dot Records Volume Two.

STANLEY CLARKE/GEORGE DUKE
1981 SWEET BABY
- (S) (3:47) Epic 36918 Clarke/Duke Project.
- (S) (3:46) Epic 66146 George Duke - Greatest Hits.

TONY CLARKE
1965 THE ENTERTAINER
- (S) (2:32) Rhino 75757 Soul Shots Volume 3.
- (S) (2:33) Chess 31318 Best Of Chess Rhythm & Blues Volume 2.
- (S) (2:32) Ripete 2392192 Beach Music Anthology Box Set.
- (S) (2:32) Rhino 72868 Brown Eyed Soul Vol. 1.
- (S) (2:32) Rhino 72815 Beg, Scream & Shout! The Big Ol' Box Of '60s Soul.
- (S) (2:32) Chess 9388 Chess Soul - A Decade Of Chicago's Finest.

CLASH
1980 TRAIN IN VAIN (STAND BY ME)
- (S) (3:10) Epic 36328 London Calling. *(this track is not listed on the cd jacket but it is track 19)*
- (S) (3:08) Epic/Legacy 46991 On Broadway.
- (S) (3:10) Epic 44035 Story Of The Clash Volume 1.
- (S) (3:05) Time-Life R102-34 The Rolling Stone Collection.
- (S) (3:10) Priority 53759 Best Of Punk Rock Vol. 1.

1983 ROCK THE CASBAH
- (S) (3:40) Sandstone 33044 and 5010 Rock The First Volume Four.
- (S) (3:40) Epic 37689 Combat Rock.
- (S) (3:40) Epic 44035 Story Of The Clash Volume 1.
- (S) (3:41) Epic/Legacy 46991 On Broadway.

CLASSICS
1963 TILL THEN
- (M) (2:13) Collectables 2507 History Of Rock - The Doo Wop Era Part 1.
- (M) (2:13) Collectables 4507 History Of Rock/The Doo Wop Era Part One.
- (M) (2:12) Time-Life 2RNR-45 Rock 'N' Roll Era - Street Corner Serenade.
- (M) (2:13) Collectables 2509 WCBS-FM For Lovers Only Part 1.
- (M) (2:15) Rhino 72507 Doo Wop Box II.
- (M) (2:11) Time-Life R857-08 The Heart Of Rock 'n' Roll 1963.

CLASSICS IV
1968 SPOOKY
- (S) (2:52) EMI 91472 Very Best Of.
- (S) (2:51) Capitol 98138 Spring Break Volume 1. *(noisy fadeout)*
- (S) (2:49) Time-Life 2CLR-19 Classic Rock - 1968: Shakin' All Over.
- (S) (2:47) Time-Life SUD-02 Superhits - 1968.
- (S) (2:47) Time-Life OPCD-4517 Tonight's The Night.
- (S) (2:50) Risky Business 66391 Ghastly Grooves.
- (S) (2:50) Rhino 71938 Billboard Top Pop Hits, 1968.
- (S) (2:39) K-Tel 3795 Music For Your Halloween Party. *(rerecording)*
- (S) (2:39) K-Tel 3795 Spooktacular Party Songs. *(rerecording)*
- (S) (2:47) Time-Life AM1-04 AM Gold - 1968.
- (S) (2:50) K-Tel 4033 Ghasty Grooves.
- (S) (2:49) Time-Life R857-22 The Heart Of Rock 'n' Roll 1967-1969.

1968 STORMY
- (S) (2:47) EMI 91472 Very Best Of.
- (S) (2:47) Capitol 98139 Spring Break Volume 2.
- (S) (2:44) Time-Life 2CLR-27 Classic Rock - 1968: Blowin' Your Mind.
- (S) (2:43) Time-Life SUD-14 Superhits - The Late 60's.
- (S) (2:46) Time-Life 2CLR-31 Classic Rock - Totally Fantastic '60s.
- (S) (2:43) Time-Life AM1-14 AM Gold - The Late '60s.
- (S) (2:46) Varese Sarabande 5801 Sunshine Days - Pop Classics Of The '60s Volume 1.

1969 TRACES
- (S) (2:45) EMI 90603 Rock Me Gently.
- (M) (2:42) Original Sound 8861 Oldies But Goodies Vol. 11. *(this compact disc uses the "Waring - fds" noise reduction process)*
- (M) (2:42) Original Sound 2222 Oldies But Goodies Volumes 3,5,11,14 and 15 Box Set. *(this box set uses the "Waring - fds" noise reduction process)*
- (M) (2:42) Original Sound 2500 Oldies But Goodies Volumes 1-15 Box Set. *(this box set uses the "Waring - fds" noise reduction process)*
- (S) (2:45) EMI 91472 Very Best Of.
- (S) (2:43) Time-Life SUD-07 Superhits - 1969.
- (S) (2:43) Time-Life AM1-01 AM Gold - 1969.

1969 EVERYDAY WITH YOU GIRL
- (S) (2:31) EMI 91472 Very Best Of. *(truncated fade)*

released as by DENNIS YOST and THE CLASSICS IV:
1972 WHAT AM I CRYING FOR?

TOM CLAY
1971 WHAT THE WORLD NEEDS NOW IS LOVE/ABRAHAM, MARTIN AND JOHN
- (S) (6:19) Motown 6184 Hard To Find Motown Classics Volume 2.

ADAM CLAYTON & LARRY MULLEN
1996 THEME FROM MISSION: IMPOSSIBLE
    (S)   (3:27)   Mother 314531682 O.S.T. Mission: Impossible.

CLEFTONES
1961 HEART AND SOUL
    (S)   (1:50)   Rhino 70951 Best Of.
    (S)   (1:51)   Collectables 8806 For Collectors Only.
    (S)   (1:50)   MCA 8001 O.S.T. American Graffiti.
    (M)   (1:48)   Time-Life 2RNR-25 Rock 'N' Roll Era - The 60's
                   Keep On Rockin'.
    (S)   (1:50)   Rhino 72156 Doo Wop Memories, Vol. 1.
    (S)   (1:50)   Collectables 5483 Spotlite On Gee Records
                   Volume 4.
    (S)   (1:50)   Rhino 72507 Doo Wop Box II.
    (S)   (1:50)   Time-Life R857-19 The Heart Of Rock 'n' Roll
                   1960-1961 Take Three.

CLARENCE CLEMONS and JACKSON BROWNE
1986 YOU'RE A FRIEND OF MINE
    (S)   (4:49)   Risky Business 57833 Read The Hits/Best Of The
                   80's. *(LP version)*
    (S)   (4:50)   Columbia 40010 Clarence Clemons - Hero. *(LP
                   version)*
    (S)   (4:48)   Time-Life R988-17 Sounds Of The Eighties: The
                   Mid '80s Take Two. *(LP version)*

JIMMY CLIFF
1970 WONDERFUL WORLD, BEAUTIFUL PEOPLE
    (S)   (3:12)   A&M 6015 Reggae Spectacular.
    (S)   (3:14)   A&M 3189 Wonderful World, Beautiful People.
    (S)   (3:11)   Madacy Entertainment 6804 More Sun Splashin'.
1993 I CAN SEE CLEARLY NOW
    (S)   (3:14)   Chaos/Columbia 57553 O.S.T. Cool Runnings.
    (S)   (3:08)   Priority 50946 100% Party Hits Of The 90's
                   Volume One.
    (S)   (3:12)   Razor & Tie 4569 '90s Style.

BUZZ CLIFFORD
1961 BABY SITTIN' BOOGIE
    (M)   (2:01)   Time-Life SUD-19 Superhits - Early 60's Classics.
    (S)   (2:02)   K-Tel 3037 Wacky Weirdos.
    (S)   (2:01)   Collectors' Choice 002 Teen Idols....For A
                   Moment.
    (M)   (2:01)   Time-Life AM1-20 AM Gold - Early '60s Classics.

MIKE CLIFFORD
1962 CLOSE TO CATHY
    (M)   (2:52)   Collectors' Choice 002 Teen Idols....For A Moment.
    (E)   (2:52)   EMI-Capitol Special Markets 19552 Lost Hits Of
                   The '60s.
    (M)   (2:52)   Time-Life R857-18 The Heart Of Rock 'n' Roll
                   1962-1963 Take Two.

CLIMAX
1972 PRECIOUS AND FEW
    (S)   (2:44)   Rhino 70927 Super Hits Of The 70's Volume 7.
    (S)   (2:42)   Collectables 5069 History Of Rock Volume 9.
    (S)   (2:43)   Original Sound 8865 Oldies But Goodies Vol. 15.
                   *(this compact disc uses the "Waring - fds" noise
                   reduction process)*
    (S)   (2:43)   Original Sound 2222 Oldies But Goodies
                   Volumes 3,5,11,14 and 15 Box Set. *(this box set
                   uses the "Waring - fds" noise reduction process)*
    (S)   (2:43)   Original Sound 2500 Oldies But Goodies
                   Volumes 1-15 Box Set. *(this box set uses the
                   "Waring - fds" noise reduction process)*
    (S)   (2:42)   Original Sound CDGO-8 Golden Oldies Volume. 8.
    (S)   (2:42)   Original Sound 8907 Best Love Songs Vol 2.
    (S)   (2:42)   Original Sound 9326 Best Love Songs Vol. 1 & 2.
    (S)   (2:42)   Original Sound 1236 Best Love Songs Box Set.
    (S)   (2:44)   Razor & Tie 4543 The '70s Preservation Society
                   Presents: Easy '70s.
    (S)   (2:44)   Time-Life SUD-11 Superhits - 1972.

    (S)   (2:44)   Time-Life SOD-32 Sounds Of The Seventies -
                   AM Pop Classics.
    (S)   (2:42)   Collectables 2605 WCBS-FM Jukebox Giants
                   Vol. 3.
    (S)   (2:45)   LaserLight 12320 Love Songs.
    (S)   (2:45)   Curb 77773 Hard To Find Hits Of Rock 'N' Roll
                   Volume One.
    (S)   (2:44)   Madacy Entertainment 1972 Rock On 1972.
    (S)   (2:45)   K-Tel 3623 Believe In Music.
    (S)   (2:44)   K-Tel 3639 Dim The Lights - Soft Rock Hits Of
                   The 70's.
    (S)   (2:44)   Eclipse Music Group 64893 Rock 'n Roll Relix
                   1972-1973.
    (S)   (2:44)   Eclipse Music Group 64897 Rock 'n Roll Relix
                   1970-1979.
    (S)   (2:44)   Time-Life AM1-07 AM Gold - 1972.
    (S)   (2:44)   Time-Life R834-05 Body Talk - Sealed With A Kiss.
    (S)   (2:44)   Time-Life R840-03 Sounds Of The Seventies -
                   Pop Nuggets: Early '70s.
    (S)   (2:45)   Rhino 72812 VH1 8-Track Flashback: The One
                   Hit Wonders.
    (S)   (2:44)   Time-Life R814-02 Love Songs.

CLIMAX BLUES BAND
1977 COULDN'T GET IT RIGHT
    (S)   (3:15)   Rhino 70672 Billboard Top Hits - 1977.
    (S)   (3:15)   Rhino 71199 Super Hits Of The 70's Volume 19.
    (S)   (3:14)   Time-Life R968-03 Guitar Rock 1976-1977.
    (S)   (3:02)   Time-Life SOD-17 Sounds Of The Seventies -
                   1977: Take Two. *(:10 edited off the ending)*
    (S)   (3:15)   Rhino 72517 Mellow Rock Hits Of The 70's -
                   Ventura Highway.
    (S)   (3:15)   Time-Life AM1-24 AM Gold - 1977.
    (S)   (3:14)   K-Tel 3986 70's Heavy Hitters: Arena Rockers
                   1975-79.
    (S)   (3:15)   Thump 6020 Easyriders Volume 2.
1981 I LOVE YOU

CLIMIE FISHER
1988 LOVE CHANGES (EVERYTHING)
    (S)   (4:27)   EMI 32694 Living In Oblivion - The 80's Greatest
                   Hits Volume Five.
    (S)   (4:28)   Capitol 90514 Everything.

PATSY CLINE
1957 WALKIN' AFTER MIDNIGHT
    (M)   (1:56)   MCA 5939 Vintage Music Volumes 17 & 18.
                   (rerecording)
    (M)   (1:56)   MCA 31214 Vintage Music Volume 17.
                   (rerecording)
    (S)   (1:57)   MCA 4038 Patsy Cline Story. *(rerecording)*
    (M)   (2:32)   MCA 12 12 Greatest Hits.
    (S)   (1:57)   MCA 12 12 Greatest Hits. *(remastered edition;
                   rerecording)*
    (M)   (2:33)   MCA 4-10421 The Patsy Cline Collection.
    (S)   (1:58)   MCA 4-10421 The Patsy Cline Collection.
                   (rerecording)
    (S)   (2:00)   MCA 6149 O.S.T. Sweet Dreams. *(rerecording)*
    (S)   (1:59)   MCA 1467 Remembering. *(rerecording)*
    (M)   (2:33)   MCA 25200 Patsy Cline.
    (M)   (2:33)   MCA 8925 Commemorative Collection.
    (E)   (2:31)   Pair 1236 The Legendary.
    (M)   (2:30)   Curb 77518 Best Of.
    (E)   (2:31)   Special Music 4927 The Legendary.
    (M)   (2:30)   Rhino 71458 Walkin' After Midnight.
    (M)   (2:33)   Time-Life CTD-02 Country USA - 1957.
    (S)   (1:59)   MCA Special Products 20427 Country Hits Of
                   The 50's Vol. 1. *(rerecording)*
    (M)   (2:30)   Collectables 5059 Golden Classics.
    (M)   (2:33)   K-Tel 225 Country Music Classics Volume I.
    (M)   (2:33)   Rhino 71902 Hillbilly Fever! Vol. 3. Legends Of
                   Nashville.
    (M)   (2:33)   Time-Life R990-05 Legendary Country Singers.
    (M)   (2:33)   MCA Special Products 20915 Loretta Lynn &
                   Patsy Cline On Tour #1.

PATSY CLINE *(Continued)*

(S) (2:00) MCA Special Products 20364 Country's Greatest Hits Volume 1. *(rerecording)*
(M) (2:33) Rhino 72442 Heroes Of Country Music Vol. Three.
(M) (2:30) JCI 3152 1955 - Only Country - 1959.
(M) (2:33) MCA Special Products 20265 Heartaches.
(M) (2:33) Time-Life R857-05 The Heart Of Rock 'n' Roll 1957.
(M) (2:33) RCA 66983 The Essential.
(S) (1:59) MCA 10952 12 Greatest Hits. *(gold disc; rerecording)*
(M) (2:33) Music Club 50028 Crazy Dreams.
(S) (2:01) MCA Special Products 21036 Legends Of Country Music. *(rerecording)*
(M) (2:30) Flashback 72809 Walkin' After Midnight.
(M) (2:34) Simitar 55022 Forever. *(the printed track lineup does not match the actual track lineup)*
(M) (2:33) Time-Life R808-03 Classic Country 1950-1959.

1961 I FALL TO PIECES

(S) (2:46) MCA 4038 Patsy Cline Story.
(M) (2:47) MCA 12 12 Greatest Hits.
(S) (2:46) MCA 12 12 Greatest Hits. *(remastered edition)*
(S) (2:48) MCA 4-10421 The Patsy Cline Collection.
(S) (2:47) MCA 6149 O.S.T. Sweet Dreams.
(M) (2:47) MCA 8925 Commemorative Collection.
(S) (2:55) MCA 27069 Always. *(rerecording)*
(S) (2:47) Time-Life CTD-01 Country USA - 1961.
(S) (2:47) MCA Special Products 20435 Country's Greatest Hits Of The 60's Vol. 1.
(M) (2:47) K-Tel 320 Country Music Classics Volume II.
(S) (2:48) MCA Special Products 20879 Sings Songs Of Love.
(S) (2:48) Time-Life R990-05 Legendary Country Singers.
(S) (2:48) MCA Special Products 20365 Country's Greatest Hits Volume 2.
(S) (2:48) MCA Special Products 20915 Loretta Lynn & Patsy Cline On Tour #1.
(M) (2:47) MCA Special Products 20845 Truckers Jukebox #3.
(S) (2:47) JCI 3153 1960 - Only Country - 1964.
(S) (2:48) Hip-O 40024 Country Wildflowers.
(S) (2:48) MCA Special Products 20265 Heartaches.
(S) (2:56) Priority 50966 I Love Country Volume One: Hits Of The 60's. *(rerecording)*
(S) (2:48) Time-Life R857-10 The Heart Of Rock 'n' Roll 1960-1961.
(S) (2:48) Hip-O 40044 Country Heartaches.
(S) (2:48) MCA Special Products 21014 Patsy Cline/Conway Twitty Back To Back.
(S) (2:48) MCA 10952 12 Greatest Hits. *(gold disc)*
(S) (2:47) Time-Life R814-02 Love Songs.
(S) (2:46) Time-Life R808-01 Classic Country 1960-1964.

1961 CRAZY

(S) (2:40) MCA 5940 Vintage Music Volumes 19 & 20.
(S) (2:40) MCA 31216 Vintage Music Volume 19.
(S) (2:41) MCA 4038 Patsy Cline Story.
(M) (2:40) MCA 25019 Songwriter's Tribute.
(M) (2:39) MCA 12 12 Greatest Hits. *(truncated fade)*
(S) (2:41) MCA 12 12 Greatest Hits. *(remastered edition)*
(S) (2:42) MCA 4-10421 The Patsy Cline Collection.
(S) (2:41) MCA 6149 O.S.T. Sweet Dreams.
(M) (2:39) MCA 8925 Commemorative Collection.
(S) (2:41) Time-Life CTD-01 Country USA - 1961.
(S) (2:42) Time-Life HPD-33 Your Hit Parade - The Early 60's.
(S) (2:41) Time-Life R138/05 Look Of Love.
(S) (2:42) MCA 11120 Stardust/The Classic Decca Hits & Standards Collection.
(S) (2:40) MCA Special Products 22133 Vintage Collectibles Volume 4.
(S) (2:41) K-Tel 3085 Great Ladies Of Country.
(S) (2:41) K-Tel 3109 Country Music Classics Volume XVII.
(S) (2:42) MCA Special Products 20879 Sings Songs Of Love.
(S) (2:42) Varese Sarabande 5606 Through The Years - Country Hits Of The 60's.
(S) (2:42) Time-Life R990-05 Legendary Country Singers.

(S) (2:41) Time-Life R857-03 The Heart Of Rock 'n' Roll - 1961.
(S) (2:40) Decca 11330 The Nashville Sound....Owen Bradley.
(S) (2:42) MCA Special Products 20916 Loretta Lynn & Patsy Cline On Tour #2.
(S) (2:41) MCA Special Products 20842 Truckers Jukebox #2.
(S) (2:42) MCA Special Products 20846 Greatest Country Classics Volume One.
(S) (2:42) MCA Special Products 20265 Heartaches.
(S) (2:41) K-Tel 3355 101 Greatest Country Hits Vol. One: Forever Country.
(S) (2:42) MCA Special Products 21014 Patsy Cline/Conway Twitty Back To Back.
(S) (2:42) MCA 10952 12 Greatest Hits. *(gold disc)*
(S) (2:41) Motown 314530841 O.S.T. In & Out. *(previous selection tracks into the introduction)*
(S) (2:41) Time-Life R857-21 The Heart Of Rock 'n' Roll Slow Dancing Classics.
(S) (2:41) Time-Life R814-01 Love Songs.
(S) (2:41) Time-Life R808-01 Classic Country 1960-1964.

1962 SHE'S GOT YOU

(S) (2:57) MCA 4038 Patsy Cline Story.
(M) (2:57) MCA 12 12 Greatest Hits.
(S) (2:57) MCA 12 12 Greatest Hits. *(remastered edition)*
(M) (2:59) MCA 90 Sentimentally Yours.
(S) (3:06) MCA 4-10421 The Patsy Cline Collection. *(with countoff)*
(S) (2:58) MCA 6149 O.S.T. Sweet Dreams.
(M) (2:57) MCA 8925 Commemorative Collection.
(M) (2:57) Time-Life CTD-03 Country USA - 1962.
(S) (2:59) Time-Life R990-05 Legendary Country Singers.
(S) (2:58) MCA Special Products 20942 Trucker's Jukebox Volume 4.
(S) (2:59) MCA Special Products 20915 Loretta Lynn & Patsy Cline On Tour #1.
(S) (2:59) MCA Special Products 20265 Heartaches.
(S) (2:59) Time-Life R857-06 The Heart Of Rock 'n' Roll 1962.
(S) (2:59) MCA 10952 12 Greatest Hits. *(gold disc)*

CLIQUE

1969 SUGAR ON SUNDAY

(S) (3:07) Varese Sarabande 5719 Bubblegum Classics Volume Three.

1969 I'LL HOLD OUT MY HAND

ROSEMARY CLOONEY

1957 MANGOS

(M) (2:35) Columbia/Legacy 53569 The Essence Of.
(M) (2:36) Time-Life HPD-31 Your Hit Parade - The 50's Forever.
(M) (2:36) Risky Business 66389 Diner Mite/The Swingin' Diner.

CLOVERS

1956 LOVE, LOVE, LOVE

(M) (2:02) Atlantic 81295 Atlantic Rhythm & Blues Volume 3.
(M) (2:01) Atlantic 82305 Atlantic Rhythm And Blues 1947-1974 Box Set.
(M) (2:02) Flashback 72706 Don't You Know I Love You And Other Hits.

1959 LOVE POTION No. 9

(S) (1:51) EMI 96268 24 Greatest Hits Of All Time. *(45 version)*
(M) (1:53) Curb 77323 All Time Greatest Hits Of Rock 'N' Roll. *(45 version)*
(S) (1:51) EMI 96336 Best Of - Love Potion No. 9. *(45 version)*
(S) (2:25) EMI 96336 Best Of - Love Potion No. 9. *(LP version; includes :31 of studio talk and a false start)*
(S) (1:51) Rhino 70593 The Rock 'N' Roll Classics Of Leiber & Stoller. *(45 version)*
(S) (1:55) MCA 8001 O.S.T. American Graffiti. *(45 version)*
(M) (1:51) Time-Life 2RNR-20 Rock 'N' Roll Era - 1959 Still Rockin'. *(45 version)*

(M) (1:51) Time-Life R10513 40 Lovin' Oldies. *(45 version)*
(S) (1:56) K-Tel 3411 Tacky Tunes. *(rerecording)*
(S) (1:50) Rhino 72507 Doo Wop Box II. *(45 version)*
(M) (1:51) Nick At Nite/550 Music/Epic 67768 Fonzie's Make Out Music. *(45 version)*
(S) (1:51) Priority 50950 I Love Rock & Roll Volume 1: Hits Of The 50's. *(45 version)*
(S) (1:50) Rhino 72971 Very Best Of. *(45 version)*
(S) (1:50) Collectables 1514 and 2514 The Anniversary Album - The 50's. *(45 version)*

CLUB NOUVEAU
1987 LEAN ON ME
(S) (3:57) Original Sound 9305 Art Laboe's Dedicated To You Vol. 5. *(45 version)*
(S) (3:57) JCI 3128 1985 - Only Rock 'N Roll - 1989. *(45 version)*
(S) (5:50) Warner Brothers 25531 Life, Love & Pain. *(LP version)*
(S) (5:50) Rhino 71972 Video Soul - Best Soul Of The 80's Vol. 2. *(LP version)*
(S) (3:57) Time-Life R988-09 Sounds Of The Eighties: 1987. *(45 version)*
(S) (3:58) Rhino 72142 Billboard Hot R&B Hits 1987. *(45 version)*
(S) (3:57) Madacy Entertainment 1987 Rock On 1987. *(45 version)*
(S) (3:56) Cold Front 6246 Classic Club Mix - R&B Grooves. *(all selections on this cd are segued together; 45 version)*
(S) (3:57) Priority 50974 Premiere The Movie Magazine Presents The Greatest Soundtrack Hits. *(45 version)*

COASTERS
1957 SEARCHIN'
(M) (2:39) Atlantic 81295 Atlantic Rhythm & Blues Volume 3.
(E) (2:39) Warner Special Products 27604 Ultimate.
(M) (2:38) Atco 33111 Greatest Hits.
(M) (2:39) Atlantic 82305 Atlantic Rhythm And Blues 1947-1974 Box Set.
(M) (2:43) Rhino 71090 50 Coastin' Classics.
(M) (2:43) Rhino 71428 Yakety Yak.
(M) (2:43) Rhino 71597 Very Best Of.
(M) (2:38) Time-Life 2RNR-01 Rock 'N' Roll Era - 1957.
(M) (2:38) Time-Life RHD-08 Rhythm & Blues - 1957.
(M) (2:37) Time-Life R10513 40 Lovin' Oldies.
(M) (2:43) Flashback 72663 Yakety Yak And Other Hits.
(M) (2:43) Flashback 72084 Soul Legends Box Set.
(M) (2:43) Rhino 72961 Ultimate '50s R&B Smashes!
(M) (2:38) Time-Life R838-23 Solid Gold Soul 1957.
1957 YOUNG BLOOD
(M) (2:20) Warner Special Products 27602 20 Party Classics.
(M) (2:19) Atlantic 81295 Atlantic Rhythm & Blues Volume 3. *(first few notes truncated)*
(M) (2:20) Warner Special Products 27604 Ultimate.
(M) (2:20) Atco 33111 Greatest Hits.
(M) (2:19) Atlantic 82305 Atlantic Rhythm And Blues 1947-1974 Box Set. *(first few notes truncated)*
(M) (2:18) Rhino 71090 50 Coastin' Classics.
(M) (2:18) Rhino 71428 Yakety Yak.
(M) (2:18) Rhino 71597 Very Best Of.
(M) (2:20) Time-Life 2RNR-01 Rock 'N' Roll Era - 1957.
(M) (2:18) Rhino 71806 The R&B Box: Thirty Years Of Rhythm & Blues.
(M) (2:19) JCI 3165 #1 Radio Hits 1955 - Only Rock 'n Roll - 1959.
(M) (2:18) Flashback 72663 Yakety Yak And Other Hits.
(M) (2:18) Flashback 72084 Soul Legends Box Set.
1958 YAKETY YAK
(S) (1:48) Warner Special Products 27601 Atlantic Soul Classics. *(stereo LP version)*
(S) (1:50) Rhino 70619 Billboard's Top Rock & Roll Hits Of 1958. *(stereo LP version)*

(S) (1:50) Rhino 72004 Billboard's Top Rock & Roll Hits 1957-1961 Box Set. *(stereo LP version)*
(M) (1:48) Atlantic 81295 Atlantic Rhythm & Blues Volume 3. *(45 version)*
(M) (1:48) Atlantic 81677 O.S.T. Stand By Me. *(45 version)*
(S) (1:49) Warner Special Products 27604 Ultimate. *(stereo LP version)*
(S) (1:49) Atco 33111 Coasters Greatest Hits. *(stereo LP version)*
(S) (1:49) MCA 6171 Good Time Rock 'N' Roll. *(all selections on this cd are recorded live)*
(M) (1:48) Atlantic 82305 Atlantic Rhythm And Blues 1947-1974 Box Set. *(45 version)*
(M) (1:49) Rhino 71090 50 Coastin' Classics. *(45 version)*
(M) (1:49) Rhino 71428 Yakety Yak. *(45 version)*
(M) (1:49) Rhino 71547 Let There Be Drums Volume 1: The 50's. *(45 version)*
(M) (1:49) Rhino 71597 Very Best Of. *(45 version)*
(S) (1:50) Time-Life 2RNR-05 Rock 'N' Roll Era - 1958. *(stereo LP version)*
(S) (1:49) Time-Life RHD-16 Rhythm & Blues - 1958. *(stereo LP version)*
(M) (1:49) Motown 6763 Rites Of Rhythm & Blues Volume Two. *(45 version)*
(M) (1:49) JCI 3129 1955 - Only Rock 'N Roll - 1959. *(45 version)*
(M) (1:49) Music For Little People 42581 A Child's Celebration Of Rock 'N' Roll. *(45 version)*
(M) (1:49) Rhino 71802 O.S.T. Andre. *(45 version)*
(S) (1:46) Collectors' Choice 7209 All Night Boogie - The Great Atlantic Vocal Groups Vol. Two. *(45 version)*
(M) (1:49) Flashback 72663 Yakety Yak And Other Hits. *(45 version)*
(M) (1:49) Flashback 72084 Soul Legends Box Set. *(45 version)*
(M) (1:49) Flashback 72857 Grease And Other Golden Oldies. *(45 version)*
(M) (1:48) Atlantic 83088 Atlantic Records: 50 Years - The Gold Anniversary Collection. *(45 version)*
(S) (1:49) Time-Life R838-22 Solid Gold Soul 1958. *(stereo LP version)*

1959 CHARLIE BROWN
(S) (2:22) Rhino 70620 Billboard's Top Rock & Roll Hits Of 1959. *(LP version)*
(S) (2:22) Rhino 72004 Billboard's Top Rock & Roll Hits 1957-1961 Box Set. *(LP version)*
(M) (2:17) Atlantic 81296 Atlantic Rhythm & Blues Volume 4. *(45 version)*
(M) (2:17) Original Sound 8858 Oldies But Goodies Vol. 8. *(this compact disc uses the "Waring - fds" noise reduction process; 45 version)*
(M) (2:17) Original Sound 2221 Oldies But Goodies Volumes 1,4,6,8 and 10 Box Set. *(this box set uses the "Waring - fds" noise reduction process; 45 version)*
(M) (2:17) Original Sound 2500 Oldies But Goodies Volumes 1-15 Box Set. *(this box set uses the "Waring - fds" noise reduction process; 45 version)*
(M) (2:18) Warner Special Products 27604 Ultimate. *(45 version; truncated fade)*
(M) (2:17) Atco 33111 Greatest Hits. *(LP version; truncated fade)*
(M) (2:15) Rhino 70593 The Rock 'N' Roll Classics Of Leiber & Stoller. *(45 version)*
(S) (2:10) MCA 6171 Good Time Rock 'N' Roll. *(all selections on this cd are recorded live)*
(M) (2:17) Atlantic 82305 Atlantic Rhythm And Blues 1947-1974 Box Set. *(45 version)*
(M) (2:18) Rhino 71090 50 Coastin' Classics. *(45 version)*
(S) (2:16) K-Tel 3150 Dumb Ditties. *(rerecording)*
(M) (2:18) Rhino 71597 Very Best Of. *(45 version)*
(S) (2:22) Time-Life 2RNR-13 Rock 'N' Roll Era - 1959. *(LP version)*

COASTERS *(Continued)*

- (S) (2:20) Time-Life RHD-03 Rhythm & Blues - 1959. *(LP version)*
- (M) (2:17) DCC Compact Classics 077 Too Cute! *(45 version)*
- (M) (2:18) Music For Little People 42581 A Child's Celebration Of Rock 'N' Roll. *(45 version)*
- (S) (2:19) Collectors' Choice 7209 All Night Boogie - The Great Atlantic Vocal Groups Vol. Two. *(45 version)*
- (M) (2:18) Flashback 72663 Yakety Yak And Other Hits. *(45 version)*
- (M) (2:18) Flashback 72084 Soul Legends Box Set. *(45 version)*
- (S) (2:20) Time-Life R838-21 Solid Gold Soul 1959. *(LP version)*

1959 ALONG CAME JONES
- (M) (2:55) Atlantic 81296 Atlantic Rhythm & Blues Volume 4.
- (M) (2:53) Warner Special Products 27604 Ultimate.
- (M) (2:55) Atco 33111 Greatest Hits.
- (M) (2:55) Atlantic 82305 Atlantic Rhythm And Blues 1947-1974 Box Set.
- (M) (2:55) Rhino 71090 50 Coastin' Classics.
- (M) (2:56) Rhino 71597 Very Best Of.
- (M) (2:55) Time-Life 2RNR-20 Rock 'N' Roll Era - 1959 Still Rockin'.
- (M) (2:55) Rhino 71802 O.S.T. Andre.

1959 POISON IVY
- (S) (2:40) Rhino 70645 Billboard's Top R&B Hits Of 1959. *(stereo LP version)*
- (S) (2:40) Atlantic 81296 Atlantic Rhythm & Blues Volume 4. *(stereo LP version)*
- (M) (2:40) Warner Special Products 27604 Ultimate. *(45 version)*
- (S) (2:40) Atco 33111 Greatest Hits. *(stereo LP version)*
- (S) (2:40) Atlantic 82305 Atlantic Rhythm And Blues 1947-1974 Box Set. *(stereo LP version)*
- (M) (2:40) Rhino 71090 50 Coastin' Classics. *(45 version)*
- (M) (2:41) Rhino 71597 Very Best Of. *(45 version)*
- (M) (2:39) Time-Life 2RNR-13 Rock 'N' Roll Era - 1959. *(45 version)*
- (M) (2:35) Time-Life RHD-03 Rhythm & Blues - 1959. *(45 version)*
- (M) (2:39) Time-Life R962-01 History Of Rock 'N' Roll: Rock 'N' Roll Classics 1957-1959. *(45 version)*
- (M) (2:35) Time-Life R838-21 Solid Gold Soul 1959. *(45 version)*

1961 LITTLE EGYPT
- (M) (2:50) Atlantic 81296 Atlantic Rhythm & Blues Volume 4. *(45 version)*
- (S) (2:50) Warner Special Products 27604 Ultimate. *(alternate take)*
- (S) (2:45) Atlantic 82305 Atlantic Rhythm And Blues 1947-1974 Box Set. *(45 version)*
- (M) (2:49) Rhino 71090 50 Coastin' Classics. *(45 version)*
- (M) (2:50) Rhino 71597 Very Best Of. *(45 version)*
- (M) (2:50) Time-Life 2RNR-18 Rock 'N' Roll Era - 1961 Still Rockin'. *(45 version)*
- (M) (2:50) Flashback 72663 Yakety Yak And Other Hits. *(45 version)*
- (M) (2:50) Flashback 72084 Soul Legends Box Set. *(45 version)*

EDDIE COCHRAN
1957 SITTIN' IN THE BALCONY
- (M) (1:57) EMI 46580 Best Of.
- (M) (1:58) EMI 92809 Legendary Masters Series Volume 1.
- (M) (1:57) Curb 77371 Greatest Hits.
- (M) (1:57) EMI 80240 Singin' To My Baby/Never To Be Forgotten.
- (M) (1:57) Time-Life 2RNR-17 Rock 'N' Roll Era - 1957 Still Rockin'.
- (M) (1:58) Razor & Tie 2162 Somethin' Else: The Fine Lookin' Hits Of Eddie Cochran.

1958 SUMMERTIME BLUES
- (M) (1:56) Rhino 70906 American Bandstand Greatest Hits Collection.
- (M) (1:56) Rhino 70087 Summer & Fun.

- (M) (1:55) Original Sound 8858 Oldies But Goodies Vol. 8. *(this compact disc uses the "Waring - fds" noise reduction process)*
- (M) (1:55) Original Sound 2221 Oldies But Goodies Volumes 1,4,6,8 and 10 Box Set. *(this box set uses the "Waring - fds" noise reduction process)*
- (M) (1:55) Original Sound 2500 Oldies But Goodies Volumes 1-15 Box Set. *(this box set uses the "Waring - fds" noise reduction process)*
- (M) (1:58) EMI 96268 24 Greatest Hits Of All Time. *(with cold ending; missing reverb on the character "responses")*
- (E) (1:56) EMI 90614 Non Stop Party Rock.
- (M) (1:56) EMI 46580 Best Of.
- (M) (1:58) EMI 92809 Legendary Masters Series Volume 1. *(with cold ending; missing reverb on the character "responses")*
- (M) (1:55) Curb 77323 All Time Greatest Hits Of Rock 'N' Roll.
- (M) (1:56) Curb 77371 Greatest Hits.
- (M) (1:55) Capitol 48993 Spuds Mackenzie's Party Faves.
- (M) (1:56) Capitol 98138 Spring Break Volume 1.
- (M) (1:54) Time-Life 2RNR-05 Rock 'N' Roll Era - 1958.
- (M) (1:55) Time-Life R962-01 History Of Rock 'N' Roll: Rock 'N' Roll Classics 1957-1959.
- (M) (1:56) K-Tel 3062 Rockin' Rebels.
- (M) (1:55) Nouveau 1060 O.S.T. This Boy's Life.
- (M) (1:57) K-Tel 3437 Summer Songs.
- (M) (1:55) JCI 3188 1955 - Only Dance - 1959.
- (M) (1:55) Priority 50950 I Love Rock & Roll Volume 1: Hits Of The 50's.
- (M) (1:56) Right Stuff 53319 Hot Rod Rock Volume 4: Hot Rod Rebels.
- (M) (1:58) Razor & Tie 2162 Somethin' Else: The Fine Lookin' Hits Of Eddie Cochran. *(with cold ending; missing reverb on the character "responses")*
- (M) (1:54) K-Tel 4018 Forefathers Of Rock.

1959 C'MON EVERYBODY
- (M) (1:57) Capitol 98139 Spring Break Volume 2. *(with countoff)*
- (M) (1:55) Rhino 70742 Rock This Town: Rockabilly Hits Vol. 2.
- (M) (1:54) Time-Life 2RNR-20 Rock 'N' Roll Era - 1959: Still Rockin'. *(fadeout distorted)*
- (M) (1:54) Curb 77371 Greatest Hits.
- (M) (1:57) EMI 92809 Legendary Masters Series Volume 1. *(with countoff)*
- (M) (1:55) EMI 46580 Best Of.
- (M) (1:54) Nouveau 1060 O.S.T. This Boy's Life.
- (M) (1:54) Razor & Tie 2162 Somethin' Else: The Fine Lookin' Hits Of Eddie Cochran.

TOM COCHRANE
1992 LIFE IS A HIGHWAY
- (S) (4:25) Capitol 97723 Mad Mad World.

BRUCE COCKBURN
1980 WONDERING WHERE THE LIONS ARE
- (S) (3:42) Columbia 48736 Dancing In The Dragon's Jaws.
- (S) (3:39) Gold Mountain 1005 Waiting For A Miracle: Singles 1970-1987.
- (S) (3:40) Rhino 71891 Radio Daze: Pop Hits Of The 80's Volume Two.

JOE COCKER
1970 SHE CAME IN THROUGH THE BATHROOM WINDOW
- (S) (2:37) A&M 2503 Classics Volume 4.
- (S) (2:36) A&M 3326 Joe Cocker!
- (S) (2:36) Time-Life 2CLR-12 Classic Rock - 1969: The Beat Goes On.
- (S) (2:36) Time-Life OPCD-4521 Guitar Rock.
- (S) (2:36) Time-Life R968-15 Guitar Rock - FM Classics.
- (S) (2:36) A&M 314540236 The Long Voyage Home - Silver Anniversary Collection.

1970 THE LETTER
- (S) (4:20) A&M 2503 Classics Volume 4. *(from "Mad Dogs & Englishmen" - not the hit single version)*

(S) (4:16) A&M 3257 Greatest Hits. *(from "Mad Dogs & Englishmen" - not the hit single version)*

(S) (4:09) A&M 6002 Mad Dogs & Englishmen. *(not the hit single version)*

(S) (4:15) Priority 7065 70's Greatest Rock Hits Volume 13: Request Line. *(from "Mad Dogs & Englishmen" - not the hit single version)*

(S) (4:14) Time-Life SOD-01 Sounds Of The Seventies - 1970. *(from "Mad Dogs & Englishmen" - not the hit single version)*

(S) (4:16) Rebound 3145200320 Class Reunion 1970. *(from "Mad Dogs & Englishmen" - not the hit single version)*

(S) (4:22) A&M 314540236 The Long Voyage Home - Silver Anniversary Collection. *(from "Mad Dogs & Englishmen" - not the hit single version)*

(S) (4:21) Rebound 314520437 Classic Rock - 70's. *(from "Mad Dogs & Englishmen" - not the hit single version)*

1970 CRY ME A RIVER

(S) (4:03) Warner Special Products 27616 Classic Rock. *(with LP version intro and outro)*

(S) (4:01) JCI 3401 Live Volume 1. *(slight edit of LP version intro)*

(S) (3:53) A&M 2503 Classics Volume 4. *(with 45 version intro and LP version outro)*

(S) (3:47) A&M 6002 Mad Dogs & Englishmen. *(LP introduction is found at the end of the previous track; longer outro than the LP version)*

(S) (4:03) A&M 3257 Greatest Hits. *(with LP version intro and outro)*

(S) (3:53) Time-Life SOD-11 Sounds Of The Seventies - 1970: Take Two. *(45 version intro; LP version outro)*

(S) (3:57) A&M 314540236 The Long Voyage Home - Silver Anniversary Collection. *(slight edit of LP version intro)*

1971 HIGH TIME WE WENT

(S) (4:28) A&M 2503 Classics Volume 4.

(S) (4:26) A&M 3257 Greatest Hits.

(S) (4:27) Time-Life SOD-12 Sounds Of The Seventies - 1971: Take Two.

(S) (4:27) Time-Life R968-19 Guitar Rock - The Early '70s: Take Two.

(S) (4:26) A&M 314540236 The Long Voyage Home - Silver Anniversary Collection.

(S) (4:25) Rebound 314520364 Class Reunion '71.

1972 FEELING ALRIGHT

(S) (4:01) JCI 3101 Rockin' Sixties.

(S) (4:11) A&M 2503 Classics Volume 4.

(S) (4:08) A&M 3106 With A Little Help From My Friends.

(S) (4:09) A&M 3257 Greatest Hits.

(S) (3:59) Priority 8662 Hard 'N Heavy/70's Greatest Rock Hits Volume 1.

(S) (4:06) Time-Life 2CLR-17 Classic Rock - Rock Renaissance.

(S) (4:57) A&M 314540236 The Long Voyage Home - Silver Anniversary Collection. *(previously unreleased live version)*

released as by JOE COCKER and THE CHRIS STAINTON BAND:
1972 MIDNIGHT RIDER

(S) (4:00) A&M 2503 Classics Volume 4.

(S) (3:57) A&M 314540236 The Long Voyage Home - Silver Anniversary Collection.

released as by JOE COCKER:
1975 YOU ARE SO BEAUTIFUL

(S) (2:41) A&M 3175 I Can Stand A Little Rain.

(S) (2:41) A&M 2503 Classics Volume 4.

(S) (2:40) A&M 3257 Greatest Hits.

(S) (2:41) Time-Life SOD-08 Sounds Of The Seventies - 1975.

(S) (2:40) Rebound 314520237 I Can Stand A Little Rain.

(S) (2:41) LaserLight 12311 and 15936 The Wonder Years - First Love.

(S) (2:40) A&M 314540236 The Long Voyage Home - Silver Anniversary Collection.

released as by JOE COCKER and JENNIFER WARNES:
1982 UP WHERE WE BELONG

(S) (3:51) Island 90017 and 422842715 O.S.T. An Officer And A Gentleman.

(S) (3:55) Island 90684 and 842901 The Island Story.

(S) (3:57) Rhino 70677 Billboard Top Hits - 1982.

(S) (3:53) Sandstone 33048 and 5016 Cosmopolitan Volume 2.

(S) (3:56) Rhino 71868 Academy Award Winning Songs.

(S) (3:53) DCC Compact Classics 087 Night Moves Volume 5.

(S) (3:52) Capitol 81243 Joe Cocker - Best Of.

(S) (3:56) Time-Life R988-05 Sounds Of The Eighties: 1982.

(S) (3:56) Time-Life R138-18 Body Talk.

(S) (3:54) A&M 314540236 Joe Cocker - The Long Voyage Home - Silver Anniversary Collection.

(S) (3:56) Rhino 72280 Academy Award Winning Songs Volume 5.

(S) (3:52) Rebound 314520372 The Roots Of Rock: Soft Rock.

(S) (3:51) Rebound 314520438 No. 1 Hits Of The 80's.

(S) (3:56) Time-Life R988-31 Sounds Of The Eighties: Cinemax Movie Hits Of The '80s.

(S) (3:56) Time-Life R834-04 Body Talk - Together Forever.

(S) (3:50) Priority 50974 Premiere The Movie Magazine Presents The Greatest Soundtrack Love Songs.

(S) (3:55) Hip-O 40079 Essential '80s: 1980-1984.

(S) (3:54) Polygram TV 314555610 The One And Only Love Album.

(S) (3:51) Rebound 314520519 Love At The Movies.

released as by JOE COCKER:
1990 WHEN THE NIGHT COMES

(S) (4:47) Capitol 92861 One Night Of Sin. *(LP version)*

(S) (3:57) Capitol 81243 Best Of. *(45 version)*

(S) (4:44) A&M 314540236 The Long Voyage Home - Silver Anniversary Collection. *(LP version)*

COCK ROBIN
1985 WHEN YOUR HEART IS WEAK

(S) (4:36) Risky Business 57469 Don't Touch My 45's/Great Lost Singles Of The 80's.

(S) (4:37) EMI 32694 Living In Oblivion - The 80's Greatest Hits Volume Five.

(S) (4:38) Columbia 39582 Cock Robin.

DENNIS COFFEY and THE DETROIT GUITAR BAND
1972 SCORPIO

(S) (4:03) Rhino 70787 Soul Hits Of The 70's Volume 7. *(45 length)*

(S) (4:04) Rhino 71209 70's Smash Hits Volume 5. *(45 length)*

(S) (4:03) Time-Life R840-04 Sounds Of The Seventies: A Loss For Words. *(45 length)*

(S) (4:03) Flashback 72685 '70s Radio Hits Volume 5. *(45 length)*

(S) (4:21) Rhino 72851 Kurtis Blow Presents The History Of Rap Vol. 1. *(LP length)*

1972 TAURUS

MARC COHN
1991 WALKING IN MEMPHIS

(S) (4:14) JCI 3123 Harvest.

(S) (4:16) Atlantic 82178 Marc Cohn.

COZY COLE
1958 TOPSY II

(M) (3:33) Rhino 70644 Billboard's Top R&B Hits Of 1958.

(M) (3:33) Capitol Special Markets 57272 Great Instrumental Hits From Rock's Golden Years.

(M) (3:34) Curb 77402 All-Time Great Instrumental Hits Volume 2.

(M) (3:34) Rhino 71547 Let There Be Drums Volume 1: The 50's.

COZY COLE *(Continued)*
- (M) (3:33) Rhino 71601 Rock Instrumental Classics Volume 1: The Fifties.
- (M) (3:33) Rhino 72035 Rock Instrumental Classics Vols. 1-5 Box Set.
- (M) (3:32) Time-Life 2RNR-36 Rock 'N' Roll Era - Axes & Saxes/The Great Instrumentals.
- (M) (3:33) Time-Life HPD-30 Your Hit Parade - 50's Instrumentals.

1958 TURVY II

JUDE COLE
1990 BABY, IT'S TONIGHT
- (S) (3:38) Reprise 26164 A View From 3rd Street.

1990 TIME FOR LETTING GO
- (S) (4:17) Reprise 26164 A View From 3rd Street.

NATALIE COLE
1975 THIS WILL BE
- (S) (2:48) Capitol 46619 Collection.
- (S) (2:48) Capitol 97769 Inseparable.
- (S) (2:48) Sandstone 33048 and 5016 Cosmopolitan Volume 2.
- (S) (2:48) Rhino 71618 Soul Train Hall Of Fame/20th Anniversary.
- (S) (2:47) Razor & Tie 22047 Sweet 70's Soul.
- (S) (2:48) DCC Compact Classics 087 Night Moves Volume 5.
- (S) (2:47) Madacy Entertainment 1975 Rock On 1975.
- (S) (2:49) Hip-O 40030 The Glory Of Love - '70s Sweet & Soulful Love Songs.
- (S) (2:48) Capitol 35962 I've Got Love On My Mind.
- (S) (2:48) Time-Life R838-10 Solid Gold Soul - 1975.
- (S) (2:48) Capitol 38308 This Will Be: Natalie Cole's Everlasting Love.
- (S) (2:48) Time-Life R834-15 Body Talk - Once In Lifetime.

1976 INSEPARABLE
- (S) (2:24) Capitol 46619 Collection.
- (S) (2:24) Capitol 97769 Inseparable.
- (S) (2:23) Original Sound 8908 Best Love Songs Vol 3.
- (S) (2:23) Original Sound 9327 Best Love Songs Vol. 3 & 4.
- (S) (2:23) Original Sound 1236 Best Love Songs Box Set.
- (S) (2:24) Capitol 35962 I've Got Love On My Mind.
- (S) (2:24) Capitol 38308 This Will Be: Natalie Cole's Everlasting Love.

1976 SOPHISTICATED LADY (SHE'S A DIFFERENT LADY)
- (S) (3:26) Capitol 46619 Collection.
- (S) (3:26) Rhino 71433 In Yo Face! History Of Funk Volume 3.
- (S) (3:26) Priority 53789 Disco Attack.
- (S) (3:26) Capitol 38308 This Will Be: Natalie Cole's Everlasting Love.

1977 I'VE GOT LOVE ON MY MIND
- (S) (4:20) Capitol 46619 Collection.
- (S) (4:18) Right Stuff 30576 Slow Jams: The 70's Volume 4.
- (S) (4:19) Time-Life R138-18 Body Talk.
- (S) (4:17) DCC Compact Classics 142 Groove On! Volume 2.
- (S) (4:18) Capitol 35962 I've Got Love On My Mind.
- (S) (4:18) Time-Life R834-08 Body Talk - On My Mind.
- (S) (4:20) Capitol 38308 This Will Be: Natalie Cole's Everlasting Love.
- (S) (4:19) Time-Life R838-16 Solid Gold Soul 1977.

1978 OUR LOVE
- (S) (5:22) Capitol 46619 Collection. *(LP version)*
- (S) (4:00) Priority 53796 Hot And Sexy - Love And Romance Volume 3. *(45 version)*
- (S) (4:01) Rhino 72129 Soul Hits Of The 70's Vol. 19. *(45 version)*
- (S) (4:01) Madacy Entertainment 1978 Rock On 1978. *(45 version)*
- (S) (5:22) One Way 19084 Thankful. *(LP version)*
- (S) (5:21) Capitol 35962 I've Got Love On My Mind. *(LP version)*
- (S) (5:26) Capitol 38308 This Will Be: Natalie Cole's Everlasting Love. *(LP version)*

- (S) (3:59) Time-Life R838-17 Solid Gold Soul 1978. *(45 version)*
- (S) (5:20) Time-Life R834-12 Body Talk - By Candlelight. *(LP version)*

1980 SOMEONE THAT I USED TO LOVE
- (S) (4:03) Capitol 46619 Collection.
- (S) (4:03) Priority 7040 Making Love.
- (S) (4:03) Priority 53700 80's Greatest Rock Hits Volume 13 - Soft Sounds.
- (S) (4:04) One Way 19083 Don't Look Back.
- (S) (4:03) Capitol 35962 I've Got Love On My Mind.
- (S) (4:03) Time-Life R834-18 Body Talk - Romantic Moments.

1987 JUMP START
- (S) (4:21) EMI 91419 MTV, BET, VH-1 Power Players. *(45 version)*
- (S) (6:26) Manhattan 46759 Everlasting. *(LP version)*
- (S) (6:26) Elektra 61114 Everlasting. *(LP version)*

1988 I LIVE FOR YOUR LOVE
- (S) (4:23) JCI 2701 Slow Grooves.
- (S) (4:25) Elektra 61114 Everlasting.
- (S) (4:25) Manhattan 46759 Everlasting.

1988 PINK CADILLAC
- (S) (4:27) Manhattan 46759 Everlasting.
- (S) (4:27) Elektra 61114 Everlasting.

1989 MISS YOU LIKE CRAZY
- (S) (3:53) JCI 3124 Rhythm Of The Night.
- (S) (3:53) Elektra 61115 Good To Be Back.
- (S) (3:53) EMI 48902 Good To Be Back.
- (S) (3:53) Priority 53681 80's Greatest Rock Hits - Agony & Ecstasy.

1990 WILD WOMEN DO
- (S) (4:01) EMI 93492 O.S.T. Pretty Woman.

released as by NATALIE COLE with NAT KING COLE:
1991 UNFORGETTABLE
- (S) (3:27) Capitol 29687 Nat King Cole - The Greatest Hits.
- (S) (3:27) Elektra 61049 and 61243 Natalie Cole - Unforgettable With Love.

NAT KING COLE
1955 DARLING JE VOUS AIME BEAUCOUP
- (M) (2:48) Capitol 93590 Capitol Collector's Series.
- (S) (2:48) Capitol 95129 Story. *(rerecording)*
- (M) (2:48) Capitol 99230 The Unforgettable.
- (M) (2:48) Capitol 99777 Nat King Cole Box Set.
- (M) (2:48) Time-Life HPD-23 Your Hit Parade - The Late 50's.
- (M) (2:48) Capitol 29687 The Greatest Hits.
- (M) (2:47) Time-Life R974-04 Many Moods Of Romance - As Time Goes By.

1955 A BLOSSOM FELL
- (M) (2:30) Capitol 93590 Capitol Collector's Series.
- (M) (2:30) Capitol 99777 Nat King Cole Box Set.
- (M) (2:31) Time-Life HPD-09 Your Hit Parade 1955.
- (M) (2:48) Capitol 29687 The Greatest Hits.

1955 IF I MAY
- (S) (2:56) Capitol 95129 Story. *(rerecording)*
- (M) (3:02) Capitol 99777 Nat King Cole Box Set.
- (S) (2:56) Pair 1222 Let's Fall In Love. *(rerecording)*
- (M) (3:02) Capitol 29687 The Greatest Hits.

1955 SOMEONE YOU LOVE
1955 FORGIVE MY HEART
1956 ASK ME
1956 TOO YOUNG TO GO STEADY
1956 THAT'S ALL THERE IS TO THAT
1956 NIGHT LIGHTS
- (M) (2:47) Capitol 99777 Nat King Cole Box Set.
- (S) (2:47) Capitol 95129 Story. *(rerecording)*
- (S) (2:48) Pair 1222 Let's Fall In Love. *(rerecording)*
- (M) (2:47) Time-Life HPD-36 Your Hit Parade - The 50's Pop Revival.

1956 TO THE ENDS OF THE EARTH
- (S) (2:24) Capitol 95129 Story. *(rerecording)*
- (M) (2:17) Capitol 99777 Nat King Cole Box Set.

1957 BALLERINA
- (S) (2:40) Capitol 95129 Story. *(rerecording)*
- (M) (2:50) Capitol 99777 Nat King Cole Box Set.
- (S) (2:40) Pair 1222 Let's Fall In Love. *(rerecording)*

1957 SEND FOR ME
(S) (2:29) Capitol 95129 Story. *(rerecording)*
(M) (2:36) Capitol 93590 Capitol Collector's Series.
(M) (2:35) Capitol 99777 Nat King Cole Box Set.
(S) (2:28) Pair 1222 Let's Fall In Love. *(rerecording)*
(M) (2:36) Time-Life HPD-17 Your Hit Parade - 1957.
(M) (2:35) Capitol 29687 The Greatest Hits.
(M) (2:36) Capitol 89545 The Billy May Sessions.

1957 MY PERSONAL POSSESSION
1957 WITH YOU ON MY MIND
(M) (2:36) Capitol 89545 The Billy May Sessions.

1958 ANGEL SMILE
1958 LOOKING BACK
(S) (2:24) Capitol 95129 Story. *(rerecording)*
(M) (2:11) Time-Life HPD-11 Your Hit Parade 1958.
(S) (2:24) Capitol 29687 The Greatest Hits. *(rerecording)*

1958 COME CLOSER TO ME
1958 NON DIMENTICAR (DON'T FORGET)
(S) (3:06) Capitol 95129 Story. *(rerecording)*
(S) (3:37) Capitol 93590 Capitol Collector's Series.
(includes :49 of studio talk)
(M) (2:47) Capitol 99230 The Unforgettable.
(S) (2:47) Capitol 99777 Nat King Cole Box Set.
(S) (3:06) Pair 1222 Let's Fall In Love. *(rerecording)*

1962 RAMBLIN' ROSE
(S) (2:47) Capitol 93590 Capitol Collector's Series.
(S) (2:47) Capitol 46651 Ramblin' Rose.
(S) (2:47) Capitol 98670 Memories Are Made Of This.
(S) (2:47) Capitol 99777 Nat King Cole Box Set.
(S) (2:46) Time-Life HPD-32 Your Hit Parade - Into The 60's.
(S) (2:45) Time-Life R138/05 Look Of Love.
(S) (2:47) Capitol 29687 The Greatest Hits.
(S) (2:47) JCI 7022 Those Wonderful Years - It Must Be Him.

1962 DEAR LONELY HEARTS
(S) (3:07) Capitol 93590 Capitol Collector's Series.
(S) (3:06) Capitol 46651 Ramblin' Rose.

1963 THOSE LAZY HAZY CRAZY DAYS OF SUMMER
(S) (2:53) Capitol 93590 Capitol Collector's Series.
(includes :30 of studio talk)
(S) (2:23) Enigma 73531 O.S.T. Scandal.
(S) (2:22) Time-Life HPD-33 Your Hit Parade - The Early 60's.
(S) (2:22) Capitol 29687 The Greatest Hits.
(S) (2:22) Nick At Nite/550 Music 63436 Patio Pool Party.

1963 THAT SUNDAY, THAT SUMMER
(S) (3:09) Capitol 99230 The Unforgettable.
(S) (3:10) Capitol 99777 Nat King Cole Box Set.

1964 I DON'T WANT TO BE HURT ANYMORE
1964 I DON'T WANT TO SEE TOMORROW
(S) (2:35) Capitol 99777 Nat King Cole Box Set.

released as by NATALIE COLE with NAT KING COLE:
1991 UNFORGETTABLE
(S) (3:27) Capitol 29687 Nat King Cole - The Greatest Hits.
(S) (3:27) Elektra 61049 and 61243 Natalie Cole - Unforgettable With Love.

PAULA COLE
1997 WHERE HAVE ALL THE COWBOYS GONE?
(S) (4:26) Imago/Warner Brothers 46424 and 46646 This Fire.
(S) (4:16) Cold Front 6254 Club Mix '98. *(all selections on this cd are segued together)*
(S) (4:25) MCA 11752 1998 Grammy Nominees.

1998 I DON'T WANT TO WAIT
(S) (5:18) Imago/Warner Brothers 46424 and 46646 This Fire.

COLLECTIVE SOUL
1994 SHINE
(S) (5:05) Atlantic 82596 Hints Allegations And Things Left Unsaid.

1995 DECEMBER
(S) (4:45) Atlantic 82745 Collective Soul.

1996 THE WORLD I KNOW
(S) (4:15) Atlantic 82745 Collective Soul.

DAVE and ANSIL COLLINS
1971 DOUBLE BARREL
(M) (2:47) Rhino 70785 Soul Hits Of The 70's Volume 5.
(M) (2:47) Rhino 72028 Soul Hits Of The 70's Volumes 1-5 Box Set.
(M) (2:46) Mango 162539935 Story Of Jamaican Music.
(M) (2:48) Ras 3225 Double Barrel.
(M) (2:48) Simitar 55112 Great Reggae.

EDWYN COLLINS
1995 A GIRL LIKE YOU
(S) (3:55) Bar/None 058 Gorgeous George.
(S) (3:55) A&M 314540384 O.S.T. Empire Records.

JUDY COLLINS
1968 BOTH SIDES NOW
(S) (3:13) Elektra 74012 Wildflowers. *(LP version)*
(S) (3:12) Elektra 75030 Colors Of The Day/Best Of. *(45 version)*
(S) (3:10) Time-Life R103-33 Singers & Songwriters. *(45 version)*
(S) (3:13) Elektra 62104 Forever - An Anthology. *(LP version)*

1969 SOMEDAY SOON
(S) (3:41) Elektra 74033 Who Knows Where The Time Goes.
(S) (3:41) Time-Life R105-26 Our Songs: Singers & Songwriters Encore.
(S) (3:44) K-Tel 3319 Rodeo's Greatest Hits.
(S) (3:42) Elektra 62104 Forever - An Anthology.

1971 AMAZING GRACE
(S) (4:03) Elektra 75010 Whales & Nightingales.
(S) (4:06) Elektra 75030 Colors Of The Day/Best Of.
(S) (4:06) Elektra 62104 Forever - An Anthology.

1973 COOK WITH HONEY
(S) (3:28) Elektra 75053 True Stories And Other Dreams.

1977 SEND IN THE CLOWNS
(S) (3:58) Elektra 111 Judith.
(S) (4:01) Time-Life R103-33 Singers & Songwriters.
(S) (4:01) JCI 3146 1975 - Only Love - 1979.
(S) (3:59) Elektra 62104 Forever - An Anthology.

PHIL COLLINS
1981 I MISSED AGAIN
(S) (3:41) Atlantic 16029 Face Value.
(S) (3:42) Atlantic 82520 Face Value. *(gold disc)*

1981 IN THE AIR TONIGHT
(S) (5:26) MCA 6150 Music From The Television Series "Miami Vice". *(LP version)*
(S) (5:28) Atlantic 81908 Classic Rock 1966-1988. *(LP version)*
(S) (5:28) Atlantic 82306 Atlantic Rock & Roll Box Set. *(LP version)*
(S) (5:31) Atlantic 16029 Face Value. *(LP version)*
(S) (5:30) Atlantic 82520 Face Value (Gold Disc). *(LP version)*
(S) (5:20) Time-Life R988-25 Sounds Of The Eighties: The Rolling Stone Collection 1980-1981. *(LP version)*
(S) (5:23) Time-Life R13610 Gold And Platinum Box Set - The Ultimate Rock Collection. *(LP version)*
(S) (4:57) Atlantic 83088 Atlantic Records: 50 Years - The Gold Anniversary Collection. *(45 version)*

1983 YOU CAN'T HURRY LOVE
(S) (2:52) Atlantic 80035 Hello, I Must Be Going.

1983 I DON'T CARE ANYMORE
(S) (5:00) Atlantic 80035 Hello, I Must Be Going. *(LP version)*

1984 AGAINST ALL ODDS
(S) (3:23) Atlantic 81910 Hit Singles 1980-1988.
(S) (3:23) Atlantic 80152 O.S.T. Against All Odds.
(S) (3:23) Time-Life R988-31 Sounds Of The Eighties: Cinemax Movie Hits Of The '80s.

released as by PHILIP BAILEY with PHIL COLLINS:
1985 EASY LOVER
(actual 45 time is (4:47) not (4:40) as stated on the record label)
(S) (5:04) Columbia 39542 Philip Bailey - Chinese Wall. *(LP length)*

PHIL COLLINS (Continued)

    (S) (4:40)   Time-Life R988-17 Sounds Of The Eighties: The Mid '80s Take Two. *(:07 shorter than the 45 length)*

released as by PHIL COLLINS:

1985 ONE MORE NIGHT

    (S) (6:20)   Atlantic 81847 12" Er's. *(12" single version)*
    (S) (4:46)   Atlantic 81240 No Jacket Required. *(LP length)*
    (S) (4:44)   Madacy Entertainment 6803 Power Of Love. *(LP length)*

1985 SUSSUDIO

    (S) (6:32)   JCI 3122 Lost Mixes. *(12" single version)*
    (S) (6:33)   Atlantic 81847 12" Er's. *(12" single version)*
    (S) (4:22)   Atlantic 81240 No Jacket Required.

1985 DON'T LOSE MY NUMBER
(dj copies of this song ran (4:11) and (4:46); commercial copies were all (4:46))

    (S) (6:33)   Atlantic 81847 12" Er's. *(12" single version)*
    (S) (4:48)   Atlantic 81240 No Jacket Required.

released as by PHIL COLLINS and MARYLIN MARTIN:

1985 SEPARATE LIVES (LOVE THEME FROM WHITE KNIGHTS)

    (S) (4:05)   Atlantic 81273 O.S.T. White Knights.
    (S) (4:06)   Madacy Entertainment 6806 Best Of Love.

released as by PHIL COLLINS:

1986 TAKE ME HOME

    (S) (5:49)   MCA 6192 Miami Vice II. *(LP version)*
    (S) (8:03)   Atlantic 81847 12" Er's. *(12" single version)*
    (S) (5:50)   Atlantic 81240 No Jacket Required. *(LP version)*

1988 GROOVY KIND OF LOVE

    (S) (3:27)   Atlantic 81905 O.S.T. Buster.
    (S) (3:27)   Foundation/WEA 26097 Super Sessions Volume Two.

1989 TWO HEARTS

    (S) (3:22)   Atlantic 81905 O.S.T. Buster.

1989 ANOTHER DAY IN PARADISE

    (S) (5:21)   Atlantic 82050 ...But Seriously. *(LP version)*

1990 I WISH IT WOULD RAIN DOWN

    (S) (5:27)   Atlantic 82050 ...But Seriously.

1990 DO YOU REMEMBER?

    (S) (4:35)   Atlantic 82050 ...But Seriously.

1990 SOMETHING HAPPENED ON THE WAY TO HEAVEN

    (S) (4:50)   Atlantic 82050 ...But Seriously. *(LP version)*

1990 HANG IN LONG ENOUGH

    (S) (4:44)   Atlantic 82050 ...But Seriously.

released as by DAVID CROSBY & PHIL COLLINS:

1993 HERO

    (S) (4:38)   Atlantic 82484 David Crosby - Thousand Roads.

released as by PHIL COLLINS:

1993 BOTH SIDES OF THE STORY

    (S) (6:38)   Atlantic 82550 Both Sides.

1994 EVERYDAY

    (S) (5:41)   Atlantic 82550 Both Sides.

TYLER COLLINS

1990 GIRLS NITE OUT

    (S) (4:38)   RCA 61144 The RCA Records Label: The 1st Note In Black Music.
    (S) (4:37)   RCA 9642 Girls Nite Out.

COLOR ME BADD

1991 I WANNA SEX YOU UP

    (S) (4:03)   Giant 24409 O.S.T. New Jack City.
    (S) (4:22)   Giant 24480 Young, Gifted And Badd. *(remixed)*
    (S) (4:05)   Giant 24429 C.M.B.
    (S) (4:05)   MCA 11329 Soul Train 25th Anniversary Box Set.
    (S) (4:04)   Cold Front 6247 Classic Club Mix - Dance Jams. *(all selections on this cd are segued together)*
    (S) (4:05)   Razor & Tie 4569 '90s Style.

1991 I ADORE MI AMOR

    (S) (4:49)   Foundation/RCA 66563 Number 1 Hit Mix.
    (S) (5:16)   Giant 24480 Young, Gifted And Badd. *(remixed)*

1992 ALL-4-LOVE

    (S) (3:13)   Tommy Boy 1053 MTV Party To Go Volume 2. *(all tracks on this cd are segued together)*

    (S) (4:18)   Giant 24480 Young, Gifted And Badd. *(remixed)*
    (S) (4:48)   Giant 24429 C.M.B. *(LP version)*
    (S) (3:29)   Rhino 72409 New Jack Hits. *(45 version)*
    (S) (3:14)   JCI 3132 1990 - Only Rock 'n Roll - 1994. *(edit of 45 version)*
    (S) (3:29)   K-Tel 3848 90s Now Volume 2. *(45 version)*

1992 THINKIN' BACK

    (S) (5:27)   Giant 24480 Young, Gifted And Badd. *(remixed)*
    (S) (5:21)   Giant 24429 C.M.B.

1992 SLOW MOTION

    (S) (4:34)   Giant 24480 Young, Gifted And Badd. *(remixed)*
    (S) (4:24)   Giant 24429 C.M.B.

1992 FOREVER LOVE

    (S) (5:09)   Perspective 1004 O.S.T. Mo' Money.
    (S) (5:09)   Giant 24480 Young, Gifted And Badd. *(remixed)*

1993 TIME AND CHANCE

    (S) (4:20)   Giant 24524 Time And Chance.

1994 CHOOSE

    (S) (4:22)   Giant 24524 Time And Chance.

1996 THE EARTH, THE SUN, THE RAIN

    (S) (4:15)   Giant 24622 Now & Forever.

JESSI COLTER

1975 I'M NOT LISA

    (S) (3:19)   Rhino 70762 Super Hits Of The 70's Volume 15.
    (S) (3:20)   EMI 90602 Heartbreak Hotel.
    (S) (3:20)   Curb 77344 70's Hits - Country Volume 1.
    (S) (3:19)   Time-Life CCD-04 Contemporary Country - The Mid 70's.
    (S) (3:19)   K-Tel 567 Country Music Classics Volume IV.
    (S) (3:19)   Liberty 32071 Collection.
    (S) (3:19)   K-Tel 3471 Desperados.
    (S) (3:19)   K-Tel 3358 101 Greatest Country Hits Vol. Four: Mellow Country.
    (S) (3:19)   Time-Life AM1-22 AM Gold - 1975.
    (S) (3:19)   Hip-O 40086 The Class Of Country 1975-1979.
    (S) (3:19)   EMI-Capitol Music Special Markets 19545 Lost Hits Of The '70s.

CHI COLTRANE

1972 THUNDER AND LIGHTNING
(actual 45 time is (3:00) not (2:56) as stated on the record label)

    (S) (3:00)   Rhino 70929 Super Hits Of The 70's Volume 9.
    (S) (3:00)   Columbia/Legacy 46160 Rock Artifacts Volume 1.
    (S) (2:58)   Razor & Tie 21640 Those Fabulous 70's.
    (S) (3:00)   Time-Life SOD-21 Sounds Of The Seventies - Rock 'N' Soul Seventies.
    (S) (3:00)   Collectables 5804 Golden Classics.
    (S) (2:59)   Eclipse Music Group 64893 Rock 'n Roll Relix 1972-1973.
    (S) (2:59)   Eclipse Music Group 64897 Rock 'n Roll Relix 1970-1979.
    (S) (3:00)   K-Tel 3912 Superstars Greatest Hits Volume 1.

SHAWN COLVIN

1997 SUNNY CAME HOME

    (S) (4:24)   Columbia 67119 A Few Small Repairs.
    (S) (4:23)   MCA 11752 1998 Grammy Nominees.

COMMANDER CODY and HIS LOST PLANET AIRMEN

1972 HOT ROD LINCOLN

    (S) (2:42)   Rhino 70928 Super Hits Of The 70's Volume 8.
    (S) (2:41)   MCA 25240 Classic Rock Volume 3.
    (S) (2:41)   Rhino 70742 Rock This Town: Rockabilly Hits Volume 2.
    (S) (2:41)   MCA 10092 Too Much Fun/Best Of.
    (S) (2:41)   MCA 31185 Lost In The Ozone.
    (S) (2:41)   Priority 8670 Hitchin A Ride/70's Greatest Rock Hits Volume 10.
    (S) (2:42)   Rhino 71210 70's Smash Hits Volume 6.
    (S) (2:41)   Compose 9927 Car And Driver/Greatest Car Songs.
    (S) (2:41)   Time-Life SOD-13 Sounds Of The Seventies - 1972: Take Two.

(S) (2:41) Rhino 71750 Spy Magazine Presents: White Men Can't Wrap.
(S) (2:41) MCA 10462 The Coach Collection.
(S) (2:42) K-Tel 3095 Country Comedy Classics.
(S) (2:41) Time-Life R968-11 Guitar Rock - The Early '70s.
(S) (2:41) MCA Special Products 20893 Greatest Tour Bands Ever Recorded.
(S) (2:42) Flashback 72686 '70s Radio Hits Volume 6.
(S) (2:41) Hip-O 40062 Under My Wheels: 12 Road Trippin' Tracks.
(S) (2:42) Time-Life R830-03 The Dr. Demento Collection: The Early '70s.
(S) (2:42) K-Tel 3996 Rockin' Down The Highway.

COMMODORES
1974 MACHINE GUN
(S) (2:39) Motown 6068 Compact Command Performances.
(S) (2:41) Motown 6028 All The Great Hits.
(S) (2:40) Motown 0912 Greatest Hits.
(S) (2:38) SBR 011 Hits Volume 1. (all tracks on this cd are rerecorded)
(S) (2:40) Motown 8502 Motown Legends.
(S) (2:40) Motown 374638502 Motown Legends - Three Times A Lady.
(S) (2:39) Motown 314530358 Anthology.
(S) (2:37) Motown 314530498 Funkology Volume One - Got To Give It Up.
(S) (2:38) Motown 314530501 The Ultimate Collection.
(S) (2:38) Capitol 56312 O.S.T. Boogie Nights.

1975 SLIPPERY WHEN WET
(S) (3:18) Motown 6068 Compact Command Performances. (LP length)
(S) (3:18) Motown 5240 Caught In The Act. (LP length)
(S) (2:58) Motown 0912 Greatest Hits. (45 length)
(S) (3:10) SBR 011 Hits Volume 1. (all tracks on this cd are rerecorded)
(S) (3:19) Motown 314530358 Anthology. (LP length)
(S) (3:18) Motown 314530531 Motown Year By Year - 1975. (LP length)
(S) (3:16) Motown 314530501 The Ultimate Collection. (LP length)

1976 SWEET LOVE
(S) (6:32) Motown 6143 and 5386 The Composer Series: Lionel Richie. (LP version)
(S) (6:28) Motown 6192 You Can't Hurry Love: All The Great Love Songs Of The Past 25 Years. (LP version)
(S) (3:25) Motown 6068 Compact Command Performances. (45 version)
(S) (3:25) Motown 6107 All The Great Love Songs. (45 version)
(S) (3:23) Motown 0912 Greatest Hits. (45 version)
(S) (3:23) SBR 011 Hits Volume 1. (all tracks on this cd are rerecorded)
(S) (3:26) Motown 314530358 Anthology. (45 version)
(S) (3:25) Motown 314530531 Motown Year By Year - 1975. (45 version)
(S) (3:24) Rebound 314520367 Soul Classics - Quiet Storm/The 70's. (45 version)
(S) (6:33) Motown 314530501 The Ultimate Collection. (LP version)
(S) (3:24) Motown 314530846 Lionel Richie: Truly - The Love Songs. (45 version)
(S) (3:25) JCI 3175 1975 - Only Soul - 1979. (45 version)
(S) (3:25) Time-Life R834-13 Body Talk - Just The Two Of Us. (45 version)

1976 JUST TO BE CLOSE TO YOU
(actual 45 time is (3:27) not (3:05) as stated on the record label)
(S) (6:23) Motown 6143 and 5386 The Composer Series: Lionel Richie. (LP version)
(S) (6:23) Motown 6107 All The Great Love Songs. (LP version)
(S) (6:57) Motown 8044 and 8144 Hot On The Tracks/In The Pocket. (:36 longer than the LP version)

(S) (6:21) Motown 5257 Hot On The Tracks. (LP version)
(S) (3:18) Motown 0912 Greatest Hits. (neither the 45 or LP version)
(S) (3:23) SBR 011 Hits Volume 1. (all tracks on this cd are rerecorded)
(S) (3:19) Motown 314530358 Anthology. (neither the 45 or LP version)
(S) (3:12) Motown 314530513 Motown Year By Year 1976. (neither the 45 or LP version)
(S) (3:15) K-Tel 3535 Slow Groove Love Jams Of The 70's. (neither the 45 or LP version)
(S) (7:05) Motown 314530573 Baddest Love Jams Volume 2 - Fire And Desire. (:44 longer than the LP version)
(S) (3:19) Rebound 314520368 Class Reunion '76. (neither the 45 or LP version)
(S) (6:21) Motown 314530501 The Ultimate Collection. (LP version)
(S) (6:21) Rebound 314520447 Soul Classics - Best Of The 70's. (LP version)
(S) (3:27) Motown 314530846 Lionel Richie: Truly - The Love Songs. (45 version)
(S) (3:17) Beast 53442 Original Players Of Love. (neither the 45 or LP version)
(S) (6:21) Time-Life R834-12 Body Talk - By Candlelight. (LP version)

1977 EASY
(actual 45 time is (4:15) not (3:58) as stated on the record label)
(S) (4:15) Motown 6137 20 Greatest Songs In Motown History.
(S) (4:16) Motown 6143 and 5386 The Composer Series: Lionel Richie.
(S) (4:49) Motown 6068 Compact Command Performances. (:34 longer than either the 45 or LP)
(S) (4:16) Motown 6107 All The Great Love Songs.
(S) (4:09) Motown 8039 and 8139 Heroes/Commodores. (:06 shorter than either the 45 or LP)
(S) (4:15) Motown 5222 Commodores.
(S) (4:09) Motown 6028 All The Great Hits. (:06 shorter than either the 45 or LP)
(S) (4:14) Motown 0912 Greatest Hits.
(S) (4:10) SBR 011 Hits Volume 1. (all tracks on this cd are rerecorded)
(S) (4:20) Motown 6358 Hitsville USA Volume Two.
(S) (4:21) Motown 314530358 Anthology.
(S) (4:22) Motown 314530569 Motown Milestones - Motown Love Songs.
(S) (4:20) Time-Life AM1-24 AM Gold - 1977.
(S) (4:15) Motown 314530501 The Ultimate Collection.
(S) (4:16) Time-Life R838-16 Solid Gold Soul 1977.
(S) (4:12) Motown 314530846 Lionel Richie: Truly - The Love Songs.
(S) (4:18) Simitar 55512 The Number One's: Lovin' Feelings.
(S) (4:16) Time-Life R834-17 Body Talk - Heart To Heart.

1977 BRICK HOUSE
(S) (3:29) Motown 9072 Motown Dance Party Volume 2. (all selections on this cd are segued together)
(S) (3:43) Motown 6068 Compact Command Performances. (:15 longer than either the 45 or LP)
(S) (3:18) Motown 8039 and 8139 Heroes/Commodores. (:10 shorter than either the 45 or LP)
(S) (3:26) Motown 5222 Commodores.
(S) (3:28) Motown 6028 All The Great Hits.
(S) (3:24) Motown 0912 Greatest Hits.
(S) (3:19) SBR 011 Hits Volume 1. (all tracks on this cd are rerecorded)
(S) (3:27) Motown 374638502 Motown Legends - Three Times A Lady.
(S) (3:32) Motown 6358 Hitsville USA Volume Two.
(S) (3:26) Time-Life SOD-17 Sounds Of The Seventies - 1977: Take Two.
(S) (3:27) Priority 53730 Mega Hits Dance Classics Vol. 13.
(S) (3:43) Rebound 314520298 Disco Nights Vol. 9. (:15 longer than either the 45 or LP)
(S) (3:33) Motown 314530358 Anthology.
(S) (3:27) Thump 4040 Old School Volume 4.

COMMODORES *(Continued)*

(S) (6:11) Motown 314530498 Funkology Volume One - Got To Give It Up. *(12" single version)*

(S) (3:33) MCA 11231 O.S.T. To Wong Foo, Thanks For Everything.

(S) (3:30) Rebound 314520432 Disco Nights Vol. XI - Disco's Leading Men.

(S) (3:26) Motown 314530501 The Ultimate Collection.

(S) (3:32) Rebound 314520430 Funk Classics Of The 70's Vol. 2.

(S) (3:30) Robbins 75002 Strip Jointz - Hot Songs For Sexy Dancers.

(S) (3:32) Chronicles 314555137 Funk Of The 70's.

(S) (3:31) Time-Life R840-07 Sounds Of The Seventies: '70s Dance Party 1976-1977.

(S) (3:31) K-Tel 4065 K-Tel's Original Party Music Vol. 1.

1978 TOO HOT TA TROT

(S) (3:31) Motown 6068 Compact Command Performances. *(45 version)*

(S) (3:28) Motown 0912 Greatest Hits. *(45 version)*

(S) (3:09) SBR 011 Hits Volume 1. *(all tracks on this cd are rerecorded)*

(S) (3:30) Motown 314530358 Anthology. *(45 version)*

(S) (3:24) Rebound 314520337 Compiled From O.S.T. Thank God It's Friday. *(45 version)*

(S) (3:24) Casablanca 314534606 O.S.T. Thank God It's Friday. *(45 version)*

(S) (5:36) Motown 314530501 The Ultimate Collection. *(LP version)*

1978 THREE TIMES A LADY
(dj copies of this 45 ran (3:35) and (4:59); commercial copies were all (3:35))

(S) (6:37) Motown 6177 Endless Love. *(LP version)*

(S) (3:35) Motown 6137 20 Greatest Songs In Motown History. *(45 version)*

(S) (6:38) Motown 6143 and 5386 The Composer Series: Lionel Richie. *(LP version)*

(S) (3:36) Motown 5344 Every Great Motown Song: The First 25 Years Volume 2. *(45 version)*

(S) (3:35) Motown 9060 Motown's Biggest Pop Hits. *(45 version)*

(S) (3:35) Motown 9082 and 5385 Great Motown Love Songs. *(45 version)*

(S) (6:37) Motown 0937 20/20 Twenty No. 1 Hits From Twenty Years At Motown. *(LP version)*

(S) (3:35) Motown 8034 and 8134 Every Great Motown Song: The First 25 Years Volumes 1 & 2. *(45 version)*

(S) (3:36) Motown 9035 and 5324 Top Ten With A Bullet! *(45 version)*

(S) (3:36) Motown 6132 25 #1 Hits From 25 Years Volume 2. *(45 version)*

(S) (3:35) Motown 6068 Compact Command Performances. *(45 version)*

(S) (3:36) Motown 6107 All The Great Love Songs. *(45 version)*

(S) (3:36) Motown 8014 and 8114 Natural High/Midnight Magic. *(45 version)*

(S) (6:38) Motown 5293 Natural High. *(LP version)*

(S) (3:35) Motown 6028 All The Great Hits. *(45 version)*

(S) (6:36) Motown 0912 Greatest Hits. *(LP version)*

(S) (3:34) SBR 011 Hits Volume 1. *(all tracks on this cd are rerecorded)*

(S) (3:35) Motown 374638502 Motown Legends - Three Times A Lady. *(45 version)*

(S) (3:35) Motown 6358 Hitsville USA Volume Two. *(45 version)*

(S) (3:35) Rhino 71618 Soul Train Hall Of Fame/20th Anniversary. *(45 version)*

(S) (3:35) Polygram Special Markets 314520030 Motown Legends - Love Songs. *(45 version)*

(S) (3:36) Motown 314530358 Anthology. *(45 version)*

(S) (3:35) Right Stuff 30576 Slow Jams: The 70's Volume 4. *(45 version)*

(S) (3:36) Motown 314530569 Motown Milestones - Motown Love Songs. *(45 version)*

(S) (3:35) Time-Life R834-04 Body Talk - Together Forever. *(45 version)*

(S) (6:38) Motown 314530501 The Ultimate Collection. *(LP version)*

(S) (3:35) Motown 314530846 Lionel Richie: Truly - The Love Songs. *(45 version)*

(S) (3:35) Motown 314530849 Motown 40 Forever. *(45 version)*

(S) (3:36) Time-Life R814-03 Love Songs. *(45 version)*

(S) (3:35) Time-Life AM1-25 AM Gold - 1978. *(45 version)*

(S) (3:36) Rebound 314520492 Class Reunion '78. *(45 version)*

1979 SAIL ON
(actual LP time is (5:32) not (5:43) as stated on the record label)

(S) (5:32) Motown 6143 and 5386 The Composer Series: Lionel Richie. *(LP version)*

(S) (3:59) Motown 5344 Every Great Motown Song: The First 25 Years Volume 2. *(45 version)*

(S) (3:59) Motown 8034 and 8134 Every Great Motown Song: The First 25 Years Volumes 1 & 2. *(45 version)*

(S) (5:33) Motown 6068 Compact Command Performances. *(LP version)*

(S) (3:59) Motown 6107 All The Great Love Songs. *(45 version)*

(S) (5:31) Motown 5348 Midnight Magic. *(LP version)*

(S) (3:58) Motown 6028 All The Great Hits. *(45 version)*

(S) (3:58) Motown 374638502 Motown Legends - Three Times A Lady. *(45 version)*

(S) (3:56) Motown 6358 Hitsville USA Volume Two. *(45 version)*

(S) (3:56) Motown 314530358 Anthology. *(45 version)*

(S) (3:58) Rebound 314520370 Soul Classics - Quiet Storm/The 80's. *(45 version)*

(S) (3:55) Motown 314530846 Lionel Richie: Truly - The Love Songs. *(45 version)*

(S) (3:59) Time-Life R834-18 Body Talk - Romantic Moments. *(45 version)*

1979 STILL
(actual LP time is (5:48) not (5:43) as stated on the record label)

(S) (5:48) Motown 6137 20 Greatest Songs In Motown History. *(LP version)*

(S) (5:48) Motown 6143 and 5386 The Composer Series: Lionel Richie. *(LP version)*

(S) (5:46) Motown 0937 20/20 Twenty No. 1 Hits From Twenty Years At Motown. *(LP version)*

(S) (5:48) Motown 9035 and 5324 Top Ten With A Bullet! *(LP version)*

(S) (3:44) Motown 6132 25 #1 Hits From 25 Years Volume 2. *(45 version)*

(S) (5:48) Motown 6068 Compact Command Performances. *(LP version)*

(S) (3:44) Motown 6107 All The Great Love Songs. *(45 version)*

(S) (5:48) Motown 5348 Midnight Magic. *(LP version)*

(S) (5:48) Motown 8014 and 8114 Natural High/Midnight Magic. *(LP version)*

(S) (3:41) Motown 6028 All The Great Hits. *(45 version)*

(S) (3:45) Motown 6358 Hitsville USA Volume Two. *(45 version)*

(S) (5:46) Polygram Special Markets 314520030 Motown Legends - Love Songs. *(LP version)*

(S) (3:44) Rebound 314520270 Class Reunion 1979. *(45 version)*

(S) (3:45) Motown 314530358 Anthology. *(45 version)*

(S) (3:43) Time-Life R834-07 Body Talk - Hearts In Motion. *(45 version)*

(S) (5:48) Motown 314530501 The Ultimate Collection. *(LP version)*

(S) (3:44) Time-Life R838-15 Solid Gold Soul 1979. *(45 version)*

(S) (3:41) Motown 314530846 Lionel Richie: Truly - The Love Songs. *(45 version)*

(S) (3:42) Madacy Entertainment 6806 Best Of Love. *(45 version)*

(S) (3:42) Time-Life AM1-26 AM Gold - 1979. *(45 version)*

1980 WONDERLAND
(S) (5:25) Motown 8014 and 8114 Natural High/Midnight Magic. *(LP version)*
(S) (5:25) Motown 5348 Midnight Magic. *(LP version)*
(S) (5:24) Motown 374638502 Motown Legends - Three Times A Lady. *(LP version)*
(S) (3:48) Motown 314530358 Anthology. *(45 version)*

1980 OLD-FASHION LOVE
(S) (4:57) Motown 6068 Compact Command Performances. *(LP version)*
(S) (3:22) Motown 6107 All The Great Love Songs. *(45 version)*
(S) (4:55) Motown 5353 Heroes. *(LP version)*
(S) (3:19) Motown 8039 and 8139 Heroes/Commodores. *(45 version)*
(S) (3:23) Motown 314530358 Anthology. *(45 version)*
(S) (3:19) Motown 314530516 Motown Year By Year 1980. *(45 version)*
(S) (4:57) Motown 314530501 The Ultimate Collection. *(LP version)*

1981 LADY (YOU BRING ME UP)
(actual 45 time is (4:01) not (3:54) as stated on the record label)
(S) (4:49) Motown 6068 Compact Command Performances. *(LP version)*
(S) (4:01) Motown 6107 All The Great Love Songs. *(45 version)*
(S) (4:48) Motown 5438 In The Pocket. *(LP version)*
(S) (3:56) Motown 8044 and 8144 Hot On The Tracks/In The Pocket. *(:05 shorter than the 45 version)*
(S) (4:01) Motown 6028 All The Great Hits. *(45 version)*
(S) (3:59) Motown 6358 Hitsville USA Volume Two. *(45 version)*
(S) (4:02) Motown 314530358 Anthology. *(45 version)*
(S) (4:01) Rebound 314520361 Class Reunion '81. *(45 version)*
(S) (4:49) Motown 314530501 The Ultimate Collection. *(LP version)*

1981 OH NO
(actual LP time is (3:00) not (2:51) as stated on the record label)
(S) (3:01) Motown 6143 and 5386 The Composer Series: Lionel Richie.
(S) (3:00) Motown 9035 and 5324 Top Ten With A Bullet!
(S) (3:00) Motown 6107 All The Great Love Songs.
(S) (3:00) Motown 5438 In The Pocket.
(S) (2:59) Motown 8044 and 8144 Hot On The Tracks/In The Pocket.
(S) (2:57) Motown 6028 All The Great Hits.
(S) (2:59) Polygram Special Markets 314520030 Motown Legends - Love Songs.
(S) (3:00) Motown 314530358 Anthology.
(S) (3:00) JCI 3176 1980 - Only Soul - 1984.
(S) (3:00) Polygram Special Markets 314520445 Soul Hits Of The 80's.
(S) (2:59) Time-Life R834-15 Body Talk - Once In Lifetime.

1985 NIGHTSHIFT
(S) (5:01) Motown 9110 Motown Memories Vol. 4 - Where Were You When. *(LP length)*
(S) (5:03) Motown 314530358 Anthology. *(LP length)*
(S) (4:21) Motown 314530519 Motown Year By Year 1985. *(45 length)*
(S) (5:04) Motown 5400 Nightshift. *(LP length)*
(S) (4:21) Motown 6358 Hitsville USA Volume Two. *(45 length)*
(S) (5:04) K-Tel 3500 The 80's - Urban Countdown. *(LP length)*
(S) (4:19) Time-Life R988-02 Sounds Of The Eighties: 1985. *(45 length)*
(S) (5:03) Risky Business 66394 Gone But Not Forgotten. *(LP length)*
(S) (4:21) Rhino 72159 Black Entertainment Television - 15th Anniversary. *(45 length)*
(S) (4:21) Rhino 72140 Billboard Hot R&B Hits 1985. *(45 length)*

(S) (5:03) Motown 314530501 The Ultimate Collection. *(LP length)*
(S) (4:21) K-Tel 3864 Slow Dancin'. *(45 length)*

PERRY COMO

1955 KO KO MO (I LOVE YOU SO)
(M) (2:40) Time-Life HPD-09 Your Hit Parade 1955.

1955 TINA MARIE
(M) (2:31) RCA 66098 Yesterday & Today.
(M) (2:32) Time-Life HPD-25 Your Hit Parade - The 50's.

1956 ALL AT ONCE YOU LOVE HER

1956 HOT DIGGITY (DOG ZIGGITY BOOM)
(M) (2:21) RCA 8467 Nipper's Greatest Hits Of The 50's Volume 2.
(E) (2:21) RCA 8323 All Time Greatest Hits.
(M) (2:21) RCA 0972 Pure Gold. *(opening notes truncated)*
(M) (2:21) RCA 53802 Como's Golden Records.
(M) (2:21) RCA 52167 Round And Round & Other Hits.
(M) (2:20) RCA 51752 A Legendary Performer.
(M) (2:20) RCA 66098 Yesterday & Today.
(M) (2:20) Time-Life HPD-15 Your Hit Parade - 1956.

1956 JUKE BOX BABY
(M) (2:13) RCA 66098 Yesterday & Today.
(M) (2:10) Time-Life HPD-31 Your Hit Parade - The 50's Forever.

1956 MORE
(M) (2:34) RCA 66098 Yesterday & Today.
(M) (2:35) Time-Life HPD-15 Your Hit Parade - 1956.

1956 GLENDORA
(M) (2:42) Time-Life HPD-21 Your Hit Parade - The Mid 50's.

1956 SOMEBODY UP THERE LIKES ME
(M) (2:05) RCA 66098 Yesterday & Today.

1956 MOONLIGHT LOVE

1957 ROUND AND ROUND
(E) (2:32) RCA 9902 Nipper's #1 Hits 1956-1986.
(E) (2:33) RCA 8323 All Time Greatest Hits.
(M) (2:32) RCA 53802 Como's Golden Records.
(M) (2:32) RCA 52167 Round And Round & Other Hits.
(M) (2:31) RCA 66098 Yesterday & Today.
(M) (2:33) Time-Life HPD-17 Your Hit Parade - 1957.

1957 THE GIRL WITH THE GOLDEN BRAIDS

1957 JUST BORN (TO BE YOUR BABY)
(M) (2:30) RCA 66098 Yesterday & Today.
(M) (2:30) Time-Life HPD-28 Your Hit Parade - The Fabulous 50's.

1957 IVY ROSE

1958 CATCH A FALLING STAR
(S) (2:26) RCA 8466 Nipper's Greatest Hits Of The 50's Volume 1.
(E) (2:28) RCA 8323 All Time Greatest Hits.
(M) (2:29) RCA 0972 Pure Gold.
(M) (2:28) Special Music 2651 It's Impossible.
(M) (2:28) RCA 53802 Como's Golden Records.
(M) (2:28) RCA 52167 Round And Round & Other Hits.
(M) (2:26) RCA 66098 Yesterday & Today.
(M) (2:28) Reprise 45516 O.S.T. A Perfect World.
(S) (2:26) Time-Life HPD-11 Your Hit Parade 1958.
(M) (2:28) K-Tel 3471 High Hopes - Songs To Lift Your Spirits.
(M) (2:26) JCI 7021 Those Wonderful Years - April Love.
(M) (2:28) Hammer & Lace 697124114 Leading Men: Masters Of Style Volume Three.
(M) (2:27) Simitar 55382 The Crooners.

1958 MAGIC MOMENTS
(E) (2:38) RCA 8323 All Time Greatest Hits.
(M) (2:38) RCA 53802 Como's Golden Records.
(M) (2:38) RCA 66098 Yesterday & Today.
(M) (2:38) Time-Life HPD-11 Your Hit Parade 1958.
(E) (2:59) Geffen 25218 O.S.T. Fear And Loathing In Las Vegas. *(time includes :19 of movie dialogue; all songs and the movie dialogue are segued together)*

1958 KEWPIE DOLL
(M) (2:32) Time-Life HPD-38 Your Hit Parade - The 50's Generation.

1958 MOON TALK

1959 TOMBOY

PERRY COMO *(Continued)*
1960 DELEWARE
- (S) (2:19) RCA 66098 Yesterday & Today.
- (M) (2:20) Time-Life HPD-35 Your Hit Parade - The Fun-Times 50's & 60's.

1962 CATERINA
1965 DREAM ON LITTLE DREAMER
- (S) (2:20) RCA 8323 All Time Greatest Hits.
- (S) (2:19) Special Music 2651 It's Impossible. *(truncated fade)*
- (S) (2:19) RCA 52167 Round And Round & Other Hits.
- (S) (2:18) RCA 66098 Yesterday & Today.

1971 IT'S IMPOSSIBLE
- (S) (3:14) RCA 8476 and 9684 Nipper's Greatest Hits Of The 70's.
- (S) (3:13) RCA 8323 All Time Greatest Hits.
- (S) (3:13) RCA 0972 Pure Gold.
- (S) (3:13) Special Music 2651 It's Impossible.
- (S) (3:13) RCA 51752 A Legendary Performer.
- (S) (3:13) RCA 66098 Yesterday & Today.
- (S) (3:13) Time-Life R974-01 Many Moods Of Romance - That's My Desire.
- (S) (3:13) JCI 7022 Those Wonderful Years - It Must Be Him.
- (S) (3:13) RCA 66859 To Mom With Love.
- (S) (3:13) Rhino 72736 Billboard Top Soft Rock Hits - 1970.
- (S) (3:13) Time-Life R814-03 Love Songs.

1973 AND I LOVE YOU SO
- (S) (3:17) Special Music 2651 It's Impossible.
- (S) (3:12) RCA 51752 A Legendary Performer.
- (S) (3:17) RCA 66098 Yesterday & Today.
- (S) (3:17) RCA 66859 To Mom With Love.
- (S) (3:17) Rhino 72739 Billboard Top Soft Rock Hits - 1973.

COMPANY B
1987 FASCINATED
- (S) (5:23) Atlantic 81763 Company B. *(LP version)*
- (S) (3:49) Elektra 62161 Maximum Dance Hits Vol. 1. *(45 version)*
- (S) (3:44) Cold Front 6330 Club Mix: The 80s. *(all selections on this cd are segued together)*

CONCRETE BLONDE
1990 JOEY
- (S) (4:07) IRS 29695 On The Charts: IRS Records 1979-1994.
- (S) (4:07) Sandstone 33044 and 5010 Rock The First Volume Four.
- (S) (4:08) IRS 13037 Bloodletting.
- (S) (4:06) I.R.S. 37072 Recollection.
- (S) (4:06) Rhino 72650 Billboard Top Modern Rock Tracks, 1990.

CON FUNK SHUN
1978 FFUN
(dj copies of this 45 ran (3:31) and (4:08); commercial copies were all (3:31))
- (S) (4:08) Mercury 314510275 Best Of. *(LP length)*
- (S) (3:34) Rhino 71435 In Yo Face! History Of Funk Volume 5. *(45 length)*
- (S) (4:07) Mercury 314514821 Funky Stuff: The Best Of Funk Essentials. *(LP length)*
- (S) (4:08) Special Music/Essex 5033 Ffun. *(LP length)*
- (S) (4:09) Rebound 314520265 Dance Fever. *(LP length)*
- (S) (4:09) Rebound 314520321 Secrets. *(LP length)*
- (S) (3:34) Rhino 72129 Soul Hits Of The 70's Vol. 19. *(45 length)*
- (S) (4:07) Polygram Special Markets 314520391 Greatest Hits. *(LP length)*
- (S) (4:07) Rebound 314520430 Funk Classics Of The 70's Vol. 2. *(LP length)*
- (S) (3:33) K-Tel 4020 Great R&B Funk Bands Of The 70's. *(45 length)*
- (S) (3:33) Time-Life R838-16 Solid Gold Soul 1977. *(45 length)*

1981 TOO TIGHT
- (S) (3:10) Mercury 314510275 Best Of.

- (S) (3:11) Special Music/Essex 5033 Ffun.
- (S) (7:09) Mercury 314532470 Best Of Volume 2. *(complete recording session)*
- (S) (3:10) Polygram Special Markets 314520391 Greatest Hits.
- (S) (3:10) JCI 3176 1980 - Only Soul - 1984.

ARTHUR CONLEY
1967 SWEET SOUL MUSIC
- (E) (2:19) Warner Special Products 27601 Atlantic Soul Classics.
- (M) (2:20) Atlantic 81911 Golden Age Of Black Music (1960-1970).
- (M) (2:20) Atlantic 81298 Atlantic Rhythm & Blues Volume 6.
- (M) (2:19) Atlantic 82305 Atlantic Rhythm And Blues 1947-1974 Box Set.
- (M) (2:19) Rhino 71459 Soul Hits, Volume 1.
- (M) (2:16) Time-Life RHD-10 Rhythm & Blues - 1967.
- (M) (2:17) Time-Life 2CLR-05 Classic Rock - 1967.
- (M) (2:19) Rhino 71517 The Muscle Shoals Sound.
- (M) (2:20) Rhino 71937 Billboard Top Pop Hits, 1967.
- (M) (2:20) Ichiban 2105 Sweet Soul Music/Best Of.
- (M) (2:16) Time-Life R838-02 Solid Gold Soul - 1967.
- (M) (2:19) Flashback 72657 '60s Soul: Try A Little Tenderness.
- (M) (2:19) Flashback 72091 '60s Soul Hits Box Set.
- (M) (2:20) Rhino 72815 Beg, Scream & Shout! The Big Ol' Box Of '60s Soul.
- (M) (2:20) Flashback 72897 25 Years Of R&B - 1967.
- (M) (2:20) Rhino 72962 Ultimate '60s Soul Sensations.

1967 SHAKE, RATTLE & ROLL
- (M) (2:22) Ichiban 2105 Sweet Soul Music/Best Of.

1968 FUNKY STREET
- (S) (2:23) Ichiban 2105 Sweet Soul Music/Best Of.

RAY CONNIFF and THE SINGERS
1966 SOMEWHERE MY LOVE
- (S) (3:45) Columbia 40214 16 Most Requested Songs. *(rerecording; titled "LARA'S THEME FROM DR. ZHIVAGO" on the cd and cd jacket)*
- (S) (2:28) Columbia 9319 Somewhere My Love.
- (S) (2:20) Columbia/Legacy 48987 'S Always Conniff. *(live)*
- (S) (2:28) Columbia/Legacy 53574 Essence Of.
- (S) (2:28) Time-Life R986-03 Instrumental Favorites.
- (S) (2:28) Nick At Nite/Epic 67148 Donna Reed's Dinner Party.
- (S) (2:28) K-Tel 3822 Percy Faith/Ray Conniff Back To Back.
- (S) (2:28) Time-Life R814-03 Love Songs.

NORMAN CONNORS
1976 YOU ARE MY STARSHIP
- (S) (3:21) Essex 7060 The Buddah Box. *(edited)*
- (S) (4:31) Right Stuff 27307 Slow Jams: The 70's Volume One.
- (S) (4:29) Rhino 71861 Smooth Grooves Volume 3.
- (S) (4:29) Right Stuff 30582 You Are My Starship.
- (S) (4:30) Rhino 72128 Hot Soul Hits Of The 70's Vol. 18.
- (S) (4:29) Rebound 314520367 Soul Classics - Quiet Storm/The 70's.
- (S) (4:29) Hip-O 40030 The Glory Of Love - '70s Sweet & Soulful Love Songs.
- (S) (4:31) Time-Life R834-05 Body Talk - Sealed With A Kiss.
- (S) (4:32) Right Stuff 59939 Best Of Norman Connors & Friends.
- (S) (4:29) Chronicles 314555138 Funk Ballads.

BILL CONTI
1977 GONNA FLY NOW
- (S) (2:46) EMI 46081 O.S.T. Rocky.
- (S) (2:46) Rhino 71199 Super Hits Of The 70's Volume 19. *(hissy)*
- (S) (2:46) Rhino 72424 Billboard Top Movie Hits - 1970s. *(hissy)*

DICK CONTINO
1957 PLEDGE OF LOVE

CONTOURS
1962 DO YOU LOVE ME
- (M) (2:51) Rhino 75778 Frat Rock.
- (M) (2:53) Rhino 70648 Billboard's Top R&B Hits Of 1962.
- (E) (2:51) RCA 6965 More Dirty Dancing.
- (M) (2:51) Motown 9104 and 5409 Motown Memories Volume 1.
- (M) (2:51) Motown 6219 Hard To Find Motown Classics Volume 3.
- (M) (2:51) Original Sound 8862 Oldies But Goodies Vol. 12. *(this compact disc uses the "Waring - fds" noise reduction process)*
- (M) (2:51) Original Sound 2223 Oldies But Goodies Volumes 2,7,9,12 and 13 Box Set. *(this box set uses the "Waring - fds" noise reduction process)*
- (M) (2:51) Original Sound 2500 Oldies But Goodies Volumes 1-15 Box Set. *(this box set uses the "Waring - fds" noise reduction process)*
- (M) (2:51) Motown 6160 The Good-Feeling Music Of The Big Chill Generation Volume 2.
- (M) (2:51) DCC Compact Classics 043 Toga Rock II.
- (M) (2:52) Rhino 70243 Greatest Movie Rock Hits.
- (M) (2:51) Motown 9017 and 5248 16 #1 Hits From The Early 60's.
- (S) (2:49) Motown 5448 A Collection Of 16 Big Hits Volume 1. *(alternate take)*
- (S) (2:51) Warner Brothers 3359 O.S.T. The Wanderers. *(alternate take)*
- (S) (6:36) Motown 5415 Do You Love Me. *(remixed disco version from the movie "Dirty Dancing")*
- (M) (2:50) Motown 9071 Motown Dance Party Volume 1. *(all selections on this cd are segued together)*
- (M) (2:51) Motown 6312 Hitsville USA.
- (M) (2:50) Time-Life 2RNR-16 Rock 'N' Roll Era - 1962 Still Rockin'.
- (M) (2:51) Time-Life RHD-11 Rhythm & Blues - 1962.
- (M) (2:51) Private Music 82119 O.S.T. Getting Even With Dad.
- (M) (2:51) Motown 314530403 Motown Classic Hits Vol. 1.
- (M) (2:51) Polygram Special Markets 314520284 Motown Legends Volume 3.
- (M) (2:52) Polygram Special Markets 314520300 Motown Legends - Guy Groups.
- (M) (2:51) Nick At Nite/Epic 67149 Dick Van Dyke's Dance Party.
- (M) (2:52) Priority 50951 I Love Rock & Roll Volume 2: Hits Of The 60's.
- (M) (2:51) Rebound 314520420 Soul Classics - Best Of The 60's.
- (M) (2:51) Time-Life R838-18 Solid Gold Soul 1962.

1988 DO YOU LOVE ME
(this song charted in two different years: 1962 & 1988; see 1962 listings)

SAM COOKE
1957 YOU SEND ME
- (E) (2:45) RCA 3863 Best Of.
- (E) (2:44) RCA 7127 The Man And His Music.
- (M) (2:42) Pair 1006 You Send Me.
- (M) (2:44) Time-Life 2RNR-17 Rock 'N' Roll Era - 1957 Still Rockin'.
- (M) (1:41) Abkco 2231 Sam Cooke's Sar Records Story. *(demo version)*
- (M) (2:42) RCA 67605 Greatest Hits.

1958 I'LL COME RUNNING BACK TO YOU
- (M) (2:10) RCA 7127 The Man And His Music.
- (M) (2:10) Time-Life 2RNR-41 Rock 'N' Roll Era - R&B Gems.

1958 (I LOVE YOU) FOR SENTIMENTAL REASONS
- (M) (2:36) RCA 3863 Best Of.
- (M) (2:37) RCA 67605 Greatest Hits.

1958 LONELY ISLAND
1958 YOU WERE MADE FOR ME
- (M) (2:55) RCA 67605 Greatest Hits.

1958 WIN YOUR LOVE FOR ME
- (S) (2:54) RCA 7127 The Man And His Music. *(rerecording)*
- (M) (2:55) RCA 67605 Greatest Hits. *(rerecording)*

1958 LOVE YOU MOST OF ALL
- (M) (2:16) RCA 67605 Greatest Hits.

1959 EVERYBODY LIKES TO CHA CHA CHA
- (M) (2:34) RCA 3863 Best Of.
- (M) (2:36) RCA 7127 The Man And His Music.
- (S) (2:40) RCA 67605 Greatest Hits.

1959 ONLY SIXTEEN
- (S) (1:53) RCA 3863 Best Of. *(:07 shorter than the 45)*
- (S) (1:53) RCA 7127 The Man And His Music. *(:07 shorter than the 45)*
- (S) (1:53) Time-Life 2RNR-20 Rock 'N' Roll Era - 1959 Still Rockin'. *(:07 shorter than the 45)*
- (S) (2:12) RCA 67605 Greatest Hits. *(:12 longer fade than the 45)*

1960 WONDERFUL WORLD
- (M) (2:04) RCA 3863 Best Of.
- (M) (2:04) RCA 7127 The Man And His Music.
- (E) (2:05) MCA 31023 O.S.T. Animal House. *(all selections on this cd are segued together)*
- (E) (2:04) Special Music 2610 The Unforgettable.
- (E) (2:06) Time-Life 2RNR-11 Rock 'N' Roll Era - 1960. *(found only on original pressings of this cd)*
- (M) (2:05) RCA 67605 Greatest Hits.

1960 CHAIN GANG
- (S) (2:35) RCA 8474 Nipper's Greatest Hits Of The 60's Volume 1.
- (S) (2:33) RCA 3863 Best Of.
- (S) (2:33) RCA 7127 The Man And His Music.
- (S) (2:34) Pair 1186 An Original.
- (E) (2:33) Time-Life 2RNR-11 Rock 'N' Roll Era - 1960. *(found only on original pressings of this cd)*
- (S) (2:39) RCA 67605 Greatest Hits.

1960 SAD MOOD
- (S) (2:27) RCA 3863 Best Of.
- (S) (2:28) RCA 7127 The Man And His Music.
- (S) (2:37) RCA 67605 Greatest Hits.

1961 THAT'S IT-I QUIT-I'M MOVIN' ON
- (S) (2:36) RCA 67605 Greatest Hits.

1961 CUPID
- (S) (2:28) RCA 3863 Best Of.
- (S) (2:29) RCA 7127 The Man And His Music.
- (S) (2:34) RCA 67605 Greatest Hits.

1962 TWISTIN' THE NIGHT AWAY
- (S) (2:38) RCA 8475 Nipper's Greatest Hits Of The 60's Volume 2.
- (S) (2:39) RCA 3863 Best Of.
- (S) (2:39) RCA 7127 The Man And His Music.
- (E) (2:38) MCA 31023 O.S.T. Animal House. *(all selections on this cd are segued together)*
- (S) (2:40) RCA 67605 Greatest Hits.

1962 HAVING A PARTY
- (E) (2:22) RCA 3863 Best Of.
- (E) (2:26) RCA 7127 The Man And His Music.
- (S) (2:34) RCA 67605 Greatest Hits.

1962 BRING IT ON HOME TO ME
- (E) (2:39) RCA 3863 Best Of.
- (E) (2:41) RCA 7127 The Man And His Music.
- (S) (2:42) RCA 67605 Greatest Hits.

1962 NOTHING CAN CHANGE THIS LOVE
- (S) (2:35) RCA 7127 The Man And His Music.
- (S) (2:36) RCA 67605 Greatest Hits.

1963 SEND ME SOME LOVIN'
- (S) (2:45) RCA 67605 Greatest Hits.

1963 ANOTHER SATURDAY NIGHT
- (S) (2:25) RCA 7127 The Man And His Music.
- (S) (2:39) RCA 67605 Greatest Hits. *(found only on initial pressings of this cd; :21 longer than the 45 or LP)*

1963 FRANKIE AND JOHNNY
- (S) (2:43) RCA 67605 Greatest Hits.

1963 LITTLE RED ROOSTER
- (S) (2:51) RCA 66760 The Rhythm And The Blues.
- (S) (2:50) RCA 67605 Greatest Hits.

125

SAM COOKE *(Continued)*
1964 GOOD NEWS
　　(S) (2:29) RCA 7127 The Man And His Music.
1964 GOOD TIMES
　　(S) (2:27) RCA 7127 The Man And His Music.
1964 TENNESSEE WALTZ
1964 COUSIN OF MINE
1965 SHAKE
　　(S) (2:48) RCA 7127 The Man And His Music.
1965 A CHANGE IS GONNA COME
　　(S) (3:12) RCA 7127 The Man And His Music.
1965 IT'S GOT THE WHOLE WORLD SHAKIN'
1965 SUGAR DUMPLING
　　(E) (2:37) Special Music 2610 The Unforgettable.

COOKIES
1962 CHAINS
　　(M) (2:29) Rhino 70989 Best Of The Girl Groups Volume 2.
　　(M) (2:33) Collectables 5414 Carole King Plus. *(truncated fade)*
　　(M) (2:29) Era 5025 The Brill Building Sound.
　　(M) (2:32) Time-Life 2RNR-29 Rock 'N' Roll Era - The 60's Rave On.
　　(M) (2:30) Rhino 71650 Colpix-Dimension Story.
　　(M) (2:29) Eclipse Music Group 64868 Rock 'n Roll Relix 1962-1963.
　　(M) (2:29) Eclipse Music Group 64872 Rock 'n Roll Relix 1960-1969.
1963 DON'T SAY NOTHIN' BAD (ABOUT MY BABY)
　　(M) (2:42) Rhino 70989 Best Of The Girl Groups Volume 2.
　　(M) (2:45) Collectables 5414 Carole King Plus. *(truncated fade)*
　　(M) (2:42) Era 5025 The Brill Building Sound.
　　(M) (2:45) Time-Life 2RNR-19 Rock 'N' Roll Era - 1963 Still Rockin'.
　　(M) (2:42) Time-Life R962-08 History Of Rock 'N' Roll: Sound Of The City 1959-1965.
　　(M) (2:43) Rhino 71650 Colpix-Dimension Story.
　　(M) (2:42) Rhino 71802 O.S.T. Andre.
1964 GIRLS GROW UP FASTER THAN BOYS
　　(M) (2:48) Rhino 71650 Colpix-Dimension Story.

EDDIE COOLEY and THE DIMPLES
1956 PRISCILLA
　　(M) (2:28) Time-Life 2RNR-48 Rock 'N' Roll Era - R&B Gems II.

RITA COOLIDGE
1977 (YOUR LOVE HAS LIFTED ME) HIGHER AND HIGHER
　　(S) (3:57) A&M 2504 Classics Volume 5.
　　(S) (3:59) A&M 3238 Greatest Hits.
　　(S) (3:59) Time-Life R834-13 Body Talk - Just The Two Of Us.
1977 WE'RE ALL ALONE
　　(S) (3:36) Priority 8664 High Times/70's Greatest Rock Hits Volume 3.
　　(S) (3:35) A&M 2504 Classics Volume 5.
　　(S) (3:38) A&M 3238 Greatest Hits.
　　(S) (3:36) Time-Life R103-33 Singers & Songwriters.
　　(S) (3:37) Time-Life R834-04 Body Talk - Together Forever.
　　(S) (3:36) Time-Life R814-04 Love Songs.
1978 THE WAY YOU DO THE THINGS YOU DO
　　(S) (3:35) A&M 2504 Classics Volume 5.
　　(S) (3:34) A&M 3238 Greatest Hits.
1978 YOU
　　(S) (3:11) A&M 2504 Classics Volume 5.
1980 I'D RATHER LEAVE WHILE I'M IN LOVE
　　(S) (3:24) A&M 2504 Classics Volume 5.
　　(S) (3:24) A&M 3238 Greatest Hits.
1983 ALL TIME HIGH
　　(S) (3:00) EMI 98413 Best Of James Bond 30th Anniversary Collection.
　　(S) (3:00) EMI 98560 Best Of James Bond 30th Anniversary.
　　(S) (3:00) EMI 46079 James Bond 13 Original Themes.
　　(S) (3:01) A&M 2504 Classics Volume 5.
　　(S) (3:02) Rhino 72509 Tim Rice Collection: Stage And Screen Classics.

　　(S) (3:03) Ryko 10705 O.S.T. Octopussy.
　　(S) (3:01) Ryko 10705 O.S.T. Octopussy. *(end title version - not the hit version)*
　　(S) (3:01) Rebound 314520493 Class Reunion '83.

COOLIO
1994 FANTASTIC VOYAGE
　　(S) (5:32) Tommy Boy 1083 It Takes A Thief.
　　(S) (5:32) Boxtunes 162444068 Big Phat Ones Of Hip-Hop Volume 1.
　　(S) (4:00) Loud/RCA 67423 All That - The Album.
　　(S) (4:02) Razor & Tie 4569 '90s Style.
1995 GANGSTA'S PARADISE
　　(S) (4:00) Tommy Boy 1141 Gangsta's Paradise.
　　(S) (4:00) MCA 11228 O.S.T. Dangerous Minds.
　　(S) (3:59) Tommy Boy 1139 MTV Party To Go Volume 8. *(all selections on this cd are segued together)*
　　(S) (4:00) Grammy Recordings/Sony 67565 1996 Grammy Nominees.
　　(S) (4:00) EMI-Capitol Music Group 54555 Movie Luv.
1996 TOO HOT
　　(S) (3:38) Tommy Boy 1141 Gangsta's Paradise.
1996 1,2,3,4 (SUMPIN' NEW)
　　(S) (3:32) Tommy Boy 1141 Gangsta's Paradise.
　　(S) (4:24) Tommy Boy 1164 MTV Party To Go Volume 9. *(remix; all selections on this cd are segued together)*
　　(S) U (3:08) Tommy Boy 1163 Jock Jams Volume 2. *(all selections on this cd are segued together)*
1996 IT'S ALL THE WAY LIVE (NOW)
　　(S) (4:18) Island/Hollywood 314524243 O.S.T. Eddie.
　　(S) (3:28) Tommy Boy 1168 MTV Party To Go Volume 10. *(all songs on this cd are segued together; remix)*
released as by COOLIO featuring 40 THEVZ:
1997 C U WHEN U GET THERE
　　(S) (4:38) Tommy Boy 1169 O.S.T. Nothing To Lose.

ALICE COOPER
1971 EIGHTEEN
(LP title is "I'M EIGHTEEN")
　　(S) (2:56) Rhino 70986 Heavy Metal Memories.
　　(S) (2:53) JCI 3302 Electric Seventies.
　　(S) (2:55) Warner Special Products 27616 Classic Rock.
　　(S) (2:54) Warner Brothers 3107 Greatest Hits.
　　(S) (2:56) Warner Brothers 1883 Love It To Death.
　　(S) (2:56) RCA 8533 O.S.T. Heartbreak Hotel.
　　(S) (2:56) Time-Life SOD-02 Sounds Of The Seventies - 1971.
　　(S) (2:54) Time-Life OPCD-4521 Guitar Rock.
　　(S) (2:56) Time-Life R968-06 Guitar Rock 1970-1971.
　　(S) (2:56) JCI 3168 #1 Radio Hits 1970 - Only Rock 'n Roll - 1974.
　　(S) (2:56) Rhino 72819 16 Magazine - Who's Your Fave Rave.
　　(S) (2:55) Simitar 55502 The Number One's: Classic Rock.
1972 SCHOOL'S OUT
　　(S) (3:27) Warner Brothers 3107 Greatest Hits. *(LP version)*
　　(S) (3:26) Warner Brothers 2623 School's Out. *(LP version)*
　　(S) (3:25) Sire 6070 Rock 'N' Roll High School. *(LP version)*
　　(S) (3:27) Priority 53680 Spring Break. *(LP version)*
　　(S) (3:27) Medicine Label 24533 O.S.T. Dazed And Confused. *(LP version)*
　　(S) (3:27) Razor & Tie 22502 Those Rocking 70's. *(LP version)*
　　(S) (3:27) Time-Life R968-05 Guitar Rock 1972-1973. *(LP version)*
　　(S) (3:27) Time-Life SOD-03 Sounds Of The Seventies - 1972. *(LP version)*
　　(S) (3:27) Time-Life R105-24 Guitar Rock Monsters. *(LP version)*
　　(S) (3:27) JCI 3130 1970 - Only Rock 'N Roll - 1974. *(LP version)*
　　(S) (3:27) Rhino 72131 Frat Rock: The 70's. *(LP version)*
1972 ELECTED
　　(S) (4:05) Warner Brothers 3107 Greatest Hits. *(LP version)*
　　(S) (4:05) Warner Brothers 2685 Billion Dollar Babies. *(LP version)*

(S) (4:05) Time-Life R968-19 Guitar Rock - The Early '70s: Take Two. *(LP version)*

1973 HELLO HURRAY
(dj copies of this 45 ran (3:01) and (4:16); commercial copies were all (3:01))
(S) (4:15) Warner Brothers 3107 Greatest Hits. *(LP version)*
(S) (4:15) Warner Brothers 2685 Billion Dollar Babies.
    (tracks into the next selection; LP version)

1973 NO MORE MR. NICE GUY
(S) (3:06) Warner Brothers 3107 Greatest Hits.
(S) (3:05) Warner Brothers 2685 Billion Dollar Babies.
(S) (3:05) Time-Life SOD-22 Sounds Of The Seventies - Seventies Top Forty.
(S) (3:05) Medicine Label 24588 Even More Dazed And Confused.
(S) (3:05) Time-Life R968-08 Guitar Rock - The Mid '70s.
(S) (3:05) JCI 3140 18 Screamers From The 70's.
(S) (3:05) Thump 6010 Easyriders Volume 1.

1975 ONLY WOMEN
(LP title is "ONLY WOMEN BLEED")
(S) (5:46) Priority 7055 Heavy Hitters/70's Greatest Rock Hits Volume 11. *(LP version)*
(S) (5:45) Atlantic 19157 Welcome To My Nightmare. *(LP version)*
(M) (3:29) Time-Life SOD-16 Sounds Of The Seventies - 1975: Take Two. *(45 version)*
(M) (3:29) JCI 3169 #1 Radio Hits 1975 - Only Rock 'n Roll - 1979. *(45 version)*

1976 I NEVER CRY
(S) (3:41) Warner Brothers 2896 Goes To Hell.

1977 YOU AND ME
(S) (5:05) Metal Blade/Warner Brothers 26446 Lace And Whiskey. *(LP version)*
(S) (3:25) Time-Life SOD-35 Sounds Of The Seventies - AM Nuggets. *(45 version)*
(S) (3:25) JCI 3146 1975 - Only Love - 1979. *(45 version)*

1978 HOW YOU GONNA SEE ME NOW
(actual 45 time is (3:50) not (3:45) as stated on the record label)
(S) (3:55) Metal Blade/Warner Brothers 26445 From The Inside.

1989 POISON
(S) (4:29) Epic 45137 Trash.
(S) (4:27) Epic/Legacy 65020 Ultimate Rock 'n' Roll Collection.
(S) (4:28) Time-Life R988-21 Sounds Of The Eighties: 1986-1989.
(S) (4:28) Razor & Tie 89004 Monsters Of Rock.

LES COOPER and THE SOUL ROCKERS
1962 WIGGLE WOBBLE
(S) (2:04) Relic 7009 Raging Harlem Hit Parade.
(S) (2:04) Capricorn 42009 Fire/Fury Records Story.
(M) (2:05) Time-Life 2RNR-36 Rock 'N' Roll Era - Axes & Saxes/The Great Instrumentals.
(M) (2:00) Collectables 5157 Wiggle Wobble.
(S) (2:04) Hip-O 40008 Soulful Grooves - R&B Instrumental Classics Volume 2.

KEN COPELAND
1957 PLEDGE OF LOVE

IMANI COPPOLA
1997 LEGEND OF A COWGIRL
(S) (3:47) Columbia 68541 Chupacabra.

JILL COREY
1957 LOVE ME TO PIECES
(M) (1:51) Time-Life HPD-25 Your Hit Parade - The 50's.

CORINA
1991 TEMPTATION
(S) (3:57) Cutting Records/Atco 91752 Corina.
(S) (3:57) JCI 3132 1990 - Only Rock 'n Roll - 1994.

CORNELIUS BROTHERS & SISTER ROSE
1971 TREAT HER LIKE A LADY
(S) (2:44) Rhino 70632 Billboard's Top Rock & Roll Hits Of 1971.
(S) (2:44) Rhino 72005 Billboard's Top Rock & Roll Hits 1968-1972 Box Set.
(S) (2:44) Rhino 70785 Soul Hits Of The 70's Volume 5.
(S) (2:44) Rhino 72028 Soul Hits Of The 70's Volumes 1-5 Box Set.
(S) (2:43) EMI 90603 Rock Me Gently.
(S) (2:44) Curb 77356 70's Hits Volume 2.
(S) (2:44) Rhino 71208 70's Smash Hits Volume 4.
(S) (2:43) Razor & Tie 22047 Sweet 70's Soul.
(S) (2:41) Time-Life RHD-09 Rhythm & Blues - 1971.
(S) (2:43) Time-Life SUD-20 Superhits - Early 70's Classics.
(S) (2:44) Time-Life SOD-12 Sounds Of The Seventies - 1971: Take Two.
(S) (2:39) EMI 53966 The Story Of.
(S) (2:43) Time-Life AM1-15 AM Gold - Early '70s Classics.
(S) (2:41) Time-Life R838-06 Solid Gold Soul - 1971.
(S) (2:44) Flashback 72684 '70s Radio Hits Volume 4.
(S) (2:44) Flashback 72090 '70s Radio Hits Box Set.

1972 TOO LATE TO TURN BACK NOW
(S) (3:20) Rhino 70788 Soul Hits Of The 70's Volume 8.
(S) (3:19) Ripete 2200 Ocean Drive Volume 3.
(S) (3:20) Time-Life RHD-20 Rhythm & Blues - 1972.
(S) (3:16) Time-Life SUD-16 Superhits - The Early 70's.
(S) (3:18) Time-Life SOD-13 Sounds Of The Seventies - 1972: Take Two.
(S) (3:18) EMI 53966 The Story Of.
(S) (3:16) Time-Life AM1-13 AM Gold - The Early '70s.
(S) (3:20) Time-Life R838-07 Solid Gold Soul - 1972.
(S) (3:20) Time-Life R834-08 Body Talk - On My Mind.
(S) (3:15) Velvel/Reel Sounds 79713 O.S.T. The Ice Storm.

1972 DON'T EVER BE LONELY (A POOR LITTLE FOOL LIKE ME)
(S) (2:59) Rhino 70788 Soul Hits Of The 70's Volume 8.
(S) (2:58) EMI 53966 The Story Of.
(S) (2:58) EMI 55261 Sex & Soul Volume Two.

1973 I'M NEVER GONNA BE ALONE ANYMORE
(S) (2:36) Ripete 2219 Beach Fever.
(S) (2:33) EMI 53966 The Story Of.

DON CORNELL
1955 THE BIBLE TELLS ME SO

CORONA
1995 THE RHYTHM OF THE NIGHT
(S) (4:22) Eastwest 61817 The Rhythm Of The Night.
(S) (4:24) Tommy Boy 1139 MTV Party To Go Volume 8. *(remixed; all selections on this cd are segued together)*
(S) (4:22) EMI-Capitol Music Group 54547 Hot Luv.
(S) (4:08) Elektra 62161 Maximum Dance Hits Vol. 1.

CORSAIRS
1962 SMOKY PLACES
(M) (2:58) MCA 5938 Vintage Music Volumes 15 & 16.
(M) (2:58) MCA 31213 Vintage Music Volume 16.
(M) (2:56) Original Sound 8858 Oldies But Goodies Vol. 8. *(this compact disc uses the "Waring - fds" noise reduction process)*
(M) (2:56) Original Sound 2221 Oldies But Goodies Volumes 1,4,6,8 and 10 Box Set. *(this box set uses the "Waring - fds" noise reduction process)*
(M) (2:56) Original Sound 2500 Oldies But Goodies Volumes 1-15 Box Set. *(this box set uses the "Waring - fds" noise reduction process)*
(M) (2:56) Original Sound CDGO-8 Golden Oldies Volume. 8.
(E) (2:56) Original Sound 9602 Best Of Oldies But Goodies Vol. 2.
(M) (2:55) Chess 31317 Best Of Chess Rhythm & Blues Volume 1.
(M) (2:58) Ripete 2392192 Beach Music Anthology Box Set.
(M) (2:57) Collectables 5065 History Of Rock Volume 5.
(M) (2:57) Time-Life 2RNR-16 Rock 'N' Roll Era - 1962 Still Rockin'.

CORSAIRS (Continued)

(M) (2:55) Collectables 2500 WCBS-FM History Of Rock - The 60's Part 1.
(M) (2:55) Collectables 4500 History Of Rock/The 60s Part One.
(M) (2:57) Collectables 2603 WCBS-FM Jukebox Giants Vol. 1.
(M) (2:56) Time-Life R102-17 Lost Treasures Of Rock 'N' Roll.
(M) (2:57) LaserLight 12322 Greatest Hit Singles Collection.
(S) (3:00) Chess 9352 Chess Rhythm & Roll.
(M) (2:58) MCA Special Products 22173 Vintage Collectibles Volume 11.
(E) (3:00) Curb 77773 Hard To Find Hits Of Rock 'N' Roll Volume One.
(S) (3:00) Time-Life R857-06 The Heart Of Rock 'n' Roll 1962.

DAVE "BABY" CORTEZ
1959 THE HAPPY ORGAN

(M) (1:58) Rhino 70620 Billboard's Top Rock & Roll Hits Of 1959.
(M) (1:58) Rhino 72004 Billboard's Top Rock & Roll Hits 1957-1961 Box Set.
(M) (2:00) Rhino 71601 Rock Instrumental Classics Volume 1: The Fifties.
(M) (2:00) Rhino 72035 Rock Instrumental Classics Vols. 1-5 Box Set.
(M) (2:01) Time-Life 2RNR-28 Rock 'N' Roll Era - The 50's Rave On.
(M) (1:56) LaserLight 12316 Rebel Rousers.
(E) (2:03) Compose 131 Unforgettable - Gold For The Road.
(M) (2:01) RCA 67474 Roller Hockey - The Album.

1962 RINKY DINK

(M) (2:50) MCA 31205 Vintage Music Volume 8.
(M) (2:50) MCA 5805 Vintage Music Volumes 7 & 8.
(M) (2:50) Chess 31320 Best Of Chess Rock 'n' Roll Volume 2.
(M) (2:48) Time-Life 2RNR-35 Rock 'N' Roll Era - The 60's Last Dance.

BILL COSBY
1967 LITTLE OLE MAN (UPTIGHT-EVERYTHING'S ALRIGHT)

DON COSTA
1960 THEME FROM "THE UNFORGIVEN" (THE NEED FOR LOVE)

(S) (2:53) Collectors' Choice 003/4 Instrumental Gems Of The 60's.

1960 NEVER ON SUNDAY

(S) (2:55) Curb 77403 All-Time Great Instrumental Hits Volume 1.
(S) (2:51) Time-Life HPD-39 Your Hit Parade - 60's Instrumentals: Take Two.
(S) (2:54) K-Tel 3091 Those Wonderful Instrumentals.
(S) (2:54) Rhino 71868 Academy Award Winning Songs.
(S) (2:51) Collectors' Choice 003/4 Instrumental Gems Of The 60's.
(S) (2:54) Rhino 72278 Academy Award Winning Songs Volume 3.

ELVIS COSTELLO
1983 EVERYDAY I WRITE THE BOOK

(S) (3:52) Rykodisc 40283 Very Best Of.
(S) (3:53) Columbia 38897 Punch The Clock.
(S) (3:47) Columbia 40101 Best Of.
(S) (3:51) Maverick/Warner Brothers 46840 O.S.T. The Wedding Singer.

1989 VERONICA

(S) (3:07) Priority 53769 Rock Of The 80's Volume 10.
(S) (3:08) Warner Brothers 25848 Spike.
(S) (3:07) Warner Brothers 46801 Extreme Honey: Very Best Of The Warner Brothers Years.

GENE COTTON
1977 YOU'VE GOT ME RUNNIN'
1978 BEFORE MY HEART FINDS OUT

(S) (2:27) K-Tel 3907 Starflight Vol. 2.

released as by GENE COTTON with KIM CARNES:
1978 YOU'RE A PART OF ME

(S) (3:43) EMI 98223 Gypsy Honeymoon: Best Of Kim Carnes.

released as by GENE COTTON:
1978 LIKE A SUNDAY IN SALEM (THE AMOS & ANDY SONG)

JOHN COUGAR (see JOHN COUGAR MELLENCAMP)

COUNT FIVE
1966 PSYCHOTIC REACTION

(E) (3:04) K-Tel 713 Battle Of The Bands.
(E) (3:03) Original Sound 8895 Dick Clark's 21 All-Time Hits Vol. 4. *(mastered from vinyl)*
(E) (3:00) Original Sound CDGO-4 Golden Oldies Volume. 4.
(E) (3:05) Warner Special Products 27607 Highs Of The 60's.
(M) (3:05) Rhino 75892 Nuggets.
(E) (3:05) Novus 3077 O.S.T. Drugstore Cowboy.
(E) (3:05) JCI 3103 Electric Sixties.
(E) (2:59) Collectables 5066 History Of Rock Volume 6.
(M) (3:01) Time-Life 2CLR-02 Classic Rock - 1966.
(M) (3:05) Performance 398 The Complete Count Five.
(E) (3:04) Risky Business 66914 Party On.
(E) (3:04) Curb 77774 Hard To Find Hits Of Rock 'N' Roll Volume Two.
(M) (3:04) Time-Life R968-09 Guitar Rock 1966-1967.
(M) (3:04) K-Tel 3183 Psychedelic Mind Trip.
(E) (3:04) LaserLight 12528 Garage Band Rock. *(mastered from vinyl)*
(M) (3:03) JCI 3190 1965 - Only Dance - 1969.
(M) (3:04) Hip-O 40038 Power Chords Volume 1.
(E) (2:54) Thump 6020 Easyriders Volume 2.

DON COVAY & THE GOODTIMERS
1964 MERCY, MERCY

(M) (2:24) Atlantic 81297 Atlantic Rhythm & Blues Volume 5.
(S) (2:24) Atlantic 82305 Atlantic Rhythm And Blues 1947-1974 Box Set.
(S) (2:23) Time-Life RHD-12 Rhythm & Blues - 1964.
(M) (2:23) Time-Life 2CLR-09 Classic Rock - 1964: The Beat Goes On.
(M) (2:22) Motown 6763 Rites Of Rhythm & Blues Volume Two.
(M) (2:22) Rhino 71806 The R&B Box: Thirty Years Of Rhythm & Blues.
(S) (2:24) Razor & Tie 2053 Mercy, Mercy: The Definitive.
(S) (2:23) Time-Life R838-13 Solid Gold Soul - 1964.

released as by DON COVAY:
1973 I WAS CHECKIN' OUT, SHE WAS CHECKIN' IN

(S) (4:06) Rhino 70551 Soul Hits Of The 70's Volume 11. *(45 version but :21 longer fade)*
(S) (4:20) Mercury 836030 Checkin' In With. *(LP version)*
(S) (4:19) Mercury 836030 Checkin' In With. *(alternate take)*
(S) (4:06) Motown 6763 Rites Of Rhythm & Blues Volume Two. *(45 version but :21 longer fade)*
(S) (4:19) Ichiban 2508 Cheatin': From A Man's Point Of View. *(LP version)*
(S) (4:20) Razor & Tie 2053 Mercy, Mercy: The Definitive. *(LP version)*

COVEN
1971 ONE TIN SOLDIER, THE LEGEND OF BILLY JACK

(S) (3:20) Rhino 70927 Super Hits Of The 70's Volume 7. *(Warner Brothers hit version which was later released on MGM in a different version)*
(S) (3:10) Priority 53701 Best Of The 60's & 70's Rock: Protest Rock. *(MGM noncharting version)*
(S) (3:19) Time-Life SOD-31 Sounds Of The Seventies - AM Top Twenty. *(Warner Brothers hit version which was later released on MGM in a different version)*
(S) (3:12) Polygram Special Markets 314520272 One Hit Wonders. *(MGM noncharting version)*

COVER GIRLS
1988 BECAUSE OF YOU
   (S)   (5:20)   Columbia 48840   Clivilles & Cole's Greatest
                         Remixes Volume 1. *(remixed)*
   (S)   (4:29)   Priority 50954   Power Workout High NRG
                         Megamix Volume 1. *(remixed; all selections on
                         this cd are segued together)*
1990 WE CAN'T GO WRONG
   (S)   (5:12)   Capitol 91041   We Can't Go Wrong.
   (S)   (5:11)   Madacy Entertainment 1989   Rock On 1989.
   (S)   (4:14)   Priority 50934   Shut Up And Dance! The 90's
                         Volume One. *(all selections on this cd are segued
                         together)*
   (S)   (4:24)   K-Tel 3868   Hot Ladies Of Pop.
   (S)   (4:25)   Time-Life R834-15   Body Talk - Once In Lifetime.
1992 WISHING ON A STAR
   (S)   (4:41)   Epic 47381   Here It Is. *(LP version)*
   (S)   (4:41)   K-Tel 6101   Hot Ladies Of The 90's - Dazzling
                         Divas. *(LP version)*
   (S)   (4:41)   JCI 3132   1990 - Only Rock 'n Roll - 1994. *(LP
                         version)*
   (S)   (4:40)   Priority 50946   100% Party Hits Of The 90's
                         Volume One. *(LP version)*

COWSILLS
1967 THE RAIN, THE PARK & OTHER THINGS
   (M)   (2:56)   Mercury 834216   45's On CD Volume 3.
   (S)   (3:00)   Polydor 833344   Best Of.
   (M)   (2:59)   Rhino 71065   Summer Of Love Volume 1.
   (M)   (2:54)   Time-Life SUD-05   Superhits - 1967.
   (M)   (2:59)   Varese Sarabande 5534   Rhythm Of The Rain.
   (S)   (2:59)   Collectables 2505   History Of Rock - The 60's Part
                         5.
   (S)   (2:59)   Collectables 4505   History Of Rock/The 60s Part
                         Five.
   (S)   (3:00)   Rebound 314520204   Best Of.
   (M)   (2:56)   K-Tel 3130   60's Sound Explosion.
   (S)   (3:01)   Razor & Tie 2037   The Cowsills.
   (S)   (2:59)   Eclipse Music Group 64870   Rock 'n Roll Relix
                         1966-1967.
   (S)   (2:59)   Eclipse Music Group 64872   Rock 'n Roll Relix
                         1960-1969.
   (M)   (2:54)   Time-Life AM1-08   AM Gold - 1967.
1968 WE CAN FLY
   (S)   (2:12)   Polydor 833344   Best Of.
   (S)   (2:12)   Rebound 314520204   Best Of.
   (S)   (2:13)   LaserLight 12312 and 15936   The Wonder Years -
                         Good Times, Good Friends.
   (M)   (2:17)   Varese Sarabande 5719   Bubblegum Classics
                         Volume Three.
1968 INDIAN LAKE
   (S)   (2:41)   Polydor 833344   Best Of.
   (S)   (2:39)   Time-Life SUD-18   Superhits - Late 60's Classics.
   (S)   (2:41)   Rebound 314520204   Best Of.
   (S)   (2:39)   Time-Life AM1-12   AM Gold - Late '60s Classics.
1968 POOR BABY
   (M)   (2:56)   Polydor 833344   Best Of.
   (M)   (2:56)   Rebound 314520204   Best Of.
1969 HAIR
   (S)   (3:28)   Rhino 70630   Billboard's Top Rock & Roll Hits Of
                         1969. *(LP version)*
   (S)   (3:28)   Rhino 72005   Billboard's Top Rock & Roll Hits
                         1968-1972 Box Set. *(LP version)*
   (S)   (3:28)   Polydor 833344   Best Of. *(LP version)*
   (S)   (3:27)   Time-Life SUD-07   Superhits - 1969. *(LP version)*
   (S)   (3:28)   Rebound 314520269   Class Reunion 1969. *(LP
                         version)*
   (S)   (3:28)   Rebound 314520204   Best Of. *(LP version)*
   (S)   (3:28)   Special Music 5026   Let It All Hang Out - 60's
                         Party Hits. *(LP version)*
   (S)   (3:28)   LaserLight 12313 and 15936   The Wonder Years -
                         Summer Time. *(LP version)*
   (S)   (3:28)   Eclipse Music Group 64871   Rock 'n Roll Relix
                         1968-1969. *(LP version)*

   (S)   (3:28)   Eclipse Music Group 64872   Rock 'n Roll Relix
                         1960-1969. *(LP version)*
   (S)   (3:28)   Time-Life 2CLR-31   Classic Rock - Totally
                         Fantastic '60s. *(LP version)*
   (S)   (3:27)   Time-Life AM1-01   AM Gold - 1969. *(LP version)*
   (S)   (3:28)   Rhino 72819   16 Magazine - Who's Your Fave
                         Rave. *(LP version)*

DEBORAH COX
1995 SENTIMENTAL
   (S)   (4:27)   Arista 18781   Deborah Cox.
   (S)   (4:08)   Arista 18977   Ultimate Hip Hop Party 1998. *(all
                         selections on this cd are segued together)*
1996 WHO DO U LOVE
   (S)   (4:21)   Arista 18781   Deborah Cox.
   (S)   (4:30)   Arista 18943   Ultimate Dance Party 1997. *(all
                         selections on this cd are segued together; remix)*

CRABBY APPLETON
1970 GO BACK
   (S)   (3:03)   Rhino 70926   Super Hits Of The 70's Volume 6.
   (M)   (2:58)   Time-Life SOD-21   Sounds Of The Seventies -
                         Rock 'N' Soul Seventies.
   (S)   (3:03)   Time-Life R968-11   Guitar Rock - The Early '70s.

BILLY "CRASH" CRADDOCK
1974 RUB IT IN
(45 length is (2:14); LP length is (2:32))
   (S)   (2:14)   MCA 6421   16 Top Country Hits Volume 1.
   (S)   (2:14)   Time-Life CCD-16   Contemporary Country - The
                         Mid 70's Hot Hits.
   (S)   (2:14)   K-Tel 3163   Behind Closed Doors.
   (S)   (2:14)   MCA Special Products 20943   Trucker's Jukebox
                         Volume 5.
   (S)   (2:25)   Razor & Tie 2095   Crash's Smashes: Hits Of.
   (S)   (2:13)   JCI 3155   1970 - Only Country - 1974.
   (S)   (2:14)   Risky Business 67309   Sexy Country.
   (S)   (2:13)   Hip-O 40085   The Class Of Country 1970-1974.

FLOYD CRAMER
1960 LAST DATE
   (S)   (2:27)   RCA 8474   Nipper's Greatest Hits Of The 60's
                         Volume 1.
   (S)   (2:27)   RCA 56322 and 66403   Best Of.
   (S)   (2:27)   Pair 1210   Best Of.
   (S)   (2:26)   Time-Life 2RNR-11   Rock 'N' Roll Era - 1960.
                         (found only on remastered versions of this cd)
   (S)   (2:25)   Time-Life CTD-12   Country USA - 1960.
   (S)   (2:27)   Time-Life R103-27   Love Me Tender.
   (S)   (2:26)   K-Tel 3096   Classic Country Instrumentals.
   (S)   (2:33)   RCA 58399   Collector's Series. *(live)*
   (S)   (2:27)   RCA 66591   The Essential.
   (S)   (2:26)   Collectors' Choice 003/4   Instrumental Gems Of
                         The 60's.
   (S)   (2:25)   RCA 53745   Piano Masterpieces (1900-1975).
   (S)   (2:26)   Time-Life R857-02   The Heart Of Rock 'n' Roll -
                         1960.
   (S)   (2:26)   RCA 66818   The Essential Series Sampler.
   (S)   (2:25)   RCA 66946   Super Hits.
   (S)   (2:26)   K-Tel 3583   Those Wonderful Instrumentals
                         Volume 3.
   (S)   (2:25)   Time-Life R814-05   Love Songs.
   (S)   (2:26)   Time-Life R986-22   Instrumental Classics - Pop
                         Classics.
   (S)   (2:25)   Time-Life R808-01   Classic Country 1960-1964.
   (S)   (2:26)   Collectables 2711   Last Date/On The Rebound.
1961 ON THE REBOUND
   (S)   (2:06)   RCA 8475   Nipper's Greatest Hits Of The 60's
                         Volume 2.
   (S)   (2:06)   RCA 56322 and 66403   Best Of.
   (S)   (2:08)   Pair 1210   Best Of.
   (S)   (2:06)   Time-Life HPD-37   Your Hit Parade - The 60's.
   (S)   (2:06)   RCA 66591   The Essential.
   (S)   (2:05)   Collectables 2711   Last Date/On The Rebound.

FLOYD CRAMER *(Continued)*
1961 SAN ANTONIO ROSE
- (S) (2:19) Rhino 70682 Billboard's Top Country Hits Of 1961.
- (S) (2:20) Pair 1210 Best Of.
- (M) (2:31) Pair 1254 Magic Touch Of. *(rerecording)*
- (S) (2:19) RCA 66591 The Essential.
- (S) (2:18) RCA 66946 Super Hits.
- (S) (2:20) K-Tel 3358 101 Greatest Country Hits Vol. Four: Mellow Country.
- (S) (2:19) Collectables 2711 Last Date/On The Rebound.

CRANBERRIES
1994 LINGER
- (S) (4:34) Island 314514156 Everybody Else Is Doing It, So Why Can't We?.
1997 WHEN YOU'RE GONE
- (S) (4:54) Island 314524234 To The Faithful Departed.
1997 FREE TO DECIDE
- (S) (4:23) Island 314524234 To The Faithful Departed.

LES CRANE
1971 DESIDERATA

CRASH TEST DUMMIES
1994 MMM MMM MMM MMM
- (S) (3:54) Arista 16531 God Shuffled His Feet. *(tracks into next selection)*

JOHNNY CRAWFORD
1962 PATTI ANN
- (M) (2:09) Del-Fi 71220 Best Of.
1962 CINDY'S BIRTHDAY
- (S) (2:02) Time-Life SUD-19 Superhits - Early 60's Classics.
- (S) (2:05) Del-Fi 71220 Best Of.
- (S) (2:05) Collectors' Choice 002 Teen Idols....For A Moment.
- (S) (2:04) K-Tel 3388 TV Stars Sing.
- (S) (2:03) Time-Life AM1-20 AM Gold - Early '60s Classics.
- (S) (2:05) Rhino 72819 16 Magazine - Who's Your Fave Rave.
- (S) (2:05) Time-Life R857-17 The Heart Of Rock 'n' Roll: The Early '60s.
1962 YOUR NOSE IS GONNA GROW
- (S) (2:01) Del-Fi 71220 Best Of.
1962 RUMORS
- (S) (2:11) Era 5025 The Brill Building Sound.
- (S) (2:13) Del-Fi 70008 The Del-Fi & Donna Story.
- (S) (2:13) Del-Fi 71220 Best Of.
1963 PROUD
- (S) (2:17) Del-Fi 70008 The Del-Fi & Donna Story.
- (S) (2:17) Del-Fi 71220 Best Of.

ROBERT CRAY BAND
1987 SMOKING GUN
- (S) (4:03) Columbia 44382 Heart Of Soul.
- (S) (4:05) Polydor 314515913 Classic Rock Box.
- (S) (4:03) Time-Life R102-34 The Rolling Stone Collection.
- (S) (4:05) K-Tel 6128 Hot Rockin' Blues.
- (S) (4:05) Mercury 830568 Strong Persuader.
- (S) (4:05) MFSL 564 Strong Persuader. *(gold disc)*
- (S) (4:05) Rebound 314520444 The Roots Of Rock: Blues Rock.

CRAZY ELEPHANT
1969 GIMME GIMME GOOD LOVIN'
- (S) (2:02) K-Tel 205 Battle Of The Bands Volume 3. *(LP version)*
- (S) (2:02) Rhino 70996 One Hit Wonders Of The 60's Volume 2. *(LP version)*
- (S) (2:02) Rhino 70732 Grandson Of Frat Rock. *(LP version)*
- (S) (2:01) Time-Life 2CLR-29 Classic Rock - Bubblegum, Garage And Pop Nuggets. *(LP version)*
- (S) (2:03) Varese Sarabande 5575 Bubblegum Classics Volume Two. *(LP version)*
- (S) (2:01) K-Tel 3386 Best Of Bubblegum Music. *(LP version)*

- (S) (2:02) Time-Life 2CLR-31 Classic Rock - Totally Fantastic '60s. *(LP version)*

CRAZY WORLD OF ARTHUR BROWN
1968 FIRE
- (S) (2:49) Mercury 834216 45's On CD Volume 3.
- (S) (2:53) Rhino 70327 History Of British Rock Volume 9.
- (S) (2:53) Rhino 72022 History Of British Rock Box Set.
- (M) (3:01) Polydor 833736 The Crazy World of Arthur Brown. *(this is the U.K. mono mix; tracks into the next selection)*
- (S) (2:53) Polydor 833736 The Crazy World Of Arthur Brown.
- (S) (2:50) Time-Life 2CLR-27 Classic Rock - 1968: Blowin' Your Mind.
- (S) (2:53) Rebound 314520277 Hard Rock Essentials - The 60's.
- (S) (2:52) Time-Life 2CLR-31 Classic Rock - Totally Fantastic '60s.

CREAM
1968 SUNSHINE OF YOUR LOVE
- (S) (4:09) JCI 3103 Electric Sixties. *(LP version)*
- (S) (4:08) Original Sound 8894 Dick Clark's 21 All-Time Hits Vol. 3. *(LP version)*
- (M) (3:01) Rhino 70326 History of British Rock Volume 8. *(45 version)*
- (M) (3:01) Rhino 72022 History Of British Rock Box Set. *(45 version)*
- (S) (4:09) Polydor 823636 Disraeli Gears. *(LP version)*
- (S) (4:09) Polydor 811639 Strange Brew/Very Best Of. *(LP version)*
- (S) (4:09) Polydor 835268 Crossroads. *(LP version)*
- (S) (4:09) Atlantic 82152 O.S.T. Goodfellas. *(LP version)*
- (S) (4:10) MFSL 562 Disraeli Gears. *(LP version; gold disc)*
- (M) (4:10) MFSL 562 Disraeli Gears. *(LP version; gold disc)*
- (S) (4:08) Time-Life 2CLR-04 Classic Rock - 1968. *(LP version)*
- (S) (4:09) Time-Life OPCD-4521 Guitar Rock. *(LP version)*
- (S) (4:09) Polydor 314523752 Very Best Of. *(LP version)*
- (S) (4:09) Polydor 314527116 Cream Of Clapton. *(LP version)*
- (S) (4:09) Polydor 314539000 Those Were The Days Box Set. *(LP version)*
- (S) (7:24) Polydor 314539000 Those Were The Days Box Set. *(live)*
- (S) (4:10) Time-Life R13610 Gold And Platinum Box Set - The Ultimate Rock Collection. *(LP version)*
- (S) (4:09) Atlantic 83088 Atlantic Records: 50 Years - The Gold Anniversary Collection. *(LP version)*
1968 WHITE ROOM
- (S) (4:55) Atlantic 81908 Classic Rock 1966-1988. *(LP version)*
- (S) (4:47) Polydor 837362 O.S.T. 1969. *(LP version)*
- (M) (3:02) Rhino 70327 History Of British Rock Volume 9. *(45 version; truncated fade)*
- (M) (3:02) Rhino 72022 History Of British Rock Box Set. *(45 version; truncated fade)*
- (S) (4:57) Polydor 811639 Strange Brew/Very Best Of. *(LP version)*
- (S) (4:57) Polydor 827578 Wheels Of Fire. *(LP version)*
- (S) (4:56) Polydor 835268 Crossroads. *(LP version)*
- (S) (4:55) Atlantic 82306 Atlantic Rock & Roll Box Set. *(LP version)*
- (S) (4:57) DCC Compact Classics 1020 Wheels Of Fire. *(LP version; gold disc)*
- (S) (4:56) Time-Life 2CLR-21 Classic Rock - Rock Renaissance II. *(LP version)*
- (S) (4:56) Polydor 314523752 Very Best Of. *(LP version)*
- (S) (4:56) Polydor 314527116 Cream Of Clapton. *(LP version)*
- (S) (4:57) Polydor 314539000 Those Were The Days Box Set. *(LP version)*
- (S) (6:20) Polydor 314539000 Those Were The Days Box Set. *(live)*
1969 CROSSROADS
(dj copies of this 45 ran (2:50) and (4:13);
commercial copies were all (4:13))
- (S) (4:13) Polydor 811639 Strange Brew/Very Best Of.

(S) (4:14) Polydor 827578 Wheels Of Fire.
(S) (4:12) Polydor 835268 Crossroads.
(S) (4:14) DCC Compact Classics 1020 Wheels Of Fire. *(gold disc)*
(S) (4:11) Time-Life 2CLR-20 Classic Rock - 1969: Shakin' All Over.
(S) (4:08) Time-Life R102-34 The Rolling Stone Collection.
(S) (4:15) Polydor 314523752 Very Best Of.
(S) (4:14) Polydor 314527116 Cream Of Clapton.
(S) (4:12) Time-Life R968-15 Guitar Rock - FM Classics.
(S) (4:09) Hammer & Lace 697124017 O.S.T. The Ride.
(S) (4:23) Polydor 314539000 Those Were The Days Box Set.

CREEDENCE CLEARWATER REVIVAL
1968 SUZIE Q (PART 1)
(S) (4:34) Fantasy CCR2 Chronicle. *(Part 1)*
(S) (4:34) Fantasy CCGCD-22-2 Chronicle: 20 Greatest Hits. *(gold disc; Part 1)*
(S) (3:58) Fantasy CCR3 Chronicle Volume 2. *(Part 2)*
(S) (3:58) Fantasy CCGCD-23-2 Chronicle Volume 2: 20 Great CCR Classics. *(gold disc; Part 2)*
(S) (8:33) Fantasy 9418 Creedence Gold. *(LP version)*
(S) (8:33) Fantasy 8382 and 4512 Creedence Clearwater Revival. *(LP version)*
(S) (4:29) Time-Life 2CLR-19 Classic Rock - 1968: Shakin' All Over. *(Part 1)*

1969 PROUD MARY
(S) (3:06) Fantasy CCR2 Chronicle. *(very poor stereo separation)*
(E) (3:04) Original Sound 8854 Oldies But Goodies Vol. 4. *(this compact disc uses the "Waring - fds" noise reduction process)*
(E) (3:04) Original Sound 2221 Oldies But Goodies Volumes 1,4,6,8 and 10 Box Set. *(this box set uses the "Waring - fds" noise reduction process)*
(E) (3:04) Original Sound 2500 Oldies But Goodies Volumes 1-15 Box Set. *(this box set uses the "Waring - fds" noise reduction process)*
(E) (3:03) Original Sound 8894 Dick Clark's 21 All-Time Hits Vol. 3.
(S) (3:06) Fantasy CCGCD-22-2 Chronicle: 20 Greatest Hits. *(gold disc; very poor stereo separation)*
(S) (3:06) Fantasy 8387 and 4513 Bayou Country. *(very poor stereo separation)*
(S) (3:06) Fantasy 9418 Creedence Gold. *(very poor stereo separation)*
(S) (3:06) DCC Compact Classics 1038 Bayou Country. *(very poor stereo separation; gold disc)*
(S) (3:06) Time-Life 2CLR-18 Classic Rock - Creedence Clearwater Revival. *(very poor stereo separation)*
(S) (3:06) Time-Life R13610 Gold And Platinum Box Set - The Ultimate Rock Collection. *(very poor stereo separation)*

1969 BAD MOON RISING
(S) (2:18) Fantasy CCR2 Chronicle. *(very poor stereo separation)*
(S) (2:18) Fantasy CCGCD-22-2 Chronicle: 20 Greatest Hits. *(gold disc; very poor stereo separation)*
(S) (2:19) Fantasy 8393 and 4514 Green River. *(very poor stereo separation)*
(S) (2:17) Epic 48732 O.S.T. My Girl. *(very poor stereo separation)*
(S) (2:18) Motown 6094 More Songs From The Original Soundtrack Of The "Big Chill". *(very poor stereo separation)*
(S) (2:18) Fantasy 9418 Creedence Gold. *(very poor stereo separation)*
(S) (2:18) Time-Life 2CLR-18 Classic Rock - Creedence Clearwater Revival. *(very poor stereo separation)*
(S) (2:19) DCC Compact Classics 1064 Green River. *(gold disc; very poor stereo separation)*
(S) (2:18) TVT 8090 O.S.T. My Fellow Americans. *(very poor stereo separation)*

1969 GREEN RIVER
(S) (2:31) Polydor 837362 O.S.T. 1969. *(LP mix)*

(S) (2:33) Fantasy CCGCD-22-2 Chronicle: 20 Greatest Hits. *(LP mix; gold disc)*
(S) (2:33) Fantasy CCR2 Chronicle. *(LP mix)*
(S) (2:33) Fantasy 8393 and 4514 Green River. *(LP mix)*
(S) (2:33) DCC Compact Classics 1064 Green River. *(LP mix; gold disc)*
(S) (2:32) Time-Life 2CLR-18 Classic Rock - Creedence Clearwater Revival. *(LP mix)*

1969 COMMOTION
(S) (2:41) Fantasy CCR2 Chronicle.
(S) (2:41) Fantasy CCGCD-22-2 Chronicle: 20 Greatest Hits. *(gold disc)*
(S) (2:41) Fantasy 8393 and 4514 Green River.
(S) (2:41) DCC Compact Classics 1064 Green River. *(gold disc)*
(S) (2:39) Time-Life 2CLR-20 Classic Rock - 1969: Shakin' All Over.

1969 DOWN ON THE CORNER
(S) (2:44) Fantasy CCR2 Chronicle. *(LP version)*
(S) (2:44) Fantasy CCGCD-22-2 Chronicle: 20 Greatest Hits. *(LP version; gold disc)*
(S) (2:44) Fantasy 8397 and 4515 Willie And The Poor Boys. *(LP version)*
(S) (2:43) Fantasy 9418 Creedence Gold. *(LP version)*
(S) (2:44) Time-Life 2CLR-18 Classic Rock - Creedence Clearwater Revival. *(LP version)*
(S) (2:44) DCC Compact Classics 1070 Willie And The Poor Boys. *(LP version; gold disc)*

1969 FORTUNATE SON
(S) (2:18) Fantasy CCR2 Chronicle.
(S) (2:18) Fantasy CCGCD-22-2 Chronicle: 20 Greatest Hits. *(gold disc)*
(S) (2:19) Fantasy 8397 and 4515 Willie And The Poor Boys.
(S) (2:18) Fantasy 9430 More Creedence Gold.
(S) (2:19) DCC Compact Classics 1070 Willie And The Poor Boys. *(gold disc)*
(S) (2:18) Time-Life 2CLR-18 Classic Rock - Creedence Clearwater Revival.
(S) (2:17) Time-Life R102-34 The Rolling Stone Collection.
(S) (2:18) Epic 66329 O.S.T. Forrest Gump.

1970 TRAVELIN' BAND
(S) (2:06) Fantasy CCR2 Chronicle.
(S) (2:06) Fantasy CCGCD-22-2 Chronicle: 20 Greatest Hits. *(gold disc)*
(S) (2:06) Fantasy 8402 and 4516 Cosmos Factory.
(S) (2:06) DCC Compact Classics 1031 Cosmos Factory. *(gold disc)*
(S) (2:06) Razor & Tie 22502 Those Rocking 70's.
(S) (2:06) Time-Life 2CLR-18 Classic Rock - Creedence Clearwater Revival.

1970 WHO'LL STOP THE RAIN
(S) (2:27) Fantasy CCR2 Chronicle.
(S) (2:27) Fantasy CCGCD-22-2 Chronicle: 20 Greatest Hits. *(gold disc)*
(S) (2:27) Fantasy 8402 and 4516 Cosmos Factory.
(S) (2:26) Fantasy 9430 More Creedence Gold.
(S) (2:26) DCC Compact Classics 1031 Cosmos Factory. *(gold disc)*
(S) (2:27) Time-Life 2CLR-18 Classic Rock - Creedence Clearwater Revival.

1970 UP AROUND THE BEND
(S) (2:41) Fantasy CCR2 Chronicle.
(S) (2:41) Fantasy CCGCD-22-2 Chronicle: 20 Greatest Hits. *(gold disc)*
(S) (2:41) Fantasy 8402 and 4516 Cosmos Factory.
(S) (2:41) DCC Compact Classics 1031 Cosmos Factory. *(gold disc)*
(S) (2:40) Fantasy 9430 More Creedence Gold.
(S) (2:40) Time-Life 2CLR-18 Classic Rock - Creedence Clearwater Revival.
(S) (2:40) Time-Life SOD-01 Sounds Of The Seventies - 1970.

1970 RUN THROUGH THE JUNGLE
(S) (3:04) Fantasy 9430 More Creedence Gold.
(S) (3:04) Fantasy CCR2 Chronicle.
(S) (3:04) Fantasy CCGCD-22-2 Chronicle: 20 Greatest Hits. *(gold disc)*

CREEDENCE CLEARWATER REVIVAL (Continued)

    (S) (3:04) Fantasy 8402 and 4516 Cosmos Factory.
    (S) (3:04) DCC Compact Classics 1031 Cosmos Factory. *(gold disc)*
    (S) (3:04) Time-Life 2CLR-18 Classic Rock - Creedence Clearwater Revival.

1970 LOOKIN' OUT MY BACK DOOR
    (S) (2:31) Fantasy CCR2 Chronicle.
    (S) (2:31) Fantasy CCGCD-22-2 Chronicle: 20 Greatest Hits. *(gold disc)*
    (S) (2:31) Fantasy 9430 More Creedence Gold.
    (S) (2:32) Fantasy 8402 and 4516 Cosmos Factory.
    (S) (2:32) DCC Compact Classics 1031 Cosmos Factory. *(gold disc)*
    (S) (2:30) MCA 10925 O.S.T. Blue Chips.
    (S) (2:31) Time-Life 2CLR-18 Classic Rock - Creedence Clearwater Revival.

1970 LONG AS I CAN SEE THE LIGHT
    (S) (3:32) Fantasy 8402 and 4516 Cosmos Factory.
    (S) (3:32) DCC Compact Classics 1031 Cosmos Factory. *(gold disc)*
    (S) (3:32) Fantasy CCR2 Chronicle.
    (S) (3:32) Fantasy CCGCD-22-2 Chronicle: 20 Greatest Hits. *(gold disc)*

1971 HAVE YOU EVER SEEN THE RAIN
    (S) (2:38) Fantasy CCR2 Chronicle.
    (S) (2:38) Fantasy CCGCD-22-2 Chronicle: 20 Greatest Hits. *(gold disc)*
    (S) (2:38) Fantasy 8410 and 4517 Pendulum.
    (S) (2:38) Fantasy 9418 Creedence Gold.
    (S) (2:38) Time-Life 2CLR-18 Classic Rock - Creedence Clearwater Revival.
    (S) (2:38) Time-Life SOD-02 Sounds Of The Seventies - 1971.
    (S) (2:38) DCC Compact Classics 1097 Pendulum. *(gold disc)*

1971 HEY TONIGHT
    (S) (2:41) Fantasy CCR2 Chronicle.
    (S) (2:41) Fantasy CCGCD-22-2 Chronicle: 20 Greatest Hits. *(gold disc)*
    (S) (2:42) Fantasy 9430 More Creedence Gold.
    (S) (2:42) Fantasy 8410 and 4517 Pendulum.
    (S) (2:42) DCC Compact Classics 1097 Pendulum. *(gold disc)*

1971 SWEET HITCH-HIKER
    (S) (2:55) Fantasy CCR2 Chronicle. *(very poor stereo separation)*
    (S) (2:55) Fantasy CCGCD-22-2 Chronicle: 20 Greatest Hits. *(gold disc; very poor stereo separation)*
    (S) (2:56) Fantasy 9404 and 4518 Mardi Gras. *(very poor stereo separation)*
    (S) (2:56) Fantasy 9430 More Creedence Gold. *(very poor stereo separation)*
    (S) (2:54) Time-Life 2CLR-18 Classic Rock - Creedence Clearwater Revival. *(very poor stereo separation)*

1972 SOMEDAY NEVER COMES
    (S) (3:59) Fantasy CCR2 Chronicle.
    (S) (3:59) Fantasy CCGCD-22-2 Chronicle: 20 Greatest Hits. *(gold disc)*
    (S) (3:58) Fantasy 9404 and 4518 Mardi Gras.
    (S) (3:58) Time-Life 2CLR-18 Classic Rock - Creedence Clearwater Revival.

MARSHALL CRENSHAW
1982 SOMEDAY, SOMEWAY
    (S) (2:49) Priority 53768 Rock Of The 80's Volume 14.
    (S) (2:49) Rhino 71698 New Wave Hits Of The 80's Vol. 5.
    (S) (2:48) Warner Brothers 3673 Marshall Crenshaw.
    (S) (2:48) Time-Life R988-26 Sounds Of The Eighties: The Rolling Stone Collection 1982-1983.

CRESCENDOS
1958 OH JULIE
    (M) (2:41) Rhino 70897 Best Of Excello Records Volume 2.
    (M) (2:39) Time-Life 2RNR-24 Rock 'N' Roll Era - The 50's Keep On Rockin'.
    (M) (2:39) Time-Life R102-17 Lost Treasures Of Rock 'N' Roll.
    (M) (2:40) Time-Life R857-11 The Heart Of Rock 'n' Roll 1958-1959.

CRESTS
1959 16 CANDLES
    (M) (2:51) Rhino 70620 Billboard's Top Rock & Roll Hits Of 1959.
    (M) (2:51) Rhino 72004 Billboard's Top Rock & Roll Hits 1957-1961 Box Set.
    (M) (2:49) Rhino 75763 Best Of Doo Wop Ballads.
    (M) (2:50) Original Sound 8864 Oldies But Goodies Vol. 14. *(this compact disc uses the "Waring - fds" noise reduction process)*
    (M) (2:50) Original Sound 2222 Oldies But Goodies Volumes 3,5,11,14 and 15 Box Set. *(this box set uses the "Waring - fds" noise reduction process)*
    (M) (2:50) Original Sound 2500 Oldies But Goodies Volumes 1-15 Box Set. *(this box set uses the "Waring - fds" noise reduction process)*
    (M) (2:50) Original Sound CDGO-1 Golden Oldies Volume. 1.
    (M) (2:50) Original Sound 8891 Dick Clark's 21 All-Time Hits Vol. 1.
    (M) (2:51) Garland 012 Remember When.
    (M) (2:52) JCI 3203 Lovin' Fifties.
    (M) (2:48) Rhino 70948 Best Of.
    (M) (2:49) Collectables 5009 Golden Classics.
    (M) (2:49) MCA 8001 O.S.T. American Graffiti.
    (M) (2:50) Rhino 71463 Doo Wop Box.
    (E) (2:50) Original Sound 8905r 13 Of The Best Doo Wop Love Songs.
    (E) (2:50) Original Sound 9326 Best Love Songs Vol. 1 & 2.
    (E) (2:50) Original Sound 4001 Art Laboe's 60 Killer Oldies.
    (E) (2:50) Original Sound 1236 Best Love Songs Box Set.
    (M) (2:50) Original Sound 9603 Best Of Oldies But Goodies Vol. 3.
    (M) (2:51) Time-Life 2RNR-13 Rock 'N' Roll Era - 1959.
    (M) (2:49) Time-Life R962-06 History Of Rock 'N' Roll: Doo Wop And Vocal Group Tradition 1955-1962.
    (M) (2:50) Collectables 2506 WCBS-FM History Of Rock - The 50's Part 1.
    (M) (2:50) Collectables 4506 History Of Rock/The 50s Part One.
    (M) (2:50) Collectables 2509 WCBS-FM For Lovers Only Part 1.
    (M) (2:50) Collectables 2604 WCBS-FM Jukebox Giants Vol. 2.
    (M) (2:49) Time-Life R103-27 Love Me Tender.
    (M) (2:51) Time-Life R10513 40 Lovin' Oldies.
    (M) (2:49) LaserLight 12324 Sixteen Candles: Very Best Of The Crests And Duprees.
    (M) (2:50) Collectables 8812 For Collectors Only.
    (M) (2:48) JCI 3129 1955 - Only Rock 'N Roll - 1959.
    (M) (2:49) Time-Life R857-01 The Heart Of Rock 'n' Roll - 1959.
    (M) (2:45) Thump 7060 Low Rider Oldies Volume 6.
    (M) (2:48) Sundazed 6075 Sing All Biggies.
    (M) (2:49) Music Club 50015 Love Me Forever - 18 Rock'N' Roll Love Songs.
    (M) (2:49) Nick At Nite/550 Music 63456 Double Date With Joanie And Chachi.
    (M) (2:49) Time-Life R857-21 The Heart Of Rock 'n' Roll Slow Dancing Classics.

1959 SIX NIGHTS A WEEK
    (M) (2:45) Rhino 70948 Best Of.
    (M) (2:44) Original Sound CDGO-2 Golden Oldies Volume. 2.
    (M) (2:47) Original Sound 9329 Oldies But Goodies Doo Wop Classics.
    (M) (2:46) Collectables 5009 Golden Classics.
    (M) (2:45) Time-Life 2RNR-50 Rock 'N' Roll Era - Street Corner Serenade II.
    (M) (2:46) Collectables 2503 WCBS-FM History Of Rock - The 50's Part 2.
    (M) (2:46) Collectables 4503 History Of Rock/The 50s Part Two.
    (M) (2:46) LaserLight 12324 Sixteen Candles: Very Best Of The Crests And Duprees.
    (M) (2:50) Collectables 8812 For Collectors Only.
    (M) (2:46) Sundazed 6075 Sing All Biggies.

1959 THE ANGELS LISTENED IN
- (S) (2:00) Rhino 70948 Best Of.
- (S) (2:00) Collectables 5009 Golden Classics.
- (M) (1:56) Original Sound 8860 Oldies But Goodies Vol. 10. *(this compact disc uses the "Waring - fds" noise reduction process)*
- (M) (1:56) Original Sound 2221 Oldies But Goodies Volumes 1,4,6,8 and 10 Box Set. *(this box set uses the "Waring - fds" noise reduction process)*
- (M) (1:56) Original Sound 2500 Oldies But Goodies Volumes 1-15 Box Set. *(this box set uses the "Waring - fds" noise reduction process)*
- (M) (1:56) Original Sound CDGO-6 Golden Oldies Volume. 6.
- (S) (2:00) Time-Life 2RNR-28 Rock 'N' Roll Era - The 50's Rave On.
- (S) (2:00) Collectables 2503 WCBS-FM History Of Rock - The 50's Part 2.
- (S) (2:00) Collectables 4503 History Of Rock/The 50s Part Two.
- (S) (2:00) LaserLight 12324 Sixteen Candles: Very Best Of The Crests And Duprees.
- (S) (2:00) Collectables 8812 For Collectors Only.
- (S) (2:00) Collectables 8812 For Collectors Only. *(alternate take)*
- (S) (2:00) Scotti Bros. 75465 Angel Hits.
- (S) (2:00) Sundazed 6075 Sing All Biggies.

1960 STEP BY STEP
- (M) (2:27) Rhino 75764 Best Of Doo Wop Uptempo.
- (S) (2:26) Rhino 70948 Best Of.
- (E) (2:24) Original Sound 8859 Oldies But Goodies Vol. 9. *(this compact disc uses the "Waring - fds" noise reduction process)*
- (E) (2:23) Original Sound CDGO-14 Golden Oldies Volume. 14.
- (S) (2:26) Collectables 5009 Golden Classics.
- (M) (2:28) Time-Life 2RNR-22 Rock 'N' Roll Era - 1960 Still Rockin'.
- (S) (2:26) Collectables 2500 WCBS-FM History Of Rock - The 60's Part 1.
- (S) (2:26) Collectables 4500 History Of Rock/The 60s Part One.
- (S) (2:26) LaserLight 12324 Sixteen Candles: Very Best Of The Crests And Duprees.
- (S) (2:26) Collectables 8812 For Collectors Only. *(alternate take)*
- (S) (2:28) Collectables 8812 For Collectors Only.
- (S) (2:25) Sundazed 6076 Isn't It Amazing.
- (S) (2:27) Rhino 72507 Doo Wop Box II.

1960 TROUBLE IN PARADISE
- (M) (2:22) Rhino 70948 Best Of.
- (M) (2:15) Original Sound CDGO-14 Golden Oldies Volume. 14.
- (M) (2:23) Collectables 5009 Golden Classics.
- (M) (2:22) Time-Life 2RNR-40 Rock 'N' Roll Era - The 60's Teen Time.
- (M) (2:23) Collectables 2504 WCBS-FM History Of Rock - The 60's Part 4.
- (M) (2:23) Collectables 4504 History Of Rock/The 60s Part Four.
- (M) (2:23) LaserLight 12324 Sixteen Candles: Very Best Of The Crests And Duprees.
- (M) (2:23) Collectables 8812 For Collectors Only.
- (M) (2:22) Sundazed 6076 Isn't It Amazing.

CREW-CUTS
1955 EARTH ANGEL
- (M) (2:51) Mercury 314532731 Best Of.
- (M) (2:51) Nick At Nite/550 Music 63456 Double Date With Joanie And Chachi.

1955 KO KO MO (I LOVE YOU SO)
- (M) (2:35) Mercury 314532731 Best Of.

1955 DON'T BE ANGRY
- (M) (2:07) Special Music/Essex 5034 Prom Night - The 50's.
- (M) (2:06) Mercury 314532731 Best Of.

1955 A STORY UNTOLD
- (M) (2:22) Mercury 314532731 Best Of.

1955 GUM DROP
- (M) (2:35) Mercury 314532731 Best Of.

1956 ANGELS IN THE SKY
- (M) (2:21) Mercury 314532731 Best Of.

1956 SEVEN DAYS
- (M) (2:42) Mercury 314532731 Best Of.

1957 YOUNG LOVE
- (M) (2:27) Mercury 314532731 Best Of.

BOB CREWE GENERATION
1967 MUSIC TO WATCH GIRLS BY
- (S) (2:54) Time-Life HPD-39 Your Hit Parade - 60's Instrumentals: Take Two.
- (S) (2:53) Collectors' Choice 003/4 Instrumental Gems Of The 60's.

CRICKETS (see BUDDY HOLLY)

CRITTERS
1966 YOUNGER GIRL
- (S) (2:24) MCA 5938 Vintage Music Volumes 15 & 16.
- (S) (2:24) MCA 31213 Vintage Music Volume 16.
- (S) (2:24) JCI 3114 Easy Sixties.
- (S) (2:24) MCA Special Products 20751 Rock Around The Oldies #2.
- (S) (2:23) Taragon 1001 Anthology.
- (S) (2:24) MCA Special Products 22173 Vintage Collectibles Volume 11.
- (S) (2:23) Buddah 49506 Feelin' Groovy.
- (M) (2:25) Varese Sarabande 5802 Sunshine Days - Pop Classics Of The '60s Volume 2.

1966 MR. DIEINGLY SAD
- (S) (2:46) K-Tel 839 Battle Of The Bands Volume 2.
- (S) (2:47) MCA 5939 Vintage Music Volumes 17 & 18.
- (S) (2:47) MCA 31214 Vintage Music Volume 17.
- (S) (2:46) Time-Life 2CLR-29 Classic Rock - Bubblegum, Garage And Pop Nuggets.
- (S) (2:46) Time-Life R962-02 History Of Rock 'N' Roll: Folk Rock 1964-1967.
- (S) (2:46) Taragon 1001 Anthology.
- (M) (2:48) Varese Sarabande 5801 Sunshine Days - Pop Classics Of The '60s Volume 1.

1967 DON'T LET THE RAIN FALL DOWN ON ME
- (S) (2:38) Taragon 1001 Anthology.

JIM CROCE
1972 YOU DON'T MESS AROUND WITH JIM
- (S) (2:59) 21 Records/Atco 90467 Photographs & Memories/His Greatest Hits.
- (S) (3:00) Saja 90468 Down The Highway.
- (S) (3:00) Saja 92569 Down The Highway. *(remastered edition)*
- (S) (2:56) Time-Life SUD-11 Superhits - 1972.
- (S) (2:58) Time-Life SOD-13 Sounds Of The Seventies - 1972: Take Two.
- (S) (2:55) Time-Life R105-26 Our Songs: Singers & Songwriters Encore.
- (S) (3:01) DCC Compact Classics 1060 24 Karat Gold In A Bottle. *(gold disc)*
- (S) (2:59) Saja 92570 Photographs & Memories/His Greatest hits. *(remastered edition)*
- (S) (2:55) Time-Life AM1-07 AM Gold - 1972.
- (S) (2:59) K-Tel 3914 Superstars Greatest Hits Volume 3.
- (S) (3:00) Priority 50962 70's Greatest Rock Hits Volume 7: Southern Rock.

1972 OPERATOR (THAT'S NOT THE WAY IT FEELS)
- (S) (3:44) 21 Records/Atco 90467 Photographs & Memories/His Greatest Hits. *(LP version)*
- (S) (3:45) 21 Records/Atco 90469 Time In A Bottle/Greatest Love Songs. *(LP version)*
- (S) (3:46) Saja/Atlantic 92567 Time In A Bottle/Greatest Love Songs. *(remastered edition; LP version)*
- (S) (3:44) Time-Life SUD-20 Superhits - Early 70's Classics. *(LP version)*
- (S) (3:47) DCC Compact Classics 1060 24 Karat Gold In A Bottle. *(gold disc; LP version)*

JIM CROCE *(Continued)*

- (S) (3:46) Saja 92570 Photographs & Memories/His Greatest Hits. *(remastered edition; LP version)*
- (S) (3:44) Rhino 72519 Mellow Rock Hits Of The 70's - Sundown. *(LP version)*
- (S) (3:44) Time-Life AM1-15 AM Gold - Early '70s Classics. *(LP version)*
- (S) (3:44) K-Tel 3885 Story Songs. *(LP version)*
- (S) (3:46) Time-Life R834-18 Body Talk - Romantic Moments. *(LP version)*

1973 ONE LESS SET OF FOOTSTEPS
- (S) (2:44) 21 Records/Atco 90467 Photographs & Memories/His Greatest Hits.
- (S) (2:45) DCC Compact Classics 1060 24 Karat Gold In A Bottle. *(gold disc)*
- (S) (2:44) Saja 92570 Photographs & Memories/His Greatest Hits. *(remastered edition)*

1973 BAD, BAD LEROY BROWN
- (S) (2:58) Rhino 70634 Billboard's Top Rock & Roll Hits Of 1973.
- (S) (2:58) 21 Records/Atco 90467 Photographs & Memories/His Greatest Hits.
- (S) (2:58) Saja 90468 Down The Highway.
- (S) (2:59) Saja 92569 Down The Highway. *(remastered edition)*
- (S) (2:57) Time-Life SUD-13 Superhits - 1973.
- (S) (2:57) Time-Life SOD-14 Sounds Of The Seventies - 1973: Take Two.
- (S) (2:57) Time-Life R103-33 Singers & Songwriters.
- (S) (2:59) DCC Compact Classics 1060 24 Karat Gold In A Bottle. *(gold disc)*
- (S) (2:59) Saja 92570 Photographs & Memories/His Greatest Hits. *(remastered edition)*
- (S) (3:00) K-Tel 3626 Music Power.
- (S) (2:57) Time-Life AM1-03 AM Gold - 1973.
- (S) (2:58) Hollywood 62138 O.S.T. Home Alone 3.
- (S) (2:57) K-Tel 3987 70s Heavy Hitters: #1 Pop Hits.

1973 I GOT A NAME
- (S) (3:09) 21 Records/Atco 90467 Photographs & Memories/His Greatest Hits.
- (S) (3:10) Saja 90468 Down The Highway.
- (S) (3:10) Saja 92569 Down The Highway. *(remastered edition)*
- (S) (3:10) DCC Compact Classics 1060 24 Karat Gold In A Bottle. *(gold disc)*
- (S) (3:09) Saja 92570 Photographs & Memories/His Greatest Hits. *(remastered edition)*
- (S) (3:10) Rhino 72424 Billboard Top Movie Hits - 1970s.
- (S) (3:09) Velvel/Reel Sounds 79713 O.S.T. The Ice Storm.
- (S) (3:09) Time-Life R834-20 Body Talk - Heart And Soul.

1974 TIME IN A BOTTLE
- (S) (2:24) 21 Records/Atco 90467 Photographs & Memories/His Greatest Hits.
- (S) (2:24) 21 Records/Atco 90469 Time In A Bottle/Greatest Love Songs.
- (S) (2:23) JCI 3304 Mellow Seventies.
- (S) (2:23) Razor & Tie 4543 The '70s Preservation Society Presents: Easy '70s.
- (S) (2:23) Priority 53706 Singers/Songwriters/70's Greatest Rock Hits Volume 15.
- (S) (2:23) Time-Life SUD-16 Superhits - The Early 70's.
- (S) (2:23) Time-Life R103-33 Singers & Songwriters.
- (S) (2:25) DCC Compact Classics 1060 24 Karat Gold In A Bottle. *(gold disc)*
- (S) (2:23) K-Tel 3455 Folk Hits Around The Campfire.
- (S) (2:23) K-Tel 3454 70s Folk Rock Hits.
- (S) (2:25) Saja/Atlantic 92567 Time In A Bottle/Greatest Love Songs. *(remastered edition)*
- (S) (2:24) Saja 92570 Photographs & Memories/His Greatest Hits. *(remastered edition)*
- (S) (2:23) JCI 3145 1970 - Only Love - 1974.
- (S) (2:23) Time-Life AM1-13 AM Gold - The Early '70s.
- (S) (2:23) Time-Life R834-03 Body Talk - Moonlit Nights.
- (S) (2:23) K-Tel 4017 70s Heavy Hitters: Summer Love.
- (S) (2:24) Rhino 72739 Billboard Top Soft Rock Hits - 1973.
- (S) (2:24) Time-Life R814-04 Love Songs.

1974 I'LL HAVE TO SAY I LOVE YOU IN A SONG
- (S) (2:29) 21 Records/Atco 90467 Photographs & Memories/His Greatest Hits.
- (S) (2:28) 21 Records/Atco 90469 Time In A Bottle/Greatest Love Songs.
- (S) (2:28) JCI 3303 Love Seventies.
- (S) (2:28) Original Sound 8909 Best Love Songs Vol 4.
- (S) (2:28) Original Sound 9327 Best Love Songs Vol. 3 & 4.
- (S) (2:28) Original Sound 1236 Best Love Songs Box Set.
- (S) (2:29) Time-Life SOD-15 Sounds Of The Seventies - 1974: Take Two.
- (S) (2:29) Time-Life R105-26 Our Songs: Singers & Songwriters Encore.
- (S) (2:31) DCC Compact Classics 1060 24 Karat Gold In A Bottle. *(gold disc)*
- (S) (2:31) Saja/Atlantic 92567 Time In A Bottle/Greatest Love Songs. *(remastered edition)*
- (S) (2:30) Saja 92570 Photographs & Memories/His Greatest hits. *(remastered edition)*
- (S) (2:29) Time-Life R834-05 Body Talk - Sealed With A Kiss.
- (S) (2:30) Rhino 72740 Billboard Top Soft Rock Hits - 1974.

1974 WORKIN' AT THE CAR WASH BLUES
- (S) (2:29) 21 Records/Atco 90467 Photographs & Memories/His Greatest Hits.
- (S) (2:31) DCC Compact Classics 1060 24 Karat Gold In A Bottle. *(gold disc)*
- (S) (2:29) Saja 92570 Photographs & Memories/His Greatest Hits. *(remastered edition)*

BING CROSBY
released as by BING CROSBY and GRACE KELLY:
1956 TRUE LOVE
- (M) (3:04) Capitol 98670 Memories Are Made Of This.
- (E) (3:04) Capitol 93787 O.S.T. High Society.
- (E) (3:04) Rhino 72826 Romantic Duets From M-G-M Classics.
- (E) (3:04) Rhino 72909 Hollywood's Best: The Fifties.

released as by BING CROSBY:
1957 AROUND THE WORLD
- (M) (2:53) MCA 10887 His Legendary Years 1931-1957 Box Set.

1957 WHITE CHRISTMAS
- (M) (3:01) MCA 1620 Greatest Hits. *(1947 recording)*
- (M) (3:01) MCA 25205 O.S.T. Holiday Inn. *(1947 recording - not the 1942 recording that appeared in the movie "Holiday Inn")*
- (M) (3:02) Curb 77351 Christmas All-Time Greatest Records. *(1947 recording)*
- (M) (3:02) MCA Special Products 22000 All Time Christmas Favorites Volume 1. *(1947 recording)*
- (M) (3:01) MCA Special Products 25988 Traditional Christmas Classics. *(1947 recording)*
- (M) (3:02) Rhino 70637 Billboard Greatest Christmas Hits (1934-1954). *(1947 recording)*
- (M) (2:57) MCA 10887 His Legendary Years 1931-1957 Box Set. *(1942 recording)*
- (M) (3:02) Rhino 72175 Santamental Christmas. *(1947 recording)*
- (M) (2:59) Rhino 72171 Billboard Presents: Family Christmas Classics. *(1946 radio broadcast version)*
- (M) (2:59) Rhino 72276 Academy Award Winning Songs Volume 1. *(1946 radio broadcast version)*
- (M) (2:59) Rhino 71868 Academy Award Winning Songs. *(1946 radio broadcast version)*
- (M) (3:01) Collectables 1513 and 2513 and 3513 and 4513 The Ultimate Christmas Album Volume Three. *(1947 recording)*
- (M) (3:03) Time-Life TCD-107 A Time-Life Treasury Of Christmas. *(1947 recording)*
- (M) (2:59) MCA 11719 Bing Crosby's Gold Records. *(1942 recording)*

1960 WHITE CHRISTMAS
**(this song charted in several different years - see
1957 listings)**
1961 WHITE CHRISTMAS
**(this song charted in several different years - see
1957 listings)**

DAVID CROSBY & GRAHAM NASH
1972 IMMIGRATION MAN
  (S)   (2:57)   Atlantic 82319   Crosby, Stills & Nash Box Set.

DAVID CROSBY & PHIL COLLINS
1993 HERO
  (S)   (4:38)   Atlantic 82484   David Crosby - Thousand Roads.

CROSBY, STILLS & NASH
1969 MARRAKESH EXPRESS
**(the LP version of this song has :02 of studio talk
preceding the music)**
  (S)   (2:35)   Atlantic 19117   Crosby, Stills & Nash. *(LP
            version)*
  (S)   (2:36)   Atlantic 82651   Crosby, Stills & Nash. *(LP
            version; remastered edition)*
  (S)   (2:35)   Atlantic 82319   Crosby, Stills & Nash Box Set.
            (LP version)
  (S)   (2:36)   Atlantic 82522   Crosby, Stills & Nash. *(LP
            version; gold disc)*
1969 SUITE: JUDY BLUE EYES
  (S)   (7:23)   Atlantic 81908   Classic Rock 1966-1988. *(LP
            version)*
  (S)   (7:23)   Atlantic 19117   Crosby, Stills & Nash. *(LP
            version)*
  (S)   (7:25)   Atlantic 82651   Crosby, Stills & Nash. *(LP
            version; remastered edition)*
  (S)   (7:22)   Atlantic 19119   So Far. *(LP version)*
  (S)   (7:25)   Atlantic 82648   So Far. *(LP version; remastered
            edition)*
  (S)   (7:23)   Atlantic 82306   Atlantic Rock & Roll Box Set.
            (LP version)
  (S)   (7:27)   Atlantic 82319   Crosby, Stills & Nash Box Set.
            (alternate take with countoff)
  (S)   (7:25)   Atlantic 82522   Crosby, Stills & Nash. *(LP
            version; gold disc)*
  (S)   (7:25)   Time-Life R13610   Gold And Platinum Box Set -
            The Ultimate Rock Collection. *(LP version)*
  (S)   (7:25)   Atlantic 83088   Atlantic Records: 50 Years - The
            Gold Anniversary Collection. *(LP version)*
1977 JUST A SONG BEFORE I GO
  (S)   (2:11)   Atlantic 19104 and 82650   CSN.
  (S)   (2:11)   Atlantic 82319   Crosby, Stills & Nash Box Set.
1982 WASTED ON THE WAY
  (S)   (2:50)   Atlantic 81595   Daylight Again.
  (S)   (2:46)   Atlantic 82319   Crosby, Stills & Nash Box Set.
1982 SOUTHERN CROSS
**(dj copies of this 45 ran (3:55) and (4:40);
commercial copies were all (3:55))**
  (S)   (4:40)   Atlantic 81908   Classic Rock 1966-1988.
  (S)   (4:40)   Atlantic 81595   Daylight Again.
  (S)   (4:39)   Atlantic 82319   Crosby, Stills & Nash Box Set.

CROSBY, STILLS, NASH & YOUNG
1970 WOODSTOCK
  (S)   (3:51)   Atlantic 19119   So Far.
  (S)   (3:52)   Atlantic 82648   So Far. *(remastered edition)*
  (S)   (3:51)   Atlantic 19118   Deja Vu.
  (S)   (3:52)   Atlantic 82649   Deja Vu. *(remastered edition)*
  (S)   (3:50)   Atlantic 82319   Crosby, Stills & Nash Box Set.
1970 TEACH YOUR CHILDREN
  (S)   (2:50)   Atlantic 82032   The Wonder Years.
  (S)   (2:51)   Atlantic 19119   So Far.
  (S)   (2:52)   Atlantic 82648   So Far. *(remastered edition)*
  (S)   (2:51)   Atlantic 19118   Deja Vu.
  (S)   (2:52)   Atlantic 82649   Deja Vu. *(remastered edition)*
  (S)   (2:51)   Atlantic 82319   Crosby, Stills & Nash Box Set.

1970 OHIO
  (S)   (2:57)   Atlantic 81908   Classic Rock 1966-1988.
  (S)   (2:57)   Atlantic 19119   So Far.
  (S)   (3:01)   Atlantic 82648   So Far. *(remastered edition)*
  (S)   (2:57)   Atlantic 82306   Atlantic Rock & Roll Box Set.
  (S)   (3:01)   Atlantic 82319   Crosby, Stills & Nash Box Set.
  (S)   (2:57)   Reprise 2257   Neil Young/Decade.
  (S)   (2:56)   Time-Life R102-34   The Rolling Stone Collection.
1970 OUR HOUSE
  (S)   (2:57)   Atlantic 19119   So Far.
  (S)   (2:58)   Atlantic 82648   So Far. *(remastered edition)*
  (S)   (2:58)   Atlantic 19118   Deja Vu.
  (S)   (2:59)   Atlantic 82649   Deja Vu. *(remastered edition)*
  (S)   (2:58)   Atlantic 82319   Crosby, Stills & Nash Box Set.
  (S)   (2:57)   Epic 57871   O.S.T. My Girl 2.
  (S)   (2:59)   Giant 24609   O.S.T. Bye Bye Love.

CHRISTOPHER CROSS
1980 RIDE LIKE THE WIND
  (S)   (4:29)   Warner Brothers 3383   Christopher Cross. *(LP
            length)*
  (S)   (3:54)   JCI 3127   1980 - Only Rock 'N Roll - 1984. *(45
            length)*
  (S)   (3:55)   Rebound 314520318   Class Reunion 1980. *(45
            length)*
  (S)   (3:55)   Madacy Entertainment 1980   Rock On 1980. *(45
            length)*
  (S)   (4:29)   Time-Life R988-16   Sounds Of The Eighties: The
            Early '80s. *(LP length)*
  (S)   (4:29)   Time-Life R834-14   Body Talk - Love And
            Tenderness. *(LP length)*
1980 SAILING
  (S)   (4:15)   Warner Brothers 3383   Christopher Cross.
  (S)   (4:14)   Priority 53699   80's Greatest Rock Hits Volume 7 -
            Light & Easy.
  (S)   (4:13)   Time-Life R988-07   Sounds Of The Eighties: 1980.
  (S)   (4:13)   Time-Life R138-18   Body Talk.
  (S)   (4:14)   JCI 3147   1980 - Only Love - 1984.
  (S)   (4:16)   Time-Life R834-02   Body Talk - Just For You.
1980 NEVER BE THE SAME
  (S)   (4:41)   Warner Brothers 3383   Christopher Cross. *(LP length)*
  (S)   (4:40)   Time-Life R834-16   Body Talk - Sweet Nothings.
            (LP length)
1981 SAY YOU'LL BE MINE
  (S)   (2:53)   Warner Brothers 3383   Christopher Cross.
1981 ARTHUR'S THEME (BEST THAT YOU CAN DO)
  (S)   (3:53)   Rhino 71868   Academy Award Winning Songs.
  (S)   (3:53)   Rhino 72279   Academy Award Winning Songs
            Volume 4.
  (S)   (3:52)   JCI 3170   #1 Radio Hits 1980 - Only Rock 'n Roll -
            1984.
  (S)   (3:52)   Madacy Entertainment 6803   Power Of Love.
  (S)   (3:52)   Time-Life R988-31   Sounds Of The Eighties:
            Cinemax Movie Hits Of The '80s.
  (S)   (3:53)   Time-Life R988-14   Sounds Of The Eighties:
            1980-1982.
  (S)   (3:53)   Time-Life R834-03   Body Talk - Moonlit Nights.
  (S)   (3:53)   Priority 50974   Premiere The Movie Magazine
            Presents The Greatest Soundtrack Love Songs.
  (S)   (3:52)   Hip-O 40079   Essential '80s: 1980-1984.
  (S)   (3:51)   K-Tel 6257   The Greatest Love Songs - 16 Soft
            Rock Hits.
  (S)   (3:52)   Rebound 314520519   Love At The Movies.
1983 ALL RIGHT
  (S)   (4:14)   Warner Brothers 23757   Another Page. *(LP
            length)*
1983 NO TIME FOR TALK
  (S)   (4:19)   Warner Brothers 23757   Another Page.
1984 THINK OF LAURA
  (S)   (3:21)   Warner Brothers 23757   Another Page.
  (S)   (3:21)   Time-Life R834-06   Body Talk - Only You.

CROSS COUNTRY
1973 IN THE MIDNIGHT HOUR

CROW
1970 EVIL WOMAN DON'T PLAY YOUR GAMES WITH ME
- (S) (3:10) Era 5002 Best Of.
- (S) (3:11) Time-Life SOD-37 Sounds Of The Seventies - AM Heavy Hits.
- (S) (3:10) Risky Business 57471 Godfathers Of Grunge.
- (S) (3:10) Time-Life R968-11 Guitar Rock - The Early '70s.
- (S) (3:10) K-Tel 3463 Platinum Rock.
- (S) (3:10) K-Tel 4030 Rock Anthems.

SHERYL CROW
1994 ALL I WANNA DO
- (S) (4:31) A&M 314540126 Tuesday Night Music Club.
- (S) (4:32) Grammy Recordings/Sony Music 67043 1995 Grammy Nominees.
- (S) (4:31) Time-Life R13610 Gold And Platinum Box Set - The Ultimate Rock Collection.
1995 STRONG ENOUGH
- (S) (3:09) A&M 314540126 Tuesday Night Music Club.
1995 CAN'T CRY ANYMORE
- (S) (3:41) A&M 314540126 Tuesday Night Music Club.
- (S) (3:50) Tommy Boy 1139 MTV Party To Go Volume 8. (all selections on this cd are segued together)
1996 IF IT MAKES YOU HAPPY
- (S) (5:23) A&M 314540587 Sheryl Crow. (LP version)
1997 EVERYDAY IS A WINDING ROAD
- (S) (4:15) A&M 314540587 Sheryl Crow.
- (S) (4:15) MCA 11752 1998 Grammy Nominees.

CROWDED HOUSE
1987 DON'T DREAM IT'S OVER
- (S) (3:56) Rhino 71642 Billboard Top Hits - 1987.
- (S) (3:53) Sandstone 33041 and 5007 Rock The First Volume 1.
- (S) (3:53) Sandstone 33052 and 5020 Cosmopolitan Volume 6.
- (S) (3:53) DCC Compact Classics 084 Night Moves Volume 4.
- (S) (3:53) Capitol 46693 Crowded House.
- (S) (3:50) Time-Life R988-29 Sounds Of The Eighties: The Rolling Stone Collection 1987-1988.
- (S) (3:55) Hip-O 40005 The '80s Hit(s) Back....Again!
- (S) (3:53) Capitol 38250 Recurring Dream: Very Best Of.
- (S) (3:55) Hip-O 40022 That Sound From Down Under.
- (S) (3:55) Time-Life R834-08 Body Talk - On My Mind.
1987 SOMETHING SO STRONG
- (S) (2:51) Capitol 46693 Crowded House.
- (S) (2:51) Time-Life R988-09 Sounds Of The Eighties: 1987.
- (S) (2:50) Capitol 38250 Recurring Dream: Very Best Of.
- (S) (2:50) Priority 50953 I Love Rock & Roll Volume 4: Hits Of The 80's.

RODNEY CROWELL
1980 ASHES BY NOW
- (S) (4:07) Warner Brothers 25965 Collection. (LP version)

CRUCIAL CONFLICT
1996 HAY
- (S) (4:20) Pallas/Universal 53006 The Final Tic.
- (S) (4:19) Polygram TV 314536204 The Source Presents Hip Hop Hits Volume 1.

CRUSADERS
1979 STREET LIFE
- (S) (3:54) Priority 7983 Mega-Hits Dance Classics Volume 7. (45 version)
- (S) (11:12) GRP 5007 The Golden Years. (LP version)
- (S) (7:43) Hip-O 40091 Disco 54: Funkin' On The Floor.

CRYSTALS
1961 THERE'S NO OTHER LIKE MY BABY
- (M) (2:29) Abkco 7118 Phil Spector/Back To Mono (1958-1969).
- (M) (2:29) Abkco 7214 Best Of.
1962 UPTOWN
- (M) (2:19) Abkco 7118 Phil Spector/Back To Mono (1958-1969).

- (S) (1:48) MCA 6171 Good Time Rock 'N' Roll. (all selections on this cd are recorded live)
- (M) (2:19) Abkco 7214 Best Of.
1962 HE'S A REBEL
- (M) (2:25) Abkco 7118 Phil Spector/Back To Mono (1958-1969).
- (M) (2:25) Abkco 7214 Best Of.
- (M) (2:25) Abkco 7213 Best Of Darlene Love.
1963 HE'S SURE THE BOY I LOVE
- (M) (2:43) Abkco 7118 Phil Spector/Back To Mono (1958-1969).
- (M) (2:41) Abkco 7214 Best Of.
- (M) (2:41) Abkco 7213 Best Of Darlene Love.
1963 DA DOO RON RON (THEN HE WALKED ME HOME)
- (M) (2:16) Abkco 7118 Phil Spector/Back To Mono (1958-1969).
- (S) (1:40) MCA 6171 Good Time Rock 'N' Roll. (all selections on this cd are recorded live)
- (M) (2:16) Abkco 7214 Best Of.
1963 THEN HE KISSED ME
- (M) (2:34) Abkco 7118 Phil Spector/Back To Mono (1958-1969).
- (M) (2:34) Abkco 7214 Best Of.

CUFF LINKS
1969 TRACY
(45 time is (2:05); LP time is (2:14) and is slower in pitch than the 45)
- (S) (2:07) K-Tel 205 Battle Of The Bands Volume 3. (LP version)
- (S) (2:14) Rhino 70921 Super Hits Of The 70's Volume 1. (LP version)
- (S) (2:14) Rhino 72009 Super Hits Of The 70's Volumes 1-4 Box Set. (LP version)
- (S) (2:09) MCA 31207 Vintage Music Volume 10. (LP version)
- (S) (2:09) MCA 5806 Vintage Music Volumes 9 & 10. (LP version)
- (S) (2:04) Time-Life SUD-07 Superhits - 1969. (LP version)
- (S) (2:09) MCA Special Products 20751 Rock Around The Oldies #2. (LP version)
- (S) (2:09) MCA Special Products 22130 Vintage Collectibles Volume 1. (LP version)
- (S) (2:12) Varese Sarabande 5535 Bubblegum Classics Volume One. (LP version)
- (S) (2:12) K-Tel 3386 Best Of Bubblegum Music. (LP version)
- (S) (2:09) MCA Special Products 20981 Bubble Gum Classics. (LP version)
- (S) (2:14) Time-Life 2CLR-31 Classic Rock - Totally Fantastic '60s. (LP version)
- (S) (2:04) Time-Life AM1-01 AM Gold - 1969. (LP version)
- (S) (2:08) MCA Special Products 21017 The Rockin' Sixties. (LP version)
1970 WHEN JULIE COMES AROUND
- (S) (2:44) Varese Sarabande 5575 Bubblegum Classics Volume Two.

CULTURE BEAT
1994 MR. VAIN
- (S) (5:36) 550 Music/Epic 57591 Serenity.
- (S) (4:11) Cold Front 6279 Techno Mix '98. (all selections on this cd are segued together)
- (S) (6:33) Beast 53022 Club Hitz Of The 90's Vol. 1. (all songs on this cd are segued together)
- (S) (4:16) Interhit/Priority 51084 DMA Dance Vol. 3: Eurodance.

CULTURE CLUB
1983 DO YOU REALLY WANT TO HURT ME
(dj copies of this 45 ran (2:51), (3:10) and (3:33); commercial copies were all (4:23))
- (S) (4:20) Priority 53750 Rock Of The 80's Volume 7.
- (S) (4:21) Rhino 70678 Billboard Top Hits - 1983.
- (S) (4:21) Rhino 71699 New Wave Hits Of The 80's Vol. 6.
- (S) (4:21) Rhino 71834 Classic MTV: Class Of 1983.
- (S) (4:22) JCI 3127 1980 - Only Rock 'N Roll - 1984.

(S) (4:21) Rhino 71879 More Music From O.S.T. Valley Girl.
(S) (4:20) Rebound 314520314 Caribbean Nights II.
(S) (4:21) Virgin/Epic 40913 This Time: First Four Years.
(S) (4:20) Virgin 91390 and 86179 Kissing To Be Clever.
(S) (4:26) SBK 39014 At Worst...Best Of. *(with :04 introduction)*
(S) (4:21) Time-Life R988-26 Sounds Of The Eighties: The Rolling Stone Collection 1982-1983.
(S) (4:20) K-Tel 3473 The 80s: New Wave.
(S) (4:21) Rhino 72491 New Wave Hits, Vol. 2.
(S) (4:21) Time-Life R834-06 Body Talk - Only You.
(S) (4:21) Flashback 72714 Ultimate New Wave Hits.
(S) (4:21) Flashback 72092 New Wave Hits Box Set.
(S) (4:21) Rhino 72894 Hard Rock Cafe: New Wave.
(S) (4:19) Maverick/Warner Brothers 46840 O.S.T. The Wedding Singer.
(S) (4:20) Rebound 314520314 Reggae Dance Party II.

1983 TIME (CLOCK OF THE HEART)
(S) (3:42) Priority 53684 Rock Of The 80's Volume 4.
(S) (3:42) Virgin/Epic 40913 This Time: First Four Years.
(S) (3:42) SBK 39014 At Worst...Best Of.
(S) (3:42) Time-Life R988-03 Sounds Of The Eighties: 1983.
(S) (3:42) Rhino 72771 The Big 80's.
(S) (3:41) Time-Life R834-08 Body Talk - On My Mind.

1983 I'LL TUMBLE 4 YA
(S) (2:35) Priority 53754 Rock Of The 80's Volume 15.
(S) (2:35) Virgin/Epic 40913 This Time: First Four Years.
(S) (4:38) Virgin/Epic 40913 This Time: First Four Years. *(remix)*
(S) (2:34) Virgin 91390 and 86179 Kissing To Be Clever.
(S) (2:35) SBK 39014 At Worst...Best Of.
(S) (2:34) Hip-O 40005 The '80s Hit(s) Back....Again!
(S) (2:34) Time-Life R988-16 Sounds Of The Eighties: The Early '80s.

1983 CHURCH OF THE POISON MIND
(S) (3:30) EMI 89605 Living In Oblivion: The 80's Greatest Hits Volume Two.
(S) (3:31) Virgin/Epic 40913 This Time: First Four Years.
(S) (3:29) Virgin 91391 and 86180 Colour By Numbers.
(S) (3:29) SBK 39014 At Worst...Best Of.
(S) (3:29) Priority 53795 Best Of 80's Rock Volume 3.
(S) (3:29) K-Tel 3742 The 80's: Hot Rock.
(S) (3:28) Time-Life R988-18 Sounds Of The Eighties: The Early '80s Take Two.

1984 KARMA CHAMELEON
(S) (3:58) Priority 53752 Rock Of The 80's Volume 12. *(:13 shorter than either the 45 or LP)*
(S) (4:11) Rhino 70679 Billboard Top Hits - 1984.
(S) (4:00) Virgin/Epic 40913 This Time: First Four Years. *(:11 shorter than either the 45 or LP)*
(S) (4:12) Virgin 91391 and 86180 Colour By Numbers.
(S) (3:59) SBK 39014 At Worst...Best Of. *(:12 shorter than either the 45 or LP)*
(S) (4:06) Rhino 71975 New Wave Hits Of The 80's Vol. 12.
(S) (4:10) Time-Life R988-06 Sounds Of The Eighties: 1984.
(S) (4:11) Big Ear Music 4002 Only In The 80's Volume Two.
(S) (3:59) Madacy Entertainment 1983 Rock On 1983. *(:12 shorter than the 45 or LP)*
(S) (4:11) Hollywood 62098 O.S.T. Romy And Michele's High School Reunion.
(S) (4:11) K-Tel 3866 The 80's: Number One Pop Hits.
(S) (4:11) Hip-O 40079 Essential '80s: 1980-1984.

1984 MISS ME BLIND
(S) (4:32) Sandstone 33047 and 5015 Cosmopolitan Volume 1.
(S) (7:08) SBK 29007 Brilliant! The Global Dance Music Experience Volume 3. *(remix)*
(S) (4:29) Virgin/Epic 40913 This Time: First Four Years.
(S) (4:29) Virgin 91391 and 86180 Colour By Numbers.
(S) (4:29) SBK 39014 At Worst...Best Of.
(S) (4:29) Priority 53781 Best Of 80's Rock Volume 2.
(S) (4:32) Time-Life R988-11 Sounds Of The 80's: 1983-1984.
(S) (4:29) Madacy Entertainment 1984 Rock On 1984.
(S) (7:08) EMI 54100 Retro Dance Club Volume Three. *(remix)*

1984 IT'S A MIRACLE
(S) (3:23) Virgin/Epic 40913 This Time: First Four Years.
(S) (3:23) Virgin 91391 and 86180 Colour By Numbers.
(S) (3:23) SBK 39014 At Worst...Best Of.
(S) (3:23) Time-Life R988-23 Sounds Of The Eighties 1984-1985.

1984 THE WAR SONG
(S) (3:57) Virgin/Epic 40913 This Time: First Four Years. *(45 length)*
(S) (4:13) Virgin 91392 Waking Up With The House On Fire. *(LP length)*

1985 MISTAKE No. 3
(S) (4:33) Virgin 91392 Waking Up With The House On Fire.

1986 MOVE AWAY
(S) (4:08) Virgin/Epic 40913 This Time: First Four Years.
(S) (4:07) SBK 39014 At Worst...Best Of.
(S) (4:07) Madacy Entertainment 1986 Rock On 1986.
(S) (4:07) JCI 3171 #1 Radio Hits 1985 - Only Rock 'n Roll - 1989.
(S) (4:07) Time-Life R988-21 Sounds Of The Eighties: 1986-1989.

BURTON CUMMINGS
1976 STAND TALL
(S) (3:42) Columbia/Legacy Rock Artifacts Volume 2. *(LP length)*
(S) (3:19) Time-Life SOD-36 Sounds Of The Seventies - More AM Nuggets. *(45 length)*
(S) (3:19) Rhino 71199 Super Hits Of The 70's Volume 19. *(45 length)*
(S) (3:43) Rhino 71717 Collection. *(LP length)*
(S) (3:40) Eclipse Music Group 64895 Rock 'n Roll Relix 1976-1977. *(LP length)*
(S) (3:40) Eclipse Music Group 64897 Rock 'n Roll Relix 1970-1979. *(LP length)*
(S) (4:58) Hip-O 40067 Up Close And Alone. *(live)*

1981 YOU SAVED MY SOUL
(S) (4:19) Rhino 71717 Collection. *(LP version)*
(S) (4:30) Hip-O 40067 Up Close And Alone. *(live)*

MIKE CURB CONGREGATION
1971 BURNING BRIDGES
(S) (2:44) Rhino 70925 Super Hits Of The 70's Volume 5.
(S) (2:43) Curb 77317 70's Hits Volume 1.
(S) (2:43) Curb 77443 Greatest Hits.

released as by SAMMY DAVIS JR. with THE MIKE CURB CONGREGATION:
1972 CANDY MAN
(S) (3:08) Rhino 70928 Super Hits Of The 70's Volume 8.
(S) (3:07) Curb 77317 70's Hits Volume 1.
(S) (3:04) Curb 77443 Mike Curb Congregation Greatest Hits.
(S) (3:09) Garland 018 Sammy Davis Jr. - Greatest Hits.
(S) (3:04) Curb 77444 Best Of Sammy Davis Jr. And The Mike Curb Congregation.
(S) (3:06) Curb 77272 Sammy Davis Jr. - Greatest Songs.
(S) (3:09) DCC Compact Classics 1848 Sammy Davis Jr. - His Greatest Hits I & II.
(S) (3:09) Razor & Tie 21640 Those Fabulous 70's.
(S) (3:08) Time-Life SUD-20 Superhits - Early 70's Classics.
(S) (3:03) CBS Special Products 46850 Society Of Singers Presents A Gift Of Music Vol. 2.
(S) (3:10) Special Music/Essex 5036 Prom Night - The 70's.
(S) (3:07) Time-Life AM1-15 AM Gold - Early '70s Classics.
(S) (1:56) K-Tel 3630 Lounge Legends. *(live)*
(S) (3:07) MCA Special Products 20198 Sammy Davis Jr. - That Old Black Magic.
(S) (3:07) Rhino 75233 '70s Party (Killers) Classics.
(S) (3:10) Polygram Special Markets 314520456 #1 Radio Hits Of The 70's.

CURE
1989 LOVESONG
(S) (3:26) Elektra 60855 Disintegration.

CURE (Continued)
- (S) (6:18) Elektra 60978 Mixed Up. *(12" single version)*
- (S) (3:26) Elektra/Fiction 62117 Galore.

1992 HIGH
- (S) (3:30) Elektra 61309 Wish.
- (S) (3:31) Elektra/Fiction 62117 Galore.

1992 FRIDAY I'M IN LOVE
- (S) (3:34) Elektra 61309 Wish.
- (S) (3:33) Elektra/Fiction 62117 Galore.

CUTTING CREW
1987 (I JUST) DIED IN YOUR ARMS
(45 length is (4:24); LP length is (4:43))
- (S) (4:24) EMI 91419 MTV, BET, VH-1 Power Players.
- (S) (4:34) EMI 27674 Living In Oblivion: The 80's Greatest Hits Volume Three.
- (S) (4:35) Priority 53704 Rock Of The 80's Volume 3.
- (S) (4:37) K-Tel 3342 The 80's Pop Explosion.
- (S) (4:43) Virgin 90573 and 86002 Broadcast.
- (S) (4:32) Time-Life R988-09 Sounds Of The Eighties: 1987.
- (S) (4:24) JCI 3186 1985 - Only Love - 1989.
- (S) (4:43) Hip-O 40080 Essential '80s: 1985-1989.
- (S) (4:31) Time-Life R834-15 Body Talk - Once In Lifetime.

1987 ONE FOR THE MOCKINGBIRD
- (S) (4:27) Virgin 90573 and 86002 Broadcast.
- (S) (4:29) Priority 53781 Best Of 80's Rock Volume 2.

1987 I'VE BEEN IN LOVE BEFORE
- (S) (5:05) Priority 53750 Rock Of The 80's Volume 7. *(missing part of the LP version introduction)*
- (S) (5:31) Virgin 90573 and 86002 Broadcast. *(LP version)*
- (S) (5:05) K-Tel 3864 Slow Dancin'. *(missing part of the LP version introduction)*

CYMARRON
1971 RINGS
(actual LP time is (2:31) not (2:46) as stated on the record label; LP pitch is much faster than the 45 pitch)
- (S) (2:30) Columbia/Legacy 46763 Rock Artifacts Volume 2. *(LP pitch)*
- (S) (2:29) Rhino 71197 Super Hits Of The 70's Volume 17. *(LP pitch)*
- (S) (2:29) Time-Life SOD-31 Sounds Of The Seventies - AM Top Twenty. *(LP pitch)*

JOHNNY CYMBAL
1963 MR. BASS MAN
- (S) (2:40) MCA 31202 Vintage Music Volume 5. *(with a :02 countoff)*
- (S) (2:40) MCA 5804 Vintage Music Volumes 5 & 6. *(with a :02 countoff)*

- (S) (2:38) K-Tel 3150 Dumb Ditties. *(rerecording)*
- (S) (2:37) Time-Life 2RNR-29 Rock 'N' Roll Era - The 60's Rave On.
- (S) (2:35) Time-Life R102-17 Lost Treasures Of Rock 'N' Roll.
- (S) (2:40) MCA Special Products 22028 Cra-a-zy Hits. *(with a :02 countoff)*
- (S) (2:40) MCA Special Products 22179 Vintage Collectibles Volume 9. *(with a :02 countoff)*
- (S) (2:39) Taragon 1006 Very Best Of. *(with a :02 countoff)*
- (S) (2:32) Taragon 1006 Very Best Of. *(alternate take)*

CYPRESS HILL
1993 INSANE IN THE BRAIN
- (S) (3:31) Ruffhouse/Columbia 53931 Black Sunday.

CYRKLE
1966 RED RUBBER BALL
- (S) (2:17) Rhino 75754 Even More Nuggets.
- (S) (2:18) Columbia 45019 Pop Classics Of The 60's. *(original pressings of this song on this cd were missing an organ overdub)*
- (S) (2:17) Columbia/Legacy 47717 Red Rubber Ball. *(remixed)*
- (S) (2:17) Rhino 71195 Kid Rock!
- (S) (2:17) Time-Life 2CLR-13 Classic Rock - 1966: Shakin' All Over.
- (S) (2:16) Time-Life SUD-12 Superhits - The Mid 60's.
- (S) (2:17) Rhino 71936 Billboard Top Pop Hits, 1966.
- (S) (2:16) Time-Life AM1-05 AM Gold - The Mid '60s.

1966 TURN DOWN DAY
- (S) (2:28) Columbia 45019 Pop Classics Of The 60's.
- (S) (2:32) Columbia/Legacy 47717 Red Rubber Ball.
- (S) (2:26) Time-Life 2CLR-22 Classic Rock - 1966: Blowin' Your Mind.
- (S) (2:30) Time-Life SUD-17 Superhits - Mid 60's Classics.
- (S) (2:32) Time-Life R962-02 History Of Rock 'N' Roll: Folk Rock 1964-1967.
- (S) (2:33) Buddah 49506 Feelin' Groovy.
- (S) (2:30) Time-Life AM1-16 AM Gold - Mid '60s Classics.

BILLY RAY CYRUS
1992 ACHY BREAKY HEART
- (S) (3:23) Mercury 314510635 Some Gave All.
- (S) (3:23) Mercury 314526691 Fifty Years Of Country Music From Mercury.
- (S) (3:22) Rebound 314520338 Hot Country For The 90's.
- (S) (3:23) Mercury 314534837 Best Of.

DA BRAT
1994 FUNKDAFIED
    (S)   (3:05)   So So Def/Chaos/Columbia 66164 Funkdafied.
    (S)   (3:06)   Priority 51021 Hip Hop Coast 2 Coast.
1994 FA ALL Y'ALL
    (S)   (3:19)   So So Def/Chaos/Columbia 66164 Funkdafied.
                 (tracks into next selection)
1995 GIVE IT 2 YOU
    (S)   (3:12)   So So Def/Chaos/Columbia 66164 Funkdafied.
1996 SITTIN' ON TOP OF THE WORLD
    (S)   (4:15)   So So Def/Columbia 67813 Anuthatantrum.
released as by TOTAL featuring DA BRAT:
1996 NO ONE ELSE
    (S)   (4:20)   Bad Boy 73006 Total.
    (S)   (4:13)   Arista 18977 Ultimate Hip Hop Party 1998. *(all selections on this cd are segued together; remix)*
released as by DA BRAT featuring T-BOZ:
1997 GHETTO LOVE
    (S)   (3:21)   So So Def/Columbia 67813 Anuthatantrum.
released as by MISSY "MISDEMEANOR" ELLIOTT featuring DA BRAT:
1997 SOCK IT 2 ME
    (S)   (4:17)   EastWest 62062 Missy "Misdemeanor" Elliott - Supa Dupa Fly.

DADDY DEWDROP
1971 CHICK-A-BOOM (DON'T YA JES' LOVE IT)
    (S)   (2:49)   Rhino 71208 70's Smash Hits Volume 4.
    (S)   (2:50)   Rhino 70925 Superhits Of The 70's Volume 5.
    (M)   (2:57)   K-Tel 3629 Madcap Melodies. *(rerecording)*
    (S)   (2:49)   Flashback 72684 '70s Radio Hits Volume 4.
    (S)   (2:49)   Flashback 72090 '70s Radio Hits Box Set.
    (S)   (2:48)   Time-Life R830-03 The Dr. Demento Collection: The Early '70s.

DADDY-0'S
1958 GOT A MATCH

ALAN DALE
1955 CHERRY PINK (AND APPLE BLOSSOM WHITE)
    (M)   (2:42)   Varese Sarabande 5782 The '50s Remembered: Haymes, Dale, Desmond & Cherry.
1955 SWEET AND GENTLE
    (M)   (2:50)   Time-Life HPD-28 Your Hit Parade - The Fabulous 50's.
    (M)   (2:48)   Varese Sarabande 5782 The '50s Remembered: Haymes, Dale, Desmond & Cherry.

DALE & GRACE
1963 I'M LEAVING IT UP TO YOU
    (M)   (2:08)   Time-Life 2RNR-07 Rock 'N' Roll Era - 1963.
    (M)   (2:04)   Time-Life SUD-08 Superhits - 1963.
    (E)   (2:04)   Original Sound 8861 Oldies But Goodies Vol. 11. *(this compact disc uses the "Waring - fds" noise reduction process)*
    (E)   (2:04)   Original Sound 2222 Oldies But Goodies Volumes 3,5,11,14 and 15 Box Set. *(this box set uses the "Waring - fds" noise reduction process)*
    (E)   (2:04)   Original Sound 2500 Oldies But Goodies Volumes 1-15 Box Set. *(this box set uses the "Waring - fds" noise reduction process)*
    (M)   (2:08)   Rhino 71584 Billboard Top Pop Hits, 1963.
    (M)   (2:05)   LaserLight 12323 American Dreams.
    (M)   (2:09)   MCA Special Products 22179 Vintage Collectibles Volume 9.

    (M)   (2:08)   Time-Life R857-08 The Heart Of Rock 'n' Roll 1963.
    (M)   (2:04)   Time-Life AM1-17 AM Gold - 1963.
    (M)   (2:11)   Jewel 5057 Rockin' 50's & 60's. *(track lineup on the cd jacket is incorrect)*
    (E)   (2:06)   JCI 3184 1960 - Only Love - 1964. *(mastered from vinyl)*
1964 STOP AND THINK IT OVER
    (M)   (2:32)   Time-Life 2CLR-03 Classic Rock - 1964.
    (M)   (2:31)   Time-Life R857-09 The Heart Of Rock 'n' Roll 1964.
    (E)   (2:31)   Jewel 5057 Rockin' 50's & 60's. *(mastered from vinyl; track lineup on the cd jacket is incorrect)*

ROGER DALTREY
1980 WITHOUT YOUR LOVE
    (S)   (3:16)   Rhino 72846 Martyrs & Madmen: The Best Of.

MICHAEL DAMIAN
1989 ROCK ON
    (S)   (3:20)   Rhino 70243 Greatest Movie Rock Hits.
    (S)   (3:20)   Cypress 9-0130 Where Do We Go From Here.
    (S)   (3:20)   Priority 53773 80's Greatest Rock Hits Volume II - Teen Idols.
    (S)   (3:20)   JCI 3171 #1 Radio Hits 1985 - Only Rock 'n Roll - 1989.
    (S)   (3:20)   Time-Life R988-13 Sounds Of The Eighties: 1989.
1989 COVER OF LOVE
    (S)   (3:57)   Cypress 9-0130 Where Do We Go From Here.
1990 WAS IT NOTHING AT ALL
    (S)   (4:32)   Cypress 9-0130 Where Do We Go From Here.

DAMN YANKEES
1991 HIGH ENOUGH
    (S)   (4:44)   JCI 3135 14 Original Metal Ballads. *(LP version)*
    (S)   (4:43)   Warner Brothers 26159 Damn Yankees. *(LP version)*
    (S)   (4:44)   Time-Life R968-25 Guitar Rock - The '90s. *(LP version)*
1992 WHERE YOU GOIN' NOW
    (S)   (4:38)   Warner Brothers 45025 Don't Tread.

LIZ DAMON'S ORIENT EXPRESS
1971 1900 YESTERDAY
    (S)   (2:56)   Varese Sarabande 5706 Dick Bartley Presents Collector's Essentials: The 70's.

VIC DAMONE
1956 ON THE STREET WHERE YOU LIVE
    (S)   (2:36)   Curb 77476 Best Of. *(rerecording)*
    (S)   (2:33)   Pair 1303 Let's Face The Music And Sing. *(live)*
    (M)   (2:40)   Rhino 71252 Sentimental Journey: Pop Vocal Classics Volume 4 (1954-1959).
    (M)   (2:40)   Rhino 72034 Sentimental Journey Pop Vocal Classics Volumes 1-4 Box Set.
    (M)   (2:42)   Columbia/Legacy 48975 16 Most Requested Songs.
    (M)   (2:40)   Time-Life HPD-15 Your Hit Parade - 1956.
    (M)   (2:42)   Time-Life R135-04 Broadway Hit Parade.
    (S)   (2:36)   Time-Life R974-14 Many Moods Of Romance - The Very Thought Of You. *(rerecording)*
    (E)   (2:42)   JCI 7022 Those Wonderful Years - It Must Be Him.
    (M)   (2:40)   Time-Life R132-10 Love Songs Of Your Hit Parade.
1957 AN AFFAIR TO REMEMBER (OUR LOVE AFFAIR)
    (M)   (2:45)   Columbia 45111 16 Most Requested Songs Of The 50's Volume 2.
    (M)   (2:45)   Columbia/Legacy 48975 16 Most Requested Songs.
    (M)   (2:45)   Epic 57682 More Songs For Sleepless Nights.
    (M)   (2:45)   Time-Life HPD-36 Your Hit Parade - The 50's Pop Revival.

VIC DAMONE *(Continued)*
    (M) (2:45)   Time-Life R138-32 Hollywood Hit Parade.
    (M) (2:45)   Time-Life R974-03 Many Moods Of Romance - I Wish You Love.
    (M) (2:45)   Simitar 55382 The Crooners.
1965 YOU WERE ONLY FOOLING (WHILE I WAS FALLING IN LOVE)

VIC DANA
1963 MORE
    (S) (2:18)   EMI 91678 Golden Greats.
    (S) (2:17)   Compose 9928 Now That's Italian.
    (S) (2:17)   K-Tel 3209 Italian Love Songs.
1964 SHANGRI-LA
    (S) (2:03)   EMI 91678 Golden Greats.
1965 RED ROSES FOR A BLUE LADY
    (S) (2:47)   EMI 91678 Golden Greats.
    (S) (2:46)   Time-Life R138/05 Look Of Love.
    (S) (2:46)   Time-Life R974-10 Many Moods Of Romance - Dream Along With Me.
1966 I LOVE YOU DROPS

DANCER, PRANCER & NERVOUS (THE SINGING REINDEER)
1960 THE HAPPY REINDEER
    (M) (2:20)   Priority 9306 Christmas Comedy Classics.

D'ANGELO
1995 BROWN SUGAR
    (S) (4:22)   EMI 32629 and 35499 Brown Sugar.
    (S) (4:02)   Mammoth 354980168 MTV Buzz Bin Volume 2.
1996 LADY
    (S) (5:46)   EMI 32629 and 35499 Brown Sugar.
    (S) (5:45)   EMI-Capitol Music Group 54548 Smooth Luv.
    (S) (4:32)   Arista 18977 Ultimate Hip Hop Party 1998. *(all selections on this cd are segued together)*
    (S) (4:05)   Polygram TV 314553641 Pure Soul 1997.

CHARLIE DANIELS BAND
released as by CHARLIE DANIELS:
1973 UNEASY RIDER
    (dj copies of this 45 ran (3:53) and (5:19); commercial copies were all (5:19))
    (S) (5:19)   Rhino 70758 Super Hits Of The 70's Volume 11. *(LP version)*
    (S) (5:18)   Epic 38795 Decade Of Hits. *(LP version)*
    (S) (5:19)   Epic 53743 All-Time Greatest Hits. *(LP version)*
    (S) (5:18)   Epic 64182 Super Hits. *(LP version)*
    (S) (5:18)   Right Stuff 36476 Harley Davidson Country Road Songs. *(LP version)*
    (S) (5:17)   Epic/Legacy 65023 The Roots Remain. *(LP version)*
    (S) (5:18)   K-Tel 3912 Superstars Greatest Hits Volume 1. *(LP version)*
    (S) (5:19)   Time-Life R830-03 The Dr. Demento Collection: The Early '70s. *(LP version)*
released as by THE CHARLIE DANIELS BAND:
1975 THE SOUTH'S GONNA DO IT
    (S) (3:58)   Priority 8668 Rough And Rowdy/70's Greatest Rock Hits Volume 7. *(LP version)*
    (S) (3:58)   Epic 38795 Decade Of Hits. *(LP version)*
    (S) (3:57)   Epic 34365 Fire On The Mountain. *(LP version)*
    (S) (3:58)   K-Tel 3099 Charlie Daniels Band/Marshall Tucker Band. *(LP version)*
    (S) (3:58)   Epic 53743 All-Time Greatest Hits. *(LP version)*
    (S) (3:58)   Epic 64182 Super Hits. *(LP version)*
    (S) (3:57)   Epic/Legacy 65023 The Roots Remain. *(LP version)*
    (S) (3:58)   K-Tel 3972 Southern Rockin' Rebels: The South's Gone And Done It. *(LP version)*
    (S) (3:57)   Epic 65370 Fire On The Mountain/Million Mile Reflections/Full Moon. *(LP version)*
1979 THE DEVIL WENT DOWN TO GEORGIA
    (S) (3:35)   Rhino 70674 Billboard Top Hits - 1979. *(45 version with "son of a gun" lyric)*
    (S) (3:34)   Epic 40248 Hot Country Rock Volume 1. *(45 version with "son of a gun" lyric)*
    (S) (3:35)   Columbia 46031 Columbia Country Classics Volume 3. *(45 version with "son of a gun" lyric)*

    (S) (3:35)   Epic 38795 Decade Of Hits. *(LP version with "son of a bitch" lyric)*
    (S) (3:35)   Epic 35751 Million Mile Reflections. *(LP version with "son of a bitch" lyric)*
    (S) (3:35)   Priority 53695 Country Rockers. *(45 version with "son of a gun" lyric)*
    (S) (3:34)   K-Tel 3099 Charlie Daniels Band/Marshall Tucker Band. *(LP version with "son of a bitch" lyric)*
    (S) (3:35)   Epic/Legacy 53323 Trucker's Jukebox Volume 3. *(LP version with "son of a bitch" lyric)*
    (S) (3:34)   Epic 53743 All-Time Greatest Hits. *(LP version with "son of a bitch" lyric)*
    (S) (3:35)   Time-Life CCD-02 Contemporary Country - The Late 70's. *(45 version with "son of a gun" lyric)*
    (S) (3:34)   Columbia 64185 Country Super Hits. *(LP version with "son of a bitch" lyric)*
    (S) (3:34)   Epic 64182 Super Hits. *(LP version with "son of a bitch" lyric)*
    (S) (3:34)   Right Stuff 31324 and 31327 Harley-Davidson Road Songs. *(LP version with "son of a bitch" lyric)*
    (S) (3:34)   K-Tel 831 Country Music Classics Volume XIII. *(LP version with "son of a bitch" lyric)*
    (S) (3:34)   K-Tel 3299 Country 'Round The Country. *(LP version with "son of a bitch" lyric)*
    (S) (3:34)   K-Tel 6083 Southern Fried Rock - Second Helping. *(LP version with "son of a bitch" lyric)*
    (S) (3:35)   Full Moon/Elektra 60690 O.S.T. Urban Cowboy. *(LP version with "son of a bitch" lyric)*
    (S) (3:34)   DCC Compact Classics 139 Rock The First Volume 9. *(LP version with "son of a bitch" lyric)*
    (S) (3:35)   JCI 3156 1975 - Only Country - 1979. *(45 version with "son of a gun" lyric)*
    (S) (3:34)   Epic/Legacy 65023 The Roots Remain. *(LP version with "son of a bitch" lyric)*
    (S) (3:35)   Epic 65370 Fire On The Mountain/Million Mile Reflections/Full Moon. *(LP version with "son of a bitch" lyric)*
    (S) (3:35)   Epic/Legacy 65396 Trucker's Jukebox/Trucker's Jukebox - Top Radio Requests/Trucker's Jukebox Volume 2. *(LP version with "son of a bitch" lyric)*
    (S) (3:35)   Sony Music Special Products 26069 Rock Hits Of The 70's. *(45 version with "son of a gun" lyric)*
    (S) (3:34)   Thump 6010 Easyriders Volume 1. *(LP version with "son of a bitch" lyric)*
1980 IN AMERICA
    (S) (3:18)   Epic 38795 Decade Of Hits.
    (S) (3:18)   Epic 36571 Full Moon.
    (S) (3:18)   K-Tel 3099 Charlie Daniels Band/Marshall Tucker Band.
    (S) (3:17)   Epic 53743 All-Time Greatest Hits.
    (S) (3:17)   Epic 64182 Super Hits.
    (S) (3:18)   Epic/Legacy 65023 The Roots Remain.
    (S) (3:18)   Epic 65370 Fire On The Mountain/Million Mile Reflections/Full Moon.
1980 THE LEGEND OF WOOLEY SWAMP
    (S) (4:14)   Epic 38795 Decade Of Hits.
    (S) (4:15)   Epic 36571 Full Moon.
    (S) (4:14)   K-Tel 3099 Charlie Daniels Band/Marshall Tucker Band.
    (S) (4:14)   Epic/Legacy 65023 The Roots Remain.
    (S) (4:15)   Epic 65370 Fire On The Mountain/Million Mile Reflections/Full Moon.
1982 STILL IN SAIGON
    (S) (3:51)   Epic 64182 Super Hits.
    (S) (3:51)   Epic 53743 All-Time Greatest Hits.
    (S) (3:51)   Epic 38795 A Decade Of Hits.
    (S) (3:51)   Epic/Legacy 65023 The Roots Remain.
    (S) (3:51)   Epic/Legacy 65228 Windows.

DANLEERS
1958 ONE SUMMER NIGHT
    (M) (2:11)   Garland 012 Remember When.
    (E) (2:12)   Collectables 2508 History Of Rock - The Doo Wop Era Part 2.
    (E) (2:12)   Collectables 4508 History Of Rock/The Doo Wop Era Part Two.
    (M) (2:11)   Rhino 71463 Doo Wop Box.

(E)	(2:12)	Time-Life 2RNR-21 Rock 'N' Roll Era - 1958 Still Rockin'.
(M)	(2:11)	Time-Life RHD-16 Rhythm & Blues - 1958.
(M)	(2:12)	Time-Life R962-06 History Of Rock 'N' Roll: Doo Wop And Vocal Group Tradition 1955-1962.
(M)	(2:12)	Collectables 2506 WCBS-FM History Of Rock - The 50's Part 1.
(M)	(2:12)	Collectables 4506 History Of Rock/The 50s Part One.
(M)	(2:12)	Collectables 2509 WCBS-FM For Lovers Only Part 1.
(M)	(2:11)	Time-Life R103-27 Love Me Tender.
(M)	(2:11)	Time-Life R10513 40 Lovin' Oldies.
(M)	(2:11)	Polygram Special Markets 314520259 Doo Wop Classics.
(M)	(2:11)	Time-Life R857-04 The Heart Of Rock 'n' Roll - 1958.
(M)	(2:11)	Thump 7050 Low Rider Oldies Volume 5.
(M)	(2:12)	Mercury 314532732 Best Of.
(M)	(2:12)	Eric 11502 Hard To Find 45's On CD (Volume I) 1955-60.
(M)	(2:11)	Time-Life R838-22 Solid Gold Soul 1958.

DANNY & THE JUNIORS
1958 AT THE HOP

(M)	(2:30)	Rhino 70619 Billboard's Top Rock & Roll Hits Of 1958.
(M)	(2:30)	Rhino 72004 Billboard's Top Rock & Roll Hits 1957-1961 Box Set.
(M)	(2:30)	MCA 31198 Vintage Music Volume 1.
(M)	(2:30)	MCA 5777 Vintage Music Volumes 1 & 2.
(M)	(2:30)	JCI 3201 Party Time Fifties.
(M)	(2:29)	Original Sound 8852 Oldies But Goodies Vol. 2. *(this compact disc uses the "Waring - fds" noise reduction process)*
(M)	(2:29)	Original Sound 2223 Oldies But Goodies Volumes 2,7,9,12 and 13 Box Set. *(this box set uses the "Waring - fds" noise reduction process)*
(M)	(2:29)	Original Sound 2500 Oldies But Goodies Volumes 1-15 Box Set. *(this box set uses the "Waring - fds" noise reduction process)*
(M)	(2:27)	MCA 31060 Rockin' With. *(truncated fade)*
(M)	(2:29)	Curb 77637 All Time Greatest Hits Of Rock 'N' Roll Volume 3.
(M)	(2:29)	Time-Life 2RNR-01 Rock 'N' Roll Era - 1957.
(M)	(2:29)	MCA Special Products 20580 Teen Idols.
(M)	(2:29)	MCA Special Products 20783 Rock Around The Oldies #1.
(M)	(2:28)	Era 511 Ultimate 50's Party.
(M)	(2:28)	K-Tel 3007 50's Sock Hop.
(M)	(2:29)	JCI 3129 1955 - Only Rock 'N Roll - 1959.
(M)	(2:28)	Collectables 5670 A Golden Classics Edition.
(M)	(2:29)	Nick At Nite/550 Music 63456 Double Date With Joanie And Chachi.
(M)	(2:26)	Collectables 1514 and 2514 The Anniversary Album - The 50's.

1958 ROCK AND ROLL IS HERE TO STAY

(M)	(2:28)	MCA 31199 Vintage Music Volume 2.
(M)	(2:28)	MCA 5777 Vintage Music Volumes 1 & 2.
(M)	(2:27)	MCA 31060 Rockin' With.
(M)	(2:27)	Time-Life 2RNR-21 Rock 'N' Roll Era - 1958 Still Rockin'.
(M)	(2:27)	MCA Special Products 22165 Vintage Collectibles Volume 7.
(M)	(2:27)	Collectables 5670 A Golden Classics Edition.

1960 TWISTIN' U.S.A.

(M)	(2:20)	Collectables 5670 A Golden Classics Edition.

DANNY WILSON
1987 MARY'S PRAYER

(S)	(3:53)	Virgin 90596 Meet.

DANTE and THE EVERGREENS
1960 ALLEY-OOP

(M)	(2:52)	Clifton 3103 Dante: Evergreen's & Friends. *(mastered from vinyl)*

TERENCE TRENT D'ARBY
1988 WISHING WELL

(S)	(3:30)	Foundation/WEA 26097 Super Sessions Volume Two.
(S)	(3:31)	Rhino 71643 Billboard Top Hits - 1988.
(S)	(3:30)	Columbia 40964 Introducing The Hardline.

1988 SIGN YOUR NAME

(S)	(4:36)	Columbia 40964 Introducing The Hardline.
(S)	(4:35)	Simitar 55562 The Number One's: Smooth Love.

1988 DANCE LITTLE SISTER (PART 1)

(S)	(3:54)	Columbia 40964 Introducing The Hardline.
(S)	(3:54)	Priority 53731 80's Greatest Rock Hits Volume 10 - Dance All Night.

BOBBY DARIN
1958 SPLISH SPLASH
(the stereo mix of this song differs slightly from the mono or 45 mix)

(M)	(2:10)	Atlantic 81909 Hit Singles 1958-1977.
(S)	(2:48)	Atco 33131 Story. *(includes :43 of talk preceding and overlapping the song)*
(M)	(2:11)	Warner Special Products 27606 Ultimate.
(M)	(2:08)	Original Sound 8858 Oldies But Goodies Vol. 8. *(this compact disc uses the "Waring - fds" noise reduction process)*
(M)	(2:08)	Original Sound 2221 Oldies But Goodies Volumes 1,4,6,8 and 10 Box Set. *(this box set uses the "Waring - fds" noise reduction process)*
(M)	(2:08)	Original Sound 2500 Oldies But Goodies Volumes 1-15 Box Set. *(this box set uses the "Waring - fds" noise reduction process)*
(S)	(2:05)	Curb 77325 Greatest Hits.
(S)	(2:06)	Atco 91794 Splish Splash.
(S)	(2:06)	Era 5025 The Brill Building Sound.
(M)	(2:09)	Time-Life 2RNR-05 Rock 'N' Roll Era - 1958.
(M)	(2:10)	Atlantic 82626 Bobby Darin.
(M)	(2:10)	Rhino 72206 As Long As I'm Singing - The Bobby Darin Collection.
(S)	(2:03)	Music For Little People 42581 A Child's Celebration Of Rock 'N' Roll.
(S)	(2:04)	Nick At Nite/550 Music/Epic 67770 Happy Days Jukebox.
(M)	(2:09)	JCI 3188 1955 - Only Dance - 1959.

1958 QUEEN OF THE HOP

(S)	(2:10)	Atco 33131 Bobby Darin Story.
(M)	(2:05)	Warner Special Products 27602 20 Party Classics.
(S)	(2:10)	Warner Special Products 27606 Ultimate.
(S)	(2:10)	Atco 91794 Splish Splash.
(M)	(2:04)	Time-Life 2RNR-28 Rock 'N' Roll Era - The 50's Rave On.
(M)	(2:05)	Rhino 72206 As Long As I'm Singing - The Bobby Darin Collection.

1959 PLAIN JANE

(S)	(1:57)	Atco 33131 Bobby Darin Story.
(M)	(1:54)	Warner Special Products 27606 Ultimate.
(M)	(1:54)	Rhino 72206 As Long As I'm Singing - The Bobby Darin Collection.

1959 DREAM LOVER

(M)	(2:30)	Elektra 60107 O.S.T. Diner.
(S)	(2:30)	Atco 33131 Bobby Darin Story.
(M)	(2:29)	Warner Special Products 27606 Ultimate.
(M)	(2:28)	Curb 77325 Greatest Hits.
(S)	(2:30)	Atco 91794 Splish Splash.
(S)	(2:31)	Era 5025 The Brill Building Sound.
(M)	(2:28)	Time-Life 2RNR-13 Rock 'N' Roll Era - 1959.
(S)	(2:30)	Time-Life R962-05 History Of Rock 'N' Roll: The Teenage Years 1957-1964.
(S)	(2:30)	Time-Life R857-01 The Heart Of Rock 'n' Roll - 1959.
(S)	(2:54)	Rhino 72206 As Long As I'm Singing - The Bobby Darin Collection. *(alternate take with studio talk)*
(M)	(2:29)	Rhino 72206 As Long As I'm Singing - The Bobby Darin Collection.
(M)	(2:28)	JCI 3183 1955 - Only Love - 1959.

BOBBY DARIN *(Continued)*

1959 MACK THE KNIFE
(the stereo mix of this song differs slightly from the mono or 45 mix)

- (S) (3:07) Rhino 70620 Billboard's Top Rock & Roll Hits Of 1959.
- (S) (3:07) Rhino 72004 Billboard's Top Rock & Roll Hits 1957-1961 Box Set.
- (M) (3:03) Atlantic 81909 Hit Singles 1958-1977.
- (S) (3:05) Atlantic 81769 O.S.T. Big Town.
- (S) (3:06) JCI 3201 Party Time Fifties.
- (S) (3:24) Atco 33131 Bobby Darin Story. *(with :22 of talk preceding and running into the music)*
- (S) (3:05) Warner Special Products 27606 Ultimate. *(bad dropout at 2:53)*
- (S) (3:31) Curb 77325 Greatest Hits. *(live)*
- (S) (3:06) Atco 91795 Mack The Knife.
- (S) (3:07) Rhino 71252 Sentimental Journey: Pop Vocal Classics Volume 4 (1954-1959).
- (S) (3:07) Rhino 72034 Sentimental Journey Pop Vocal Classics Volumes 1-4 Box Set.
- (S) (3:07) Time-Life HPD-13 Your Hit Parade - 1959.
- (S) (3:06) Atlantic 82627 That's All.
- (S) (3:07) Time-Life R135-04 Broadway Hit Parade.
- (M) (3:03) Rhino 72206 As Long As I'm Singing - The Bobby Darin Collection.
- (S) (3:07) Time-Life R132-12 Your Hit Parade - #1 Hits Of The '50s.
- (S) (3:05) Hammer & Lace 697124114 Leading Men: Masters Of Style Volume Two.
- (M) (3:03) Rhino 72819 16 Magazine - Who's Your Fave Rave.
- (S) (3:05) Atlantic 83088 Atlantic Records: 50 Years - The Gold Anniversary Collection.
- (S) (3:06) K-Tel 4066 K-Tel's Original Party Music Vol. 2.

1960 BEYOND THE SEA

- (M) (2:49) Elektra 60107 O.S.T. Diner.
- (S) (2:53) Capitol 91185 O.S.T. Tequila Sunrise.
- (S) (3:01) Atco 33131 Bobby Darin Story. *(talk over the introduction which is mono and runs longer than either the LP or 45 version; the rest of the song is in stereo!)*
- (S) (2:52) Atlantic 82152 O.S.T. Goodfellas.
- (S) (2:53) Warner Special Products 27606 Ultimate.
- (M) (2:48) Atco 91795 Mack The Knife.
- (S) (2:46) Time-Life HPD-32 Your Hit Parade - Into The 60's.
- (S) (2:52) Atlantic 82627 That's All.
- (M) (2:48) Rhino 72206 As Long As I'm Singing - The Bobby Darin Collection.
- (S) (2:52) Innerstate/London 314540809 O.S.T. A Life Less Ordinary.
- (S) (2:52) Play-Tone/Epic 69179 Music From The HBO Miniseries "From The Earth To The Moon". *(hum noticeable at the end of every song on this cd)*

1960 CLEMENTINE

- (S) (3:11) Atco 33131 Bobby Darin Story. *(alternate take)*
- (S) (3:11) Warner Special Products 27606 Ultimate.
- (M) (3:13) Atco 91795 Mack The Knife.
- (S) (3:12) Atlantic 82628 This Is Darin.
- (S) (3:12) Rhino 72206 As Long As I'm Singing - The Bobby Darin Collection.

1960 WON'T YOU COME HOME BILL BAILEY

- (S) (2:04) Atco 33131 Bobby Darin Story.
- (M) (2:04) Warner Special Products 27606 Ultimate.
- (S) (2:03) Atco 91795 Mack The Knife.
- (M) (2:04) Rhino 72206 As Long As I'm Singing - The Bobby Darin Collection.

1960 ARTIFICIAL FLOWERS

- (S) (3:14) Atco 33131 Bobby Darin Story.
- (M) (3:15) Warner Special Products 27606 Ultimate.
- (M) (3:15) Atco 91795 Mack The Knife.
- (M) (3:15) Rhino 72206 As Long As I'm Singing - The Bobby Darin Collection.

1961 LAZY RIVER

- (S) (2:46) Atco 33131 Bobby Darin Story. *(preceded by :15 of talk but at least the talk does not overlap the music)*
- (M) (2:31) Warner Special Products 27606 Ultimate.

- (M) (2:30) Atco 91795 Mack The Knife.
- (S) (2:30) Time-Life HPD-37 Your Hit Parade - The 60's.
- (M) (2:31) Rhino 72206 As Long As I'm Singing - The Bobby Darin Collection.
- (M) (2:31) Rhino 72557 Jackpot! The Las Vegas Story.

1961 NATURE BOY

- (S) (2:32) Atco 91794 Splish Splash.
- (S) (2:33) Rhino 72206 As Long As I'm Singing - The Bobby Darin Collection.

1961 YOU MUST HAVE BEEN A BEAUTIFUL BABY

- (M) (2:12) Warner Special Products 27606 Ultimate.
- (S) (2:04) Atco 91794 Splish Splash.
- (M) (2:12) Rhino 71504 Great American Songwriters Volume 2: Johnny Mercer.
- (M) (2:12) Rhino 72033 Great American Songwriters Vol. 1-5 Box Set.
- (M) (2:12) Rhino 72206 As Long As I'm Singing - The Bobby Darin Collection.

1962 IRRESISTIBLE YOU

- (S) (2:31) Warner Special Products 27606 Ultimate.
- (S) (2:31) Atco 91794 Splish Splash.
- (M) (2:33) Rhino 72206 As Long As I'm Singing - The Bobby Darin Collection.

1962 MULTIPLICATION

- (S) (2:15) Warner Special Products 27606 Ultimate.
- (S) (2:15) Atco 91794 Splish Splash.
- (M) (2:13) Rhino 72206 As Long As I'm Singing - The Bobby Darin Collection.

1962 WHAT'D I SAY (PART 1)

- (S) (4:04) Atco 91794 Splish Splash. *(Parts 1 & 2)*
- (M) (4:03) Rhino 72206 As Long As I'm Singing - The Bobby Darin Collection. *(Parts 1 & 2)*

1962 THINGS

- (S) (2:32) Warner Special Products 27606 Ultimate. *(noise on fadeout)*
- (S) (2:33) Atco 91794 Splish Splash. *(noise on fadeout)*
- (S) (2:29) Time-Life 2RNR-47 Rock 'N' Roll Era - Teen Idols II.
- (S) (2:30) Time-Life SUD-06 Superhits - 1962.
- (S) (2:32) Rhino 72206 As Long As I'm Singing - The Bobby Darin Collection.
- (S) (2:30) Time-Life AM1-18 AM Gold - 1962.

1962 IF A MAN ANSWERS

- (S) (2:20) Capitol 91625 Capitol Collector's Series.
- (M) (2:21) Rhino 72206 As Long As I'm Singing - The Bobby Darin Collection.

1962 BABY FACE

- (M) (2:05) Atco 91794 Splish Splash.
- (M) (2:06) Rhino 72206 As Long As I'm Singing - The Bobby Darin Collection.

1963 YOU'RE THE REASON I'M LIVING

- (S) (2:26) Capitol 91625 Capitol Collector's Series.
- (S) (2:26) Capitol 98665 When AM Was King.
- (S) (2:24) Time-Life SUD-08 Superhits - 1963.
- (S) (2:26) Rhino 72206 As Long As I'm Singing - The Bobby Darin Collection.
- (S) (2:25) JCI 7022 Those Wonderful Years - It Must Be Him.
- (S) (2:24) Time-Life AM1-17 AM Gold - 1963.

1963 18 YELLOW ROSES

- (S) (2:16) Curb 77355 60's Hits Volume 1.
- (S) (2:16) Capitol 91625 Capitol Collector's Series.
- (S) (2:16) Curb 77325 Greatest Hits.
- (S) (2:15) Time-Life HPD-33 Your Hit Parade - The Early 60's.
- (S) (2:16) Rhino 72206 As Long As I'm Singing - The Bobby Darin Collection.
- (S) (2:16) Time-Life R857-17 The Heart Of Rock 'n' Roll: The Early '60s.

1966 IF I WERE A CARPENTER

- (S) (3:21) Curb 77325 Greatest Hits. *(live)*
- (S) (2:20) Atco 91794 Splish Splash. *(LP version)*
- (S) (2:19) Rhino 72206 As Long As I'm Singing - The Bobby Darin Collection. *(LP version)*

1967 LOVIN' YOU

- (S) (2:11) Atco 91794 Splish Splash.
- (M) (2:11) Rhino 72206 As Long As I'm Singing - The Bobby Darin Collection.

JAMES DARREN
1959 GIDGET
    (S) (2:31)   Rhino 71664 Best Of.
1961 GOODBYE CRUEL WORLD
    (S) (2:18)   Rhino 70622 Billboard's Top Rock & Roll Hits Of 1961. *(found only on the 1993 reissue of this cd)*
    (S) (2:22)   Time-Life 2RNR-47 Rock 'N' Roll Era - Teen Idols II.
    (S) (2:22)   Rhino 71650 Colpix-Dimension Story.
    (S) (2:22)   Rhino 71664 Best Of.
1962 HER ROYAL MAJESTY
    (M) (2:11)   Era 5025 The Brill Building Sound.
    (S) (2:11)   Rhino 71650 Colpix-Dimension Story.
    (S) (2:11)   Rhino 71664 Best Of.
1962 CONSCIENCE
    (M) (2:32)   Rhino 71650 Colpix-Dimension Story.
    (M) (2:32)   Rhino 71664 Best Of.
1967 ALL
    (S) (2:47)   Rhino 71664 Best Of.

DARTELLS
1963 HOT PASTRAMI
(actual 45 time is (1:53) not (2:18) as stated on the record label)
    (M) (1:44)   Rhino 75772 Son Of Frat Rock. *(LP version)*
    (S) (1:44)   MCA 5936 Vintage Music Volumes 11 & 12. *(LP version)*
    (S) (1:44)   MCA 31208 Vintage Music Volume 11. *(LP version)*
    (M) (1:53)   Time-Life 2RNR-19 Rock 'N' Roll Era - 1963 Still Rockin'. *(45 version)*
    (M) (1:44)   K-Tel 3453 Rockin' Instrumentals. *(LP version)*
    (S) (1:45)   MCA Special Products 20900 Rock Around The Oldies #3. *(LP version)*
    (S) (1:46)   MCA Special Products 20902 Classic Rock & Roll Instrumental Hits, Volume 1. *(LP version; mastered from vinyl)*
    (S) (1:46)   MCA Special Products 21742 Vintage Collectibles Volume 12. *(LP version)*
    (S) (1:46)   MCA Special Products 21017 The Rockin' Sixties. *(LP version)*

DAS EFX
1992 THEY WANT EFX
    (S) (3:38)   JCI 2714 Bust It 2.
    (S) (3:38)   Tommy Boy 1075 MTV Party To Go Volume 4. *(remix; all tracks on this cd are segued together)*
    (S) (3:39)   Eastwest 91827 Dead Serious.
    (S) (3:38)   Elektra 62091 Maximum Rap.
released as by ICE CUBE featuring DAS EFX:
1993 CHECK YO SELF
    (S) (3:42)   Priority 57185 Ice Cube - The Predator.

DAVID & DAVID
1986 WELCOME TO THE BOOMTOWN
    (S) (5:31)   A&M 5134 Boomtown.

DAVID & JONATHAN
1966 MICHELLE

MAC DAVIS
1972 BABY DON'T GET HOOKED ON ME
    (S) (3:02)   Columbia 36317 Greatest Hits.
    (S) (3:03)   Rhino 71200 Super Hits Of The 70's Volume 20.
    (S) (3:01)   Razor & Tie 21640 Those Fabulous 70's.
    (S) (3:00)   Time-Life SUD-11 Superhits - 1972.
    (S) (3:00)   Time-Life AM1-07 AM Gold - 1972.
    (S) (3:03)   Collectables 5851 Baby Don't Get Hooked On Me/Stop And Smell The Roses.
1974 ONE HELL OF A WOMAN
    (S) (2:50)   Columbia 36317 Greatest Hits.
    (S) (2:51)   Collectables 5851 Baby Don't Get Hooked On Me/Stop And Smell The Roses.
1974 STOP AND SMELL THE ROSES
    (S) (2:54)   Columbia 36317 Greatest Hits.

    (S) (3:21)   Collectables 5851 Baby Don't Get Hooked On Me/Stop And Smell The Roses. *(neither the 45 or LP version)*
1975 ROCK N' ROLL (I GAVE YOU THE BEST YEARS OF MY LIFE)
    (S) (3:26)   Collectables 5851 Baby Don't Get Hooked On Me/Stop And Smell The Roses.
1980 IT'S HARD TO BE HUMBLE
    (S) (4:22)   Casablanca 422822638 Very Best And More.
    (S) (4:16)   Collectables 5851 Baby Don't Get Hooked On Me/Stop And Smell The Roses.

PAUL DAVIS
1975 RIDE 'EM COWBOY
    (S) (3:55)   Epic/Bang 66869 Greatest Hits.
1976 SUPERSTAR
1978 I GO CRAZY
(actual 45 time is (3:54) not (3:37) as stated on the record label; LP length is (3:51))
    (S) (3:53)   Columbia/Legacy 46763 Rock Artifacts Volume 2.
    (S) (3:41)   Rhino 70673 Billboard Top Hits - 1978.
    (S) (3:51)   Razor & Tie 4543 The '70s Preservation Society Presents: Easy '70s.
    (S) (3:38)   Time-Life SOD-34 Sounds Of The Seventies - The Late 70's.
    (S) (3:52)   Epic/Bang 66869 Greatest Hits.
    (S) (3:40)   Time-Life R138-18 Body Talk.
    (S) (3:41)   Rhino 72446 Listen To The Music: 70's Male Singer/Songwriters.
    (S) (3:37)   JCI 3146 1975 - Only Love - 1979.
    (S) (3:52)   Eclipse Music Group 64895 Rock 'n Roll Relix 1976-1977.
    (S) (3:52)   Eclipse Music Group 64897 Rock 'n Roll Relix 1970-1979.
    (S) (3:51)   Time-Life R834-01 Body Talk - Forever Yours.
    (S) (3:50)   K-Tel 4017 70s Heavy Hitters: Summer Love.
1978 SWEET LIFE
    (S) (3:30)   Epic/Bang 66869 Greatest Hits.
1980 DO RIGHT
    (S) (4:01)   Epic/Bang 66869 Greatest Hits.
    (S) (3:58)   Rhino 71891 Radio Daze: Pop Hits Of The 80's Volume Two.
1982 COOL NIGHT
    (S) (3:37)   Era 5016 Cool Night.
    (S) (3:37)   Time-Life R834-17 Body Talk - Heart To Heart.
1982 '65 LOVE AFFAIR
    (S) (3:52)   Era 5016 Cool Night. *(LP pitch and length)*
    (S) (3:39)   Madacy Entertainment 1982 Rock On 1982. *(45 pitch and length)*
    (S) (3:50)   Time-Life R988-18 Sounds Of The Eighties: The Early '80s Take Two. *(LP pitch and length)*

SAMMY DAVIS JR.
1955 SOMETHING'S GOTTA GIVE
    (M) (2:03)   Garland 018 Greatest Hits.
    (M) (2:03)   MCA 10101 The Decca Years.
    (M) (2:03)   Time-Life HPD-21 Your Hit Parade - The Mid 50's.
    (M) (2:03)   MCA Special Products 20198 That Old Black Magic.
1955 LOVE ME OR LEAVE ME
    (M) (2:55)   MCA 10101 The Decca Years.
    (M) (2:56)   Time-Life HPD-31 Your Hit Parade - The 50's Forever.
    (M) (2:56)   MCA Special Products 20198 That Old Black Magic.
1955 THAT OLD BLACK MAGIC
    (M) (3:16)   Garland 018 Greatest Hits.
    (S) (3:29)   Curb 77444 Best Of. *(rerecording)*
    (S) (1:53)   Pair 1321 What Kind Of Fool Am I. *(rerecording)*
    (M) (3:17)   MCA 10101 The Decca Years.
    (M) (3:18)   Rhino 71252 Sentimental Journey: Pop Vocal Classics Vol. 4.
    (M) (3:17)   MCA Special Products 20198 That Old Black Magic.
    (M) (3:17)   MCA Special Products 20936 Legends Of Stage And Screen.
1962 WHAT KIND OF FOOL AM I
    (S) (3:21)   Garland 018 Greatest Hits. *(LP version)*
    (S) (3:38)   Curb 77272 Greatest Songs. *(rerecording)*

SAMMY DAVIS JR. *(Continued)*

(S) (3:20) Columbia/Legacy 52454 A Tribute To Black Entertainers. *(LP version)*
(S) (3:21) DCC Compact Classics 1848 His Greatest Hits I & II. *(LP version)*
(S) (3:21) Pair 1321 What Kind Of Fool Am I. *(LP version)*
(M) (2:58) Time-Life HPD-32 Your Hit Parade - Into The 60's. *(45 version)*
(S) (3:19) Time-Life R138/05 Look Of Love. *(LP version)*
(S) (3:21) Time-Life R135-04 Broadway Hit Parade. *(LP version)*
(S) (3:21) JCI 7022 Those Wonderful Years - It Must Be Him. *(LP version)*
(S) (3:22) Reprise 46416 I've Gotta Be Me: The Best Of Sammy Davis Jr. On Reprise. *(LP version)*

1964 THE SHELTER OF YOUR ARMS
(S) (2:47) DCC Compact Classics 048 Greatest Hits Volume 2.
(S) (2:47) DCC Compact Classics 1848 His Greatest Hits I & II.
(S) (2:48) Time-Life HPD-37 Your Hit Parade - The 60's.
(S) (2:50) Reprise 46416 I've Gotta Be Me: The Best Of Sammy Davis Jr. On Reprise.

1967 DON'T BLAME THE CHILDREN
1969 I'VE GOTTA BE ME
(S) (2:55) Garland 018 Greatest Hits.
(S) (2:15) Curb 77272 Greatest Songs. *(live)*
(S) (2:55) DCC Compact Classics 1848 His Greatest Hits I & II.
(S) (2:54) Rhino 72557 Jackpot! The Las Vegas Story.
(S) (2:54) Reprise 46416 I've Gotta Be Me: The Best Of Sammy Davis Jr. On Reprise.

released as by SAMMY DAVIS JR. with THE MIKE CURB CONGREGATION:
1972 CANDY MAN
(S) (3:08) Rhino 70928 Super Hits Of The 70's Volume 8.
(S) (3:07) Curb 77317 70's Hits Volume 1.
(S) (3:04) Curb 77443 Mike Curb Congregation Greatest Hits.
(S) (3:09) Garland 018 Sammy Davis Jr. - Greatest Hits.
(S) (3:04) Curb 77444 Best Of Sammy Davis Jr. And The Mike Curb Congregation.
(S) (3:06) Curb 77272 Sammy Davis Jr. - Greatest Songs.
(S) (3:09) DCC Compact Classics 1848 Sammy Davis Jr. - His Greatest Hits I & II.
(S) (3:09) Razor & Tie 21640 Those Fabulous 70's.
(S) (3:08) Time-Life SUD-20 Superhits - Early 70's Classics.
(S) (3:03) CBS Special Products 46850 Society Of Singers Presents A Gift Of Music Vol. 2.
(S) (3:10) Special Music/Essex 5036 Prom Night - The 70's.
(S) (3:07) Time-Life AM1-15 AM Gold - Early '70s Classics.
(S) (1:56) K-Tel 3630 Lounge Legends. *(live)*
(S) (3:07) MCA Special Products 20198 Sammy Davis Jr. - That Old Black Magic.
(S) (3:07) Rhino 75233 '70s Party (Killers) Classics.
(S) (3:10) Polygram Special Markets 314520456 #1 Radio Hits Of The 70's.

SKEETER DAVIS
1960 (I CAN'T HELP YOU) I'M FALLING TOO
(S) (2:43) Rhino 70681 Billboard's Top Country Hits Of 1960.
(S) (2:41) Time-Life CTD-12 Country USA - 1960.
(S) (2:43) RCA 66536 Essential.

1961 MY LAST DATE (WITH YOU)
(S) (2:32) RCA 66536 Essential.
(S) (2:31) Time-Life CTD-01 Country U.S.A. - 1961.

1963 THE END OF THE WORLD
(S) (2:36) RCA 8474 Nipper's Greatest Hits Of The 60's Volume 1.
(S) (2:36) Rhino 70684 Billboard's Top Country Hits Of 1963.
(S) (2:36) RCA 5802 Best Of The 60's.
(S) (2:35) Time-Life 2RNR-29 Rock 'N' Roll Era - The 60's Rave On.
(S) (2:35) Time-Life CTD-03 Country USA - 1962.
(S) (2:35) Time-Life SUD-08 Superhits - 1963.
(S) (2:35) Time-Life R103-27 Love Me Tender.
(S) (2:35) Time-Life R138/05 Look Of Love.
(S) (2:35) RCA 66536 Essential.

(S) (2:36) DCC Compact Classics 078 Best Of Tragedy.
(S) (2:36) K-Tel 3357 101 Greatest Country Hits Vol. Three: Easy Country. *(rerecording)*
(S) (2:35) Time-Life R857-08 The Heart Of Rock 'n' Roll 1963.
(S) (2:35) Time-Life AM1-17 AM Gold - 1963.
(S) (2:35) Time-Life R814-02 Love Songs.
(S) (2:35) Time-Life R808-01 Classic Country 1960-1964.

1963 I CAN'T STAY MAD AT YOU
(S) (2:06) Rhino 70988 Best Of The Girl Groups Volume 1.
(S) (2:06) RCA 8475 Nipper's Greatest Hits Of The 60's Volume 2.
(S) (2:56) Era 5025 The Brill Building Sound. *(previously unreleased extended version)*
(S) (2:04) Time-Life 2RNR-35 Rock 'N' Roll Era - The 60's Last Dance.
(S) (2:05) RCA 66536 Essential.

1964 GONNA GET ALONG WITHOUT YOU NOW
(S) (2:20) RCA 66536 Essential.

SPENCER DAVIS GROUP
1967 GIMME SOME LOVIN'
(M) (2:56) Rhino 70322 History Of British Rock Volume 4.
(M) (2:56) Rhino 72022 History Of British Rock Box Set.
(M) (2:56) Rhino 72008 History Of British Rock Volumes 1-4 Box Set.
(E) (2:51) Original Sound 8894 Dick Clark's 21 All-Time Hits Vol. 3.
(M) (2:56) Rhino 75778 Frat Rock.
(M) (2:56) Rhino 70628 Billboard's Top Rock & Roll Hits Of 1967.
(M) (2:55) DCC Compact Classics 043 Toga Rock II.
(M) (2:52) Capitol 48993 Spuds Mackenzie's Party Faves.
(M) (2:53) EMI 46598 Best Of.
(M) (2:51) Motown 6094 More Songs From The Original Soundtrack Of The "Big Chill".
(M) (2:52) Capitol 98138 Spring Break Volume 1.
(E) (2:50) JCI 3111 Good Time Sixties.
(M) (2:52) Time-Life 2CLR-10 Classic Rock - 1967: The Beat Goes On.
(M) (2:54) Island 314516860 Steve Winwood - The Finer Things.
(M) (2:52) Risky Business 67310 We Came To Play.
(M) (2:56) Varese 5635 and 5654 and 5655 and 5657 Arrow: All Rock & Roll Oldies Volume Two.
(M) (2:56) EMI 52498 O.S.T. Striptease.
(M) (2:56) Varese Sarabande 5708 All Rock & Roll Hits Vol. One.
(M) (2:52) Island 314524394 Island Records 40th Anniversary Volume 2 1964-1969: Rhythm & Blues.

1967 I'M A MAN
(LP length is (2:38) not (2:48) as stated on the record label; 45 length is (2:38) not (2:28) as stated on the record label)
(M) (2:39) Rhino 70326 History Of British Rock Volume 8.
(M) (2:39) Rhino 72022 History Of British Rock Box Set.
(M) (2:49) EMI 46598 Best Of. *(neither the 45 or LP version)*
(M) (2:48) Time-Life 2CLR-15 Classic Rock - 1967: Shakin' All Over. *(neither the 45 or LP version)*
(M) (2:55) Island 314516860 Steve Winwood - The Finer Things. *(neither the 45 or LP version)*
(M) (2:39) Cabin Fever Music 973 Harley Davidson: The American Motorcycle Soundtrack.

TYRONE DAVIS
1969 CAN I CHANGE MY MIND
(S) (2:47) Rhino 75770 Soul Shots Volume 2.
(S) (2:46) Rhino 70655 Billboard's Top R&B Hits Of 1969.
(S) (2:46) Rhino 72006 Billboard's Top R&B Hits 1965-1969 Box Set.
(S) (2:46) Atlantic 81911 Golden Age Of Black Music (1960-1970).
(S) (2:52) Epic 38626 Greatest Hits. *(truncated fade)*
(S) (2:46) Atlantic 82305 Atlantic Rhythm And Blues 1947-1974 Box Set.
(S) (2:46) Rhino 70533 Greatest Hits.
(S) (2:44) Time-Life RHD-13 Rhythm & Blues - 1969.
(S) (2:44) Time-Life 2CLR-12 Classic Rock - 1969: The Beat Goes On.

(S) (2:46) Brunswick 81009 The Brunswick Years Volume One.
(S) (2:44) Time-Life R838-04 Solid Gold Soul - 1969.
(S) (2:46) Rhino 72815 Beg, Scream & Shout! The Big Ol' Box Of '60s Soul.
(S) (2:45) Repeat/Relativity 1609 Tell It Like It Is: #1 Soul Hits Of The 60's Volume 1.

1969 IS IT SOMETHING YOU'VE GOT
(S) (2:33) Epic 38626 Greatest Hits.
(S) (2:35) Rhino 70533 Greatest Hits.
(S) (2:35) Rhino 72412 Turn Back The Hands Of Time.

1970 TURN BACK THE HANDS OF TIME
(the 45 and LP length was originally (2:39); the extended version running (2:54) first appeared on a Tyrone Davis "Greatest Hits" vinyl LP in the 80's)
(S) (2:55) Rhino 70658 Billboard's Top R&B Hits Of 1970.
(S) (2:53) DCC Compact Classics 028 Sock Hop.
(S) (2:55) Rhino 70782 Soul Hits Of The 70's Volume 2.
(S) (2:55) Rhino 72028 Soul Hits Of The 70's Volumes 1-5 Box Set.
(S) (2:37) Atlantic 81299 Atlantic Rhythm & Blues Volume 7.
(S) (2:54) Epic 38626 Greatest Hits.
(S) (2:37) Atlantic 82305 Atlantic Rhythm And Blues 1947-1974 Box Set.
(S) (2:37) Rhino 70533 Greatest Hits.
(S) (2:37) Rhino 71206 70's Smash Hits Volume 2.
(S) (2:52) Time-Life RHD-18 Rhythm & Blues - 1970.
(S) (2:55) Time-Life SOD-11 Sounds Of The Seventies - 1970: Take Two.
(S) (2:37) Milan 35726 O.S.T. Nine Months.
(S) (2:36) K-Tel 3518 Sweet Soul Music.
(S) (2:37) Rhino 72112 Billboard Hot Soul Hits - 1970.
(S) (2:55) Brunswick 81009 The Brunswick Years Volume One.
(S) (2:37) Rhino 72412 Turn Back The Hands Of Time.
(S) (2:36) Right Stuff 52660 Flick Hits - Old School Tracks.
(S) (2:52) Time-Life R838-05 Solid Gold Soul - 1970.
(S) (2:54) Rebound 314520420 Soul Classics - Best Of The 60's.
(S) (2:37) Flashback 72682 '70s Radio Hits Volume 2.
(S) (2:37) Flashback 72090 '70s Radio Hits Box Set.

1973 THERE IT IS
(both the dj and commercial 45 length was (3:39) even though the label of the dj 45 stated (3:25))
(S) (4:05) Epic 38626 Greatest Hits. *(LP version)*
(S) (4:07) Rhino 70533 Greatest Hits. *(LP version)*
(S) (4:07) Rhino 72412 Turn Back The Hands Of Time. *(LP version)*

1976 GIVE IT UP (TURN IT LOOSE)
(S) (4:19) Columbia/Legacy 64831 Best Of: In The Mood. *(LP version)*

DAWN
1970 CANDIDA
(E) (3:04) Time-Life SUD-04 Superhits - 1970.
(S) (3:04) Rhino 71691 Best Of.
(S) (3:06) Razor & Tie 2119 Candida.
(S) (3:04) Time-Life AM1-02 AM Gold - 1970.
1971 KNOCK THREE TIMES
(S) (2:57) Rhino 70632 Billboard's Top Rock & Roll Hits Of 1971.
(S) (2:57) Rhino 72005 Billboard's Top Rock & Roll Hits 1968-1972 Box Set.
(S) (2:56) Priority 8669 Hits/70's Greatest Rock Hits Volume 9.
(S) (2:52) Time-Life SUD-10 Superhits - 1971.
(S) (2:56) Rhino 71691 Best Of.
(S) (2:56) Varese Sarabande 5535 Bubblegum Classics Volume One. *(noise on fadeout)*
(M) (2:56) K-Tel 3130 60's Sound Explosion.
(S) (2:56) Razor & Tie 2119 Candida.
(S) (2:55) Columbia 67380 O.S.T. Now And Then.
(S) (2:52) Time-Life AM1-06 AM Gold - 1971.
(S) (2:56) Collectables 1516 and 2516 The Anniversary Album - The 70's. *(noisy fadeout)*
1971 I PLAY AND SING
(S) (2:20) Rhino 71691 Best Of.
1971 SUMMER SAND
(S) (2:55) Rhino 71691 Best Of.

released as by DAWN featuring TONY ORLANDO:
1971 WHAT ARE YOU DOING SUNDAY
(S) (2:33) Rhino 71691 Best Of.
(S) (2:33) Razor & Tie 2119 Candida.
1973 TIE A YELLOW RIBBON ROUND THE OLD OAK TREE
(S) (3:18) Time-Life SUD-13 Superhits - 1973.
(M) (3:17) Original Sound 8853 Oldies But Goodies Vol. 3. *(this compact disc uses the "Waring - fds" noise reduction process)*
(M) (3:17) Original Sound 2222 Oldies But Goodies Volumes 3,5,11,14 and 15 Box Set. *(this box set uses the "Waring - fds" noise reduction process)*
(M) (3:17) Original Sound 2500 Oldies But Goodies Volumes 1-15 Box Set. *(this box set uses the "Waring - fds" noise reduction process)*
(S) (3:23) Rhino 71691 Best Of.
(S) (3:23) Eclipse Music Group 64893 Rock 'n Roll Relix 1972-1973.
(S) (3:23) Eclipse Music Group 64897 Rock 'n Roll Relix 1970-1979.
(S) (3:18) Time-Life AM1-03 AM Gold - 1973.
(S) (3:23) K-Tel 3910 Fantastic Volume 1.
(S) (3:18) K-Tel 3913 Superstars Greatest Hits Volume 2.
(S) (3:23) Rhino 75233 '70s Party (Killers) Classics.
1973 SAY, HAS ANYBODY SEEN MY SWEET GYPSY ROSE
(S) (2:52) Time-Life SOD-33 Sounds Of The Seventies - AM Pop Classics II.
(S) (2:52) Rhino 71691 Best Of.
(S) (2:52) Madacy Entertainment 1973 Rock On 1973.
(S) (2:52) K-Tel 3626 Music Power.

released as by TONY ORLANDO & DAWN:
1973 WHO'S IN THE STRAWBERRY PATCH WITH SALLY
(S) (2:22) Rhino 71691 Best Of.
1974 STEPPIN' OUT (GONNA BOOGIE TONIGHT)
(S) (2:51) Rhino 71691 Best Of.
1975 LOOK IN MY EYES PRETTY WOMAN
(S) (3:04) Rhino 71691 Best Of.
1975 HE DON'T LOVE YOU (LIKE I LOVE YOU)
(S) (3:36) Priority 8669 Hits/70's Greatest Rock Hits Volume 9.
(S) (3:36) Rhino 71691 Best Of.
(S) (3:36) Rhino 72516 Behind Closed Doors - '70s Swingers.
1975 MORNIN' BEAUTIFUL
(S) (3:13) Rhino 71691 Best Of.
1975 YOU'RE ALL I NEED TO GET BY
1976 CUPID
(S) (3:02) Rhino 71691 Best Of.

BOBBY DAY
released as by BOBBY DAY and THE SATELLITES:
1957 LITTLE BITTY PRETTY ONE
(M) (2:26) Collectables 5074 Golden Classics.
(M) (2:25) Collectables 5651 Spotlite On Class Records Volume 1.
(M) (2:25) Relic 7139 Golden Era Of Doo-Wops - Class Records.
released as by BOBBY DAY:
1958 ROCK-IN ROBIN
(M) (2:33) Rhino 70644 Billboard's Top R&B Hits Of 1958.
(E) (2:33) Original Sound 8855 Oldies But Goodies Vol. 5. *(this compact disc uses the "Waring - fds" noise reduction process; ambient background noise throughout the disc)*
(E) (2:33) Original Sound 2222 Oldies But Goodies Volumes 3,5,11,14 and 15 Box Set. *(this box set uses the "Waring - fds" noise reduction process; ambient background noise throughout the song)*
(E) (2:33) Original Sound 2500 Oldies But Goodies Volumes 1-15 Box Set. *(this box set uses the "Waring - fds" noise reduction process; ambient background noise throughout the song)*
(E) (2:33) Original Sound CDGO-3 Golden Oldies Volume. 3.
(E) (2:34) Original Sound 8881 Twenty-One #1 Hits. *(this compact disc uses the "Waring - fds" noise reduction process)*
(E) (2:33) Original Sound 8891 Dick Clark's 21 All-Time Hits Vol. 1.

BOBBY DAY *(Continued)*

- (E) (2:34) Original Sound 9603 Best Of Oldies But Goodies Vol. 3.
- (M) (2:34) Collectables 5074 Golden Classics.
- (M) (2:32) Virgin 92153 and 86289 O.S.T. American Me.
- (M) (2:33) Rhino 70495 Fun Rock!
- (M) (2:32) Collectables 5061 History Of Rock Volume 1.
- (M) (2:33) Time-Life 2RNR-05 Rock 'N' Roll Era - 1958.
- (M) (2:32) Time-Life RHD-16 Rhythm & Blues - 1958.
- (E) (2:33) Collectables 2503 WCBS-FM History Of Rock - The 50's Part 2.
- (M) (2:31) Collectables 4503 History Of Rock/The 50s Part Two.
- (M) (2:32) Collectables 2603 WCBS-FM Jukebox Giants Vol. 1.
- (M) (2:32) JCI 3129 1955 - Only Rock 'N Roll - 1959.
- (M) (2:32) Collectables 5652 Spotlite On Class Records Volume 2.
- (S) (2:30) King 499 Classic Rock & Roll. *(rerecording)*
- (M) (2:32) Music For Little People 42581 A Child's Celebration Of Rock 'N' Roll.
- (M) (2:32) Relic 7139 Golden Era Of Doo-Wops - Class Records.
- (M) (2:33) Nick At Nite/550 Music/Epic 67770 Happy Days Jukebox.
- (M) (2:33) Priority 50950 I Love Rock & Roll Volume 1: Hits Of The 50's.
- (M) (2:32) Time-Life R838-22 Solid Gold Soul 1958.

DORIS DAY
1955 I'LL NEVER STOP LOVING YOU
- (M) (3:05) Columbia 45111 16 Most Requested Songs Of The 50's, Vol. 2.
- (M) (3:03) Columbia/Legacy 48987 16 Most Requested Songs.
- (M) (3:02) Time-Life HPD-31 Your Hit Parade - The 50's Forever.
- (M) (3:03) Time-Life HPD-09 Your Hit Parade - 1955.
- (M) (3:05) Columbia 44371 A Day At The Movies.
- (E) (1:54) Nick At Nite/550 Music/Epic 67689 Stand By Your Man. *(live)*
- (E) (1:55) Columbia/Legacy 47503 O.S.T. Love Me Or Leave Me. *(live)*
- (M) (3:02) Columbia/Legacy 47503 O.S.T. Love Me Or Leave Me.
- (E) (1:54) Time-Life R855-01 The Best Of Broadway - The Late '50s. *(live)*

1956 WHATEVER WILL BE, WILL BE (QUE SERA, SERA)
- (M) (2:03) Columbia 45111 16 Most Requested Songs Of The 50's Volume 2.
- (M) (2:03) Columbia 44371 A Day At The Movies.
- (M) (2:03) Columbia 45017 Radio Classics Of The 50's.
- (M) (2:03) Columbia 8635 Greatest Hits.
- (M) (2:04) Columbia/Legacy 48987 16 Most Requested Songs.
- (M) (2:04) Rhino 71252 Sentimental Journey: Pop Vocal Classics Volume 4 (1954-1959).
- (M) (2:04) Rhino 72034 Sentimental Journey Pop Vocal Classics Volumes 1-4 Box Set.
- (M) (2:04) Time-Life HPD-15 Your Hit Parade - 1956.
- (M) (2:04) Columbia/Legacy 57741 Academy Award Winners: 16 Most Requested Songs.
- (M) (2:03) Rhino 71868 Academy Award Winning Songs.
- (M) (2:03) K-Tel 3471 High Hopes - Songs To Lift Your Spirits.
- (M) (2:03) Time-Life R138-32 Hollywood Hit Parade.
- (M) (2:02) Nick At Nite/Epic 67148 Donna Reed's Dinner Party.
- (M) (2:03) Rhino 72277 Academy Award Winning Songs Volume 2.
- (M) (2:04) Rhino 72422 Billboard Top Movie Hits 1955-1959.
- (M) (2:03) JCI 7011 Those Wonderful Years - That's Hollywood.

1958 EVERYBODY LOVES A LOVER
- (M) (2:41) Columbia 8635 Greatest Hits.
- (M) (2:42) Columbia/Legacy 48987 16 Most Requested Songs.
- (M) (2:40) Columbia/Legacy 53575 The Essence Of.
- (M) (2:42) Time-Life HPD-11 Your Hit Parade 1958.

MORRIS DAY
1988 FISHNET
(actual 45 time is (4:06) not (3:58) as stated on the record label)
- (S) (6:04) Warner Brothers 25651 Daydreaming. *(LP version)*
- (S) (4:07) Cold Front 6246 Classic Club Mix - R&B Grooves. *(all selections on this cd are segued together; 45 version)*

TAYLOR DAYNE
1988 TELL IT TO MY HEART
(actual 45 time is (3:39) not (3:31) as stated on the record label)
- (S) (3:37) Foundation/WEA 26097 Super Sessions Volume Two.
- (S) (3:38) JCI 2720 Rockin' Ladies Of The 80's.
- (S) (3:36) JCI 2702 Hot Moves.
- (S) (3:38) Priority 53732 80's Greatest Rock Hits Volume 8 - Dance Party.
- (S) (3:38) Sandstone 33046 and 5012 Rock The First Volume Six.
- (S) (3:39) Arista 8529 Tell It To My Heart.
- (S) (3:38) Arista 18774 Greatest Hits.
- (S) (3:45) Arista 18774 Greatest Hits. *(remixed)*
- (S) (3:38) Madacy Entertainment 1987 Rock On 1987.
- (S) (3:38) JCI 3171 #1 Radio Hits 1985 - Only Rock 'n Roll - 1989.
- (S) (3:21) Arista 18943 Ultimate Dance Party 1997. *(all selections on this cd are segued together; remix)*
- (S) (3:32) Quality 5008 Dance Box Set. *(all selections on this cd are segued together)*
- (S) (3:26) Priority 50941 Shut Up And Dance! Volume Two - The 80's. *(all songs on this cd are segued together)*
- (S) (3:38) Time-Life R988-19 Sounds Of The Eighties: The Late '80s.
- (S) (3:37) Rhino 72838 Disco Queens: The 80's.
- (S) (3:37) Cold Front 3865 Club Mix - Women Of Dance Vol. 2.
- (S) (3:38) Hip-O 40075 Rock She Said: On The Pop Side.

1988 PROVE YOUR LOVE
- (S) (3:26) Arista 8529 Tell It To My Heart.
- (S) (3:25) Arista 18774 Greatest Hits.

1988 I'LL ALWAYS LOVE YOU
- (S) (4:29) Sandstone 33048 and 5016 Cosmopolitan Volume 2. *(LP length)*
- (S) (4:29) DCC Compact Classics 087 Night Moves Volume 5. *(LP length)*
- (S) (4:30) Arista 8529 Tell It To My Heart. *(LP length)*
- (S) (4:29) Priority 53700 80's Greatest Rock Hits Volume 13 - Soft Sounds. *(LP length)*
- (S) (4:16) Arista 18774 Greatest Hits. *(45 length)*
- (S) (4:28) Madacy Entertainment 6803 Power Of Love. *(LP length)*
- (S) (4:16) Rhino 72580 Soul Serenade - Intimate R&B. *(45 length)*
- (S) (4:16) Time-Life R988-20 Sounds Of The Eighties: The Late '80s Take Two. *(45 length)*
- (S) (4:29) Time-Life R834-02 Body Talk - Just For You. *(LP length)*

1989 DON'T RUSH ME
- (S) (3:46) K-Tel 842 Hot Ladies Of The 80's.
- (S) (3:47) Arista 8529 Tell It To My Heart.
- (S) (3:47) Arista 18774 Greatest Hits.
- (S) (3:46) Time-Life R988-21 Sounds Of The Eighties: 1986-1989.

1989 WITH EVERY BEAT OF MY HEART
(actual 45 time is (4:21) not (4:12) as stated on the record label)
- (S) (4:21) JCI 3128 1985 - Only Rock 'N Roll - 1989.
- (S) (4:21) Arista 8581 Can't Fight Fate.
- (S) (4:21) Arista 18774 Greatest Hits.
- (S) (4:21) Scotti Bros. 75504 Club Ladies Night.

1990 LOVE WILL LEAD YOU BACK
(actual 45 time is (4:23) not (4:17) as stated on the record label)
- (S) (4:36) Foundation/Capitol 96427 Hearts Of Gold: The Pop Collection. *(LP version)*
- (S) (4:36) Priority 7040 Making Love. *(LP version)*

(S) (4:36) K-Tel 6006 Lite Rock. *(LP version)*
(S) (4:36) Arista 8581 Can't Fight Fate. *(LP version)*
(S) (4:23) Arista 18774 Greatest Hits. *(45 version)*
(S) (4:23) Time-Life R834-12 Body Talk - By Candlelight. *(45 version)*

1990 I'LL BE YOUR SHELTER
(actual 45 time is (4:06) not (3:59) as stated on the record label)
(S) (4:41) K-Tel 3263 The 80's Love Jams. *(LP length)*
(S) (4:42) Mercury 314525354 Women For Women. *(LP length)*
(S) (4:42) Arista 8581 Can't Fight Fate. *(LP length)*
(S) (4:06) Arista 18774 Greatest Hits. *(45 length)*
(S) (4:05) Hip-O 40000 Thinking About You - A Collection Of Modern Love Songs. *(45 length)*
(S) (4:06) Rhino 72915 Lesbian Favorites: Women Like Us. *(45 length)*
(S) (4:42) K-Tel 3848 90s Now Volume 2. *(LP length)*

1990 HEART OF STONE
(S) (4:16) Arista 8581 Can't Fight Fate. *(LP length)*
(S) (4:01) Arista 18774 Greatest Hits. *(45 length)*

1993 CAN'T GET ENOUGH OF YOUR LOVE
(S) (4:25) Arista 18705 Soul Dancing.
(S) (4:25) Arista 18774 Greatest Hits.
(S) (6:05) Rhino 72839 Disco Queens: The 90's. *(remix)*

DAZZ BAND
1982 LET IT WHIP
(S) (4:02) Motown 9021 and 5309 25 Years Of Grammy Greats. *(45 version)*
(S) (4:02) Priority 7057 Mega-Hits Dance Classics (Volume 8). *(45 version)*
(S) (4:02) Thump 4020 Old School Volume 2. *(45 version)*
(S) (4:41) Motown/Essex 374638514 Motown Legends - Let It Whip. *(LP version)*
(S) (4:28) Rebound 314520218 Disco Nights Vol. 2. *(45 version but :26 longer fade)*
(S) (4:40) Rebound 314520298 Disco Nights Vol. 9. *(LP version)*
(S) (4:26) Motown 314530436 A Tribute To Berry Gordy. *(45 version but :24 longer fade)*
(S) (4:28) Motown 314530418 Funkology: Definitive Dazz Band. *(45 version but :26 longer fade)*
(S) (4:02) Motown 5387 Greatest Hits. *(45 version)*
(S) (4:05) Motown 6358 Hitsville USA Volume Two. *(45 version)*
(S) (4:28) Motown 314530534 Motown Year By Year - 1982. *(45 version but :26 longer fade)*
(S) (6:09) Motown 314530498 Funkology Volume One - Got To Give It Up. *(12" single version)*
(S) (4:05) Rhino 72159 Black Entertainment Television - 15th Anniversary. *(45 version)*
(S) (4:05) K-Tel 3581 Roller Disco - Boogie From The Skating Rinks. *(45 version)*
(S) (4:22) London 422828944 More Music From O.S.T. Grosse Pointe Blank. *(45 version but :22 longer fade)*
(S) (4:03) Motown 314530849 Motown 40 Forever. *(45 version)*
(S) (4:07) Cold Front 6330 Club Mix: The 80s. *(all selections on this cd are segued together)*

DC TALK
1996 JUST BETWEEN YOU AND ME
(S) (4:58) Forefront 25140 Jesus Freak.

DEADEYE DICK
1995 NEW AGE GIRL
(S) (3:26) RCA 66523 O.S.T. Dumb And Dumber.
(S) (3:29) Ichiban 6501 A Different Story.
(S) (3:26) K-Tel 3850 90s Now Volume 3.
(S) (3:26) Boxtunes 162531028 Big Ones Of Alternative Rock.

DEAD OR ALIVE
1985 YOU SPIN ME AROUND (LIKE A RECORD)
(S) (7:59) Epic 66155 Club Epic Volume 2. *(remix)*

(S) (3:16) Risky Business 57468 This Ain't No Disco/New Wave Dance Hits.
(S) (3:17) Epic 40119 Youthquake.
(S) (7:12) Oglio 81584 Hit That Perfect Beat Volume 2. *(remix; all songs on this cd are segued together)*
(S) (7:59) DCC Compact Classics 131 HI-NRG Dance Classics Volume 1. *(12" single version)*
(S) (3:15) JCI 3159 18 Modern Rock Classics From The 80's.
(S) (3:15) Time-Life R988-17 Sounds Of The Eighties: The Mid '80s Take Two.
(S) (3:16) Epic/Legacy 65254 Fizz Pop Modern Rock Volume 1.
(S) (3:53) Thump 4802 Thump'n Disco Quick Mixx. *(all selections on this cd are segued together)*
(S) (2:58) Priority 50940 Shut Up And Dance! The 80's Volume One. *(all selections on this cd are segued together)*

1987 BRAND NEW LOVER
(S) (5:18) Epic 40572 Mad, Bad And Dangerous To Know. *(LP version)*
(S) (4:33) Risky Business 66390 Hazy Shade Of 80's. *(neither the 45, LP or 12" single version)*
(S) (3:35) Rhino 72771 The Big 80's. *(45 version)*
(S) (9:03) Epic 67534 Club Epic Volume 5. *(12" single version)*
(S) (4:33) Epic/Legacy 65255 Fizz Pop Modern Rock Volume 2. *(neither the 45, LP or 12" single version)*

BILL DEAL & THE RHONDELS
1969 MAY I
(M) (2:29) JCI 3115 Groovin' Sixties
(E) (2:28) Ripete 2392193 Bill Deal & Ammon Tharp (The Original Rhondels).
(E) (2:27) Ripete 0001 Coolin' Out/24 Carolina Classics Volume 1.
(M) (2:31) Varese Sarabande 5785 Vintage Rock.

1969 I'VE BEEN HURT
(M) (2:09) Rhino 75770 Soul Shots Volume 2.
(M) (2:07) JCI 3115 Groovin' Sixties.
(E) (2:08) Original Sound 8857 Oldies But Goodies Vol. 7. *(this compact disc uses the "Waring - fds" noise reduction process)*
(E) (2:08) Original Sound 2223 Oldies But Goodies Volumes 2,7,9,12 and 13 Box Set. *(this box set uses the "Waring - fds" noise reduction process)*
(E) (2:08) Original Sound 2500 Oldies But Goodies Volumes 1-15 Box Set. *(this box set uses the "Waring - fds" noise reduction process)*
(E) (2:06) Original Sound CDGO-7 Golden Oldies Volume. 7.
(E) (2:08) Ripete 2392192 Beach Music Anthology Box Set.
(E) (2:07) Ripete 2392193 Bill Deal & Ammon Tharp (The Original Rhondels).
(M) (2:08) Ripete 0003 Coolin' Out/24 Carolina Classics Vol. 3.
(M) (2:01) K-Tel 3269 Carolina Beach Music.
(E) (2:08) Varese Sarabande 5785 Vintage Rock. *(dropout at :03)*
(M) (2:25) MCA 11539 O.S.T. Trees Lounge. *(time includes a :17 instrumental coda)*

1969 WHAT KIND OF FOOL DO YOU THINK I AM
(M) (2:13) Rhino 75772 Son Of Frat Rock.
(M) (2:11) JCI 3115 Groovin' Sixties.
(E) (2:11) Original Sound 8865 Oldies But Goodies Vol. 15. *(this compact disc uses the "Waring - fds" noise reduction process)*
(E) (2:11) Original Sound 2222 Oldies But Goodies Volumes 3,5,11,14 and 15 Box Set. *(this box set uses the "Waring - fds" noise reduction process)*
(E) (2:11) Original Sound 2500 Oldies But Goodies Volumes 1-15 Box Set. *(this box set uses the "Waring - fds" noise reduction process)*
(E) (2:11) Original Sound CDGO-9 Golden Oldies Volume. 9.
(M) (2:13) Ripete 2392192 Beach Music Anthology Box Set.
(E) (2:11) Ripete 2392193 Bill Deal & Ammon Tharp (The Original Rhondels).
(E) (2:11) Ripete 0002 Coolin' Out/24 Carolina Classics Vol. 2.
(M) (2:13) Varese Sarabande 5785 Vintage Rock. *(dropout at :01)*

JIMMY DEAN
1961 BIG BAD JOHN
(the very first pressings of this 45 included the
words "hell of a man" which were quickly replaced
by "a big big man")
- (M) (2:59) Rhino 70682 Billboard's Top Country Hits Of 1961. *("hell of a man" version)*
- (S) (3:00) Columbia 46031 Columbia Country Classics Volume 3. *("big big man" version)*
- (S) (3:00) Columbia 45077 American Originals. *("big big man" version)*
- (S) (3:00) Columbia 9285 Greatest Hits. *("big big man" version)*
- (M) (2:59) Time-Life CTD-01 Country USA - 1961. *("hell of a man" version)*
- (M) (2:59) Rhino 71750 Spy Magazine Presents: White Men Can't Wrap. *("hell of a man" version)*
- (S) (2:58) Curb 77764 Greatest Songs. *(rerecording)*
- (M) (2:59) Priority 50966 I Love Country Volume One: Hits Of The 60's. *("hell of a man" version)*
- (S) (3:00) Epic 67941 Super Hits Of The 60's. *("big big man" version)*
- (S) (2:58) K-Tel 3359 101 Greatest Country Hits Vol. Five: Country Memories. *(rerecording)*
- (S) (3:00) Columbia/Legacy 65256 Greatest Hits. *("big big man" version)*

1962 DEAR IVAN
- (M) (3:45) Columbia 45077 American Originals.
- (S) (3:59) Curb 77764 Greatest Songs. *(rerecording)*
- (S) (3:49) Columbia/Legacy 65256 Greatest Hits.

1962 THE CAJUN QUEEN
- (M) (2:35) Columbia 45077 American Originals.
- (S) (2:36) Columbia 9285 Greatest Hits.
- (S) (2:32) Curb 77764 Greatest Songs. *(rerecording)*
- (S) (2:36) Columbia/Legacy 65256 Greatest Hits.

1962 TO A SLEEPING BEAUTY
- (S) (5:14) Columbia 9285 Greatest Hits.
- (S) (5:58) Curb 77764 Greatest Songs. *(rerecording)*
- (S) (5:12) Columbia/Legacy 65256 Greatest Hits.

1962 P.T. 109
- (M) (3:07) Columbia 45077 American Originals.
- (S) (3:10) Rhino 70683 Billboard's Top Country Hits Of 1962.
- (S) (3:10) Columbia 9285 Greatest Hits.
- (S) (3:20) Curb 77764 Greatest Songs. *(rerecording)*
- (S) (3:10) Columbia/Legacy 65256 Greatest Hits.

1962 LITTLE BLACK BOOK
- (S) (2:23) Columbia 45077 American Originals.
- (S) (2:23) Columbia 9285 Greatest Hits.
- (S) (2:24) Curb 77764 Greatest Songs. *(rerecording)*
- (S) (2:23) Columbia/Legacy 65256 Greatest Hits.

1976 I.O.U.
- (S) (6:03) Curb 77764 Greatest Songs. *(rerecording)*

DEAN and JEAN
1964 TRA LA LA LA SUZY
- (S) (2:43) Time-Life 2RNR-42 Rock 'N' Roll Era - The 60's Sock Hop.

1964 HEY JEAN, HEY DEAN
- (S) (2:33) Time-Life 2RNR-40 Rock 'N' Roll Era - The 60's Teen Time.

DeBARGE
1983 I LIKE IT
- (S) (4:38) Motown 6173 Greatest Hits. *(LP version)*
- (S) (4:38) Motown 5392 All This Love. *(LP version)*
- (S) (3:42) Motown 314530534 Motown Year By Year - 1982. *(45 version)*
- (S) (4:38) Motown 314530561 The Ultimate Collection. *(LP version)*

1983 ALL THIS LOVE
- (S) (4:08) Motown 9082 and 5385 Three Times A Lady - Great Motown Love Songs. *(45 version)*
- (S) (5:52) Motown 6177 Endless Love: 15 Of Motown's Greatest Love Songs. *(LP version)*
- (S) (5:50) Motown 6192 You Can't Hurry Love. *(LP version)*
- (S) (5:52) Motown 6173 Greatest Hits. *(LP version)*
- (S) (5:51) Motown 5392 All This Love. *(LP version)*

- (S) (5:52) Motown 314530561 The Ultimate Collection. *(LP version)*
- (S) (5:53) Rhino 72757 Smooth Grooves - Wedding Songs. *(LP version)*
- (S) (4:07) Motown 314530849 Motown 40 Forever. *(45 version)*
- (S) (5:52) Time-Life R834-18 Body Talk - Romantic Moments. *(LP version)*

1984 TIME WILL REVEAL
- (S) (4:09) Motown 6173 Greatest Hits.
- (S) (4:16) Motown 5393 In A Special Way.
- (S) (4:05) Motown 6358 Hitsville USA Volume Two.
- (S) (4:15) Motown 314530561 The Ultimate Collection.

1985 RHYTHM OF THE NIGHT
- (S) (3:54) Motown 314530519 Motown Year By Year 1985.
- (S) (3:47) Motown 6123 Rhythm Of The Night.
- (S) (3:47) Motown 6173 Greatest Hits.
- (S) (3:53) Motown 6358 Hitsville USA Volume Two.
- (S) (3:53) Time-Life R988-12 Sounds Of The 80's: 1985-1986.
- (S) (3:53) Rhino 72140 Billboard Hot R&B Hits 1985.
- (S) (3:52) Hip-O 40005 The '80s Hit(s) Back....Again!
- (S) (3:53) Rebound 314520431 Soul Classics - Best Of The 80's.
- (S) (5:43) Motown 314530561 The Ultimate Collection. *("Last Dragon" soundtrack LP version)*
- (S) (3:52) Priority 50974 Premiere The Movie Magazine Presents The Greatest Soundtrack Hits.

1985 WHO'S HOLDING DONNA NOW
- (S) (4:25) Motown 314530519 Motown Year By Year 1985. *(LP length)*
- (S) (4:27) Motown 6123 Rhythm Of The Night. *(LP length)*
- (S) (4:26) Motown 6173 Greatest Hits. *(LP length)*
- (S) (4:06) Rhino 72140 Billboard Hot R&B Hits 1985. *(45 length)*
- (S) (4:27) Motown 314530561 The Ultimate Collection. *(LP length)*
- (S) (4:25) K-Tel 3864 Slow Dancin'. *(LP length)*
- (S) (4:06) Time-Life R834-11 Body Talk - After Dark. *(45 length)*
- (S) (4:06) Time-Life R988-23 Sounds Of The Eighties 1984-1985. *(45 length)*

CHICO DeBARGE
1987 TALK TO ME
- (S) (3:50) Motown 6358 Hitsville USA Volume Two.
- (S) (3:49) Motown 314530561 DeBarge - The Ultimate Collection.

EL DeBARGE
1986 WHO'S JOHNNY
- (S) (4:08) Motown 6181 El DeBarge.
- (S) (4:08) Motown 6358 Hitsville USA Volume Two.
- (S) (4:08) Rhino 72141 Billboard Hot R&B Hits 1986.
- (S) (4:09) Motown 314530561 DeBarge - The Ultimate Collection.

released as by QUINCY JONES featuring AL B.SURE!/
JAMES INGRAM/EL DeBARGE/BARRY WHITE:
1990 THE SECRET GARDEN
- (S) (6:39) Qwest/Warner Brothers 26020 Quincy Jones - Back On The Block.
- (S) (6:45) Mercury 314514143 Barry White - Just For You. *(includes a :06 previously unreleased introduction by Barry White)*

CHRIS DeBURGH
1983 DON'T PAY THE FERRYMAN
- (S) (3:47) A&M 4929 The Getaway.
1987 THE LADY IN RED
- (S) (4:15) Arista 8593 O.S.T. Working Girl.
- (S) (4:15) Rhino 71642 Billboard Top Hits - 1987.
- (S) (4:15) A&M 5121 Into The Light.
- (S) (4:03) JCI 3186 1985 - Only Love - 1989.
- (S) (4:14) Madacy Entertainment 6803 Power Of Love.
- (S) (4:14) Time-Life R103-18 Great Love Songs Of The '70s & '80s.
- (S) (4:15) Rebound 314520438 No. 1 Hits Of The 80's.

JOEY DEE & THE STARLITERS
1962 PEPPERMINT TWIST (PART 1)
    (S) (2:00) Rhino 70623 Billboard's Top Rock & Roll Hits Of 1962.
    (S) (2:00) Rhino 72007 Billboard's Top Rock & Roll Hits 1962-1966 Box Set.
    (S) (1:58) Rhino 70992 Groove 'N' Grind.
    (S) (1:58) Rhino 70965 Best Of.
    (S) (1:58) Essex 7052 All Time Rock Classics.
    (S) (2:01) MCA 8001 O.S.T. American Graffiti.
    (S) (1:58) Time-Life 2RNR-04 Rock 'N' Roll Era - 1961. *(original pressings of this song on this cd were (E))*
    (S) (1:58) K-Tel 3241 Let's Twist.
    (S) (1:58) Nick At Nite/Epic 67149 Dick Van Dyke's Dance Party.
    (S) (2:01) Rhino 71802 O.S.T. Andre.
    (S) (1:58) JCI 3189 1960 - Only Dance - 1964.
    (S) (2:00) Sony Music Special Products 22210 Fun Rock.
1962 HEY LET'S TWIST
    (M) (1:58) Rhino 70965 Best Of.
    (M) (1:58) K-Tel 3241 Let's Twist.
1962 SHOUT (PART 1)
    (E) (2:29) JCI 3110 Sock Hoppin' Sixties.
    (S) (2:31) Rhino 70965 Best Of.
    (S) (2:32) Rhino 72213 Stadium Rock.
    (E) (2:28) Cypress 71334 O.S.T. Coupe De Ville.
    (S) (2:32) Flashback 72711 Sports Rock.
1962 WHAT KIND OF LOVE IS THIS
    (S) (2:06) Rhino 70965 Best Of.
1963 HOT PASTRAMI WITH MASHED POTATOES (PART 1)
    (S) (4:45) Rhino 70965 Best Of. *(Parts 1 & 2)*

JOHNNY DEE
1957 SITTIN' IN THE BALCONY

KIKI DEE
1974 I'VE GOT THE MUSIC IN ME
(dj copies of this 45 ran (3:06) and (5:00); commercial copies were all (5:00))
    (S) (4:58) Rhino 72297 Superhits Of The 70's Volume 23.
    (S) (4:58) K-Tel 3627 Out Of Sight.
released as by ELTON JOHN and KIKI DEE:
1976 DON'T GO BREAKING MY HEART
    (S) (4:22) Rhino 70671 Billboard Top Hits - 1976.
    (S) (4:20) Priority 7059 Mega-Hits Dance Classics Volume 10.
    (S) (4:24) MCA 37216 Elton John - Greatest Hits Volume 2.
    (S) (4:30) MCA 10693 Elton John - Greatest Hits 1976-1986.
    (S) (4:30) MCA 10110 Elton John - To Be Continued.
    (S) (4:21) Time-Life SOD-04 Sounds Of The Seventies - 1976.

TOMMY DEE
1959 THREE STARS

DEEE-LITE
1990 GROOVE IS IN THE HEART
    (S) (3:51) Elektra 60957 World Clique.
    (S) (5:11) Rebound 314520359 World Of Dance - The 90's. *(remix)*
    (S) (4:25) Elektra 61872 Sampladelic Relics & Dancefloor Oddities. *(remix)*
    (S) (3:51) Razor & Tie 4569 '90s Style.
    (S) (3:51) Elektra 62089 Maximum R&B.

DEELE
1988 TWO OCCASIONS
    (S) (4:16) Solar 72555 Eyes Of A Stranger.
    (S) (4:10) Thump 9956 Old School Funk. *(all selections on this cd are segued together)*
    (S) (5:50) Solar/Right Stuff 54489 Eyes Of A Stranger. *(live; this is not the version that appeared on the vinyl LP "Eyes Of A Stranger")*

DEEP BLUE SOMETHING
1996 BREAKFAST AT TIFFANY'S
    (S) (4:19) Interscope 92608 Home.
    (S) (4:10) Atlantic 82895 VH1 Crossroads. *(live)*

DEEP PURPLE
1968 HUSH
(the LP version of this song includes 3 wolf calls - the 45 version includes 2)
    (S) (4:18) Rhino 70327 History Of British Rock Volume 9. *(45 version)*
    (S) (4:18) Rhino 72022 History Of British Rock Box Set. *(45 version)*
    (S) (4:22) Warner Brothers 3223 When We Rock, We Rock. *(LP version)*
    (M) (4:23) Time-Life 2CLR-11 Classic Rock - 1968: The Beat Goes On. *(LP version)*
    (S) (4:17) Rhino 71938 Billboard Top Pop Hits, 1968. *(45 version)*
    (S) (4:17) Time-Life R968-07 Guitar Rock 1968-1969. *(45 version)*
    (S) (3:30) Polygram Special Markets 314520503 Smoke On The Water. *(rerecording)*
1968 KENTUCKY WOMAN
    (S) (4:43) Warner Brothers 3223 When We Rock, We Rock. *(LP version)*
    (S) (4:42) Time-Life 2CLR-17 Classic Rock - Rock Renaissance. *(LP version)*
    (S) (4:42) Time-Life R968-12 Guitar Rock - The Late '60s. *(LP version)*
1973 SMOKE ON THE WATER
    (S) (6:26) Warner Brothers 3223 When We Rock, We Rock. *(live; an edit from the "Made In Japan" LP)*
    (S) (5:40) Warner Brothers 3100 Machine Head. *(LP version)*
    (S) (5:38) Warner Brothers 3486 Deepest Purple/Very Best Of. *(LP version)*
    (S) (5:39) Foundation/Capitol 96647 Hearts Of Gold - The Classic Rock Collection. *(LP version)*
    (S) (5:38) Time-Life R968-05 Guitar Rock 1972-1973. *(LP version)*
    (S) (4:30) Time-Life SOD-06 Sounds Of The Seventies - 1973. *(this live version was the flip side of the studio version 45, and was an edit from the "Made In Japan" LP)*
    (S) (3:55) Time-Life OPCD-4521 Guitar Rock. *(45 version)*
    (S) (5:38) Elektra 61498 O.S.T. Made In America. *(LP version)*
    (S) (5:40) Rhino 72132 Frat Rock: More Of The 70's. *(LP version)*
    (S) (5:38) Pointblank 42088 Fender 50th Anniversary Guitar Legends. *(LP version)*
    (S) (3:55) JCI 3168 #1 Radio Hits 1970 - Only Rock 'n Roll - 1974. *(45 version)*
    (S) (5:34) Warner Brothers 46477 Howard Stern Private Parts: The Album. *(LP version)*
    (S) (5:40) Priority 50991 The Best Of The 70's - Rock Chart Toppers. *(LP version)*
    (S) (5:39) Rhino 72893 Hard Rock Cafe: Classic Rock. *(LP version)*
    (S) (7:23) Polygram Special Markets 314520503 Smoke On The Water. *(live)*

RICK DEES
1976 DISCO DUCK (PART 1)
    (S) (3:14) Rhino 71200 Super Hits Of The 70's Volume 20.
    (S) (3:13) Time-Life R830-01 The Dr. Demento Collection - The Mid 70's.

DEF LEPPARD
1983 PHOTOGRAPH
    (S) (4:07) Mercury 810308 Pyromania. *(LP length)*
    (S) (4:07) MFSL 520 Pyromania. *(LP length; gold disc)*
    (S) (4:07) Time-Life R988-26 Sounds Of The Eighties: The Rolling Stone Collection 1982-1983. *(LP length)*
    (S) (4:07) Mercury 314528718 Greatest Hits. *(LP length)*
1983 ROCK OF AGES
    (S) (4:07) Mercury 810308 Pyromania.
    (S) (4:07) MFSL 520 Pyromania. *(gold disc)*
    (S) (4:07) Time-Life R968-10 Guitar Rock Classics.
    (S) (4:07) Mercury 314528718 Greatest Hits.
1983 FOOLIN'
    (S) (4:33) Mercury 810308 Pyromania.
    (S) (4:33) MFSL 520 Pyromania. *(gold disc)*

DEF LEPPARD (Continued)
- (S) (4:33)   Mercury 314528718   Greatest Hits.

1987 ANIMAL
- (S) (4:03)   Mercury 830675   Hysteria.
- (S) (4:03)   MFSL 580   Hysteria. *(gold disc)*
- (S) (4:03)   Mercury 314528718   Greatest Hits.

1988 HYSTERIA
- (S) (5:54)   Mercury 830675   Hysteria.
- (S) (5:54)   MFSL 580   Hysteria. *(gold disc)*
- (S) (5:54)   Mercury 314528718   Greatest Hits.

1988 POUR SOME SUGAR ON ME
- (S) (4:25)   Mercury 830675   Hysteria.
- (S) (4:25)   MFSL 580   Hysteria. *(gold disc)*
- (S) (4:51)   Mercury 314528718   Greatest Hits. *(video version)*

1988 LOVE BITES
- (S) (5:46)   Mercury 830675   Hysteria.
- (S) (5:46)   MFSL 580   Hysteria. *(gold disc)*
- (S) (5:46)   Mercury 314528718   Greatest Hits.
- (S) (5:46)   Time-Life R13610   Gold And Platinum Box Set - The Ultimate Rock Collection.

1989 ARMAGEDDON IT
- (S) (5:20)   Polydor 314515913   Classic Rock Box.
- (S) (5:21)   Mercury 830675   Hysteria.
- (S) (5:21)   MFSL 580   Hysteria. *(gold disc)*
- (S) (5:21)   Mercury 314528718   Greatest Hits.

1989 ROCKET
- (S) (6:35)   Mercury 830675   Hysteria. *(LP version)*
- (S) (6:35)   MFSL 580   Hysteria. *(LP version; gold disc)*
- (S) (4:06)   Mercury 314528718   Greatest Hits. *(video version)*

1992 LET'S GET ROCKED
- (S) (4:55)   Mercury 314512185   Adrenalize.
- (S) (4:55)   Mercury 314528718   Greatest Hits.

1992 MAKE LOVE LIKE A MAN
- (S) (4:14)   Mercury 314512185   Adrenalize.

1992 HAVE YOU EVER NEEDED SOMEONE SO BAD
- (S) (5:21)   Mercury 314512185   Adrenalize.
- (S) (5:19)   Mercury 314528718   Greatest Hits.

1993 STAND UP (KICK LOVE INTO MOTION)
- (S) (4:32)   Mercury 314512185   Adrenalize.

1993 TWO STEPS BEHIND
- (S) (4:17)   Columbia 57127   O.S.T. Last Action Hero. *(acoustic version)*
- (S) (4:16)   Mercury 314518305   Retroactive. *(acoustic version)*
- (S) (4:56)   Mercury 314518305   Retroactive. *(electric version)*
- (S) (4:18)   Mercury 314528718   Greatest Hits. *(acoustic version)*

1994 MISS YOU IN A HEARTBEAT
- (S) (4:04)   Mercury 314518305   Retroactive.
- (S) (4:04)   Mercury 314528718   Greatest Hits.

DeFRANCO FAMILY featuring TONY DeFRANCO
1973 HEARTBEAT - IT'S A LOVEBEAT
- (S) (3:09)   Rhino 70930   Super Hits Of The 70's Volume 10.
- (S) (3:10)   Rhino 71228   Yesterday's Heroes: 70's Teen Idols.
- (S) (3:08)   Razor & Tie 21640   Those Fabulous 70's.
- (S) (3:08)   Time-Life SUD-20   Superhits - Early 70's Classics.
- (S) (3:08)   Time-Life SOD-33   Sounds Of The Seventies - AM Pop Classics II.
- (S) (3:11)   K-Tel 3211   70's Teen Heart-Throbs.
- (S) (3:08)   Time-Life AM1-15   AM Gold - Early '70s Classics.
- (S) (3:08)   Time-Life R840-03   Sounds Of The Seventies - Pop Nuggets: Early '70s.
- (S) (3:09)   K-Tel 3914   Superstars Greatest Hits Volume 3.

1974 ABRA-CA-DABRA
- (S) (3:07)   Varese Sarabande 5535   Bubblegum Classics Volume One.

1974 SAVE THE LAST DANCE FOR ME

DeJOHN SISTERS
1955 (MY BABY DON'T LOVE ME) NO MORE
- (M) (2:00)   Time-Life HPD-27   Your Hit Parade - The Unforgettable 50's.
- (M) (1:59)   JCI 7014   Those Wonderful Years - Mr. Sandman.

DESMOND DEKKER & THE ACES
1969 ISRAELITES
(the original 45 and LP length was (2:35))
- (M) (2:46)   Island 90684 and 842901   The Island Story.
- (E) (2:46)   Novus 3077   O.S.T. Drugstore Cowboy.
- (M) (2:35)   Rhino 70271   Best Of.
- (S) (3:07)   Rhino 71062   Stiff Records Box Set. *(rerecorded)*
- (S) (2:34)   Time-Life 2CLR-12   Classic Rock - 1969: The Beat Goes On.
- (E) (2:47)   Mango 162539935   Story Of Jamaican Music.
- (M) (2:35)   K-Tel 6067   Best Of Reggae.
- (M) (2:47)   Island 314524394   Island Records 40th Anniversary Volume 2 1964-1969: Rhythm & Blues.
- (M) (2:31)   Music Club 50024   The Original Rude Boy - Best Of. *(distorted)*
- (M) (2:35)   Simitar 55112   Great Reggae.

DEL AMITRI
1990 KISS THIS THING GOODBYE
- (S) (4:34)   A&M 5287   Waking Hours.

1992 ALWAYS THE LAST TO KNOW
- (S) (4:20)   A&M 5385   Change Everything.

1995 ROLL TO ME
- (S) (2:12)   A&M 314540311   Twisted.
- (S) (2:06)   Atlantic 82895   VH1 Crossroads. *(live)*

DELANEY & BONNIE & FRIENDS
1971 NEVER ENDING SONG OF LOVE
- (S) (3:19)   Rhino 70777   Best Of. *(LP version)*
- (S) (2:40)   Rhino 71196   Super Hits Of The 70's Volume 16. *(45 version)*
- (S) (2:33)   Time-Life SUD-16   Superhits - The Early 70's. *(45 version)*
- (S) (2:40)   Time-Life SOD-12   Sounds Of The Seventies - 1971: Take Two. *(45 version)*
- (S) (3:13)   K-Tel 6137   Peaceful Easy Feeling - The Best Of Country Rock. *(LP version)*
- (S) (3:19)   Scotti Brothers 75434   Romantic Duets. *(LP version)*
- (M) (2:36)   Rhino 71904   Hillbilly Fever Vol. 5. - Legends Of Country Rock. *(45 version)*
- (M) (2:36)   Rhino 72444   Heroes Of Country Music Vol. Five. *(45 version)*
- (S) (2:33)   Time-Life AM1-13   AM Gold - The Early '70s. *(45 version)*

released as by DELANEY & BONNIE:
1971 ONLY YOU KNOW AND I KNOW
- (S) (3:24)   Rhino 70777   Best Of.
- (S) (4:42)   Atco 33326   On Tour With Eric Clapton. *(live)*

DE LA SOUL
1989 ME MYSELF AND I
- (S) (3:40)   JCI 2714   Bust It 2.
- (S) (3:43)   Luke/Atlantic 91598   Bass Waves Volume Three.
- (S) (3:40)   Priority 7940   On The Rap Tip.
- (S) (3:43)   K-Tel 315   Rap's Biggest Hits.
- (S) (3:40)   Tommy Boy 1019   3 Feet High And Rising.
- (S) (3:39)   Time-Life R988-30   Sounds Of The Eighties: The Rolling Stone Collection 1988-1989.
- (S) (3:39)   Rhino 72144   Billboard Hot R&B Hits 1989.

DELEGATES
1972 CONVENTION '72
- (M) (5:07)   Time-Life R830-03   The Dr. Demento Collection: The Early '70s.

DELFONICS
1968 LA-LA MEANS I LOVE YOU
- (S) (3:17)   Rhino 75774   Soul Shots.
- (S) (3:18)   Rhino 70654   Billboard's Top R&B Hits Of 1968.
- (S) (3:18)   Rhino 72006   Billboard's Top R&B Hits 1965-1969 Box Set.
- (M) (3:16)   Original Sound 8862   Oldies But Goodies Vol. 12. *(this compact disc uses the "Waring - fds" noise reduction process)*

(M) (3:16) Original Sound 2223 Oldies But Goodies Volumes 2,7,9,12 and 13 Box Set. *(this box set uses the "Waring - fds" noise reduction process)*

(M) (3:16) Original Sound 2500 Oldies But Goodies Volumes 1-15 Box Set. *(this box set uses the "Waring - fds" noise reduction process)*

(M) (3:15) Original Sound CDGO-12 Golden Oldies Volume. 12.

(S) (3:17) JCI 3102 Love Sixties.

(S) (3:19) Arista 8333 Best Of.

(S) (3:15) Time-Life RHD-04 Rhythm & Blues - 1968.

(S) (3:17) Time-Life 2CLR-04 Classic Rock - 1968.

(S) (3:18) Right Stuff 27306 Slow Jams: The 60's Volume One.

(S) (3:16) Time-Life OPCD-4517 Tonight's The Night.

(S) (3:19) Thump 7010 Low Rider Oldies Volume 1.

(S) (3:18) MCA 11065 O.S.T. Crooklyn Volume II.

(S) (3:17) Hip-O 40001 The Glory Of Love - Sweet & Soulful Love Songs.

(S) (3:15) JCI 3185 1965 - Only Love - 1969.

(M) (3:15) Rhino 72620 Smooth Grooves: The '60s Volume 3 Late '60s.

(S) (3:15) Time-Life R838-03 Solid Gold Soul - 1968.

(S) (3:18) Time-Life R834-02 Body Talk - Just For You.

(M) (3:15) Rhino 72815 Beg, Scream & Shout! The Big Ol' Box Of '60s Soul.

(S) (3:17) Arista 18979 La-La Means I Love You: Definitive Collection.

(S) (3:18) Time-Life R857-22 The Heart Of Rock 'n' Roll 1967-1969.

(S) (3:14) K-Tel 3886 Great R&B Male Groups: Hits Of The 60's.

1968 BREAK YOUR PROMISE

(S) (3:01) Arista 8333 Best Of.

(S) (3:00) Arista 18979 La-La Means I Love You: Definitive Collection.

1969 READY OR NOT HERE I COME (CAN'T HIDE FROM LOVE) (actual 45 time is (1:59) not (2:55) as stated on the record label)

(S) (1:59) Arista 8333 Best Of.

(S) (1:59) JCI 3190 1965 - Only Dance - 1969.

(S) (1:58) Arista 18979 La-La Means I Love You: Definitive Collection.

1969 YOU GOT YOURS AND I'LL GET MINE

(S) (3:17) Arista 8333 Best Of.

(S) (3:16) Arista 18979 La-La Means I Love You: Definitive Collection.

1970 DIDN'T I (BLOW YOUR MIND THIS TIME)

(S) (3:20) Epic 46940 O.S.T. Queenslogic.

(S) (3:20) Rhino 70781 Soul Hits Of The 70's Volume 1.

(S) (3:20) Rhino 72028 Soul Hits Of The 70's Volumes 1-5 Box Set.

(S) (3:20) Arista 8333 Best Of.

(S) (3:20) Rhino 71205 70's Smash Hits Volume 1.

(S) (3:19) Time-Life RHD-18 Rhythm & Blues - 1970.

(S) (3:20) Time-Life SOD-22 Sounds Of The Seventies - Seventies Top Forty.

(S) (3:20) Right Stuff 28372 Slow Jams: The 70's Volume Two.

(S) (3:20) Thump 7020 Low Rider Oldies Volume II.

(S) (3:20) Rhino 72112 Billboard Hot Soul Hits - 1970.

(S) (3:20) Priority 53130 Deep Soul Volume Three.

(S) (3:19) JCI 3145 1970 - Only Love - 1974.

(S) (3:19) JCI 3173 1970 - Only Soul - 1974.

(S) (3:18) Eclipse Music Group 64892 Rock 'n Roll Relix 1970-1971.

(S) (3:18) Eclipse Music Group 64897 Rock 'n Roll Relix 1970-1979.

(S) (3:19) Time-Life R838-05 Solid Gold Soul - 1970.

(S) (3:20) Flashback 72681 '70s Radio Hits Volume 1.

(S) (3:20) Flashback 72090 '70s Radio Hits Box Set.

(S) (3:19) Arista 18979 La-La Means I Love You: Definitive Collection.

(S) (3:19) Maverick 46841 O.S.T. Jackie Brown.

(S) (3:20) Right Stuff 52274 Flick Hits Take 2.

(S) (3:20) Beast 53442 Original Players Of Love.

(S) (3:20) Time-Life R834-17 Body Talk - Heart To Heart.

1970 TRYING TO MAKE A FOOL OF ME

(S) (2:59) Arista 8333 Best Of.

DELINQUENT HABITS
1996 TRES DELINQUENTES

(S) (4:15) Loud/RCA 66951 and 66929 Delinquent Habits.

(S) (3:26) Boxtunes 314524387 Big Phat Ones Of Hip-Hop Volume 2. *(all songs on this cd are segued together)*

DELLS
1968 THERE IS

(S) (3:30) Chess 9283 Best Of Chess Vocal Groups Volume 2.

(S) (3:31) Chess 9288 There Is.

(S) (3:30) JCI/Telstar 3515 Best Of.

(S) (3:31) Chess 9333 On Their Corner/The Best Of.

(S) (3:30) Ripete 2392192 Beach Music Anthology Box Set.

(M) (3:28) Time-Life 2CLR-11 Classic Rock - 1968: The Beat Goes On.

(S) (3:30) MCA Special Products 21030 Beach Music Hits.

1968 STAY IN MY CORNER
(dj copies of this 45 ran (3:05) and (6:10); commercial copies were all (6:10); this song was originally released in 1965 but never charted - rerecorded and released again in 1968)

(S) (3:05) Rhino 75757 Soul Shots Volume 3.

(S) (6:09) Rhino 70654 Billboard's Top R&B Hits Of 1968.

(S) (6:09) Rhino 72006 Billboard's Top R&B Hits 1965-1969 Box Set.

(S) (6:09) Chess 9288 There Is.

(S) (3:04) Original Sound 9329 Oldies But Goodies Doo Wop Classics.

(S) (6:10) Motown 6215 and 9067 Hits From The Legendary Vee-Jay Records. *(this is a recording made for Vee-Jay Records and is not the hit version)*

(S) (6:09) MCA 5936 Vintage Music Volumes 11 & 12.

(S) (6:09) MCA 31208 Vintage Music Volume 11.

(S) (4:45) Original Sound 9307 Dedicated To You Vol. 7. *(faded 1:25 earlier than the 45 or LP)*

(S) (6:10) Chess 31318 Best Of Chess Rhythm & Blues Volume 2.

(S) (6:08) JCI/Telstar 3515 Best Of.

(S) (6:09) MCA 10288 Classic Soul.

(S) (6:10) Chess 9333 On Their Corner/The Best Of.

(S) (2:51) Collectables 5061 History Of Rock Volume 1. *(1965 noncharting version)*

(S) (2:51) Vee Jay 710 A Taste Of Soul Volume 1. *(1965 noncharting version)*

(S) (2:51) Vee Jay 3-400 Celebrating 40 Years Of Classic Hits (1953-1993). *(1965 noncharting version)*

(S) (6:06) Time-Life RHD-04 Rhythm & Blues - 1968.

(S) (6:06) Time-Life 2CLR-19 Classic Rock - 1968: Shakin' All Over.

(S) (6:11) Right Stuff 27306 Slow Jams: The 60's Volume One.

(M) (2:51) Thump 7020 Low Rider Oldies Volume II. *(1965 noncharting version)*

(S) (6:23) Varese Sarabande 5486 A Celebration Of Soul Vol. 1: The Chi-Sound Records Collection. *(rerecording)*

(S) (6:09) Virgin 91609 O.S.T. The Five Heartbeats.

(M) (2:53) Scotti Bros. 75481 Quiet Storm Memories. *(1965 noncharting version)*

(S) (6:09) MCA Special Products 21742 Vintage Collectibles Volume 12.

(S) (6:09) MCA Special Products 20857 Classic Soul Greatest Hits.

(S) (6:10) Priority 53131 Deep Soul Volume Two.

(S) (6:06) JCI 3185 1965 - Only Love - 1969.

(S) (6:07) MCA Special Products 20972 The Dells Vs. The Dramatics.

(S) (6:09) Hip-O 40029 The Glory Of Love - '60s Sweet & Soulful Love Songs.

(S) (6:10) MCA Special Products 20979 Soul Hits Volume 1.

(S) (6:10) Rhino 72620 Smooth Grooves: The '60s Volume 3 Late '60s.

(S) (6:06) Time-Life R838-03 Solid Gold Soul - 1968.

(S) (6:08) Time-Life R834-05 Body Talk - Sealed With A Kiss.

(M) (2:50) Rhino 72815 Beg, Scream & Shout! The Big Ol' Box Of '60s Soul. *(1965 noncharting version)*

(S) (6:10) Repeat/Relativity 1610 Tighten Up: #1 Soul Hits Of The 60's Volume 2.

(S) (6:09) Chess 9395 Oh, What A Night!/The Great Ballads.

(S) (6:08) Time-Life R857-22 The Heart Of Rock 'n' Roll 1967-1969.

(S) (6:09) K-Tel 3886 Great R&B Male Groups: Hits Of The 60's.

1968 ALWAYS TOGETHER

(S) (2:58) JCI/Telstar 3515 Best Of.

(S) (3:03) Chess 9333 On Their Corner/The Best Of.

(S) (3:02) Chess 9395 Oh, What A Night!/The Great Ballads.

1969 I CAN SING A RAINBOW/LOVE IS BLUE

(S) (3:17) JCI/Telstar 3515 Best Of. *(dropouts near the end of the song)*

(S) (3:23) Chess 9333 On Their Corner/The Best Of. *(noisy fadeout)*

(S) (3:22) Chess 9395 Oh, What A Night!/The Great Ballads.

1969 OH, WHAT A NIGHT
(this song was originally released in 1956 but never charted - rerecorded and released again in 1969)

(M) (2:52) Rhino 75763 Best Of Doo Wop Ballads. *(1956 noncharting version)*

(M) (2:51) Original Sound CDGO-2 Golden Oldies Volume 2. *(1956 noncharting version)*

(M) (2:51) Original Sound 8853 Oldies But Goodies Vol. 3. *(this compact disc uses the "Waring - fds" noise reduction process; 1956 noncharting version)*

(M) (2:51) Original Sound 2222 Oldies But Goodies Volumes 3,5,11,14 and 15 Box Set. *(this box set uses the "Waring - fds" noise reduction process; 1956 noncharting version)*

(M) (2:51) Original Sound 2500 Oldies But Goodies Volumes 1-15 Box Set. *(this box set uses the "Waring - fds" noise reduction process; 1956 noncharting version)*

(M) (2:51) Original Sound 9601 Best Of Oldies But Goodies Vol. 1. *(1956 noncharting version)*

(S) (4:03) Rhino 75770 Soul Shots Volume 2. *(1969 hit version)*

(S) (4:03) Rhino 70655 Billboard's Top R&B Hits Of 1969. *(1969 hit version)*

(S) (4:03) Rhino 72006 Billboard's Top R&B Hits 1965-1969 Box Set. *(1969 hit version)*

(S) (4:02) Chess 9283 Best Of Chess Vocal Groups Volume 2. *(1969 hit version)*

(S) (4:02) MCA 5937 Vintage Music Volumes 13 & 14. *(1969 hit version)*

(S) (4:02) MCA 31211 Vintage Music Volume 14. *(1969 hit version)*

(M) (2:51) DCC Compact Classics 031 Back Seat Jams. *(1956 noncharting version)*

(M) (2:51) DCC Compact Classics 028 Sock Hop. *(1956 noncharting version)*

(M) (2:51) Motown 6215 and 9067 Hits From The Legendary Vee-Jay Records. *(1956 noncharting version)*

(S) (3:57) JCI/Telstar 3515 Best Of. *(1969 hit version)*

(S) (4:03) Chess 9333 On Their Corner/The Best Of. *(1969 hit version)*

(M) (2:53) Vee Jay 701 Dreams Of Contentment. *(1956 noncharting version)*

(M) (2:51) Collectables 5069 History Of Rock Volume 9. *(1956 noncharting version)*

(M) (2:51) Rhino 71463 Doo Wop Box. *(1956 noncharting version)*

(M) (2:53) Vee Jay 3-400 Celebrating 40 Years Of Classic Hits (1953-1993). *(1956 noncharting version)*

(E) (2:51) Original Sound 8905r 13 Of The Best Doo Wop Love Songs. *(1956 noncharting version)*

(E) (2:51) Original Sound 9326 Best Love Songs Vol. 1 & 2. *(1956 noncharting version)*

(E) (2:51) Original Sound 4001 Art Laboe's 60 Killer Oldies. *(1956 noncharting version)*

(E) (2:51) Original Sound 1236 Best Love Songs Box Set. *(1956 noncharting version)*

(M) (2:51) Time-Life 2RNR-23 Rock 'N' Roll Era - 1956 Still Rockin'. *(1956 noncharting version)*

(M) (2:50) Time-Life RHD-05 Rhythm & Blues - 1956. *(1956 noncharting version)*

(S) (3:59) Time-Life RHD-13 Rhythm & Blues - 1969. *(1969 hit version)*

(S) (4:02) Time-Life 2CLR-06 Classic Rock - 1969. *(1969 hit version)*

(M) (2:52) Time-Life R962-03 History Of Rock 'N' Roll: Rock 'N' Roll Classics 1954-1956. *(1956 noncharting version)*

(M) (2:50) Collectables 2506 WCBS-FM History Of Rock - The 50's Part 1. *(1956 noncharting version)*

(M) (2:50) Collectables 4506 History Of Rock/The 50s Part One. *(1956 noncharting version)*

(M) (2:51) Collectables 2509 WCBS-FM For Lovers Only Part 1. *(1956 noncharting version)*

(M) (2:51) Collectables 2552 WOGL History Of Rock Vol. 2. *(1956 noncharting version)*

(M) (2:51) Time-Life R10513 40 Lovin' Oldies. *(1956 noncharting version)*

(S) (4:03) Time-Life OPCD-4517 Tonight's The Night. *(1969 hit version)*

(S) (4:02) MCA Special Products 20753 Classic R&B Oldies From The 60's. *(1969 hit version)*

(S) (4:02) MCA Special Products 20639 Oh, What A Night. *(1969 hit version)*

(M) (2:51) Thump 7010 Low Rider Oldies Volume 1. *(1956 noncharting version)*

(M) (2:53) Ripete 2163-RE Ebb Tide. *(1956 noncharting version)*

(M) (2:52) Rhino 71806 The R&B Box: Thirty Years Of Rhythm & Blues. *(1956 noncharting version)*

(S) (4:02) MCA Special Products 20899 Rock Around The Oldies #4. *(1969 hit version)*

(M) (2:52) Collectables 5543 More Memories Of Times Square Records Volume 8. *(1956 noncharting version)*

(S) (4:02) MCA Special Products 20857 Classic Soul Greatest Hits. *(1969 hit version)*

(M) (2:53) Hip-O 40028 The Glory Of Love - '50s Sweet & Soulful Love Songs. *(1956 noncharting version)*

(M) (2:50) K-Tel 3812 Doo Wop's Greatest Hits. *(1956 noncharting version)*

(M) (2:52) Time-Life R857-07 The Heart Of Rock 'n' Roll 1956. *(1956 noncharting version)*

(S) (3:59) Time-Life R838-04 Solid Gold Soul - 1969. *(1969 hit version)*

(S) (4:02) Repeat/Relativity 1611 A Brand New Bag: #1 Soul Hits Of The 60's Volume 3. *(1969 hit version)*

(S) (4:02) Chess 9395 Oh, What A Night!/The Great Ballads. *(1969 hit version)*

(S) (4:03) Time-Life R834-12 Body Talk - By Candlelight. *(1969 hit version)*

(M) (2:50) Time-Life R838-24 Solid Gold Soul 1956. *(1956 noncharting version)*

1971 THE LOVE WE HAD (STAYS ON MY MIND)

(S) (4:47) Rhino 70786 Soul Hits Of The 70's Volume 6.

(S) (4:14) JCI/Telstar 3515 Best Of. *(edited)*

(S) (4:48) Chess 9333 On Their Corner/The Best Of.

(S) (4:48) Chess 9395 Oh, What A Night!/The Great Ballads.

1973 GIVE YOUR BABY A STANDING OVATION
(actual commercial 45 time is (4:33) not (3:52) as stated on the record label; some dj copies stated a time of (3:35) but ran (3:30), others stated a time of (3:52) and actually ran (4:33) just like the commercial copies)

(S) (4:02) Rhino 70551 Soul Hits Of The 70's Volume 11. *(neither the 45 or LP version)*

(S) (3:57) JCI/Telstar 3515 Best Of. *(neither the 45 or LP version)*

(S) (4:35) Chess 9333 On Their Corner/The Best Of.

(S) (4:35) Time-Life R838-08 Solid Gold Soul - 1973.

(S) (4:34) Angel 56344 O.S.T. The People Vs. Larry Flynt.

(S) (4:35) K-Tel 3900 Great R&B Male Groups: Hits Of The 70's.

DELL-VIKINGS

1957 COME GO WITH ME

(M) (2:40) Rhino 75764 Best Of Doo Wop Uptempo.

(M) (2:40) Rhino 70643 Billboard's Top R&B Hits Of 1957.

(M) (2:40) MCA 31198 Vintage Music Volume 1.

(M) (2:40) MCA 5777 Vintage Music Volumes 1 & 2.

(M) (2:37)   Original Sound 8853   Oldies But Goodies Vol. 3. *(this compact disc uses the "Waring - fds" noise reduction process)*
(M) (2:37)   Original Sound 2222   Oldies But Goodies Volumes 3,5,11,14 and 15 Box Set. *(this box set uses the "Waring - fds" noise reduction process)*
(M) (2:37)   Original Sound 2500   Oldies But Goodies Volumes 1-15 Box Set. *(this box set uses the "Waring - fds" noise reduction process)*
(M) (2:38)   Atlantic 81677   O.S.T. Stand By Me.
(M) (2:39)   Elektra 60107   O.S.T. Diner.
(M) (2:37)   Collectables 5065   History Of Rock Volume 5.
(M) (2:38)   Collectables 8809   For Collectors Only.
(M) (2:39)   MCA 8001   O.S.T. American Graffiti.
(M) (2:38)   Rhino 71463   Doo Wop Box.
(M) (2:40)   Time-Life 2RNR-01   Rock 'N' Roll Era - 1957. *(original pressings of this song on this cd were (E))*
(M) (2:39)   Time-Life RHD-08   Rhythm & Blues - 1957.
(M) (2:40)   Time-Life R962-01   History Of Rock 'N' Roll: Rock 'N' Roll Classics 1957-1959.
(M) (2:37)   Collectables 2506   WCBS-FM History Of Rock - The 50's Part 1.
(M) (2:37)   Collectables 4506   History Of Rock/The 50s Part One.
(M) (2:38)   Collectables 2603   WCBS-FM Jukebox Giants Vol. 1.
(M) (2:37)   Collectables 2552   WOGL History Of Rock Vol. 2.
(M) (2:36)   Collectables 5010   Golden Classics.
(E) (2:35)   Time-Life R10513   40 Lovin' Oldies.
(M) (2:39)   MCA Special Products 20783   Rock Around The Oldies #1.
(E) (2:34)   Columbia 57317   O.S.T. Calendar Girl. *(truncated fade)*
(M) (2:36)   K-Tel 3007   50's Sock Hop.
(M) (2:37)   Collectables 2554   CBS-FM History Of Rock Volume 2.
(S) (2:36)   Ripete 2184-RE   Ocean Drive Vol. 2. *(rerecording)*
(M) (2:36)   Varese Sarabande 5687   History Of Dot Records Volume Two.
(M) (2:39)   JCI 3183   1955 - Only Love - 1959.
(M) (2:39)   Priority 50950   I Love Rock & Roll Volume 1: Hits Of The 50's.
(E) (2:36)   K-Tel 3812   Doo Wop's Greatest Hits.
(M) (2:40)   Hip-O 40059   Come Go With Me: The Dot/ABC Recordings.
(M) (2:40)   Nick At Nite/550 Music 63456   Double Date With Joanie And Chachi.
(M) (2:39)   Time-Life R838-23   Solid Gold Soul 1957.

1957   WHISPERING BELLS
(M) (2:23)   Rhino 75764   Best Of Doo Wop Uptempo.
(M) (2:27)   MCA 31199   Vintage Music Volume 2.
(M) (2:27)   MCA 5777   Vintage Music Volumes 1 & 2.
(M) (2:22)   Atlantic 81677   O.S.T. Stand By Me.
(E) (2:21)   Collectables 2508   History Of Rock - The Doo Wop Era Part 2.
(E) (2:21)   Collectables 4508   History Of Rock/The Doo Wop Era Part Two.
(M) (2:23)   Collectables 5062   History Of Rock Volume 2.
(M) (2:22)   Collectables 8809   For Collectors Only.
(M) (2:25)   Rhino 71463   Doo Wop Box.
(M) (2:26)   Time-Life 2RNR-17   Rock 'N' Roll Era - 1957 Still Rockin'.
(M) (2:21)   Collectables 2503   WCBS-FM History Of Rock - The 50's Part 2.
(M) (2:21)   Collectables 4503   History Of Rock/The 50s Part Two.
(M) (2:23)   Collectables 5010   Golden Classics.
(M) (2:23)   Collectables 2605   WCBS-FM Jukebox Giants Vol. 3.
(M) (2:22)   Time-Life R102-17   Lost Treasures Of Rock 'N' Roll.
(M) (2:26)   MCA Special Products 22165   Vintage Collectibles Volume 7.
(M) (2:23)   Hip-O 40059   Come Go With Me: The Dot/ABC Recordings.

1957   COOL SHAKE
(M) (2:11)   Mercury 830283   The Vocal Group Collection.
(M) (2:10)   Mercury 314532722   Best Of.

DEMENSIONS
1960   OVER THE RAINBOW
(M) (3:14)   Collectables 2508   History Of Rock - The Doo Wop Era Part 2.
(M) (3:14)   Collectables 4508   History Of Rock/The Doo Wop Era Part Two.
(M) (3:14)   Relic 7032   Over The Rainbow.
(M) (3:14)   Relic 7122   Golden Era Of Doo Wops - Mohawk Records.
(M) (3:14)   Collectables 2607   WCBS-FM For Lovers Only Vol. 3.

CATHY DENNIS
released as by D-MOB introducing CATHY DENNIS:
1990   C'MON AND GET MY LOVE
(S) (3:47)   Mercury 841583   O.S.T. She-Devil.
(S) (3:48)   Polydor 847267   Cathy Dennis - Move To This.
(S) (3:51)   FFRR/Polygram 828159   A Little Bit Of This, A Little Bit Of That.
(S) (3:47)   Rebound 314520357   World Of Dance - The 80's.
(S) (3:48)   Rebound 314520438   No. 1 Hits Of The 80's.
(S) (3:47)   Cold Front 3832   Club Mix - Women Of Dance Vol. 1.
(S) (3:42)   Cold Front 6284   More Of! Club Mix's Biggest Jams. *(all selections on this cd are segued together)*

released as by CATHY DENNIS:
1991   JUST ANOTHER DREAM
(S) (4:01)   Polydor 847267   Move To This.
1991   TOUCH ME (ALL NIGHT LONG)
(S) (5:55)   Rebound 314520246   Disco Nights Vol. 5 - Best Of Housemusic. *(remix)*
(S) (4:08)   Polydor 847267   Move To This.
(S) (3:59)   Rebound 314520359   World Of Dance - The 90's.
(S) (7:12)   Mercury 314532494   100% Pure Dance. *(remix; all songs on this cd are segued together)*
1991   TOO MANY WALLS
(S) (4:26)   Mercury 314525354   Women For Women.
(S) (4:30)   Polydor 847267   Move To This.
1992   YOU LIED TO ME
(S) (5:26)   Polydor 314513935   Into The Skyline.

MARTIN DENNY
1959   QUIET VILLAGE
(actual 45 time is (2:58) not (2:42) as stated on the record label)
(M) (3:38)   Rhino 70774   Best Of. *(neither the 45 or LP version)*
(S) (3:46)   Pair 1267   Paradise. *("Exotica" vinyl LP version)*
(M) (3:17)   Time-Life HPD-13   Your Hit Parade - 1959. *(neither the 45 or LP version)*
(S) (3:46)   Curb 77685   Greatest Hits. *("Exotica" vinyl LP version)*
(S) (3:46)   JCI 7010   Those Wonderful Years - Melodies Of Love. *("Exotica" vinyl LP version)*
(M) (3:38)   DCC Compact Classics 079   Music For A Bachelor's Den. *(neither the 45 or LP version)*
(S) (3:42)   Pair 1351   Best Of: Bachelor In Paradise. *("Exotica" vinyl LP version)*
(S) (3:45)   K-Tel 3583   Those Wonderful Instrumentals Volume 3. *("Exotica" vinyl LP version)*
(M) (3:39)   Capitol 38374   The Exotic Sounds Of. *(neither the 45 or LP version)*
(S) (3:44)   Capitol 32563   Ultra Lounge Volume One: Mondo Exotica. *("Exotica" vinyl LP version)*
(S) (3:46)   Time-Life R986-19   Instrumental Favorites - Exotic Moods. *("Exotica" vinyl LP version)*
(M) (3:16)   Collectors' Choice 5190   More Instrumental Gems Of The 60's. *(neither the 45 or LP version)*
1959   THE ENCHANTED SEA
(S) (1:57)   Rhino 70774   Best Of.
(S) (1:56)   Pair 1267   Paradise.
(S) (1:56)   Curb 77685   Greatest Hits.
(S) (1:54)   Pair 1351   Best Of: Bachelor In Paradise.
(S) (1:56)   Capitol 38374   The Exotic Sounds Of.

JOHN DENVER

1971 TAKE ME HOME, COUNTRY ROADS
- (S) (3:09)   RCA 0374   Greatest Hits.
- (S) (3:07)   RCA 5189   Poems, Prayers And Promises.
- (S) (3:07)   RCA 52160   Take Me Home, Country Roads & Other Hits.
- (S) (3:08)   RCA 66837   Rocky Mountain Collection.
- (S) (3:08)   RCA 67437   The Country Roads Collection.
- (S) (3:08)   RCA 67604   Greatest Country Hits.

1973 ROCKY MOUNTAIN HIGH
- (S) (4:43)   RCA 0374   Greatest Hits.
- (S) (4:40)   RCA 5190   Rocky Mountain High.
- (S) (4:42)   RCA 52160   Take Me Home, Country Roads & Other Hits.
- (S) (4:42)   RCA 66837   Rocky Mountain Collection.
- (S) (4:42)   RCA 67437   The Country Roads Collection.

1974 SUNSHINE ON MY SHOULDERS
- (S) (5:09)   RCA 5189   Poems, Prayers And Promises. *(LP version)*
- (S) (5:09)   RCA 52160   Take Me Home, Country Roads & Other Hits. *(LP version)*
- (S) (5:10)   RCA 0374   Greatest Hits. *(LP version)*
- (S) (5:11)   RCA 66837   Rocky Mountain Collection. *(LP version)*
- (S) (5:11)   RCA 66987   Reflections: Songs Of Love & Life. *(LP version)*
- (S) (5:09)   RCA 67437   The Country Roads Collection. *(LP version)*
- (S) (5:10)   RCA 67604   Greatest Country Hits. *(LP version)*

1974 ANNIE'S SONG
- (S) (2:59)   RCA 5193   Back Home Again.
- (S) (2:59)   RCA 2195   Greatest Hits Volume 2.
- (S) (2:58)   RCA 66837   Rocky Mountain Collection.
- (S) (2:58)   RCA 66987   Reflections: Songs Of Love & Life.
- (S) (2:58)   RCA 67437   The Country Roads Collection.
- (S) (2:58)   RCA 67604   Greatest Country Hits.
- (S) (2:58)   Time-Life R814-05   Love Songs.

1974 BACK HOME AGAIN
- (S) (4:43)   RCA 5193   Back Home Again.
- (S) (4:44)   RCA 2195   Greatest Hits Volume 2.
- (S) (4:42)   RCA 66837   Rocky Mountain Collection.
- (S) (4:43)   RCA 67437   The Country Roads Collection.
- (S) (4:43)   RCA 67604   Greatest Country Hits.

1975 SWEET SURRENDER
- (S) (5:24)   RCA 5193   Back Home Again. *("Back Home Again" LP version - not the hit version)*
- (S) (5:03)   RCA 50764   An Evening With John Denver. *("An Evening With John Denver" LP version - the hit LP version)*
- (S) (5:25)   RCA 66837   Rocky Mountain Collection. *("Back Home Again" LP version - not the hit version)*
- (S) (5:26)   RCA 67437   The Country Roads Collection. *("Back Home Again" LP version - not the hit version)*
- (S) (5:08)   RCA 67604   Greatest Country Hits. *("An Evening With John Denver" LP version - the hit LP version)*

1975 THANK GOD I'M A COUNTRY BOY
- (S) (3:05)   RCA 5193   Back Home Again. *("Back Home Again" LP version - not the hit version)*
- (S) (3:20)   RCA 2195   Greatest Hits Volume 2. *("An Evening With" LP version but missing :20 of audience applause and stage banter at the end of the song)*
- (S) (3:40)   RCA 50764   An Evening With John Denver. *(LP version)*
- (S) (3:06)   RCA 66837   Rocky Mountain Collection. *("Back Home Again" LP version - not the hit version)*
- (S) (2:47)   RCA 67437   The Country Roads Collection. *(45 version)*
- (S) (3:26)   RCA 67604   Greatest Country Hits. *("An Evening With John Denver" LP version but missing :14 of audience applause and stage banter at the end of the song)*

1975 I'M SORRY
- (S) (3:30)   RCA 2195   Greatest Hits Volume 2.
- (S) (3:29)   RCA 66837   Rocky Mountain Collection.
- (S) (3:29)   RCA 66987   Reflections: Songs Of Love & Life.
- (S) (3:29)   RCA 67437   The Country Roads Collection.
- (S) (3:29)   RCA 67604   Greatest Country Hits.

1975 CALYPSO
- (S) (3:35)   RCA 2195   Greatest Hits Volume 2.
- (S) (3:34)   RCA 66837   Rocky Mountain Collection.
- (S) (3:34)   RCA 66987   Reflections: Songs Of Love & Life.
- (S) (3:34)   RCA 67437   The Country Roads Collection.

1976 FLY AWAY
- (S) (4:09)   RCA 2195   Greatest Hits Volume 2. *(LP version)*
- (S) (4:08)   RCA 66837   Rocky Mountain Collection. *(LP version)*
- (S) (4:08)   RCA 67437   The Country Roads Collection. *(LP version)*
- (S) (4:08)   RCA 67604   Greatest Country Hits. *(LP version)*

1976 LOOKING FOR SPACE
- (S) (3:59)   RCA 2195   Greatest Hits Volume 2.
- (S) (3:58)   RCA 66837   Rocky Mountain Collection.
- (S) (3:58)   RCA 67604   Greatest Country Hits.

1977 MY SWEET LADY
- (S) (4:22)   RCA 5189   Poems, Prayers And Promises. *(original version but not the hit version)*
- (S) (4:48)   RCA 2195   Greatest Hits Volume 2.
- (S) (4:24)   RCA 66837   Rocky Mountain Collection. *(original version but not the hit version)*
- (S) (4:22)   RCA 66987   Reflections: Songs Of Love & Life. *(original version but not the hit version)*

1982 SHANGHAI BREEZES
- (S) (3:09)   RCA 66837   Rocky Mountain Collection.
- (S) (3:09)   RCA 67437   The Country Roads Collection.

DEODATO

1973 ALSO SPRACH ZARATHUSTRA (2001)
- (S) (5:03)   Rhino 70758   Super Hits Of The 70's Volume 11. *(45 version)*
- (S) (8:57)   CBS Associated 40695 and 65129. *(LP version)*
- (S) (8:57)   Verve 314521007   Playboy's 40th Anniversary: Four Decades Of Jazz (1953-1993). *(LP version)*
- (S) (5:03)   Rhino 71603   Rock Instrumental Classics Volume 3: The Seventies. *(45 version)*
- (S) (5:03)   Rhino 72035   Rock Instrumental Classics Vols. 1-5 Box Set. *(45 version)*
- (S) (5:03)   Time-Life R840-04   Sounds Of The Seventies: A Loss For Words. *(45 version)*

DEPECHE MODE

1985 PEOPLE ARE PEOPLE
- (S) (3:51)   Sire 25194   Some Great Reward. *(not the hit version)*
- (S) (3:43)   Sire 25124   People Are People.

1990 PERSONAL JESUS
- (S) (4:53)   Rhino 70546   Best Of MTV's 120 Minutes Vol. 2. *(LP version)*
- (S) (5:40)   Tommy Boy 1037   MTV Party To Go Volume 1. *(remix; all tracks on this cd are segued together)*
- (S) (4:53)   Sire 26081   Violator. *(LP version)*
- (S) (4:53)   Time-Life R988-30   Sounds Of The Eighties: The Rolling Stone Collection 1988-1989. *(LP version)*

1990 ENJOY THE SILENCE
- (S) (6:12)   Sire 26081   Violator. *(LP version)*

1990 POLICY OF TRUTH
- (S) (4:52)   Sire 26081   Violator. *(LP version)*

1993 I FEEL YOU
- (S) (4:34)   Sire 45243   Songs Of Faith And Devotion.

1997 IT'S NO GOOD
- (S) (5:57)   Mute/Reprise 46522   Ultra.
- (S) (3:42)   Tommy Boy 1207   MTV Grind Volume One. *(all selections on this cd are segued together)*

DEREK

1969 CINNAMON
- (M) (2:42)   Rhino 70996   One Hit Wonders Of The 60's Volume 2.
- (S) (2:43)   Columbia/Legacy 46983   Rock Artifacts Volume 3.
- (M) (2:42)   Time-Life 2CLR-27   Classic Rock - 1968: Blowin' Your Mind.
- (S) (2:34)   K-Tel 3409   Funniest Food Songs. *(rerecording)*

DEREK and THE DOMINOS
1972 LAYLA
(dj and commercial copies of this 45 ran were
pressed with times of either (2:43) or (7:10))
- (S) (7:05) Atlantic 81908 Classic Rock 1966-1988.
- (S) (7:03) Polydor 823277 Layla And Other Assorted Love Songs.
- (S) (7:06) Polydor 835269 Crossroads. *(remixed)*
- (S) (7:03) Sandstone 33004 Reelin' In The Years Volume 5.
- (S) (7:04) Polydor 847083 Layla Sessions. *(remixed)*
- (S) (7:04) Polydor 847090 Layla And Other Assorted Love Songs. *(remixed)*
- (S) (3:52) Atlantic 82152 O.S.T. Goodfellas. *(this is only the piano exit)*
- (S) (7:05) Atlantic 82306 Atlantic Rock & Roll Box Set.
- (S) (7:03) Polydor 800014 Time Pieces.
- (S) (7:02) Priority 7065 70's Greatest Rock Hits Volume 13: Request Line.
- (S) (7:03) DCC Compact Classics 066 Rock Of The 70's Volume Five.
- (S) (7:05) Time-Life SOD-03 Sounds Of The Seventies - 1972.
- (S) (7:05) Time-Life OPCD-4521 Guitar Rock.
- (S) (7:02) Polydor 314527116 Cream Of Clapton.
- (S) (7:04) MFSL 585 Layla And Other Assorted Love Songs. *(gold disc)*
- (S) (7:02) Polydor 314531820 Layla. *(remastered edition)*
- (S) (7:05) Time-Life R13610 Gold And Platinum Box Set - The Ultimate Rock Collection.
- (S) (7:02) Atlantic 83088 Atlantic Records: 50 Years - The Gold Anniversary Collection.

RICK DERRINGER
1974 ROCK AND ROLL, HOOCHIE KOO
- (S) (3:41) Priority 7055 Heavy Hitters/70's Greatest Rock Hits Volume 11. *(LP version)*
- (S) (3:41) Priority 7942 Hard Rockin' 70's. *(LP version)*
- (S) (3:42) Rhino 70721 Legends Of Guitar: The 70's Volume 1. *(LP version)*
- (S) (3:41) Rhino 70759 Super Hits Of The 70's Volume 12. *(LP version)*
- (S) (3:42) Sandstone 33002 Reelin' In The Years Volume 3. *(LP version)*
- (S) (3:42) Blue Sky/Epic 32481 All American Boy. *(LP version)*
- (S) (3:42) Priority 53680 Spring Break. *(LP version)*
- (S) (3:42) DCC Compact Classics 064 Rock Of The 70's Volume Three. *(LP version)*
- (S) (3:41) Medicine Label 24533 O.S.T. Dazed And Confused. *(LP version)*
- (S) (3:41) JCI 4510 Masters Of Metal: Crankin' Up 1970-1980. *(LP version)*
- (S) (3:41) Razor & Tie 22502 Those Rocking 70's. *(LP version)*
- (S) (3:41) Time-Life R968-01 Guitar Rock 1974-1975. *(LP version)*
- (S) (2:54) Time-Life SOD-15 Sounds Of The Seventies - 1974: Take Two. *(45 version)*
- (S) (2:53) Time-Life OPCD-4521 Guitar Rock. *(45 version)*
- (S) (3:41) Risky Business 67310 We Came To Play. *(LP version)*
- (S) (3:41) K-Tel 3510 Platinum Rock Volume 2. *(LP version)*
- (S) (3:43) Epic Associated/Legacy 57166 Rock And Roll Hoochie Koo: Best Of. *(LP version)*
- (S) (3:41) Hip-O 40039 Power Chords Volume 2. *(LP version)*
- (S) (3:41) K-Tel 3985 70s Heavy Hitters: Arena Rockers 1970-74. *(LP version)*
- (S) (2:54) Simitar 55772 Stud Rock - Rock Me. *(45 version)*
- (S) (2:54) Thump 6010 Easyriders Volume 1. *(45 version)*
- (S) (3:41) K-Tel 4030 Rock Anthems. *(LP version)*

TERI DeSARIO with K.C.
1980 YES, I'M READY
- (S) (3:15) Casablanca 314516918 Casablanca Records Story.
- (S) (3:16) Time-Life R138-18 Body Talk.
- (S) (3:15) Casablanca 314526253 Casablanca Records Greatest Hits.
- (S) (3:15) Time-Life R834-04 Body Talk - Together Forever.

- (S) (3:13) Rebound 314520440 No. 1 Hits Of The 70's.
- (S) (3:08) Polygram Special Markets 314520456 #1 Radio Hits Of The 70's.

JACKIE DeSHANNON
1965 WHAT THE WORLD NEEDS NOW IS LOVE
- (S) (3:11) Rhino 70738 Best Of.
- (S) (3:04) EMI 91473 Very Best Of.
- (S) (3:11) Pair 1284 Good As Gold.
- (S) (3:11) K-Tel 666 Flower Power.
- (E) (3:03) Original Sound 8864 Oldies But Goodies Vol. 14. *(this compact disc uses the "Waring - fds" noise reduction process)*
- (E) (3:03) Original Sound 2222 Oldies But Goodies Volumes 3,5,11,14 and 15 Box Set. *(this box set uses the "Waring - fds" noise reduction process)*
- (E) (3:03) Original Sound 2500 Oldies But Goodies Volumes 1-15 Box Set. *(this box set uses the "Waring - fds" noise reduction process)*
- (M) (3:03) Time-Life 2CLR-14 Classic Rock - 1965: Shakin' All Over.
- (S) (3:08) Time-Life SUD-03 Superhits - 1965.
- (S) (3:09) Time-Life R962-04 History Of Rock 'N' Roll: California Pop 1963-1967.
- (S) (3:11) Time-Life R921-38 Get Together.
- (S) (3:13) EMI 29786 Definitive Collection.
- (S) (3:11) Epic 66329 O.S.T. Forrest Gump.
- (S) (3:05) Collectables 5668 Very Best Of.
- (S) (3:08) JCI 3185 1965 - Only Love - 1969.
- (S) (3:08) Time-Life AM1-10 AM Gold - 1965.
- (S) (3:11) Work 68166 O.S.T. My Best Friend's Wedding.
- (S) (3:13) Varese Sarabande 5873 The Burt Bacharach Songbook.
- (S) (3:10) Time-Life R857-20 The Heart Of Rock 'n' Roll 1965-1966.
- (S) (3:09) Time-Life R814-02 Love Songs.
1969 PUT A LITTLE LOVE IN YOUR HEART
- (S) (2:31) Rhino 70738 Best Of.
- (S) (2:37) Novus 3077 O.S.T. Drugstore Cowboy.
- (S) (2:34) Curb 77355 60's Hits Volume 1. *(truncated fade)*
- (S) (2:34) EMI 91473 Very Best Of. *(truncated fade)*
- (S) (2:34) Time-Life 2CLR-06 Classic Rock - 1969.
- (S) (2:29) Time-Life SUD-07 Superhits - 1969.
- (S) (2:31) Time-Life R921-38 Get Together.
- (S) (2:34) EMI 29786 Definitive Collection.
- (S) (2:34) Collectables 5668 Very Best Of. *(truncated fade)*
- (S) (2:28) Time-Life AM1-01 AM Gold - 1969.
- (S) (2:29) Time-Life R814-04 Love Songs.
1969 LOVE WILL FIND A WAY
- (S) (2:33) Rhino 70738 Best Of.
- (S) (2:37) EMI 91473 Very Best Of.
- (S) (2:35) Pair 1284 Good As Gold.
- (S) (2:34) EMI 29786 Definitive Collection.
- (S) (2:37) Collectables 5668 Very Best Of.

JOHNNY DESMOND
1955 PLAY ME HEARTS AND FLOWERS
- (M) (2:45) Time-Life HPD-25 Your Hit Parade - The 50's.
- (M) (2:44) Varese Sarabande 5782 The '50s Remembered: Haymes, Dale, Desmond & Cherry.
1955 THE YELLOW ROSE OF TEXAS

DES'REE
1995 YOU GOTTA BE
- (S) (4:04) 550 Music/Epic 64324 I Ain't Movin'.
- (S) (4:02) Priority 50946 100% Party Hits Of The 90's Volume One.
- (S) (3:59) Columbia 69012 Diana Princess Of Wales Tribute.

DESTINY'S CHILD
1998 NO, NO, NO
- (S) (4:06) Columbia 67728 Destiny's Child.

DETERGENTS
1965 LEADER OF THE LAUNDROMAT
- (M) (3:10) K-Tel 3036 Silly Songs.

DETERGENTS *(Continued)*

- (M) (3:10) Time-Life 2RNR-37 Rock 'N' Roll Era - Weird, Wild & Wacky.
- (M) (3:12) Rhino 72124 Dr. Demento 25th Anniversary Collection.
- (E) (3:10) Sony Music Special Products 22210 Fun Rock.

DETROIT EMERALDS
1972 YOU WANT IT, YOU GOT IT
1972 BABY LET ME TAKE YOU (IN MY ARMS)

WILLIAM DeVAUGHN
1974 BE THANKFUL FOR WHAT YOU GOT

- (S) (3:20) Rhino 70662 Billboard's Top R&B Hits Of 1974. *(LP version edited in an unsuccessful attempt to recreate the 45 version)*
- (S) (3:20) Rhino 70552 Soul Hits Of The 70's Volume 12. *(LP version edited in an unsuccessful attempt to recreate the 45 version)*
- (S) (7:11) Collectables 5271 Be Thankful For What You Got. *(LP version)*
- (S) (3:20) Time-Life SOD-32 Sounds Of The Seventies - AM Pop Classics. *(LP version edited in an unsuccessful attempt to recreate the 45 version)*
- (S) (3:25) Original Sound 8861 Oldies But Goodies Vol. 11. *(this compact disc uses the "Waring - fds" noise reduction process; 45 version)*
- (S) (3:25) Original Sound 2222 Oldies But Goodies Volumes 3,5,11,14 and 15 Box Set. *(this box set uses the "Waring - fds" noise reduction process; 45 version)*
- (S) (3:25) Original Sound 2500 Oldies But Goodies Volumes 1-15 Box Set. *(this box set uses the "Waring - fds" noise reduction process; 45 version)*
- (S) (3:25) Original Sound CDGO-11 Golden Oldies Volume. 11. *(45 version)*
- (S) (3:25) Thump 7040 Low Rider Oldies Volume 4. *(45 version)*
- (S) (3:25) Original Sound 9305 Art Laboe's Dedicated To You Volume 5. *(45 version)*
- (S) (3:26) Coldfront 3517 Players & Hustlers Of The 70's - Can You Dig It?. *(45 version)*
- (S) (3:26) K-Tel 3625 Dynamite. *(45 version)*
- (S) (3:26) Priority 50928 Rare Grooves Volume 1. *(45 version)*
- (S) (5:00) WMOT/Hot Productions 38 Best Of WMOT Records. *(rerecording)*
- (S) (3:20) Time-Life R838-09 Solid Gold Soul - 1974. *(LP version edited in an unsuccessful attempt to recreate the 45 version)*
- (S) (3:25) K-Tel 3914 Superstars Greatest Hits Volume 3. *(45 version)*
- (S) (3:25) Cold Front 4024 Old School Mega Mix Volume 2. *(45 version)*
- (S) (3:20) Time-Life R834-14 Body Talk - Love And Tenderness. *(LP version edited in an unsuccessful attempt to recreate the 45 version)*

DEVICE
1986 HANGING ON A HEART ATTACK

- (S) (4:00) EMI 27674 Living In Oblivion: The 80's Greatest Hits Volume Three.

DEVO
1980 WHIP IT

- (S) (2:37) Warner Brothers 26449 Greatest Hits.
- (S) (2:37) Warner Brothers 3435 Freedom Of Choice.
- (S) (2:37) Priority 7994 Rock Of The 80's.
- (S) (2:38) Rhino 71695 New Wave Hits Of The 80's Vol. 2.
- (S) (2:37) Sandstone 33043 and 5009 Rock The First Volume Three.
- (S) (2:37) Rebound 314520323 Alterno-Daze: Origin Of The Species.
- (S) (2:38) Rhino 72133 Frat Rock: The 80's.
- (S) (2:38) Time-Life R988-25 Sounds Of The Eighties: The Rolling Stone Collection 1980-1981.
- (S) (2:37) JCI 3149 1980 - Only Dance - 1984.

- (S) (2:38) Rhino 72490 New Wave Hits, Vol. 1.
- (S) (2:39) Flashback 72713 Essential New Wave Hits.
- (S) (2:39) Flashback 72092 New Wave Hits Box Set.
- (S) (2:38) Rhino 72820 VH1 - More Of The Big 80's.
- (S) (2:38) Hollywood 62123 More Music From The Motion Picture "Romy And Michele's High School Reunion".
- (S) (2:38) Rhino 75200 Basketball's Greatest Hits.
- (S) (2:37) JCI 3193 18 Rock Classics Volume 3.

1981 WORKING IN THE COAL MINE

- (S) (2:47) Warner Brothers 26449 Greatest Hits.
- (S) (2:47) Full Moon/Elektra 60691 O.S.T. Heavy Metal.
- (S) (2:47) JCI 3163 18 Disco Superhits.
- (S) (2:47) Time-Life R988-31 Sounds Of The Eighties: Cinemax Movie Hits Of The '80s.
- (S) (2:48) Infinite Zero/American 43111 New Traditionalists.

DEVOTIONS
1964 RIP VAN WINKLE

- (M) (2:17) Time-Life 2RNR-40 Rock 'N' Roll Era - The 60's Teen Time.
- (M) (2:16) Time-Life HPD-40 Your Hit Parade - Golden Goofers.
- (M) (2:16) Collectables 5467 The Spotlight Series - Roulette Records Vol. 2.
- (M) (2:16) Collectables 7005 Harlem N.Y. - The Doo Wop Era Part 2.
- (M) (2:16) Collectables 2601 WCBS-FM History Of Rock - The Group Sounds Vol. 2.
- (M) (2:16) Collectables 5542 More Memories Of Times Square Records Volume 7.
- (M) (2:16) Rhino 72507 Doo Wop Box II.

DEXY'S MIDNIGHT RUNNERS
1983 COME ON EILEEN
(dj copies of this 45 ran (3:28) and (4:12); commercial copies were all (4:12))

- (S) (4:12) Priority 53754 Rock Of The 80's Volume 15. *(45 version)*
- (S) (4:12) Rhino 71701 New Wave Hits Of The 80's Vol. 8. *(45 version)*
- (S) (4:11) Rhino 71834 Classic MTV: Class Of 1983. *(45 version)*
- (S) (4:31) Mercury 810054 Too-Rye-Ay. *(with LP introduction but with ending not found on the 45 or vinyl LP)*
- (S) (4:11) EMI 28339 Living In Oblivion: The 80's Greatest Hits - Volume Four. *(45 version)*
- (S) (4:12) Time-Life R988-03 Sounds Of The Eighties: 1983. *(45 version)*
- (S) (4:00) Rebound 314520354 World Of Dance: New Wave - The 80's. *(LP version)*
- (S) (4:05) Warner Brothers 45904 O.S.T. Tommy Boy (The Movie). *(LP version)*
- (S) (4:12) Priority 50953 I Love Rock & Roll Volume 4: Hits Of The 80's. *(45 version)*
- (S) (3:59) Rebound 314520442 The Roots Of Rock: 80's New Wave. *(LP version)*
- (S) (4:12) Rhino 72820 VH1 - More Of The Big 80's. *(45 version)*
- (S) (4:00) Rebound 314520493 Class Reunion '83. *(LP version)*

CLIFF DeYOUNG
1974 MY SWEET LADY

DENNIS DeYOUNG
1984 DESERT MOON

NEIL DIAMOND
1966 CHERRY CHERRY (studio version)

- (S) (2:41) Columbia 38792 Classics - The Early Years. *(contains some additional vocals by Neil Diamond not found on the original 45 or LP)*
- (M) (2:42) Columbia 52703 Greatest Hits 1966-1992.
- (M) (2:42) MCA 11373 O.S.T. How To Make An American Quilt.

(M) (2:40) Columbia 65013 In My Lifetime Box Set.
(M) (2:54) Columbia 65013 In My Lifetime Box Set. *(alternate version)*
(S) (2:41) Columbia 65371 The Early Years/The Jazz Singer/Beautiful Noise. *(contains some additional vocals by Neil Diamond not found on the original 45 or LP)*

1966 I GOT THE FEELIN' (OH NO NO)
(S) (2:09) Columbia 38792 Classics - The Early Years.
(M) (2:18) Columbia 52703 Greatest Hits 1966-1992. *(:06 longer than the 45 or LP length)*
(M) (2:11) Columbia 65013 In My Lifetime Box Set.
(S) (2:09) Columbia 65371 The Early Years/The Jazz Singer/Beautiful Noise.

1967 YOU GOT TO ME
(S) (2:44) Columbia 38792 Classics - The Early Years.
(M) (2:48) Columbia 52703 Greatest Hits 1966-1992.
(M) (2:46) Columbia 65013 In My Lifetime Box Set.
(S) (2:44) Columbia 65371 The Early Years/The Jazz Singer/Beautiful Noise.

1967 GIRL, YOU'LL BE A WOMAN SOON
(S) (3:20) Columbia 38792 Classics - The Early Years. *(:24 longer than the 45 or LP; this extended version first showed up in 1978 on the "Neil Diamond - Early Classics" vinyl LP)*
(M) (2:53) Columbia 52703 Greatest Hits 1966-1992.
(M) (2:53) Columbia 65013 In My Lifetime Box Set.
(S) (3:20) Columbia 65371 The Early Years/The Jazz Singer/Beautiful Noise. *(:24 longer than the 45 or LP; this extended version first showed up in 1978 on the "Neil Diamond - Early Classics" vinyl LP)*

1967 THANK THE LORD FOR THE NIGHT TIME
(S) (3:02) Columbia 38792 Classics - The Early Years.
(M) (3:01) Columbia 52703 Greatest Hits 1966-1992.
(S) (3:03) MCA 10502 Glory Road 1968-1972. *(live)*
(M) (3:00) Columbia 65013 In My Lifetime Box Set.
(S) (3:02) Columbia 65371 The Early Years/The Jazz Singer/Beautiful Noise.

1967 KENTUCKY WOMAN
(E) (2:24) Columbia 38792 Classics - The Early Years.
(M) (2:24) Columbia 52703 Greatest Hits 1966-1992.
(S) (2:41) MCA 10502 Glory Road 1968-1972. *(live)*
(M) (2:23) Columbia 65013 In My Lifetime Box Set.
(E) (2:24) Columbia 65371 The Early Years/The Jazz Singer/Beautiful Noise.

1969 BROTHER LOVE'S TRAVELLING SALVATION SHOW
(S) (3:28) MCA 31050 Sweet Caroline.
(S) (3:25) MCA 37252 His 12 Greatest Hits. *(remix)*
(S) (5:55) Columbia 52703 Greatest Hits 1966-1992. *(live)*
(S) (3:28) MCA 10502 Glory Road 1968-1972.
(S) (3:28) MCA 11540 His 12 Greatest Hits.
(S) (3:32) Columbia 65013 In My Lifetime Box Set. *(time includes 3:26 for the song and :06 for a stop watch sound effect at the end of the song)*
(S) (3:28) MCA 10955 His 12 Greatest Hits. *(gold disc)*

1969 SWEET CAROLINE (GOOD TIMES NEVER SEEMED SO GOOD)
(actual 45 time is (3:23) not (2:50) as stated on the record label)
(S) (3:22) MCA 31050 Sweet Caroline.
(S) (3:30) MCA 37252 His 12 Greatest Hits. *(remixed; :07 longer fade than the 45 or LP)*
(S) (4:06) Columbia 52703 Greatest Hits 1966-1992. *(live)*
(S) (3:19) MCA 10502 Glory Road 1968-1972.
(S) (3:22) Elektra 61888 O.S.T. Beautiful Girls.
(S) (4:12) MCA 11540 His 12 Greatest Hits. *(live)*
(S) (3:20) Columbia 65013 In My Lifetime Box Set.
(S) (4:13) MCA 10955 His 12 Greatest Hits. *(gold disc; live)*

1969 HOLLY HOLY
(S) (4:40) MCA 37252 His 12 Greatest Hits.
(S) (4:38) MCA 31052 Touching You, Touching Me.
(S) (5:26) Columbia 52703 Greatest Hits 1966-1992. *(live)*
(S) (4:40) MCA 10502 Glory Road 1968-1972.
(S) (5:44) MCA 11540 His 12 Greatest Hits. *(live)*
(S) (4:29) Columbia 65013 In My Lifetime Box Set.
(S) (5:44) MCA 10955 His 12 Greatest Hits. *(gold disc; live)*

1970 SHILO
(S) (2:55) MCA 37252 His 12 Greatest Hits. *(rerecording)*
(S) (3:48) Columbia 38792 Classics - The Early Years. *(hit single version; released earlier as a 45 in a different version which never charted)*
(M) (3:23) Columbia 52703 Greatest Hits 1966-1992. *(original recording but not the hit single version)*
(S) (2:58) MCA 10502 Glory Road 1968-1972. *(rerecording)*
(S) (2:55) MCA 31051 Velvet Gloves And Spit. *(rerecording)*
(S) (2:58) MCA 11540 His 12 Greatest Hits. *(rerecording)*
(M) (3:22) Columbia 65013 In My Lifetime Box Set. *(original recording but not the hit single version)*
(S) (2:58) MCA 10955 His 12 Greatest Hits. *(gold disc; rerecording)*

1970 SOOLAIMON (AFRICAN TRILOGY II)
(S) (4:16) MCA 37252 His 12 Greatest Hits.
(S) (4:25) MCA 31071 Tap Root Manuscript. *(LP version; drum beat tracks into next selection)*
(S) (4:36) Columbia 52703 Greatest Hits 1966-1992. *(live)*
(S) (4:12) MCA 10502 Glory Road 1968-1972.
(S) (4:12) MCA 11540 His 12 Greatest Hits.
(S) (4:10) Columbia 65013 In My Lifetime Box Set.
(S) (4:12) MCA 10955 His 12 Greatest Hits. *(gold disc)*

1970 SOLITARY MAN
(S) (2:33) Columbia 38792 Classics - The Early Years. *(alternate take)*
(M) (2:32) Columbia 52703 Greatest Hits 1966-1992.
(S) (3:18) MCA 10502 Glory Road 1968-1972. *(live; includes a :21 spoken introduction)*
(M) (2:31) Columbia 65013 In My Lifetime Box Set.

1970 CRACKLIN' ROSIE
(S) (2:56) MCA 37252 His 12 Greatest Hits.
(S) (3:00) MCA 31071 Tap Root Manuscript.
(S) (3:06) Columbia 52703 Greatest Hits 1966-1992. *(live)*
(S) (3:02) MCA 10502 Glory Road 1968-1972. *(includes :04 of studio talk)*
(S) (2:57) MCA 11540 His 12 Greatest Hits.
(S) (2:57) Columbia 65013 In My Lifetime Box Set.
(S) (2:57) MCA 10955 His 12 Greatest Hits. *(gold disc)*

1970 HE AIN'T HEAVY...HE'S MY BROTHER
(S) (4:09) MCA 1606 Rainbow.
(S) (4:09) MCA 31071 Tap Root Manuscript.
(S) (4:10) MCA 10502 Glory Road 1968-1972.
(S) (4:09) Columbia 65013 In My Lifetime Box Set.

1970 DO IT
(M) (2:21) Columbia 38792 Classics - The Early Years. *(hit 45 version)*

1971 I AM I SAID
(S) (3:31) MCA 37252 His 12 Greatest Hits.
(S) (5:05) Columbia 52703 Greatest Hits 1966-1992. *(live)*
(S) (3:32) MCA 10502 Glory Road 1968-1972.
(S) (3:32) MCA 11540 His 12 Greatest Hits.
(S) (3:32) Columbia 65013 In My Lifetime Box Set.
(S) (3:33) Rhino 72737 Billboard Top Soft Rock Hits - 1971.
(S) (3:33) MCA 10955 His 12 Greatest Hits. *(gold disc)*

1971 STONES
(S) (3:03) MCA 37252 His 12 Greatest Hits.
(S) (3:02) MCA 1607 And The Singer Sings His Song.
(S) (3:02) MCA 1490 Love Songs.
(S) (3:03) MCA 10502 Glory Road 1968-1972.
(S) (3:04) MCA 11540 His 12 Greatest Hits.
(S) (3:04) MCA 10955 His 12 Greatest Hits. *(gold disc)*

1972 SONG SUNG BLUE
(S) (3:12) MCA 37252 His 12 Greatest Hits.
(S) (3:14) MCA 31061 Moods.
(S) (3:05) Columbia 52703 Greatest Hits 1966-1992. *(live)*
(S) (3:14) MCA 10502 Glory Road 1968-1972.
(S) (3:12) MCA 11540 His 12 Greatest Hits.
(S) (3:11) Columbia 65013 In My Lifetime Box Set.
(S) (3:12) Rhino 72738 Billboard Top Soft Rock Hits - 1972.
(S) (3:12) MCA 10955 His 12 Greatest Hits. *(gold disc)*

1972 PLAY ME
(S) (3:49) MCA 37252 His 12 Greatest Hits.
(S) (3:51) MCA 31061 Moods.
(S) (3:50) MCA 1490 Love Songs.
(S) (4:01) Columbia 52703 Greatest Hits 1966-1992. *(rerecording)*

NEIL DIAMOND *(Continued)*

 (S) (3:49) MCA 10502 Glory Road 1968-1972.
 (S) (3:49) MCA 11540 His 12 Greatest Hits.
 (S) (3:48) Columbia 65013 In My Lifetime Box Set.
 (S) (3:49) MCA 10955 His 12 Greatest Hits. *(gold disc)*

1972 WALK ON WATER
(the original commercial 45 and LP version both
included a (1:37) instrumental ending titled "THEME")

 (S) (3:03) MCA 1607 And The Singer Sings His Song.
 (does not include "THEME")
 (S) (3:05) MCA 31061 Moods. *(tracks into "THEME")*
 (S) (3:05) MCA 10502 Glory Road 1968-1972. *(tracks into "THEME")*

1973 CHERRY CHERRY from HOT AUGUST NIGHT
(live version)

 (S) (4:43) MCA 6896 Hot August Night. *(LP version)*
 (S) (4:43) MFSL 584 Hot August Night. *(LP version; gold disc)*
 (S) (4:44) MCA 10502 Glory Road 1968-1972. *(LP version)*

1973 BE

 (S) (6:29) Columbia 32550 O.S.T. Jonathan Livingston Seagull. *(there are 2 vocal versions of "BE" on the "O.S.T. Jonathan Livingston Seagull" album and this is the 1st LP version)*
 (S) (3:30) Columbia 32550 O.S.T. Jonathan Livingston Seagull. *(there are 2 vocal versions of "BE" on the "O.S.T. Jonathan Livingston Seagull" album and this is the 2nd LP version)*
 (S) (6:29) Columbia 52703 Greatest Hits 1966-1992. *(there are 2 vocal versions of "BE" on the "O.S.T. Jonathan Livingston Seagull album and this is the 1st LP version)*
 (S) (5:04) Columbia 38068 12 Greatest Hits Volume II. *(:24 shorter than the 45 version)*
 (S) (3:12) Columbia 65013 In My Lifetime Box Set. *(there are 2 vocal versions of "BE" on the "O.S.T. Jonathan Livingston Seagull" album and this is the 2nd LP version but missing the wind sound effects at the end)*

1974 LONGFELLOW SERENADE
(actual 45 time is (3:44) not (3:22) as stated on the
record label; LP length is (3:49))

 (S) (3:50) Columbia 52703 Greatest Hits 1966-1992.
 (S) (3:49) Columbia 32919 Serenade.
 (S) (3:51) Columbia 38068 12 Greatest Hits Volume II.
 (S) (3:47) Columbia 65013 In My Lifetime Box Set.

1976 IF YOU KNOW WHAT I MEAN

 (S) (3:40) Columbia 52703 Greatest Hits 1966-1992.
 (S) (3:40) Columbia 33965 Beautiful Noise.
 (S) (3:40) Columbia 38068 12 Greatest Hits Volume II.
 (S) (3:39) Columbia 65013 In My Lifetime Box Set.
 (S) (3:40) Columbia 65371 The Early Years/The Jazz Singer/Beautiful Noise.

1978 DESIREE

 (S) (3:14) Columbia 34990 I'm Glad You're Here With Me Tonight.
 (S) (3:17) Columbia 52703 Greatest Hits 1966-1992.
 (S) (3:17) Columbia 38068 12 Greatest Hits Volume II.
 (S) (3:16) Columbia 65013 In My Lifetime Box Set.

released as by BARBRA & NEIL (BARBRA STREISAND &
NEIL DIAMOND):
1978 YOU DON'T BRING ME FLOWERS

 (S) (3:56) Columbia 35375 Barbra Streisand: Songbird. *(Barbra Streisand solo)*
 (S) (3:23) Columbia 35679 Barbra Streisand: Greatest Hits Volume 2. *(LP length)*
 (S) (3:22) Columbia 37678 Barbra Streisand: Memories. *(LP length)*
 (S) (3:36) Columbia 44111 Barbra Streisand: Just For The Record. *(live)*
 (S) (3:35) Columbia 52849 Barbra Streisand: Highlights From Just For The Record. *(live)*
 (S) (3:14) Columbia 35625 Neil Diamond: You Don't Bring Me Flowers. *(45 length)*
 (S) (3:07) Columbia 34990 Neil Diamond: I'm Glad You're Here With Me Tonight. *(Neil Diamond solo)*

 (S) (3:22) Columbia 52703 Neil Diamond: Greatest Hits 1966-1992. *(LP length)*
 (S) (3:23) Columbia 38068 Neil Diamond: 12 Greatest Hits Volume II. *(LP length)*
 (S) (3:13) Columbia 65013 Neil Diamond: In My Lifetime Box Set. *(45 length)*

released as by NEIL DIAMOND:
1979 FOREVER IN BLUE JEANS
(actual 45 time is (3:22) not (3:30) as stated on the
record label)

 (S) (3:36) Columbia 52703 Greatest Hits 1966-1992. *(LP length)*
 (S) (3:36) Columbia 35625 You Don't Bring Me Flowers. *(LP length)*
 (S) (3:23) Columbia 38068 12 Greatest Hits Volume II. *(45 length)*
 (S) (3:36) Columbia 65013 In My Lifetime Box Set. *(LP length)*

1980 SEPTEMBER MORN'

 (S) (3:51) Columbia 52703 Greatest Hits 1966-1992. *(LP version)*
 (S) (3:51) Columbia 36121 September Morn. *(LP version)*
 (S) (3:51) Columbia 38068 12 Greatest Hits Volume II. *(LP version)*
 (S) (3:49) Columbia 65013 In My Lifetime Box Set. *(LP version)*

1981 LOVE ON THE ROCKS

 (S) (3:38) Columbia 52703 Greatest Hits 1966-1992.
 (S) (3:38) Columbia 38068 12 Greatest Hits Volume II.
 (S) (3:37) Capitol 46026 Jazz Singer.
 (S) (3:37) Columbia 67569 Jazz Singer.
 (S) (3:37) Columbia 65013 In My Lifetime Box Set.
 (S) (3:38) Time-Life R834-01 Body Talk - Forever Yours.
 (S) (3:37) Columbia 65371 The Early Years/The Jazz Singer/Beautiful Noise.

1981 HELLO AGAIN

 (S) (4:04) Columbia 52703 Greatest Hits 1966-1992. *(LP version)*
 (S) (4:06) Columbia 38068 12 Greatest Hits Volume II. *(LP version)*
 (S) (4:02) Capitol 46026 Jazz Singer. *(LP version)*
 (S) (4:02) Columbia 67569 Jazz Singer. *(LP version)*
 (S) (3:37) Columbia 65013 In My Lifetime Box Set. *(45 version)*
 (S) (4:02) Columbia 65371 The Early Years/The Jazz Singer/Beautiful Noise. *(LP version)*

1981 AMERICA

 (S) (4:18) Columbia 52703 Greatest Hits 1966-1992. *(LP version)*
 (S) (4:18) Columbia 38068 12 Greatest Hits Volume II. *(LP version)*
 (S) (4:17) Capitol 46026 Jazz Singer. *(tracks into next selection; LP version)*
 (S) (4:17) Columbia 67569 Jazz Singer. *(tracks into next selection; LP version)*
 (S) (4:17) Columbia 65013 In My Lifetime Box Set. *(LP version)*
 (S) (4:17) Columbia 65371 The Early Years/The Jazz Singer/Beautiful Noise. *(tracks into next selection; LP version)*

1982 YESTERDAY'S SONGS

 (S) (2:52) Columbia 37628 On The Way To The Sky.
 (S) (2:49) Columbia 38068 12 Greatest Hits Volume II.
 (S) (2:48) Columbia 65013 In My Lifetime Box Set.

1982 ON THE WAY TO THE SKY

 (S) (3:47) Columbia 37628 On The Way To The Sky.

1982 BE MINE TONIGHT

 (S) (2:38) Columbia 37628 On The Way To The Sky.

1982 HEARTLIGHT

 (S) (4:25) Columbia 38359 Heartlight.
 (S) (4:23) Columbia 65013 In My Lifetime Box Set.
 (S) (4:24) Time-Life R814-03 Love Songs.

1983 I'M ALIVE

 (S) (3:47) Columbia 38359 Heartlight.
 (S) (3:42) Columbia 65013 In My Lifetime Box Set.

DIAMONDS
1955 WHY DO FOOLS FALL IN LOVE
    (M) (2:24) Mercury 314532734 Best Of.
1955 THE CHURCH BELLS MAY RING
    (M) (2:17) Mercury 314532734 Best Of.
1956 LOVE, LOVE, LOVE
1956 SOFT SUMMER BREEZE
1956 KA-DING-DONG
    (M) (1:57) Mercury 314532734 Best Of.
1957 LITTLE DARLIN'
    (M) (2:06) Rhino 70618 Billboard's Top Rock & Roll Hits Of 1957.
    (M) (2:06) Rhino 72004 Billboard's Top Rock & Roll Hits 1957-1961 Box Set.
    (M) (2:06) Mercury 832041 45's On CD Volume 1.
    (M) (2:07) Mercury 826448 Oldies Golden Million Sellers.
    (M) (2:06) Original Sound 8861 Oldies But Goodies Vol. 11. *(this compact disc uses the "Waring - fds" noise reduction process)*
    (M) (2:06) Original Sound 2222 Oldies But Goodies Volumes 3,5,11,14 and 15 Box Set. *(this box set uses the "Waring - fds" noise reduction process)*
    (M) (2:06) Original Sound 2500 Oldies But Goodies Volumes 1-15 Box Set. *(this box set uses the "Waring - fds" noise reduction process)*
    (S) (2:01) MCA 6171 Good Time Rock 'N' Roll. *(all selections on this cd are recorded live)*
    (M) (2:06) Atlantic 82155 O.S.T. Book Of Love.
    (M) (2:06) MCA 8001 O.S.T. American Graffiti.
    (M) (2:06) Time-Life 2RNR-01 Rock 'N' Roll Era - 1957.
    (M) (2:06) Time-Life R962-06 History Of Rock 'N' Roll: Doo Wop And Vocal Group Tradition 1955-1962.
    (M) (2:05) Time-Life R10513 40 Lovin' Oldies.
    (M) (2:05) Polygram Special Markets 314520259 Doo Wop Classics.
    (M) (2:06) Special Music/Essex 5034 Prom Night - The 50's.
    (M) (2:06) Mercury 314532734 Best Of.
    (M) (2:06) JCI 3165 #1 Radio Hits 1955 - Only Rock 'n Roll - 1959.
    (M) (2:06) Polygram Special Markets 314520478 50's Jukebox Hits.
1957 WORDS OF LOVE
    (M) (2:12) Mercury 314532734 Best Of.
1957 ZIP ZIP
    (M) (2:03) Mercury 314532734 Best Of.
1957 SILHOUETTES
    (M) (2:40) Mercury 314532734 Best Of.
    (M) (2:41) Time-Life R857-05 The Heart Of Rock 'n' Roll 1957.
1958 THE STROLL
    (M) (2:26) Rhino 70992 Groove 'n' Grind.
    (M) (2:28) Mercury 832041 45's On CD Volume 1.
    (M) (2:25) JCI 3201 Party Time Fifties.
    (M) (2:24) Original Sound 8891 Dick Clark's 21 All-Time Hits Vol. 1.
    (M) (2:26) MCA 8001 O.S.T. American Graffiti.
    (M) (2:27) Time-Life 2RNR-17 Rock 'N' Roll Era - 1957 Still Rockin'.
    (M) (2:25) K-Tel 3331 Do You Wanna Dance.
    (E) (2:26) Era 511 Ultimate 50's Party.
    (M) (2:25) Risky Business 67311 The Ultimate Party Survival Kit.
    (M) (2:27) Elektra 61888 O.S.T. Beautiful Girls.
    (M) (2:26) Mercury 314532734 Best Of.
    (M) (2:27) JCI 3188 1955 - Only Dance - 1959.
    (M) (2:26) Nick At Nite/550 Music 63407 Dancing At The Nick At Niteclub.
    (M) (2:26) Polygram Special Markets 314520462 50's Soul.
    (M) (2:26) K-Tel 4066 K-Tel's Original Party Music Vol. 2.
1958 HIGH SIGN
    (M) (2:21) Mercury 314532734 Best Of.
1958 KATHY-O
1958 WALKING ALONG
    (M) (2:17) Mercury 314532734 Best Of.
1959 SHE SAY (OOM DOOBY DOOM)
    (M) (2:02) Time-Life 2RNR-33 Rock 'N' Roll Era - The 50's Last Dance.
    (M) (2:05) Mercury 314532734 Best Of.

1961 ONE SUMMER NIGHT
    (S) (2:31) Mercury 314532734 Best Of.

MANU DIBANGO
1973 SOUL MAKOSSA
    (S) (4:27) Rhino 70552 Soul Hits Of The 70's Volume 12.
    (S) (4:27) Rhino 70274 The Disco Years Volume 3.
    (S) (4:24) Turnstyle/Atlantic 14215 Atlantic Dance Classics.
    (S) (4:27) Rhino 70274 The Disco Years Volume 3.
    (S) (4:27) Rhino 71604 Rock Instrumental Classics Vol. 4: Soul.
    (S) (4:27) Rhino 72035 Rock Instrumental Classics Vols. 1-5 Box Set.
    (S) (4:25) MCA 11065 O.S.T. Crooklyn Volume II.

DICK and DEEDEE
1961 THE MOUNTAIN'S HIGH
    (M) (2:09) Time-Life 2RNR-04 Rock 'N' Roll Era - 1961.
    (M) (2:12) Rhino 71582 Billboard Top Pop Hits, 1961.
    (M) (2:12) Varese Sarabande 5576 Best Of.
1962 TELL ME
    (M) (2:12) Varese Sarabande 5576 Best Of.
1963 YOUNG AND IN LOVE
    (S) (2:17) Time-Life 2RNR-47 Rock 'N' Roll Era - Teen Idols II.
    (S) (2:18) Varese Sarabande 5576 Best Of.
1964 TURN AROUND
    (S) (2:39) Varese Sarabande 5576 Best Of.
1965 THOU SHALT NOT STEAL
    (S) (1:54) Time-Life 2RNR-40 Rock 'N' Roll Era - The 60's Teen Time.
    (S) (1:56) Time-Life SUD-17 Superhits - Mid 60's Classics.
    (S) (1:59) Varese Sarabande 5576 Best Of.
    (S) (1:56) Time-Life AM1-16 AM Gold - Mid '60s Classics.

"LITTLE" JIMMY DICKENS
1965 MAY THE BIRD OF PARADISE FLY UP YOUR NOSE
    (S) (2:26) Columbia 46031 Columbia Country Classics Volume 3.
    (S) (2:23) Time-Life HPD-35 Your Hit Parade - The Fun-Times 50's & 60's.
    (S) (2:17) K-Tel 3243 Kooky Kountry. *(rerecording)*
    (S) (2:21) K-Tel 771 Country Music Classics Volume IX.
    (S) (2:24) Rhino 72125 Dr. Demento's Country Corn.
    (S) (2:25) Epic 67941 Super Hits Of The 60's.
    (S) (2:17) K-Tel 3368 101 Greatest Country Hits Vol. Nine: Country Classics. *(rerecording)*

DICKY DOO and THE DON'TS
1958 CLICK CLACK
    (M) (2:26) LaserLight 12322 Greatest Hit Singles Collection.
    (M) (2:19) Relic 7108 The Gerry Granahan Scrapbook.
    (M) (2:29) Forevermore 5008 Oldies I Forgot To Buy.

BO DIDDLEY
1959 SAY MAN
    (M) (3:10) Chess 19502 The Chess Box.
    (M) (3:09) Telstar/JCI 3506 Best Of.
    (M) (3:09) Chess 5904 Bo Diddley/Go Bo Diddley.
    (M) (3:08) Time-Life 2RNR-28 Rock 'N' Roll Era - The 50's Rave On.
    (M) (3:12) Chess 9352 Chess Rhythm & Roll.
    (M) (3:12) Chess 9373 His Best.

DIESEL
1981 SAUSALITO SUMMERNIGHT

DIGABLE PLANETS
1993 REBIRTH OF SLICK (COOL LIKE DAT)
    (S) (4:21) Pendulum 61414 and 27758 Reachin'.
    (S) (4:21) Razor & Tie 4569 '90s Style.

DIGITAL UNDERGROUND
1990 HUMPTY DANCE
    (S) (4:43) JCI 2717 Shake It Up. *(hum noticeable on the fadeout; 45 version)*

DIGITAL UNDERGROUND (Continued)

- (S) (4:39) Priority 7053 Best Of Hip Hop. *(45 version)*
- (S) (5:50) Tommy Boy 1037 MTV Party To Go Volume 1. *(remix; all tracks on this cd are segued together)*
- (S) (6:30) Tommy Boy 1026 Sex Packets. *(LP version)*
- (S) (6:29) Rebound 314520449 Hip Hop With R&B Flava. *(LP version)*

MARK DINNING
1960 TEEN ANGEL
- (M) (2:39) Mercury 832041 45's On CD Volume 1.
- (M) (2:39) JCI 3203 Lovin' Fifties.
- (S) (2:39) Original Sound 8857 Oldies But Goodies Vol. 7. *(this compact disc uses the "Waring - fds" noise reduction process)*
- (S) (2:39) Original Sound 2223 Oldies But Goodies Volumes 2,7,9,12 and 13 Box Set. *(this box set uses the "Waring - fds" noise reduction process)*
- (S) (2:39) Original Sound 2500 Oldies But Goodies Volumes 1-15 Box Set. *(this box set uses the "Waring - fds" noise reduction process)*
- (M) (2:39) MCA 8001 O.S.T. American Graffiti.
- (E) (2:39) Time-Life 2RNR-22 Rock 'N' Roll Era - 1960 Still Rockin'.
- (S) (2:39) Rhino 71581 Billboard Top Pop Hits, 1960.
- (M) (2:39) Polygram Special Markets 314520258 No. 1 Hits Of The 50's.
- (M) (2:39) Special Music 5026 Let It All Hang Out - 60's Party Hits.
- (S) (2:39) DCC Compact Classics 078 Best Of Tragedy.
- (M) (2:39) Special Music/Essex 5034 Prom Night - The 50's.
- (S) (2:39) Collectors' Choice 002 Teen Idols....For A Moment.
- (S) (2:38) Eric 11502 Hard To Find 45's On CD (Volume I) 1955-60.
- (M) (2:39) Time-Life R857-14 The Heart Of Rock 'n' Roll 1960-1961 Take Two.
- (S) (2:38) Polygram Special Markets 314520478 50's Jukebox Hits.

DINO
1989 I LIKE IT
- (S) (5:05) 4th B'Way 4011 24/7. *(LP version)*
- (S) (3:55) Priority 53773 80's Greatest Rock Hits Volume II - Teen Idols. *(45 version)*
- (S) (3:54) Rhino 75217 Heartthrob Hits. *(45 version)*
1989 SUNSHINE
- (S) (3:46) 4th B'Way 4011 24/7.
1990 ROMEO
- (S) (4:41) Island 422846481 Swingin'. *(LP version)*
1990 GENTLE
- (S) (5:21) Island 422846481 Swingin'.
1993 OOH CHILD
- (S) (4:12) EastWest 92253 The Way I Am.

KENNY DINO
1961 YOUR MA SAID YOU CRIED IN YOUR SLEEP LAST NIGHT

DINO, DESI & BILLY
1965 I'M A FOOL
- (S) (2:53) Rhino 75754 Even More Nuggets.
- (S) (2:48) Time-Life 2CLR-23 Classic Rock - 1965: Blowin' Your Mind.
- (S) (2:48) Time-Life SUD-17 Superhits - Mid 60's Classics.
- (S) (2:51) Time-Life R962-04 History Of Rock 'N' Roll: California Pop 1963-1967.
- (S) (2:46) Sundazed 11034 Best Of.
- (S) (2:48) JCI 3185 1965 - Only Love - 1969.
- (S) (2:49) Time-Life AM1-16 AM Gold - Mid '60s Classics.
1965 NOT THE LOVIN' KIND
- (S) (2:01) Sundazed 11034 Best Of.

DION
1960 LONELY TEENAGER
- (S) (2:14) 3C/Laurie 105 The Wanderer.
- (S) (2:17) Arista 8206 24 Original Classics.

- (S) (2:14) 3C/Laurie 103 Classic Old & Gold Volume 4.
- (S) (2:17) Collectables 5064 History Of Rock Volume 4.
- (S) (2:13) Time-Life 2RNR-22 Rock 'N' Roll Era - 1960 Still Rockin'.
- (S) (2:14) Collectables 2505 History Of Rock - The 60's Part 5.
- (S) (2:14) Collectables 4505 History Of Rock/The 60s Part Five.
- (S) (2:17) Time-Life R857-10 The Heart Of Rock 'n' Roll 1960-1961.

1961 RUNAROUND SUE
- (S) (2:41) Arista 8206 24 Original Classics.
- (S) (2:41) Rhino 70622 Billboard's Top Rock & Roll Hits Of 1961.
- (S) (2:41) Rhino 72004 Billboard's Top Rock & Roll Hits 1957-1961 Box Set.
- (E) (2:39) Original Sound 8857 Oldies But Goodies Vol. 7. *(this compact disc uses the "Waring - fds" noise reduction process)*
- (E) (2:39) Original Sound 2223 Oldies But Goodies Volumes 2,7,9,12 and 13 Box Set. *(this box set uses the "Waring - fds" noise reduction process)*
- (E) (2:39) Original Sound 2500 Oldies But Goodies Volumes 1-15 Box Set. *(this box set uses the "Waring - fds" noise reduction process)*
- (E) (2:38) Original Sound CDGO-6 Golden Oldies Volume. 6.
- (E) (2:39) Original Sound 8881 Twenty-One #1 Hits. *(this compact disc uses the "Waring - fds" noise reduction process)*
- (S) (2:38) Original Sound 1081 All #1 Hits.
- (S) (2:34) Warner Brothers 3359 O.S.T. The Wanderers.
- (S) (2:36) Warner Special Products 27602 20 Party Classics.
- (S) (2:42) 3C/Laurie 105 The Wanderer.
- (S) (2:39) CBS Special Products 46200 Rock Goes To The Movies Volume 3.
- (S) (2:42) 3C/Laurie 103 Classic Old & Gold Volume 4.
- (S) (2:42) Essex 7052 All Time Rock Classics.
- (S) (2:40) Collectables 5062 History Of Rock Volume 2.
- (M) (2:37) JCI 3112 Pop Sixties.
- (S) (2:40) Time-Life 2RNR-04 Rock 'N' Roll Era - 1961.
- (S) (2:38) Time-Life R962-05 History Of Rock 'N' Roll: The Teenage Years 1957-1964.
- (S) (2:42) Collectables 2500 WCBS-FM History Of Rock - The 60's Part 1.
- (S) (2:42) Collectables 4500 History Of Rock/The 60s Part One.
- (S) (2:50) Right Stuff 27304 Runaround Sue.
- (S) (2:40) RCA 66460 O.S.T. Little Big League.
- (S) (2:40) Original Sound 9603 Best Of Oldies But Goodies Vol. 3.
- (S) (2:38) K-Tel 4066 K-Tel's Original Party Music Vol. 2.

1962 THE WANDERER
- (S) (2:42) 3C/Laurie 105 The Wanderer.
- (E) (2:40) Original Sound 8855 Oldies But Goodies Vol. 5. *(this compact disc uses the "Waring - fds" noise reduction process; ambient background noise throughout the disc)*
- (E) (2:40) Original Sound 2222 Oldies But Goodies Volumes 3,5,11,14 and 15 Box Set. *(this box set uses the "Waring - fds" noise reduction process; ambient background noise throughout the song)*
- (E) (2:40) Original Sound 2500 Oldies But Goodies Volumes 1-15 Box Set. *(this box set uses the "Waring - fds" noise reduction process; ambient background noise throughout the song)*
- (E) (2:39) Original Sound CDGO-3 Golden Oldies Volume. 3.
- (E) (2:40) Original Sound 8892 Dick Clark's 21 All-Time Hits Vol. 2.
- (S) (2:44) Original Sound 9601 Best Of Oldies But Goodies Vol. 1.
- (S) (2:46) Arista 8206 24 Original Classics.
- (S) (2:46) Rhino 70623 Billboard's Top Rock & Roll Hits Of 1962.
- (S) (2:46) Rhino 72007 Billboard's Top Rock & Roll Hits 1962-1966 Box Set.
- (S) (2:46) Capitol 48993 Spuds Mackenzie's Party Faves.

(S) (2:46) JCI 3110 Sock Hoppin' Sixties.
(S) (2:41) Warner Brothers 3359 O.S.T. The Wanderers.
(S) (2:42) 3C/Laurie 103 Classic Old & Gold Volume 4.
(S) (2:45) Collectables 5070 History Of Rock Volume 10.
(S) (2:45) Rhino 71547 Let There Be Drums Volume 1: The 50's.
(S) (2:46) Compose 9923 James Dean/Tribute To A Rebel.
(S) (2:46) Time-Life 2RNR-02 Rock 'N' Roll Era - 1962.
(S) (2:41) Collectables 2502 WCBS-FM History Of Rock - The 60's Part 3.
(S) (2:41) Collectables 4502 History Of Rock/The 60s Part Three.
(S) (2:47) Right Stuff 27304 Runaround Sue.
(S) (2:44) Original Sound 8883 21 Legendary Superstars.
(S) (2:46) JCI 3125 1960 - Only Rock 'N Roll - 1964.
(S) (2:46) Cypress 71334 O.S.T. Coupe De Ville.
(S) (2:46) Right Stuff 53319 Hot Rod Rock Volume 4: Hot Rod Rebels.

1962 LOVERS WHO WANDER
(S) (2:22) 3C/Laurie 105 The Wanderer.
(S) (2:29) Arista 8206 24 Original Classics.
(S) (2:22) 3C/Laurie 103 Classic Old & Gold Volume 4.
(S) (2:21) Time-Life 2RNR-16 Rock 'N' Roll Era - 1962 Still Rockin'.
(S) (2:21) Collectables 2504 WCBS-FM History Of Rock - The 60's Part 4.
(S) (2:21) Collectables 4504 History Of Rock/The 60s Part Four.
(S) (2:30) Right Stuff 27305 Lovers Who Wander.
(S) (2:29) Rhino 71583 Billboard Top Pop Hits, 1962.

1962 LITTLE DIANE
(S) (2:40) 3C/Laurie 105 The Wanderer.
(S) (2:45) Arista 8206 24 Original Classics.
(S) (2:40) 3C/Laurie 103 Classic Old & Gold Volume 4.
(S) (2:38) Time-Life 2RNR-25 Rock 'N' Roll Era - The 60's Keep On Rockin'.
(S) (2:46) Right Stuff 27305 Lovers Who Wander.

1962 LOVE CAME TO ME
(M) (2:37) 3C/Laurie 105 The Wanderer. *(truncated fade)*
(S) (2:44) Arista 8206 24 Original Classics.
(M) (2:37) 3C/Laurie 103 Classic Old & Gold Volume 4. *(truncated fade)*
(S) (2:37) Time-Life 2RNR-40 Rock 'N' Roll Era - The 60's Teen Time.

1963 RUBY BABY
(S) (2:36) Columbia/Legacy 46972 Bronx Blues: The Columbia Recordings (1962-1965).
(S) (2:36) Arista 8206 24 Original Classics.
(S) (2:36) Rhino 70593 The Rock 'N' Roll Classics Of Leiber & Stoller.
(S) (2:36) Time-Life 2RNR-29 Rock 'N' Roll Era - The 60's Rave On.
(S) (2:34) Columbia/Legacy 64889 The Road I'm On: A Retrospective.
(S) (2:25) Columbia/Legacy 64889 The Road I'm On: A Retrospective. *(alternate take)*

1963 SANDY
(S) (2:19) Arista 8206 24 Original Classics.
(S) (2:19) 3C/Laurie 105 The Wanderer. *(truncated fade)*
(S) (2:19) 3C/Laurie 103 Classic Old & Gold Volume 4. *(truncated fade)*
(S) (2:14) Time-Life 2RNR-42 Rock 'N' Roll Era - The 60's Sock Hop.

1963 THIS LITTLE GIRL
(S) (2:35) Columbia/Legacy 46972 Bronx Blues: The Columbia Recordings (1962-1965).
(S) (2:33) Arista 8206 24 Original Classics.
(S) (2:35) Columbia/Legacy 64889 The Road I'm On: A Retrospective.

1963 BE CAREFUL OF STONES THAT YOU THROW
1963 DONNA THE PRIMA DONNA
(S) (2:52) Columbia/Legacy 46972 Bronx Blues: The Columbia Recordings (1962-1965). *(remixed and in portions does not resemble the previously released 45 or LP version; truncated fade)*
(S) (2:47) Arista 8206 24 Original Classics.
(S) (2:48) Time-Life 2RNR-47 Rock 'N' Roll Era - Teen Idols II. *(remixed and in portions does not resemble the previously released 45 or LP version)*

(S) (2:51) Columbia/Legacy 64889 The Road I'm On: A Retrospective.
(M) (2:42) Columbia/Legacy 64889 The Road I'm On: A Retrospective. *(Italian version)*
(S) (2:52) Collectables 1515 and 2515 The Anniversary Album - The 60's. *(remixed and in portions does not resemble the previously released 45 or LP version; truncated fade)*

1963 DRIP DROP
(S) (2:35) Columbia/Legacy 46972 Bronx Blues: The Columbia Recordings (1962-1965).
(S) (2:34) Arista 8206 24 Original Classics.
(S) (2:35) Rhino 70593 The Rock 'N' Roll Classics Of Leiber & Stoller.
(S) (2:31) Time-Life 2RNR-46 Rock 'N' Roll Era - 60's Juke Box Memories.
(S) (2:34) Columbia/Legacy 64889 The Road I'm On: A Retrospective.

1968 ABRAHAM, MARTIN AND JOHN
(S) (3:17) Arista 8206 24 Original Classics.
(S) (3:18) Rhino 70734 Songs Of Protest.
(S) (3:16) Collectables 5063 History Of Rock Volume 3.
(S) (3:18) Time-Life 2CLR-04 Classic Rock - 1968.
(S) (3:15) Time-Life SUD-02 Superhits - 1968.
(S) (3:18) Collectables 2510 WCBS-FM History Of Rock - The Rockin' 60's.
(S) (3:18) Collectables 4510 History Of Rock/The Rockin' 60s.
(S) (3:17) Collectables 2501 WCBS-FM History Of Rock - The 60's Part 2.
(S) (3:17) Collectables 4501 History Of Rock/The 60s Part Two.
(E) (3:15) Time-Life R103-33 Singers & Songwriters.
(S) (3:17) Time-Life R921-38 Get Together.
(S) (3:19) Right Stuff 29667 Dion.
(S) (3:17) Rhino 71938 Billboard Top Pop Hits, 1968.
(S) (3:15) Time-Life AM1-04 AM Gold - 1968.
(S) (3:17) Time-Life R132-22 Treasury Of Folk Music Volume Two.

DION & THE BELMONTS
1958 I WONDER WHY
(M) (2:19) 3C/Laurie 105 The Wanderer.
(M) (2:17) Arista 8206 24 Original Classics.
(M) (2:17) Rhino 75764 Best Of Doo Wop Uptempo.
(M) (2:15) Original Sound 8862 Oldies But Goodies Vol. 12. *(this compact disc uses the "Waring - fds" noise reduction process)*
(M) (2:15) Original Sound 2223 Oldies But Goodies Volumes 2,7,9,12 and 13 Box Set. *(this box set uses the "Waring - fds" noise reduction process)*
(M) (2:15) Original Sound 2500 Oldies But Goodies Volumes 1-15 Box Set. *(this box set uses the "Waring - fds" noise reduction process)*
(M) (2:20) Elektra 60107 O.S.T. Diner.
(M) (2:20) 3C/Laurie 102 Classic Old & Gold Volume 3.
(M) (2:19) Collectables 2507 History Of Rock - The Doo Wop Era Part 1.
(M) (2:19) Collectables 4507 History Of Rock/The Doo Wop Era Part One.
(M) (2:16) Rhino 71463 Doo Wop Box.
(M) (2:16) Time-Life 2RNR-21 Rock 'N' Roll Era - 1958 Still Rockin'.
(M) (2:15) Time-Life R962-06 History Of Rock 'N' Roll: Doo Wop And Vocal Group Tradition 1955-1962.
(M) (2:18) Collectables 2503 WCBS-FM History Of Rock - The 50's Part 2.
(M) (2:17) Collectables 4503 History Of Rock/The 50s Part Two.
(M) (2:20) Collectables 2552 WOGL History Of Rock Vol. 2.
(M) (2:17) Nick At Nite/550 Music 63456 Double Date With Joanie And Chachi.

1958 NO ONE KNOWS
(M) (2:34) 3C/Laurie 105 The Wanderer.
(M) (2:34) 3C/Laurie 102 Classic Old & Gold Volume 3.

1959 DON'T PITY ME
(M) (2:35) 3C/Laurie 105 The Wanderer.
(M) (2:36) 3C/Laurie 102 Classic Old & Gold Volume 3.

DION & THE BELMONTS *(Continued)*
1959 TEENAGER IN LOVE
    (S) (2:36)   Arista 8206   24 Original Classics.
    (S) (2:36)   Rhino 70906   American Bandstand Greatest Hits Collection.
    (M) (2:29)   Original Sound 8856   Oldies But Goodies Vol. 6. *(this compact disc uses the "Waring - fds" noise reduction process)*
    (M) (2:29)   Original Sound 2221   Oldies But Goodies Volumes 1,4,6,8 and 10 Box Set. *(this box set uses the "Waring - fds" noise reduction process)*
    (M) (2:29)   Original Sound 2500   Oldies But Goodies Volumes 1-15 Box Set. *(this box set uses the "Waring - fds" noise reduction process)*
    (S) (2:31)   Original Sound CDGO-6   Golden Oldies Volume. 6.
    (S) (2:31)   Original Sound 8891   Dick Clark's 21 All-Time Hits Vol. 1.
    (S) (2:31)   Original Sound 9602   Best Of Oldies But Goodies Vol. 2.
    (S) (2:29)   Elektra 60107   O.S.T. Diner.
    (E) (2:36)   JCI 3201   Party Time Fifties.
    (S) (2:35)   3C/Laurie 105   The Wanderer.
    (S) (2:36)   3C/Laurie 102   Classic Old & Gold Volume 3.
    (S) (2:34)   Collectables 5066   History Of Rock Volume 6.
    (S) (2:35)   Era 5025   The Brill Building Sound.
    (S) (2:33)   Rhino 71463   Doo Wop Box.
    (S) (2:35)   Time-Life 2RNR-13   Rock 'N' Roll Era - 1959.
    (S) (2:33)   Time-Life R962-08   History Of Rock 'N' Roll: Sound Of The City 1959-1965.
    (S) (2:36)   Collectables 2506   WCBS-FM History Of Rock - The 50's Part 1.
    (S) (2:36)   Collectables 4506   History Of Rock/The 50s Part One.
    (S) (2:35)   Time-Life R10513   40 Lovin' Oldies.
    (S) (2:35)   Nick At Nite/550 Music/Epic 67770   Happy Days Jukebox.
    (E) (2:37)   Right Stuff 53320   Hot Rod Rock Volume 5: Back Seat Movers.
1960 WHERE OR WHEN
    (M) (2:36)   3C/Laurie 105   The Wanderer.
    (M) (2:36)   Rhino 75763   Best Of Doo Wop Ballads.
    (M) (2:36)   Arista 8206   24 Original Classics.
    (M) (2:36)   3C/Laurie 102   Classic Old & Gold Volume 3.
    (M) (2:35)   Collectables 5068   History Of Rock Volume 8.
    (E) (2:36)   Time-Life 2RNR-22   Rock 'N' Roll Era - 1960 Still Rockin'.
    (M) (2:35)   Time-Life SUD-15   Superhits - The Early 60's.
    (M) (2:36)   Collectables 2502   WCBS-FM History Of Rock - The 60's Part 3.
    (M) (2:36)   Collectables 4502   History Of Rock/The 60s Part Three.
    (M) (2:35)   Time-Life R103-27   Love Me Tender.
    (M) (2:36)   Time-Life R857-02   The Heart Of Rock 'n' Roll - 1960.
    (M) (2:36)   Rhino 72507   Doo Wop Box II.
    (M) (2:35)   Time-Life AM1-19   AM Gold - The Early '60s.
1960 WHEN YOU WISH UPON A STAR
    (S) (2:25)   3C/Laurie 105   The Wanderer.
    (S) (2:26)   3C/Laurie 102   Classic Old & Gold Volume 3.
1960 IN THE STILL OF THE NIGHT
    (S) (2:35)   3C/Laurie 105   The Wanderer.
    (S) (2:36)   3C/Laurie 102   Classic Old & Gold Volume 3.

CELINE DION
1991 WHERE DOES MY HEART BEAT NOW
    (S) (4:32)   Epic 46893   Unison.
1991 (IF THERE WAS) ANY OTHER WAY
    (S) (3:59)   Sandstone 33053 and 5021   Cosmopolitan Volume 7.
    (S) (3:58)   DCC Compact Classics 081   Night Moves Volume 1.
    (S) (4:00)   Epic 46893   Unison.
released as by CELINE DION and PEABO BRYSON:
1992 BEAUTY AND THE BEAST
    (S) (4:02)   Walt Disney 60618   O.S.T. Beauty And The Beast.
    (S) (4:03)   Epic 52473   Celine Dion.

released as by CELINE DION:
1992 IF YOU ASKED ME TO
    (S) (3:53)   Epic 52473   Celine Dion.
1992 NOTHING BROKEN BUT MY HEART
    (S) (5:54)   Epic 52473   Celine Dion. *(LP version)*
1993 LOVE CAN MOVE MOUNTAINS
    (S) (6:07)   Epic 52473   Celine Dion.
released as by CELINE DION and CLIVE GRIFFIN:
1993 WHEN I FALL IN LOVE
    (S) (4:19)   Epic 53439   O.S.T. Peter's Friends.
    (S) (4:19)   Epic 53764   O.S.T. Sleepless In Seattle.
    (S) (4:19)   550 Music/Epic 57555   Celine Dion - Colour Of My Love.
released as by CELINE DION:
1994 THE POWER OF LOVE
    (S) (5:41)   550 Music/Epic 57555   Colour Of My Love.
    (S) (5:41)   Grammy Recordings/Sony Music 67043   1995 Grammy Nominees.
1994 MISLED
    (S) (3:30)   550 Music/Epic 57555   Colour Of My Love.
1996 BECAUSE YOU LOVED ME
    (S) (4:32)   550 Music/Epic 67541   Falling Into You.
    (S) (4:32)   Grammy Recordings/Chronicles 314553292   1997 Grammy Nominees.
    (S) (4:31)   Columbia 69012   Diana Princess Of Wales Tribute.
1996 IT'S ALL COMING BACK TO ME NOW
    (S) (7:35)   550 Music/Epic 67541   Falling Into You.
1997 ALL BY MYSELF
    (S) (5:10)   550 Music/Epic 67541   Falling Into You.

DIRE STRAITS
1979 SULTANS OF SWING
(dj copies of this 45 ran (4:38), (4:44), (5:49) and (5:52); commercial copies were all (5:49))
    (S) (5:46)   Warner Brothers 25794   Money For Nothing.
    (S) (5:46)   Warner Brothers 3266   Dire Straits.
    (S) (5:43)   Time-Life R102-34   The Rolling Stone Collection.
    (S) (5:43)   Time-Life R968-02   Guitar Rock 1978-1979.
    (S) (5:47)   Pointblank 42088   Fender 50th Anniversary Guitar Legends.
1985 MONEY FOR NOTHING
(dj copies of this 45 ran (4:05); commercial copies were all (4:38))
    (S) (4:04)   Warner Brothers 25794   Money For Nothing.
    (S) (8:20)   Warner Brothers 25264   Brothers In Arms. *(neither the 45 or LP version)*
    (S) (4:04)   Time-Life R13610   Gold And Platinum Box Set - The Ultimate Rock Collection.
1986 WALK OF LIFE
    (S) (4:06)   Warner Brothers 25794   Money For Nothing.
    (S) (4:06)   Warner Brothers 25264   Brothers In Arms.
    (S) (4:06)   Time-Life R988-01   Sounds Of The Eighties: The Rockin' Eighties.
    (S) (4:04)   Time-Life R988-27   Sounds Of The Eighties: The Rolling Stone Collection 1983-1985.
    (S) (4:05)   Pyramid 71830   Earthrise - The Rainforest Album.
1986 SO FAR AWAY
    (S) (5:05)   Warner Brothers 25264   Brothers In Arms. *(LP version)*
    (S) (5:05)   Time-Life R988-04   Sounds Of The Eighties: 1986. *(LP version)*

SENATOR EVERETT McKINLEY DIRKSEN
1967 GALLANT MEN
    (S) (2:38)   Capitol 95859   Gallant Men.

DIRT BAND (see NITTY GRITTY DIRT BAND)

DISCO TEX & THE SEX-O-LETTES
1975 GET DANCIN'
(actual 45 time is (3:48) not (3:53) as stated on the record label)
    (S) (3:54)   Priority 7973   Mega-Hits Dance Classics Volume 3. *(45 version)*
    (S) (3:52)   Rhino 71094   Disco Hits Volume 1. *(45 version)*

(S) (4:10) Collectables 5075 Get Dancin'. *(most selections on this cd are segued together; cd jacket track listing does not match the actual cd tracking; LP version)*

(S) (3:14) Curb 77774 Hard To Find Hits Of Rock 'N' Roll Volume Two. *(45 version faded :34 early)*

(S) (3:52) K-Tel 3371 Hot Nights - Disco Lights. *(45 version)*

(S) (3:50) K-Tel 3624 Music Express. *(45 version)*

(S) (3:52) JCI 3163 18 Disco Superhits. *(45 version)*

(S) (3:52) Priority 53129 Deep Soul Volume One. *(45 version)*

(S) (3:52) Flashback 72688 Disco Hits: Get Down Tonight. *(45 version)*

(S) (3:52) Flashback 72086 Disco Hits Box Set. *(45 version)*

1975 I WANNA DANCE WIT' CHOO (DOO DAT DANCE) PART 1

(S) (5:07) Collectables 5075 Get Dancin'. *(most selections on this cd are segued together; cd jacket track listing does not match the actual cd tracking; LP version)*

(M) (3:40) Curb 77774 Hard To Find Hits Of Rock 'N' Roll Volume Two. *(45 version)*

(S) (5:09) Priority 53789 Disco Attack. *(LP version)*

DISHWALLA
1996 COUNTING BLUE CARS

(S) (4:49) A&M 314540319 Pet Your Friends.

DIVINYLS
1991 I TOUCH MYSELF

(S) (3:45) Priority 53741 Cutting Edge Vol. 1 - Best Of Modern Rock Hits.

(S) (3:45) Virgin 91397 and 86185 Divinyls.

(S) (3:45) K-Tel 6101 Hot Ladies Of The 90's - Dazzling Divas.

(S) (3:45) DCC Compact Classics 140 Rock The First Volume 10.

(S) (3:44) Hip-O 40022 That Sound From Down Under.

(S) (3:45) Priority 50947 A Bunch O' Hits: The Best Rock Of The 90's Volume 1.

(S) (3:44) Hollywood 62112 O.S.T. Austin Roberts.

(S) (3:45) Rhino 72651 Billboard Top Modern Rock Tracks, 1991.

(S) (3:45) Rhino 72856 Just Can't Get Enough: New Wave Women.

(S) (3:42) Boxtunes 162531028 Big Ones Of Alternative Rock.

(S) (3:45) K-Tel 3847 90s Now Volume 1.

DIXIEBELLES
1963 (DOWN AT) PAPA JOE'S

(M) (2:30) Time-Life SUD-15 Superhits - The Early 60's.

(M) (2:30) Collectables 2502 WCBS-FM History Of Rock - The 60's Part 3.

(M) (2:30) Collectables 4502 History Of Rock/The 60s Part Three.

(E) (2:31) Sony Music Special Products 66106 The Monument Story.

(M) (2:30) Time-Life AM1-19 AM Gold - The Early '60s.

(E) (2:31) Collectables 5829 Golden Classics.

1964 SOUTHTOWN U.S.A.

(E) (2:10) Collectables 5829 Golden Classics.

DIXIE CUPS
1964 CHAPEL OF LOVE

(M) (2:46) Warner Brothers 25613 O.S.T. Full Metal Jacket.

(M) (2:45) Original Sound 8861 Oldies But Goodies Vol. 11. *(this compact disc uses the "Waring - fds" noise reduction process)*

(M) (2:45) Original Sound 2222 Oldies But Goodies Volumes 3,5,11,14 and 15 Box Set. *(this box set uses the "Waring - fds" noise reduction process)*

(M) (2:45) Original Sound 2500 Oldies But Goodies Volumes 1-15 Box Set. *(this box set uses the "Waring - fds" noise reduction process)*

(M) (2:45) Original Sound 8881 Twenty-One #1 Hits. *(this compact disc uses the "Waring - fds" noise reduction process)*

(M) (2:44) Original Sound 8892 Dick Clark's 21 All-Time Hits Vol. 2.

(M) (2:45) Original Sound 1081 All #1 Hits.

(M) (2:47) Rhino 75891 Wonder Women.

(M) (2:46) Rhino 70988 Best Of The Girl Groups Volume 1.

(M) (2:47) Rhino 70650 Billboard's Top R&B Hits Of 1964.

(M) (2:46) Rhino 70588 Rockin' & Rollin' Wedding Songs Volume 1.

(E) (2:44) Motown 5322 and 9087 Girl Groups: The Story Of A Sound.

(M) (2:46) Era 5025 The Brill Building Sound.

(M) (2:46) Time-Life 2RNR-10 Rock 'N' Roll Era - 1964.

(M) (2:44) Collectables 2500 WCBS-FM History Of Rock - The 60's Part 1.

(M) (2:44) Collectables 4500 History Of Rock/The 60s Part One.

(M) (2:47) MCA Special Products 20783 Rock Around The Oldies #1.

(S) (2:51) DCC Compact Classics 077 Too Cute! *(alternate take)*

(M) (2:45) Priority 50951 I Love Rock & Roll Volume 2: Hits Of The 60's.

(S) (2:51) Eclipse Music Group 64869 Rock 'n Roll Relix 1964-1965. *(alternate take)*

(S) (2:51) Eclipse Music Group 64872 Rock 'n Roll Relix 1960-1969. *(alternate take)*

(M) (2:46) Time-Life R857-09 The Heart Of Rock 'n' Roll 1964.

(S) (2:48) Collectables 5742 Ad Libs & Friends. *(alternate take)*

(M) (2:47) K-Tel 3888 Great R&B Female Groups Hits Of The 60's.

(E) (2:45) JCI 3184 1960 - Only Love - 1964.

(S) (2:49) Taragon 1029 Very Best Of Red Bird/Blue Cat Records. *(alternate take)*

1964 PEOPLE SAY

(M) (2:32) Rhino 75891 Wonder Women. *(:13 longer than the 45 or LP)*

(M) (2:43) Rhino 70988 Best Of The Girl Groups Volume 1. *(:24 longer than the 45 or LP)*

(M) (2:31) Time-Life 2CLR-09 Classic Rock - 1964: The Beat Goes On. *(:12 longer than the 45 or LP)*

(M) (2:30) Collectables 2501 WCBS-FM History Of Rock - The 60's Part 2. *(:11 longer than the 45 or LP)*

(M) (2:30) Collectables 4501 History Of Rock/The 60s Part Two. *(:11 longer than the 45 or LP)*

(E) (2:28) Collectables 5742 Ad Libs & Friends. *(:09 longer than the 45 or LP)*

(S) (2:36) Taragon 1029 Very Best Of Red Bird/Blue Cat Records. *(:17 longer than the 45 or LP)*

1965 IKO IKO

(M) (2:02) Rhino 75766 Best Of New Orleans Rhythm & Blues Volume 2.

(M) (2:04) Rhino 75891 Wonder Women.

(M) (2:02) Rhino 70243 Greatest Movie Rock Hits.

(M) (2:00) Mango 539909 O.S.T. The Big Easy.

(M) (2:01) Time-Life 2CLR-23 Classic Rock - 1965: Blowin' Your Mind.

(M) (2:00) Collectables 2502 WCBS-FM History Of Rock - The 60's Part 3.

(M) (2:00) Collectables 4502 History Of Rock/The 60s Part Three.

(M) (2:02) K-Tel 3680 Mardi Gras Party Time!

(E) (1:54) Collectables 5742 Ad Libs & Friends. *(missing :04 of the introduction)*

(S) (2:04) Taragon 1029 Very Best Of Red Bird/Blue Cat Records.

D.J. JAZZY JEFF & THE FRESH PRINCE
1988 PARENTS JUST DON'T UNDERSTAND

(S) (5:12) RCA 61144 The RCA Records Label: The 1st Note In Black Music.

(S) (5:11) Jive 1091 He's The DJ, I'm The Rapper.

(S) (5:12) Priority 50982 Rap's Greatest Hits Volume Two.

(S) (5:10) Time-Life R988-20 Sounds Of The Eighties: The Late '80s Take Two.

D.J. JAZZY JEFF & THE FRESH PRINCE *(Continued)*
1988 A NIGHTMARE ON MY STREET
    (S) (4:50) Rhino 71777 Dr. Demento Presents: Spooky Tunes & Scary Melodies.
    (S) (4:53) Rhino 71778 Elvira Presents Monster Hits.
    (S) (4:54) Jive 1091 He's The DJ, I'm The Rapper.
    (S) (4:50) Rhino 72481 Haunted Hits.

1991 SUMMERTIME
    (S) (4:30) JCI 2714 Bust It 2.
    (S) (5:22) Tommy Boy 1053 MTV Party To Go Volume 2. *(remix; all tracks on this cd are segued together)*
    (S) (4:30) Jive 1392 Homebase.
    (S) (4:30) K-Tel 3751 History Of Rap Volume 3.
    (S) (4:29) Priority 50946 100% Party Hits Of The 90's Volume One.
    (S) (4:30) Cold Front 6246 Classic Club Mix - R&B Grooves. *(all selections on this cd are segued together)*
    (S) (4:28) Rhino 72917 Beats & Rhymes: Hip-Hop Of The 90's Part II.
    (S) (4:30) K-Tel 3847 90s Now Volume 1.
    (S) (4:30) Beast 53302 Summer Jammin'.

1991 RING MY BELL
    (S) (4:45) K-Tel 6102 Funk-Tastic Jams.
    (S) (4:44) Jive 1392 Homebase.

released as by JAZZY JEFF & FRESH PRINCE:
1993 BOOM! SHAKE THE ROOM
    (S) (6:31) Tommy Boy 1097 MTV Party To Go Volume 5. *(remix; all tracks on this cd are segued together)*
    (S) (3:46) Jive 41489 Code Red.
    (S) (4:29) Jive 41489 Code Red. *(remix)*
    (S) (3:46) Rhino 71916 Whats Up? Rap Hits Of The 90's.
    (S) (3:46) Hollywood 62121 Monday Night Football Jamz.
    (S) (3:45) K-Tel 3849 90s Now Volume 4.
    (S) (3:31) Priority 50935 100% Party Hits Of The 90's Volume Two. *(all selections on this cd are segued together)*

DJ KOOL
1997 LET ME CLEAR MY THROAT
    (S) (4:47) American 43105 Let Me Clear My Throat. *(all selections on this cd are segued together)*
    (S) (3:50) Tommy Boy 1214 ESPN Presents Jock Jams Volume 3. *(all selections on this cd are segued together)*

D-MOB introducing CATHY DENNIS
1990 C'MON AND GET MY LOVE
    (S) (3:47) Mercury 841583 O.S.T. She-Devil.
    (S) (3:48) Polydor 847267 Cathy Dennis - Move To This.
    (S) (3:51) FFRR/Polygram 828159 A Little Bit Of This, A Little Bit Of That.
    (S) (3:47) Rebound 314520357 World Of Dance - The 80's.
    (S) (3:48) Rebound 314520438 No. 1 Hits Of The 80's.
    (S) (3:47) Cold Front 3832 Club Mix - Women Of Dance Vol. 1.
    (S) (3:42) Cold Front 6284 More Of! Club Mix's Biggest Jams. *(all selections on this cd are segued together)*

D.N.A. featuring SUZANNE VEGA
1990 TOM'S DINER
    (S) (3:47) Foundation/Capitol 96427 Hearts Of Gold: The Pop Collection.
    (S) (5:27) A&M 5339 The A&M Underground Dance Compilation. *(remix)*
    (S) (5:07) Tommy Boy 1037 MTV Party To Go Volume 1. *(remix; all tracks on this cd are segued together)*
    (S) (3:47) A&M 5363 Tom's Album.
    (M) (2:08) A&M 5136 Suzanne Vega - Solitude Standing. *(a cappella version)*
    (M) (2:05) A&M 5363 Tom's Album. *(a cappella version)*
    (S) (3:47) Razor & Tie 4569 '90s Style.

CARL DOBKINS JR.
1959 MY HEART IS AN OPEN BOOK
    (M) (2:07) MCA 5936 Vintage Music Volumes 11 & 12.
    (M) (2:07) MCA 31209 Vintage Music Volume 12.

    (M) (2:07) Time-Life 2RNR-20 Rock 'N' Roll Era - 1959 Still Rockin'.
    (S) (2:06) Collectors' Choice 002 Teen Idols....For A Moment.
    (S) (2:06) Time-Life R857-16 The Heart Of Rock 'n' Roll The Late '50s.

1960 LUCKY DEVIL

DR. BUZZARD'S ORIGINAL "SAVANNAH" BAND
1977 WHISPERING/CHERCHEZ LA FEMME/SE SI BON
    (S) (5:45) RCA 7639 Dance! Dance! Dance! *(LP version)*
    (S) (5:46) RCA 9684 Nipper's Greatest Hits - The 70's. *(LP version)*
    (S) (5:51) RCA 1504 Dr. Buzzard's Original "Savannah" Band. *(the timing index on every track of this cd is out of synchronization with the music)*
    (S) (5:45) RCA 66903 Very Best Of. *(LP version)*
    (S) (5:44) Hip-O 40041 The Studio Collection Disco 54. *(LP version)*

DR. DRE
1993 NUTHIN' BUT A "G" THANG
    (S) (3:58) Interscope 57128 The Chronic.
    (S) (3:58) Death Row/Interscope 50611 The Chronic.
    (S) (3:58) Priority 53777 Rap G Style.
    (S) (3:40) Death Row/Interscope 50677 Death Row Greatest Hits. *(all songs on this cd are segued together)*
    (S) (4:33) Death Row/Interscope 50677 Death Row Greatest Hits. *(all songs on this cd are segued together; remixed)*

1993 DRE DAY
    (S) (4:51) Interscope 57128 The Chronic.
    (S) (4:51) Death Row/Interscope 50611 The Chronic.

1993 LET ME RIDE
    (S) (3:54) Tommy Boy 1097 MTV Party To Go Volume 5. *(remix; all tracks on this cd are segued together)*
    (S) (4:21) Interscope 57128 The Chronic.
    (S) (4:21) Death Row/Interscope 50611 The Chronic.
    (S) (6:01) Death Row/Interscope 50677 Death Row Greatest Hits. *(all songs on this cd are segued together; remix)*
    (S) (11:01) Priority 50927 Da Underground Sound: West Side Volume 2. *(all selections on this cd are segued together; remix)*

1995 KEEP THEIR HEADS RINGIN'
    (S) (5:05) Priority 53959 O.S.T. Friday.
    (S) (3:58) Death Row/Interscope 50677 Death Row Greatest Hits. *(all songs on this cd are segued together)*

released as by BLACKSTREET featuring DR. DRE:
1996 NO DIGGITY
    (S) (5:04) Interscope 90071 Blackstreet - Another Level.
    (S) (3:41) Tommy Boy 1214 Jock Jams Volume 3. *(all selections on this cd are segued together)*
    (S) (5:00) Tommy Boy 1234 MTV Party To Go '98. *(all songs on this cd are segued together)*
    (M) (4:54) Elektra 62088 Party Over Here '98. *(all tracks on this cd are segued together)*
    (S) (5:05) Priority 51021 Hip Hop Coast 2 Coast.

DR. HOOK and THE MEDICINE SHOW
1972 SYLVIA'S MOTHER
    (S) (3:39) Rhino 70928 Super Hits Of The 70's Volume 8. *(45 version)*
    (S) (3:46) Columbia 45047 Pop Classics Of The 70's. *(LP version)*
    (S) (3:49) Capitol 46620 Greatest Hits (And More). *(LP version)*
    (S) (3:49) Columbia 34147 Revisited. *(LP version)*
    (S) (3:48) Columbia 30898 Dr. Hook. *(LP version)*
    (S) (3:48) Razor & Tie 21640 Those Fabulous 70's. *(LP version)*
    (S) (3:37) Time-Life SUD-11 Superhits - 1972. *(45 version)*
    (S) (3:40) Time-Life SOD-22 Sounds Of The Seventies - Seventies Top Forty. *(45 version)*
    (S) (3:48) K-Tel 3181 Countryside. *(LP version)*
    (S) (3:49) Eclipse Music Group 64893 Rock 'n Roll Relix 1972-1973. *(LP version)*

(S) (3:49) Eclipse Music Group 64897 Rock 'n Roll Relix 1970-1979. *(LP version)*

(S) (3:37) Time-Life AM1-07 AM Gold - 1972. *(45 version)*

1973 THE COVER OF "ROLLING STONE"

(S) (2:53) Rhino 70930 Super Hits Of The 70's Volume 10.

(S) (2:51) Priority 8665 Southern Comfort/70's Greatest Hits Volume 4.

(S) (2:51) Capitol 46620 Greatest Hits (And More).

(S) (2:51) Columbia 34147 Revisited.

(S) (2:51) Columbia 40695 Sloppy Seconds.

(S) (2:52) Time-Life SUD-13 Superhits - 1973.

(S) (2:51) Risky Business 66871 Polyester Dreams/Greatest Hits Of The 70's.

(S) (2:52) Time-Life AM1-03 AM Gold - 1973.

(S) (2:52) K-Tel 3912 Superstars Greatest Hits Volume 1.

(S) (2:52) Time-Life R830-03 The Dr. Demento Collection: The Early '70s.

(S) (2:51) Priority 50962 70's Greatest Rock Hits Volume 7: Southern Rock.

released as by DR. HOOK:

1976 ONLY SIXTEEN

(S) (2:41) Curb 77356 70's Hits Volume 2.

(S) (2:43) Capitol 46620 Greatest Hits (And More).

(S) (2:43) Madacy Entertainment 1976 Rock On 1976.

1976 A LITTLE BIT MORE

(S) (3:14) EMI 90603 Rock Me Gently. *(LP version)*

(S) (2:53) Capitol 46620 Greatest Hits (And More). *(45 version)*

(M) (3:11) K-Tel 3181 Countryside. *(LP version)*

(S) (2:52) Rhino 72517 Mellow Rock Hits Of The 70's - Ventura Highway. *(45 version)*

(S) (2:53) Time-Life R834-14 Body Talk - Love And Tenderness. *(45 version)*

1978 SHARING THE NIGHT TOGETHER

(S) (2:54) Capitol 46620 Greatest Hits (And More).

(S) (2:52) Time-Life SOD-34 Sounds Of The Seventies - The Late 70's.

(S) (2:52) JCI 3131 1975 - Only Rock 'N Roll - 1979.

(S) (2:52) K-Tel 3163 Behind Closed Doors.

(S) (2:51) Madacy Entertainment 1978 Rock On 1978.

(S) (2:53) Capitol 38209 Pleasure And Pain.

(S) (2:52) K-Tel 3639 Dim The Lights - Soft Rock Hits Of The 70's.

(S) (2:52) Priority 50967 I Love Country Volume Two: Hits Of The 70's.

(S) (2:53) Time-Life R834-08 Body Talk - On My Mind.

(S) (2:52) Time-Life AM1-26 AM Gold - 1979.

1979 WHEN YOU'RE IN LOVE WITH A BEAUTIFUL WOMAN

(S) (2:56) Capitol 46620 Greatest Hits (And More).

(S) (2:54) Time-Life SOD-35 Sounds Of The Seventies - AM Nuggets.

(S) (2:55) K-Tel 3181 Countryside.

(S) (2:53) Madacy Entertainment 1979 Rock On 1979.

(S) (2:57) Capitol 38209 Pleasure And Pain.

(S) (2:56) Time-Life R840-01 Sounds Of The Seventies - Pop Nuggets: Late '70s.

(S) (2:54) K-Tel 3907 Starflight Vol. 2.

(S) (2:56) Time-Life R834-19 Body Talk - Always And Forever.

1980 BETTER LOVE NEXT TIME

(S) (3:00) Capitol 46620 Greatest Hits (And More).

(S) (3:00) Time-Life R834-17 Body Talk - Heart To Heart.

1980 SEXY EYES

(S) (2:57) Capitol 46620 Greatest Hits (And More).

(S) (2:57) Madacy Entertainment 1980 Rock On 1980.

(S) (2:57) Time-Life R988-18 Sounds Of The Eighties: The Early '80s Take Two.

(S) (2:57) Time-Life R834-15 Body Talk - Once In Lifetime.

1980 GIRLS CAN GET IT

1982 BABY MAKES HER BLUE JEANS TALK

DR. JOHN

1973 RIGHT PLACE WRONG TIME

(S) (2:50) Warner Special Products 27616 Classic Rock.

(S) (2:51) Atco 7018 In The Right Place.

(S) (2:51) Warner Special Products 27612 Ultimate Dr. John.

(S) (2:51) Sandstone 33001 Reelin' In The Years Volume 2.

(S) (2:51) DCC Compact Classics 063 Rock Of The 70's Volume 2.

(S) (2:51) Rhino 71450 Anthology.

(S) (2:49) Razor & Tie 22045 Those Funky 70's.

(M) (2:49) Time-Life SOD-06 Sounds Of The Seventies - 1973.

(S) (2:51) Medicine Label 24588 Even More Dazed And Confused.

(S) (2:51) Rhino 71924 Very Best Of.

(S) (2:51) MFSL 619 In The Right Place/Gumbo. *(gold disc)*

(S) (2:50) EMI 37350 Crescent City Soul: The Sound Of New Orleans 1947-1974.

(S) (2:51) Hollywood 62077 Official Party Album - ABC's Monday Night Football.

(S) (2:51) Rhino 72964 Ultimate '70s R&B Smashes!

BILL DOGGETT

1956 HONKY TONK (PARTS 1 & 2)

(M) (2:32) Time-Life 2RNR-14 Rock 'N' Roll Era - 1956. *(Part 2)*

(M) (2:32) Time-Life RHD-05 Rhythm & Blues - 1956. *(Part 2)*

(M) (2:32) Time-Life R962-03 History Of Rock 'N' Roll: Rock 'N' Roll Classics 1954-1956. *(Part 2)*

(E) (3:02) Original Sound 8856 Oldies But Goodies Vol. 6. *(this compact disc uses the "Waring - fds" noise reduction process; Part 1)*

(E) (3:02) Original Sound 2221 Oldies But Goodies Volumes 1,4,6,8 and 10 Box Set. *(this box set uses the "Waring - fds" noise reduction process; Part 1)*

(E) (3:02) Original Sound 2500 Oldies But Goodies Volumes 1-15 Box Set. *(this box set uses the "Waring - fds" noise reduction process; Part 1)*

(E) (2:32) Original Sound 8856 Oldies But Goodies Vol. 6. *(this compact disc uses the "Waring - fds" noise reduction process; Part 2)*

(E) (2:32) Original Sound 2221 Oldies But Goodies Volumes 1,4,6,8 and 10 Box Set. *(this box set uses the "Waring - fds" noise reduction process; Part 2)*

(E) (2:32) Original Sound 2500 Oldies But Goodies Volumes 1-15 Box Set. *(this box set uses the "Waring - fds" noise reduction process; Part 2)*

(E) (2:32) Original Sound CDGO-6 Golden Oldies Volume. 6. *(Part 2)*

(E) (2:33) Original Sound 8881 Twenty-One #1 Hits. *(this compact disc uses the "Waring - fds" noise reduction process; Part 2)*

(M) (3:06) Motown 6763 Rites Of Rhythm & Blues Volume 2. *(Part 1)*

(S) (5:16) Wild Dog/Ichiban 9104 Beach Blast. *(live)*

(M) (3:05) King 7002 King R&B Box Set. *(Part 1)*

(M) (2:34) King 7002 King R&B Box Set. *(Part 2)*

(M) (3:10) King 1407 Original Blues. *(Part 1)*

(M) (2:25) King 778 Many Moods Of. *(rerecorded; vocal version)*

(M) (3:01) King 5009 All His Hits. *(Part 1)*

(M) (2:32) JCI 3165 #1 Radio Hits 1955 - Only Rock 'n Roll - 1959. *(Part 2)*

(M) (2:32) Time-Life R838-24 Solid Gold Soul 1956. *(Part 2)*

1956 SLOW WALK

(M) (2:31) King 1407 Original Blues.

THOMAS DOLBY

1983 SHE BLINDED ME WITH SCIENCE
(dj copies of this 45 ran (3:40) and (5:09);
commercial copies were all (5:09))

(S) (3:40) EMI 81417 Living In Oblivion: The 80's Greatest Hits Volume One.

(S) (5:06) Priority 53705 Rock Of The 80's Volume 2.

(S) (5:07) K-Tel 3262 The 80's Video Stars.

(S) (3:40) Rhino 71701 New Wave Hits Of The 80's Vol. 8.

(S) (5:06) Rhino 71834 Classic MTV: Class Of 1983.

THOMAS DOLBY (Continued)

(S) (3:40) Capitol 27642 Best Of/Retrospectacle.
(S) (5:06) Time-Life R988-03 Sounds Of The Eighties: 1983.
(S) (3:39) Rebound 314520354 World Of Dance: New Wave - The 80's.
(S) (5:06) Madacy Entertainment 1983 Rock On 1983.
(S) (3:39) Hip-O 40023 Smash Alternatives - 14 Classic New Wave Hits.
(S) (3:39) Rebound 314520442 The Roots Of Rock: 80's New Wave.
(S) (5:07) Hollywood 62123 More Music From The Motion Picture "Romy And Michele's High School Reunion".
(S) (4:19) Arista 18985 Ultimate New Wave Party 1998. *(all selections on this cd are segued together)*

MICKEY DOLENZ and PETER TORK of THE MONKEES
(see also THE MONKEES)
1986 THAT WAS THEN, THIS IS NOW

(S) (4:00) Arista 8432 Then & Now...The Best Of The Monkees.
(S) (4:00) Rhino 70566 Monkees - Listen To The Band.
(S) (4:00) Rhino 72190 Monkees - Greatest Hits.
(S) (4:01) Rhino 75269 Anthology.

DOMINO
1994 GETTO JAM

(S) (4:48) Tommy Boy 1109 MTV Party To Go Volume 6. *(all tracks on this cd are segued together; remix)*
(S) (4:17) OutBurst/Chaos 57701 Domino.
(S) (4:18) Def Jam 314523848 Def Jam Music Group 10th Year Anniversary.
(S) (4:17) Priority 50927 Da Underground Sound: West Side Volume 2. *(all selections on this cd are segued together)*
(S) (4:17) Def Jam 314536377 Def Jam's Greatest Hits.

1994 SWEET POTATOE PIE

(S) (3:29) OutBurst/Chaos 57701 Domino.
(S) (3:59) Def Jam 314523848 Def Jam Music Group 10th Year Anniversary.

FATS DOMINO
1955 AIN'T THAT A SHAME

(M) (2:31) Rhino 70598 Billboard's Top Rock & Roll Hits Of 1955.
(M) (2:32) EMI 92808 My Blue Heaven - The Best Of.
(M) (2:24) JCI 3202 Rockin' Fifties.
(M) (2:24) EMI 46581 Best Of.
(S) (2:32) MCA 6170 His Greatest Hits. *(all selections on this cd are recorded live)*
(M) (2:23) EMI 96784 They Call Me The Fat Man.
(S) (2:21) Rhino/Tomato 70391 Antoine "Fats" Domino. *(all selections on this cd are live recordings)*
(M) (2:24) Pair 1123 Whole Lotta Rock 'N' Roll.
(M) (2:23) EMI 80184 Genius Of Dave Bartholomew.
(S) (2:28) Special Music 4817 Greatest Hits. *(all selections on this cd are recorded live)*
(M) (2:24) MCA 8001 O.S.T. American Graffiti.
(M) (2:24) Time-Life 2RNR-08 Rock 'N' Roll Era - 1954-1955.
(M) (2:23) Time-Life RHD-17 Rhythm & Blues - 1955.
(M) (2:25) EMI 37350 Crescent City Soul: The Sound Of New Orleans 1947-1974.
(M) (2:25) EMI 37355 Highlights From Crescent City Soul: The Sound Of New Orleans 1947-1974.
(M) (2:23) EMI 52326 25 Classic Performances.
(M) (2:24) EMI 55905 Greatest Hits.
(M) (2:32) Right Stuff 53319 Hot Rod Rock Volume 4: Hot Rod Rebels.

1956 I'M IN LOVE AGAIN

(M) (1:56) Rhino 70599 Billboard's Top Rock & Roll Hits Of 1956.
(M) (2:00) Sire 26617 Music From The Film A Rage In Harlem.
(M) (1:56) EMI 92808 My Blue Heaven - The Best Of.
(M) (2:00) EMI 46581 Best Of.

(M) (1:52) EMI 96784 They Call Me The Fat Man.
(S) (3:12) MCA 6170 His Greatest Hits. *(all selections on this cd are recorded live)*
(S) (3:31) Rhino/Tomato 70391 Antoine "Fats" Domino. *(all selections on this cd are live recordings)*
(M) (1:56) Pair 1123 Whole Lotta Rock 'N' Roll.
(S) (3:11) Special Music 4817 Greatest Hits. *(all selections on this cd are recorded live)*
(M) (2:00) Curb 77637 All Time Greatest Hits Of Rock 'N' Roll Volume 3.
(M) (2:00) Time-Life 2RNR-14 Rock 'N' Roll Era - 1956.
(M) (1:55) Time-Life RHD-05 Rhythm & Blues - 1956.
(M) (1:59) Original Sound 8883 21 Legendary Superstars.
(M) (1:56) Rhino 71806 The R&B Box: Thirty Years Of Rhythm & Blues.
(M) (1:54) EMI 37350 Crescent City Soul: The Sound Of New Orleans 1947-1974.
(M) (1:51) EMI 52326 25 Classic Performances.
(M) (2:00) JCI 3165 #1 Radio Hits 1955 - Only Rock 'n Roll - 1959.
(M) (2:00) EMI 55905 Greatest Hits.
(M) (1:55) Time-Life R838-24 Solid Gold Soul 1956.

1956 MY BLUE HEAVEN

(M) (2:04) Time-Life 2RNR-23 The Rock 'N' Roll Era - 1956: Still Rockin'.
(M) (2:06) EMI 96784 They Call Me The Fat Man.
(M) (2:04) Original Sound 8860 Oldies But Goodies Vol. 10. *(this compact disc uses the "Waring - fds" noise reduction process)*
(M) (2:04) Original Sound 2221 Oldies But Goodies Volumes 1,4,6,8 and 10 Box Set. *(this box set uses the "Waring - fds" noise reduction process)*
(M) (2:04) Original Sound 2500 Oldies But Goodies Volumes 1-15 Box Set. *(this box set uses the "Waring - fds" noise reduction process)*
(M) (2:04) Curb 77378 All-Time Greatest Hits.
(M) (2:07) Pair 1123 Whole Lotta Rock 'N' Roll.
(M) (2:07) EMI 92808 My Blue Heaven - The Best Of.
(M) (2:04) EMI 46581 Best Of.
(M) (2:05) EMI 52326 25 Classic Performances.

1956 WHEN MY DREAMBOAT COMES HOME

(M) (2:19) EMI 92808 My Blue Heaven - The Best Of.
(M) (2:22) EMI 46581 Best Of.
(M) (2:17) EMI 96784 They Call Me The Fat Man.
(M) (2:20) Pair 1123 Whole Lotta Rock 'N' Roll.

1956 BLUEBERRY HILL

(M) (2:20) Rhino 70642 Billboard's Top R&B Hits Of 1956.
(M) (2:18) JCI 3204 Heart & Soul Fifties.
(M) (2:19) Original Sound 8852 Oldies But Goodies Vol. 2. *(this compact disc uses the "Waring - fds" noise reduction process)*
(M) (2:19) Original Sound 2223 Oldies But Goodies Volumes 2,7,9,12 and 13 Box Set. *(this box set uses the "Waring - fds" noise reduction process)*
(M) (2:19) Original Sound 2500 Oldies But Goodies Volumes 1-15 Box Set. *(this box set uses the "Waring - fds" noise reduction process)*
(M) (2:18) EMI 96268 24 Greatest Hits Of All Time.
(M) (2:18) Curb 77354 50's Hits Volume 1.
(M) (2:18) EMI 92808 My Blue Heaven - The Best Of.
(M) (2:19) EMI 46581 Best Of.
(M) (2:18) Curb 77378 All Time Greatest Hits.
(M) (2:20) EMI 96784 They Call Me The Fat Man.
(M) (2:18) Curb 77525 Greatest Hits Of Rock 'N' Roll Volume 2.
(S) (2:40) MCA 6170 His Greatest Hits. *(all selections on this cd are recorded live)*
(S) (2:34) Rhino/Tomato 70391 Antoine "Fats" Domino. *(all selections on this cd are live recordings)*
(M) (2:19) Pair 1123 Whole Lotta Rock 'N' Roll.
(E) (3:01) Special Music 4817 Greatest Hits. *(all selections on this cd are recorded live)*
(M) (2:18) Time-Life 2RNR-14 Rock 'N' Roll Era - 1956.
(M) (2:20) Time-Life RHD-05 Rhythm & Blues - 1956.
(M) (2:20) Time-Life R962-03 History Of Rock 'N' Roll: Rock 'N' Roll Classics 1954-1956.
(M) (2:18) MCA 11392 O.S.T. 12 Monkeys.

(M) (2:19) EMI 52326 25 Classic Performances.
(M) (2:18) Nick At Nite/550 Music/Epic 67768 Fonzie's Make Out Music.
(M) (2:18) EMI 55905 Greatest Hits.
(M) (2:19) Time-Life R857-07 The Heart Of Rock 'n' Roll 1956.
(M) (2:18) K-Tel 4018 Forefathers Of Rock.
(S) (2:24) Jewel 5057 Rockin' 50's & 60's. *(live; track lineup on the cd jacket is incorrect)*
(M) (2:19) Time-Life R838-24 Solid Gold Soul 1956.
(M) (2:17) Collectables 1514 and 2514 The Anniversary Album - The 50's.

1957 BLUE MONDAY
(M) (2:14) Rhino 70643 Billboard's Top R&B Hits Of 1957.
(M) (2:15) EMI 92808 My Blue Heaven - The Best Of.
(M) (2:14) EMI 46581 Best Of.
(M) (2:14) Curb 77378 All Time Greatest Hits.
(M) (2:14) EMI 96784 They Call Me The Fat Man.
(S) (2:33) MCA 6170 His Greatest Hits. *(all selections on this cd are recorded live)*
(S) (2:40) Rhino/Tomato 70391 Antoine "Fats" Domino. *(all selections on this cd are live recordings)*
(S) (2:23) Special Music 4817 Greatest Hits. *(all selections on this cd are recorded live)*
(M) (2:14) Time-Life 2RNR-17 Rock 'N' Roll Era - 1957 Still Rockin'.
(M) (2:14) Nouveau 1060 O.S.T. This Boy's Life.
(M) (2:14) EMI 52326 25 Classic Performances.

1957 WHAT'S THE REASON I'M NOT PLEASING YOU
(M) (2:01) EMI 96784 They Call Me The Fat Man.

1957 I'M WALKIN'
(M) (2:08) Rhino 70643 Billboard's Top R&B Hits Of 1957.
(M) (2:11) EMI 92808 My Blue Heaven - The Best Of.
(M) (2:02) EMI 46581 Best Of.
(M) (2:02) Curb 77378 All Time Greatest Hits.
(M) (2:11) EMI 96784 They Call Me The Fat Man.
(S) (2:44) MCA 6170 His Greatest Hits. *(all selections on this cd are recorded live)*
(M) (2:11) Capitol 98139 Spring Break Volume 2.
(S) (2:53) Rhino/Tomato 70391 Antoine "Fats" Domino. *(all selections on this cd are live recordings)*
(M) (2:07) Rhino 71547 Let There Be Drums Volume 1: The 50's.
(M) (2:07) Time-Life 2RNR-01 Rock 'N' Roll Era - 1957. *(original pressings of this song on this cd were (E))*
(M) (2:05) Time-Life RHD-08 Rhythm & Blues - 1957.
(M) (2:08) Motown 6763 Rites Of Rhythm & Blues Volume 2.
(M) (2:11) K-Tel 3007 50's Sock Hop.
(M) (2:01) EMI 37350 Crescent City Soul: The Sound Of New Orleans 1947-1974.
(M) (2:10) EMI 37356 That's Fats! - A Tribute To Fats Domino.
(M) (2:00) EMI 37355 Highlights From Crescent City Soul: The Sound Of New Orleans 1947-1974.
(M) (2:10) EMI 52326 25 Classic Performances.
(M) (2:01) Nick At Nite/550 Music/Epic 67770 Happy Days Jukebox.
(E) (2:01) JCI 3188 1955 - Only Dance - 1959.
(M) (2:01) EMI 55905 Greatest Hits.
(M) (2:05) Time-Life R838-23 Solid Gold Soul 1957.

1957 VALLEY OF TEARS
(M) (2:05) EMI 92808 My Blue Heaven - The Best Of. *(includes :09 of studio talk)*
(M) (1:51) EMI 46581 Best Of.
(M) (1:51) EMI 96784 They Call Me The Fat Man.
(S) (2:42) Rhino/Tomato 70391 Antoine "Fats" Domino. *(all selections on this cd are live recordings)*
(M) (1:52) EMI 80184 Genius Of Dave Bartholomew.
(S) (1:54) EMI 52326 25 Classic Performances.
(M) (1:52) EMI 55905 Greatest Hits.

1957 IT'S YOU I LOVE
(M) (2:01) EMI 96784 They Call Me The Fat Man.
(S) (2:05) EMI 52326 25 Classic Performances.
(M) (2:01) EMI 55905 Greatest Hits.

1957 WHEN I SEE YOU
(M) (2:10) EMI 96784 They Call Me The Fat Man.

1957 WAIT AND SEE
(M) (1:53) EMI 96784 They Call Me The Fat Man.
(S) (1:56) EMI 52326 25 Classic Performances.

1957 I WANT YOU TO KNOW
(M) (1:58) EMI 96784 They Call Me The Fat Man.

1958 THE BIG BEAT
(M) (1:57) EMI 96784 They Call Me The Fat Man.
(M) (2:01) EMI 92808 My Blue Heaven - The Best Of.
(S) (1:59) EMI 52326 25 Classic Performances.

1958 SICK AND TIRED
(M) (2:36) EMI 96784 They Call Me The Fat Man.
(S) (2:32) EMI 52326 25 Classic Performances.

1959 WHOLE LOTTA LOVING
(M) (1:38) Rhino 70644 Billboard's Top R&B Hits Of 1958.
(M) (1:39) Elektra 60107 O.S.T. Diner.
(M) (1:38) EMI 92808 My Blue Heaven - The Best Of.
(M) (1:37) EMI 46581 Best Of.
(M) (1:37) Curb 77323 All Time Greatest Hits Of Rock 'N' Roll.
(M) (1:37) Curb 77378 All Time Greatest Hits.
(M) (1:37) EMI 96784 They Call Me The Fat Man.
(S) (1:31) MCA 6170 His Greatest Hits. *(all selections on this cd are recorded live)*
(M) (1:37) Pair 1123 Whole Lotta Rock 'N' Roll.
(M) (1:00) Special Music 4817 Greatest Hits. *(all selections on this cd are recorded live)*
(M) (1:37) Time-Life 2RNR-21 Rock 'N' Roll Era - 1958 Still Rockin'.
(M) (1:38) Time-Life R962-01 History Of Rock 'N' Roll: Rock 'N' Roll Classics 1957-1959.
(M) (1:35) EMI 52326 25 Classic Performances.
(M) (1:37) EMI 55905 Greatest Hits.

1959 I'M READY
(M) (2:03) EMI 92808 My Blue Heaven - The Best Of.
(E) (2:03) EMI 90614 Non Stop Party Rock.
(M) (2:02) Rhino 70794 KFOG Presents M. Dung's Idiot Show.
(M) (2:02) Curb 77378 All Time Greatest Hits.
(M) (2:02) EMI 96784 They Call Me The Fat Man.
(S) (1:53) MCA 6170 His Greatest Hits. *(all selections on this cd are recorded live)*
(M) (2:02) Pair 1123 Whole Lotta Rock 'N' Roll.
(S) (1:52) Special Music 4817 Greatest Hits. *(all selections on this cd are recorded live)*
(M) (2:02) Time-Life 2RNR-24 Rock 'N' Roll Era - The 50's Keep On Rockin'.
(M) (2:01) EMI 55905 Greatest Hits.

1959 I WANT TO WALK YOU HOME
(S) (2:16) Rhino 70645 Billboard's Top R&B Hits Of 1959.
(S) (2:18) EMI 92808 My Blue Heaven - The Best Of.
(M) (2:20) EMI 46581 Best Of.
(M) (2:20) Curb 77378 All Time Greatest Hits.
(S) (2:17) EMI 96784 They Call Me The Fat Man.
(S) (2:34) MCA 6170 His Greatest Hits. *(all selections on this cd are recorded live)*
(S) (2:38) Rhino/Tomato 70391 Antoine "Fats" Domino. *(all selections on this cd are live recordings)*
(M) (2:26) Special Music 4817 Greatest Hits. *(all selections on this cd are recorded live)*
(M) (2:19) Time-Life 2RNR-13 Rock 'N' Roll Era - 1959.
(S) (2:14) Time-Life RHD-03 Rhythm & Blues - 1959.
(S) (2:15) Time-Life R857-01 The Heart Of Rock 'n' Roll - 1959.
(M) (2:19) EMI 37350 Crescent City Soul: The Sound Of New Orleans 1947-1974.
(S) (2:17) EMI 52326 25 Classic Performances.
(M) (2:17) EMI 55905 Greatest Hits.
(S) (2:14) Time-Life R838-21 Solid Gold Soul 1959.

1959 I'M GONNA BE A WHEEL SOME DAY
(M) (2:01) EMI 92808 My Blue Heaven - The Best Of.
(M) (2:01) EMI 46581 Best Of.
(M) (2:01) EMI 96784 They Call Me The Fat Man.
(S) (2:13) MCA 6170 His Greatest Hits. *(all selections on this cd are recorded live)*
(S) (2:25) Rhino/Tomato 70391 Antoine "Fats" Domino. *(all selections on this cd are live recordings)*

FATS DOMINO *(Continued)*

- (M) (2:17) Special Music 4817 Greatest Hits. *(all selections on this cd are recorded live)*
- (M) (2:01) Time-Life 2RNR-28 Rock 'N' Roll Era - The 50's Rave On.

1959 BE MY GUEST
- (S) (2:14) EMI 92808 My Blue Heaven - The Best Of.
- (M) (1:59) EMI 46581 Best Of.
- (M) (1:59) Curb 77378 All Time Greatest Hits.
- (S) (2:13) EMI 96784 They Call Me The Fat Man.
- (S) (1:54) Rhino/Tomato 70391 Antoine "Fats" Domino. *(all selections on this cd are live recordings)*
- (M) (2:00) Time-Life 2RNR-33 Rock 'N' Roll Era - The 50's Last Dance.

1960 COUNTRY BOY
- (S) (2:14) EMI 96784 They Call Me The Fat Man.

1960 WALKING TO NEW ORLEANS
- (S) (1:59) Rhino 70646 Billboard's Top R&B Hits Of 1960.
- (S) (1:58) EMI 92808 My Blue Heaven - The Best Of.
- (M) (1:54) EMI 46581 Best Of.
- (M) (1:54) Curb 77378 All Time Greatest Hits.
- (S) (1:58) EMI 96784 They Call Me The Fat Man.
- (S) (2:21) MCA 6170 His Greatest Hits. *(all selections on this cd are recorded live)*
- (S) (3:07) Rhino/Tomato 70391 Antoine "Fats" Domino. *(all selections on this cd are live recordings)*
- (S) (1:57) EMI 80184 Genius Of Dave Bartholomew. *(missing some overdubs; truncated fade)*
- (S) (2:21) Ripete 2199 Walkin' To New Orleans. *(live)*
- (S) (1:57) Time-Life 2RNR-11 Rock 'N' Roll Era - 1960. *(original pressings of this song on this cd were (M))*
- (S) (1:56) Time-Life RHD-15 Rhythm & Blues - 1960.
- (S) (1:58) Time-Life R857-02 The Heart Of Rock 'n' Roll - 1960.
- (M) (1:54) EMI 37350 Crescent City Soul: The Sound Of New Orleans 1947-1974.
- (M) (1:54) EMI 37355 Highlights From Crescent City Soul: The Sound Of New Orleans 1947-1974.
- (S) (1:55) JCI 3166 #1 Radio Hits 1960 - Only Rock 'n Roll - 1964.
- (M) (1:55) EMI 55905 Greatest Hits.
- (S) (1:55) Time-Life R838-20 Solid Gold Soul 1960.

1960 DON'T COME KNOCKIN'
- (S) (1:55) EMI 96784 They Call Me The Fat Man.
- (M) (1:55) Pair 1123 Whole Lotta Rock 'N' Roll.

1960 THREE NIGHTS A WEEK
- (S) (1:43) EMI 96784 They Call Me The Fat Man.
- (M) (1:43) Pair 1123 Whole Lotta Rock 'N' Roll.
- (S) (1:43) EMI 52326 25 Classic Performances.

1960 MY GIRL JOSEPHINE
- (M) (2:00) Curb 77378 All Time Greatest Hits.
- (S) (2:03) EMI 96784 They Call Me The Fat Man.
- (S) (1:51) MCA 6170 His Greatest Hits. *(all selections on this cd are recorded live)*
- (M) (2:00) Pair 1123 Whole Lotta Rock 'N' Roll.
- (S) (2:02) EMI 81128 Rock Is Dead But It Won't Lie Down.
- (M) (1:58) Time-Life 2RNR-22 Rock 'N' Roll Era - 1960 Still Rockin'.
- (S) (2:01) EMI 52326 25 Classic Performances.

1961 WHAT A PRICE
- (S) (2:21) EMI 96784 They Call Me The Fat Man.
- (S) (2:12) Rhino/Tomato 70391 Antoine "Fats" Domino. *(all selections on this cd are live recordings)*
- (S) (2:20) EMI 52326 25 Classic Performances.

1961 AIN'T THAT JUST LIKE A WOMAN
- (S) (2:39) EMI 96784 They Call Me The Fat Man.

1961 SHU RAH
- (S) (1:41) EMI 96784 They Call Me The Fat Man.

1961 IT KEEPS RAININ'
- (S) (2:44) EMI 96784 They Call Me The Fat Man.
- (S) (2:42) EMI 37350 Crescent City Soul: The Sound Of New Orleans 1947-1974.

1961 LET THE FOUR WINDS BLOW
- (S) (2:15) Rhino 70647 Billboard's Top R&B Hits Of 1961. *(:15 longer than the 45 length)*
- (S) (2:15) EMI 92808 My Blue Heaven EMI 52326 25 Classic Performances.- The Best Of. *(:15 longer than the 45 length)*

- (M) (2:00) EMI 46581 Best Of.
- (M) (2:00) Curb 77378 All Time Greatest Hits.
- (S) (2:15) EMI 96784 They Call Me The Fat Man. *(:15 longer than the 45 length)*
- (S) (4:23) MCA 6170 His Greatest Hits. *(all selections on this cd are recorded live)*
- (S) (6:49) Rhino/Tomato 70391 Antoine "Fats" Domino. *(all selections on this cd are live recordings)*
- (M) (2:01) Pair 1123 Whole Lotta Rock 'N' Roll.
- (E) (2:38) Special Music 4817 Greatest Hits. *(all selections on this cd are recorded live)*
- (M) (2:01) Time-Life 2RNR-18 Rock 'N' Roll Era - 1961 Still Rockin'.

1961 WHAT A PARTY
- (S) (1:57) EMI 92808 My Blue Heaven - The Best Of.
- (S) (1:57) EMI 96784 They Call Me The Fat Man.

1962 JAMBALAYA (ON THE BAYOU)
- (M) (2:21) Enigma 73531 O.S.T. Scandal.
- (M) (2:20) EMI 96784 They Call Me The Fat Man.
- (M) (2:20) Rhino 70587 New Orleans Party Classics.
- (S) (4:37) MCA 6170 His Greatest Hits. *(all selections on this cd are recorded live)*
- (S) (8:57) Rhino/Tomato 70391 Antoine "Fats" Domino. *(all selections on this cd are live recordings)*
- (M) (2:22) Pair 1123 Whole Lotta Rock 'N' Roll.
- (S) (3:21) Special Music 4817 Greatest Hits. *(all selections on this cd are recorded live)*
- (M) (2:20) EMI 52326 25 Classic Performances.

1962 YOU WIN AGAIN
- (S) (2:12) EMI 96784 They Call Me The Fat Man.
- (E) (2:12) Pair 1123 Whole Lotta Rock 'N' Roll.
- (S) (2:11) EMI 52326 25 Classic Performances.

ANDRU DONALDS
1995 MISHALE
- (S) (3:59) Metro Blue 28065 Andru Donalds.

BO DONALDSON and THE HEYWOODS
1974 BILLY, DON'T BE A HERO
(45 length is (3:22); LP length is (3:38))
- (S) (3:38) Rhino 70760 Super Hits Of The 70's Volume 13.
- (S) (3:22) Razor & Tie 21640 Those Fabulous 70's.
- (S) (3:37) Time-Life SOD-31 Sounds Of The Seventies - AM Top Twenty.
- (S) (3:23) K-Tel 3211 70's Teen Heart-Throbs.
- (S) (3:23) MCA Special Products 20949 Rockin' 70's Volume 2.
- (S) (3:40) Varese Sarabande 5724 Best Of.
- (S) (3:23) MCA Special Products 20981 Bubble Gum Classics.
- (S) (3:37) Time-Life AM1-21 AM Gold - 1974.
- (S) (3:38) Rhino 75233 '70s Party (Killers) Classics.

1974 WHO DO YOU THINK YOU ARE
- (S) (3:15) Rhino 70760 Super Hits Of The 70's Volume 13. *(LP length)*
- (S) (2:59) MCA Special Products 22105 Greatest Classic Rock Hits. *(45 length)*
- (S) (3:18) Varese Sarabande 5724 Best Of. *(LP length)*

DON & JUAN
1962 WHAT'S YOUR NAME
- (M) (2:12) Time-Life 2RNR-02 Rock 'N' Roll Era - 1962.
- (M) (2:10) Collectables 2502 WCBS-FM History Of Rock - The 60's Part 3.
- (M) (2:10) Collectables 4502 History Of Rock/The 60s Part Three.
- (M) (2:12) Collectables 2606 WCBS-FM For Lovers Only Vol. 2.
- (E) (2:11) Original Sound 8859 Oldies But Goodies Vol. 9. *(this compact disc uses the "Waring - fds" noise reduction process)*
- (M) (2:11) Original Sound 8859r Oldies But Goodies Vol. 9. *(remastered edition)*
- (M) (2:11) Original Sound 2223 Oldies But Goodies Volumes 2,7,9,12 and 13 Box Set. *(Volumes 2, 7 and 12 of this box set use the "Waring - fds" noise reduction process)*

(M)	(2:11)	Original Sound 2500 Oldies But Goodies Volumes 1-15 Box Set. *(most volumes in this box set use the "Waring - fds" noise reduction process)*
(E)	(2:09)	Original Sound CDGO-12 Golden Oldies Volume. 12.
(M)	(2:12)	Time-Life R102-17 Lost Treasures Of Rock 'N' Roll.
(M)	(2:12)	LaserLight 12322 Greatest Hit Singles Collection.
(M)	(2:12)	Collectables 5519 What's Your Name.
(M)	(2:12)	Thump 7060 Low Rider Oldies Volume 6.
(M)	(2:12)	Rhino 72507 Doo Wop Box II.
(M)	(2:12)	JCI 3164 Eighteen Soulful Ballads.
(M)	(2:12)	Time-Life R857-06 The Heart Of Rock 'n' Roll 1962.
(M)	(2:13)	Right Stuff 53320 Hot Rod Rock Volume 5: Back Seat Movers.

LONNIE DONEGAN and HIS SKIFFLE GROUP
1956 ROCK ISLAND LINE
(M)	(2:26)	Time-Life HPD-36 Your Hit Parade - The 50's Pop Revival.
(M)	(2:26)	Rhino 72160 Troubadours Of British Folk Volume 1.
(M)	(2:26)	Time-Life R132-22 Treasury Of Folk Music Volume One.

1961 DOES YOUR CHEWING GUM LOSE ITS FLAVOR (ON THE BEDPOST OVERNIGHT)
(M)	(2:28)	Rhino 75768 Dr. Demento Presents.
(M)	(2:27)	Rhino 70743 Dr. Demento 20th Anniversary Collection.
(S)	(3:31)	K-Tel 3036 Silly Songs. *(rerecording)*
(M)	(2:26)	Time-Life HPD-35 Your Hit Parade - The Fun-Times 50's & 60's.
(S)	(3:27)	K-Tel 3409 Funniest Food Songs. *(rerecording)*
(M)	(2:27)	Music For Little People 42581 A Child's Celebration Of Rock 'N' Roll.

RAL DONNER
1961 GIRL OF MY BEST FRIEND
(M)	(2:12)	Time-Life 2RNR-42 Rock 'N' Roll Era - The 60's Sock Hop.
(M)	(2:14)	Collectables 5627 Golden Classics.

1961 YOU DON'T KNOW WHAT YOU'VE GOT (UNTIL YOU LOSE IT)
(S)	(2:10)	Time-Life 2RNR-04 Rock 'N' Roll Era - 1961. *(original pressings of this song on this cd were (M))*
(S)	(2:11)	Time-Life SUD-15 Superhits - The Early 60's.
(S)	(2:10)	Time-Life R102-17 Lost Treasures Of Rock 'N' Roll.
(S)	(2:11)	Time-Life R857-10 The Heart Of Rock 'n' Roll 1960-1961.
(S)	(2:13)	Collectables 5627 Golden Classics.
(S)	(2:11)	Time-Life AM1-19 AM Gold - The Early '60s.

1961 PLEASE DON'T GO
(S)	(2:14)	Collectables 5627 Golden Classics.

1962 SHE'S EVERYTHING (I WANTED YOU TO BE)
(S)	(2:28)	Collectables 5627 Golden Classics.

DONOVAN
1965 CATCH THE WIND
(M)	(2:16)	Rhino 70320 History Of British Rock Volume 2. *(45 version)*
(M)	(2:16)	Rhino 72022 History Of British Rock Box Set. *(45 version)*
(M)	(2:16)	Rhino 72008 History Of British Rock Volumes 1-4 Box Set. *(45 version)*
(M)	(2:53)	Garland 016 Catch The Wind. *(LP version)*
(M)	(2:16)	Rhino 70262 Troubadours Of The Folk Era Volume 1. *(45 version)*
(S)	(5:01)	Epic 26439 Greatest Hits. *(rerecording)*
(M)	(2:53)	Epic/Legacy 46986 Troubadour. *(LP version)*
(M)	(2:53)	Sandstone 33077 Catch The Wind. *(LP version)*
(M)	(2:15)	JCI 3107 British Sixties. *(45 version)*
(M)	(2:15)	Time-Life 2CLR-17 Classic Rock - Rock Renaissance. *(45 version)*
(M)	(2:15)	Time-Life R962-02 History Of Rock 'N' Roll: Folk Rock 1964-1967. *(45 version)*

(M)	(2:15)	Time-Life R103-33 Singers & Songwriters. *(45 version)*
(M)	(2:52)	K-Tel 3438 Best Of Folk Rock. *(LP version)*
(M)	(2:16)	LaserLight 12312 and 15936 The Wonder Years - Good Times, Good Friends. *(45 version)*
(M)	(2:16)	Time-Life R132-22 Treasury Of Folk Music Volume One. *(45 version)*

1966 SUNSHINE SUPERMAN
(45 and LP length is (3:15))
(S)	(3:29)	Rhino 70323 History Of British Rock Volume 5.
(S)	(3:29)	Rhino 72022 History Of British Rock Box Set.
(M)	(3:15)	Epic 26217 Sunshine Superman.
(S)	(4:31)	Epic 26439 Greatest Hits. *(this version first appeared on Donovan's "Greatest Hits" vinyl LP)*
(M)	(3:12)	Epic/Legacy 46986 Troubadour.
(S)	(4:31)	Time-Life 2CLR-02 Classic Rock - 1966. *(this version first appeared on Donovan's "Greatest Hits" vinyl LP)*
(S)	(3:21)	Time-Life R962-07 History Of Rock 'N' Roll: The British Invasion 1964-1966.
(S)	(3:29)	Rhino 71936 Billboard Top Pop Hits, 1966.
(M)	(3:14)	Nick At Nite/550 Music 63436 Patio Pool Party.

1966 MELLOW YELLOW
(M)	(3:41)	Rhino 70325 History Of British Rock Volume 7.
(M)	(3:41)	Rhino 72022 History Of British Rock Box Set.
(E)	(3:38)	Epic 26439 Greatest Hits.
(M)	(3:39)	Epic/Legacy 46986 Troubadour.
(M)	(3:42)	Time-Life 2CLR-07 Classic Rock - 1966: The Beat Goes On.

1967 EPISTLE TO DIPPY
(S)	(3:09)	Epic 26439 Greatest Hits.
(M)	(3:07)	Epic/Legacy 46986 Troubadour.
(M)	(3:08)	Rhino 71066 Summer Of Love Volume 2.

1967 THERE IS A MOUNTAIN
(S)	(2:33)	Epic 26439 Greatest Hits.
(M)	(2:32)	Epic/Legacy 46986 Troubadour.

1967 WEAR YOUR LOVE LIKE HEAVEN
(S)	(2:23)	Epic 26439 Greatest Hits.
(S)	(2:23)	Epic/Legacy 46986 Troubadour.

1968 JENNIFER JUNIPER
(S)	(2:39)	Epic 26439 Greatest Hits.
(S)	(2:40)	Epic 26420 Hurdy Gurdy Man.
(S)	(2:39)	Epic/Legacy 46986 Troubadour.
(S)	(2:39)	Time-Life 2CLR-19 Classic Rock - 1968: Shakin' All Over.

1968 HURDY GURDY MAN
(S)	(3:11)	DCC Compact Classics 045 Golden Age Of Underground Radio.
(M)	(3:15)	Rhino 70326 History Of British Rock Volume 8.
(M)	(3:15)	Rhino 72022 History Of British Rock Box Set.
(S)	(3:16)	Epic 26439 Greatest Hits.
(S)	(3:13)	Epic 26420 Hurdy Gurdy Man.
(S)	(3:13)	Epic/Legacy 46986 Troubadour.
(S)	(3:14)	Priority 53701 Best Of The 60's & 70's Rock: Protest Rock.
(S)	(3:12)	JCI 3116 Psychedelic Sixties.
(S)	(3:10)	Time-Life 2CLR-04 Classic Rock - 1968.
(S)	(3:12)	Time-Life R968-07 Guitar Rock 1968-1969.
(S)	(3:13)	K-Tel 3183 Psychedelic Mind Trip.
(S)	(3:15)	Thump 6010 Easyriders Volume 1.

1968 LALENA
(S)	(2:54)	Rhino 70327 History Of British Rock Volume 9.
(S)	(2:54)	Rhino 72022 History Of British Rock Box Set.
(S)	(2:53)	Epic 26439 Greatest Hits.
(M)	(2:54)	Epic/Legacy 46986 Troubadour.

1969 TO SUSAN ON THE WEST COAST WAITING
(S)	(3:11)	Epic 26481 Barabajagal.
(S)	(3:10)	Epic/Legacy 46986 Troubadour.

1969 ATLANTIS
(S)	(4:56)	DCC Compact Classics 045 Golden Age Of Underground Radio.
(S)	(5:02)	Rhino 70327 History Of British Rock Volume 9.
(S)	(5:02)	Rhino 72022 History Of British Rock Box Set.
(S)	(5:01)	Epic 26481 Barabajagal.
(S)	(4:59)	Epic/Legacy 46986 Troubadour.
(S)	(4:57)	Time-Life 2CLR-20 Classic Rock - 1969: Shakin' All Over.

169

DONOVAN *(Continued)*
released as by DONOVAN with THE JEFF BECK GROUP:
1969 GOO GOO BARABAJAGAL (LOVE IS HOT)
    (the album title was simply "BARABAJAGAL")
    (S) (3:19) Epic 26481 Barabajagal.
    (S) (3:17) Epic/Legacy 46986 Troubadour.

DOOBIE BROTHERS
1972 LISTEN TO THE MUSIC
    (S) (3:46) Priority 8667 FM Hits/70's Greatest Rock Hits Volume 6. *(45 version with :20 additional music before fadeout)*
    (S) (3:46) Warner Brothers 3112 Best Of. *(45 version with :20 additional music before fadeout)*
    (S) (4:32) Warner Brothers 2634 Toulous Street. *(LP version)*
    (S) (3:23) Time-Life SUD-16 Superhits - The Early 70's. *(45 version)*
    (S) (3:25) Time-Life SOD-03 Sounds Of The Seventies - 1972. *(45 version)*
    (S) (3:46) Time-Life R968-11 Guitar Rock - The Early '70s. *(45 version with :20 additional music before fadeout)*
    (S) (4:43) Rhino 72445 Listen To The Music: The 70's California Sound. *(LP version)*
    (S) (3:23) Time-Life AM1-13 AM Gold - The Early '70s. *(45 version)*
    (S) (3:22) Madacy Entertainment 6804 More Sun Splashin'. *(45 version)*
    (S) (3:26) Rhino 72893 Hard Rock Cafe: Classic Rock. *(45 version)*
    (S) (3:46) Simitar 55502 The Number One's: Classic Rock. *(45 version with :20 additional music before fadeout)*

1973 JESUS IS JUST ALRIGHT
    (S) (4:33) Warner Brothers 3112 Best Of. *(LP version)*
    (S) (4:32) Warner Brothers 2634 Toulous Street. *(LP version)*
    (S) (4:34) Time-Life SOD-37 Sounds Of The Seventies - AM Heavy Hits. *(LP version)*

1973 LONG TRAIN RUNNIN'
    (S) (3:25) Warner Brothers 3112 Best Of.
    (S) (3:25) Warner Brothers 2694 The Captain And Me.
    (S) (3:24) Time-Life SOD-06 Sounds Of The Seventies - 1973.
    (S) (3:24) Time-Life R105-24 Guitar Rock Monsters.
    (S) (7:55) JCI 3122 Lost Mixes: Rare Rock Mixes. *(rerecorded)*
    (S) (3:25) Time-Life R968-08 Guitar Rock - The Mid '70s.
    (S) (3:24) JCI 3140 18 Screamers From The 70's.
    (S) (3:25) JCI 3191 1970 - Only Dance - 1974.
    (S) (3:24) Madacy Entertainment 6805 The Power Of Rock.

1973 CHINA GROVE
    (S) (3:13) Warner Brothers 3112 Best Of.
    (S) (3:13) Warner Brothers 2694 The Captain And Me.
    (S) (3:14) Sandstone 33001 Reelin' In The Years Volume 2.
    (S) (3:14) DCC Compact Classics 063 Rock Of The 70's Volume 2.
    (S) (3:13) Time-Life R968-05 Guitar Rock 1972-1973.
    (S) (3:13) Time-Life SOD-14 Sounds Of The Seventies - 1973: Take Two.
    (S) (3:14) Time-Life OPCD-4521 Guitar Rock.
    (S) (3:13) JCI 3192 18 Rock Classics Volume 2.
    (S) (3:12) Simitar 55752 Stud Rock - Heart Breakers.

1974 ANOTHER PARK, ANOTHER SUNDAY
    (S) (4:25) Warner Brothers 2750 What Were Once Vices Are Now Habits. *(LP version)*
    (S) (4:23) JCI 3307 Easy Seventies. *(LP version)*

1975 BLACK WATER
    (S) (4:17) Warner Brothers 3112 Best Of.
    (S) (4:16) Warner Brothers 2750 What Were Once Vices Are Now Habits.
    (S) (4:17) Time-Life SOD-08 Sounds Of The Seventies - 1975.
    (S) (4:12) Time-Life R105-26 Our Songs: Singers & Songwriters Encore.
    (S) (4:17) Rebound 314520317 Class Reunion 1975.

    (S) (4:13) JCI 3169 #1 Radio Hits 1975 - Only Rock 'n Roll - 1979.
    (S) (4:16) Rhino 72517 Mellow Rock Hits Of The 70's - Ventura Highway.
    (S) (4:15) Priority 50952 I Love Rock & Roll Volume 3: Hits Of The 70's.
    (S) (4:15) Time-Life AM1-22 AM Gold - 1975.
    (S) (4:16) Hip-O 40096 '70s Hit(s) Back Again.
    (S) (4:13) Thump 6010 Easyriders Volume 1.

1975 TAKE ME IN YOUR ARMS (ROCK ME)
    (S) (3:39) Warner Brothers 3112 Best Of.
    (S) (3:37) Warner Brothers 2835 Stampede.
    (S) (3:39) Time-Life R968-01 Guitar Rock 1974-1975.
    (S) (3:40) Time-Life SOD-16 Sounds Of The Seventies - 1975: Take Two.
    (S) (3:37) Simitar 55772 Stud Rock - Rock Me.

1976 TAKIN' IT TO THE STREETS
    (S) (3:38) Warner Brothers 3112 Best Of. *(45 version but :18 longer than the 45)*
    (S) (3:55) Warner Brothers 2899 Takin' It To The Streets. *(LP version)*
    (S) (3:44) Time-Life SOD-04 Sounds Of The Seventies - 1976. *(45 version but :24 longer than the 45)*

1979 WHAT A FOOL BELIEVES
    (S) (3:43) Warner Brothers 3193 Minute By Minute.
    (S) (3:43) Warner Brothers 3612 Best Of Volume II.
    (S) (3:40) Original Sound 9308 Dedicated To You Vol. 8. *(truncated fade)*
    (S) (3:41) Time-Life SOD-09 Sounds Of The Seventies - 1979.
    (S) (3:36) JCI 3131 1975 - Only Rock 'N Roll - 1979.
    (S) (3:43) Curb 77534 O.S.T. Frankie & Johnny.
    (S) (3:43) Eclipse Music Group 64896 Rock 'n Roll Relix 1978-1979.
    (S) (3:43) Eclipse Music Group 64897 Rock 'n Roll Relix 1970-1979.
    (S) (3:40) Time-Life R834-09 Body Talk - Magic Moments.
    (S) (3:41) Time-Life R840-10 Sounds Of The Seventies: '70s Dance Party 1979.
    (S) (3:39) Time-Life AM1-26 AM Gold - 1979.

1979 MINUTE BY MINUTE
    (S) (3:25) Warner Brothers 3193 Minute By Minute.
    (S) (3:26) Sandstone 33049 and 5017 Cosmopolitan Volume 3.
    (S) (3:25) Time-Life SOD-19 Sounds Of The Seventies - 1979: Take Two.
    (S) (3:26) Sandstone 33049 and 5017 Cosmopolitan Volume 3.
    (S) (3:26) DCC Compact Classics 088 Night Moves Volume 6.
    (S) (3:26) Warner Brothers 3612 Best Of Volume II.
    (S) (3:25) Madacy Entertainment 1979 Rock On 1979.
    (S) (3:24) JCI 3193 18 Rock Classics Volume 3.
    (S) (3:25) Time-Life R834-13 Body Talk - Just The Two Of Us.

1979 DEPENDIN' ON YOU
    (S) (3:43) Warner Brothers 3193 Minute By Minute. *(LP version)*
    (S) (3:46) Warner Brothers 3612 Best Of Volume II. *(LP version)*

1980 REAL LOVE
    (S) (4:19) Warner Brothers 26628 One Step Closer.
    (S) (4:20) Warner Brothers 3612 Best Of Volume II.
    (S) (4:16) Madacy Entertainment 1980 Rock On 1980.
    (S) (4:17) JCI 3147 1980 - Only Love - 1984.
    (S) (4:17) Time-Life R103-18 Great Love Songs Of The '70s & '80s.
    (S) (4:16) Time-Life R988-14 Sounds Of The Eighties: 1980-1982.
    (S) (4:15) Time-Life R834-07 Body Talk - Hearts In Motion.

1981 ONE STEP CLOSER
    (S) (4:09) Warner Brothers 26628 One Step Closer.
    (S) (4:09) Warner Brothers 3612 Best Of Volume II.

1989 THE DOCTOR
    (S) (3:44) Capitol 90371 Cycles.
    (S) (3:43) Madacy Entertainment 1989 Rock On 1989.
    (S) (3:43) K-Tel 3849 90s Now Volume 4.

DO OR DIE featuring TUNG TWISTA
1996 PO PIMP
   (S) (3:54)   Neighborhood Watch/Rap-A-Lot/Noo Trybe 42058
                 Picture This.

DOORS
1967 LIGHT MY FIRE
   (S) (7:05)   Elektra 60345 Best Of. *(LP version)*
   (S) (7:05)   Elektra 74007 The Doors. *(LP version)*
   (S) (7:05)   Elektra 61047 O.S.T. The Doors. *(LP version)*
   (S) (7:05)   DCC Compact Classics 1023 The Doors. *(LP
                 version; gold disc)*
   (S) (7:04)   Elektra 61996 Greatest Hits. *(LP version)*
   (S) (7:05)   Elektra 62123 The Doors Box Set. *(LP version)*
1967 PEOPLE ARE STRANGE
   (S) (2:08)   Elektra 60345 Best Of.
   (S) (2:08)   Elektra 74014 Strange Days.
   (S) (2:08)   DCC Compact Classics 1026 Strange Days.
                 (gold disc)
   (S) (2:08)   Elektra 61996 Greatest Hits.
1968 LOVE ME TWO TIMES
   (S) (3:13)   Elektra 74014 Strange Days. *(LP version)*
   (S) (3:13)   Elektra 60345 Best Of. *(LP version)*
   (S) (3:13)   DCC Compact Classics 1026 Strange Days.
                 (gold disc; LP version)
   (S) (3:13)   Elektra 61996 Greatest Hits. *(LP version)*
   (S) (3:13)   Elektra 62123 The Doors Box Set. *(LP version)*
1968 THE UNKNOWN SOLDIER
   (S) (3:21)   Elektra 60345 Best Of. *(LP version)*
   (S) (3:19)   Elektra 74024 Waiting For The Sun. *(LP version)*
   (S) (3:19)   DCC Compact Classics 1045 Waiting For The
                 Sun. *(LP version; gold disc)*
   (S) (3:20)   Elektra 62123 The Doors Box Set. *(LP version)*
1968 HELLO, I LOVE YOU
   (S) (2:12)   Elektra 74024 Waiting For The Sun.
   (S) (2:10)   Atlantic 81742 O.S.T. Platoon.
   (S) (2:13)   Elektra 60345 Best Of.
   (S) (2:13)   DCC Compact Classics 1045 Waiting For The
                 Sun. *(gold disc)*
   (M) (2:27)   Elektra 62123 The Doors Box Set. *(demo version)*
   (S) (2:11)   Elektra 61996 Greatest Hits.
   (S) (2:12)   Time-Life R13610 Gold And Platinum Box Set -
                 The Ultimate Rock Collection.
1969 TOUCH ME
   (S) (3:10)   Elektra 60345 Best Of. *(LP version)*
   (S) (3:10)   Elektra 75005 The Soft Parade. *(LP version)*
   (S) (3:10)   Elektra 61996 Greatest Hits. *(LP version)*
1969 WISHFUL SINFUL
   (S) (2:54)   Elektra 75007 The Soft Parade. *(LP mix)*
   (S) (2:55)   Elektra 62123 The Doors Box Set. *(LP mix)*
1971 LOVE HER MADLY
   (S) (3:16)   Elektra 60345 Best Of. *(LP length)*
   (S) (3:17)   Elektra 75011 L.A. Woman. *(LP length)*
   (S) (3:17)   DCC Compact Classics 1034 L.A. Woman. *(LP
                 length; gold disc)*
   (S) (3:16)   Elektra 61996 Greatest Hits. *(LP length)*
1971 RIDERS ON THE STORM
   (S) (7:08)   Elektra 60345 Best Of. *(LP version)*
   (S) (7:06)   Elektra 75011 L.A. Woman. *(LP version)*
   (S) (7:00)   Elektra 61047 O.S.T. The Doors. *(LP version)*
   (S) (7:06)   DCC Compact Classics 1034 L.A. Woman. *(LP
                 version; gold disc)*
   (S) (7:06)   Elektra 61996 Greatest Hits. *(LP version)*
   (S) (6:55)   Island 314524093 O.S.T. Basketball Diaries. *(LP
                 version)*
   (S) (7:07)   Elektra 62123 The Doors Box Set. *(LP version)*

CHARLIE DORE
1980 PILOT OF THE AIRWAVES
   (S) (3:16)   K-Tel 3342 The 80's Pop Explosion. *(45 version)*
   (S) (3:18)   Rhino 71891 Radio Daze: Pop Hits Of The 80's
                 Volume Two. *(45 version)*
   (S) (3:53)   Rebound 314520438 No. 1 Hits Of The 80's. *(LP
                 version)*
   (S) (3:52)   Polygram Special Markets 314520457 #1 Radio
                 Hits Of The 80's. *(LP version)*

HAROLD DORMAN
1960 MOUNTAIN OF LOVE
   (M) (2:23)   Collectables 5070 History Of Rock Volume 10.
   (M) (2:24)   Vee Jay 708 The Unavailable 16/The Original
                 Nitty Gritty.
   (M) (2:24)   Time-Life 2RNR-22 Rock 'N' Roll Era - 1960 Still
                 Rockin'.
   (M) (2:23)   Collectables 2603 WCBS-FM Jukebox Giants
                 Vol. 1.
   (M) (2:23)   Time-Life R102-17 Lost Treasures Of Rock 'N'
                 Roll.
   (E) (2:25)   Compose 131 Unforgettable - Gold For The Road.
   (E) (2:21)   JCI 3184 1960 - Only Love - 1964.

JIMMY DORSEY
1957 SO RARE
   (M) (2:35)   Time-Life HPD-17 Your Hit Parade - 1957.
   (M) (2:34)   DCC Compact Classics 079 Music For A
                 Bachelor's Den.
   (E) (2:42)   Curb 77775 Hard To Find Original Recordings -
                 Classic Hits.
   (M) (2:32)   Curb 77411 Greatest Hits.
1957 JUNE NIGHT
   (M) (2:07)   K-Tel 3406 Swingin' Big Bands. *(rerecording)*

LEE DORSEY
1961 YA YA
   (M) (2:25)   Rhino 70647 Billboard's Top R&B Hits Of 1961.
                 (mastered from vinyl)
   (M) (1:54)   Warner Brothers 3359 O.S.T. The Wanderers.
                 (mastered from a scratchy record; edited)
   (M) (2:25)   Relic 7009 Raging Harlem Hit Parade.
   (M) (2:26)   Relic 7013 Ya Ya.
   (M) (2:25)   Collectables 5062 History Of Rock Volume 2.
   (M) (2:22)   Capricorn 42009 Fire/Fury Records Story.
                 (mastered from vinyl)
   (M) (2:24)   MCA 8001 O.S.T. American Graffiti.
   (M) (2:25)   Ripete 0002 Coolin' Out/24 Carolina Classics Vol.
                 2.
   (M) (2:25)   Time-Life 2RNR-18 Rock 'N' Roll Era - 1961 Still
                 Rockin'.
   (M) (2:24)   Time-Life RHD-14 Rhythm & Blues - 1961.
   (M) (2:23)   Collectables 2501 WCBS-FM History Of Rock -
                 The 60's Part 2.
   (M) (2:23)   Collectables 4501 History Of Rock/The 60s Part
                 Two.
   (M) (2:25)   Collectables 2604 WCBS-FM Jukebox Giants
                 Vol. 2.
   (M) (2:25)   Collectables 5082 Golden Classics.
   (M) (2:25)   Arista 18980 Wheelin' And Deelin' - The
                 Definitive Collection.
   (M) (2:24)   Time-Life R838-19 Solid Gold Soul 1961.
1962 DO-RE-MI
   (S) (2:10)   Relic 7009 Raging Harlem Hit Parade.
   (S) (2:12)   Relic 7013 Ya Ya.
   (S) (2:10)   Capricorn 42009 Fire/Fury Records Story.
   (S) (2:16)   Time-Life 2RNR-44 Rock 'N' Roll Era - Lost
                 Treasures.
   (M) (2:05)   Collectables 5082 Golden Classics.
   (S) (2:12)   Arista 18980 Wheelin' And Deelin' - The
                 Definitive Collection.
1965 RIDE YOUR PONY
   (M) (2:51)   Rhino 75766 Best Of New Orleans Rhythm &
                 Blues Volume 2.
   (S) (2:50)   Time-Life RHD-07 Rhythm & Blues - 1965.
   (M) (2:47)   Time-Life 2CLR-14 Classic Rock - 1965: Shakin'
                 All Over.
   (S) (3:18)   Collectables 5082 Golden Classics. *(:26 longer
                 than the 45 or LP)*
   (S) (2:53)   Ripete 2220 Soul Patrol Vol. 2.
   (S) (2:50)   Time-Life R838-12 Solid Gold Soul - 1965.
   (S) (2:51)   Arista 18980 Wheelin' And Deelin' - The
                 Definitive Collection.
1966 WORKING IN THE COAL MINE
   (M) (2:47)   Rhino 75766 Best Of New Orleans Rhythm &
                 Blues Volume 2.

LEE DORSEY *(Continued)*

- (S) (2:49) Warner Special Products 27610 More Party Classics.
- (S) (3:05) Ripete 2199 Walkin' To New Orleans. *(sound effects added to the introduction)*
- (S) (2:45) Time-Life RHD-01 Rhythm & Blues - 1966.
- (M) (2:45) Time-Life 2CLR-13 Classic Rock - 1966: Shakin' All Over.
- (M) (2:47) Collectables 2502 WCBS-FM History Of Rock - The 60's Part 3.
- (M) (2:47) Collectables 4502 History Of Rock/The 60s Part Three.
- (M) (2:43) Collectables 5082 Golden Classics.
- (M) (2:43) MCA 11389 O.S.T. Casino.
- (S) (2:49) EMI 37350 Crescent City Soul: The Sound Of New Orleans 1947-1974.
- (S) (2:45) Time-Life R838-01 Solid Gold Soul - 1966.
- (S) (2:48) Arista 18980 Wheelin' And Deelin' - The Definitive Collection.
- (S) (2:48) Simitar 55532 The Number One's: The '60s.

1966 HOLY COW
- (S) (2:31) Ripete 2199 Walkin' To New Orleans.
- (S) (2:29) Time-Life 2CLR-22 Classic Rock - 1966: Blowin' Your Mind.
- (M) (2:27) Collectables 5082 Golden Classics.
- (S) (2:30) Arista 18980 Wheelin' And Deelin' - The Definitive Collection.

TOMMY DORSEY ORCHESTRA starring WARREN COVINGTON
1958 TEA FOR TWO CHA CHA CHA
- (S) (2:56) Time-Life HPD-23 Your Hit Parade - The Late 50's.

DOUBLE
1986 THE CAPTAIN OF HER HEART
- (S) (4:31) K-Tel 898 Romantic Hits Of The 80's.
- (S) (4:31) EMI 32694 Living In Oblivion - The 80's Greatest Hits Volume Five.
- (S) (4:31) A&M 5133 Blue.

CARL DOUGLAS
1974 KUNG FU FIGHTING
- (S) (3:14) Rhino 70761 Super Hits Of The 70's Volume 14.
- (S) (3:14) Rhino 70799 O.S.T. Spirit Of '76.
- (M) (3:06) Razor & Tie 22045 Those Funky 70's.
- (S) (3:15) Time-Life SOD-07 Sounds Of The Seventies - 1974.
- (S) (3:12) Hot Productions 51 Best Of.
- (S) (3:14) Rhino 72258 Dumb And Dumber: Get Down, Get Dumb.
- (S) (3:15) Madacy Entertainment 1974 Rock On 1974.
- (S) (3:13) K-Tel 3627 Out Of Sight.
- (S) (3:10) EMI 55204 O.S.T. Beverly Hills Ninja.
- (S) (3:12) Priority 53142 Mega Hits - Disco Express.
- (S) (3:13) Cold Front 4024 Old School Mega Mix Volume 2.
- (S) (3:13) K-Tel 4065 K-Tel's Original Party Music Vol. 1.

CAROL DOUGLAS
1975 DOCTOR'S ORDERS
- (S) (3:28) Rhino 70554 Soul Hits Of The 70's Volume 14. *(neither the 45 or LP version)*
- (S) (2:57) Rhino 70274 The Disco Years Volume 3. *(45 version)*
- (S) (3:28) Time-Life SOD-36 Sounds Of The Seventies - More AM Nuggets. *(neither the 45 or LP version)*
- (S) (4:58) Hot Productions 24 Best Of. *(LP version with :28 longer fade)*
- (S) (3:28) Priority 53141 Mega Hits Disco Locomotion Volume 2. *(neither the 45 or LP version)*
- (S) (3:28) Rhino 72837 Disco Queens: The 70's. *(neither the 45 or LP version)*
- (S) (2:56) Time-Life R840-05 Sounds Of The Seventies: '70s Dance Party 1972-1974. *(45 version)*

MIKE DOUGLAS
1966 THE MEN IN MY LITTLE GIRL'S LIFE
- (S) (3:43) Collectables 5671 The Men In My Little Girl's Life.
- (S) (3:44) Nick At Nite/Epic 67148 Donna Reed's Dinner Party.

RONNIE DOVE
1964 SAY YOU
- (S) (2:28) Collectables 5510 Golden Classics.
- (S) (2:28) Collectables 8830 For Collectors Only.
- (S) (2:28) Collectables 5699 Ronnie Dove Collection Part 3.

1964 RIGHT OR WRONG
- (M) (2:11) Collectables 5510 Golden Classics.
- (M) (2:11) Collectables 8830 For Collectors Only.
- (M) (2:11) Collectables 5699 Ronnie Dove Collection Part 3.

1965 ONE KISS FOR OLD TIMES SAKE
- (M) (3:00) Time-Life HPD-37 Your Hit Parade - The 60's.
- (M) (3:00) Collectables 5510 Golden Classics.
- (M) (3:00) Collectables 8830 For Collectors Only.
- (E) (2:58) Collectables 5697 Ronnie Dove Collection Part 1.

1965 A LITTLE BIT OF HEAVEN
- (S) (2:45) Collectables 5510 Golden Classics.
- (S) (2:45) Collectables 8830 For Collectors Only.
- (E) (2:41) Collectables 5697 Ronnie Dove Collection Part 1.

1965 I'LL MAKE ALL YOUR DREAMS COME TRUE
- (M) (2:37) Collectables 5510 Golden Classics. *(mastered from vinyl)*
- (M) (2:37) Collectables 8830 For Collectors Only. *(mastered from vinyl)*
- (E) (2:38) Collectables 5697 Ronnie Dove Collection Part 1.

1965 KISS AWAY
- (S) (2:49) Collectables 5510 Golden Classics.
- (S) (2:49) Collectables 8830 For Collectors Only.
- (E) (2:39) Collectables 5697 Ronnie Dove Collection Part 1.

1966 WHEN LIKING TURNS TO LOVING
- (S) (2:53) Collectables 5510 Golden Classics.
- (S) (2:53) Collectables 8830 For Collectors Only.

1966 LET'S START ALL OVER AGAIN
- (S) (2:38) Collectables 5510 Golden Classics.
- (S) (2:38) Collectables 8830 For Collectors Only.
- (E) (2:38) Collectables 5698 Ronnie Dove Collection Part 2.

1966 HAPPY SUMMER DAYS
- (S) (2:18) Collectables 5510 Golden Classics.
- (S) (2:18) Collectables 8830 For Collectors Only.
- (E) (2:15) Collectables 5698 Ronnie Dove Collection Part 2.

1966 I REALLY DON'T WANT TO KNOW
- (S) (3:04) Collectables 5510 Golden Classics.
- (S) (3:04) Collectables 8830 For Collectors Only.
- (E) (3:02) Collectables 5698 Ronnie Dove Collection Part 2.

1966 CRY
- (M) (2:57) Collectables 5510 Golden Classics. *(mastered from vinyl)*
- (M) (2:57) Collectables 8830 For Collectors Only. *(mastered from vinyl)*
- (E) (2:56) Collectables 5698 Ronnie Dove Collection Part 2.

DOVELLS
1961 BRISTOL STOMP
1962 (DO THE NEW) CONTINENTAL
1962 BRISTOL TWISTIN' ANNIE
1962 HULLY GULLY BABY
1963 YOU CAN'T SIT DOWN
- (S) (2:21) King 499 Classic Rock & Roll. *(rerecording)*

JOE DOWELL
1961 WOODEN HEART
- (S) (2:01) Mercury 826448 Oldies Golden Million Sellers. *(includes reverb not found on the original 45 version)*
- (S) (1:59) Time-Life SUD-19 Superhits - Early 60's Classics. *(includes reverb not found on the original 45 version)*
- (M) (2:01) Rhino 71582 Billboard Top Pop Hits, 1961.
- (S) (1:59) Polygram Special Markets 314520260 Number One Hits Of The Sixties. *(contains reverb not found on the original 45 version)*

(S) (2:00) Eric 11503 Hard To Find 45's On CD (Volume II) 1961-64. *(contains reverb not found on the original 45 version)*

(S) (2:00) Time-Life AM1-20 AM Gold - Early '60s Classics. *(contains reverb not found on the original 45 version)*

1962 LITTLE RED RENTED ROWBOAT

(M) (2:29) Eric 11503 Hard To Find 45's On CD (Volume II) 1961-64.

LAMONT DOZIER
1974 TRYING TO HOLD ON TO MY WOMAN

(S) (4:23) Rhino 72126 Soul Hits Of The 70's Vol. 16.

(S) (4:30) Hip-O 40010 ABC's Of Soul Volume 2.

(S) (4:30) Hip-O 40030 The Glory Of Love - '70s Sweet & Soulful Love Songs.

1974 FISH AIN'T BITIN'

(S) (3:39) Priority 53131 Deep Soul Volume Two.

CHARLIE DRAKE
1962 MY BOOMERANG WON'T COME BACK

(M) (3:37) K-Tel 3150 Dumb Ditties. *("black in the face" lyrics; complete session recording which was not the hit version)*

(S) (2:45) Time-Life HPD-35 Your Hit Parade - The Fun-Times 50's & 60's. *(original "black in the face" version)*

PETE DRAKE
1964 FOREVER

(S) (2:38) Polygram Special Markets 314520273 Great Instrumental Hits.

(S) (2:38) Collectors' Choice 003/4 Instrumental Gems Of The 60's.

DRAMATICS
1971 WHATCHA SEE IS WHATCHA GET

(S) (3:31) Rhino 70786 Soul Hits Of The 70's Volume 6. *(45 version)*

(S) (3:55) Stax 60-003 Best Of. *(LP version)*

(S) (3:55) Stax 4111 Whatcha See Is Whatcha Get. *(LP version)*

(S) (3:53) Original Sound 8864 Oldies But Goodies Vol. 14. *(this compact disc uses the "Waring - fds" noise reduction process; LP version)*

(S) (3:53) Original Sound 2222 Oldies But Goodies Volumes 3,5,11,14 and 15 Box Set. *(this box set uses the "Waring - fds" noise reduction process; LP version)*

(S) (3:53) Original Sound 2500 Oldies But Goodies Volumes 1-15 Box Set. *(this box set uses the "Waring - fds" noise reduction process; LP version)*

(S) (3:52) Original Sound CDGO-11 Golden Oldies Volume. 11. *(LP version)*

(S) (3:32) Stax 88008 Top Of The Stax Volume 2. *(45 version)*

(S) (3:33) Stax 4411 Complete Stax/Volt Soul Singles 1968 - 1971. *(45 version)*

(S) (3:31) Time-Life RHD-09 Rhythm & Blues - 1971. *(45 version)*

(S) (3:34) Time-Life SOD-12 Sounds Of The Seventies - 1971: Take Two. *(45 version)*

(S) (3:33) Thump 7040 Low Rider Oldies Volume 4. *(45 version)*

(S) (3:56) Priority 53130 Deep Soul Volume Three. *(LP version)*

(S) (3:31) Time-Life R838-06 Solid Gold Soul - 1971. *(45 version)*

1972 IN THE RAIN
(dj copies of this 45 ran (3:15) and (5:08); commercial copies were all (5:08))

(S) (5:06) Stax 88005 Top Of The Stax.

(S) (4:30) Rhino 70787 Soul Hits Of The 70's Volume 7. *(neither the LP or 45 version)*

(S) (5:06) Original Sound 8857 Oldies But Goodies Vol. 7. *(this compact disc uses the "Waring - fds" noise reduction process)*

(S) (5:06) Original Sound 2223 Oldies But Goodies Volumes 2,7,9,12 and 13 Box Set. *(this box set uses the "Waring - fds" noise reduction process)*

(S) (5:06) Original Sound 2500 Oldies But Goodies Volumes 1-15 Box Set. *(this box set uses the "Waring - fds" noise reduction process)*

(S) (5:05) Original Sound CDGO-9 Golden Oldies Volume. 9.

(S) (5:06) Stax 60-003 Best Of.

(S) (5:06) Stax 4111 Whatcha See Is Whatcha Get.

(S) (5:06) Time-Life RHD-20 Rhythm & Blues - 1972.

(S) (5:07) Time-Life SOD-25 Sounds Of The Seventies - Seventies Generation.

(S) (4:30) Varese Sarabande 5534 Rhythm Of The Rain. *(neither the LP or 45 version)*

(S) (3:24) Stax 4415 Complete Stax/Volt Soul Singles Volume 3 1972-1975.

(S) (5:07) Thump 7060 Low Rider Oldies Volume 6.

(S) (4:29) MCA 11329 Soul Train 25th Anniversary Box Set. *(neither the 45 or LP version)*

(S) (4:30) Rhino 72114 Billboard Hot Soul Hits - 1972. *(neither the 45 or LP version)*

(S) (5:06) JCI 3173 1970 - Only Soul - 1974.

(S) (5:06) Time-Life R838-07 Solid Gold Soul - 1972.

(S) (5:06) Time-Life R834-06 Body Talk - Only You.

RUSTY DRAPER
1955 THE SHIFTING, WHISPERING SANDS

(M) (2:41) Time-Life HPD-09 Your Hit Parade 1955.

1956 ARE YOU SATISFIED?
1956 IN THE MIDDLE OF THE HOUSE

(M) (1:56) Time-Life HPD-35 Your Hit Parade - The Fun-Times 50's & 60's.

1957 FREIGHT TRAIN

DREAM ACADEMY
1986 LIFE IN A NORTHERN TOWN

(S) (4:14) EMI 27674 Living In Oblivion: The 80's Greatest Hits Volume Three.

(S) (4:15) Sandstone 33045 and 5011 Rock The First Volume Five.

(S) (4:15) JCI 3128 1985 - Only Rock 'N Roll - 1989.

(S) (4:15) Warner Brothers 25265 The Dream Academy.

(S) (4:15) Rhino 71978 New Wave Hits Of The 80's Vol. 15.

(S) (4:16) Priority 53765 Rock Of The 80's Volume 9.

(S) (4:15) Time-Life R988-04 Sounds Of The Eighties: 1986.

1986 THE LOVE PARADE

(S) (3:45) Warner Brothers 25265 The Dream Academy.

(S) (3:45) Priority 53798 Best Of 80's Rock Volume 5.

DREAMLOVERS
1961 WHEN WE GET MARRIED

(M) (2:25) JCI 3115 Groovin' Sixties.

(E) (2:25) Original Sound 8855 Oldies But Goodies Vol. 5. *(this compact disc uses the "Waring - fds" noise reduction process; ambient background noise throughout the disc)*

(E) (2:25) Original Sound 2222 Oldies But Goodies Volumes 3,5,11,14 and 15 Box Set. *(this box set uses the "Waring - fds" noise reduction process; ambient background noise throughout the song)*

(E) (2:25) Original Sound 2500 Oldies But Goodies Volumes 1-15 Box Set. *(this box set uses the "Waring - fds" noise reduction process; ambient background noise throughout the song)*

(E) (2:24) Original Sound CDGO-1 Golden Oldies Volume. 1.

(M) (2:25) DCC Compact Classics 031 Back Seat Jams.

(M) (2:26) Rhino 70588 Rockin' & Rollin' Wedding Songs Volume 1.

(E) (2:24) Collectables 2508 History Of Rock - The Doo Wop Era Part 2.

(E) (2:24) Collectables 4508 History Of Rock/The Doo Wop Era Part Two.

(M) (2:25) Collectables 5004 Best Of.

(M) (2:25) Time-Life 2RNR-25 Rock 'N' Roll Era - The 60's Keep On Rockin'.

DREAMLOVERS (Continued)

- (E) (2:24) Collectables 2500 WCBS-FM History Of Rock - The 60's Part 1.
- (E) (2:24) Collectables 4500 History Of Rock/The 60s Part One.
- (M) (2:24) Collectables 2608 WCBS-FM For Lovers Only Vol. 4.
- (E) (2:25) Original Sound 8911 Art Laboe's Dedicated To You Vol. 2.
- (E) (2:25) Original Sound 4001 Art Laboe's 60 Killer Oldies.
- (M) (2:25) Time-Life R102-17 Lost Treasures Of Rock 'N' Roll.
- (M) (2:26) Polygram Special Markets 314520258 No. 1 Hits Of The 50's.
- (M) (2:26) Collectables 5476 Golden Classics.
- (M) (2:24) Rhino 72507 Doo Wop Box II.
- (M) (2:26) Time-Life R857-10 The Heart Of Rock 'n' Roll 1960-1961.
- (M) (2:25) Thump 7070 Lowrider Oldies Volume 7.

DREAM WEAVERS
1956 IT'S ALMOST TOMORROW
- (M) (2:45) Time-Life HPD-23 Your Hit Parade - The Late 50's.

DRIFTERS
1959 THERE GOES MY BABY
- (M) (2:09) Rhino 70906 American Bandstand Greatest Hits Collection.
- (M) (2:09) Atlantic 81296 Atlantic Rhythm & Blues Volume 4.
- (M) (2:09) Atlantic 8153 Golden Hits.
- (M) (2:08) Atlantic 81931 1959-1965 All Time Greatest Hits.
- (M) (2:09) Atlantic 82305 Atlantic Rhythm And Blues 1947-1974 Box Set.
- (M) (2:09) Curb 77594 Best Of Ben E King.
- (M) (2:10) Rhino 71211 Very Best Of.
- (M) (2:10) Rhino 71215 Ben E. King Anthology.
- (M) (2:08) Time-Life 2RNR-13 Rock 'N' Roll Era - 1959.
- (M) (2:07) Time-Life RHD-03 Rhythm & Blues - 1959.
- (M) (2:11) Motown 6763 Rites Of Rhythm & Blues Volume 2.
- (M) (2:07) Original Sound 8863 Oldies But Goodies Vol. 13.
- (M) (2:07) Original Sound 2223 Oldies But Goodies Volumes 2,7,9,12 and 13 Box Set. *(Volumes 2, 7 and 12 of this box set use the "Waring - fds" noise reduction process)*
- (M) (2:07) Original Sound 2500 Oldies But Goodies Volumes 1-15 Box Set. *(most volumes in this box set use the "Waring - fds" noise reduction process)*
- (M) (2:08) Time-Life R857-01 The Heart Of Rock 'n' Roll - 1959.
- (M) (2:10) Rhino 72156 Doo Wop Memories, Vol. 1.
- (M) (2:10) Rhino 72417 Rockin' & Driftin' The Drifters Box Set.
- (M) (2:08) JCI 3166 #1 Radio Hits 1960 - Only Rock 'n Roll - 1964.
- (M) (2:11) Flashback 72666 There Goes My Baby And Other Hits.
- (M) (2:07) Time-Life R838-21 Solid Gold Soul 1959.
- (M) (2:11) Rhino 72961 Ultimate '50s R&B Smashes!
- (M) (2:11) Rhino 72970 Very Best Of Ben E. King.

1959 DANCE WITH ME
- (M) (2:23) Atlantic 81296 Atlantic Rhythm & Blues Volume 4.
- (M) (2:22) Atlantic 8153 Golden Hits. *(truncated fade)*
- (S) (2:24) Atlantic 81931 1959-1965 All Time Greatest Hits. *(original pressings of this song on this cd were (M); truncated fade)*
- (S) (2:24) Atlantic 82305 Atlantic Rhythm And Blues 1947-1974 Box Set.
- (M) (2:22) Rhino 71211 Very Best Of.
- (M) (2:22) Rhino 71215 Ben E. King Anthology.
- (M) (2:22) Time-Life 2RNR-20 Rock 'N' Roll Era - 1959 Still Rockin'.
- (M) (2:22) Rhino 72417 Rockin' & Driftin' The Drifters Box Set.
- (M) (2:22) Time-Life R857-11 The Heart Of Rock 'n' Roll 1958-1959.
- (M) (2:22) Flashback 72666 There Goes My Baby And Other Hits.

- (M) (2:22) Rhino 72970 Very Best Of Ben E. King.

1959 (IF YOU CRY) TRUE LOVE, TRUE LOVE
- (S) (2:19) Atlantic 8153 Golden Hits.
- (S) (2:19) Atlantic 81931 1959-1965 All Time Greatest Hits.
- (M) (2:16) Rhino 71211 Very Best Of.
- (M) (2:16) Rhino 72417 Rockin' & Driftin' The Drifters Box Set.
- (M) (2:16) Flashback 72666 There Goes My Baby And Other Hits.

1960 THIS MAGIC MOMENT
- (M) (2:28) Atlantic 81296 Atlantic Rhythm & Blues Volume 4.
- (S) (2:26) Atlantic 8153 Golden Hits.
- (S) (2:25) Atlantic 81931 1959-1965 All Time Greatest Hits.
- (S) (2:25) Atlantic 80213 Ultimate Ben E King Collection.
- (S) (2:30) Atlantic 82305 Atlantic Rhythm And Blues 1947-1974 Box Set.
- (S) (2:25) Curb 77594 Best Of Ben E King.
- (M) (2:28) Rhino 71211 Very Best Of.
- (M) (2:28) Rhino 71215 Ben E. King Anthology.
- (S) (2:25) Time-Life 2RNR-22 Rock 'N' Roll Era - 1960 Still Rockin'.
- (M) (2:28) Motown 6763 Rites Of Rhythm & Blues Volume 2.
- (S) (2:25) Time-Life OPCD-4517 Tonight's The Night.
- (M) (2:28) Rhino 71802 O.S.T. Andre.
- (M) (2:28) Rhino 72417 Rockin' & Driftin' The Drifters Box Set.
- (S) (2:25) Time-Life R857-14 The Heart Of Rock 'n' Roll 1960-1961 Take Two.
- (M) (2:28) Flashback 72666 There Goes My Baby And Other Hits.
- (M) (2:28) Rhino 72970 Very Best Of Ben E. King.

1960 SAVE THE LAST DANCE FOR ME
- (S) (2:28) Rhino 70621 Billboard's Top Rock & Roll Hits Of 1960.
- (S) (2:28) Rhino 72004 Billboard's Top Rock & Roll Hits 1957-1961 Box Set.
- (S) (2:26) Atlantic 81296 Atlantic Rhythm & Blues Volume 4.
- (S) (2:25) Atlantic 8153 Golden Hits.
- (S) (2:26) Atlantic 81931 1959-1965 All Time Greatest Hits.
- (S) (2:26) Atlantic 80213 Ultimate Ben E King Collection.
- (S) (2:26) Atlantic 82305 Atlantic Rhythm And Blues 1947-1974 Box Set.
- (M) (2:32) Rhino 71211 Very Best Of.
- (M) (2:32) Rhino 71215 Ben E. King Anthology.
- (M) (2:25) Time-Life 2RNR-11 Rock 'N' Roll Era - 1960.
- (S) (2:25) Time-Life RHD-15 Rhythm & Blues - 1960.
- (S) (2:26) Time-Life SUD-15 Superhits - The Early 60's.
- (S) (2:25) Time-Life R10513 40 Lovin' Oldies.
- (S) (2:25) JCI 3125 1960 - Only Rock 'N Roll - 1964.
- (S) (2:28) Time-Life R857-02 The Heart Of Rock 'n' Roll - 1960.
- (S) (2:25) Nick At Nite/Epic 67149 Dick Van Dyke's Dance Party.
- (M) (2:33) Rhino 72417 Rockin' & Driftin' The Drifters Box Set.
- (S) (2:25) JCI 3164 Eighteen Soulful Ballads.
- (S) (2:26) Time-Life AM1-19 AM Gold - The Early '60s.
- (M) (2:32) Flashback 72666 There Goes My Baby And Other Hits.
- (S) (2:26) Repeat/Relativity 1610 Tighten Up: #1 Soul Hits Of The 60's Volume 2.
- (S) (2:25) Time-Life R838-20 Solid Gold Soul 1960.
- (M) (2:32) Flashback 72857 Grease And Other Golden Oldies.
- (M) (2:33) Rhino 72970 Very Best Of Ben E. King.
- (S) (2:26) K-Tel 3886 Great R&B Male Groups: Hits Of The 60's.

1961 I COUNT THE TEARS
- (S) (2:11) Atlantic 8153 Golden Hits.
- (S) (2:11) Atlantic 81931 1959-1965 All Time Greatest Hits.
- (S) (2:11) Atlantic 80213 Ultimate Ben E King Collection.
- (M) (2:07) Rhino 71211 Very Best Of.
- (M) (2:07) Rhino 71215 Ben E. King Anthology.
- (S) (2:09) Time-Life 2RNR-25 Rock 'N' Roll Era - The 60's Keep On Rockin'.
- (M) (2:07) Rhino 72417 Rockin' & Driftin' The Drifters Box Set.
- (M) (2:07) Flashback 72666 There Goes My Baby And Other Hits.

(M) (2:07)   Time-Life R857-17   The Heart Of Rock 'n' Roll: The Early '60s.

(M) (2:07)   Rhino 72970   Very Best Of Ben E. King.

1961 SOME KIND OF WONDERFUL

(S) (2:35)   RCA 6965   More Dirty Dancing. *(LP version)*

(S) (2:35)   Atlantic 8153   Golden Hits. *(LP version)*

(S) (2:35)   Atlantic 81931   1959-1965 All Time Greatest Hits. *(LP version)*

(M) (2:17)   Rhino 71211   Very Best Of. *(45 version)*

(M) (2:16)   Rhino 72417   Rockin' & Driftin' The Drifters Box Set. *(45 version)*

(M) (2:16)   Flashback 72666   There Goes My Baby And Other Hits. *(45 version)*

(S) (2:34)   Time-Life R857-19   The Heart Of Rock 'n' Roll 1960-1961 Take Three. *(LP version)*

1961 PLEASE STAY

(S) (2:13)   Atlantic 81931   1959-1965 All Time Greatest Hits.

(M) (2:15)   Rhino 71211   Very Best Of.

(S) (2:13)   Time-Life 2RNR-18   Rock 'N' Roll Era - 1961 Still Rockin'.

(M) (2:15)   Rhino 72417   Rockin' & Driftin' The Drifters Box Set.

(S) (2:13)   Time-Life R857-10   The Heart Of Rock 'n' Roll 1960-1961.

(M) (2:14)   Flashback 72666   There Goes My Baby And Other Hits.

1961 SWEETS FOR MY SWEET

(S) (2:27)   Atlantic 81931   1959-1965 All Time Greatest Hits.

(M) (2:34)   Rhino 71211   Very Best Of.

(S) (2:25)   Time-Life 2RNR-35   Rock 'N' Roll Era - The 60's Last Dance.

(M) (2:34)   Rhino 72417   Rockin' & Driftin' The Drifters Box Set.

(M) (2:34)   Flashback 72666   There Goes My Baby And Other Hits.

1962 WHEN MY LITTLE GIRL IS SMILING

(S) (2:29)   Atlantic 81931   1959-1965 All Time Greatest Hits.

(M) (2:32)   Rhino 71211   Very Best Of.

(S) (2:24)   Time-Life 2RNR-42   Rock 'N' Roll Era - The 60's Sock Hop.

(M) (2:31)   Rhino 72417   Rockin' & Driftin' The Drifters Box Set.

1963 UP ON THE ROOF

(S) (2:34)   Atlantic 81297   Atlantic Rhythm & Blues Volume 5. *(LP version)*

(S) (2:35)   Atlantic 8153   Golden Hits. *(LP version)*

(S) (2:35)   Atlantic 81931   1959-1965 All Time Greatest Hits. *(LP version)*

(S) (2:35)   Atlantic 82305   Atlantic Rhythm And Blues 1947-1974 Box Set. *(LP version)*

(M) (2:35)   Rhino 71211   Very Best Of. *(45 version)*

(M) (2:35)   Era 5025   The Brill Building Sound. *(45 version)*

(M) (2:35)   Rhino 71230   Up On The Roof, On Broadway & Under The Boardwalk. *(45 version)*

(M) (2:35)   Time-Life 2RNR-02   Rock 'N' Roll Era - 1962. *(45 version)*

(S) (2:33)   Time-Life RHD-11   Rhythm & Blues - 1962. *(LP version)*

(S) (2:32)   Time-Life SUD-06   Superhits - 1962. *(LP version)*

(M) (2:35)   Time-Life R962-08   History Of Rock 'N' Roll: Sound Of The City 1959-1965. *(45 version)*

(M) (2:35)   Rhino 72417   Rockin' & Driftin' The Drifters Box Set. *(45 version)*

(S) (2:33)   Time-Life R857-08   The Heart Of Rock 'n' Roll 1963. *(LP version)*

(S) (2:32)   Time-Life AM1-18   AM Gold - 1962. *(LP version)*

(M) (2:35)   Flashback 72665   Under The Boardwalk And Other Hits. *(45 version)*

(M) (2:35)   Flashback 72084   Soul Legends Box Set. *(45 version)*

(S) (2:33)   Time-Life R838-18   Solid Gold Soul 1962. *(LP version)*

(S) (2:35)   JCI 3184   1960 - Only Love - 1964. *(LP version)*

1963 ON BROADWAY

(M) (2:59)   Atlantic 81297   Atlantic Rhythm & Blues Volume 5.

(S) (2:59)   Warner Special Products 27601   Atlantic Soul Classics.

(S) (2:56)   Original Sound 8858   Oldies But Goodies Vol. 8. *(this compact disc uses the "Waring - fds" noise reduction process)*

(S) (2:56)   Original Sound 2221   Oldies But Goodies Volumes 1,4,6,8 and 10 Box Set. *(this box set uses the "Waring - fds" noise reduction process)*

(S) (2:56)   Original Sound 2500   Oldies But Goodies Volumes 1-15 Box Set. *(this box set uses the "Waring - fds" noise reduction process)*

(S) (2:59)   Atlantic 8153   Golden Hits.

(S) (2:58)   Atlantic 81931   1959-1965 All Time Greatest Hits.

(M) (2:59)   Rhino 70593   The Rock 'N' Roll Classics Of Leiber & Stoller.

(S) (2:58)   Atlantic 82305   Atlantic Rhythm And Blues 1947-1974 Box Set.

(M) (3:01)   Rhino 71211   Very Best Of.

(M) (3:01)   Era 5025   The Brill Building Sound.

(M) (3:00)   Rhino 71230   Up On The Roof, On Broadway & Under The Boardwalk.

(M) (2:59)   Time-Life 2RNR-07   Rock 'N' Roll Era - 1963.

(S) (2:56)   Time-Life SUD-08   Superhits - 1963.

(M) (3:01)   Rhino 72417   Rockin' & Driftin' The Drifters Box Set.

(S) (2:58)   Eclipse Music Group 64868   Rock 'n Roll Relix 1962-1963.

(S) (2:58)   Eclipse Music Group 64872   Rock 'n Roll Relix 1960-1969.

(S) (2:56)   Time-Life AM1-17   AM Gold - 1963.

(M) (3:00)   Flashback 72665   Under The Boardwalk And Other Hits.

(M) (3:00)   Flashback 72084   Soul Legends Box Set.

(M) (3:01)   Rhino 72963   Ultimate '60s Soul Smashes.

1963 I'LL TAKE YOU HOME

(S) (2:35)   Atlantic 81931   1959-1965 All Time Greatest Hits.

(M) (2:41)   Rhino 71211   Very Best Of.

(M) (2:40)   Rhino 71230   Up On The Roof, On Broadway & Under The Boardwalk.

(M) (2:41)   Rhino 72417   Rockin' & Driftin' The Drifters Box Set.

(M) (2:40)   Flashback 72665   Under The Boardwalk And Other Hits.

(M) (2:40)   Flashback 72084   Soul Legends Box Set.

1964 UNDER THE BOARDWALK

(S) (2:39)   Atlantic 81297   Atlantic Rhythm & Blues Volume 5. *(LP version)*

(S) (2:39)   Atlantic 8153   Golden Hits. *(LP version)*

(S) (2:39)   Atlantic 81931   1959-1965 All Time Greatest Hits. *(LP version)*

(S) (2:39)   Atlantic 82305   Atlantic Rhythm And Blues 1947-1974 Box Set. *(LP version)*

(M) (2:41)   Rhino 71211   Very Best Of. *(45 version)*

(M) (2:41)   Rhino 71230   Up On The Roof, On Broadway & Under The Boardwalk. *(45 version)*

(S) (2:38)   Time-Life 2RNR-10   Rock 'N' Roll Era - 1964. *(LP version)*

(S) (2:39)   Time-Life RHD-12   Rhythm & Blues - 1964. *(LP version)*

(S) (2:39)   Time-Life SUD-09   Superhits - 1964. *(LP version)*

(S) (2:39)   Ripete 2183-RE   Ocean Drive Volume 1. *(LP version)*

(M) (2:41)   Rhino 72417   Rockin' & Driftin' The Drifters Box Set. *(45 version)*

(S) (2:39)   Time-Life R857-09   The Heart Of Rock 'n' Roll 1964. *(LP version)*

(S) (2:39)   Time-Life AM1-11   AM Gold - 1964. *(LP version)*

(S) (2:39)   Time-Life R838-13   Solid Gold Soul - 1964. *(LP version)*

(M) (2:41)   Flashback 72665   Under The Boardwalk And Other Hits. *(45 version)*

(M) (2:41)   Flashback 72084   Soul Legends Box Set. *(45 version)*

DRIFTERS *(Continued)*
1964 I'VE GOT SAND IN MY SHOES
- (S) (2:45) Atlantic 8153 Golden Hits.
- (S) (2:45) Atlantic 81931 1959-1965 All Time Greatest Hits.
- (S) (2:45) Rhino 70279 Rare Soul: Beach Music Classics Volume 3.
- (M) (2:48) Rhino 71211 Very Best Of.
- (M) (2:48) Rhino 71230 Up On The Roof, On Broadway & Under The Boardwalk.
- (S) (2:44) Time-Life 2RNR-46 Rock 'N' Roll Era - 60's Juke Box Memories.
- (M) (2:47) Rhino 72417 Rockin' & Driftin' The Drifters Box Set.
- (M) (2:47) Flashback 72665 Under The Boardwalk And Other Hits.
- (M) (2:47) Flashback 72084 Soul Legends Box Set.

1964 SATURDAY NIGHT AT THE MOVIES
- (S) (2:29) Atlantic 8153 Golden Hits.
- (S) (2:28) Atlantic 81931 1959-1965 All Time Greatest Hits.
- (M) (2:28) Rhino 71211 Very Best Of.
- (M) (2:28) Rhino 71230 Up On The Roof, On Broadway & Under The Boardwalk.
- (S) (2:25) Time-Life 2RNR-44 Rock 'N' Roll Era - Lost Treasures.
- (M) (2:28) Rhino 72417 Rockin' & Driftin' The Drifters Box Set.
- (M) (2:28) Flashback 72665 Under The Boardwalk And Other Hits.
- (M) (2:28) Flashback 72084 Soul Legends Box Set.

D.R.S
1993 GANGSTA LEAN
- (S) (5:23) Capitol 81445 Gangsta Lean.
- (S) (4:05) Rhino 72159 Black Entertainment Television - 15th Anniversary.

DRU HILL
1996 TELL ME
- (S) (4:12) Island/Hollywood 314524243 O.S.T. Eddie.
- (S) (4:12) Island 314524306 Dru Hill.
1997 IN MY BED
- (S) (4:44) Island 314524306 Dru Hill.
- (S) (4:07) Tommy Boy 1234 MTV Party To Go '98. *(all songs on this cd are segued together)*
- (S) (3:56) Boxtunes 314524387 Big Phat Ones Of Hip-Hop Volume 2. *(all songs on this cd are segued together)*
1997 NEVER MAKE A PROMISE
- (S) (5:26) Island 314524306 Dru Hill.
1998 WE'RE NOT MAKING LOVE NO MORE
- (S) (4:49) LaFace 26041 O.S.T. Soul Food.

DUALS
1961 STICK SHIFT
- (E) (2:28) Capitol 96862 Monster Summer Hits - Drag City.
- (M) (2:28) Collectables 5123 Best Of Sue Records.
- (M) (2:28) Era 840 Rock N' Roll Guitar Classics.
- (M) (2:29) EMI 80932 Sue Records Story.
- (M) (2:28) Collectables 0680 Stick Shift.

DUBS
1957 COULD THIS BE MAGIC
- (M) (2:15) Collectables 5402 Best Of.
- (M) (2:16) Time-Life 2RNR-01 Rock 'N' Roll Era - 1957.
- (M) (2:16) Time-Life R962-06 History Of Rock 'N' Roll: Doo Wop And Vocal Group Tradition 1955-1962.
- (M) (2:15) Collectables 5461 The Spotlight Series - Gone Records Vol. 2.
- (M) (2:16) Collectables 2602 WCBS-FM History Of Rock - The Group Sounds Vol. 3.
- (M) (2:15) Collectables 2608 WCBS-FM For Lovers Only Vol. 4.
- (M) (2:15) Time-Life R10513 40 Lovin' Oldies.
- (M) (2:14) Thump 7050 Low Rider Oldies Volume 5.
- (M) (2:16) Rhino 72156 Doo Wop Memories, Vol. 1.
- (M) (2:15) Rhino 72507 Doo Wop Box II.

- (M) (2:16) Time-Life R857-05 The Heart Of Rock 'n' Roll 1957.

DAVE DUDLEY
1963 SIX DAYS ON THE ROAD
- (M) (2:20) Rhino 70723 Legends Of Guitar: Country Volume 2.
- (M) (2:20) Rhino 70684 Billboard's Top Country Hits Of 1963.
- (M) (2:20) Time-Life CTD-11 Country USA - 1963.
- (M) (2:20) Rhino 71671 Country Shots: Gear-Jammin' Greats.
- (S) (2:12) K-Tel 3151 Working Man's Country. *(rerecording)*
- (M) (2:15) K-Tel 320 Country Music Classics Volume II.
- (E) (2:16) K-Tel 3369 101 Greatest Country Hits Vol. Ten: Country Roads.
- (S) (2:12) Right Stuff 53317 Hot Rod Rock Volume 2: Hot Rod Cowboys. *(rerecording)*
- (M) (2:20) Time-Life R808-01 Classic Country 1960-1964.

DUICE
1993 DAZZY DUKS
- (S) (4:01) Bellmark 71000 Dazzey Duks.
- (S) (5:11) Bellmark 71000 Dazzey Duks. *(remix)*
- (S) (4:01) Cold Front 6285 Bass Mix USA.

PATTY DUKE
1965 DON'T JUST STAND THERE
- (S) (2:39) EMI 29787 Best Of.
1965 SAY SOMETHING FUNNY
- (S) (2:17) EMI 29787 Best Of.

CANDY DULFER (see DAVID A. STEWART)

DAVID DUNDAS
1977 JEANS ON
- (M) (2:34) Rhino 71199 Super Hits Of The 70's Volume 19.

ROBBIE DUPREE
1980 STEAL AWAY
- (S) (3:23) Priority 53699 80's Greatest Rock Hits Volume 7 - Light & Easy. *(noisy fadeout)*
- (S) (3:28) Rhino 71892 Radio Daze: Pop Hits Of The 80's Volume Three.
- (S) (3:26) Madacy Entertainment 1980 Rock On 1980.
- (S) (3:28) JCI 3170 #1 Radio Hits 1980 - Only Rock 'n Roll - 1984.
- (S) (3:28) Time-Life R834-16 Body Talk - Sweet Nothings.
1980 HOT ROD HEARTS
- (S) (3:38) Rhino 71893 Radio Daze: Pop Hits Of The 80's Volume Four.

DUPREES
1962 YOU BELONG TO ME
- (S) (2:42) Rhino 71004 Best Of.
- (S) (2:42) Collectables 5008 Best Of.
- (M) (2:34) Original Sound 8860 Oldies But Goodies Vol. 10. *(this compact disc uses the "Waring - fds" noise reduction process)*
- (M) (2:34) Original Sound 2221 Oldies But Goodies Volumes 1,4,6,8 and 10 Box Set. *(this box set uses the "Waring - fds" noise reduction process)*
- (M) (2:34) Original Sound 2500 Oldies But Goodies Volumes 1-15 Box Set. *(this box set uses the "Waring - fds" noise reduction process)*
- (S) (2:34) Original Sound CDGO-12 Golden Oldies Volume. 12.
- (S) (2:34) Original Sound 8892 Dick Clark's 21 All-Time Hits Vol. 2.
- (S) (2:34) Original Sound 9601 Best Of Oldies But Goodies Vol. 1.
- (S) (2:34) Original Sound 9328 13 Of The Best Doo Wop Love Songs Vol. 2.
- (S) (2:35) Time-Life 2RNR-16 Rock 'N' Roll Era - 1962 Still Rockin'.
- (S) (2:42) Time-Life SUD-06 Superhits - 1962.

(S) (2:42) Collectables 2500 WCBS-FM History Of Rock - The 60's Part 1.
(S) (2:42) Collectables 4500 History Of Rock/The 60s Part One.
(M) (2:34) Collectables 2509 WCBS-FM For Lovers Only Part 1.
(S) (2:42) Time-Life R103-27 Love Me Tender.
(S) (2:35) Time-Life OPCD-4517 Tonight's The Night.
(S) (2:42) LaserLight 12324 Sixteen Candles: Very Best Of The Crests And Duprees.
(S) (2:42) Sundazed 6072 You Belong To Me.
(S) (2:46) Rhino 72507 Doo Wop Box II. *(with cold ending)*
(S) (2:42) Music Club 50015 Love Me Forever - 18 Rock'N' Roll Love Songs.
(S) (2:42) Time-Life R857-06 The Heart Of Rock 'n' Roll 1962.
(S) (2:42) Time-Life AM1-18 AM Gold - 1962.
(S) (2:46) Collectables 8814 For Collectors Only.
(S) (2:42) JCI 3184 1960 - Only Love - 1964.
(S) (2:35) Time-Life R814-05 Love Songs.

1962 MY OWN TRUE LOVE
(S) (2:27) Rhino 71004 Best Of.
(S) (2:27) Collectables 5008 Best Of.
(S) (2:27) Time-Life 2RNR-46 Rock 'N' Roll Era - 60's Juke Box Memories.
(S) (2:28) LaserLight 12324 Sixteen Candles: Very Best Of The Crests And Duprees.
(S) (2:27) Sundazed 6072 You Belong To Me.
(S) (2:28) Music Club 50015 Love Me Forever - 18 Rock'N' Roll Love Songs.
(S) (2:28) Time-Life R857-12 The Heart Of Rock 'n' Roll 1962-1963.
(S) (2:30) Collectables 8814 For Collectors Only.

1963 WHY DON'T YOU BELIEVE ME
(S) (2:36) Rhino 71004 Best Of.
(S) (2:36) Collectables 5008 Best Of.
(S) (2:38) Collectables 2608 WCBS-FM For Lovers Only Vol. 4.
(S) (2:36) LaserLight 12324 Sixteen Candles: Very Best Of The Crests And Duprees.
(S) (2:36) Sundazed 6072 You Belong To Me.
(S) (2:40) Collectables 8814 For Collectors Only.

1963 HAVE YOU HEARD
(M) (2:28) Rhino 71004 Best Of.
(M) (2:25) Original Sound CDGO-2 Golden Oldies Volume. 2.
(M) (2:28) Collectables 5008 Best Of.
(M) (2:27) Time-Life 2RNR-40 Rock 'N' Roll Era - The 60's Teen Time.
(M) (2:28) Collectables 2502 WCBS-FM History Of Rock - The 60's Part 3.
(M) (2:28) Collectables 4502 History Of Rock/The 60s Part Three.
(M) (2:28) LaserLight 12324 Sixteen Candles: Very Best Of The Crests And Duprees.
(M) (2:28) Sundazed 6073 Have You Heard.
(M) (2:43) Sundazed 6073 Have You Heard. *(alternate take)*
(M) (2:27) Collectables 8814 For Collectors Only.
(M) (2:28) Time-Life R857-18 The Heart Of Rock 'n' Roll 1962-1963 Take Two.

DURAN DURAN
1983 HUNGRY LIKE THE WOLF
(dj copies of this 45 ran (3:23), (4:11) and (5:14); commercial copies were also (4:11) and (5:14); there were two different pressings of the "Rio" LP on which this song appeared with running times of (3:40) and (5:14))
(S) (4:03) Sandstone 33042 and 5008 Rock The First Volume 2. *(45 version)*
(S) (3:24) Capitol 93178 Decade. *(this is one of the dj edits of the 45)*
(S) (3:39) Capitol 46003 Rio. *(LP version)*
(S) (3:09) Arista 18985 Ultimate New Wave Party 1998. *(all selections on this cd are segued together)*
(S) (5:14) EMI-Capitol Entertainment Properties 93922 Essential. *(remix)*

1983 RIO
(dj copies of this 45 ran (4:34); commercial copies were all (3:57))
(S) (3:58) Rhino 71702 New Wave Hits Of The 80's Vol. 9. *(commercial 45 version)*
(S) (5:33) Capitol 93178 Decade. *(LP version)*
(S) (5:36) Capitol 46003 Rio. *(LP version)*
(S) (6:43) EMI-Capitol Entertainment Properties 93922 Essential. *(remix)*

1983 IS THERE SOMETHING I SHOULD KNOW
(S) (4:08) Priority 53704 Rock Of The 80's Volume 3.
(S) (4:08) Capitol 93178 Decade.
(S) (4:07) Capitol 46042 Duran Duran.
(S) (6:40) EMI-Capitol Entertainment Properties 93922 Essential. *(remix)*

1983 UNION OF THE SNAKE
(S) (4:19) Capitol 93178 Decade.
(S) (4:19) Capitol 46015 Seven And The Ragged Tiger.
(S) (6:24) EMI-Capitol Entertainment Properties 93922 Essential. *(remix)*

1984 NEW MOON ON MONDAY
(S) (4:14) Capitol 46015 Seven And The Ragged Tiger.
(S) (4:14) Chrysalis 21750 After The Hurricane - Songs For Montserrat.
(S) (6:14) EMI-Capitol Entertainment Properties 93922 Essential. *(remix)*

1984 THE REFLEX
(S) (4:23) Capitol 93178 Decade. *(45 version)*
(S) (5:27) Capitol 46015 Seven And The Ragged Tiger. *(LP version)*
(S) (4:23) Time-Life R13610 Gold And Platinum Box Set - The Ultimate Rock Collection. *(45 version)*
(S) (6:34) EMI-Capitol Entertainment Properties 93922 Essential. *(remix)*

1984 THE WILD BOYS
(S) (4:16) Capitol 93178 Decade.
(S) (4:16) Capitol 46048 Arena.
(S) (8:00) EMI-Capitol Entertainment Properties 93922 Essential. *(remix)*

1985 SAVE A PRAYER
(commercial copies of this 45 had no time stated on the record label but the actual time is (3:43); dj copies state a time of (3:59) but the actual time is (3:43))
(S) (5:24) Capitol 93178 Decade. *(LP version)*
(S) (5:25) Capitol 46003 Rio. *(LP version)*

1985 A VIEW TO A KILL
(S) (3:33) EMI 98413 Best Of James Bond 30th Anniversary Collection.
(S) (3:33) EMI 98560 Best Of James Bond 30th Anniversary.
(S) (3:33) Capitol 93178 Decade.

1986 NOTORIOUS
(S) (4:17) Capitol 46415 Notorious. *(LP version)*
(S) (3:58) Capitol 93178 Decade. *(45 version)*

1988 I DON'T WANT YOUR LOVE
(S) (3:47) Capitol 93178 Decade. *(45 version)*
(S) (4:05) Capitol 90958 Big Thing. *(LP version)*

1989 ALL SHE WANTS IS
(S) (4:30) Capitol 93178 Decade.
(S) (4:32) Capitol 90958 Big Thing.

1993 ORDINARY WORLD
(S) (5:40) Capitol 98876 Duran Duran. *(LP version)*

1993 COME UNDONE
(S) (7:16) EMI 32393 Loaded Volume 1. *(live)*
(S) (4:38) Capitol 98876 Duran Duran.

BOB DYLAN
1965 SUBTERRANEAN HOMESICK BLUES
(S) (2:17) Columbia 9463 Greatest Hits.
(S) (2:16) Columbia 38830 and 65295 Biograph.
(S) (2:21) Columbia 9128 Bringing It All Back Home.

1965 LIKE A ROLLING STONE
(dj copies of this 45 were issued in two different configurations; Part 1 (3:02) with Part 2 (3:02) on the flip side and another with the complete version running (6:00); commercial copies of the 45 were all (6:00))
(S) (6:06) Columbia 9463 Greatest Hits.

BOB DYLAN *(Continued)*

    (S) (6:07)   Columbia 38830 and 65295 Biograph.
    (S) (6:08)   Columbia 9189 Highway 61 Revisited.
    (S) (5:15)   Columbia 30050 Self Portrait. *(Live)*
    (S) (6:07)   Polydor 314515913 Classic Rock Box.
    (S) (6:08)   DCC Compact Classics 1021 Highway 61
                  Revisited. *(gold disc)*
    (S) (6:05)   Time-Life R102-34 The Rolling Stone Collection.

1965 POSITIVELY 4TH STREET

    (S) (3:52)   Columbia 9463 Greatest Hits.
    (S) (3:52)   Columbia 38830 and 65295 Biograph.

1966 RAINY DAY WOMEN #12 & 35

    (S) (4:32)   Columbia 45018 Rock Classics Of The 60's. *(LP
                  version)*
    (S) (4:34)   Columbia 9463 Greatest Hits. *(LP version)*
    (S) (4:35)   Columbia 0841 and 53016 and 64411 Blonde On
                  Blonde. *(LP version)*
    (S) (4:33)   Elektra 60873 O.S.T. Rude Awakening. *(LP
                  version)*
    (S) (4:33)   Epic 66329 O.S.T. Forrest Gump. *(LP version)*

1966 I WANT YOU

    (S) (3:04)   Columbia 9463 Greatest Hits.
    (S) (3:04)   Columbia 38830 and 65295 Biograph.
    (S) (3:05)   Columbia 0841 and 53016 Blonde On Blonde.

1966 JUST LIKE A WOMAN

    (S) (4:52)   Columbia 9463 Greatest Hits. *(LP version)*
    (S) (4:53)   Columbia 38830 and 65295 Biograph. *(LP
                  version)*
    (S) (4:50)   Columbia 0841 and 53016 Blonde On Blonde.
                  (LP version)
    (S) (4:50)   Time-Life R13610 Gold And Platinum Box Set -
                  The Ultimate Rock Collection. *(LP version)*

1969 LAY LADY LAY

    (S) (3:14)   Columbia 31120 Greatest Hits Volume 2.
    (S) (3:16)   Columbia 38830 and 65295 Biograph.
    (S) (3:16)   Columbia 9825 Nashville Skyline.
    (S) (3:15)   Time-Life R102-34 The Rolling Stone Collection.
    (S) (3:16)   Columbia 65373 Nashville Skyline/New
                  Morning/John Wesley Harding.

1970 WIGWAM

    (S) (3:06)   Columbia 30050 Self Portrait.

1971 WATCHING THE RIVER FLOW

    (S) (3:32)   Columbia 31120 Greatest Hits Volume 2.

1972 GEORGE JACKSON

1973 KNOCKIN' ON HEAVEN'S DOOR

    (S) (2:28)   Columbia 45048 Rock Classics Of The 70's.
    (S) (2:29)   Columbia 38830 and 65295 Biograph.
    (S) (2:29)   Columbia 32460 O.S.T. Pat Garrett & Billy The Kid.
    (S) (2:28)   Time-Life R102-34 The Rolling Stone Collection.
    (S) (2:29)   Columbia 66783 Greatest Hits Volume 3.

1974 ON A NIGHT LIKE THIS

    (S) (2:55)   Columbia 37637 Planet Waves.
    (S) (2:54)   Columbia 38830 and 65295 Biograph.

1975 TANGLED UP IN BLUE
(dj copies of this 45 ran (3:27) and (5:31);
commercial copies were all (5:31))

    (S) (5:40)   Columbia 38830 and 65295 Biograph.
    (S) (5:40)   Columbia 66783 Greatest Hits Volume 3.
    (S) (5:40)   Columbia 33235 Blood On The Tracks.

1976 HURRICANE (PART 1)

    (S) (8:31)   Columbia 33893 Desire. *(Parts 1 & 2)*
    (S) (8:32)   Columbia 66783 Greatest Hits Volume 3. *(Parts
                  1 & 2)*

1979 GOTTA SERVE SOMEBODY
(dj copies of this 45 ran (3:57) and (5:22);
commercial copies were all (3:57))

    (S) (5:23)   Columbia 38830 and 65295 Biograph. *(LP version)*
    (S) (5:21)   Columbia 36120 Slow Train Coming. *(LP version)*
    (S) (5:23)   Columbia 66783 Greatest Hits Volume 3. *(LP
                  version)*

RONNIE DYSON

1970 (IF YOU LET ME MAKE LOVE TO YOU) WHY CAN'T I
TOUCH YOU?

    (S) (3:24)   Rhino 70783 Soul Hits Of The 70's Volume 3.
    (S) (3:24)   Rhino 72028 Soul Hits Of The 70's Volumes 1-5
                  Box Set.
    (S) (3:23)   Collectables 5648 His All Time Golden Classics.
    (S) (3:23)   Priority 53129 Deep Soul Volume One.
    (S) (3:23)   Eclipse Music Group 64892 Rock 'n Roll Relix
                  1970-1971.
    (S) (3:23)   Eclipse Music Group 64897 Rock 'n Roll Relix
                  1970-1979.

1973 ONE MAN BAND (PLAYS ALL ALONE)

    (S) (3:38)   Collectables 5648 His All Time Golden Classics.

EAGLES
1972 TAKE IT EASY
- (S)   (3:31)   Asylum 5054   The Eagles. *(LP version)*
- (S)   (3:28)   Asylum 105   Their Greatest Hits. *(LP version)*
- (S)   (3:28)   DCC Compact Classics 1039   Their Greatest Hits. *(LP version; gold disc)*
- (S)   (3:27)   Time-Life R102-34   The Rolling Stone Collection. *(LP version)*

1972 WITCHY WOMAN
- (S)   (4:12)   Asylum 5054   The Eagles. *(LP version)*
- (S)   (4:09)   Asylum 105   Their Greatest Hits. *(LP version)*
- (S)   (4:09)   DCC Compact Classics 1039   Their Greatest Hits. *(LP version; gold disc)*

1973 PEACEFUL EASY FEELING
- (S)   (4:19)   Asylum 5054   The Eagles.
- (S)   (4:14)   Asylum 105   Their Greatest Hits.
- (S)   (4:14)   DCC Compact Classics 1039   Their Greatest Hits. *(gold disc)*

1974 ALREADY GONE
- (S)   (4:11)   Asylum 105   Their Greatest Hits. *(LP length)*
- (S)   (4:13)   DCC Compact Classics 1039   Their Greatest Hits. *(gold disc; LP length)*
- (S)   (4:13)   Asylum 1004   On The Border. *(LP length)*

1975 BEST OF MY LOVE
- (S)   (4:32)   Asylum 105   Their Greatest Hits. *(LP version)*
- (S)   (4:31)   Asylum 1004   On The Border. *(LP version)*
- (S)   (4:31)   DCC Compact Classics 1039   Their Greatest Hits. *(gold disc; LP version)*

1975 ONE OF THESE NIGHTS
- (S)   (4:51)   Asylum 105   Their Greatest Hits. *(LP version)*
- (S)   (4:46)   Asylum 1039   One Of These Nights. *(LP version)*
- (S)   (4:51)   DCC Compact Classics 1039   Their Greatest Hits. *(gold disc; LP version)*
- (S)   (4:45)   Time-Life R13610   Gold And Platinum Box Set - The Ultimate Rock Collection. *(LP version)*

1975 LYIN' EYES
(dj copies of this 45 ran (6:20) and (3:58); commercial copies were all (6:20))
- (S)   (6:21)   Asylum 105   Their Greatest Hits. *(LP version)*
- (S)   (6:20)   Asylum 1039   One Of These Nights. *(LP version)*
- (S)   (6:21)   DCC Compact Classics 1039   Their Greatest Hits. *(gold disc; LP version)*
- (S)   (6:21)   Full Moon/Elektra 60690   O.S.T. Urban Cowboy. *(LP version)*

1976 TAKE IT TO THE LIMIT
- (S)   (4:48)   Asylum 105   Greatest Hits. *(LP length)*
- (S)   (4:47)   Asylum 1039   One Of These Nights. *(LP length)*

1977 NEW KID IN TOWN
- (S)   (5:02)   Asylum 60205   Greatest Hits Volume 2. *(LP length)*
- (S)   (5:04)   Asylum 103   Hotel California. *(LP length)*
- (S)   (5:04)   DCC Compact Classics 1039   Their Greatest Hits. *(gold disc; LP length)*

1977 HOTEL CALIFORNIA
- (S)   (6:27)   Asylum 60205   Greatest Hits Volume 2. *(LP length)*
- (S)   (6:29)   Asylum 103   Hotel California. *(LP length)*
- (S)   (6:29)   DCC Compact Classics 1024   Hotel California. *(LP length; gold disc)*
- (S)   (6:23)   Time-Life R102-34   The Rolling Stone Collection. *(LP length)*

1977 LIFE IN THE FAST LANE
- (S)   (4:43)   Asylum 60205   Greatest Hits Volume 2.
- (S)   (4:44)   Asylum 103   Hotel California.

- (S)   (4:44)   DCC Compact Classics 1024   Hotel California. *(gold disc)*

1978 PLEASE COME HOME FOR CHRISTMAS
- (S)   (2:57)   Columbia 67407   Christmas Of Hope.

1979 HEARTACHE TONIGHT
- (S)   (4:24)   Asylum 60205   Greatest Hits Volume 2.
- (S)   (4:25)   Asylum 508   The Long Run.

1980 THE LONG RUN
- (S)   (3:39)   Asylum 60205   Greatest Hits Volume 2.
- (S)   (3:40)   Asylum 508   The Long Run.

1980 I CAN'T TELL YOU WHY
- (S)   (4:53)   Asylum 60205   Greatest Hits Volume 2. *(LP length)*
- (S)   (4:53)   Asylum 508   The Long Run. *(LP length)*

1981 SEVEN BRIDGES ROAD
- (S)   (2:57)   Asylum 60205   Greatest Hits Volume 2. *(45 version)*
- (S)   (3:26)   Elektra 705   Live. *(LP version)*

1994 GET OVER IT
- (S)   (3:30)   Geffen 24725   Hell Freezes Over.

STACY EARL
1992 LOVE ME ALL UP
- (S)   (4:55)   RCA 61003   Stacy Earl.

1992 ROMEO AND JULIET
- (S)   (4:13)   RCA 61003   Stacy Earl.

EARLS
1963 REMEMBER THEN
- (S)   (2:06)   Collectables 5058   Remember Me Baby.
- (S)   (2:06)   Rhino 71463   Doo Wop Box.
- (M)   (2:08)   Time-Life 2RNR-19   Rock 'N' Roll Era - 1963 Still Rockin'.
- (S)   (1:57)   K-Tel 3812   Doo Wop's Greatest Hits. *(much faster than the orignal recording speed)*

EARTH, WIND & FIRE
1974 MIGHTY MIGHTY
- (S)   (3:03)   Columbia 32712   Open Our Eyes.
- (S)   (3:03)   Columbia/Legacy 52439   The Eternal Dance.
- (S)   (3:03)   Rhino 71431   In Yo Face! History Of Funk Volume 1.
- (S)   (3:01)   Time-Life SOD-27   Sounds Of The Seventies - Dance Fever.
- (S)   (3:03)   Time-Life R838-09   Solid Gold Soul - 1974.

1975 SHINING STAR
- (S)   (2:50)   Epic 46940   O.S.T. Queens Logic.
- (S)   (2:50)   Priority 7057   Mega-Hits Dance Classics Volume 8.
- (S)   (2:50)   Columbia 35647   Best Of Volume I. *(tracks into next selection)*
- (S)   (2:50)   Columbia 33280   That's The Way Of The World. *(tracks into next selection)*
- (S)   (4:54)   Columbia 33694   Gratitude. *(live)*
- (S)   (3:23)   Columbia/Legacy 52439   The Eternal Dance. *(alternate mix; unedited)*
- (S)   (2:50)   Columbia/Legacy 52439   The Eternal Dance. *(tracks into next selection)*
- (S)   (2:50)   Rhino 71432   In Yo Face! History Of Funk Volume 2.
- (S)   (2:51)   Razor & Tie 22045   Those Funky 70's.
- (S)   (2:50)   Time-Life SOD-16   Sounds Of The Seventies - 1975: Take Two.
- (S)   (2:51)   Risky Business 53921   Double Knit Dance Hits.
- (S)   (2:50)   Rebound 314520317   Class Reunion 1975.
- (S)   (2:50)   JCI 3146   1975 - Only Love - 1979.

EARTH, WIND & FIRE (Continued)

- (S) (2:51) Eclipse Music Group 64894 Rock 'n Roll Relix 1974-1975.
- (S) (2:51) Eclipse Music Group 64897 Rock 'n Roll Relix 1970-1979.
- (S) (2:51) Time-Life AM1-22 AM Gold - 1975.
- (S) (2:50) Time-Life R838-10 Solid Gold Soul - 1975.
- (S) (2:50) Columbia/Legacy 65374 That's The Way Of The World/Spirit/All In All. *(tracks into the next selection)*
- (S) (2:50) Nick At Nite/550 Music 63437 Nick At Nite Goes To Outer Space.
- (S) (2:50) JCI 3175 1975 - Only Soul - 1979.
- (S) (2:50) Time-Life R840-06 Sounds Of The Seventies: '70s Dance Party 1975-1976.

1975 THAT'S THE WAY OF THE WORLD
- (S) (5:44) Columbia 35647 Best Of Volume I. *(LP version)*
- (S) (5:45) Columbia 33280 That's The Way Of The World. *(tracks into next selection; LP version)*
- (S) (5:45) Columbia/Legacy 52439 The Eternal Dance. *(LP version)*
- (S) (7:36) Columbia/Legacy 52439 The Eternal Dance. *(live)*
- (S) (3:07) MCA 11329 Soul Train 25th Anniversary Box Set. *(45 version)*
- (S) (5:45) Columbia/Legacy 65374 That's The Way Of The World/Spirit/All In All. *(tracks into the next selection; LP version)*
- (S) (5:43) Time-Life R834-16 Body Talk - Sweet Nothings. *(LP version)*

1976 SING A SONG
- (S) (3:21) Columbia 35647 Best Of Volume I.
- (S) (3:23) Columbia 33694 Gratitude. *(tracks into next selection)*
- (S) (3:22) Columbia/Legacy 52439 The Eternal Dance.
- (S) (3:21) Time-Life R838-11 Solid Gold Soul - 1976.

1976 GETAWAY
- (S) (3:45) Columbia 35647 Best Of Volume I.
- (S) (3:44) Columbia 34241 Spirit.
- (S) (3:54) Columbia/Legacy 52439 The Eternal Dance. *(includes a :10 previously unreleased introduction)*
- (S) (3:44) Columbia/Legacy 65374 That's The Way Of The World/Spirit/All In All.

1977 SATURDAY NITE
- (S) (4:02) Columbia 45013 Best Of Volume II. *(LP length)*
- (S) (4:02) Columbia 34241 Spirit. *(LP length)*
- (S) (4:02) Columbia/Legacy 52439 The Eternal Dance. *(LP length)*
- (S) (4:02) Columbia/Legacy 65374 That's The Way Of The World/Spirit/All In All. *(LP length)*

1978 SERPENTINE FIRE
- (S) (3:51) Columbia 45013 Best Of Volume II. *(LP length)*
- (S) (3:50) Columbia 34905 All 'N All. *(LP length; tracks into next selection)*
- (S) (3:50) Columbia/Legacy 52439 The Eternal Dance. *(LP length)*
- (S) (3:43) Rhino 71434 In Yo Face! History Of Funk Volume 4. *(45 length)*
- (S) (3:51) Time-Life SOD-05 Sounds Of The Seventies - 1977. *(LP length)*
- (S) (3:42) Time-Life R838-16 Solid Gold Soul 1977. *(45 length)*
- (S) (3:50) Columbia/Legacy 65374 That's The Way Of The World/Spirit/All In All. *(LP length; tracks into the next selection)*

1978 FANTASY
- (S) (3:46) Columbia 45013 Best Of Volume II. *(45 version)*
- (S) (3:45) Columbia 35647 Best Of Volume I. *(45 version)*
- (S) (4:37) Columbia 34905 All 'N All. *(LP version)*
- (S) (4:37) Columbia/Legacy 52439 The Eternal Dance. *(LP version)*
- (S) (4:37) Columbia/Legacy 65374 That's The Way Of The World/Spirit/All In All. *(LP version)*

1978 GOT TO GET YOU INTO MY LIFE
(actual commercial 45 time is (4:03) not (4:08) as stated on the record label; the dj copies of this song ran (4:11) and featured a completely different ending)
- (S) (4:03) Columbia 35647 Best Of Volume I. *(commercial 45 version)*
- (S) (4:09) Columbia/Legacy 52439 The Eternal Dance. *(dj promotional 45 version)*
- (S) (4:11) Rhino 71227 Black On White: Great R&B Covers Of Rock Classics. *(dj promotional 45 version)*
- (S) (4:02) Hip-O 40064 Meet The Covers. *(commercial 45 version)*
- (S) (3:34) Polydor 314557076 O.S.T. Sgt. Pepper's Lonely Hearts Club Band. *(soundtrack length)*

1979 SEPTEMBER
- (S) (3:34) Priority 7983 Mega-Hits Dance Classics Volume 7.
- (S) (3:34) Sandstone 33002 Reelin' In The Years Volume 3.
- (S) (3:34) Columbia 35647 Best Of Volume I.
- (S) (3:35) Columbia/Legacy 52439 The Eternal Dance.
- (S) (3:34) DCC Compact Classics 064 Rock Of The 70's Volume Three.
- (S) (3:35) Time-Life SOD-20 Sounds Of The Seventies - 1978: Take Two.
- (S) (3:34) DCC Compact Classics 141 Groove On! Volume 1.
- (S) (3:34) Time-Life R838-17 Solid Gold Soul 1978.
- (S) (3:35) LaFace 26041 O.S.T. Soul Food.
- (S) (3:34) Time-Life R834-20 Body Talk - Heart And Soul.
- (S) (3:34) Priority 50998 70's Greatest Rock Hits Volume 2: Rock & Soul.

released as by EARTH, WIND & FIRE with THE EMOTIONS:
1979 BOOGIE WONDERLAND
(actual 12" single time is (8:21) not (9:21) as stated on the record label)
- (S) (4:52) Columbia 46088 Club Columbia.
- (S) (4:49) Columbia 45013 Earth, Wind & Fire - Best Of Volume II.
- (S) (4:50) Priority 7974 Mega-Hits Dance Classics Volume 4.
- (S) (4:48) Columbia 35730 Earth, Wind & Fire - I Am.
- (S) (4:48) Columbia/Legacy 52439 Earth, Wind & Fire - The Eternal Dance.
- (S) (4:48) Razor & Tie 22496 Disco Fever.
- (S) (4:54) Thump 4099 Old School Boogie.
- (S) (4:48) K-Tel 3581 Roller Disco - Boogie From The Skating Rinks.
- (S) (4:48) Columbia/Legacy 64832 Best Of My Love: Best Of The Emotions.
- (S) (4:48) JCI 3148 1975 - Only Dance - 1979.
- (S) (8:20) Rhino 72588 Phat Trax: The Best Of Old School, Vol. 7. *(12" single version)*
- (S) (4:47) K-Tel 3906 Starflight Vol. 1.
- (S) (4:49) Time-Life R840-08 Sounds Of The Seventies: '70s Dance Party 1978-1979.

released as by EARTH, WIND & FIRE:
1979 AFTER THE LOVE HAS GONE
- (S) (3:55) Columbia 45013 Best Of Volume II. *(45 version)*
- (S) (4:26) Columbia 35730 I Am. *(LP version; tracks into ext selection)*
- (S) (4:26) Columbia/Legacy 52439 The Eternal Dance. *(LP version)*
- (S) (3:54) Time-Life SOD-19 Sounds Of The Seventies - 1979: Take Two. *(45 version)*
- (S) (4:27) Right Stuff 29138 Slow Jams: The 70's Vol. 3. *(LP version)*
- (S) (4:22) Thump 4720 Old School Love Songs Volume 2. *(LP version)*
- (S) (4:25) Columbia/Legacy 64899 Elements Of Love: The Ballads. *(LP version)*
- (S) (3:55) Time-Life R834-01 Body Talk - Forever Yours. *(45 version)*
- (S) (3:55) Time-Life R838-15 Solid Gold Soul 1979. *(45 version)*
- (S) (3:55) Time-Life AM1-26 AM Gold - 1979. *(45 version)*

1981 LET'S GROOVE
(dj copies of this 45 ran (3:30) and (3:55); commercial copies all stated (3:55) but the actual 45 time is (4:04) not (3:55) as stated on the record label)
- (S) (3:31) EMI 91419 MTV, BET, VH-1 Power Players. *(this is the dj 45 edit)*
- (S) (4:03) CBS Special Products 44363 Rock Of The 80's. *(45 version)*
- (S) (5:37) Columbia 37548 Raise. *(LP version)*
- (S) (5:37) Columbia 45013 Best Of Volume II. *(LP version)*
- (S) (5:31) Columbia/Legacy 52439 The Eternal Dance. *(LP version)*
- (S) (5:37) Priority 53730 Mega Hits Dance Classics Vol. 13. *(LP version)*
- (S) (5:33) Thump 4030 Old School Vol. 3. *(LP version; tracks into next selection)*
- (S) (5:28) Epic 66155 Club Epic Volume 3. *(LP version; tracks into next selection)*
- (S) (5:36) Risky Business 57833 Read The Hits/Best Of The 80's. *(LP version)*
- (S) (5:37) Time-Life R988-08 Sounds Of The Eighties: 1981. *(LP version)*
- (S) (4:04) Rhino 72159 Black Entertainment Television - 15th Anniversary. *(45 version)*
- (S) (4:03) Rhino 72136 Billboard Hot R&B Hits 1981. *(45 version)*
- (S) (4:03) K-Tel 3673 The 80's - Funky Love. *(45 version)*
- (S) (5:36) Time-Life R840-09 Sounds Of The Seventies: '70s Dance Party 1979-1981. *(LP version)*

1983 FALL IN LOVE WITH ME
- (S) (5:52) Columbia 38367 Powerlight. *(LP version)*
- (S) (5:21) Columbia/Legacy 52439 The Eternal Dance. *(neither the 45 or LP version)*

SHEENA EASTON
1981 MORNING TRAIN (NINE TO FIVE)
- (S) (3:19) EMI/Manhattan 90267 Sheena Easton.
- (S) (3:18) EMI 91754 Best Of.
- (S) (3:20) EMI 81491 World Of: The Singles Collection.
- (S) (3:18) Priority 53699 80's Greatest Rock Hits Volume 7 - Light & Easy.
- (S) (3:18) Time-Life R988-08 Sounds Of The Eighties: 1981.
- (S) (3:18) EMI 55904 Greatest Hits.
- (S) (3:18) Hip-O 40079 Essential '80s: 1980-1984.

1981 MODERN GIRL
- (S) (3:35) EMI/Manhattan 90267 Sheena Easton.
- (S) (3:36) EMI 91754 Best Of.
- (S) (3:37) EMI 81491 World Of: The Singles Collection.
- (S) (3:34) EMI 55904 Greatest Hits.

1981 FOR YOUR EYES ONLY
- (S) (3:03) EMI 46079 James Bond 13 Original Themes.
- (S) (3:03) EMI 98560 Best Of James Bond 30th Anniversary.
- (S) (3:03) EMI 91754 Best Of.
- (S) (3:03) EMI 98413 Best Of James Bond 30th Anniversary Collection.
- (S) (2:58) EMI 81491 World Of: The Singles Collection.

1982 YOU COULD HAVE BEEN WITH ME
- (S) (3:45) EMI 90268 You Could Have Been With Me.
- (S) (3:44) EMI 81491 World Of: The Singles Collection.
- (S) (3:43) Priority 53700 80's Greatest Rock Hits Volume 13 - Soft Sounds.
- (S) (3:44) EMI 55904 Greatest Hits.
- (S) (3:43) Time-Life R834-15 Body Talk - Once In Lifetime.

1982 WHEN HE SHINES
- (S) (3:52) EMI 90268 You Could Have Been With Me.
- (S) (3:52) EMI 91754 Best Of.
- (S) (3:51) EMI 81491 World Of: The Singles Collection.
- (S) (3:52) EMI 55904 Greatest Hits.

released as by KENNY ROGERS and SHEENA EASTON:
1983 WE'VE GOT TONIGHT
- (S) (3:49) EMI 91754 Sheena Easton - Best Of.
- (S) (3:49) EMI 81491 Sheena Easton - World Of: The Singles Collection.
- (S) (3:49) Razor & Tie 2050 Kenny Rogers - We've Got Tonight.
- (S) (3:49) EMI 48405 Kenny Rogers - We've Got Tonight.
- (S) (3:48) Curb 77358 Kenny Rogers - Greatest Country Hits.
- (S) (3:48) EMI 46106 Kenny Rogers - 20 Greatest Hits.
- (S) (3:50) EMI 46595 Kenny Rogers - Duets.
- (S) (3:48) EMI 46673 Kenny Rogers - 25 Greatest Hits.
- (S) (3:48) Capitol 35779 Kenny Rogers - Best Of.

released as by SHEENA EASTON:
1983 TELEFONE (LONG DISTANCE LOVE AFFAIR)
- (S) (3:43) EMI 91754 Best Of.
- (S) (3:42) EMI 90265 Best Kept Secret.
- (S) (3:41) EMI 81491 World Of: The Singles Collection.
- (S) (3:42) Madacy Entertainment 1983 Rock On 1983.
- (S) (3:42) EMI 55904 Greatest Hits.
- (S) (3:42) Time-Life R988-22 Sounds Of The Eighties 1980-1983.

1984 ALMOST OVER YOU
- (S) (3:38) EMI 91754 Best Of.
- (S) (3:38) EMI 90265 Best Kept Secret.
- (S) (3:36) EMI 81491 World Of: The Singles Collection.
- (S) (3:38) EMI 55904 Greatest Hits.

1984 STRUT
- (S) (4:00) JCI 2720 Rockin' Ladies Of The 80's.
- (S) (4:00) Priority 53728 Mega-Hits Dance Classics (Volume 12).
- (S) (3:59) K-Tel 842 Hot Ladies Of The 80's.
- (S) (4:01) EMI 46054 A Private Heaven.
- (S) (3:59) EMI 91754 Best Of.
- (S) (3:59) EMI 81491 World Of: The Singles Collection.
- (S) (4:00) JCI 3149 1980 - Only Dance - 1984.
- (S) (3:59) Madacy Entertainment 1984 Rock On 1984.
- (S) (3:59) EMI 55904 Greatest Hits.
- (S) (3:59) K-Tel 3867 The 80's: Hot Ladies.
- (S) (3:59) Time-Life R988-23 Sounds Of The Eighties 1984-1985.

1985 SUGAR WALLS
- (S) (3:59) EMI 46054 A Private Heaven.
- (S) (4:00) EMI 91754 Best Of.
- (S) (3:56) EMI 81491 World Of: The Singles Collection.
- (S) (4:00) Madacy Entertainment 1985 Rock On 1985.
- (S) (3:55) Thump 9956 Old School Funk. *(all selections on this cd are segued together)*
- (S) (3:59) EMI 55904 Greatest Hits.

1985 DO IT FOR LOVE
- (S) (5:03) EMI 46200 Do You. *(LP version)*
- (S) (3:48) EMI 81491 World Of: The Singles Collection. *(45 version)*
- (S) (5:02) EMI 55904 Greatest Hits. *(LP version)*

1989 THE LOVER IN ME
- (S) (4:57) Foundation/Capitol 96427 Hearts Of Gold: The Pop Collection. *(LP version)*
- (S) (5:00) MCA 44249 The Lover In Me. *(LP version)*
- (S) (5:00) Madacy Entertainment 1989 Rock On 1989. *(LP version)*
- (S) (5:26) MCA Special Products 21034 Club Disco Dance Hits. *(remix)*

released as by PRINCE with SHEENA EASTON:
1989 THE ARMS OF ORION
- (S) (5:02) Warner Brothers 25936 and 25978 O.S.T. Batman.

released as by SHEENA EASTON:
1991 WHAT COMES NATURALLY
- (S) (4:30) MCA 10131 What Comes Naturally.

EASYBEATS
1967 FRIDAY ON MY MIND
- (M) (2:49) K-Tel 839 Battle Of The Bands Volume 2. *(45 version but slower than the 45 and LP)*
- (S) (2:41) Rhino 75892 Nuggets. *(LP version)*
- (S) (2:41) Rhino 70325 History Of British Rock Volume 7. *(LP version)*
- (S) (2:41) Rhino 72022 History Of British Rock Box Set. *(LP version)*
- (S) (2:41) Time-Life 2CLR-15 Classic Rock - 1967: Shakin' All Over. *(LP version)*

(S) (2:41) Time-Life R968-09 Guitar Rock 1966-1967. *(LP version)*

(S) (2:41) Rhino 72478 Beverly Hills 90210: Songs From The Peach Pit. *(LP version)*

(M) (2:48) Varese Sarabande 5847 On The Radio Volume Two. *(45 version)*

ECHOES
1961 BABY BLUE
(S) (2:28) Time-Life 2RNR-45 Rock 'N' Roll Era - Street Corner Serenade.

(S) (2:29) Time-Life R857-14 The Heart Of Rock 'n' Roll 1960-1961 Take Two.

DUANE EDDY
1958 REBEL-'ROUSER
(M) (1:56) Rhino 70719 Legends Of Guitar - Rock; The 50's. *(missing the first :18 of the song)*

(M) (2:21) Motown 9068 21 Compact Command Performances.

(M) (2:21) Motown 5431 Have "Twangy" Guitar Will Travel.

(M) (2:21) Motown 8058 and 8158 Have "Twangy" Guitar Will Travel/$1,000,000 Worth Of Twang.

(M) (2:21) Rhino 71223 Anthology.

(M) (2:20) Rhino 71601 Rock Instrumental Classics Volume 1: The Fifties.

(M) (2:20) Rhino 72035 Rock Instrumental Classics Vols. 1-5 Box Set.

(M) (2:21) Compose 9923 James Dean/Tribute To A Rebel.

(M) (2:20) Time-Life 2RNR-05 Rock 'N' Roll Era - 1958.

(E) (2:18) Era 840 Rock N' Roll Guitar Classics.

(M) (2:21) LaserLight 12316 Rebel Rousers.

(M) (2:21) Epic 66329 O.S.T. Forrest Gump.

(E) (2:18) K-Tel 3062 Rockin' Rebels.

(E) (2:22) K-Tel 3096 Classic Country Instrumentals.

(E) (2:18) K-Tel 3453 Rockin' Instrumentals.

(S) (3:30) Curb 77801 Ghostrider/Great Guitar Hits. *(all selections on this cd are rerecorded)*

(M) (2:20) JCI 3188 1955 - Only Dance - 1959.

(E) (2:17) K-Tel 4018 Forefathers Of Rock.

1958 RAMROD
(M) (1:38) Motown 9068 21 Compact Command Performances.

(M) (1:39) Motown 5431 Have "Twangy" Guitar Will Travel.

(M) (1:39) Motown 8058 and 8158 Have "Twangy" Guitar Will Travel/$1,000,000 Worth Of Twang.

(M) (1:40) Rhino 71223 Anthology.

(S) (7:03) Curb 77801 Ghostrider/Great Guitar Hits. *(all selections on this cd are rerecorded; medley with "Fanny Mae")*

1958 CANNONBALL
(M) (1:53) Motown 9068 21 Compact Command Performances.

(M) (1:53) Motown 5431 Have "Twangy" Guitar Will Travel.

(M) (1:52) Rhino 71223 Anthology.

(M) (1:53) Time-Life 2RNR-33 Rock 'N' Roll Era - The 50's Last Dance.

(M) (1:53) Motown 8058 and 8158 Have "Twangy" Guitar Will Travel/$1,000,000 Worth Of Twang.

(S) (3:08) Curb 77801 Ghostrider/Great Guitar Hits. *(all selections on this cd are rerecorded)*

1959 THE LONELY ONE
(M) (1:40) Motown 9068 21 Compact Command Performances.

(M) (1:40) Motown 5431 Have "Twangy" Guitar Will Travel.

(M) (1:40) Motown 8058 and 8158 Have "Twangy" Guitar Will Travel/$1,000,000 Worth Of Twang.

(M) (1:39) Rhino 71223 Anthology.

1959 "YEP!"
(M) (2:06) Motown 9068 21 Compact Command Performances.

(M) (2:09) Rhino 71223 Anthology.

1959 FORTY MILES OF BAD ROAD
(M) (2:03) Motown 9068 21 Compact Command Performances.

(M) (2:04) Motown 5424 $1,000,000 Worth Of Twang.

(M) (2:03) Motown 8058 and 8158 Have "Twangy" Guitar Will Travel/$1,000,000 Worth Of Twang.

(M) (2:03) Rhino 71223 Anthology.

(M) (2:04) Rhino 71601 Rock Instrumental Classics Volume 1: The Fifties.

(M) (2:04) Rhino 72035 Rock Instrumental Classics Vols. 1-5 Box Set.

(M) (2:02) Time-Life 2RNR-20 Rock 'N' Roll Era - 1959 Still Rockin'.

(S) (3:24) Curb 77801 Ghostrider/Great Guitar Hits. *(all selections on this cd are rerecorded)*

1959 SOME KIND-A-EARTHQUAKE
(M) (1:17) Motown 9068 21 Compact Command Performances.

(M) (1:17) Motown 5424 $1,000,000 Worth Of Twang.

(M) (1:17) Motown 8058 and 8158 Have "Twangy" Guitar Will Travel/$1,000,000 Worth Of Twang.

(S) (1:16) Rhino 71223 Anthology.

1960 BONNIE CAME BACK
(M) (2:16) Motown 9068 21 Compact Command Performances.

(M) (2:16) Motown 5424 $1,000,000 Worth Of Twang.

(M) (2:16) Motown 8058 and 8158 Have "Twangy" Guitar Will Travel/$1,000,000 Worth Of Twang.

1960 BECAUSE THEY'RE YOUNG
(M) (1:56) Motown 9068 21 Compact Command Performances.

(M) (1:56) Motown 5424 $1,000,000 Worth Of Twang.

(M) (1:56) Motown 8058 and 8158 Have "Twangy" Guitar Will Travel/$1,000,000 Worth Of Twang.

(M) (1:56) Rhino 71223 Anthology.

(S) (1:56) Rhino 71602 Rock Instrumental Classics Volume 2: The Sixties.

(S) (1:56) Rhino 72035 Rock Instrumental Classics Vols. 1-5 Box Set.

(M) (1:55) Time-Life 2RNR-22 Rock 'N' Roll Era - 1960 Still Rockin'.

(M) (1:54) Time-Life SUD-19 Superhits - Early 60's Classics.

(S) (1:57) Rhino 71581 Billboard Top Pop Hits, 1960.

(S) (1:54) Curb 77801 Ghostrider/Great Guitar Hits. *(all selections on this cd are rerecorded)*

(M) (1:54) K-Tel 3583 Those Wonderful Instrumentals Volume 3.

(M) (1:54) Time-Life AM1-20 AM Gold - Early '60s Classics.

1960 PETER GUNN
(M) (2:17) Motown 9068 21 Compact Command Performances.

(S) (2:19) Rhino 71223 Anthology.

(M) (2:17) Time-Life 2RNR-36 Rock 'N' Roll Era - Axes & Saxes/The Great Instrumentals.

(S) (4:45) Curb 77801 Ghostrider/Great Guitar Hits. *(all selections on this cd are rerecorded)*

1961 "PEPE"
(M) (2:02) Motown 9068 21 Compact Command Performances.

(M) (2:03) Motown 5424 $1,000,000 Worth Of Twang.

(M) (2:02) Motown 8058 and 8158 Have "Twangy" Guitar Will Travel/$1,000,000 Worth Of Twang.

(S) (2:02) Rhino 71223 Anthology.

1961 THEME FROM DIXIE
(M) (1:54) Motown 9068 21 Compact Command Performances.

(M) (1:54) Motown 5424 $1,000,000 Worth Of Twang.

(M) (1:54) Motown 8058 and 8158 Have "Twangy" Guitar Will Travel/$1,000,000 Worth Of Twang.

1962 THE BALLAD OF PALLADIN
(M) (1:54) Rhino 71223 Anthology.

1962 (DANCE WITH THE) GUITAR MAN
(S) (2:36) RCA 8475 Nipper's Greatest Hits Of The 60's Volume 2.

(S) (2:40) Rhino 71223 Anthology.

1963 BOSS GUITAR
(M) (2:26) Rhino 71223 Anthology.

EDISON LIGHTHOUSE
1970 LOVE GROWS (WHERE MY ROSEMARY GOES)
- (S) (2:48) Rhino 70922 Super Hits Of The 70's Volume 2.
- (S) (2:48) Rhino 72009 Super Hits Of The 70's Volumes 1-4 Box Set.
- (S) (2:46) Collectables 5066 History Of Rock Volume 6.
- (S) (2:48) Rhino 71205 70's Smash Hits Volume 1.
- (S) (2:44) Time-Life SUD-04 Superhits - 1970.
- (S) (2:46) Time-Life SOD-32 Sounds Of The Seventies - AM Pop Classics.
- (S) (2:48) Varese Sarabande 5535 Bubblegum Classics Volume One.
- (S) (2:47) Ripete 2187-RE Preppy Deluxe.
- (S) (2:51) Varese Sarabande 5725 Love Grows (Where My Rosemary Goes) - The Voice Of Tony Burrows.
- (S) (2:48) LaserLight 12317 The British Invasion.
- (S) (2:44) Time-Life AM1-02 AM Gold - 1970.
- (S) (2:47) Time-Life R840-03 Sounds Of The Seventies - Pop Nuggets: Early '70s.
- (S) (2:48) Flashback 72681 '70s Radio Hits Volume 1.
- (S) (2:48) Flashback 72090 '70s Radio Hits Box Set.

DAVE EDMUNDS
1971 I HEAR YOU KNOCKING
- (S) (2:47) Rhino 70742 Rock This Town: Rockabilly Hits Volume 2.
- (S) (2:48) Rhino 71191 Anthology (1968-1990).
- (S) (2:47) Time-Life R968-11 Guitar Rock - The Early '70s.

1983 SLIPPING AWAY
- (S) (4:19) Risky Business 57833 Read The Hits/Best Of The 80's.

EDSELS
1961 RAMA LAMA DING DONG
- (M) (2:23) Collectables 2507 History Of Rock - The Doo Wop Era Part 1.
- (M) (2:23) Collectables 4507 History Of Rock/The Doo Wop Era Part One.
- (M) (2:25) Relic 2050 Rama Lama Ding Dong.
- (M) (2:22) Original Sound 8852 Oldies But Goodies Vol. 2. *(this compact disc uses the "Waring - fds" noise reduction process)*
- (M) (2:22) Original Sound 2223 Oldies But Goodies Volumes 2,7,9,12 and 13 Box Set. *(this box set uses the "Waring - fds" noise reduction process)*
- (M) (2:22) Original Sound 2500 Oldies But Goodies Volumes 1-15 Box Set. *(this box set uses the "Waring - fds" noise reduction process)*
- (M) (2:24) Rhino 71463 Doo Wop Box.
- (M) (2:23) Time-Life 2RNR-18 Rock 'N' Roll Era - 1961 Still Rockin'.
- (M) (2:23) Collectables 2504 WCBS-FM History Of Rock - The 60's Part 4.
- (M) (2:23) Collectables 4504 History Of Rock/The 60s Part Four.
- (M) (2:23) Time-Life R10513 40 Lovin' Oldies.
- (M) (2:24) Rhino 71802 O.S.T. Andre.

EDWARD BEAR
1973 LAST SONG
- (S) (3:11) Rhino 70930 Super Hits Of The 70's Volume 10.
- (S) (3:11) EMI 90603 Rock Me Gently.
- (S) (3:11) Capitol 98665 When AM Was King.
- (S) (3:11) Time-Life SUD-20 Superhits - Early 70's Classics.
- (S) (3:11) Time-Life AM1-15 AM Gold - Early '70s Classics.
- (S) (3:04) EMI-Capitol Music Special Markets 19545 Lost Hits Of The '70s.

1973 CLOSE YOUR EYES

BOBBY EDWARDS
1961 YOU'RE THE REASON

JONATHAN EDWARDS
1972 SUNSHINE
- (S) (2:14) Rhino 70927 Super Hits Of The 70's Volume 7.
- (S) (2:15) Atco 862 Jonathan Edwards.
- (S) (2:13) Time-Life SUD-10 Superhits - 1971.
- (S) (2:13) Time-Life R105-26 Our Songs: Singers & Songwriters Encore.
- (S) (2:14) JCI 3168 #1 Radio Hits 1970 - Only Rock 'n Roll - 1974.
- (S) (2:13) Time-Life AM1-06 AM Gold - 1971.

TOMMY EDWARDS
1958 IT'S ALL IN THE GAME
- (S) (2:35) Mercury 832041 45's On CD Volume 1.
- (S) (2:35) JCI 3203 Lovin' Fifties.
- (E) (2:37) Elektra 60107 O.S.T. Diner.
- (S) (2:35) Time-Life 2RNR-33 Rock 'N' Roll Era - The 50's Last Dance.
- (S) (2:34) Time-Life RHD-16 Rhythm & Blues - 1958.
- (M) (2:36) Time-Life HPD-11 Your Hit Parade 1958.
- (E) (2:34) Original Sound 8857 Oldies But Goodies Vol. 7. *(this compact disc uses the "Waring - fds" noise reduction process)*
- (E) (2:34) Original Sound 2223 Oldies But Goodies Volumes 2,7,9,12 and 13 Box Set. *(this box set uses the "Waring - fds" noise reduction process)*
- (E) (2:34) Original Sound 2500 Oldies But Goodies Volumes 1-15 Box Set. *(this box set uses the "Waring - fds" noise reduction process)*
- (E) (2:34) Original Sound 8907 Best Love Songs Vol. 2.
- (E) (2:34) Original Sound 9326 Best Love Songs Vol. 1 & 2.
- (E) (2:34) Original Sound 1236 Best Love Songs Box Set.
- (S) (2:35) Time-Life R103-27 Love Me Tender.
- (S) (2:25) Eric 11501 Complete Hits Of.
- (M) (2:58) Eric 11501 Complete Hits Of. *(1951 noncharting version)*
- (M) (2:35) Rhino 71580 Billboard Pop Memories 1955-1959.
- (S) (2:35) Polygram Special Markets 314520258 No. 1 Hits Of The 50's.
- (S) (2:35) Time-Life R857-04 The Heart Of Rock 'n' Roll - 1958.
- (S) (2:35) Polygram Special Markets 314520393 Best Of.
- (M) (2:35) Hammer & Lace 697124114 Leading Men: Masters Of Style Volume Two.
- (M) (2:35) Compose 131 Unforgettable - Gold For The Road.
- (S) (2:35) Polygram Special Markets 314520462 50's Soul.
- (S) (2:35) Polygram Special Markets 314520478 50's Jukebox Hits.
- (S) (2:34) Time-Life R838-22 Solid Gold Soul 1958.
- (M) (2:35) Collectables 1514 and 2514 The Anniversary Album - The 50's.

1958 LOVE IS ALL WE NEED
- (S) (2:38) Time-Life HPD-38 Your Hit Parade - The 50's Generation.
- (S) (2:38) Eric 11501 Complete Hits Of.
- (S) (2:38) Polygram Special Markets 314520393 Best Of.
- (S) (2:37) Time-Life R857-11 The Heart Of Rock 'n' Roll 1958-1959.

1959 PLEASE MR. SUN
- (S) (2:18) Eric 11501 Complete Hits Of.
- (S) (2:10) Polygram Special Markets 314520393 Best Of.

1959 THE MORNING SIDE OF THE MOUNTAIN
- (S) (2:36) Eric 11501 Complete Hits Of.

1959 MY MELANCHOLY BABY
- (S) (2:38) Eric 11501 Complete Hits Of.
- (S) (2:38) Time-Life R974-09 Many Moods Of Romance - True Love.

1960 I REALLY DON'T WANT TO KNOW
- (S) (2:15) Eric 11501 Complete Hits Of.

E-40
1997 THINGS'LL NEVER CHANGE
- (S) (5:04) Jive 41591 and 41600 Tha Hall Of Game.

1997 RAPPER'S BALL
- (S) (5:27) Jive 41591 and 41600 Tha Hall Of Game.
- (S) (4:34) Boxtunes 314524387 Big Phat Ones Of Hip-Hop Volume 2. *(all songs on this cd are segued together)*
- (S) (5:27) Priority 51021 Hip Hop Coast 2 Coast.

WALTER EGAN
1978 MAGNET AND STEEL

(S)	(3:23)	Columbia/Legacy 46763 Rock Artifacts Volume 2.
(S)	(3:23)	Rhino 71201 Super Hits Of The 70's Volume 21.
(S)	(3:18)	Time-Life SOD-34 Sounds Of The Seventies - The Late 70's.
(S)	(3:24)	Sony Music Distribution 57854 For Your Love.
(S)	(3:23)	Razor & Tie 2027 Not Shy.
(S)	(3:25)	Rhino 72445 Listen To The Music: The 70's California Sound.
(S)	(3:20)	Eclipse Music Group 64896 Rock 'n Roll Relix 1978-1979.
(S)	(3:20)	Eclipse Music Group 64897 Rock 'n Roll Relix 1970-1979.
(S)	(3:22)	Capitol 56312 O.S.T. Boogie Nights.
(S)	(3:18)	Rebound 314520492 Class Reunion '78.

8TH DAY
1971 SHE'S NOT JUST ANOTHER WOMAN

(M)	(3:02)	Rhino 70785 Soul Hits Of The 70's Volume 5. *(45 version)*
(S)	(3:11)	HDH 3910 Best Of. *(LP version)*
(M)	(3:01)	Time-Life RHD-09 Rhythm & Blues - 1971. *(45 version)*
(S)	(3:13)	Time-Life SOD-21 Sounds Of The Seventies - Rock 'N' Soul Seventies. *(LP version)*
(M)	(3:02)	Rhino 71615 In Yo Face! The Roots Of Funk Vol. 1/2. *(45 version)*
(M)	(3:01)	Time-Life R838-06 Solid Gold Soul - 1971. *(45 version)*

1971 YOU'VE GOT TO CRAWL (BEFORE YOU WALK)

(S)	(2:46)	Rhino 70786 Soul Hits Of The 70's Volume 6.
(S)	(2:50)	HDH 3910 Best Of.

DONNIE ELBERT
1971 WHERE DID OUR LOVE GO

(S)	(3:20)	Rhino 70786 Soul Hits Of The 70's Volume 6. *(LP version)*
(S)	(3:20)	Ripete 2392156 Grand Stand Gold. *(LP version)*
(S)	(3:18)	Original Sound 9303 Art Laboe's Dedicated To You Vol. 3. *(tracks into next selection; LP version)*
(S)	(3:20)	Ripete 2156-RE Grand Stand Gold Vol. 1. *(LP version)*

1972 I CAN'T HELP MYSELF (SUGAR PIE, HONEY BUNCH)

(S)	(2:33)	Ripete 0001 Coolin' Out/24 Carolina Classics Volume 1.

EL CHICANO
1970 VIVA TIRADO (PART 1)

(S)	(4:40)	Rhino 70782 Soul Hits Of The 70's Volume 2.
(S)	(4:40)	Rhino 72028 Soul Hits Of The 70's Volumes 1-5 Box Set.
(S)	(4:40)	MCA 25197 Viva El Chicano/Their Very Best.
(M)	(4:40)	Rhino 71604 Rock Instrumental Classics Vol. 4: Soul.
(M)	(4:40)	Rhino 72035 Rock Instrumental Classics Vols. 1-5 Box Set.
(S)	(4:40)	Hip-O 40007 Soulful Grooves - R&B Instrumental Classics Volume 1.
(S)	(4:40)	Miramax/Hollywood 62058 O.S.T. The Pallbearer.
(S)	(4:40)	Thump 7100 Latin Oldies.
(S)	(4:40)	MCA Special Products 21035 Classic Rock & Roll Instrumental Hits, Volume 2.
(S)	(4:40)	Rhino 72920 Raza Rock Of The '70s & '80s.

1974 TELL HER SHE'S LOVELY

(S)	(3:13)	Rhino 70758 Super Hits Of The 70's Volume 11. *(:14 longer than the 45 version)*
(S)	(3:52)	MCA 25197 Viva El Chicano/Their Very Best. *(LP version)*
(S)	(3:47)	Thump 7200 Latin Oldies Volume Two. *(LP version)*
(S)	(3:51)	Rhino 72870 Brown Eyed Soul Vol. 3. *(LP version)*

EL DORADOS
1955 AT MY FRONT DOOR

(M)	(2:34)	Rhino 75764 Best Of Doo Wop Uptempo.
(M)	(2:34)	Rhino 70598 Billboard's Top Rock & Roll Hits Of 1955.
(M)	(2:34)	Motown 6215 and 9067 Hits From The Legendary Vee-Jay Records.
(M)	(2:34)	DCC Compact Classics 028 Sock Hop. *(song title is incorrectly identified on the cd jacket as "CRAZY LITTLE MAMA")*
(M)	(2:34)	Vee Jay 702 Bim Bam Boom. *(this song originally ended cold but it is slowly faded out on this compact disc)*
(M)	(2:35)	Collectables 5061 History Of Rock Volume 1.
(M)	(2:34)	Vee Jay 715 A Taste Of Doo Wop Volume Two.
(M)	(2:34)	Rhino 71463 Doo Wop Box.
(M)	(2:34)	Vee Jay 3-400 Celebrating 40 Years Of Classic Hits (1953-1993).
(M)	(2:34)	Time-Life 2RNR-24 Rock 'N' Roll Era - The 50's Keep On Rockin'.
(M)	(2:33)	Time-Life RHD-17 Rhythm & Blues - 1955.
(M)	(2:34)	Time-Life R962-03 History Of Rock 'N' Roll: Rock 'N' Roll Classics 1954-1956.
(M)	(2:35)	Collectables 5038 Great Groups Of The Fifties Volume II.
(M)	(2:34)	Time-Life R10513 40 Lovin' Oldies.
(M)	(2:34)	Rhino 71806 The R&B Box: Thirty Years Of Rhythm & Blues.
(M)	(2:34)	Collectables 5542 More Memories Of Times Square Records Volume 7.
(M)	(2:33)	JCI 3165 #1 Radio Hits 1955 - Only Rock 'n Roll - 1959.
(M)	(2:34)	Collectables 4503 History Of Rock/The 50s Part Two.

ELECTRIC INDIAN
1969 KEEM-O-SABE

(S)	(2:08)	Capitol Special Markets 57272 Great Instrumental Hits From Rock's Golden Years.
(S)	(2:07)	EMI-Capitol Special Markets 19552 Lost Hits Of The '60s.

ELECTRIC LIGHT ORCHESTRA
1975 CAN'T GET IT OUT OF MY HEAD

(S)	(4:21)	Jet 35526 Eldorado. *(LP version)*
(S)	(4:22)	Jet 35528 Ole ELO. *(LP version)*
(S)	(4:21)	Jet 36310 Greatest Hits. *(LP version)*
(S)	(4:24)	Epic Associated 46090 Afterglow. *(LP version)*
(S)	(4:21)	DCC Compact Classics 1041 Eldorado. *(LP version; gold disc)*
(S)	(3:06)	Time-Life SOD-16 Sounds Of The Seventies - 1975: Take Two. *(45 version)*
(S)	(4:21)	Legacy/Epic 64157 Strange Magic - Best Of. *(LP version)*

1976 EVIL WOMAN

(S)	(4:18)	Sandstone 33000 Reelin' In The Years Volume 1. *(LP version)*
(S)	(4:18)	Jet 35527 Face The Music. *(LP version)*
(S)	(4:14)	Jet 35528 Ole ELO. *(LP version)*
(S)	(4:11)	Jet 36310 Greatest Hits. *(LP version)*
(S)	(4:18)	Epic Associated 46090 Afterglow. *(LP version)*
(S)	(4:18)	DCC Compact Classics 062 Rock Of The 70's Volume 1. *(LP version)*
(S)	(4:15)	Razor & Tie 22502 Those Rocking 70's. *(LP version)*
(S)	(3:25)	Time-Life SOD-18 Sounds Of The Seventies - 1976: Take Two. *(45 version)*
(S)	(4:16)	Risky Business 66662 Swingin' Singles/Greatest Hits Of The 70's. *(LP version)*
(S)	(4:18)	Legacy/Epic 64157 Strange Magic - Best Of. *(LP version)*
(S)	(4:18)	Epic 64813 Face The Music/A New World Record/Discovery. *(LP version)*
(S)	(4:14)	K-Tel 3510 Platinum Rock Volume 2. *(LP version)*
(S)	(4:18)	Epic/Legacy 57184 Face The Music. *(gold disc; LP version)*

(S)　(4:25)　CMC International 86233　Superstar Hits. *(live)*

(S)　(4:13)　Thump 6010　Easyriders Volume 1. *(LP version)*

1976　STRANGE MAGIC

(S)　(4:29)　Jet 35527　Face The Music. *(LP version; tracks into next selection)*

(S)　(4:01)　Jet 35528　Ole ELO. *(LP version but missing the :21 introduction)*

(S)　(4:06)　Jet 36310　Greatest Hits. *(LP version but missing the :21 introduction)*

(S)　(4:29)　Epic Associated 46090　Afterglow. *(LP version)*

(S)　(4:29)　Time-Life SOD-21　Sounds Of The Seventies - Rock 'N' Soul Seventies. *(LP version)*

(S)　(4:29)　Legacy/Epic 64157　Strange Magic - Best Of. *(LP version)*

(S)　(4:29)　Epic 64813　Face The Music/A New World Record/Discovery. *(LP version; tracks into next selection)*

(S)　(4:29)　Epic/Legacy 57184　Face The Music. *(gold disc; LP version; tracks into the next selection)*

1976　LIVIN' THING

(S)　(3:30)　Jet 35529　A New World Record.

(S)　(3:30)　Jet 36310　Greatest Hits.

(S)　(3:30)　Epic Associated 46090　Afterglow.

(S)　(3:31)　Legacy/Epic 64157　Strange Magic - Best Of.

(S)　(3:30)　Epic 64813　Face The Music/A New World Record/Discovery.

(S)　(3:29)　Capitol 56312　O.S.T. Boogie Nights.

1977　DO YA

(S)　(3:42)　Jet 35529　A New World Record.

(S)　(3:43)　Epic Associated 46090　Afterglow.

(S)　(3:44)　Time-Life R968-03　Guitar Rock 1976-1977.

(S)　(3:44)　Time-Life SOD-17　Sounds Of The Seventies - 1977: Take Two.

(S)　(3:44)　Time-Life R105-24　Guitar Rock Monsters.

(S)　(3:44)　Legacy/Epic 64157　Strange Magic - Best Of.

(S)　(3:42)　Epic 64813　Face The Music/A New World Record/Discovery.

1977　TELEPHONE LINE

(S)　(4:37)　Jet 35529　A New World Record. *(LP version)*

(S)　(4:36)　Jet 36310　Greatest Hits. *(LP version)*

(S)　(4:38)　Epic Associated 46090　Afterglow. *(LP version)*

(S)　(4:40)　Time-Life SOD-17　Sounds Of The Seventies - 1977: Take Two. *(LP version)*

(S)　(4:39)　Legacy/Epic 64157　Strange Magic - Best Of. *(LP version)*

(S)　(4:39)　JCI 3119　18 Rock Classics. *(LP version)*

(S)　(4:37)　Epic 64813　Face The Music/A New World Record/Discovery. *(LP version)*

1978　TURN TO STONE

(S)　(3:45)　Jet 35530　Out Of The Blue.

(S)　(3:46)　Jet 36310　Greatest Hits.

(S)　(3:47)　Epic Associated 46090　Afterglow.

(S)　(3:47)　Legacy/Epic 64157　Strange Magic - Best Of.

(S)　(3:45)　MCA Special Products 20893　Greatest Tour Bands Ever Recorded.

(S)　(3:47)　Eclipse Music Group 64895　Rock 'n Roll Relix 1976-1977.

(S)　(3:47)　Eclipse Music Group 64897　Rock 'n Roll Relix 1970-1979.

(S)　(3:47)　Sony Music Special Products 26069　Rock Hits Of The 70's.

1978　SWEET TALKIN' WOMAN

(S)　(3:47)　Jet 35530　Out Of The Blue.

(S)　(3:46)　Jet 36310　Greatest Hits.

(S)　(3:47)　Epic Associated 46090　Afterglow.

(S)　(3:47)　Legacy/Epic 64157　Strange Magic - Best Of.

1978　MR. BLUE SKY

(S)　(5:04)　Jet 35530　Out Of The Blue. *(LP version)*

(S)　(5:03)　Jet 36310　Greatest Hits. *(LP version)*

(S)　(3:46)　Epic Associated 46090　Afterglow. *(45 version)*

(S)　(5:01)　Legacy/Epic 64157　Strange Magic - Best Of. *(LP version)*

1979　SHINE A LITTLE LOVE

(S)　(4:39)　Jet 35769 and 64646　Discovery. *(LP version)*

(S)　(4:38)　Epic Associated 46090　Afterglow. *(LP version)*

(S)　(4:39)　Legacy/Epic 64157　Strange Magic - Best Of. *(LP version)*

(S)　(4:39)　Epic 64813　Face The Music/A New World Record/Discovery. *(LP version)*

1979　DON'T BRING ME DOWN (actual 45 and LP time is (4:01) not (4:08) as stated on the record label)

(S)　(4:01)　Jet 35769 and 64646　Discovery.

(S)　(4:01)　Epic Associated 46090　Afterglow.

(S)　(4:02)　Time-Life R968-02　Guitar Rock 1978-1979.

(S)　(4:02)　Time-Life SOD-09　Sounds Of The Seventies - 1979.

(S)　(4:03)　MCA Special Products 22105　Greatest Classic Rock Hits.

(S)　(4:01)　Legacy/Epic 64157　Strange Magic - Best Of.

(S)　(4:01)　Epic 64813　Face The Music/A New World Record/Discovery.

(S)　(4:03)　K-Tel 3463　Platinum Rock.

(S)　(4:01)　Epic/Legacy 65020　Ultimate Rock 'n' Roll Collection.

(S)　(4:02)　Eclipse Music Group 64896　Rock 'n Roll Relix 1978-1979.

(S)　(4:02)　Eclipse Music Group 64897　Rock 'n Roll Relix 1970-1979.

(S)　(4:02)　K-Tel 3904　The Rock Album Volume 1.

(S)　(4:01)　Time-Life R840-10　Sounds Of The Seventies: '70s Dance Party 1979.

(S)　(4:01)　Priority 53139　The Best Of 70's: Rock Chart Toppers.

1980　LAST TRAIN TO LONDON

(S)　(4:30)　Jet 35769 and 64646　Discovery.

(S)　(4:30)　Legacy/Epic 64157　Strange Magic - Best Of.

(S)　(4:30)　Epic 64813　Face The Music/A New World Record/Discovery.

1980　I'M ALIVE

1980　ALL OVER THE WORLD

released as by OLIVIA NEWTON-JOHN/ELECTRIC LIGHT ORCHESTRA:

1980　XANADU

(S)　(3:28)　MCA 5347　Olivia Newton-John's Greatest Hits Volume 2.

released as by ELO:

1981　HOLD ON TIGHT

(S)　(3:06)　Jet 37371　Time.

(S)　(3:05)　Epic Associated 46090　Afterglow.

(S)　(3:05)　Legacy/Epic 64157　Strange Magic - Best Of.

(S)　(3:05)　Rhino 72594　Billboard Top Album Rock Hits, 1981.

(S)　(3:05)　Time-Life R988-22　Sounds Of The Eighties 1980-1983.

1981　TWILIGHT (actual 45 time is (3:24) not (3:29) as stated on the record label)

(S)　(3:41)　Jet 37371　Time. *(LP version)*

(S)　(3:32)　Epic Associated 46090　Afterglow. *(LP version faded :09 early)*

(S)　(3:41)　Legacy/Epic 64157　Strange Magic - Best Of. *(LP version)*

1983　ROCK 'N' ROLL IS KING

(S)　(3:15)　Legacy/Epic 64157　Strange Magic - Best Of. *(neither the 45 or LP version)*

(S)　(3:44)　Jet 38490　Secret Messages. *(LP version)*

released as by ELECTRIC LIGHT ORCHESTRA:

1986　CALLING AMERICA

(S)　(3:27)　Legacy/Epic 64157　Strange Magic - Best Of.

(S)　(3:27)　CBS Associated 40048　Balance Of Power.

ELECTRIC PRUNES

1967　I HAD TOO MUCH TO DREAM (LAST NIGHT)

(S)　(2:56)　Warner Special Products 27607　Highs Of The 60's.

(S)　(2:56)　Rhino 75754　Even More Nuggets.

(S)　(2:55)　JCI 3103　Electric Sixties.

(M)　(2:57)　Rhino 71066　Summer Of Love Volume 2.

(S)　(2:54)　Time-Life 2CLR-05　Classic Rock - 1967.

(S)　(2:54)　Time-Life R968-09　Guitar Rock 1966-1967.

(S)　(2:56)　K-Tel 3183　Psychedelic Mind Trip.

(S)　(2:55)　Buddah 49507　Psychedelic Pop.

(S)　(2:53)　Hip-O 40038　Power Chords Volume 1.

ELECTRIC PRUNES *(Continued)*
1967 GET ME TO THE WORLD ON TIME
- (S) (2:27) Time-Life 2CLR-17 Classic Rock - Rock Renaissance.
- (S) (2:29) Time-Life R968-22 Guitar Rock - The Late '60s Take Two.

ELECTRONIC
1990 GETTING AWAY WITH IT
- (S) (5:13) Warner Brothers 26387 Electronic.

ELEGANTS
1958 LITTLE STAR
- (M) (2:38) Rhino 75764 Best Of Doo Wop Uptempo.
- (M) (2:38) Rhino 70619 Billboard Top Rock & Roll Hits Of 1958.
- (M) (2:38) Rhino 72004 Billboard Top Rock & Roll Hits 1957-1961 Box Set.
- (E) (2:36) Original Sound 8855 Oldies But Goodies Vol. 5. *(this compact disc uses the "Waring - fds" noise reduction process; ambient background noise throughout the disc)*
- (E) (2:36) Original Sound 2222 Oldies But Goodies Volumes 3,5,11,14 and 15 Box Set. *(this box set uses the "Waring - fds" noise reduction process; ambient background noise throughout the song)*
- (E) (2:36) Original Sound 2500 Oldies But Goodies Volumes 1-15 Box Set. *(this box set uses the "Waring - fds" noise reduction process; ambient background noise throughout the song)*
- (M) (2:38) MCA 5937 Vintage Music Volumes 13 & 14.
- (M) (2:36) JCI 3203 Lovin' Fifties. *(sounds like it was mastered from vinyl)*
- (M) (2:40) Collectables 5420 Best Of.
- (M) (2:40) Rhino 71463 Doo Wop Box.
- (M) (2:38) Curb 77637 All Time Greatest Hits Of Rock 'N' Roll Volume 3.
- (M) (2:40) Time-Life 2RNR-05 Rock 'N' Roll Era - 1958.
- (M) (2:40) Time-Life R962-06 History Of Rock 'N' Roll: Doo Wop And Vocal Group Tradition 1955-1962.
- (M) (2:40) Collectables 2602 WCBS-FM History Of Rock - The Group Sounds Vol. 3.
- (M) (2:40) Time-Life R10513 40 Lovin' Oldies.
- (M) (2:38) Polygram Special Markets 314520259 Doo Wop Classics.
- (M) (2:39) Time-Life R857-04 The Heart Of Rock 'n' Roll - 1958.
- (M) (2:40) Rhino 72157 Doo Wop Memories, Vol. 2.
- (M) (2:40) JCI 3183 1955 - Only Love - 1959.

LARRY ELGART and HIS MANHATTAN SWING ORCHESTRA
1982 HOOKED ON SWING
- (S) (6:33) RCA 4343 Hooked On Swing. *(LP version)*
- (S) (6:32) K-Tel 7853 Hooked On Swing. *(LP version)*

JIMMY ELLEDGE
1962 FUNNY HOW TIME SLIPS AWAY
- (S) (2:48) RCA 8475 Nipper's Greatest Hits Of The 60's Volume 2.
- (S) (2:47) Time-Life HPD-37 Your Hit Parade - The 60's.
- (S) (2:47) RCA 66881 RCA's Greatest One-Hit Wonders.
- (S) (2:48) Time-Life R857-12 The Heart Of Rock 'n' Roll 1962-1963.

YVONNE ELLIMAN
1971 I DON'T KNOW HOW TO LOVE HIM
- (S) (3:38) MCA 2-10000 Jesus Christ Superstar. *(previous selection tracks over introduction; LP version)*
- (S) (3:58) Taragon 1003 Very Best Of. *(LP version; includes "Everything's Alright" prelude)*
- (S) (3:53) Rhino 72509 Tim Rice Collection: Stage And Screen Classics. *(movie soundtrack version)*
- (S) (3:38) MCA 11542 Jesus Christ Superstar - A Rock Opera. *(previous selection tracks over introduction; LP version; remastered edition)*
- (S) (3:32) Polydor 314553336 Best Of. *(45 version)*
- (S) (3:33) Varese Sarabande 5847 On The Radio Volume Two. *(45 version)*
- (S) (3:53) MCA 11757 O.S.T. Jesus Christ Superstar. *(movie soundtrack version)*

1977 LOVE ME
- (S) (3:37) Taragon 1003 Very Best Of. *(:16 longer fade than the 45 or LP)*
- (S) (3:21) Rhino 72297 Superhits Of The 70's Volume 23.
- (S) (3:40) Polydor 314553336 Best Of. *(:19 longer fade than the 45 or LP)*
- (S) (3:40) Simitar 55562 The Number One's: Smooth Love. *(:19 longer fade than the 45 or LP)*
- (S) (3:37) Time-Life R834-20 Body Talk - Heart And Soul. *(:16 longer fade than the 45 or LP)*

1977 HELLO STRANGER
- (S) (3:09) Taragon 1003 Very Best Of.
- (S) (3:08) Polydor 314535195 The Power Of Love - Best Of The "Soul Essentials" Ballads.
- (S) (3:09) Special Music 5041 Great Britons! Volume Three.
- (S) (3:09) Special Music 5039 Great Britons! Volume One.
- (S) (3:08) Polydor 314553336 Best Of.
- (S) (3:09) Time-Life R834-16 Body Talk - Sweet Nothings.

1978 IF I CAN'T HAVE YOU
- (S) (2:55) Priority 7973 Mega-Hits Dance Classics Volume 3. *(truncated fade)*
- (S) (2:56) Rhino 70673 Billboard Top Hits - 1978.
- (S) (2:57) Polydor 800068 O.S.T. Saturday Night Fever.
- (S) (2:56) Razor & Tie 22496 Disco Fever.
- (S) (2:58) Time-Life SOD-27 Sounds Of The Seventies - Dance Fever.
- (S) (2:58) Taragon 1003 Very Best Of.
- (S) (3:59) Rebound 314520217 Disco Nights Vol. 1 - Divas Of Dance. *(neither the 45 or LP version; this version first appeared on a promotional only vinyl album titled "O.S.T. Saturday Night Fever - Special Disco Versions")*
- (S) (3:59) Rebound 314520366 Disco Nights Vol. 10 - Disco's Greatest Movie Hits. *(neither the 45 or LP version; this version first appeared on a promotional only vinyl album titled "O.S.T. Saturday Night Fever - Special Disco Versions")*
- (S) (2:56) Polydor 422825389 O.S.T. Saturday Night Fever. *(remastered edition)*
- (S) (2:54) Polydor 314535877 Pure Disco.
- (S) (2:56) Right Stuff 35600 Soul Of The Bee Gees.
- (S) (2:56) Eclipse Music Group 64896 Rock 'n Roll Relix 1978-1979.
- (S) (2:56) Eclipse Music Group 64897 Rock 'n Roll Relix 1970-1979.
- (S) (3:59) Rebound 314520440 No. 1 Hits Of The 70's. *(neither the 45 or LP version; this version first appeared on a promotional only vinyl album titled "O.S.T. Saturday Night Fever - Special Disco Versions")*
- (S) (2:56) Polydor 314553336 Best Of.
- (S) (2:58) Mobile Fidelity 716 O.S.T. Saturday Night Fever. *(gold disc)*
- (S) (2:56) Time-Life R840-08 Sounds Of The Seventies: '70s Dance Party 1978-1979.
- (S) (2:56) Time-Life AM1-25 AM Gold - 1978.
- (S) (2:54) Rebound 314520492 Class Reunion '78.

MISSY "MISDEMEANOR" ELLIOTT featuring DA BRAT
1997 SOCK IT 2 ME
- (S) (4:17) EastWest 62062 Missy "Misdemeanor" Elliott - Supa Dupa Fly.

SHIRLEY ELLIS
1964 THE NITTY GRITTY
- (S) (2:15) Rhino 70650 Billboard's Top R&B Hits Of 1964.
- (S) (2:14) MCA 31205 Vintage Music Volume 8. *(missing the fake audience noise overdub that appeared on the original hit version)*
- (S) (2:14) MCA 5805 Vintage Music Volumes 7 & 8. *(missing the fake audience noise overdub that appeared on the original hit version)*

(S) (2:14) Time-Life 2RNR-35 Rock 'N' Roll Era - The 60's Last Dance.

(S) (2:50) Taragon 1005 Very Best Of. *(neither the 45 or LP version)*

(M) (2:13) Rhino 72815 Beg, Scream & Shout! The Big Ol' Box Of '60s Soul. *(mistakenly titled "THE REAL NITTY GRITTY" on the cd packaging)*

1965 THE NAME GAME

(S) (3:00) MCA 31204 Vintage Music Volume 7. *(:20 longer than either the 45 or LP)*

(S) (3:00) MCA 5805 Vintage Music Volumes 7 & 8. *(:20 longer than either the 45 or LP)*

(S) (2:59) Rhino 70626 Billboard's Top Rock & Roll Hits Of 1965. *(:19 longer than either the 45 or LP; found only on the 2nd pressings of this compact disc)*

(S) (3:00) Rhino 70495 Fun Rock! *(:20 longer than either the 45 or LP)*

(S) (2:59) Rhino 71195 Kid Rock! *(:19 longer than either the 45 or LP)*

(S) (2:59) Time-Life 2CLR-09 Classic Rock - 1964: The Beat Goes On. *(:19 longer than either the 45 or LP)*

(S) (3:00) MCA Special Products 22135 Vintage Collectibles Volume 6. *(:20 longer than either the 45 or LP)*

(S) (3:00) DCC Compact Classics 077 Too Cute! *(:20 longer than either the 45 or LP)*

(S) (4:37) Taragon 1005 Very Best Of. *(1:57 longer than either the 45 or LP)*

(S) (2:58) Music For Little People 42581 A Child's Celebration Of Rock 'N' Roll. *(:18 longer than either the 45 or LP)*

(S) (4:37) JCI 3189 1960 - Only Dance - 1964. *(1:57 longer than either the 45 or LP)*

1965 THE CLAPPING SONG (CLAP PAT CLAP SLAP)

(S) (3:10) Taragon 1005 Very Best Of. *(this is not the hit version)*

EMBERS
1961 SOLITAIRE

(M) (2:46) Collectables 2608 WCBS-FM For Lovers Only Vol. 4.

EMERSON, LAKE & PALMER
1972 FROM THE BEGINNING

(S) (4:12) Atlantic 19123 Trilogy. *(LP version)*
(S) (4:12) Atlantic 82403 The Atlantic Years. *(LP version)*
(S) (4:12) Victory 383480019 Trilogy. *(LP version)*
(S) (4:12) Victory 383484004 Return Of The Manticore. *(LP version)*
(S) (4:12) MFSL 621 Trilogy. *(LP version; gold disc)*
(S) (4:12) Rhino 72234 Return Of The Manticore. *(LP version)*
(S) (4:13) Rhino 72233 Best Of. *(LP version)*
(S) (4:12) Rhino 72226 Trilogy. *(LP version)*
(S) (4:12) Rhino 72627 Greg Lake Retrospective - From The Beginning. *(LP version)*

EMF
1991 UNBELIEVABLE

(S) (5:03) Columbia 52826 Red Hot + Dance. *(remix)*
(S) (3:28) EMI 32393 Loaded Volume 1.
(S) (3:28) EMI 96238 Schubert Dip.
(S) (3:27) Tommy Boy 1137 ESPN Presents Jock Jams. *(all songs on this cd are segued together with crowd sound effects added)*
(S) (3:28) Risky Business 67310 We Came To Play.
(M) (4:23) Priority 50934 Shut Up And Dance! The 90's Volume One. *(remixed; all selections on this cd are segued together)*
(S) (3:28) K-Tel 3849 90s Now Volume 4.

1991 LIES

(S) (4:27) EMI 96238 Schubert Dip.

EMOTIONS
1969 SO I CAN LOVE YOU

(S) (2:49) Stax 88005 Top Of The Stax.
(S) (2:48) Stax 4121 Chronicle: Greatest Hits.

(S) (2:49) Stax 4411 Complete Stax/Volt Soul Singles 1968 - 1971.

(S) (2:49) Stax 88029 So I Can Love You/Untouched.

1977 BEST OF MY LOVE

(S) (3:40) Columbia 46088 Club Columbia.
(S) (3:39) Columbia 34762 Rejoice.
(S) (3:40) Time-Life SOD-17 Sounds Of The Seventies - 1977: Take Two.
(S) (3:39) Priority 53729 Mega Hits Dance Classics Vol 11.
(S) (3:39) Rhino 71756 and 72833 Phat Trax: The Best Of Old School Volume 5.
(S) (3:37) JCI 3131 1975 - Only Rock 'N Roll - 1979.
(S) (3:39) Rhino 72128 Hot Soul Hits Of The 70's Vol. 18.
(S) (3:39) DCC Compact Classics 141 Groove On! Volume 1.
(S) (3:39) Rhino 72414 Dance Floor Divas: The 70's.
(S) (3:40) Columbia/Legacy 64832 Best Of My Love: Best Of.
(S) (3:27) Coldfront 3375 Old School Megamix. *(all selections on this cd are sequed together)*
(S) (3:39) Eclipse Music Group 64895 Rock 'n Roll Relix 1976-1977.
(S) (3:39) Eclipse Music Group 64897 Rock 'n Roll Relix 1970-1979.
(S) (3:38) Capitol 56312 O.S.T. Boogie Nights.
(S) (3:39) Simitar 55602 The Number One's: Silky Soul.
(S) (3:39) Time-Life R834-20 Body Talk - Heart And Soul.
(S) (3:38) K-Tel 3889 Great R&B Female Groups: Hits Of The 70s.

released as by EARTH, WIND & FIRE with THE EMOTIONS:
1979 BOOGIE WONDERLAND
(actual 12" single time is (8:21) not (9:21) as stated on the record label)

(S) (4:52) Columbia 46088 Club Columbia.
(S) (4:49) Columbia 45013 Earth, Wind & Fire - Best Of Volume II.
(S) (4:50) Priority 7974 Mega-Hits Dance Classics Volume 4.
(S) (4:48) Columbia 35730 Earth, Wind & Fire - I Am.
(S) (4:48) Columbia/Legacy 52439 Earth, Wind & Fire - The Eternal Dance.
(S) (4:48) Razor & Tie 22496 Disco Fever.
(S) (4:54) Thump 4099 Old School Boogie.
(S) (4:48) K-Tel 3581 Roller Disco - Boogie From The Skating Rinks.
(S) (4:48) Columbia/Legacy 64832 Best Of My Love: Best Of.
(S) (4:48) JCI 3148 1975 - Only Dance - 1979.
(S) (8:20) Rhino 72588 Phat Trax: The Best Of Old School, Vol. 7. *(12" single version)*
(S) (4:47) K-Tel 3906 Starflight Vol. 1.
(S) (4:49) Time-Life R840-08 Sounds Of The Seventies: '70s Dance Party 1978-1979.

ENCHANTMENT
1977 GLORIA
(dj copies of this 45 ran (3:25) and (5:20); commercial copies were all (3:25))

(S) (5:36) Collectables 5238 Golden Classics. *(LP version)*
(S) (5:35) Right Stuff 30576 Slow Jams: The 70's Volume 4. *(LP version)*
(S) (3:26) Rhino 72129 Soul Hits Of The 70's Vol. 19. *(45 version)*
(S) (5:35) EMI 34401 If You're Ready....Best Of. *(LP version)*

1978 IT'S YOU THAT I NEED

(S) (5:58) Collectables 5238 Golden Classics. *(LP version)*
(S) (5:57) Right Stuff 31974 Slow Jams: The Timeless Collection Volume 4. *(LP version)*
(S) (6:00) EMI 34401 If You're Ready....Best Of. *(LP version)*
(S) (6:00) EMI 38310 Sex & Soul Volume One. *(LP version)*

ENGLAND DAN & JOHN FORD COLEY
1976 I'D REALLY LOVE TO SEE YOU TONIGHT

(S) (2:37) Atlantic 81909 Hit Singles 1958-1977.
(S) (2:37) Rhino 70671 Billboard Top Hits - 1976.
(S) (2:36) Atlantic 76018 Best Of.

ENGLAND DAN & JOHN FORD COLEY *(Continued)*

- (S) (2:37) Razor & Tie 4543 The '70s Preservation Society Presents: Easy '70s.
- (S) (2:36) Rhino 71198 Super Hits Of The 70's Volume 18.
- (S) (2:33) Time-Life SOD-33 Sounds Of The Seventies - AM Pop Classics II.
- (S) (2:36) Rhino 72568 Very Best Of.
- (S) (2:33) JCI 3146 1975 - Only Love - 1979.
- (S) (2:35) Time-Life AM1-23 AM Gold - 1976.
- (S) (2:36) Time-Life R834-05 Body Talk - Sealed With A Kiss.
- (S) (2:35) Time-Life R840-01 Sounds Of The Seventies - Pop Nuggets: Late '70s.
- (S) (2:36) Polygram TV 314555610 The One And Only Love Album.
- (S) (2:36) Time-Life R814-05 Love Songs.

1976 NIGHTS ARE FOREVER WITHOUT YOU

- (S) (2:51) Atlantic 76018 Best Of.
- (S) (2:51) Rhino 72568 Very Best Of.
- (S) (2:49) JCI 3169 #1 Radio Hits 1975 - Only Rock 'n Roll - 1979.
- (S) (2:51) Rhino 72517 Mellow Rock Hits Of The 70's - Ventura Highway.
- (S) (2:51) Time-Life R834-14 Body Talk - Love And Tenderness.
- (S) (2:51) Priority 50962 70's Greatest Rock Hits Volume 7: Southern Rock.

1977 IT'S SAD TO BELONG

- (S) (2:47) Atlantic 76018 Best Of.
- (S) (2:50) Rhino 72568 Very Best Of.
- (S) (2:51) Time-Life R834-17 Body Talk - Heart To Heart.

1977 GONE TOO FAR

- (S) (2:55) Atlantic 76018 Best Of.
- (S) (2:55) Rhino 72568 Very Best Of.

1978 WE'LL NEVER HAVE TO SAY GOODBYE AGAIN

- (S) (2:45) Atlantic 76018 Best Of.
- (S) (2:49) Rhino 72568 Very Best Of.
- (S) (2:48) Time-Life R834-10 Body Talk - From The Heart.
- (S) (2:48) Time-Life R814-01 Love Songs.

1979 LOVE IS THE ANSWER

- (S) (4:40) Atlantic 76018 Best Of.
- (S) (4:36) JCI 3307 Easy Seventies.
- (S) (4:40) Rhino 72568 Very Best Of.
- (S) (4:36) Time-Life R834-06 Body Talk - Only You.

ENGLISH CONGREGATION

1972 SOFTLY WHISPERING I LOVE YOU

- (S) (2:57) Rhino 70927 Super Hits Of The 70's Volume 7.
- (S) (2:56) Time-Life SOD-33 Sounds Of The Seventies - AM Pop Classics II.

ENIGMA

1991 SADENESS (PART 1)

- (S) (4:46) Tommy Boy 1053 MTV Party To Go Volume 2. *(remix; all tracks on this cd are segued together)*
- (S) (11:43) Charisma 91642 and 86224 MCMXC a.D.. *(LP version)*
- (S) (4:13) Virgin 42186 Pure Moods. *(45 version)*

1994 RETURN TO INNOCENCE

- (S) (4:15) Charisma 39236 The Cross Of Changes. *(tracks into next selection)*

EN VOGUE

1990 HOLD ON

- (S) (3:44) Sandstone 33047 and 5015 Cosmopolitan Volume 1. *(45 version)*
- (S) (5:03) Atlantic 82084 Born To Sing. *(LP version)*
- (S) (5:27) Eastwest 91814 Remix To Sing. *(remix)*

1990 LIES

- (S) (4:15) JCI 3124 Rhythm Of The Night.
- (S) (4:15) Atlantic 82084 Born To Sing.
- (S) (5:43) Eastwest 91814 Remix To Sing. *(remix)*
- (S) (4:15) Rhino 72409 New Jack Hits.

1992 MY LOVIN' (YOU'RE NEVER GONNA GET IT)

- (S) (6:55) Tommy Boy 1075 MTV Party To Go Volume 4. *(remix; all tracks on this cd are segued together)*

- (S) (4:42) Foundation/RCA 66563 Number 1 Hit Mix.
- (S) (4:41) Eastwest 92121 Funky Divas.
- (S) (4:40) Razor & Tie 4569 '90s Style.
- (S) (4:41) Elektra 62089 Maximum R&B.

1992 GIVING HIM SOMETHING HE CAN FEEL

- (S) (3:56) Eastwest 92121 Funky Divas.
- (S) (3:55) Elektra 62090 Maximum Slow Jams.

1992 FREE YOUR MIND

- (S) (4:44) Warner Brothers 26974 Barcelona Gold.
- (S) (4:51) Eastwest 92121 Funky Divas.

1993 GIVE IT UP, TURN IT LOOSE

- (S) (5:09) Eastwest 92121 Funky Divas.

1993 LOVE DON'T LOVE YOU

- (S) (3:56) Eastwest 92121 Funky Divas.

released as by SALT-N-PEPA featuring EN VOGUE:

1994 WHATTA MAN

- (S) (5:07) Next Plateau 828392 Salt-N-Pepa - Very Necessary.
- (S) (4:53) Eastwest 92296 En Vogue - Runaway Love.

released as by EN VOGUE:

1997 DON'T LET GO (LOVE)

- (S) (4:51) EastWest 61951 O.S.T. Set It Off.
- (S) (4:50) EastWest 62057 EV3.

1997 WHATEVER

- (S) (4:19) EastWest 62057 EV3.
- (S) (3:45) Elektra 62088 Party Over Here '98. *(all tracks on this cd are segued together)*

1997 TOO GONE, TOO LONG

- (S) (4:41) EastWest 62057 EV3.

ENYA

1989 ORINOCO FLOW (SAIL AWAY)

- (S) (4:25) Geffen 24233 Watermark. *(LP version)*
- (S) (4:25) Reprise 26774 Watermark. *(LP version)*
- (S) (3:43) Virgin 42186 Pure Moods. *(45 version)*
- (S) (4:25) Reprise 46835 Paint The Sky With Stars - Best Of. *(LP version)*

EPMD

1992 CROSSOVER

- (S) (3:48) RAL/Chaos/Columbia 52848 Business Never Personal.
- (S) (3:48) RAL 314523512 Business Never Personal.

PRESTON EPPS

1959 BONGO ROCK

- (M) (2:05) Rhino 71547 Let There Be Drums Volume 1: The 50's.
- (M) (2:08) Original Sound 8853 Oldies But Goodies Vol. 3. *(this compact disc uses the "Waring - fds" noise reduction process)*
- (M) (2:08) Original Sound 2222 Oldies But Goodies Volumes 3,5,11,14 and 15 Box Set. *(this box set uses the "Waring - fds" noise reduction process)*
- (M) (2:08) Original Sound 2500 Oldies But Goodies Volumes 1-15 Box Set. *(this box set uses the "Waring - fds" noise reduction process)*
- (M) (2:07) Original Sound CDGO-4 Golden Oldies Volume. 4.
- (M) (2:38) Original Sound 9601 Best Of Oldies But Goodies Vol. 1. *(extended version)*
- (M) (2:07) Rhino 71601 Rock Instrumental Classics Volume 1: The Fifties.
- (M) (2:07) Rhino 72035 Rock Instrumental Classics Vols. 1-5 Box Set.
- (M) (2:07) Time-Life 2RNR-33 Rock 'N' Roll Era - The 50's Last Dance.
- (E) (2:06) Era 511 Ultimate 50's Party.
- (M) (3:10) Nouveau 1060 O.S.T. This Boy's Life. *(previously unreleased version)*
- (M) (3:10) K-Tel 3453 Rockin' Instrumentals. *(previously unreleased version)*
- (M) (2:08) K-Tel 6256 Kahuna Classics.
- (M) (2:06) I.D. 90072 Jenny McCarthy's Surfin' Safari.

EQUALS
1968 BABY, COME BACK
- (S) (2:39) MCA Special Products 20941 R&B Crossover Oldies Vol. 1.
- (S) (2:39) Varese Sarabande 5705 Dick Bartley Presents Collector's Essentials: The 60's.

ERASURE
1988 CHAINS OF LOVE
- (S) (3:33) JCI 2703 Cutting Edge.
- (S) (3:34) Sire/Reprise 25730 The Innocents.
- (S) (3:35) Rhino 72502 Modern Rock 1988 - Hang The DJ.
- (S) (3:32) Time-Life R988-21 Sounds Of The Eighties: 1986-1989.

1989 A LITTLE RESPECT
(dj copies of this 45 ran (3:33) and (3:55);
commercial copies were all (3:33))
- (S) (6:32) JCI 3117 Lost Mixes - Extended Ecstasy. *(remix)*
- (S) (3:33) Sire/Reprise 25730 The Innocents.

1994 ALWAYS
- (S) (3:57) Mute/Elektra 61633 I Say I Say I Say.

ERNIE (real name JIM HENSON)
1970 RUBBER DUCKIE

ERUPTION
1978 I CAN'T STAND THE RAIN
- (S) (3:05) Rhino 72123 Disco Years, Vol. 7.

ESCAPE CLUB
1988 WILD, WILD WEST
- (S) (5:41) Priority 53684 Rock Of The 80's Volume 4. *(LP version)*
- (S) (4:04) Rhino 71643 Billboard Top Hits - 1988. *(45 version)*
- (S) (5:41) Sandstone 33043 and 5009 Rock The First Volume Three. *(LP version)*
- (S) (5:41) Sandstone 5023 Cosmopolitan Volume 9. *(LP version)*
- (S) (3:58) JCI 3128 1985 - Only Rock 'N Roll - 1989. *(45 version)*
- (S) (5:41) K-Tel 3342 The 80's Pop Explosion. *(LP version)*
- (S) (5:41) Atlantic 81871 Wild Wild West. *(LP version)*
- (S) (4:04) Time-Life R988-10 Sounds Of The 80's: 1988. *(45 version)*
- (S) (3:57) Cold Front 6245 Greatest Sports Rock And Jams. *(all selections on this cd are segued together)*
- (S) (3:58) Madacy Entertainment 6804 More Sun Splashin'. *(45 version)*
- (S) (4:04) Intersound 9521 Retro Lunch Box - Squeeze The Cheese. *(45 version)*

1989 SHAKE FOR THE SHEIK
- (S) (3:59) Atlantic 81871 Wild Wild West.

1991 CALL IT POISON
- (S) (4:51) Atlantic 82198 Dollars And Sex.

1991 I'LL BE THERE
- (S) (5:46) Atlantic 82198 Dollars And Sex. *(LP version)*
- (S) (4:55) JCI 3132 1990 - Only Rock 'n Roll - 1994. *(45 version)*
- (S) (5:46) Time-Life R834-19 Body Talk - Always And Forever. *(LP version)*

ESQUIRES
1967 GET ON UP
- (M) (2:21) Rhino 70653 Billboard's Top R&B Hits Of 1967.
- (M) (2:21) Rhino 72006 Billboard's Top R&B Hits 1965-1969 Box Set.
- (S) (2:24) Capricorn 42003 The Scepter Records Story.
- (S) (2:20) Ripete 2392192 Beach Music Anthology Box Set.
- (S) (2:22) Collectables 5069 History Of Rock Volume 9.
- (S) (2:21) Ripete 0002 Coolin' Out/24 Carolina Classics Vol. 2.
- (S) (2:20) Time-Life RHD-10 Rhythm & Blues - 1967.
- (S) (2:20) Time-Life 2CLR-10 Classic Rock - 1967: The Beat Goes On.

- (S) (2:22) Collectables 5517 Get On Up.
- (S) (2:20) Time-Life R838-02 Solid Gold Soul - 1967.
- (M) (2:21) Rhino 72815 Beg, Scream & Shout! The Big Ol' Box Of '60s Soul.
- (S) (2:22) TVT 4010 Rhythm Revue.

1968 AND GET AWAY
- (S) (2:40) Capricorn 42003 The Scepter Records Story.
- (S) (2:40) Collectables 5517 Get On Up.
- (S) (2:40) Ripete 2148-RE Beach Beat Classics Volume III.

ESSEX
1963 EASIER SAID THAN DONE
- (S) (2:07) Rhino 70624 Billboard's Top Rock & Roll Hits Of 1963.
- (S) (2:07) Rhino 72007 Billboard's Top Rock & Roll Hits 1962-1966 Box Set.
- (S) (2:07) Rhino 70989 Best Of The Girl Groups Volume 2.
- (S) (2:05) Time-Life 2RNR-07 Rock 'N' Roll Era - 1963.
- (S) (2:05) Time-Life RHD-02 Rhythm & Blues - 1963.
- (S) (2:07) Time-Life R962-08 History Of Rock 'N' Roll: Sound Of The City 1959-1965.
- (S) (2:05) Time-Life R838-14 Solid Gold Soul - 1963.

1963 A WALKIN' MIRACLE
- (M) (2:16) Time-Life 2RNR-19 Rock 'N' Roll Era - 1963 Still Rockin'.

DAVID ESSEX
1974 ROCK ON
- (S) (3:24) JCI 3301 Rockin' Seventies. *(LP version)*
- (S) (3:23) Rhino 70635 Billboard's Top Rock & Roll Hits Of 1974. *(LP version)*
- (S) (3:23) Rhino 70759 Super Hits Of The 70's Volume 12. *(LP version)*
- (S) (3:22) Columbia 32560 Rock On. *(LP version)*
- (S) (3:23) Compose 9923 James Dean/Tribute To A Rebel. *(LP version)*
- (S) (3:23) Razor & Tie 22502 Those Rocking 70's. *(LP version)*
- (S) (3:24) Time-Life SOD-07 Sounds Of The Seventies - 1974. *(LP version)*
- (S) (3:22) Risky Business 57470 Wham Bam, Thank You Glam! *(LP version)*
- (S) (3:23) Time-Life R968-16 Guitar Rock - The Mid '70s: Take Two. *(LP version)*
- (S) (3:22) Time-Life AM1-21 AM Gold - 1974. *(LP version)*
- (S) (3:24) Rhino 72812 VH1 8-Track Flashback: The One Hit Wonders. *(LP version)*

GLORIA ESTEFAN
released as by MIAMI SOUND MACHINE:
1986 CONGA
- (S) (4:14) Elektra 60873 O.S.T. Rude Awakening.
- (S) (4:14) Sandstone 33053 and 5021 Cosmopolitan Volume 7.
- (S) (4:14) DCC Compact Classics 081 Night Moves Volume 1.
- (S) (4:14) Epic 40131 Primitive Love.
- (S) (4:14) Epic 53046 Greatest Hits.
- (S) (3:51) Edel America 29782 O.S.T. The Birdcage. *(edited; neither the 45 or LP version)*

1986 BAD BOY
- (S) (3:55) Epic 40131 Primitive Love. *(LP version)*

1986 WORDS GET IN THE WAY
- (S) (3:27) Epic 40131 Primitive Love.
- (S) (3:25) Epic 53046 Greatest Hits.

1987 FALLING IN LOVE (UH-OH)
- (S) (3:58) Sony Music Distribution 57854 For Your Love.
- (S) (3:57) Epic 40131 Primitive Love.

released as by GLORIA ESTEFAN and MIAMI SOUND MACHINE:
1987 RHYTHM IS GONNA GET YOU
- (S) (3:56) Columbia 44382 Heart Of Soul.
- (S) (3:55) Sandstone 33051 and 5019 Cosmopolitan Volume 5.
- (S) (3:55) DCC Compact Classics 083 Night Moves Volume 3.
- (S) (3:55) Epic 40769 Let It Loose.

GLORIA ESTEFAN *(Continued)*
- (S) (3:55)   Epic 53046   Greatest Hits.
- (S) (7:04)   Epic/Legacy 65035   Club Epic Volume 6. *(12" single version)*
- (S) (3:55)   Epic/Legacy 64680   Let It Loose. *(gold disc)*

1987 BETCHA SAY THAT
- (S) (4:37)   Epic 40769   Let It Loose.
- (S) (4:37)   Epic/Legacy 64680   Let It Loose. *(gold disc)*

1988 CAN'T STAY AWAY FROM YOU
- (S) (3:55)   Epic 40769   Let It Loose.
- (S) (3:55)   Epic 53046   Greatest Hits.
- (S) (3:55)   Epic/Legacy 64680   Let It Loose. *(gold disc)*

1988 ANYTHING FOR YOU
- (S) (4:02)   Rhino 71643   Billboard Top Hits - 1988. *(45 length)*
- (S) (3:41)   Epic 40769   Let It Loose. *(LP length)*
- (S) (4:01)   Epic 53046   Greatest Hits. *(45 length)*
- (S) (4:01)   Time-Life R834-01   Body Talk - Forever Yours. *(45 length)*
- (S) (3:41)   Epic/Legacy 64680   Let It Loose. *(gold disc; LP length)*

1988 1-2-3
- (S) (3:28)   Epic 40769   Let It Loose.
- (S) (3:33)   Epic 53046   Greatest Hits. *(remix)*
- (S) (3:28)   Epic/Legacy 64680   Let It Loose. *(gold disc)*

released as by GLORIA ESTEFAN:
1989 DON'T WANNA LOSE YOU
- (S) (4:03)   Rhino 71644   Billboard Top Hits - 1989.
- (S) (4:07)   Epic 45217   Cuts Both Ways.
- (S) (4:08)   Epic 53046   Greatest Hits.
- (S) (4:01)   Columbia 69012   Diana Princess Of Wales Tribute.

1989 GET ON YOUR FEET
- (S) (3:37)   Epic 45217   Cuts Both Ways.
- (S) (3:37)   Epic 53046   Greatest Hits.

1990 HERE WE ARE
- (S) (4:43)   Foundation/Capitol 96427   Hearts Of Gold: The Pop Collection.
- (S) (4:48)   Epic 45217   Cuts Both Ways.
- (S) (4:48)   Epic 53046   Greatest Hits.

1991 COMING OUT OF THE DARK
- (S) (4:02)   Foundation/RCA 66104   Hot #1 Hits.
- (S) (4:02)   Epic 46988   Into The Light.
- (S) (4:02)   Epic 53046   Greatest Hits.

1991 LIVE FOR LOVING YOU
- (S) (4:36)   Epic 46988   Into The Light.

1994 TURN THE BEAT AROUND
- (S) (3:51)   Crescent Moon/Epic 66384   O.S.T. The Specialist.
- (S) (3:51)   Epic 66205   Hold Me, Thrill Me, Kiss Me.
- (S) (7:22)   Priority 50960   Work It! Dance = Life. *(remix; all selections on this cd are segued together)*

1995 EVERLASTING LOVE
- (S) (4:00)   Epic 66205   Hold Me, Thrill Me, Kiss Me.
- (S) (4:00)   Epic 65034   Dancin Divas.

DEON ESTUS with GEORGE MICHAEL
1989 HEAVEN HELP ME
- (S) (4:38)   Mika/Polydor 835713   Deon Estus - Spell.
- (S) (4:37)   Polydor 314535195   The Power Of Love - Best Of The "Soul Essentials" Ballads.

ETERNAL
1994 STAY
- (S) (3:56)   EMI 28212   Always & Forever.
- (S) (3:54)   Right Stuff 52287   Free To Be Volume 3.
- (S) (7:23)   EMI 54097   Retro Dance Club Volume One. *(remix)*

MELISSA ETHERIDGE
1994 COME TO MY WINDOW
- (S) (3:54)   Island 422848660   Yes I Am.

1994 I'M THE ONLY ONE
- (S) (4:54)   Island 422848660   Yes I Am.

1995 IF I WANTED TO
- (S) (3:54)   Island 422848660   Yes I Am.

1995 LIKE THE WAY I DO
- (S) (5:21)   Island 90875 and 422842303   Melissa Etheridge.
- (S) (5:24)   Island 314524154   Your Little Secret.

1996 NOWHERE TO GO
- (S) (5:52)   Island 314524154   Your Little Secret.

E.U.
1988 DA'BUTT
- (S) (5:11)   EMI Manhattan 48680   O.S.T. School Daze. *(LP version)*
- (S) (3:53)   Rebound 314520365   Funk Classics - The 80's. *(45 version)*
- (S) (5:09)   Thump 9956   Old School Funk. *(all selections on this cd are segued together)*

EUROPE
1987 THE FINAL COUNTDOWN
- (S) (3:59)   Columbia 44381   Heart Of Rock. *(45 version)*
- (S) (5:08)   Epic 40241   The Final Countdown. *(LP version)*
- (S) (5:08)   Rhino 72292   Heavy Metal Hits Of The 80's Volume 2. *(LP version)*
- (S) (5:08)   Epic 57445   1982-1992. *(LP version)*
- (S) (5:09)   Priority 50937   Best Of 80's Metal Volume Two: Bang Your Head. *(LP version)*
- (S) (5:07)   Time-Life R968-24   Guitar Rock - The '80s Take Two. *(LP version)*
- (S) (5:09)   Epic/Legacy 65440   Super Hits. *(LP version)*
- (S) (5:08)   Razor & Tie 89004   Monsters Of Rock. *(LP version)*

1987 ROCK THE NIGHT
- (S) (4:03)   Priority 53733   80's Greatest Rock Hits Vol. 9.
- (S) (4:03)   Epic 40241   The Final Countdown.
- (S) (4:03)   Epic 57445   1982-1992.
- (S) (4:03)   Time-Life R968-20   Guitar Rock - The '80s.

1987 CARRIE
- (S) (4:29)   Priority 7965   Heavy Metal Love.
- (S) (4:29)   Epic 40241   The Final Countdown.
- (S) (4:29)   Epic 57445   1982-1992.
- (S) (4:29)   Time-Life R988-19   Sounds Of The Eighties: The Late '80s.
- (S) (4:29)   Epic/Legacy 65440   Super Hits.
- (S) (4:29)   Time-Life R834-20   Body Talk - Heart And Soul.

1988 SUPERSTITIOUS
- (S) (4:33)   Foundation/WEA 26096   Super Sessions Volume One.
- (S) (4:33)   Epic 44185   Out Of This World.
- (S) (4:33)   Epic 57445   1982-1992.

EURYTHMICS
1983 SWEET DREAMS (ARE MADE OF THIS)
- (S) (4:48)   Time-Life R102-34   The Rolling Stone Collection. *(12" single version)*
- (S) (4:51)   Arista 8680   Greatest Hits. *(12" single version)*
- (S) (3:36)   RCA 4681   Sweet Dreams (Are Made Of This).
- (S) (3:35)   EMI 52498   O.S.T. Striptease.
- (S) (3:36)   Rebound 314520434   Classic Rock - 80's.
- (S) (3:35)   Rhino 72856   Just Can't Get Enough: New Wave Women.
- (S) (3:03)   Arista 18985   Ultimate New Wave Party 1998. *(all selections on this cd are segued together)*
- (S) (4:50)   K-Tel 3866   The 80's: Number One Pop Hits. *(12" single version)*

1983 LOVE IS A STRANGER
- (S) (3:39)   Arista 8680   Greatest Hits.
- (S) (3:44)   RCA 4681   Sweet Dreams (Are Made Of This).

1984 HERE COMES THE RAIN AGAIN
(dj copies of this 45 ran (3:50) and (5:05); commercial copies were all (5:05))
- (S) (5:03)   Arista 8680   Greatest Hits.
- (S) (4:53)   RCA 4917   Touch.
- (S) (5:02)   Time-Life R988-27   Sounds Of The Eighties: The Rolling Stone Collection 1983-1985.
- (S) (5:03)   Pyramid R71830   Earthrise - The Rainforest Album.

1984 WHO'S THAT GIRL?
(dj copies of this 45 ran (3:45) and (4:46); commercial copies were all (4:46))
- (S) (3:44)   Arista 8680   Greatest Hits.
- (S) (4:45)   RCA 4917   Touch.

1984 RIGHT BY YOUR SIDE
    (S) (4:04) RCA 4917 Touch.

1985 WOULD I LIE TO YOU?
    (S) (4:22) Arista 8680 Greatest Hits. *(LP length)*
    (S) (4:24) RCA 5429 Be Yourself Tonight. *(LP length)*
    (S) (4:22) Time-Life R13610 Gold And Platinum Box Set - The Ultimate Rock Collection. *(LP length)*
    (S) (4:13) Cold Front 6330 Club Mix: The 80s. *(all selections on this cd are segued together)*

1985 THERE MUST BE AN ANGEL (PLAYING WITH MY HEART)
    (S) (5:19) Arista 8680 Greatest Hits. *(LP version)*
    (S) (5:20) RCA 5429 Be Yourself Tonight. *(LP version)*
    (S) (4:32) Rhino 75234 Rupaul's Go-Go Box Classics. *(45 version)*

released as by THE EURYTHMICS and ARETHA FRANKLIN:
1985 SISTERS ARE DOIN' IT FOR THEMSELVES
    (S) (5:55) Arista 8680 Eurythmics - Greatest Hits. *(LP version)*
    (S) (5:55) RCA 5429 Eurythmics - Be Yourself Tonight. *(LP version)*
    (S) (5:52) Arista 8286 Aretha Franklin - Who's Zoomin' Who. *(LP version)*
    (S) (5:52) Work 67814 O.S.T. First Wives Club. *(LP version)*

released as by THE EURYTHMICS:
1986 MISSIONARY MAN
    (S) (3:45) Arista 8680 Greatest Hits. *(45 version)*
    (S) (4:28) RCA 5847 Revenge. *(LP version)*
    (S) (4:26) RCA 66862 Hi Octane Hard Drivin' Hits. *(LP version)*
    (S) (4:25) Rhino 72500 Modern Rock 1986 - Hang The DJ. *(LP version)*

1989 DON'T ASK ME WHY
    (S) (4:11) Arista 8680 Greatest Hits.
    (S) (4:20) Arista 8606 We Too Are One.

FAITH EVANS (see FAITH)

PAUL EVANS
1959 SEVEN LITTLE GIRLS SITTING IN THE BACK SEAT
1960 MIDNITE SPECIAL
1960 HAPPY-GO-LUCKY-ME

BETTY EVERETT
1964 THE SHOOP SHOOP SONG (IT'S IN HIS KISS)
    (S) (2:15) Rhino 75891 Wonder Women.
    (S) (2:14) Rhino 70988 Best Of The Girl Groups Volume 1.
    (S) (2:09) Original Sound 8853 Oldies But Goodies Vol. 3. *(this compact disc uses the "Waring - fds" noise reduction process)*
    (S) (2:09) Original Sound 2222 Oldies But Goodies Volumes 3,5,11,14 and 15 Box Set. *(this box set uses the "Waring - fds" noise reduction process)*
    (S) (2:09) Original Sound 2500 Oldies But Goodies Volumes 1-15 Box Set. *(this box set uses the "Waring - fds" noise reduction process)*
    (S) (2:09) Original Sound CDGO-3 Golden Oldies Volume 3.
    (S) (2:09) Original Sound 8892 Dick Clark's 21 All-Time Hits Vol. 2.
    (S) (2:14) Rhino 70650 Billboard's Top R&B Hits Of 1964.
    (S) (2:12) DCC Compact Classics 028 Sock Hop.
    (S) (2:11) Motown 6215 and 9067 Hits From The Legendary Vee-Jay Records. *(song incorrectly identified on the cd jacket by its subtitle only, "IT'S IN HIS KISS")*
    (S) (2:13) Ripete 2392192 Beach Music Anthology Box Set.
    (S) (2:13) Collectables 5063 History Of Rock Volume 3.
    (S) (2:13) Vee Jay 707 The Shoop Shoop Song.
    (S) (2:12) Vee Jay 3-400 Celebrating 40 Years Of Classic Hits (1953-1993). *(starts slowly fading out midway through song)*
    (S) (2:11) Ripete 0001 Coolin' Out/24 Carolina Classics Volume 1.
    (S) (2:13) Time-Life 2RNR-10 Rock 'N' Roll Era - 1964.

    (S) (2:13) Time-Life RHD-12 Rhythm & Blues - 1964.
    (S) (2:10) Collectables 2502 WCBS-FM History Of Rock - The 60's Part 3.
    (S) (2:10) Collectables 4502 History Of Rock/The 60s Part Three.
    (S) (2:13) Collectables 2605 WCBS-FM Jukebox Giants Vol. 3.
    (S) (2:14) K-Tel 3008 60's Sock Hop.
    (S) (2:13) Time-Life R838-13 Solid Gold Soul - 1964.
    (S) (2:09) JCI 3184 1960 - Only Love - 1964.

released as by BETTY EVERETT & JERRY BUTLER:
1964 LET IT BE ME
    (M) (2:48) DCC Compact Classics 028 Sock Hop.
    (M) (2:47) JCI 3102 Love Sixties.
    (S) (2:39) Original Sound 8860 Oldies But Goodies Vol. 10. *(this compact disc uses the "Waring - fds" noise reduction process; :08 shorter and faster than the 45 or LP)*
    (S) (2:39) Original Sound 2221 Oldies But Goodies Volumes 1,4,6,8 and 10 Box Set. *(this box set uses the "Waring - fds" noise reduction process; :08 shorter and faster than the 45 or LP)*
    (S) (2:39) Original Sound 2500 Oldies But Goodies Volumes 1-15 Box Set. *(this box set uses the "Waring - fds" noise reduction process; :08 shorter and faster than the 45 or LP)*
    (S) (2:42) Motown 6215 and 9067 Hits From The Legendary Vee-Jay Records. *(much faster than the 45 or LP)*
    (M) (2:48) Rhino 75881 Best Of Jerry Butler.
    (M) (2:47) Curb 77419 Jerry Butler's Greatest Hits.
    (S) (2:37) Vee Jay 700 The Ice Man. *(:10 shorter and faster than the 45 or LP)*
    (S) (2:41) Collectables 5061 History Of Rock Volume 1. *(:06 shorter and faster than the 45 or LP)*
    (S) (2:37) Vee Jay 3-400 Celebrating 40 Years Of Classic Hits (1953-1993). *(:10 shorter and faster than the 45 or LP)*
    (M) (2:47) Time-Life RHD-12 Rhythm & Blues - 1964.
    (S) (2:41) Time-Life SUD-09 Superhits - 1964. *(:06 shorter and faster than the 45 or LP)*
    (S) (2:40) Collectables 2502 WCBS-FM History Of Rock - The 60's Part 3. *(:07 shorter and faster than the 45 or LP)*
    (S) (2:40) Collectables 4502 History Of Rock/The 60s Part Three. *(:07 shorter and faster than the 45 or LP)*
    (S) (2:39) Collectables 2509 WCBS-FM For Lovers Only Part 1. *(:08 shorter and faster than the 45 or LP)*
    (S) (2:41) Collectables 2603 WCBS-FM Jukebox Giants Vol. 1. *(:06 shorter and faster than the 45 or LP)*
    (M) (2:49) Right Stuff 28371 Slow Jams: The 60's Volume Two.
    (M) (2:48) Time-Life OPCD-4517 Tonight's The Night.
    (S) (2:42) LaserLight 12321 Soulful Love. *(:05 shorter and faster than the 45 or LP)*
    (S) (2:38) Ripete 2163-RE Ebb Tide. *(:09 shorter and faster than the 45 or LP)*
    (S) (2:37) Ichiban 2512 Soulful Love - Duets Vol. 1. *(:10 shorter and faster than the 45 or LP)*
    (S) (2:40) JCI 3164 Eighteen Soulful Ballads. *(:07 shorter and faster than the 45 or LP)*
    (S) (2:37) Hip-O 40029 The Glory Of Love - '60s Sweet & Soulful Love Songs. *(:10 shorter and faster than the 45 or LP)*
    (M) (2:49) Rhino 72618 Smooth Grooves: The '60s Volume 1 Early '60s.
    (M) (2:47) Time-Life R857-09 The Heart Of Rock 'n' Roll 1964.
    (S) (2:41) Time-Life AM1-11 AM Gold - 1964. *(:06 shorter and faster than the 45 or LP)*
    (M) (2:47) Time-Life R838-13 Solid Gold Soul - 1964.

released as by BETTY EVERETT:
1969 THERE'LL COME A TIME
    (S) (2:41) Varese Sarabande 5619 There'll Come A Time.
    (S) (2:40) MCA Special Products 21010 R&B Crossover Hits Volume 2.

EVERLY BROTHERS
1957 BYE BYE LOVE
- (M) (2:25) Rhino 75893 Jukebox Classics Volume 1.
- (M) (2:23) Rhino 5258 Cadence Classics.
- (M) (2:23) Arista 8207 24 Original Classics.
- (M) (2:22) Original Sound 8852 Oldies But Goodies Vol. 2. *(this compact disc uses the "Waring - fds" noise reduction process)*
- (M) (2:22) Original Sound 2223 Oldies But Goodies Volumes 2,7,9,12 and 13 Box Set. *(this box set uses the "Waring - fds" noise reduction process)*
- (M) (2:22) Original Sound 2500 Oldies But Goodies Volumes 1-15 Box Set. *(this box set uses the "Waring - fds" noise reduction process)*
- (S) (2:14) Warner Brothers 1554 Very Best Of. *(rerecorded)*
- (M) (2:24) Rhino 70211 The Everly Brothers.
- (M) (2:19) Curb 77311 All Time Greatest Hits.
- (M) (2:21) Essex 7052 All Time Rock Classics. *(some major dropouts from :53 - :59)*
- (M) (2:18) Time-Life 2RNR-09 Rock 'N' Roll Era - Everly Brothers 1957-1962.
- (E) (2:21) Time-Life CTD-02 Country USA - 1957.
- (M) (2:21) Time-Life R962-01 History Of Rock 'N' Roll: Rock 'N' Roll Classics 1957-1959.
- (M) (2:22) Original Sound 8883 21 Legendary Superstars.
- (M) (2:19) Rhino 71779 Heartaches & Harmonies.
- (M) (2:18) ouveau 1060 O.S.T. This Boy's Life.
- (M) (2:19) Varese Sarabande 5579 History Of Cadence Records Volume 2.
- (M) (2:18) LaserLight 12420 Bye Bye Love.
- (M) (2:18) JCI 3165 #1 Radio Hits 1955 - Only Rock 'n Roll - 1959.
- (M) (2:17) Priority 50950 I Love Rock & Roll Volume 1: Hits Of The 50's.
- (M) (2:19) Music Club 50038 This Is - 16 Of Their Greatest Recordings.
- (M) (2:22) Nick At Nite/550 Music 63456 Double Date With Joanie And Chachi.
- (M) (2:20) Time-Life R808-03 Classic Country 1950-1959.
- (M) (2:19) Collectables 1514 and 2514 The Anniversary Album - The 50's.

1957 WAKE UP LITTLE SUSIE
- (M) (2:00) Rhino 70618 Billboard's Top Rock & Roll Hits Of 1957.
- (M) (2:00) Rhino 72004 Billboard's Top Rock & Roll Hits 1957-1961 Box Set.
- (M) (1:59) Rhino 75894 Jukebox Classics Volume 2.
- (M) (1:57) JCI 3201 Party Time Fifties. *(truncated fade)*
- (E) (2:02) Original Sound 8857 Oldies But Goodies Vol. 7. *(this compact disc uses the "Waring - fds" noise reduction process)*
- (E) (2:02) Original Sound 2223 Oldies But Goodies Volumes 2,7,9,12 and 13 Box Set. *(this box set uses the "Waring - fds" noise reduction process)*
- (E) (2:02) Original Sound 2500 Oldies But Goodies Volumes 1-15 Box Set. *(this box set uses the "Waring - fds" noise reduction process)*
- (E) (2:00) Original Sound 8891 Dick Clark's 21 All-Time Hits Vol. 1.
- (M) (2:00) Rhino 5258 Cadence Classics.
- (M) (2:01) Arista 8207 24 Original Classics.
- (S) (2:00) Warner Brothers 1554 Very Best Of. *(rerecorded)*
- (M) (2:01) Rhino 70211 The Everly Brothers.
- (M) (1:59) Curb 77311 All Time Greatest Hits.
- (M) (2:00) Time-Life 2RNR-01 Rock 'N' Roll Era - 1957.
- (M) (1:58) Collectables 2503 WCBS-FM History Of Rock - The 50's Part 2.
- (M) (1:59) Collectables 4503 History Of Rock/The 50s Part Two.
- (M) (2:01) Rhino 71779 Heartaches & Harmonies.
- (M) (1:59) K-Tel 3007 50's Sock Hop.
- (M) (1:59) JCI 3129 1955 - Only Rock 'N Roll - 1959.
- (M) (2:01) Varese Sarabande 5605 Through The Years - Country Hits Of The 50's.
- (M) (2:01) Varese Sarabande 5579 History Of Cadence Records Volume 2.
- (M) (2:00) LaserLight 12313 and 15936 The Wonder Years - Summer Time.

- (M) (2:00) LaserLight 12419 Wake Up Little Susie.
- (M) (2:00) Music Club 50038 This Is - 16 Of Their Greatest Recordings.

1958 THIS LITTLE GIRL OF MINE
- (M) (2:15) Rhino 70211 The Everly Brothers.
- (M) (2:15) Rhino 5258 Cadence Classics.
- (M) (2:14) Time-Life 2RNR-09 Rock 'N' Roll Era - Everly Brothers 1957-1962.
- (M) (2:15) LaserLight 12419 Wake Up Little Susie.

1958 ALL I HAVE TO DO IS DREAM
- (M) (2:18) Rhino 75894 Jukebox Classics Volume 2. *(truncated fade)*
- (M) (2:19) JCI 3203 Lovin' Fifties.
- (M) (2:17) Original Sound 8862 Oldies But Goodies Vol. 12. *(this compact disc uses the "Waring - fds" noise reduction process)*
- (M) (2:17) Original Sound 2223 Oldies But Goodies Volumes 2,7,9,12 and 13 Box Set. *(this box set uses the "Waring - fds" noise reduction process)*
- (M) (2:17) Original Sound 2500 Oldies But Goodies Volumes 1-15 Box Set. *(this box set uses the "Waring - fds" noise reduction process)*
- (E) (2:16) Original Sound 8881 Twenty-One #1 Hits. *(this compact disc uses the "Waring - fds" noise reduction process)*
- (M) (2:18) Rhino 5258 Cadence Classics.
- (M) (2:18) Arista 8207 24 Original Classics.
- (S) (2:20) Warner Brothers 1554 Very Best Of. *(rerecorded)*
- (M) (2:18) Rhino 70213 Fabulous Style Of.
- (M) (2:21) Curb 77311 All Time Greatest Hits.
- (S) (2:20) Atlantic 81885 O.S.T. Stealing Home. *(rerecorded)*
- (M) (2:20) Time-Life 2RNR-09 Rock 'N' Roll Era - Everly Brothers 1957-1962.
- (M) (2:18) Time-Life CTD-07 Country USA - 1958.
- (M) (2:18) Time-Life HPD-11 Your Hit Parade 1958.
- (M) (2:18) Collectables 2503 WCBS-FM History Of Rock - The 50's Part 2.
- (M) (2:16) Collectables 4503 History Of Rock/The 50s Part Two. *(truncated fade)*
- (M) (2:19) LaserLight 12323 American Dreams.
- (M) (2:18) Rhino 71779 Heartaches & Harmonies.
- (M) (2:18) Time-Life R857-04 The Heart Of Rock 'n' Roll - 1958.
- (M) (2:18) Varese Sarabande 5578 History Of Cadence Records Volume 1.
- (M) (2:19) LaserLight 12418 All I Have To Do Is Dream.
- (M) (2:16) Music Club 50015 Love Me Forever - 18 Rock 'N' Roll Love Songs.
- (M) (2:18) Right Stuff 53320 Hot Rod Rock Volume 5: Back Seat Movers.
- (M) (2:15) Priority 50974 Premiere The Movie Magazine Presents The Greatest Soundtrack Love Songs.
- (M) (2:19) Music Club 50038 This Is - 16 Of Their Greatest Recordings.
- (M) (2:18) Nick At Nite/550 Music 63456 Double Date With Joanie And Chachi.

1958 CLAUDETTE
- (M) (2:12) Rhino 71779 Heartaches & Harmonies.
- (M) (2:12) Rhino 5258 Cadence Classics.
- (M) (2:12) Rhino 70213 Fabulous Style Of.
- (M) (2:13) LaserLight 12419 Wake Up Little Susie.
- (M) (2:13) Music Club 50038 This Is - 16 Of Their Greatest Recordings.

1958 BIRD DOG
- (M) (2:14) Rhino 70619 Billboard's Top Rock & Roll Hits Of 1958.
- (M) (2:14) Rhino 72004 Billboard's Top Rock & Roll Hits 1957-1964 Box Set.
- (M) (2:14) Rhino 5258 Cadence Classics.
- (M) (2:10) Original Sound 8854 Oldies But Goodies Vol. 4. *(this compact disc uses the "Waring - fds" noise reduction process)*
- (M) (2:10) Original Sound 2221 Oldies But Goodies Volumes 1,4,6,8 and 10 Box Set. *(this box set uses the "Waring - fds" noise reduction process)*

(M) (2:10) Original Sound 2500 Oldies But Goodies Volumes 1-15 Box Set. *(this box set uses the "Waring - fds" noise reduction process)*
(M) (2:13) Arista 8207 24 Original Classics.
(S) (2:13) Warner Brothers 1554 Very Best Of. *(rerecorded)*
(M) (2:13) Rhino 70213 Fabulous Style Of.
(E) (2:14) Curb 77311 All Time Greatest Hits.
(M) (2:15) Time-Life 2RNR-09 Rock 'N' Roll Era - Everly Brothers 1957-1962.
(M) (2:12) Time-Life CTD-07 Country USA - 1958.
(M) (2:14) Rhino 71779 Heartaches & Harmonies.
(M) (2:12) K-Tel 3436 Rockabilly Riot.
(M) (2:13) LaserLight 12419 Wake Up Little Susie.
(M) (2:14) JCI 3188 1955 - Only Dance - 1959.
(M) (2:13) Walt Disney 60870 Dog Songs.
(M) (2:13) Music Club 50038 This Is - 16 Of Their Greatest Recordings.

1958 DEVOTED TO YOU
(M) (2:21) Rhino 5258 Cadence Classics.
(M) (2:21) Arista 8207 24 Original Classics.
(S) (2:20) Warner Brothers 1554 Very Best Of. *(rerecorded)*
(M) (2:21) Rhino 70213 Fabulous Style Of.
(M) (2:25) Time-Life 2RNR-09 Rock 'N' Roll Era - Everly Brothers 1957-1962.
(M) (2:24) LaserLight 12320 Love Songs.
(M) (2:21) Rhino 71779 Heartaches & Harmonies.
(M) (2:21) Scotti Brothers 75434 Romantic Duets.
(M) (2:22) K-Tel 478 More 50's Jukebox Favorites.
(M) (2:23) K-Tel 3289 The Ties That Bind - Country Love Songs.
(M) (2:24) LaserLight 12420 Bye Bye Love.
(M) (2:22) Music Club 50015 Love Me Forever - 18 Rock'N' Roll Love Songs.
(M) (2:21) Time-Life R857-11 The Heart Of Rock 'n' Roll 1958-1959.
(M) (2:23) Music Club 50038 This Is - 16 Of Their Greatest Recordings.
(M) (2:21) Time-Life R857-21 The Heart Of Rock 'n' Roll Slow Dancing Classics.

1958 PROBLEMS
(M) (1:55) Rhino 5258 Cadence Classics.
(M) (1:55) Arista 8207 24 Original Classics.
(M) (1:55) Rhino 70213 Fabulous Style Of.
(M) (1:55) Curb 77311 All Time Greatest Hits.
(M) (1:55) Time-Life 2RNR-09 Rock 'N' Roll Era - Everly Brothers 1957-1962.
(M) (1:56) Rhino 71779 Heartaches & Harmonies.
(M) (1:56) LaserLight 12420 Bye Bye Love.
(M) (1:56) Music Club 50038 This Is - 16 Of Their Greatest Recordings. *(missing the first few seconds of the song which are replaced with silence)*

1959 TAKE A MESSAGE TO MARY
(S) (2:23) Rhino 5258 Cadence Classics.
(S) (2:24) Arista 8207 24 Original Classics.
(S) (2:24) Rhino 70213 Fabulous Style Of.
(S) (2:27) Time-Life 2RNR-09 Rock 'N' Roll Era - Everly Brothers 1957-1962.
(S) (2:24) Rhino 71779 Heartaches & Harmonies.
(M) (2:26) LaserLight 12418 All I Have To Do Is Dream.
(M) (2:25) Music Club 50038 This Is - 16 Of Their Greatest Recordings.

1959 POOR JENNY
(S) (2:07) Rhino 5258 Cadence Classics.
(S) (2:08) Arista 8207 24 Original Classics.
(S) (2:08) Rhino 70211 The Everly Brothers.
(S) (2:16) Rhino 70213 Fabulous Style Of. *(alternate take)*
(S) (2:10) Time-Life 2RNR-09 Rock 'N' Roll Era - Everly Brothers 1957-1962.
(S) (2:08) Rhino 71779 Heartaches & Harmonies.
(M) (2:06) LaserLight 12419 Wake Up Little Susie.
(M) (2:05) Music Club 50038 This Is - 16 Of Their Greatest Recordings.

1959 ('TIL) I KISSED YOU
(S) (2:23) Rhino 5258 Cadence Classics.
(S) (2:23) Arista 8207 24 Original Classics.

(S) (2:21) Original Sound 8892 Dick Clark's 21 All-Time Hits Vol. 2.
(S) (2:21) Warner Brothers 1554 Very Best Of. *(rerecorded)*
(S) (2:23) Rhino 70213 Fabulous Style Of.
(S) (2:22) Curb 77311 All Time Greatest Hits.
(S) (2:22) Essex 7053 A Hot Summer Night In '59.
(S) (2:22) Time-Life 2RNR-09 Rock 'N' Roll Era - Everly Brothers 1957-1962.
(S) (2:21) Rhino 71779 Heartaches & Harmonies.
(S) (2:22) Varese Sarabande 5578 History Of Cadence Records Volume 1.
(M) (2:25) LaserLight 12420 Bye Bye Love.
(S) (2:22) JCI 3183 1955 - Only Love - 1959.
(M) (2:24) Music Club 50038 This Is - 16 Of Their Greatest Recordings.

1960 LET IT BE ME
(S) (2:35) Rhino 75893 Jukebox Classics Volume 1.
(S) (2:34) Rhino 5258 Cadence Classics.
(S) (2:34) Arista 8207 24 Original Classics.
(S) (2:34) Rhino 70213 Fabulous Style Of.
(S) (2:40) Curb 77311 All Time Greatest Hits.
(S) (2:40) Time-Life 2RNR-09 Rock 'N' Roll Era - Everly Brothers 1957-1962.
(S) (2:34) Time-Life HPD-33 Your Hit Parade - The Early 60's.
(S) (2:34) Time-Life R103-27 Love Me Tender.
(S) (2:35) LaserLight 12320 Love Songs.
(S) (2:34) Rhino 71779 Heartaches & Harmonies.
(S) (2:34) Time-Life R857-02 The Heart Of Rock 'n' Roll - 1960.
(S) (2:34) Time-Life R974-04 Many Moods Of Romance - As Time Goes By.
(M) (2:37) LaserLight 12418 All I Have To Do Is Dream
(M) (2:37) Music Club 50038 This Is - 16 Of Their Greatest Recordings.
(S) (2:35) JCI 3184 1960 - Only Love - 1964.
(S) (2:34) Time-Life R814-04 Love Songs.

1960 CATHY'S CLOWN
(S) (2:23) Rhino 70621 Billboard's Top Rock & Roll Hits Of 1960.
(S) (2:23) Rhino 72004 Billboard's Top Rock & Roll Hits 1957-1961 Box Set.
(S) (2:22) Arista 8207 24 Original Classics.
(S) (2:22) Warner Brothers 1471 Golden Hits Of.
(S) (2:22) Warner Brothers 1554 Very Best Of.
(S) (2:23) Curb 77311 All Time Greatest Hits.
(S) (2:22) Warner Brothers 45164 Walk Right Back: The Everly Brothers On Warner Brothers 1960-1969.
(S) (2:20) JCI 3112 Pop Sixties.
(S) (2:22) Time-Life 2RNR-09 Rock 'N' Roll Era - Everly Brothers 1957-1962.
(S) (2:22) Time-Life 2RNR-11 Rock 'N' Roll Era - 1960. *(this song appears only on remastered versions of this cd)*
(S) (2:22) Time-Life R962-05 History Of Rock 'N' Roll: The Teenage Years 1957-1964.
(S) (2:23) Rhino 71779 Heartaches & Harmonies.
(S) (2:22) Time-Life R808-01 Classic Country 1960-1964.

1960 WHEN WILL I BE LOVED
(M) (1:57) JCI 3102 Love Sixties.
(S) (2:00) Original Sound 8861 Oldies But Goodies Vol. 11. *(this compact disc uses the "Waring - fds" noise reduction process)*
(S) (2:00) Original Sound 2222 Oldies But Goodies Volumes 3,5,11,14 and 15 Box Set. *(this box set uses the "Waring - fds" noise reduction process)*
(S) (2:00) Original Sound 2500 Oldies But Goodies Volumes 1-15 Box Set. *(this box set uses the "Waring - fds" noise reduction process)*
(S) (2:01) Rhino 5258 Cadence Classics.
(S) (2:01) Arista 8207 24 Original Classics.
(S) (2:01) Rhino 70213 Fabulous Style Of.
(M) (1:57) Curb 77311 All Time Greatest Hits.
(M) (1:57) Time-Life 2RNR-09 Rock 'N' Roll Era - Everly Brothers 1957-1962.
(S) (2:01) Columbia 57317 O.S.T. Calendar Girl.

EVERLY BROTHERS (Continued)
- (S) (2:00) Rhino 71779 Heartaches & Harmonies.
- (M) (1:57) LaserLight 12418 All I Have To Do Is Dream.
- (M) (1:56) Music Club 50038 This Is - 16 Of Their Greatest Recordings.

1960 SO SAD (TO WATCH GOOD LOVE GO BAD)
- (S) (2:32) Arista 8207 24 Original Classics.
- (S) (2:32) Warner Brothers 1471 Golden Hits Of.
- (S) (2:32) Warner Brothers 1554 Very Best Of.
- (S) (2:32) Warner Brothers 45164 Walk Right Back: The Everly Brothers On Warner Brothers 1960-1969.
- (S) (2:32) Time-Life 2RNR-09 Rock 'N' Roll Era - Everly Brothers 1957-1962.
- (S) (2:32) Rhino 71779 Heartaches & Harmonies.
- (S) (2:32) Giant 24609 O.S.T. Bye Bye Love.
- (S) (2:32) Time-Life R857-10 The Heart Of Rock 'n' Roll 1960-1961.

1960 LIKE STRANGERS
- (S) (2:00) Rhino 5258 Cadence Classics.
- (S) (1:59) Rhino 70213 Fabulous Style Of.
- (S) (1:59) Time-Life 2RNR-09 Rock 'N' Roll Era - Everly Brothers 1957-1962.
- (M) (1:59) LaserLight 12419 Wake Up Little Susie.
- (M) (1:59) Music Club 50038 This Is - 16 Of Their Greatest Recordings.
- (S) (1:59) Time-Life R857-19 The Heart Of Rock 'n' Roll 1960-1961 Take Three.

1961 WALK RIGHT BACK
- (S) (2:15) Arista 8207 24 Original Classics.
- (S) (2:17) Warner Brothers 1471 Golden Hits Of.
- (S) (2:17) Warner Brothers 1554 Very Best Of.
- (S) (2:17) Warner Brothers 45164 Walk Right Back: The Everly Brothers On Warner Brothers 1960-1969.
- (S) (2:16) Time-Life 2RNR-09 Rock 'N' Roll Era - Everly Brothers 1957-1962.
- (S) (2:17) Time-Life 2RNR-18 Rock 'N' Roll Era - 1961 Still Rockin'.
- (S) (2:15) Rhino 71779 Heartaches & Harmonies.

1961 EBONY EYES
- (E) (3:03) Warner Brothers 1471 Golden Hits Of.
- (E) (3:03) Warner Brothers 1554 Very Best Of.
- (S) (3:03) Warner Brothers 45164 Walk Right Back: The Everly Brothers On Warner Brothers 1960-1969. *(original pressings of this song on this cd were (E))*
- (S) (3:04) Time-Life 2RNR-09 Rock 'N' Roll Era - Everly Brothers 1957-1962.
- (S) (3:03) Time-Life SUD-19 Superhits - Early 60's Classics.
- (S) (3:04) Rhino 71779 Heartaches & Harmonies.
- (S) (3:03) Time-Life R857-14 The Heart Of Rock 'n' Roll 1960-1961 Take Two.
- (S) (3:03) Time-Life AM1-20 AM Gold - Early '60s Classics.

1961 TEMPTATION
- (S) (2:11) Warner Brothers 1471 Golden Hits Of.
- (S) (2:11) Warner Brothers 45164 Walk Right Back: The Everly Brothers On Warner Brothers 1960-1969.
- (S) (2:11) Rhino 71779 Heartaches & Harmonies.

1961 DON'T BLAME ME
- (S) (3:23) Warner Brothers 1471 Golden Hits Of. *(lots of tape hiss; "Golden Hits Of" vinyl LP version)*
- (S) (3:22) Warner Brothers 45164 Walk Right Back: The Everly Brothers On Warner Brothers 1960-1969. *(lots of tape hiss; "Golden Hits Of" vinyl LP version)*
- (S) (3:22) Time-Life 2RNR-09 Rock 'N' Roll Era - Everly Brothers 1957-1962. *("Golden Hits Of" vinyl LP version)*
- (S) (3:24) Rhino 71779 Heartaches & Harmonies. *("Golden Hits Of" vinyl LP version)*
- (S) (3:24) Time-Life R857-17 The Heart Of Rock 'n' Roll: The Early '60s. *(lots of tape hiss; "Golden Hits Of" vinyl LP version)*

1962 CRYING IN THE RAIN
- (S) (1:59) Arista 8207 24 Original Classics.
- (S) (1:57) Warner Brothers 1471 Golden Hits Of.
- (S) (1:57) Warner Brothers 1554 Very Best Of.

- (S) (1:59) Curb 77311 All Time Greatest Hits.
- (S) (1:57) Era 5025 The Brill Building Sound.
- (S) (1:57) Warner Brothers 45164 Walk Right Back: The Everly Brothers On Warner Brothers 1960-1969.
- (S) (1:59) Time-Life 2RNR-09 Rock 'N' Roll Era - Everly Brothers 1957-1962.
- (S) (1:59) Time-Life 2RNR-16 Rock 'N' Roll Era - 1962 Still Rockin'.
- (S) (1:58) Time-Life SUD-06 Superhits - 1962.
- (S) (1:59) Varese Sarabande 5534 Rhythm Of The Rain.
- (S) (1:59) Rhino 71779 Heartaches & Harmonies.
- (S) (1:58) Cypress 71334 O.S.T. Coupe De Ville.
- (S) (1:59) Time-Life R857-06 The Heart Of Rock 'n' Roll 1962.
- (S) (1:58) Time-Life AM1-18 AM Gold - 1962.

1962 THAT'S OLD FASHIONED (THAT'S THE WAY LOVE SHOULD BE)
- (S) (2:20) Warner Brothers 1471 Golden Hits Of.
- (S) (2:20) Warner Brothers 45164 Walk Right Back: The Everly Brothers On Warner Brothers 1960-1969.
- (S) (2:21) Time-Life 2RNR-09 Rock 'N' Roll Era - Everly Brothers 1957-1962.
- (S) (2:21) Rhino 71779 Heartaches & Harmonies.
- (S) (2:21) Time-Life R857-12 The Heart Of Rock 'n' Roll 1962-1963.

1964 GONE, GONE, GONE
- (S) (2:01) Arista 8207 24 Original Classics.
- (S) (2:01) Warner Brothers 45164 Walk Right Back: The Everly Brothers On Warner Brothers 1960-1969.
- (S) (2:01) Rhino 71779 Heartaches & Harmonies.

1967 BOWLING GREEN
- (S) (2:44) Rhino 71779 Heartaches & Harmonies.
- (S) (2:51) Warner Brothers 45164 Walk Right Back: The Everly Brothers On Warner Brothers 1960-1969.
- (S) (2:46) Arista 8207 24 Original Classics.
- (S) (2:51) Rhino 71904 Hillbilly Fever! Vol. 5: Legends Of Country Rock.
- (S) (2:51) Rhino 72444 Heroes Of Country Music Vol. Five.
- (S) (2:43) JCI 3185 1965 - Only Love - 1969.

EVERY MOTHERS' SON
1967 COME ON DOWN TO MY BOAT
- (S) (2:33) K-Tel 205 Battle Of The Bands Volume 3.
- (S) (2:33) Mercury 834216 45's On CD Volume 3.
- (S) (2:33) Time-Life SUD-14 Superhits - The Late 60's.
- (S) (2:34) Polygram Special Markets 314520272 One Hit Wonders.
- (S) (2:33) Special Music 5026 Let It All Hang Out - 60's Party Hits.
- (S) (2:33) Eclipse Music Group 64870 Rock 'n Roll Relix 1966-1967.
- (S) (2:33) Eclipse Music Group 64872 Rock 'n Roll Relix 1966-1969.
- (S) (2:33) Time-Life 2CLR-31 Classic Rock - Totally Fantastic '60s.
- (S) (2:33) Time-Life AM1-14 AM Gold - The Late '60s.
- (S) (2:33) Collectables 5867 Very Best Of.

EVERYTHING BUT THE GIRL
1996 MISSING
- (S) (4:03) Atlantic 82605 Amplified Heart.
- (S) (4:28) Tommy Boy 1164 MTV Party To Go Volume 9. *(remix; all selections on this cd are segued together)*
- (S) (4:47) Arista 18943 Ultimate Dance Party 1997. *(all selections on this cd are segued together; remix)*
- (S) (4:56) EMI-Capitol Music Group 54547 Hot Luv. *(remix)*

EXCITERS
1963 TELL HIM
- (S) (2:36) Rhino 70989 Best Of The Girl Groups Volume 2. *(LP version)*
- (S) (2:29) Motown 6120 and 6062 O.S.T. The Big Chill. *(LP version)*
- (S) (2:33) EMI 96268 24 Greatest Hits Of All Time. *(45 version)*

(S)	(2:33)	EMI 95202 Tell Him. *(45 version)*
(S)	(2:48)	EMI 95202 Tell HIm. *(LP version; includes :11 of studio talk)*
(S)	(2:33)	Capitol 98138 Spring Break Volume 1. *(45 version)*
(M)	(2:28)	Curb 77637 All Time Greatest Hits Of Rock 'N' Roll Volume 3. *(LP version)*
(S)	(2:27)	Time-Life 2RNR-07 Rock 'N' Roll Era - 1963. *(LP version)*
(S)	(2:26)	Time-Life RHD-02 Rhythm & Blues - 1963. *(LP version)*
(S)	(2:33)	Time-Life R962-08 History Of Rock 'N' Roll: Sound Of The City 1959-1965. *(45 version)*
(S)	(2:33)	Collectables 5672 Tell Him. *(45 version)*
(S)	(2:48)	Collectables 5672 Tell Him. *(LP version; includes :11 of studio talk)*
(S)	(2:26)	Time-Life R838-14 Solid Gold Soul - 1963. *(LP version)*
(S)	(2:32)	Work 68166 O.S.T. My Best Friend's Wedding. *(LP version)*

EXILE
1978 KISS YOU ALL OVER
(dj copies of this 45 ran (3:20), (3:30) and (4:54); commercial copies were all (3:30))

(S)	(4:54)	Curb 77317 70's Hits Volume 1. *(LP version)*
(S)	(3:27)	Rhino 70673 Billboard Top Hits - 1978. *(45 version)*
(S)	(3:28)	Priority 7058 Mega-Hits Dance Classics Volume 9. *(45 version)*
(S)	(3:27)	Razor & Tie 4543 The '70s Preservation Society Presents: Easy '70s. *(45 version)*
(S)	(4:52)	Curb 77296 Best Of. *(LP version)*
(S)	(4:51)	Curb 77503 The Complete Collection. *(LP version)*
(S)	(3:27)	Rhino 71201 Super Hits Of The 70's Volume 21. *(45 version)*
(S)	(3:27)	Time-Life SOD-10 Sounds Of The Seventies - 1978. *(45 version)*
(S)	(4:52)	Curb 77651 Retro Rock Dance Hits. *(all selections on this cd are remixed with extra instrumentation added)*
(S)	(3:34)	Columbia 64185 Country Super Hits. *(45 version)*
(S)	(3:34)	Epic 53313 Super Hits. *(rerecording)*
(S)	(3:27)	K-Tel 3639 Dim The Lights - Soft Rock Hits Of The 70's. *(45 version)*
(S)	(3:33)	Risky Business 67309 Sexy Country. *(rerecording)*
(S)	(4:48)	MCA Special Products 21011 70's Biggest Hits. *(alternate take)*
(S)	(3:27)	K-Tel 3907 Starflight Vol. 2. *(45 version)*
(S)	(3:27)	Time-Life AM1-25 AM Gold - 1978. *(45 version)*
(S)	(3:27)	K-Tel 3987 70s Heavy Hitters: #1 Pop Hits. *(45 version)*

EXPOSE
1987 COME GO WITH ME
(actual 45 time is (3:36) not (3:29) as stated on the record label)

(S)	(4:16)	K-Tel 842 Hot Ladies Of The 80's. *(LP version)*
(S)	(4:16)	Arista 8441 Exposure. *(LP version)*
(S)	(4:16)	Arista 18773 Greatest Hits. *(LP version)*
(S)	(4:13)	JCI 3186 1985 - Only Love - 1989. *(LP version)*
(S)	(4:55)	Cold Front 6242 Club Mix '97. *(all selections on this cd are segued together; remix)*
(S)	(3:35)	Rhino 75217 Heartthrob Hits. *(45 version)*
(S)	(4:07)	Priority 50940 Shut Up And Dance! The 80's Volume One. *(all selections on this cd are segued together)*

1987 POINT OF NO RETURN

(S)	(3:27)	Arista 8441 Exposure.
(S)	(3:27)	Arista 18773 Greatest Hits.
(S)	(3:27)	JCI 3171 #1 Radio Hits 1985 - Only Rock 'n Roll - 1989.
(S)	(3:26)	Scotti Bros. 75504 Club Ladies Night.

(S)	(3:26)	Quality 5008 Dance Box Set. *(all selections on this cd are segued together)*
(S)	(4:31)	Priority 50955 Power Workout High NRG Megamix Volume 2. *(all selections on this cd are segued together; remixed)*

1987 LET ME BE THE ONE
(actual 45 time is (4:07) not (3:56) as stated on the record label)

(S)	(4:07)	EMI 91419 MTV, BET, VH-1 Power Players. *(45 version)*
(S)	(4:19)	Arista 8441 Exposure. *(LP version)*
(S)	(4:07)	Arista 18773 Greatest Hits. *(45 version)*
(S)	(4:06)	Cold Front 3865 Club Mix - Women Of Dance Vol. 2. *(45 version)*

1988 SEASONS CHANGE
(actual 45 time is (4:11) not (3:58) as stated on the record label)

(S)	(4:52)	K-Tel 898 Romantic Hits Of The 80's. *(LP version)*
(S)	(4:52)	Priority 7040 Making Love. *(LP version)*
(S)	(4:15)	Rhino 71643 Billboard Top Hits - 1988. *(45 version)*
(S)	(4:52)	Sandstone 33043 and 5009 Rock The First Volume Three. *(LP version)*
(S)	(4:52)	Arista 8441 Exposure. *(LP version)*
(S)	(4:15)	Arista 18773 Greatest Hits. *(45 version)*
(S)	(4:52)	Madacy Entertainment 1988 Rock On 1988. *(LP version)*
(S)	(4:15)	Time-Life R988-21 Sounds Of The Eighties: 1986-1989. *(45 version)*
(S)	(4:52)	Time-Life R834-02 Body Talk - Just For You. *(LP version)*
(S)	(4:51)	K-Tel 3867 The 80's: Hot Ladies. *(LP version)*

1989 WHAT YOU DON'T KNOW
(actual 45 time is (4:10) not (3:58) as stated on the record label)

(S)	(4:46)	Arista 8532 What You Don't Know. *(LP version)*
(S)	(4:44)	Priority 53773 80's Greatest Rock Hits Volume II - Teen Idols. *(LP version)*
(S)	(4:10)	Arista 18773 Greatest Hits. *(45 version)*
(S)	(4:10)	JCI 3150 1985 - Only Dance - 1989. *(45 version)*

1989 WHEN I LOOKED AT HIM

(S)	(5:31)	Arista 8532 What You Don't Know. *(LP version)*
(S)	(4:16)	Arista 18773 Greatest Hits. *(45 version)*
(S)	(5:31)	Madacy Entertainment 1989 Rock On 1989. *(LP version)*

1990 TELL ME WHY

(S)	(5:22)	Arista 8532 What You Don't Know. *(LP version)*
(S)	(4:24)	Arista 18773 Greatest Hits. *(45 version)*
(S)	(10:22)	DCC Compact Classics 121 Divas Of Dance Volume 1. *(remix)*

1990 YOUR BABY NEVER LOOKED GOOD IN BLUE

(S)	(3:53)	Arista 8532 What You Don't Know.
(S)	(3:59)	Arista 18773 Greatest Hits.

1992 I WISH THE PHONE WOULD RING

(S)	(4:05)	Arista 18577 Expose.

1993 I'LL NEVER GET OVER YOU (GETTING OVER ME)

(S)	(3:48)	Arista 18577 Expose.
(S)	(3:48)	Original Sound 9307 Dedicated To You Vol. 7.
(S)	(3:48)	Arista 18773 Greatest Hits.
(S)	(3:48)	JCI 3132 1990 - Only Rock 'n Roll - 1994.
(S)	(3:46)	Priority 50946 100% Party Hits Of The 90's Volume One.
(S)	(3:47)	Time-Life R834-17 Body Talk - Heart To Heart.

EXTREME
1991 MORE THAN WORDS

(S)	(5:33)	A&M 5313 Pornograffitti. *(LP version)*
(S)	(5:37)	Polygram TV 314555610 The One And Only Love Album. *(LP version)*

1991 HOLE HEARTED

(S)	(3:37)	A&M 5313 Pornograffitti.

EYE TO EYE
1982 NICE GIRLS

SHELLEY FABARES
1962 JOHNNY ANGEL
- (S) (2:21) Rhino 70623 Billboard's Top Rock & Roll Hits Of 1962.
- (S) (2:21) Rhino 72007 Billboard's Top Rock & Roll Hits 1962-1966 Box Set.
- (S) (2:21) Geffen 24310 O.S.T. Mermaids.
- (S) (2:18) Time-Life 2RNR-27 Rock 'N' Roll Era - Teen Idols.
- (S) (2:19) Time-Life SUD-06 Superhits - 1962.
- (S) (2:19) Rhino 71650 Colpix-Dimension Story.
- (S) (2:19) Rhino 71651 Best Of.
- (S) (2:20) Polygram Special Markets 314520260 Number One Hits Of The Sixties.
- (S) (2:20) DCC Compact Classics 077 Too Cute!
- (S) (2:19) Scotti Bros. 75465 Angel Hits.
- (S) (2:19) Nick At Nite/Epic 67148 Donna Reed's Dinner Party.
- (S) (2:19) Rhino 71802 O.S.T. Andre.
- (S) (2:18) K-Tel 3388 TV Stars Sing.
- (S) (2:19) JCI 3166 #1 Radio Hits 1960 - Only Rock 'n Roll - 1964.
- (S) (2:18) Eclipse Music Group 64868 Rock 'n Roll Relix 1962-1963.
- (S) (2:18) Eclipse Music Group 64872 Rock 'n Roll Relix 1960-1969.
- (S) (2:21) Time-Life R857-12 The Heart Of Rock 'n' Roll 1962-1963.
- (S) (2:19) Time-Life AM1-18 AM Gold - 1962.
- (S) (2:18) Collectables 1515 and 2515 The Anniversary Album - The 60's. *(truncated fade)*

1962 JOHNNY LOVES ME
- (M) (2:19) Era 5025 The Brill Building Sound. *(no fidelity)*
- (S) (2:21) Rhino 71650 Colpix-Dimension Story.
- (S) (2:21) Rhino 71651 Best Of.

FABIAN
1959 I'M A MAN
- (M) (2:09) LaserLight 12319 Frankie Avalon/Fabian/Ritchie Valens - Their Greatest Hits.
- (M) (2:08) Varese Sarabande 5576 Best Of.
- (M) (2:08) Taragon 1019 Chancellor Records Story, Volume 2.
- (M) (2:08) Music Club 50030 The Teen Idols: Very Best Of Frankie Avalon & Fabian.

1959 TURN ME LOOSE
- (S) (2:23) Rhino 75893 Jukebox Classics Volume 1.
- (S) (2:21) Garland 012 Remember When.
- (S) (2:19) MCA 6171 Good Time Rock 'N' Roll. *(all selections on this cd are recorded live)*
- (S) (2:21) Collectables 5066 History Of Rock Volume 6.
- (M) (2:19) Era 5025 The Brill Building Sound. *(this version sounds like it was originally (E) mixed to (M))*
- (S) (2:21) Time-Life 2RNR-27 Rock 'N' Roll Era - Teen Idols.
- (M) (2:19) Collectables 2503 WCBS-FM History Of Rock - The 50's Part 2.
- (S) (2:22) Collectables 4503 History Of Rock/The 50s Part Two.
- (S) (2:21) LaserLight 12319 Frankie Avalon/Fabian/Ritchie Valens - Their Greatest Hits.
- (S) (2:22) Varese Sarabande 5576 Best Of.
- (S) (2:21) Taragon 1018 Chancellor Records Story, Volume 1.
- (S) (2:21) Music Club 50030 The Teen Idols: Very Best Of Frankie Avalon & Fabian.

1959 TIGER
- (S) (2:31) Rhino 75894 Jukebox Classics Volume 2.
- (S) (2:29) Time-Life 2RNR-27 Rock 'N' Roll Era - Teen Idols.
- (S) (2:30) Time-Life R962-05 History Of Rock 'N' Roll: The Teenage Years 1957-1964.
- (S) (2:31) LaserLight 12319 Frankie Avalon/Fabian/Ritchie Valens - Their Greatest Hits.
- (S) (2:30) Varese Sarabande 5576 Best Of.
- (S) (2:28) Taragon 1019 Chancellor Records Story, Volume 2.
- (S) (2:30) Music Club 50030 The Teen Idols: Very Best Of Frankie Avalon & Fabian.

1959 COME ON AND GET ME
- (M) (1:53) Varese Sarabande 5576 Best Of.
- (S) (1:52) Taragon 1018 Chancellor Records Story, Volume 1.
- (M) (1:53) Music Club 50030 The Teen Idols: Very Best Of Frankie Avalon & Fabian.

1960 HOUND DOG MAN
- (M) (2:12) Time-Life 2RNR-47 Rock 'N' Roll Era - Teen Idols II.
- (M) (2:12) LaserLight 12319 Frankie Avalon/Fabian/Ritchie Valens - Their Greatest Hits.
- (S) (2:12) Varese Sarabande 5576 Best Of.
- (S) (2:11) Taragon 1018 Chancellor Records Story, Volume 1.
- (S) (2:12) Music Club 50030 The Teen Idols: Very Best Of Frankie Avalon & Fabian.

1960 THIS FRIENDLY WORLD
- (S) (2:00) Varese Sarabande 5576 Best Of.
- (S) (2:00) Music Club 50030 The Teen Idols: Very Best Of Frankie Avalon & Fabian.

1960 ABOUT THIS THING CALLED LOVE
- (S) (2:34) Varese Sarabande 5576 Best Of.
- (S) (2:33) Music Club 50030 The Teen Idols: Very Best Of Frankie Avalon & Fabian.

1960 STRING ALONG
- (S) (2:19) Varese Sarabande 5576 Best Of.
- (S) (2:18) Music Club 50030 The Teen Idols: Very Best Of Frankie Avalon & Fabian.

BENT FABRIC
1962 ALLEY CAT
- (S) (2:30) Time-Life HPD-39 Your Hit Parade - 60's Instrumentals: Take Two.
- (S) (2:29) Collectors' Choice 003/4 Instrumental Gems Of The 60's.
- (S) (2:29) Risky Business 67311 The Ultimate Party Survival Kit.
- (S) (2:29) K-Tel 3583 Those Wonderful Instrumentals Volume 3.
- (S) (2:29) Taragon 1028 Very Best Of.

FABULOUS THUNDERBIRDS
1986 TUFF ENOUGH
- (S) (3:21) Priority 53712 Classic Rock Volume 3 - Wild Weekend.
- (S) (3:22) Sandstone 33042 and 5008 Rock The First Volume 2.
- (S) (3:21) Epic 53007 Hot Stuff: Their Greatest Hits.
- (S) (3:22) Epic Associated 40304 Tuff Enuff.
- (S) (3:21) Time-Life R988-17 Sounds Of The Eighties: The Mid '80s Take Two.
- (S) (3:22) Time-Life R968-24 Guitar Rock - The '80s Take Two.
- (S) (3:21) Rhino 72820 VH1 - More Of The Big 80's.
- (S) (3:22) Scotti Bros. 75518 Big Screen Rock.
- (S) (3:20) Thump 6010 Easyriders Volume 1.

TOMMY FACENDA
1959 HIGH SCHOOL U.S.A.
(there were 29 different 45 versions of this song each mentioning high schools in different cities)
    (M) (2:07)   Collectors' Choice 002 Teen Idols....For A Moment. *(national version)*

FACES
released as by ROD STEWART with FACES:
1972 (I KNOW) I'M LOSING YOU
    (S) (3:40)   Rhino 70327 History Of British Rock Volume 9. *(45 version)*
    (S) (3:40)   Rhino 70319 History Of British Rock Box Set. *(45 version)*
    (S) (5:03)   Mercury 824882 Rod Stewart - Sing It Again Rod. *(edit of LP version; preceding selection, this song, and the following selection are all segued together)*
    (S) (5:20)   Mercury 822385 Rod Stewart - Every Picture Tells A Story. *(LP version)*
    (S) (5:19)   Warner Brothers 25987 Rod Stewart - Storyteller. *(LP version)*
    (S) (5:20)   MFSL 532 Rod Stewart - Every Picture Tells A Story. *(LP version)*
    (S) (5:20)   Special Music 836739 Rod Stewart - You Wear It Well. *(LP version)*
    (S) (3:38)   Time-Life R968-10 Guitar Rock Classics. *(45 version)*
    (S) (5:19)   Mercury 314512805 Rod Stewart - Mercury Anthology. *(LP version)*
    (S) (3:41)   Priority 7065 70's Greatest Rock Hits Volume 12: Request Line. *(45 version)*
    (S) (4:48)   Special Music 846495 Rod Stewart - Stay With Me. *(edit of LP version)*
    (S) (3:38)   Time-Life SOD-02 Sounds Of The Seventies - 1971. *(45 version)*
    (S) (3:38)   Time-Life OPCD-4521 Guitar Rock. *(45 version)*
    (S) (5:19)   Rebound 314520278 Hard Rock Essentials - The 70's. *(LP version)*
    (S) (3:39)   Rebound 314520231 Rod Stewart - Best Of. *(45 version)*
    (S) (5:19)   Varese 5635 and 5654 and 5655 and 5657 Arrow: All Rock & Roll Oldies Volume Two. *(LP version)*
    (S) (3:39)   Special Music 5041 Great Britons! Volume Three. *(45 version)*
    (S) (5:20)   Varese Sarabande 5708 All Rock & Roll Hits Vol. One. *(LP version)*
    (S) (3:39)   Rebound 314520390 Rod Stewart - Legendary Hits. *(45 version)*
    (S) (3:39)   Rebound 314520440 No. 1 Hits Of The 70's. *(45 version)*
    (S) (5:20)   Mercury 314558060 Every Picture Tells A Story. *(LP version; remastered edition)*
    (S) (5:04)   Mercury 314558062 Sing It Again Rod. *(remastered edition; previous selection tracks into the introduction; edit of the LP version)*

released as by FACES:
1972 STAY WITH ME
    (S) (4:36)   Warner Brothers 25987 Storyteller.
    (S) (5:03)   Special Music 846495 Stay With Me. *(live)*
    (S) (4:37)   Warner Brothers 2574 A Nod Is As Good As A Wink.

FACE TO FACE
1984 10-9-8
    (S) (3:52)   Risky Business 66390 Hazy Shade Of 80's.
    (S) (5:41)   Epic 67534 Club Epic Volume 5. *(12" single version)*

DONALD FAGEN
1982 I.G.Y. (WHAT A BEAUTIFUL WORLD)
    (S) (6:02)   Warner Brothers 23696 The Nightfly. *(LP version)*

BARBARA FAIRCHILD
1973 TEDDY BEAR SONG
    (S) (3:04)   K-Tel 3357 101 Greatest Country Hits Vol. Three: Easy Country. *(rerecording)*
    (S) (3:01)   Columbia 69083 Ladies Choice Super Hits.

FAITH
1995 YOU USED TO LOVE ME
    (S) (4:28)   Bad Boy 73003 Faith.
    (S) (4:27)   Loud/RCA 67423 All That - The Album.
    (S) (4:26)   Arista 18977 Ultimate Hip Hop Party 1998. *(all selections on this cd are segued together)*
released as by FAITH EVANS:
1996 SOON AS I GET HOME
    (S) (5:21)   Bad Boy 73003 Faith.
released as by PUFF DADDY & FAITH EVANS featuring 112:
1997 I'LL BE MISSING YOU
    (S) (5:42)   Bad Boy 73012 and 73014 No Way Out.

ADAM FAITH
1965 IT'S ALRIGHT
    (S) (2:32)   Rhino 70319 History Of British Rock Volume 1.
    (S) (2:32)   Rhino 72022 History Of British Rock Box Set.
    (S) (2:32)   Rhino 72008 History Of British Rock Volumes 1-4 Box Set.

PERCY FAITH
1960 THE THEME FROM "A SUMMER PLACE"
    (M) (2:25)   Columbia 44374 Hollywood Magic - The 50's.
    (S) (2:25)   Columbia 44398 16 Most Requested Songs.
    (M) (2:25)   Columbia 8637 Greatest Hits.
    (S) (2:20)   Original Sound 8907 Best Love Songs Vol 2.
    (S) (2:20)   Original Sound 9326 Best Love Songs Vol. 1 & 2.
    (S) (2:20)   Original Sound 1236 Best Love Songs Box Set.
    (S) (2:21)   Time-Life HPD-34 Your Hit Parade - 60's Instrumentals.
    (S) (2:22)   Time-Life R138/05 Look Of Love.
    (M) (2:25)   K-Tel 3091 Those Wonderful Instrumentals.
    (S) (2:21)   Rhino 71581 Billboard Top Pop Hits, 1960.
    (S) (2:21)   JCI 7010 Those Wonderful Years - Melodies Of Love.
    (S) (2:20)   Collectors' Choice 003/4 Instrumental Gems Of The 60's.
    (S) (2:19)   Time-Life R986-02 Instrumental Favorites.
    (S) (2:21)   Time-Life R857-02 The Heart Of Rock 'n' Roll - 1960.
    (S) (2:21)   Time-Life R138-32 Hollywood Hit Parade.
    (S) (2:21)   Nick At Nite/Epic 67148 Donna Reed's Dinner Party.
    (S) (2:21)   Rhino 72423 Billboard Top Movie Hits - 1960s.
    (S) (2:19)   K-Tel 3822 Percy Faith/Ray Conniff Back To Back.
    (S) (2:22)   Collectables 5843 Tara's Theme From Gone With The Wind/Jealousy.
    (S) (2:21)   Time-Life R857-21 The Heart Of Rock 'n' Roll Slow Dancing Classics.
    (S) (2:19)   Time-Life R814-03 Love Songs.
    (S) (2:19)   Time-Life R986-22 Instrumental Classics - Pop Classics.
    (S) (2:21)   Collectables 1515 and 2515 The Anniversary Album - The 60's.

MARIANNE FAITHFULL
1965 AS TEARS GO BY
    (M) (2:36)   Abkco 7547 Greatest Hits.
    (E) (2:36)   Island 314524004 A Collection Of Her Best Recordings.
1965 COME AND STAY WITH ME
    (M) (2:22)   Abkco 7547 Greatest Hits.
1965 THIS LITTLE BIRD
    (M) (2:00)   Abkco 7547 Greatest Hits.
1965 SUMMER NIGHTS
    (M) (1:44)   Abkco 7547 Greatest Hits.

FAITH NO MORE
1990 EPIC
    (S) (4:51)   Slash/Reprise 25878 The Real Thing.
    (S) (4:50)   Tommy Boy 1173 ESPN Presents X Games Vol. 1.
    (S) (4:50)   Razor & Tie 4569 '90s Style.

FALCO
1986 ROCK ME AMADEUS
    (S) (3:11)   K-Tel 3342 The 80's Pop Explosion. *(45 version)*
    (S) (8:21)   A&M 5105 Falco. *(LP version)*
    (S) (6:46)   Sire/Warner Brothers 26796 Remix Hit Collection. *(remix)*
    (S) (3:19)   Time-Life R988-04 Sounds Of The Eighties: 1986. *(45 version)*
    (S) (3:18)   JCI 3150 1985 - Only Dance - 1989. *(45 version)*
1986 VIENNA CALLING
    (S) (7:38)   A&M 5105 Falco. *(LP version)*
    (S) (4:02)   Sire/Warner Brothers 26796 Remix Hit Collection. *(remix)*

BILLY FALCON
1991 POWER WINDOWS
    (S) (4:00)   Jambco/Mercury 848800 Pretty Blue World.

FALCONS
1959 YOU'RE SO FINE
    (M) (2:25)   Rhino 70645 Billboard's Top R&B Hits Of 1959.
    (M) (2:23)   Relic 7003 You're So Fine.
    (M) (2:23)   Curb 77323 All Time Greatest Hits Of Rock 'N' Roll.
    (E) (2:25)   Ripete 2200 Ocean Drive Volume 3.
    (M) (2:25)   Time-Life 2RNR-20 Rock 'N' Roll Era - 1959 Still Rockin'.
    (M) (2:24)   Time-Life RHD-03 Rhythm & Blues - 1959.
    (M) (2:23)   Rhino 72507 Doo Wop Box II.
    (M) (2:24)   Time-Life R838-21 Solid Gold Soul 1959.
    (M) (2:23)   Time-Life R857-16 The Heart Of Rock 'n' Roll The Late '50s.

HAROLD FALTERMEYER
1985 AXEL F
    (S) (2:59)   MCA 6330 Soundtrack Smashes - The 80's.
    (S) (3:00)   MCA 5553 O.S.T. Beverly Hills Cop.
    (S) (3:00)   Priority 53767 Rock Of The 80's Volume 11.
    (S) (3:00)   Time-Life R988-12 Sounds Of The 80's: 1985-1986.
    (S) (2:59)   Madacy Entertainment 1985 Rock On 1985.
    (S) (2:59)   Hip-O 40004 The '80s Hit(s) Back!
    (S) (3:00)   Hip-O 40017 Mission Accomplished: Themes For Spies & Cops.
    (S) (3:00)   JCI 3171 #1 Radio Hits 1985 - Only Rock 'n Roll - 1989.
    (S) (2:59)   K-Tel 3798 The 80's Mega Hits.
    (S) (2:59)   Hip-O 40013 Synth Me Up - 14 Classic Electronic Hits.

AGNETHA FALTSKOG
1983 CAN'T SHAKE LOOSE

GEORGIE FAME
1965 YEH, YEH
    (M) (2:19)   Rhino 70323 History Of British Rock Volume 5.
    (M) (2:19)   Rhino 72022 History Of British Rock Box Set.
    (M) (2:44)   Time-Life SUD-17 Superhits - Mid 60's Classics. *(neither the 45 or LP version)*
    (M) (2:19)   Time-Life R962-07 History Of Rock 'N' Roll: The British Invasion 1964-1966.
    (M) (2:44)   Time-Life AM1-16 AM Gold - Mid '60s Classics. *(neither the 45 or LP version)*
1968 THE BALLAD OF BONNIE AND CLYDE
    (M) (3:08)   Columbia/Legacy 46984 Rock Artifacts Volume 4.
    (M) (3:08)   Rhino 70326 History Of British Rock Volume 8.
    (M) (3:08)   Rhino 72022 History Of British Rock Box Set.

FANCY
1974 WILD THING
1974 TOUCH ME

FANNY
1971 CHARITY BALL
1975 BUTTER BOY

FANTASTIC JOHNNY C
1967 BOOGALOO DOWN BROADWAY
    (S) (2:30)   Time-Life 2CLR-15 Classic Rock - 1967: Shakin' All Over.
    (S) (2:31)   Rhino 71615 In Yo Face! The Roots Of Funk Vol. 1/2.
    (M) (2:41)   Rhino 72815 Beg, Scream & Shout! The Big Ol' Box Of '60s Soul.
    (S) (2:38)   TVT 4010 Rhythm Revue.
    (S) (2:30)   Jamie/Guyden 4003 Philly Original Soul Classics Volume One: Storm Warning.
1968 HITCH IT TO THE HORSE

DON FARDON
1968 INDIAN RESERVATION
    (S) (3:23)   Varese Sarabande 5705 Dick Bartley Presents Collector's Essentials: The 60's.

DONNA FARGO
1972 THE HAPPIEST GIRL IN THE WHOLE U.S.A.
    (S) (2:30)   MCA 6421 16 Top Country Hits Volume 1.
    (S) (2:28)   Time-Life CTD-18 Country USA - 1972.
    (S) (2:29)   Time-Life CCD-06 Contemporary Country - The Early 70's.
    (S) (2:29)   Varese Sarabande 5567 Best Of.
    (S) (2:28)   K-Tel 567 Country Music Classics Volume IV.
    (S) (2:30)   MCA Special Products 20364 Country's Greatest Hits Volume 1.
    (S) (2:29)   MCA Special Products 20980 Country Sweethearts.
    (S) (2:29)   JCI 3155 1970 - Only Country - 1974.
    (S) (2:33)   K-Tel 3357 101 Greatest Country Hits Vol. Three: Easy Country. *(rerecording)*
    (S) (2:28)   MCA Special Products 20802 Country Hits Of The 70's.
    (S) (2:29)   Curb 77876 Best Of.
    (S) (2:29)   Hip-O 40085 The Class Of Country 1970-1974.
    (S) (2:29)   Time-Life R808-04 Classic Country 1970-1974.
1973 FUNNY FACE
    (S) (2:46)   Rhino 70758 Super Hits Of The 70's Volume 11.
    (S) (2:46)   MCA 6421 16 Top Country Hits Volume 1.
    (S) (2:45)   Varese Sarabande 5567 Best Of.
    (S) (2:37)   K-Tel 3253 Old-Fashioned Love: Country Style.
    (S) (2:44)   MCA Special Products 20980 Country Sweethearts.
    (S) (2:46)   Priority 50967 I Love Country Volume Two: Hits Of The 70's.
    (S) (2:44)   Curb 77876 Best Of.
    (S) (2:45)   Time-Life R808-04 Classic Country 1970-1974.
1973 SUPERMAN
    (S) (2:25)   Varese Sarabande 5567 Best Of.

FARM
1991 GROOVY TRAIN
    (S) (4:07)   Sire/Reprise 26600 Spartacus.

DIONNE FARRIS
1995 I KNOW
    (S) (3:46)   Columbia 57359 Wild Seed - Wild Flower.

FASTER PUSSYCAT
1990 HOUSE OF PAIN
    (S) (5:44)   JCI 3135 14 Original Metal Ballads.
    (S) (5:44)   Elektra 60883 Wake Me When It's Over.
    (S) (5:44)   K-Tel 3999 Glam Rock Vol. 2: The 80's And Beyond.

FAT BOYS
released as by THE FAT BOYS with THE BEACH BOYS:
1987 WIPEOUT
(actual 45 time is (3:57) not (3:50) as stated on the record label)
- (S) (4:27) Tin Pan Apple/Polydor 831948 Fat Boys - Crushin'. *(LP version)*
- (S) (3:59) Capitol 92639 Beach Boys - Still Cruisin'. *(45 version)*
- (S) (3:59) Capitol 21277 Essential Beach Boys - Perfect Harmony. *(45 version)*
- (S) (3:59) Rhino 72632 Fat Boys - Best Of. *(45 version)*
- (S) (4:27) Polygram Special Markets 314520445 Soul Hits Of The 80's. *(LP version)*

released as by THE FAT BOYS with CHUBBY CHECKER:
1988 THE TWIST (YO, TWIST!)
- (S) (4:04) Tin Pan Apple/Polydor 835809 Fat Boys - Coming Back Hard Again.
- (S) (4:05) Rhino 72632 Fat Boys - Best Of.

FATHER M.C.
1991 I'LL DO 4 U
- (S) (3:05) Uptown/MCA 10061 Father's Day.
- (S) (3:02) Uptown 53025 Uptown's Block Party Volume 2.
1993 EVERYTHING'S GONNA BE ALRIGHT
- (S) (3:41) Uptown/MCA 10542 Close To You.

JOSE FELICIANO
1968 LIGHT MY FIRE
- (S) (3:32) RCA 8474 Nipper's Greatest Hits Of The 60's Volume 1. *(LP length)*
- (S) (3:34) RCA 6903 All Time Greatest Hits. *(LP length)*
- (S) (3:34) RCA 66024 Light My Fire. *(LP length)*
- (S) (3:27) Time-Life SUD-02 Superhits - 1968. *(LP length)*
- (S) (3:29) Time-Life OPCD-4517 Tonight's The Night. *(LP length)*
- (S) (3:34) RCA 53957 Feliciano! *(LP length)*
- (S) (3:34) RCA 66595 Feliciano! *(LP length; gold disc)*
- (S) (3:27) Time-Life AM1-04 AM Gold - 1968. *(LP length)*
1968 HI-HEEL SNEAKERS
- (S) (2:18) RCA 6903 All Time Greatest Hits. *(1964 recording -- not the hit version)*

FREDDY FENDER
1975 BEFORE THE NEXT TEARDROP FALLS
- (S) (2:32) MCA 6421 16 Top Country Hits Volume 1.
- (S) (2:36) Reprise 26638 Collection. *(rerecording)*
- (S) (2:31) Original Sound 8852 Oldies But Goodies Vol. 2. *(this compact disc uses the "Waring - fds" noise reduction process)*
- (S) (2:31) Original Sound 2223 Oldies But Goodies Volumes 2,7,9,12 and 13 Box Set. *(this box set uses the "Waring - fds" noise reduction process)*
- (S) (2:31) Original Sound 2500 Oldies But Goodies Volumes 1-15 Box Set. *(this box set uses the "Waring - fds" noise reduction process)*
- (S) (2:33) Rhino 71197 Super Hits Of The 70's Volume 17. *(hissy)*
- (S) (2:32) Time-Life CCD-04 Contemporary Country - The Mid 70's.
- (S) (2:32) MCA Special Products 20257 Before The Next Teardrop Falls.
- (S) (2:32) K-Tel 605 Country Music Classics Volume V.
- (S) (2:33) MCA Special Products 20364 Country's Greatest Hits Volume 1.
- (S) (2:31) JCI 3156 1975 - Only Country - 1979.
- (S) (2:32) MCA 11464 Best Of.
- (S) (2:31) K-Tel 3367 101 Greatest Country Hits Vol. Eight: Country Romance. *(rerecording)*
- (S) (2:33) Hip-O 40086 The Class Of Country 1975-1979.
1975 WASTED DAYS AND WASTED NIGHTS
- (S) (2:44) Reprise 26638 Collection. *(rerecording)*
- (S) (2:41) Rhino 71198 Super Hits Of The 70's Volume 18.
- (S) (2:42) Time-Life CCD-08 Contemporary Country - The Mid 70's Pure Gold.
- (S) (2:42) MCA Special Products 20257 Before The Next Teardrop Falls.

- (S) (2:42) K-Tel 3111 Country Music Classics Vol. XIX.
- (S) (2:52) MCA 11464 Best Of. *(time includes a :10 introduction)*
- (S) (2:52) MCA Special Products 20802 Country Hits Of The 70's. *(time includes a :10 introduction)*
- (S) (2:41) Simitar 55632 This Is Outlaw Country.
1975 SECRET LOVE
- (S) (3:43) Reprise 26638 Collection. *(rerecording)*
- (S) (3:38) Time-Life CCD-20 Contemporary Country - The 70's Pure Gold.
- (S) (3:38) MCA Special Products 20257 Before The Next Teardrop Falls.
- (S) (3:37) MCA 11464 Best Of.
1976 YOU'LL LOSE A GOOD THING
- (S) (2:48) Reprise 26638 Collection. *(rerecording)*
- (S) (2:49) Time-Life CCD-16 Contemporary Country - The Mid 70's Hot Hits.
- (S) (2:50) MCA Special Products 20257 Before The Next Teardrop Falls.
- (S) (2:50) MCA 11464 Best Of.

FENDERMEN
1960 MULE SKINNER BLUES
- (M) (2:22) Rhino 70495 Fun Rock!
- (M) (2:21) Collectables 5064 History Of Rock Volume 4.
- (M) (2:22) Time-Life 2RNR-22 Rock 'N' Roll Era - 1960 Still Rockin'.
- (E) (2:22) K-Tel 3243 Kooky Kountry. *(mastered from vinyl)*
- (M) (2:22) Rhino 71581 Billboard Top Pop Hits, 1960.
- (E) (2:22) Curb 77773 Hard To Find Hits Of Rock 'N' Roll Volume One.

JAY FERGUSON
1977 THUNDER ISLAND
- (S) (3:28) Rhino 71201 Super Hits Of The 70's Volume 21. *(45 length)*
- (S) (3:23) Time-Life SOD-35 Sounds Of The Seventies - AM Nuggets. *(45 length)*
- (S) (3:23) JCI 3169 #1 Radio Hits 1975 - Only Rock 'n Roll - 1979. *(45 length)*
- (S) (3:59) Rhino 72518 Mellow Rock Hits Of The 70's - Summer Breeze. *(LP length)*
- (S) (3:27) Time-Life R840-01 Sounds Of The Seventies - Pop Nuggets: Late '70s. *(45 length)*
- (S) (3:23) K-Tel 3909 High Energy Volume 2. *(45 length)*
- (S) (3:27) Time-Life AM1-25 AM Gold - 1978. *(45 length)*
1979 SHAKEDOWN CRUISE

JOHNNY FERGUSON
1960 ANGELA JONES
- (M) (2:24) Collectors' Choice 002 Teen Idols....For A Moment.

MAYNARD FERGUSON
1977 GONNA FLY NOW (THEME FROM "ROCKY")
- (S) (4:22) Columbia 34457 Conquistador. *(LP version)*
- (S) (4:21) Risky Business 66662 Swingin' Singles/Greatest Hits Of The 70's. *(LP version)*
- (S) (4:21) Risky Business 67310 We Came To Play. *(LP version)*

FERRANTE & TEICHER
1960 THEME FROM THE APARTMENT
- (S) (2:58) Curb 77338 Greatest Hits.
- (S) (2:59) EMI 98823 All Time Great Movie Themes.
- (S) (2:59) Time-Life HPD-33 Your Hit Parade - The Early 60's.
- (S) (3:00) Pair 1157 Grand Pianos.
- (S) (2:59) Collectors' Choice 003/4 Instrumental Gems Of The 60's.
- (S) (2:59) Time-Life R986-08 Instrumental Favorites.
- (S) (3:00) EMI 35965 All-Time Greatest Hits.
- (S) (3:09) Varese Sarabande 5919 The Ferrante & Teicher Collection. *(rerecorded)*

FERRANTE & TEICHER *(Continued)*
1961 EXODUS
    (S) (2:53)   Curb 77403 All-Time Great Instrumental Hits Volume 1.
    (S) (2:53)   Curb 77338 Greatest Hits.
    (S) (2:54)   EMI 98823 All Time Great Movie Themes.
    (S) (2:54)   Time-Life HPD-34 Your Hit Parade - 60's Instrumentals.
    (S) (2:54)   K-Tel 3091 Those Wonderful Instrumentals.
    (S) (2:54)   Rhino 71582 Billboard Top Pop Hits, 1961.
    (S) (2:54)   Pair 1157 Grand Pianos.
    (S) (2:53)   Collectors' Choice 003/4 Instrumental Gems Of The 60's.
    (S) (2:53)   Time-Life R986-08 Instrumental Favorites.
    (S) (2:54)   EMI 35965 All-Time Greatest Hits.
    (S) (2:54)   Rhino 72423 Billboard Top Movie Hits - 1960s.
    (S) (3:09)   Varese Sarabande 5919 The Ferrante & Teicher Collection. *(rerecorded)*

1961 LOVE THEME FROM ONE EYED JACKS
    (S) (3:00)   Curb 77338 Greatest Hits.
    (S) (3:01)   EMI 98823 All Time Great Movie Themes.
    (S) (3:01)   Time-Life R986-08 Instrumental Favorites.

1961 TONIGHT
(actual 45 time is (2:59) not (2:52) as stated on the record label)
    (S) (3:11)   Curb 77338 Greatest Hits. *(LP version; no fidelity)*
    (S) (2:59)   EMI 98823 All Time Great Movie Themes. *(45 version)*
    (S) (2:58)   Time-Life HPD-39 Your Hit Parade - 60's Instrumentals: Take Two. *(45 version)*
    (S) (3:13)   Pair 1157 Grand Pianos. *(LP version)*
    (S) (3:12)   K-Tel 3472 Those Wonderful Instrumentals Volume 2. *(LP version)*
    (S) (2:58)   Time-Life R986-08 Instrumental Favorites. *(45 version)*
    (S) (3:13)   EMI 35965 All-Time Greatest Hits. *(LP version)*
    (S) (2:59)   Time-Life R986-22 Instrumental Classics - Pop Classics. *(45 version)*

1970 MIDNIGHT COWBOY
    (S) (3:14)   Curb 77338 Greatest Hits.
    (S) (3:17)   EMI 91682 Best Of.
    (S) (3:16)   EMI 98823 All Time Great Movie Themes.
    (S) (3:17)   Rhino 71196 Super Hits Of The 70's Volume 16.
    (S) (3:18)   Pair 1157 Grand Pianos.
    (S) (3:14)   Collectors' Choice 003/4 Instrumental Gems Of The 60's.
    (S) (3:16)   Time-Life R986-08 Instrumental Favorites.
    (S) (3:18)   EMI 35965 All-Time Greatest Hits.
    (S) (3:16)   Rhino 72424 Billboard Top Movie Hits - 1970s.

BRYAN FERRY
1988 KISS AND TELL
    (S) (3:56)   Time-Life R105-40 Rock Dreams. *(45 version)*
    (S) (4:03)   Warner Brothers 25688 O.S.T. Bright Lights, Big City. *(45 version)*
    (S) (7:05)   JCI 3117 Lost Mixes - Extended Ecstasy. *(remix)*
    (S) (4:51)   Reprise 25598 Bete Noire. *(LP version)*

ERNIE FIELDS
1959 IN THE MOOD
    (S) (2:39)   Curb 77402 All-Time Great Instrumental Hits Volume 2. *(rerecording)*
    (M) (2:32)   Original Sound 8860 Oldies But Goodies Vol. 10. *(this compact disc uses the "Waring - fds" noise reduction process)*
    (M) (2:32)   Original Sound 2221 Oldies But Goodies Volumes 1,4,6,8 and 10 Box Set. *(this box set uses the "Waring - fds" noise reduction process)*
    (M) (2:32)   Original Sound 2500 Oldies But Goodies Volumes 1-15 Box Set. *(this box set uses the "Waring - fds" noise reduction process)*
    (M) (2:33)   Rhino 71601 Rock Instrumental Classics Volume 1: The Fifties.
    (M) (2:33)   Rhino 72035 Rock Instrumental Classics Vols. 1-5 Box Set.

    (M) (2:34)   Time-Life HPD-30 Your Hit Parade - 50's Instrumentals.
    (M) (2:33)   LaserLight 12316 Rebel Rousers.
    (M) (2:36)   Collectables 5579 In The Mood - A Golden Classics Edition.

FIESTAS
1959 SO FINE
    (M) (2:20)   JCI 3201 Party Time Fifties.
    (M) (2:18)   Rhino 71463 Doo Wop Box.
    (M) (2:17)   Time-Life 2RNR-13 Rock 'N' Roll Era - 1959.
    (M) (2:13)   Time-Life RHD-03 Rhythm & Blues - 1959.
    (M) (2:25)   Ripete 2183-RE Ocean Drive Volume 1.
    (M) (2:18)   Thump 7050 Low Rider Oldies Volume 5.
    (M) (2:18)   Time-Life R857-11 The Heart Of Rock 'n' Roll 1958-1959.
    (M) (2:13)   Time-Life R838-21 Solid Gold Soul 1959.

FIFTH DIMENSION
1967 GO WHERE YOU WANNA GO
    (S) (2:21)   Arista 18961 Up-Up And Away: The Definitive Collection.
    (S) (2:21)   Varese Sarabande 5801 Sunshine Days - Pop Classics Of The '60s Volume 1.

1967 UP-UP AND AWAY
    (S) (2:38)   Arista 8335 Greatest Hits On Earth.
    (M) (2:38)   Rhino 71065 Summer Of Love Volume 1. *(noise noticeable on fadeout)*
    (S) (2:37)   Rhino 71093 Better Days.
    (S) (2:36)   Time-Life SUD-05 Superhits - 1967.
    (S) (2:36)   Time-Life AM1-08 AM Gold - 1967.
    (S) (2:37)   Flashback 72687 '60s Rock: Feelin' Groovy.
    (S) (2:37)   Flashback 72088 '60s Rock Hits Box Set.
    (S) (2:36)   Arista 18961 Up-Up And Away: The Definitive Collection.

1967 PAPER CUP
    (S) (2:40)   Arista 18961 Up-Up And Away: The Definitive Collection.

1968 CARPET MAN
    (S) (3:03)   Arista 18961 Up-Up And Away: The Definitive Collection.

1968 STONED SOUL PICNIC
    (S) (3:25)   Arista 8335 Greatest Hits On Earth.
    (S) (3:24)   Time-Life 2CLR-19 Classic Rock - 1968: Shakin' All Over.
    (S) (3:22)   Time-Life SUD-02 Superhits - 1968.
    (S) (3:25)   Buddah 49506 Feelin' Groovy.
    (S) (3:24)   JCI 3190 1965 - Only Dance - 1969.
    (S) (3:23)   Time-Life AM1-04 AM Gold - 1968.
    (S) (3:25)   Arista 18961 Up-Up And Away: The Definitive Collection.
    (S) (3:25)   Simitar 55572 The Number One's: Hot In The '60s.

1968 SWEET BLINDNESS
    (S) (3:21)   Arista 18961 Up-Up And Away: The Definitive Collection.

1969 CALIFORNIA SOUL
    (S) (3:11)   Arista 18961 Up-Up And Away: The Definitive Collection.

1969 AQUARIUS/LET THE SUNSHINE IN
(dj copies of this 45 ran (3:02) and (4:49); commercial copies were all (4:49))
    (S) (4:49)   Rhino 70630 Billboard's Top Rock & Roll Hits Of 1969.
    (S) (4:49)   Rhino 72005 Billboard's Top Rock & Roll Hits 1968-1972 Box Set.
    (S) (4:47)   K-Tel 666 Flower Power.
    (S) (4:46)   Arista 8335 Greatest Hits On Earth.
    (S) (4:49)   Polygram 837362 O.S.T. 1969.
    (S) (4:47)   JCI 3104 Mellow Sixties.
    (S) (4:44)   Time-Life 2CLR-20 Classic Rock - 1969: Shakin' All Over.
    (S) (4:46)   Time-Life R921-38 Get Together.
    (S) (4:46)   Epic 66329 O.S.T. Forrest Gump.
    (S) (4:47)   K-Tel 3130 60's Sound Explosion.
    (S) (4:46)   Arista 18961 Up-Up And Away: The Definitive Collection.

(S) (4:45) K-Tel 3901 Soul Brothers & Sisters Of The 60's.
1969 WORKIN' ON A GROOVY THING
   (S) (3:07) Arista 18961 Up-Up And Away: The Definitive Collection.
   (S) (3:08) Varese Sarabande 5803 Sunshine Days - Pop Classics Of The '60s Volume 3.
1969 WEDDING BELL BLUES
   (S) (2:42) Arista 8335 Greatest Hits On Earth. *(truncated fade)*
   (S) (2:42) Epic 48732 O.S.T. My Girl.
   (S) (2:42) Rhino 70588 Rockin' & Rollin' Wedding Songs Volume 1.
   (S) (2:41) Time-Life SUD-07 Superhits - 1969.
   (S) (2:41) Time-Life R138/05 Look Of Love.
   (S) (2:42) Rhino 71939 Billboard Top Pop Hits, 1969.
   (S) (2:40) Time-Life AM1-01 AM Gold - 1969.
   (S) (2:41) Arista 18961 Up-Up And Away: The Definitive Collection.
   (S) (2:41) Time-Life R814-01 Love Songs.
1970 BLOWING AWAY
   (S) (2:28) Arista 18961 Up-Up And Away: The Definitive Collection.
1970 PUPPET MAN
   (S) (2:55) Arista 8335 Greatest Hits On Earth.
   (S) (2:56) Arista 18961 Up-Up And Away: The Definitive Collection.
1970 SAVE THE COUNTRY
   (S) (2:38) Arista 8335 Greatest Hits On Earth.
   (S) (2:37) Arista 18961 Up-Up And Away: The Definitive Collection.
1970 ONE LESS BELL TO ANSWER
   (S) (3:29) Arista 8335 Greatest Hits On Earth.
   (S) (3:28) Time-Life SUD-04 Superhits - 1970.
   (S) (3:28) Rebound 3145200320 Class Reunion 1970.
   (S) (3:28) Madacy Entertainment 1971 Rock On 1971.
   (S) (3:28) JCI 3145 1970 - Only Love - 1974.
   (S) (3:28) Time-Life AM1-02 AM Gold - 1970.
   (S) (3:27) Arista 18961 Up-Up And Away: The Definitive Collection.
   (S) (3:29) Varese Sarabande 5873 The Burt Bacharach Songbook.
   (S) (3:28) Time-Life R834-12 Body Talk - By Candlelight.
   (S) (3:28) Time-Life R814-03 Love Songs.
1971 LOVE'S LINES, ANGLES AND RHYMES
   (S) (4:10) Arista 8335 Greatest Hits On Earth. *(truncated fade; LP version)*
   (S) (4:08) Arista 18961 Up-Up And Away: The Definitive Collection. *(LP version)*
1971 LIGHT SINGS
   (S) (3:27) Arista 18961 Up-Up And Away: The Definitive Collection.
1971 NEVER MY LOVE
(dj copies of this 45 stated times of (3:26) and (3:45) but actually ran (3:50) and (4:15); commercial copies all stated a time of (3:45) but actually ran (4:15))
   (S) (3:54) Arista 8335 Greatest Hits On Earth. *(tracks into next selection; slight edit of both the 45 and LP version because of the length of audience applause used)*
   (S) (3:54) Arista 18961 Up-Up And Away: The Definitive Collection. *(slight edit of both the 45 and LP version because of the length of audience applause used)*
1972 TOGETHER LET'S FIND LOVE
   (S) (3:35) Arista 8335 Greatest Hits On Earth. *(previous selection tracks over introduction)*
   (S) (3:35) Arista 18961 Up-Up And Away: The Definitive Collection.
1972 (LAST NIGHT) I DIDN'T GET TO SLEEP AT ALL
   (S) (3:11) Arista 8335 Greatest Hits On Earth.
   (S) (3:07) Razor & Tie 4543 The '70s Preservation Society Presents: Easy '70s.
   (S) (3:07) Time-Life SUD-11 Superhits - 1972.
   (S) (3:11) DCC Compact Classics 142 Groove On! Volume 2.
   (S) (3:07) Time-Life AM1-07 AM Gold - 1972.

   (S) (3:08) Arista 18961 Up-Up And Away: The Definitive Collection.
   (S) (3:10) Time-Life R834-11 Body Talk - After Dark.
   (S) (3:07) Time-Life R814-05 Love Songs.
1972 IF I COULD REACH YOU
   (S) (3:05) Arista 18961 Up-Up And Away: The Definitive Collection.
   (S) (3:20) Time-Life R834-17 Body Talk - Heart To Heart. *(much slower than the 45 or LP)*
1973 LIVING TOGETHER, GROWING TOGETHER
   (S) (3:48) Arista 18961 Up-Up And Away: The Definitive Collection.

FIFTH ESTATE
1967 DING DONG! THE WITCH IS DEAD
   (S) (2:04) Rhino 70996 One Hit Wonders Of The 60's Volume 2.
   (S) (2:04) Boston Skyline 116 Ding Dong! The Witch Is Back!
   (M) (2:13) Boston Skyline 116 Ding Dong! The Witch Is Back! *(alternate take)*
   (S) (2:02) Time-Life SUD-18 Superhits - Late 60's Classics.
   (S) (2:04) Rhino 71728 '60s Rock Classics, Vol. 1.
   (S) (2:05) Varese Sarabande 5535 Bubblegum Classics Volume One.
   (S) (2:02) Time-Life AM1-12 AM Gold - Late '60s Classics.
   (S) (2:04) Flashback 72701 '60s Rock: Mony Mony.
   (S) (2:04) Flashback 72088 '60s Rock Hits Box Set.
   (M) (2:06) Sony Music Special Products 22210 Fun Rock.

FINE YOUNG CANNIBALS
1989 SHE DRIVES ME CRAZY
   (S) (3:35) IRS 29695 On The Charts: IRS Records 1979-1994.
   (S) (3:35) Sandstone 33041 and 5007 Rock The First Volume 1.
   (S) (7:04) IRS/MCA 10125 The Raw & The Remix. *(12" single version)*
   (S) (4:53) IRS/MCA 10125 The Raw & The Remix. *(remix)*
   (S) (3:34) IRS 6273 The Raw & The Cooked.
   (S) (3:34) Hip-O 40004 The '80s Hit(s) Back!
   (S) (3:35) MCA 11525 The Finest.
   (S) (3:27) Arista 18985 Ultimate New Wave Party 1998. *(all selections on this cd are segued together)*
   (S) (3:34) Time-Life R13610 Gold And Platinum Box Set - The Ultimate Rock Collection.
1989 GOOD THING
   (S) (4:37) IRS/MCA 10125 The Raw & The Remix. *(12" single version)*
   (S) (3:21) IRS 6273 The Raw & The Cooked.
   (S) (3:21) MCA 11525 The Finest.
1989 DON'T LOOK BACK
   (S) (3:36) IRS 6273 The Raw & The Cooked.
   (S) (3:42) MCA 11525 The Finest.

LARRY FINNEGAN
1962 DEAR ONE
   (M) (3:00) Time-Life 2RNR-46 Rock 'N' Roll Era - 60's Juke Box Memories.
   (M) (3:00) Eric 11503 Hard To Find 45's On CD (Volume II) 1961-64.

ELISA FIORILLO
released as by JELLYBEAN/ELISA FIORILLO:
1987 WHO FOUND WHO
   (S) (4:47) Chrysalis 21569 and 41569 Just Visiting This Planet. *(LP version)*
   (S) (6:40) Chrysalis 21652 and 41652 Rocks The House. *(12" single version)*
   (S) (6:15) Priority 53731 80's Greatest Rock Hits Volume 10 - Dance All Night. *(edit of 12" single version)*
   (S) (6:40) Right Stuff 52288 Free To Be Volume 4. *(12" single version)*

ELISA FIORILLO (Continued)
released as by ELISA FIORILLO:
1990 ON THE WAY UP
    (S) (4:17) Chrysalis 21678 I Am. *(tracks into next selection)*

FIREBALLS
1959 TORQUAY
    (S) (1:51) Sundazed 6089 Torquay. *(rerecording)*
    (M) (1:54) Sundazed 6088 The Fireballs.
1960 BULLDOG
    (M) (2:10) Rhino 71602 Rock Instrumental Classics Volume 2: The Sixties.
    (M) (2:10) Rhino 72035 Rock Instrumental Classics Vols. 1-5 Box Set.
    (M) (2:09) Rhino 72418 Cowabunga! The Surf Box.
    (M) (2:08) Sundazed 6088 The Fireballs.
    (M) (2:09) K-Tel 6256 Kahuna Classics.
1961 QUITE A PARTY
    (S) (1:43) Sundazed 6089 Torquay. *(rerecording)*
1968 BOTTLE OF WINE
    (M) (2:08) Rhino 75772 Son Of Frat Rock.
    (M) (2:08) Time-Life 2CLR-11 Classic Rock - 1968: The Beat Goes On.
    (S) (2:09) Varese Sarabande 5697 Best Of Jimmy Gilmer & The Fireballs.
    (M) (3:08) JCI 3167 #1 Radio Hits 1965 - Only Rock 'n Roll - 1969.

FIREFALL
1976 YOU ARE THE WOMAN
    (S) (2:41) Atlantic 82306 Atlantic Rock & Roll Box Set.
    (S) (2:41) Atlantic 81908 Classic Rock 1966-1988.
    (S) (2:35) Razor & Tie 4543 The '70s Preservation Society Presents: Easy '70s.
    (S) (2:34) Priority 8666 Kickin' Back/70's Greatest Rock Hits Volume 5.
    (S) (2:42) Rhino 70379 Firefall.
    (S) (2:39) Rhino 71231 You Are The Woman.
    (S) (2:35) Time-Life SOD-35 Sounds Of The Seventies - AM Nuggets.
    (S) (2:40) Rhino 71055 Greatest Hits.
    (S) (2:34) JCI 3169 #1 Radio Hits 1975 - Only Rock 'n Roll - 1979.
    (S) (2:35) Time-Life R103-18 Great Love Songs Of The '70s & '80s.
    (S) (2:42) Time-Life AM1-23 AM Gold - 1976.
    (S) (2:41) Time-Life R834-06 Body Talk - Only You.
    (S) (2:40) Flashback 72678 You Are The Woman And Other Hits.
1977 CINDERELLA
    (S) (3:50) Rhino 70379 Firefall. *(LP version)*
    (S) (3:31) Rhino 71231 You Are The Woman. *(45 version)*
    (S) (3:31) Rhino 71055 Greatest Hits. *(45 version)*
    (S) (3:31) Flashback 72678 You Are The Woman And Other Hits. *(45 version)*
1977 JUST REMEMBER I LOVE YOU
    (S) (3:13) Priority 8664 High Times/70's Greatest Rock Hits Volume 3.
    (S) (3:14) Rhino 71231 You Are The Woman.
    (S) (3:14) Rhino 71055 Greatest Hits.
    (S) (3:15) Rhino 71925 Luna Sea.
    (S) (3:14) K-Tel 3697 Best Of Country Rock.
    (S) (3:12) Time-Life AM1-24 AM Gold - 1977.
    (S) (3:12) Time-Life R834-03 Body Talk - Moonlit Nights.
    (S) (3:14) Flashback 72678 You Are The Woman And Other Hits.
1978 STRANGE WAY
    (S) (3:54) Time-Life SOD-20 Sounds Of The Seventies - 1978: Take Two. *(45 version)*
    (S) (3:22) Rhino 71055 Greatest Hits. *(edit of the 45 version)*
    (S) (4:43) Rhino 71926 Elan. *(LP version)*
    (S) (3:22) Rhino 72478 Beverly Hills 90210: Songs From The Peach Pit. *(edit of the 45 version)*
    (S) (3:22) Flashback 72678 You Are The Woman And Other Hits. *(edit of the 45 version)*
    (S) (4:42) Time-Life R834-15 Body Talk - Once In Lifetime. *(LP version)*

1979 GOODBYE, I LOVE YOU
**(dj copies of this 45 ran (3:23) and (4:19);
commercial copies were all (4:19))**
    (S) (4:20) Rhino 71231 You Are The Woman.
    (S) (4:20) Rhino 71055 Greatest Hits.
    (S) (4:19) Rhino 71926 Elan.
    (S) (4:20) Flashback 72678 You Are The Woman And Other Hits.
1980 HEADED FOR A FALL
    (S) (4:07) Rhino 71055 Greatest Hits.
    (S) (4:08) Rhino 71927 Undertow.
    (S) (4:12) Rhino 71926 Elan. *(acoustic version)*

FIREFLIES
1959 YOU WERE MINE
    (M) (1:54) DCC Compact Classics 031 Back Seat Jams.
    (M) (1:53) Collectables 2508 History Of Rock - The Doo Wop Era Part 2.
    (M) (1:53) Collectables 4508 History Of Rock/The Doo Wop Era Part Two.
    (M) (1:53) Original Sound 8856 Oldies But Goodies Vol. 6. *(this compact disc uses the "Waring - fds" noise reduction process)*
    (M) (1:53) Original Sound 2221 Oldies But Goodies Volumes 1,4,6,8 and 10 Box Set. *(this box set uses the "Waring - fds" noise reduction process)*
    (M) (1:53) Original Sound 2500 Oldies But Goodies Volumes 1-15 Box Set. *(this box set uses the "Waring - fds" noise reduction process)*
    (M) (1:53) Time-Life 2RNR-24 Rock 'N' Roll Era - The 50's Keep On Rockin'.
    (M) (1:53) Collectables 2509 WCBS-FM For Lovers Only Part 1.
    (M) (1:55) LaserLight 12320 Love Songs.
    (M) (1:55) Relic 7108 The Gerry Granahan Scrapbook.
    (M) (1:53) Time-Life R857-16 The Heart Of Rock 'n' Roll The Late '50s.

FIREHOUSE
1991 DON'T TREAT ME BAD
    (S) (3:55) Epic 46186 Firehouse.
1991 LOVE OF A LIFETIME
    (S) (4:46) Epic 46186 Firehouse.
1992 WHEN I LOOK INTO YOUR EYES
    (S) (3:59) Epic 48615 Hold Your Fire.
1995 I LIVE MY LIFE FOR YOU
    (S) (4:22) Epic 57459 Firehouse 3.

FIRM
1985 RADIOACTIVE
    (S) (2:48) Atlantic 81239 The Firm.
    (S) (2:48) Time-Life R968-18 Guitar Rock - The Heavy '80s.

FIRST CHOICE
1973 ARMED AND EXTREMELY DANGEROUS
    (S) (2:47) Rhino 70790 Soul Hits Of The 70's Volume 10.
    (S) (2:46) Salsoul 2005 and 2018 Greatest Hits.
    (S) (2:46) Collectables 5500 Philly Golden Classics.
    (S) (2:46) Salsoul/Right Stuff 52192 Greatest Hits.
    (S) (2:46) K-Tel 3910 Fantastic Volume 1.
    (S) (4:54) Hip-O 40092 Disco 54: Where We Started From. *(previously unreleased version)*
    (S) (2:47) K-Tel 3889 Great R&B Female Groups: Hits Of The 70s.

FIRST CLASS
1974 BEACH BABY
**(dj copies of this 45 ran (3:08) and (4:59);
commercial copies were all (4:59))**
    (S) (4:59) Rhino 70760 Super Hits Of The 70's Volume 13.
    (S) (4:53) Collectables 0561 Golden Classics. *(truncated fade)*
    (S) (4:59) Time-Life SOD-31 Sounds Of The Seventies - AM Top Twenty.

(S) (4:48) MCA Special Products 20751 Rock Around The Oldies #2.
(S) (4:49) MCA Special Products 22105 Greatest Classic Rock Hits.
(S) (4:59) Ripete 2187-RE Preppy Deluxe.
(S) (4:49) MCA Special Products 20948 Biggest Summer Hits.
(S) (3:08) Varese Sarabande 5706 Dick Bartley Presents Collector's Essentials: The 70's. *(this is the dj 45 edit)*
(S) (4:48) K-Tel 3627 Out Of Sight.
(S) (4:53) Varese Sarabande 5725 Love Grows (Where My Rosemary Goes) - The Voice Of Tony Burrows.
(S) (4:59) Eclipse Music Group 64894 Rock 'n Roll Relix 1974-1975.
(S) (4:59) Eclipse Music Group 64897 Rock 'n Roll Relix 1970-1979.
(S) (4:58) Time-Life AM1-21 AM Gold - 1974.
(S) (4:59) Nick At Nite/550 Music 63435 Beach Blanket Bash.

FIRST EDITION (see KENNY ROGERS and THE FIRST EDITION)

LISA FISCHER
1991 HOW CAN I EASE THE PAIN
(S) (5:24) Elektra 60889 So Intense.
(S) (5:24) Elektra 62090 Maximum Slow Jams.

EDDIE FISHER
1955 HEART
(M) (2:36) RCA 9592 All Time Greatest Hits Volume 1.
(S) (2:25) MCA 31174 Very Best Of. *(rerecording)*
(M) (2:35) Time-Life HPD-36 Your Hit Parade - The 50's Pop Revival.
(M) (2:35) Taragon 1031 Very Best Of.
1956 DUNGAREE DOLL
(M) (2:00) RCA 8466 Nipper's Greatest Hits Of The 50's Volume 1.
(M) (1:59) RCA 9592 All Time Greatest Hits Volume 1.
(M) (2:00) Time-Life HPD-31 Your Hit Parade - The 50's Forever.
(M) (2:00) Taragon 1031 Very Best Of.
1956 CINDY, OH CINDY
(M) (2:58) RCA 9592 All Time Greatest Hits Volume 1.
(M) (2:58) Taragon 1031 Very Best Of.

MISS TONI FISHER
1960 THE BIG HURT
(M) (2:09) Collectables 5063 History Of Rock Volume 3.
(E) (2:10) Original Sound 8854 Oldies But Goodies Vol. 4. *(this compact disc uses the "Waring - fds" noise reduction process)*
(E) (2:10) Original Sound 2221 Oldies But Goodies Volumes 1,4,6,8 and 10 Box Set. *(this box set uses the "Waring - fds" noise reduction process)*
(E) (2:10) Original Sound 2500 Oldies But Goodies Volumes 1-15 Box Set. *(this box set uses the "Waring - fds" noise reduction process)*
(M) (2:10) Time-Life HPD-13 Your Hit Parade - 1959.
(M) (2:10) Collectables 2500 WCBS-FM History Of Rock - The 60's Part 1.
(M) (2:10) Collectables 4500 History Of Rock/The 60s Part One.
(M) (2:10) Risky Business 66388 The Big Hurt/Songs To Cry By.
(E) (2:07) Curb 77775 Hard To Find Original Recordings - Classic Hits.
(M) (2:11) Time-Life R857-16 The Heart Of Rock 'n' Roll The Late '50s.
1962 WEST OF THE WALL

ELLA FITZGERALD
1960 MACK THE KNIFE
(E) (5:12) Verve 825670 Mack The Knife: Ella In Berlin. *(LP version)*
(E) (5:05) Verve 841765 For The Love Of Ella. *(LP version)*
(E) (5:04) Verve 314517170 The Essential. *(LP version)*
(E) (5:05) Verve 314517898 First Lady Of Song. *(LP version)*
(M) (4:40) Verve 314521737 The Verve Story 1944-1994. *(45 version)*
(M) (4:40) Verve 314521485 Verve Grammy Winners. *(45 version)*
(M) (4:38) Verve 314519564 The Complete Ella In Berlin. *(45 version but this track segues into the next track which includes the :24 stage banter included on the LP version)*

FIVE AMERICANS
1966 I SEE THE LIGHT
(S) (2:07) Sundazed 6018 I See The Light. *(with drum beat at the end of the song)*
(S) (2:07) Sundazed 11004 The Five Americans. *(with drum beat at the end of the song)*
(S) (2:06) Time-Life 2CLR-26 Classic Rock - Rock Renaissance III. *(with drum beat at the end of the song)*
(S) (2:06) Rhino 75892 Nuggets. *(no drum beat at the end of the song)*
1967 WESTERN UNION
(45 and LP length is (2:26))
(S) (2:32) K-Tel 205 Battle Of The Bands Volume 3. *(very poor stereo separation)*
(M) (2:25) Rhino 75777 More Nuggets. *(truncated fade)*
(S) (2:34) Sundazed 11004 Western Union.
(M) (2:25) Time-Life 2CLR-10 Classic Rock - 1967: The Beat Goes On.
(S) (2:34) Collectables 2510 WCBS-FM History Of Rock - The Rockin' 60's.
(S) (2:34) Collectables 4510 History Of Rock/The Rockin' 60s.
(S) (2:33) Collectables 2501 WCBS-FM History Of Rock - The 60's Part 2.
(S) (2:33) Collectables 4501 History Of Rock/The 60s Part Two.
(S) (2:27) Varese Sarabande 5575 Bubblegum Classics Volume Two.
(S) (2:34) Time-Life 2CLR-31 Classic Rock - Totally Fantastic '60s.
1967 SOUND OF LOVE
(S) (2:24) Sundazed 11004 Western Union. *(with countoff)*
1967 ZIP CODE
(S) (3:13) Sundazed 11004 Western Union. *(complete session recording)*

FIVE BLOBS
1958 THE BLOB
(M) (2:39) Rhino 71492 Elvira Presents Haunted Hits.
(M) (2:38) Rhino 70535 Halloween Hits.
(M) (2:38) CBS Special Products 46200 Rock Goes To The Movies Volume 3.
(M) (2:37) Time-Life 2RNR-37 Rock 'N' Roll Era - Weird, Wild & Wacky.
(E) (2:37) Risky Business 66391 Ghastly Grooves.
(E) (2:37) K-Tel 4033 Ghasty Grooves.
(M) (2:38) Varese Sarabande 5882 They Came From Outer Space.

FIVE FLIGHTS UP
1970 DO WHAT YOU WANNA DO

FIVE KEYS
1956 OUT OF SIGHT, OUT OF MIND
(M) (2:15) Capitol 92709 Capitol Collector's Series.
(M) (2:14) Time-Life 2RNR-23 Rock 'N' Roll Era - 1956 Still Rockin'.
(M) (2:15) Collectables 5472 Golden Classics.
(M) (2:15) Time-Life R857-07 The Heart Of Rock 'n' Roll 1956.
1956 WISDOM OF A FOOL
(M) (2:35) Capitol 92709 Capitol Collector's Series. *(includes :06 of studio talk)*
(M) (2:35) Collectables 5472 Golden Classics. *(includes :06 of studio talk)*

FIVE MAN ELECTRICAL BAND
1971 SIGNS
(this 45 was issued in two versions: one with a printed label time of (4:05) which actually ran (3:25) and another with a printed label time of (3:20) which actually ran (3:02))

(M) (4:01) Rhino 70926 Super Hits Of The 70's Volume 6. *(LP version)*

(M) (4:01) Rhino 70734 Songs Of Protest. *(LP version)*

(M) (3:59) Priority 8670 Hitchin A Ride/70's Greatest Rock Hits Volume 10. *(LP version)*

(M) (4:00) Rhino 71209 70's Smash Hits Volume 5. *(LP version)*

(M) (3:59) Razor & Tie 22505 More Fabulous 70's Volume 2. *(LP version)*

(M) (4:00) Time-Life SUD-10 Superhits - 1971. *(LP version)*

(M) (4:00) Rhino 72131 Frat Rock: The 70's. *(LP version)*

(S) (3:02) Rebound 314520364 Class Reunion '71. *(very poor stereo separation)*

(M) (4:00) Time-Life AM1-06 AM Gold - 1971. *(LP version)*

(S) (3:02) Rebound 314520440 No. 1 Hits Of The 70's. *(very poor stereo separation)*

(M) (4:00) Flashback 72685 '70s Radio Hits Volume 5. *(LP version)*

(S) (3:01) Polygram Special Markets 314520456 #1 Radio Hits Of The 70's. *(very poor stereo separation)*

1971 ABSOLUTELY RIGHT

(S) (2:17) Rhino 70926 Super Hits Of The 70's Volume 6.

FIVE SATINS
1956 IN THE STILL OF THE NIGHT

(M) (3:03) Rhino 75763 Best Of Doo Wop Ballads.

(M) (3:04) Rhino 70642 Billboard's Top R&B Hits Of 1956.

(M) (3:04) RCA 6408 O.S.T. Dirty Dancing.

(M) (3:03) Arista 8605 16 Original Doo-Wop Classics.

(M) (3:00) Relic 7001 Greatest Hits.

(M) (2:58) Collectables 2508 History Of Rock - The Doo Wop Era Volume 2.

(M) (2:58) Collectables 4508 History Of Rock/The Doo Wop Era Part Two.

(M) (3:00) Collectables 5017 Sing Their Greatest Hits.

(M) (3:02) Collectables 5064 History Of Rock Volume 4.

(S) (4:17) Special Music 4913 Rock & Roll Revival. *(live)*

(M) (3:01) Rhino 71463 Doo Wop Box.

(E) (3:04) Original Sound 8905r 13 Of The Best Doo Wop Love Songs.

(E) (3:04) Original Sound 9326 Best Love Songs Vol. 1 & 2.

(E) (3:04) Original Sound 4001 Art Laboe's 60 Killer Oldies.

(E) (3:04) Original Sound 1236 Best Love Songs Box Set.

(M) (3:05) Original Sound 9329 Oldies But Goodies Doo Wop Classics.

(M) (2:53) Relic 7056 Lost Treasures. *(distorted; alternate take; mastered from vinyl)*

(M) (3:01) Time-Life 2RNR-14 Rock 'N' Roll Era - 1956.

(M) (2:58) Time-Life RHD-05 Rhythm & Blues - 1956.

(M) (3:03) Time-Life R962-06 History Of Rock 'N' Roll: Doo Wop And Vocal Group Tradition 1955-1962.

(M) (2:58) Collectables 2506 WCBS-FM History Of Rock - The 50's Part 1.

(M) (2:58) Collectables 4506 History Of Rock/The 50s Part One.

(M) (3:01) Collectables 5055 Harlem Holiday - N.Y. Rhythm & Blues Vol. 5.

(M) (3:01) Collectables 5037 Great Groups Of The Fifties Volume I.

(M) (2:59) Collectables 2509 WCBS-FM For Lovers Only Part 1.

(M) (3:02) Collectables 2604 WCBS-FM Jukebox Giants Vol. 2.

(M) (3:01) Time-Life R103-27 Love Me Tender.

(M) (3:01) Time-Life R10513 40 Lovin' Oldies.

(M) (3:02) Rhino 71806 The R&B Box: Thirty Years Of Rhythm & Blues.

(M) (3:01) Thump 7060 Low Rider Oldies Volume 6.

(M) (3:00) Collectables 5653 Spotlite On Ember Records Volume 1.

(M) (3:02) JCI 3183 1955 - Only Love - 1959.

(M) (3:03) K-Tel 3812 Doo Wop's Greatest Hits.

(M) (3:02) Time-Life R857-07 The Heart Of Rock 'n' Roll 1956.

(M) (2:59) Relic 7100 The Golden Era Of Doo Wops: Ember Records Part 2.

(M) (3:02) Time-Life R857-21 The Heart Of Rock 'n' Roll Slow Dancing Classics.

(M) (2:58) Time-Life R838-24 Solid Gold Soul 1956.

1957 TO THE AISLE

(M) (2:43) Arista 8605 16 Original Doo-Wop Classics.

(M) (2:43) Relic 7001 Greatest Hits.

(M) (2:42) Rhino 70588 Rockin' & Rollin' Wedding Songs Volume 1.

(M) (2:43) Collectables 5017 Sing Their Greatest Hits.

(M) (2:44) Collectables 5067 History Of Rock Volume 7.

(S) (3:32) Special Music 4913 Rock & Roll Revival. *(live)*

(M) (2:42) MCA 8001 O.S.T. American Graffiti. *(Wolfman Jack talks over the introduction)*

(M) (2:43) Relic 7056 Lost Treasures. *(alternate take)*

(M) (2:42) Time-Life 2RNR-41 Rock 'N' Roll Era - R&B Gems.

(M) (2:42) Time-Life RHD-08 Rhythm & Blues - 1957.

(M) (2:44) Original Sound 9328 13 Of The Best Doo Wop Love Songs Vol. 2.

(M) (2:42) Collectables 2506 WCBS-FM History Of Rock - The 50's Part 1.

(M) (2:42) Collectables 4506 History Of Rock/The 50s Part One.

(M) (2:44) Collectables 5057 Harlem Holiday - N.Y. Rhythm & Blues Vol. 7.

(M) (2:44) Collectables 5038 Great Groups Of The Fifties Volume II.

(M) (2:44) Collectables 2608 WCBS-FM For Lovers Only Vol. 4.

(M) (2:47) Collectables 2552 WOGL History Of Rock Vol. 2.

(M) (2:42) Time-Life R102-17 Lost Treasures Of Rock 'N' Roll.

(M) (2:44) Collectables 5653 Spotlite On Ember Records Volume 1.

(M) (2:44) Rhino 72507 Doo Wop Box II.

(M) (2:42) Time-Life R857-05 The Heart Of Rock 'n' Roll 1957.

(M) (2:44) Relic 7060 The Golden Era Of Doo Wops: Ember Records.

(M) (2:42) Time-Life R838-23 Solid Gold Soul 1957.

FIVE STAIRSTEPS
1970 O-o-h CHILD
(the LP time is (3:14); the 45 time is (3:11))

(S) (2:54) Pair 1202 Best Of Buddah. *(mistakenly identifies the group only as the "Stairsteps"; edited)*

(S) (2:54) Pair 1199 Best Of Bubblegum Music. *(mistakenly identifies the group only as the "Stairsteps"; edited)*

(S) (3:14) Rhino 70782 Soul Hits Of The 70's Volume 2.

(S) (3:14) Rhino 72028 Soul Hits Of The 70's Volumes 1-5 Box Set.

(S) (3:16) Collectables 5023 Greatest Hits.

(S) (3:14) Rhino 71206 70's Smash Hits Volume 2.

(S) (2:53) Essex 7060 The Buddah Box. *(edited)*

(S) (3:12) Razor & Tie 22047 Sweet 70's Soul.

(S) (3:12) Time-Life RHD-18 Rhythm & Blues - 1970.

(S) (2:53) Time-Life SUD-04 Superhits - 1970. *(edited)*

(S) (3:16) MCA 11036 O.S.T. Crooklyn.

(S) (3:15) JCI 3130 1970 - Only Rock 'N Roll - 1974.

(S) (3:14) Ichiban 2510 Lifting The Spirit.

(S) (3:13) Varese Sarabande 5718 Soulful Pop.

(S) (2:53) Time-Life AM1-02 AM Gold - 1970. *(edited)*

(S) (3:12) Time-Life R838-05 Solid Gold Soul - 1970.

(S) (3:14) Flashback 72682 '70s Radio Hits Volume 2.

(S) (3:14) Flashback 72090 '70s Radio Hits Box Set.

(S) (3:13) K-Tel 3887 Soul Brothers & Sisters Of The 70's.

(S) (2:53) BMG Special Products 44643 The Best Of Buddah. *(edited)*

(S) (3:14) Varese Sarabande 5890 Bubblegum Classics Volume Four - Soulful Pop.

5000 VOLTS
1975 I'M ON FIRE
    (S) (2:47) Rhino 70276 The Disco Years Volume 5.

FIXX
1983 SAVED BY ZERO
    (S) (3:39) Priority 53721 Rock Of The 80's Volume 5. *(LP version)*
    (S) (3:40) Right Stuff 27754 Sedated In The Eighties. *(LP version)*
    (S) (3:36) K-Tel 3342 The 80's Pop Explosion. *(LP version)*
    (S) (3:39) MCA 42316 Greatest Hits. *(LP version)*
    (S) (3:38) MCA 31025 Reach The Beach. *(LP version)*
    (S) (3:38) Time-Life R988-18 Sounds Of The Eighties: The Early '80s Take Two. *(LP version)*
    (S) (3:38) Hip-O 40047 The '80s Hit(s) Back 3. *(LP version)*
    (S) (3:37) Intersound 9521 Retro Lunch Box - Squeeze The Cheese. *(LP version)*
    (S) (3:39) Simitar 55552 The Number One's: Eighties Rock. *(LP version)*
1983 ONE THING LEADS TO ANOTHER
    (S) (3:16) Priority 7994 Rock Of The 80's.
    (S) (3:14) K-Tel 3262 The 80's Video Stars.
    (S) (3:16) Sandstone 33046 and 5012 Rock The First Volume Six.
    (S) (3:17) Rhino 71834 Classic MTV: Class Of 1983.
    (S) (3:17) MCA 42316 Greatest Hits.
    (S) (3:17) MCA 31025 Reach The Beach.
    (S) (3:16) EMI 28339 Living In Oblivion: The 80's Greatest Hits - Volume Four.
    (S) (3:22) Rhino 71974 New Wave Hits Of The 80's Vol. 11.
    (S) (3:15) Time-Life R988-03 Sounds Of The Eighties: 1983.
    (S) (3:13) JCI 3149 1980 - Only Dance - 1984.
    (S) (3:17) Risky Business 66390 Hazy Shade Of 80's.
    (S) (7:48) Oglio 81584 Hit That Perfect Beat Volume 2. *(12" single version; all songs on this cd are segued together)*
    (S) (3:15) Madacy Entertainment 1983 Rock On 1983.
    (S) (3:16) Hip-O 40004 The '80s Hit(s) Back!
    (S) (3:13) JCI 3159 18 Modern Rock Classics From The 80's.
    (S) (3:18) Rhino 72596 Billboard Top Album Rock Hits, 1983.
1984 THE SIGN OF FIRE
    (S) (3:48) Priority 53751 Rock Of The 80's Volume 13.
    (S) (3:48) MCA 42316 Greatest Hits.
    (S) (3:49) MCA 31025 Reach The Beach.
1984 ARE WE OURSELVES?
    (S) (2:43) Priority 53748 Rock Of The 80's Volume 8. *(live)*
    (S) (2:27) MCA 31063 Phantoms.
    (S) (2:27) MCA 42316 Greatest Hits.
    (S) (2:26) Hip-O 40023 Smash Alternatives - 14 Classic New Wave Hits.
    (S) (2:27) Time-Life R988-15 Sounds Of The Eighties: The Mid 80's.
    (S) (2:28) Rhino 72597 Billboard Top Album Rock Hits, 1984.
1986 SECRET SEPARATION
    (S) (3:48) Priority 53754 Rock Of The 80's Volume 15.
    (S) (3:48) MCA 42316 Greatest Hits.
    (S) (3:50) MCA 5705 Walkabout.
1991 HOW MUCH IS ENOUGH
    (S) (4:02) MCA 10205 Ink.
    (S) (4:02) Rhino 72651 Billboard Top Modern Rock Tracks, 1991.

ROBERTA FLACK
released as by ROBERTA FLACK & DONNY HATHAWAY:
1971 YOU'VE GOT A FRIEND
    (S) (3:23) Atlantic 81299 Atlantic Rhythm & Blues Volume 7.
    (S) (3:22) Atlantic 19317 Best Of Roberta Flack.
    (S) (3:23) Atlantic 7216 Roberta Flack & Donny Hathaway.
    (S) (3:23) Atlantic 82794 Roberta Flack & Donny Hathaway. *(remastered edition)*
    (S) (3:23) Atlantic 82092 Donny Hathaway Collection.
    (S) (3:23) Atlantic 82305 Atlantic Rhythm And Blues 1947-1974 Box Set.

released as by ROBERTA FLACK:
1972 THE FIRST TIME EVER I SAW YOUR FACE
    (S) (4:17) Atlantic 81912 Golden Age Of Black Music (1970-1975). *(45 version)*
    (S) (5:20) Atlantic 8230 First Take. *(LP version)*
    (S) (5:19) Atlantic 82792 First Take. *(remastered edition; LP version)*
    (S) (4:17) Atlantic 81298 Atlantic Rhythm & Blues Volume 6. *(45 version)*
    (S) (4:16) Atlantic 19317 Best Of. *(45 version)*
    (S) (4:17) Atlantic 82305 Atlantic Rhythm And Blues 1947-1974 Box Set. *(45 version)*
    (S) (5:20) Atlantic 82498 Softly With These Songs: Best Of. *(LP version)*
released as by ROBERTA FLACK & DONNY HATHAWAY:
1972 WHERE IS THE LOVE
    (S) (2:41) Atlantic 81299 Atlantic Rhythm & Blues Volume 7.
    (S) (2:41) Atlantic 19317 Best Of Roberta Flack.
    (S) (2:43) Atlantic 7216 Roberta Flack & Donny Hathaway.
    (S) (2:43) Atlantic 82794 Roberta Flack & Donny Hathaway. *(remastered edition)*
    (S) (2:43) Atlantic 82092 Donny Hathaway Collection.
    (S) (2:43) Atlantic 82305 Atlantic Rhythm And Blues 1947-1974 Box Set.
    (S) (2:43) Atlantic 82498 Roberta Flack - Softly With These Songs: Best Of.
released as by ROBERTA FLACK:
1973 KILLING ME SOFTLY WITH HIS SONG
    (S) (4:45) Atlantic 81299 Atlantic Rhythm & Blues Volume 7.
    (S) (4:45) Atlantic 81912 Golden Age Of Black Music (1970-1975).
    (S) (4:45) Atlantic 19154 Killing Me Softly.
    (S) (4:46) Atlantic 82793 Killing Me Softly. *(remastered edition)*
    (S) (4:45) Atlantic 19317 Best Of.
    (S) (4:44) Atlantic 82305 Atlantic Rhythm And Blues 1947-1974 Box Set.
    (S) (4:45) Atlantic 82498 Softly With These Songs: Best Of.
1973 JESSE
    (S) (3:59) Atlantic 19154 Killing Me Softly.
    (S) (4:00) Atlantic 82793 Killing Me Softly. *(remastered edition)*
    (S) (3:59) Atlantic 19317 Best Of.
1974 FEEL LIKE MAKIN' LOVE
    (S) (2:54) Atlantic 81299 Atlantic Rhythm & Blues Volume 7.
    (S) (2:54) Atlantic 82305 Atlantic Rhythm And Blues (1947-1974) Box Set.
    (S) (2:54) Atlantic 81912 Golden Age Of Black Music (1970-1975).
    (S) (2:54) Atlantic 80333 Feel Like Makin' Love.
    (S) (2:52) Atlantic 19317 Best Of.
    (S) (2:52) Atlantic 82498 Softly With These Songs: Best Of.
1978 IF EVER I SEE YOU AGAIN
    (S) (3:31) Atlantic 19317 Best Of.
released as by ROBERTA FLACK & DONNY HATHAWAY:
1979 THE CLOSER I GET TO YOU
(dj copies of this 45 ran (3:27) and (4:39); commercial copies were all (4:39))
    (S) (4:38) Atlantic 81913 Golden Age Of Black Music (1977-1988).
    (S) (4:37) Atlantic 19317 Roberta Flack - Best Of.
    (S) (4:38) Atlantic 19149 Roberta Flack - Blue Lights In The Basement.
    (S) (4:38) Atlantic 82791 Roberta Flack - Blue Lights In The Basement. *(remastered edition)*
    (S) (4:39) Atlantic 82498 Roberta Flack - Softly With These Songs: Best Of.
released as by ROBERTA FLACK:
1982 MAKING LOVE
    (S) (3:41) Atlantic 82498 Softly With These Songs: Best Of.
    (S) (3:41) Atlantic 19354 I'm The One.

ROBERTA FLACK (Continued)
released as by PEABO BRYSON/ROBERTA FLACK:
1983 TONIGHT I CELEBRATE MY LOVE
- (S) (3:29) Priority 7040 Making Love.
- (S) (3:29) Scotti Brothers 75434 Romantic Duets.
- (S) (3:28) Capitol 46071 Peabo Bryson Collection.
- (S) (3:29) Atlantic 82498 Roberta Flack - Softly With These Songs: Best Of.
- (S) (3:29) CEMA Special Markets 35966 Tonight I Celebrate My Love.
- (S) (3:29) DCC Compact Classics 104 Duets - A Man & A Woman.
- (S) (3:29) MCA 11431 Quiet Storms 2.
- (S) (3:28) Madacy Entertainment 6803 Power Of Love.
- (S) (3:29) Time-Life R834-08 Body Talk - On My Mind.
- (S) (3:29) Angel 56580 Men Are From Mars, Women Are From Venus - Songs For Loving Couples.

released as by ROBERTA FLACK with MAXI PRIEST:
1991 SET THE NIGHT TO MUSIC
- (S) (5:21) Atlantic 82498 Roberta Flack - Softly With These Songs: Best Of. *(LP version)*
- (S) (5:20) Atlantic 82321 Roberta Flack - Set The Night To Music. *(LP version)*

FLAMING EMBER
1969 MIND, BODY AND SOUL
- (M) (2:58) Rhino 70781 Soul Hits Of The 70's Volume 1.
- (M) (2:58) Rhino 72028 Soul Hits Of The 70's Volumes 1-5 Box Set.
- (S) (2:53) HDH 3906 Best Of.
1970 WESTBOUND #9
- (M) (2:48) Rhino 70783 Soul Hits Of The 70's Volume 3. *(this is a highly edited version that bears no resemblence to the original hit version)*
- (M) (2:48) Rhino 72028 Soul Hits Of The 70's Volumes 1-5 Box Set. *(this is a highly edited version that bears no resemblance to the original hit version)*
- (E) (3:28) HDH 3906 Best Of.
1970 I'M NOT MY BROTHERS KEEPER
- (S) (3:01) Rhino 70783 Soul Hits Of The 70's Volume 3.
- (S) (3:01) Rhino 72028 Soul Hits Of The 70's Volumes 1-5 Box Set.
- (S) (4:08) HDH 3906 Best Of.

FLAMINGOS
1959 I ONLY HAVE EYES FOR YOU
- (S) (3:19) Rhino 70906 American Bandstand Greatest Hits Collection.
- (S) (3:21) Rhino 75763 Best Of Doo Wop Ballads.
- (S) (3:20) Rhino 70967 Best Of.
- (S) (3:21) Epic 48732 O.S.T. My Girl.
- (S) (3:21) Collectables 5424 Flamingo Serenade.
- (S) (3:20) Collectables 8803 For Collectors Only.
- (S) (3:19) Essex 7053 A Hot Summer Night In '59.
- (S) (3:21) Collectables 5426 The Sound Of. *(truncated fade)*
- (S) (3:20) MCA 8001 O.S.T. American Graffiti.
- (S) (3:20) Scotti Brothers 75405 There Is Still Love (The Anniversary Songs).
- (S) (3:20) Original Sound 8905r 13 Of The Best Doo Wop Love Songs.
- (S) (3:20) Original Sound 9326 Best Love Songs Vol. 1 & 2.
- (S) (3:20) Original Sound 4001 Art Laboe's 60 Killer Oldies.
- (S) (3:20) Original Sound 1236 Best Love Songs Box Set.
- (S) (3:20) Original Sound 8863 Oldies But Goodies Vol. 13.
- (S) (3:20) Original Sound 2223 Oldies But Goodies Volumes 2,7,9,12 and 13 Box Set. *(Volumes 2, 7 and 12 of this box set use the "Waring - fds" noise reduction process)*
- (S) (3:20) Original Sound 2500 Oldies But Goodies Volumes 1-15 Box Set. *(most volumes in this box set use the "Waring - fds" noise reduction process)*
- (S) (3:18) Rhino 71463 Doo Wop Box.
- (S) (3:15) Time-Life 2RNR-20 Rock 'N' Roll Era - 1959 Still Rockin'.
- (S) (3:15) Time-Life RHD-03 Rhythm & Blues - 1959.
- (S) (3:20) Time-Life R962-06 History Of Rock 'N' Roll: Doo Wop And Vocal Group Tradition 1955-1962.
- (S) (3:18) Collectables 5470 The Spotlight Series - End Records Vol. 1. *(alternate take; includes countoff)*
- (S) (3:21) Collectables 2602 WCBS-FM History Of Rock - The Group Sounds Vol. 3.
- (S) (3:18) Collectables 2608 WCBS-FM For Lovers Only Vol. 4.
- (S) (3:19) Time-Life R103-27 Love Me Tender.
- (S) (3:15) Time-Life R10513 40 Lovin' Oldies.
- (S) (3:20) Rhino 71806 The R&B Box: Thirty Years Of Rhythm & Blues.
- (S) (3:20) Pyramid 71888 A Future To This Life - Robocop: The Series Soundtrack.
- (S) (3:20) Polygram Special Markets 314520259 Doo Wop Classics.
- (S) (3:20) Time-Life R857-01 The Heart Of Rock 'n' Roll - 1959.
- (S) (3:20) Time-Life R138-32 Hollywood Hit Parade.
- (S) (3:18) Rhino 72157 Doo Wop Memories, Vol. 2.
- (S) (3:20) Rhino 71802 O.S.T. Andre.
- (S) (3:15) Nick At Nite/550 Music/Epic 67768 Fonzie's Make Out Music.
- (M) (3:09) Cypress 71334 O.S.T. Coupe De Ville.
- (S) (3:18) Hip-O 40028 The Glory Of Love - '50s Sweet & Soulful Love Songs.
- (S) (3:20) Rhino 72580 Soul Serenade - Intimate R&B.
- (S) (3:19) Angel 56580 Men Are From Mars, Women Are From Venus - Songs For Loving Couples.
- (S) (3:18) Flashback 72716 Doo Wop - Sh-Boom.
- (S) (3:15) Time-Life R838-21 Solid Gold Soul 1959.
- (S) (3:15) Time-Life R132-14 Golden Groups Of Your Hit Parade.

FLARES
1961 FOOT STOMPING (PART 1)
- (E) (2:15) Rhino 75764 Best Of Doo Wop Uptempo.
- (S) (2:15) MCA 6228 O.S.T. Hairspray. *(missing some footstomps and an organ overdub)*
- (M) (2:14) Time-Life 2RNR-41 Rock 'N' Roll Era - R&B Gems.
- (M) (2:14) Eric 11503 Hard To Find 45's On CD (Volume II) 1961-64.

FLASH
1972 SMALL BEGINNINGS
- (S) (3:10) Rhino 71196 Super Hits Of The 70's Volume 16.
- (S) (9:19) EMI-Capitol Music Special Markets 19545 Lost Hits Of The '70s.

FLASH CADILLAC & THE CONTINENTAL KIDS
1976 DID YOU BOOGIE (WITH YOUR BABY)
(dj copies of this 45 featured Wolfman Jack narration with Flash Cadillac on one side and Flash Cadillac only on the other side; commercial copies all featured Wolfman Jack with Flash Cadillac)
- (S) (2:53) Rhino 72298 Superhits Of The 70's Volume 24. *(with Wolfman Jack)*

FLEETWOOD MAC
1976 OVER MY HEAD
- (S) (3:34) Reprise 2281 Fleetwood Mac. *(LP version)*
- (S) (3:33) Warner Brothers 25801 Greatest Hits. *(LP version)*
- (S) (3:33) Warner Brothers 45129 The Chain. *(LP version)*
- (S) (3:33) Time-Life R834-09 Body Talk - Magic Moments. *(LP version)*
1976 RHIANNON (WILL YOU EVER WIN)
- (S) (4:11) Reprise 2281 Fleetwood Mac. *(LP version; tracks into next selection)*
- (S) (4:09) Warner Brothers 25801 Greatest Hits. *(LP version)*
- (S) (4:09) Warner Brothers 45129 The Chain. *(LP version; tracks into next selection)*
- (S) (4:08) JCI 3146 1975 - Only Love - 1979. *(LP version)*

1976 SAY YOU LOVE ME
(S) (4:11) Reprise 2281 Fleetwood Mac. *(LP version)*
(S) (4:09) Warner Brothers 25801 Greatest Hits. *(LP version)*
(S) (3:44) Warner Brothers 45129 The Chain. *(45 version)*
(S) (3:58) Time-Life SOD-04 Sounds Of The Seventies - 1976. *(LP version faded :11 early)*
(S) (3:43) Time-Life AM1-23 AM Gold - 1976. *(45 version)*

1977 GO YOUR OWN WAY
(S) (3:38) Warner Brothers 3010 Rumours.
(S) (3:36) Warner Brothers 25801 Greatest Hits.
(S) (3:38) Warner Brothers 45129 The Chain.
(S) (3:35) Time-Life R102-34 The Rolling Stone Collection.
(S) (3:36) MCA 11389 O.S.T. Casino.

1977 DREAMS
(S) (4:14) Warner Brothers 3010 Rumours.
(S) (4:13) Warner Brothers 25801 Greatest Hits.
(S) (4:13) Warner Brothers 45129 The Chain.
(S) (4:14) Time-Life SOD-05 Sounds Of The Seventies - 1977.
(S) (4:13) JCI 3131 1975 - Only Rock 'N Roll - 1979.
(S) (4:14) Rhino 72518 Mellow Rock Hits Of The 70's - Summer Breeze.
(S) (4:13) Time-Life R834-03 Body Talk - Moonlit Nights.

1977 DON'T STOP
(S) (3:11) Warner Brothers 3010 Rumours.
(S) (3:09) Warner Brothers 25801 Greatest Hits.
(S) (3:10) Warner Brothers 45129 The Chain.
(S) (3:09) Time-Life R968-14 Guitar Rock - The Late '70s.
(S) (3:09) JCI 3169 #1 Radio Hits 1975 - Only Rock 'n Roll - 1979.
(S) (3:09) Time-Life AM1-24 AM Gold - 1977.
(S) (3:09) Time-Life R13610 Gold And Platinum Box Set - The Ultimate Rock Collection.
(S) (3:09) Madacy Entertainment 6805 The Power Of Rock.

1977 YOU MAKE LOVING FUN
(S) (3:31) Warner Brothers 3010 Rumours.
(S) (3:30) Warner Brothers 25801 Greatest Hits.
(S) (3:29) Warner Brothers 45129 The Chain.

1979 TUSK
(S) (3:34) Warner Brothers 3350 Tusk.
(S) (3:29) Warner Brothers 25801 Greatest Hits.
(S) (3:12) Warner Brothers 45129 The Chain. *(alternate take)*

1980 SARA
(S) (4:34) Warner Brothers 3350 Tusk. *(45 version)*
(S) (6:21) Warner Brothers 25801 Greatest Hits. *(LP version)*
(S) (6:23) Warner Brothers 45129 The Chain. *(LP version)*
(S) (4:34) Time-Life R988-07 Sounds Of The Eighties: 1980. *(45 version)*

1980 THINK ABOUT ME
(S) (2:39) Warner Brothers 3350 Tusk.
(S) (2:39) Warner Brothers 45129 The Chain.

1982 HOLD ME
(S) (3:44) Warner Brothers 23607 Mirage.
(S) (3:43) Warner Brothers 25801 Greatest Hits.
(S) (3:43) Time-Life R988-01 Sounds Of The Eighties: The Rockin' Eighties.
(S) (3:43) Time-Life R834-10 Body Talk - From The Heart.
(S) (3:43) Rhino 72595 Billboard Top Album Rock Hits, 1982.

1982 GYPSY
(S) (4:24) Warner Brothers 23607 Mirage. *(LP version)*
(S) (4:23) Warner Brothers 25801 Greatest Hits. *(LP version)*
(S) (5:20) Warner Brothers 45129 The Chain. *(previously unreleased version)*
(S) (4:22) Time-Life R988-14 Sounds Of The Eighties: 1980-1982. *(LP version)*

1983 LOVE IN STORE
(S) (3:13) Warner Brothers 23607 Mirage.
(S) (3:21) Warner Brothers 45129 The Chain.

1987 BIG LOVE
(S) (3:37) Warner Brothers 25471 Tango In The Night.
(S) (3:37) Warner Brothers 25801 Greatest Hits.
(S) (3:38) Warner Brothers 45129 The Chain.
(S) (3:37) Time-Life R988-28 Sounds Of The Eighties: The Rolling Stone Collection 1986-1987.

1987 SEVEN WONDERS
(S) (3:37) Warner Brothers 25471 Tango In The Night.

1987 LITTLE LIES
(S) (6:14) JCI 3122 Lost Mixes. *(remixed)*
(S) (3:38) JCI 3128 1985 - Only Rock 'N Roll - 1989.
(S) (3:38) Warner Brothers 25471 Tango In The Night.
(S) (3:37) Warner Brothers 25801 Greatest Hits.
(S) (3:36) Time-Life R988-09 Sounds Of The Eighties: 1987.
(S) (3:36) Time-Life R834-06 Body Talk - Only You.

1988 EVERYWHERE
(S) (3:40) Warner Brothers 25471 Tango In The Night.
(S) (3:41) Warner Brothers 45129 The Chain.
(S) (3:39) JCI 3186 1985 - Only Love - 1989.
(S) (3:40) Time-Life R988-20 Sounds Of The Eighties: The Late '80s Take Two.

1989 AS LONG AS YOU FOLLOW
(S) (4:08) Warner Brothers 25801 Greatest Hits.

1990 SAVE ME
(S) (4:13) Warner Brothers 26206 and 26111 Behind The Mask.
(S) (4:12) Warner Brothers 45129 The Chain.

FLEETWOODS
1959 COME SOFTLY TO ME
(M) (2:21) Enigma 73531 O.S.T. Scandal.
(M) (2:24) Rhino 70980 Best Of.
(M) (2:19) EMI 81128 Rock Is Dead But It Won't Lie Down.
(M) (2:23) EMI 98830 Come Softly To Me: Very Best Of.
(M) (2:19) Time-Life 2RNR-13 Rock 'N' Roll Era - 1959.
(M) (2:23) Time-Life R962-05 History Of Rock 'N' Roll: The Teenage Years 1957-1964.
(M) (2:19) Time-Life R10513 40 Lovin' Oldies.
(M) (2:23) Time-Life R857-01 The Heart Of Rock 'n' Roll - 1959.
(S) (2:34) EMI 98830 Come Softly To Me: Very Best Of. *(a cappella version; includes :08 of studio talk)*
(M) (2:18) JCI 3183 1955 - Only Love - 1959.
(M) (2:23) Van Meter 3001 Mr. Blue.
(S) (2:11) Van Meter 3001 Mr. Blue. *(includes additional percussion)*
(M) (2:19) Time-Life R132-14 Golden Groups Of Your Hit Parade.

1959 GRADUATION'S HERE
(S) (1:57) Rhino 70980 Best Of.
(S) (1:57) EMI 98830 Come Softly To Me: Very Best Of.

1959 MR. BLUE
(M) (2:23) Elektra 60107 O.S.T. Diner.
(E) (2:21) JCI 3203 Lovin' Fifties.
(M) (2:23) Rhino 70980 Best Of.
(M) (2:23) EMI 98830 Come Softly To Me: Very Best Of.
(M) (2:22) Time-Life 2RNR-20 Rock 'N' Roll Era - 1959 Still Rockin'.
(M) (2:25) Time-Life HPD-13 Your Hit Parade - 1959.
(M) (2:23) Risky Business 66388 The Big Hurt/Songs To Cry By.
(S) (2:26) EMI 98830 Come Softly To Me: Very Best Of. *(a cappella version)*
(M) (2:22) Time-Life R857-11 The Heart Of Rock 'n' Roll 1958-1959.
(M) (2:23) Van Meter 3001 Mr. Blue.
(M) (2:23) Time-Life R857-21 The Heart Of Rock 'n' Roll Slow Dancing Classics.

1960 OUTSIDE MY WINDOW
(S) (2:05) Rhino 70980 Best Of.
(S) (2:07) EMI 98830 Come Softly To Me: Very Best Of.

1960 RUNAROUND
(S) (2:32) Rhino 70980 Best Of.
(S) (2:31) EMI 98830 Come Softly To Me: Very Best Of.
(S) (2:32) Time-Life 2RNR-46 Rock 'N' Roll Era - 60's Juke Box Memories.
(S) (2:32) Time-Life R857-19 The Heart Of Rock 'n' Roll 1960-1961 Take Three.

FLEETWOODS *(Continued)*
1961 TRAGEDY
(S) (2:43) Rhino 70980 Best Of.
(S) (2:44) EMI 98830 Come Softly To Me: Very Best Of.
(S) (2:42) Time-Life 2RNR-35 Rock 'N' Roll Era - The 60's Last Dance.
(S) (2:44) DCC Compact Classics 078 Best Of Tragedy.
(S) (2:43) Time-Life R857-17 The Heart Of Rock 'n' Roll: The Early '60s.

1961 HE'S THE GREAT IMPOSTER
(S) (2:10) EMI 98830 Come Softly To Me: Very Best Of.
(S) (2:10) Rhino 70980 Best Of.
(S) (2:06) Time-Life 2RNR-42 Rick 'N' Roll Era - The 60's Sock Hop.
(S) (2:10) MCA 8001 O.S.T. American Graffiti.

1962 LOVERS BY NIGHT, STRANGERS BY DAY
(S) (2:09) Rhino 70980 Best Of.
(S) (2:11) EMI 98830 Come Softly To Me: Very Best Of.

1963 GOODNIGHT MY LOVE
(S) (2:21) EMI 98830 Come Softly To Me: Very Best Of.
(S) (2:21) Rhino 70980 Best Of.

SHELBY FLINT
1961 ANGEL ON MY SHOULDER
(M) (2:15) Time-Life HPD-32 Your Hit Parade - Into The 60's.

FLIRTATIONS
1969 NOTHING BUT A HEARTACHE
(S) (2:42) Rhino 75770 Soul Shots Volume 2.
(S) (2:40) Time-Life 2CLR-20 Classic Rock - 1969: Shakin' All Over.
(S) (2:41) Ripete 5151 Ocean Drive 4.
(M) (2:41) Rhino 72815 Beg, Scream & Shout! The Big Ol' Box Of '60s Soul.

FLOATERS
1977 FLOAT ON
(dj copies of this 45 ran (3:51) and (4:13); commercial copies were all (4:13))
(S) (4:10) Time-Life SOD-17 Sounds Of The Seventies - 1977: Take Two. *(45 version)*
(S) (4:11) MCA Special Products 20752 Classic R&B Oldies From The 70's Vol. 2. *(45 version)*
(S) (11:41) Right Stuff 27307 Slow Jams: The 70's Volume One. *(LP version)*
(S) (11:46) MCA Special Products 20543 Float On. *(LP version)*
(S) (5:51) Thump 7030 Low Rider Oldies Volume III. *(neither the 45 or LP version)*
(S) (11:42) Rhino 71861 Smooth Grooves Volume 3. *(LP version)*
(S) (4:12) Rhino 72129 Soul Hits Of The 70's Vol. 19. *(45 version)*
(S) (4:11) MCA Special Products 20948 Biggest Summer Hits. *(45 version)*
(S) (4:11) Madacy Entertainment 1977 Rock On 1977. *(45 version)*
(S) (4:12) Hip-O 40011 ABC's Of Soul Volume 3. *(45 version)*
(S) (11:46) MCA Special Products 20979 Soul Hits Volume 1. *(LP version)*
(S) (11:42) Priority 50929 Rare Grooves Volume 2. *(LP version)*
(S) (4:10) Time-Life R834-04 Body Talk - Together Forever. *(45 version)*
(S) (11:42) Thump 4740 Old School Love Songs Volume 4. *(LP version)*
(S) (4:11) Time-Life R838-16 Solid Gold Soul 1977. *(45 version)*

FLOCK OF SEAGULLS
1982 I RAN (SO FAR AWAY)
(S) (3:57) Arista 8308 Arista's Perfect 10 Rides Again. *(neither the 45 or LP version)*
(S) (5:06) Priority 7994 Rock Of The 80's. *(LP version)*

(S) (5:03) K-Tel 3262 The 80's Video Stars. *(LP version)*
(S) (3:43) Rhino 71698 New Wave Hits Of The 80's Vol. 5. *(45 version)*
(S) (5:07) Jive 1007 A Flock Of Seagulls. *(LP version)*
(S) (5:03) Jive 1034 Best Of. *(LP version)*
(S) (3:42) Time-Life R988-05 Sounds Of The Eighties: 1982. *(45 version)*
(S) (3:43) Rhino 72490 New Wave Hits, Vol. 1. *(45 version)*
(S) (3:43) Flashback 72713 Essential New Wave Hits. *(45 version)*
(S) (3:43) Flashback 72092 New Wave Hits Box Set. *(45 version)*
(S) (3:43) Rhino 72820 VH1 - More Of The Big 80's. *(45 version)*
(S) (3:33) Arista 18985 Ultimate New Wave Party 1998. *(all selections on this cd are segued together)*
(S) (5:03) Intersound 9521 Retro Lunch Box - Squeeze The Cheese. *(LP version)*
(S) (3:43) Scotti Bros. 75512 New Wave Dance Hits! *(45 version)*
(S) (5:02) Simitar 55612 The Number One's: The '80s. *(LP version)*

1983 SPACE AGE LOVE SONG
(S) (3:45) Priority 53749 Rock Of The 80's Volume 6. *(LP version)*
(S) (3:45) Risky Business 57467 Big Hits, Skinny Ties - New Wave In The UK. *(LP version)*
(S) (3:47) Jive 1007 A Flock Of Seagulls. *(LP version)*
(S) (3:45) Jive 1034 Best Of. *(LP version)*

1983 WISHING (IF I HAD A PHOTOGRAPH OF YOU)
(S) (4:11) Rhino 71703 New Wave Hits Of The 80's Vol. 10. *(45 version)*
(S) (5:29) Jive 1034 Best Of. *(LP version)*
(S) (5:30) Priority 53765 Rock Of The 80's Volume 9. *(LP version)*

EDDIE FLOYD
1966 KNOCK ON WOOD
(M) (3:02) Atlantic Group 88218 Complete Stax/Volt Singles.
(S) (3:02) Stax 88005 Top Of The Stax.
(S) (3:02) Warner Special Products 27609 Memphis Soul Classics.
(S) (3:02) JCI 3100 Dance Sixties.
(S) (3:02) Atlantic 81298 Atlantic Rhythm & Blues Volume 6.
(S) (3:04) Atlantic 80283 Knock On Wood. *(truncated fade)*
(S) (3:07) Stax 4122 Chronicle: Greatest Hits.
(M) (3:02) Atlantic 82305 Atlantic Rhythm And Blues 1947-1974 Box Set.
(S) (3:07) Stax 88013 Rare Stamps.
(M) (3:03) Rhino 71461 Soul Hits, Volume 3.
(S) (3:01) Time-Life RHD-01 Rhythm & Blues - 1966.
(S) (3:01) Time-Life 2CLR-13 Classic Rock - 1966: Shakin' All Over.
(M) (3:03) Rhino 71806 The R&B Box: Thirty Years Of Rhythm & Blues.
(M) (3:03) Rhino 72478 Beverly Hills 90210: Songs From The Peach Pit.
(S) (3:00) Time-Life R838-01 Solid Gold Soul - 1966.
(M) (3:03) Flashback 72659 '60s Soul: When A Man Loves A Woman.
(M) (3:03) Flashback 72091 '60s Soul Hits Box Set.
(M) (3:02) TVT 4010 Rhythm Revue.
(S) (3:02) Repeat/Relativity 1609 Tell It Like It Is: #1 Soul Hits Of The 60's Volume 1.
(M) (3:03) Flashback 72896 25 Years Of R&B - 1966.
(M) (3:03) Rhino 72963 Ultimate '60s Soul Smashes.

1968 BRING IT ON HOME TO ME
(S) (2:29) Stax 4122 Chronicle: Greatest Hits.
(S) (2:29) Stax 8548 Stax Soul Brothers.
(S) (2:30) Stax 88013 Rare Stamps.
(S) (2:30) Stax 4411 Complete Stax/Volt Soul Singles 1968 - 1971.

KING FLOYD
1971 GROOVE ME
    (S)   (2:59)   Rhino 70659 Billboard's Top R&B Hits Of 1971.
    (S)   (2:58)   Rhino 70784 Soul Hits Of The 70's Volume 4.
    (S)   (2:58)   Rhino 72028 Soul Hits Of The 70's Volumes 1-5 Box Set.
    (S)   (3:00)   Atlantic 81299 Atlantic Rhythm & Blues Volume 7.
    (S)   (3:00)   Atlantic 81912 Golden Age Of Black Music (1970-1975).
    (S)   (2:59)   Atlantic 82305 Atlantic Rhythm And Blues 1947-1974 Box Set.
    (S)   (2:58)   Rhino 71431 In Yo Face! History Of Funk Volume 1.
    (S)   (2:58)   Time-Life RHD-09 Rhythm & Blues - 1971.
    (S)   (2:56)   Time-Life SOD-22 Sounds Of The Seventies - Seventies Top Forty.
    (S)   (2:58)   Elektra 61888 O.S.T. Beautiful Girls.
    (S)   (2:58)   Ripete 2222 Soul Patrol Vol. 4.
    (S)   (2:56)   JCI 3191 1970 - Only Dance - 1974.
    (S)   (2:58)   Priority 53129 Deep Soul Volume One.
    (S)   (2:58)   Time-Life R838-06 Solid Gold Soul - 1971.
    (S)   (2:58)   Miramax/Hollywood 206162091 O.S.T. Swingers.
    (S)   (2:58)   Flashback 72900 25 Years Of Soul - 1970.
1971 BABY LET ME KISS YOU
    (S)   (2:49)   Rhino 70785 Soul Hits Of The 70's Volume 5.
    (S)   (2:49)   Rhino 72028 Soul Hits Of The 70's Volumes 1-5 Box Set.

FLYING MACHINE
1969 SMILE A LITTLE SMILE FOR ME
    (S)   (2:56)   Rhino 70921 Super Hits Of The 70's Volume 1. *(neither the 45 or LP version)*
    (S)   (2:56)   Rhino 72009 Super Hits Of The 70's Volumes 1-4 Box Set. *(neither the 45 or LP version)*
    (M)   (2:57)   Rhino 70327 History Of British Rock Volume 9. *(neither the 45 or LP version)*
    (M)   (2:57)   Rhino 72022 History Of British Rock Box Set. *(neither the 45 or LP version)*
    (S)   (2:55)   Time-Life 2CLR-29 Classic Rock - Bubblegum, Garage And Pop Nuggets. *(neither the 45 or LP version)*
    (S)   (2:55)   Time-Life SUD-07 Superhits - 1969. *(neither the 45 or LP version)*
    (S)   (2:57)   Varese Sarabande 5575 Bubblegum Classics Volume Two. *(neither the 45 or LP version)*
    (S)   (2:56)   LaserLight 12317 The British Invasion. *(neither the 45 or LP version)*
    (S)   (2:55)   Time-Life AM1-01 AM Gold - 1969. *(neither the 45 or LP version)*

FOCUS
1973 HOCUS POCUS
    (S)   (3:27)   JCI 3302 Electric Seventies. *(45 version but :09 longer fade than the 45)*
    (S)   (6:39)   IRS 13060 Moving Waves. *(LP version)*
    (S)   (3:26)   Time-Life R968-05 Guitar Rock 1972-1973. *(45 version but :08 longer fade than the 45)*
    (S)   (6:40)   IRS 28162 Best Of: Hocus Pocus. *(LP version)*
    (S)   (3:16)   Rhino 72297 Superhits Of The 70's Volume 23. *(45 version)*
    (S)   (6:40)   Rhino 72451 Supernatural Fairy Tales - The Progressive Rock Era. *(LP version)*
    (S)   (6:38)   K-Tel 3610 Psychedelic Mind Trip Vol. 2: Another Flashback. *(LP version)*
    (S)   (3:22)   Popular/Critique 12009 Dutch Treats. *(rerecording)*
    (S)   (3:26)   Hip-O 40038 Power Chords Volume 1. *(45 version but :08 longer fade than the 45)*
    (S)   (6:38)   K-Tel 3910 Fantastic Volume 1. *(LP version)*

DAN FOGELBERG
1975 PART OF THE PLAN
    (S)   (3:17)   Epic 38308 Greatest Hits.
    (S)   (3:18)   Epic 33137 Souvenirs.
    (S)   (3:18)   Epic 64814 Souvenirs/Captured Angel/Nether Lands.

    (S)   (3:17)   Rhino 72519 Mellow Rock Hits Of The 70's - Sundown.
    (S)   (3:16)   Epic/Legacy 67949 Portrait - The Music Of 1972-1997.
released as by DAN FOGELBERG/TIM WEISBERG:
1978 THE POWER OF GOLD
    (S)   (4:27)   Epic 38308 Greatest Hits.
    (S)   (4:30)   Epic 35339 Twin Sons Of Different Mothers.
    (S)   (4:30)   Epic/Legacy 67949 Portrait - The Music Of 1972-1997.
    (S)   (4:30)   Epic/Legacy 65444 Super Hits.
released as by DAN FOGELBERG:
1980 LONGER
    (S)   (3:14)   Epic 38308 Greatest Hits.
    (S)   (3:14)   Epic 35634 Phoenix.
    (S)   (3:15)   Rhino 72446 Listen To The Music: 70's Male Singer/Songwriters.
    (S)   (3:11)   Time-Life R988-16 Sounds Of The Eighties: The Early '80s.
    (S)   (3:12)   Time-Life R834-01 Body Talk - Forever Yours.
    (S)   (3:14)   Epic/Legacy 67949 Portrait - The Music Of 1972-1997.
    (S)   (3:13)   Epic/Legacy 65444 Super Hits.
    (S)   (3:13)   Madacy Entertainment 6806 Best Of Love.
    (S)   (3:12)   Time-Life R814-03 Love Songs.
1980 HEART HOTELS
    (S)   (4:13)   Epic 38308 Greatest Hits. *(LP version)*
    (S)   (4:14)   Epic 35634 Phoenix. *(LP version)*
    (S)   (4:13)   Epic/Legacy 67949 Portrait - The Music Of 1972-1997. *(LP version)*
1981 SAME OLD LANG SYNE
    (S)   (5:17)   Epic 38308 Greatest Hits.
    (S)   (5:18)   Epic 37393 The Innocent Age.
    (S)   (5:19)   Epic/Legacy 67949 Portrait - The Music Of 1972-1997.
    (S)   (5:15)   Time-Life R834-20 Body Talk - Heart And Soul.
1981 HARD TO SAY
    (S)   (3:58)   Epic 38308 Greatest Hits.
    (S)   (3:59)   Epic 37393 The Innocent Age.
    (S)   (3:56)   Time-Life R834-09 Body Talk - Magic Moments.
    (S)   (3:55)   Epic/Legacy 67949 Portrait - The Music Of 1972-1997.
1982 LEADER OF THE BAND
    (S)   (4:16)   Epic 38308 Greatest Hits.
    (S)   (4:52)   Epic/Legacy 67949 Portrait - The Music Of 1972-1997. *(live)*
1982 RUN FOR THE ROSES
    (S)   (4:15)   Epic 38308 Greatest Hits.
    (S)   (4:17)   Epic 37393 The Innocent Age.
    (S)   (4:17)   Epic/Legacy 67949 Portrait - The Music Of 1972-1997.
1982 MISSING YOU
    (S)   (4:36)   Epic 38308 Greatest Hits.
    (S)   (4:33)   Epic/Legacy 67949 Portrait - The Music Of 1972-1997.
1983 MAKE LOVE STAY
    (S)   (4:33)   Epic 38308 Greatest Hits.
    (S)   (4:32)   Epic/Legacy 67949 Portrait - The Music Of 1972-1997.
1984 LANGUAGE OF LOVE
    (S)   (3:43)   Epic 39004 Windows And Walls.
    (S)   (3:41)   Epic/Legacy 67949 Portrait - The Music Of 1972-1997.
    (S)   (3:40)   Epic/Legacy 65444 Super Hits.

JOHN FOGERTY
1975 ROCKIN' ALL OVER THE WORLD
1985 THE OLD MAN DOWN THE ROAD
    (S)   (3:32)   Warner Brothers 25203 Centerfield.
1985 ROCK AND ROLL GIRLS
    (S)   (3:25)   Warner Brothers 25203 Centerfield.

FOGHAT
1976 SLOW RIDE
(actual 45 time is (3:53) not (3:45) as stated on the record label)
    (S)   (3:55)   JCI 3301 Rockin' Seventies. *(45 version)*

FOGHAT *(Continued)*

(S)	(8:12)	Priority 8662 Hard N' Heavy/70's Greatest Rock Hits Volume 1. *(LP version)*
(S)	(8:12)	Sandstone 33002 Reelin' In The Years Volume 3. *(LP version)*
(S)	(3:55)	Rhino 70088 Best Of. *(45 version)*
(S)	(8:11)	Rhino 70882 Fool For The City. *(LP version)*
(S)	(8:12)	DCC Compact Classics 064 Rock Of The 70's Volume Three. *(LP version)*
(S)	(3:55)	Reprise 45516 O.S.T. A Perfect World. *(45 version)*
(S)	(3:55)	Rhino 71030 Best Of/Rhino Special Editions. *(45 version)*
(S)	(3:53)	Time-Life R968-01 Guitar Rock 1974-1975. *(45 version)*
(S)	(3:55)	Time-Life SOD-18 Sounds Of The Seventies - 1976: Take Two. *(45 version)*
(S)	(3:54)	Time-Life R105-24 Guitar Rock Monsters. *(45 version)*
(S)	(8:12)	Varese Sarabande 5503 and 5504 and 5505 and 5506 and 5507 and 5508 and 5509 and 5513 and 5571 Arrow: All Rock & Roll Oldies Volume One. *(LP version)*
(S)	(8:12)	Risky Business 57471 Godfathers Of Grunge. *(LP version)*
(S)	(8:12)	Rhino 72132 Frat Rock: More Of The 70's. *(LP version)*
(S)	(3:55)	K-Tel 3463 Platinum Rock. *(45 version)*
(S)	(8:10)	Epic/Legacy 65020 Ultimate Rock 'n' Roll Collection. *(LP version)*
(S)	(3:53)	JCI 3140 18 Screamers From The 70's. *(45 version)*
(S)	(3:55)	Rhino 72478 Beverly Hills 90210: Songs From The Peach Pit. *(45 version)*
(S)	(8:14)	Time-Life R968-23 Guitar Rock - Live! *(LP version)*
(S)	(3:55)	Flashback 72675 Slow Ride And Other Hits. *(45 version)*
(S)	(3:55)	Flashback 72089 '70s Rock Legends Box Set. *(45 version)*
(S)	(3:52)	Rhino 72893 Hard Rock Cafe: Classic Rock. *(45 version)*
(S)	(8:11)	Hip-O 40070 Rock For The Ages. *(LP version)*
(S)	(3:55)	K-Tel 3996 Rockin' Down The Highway. *(45 version)*
(S)	(3:55)	K-Tel 3986 70's Heavy Hitters: Arena Rockers 1975-79. *(45 version)*
(S)	(3:53)	Simitar 55752 Stud Rock - Heart Breakers. *(45 version)*
(S)	(8:12)	K-Tel 4030 Rock Anthems. *(LP version)*

1977 DRIVIN' WHEEL

(S)	(4:28)	Rhino 70088 Best Of. *(neither the 45 or LP version)*
(S)	(5:11)	Rhino 70888 Night Shift. *(LP version)*
(S)	(4:28)	Rhino 71030 Best Of/Rhino Special Editions. *(neither the 45 or LP version)*
(S)	(5:10)	Time-Life R968-03 Guitar Rock 1976-1977. *(LP version)*
(S)	(5:10)	Time-Life SOD-37 Sounds Of The Seventies - AM Heavy Hits. *(LP version)*
(S)	(4:28)	Priority 53713 Classic Rock Volume 1 - Highway Rockers. *(neither the 45 or LP version)*
(S)	(4:28)	Flashback 72675 Slow Ride And Other Hits. *(neither the 45 or LP version)*
(S)	(4:28)	Flashback 72089 '70s Rock Legends Box Set. *(neither the 45 or LP version)*
(S)	(5:10)	Hip-O 40062 Under My Wheels: 12 Road Trippin' Tracks. *(LP version)*

1977 I JUST WANT TO MAKE LOVE TO YOU (live version)

(S)	(8:34)	JCI 3402 Live Volume 2. *(LP version)*
(S)	(3:49)	Rhino 70986 Heavy Metal Memories. *(45 version)*
(S)	(4:18)	Rhino 70088 Best Of. *(studio version from the "Foghat" LP)*
(S)	(3:49)	Rhino 70516 Best Of Volume 2. *(45 version)*
(S)	(8:34)	Rhino 70884 Live. *(LP version)*
(S)	(4:18)	Rhino 70887 Foghat. *(studio version from the "Foghat" LP)*

(S)	(3:46)	Rhino 71030 Best Of/Rhino Special Editions. *(45 version)*
(S)	(4:18)	Medicine Label 24588 Even More Dazed And Confused. *(studio version from the "Foghat" LP)*
(S)	(4:18)	Time-Life R968-21 Guitar Rock - The Early '70s: The Hard Stuff. *(studio version from the "Foghat" LP)*
(S)	(4:18)	Flashback 72675 Slow Ride And Other Hits. *(studio version from the "Foghat" LP)*
(S)	(4:18)	Flashback 72089 '70s Rock Legends Box Set. *(studio version from the "Foghat" LP)*
(S)	(4:18)	Thump 6010 Easyriders Volume 1. *(studio version from the "Foghat" LP)*

1980 THIRD TIME LUCKY (FIRST TIME I WAS A FOOL)

(S)	(4:10)	Rhino 70088 Best Of. *(LP version)*
(S)	(4:10)	Rhino 71030 Best Of/Rhino Special Editions. *(LP version)*
(S)	(4:10)	Rebound 314520257 Hard Rock Essentials - The 80's. *(LP version)*
(S)	(4:10)	Flashback 72675 Slow Ride And Other Hits. *(LP version)*
(S)	(4:10)	Flashback 72089 '70s Rock Legends Box Set. *(LP version)*

FOLK IMPLOSION
1996 NATURAL ONE

(S)	(3:08)	London 422828640 O.S.T. Kids.
(S)	(3:04)	Mammoth 354980168 MTV Buzz Bin Volume 2.

WAYNE FONTANA & THE MINDBENDERS (see MINDBENDERS)

FONTANE SISTERS
1955 HEARTS OF STONE

(M)	(2:03)	Rhino 70598 Billboard's Top Rock & Roll Hits Of 1955.
(M)	(2:03)	MCA 31201 Vintage Music Volume 4. *(background vocals differ from the hit version)*
(M)	(2:03)	MCA 5778 Vintage Music Volumes 3 & 4. *(background vocals differ from the hit version)*
(M)	(2:02)	Atlantic 82155 O.S.T. Book Of Love. *(background vocals differ from the hit version)*
(M)	(2:03)	Time-Life HPD-09 Your Hit Parade 1955.
(M)	(2:04)	Varese Sarabande 5526 Hearts Of Stone: Best Of.
(M)	(2:03)	MCA Special Products 22166 Vintage Collectibles Volume 8. *(background vocals differ from the hit version)*
(M)	(2:03)	JCI 7014 Those Wonderful Years - Mr. Sandman. *(background vocals differ from the hit version)*
(M)	(2:03)	Time-Life R132-14 Golden Groups Of Your Hit Parade.

1955 ROCK LOVE

(M)	(1:52)	Varese Sarabande 5526 Hearts Of Stone: Best Of.

1955 SEVENTEEN

(M)	(2:03)	Time-Life HPD-38 Your Hit Parade - The 50's Generation.
(M)	(2:02)	Varese Sarabande 5526 Hearts Of Stone: Best Of.
(M)	(2:03)	Time-Life R132-14 Golden Groups Of Your Hit Parade.

1956 DADDY-O

(M)	(1:56)	Time-Life HPD-35 Your Hit Parade - The Fun-Times 50's & 60's.
(M)	(1:55)	Varese Sarabande 5526 Hearts Of Stone: Best Of.

1956 EDDIE MY LOVE

(M)	(2:20)	Varese Sarabande 5526 Hearts Of Stone: Best Of.
(M)	(2:20)	Varese Sarabande 5686 History Of Dot Records Volume One.

1956 THE BANANA BOAT SONG
1958 CHANSON d'AMOUR (SONG OF LOVE)

(M)	(2:11)	Varese Sarabande 5526 Hearts Of Stone: Best Of.

STEVE FORBERT
1980 ROMEO'S TUNE

(S)	(3:29)	Rhino 71890 Radio Daze: Pop Hits Of The 80's Volume One.
(S)	(3:29)	Nemperor/Epic Associated/Legacy 64888 Jackrabbit Slim.

(S) (3:29) Rhino 72519 Mellow Rock Hits Of The 70's - Sundown.

(S) (3:29) Time-Life R988-16 Sounds Of The Eighties: The Early '80s.

FORCE M.D.'S
1986 TENDER LOVE
(actual 45 time is (4:13) not (4:19) as stated on the record label)

(S) (4:12) JCI 2701 Slow Grooves. *(45 version)*

(S) (3:54) Scotti Brothers 75419 Fabio After Dark. *(LP version)*

(S) (3:54) Rhino 71860 Smooth Grooves Volume 2. *(12" single version)*

(S) (3:55) Tommy Boy 1010 Chillin'. *(LP version)*

(S) (4:09) JCI 3186 1985 - Only Love - 1989. *(45 version)*

(S) (3:55) K-Tel 3673 The 80's - Funky Love. *(LP version)*

(S) (3:59) Rhino 72978 Smooth Grooves - New Jack Ballads Volume 2. *(neither the 45, LP or 12" single version)*

(S) (3:53) Time-Life R834-14 Body Talk - Love And Tenderness. *(12" single version)*

FRANKIE FORD
1959 SEA CRUISE
(actual 45 time is (2:45) not (2:10) as stated on the record label)

(M) (2:40) Rhino 75766 Best Of New Orleans Rhythm & Blues Volume 2.

(M) (2:44) JCI 3202 Rockin' Fifties.

(M) (2:43) Original Sound 8853 Oldies But Goodies Vol. 3. *(this compact disc uses the "Waring - fds" noise reduction process)*

(M) (2:43) Original Sound 2222 Oldies But Goodies Volumes 3,5,11,14 and 15 Box Set. *(this box set uses the "Waring - fds" noise reduction process)*

(M) (2:43) Original Sound 2500 Oldies But Goodies Volumes 1-15 Box Set. *(this box set uses the "Waring - fds" noise reduction process)*

(M) (2:42) Original Sound CDGO-3 Golden Oldies Volume. 3.

(M) (2:43) Original Sound 8891 Dick Clark's 21 All-Time Hits Vol. 1.

(M) (2:43) Original Sound 9601 Best Of Oldies But Goodies Vol. 1.

(M) (2:44) Ace 2036 Let's Take A Sea Cruise. *(mastered from vinyl)*

(M) (2:40) Rhino 70587 New Orleans Party Classics.

(M) (2:38) Rock N' Roll/Scotti Brothers 75266 Best Of Ace Records Volume 1. *(mastered from vinyl)*

(M) (2:40) Time-Life 2RNR-13 Rock 'N' Roll Era - 1959.

(M) (2:39) Time-Life R962-01 History Of Rock 'N' Roll: Rock 'N' Roll Classics 1957-1959.

(M) (2:40) Collectables 2503 WCBS-FM History Of Rock - The 50's Part 2.

(S) (2:36) Music For Little People 42581 A Child's Celebration Of Rock 'N' Roll. *(rerecording)*

(M) (2:38) JCI 3188 1955 - Only Dance - 1959.

(M) (2:40) K-Tel 3680 Mardi Gras Party Time!

LITA FORD
1988 KISS ME DEADLY

(S) (3:58) Foundation/WEA 26096 Super Sessions Volume One.

(S) (3:59) Priority 7963 First Degree Metal.

(S) (3:59) RCA 6397 Lita Ford.

(S) (3:58) RCA 66037 Best Of.

(S) (3:55) RCA 66199 Greatest Hits.

(S) (3:59) RCA 66862 Hi Octane Hard Drivin' Hits.

(S) (3:59) Priority 50937 Best Of 80's Metal Volume Two: Bang Your Head.

(S) (3:59) Time-Life R968-20 Guitar Rock - The '80s.

(S) (3:57) K-Tel 3883 The 80's: Glam Rock.

(S) (3:58) Hip-O 40077 Rock She Said: Guitars + Attitudes.

released as by LITA FORD with OZZY OSBORNE:
1989 CLOSE MY EYES FOREVER

(S) (4:41) RCA 6397 Lita Ford.

(S) (4:40) RCA 66037 Lita Ford - Best Of.

TENNESSEE ERNIE FORD
1955 BALLAD OF DAVY CROCKETT

(M) (2:51) Capitol 95291 Capitol Collector's Series.

(M) (2:51) Razor & Tie 2134 The Ultimate Collection.

1955 SIXTEEN TONS

(E) (2:33) Capitol 90592 Memories Are Made Of This.

(M) (2:33) Curb 77330 50's Hits - Country Volume 1.

(M) (2:33) Rhino 70975 Best Of.

(M) (2:34) Capitol 95291 Capitol Collector's Series.

(M) (2:34) Capitol 98665 When AM Was King.

(M) (2:34) Capitol 95916 Golden Country Jukebox Favorites.

(M) (2:33) Time-Life CTD-19 Country USA - 1955.

(M) (2:35) Time-Life HPD-09 Your Hit Parade 1955.

(E) (2:34) Curb 77625 Greatest Hits.

(M) (2:33) Liberty 30292 Masters 1949-1976.

(M) (2:34) K-Tel 3151 Working Man's Country.

(M) (2:33) K-Tel 225 Country Music Classics Volume I.

(M) (2:34) Capitol 33833 Sixteen Tons.

(E) (2:33) JCI 7003 Those Wonderful Years - Fever!

(M) (2:34) JCI 3152 1955 - Only Country - 1959.

(M) (2:34) Capitol 54319 Vintage Collections.

(E) (2:33) K-Tel 3365 101 Greatest Country Hits Vol. Six: Timeless Country.

(M) (2:34) Razor & Tie 2134 The Ultimate Collection.

(M) (2:34) Time-Life R808-03 Classic Country 1950-1959.

1956 THAT'S ALL

(M) (2:45) Capitol 95291 Capitol Collector's Series.

(M) (2:45) Liberty 30292 Masters 1949-1976.

(M) (2:45) Razor & Tie 2134 The Ultimate Collection.

1957 IN THE MIDDLE OF AN ISLAND

(M) (2:20) Capitol 95291 Capitol Collector's Series.

FOREIGNER
1977 FEELS LIKE THE FIRST TIME

(S) (3:49) Atlantic 82306 Atlantic Rock & Roll Box Set. *(LP version)*

(S) (3:49) Atlantic 81908 Classic Rock 1966-1988. *(LP version)*

(S) (3:27) Atlantic 80999 Records. *(neither the 45 or LP version)*

(S) (3:50) Atlantic 19109 Foreigner. *(LP version)*

(S) (3:50) Atlantic 82798 Foreigner. *(remastered edition; LP version)*

(S) (3:26) Time-Life R968-03 Guitar Rock 1976-1977. *(neither the 45 or LP version)*

(S) (3:27) Time-Life SOD-05 Sounds Of The Seventies - 1977. *(neither the 45 or LP version)*

(S) (3:26) Time-Life R105-24 Guitar Rock Monsters. *(neither the 45 or LP version)*

(S) (3:28) Atlantic 82800 Records. *(remastered edition; neither the 45 or LP version)*

(S) (3:26) JCI 3169 #1 Radio Hits 1975 - Only Rock 'n Roll - 1979. *(neither the 45 or LP version)*

(S) (3:49) Priority 50952 I Love Rock & Roll Volume 3: Hits Of The 70's. *(LP version)*

(S) (3:28) Hip-O 40095 '70s Hit(s) Back. *(neither the 45 or LP version)*

1977 COLD AS ICE

(S) (3:17) Atlantic 80999 Records.

(S) (3:19) Atlantic 82800 Records. *(remastered edition)*

(S) (3:19) Atlantic 89999 Very Best......And Beyond.

(S) (3:20) Atlantic 19109 Foreigner.

(S) (3:20) Atlantic 82798 Foreigner. *(remastered edition)*

(S) (3:17) Time-Life R968-03 Guitar Rock 1976-1977.

(S) (3:18) Time-Life SOD-05 Sounds Of The Seventies - 1977.

(S) (3:16) Eclipse Music Group 64895 Rock 'n Roll Relix 1976-1977.

(S) (3:16) Eclipse Music Group 64897 Rock 'n Roll Relix 1970-1979.

FOREIGNER *(Continued)*
- (S) (3:19) Rhino 72893 Hard Rock Cafe: Classic Rock.
- (S) (3:18) Simitar 55502 The Number One's: Classic Rock.

1978 LONG, LONG WAY FROM HOME
- (S) (2:48) Atlantic 80999 Records.
- (S) (2:49) Atlantic 82800 Records. *(remastered edition)*
- (S) (2:54) Atlantic 19109 Foreigner.
- (S) (2:55) Atlantic 82798 Foreigner. *(remastered edition)*
- (S) (2:49) Time-Life SOD-21 Sounds Of The Seventies - Rock 'N' Soul Seventies.
- (S) (2:49) Time-Life R968-17 Guitar Rock - The Late '70s: Take Two.

1978 HOT BLOODED
- (S) (4:26) Geffen 24063 O.S.T. Vision Quest. *(LP version)*
- (S) (4:22) Foundation/Capitol 96647 Hearts Of Gold - The Classic Rock Collection. *(LP version)*
- (S) (6:54) Atlantic 80999 Records. *(live)*
- (S) (6:54) Atlantic 82800 Records. *(remastered edition; live)*
- (S) (4:23) Atlantic 89999 Very Best......And Beyond. *(LP version)*
- (S) (4:22) Atlantic 19999 Double Vision. *(LP version)*
- (S) (4:24) Atlantic 82797 Double Vison. *(remastered edition; LP version)*
- (S) (4:22) JCI 4520 Masters Of Metal - Wrecking Havoc 1975-1985 Volume 1. *(LP version)*
- (S) (4:19) Time-Life R968-02 Guitar Rock 1978-1979. *(LP version)*
- (S) (3:02) Time-Life SOD-10 Sounds Of The Seventies - 1978. *(45 version)*
- (S) (2:59) Time-Life OPCD-4521 Guitar Rock. *(45 version)*
- (S) (4:22) Right Stuff 31324 and 31327 Harley-Davidson Road Songs. *(LP version)*
- (S) (4:22) Rhino 72131 Frat Rock: The 70's. *(LP version)*
- (S) (4:25) Scotti Bros. 75518 Big Screen Rock. *(LP version)*
- (S) (3:02) Madacy Entertainment 6805 The Power Of Rock. *(45 version)*
- (S) (3:02) JCI 3192 18 Rock Classics Volume 2. *(45 version)*
- (S) (3:02) Simitar 55752 Stud Rock - Heart Breakers. *(45 version)*
- (S) (3:03) Priority 53139 The Best Of 70's: Rock Chart Toppers. *(45 version)*

1978 DOUBLE VISION
- (S) (3:28) Atlantic 80999 Records. *(45 version)*
- (S) (3:29) Atlantic 82800 Records. *(remastered edition; 45 version)*
- (S) (3:42) Atlantic 89999 Very Best......And Beyond. *(LP version)*
- (S) (3:41) Atlantic 19999 Double Vision. *(LP version)*
- (S) (3:29) Time-Life R968-02 Guitar Rock 1978-1979. *(45 version)*
- (S) (3:29) Time-Life SOD-10 Sounds Of The Seventies - 1978. *(45 version)*
- (S) (3:39) JCI 3131 1975 - Only Rock 'N Roll - 1979. *(LP version)*
- (S) (3:43) Atlantic 82797 Double Vison. *(remastered edition; LP version)*
- (S) (3:30) K-Tel 3909 High Energy Volume 2. *(45 version)*
- (S) (3:28) Thump 6010 Easyriders Volume 1. *(45 version)*

1979 BLUE MORNING, BLUE DAY
- (S) (3:08) Atlantic 19999 Double Vision.
- (S) (3:09) Time-Life SOD-23 Sounds Of The Seventies - Guitar Power.
- (S) (3:10) Atlantic 82797 Double Vison. *(remastered edition)*
- (S) (3:09) K-Tel 3907 Starflight Vol. 2.

1979 DIRTY WHITE BOY
- (S) (3:11) Atlantic 80999 Records. *(45 version)*
- (S) (3:12) Atlantic 82800 Records. *(remastered edition; 45 version)*
- (S) (3:38) Atlantic 29999 Head Games. *(LP version; tracks into next selection)*
- (S) (3:38) Atlantic 82799 Head Games. *(remastered edition; LP version; tracks into next selection)*

- (S) (3:37) Atlantic 89999 Very Best......And Beyond. *(LP version)*
- (S) (3:38) Time-Life SOD-19 Sounds Of The Seventies - 1979: Take Two. *(LP version)*
- (S) (3:37) Time-Life R968-14 Guitar Rock - The Late '70s. *(LP version)*
- (S) (3:38) K-Tel 3904 The Rock Album Volume 1. *(LP version)*
- (S) (3:38) Simitar 55772 Stud Rock - Rock Me. *(LP version)*

1980 HEAD GAMES
- (S) (3:36) Atlantic 80999 Records. *(LP length)*
- (S) (3:37) Atlantic 82800 Records. *(remastered edition; LP length)*
- (S) (3:37) Atlantic 29999 Head Games. *(LP length)*
- (S) (3:37) Atlantic 82799 Head Games. *(remastered edition; LP length)*
- (S) (3:37) Atlantic 89999 Very Best......And Beyond. *(LP length)*
- (S) (3:33) Time-Life R968-04 Guitar Rock 1980-1981. *(LP length)*
- (S) (3:36) Time-Life SOD-19 Sounds Of The Seventies - 1979: Take Two. *(LP length)*
- (S) (3:33) JCI 3140 18 Screamers From The 70's. *(LP length)*

1981 URGENT
- (S) (3:58) Atlantic 80999 Records. *(45 version)*
- (S) (3:56) Atlantic 82800 Records. *(remastered edition; 45 version)*
- (S) (4:28) Atlantic 89999 Very Best......And Beyond. *(LP version)*
- (S) (4:28) Atlantic 16999 Foreigner 4. *(LP version)*
- (S) (4:24) Time-Life R968-04 Guitar Rock 1980-1981. *(LP version)*
- (S) (4:25) Time-Life R105-24 Guitar Rock Monsters. *(LP version)*
- (S) (4:31) Atlantic 82545 Foreigner 4. *(gold disc; LP version)*
- (S) (4:29) Time-Life R988-01 Sounds Of The Eighties: The Rockin' Eighties. *(LP version)*
- (S) (4:31) Atlantic 82795 Foreigner 4. *(remastered edition; LP version)*
- (S) (4:27) JCI 3143 18 Screamers From The 80's. *(LP version)*
- (S) (4:28) JCI 3170 #1 Radio Hits 1980 - Only Rock 'n Roll - 1984. *(LP version)*
- (S) (4:29) Simitar 55762 Stud Rock - Wild Ride. *(LP version)*

1981 WAITING FOR A GIRL LIKE YOU
- (S) (4:47) Atlantic 81910 Hit Singles 1980-1988. *(LP version)*
- (S) (4:32) Atlantic 80999 Records. *(45 version)*
- (S) (4:32) Atlantic 82800 Records. *(remastered edition; 45 version)*
- (S) (4:48) Atlantic 89999 Very Best......And Beyond. *(LP version)*
- (S) (4:48) Atlantic 16999 Foreigner 4. *(LP version)*
- (S) (4:33) Sandstone 33047 and 5015 Cosmopolitan Volume 1. *(45 version)*
- (S) (4:28) Time-Life R105-40 Rock Dreams. *(45 version)*
- (S) (4:50) Atlantic 82545 Foreigner 4. *(gold disc; LP version)*
- (S) (4:33) Time-Life R988-08 Sounds Of The Eighties: 1981. *(45 version)*
- (S) (4:32) Time-Life R138-18 Body Talk. *(45 version)*
- (S) (4:50) Atlantic 82795 Foreigner 4. *(remastered edition; LP version)*
- (S) (4:34) Madacy Entertainment 1981 Rock On 1981. *(45 version)*
- (S) (4:31) JCI 3147 1980 - Only Love - 1984. *(45 version)*
- (S) (4:48) Time-Life R834-03 Body Talk - Moonlit Nights. *(LP version)*
- (S) (4:47) Rhino 72594 Billboard Top Album Rock Hits, 1981. *(LP version)*
- (S) (4:32) K-Tel 6257 The Greatest Love Songs - 16 Soft Rock Hits. *(45 version)*

1982 JUKE BOX HERO
- (S) (4:19) Atlantic 81908 Classic Rock 1966-1988. *(LP version)*

(S) (4:19) Atlantic 82545 Foreigner 4. *(gold disc; LP version)*
(S) (4:19) Atlantic 16999 Foreigner 4. *(LP version)*
(S) (4:01) Atlantic 80999 Records. *(45 version)*
(S) (4:03) Atlantic 82800 Records. *(remastered edition; 45 version)*
(S) (4:19) Atlantic 89999 Very Best......And Beyond. *(LP version)*
(S) (4:19) Time-Life R988-25 Sounds Of The Eighties: The Rolling Stone Collection 1980-1981. *(LP version)*
(S) (4:19) Time-Life R968-13 Guitar Rock - The Early '80s. *(LP version)*
(S) (4:19) Atlantic 82795 Foreigner 4. *(remastered edition; LP version)*
(S) (4:18) Madacy Entertainment 1982 Rock On 1982. *(LP version)*
(S) (4:19) Hip-O 40040 Power Chords Volume 3. *(LP version)*

1982 BREAK IT UP
(S) (4:12) Atlantic 82545 Foreigner 4. *(gold disc; LP version)*
(S) (4:11) Atlantic 16999 Foreigner 4. *(LP version)*
(S) (4:12) Atlantic 82795 Foreigner 4. *(remastered edition; LP version)*

1985 I WANT TO KNOW WHAT LOVE IS
(S) (5:03) Atlantic 81910 Hit Singles 1980-1988.
(S) (4:57) Time-Life R102-34 The Rolling Stone Collection.
(S) (4:57) JCI 3128 1985 - Only Rock 'N Roll - 1989.
(S) (4:59) JCI 3119 18 Rock Classics.
(S) (5:02) Atlantic 81999 Agent Provocateur.
(S) (5:03) Atlantic 82796 Agent Provocateur. *(remastered edition)*
(S) (5:03) Atlantic 89999 Very Best......And Beyond.
(S) (4:58) Time-Life R988-02 Sounds Of The Eighties: 1985.
(S) (4:57) Hip-O 40005 The '80s Hit(s) Back....Again!
(S) (5:02) Rhino 72579 Feel Like Makin' Love - Romantic Power Ballads.
(S) (5:03) Time-Life R834-06 Body Talk - Only You.
(S) (4:58) Madacy Entertainment 6806 Best Of Love.
(S) (5:02) Polygram TV 314555610 The One And Only Love Album.
(S) (5:03) Atlantic 83088 Atlantic Records: 50 Years - The Gold Anniversary Collection.

1985 THAT WAS YESTERDAY
(S) (6:14) JCI 3122 Lost Mixes. *(remixed)*
(S) (3:47) Atlantic 81999 Agent Provocateur.
(S) (3:47) Atlantic 82796 Agent Provocateur. *(remastered edition)*
(S) (3:46) Atlantic 89999 Very Best......And Beyond.

1988 SAY YOU WILL
(S) (4:11) Foundation/WEA 26096 Super Sessions Volume One.
(S) (4:11) Atlantic 81808 Inside Information.
(S) (4:11) Atlantic 89999 Very Best......And Beyond.
(S) (4:12) JCI 3171 #1 Radio Hits 1985 - Only Rock 'n Roll - 1989.
(S) (4:11) Time-Life R988-20 Sounds Of The Eighties: The Late '80s Take Two.
(S) (4:11) JCI 3193 18 Rock Classics Volume 3.
(S) (4:11) Time-Life R834-19 Body Talk - Always And Forever.

1988 I DON'T WANT TO LIVE WITHOUT YOU
(S) (3:54) Time-Life R105-40 Rock Dreams. *(45 version)*
(S) (4:52) Atlantic 81808 Inside Information. *(LP version)*
(S) (4:53) Atlantic 89999 Very Best......And Beyond. *(LP version)*
(S) (4:50) Time-Life R988-10 Sounds Of The 80's: 1988. *(LP version)*
(S) (3:53) JCI 3186 1985 - Only Love - 1989. *(45 version)*
(S) (4:51) Time-Life R834-08 Body Talk - On My Mind. *(LP version)*

FORTUNES
1965 YOU'VE GOT YOUR TROUBLES
(S) (3:21) Rhino 70323 History Of British Rock Volume 5. *(LP version)*
(S) (3:21) Rhino 72022 History Of British Rock Box Set. *(LP version)*
(S) (3:19) Time-Life SUD-03 Superhits - 1965. *(LP version)*
(S) (3:19) JCI 3167 #1 Radio Hits 1965 - Only Rock 'n Roll - 1969. *(LP version)*
(S) (3:19) Time-Life AM1-10 AM Gold - 1965. *(LP version)*
(S) (3:21) Polygram Special Markets 314520495 45's On CD Volume 2. *(LP version)*

1965 HERE IT COMES AGAIN
1971 HERE COMES THAT RAINY DAY FEELING AGAIN
(S) (2:48) Rhino 70925 Super Hits Of The 70's Volume 5.
(S) (2:49) EMI 90603 Rock Me Gently.
(S) (2:46) Curb 77356 70's Hits Volume 2.
(S) (2:49) Capitol 98665 When AM Was King.
(S) (2:48) Rhino 71208 70's Smash Hits Volume 4.
(S) (2:46) Time-Life SOD-32 Sounds Of The Seventies - AM Pop Classics.
(S) (2:48) Varese Sarabande 5534 Rhythm Of The Rain.
(S) (2:48) Taragon 1010 Very Best Of (1967-1972).
(S) (2:48) Flashback 72684 '70s Radio Hits Volume 4.
(S) (2:48) Flashback 72090 '70s Radio Hits Box Set.

DAVID FOSTER
1985 LOVE THEME FROM ST. ELMO'S FIRE
(S) (3:29) Atlantic 81642 David Foster.
(S) (3:28) Atlantic 81261 O.S.T. St. Elmo's Fire.

FOUNDATIONS
1968 BABY, NOW THAT I'VE FOUND YOU
(M) (2:34) Rhino 70324 History Of British Rock Volume 6.
(M) (2:34) Rhino 72022 History Of British Rock Box Set.
(M) (2:32) JCI 3107 British Sixties.
(M) (2:32) Time-Life 2CLR-19 Classic Rock - 1968: Shakin' All Over.
(M) (2:33) Ripete 0003 Coolin' Out/24 Carolina Classics Vol. 3.
(M) (2:46) Taragon 1009 Very Best Of. *(:12 longer than either the 45 or LP)*
(S) (2:51) Taragon 1009 Very Best Of. *(alternate take)*
(M) (2:35) Varese Sarabande 5718 Soulful Pop.
(M) (2:35) Varese Sarabande 5890 Bubblegum Classics Volume Four - Soulful Pop.

1969 BUILD ME UP BUTTERCUP
(M) (2:58) Rhino 70630 Billboard's Top Rock & Roll Hits Of 1969.
(M) (2:58) Rhino 72005 Billboard's Top Rock & Roll Hits 1968-1972 Box Set.
(S) (2:57) Rhino 70327 History Of British Rock Volume 9. *(hum noticeable on the fadeout)*
(S) (2:57) Rhino 72022 History Of British Rock Box Set. *(hum noticeable on the fadeout)*
(S) (2:57) Ripete 2392192 Beach Music Anthology Box Set. *(hum noticeable on the fadeout)*
(S) (2:55) Ripete 0002 Coolin' Out/24 Carolina Classics Vol. 2.
(M) (2:55) Time-Life 2CLR-06 Classic Rock - 1969.
(S) (2:55) Time-Life SUD-18 Superhits - Late 60's Classics.
(S) (2:54) Taragon 1009 Very Best Of.
(S) (2:55) Ripete 2187-RE Preppy Deluxe.
(S) (2:57) Varese Sarabande 5718 Soulful Pop.
(S) (2:57) LaserLight 12317 The British Invasion. *(hum noticeable on the fadeout)*
(S) (2:55) Time-Life AM1-12 AM Gold - Late '60s Classics.
(S) (2:57) Varese Sarabande 5890 Bubblegum Classics Volume Four - Soulful Pop.
(S) (2:57) Collectables 1515 and 2515 The Anniversary Album - The 60's. *(hum noticeable on the fadeout)*

1969 IN THE BAD BAD OLD DAYS (BEFORE YOU LOVED ME)
(S) (3:21) Taragon 1009 Very Best Of.

FOUR ACES
1955 MELODY OF LOVE
    (M) (2:44)   MCA 10886 Greatest Hits.
1955 HEART
    (M) (2:43)   MCA 10886 Greatest Hits.
1955 LOVE IS A MANY-SPLENDORED THING
    (M) (2:58)   Uni 600 O.S.T. Cookie.
    (M) (2:57)   MCA 10886 Greatest Hits.
    (M) (2:58)   Time-Life HPD-09 Your Hit Parade 1955.
    (M) (2:57)   MCA 11120 Stardust/The Classic Decca Hits & Standards Collection.
    (E) (2:55)   CBS Special Products 46850 Society Of Singers Presents A Gift Of Music Vol. 2.
    (M) (2:58)   Rhino 71580 Billboard Pop Memories 1955-1959.
    (M) (2:58)   Rhino 71868 Academy Award Winning Songs.
    (M) (2:57)   Time-Life R138-32 Hollywood Hit Parade.
    (M) (2:58)   Rhino 72277 Academy Award Winning Songs Volume 2.
    (M) (2:58)   Rhino 72422 Billboard Top Movie Hits 1955-1959.
    (M) (2:58)   JCI 7011 Those Wonderful Years - That's Hollywood.
    (M) (2:58)   Rhino 72577 Eh, Paisano! Italian-American Classics.
    (M) (2:58)   Time-Life R132-10 Love Songs Of Your Hit Parade.
1956 A WOMAN IN LOVE
    (M) (3:17)   MCA 10886 Greatest Hits.
1956 I ONLY KNOW I LOVE YOU
    (M) (2:58)   Varese Sarabande 5617 More Greatest Hits.
1956 YOU CAN'T RUN AWAY FROM IT
    (M) (2:24)   Varese Sarabande 5617 More Greatest Hits.

FOUR COINS
1955 I LOVE YOU MADLY
    (E) (1:56)   Collectables 5498 In Shangri-La.
1956 MEMORIES OF YOU
    (E) (2:39)   Collectables 5498 In Shangri-La.
1957 SHANGRI-LA
    (M) (2:45)   Time-Life HPD-17 Your Hit Parade - 1957.
    (E) (2:45)   Collectables 5498 In Shangri-La.
    (M) (2:45)   Time-Life R132-10 Love Songs Of Your Hit Parade.
    (M) (2:45)   Time-Life R132-14 Golden Groups Of Your Hit Parade.
1957 MY ONE SIN
    (E) (2:14)   Collectables 5498 In Shangri-La.
1958 THE WORLD OUTSIDE
    (S) (2:52)   Collectables 5498 In Shangri-La.

FOUR ESQUIRES
1957 LOVE ME FOREVER
1958 HIDEAWAY

FOUR FRESHMEN
1956 GRADUATION DAY
    (M) (3:04)   Capitol 93197 Capitol Collector's Series.
    (includes :02 of studio noise preceding music)
    (M) (3:01)   Curb 77612 Greatest Hits.
    (M) (3:01)   Time-Life HPD-31 Your Hit Parade - The 50's Forever.
    (M) (3:01)   Time-Life R857-13 The Heart Of Rock 'n' Roll 1956-1957.
    (M) (3:01)   Time-Life R132-14 Golden Groups Of Your Hit Parade.

FOUR JACKS and A JILL
1968 MASTER JACK
    (S) (2:42)   Varese Sarabande 5705 Dick Bartley Presents Collector's Essentials: The 60's. *(LP version)*

FOUR LADS
1955 MOMENTS TO REMEMBER
    (M) (3:14)   Columbia 45110 16 Most Requested Songs Of The 50's Volume 1.
    (M) (3:15)   Columbia 45017 Radio Classics Of The 50's.
    (M) (3:14)   Columbia/Legacy 46158 16 Most Requested Songs.

    (E) (3:16)   Columbia 11369 Moments To Remember.
    (M) (3:16)   Time-Life HPD-09 Your Hit Parade 1955.
1956 NO, NOT MUCH!
    (M) (3:16)   Columbia/Legacy 46158 16 Most Requested Songs.
    (E) (3:17)   Columbia 11369 Moments To Remember.
    (M) (3:17)   Time-Life HPD-15 Your Hit Parade - 1956.
    (M) (3:16)   JCI 7014 Those Wonderful Years - Mr. Sandman.
    (M) (3:17)   Time-Life R132-14 Golden Groups Of Your Hit Parade.
1956 STANDING ON THE CORNER
    (M) (2:50)   Columbia 45111 16 Most Requested Songs Of The 50's Volume 2.
    (M) (2:51)   Columbia/Legacy 46158 16 Most Requested Songs.
    (M) (2:51)   Time-Life HPD-15 Your Hit Parade - 1956.
    (M) (2:50)   JCI 7021 Those Wonderful Years - April Love.
    (M) (2:50)   Time-Life R132-14 Golden Groups Of Your Hit Parade.
1956 THE BUS STOP SONG (A PAPER OF PINS)
    (M) (2:10)   Columbia 44374 Hollywood Magic - The 1950's.
1956 A HOUSE WITH LOVE IN IT
1957 WHO NEEDS YOU
    (M) (2:57)   Columbia/Legacy 46158 16 Most Requested Songs.
    (E) (2:56)   Columbia 11369 Moments To Remember.
    (M) (2:57)   Time-Life HPD-36 Your Hit Parade - The 50's Pop Revival.
1957 I JUST DON'T KNOW
1958 PUT A LIGHT IN THE WINDOW
    (M) (2:23)   Time-Life HPD-11 Your Hit Parade 1958.
1958 THERE'S ONLY ONE OF YOU
    (S) (2:52)   Columbia/Legacy 46158 16 Most Requested Songs.
    (E) (2:54)   Columbia 11369 Moments To Remember.
1958 ENCHANTED ISLAND

4 NON BLONDES
1993 WHAT'S UP
    (S) (4:55)   Interscope 92112 Bigger, Better, Faster, More.
    (S) (4:53)   Priority 50947 A Bunch O' Hits: The Best Rock Of The 90's Volume 1.
    (S) (4:51)   Razor & Tie 4569 '90s Style.

4 P.M. (FOR POSITIVE MUSIC)
1995 SUKIYAKI
    (S) (2:41)   Next Plateau/London 422828579 and 422828595 Now's The Time.
    (S) (2:41)   Razor & Tie 4569 '90s Style.
    (S) (2:41)   Beast 53012 Smooth Love Of The 90's Vol. 1.

FOUR PREPS
1958 26 MILES (SANTA CATALINA)
    (E) (2:27)   Capitol 90592 Memories Are Made Of This.
    (M) (2:26)   Curb 77354 50's Hits Volume 1.
    (M) (2:26)   Capitol 91626 Capitol Collector's Series.
    (M) (2:27)   Capitol 98665 When AM Was King.
    (M) (2:26)   Curb 77590 Best Of.
    (M) (2:27)   Time-Life HPD-11 Your Hit Parade 1958.
    (M) (2:26)   Collectables 5685 A Golden Classics Edition.
    (M) (2:26)   JCI 7014 Those Wonderful Years - Mr. Sandman.
1958 BIG MAN
    (M) (2:21)   Capitol 91626 Capitol Collector's Series.
    (M) (2:20)   Curb 77590 Best Of.
    (M) (2:22)   Time-Life HPD-23 Your Hit Parade - The Late 50's.
    (M) (2:21)   Collectables 5685 A Golden Classics Edition.
1958 LAZY SUMMER NIGHT
    (M) (2:09)   Capitol 91626 Capitol Collector's Series.
    (M) (2:10)   Curb 77590 Best Of.
    (M) (2:10)   Collectables 5685 A Golden Classics Edition.
1960 DOWN BY THE STATION
    (S) (2:47)   Capitol 91626 Capitol Collector's Series. *(with countoff)*
    (S) (2:45)   Curb 77590 Best Of. *(with countoff)*
    (S) (2:47)   Collectables 5685 A Golden Classics Edition. *(with countoff)*

1960 GOT A GIRL
- (S) (2:27) Capitol 91626 Capitol Collector's Series.
- (S) (2:27) Collectables 5685 A Golden Classics Edition.

1961 MORE MONEY FOR YOU AND ME
- (S) (6:24) Capitol 91626 Capitol Collector's Series. *(LP version)*
- (S) (6:24) Collectables 5685 A Golden Classics Edition. *(LP version)*

FOUR SEASONS (see also FRANKIE VALLI)
1962 SHERRY
- (S) (2:30) Warner Brothers 3359 O.S.T. The Wanderers. *(very poor stereo separation)*
- (S) (2:31) Rhino 72998 25th Anniversary Collection.
- (S) (2:30) Rhino 71490 Anthology.
- (S) (2:29) Atlantic 81885 O.S.T. Stealing Home. *(truncated fade)*
- (S) (2:30) Rhino 70594 Greatest Hits Volume 1.
- (S) (2:30) Curb 77525 Greatest Hits Of Rock 'N' Roll Volume 2.
- (S) (2:29) Curb 77304 Hits Digitally Enhanced. *(remixed)*
- (S) (2:30) MCA/Curb 39114 Hits Digitally Enhanced. *(remixed)*
- (S) (2:29) Time-Life 2RNR-02 Rock 'N' Roll Era - 1962.
- (S) (2:29) Time-Life 2RNR-15 Rock 'N' Roll Era - Frankie Valli & The Four Seasons 1962-1967.
- (S) (2:29) Time-Life SUD-15 Superhits - The Early 60's.
- (S) (2:29) Time-Life R10513 40 Lovin' Oldies.
- (S) (2:30) Rhino 71583 Billboard Top Pop Hits, 1962.
- (S) (2:29) Warner Special Products 1625 Sing For You.
- (S) (2:30) Curb 77695 Sherry And 11 Other Hits.
- (S) (2:30) JCI 3166 #1 Radio Hits 1960 - Only Rock 'n Roll - 1964.
- (S) (2:29) Time-Life AM1-19 AM Gold - The Early '60s.
- (S) (2:30) Curb 77892 2nd Gold Vault Of Hits.

1962 BIG GIRLS DON'T CRY
- (S) (2:24) Rhino 70623 Billboard's Top Rock & Roll Hits Of 1962.
- (S) (2:24) Rhino 72007 Billboard's Top Rock & Roll Hits 1962-1966 Box Set.
- (S) (2:23) RCA 6965 More Dirty Dancing.
- (S) (2:23) Geffen 24310 O.S.T. Mermaids.
- (S) (2:25) Warner Brothers 3359 O.S.T. The Wanderers. *(very poor stereo separation)*
- (S) (2:23) Rhino 72998 25th Anniversary Collection.
- (S) (2:23) Rhino 71490 Anthology.
- (S) (2:23) Rhino 70594 Greatest Hits Volume 1.
- (S) (2:23) Curb 77304 Hits Digitally Enhanced. *(remixed; additional instrumentation added)*
- (S) (5:16) Curb 77304 Hits Digitally Enhanced. *(remixed; additional instrumentation added)*
- (S) (2:23) MCA/Curb 39114 Hits Digitally Enhanced. *(remixed; additional instrumentation added)*
- (S) (5:07) MCA/Curb 39114 Hits Digitally Enhanced. *(remixed; additional instrumentation added)*
- (S) (2:23) Warner Brothers 26491 O.S.T. Nothing But Trouble.
- (S) (2:22) JCI 3112 Pop Sixties.
- (S) (2:23) Time-Life 2RNR-15 Rock 'N' Roll Era - Frankie Valli & The Four Seasons 1962-1967.
- (S) (2:23) Time-Life 2RNR-16 Rock 'N' Roll Era - 1962 Still Rockin'.
- (S) (5:16) Curb 77651 Retro Rock Dance Hits. *(all selections on this cd are remixed with extra instrumentation added)*
- (S) (2:24) Columbia 57376 O.S.T. The Main Event.
- (S) (2:23) Warner Special Products 1625 Sing For You.
- (S) (2:23) JCI 3125 1960 - Only Rock 'N Roll - 1964.
- (S) (2:23) Curb 77696 Big Girls Don't Cry And 12 Other Hits.
- (S) (2:25) Curb 77695 Sherry And 11 Other Hits.
- (S) (2:24) Curb 77892 2nd Gold Vault Of Hits.
- (S) (2:24) JCI 3189 1960 - Only Dance - 1964.

1963 SANTA CLAUS IS COMING TO TOWN
- (S) (1:47) Rhino 70234 The Four Seasons Christmas Album.

1963 WALK LIKE A MAN
- (S) (2:15) Rhino 70624 Billboard's Top Rock & Roll Hits Of 1963. *(found only on the original 1988 release of this cd)*
- (S) (2:15) Rhino 72007 Billboard's Top Rock & Roll Hits 1962-1966 Box Set.
- (S) (2:15) Warner Brothers 3359 O.S.T. The Wanderers. *(very poor stereo separation)*
- (S) (2:15) Rhino 72998 25th Anniversary Collection.
- (S) (2:15) Rhino 71490 Anthology.
- (M) (2:15) Rhino 70594 Greatest Hits Volume 1.
- (S) (2:14) MCA 10919 O.S.T. Heart And Souls.
- (S) (2:14) Time-Life 2RNR-15 Rock 'N' Roll Era - Frankie Valli & The Four Seasons 1962-1967.
- (S) (2:12) Time-Life SUD-19 Superhits - Early 60's Classics.
- (S) (2:15) Time-Life R962-08 History Of Rock 'N' Roll: Sound Of The City 1959-1965.
- (S) (2:15) Curb 77696 Big Girls Don't Cry And 12 Other Hits.
- (S) (2:12) Time-Life AM1-20 AM Gold - Early '60s Classics.
- (M) (2:15) Curb 77892 2nd Gold Vault Of Hits.

1963 AIN'T THAT A SHAME
- (S) (2:34) Rhino 72998 25th Anniversary Collection. *(LP version)*
- (M) (2:36) Rhino 70594 Greatest Hits Volume 1. *(45 version)*
- (S) (2:34) Time-Life 2RNR-15 Rock 'N' Roll Era - Frankie Valli & The Four Seasons 1962-1967. *(LP version)*
- (S) (2:34) Curb 77697 Ain't That A Shame And 11 Other Hits. *(LP version)*

1963 CANDY GIRL
- (S) (2:37) Rhino 72998 25th Anniversary Collection.
- (S) (2:34) Rhino 71490 Anthology.
- (S) (2:37) Rhino 70594 Greatest Hits Volume 1.
- (S) (2:33) Time-Life 2RNR-15 Rock 'N' Roll Era - Frankie Valli & The Four Seasons 1962-1967.
- (S) (2:34) Warner Special Products 1625 Sing For You.
- (S) (2:37) Curb 77697 Ain't That A Shame And 11 Other Hits.
- (S) (2:34) Curb 77892 2nd Gold Vault Of Hits.

1963 MARLENA
- (S) (2:33) Rhino 72998 25th Anniversary Collection.
- (S) (2:33) Rhino 71490 Anthology.
- (S) (2:33) Rhino 70594 Greatest Hits Volume 1.
- (S) (2:31) Curb 77304 Hits Digitally Enhanced. *(remixed)*
- (S) (2:32) MCA/Curb 39114 Hits Digitally Enhanced. *(remixed)*
- (S) (2:31) Time-Life 2RNR-15 Rock 'N' Roll Era - Frankie Valli & The Four Seasons 1962-1967.
- (S) (2:33) Warner Special Products 1625 Sing For You.
- (S) (2:33) Curb 77697 Ain't That A Shame And 11 Other Hits.
- (S) (2:33) Curb 77892 2nd Gold Vault Of Hits.

1963 NEW MEXICAN ROSE
- (M) (2:46) Rhino 72998 25th Anniversary Collection.
- (M) (2:46) Curb 77697 Ain't That A Shame And 11 Other Hits.

1964 DAWN (GO AWAY)
- (M) (2:45) Rhino 72998 25th Anniversary Collection.
- (M) (2:45) Rhino 71490 Anthology.
- (M) (2:45) Rhino 70594 Greatest Hits Volume 1.
- (M) (2:44) Time-Life 2RNR-15 Rock 'N' Roll Era - Frankie Valli & The Four Seasons 1962-1967.
- (M) (2:42) Time-Life SUD-12 Superhits - The Mid 60's.
- (M) (2:44) Warner Special Products 1625 Sing For You.
- (M) (2:45) Curb 77698 Dawn (Go Away) And 11 Other Hits.
- (M) (2:42) Time-Life AM1-05 AM Gold - The Mid '60s.
- (M) (2:45) Curb 77891 Gold Vault Of Hits.

1964 STAY
- (S) (1:55) Rhino 72998 25th Anniversary Collection.
- (S) (1:55) Rhino 71490 Anthology.
- (S) (1:54) Rhino 70594 Greatest Hits Volume 1.
- (S) (1:53) Curb 77304 Hits Digitally Enhanced. *(remixed; extra instrumentation added)*

FOUR SEASONS *(Continued)*

    (S) (1:53) MCA/Curb 39114 Hits Digitally Enhanced. *(remixed; additional instrumentation added)*

    (S) (1:52) Time-Life 2RNR-15 Rock 'N' Roll Era - Frankie Valli & The Four Seasons 1962-1967.

    (S) (1:54) Curb 77697 Ain't That A Shame And 11 Other Hits.

    (S) (1:54) Curb 77892 2nd Gold Vault Of Hits.

1964 RONNIE

    (M) (2:56) Rhino 72998 25th Anniversary Collection.

    (M) (2:56) Rhino 71490 Anthology.

    (M) (2:56) Rhino 70594 Greatest Hits Volume 1.

    (M) (2:53) Time-Life 2RNR-15 Rock 'N' Roll Era - Frankie Valli & The Four Seasons 1962-1967.

    (M) (2:56) Warner Special Products 1625 Sing For You.

    (M) (2:56) Curb 77891 Gold Vault Of Hits.

1964 RAG DOLL

    (M) (2:59) Rhino 70625 Billboard's Top Rock & Roll Hits Of 1964.

    (M) (2:59) Rhino 72007 Billboard's Top Rock & Roll Hits 1962-1966 Box Set.

    (M) (2:59) Rhino 72998 25th Anniversary Collection.

    (M) (2:59) Rhino 71490 Anthology.

    (S) (2:55) Rhino 70595 Greatest Hits Volume 2.

    (S) (2:54) Time-Life 2RNR-15 Rock 'N' Roll Era - Frankie Valli & The Four Seasons 1962-1967.

    (S) (2:53) Time-Life SUD-09 Superhits - 1964.

    (M) (2:59) Warner Special Products 1625 Sing For You.

    (S) (2:55) Curb 77699 Rag Doll And 11 Other Hits.

    (S) (2:53) Time-Life AM1-11 AM Gold - 1964.

    (S) (2:55) Curb 77891 Gold Vault Of Hits.

1964 ALONE

    (S) (2:50) Rhino 72998 25th Anniversary Collection.

    (S) (2:50) Rhino 70594 Greatest Hits Volume 1.

    (S) (2:49) Time-Life 2RNR-15 Rock 'N' Roll Era - Frankie Valli & The Four Seasons 1962-1967.

    (S) (2:49) Curb 77696 Big Girls Don't Cry And 12 Other Hits.

    (S) (2:50) Curb 77892 2nd Gold Vault Of Hits.

1964 SAVE IT FOR ME

    (S) (2:35) Rhino 72998 25th Anniversary Collection.

    (S) (2:35) Rhino 71490 Anthology.

    (S) (2:35) Rhino 70594 Greatest Hits Volume 1.

    (S) (2:34) Time-Life 2RNR-15 Rock 'N' Roll Era - Frankie Valli & The Four Seasons 1962-1967.

    (S) (2:35) Curb 77699 Rag Doll And 11 Other Hits.

    (S) (2:35) Curb 77891 Gold Vault Of Hits.

1964 BIG MAN IN TOWN

    (S) (2:44) Rhino 72998 25th Anniversary Collection.

    (S) (2:44) Rhino 71490 Anthology.

    (S) (2:44) Rhino 70594 Greatest Hits Volume 1.

    (S) (2:43) Time-Life 2RNR-15 Rock 'N' Roll Era - Frankie Valli & The Four Seasons 1962-1967.

    (S) (2:43) Time-Life SUD-17 Superhits - Mid 60's Classics.

    (S) (2:43) Time-Life AM1-16 AM Gold - Mid '60s Classics.

    (S) (2:44) Curb 77891 Gold Vault Of Hits.

1965 BYE, BYE, BABY (BABY GOODBYE)

    (S) (2:31) Rhino 72998 25th Anniversary Collection.

    (S) (2:30) Rhino 71490 Anthology.

    (S) (2:30) Rhino 70594 Greatest Hits Volume 1.

    (S) (2:28) Time-Life 2RNR-15 Rock 'N' Roll Era - Frankie Valli & The Four Seasons 1962-1967.

    (S) (2:30) Curb 77712 New Gold Hits.

    (S) (2:30) Curb 77891 Gold Vault Of Hits.

1965 GIRL COME RUNNING

    (M) (2:58) Rhino 72998 25th Anniversary Collection.

    (M) (2:58) Rhino 71490 Anthology.

    (M) (2:58) Rhino 70594 Greatest Hits Volume 1.

    (S) (2:57) Time-Life 2RNR-15 Rock 'N' Roll Era - Frankie Valli & The Four Seasons 1962-1967.

    (M) (2:57) Warner Special Products 1625 Sing For You.

    (M) (2:58) Curb 77891 Gold Vault Of Hits.

1965 LET'S HANG ON!

    (M) (3:15) Rhino 72998 25th Anniversary Collection.

    (M) (3:15) Rhino 71490 Anthology.

    (M) (3:15) Rhino 70595 Greatest Hits Volume 2.

    (M) (3:14) Time-Life 2RNR-15 Rock 'N' Roll Era - Frankie Valli & The Four Seasons 1962-1967.

    (M) (3:12) Time-Life SUD-12 Superhits - The Mid 60's.

    (M) (3:15) Warner Special Products 1625 Sing For You.

    (M) (3:15) Curb 77711 Let's Hang On And 11 Other Hits.

    (M) (3:12) Time-Life AM1-05 AM Gold - The Mid '60s.

    (M) (3:15) Curb 77891 Gold Vault Of Hits.

    (M) (3:15) Simitar 55532 The Number One's: The '60s.

1966 WORKING MY WAY BACK TO YOU

    (S) (3:03) Rhino 72998 25th Anniversary Collection.

    (S) (3:03) Rhino 70247 Working My Way Back To You.

    (S) (3:03) Rhino 71490 Anthology.

    (S) (3:02) Rhino 70595 Greatest Hits Volume 2.

    (S) (3:03) Time-Life 2RNR-15 Rock 'N' Roll Era - Frankie Valli & The Four Seasons 1962-1967.

    (S) (3:03) Curb 77711 Let's Hang On And 11 Other Hits.

    (S) (3:03) Curb 77892 2nd Gold Vault Of Hits.

1966 OPUS 17 (DON'T YOU WORRY 'BOUT ME)

    (S) (2:31) Rhino 72998 25th Anniversary Collection.

    (S) (2:31) Rhino 71490 Anthology.

    (S) (2:31) Rhino 70595 Greatest Hits Volume 2.

    (S) (2:30) Time-Life 2RNR-15 Rock 'N' Roll Era - Frankie Valli & The Four Seasons 1962-1967.

    (S) (2:31) Curb 77711 Let's Hang On And 11 Other Hits.

    (S) (2:31) Curb 77892 2nd Gold Vault Of Hits.

1966 I'VE GOT YOU UNDER MY SKIN

    (S) (3:37) Rhino 72998 25th Anniversary Collection.

    (S) (3:37) Rhino 71490 Anthology.

    (S) (3:37) Rhino 70595 Greatest Hits Volume 2.

    (S) (3:38) Time-Life 2RNR-15 Rock 'N' Roll Era - Frankie Valli & The Four Seasons 1962-1967.

    (S) (3:37) Curb 77699 Rag Doll And 11 Other Hits.

    (S) (3:38) Curb 77892 2nd Gold Vault Of Hits.

1967 TELL IT TO THE RAIN

    (S) (2:34) Rhino 72998 25th Anniversary Collection.

    (S) (2:35) Rhino 71490 Anthology.

    (S) (2:34) Rhino 70595 Greatest Hits Volume 2.

    (S) (2:29) Time-Life 2RNR-15 Rock 'N' Roll Era - Frankie Valli & The Four Seasons 1962-1967.

    (S) (2:34) Curb 77712 New Gold Hits.

1967 BEGGIN'

    (S) (2:46) Rhino 72998 25th Anniversary Collection.

    (S) (2:45) Rhino 71490 Anthology.

    (S) (2:46) Rhino 70595 Greatest Hits Volume 2.

    (S) (2:46) Time-Life 2RNR-15 Rock 'N' Roll Era - Frankie Valli & The Four Seasons 1962-1967.

    (S) (2:46) Curb 77712 New Gold Hits.

1967 C'MON MARIANNE

    (S) (2:33) Rhino 72998 25th Anniversary Collection.

    (S) (2:33) Rhino 71490 Anthology.

    (S) (2:33) Rhino 70595 Greatest Hits Volume 2.

    (S) (2:33) Time-Life 2RNR-15 Rock 'N' Roll Era - Frankie Valli & The Four Seasons 1962-1967.

    (S) (2:31) Time-Life SUD-18 Superhits - Late 60's Classics.

    (S) (2:32) Warner Special Products 1625 Sing For You.

    (S) (2:33) Curb 77712 New Gold Hits.

    (S) (2:30) Time-Life AM1-12 AM Gold - Late '60s Classics.

1967 WATCH THE FLOWERS GROW

    (S) (3:17) Rhino 72998 25th Anniversary Collection.

1968 WILL YOU LOVE ME TOMORROW

    (S) (3:16) Rhino 72998 25th Anniversary Collection.

    (S) (3:16) Rhino 71490 Anthology.

    (S) (3:16) Rhino 70595 Greatest Hits Volume 2.

    (S) (3:15) Curb 77712 New Gold Hits.

1969 AND THAT REMINDS ME

    (S) (3:30) Rhino 72998 25th Anniversary Collection.

1975 WHO LOVES YOU

    (S) (4:06) MCA/Curb 39114 Hits Digitally Enhanced. *(remixed; additional instrumentation added)*

    (S) (4:18) Rhino 72998 25th Anniversary Collection. *(LP length)*

    (S) (4:49) Curb 77304 Hits Digitally Enhanced. *(remixed; additional instrumentation added)*

    (S) (4:14) Rhino 71490 Anthology. *(:04 shorter than the LP length)*

    (S) (4:18) Rhino 70595 Greatest Hits Volume 2. *(LP length)*

    (S) (4:05) Curb 77634 The Dance Album. *(remixed with completely new instrumentation)*

(S) (4:28) Curb 77693 Oh What A Night. *(remixed; additional instrumentation added)*
(S) (4:21) Curb 77713 Who Loves You. *(LP length)*

1976 DECEMBER, 1963 (OH, WHAT A NIGHT)
(45 length is (3:21); LP length is (3:32))
(S) (3:26) Curb 77317 70's Hits Volume 1.
(S) (3:33) Rhino 72998 25th Anniversary Collection.
(S) (3:26) Curb 77304 Hits Digitally Enhanced. *(remixed; additional instrumentation added)*
(S) (3:16) Rhino 71490 Anthology.
(S) (3:33) Rhino 70595 Greatest Hits Volume 2.
(S) (3:33) Time-Life SOD-36 Sounds Of The Seventies - More AM Nuggets.
(S) (3:32) Curb 77713 Who Loves You.
(S) (3:33) JCI 3163 18 Disco Superhits.
(S) (3:32) Time-Life AM1-23 AM Gold - 1976.
(S) (3:33) Time-Life R840-06 Sounds Of The Seventies: '70s Dance Party 1975-1976.

1994 DECEMBER, 1963 (OH, WHAT A NIGHT)
(this is a remixed version of the original 1976 hit)
(S) (6:13) MCA/Curb 39114 Hits Digitally Enhanced. *(full length version)*
(S) (4:20) Curb 77693 Oh What A Night. *(radio edit)*
(S) (3:38) Curb 77693 Oh What A Night. *(European mix)*
(S) (6:13) Curb 77634 The Dance Album. *(full length version)*
(S) (6:12) Curb 77304 Hits Digitally Enhanced. *(full length version)*
(S) (4:20) Curb 77934 Absolute Dance Hits: How Do I Live. *(all songs on this cd are remixed; radio edit)*

FOUR TOPS
1964 BABY I NEED YOUR LOVING
(S) (2:43) Rhino 70650 Billboard's Top R&B Hits Of 1964.
(S) (2:45) Motown 6138 The Composer Series: Holland/Dozier/Holland.
(S) (2:46) Motown 5451 A Collection Of 16 Big Hits Volume 4.
(S) (2:43) Motown 0809 and 6188 Anthology.
(S) (2:44) Motown 9042 and 6106 Compact Command Performances. *(almost all tracks on this cd have a buzz audible as each song reaches the end of its fade)*
(S) (2:44) MCA 6467 O.S.T. Air America.
(S) (2:44) Motown 9097 The Most Played Oldies On America's Jukeboxes. *(buzz noticeable on fadeout)*
(S) (2:46) Motown 5209 Greatest Hits.
(S) (2:43) Motown 5314 and 9022 Great Songs And Performances That Inspired The Motown 25th Anniversary TV Special.
(S) (2:44) Motown 5122 Four Tops.
(S) (2:44) Motown 9098 Radio's #1 Hits. *(buzz noticeable on fadeout)*
(S) (2:44) Motown 8027 and 8127 Four Tops/Four Tops Second Album.
(S) (2:42) Motown 6192 You Can't Hurry Love: All The Great Love Songs Of The Past 25 Years.
(S) (2:43) Ripete 392183 Ocean Drive.
(S) (2:43) Motown 5114 Superstar Series Volume 14.
(M) (2:43) Motown 6312 Hitsville USA.
(S) (2:42) K-Tel 3065 Temptations/Four Tops.
(S) (2:43) Time-Life RHD-12 Rhythm & Blues - 1964.
(S) (2:43) Time-Life 2CLR-09 Classic Rock - 1964: The Beat Goes On.
(S) (4:40) MCA Special Products 20388 Ain't No Woman (Like The One I Got). *(live)*
(M) (2:43) Motown/Essex 374638528 Motown Legends - It's The Same Old Song.
(M) (2:41) Motown 314530422 Motown Classics Vol. V.
(S) (2:45) Motown 314530504 Motown Year By Year 1964.
(S) (2:43) Eclipse Music Group 64869 Rock 'n Roll Relix 1964-1965.
(S) (2:43) Eclipse Music Group 64872 Rock 'n Roll Relix 1960-1969.

(S) (2:43) Time-Life R838-13 Solid Gold Soul - 1964.
(M) (2:42) Motown 314530825 The Ultimate Collection.

1965 ASK THE LONELY
(the 45 length is (2:55); LP length is (2:38))
(S) (2:36) Motown 0809 and 6188 Anthology.
(S) (2:39) Motown 9042 and 6106 Compact Command Performances.
(S) (2:57) Motown 5209 Greatest Hits.
(S) (2:38) Motown 5122 Four Tops.
(S) (2:37) Motown 8027 and 8127 Four Tops/Four Tops Second Album.
(S) (2:39) Motown 5114 Superstar Series Volume 14.
(M) (2:45) Motown 6312 Hitsville USA.
(S) (2:36) K-Tel 3065 Temptations/Four Tops.
(S) (2:36) Time-Life 2CLR-23 Classic Rock - 1965: Blowin' Your Mind.
(M) (2:45) Motown/Essex 374638528 Motown Legends - It's The Same Old Song.
(S) (2:39) Rebound 314520369 Soul Classics - Quiet Storm/The 60's.
(M) (2:45) Motown 314530825 The Ultimate Collection.

1965 I CAN'T HELP MYSELF
(S) (2:42) Rhino 70651 Billboard's Top R&B Hits Of 1965.
(S) (2:42) Rhino 72006 Billboard's Top R&B Hits 1965-1969 Box Set.
(S) (2:41) Motown 6132 25 #1 Hits From 25 Years.
(S) (2:40) Motown 6159 The Good-Feeling Music Of The Big Chill Generation Volume 1.
(S) (2:41) Motown 5452 A Collection Of 16 Big Hits Volume 5.
(S) (2:41) Motown 6138 The Composer Series: Holland/Dozier/Holland.
(S) (2:40) Motown 0809 and 6188 Anthology.
(S) (2:40) Motown 9042 and 6106 Compact Command Performances.
(S) (2:40) MCA 10063 Original Television Soundtrack "The Sounds Of Murphy Brown".
(S) (2:40) Motown 9017 and 5248 16 #1 Hits From The Early 60's. *(buzz noticeable on fadeout)*
(S) (2:40) Motown 9097 The Most Played Oldies On America's Jukeboxes. *(buzz noticeable on fadeout)*
(S) (2:41) Motown 5209 Greatest Hits.
(S) (2:40) Motown 5314 and 9022 Great Songs And Performances That Inspired The Motown 25th Anniversary TV Special.
(S) (2:40) Motown 5264 Second Album.
(S) (2:40) Motown 9098 Radio's #1 Hits. *(buzz noticeable on fadeout)*
(S) (2:39) Motown 8027 and 8127 Four Tops/Four Tops Second Album.
(S) (2:40) Motown 9060 Motown's Biggest Pop Hits. *(buzz noticeable on fadeout)*
(S) (2:39) Motown 9071 Motown Dance Party Volume 1. *(all selections on this cd are segued together)*
(S) (2:40) Ripete 392183 Ocean Drive.
(M) (2:43) Motown 6312 Hitsville USA.
(S) (2:39) K-Tel 3065 Temptations/Four Tops.
(S) (2:41) Time-Life RHD-07 Rhythm & Blues - 1965.
(S) (2:40) Time-Life 2CLR-01 Classic Rock - 1965.
(S) (2:40) Epic 66329 O.S.T. Forrest Gump.
(M) (2:43) Rhino 71806 The R&B Box: Thirty Years Of Rhythm & Blues.
(S) (2:40) Polygram Special Markets 314520282 Motown Legends - Volume 1.
(M) (2:41) Right Stuff 52660 Flick Hits - Old School Tracks.
(S) (2:41) Time-Life R838-12 Solid Gold Soul - 1965.
(M) (2:43) Rebound 314520420 Soul Classics - Best Of The 60's.
(M) (2:42) Motown 314530825 The Ultimate Collection.
(S) (2:41) Motown 314530849 Motown 40 Forever.

1965 IT'S THE SAME OLD SONG
(S) (2:46) Rhino 70651 Billboard's Top R&B Hits Of 1965.
(S) (2:46) Rhino 72006 Billboard's Top R&B Hits 1965-1969 Box Set.

FOUR TOPS (Continued)

(S) (2:47) Motown 6138 The Composer Series: Holland/Dozier/Holland.
(S) (2:45) Motown 5453 A Collection Of 16 Big Hits Volume 6.
(S) (2:45) Motown 6120 and 6062 O.S.T. The Big Chill.
(S) (2:45) Motown 0809 and 6188 Anthology.
(S) (2:46) Motown 9042 and 6106 Compact Command Performances.
(S) (2:45) Motown 5209 Greatest Hits.
(S) (2:46) Motown 5314 and 9022 Great Songs And Performances That Inspired The Motown 25th Anniversary TV Special.
(S) (2:46) Motown 5264 Second Album.
(S) (2:45) Motown 6094 More Songs From The Original Soundtrack Of The "Big Chill".
(S) (2:46) Motown 8027 and 8127 Four Tops/Four Tops Second Album.
(S) (2:46) Motown 9071 Motown Dance Party Volume 1. *(all selections on this cd are segued together)*
(S) (2:45) Motown 5114 Superstar Series Volume 14.
(M) (2:44) Motown 6312 Hitsville USA.
(S) (2:45) Time-Life 2CLR-08 Classic Rock - 1965: The Beat Goes On.
(M) (2:43) Motown/Essex 374638528 Motown Legends - It's The Same Old Song.
(M) (2:43) Motown 314530825 The Ultimate Collection.

1965 SOMETHING ABOUT YOU
(45 length is (2:48); LP length is (2:40))

(S) (2:39) Motown 0809 and 6188 Anthology.
(S) (2:41) Motown 9042 and 6106 Compact Command Performances.
(S) (2:40) Motown 5209 Greatest Hits.
(S) (2:48) Motown 5264 Second Album.
(S) (2:48) Motown 8027 and 8127 Four Tops/Four Tops Second Album.
(M) (2:47) Motown 314530825 The Ultimate Collection.

1966 SHAKE ME, WAKE ME (WHEN IT'S OVER)

(S) (2:37) Motown 5454 A Collection Of 16 Big Hits Volume 7.
(S) (2:38) Motown 0809 and 6188 Anthology.
(S) (2:38) Motown 9042 and 6106 Compact Command Performances.
(S) (2:38) Motown 5209 Greatest Hits.
(S) (2:38) Motown 5444 On Top. *(truncated fade)*
(S) (2:38) Motown 314530522 Motown Year By Year - 1966.
(M) (2:41) Motown 314530825 The Ultimate Collection.

1966 REACH OUT I'LL BE THERE

(S) (2:58) Rhino 70627 Billboard's Top Rock & Roll Hits Of 1966.
(S) (2:58) Rhino 72007 Billboard's Top Rock & Roll Hits 1962-1966 Box Set.
(S) (2:59) Motown 6132 25 #1 Hits From 25 Years.
(S) (2:57) Motown 6160 The Good-Feeling Music Of The Big Chill Generation Volume 2.
(S) (2:58) Motown 6137 20 Greatest Songs In Motown History.
(S) (2:58) Motown 6138 The Composer Series: Holland/Dozier/Holland.
(S) (2:57) Motown 5456 A Collection Of 16 Big Hits Volume 9.
(S) (2:57) Priority 7909 Vietnam: Rockin' The Delta.
(S) (2:54) Motown 0809 and 6188 Anthology.
(S) (2:58) Motown 9042 and 6106 Compact Command Performances.
(S) (2:55) Motown 9072 Motown Dance Party Volume 2. *(all selections on this cd are segued together)*
(S) (2:57) Motown 9097 The Most Played Oldies On America's Jukeboxes. *(buzz noticeable on fadeout)*
(S) (2:57) Motown 9018 and 5249 16 #1 Hits From The Late 60's.
(S) (2:59) Motown 5149 Reach Out.
(S) (2:57) Motown 5209 Greatest Hits.
(S) (2:58) Motown 5314 and 9022 Great Songs And Performances That Inspired The Motown 25th Anniversary TV Special.

(S) (2:58) Motown 5343 Every Great Motown Song: The First 25 Years Volume 1. *(most selections on this cd have noise on the fadeout)*
(S) (2:58) Motown 8034 and 8134 Every Great Motown Song: The First 25 Years Volumes 1 & 2. *(most selections on this cd have noise on the fadeout)*
(S) (2:59) Motown 8007 and 8107 Reach Out/Still Waters Run Deep.
(M) (2:58) Motown 6312 Hitsville USA.
(S) (2:53) Motown 374638503 Motown Legends - Bernadette.
(S) (2:55) Time-Life RHD-01 Rhythm & Blues - 1966.
(S) (2:57) Time-Life 2CLR-02 Classic Rock - 1966.
(S) (2:58) Time-Life R921-38 Get Together.
(S) (2:54) MCA Special Products 20753 Classic R&B Oldies From The 60's.
(S) (2:58) Polygram Special Markets 314520283 Motown Legends Volume 2.
(S) (2:55) Time-Life R838-01 Solid Gold Soul - 1966.
(M) (2:59) Motown 314530825 The Ultimate Collection.
(S) (2:57) Simitar 55572 The Number One's: Hot In The '60s.

1967 STANDING IN THE SHADOWS OF LOVE

(S) (2:34) Motown 9105 and 5410 Motown Memories Volume 2.
(S) (2:34) Motown 6137 20 Greatest Songs In Motown History.
(S) (2:35) Motown 6138 The Composer Series: Holland/Dozier/Holland.
(S) (2:34) Motown 5457 A Collection Of 16 Big Hits Volume 10.
(S) (2:34) Motown 0809 and 6188 Anthology.
(S) (2:34) Motown 9042 and 6106 Compact Command Performances.
(S) (2:33) Motown 9072 Motown Dance Party Volume 2. *(all selections on this cd are segued together)*
(S) (2:35) Motown 5149 Reach Out.
(S) (2:36) Motown 5209 Greatest Hits.
(S) (2:34) Motown 5314 and 9022 Great Songs And Performances That Inspired The Motown 25th Anniversary TV Special.
(S) (2:34) Motown 8034 and 8134 Every Great Motown Song: The First 25 Years Volumes 1 & 2. *(most selections on this cd have noise on the fadeout)*
(S) (2:34) Motown 5343 Every Great Motown Song: The First 25 Years Volume 1. *(most selections on this cd have noise on the fadeout)*
(S) (2:35) Motown 8007 and 8107 Reach Out/Still Waters Run Deep.
(M) (2:36) Motown 6312 Hitsville USA.
(S) (2:34) K-Tel 3065 Temptations/Four Tops.
(S) (2:34) Time-Life 2CLR-02 Classic Rock - 1966.
(M) (2:35) Motown 314530825 The Ultimate Collection.

1967 BERNADETTE

(S) (3:01) Motown 6161 The Good-Feeling Music Of The Big Chill Generation Volume 3.
(S) (3:00) Motown 5456 A Collection Of 16 Big Hits Volume 9.
(S) (3:00) Motown 0809 and 6188 Anthology.
(S) (3:01) Motown 9042 and 6106 Compact Command Performances.
(S) (3:00) Motown 5149 Reach Out.
(S) (3:00) Motown 5209 Greatest Hits.
(S) (3:01) Motown 5314 and 9022 Great Songs And Performances That Inspired The Motown 25th Anniversary TV Special.
(S) (3:00) Motown 8007 and 8107 Reach Out/Still Waters Run Deep.
(M) (2:59) Motown 6312 Hitsville USA.
(S) (3:00) Motown 374638503 Motown Legends - Bernadette.
(S) (2:59) Time-Life RHD-10 Rhythm & Blues - 1967.
(S) (3:00) Time-Life 2CLR-05 Classic Rock - 1967.
(S) (3:01) Polygram Special Markets 314520292 Motown Legends - Volume 4.
(S) (2:59) Time-Life R838-02 Solid Gold Soul - 1967.
(M) (2:59) Motown 314530825 The Ultimate Collection.

1967 7 ROOMS OF GLOOM
- (S) (2:30) Motown 5457 A Collection Of 16 Big Hits Volume 10.
- (S) (2:29) Motown 0809 and 6188 Anthology.
- (S) (2:33) Motown 5149 Reach Out.
- (S) (2:33) Motown 5209 Greatest Hits.
- (S) (2:33) Motown 8007 and 8107 Reach Out/Still Waters Run Deep.
- (S) (2:29) Time-Life 2CLR-24 Classic Rock - 1967: Blowin' Your Mind.
- (S) (2:33) Polygram Special Markets 314520300 Motown Legends - Guy Groups.
- (M) (2:32) Rhino 72815 Beg, Scream & Shout! The Big Ol' Box Of '60s Soul.
- (M) (2:31) Motown 314530825 The Ultimate Collection.

1967 YOU KEEP RUNNING AWAY
- (S) (2:48) Motown 0809 and 6188 Anthology.
- (M) (2:48) Motown 9042 and 6106 Compact Command Performances.
- (M) (2:47) Motown 314530825 The Ultimate Collection.

1968 WALK AWAY RENEE
- (S) (2:42) Motown 0809 and 6188 Anthology.
- (S) (2:43) Motown 9042 and 6106 Compact Command Performances.
- (S) (2:43) Motown 5149 Reach Out.
- (S) (2:42) Motown 5314 and 9022 Great Songs And Performances That Inspired The Motown 25th Anniversary TV Special.
- (S) (2:42) Motown 8007 and 8107 Reach Out/Still Waters Run Deep.
- (M) (2:43) Rhino 71227 Black On White: Great R&B Covers Of Rock Classics.
- (S) (2:42) Motown 374638503 Motown Legends - Bernadette.
- (S) (2:42) LaserLight 12315 and 15936 The Wonder Years - Movin' On.
- (M) (2:43) Motown 314530825 The Ultimate Collection.

1968 IF I WERE A CARPENTER
- (S) (2:47) Motown 0809 and 6188 Anthology.
- (S) (2:49) Motown 9042 and 6106 Compact Command Performances.
- (S) (2:48) Motown 5149 Reach Out.
- (S) (2:48) Motown 8007 and 8107 Reach Out/Still Waters Run Deep.
- (M) (2:48) Motown/Essex 374638528 Motown Legends - It's The Same Old Song.
- (S) (2:47) Eclipse Music Group 64871 Rock 'n Roll Relix 1968-1969.
- (S) (2:47) Eclipse Music Group 64872 Rock 'n Roll Relix 1960-1969.

1968 YESTERDAY'S DREAMS
- (S) (2:56) Motown 9042 and 6106 Compact Command Performances.
- (S) (2:54) Motown 0809 and 6188 Anthology.
- (S) (2:54) Motown 314530507 Motown Year By Year 1968.
- (M) (2:56) Motown 314530825 The Ultimate Collection.

1970 IT'S ALL IN THE GAME
- (S) (2:44) Motown 6110 Motown Grammy R&B Performances Of The 60's & 70's.
- (S) (2:42) Motown 0809 and 6188 Anthology. *(truncated fade)*
- (S) (2:44) Motown 9042 and 6106 Compact Command Performances.
- (S) (2:44) Motown 5314 and 9022 Great Songs And Performances That Inspired The Motown 25th Anniversary TV Special.
- (S) (2:43) Motown 8007 and 8107 Reach Out/Still Waters Run Deep.
- (S) (2:44) Motown 5224 Still Waters Run Deep.
- (S) (2:42) Motown 5114 Superstar Series Volume 14.
- (E) (2:34) Original Sound 8907 Best Love Songs Vol 2.
- (E) (2:34) Original Sound 9326 Best Love Songs Vol. 1 & 2.
- (E) (2:34) Original Sound 1236 Best Love Songs Box Set.
- (M) (2:49) Motown 314530825 The Ultimate Collection.

1970 STILL WATER (LOVE)
- (S) (3:05) Motown 0809 and 6188 Anthology.
- (S) (3:08) Motown 9042 and 6106 Compact Command Performances.
- (S) (3:08) Motown 5314 and 9022 Great Songs And Performances That Inspired The Motown 25th Anniversary TV Special.
- (S) (3:08) Motown 8007 and 8107 Reach Out/Still Waters Run Deep.
- (S) (3:08) Motown 5224 Still Waters Run Deep.
- (M) (3:11) Motown 6312 Hitsville USA.
- (S) (3:08) Motown 314530528 Motown Year By Year - 1970.
- (S) (3:11) Motown 314530825 The Ultimate Collection.

released as by THE SUPREMES & FOUR TOPS:
1971 RIVER DEEP - MOUNTAIN HIGH
(actual 45 time is (3:13) not (3:05) as stated on the record label)
- (S) (4:47) Motown 6184 20 Hard To Find Motown Classics Volume 2. *(LP version)*
- (M) (3:13) Motown 5491 Best Of The Supremes & Four Tops. *(45 version)*
- (S) (4:50) Motown 5123 Magnificent 7. *(LP version)*
- (E) (4:29) Motown 0809 and 6188 Four Tops Anthology. *(edit of LP version)*
- (M) (3:13) Motown 314530511 Diana Ross & The Supremes Anthology. *(45 version)*

released as by THE FOUR TOPS:
1971 JUST SEVEN NUMBERS (CAN STRAIGHTEN OUT MY LIFE)
- (S) (3:03) Motown 0809 and 6188 Anthology.
- (S) (3:05) Motown 9042 and 6106 Compact Command Performances.
- (S) (3:04) Motown 5478 Changing Times. *(tracks into next selection; actual time is (3:04) but the track plays to (3:11) because :07 of the introduction to the next track was mistakenly added to the end of this song)*

1971 MAC ARTHUR PARK (PART 2)
- (S) (6:31) Motown 9042 and 6106 Compact Command Performances. *(LP version which is Parts 1 & 2)*
- (S) (6:30) Motown 5466 Now! *(LP version which is Parts 1 & 2)*

1973 KEEPER OF THE CASTLE
- (S) (2:52) Rhino 70789 Soul Hits Of The 70's Volume 9.
- (S) (2:54) MCA 27019 Greatest Hits.
- (S) (2:56) Motown 5428 Keeper Of The Castle.
- (S) (2:55) Motown 8046 and 8146 Keeper Of The Castle/Nature Planned It.
- (S) (2:54) MCA Special Products 20388 Ain't No Woman (Like The One I Got).
- (S) (2:55) MCA Special Products 20949 Rockin' 70's Volume 2.
- (S) (2:55) Madacy Entertainment 1972 Rock On 1972.
- (S) (2:54) K-Tel 3626 Music Power.
- (S) (2:56) MCA 11647 Keepers Of The Castle/Their Best 1972-1978.

1973 AIN'T NO WOMAN (LIKE THE ONE I'VE GOT)
- (S) (3:05) Rhino 70790 Soul Hits Of The 70's Volume 10.
- (S) (3:00) Rhino 70661 Billboard's Top R&B Hits Of 1973.
- (S) (3:05) MCA 27019 Greatest Hits.
- (S) (2:58) Motown 5428 Keeper Of The Castle.
- (S) (2:58) Motown 8046 and 8146 Keeper Of The Castle/Nature Planned It.
- (S) (3:05) MCA 10288 Classic Soul.
- (S) (3:05) Original Sound 8863 Oldies But Goodies Vol. 13. *(noisy fadeout)*
- (S) (3:05) Original Sound 2223 Oldies But Goodies Volumes 2,7,9,12 and 13 Box Set. *(Volumes 2, 7 and 12 of this box set use the "Waring - fds" noise reduction process; noisy fadeout)*
- (S) (3:05) Original Sound 2500 Oldies But Goodies Volumes 1-15 Box Set. *(most volumes in this box set use the "Waring - fds" noise reduction process; noisy fadeout)*
- (S) (3:04) Original Sound 9306 Dedicated To You Vol. 6.
- (S) (3:04) Rhino 71618 Soul Train Hall Of Fame/20th Anniversary.

FOUR TOPS *(Continued)*

- (S) (3:04) Razor & Tie 22047 Sweet 70's Soul.
- (S) (3:03) Time-Life SUD-13 Superhits - 1973.
- (S) (3:06) Time-Life SOD-06 Sounds Of The Seventies - 1973.
- (S) (3:05) MCA Special Products 20752 Classic R&B Oldies From The 70's Vol. 2.
- (S) (3:02) MCA Special Products 20388 Ain't No Woman (Like The One I Got).
- (S) (3:03) Ripete 2183-RE Ocean Drive Volume 1.
- (S) (3:04) JCI 3130 1970 - Only Rock 'N Roll - 1974.
- (S) (3:02) MCA Special Products 20899 Rock Around The Oldies #4.
- (S) (3:04) Priority 53790 Disco Nice And Nasty.
- (S) (3:02) MCA Special Products 20910 Rockin' 70's.
- (S) (3:04) Madacy Entertainment 1973 Rock On 1973.
- (S) (3:04) Hip-O 40001 The Glory Of Love - Sweet & Soulful Love Songs.
- (S) (3:05) Hip-O 40010 ABC's Of Soul Volume 2.
- (S) (3:03) Time-Life AM1-03 AM Gold - 1973.
- (S) (3:04) Time-Life R838-08 Solid Gold Soul - 1973.
- (S) (3:04) MCA Special Products 21017 The Rockin' Sixties.
- (S) (3:03) Elektra 62093 O.S.T. A Smile Like Yours.
- (S) (3:06) MCA 11647 Keepers Of The Castle/Their Best 1972-1978.
- (S) (3:05) Rhino 72943 VH1 8-Track Flashback: Classic '70s Soul.
- (S) (3:04) Time-Life R834-12 Body Talk - By Candlelight.

1973 ARE YOU MAN ENOUGH

- (S) (3:23) MCA 27019 Greatest Hits.
- (S) (3:23) MCA Special Products 20388 Ain't No Woman (Like The One I Got).
- (S) (3:24) Coldfront 3517 Players & Hustlers Of The 70's - Can You Dig It?.
- (S) (3:25) MCA 11647 Keepers Of The Castle/Their Best 1972-1978.
- (S) (3:22) K-Tel 3900 Great R&B Male Groups: Hits Of The 70's.
- (S) (3:23) Hip-O 40107 Super Bad On Celluloid: Music From '70s Black Cinema.

1973 SWEET UNDERSTANDING LOVE

- (S) (2:58) MCA 27019 Greatest Hits.
- (S) (2:58) MCA Special Products 20388 Ain't No Woman (Like The One I Got).
- (S) (3:00) MCA 11647 Keepers Of The Castle/Their Best 1972-1978.

1974 ONE CHAIN DON'T MAKE NO PRISON

- (S) (4:03) MCA 27019 Greatest Hits. *(LP version)*
- (S) (4:05) Hip-O 40010 ABC's Of Soul Volume 2. *(LP version)*
- (S) (4:05) Hip-O 40035 Cigar Classics Volume 2 - Urban Fire. *(LP version)*
- (S) (4:06) MCA 11647 Keepers Of The Castle/Their Best 1972-1978. *(LP version)*

1981 WHEN SHE WAS MY GIRL

- (S) (3:18) Casablanca 800049 Tonight.
- (S) (3:21) Casablanca 314514127 When She Was My Girl.
- (S) (3:21) Casablanca 314516918 Casablanca Records Story.
- (S) (3:21) Rhino 71972 Video Soul - Best Soul Of The 80's Vol. 2.
- (S) (3:21) Time-Life R988-08 Sounds Of The Eighties: 1981.
- (S) (3:21) Ripete 5151 Ocean Drive 4.
- (S) (3:24) Rhino 72136 Billboard Hot R&B Hits 1981.
- (S) (3:21) Polygram Special Markets 314520445 Soul Hits Of The 80's.

1988 INDESTRUCTABLE

- (S) (4:26) Arista 8551 The Summer Olympics: One Moment In Time.
- (S) (4:29) Arista 8492 Indestructable.

SAMANTHA FOX
1987 TOUCH ME (I WANT YOUR BODY)

- (S) (3:46) Priority 53703 Hot And Sexy - Passion And Soul.
- (S) (3:46) Jive 1012 Touch Me.

- (S) (3:39) Jive 41478 Greatest Hits.
- (S) (3:38) Madacy Entertainment 1987 Rock On 1987.
- (S) (3:38) Robbins 75002 Strip Jointz - Hot Songs For Sexy Dancers.

1988 NAUGHTY GIRLS (NEED LOVE TOO)

- (S) (3:21) Jive 41478 Greatest Hits. *(neither the 45, LP or 12" single version)*
- (S) (5:10) Jive 1061 Samantha Fox. *(LP version)*
- (S) (3:38) Scotti Bros. 75504 Club Ladies Night. *(neither the 45, LP or 12" single version)*
- (M) (2:59) Priority 51002 Shut Up And Dance! The Best Of Freestyle Volume One. *(all selections on this cd are segued together)*

1988 I WANNA HAVE SOME FUN

- (S) (4:05) K-Tel 842 Hot Ladies Of The 80's. *(45 version)*
- (S) (5:00) Jive 1150 I Wanna Have Some Fun. *(LP version)*
- (S) (3:54) Jive 41478 Greatest Hits. *(45 version)*
- (S) (3:55) Priority 53731 80's Greatest Rock Hits Volume 10 - Dance All Night. *(45 version)*
- (S) (3:54) Madacy Entertainment 1989 Rock On 1989. *(45 version)*
- (S) (4:03) Cold Front 6245 Greatest Sports Rock And Jams. *(all songs on this cd are segued together)*
- (S) (3:55) Rhino 72838 Disco Queens: The 80's. *(45 version)*
- (S) (4:05) Cold Front 3865 Club Mix - Women Of Dance Vol. 2. *(45 version)*

1989 I ONLY WANNA BE WITH YOU

- (S) (2:43) Jive 1150 I Wanna Have Some Fun.
- (S) (2:42) Jive 41478 Greatest Hits.

INEZ FOXX
1963 MOCKINGBIRD

- (M) (2:37) Rhino 70649 Billboard's Top R&B Hits Of 1963.
- (E) (2:37) EMI 90614 Non Stop Party Rock.
- (M) (2:35) Curb 77323 All Time Greatest Hits Of Rock 'N' Roll.
- (M) (2:35) Time-Life 2RNR-07 Rock 'N' Roll Era - 1963.
- (M) (2:34) Time-Life RHD-02 Rhythm & Blues - 1963.
- (M) (2:36) Collectables 5123 Best Of Sue Records.
- (M) (2:37) Ripete 0003 Coolin' Out/24 Carolina Classics Vol. 3.
- (M) (2:37) EMI 80932 Sue Records Story.
- (M) (2:35) Collectables 5301 Mockingbird.
- (M) (2:34) Time-Life R838-14 Solid Gold Soul - 1963.
- (E) (2:35) Compose 131 Unforgettable - Gold For The Road.
- (M) (2:37) Island 314524394 Island Records 40th Anniversary Volume 2 1964-1969: Rhythm & Blues.
- (M) (2:37) JCI 3189 1960 - Only Dance - 1964.

FOXY
1978 GET OFF

- (S) (5:41) Priority 7976 Mega-Hits Dance Classics Volume 6. *(12" single version)*
- (S) (3:30) Rhino 71003 Get Down Tonight: The Best Of T.K. Records. *(45 version)*
- (S) (3:35) Rhino 70274 The Disco Years Volume 3. *(:05 longer than the 45 version)*
- (S) (3:30) Rhino 71096 Disco Hits Volume 3. *(45 version)*
- (S) (3:30) Essex 7051 Non-Stop Dance Hits. *(45 version; mistakenly identified on the cd jacket as "HOLD BACK THE NIGHT" by THE TRAMMPS)*
- (S) (3:31) Time-Life SOD-27 Sounds Of The Seventies - Dance Fever. *(45 version)*
- (S) (5:44) Rhino 71756 and 72833 Phat Trax: The Best Of Old School Volume 5. *(12" single version)*
- (S) (4:01) Hot Productions 11 Best Of The Sound Of Sunshine. *(LP version)*
- (S) (5:44) Hot Productions 31 Best Of. *(12" single version; loud pop at 5:43)*
- (S) (3:31) K-Tel 3371 Hot Nights - Disco Lights. *(45 version)*
- (S) (3:31) JCI 3148 1975 - Only Dance - 1979. *(45 version)*
- (S) (3:31) JCI 3163 18 Disco Superhits. *(45 version)*

(S) (3:31) Flashback 72691 Disco Hits: Le Freak. *(45 version)*

(S) (3:31) Flashback 72086 Disco Hits Box Set. *(45 version)*

(S) (3:34) Time-Life R838-17 Solid Gold Soul 1978. *(45 version)*

(S) (3:35) Time-Life R840-08 Sounds Of The Seventies: '70s Dance Party 1978-1979. *(45 version)*

1979 HOT NUMBER

(S) (3:44) Rhino 71003 Get Down Tonight: The Best Of T.K. Records.

(S) (3:44) Rhino 71669 Disco Hits Vol. 6.

(S) (6:05) Hot Productions 31 Best Of.

(S) (3:44) Priority 53790 Disco Nice And Nasty.

(S) (3:44) Flashback 72693 Disco Hits: Good Times.

(S) (3:44) Flashback 72086 Disco Hits Box Set.

(S) (3:44) K-Tel 3909 High Energy Volume 2.

PETER FRAMPTON
1976 SHOW ME THE WAY
(actual 45 time is (3:33) not (3:25) as stated on the record label)

(S) (3:34) Priority 7997 Super Songs/70's Greatest Rock Hits Volume 8. *(45 version)*

(S) (4:33) A&M 2510 Classics Volume 12. *(LP version)*

(S) (4:34) A&M 6505 Frampton Comes Alive. *(LP version)*

(S) (4:39) A&M 314540015 Shine On: A Collection. *(LP version)*

(S) (3:32) Priority 7080 70's Greatest Rock Hits Volume 14: Kings Of Rock. *(45 version)*

(S) (3:32) Time-Life R968-03 Guitar Rock 1976-1977. *(45 version)*

(S) (3:33) Time-Life SOD-04 Sounds Of The Seventies - 1976. *(45 version)*

(S) (3:30) Time-Life OPCD-4521 Guitar Rock. *(45 version)*

(S) (4:39) Medicine Label 24588 Even More Dazed And Confused. *(LP version)*

(S) (4:02) Rebound 314520289 Frampton. *(this is the studio recording which was not the hit version)*

(S) (4:35) Varese 5635 and 5654 and 5655 and 5657 Arrow: All Rock & Roll Oldies Volume Two. *(LP version)*

(S) (4:35) MFSL 678 Frampton Comes Alive. *(LP version; gold disc)*

(S) (4:35) Varese Sarabande 5708 All Rock & Roll Hits Vol. One. *(LP version)*

(S) (4:37) A&M 314540557 Greatest Hits. *(LP version)*

(S) (3:32) Time-Life AM1-23 AM Gold - 1976. *(45 version)*

(S) (3:33) Rhino 72893 Hard Rock Cafe: Classic Rock. *(45 version)*

1976 BABY, I LOVE YOUR WAY

(S) (4:42) Priority 8667 FM Hits/70's Greatest Rock Hits Volume 6. *(LP version)*

(S) (4:42) A&M 2510 Classics Volume 12. *(LP version)*

(S) (4:37) A&M 6505 Frampton Comes Alive. *(LP version)*

(S) (5:49) A&M 314540015 Shine On: A Collection. *(rerecording; medley with "NASSAU")*

(S) (3:36) Time-Life SOD-18 Sounds Of The Seventies - 1976: Take Two. *(45 version)*

(S) (4:41) Rebound 314520289 Frampton. *(this is the studio recording which was not the hit version)*

(S) (4:42) MFSL 678 Frampton Comes Alive. *(LP version; gold disc)*

(S) (4:48) A&M 314540557 Greatest Hits. *(LP version)*

(S) (4:41) Rebound 314520437 Classic Rock - 70's. *(LP version)*

(S) (3:36) Time-Life R13610 Gold And Platinum Box Set - The Ultimate Rock Collection. *(45 version)*

(S) (5:49) Polygram TV 314555610 The One And Only Love Album. *(rerecording; medley with "NASSAU")*

(S) (3:35) Time-Life R834-13 Body Talk - Just The Two Of Us. *(45 version)*

1976 DO YOU FEEL LIKE WE DO

(S) (13:44) A&M 2510 Classics Volume 12. *(:30 of audience applause edited from the LP version)*

(S) (14:14) A&M 6505 Frampton Comes Alive. *(LP version)*

(S) (13:54) A&M 314540015 Shine On: A Collection. *(:20 of audience applause edited from the LP version)*

(S) (13:56) Polydor 314515913 Classic Rock Box. *(:18 of audience applause edited from the LP version)*

(S) (13:44) K-Tel 3221 Axe Gods. *(:30 of audience applause edited from the LP version)*

(S) (7:11) Medicine Label 24588 Even More Dazed And Confused. *(45 version)*

(S) (13:53) Rebound 314520278 Hard Rock Essentials - The 70's. *(:21 of audience applause edited from the LP version)*

(S) (13:44) Rhino 72131 Frat Rock: The 70's. *(:30 of audience applause edited from the LP version)*

(S) (7:18) Time-Life R968-08 Guitar Rock - The Mid '70s. *(45 version)*

(S) (14:14) MFSL 678 Frampton Comes Alive. *(LP version; gold disc)*

(S) (13:54) A&M 314540557 Greatest Hits. *(:20 of audience applause edited from the LP version)*

(S) (14:15) MCA Special Products 22142 Classic Live Performances. *(LP version)*

1977 I'M IN YOU
(actual 45 time is (4:08) not (3:57) as stated on the record label)

(S) (4:08) Rhino 70672 Billboard Top Hits - 1977.

(S) (4:08) A&M 2510 Classics Volume 12.

(S) (4:09) A&M 314540015 Shine On: A Collection.

(S) (4:08) Priority 7065 70's Greatest Rock Hits Volume 13: Request Line.

(S) (4:08) Time-Life SOD-05 Sounds Of The Seventies - 1977.

(S) (4:08) A&M 314540557 Greatest Hits.

(S) (4:09) Time-Life R834-11 Body Talk - After Dark.

1977 SIGNED, SEALED, DELIVERED (I'M YOURS)

(S) (3:46) A&M 314540015 Shine On: A Collection.

(S) (3:46) A&M 314540557 Greatest Hits.

1979 I CAN'T STAND IT NO MORE
(actual 45 time is (3:49) not (3:40) as stated on the record label)

(S) (4:10) A&M 2510 Classics Volume 12. *(LP version)*

(S) (4:13) A&M 314540015 Shine On: A Collection. *(LP version)*

(S) (3:49) Time-Life SOD-19 Sounds Of The Seventies - 1979: Take Two. *(45 version)*

(S) (4:12) Rebound 314520270 Class Reunion 1979. *(LP version)*

(S) (4:12) A&M 314540557 Greatest Hits. *(LP version)*

(S) (4:10) K-Tel 3906 Starflight Vol. 1. *(LP version)*

CONNIE FRANCIS
1958 WHO'S SORRY NOW

(M) (2:16) JCI 3203 Lovin' Fifties.

(M) (2:15) Original Sound 8891 Dick Clark's 21 All-Time Hits Vol. 1.

(M) (2:15) Polydor 827569 Very Best Of.

(S) (2:11) Malaco 2003 Where The Hits Are. *(all selections on this cd are rerecorded)*

(M) (2:16) Time-Life 2RNR-27 Rock 'N' Roll Era - Teen Idols.

(M) (2:16) Time-Life HPD-11 Your Hit Parade 1958.

(M) (2:16) Time-Life R103-27 Love Me Tender.

(M) (2:16) JCI 3129 1955 - Only Rock 'N Roll - 1959.

(M) (2:16) Polygram Special Markets 314520267 Hits To Remember.

(M) (2:16) Time-Life R857-04 The Heart Of Rock 'n' Roll - 1958.

(M) (2:15) Polydor 314533382 Souvenirs Box Set.

(M) (2:16) Time-Life R133-34 Best Of.

1958 I'M SORRY I MADE YOU CRY

(M) (2:27) Polydor 827569 Very Best Of.

(M) (2:27) Polydor 314533382 Souvenirs Box Set.

(M) (2:27)   Time-Life R132-04   From The Heart.

(M) (2:27)   Time-Life R133-34   Best Of.

1958 STUPID CUPID

(M) (2:12)   Mercury 832041   45's On CD Volume 1.

(M) (2:12)   Polydor 827569   Very Best Of.

(S) (2:10)   Malaco 2003   Where The Hits Are. *(all selections on this cd are rerecorded)*

(M) (2:13)   Era 5025   The Brill Building Sound.

(M) (2:11)   Time-Life 2RNR-47   Rock 'N' Roll Era - Teen Idols II.

(M) (2:13)   Special Music/Essex 5034   Prom Night - The 50's.

(M) (2:13)   Polydor 314533382   Souvenirs Box Set.

(M) (2:13)   Polygram Special Markets 314520377   Best Of.

(M) (2:12)   Time-Life R133-34   Best Of.

1958 FALLIN'

(M) (2:12)   Polydor 827569   Very Best Of.

(M) (2:13)   Polydor 314533382   Souvenirs Box Set.

(M) (2:12)   Time-Life R133-34   Best Of.

1959 MY HAPPINESS

(S) (2:26)   Polydor 827569   Very Best Of.

(S) (2:18)   Malaco 2003   Where The Hits Are. *(all selections on this cd are rerecorded)*

(S) (2:27)   Time-Life HPD-25   Your Hit Parade - The 50's.

(S) (2:26)   Time-Life R857-01   The Heart Of Rock 'n' Roll - 1959.

(S) (2:27)   Polydor 314533382   Souvenirs Box Set.

(S) (2:26)   JCI 3183   1955 - Only Love - 1959.

(S) (2:26)   Time-Life R133-34   Best Of.

1959 IF I DIDN'T CARE

(M) (2:36)   Polydor 827569   Very Best Of.

(S) (2:47)   Malaco 2003   Where The Hits Are. *(all selections on this cd are rerecorded)*

(M) (2:36)   Polydor 314533382   Souvenirs Box Set.

(M) (2:37)   Time-Life R133-34   Best Of.

1959 LIPSTICK ON YOUR COLLAR

(S) (2:16)   Polydor 827569   Very Best Of.

(S) (2:14)   Essex 7053   A Hot Summer Night In '59.

(S) (2:18)   Malaco 2003   Where The Hits Are. *(all selections on this cd are rerecorded)*

(S) (2:15)   Time-Life 2RNR-33   Rock 'N' Roll Era - The 50's Last Dance.

(S) (2:18)   Polydor 314533382   Souvenirs Box Set.

(S) (2:18)   Polygram Special Markets 314520377   Best Of.

(S) (2:16)   Time-Life R133-34   Best Of.

1959 FRANKIE

(S) (2:30)   Polydor 827569   Very Best Of.

(S) (2:45)   Malaco 2003   Where The Hits Are. *(all selections on this cd are rerecorded)*

(S) (2:30)   Polydor 314533382   Souvenirs Box Set.

(S) (2:30)   Time-Life R133-34   Best Of.

1959 YOU'RE GONNA MISS ME

(M) (2:43)   Polydor 827569   Very Best Of.

(M) (2:43)   Polydor 314533382   Souvenirs Box Set.

1959 AMONG MY SOUVENIRS

(M) (2:29)   Polydor 827569   Very Best Of.

(S) (2:18)   Malaco 2003   Where The Hits Are. *(all selections on this cd are rerecorded)*

(M) (2:29)   Time-Life HPD-13   Your Hit Parade - 1959.

(E) (2:30)   Polydor 314533382   Souvenirs Box Set.

(M) (2:29)   Time-Life R857-11   The Heart Of Rock 'n' Roll 1958-1959.

(M) (2:29)   Time-Life R133-34   Best Of.

1959 GOD BLESS AMERICA

(S) (2:44)   Polydor 831699   Very Best Of Volume 2.

(S) (2:43)   Polydor 314533382   Souvenirs Box Set.

(S) (2:44)   Time-Life R132-04   From The Heart.

1960 MAMA

(S) (3:55)   Polydor 831699   Very Best Of Volume 2.

(S) (3:55)   Compose 9928   Now That's Italian.

(S) (3:54)   Polydor 314533382   Souvenirs Box Set.

(S) (3:55)   Rhino 72577   Eh, Paisano! Italian-American Classics.

(S) (3:55)   Time-Life R133-34   Best Of.

(S) (3:55)   Polydor 314539556   The Italian Collection Volume One.

1960 TEDDY

(M) (2:44)   Polydor 827569   Very Best Of.

(M) (2:44)   Polydor 314533382   Souvenirs Box Set.

(M) (2:44)   Time-Life R133-34   Best Of.

1960 EVERYBODY'S SOMEBODY'S FOOL

(S) (2:37)   Polydor 827569   Very Best Of.

(S) (2:31)   Malaco 2003   Where The Hits Are. *(all selections on this cd are rerecorded)*

(S) (2:37)   Era 5025   The Brill Building Sound.

(S) (2:36)   Time-Life SUD-19   Superhits - Early 60's Classics.

(S) (2:37)   Rhino 71581   Billboard Top Pop Hits, 1960.

(S) (2:37)   Polygram Special Markets 314520260   Number One Hits Of The Sixties.

(S) (2:37)   Polydor 314533382   Souvenirs Box Set.

(S) (2:37)   Eclipse Music Group 64867   Rock 'n Roll Relix 1960-1961.

(S) (2:37)   Eclipse Music Group 64872   Rock 'n Roll Relix 1960-1969.

(S) (2:37)   Polygram Special Markets 314520377   Best Of.

(S) (2:36)   Time-Life AM1-20   AM Gold - Early '60s Classics.

(S) (2:37)   Time-Life R133-34   Best Of.

1960 JEALOUS OF YOU

(M) (2:23)   Polydor 831699   Very Best Of Volume 2.

(S) (2:23)   Polydor 314533382   Souvenirs Box Set.

(S) (2:23)   Time-Life R133-34   Best Of.

1960 MY HEART HAS A MIND OF ITS OWN

(S) (2:30)   Polydor 827569   Very Best Of.

(S) (2:24)   Malaco 2003   Where The Hits Are. *(all selections on this cd are rerecorded)*

(S) (2:30)   Time-Life HPD-32   Your Hit Parade - Into The 60's.

(S) (2:30)   Polydor 314533382   Souvenirs Box Set.

(S) (2:30)   Polygram Special Markets 314520377   Best Of.

(S) (2:30)   Time-Life R133-34   Best Of.

1960 MANY TEARS AGO

(S) (1:54)   Polydor 827569   Very Best Of.

(S) (1:56)   Malaco 2003   Where The Hits Are. *(all selections on this cd are rerecorded)*

(S) (1:53)   Polydor 314533382   Souvenirs Box Set.

(S) (1:54)   Polygram Special Markets 314520377   Best Of.

(S) (1:54)   Time-Life R133-34   Best Of.

1961 WHERE THE BOYS ARE

(S) (2:36)   Polydor 827569   Very Best Of.

(S) (2:35)   Malaco 2003   Where The Hits Are. *(all selections on this cd are rerecorded)*

(S) (2:36)   Era 5025   The Brill Building Sound.

(S) (2:36)   Time-Life 2RNR-27   Rock 'N' Roll Era - Teen Idols.

(S) (2:36)   Time-Life SUD-15   Superhits - The Early 60's.

(S) (2:36)   Time-Life R962-05   History Of Rock 'N' Roll: The Teenage Years 1957-1964.

(S) (2:36)   Collectables 2505   History Of Rock - The 60's Part 5.

(S) (2:36)   Collectables 4505   History Of Rock/The 60s Part Five.

(S) (2:36)   Time-Life R857-03   The Heart Of Rock 'n' Roll - 1961.

(S) (2:36)   Polydor 314533382   Souvenirs Box Set.

(S) (2:36)   Eclipse Music Group 64867   Rock 'n Roll Relix 1960-1961.

(S) (2:36)   Eclipse Music Group 64872   Rock 'n Roll Relix 1960-1969.

(S) (2:36)   Polygram Special Markets 314520377   Best Of.

(S) (2:36)   Time-Life AM1-19   AM Gold - The Early '60s.

(S) (2:36)   Rhino 72774   Where The Boys Are: Connie Francis In Hollywood. *(medley with "MAIN TITLE" from the soundtrack "Where The Boys Are")*

(S) (3:30)   Rhino 72774   Where The Boys Are: Connie Francis In Hollywood. *(finale from the soundtrack "Where The Boys Are")*

(S) (2:36)   Time-Life R133-34   Best Of.

(S) (2:36)   JCI 3184   1960 - Only Love - 1964.

(S) (2:36)   Time-Life R814-04   Love Songs.

1961 BREAKIN' IN A BRAND NEW BROKEN HEART

(S) (2:36)   Polydor 827569   Very Best Of.

(S) (2:28)   Malaco 2003   Where The Hits Are. *(all selections on this cd are rerecorded)*

(S) (2:36) Polydor 314533382 Souvenirs Box Set.
(S) (2:36) Polygram Special Markets 314520377 Best Of.
(S) (2:36) Time-Life R133-34 Best Of.
(S) (2:36) Time-Life R857-19 The Heart Of Rock 'n' Roll 1960-1961 Take Three.

1961 TOGETHER
(S) (2:53) Polydor 831699 Very Best Of Volume 2.
(S) (2:45) Malaco 2003 Where The Hits Are. *(all selections on this cd are rerecorded)*
(S) (2:53) Time-Life R974-16 Many Moods Of Romance - The Look Of Love.
(S) (2:52) Polydor 314533382 Souvenirs Box Set.
(S) (2:53) Time-Life R857-14 The Heart Of Rock 'n' Roll 1960-1961 Take Two.
(S) (2:53) Time-Life R133-34 Best Of.

1961 (HE'S MY) DREAMBOAT
(S) (2:41) Polydor 831698 Rocksides.
(S) (2:41) Polydor 314533382 Souvenirs Box Set.
(S) (2:41) Time-Life R133-34 Best Of.

1961 HOLLYWOOD
(M) (2:13) Polydor 831698 Rocksides.
(M) (2:13) Polydor 314533382 Souvenirs Box Set.

1962 WHEN THE BOY IN YOUR ARMS (IS THE BOY IN YOUR HEART)
(S) (2:42) Polydor 831699 Very Best Of Volume 2.
(M) (2:42) Special Music/Essex 5035 Prom Night - The 60's.
(S) (2:42) Polydor 314533382 Souvenirs Box Set.
(S) (2:42) Polygram Special Markets 314520377 Best Of.
(S) (2:42) Time-Life R857-17 The Heart Of Rock 'n' Roll: The Early '60s.
(S) (2:42) Time-Life R133-34 Best Of.

1962 DON'T BREAK THE HEART THAT LOVES YOU
(S) (3:01) Polydor 827569 Very Best Of.
(S) (2:56) Malaco 2003 Where The Hits Are. *(all selections on this cd are rerecorded)*
(S) (3:01) Time-Life SUD-06 Superhits - 1962.
(S) (3:01) Time-Life HPD-33 Your Hit Parade - The Early 60's.
(S) (3:01) Time-Life R138/05 Look Of Love.
(S) (3:00) Rhino 71583 Billboard Top Pop Hits, 1962.
(S) (3:02) Polydor 314533382 Souvenirs Box Set.
(S) (3:02) Time-Life R857-06 The Heart Of Rock 'n' Roll 1962.
(S) (3:01) Time-Life AM1-18 AM Gold - 1962.
(S) (3:02) Time-Life R133-34 Best Of.
(S) (3:01) Time-Life R814-03 Love Songs.

1962 SECOND HAND LOVE
(S) (2:49) Polydor 827569 Very Best Of.
(S) (2:53) Malaco 2003 Where The Hits Are. *(all selections on this cd are rerecorded)*
(S) (2:49) Polydor 314533382 Souvenirs Box Set.
(S) (2:49) Polygram Special Markets 314520377 Best Of.
(S) (2:50) Time-Life R133-34 Best Of.

1962 VACATION
(S) (2:21) Polydor 827569 Very Best Of.
(S) (2:39) Malaco 2003 Where The Hits Are. *(all selections on this cd are rerecorded)*
(S) (2:21) Polydor 314533382 Souvenirs Box Set.
(S) (2:22) Time-Life R133-34 Best Of.

1962 I WAS SUCH A FOOL (TO FALL IN LOVE WITH YOU)
(M) (2:44) Polydor 831699 Very Best Of Volume 2.
(M) (2:44) Polydor 314533382 Souvenirs Box Set.
(M) (2:44) Time-Life R133-34 Best Of.

1963 I'M GONNA BE WARM THIS WINTER
(M) (2:23) Polydor 827569 Very Best Of.
(S) (2:27) Malaco 2003 Where The Hits Are. *(all selections on this cd are rerecorded)*
(M) (2:22) Polydor 314533382 Souvenirs Box Set.
(M) (2:23) Time-Life R133-34 Best Of.

1963 FOLLOW THE BOYS
(E) (2:38) Polydor 827569 Very Best Of.
(S) (2:38) Polydor 314533382 Souvenirs Box Set.
(S) (2:38) Polygram Special Markets 314520377 Best Of.
(S) (2:38) Rhino 72774 Where The Boys Are: Connie Francis In Hollywood.

(S) (2:38) Rhino 72819 16 Magazine - Who's Your Fave Rave.
(M) (2:39) Time-Life R133-34 Best Of.
(S) (2:38) Polygram Special Markets 314520516 45's On CD Volume 1.

1963 IF MY PILLOW COULD TALK
(M) (2:06) Polydor 314533382 Souvenirs Box Set.
(M) (2:06) Time-Life R133-34 Best Of.

1963 DROWNIN' MY SORROWS
(M) (2:03) Polydor 314533382 Souvenirs Box Set.

1963 YOUR OTHER LOVE
(M) (2:09) Polydor 314533382 Souvenirs Box Set.
(M) (2:08) Time-Life R133-34 Best Of.

1964 IN THE SUMMER OF HIS YEARS
(S) (2:31) Polydor 314533382 Souvenirs Box Set.

1964 BLUE WINTER
(M) (2:24) Polydor 831699 Very Best Of Volume 2.
(M) (2:24) Polydor 314533382 Souvenirs Box Set.
(M) (2:24) Time-Life R133-34 Best Of.

1964 BE ANYTHING (BUT BE MINE)
(M) (2:08) Polydor 831699 Very Best Of Volume 2.
(M) (2:08) Polydor 314533382 Souvenirs Box Set.
(M) (2:08) Time-Life R133-34 Best Of.

1964 LOOKING FOR LOVE
(M) (2:18) Polydor 831698 Rocksides. *(45 version)*
(S) (2:04) CBS Special Products 46200 Rock Goes To The Movies Volume 3. *(soundtrack version 2)*
(M) (2:19) Polydor 314533382 Souvenirs Box Set. *(45 version)*
(S) (2:05) Rhino 72774 Where The Boys Are: Connie Francis In Hollywood. *(soundtrack version 1)*
(S) (2:20) Rhino 72774 Where The Boys Are: Connie Francis In Hollywood. *(soundtrack version 2)*
(M) (2:25) Rhino 72774 Where The Boys Are: Connie Francis In Hollywood. *(demo version)*
(M) (2:04) Rhino 72774 Where The Boys Are: Connie Francis In Hollywood. *(demo version)*

1964 DON'T EVER LEAVE ME
(M) (2:43) Polydor 831698 Rocksides.
(M) (2:44) Mercury 314528171 Growin' Up Too Fast - The Girl Group Anthology.
(M) (2:44) Polydor 314533382 Souvenirs Box Set.

1965 FOR MAMA (LA MAMMA)
(S) (3:25) Polydor 831699 Very Best Of Volume 2.
(S) (3:25) Polydor 314533382 Souvenirs Box Set.
(S) (3:25) Time-Life R132-04 From The Heart.
(S) (3:25) Polydor 314539557 The Italian Collection Volume Two.

1965 JEALOUS HEART
(S) (2:33) Polydor 314533382 Souvenirs Box Set.
(E) (2:33) Time-Life R132-04 From The Heart.

FRANKE & THE KNOCKOUTS
1981 SWEETHEART
(S) (3:47) Rhino 71894 Radio Daze: Pop Hits Of The 80's Volume Five.

1981 YOU'RE MY GIRL
1982 WITHOUT YOU (NOT ANOTHER LONELY NIGHT)

FRANKIE GOES TO HOLLYWOOD
1985 RELAX
(S) (3:54) Rebound 314520324 Alterno-Daze: Survival Of 80's The Fittest.
(S) (3:55) Island 824052 Welcome To The Pleasuredome.
(S) (3:54) Atlantic 82587 Bang!....Greatest Hits Of.
(S) (3:58) Rhino 71976 New Wave Hits Of The 80's Vol. 13.
(S) (3:54) Time-Life R988-02 Sounds Of The Eighties: 1985.
(S) (3:53) Rebound 314520354 World Of Dance: New Wave - The 80's.
(S) (3:02) Island 90684 and 842901 The Island Story. *(edited)*
(S) (3:52) Cold Front 6284 More Of! Club Mix's Biggest Jams. *(all selections on this cd are segued together)*

ARETHA FRANKLIN
1961 ROCK-A-BYE YOUR BABY WITH A DIXIE MELODY
1967 I NEVER LOVED A MAN (THE WAY I LOVE YOU)
(45 length is (2:47); LP length is (2:41))

(M)	(2:47)	Rhino 70653 Billboard's Top R&B Hits Of 1967.
(M)	(2:47)	Rhino 72006 Billboard's Top R&B Hits 1965-1969 Box Set.
(S)	(2:40)	Atlantic 81911 Golden Age Of Black Music (1960-1970).
(M)	(2:41)	Atlantic 81298 Atlantic Rhythm & Blues Volume 6.
(S)	(2:41)	Atlantic 81668 30 Greatest Hits.
(S)	(2:41)	Atlantic 8139 I Never Loved A Man The Way I Love You.
(M)	(2:48)	Rhino 71934 I Never Loved A Man The Way I Love You.
(S)	(2:41)	Rhino 71934 I Never Loved A Man The Way I Love You.
(S)	(2:41)	MFSL 574 I Never Loved A Man The Way I Love You. (gold disc)
(S)	(2:41)	Atlantic 81280 Best Of.
(S)	(2:41)	Atlantic 8227 Aretha's Gold.
(S)	(2:42)	Atco 91813 Classic Recordings.
(S)	(2:40)	Atlantic 82305 Atlantic Rhythm And Blues 1947-1974 Box Set.
(M)	(2:48)	Rhino 71063 Queen Of Soul.
(M)	(2:41)	Scotti Brothers 75402 There Was Love (The Divorce Songs).
(M)	(2:48)	Rhino 71429 Chain Of Fools.
(M)	(2:47)	Rhino 71517 The Muscle Shoals Sound.
(M)	(2:48)	Rhino 71598 Very Best Of Vol. 1.
(S)	(2:39)	Time-Life RHD-10 Rhythm & Blues - 1967.
(S)	(2:39)	Time-Life 2CLR-24 Classic Rock - 1967: Blowin' Your Mind.
(S)	(2:41)	Atlantic 82848 O.S.T. Heaven's Prisoners.
(M)	(2:39)	JCI 3185 1965 - Only Love - 1969.
(S)	(2:39)	Time-Life R838-02 Solid Gold Soul - 1967.
(M)	(2:48)	Flashback 72660 Respect And Other Hits.
(M)	(2:48)	Flashback 72083 Kings And Queens Of Soul Box Set.
(M)	(2:48)	Flashback 72897 25 Years Of R&B - 1967.

1967 RESPECT

(M)	(2:22)	Atlantic 81298 Atlantic Rhythm & Blues Volume 6.
(S)	(2:25)	Atlantic 81742 O.S.T. Platoon.
(S)	(2:22)	Atlantic 81911 Golden Age Of Black Music (1960-1970).
(S)	(2:25)	JCI 3105 Soul Sixties.
(S)	(2:25)	Warner Special Products 27601 Atlantic Soul Classics.
(S)	(2:25)	Atlantic 81668 30 Greatest Hits.
(S)	(2:24)	Atlantic 8139 I Never Loved A Man The Way I Love You.
(S)	(2:24)	MFSL 574 I Never Loved A Man The Way I Love You. (gold disc)
(M)	(2:23)	Rhino 71934 I Never Loved A Man The Way I Love You.
(S)	(2:25)	Rhino 71934 I Never Loved A Man The Way I Love You. (noisy fadeout)
(S)	(2:25)	Atlantic 81280 Best Of.
(S)	(2:25)	Atlantic 8227 Aretha's Gold.
(S)	(2:23)	MCA 10063 Original Television Soundtrack "The Sounds Of Murphy Brown". (previous selection tracks over the introduction)
(S)	(2:24)	Atlantic 82305 Atlantic Rhythm And Blues 1947-1974 Box Set.
(M)	(2:22)	Rhino 71063 Queen Of Soul.
(M)	(2:22)	Rhino 71429 Chain Of Fools.
(M)	(2:22)	Rhino 71459 Soul Hits, Volume 1.
(M)	(2:22)	Rhino 71598 Very Best Of Vol. 1.
(S)	(2:23)	Time-Life RHD-10 Rhythm & Blues - 1967.
(S)	(2:24)	Time-Life 2CLR-05 Classic Rock - 1967.
(S)	(2:25)	Epic 66329 O.S.T. Forrest Gump.
(S)	(2:25)	Ripete 2183-RE Ocean Drive Volume 1.
(S)	(2:24)	JCI 3126 1965 - Only Rock 'N Roll - 1969.
(S)	(2:25)	MCA 11329 Soul Train 25th Anniversary Box Set.
(M)	(2:17)	Tommy Boy 1136 ESPN Presents Jock Rock Vol. 2. (all songs on this cd are segued together with crowd sound effects added)

(M)	(2:22)	Rhino 72275 More Stadium Rock.
(S)	(2:24)	Nick At Nite/550 Music 67690 I Am Woman.
(S)	(2:23)	Time-Life R838-02 Solid Gold Soul - 1967.
(M)	(2:22)	Flashback 72712 Arena Rock.
(M)	(2:23)	Flashback 72657 '60s Soul: Try A Little Tenderness.
(M)	(2:23)	Flashback 72091 '60s Soul Hits Box Set.
(M)	(2:22)	Flashback 72660 Respect And Other Hits.
(M)	(2:22)	Flashback 72083 Kings And Queens Of Soul Box Set.
(M)	(2:21)	TVT 4010 Rhythm Revue.
(M)	(2:22)	Flashback 72897 25 Years Of R&B - 1967.
(S)	(2:59)	Universal 53116 O.S.T. Blues Brothers 2000. (rerecording)
(S)	(2:25)	Rhino 72506 Go Girl! Soul Sisters Tellin' It Like It Is. (noisy fadeout)
(M)	(2:23)	Rhino 72963 Ultimate '60s Soul Smashes.
(M)	(2:22)	Atlantic 83088 Atlantic Records: 50 Years - The Gold Anniversary Collection.

1967 BABY I LOVE YOU

(M)	(2:39)	Atlantic 81298 Atlantic Rhythm & Blues Volume 6.
(S)	(2:36)	Atlantic 81911 Golden Age Of Black Music (1960-1970).
(S)	(2:36)	Atlantic 81668 30 Greatest Hits.
(S)	(2:36)	Atlantic 8227 Aretha's Gold.
(S)	(2:36)	Atlantic 82152 O.S.T. Goodfellas.
(S)	(2:36)	Atlantic 82305 Atlantic Rhythm And Blues 1947-1974 Box Set.
(M)	(2:39)	Rhino 71063 Queen Of Soul.
(M)	(2:40)	Rhino 71274 Aretha Arrives.
(M)	(2:40)	Rhino 71429 Chain Of Fools.
(M)	(2:40)	Rhino 71460 Soul Hits, Volume 2.
(M)	(2:40)	Rhino 71598 Very Best Of Vol. 1.
(S)	(2:35)	Time-Life 2CLR-15 Classic Rock - 1967: Shakin' All Over.
(M)	(2:40)	Rhino 72576 Love Songs.
(M)	(2:40)	Flashback 72658 '60s Soul: Baby I Love You.
(M)	(2:40)	Flashback 72091 '60s Soul Hits Box Set.
(M)	(2:40)	Flashback 72660 Respect And Other Hits.
(M)	(2:40)	Flashback 72083 Kings And Queens Of Soul Box Set.

1967 A NATURAL WOMAN (YOU MAKE ME FEEL LIKE)

(S)	(2:41)	JCI 3102 Love Sixties. (LP version)
(S)	(2:41)	Atlantic 81298 Atlantic Rhythm & Blues Volume 6. (LP version)
(S)	(2:42)	Motown 6120 and 6062 O.S.T. The Big Chill. (LP version)
(S)	(2:40)	Atlantic 81668 30 Greatest Hits. (LP version)
(S)	(2:41)	Atlantic 8176 Lady Soul. (LP version)
(S)	(2:40)	Atlantic 81280 Best Of. (LP version)
(S)	(2:40)	Atlantic 8227 Aretha's Gold. (LP version)
(S)	(2:40)	Atlantic 82305 Atlantic Rhythm And Blues 1947-1974 Box Set. (LP version)
(M)	(2:43)	Rhino 71063 Queen Of Soul. (45 version)
(S)	(2:39)	Original Sound 8908 Best Love Songs Vol 3. (LP version)
(S)	(2:39)	Original Sound 9327 Best Love Songs Vol. 3 & 4. (LP version)
(S)	(2:39)	Original Sound 1236 Best Love Songs Box Set. (LP version)
(M)	(2:41)	Rhino 71598 Very Best Of Vol. 1. (LP version)
(S)	(2:41)	Time-Life 2CLR-10 Classic Rock - 1967: The Beat Goes On. (LP version)
(S)	(2:40)	Right Stuff 30577 Slow Jams: The 60's Volume 3. (LP version)
(M)	(2:43)	Rhino 71933 Lady Soul. (45 version)
(S)	(2:42)	Rhino 71933 Lady Soul. (LP version)
(S)	(2:42)	Rebound 314520369 Soul Classics - Quiet Storm/The 60's. (LP version)
(S)	(2:41)	JCI 3164 Eighteen Soulful Ballads. (LP version)
(M)	(2:43)	Rhino 72619 Smooth Grooves: The '60s Volume 2 Mid '60s. (45 version)
(S)	(2:41)	Rhino 72580 Soul Serenade - Intimate R&B. (LP version)
(M)	(2:44)	Rhino 72576 Love Songs. (45 version)

(S)	(2:43)	Time-Life R834-06 Body Talk - Only You. *(LP version)*	
(S)	(2:41)	Flashback 72661 A Natural Woman And Other Hits. *(LP version)*	
(S)	(2:41)	Flashback 72084 Soul Legends Box Set. *(LP version)*	
(M)	(2:44)	Time-Life R857-22 The Heart Of Rock 'n' Roll 1967-1969. *(45 version)*	

1968 CHAIN OF FOOLS

(M)	(2:45)	Warner Special Products 27602 20 Party Classics. *(LP version)*
(M)	(2:44)	Atlantic 81298 Atlantic Rhythm & Blues Volume 6. *(LP version)*
(S)	(2:44)	Atlantic 81911 Golden Age Of Black Music (1960-1970). *(LP version)*
(S)	(2:42)	Original Sound 8863 Oldies But Goodies Vol. 13. *(LP version)*
(S)	(2:42)	Original Sound 2223 Oldies But Goodies Volumes 2,7,9,12 and 13 Box Set. *(Volumes 2, 7 and 12 of this box set use the "Waring - fds" noise reduction process; LP version)*
(S)	(2:42)	Original Sound 2500 Oldies But Goodies Volumes 1-15 Box Set. *(most volumes in this box set use the "Waring - fds" noise reduction process; LP version)*
(S)	(2:44)	Atlantic 81668 30 Greatest Hits. *(LP version)*
(S)	(2:44)	Atlantic 8176 Lady Soul. *(LP version)*
(S)	(2:44)	Atlantic 81280 Best Of. *(LP version)*
(S)	(2:44)	Atlantic 8227 Aretha's Gold. *(LP version)*
(S)	(2:45)	Atco 91813 Classic Recordings. *(LP version)*
(S)	(2:44)	Atlantic 82305 Atlantic Rhythm And Blues 1947-1974 Box Set. *(truncated fade; LP version)*
(M)	(2:45)	Rhino 71063 Queen Of Soul. *(45 version)*
(M)	(2:45)	Rhino 71429 Chain Of Fools. *(45 version)*
(M)	(2:45)	Rhino 71461 Soul Hits, Volume 3. *(45 version)*
(M)	(2:45)	Rhino 71598 Very Best Of Vol. 1. *(45 version)*
(S)	(2:43)	Time-Life RHD-04 Rhythm & Blues - 1968. *(LP version)*
(S)	(2:43)	Time-Life 2CLR-11 Classic Rock - 1968: The Beat Goes On. *(LP version)*
(S)	(2:44)	Rhino 71933 Lady Soul. *(LP version)*
(S)	(4:18)	Rhino 71933 Lady Soul. *(complete recording session)*
(S)	(2:44)	Revolution 24666 O.S.T. Michael. *(LP version)*
(S)	(2:43)	Time-Life R838-03 Solid Gold Soul - 1968. *(LP version)*
(M)	(2:45)	Flashback 72659 '60s Soul: When A Man Loves A Woman. *(45 version)*
(M)	(2:45)	Flashback 72091 '60s Soul Hits Box Set. *(45 version)*
(M)	(2:45)	Flashback 72660 Respect And Other Hits. *(45 version)*
(M)	(2:45)	Flashback 72083 Kings And Queens Of Soul Box Set. *(45 version)*
(S)	(2:45)	Rhino 72874 Let's Dance! The Best Of Ballroom: Swing, Lindy, Jitterbug And Jive. *(LP version)*
(M)	(2:45)	Flashback 72898 25 Years Of R&B - 1968. *(45 version)*
(M)	(2:45)	Rhino 72962 Ultimate '60s Soul Sensations. *(45 version)*

1968 (SWEET SWEET BABY) SINCE YOU'VE BEEN GONE

(S)	(2:22)	Atlantic 81911 Golden Age Of Black Music (1960-1970).
(S)	(2:22)	Atlantic 81668 30 Greatest Hits.
(S)	(2:21)	Atlantic 8176 Lady Soul.
(S)	(2:22)	Atlantic 8227 Aretha's Gold.
(S)	(2:22)	Atlantic 82305 Atlantic Rhythm And Blues 1947-1974 Box Set.
(S)	(2:22)	Rhino 71063 Queen Of Soul.
(S)	(2:22)	Rhino 71548 Let There Be Drums Volume 2: The 60's.
(S)	(2:22)	Rhino 71598 Very Best Of Vol. 1.
(S)	(2:21)	Time-Life RHD-04 Rhythm & Blues - 1968.
(S)	(2:20)	Time-Life 2CLR-04 Classic Rock - 1968.
(S)	(2:22)	Rhino 71933 Lady Soul.
(M)	(2:23)	Rhino 71933 Lady Soul. *(dropout at :01; 45 mix)*

(S)	(2:21)	JCI 3161 18 Soul Hits From The 60's.
(S)	(2:21)	Time-Life R838-03 Solid Gold Soul - 1968.
(M)	(2:23)	Rhino 72815 Beg, Scream & Shout! The Big Ol' Box Of '60s Soul. *(dropout at :01; 45 mix)*

1968 THINK

(S)	(2:15)	Atlantic 81298 Atlantic Rhythm & Blues Volume 6.
(S)	(2:16)	Atlantic 81911 Golden Age Of Black Music (1960-1970).
(S)	(2:16)	JCI 3100 Dance Sixties.
(S)	(2:15)	Atlantic 81668 30 Greatest Hits.
(S)	(2:16)	Atlantic 81280 Best Of.
(S)	(2:16)	Atlantic 8227 Aretha's Gold.
(S)	(2:16)	Atlantic 82305 Atlantic Rhythm And Blues 1947-1974 Box Set.
(S)	(2:15)	Rhino 71063 Queen Of Soul.
(S)	(2:15)	Rhino 71273 Aretha Now.
(S)	(2:15)	Rhino 71461 Soul Hits, Volume 3.
(S)	(2:15)	Right Stuff 28373 Movin' On Up.
(S)	(2:16)	Rhino 71598 Very Best Of Vol. 1.
(S)	(2:13)	Time-Life 2CLR-04 Classic Rock - 1968.
(S)	(2:15)	Hollywood 62032 O.S.T. Operation Dumbo Drop.
(S)	(2:15)	Work 67814 O.S.T. First Wives Club.
(S)	(2:13)	JCI 3190 1965 - Only Dance - 1969.
(S)	(2:15)	Flashback 72659 '60s Soul: When A Man Loves A Woman.
(S)	(2:15)	Flashback 72091 '60s Soul Hits Box Set.
(S)	(2:14)	TVT 4010 Rhythm Revue.
(S)	(2:16)	Rhino 72874 Let's Dance! The Best Of Ballroom: Swing, Lindy, Jitterbug And Jive.
(S)	(2:15)	Flashback 72898 25 Years Of R&B - 1968.

1968 THE HOUSE THAT JACK BUILT

(S)	(2:17)	Atlantic 81668 30 Greatest Hits.
(S)	(2:17)	Atlantic 8227 Aretha's Gold.
(M)	(2:18)	Rhino 71063 Queen Of Soul.
(M)	(2:19)	Rhino 71598 Very Best Of Vol. 1.
(S)	(2:16)	Time-Life 2CLR-19 Classic Rock - 1968: Shakin' All Over.
(M)	(2:18)	Flashback 72661 A Natural Woman And Other Hits.
(M)	(2:18)	Flashback 72084 Soul Legends Box Set.

1968 I SAY A LITTLE PRAYER

(S)	(3:30)	Atlantic 81911 Golden Age Of Black Music (1960-1970). *(LP version)*
(S)	(3:30)	Atlantic 81668 30 Greatest Hits. *(LP version)*
(S)	(3:30)	Atlantic 81280 Best Of. *(LP version)*
(S)	(3:30)	Atlantic 8227 Aretha's Gold. *(LP version)*
(S)	(3:32)	Rhino 71063 Queen Of Soul. *(LP version)*
(S)	(3:32)	Rhino 71273 Aretha Now. *(LP version)*
(S)	(3:32)	Rhino 71598 Very Best Of Vol. 1. *(LP version)*
(S)	(3:32)	Rhino 72576 Love Songs. *(LP version)*
(S)	(3:32)	Flashback 72661 A Natural Woman And Other Hits. *(LP version)*
(S)	(3:32)	Flashback 72084 Soul Legends Box Set. *(LP version)*

1968 SEE SAW

(S)	(2:40)	Atlantic 81668 30 Greatest Hits.
(S)	(2:40)	Atlantic 8227 Aretha's Gold.
(S)	(2:42)	Rhino 71063 Queen Of Soul.
(S)	(2:42)	Rhino 71273 Aretha Now.
(S)	(2:42)	Rhino 71598 Very Best Of Vol. 1.

1969 THE WEIGHT

(S)	(2:55)	Atlantic 81668 30 Greatest Hits.
(M)	(2:51)	Rhino 71063 Queen Of Soul.
(M)	(2:51)	Rhino 71227 Black On White: Great R&B Covers Of Rock Classics.
(M)	(2:51)	Rhino 71429 Chain Of Fools.
(M)	(2:51)	Rhino 71598 Very Best Of Vol. 1.
(M)	(2:51)	Flashback 72660 Respect And Other Hits.
(M)	(2:51)	Flashback 72083 Kings And Queens Of Soul Box Set.

1969 I CAN'T SEE MYSELF LEAVING YOU

(S)	(2:59)	Rhino 71063 Queen Of Soul.

1969 SHARE YOUR LOVE WITH ME

(S)	(3:17)	Atlantic 81668 30 Greatest Hits.
(S)	(3:17)	Rhino 71063 Queen Of Soul.
(S)	(3:18)	Rhino 71598 Very Best Of Vol. 1.

ARETHA FRANKLIN *(Continued)*

(S) (3:17) Rhino 71524 This Girl's In Love With You.
(S) (3:14) Time-Life RHD-13 Rhythm & Blues - 1969.
(S) (3:19) Rhino 72620 Smooth Grooves: The '60s Volume 3 Late '60s.
(S) (3:14) Time-Life R838-04 Solid Gold Soul - 1969.
(S) (3:17) Flashback 72899 25 Years Of Soul - 1969.

1969 ELEANOR RIGBY

(S) (2:32) Atlantic 81668 30 Greatest Hits.
(S) (2:34) Rhino 71063 Queen Of Soul.
(S) (2:34) Rhino 71598 Very Best Of Vol. 1.
(S) (2:34) Rhino 71524 This Girl's In Love With You.
(S) (2:34) Flashback 72661 A Natural Woman And Other Hits.
(S) (2:34) Flashback 72084 Soul Legends Box Set.

1970 CALL ME

(S) (3:52) Atlantic 81668 30 Greatest Hits. *(LP version)*
(S) (3:51) Atlantic 82305 Atlantic Rhythm And Blues 1947-1974 Box Set. *(LP version)*
(S) (3:53) Rhino 71063 Queen Of Soul. *(LP version)*
(S) (3:54) Rhino 71598 Very Best Of Vol. 1. *(LP version)*
(S) (3:53) Rhino 71524 This Girl's In Love With You. *(LP version)*
(M) (3:15) Rhino 72112 Billboard Hot Soul Hits - 1970. *(45 version)*
(S) (3:54) Rhino 72576 Love Songs. *(LP version)*
(S) (3:54) Flashback 72900 25 Years Of Soul - 1970. *(LP version)*

1970 SPIRIT IN THE DARK

(S) (3:59) Atlantic 81668 30 Greatest Hits. *(LP version)*
(S) (3:59) Rhino 71063 Queen Of Soul. *(LP version)*
(S) (4:00) Rhino 71599 Very Best Of Vol. 2. *(LP version)*
(S) (4:00) Rhino 71525 Spirit In The Dark. *(LP version)*
(S) (3:59) Flashback 72661 A Natural Woman And Other Hits. *(LP version)*
(S) (3:59) Flashback 72084 Soul Legends Box Set. *(LP version)*

1970 DON'T PLAY THAT SONG

(S) (2:57) Atlantic 81299 Atlantic Rhythm & Blues Volume 7.
(S) (2:57) Atlantic 81912 Golden Age Of Black Music (1970-1975).
(S) (2:56) Atlantic 81668 30 Greatest Hits.
(S) (2:56) Atlantic 82305 Atlantic Rhythm And Blues 1947-1974 Box Set.
(S) (2:57) Rhino 71063 Queen Of Soul.
(S) (2:58) Rhino 71599 Very Best Of Vol. 2.
(S) (2:58) Rhino 71525 Spirit In The Dark.
(S) (2:54) Time-Life RHD-18 Rhythm & Blues - 1970.
(S) (2:56) Time-Life SOD-11 Sounds Of The Seventies - 1970: Take Two.
(S) (2:54) Time-Life R838-05 Solid Gold Soul - 1970.
(S) (2:58) Flashback 72900 25 Years Of Soul - 1970.

1970 BORDER SONG (HOLY MOSES)

(S) (3:18) Rhino 71063 Queen Of Soul.
(S) (3:19) Rhino 71599 Very Best Of Vol. 2.

1971 YOU'RE ALL I NEED TO GET BY

(S) (3:33) Atlantic 81668 30 Greatest Hits.
(S) (3:33) Rhino 71063 Queen Of Soul.
(S) (3:33) Rhino 71599 Very Best Of Vol. 2.
(S) (3:34) Angel 56580 Men Are From Mars, Women Are From Venus - Songs For Loving Couples.

1971 BRIDGE OVER TROUBLED WATER

(S) (5:27) Atlantic 81668 30 Greatest Hits. *(LP version)*
(S) (5:30) Rhino 71063 Queen Of Soul. *(LP version)*
(S) (5:30) Rhino 71599 Very Best Of Vol. 2. *(LP version)*
(S) (5:27) Time-Life R921-38 Get Together. *(LP version)*
(S) (5:30) Rhino 72113 Billboard Hot Soul Hits - 1971. *(LP version)*
(S) (5:30) Flashback 72661 A Natural Woman And Other Hits. *(LP version)*
(S) (5:30) Flashback 72084 Soul Legends Box Set. *(LP version)*

1971 SPANISH HARLEM

(S) (3:26) Rhino 70659 Billboard's Top R&B Hits Of 1971.
(S) (3:29) Atlantic 81668 30 Greatest Hits.
(S) (3:29) Atlantic 81280 Best Of.
(S) (3:28) Rhino 71063 Queen Of Soul.
(S) (3:30) Rhino 71599 Very Best Of Vol. 2.

(S) (3:26) Time-Life RHD-09 Rhythm & Blues - 1971.
(S) (3:26) Time-Life SUD-10 Superhits - 1971.
(S) (3:26) Time-Life AM1-06 AM Gold - 1971.
(S) (3:26) Time-Life R838-06 Solid Gold Soul - 1971.

1971 ROCK STEADY

(S) (3:10) Atlantic 81299 Atlantic Rhythm & Blues Volume 7.
(S) (3:11) Atlantic 81668 30 Greatest Hits.
(S) (3:11) Atlantic 81280 Best Of.
(S) (3:10) Atlantic 82305 Atlantic Rhythm And Blues 1947-1974 Box Set.
(S) (3:11) Rhino 71063 Queen Of Soul.
(S) (3:11) Rhino 71599 Very Best Of Vol. 2.
(S) (3:10) JCI 3306 Dance Seventies.
(S) (3:11) Rhino 71549 Let There Be Drums Vol. 3: The 70's.
(S) (3:09) Razor & Tie 22045 Those Funky 70's.
(S) (3:11) Rhino 71527 Young, Gifted And Black.
(S) (3:10) JCI 3168 #1 Radio Hits 1970 - Only Rock 'n Roll - 1974.
(S) (3:11) Flashback 72661 A Natural Woman And Other Hits.
(S) (3:11) Flashback 72084 Soul Legends Box Set.
(S) (3:11) Rhino 72964 Ultimate '70s R&B Smashes!

1972 DAY DREAMING

(S) (3:57) Atlantic 81912 Golden Age Of Black Music (1970-1975). *(LP version)*
(S) (3:57) Atlantic 81668 30 Greatest Hits. *(LP version)*
(S) (3:59) Atlantic 82305 Atlantic Rhythm And Blues 1947-1974 Box Set. *(LP version)*
(S) (3:57) Rhino 71063 Queen Of Soul. *(LP version)*
(S) (3:57) Rhino 71599 Very Best Of Vol. 2. *(LP version)*
(S) (3:57) Time-Life RHD-20 Rhythm & Blues - 1972. *(LP version)*
(S) (3:58) Rhino 71527 Young, Gifted And Black. *(LP version)*
(S) (2:43) Rhino 72114 Billboard Hot Soul Hits - 1972. *(45 version)*
(S) (3:57) Rhino 72576 Love Songs. *(LP version)*
(S) (3:57) Time-Life R838-07 Solid Gold Soul - 1972. *(LP version)*
(S) (3:57) Time-Life R834-10 Body Talk - From The Heart. *(LP version)*

1972 ALL THE KING'S HORSES

(S) (3:51) Rhino 71063 Queen Of Soul.
(S) (3:52) Rhino 71599 Very Best Of Vol. 2.
(S) (3:52) Rhino 71527 Young, Gifted And Black.

1973 MASTER OF EYES (THE DEEPNESS OF YOUR EYES)

(S) (3:23) Rhino 71063 Queen Of Soul.
(S) (3:23) Rhino 71599 Very Best Of Vol. 2.
(S) (3:23) Rhino 71853 Hey Hey Now (The Other Side Of The Sky).

1973 ANGEL

(S) (4:25) Atlantic 81668 30 Greatest Hits. *(LP version)*
(S) (4:26) Rhino 71063 Queen Of Soul. *(LP version)*
(S) (3:32) Rhino 71599 Very Best Of Vol. 2. *(45 version)*
(S) (4:26) Rhino 71853 Hey Hey Now (The Other Side Of The Sky). *(LP version)*
(S) (3:32) Rhino 72115 Billboard Hot Soul Hits - 1973. *(45 version)*
(S) (3:31) Time-Life R838-08 Solid Gold Soul - 1973. *(45 version)*
(S) (4:26) Time-Life R834-19 Body Talk - Always And Forever. *(LP version)*

1974 UNTIL YOU COME BACK TO ME (THAT'S WHAT I'M GONNA DO)

(S) (3:24) Atlantic 81912 Golden Age Of Black Music (1970-1975).
(S) (3:24) Atlantic 81668 30 Greatest Hits.
(S) (3:24) Atlantic 81280 Best Of.
(S) (3:24) Rhino 71063 Queen Of Soul.
(S) (3:23) Rhino 71599 Very Best Of Vol. 2.
(S) (3:22) Time-Life SUD-13 Superhits - 1973.
(S) (3:24) Time-Life SOD-15 Sounds Of The Seventies - 1974: Take Two.
(S) (3:25) Rhino 71854 Let Me In Your Life.
(S) (3:23) JCI 3145 1970 - Only Love - 1974.

(S)	(3:22)	Time-Life AM1-03 AM Gold - 1973.	
(S)	(3:24)	Time-Life R838-09 Solid Gold Soul - 1974.	
(S)	(3:23)	Time-Life R834-03 Body Talk - Moonlit Nights.	
(S)	(3:23)	Rhino 72943 VH1 8-Track Flashback: Classic '70s Soul.	

1974 I'M IN LOVE

(S)	(2:47)	Atlantic 81668 30 Greatest Hits.
(S)	(2:48)	Rhino 71063 Queen Of Soul.
(S)	(2:46)	Rhino 71599 Very Best Of Vol. 2.
(S)	(2:48)	Rhino 71854 Let Me In Your Life.
(S)	(2:46)	Rhino 72116 Billboard Hot Soul Hits - 1974.
(S)	(2:48)	Rhino 72576 Love Songs.

1976 SOMETHING HE CAN FEEL

(S)	(6:17)	Rhino 71063 Queen Of Soul. *(LP version)*
(S)	(6:18)	Rhino 71148 Sparkle. *(LP version)*
(S)	(3:25)	Rhino 71599 Very Best Of Vol. 2. *(45 version)*
(S)	(3:26)	Rhino 71618 Soul Train Hall Of Fame/20th Anniversary. *(45 version)*
(S)	(6:17)	Rhino 71861 Smooth Grooves Volume 3. *(LP version)*
(S)	(6:19)	Rhino 72576 Love Songs. *(LP version)*
(S)	(6:17)	Time-Life R834-14 Body Talk - Love And Tenderness. *(LP version)*
(S)	(3:26)	Hip-O 40107 Super Bad On Celluloid: Music From '70s Black Cinema. *(45 version)*

1982 JUMP TO IT

(S)	(6:38)	Arista 8416 Perfect 10 III. *(LP version)*
(S)	(6:39)	Arista 8222 and 19013 Jump To It. *(LP version)*
(S)	(4:14)	Arista 18722 Greatest Hits (1980-1994). *(45 version)*
(S)	(4:14)	Rhino 71972 Video Soul - Best Soul Of The 80's Vol. 2. *(45 version)*
(S)	(4:14)	Rhino 72137 Billboard Hot R&B Hits 1982. *(45 version)*
(S)	(4:14)	Rebound 314520431 Soul Classics - Best Of The 80's. *(45 version)*
(S)	(4:15)	JCI 3176 1980 - Only Soul - 1984. *(45 version)*

1985 FREEWAY OF LOVE
(dj copies of this 45 ran (4:08) even though the label stated (3:58) and the flip side ran (5:49); commercial copies were all (5:49))

(S)	(5:48)	MCA Special Products 20767 Classic R&B Oldies From The 80's Volume 3.
(S)	(5:50)	Sandstone 33046 and 5012 Rock The First Volume Six.
(S)	(4:09)	JCI 3128 1985 - Only Rock 'N Roll - 1989. *(this is the dj 45 edit)*
(S)	(5:50)	Arista 8286 Who's Zoomin' Who.
(S)	(5:53)	Arista 18722 Greatest Hits (1980-1994).
(S)	(5:51)	Priority 53731 80's Greatest Rock Hits Volume 10 - Dance All Night.
(S)	(5:48)	Time-Life R988-02 Sounds Of The Eighties: 1985.
(S)	(4:07)	Rhino 72159 Black Entertainment Television - 15th Anniversary. *(this is the dj 45 edit)*
(S)	(5:50)	Rhino 72140 Billboard Hot R&B Hits 1985.
(S)	(5:49)	Hip-O 40015 Soulful Ladies Of The 80's.
(S)	(4:07)	K-Tel 3673 The 80's - Funky Love. *(this is the dj 45 edit)*
(S)	(5:50)	Scotti Bros. 75504 Club Ladies Night.
(S)	(4:08)	Madacy Entertainment 6804 More Sun Splashin'. *(this is the dj 45 edit)*
(S)	(3:50)	Cold Front 6330 Club Mix: The 80s. *(all selections on this cd are segued together)*

1985 WHO'S ZOOMIN' WHO
(dj copies of this 45 ran (3:59); commercial copies were all (4:42))

(S)	(4:42)	Arista 8416 Perfect 10 III.
(S)	(4:42)	Arista 8286 Who's Zoomin' Who.
(S)	(4:43)	Arista 18722 Greatest Hits (1980-1994).
(S)	(4:42)	Madacy Entertainment 1985 Rock On 1985.
(S)	(4:36)	JCI 3177 1985 - Only Soul - 1989.
(S)	(4:42)	Time-Life R988-15 Sounds Of The Eighties: The Mid 80's.

released as by THE EURYTHMICS and ARETHA FRANKLIN:
1985 SISTERS ARE DOIN' IT FOR THEMSELVES

(S)	(5:55)	Arista 8680 Eurythmics - Greatest Hits. *(LP version)*

(S)	(5:55)	RCA 5429 Eurythmics - Be Yourself Tonight. *(LP version)*
(S)	(5:52)	Arista 8286 Aretha Franklin - Who's Zoomin' Who. *(LP version)*
(S)	(5:52)	Work 67814 O.S.T. First Wives Club. *(LP version)*

released as by ARETHA FRANKLIN:
1986 ANOTHER NIGHT

(S)	(4:28)	Arista 18722 Greatest Hits (1980-1994).
(S)	(4:29)	Arista 8286 Aretha Franklin - Who's Zoomin' Who.

1986 JUMPIN' JACK FLASH
(dj copies of this 45 ran (4:16) and (4:56); commercial copies ran (4:25) and (4:56))

(S)	(5:01)	Arista 8442 Aretha.

1987 JIMMY LEE
(dj copies of this 45 ran (4:10) and (5:47); commercial copies were all (5:47))

(S)	(5:44)	Arista 8442 Aretha.
(S)	(5:44)	Arista 18722 Greatest Hits (1980-1994).

released as by ARETHA FRANKLIN and GEORGE MICHAEL:
1987 I KNEW YOU WERE WAITING (FOR ME)

(S)	(3:58)	Rhino 71642 Billboard Top Hits - 1987.
(S)	(3:59)	Arista 8442 Aretha.
(S)	(3:59)	Arista 18722 Aretha Franklin - Greatest Hits (1980-1994).
(S)	(3:59)	Time-Life R103-18 Great Love Songs Of The '70s & '80s.
(S)	(3:59)	Time-Life R988-19 Sounds Of The Eighties: The Late '80s.
(S)	(3:59)	Time-Life R834-02 Body Talk - Just For You.
(S)	(3:57)	K-Tel 3868 Hot Ladies Of Pop.

released as by ARETHA FRANKLIN and ELTON JOHN:
1989 THROUGH THE STORM

(S)	(4:20)	Arista 8572 Aretha Franklin - Through The Storm.
(S)	(4:20)	DCC Compact Classics 104 Duets - A Man & A Woman.

released as by ARETHA FRANKLIN and WHITNEY HOUSTON:
1989 IT ISN'T, IT WASN'T, IT AIN'T NEVER GONNA BE

(S)	(5:36)	Arista 8572 Aretha Franklin - Through The Storm.

released as by ARETHA FRANKLIN:
1994 WILLING TO FORGIVE

(S)	(4:11)	Arista 18722 Greatest Hits (1980-1994).

FREAK NASTY
1997 DA' DIP

(S)	(3:56)	Hard Hood/Power/Triad 2111 Controversee...That's Life...And That's The Way It Is.
(S)	(3:34)	Tommy Boy 1214 ESPN Presents Jock Jams Volume 3. *(all selections on this cd are segued together)*
(S)	(3:50)	Cold Front 6254 Club Mix '98. *(all selections on this cd are segued together)*
(S)	(3:39)	Polygram TV 314553847 Pure Dance 1998. *(all songs on this cd are segued together)*
(S)	(3:47)	Robbins Entertainment 75008 Dance Party (Like It's 1998). *(remix; all songs on this cd are segued together)*
(S)	(3:56)	Cold Front 6299 Da Booty - 17 Smash Bass Hits.
(S)	(3:56)	Cold Front 6250 Crucial Rap.

STAN FREBERG
1955 THE YELLOW ROSE OF TEXAS

(M)	(3:23)	Capitol 91627 Capitol Collector's Series.
(M)	(3:23)	Curb 77615 Greatest Hits.

1957 BANANA BOAT (DAY-O)

(M)	(3:27)	Capitol 91627 Capitol Collector's Series.
(M)	(3:27)	Curb 77615 Greatest Hits.

1957 WUN'ERFUL WUN'ERFUL! (PARTS 1 & 2)

(M)	(3:39)	Capitol 91627 Capitol Collector's Series. *(Part 1)*
(M)	(3:25)	Capitol 91627 Capitol Collector's Series. *(Part 2)*
(M)	(7:04)	Curb 77615 Greatest Hits.

1959 GREEN CHRITMA

(M)	(6:52)	Rhino 75755 Dr. Demento Presents The Greatest Christmas Novelty CD.
(M)	(6:50)	Capitol 91627 Capitol Collector's Series.
(M)	(6:52)	Priority 9306 Christmas Comedy Classics.

JOHN FRED & HIS PLAYBOY BAND
1968 JUDY IN DISGUISE (WITH GLASSES)
    (S)   (2:55)   Rhino 70629 Billboard's Top Rock & Roll Hits Of 1968. *(mastered from vinyl; very poor stereo separation)*

    (S)   (2:55)   Rhino 72006 Billboard's Top R&B Hits 1965-1969 Box Set. *(mastered from vinyl; very poor stereo separation)*

    (S)   (2:55)   Novus 3077 O.S.T. Drugstore Cowboy. *(mastered from vinyl; very poor stereo separation)*

    (S)   (2:54)   Paula 9000 History Of. *(very poor stereo separation)*

    (S)   (2:53)   Time-Life 2CLR-19 Classic Rock - 1968: Shakin' All Over. *(very poor stereo separation)*

    (S)   (2:51)   Collectables 2504 WCBS-FM History Of Rock - The 60's Part 4. *(very poor stereo separation)*

    (S)   (2:51)   Collectables 4504 History Of Rock/The 60s Part Four. *(very poor stereo separation)*

    (S)   (2:54)   MCA Special Products 20900 Rock Around The Oldies #3. *(very poor stereo separation)*

    (S)   (2:52)   LaserLight 12313 and 15936 The Wonder Years - Summer Time. *(very poor stereo separation)*

    (S)   (2:54)   Time-Life 2CLR-31 Classic Rock - Totally Fantastic '60s. *(very poor stereo separation)*

    (S)   (2:55)   Varese Sarabande 5846 On The Radio Volume One. *(very poor stereo separation)*

    (S)   (2:54)   Jewel 5057 Rockin' 50's & 60's. *(very poor stereo separation; mastered from vinyl; track lineup on the cd jacket is incorrect)*

    (S)   (2:54)   Simitar 55572 The Number One's: Hot In The '60s. *(very poor stereo separation)*

FREDDIE and THE DREAMERS
1965 I'M TELLING YOU NOW
    (S)   (2:06)   Rhino 70319 History Of British Rock Volume 1.

    (S)   (2:06)   Rhino 72022 History Of British Rock Box Set.

    (S)   (2:06)   Rhino 72008 History Of British Rock Volumes 1-4 Box Set.

    (S)   (2:05)   EMI 96979 Best Of.

    (S)   (2:04)   EMI 81128 Rock Is Dead But It Won't Lie Down.

    (S)   (2:06)   Time-Life 2CLR-14 Classic Rock - 1965: Shakin' All Over.

    (S)   (2:07)   Time-Life R962-07 History Of Rock 'N' Roll: The British Invasion 1964-1966.

    (S)   (2:07)   Rhino 71935 Billboard Top Pop Hits, 1965.

1965 DO THE FREDDIE
    (S)   (2:03)   Rhino 70321 History Of British Rock Volume 3.

    (S)   (2:03)   Rhino 72022 History Of British Rock Box Set.

    (S)   (2:03)   Rhino 72008 History Of British Rock Volumes 1-4 Box Set.

    (S)   (2:04)   EMI 96979 Best Of.

1965 YOU WERE MADE FOR ME
    (S)   (2:08)   Rhino 70320 History Of British Rock Volume 2. *(LP version)*

    (S)   (2:08)   Rhino 72022 History Of British Rock Box Set. *(LP version)*

    (S)   (2:08)   Rhino 72008 History Of British Rock Volumes 1-4 Box Set. *(LP version)*

    (S)   (2:17)   EMI 96979 Best Of. *(45 version)*

FREE
1970 ALL RIGHT NOW
(dj copies of this 45 were issued with times of either (4:13), (3:32) or (3:12); commercial copies were all (4:13); reissue copies are (3:45))
    (S)   (4:12)   Island 90684 and 842901 The Island Story.

    (S)   (5:30)   Priority 8668 Rough And Ready/70's Greatest Rock Hits Volume 7. *(LP version)*

    (S)   (5:30)   A&M 3663 Best Of. *(LP version)*

    (S)   (5:29)   A&M 3126 Fire And Water. *(LP version)*

    (S)   (5:31)   Polydor 314515913 Classic Rock Box. *(LP version)*

    (S)   (5:31)   A&M 314518456 Molten Gold: The Anthology. *(LP version)*

    (S)   (5:29)   Razor & Tie 22502 Those Rocking 70's. *(LP version)*

    (S)   (3:48)   Time-Life SOD-01 Sounds Of The Seventies - 1970.

    (S)   (3:45)   Time-Life OPCD-4521 Guitar Rock.

    (S)   (5:29)   K-Tel 3221 Axe Gods. *(LP version)*

    (S)   (5:29)   Right Stuff 31324 and 31327 Harley-Davidson Road Songs. *(LP version)*

    (S)   (5:29)   Rebound 314520278 Hard Rock Essentials - The 70's. *(LP version)*

    (S)   (5:30)   Time-Life R968-10 Guitar Rock Classics. *(LP version)*

    (S)   (5:31)   Varese 5635 and 5654 and 5655 and 5657 Arrow: All Rock & Roll Oldies Volume Two. *(LP version)*

    (S)   (5:31)   Varese Sarabande 5708 All Rock & Roll Hits Vol. One. *(LP version)*

    (S)   (5:28)   Columbia 67380 O.S.T. Now And Then. *(LP version)*

    (S)   (5:31)   Mercury 314535648 O.S.T. Bordello Of Blood. *(LP version)*

    (S)   (3:32)   Hip-O 40070 Rock For The Ages.

    (S)   (3:45)   Madacy Entertainment 6805 The Power Of Rock.

    (S)   (3:45)   Simitar 55762 Stud Rock - Wild Ride.

BOBBY FREEMAN
1958 DO YOU WANT TO DANCE
    (M)   (2:32)   Rhino 70644 Billboard's Top R&B Hits Of 1958.

    (M)   (2:32)   Collectables 5417 Do You Wanna Dance.

    (M)   (2:32)   MCA 8001 O.S.T. American Graffiti.

    (M)   (2:32)   Time-Life 2RNR-05 Rock 'N' Roll Era - 1958.

    (M)   (2:31)   Time-Life RHD-16 Rhythm & Blues - 1958.

    (M)   (2:33)   Flashback 72857 Grease And Other Golden Oldies.

    (M)   (2:31)   Time-Life R838-22 Solid Gold Soul 1958.

1958 BETTY LOU GOT A NEW PAIR OF SHOES
    (S)   (2:26)   Collectables 5417 Do You Wanna Dance.

    (M)   (2:22)   Time-Life 2RNR-48 Rock 'N' Roll Era - R&B Gems II.

    (M)   (2:22)   JCI 3188 1955 - Only Dance - 1959.

    (S)   (2:24)   Sony Music Special Products 22210 Fun Rock.

1964 C'MON AND SWIM
    (M)   (2:44)   Rhino 70992 Groove 'n' Grind.

    (S)   (3:04)   Collectables 5417 Do You Wanna Dance. *(Part 1 and Part 2)*

    (S)   (3:03)   Collectables 5064 History Of Rock Volume 4. *(Part 1 and Part 2)*

    (M)   (2:42)   Time-Life 2RNR-10 Rock 'N' Roll Era - 1964.

    (M)   (2:44)   Rhino 71729 '60s Rock Classics, Vol. 2.

    (M)   (2:43)   K-Tel 3331 Do You Wanna Dance.

    (M)   (2:44)   K-Tel 3008 60's Sock Hop.

    (M)   (2:44)   Flashback 72702 '60s Rock: The Beat Goes On.

    (M)   (2:44)   Flashback 72088 '60s Rock Hits Box Set.

    (S)   (3:04)   JCI 3189 1960 - Only Dance - 1964. *(Part 1 and Part 2)*

ERNIE FREEMAN
1957 RAUNCHY
    (M)   (2:14)   Rhino 70644 Billboard's Top R&B Hits Of 1958.

    (M)   (2:15)   Curb 77402 All-Time Great Instrumental Hits Volume 2.

    (M)   (2:14)   Curb 77637 All Time Greatest Hits Of Rock 'N' Roll Volume 3.

    (M)   (2:12)   Time-Life RHD-08 Rhythm & Blues - 1957.

    (M)   (2:12)   Time-Life R838-23 Solid Gold Soul 1957.

FREE MOVEMENT
1971 I'VE FOUND SOMEONE OF MY OWN
    (S)   (3:38)   Rhino 70786 Soul Hits Of The 70's Volume 6.

    (S)   (3:37)   Razor & Tie 22047 Sweet 70's Soul.

    (S)   (3:39)   Time-Life SOD-36 Sounds Of The Seventies - More AM Nuggets.

    (S)   (3:42)   Collectables 5803 Golden Classics.

ACE FREHLEY
1978 NEW YORK GROOVE
    (S)   (2:58)   Rhino 72299 Superhits Of The 70's Volume 25.

    (S)   (2:59)   Casablanca 826916 Ace Frehley.

    (S)   (2:59)   Special Music 5038 Guitar Heroes.

    (S)   (3:00)   Mercury 314532385 Ace Frehley. *(remastered edition)*

NICKI FRENCH
1995 TOTAL ECLIPSE OF THE HEART
    (S)   (3:52)   Critique 15436 Secrets.

(S) (3:42) Arista 18943 Ultimate Dance Party 1997. *(all selections on this cd are segued together)*
(S) (3:50) EMI-Capitol Music Group 54547 Hot Luv.
(S) (5:14) Cold Front 6242 Club Mix '97. *(all selections on this cd are segued together; remix)*
(S) (4:14) Rhino 72839 Disco Queens: The 90's.
(S) (3:50) Cold Front 3865 Club Mix - Women Of Dance Vol. 2.
(S) (5:16) Priority 51086 Club NRG Volume 1. *(remix)*

GLENN FREY
1982 I FOUND SOMEBODY
(S) (4:04) Elektra 60129 No Fun Aloud.
1982 THE ONE YOU LOVE
(S) (4:34) Elektra 60129 No Fun Aloud.
(S) (4:33) MCA 11227 Solo Collection.
(S) (4:33) K-Tel 6257 The Greatest Love Songs - 16 Soft Rock Hits.
1983 ALL THOSE LIES
(S) (4:43) Elektra 60129 No Fun Aloud.
1984 SEXY GIRL
(S) (3:28) MCA 31158 The Allnighter.
(S) (3:28) MCA 11227 Solo Collection.
1985 THE HEAT IS ON
(S) (3:45) MCA 6330 Soundtrack Smashes - The 80's.
(S) (3:44) MCA 6435 Soundtrack Smashes - The 80's And More.
(S) (3:45) MCA 5553 O.S.T. Beverly Hills Cop.
(S) (3:44) Rhino 71640 Billboard Top Hits - 1985.
(S) (3:44) MCA 11227 Solo Collection.
(S) (3:44) Rhino 72133 Frat Rock: The 80's.
(S) (3:44) Time-Life R988-02 Sounds Of The Eighties: 1985.
(S) (3:44) Madacy Entertainment 1985 Rock On 1985.
(S) (3:45) Hollywood 62077 Official Party Album - ABC's Monday Night Football.
(S) (3:44) JCI 3150 1985 - Only Dance - 1989.
(S) (3:44) Time-Life R988-31 Sounds Of The Eighties: Cinemax Movie Hits Of The '80s.
(S) (3:43) Madacy Entertainment 6804 More Sun Splashin'.
(S) (3:44) Priority 50974 Premiere The Movie Magazine Presents The Greatest Soundtrack Hits.
(S) (3:41) Cold Front 6255 Greatest Sports Rock And Jams Volume 2. *(all selections on this cd are segued together)*
(S) (3:45) Rhino 75200 Basketball's Greatest Hits.
1985 SMUGGLER'S BLUES
(S) (3:48) MCA 6150 Music From The Television Series Miami Vice.
(S) (3:47) Sandstone 33042 and 5008 Rock The First Volume 2.
(S) (3:49) MCA 11227 Solo Collection.
(S) (3:47) Time-Life R988-15 Sounds Of The Eighties: The Mid 80's.
1985 YOU BELONG TO THE CITY
(dj copies of this 45 ran (4:22) and (5:51); commercial copies were all (5:51))
(S) (5:49) MCA 6150 Music From The Television Series Miami Vice.
(S) (5:49) MCA 6330 Soundtrack Smashes - The 80's.
(S) (4:23) Priority 53714 80's Greatest Rock Hits Volume 1 - Passion & Power.
(S) (5:48) Sandstone 33050 and 5018 Cosmopolitan Volume 4.
(S) (5:49) DCC Compact Classics 089 Night Moves Volume 7.
(S) (5:49) MCA 11227 Solo Collection.
(S) (5:48) Time-Life R988-01 Sounds Of The Eighties: The Rockin' Eighties.
(S) (5:49) Hip-O 40005 The '80s Hit(s) Back....Again!
(S) (5:48) Time-Life R834-05 Body Talk - Sealed With A Kiss.
1988 TRUE LOVE
(S) (4:39) MCA 6239 Soul Searchin'. *(LP length)*
(S) (4:39) MCA 11227 Solo Collection. *(LP length)*
(S) (4:38) Hip-O 40000 Thinking About You - A Collection Of Modern Love Songs. *(LP length)*
(S) (4:39) Time-Life R834-12 Body Talk - By Candlelight. *(LP length)*

FRIDA
1983 I KNOW THERE'S SOMETHING GOING ON
(dj copies of this 45 ran (3:18) and (4:06); commercial copies were all (4:06))
(S) (4:03) Rhino 72771 The Big 80's. *(45 version)*
(S) (4:02) Time-Life R988-22 Sounds Of The Eighties 1980-1983. *(45 version)*
(S) (5:27) Rebound 314520493 Class Reunion '83. *(LP version)*

DEAN FRIEDMAN
1977 ARIEL
(S) (4:18) Rhino 71200 Super Hits Of The 70's Volume 20. *(LP version)*

FRIEND AND LOVER
1968 REACH OUT OF THE DARKNESS
(S) (3:05) Mercury 834216 45's On CD Volume 3.
(S) (3:07) K-Tel 666 Flower Power.
(M) (3:15) Rhino 71065 Summer Of Love Volume 1.
(S) (3:06) JCI 3114 Easy Sixties. *(sounds like it was mastered from vinyl)*
(S) (3:04) Time-Life 2CLR-19 Classic Rock - 1968: Shakin' All Over.
(S) (3:04) Time-Life SUD-14 Superhits - The Late 60's.
(S) (3:05) Time-Life R921-38 Get Together.
(S) (3:07) Polygram Special Markets 314520272 One Hit Wonders.
(S) (3:06) Eclipse Music Group 64871 Rock 'n Roll Relix 1968-1969.
(S) (3:06) Eclipse Music Group 64872 Rock 'n Roll Relix 1960-1969.
(S) (3:04) Time-Life AM1-14 AM Gold - The Late '60s.

FRIENDS OF DISTINCTION
1969 GRAZING IN THE GRASS
(S) (2:52) RCA 8474 Nipper's Greatest Hits Of The 60's Volume 1.
(S) (2:55) Rhino 70781 Soul Hits Of The 70's Volume 1.
(S) (2:55) Rhino 72028 Soul Hits Of The 70's Volumes 1-5 Box Set.
(S) (2:56) Collectables 5102 Golden Classics.
(S) (2:57) RCA 66906 Best Of.
(S) (2:54) Varese Sarabande 5802 Sunshine Days - Pop Classics Of The '60s Volume 2.
(S) (2:51) K-Tel 3901 Soul Brothers & Sisters Of The 60's.
(S) (2:54) Simitar 55532 The Number One's: The '60s.
1969 GOING IN CIRCLES
(actual 45 time is (4:25) not (4:32) as stated on the record label; actual LP time is (4:18) not (4:28) as stated on the record label)
(S) (4:13) Rhino 70781 Soul Hits Of The 70's Volume 1. *(faster than either the LP or 45)*
(S) (4:13) Rhino 72028 Soul Hits Of The 70's Volumes 1-5 Box Set. *(faster than either the LP or 45)*
(S) (4:13) Collectables 5102 Golden Classics. *(faster than either the 45 or LP)*
(S) (4:11) Time-Life RHD-13 Rhythm & Blues - 1969. *(faster than either the 45 or LP)*
(S) (4:10) Time-Life 2CLR-20 Classic Rock - 1969: Shakin' All Over. *(faster than either the 45 or LP)*
(S) (4:10) Original Sound 9307 Dedicated To You Vol. 7. *(faster than either the 45 or LP)*
(S) (4:11) Right Stuff 28371 Slow Jams: The 60's Volume Two. *(faster than either the 45 or LP)*
(S) (4:11) RCA 66812 Do You Love Me? (All-Time Best Love Songs). *(faster than either the 45 or LP)*
(S) (4:10) Priority 53131 Deep Soul Volume Two. *(faster than either the 45 or LP)*
(S) (4:14) RCA 66906 Best Of. *(faster than either the 45 or LP)*
(S) (4:10) Hip-O 40029 The Glory Of Love - '60s Sweet & Soulful Love Songs. *(faster than either the 45 or LP)*
(S) (4:13) Rhino 72620 Smooth Grooves: The '60s Volume 3 Late '60s. *(faster than either the 45 or LP)*
(S) (4:11) Time-Life R838-04 Solid Gold Soul - 1969. *(faster than either the 45 or LP)*

FRIENDS OF DISTINCTION *(Continued)*

    (S)   (4:13)   Time-Life R834-09 Body Talk - Magic Moments.
                  (faster than either the 45 or LP)

1970 LOVE OR LET ME BE LONELY
(actual 45 time is (3:11) not (3:15) as stated on the record label)

    (S)   (3:21)   RCA 8476 and 9684 Nipper's Greatest Hits Of The 70's. *(LP length)*
    (S)   (3:11)   Rhino 70782 Soul Hits Of The 70's Volume 2. *(45 length)*
    (S)   (3:11)   Rhino 72028 Soul Hits Of The 70's Volumes 1-5 Box Set. *(45 length)*
    (S)   (3:19)   Collectables 5102 Golden Classics. *(LP length)*
    (S)   (3:11)   Rhino 71205 70's Smash Hits Volume 1. *(45 length)*
    (S)   (3:18)   Time-Life SUD-16 Superhits - The Early 70's. *(LP length)*
    (S)   (3:19)   RCA 66906 Best Of. *(LP length)*
    (S)   (3:18)   Time-Life AM1-13 AM Gold - The Early '70s. *(LP length)*
    (S)   (3:11)   Flashback 72681 '70s Radio Hits Volume 1. *(45 length)*
    (S)   (3:11)   Flashback 72090 '70s Radio Hits Box Set. *(45 length)*

FRIJID PINK
1970 HOUSE OF THE RISING SUN

    (S)   (4:42)   Rebound 314520278 Hard Rock Essentials - The 70's.
    (S)   (4:42)   Time-Life R968-10 Guitar Rock Classics.
    (S)   (4:42)   Special Music 5041 Great Britons! Volume Three.

1970 SING A SONG FOR FREEDOM

FROGMEN
1961 UNDERWATER

    (M)   (2:24)   DCC Compact Classics 030 Beach Classics. *(alternate take)*
    (M)   (2:05)   Rhino 71605 Rock Instrumental Classics Volume 5: Surf.
    (M)   (2:05)   Rhino 72035 Rock Instrumental Classics Vols. 1-5 Box Set.
    (M)   (2:05)   Rhino 72418 Cowabunga! The Surf Box.

MAX FROST and THE TROOPERS
1968 SHAPE OF THINGS TO COME

    (S)   (1:54)   K-Tel 686 Battle Of The Bands Volume 4.
    (S)   (1:54)   Rhino 75754 Even More Nuggets.
    (S)   (1:54)   Time-Life R968-07 Guitar Rock 1968-1969.
    (S)   (1:54)   Varese Sarabande 5846 On The Radio Volume One.
    (S)   (1:54)   Simitar 55362 Garage Band Classics.

FUGEES
1996 FU-GEE-LA

    (S)   (4:19)   Ruffhouse/Columbia 67147 The Score.

BOBBY FULLER FOUR
1966 I FOUGHT THE LAW
(actual 45 time is (2:17) not (2:07) as stated on the record label)

    (S)   (2:19)   K-Tel 713 Battle Of The Bands. *(LP veresion)*
    (S)   (2:16)   DCC Compact Classics 029 Toga Rock. *(LP version)*
    (S)   (2:16)   Original Sound 8859 Oldies But Goodies Vol. 9. *(this compact disc uses the "Waring - fds" noise reduction process; LP version)*
    (S)   (2:15)   Original Sound 8859r Oldies But Goodies Vol. 9. *(remastered edition; LP version)*
    (S)   (2:15)   Original Sound 2223 Oldies But Goodies Volumes 2,7,9,12 and 13 Box Set. *(Volumes 2, 7 and 12 of this box set use the "Waring - fds" noise reduction process; LP version)*
    (S)   (2:15)   Original Sound 2500 Oldies But Goodies Volumes 1-15 Box Set. *(most volumes in this box set use the "Waring - fds" noise reduction process; LP version)*
    (S)   (2:15)   Original Sound CDGO-9 Golden Oldies Volume 9. *(LP version)*

    (M)   (2:16)   Rhino 75772 Son Of Frat Rock. *(LP version)*
    (E)   (2:12)   Warner Special Products 27607 Highs Of The 60's. *(45 version but faster than the 45 or LP)*
    (S)   (2:16)   Rhino 70174 Best Of. *(LP version)*
    (S)   (2:16)   Del Fi 70174 Best Of. *(LP version)*
    (S)   (2:16)   Time-Life 2CLR-02 Classic Rock - 1966. *(LP version)*
    (S)   (2:16)   Time-Life R962-04 History Of Rock 'N' Roll: California Pop 1963-1967. *(LP version)*
    (S)   (2:16)   Time-Life OPCD-4521 Guitar Rock. *(LP version)*
    (S)   (2:16)   Rhino 71729 '60s Rock Classics, Vol. 2. *(LP version)*
    (S)   (2:17)   Risky Business 66393 Jailhouse Rock. *(LP version)*
    (S)   (2:16)   Time-Life R968-09 Guitar Rock 1966-1967. *(LP version)*
    (S)   (2:16)   Del Fi 9010 The Bobby Fuller Four. *(LP version)*
    (M)   (2:12)   Del-Fi 2902 Shakedown! The Texas Tapes Revisited. *(alternate take)*
    (M)   (2:17)   Del-Fi 2902 Shakedown! The Texas Tapes Revisited. *(alternate take)*
    (S)   (2:16)   Flashback 72702 '60s Rock: The Beat Goes On. *(LP version)*
    (S)   (2:16)   Flashback 72088 '60s Rock Hits Box Set. *(LP version)*
    (S)   (2:17)   Right Stuff 53319 Hot Rod Rock Volume 4: Hot Rod Rebels. *(LP version)*
    (S)   (2:16)   Mustang 3903 Never To Be Forgotten. *(LP version)*
    (M)   (2:16)   Mustang 3903 Never To Be Forgotten. *(45 version)*
    (S)   (2:16)   Thump 6020 Easyriders Volume 2. *(LP version)*

1966 LOVE'S MADE A FOOL OF YOU

    (S)   (1:58)   Time-Life 2CLR-26 Classic Rock - Rock Renaissance III.
    (S)   (1:59)   Rhino 70174 Best Of.
    (S)   (1:59)   Del Fi 70174 Best Of.
    (S)   (1:59)   Del Fi 9010 The Bobby Fuller Four.
    (S)   (1:58)   Mustang 3903 Never To Be Forgotten.

FUNKADELIC
1978 ONE NATION UNDER A GROOVE (PART 1)

    (S)   (7:27)   Priority 53872 One Nation Under A Groove. *(LP version)*
    (S)   (4:13)   Time-Life SOD-27 Sounds Of The Seventies - Dance Fever. *(45 version)*
    (S)   (11:25)   Rhino 71753 and 72830 Phat Trax: The Best Of Old School Volume 2. *(12" single version)*
    (S)   (7:26)   Chronicles 314553403 Cosmic Funk. *(LP version)*
    (S)   (4:13)   Time-Life R838-17 Solid Gold Soul 1978. *(45 version)*

RICHIE FURAY
1979 I STILL HAVE DREAMS

    (S)   (3:23)   Rhino 71891 Radio Daze: Pop Hits Of The 80's Volume Two.

FU-SCHNICKENS with SHAQUILLE O'NEAL
1993 WHAT'S UP DOC? (CAN WE ROCK)

    (S)   (3:52)   Jive 41529 Shaquille O'Neal - Shaq Diesel.
    (S)   (3:56)   Jive 41519 Fu-Schnickens - Nervous Breakdown.
    (S)   (3:51)   Jive 41582 Fu-Schnickens - Greatest Hits.
    (S)   (3:52)   Jive 41599 Shaquille O'Neal - Best Of.

FUZZ
1971 I LOVE YOU FOR ALL SEASONS

    (S)   (3:06)   Rhino 70784 Soul Hits Of The 70's Volume 4.
    (S)   (3:06)   Rhino 72028 Soul Hits Of The 70's Volumes 1-5 Box Set.
    (S)   (3:05)   Original Sound 8911 Art Laboe's Dedicated To You Vol. 2.
    (S)   (3:05)   Original Sound 4001 Art Laboe's 60 Killer Oldies.

PETER GABRIEL
1983 SHOCK THE MONKEY
> (S) (3:55)   Geffen 24326 Shaking The Tree - Sixteen Golden Greats. *(45 version)*
> (S) (5:23)   Geffen 2011 Security. *(LP version)*

1986 SLEDGEHAMMER
(dj copies of this 45 ran (4:02);commercial copies were all (4:58); LP length is (5:08))
> (S) (4:53)   Geffen 24326 Shaking The Tree - Sixteen Golden Greats.
> (S) (5:08)   Geffen 24088 So.
> (S) (5:07)   Time-Life R988-28 Sounds Of The Eighties: The Rolling Stone Collection 1986-1987.

1986 IN YOUR EYES
(dj copies of this 45 ran (4:36) and (6:15); commercial copies were all (6:15))
> (S) (5:23)   Geffen 24088 So. *(LP version)*
> (S) (5:21)   WTG 45140 O.S.T. Say Anything. *(LP version)*

1987 BIG TIME
(dj copies of this 45 ran (3:12) and (4:24); commercial copies were all (4:24))
> (S) (4:24)   Geffen 24326 Shaking The Tree - Sixteen Golden Greats.
> (S) (4:25)   Geffen 24088 So.

1993 STEAM
> (S) (6:00)   Geffen 24473 Us.

GABRIELLE
1994 DREAMS
> (S) (3:42)   Go! Discs/London 828443 Gabrielle.

GALLERY
1972 NICE TO BE WITH YOU
> (S) (2:36)   Rhino 70928 Super Hits Of The 70's Volume 8.
> (S) (2:37)   Rhino 71210 70's Smash Hits Volume 6.
> (S) (2:33)   Razor & Tie 22505 More Fabulous 70's Volume 2.
> (S) (2:36)   Time-Life SUD-11 Superhits - 1972.
> (S) (2:36)   Time-Life SOD-32 Sounds Of The Seventies - AM Pop Classics.
> (S) (2:36)   Time-Life AM1-07 AM Gold - 1972.
> (S) (2:36)   Flashback 72686 '70s Radio Hits Volume 6.

1972 I BELIEVE IN MUSIC
> (S) (2:35)   Rhino 70929 Super Hits Of The 70's Volume 9.
> (S) (2:34)   K-Tel 3623 Believe In Music.

1973 BIG CITY MISS RUTH ANN
> (S) (2:23)   Rhino 70758 Super Hits Of The 70's Volume 11.

FRANK GALLOP
1958 GOT A MATCH?
1966 BALLAD OF IRVING
> (S) (3:26)   Rhino 70743 Dr. Demento 20th Anniversary Collection.

GAP BAND
1982 EARLY IN THE MORNING
> (S) (7:34)   Casablanca 838811 Let's Start The Dance (Polygram Dance Classics) Vol. 2. *(12" single version)*
> (S) (6:24)   Thump 4030 Old School Volume 3. *(tracks into next selection; LP version)*
> (S) (6:27)   Rebound 314520034 Funk Classics Of The 70's. *(LP version)*

> (S) (6:29)   Mercury 824343 Gap Gold/Best Of. *(LP version)*
> (S) (7:34)   Mercury 314522457 Best Of. *(12" single version)*
> (S) (6:27)   Mercury 822794 Gap Band IV. *(LP version)*
> (S) (6:27)   Rebound 314520431 Soul Classics - Best Of The 80's. *(LP version)*
> (S) (3:37)   Thump 4100 Old School Mix. *(all selections on this cd are segued together and remixed)*

1982 YOU DROPPED A BOMB ON ME
> (S) (13:07) Mercury 314522460 Funk Funk: Best Of Funk Essentials 2. *(12" single version)*
> (S) (5:11)   Original Sound 9305 Art Laboe's Dedicated To You Vol. 5. *(LP version)*
> (S) (5:13)   Priority 53729 Mega-Hits Dance Classics (Volume 11). *(LP version)*
> (S) (13:11) Rhino 71756 and 72833 Phat Trax: The Best Of Old School Vol. 5. *(12" single version)*
> (S) (5:10)   Thump 4010 Old School. *(LP version)*
> (S) (5:11)   Mercury 824343 Gap Gold/Best Of. *(LP version)*
> (S) (5:11)   Mercury 314522457 Best Of. *(LP version)*
> (S) (5:10)   Mercury 822794 Gap Band IV. *(LP version)*
> (S) (4:02)   JCI 3149 1980 - Only Dance - 1984. *(45 version)*
> (S) (5:10)   Rebound 314520357 World Of Dance - The 80's. *(LP version)*
> (S) (5:11)   Rebound 314520365 Funk Classics - The 80's. *(LP version)*
> (S) (5:11)   Rebound 314520522 Rockin' Sports Jams. *(LP version)*

GARBAGE
1996 STUPID GIRL
> (S) (4:18)   Almo 80004 Garbage.
> (S) (4:18)   Grammy Recordings/Chronicles 314553292 1997 Grammy Nominees.
> (S) (4:34)   Tommy Boy 1207 MTV Grind Volume One. *(remixed; all selections on this cd are segued together)*

DAVE GARDNER
1957 WHITE SILVER SANDS

DON GARDNER and DEE DEE FORD
1962 I NEED YOUR LOVING
> (S) (2:53)   Relic 7009 Raging Harlem Hit Parade.
> (S) (5:43)   Ripete 2392192 Beach Music Anthology Box Set. *(rerecording)*
> (M) (2:48)   Capitol 91184 O.S.T. Everybody's All-American. *(mastered from vinyl)*
> (S) (2:54)   Collectables 5065 History Of Rock Volume 5.
> (S) (2:53)   Capricorn 42009 Fire/Fury Records Story.
> (S) (2:53)   Time-Life 2RNR-16 Rock 'N' Roll Era - 1962 Still Rockin'.
> (S) (2:50)   Time-Life RHD-11 Rhythm & Blues - 1962.
> (E) (2:50)   Collectables 5155 I Need Your Lovin'.
> (M) (2:48)   Capitol 89098 O.S.T. Wild Palms. *(mastered from vinyl)*
> (S) (2:53)   Ichiban 2512 Soulful Love - Duets Vol. 1.
> (S) (5:42)   Ripete 2223 Soul Patrol Vol. 5. *(rerecording)*
> (M) (2:51)   K-Tel 3901 Soul Brothers & Sisters Of The 60's. *(mastered from vinyl)*
> (S) (2:50)   Time-Life R838-18 Solid Gold Soul 1962.

ART GARFUNKEL
1973 ALL I KNOW
- (S) (3:47) Columbia 45008 Garfunkel.
- (S) (3:43) Columbia 31474 Angel Clare.
- (S) (2:25) Columbia 47113 Up 'Til Now. *(rerecording)*
- (S) (3:42) Time-Life SUD-13 Superhits - 1973.
- (S) (3:42) Time-Life AM1-03 AM Gold - 1973.
- (S) (3:42) Time-Life R834-09 Body Talk - Magic Moments.

released as by GARFUNKEL:
1974 I SHALL SING
- (S) (3:30) Columbia 31474 Angel Clare.

1974 SECOND AVENUE
- (S) (2:45) Columbia 45008 Garfunkel. *(tracks into next selection)*

released as by ART GARFUNKEL:
1975 I ONLY HAVE EYES FOR YOU
- (S) (3:38) Columbia 45008 Garfunkel.
- (S) (3:39) Columbia 33700 Breakaway.
- (S) (3:38) Time-Life R834-16 Body Talk - Sweet Nothings.

1976 BREAKAWAY
- (S) (3:30) Columbia 45008 Garfunkel.
- (S) (3:34) Columbia 33700 Breakaway.

released as by ART GARFUNKEL with JAMES TAYLOR & PAUL SIMON:
1978 (WHAT A) WONDERFUL WORLD
- (S) (3:28) Columbia 45008 Art Garfunkel - Garfunkel.
- (S) (3:29) Columbia 34975 Art Garfunkel - Watermark.

FRANK GARI
1961 UTOPIA
1961 LULLABY OF LOVE

GALE GARNETT
1964 WE'LL SING IN THE SUNSHINE
- (S) (2:56) RCA 8475 Nipper's Greatest Hits Of The 60's Volume 2.
- (S) (2:56) Time-Life SUD-09 Superhits - 1964.
- (S) (2:55) JCI 3160 18 Free & Easy Hits From The 60's.
- (S) (2:55) Time-Life R857-09 The Heart Of Rock 'n' Roll 1964.
- (S) (2:55) Time-Life AM1-11 AM Gold - 1964.
- (S) (2:55) Time-Life R132-22 Treasury Of Folk Music Volume One.
- (S) (2:55) Collectables 5864 We'll Sing In The Sunshine. *(alternate take)*
- (S) (2:56) Collectables 5864 We'll Sing In The Sunshine.
- (S) (2:55) Time-Life R814-05 Love Songs.

LEIF GARRETT
1977 SURFIN' USA
- (S) (2:22) Rock 'n' Roll 75538 Collection.
1978 RUNAROUND SUE
- (S) (2:23) K-Tel 3211 70's Teen Heart-Throbs.
- (S) (2:22) Rock 'n' Roll 75538 Collection.
1978 I WAS MADE FOR DANCIN'
(dj copies of this 45 ran (3:14) and (4:51); commercial copies were all (3:14))
- (S) (3:15) Rhino 71228 Yesterday's Heroes: 70's Teen Idols.
- (S) (3:15) Rhino 72819 16 Magazine - Who's Your Fave Rave.
- (S) (3:15) Rock 'n' Roll 75538 Collection.
- (S) (3:14) Time-Life AM1-26 AM Gold - 1979.

GARY'S GANG
1979 KEEP ON DANCIN'
(actual 45 time is (3:38) not (3:45) as stated on the record label)
- (S) (7:08) Columbia 46088 Club Columbia. *(LP version)*
- (S) (4:18) Columbia 40517 Let's Dance. *(edit of LP version and slightly faster)*
- (S) (4:18) Risky Business 66662 Swingin' Singles/Greatest Hits Of The 70's. *(edit of LP version and slightly faster)*

DAVID GATES
1975 NEVER LET HER GO
- (S) (3:05) Rhino 72519 Mellow Rock Hits Of The 70's - Sundown.
- (S) (3:05) Rhino 73509 Bread Retrospective.

1978 GOODBYE GIRL
- (S) (2:45) Rhino 71201 Super Hits Of The 70's Volume 21.
- (S) (2:44) Time-Life R105-26 Our Songs: Singers & Songwriters Encore.
- (S) (2:44) Rhino 73509 Bread Retrospective.
1978 TOOK THE LAST TRAIN
- (S) (4:29) Rhino 73509 Bread Retrospective.

MARVIN GAYE
1962 STUBBORN KIND OF FELLOW
- (E) (2:47) Motown 5448 A Package Of 16 Big Hits.
- (S) (2:45) Motown 0791 and 6199 Anthology.
- (S) (2:43) Motown 6201 Compact Command Performances Volume 2.
- (M) (2:49) Motown 6311 The Marvin Gaye Collection.
- (S) (2:43) Motown 5218 That Stubborn Kind Of Fellow.
- (S) (2:46) Motown 5301 Super Hits.
- (E) (2:42) Motown 8057 and 8157 How Sweet It Is To Be Loved By You/That Stubborn Kind Of Fellow. *(truncated fade)*
- (S) (2:42) Ripete 392183 Ocean Drive.
- (M) (2:43) Motown 6312 Hitsville USA.
- (M) (2:40) Motown 314530403 Motown Classic Hits Vol. 1.
- (M) (2:42) Motown/Essex 374638515 Motown Legends - I'll Be Doggone.
- (M) (2:43) Motown 314530492 The Master 1961-1984.
- (M) (2:43) Motown 314530529 Anthology.
- (S) (2:46) MCA 11526 O.S.T. The Long Kiss Goodnight.
- (S) (2:45) Right Stuff 52274 Flick Hits Take 2.
1963 HITCH HIKE
- (E) (2:25) K-Tel 3331 Do You Wanna Dance.
- (S) (2:28) Motown 5301 Super Hits.
- (M) (2:31) Motown 6311 The Marvin Gaye Collection.
- (M) (2:31) Motown 314530420 Motown Classic Hits Vol. III.
- (M) (2:31) Motown 314530492 The Master 1961-1984.
- (M) (2:32) Motown 314530529 Anthology.
- (S) (2:28) Motown 5449 A Collection Of 16 Big Hits Vol. 2.
- (E) (2:26) Time-Life 2RNR-19 The Rock 'N' Roll Era - 1963: Still Rockin'.
- (E) (2:31) Motown 6161 The Good Feeling Music Of The Big Chill Generation Volume Three.
- (S) (2:27) Motown 5218 That Stubborn Kind Of Fellow.
- (E) (2:28) Motown 8057 and 8157 How Sweet It Is To Be Loved By You/That Stubborn Kind Of Fellow.
- (S) (2:27) Motown 0791 and 6199 Anthology.
- (E) (2:26) Motown 6201 Compact Command Performances Volume 2.
- (E) (2:31) Polygram Special Markets 314520292 Motown Legends - Volume 4.
1963 PRIDE AND JOY
- (S) (2:06) Rhino 70649 Billboard's Top R&B Hits Of 1963. *(45 version)*
- (S) (2:04) Motown 5448 A Package Of 16 Original Big Hits. *(45 version)*
- (S) (2:05) Motown 0791 and 6199 Anthology. *(45 version with first note truncated)*
- (M) (2:26) Motown 6201 Compact Command Performances Volume 2. *(LP version)*
- (M) (2:28) Motown 6311 The Marvin Gaye Collection. *(alternate take)*
- (S) (2:05) Motown 5218 That Stubborn Kind Of Fellow. *(45 version with first note truncated)*
- (S) (2:06) Motown 5301 Super Hits. *(45 version)*
- (E) (2:35) Motown 8057 and 8157 How Sweet It Is To Be Loved By You/That Stubborn Kind Of Fellow. *(LP version)*
- (M) (2:05) Motown 6312 Hitsville USA. *(45 version)*
- (S) (2:05) K-Tel 3063 Marvin Gaye/Smokey Robinson & The Miracles. *(45 version with first note truncated)*
- (M) (2:25) Time-Life 2RNR-19 Rock 'N' Roll Era - 1963 Still Rockin'. *(LP version)*
- (S) (2:04) Time-Life RHD-02 Rhythm & Blues - 1963. *(45 version)*
- (M) (2:04) Motown 314530403 Motown Classic Hits Vol. 1. *(45 version)*

(M) (2:05) Rhino 71806 The R&B Box: Thirty Years Of Rhythm & Blues. *(45 version)*

(M) (2:04) Motown 314530492 The Master 1961-1984. *(45 version)*

(M) (2:05) Motown 314530529 Anthology. *(45 version)*

(S) (2:04) Time-Life R838-14 Solid Gold Soul - 1963. *(45 version)*

1963 CAN I GET A WITNESS

(S) (2:48) Motown 6138 The Composer Series: Holland/Dozier/Holland.

(S) (2:46) Motown 5450 A Collection Of 16 Big Hits Volume 3.

(S) (2:46) Motown 0791 and 6199 Anthology.

(S) (2:47) Motown 6201 Compact Command Performances Volume 2.

(M) (2:46) Motown 6311 The Marvin Gaye Collection.

(S) (2:47) Motown 5191 Greatest Hits.

(S) (2:49) Motown 5301 Super Hits.

(S) (2:46) Time-Life 2RNR-19 Rock 'N' Roll Era - 1963 Still Rockin'.

(M) (2:45) Motown 314530492 The Master 1961-1984.

(M) (2:46) Motown 314530421 Motown Classics Vol. IV.

(M) (2:46) Motown 314530529 Anthology.

(M) (2:46) Rhino 72815 Beg, Scream & Shout! The Big Ol' Box Of '60s Soul.

1964 YOU'RE A WONDERFUL ONE

(S) (2:45) Motown 5450 A Collection Of 16 Big Hits Volume 3.

(S) (2:46) Motown 0791 and 6199 Anthology.

(S) (2:43) Motown 6201 Compact Command Performances Volume 2.

(M) (2:45) Motown 6311 The Marvin Gaye Collection.

(S) (2:44) Motown 5419 How Sweet It Is To Be Loved By You.

(S) (2:43) Motown 5301 Super Hits.

(S) (2:41) Motown 8057 and 8157 How Sweet It Is To Be Loved By You/That Stubborn Kind Of Fellow. *(badly distorted)*

(S) (2:44) Time-Life 2CLR-09 Classic Rock - 1964: The Beat Goes On.

(M) (2:44) Motown 314530492 The Master 1961-1984.

(M) (2:45) Motown 314530421 Motown Classics Vol. IV.

(S) (2:46) Motown 314530504 Motown Year By Year 1964.

1964 TRY IT BABY

(S) (2:57) Motown 5451 A Collection Of 16 Big Hits Volume 4. *(45 length)*

(S) (2:45) Motown 0791 and 6199 Anthology. *(LP length)*

(S) (2:46) Motown 6201 Compact Command Performances Volume 2. *(LP length)*

(M) (2:58) Motown 6311 The Marvin Gaye Collection. *(45 length)*

(S) (2:46) Motown 6255 A Musical Testament 1964 - 1984. *(LP length)*

(S) (2:49) Motown 5419 How Sweet It Is To Be Loved By You. *(LP length)*

(S) (2:57) Motown 5301 Super Hits. *(45 length)*

(S) (2:50) Motown 8057 and 8157 How Sweet It Is To Be Loved By You/That Stubborn Kind Of Fellow. *(LP length)*

(M) (2:58) Motown 314530492 The Master 1961-1984. *(45 length)*

(M) (2:56) Motown 314530422 Motown Classics Vol. V. *(45 length)*

(M) (2:58) Motown 314530436 A Tribute To Berry Gordy. *(45 length)*

(M) (2:59) Motown 314530529 Anthology. *(45 length)*

1964 BABY DON'T YOU DO IT

(S) (2:37) Motown 0791 and 6199 Anthology.

(S) (2:37) Motown 6201 Compact Command Performances Volume 2.

(S) (2:37) Motown 6255 A Musical Testament 1964 - 1984.

(S) (2:37) Motown 5419 How Sweet It Is To Be Loved By You.

(S) (2:33) Motown 5301 Super Hits.

(S) (2:38) Motown 8057 and 8157 How Sweet It Is To Be Loved By You/That Stubborn Kind Of Fellow.

(S) (2:37) K-Tel 3063 Marvin Gaye/Smokey Robinson & The Miracles.

(M) (2:32) Motown 314530492 The Master 1961-1984.

(S) (2:32) Motown 314530504 Motown Year By Year 1964.

(M) (2:32) Motown 314530529 Anthology.

1965 HOW SWEET IT IS TO BE LOVED BY YOU

(S) (2:58) Motown 6138 The Composer Series: Holland/Dozier/Holland.

(S) (2:57) Motown 6137 20 Greatest Songs In Motown History.

(S) (2:50) Motown 5452 A Collection Of 16 Big Hits Volume 5.

(S) (2:56) Original Sound 8858 Oldies But Goodies Vol. 8. *(this compact disc uses the "Waring - fds" noise reduction process)*

(S) (2:56) Original Sound 2221 Oldies But Goodies Volumes 1,4,6,8 and 10 Box Set. *(this box set uses the "Waring - fds" noise reduction process)*

(S) (2:56) Original Sound 2500 Oldies But Goodies Volumes 1-15 Box Set. *(this box set uses the "Waring - fds" noise reduction process)*

(S) (2:57) Motown 6069 Compact Command Performances.

(S) (2:54) Motown 0791 and 6199 Anthology.

(S) (2:57) Motown 9098 Radio's #1 Hits.

(M) (2:55) Motown 6311 The Marvin Gaye Collection.

(S) (2:57) Motown 5324 and 9035 Top Ten With A Bullet: Motown Love Songs.

(S) (2:58) Motown 5359 and 9084 Motown Legends.

(S) (2:57) Motown 5191 Greatest Hits.

(S) (2:56) Motown 5419 How Sweet It Is To Be Loved By You.

(S) (2:57) Motown 5343 Every Great Motown Song: The First 25 Years Volume 1. *(most selections on this cd have noise on the fadeout)*

(S) (2:57) Motown 8034 and 8134 Every Great Motown Song: The First 25 Years Volumes 1 & 2. *(most selections on this cd have noise on the fadeout)*

(S) (2:50) Motown 5301 Super Hits. *(buzz noticeable on the fadeout)*

(S) (2:58) Motown 6058 Every Great Motown Hit.

(S) (2:57) Motown 8057 and 8157 How Sweet It Is To Be Loved By You/That Stubborn Kind Of Fellow.

(S) (2:56) Motown 6192 You Can't Hurry Love: All The Great Love Songs Of The Past 25 Years.

(M) (2:57) Motown 6312 Hitsville USA.

(S) (2:57) Time-Life 2CLR-09 Classic Rock - 1964: The Beat Goes On.

(S) (2:56) Time-Life SUD-12 Superhits - The Mid 60's.

(S) (2:56) Original Sound 8883 21 Legendary Superstars.

(S) (2:56) Polygram Special Markets 314520030 Motown Legends - Love Songs.

(M) (2:57) Motown 314530492 The Master 1961-1984.

(M) (2:57) Motown 314530529 Anthology.

(S) (2:53) LaserLight 12311 and 15936 The Wonder Years - First Love.

(S) (2:56) Time-Life AM1-05 AM Gold - The Mid '60s.

(M) (2:56) Time-Life R857-20 The Heart Of Rock 'n' Roll 1965-1966.

1965 I'LL BE DOGGONE

(S) (2:46) Rhino 70651 Billboard's Top R&B Hits Of 1965.

(S) (2:46) Rhino 72006 Billboard's Top R&B Hits 1965-1969 Box Set.

(S) (2:45) Motown 6159 The Good-Feeling Music Of The Big Chill Generation Volume 1.

(S) (2:47) Motown 5452 A Collection Of 16 Big Hits Volume 5.

(S) (2:43) Motown 5454 A Collection Of 16 Big Hits Volume 7.

(S) (2:44) Motown 0791 and 6199 Anthology.

(S) (2:44) Motown 6201 Compact Command Performances Volume 2.

(M) (2:47) Motown 6311 The Marvin Gaye Collection.

(S) (2:46) Motown 5296 Moods Of.

MARVIN GAYE *(Continued)*

- (S) (2:45) Motown 5359 and 9084 Motown Legends.
- (S) (2:48) Motown 5301 Super Hits. *(buzz noticeable on the fadeout)*
- (S) (2:44) Motown 8161 and 8061 Moods Of/That's The Way Love Is.
- (S) (2:44) Time-Life 2CLR-08 Classic Rock - 1965: The Beat Goes On.
- (M) (2:44) Motown/Essex 374638515 Motown Legends - I'll Be Doggone.
- (S) (2:45) Polygram Special Markets 314520283 Motown Legends Volume 2.
- (M) (2:49) Motown 314530492 The Master 1961-1984.
- (M) (2:49) Motown 314530529 Anthology.

1965 PRETTY LITTLE BABY
- (S) (2:35) Motown 0791 and 6199 Anthology.
- (S) (2:35) Motown 6201 Compact Command Performances Volume 2.
- (M) (2:34) Motown 314530492 The Master 1961-1984.

1965 AIN'T THAT PECULIAR
- (S) (2:59) Rhino 70651 Billboard's Top R&B Hits Of 1965.
- (S) (2:59) Rhino 72006 Billboard's Top R&B Hits 1965-1969 Box Set.
- (S) (2:59) Motown 6159 The Good-Feeling Music Of The Big Chill Generation Volume 1.
- (S) (3:00) Motown 6139 The Composer Series: Smokey Robinson.
- (S) (2:57) Motown 5453 A Collection Of 16 Big Hits Volume 6.
- (S) (2:59) Motown 6069 Compact Command Performances.
- (S) (2:57) Motown 0791 and 6199 Anthology.
- (M) (2:56) Motown 6311 The Marvin Gaye Collection.
- (S) (2:59) Motown 5296 Moods Of.
- (S) (2:59) Motown 5359 and 9084 Motown Legends.
- (S) (2:58) Motown 5301 Super Hits.
- (S) (2:58) Motown 8161 and 8061 Moods Of/That's The Way Love Is.
- (S) (2:59) Motown 5311 Great Songs And Performances That Inspired The Motown 25th Anniversary TV Special.
- (S) (2:58) Motown 9071 Motown Dance Party Volume 1. *(all selections on this cd are segued together)*
- (S) (2:57) K-Tel 3063 Marvin Gaye/Smokey Robinson & The Miracles.
- (S) (2:58) Time-Life RHD-07 Rhythm & Blues - 1965.
- (S) (2:59) Time-Life 2CLR-14 Classic Rock - 1965: Shakin' All Over.
- (S) (2:59) Polygram Special Markets 314520282 Motown Legends - Volume 1.
- (M) (2:57) Motown 314530492 The Master 1961-1984.
- (M) (2:58) Motown 314530529 Anthology.
- (S) (2:58) Time-Life R838-12 Solid Gold Soul - 1965.

1966 ONE MORE HEARTACHE
- (S) (2:39) Motown 0791 and 6199 Anthology.
- (S) (2:39) Motown 6201 Compact Command Performances Volume 2.
- (S) (2:39) Motown 5296 Moods Of.
- (S) (2:39) Motown 5359 and 9084 Motown Legends.
- (S) (2:39) Motown 8161 and 8061 Moods Of/That's The Way Love Is.
- (M) (2:33) Motown 314530492 The Master 1961-1984.
- (M) (2:40) Motown 314530529 Anthology.
- (S) (2:39) Motown 314530522 Motown Year By Year - 1966.

1966 TAKE THIS HEART OF MINE
- (S) (2:45) Motown 0791 and 6199 Anthology.
- (S) (2:45) Motown 6201 Compact Command Performances Volume 2.
- (S) (2:46) Motown 5296 Moods Of.
- (S) (2:46) Motown 5359 and 9084 Motown Legends.
- (S) (2:45) Motown 8161 and 8061 Moods Of/That's The Way Love Is.
- (M) (2:41) Motown 314530492 The Master 1961-1984.
- (M) (2:42) Motown 314530529 Anthology.

1967 YOUR UNCHANGING LOVE
(actual 45 time is (3:17) not (2:58) as stated on the record label; LP length is (3:10))
- (S) (3:17) Motown 5455 A Collection Of 16 Big Hits Volume 8.

- (S) (3:09) Motown 0791 and 6199 Anthology.
- (S) (3:09) Motown 6201 Compact Command Performances Volume 2.
- (S) (3:10) Motown 5296 Moods Of.
- (S) (3:11) Motown 5359 and 9084 Motown Legends.
- (S) (3:10) Motown 8161 and 8061 Moods Of/That's The Way Love Is.
- (M) (3:02) Motown 314530492 The Master 1961-1984.
- (M) (3:02) Motown 314530529 Anthology.

1968 YOU
- (S) (2:23) Motown 5457 A Collection Of 16 Big Hits Volume 10.
- (S) (2:24) Motown 0791 and 6199 Anthology.
- (S) (2:24) Motown 6201 Compact Command Performances Volume 2.
- (S) (2:24) Motown 5395 I Heard It Through The Grapevine.
- (S) (2:25) Motown 5301 Super Hits. *(truncated fade)*
- (S) (2:25) Motown 8010 and 8110 I Heard It Through The Grapevine/I Want You.
- (S) (2:24) K-Tel 3063 Marvin Gaye/Smokey Robinson & The Miracles.
- (M) (2:23) Motown 314530492 The Master 1961-1984.
- (M) (2:23) Motown 314530529 Anthology.

1968 CHAINED
- (S) (2:37) Motown 0791 and 6199 Anthology.
- (S) (2:37) Motown 6201 Compact Command Performances Volume 2.
- (S) (2:37) Motown 5395 I Heard It Through The Grapevine.
- (S) (2:37) Motown 5301 Super Hits.
- (S) (2:37) Motown 8010 and 8110 I Heard It Through The Grapevine/I Want You.
- (M) (2:34) Motown 314530492 The Master 1961-1984.
- (S) (2:33) Motown 314530507 Motown Year By Year 1968.
- (M) (2:35) Motown 314530529 Anthology.

1968 I HEARD IT THROUGH THE GRAPEVINE
- (S) (3:14) Rhino 70629 Billboard's Top Rock & Roll Hits Of 1968.
- (S) (3:14) Rhino 72005 Billboard's Top Rock & Roll Hits 1968-1972 Box Set.
- (S) (3:15) Motown 6132 25 #1 Hits From 25 Years.
- (S) (3:15) Motown 6161 The Good-Feeling Music Of The Big Chill Generation Volume 3.
- (S) (3:14) Motown 6137 20 Greatest Songs In Motown History.
- (S) (5:01) Motown 6120 and 6062 O.S.T. The Big Chill. *(this extended version made its debut on this cd)*
- (S) (3:14) Motown 6069 Compact Command Performances.
- (S) (3:14) Motown 0791 and 6199 Anthology.
- (M) (3:12) Motown 6311 The Marvin Gaye Collection.
- (S) (3:14) Motown 9097 The Most Played Oldies On America's Jukeboxes.
- (S) (3:14) Motown 5395 I Heard It Through The Grapevine.
- (S) (3:14) Motown 6255 A Musical Testament 1964 - 1984.
- (S) (3:14) Motown 5191 Greatest Hits.
- (S) (3:14) Motown 9098 Radio's #1 Hits.
- (S) (3:14) Motown 5301 Super Hits.
- (S) (3:14) Motown 6058 Every Great Motown Hit.
- (S) (3:13) Motown 8010 and 8110 I Heard It Through The Grapevine/I Want You.
- (S) (3:15) Motown 9060 Motown's Biggest Pop Hits.
- (S) (3:14) Motown 5311 Great Songs And Performances That Inspired The Motown 25th Anniversary TV Special.
- (S) (3:13) Motown 9071 Motown Dance Party Volume 1. *(all selections on this cd are segued together)*
- (S) (3:13) Ripete 392183 Ocean Drive.
- (M) (3:12) Motown 6312 Hitsville USA.
- (S) (3:14) K-Tel 3063 Marvin Gaye/Smokey Robinson & The Miracles.
- (S) (3:13) Time-Life RHD-04 Rhythm & Blues - 1968.
- (S) (3:14) Time-Life 2CLR-11 Classic Rock - 1968: The Beat Goes On.
- (S) (3:12) Time-Life SUD-02 Superhits - 1968.
- (S) (3:13) Motown 314530355 The Norman Whitfield Sessions.
- (M) (3:11) Motown 314530492 The Master 1961-1984.
- (S) (3:13) Motown 314530507 Motown Year By Year 1968.
- (M) (3:11) Motown 314530529 Anthology.

(M) (3:12) Motown 314530478 O.S.T. The Walking Dead.
(S) (3:14) Polygram Special Markets 314520293 Motown Legends - Volume 5.
(S) (3:12) Time-Life AM1-04 AM Gold - 1968.
(S) (3:12) Time-Life R838-03 Solid Gold Soul - 1968.
(M) (3:11) Time-Life R13610 Gold And Platinum Box Set - The Ultimate Rock Collection.

1969 TOO BUSY THINKING ABOUT MY BABY
(S) (2:56) Motown 6161 The Good-Feeling Music Of The Big Chill Generation Volume 3.
(S) (2:56) Rhino 70655 Billboard's Top R&B Hits Of 1969.
(S) (2:56) Rhino 72006 Billboard's Top R&B Hits 1965-1969 Box Set.
(S) (2:56) Motown 6069 Compact Command Performances.
(S) (2:55) Motown 0791 and 6199 Anthology.
(M) (2:53) Motown 6311 The Marvin Gaye Collection.
(S) (2:56) Motown 5359 and 9084 Motown Legends.
(S) (2:55) Motown 5125 M.P.G.
(S) (2:54) Motown 5301 Super Hits.
(S) (2:55) Motown 6058 Every Great Motown Hit.
(S) (2:55) Motown 5311 Great Songs And Performances That Inspired The Motown 25th Anniversary TV Special.
(S) (2:54) Motown 8036 and 8136 Trouble Man/M.P.G.
(S) (2:54) Motown 374638504 Motown Legends - Mercy Mercy Me.
(S) (2:55) Time-Life RHD-13 Rhythm & Blues - 1969.
(S) (2:55) Time-Life 2CLR-12 Classic Rock - 1969: The Beat Goes On.
(S) (2:55) Motown 314530355 The Norman Whitfield Sessions.
(M) (2:55) Motown 314530492 The Master 1961-1984.
(M) (2:55) Motown 314530529 Anthology.
(S) (2:55) Motown 314530525 Motown Year By Year - 1969.
(S) (2:56) Polygram Special Markets 314520292 Motown Legends - Volume 4.
(S) (2:55) Time-Life R838-04 Solid Gold Soul - 1969.
(S) (2:55) Elektra 62093 O.S.T. A Smile Like Yours.

1969 THAT'S THE WAY LOVE IS
(actual 45 time is (3:35) not (3:15) as stated on the record label)
(E) (3:35) Motown 6069 Compact Command Performances.
(S) (3:41) Motown 0791 and 6199 Anthology.
(M) (3:38) Motown 6311 The Marvin Gaye Collection.
(E) (3:41) Motown 6255 A Musical Testament 1964 - 1984.
(S) (3:41) Motown 5125 M.P.G.
(E) (3:32) Motown 5422 That's The Way Love Is.
(E) (3:36) Motown 5301 Super Hits.
(E) (3:35) Motown 6058 Every Great Motown Hit.
(E) (3:32) Motown 8161 and 8061 Moods Of/That's The Way Love Is.
(S) (3:41) Motown 8036 and 8136 Trouble Man/M.P.G.
(S) (3:40) Motown 374638504 Motown Legends - Mercy Mercy Me.
(E) (3:28) Time-Life 2CLR-20 Classic Rock - 1969: Shakin' All Over.
(S) (3:41) Motown 314530355 The Norman Whitfield Sessions.
(M) (3:34) Motown 314530492 The Master 1961-1984.
(M) (3:35) Motown 314530529 Anthology.

1970 HOW CAN I FORGET
(S) (1:55) Motown 0791 and 6199 Anthology.
(S) (1:55) Motown 6201 Compact Command Performances Volume 2.
(S) (1:57) Motown 5422 That's The Way Love Is.
(S) (1:57) Motown 8161 and 8061 Moods Of/That's The Way Love Is.
(M) (2:02) Motown 314530492 The Master 1961-1984.
(S) (2:02) Motown 314530528 Motown Year By Year - 1970.

1970 THE END OF OUR ROAD
(S) (2:48) Motown 0791 and 6199 Anthology.
(S) (2:48) Motown 6201 Compact Command Performances Volume 2.

(S) (2:44) Motown 6255 A Musical Testament 1964 - 1984.
(S) (2:44) Motown 5125 M.P.G.
(S) (2:50) Motown 5301 Super Hits.
(M) (2:44) Motown 314530492 The Master 1961-1984.

1971 WHAT'S GOING ON
(S) (3:52) Motown 6132 25 #1 Hits From 25 Years. *(LP version)*
(S) (3:51) Motown 6120 and 6062 O.S.T. The Big Chill. *(LP version)*
(S) (3:52) Rhino 70659 Billboard's Top R&B Hits Of 1971. *(LP version)*
(S) (3:51) Motown 6069 Compact Command Performances. *(LP version)*
(S) (3:48) Motown 0791 and 6199 Anthology. *(LP version)*
(S) (3:50) Motown 6311 The Marvin Gaye Collection. *(LP version)*
(S) (3:52) Motown 5339 and 314530022 What's Going On. *(all selections on this cd are segued together; LP version)*
(S) (3:51) Motown 5191 Greatest Hits. *(LP version)*
(S) (3:49) Motown 6094 More Songs From The Original Soundtrack Of The "Big Chill". *(LP version)*
(S) (3:51) Motown 6058 Every Great Motown Hit. *(LP version)*
(S) (3:50) Motown 0937 20/20 Twenty No. 1 Hits From Twenty Years At Motown. *(LP version)*
(S) (3:49) Motown 5311 Great Songs And Performances That Inspired The Motown 25th Anniversary TV Special. *(LP version)*
(M) (3:54) Motown 6312 Hitsville USA. *(45 version)*
(S) (3:50) Time-Life RHD-09 Rhythm & Blues - 1971. *(LP version)*
(S) (3:44) Time-Life R102-34 The Rolling Stone Collection. *(LP version)*
(S) (3:46) Time-Life SOD-02 Sounds Of The Seventies - 1971. *(LP version)*
(S) (3:51) Motown 314530492 The Master 1961-1984. *(LP version)*
(S) (3:57) Motown 314530529 Anthology. *(45 version; very poor stereo separation)*
(S) (3:50) Motown 314530478 O.S.T. The Walking Dead. *(LP version)*
(S) (3:50) Thump 9947 Cruizin' To Motown. *(LP version)*
(S) (3:52) Motown 314530022 What's Going On. *(LP version)*
(S) (3:50) Time-Life R838-06 Solid Gold Soul - 1971. *(LP version)*
(S) (3:50) Motown 314530849 Motown 40 Forever. *(LP version)*
(S) (3:52) Motown 314530883 What's Going On. *(remastered edition; most songs on this cd are segued together; LP version)*

1971 MERCY MERCY ME (THE ECOLOGY)
(actual 45 time is (2:29) not (2:39) as stated on the record label; LP time is (3:11))
(S) (3:12) Motown 6069 Compact Command Performances.
(S) (3:11) Motown 0791 and 6199 Anthology.
(S) (3:12) Motown 6311 The Marvin Gaye Collection.
(S) (3:12) MCA 10063 Original Television Soundtrack "The Sounds Of Murphy Brown".
(S) (3:12) Motown 5339 and 314530022 What's Going On. *(all selections on this cd are segued together)*
(S) (3:12) Motown 5191 Greatest Hits.
(S) (3:12) Motown 6058 Every Great Motown Hit.
(S) (3:12) Motown 5311 Great Songs And Performances That Inspired The Motown 25th Anniversary TV Special.
(M) (2:28) Motown 6312 Hitsville USA.
(S) (3:11) Motown 374638504 Motown Legends - Mercy Mercy Me.
(S) (3:12) Time-Life RHD-09 Rhythm & Blues - 1971.
(S) (3:12) Time-Life SOD-12 Sounds Of The Seventies - 1971: Take Two.
(S) (3:13) Motown 314530492 The Master 1961-1984. *(previous selection blends into the introduction)*
(S) (2:33) Motown 314530529 Anthology.

MARVIN GAYE _(Continued)_

(S) (3:12) Motown 314530022 What's Going On.
(S) (3:12) Time-Life R838-06 Solid Gold Soul - 1971.
(S) (3:12) Rebound 314520447 Soul Classics - Best Of The 70's.
(S) (3:13) Motown 314530883 What's Going On. _(remastered edition; most songs on this cd are segued together)_

1971 INNER CITY BLUES (MAKE ME WANNA HOLLER)

(S) (3:05) Motown 6069 Compact Command Performances. _(45 version)_
(S) (3:01) Motown 0791 and 6199 Anthology. _(45 version)_
(S) (3:04) Motown 6311 The Marvin Gaye Collection. _(45 version)_
(S) (5:25) Motown 5339 and 314530022 What's Going On. _(all selections on this cd are segued together; LP version)_
(S) (3:05) Motown 6058 Every Great Motown Hit. _(45 version)_
(S) (3:04) Motown 5311 Great Songs And Performances That Inspired The Motown 25th Anniversary TV Special. _(45 version)_
(S) (5:26) Motown 314530492 The Master 1961-1984. _(LP version)_
(S) (3:05) Right Stuff 29669 Movin' On Up Vol. 2. _(45 version)_
(S) (2:57) Razor & Tie 22047 Anthology. _(45 version)_
(S) (5:25) Motown 314530022 What's Going On. _(LP version)_
(S) (5:25) Motown 314530883 What's Going On. _(remastered edition; most songs on this cd are segued together; LP version)_

1973 TROUBLE MAN

(S) (3:49) Motown 9104 and 5409 Motown Memories Volume 1.
(S) (3:48) Motown 6069 Compact Command Performances.
(S) (3:45) Motown 0791 and 6199 Anthology.
(S) (3:48) Motown 6311 The Marvin Gaye Collection.
(S) (3:48) Motown 5191 Greatest Hits.
(S) (3:48) Motown 6058 Every Great Motown Hit.
(S) (3:49) Motown 5241 O.S.T. Trouble Man. _(the previous and following tracks are segued together)_
(S) (3:49) Motown 8036 and 8136 Trouble Man/M.P.G. _(the previous and following tracks are segued together)_
(S) (3:44) Motown 374638504 Motown Legends - Mercy Mercy Me.
(S) (3:48) Time-Life SOD-14 Sounds Of The Seventies - 1973: Take Two.
(S) (3:53) Motown 314530320 Classics Collection. _(the previous and following tracks are segued together)_
(S) (3:48) Motown 314530492 The Master 1961-1984.
(S) (3:57) Motown 314530529 Anthology.
(S) (3:48) TVT 6510 O.S.T. Seven.
(S) (3:48) Motown 314530884 O.S.T. Trouble Man. _(remastered edition; the previous and following tracks are segued together)_
(S) (3:48) Hip-O 40107 Super Bad On Celluloid: Music From '70s Black Cinema.

1973 LET'S GET IT ON

(S) (4:00) Rhino 70634 Billboard's Top Rock & Roll Hits Of 1973. _(45 version)_
(S) (4:01) Motown 6132 25 #1 Hits From 25 Years. _(45 version)_
(S) (3:59) Epic 46940 O.S.T. Queenslogic. _(45 version)_
(S) (3:59) Priority 7909 Vietnam: Rockin' The Delta. _(45 version)_
(S) (4:01) Motown 6069 Compact Command Performances. _(45 version)_
(S) (3:56) Motown 0791 and 6199 Anthology. _(45 version)_
(S) (4:00) Motown 6311 The Marvin Gaye Collection. _(45 version)_
(S) (3:59) Motown 5191 Greatest Hits. _(45 version)_
(S) (4:00) Motown 6058 Every Great Motown Hit. _(45 version)_
(S) (4:51) Motown 5192 Let's Get It On. _(LP version)_
(S) (4:00) Motown 9060 Motown's Biggest Pop Hits. _(45 version)_

(S) (4:00) Motown 0937 20/20 Twenty No. 1 Hits From Twenty Years At Motown. _(45 version)_
(S) (3:59) Motown 5311 Great Songs And Performances That Inspired The Motown 25th Anniversary TV Special. _(45 version)_
(S) (3:56) Priority 53703 Hot And Sexy: Passion And Soul. _(45 version)_
(S) (3:59) Original Sound 8908 Best Love Songs Vol 3. _(45 version)_
(S) (3:59) Original Sound 9327 Best Love Songs Vol. 3 & 4. _(45 version)_
(S) (3:59) Original Sound 1236 Best Love Songs Box Set. _(45 version)_
(S) (3:58) Original Sound 8863 Oldies But Goodies Vol. 13. _(45 version)_
(S) (3:58) Original Sound 2223 Oldies But Goodies Volumes 2,7,9,12 and 13 Box Set. _(Volumes 2, 7 and 12 of this box set use the "Waring - fds" noise reduction process; 45 version)_
(S) (3:58) Original Sound 2500 Oldies But Goodies Volumes 1-15 Box Set. _(most volumes in this box set use the "Waring - fds" noise reduction process; 45 version)_
(S) (4:02) Motown 6358 Hitsville USA Volume Two. _(45 version)_
(S) (3:58) Razor & Tie 22047 Sweet 70's Soul. _(45 version)_
(S) (4:00) Time-Life SOD-06 Sounds Of The Seventies - 1973. _(45 version)_
(S) (4:51) Motown 314530320 Classics Collection. _(LP version)_
(S) (4:51) Right Stuff 29139 Slow Jams: The Timeless Collection Volume 1. _(LP version)_
(S) (4:50) Motown 314530492 The Master 1961-1984. _(LP version; preceded by (1:06) of "hidden" studio talk)_
(S) (4:51) K-Tel 6013 70's Soul - Sexy Ballads. _(LP version)_
(S) (4:01) Motown 314530510 Motown Year By Year 1973. _(45 version)_
(S) (3:59) Milan 35726 O.S.T. Nine Months. _(45 version)_
(S) (4:01) Motown 314530529 Anthology. _(45 version)_
(S) (4:01) Thump 9947 Cruizin' To Motown. _(45 version)_
(S) (4:01) MCA 11329 Soul Train 25th Anniversary Box Set. _(45 version)_
(S) (3:57) Giant 24571 O.S.T. Inkwell. _(45 version)_
(S) (4:00) Time-Life R838-08 Solid Gold Soul - 1973. _(45 version)_
(S) (4:50) Time-Life R834-04 Body Talk - Together Forever. _(LP version)_
(S) (4:51) Cold Front 4025 Old School Mega Mix Volume 3. _(LP version)_
(S) (3:58) Motown 314530849 Motown 40 Forever. _(45 version)_
(S) (4:51) Motown 314530885 Let's Get It On. _(remastered edition; LP version)_

1973 COME GET TO THIS

(S) (2:39) Motown 0791 and 6199 Anthology.
(S) (2:39) Motown 6201 Compact Command Performances Volume 2.
(S) (2:40) Motown 5192 Let's Get It On.
(S) (2:39) Ripete 392183 Ocean Drive.
(S) (2:40) Motown 314530320 Classics Collection.
(S) (2:39) Motown 314530492 The Master 1961-1984.
(S) (2:40) Motown 314530529 Anthology.
(S) (2:38) Time-Life R834-19 Body Talk - Always And Forever.
(S) (2:40) Motown 314530885 Let's Get It On. _(remastered edition)_

1974 YOU SURE LOVE TO BALL

(S) (4:42) Motown 5192 Let's Get It On. _(LP version)_
(S) (4:45) Motown 314530320 Classics Collection. _(LP version)_
(S) (4:41) Motown/Essex 374638515 Motown Legends - I'll Be Doggone. _(LP version)_
(S) (4:45) Motown 314530885 Let's Get It On. _(remastered edition; LP version)_

1974 DISTANT LOVER
(actual 45 time is (3:54) not (3:28) as stated on the record label)

(S) (5:58) Motown 5191 Greatest Hits. *(LP version)*
(S) (5:58) Motown 6201 Compact Command Performances Volume 2. *(LP version)*
(S) (3:53) Motown 0791 and 6199 Anthology. *(45 version)*
(S) (4:15) Motown 5192 Let's Get It On. *(studio recording which was not the hit version)*
(S) (4:05) Motown 6255 A Musical Testament 1964 - 1984. *(neither the LP or 45 version)*
(S) (6:15) Motown 9004 and 5181 Live. *(LP version)*
(S) (4:15) Motown 314530320 Classics Collection. *(studio recording which was not the hit version)*
(S) (5:15) Original Sound 9304 Art Laboe's Dedicated To You Vol. 4. *(LP version but missing the first :38)*
(S) (6:20) Motown 314530492 The Master 1961-1984. *(LP version)*
(S) (3:55) Motown 314530529 Anthology. *(45 version)*
(S) (5:58) Thump 9947 Cruizin' To Motown. *(LP version)*
(S) (4:13) Motown 314530560 Baddest Love Jams Volume 1 - Quiet Storm. *(studio recording which was not the hit version)*
(S) (3:55) Chronicles 314555138 Funk Ballads. *(45 version)*
(S) (4:13) Time-Life R834-18 Body Talk - Romantic Moments. *(studio recording which was not the hit version)*
(S) (4:15) Motown 314530885 Let's Get It On. *(remastered edition; studio recording which was not the hit version)*
(S) (6:14) Motown 314530886 Live. *(remastered edition; LP version)*

1976 I WANT YOU
(S) (3:55) Motown 5191 Greatest Hits. *(45 version)*
(S) (4:33) Motown 8010 and 8110 I Heard It Through The Grapevine/I Want You. *(LP version)*
(S) (4:33) Motown 5292 I Want You. *(LP version)*
(S) (3:55) Motown 6311 The Marvin Gaye Collection. *(45 version)*
(S) (3:55) Motown 6358 Hitsville USA Volume Two. *(45 version)*
(S) (3:53) Time-Life SOD-34 Sounds Of The Seventies - The Late 70's. *(45 version)*
(S) (4:34) Motown 314530320 Classics Collection. *(LP version)*
(S) (4:31) Motown 314530492 The Master 1961-1984. *(LP version)*
(S) (3:50) Motown 314530513 Motown Year By Year 1976. *(45 version)*
(S) (3:55) Motown 314530529 Anthology. *(45 version)*
(S) (3:55) Motown 0791 and 6199 Anthology. *(45 version)*
(S) (4:31) Time-Life R834-07 Body Talk - Hearts In Motion. *(LP version)*
(S) (4:33) Motown 314530887 I Want You. *(remastered edition; LP version)*

1977 GOT TO GIVE IT UP (PART 1)
(actual 45 time is (4:06) not (3:58) as stated on the record label)

(S) (4:08) Rhino 70672 Billboard Top Hits - 1977. *(45 version)*
(S) (4:11) Motown 5344 Every Great Motown Song: The First 25 Years Volume 2. *(45 version)*
(S) (11:53) Motown 0937 20/20 Twenty No. 1 Hits From Twenty Years At Motown. *(LP version)*
(S) (4:11) Motown 6110 Motown Grammy Rhythm & Blues Performances Of The 60's & 70's. *(45 version)*
(S) (4:11) Motown 8034 & 8134 Every Great Motown Song: The First 25 Years Volumes 1 & 2. *(45 version)*
(S) (4:06) Motown 9072 Motown Dance Party Volume 2. *(all selections on this cd are segued together; 45 version)*
(S) (4:13) Motown 6132 25 #1 Hits From 25 Years Volume 2. *(45 version)*
(S) (4:09) Rhino 70491 Billboard Top Dance Hits - 1977. *(45 version)*
(S) (11:53) Motown 5259 and 6191 Live At The London Palladium. *(LP version)*

(S) (4:12) Motown 6311 The Marvin Gaye Collection. *(45 version)*
(S) (4:12) Rhino 71434 In Yo Face! History Of Funk Volume 4. *(45 version)*
(S) (4:11) Motown 6358 Hitsville USA Volume Two. *(45 version)*
(S) (4:08) Razor & Tie 22496 Disco Fever. *(45 version)*
(S) (4:12) Time-Life SOD-05 Sounds Of The Seventies - 1977. *(45 version)*
(S) (6:00) Rebound 314520218 Disco Nights Vol. 2. *(neither the 45 or LP version)*
(S) (4:13) Motown 314530492 The Master 1961-1984. *(45 version)*
(S) (4:12) Motown 314530529 Anthology. *(45 version)*
(S) (11:52) Motown 314530498 Funkology Volume One - Got To Give It Up. *(LP version)*
(S) (4:07) Polydor 314535877 Pure Disco. *(45 version)*
(S) (4:12) Time-Life R838-16 Solid Gold Soul 1977. *(45 version)*
(S) (4:07) Capitol 56312 O.S.T. Boogie Nights. *(45 version)*

1983 SEXUAL HEALING
(S) (3:59) MCA Special Products 20767 Classic R&B Oldies From The 80's Volume 3.
(S) (3:58) Sandstone 33051 and 5019 Cosmopolitan Volume 5.
(S) (3:58) Thump 4710 Old School Love Songs.
(S) (3:58) Rhino 71862 Smooth Grooves Volume 4.
(S) (3:58) Motown 6311 The Marvin Gaye Collection.
(S) (3:58) Motown 314530492 The Master 1961-1984.
(S) (3:59) K-Tel 3263 The 80's Love Jams.
(S) (3:58) DCC Compact Classics 083 Night Moves Volume 3.
(S) (3:56) Time-Life R988-03 Sounds Of The Eighties: 1983.
(S) (3:57) Time-Life R988-26 Sounds Of The Eighties: The Rolling Stone Collection 1982-1983.
(S) (3:57) Time-Life R138-18 Body Talk.
(S) (4:06) Rhino 72159 Black Entertainment Television - 15th Anniversary.
(S) (3:57) JCI 3147 1980 - Only Love - 1984.
(S) (4:06) Time-Life R834-01 Body Talk - Forever Yours.

MARVIN GAYE & DIANA ROSS
1973 YOU'RE A SPECIAL PART OF ME
(actual 45 time is (3:37) not (3:15) as stated on the record label)

(S) (3:36) Motown 9109 and 5413 Motown Memories Volume 3.
(S) (3:37) Motown 6153 and 9053 Marvin Gaye & His Women.
(S) (3:36) Motown 8015 and 8115 Marvin Gaye & Tami Terrell's Greatest Hits/Diana & Marvin.
(S) (4:36) Motown 6311 The Marvin Gaye Collection. *(previously unreleased extended version)*
(S) (3:36) Motown 6197 and 6049 Diana Ross Anthology.
(S) (3:36) Motown 9090 and 5124 Diana & Marvin.
(S) (4:31) Motown 314530510 Motown Year By Year 1973. *(with countoff; previously unreleased extended version)*

1974 MY MISTAKE (WAS TO LOVE YOU)
(S) (2:54) Motown 6153 and 9053 Marvin Gaye & His Women.
(S) (3:02) Motown 6311 The Marvin Gaye Collection. *(:07 longer than either the 45 or LP)*
(S) (2:54) Motown 9090 and 5124 Diana & Marvin.
(S) (2:52) Motown 9031 and 5214 Diana's Duets.
(S) (2:53) Motown 6197 and 6049 Diana Ross Anthology.
(S) (2:54) Motown 8015 and 8115 Marvin Gaye & Tami Terrell's Greatest Hits/Diana & Marvin.
(S) (2:53) Motown 6357 Diana Ross Forever: Musical Memories.
(S) (2:54) Motown 314530492 Marvin Gaye The Master 1961 - 1984.
(S) (2:54) Motown 314530529 Marvin Gaye - Anthology.

MARVIN GAYE & TAMMI TERRELL
1967 AIN'T NO MOUNTAIN HIGH ENOUGH

    (S)   (2:26)   Motown 6137 20 Greatest Songs In Motown History.

    (S)   (2:25)   Motown 5456 A Collection Of 16 Big Hits Volume 9.

    (S)   (2:26)   Motown 8015 and 8115 Marvin Gaye & Tami Terrell's Greatest Hits/Diana & Marvin.

    (S)   (2:27)   Motown 6110 Motown Grammy R&B Performances Of The 60's & 70's.

    (S)   (2:24)   Motown 0791 and 6199 Marvin Gaye Anthology.

    (S)   (2:26)   Motown 6153 and 9053 Marvin Gaye & His Women.

    (M)   (2:25)   Motown 6311 The Marvin Gaye Collection.

    (S)   (2:27)   Motown 9009 and 5200 United.

    (S)   (2:27)   Motown 8047 and 8147 You're All I Need/United.

    (S)   (2:27)   Motown 5225 Marvin Gaye & Tammi Terrell - Greatest Hits.

    (M)   (2:26)   Motown 6312 Hitsville USA.

    (S)   (2:25)   Time-Life 2CLR-15 Classic Rock - 1967: Shakin' All Over.

    (S)   (2:25)   Time-Life SUD-18 Superhits - Late 60's Classics.

    (M)   (2:27)   Motown 314530492 Marvin Gaye The Master 1961 - 1984.

    (M)   (2:27)   Motown 314530529 Marvin Gaye - Anthology.

    (S)   (2:25)   Time-Life AM1-12 AM Gold - Late '60s Classics.

    (S)   (2:26)   Motown 314530882 Marvin Gaye & Tammi Terrell - Greatest Hits. *(remastered edition)*

1967 YOUR PRECIOUS LOVE

    (S)   (3:01)   Rhino 70653 Billboard's Top R&B Hits Of 1967.

    (S)   (3:01)   Rhino 72006 Billboard's Top R&B Hits 1965-1969 Box Set.

    (S)   (3:02)   Motown 8015 and 8115 Marvin Gaye & Tami Terrell's Greatest Hits/Diana & Marvin.

    (S)   (3:00)   Motown 5456 A Collection Of 16 Big Hits Volume 9.

    (S)   (3:02)   Motown 6140 The Composer Series: Ashford & Simpson.

    (S)   (3:01)   Motown 6160 The Good-Feeling Music Of The Big Chill Generation Volume 2.

    (S)   (3:01)   Motown 6069 Compact Command Performances.

    (S)   (2:59)   Motown 0791 and 6199 Marvin Gaye Anthology.

    (S)   (3:01)   Motown 6153 and 9053 Marvin Gaye & His Women.

    (M)   (2:58)   Motown 6311 The Marvin Gaye Collection.

    (S)   (3:01)   Motown 5324 and 9035 Top Ten With A Bullet: Motown Love Songs.

    (S)   (3:02)   Motown 9009 and 5200 United.

    (S)   (2:58)   Motown 6058 Every Great Motown Hit.

    (S)   (2:58)   Motown 5246 Marvin Gaye And His Girls.

    (S)   (3:02)   Motown 8047 and 8147 You're All I Need/United.

    (S)   (3:02)   Motown 5225 Marvin Gaye & Tammi Terrell - Greatest Hits.

    (S)   (2:59)   Time-Life RHD-10 Rhythm & Blues - 1967.

    (S)   (2:58)   Time-Life 2CLR-10 Classic Rock - 1967: The Beat Goes On.

    (S)   (3:00)   Time-Life SUD-14 Superhits - The Late 60's.

    (S)   (2:59)   Time-Life OPCD-4517 Tonight's The Night.

    (S)   (3:00)   Polygram Special Markets 314520030 Motown Legends - Love Songs.

    (M)   (2:58)   Motown 314530492 Marvin Gaye The Master 1961 - 1984.

    (M)   (2:58)   Motown 314530529 Marvin Gaye - Anthology.

    (S)   (3:02)   Motown 314530560 Baddest Love Jams Volume 1 - Quiet Storm.

    (S)   (3:01)   Polygram Special Markets 314520292 Motown Legends - Volume 4.

    (S)   (2:59)   Time-Life AM1-14 AM Gold - The Late '60s.

    (S)   (2:59)   Time-Life R838-02 Solid Gold Soul - 1967.

    (S)   (3:01)   Time-Life R834-08 Body Talk - On My Mind.

    (S)   (3:01)   Time-Life R857-22 The Heart Of Rock 'n' Roll 1967-1969.

    (S)   (3:01)   Motown 314530882 Marvin Gaye & Tammi Terrell - Greatest Hits. *(remastered edition)*

1968 IF I COULD BUILD MY WHOLE WORLD AROUND YOU

    (S)   (2:17)   Motown 5457 A Collection Of 16 Big Hits Volume 10.

    (S)   (2:18)   Motown 0791 and 6199 Marvin Gaye Anthology.

    (S)   (2:19)   Motown 6153 and 9053 Marvin Gaye & His Women.

    (S)   (2:20)   Motown 8015 and 8115 Marvin Gaye & Tami Terrell's Greatest Hits/Diana & Marvin.

    (M)   (2:20)   Motown 6311 The Marvin Gaye Collection.

    (S)   (2:20)   Motown 9009 and 5200 United.

    (S)   (2:19)   Motown 6058 Every Great Motown Hit.

    (S)   (2:20)   Motown 8047 and 8147 You're All I Need/United.

    (S)   (2:20)   Motown 5225 Marvin Gaye & Tammi Terrell - Greatest Hits.

    (S)   (2:16)   Time-Life 2CLR-27 Classic Rock - 1968: Blowin' Your Mind.

    (M)   (2:21)   Motown 314530492 Marvin Gaye The Master 1961 - 1984.

    (M)   (2:21)   Motown 314530529 Marvin Gaye - Anthology.

    (S)   (2:20)   Motown 314530882 Marvin Gaye & Tammi Terrell - Greatest Hits. *(remastered edition)*

1968 AIN'T NOTHING LIKE THE REAL THING

    (S)   (2:13)   Motown 6160 The Good-Time Feeling Of The Big Chill Generation Volume 2.

    (S)   (2:13)   Motown 6140 The Composer Series: Ashford & Simpson.

    (S)   (2:12)   Motown 0791 and 6199 Marvin Gaye Anthology.

    (S)   (2:13)   Motown 6153 and 9053 Marvin Gaye & His Women.

    (S)   (2:13)   Motown 8015 and 8115 Marvin Gaye & Tami Terrell's Greatest Hits/Diana & Marvin.

    (M)   (2:15)   Motown 6311 The Marvin Gaye Collection.

    (S)   (2:13)   Motown 5142 You're All I Need.

    (S)   (2:13)   Motown 6058 Every Great Motown Hit.

    (S)   (2:13)   Motown 8047 and 8147 You're All I Need/United.

    (S)   (2:13)   Motown 5225 Marvin Gaye & Tammi Terrell - Greatest Hits.

    (M)   (2:16)   Motown 6312 Hitsville USA.

    (S)   (2:13)   Time-Life 2CLR-11 Classic Rock - 1968: The Beat Goes On.

    (S)   (2:12)   Time-Life SUD-02 Superhits - 1968.

    (M)   (2:16)   Polygram Special Markets 314520284 Motown Legends Volume 3.

    (M)   (2:15)   Motown 314530492 Marvin Gaye The Master 1961 - 1984.

    (M)   (2:16)   Motown 314530529 Marvin Gaye - Anthology.

    (S)   (2:12)   Polygram Special Markets 314520031 Motown Legends - Duets.

    (S)   (2:12)   Time-Life AM1-04 AM Gold - 1968.

    (S)   (2:12)   Motown 314530849 Motown 40 Forever.

    (M)   (2:15)   Time-Life R834-13 Body Talk - Just The Two Of Us.

    (S)   (2:12)   Motown 314530882 Marvin Gaye & Tammi Terrell - Greatest Hits. *(remastered edition)*

1968 YOU'RE ALL I NEED TO GET BY

    (S)   (2:47)   Motown 6161 The Good-Time Feeling Of The Big Chill Generation Volume 3. *(LP length)*

    (S)   (2:47)   Motown 6177 Endless Love. *(LP length)*

    (S)   (2:48)   Motown 6140 The Composer Series: Ashford & Simpson. *(LP length)*

    (S)   (2:46)   SBK 93744 China Beach - Music & Memories. *(LP length)*

    (S)   (2:48)   Rhino 70654 Billboard's Top R&B Hits Of 1968. *(LP length)*

    (S)   (2:48)   Rhino 72006 Billboard's Top R&B Hits 1965-1969 Box Set. *(LP length)*

    (S)   (2:47)   Motown 6069 Compact Command Performances. *(LP length)*

    (S)   (2:48)   Motown 0791 and 6199 Marvin Gaye Anthology. *(LP length)*

    (S)   (2:47)   Motown 6153 and 9053 Marvin Gaye & His Women. *(LP length)*

    (S)   (2:47)   Motown 8015 and 8115 Marvin Gaye & Tami Terrell's Greatest Hits/Diana & Marvin. *(LP length)*

(M) (2:39) Motown 6311   The Marvin Gaye Collection. *(45 length)*
(S) (2:48) Motown 5142   You're All I Need. *(LP length)*
(S) (2:47) Motown 6058   Every Great Motown Hit. *(LP length)*
(S) (2:48) Motown 8047 and 8147   You're All I Need/United. *(LP length)*
(S) (2:47) Motown 5225   Marvin Gaye & Tammi Terrell - Greatest Hits. *(LP length)*
(S) (2:47) Time-Life RHD-04   Rhythm & Blues - 1968. *(LP length)*
(S) (2:48) Time-Life 2CLR-19   Classic Rock - 1968: Shakin' All Over. *(LP length)*
(S) (2:46) Time-Life OPCD-4517   Tonight's The Night. *(LP length)*
(M) (2:37) Motown 314530492   Marvin Gaye The Master 1961 - 1984. *(45 length)*
(S) (2:47) Motown 314530507   Motown Year By Year 1968. *(LP length)*
(M) (2:38) Motown 314530529   Marvin Gaye - Anthology. *(45 length)*
(S) (2:47) Polygram Special Markets 314520293   Motown Legends - Volume 5. *(LP length)*
(S) (2:48) Hip-O 40001   The Glory Of Love - Sweet & Soulful Love Songs. *(LP length)*
(S) (2:48) Rhino 72580   Soul Serenade - Intimate R&B. *(LP length)*
(S) (2:47) Time-Life R838-03   Solid Gold Soul - 1968. *(LP length)*
(S) (2:48) Time-Life R834-18   Body Talk - Romantic Moments. *(LP length)*
(S) (2:47) Motown 314530882   Marvin Gaye & Tammi Terrell - Greatest Hits. *(remastered edition; LP length)*

1968 KEEP ON LOVIN' ME HONEY
(S) (2:29) Motown 6153 and 9053   Marvin Gaye & His Women.
(S) (2:29) Motown 5142   You're All I Need.
(S) (2:29) Motown 8047 and 8147   You're All I Need/United.
(S) (2:29) Motown 8015 and 8115   Marvin Gaye & Tami Terrell's Greatest Hits/Diana & Marvin.
(S) (2:29) Motown 5225   Marvin Gaye & Tammi Terrell - Greatest Hits.
(M) (2:28) Motown 314530492   Marvin Gaye The Master 1961 - 1984.
(S) (2:28) Motown 314530882   Marvin Gaye & Tammi Terrell - Greatest Hits. *(remastered edition)*

MARVIN GAYE & MARY WELLS
1964 ONCE UPON A TIME
(S) (2:29) Motown 0791 and 6199   Marvin Gaye Anthology.
(S) (2:29) Motown 6153 and 9053   Marvin Gaye & His Women.
(M) (2:29) Motown 6311   The Marvin Gaye Collection.
(S) (2:27) Motown 5451   A Collection Of 16 Big Hits Volume 4.
(S) (2:30) Motown 5246   Marvin Gaye And His Girls.
(S) (2:28) Motown 5260   Marvin Gaye & Mary Wells Together.
(M) (2:30) Motown 6253   Mary Wells: Looking Back 1961-1964.
(M) (2:30) Motown 314530492   Marvin Gaye The Master 1961-1984.
(M) (2:29) Motown 314530422   Motown Classics Vol. V.
(M) (2:26) Motown 314530859   Mary Wells Ultimate Collection.

1964 WHAT'S THE MATTER WITH YOU BABY
(S) (2:21) Motown 5451   A Collection Of 16 Big Hits Volume 4.
(S) (2:25) Motown 0791 and 6199   Marvin Gaye Anthology.
(S) (2:26) Motown 6153 and 9053   Marvin Gaye & His Women.
(M) (2:21) Motown 6311   The Marvin Gaye Collection.
(S) (2:24) Motown 5246   Marvin Gaye And His Girls.
(S) (2:21) Motown 5260   Marvin Gaye & Mary Wells Together.

(M) (2:21) Motown 6253   Mary Wells: Looking Back 1961-1964.
(M) (2:19) Motown 314530422   Motown Classics Vol. V.
(M) (2:21) Motown 314530492   Marvin Gaye The Master 1961-1984.
(M) (2:21) Motown 314530529   Marvin Gaye - Anthology.
(M) (2:21) Motown 314530859   Mary Wells Ultimate Collection.

MARVIN GAYE & KIM WESTON
1967 IT TAKES TWO
(M) (2:56) Motown 314530492   The Master 1961-1984.
(S) (2:56) Motown 0791   Marvin Gaye - Anthology.
(S) (2:54) Motown 5246   Marvin Gaye And His Girls.
(M) (2:55) Motown 5486   Kim Weston - Greateset Hits And Rare Classics.
(M) (2:57) Motown 6312   Hitsville USA.
(S) (2:57) Motown 6153 and 9053   Marvin Gaye & His Women.
(M) (2:56) Motown 6311   The Marvin Gaye Collection.
(M) (2:55) Motown 314530529   Marvin Gaye - Anthology.
(S) (2:57) Motown 9104   Motown Memories Vol. 1.
(S) (2:55) Motown 5454   A Collection Of 16 Big Hits Vol. 7.
(S) (2:55) Time-Life 2CLR-24   Classic Rock - 1967: Blowin' Your Mind.

CRYSTAL GAYLE
1977 DON'T IT MAKE MY BROWN EYES BLUE
(S) (2:35) EMI 90602   Heartbreak Hotel.
(S) (2:36) EMI-Manhattan 48380   We Must Believe In Magic.
(S) (2:35) Curb 77344   70's Hits - Country Volume 1.
(S) (2:32) Razor & Tie 4543   The '70s Preservation Society Presents: Easy '70s.
(S) (2:37) EMI 46549   Classic Crystal.
(S) (2:37) Curb 77360   All-Time Greatest Hits.
(S) (2:30) Time-Life CCD-02   Contemporary Country - The Late 70's.
(S) (2:35) K-Tel 3085   Great Ladies Of Country.
(S) (2:34) K-Tel 605   Country Music Classics Volume V.
(S) (2:36) Priority 53717   Branson USA Vol. 2.
(S) (2:34) Madacy Entertainment 1977   Rock On 1977.
(S) (2:38) Priority 53140   Best Of The 70's: Legendary Ladies.
(S) (2:32) K-Tel 3366   101 Greatest Country Hits Vol. Seven: Country Nights. *(truncated fade)*
(S) (2:30) Time-Life R834-08   Body Talk - On My Mind.
(S) (2:30) Time-Life R814-02   Love Songs.

1978 TALKING IN YOUR SLEEP
(S) (2:53) EMI 46549   Classic Crystal.
(S) (2:53) Curb 77360   All-Time Greatest Hits.
(S) (2:52) Priority 9305   Country Gold.
(S) (2:53) Time-Life CCD-10   Contemporary Country - The Late 70's Pure Gold.
(S) (2:53) Priority 53762   Three Decades Of Country.
(S) (2:53) K-Tel 3111   Country Music Classics Vol. XIX.
(S) (2:52) JCI 3156   1975 - Only Country - 1979.
(S) (2:53) Time-Life R834-19   Body Talk - Always And Forever.

1979 HALF THE WAY
(S) (4:03) Capitol 95563   Miss The Mississippi.
(S) (4:03) Capitol 95886   Greatest Hits.
(S) (4:03) Columbia 38803   Greatest Hits.
(S) (4:02) Columbia 69098   Super Hits.

released as by EDDIE RABBITT with CRYSTAL GAYLE:
1983 YOU AND I
(S) (3:53) Priority 8674   Country's Greatest Hits - 80's Country Duets.
(S) (3:57) Warner Brothers 45512   Great Wedding Songs.
(S) (3:57) Warner Brothers 45668   Greatest Country Hits Of The 80's Volume II.
(S) (3:57) Capitol 94652   Radio Romance.
(S) (3:52) Priority 50968   I Love Country Volume Three: Hits Of The 80's.
(S) (3:52) K-Tel 3358   101 Greatest Country Hits Vol. Four: Mellow Country.
(S) (3:57) Time-Life R834-15   Body Talk - Once In Lifetime.

GLORIA GAYNOR
1975 NEVER CAN SAY GOODBYE

(S) (2:56) Priority 7972 Mega-Hits Dance Classics Volume 2. *(45 version)*
(S) (2:56) Rhino 70984 The Disco Years Volume 1. *(45 version)*
(S) (2:58) Rhino 70554 Soul Hits Of The 70's Volume 14. *(45 version)*
(S) (6:18) Polydor 833433 Greatest Hits. *(LP version; tracks into next selection)*
(S) (2:56) Essex 7051 Non-Stop Dance Hits. *(45 version)*
(S) (6:18) Rebound 314520247 Class Reunion 1974. *(LP version)*
(S) (2:58) Rebound 314520265 Dance Fever. *(45 version)*
(S) (2:57) Rebound 314520309 Disco Nights Vol. VII - D.J. Pix. *(45 version)*
(S) (4:08) Radikal/Critique 15444 I'll Be There. *(rerecording)*
(S) (2:57) Eclipse Music Group 64894 Rock 'n Roll Relix 1974-1975. *(45 version)*
(S) (2:57) Eclipse Music Group 64897 Rock 'n Roll Relix 1970-1979. *(45 version)*
(S) (6:18) Polygram Special Markets 314520378 Best Of. *(LP version)*
(S) (3:47) Thump 4840 Flashback Disco. *(all selections on this cd are segued together)*
(S) (2:57) Time-Life R834-16 Body Talk - Sweet Nothings. *(45 version)*
(S) (2:56) Time-Life R840-05 Sounds Of The Seventies: '70s Dance Party 1972-1974. *(45 version)*
(S) (6:18) Polydor 314557236 I Will Survive: The Anthology. *(the previous and following selection are segued together; LP version)*

1979 I WILL SURVIVE

(S) (3:16) Priority 7973 Mega-Hits Dance Classics Volume 3. *(45 version)*
(S) (3:15) Rhino 70985 The Disco Years Volume 2. *(45 version)*
(S) (3:16) Rhino 70674 Billboard Top Hits - 1979. *(45 version)*
(S) (3:16) Rhino 70493 Billboard Top Dance Hits - 1979. *(45 version)*
(S) (7:56) Polydor 833433 Greatest Hits. *(12" single version)*
(S) (3:46) London 828509 O.S.T. Four Weddings And A Funeral. *(neither the 45 or LP version)*
(S) (3:15) Razor & Tie 22496 Disco Fever. *(45 version)*
(S) (3:15) Time-Life SOD-09 Sounds Of The Seventies - 1979. *(45 version)*
(S) (6:26) Rebound 314520270 Class Reunion 1979. *(neither the 45, LP or 12" single version)*
(S) (6:26) Rebound 314520217 Disco Nights Vol. 1 - Divas Of Dance. *(neither the 45, LP or 12" single version)*
(S) (3:17) Polygram Special Markets 314520271 Hits Of The 70's. *(45 version)*
(S) (3:16) K-Tel 3126 Disco Mania. *(45 version)*
(S) (3:16) Mother 314516937 O.S.T. The Adventures Of Priscilla - Queen Of The Desert. *(45 version)*
(S) (4:50) Mother 314516937 O.S.T. The Adventures Of Priscilla - Queen Of The Desert. *(1993 remix)*
(S) (3:15) MCA 11329 Soul Train 25th Anniversary Box Set. *(45 version)*
(S) (3:42) Radikal/Critique 15444 I'll Be There. *(rerecording)*
(S) (3:16) Nick At Nite/550 Music 67690 I Am Woman. *(45 version)*
(S) (3:15) Polydor 314535877 Pure Disco. *(45 version)*
(S) (3:15) Eclipse Music Group 64896 Rock 'n Roll Relix 1978-1979. *(45 version)*
(S) (3:15) Eclipse Music Group 64897 Rock 'n Roll Relix 1970-1979. *(45 version)*
(S) (3:46) Polygram Special Markets 314520378 Best Of. *(neither the 45 or LP version)*
(S) (2:26) Popular 12011 Disco Dance Hits. *(rerecorded)*
(S) (3:58) Polydor 314555120 Pure Disco 2. *(remixed)*

(S) (3:16) Time-Life R840-10 Sounds Of The Seventies: '70s Dance Party 1979. *(45 version)*
(S) (8:00) Polydor 314557236 I Will Survive: The Anthology. *(12" single version)*
(S) (3:45) Polydor 314557236 I Will Survive: The Anthology. *(remix)*

G-CLEFS
1956 KA-DING DONG

(M) (1:57) Time-Life 2RNR-45 Rock 'N' Roll Era - Street Corner Serenade.
(M) (1:57) Collectables 7007 Harlem New York - The Doo Wop Era Part 3.
(M) (1:57) Relic 7105 Ka-Ding-Dong.
(M) (1:57) Rhino 72507 Doo Wop Box II.
(M) (1:57) Flashback 72716 Doo Wop - Sh-Boom.

1961 I UNDERSTAND (JUST HOW YOU FEEL)

(M) (2:43) Relic 7105 Ka-Ding-Dong.

DAVID GEDDES
1975 RUN JOEY RUN

(S) (2:51) Rhino 70762 Super Hits Of The 70's Volume 15.
(S) (2:49) Razor & Tie 21640 Those Fabulous 70's.
(S) (2:51) Time-Life SOD-31 Sounds Of The Seventies - AM Top Twenty.

1975 THE LAST GAME OF THE SEASON (A BLIND MAN IN THE BLEACHERS)

(S) (3:34) Rhino 71200 Super Hits Of The 70's Volume 20.

J. GEILS BAND
1972 LOOKING FOR A LOVE

(S) (3:45) Warner Special Products 27614 Highs Of The Seventies. *(LP version)*
(S) (3:42) JCI 3301 Rockin' 70's. *(LP version)*
(S) (3:45) Atlantic 8297 The Morning After. *(LP version)*
(S) (3:45) Atlantic 82807 The Morning After. *(LP version; remastered edition)*
(S) (5:01) Atlantic 19234 Best Of. *(live)*
(S) (3:45) Rhino 71164 Anthology. *(LP version)*
(S) (3:42) Time-Life SOD-37 Sounds Of The Seventies - AM Heavy Hits. *(LP version)*
(S) (3:45) Rhino 71875 Must Of Got Lost. *(LP version)*
(S) (3:42) Time-Life R968-19 Guitar Rock - The Early '70s: Take Two. *(LP version)*
(S) (3:44) Flashback 72679 Looking For A Love And Other Hits. *(LP version)*
(S) (3:44) Flashback 72089 '70s Rock Legends Box Set. *(LP version)*

1973 GIVE IT TO ME
(45's were pressed in lengths of (3:07) and (6:28) even though the labels always stated (3:07))

(S) (6:28) Atlantic 81908 Classic Rock 1966-1988.
(S) (6:28) Atlantic 7260 Bloodshot.
(S) (6:27) Atlantic 82801 Bloodshot. *(remastered edition)*
(S) (6:26) Atlantic 19234 Best Of.
(S) (6:27) Atlantic 82306 Atlantic Rock & Roll Box Set.
(S) (3:09) Rhino 71164 Anthology.
(S) (3:09) Rhino 71875 Must Of Got Lost.
(S) (3:09) Time-Life R968-16 Guitar Rock - The Mid 70s: Take Two.
(S) (3:09) Flashback 72679 Looking For A Love And Other Hits.
(S) (3:09) Flashback 72089 '70s Rock Legends Box Set.
(S) (3:08) Simitar 55772 Stud Rock - Rock Me.

1975 MUST OF GOT LOST

(S) (5:05) Priority 8668 Rough And Rowdy/70's Greatest Rock Hits Volume 7. *(truncated fade; LP version)*
(S) (2:56) Warner Special Products 27616 Classic Rock. *(45 version)*
(S) (5:04) Atlantic 18107 Nightmares.......And Other Tales From The Vinyl Jungle. *(LP version)*
(S) (5:05) Atlantic 82805 Nightmares.......And Other Tales From The Vinyl Jungle. *(LP version; remastered edition)*
(S) (2:55) Atlantic 19234 Best Of. *(45 version)*
(S) (2:57) Rhino 71164 Anthology. *(45 version)*

(S) (2:56) Time-Life R968-01 Guitar Rock 1974-1975. *(45 version)*

(S) (2:56) Time-Life SOD-08 Sounds Of The Seventies - 1975. *(45 version)*

(S) (2:57) Rhino 71875 Must Of Got Lost. *(45 version)*

(S) (2:56) JCI 3140 18 Screamers From The 70's. *(45 version)*

(S) (2:56) Flashback 72679 Looking For A Love And Other Hits. *(45 version)*

(S) (2:56) Flashback 72089 '70s Rock Legends Box Set. *(45 version)*

(S) (2:56) JCI 3192 18 Rock Classics Volume 2. *(45 version)*

(S) (2:54) Simitar 55152 Blue Eyed Soul. *(45 version)*

(S) (2:56) Thump 6010 Easyriders Volume 1. *(45 version)*

1979 ONE LAST KISS

(S) (4:20) EMI 46551 Flashback - Best Of.

(S) (4:21) Rhino 71164 Anthology.

1980 COME BACK

(S) (3:33) EMI 46551 Flashback - Best Of. *(45 version)*

(S) (5:11) EMI 92703 Love Stinks. *(LP version)*

(S) (3:33) Time-Life R968-20 Guitar Rock - The '80s. *(45 version)*

1980 LOVE STINKS

(S) (3:34) EMI 46551 Flashback - Best Of. *(45 length)*

(S) (3:44) EMI 92703 Love Stinks. *(LP length; tracks into next selection)*

(S) (3:44) Rhino 71164 Anthology. *(LP length)*

(S) (3:44) Time-Life R968-04 Guitar Rock 1980-1981. *(LP length)*

(S) (3:34) Time-Life R988-18 Sounds Of The Eighties: The Early '80s Take Two. *(45 length)*

1982 CENTERFOLD

(S) (3:36) Rhino 70677 Billboard Top Hits - 1982.

(S) (3:36) Varese Sarabande 5503 and 5504 and 5505 and 5506 and 5507 and 5508 and 5509 and 5513 and 5571 Arrow: All Rock & Roll Oldies Volume One.

(S) (3:35) JCI 3127 1980 - Only Rock 'N Roll - 1984.

(S) (3:35) K-Tel 3261 The 80's Rock On.

(S) (3:36) EMI America 46014 Freeze Frame.

(S) (3:35) EMI 46551 Flashback - Best Of.

(S) (3:36) Rhino 71164 Anthology.

(S) (3:36) Rhino 72133 Frat Rock: The 80's.

(S) (3:36) Time-Life R988-25 Sounds Of The Eighties: The Rolling Stone Collection 1980-1981.

(S) (3:36) Time-Life R968-13 Guitar Rock - The Early '80s.

(S) (3:35) Madacy Entertainment 1981 Rock On 1981.

(S) (3:36) Rhino 72771 The Big 80's.

(S) (3:35) K-Tel 3997 Arena Rock - The 80's.

(S) (3:36) Hip-O 40079 Essential '80s: 1980-1984.

(S) (3:35) Simitar 55762 Stud Rock - Wild Ride.

1982 FREEZE-FRAME

(S) (3:56) Priority 53715 80's Greatest Rock Hits Volume 3 - Arena Rock.

(S) (3:54) Time-Life R102-34 The Rolling Stone Collection.

(S) (3:57) EMI America 46014 Freeze Frame.

(S) (3:55) EMI 46551 Flashback - Best Of.

(S) (3:56) Rhino 71164 Anthology.

(S) (3:56) Time-Life R988-05 Sounds Of The Eighties: 1982.

(S) (3:55) Big Ear Music 4001 Only In The 80's Volume One.

(S) (3:56) Risky Business 67310 We Came To Play.

(S) (3:55) Madacy Entertainment 1982 Rock On 1982.

(S) (3:55) Priority 50953 I Love Rock & Roll Volume 4: Hits Of The 80's.

(S) (3:55) K-Tel 3798 The 80's Mega Hits.

(S) (3:55) Simitar 55582 The Number One's: Rock It Up.

1982 ANGEL IN BLUE
(dj copies of this 45 ran (3:54) and (4:51); commercial copies were all (4:51))

(S) (4:50) Scotti Bros. 75465 Angel Hits.

(S) (4:50) EMI America 46014 Freeze Frame.

1983 I DO (live version)

(S) (3:08) EMI 46551 Flashback - Best Of. *(live hit version; :08 longer than the 45 or LP)*

(S) (3:16) Rhino 71164 Anthology. *(live hit version; :16 longer than the 45 or LP)*

(S) (3:07) Rhino 71875 Must Of Got Lost. *(1977 studio recording from the "Monkey Island" LP - not the hit version)*

(S) (3:07) Flashback 72679 Looking For A Love And Other Hits. *(1977 studio recording from the "Monkey Island" LP - not the hit version)*

(S) (3:07) Flashback 72089 '70s Rock Legends Box Set. *(1977 studio recording from the "Monkey Island" LP - not the hit version)*

(S) (3:06) Atlantic 81557 Best Of. *(1977 studio recording from the "Monkey Island" LP - not the hit version)*

GENE & DEBBE
1968 PLAYBOY

(M) (2:46) Collectables 5064 History Of Rock Volume 4.

(S) (2:51) Collectables 5817 Golden Classics.

GENERAL PUBLIC
1985 TENDERNESS

(S) (3:35) IRS 29695 On The Charts: IRS Records 1979-1994.

(S) (3:36) IRS 13086 The Beat Goes On.

(S) (3:35) Priority 7994 Rock Of The 80's.

(S) (3:33) K-Tel 3342 The 80's Pop Explosion.

(S) (3:36) EMI 28339 Living In Oblivion: The 80's Greatest Hits - Volume Four.

(S) (3:35) Rhino 71977 New Wave Hits Of The 80's Vol. 14.

(S) (3:32) K-Tel 3473 The 80s: New Wave.

(S) (3:35) Madacy Entertainment 1985 Rock On 1985.

(S) (3:29) JCI 3186 1985 - Only Love - 1989.

1994 I'LL TAKE YOU THERE

(S) (4:02) Epic 57881 O.S.T. Threesome.

(S) (4:00) Priority 50946 100% Party Hits Of The 90's Volume One.

GENESIS
1978 FOLLOW YOU FOLLOW ME

(S) (3:54) Atlantic 19173 And Then There Were Three. *(LP version)*

(S) (3:20) Time-Life SOD-20 Sounds Of The Seventies - 1978: Take Two. *(45 version)*

(S) (3:57) Atlantic 82691 And Then There Were Three. *(remastered edition; LP version)*

1980 MISUNDERSTANDING

(S) (3:12) Atlantic 16014 Duke.

(S) (3:11) Atlantic 82692 Duke. *(remastered edition)*

(S) (3:11) Time-Life R988-18 Sounds Of The Eighties: The Early '80s Take Two.

1981 NO REPLY AT ALL
(dj copies of this 45 ran (4:00) and (4:37); commercial copies were all (4:37))

(S) (4:37) Atlantic 19313 Abacab.

(S) (4:38) Atlantic 82693 Abacab. *(remastered edition)*

(S) (4:40) Atlantic 82521 Abacab. *(gold disc edition)*

1982 ABACAB

(S) (6:56) Atlantic 19313 Abacab. *(LP version)*

(S) (7:00) Atlantic 82693 Abacab. *(remastered edition; LP version)*

(S) (7:02) Atlantic 82521 Abacab. *(gold disc edition; LP version)*

1982 PAPERLATE

(S) (3:14) Atlantic 2000 Three Sides Live.

1984 THAT'S ALL

(S) (4:22) Atlantic 80116 Genesis.

(S) (4:22) Time-Life R988-06 Sounds Of The Eighties: 1984.

1986 INVISIBLE TOUCH

(S) (3:26) Atlantic 81910 Hit Singles 1980-1988.

(S) (3:26) Atlantic 81641 Invisible Touch.

(S) (3:26) Time-Life R988-04 Sounds Of The Eighties: 1986.

GENESIS (Continued)

(S) (3:26) Time-Life R13610 Gold And Platinum Box Set - The Ultimate Rock Collection.

1986 THROWING IT ALL AWAY
(S) (3:48) Atlantic 81641 Invisible Touch.
(S) (3:48) Time-Life R988-12 Sounds Of The 80's: 1985-1986.

1987 LAND OF CONFUSION
(S) (4:43) Atlantic 81641 Invisible Touch.

1987 TONIGHT, TONIGHT, TONIGHT
(S) (8:49) Atlantic 81908 Classic Rock 1966-1988. *(LP version)*
(S) (8:49) Atlantic 81641 Invisible Touch. *(LP version)*

1987 IN TOO DEEP
(S) (4:56) Atlantic 81641 Invisible Touch.

1992 NO SON OF MINE
(dj copies of this 45 ran (4:41) and (6:38); commercial copies were all (6:29))
(S) (6:37) Atlantic 82344 We Can't Dance.

1992 I CAN'T DANCE
(S) (3:58) Atlantic 82344 We Can't Dance.

1992 HOLD ON MY HEART
(S) (4:36) Atlantic 82344 We Can't Dance.

1992 JESUS HE KNOWS ME
(S) (4:14) Atlantic 82344 We Can't Dance.

1993 NEVER A TIME
(S) (3:48) Atlantic 82344 We Can't Dance.

BOBBIE GENTRY
1967 ODE TO BILLIE JOE
(S) (4:13) Curb 77355 60's Hits Volume 1.
(S) (4:13) Curb 77343 60's Hits - Country Volume 1.
(S) (4:12) Curb 77387 Greatest Hits.
(S) (4:12) Capitol 95848 All Time Country Classics.
(S) (4:13) Capitol 91628 Greatest.
(S) (4:12) Capitol 98665 When AM Was King.
(S) (4:11) Time-Life CTD-17 Country USA - 1967.
(S) (4:11) Time-Life 2CLR-15 Classic Rock - 1967: Shakin' All Over.
(S) (4:11) Time-Life SUD-05 Superhits - 1967.
(S) (4:13) DCC Compact Classics 078 Best Of Tragedy.
(S) (4:13) Rhino 71937 Billboard Top Pop Hits, 1967.
(S) (4:14) Priority 50966 I Love Country Volume One: Hits Of The 60's.
(S) (4:12) K-Tel 3369 101 Greatest Country Hits Vol. Ten: Country Roads.
(S) (4:11) Time-Life AM1-08 AM Gold - 1967.
(S) (4:11) K-Tel 3885 Story Songs.
(S) (4:13) Collectables 5862 Golden Classics.

1970 FANCY
(S) (4:14) Capitol 95848 All Time Country Classics. *(LP version)*
(E) (4:03) Curb 77387 Greatest Hits. *(45 version)*
(S) (4:14) Collectables 5862 Golden Classics. *(LP version)*

released as by BOBBIE GENTRY & GLEN CAMPBELL:
1970 ALL I HAVE TO DO IS DREAM
(S) (2:33) Capitol 46483 Very Best Of Glen Campbell.
(S) (2:32) Priority 8675 Country's Greatest Hits Volume 10: Duets Of The 70's.
(S) (2:32) Capitol 33829 Glen Campbell - Essential Volume Two.
(S) (2:31) Razor & Tie 2129 Glen Campbell Collection (1962-1989).
(S) (2:32) Priority 50967 I Love Country Volume Two: Hits Of The 70's.
(S) (2:32) Collectables 5862 Bobbie Gentry - Golden Classics.

GENTRYS
1965 KEEP ON DANCING
(M) (2:08) K-Tel 713 Battle Of The Bands.
(M) (2:09) Warner Special Products 27610 More Party Classics.
(M) (2:09) Rhino 75778 Frat Rock.
(M) (2:09) Mercury 816555 45's On CD Volume 2.
(M) (2:08) Time-Life 2CLR-08 Classic Rock - 1965: The Beat Goes On.

(M) (2:09) Collectables 5622 Keep On Dancing.
(M) (2:08) Special Music 5026 Let It All Hang Out - 60's Party Hits.
(M) (2:08) Special Music 5025 Rebel Rousers! Best Of Southern Rock.
(M) (2:08) JCI 3190 1965 - Only Dance - 1969.
(M) (2:08) Eclipse Music Group 64869 Rock 'n Roll Relix 1964-1965.
(M) (2:08) Eclipse Music Group 64872 Rock 'n Roll Relix 1960-1969.
(M) (2:08) Polygram Special Markets 314520495 45's On CD Volume 2.

1966 SPREAD IT ON THICK
(M) (2:23) K-Tel 839 Battle Of The Bands Volume 2.
(M) (2:23) Collectables 5622 Keep On Dancing.

BARBARA GEORGE
1962 I KNOW (YOU DON'T LOVE ME NO MORE)
(M) (2:22) Rhino 75766 Best Of New Orleans Rhythm & Blues Volume 2.
(M) (2:22) Rhino 70648 Billboard's Top R&B Hits Of 1962.
(M) (2:21) Collectables 5063 History Of Rock Volume 3.
(M) (2:23) Ripete 2199 Walkin' To New Orleans.
(M) (2:22) Time-Life 2RNR-02 Rock 'N' Roll Era - 1962.
(M) (2:20) Time-Life RHD-11 Rhythm & Blues - 1962.
(M) (2:22) Collectables 5123 Best Of Sue Records.
(M) (2:22) Collectables 2500 WCBS-FM History Of Rock - The 60's Part 1.
(M) (2:22) Collectables 4500 History Of Rock/The 60s Part One.
(M) (2:22) Collectables 2603 WCBS-FM Jukebox Giants Vol. 1.
(M) (2:21) Collectables 5141 Golden Classics. *(originally issued in 1988, this cd was remastered in 1994)*
(M) (2:22) EMI 80932 Sue Records Story.
(M) (2:21) EMI 37350 Crescent City Soul: The Sound Of New Orleans 1947-1974.
(M) (2:20) EMI 37355 Highlights From Crescent City Soul: The Sound Of New Orleans 1947-1974.
(M) (2:22) Repeat/Relativity 1611 A Brand New Bag: #1 Soul Hits Of The 60's Volume 3.
(M) (2:20) Time-Life R838-18 Solid Gold Soul 1962.

GEORGIA SATELLITES
1987 KEEP YOUR HANDS TO YOURSELF
(S) (3:26) Sandstone 5023 Cosmopolitan Volume 9.
(S) (3:22) Time-Life R105-24 Guitar Rock Monsters.
(S) (3:22) JCI 3128 1985 - Only Rock 'N Roll - 1989.
(S) (3:25) Elektra 60496 Georgia Satellites.
(S) (3:26) Elektra 61336 Let It Rock: Best Of.
(S) (3:22) Time-Life R988-28 Sounds Of The Eighties: The Rolling Stone Collection 1986-1987.
(S) (3:22) Time-Life R968-18 Guitar Rock - The Heavy '80s.
(S) (3:25) Hollywood 62077 Official Party Album - ABC's Monday Night Football.
(S) (3:23) JCI 3143 18 Screamers From The 80's.
(S) (3:22) Hip-O 40047 The '80s Hit(s) Back 3.
(S) (3:22) Simitar 55772 Stud Rock - Rock Me.

GERARDO
1991 RICO SUAVE
(S) (4:50) Interscope 91619 Mo' Ritmo.
(S) (3:57) Priority 50934 Shut Up And Dance! The 90's Volume One. *(all selections on this cd are segued together)*

1991 WE WANT THE FUNK
(S) (4:10) Interscope 91619 Mo' Ritmo.

GERRY and THE PACEMAKERS
1964 DON'T LET THE SUN CATCH YOU CRYING
(S) (2:34) Rhino 70319 History Of British Rock Volume 1.
(S) (2:34) Rhino 72022 History Of British Rock Box Set.
(S) (2:34) Rhino 72008 History Of British Rock Volumes 1-4 Box Set.
(S) (2:34) EMI 46583 Great Hits.
(S) (2:34) EMI 96093 Best Of.
(S) (2:34) EMI 81128 Rock Is Dead But It Won't Lie Down.

(S) (2:34) JCI 3107 British Sixties.
(S) (2:34) Time-Life 2CLR-16 Classic Rock - 1964: Shakin' All Over.
(S) (2:34) Time-Life SUD-09 Superhits - 1964.
(S) (2:35) Razor & Tie 2084 Gerry Cross The Mersey.
(S) (2:34) Collectables 5629 Best Of/The Definitive Collection.
(S) (2:33) Varese Sarabande 5717 Magic Moments. *(all selections on this cd are rerecordings)*
(S) (2:34) Time-Life AM1-11 AM Gold - 1964.
(S) (2:33) Simitar 55532 The Number One's: The '60s.

1964 HOW DO YOU DO IT?
(S) (1:53) Rhino 70319 History Of British Rock Volume 1.
(S) (1:53) Rhino 72022 History Of British Rock Box Set.
(S) (1:53) Rhino 72008 History Of British Rock Volumes 1-4 Box Set.
(M) (1:52) Atlantic 81905 O.S.T. Buster.
(S) (1:53) EMI 46583 Great Hits.
(S) (1:53) EMI 96093 Best Of.
(S) (1:52) Time-Life 2CLR-03 Classic Rock - 1964.
(S) (1:53) Razor & Tie 2084 Gerry Cross The Mersey.
(S) (1:53) Collectables 5629 Best Of/The Definitive Collection.
(S) (1:51) Varese Sarabande 5717 Magic Moments. *(all selections on this cd are rerecordings)*

1964 I LIKE IT
(M) (2:13) Rhino 70320 History Of British Rock Volume 2.
(M) (2:13) Rhino 72022 History Of British Rock Box Set.
(M) (2:13) Rhino 72008 History Of British Rock Volumes 1-4 Box.
(M) (2:12) EMI 46583 Great Hits.
(S) (2:44) EMI 96093 Best Of. *(includes a :31 false start)*
(M) (2:12) Time-Life 2CLR-03 Classic Rock - 1964.
(S) (2:14) Razor & Tie 2084 Gerry Cross The Mersey. *(with countoff)*
(S) (2:44) Collectables 5629 Best Of/The Definitive Collection. *(includes a :31 false start and countoff)*
(S) (2:09) Varese Sarabande 5717 Magic Moments. *(all selections on this cd are rerecordings)*

1965 I'LL BE THERE
(S) (3:12) Rhino 70320 History Of British Rock Volume 2. *(alternate take)*
(S) (3:12) Rhino 72022 History Of British Rock Box Set. *(alternate take)*
(S) (3:12) Rhino 72008 History Of British Rock Volumes 1-4 Box Set. *(alternate take)*
(S) (3:09) EMI 46583 Great Hits. *(alternate take)*
(S) (3:12) EMI 96093 Best Of. *(alternate take)*
(S) (3:12) Razor & Tie 2084 Gerry Cross The Mersey. *(alternate take)*
(S) (3:12) Collectables 5629 Best Of/The Definitive Collection. *(alternate take)*
(S) (3:03) Varese Sarabande 5717 Magic Moments. *(all selections on this cd are rerecordings)*

1965 FERRY ACROSS THE MERSEY
(S) (2:22) Rhino 70322 History Of British Rock Volume 4.
(S) (2:22) Rhino 72022 History Of British Rock Box Set.
(S) (2:22) Rhino 72008 History Of British Rock Volumes 1-4 Set.
(S) (2:22) EMI 46583 Great Hits.
(S) (2:22) EMI 96093 Best Of.
(S) (2:22) Time-Life 2CLR-23 Classic Rock - 1965: Blowin' Your Mind.
(S) (2:21) Time-Life SUD-12 Superhits - The Mid 60's.
(S) (2:22) Time-Life R962-07 History Of Rock 'N' Roll: The British Invasion 1964-1966.
(S) (2:22) Razor & Tie 2084 Gerry Cross The Mersey.
(S) (2:22) Collectables 5629 Best Of/The Definitive Collection.
(S) (2:21) Varese Sarabande 5717 Magic Moments. *(all selections on this cd are rerecordings)*
(S) (2:21) Time-Life AM1-05 AM Gold - The Mid '60s.

1965 IT'S GONNA BE ALRIGHT
(S) (2:09) Rhino 70321 History Of British Rock Volume 3.
(S) (2:09) Rhino 72022 History Of British Rock Box Set.

(S) (2:09) Rhino 72008 History Of British Rock Volumes 1-4 Box Set.
(S) (2:08) EMI 46583 Great Hits.
(S) (2:23) EMI 96093 Best Of. *(neither the 45 or LP version)*
(S) (2:08) Razor & Tie 2084 Gerry Cross The Mersey.
(S) (2:23) Collectables 5629 Best Of/The Definitive Collection. *(neither the 45 or LP version)*

1966 GIRL ON A SWING
(S) (2:04) EMI 96093 Best Of.
(S) (2:04) Rhino 70325 History Of British Rock Volume 7.
(S) (2:04) Rhino 72022 History Of British Rock Box Set.
(S) (2:03) Razor & Tie 2084 Gerry Cross The Mersey.
(S) (2:04) Collectables 5629 Best Of/The Definitive Collection.

GETO BOYS
1992 MIND PLAYING TRICKS ON ME
(M) (5:07) Rap-A-Lot 57161 We Can't Be Stopped.
(M) (5:05) Rap-A-Lot/Noo Trybe 42510 10th Anniversary - Rap-A-Lot Records.

STAN GETZ/CHARLIE BYRD
1962 DESAFINADO
(S) (5:48) Verve 810061 Jazz Samba. *(LP version)*
(S) (5:49) Verve 823611 The Girl From Ipanema/The Bossa Nova Years. *(LP version)*
(S) (4:00) Verve 833289 Best Of Bossa Nova. *(rerecording)*
(S) (5:48) Verve 831368 Stan Getz: Compact Jazz. *(LP version)*
(S) (5:49) Verve 314521737 The Verve Story 1944-1994. *(LP version)*
(S) (2:04) Time-Life HPD-39 Your Hit Parade - 60's Instrumentals: Take Two. *(45 version)*
(S) (5:49) Verve 314521485 Verve Grammy Winners. *(LP version)*
(S) (5:48) Polygram Special Markets 314520262 Great Jazz Soloists. *(LP version)*
(S) (2:03) Collectors' Choice 003/4 Instrumental Gems Of The 60's. *(45 version)*
(S) (5:49) DCC Compact Classics 1069 Jazz Samba. *(gold disc; LP version)*
(S) (2:00) DCC Compact Classics 1069 Jazz Samba. *(gold disc; 45 version)*
(S) (4:10) Verve 314525880 Antonio Carlos Jobim - The Man From Ipanema. *(rerecording)*
(S) (2:03) Rhino 72474 Masters Of Jazz, Vol. 7: Jazz Hit Singles. *(45 version)*
(S) (5:47) Verve 314535884 Novabossa: Red Hot On Verve. *(LP version)*
(S) (2:03) Time-Life R986-12 Instrumental Favorites - Latin Rhythms. *(45 version)*
(S) (5:48) Verve 314521413 Jazz Samba. *(LP version; remastered edition)*

STAN GETZ/ASTRUD GILBERTO
1964 THE GIRL FROM IPANEMA
(S) (2:45) Rhino 70995 One Hit Wonders Of The 60's Volume 1. *(45 version)*
(S) (5:12) Verve 810048 Stan Getz/Joao Gilberto. *(LP version)*
(S) (5:21) Verve 823611 The Girl From Ipanema/The Bossa Nova Years. *(LP version)*
(S) (2:52) Sony Music Special Products 52420 Get Yourself A College Girl. *(rerecording)*
(S) (6:35) Verve 831368 Stan Getz: Compact Jazz. *(live)*
(S) (5:12) Verve 831369 Astrud Gilberto: Compact Jazz. *(LP version)*
(S) (5:21) Verve 314517171 The Essential. *(LP version)*
(S) (5:21) Verve 314521007 Playboy's 40th Anniversary: Four Decades Of Jazz (1953-1993). *(LP version)*
(S) (5:21) Verve 314521737 The Verve Story 1944-1994. *(LP version)*
(S) (2:43) Time-Life SUD-09 Superhits - 1964. *(45 version)*

STAN GETZ/ASTRUD GILBERTO *(Continued)*

(S) (5:21) Verve 314521485 Verve Grammy Winners. *(LP version)*
(S) (2:43) Time-Life HPD-32 Your Hit Parade - Into The 60's. *(45 version)*
(S) (2:43) Time-Life R138/05 Look Of Love. *(45 version)*
(S) (6:35) Polygram Special Markets 314520262 Great Jazz Soloists. *(live)*
(S) (5:21) Verve 314525472 Firl From Ipanema - Antonio Carlos Jobim Songbook. *(LP version)*
(S) (5:21) Verve 843273 Antonio Carlos Jobim - Compact Jazz. *(LP version)*
(S) (5:21) K-Tel 3575 Hot, Hot Vacation Jams - Week One. *(LP version)*
(S) (5:21) Verve 314525880 Antonio Carlos Jobim - The Man From Ipanema. *(LP version)*
(M) (2:44) Chronicles 314535882 Lounge Music Goes Latin. *(45 version)*
(M) (2:44) Chronicles 314535875 Bachelor Pad Favorites. *(45 version)*
(S) (5:12) Verve 314535884 Novabossa: Red Hot On Verve. *(LP version)*
(S) (2:43) Time-Life AM1-11 AM Gold - 1964. *(45 version)*
(S) (5:21) Verve 314521414 Stan Getz/Joao Gilberto. · *(LP version; remastered edition)*
(S) (2:52) Rhino 72910 Hollywood's Best: The Sixties. *(rerecording)*
(S) (2:43) Time-Life R814-04 Love Songs. *(45 version)*

GHOST TOWN DJ's
1996 MY BOO
(S) (5:46) So So Def/Columbia 67532 So So Def Bass All Stars. *(all selections on this cd are segued together)*
(S) (5:31) So So Def/Columbia 67998 So So Def Bass All-Stars Vol. II. *(remix; all selections on this cd are segued together)*
(S) (5:02) Beast 54112 Boom!
(S) (4:08) Columbia 68602 Total Dance Explosion. *(all songs on this cd are segued together)*

GIANT
1990 I'LL SEE YOU IN MY DREAMS
(S) (4:44) Priority 7049 Metal Heat. *(LP version)*
(S) (4:45) A&M 5272 Last Of The Runaways. *(LP version)*

GIANT STEPS
1988 ANOTHER LOVER
(actual 45 time is (4:10) not (3:40) as stated on the record label)
(S) (4:12) A&M 5190 The Book Of Pride.

ANDY GIBB
1977 I JUST WANT TO BE YOUR EVERYTHING
(S) (3:45) Priority 7971 Mega-Hits Dance Classics Volume 1. *(LP length)*
(S) (3:44) Polydor 511585 Andy Gibb. *(LP length)*
(S) (3:42) Rebound 314520432 Disco Nights Vol. XI - Disco's Leading Men. *(LP length)*
(S) (3:44) Time-Life R834-07 Body Talk - Hearts In Motion. *(LP length)*
(S) (3:44) Polydor 314555120 Pure Disco 2. *(LP length)*
(S) (3:44) Polydor 314539921 Flowing Rivers. *(LP length)*
(S) (3:44) Time-Life R840-07 Sounds Of The Seventies: '70s Dance Party 1976-1977. *(LP length)*
1978 (LOVE IS) THICKER THAN WATER
(S) (4:13) Polydor 511585 Andy Gibb. *(LP version)*
(S) (3:20) Special Music 5041 Great Britons! Volume Three. *(45 version)*
(S) (4:14) Polydor 314539921 Flowing Rivers. *(LP version)*
(S) (4:13) Time-Life R834-13 Body Talk - Just The Two Of Us. *(LP version)*

1978 SHADOW DANCING
(dj copies of this 45 were issued in two different lengths; one stated a time of (3:35) but actually ran (3:55) and the other stated a time of (4:12) but actually ran (4:32); commercial copies all stated a time of (4:34) on the record label and actually ran (4:32))
(S) (4:29) Polydor 511585 Andy Gibb.
(S) (4:29) Time-Life R138-38 Celebration.
(S) (4:29) Rebound 314520440 No. 1 Hits Of The 70's.
(S) (4:32) Polydor 422847916 Shadow Dancing.
(S) (4:29) Time-Life R840-08 Sounds Of The Seventies: '70s Dance Party 1978-1979.
(S) (4:29) Time-Life AM1-25 AM Gold - 1978.
1978 AN EVERLASTING LOVE
(S) (4:04) Polydor 511585 Andy Gibb. *(LP length)*
(S) (4:06) Polydor 422847916 Shadow Dancing. *(LP length)*
1978 (OUR LOVE) DON'T THROW IT ALL AWAY
(S) (4:05) Polydor 511585 Andy Gibb. *(LP length)*
(S) (4:07) Polydor 422847916 Shadow Dancing. *(LP length)*
(S) (4:04) Time-Life R834-20 Body Talk - Heart And Soul. *(LP length)*
1980 DESIRE
(actual 45 time is (3:59) not (3:36) as stated on the record label)
(S) (4:27) Polydor 511585 Andy Gibb. *(LP length)*
(S) (4:26) Rebound 314520318 Class Reunion 1980. *(LP length)*
(S) (4:27) JCI 3170 #1 Radio Hits 1980 - Only Rock 'n Roll - 1984. *(LP length)*
(S) (4:27) Rebound 314520438 No. 1 Hits Of The 80's. *(LP length)*
(S) (4:28) Polydor 314539922 After Dark. *(LP length)*
(S) (4:27) Time-Life R840-09 Sounds Of The Seventies: '70s Dance Party 1979-1981. *(LP length)*
(S) (4:27) Time-Life R834-18 Body Talk - Romantic Moments. *(LP length)*
(S) (4:27) Polygram Special Markets 314520457 #1 Radio Hits Of The 80's. *(LP length)*
released as by ANDY GIBB and OLIVIA NEWTON-JOHN:
1980 I CAN'T HELP IT
(dj copies of this 45 ran (3:46) and (4:07) even though the label stated (3:33) and (3:54); commercial copies were all (4:07))
(S) (4:06) Polydor 511585 Andy Gibb.
(S) (4:06) Polydor 314539922 Andy Gibb - After Dark.
(S) (4:06) Time-Life R834-20 Body Talk - Heart And Soul.
released as by ANDY GIBB:
1981 TIME IS TIME
(S) (3:39) Polydor 511585 Andy Gibb. *(edit of LP version)*

BARRY GIBB
released as by BARBRA STREISAND & BARRY GIBB:
1981 GUILTY
(S) (4:22) Columbia 36750 Barbra Streisand: Guilty.
(S) (4:22) Columbia 45369 Barbra Streisand: A Collection/Greatest Hits And More.
(S) (4:26) Columbia 44111 Barbra Streisand: Just For The Record. *(with countoff and studio talk on the ending)*
1981 WHAT KIND OF FOOL
(S) (4:03) Columbia 36750 Barbra Streisand: Guilty.
(S) (4:03) Columbia 45369 Barbra Streisand: A Collection/Greatest Hits And More.
released as by BARRY GIBB:
1984 SHINE SHINE

ROBIN GIBB
1978 OH! DARLING
(S) (3:27) Polydor 314557076 O.S.T. Sgt. Pepper's Lonely Hearts Club Band.

GEORGIA GIBBS
1955 TWEEDLEE DEE
(M) (2:29) Time-Life HPD-23 Your Hit Parade - The Late 50's.
(M) (2:30) Mercury 314532872 Best Of.

1955 DANCE WITH ME HENRY (WALLFLOWER)
- (M) (2:17)   Time-Life HPD-09   Your Hit Parade 1955.
- (M) (2:17)   Mercury 314532872   Best Of.
- (M) (2:17)   Polygram Special Markets 314520458   Golden Greats.

1955 SWEET AND GENTLE
- (M) (2:29)   Mercury 314532872   Best Of.

1955 I WANT YOU TO BE MY BABY
- (M) (2:28)   Mercury 314532872   Best Of.

1956 HAPPINESS STREET
- (M) (2:33)   Mercury 314532872   Best Of.

1956 TRA LA LA
1958 THE HULA HOOP SONG

TERRI GIBBS
1981 SOMEBODY'S KNOCKIN'
- (S) (2:57)   MCA 6422   16 Top Country Hits Volume 2.
- (S) (2:57)   Priority 9305   Country Gold.
- (S) (2:52)   Time-Life CCD-09   Contemporary Country - The Early 80's Pure Gold.
- (S) (2:59)   Rhino 71894   Radio Daze: Pop Hits Of The 80's Volume Five.
- (S) (2:57)   K-Tel 3047   Country Music Classics Volume VI.
- (S) (3:00)   MCA Special Products 20365   Country's Greatest Hits Volume 2.
- (S) (2:58)   Madacy Entertainment 1981   Rock On 1981.
- (S) (2:58)   Hip-O 40005   The '80s Hit(s) Back....Again!
- (S) (2:57)   Varese Sarabande 5615   Best Of.
- (S) (2:51)   JCI 3157   1980 - Only Country - 1984.
- (S) (2:58)   MCA Special Products 20997   Mellow Rock.
- (S) (2:57)   K-Tel 4004   Country Favorites Of The 80s.
- (S) (2:58)   Simitar 55082   80's Country 1980-82.

DEBBIE GIBSON
1987 ONLY IN MY DREAMS
- (S) (3:51)   Foundation/WEA 26097   Super Sessions Volume Two.
- (S) (3:53)   Atlantic 81780   Out Of The Blue.
- (S) (3:50)   Priority 53773   80's Greatest Rock Hits Volume II - Teen Idols.
- (S) (3:52)   Atlantic 82624   Greatest Hits.
- (S) (3:50)   JCI 3171   #1 Radio Hits 1985 - Only Rock 'n Roll - 1989.
- (S) (3:49)   Time-Life R988-21   Sounds Of The Eighties: 1986-1989.
- (S) (3:49)   K-Tel 3867   The 80's: Hot Ladies.
- (S) (3:53)   Hip-O 40075   Rock She Said: On The Pop Side.

1987 SHAKE YOUR LOVE
- (S) (3:42)   Atlantic 81780   Out Of The Blue.
- (S) (3:41)   Time-Life R988-09   Sounds Of The Eighties: 1987.
- (S) (3:42)   Atlantic 82624   Greatest Hits.
- (S) (3:43)   JCI 3150   1985 - Only Dance - 1989.

1988 OUT OF THE BLUE
- (S) (3:53)   Atlantic 81780   Out Of The Blue.
- (S) (3:53)   Atlantic 82624   Greatest Hits.
- (S) (3:52)   JCI 3186   1985 - Only Love - 1989.
- (S) (3:52)   Time-Life R988-19   Sounds Of The Eighties: The Late '80s.

1988 FOOLISH BEAT
- (S) (4:22)   Atlantic 81910   Hit Singles 1980-1988.
- (S) (4:22)   Atlantic 81780   Out Of The Blue.
- (S) (4:22)   Time-Life R988-10   Sounds Of The 80's: 1988.
- (S) (4:22)   Atlantic 82624   Greatest Hits.
- (S) (4:22)   Rhino 75217   Heartthrob Hits.
- (S) (4:22)   Time-Life R834-19   Body Talk - Always And Forever.

1988 STAYING TOGETHER
- (S) (4:04)   Atlantic 81780   Out Of The Blue.
- (S) (4:04)   Atlantic 82624   Greatest Hits.

1989 LOST IN YOUR EYES
- (S) (3:32)   Atlantic 81932   Electric Youth.
- (S) (3:32)   Rhino 71644   Billboard Top Hits - 1989.
- (S) (3:32)   Atlantic 82624   Greatest Hits.
- (S) (3:32)   Time-Life R988-13   Sounds Of The Eighties: 1989.
- (S) (3:32)   Time-Life R834-10   Body Talk - From The Heart.

1989 ELECTRIC YOUTH
- (S) (4:55)   Atlantic 81932   Electric Youth.
- (S) (4:55)   Atlantic 82624   Greatest Hits.

1989 NO MORE RHYME
- (S) (4:12)   Atlantic 81932   Electric Youth.
- (S) (4:12)   Atlantic 82624   Greatest Hits.

1991 ANYTHING IS POSSIBLE
- (S) (3:43)   Atlantic 82167   Anything Is Possible.
- (S) (3:42)   Atlantic 82624   Greatest Hits.

DON GIBSON
1958 OH LONESOME ME
- (M) (2:28)   RCA 8466   Nipper's Greatest Hits Of The 50's Volume 1.
- (E) (2:29)   RCA 2295   All Time Greatest Hits.
- (S) (2:34)   Curb 77440   Best Of Volume 1. *(rerecording)*
- (S) (2:34)   Curb 77474   18 Greatest Hits. *(rerecording)*
- (M) (2:29)   Time-Life CTD-07   Country USA - 1958.
- (M) (2:30)   Time-Life HPD-27   Your Hit Parade - The Unforgettable 50's.
- (S) (2:26)   K-Tel 3357   101 Greatest Country Hits Vol. Three: Easy Country. *(rerecording)*
- (M) (2:29)   Collectables 5874   Oh Lonesome Me.
- (M) (2:30)   Time-Life R808-03   Classic Country 1950-1959.

1958 BLUE BLUE DAY
- (E) (1:52)   RCA 2295   All Time Greatest Hits.
- (S) (1:56)   Curb 77440   Best Of Volume 1. *(rerecording)*
- (S) (1:56)   Curb 77474   18 Greatest Hits. *(rerecording)*
- (M) (1:52)   Reprise 45516   O.S.T. A Perfect World.
- (M) (1:53)   Time-Life CTD-07   Country USA - 1958.
- (M) (1:53)   Collectables 5874   Oh Lonesome Me.

1960 JUST ONE TIME
- (S) (2:42)   RCA 2295   All Time Greatest Hits.
- (S) (2:18)   Curb 77474   18 Greatest Hits. *(rerecording)*
- (S) (2:00)   Collectables 5874   Oh Lonesome Me. *(rerecording)*

1961 SEA OF HEARTBREAK
- (S) (2:31)   RCA 2295   All Time Greatest Hits.
- (S) (2:15)   Curb 77474   18 Greatest Hits. *(rerecording)*
- (S) (2:31)   Reprise 45516   O.S.T. A Perfect World.
- (S) (2:31)   Time-Life CTD-01   Country USA - 1961.
- (S) (2:30)   Collectables 5874   Oh Lonesome Me.
- (S) (2:31)   Time-Life R808-01   Classic Country 1960-1964.

NICK GILDER
1978 HOT CHILD IN THE CITY
- (S) (3:06)   Priority 7997   Super Songs/70's Greatest Rock Hits Volume 8. *(45 version)*
- (S) (3:06)   Original Sound 8895   Dick Clark's 21 All-Time Hits Vol. 4. *(45 version)*
- (S) (3:06)   Rhino 70673   Billboard Top Hits - 1978. *(45 version)*
- (S) (3:06)   Rhino 71202   Super Hits Of The 70's Volume 22. *(45 version)*
- (S) (3:05)   Time-Life SOD-10   Sounds Of The Seventies - 1978. *(45 version)*
- (S) (3:05)   Madacy Entertainment 1978   Rock On 1978. *(45 version)*
- (S) (3:05)   Priority 50952   I Love Rock & Roll Volume 3: Hits Of The 70's. *(45 version)*
- (S) (3:06)   Simitar 55582   The Number One's: Rock It Up. *(45 version)*
- (S) (3:06)   Time-Life AM1-25   AM Gold - 1978. *(45 version)*
- (S) (3:05)   K-Tel 3987   70s Heavy Hitters: #1 Pop Hits. *(45 version)*

TERRY GILKYSON and THE EASY RIDERS
1957 MARIANNE
- (M) (2:22)   Columbia 45111   16 Most Requested Songs Of The 50's Volume 2.
- (M) (2:22)   Columbia 45017   Radio Classics Of The 50's.
- (M) (2:21)   Time-Life HPD-17   Your Hit Parade - 1957.
- (M) (2:21)   Time-Life R132-22   Treasury Of Folk Music Volume One.

JOHNNY GILL
1990 RUB YOU THE RIGHT WAY
- (S) (5:30) Motown 6283 Johnny Gill. *(LP version)*
- (S) (4:15) Motown 6358 Hitsville USA Volume Two. *(45 version)*
- (S) (5:29) Rhino 72409 New Jack Hits. *(LP version)*
- (S) (4:11) Motown 314530849 Motown 40 Forever. *(45 version)*

1990 MY, MY, MY
- (S) (4:05) Priority 7040 Making Love. *(45 version)*
- (S) (5:19) Motown 6283 Johnny Gill. *(LP version)*
- (S) (4:05) MCA 11329 Soul Train 25th Anniversary Box Set. *(45 version)*
- (S) (4:14) Rhino 72159 Black Entertainment Television - 15th Anniversary. *(45 version)*
- (S) (5:20) Rebound 314520439 Soul Classics - Best Of The 90's. *(LP version)*
- (S) (5:19) Beast 53012 Smooth Love Of The 90's Vol. 1. *(LP version)*

1990 FAIRWEATHER FRIEND
- (S) (4:34) Motown 6283 Johnny Gill. *(LP version)*

released as by SHANICE featuring JOHNNY GILL:
1992 SILENT PRAYER
- (S) (5:03) Motown 6319 Shanice - Inner Child.

released as by SHABBA RANKS featuring JOHNNY GILL:
1993 SLOW AND SEXY
- (S) (5:19) Epic 52464 Shabba Ranks - X-Tra Naked.

MICKEY GILLEY
1980 STAND BY ME
- (S) (3:35) Epic 38320 Biggest Hits.
- (S) (3:34) Epic 39867 Ten Years Of Hits.
- (S) (3:34) Priority 7999 Country's Greatest Hits: Country Crossroads.
- (S) (3:35) Columbia 53060 30 Years Of Hits Volume 15.
- (S) (3:34) Risky Business 57473 Country Goes To The Movies.
- (S) (3:35) Full Moon/Elektra 60690 O.S.T. Urban Cowboy.
- (S) (3:35) K-Tel 3511 Jerry Lee Lewis/Mickey Gilley - Back To Back.
- (S) (3:35) JCI 3137 Rock Your Boots Off.

JIMMY GILMER & THE FIREBALLS
1963 SUGAR SHACK
- (S) (1:59) Rhino 70624 Billboard's Top Rock & Roll Hits Of 1963. *(stereo LP version)*
- (S) (1:59) Rhino 72007 Billboard's Top Rock & Roll Hits 1962-1966 Box Set. *(stereo LP version)*
- (S) (1:58) JCI 3112 Pop Sixties. *(stereo LP version)*
- (S) (1:58) Time-Life 2RNR-40 Rock 'N' Roll Era - The 60's Teen Time. *(stereo LP version)*
- (S) (1:57) Time-Life SUD-08 Superhits - 1963. *(stereo LP version)*
- (S) (1:59) Varese Sarabande 5697 Best Of. *(stereo LP version)*
- (M) (2:00) Varese Sarabande 5687 History Of Dot Records Volume Two. *(45 version)*
- (S) (1:58) JCI 3166 #1 Radio Hits 1960 - Only Rock 'n Roll - 1964. *(stereo LP version)*
- (M) (1:59) Eric 11503 Hard To Find 45's On CD (Volume II) 1961-64. *(45 version)*
- (S) (1:57) Time-Life AM1-17 AM Gold - 1963. *(LP version)*

1964 DAISY PETAL PICKIN'
- (M) (2:12) Varese Sarabande 5697 Best Of.

JAMES GILREATH
1963 LITTLE BAND OF GOLD

GINA G
1997 OOH AH...JUST A LITTLE BIT
- (S) (3:22) Eternal/Warner Brothers 46517 Fresh!
- (S) (3:14) Arista 18988 Ultimate Dance Party 1998. *(all selections on this cd are segued together)*
- (S) (3:00) Tommy Boy 1207 MTV Grind Volume One. *(all selections on this cd are segued together)*

GIN BLOSSOMS
1993 HEY JEALOUSY
- (S) (3:55) A&M 750215403 New Miserable Experience.
- (S) (3:54) Mammoth 92672 and 354980125 MTV Buzz Bin Volume 1.

1994 FOUND OUT ABOUT YOU
- (S) (3:51) A&M 750215403 New Miserable Experience.

1996 TIL I HEAR IT FROM YOU
- (S) (3:46) A&M 314540384 O.S.T. Empire Records.
- (S) (3:44) Atlantic 82895 VH1 Crossroads.

1996 FOLLOW YOU DOWN
- (S) (4:28) A&M 314540469 Congratulations I'm Sorry.

GINO & GINA
1958 (IT'S BEEN A LONG TIME) PRETTY BABY
- (M) (1:56) Eric 11502 Hard To Find 45's On CD (Volume I) 1955-60.

GINUWINE
1996 PONY
- (S) (5:24) 550 Music/Epic 67685 Ginuwine...The Bachelor.
- (S) (5:02) Tommy Boy 1234 MTV Party To Go '98. *(all songs on this cd are segued together)*

GIORGIO
1972 SON OF MY FATHER
- (S) (3:42) Rhino 70927 Super Hits Of The 70's Volume 7.

GIUFFRIA
1985 CALL TO THE HEART
(actual 45 time is (4:10) not (3:59) as stated on the record label)
- (S) (4:35) K-Tel 3999 Glam Rock Vol. 2: The 80's And Beyond. *(LP version)*

WILL GLAHE
1958 LIECHTENSTEINER POLKA

GLASS BOTTLE
1971 I AIN'T GOT TIME ANYMORE
- (S) (2:25) Rhino 70924 Super Hits Of The 70's Volume 4.
- (S) (2:25) Rhino 72009 Super Hits Of The 70's Volumes 1-4 Box Set.
- (S) (2:23) Time-Life SOD-32 Sounds Of The Seventies - AM Pop Classics.

GLASS TIGER
1986 DON'T FORGET ME WHEN I'M GONE
- (S) (4:04) EMI Manhattan 46313 Thin Red Line.
- (S) (4:05) EMI 27022 Best Of.
- (S) (4:04) Madacy Entertainment 1986 Rock On 1986.
- (S) (4:05) Time-Life R988-15 Sounds Of The Eighties: The Mid 80's.
- (S) (4:05) Rhino 75217 Heartthrob Hits.

1987 SOMEDAY
- (S) (3:34) EMI Manhattan 46313 Thin Red Line.
- (S) (3:35) EMI 27022 Best Of.
- (S) (3:35) EMI-Capitol Music Special Markets 19460 Lost Hits Of The '80s.

1987 I WILL BE THERE
- (S) (3:26) EMI Manhattan 46313 Thin Red Line.
- (S) (3:26) EMI 27022 Best Of.

1988 I'M STILL SEARCHING
- (S) (3:56) EMI Manhattan 48684 Diamond Sun.
- (S) (3:56) EMI 27022 Best Of.

TOM GLAZER and THE DO-RE-MI CHILDREN'S CHORUS
1963 ON TOP OF SPAGHETTI
- (S) (2:38) K-Tel 3036 Silly Songs.
- (S) (2:39) K-Tel 3409 Funniest Food Songs.

GLENCOVES
1963 HOOTENANNY

GARY GLITTER
1972 ROCK AND ROLL (PART 2)
(45 length is (3:10); LP length is (3:00))
- (S) (2:55) Rhino 70929 Super Hits Of The 70's Volume 9.
- (S) (2:59) DCC Compact Classics 043 Toga Rock II.
- (S) (3:01) Rhino 70729 and 75201 Greatest Hits.
- (S) (3:00) Rhino 71603 Rock Instrumental Classics Volume 3: The Seventies.
- (S) (3:00) Rhino 72035 Rock Instrumental Classics Vols. 1-5 Box Set.
- (S) (2:55) Razor & Tie 22502 Those Rocking 70's.
- (S) (3:00) Time-Life R968-05 Guitar Rock 1972-1973.
- (S) (2:58) Time-Life SOD-13 Sounds Of The Seventies - 1972: Take Two.
- (S) (2:51) Tommy Boy 1100 ESPN Presents Jock Rock. *(sound effects added to the ending)*
- (S) (3:40) Mercury 314522367 Soccer Rocks The Globe. *(1994 version)*
- (S) (2:58) Priority 53720 Classic Rock Volume 5 - Glitter Bands.
- (S) (3:00) Varese Sarabande 5503 and 5504 and 5505 and 5506 and 5507 and 5508 and 5509 and 5513 and 5571 Arrow: All Rock & Roll Oldies Volume One.
- (S) (2:59) Risky Business 57470 Wham Bam, Thank You Glam!
- (S) (3:00) Rhino 72132 Frat Rock: More Of The 70's.
- (S) (2:57) Tommy Boy 1137 ESPN Presents Jock Jams. *(all songs on this cd are segued together with crowd sound effects added)*
- (S) (2:55) Rhino 72275 More Stadium Rock.
- (S) (2:58) Madacy Entertainment 1972 Rock On 1972.
- (S) (2:59) LaserLight 12317 The British Invasion.
- (S) (2:55) Eclipse Music Group 64893 Rock 'n Roll Relix 1972-1973.
- (S) (2:55) Eclipse Music Group 64897 Rock 'n Roll Relix 1970-1979.
- (S) (2:54) Cold Front 6245 Greatest Sports Rock And Jams. *(all selections on this cd are segued together)*
- (S) (2:55) Flashback 72712 Arena Rock.
- (S) (2:55) Rhino 72812 VH1 8-Track Flashback: The One Hit Wonders.
- (S) (2:55) K-Tel 3910 Fantastic Volume 1.
- (S) (2:54) Cold Front 6255 Greatest Sports Rock And Jams Volume 2. *(all selections on this cd are segued together)*
- (S) (3:00) RCA 68904 O.S.T. The Full Monty.
- (S) (3:00) Rhino 75200 Basketball's Greatest Hits.
- (S) (2:58) Priority 53139 The Best Of 70's: Rock Chart Toppers.

1972 I DIDN'T KNOW I LOVED YOU (TILL I SAW YOU ROCK AND ROLL)
- (S) (3:23) Rhino 70729 Greatest Hits.

GODLEY & CREME
1985 CRY
- (S) (18:52) Polydor 825981 History Mix Volume 1. *(LP version)*
- (S) (3:54) Special Music 5041 Great Britons! Volume Three. *(45 version)*
- (S) (3:58) Rhino 72820 VH1 - More Of The Big 80's. *(45 version)*

GODSPELL
1972 DAY BY DAY
- (S) (3:14) Rhino 70928 Super Hits Of The 70's Volume 8.
- (S) (3:13) Arista 8304 A Musical Based On The Gospel According To St. Matthew.
- (S) (3:13) Rhino 71885 Best Of Broadway.
- (S) (3:12) K-Tel 3455 Folk Hits Around The Campfire.
- (S) (3:13) Madacy Entertainment 1972 Rock On 1972.
- (S) (3:13) K-Tel 3913 Superstars Greatest Hits Volume 2.

GO GO's
1981 OUR LIPS ARE SEALED
- (S) (2:44) IRS 0059 Greatest.

- (S) (2:45) IRS 75021 Beauty And The Beat.
- (S) (2:44) Right Stuff 27754 Sedated In The Eighties.
- (S) (2:44) IRS 29694 Return To The Valley Of The Go-Go's.
- (S) (2:45) IRS 29695 On The Charts: IRS Records 1979-1994.
- (S) (2:44) Rebound 314520324 Alterno-Daze: Survival Of 80's The Fittest.
- (S) (2:43) K-Tel 3742 The 80's: Hot Rock.
- (S) (2:43) Time-Life R988-18 Sounds Of The Eighties: The Early '80s Take Two.
- (S) (2:44) Hollywood 62098 O.S.T. Romy And Michele's High School Reunion.

1982 WE GOT THE BEAT
- (S) (2:29) IRS 82010 These People Are Nuts.
- (S) (2:29) A&M 3245 O.S.T. Brimstone & Treacle.
- (S) (2:30) Priority 7076 80's Greatest Rock Hits Volume 2 - Leather And Lace.
- (S) (2:29) K-Tel 3261 The 80's Rock On.
- (S) (2:30) IRS 75021 Beauty And The Beat.
- (S) (2:29) IRS 0059 Greatest.
- (S) (2:30) IRS 29694 Return To The Valley Of The Go-Go's.
- (S) (2:29) Time-Life R988-25 Sounds Of The Eighties: The Rolling Stone Collection 1980-1981.
- (S) (2:30) Big Ear Music 4001 Only In The 80's Volume One.
- (S) (2:29) JCI 3149 1980 - Only Dance - 1984.
- (S) (2:30) Rhino 72771 The Big 80's.
- (S) (2:29) JCI 3170 #1 Radio Hits 1980 - Only Rock 'n Roll - 1984.
- (S) (2:29) Hollywood 62098 O.S.T. Romy And Michele's High School Reunion.
- (S) (2:29) Time-Life R13610 Gold And Platinum Box Set - The Ultimate Rock Collection.

1982 VACATION
- (S) (2:58) Priority 53752 Rock Of The 80's Volume 12.
- (S) (2:59) Rhino 71698 New Wave Hits Of The 80's Vol. 5.
- (S) (2:58) IRS 75031 Vacation.
- (S) (2:58) IRS 0059 Greatest.
- (S) (2:58) IRS 29694 Return To The Valley Of The Go-Go's.
- (S) (2:58) Time-Life R988-01 Sounds Of The Eighties: The Rockin' Eighties.
- (S) (2:57) Rebound 314520354 World Of Dance: New Wave - The 80's.
- (S) (2:58) Nick At Nite/550 Music 63435 Beach Blanket Bash.

1984 HEAD OVER HEELS
- (S) (3:35) IRS 75041 Talk Show.
- (S) (3:35) IRS 0059 Greatest.
- (S) (3:36) IRS 29694 Return To The Valley Of The Go-Go's.
- (S) (3:35) Priority 53798 Best Of 80's Rock Volume 5.
- (S) (3:35) Time-Life R988-11 Sounds Of The 80's: 1983-1984.
- (S) (3:35) K-Tel 3473 The 80s: New Wave.

1984 TURN TO YOU
- (S) (3:48) IRS 75041 Talk Show.
- (S) (3:48) IRS 0059 Greatest.
- (S) (3:49) IRS 29694 Return To The Valley Of The Go-Go's.
- (S) (3:48) Priority 53797 Best Of 80's Rock Volume 4.

ANDREW GOLD
1977 LONELY BOY
(dj copies of this 45 ran (3:54) and (4:22); commercial copies were all (4:22))
- (S) (3:59) Rhino 71199 Super Hits Of The 70's Volume 19.
- (S) (3:55) Time-Life SOD-34 Sounds Of The Seventies - The Late 70's.
- (S) (4:20) Rhino 72445 Listen To The Music: The 70's California Sound.
- (S) (3:57) JCI 3169 #1 Radio Hits 1975 - Only Rock 'n Roll - 1979.
- (S) (3:58) Time-Life AM1-24 AM Gold - 1977.
- (S) (3:59) Time-Life R840-01 Sounds Of The Seventies - Pop Nuggets: Late '70s.
- (S) (4:20) Rhino 73511 Thank You For Being A Friend: Best Of.

1978 THANK YOU FOR BEING A FRIEND
(dj copies of this 45 ran (3:56); commercial
copies were all (4:41))

- (S) (3:57) Rhino 71911 Tube Tunes Volume Two - The 70's & 80's.
- (S) (3:57) Rhino 72298 Superhits Of The 70's Volume 24.
- (S) (4:39) Rhino 73511 Thank You For Being A Friend: Best Of.

GOLDEN EARRING
1974 RADAR LOVE
(dj copies of this 45 ran (2:53) and (5:01);
commercial copies were all (5:01))

- (S) (6:22) JCI 3301 Rockin' Seventies. *(LP version)*
- (S) (6:24) MCA 31273 Classic Rock Volume 1. *(LP version)*
- (S) (5:02) Priority 8662 Hard N' Heavy/70's Greatest Rock Hits Volume 1. *(45 version)*
- (S) (5:03) Rhino 70760 Super Hits Of The 70's Volume 13. *(45 version)*
- (S) (6:24) Sandstone 33004 Reelin' In The Years Volume 5. *(LP version)*
- (S) (6:25) MCA 31014 Moontan. *(LP version)*
- (S) (5:04) Priority 53680 Spring Break. *(45 version)*
- (S) (6:24) DCC Compact Classics 066 Rock Of The 70's Volume Five. *(LP version)*
- (S) (6:23) MCA 6355 The Continuing Story Of Radar Love. *(LP version)*
- (S) (5:02) Reprise 45485 O.S.T. Wayne's World 2. *(45 version)*
- (S) (5:03) Razor & Tie 22502 Those Rocking 70's. *(45 version)*
- (S) (5:03) Time-Life R968-01 Guitar Rock 1974-1975. *(45 version)*
- (S) (5:01) Time-Life SOD-15 Sounds Of The Seventies - 1974: Take Two. *(45 version)*
- (S) (5:03) Time-Life OPCD-4521 Guitar Rock. *(45 version)*
- (S) (6:24) Right Stuff 31324 and 31327 Harley-Davidson Road Songs. *(LP version)*
- (S) (6:23) Rhino 72132 Frat Rock: More Of The 70's. *(LP version)*
- (S) (6:24) MCA Special Products 20899 Rock Around The Oldies #4. *(LP version)*
- (S) (6:24) MCA Special Products 20903 The 70's Come Alive Again. *(LP version)*
- (S) (5:02) K-Tel 3463 Platinum Rock. *(45 version)*
- (S) (2:55) Varese Sarabande 5706 Dick Bartley Presents Collector's Essentials: The 70's. *(this is the dj 45 edit)*
- (S) (6:25) Rhino 72451 Supernatural Fairy Tales - The Progressive Rock Era. *(LP version)*
- (S) (6:22) Epic/Legacy 65020 Ultimate Rock 'n' Roll Collection. *(LP version)*
- (S) (5:03) JCI 3191 1970 - Only Dance - 1974. *(45 version)*
- (S) (4:22) Popular/Critique 12009 Dutch Treats. *(live)*
- (S) (5:03) MCA Special Products 20956 Rockin' Guitars. *(45 version)*
- (S) (6:22) Hip-O 40039 Power Chords Volume 2. *(LP version)*
- (S) (6:22) MCA Special Products 21011 70's Biggest Hits. *(LP version)*
- (S) (5:03) Rhino 72893 Hard Rock Cafe: Classic Rock. *(45 version)*
- (S) (6:22) Hip-O 40062 Under My Wheels: 12 Road Trippin' Tracks. *(LP version)*
- (S) (3:41) K-Tel 3985 70s Heavy Hitters: Arena Rockers 1970-74. *(edited)*
- (S) (5:02) Simitar 55752 Stud Rock - Heart Breakers. *(45 version)*
- (S) (5:02) Rebound 314520521 Highway Rockin'. *(45 version)*
- (S) (6:22) Priority 53139 The Best Of 70's: Rock Chart Toppers. *(LP version)*

1983 TWILIGHT ZONE

- (S) (4:48) Rhino 71699 New Wave Hits Of The 80's Vol. 6. *(45 version)*
- (S) (4:48) Rhino 71834 Classic MTV: Class Of 1983. *(45 version)*
- (S) (7:54) First Quake Entertainment 4480 Cut. *(LP version)*
- (S) (4:48) Time-Life R988-11 Sounds Of The 80's: 1983-1984. *(45 version)*
- (S) (4:48) Time-Life R968-18 Guitar Rock - The Heavy '80s. *(45 version)*
- (S) (7:50) Hip-O 40047 The '80s Hit(s) Back 3. *(LP version)*
- (S) (7:54) Rhino 72596 Billboard Top Album Rock Hits, 1983. *(LP version)*

BOBBY GOLDSBORO
1964 SEE THE FUNNY LITTLE CLOWN

- (S) (2:34) Curb 77327 All Time Greatest Hits.
- (S) (2:35) EMI 48055 Greatest Hits.
- (S) (2:35) EMI 96094 Best Of Bobby Goldsboro/Honey.
- (S) (2:35) Time-Life SUD-09 Superhits - 1964.
- (S) (2:34) Collectables 5690 Best Of - Honey.
- (S) (2:34) Time-Life AM1-11 AM Gold - 1964.

1965 LITTLE THINGS

- (S) (2:24) Novus 3077 O.S.T. Drugstore Cowboy.
- (S) (2:24) Curb 77327 All Time Greatest Hits.
- (S) (2:24) EMI 96094 Best Of Bobby Goldsboro/Honey.
- (S) (2:24) Time-Life SUD-03 Superhits - 1965.
- (S) (2:24) Collectables 5690 Best Of - Honey.
- (S) (2:24) Time-Life AM1-10 AM Gold - 1965.

1965 VOODOO WOMAN

- (S) (2:19) EMI 96094 Best Of Bobby Goldsboro/Honey. *(alternate take)*
- (S) (2:12) Collectables 5690 Best Of - Honey.

1966 IT'S TOO LATE

- (S) (2:27) Curb 77327 All Time Greatest Hits.
- (S) (2:28) EMI 48055 Greatest Hits.
- (S) (2:32) EMI 96094 Best Of Bobby Goldsboro/Honey.
- (S) (2:32) Collectables 5690 Best Of - Honey.

1967 BLUE AUTUMN

- (S) (3:05) EMI 48055 Greatest Hits. *(rerecording)*
- (S) (2:27) EMI 96094 Best Of Bobby Goldsboro/Honey.
- (S) (2:28) Collectables 5690 Best Of - Honey.

1968 HONEY

- (S) (3:58) EMI 96268 24 Greatest Hits Of All Time.
- (S) (3:58) Curb 77343 60's Hits - Country Volume 1.
- (S) (3:57) Curb 77327 All Time Greatest Hits.
- (S) (3:58) EMI 48055 Greatest Hits.
- (S) (3:56) EMI 96094 Best Of Bobby Goldsboro/Honey.
- (S) (3:56) Time-Life SUD-02 Superhits - 1968.
- (S) (3:58) Time-Life R138/05 Look Of Love.
- (S) (3:58) DCC Compact Classics 078 Best Of Tragedy.
- (S) (3:55) Rhino 71938 Billboard Top Pop Hits, 1968.
- (S) (3:56) Collectables 5690 Best Of - Honey.
- (S) (3:55) Priority 50966 I Love Country Volume One: Hits Of The 60's.
- (S) (3:56) Time-Life AM1-04 AM Gold - 1968.
- (S) (3:56) Hammer & Lace 697124114 Leading Men: Masters Of Style Volume Three.
- (S) (3:57) K-Tel 3885 Story Songs.
- (S) (3:57) Time-Life R814-01 Love Songs.
- (S) (3:57) Time-Life R808-02 Classic Country 1965-1969.

1968 AUTUMN OF MY LIFE

- (S) (3:26) Curb 77327 All Time Greatest Hits.
- (S) (3:25) EMI 48055 Greatest Hits.
- (S) (3:24) EMI 96094 Best Of Bobby Goldsboro/Honey.
- (S) (3:25) Collectables 5690 Best Of - Honey.

1968 THE STRAIGHT LIFE

- (S) (2:38) Curb 77327 All Time Greatest Hits.
- (S) (2:37) EMI 96094 Best Of Bobby Goldsboro/Honey.
- (S) (2:38) Collectables 5690 Best Of - Honey.

1971 WATCHING SCOTTY GROW

- (S) (2:33) Curb 77327 All Time Greatest Hits.
- (S) (2:33) EMI 96094 Best Of Bobby Goldsboro/Honey.
- (S) (2:34) Collectables 5690 Best Of - Honey.

(S) (2:33) Priority 50967 I Love Country Volume Two: Hits Of The 70's.

(S) (2:33) Rhino 72737 Billboard Top Soft Rock Hits - 1971.

1973 SUMMER (THE FIRST TIME)
(S) (4:36) Curb 77327 All Time Greatest Hits.

(S) (4:38) EMI 96094 Best Of Bobby Goldsboro/Honey.

(S) (4:38) K-Tel 3163 Behind Closed Doors.

(S) (4:39) Collectables 5690 Best Of - Honey.

(S) (4:36) Nick At Nite/550 Music 63436 Patio Pool Party.

IAN GOMM
1979 HOLD ON
(S) (2:57) Rhino 71202 Super Hits Of The 70's Volume 22.

GONE ALL STARS
1958 7-11

GONZALEZ
1979 HAVEN'T STOPPED DANCING YET

GOODIE MOB
1995 CELL THERAPY
(S) (4:36) LaFace 26018 Soul Food.

DICKIE GOODMAN
1974 ENERGY CRISIS '74
(S) (1:41) Hot 33205 Greatest Fables. *(distorted; incorrectly titled "ENERGY CRISIS" on the cd jacket)*

1975 MR. JAWS
(M) (2:04) Time-Life R830-01 The Dr. Demento Collection - The Mid 70's.

(M) (2:01) Hot 33205 Greatest Fables.

GOO GOO DOLLS
1996 NAME
(S) (4:29) Warner Brothers/Metal Blade 45750 A Boy Named Goo.

(S) (4:42) Atlantic 82895 VH1 Crossroads. *(live)*

LESLEY GORE
1963 IT'S MY PARTY
(S) (2:19) Rhino 70624 Billboard's Top Rock & Roll Hits Of 1963.

(S) (2:19) Rhino 72007 Billboard's Top Rock & Roll Hits 1962-1966 Box Set.

(S) (2:19) Geffen 24310 O.S.T. Mermaids.

(S) (2:19) Mercury 826448 Oldies Golden Million Sellers.

(S) (2:15) Original Sound 8853 Oldies But Goodies Vol. 3. *(this compact disc uses the "Waring - fds" noise reduction process; :04 shorter than the 45 or LP)*

(S) (2:15) Original Sound 2222 Oldies But Goodies Volumes 3,5,11,14 and 15 Box Set. *(this box set uses the "Waring - fds" noise reduction process; :04 shorter than the 45 or LP)*

(S) (2:15) Original Sound 2500 Oldies But Goodies Volumes 1-15 Box Set. *(this box set uses the "Waring - fds" noise reduction process; :04 shorter than the 45 or LP)*

(S) (2:14) Mercury 810370 Golden Hits Of. *(:05 shorter than the 45 and LP)*

(S) (2:09) MCA 6171 Good Time Rock 'N' Roll. *(all selections on this cd are recorded live)*

(S) (2:14) Special Music 836688 It's My Party. *(:05 shorter than the 45 and LP)*

(S) (2:19) K-Tel 3051 Lesley Gore/Angels.

(S) (2:18) Time-Life 2RNR-07 Rock 'N' Roll Era - 1963.

(S) (2:17) Collectables 2505 History Of Rock - The 60's Part 5.

(S) (2:17) Collectables 4505 History Of Rock/The 60s Part Five.

(S) (2:13) Polygram Special Markets 314520260 Number One Hits Of The Sixties.

(S) (2:14) DCC Compact Classics 077 Too Cute!

(S) (2:13) Special Music/Essex 5035 Prom Night - The 60's.

(S) (2:19) Mercury 314532517 It's My Party - The Mercury Anthology.

(S) (2:14) LaserLight 12314 and 15936 The Wonder Years - Party Time.

(S) (2:13) Eclipse Music Group 64868 Rock 'n Roll Relix 1962-1963.

(S) (2:13) Eclipse Music Group 64872 Rock 'n Roll Relix 1960-1969.

(S) (2:17) Polygram Special Markets 314520388 Best Of.

(S) (2:09) K-Tel 4046 More Music For Your Party. *(rerecording)*

(S) (2:14) JCI 3189 1960 - Only Dance - 1964.

(S) (2:19) Polygram Special Markets 314520460 #1 Radio Hits Of The 60's.

(S) (2:19) Polygram Special Markets 314520516 45's On CD Volume 1.

1963 JUDY'S TURN TO CRY
(S) (2:10) Mercury 810370 Golden Hits Of.

(S) (2:11) K-Tel 3051 Lesley Gore/Angels.

(S) (2:09) Time-Life 2RNR-29 Rock 'N' Roll Era - The 60's Rave On.

(S) (2:08) K-Tel 3008 60's Sock Hop.

(S) (2:11) Mercury 314532517 It's My Party - The Mercury Anthology.

(S) (2:09) Eclipse Music Group 64868 Rock 'n Roll Relix 1962-1963.

(S) (2:09) Eclipse Music Group 64872 Rock 'n Roll Relix 1960-1969.

1963 SHE'S A FOOL
(S) (2:10) Mercury 810370 Golden Hits Of.

(S) (2:07) K-Tel 3051 Lesley Gore/Angels.

(S) (2:08) Time-Life 2RNR-19 Rock 'N' Roll Era - 1963 Still Rockin'.

(S) (2:08) Mercury 314532517 It's My Party - The Mercury Anthology.

1964 YOU DON'T OWN ME
(S) (2:30) Mercury 826448 Oldies Golden Million Sellers.

(S) (2:28) Mercury 810370 Golden Hits Of.

(S) (2:08) MCA 6171 Good Time Rock 'N' Roll. *(all selections on this cd are recorded live)*

(S) (2:28) Special Music 836688 It's My Party.

(S) (2:29) K-Tel 3051 Lesley Gore/Angels.

(S) (2:28) Time-Life 2RNR-10 Rock 'N' Roll Era - 1964.

(S) (2:25) Time-Life SUD-09 Superhits - 1964.

(S) (2:30) Rhino 71585 Billboard Top Pop Hits, 1964.

(S) (2:29) Mercury 314532517 It's My Party - The Mercury Anthology.

(S) (2:27) Polygram Special Markets 314520388 Best Of.

(S) (2:28) Time-Life R857-09 The Heart Of Rock 'n' Roll 1964.

(S) (2:25) Time-Life AM1-11 AM Gold - 1964.

(S) (2:30) Polygram Special Markets 314520495 45's On CD Volume 2.

1964 THAT'S THE WAY BOYS ARE
(S) (2:13) Mercury 810370 Golden Hits Of.

(S) (2:13) Special Music 836688 It's My Party.

(S) (2:11) Time-Life 2RNR-46 Rock 'N' Roll Era - 60's Juke Box Memories.

(S) (2:13) Mercury 314532517 It's My Party - The Mercury Anthology.

(M) (2:13) Mercury 314528171 Growin' Up Too Fast - The Girl Group Anthology.

(M) (2:12) Polygram Special Markets 314520388 Best Of.

1964 MAYBE I KNOW
(S) (2:35) Mercury 810370 Golden Hits Of.

(S) (2:35) Special Music 836688 It's My Party.

(S) (2:35) Era 5025 The Brill Building Sound.

(S) (2:33) Time-Life 2RNR-25 Rock 'N' Roll Era - The 60's Keep On Rockin'.

(S) (2:35) Mercury 314532517 It's My Party - The Mercury Anthology.

(M) (2:32) Mercury 314528171 Growin' Up Too Fast - The Girl Group Anthology.

(S) (2:34) Eclipse Music Group 64869 Rock 'n Roll Relix 1964-1965.

(S) (2:34) Eclipse Music Group 64872 Rock 'n Roll Relix 1960-1969.

(S) (2:32) Polygram Special Markets 314520388 Best Of.

LESLEY GORE *(Continued)*
1965 LOOK OF LOVE
    (S) (2:07) Mercury 810370 Golden Hits Of. *(LP version)*
    (S) (2:07) Special Music 836688 It's My Party. *(LP version)*
    (S) (2:07) Era 5025 The Brill Building Sound. *(LP version)*
    (S) (1:55) Mercury 314532517 It's My Party - The Mercury Anthology. *(45 version)*
    (M) (1:59) Mercury 314528171 Growin' Up Too Fast - The Girl Group Anthology. *(45 version)*
    (S) (2:07) Polygram Special Markets 314520388 Best Of. *(LP version)*

1965 SUNSHINE, LOLLIPOPS AND RAINBOWS
    (S) (1:36) Mercury 810370 Golden Hits Of. *(slower in pitch than the 45 or LP)*
    (S) (1:34) Mercury 314532517 It's My Party - The Mercury Anthology.

1965 MY TOWN, MY GUY AND ME
    (S) (2:25) Mercury 810370 Golden Hits Of.
    (S) (2:25) Mercury 314532517 It's My Party - The Mercury Anthology. *(noisy fadeout)*

1967 CALIFORNIA NIGHTS
    (S) (2:45) Rhino 70087 Summer & Sun.
    (S) (2:45) Mercury 810370 Golden Hits Of.
    (S) (2:46) Special Music 836688 It's My Party.
    (S) (2:45) K-Tel 3051 Lesley Gore/Angels.
    (S) (2:48) Mercury 314532517 It's My Party - The Mercury Anthology.
    (S) (2:42) Polygram Special Markets 314520388 Best Of.
    (S) (2:46) Simitar 55572 The Number One's: Hot In The '60s.

EYDIE GORME
1956 MAMA, TEACH ME TO DANCE
1957 LOVE ME FOREVER
1958 YOU NEED HANDS
    (E) (2:26) Curb 77413 Best Of. *(faster than the original recording)*

1963 BLAME IT ON THE BOSSA NOVA
released as by STEVE & EYDIE (STEVE LAWRENCE & EYDIE GORME):
1963 I WANT TO STAY HERE

ROBERT GOULET
1965 MY LOVE, FORGIVE ME (AMORE, SCUSAMI)
    (S) (2:45) Columbia 9815 Greatest Hits.
    (S) (2:46) Columbia 44402 16 Most Requested Songs.
    (S) (2:46) Time-Life HPD-37 Your Hit Parade - The 60's.
    (S) (2:45) K-Tel 3209 Italian Love Songs.
    (S) (2:46) JCI 7022 Those Wonderful Years - It Must Be Him.
    (S) (2:45) K-Tel 3630 Lounge Legends.
    (S) (2:47) Collectables 5847 My Love Forgive Me/Sincerely Yours.

GO WEST
1987 DON'T LOOK DOWN - THE SEQUEL
    (S) (4:21) Chrysalis 41550 Dancing On The Couch.
    (S) (4:19) EMI 27196 Aces And Kings - Best Of.
1990 KING OF WISHFUL THINKING
    (S) (3:59) EMI 93492 O.S.T. Pretty Woman.
    (S) (4:01) Chrysalis 94230 Indian Summer.
    (S) (4:00) EMI 27196 Aces And Kings - Best Of.
1993 FAITHFUL
    (S) (4:23) Chrysalis 94230 Indian Summer.
    (S) (4:23) EMI 27196 Aces And Kings - Best Of.

GQ
1979 DISCO NIGHTS (ROCK-FREAK)
(actual 45 time is (3:55) not (3:46) as stated on the record label)
    (S) (3:48) Priority 7973 Mega-Hits Dance Classics Volume 3. *(considerably faster than the 45)*
    (S) (3:55) Rhino 70985 The Disco Years Volume 2.
    (S) (3:54) Razor & Tie 22496 Disco Fever.

    (S) (3:55) Rhino 71667 Disco Hits Vol. 4.
    (S) (7:54) Rhino 71756 and 72833 Phat Trax: The Best Of Old School Volume 5. *(sped up considerably; remixed; neither the LP, 45 or 12" single version)*
    (S) (3:55) Thump 4050 Old School Volume 5.
    (S) (3:54) Rebound 314520220 Disco Nights Vol. 4 - Greatest Disco Groups.
    (S) (3:53) K-Tel 3371 Hot Nights - Disco Lights.
    (S) (3:50) JCI 3148 1975 - Only Dance - 1979.
    (S) (3:53) Priority 50956 Mega Hits - Disco Heat.
    (S) (3:54) Flashback 72690 Disco Hits: That's The Way I Like It.
    (S) (3:55) Time-Life R838-15 Solid Gold Soul 1979.
    (S) (3:50) K-Tel 3909 High Energy Volume 2.
    (S) (3:52) Cold Front 4025 Old School Mega Mix Volume 3.
    (S) (3:49) Hip-O 40091 Disco 54: Funkin' On The Floor.
    (S) (3:55) Time-Life R840-08 Sounds Of The Seventies: '70s Dance Party 1978-1979.

1979 I DO LOVE YOU
(actual 45 time is (4:20) not (4:11) as stated on the record label)
    (S) (4:20) Thump 7030 Low Rider Oldies Volume III. *(45 version)*
    (S) (4:44) Rhino 72130 Soul Hits Of The 70's Vol. 20. *(LP version)*
    (S) (4:41) Rhino 71863 Smooth Grooves Volume 5. *(LP version)*
    (S) (4:43) RCA 66812 Do You Love Me? (All-Time Best Love Songs). *(LP version)*
    (S) (4:41) Hip-O 40030 The Glory Of Love - '70s Sweet & Soulful Love Songs. *(LP version)*
    (S) (4:44) Time-Life R834-17 Body Talk - Heart To Heart. *(LP version)*

CHARLIE GRACIE
1957 BUTTERFLY
1957 FABULOUS

LARRY GRAHAM
1980 ONE IN A MILLION YOU
    (S) (4:10) Rhino 71859 Smooth Grooves Volume 1.
    (S) (4:09) Rhino 71893 Radio Daze: Pop Hits Of The 80's Volume Four.
    (S) (4:07) Rhino 71971 Video Soul - Best Soul Of The 80's Vol. 1.
    (S) (4:09) Priority 53796 Hot And Sexy - Love And Romance Volume 3.
    (S) (4:09) Scotti Bros. 75481 Quiet Storm Memories.
    (S) (4:09) Rhino 72135 Billboard Hot R&B Hits 1980.
    (S) (4:09) MCA 11431 Quiet Storms 2.
    (S) (4:09) Warner Brothers 46024 Love Jams......Volume One.
    (S) (4:08) JCI 3147 1980 - Only Love - 1984.
    (S) (4:08) K-Tel 3673 The 80's - Funky Love.
    (S) (4:10) Rhino 72580 Soul Serenade - Intimate R&B.
    (S) (4:10) Time-Life R834-06 Body Talk - Only You.
    (S) (4:09) Warner Brothers 46043 Best Of.

LOU GRAMM
1987 MIDNIGHT BLUE
    (S) (3:43) Time-Life R105-40 Rock Dreams.
    (S) (3:53) Atlantic 81728 Ready Or Not.
    (S) (3:54) Priority 53681 80's Greatest Rock Hits - Agony & Ecstasy.
    (S) (3:52) Time-Life R988-09 Sounds Of The Eighties: 1987.
    (S) (3:44) JCI 3171 #1 Radio Hits 1985 - Only Rock 'n Roll - 1989.

1990 JUST BETWEEN YOU AND ME
    (S) (4:53) Sandstone 33049 and 5017 Cosmopolitan Volume 3.
    (S) (4:53) K-Tel 6006 Lite Rock.
    (S) (4:53) DCC Compact Classics 088 Night Moves Volume 6.
    (S) (4:53) Atlantic 81915 Long Hard Look.
    (S) (4:52) Time-Life R988-19 Sounds Of The Eighties: The Late '80s.

1990 TRUE BLUE LOVE
- (S) (4:55) Atlantic 81915 Long Hard Look.

BILLY GRAMMER
1959 GOTTA TRAVEL ON
- (M) (2:28) Time-Life CTD-09 Country USA - 1959.
- (E) (2:27) Time-Life HPD-28 Your Hit Parade - The Fabulous 50's.
- (E) (2:28) Sony Music Special Products 66106 The Monument Story.

GERRY GRANAHAN
1958 NO CHEMISE, PLEASE
- (M) (2:28) Relic 7108 The Gerry Granahan Scrapbook.

ROCCO GRANATA
1959 MARINA

GRAND FUNK RAILROAD
1970 CLOSER TO HOME
(the LP title of this song was "I'M YOUR CAPTAIN")
- (S) (10:08) Capitol 90608 Capitol Collector's Series. *(includes :16 of studio talk; LP version)*
- (S) (9:54) Capitol 48429 Closer To Home. *(LP version)*
- (S) (9:50) Polydor 314515913 Classic Rock Box. *(LP version)*
- (S) (5:29) Time-Life SOD-11 Sounds Of The Seventies - 1970: Take Two. *(45 version)*
- (S) (5:28) Time-Life R968-11 Guitar Rock - The Early '70s. *(45 version)*

1972 FOOTSTOMPIN' MUSIC
(dj copies of this 45 ran (2:34) and (3:45); commercial copies were all (3:45))
- (S) (3:45) Sandstone 33004 Reelin' In The Years Volume 5.
- (S) (3:44) Capitol 90608 Capitol Collector's Series.
- (S) (3:44) Capitol 98138 Spring Break Volume 1.
- (S) (3:46) Pair 1178 Great!
- (S) (3:45) DCC Compact Classics 066 Rock Of The 70's Volume Five.
- (S) (3:45) Time-Life SOD-22 Sounds Of The Seventies - Seventies Top Forty.
- (S) (3:45) Time-Life R968-06 Guitar Rock 1970-1971.
- (S) (3:45) Capitol 31928 E Pluribus Funk.

1972 ROCK 'N ROLL SOUL
- (S) (3:24) Capitol 90608 Capitol Collector's Series.
- (S) (3:28) Capitol 46623 Grand Funk Hits.

released as by GRAND FUNK:
1973 WE'RE AN AMERICAN BAND
- (S) (3:24) Rhino 70799 O.S.T. Spirit Of '76.
- (S) (3:24) JCI 3302 Electric Seventies.
- (S) (3:24) Sandstone 33001 Reelin' In The Years Volume 2.
- (S) (3:24) Capitol 90608 Capitol Collector's Series.
- (S) (3:24) Capitol 46623 Grand Funk Hits.
- (S) (3:23) Rhino 70519 Todd Rundgren: An Elpees Worth Of Productions.
- (S) (3:25) Capitol 98665 When AM Was King.
- (S) (3:24) DCC Compact Classics 063 Rock Of The 70's Volume 2.
- (S) (3:24) Razor & Tie 22502 Those Rocking 70's.
- (S) (3:24) Time-Life R968-05 Guitar Rock 1972-1973.
- (S) (3:25) Time-Life SOD-06 Sounds Of The Seventies - 1973.
- (S) (3:24) Time-Life OPCD-4521 Guitar Rock.
- (S) (3:25) Priority 53683 Classic Rock Volume 2 - Men At Work.
- (S) (3:23) Rhino 72131 Frat Rock: The 70's.
- (S) (3:24) MCA 11239 You Can Still Rock In America.
- (S) (3:25) Capitol 31929 We're An American Band.

1974 WALK LIKE A MAN
- (S) (3:23) Capitol 46623 Grand Funk Hits. *(45 version)*
- (S) (4:03) Capitol 90608 Capitol Collector's Series. *(LP version)*
- (S) (3:23) Time-Life SOD-25 Sounds Of The Seventies - Seventies Generation. *(45 version)*
- (S) (4:03) Time-Life R968-08 Guitar Rock - The Mid '70s. *(LP version)*

- (S) (4:03) Capitol 31929 We're An American Band. *(LP version)*

1974 THE LOCO-MOTION
- (S) (2:45) Rhino 70635 Billboard's Top Rock & Roll Hits Of 1974.
- (S) (2:56) Capitol 98139 Spring Break Volume 2. *(includes :12 of studio talk)*
- (S) (2:43) Priority 7961 Three Decades Of Rock.
- (S) (2:44) Sandstone 33000 Reelin' In The Years Volume 1.
- (S) (2:45) Capitol 46623 Grand Funk Hits.
- (S) (2:56) Capitol 90608 Capitol Collector's Series. *(includes:12 of studio talk)*
- (S) (2:44) DCC Compact Classics 062 Rock Of The 70's Volume 1.
- (S) (2:45) Time-Life R968-01 Guitar Rock 1974-1975.
- (S) (2:45) Time-Life SOD-07 Sounds Of The Seventies - 1974.
- (S) (2:45) Time-Life R105-24 Guitar Rock Monsters.
- (S) (2:45) Rhino 72132 Frat Rock: More Of The 70's.
- (S) (2:44) JCI 3140 18 Screamers From The 70's.

1974 SHININ' ON
- (S) (3:27) Priority 7942 Hard Rockin' 70's. *(45 version)*
- (S) (3:27) Capitol 46623 Grand Funk Hits. *(45 version)*
- (S) (5:54) Capitol 90608 Capitol Collector's Series. *(LP version)*
- (S) (3:26) Time-Life SOD-15 Sounds Of The Seventies - 1974: Take Two. *(45 version)*
- (S) (3:25) Time-Life R968-15 Guitar Rock - FM Classics. *(45 version)*

1975 SOME KIND OF WONDERFUL
- (S) (3:20) Capitol 46623 Grand Funk Hits.
- (S) (3:15) Capitol 90608 Capitol Collector's Series.
- (S) (3:15) Priority 7080 70's Greatest Rock Hits Volume 14: Kings Of Rock.
- (S) (3:20) Time-Life SOD-08 Sounds Of The Seventies - 1975.
- (S) (3:15) Time-Life R968-16 Guitar Rock - The Mid '70s: Take Two.

1975 BAD TIME
- (S) (2:53) Priority 8668 Rough And Rowdy/70's Greatest Rock Hits Volume 7.
- (S) (2:54) Capitol 46623 Grand Funk Hits.
- (S) (2:53) Capitol 90608 Capitol Collector's Series.
- (S) (2:53) Time-Life R968-01 Guitar Rock 1974-1975.
- (S) (2:54) Time-Life SOD-16 Sounds Of The Seventies - 1975: Take Two.
- (S) (2:53) Madacy Entertainment 1975 Rock On 1975.

AMY GRANT
1985 FIND A WAY
- (S) (3:27) RCA 66258 The Collection.
- (S) (3:26) Reunion 24339 Unguarded.
- (S) (3:27) A&M 5060 Unguarded.
- (S) (3:26) Myrrh 680627-8 Unguarded.
- (S) (3:26) RCA/Reunion 66257 Unguarded.

released as by PETER CETERA with AMY GRANT:
1986 THE NEXT TIME I FALL
- (S) (3:43) Warner Brothers 25474 Peter Cetera - Solitude/Solitaire.
- (S) (3:43) Time-Life R138-18 Body Talk.
- (S) (3:43) Time-Life R834-06 Body Talk - Only You.
- (S) (3:39) River North 514161250 Peter Cetera - You're The Inspiration - A Collection.

released as by AMY GRANT:
1991 BABY BABY
- (S) (3:56) A&M 5321 Heart In Motion.

1991 EVERY HEARTBEAT
- (S) (3:31) A&M 5321 Heart In Motion.

1991 THAT'S WHAT LOVE IS FOR
- (S) (4:16) Mercury 314525354 Women For Women.
- (S) (4:16) A&M 5321 Heart In Motion.

1992 GOOD FOR ME
- (S) (3:58) A&M 5321 Heart In Motion.

1992 I WILL REMEMBER YOU
- (S) (4:59) A&M 5321 Heart In Motion.

1994 LUCKY ONE
- (S) (4:10) A&M 314540230 House Of Love.

AMY GRANT *(Continued)*
released as by AMY GRANT with VINCE GILL:
1995 HOUSE OF LOVE
    (S) (4:38) A&M 314540230 Amy Grant - House Of Love.

EARL GRANT
1958 THE END
    (M) (2:18) Time-Life HPD-23 Your Hit Parade - The Late 50's.
    (M) (2:18) Time-Life R857-04 The Heart Of Rock 'n' Roll - 1958.
    (M) (2:18) Hip-O 40028 The Glory Of Love - '50s Sweet & Soulful Love Songs.

EDDY GRANT
1983 ELECTRIC AVENUE
    (S) (3:46) Rhino 70678 Billboard Top Hits - 1983.
    (S) (3:47) JCI 3127 1980 - Only Rock 'N Roll - 1984.
    (S) (3:48) Portrait 38554 Killer On The Rampage.
    (S) (3:47) Time-Life R988-11 Sounds Of The 80's: 1983-1984.
    (S) (3:46) Madacy Entertainment 6804 More Sun Splashin'.
    (S) (3:46) Beast 53302 Summer Jammin'.
1984 ROMANCING THE STONE
    (S) (4:51) Portrait 39261 Going For Broke. *(LP version)*

GOGI GRANT
1955 SUDDENLY THERE'S A VALLEY
    (M) (2:55) Era 5011 The Wayward Wind - Best Of.
    (M) (2:54) Time-Life HPD-38 Your Hit Parade - The 50's Generation.
1956 THE WAYWARD WIND
    (M) (2:57) Era 5011 The Wayward Wind - Best Of.
    (M) (3:13) Era 5011 The Wayward Wind - Best Of. *(includes :16 of studio talk; alternate take)*
    (M) (2:55) Collectables 5067 History Of Rock Volume 7.
    (M) (2:56) Rhino 71252 Sentimental Journey: Pop Vocal Classics Volume 4 (1954-1959).
    (M) (2:56) Rhino 72034 Sentimental Journey Pop Vocal Classics Volumes 1-4 Box Set.
    (M) (2:56) Time-Life HPD-15 Your Hit Parade - 1956.
    (E) (2:55) CBS Special Products 46850 Society Of Singers Presents A Gift Of Music Vol. 2.
    (M) (2:56) Rhino 71580 Billboard Pop Memories 1955-1959.
    (E) (2:55) Curb 77775 Hard To Find Original Recordings - Classic Hits.
    (M) (2:56) JCI 7003 Those Wonderful Years - Fever!
    (M) (2:56) Time-Life R132-12 Your Hit Parade - #1 Hits Of The '50s.

JANIE GRANT
1961 TRIANGLE
    (M) (2:25) Collectors' Choice 5189 I Wish I Were A Princess - The Great Lost Female Teen Idols.

GRASS ROOTS
1966 WHERE WERE YOU WHEN I NEEDED YOU
    (S) (2:57) MCA 5938 Vintage Music Volumes 15 & 16 *("Let's Live For Today" vinyl LP version)*
    (S) (2:57) MCA 31212 Vintage Music Volume 15. *("Let's Live For Today" vinyl LP version)*
    (S) (2:58) MCA 31132 Greatest Hits Volume 1. *("Let's Live For Today" vinyl LP version)*
    (S) (2:59) Rhino 70746 Anthology (1965-1975).
    (S) (2:58) MCA 31325 Let's Live For Today. *("Let's Live For Today" vinyl LP version)*
    (S) (3:00) Time-Life R962-02 History Of Rock 'N' Roll: Folk Rock 1964-1967.
    (S) (2:58) MCA Special Products 20194 Temptation Eyes. *("Let's Live For Today" vinyl LP version)*
    (S) (3:00) Varese Sarabande 5511 Where Were You When I Needed You.
    (S) (3:01) K-Tel 3438 Best Of Folk Rock. *("Let's Live For Today" vinyl LP version; includes :03 of studio talk)*

    (S) (2:59) MCA 11467 All Time Greatest Hits.
1967 LET'S LIVE FOR TODAY
    (S) (2:45) K-Tel 839 Battle Of The Bands Volume 2.
    (S) (2:46) Rhino 75754 Even More Nuggets.
    (S) (3:04) MCA 31207 Vintage Music Volume 10. *(:19 longer ending than either the 45 or LP)*
    (S) (3:04) MCA 5806 Vintage Music Volumes 9 & 10. *(:19 longer ending than either the 45 or LP)*
    (S) (2:46) MCA 31132 Greatest Hits Volume 1.
    (S) (2:46) Rhino 70746 Anthology (1965-1975).
    (S) (2:46) MCA 31325 Let's Live For Today.
    (S) (2:46) Rhino 71066 Summer Of Love Volume 2.
    (S) (2:48) Time-Life 2CLR-10 Classic Rock - 1967: The Beat Goes On.
    (S) (2:44) Time-Life R962-04 History Of Rock 'N' Roll: California Pop 1963-1967.
    (S) (3:04) MCA Special Products 22130 Vintage Collectibles Volume 1. *(:19 longer ending than either the 45 or LP)*
    (S) (2:46) Time-Life R968-09 Guitar Rock 1966-1967.
    (S) (2:45) MCA 11467 All Time Greatest Hits.
1967 THINGS I SHOULD HAVE SAID
    (S) (2:30) MCA 5936 Vintage Music Volumes 11 & 12.
    (S) (2:30) MCA 31208 Vintage Music Volume 11.
    (S) (2:27) MCA 31133 Greatest Hits Volume 2.
    (S) (2:29) Rhino 70746 Anthology (1965-1975).
    (S) (2:29) MCA 31325 Let's Live For Today.
    (S) (2:29) MCA Special Products 20194 Temptation Eyes.
    (S) (2:28) Risky Business 53924 Oh, Split! *(includes a drum stick "tap" before the song begins)*
    (S) (2:30) MCA Special Products 21742 Vintage Collectibles Volume 12.
    (S) (2:29) MCA 11467 All Time Greatest Hits.
1968 MIDNIGHT CONFESSIONS
    (S) (2:49) MCA 31206 Vintage Music Volume 9.
    (S) (2:49) MCA 5806 Vintage Music Volumes 9 & 10.
    (S) (2:44) MCA 31133 Greatest Hits Volume 2.
    (S) (2:43) Rhino 70746 Anthology (1965-1975).
    (S) (2:48) Time-Life 2CLR-04 Classic Rock - 1968.
    (S) (2:42) Time-Life SUD-14 Superhits - The Late 60's.
    (S) (2:44) MCA Special Products 20194 Temptation Eyes.
    (S) (2:49) MCA Special Products 22131 Vintage Collectibles Volume 2.
    (S) (2:48) MCA Special Products 20900 Rock Around The Oldies #3.
    (S) (2:43) MCA 11467 All Time Greatest Hits.
    (S) (2:42) Time-Life AM1-14 AM Gold - The Late '60s.
    (S) (2:44) MCA Special Products 21017 The Rockin' Sixties.
    (S) (2:42) Maverick 46841 O.S.T. Jackie Brown.
    (S) (2:48) MCA Special Products 21046 Top Singles Of The Sixties.
1969 BELLA LINDA
(actual 45 time is (2:53) not (2:47) as stated on the record label; LP length is (3:03))
    (S) (2:56) MCA 5940 Vintage Music Volumes 19 & 20.
    (S) (2:56) MCA 31217 Vintage Music Volume 20.
    (S) (2:51) MCA 31132 Greatest Hits Volume 1.
    (S) (3:03) Rhino 70746 Anthology (1965-1975).
    (S) (2:56) MCA Special Products 20194 Temptation Eyes.
    (S) (2:56) MCA Special Products 22134 Vintage Collectibles Volume 5.
    (S) (3:03) MCA 11467 All Time Greatest Hits.
1969 LOVIN' THINGS
    (S) (2:48) Rhino 70746 Anthology (1965-1975).
    (S) (2:42) MCA 31133 Greatest Hits Volume 2.
    (S) (2:43) MCA 11467 All Time Greatest Hits.
1969 THE RIVER IS WIDE
    (S) (2:44) MCA 31132 Greatest Hits Volume 1. *(LP version)*
    (S) (2:50) Rhino 70746 Anthology (1965-1975). *(45 version)*
    (S) (2:38) MCA 11467 All Time Greatest Hits. *(LP version)*
1969 I'D WAIT A MILLION YEARS
(the LP title of this song was "WAIT A MILLION YEARS")
    (S) (2:41) MCA 31133 Greatest Hits Volume 2. *(45 version)*

(S)　(2:44)　Rhino 70746　Anthology (1965-1975). *(45 version)*

(S)　(2:41)　MCA Special Products 20194　Temptation Eyes. *(45 version)*

(S)　(3:18)　MCA 11467　All Time Greatest Hits. *(LP version)*

1969　HEAVEN KNOWS

(S)　(2:21)　MCA 31133　Greatest Hits Volume 2.

(S)　(2:25)　Rhino 70746　Anthology (1965-1975).

(S)　(2:21)　MCA Special Products 20194　Temptation Eyes.

(S)　(2:25)　MCA 11467　All Time Greatest Hits.

1970　WALKING THROUGH THE COUNTRY

(S)　(2:58)　Rhino 70746　Anthology (1965-1975).

(S)　(2:58)　MCA 31132　Greatest Hits Volume 1.

1970　BABY HOLD ON

(S)　(2:32)　MCA 31133　Greatest Hits Volume 2.

(S)　(2:37)　Rhino 70746　Anthology (1965-1975).

(S)　(2:37)　MCA 11467　All Time Greatest Hits.

1970　COME ON AND SAY IT

(S)　(2:26)　MCA 31133　Greatest Hits Volume 2.

(S)　(2:28)　Rhino 70746　Anthology (1965-1975).

(S)　(2:27)　MCA 11467　All Time Greatest Hits.

1971　TEMPTATION EYES

(S)　(2:31)　MCA 31132　Greatest Hits Volume 1.

(S)　(2:37)　Rhino 70746　Anthology (1965-1975).

(S)　(2:32)　Time-Life SUD-10　Superhits - 1971.

(S)　(2:31)　MCA Special Products 20194　Temptation Eyes.

(S)　(2:37)　Madacy Entertainment 1970　Rock On 1970.

(S)　(2:38)　MCA 11467　All Time Greatest Hits.

(S)　(2:32)　Priority 50952　I Love Rock & Roll Volume 3: Hits Of The 70's.

(S)　(2:32)　Time-Life AM1-06　AM Gold - 1971.

(S)　(2:31)　MCA Special Products 21011　70's Biggest Hits.

1971　SOONER OR LATER

(S)　(2:39)　MCA 31132　Greatest Hits Volume 1.

(S)　(2:38)　Rhino 70746　Anthology (1965-1975).

(S)　(2:39)　Priority 7066　#1 Groups/70's Greatest Rock Hits Volume 12.

(S)　(2:33)　Time-Life SUD-16　Superhits - The Early 70's.

(S)　(2:39)　Time-Life SOD-12　Sounds Of The Seventies - 1971: Take Two.

(S)　(2:40)　MCA Special Products 22105　Greatest Classic Rock Hits.

(S)　(2:39)　MCA Special Products 20194　Temptation Eyes.

(S)　(2:40)　MCA Special Products 20903　The 70's Come Alive Again.

(S)　(2:39)　MCA Special Products 20948　Biggest Summer Hits.

(S)　(2:39)　MCA Special Products 20910　Rockin' 70's.

(S)　(2:39)　Madacy Entertainment 1971　Rock On 1971.

(S)　(2:39)　MCA 11467　All Time Greatest Hits.

(S)　(2:39)　MCA Special Products 20981　Bubble Gum Classics.

(S)　(2:33)　Time-Life AM1-13　AM Gold - The Early '70s.

(S)　(2:39)　Milan 35788　O.S.T. Hotel De Love.

(S)　(2:39)　Priority 50989　70's Greatest Rock Hits Volume 2: Rock & Soul.

1971　TWO DIVIDED BY LOVE

(S)　(2:34)　MCA 31132　Greatest Hits Volume 1.

(S)　(2:34)　Rhino 70746　Anthology (1965-1975).

(S)　(2:34)　MCA 11467　All Time Greatest Hits.

1972　GLORY BOUND

(S)　(2:33)　Rhino 70746　Anthology (1965-1975).

(S)　(2:34)　Madacy Entertainment 1972　Rock On 1972.

(S)　(2:34)　MCA 11467　All Time Greatest Hits.

1972　THE RUNWAY

(S)　(2:51)　Rhino 70746　Anthology (1965-1975).

(S)　(2:51)　MCA 11467　All Time Greatest Hits.

GRATEFUL DEAD

1987　TOUCH OF GREY
(actual 45 time is (4:33) not (4:14) as stated on the record label)

(S)　(4:30)　Columbia 44381　Heart Of Rock. *(45 version)*

(S)　(5:42)　Time-Life R105-24　Guitar Rock Monsters. *(LP version)*

(S)　(5:44)　Time-Life R102-34　The Rolling Stone Collection. *(LP version)*

(S)　(5:46)　Arista 8452　In The Dark. *(LP version)*

(S)　(5:48)　Arista 18934　The Arista Years. *(LP version)*

(S)　(4:30)　Time-Life R13610　Gold And Platinum Box Set - The Ultimate Rock Collection. *(45 version)*

DOBIE GRAY

1965　THE "IN" CROWD

(M)　(2:49)　Time-Life 2CLR-23　Classic Rock - 1965: Blowin' Your Mind.

(E)　(2:48)　Original Sound 8859　Oldies But Goodies Vol. 9. *(this compact disc uses the "Waring - fds" noise reduction process)*

(E)　(2:47)　Original Sound CDGO-5　Golden Oldies Volume 5.

(M)　(2:49)　Collectables 5072　Sings For "In" Crowders That "Go Go".

(M)　(2:42)　Razor & Tie 2112　Drift Away - His Very Best.

(M)　(2:49)　Rhino 72815　Beg, Scream & Shout! The Big Ol' Box Of '60s Soul.

(S)　(2:47)　Columbia 69059　Party Super Hits. *(rerecording)*

1973　DRIFT AWAY

(S)　(3:54)　Rhino 70930　Super Hits Of The 70's Volume 10.

(S)　(3:55)　MCA 31273　Classic Rock Volume 1.

(S)　(3:49)　RCA 8533　O.S.T. Heartbreak Hotel.

(S)　(3:49)　Original Sound 8860　Oldies But Goodies Vol. 10. *(this compact disc uses the "Waring - fds" noise reduction process)*

(S)　(3:49)　Original Sound 2221　Oldies But Goodies Volumes 1,4,6,8 and 10 Box Set. *(this box set uses the "Waring - fds" noise reduction process)*

(S)　(3:49)　Original Sound 2500　Oldies But Goodies Volumes 1-15 Box Set. *(this box set uses the "Waring - fds" noise reduction process)*

(S)　(3:48)　Razor & Tie 22047　Sweet 70's Soul.

(S)　(3:52)　Time-Life SUD-13　Superhits - 1973.

(S)　(3:54)　Time-Life SOD-14　Sounds Of The Seventies - 1973: Take Two.

(S)　(3:54)　Time-Life R921-38　Get Together.

(S)　(3:55)　MCA Special Products 22105　Greatest Classic Rock Hits.

(S)　(3:55)　MCA Special Products 20899　Rock Around The Oldies #4.

(S)　(3:55)　MCA Special Products 20941　R&B Crossover Oldies Vol. 1.

(S)　(3:55)　MCA Special Products 20910　Rockin' 70's.

(S)　(3:52)　Madacy Entertainment 1973　Rock On 1973.

(S)　(3:53)　K-Tel 3626　Music Power.

(S)　(3:55)　Razor & Tie 2112　Drift Away - His Very Best.

(S)　(3:55)　MCA Special Products 20958　Mellow Classics.

(S)　(3:52)　Time-Life AM1-03　AM Gold - 1973.

(S)　(3:56)　MCA Special Products 21011　70's Biggest Hits.

(S)　(3:54)　Priority 50991　The Best Of The 70's - Rock Chart Toppers.

(S)　(3:55)　Hip-O 40096　'70s Hit(s) Back Again.

(S)　(3:48)　Rebound 314520507　Class Reunion '73.

CHARLES RANDOLPH GREAN SOUNDE

1969　QUENTIN'S THEME

(S)　(1:58)　Varese Sarabande 5702　Dark Shadows: The 30th Anniversary Collection.

GREAT WHITE

1989　ONCE BITTEN TWICE SHY
(actual commercial 45 time is (5:21) not (5:02) as stated on the record label; dj copies were all (4:00))

(S)　(5:22)　Sandstone 33042 and 5008　Rock The First Volume 2.

(S)　(5:18)　Right Stuff 31324 and 31327　Harley-Davidson Road Songs.

(S)　(5:22)　Capitol 90640　Twice Shy.

(S)　(5:22)　Capitol 27185　Best Of 1986-1992.

(S)　(5:20)　Time-Life R968-18　Guitar Rock - The Heavy '80s.

(S)　(3:58)　Madacy Entertainment 1989　Rock On 1989. *(this is the dj 45 edit)*

GREAT WHITE (Continued)

    (S) (5:22) Priority 50937 Best Of 80's Metal Volume Two: Bang Your Head.

    (S) (5:22) Time-Life R988-13 Sounds Of The Eighties: 1989.

    (S) (5:19) Razor & Tie 89004 Monsters Of Rock.

1989 THE ANGEL SONG

    (S) (4:50) JCI 3135 14 Original Metal Ballads. *(LP version)*

    (S) (4:50) Capitol 90640 Twice Shy. *(LP version)*

R.B. GREAVES
1969 TAKE A LETTER MARIA

    (S) (2:40) Atlantic 81298 Atlantic Rhythm & Blues Volume 6.

    (S) (2:42) Rhino 70781 Soul Hits Of The 70's Volume 1.

    (S) (2:42) Rhino 72028 Soul Hits Of The 70's Volumes 1-5 Box Set.

    (S) (2:40) Atlantic 82305 Atlantic Rhythm And Blues 1947-1974 Box Set.

    (S) (2:42) Rhino 71205 70's Smash Hits Volume 1.

    (S) (2:39) Time-Life 2CLR-12 Classic Rock - 1969: The Beat Goes On.

    (S) (2:39) Time-Life SUD-14 Superhits - The Late 60's.

    (S) (2:38) Rhino 71517 The Muscle Shoals Sound.

    (S) (2:42) Mother 314516937 O.S.T. The Adventures Of Priscilla - Queen Of The Desert.

    (S) (2:39) Time-Life AM1-14 AM Gold - The Late '60s.

    (S) (2:43) Flashback 72681 '70s Radio Hits Volume 1.

    (S) (2:43) Flashback 72090 '70s Radio Hits Box Set.

    (S) (2:41) Flashback 72899 25 Years Of Soul - 1969.

1970 ALWAYS SOMETHING THERE TO REMIND ME

CYNDI GRECCO
1976 MAKING OUR DREAMS COME TRUE

    (S) (2:28) Rhino 71198 Super Hits Of The 70's Volume 18. *(mastered from vinyl)*

    (S) (2:28) Time-Life SOD-34 Sounds Of The Seventies - The Late 70's.

    (S) (2:29) Rhino 71910 Tube Tunes Volume One - The 70's.

    (S) (2:29) Time-Life R840-02 Sounds Of The Seventies - TV Themes.

AL GREEN
1971 TIRED OF BEING ALONE

    (S) (2:51) Motown 6111 Compact Command Performances.

    (S) (2:50) Motown 5283 and 9019 Greatest Hits Volume 1.

    (S) (2:48) Right Stuff 66709 Gets Next To You. *(initial pressings of this cd mistakenly substituted "THE LETTER" for "TIRED OF BEING ALONE")*

    (S) (2:49) Time-Life RHD-09 Rhythm & Blues - 1971.

    (S) (2:50) Time-Life SOD-02 Sounds Of The Seventies - 1971.

    (M) (2:41) Right Stuff 30584 Hi Times - The Hi Records R&B Years.

    (M) (2:41) Right Stuff 30800 Greatest Hits.

    (S) (2:46) Capitol 32438 O.S.T. Dead Presidents.

    (M) (2:40) Right Stuff 53033 Anthology.

    (S) (2:49) Time-Life R838-06 Solid Gold Soul - 1971.

    (M) (2:40) Time-Life R834-18 Body Talk - Romantic Moments.

1972 LET'S STAY TOGETHER
(both the LP and 45 originally ran (3:16); the (4:46) version first appeared on Al Green's "Greatest Hits" vinyl LP)

    (S) (3:16) MCA 25226 History Of Hi Records Rhythm & Blues Volume 1.

    (S) (3:38) Rhino 70660 Billboard's Top R&B Hits Of 1972. *(:22 longer than either the 45 or LP)*

    (S) (3:16) Motown 6111 Compact Command Performances.

    (S) (4:46) Motown 5283 and 9019 Greatest Hits Volume 1.

    (S) (3:13) JCI 3303 Love Seventies.

    (S) (3:16) Motown 5290 Let's Stay Together.

    (S) (3:15) Motown 8018 and 8118 Let's Stay Together/I'm Still In Love With You.

    (S) (3:15) Original Sound 8908 Best Love Songs Vol 3.

    (S) (3:15) Original Sound 9327 Best Love Songs Vol. 3 & 4.

    (S) (3:15) Original Sound 1236 Best Love Songs Box Set.

    (S) (3:13) Right Stuff 27121 Let's Stay Together.

    (S) (3:13) MCA 10925 O.S.T. Blue Chips.

    (S) (3:38) Razor & Tie 22047 Sweet 70's Soul. *(:22 longer than either the 45 or LP)*

    (S) (3:38) Time-Life RHD-20 Rhythm & Blues - 1972. *(:22 longer than either the 45 or LP)*

    (S) (3:36) Time-Life SUD-16 Superhits - The Early 70's. *(:20 longer than either the 45 or LP)*

    (S) (3:16) Time-Life SOD-03 Sounds Of The Seventies - 1972.

    (S) (4:47) MCA Special Products 20752 Classic R&B Oldies From The 70's Vol. 2.

    (S) (3:18) Ripete 2198 Soul Patrol.

    (S) (3:15) Original Sound 9304 Art Laboe's Dedicated To You Vol. 4.

    (S) (3:15) MCA 11103 and 11188 O.S.T. Pulp Fiction.

    (M) (3:15) Right Stuff 30584 Hi Times - The Hi Records R&B Years.

    (S) (3:15) K-Tel 6013 70's Soul - Sexy Ballads.

    (M) (3:15) Right Stuff 30800 Greatest Hits.

    (S) (3:13) MCA 11329 Soul Train 25th Anniversary Box Set.

    (M) (3:17) Right Stuff 52660 Flick Hits - Old School Tracks.

    (S) (3:16) Right Stuff 53033 Anthology.

    (S) (3:37) Time-Life AM1-13 AM Gold - The Early '70s. *(:21 longer than either the 45 or LP)*

    (S) (3:38) Time-Life R838-07 Solid Gold Soul - 1972. *(:22 longer than either the 45 or LP)*

    (S) (3:38) Time-Life R834-04 Body Talk - Together Forever. *(:22 longer than either the 45 or LP)*

    (S) (4:48) Right Stuff 57074 More Greatest Hits.

1972 LOOK WHAT YOU DONE FOR ME

    (S) (3:04) Motown 6111 Compact Command Performances.

    (S) (3:03) Motown 5283 and 9019 Greatest Hits Volume 1.

    (S) (3:03) Motown 5284 I'm Still In Love With You.

    (S) (3:01) Motown 8018 and 8118 Let's Stay Together/I'm Still In Love With You.

    (S) (3:04) Right Stuff 27627 I'm Still In Love With You.

    (S) (3:03) Right Stuff 30800 Greatest Hits.

    (S) (3:03) Right Stuff 53033 Anthology.

    (S) (3:03) Time-Life R834-15 Body Talk - Once In Lifetime.

1972 I'M STILL IN LOVE WITH YOU

    (S) (3:10) MCA 25227 History Of Hi Records Rhythm & Blues Volume 2.

    (S) (3:12) Motown 6111 Compact Command Performances.

    (S) (3:12) Motown 5283 and 9019 Greatest Hits Volume 1.

    (S) (3:11) Motown 5284 I'm Still In Love With You.

    (S) (3:09) Motown 6192 You Can't Hurry Love: All The Great Love Songs Of The Past 25 Years.

    (S) (3:10) Motown 8018 and 8118 Let's Stay Together/I'm Still In Love With You.

    (S) (3:13) Right Stuff 27627 I'm Still In Love With You.

    (S) (3:11) Time-Life RHD-20 Rhythm & Blues - 1972.

    (S) (3:09) Time-Life SUD-11 Superhits - 1972.

    (S) (3:11) Time-Life SOD-13 Sounds Of The Seventies - 1972: Take Two.

    (S) (3:13) Right Stuff 28372 Slow Jams: The 70's Volume Two.

    (S) (3:11) Right Stuff 30584 Hi Times - The Hi Records R&B Years.

    (S) (3:11) Right Stuff 30800 Greatest Hits.

    (S) (3:11) Rhino 72114 Billboard Hot Soul Hits - 1972.

    (S) (3:11) Right Stuff 53033 Anthology.

    (S) (3:11) Hip-O 40030 The Glory Of Love - '70s Sweet & Soulful Love Songs.

    (S) (3:09) Time-Life AM1-07 AM Gold - 1972.

    (S) (3:11) Time-Life R838-07 Solid Gold Soul - 1972.

    (S) (3:13) Time-Life R834-08 Body Talk - On My Mind.

1972 YOU OUGHT TO BE WITH ME

    (S) (3:14) Motown 6111 Compact Command Performances.

    (S) (3:16) Motown 5283 and 9019 Greatest Hits Volume 1.

    (S) (3:14) Motown 5286 Call Me.

    (S) (3:13) Motown 8040 and 8140 Call Me/Livin' For You.

    (S) (3:16) Right Stuff 28538 Call Me.

    (S) (3:17) Right Stuff 30584 Hi Times - The Hi Records R&B Years.

(S) (3:17) Right Stuff 30800 Greatest Hits.
(S) (4:52) Right Stuff 53033 Anthology. *(live)*
(S) (3:16) Right Stuff 52274 Flick Hits Take 2.
(S) (3:13) Time-Life R834-12 Body Talk - By Candlelight.

1973 CALL ME (COME BACK HOME)
(S) (3:01) MCA 25227 History Of Hi Records Rhythm & Blues Volume 2.
(S) (3:04) Motown 6111 Compact Command Performances.
(S) (3:03) Motown 5283 and 9019 Greatest Hits Volume 1.
(S) (3:00) Motown 5286 Call Me.
(S) (3:01) Motown 8040 and 8140 Call Me/Livin' For You.
(S) (3:02) Right Stuff 28538 Call Me.
(S) (3:00) Time-Life SUD-13 Superhits - 1973.
(S) (3:02) Time-Life SOD-14 Sounds Of The Seventies - 1973: Take Two.
(S) (3:01) Right Stuff 30584 Hi Times - The Hi Records R&B Years.
(S) (3:01) Right Stuff 30800 Greatest Hits.
(S) (3:01) Right Stuff 53033 Anthology.
(S) (3:01) Time-Life AM1-03 AM Gold - 1973.
(S) (2:58) Thump 9960 Old School Funk II.
(S) (3:01) Time-Life R834-13 Body Talk - Just The Two Of Us.

1973 HERE I AM (COME AND TAKE ME)
(dj copies of this 45 ran (3:04) and (4:14);
commercial copies were all (4:14) even though the
label states (4:10))
(S) (4:14) Rhino 70661 Billboard's Top R&B Hits Of 1973.
(S) (3:11) Motown 6111 Compact Command Performances.
(S) (3:10) Motown 5283 and 9019 Greatest Hits Volume 1.
(S) (4:13) Motown 5286 Call Me.
(S) (4:14) Motown 8040 and 8140 Call Me/Livin' For You.
(S) (4:14) Right Stuff 28538 Call Me.
(S) (4:16) Time-Life SOD-21 Sounds Of The Seventies - Rock 'N' Soul Seventies.
(S) (4:12) Right Stuff 30584 Hi Times - The Hi Records R&B Years.
(S) (4:12) Right Stuff 30800 Greatest Hits.
(S) (4:12) Right Stuff 53033 Anthology.
(S) (4:14) Time-Life R838-08 Solid Gold Soul - 1973.
(S) (4:13) Time-Life R834-19 Body Talk - Always And Forever.

1974 LIVIN' FOR YOU
(S) (3:08) Rhino 70662 Billboard's Top R&B Hits Of 1974.
(S) (3:09) Motown 6111 Compact Command Performances.
(S) (3:08) Motown 8040 and 8140 Call Me/Livin' For You.
(S) (3:07) Motown 5291 and 9020 Greatest Hits Volume 2.
(S) (3:08) Motown 5304 Livin' For You.
(S) (3:08) Right Stuff 29791 Livin' For You.
(S) (3:08) Right Stuff 30800 Greatest Hits.
(S) (3:09) Right Stuff 53033 Anthology.
(S) (3:08) Time-Life R838-09 Solid Gold Soul - 1974.

1974 LET'S GET MARRIED
(S) (3:19) Rhino 70589 Rockin' & Rollin' Wedding Songs Volume 2. *(45 version)*
(S) (4:24) Motown 6111 Compact Command Performances. *(neither the 45 or LP version; this version first appeared on Al Green's "Greatest Hits" vinyl LP)*
(S) (4:23) Motown 5283 and 9019 Greatest Hits Volume 1. *(neither the 45 or LP version; this version first appeared on Al Green's "Greatest Hits" vinyl LP)*
(S) (5:26) Motown 8040 and 8140 Call Me/Livin' For You. *(LP version)*
(S) (5:26) Motown 5304 Livin' For You. *(LP version)*
(S) (5:32) Right Stuff 29791 Livin' For You. *(LP version)*
(S) (3:20) Right Stuff 30584 Hi Times - The Hi Records R&B Years. *(45 version)*
(S) (3:20) Right Stuff 30800 Greatest Hits. *(45 version)*
(S) (5:27) Time-Life R834-17 Body Talk - Heart To Heart. *(LP version)*

1974 SHA-LA-LA (MAKE ME HAPPY)
(S) (2:57) Motown 5291 and 9020 Greatest Hits Volume 2.
(S) (2:57) Motown 5287 Explores Your Mind.
(S) (2:56) Time-Life SOD-07 Sounds Of The Seventies - 1974.
(S) (2:57) Right Stuff 30581 Explores Your Mind.

(S) (2:59) Right Stuff 30584 Hi Times - The Hi Records R&B Years.
(S) (2:59) Right Stuff 30800 Greatest Hits.
(S) (2:59) Rhino 72126 Soul Hits Of The 70's Vol. 16.
(S) (5:07) Right Stuff 53033 Anthology. *(live)*
(S) (2:58) Time-Life R834-11 Body Talk - After Dark.

1975 L-O-V-E (LOVE)
(S) (3:01) Motown 6192 You Can't Hurry Love: All The Great Love Songs Of The Past 25 Years.
(S) (3:00) Motown 5432 Al Green Is Love.
(S) (3:02) Motown 5291 and 9020 Greatest Hits Volume 2.
(S) (3:00) Motown 8048 and 8148 Al Green Is Love/Full Of Fire.
(S) (3:03) Time-Life SOD-16 Sounds Of The Seventies - 1975: Take Two.
(S) (3:02) Right Stuff 30580 Is Love.
(S) (3:06) Right Stuff 30584 Hi Times - The Hi Records R&B Years.
(S) (3:06) Right Stuff 30800 Greatest Hits.
(S) (3:00) EMI 55334 Sex & Soul Volume Three.
(S) (3:50) Right Stuff 53033 Anthology. *(live)*
(S) (3:03) Time-Life R838-10 Solid Gold Soul - 1975.
(S) (3:00) Time-Life R834-06 Body Talk - Only You.

1975 FULL OF FIRE
(S) (5:10) Motown 5285 Full Of Fire. *(LP version)*
(S) (5:10) Motown 5291 and 9020 Greatest Hits Volume 2. *(LP version)*
(S) (5:11) Motown 8048 and 8148 Al Green Is Love/Full Of Fire. *(LP version)*
(M) (3:26) Right Stuff 30800 Greatest Hits. *(45 version)*
(S) (5:11) Right Stuff 36592 Full Of Fire. *(LP version)*
(S) (5:12) Right Stuff 53033 Anthology. *(LP version)*

released as by ANNIE LENNOX & AL GREEN:
1989 PUT A LITTLE LOVE IN YOUR HEART
(S) (3:48) A&M 3921 O.S.T. Scrooged.

GARLAND GREEN
1969 JEALOUS KIND OF FELLA
(S) (2:50) Time-Life RHD-13 Rhythm & Blues - 1969.
(S) (2:50) Ripete 2198 Soul Patrol.
(S) (2:51) Varese Sarabande 5611 Jealous Kind Of Fella.
(S) (2:50) Time-Life R838-04 Solid Gold Soul - 1969.
(S) (2:51) MCA Special Products 21010 R&B Crossover Hits Volume 2.

NORMAN GREENBAUM
1970 SPIRIT IN THE SKY
(S) (4:00) Rhino 70922 Super Hits Of The 70's Volume 2.
(S) (4:00) Rhino 72009 Super Hits Of The 70's Volumes 1-4 Box Set.
(S) (4:00) Rhino 70631 Billboard's Top Rock & Roll Hits Of 1970.
(S) (4:00) Rhino 72005 Billboard's Top Rock & Roll Hits 1968-1972 Box Set.
(S) (3:57) Original Sound CDGO-9 Golden Oldies Volume. 9.
(S) (3:59) Original Sound 8895 Dick Clark's 21 All-Time Hits Vol. 4.
(S) (3:59) Warner Special Products 27610 More Party Classics.
(S) (3:57) JCI 3304 Mellow Seventies.
(S) (3:59) Rhino 71206 70's Smash Hits Volume 2.
(S) (3:59) Reprise 45485 O.S.T. Wayne's World 2.
(S) (3:59) Time-Life SOD-01 Sounds Of The Seventies - 1970.
(S) (3:59) Time-Life R921-38 Get Together.
(S) (3:50) MCA 11241 O.S.T. Apollo 13. *(all selections on this cd are segued together; track selection numbers on the cd jacket are incorrect; this cd is a disaster)*
(S) (4:00) Varese Sarabande 5668 Best Of.
(S) (3:59) Time-Life R968-06 Guitar Rock 1970-1971.
(S) (3:59) Varese 5635 and 5654 and 5655 and 5657 Arrow: All Rock & Roll Oldies Volume Two.
(S) (3:59) Madacy Entertainment 1970 Rock On 1970.
(S) (3:59) Varese Sarabande 5708 All Rock & Roll Hits Vol. One.
(S) (3:59) LaserLight 12528 Garage Band Rock.

NORMAN GREENBAUM *(Continued)*

- (S) (3:59) JCI 3168 #1 Radio Hits 1970 - Only Rock 'n Roll - 1974.
- (S) (4:00) Flashback 72682 '70s Radio Hits Volume 2.
- (S) (4:00) Flashback 72090 '70s Radio Hits Box Set.
- (S) (3:59) Revolution 24666 O.S.T. Michael.
- (S) (3:59) Milan 35786 O.S.T. Angel Baby.
- (S) (3:59) Varese Sarabande 5906 God, Love And Rock & Roll.

1970 CANNED HAM

- (S) (2:51) Varese Sarabande 5668 Best Of.

LORNE GREENE
1964 RINGO

- (S) (3:13) RCA 8475 Nipper's Greatest Hits Of The 60's Volume 2.
- (S) (3:13) RCA 9902 Nipper's #1 Hits (1956-1986).
- (S) (3:12) Rhino 71750 Spy Magazine Presents: White Men Can't Wrap.
- (S) (3:11) RCA 66881 RCA's Greatest One-Hit Wonders.
- (S) (3:33) Razor & Tie 8157 On The Ponderosa. *(time includes the :20 LP introduction)*

GREEN JELLO (group was later forced to change their name to GREEN JELLY)
1993 THREE LITTLE PIGS

- (S) (5:53) Zoo 11038 and 31038 Cereal Killer Soundtrack.
- (S) (4:20) Rhino 72124 Dr. Demento 25th Anniversary Collection.
- (S) (4:33) Razor & Tie 4569 '90s Style.

BOBBY GREGG and HIS FRIENDS
1962 THE JAM (PART 1)

- (M) (3:54) Rhino 70562 Legends Of Guitar - Rock: The 60's Volume 2.

LARRY GROCE
1976 JUNK FOOD JUNKIE

- (S) (3:03) Rhino 75768 Dr. Demento Presents The Greatest Novelty CD Of All Time. *(the music is recorded (M) but the intermittent audience applause is (S))*
- (S) (3:03) Rhino 70743 Dr. Demento 20th Anniversary Collection. *(the music is recorded (M) but the intermittent audience applause is (S))*
- (S) (3:01) K-Tel 3150 Dumb Ditties. *(the music is recorded (E) but the intermittent audience applause is (S))*
- (S) (3:03) Priority 53747 Wild & Crazy Tunes. *(the music is recorded (M) but the intermittent audience applause is (S))*
- (S) (3:03) Time-Life R830-01 The Dr. Demento Collection - The Mid 70's. *(the music is recorded (M) but the intermittent audience applause is (S))*

GROOVE THEORY
1995 TELL ME

- (S) (3:54) Epic 57421 Groove Theory.
- (S) (3:51) Epic 65034 Dancin Divas.
- (S) (4:44) Tommy Boy 1164 MTV Party To Go Volume 9. *(all selections on this cd are segued together)*
- (S) (3:55) Cold Front 6242 Club Mix '97. *(all selections on this cd are segued together)*

HENRY GROSS
1976 SHANNON

- (S) (3:49) Rhino 71198 Super Hits Of The 70's Volume 18.
- (S) (3:48) Time-Life SOD-31 Sounds Of The Seventies - AM Top Twenty.
- (S) (3:51) Varese Sarabande 5737 Best Of.
- (S) (3:49) Time-Life AM1-23 AM Gold - 1976.
- (S) (3:48) Time-Life R834-19 Body Talk - Always And Forever.

1976 SPRINGTIME MAMA

- (S) (3:38) Varese Sarabande 5737 Best Of.

GTR
1986 WHEN THE HEART RULES THE MIND

- (S) (5:24) Priority 53754 Rock Of The 80's Volume 15.
- (S) (5:26) Arista 8400 GTR.

VINCE GUARALDI TRIO
1963 CAST YOUR FATE TO THE WIND

- (S) (3:04) Fantasy 7706 Greatest Hits.
- (S) (3:04) Fantasy 437 Jazz Impressions Of Black Orpheus.
- (S) (3:04) DCC Compact Classics 1042 Jazz Impressions Of Black Orpheus. *(gold disc)*
- (S) (3:04) Time-Life HPD-34 Your Hit Parade - 60's Instrumentals.
- (S) (3:04) Collectors' Choice 003/4 Instrumental Gems Of The 60's.
- (S) (3:05) Rhino 72474 Masters Of Jazz, Vol. 7: Jazz Hit Singles.

GUESS WHO
1965 SHAKIN' ALL OVER

- (M) (2:41) Rhino 70732 Grandson Of Frat Rock.
- (M) (2:40) Time-Life 2CLR-14 Classic Rock - 1965: Shakin' All Over.
- (M) (2:35) Simitar 55362 Garage Band Classics.

1969 THESE EYES

- (S) (3:41) RCA 8474 Nipper's Greatest Hits Of The 60's Volume 1.
- (S) (3:43) RCA 4141 Wheatfield Soul.
- (S) (3:43) RCA 2076 American Woman, These Eyes & Other Hits.
- (S) (3:44) RCA 3746 Greatest Of.
- (S) (3:44) RCA 3662 Best Of.
- (S) (3:36) RCA 61077 Track Record. *(faster pitch than the 45 or LP)*
- (S) (3:44) RCA 61133 and 61152 These Eyes.
- (S) (3:39) Time-Life 2CLR-20 Classic Rock - 1969: Shakin' All Over.
- (S) (3:38) Time-Life SUD-07 Superhits - 1969.
- (S) (3:41) K-Tel 3463 Platinum Rock.
- (S) (3:38) JCI 3167 #1 Radio Hits 1965 - Only Rock 'n Roll - 1969.
- (S) (3:37) RCA 67300 The Ultimate Collection. *(faster pitch than the 45 or LP)*
- (S) (3:38) Time-Life AM1-01 AM Gold - 1969.

1969 LAUGHING

- (S) (2:34) RCA 4157 Canned Wheat.
- (S) (2:38) RCA 2076 American Woman, These Eyes & Other Hits.
- (S) (2:38) RCA 3746 Greatest Of.
- (S) (2:37) RCA 3662 Best Of.
- (S) (2:42) RCA 61077 Track Record.
- (S) (2:40) RCA 67300 The Ultimate Collection.

1969 UNDUN

- (S) (3:41) Sandstone 33001 Reelin' In The Years Volume 2. *(LP version)*
- (S) (3:41) RCA 4157 Canned Wheat. *(LP version)*
- (S) (3:26) RCA 2076 American Woman, These Eyes & Other Hits. *(45 version)*
- (S) (3:26) RCA 3746 Greatest Of. *(45 version)*
- (S) (3:26) RCA 3662 Best Of. *(45 version)*
- (S) (3:28) RCA 61077 Track Record. *(45 version)*
- (S) (3:25) RCA 61133 and 61152 These Eyes. *(45 version)*
- (S) (3:41) DCC Compact Classics 063 Rock Of The 70's Volume 2. *(LP version)*
- (S) (3:28) RCA 67300 The Ultimate Collection. *(45 version)*

1970 NO TIME

- (S) (3:37) Priority 8668 Rough And Ready/70's Greatest Rock Hits Volume 7.
- (S) (5:30) RCA 4157 Canned Wheat. *("Canned Wheat" vinyl LP version)*
- (S) (3:28) RCA 2076 American Woman, These Eyes & Other Hits. *(edited)*
- (S) (3:40) RCA 3746 Greatest Of.
- (S) (3:39) RCA 3662 Best Of.
- (S) (3:46) RCA 4266 American Woman.

(S) (3:43) RCA 61077 Track Record.

(S) (3:38) Priority 7080 70's Greatest Rock Hits Volume 14: Kings Of Rock.

(S) (3:33) Time-Life 2CLR-06 Classic Rock - 1969.

(S) (3:47) Time-Life SOD-11 Sounds Of The Seventies - 1970: Take Two.

(S) (3:38) Time-Life R968-07 Guitar Rock 1968-1969.

(S) (3:43) RCA 67300 The Ultimate Collection.

(S) (3:18) RCA 67474 Roller Hockey - The Album. *(sped up considerably and faded much sooner than the 45 or LP)*

(S) (3:39) Priority 50991 The Best Of The 70's - Rock Chart Toppers.

1970 AMERICAN WOMAN

(S) (3:51) Rhino 70906 American Bandstand Greatest Hits Collection. *(45 version)*

(S) (3:48) Original Sound 8895 Dick Clark's 21 All-Time Hits Vol. 4. *(45 version)*

(S) (3:48) RCA 9902 Nipper's #1 Hits 1956-1986. *(45 version)*

(S) (3:49) RCA 8476 and 9684 Nipper's Greatest Hits Of The 70's. *(45 version)*

(S) (5:05) RCA 2076 American Woman, These Eyes & Other Hits. *(LP version)*

(S) (5:05) RCA 3746 Greatest Of. *(LP version)*

(S) (5:05) RCA 3662 Best Of. *(LP version)*

(S) (5:06) RCA 4266 American Woman. *(LP version)*

(S) (5:05) RCA 61077 Track Record. *(LP version)*

(S) (5:05) RCA 61133 and 61152 These Eyes. *(LP version)*

(S) (5:05) Priority 7066 #1 Groups/70's Greatest Rock Hits Volume 12. *(LP version)*

(S) (5:06) RCA 66200 At Their Best. *(LP version)*

(S) (3:51) Time-Life SOD-01 Sounds Of The Seventies - 1970. *(45 version)*

(S) (3:50) Time-Life OPCD-4521 Guitar Rock. *(45 version)*

(S) (5:06) K-Tel 621 Rock Classics. *(LP version)*

(S) (5:03) JCI 3130 1970 - Only Rock 'N Roll - 1974. *(LP version)*

(S) (3:51) Time-Life R968-06 Guitar Rock 1970-1971. *(45 version)*

(S) (5:04) K-Tel 3510 Platinum Rock Volume 2. *(LP version)*

(S) (3:50) RCA 66862 Hi Octane Hard Drivin' Hits. *(45 version)*

(S) (5:06) Epic/Legacy 65020 Ultimate Rock 'n' Roll Collection. *(LP version)*

(S) (5:05) RCA 67300 The Ultimate Collection. *(LP version)*

(S) (4:21) RCA 67300 The Ultimate Collection. *(alternate take)*

(S) (5:05) Priority 50952 I Love Rock & Roll Volume 3: Hits Of The 70's. *(LP version)*

(S) (3:48) Eclipse Music Group 64892 Rock 'n Roll Relix 1970-1971. *(45 version)*

(S) (3:48) Eclipse Music Group 64897 Rock 'n Roll Relix 1970-1979. *(45 version)*

(S) (3:50) Madacy Entertainment 6805 The Power Of Rock. *(45 version)*

(S) (3:50) Simitar 55752 Stud Rock - Heart Breakers. *(45 version)*

(S) (3:48) Thump 6020 Easyriders Volume 2. *(45 version)*

1970 NO SUGAR TONIGHT
(the LP version of this song is actually a medley of "NO SUGAR TONIGHT" and "NEW MOTHER NATURE")

(S) (4:49) RCA 3662 Best Of. *(LP version)*

(S) (4:51) RCA 4266 American Woman. *(LP version)*

(S) (4:51) RCA 61077 Track Record. *(LP version)*

(S) (4:49) RCA 61133 and 61152 These Eyes. *(LP version)*

(S) (4:51) RCA 66200 At Their Best. *(LP version)*

(S) (2:04) JCI 3140 18 Screamers From The 70's. *(45 version)*

(S) (4:50) RCA 67300 The Ultimate Collection. *(LP version)*

(S) (4:46) RCA 67300 The Ultimate Collection. *(alternate take)*

(S) (2:06) Varese Sarabande 5846 On The Radio Volume One. *(45 version)*

1970 HAND ME DOWN WORLD

(S) (3:21) RCA 2076 American Woman, These Eyes & Other Hits.

(S) (3:21) RCA 3746 Greatest Of.

(S) (3:21) RCA 3662 Best Of.

(S) (3:25) RCA 61077 Track Record.

(S) (3:25) RCA 54359 Share The Land.

(S) (3:24) RCA 67300 The Ultimate Collection.

1970 SHARE THE LAND

(S) (3:52) RCA 2076 American Woman, These Eyes & Other Hits.

(S) (3:52) RCA 3662 Best Of.

(S) (3:30) RCA 61077 Track Record. *(fades :22 earlier than the 45 or LP)*

(S) (3:52) RCA 61133 and 61152 These Eyes.

(S) (3:52) RCA 66200 At Their Best.

(S) (3:52) Priority 7065 70's Greatest Rock Hits Volume 13: Request Line.

(S) (3:45) Time-Life SUD-04 Superhits - 1970.

(S) (3:51) RCA 54359 Share The Land.

(S) (3:44) JCI 3168 #1 Radio Hits 1970 - Only Rock 'n Roll - 1974.

(S) (3:30) RCA 67300 The Ultimate Collection. *(fades :22 earlier than the 45 or LP)*

(S) (3:44) Time-Life AM1-02 AM Gold - 1970.

(S) (3:53) Priority 50962 70's Greatest Rock Hits Volume 7: Southern Rock.

1971 HANG ON TO YOUR LIFE

(S) (4:09) RCA 3662 Best Of. *(LP version)*

(S) (4:07) RCA 61077 Track Record. *(LP version)*

(S) (4:08) RCA 54359 Share The Land. *(LP version)*

(S) (4:07) RCA 67300 The Ultimate Collection. *(LP version)*

1971 ALBERT FLASHER

(S) (2:25) RCA 3746 Greatest Of.

(S) (2:23) RCA 61077 Track Record.

(S) (2:23) RCA 66200 At Their Best.

(S) (2:23) RCA 67300 The Ultimate Collection.

1971 RAIN DANCE

(S) (2:40) RCA 61077 Track Record.

(S) (2:43) RCA 66200 At Their Best.

(S) (2:40) RCA 67300 The Ultimate Collection.

1972 HEARTBROKEN BOPPER

(S) (4:54) RCA 61077 Track Record. *(LP version)*

(S) (4:53) RCA 66200 At Their Best. *(LP version)*

(S) (4:52) RCA 67300 The Ultimate Collection. *(LP version)*

(S) (4:07) JCI 3192 18 Rock Classics Volume 2. *(neither the 45 or LP version)*

1974 STAR BABY

(S) (2:34) RCA 3746 Greatest Of.

(S) (2:38) RCA 61077 Track Record.

(S) (2:35) RCA 67300 The Ultimate Collection.

1974 CLAP FOR THE WOLFMAN

(S) (3:24) RCA 3746 Greatest Of. *(45 version)*

(S) (3:26) RCA 61133 These Eyes. *(45 version)*

(S) (4:05) RCA 61077 Track Record. *(LP version)*

(S) (3:23) JCI 3191 1970 - Only Dance - 1974. *(45 version)*

(S) (4:01) RCA 67300 The Ultimate Collection. *(LP version)*

1975 DANCIN' FOOL

(S) (3:21) RCA 3746 Greatest Of.

(S) (3:17) RCA 61077 Track Record.

(S) (3:22) RCA 67300 The Ultimate Collection.

GREGG GUIDRY
1982 GOIN' DOWN

BONNIE GUITAR
1957 DARK MOON

(M) (2:40) Time-Life 2RNR-49 Rock 'N' Roll Era - Lost Treasures II.

(M) (2:40) Varese Sarabande 5686 History Of Dot Records Volume One.

GUNHILL ROAD
1973 BACK WHEN MY HAIR WAS SHORT
    (S)   (2:38)   Essex 7060 The Buddah Box.
    (S)   (2:37)   Rhino 72297 Superhits Of The 70's Volume 23.
    (S)   (2:36)   K-Tel 3910 Fantastic Volume 1.

GUNS N' ROSES
1988 SWEET CHILD O' MINE
    (S)   (5:54)   Geffen 24148 Appetite For Destruction.
    (S)   (5:54)   MFSL 699 Appetite For Destruction.
1988 WELCOME TO THE JUNGLE
    (S)   (4:31)   Warner Brothers 25843 O.S.T. Lean On Me.
    (S)   (4:30)   Geffen 24148 Appetite For Destruction.
    (S)   (4:31)   MFSL 699 Appetite For Destruction.
1989 PARADISE CITY
    (S)   (6:44)   Geffen 24148 Appetite For Destruction.
    (S)   (6:44)   MFSL 699 Appetite For Destruction.
1989 PATIENCE
    (S)   (5:54)   Geffen 24198 G N' R Lies.
1991 YOU COULD BE MINE
    (S)   (5:41)   Varese Sarabande 5335 O.S.T. Terminator 2 - Judgment Day. *(LP version)*
    (S)   (5:41)   Geffen 24420 Use Your Illusion II. *(LP version)*
    (S)   (5:41)   MFSL 712 Use Your Illusion II. *(gold disc)*
1991 DON'T CRY
    (S)   (4:42)   Geffen 24420 Use Your Illusion II. *(alternate lyrics)*
    (S)   (4:42)   Geffen 24415 Use Your Illusion I. *(original version)*
    (S)   (4:42)   MFSL 712 Use Your Illusion II. *(gold disc; alternate lyrics)*
    (S)   (4:42)   MFSL 711 Use Your Illusion I. *(gold disc; original version)*

1992 LIVE AND LET DIE
    (S)   (3:01)   Geffen 24415 Use Your Illusion I.
    (S)   (3:01)   London 422828867 O.S.T. Grosse Pointe Blank.
1992 NOVEMBER RAIN
    (S)   (8:55)   Geffen 24415 Use Your Illusion I. *(LP version)*

ARLO GUTHRIE
1972 THE CITY OF NEW ORLEANS
    (S)   (4:28)   Warner Special Products 27615 Storytellers: Singers & Songwriters.
    (S)   (4:28)   Priority 8670 Hitchin A Ride/70's Greatest Rock Hits Volume 10.
    (S)   (4:29)   Warner Brothers 3117 Best Of.
    (S)   (4:27)   JCI 3304 Mellow Seventies.
    (S)   (4:30)   Rising Son 2060 Hobo's Lullaby.
    (S)   (4:29)   Rhino 71196 Super Hits Of The 70's Volume 16.
    (S)   (4:29)   Time-Life SOD-21 Sounds Of The Seventies - Rock 'N' Soul Seventies.
    (S)   (4:28)   Time-Life R103-33 Singers & Songwriters.
    (S)   (4:29)   K-Tel 6137 Peaceful Easy Feeling - The Best Of Country Rock.
    (S)   (4:30)   Rhino 71931 Ben & Jerry's One World One Heart.
    (S)   (4:29)   Rhino 72738 Billboard Top Soft Rock Hits - 1972.
    (S)   (4:31)   Koch 7951 Hobo's Lullaby.

JASMINE GUY
1991 JUST WANT TO HOLD YOU
    (S)   (4:09)   Warner Brothers 26021 Jasmine Guy.

HADDAWAY
1993 WHAT IS LOVE
- (S) (5:29) Arista 18735 House Of Groove. *(remix)*
- (S) (6:33) Tommy Boy 1097 MTV Party To Go Volume 5. *(remix; all tracks on this cd are segued together)*
- (S) (4:27) Arista 18743 Haddaway.
- (S) (4:27) Logic 59504 Logic Euro-Dance Compilation Vol. 1.
- (S) (4:27) Razor & Tie 4569 '90s Style.
- (S) (4:24) Arista 18988 Ultimate Dance Party 1998. *(all selections on this cd are segued together)*

SAMMY HAGAR
1983 YOUR LOVE IS DRIVING ME CRAZY
- (S) (3:28) Geffen 2021 Three Lock Box.
- (S) (3:28) Time-Life R968-20 Guitar Rock - The '80s.
- (S) (3:28) Geffen 25151 Geffen Vintage 80s Vol. II.
- (S) (3:28) K-Tel 3997 Arena Rock - The 80's.
- (S) (3:28) Simitar 55142 80's Rock Classics - Party Town.
- (S) (3:28) Time-Life R988-22 Sounds Of The Eighties 1980-1983.

1984 TWO SIDES OF LOVE
- (S) (3:40) Geffen 24043 VOA.

1984 I CAN'T DRIVE 55
- (S) (4:08) Priority 53713 Classic Rock Volume 1 - Highway Rockers.
- (S) (4:09) Right Stuff 31324 and 31327 Harley-Davidson Road Songs.
- (S) (4:10) Rebound 314520257 Hard Rock Essentials - The 80's.
- (S) (4:11) Geffen 24043 VOA.
- (S) (4:11) Time-Life R968-13 Guitar Rock - The Early '80s.
- (S) (4:10) JCI 3143 18 Screamers From The 80's.

1987 GIVE TO LIVE
- (S) (4:22) Geffen 24144 I Never Said Goodbye.
- (S) (4:21) Time-Life R968-18 Guitar Rock - The Heavy '80s.

MERLE HAGGARD
1974 IF WE MAKE IT THROUGH DECEMBER
- (S) (2:40) Rhino 70917 More Of The Best.
- (S) (2:40) Capitol 46484 Very Best Of.
- (S) (2:40) Time-Life CCD-04 Contemporary Country - The Mid 70's.
- (S) (2:40) Curb 77647 Greatest Hits Volume 2.
- (S) (2:40) K-Tel 567 Country Music Classics Volume IV.
- (S) (2:40) Razor & Tie 2059 Anthology (1963-1977).
- (S) (2:41) Time-Life R990-07 Legendary Country Singers.
- (S) (2:40) Capitol 35711 Down Every Road 1962-1994.
- (S) (2:40) Time-Life TCD-109B Country Christmas.
- (S) (2:43) Simitar 55042 My Best. *(rerecording; the printed track lineup does not match the actual track lineup)*
- (S) (2:41) Time-Life R808-04 Classic Country 1970-1974.

K-CI HAILEY
1995 IF YOU THINK YOU'RE LONELY NOW
- (S) (3:56) Mercury 314522915 and 314526211 O.S.T. Jason's Lyric.

HAIRCUT ONE HUNDRED
1982 LOVE PLUS ONE
- (S) (5:36) EMI 89605 Living In Oblivion: The 80's Greatest Hits Volume Two. *(neither the 45 or LP version)*
- (S) (3:31) Priority 7994 Rock Of The 80's.
- (S) (3:36) Rhino 71698 New Wave Hits Of The 80's Vol. 5.

- (S) (3:37) Risky Business 66392 Get Into The Greed: Greatest Hits Of The 80's.
- (S) (3:32) Arista 8330 Pelican West Plus.
- (S) (3:36) TVT 6510 O.S.T. Seven.
- (S) (3:36) Rhino 72492 New Wave Hits, Vol. 3.
- (S) (3:35) JCI 3159 18 Modern Rock Classics From The 80's.
- (S) (3:36) Flashback 72715 Definitive New Wave Hits.
- (S) (3:36) Flashback 72092 New Wave Hits Box Set.
- (S) (3:06) Arista 18985 Ultimate New Wave Party 1998. *(all selections on this cd are segued together)*
- (S) (3:35) Intersound 9521 Retro Lunch Box - Squeeze The Cheese.
- (S) (3:30) Simitar 55552 The Number One's: Eighties Rock.

BILL HALEY and HIS COMETS
1955 DIM, DIM THE LIGHTS
- (M) (2:30) MCA 5539 From The Original Master Tapes.

1955 BIRTH OF THE BOOGIE
- (M) (2:13) MCA 5539 From The Original Master Tapes.

1955 MAMBO ROCK
- (M) (2:37) MCA 5539 From The Original Master Tapes.

1955 (WE'RE GONNA) ROCK AROUND THE CLOCK
- (M) (2:10) Rhino 70598 Billboard's Top Rock & Roll Hits Of 1955. *(with countoff)*
- (M) (2:06) Original Sound 8864 Oldies But Goodies Vol. 14. *(this compact disc uses the "Waring - fds" noise reduction process)*
- (M) (2:06) Original Sound 2222 Oldies But Goodies Volumes 3,5,11,14 and 15 Box Set. *(this box set uses the "Waring - fds" noise reduction process)*
- (M) (2:06) Original Sound 2500 Oldies But Goodies Volumes 1-15 Box Set. *(this box set uses the "Waring - fds" noise reduction process)*
- (M) (2:10) RCA 5463 Rock & Roll - The Early Days.
- (M) (2:10) MCA 31200 Vintage Music Volume 3. *(with countoff)*
- (M) (2:10) MCA 5778 Vintage Music Volumes 3 & 4. *(with countoff)*
- (M) (2:10) JCI 3201 Partytime 50's.
- (M) (2:11) Curb 77323 All Time Greatest Hits Of Rock 'N' Roll. *(with countoff)*
- (M) (2:11) MCA 5539 From The Original Master Tapes. *(with countoff)*
- (M) (2:10) MCA 0161 Greatest Hits. *(with countoff)*
- (S) (3:13) Special Music 4913 Rock & Roll Revival. *(live)*
- (M) (2:09) MCA 8001 O.S.T. American Graffiti.
- (M) (2:08) Rhino 71547 Let There Be Drums Volume 1: The 50's.
- (M) (2:09) Time-Life 2RNR-08 Rock 'N' Roll Era - 1954-1955. *(missing the opening drum beats)*
- (M) (2:09) Time-Life R962-03 History Of Rock 'N' Roll: Rock 'N' Roll Classics 1954-1956.
- (M) (2:10) MCA Special Products 20751 Rock Around The Oldies #2. *(with countoff)*
- (M) (2:09) MCA 11119 The Decca Rock 'N' Roll Collection.
- (M) (2:06) Original Sound 8883 21 Legendary Superstars.
- (M) (2:08) Era 511 Ultimate 50's Party.
- (M) (2:09) Risky Business 66387 Rock Around The Clock. *(missing the opening drum beats)*
- (M) (2:11) JCI 3129 1955 - Only Rock 'N Roll - 1959. *(with countoff)*
- (M) (2:08) Music For Little People 42581 A Child's Celebration Of Rock 'N' Roll.
- (M) (2:10) K-Tel 3796 Music For Your Party. *(with countoff)*

BILL HALEY and HIS COMETS *(Continued)*

    (M) (2:09)   Nick At Nite/550 Music/Epic 67770 Happy Days Jukebox. *(missing the opening drum beats)*
    (M) (2:08)   K-Tel 4018 Forefathers Of Rock.

1956 RAZZLE-DAZZLE

    (M) (2:41)   MCA 5539 From The Original Master Tapes.
    (M) (2:41)   MCA 0161 Greatest Hits.

1956 BURN THAT CANDLE

    (M) (2:44)   MCA 5539 From The Original Master Tapes.
    (M) (2:43)   MCA 0161 Greatest Hits.

1956 ROCK-A-BEATIN' BOOGIE

    (M) (2:18)   MCA 5539 From The Original Master Tapes.
    (M) (2:17)   MCA 11119 The Decca Rock 'N' Roll Collection.

1956 SEE YOU LATER, ALLIGATOR

    (M) (2:44)   Rhino 70599 Billboard's Top Rock & Roll Hits Of 1956. *(noise at the very end of the song)*
    (M) (2:45)   MCA 5936 Vintage Music Volumes 11 & 12.
    (M) (2:45)   MCA 31208 Vintage Music Volume 11.
    (M) (2:44)   MCA 5539 From The Original Master Tapes.
    (M) (2:44)   MCA 0161 Greatest Hits.
    (M) (2:44)   Rhino 70495 Fun Rock!
    (M) (2:43)   Time-Life 2RNR-14 Rock 'N' Roll Era - 1956.
    (M) (2:44)   MCA Special Products 22028 Cra-a-zy Hits.
    (M) (2:44)   MCA Special Products 21742 Vintage Collectibles Volume 12.
    (M) (2:44)   JCI 3188 1955 - Only Dance - 1959.

1956 R-O-C-K

    (M) (2:19)   MCA 5539 From The Original Master Tapes.
    (M) (2:19)   Priority 50950 I Love Rock & Roll Volume 1: Hits Of The 50's.

1956 THE SAINTS ROCK 'N ROLL

    (M) (3:26)   MCA 5539 From The Original Master Tapes.
    (M) (3:27)   MCA 0161 Greatest Hits.

1956 RIP IT UP

    (M) (2:23)   MCA 5539 From The Original Master Tapes.

1956 RUDY'S ROCK

    (M) (2:40)   MCA 5939 Vintage Music Volumes 17 & 18.
    (M) (2:40)   MCA 31214 Vintage Music Volume 17.
    (M) (2:47)   MCA 5539 From The Original Master Tapes.

1958 SKINNY MINNIE

    (M) (2:56)   MCA 0161 Greatest Hits.
    (M) (2:56)   MCA Special Products 20957 Solid Gold Rock & Roll.

1959 JOEY'S SONG

    (M) (2:54)   MCA 0161 Greatest Hits.

1974 (WE'RE GONNA) ROCK AROUND THE CLOCK (this song charted in two different years: 1955 & 1974; see 1955 listings)

AARON HALL

1994 I MISS YOU

    (S) (6:20)   Silas/MCA 10810 The Truth.

DARYL HALL

1986 DREAMTIME (dj copies of this 45 ran (3:57) and (4:48); commercial copies were all (4:48))

    (S) (4:44)   RCA 7196 Three Hearts In The Happy Ending Machine.
    (S) (4:43)   Razor & Tie 1474 Greatest Hits.

1986 FOOLISH PRIDE

    (S) (3:55)   RCA 7196 Three Hearts In The Happy Ending Machine.

DARYL HALL & JOHN OATES

1976 SARA SMILE

    (S) (3:07)   RCA 4858 Greatest Hits.
    (S) (3:06)   RCA 61132 Soulful Sounds.
    (S) (3:08)   Time-Life SOD-04 Sounds Of The Seventies - 1976.
    (S) (3:06)   RCA 51144 Daryl Hall & John Oates.
    (S) (3:08)   Time-Life R138-18 Body Talk.
    (S) (3:07)   RCA 66812 Do You Love Me? (All-Time Best Love Songs).
    (S) (3:06)   Rebound 314520368 Class Reunion '76.
    (S) (3:06)   Rhino 72517 Mellow Rock Hits Of The 70's - Ventura Highway.

    (S) (3:05)   Razor & Tie 1474 Greatest Hits.
    (S) (3:07)   Time-Life AM1-23 AM Gold - 1976.
    (S) (3:08)   Time-Life R834-02 Body Talk - Just For You.
    (S) (3:06)   Simitar 55512 The Number One's: Lovin' Feelings.
    (S) (3:06)   Hip-O 40096 '70s Hit(s) Back Again.
    (S) (3:08)   Time-Life R814-05 Love Songs.
    (S) (3:07)   Priority 50989 70's Greatest Rock Hits Volume 2: Rock & Soul.

1976 SHE'S GONE

    (S) (5:12)   Atlantic 19139 Abandoned Luncheonette. *(LP version)*
    (S) (3:26)   RCA 4858 Greatest Hits. *(45 version)*
    (S) (5:13)   Rhino 71549 Let There Be Drums Vol. 3: The 70's. *(LP version)*
    (S) (3:25)   Time-Life SOD-18 Sounds Of The Seventies - 1976: Take Two. *(45 version)*
    (S) (5:14)   Rhino 72205 The Atlantic Collection. *(LP version)*
    (S) (3:25)   Time-Life R834-05 Body Talk - Sealed With A Kiss. *(45 version)*
    (S) (3:25)   Collectables 1516 and 2516 The Anniversary Album - The 70's. *(45 version)*

1977 RICH GIRL

    (S) (2:22)   RCA 9902 Nippers #1 Hits 1956-1986.
    (S) (2:22)   RCA 9684 and 8476 Nipper's Greatest Hits - The 70's.
    (S) (2:23)   Rhino 70672 Billboard Top Hits - 1977.
    (S) (2:24)   RCA 1467 Bigger Than Both Of Us.
    (S) (2:23)   RCA 4858 Greatest Hits.
    (S) (2:23)   RCA 61132 Soulful Sounds.
    (S) (2:21)   Time-Life SOD-05 Sounds Of The Seventies - 1977.
    (S) (2:22)   JCI 3131 1975 - Only Rock 'N Roll - 1979.
    (S) (2:23)   Razor & Tie 1474 Greatest Hits.
    (S) (2:21)   Eclipse Music Group 64895 Rock 'n Roll Relix 1976-1977.
    (S) (2:21)   Eclipse Music Group 64897 Rock 'n Roll Relix 1970-1979.
    (S) (2:24)   Time-Life AM1-24 AM Gold - 1977.
    (S) (2:21)   Time-Life R13610 Gold And Platinum Box Set - The Ultimate Rock Collection.
    (S) (2:21)   Simitar 55152 Blue Eyed Soul.
    (S) (2:22)   K-Tel 3987 70s Heavy Hitters: #1 Pop Hits.
    (S) (2:23)   Priority 53139 The Best Of 70's: Rock Chart Toppers.

1977 BACK TOGETHER AGAIN

    (S) (3:24)   RCA 1467 Bigger Than Both Of Us.
    (S) (3:24)   Razor & Tie 1474 Greatest Hits.

1978 IT'S A LAUGH

    (S) (3:50)   RCA 66939 Along The Red Ledge. *(tracks into the next selection)*
    (S) (3:49)   Razor & Tie 1474 Greatest Hits.

1980 WAIT FOR ME

    (S) (6:04)   RCA 4858 Greatest Hits. *(live version - not the hit version)*
    (S) (4:05)   Razor & Tie 1474 Greatest Hits.

1980 HOW DOES IT FEEL TO BE BACK (actual 45 time is (4:16) not (3:58) as stated on the record label)

    (S) (4:34)   RCA 3646 Voices. *(LP length)*
    (S) (4:32)   RCA 61132 Soulful Sounds. *(LP length)*
    (S) (4:33)   Razor & Tie 1474 Greatest Hits. *(LP length)*

1980 YOU'VE LOST THAT LOVIN' FEELING

    (S) (4:35)   RCA 3646 Voices. *(LP length)*
    (S) (4:34)   Razor & Tie 1474 Greatest Hits. *(LP length)*

1981 KISS ON MY LIST

    (S) (3:48)   Rhino 70676 Billboard Top Hits - 1981. *(45 version)*
    (S) (4:24)   RCA 3646 Voices. *(LP version)*
    (S) (3:52)   RCA 4858 Greatest Hits. *(edit of LP version)*
    (S) (3:46)   Time-Life R988-08 Sounds Of The Eighties: 1981. *(45 version)*
    (S) (4:17)   Rebound 314520361 Class Reunion '81. *(LP version)*
    (S) (3:34)   JCI 3163 18 Disco Superhits. *(45 version faded :14 early)*
    (S) (4:23)   Razor & Tie 1474 Greatest Hits. *(LP version)*

(S) (4:22) Hip-O 40079 Essential '80s: 1980-1984. *(LP version)*
(S) (4:22) Simitar 55562 The Number One's: Smooth Love. *(LP version)*
(S) (3:47) Time-Life R834-11 Body Talk - After Dark. *(45 version)*

1981 YOU MAKE MY DREAMS
(S) (3:10) RCA 3646 Voices.
(S) (3:08) RCA 4858 Greatest Hits.
(S) (3:07) Big Ear Music 4001 Only In The 80's Volume One.
(S) (3:04) JCI 3149 1980 - Only Dance - 1984.
(S) (3:09) Razor & Tie 1474 Greatest Hits.

1981 PRIVATE EYES
(S) (3:37) RCA 4028 Private Eyes. *(LP length)*
(S) (3:26) RCA 4858 Greatest Hits. *(45 length)*
(S) (3:36) Razor & Tie 1474 Greatest Hits. *(LP length)*
(S) (3:26) Time-Life R988-16 Sounds Of The Eighties: The Early '80s. *(45 length)*
(S) (3:36) Simitar 55612 The Number One's: The '80s. *(LP length)*

1982 I CAN'T GO FOR THAT (NO CAN DO)
(S) (3:43) RCA 9902 Nipper's #1 Hits 1956-1986. *(45 version)*
(S) (6:01) RCA 2357 Dance, Dance, Dance Volume II. *(12" single version)*
(S) (3:42) JCI 3127 1980 - Only Rock 'N Roll - 1984. *(45 version)*
(S) (3:44) RCA 4858 Greatest Hits. *(45 version)*
(S) (5:07) RCA 4028 Private Eyes. *(LP version)*
(S) (3:43) Rhino 72137 Billboard Hot R&B Hits 1982. *(45 version)*
(S) (5:05) Razor & Tie 1474 Greatest Hits. *(LP version)*
(S) (3:42) Time-Life R988-14 Sounds Of The Eighties: 1980-1982. *(45 version)*
(S) (3:42) Time-Life R834-09 Body Talk - Magic Moments. *(45 version)*

1982 DID IT IN A MINUTE
(S) (3:36) RCA 4028 Private Eyes.
(S) (3:36) Razor & Tie 1474 Greatest Hits.

1982 YOUR IMAGINATION
(S) (3:33) RCA 4028 Private Eyes. *(LP mix)*
(S) (5:40) Razor & Tie 1474 Greatest Hits.

1983 MANEATER
(dj copies of this 45 ran (3:28) and (4:30); commercial copies were all (4:30))
(S) (4:29) RCA 9970 Nipper's Greatest Hits - The 80's.
(S) (4:30) Rhino 70677 Billboard Top Hits - 1982.
(S) (4:30) Original Sound 8895 Dick Clark's 21 All-Time Hits Vol. 4.
(S) (4:31) RCA 4383 H2O.
(S) (4:31) RCA 4858 Greatest Hits.
(S) (4:29) Time-Life R988-05 Sounds Of The Eighties: 1982.
(S) (4:30) Big Ear Music 4002 Only In The 80's Volume Two.
(S) (4:31) Razor & Tie 1474 Greatest Hits.
(S) (4:30) K-Tel 3798 The 80's Mega Hits.
(S) (4:29) Simitar 55552 The Number One's: Eighties Rock.

1983 ONE ON ONE
(dj copies of this 45 ran (3:45) and (3:53); commercial copies were all (3:53); actual LP time is (4:15) not (4:28) as stated on the record label)
(S) (4:15) RCA 4383 H2O. *(LP length)*
(S) (3:56) RCA 4858 Greatest Hits. *(45 length)*
(S) (4:13) RCA 61132 Soulful Sounds. *(LP length)*
(S) (3:50) Rebound 314520372 The Roots Of Rock: Soft Rock. *(45 length)*
(S) (4:15) Razor & Tie 1474 Greatest Hits. *(LP length)*
(S) (3:53) Time-Life R834-07 Body Talk - Hearts In Motion. *(45 length)*
(S) (4:13) K-Tel 3864 Slow Dancin'. *(LP length)*
(S) (3:54) K-Tel 6257 The Greatest Love Songs - 16 Soft Rock Hits. *(45 length)*

1983 FAMILY MAN
(S) (3:25) RCA 4383 H2O.
(S) (3:24) RCA 66862 Hi Octane Hard Drivin' Hits.

(S) (3:24) Razor & Tie 1474 Greatest Hits.
(S) (3:24) Time-Life R988-22 Sounds Of The Eighties 1980-1983.

1983 SAY IT ISN'T SO
(S) (4:16) RCA 4858 Greatest Hits. *(LP length)*
(S) (4:17) Time-Life R988-11 Sounds Of The 80's: 1983-1984. *(LP length)*
(S) (4:00) Time-Life R988-03 Sounds Of The Eighties: 1983. *(45 length)*
(S) (4:16) Razor & Tie 1474 Greatest Hits. *(LP length)*
(S) (4:14) Time-Life R834-13 Body Talk - Just The Two Of Us. *(LP length)*

1984 ADULT EDUCATION
(S) (5:23) RCA 4858 Greatest Hits. *(LP version)*
(S) (5:22) Razor & Tie 1474 Greatest Hits. *(LP version)*

1984 OUT OF TOUCH
(S) (3:55) T.J. Martell Foundation/Columbia 40315 Music For The Miracle. *(45 version)*
(S) (4:16) RCA 5336 Big Bam Boom. *(LP version)*
(S) (3:53) Time-Life R988-06 Sounds Of The Eighties: 1984. *(45 version)*
(S) (4:19) RCA 66937 Big Bam Boom. *(LP version)*
(S) (4:20) Razor & Tie 1474 Greatest Hits. *(LP version)*
(S) (3:53) Priority 50953 I Love Rock & Roll Volume 4: Hits Of The 80's. *(45 version)*
(S) (4:20) K-Tel 3866 The 80's: Number One Pop Hits. *(LP version)*

1985 METHOD OF MODERN LOVE
(S) (5:33) RCA 5336 Big Bam Boom. *(LP version)*
(S) (5:21) JCI 3186 1985 - Only Love - 1989. *(LP version faded :12 early)*
(S) (5:29) RCA 66937 Big Bam Boom. *(LP version)*
(S) (5:29) Razor & Tie 1474 Greatest Hits. *(LP version)*

1985 SOME THINGS ARE BETTER LEFT UNSAID
(S) (5:25) RCA 5336 Big Bam Boom. *(LP version)*
(S) (5:23) RCA 66937 Big Bam Boom. *(LP version)*
(S) (5:24) Razor & Tie 1474 Greatest Hits. *(LP version)*

1985 POSSESSION OBSESSION
(S) (4:34) RCA 5336 Big Bam Boom. *(LP version)*
(S) (4:34) RCA 66937 Big Bam Boom. *(LP version)*
(S) (4:35) Razor & Tie 1474 Greatest Hits. *(LP version)*

released as by DARY HALL/JOHN OATES with DAVID RUFFIN and EDDIE KENDRICK:
1985 THE WAY YOU DO THE THINGS YOU DO/MY GIRL
(S) (12:35) RCA 7035 Live At The Apollo. *(LP version which is a medley of a number of different songs)*
(S) (5:42) RCA 66862 Hi Octane Hard Drivin' Hits. *(edit of LP version)*

released as by DARYL HALL & JOHN OATES:
1988 EVERYTHING YOUR HEART DESIRES
(S) (4:59) Arista 8539 Ooh Yeah! *(LP version)*
1988 MISSED OPPORTUNITY
(S) (4:46) Arista 8539 Ooh Yeah! *(LP length)*
1988 DOWNTOWN LIFE
(S) (4:26) Arista 8539 Ooh Yeah! *(LP version)*
1990 SO CLOSE
(S) (4:39) Arista 8614 Change Of Season. *(LP version)*
1991 DON'T HOLD BACK YOUR LOVE
(S) (5:11) Arista 8614 Change Of Season.

JIMMY HALL
1980 I'M HAPPY THAT LOVE HAS FOUND YOU
(S) (3:59) Rhino 71893 Radio Daze: Pop Hits Of The 80's Volume Four. *(LP version)*
(S) (3:56) Sony Music Special Products 75066 Endless Beach. *(LP version)*
(S) (3:56) CBS Special Products 37915 Endless Beach. *(LP version)*

LARRY HALL
1960 SANDY
(M) (2:22) Time-Life SUD-15 Superhits - The Early 60's.
(E) (2:27) Collectables 5582 Sandy.
(M) (2:22) Time-Life AM1-19 AM Gold - The Early '60s.

TOM T. HALL
1974 I LOVE
- (S) (2:06) Mercury 422824144 Greatest Hits Volume 2.
- (S) (2:04) Time-Life CCD-04 Contemporary Country - The Mid 70's.
- (S) (2:05) K-Tel 3111 Country Music Classics Vol. XIX.
- (S) (2:05) Polygram Special Markets 314520316 Country Classics.
- (S) (2:05) K-Tel 3253 Old-Fashioned Love: Country Style.
- (S) (2:05) Mercury 810462 Greatest Hits Volumes I & II.
- (S) (2:06) Priority 50967 I Love Country Volume Two: Hits Of The 70's.
- (S) (2:04) Mercury 314534666 The Hits.
- (S) (2:06) Hip-O 40085 The Class Of Country 1970-1974.
- (S) (2:04) Time-Life R808-04 Classic Country 1970-1974.

HALOS
1961 "NAG"
- (M) (2:48) Rhino 71463 Doo Wop Box.
- (M) (2:44) Time-Life 2RNR-42 Rock 'N' Roll Era - The 60's Sock Hop.
- (M) (2:48) Collectables 5580 Nag.
- (M) (2:50) Forevermore 5008 Oldies I Forgot To Buy.

GEORGE HAMILTON IV
1956 A ROSE AND A BABY RUTH
- (E) (1:58) MCA 5936 Vintage Music Volumes 11 & 12.
- (E) (1:58) MCA 31209 Vintage Music Volume 12.
- (M) (1:58) Time-Life HPD-38 Your Hit Parade - The 50's Generation.
- (M) (1:58) Collectors' Choice 002 Teen Idols....For A Moment.
- (M) (1:58) Time-Life R857-07 The Heart Of Rock 'n' Roll 1956.
- (M) (1:58) Collectables 5875 Abilene Plus More Great Folk Hits.

1957 ONLY ONE LOVE
1958 WHY DON'T THEY UNDERSTAND
- (M) (2:30) Time-Life HPD-28 Your Hit Parade - The Fabulous 50's.
- (E) (2:32) MCA Special Products 20580 Teen Idols.
- (M) (2:31) Collectables 5875 Abilene Plus More Great Folk Hits.

1958 NOW AND FOR ALWAYS
- (M) (2:22) Collectables 5875 Abilene Plus More Great Folk Hits.

released as by PAUL ANKA-GEORGE HAMILTON IV-JOHNNY NASH:
1959 THE TEEN COMMANDMENTS
- (M) (1:41) Rhino 71489 Paul Anka - 30th Anniversary Collection.

released as by GEORGE HAMILTON IV:
1963 ABILENE
- (S) (2:11) RCA 8475 Nipper's Greatest Hits Of The 60's Volume 2.
- (S) (2:11) Rhino 70684 Billboard's Top Country Hits Of 1963.
- (S) (2:11) RCA 5802 Best Of The 60's.
- (S) (2:09) Reprise 45516 O.S.T. A Perfect World.
- (S) (2:10) Time-Life CTD-11 Country USA - 1963.
- (S) (2:16) K-Tel 3357 101 Greatest Country Hits Vol. Three: Easy Country. *(rerecording)*
- (S) (2:11) Collectables 5875 Abilene Plus More Great Folk Hits.
- (S) (2:10) Time-Life R808-01 Classic Country 1960-1964.

ROY HAMILTON
1955 UNCHAINED MELODY
- (E) (2:57) Collectables 5150 Golden Classics.
- (E) (2:57) Collectables 8823 Anthology.
- (M) (2:55) Nick At Nite/Epic 67148 Donna Reed's Dinner Party.

1958 DON'T LET GO
- (S) (2:30) Collectables 5150 Golden Classics.
- (S) (2:27) Time-Life 2RNR-44 Rock 'N' Roll Era - Lost Treasures.

- (S) (2:26) Time-Life RHD-16 Rhythm & Blues - 1958.
- (S) (2:28) Time-Life HPD-36 Your Hit Parade - The 50's Pop Revival.
- (S) (2:30) Collectables 8823 Anthology.
- (S) (2:26) Time-Life R838-22 Solid Gold Soul 1958.

1961 YOU CAN HAVE HER
- (S) (2:44) Collectables 5150 Golden Classics.
- (S) (2:43) Time-Life 2RNR-49 Rock 'N' Roll Era - Lost Treasures II.
- (S) (2:44) Time-Life HPD-37 Your Hit Parade - The 60's.
- (S) (2:45) Collectables 8823 Anthology.

RUSS HAMILTON
1957 RAINBOW
- (M) (2:40) Time-Life HPD-17 Your Hit Parade - 1957.

HAMILTON, JOE FRANK & REYNOLDS
1971 DON'T PULL YOUR LOVE
- (S) (2:40) Rhino 70925 Super Hits Of The 70's Volume 5.
- (S) (2:41) Priority 8666 Kickin' Back/70's Greatest Rock Hits Volume 5.
- (S) (2:40) Rhino 71209 70's Smash Hits Volume 5.
- (S) (2:38) Razor & Tie 21640 Those Fabulous 70's.
- (S) (2:38) Time-Life SUD-10 Superhits - 1971.
- (S) (2:40) MCA Special Products 20839 Greatest Hits.
- (S) (2:39) MCA Special Products 20899 Rock Around The Oldies #4.
- (S) (2:40) MCA Special Products 20949 Rockin' 70's Volume 2.
- (S) (2:38) Madacy Entertainment 1971 Rock On 1971.
- (S) (2:38) JCI 3191 1970 - Only Dance - 1974.
- (S) (2:38) Time-Life AM1-06 AM Gold - 1971.
- (S) (2:40) MCA Special Products 20997 Mellow Rock.
- (S) (2:40) Flashback 72685 '70s Radio Hits Volume 5.
- (S) (2:39) MCA Special Products 21011 70's Biggest Hits.

1972 DAISY MAE
- (S) (2:58) MCA Special Products 20839 Greatest Hits.

1975 FALLIN' IN LOVE
- (S) (2:59) Rhino 70670 Billboard Top Hits - 1975. *(LP length)*
- (S) (2:59) Rhino 70762 Super Hits Of The 70's Volume 15. *(LP length)*
- (S) (2:59) Razor & Tie 4543 The '70s Preservation Society Presents: Easy '70s. *(LP length)*
- (S) (2:59) Time-Life R840-03 Sounds Of The Seventies - Pop Nuggets: Early '70s. *(LP length)*

1975 WINNERS AND LOSERS

MARVIN HAMLISCH
1974 THE ENTERTAINER
- (S) (3:03) MCA 31034 O.S.T. The Sting.
- (S) (3:03) Rhino 70759 Super Hits Of The 70's Volume 12.
- (S) (3:03) Rhino 72424 Billboard Top Movie Hits - 1970s.
- (M) (2:32) K-Tel 3627 Out Of Sight. *(this is the "piano version" from O.S.T. "The Sting")*
- (S) (3:02) Time-Life R840-04 Sounds Of The Seventies: A Loss For Words.
- (S) (3:02) Time-Life AM1-21 AM Gold - 1974.
- (S) (3:01) Time-Life R986-22 Instrumental Classics - Pop Classics.

HAMMER (see M.C. HAMMER)

JAN HAMMER
1985 "MIAMI VICE" THEME
- (S) (2:26) MCA 6150 Music From The Television Series Miami Vice.
- (S) (2:25) MCA 6330 Soundtrack Smashes - The 80's.
- (S) (2:25) Rhino 71640 Billboard Top Hits - 1985.
- (S) (2:25) Rhino 71912 Tube Tunes Volume Three - The 80's.
- (S) (2:25) Time-Life R988-02 Sounds Of The Eighties: 1985.
- (S) (2:26) Madacy Entertainment 1985 Rock On 1985.
- (S) (2:26) Hip-O 40005 The '80s Hit(s) Back....Again!

(S) (2:26) Hip-O 40017 Mission Accomplished: Themes For Spies & Cops.
(S) (2:25) JCI 3171 #1 Radio Hits 1985 - Only Rock 'n Roll - 1989.
(S) (2:25) Time-Life R988-32 Sounds Of The Eighties: TV Themes Of The '80s.
(S) (2:25) Hip-O 40013 Synth Me Up - 14 Classic Electronic Hits.
(S) (2:26) Hip-O 40080 Essential '80s: 1985-1989.

ALBERT HAMMOND
1972 IT NEVER RAINS IN SOUTHERN CALIFORNIA
(45 length is (3:12); LP length is (3:50))
(S) (3:36) Rhino 70930 Super Hits Of The 70's Volume 10.
(S) (3:49) Columbia/Legacy 46763 Rock Artifacts Volume 2.
(S) (3:28) Time-Life SUD-16 Superhits - The Early 70's.
(S) (3:35) Varese Sarabande 5534 Rhythm Of The Rain.
(S) (3:49) Risky Business 66662 Swingin' Singles/Greatest Hits Of The 70's.
(S) (3:50) Collectables 5819 It Never Rains In Southern California - A Golden Classics Edition.
(S) (3:51) Eclipse Music Group 64893 Rock 'n Roll Relix 1972-1973.
(S) (3:51) Eclipse Music Group 64897 Rock 'n Roll Relix 1970-1979.
(S) (3:28) Time-Life AM1-13 AM Gold - The Early '70s.
(S) (3:34) K-Tel 3912 Superstars Greatest Hits Volume 1.
1974 I'M A TRAIN
(S) (3:20) Columbia/Legacy 46763 Rock Artifacts Volume 2.
(S) (3:18) Collectables 5819 It Never Rains In Southern California - A Golden Classics Edition.

HANSON
1997 MMMBOP
(S) (4:26) Mercury 314534615 Middle Of Nowhere.
(S) (4:27) MCA 11752 1998 Grammy Nominees.
1997 I WILL COME TO YOU
(S) (4:09) Mercury 314534615 Middle Of Nowhere.

HAPPENINGS
1966 SEE YOU IN SEPTEMBER
(S) (2:31) Time-Life SUD-01 Superhits - 1966.
(S) (2:27) Rhino 71730 '60s Rock Classics, Vol. 3.
(S) (2:31) Time-Life AM1-09 AM Gold - 1966.
(S) (2:27) Flashback 72703 '60s Rock: It's A Beautiful Morning.
(S) (2:27) Flashback 72088 '60s Rock Hits Box Set.
(S) (2:31) Time-Life R857-20 The Heart Of Rock 'n' Roll 1965-1966.
(S) (2:27) Collectables 1515 and 2515 The Anniversary Album - The 60's.
1966 GO AWAY LITTLE GIRL
1967 I GOT RHYTHM
(S) (2:56) Time-Life SUD-18 Superhits - Late 60's Classics.
(S) (2:58) Rhino 71728 '60s Rock Classics, Vol. 1.
(S) (2:56) Time-Life AM1-12 AM Gold - Late '60s Classics.
(S) (2:58) Flashback 72701 '60s Rock: Mony Mony.
(S) (2:58) Flashback 72088 '60s Rock Hits Box Set.
(S) (2:54) Varese Sarabande 5801 Sunshine Days - Pop Classics Of The '60s Volume 1.
1967 MY MAMMY

PAUL HARDCASLE
1985 19
(S) (3:36) EMI 81417 Living In Oblivion: The 80's Greatest Hits Volume One. *(45 version)*
(S) (6:18) Priority 53754 Rock Of The 80's Volume 15. *(LP version)*
(S) (6:18) Chrysalis 41549 and 21549 No Winners. *(LP version)*
(S) (3:37) Rhino 71978 New Wave Hits Of The 80's Vol. 15. *(45 version)*

JOE HARNELL
1963 FLY ME TO THE MOON – BOSSA NOVA
(S) (2:29) Time-Life HPD-34 Your Hit Parade - 60's Instrumentals.
(S) (2:25) Collectors' Choice 003/4 Instrumental Gems Of The 60's.
(S) (2:28) K-Tel 3472 Those Wonderful Instrumentals Volume 2.
(S) (2:26) Hip-O 40034 Cigar Classics Volume 4 - Smokin' Lounge.
(S) (2:24) Time-Life R986-12 Instrumental Favorites - Latin Rhythms. *(noisy fadeout)*
(S) (2:28) MCA Special Products 21035 Classic Rock & Roll Instrumental Hits, Volume 2.
(S) (2:22) MCA Special Products 21025 The Best Of Easy Listening.

JIMMY HARNEN with SYNCH
1989 WHERE ARE YOU NOW?
(S) (4:28) Priority 53767 Rock Of The 80's Volume 11.
(S) (4:28) WTG 45243 Can't Fight The Midnight.

HARPERS BIZARRE
1967 THE 59TH STREET BRIDGE SONG (FEELIN' GROOVY)
(M) (2:33) Rhino 71065 Summer Of Love Volume 1.
(M) (2:33) Rhino 71093 Better Days.
(S) (2:34) JCI 3114 Easy Sixties.
(S) (2:33) Time-Life SUD-05 Superhits - 1967.
(S) (2:33) Time-Life R962-02 History Of Rock 'N' Roll: Folk Rock 1964-1967.
(S) (2:34) Buddah 49506 Feelin' Groovy.
(S) (2:32) Time-Life AM1-08 AM Gold - 1967.
(M) (2:33) Flashback 72687 '60s Rock: Feelin' Groovy.
(M) (2:33) Flashback 72088 '60s Rock Hits Box Set.
(S) (2:35) Warner Brothers 46261 Feelin' Groovy: The Best Of.
(S) (2:32) Madacy Entertainment 6804 More Sun Splashin'.

SLIM HARPO
1961 RAININ' IN MY HEART
(M) (2:31) Rhino 70896 Best Of Excello Records Volume 1.
(M) (2:31) Rhino 70169 Best Of.
(M) (2:31) Time-Life 2RNR-41 Rock 'N' Roll Era - R&B Gems.
(M) (2:32) Excello 2001 The Excello Collection.
(M) (2:31) Time-Life R859-05 Living The Blues: 1960-1964 Blues Classics.
(M) (2:32) Hip-O 40072 Best Of.
(M) (2:31) Time-Life R857-19 The Heart Of Rock 'n' Roll 1960-1961 Take Three.
1966 BABY SCRATCH MY BACK
(M) (2:51) Rhino 70896 Best Of Excello Records Volume 1.
(M) (2:52) Rhino 70169 Best Of.
(M) (2:51) Rhino 71128 Blues Masters Volume 7: Blues Revival.
(M) (2:51) Time-Life RHD-01 Rhythm & Blues - 1966.
(M) (2:51) Time-Life 2CLR-22 Classic Rock - 1966: Blowin' Your Mind.
(M) (2:51) Excello 3001 Excello Story.
(M) (2:52) Excello 2001 The Excello Collection.
(M) (2:51) Time-Life R859-02 Living The Blues - Blues Masters.
(M) (2:52) Hip-O 40008 Soulful Grooves - R&B Instrumental Classics Volume 2.
(M) (2:51) Time-Life R838-01 Solid Gold Soul - 1966.
(M) (2:51) Hip-O 40072 Best Of.

BETTY HARRIS
1963 CRY TO ME
(M) (3:10) Time-Life 2RNR-19 Rock 'N' Roll Era - 1963 Still Rockin'.
(M) (3:10) Time-Life R857-17 The Heart Of Rock 'n' Roll: The Early '60s.

EMMYLOU HARRIS
1981 MISTER SANDMAN
- (S) (2:19)   Warner Brothers 25161 Profile II. *(45 version)*
- (S) (2:19)   Rhino 72265 Lullabies For Little Dreamers. *(LP version with backup vocals by Linda Ronstadt and Dolly Parton)*
- (S) (2:18)   JCI 3137 Rock Your Boots Off. *(45 version)*
- (S) (2:19)   Reprise 45308 Portraits. *(LP version with backup vocals by Linda Ronstadt and Dolly Parton)*
- (S) (2:17)   K-Tel 3366 101 Greatest Country Hits Vol. Seven: Country Nights. *(LP version with backup vocals by Linda Ronstadt and Dolly Parton)*

MAJOR HARRIS
1975 LOVE WON'T LET ME WAIT
- (S) (5:30)   Atlantic 81299 Atlantic Rhythm & Blues Volume 7. *(LP version)*
- (S) (5:30)   Atlantic 82305 Atlantic Rhythm And Blues (1947-1974) Box Set. *(LP version)*
- (S) (3:45)   Rhino 70555 Soul Hits Of The 70's Volume 15. *(45 version)*
- (S) (3:44)   Right Stuff 27307 Slow Jams: The 70's Volume One. *(45 version)*
- (S) (3:44)   Scotti Bros. 75481 Quiet Storm Memories. *(45 version)*
- (S) (3:43)   Thump 4730 Old School Love Songs Volume 3. *(45 version)*
- (S) (3:42)   WMOT 6633 Best Of Now And Then. *(45 version)*
- (S) (3:45)   Time-Life R838-10 Solid Gold Soul - 1975. *(45 version)*
- (S) (5:29)   Time-Life R834-03 Body Talk - Moonlit Nights. *(LP version)*
- (S) (5:29)   JCI 3175 1975 - Only Soul - 1979. *(LP version)*
- (S) (3:43)   Beast 53442 Original Players Of Love. *(45 version)*

RICHARD HARRIS
1968 MacARTHUR PARK
- (S) (7:23)   MCA 10780 A Tramp Shining.

ROLF HARRIS
1963 TIE ME KANGAROO DOWN, SPORT
- (S) (3:03)   Time-Life HPD-35 Your Hit Parade - The Fun-Times 50's & 60's.
- (S) (3:03)   K-Tel 3411 Tacky Tunes.

SAM HARRIS
1984 SUGAR DON'T BITE
- (S) (4:04)   Motown 9103 and 5408 Sam Harris.

THURSTON HARRIS
1957 LITTLE BITTY PRETTY ONE
- (M) (2:21)   Rhino 70643 Billboard's Top R&B Hits Of 1957.
- (M) (2:21)   JCI 3204 Heart & Soul Fifties.
- (M) (2:21)   Ripete 0002 Coolin' Out/24 Carolina Classics Vol. 2.
- (M) (2:21)   Time-Life 2RNR-01 Rock 'N' Roll Era - 1957.
- (M) (2:21)   Time-Life RHD-08 Rhythm & Blues - 1957.
- (M) (2:21)   Time-Life R962-01 History Of Rock 'N' Roll: Rock 'N' Roll Classics 1957-1959.
- (M) (2:21)   RCA 66443 O.S.T. Corrina, Corrina.
- (M) (2:21)   EMI 30882 Aladdin Records Story.
- (M) (2:21)   Rhino 71806 The R&B Box: Thirty Years Of Rhythm & Blues.
- (M) (2:21)   JCI 3188 1955 - Only Dance - 1959.
- (M) (2:21)   Time-Life R838-23 Solid Gold Soul 1957.

GEORGE HARRISON
1970 MY SWEET LORD
- (S) (4:36)   Capitol 46682 Best Of.
- (S) (4:36)   Capitol 46688 All Things Must Pass.
1971 WHAT IS LIFE
- (S) (4:14)   Capitol 46682 Best Of.

- (S) (4:15)   Capitol 46688 All Things Must Pass.
1971 BANGLA-DESH
- (S) (3:55)   Capitol 46682 Best Of. *(45 version)*
1973 GIVE ME LOVE (GIVE ME PEACE ON EARTH)
- (S) (3:33)   Capitol 46682 Best Of.
- (S) (3:34)   Capitol 94110 Living In The Material World.
1975 DARK HORSE
- (S) (3:51)   Capitol 46682 Best Of.
- (S) (3:53)   Capitol 98079 Dark Horse.
1975 DING DONG; DING DONG
- (S) (3:39)   Capitol 98079 Dark Horse. *(LP version)*
1975 YOU
- (S) (3:40)   Capitol 46682 Best Of.
- (S) (3:40)   Capitol 98080 Extra Texture.
1977 THIS SONG
- (S) (4:11)   Dark Horse/Warner Brothers 26612 Thirty Three & 1/3. *(LP version)*
1977 CRACKERBOX PALACE
- (S) (3:54)   Dark Horse/Warner Brothers 25726 Best Of Dark Horse 1976-1989.
- (S) (3:55)   Dark Horse/Warner Brothers 26612 Thirty Three & 1/3.
1979 BLOW AWAY
- (S) (3:57)   Dark Horse/Warner Brothers 25726 Best Of Dark Horse 1976-1989.
- (S) (3:58)   Dark Horse/Warner Brothers 26613 George Harrison.
- (S) (3:56)   Mercury 846043 O.S.T. Nuns On The Run.
1981 ALL THOSE YEARS AGO
- (S) (3:42)   Dark Horse/Warner Brothers 25726 Best Of Dark Horse 1976-1989.
- (S) (3:44)   Dark Horse/Warner Brothers 26614 Somewhere In England.
- (S) (3:42)   Time-Life R13610 Gold And Platinum Box Set - The Ultimate Rock Collection.
1988 GOT MY MIND SET ON YOU
- (S) (3:50)   Dark Horse 25643 Cloud Nine.
1988 WHEN WE WAS FAB
- (S) (3:54)   Dark Horse 25643 Cloud Nine.

WILBERT HARRISON
1959 KANSAS CITY
- (M) (2:24)   Rhino 70620 Billboard's Top Rock & Roll Hits Of 1959.
- (M) (2:24)   Rhino 72004 Billboard's Top Rock & Roll Hits 1957-1961 Box Set.
- (M) (2:22)   Rhino 70719 Legends Of Guitar - Rock; The 50's. *(first note truncated)*
- (M) (2:26)   Relic 7009 Raging Harlem Hit Parade.
- (S) (2:42)   Grudge 4510 Greatest Classic R&B Hits. *(rerecording)*
- (M) (2:25)   Rhino 70593 The Rock 'N' Roll Classics Of Leiber & Stoller.
- (M) (2:26)   Relic 7035 Kansas City.
- (M) (2:25)   Ripete 2392192 Beach Music Anthology Box Set.
- (E) (2:24)   Capricorn 42009 Fire/Fury Records Story.
- (M) (2:26)   Ripete 0002 Coolin' Out/24 Carolina Classics Vol. 2.
- (M) (2:22)   Time-Life 2RNR-13 Rock 'N' Roll Era - 1959. *(first note truncated)*
- (M) (2:21)   Time-Life RHD-03 Rhythm & Blues - 1959. *(first note truncated)*
- (M) (2:25)   Rhino 71806 The R&B Box: Thirty Years Of Rhythm & Blues.
- (E) (2:24)   K-Tel 3271 Best Of Kansas City.
- (M) (2:28)   Collectables 5294 Kansas City.
- (M) (2:24)   JCI 3129 1955 - Only Rock 'N Roll - 1959.
- (M) (2:25)   Priority 50950 I Love Rock & Roll Volume 1: Hits Of The 50's.
- (E) (2:24)   Time-Life R859-04 Living The Blues: 1957-1959 Blues Classics.
- (M) (2:21)   Time-Life R838-21 Solid Gold Soul 1959. *(first note truncated)*
1970 LET'S WORK TOGETHER (PART 1)
- (M) (5:24)   Grudge 4510 Greatest Classic R&B Hits. *(LP version which is Parts 1 & 2)*

| (M) | (2:39) | Time-Life 2CLR-06 Classic Rock - 1969. *(45 version)* |

(M) (2:39) Time-Life 2CLR-06 Classic Rock - 1969. *(45 version)*

(M) (5:19) Collectables 5123 Best Of Sue Records. *(LP version which is Parts 1 & 2)*

(M) (5:19) Collectables 5294 Kansas City. *(LP version which is Parts 1 & 2)*

COREY HART
1984 SUNGLASSES AT NIGHT
(S) (3:54) EMI 27674 Living In Oblivion: The 80's Greatest Hits Volume Three. *(45 version)*

(S) (5:16) EMI 94974 The Singles. *(LP version)*

(S) (5:15) EMI 46077 First Offense. *(LP version)*

(S) (3:52) Rhino 71977 New Wave Hits Of The 80's Vol. 14. *(45 version)*

(S) (3:54) Time-Life R988-11 Sounds Of The 80's: 1983-1984. *(45 version)*

(S) (3:53) Madacy Entertainment 1984 Rock On 1984. *(45 version)*

(S) (5:17) RCA 66862 Hi Octane Hard Drivin' Hits. *(LP version)*

(S) (5:15) Simitar 55612 The Number One's: The '80s. *(LP version)*

1984 IT AIN'T ENOUGH
(S) (3:26) EMI 94974 The Singles.

(S) (3:29) EMI 46077 First Offense.

1985 NEVER SURRENDER
(actual 45 time is (4:23) not (4:18) as stated on the record label)
(S) (4:55) EMI 94974 The Singles. *(LP version)*

(S) (4:55) EMI 46166 Boy In The Box. *(LP version)*

(S) (4:53) Madacy Entertainment 1985 Rock On 1985. *(LP version)*

(S) (4:51) Rhino 75217 Heartthrob Hits. *(LP version)*

(S) (4:23) Time-Life R988-23 Sounds Of The Eighties 1984-1985. *(45 version)*

1985 BOY IN THE BOX
(S) (4:25) EMI 94974 The Singles. *(LP version)*

(S) (4:26) EMI 46166 Boy In The Box. *(LP version)*

1986 EVERYTHING IN MY HEART
(S) (4:51) EMI 94974 The Singles. *(LP version)*

(S) (4:51) EMI 46166 Boy In The Box. *(LP version)*

1986 I AM BY YOUR SIDE
(S) (4:35) EMI 94974 The Singles. *(LP version)*

(S) (4:36) EMI 46331 Fields Of Fire. *(LP version)*

(S) (4:34) Madacy Entertainment 1986 Rock On 1986. *(LP version)*

1987 CAN'T HELP FALLING IN LOVE
(S) (3:24) Scotti Brothers 75262 There Is Love (The Wedding Songs).

(S) (3:24) EMI 94974 The Singles.

(S) (3:25) EMI 46331 Fields Of Fire.

FREDDIE HART
1971 EASY LOVING
(S) (2:26) Time-Life CTD-05 Country USA - 1971.

(S) (2:26) Time-Life CCD-06 Contemporary Country - The Early 70's.

(S) (2:25) Scotti Bros. 75483 Country Favorites - The Number One Hits.

(S) (2:25) JCI 3155 1970 - Only Country - 1974.

DAN HARTMAN
1978 INSTANT REPLAY
(S) (3:24) Priority 7974 Mega-Hits Dance Classics Volume 4. *(45 version)*

(S) (5:19) Blue Sky 35641 Instant Replay. *(LP version)*

(S) (8:14) Epic 66155 Club Epic Volume 3. *(12" single version)*

(S) (5:19) Risky Business 66871 Polyester Dreams/Greatest Hits Of The 70's. *(LP version)*

(S) (3:24) Rhino 72122 Disco Years, Vol. 6. *(45 version)*

(S) (5:19) K-Tel 3470 Get Up And Disco. *(LP version)*

(S) (5:18) Hip-O 40041 The Studio Collection Disco 54. *(LP version)*

(S) (8:00) Chronicles 314553405 Non-Stop Disco Vol. 2. *(all songs on this cd are segued together)*

(S) (5:07) Rebound 314520520 Body Moves - Non-Stop Disco Workout Vol. 1. *(all selections on this cd are segued together)*

1984 I CAN DREAM ABOUT YOU
(45 length is (3:49); LP length is (4:09))
(S) (4:08) MCA 6330 Soundtrack Smashes - The 80's.

(S) (4:09) MCA 5492 O.S.T. Streets Of Fire.

(S) (4:21) MCA 6435 Soundtrack Smashes - The 80's And More.

(S) (4:08) Sandstone 33050 and 5018 Cosmopolitan Volume 4.

(S) (4:08) Sandstone 33045 and 5011 Rock The First Volume Five.

(S) (4:10) JCI 3127 1980 - Only Rock 'N Roll - 1984.

(S) (4:08) DCC Compact Classics 089 Night Moves Volume 7.

(S) (4:10) MCA 5525 I Can Dream About You.

(S) (4:09) Priority 53681 80's Greatest Rock Hits - Agony & Ecstasy.

(S) (4:09) MCA Special Products 20897 Greatest Rock Hits Of The 80's.

(S) (3:49) Madacy Entertainment 1984 Rock On 1984.

(S) (4:21) MCA Special Products 20958 Mellow Classics.

(S) (4:07) Madacy Entertainment 6803 Power Of Love.

(S) (4:08) K-Tel 3798 The 80's Mega Hits.

(S) (4:08) Time-Life R988-15 Sounds Of The Eighties: The Mid 80's.

(S) (4:08) Time-Life R834-05 Body Talk - Sealed With A Kiss.

(S) (4:10) Priority 50974 Premiere The Movie Magazine Presents The Greatest Soundtrack Love Songs.

(S) (4:09) Rebound 314520519 Love At The Movies.

1984 WE ARE THE YOUNG
(S) (4:18) MCA 5525 I Can Dream About You. *(LP version)*

1985 SECOND NATURE
(S) (3:57) MCA 5525 I Can Dream About You.

HARVEY and THE MOONGLOWS (see THE MOONGLOWS)

DONNY HATHAWAY (see Roberta Flack)

RICHIE HAVENS
1971 HERE COMES THE SUN
(some dj copies of this 45 ran (2:36) and others (3:43); commercial copies were all (3:43))
(M) (2:30) Rhino 70925 Super Hits Of The 70's Volume 5.

(S) (2:42) Rykodisc 20035 Sings Beatles And Dylan. *(rerecording)*

(E) (3:47) Rykodisc 20036 Collection. *(with audience applause in stereo on introduction but there was no audience applause on the introduction of the 45 or LP version; stereo audience applause on the ending but not the same applause as found on the 45 and LP)*

(M) (3:45) Rhino 71187 Resume: The Best Of.

(E) (3:47) Time-Life SOD-12 Sounds Of The Seventies - 1971: Take Two. *(same comments as for Rykodisc 20036)*

(E) (3:47) Time-Life R103-33 Singers & Songwriters. *(same comments as for Rykodisc 20036)*

(M) (3:44) K-Tel 3454 70s Folk Rock Hits.

(M) (3:42) Hip-O 40064 Meet The Covers.

CHESNEY HAWKES
1991 THE ONE AND ONLY
(S) (3:40) Chrysalis 21861 The One And Only.

DALE HAWKINS
1957 SUSIE-Q
(M) (2:17) MCA 5777 Vintage Music Volumes 1 & 2.

(M) (2:17) MCA 31198 Vintage Music Volume 1.

(M) (2:16) Time-Life R102-17 Lost Treasures Of Rock 'N' Roll.

(M) (2:16) Time-Life 2RNR-01 The Rock 'N' Roll Era - 1957.

DALE HAWKINS *(Continued)*
   (M) (2:12) Rhino 70719 Legends Of Guitar - Rock: The 50's, Vol. 1.
   (M) (2:18) Rhino 70741 Rock This town: Rockabilly Hits, Vol. 1.
   (M) (2:16) Collectables 2503 History Of Rock - The 50's Part 2.
   (M) (2:15) Collectables 4503 History Of Rock/The 50s Part Two.
   (M) (2:16) Chess 31319 Best Of Chess Rock 'N' Roll Volume One.
   (M) (2:12) Chess 9352 Chess Rhythm & Roll.
   (M) (2:12) Chess 9347 Stone Rock Blues.
   (M) (2:14) Garland 011 Footstompin' Oldies.
   (M) (2:16) Time-Life R102-17 Lost Treasures Of Rock 'N' Roll.
   (M) (2:15) Chess 9356 Oh! Susie Q - The Best Of.
   (M) (2:15) Chess 9389 The Chess Blues-Rock Songbook.

1958 LA-DO-DADA
   (M) (2:32) Chess 9352 Chess Rhythm & Roll.
   (M) (2:34) Chess 9356 Oh! Susie Q - The Best Of.

EDWIN HAWKINS SINGERS
1969 OH HAPPY DAY
   (S) (3:06) Pair 1202 Best Of Buddah. *(edited)*
   (S) (5:08) Rhino 70781 Soul Hits Of The 70's Volume 1.
   (S) (5:08) Rhino 72028 Soul Hits Of The 70's Volumes 1-5 Box Set.
   (S) (5:07) Pair 3301 Oh Happy Day.
   (S) (5:08) Rhino 70288 Jubilation! Great Gospel Performances Volume 1: Black Gospel.
   (S) (5:07) Essex 7060 The Buddah Box.
   (S) (5:07) JCI 3114 Easy Sixties.
   (S) (5:05) Time-Life 2CLR-12 Classic Rock - 1969: The Beat Goes On.
   (S) (5:08) Time-Life R921-38 Get Together.
   (S) (5:05) Buddah 49514 Let Us Go Into The House Of The Lord.
   (S) (5:07) Right Stuff/Buddah 56442 Best Of.
   (S) (5:08) Varese Sarabande 5906 God, Love And Rock & Roll.

released as by MELANIE with THE EDWIN HAWKINS SINGERS:
1970 LAY DOWN (CANDLES IN THE RAIN)
   (S) (3:59) Rhino 70923 Super Hits Of The 70's Volume 3. *(:13 longer than the 45 and "Candles In The Rain" LP)*
   (S) (3:59) Rhino 72009 Super Hits Of The 70's Volumes 1-4 Box Set. *(:13 longer than the 45 and "Candles In The Rain" LP)*
   (S) (3:47) Pair 1202 Best Of Buddah.
   (S) (3:45) Rhino 70991 Melanie - Best Of.
   (S) (3:47) Pair 1203 Melanie - Best Of.
   (S) (3:46) Pair 3302 Melanie - Candles In The Rain. *(truncated fade)*
   (S) (3:45) Rhino 71206 70's Smash Hits Volume 2.
   (S) (3:47) Pair 4915 Melanie - Best Of.
   (S) (3:46) Essex 7060 The Buddah Box.
   (S) (3:52) Time-Life SUD-04 Superhits - 1970.
   (S) (3:47) Time-Life R103-33 Singers & Songwriters.
   (S) (3:45) Time-Life R921-38 Get Together.
   (S) (3:46) JCI 3130 1970 - Only Rock 'N Roll - 1974.
   (S) (3:45) Buddah 49509 Melanie - Candles In The Rain.
   (S) (3:47) Eclipse Music Group 64892 Rock 'n Roll Relix 1970-1971.
   (S) (3:47) Eclipse Music Group 64897 Rock 'n Roll Relix 1970-1979.
   (S) (3:52) Time-Life AM1-02 AM Gold - 1970.
   (S) (3:45) Flashback 72682 '70s Radio Hits Volume 2.
   (S) (3:45) Flashback 72090 '70s Radio Hits Box Set.

RONNIE HAWKINS & THE HAWKS
1959 MARY LOU
   (S) (2:08) Rhino 70742 Rock This Town: Rockabilly Hits Volume 2.
   (S) (2:08) Rhino 70966 Best Of.
   (M) (2:04) Time-Life 2RNR-28 Rock 'N' Roll Era - The 50's Rave On.

   (S) (2:08) K-Tel 3062 Rockin' Rebels.
   (S) (2:08) K-Tel 4018 Forefathers Of Rock.

SOPHIE B. HAWKINS
1992 DAMN I WISH I WAS YOUR LOVER
   (S) (5:22) Sandstone 33053 and 5021 Cosmopolitan Volume 7.
   (S) (5:22) DCC Compact Classics 081 Night Moves Volume 1.

1995 AS I LAY ME DOWN
   (S) (4:08) Columbia 53300 Whaler.

DEANE HAWLEY
1960 LOOK FOR A STAR

BILL HAYES
1955 THE BALLAD OF DAVY CROCKETT
   (M) (2:23) Rhino 71263 and 71451 Songs Of The West. *(alternate take)*
   (M) (2:23) Time-Life HPD-09 Your Hit Parade 1955. *(alternate take)*
   (M) (2:23) Rhino 71684 Songs Of The West Vol. Four: Movie And Television Themes. *(alternate take)*
   (M) (2:23) Varese Sarabande 5578 History Of Cadence Records Volume 1. *(alternate take)*

1957 WRINGLE, WRANGLE

ISAAC HAYES
1969 WALK ON BY
   (S) (4:31) Stax 4411 Complete Stax/Volt Soul Singles 1968 - 1971. *(45 version)*
   (S) (12:01) Stax 4114 Hot Buttered Soul. *(LP version)*
   (S) (12:01) Stax 60001 Best Of Volume 1. *(LP version)*
   (S) (4:32) Stax 8515 Greatest Hit Singles. *(45 version)*
   (S) (4:31) Capitol 32438 O.S.T. Dead Presidents. *(45 version)*

1970 I STAND ACCUSED
   (S) (11:34) Stax 60001 Best Of Volume 1. *(LP version)*
   (S) (4:02) Stax 8515 Greatest Hit Singles. *(45 version)*
   (S) (11:36) Stax 4129 Isaac Hayes Movement. *(LP version)*
   (S) (4:03) Stax 4411 Complete Stax/Volt Soul Singles 1968 - 1971. *(45 version)*

1971 NEVER CAN SAY GOODBYE
   (S) (3:35) Stax 8515 Greatest Hit Singles. *(45 version)*
   (S) (5:06) Stax 88006 Black Moses. *(LP version)*
   (S) (3:36) Stax 60-002 Best Of Volume 2. *(45 version)*
   (S) (3:35) Stax 88008 Top Of The Stax Volume 2. *(45 version)*

1971 THEME FROM SHAFT
(the true 45 version of this song edited out the word "mother" at 2:31)
   (S) (3:15) Rhino 70786 Soul Hits Of The 70's Volume 6. *(not the "true" 45 version)*
   (S) (4:35) Stax 88005 Top Of The Stax. *(LP version)*
   (S) (3:15) Stax 8515 Greatest Hit Singles. *(not the "true" 45 version)*
   (S) (4:35) Stax 60-001 Best Of Volume 1. *(LP version)*
   (S) (4:35) Stax 88002 Shaft. *(LP version)*
   (S) (3:15) Atco 91813 Classic Recordings. *(not the "true" 45 version)*
   (S) (3:15) Stax 4411 Complete Stax/Volt Soul Single 1968 - 1971. *(not the "true" 45 version)*
   (S) (4:34) Razor & Tie 22045 Those Funky 70's. *(LP version)*
   (S) (3:14) Time-Life RHD-09 Rhythm & Blues - 1971. *(not the "true" 45 version)*
   (S) (3:14) Time-Life SOD-12 Sounds Of The Seventies - 1971: Take Two. *(not the "true" 45 version)*
   (S) (3:15) Rhino 71868 Academy Award Winning Songs. *(not the "true" 45 version)*
   (S) (3:17) MCA 11065 O.S.T. Crooklyn Volume II. *(not the "true" 45 version)*
   (S) (3:15) MCA 11329 Soul Train 25th Anniversary Box Set. *(not the "true" 45 version)*
   (S) (3:15) Rhino 72279 Academy Award Winning Songs Volume 4. *(not the "true" 45 version)*

(S) (3:15) Rhino 72424 Billboard Top Movie Hits - 1970s. *(not the "true" 45 version)*

(S) (3:14) JCI 3168 #1 Radio Hits 1970 - Only Rock 'n Roll - 1974. *(not the "true" 45 version)*

(S) (3:14) JCI 3173 1970 - Only Soul - 1974. *(not the "true" 45 version)*

(S) (3:14) Time-Life R838-06 Solid Gold Soul - 1971. *(not the "true" 45 version)*

(S) (3:15) Varese Sarabande 5847 On The Radio Volume Two. *(not the "true" 45 version)*

(S) (4:35) Hip-O 40107 Super Bad On Celluloid: Music From '70s Black Cinema. *(LP version)*

1972 DO YOUR THING
(S) (3:17) Rhino 70788 Soul Hits Of The 70's Volume 8. *(45 version)*

(S) (3:16) Stax 8515 Greatest Hit Singles. *(45 version)*

(S) (19:30) Stax 60-001 Best Of Volume 1. *(LP version)*

(S) (19:30) Stax 88002 Shaft. *(LP version)*

(S) (3:16) Time-Life RHD-20 Rhythm & Blues - 1972. *(45 version)*

(S) (3:18) Stax 4415 Complete Stax/Volt Soul Singles Volume 3 1972-1975. *(45 version)*

(S) (3:16) Time-Life R838-07 Solid Gold Soul - 1972. *(45 version)*

1972 THEME FROM THE MEN
(S) (3:58) Stax 8515 Greatest Hit Singles.

(S) (4:02) Stax 60-002 Best Of Volume 2.

(S) (4:01) Stax 4415 Complete Stax/Volt Soul Singles Volume 3 1972-1975.

(S) (3:58) Rhino 71910 Tube Tunes Volume One - The 70's.

1974 JOY (PART 1)
(S) (15:55) Stax 8530 Joy. *(LP version)*

(S) (15:53) Stax 60-002 Best Of Volume 2. *(LP version)*

(S) (4:35) Stax 8515 Greatest Hit Singles. *(45 version)*

(S) (4:35) Stax 4415 Complete Stax/Volt Soul Singles Volume 3 1972-1975. *(45 version)*

(S) (4:33) Priority 53131 Deep Soul Volume Two. *(45 version)*

1980 DON'T LET GO
(S) (12:52) Casablanca 838811 Let's Start The Dance (Polygram Dance Classics) Volume 2. *(12" single version)*

(S) (3:55) K-Tel 30572 Barry White/Isaac Hayes. *(45 version)*

(S) (7:17) Rebound 314520218 Disco Nights Vol. 2. *(LP version)*

(S) (3:55) Ripete 5151 Ocean Drive 4. *(45 version)*

(S) (7:15) Hollywood 62042 Greatest Hits I & II. *(LP version)*

RICHARD HAYMAN
1956 (A THEME FROM) THE THREE PENNY OPERA (MORITAT)

LEON HAYWOOD
1975 I WANT'A DO SOMETHING FREAKY TO YOU
(actual 45 time is (3:46) not (3:35) as stated on the record label)

(S) (5:52) Mercury 314514821 Funky Stuff: The Best Of Funk Essentials. *(LP version)*

(S) (3:57) Rebound 314520265 Dance Fever. *(neither the 45 or LP version)*

(S) (3:46) Thump 4040 Old School Volume 4. *(45 version)*

(S) (5:51) Mercury 314532469 Best Of. *(LP version)*

(S) (5:52) Priority 50929 Rare Grooves Volume 2. *(LP version)*

(S) (3:55) Beast 53442 Original Players Of Love. *(neither the 45 or LP version)*

MURRAY HEAD
1971 SUPERSTAR
(S) (4:15) Rhino 70925 Super Hits Of The 70's Volume 5.

(S) (4:15) MCA 2-10000 Jesus Christ Superstar. *(previous selection barely tracks over the introduction)*

(S) (4:16) Rhino 71885 Best Of Broadway.

(S) (4:16) Rhino 72509 Tim Rice Collection: Stage And Screen Classics.

(S) (4:15) MCA 11542 Jesus Christ Superstar - A Rock Opera. *(remastered edition; previous selection barely tracks over the introduction)*

(S) (3:54) MCA 11757 O.S.T. Jesus Christ Superstar. *(movie soundtrack version)*

1985 ONE NIGHT IN BANGKOK
(S) (5:00) RCA 5340 Chess - The Musical. *(LP version)*

(S) (4:06) Rhino 71977 New Wave Hits Of The 80's Vol. 14. *(45 version)*

(S) (4:06) Rhino 72509 Tim Rice Collection: Stage And Screen Classics. *(45 version)*

(S) (4:05) Intersound 9521 Retro Lunch Box - Squeeze The Cheese. *(45 version)*

ROY HEAD
released as by ROY HEAD and THE TRAITS:
1965 TREAT HER RIGHT
(M) (2:03) Rhino 70626 Billboard's Top Rock & Roll Hits Of 1965.

(M) (2:03) Rhino 72007 Billboard's Top Rock & Roll Hits 1962-1966 Box Set.

(S) (2:03) Original Sound 8865 Oldies But Goodies Vol. 15. *(this compact disc uses the "Waring - fds" noise reduction process; missing some overdubs)*

(S) (2:03) Original Sound 2222 Oldies But Goodies Volumes 3,5,11,14 and 15 Box Set. *(this box set uses the "Waring - fds" noise reduction process; missing some overdubs)*

(S) (2:03) Original Sound 2500 Oldies But Goodies Volumes 1-15 Box Set. *(this box set uses the "Waring - fds" noise reduction process; missing some overdubs)*

(S) (2:03) Original Sound CDGO-4 Golden Oldies Volume. 4. *(alternate take)*

(S) (2:03) MCA 31204 Vintage Music Volume 7. *(missing some overdubs)*

(S) (2:03) MCA 5805 Vintage Music Volumes 7 & 8. *(missing some overdubs)*

(M) (2:03) MCA 10666 Duke-Peacock's Greatest Hits.

(S) (3:00) Rhino/Tomato 70667 Texas - A Musical Celebration 150 Years. *(live)*

(S) (2:03) Time-Life 2CLR-08 Classic Rock - 1965: The Beat Goes On. *(missing some overdubs)*

(S) (2:03) MCA Special Products 22135 Vintage Collectibles Volume 6. *(missing some overdubs)*

(M) (2:02) Rhino 71783 Texas Music Volume 3: Garage Bands & Psychedelia.

(M) (2:05) Varese Sarabande 5618 Treat Her Right - Best Of.

(S) (2:03) MCA Special Products 20941 R&B Crossover Oldies Vol. 1. *(missing some overdubs)*

(S) (2:03) JCI 3190 1965 - Only Dance - 1969. *(missing some overdubs)*

released as by ROY HEAD:
1965 JUST A LITTLE BIT
(S) (1:42) Capricorn 42003 The Scepter Records Story.

(M) (1:41) Varese Sarabande 5618 Treat Her Right - Best Of.

(S) (1:42) King 499 Classic Rock & Roll.

released as by ROY HEAD and THE TRAITS:
1965 APPLE OF MY EYE
(M) (2:18) Varese Sarabande 5618 Treat Her Right - Best Of.

JEFF HEALEY BAND
1989 ANGEL EYES
(S) (4:39) Priority 7077 80's Greatest Rock Hits Volume 5 - From The Heart. *(LP length)*

(S) (4:39) K-Tel 6006 Lite Rock. *(LP length)*

(S) (4:39) Arista 8553 See The Light. *(LP length)*

(S) (4:39) Rhino 71267 Love Gets Strange: The Songs Of John Hiatt. *(LP length)*

(S) (4:39) Time-Life R988-13 Sounds Of The Eighties: 1989. *(LP length)*

(S) (4:39) Time-Life R834-09 Body Talk - Magic Moments. *(LP length)*

HEART
1976 CRAZY ON YOU
(dj copies of this 45 ran either (4:10), (3:09) or
(2:58); commercial 45's ran (4:16))
- (S) (4:53)   Epic 36888   Greatest Hits. *(LP version)*
- (S) (4:53)   Capitol 46491   Dreamboat Annie. *(LP version)*
- (S) (4:53)   DCC Compact Classics 1058   Dreamboat Annie. *(LP version; gold disc)*
- (S) (4:50)   Capitol 53376   These Dreams - Heart's Greatest Hits. *(LP version)*

1976 MAGIC MAN
(dj copies of this 45 ran (2:45) and (5:35);
commercial copies were all (5:35); actual time is
(5:27) not (5:35) as the dj and commercial record
labels stated)
- (S) (5:27)   Epic 36888   Greatest Hits.
- (S) (5:27)   Capitol 46491   Dreamboat Annie.
- (S) (5:27)   DCC Compact Classics 1058   Dreamboat Annie. *(gold disc)*
- (S) (5:27)   Capitol 53376   These Dreams - Heart's Greatest Hits.
- (S) (5:28)   Time-Life R13610   Gold And Platinum Box Set - The Ultimate Rock Collection.

1977 DREAMBOAT ANNIE
- (S) (2:05)   Epic 36888   Greatest Hits. *(LP version)*
- (S) (2:01)   Capitol 46491   Dreamboat Annie. *(LP version)*
- (S) (2:01)   DCC Compact Classics 1058   Dreamboat Annie. *(gold disc; LP version)*
- (S) (2:03)   Capitol 53376   These Dreams - Heart's Greatest Hits. *(LP version)*

1977 BARRACUDA
- (S) (4:21)   Epic 36888   Greatest Hits. *(LP length)*
- (S) (4:22)   Portrait 34799   Little Queen. *(LP length)*
- (S) (4:25)   Capitol 53376   These Dreams - Heart's Greatest Hits. *(live)*
- (S) (4:22)   Epic/Legacy 65377   Little Queen/Dog & Butterfly/Bebe Le Strange. *(LP length)*

1978 HEARTLESS
- (S) (5:00)   Epic 36888   Greatest Hits. *(LP version)*
- (S) (5:01)   Capitol 46492   Magazine. *(LP version)*
- (S) (5:00)   Capitol 53376   These Dreams - Heart's Greatest Hits. *(LP version)*

1978 STRAIGHT ON
(actual 45 time is (5:00) not (5:09) as stated on the
record label)
- (S) (4:52)   Epic 36888   Greatest Hits. *(slight edit of both the 45 and LP)*
- (S) (5:07)   Portrait 35555   Dog & Butterfly. *(LP length)*
- (S) (4:47)   Polydor 314515913   Classic Rock Box. *(slight edit of both the 45 and LP)*
- (S) (4:48)   Capitol 53376   These Dreams - Heart's Greatest Hits. *(live acoustic version)*
- (S) (5:07)   Epic/Legacy 65377   Little Queen/Dog & Butterfly/Bebe Le Strange. *(LP length)*

1979 DOG & BUTTERFLY
- (S) (5:19)   Epic 36888   Greatest Hits. *(LP length)*
- (S) (5:19)   Portrait 35555   Dog & Butterfly. *(LP length)*
- (S) (6:02)   Capitol 53376   These Dreams - Heart's Greatest Hits. *(live acoustic version)*
- (S) (5:19)   Epic/Legacy 65377   Little Queen/Dog & Butterfly/Bebe Le Strange. *(LP length)*

1980 EVEN IT UP
(dj copies ran (5:10) and (3:45); commercial copies
were all (5:10))
- (S) (5:09)   Epic 36888   Greatest Hits.
- (S) (5:08)   Epic 36371   Bebe Le Strange.
- (S) (5:08)   Epic/Legacy 65377   Little Queen/Dog & Butterfly/Bebe Le Strange.

1981 TELL IT LIKE IT IS
(dj copies of this 45 ran (3:47) and (4:28);
commercial copies were all (3:47))
- (S) (4:28)   Epic 36888   Greatest Hits. *(LP length)*

1982 THIS MAN IS MINE
- (S) (2:58)   Epic 38049   Private Audition.

1985 WHAT ABOUT LOVE?
- (S) (3:39)   Capitol 46157   Heart.
- (S) (3:39)   MFSL 597   Heart. *(gold disc)*
- (S) (3:39)   Capitol 53376   These Dreams - Heart's Greatest Hits.

1985 NEVER
- (S) (4:04)   Capitol 46157   Heart. *(LP version)*
- (S) (4:04)   MFSL 597   Heart. *(LP version; gold disc)*
- (S) (4:03)   Capitol 53376   These Dreams - Heart's Greatest Hits. *(45 version)*

1986 THESE DREAMS
- (S) (4:14)   Capitol 46157   Heart. *(LP version)*
- (S) (4:14)   MFSL 597   Heart. *(LP version; gold disc)*
- (S) (4:12)   Capitol 53376   These Dreams - Heart's Greatest Hits. *(LP version)*

1986 NOTHIN' AT ALL
- (S) (4:12)   Capitol 46157   Heart. *(LP mix)*
- (S) (4:12)   MFSL 597   Heart. *(LP mix; gold disc)*
- (S) (4:08)   Capitol 53376   These Dreams - Heart's Greatest Hits. *(LP mix)*

1987 ALONE
- (S) (3:38)   Capitol 46676   Bad Animals.
- (S) (3:37)   Capitol 53376   These Dreams - Heart's Greatest Hits.

1987 WHO WILL YOU RUN TO
- (S) (4:06)   Capitol 46676   Bad Animals. *(LP length)*
- (S) (4:04)   Capitol 53376   These Dreams - Heart's Greatest Hits.

1988 THERE'S THE GIRL
- (S) (3:49)   Capitol 46676   Bad Animals. *(LP version)*

1990 ALL I WANNA DO IS MAKE LOVE TO YOU
- (S) (5:07)   Capitol 91820   Brigade. *(LP version)*
- (S) (5:06)   Capitol 53376   These Dreams - Heart's Greatest Hits. *(LP version)*

1990 I DIDN'T WANT TO NEED YOU
- (S) (4:05)   Capitol 91820   Brigade.

1990 STRANDED
- (S) (3:55)   Capitol 91820   Brigade.
- (S) (3:53)   Capitol 53376   These Dreams - Heart's Greatest Hits.

1994 WILL YOU BE THERE (IN THE MORNING)
- (S) (4:29)   Capitol 99627   Desire Walks On.
- (S) (4:23)   Capitol 53376   These Dreams - Heart's Greatest Hits.

HEARTBEATS
1956 A THOUSAND MILES AWAY
- (M) (2:24)   Rhino 75763   Best Of The Doo Wop Ballads.
- (M) (2:26)   Elektra 60107   O.S.T. Diner.
- (M) (2:24)   Rhino 70952   Best Of.
- (M) (2:25)   Collectables 5416   Murray The K - Sing Along With The Golden Greats. *(truncated fade)*
- (M) (2:23)   Original Sound 9329   Oldies But Goodies Doo Wop Classics.
- (M) (2:23)   Original Sound 9328   13 Of The Best Doo Wop Love Songs Vol. 2.
- (M) (2:24)   Collectables 8805   Heartbeats/Shep & The Limelights For Collectors Only.
- (M) (2:24)   MCA 8001   O.S.T. American Graffiti.
- (M) (2:24)   Rhino 71463   Doo Wop Box.
- (M) (2:22)   Time-Life 2RNR-23   Rock 'N' Roll Era - 1956 Still Rockin'.
- (M) (2:23)   Time-Life RHD-05   Rhythm & Blues - 1956.
- (M) (2:24)   Time-Life R962-06   History Of Rock 'N' Roll: Doo Wop And Vocal Group Tradition 1955-1962.
- (M) (2:24)   Collectables 2600   WCBS-FM History Of Rock - The Group Sounds Volume 1.
- (M) (2:24)   Thump 7050   Low Rider Oldies Volume 5.
- (M) (2:24)   Rhino 72157   Doo Wop Memories, Vol. 2.
- (M) (2:24)   Collectables 5488   Spotlite On Hull Records Volume 2.
- (M) (2:24)   Time-Life R857-07   The Heart Of Rock 'n' Roll 1956.
- (M) (2:24)   Flashback 72717   Doo Wop - Blue Moon.
- (M) (2:23)   Time-Life R838-24   Solid Gold Soul 1956.

JOEY HEATHERTON
1972 GONE

HEATWAVE
1977 BOOGIE NIGHTS
(dj copies of this 45 ran (3:06) and (3:36);
commercial copies were all (3:36))
- (S) (3:38)   Rhino 70672   Billboard Top Hits - 1977. *(45 version)*
- (S) (5:02)   Priority 7058   Mega-Hits Dance Classics Volume 9. *(LP version)*

(S)	(3:38)	Rhino 70276 The Disco Years Volume 5. (45 version)
(S)	(3:36)	Epic 39279 Greatest Hits. (45 version)
(S)	(5:03)	Epic 34761 Too Hot To Handle. (LP version)
(S)	(3:38)	Razor & Tie 22496 Disco Fever. (45 version)
(S)	(3:36)	Time-Life SOD-17 Sounds Of The Seventies - 1977: Take Two. (45 version)
(S)	(4:43)	Epic 66155 Club Epic Volume 3. (12" single version)
(S)	(5:03)	Risky Business 53921 Double Knit Dance Hits. (LP version)
(S)	(3:38)	K-Tel 3126 Disco Mania. (45 version)
(S)	(3:34)	Thump 4099 Old School Boogie. (45 version)
(S)	(5:02)	Epic/Legacy 64914 Best Of - Always And Forever. (LP version)
(S)	(3:38)	Eclipse Music Group 64895 Rock 'n Roll Relix 1976-1977. (45 version)
(S)	(3:38)	Eclipse Music Group 64897 Rock 'n Roll Relix 1970-1979. (45 version)

1978 ALWAYS AND FOREVER

(S)	(4:46)	Epic 39279 Greatest Hits. (neither the 45 or LP version)
(S)	(6:14)	Epic 34761 Too Hot To Handle. (LP version)
(S)	(6:13)	Original Sound 8909 Best Love Songs Vol 4. (LP version)
(S)	(6:13)	Original Sound 9327 Best Love Songs Vol. 3 & 4. (LP version)
(S)	(6:13)	Original Sound 1236 Best Love Songs Box Set. (LP version)
(S)	(4:46)	Original Sound 8863 Oldies But Goodies Vol. 13. (neither the 45 or LP version)
(S)	(4:46)	Original Sound 2223 Oldies But Goodies Volumes 2,7,9,12 and 13 Box Set. (Volumes 2, 7 and 12 of this box set use the "Waring - fds" noise reduction process; neither the 45 or LP version)
(S)	(4:46)	Original Sound 2500 Oldies But Goodies Volumes 1-15 Box Set. (most volumes in this box set use the "Waring - fds" noise reduction process; neither the 45 or LP version)
(S)	(4:46)	Razor & Tie 22047 Sweet 70's Soul. (neither the 45 or LP version)
(S)	(6:13)	MCA Special Products 20752 Classic R&B Oldies From The 70's Vol. 2. (LP version)
(S)	(6:13)	Right Stuff 27307 Slow Jams: The 70's Volume One. (LP version)
(S)	(6:13)	Original Sound 9303 Art Laboe's Dedicated To You Vol. 3. (LP version)
(S)	(6:13)	Thump 4710 Old School Love Songs. (LP version)
(S)	(6:13)	Rhino 71859 Smooth Grooves Volume 1. (LP version)
(S)	(3:31)	Rhino 72129 Soul Hits Of The 70's Vol. 19. (45 version)
(S)	(6:13)	Epic/Legacy 64914 Best Of - Always And Forever. (LP version)
(S)	(3:30)	Time-Life R838-17 Solid Gold Soul 1978. (45 version)
(S)	(3:30)	Time-Life R834-11 Body Talk - After Dark. (45 version)
(S)	(3:31)	Collectables 1516 and 2516 The Anniversary Album - The 70's. (45 version)

1978 THE GROOVE LINE

(S)	(7:26)	Epic 46087 Club Epic. (12" single version)
(S)	(4:19)	Priority 7057 Mega-Hits Dance Classics Volume 8. (45 version)
(S)	(4:13)	Epic 39279 Greatest Hits. (45 version)
(S)	(4:16)	Time-Life SOD-20 Sounds Of The Seventies - 1978: Take Two. (45 version)
(S)	(7:26)	Rhino 71756 and 72833 Phat Trax: The Best Of Old School Volume 5. (12" single version)
(S)	(7:25)	Epic/Legacy 64914 Best Of - Always And Forever. (12" single version)
(S)	(4:16)	JCI 3148 1975 - Only Dance - 1979. (45 version)
(S)	(7:25)	Epic/Legacy 65504 Disco Super Hits. (12" single version)
(S)	(4:16)	Time-Life R840-08 Sounds Of The Seventies: '70s Dance Party 1978-1979. (45 version)

HEAVY D. & THE BOYZ
1991 NOW THAT WE FOUND LOVE

(S)	(5:26)	Tommy Boy 1053 MTV Party To Go Volume 2. (remix; all tracks on this cd are segued together)
(S)	(4:16)	MCA/Uptown 10289 Peaceful Journey.
(S)	(4:16)	Uptown 53025 Uptown's Block Party Volume 2.
(S)	(4:16)	Rhino 72917 Beats & Rhymes: Hip-Hop Of The 90's Part II.

1992 IS IT GOOD TO YOU

(S)	(4:50)	MCA/Uptown 10289 Peaceful Journey.

1994 GOT ME WAITING

(S)	(4:31)	MCA/Uptown 10998 Nuttin' But Love.
(S)	(4:39)	Uptown 53022 Uptown's Block Party Volume 1.

1994 NUTTIN' BUT LOVE

(S)	(3:33)	MCA/Uptown 10998 Nuttin' But Love.

released as by HEAVY D:
1997 BIG DADDY

(S)	(4:09)	Universal 53033 Waterbed Hev.
(M)	(2:41)	Elektra 62088 Party Over Here '98. (all tracks on this cd are segued together)

BOBBY HEBB
1966 SUNNY

(S)	(2:45)	Rhino 70652 Billboard's Top R&B Hits Of 1966.
(S)	(2:45)	Rhino 72006 Billboard's Top R&B Hits 1965-1969 Box Set.
(S)	(2:43)	Mercury 826448 Oldies Golden Million Sellers.
(S)	(2:44)	Mercury 816555 45's On CD Volume 2.
(S)	(2:40)	Original Sound 8861 Oldies But Goodies Vol. 11. (this compact disc uses the "Waring - fds" noise reduction process)
(S)	(2:40)	Original Sound 2222 Oldies But Goodies Volumes 3,5,11,14 and 15 Box Set. (this box set uses the "Waring - fds" noise reduction process)
(S)	(2:40)	Original Sound 2500 Oldies But Goodies Volumes 1-15 Box Set. (this box set uses the "Waring - fds" noise reduction process)
(M)	(2:45)	Rhino 71093 Better Days.
(S)	(2:39)	Time-Life RHD-01 Rhythm & Blues - 1966.
(S)	(2:38)	Time-Life 2CLR-22 Classic Rock - 1966: Blowin' Your Mind.
(S)	(2:40)	Time-Life SUD-01 Superhits - 1966.
(S)	(2:43)	Polygram Special Markets 314520264 Soul Hits Of The 60's.
(S)	(2:40)	Time-Life AM1-09 AM Gold - 1966.
(S)	(2:40)	Time-Life R838-01 Solid Gold Soul - 1966.
(S)	(2:43)	Hammer & Lace 697124114 Leading Men: Masters Of Style Volume Three.
(M)	(2:46)	Flashback 72687 '60s Rock: Feelin' Groovy.
(M)	(2:46)	Flashback 72088 '60s Rock Hits Box Set.
(M)	(2:45)	Rhino 72815 Beg, Scream & Shout! The Big Ol' Box Of '60s Soul.
(S)	(2:41)	Polygram Special Markets 314520460 #1 Radio Hits Of The 60's.

1966 A SATISFIED MIND

NEAL HEFTI
1966 BATMAN THEME

(S)	(2:17)	RCA 3573 Neal Hefti.
(S)	(2:17)	Time-Life HPD-39 Your Hit Parade - 60's Instrumentals: Take Two.
(S)	(2:17)	Collectors' Choice 003/4 Instrumental Gems Of The 60's.
(S)	(2:17)	RCA 66881 RCA's Greatest One-Hit Wonders.
(S)	(2:17)	Razor & Tie 2153 Batman Theme And 19 Hefti Bat Songs.
(S)	(2:17)	Time-Life AM1-27 AM Gold 60's TV Themes.
(S)	(2:17)	Varese Sarabande 5821 Batmania.

HEIGHTS
1992 HOW DO YOU TALK TO AN ANGEL

(S)	(3:45)	Foundation/RCA 66563 Number 1 Hit Mix.
(S)	(3:45)	Capitol 80328 Music From The Television Show "The Heights".
(S)	(3:44)	Hip-O 40000 Thinking About You - A Collection Of Modern Love Songs.

HEIGHTS (Continued)
- (S) (3:23) JCI 3132 1990 - Only Rock 'n Roll - 1994. *(edited)*
- (S) (3:44) K-Tel 3849 90s Now Volume 4.

BOBBY HELMS
1957 MY SPECIAL ANGEL
- (M) (2:57) MCA 31199 Vintage Music Volume 2.
- (M) (2:57) MCA 5777 Vintage Music Volumes 1 & 2.
- (M) (2:56) Original Sound 8864 Oldies But Goodies Vol. 14. *(this compact disc uses the "Waring - fds" noise reduction process)*
- (M) (2:56) Original Sound 2222 Oldies But Goodies Volumes 3,5,11,14 and 15 Box Set. *(this box set uses the "Waring - fds" noise reduction process)*
- (M) (2:56) Original Sound 2500 Oldies But Goodies Volumes 1-15 Box Set. *(this box set uses the "Waring - fds" noise reduction process)*
- (M) (2:56) Time-Life 2RNR-23 Rock 'N' Roll Era - 1956 Still Rockin'.
- (M) (2:56) Time-Life CTD-02 Country USA - 1957.
- (M) (2:56) MCA Special Products 22165 Vintage Collectibles Volume 7.
- (M) (2:56) Scotti Bros. 75465 Angel Hits.
- (M) (2:56) K-Tel 3289 The Ties That Bind - Country Love Songs.
- (S) (2:52) K-Tel 3367 101 Greatest Country Hits Vol. Eight: Country Romance. *(rerecording)*
- (M) (2:56) Time-Life R857-05 The Heart Of Rock 'n' Roll 1957.
- (M) (2:56) Time-Life R808-03 Classic Country 1950-1959.

1958 JINGLE BELL ROCK
- (M) (2:09) Rhino 70192 Christmas Classics.
- (M) (2:09) Rhino 70636 Billboard's Greatest Christmas Hits.
- (M) (2:09) Rhino 70639 Billboard's Greatest Country Christmas Hits.
- (M) (2:09) MCA 25991 Christmas Hits.
- (M) (2:09) Curb 77515 Christmas All-Time Greatest Records Volume 2.
- (M) (2:09) Uni 600 O.S.T. Cookie.
- (M) (2:09) Time-Life 2RNR-XM Rock 'N' Roll Era - Jingle Bell Rock.
- (M) (2:08) MCA 25084 Rockin' Little Christmas.
- (M) (2:08) Collectables 1511 and 2511 and 3511 and 4511 and 9611 and 9711 The Ultimate Christmas Album.
- (M) (2:08) LaserLight 12780 A Very Cherry Christmas.
- (M) (2:09) Time-Life TCD-107 A Time-Life Treasury Of Christmas.
- (M) (2:08) Right Stuff 21181 Hot Rod Holiday.
- (M) (2:09) Time-Life R135-12 The Spirit Of Christmas.
- (S) (1:55) Collectables 5798 Jingle Bell Rock. *(rerecording)*

JOE HENDERSON
1962 SNAP YOUR FINGERS
- (M) (2:57) Time-Life 2RNR-29 Rock 'N' Roll Era - The 60's Rave On.
- (M) (2:57) Time-Life RHD-11 Rhythm & Blues - 1962.
- (M) (2:57) Time-Life R102-17 Lost Treasures Of Rock 'N' Roll.
- (S) (2:57) Ripete 2222 Soul Patrol Vol. 4. *(mastered from vinyl)*
- (S) (2:57) Time-Life R857-12 The Heart Of Rock 'n' Roll 1962-1963.
- (M) (2:57) Time-Life R838-18 Solid Gold Soul 1962.

BOBBY HENDRICKS
1958 ITCHY TWITCHY FEELING
- (M) (2:27) Time-Life 2RNR-28 The Rock 'N' Roll Era - The 50's: Rave On.
- (M) (2:32) Collectables 5123 Best Of "Sue" Records.
- (M) (2:32) Collectables 5738 Itchy Twitchy Feeling.

JIMI HENDRIX EXPERIENCE
1968 ALL ALONG THE WATCHTOWER
- (S) (3:59) Polydor 837362 O.S.T. 1969.
- (S) (3:57) Reprise 6307 Electric Ladyland.
- (S) (3:57) Reprise 2276 Smash Hits.
- (S) (3:57) Reprise 26035 Essential Volumes One & Two.
- (S) (3:57) Reprise 25119 Kiss The Sky.
- (S) (3:57) WTG 46042 O.S.T. Flashback.
- (S) (3:58) MCA 10829 The Ultimate Experience.
- (S) (3:57) MCA 10895 Electric Ladyland.
- (S) (3:57) MCA 10936 Gift Set.
- (S) (3:57) MCA 10925 O.S.T. Blue Chips.
- (S) (3:55) Time-Life 2CLR-19 Classic Rock - 1968: Shakin' All Over.
- (S) (3:56) Time-Life R102-34 The Rolling Stone Collection.
- (S) (3:58) Experience Hendrix/MCA 11600 Electric Ladyland. *(remastered edition)*
- (S) (3:59) Experience Hendrix/MCA 11684 South Saturn Delta. *(alternate take)*

1968 CROSSTOWN TRAFFIC
- (S) (2:16) Reprise 2276 Smash Hits.
- (S) (2:24) Reprise 6307 Electric Ladyland. *(LP length with ending audience applause)*
- (S) (2:16) Reprise 26035 Essential Volumes One & Two.
- (S) (2:16) Reprise 25119 Kiss The Sky.
- (S) (2:11) MCA 10829 The Ultimate Experience.
- (S) (2:26) MCA 10895 Electric Ladyland. *(LP length with ending audience applause)*
- (S) (2:26) MCA 10936 Gift Set. *(LP length with ending audience applause)*
- (S) (2:26) Experience Hendrix/MCA 11600 Electric Ladyland. *(remastered edition; LP length with ending audience applause)*

HENHOUSE FIVE PLUS TOO
1977 IN THE MOOD
- (S) (2:40) MCA 46062 Ray Stevens Greatest Hits Volume 2.
- (S) (2:40) Curb 77312 Ray Stevens All-Time Greatest Comic Hits.
- (S) (2:40) K-Tel 3243 Kooky Kountry.
- (S) (2:39) Warner Brothers 45890 Ray Stevens - Cornball.
- (S) (2:40) Time-Life R830-02 The Dr. Demento Collection - The Late 70's.

DON HENLEY
released as by STEVIE NICKS with DON HENLEY:
1982 LEATHER AND LACE
- (S) (3:41) Modern 38139 Stevie Nicks - Bella Donna. *(LP version)*
- (S) (3:47) Modern 91711 Timespace - Best Of Stevie Nicks. *(LP version)*
- (S) (3:54) Atlantic 83093 Stevie Nicks - Enchanted (Box Set). *(LP version but with a :13 longer fade)*

released as by DON HENLEY:
1982 JOHNNY CAN'T READ
- (S) (3:31) Asylum 60048 I Can't Stand Still.
1983 DIRTY LAUNDRY
- (S) (5:35) Asylum 60048 I Can't Stand Still.
- (S) (5:35) Geffen 24834 Actual Miles - Greatest Hits.
1983 I CAN'T STAND STILL
- (S) (3:33) Asylum 60048 I Can't Stand Still.
1985 THE BOYS OF SUMMER (AFTER THE BOYS OF SUMMER HAVE GONE)
(dj copies of this 45 ran (3:54) and (4:47); commercial copies were all (4:47))
- (S) (4:44) Time-Life R102-34 The Rolling Stone Collection.
- (S) (4:48) Geffen 24026 Building The Perfect Beast.
- (S) (4:45) Geffen 24834 Actual Miles - Greatest Hits.
- (S) (4:48) MFSL 705 Building The Perfect Beast. *(gold disc)*
1985 ALL SHE WANTS TO DO IS DANCE
- (S) (4:28) Geffen 24026 Building The Perfect Beast.
- (S) (4:28) MFSL 705 Building The Perfect Beast. *(gold disc)*
- (S) (4:27) Geffen 24834 Actual Miles - Greatest Hits.
1985 NOT ENOUGH LOVE IN THE WORLD
- (S) (3:53) Geffen 24026 Building The Perfect Beast.
- (S) (3:53) MFSL 705 Building The Perfect Beast. *(gold disc)*
- (S) (3:52) Geffen 24834 Actual Miles - Greatest Hits.

1985 **SUNSET GRILL**
(dj copies of this 45 ran (4:26) and (6:22);
commercial copies were all (6:22))
 (S) (6:18) Geffen 24026 Building The Perfect Beast.
 (S) (6:18) MFSL 705 Building The Perfect Beast. *(gold disc)*
 (S) (6:26) Geffen 24834 Actual Miles - Greatest Hits.
1989 **THE END OF THE INNOCENCE**
 (S) (5:11) Time-Life R102-34 The Rolling Stone Collection.
 (S) (5:14) Geffen 24217 End Of The Innocence.
 (S) (5:13) Geffen 24834 Actual Miles - Greatest Hits.
 (S) (5:14) Time-Life R13610 Gold And Platinum Box Set - The Ultimate Rock Collection.
 (S) (5:14) MFSL 721 End Of The Innocence. *(gold disc)*
1989 **THE LAST WORTHLESS EVENING**
 (S) (6:01) Geffen 24217 End Of The Innocence.
 (S) (6:01) Geffen 24834 Actual Miles - Greatest Hits.
 (S) (6:01) MFSL 721 End Of The Innocence. *(gold disc)*
1990 **THE HEART OF THE MATTER**
 (S) (5:21) Geffen 24217 End Of The Innocence.
 (S) (5:19) Geffen 24834 Actual Miles - Greatest Hits.
 (S) (5:21) MFSL 721 End Of The Innocence. *(gold disc)*
1990 **HOW BAD DO YOU WANT IT?**
 (S) (3:45) Geffen 24217 End Of The Innocence.
 (S) (3:45) MFSL 721 End Of The Innocence. *(gold disc)*

CLARENCE HENRY
1957 **AIN'T GOT NO HOME**
 (M) (2:19) Rhino 75766 Best Of New Orleans Rhythm & Blues Volume 2.
 (M) (2:18) MCA 31199 Vintage Music Volume 2.
 (M) (2:18) MCA 5777 Vintage Music Volumes 1 & 2.
 (M) (2:18) Garland 011 Footstompin' Oldies.
 (M) (2:18) Chess 31319 Best Of Chess Rock 'n' Roll Volume 1.
 (M) (2:20) Elektra 60107 O.S.T. Diner.
 (M) (2:18) Sire 26617 Music From The Film A Rage In Harlem.
 (M) (2:18) Time-Life 2RNR-17 Rock 'N' Roll Era - 1957 Still Rockin'.
 (M) (2:19) Time-Life RHD-08 Rhythm & Blues - 1957.
 (M) (2:19) Chess 9346 Best Of.
 (M) (2:19) Chess 9352 Chess Rhythm & Roll.
 (M) (2:18) MCA Special Products 22165 Vintage Collectibles Volume 7.
 (M) (2:19) Chess 9355 Chess New Orleans.
 (M) (2:19) K-Tel 3035 Goofy Greats. *(rerecording)*
 (M) (2:19) MCA 11389 O.S.T. Casino.
 (M) (2:19) EMI 37350 Crescent City Soul: The Sound Of New Orleans 1947-1974.
 (M) (2:19) Time-Life R838-23 Solid Gold Soul 1957.
1961 **BUT I DO**
 (M) (2:17) Rhino 75766 Best Of New Orleans Rhythm & Blues Volume 2.
 (S) (2:17) MCA 31203 Vintage Music Volume 6.
 (S) (2:17) MCA 5804 Vintage Music Volumes 5 & 6.
 (S) (2:17) Garland 012 Remember When.
 (S) (2:17) Chess 31317 Best Of Chess Rhythm & Blues Volume 1.
 (S) (2:17) Epic 57682 More Songs For Sleepless Nights.
 (S) (2:17) Time-Life 2RNR-29 Rock 'N' Roll Era - The 60's Rave On.
 (S) (2:18) Chess 9346 Best Of.
 (S) (2:18) Epic 66329 O.S.T. Forrest Gump.
 (S) (2:17) Collectables 2505 History Of Rock - The 60's Part 5.
 (S) (2:17) Collectables 4505 History Of Rock/The 60s Part Five.
 (S) (2:18) MCA Special Products 22172 Vintage Collectibles Volume 10.
 (S) (2:17) Chess 9355 Chess New Orleans.

1961 **YOU ALWAYS HURT THE ONE YOU LOVE**
 (M) (2:26) Time-Life 2RNR-40 Rock 'N' Roll Era - The 60's Teen Time.
 (M) (2:27) Chess 9346 Best Of.

JIM HENSON (see either ERNIE or KERMIT)

HERMAN'S HERMITS
1964 **I'M INTO SOMETHING GOOD**
 (M) (2:31) Abkco 4227 Their Greatest Hits.
1965 **CAN'T YOU HEAR MY HEARTBEAT**
 (M) (2:13) Abkco 4227 Their Greatest Hits.
1965 **SILHOUETTES**
 (M) (1:57) Abkco 4227 Their Greatest Hits.
1965 **MRS. BROWN YOU'VE GOT A LOVELY DAUGHTER**
 (M) (2:44) Abkco 4227 Their Greatest Hits.
1965 **WONDERFUL WORLD**
 (M) (1:58) Abkco 4227 Their Greatest Hits.
1965 **I'M HENRY VIII I AM**
 (M) (1:48) Abkco 4227 Their Greatest Hits.
1965 **JUST A LITTLE BIT BETTER**
 (M) (2:51) Abkco 4227 Their Greatest Hits.
1966 **A MUST TO AVOID**
 (M) (1:54) Abkco 4227 Their Greatest Hits.
1966 **LISTEN PEOPLE**
 (M) (2:29) Abkco 4227 Their Greatest Hits.
 (S) (2:33) Rhino 72910 Hollywood's Best: The Sixties. *(rerecording)*
1966 **LEANING ON THE LAMP POST**
 (M) (2:32) Abkco 4227 Their Greatest Hits. *(LP version)*
1966 **THIS DOOR SWINGS BOTH WAYS**
 (M) (2:05) Abkco 4227 Their Greatest Hits.
1966 **DANDY**
 (M) (1:57) Abkco 4227 Their Greatest Hits.
1967 **EAST WEST**
1967 **THERE'S A KIND OF HUSH**
 (M) (2:33) Abkco 4227 Their Greatest Hits.
1967 **NO MILK TODAY**
 (M) (2:52) Abkco 4227 Their Greatest Hits.
1967 **DON'T GO OUT INTO THE RAIN (YOU'RE GOING TO MELT)**
1967 **MUSEUM**
1968 **I CAN TAKE OR LEAVE YOUR LOVING**

PATRICK HERNANDEZ
1979 **BORN TO BE ALIVE**
 (S) (6:04) Columbia 40517 Let's Dance. *(12" single version)*
 (S) (3:18) Priority 7058 Mega-Hits Dance Classics Volume 9. *(45 version)*
 (S) (3:23) Rhino 70493 Billboard Top Dance Hits - 1979. *(45 version)*
 (S) (3:18) Razor & Tie 22496 Disco Fever. *(45 version)*
 (S) (7:24) Risky Business 53921 Double Knit Dance Hits. *(LP version)*
 (S) (6:04) Rebound 314520245 Disco Nights Vol. 6 - #1 Disco Hits. *(12" single version)*
 (S) (6:04) Hot Productions 64 Best Of. *(12" single version)*

HESITATIONS
1968 **BORN FREE**

EDDIE HEYWOOD
1956 **SOFT SUMMER BREEZE**
 (M) (2:41) Time-Life HPD-30 Your Hit Parade - 50's Instrumentals.
 (M) (2:42) Polygram Special Markets 314520273 Great Instrumental Hits.
released as by HUGO WINTERHALTER/EDDIE HEYWOOD:
1956 **CANADIAN SUNSET**
 (M) (2:52) RCA 8467 Nipper's Greatest Hits Of The 50's Volume 2.
 (M) (2:52) Time-Life HPD-27 Your Hit Parade - The Unforgettable 50's.
 (E) (2:51) JCI 7010 Those Wonderful Years - Melodies Of Love.

EDDIE HEYWOOD (Continued)
    (M) (2:51)   K-Tel 3472 Those Wonderful Instrumentals Volume 2.
    (M) (2:51)   Time-Life R986-17 Instrumental Favorites - Around The World.

AL HIBBLER
1955 UNCHAINED MELODY
    (M) (2:53)   MCA 5937 Vintage Music Volumes 13 & 14.
    (M) (2:53)   MCA 31211 Vintage Music Volume 14.
    (M) (2:52)   Time-Life RHD-17 Rhythm & Blues - 1955.
    (M) (2:53)   Time-Life HPD-09 Your Hit Parade 1955.
    (M) (2:53)   MCA 11120 Stardust/The Classic Decca Hits & Standards Collection.
    (M) (2:53)   Time-Life R138-32 Hollywood Hit Parade.
    (M) (2:54)   JCI 7011 Those Wonderful Years - That's Hollywood.
    (M) (2:53)   Time-Life R857-15 The Heart Of Rock 'n' Roll 1953-1955.
    (M) (2:53)   Time-Life R132-10 Love Songs Of Your Hit Parade.
1955 HE
    (M) (3:07)   Time-Life HPD-27 Your Hit Parade - The Unforgettable 50's.
1956 11TH HOUR MELODY
1956 NEVER TURN BACK
1956 AFTER THE LIGHTS GO DOWN LOW
    (M) (2:38)   Atlantic 82305 Atlantic Rhythm And Blues 1947-1974 Box Set. *(earlier recording than the hit version; no fidelity)*
    (M) (2:38)   Atlantic 1251 After The Lights Go Down Low. *(earlier recording than the hit version)*
    (M) (2:34)   Time-Life HPD-15 Your Hit Parade - 1956.

HI-FIVE
1991 I LIKE THE WAY (KISSING GAME)
    (S) (5:43)   RCA 61144 The RCA Records Label: The 1st Note In Black Music.
    (S) (5:41)   K-Tel 6102 Funk-Tastic Jams.
    (S) (5:48)   Jive 41544 Greatest Hits.
    (S) (5:47)   Jive 1328 Hi-Five.
    (S) (5:47)   Rebound 314520439 Soul Classics - Best Of The 90's.
    (S) (3:50)   Razor & Tie 4569 '90s Style.
    (S) (5:41)   K-Tel 3847 90s Now Volume 1.
    (S) (5:46)   Simitar 55562 The Number One's: Smooth Love.
    (S) (5:47)   Beast 53012 Smooth Love Of The 90's Vol. 1.
    (S) (5:42)   Time-Life R834-18 Body Talk - Romantic Moments.
1991 I CAN'T WAIT ANOTHER MINUTE
    (S) (4:59)   Scotti Brothers 75419 Fabio After Dark.
    (S) (5:00)   Jive 41544 Greatest Hits.
    (S) (4:59)   Jive 1328 Hi-Five.
    (S) (4:59)   K-Tel 3850 90s Now Volume 3.
1992 SHE'S PLAYING HARD TO GET
    (S) (4:34)   Jive 41544 Greatest Hits.
    (S) (4:34)   Jive 41474 Keep It Goin' On.
1993 QUALITY TIME
    (S) (4:41)   Jive 41544 Greatest Hits.
    (S) (4:41)   Jive 41474 Keep It Goin' On.
1993 NEVER SHOULD'VE LET YOU GO
    (S) (4:38)   Hollywood 61562 O.S.T. Sister Act 2.
    (S) (4:40)   Jive 41544 Greatest Hits.
    (S) (4:39)   Scotti Bros. 75481 Quiet Storm Memories.

BERTIE HIGGINS
1982 KEY LARGO
    (actual 45 time is (3:05) not (2:59) as stated on the record label and is slower than the LP version)
    (S) (3:13)   Original Sound 8909 Best Love Songs Vol. 4. *(LP speed and length)*
    (S) (3:13)   Original Sound 9322 Best Love Songs Vol. 3 & 4. *(LP speed and length)*
    (S) (3:13)   Original Sound 1236 Best Love Songs Box Set. *(LP speed and length)*
    (S) (3:17)   Epic 66780 Best Of. *(LP speed and length)*

    (S) (3:17)   Collectables 5814 Golden Classics. *(LP speed and length)*
    (S) (3:18)   Epic 37901 Just Another Day In Paradise. *(LP speed and length)*
    (S) (3:16)   Time-Life R988-14 Sounds Of The Eighties: 1980-1982. *(LP speed and length)*

HIGH INERGY
1978 YOU CAN'T TURN ME OFF (IN THE MIDDLE OF TURNING ME ON)
    (S) (3:32)   Motown 9105 and 5410 Motown Memories Volume 2.
    (S) (3:31)   Motown 6358 Hitsville USA Volume Two.
    (S) (3:31)   Rhino 72129 Soul Hits Of The 70's Vol. 19.
    (S) (3:30)   Time-Life R838-16 Solid Gold Soul 1977.
    (S) (3:30)   K-Tel 3889 Great R&B Female Groups: Hits Of The 70s.

HIGHLIGHTS
1956 CITY OF ANGELS

HIGHWAYMEN
1961 MICHAEL
    (S) (2:45)   EMI 96268 24 Greatest Hits Of All Time.
    (S) (2:43)   Rhino 70264 Troubadours Of The Folk Era Volume 3.
    (S) (2:44)   EMI 96334 Michael Row The Boat Ashore: Best Of.
    (S) (2:42)   JCI 3109 Folk Sixties.
    (S) (2:42)   Time-Life HPD-32 Your Hit Parade - Into The 60's.
    (S) (2:43)   Rhino 71582 Billboard Top Pop Hits, 1961.
    (S) (2:43)   Time-Life R132-22 Treasury Of Folk Music Volume One.
1962 COTTON FIELDS
    (S) (2:30)   EMI 96334 Michael Row The Boat Ashore: Best Of. *(includes :18 of studio talk)*
    (S) (2:11)   Time-Life R132-22 Treasury Of Folk Music Volume Two.

BUNKER HILL
1962 HIDE & GO SEEK (PART 1)

DAN HILL
1978 SOMETIMES WHEN WE TOUCH
    (dj copies of this 45 ran (3:31) and (4:03); commercial copies were all (3:31))
    (S) (3:31)   Rhino 71201 Super Hits Of The 70's Volume 21. *(45 version)*
    (S) (4:00)   Razor & Tie 4543 The '70s Preservation Society Presents: Easy '70s. *(LP version)*
    (S) (4:02)   Spontaneous 5001 Greatest Hits And More. *(LP version)*
    (S) (3:31)   Rhino 75233 '70s Party (Killers) Classics. *(45 version)*
1978 ALL I SEE IS YOUR FACE
    (S) (3:24)   Spontaneous 5001 Greatest Hits And More.
released as by DAN HILL with VONDA SHEPPARD:
1987 CAN'T WE TRY
    (S) (3:58)   Columbia 40456 Dan Hill.
    (S) (3:50)   Spontaneous 5001 Greatest Hits And More. *(new recording as a duet with RIQUE FRANKS)*
    (S) (3:55)   DCC Compact Classics 104 Duets - A Man & A Woman.
    (S) (3:57)   Time-Life R834-01 Body Talk - Forever Yours.

JESSE HILL
1960 OOH POO PAH DOO (PART 2)
    (M) (2:19)   Rhino 75765 Best Of New Orleans Rhythm & Blues Volume 1. *(this is Part 1 but Part 2 was the hit side)*
    (M) (2:18)   Capitol 91184 O.S.T. Everybody's All American. *(this is Part 1 but Part 2 was the hit side)*
    (M) (3:53)   Ripete 2199 Walkin' To New Orleans. *(edit of Parts 1 & 2)*

(M) (2:16) Time-Life 2RNR-22 Rock 'N' Roll Era - 1960 Still Rockin'. *(this is Part 1 but Part 2 was the hit side)*
(M) (2:15) Time-Life RHD-15 Rhythm & Blues - 1960. *(Part 2)*
(E) (2:16) Collectables 5164 Golden Classics. *(this is Part 1 but Part 2 was the hit side; mastered from vinyl)*
(M) (4:35) EMI 30879 Minit Records Story. *(Parts 1 & 2)*
(M) (2:16) EMI 37350 Crescent City Soul: The Sound Of New Orleans 1947-1974. *(Part 1)*
(M) (2:18) EMI 37355 Highlights From Crescent City Soul: The Sound Of New Orleans 1947-1974. *(Part 1)*
(M) (2:15) Time-Life R838-20 Solid Gold Soul 1960. *(Part 2)*

HILLSIDE SINGERS
1972 I'D LIKE TO TEACH THE WORLD TO SING (IN PERFECT HARMONY)
(S) (2:11) Varese Sarabande 5801 Sunshine Days - Pop Classics Of The '60s Volume 1.

HILLTOPPERS
1956 ONLY YOU (AND YOU ALONE)
(M) (2:41) Varese Sarabande 5524 P.S. I Love You: Best Of.
1956 MY TREASURE
(M) (2:10) Varese Sarabande 5524 P.S. I Love You: Best Of.
1956 KA-DING-DONG
1957 MARIANNE
(M) (2:12) Varese Sarabande 5524 P.S. I Love You: Best Of.
(M) (2:12) JCI 7014 Those Wonderful Years - Mr. Sandman.
1957 THE JOKER (THAT'S WHAT THEY CALL ME)
(M) (2:23) Varese Sarabande 5524 P.S. I Love You: Best Of.

JOE HINTON
1964 FUNNY
(M) (3:02) MCA 5938 Vintage Music Volumes 15 & 16.
(M) (3:02) MCA 31212 Vintage Music Volume 15.
(S) (3:01) Original Sound 8865 Oldies But Goodies Vol. 15. *(this compact disc uses the "Waring - fds" noise reduction process)*
(S) (3:01) Original Sound 2222 Oldies But Goodies Volumes 3,5,11,14 and 15 Box Set. *(this box set uses the "Waring - fds" noise reduction process)*
(S) (3:01) Original Sound 2500 Oldies But Goodies Volumes 1-15 Box Set. *(this box set uses the "Waring - fds" noise reduction process)*
(M) (3:02) Stax 8559 Superblues Volume 2.
(S) (3:02) MCA 10288 Classic Soul.
(S) (3:02) MCA 10666 Duke-Peacock's Greatest Hits.
(S) (3:02) Time-Life RHD-12 Rhythm & Blues - 1964.
(S) (3:02) Hip-O 40009 ABC's Of Soul Volume 1.
(S) (3:02) MCA 11526 O.S.T. The Long Kiss Goodnight.
(S) (3:02) Time-Life R857-09 The Heart Of Rock 'n' Roll 1964.
(S) (3:02) Time-Life R838-13 Solid Gold Soul - 1964.
(M) (3:01) Rhino 72815 Beg, Scream & Shout! The Big Ol' Box Of '60s Soul.

HIPSWAY
1987 THE HONEYTHIEF
(S) (3:10) Risky Business 57469 Don't Touch My 45's/Great Lost Singles Of The 80's.
(S) (3:09) EMI 32694 Living In Oblivion - The 80's Greatest Hits Volume Five.
(S) (3:09) Columbia 40522 Hipsway.

AL HIRT
1964 JAVA
(S) (1:56) RCA 8474 Nipper's Greatest Hits Of The 60's Volume 1.
(S) (1:55) RCA 9593 All Time Greatest Hits.
(S) (1:55) Time-Life SUD-17 Superhits - Mid 60's Classics.
(S) (1:55) Time-Life HPD-34 Your Hit Parade - 60's Instrumentals.
(S) (1:55) Collectors' Choice 003/4 Instrumental Gems Of The 60's.

(S) (1:55) K-Tel 3583 Those Wonderful Instrumentals Volume 3.
(S) (1:55) Time-Life AM1-16 AM Gold - Mid '60s Classics.
(S) (1:55) Razor & Tie 2148 The Al Hirt Collection Featuring Beauty And The Beard With Ann-Margret.
1964 COTTON CANDY
(S) (2:13) RCA 9593 All Time Greatest Hits.
(S) (2:13) Time-Life HPD-39 Your Hit Parade - 60's Instrumentals: Take Two.
(S) (2:13) Razor & Tie 2148 The Al Hirt Collection Featuring Beauty And The Beard With Ann-Margret.
1964 SUGAR LIPS
(S) (2:00) RCA 9593 All Time Greatest Hits.
(S) (1:59) Razor & Tie 2148 The Al Hirt Collection Featuring Beauty And The Beard With Ann-Margret.

EDDIE HODGES
1961 I'M GONNA KNOCK ON YOUR DOOR
(M) (2:02) Collectors' Choice 002 Teen Idols....For A Moment.
(M) (2:02) Varese Sarabande 5578 History Of Cadence Records Volume 1.
1962 (GIRLS, GIRLS, GIRLS) MADE TO LOVE
(M) (2:23) Time-Life 2RNR-46 Rock 'N' Roll Era - 60's Juke Box Memories.
(M) (2:23) Collectors' Choice 002 Teen Idols....For A Moment.
(M) (2:25) Varese Sarabande 5579 History Of Cadence Records Volume 2.

SUSANNA HOFFS
1991 MY SIDE OF THE BED
(S) (3:27) Columbia 46076 When You're A Boy.

RON HOLDEN
1960 LOVE YOU SO
(actual 45 time is (3:25) not (2:58) as stated on the record label)
(M) (3:06) Original Sound 1960 Memories Of El Monte. *(faded :19 early)*
(M) (3:06) Original Sound 4001 Art Laboe's 60 Killer Oldies. *(faded :19 early)*
(M) (3:25) Time-Life 2RNR-22 Rock 'N' Roll Era - 1960 Still Rockin'.
(M) (3:25) Time-Life R102-17 Lost Treasures Of Rock 'N' Roll.
(M) (3:25) Del-Fi 71219 A Barrel Of Oldies.
(E) (3:25) Del-Fi 72111 Love You So.
(M) (3:24) Del-Fi 70008 The Del-Fi & Donna Story.
(M) (3:24) Time-Life R857-02 The Heart Of Rock 'n' Roll - 1960.

AMY HOLLAND
1980 HOW DO I SURVIVE
(S) (3:57) Rhino 71893 Radio Daze: Pop Hits Of The 80's Volume Four.
(S) (3:57) Madacy Entertainment 1980 Rock On 1980.
(S) (3:57) EMI-Capitol Music Special Markets 19460 Lost Hits Of The '80s.

EDDIE HOLLAND
1962 JAMIE
(E) (2:25) Motown 6184 Hard To Find Motown Classics Volume 2.
(E) (2:25) Motown 5448 A Collection Of 16 Big Hits Volume 1.
(M) (2:22) Motown 6312 Hitsville USA.
(E) (2:25) Time-Life 2RNR-40 Rock 'N' Roll Era - The 60's Teen Time.
(M) (2:20) Motown 314530403 Motown Classic Hits Vol. 1.

JENNIFER HOLLIDAY
1982 AND I'M TELLING YOU I'M NOT GOING
    (S) (4:03) Geffen 2007 Original Broadway Cast -
                     Dreamgirls.
    (S) (4:04) Geffen 25004 Best Of.

HOLLIES
1966 LOOK THROUGH ANY WINDOW
    (M) (2:15) Rhino 70324 History Of British Rock Volume 6.
                     (45 version)
    (M) (2:15) Rhino 72022 History Of British Rock Box Set.
                     (45 version)
    (S) (2:16) Curb 77377 All Time Greatest Hits. *(LP version)*
    (S) (2:16) Epic 32061 Greatest Hits. *(LP version)*
    (S) (2:16) EMI 46584 Best Of Volume 1. *(LP version)*
    (S) (2:14) EMI 99917 30th Anniversary Collection. *(45
                     version; remixed)*
    (M) (2:15) Rhino 71548 Let There Be Drums Volume 2: The
                     60's. *(45 version)*
    (M) (2:14) JCI 3107 British Sixties. *(45 version)*
    (S) (2:15) EMI 35985 Best Of. *(LP version)*
1966 BUS STOP
    (E) (2:52) JCI 3101 Rockin' Sixties.
    (S) (2:52) Rhino 70321 History Of British Rock Volume 3.
    (S) (2:52) Rhino 72022 History Of British Rock Box Set.
    (S) (2:52) Rhino 72008 History Of British Rock Volumes 1-
                     4 Box Set.
    (S) (2:53) Curb 77377 All Time Greatest Hits.
    (S) (2:54) Epic 32061 Greatest Hits.
    (S) (2:53) EMI 46584 Best Of Volume 1.
    (S) (2:54) EMI 81128 Rock Is Dead But It Won't Lie Down.
    (S) (2:54) EMI 99917 30th Anniversary Collection.
    (S) (2:51) Time-Life 2CLR-22 Classic Rock - 1966: Blowin'
                     Your Mind.
    (S) (2:51) Time-Life SUD-12 Superhits - The Mid 60's.
    (S) (2:52) Time-Life R962-07 History Of Rock 'N' Roll: The
                     British Invasion 1964-1966.
    (S) (2:52) EMI 35985 Best Of.
    (S) (2:51) Time-Life AM1-05 AM Gold - The Mid '60s.
1966 STOP STOP STOP
    (S) (2:48) Rhino 70322 History Of British Rock Volume 4.
    (S) (2:48) Rhino 72022 History Of British Rock Box Set.
    (S) (2:48) Rhino 72008 History Of British Rock Volumes 1-
                     4 Box Set.
    (S) (2:48) Curb 77377 All Time Greatest Hits.
    (S) (2:49) Epic 32061 Greatest Hits.
    (S) (2:48) EMI 46584 Best Of Volume 1.
    (S) (2:59) EMI 99917 30th Anniversary Collection.
                     (previously unreleased extended version)
    (S) (2:47) Time-Life 2CLR-13 Classic Rock - 1966: Shakin'
                     All Over.
    (S) (2:47) EMI 35985 Best Of.
1967 ON A CAROUSEL
    (S) (3:12) Rhino 70324 History Of British Rock Volume 6.
    (S) (3:12) Rhino 72022 History Of British Rock Box Set.
    (S) (3:12) Curb 77377 All Time Greatest Hits.
    (S) (3:10) Epic 32061 Greatest Hits.
    (S) (3:12) EMI 46584 Best Of Volume 1.
    (S) (3:12) EMI 99917 30th Anniversary Collection.
    (S) (3:10) Time-Life 2CLR-15 Classic Rock - 1967: Shakin'
                     All Over.
    (S) (3:11) EMI 35985 Best Of.
1967 PAY YOU BACK WITH INTEREST
    (S) (2:39) Rhino 70322 History Of British Rock Volume 4.
    (S) (2:39) Rhino 72022 History Of British Rock Box Set.
    (S) (2:39) Rhino 72008 History Of British Rock Volumes 1-
                     4 Box Set.
    (S) (2:40) Epic 32061 Greatest Hits.
    (S) (2:40) EMI 46584 Best Of Volume 1.
    (S) (2:41) EMI 99917 30th Anniversary Collection.
    (S) (2:38) Time-Life 2CLR-21 Classic Rock - Rock
                     Renaissance II.
    (S) (2:39) EMI 35985 Best Of.
1967 CARRIE-ANNE
    (S) (2:54) JCI 3104 Mellow Sixties.
    (M) (2:54) Rhino 70325 History Of British Rock Volume 7.

    (M) (2:54) Rhino 72022 History Of British Rock Box Set.
    (S) (2:53) Curb 77377 All Time Greatest Hits.
    (S) (3:03) Epic Anthology. *(with :09 of studio
                     talk and a countoff)*
    (S) (2:55) Epic 32061 Greatest Hits.
    (S) (2:54) EMI 46584 Best Of Volume 1.
    (S) (3:00) EMI 99917 30th Anniversary Collection.
                     (includes an :08 countoff)
    (S) (2:53) Time-Life 2CLR-10 Classic Rock - 1967: The
                     Beat Goes On.
    (S) (2:54) EMI 35985 Best Of.
1970 HE AIN'T HEAVY, HE'S MY BROTHER
    (S) (4:19) Rhino 70327 History Of British Rock Volume 9.
    (S) (4:19) Rhino 72022 History Of British Rock Box Set.
    (S) (4:18) Curb 77377 All Time Greatest Hits.
    (S) (4:17) Epic 46161 Epic Anthology.
    (S) (4:18) Epic 32061 Greatest Hits.
    (S) (4:18) EMI 48831 Best Of Volume 2.
    (S) (4:17) Priority 53701 Best Of The 60's & 70's Rock:
                     Protest Rock.
    (S) (4:18) EMI 99917 30th Anniversary Collection.
    (S) (4:13) Time-Life SOD-01 Sounds Of The Seventies -
                     1970.
    (S) (4:19) Time-Life R921-38 Get Together.
    (S) (4:18) Risky Business 53919 Songs Of Peacemakers,
                     Protesters And Potheads.
    (S) (4:13) Madacy Entertainment 1970 Rock On 1970.
    (S) (4:16) Simitar 55532 The Number One's: The '60s.
    (S) (4:19) Time-Life R834-16 Body Talk - Sweet Nothings.
1972 LONG COOL WOMAN (IN A BLACK DRESS)
    (S) (3:16) Rhino 70633 Billboard's Top Rock & Roll Hits Of
                     1972.
    (S) (3:16) Rhino 72005 Billboard's Top Rock & Roll Hits
                     1968-1972 Box Set.
    (S) (3:15) Rhino 70327 History Of British Rock Volume 9.
    (S) (3:15) Rhino 72022 History Of British Rock Box Set.
    (S) (3:16) JCI 3301 Rockin' Seventies.
    (S) (3:15) Sandstone 33004 Reelin' In The Years Volume 5.
    (S) (3:16) Curb 77377 All Time Greatest Hits.
    (S) (3:15) Epic 30958 Distant Light.
    (S) (3:15) Epic 46161 Epic Anthology.
    (S) (3:16) Epic 32061 Greatest Hits.
    (S) (3:15) EMI 48831 Best Of Volume 2.
    (S) (3:16) EMI 99917 30th Anniversary Collection.
    (S) (3:15) DCC Compact Classics 066 Rock Of The 70's
                     Volume Five.
    (S) (3:15) Razor & Tie 22502 Those Rocking 70's.
    (S) (3:16) Time-Life SOD-03 Sounds Of The Seventies -
                     1972.
    (S) (3:14) Time-Life R968-11 Guitar Rock - The Early '70s.
    (S) (3:14) Epic/Legacy 65020 Ultimate Rock 'n' Roll
                     Collection.
    (S) (3:16) Eclipse Music Group 64893 Rock 'n Roll Relix
                     1972-1973.
    (S) (3:16) Eclipse Music Group 64897 Rock 'n Roll Relix
                     1970-1979.
    (S) (3:16) K-Tel 3912 Superstars Greatest Hits Volume 1.
    (S) (3:16) Collectables 1516 and 2516 The Anniversary
                     Album - The 70's.
1972 LONG DARK ROAD
    (S) (4:15) Curb 77377 All Time Greatest Hits. *(LP version)*
    (S) (4:14) Epic 30958 Distant Light. *(LP version)*
    (S) (4:15) Epic 46161 Epic Anthology. *(LP version)*
    (S) (3:24) Epic 32061 Greatest Hits. *(45 version)*
    (S) (4:16) EMI 48831 Best Of Volume 2. *(LP version)*
    (S) (4:15) EMI 99917 30th Anniversary Collection. *(LP
                     version)*
1974 THE AIR THAT I BREATHE
    (S) (4:09) Curb 77356 70's Hits Volume 2. *(LP length)*
    (S) (4:09) EMI 48831 Best Of Volume 2. *(LP length)*
    (S) (4:08) Razor & Tie 4543 The '70s Preservation Society
                     Presents: Easy '70s. *(LP length)*
    (S) (4:08) Epic 46161 Epic Anthology. *(LP length)*
    (S) (4:09) Curb 77377 All-Time Greatest Hits. *(LP length)*
    (S) (4:10) Epic 32574 Hollies. *(LP length)*
    (S) (4:08) Priority 7065 70's Greatest Rock Hits Volume 13:
                     Request Line. *(LP length)*

(S) (4:09) EMI 99917 30th Anniversary Collection. *(LP length)*
(S) (3:46) Time-Life SOD-25 Sounds Of The Seventies - Seventies Generation. *(45 length)*
(S) (3:45) Madacy Entertainment 1974 Rock On 1974. *(45 length)*
(S) (4:08) JCI 3145 1970 - Only Love - 1974. *(LP length)*
(S) (4:06) Eclipse Music Group 64894 Rock 'n Roll Relix 1974-1975. *(LP length)*
(S) (4:06) Eclipse Music Group 64897 Rock 'n Roll Relix 1970-1979. *(LP length)*
(S) (3:45) Time-Life AM1-21 AM Gold - 1974. *(45 length)*
(S) (4:02) Time-Life R834-09 Body Talk - Magic Moments. *(:06 shorter than LP length)*
(S) (4:09) Rhino 72740 Billboard Top Soft Rock Hits - 1974. *(LP length)*
(S) (4:07) Simitar 55512 The Number One's: Lovin' Feelings. *(LP length)*

1983 STOP IN THE NAME OF LOVE

BRENDA HOLLOWAY
1964 EVERY LITTLE BIT HURTS
(S) (2:51) Motown 9105 and 5410 Motown Memories Volume 2.
(E) (2:53) Motown 6184 Hard To Find Motown Classics Volume 2.
(S) (2:48) Motown 5450 A Collection Of 16 Big Hits Volume 3.
(M) (2:54) Motown 5485 Greatest Hits And Rare Classics.
(M) (2:56) Motown 6312 Hitsville USA.
(M) (2:48) Time-Life RHD-12 Rhythm & Blues - 1964.
(E) (2:50) Time-Life 2CLR-16 Classic Rock - 1964: Shakin' All Over.
(M) (2:53) Motown 314530420 Motown Classic Hits Vol. III.
(M) (2:56) Motown 314530409 Motown Milestones - Motown's Leading Ladies.
(M) (2:55) Motown 314530573 Baddest Love Jams Volume 2 - Fire And Desire.
(M) (2:48) Time-Life R838-13 Solid Gold Soul - 1964.
(M) (2:56) Rhino 72815 Beg, Scream & Shout! The Big Ol' Box Of '60s Soul.

1965 WHEN I'M GONE
(S) (2:06) Rhino 75757 Soul Shots Volume 3.
(E) (2:10) Motown 6184 Hard To Find Motown Classics Volume 2.
(E) (2:09) Motown 5452 A Collection Of 16 Big Hits Volume 5.
(S) (2:04) Motown 5485 Greatest Hits And Rare Classics.
(M) (2:06) Motown 6312 Hitsville USA.
(M) (2:07) Motown 314530409 Motown Milestones - Motown's Leading Ladies.

BUDDY HOLLY (also CRICKETS)
released as by THE CRICKETS:
1957 THAT'LL BE THE DAY
(M) (2:14) Rhino 70618 Billboard's Top Rock & Roll Hits Of 1957.
(M) (2:14) Rhino 72004 Billboard's Top Rock & Roll Hits 1957-1961 Box Set.
(M) (2:14) MCA 31198 Vintage Music Volume 1.
(M) (2:14) MCA 5777 Vintage Music Volumes 1 & 2.
(M) (2:14) Original Sound 8850 Oldies But Goodies Vol. 1. *(this compact disc uses the "Waring - fds" noise reduction process)*
(M) (2:14) Original Sound 2221 Oldies But Goodies Volumes 1,4,6,8 and 10 Box Set. *(this box set uses the "Waring - fds" noise reduction process)*
(M) (2:14) Original Sound 2500 Oldies But Goodies Volumes 1-15 Box Set. *(this box set uses the "Waring - fds" noise reduction process)*
(M) (2:14) JCI 3201 Party Time Favorites.
(M) (2:15) MCA 5540 Buddy Holly From The Original Master Tapes.
(E) (2:27) MCA 31037 The Great Buddy Holly. *(rerecording)*
(M) (2:14) MCA 31182 The "Chirping" Crickets.

(M) (2:15) MCA 8001 O.S.T. American Graffiti. *(Wolfman Jack talks over the introduction)*
(M) (2:14) MCA 10883 The Buddy Holly Collection.
(M) (2:14) Time-Life 2RNR-17 Rock 'N' Roll Era - 1957 Still Rockin'.
(M) (2:15) Time-Life R962-01 History Of Rock 'N' Roll: Rock 'N' Roll Classics 1957-1959.
(M) (2:14) MCA Special Products 20751 Rock Around The Oldies #2.
(M) (2:15) MCA 11119 The Decca Rock 'N' Roll Collection.
(M) (2:15) MCA 11213 Greatest Hits. *(gold disc)*
(M) (2:14) JCI 3129 1955 - Only Rock 'N Roll - 1959.
(M) (2:15) Pointblank 42088 Fender 50th Anniversary Guitar Legends.
(M) (2:15) MCA 11536 Greatest Hits.

released as by BUDDY HOLLY:
1958 PEGGY SUE
(M) (2:28) Rhino 70618 Billboard's Top Rock & Roll Hits Of 1957.
(M) (2:28) Rhino 72004 Billboard's Top Rock & Roll Hits 1957-1961 Box Set.
(M) (2:28) MCA 31199 Vintage Music Volume 2.
(M) (2:28) MCA 5777 Vintage Music Volumes 1 & 2.
(E) (2:29) Original Sound 8854 Oldies But Goodies Vol. 4. *(this compact disc uses the "Waring - fds" noise reduction process)*
(E) (2:29) Original Sound 2221 Oldies But Goodies Volumes 1,4,6,8 and 10 Box Set. *(this box set uses the "Waring - fds" noise reduction process)*
(E) (2:29) Original Sound 2500 Oldies But Goodies Volumes 1-15 Box Set. *(this box set uses the "Waring - fds" noise reduction process)*
(M) (2:28) JCI 3202 Rockin' Fifties. *(no fidelity)*
(M) (2:28) Curb 77323 All Time Greatest Hits Of Rock 'N' Roll.
(M) · (2:29) MCA 5540 From The Original Master Tapes.
(M) (2:28) MCA 25239 Buddy Holly.
(M) (2:28) MCA 10883 The Buddy Holly Collection.
(M) (2:28) Rhino 71547 Let There Be Drums Volume 1: The 50's.
(M) (2:28) Time-Life 2RNR-01 Rock 'N' Roll Era - 1957.
(M) (2:29) Time-Life R962-01 History Of Rock 'N' Roll: Rock 'N' Roll Classics 1957-1959.
(M) (2:29) K-Tel 3007 50's Sock Hop.
(M) (2:28) MCA 11213 Greatest Hits. *(gold disc)*
(M) (2:28) MCA Special Products 22165 Vintage Collectibles Volume 7.
(M) (2:28) JCI 3129 1955 - Only Rock 'N Roll - 1959.
(M) (2:29) K-Tel 3125 Solid Gold Rock N' Roll.
(M) (2:28) MCA 11536 Greatest Hits.
(M) (2:28) Nick At Nite/550 Music/Epic 67770 Happy Days Jukebox.
(M) (2:28) Collectables 1514 and 2514 The Anniversary Album - The 50's.

released as by THE CRICKETS:
1958 OH BOY!
(M) (2:06) MCA 31200 Vintage Music Volume 3.
(M) (2:06) MCA 5778 Vintage Music Volumes 3 & 4.
(M) (2:06) Rhino 70741 Rock This Town: Rockabilly Hits Volume 1.
(M) (2:07) MCA 5540 Buddy Holly From The Original Master Tapes.
(M) (2:06) MCA 31182 The "Chirping" Crickets.
(M) (2:06) MCA 10883 The Buddy Holly Collection.
(M) (2:06) Time-Life 2RNR-05 Rock 'N' Roll Era - 1958.
(M) (2:06) MCA Special Products 20425 Oh Boy.
(M) (2:06) MCA 11213 Greatest Hits. *(gold disc)*
(M) (2:06) MCA 11536 Greatest Hits.
(M) (2:06) JCI 3188 1955 - Only Dance - 1959.

1958 MAYBE BABY
(M) (2:00) MCA 31201 Vintage Music Volume 4.
(M) (2:00) MCA 5778 Vintage Music Volumes 3 & 4.
(M) (2:01) MCA 5540 Buddy Holly From The Original Master Tapes.
(M) (2:01) MCA 31182 The "Chirping" Crickets.
(M) (2:00) MCA 8001 O.S.T. American Graffiti.

BUDDY HOLLY *(Continued)*
- (M) (2:01) MCA 10883 The Buddy Holly Collection.
- (M) (2:01) Time-Life 2RNR-21 Rock 'N' Roll Era - 1958 Still Rockin'.
- (M) (1:59) Original Sound 8883 21 Legendary Superstars.
- (M) (2:01) MCA 11213 Greatest Hits. *(gold disc)*
- (M) (2:00) MCA Special Products 22166 Vintage Collectibles Volume 8.
- (M) (2:01) MCA 11536 Greatest Hits.

released as by BUDDY HOLLY:
1958 RAVE ON
- (M) (1:47) MCA 5805 Vintage Music Volumes 7 & 8.
- (M) (1:47) MCA 31204 Vintage Music Volume 7.
- (M) (1:47) Time-Life 2RNR-21 The Rock 'N' Roll Era - 1958: Still Rockin'.
- (M) (1:47) MCA 25239 Buddy Holly.
- (M) (1:48) MCA 5540 Buddy Holly From The Original Master Tapes.
- (M) (1:47) MCA 11213 Greatest Hits. *(gold disc)*
- (M) (1:47) MCA 10883 The Buddy Holly Collection.
- (M) (1:47) MCA Special Products 22135 Vintage Collectibles Volume 6.
- (M) (1:47) MCA Special Products 20957 Solid Gold Rock & Roll.
- (M) (1:47) MCA 11536 Greatest Hits.

released as by THE CRICKETS:
1958 THINK IT OVER
- (M) (1:45) MCA Special Products 20580 Teen Idols.
- (M) (1:45) Time-Life 2RNR-24 The Rock 'N' Roll Era - The 50's: Keep On Rockin'.
- (M) (1:45) MCA 5540 Buddy Holly From The Original Master Tapes.
- (M) (1:44) MCA 11213 Greatest Hits. *(gold disc)*
- (M) (1:45) MCA 10883 The Buddy Holly Collection.
- (M) (1:44) MCA 11536 Greatest Hits.

released as by BUDDY HOLLY:
1958 EARLY IN THE MORNING
- (M) (2:05) MCA 10883 The Buddy Holly Collection.
- (M) (2:05) MCA Special Products 20425 Oh Boy.
- (M) (2:05) MCA 11213 Greatest Hits. *(gold disc)*
- (M) (2:05) MCA 11536 Greatest Hits.

1959 IT DOESN'T MATTER ANYMORE
- (S) (2:05) MCA 5540 From The Original Master Tapes. *(with countoff)*
- (S) (2:02) MCA 10883 The Buddy Holly Collection.
- (S) (2:02) Time-Life 2RNR-20 Rock 'N' Roll Era - 1959 Still Rockin'.
- (S) (2:02) MCA Special Products 22019 Summer Hits Of The 50's And 60's.
- (S) (2:02) MCA Special Products 20425 Oh Boy.
- (S) (2:02) MCA 11213 Greatest Hits. *(gold disc)*
- (S) (2:02) MCA 11536 Greatest Hits.

HOLLYWOOD ARGYLES
1960 ALLEY-OOP
- (M) (2:42) Rhino 70621 Billboard's Top Rock & Roll Hits Of 1960.
- (M) (2:42) Rhino 72004 Billboard's Top Rock & Roll Hits 1957-1961 Box Set.
- (E) (2:41) Original Sound 8855 Oldies But Goodies Vol. 5. *(this compact disc uses the "Waring - fds" noise reduction process; ambient background noise throughout the disc)*
- (E) (2:41) Original Sound 2222 Oldies But Goodies Volumes 3,5,11,14 and 15 Box Set. *(this box set uses the "Waring - fds" noise reduction process; ambient background noise throughout the song)*
- (E) (2:41) Original Sound 2500 Oldies But Goodies Volumes 1-15 Box Set. *(this box set uses the "Waring - fds" noise reduction process; ambient background noise throughout the song)*
- (E) (2:40) Original Sound CDGO-6 Golden Oldies Volume. 6.
- (M) (2:42) Rhino 70794 KFOG Presents M. Dung's Idiot Show.
- (M) (2:42) Rhino 70495 Fun Rock!
- (M) (2:41) Collectables 5065 History Of Rock Volume 5.

- (M) (2:41) Time-Life 2RNR-11 Rock 'N' Roll Era - 1960.
- (E) (2:40) Collectables 2500 WCBS-FM History Of Rock - The 60's Part 1.
- (E) (2:40) Collectables 4500 History Of Rock/The 60s Part One.
- (E) (2:42) K-Tel 3035 Goofy Greats.
- (E) (2:42) Curb 77773 Hard To Find Hits Of Rock 'N' Roll Volume One.
- (E) (2:41) Music For Little People 42581 A Child's Celebration Of Rock 'N' Roll.
- (M) (2:42) Nick At Nite/550 Music/Epic 67770 Happy Days Jukebox.

HOLLYWOOD FLAMES
1958 BUZZ BUZZ BUZZ
- (M) (2:13) Rhino 75764 Best Of Doo Wop Uptempo.
- (M) (2:15) Specialty 7021 The Hollywood Flames.
- (M) (2:16) Rhino 71463 Doo Wop Box.
- (M) (2:14) Time-Life 2RNR-17 Rock 'N' Roll Era - 1957 Still Rockin'.
- (M) (2:12) Time-Life RHD-16 Rhythm & Blues - 1958.
- (M) (2:13) Time-Life R962-06 History Of Rock 'N' Roll: Doo Wop And Vocal Group Tradition 1955-1962.
- (M) (2:12) Time-Life R102-17 Lost Treasures Of Rock 'N' Roll.
- (M) (2:12) Time-Life R838-22 Solid Gold Soul 1958.

EDDIE HOLMAN
1970 HEY THERE LONELY GIRL
- (S) (3:33) Rhino 75770 Soul Shots Volume 2. *(LP version)*
- (S) (3:33) Rhino 70781 Soul Hits Of The 70's Volume 1. *(LP version)*
- (S) (3:33) Rhino 72028 Soul Hits Of The 70's Volumes 1-5 Box Set. *(LP version)*
- (S) (3:31) Original Sound 8858 Oldies But Goodies Vol. 8. *(this compact disc uses the "Waring - fds" noise reduction process)*
- (S) (3:31) Original Sound 2221 Oldies But Goodies Volumes 1,4,6,8 and 10 Box Set. *(this box set uses the "Waring - fds" noise reduction process)*
- (S) (3:31) Original Sound 2500 Oldies But Goodies Volumes 1-15 Box Set. *(this box set uses the "Waring - fds" noise reduction process)*
- (S) (3:33) MCA 5938 Vintage Music Volumes 15 & 16. *(LP version)*
- (S) (3:33) MCA 31213 Vintage Music Volume 16. *(LP version)*
- (S) (3:32) MCA 10288 Classic Soul. *(LP version)*
- (S) (3:33) Rhino 71205 70's Smash Hits Volume 1. *(LP version)*
- (S) (3:32) Time-Life RHD-18 Rhythm & Blues - 1970. *(LP version)*
- (S) (3:32) Time-Life 2CLR-06 Classic Rock - 1969. *(LP version)*
- (S) (3:32) Time-Life SUD-04 Superhits - 1970. *(LP version)*
- (S) (3:32) Time-Life SOD-11 Sounds Of The Seventies - 1970: Take Two. *(LP version)*
- (S) (3:33) Right Stuff 27306 Slow Jams: The 60's Volume One. *(LP version)*
- (S) (3:33) Varese Sarabande 5492 I Love You. *(LP version)*
- (S) (3:32) Time-Life OPCD-4517 Tonight's The Night. *(LP version)*
- (S) (3:33) MCA Special Products 20753 Classic R&B Oldies From The 60's. *(LP version)*
- (S) (3:32) Thump 7040 Low Rider Oldies Volume 4. *(LP version)*
- (S) (3:33) MCA Special Products 22173 Vintage Collectibles Volume 11. *(LP version)*
- (S) (3:33) MCA Special Products 20899 Rock Around The Oldies #4. *(LP version)*
- (S) (3:32) Madacy Entertainment 1970 Rock On 1970. *(LP version)*
- (S) (3:33) Hip-O 40009 ABC's Of Soul Volume 1. *(LP version)*
- (S) (3:32) JCI 3145 1970 - Only Love - 1974. *(LP version)*
- (S) (3:34) Hip-O 40029 The Glory Of Love - '60s Sweet & Soulful Love Songs. *(LP version)*

(S) (3:33) Rhino 72620 Smooth Grooves: The '60s Volume 3 Late '60s. *(LP version)*

(S) (3:32) Time-Life R103-18 Great Love Songs Of The '70s & '80s. *(LP version)*

(S) (3:32) Time-Life AM1-02 AM Gold - 1970. *(LP version)*

(S) (3:32) Time-Life R838-05 Solid Gold Soul - 1970. *(LP version)*

(S) (3:32) Time-Life R834-05 Body Talk - Sealed With A Kiss. *(LP version)*

(S) (3:33) Flashback 72681 '70s Radio Hits Volume 1. *(LP version)*

(S) (3:33) Flashback 72090 '70s Radio Hits Box Set. *(LP version)*

(S) (3:33) Rhino 72815 Beg, Scream & Shout! The Big Ol' Box Of '60s Soul. *(LP version)*

CLINT HOLMES
1973 PLAYGROUND IN MY MIND

(S) (2:55) Rhino 70758 Super Hits Of The 70's Volume 11.

(S) (2:53) Columbia/Legacy 46763 Rock Artifacts Volume 2.

(S) (2:52) Razor & Tie 21640 Those Fabulous 70's.

(S) (2:54) Time-Life SOD-36 Sounds Of The Seventies - More AM Nuggets.

(S) (2:52) Risky Business 66871 Polyester Dreams/Greatest Hits Of The 70's.

(S) (2:53) Collectables 5841 A Golden Classics Edition.

(S) (2:53) K-Tel 3912 Superstars Greatest Hits Volume 1.

(S) (2:54) Rhino 75233 '70s Party (Killers) Classics.

RICHARD "GROOVE" HOLMES
1966 MISTY

(S) (1:55) Prestige 724 Richard "Groove" Holmes.

(S) (1:55) Hip-O 40007 Soulful Grooves - R&B Instrumental Classics Volume 1.

RUPERT HOLMES
1979 ESCAPE (THE PINA COLADA SONG)
(actual LP time is (4:35) not (4:40) as stated on the record label; dj copies of this 45 ran (3:50) and (4:40); commercial copies were all (3:50))

(S) (4:33) Priority 8669 Hits/70's Greatest Rock Hits Volume 9. *(LP version)*

(S) (4:09) Rhino 70674 Billboard Top Hits - 1979. *(edit of the LP version)*

(S) (4:33) MCA 10841 Partners In Crime. *(LP version)*

(S) (4:35) K-Tel 852 100 Proof Hits. *(LP version)*

(S) (4:33) Priority 53699 80's Greatest Rock Hits Volume 7 - Light & Easy. *(LP version)*

(S) (3:52) Rhino 71890 Radio Daze: Pop Hits Of The 80's Volume One. *(45 version)*

(S) (4:35) K-Tel 3575 Hot, Hot Vacation Jams - Week One. *(LP version)*

(S) (4:08) Madacy Entertainment 26927 Sun Splashin'. *(edit of the LP version)*

(S) (3:52) Time-Life R840-01 Sounds Of The Seventies - Pop Nuggets: Late '70s. *(45 version)*

(S) (4:33) MCA Special Products 20997 Mellow Rock. *(LP version)*

(S) (4:35) K-Tel 3907 Starflight Vol. 2. *(LP version)*

(S) (4:09) Rhino 75233 '70s Party (Killers) Classics. *(edit of the LP version)*

(S) (3:51) Time-Life AM1-26 AM Gold - 1979. *(45 version)*

1980 HIM
(actual 45 time is (3:40) not (3:34) as stated on the record label)

(S) (4:04) MCA 10841 Partners In Crime. *(LP length)*

(S) (3:37) Rhino 71891 Radio Daze: Pop Hits Of The 80's Volume Two. *(45 length)*

(S) (4:02) Madacy Entertainment 1980 Rock On 1980. *(LP length)*

(S) (4:01) JCI 3147 1980 - Only Love - 1984. *(LP length)*

(S) (3:36) Time-Life R834-05 Body Talk - Sealed With A Kiss. *(45 length)*

1980 ANSWERING MACHINE

(S) (3:32) MCA 10841 Partners In Crime.

HOMBRES
1967 LET IT OUT (LET IT ALL HANG OUT)

(S) (2:06) K-Tel 205 Battle Of The Bands Volume 3.

(M) (2:02) Mercury 834216 45's On CD Volume 3.

(S) (2:06) Rhino 70996 One Hit Wonders Of The 60's Volume 2.

(M) (2:08) Rhino 71066 Summer Of Love Volume 2.

(M) (2:02) Time-Life 2CLR-24 Classic Rock - 1967: Blowin' Your Mind.

(M) (2:03) Special Music 5026 Let It All Hang Out - 60's Party Hits.

(M) (2:03) Special Music 5025 Rebel Rousers! Best Of Southern Rock.

(M) (2:06) Rebound 314520435 Classic Rock - 60's.

(M) (2:03) Time-Life 2CLR-31 Classic Rock - Totally Fantastic '60s.

HOMER and JETHRO
1959 THE BATTLE OF KOOKAMONGA

(S) (2:36) RCA 8467 Nipper's Greatest Hits Of The 50's Volume 2.

(S) (2:36) Rhino 70743 Dr. Demento 20th Anniversary Collection.

(M) (2:36) Time-Life HPD-40 Your Hit Parade - Golden Goofers.

(E) (2:38) K-Tel 3640 Corny Country.

(E) (2:38) Razor & Tie 2130 America's Song Butchers.

HONDELLS
1964 LITTLE HONDA
(45 pressings were faster than the LP pressings of this song; actual 45 time is (2:00) not (2:03) as stated on the record label)

(S) (2:03) Mercury 826448 Oldies Golden Million Sellers. *(LP speed)*

(S) (2:03) Mercury 816555 45's On CD Volume 2. *(LP speed)*

(S) (2:03) DCC Compact Classics 030 Beach Classics. *(LP speed)*

(S) (2:02) Time-Life 2CLR-16 Classic Rock - 1964: Shakin' All Over. *(LP speed)*

(S) (2:02) Time-Life R962-04 History Of Rock 'N' Roll: California Pop 1963-1967. *(LP speed)*

(S) (2·02) K-Tel 3130 60's Sound Explosion. *(LP speed)*

(S) (2:03) Curb 77819 Greatest Hits. *(LP speed)*

(S) (2:03) Eric 11503 Hard To Find 45's On CD (Volume II) 1961-64. *(LP speed)*

(S) (2:04) Polygram Special Markets 314520495 45's On CD Volume 2. *(LP speed)*

1966 YOUNGER GIRL

(M) (2:25) Curb 77819 Greatest Hits.

(M) (2:27) Simitar 55572 The Number One's: Hot In The '60s.

HONEYCOMBS
1964 HAVE I THE RIGHT?

(M) (2:55) Rhino 70906 American Bandstand Greatest Hits Collection.

(M) (2:56) Rhino 70319 History Of British Rock Volume 1.

(M) (2:56) Rhino 72022 History Of British Rock Box Set.

(M) (2:56) Rhino 72008 History Of British Rock Volumes 1-4 Box Set.

(M) (2:55) JCI 3107 British Sixties.

(M) (2:54) Time-Life 2CLR-09 Classic Rock - 1964: The Beat Goes On.

(M) (2:55) Time-Life R962-07 History Of Rock 'N' Roll: The British Invasion 1964-1966.

(M) (2:55) Razor & Tie 2080 It's Hard To Believe It: The Amazing World Of Joe Meek.

(M) (2:55) Collectables 0565 Watch Your Step - The Beat Era Vol. 1. *(no fidelity)*

HONEY CONE
1971 WANT ADS
- (M) (2:33) Pair 1202 Best Of Buddah. *(cd jacket mistakenly identifies the group as "HONEYCOMB"; 45 length)*
- (S) (2:45) Rhino 70785 Soul Hits Of The 70's Volume 5. *("Sweet Replies" vinyl LP length; :09 longer fade than the 45)*
- (S) (2:45) Rhino 72028 Soul Hits Of The 70's Volumes 1-5 Box Set. *("Sweet Replies" vinyl LP length; :09 longer fade than the 45)*
- (S) (3:46) H-D-H 3902 Greatest Hits. *("Soulful Tapestry" vinyl LP version)*
- (S) (2:44) Essex 7060 The Buddah Box. *("Sweet Replies" vinyl LP length; :08 longer fade than the 45)*
- (S) (2:43) Time-Life RHD-09 Rhythm & Blues - 1971. *("Sweet Replies" vinyl LP length; :07 longer fade than the 45)*
- (S) (2:42) Time-Life SUD-10 Superhits - 1971. *("Sweet Replies" vinyl LP length; :06 longer fade than the 45)*
- (S) (2:44) Time-Life SOD-25 Sounds Of The Seventies - Seventies Generation. *("Sweet Replies" vinyl LP length; :08 longer fade than the 45)*
- (S) (2:45) Rhino 72113 Billboard Hot Soul Hits - 1971. *("Sweet Replies" vinyl LP length; :09 longer fade than the 45)*
- (S) (2:42) Time-Life AM1-06 AM Gold - 1971. *("Sweet Replies" vinyl LP length; :06 longer fade than the 45)*
- (S) (2:43) Time-Life R838-06 Solid Gold Soul - 1971. *("Sweet Replies" vinyl LP length; :07 longer fade than the 45)*
- (S) (3:46) Thump 7070 Lowrider Oldies Volume 7. *("Soulful Tapestry" vinyl LP version)*
- (S) (2:44) K-Tel 3889 Great R&B Female Groups: Hits Of The 70s. *("Sweet Replies" vinyl LP length; :08 longer fade than the 45)*

1971 STICK UP
- (S) (2:49) Rhino 70785 Soul Hits Of The 70's Volume 5. *(45 version)*
- (S) (2:49) Rhino 72028 Soul Hits Of The 70's Volumes 1-5 Box Set. *(45 version)*
- (S) (3:00) H-D-H 3902 Greatest Hits. *(LP version)*

1972 ONE MONKEY DON'T STOP NO SHOW (PART 1)
- (S) (3:42) Rhino 70787 Soul Hits Of The 70's Volume 7. *(45 version but :11 longer than the 45)*
- (S) (3:27) H-D-H 3902 Greatest Hits. *(LP version)*
- (S) (3:28) Priority 53130 Deep Soul Volume Three. *(LP version)*
- (S) (3:42) Varese Sarabande 5718 Soulful Pop. *(45 version but :11 longer than the 45)*
- (S) (3:42) K-Tel 3913 Superstars Greatest Hits Volume 2. *(45 version but :11 longer than the 45)*
- (S) (3:42) Varese Sarabande 5890 Bubblegum Classics Volume Four - Soulful Pop. *(45 version but :11 longer than the 45)*

1972 THE DAY I FOUND MYSELF
- (S) (3:06) Rhino 70788 Soul Hits Of The 70's Volume 8. *(45 version)*
- (S) (4:14) H-D-H 3902 Greatest Hits. *(LP version)*

HONEYDRIPPERS
1985 SEA OF LOVE
- (S) (3:02) JCI 3128 1985 - Only Rock 'N Roll - 1989.
- (S) (3:02) Es Paranza 90220 Volume One.
- (S) (3:02) Time-Life R988-02 Sounds Of The Eighties: 1985.
- (S) (3:02) Time-Life R834-03 Body Talk - Moonlit Nights.

1985 ROCKIN' AT MIDNIGHT
(dj copies of this 45 ran (4:34) and (5:57); commercial copies were all (5:57))
- (S) (5:56) Es Paranza 90220 Volume One.

HONEYMOON SUITE
1986 FEEL IT AGAIN
- (S) (4:05) Time-Life R105-40 Rock Dreams. *(45 version)*
- (S) (4:35) Warner Brothers 25293 Big Prize. *(LP version)*

HOOTERS
1985 AND WE DANCED
- (S) (3:47) Priority 53768 Rock Of The 80's Volume 14.
- (S) (3:48) Risky Business 57833 Read The Hits/Best Of The 80's.
- (S) (3:48) Columbia 39912 Nervous Night.
- (S) (3:47) Risky Business 67310 We Came To Play.
- (S) (3:49) Columbia/Legacy 64945 Hooterization: A Retrospective.
- (S) (3:43) Time-Life R988-23 Sounds Of The Eighties 1984-1985.

1986 DAY BY DAY
- (S) (3:23) Columbia 39912 Nervous Night.
- (S) (3:23) Columbia/Legacy 64945 Hooterization: A Retrospective.
- (S) (3:22) Time-Life R988-17 Sounds Of The Eighties: The Mid '80s Take Two.

1986 WHERE DO THE CHILDREN GO
- (S) (5:26) Columbia 39912 Nervous Night. *(LP version)*
- (S) (5:27) Columbia/Legacy 64945 Hooterization: A Retrospective. *(LP version)*

HOOTIE & THE BLOWFISH
1995 HOLD MY HAND
- (S) (4:14) Atlantic 82613 Cracked Rear View.
- (S) (4:13) Time-Life R13610 Gold And Platinum Box Set - The Ultimate Rock Collection.
- (S) (4:15) Atlantic 83088 Atlantic Records: 50 Years - The Gold Anniversary Collection.

1995 LET HER CRY
- (S) (5:07) Atlantic 82613 Cracked Rear View.
- (S) (5:06) Grammy Recordings/Sony 67565 1996 Grammy Nominees.

1995 ONLY WANNA BE WITH YOU
- (S) (3:45) Atlantic 82613 Cracked Rear View.

1996 TIME
- (S) (4:52) Atlantic 82613 Cracked Rear View.

1996 OLD MAN & ME (WHEN I GET TO HEAVEN)
- (S) (4:24) Atlantic 82886 Fairweather Johnson.

1996 TUCKER'S TOWN
- (S) (3:44) Atlantic 82886 Fairweather Johnson.

MARY HOPKIN
1968 THOSE WERE THE DAYS
- (S) (5:07) Capitol 97578 Post Card.

1969 GOODBYE

BRUCE HORNSBY
1986 THE WAY IT IS
- (S) (4:55) Columbia 44381 Heart Of Rock. *(LP length)*
- (S) (4:54) RCA 9970 Nipper's Greatest Hits - The 80's. *(LP length)*
- (S) (4:56) RCA 9902 Nipper's #1 Hits 1956-1986. *(LP length)*
- (S) (4:56) RCA 5904 The Way It Is. *(LP length)*
- (S) (4:56) Time-Life R13610 Gold And Platinum Box Set - The Ultimate Rock Collection. *(LP length)*

1987 MANDOLIN RAIN
- (S) (5:17) RCA 5904 The Way It Is. *(LP version)*

1987 EVERY LITTLE KISS
- (S) (5:47) RCA 5904 The Way It Is. *(LP version)*

1988 THE VALLEY ROAD
- (S) (4:41) Foundation/WEA 26096 Super Sessions Volume One.
- (S) (4:42) RCA 6686 Scenes From The Southside.

1988 LOOK OUT ANY WINDOW
(dj copies of this 45 ran (4:45) and (5:28); commercial copies were all (4:45))
- (S) (5:27) Geffen 24236 Greenpeace - Rainbow Warriors.
- (S) (5:27) RCA 6686 Scenes From The Southside.

1990 ACROSS THE RIVER
- (S) (5:09) RCA 52041 Night On The Town. *(LP version)*

JOHNNY HORTON
1959 THE BATTLE OF NEW ORLEANS
- (S) (2:30) Rhino 70680 Billboard's Top Country Hits Of 1959.

(S) (2:29) Columbia 45017 Radio Classics Of The 50's.
(S) (2:29) Columbia 46031 Columbia Country Classics Volume 3.
(S) (2:31) Columbia 45071 American Originals.
(S) (2:31) Columbia 40665 Greatest Hits.
(S) (2:30) Rhino 71547 Let There Be Drums Volume 1: The 50's.
(S) (2:30) Time-Life CTD-09 Country USA - 1959.
(S) (2:30) Time-Life HPD-13 Your Hit Parade - 1959.
(S) (2:30) K-Tel 794 Marty Robbins/Johnny Horton.
(S) (2:31) K-Tel 225 Country Music Classics Volume I.
(S) (2:28) Columbia/Legacy 64761 Honky Tonk Man - Essential 1956-1960.
(S) (2:31) K-Tel 3365 101 Greatest Country Hits Vol. Six: Timeless Country.
(S) (2:30) Time-Life R808-03 Classic Country 1950-1959.

1960 SINK THE BISMARCK
(some pressings of this 45 used the spelling "Bismarck" and others "Bismark")
(S) (3:12) Rhino 70681 Billboard's Top Country Hits Of 1960.
(S) (3:14) Columbia 45071 American Originals.
(S) (3:14) Columbia 40665 Greatest Hits.
(S) (3:14) CBS Special Products 46200 Rock Goes To The Movies Volume 3.
(S) (3:12) K-Tel 794 Marty Robbins/Johnny Horton.
(S) (3:14) K-Tel 763 Country Music Classics Volume VIII.
(S) (3:11) Columbia/Legacy 64761 Honky Tonk Man - Essential 1956-1960.

1960 NORTH TO ALASKA
(S) (2:48) Rhino 70682 Billboard's Top Country Hits Of 1961.
(M) (2:48) Columbia 44373 Hollywood Magic - The 1960's.
(M) (2:46) Columbia 46031 Columbia Country Classics Volume 3.
(S) (2:49) Columbia 45071 American Originals.
(S) (2:49) Columbia 40665 Greatest Hits.
(S) (2:49) CBS Special Products 46200 Rock Goes To The Movies Volume 3.
(S) (2:48) Time-Life CTD-12 Country USA - 1960.
(M) (2:46) Risky Business 57473 Country Goes To The Movies.
(S) (2:49) K-Tel 3108 Country Music Classics Volume XVI.
(S) (2:48) K-Tel 794 Marty Robbins/Johnny Horton.
(S) (2:46) Columbia/Legacy 64761 Honky Tonk Man - Essential 1956-1960.
(S) (2:49) Epic 67941 Super Hits Of The 60's.
(S) (2:48) Columbia 69069 Super Hits Goes To The Movies.
(S) (2:48) Time-Life R808-01 Classic Country 1960-1964.

HOT
1977 ANGEL IN YOUR ARMS
(S) (2:55) Atlantic 81909 Hit Singles 1958-1977.
(S) (2:53) Rhino 71200 Super Hits Of The 70's Volume 20.
(S) (2:53) Scotti Bros. 75465 Angel Hits.
(S) (2:56) Priority 53796 Hot And Sexy - Love And Romance Volume 3.
(S) (2:52) DCC Compact Classics 142 Groove On! Volume 2.
(S) (2:53) Time-Life R834-15 Body Talk - Once In Lifetime.

HOT BUTTER
1972 POPCORN
(S) (2:30) Rhino 70929 Super Hits Of The 70's Volume 9.
(S) (2:31) Rhino 71603 Rock Instrumental Classics Volume 3: The Seventies.
(S) (2:31) Rhino 72035 Rock Instrumental Classics Vols. 1-5 Box Set.
(S) (2:31) Time-Life SOD-32 Sounds Of The Seventies - AM Pop Classics.
(S) (2:31) King 1421 Party Time Rock & Roll.
(S) (2:30) Madacy Entertainment 1972 Rock On 1972.
(S) (2:30) JCI 3191 1970 - Only Dance - 1974.
(S) (2:30) Hip-O 40035 Cigar Classics Volume 2 - Urban Fire.

(S) (2:30) Time-Life R840-04 Sounds Of The Seventies: A Loss For Words.
(S) (2:30) Hip-O 40013 Synth Me Up - 14 Classic Electronic Hits.

HOT CHOCOLATE
1975 EMMA
(S) (3:50) Rhino 70761 Super Hits Of The 70's Volume 14.
(S) (3:51) EMI 89068 Very Best Of.

1975 DISCO QUEEN
(S) (3:07) EMI 89068 Very Best Of. *(missing the :24 coda)*
(S) (3:07) Rhino 71668 Disco Hits Vol. 5. *(missing the :24 coda)*
(S) (3:07) Flashback 72692 Disco Hits: We Are Family. *(missing the :24 coda)*
(S) (3:07) Flashback 72086 Disco Hits Box Set. *(missing the :24 coda)*

1976 YOU SEXY THING
(S) (4:04) Rhino 70762 Super Hits Of The 70's Volume 15. *(LP length)*
(S) (3:30) Priority 7057 Mega-Hits Dance Classics Volume 8. *(45 length)*
(S) (4:03) EMI 89068 Very Best Of. *(LP length)*
(S) (3:30) Time-Life SOD-18 Sounds Of The Seventies - 1976: Take Two. *(45 length)*
(S) (4:04) Risky Business 66663 Sex In The Seventies. *(LP length)*
(S) (4:03) Rhino 72123 Disco Years, Vol. 7. *(LP length)*
(S) (3:30) Madacy Entertainment 1975 Rock On 1975. *(45 length)*
(S) (3:30) JCI 3148 1975 - Only Dance - 1979. *(45 length)*
(S) (3:30) Priority 50957 Mega Hits Disco Explosion Volume 4. *(45 length)*
(S) (4:02) RCA 68904 O.S.T. The Full Monty. *(LP length)*
(S) (4:01) Capitol 93076 More Music From O.S.T. Boogie Nights. *(LP length)*
(S) (3:30) Right Stuff 52274 Flick Hits Take 2. *(45 length)*
(S) (4:02) Time-Life R840-07 Sounds Of The Seventies: '70s Dance Party 1976-1977. *(LP length)*

1979 EVERY 1'S A WINNER
(S) (4:00) EMI 89068 Very Best Of. *(edit of the LP version)*
(S) (3:39) Rhino 71202 Super Hits Of The 70's Volume 22. *(45 version)*
(S) (3:54) Time-Life SOD-19 Sounds Of The Seventies - 1979: Take Two. *(edit of the LP version)*
(S) (3:39) Rhino 71667 Disco Hits Vol. 4. *(45 version)*
(S) (3:39) Rhino 72122 Disco Years, Vol. 6. *(45 version)*
(S) (3:53) Madacy Entertainment 1978 Rock On 1978. *(edit of the LP version)*
(S) (3:39) Flashback 72690 Disco Hits: That's The Way I Like It. *(45 version)*

HOTLEGS
1970 NEANDERTHAL MAN
(actual 45 time is (4:18) not (4:29) as stated on the record label; the LP version is the same as the 45 version except that it fades out instead of ending cold)
(S) (4:18) Rhino 70923 Super Hits Of The 70's Volume 3. *(LP version)*
(S) (4:18) Rhino 72009 Super Hits Of The 70's Volumes 1-4 Box Set. *(LP version)*
(S) (4:17) Time-Life SOD-37 Sounds Of The Seventies - AM Heavy Hits. *(LP version)*
(S) (4:12) EMI-Capitol Music Special Markets 19545 Lost Hits Of The '70s. *(LP version)*

HOUSE OF PAIN
1992 JUMP AROUND
(S) (3:40) Tommy Boy 1074 MTV Party To Go Volume 3. *(remix; all tracks on this cd are segued together)*
(S) (3:36) Tommy Boy 1056 House Of Pain.

DAVID HOUSTON
1966 ALMOST PERSUADED

    (S) (2:54) Rhino 70687 Billboard's Top Country Hits Of 1966.

    (S) (2:53) Columbia 46032 Columbia Country Classics Volume 4.

    (S) (2:56) Columbia 45074 American Originals.

    (S) (2:52) Time-Life CTD-21 Country USA - 1966.

    (S) (2:53) Rhino 71647 Country Shots: Two-Timing Tunes.

    (S) (2:56) K-Tel 413 Country Music Classics Volume III.

    (S) (2:55) Scotti Bros. 75483 Country Favorites - The Number One Hits. *(rerecorded)*

    (S) (2:54) Varese Sarabande 5606 Through The Years - Country Hits Of The 60's.

    (S) (2:56) Epic 67941 Super Hits Of The 60's.

    (S) (2:57) K-Tel 3357 101 Greatest Country Hits Vol. Three: Easy Country. *(rerecording)*

    (S) (2:53) Time-Life R808-02 Classic Country 1965-1969.

THELMA HOUSTON
1977 DON'T LEAVE ME THIS WAY

    (S) (3:37) Motown 9105 and 5410 Motown Memories Volume 2. *(45 version)*

    (S) (3:37) Motown 9021 and 5309 25 Years Of Grammy Greats. *(45 version)*

    (S) (3:37) Priority 7973 Mega-Hits Dance Classics Volume 3. *(45 version)*

    (S) (3:37) Rhino 70984 The Disco Years Volume 1. *(45 version)*

    (S) (3:37) Rhino 70672 Billboard Top Hits - 1977. *(45 version)*

    (S) (3:37) Motown 6110 Motown Grammy Rhythm & Blues Performances Of The 60's & 70's. *(45 version)*

    (S) (3:37) Motown 9072 Motown Dance Party Volume 2. *(all selections on this cd are segued together; 45 version)*

    (S) (3:38) Motown 6132 25 #1 Hits From 25 Years Volume 2. *(45 version)*

    (S) (3:37) Rhino 70490 Billboard Top Dance Hits - 1976. *(45 version)*

    (S) (5:40) Motown 5226 Any Way You Like It. *(LP version)*

    (S) (5:39) Motown 5492 Best Of. *(LP version)*

    (S) (3:37) Motown 6358 Hitsville USA Volume Two. *(45 version)*

    (S) (3:37) Razor & Tie 22496 Disco Fever. *(45 version)*

    (S) (3:37) Time-Life SOD-17 Sounds Of The Seventies - 1977: Take Two. *(45 version)*

    (S) (5:40) Priority 53728 Mega Hits Dance Classics Vol 12. *(LP version)*

    (S) (5:44) Rebound 314520298 Disco Nights Vol. 9. *(LP version)*

    (S) (5:39) Rebound 314520245 Disco Nights Vol. 6 - #1 Disco Hits. *(LP version)*

    (S) (3:37) Motown 314530513 Motown Year By Year 1976. *(45 version)*

    (S) (3:37) Motown 314530409 Motown Milestones - Motown's Leading Ladies. *(45 version)*

    (S) (5:41) Motown 314530608 Funkology Volume Three: Dance Divas. *(LP version)*

    (S) (3:37) Rebound 314520368 Class Reunion '76. *(45 version)*

    (S) (3:35) Polydor 314535877 Pure Disco. *(45 version)*

    (S) (4:40) Chronicles 314553405 Non-Stop Disco Vol. 2. *(all songs on this cd are segued together)*

    (S) (3:37) Rhino 72812 VH1 8-Track Flashback: The One Hit Wonders. *(45 version)*

    (S) (2:29) Popular 12011 Disco Dance Hits. *(rerecorded)*

    (S) (3:37) Time-Life R838-16 Solid Gold Soul 1977. *(45 version)*

    (S) (3:37) JCI 3175 1975 - Only Soul - 1979. *(45 version)*

    (S) (3:37) Time-Life R840-07 Sounds Of The Seventies: '70s Dance Party 1976-1977. *(45 version)*

WHITNEY HOUSTON
1985 YOU GIVE GOOD LOVE TO ME
(actual 45 time is (4:12) not (3:58) as stated on the record label)

    (S) (4:35) Arista 8416 Perfect 10 III. *(LP length)*

    (S) (4:35) Arista 8212 Whitney Houston. *(LP length)*

1985 SAVING ALL MY LOVE FOR YOU

    (S) (3:57) Arista 8212 Whitney Houston.

1986 HOW WILL I KNOW
(actual 45 time is (4:34) not (4:10) as stated on the record label)

    (S) (4:34) Arista 8212 Whitney Houston.

    (S) (4:32) MCA 11329 Soul Train 25th Anniversary Box Set.

1986 GREATEST LOVE OF ALL
(actual 45 time is (4:48) not (4:30) as stated on the record label)

    (S) (4:49) Arista 8212 Whitney Houston.

    (S) (4:47) Time-Life R834-02 Body Talk - Just For You.

1987 I WANNA DANCE WITH SOMEBODY
(actual 45 time is (4:49) not (4:36) as stated on the record label)

    (S) (4:49) Arista 8405 Whitney.

1987 DIDN'T WE ALMOST HAVE IT ALL
(actual 45 time is (4:34) not (3:59) as stated on the record label)

    (S) (5:03) Arista 8405 Whitney. *(LP version)*

1987 SO EMOTIONAL
(actual 45 time is (3:59) not (3:46) as stated on the record label)

    (S) (4:34) Arista 8405 Whitney. *(LP version)*

1988 WHERE DO BROKEN HEARTS GO

    (S) (4:36) Arista 8405 Whitney.

1988 LOVE WILL SAVE THE DAY

    (S) (5:20) Arista 8405 Whitney. *(LP version)*

1988 ONE MOMENT IN TIME

    (S) (4:43) Arista 8551 The Summer Olympics: On Moment In Time.

released as by ARETHA FRANKLIN and WHITNEY HOUSTON:
1989 IT ISN'T, IT WASN'T, IT AIN'T NEVER GONNA BE

    (S) (5:36) Arista 8572 Aretha Franklin - Through The Storm.

released as by WHITNEY HOUSTON:
1990 I'M YOUR BABY TONIGHT

    (S) (4:58) Arista 8616 I'm Your Baby Tonight.

1991 ALL THE MAN THAT I NEED

    (S) (4:09) Arista 8616 I'm Your Baby Tonight.

1991 MIRACLE

    (S) (5:41) Arista 8616 I'm Your Baby Tonight.

1991 MY NAME IS NOT SUSAN

    (S) (4:37) Arista 8616 I'm Your Baby Tonight.

1993 I WILL ALWAYS LOVE YOU

    (S) (4:30) Arista 18699 O.S.T. The Bodyguard.

1993 I'M EVERY WOMAN

    (S) (4:44) Foundation/RCA 66563 Number 1 Hit Mix.

    (S) (4:44) Arista 18699 O.S.T. The Bodyguard.

1993 I HAVE NOTHING

    (S) (4:49) Arista 18699 O.S.T. The Bodyguard.

1993 RUN TO YOU

    (S) (4:23) Arista 18699 O.S.T. The Bodyguard.

1995 EXHALE (SHOOP SHOOP)

    (S) (3:23) Arista 18796 O.S.T. Waiting To Exhale.

released as by WHITNEY HOUSTON & CECE WINANS:
1996 COUNT ON ME

    (S) (4:25) Arista 18796 O.S.T. Waiting To Exhale.

1996 WHY DOES IT HURT SO BAD

    (S) (4:36) Arista 18796 O.S.T. Waiting To Exhale.

1997 I BELIEVE IN YOU AND ME

    (S) (3:59) Arista 18951 O.S.T. The Preacher's Wife.

1997 STEP BY STEP

    (S) (4:32) Arista 18951 O.S.T. The Preacher's Wife.

    (S) (3:51) Arista 18988 Ultimate Dance Party 1998. *(all selections on this cd are segued together)*

ADINA HOWARD
1995 FREAK LIKE ME
- (S) (4:12) EastWest 61757 Do You Wanna Ride.
- (S) (4:10) Razor & Tie 4569 '90s Style.
- (S) (4:12) Elektra 62089 Maximum R&B.

released as by WARREN G featuring ADINA HOWARD:
1996 WHAT'S LOVE GOT TO DO WITH IT
- (S) (4:16) Interscope 90088 O.S.T. Supercop.

H-TOWN
1993 KNOCKIN' DA BOOTS
- (S) (4:50) Tommy Boy 1097 MTV Party To Go Volume 5. *(all tracks on this cd are segued together)*
- (S) (5:27) Luke 126 Fever For Da Flavor.
- (S) (4:26) Robbins 75002 Strip Jointz - Hot Songs For Sexy Dancers.

1996 A THIN LINE BETWEEN LOVE & HATE
- (S) (4:57) Jac-Mac/Warner Brothers 46134 O.S.T. A Thin Line Between Love & Hate.

HUDSON BROTHERS
1974 SO YOU ARE A STAR
- (S) (3:46) Rhino 70761 Super Hits Of The 70's Volume 14.
- (S) (3:46) Rhino 71228 Yesterday's Heroes: 70's Teen Idols.
- (S) (3:48) Varese Sarabande 5572 Best Of.

1975 RENDEZVOUS
- (S) (3:19) Rhino 71197 Super Hits Of The 70's Volume 17. *(faded :10 earlier than the 45 or LP; mastered from vinyl)*
- (S) (3:17) Time-Life SOD-33 Sounds Of The Seventies - AM Pop Classics II. *(faded :12 earlier than the 45 or LP)*
- (S) (3:27) Varese Sarabande 5572 Best Of.

HUES CORPORATION
1974 ROCK THE BOAT
- (S) (3:21) RCA 7639 Dance! Dance! Dance! *(LP length)*
- (S) (3:06) RCA 9902 Nippers #1 Hits 1956-1986. *(45 length)*
- (S) (3:06) RCA 9684 and 8476 Nipper's Greatest Hits - The 70's. *(45 length)*
- (S) (3:06) Rhino 70553 Soul Hits Of The 70's Volume 13. *(45 length)*
- (S) (3:06) Rhino 70799 O.S.T. Spirit Of '76. *(45 length)*
- (S) (3:05) RCA 61144 The RCA Records Label: The 1st Note In Black Music. *(45 length)*
- (S) (3:06) Rhino 70274 The Disco Years Volume 3. *(45 length)*
- (S) (3:17) Collectables 5215 Rock The Boat. *(LP length)*
- (S) (3:20) RCA 66205 Rock The Boat - Best Of. *(LP length)*
- (S) (3:06) Epic 57620 O.S.T. Carlito's Way. *(45 length)*
- (S) (3:04) Razor & Tie 22047 Sweet 70's Soul. *(45 length)*
- (S) (3:06) Time-Life SOD-07 Sounds Of The Seventies - 1974. *(45 length)*
- (S) (3:19) Rebound 314520220 Disco Nights Vol. 4 - Greatest Disco Groups. *(LP length)*
- (S) (3:04) K-Tel 3627 Out Of Sight. *(45 length)*
- (S) (3:06) JCI 3191 1970 - Only Dance - 1974. *(45 length)*
- (S) (3:06) Time-Life AM1-21 AM Gold - 1974. *(45 length)*
- (S) (3:06) Time-Life R838-09 Solid Gold Soul - 1974. *(45 length)*
- (S) (3:05) Time-Life R840-03 Sounds Of The Seventies - Pop Nuggets: Early '70s. *(45 length)*
- (S) (3:04) K-Tel 3887 Soul Brothers & Sisters Of The 70's. *(45 length)*
- (S) (3:04) Cold Front 4024 Old School Mega Mix Volume 2. *(all songs on this cd are segued together)*
- (S) (3:06) Polydor 314555120 Pure Disco 2. *(45 length)*
- (S) (3:06) Time-Life R840-05 Sounds Of The Seventies: '70s Dance Party 1972-1974. *(45 length)*

1974 ROCKIN' SOUL
- (S) (2:54) Collectables 5215 Rock The Boat.
- (S) (2:55) RCA 66205 Rock The Boat - Best Of.
- (S) (2:56) Rhino 72127 Soul Hits Of The 70's Vol. 17.

GRAYSON HUGH
1989 TALK IT OVER
- (S) (4:16) RCA 2171 Blind To Reason.

FRED HUGHES
1965 OO WEE BABY, I LOVE YOU
- (E) (2:17) Motown 6215 and 9067 Hits From The Legendary Vee-Jay Records.
- (M) (2:22) Vee Jay 710 A Taste Of Soul Volume 1. *(mastered from vinyl)*
- (M) (2:22) Vee Jay 3-400 Celebrating 40 Years Of Classic Hits (1953-1993). *(no high end)*
- (M) (2:17) Time-Life RHD-07 Rhythm & Blues - 1965.
- (M) (2:17) Ripete 2223 Soul Patrol Vol. 5.
- (M) (2:17) Time-Life R838-12 Solid Gold Soul - 1965.

JIMMY HUGHES
1964 STEAL AWAY
- (M) (2:24) Stax 8559 Superblues Volume 2.
- (M) (2:25) Time-Life 2CLR-16 Classic Rock - 1964: Shakin' All Over.
- (M) (2:21) Rhino 71517 The Muscle Shoals Sound.
- (M) (2:25) Ripete 2198 Soul Patrol.
- (M) (2:25) Right Stuff 30577 Slow Jams: The 60's Volume 3.

HUMAN BEINZ
1968 NOBODY BUT ME
- (E) (2:18) K-Tel 839 Battle Of The Bands Volume 2. *(slightly longer intro than the LP or 45)*
- (M) (2:15) Rhino 75772 Frat Rock.
- (E) (2:16) EMI 90614 Non-Stop Party Rock.
- (S) (2:16) DCC Compact Classics 029 Toga Rock.
- (M) (2:15) Capitol 48993 Spuds Mackenzie's Party Faves.
- (M) (2:15) Capitol 98138 Spring Break Volume 1.
- (E) (2:16) JCI 3111 Good Time Sixties.
- (S) (2:15) Time-Life 2CLR-11 Classic Rock - 1968: The Beat Goes On.
- (S) (2:18) Collectables 0547 Golden Classics.
- (S) (2:10) Tommy Boy 1136 ESPN Presents Jock Rock Vol. 2. *(all songs on this cd are segued together with crowd sound effects added)*
- (M) (2:16) Right Stuff 53319 Hot Rod Rock Volume 4: Hot Rod Rebels.

HUMAN LEAGUE
1982 DON'T YOU WANT ME
- (S) (3:56) A&M 5227 Greatest Hits.
- (S) (3:57) A&M 4892 Dare.

1983 (KEEP FEELING) FASCINATION
- (S) (3:43) EMI 27674 Living In Oblivion: The 80's Greatest Hits Volume Three. *(45 version)*
- (S) (3:42) Rhino 71703 New Wave Hits Of The 80's Vol. 10. *(45 version)*
- (S) (3:42) A&M 5227 Greatest Hits. *(45 version)*
- (S) (3:42) Time-Life R988-11 Sounds Of The 80's: 1983-1984. *(45 version)*

1983 MIRROR MAN
- (S) (3:49) Rhino 71834 Classic MTV: Class Of 1983.
- (S) (3:49) A&M 5227 Greatest Hits.

1986 HUMAN
- (S) (3:46) A&M 5227 Greatest Hits. *(45 length)*
- (S) (4:25) A&M 5129 Crash. *(LP length)*

1990 HEART LIKE A WHEEL
- (S) (4:27) A&M 5316 Romantic?.

1995 TELL ME WHEN
- (S) (4:50) EastWest 61788 Octopus.

ENGELBERT HUMPERDINCK
1967 RELEASE ME (AND LET ME LOVE AGAIN)
- (S) (3:20) London 820367 Greatest Hits.
- (S) (3:20) London 820459 Release Me.
- (S) (3:16) Time-Life SUD-14 Superhits - The Late 60's.
- (S) (3:17) Time-Life R138/05 Look Of Love.
- (S) (3:17) Special Music/Essex 5028 At His Best.

ENGELBERT HUMPERDINCK (Continued)

- (S) (3:17) Rebound 314520243 Tom Jones/Engelbert Humperdinck Back To Back.
- (S) (2:26) Epic/Legacy 65006 16 Most Requested Songs. *(live)*
- (S) (3:18) Rhino 72557 Jackpot! The Las Vegas Story.
- (S) (3:16) Time-Life AM1-14 AM Gold - The Late '60s.
- (S) (3:17) Rebound 314520450 Tom Jones/Engelbert Humperdinck Sing Country Favorites.
- (S) (2:26) Epic/Legacy 65442 Super Hits. *(live)*
- (S) (3:17) Polygram Special Markets 314520459 Vocal Treasures.
- (S) (3:17) Time-Life R814-01 Love Songs.

1967 THERE GOES MY EVERYTHING
- (S) (2:53) London 820367 Greatest Hits.
- (S) (2:52) Special Music/Essex 5028 At His Best.
- (S) (2:52) Rebound 314520243 Tom Jones/Engelbert Humperdinck Back To Back.
- (S) (2:46) Epic/Legacy 65006 16 Most Requested Songs. *(rerecorded)*
- (S) (2:51) Hammer & Lace 697124114 Leading Men: Masters Of Style Volume Three.
- (S) (2:51) Rebound 314520450 Tom Jones/Engelbert Humperdinck Sing Country Favorites.

1967 THE LAST WALTZ
- (S) (2:58) London 820367 Greatest Hits.
- (S) (3:24) Epic/Legacy 65006 16 Most Requested Songs. *(rerecorded)*
- (S) (2:57) Special Music 5039 Great Britons! Volume One.
- (S) (2:57) Time-Life R814-04 Love Songs.

1968 AM I THAT EASY TO FORGET
- (S) (3:07) London 820367 Greatest Hits.
- (S) (3:11) Epic/Legacy 65006 16 Most Requested Songs. *(rerecorded)*

1968 A MAN WITHOUT LOVE
- (S) (3:19) London 820367 Greatest Hits.
- (S) (3:19) Pair 1326 Step Into My Life. *(rerecorded)*
- (S) (3:24) Epic/Legacy 65006 16 Most Requested Songs. *(rerecorded)*

1968 LES BICYCLETTES DE BELSIZE
- (S) (3:11) London 820367 Greatest Hits.
- (S) (3:09) Epic/Legacy 65006 16 Most Requested Songs. *(rerecorded)*
- (S) (3:09) Rhino 72873 Let's Dance! The Best Of Ballroom: Fox Trots And Waltzes.

1969 THE WAY IT USED TO BE
- (S) (3:09) London 820367 Greatest Hits.

1969 I'M A BETTER MAN
- (S) (2:48) London 820367 Greatest Hits.

1970 WINTER WORLD OF LOVE
- (S) (3:20) London 820367 Greatest Hits.
- (S) (3:16) Epic/Legacy 65006 16 Most Requested Songs. *(rerecorded)*

1970 MY MARIE
- (S) (3:05) Rhino 72736 Billboard Top Soft Rock Hits - 1970.

1977 AFTER THE LOVIN'
- (S) (3:54) Rhino 71200 Super Hits Of The 70's Volume 20.
- (S) (3:25) Epic/Legacy 65006 16 Most Requested Songs. *(live)*
- (S) (3:54) Razor & Tie 4543 The '70s Preservation Society Presents: Easy '70s.
- (S) (3:53) K-Tel 3630 Lounge Legends.
- (S) (3:54) Time-Life R834-09 Body Talk - Magic Moments.
- (S) (3:53) Rhino 72516 Behind Closed Doors - '70s Swingers.
- (S) (3:53) Rebound 314520450 Tom Jones/Engelbert Humperdinck Sing Country Favorites.
- (S) (3:24) Epic/Legacy 65442 Super Hits. *(live)*
- (S) (3:54) Time-Life R814-02 Love Songs.

PAUL HUMPHREY & HIS COOL AID CHEMISTS
1971 COOL AID
- (S) (2:41) Rhino 70785 Soul Hits Of The 70's Volume 5.
- (S) (2:41) Rhino 72028 Soul Hits Of The 70's Volumes 1-5 Box Set.

IVORY JOE HUNTER
1956 SINCE I MET YOU BABY
- (M) (2:42) JCI 3204 Heart & Soul Fifties. *(no fidelity)*
- (M) (2:42) Atlantic 81295 Atlantic Rhythm & Blues Volume 3.
- (M) (2:41) Atlantic 81769 O.S.T. Big Town.
- (M) (2:41) Atlantic 82305 Atlantic Rhythm And Blues 1947-1974 Box Set.
- (M) (2:42) A&M 3930 O.S.T. Heart Of Dixie.
- (M) (2:42) Time-Life 2RNR-14 Rock 'N' Roll Era - 1956.
- (M) (2:42) Time-Life RHD-08 Rhythm & Blues - 1957.
- (M) (2:42) Rhino 71806 The R&B Box: Thirty Years Of Rhythm & Blues.
- (M) (2:48) Razor & Tie 2052 Since I Met You Baby: Best Of.
- (M) (2:42) JCI 3165 #1 Radio Hits 1955 - Only Rock 'n Roll - 1959.
- (M) (2:42) Hip-O 40028 The Glory Of Love - '50s Sweet & Soulful Love Songs.
- (M) (2:48) Time-Life R857-07 The Heart Of Rock 'n' Roll 1956.
- (M) (2:42) Rhino 72961 Ultimate '50s R&B Smashes!
- (M) (2:42) Time-Life R838-23 Solid Gold Soul 1957.

1957 EMPTY ARMS
- (M) (2:40) Atlantic 81295 Atlantic Rhythm & Blues Volume 3.
- (M) (2:40) Atlantic 82305 Atlantic Rhythm And Blues 1947-1974 Box Set.
- (S) (1:57) Collectables 5226 I'm Coming Down With The Blues. *(rerecorded)*
- (M) (2:42) Razor & Tie 2052 Since I Met You Baby: Best Of.
- (M) (2:42) Time-Life R857-13 The Heart Of Rock 'n' Roll 1956-1957.

JOHN HUNTER
1985 TRAGEDY

TAB HUNTER
1957 YOUNG LOVE
- (M) (2:24) Time-Life 2RNR-47 Rock 'N' Roll Era - Teen Idols II.
- (M) (2:17) MCA Special Products 20580 Teen Idols. *(rerecording)*
- (M) (2:24) Collectors' Choice 002 Teen Idols....For A Moment.
- (M) (2:23) Varese Sarabande 5686 History Of Dot Records Volume One.
- (S) (2:15) Nick At Nite/550 Music/Epic 67768 Fonzie's Make Out Music. *(rerecording)*

1957 NINETY-NINE WAYS
- (M) (1:45) Varese Sarabande 5687 History Of Dot Records Volume Two.

1959 (I'LL BE WITH YOU IN) APPLE BLOSSOM TIME

FERLIN HUSKY
1957 GONE
- (M) (2:22) Curb 77330 50's Hits - Country Volume 1.
- (M) (2:22) Curb 77341 Greatest Hits.
- (M) (2:22) Capitol 91629 Capitol Collector's Series.
- (M) (2:21) Capitol 95917 Opry Legends.
- (M) (2:18) Time-Life CTD-02 Country USA - 1957.
- (M) (2:22) K-Tel 225 Country Music Classics Volume I.
- (M) (2:20) Rhino 71903 Hillbilly Fever! Vol. 4: Legends Of The West Coast.
- (M) (2:21) Capitol 36593 Vintage Collections.
- (M) (2:20) Rhino 72443 Heroes Of Country Music Vol. Four.
- (M) (2:21) JCI 3152 1955 - Only Country - 1959.
- (M) (2:17) Priority 50966 I Love Country Volume One: Hits Of The 60's.
- (M) (2:21) Time-Life R857-05 The Heart Of Rock 'n' Roll 1957.
- (M) (2:21) Time-Life R808-03 Classic Country 1950-1959.

1957 A FALLEN STAR
- (M) (2:22) Capitol 91629 Capitol Collector's Series.
- (M) (2:21) Pair 1301 With Feelin'.
- (M) (2:21) Capitol 36593 Vintage Collections.

1961 WINGS OF A DOVE
- (S) (2:17) Curb 77343 60's Hits - Country Volume 1.
- (S) (2:17) Curb 77341 Greatest Hits.
- (S) (2:16) Capitol 91629 Capitol Collector's Series.
- (M) (2:16) Capitol 95916 Golden Country Jukebox Favorites. *(truncated fade)*
- (M) (2:17) Capitol 95917 Opry Legends. *(truncated fade)*
- (S) (2:16) Time-Life CTD-12 Country USA - 1960.
- (S) (2:17) K-Tel 320 Country Music Classics Volume II.
- (S) (2:16) Scotti Bros. 75483 Country Favorites - The Number One Hits. *(rerecorded)*
- (M) (2:17) Capitol 36593 Vintage Collections.
- (M) (2:15) JCI 3153 1960 - Only Country - 1964.
- (S) (2:21) K-Tel 3359 101 Greatest Country Hits Vol. Five: Country Memories. *(rerecording)*
- (S) (2:16) Time-Life R808-01 Classic Country 1960-1964.

BRIAN HYLAND
1960 ITSY BITSY TEENIE WEENIE YELLOW POLKADOT BIKINI
- (S) (2:20) MCA 31202 Vintage Music Volume 5.
- (S) (2:20) MCA 5804 Vintage Music Volumes 5 & 6.
- (S) (2:20) K-Tel 3036 Silly Songs.
- (S) (2:19) Time-Life 2RNR-37 Rock 'N' Roll Era - Weird, Wild & Wacky.
- (S) (2:21) MCA 11034 Greatest Hits.
- (S) (2:19) MCA Special Products 22019 Summer Hits Of The 50's And 60's.
- (S) (2:19) MCA Special Products 22028 Cra-a-zy Hits.
- (S) (2:21) Rhino 71581 Billboard Top Pop Hits, 1960.
- (S) (2:20) MCA Special Products 22179 Vintage Collectibles Volume 9.
- (S) (2:19) DCC Compact Classics 077 Too Cute!
- (S) (2:21) MCA Special Products 21023 Tommy Roe/Brian Hyland Sing The Big Hits.

1961 LET ME BELONG TO YOU
- (S) (3:03) MCA 11034 Greatest Hits.

1962 GINNY COME LATELY
- (S) (2:49) MCA 11034 Greatest Hits.
- (S) (2:49) MCA Special Products 21023 Tommy Roe/Brian Hyland Sing The Big Hits.

1962 SEALED WITH A KISS
- (M) (2:40) MCA 31207 Vintage Music Volume 10. *(noisy intro)*
- (M) (2:40) MCA 5806 Vintage Music Volumes 9 & 10. *(noisy intro)*
- (M) (2:39) Time-Life 2RNR-27 Rock 'N' Roll Era - Teen Idols. *(noisy intro)*
- (M) (2:39) Time-Life SUD-06 Superhits - 1962. *(noisy intro)*
- (E) (2:39) Original Sound 8852 Oldies But Goodies Vol. 2. *(this compact disc uses the "Waring - fds" noise reduction process; noisy intro)*
- (E) (2:39) Original Sound 2223 Oldies But Goodies Volumes 2,7,9,12 and 13 Box Set. *(this box set uses the "Waring - fds" noise reduction process; noisy intro)*
- (E) (2:39) Original Sound 2500 Oldies But Goodies Volumes 1-15 Box Set. *(this box set uses the "Waring - fds" noise reduction process; noisy intro)*
- (M) (2:38) MCA 11034 Greatest Hits. *(noisy intro)*
- (M) (2:40) MCA Special Products 22019 Summer Hits Of The 50's And 60's. *(noisy intro)*
- (M) (2:40) MCA Special Products 20751 Rock Around The Oldies #2. *(noisy intro)*
- (M) (2:40) MCA Special Products 20580 Teen Idols. *(noisy intro)*
- (M) (2:40) MCA Special Products 22130 Vintage Collectibles Volume 1. *(noisy intro)*
- (M) (2:40) LaserLight 12315 and 15936 The Wonder Years - Movin' On. *(noisy intro)*
- (M) (2:40) Time-Life R857-06 The Heart Of Rock 'n' Roll 1962. *(noisy intro)*
- (M) (2:39) Time-Life AM1-18 AM Gold - 1962. *(noisy intro)*
- (M) (2:38) MCA Special Products 21023 Tommy Roe/Brian Hyland Sing The Big Hits. *(noisy intro)*
- (M) (2:38) JCI 3184 1960 - Only Love - 1964. *(noisy intro)*

1962 WARMED OVER KISSES (LEFT OVER LOVE)
- (S) (2:18) MCA 11034 Greatest Hits.

1966 THE JOKER WENT WILD
- (S) (2:41) MCA 11034 Greatest Hits.

1966 RUN, RUN, LOOK AND SEE
- (S) (2:37) MCA 11034 Greatest Hits.

1970 GYPSY WOMAN
- (M) (2:33) Rhino 70923 Super Hits Of The 70's Volume 3.
- (M) (2:33) Rhino 72009 Super Hits Of The 70's Volumes 1-4 Box Set.
- (M) (2:34) Rhino 71207 70's Smash Hits Volume 3.
- (M) (2:31) Time-Life SUD-04 Superhits - 1970.
- (M) (2:33) MCA 11034 Greatest Hits.
- (M) (2:33) MCA Special Products 20900 Rock Around The Oldies #3.
- (M) (2:33) MCA Special Products 20910 Rockin' 70's.
- (M) (2:32) Madacy Entertainment 1970 Rock On 1970.
- (M) (2:31) Time-Life AM1-02 AM Gold - 1970.
- (M) (2:33) MCA Special Products 20997 Mellow Rock.
- (M) (2:33) Flashback 72683 '70s Radio Hits Volume 3.
- (M) (2:33) Flashback 72090 '70s Radio Hits Box Set.
- (M) (2:33) MCA Special Products 21023 Tommy Roe/Brian Hyland Sing The Big Hits.

DICK HYMAN TRIO
1956 MORITAT (A THEME FROM THE "THREE PENNY OPERA")
- (M) (2:14) Time-Life HPD-30 Your Hit Parade - 50's Instrumentals.
- (M) (2:14) DCC Compact Classics 079 Music For A Bachelor's Den.

released as by DICK HYMAN & HIS ELECTRIC ECLECTICS:
1969 THE MINOTAUR
- (S) (8:29) Varese Sarabande 5788 Moog: The Electric Eclectics Of. *(complete recording session)*
- (S) (8:31) Hip-O 40013 Synth Me Up - 14 Classic Electronic Hits. *(complete recording session)*

JANIS IAN
1967 SOCIETY'S CHILD
    (M) (3:10)   Rhino 70734 Songs Of Protest.
    (M) (3:11)   Warner Special Products 27615 Storytellers: Singers & Songwriters.
    (M) (3:11)   Mercury 834216 45's On CD Volume 3.
    (M) (3:11)   Time-Life 2CLR-15 Classic Rock - 1967: Shakin' All Over.
    (M) (3:10)   Time-Life R103-33 Singers & Songwriters.
    (M) (3:10)   Special Music 5026 Let It All Hang Out - 60's Party Hits.
    (M) (3:11)   Polydor 314527591 Society's Child: The Verve Recordings.
1975 AT SEVENTEEN
    (S) (3:55)   Rhino 70762 Super Hits Of The 70's Volume 15. *(45 version)*
    (S) (4:40)   Columbia 33394 Between The Lines. *(LP version)*
    (S) (3:55)   Time-Life R105-26 Our Songs: Singers & Songwriters Encore. *(45 version)*
    (S) (4:40)   Right Stuff 57092 Free To Be Volume 9. *(LP version)*

ICE CUBE
1993 IT WAS A GOOD DAY
    (S) (4:19)   Priority 57185 Ice Cube - The Predator.
released as by ICE CUBE featuring DAS EFX:
1993 CHECK YO SELF
    (S) (3:42)   Priority 57185 Ice Cube - The Predator.
released as by ICE CUBE:
1994 REALLY DOE
    (S) (4:27)   Priority 53876 Lethal Injection.
1994 YOU KNOW HOW WE DO IT
    (S) (3:52)   Priority 53876 Lethal Injection.
1994 BOP GUN (ONE NATION)
    (S) (11:04)   Priority 53876 Lethal Injection.

ICEHOUSE
1988 CRAZY
    (S) (4:47)   Chrysalis 41592 and 21592 Man Of Colours. *(LP version)*
    (S) (3:21)   K-Tel 3742 The 80's: Hot Rock. *(45 version)*
1988 ELECTRIC BLUE
    (S) (4:23)   Foundation/WEA 26097 Super Sessions Volume Two.
    (S) (4:31)   Chrysalis 41592 and 21592 Man Of Colours.
    (S) (4:21)   K-Tel 3798 The 80's Mega Hits.
    (S) (4:21)   Time-Life R988-20 Sounds Of The Eighties: The Late '80s Take Two.

ICICLE WORKS
1984 WHISPER TO A SCREAM (BIRDS FLY)
    (S) (3:43)   Priority 53750 Rock Of The 80's Volume 7.
    (S) (3:42)   EMI 32694 Living In Oblivion - The 80's Greatest Hits Volume Five.
    (S) (3:45)   Rhino 71976 New Wave Hits Of The 80's Vol. 13.

IDES OF MARCH
1970 VEHICLE
    (S) (2:53)   Rhino 70631 Billboard's Top Rock & Roll Hits Of 1970.
    (S) (2:53)   Rhino 72005 Billboard's Top Rock & Roll Hits 1968-1972 Box Set.
    (S) (2:53)   JCI 3101 Rockin' Sixties.
    (S) (2:53)   Rhino 71196 Super Hits Of The 70's Volume 16.

    (S) (2:53)   Time-Life SOD-11 Sounds Of The Seventies - 1970: Take Two.
    (S) (2:53)   K-Tel 3585 Horn Rock Bands.
    (S) (2:53)   JCI 3191 1970 - Only Dance - 1974.
    (S) (2:53)   Rebound 314520521 Highway Rockin'.

BILLY IDOL
1982 HOT IN THE CITY
    (S) (3:37)   Chrysalis 21377 and 41377 Billy Idol.
    (S) (5:09)   Chrysalis 21620 and 41620 Vital Idol. *(remix)*
1983 WHITE WEDDING
    (S) (4:10)   Right Stuff 28996 Sedated In The Eighties No. 2. *(LP version)*
    (S) (4:11)   Chrysalis 21377 and 41377 Billy Idol. *(LP version)*
    (S) (8:22)   Chrysalis 21620 and 41620 Vital Idol. *(12" single version)*
    (S) (3:33)   Hip-O 40023 Smash Alternatives - 14 Classic New Wave Hits. *(45 version)*
    (S) (4:09)   Maverick/Warner Brothers 46840 O.S.T. The Wedding Singer. *(LP version)*
1984 REBEL YELL
    (S) (4:47)   Chrysalis 21450 and 41450 Rebel Yell. *(LP version)*
1984 EYES WITHOUT A FACE
    (S) (4:57)   Chrysalis 21450 and 41450 Rebel Yell. *(LP version)*
1984 FLESH FOR FANTASY
    (S) (7:02)   Chrysalis 21620 and 41620 Vital Idol. *(12" single version)*
    (S) (4:38)   Chrysalis 21450 and 41450 Rebel Yell. *(LP version)*
1986 TO BE A LOVER
    (S) (6:47)   Chrysalis 21620 and 41620 Vital Idol. *(12" single version)*
    (S) (3:51)   Chrysalis 21514 and 41514 Whiplash Smile.
    (S) (3:50)   Hip-O 40047 The '80s Hit(s) Back 3.
1987 DON'T NEED A GUN
    (S) (6:17)   Chrysalis 21514 and 41514 Whiplash Smile. *(LP version)*
1987 SWEET SIXTEEN
    (S) (4:16)   Chrysalis 21514 and 41514 Whiplash Smile.
1987 MONY MONY (live version)
(dj copies of this 45 ran (4:15); commercial copies were all (4:00))
    (S) (5:00)   Chrysalis 21620 and 41620 Vital Idol. *(studio version)*
    (S) (5:01)   Chrysalis 21729 Don't Stop. *(studio version)*
    (S) (2:51)   Rhino 72213 Stadium Rock. *(edit of the studio version)*
    (S) (5:00)   EMI 52498 O.S.T. Striptease. *(studio version)*
    (S) (4:52)   Cold Front 6255 Greatest Sports Rock And Jams Volume 2. *(all selections on this cd are segued together; studio version)*
    (S) (4:59)   Simitar 55582 The Number One's: Rock It Up. *(studio version)*
1990 CRADLE OF LOVE
    (S) (4:38)   Elektra 60952 O.S.T. Adventures Of Ford Fairlane.
    (S) (4:40)   Chrysalis 21735 Charmed Life.

FRANK IFIELD
1962 I REMEMBER YOU
    (M) (2:02)   Enigma 73531 O.S.T. Scandal.
    (E) (2:02)   Curb 77453 Best Of.
    (M) (2:01)   Collectables 5068 History Of Rock Volume 8.

(S) (1:57) Time-Life SUD-06 Superhits - 1962. *(rerecording)*
(M) (2:03) Time-Life HPD-33 Your Hit Parade - The Early 60's.
(M) (2:02) Time-Life R857-06 The Heart Of Rock 'n' Roll 1962.
(S) (1:57) Time-Life AM1-18 AM Gold - 1962. *(rerecording)*

JULIO IGLESIAS
released as by JULIO IGLESIAS and WILLIE NELSON:
1984 TO ALL THE GIRLS I'VE LOVED BEFORE
(S) (3:32) Columbia 44428 Greatest Country Hits Of The 80's, 1984.
(S) (3:31) Columbia 39157 Julio Iglesias - 1100 Bel Air Place.
(S) (3:31) Columbia 39990 Willie Nelson - Half Nelson.
released as by JULIO IGLESIAS and DIANA ROSS:
1984 ALL OF YOU
(S) (4:01) Columbia 39157 Julio Iglesias - 1100 Bel Air Place.
(S) (3:59) RCA 5009 Diana Ross - Swept Away.

IKETTES
1962 I'M BLUE (THE GONG GONG SONG)
(M) (2:28) MCA 6228 O.S.T. Hairspray.
(M) (2:29) Atlantic 82305 Atlantic Rhythm And Blues 1947-1974 Box Set.
(M) (2:26) Original Sound 9323 Ike & Tina Turner - Legendary Superstars.
(M) (2:31) Curb 77332 Ike & Tina Turner's Greatest Hits. *(sounds like it was mastered from vinyl)*
(M) (2:04) Mogull Entertainment 35830 Ike & Tina Turner: In The Beginning. *(rerecording)*
(M) (2:27) Time-Life 2RNR-16 Rock 'N' Roll Era - 1962 Still Rockin'.
(M) (2:30) Rhino 72815 Beg, Scream & Shout! The Big Ol' Box Of '60s Soul.
(M) (2:29) K-Tel 3888 Great R&B Female Groups Hits Of The 60's.

ILLUSION
1969 DID YOU SEE HER EYES
(actual 45 time is (2:57) not (2:47) as stated on the record label)
(S) (2:58) Varese Sarabande 5705 Dick Bartley Presents Collector's Essentials: The 60's. *(45 version)*

IMMATURE
1994 NEVER LIE
(S) (4:11) MCA 11068 Playtyme Is Over.
1995 CONSTANTLY
(S) (5:42) MCA 11068 Playtyme Is Over.
1996 WE GOT IT
(S) (3:38) MCA 11385 We Got It.
(S) (2:51) Loud/RCA 67423 All That - The Album.
1996 PLEASE DON'T GO
(S) (4:31) MCA 11385 We Got It.
released as by IMMATURE featuring SMOOTH and ED from GOOD BURGER:
1997 WATCH ME DO MY THING
(S) (3:50) Loud/RCA 67423 All That - The Album. *(tracks into next selection)*

IMPALAS
1959 SORRY (I RAN ALL THE WAY HOME)
(S) (2:32) Rhino 71463 Doo Wop Box.
(S) (2:32) Time-Life 2RNR-13 Rock 'N' Roll Era - 1959.
(S) (2:30) Collectables 5625 Sorry (I Ran All The Way Home).
(S) (2:31) Eric 11502 Hard To Find 45's On CD (Volume I) 1955-60.
(S) (2:32) K-Tel 3812 Doo Wop's Greatest Hits.
(S) (2:31) Polygram Special Markets 314520478 50's Jukebox Hits.
(S) (2:30) Collectables 1514 and 2514 The Anniversary Album - The 50's.

IMPRESSIONS
released as by JERRY BUTLER and THE IMPRESSIONS:
1958 FOR YOUR PRECIOUS LOVE
(S) (2:43) Rhino 75893 Jukebox Classics Volume 1.

(E) (2:41) Original Sound 8853 Oldies But Goodies Vol. 3. *(this compact disc uses the "Waring - fds" noise reduction process)*
(E) (2:41) Original Sound 2222 Oldies But Goodies Volumes 3,5,11,14 and 15 Box Set. *(this box set uses the "Waring - fds" noise reduction process)*
(E) (2:41) Original Sound 2500 Oldies But Goodies Volumes 1-15 Box Set. *(this box set uses the "Waring - fds" noise reduction process)*
(S) (2:41) Motown 6215 and 9067 Hits From The Legendary Vee-Jay Records.
(S) (2:43) Rhino 75881 Jerry Butler: Best Of.
(E) (2:38) Curb 77419 Jerry Butler: Greatest Hits.
(S) (2:42) Ripete 2392192 Beach Music Anthology Box Set.
(S) (2:43) Vee Jay 700 Jerry Butler: The Ice Man.
(S) (2:41) Collectables 5063 History Of Rock Volume 3.
(S) (2:42) Vee Jay 719 Impressions: Their Complete Vee-Jay Recordings.
(S) (2:42) Rhino 71463 Doo Wop Box.
(S) (2:43) Vee Jay 3-400 Celebrating 40 Years Of Classic Hits (1953-1993).
(S) (2:43) Epic 57560 O.S.T. A Bronx Tale.
(S) (2:42) Time-Life 2RNR-21 Rock 'N' Roll Era - 1958 Still Rockin'.
(S) (2:42) Time-Life RHD-16 Rhythm & Blues - 1958.
(E) (2:41) Collectables 2506 WCBS-FM History Of Rock - The 50's Part 1. *(sounds like it was mastered from vinyl)*
(E) (2:41) Collectables 4506 History Of Rock/The 50s Part One. *(sounds like it was mastered from vinyl)*
(S) (2:43) Collectables 2607 WCBS-FM For Lovers Only Vol. 3.
(S) (2:43) Motown 6763 Rites Of Rhythm & Blues Volume Two.
(S) (2:43) Time-Life R103-27 Love Me Tender.
(S) (5:08) Varese Sarabande 5486 A Celebration Of Soul Vol. 1: The Chi-Sound Records Collection. *(rerecording)*
(S) (2:41) LaserLight 12321 Soulful Love.
(S) (2:42) Ripete 2163-RE Ebb Tide.
(S) (2:42) Rhino 71806 The R&B Box: Thirty Years Of Rhythm & Blues.
(S) (2:42) SBK 28336 Original Songs From The Daytime Drama "One Life To Live".
(S) (2:42) Ripete 2220 Soul Patrol Vol. 2.
(S) (2:43) Time-Life R857-04 The Heart Of Rock 'n' Roll - 1958.
(S) (2:42) JCI 3164 Eighteen Soulful Ballads.
(S) (2:43) Hip-O 40028 The Glory Of Love - '50s Sweet & Soulful Love Songs.
(S) (2:43) Rhino 72580 Soul Serenade - Intimate R&B.
(S) (2:42) Time-Life R838-22 Solid Gold Soul 1958.
released as by THE IMPRESSIONS:
1961 GYPSY WOMAN
(S) (2:18) Rhino 70647 Billboard's Top R&B Hits Of 1961.
(S) (2:18) MCA 31203 Vintage Music Volume 6.
(S) (2:18) MCA 5804 Vintage Music Volumes 5 & 6.
(S) (2:18) Original Sound 8862 Oldies But Goodies Vol. 12. *(this compact disc uses the "Waring - fds" noise reduction process)*
(S) (2:18) Original Sound 2223 Oldies But Goodies Volumes 2,7,9,12 and 13 Box Set. *(this box set uses the "Waring - fds" noise reduction process)*
(S) (2:18) Original Sound 2500 Oldies But Goodies Volumes 1-15 Box Set. *(this box set uses the "Waring - fds" noise reduction process)*
(S) (2:19) MCA 31338 Greatest Hits.
(S) (2:17) MCA 10664 Anthology 1961-1977.
(S) (2:18) Time-Life 2RNR-18 Rock 'N' Roll Era - 1961 Still Rockin'.
(S) (2:18) Rhino 71806 The R&B Box: Thirty Years Of Rhythm & Blues.
(S) (2:17) MCA Special Products 20838 Tams & Impressions Greatest Hits.
(S) (2:17) MCA Special Products 22175 It's All Right.
(S) (2:18) MCA Special Products 22172 Vintage Collectibles Volume 10.
(S) (2:18) Rhino 72262 The Curtis Mayfield Story.
(S) (2:21) Hip-O 40009 ABC's Of Soul Volume 1.
(S) (2:17) Time-Life R857-14 The Heart Of Rock 'n' Roll 1960-1961 Take Two.

IMPRESSIONS *(Continued)*

    (S) (2:18) Rhino 72583 Very Best Of.

1963 IT'S ALL RIGHT
    (S) (2:46) Rhino 70649 Billboard's Top R&B Hits Of 1963.
    (S) (2:46) Rhino 75757 Soul Shots Volume 3.
    (S) (2:48) MCA 31202 Vintage Music Volume 5.
    (S) (2:48) MCA 5804 Vintage Music Volumes 5 & 6.
    (S) (2:48) MCA 31338 Greatest Hits.
    (S) (2:48) Ripete 392183 Ocean Drive.
    (S) (2:45) MCA 10664 Anthology 1961-1977.
    (S) (2:46) Rhino 71461 Soul Hits, Volume 3.
    (S) (2:46) Time-Life 2RNR-07 Rock 'N' Roll Era - 1963.
    (S) (2:44) Time-Life RHD-02 Rhythm & Blues - 1963.
    (S) (2:48) MCA Special Products 20753 Classic R&B Oldies From The 60's.
    (S) (2:49) Ripete 2183-RE Ocean Drive Volume 1.
    (S) (2:45) MCA Special Products 20838 Tams & Impressions Greatest Hits.
    (S) (2:45) MCA Special Products 22175 It's All Right.
    (S) (2:48) MCA Special Products 22179 Vintage Collectibles Volume 9.
    (S) (2:48) MCA Special Products 20899 Rock Around The Oldies #4.
    (S) (2:47) Rhino 72262 The Curtis Mayfield Story.
    (S) (2:44) Time-Life R838-14 Solid Gold Soul - 1963.
    (S) (2:47) Rhino 72583 Very Best Of.
    (S) (2:46) Flashback 72659 '60s Soul: When A Man Loves A Woman.
    (S) (2:46) Flashback 72091 '60s Soul Hits Box Set.
    (S) (2:45) MCA Special Products 21030 Beach Music Hits.
    (S) (2:48) MCA Special Products 21010 R&B Crossover Hits Volume 2.
    (S) (2:43) TVT 4010 Rhythm Revue.
    (S) (2:45) Repeat/Relativity 1611 A Brand New Bag: #1 Soul Hits Of The 60's Volume 3.
    (S) (2:44) Columbia 69059 Party Super Hits. *(rerecording; mastered from vinyl)*
    (S) (2:46) Time-Life R857-18 The Heart Of Rock 'n' Roll 1962-1963 Take Two.
    (S) (2:48) K-Tel 3886 Great R&B Male Groups: Hits Of The 60's.

1964 TALKING ABOUT MY BABY
    (S) (2:29) MCA 5940 Vintage Music Volumes 19 & 20.
    (S) (2:29) MCA 31217 Vintage Music Volume 20.
    (S) (2:29) MCA 31338 Greatest Hits.
    (S) (2:29) MCA 10664 Anthology 1961-1977.
    (S) (2:29) Time-Life 2CLR-16 Classic Rock - 1964: Shakin' All Over.
    (S) (2:29) MCA Special Products 22134 Vintage Collectibles Volume 5.
    (S) (2:29) Ripete 2183-RE Ocean Drive Volume 1.
    (S) (2:30) MCA Special Products 20838 Tams & Impressions Greatest Hits.
    (S) (2:29) MCA Special Products 22175 It's All Right.
    (S) (2:29) Rhino 72583 Very Best Of.

1964 I'M SO PROUD
    (S) (2:47) Rhino 75757 Soul Shots Volume 3.
    (S) (2:47) MCA 5939 Vintage Music Volumes 17 & 18.
    (S) (2:47) MCA 31214 Vintage Music Volume 17.
    (S) (2:47) MCA 31338 Greatest Hits.
    (S) (2:46) MCA 10664 Anthology 1961-1977.
    (S) (2:46) Epic 57560 O.S.T. A Bronx Tale.
    (S) (2:49) Time-Life 2CLR-03 Classic Rock - 1964.
    (S) (2:46) Original Sound 9303 Art Laboe's Dedicated To You Vol. 3. *(tracks into next selection)*
    (S) (2:48) Right Stuff 30578 Slow Jams: The 60's Volume 4.
    (S) (2:46) Thump 7050 Low Rider Oldies Volume 5.
    (S) (2:48) Rhino 72262 The Curtis Mayfield Story.
    (S) (2:46) Hip-O 40029 The Glory Of Love - '60s Sweet & Soulful Love Songs.
    (S) (2:48) Rhino 72619 Smooth Grooves: The '60s Volume 2 Mid '60s.
    (S) (2:46) MCA Special Products 20998 More Of The Tams & Impressions Greatest Hits.
    (S) (2:45) Time-Life R857-09 The Heart Of Rock 'n' Roll 1964.

1964 KEEP ON PUSHING
    (S) (2:32) Rhino 70650 Billboard's Top R&B Hits Of 1964.

    (S) (2:30) MCA 5936 Vintage Music Volumes 11 & 12.
    (S) (2:30) MCA 31208 Vintage Music Volume 11.
    (S) (2:31) MCA 31338 Greatest Hits.
    (S) (2:31) MCA 10664 Anthology 1961-1977.
    (S) (2:31) Right Stuff 28373 Movin' On Up.
    (S) (2:31) Time-Life RHD-12 Rhythm & Blues - 1964.
    (M) (2:30) Time-Life 2CLR-09 Classic Rock - 1964: The Beat Goes On.
    (S) (2:31) MCA Special Products 20838 Tams & Impressions Greatest Hits.
    (S) (2:31) MCA Special Products 22175 It's All Right.
    (S) (2:31) Rhino 72262 The Curtis Mayfield Story.
    (S) (2:30) MCA Special Products 21742 Vintage Collectibles Volume 12.
    (S) (2:31) Capitol 35818 O.S.T. Dead Presidents Volume II.
    (S) (2:31) Time-Life R838-13 Solid Gold Soul - 1964.
    (S) (2:31) Rhino 72583 Very Best Of.
    (S) (2:32) Right Stuff 52274 Flick Hits Take 2.

1964 YOU MUST BELIEVE ME
    (S) (2:31) MCA 31338 Greatest Hits.
    (S) (2:30) MCA 10664 Anthology 1961-1977.
    (S) (2:26) Time-Life 2CLR-25 Classic Rock - On The Soul Side.
    (S) (2:31) Rhino 72583 Very Best Of.

1964 AMEN
    (S) (3:27) MCA 31204 Vintage Music Volume 7. *(LP version)*
    (S) (3:27) MCA 5805 Vintage Music Volumes 7 & 8. *(LP version)*
    (S) (3:26) MCA 31338 Greatest Hits. *(LP version)*
    (S) (3:25) MCA 25991 Christmas Hits. *(LP version)*
    (S) (3:27) MCA 10664 Anthology 1961-1977. *(LP version)*
    (S) (3:27) Time-Life 2CLR-09 Classic Rock - 1964: The Beat Goes On. *(LP version)*
    (S) (3:27) MCA Special Products 22135 Vintage Collectibles Volume 6. *(LP version)*
    (S) (3:27) MCA Special Products 22175 It's All Right. *(LP version)*
    (S) (3:27) Rhino 72262 The Curtis Mayfield Story. *(LP version)*
    (S) (3:27) Collectables 1513 and 2513 and 3513 and 4513 The Ultimate Christmas Album Volume Three. *(LP version)*
    (S) (3:27) MCA Special Products 20998 More Of The Tams & Impressions Greatest Hits. *(LP version)*
    (S) (3:27) Rhino 72583 Very Best Of. *(LP version)*
    (S) (3:28) Varese Sarabande 5906 God, Love And Rock & Roll. *(LP version)*

1965 PEOPLE GET READY
    (S) (2:36) MCA 31338 Greatest Hits.
    (S) (2:36) MCA 10664 Anthology 1961-1977.
    (S) (2:37) Time-Life RHD-07 Rhythm & Blues - 1965.
    (S) (2:35) Time-Life 2CLR-14 Classic Rock - 1965: Shakin' All Over.
    (S) (2:36) Risky Business 67308 Train Trax.
    (S) (2:36) Rhino 72262 The Curtis Mayfield Story.
    (S) (2:36) MCA Special Products 20998 More Of The Tams & Impressions Greatest Hits.
    (S) (2:37) Time-Life R838-12 Solid Gold Soul - 1965.
    (S) (2:37) Rhino 72583 Very Best Of.
    (S) (2:37) Varese Sarabande 5906 God, Love And Rock & Roll.

1965 WOMAN'S GOT SOUL
    (S) (2:21) MCA 31207 Vintage Music Volume 10.
    (S) (2:21) MCA 5806 Vintage Music Volumes 9 & 10.
    (S) (2:21) MCA 31338 Greatest Hits.
    (S) (2:15) MCA 10664 Anthology 1961-1977.
    (S) (2:21) MCA Special Products 22130 Vintage Collectibles Volume 1.
    (S) (2:15) MCA Special Products 22175 It's All Right.
    (S) (2:15) Rhino 72262 The Curtis Mayfield Story.
    (S) (2:15) Hip-O 40001 The Glory Of Love - Sweet & Soulful Love Songs.
    (S) (2:15) MCA Special Products 20998 More Of The Tams & Impressions Greatest Hits.
    (S) (2:15) Rhino 72583 Very Best Of.

1966 YOU'VE BEEN CHEATIN'
    (E) (2:33) MCA 31338 Greatest Hits.
    (E) (2:32) MCA 10664 Anthology 1961-1977.
    (E) (2:32) Ichiban 2508 Cheatin': From A Man's Point Of View.

1968 WE'RE A WINNER
   (S) (2:22) Rhino 70654 Billboard's Top R&B Hits Of 1968.
   (S) (2:22) Rhino 72006 Billboard's Top R&B Hits 1965-
                     1969 Box Set.
   (S) (2:21) MCA 31338 Greatest Hits.
   (S) (2:21) MCA 10288 Classic Soul.
   (S) (2:21) MCA 10664 Anthology 1961-1977.
   (S) (2:21) Right Stuff 28373 Movin' On Up.
   (S) (2:19) Time-Life RHD-04 Rhythm & Blues - 1968.
   (S) (2:21) MCA 10462 The Coach Collection.
   (S) (2:21) MCA Special Products 20838 Tams &
                     Impressions Greatest Hits.
   (S) (2:21) Rhino 72262 The Curtis Mayfield Story.
   (S) (2:21) Hip-O 40009 ABC's Of Soul Volume 1.
   (S) (2:21) MCA Special Products 20998 More Of The Tams
                     & Impressions Greatest Hits.
   (S) (2:20) Time-Life R838-03 Solid Gold Soul - 1968.
   (S) (2:21) Rhino 72583 Very Best Of.
   (S) (2:21) Repeat/Relativity 1609 Tell It Like It Is: #1 Soul
                     Hits Of The 60's Volume 1.

1968 FOOL FOR YOU
   (S) (2:51) MCA 10664 Anthology 1961-1977.
   (S) (2:52) Rhino 72262 The Curtis Mayfield Story.
   (S) (2:52) Rhino 72583 Very Best Of.

1969 THIS IS MY COUNTRY
   (S) (2:46) MCA 10664 Anthology 1961-1977.
   (S) (2:47) Rhino 72262 The Curtis Mayfield Story.
   (S) (2:46) MCA 11238 God Bless The U.S.A.
   (S) (2:47) Rhino 72583 Very Best Of.

1969 CHOICE OF COLORS
   (S) (3:15) MCA 10664 Anthology 1961-1977.
   (S) (3:16) Time-Life RHD-13 Rhythm & Blues - 1969.
   (S) (3:15) Risky Business 53917 Soul Of Vietnam.
   (S) (3:16) Rhino 72262 The Curtis Mayfield Story.
   (S) (3:16) Time-Life R838-04 Solid Gold Soul - 1969.
   (S) (3:16) Rhino 72583 Very Best Of.
   (S) (3:16) Rhino 72815 Beg, Scream & Shout! The Big Ol'
                     Box Of '60s Soul.
   (S) (3:15) Repeat/Relativity 1610 Tighten Up: #1 Soul Hits
                     Of The 60's Volume 2.

1970 CHECK OUT YOUR MIND
   (S) (3:26) MCA 10664 Anthology 1961-1977.
   (S) (3:53) Rhino 72262 The Curtis Mayfield Story. *(live)*
   (S) (3:26) Rhino 72583 Very Best Of.

1974 FINALLY GOT MYSELF TOGETHER
   (S) (3:04) Rhino 70553 Soul Hits Of The 70's Volume 13.
   (S) (3:05) Rhino 72583 Very Best Of.
   (S) (3:04) K-Tel 3900 Great R&B Male Groups: Hits Of The
                     70's.

INDECENT OBSESSION
1990 TELL ME SOMETHING
   (S) (4:30) MCA 6426 Indecent Obsession.

INDEPENDENTS
1973 LEAVING ME
   (S) (3:07) Rhino 70790 Soul Hits Of The 70's Volume 10.
   (M) (3:15) Collectables 5245 Leaving Me - Their Golden Classics.
   (S) (3:07) Ripete 2222 Soul Patrol Vol. 4.
   (S) (3:21) K-Tel 3887 Soul Brothers & Sisters Of The 70's.

1973 BABY I'VE BEEN MISSING YOU
   (M) (3:38) Collectables 5245 Leaving Me - Their Golden
                     Classics. *(very poor quality)*
   (E) (3:37) Ripete 2223 Soul Patrol Vol. 5. *(very poor quality)*

INFORMATION SOCIETY
1988 WHAT'S ON YOUR MIND (PURE ENERGY)
(dj copies of this 45 ran (3:15) and (3:40);
commercial copies were all (3:40))
   (S) (3:34) JCI 2702 Hot Moves. *(45 version)*
   (S) (4:35) Tommy Boy 25691 Information Society. *(LP version)*

1989 WALKING AWAY
   (S) (5:00) Tommy Boy 25691 Information Society. *(LP version)*

1990 THINK
   (S) (6:43) Tommy Boy 1037 MTV Party To Go Volume 1.
                     (remix; all tracks on this cd are segued together)

   (S) (5:04) Tommy Boy 26258 Hack. *(LP version)*
   (S) (3:54) Priority 53770 Techno Dance Classics Volume 1 -
                     Pump Up The Jam. *(45 version)*

JORGEN INGMANN
1961 APACHE
   (M) (3:00) Rhino 71602 Rock Instrumental Classics Volume
                     2: The Sixties.
   (M) (3:00) Rhino 72035 Rock Instrumental Classics Vols. 1-
                     5 Box Set.
   (M) (2:52) Time-Life SUD-19 Superhits - Early 60's Classics.
                     (sounds like it was mastered from vinyl)
   (M) (2:59) Rhino 71582 Billboard Top Pop Hits, 1961.
   (M) (2:52) Time-Life AM1-20 AM Gold - Early '60s
                     Classics. *(sounds like it was masterd from vinyl)*

JAMES INGRAM
released as by QUINCY JONES featuring JAMES INGRAM:
1981 JUST ONCE
   (S) (4:29) A&M 6550 Quincy Jones - Classics Volume 3.
   (S) (4:32) A&M 3248 Quincy Jones - The Dude.
   (S) (4:29) A&M 3200 Quincy Jones - The Best.
   (S) (4:32) Warner Brothers 26700 James Ingram - Greatest Hits.
   (S) (4:30) MCA 11329 Soul Train 25th Anniversary Box Set.
   (S) (4:31) A&M 314540556 Quincy Jones - Greatest Hits.
   (S) (4:32) Time-Life R834-10 Body Talk - From The Heart.

1982 ONE HUNDRED WAYS
   (S) (4:17) Rebound 314520241 Quincy Jones - The Best
                     Volume Two.
   (S) (4:17) A&M 6550 Quincy Jones - Classics Volume 3.
   (S) (4:18) A&M 3248 Quincy Jones - The Dude.
   (S) (4:17) A&M 3278 Quincy Jones - The Best Volume Two.
   (S) (4:18) Warner Brothers 26700 James Ingram - Greatest Hits.
   (S) (4:16) A&M 314540556 Quincy Jones - Greatest Hits.
   (S) (4:17) Rebound 314520431 Soul Classics - Best Of The 80's.
   (S) (4:18) Time-Life R834-13 Body Talk - Just The Two Of Us.

released as by PATTI AUSTIN with JAMES INGRAM:
1983 BABY, COME TO ME
   (S) (3:35) Original Sound 8909 Best Love Songs Vol. 4.
   (S) (3:35) Original Sound 9322 Best Love Songs Vol. 3 & 4.
   (S) (3:35) Original Sound 1236 Best Love Songs Box Set.
   (S) (3:35) Scotti Brothers 75434 Romantic Duets.
   (S) (3:35) Qwest 3591 Patti Austin - Every Home Should
                     Have One.
   (S) (3:35) K-Tel 3263 The 80's Love Jams.
   (S) (3:34) Rhino 71972 Video Soul - Best Soul Of The 80's
                     Vol. 2.
   (S) (3:35) Priority 53700 80's Greatest Rock Hits Volume 13 -
                     Soft Sounds.
   (S) (3:34) Warner Brothers 26700 James Ingram - Greatest Hits.
   (S) (3:36) Time-Life R138-18 Body Talk.
   (S) (3:34) MCA 11431 Quiet Storms 2.
   (S) (3:34) JCI 3147 1980 - Only Love - 1984.
   (S) (3:32) Madacy Entertainment 6803 Power Of Love.
   (S) (3:33) Rhino 72580 Soul Serenade - Intimate R&B.
   (S) (3:35) Time-Life R988-18 Sounds Of The Eighties: The
                     Early '80s Take Two.
   (S) (3:34) Time-Life R834-03 Body Talk - Moonlit Nights.

released as by JAMES INGRAM with MICHAEL McDONALD:
1984 YAH MO B THERE
   (S) (4:39) Qwest 23970 James Ingram - It's Your Night.
                     (LP version)
   (S) (4:29) Warner Brothers 26700 James Ingram - Greatest
                     Hits. *(LP version)*
   (S) (4:29) Time-Life R834-20 Body Talk - Heart And Soul.
                     (LP version)
   (S) (4:29) Time-Life R988-23 Sounds Of The Eighties 1984-
                     1985. *(LP version)*

**released as by KENNY ROGERS with KIM CARNES and
JAMES INGRAM:**
1984 WHAT ABOUT ME
   (S) (4:22) RCA 5335 Kenny Rogers - What About Me?.
   (S) (4:20) Reprise 46571 Kenny Rogers - A Decade Of Hits.

released as by LINDA RONSTADT and JAMES INGRAM:
1987 SOMEWHERE OUT THERE
   (S) (3:57) MCA 39096 O.S.T. An American Tail.

JAMES INGRAM (Continued)

    (S) (3:57) Warner Brothers 26700 James Ingram - Greatest Hits.

released as by QUINCY JONES featuring AL B. SURE!/ JAMES INGRAM/EL DeBARGE/BARRY WHITE:
1990 THE SECRET GARDEN

    (S) (6:39) Qwest/Warner Brothers 26020 Quincy Jones - Back On The Block.

    (S) (6:45) Mercury 314514143 Barry White - Just For You. *(includes a :06 previously unreleased introduction by Barry White)*

released as by JAMES INGRAM:
1990 I DON'T HAVE THE HEART

    (S) (4:11) Warner Brothers 25924 It's Real.

    (S) (4:12) Warner Brothers 26700 James Ingram - Greatest Hits.

    (S) (4:12) Time-Life R834-03 Body Talk - Moonlit Nights.

LUTHER INGRAM
1972 (IF LOVING YOU IS WRONG) I DON'T WANT TO BE RIGHT

    (M) (3:25) Rhino 70788 Soul Hits Of The 70's Volume 8. *(sounds like it was mastered from vinyl)*

    (M) (3:25) Original Sound 8908 Best Love Songs Vol 3.

    (M) (3:25) Original Sound 9327 Best Love Songs Vol. 3 & 4.

    (M) (3:25) Original Sound 1236 Best Love Songs Box Set.

    (M) (3:25) Time-Life RHD-20 Rhythm & Blues - 1972.

    (M) (3:23) Time-Life SOD-21 Sounds Of The Seventies - Rock 'N' Soul Seventies.

    (M) (3:30) Collectables 5192 Golden Classics.

    (S) (3:33) Ripete 2198 Soul Patrol. *(mastered from vinyl)*

    (M) (3:30) Ichiban 2508 Cheatin': From A Man's Point Of View.

    (M) (3:25) K-Tel 6013 70's Soul - Sexy Ballads.

    (M) (3:26) Rhino 72114 Billboard Hot Soul Hits - 1972.

    (M) (3:24) Rebound 314520367 Soul Classics - Quiet Storm/The 70's.

    (M) (3:23) Madacy Entertainment 1972 Rock On 1972.

    (M) (3:30) Right Stuff 35884 Greatest Hits.

    (M) (3:25) JCI 3145 1970 - Only Love - 1974.

    (M) (3:25) Time-Life R838-07 Solid Gold Soul - 1972.

    (M) (3:23) Time-Life R834-08 Body Talk - On My Mind.

    (M) (3:30) Beast 53442 Original Players Of Love.

    (M) (3:25) Priority 53108 Slow Grind Volume One.

1973 I'LL BE YOUR SHELTER (IN TIME OF STORM)

    (S) (3:17) Collectables 5192 Golden Classics.

    (S) (3:17) Right Stuff 35884 Greatest Hits.

INNER CIRCLE
1993 BAD BOYS

    (S) (3:48) Big Beat 92261 Bad Boys.

    (S) (3:48) Elektra 62210 Maximum Dancehall & Reggae Hits.

1993 SWEAT (A LA LA LA LA SONG)

    (S) (3:45) Big Beat 92261 Bad Boys.

    (S) (3:45) JCI 3132 1990 - Only Rock 'n Roll - 1994.

INNOCENTS
1960 HONEST I DO
1961 GEE WHIZ

    (M) (2:28) Time-Life R857-19 The Heart Of Rock 'n' Roll 1960-1961 Take Three.

INSTANT FUNK
1979 I GOT MY MIND MADE UP (YOU CAN GET IT GIRL)

    (S) (9:46) Salsoul 1000 and 1027 The Original Salsoul Classics. *(12" single version)*

    (S) (9:46) Salsoul 1001 The Original Salsoul Classics Volume One. *(12" single version)*

    (S) (5:18) Salsoul 1011 and 8004 Instant Funk. *(LP version)*

    (S) (5:15) Right Stuff/Salsoul 52191 Greatest Hits. *(LP version)*

    (S) (5:14) Rebound 314520430 Funk Classics Of The 70's Vol. 2. *(LP version)*

    (S) (4:41) Time-Life R838-15 Solid Gold Soul 1979. *(neither the 45, LP or 12" single version)*

    (S) (4:40) K-Tel 3908 High Energy Volume 1. *(neither the 45, LP or 12" single version)*

    (S) (5:20) Thump 9960 Old School Funk II. *(LP version)*

INTRIGUES
1969 IN A MOMENT

    (S) (2:47) Collectables 5180 In A Moment/Golden Classics.

    (S) (2:47) Ripete 2392192 Beach Music Anthology Box Set.

INTRO
1993 COME INSIDE

    (S) (8:07) Atlantic 82463 Intro.

INTRUDERS
1968 COWBOYS TO GIRLS

    (S) (2:36) Rhino 75774 Soul Shots.

    (S) (2:36) Philadelphia International 32131 Super Hits.

    (S) (2:34) Time-Life 2CLR-11 Classic Rock - 1968: The Beat Goes On.

    (S) (2:36) Thump 4710 Old School Love Songs.

    (S) (2:36) Collectables 8820 Philly Golden Classics.

    (S) (2:36) Legacy/Epic 66912 Legacy's Rhythm & Soul Revue.

    (S) (2:37) Ripete 2219 Beach Fever.

    (S) (2:36) MCA 11329 Soul Train 25th Anniversary Box Set.

    (S) (2:36) Capitol 35818 O.S.T. Dead Presidents Volume II.

    (S) (2:37) Legacy/Epic Associated 66688 Best Of: Cowboys To Girls.

    (S) (2:36) Epic/Legacy 64647 The Philly Sound Box Set.

    (M) (2:34) Rhino 72815 Beg, Scream & Shout! The Big Ol' Box Of '60s Soul.

    (S) (2:36) Repeat/Relativity 1611 A Brand New Bag: #1 Soul Hits Of The 60's Volume 3.

    (S) (2:36) Time-Life R857-22 The Heart Of Rock 'n' Roll 1967-1969.

    (S) (2:36) K-Tel 3886 Great R&B Male Groups: Hits Of The 60's.

1968 (LOVE IS LIKE A) BASEBALL GAME

    (S) (2:44) Collectables 8820 Philly Golden Classics.

    (S) (2:44) Philadelphia International 32131 Super Hits.

    (S) (2:43) Rhino 70710 Baseball's Greatest Hits.

    (S) (2:42) Thump 4720 Old School Love Songs Volume 2.

    (S) (2:44) Legacy/Epic Associated 66688 Best Of: Cowboys To Girls.

1973 I'LL ALWAYS LOVE MY MAMA (PART 1)

    (S) (9:46) Philadelphia International 34940 Philadelphia Classics. *(this version first appeared on the vinyl album "Philadelphia Classics" in 1977)*

    (S) (9:45) Original Sound 1960 Art Laboe's Memories Of El Monte. *(this version first appeared on the vinyl album "Philadelphia Classics" in 1977)*

    (S) (9:45) Original Sound 4001 Art Laboe's 60 Killer Oldies. *(this version first appeared on the vinyl album "Philadelphia Classics" in 1977)*

    (S) (9:46) Thump 4710 Old School Love Songs. *(this version first appeared on the vinyl album "Philadelphia Classics" in 1977)*

    (S) (6:36) Collectables 8820 Philly Golden Classics. *(LP version)*

    (S) (3:00) Priority 53130 Deep Soul Volume Three. *(45 version)*

    (S) (6:36) Legacy/Epic Associated 66688 Best Of: Cowboys To Girls. *(LP version)*

    (S) (6:36) Epic/Legacy 64647 The Philly Sound Box Set. *(LP version)*

    (S) (6:36) Epic Associated/Legacy 65162 A Postcard From Philly. *(LP version)*

INXS
1983 THE ONE THING

    (S) (3:23) Atlantic 82622 Greatest Hits.

    (S) (3:23) Atco 90072 Shabooh Shoobah.

    (S) (3:24) Rhino 72596 Billboard Top Album Rock Hits, 1983.

    (S) (3:22) JCI 3192 18 Rock Classics Volume 2.

1986 WHAT YOU NEED
(dj copies of this 45 ran (3:33) and (3:26); commercial copies were all (3:33))

    (S) (3:34) Polydor 314515913 Classic Rock Box.

    (S) (3:35) Atlantic 81277 Listen Like Thieves.

    (S) (3:33) Atlantic 82622 Greatest Hits.

    (S) (3:35) Rhino 72500 Modern Rock 1986 - Hang The DJ.

    (S) (3:34) JCI 3159 18 Modern Rock Classics From The 80's.

(S) (3:33) Hip-O 40022 That Sound From Down Under.
1988 NEED YOU TONIGHT
(S) (3:01) Atlantic 81910 Hit Singles 1980-1988.
(S) (3:05) Atlantic 81796 Kick. *(tracks into the next selection)*
(S) (3:00) Atlantic 82622 Greatest Hits.
(S) (3:09) Rhino 72502 Modern Rock 1988 - Hang The DJ.
(S) (3:01) JCI 3171 #1 Radio Hits 1985 - Only Rock 'n Roll - 1989.
(S) (3:01) Time-Life R988-21 Sounds Of The Eighties: 1986-1989.
(S) (3:01) Time-Life R13610 Gold And Platinum Box Set - The Ultimate Rock Collection.
1988 DEVIL INSIDE
(dj copies of this 45 ran (5:11) and (3:54); commercial copies were all (5:11))
(S) (5:11) Atlantic 81796 Kick.
(S) (5:10) Atlantic 82622 Greatest Hits.
(S) (5:10) Hip-O 40047 The '80s Hit(s) Back 3.
(S) (5:09) Rhino 72894 Hard Rock Cafe: New Wave.
1988 NEW SENSATION
(S) (3:39) Atlantic 81908 Classic Rock 1966-1988.
(S) (3:38) Atlantic 81796 Kick.
(S) (3:39) Atlantic 82622 Greatest Hits.
(S) (3:39) Rebound 314520434 Classic Rock - 80's.
(S) (3:39) Time-Life R988-21 Sounds Of The Eighties: 1986-1989.
1988 NEVER TEAR US APART
(S) (3:02) Atlantic 81796 Kick.
(S) (3:01) Atlantic 82622 Greatest Hits.
(S) (2:58) JCI 3186 1985 - Only Love - 1989.
1990 SUICIDE BLONDE
(S) (3:50) Atlantic 82140 X.
(S) (3:49) Atlantic 82622 Greatest Hits.
(S) (3:49) Time-Life R968-25 Guitar Rock - The '90s.
(S) (3:49) Rhino 72650 Billboard Top Modern Rock Tracks, 1990.
(S) (3:49) Simitar 55762 Stud Rock - Wild Ride.
1991 DISAPPEAR
(S) (4:07) Atlantic 82140 X.
(S) (4:06) Atlantic 82622 Greatest Hits.
1991 BITTER TEARS
(S) (3:49) Atlantic 82140 X.
1992 NOT ENOUGH TIME
(S) (4:19) Warner Brothers 26974 Barcelona Gold.
(S) (4:10) Atlantic 82394 Welcome To Wherever You Are.
(S) (4:09) Rhino 72652 Billboard Top Modern Rock Tracks, 1992.

DONNIE IRIS
1981 AH! LEAH!
(S) (3:41) Razor & Tie 2015 Back On The Streets.
(S) (3:41) Seathru 101 Out Of The Blue.
(S) (3:41) Rhino 71894 Radio Daze: Pop Hits Of The 80's Volume Five.
(S) (3:41) K-Tel 3742 The 80's: Hot Rock.
(S) (3:41) JCI 3143 18 Screamers From The 80's.
(S) (3:41) Hip-O 40040 Power Chords Volume 3.
1982 LOVE IS LIKE A ROCK
(S) (3:33) Priority 53775 Best Of 80's Rock Volume 1.
(S) (3:33) MCA Special Products 20897 Greatest Rock Hits Of The 80's.
(S) (3:33) Razor & Tie 2016 King Cool.
(S) (3:28) MCA Special Products 21028 The Best Of Hard Rock.
1982 MY GIRL
(S) (3:57) Razor & Tie 2016 King Cool.

IRISH ROVERS
1968 THE UNICORN
(S) (3:18) MCA 5940 Vintage Music Volumes 19 & 20.
(S) (3:18) MCA 31216 Vintage Music Volume 19.
(S) (3:18) MCA 15 The Unicorn.
(S) (3:19) Time-Life SUD-18 Superhits - Late 60's Classics.
(S) (3:18) MCA Special Products 20307 Years May Come, Years May Go.
(S) (3:17) MCA Special Products 22028 Cra-a-zy Hits.
(S) (3:18) MCA Special Products 22133 Vintage Collectibles Volume 4.

(S) (3:19) Time-Life AM1-12 AM Gold - Late '60s Classics.
(S) (3:18) Time-Life R132-22 Treasury Of Folk Music Volume One.
released as by THE ROVERS:
1981 WASN'T THAT A PARTY

IRON BUTTERFLY
1968 IN-A-GADDA-DA-VIDA
(S) (2:52) JCI 3116 Psychedelic Sixties. *(45 version)*
(S) (2:51) Original Sound 8894 Dick Clark's 21 All-Time Hits Vol. 3. *(45 version)*
(S) (2:51) Risky Business 57471 Godfathers Of Grunge. *(45 version)*
(S) (2:51) Pyramid 71888 A Future To This Life - Robocop: The Series Soundtrack. *(45 version)*
(S) (17:01) Atco 33250 In-A-Gadda-Da-Vida. *(LP version)*
(S) (2:51) Rhino 71166 Light And Heavy: Best Of. *(45 version)*
(S) (17:00) Atlantic 81908 Classic Rock 1966-1988. *(LP version)*
(S) (2:52) Time-Life 2CLR-27 Classic Rock - 1968: Blowin' Your Mind. *(45 version)*
(S) (2:52) Warner Special Products 27607 Highs Of The 60's. *(45 version)*
(S) (2:51) Rhino 71729 '60's Rock Classics, Vol. 2. *(45 version)*
(S) (2:52) Time-Life R968-07 Guitar Rock 1968-1969. *(45 version)*
(S) (17:04) Rhino 72196 In-A-Gadda-Da-Vida. *(LP version)*
(S) (18:49) Rhino 72196 In-A-Gadda-Da-Vida. *(live)*
(S) (2:51) Rhino 72196 In-A-Gadda-Da-Vida. *(45 version)*
(S) (17:02) MFSL 675 In-A-Gadda-Da-Vida. *(gold disc; LP version)*
(S) (2:52) Flashback 72702 '60s Rock: The Beat Goes On. *(45 version)*
(S) (2:52) Flashback 72088 '60s Rock Hits Box Set. *(45 version)*
(S) (2:52) Flashback 72802 Vanilla Fudge & Iron Butterfly Hits. *(45 version)*
(S) (2:52) Thump 6010 Easyriders Volume 1. *(45 version)*

BIG DEE IRWIN
1963 SWINGING ON A STAR
(M) (2:36) Collectables 5407 Best Of Little Eva.
(M) (2:37) Time-Life 2RNR-44 Rock 'N' Roll Era - Lost Treasures.
(M) (2:36) Rhino 71650 Colpix-Dimension Story.
(M) (2:36) Rhino 72273 Little Eva - The Loco-Motion.

RUSS IRWIN
1991 MY HEART BELONGS TO YOU
(S) (4:00) SBK 96915 Russ Irwin.

CHRIS ISAAK
1991 WICKED GAME
(S) (4:46) Sandstone 33048 and 5016 Cosmopolitan Volume 2.
(S) (4:47) DCC Compact Classics 087 Night Moves Volume 5.
(S) (4:46) Reprise 25837 Heart Shaped World.
(S) (4:46) Time-Life R988-30 Sounds Of The Eighties: The Rolling Stone Collection 1988-1989.

ISLANDERS
1959 THE ENCHANTED SEA
(S) (2:01) Time-Life HPD-30 Your Hit Parade - 50's Instrumentals.
(S) (2:01) Time-Life R986-19 Instrumental Favorites - Exotic Moods.

ISLEY BROTHERS
1959 SHOUT (PART 1)
(S) (4:24) RCA 8467 Nipper's Greatest Hits Of The 50's Volume 2. *(Parts 1 & 2)*
(S) (4:38) Rhino 70732 Grandson Of Frat Rock. *(Parts 1 & 2; Part 2 is :13 longer than the LP length and :08 longer than the 45 length)*
(S) (2:14) Warner Brothers 3359 O.S.T. The Wanderers.
(S) (2:14) DCC Compact Classics 043 Toga Rock II.

(S) (4:38)   Rhino 70908   Isley Brothers Story Volume 1. *(Parts 1 & 2; Part 2 is :13 longer than the LP length and :08 longer than the 45 length)*

(S) (4:40)   RCA 9901   Shout! The Complete Victor Sessions. *(Parts 1 & 2; Part 2 is :15 longer than the LP length and :10 longer than the 45 length)*

(E) (4:39)   RCA 61144   The RCA Records Label: The First Note In Black Music. *(Parts 1 & 2; Part 2 is :14 longer than the LP length and :09 longer than the 45 length)*

(S) (2:16)   Essex 7052   All Time Rock Classics.

(S) (4:25)   Collectables 5103   Shout. *(Parts 1 & 2; LP length)*

(S) (4:38)   RCA 2357   Dance! Dance! Dance! Volume 2. *(all selections on this cd are segued together; Parts 1 & 2; Part 2 is :13 longer than the LP length and :08 longer than the 45 length)*

(E) (4:30)   Time-Life 2RNR-24   Rock 'N' Roll Era - The 50's Keep On Rockin'. *(Parts 1 & 2; 45 length)*

(S) (4:38)   Tommy Boy 1100   ESPN Presents Jock Rock. *(Parts 1 & 2; Part 2 is :13 longer than the LP length and :08 longer than the 45 length)*

(S) (4:23)   RCA 66862   Hi Octane Hard Drivin' Hits. *(Parts 1 & 2; LP length)*

(S) (4:23)   RCA 66883   Shout - The RCA Sessions. *(Parts 1 & 2; LP length)*

(M) (4:29)   Nick At Nite/550 Music/Epic 67770   Happy Days Jukebox. *(Parts 1 & 2; 45 length)*

(M) (4:29)   Polygram Special Markets 314520326   Best Of The Early Years. *(Parts 1&2; 45 length)*

(S) (4:21)   RCA 67474   Roller Hockey - The Album. *(Parts 1 & 2; LP length)*

(S) (4:24)   Simitar 55522   The Number One's: Party Time. *(Parts 1 & 2; LP length)*

(S) (4:38)   Collectables 1514 and 2514   The Anniversary Album - The 50's. *(Parts 1 & 2; Part 2 is :13 longer than the LP length and :08 longer than the 45 length)*

1962   TWIST AND SHOUT

(S) (2:28)   DCC Compact Classics 029   Toga Rock.

(M) (2:29)   DCC Compact Classics 028   Sock Hop.

(M) (2:28)   Original Sound 8856   Oldies But Goodies Vol. 6. *(this compact disc uses the "Waring - fds" noise reduction process)*

(M) (2:28)   Original Sound 2221   Oldies But Goodies Volumes 1,4,6,8 and 10 Box Set. *(this box set uses the "Waring - fds" noise reduction process)*

(M) (2:28)   Original Sound 2500   Oldies But Goodies Volumes 1-15 Box Set. *(this box set uses the "Waring - fds" noise reduction process)*

(M) (2:28)   Original Sound CDGO-5   Golden Oldies Volume. 5.

(M) (2:28)   Original Sound 8895   Dick Clark's 21 All-Time Hits Vol. 4.

(S) (2:28)   Rhino 70732   Grandson Of Frat Rock.

(M) (2:28)   Curb 77333   Best Of.

(S) (2:28)   Rhino 70908   Isley Brothers Story Volume 1.

(M) (2:27)   Motown 5483   Greatest Hits And Rare Classics.

(S) (2:31)   Capricorn 42003   The Scepter Records Story.

(S) (2:31)   Special Music 4804   At Their Best.

(S) (3:32)   Sundazed 6002   Twist & Shout.

(S) (2:28)   Rhino 71548   Let There Be Drums Volume 2: The 60's.

(S) (2:26)   Time-Life 2RNR-02   Rock 'N' Roll Era - 1962.

(M) (2:26)   Time-Life RHD-11   Rhythm & Blues - 1962.

(S) (2:32)   K-Tel 3241   Let's Twist.

(S) (2:29)   Ripete 2187-RE   Preppy Deluxe.

(S) (2:26)   Tommy Boy 1136   ESPN Presents Jock Rock Vol. 2. *(all songs on this cd are segued together with crowd sound effects added)*

(S) (2:32)   Nick At Nite/Epic 67149   Dick Van Dyke's Dance Party.

(S) (2:31)   King 1421   Party Time Rock & Roll.

(S) (2:31)   King 499   Classic Rock & Roll.

(M) (2:28)   Collectables 2554   CBS-FM History Of Rock Volume 2.

(M) (2:28)   LaserLight 12528   Garage Band Rock.

(M) (2:28)   LaserLight 12725   Best Of.

(S) (2:29)   Priority 50951   I Love Rock & Roll Volume 2: Hits Of The 60's.

(S) (2:31)   Cold Front 6255   Greatest Sports Rock And Jams Volume 2. *(all selections on this cd are segued together)*

(S) (2:29)   TVT 4010   Rhythm Revue.

(M) (2:26)   Time-Life R838-18   Solid Gold Soul 1962.

(S) (2:32)   K-Tel 4046   More Music For Your Party.

(S) (2:32)   Thump 7070   Lowrider Oldies Volume 7.

1966   THIS OLD HEART OF MINE (IS WEAK FOR YOU)

(S) (2:51)   Motown 6219   Hard To Find Motown Classics Volume 3. *(LP length)*

(S) (2:51)   Motown 6159   The Good Feeling Music Of The Big Chill Generation Volume 1. *(LP length)*

(S) (2:52)   Motown 6138   The Composer Series: Holland/Dozier/Holland. *(LP length)*

(S) (2:36)   Motown 5453   A Collection Of 16 Big Hits Volume 6. *(45 length)*

(S) (2:51)   MCA 6214   Moonlighting - TV Soundtrack. *(LP length)*

(S) (2:51)   Curb 77333   Best Of. *(LP length)*

(S) (2:53)   Rhino 70908   Isley Brothers Story Volume 1. *(LP length)*

(M) (2:42)   Motown 5483   Greatest Hits And Rare Classics. *(45 length)*

(S) (2:51)   MCA 10063   Original Television Soundtrack "The Sounds Of Murphy Brown". *(LP length)*

(S) (2:51)   Motown 5128   This Old Heart Of Mine. *(LP length)*

(S) (2:49)   Motown 9071   Motown Dance Party Volume 1. *(all selections on this cd are segued together; LP length)*

(S) (2:51)   Ripete 392183   Ocean Drive. *(LP length)*

(M) (2:44)   Motown 6312   Hitsville USA. *(45 length)*

(S) (2:49)   Time-Life RHD-01   Rhythm & Blues - 1966. *(LP length)*

(S) (2:50)   Time-Life 2CLR-13   Classic Rock - 1966: Shakin' All Over. *(LP length)*

(M) (2:44)   Rhino 71806   The R&B Box: Thirty Years Of Rhythm & Blues. *(45 length)*

(S) (2:51)   Polygram Special Markets 314520283   Motown Legends Volume 2. *(LP length)*

(S) (2:50)   K-Tel 3269   Carolina Beach Music. *(LP length)*

(M) (4:42)   LaserLight 12725   Best Of. *(instrumental rerecording)*

(S) (2:51)   Eclipse Music Group 64870   Rock 'n Roll Relix 1966-1967. *(LP length)*

(S) (2:51)   Eclipse Music Group 64872   Rock 'n Roll Relix 1960-1969. *(LP length)*

(S) (2:51)   Polygram Special Markets 314520326   Best Of The Early Years. *(LP length)*

(S) (2:49)   Time-Life R838-01   Solid Gold Soul - 1966. *(LP length)*

1969   IT'S YOUR THING

(S) (2:49)   Rhino 70655   Billboard's Top R&B Hits Of 1969.

(S) (2:49)   Rhino 72006   Billboard's Top R&B Hits 1965-1969 Box Set.

(S) (2:46)   Rhino 70909   Isley Brothers Story Volume 2.

(S) (2:44)   Motown 5483   Greatest Hits And Rare Classics.

(S) (2:47)   Time-Life 2CLR-20   Classic Rock - 1969: Shakin' All Over.

(S) (2:47)   JCI 3126   1965 - Only Rock 'N Roll - 1969.

(S) (2:49)   MCA 11329   Soul Train 25th Anniversary Box Set.

(S) (2:41)   JCI 3161   18 Soul Hits From The 60's.

(M) (3:18)   LaserLight 12725   Best Of. *(instrumental rerecording)*

(S) (2:44)   Polygram Special Markets 314520326   Best Of The Early Years.

(S) (2:49)   Rhino 72815   Beg, Scream & Shout! The Big Ol' Box Of '60s Soul.

(S) (2:45)   Repeat/Relativity 1609   Tell It Like It Is: #1 Soul Hits Of The 60's Volume 1.

(S) (2:44)   K-Tel 3886   Great R&B Male Groups: Hits Of The 60's.

1969   I TURNED YOU ON

(S) (2:36)   Rhino 70909   Isley Brothers Story Volume 2.

1971   LOVE THE ONE YOU'RE WITH

(S) (3:38)   Rhino 70909   Isley Brothers Story Volume 2.

1971 SPILL THE WINE
- (S) (6:35) Rhino 70909 Isley Brothers Story Volume 2. *(LP version; truncated fade)*

1972 POP THAT THANG
- (S) (2:55) Rhino 70909 Isley Brothers Story Volume 2.

1973 THAT LADY (PART 1)
- (S) (3:18) Rhino 70661 Billboard's Top R&B Hits Of 1973.
- (S) (5:35) Columbia/Legacy 46160 Rock Artifacts Volume 1. *(Parts 1 & 2)*
- (S) (5:34) T-Neck 39240 Greatest Hits Volume 1. *(Parts 1 & 2)*
- (M) (2:47) Curb 77333 Best Of. *(1964 noncharting version)*
- (S) (2:47) Rhino 70908 Isley Brothers Story Volume 1. *(1964 noncharting version)*
- (S) (2:47) EMI 95203 The Complete UA Sessions. *(1964 noncharting version)*
- (S) (2:47) EMI 96286 24 Greatest Hits Of All Time. *(1964 noncharting version)*
- (S) (5:34) Rhino 70909 Isley Brothers Story Volume 2. *(Parts 1 & 2)*
- (S) (5:34) Razor & Tie 22047 Sweet 70's Soul. *(Parts 1 & 2)*
- (S) (5:34) Risky Business 53921 Double Knit Dance Hits. *(Parts 1 & 2)*
- (S) (3:19) Rhino 72115 Billboard Hot Soul Hits - 1973.
- (S) (5:34) DCC Compact Classics 143 Groove On! Volume 3. *(Parts 1 & 2)*
- (S) (3:18) JCI 3173 1970 - Only Soul - 1974.
- (S) (3:17) Time-Life R838-08 Solid Gold Soul - 1973.

1975 FIGHT THE POWER (PART 1)
(dj copies of this 45 ran (5:05) and (3:17) and both edited out the word "bullshit"; commercial copies were all (3:17) and were not censored)
- (S) (5:20) T-Neck 33536 The Heat Is On. *(LP version)*
- (S) (5:19) Rhino 70909 Isley Brothers Story Volume 2. *(LP version)*
- (S) (5:16) T-Neck 39240 Greatest Hits Volume 1. *(LP version)*
- (S) (3:20) Rhino 71433 In Yo Face! History Of Funk Volume 3. *(45 version)*
- (S) (3:19) Rhino 71618 Soul Train Hall Of Fame/20th Anniversary. *(45 version)*
- (S) (3:15) Time-Life SOD-16 Sounds Of The Seventies - 1975: Take Two. *(45 version)*
- (S) (5:16) K-Tel 6011 70's Soul: Super Funky Hits. *(LP version)*
- (S) (5:19) Right Stuff 29669 Movin' On Up Vol. 2. *(LP version)*
- (S) (3:19) Time-Life R838-10 Solid Gold Soul - 1975. *(45 version)*
- (S) (5:20) Epic/Legacy 65378 The Heat Is On/Go For Your Guns/Between The Sheets. *(LP version)*

1975 FOR THE LOVE OF YOU
(dj copies of this 45 ran (3:15); commercial copies were all (4:44))
- (S) (5:38) T-Neck 33536 The Heat Is On. *(LP version)*
- (S) (5:35) Rhino 70909 Isley Brothers Story Volume 2. *(LP version)*
- (S) (5:36) T-Neck 39240 Greatest Hits Volume 1. *(LP version)*
- (S) (5:37) Right Stuff 27307 Slow Jams: The 70's Volume One. *(LP version)*
- (S) (5:32) Original Sound 9305 Art Laboe's Dedicated To You Volume 5. *(LP version)*
- (S) (5:35) Sony Music Distribution 57854 For Your Love. *(LP version)*
- (S) (5:37) Thump 4710 Old School Love Songs. *(LP version)*
- (S) (5:35) Scotti Bros. 75481 Quiet Storm Memories. *(LP version)*
- (S) (5:37) Priority 50928 Rare Grooves Volume 1. *(LP version)*
- (S) (5:38) Epic/Legacy 65378 The Heat Is On/Go For Your Guns/Between The Sheets. *(LP version)*

1980 DON'T SAY GOODNIGHT (IT'S TIME FOR LOVE) PARTS 1 & 2
- (S) (5:44) Epic/Legacy 57860 Beautiful Ballads.
- (S) (5:44) Rhino 72135 Billboard Hot R&B Hits 1980.

BURL IVES
1962 A LITTLE BITTY TEAR
- (M) (2:03) MCA 2-8025 30 Years Of Hits 1958-1974.
- (M) (2:04) Time-Life HPD-33 Your Hit Parade - The Early 60's.
- (S) (2:03) MCA 11069 From The Vaults - Decca Country Classics 1934-1973.
- (M) (2:02) MCA Special Products 20435 Country's Greatest Hits Of The 60's Vol. 1.
- (S) (2:01) MCA Special Products 20280 A Little Bity Tear.
- (S) (2:01) MCA 11439 Greatest Hits.
- (M) (2:03) Time-Life R132-22 Treasury Of Folk Music Volume One.

1962 FUNNY WAY OF LAUGHIN'
- (S) (2:39) Time-Life HPD-37 Your Hit Parade - The 60's.
- (S) (2:38) MCA Special Products 20280 A Little Bity Tear.
- (S) (2:39) MCA 11439 Greatest Hits.

1962 CALL ME MR. IN-BETWEEN
- (S) (2:40) MCA Special Products 20280 A Little Bity Tear.
- (S) (2:40) MCA 11439 Greatest Hits.

1962 MARY ANN REGRETS

IVY THREE
1960 YOGI

J

TERRY JACKS
1974 SEASONS IN THE SUN
- (S) (3:27) Priority 8669 Hits/70's Greatest Rock Hits Volume 9.
- (S) (3:27) Rhino 70759 Super Hits Of The 70's Volume 12.
- (S) (3:25) Razor & Tie 21640 Those Fabulous 70's.
- (S) (3:27) Time-Life SOD-31 Sounds Of The Seventies - AM Top Twenty.
- (S) (3:26) Madacy Entertainment 1974 Rock On 1974.
- (S) (3:29) K-Tel 3625 Dynamite.
- (S) (3:27) Time-Life AM1-21 AM Gold - 1974.
- (S) (3:27) Rhino 72812 VH1 8-Track Flashback: The One Hit Wonders.
- (S) (3:27) Rhino 72740 Billboard Top Soft Rock Hits - 1974.

CHUCK JACKSON
1961 I DON'T WANT TO CRY
- (M) (2:14) Collectables 5115 Golden Classics.
- (S) (2:18) Capricorn 42003 The Scepter Records Story.
- (S) (2:17) Ripete 2392192 Beach Music Anthology Box Set.
- (S) (2:17) Time-Life 2RNR-35 Rock 'N' Roll Era - The 60's Last Dance.
- (S) (2:16) Time-Life RHD-14 Rhythm & Blues - 1961.
- (S) (2:16) Tomato 71655 The Great Recordings.
- (S) (2:17) King 1422 Greatest R & B Hits.
- (S) (2:17) Curb 77827 Greatest Hits.
- (S) (2:16) Ripete 2184-RE Ocean Drive Vol. 2.
- (S) (2:17) Varese Sarabande 5777 Very Best Of.
- (M) (2:13) Rhino 72815 Beg, Scream & Shout! The Big Ol' Box Of '60s Soul.
- (S) (2:16) Time-Life R838-19 Solid Gold Soul 1961.

1962 ANY DAY NOW (MY WILD BEAUTIFUL BIRD)
- (S) (3:18) Collectables 5115 Golden Classics.
- (S) (3:24) Capricorn 42003 The Scepter Records Story.
- (S) (3:19) Ripete 2392192 Beach Music Anthology Box Set.
- (S) (3:18) Ripete 0002 Coolin' Out/24 Carolina Classics Vol. 2.
- (S) (3:19) Time-Life 2RNR-16 Rock 'N' Roll Era - 1962 Still Rockin'.
- (S) (3:15) Time-Life RHD-11 Rhythm & Blues - 1962.
- (S) (3:23) Time-Life R962-08 History Of Rock 'N' Roll: Sound Of The City 1959-1965.
- (S) (3:19) Rhino 71806 The R&B Box: Thirty Years Of Rhythm & Blues.
- (S) (3:21) Tomato 71655 The Great Recordings.
- (S) (3:19) King 1422 Greatest R & B Hits.
- (S) (3:19) Curb 77827 Greatest Hits.
- (S) (3:22) JCI 3164 Eighteen Soulful Ballads.
- (S) (3:20) Varese Sarabande 5777 Very Best Of.
- (S) (3:22) TVT 4010 Rhythm Revue.
- (S) (3:15) Time-Life R838-18 Solid Gold Soul 1962.
- (S) (3:23) Time-Life R857-18 The Heart Of Rock 'n' Roll 1962-1963 Take Two.

DEON JACKSON
1966 LOVE MAKES THE WORLD GO ROUND
- (S) (2:28) Rhino 75770 Soul Shots Volume 2.
- (S) (2:28) Ripete 2392192 Beach Music Anthology Box Set.
- (S) (2:27) Original Sound 8865 Oldies But Goodies Vol. 15. *(this compact disc uses the "Waring - fds" noise reduction process)*
- (S) (2:27) Original Sound 2222 Oldies But Goodies Volumes 3,5,11,14 and 15 Box Set. *(this box set uses the "Waring - fds" noise reduction process)*

- (S) (2:27) Original Sound 2500 Oldies But Goodies Volumes 1-15 Box Set. *(this box set uses the "Waring - fds" noise reduction process)*
- (S) (2:26) Original Sound CDGO-8 Golden Oldies Volume. 8.
- (S) (2:29) Collectables 5068 History Of Rock Volume 8.
- (S) (2:27) Time-Life 2CLR-22 Classic Rock - 1966: Blowin' Your Mind.
- (M) (2:29) Collectables 5106 Golden Classics. *(mastered from vinyl)*
- (S) (2:27) Time-Life OPCD-4517 Tonight's The Night.
- (S) (2:28) Ripete 2163-RE Ebb Tide.
- (M) (2:26) Collectables 2505 History Of Rock - The 60's Part 5.
- (M) (2:26) Collectables 4505 History Of Rock/The 60s Part Five.
- (S) (2:27) K-Tel 3518 Sweet Soul Music.
- (S) (2:27) JCI 3164 Eighteen Soulful Ballads.
- (M) (2:33) Rhino 72815 Beg, Scream & Shout! The Big Ol' Box Of '60s Soul.

FREDDIE JACKSON
1985 ROCK ME TONIGHT (FOR OLD TIMES SAKE)
- (S) (7:10) Capitol 46170 Rock Me Tonight. *(LP version)*
- (S) (7:10) Capitol 27641 Greatest Hits Of. *(LP version)*
- (S) (7:06) Capitol 27641 Greatest Hits Of. *(remix)*
- (S) (4:01) Rhino 72159 Black Entertainment Television - 15th Anniversary. *(noisy fadeout; 45 version)*
- (S) (4:01) Rhino 72140 Billboard Hot R&B Hits 1985. *(45 version)*
- (S) (7:09) EMI 38307 For Old Times Sake: The Freddie Jackson Story. *(LP version)*
- (S) (4:00) Time-Life R834-11 Body Talk - After Dark. *(45 version)*

1985 YOU ARE MY LADY
(actual 45 time is (4:15) not (4:07) as stated on the record label)
- (S) (4:41) Capitol 46170 Rock Me Tonight. *(LP length)*
- (S) (4:41) Capitol 27641 Greatest Hits Of. *(LP length)*
- (S) (4:19) Rebound 314520370 Soul Classics - Quiet Storm/The 80's. *(45 length)*
- (S) (4:20) MCA 11431 Quiet Storms 2. *(45 length)*
- (S) (4:42) EMI 38307 For Old Times Sake: The Freddie Jackson Story. *(LP length)*
- (S) (4:18) Time-Life R834-08 Body Talk - On My Mind. *(45 length)*

1986 HE'LL NEVER LOVE YOU (LIKE I DO)
- (S) (4:43) Capitol 46170 Rock Me Tonight.

1987 JAM TONIGHT
- (S) (4:30) Capitol 46325 Just Like The First Time. *(LP length)*
- (S) (4:29) Capitol 27641 Greatest Hits Of. *(LP length)*
- (S) (4:30) EMI 38307 For Old Times Sake: The Freddie Jackson Story. *(LP length)*

JANET JACKSON
1986 WHAT HAVE YOU DONE FOR ME LATELY
- (S) (4:59) A&M 3905 Control. *(LP version)*
- (S) (4:43) A&M 314540399 Design Of A Decade 1986/1996. *(LP version but missing the :16 spoken introduction)*

1986 NASTY
- (S) (4:03) A&M 3905 Control. *(LP version)*

(S) (4:02) A&M 314540399 Design Of A Decade 1986/1996. *(LP version)*

1986 WHEN I THINK OF YOU
(S) (4:03) A&M 3905 Control.
(S) (3:54) A&M 314540399 Design Of A Decade 1986/1996.

1987 CONTROL
(dj copies of this 45 ran (3:26) and (4:35); commercial copies were all (3:26))
(S) (5:53) A&M 3905 Control. *(LP version)*
(S) (5:14) A&M 314540399 Design Of A Decade 1986/1996. *(LP version but missing the :40 introduction)*
(S) (3:26) Time-Life R13610 Gold And Platinum Box Set - The Ultimate Rock Collection. *(45 version)*

1987 LET'S WAIT A WHILE
(both dj and commercial 45's are a remix of the LP version)
(S) (4:37) A&M 3905 Control. *(LP version)*
(S) (4:36) A&M 314540399 Design Of A Decade 1986/1996. *(LP version)*

1987 THE PLEASURE PRINCIPLE
(S) (4:57) A&M 3905 Control.
(S) (4:12) A&M 314540399 Design Of A Decade 1986/1996. *(previously unreleased version)*

1989 MISS YOU MUCH
(S) (4:12) A&M 3920 Rhythm Nation 1814. *(LP version)*
(S) (4:11) A&M 314540399 Design Of A Decade 1986/1996. *(LP version)*

1989 RHYTHM NATION
(S) (5:30) A&M 3920 Rhythm Nation 1814. *(LP version)*
(S) (5:57) A&M 314540399 Design Of A Decade 1986/1996. *(neither the 45 or LP version)*
(S) (4:39) MCA 11329 Soul Train 25th Anniversary Box Set. *(neither the 45 or LP version)*

1990 ESCAPADE
(S) (4:43) A&M 3920 Rhythm Nation 1814.
(S) (4:44) A&M 314540399 Design Of A Decade 1986/1996.

1990 ALRIGHT
(S) (6:26) A&M 3920 Rhythm Nation 1814. *(LP version)*
(S) (4:37) A&M 314540399 Design Of A Decade 1986/1996. *(45 version)*

1990 COME BACK TO ME
(S) (5:32) A&M 3920 Rhythm Nation 1814.
(S) (5:36) A&M 314540399 Design Of A Decade 1986/1996.

1990 BLACK CAT
(S) (4:50) A&M 3920 Rhythm Nation 1814.
(S) (4:47) A&M 314540399 Design Of A Decade 1986/1996.

1991 LOVE WILL NEVER DO (WITHOUT YOU)
(S) (5:52) Foundation/RCA 66104 Hot #1 Hits.
(S) (5:49) A&M 3920 Rhythm Nation 1814.
(S) (4:34) A&M 314540399 Design Of A Decade 1986/1996.

1991 STATE OF THE WORLD
(S) (5:47) A&M 3920 Rhythm Nation 1814.

released as by LUTHER VANDROSS and JANET JACKSON with BBD and RALPH TRESVANT:
1992 THE BEST THINGS IN LIFE ARE FREE
(S) (4:35) Perspective 1004 O.S.T. Mo' Money.
(S) (4:01) LV Records/Epic 68220 Luther Vandross - One Night With You: The Best Of Love Volume 2.

released as by JANET JACKSON:
1993 THAT'S THE WAY LOVE GOES
(S) (4:24) Virgin 87825 Janet.
(S) (4:25) A&M 314540399 Design Of A Decade 1986/1996.
(S) (4:24) EMI-Capitol Music Group 54548 Smooth Luv.

1993 IF
(S) (4:31) Virgin 87825 Janet.

1993 AGAIN
(S) (3:46) Virgin 87825 Janet.

1994 BECAUSE OF LOVE
(S) (4:20) Virgin 87825 Janet.
(S) (3:57) Priority 50960 Work It! Dance = Life. *(remix; all selections on this cd are segued together)*

1994 ANY TIME, ANY PLACE
(S) (7:08) Virgin 87825 Janet.

1994 YOU WANT THIS
(S) (5:05) Virgin 87825 Janet.

1994 70's LOVE GROOVE
released as by MICHAEL JACKSON & JANET JACKSON:
1995 SCREAM
(S) (4:38) Epic 59000 Michael Jackson - History: Past, Present And Future.

released as by JANET JACKSON:
1995 RUNAWAY
(S) (3:33) A&M 314540399 Design Of A Decade 1986/1996.

released as by JANET:
1998 TOGETHER AGAIN
(S) (5:01) Virgin 44762 The Velvet Rope. *(tracks into the next selection)*

JERMAINE JACKSON
1973 DADDY'S HOME
(S) (2:57) Motown 0868 and 6194 Jackson Five Anthology.
(S) (3:03) Motown 5484 Greatest Hits And Rare Classics.
(S) (3:05) Motown 314530489 Jackson Five - Soulsation! 25th Anniversary Collection.
(S) (3:01) Motown 314530558 Jackson Five - Ultimate Collection.

1980 LET'S GET SERIOUS
(S) (3:33) Motown 9021 and 5309 25 Years Of Grammy Greats. *(45 version)*
(S) (3:32) Priority 7976 Mega-Hits Dance Classics Volume 6. *(45 version)*
(S) (7:57) Motown 5484 Greatest Hits And Rare Classics. *(LP version)*
(S) (7:57) Motown 5354 Let's Get Serious. *(LP version)*
(S) (3:33) Motown 0868 and 6194 Jackson Five Anthology. *(45 version)*
(S) (3:33) Motown 6358 Hitsville USA Volume Two. *(45 version)*
(S) (3:31) Motown 314530516 Motown Year By Year 1980. *(45 version)*
(S) (3:33) Time-Life R988-07 Sounds Of The Eighties: 1980. *(45 version)*
(S) (3:33) Rhino 72159 Black Entertainment Television - 15th Anniversary. *(45 version)*
(S) (3:31) K-Tel 3908 High Energy Volume 1. *(45 version)*
(S) (3:32) Motown 314530849 Motown 40 Forever. *(45 version)*
(S) (3:33) JCI 3176 1980 - Only Soul - 1984. *(45 version)*

1980 YOU'RE SUPPOSED TO KEEP YOUR LOVE FOR ME
(S) (3:48) Motown 5484 Greatest Hits And Rare Classics. *(45 version)*
(S) (5:34) Motown 5354 Let's Get Serious. *(LP version)*

1982 LET ME TICKLE YOUR FANCY
(S) (3:48) Motown 5484 Greatest Hits And Rare Classics.
(S) (3:49) Motown 314530534 Motown Year By Year - 1982.

1984 DYNAMITE
(S) (5:59) Arista 8203 Jermaine Jackson. *(LP version)*
(S) (3:58) Priority 50940 Shut Up And Dance! The 80's Volume One. *(all selections on this cd are segued together)*

1985 DO WHAT YOU DO
(S) (4:47) Arista 8203 Jermaine Jackson. *(LP version)*
(S) (4:25) Time-Life R834-02 Body Talk - Just For You. *(alternate take)*

1986 I THINK IT'S LOVE
(S) (3:52) Arista 8416 Perfect 10 III.
(S) (3:53) Arista 8277 Precious Moments.

J.J. JACKSON
1966 BUT IT'S ALRIGHT
(E) (2:47) Rhino 75774 Soul Shots.
(E) (2:47) JCI 3105 Soul Sixties.
(E) (2:47) Rhino 71461 Soul Hits, Volume 3.
(E) (2:44) Time-Life 2CLR-22 Classic Rock - 1966: Blowin' Your Mind.

J.J. JACKSON (Continued)
- (M) (2:50) Warner Brothers 45711 The Best Of Loma Records.
- (M) (2:43) AVI 5015 Soul Of The 60's Volume 1: Calla Records.
- (E) (2:44) JCI 3161 18 Soul Hits From The 60's.
- (E) (2:47) Flashback 72659 '60s Soul: When A Man Loves A Woman.
- (E) (2:47) Flashback 72091 '60s Soul Hits Box Set.
- (M) (2:51) Rhino 72815 Beg, Scream & Shout! The Big Ol' Box Of '60s Soul.
- (E) (2:47) Flashback 72896 25 Years Of R&B - 1966.

JOE JACKSON
1979 IS SHE REALLY GOING OUT WITH HIM?
- (S) (3:33) A&M 3187 Look Sharp!
- (S) (3:33) Rhino 71174 DIY: Starry Eyes - UK Pop II.
- (S) (3:33) Time-Life SOD-19 Sounds Of The Seventies - 1979: Take Two.
- (S) (3:33) Rebound 314520323 Alterno-Daze: Origin Of The Species.
- (S) (3:34) A&M 314540524 Greatest Hits.
- (S) (3:34) Rhino 72894 Hard Rock Cafe: New Wave.
1982 STEPPIN' OUT
- (S) (4:23) A&M 4906 and 3334 Night And Day. *(LP version)*
- (S) (4:17) A&M 314540524 Greatest Hits. *(LP version)*
- (S) (4:18) Hollywood 62123 More Music From The Motion Picture "Romy And Michele's High School Reunion". *(LP version)*
1983 BREAKING US IN TWO
- (S) (4:52) A&M 4906 and 3334 Night And Day.
- (S) (4:52) A&M 314540524 Greatest Hits.
1984 YOU CAN'T GET WHAT YOU WANT
- (S) (4:51) A&M 5000 and 3286 Body And Soul. *(LP version)*
- (S) (4:51) A&M 314540524 Greatest Hits. *(LP version)*

MICHAEL JACKSON
1972 GOT TO BE THERE
- (S) (3:22) Motown 0868 and 6194 Jackson Five Anthology.
- (S) (3:22) Motown 9040 Compact Command Performances.
- (S) (3:22) Motown 5402 and 6195 Anthology.
- (S) (3:22) Motown 5416 Got To Be There.
- (S) (3:21) Motown 5312 Great Songs And Performances That Inspired The Motown 25th Anniversary TV Special.
- (S) (3:21) Motown 8000 and 8100 Got To Be There/Ben.
- (S) (3:22) Motown 5194 and 9079 Best Of.
- (S) (3:21) Motown 6250 Original Soul Of.
- (S) (3:21) Motown 374638505 Motown Legends - Rockin' Robin.
- (S) (3:22) Motown 6358 Hitsville USA Volume Two.
- (S) (3:22) Motown 314530480 Anthology.
- (S) (3:21) Motown 314530489 Jackson Five - Soulsation! 25th Anniversary Collection.
- (S) (3:22) Motown 314530569 Motown Milestones - Motown Love Songs.
- (S) (3:21) Motown 314530558 Jackson Five - Ultimate Collection.
1972 ROCKIN' ROBIN
- (S) (2:30) Motown 0868 and 6194 Jackson Five Anthology.
- (S) (2:31) Motown 9040 Compact Command Performances.
- (S) (2:30) Motown 5402 and 6195 Anthology.
- (S) (2:31) Motown 5416 Got To Be There.
- (S) (2:30) Motown 5312 Great Songs And Performances That Inspired The Motown 25th Anniversary TV Special.
- (S) (2:30) Motown 8000 and 8100 Got To Be There/Ben.
- (S) (2:31) Motown 5194 and 9079 Best Of.
- (S) (2:30) Motown 6250 Original Soul Of.
- (S) (2:30) Motown 374638505 Motown Legends - Rockin' Robin.
- (S) (2:31) Motown 314530480 Anthology.
- (S) (2:31) Motown 314530489 Jackson Five - Soulsation! 25th Anniversary Collection.
- (S) (2:31) Motown 314530558 Jackson Five - Ultimate Collection.

- (S) (2:30) Polygram Special Markets 314520446 Soul Hits Of The 70's.
1972 I WANNA BE WHERE YOU ARE
- (S) (2:52) Motown 9105 and 5410 Motown Memories Volume 2.
- (S) (2:58) Motown 0868 and 6194 Jackson Five Anthology.
- (S) (2:58) Motown 9040 Compact Command Performances.
- (S) (2:54) Motown 5402 and 6195 Anthology.
- (S) (2:59) Motown 5416 Got To Be There.
- (S) (2:55) Motown 5312 Great Songs And Performances That Inspired The Motown 25th Anniversary TV Special.
- (S) (2:59) Motown 8000 and 8100 Got To Be There/Ben.
- (S) (2:55) Motown 5194 and 9079 Best Of.
- (S) (2:54) Motown 374638505 Motown Legends - Rockin' Robin.
- (S) (2:59) Motown 314530480 Anthology.
- (S) (2:58) Motown 314530489 Jackson Five - Soulsation! 25th Anniversary Collection.
- (S) (2:56) Motown 314530558 Ultimate Collection.
1972 BEN
- (S) (2:43) Motown 0868 and 6194 Jackson Five Anthology.
- (S) (2:44) Motown 9040 Compact Command Performances.
- (S) (2:43) Motown 5344 Every Great Motown Song: The First 25 Years Volume 2.
- (S) (2:43) Motown 5402 and 6195 Anthology.
- (S) (2:43) Motown 5153 Ben.
- (S) (2:43) Motown 5275 12 #1 Hits From The 70's.
- (S) (2:43) Motown 5312 Great Songs And Performances That Inspired The Motown 25th Anniversary TV Special.
- (S) (2:43) Motown 8000 and 8100 Got To Be There/Ben.
- (S) (2:43) Motown 5194 and 9079 Best Of.
- (S) (2:43) Motown 0937 20/20 Twenty No. 1 Hits From Twenty Years At Motown.
- (S) (2:44) Rhino 71228 Yesterday's Heroes: 70's Teen Idols.
- (S) (2:43) Motown 6358 Hitsville USA Volume Two.
- (S) (2:44) Motown 314530480 Anthology.
- (S) (2:43) Motown 314530489 Jackson Five - Soulsation! 25th Anniversary Collection.
- (S) (2:44) Motown 314530569 Motown Milestones - Motown Love Songs.
- (S) (2:44) Rhino 72738 Billboard Top Soft Rock Hits - 1972.
1975 JUST A LITTLE BIT OF YOU
- (S) (3:08) Motown 0868 and 6194 Jackson Five Anthology.
- (S) (3:08) Motown 5402 and 6195 Anthology.
- (S) (3:08) Rebound 314520317 Class Reunion 1975.
- (S) (3:12) Motown 314530480 Anthology.
- (S) (3:11) Motown 314530489 Jackson Five - Soulsation! 25th Anniversary Collection.
- (S) (3:09) Motown 314530531 Motown Year By Year - 1975.
- (S) (3:11) Motown 314530558 Jackson Five - Ultimate Collection.
1979 DON'T STOP 'TIL YOU GET ENOUGH
(dj copies ran (3:55) and (5:45); commercial copies were all (5:45); actual 45 time is (5:56) not (5:45) as stated on the record label)
- (S) (6:06) Epic 35745 Off The Wall. *(LP length)*
- (S) (6:03) Epic 59000 History - Past, Present And Future. *(LP length)*
1980 ROCK WITH YOU
- (S) (3:40) Epic 35745 Off The Wall. *(LP version)*
- (S) (3:39) Epic 59000 History - Past, Present And Future. *(LP version)*
1980 OFF THE WALL
- (S) (4:06) Epic 35745 Off The Wall. *(LP length)*
1980 SHE'S OUT OF MY LIFE
- (S) (3:37) Epic 35745 Off The Wall.
- (S) (3:36) Epic 59000 History - Past, Present And Future.
released as by MICHAEL JACKSON/PAUL McCARTNEY:
1983 THE GIRL IS MINE
(dj copies of this 45 ran (3:32) and (3:41); commercial copies were all (3:41))
- (S) (3:41) Epic 38112 Michael Jackson - Thriller.
- (S) (3:40) Epic 59000 Michael Jackson: History - Past, Present And Future.

released as by MICHAEL JACKSON:
1983 BILLIE JEAN
    (S)   (4:53)   Epic 38112 Thriller.
    (S)   (4:52)   Epic 59000 History - Past, Present And Future.
1983 BEAT IT
    (S)   (4:18)   Epic 38112 Thriller.
    (S)   (4:17)   Epic 59000 History - Past, Present And Future.
1983 WANNA BE STARTIN' SOMETHIN'
    (S)   (6:03)   Epic 38112 Thriller. *(LP version)*
    (S)   (6:01)   Epic 59000 History - Past, Present And Future.
               (LP version)
1983 HUMAN NATURE
    (S)   (4:06)   Epic 38112 Thriller.
    (S)   (4:04)   Time-Life R13610 Gold And Platinum Box Set - The Ultimate Rock Collection.
1983 P.Y.T. (PRETTY YOUNG THING)
    (S)   (3:58)   Epic 38112 Thriller.
released as by PAUL McCARTNEY and MICHAEL JACKSON:
1983 SAY SAY SAY
    (S)   (3:54)   Capitol 46018 Paul McCartney - Pipes Of Peace.
    (S)   (3:54)   Columbia 39149 Paul McCartney - Pipes Of Peace.
    (S)   (3:53)   Capitol 48287 Paul McCartney: All The Best.
released as by MICHAEL JACKSON:
1984 THRILLER
    (dj copies of this 45 ran (3:56) and (5:11);
    commercial copies were all (3:56))
    (S)   (5:57)   Epic 38112 Thriller. *(LP version)*
    (S)   (5:56)   Epic 59000 History - Past, Present And Future.
               (LP version)
1984 FAREWELL MY SUMMER LOVE
    (S)   (3:42)   Motown 314530480 Anthology. *(45 version)*
    (S)   (4:19)   Motown 5402 and 6195 Anthology. *(LP version)*
1987 I JUST CAN'T STOP LOVING YOU
    (S)   (4:21)   Columbia 44382 Heart Of Soul. *(LP version)*
    (S)   (4:23)   Epic 40600 Bad. *(LP version)*
    (S)   (4:11)   Epic 59000 History - Past, Present And Future.
               (45 version)
1987 BAD
    (S)   (4:05)   Epic 40600 Bad.
    (S)   (4:06)   Epic 59000 History - Past, Present And Future.
1988 THE WAY YOU MAKE ME FEEL
    (S)   (4:58)   Epic 40600 Bad. *(LP version)*
    (S)   (4:57)   Epic 59000 History - Past, Present And Future.
               (LP version)
1988 MAN IN THE MIRROR
    (S)   (5:18)   Epic 40600 Bad. *(LP version)*
    (S)   (5:18)   Epic 59000 History - Past, Present And Future.
               (LP version)
1988 DIRTY DIANA
    (S)   (4:51)   Epic 40600 Bad. *(LP length)*
    (S)   (4:49)   Time-Life R13610 Gold And Platinum Box Set - The Ultimate Rock Collection. *(LP length)*
1988 ANOTHER PART OF ME
    (S)   (3:53)   Epic 40600 Bad.
1989 SMOOTH CRIMINAL
    (S)   (4:16)   Epic 40600 Bad.
1991 BLACK OR WHITE
    (S)   (4:14)   Epic 45400 Dangerous. *(LP version)*
    (S)   (4:14)   Epic 59000 History - Past, Present And Future.
               (LP version)
1992 REMEMBER THE TIME
    (S)   (3:59)   Epic 45400 Dangerous. *(LP version)*
    (S)   (3:58)   Epic 59000 History - Past, Present And Future.
               (LP version)
1992 IN THE CLOSET
    (S)   (6:30)   Epic 45400 Dangerous. *(LP version)*
1992 JAM
    (S)   (5:38)   Epic 45400 Dangerous. *(LP version)*
1993 HEAL THE WORLD
    (S)   (6:24)   Epic 45400 Dangerous. *(LP version)*
    (S)   (6:24)   Epic 59000 History - Past, Present And Future.
               (LP version)
1993 WHO IS IT
    (S)   (6:33)   Epic 45400 Dangerous. *(LP version)*
1993 WILL YOU BE THERE
    (S)   (5:52)   MJJ/Epic 57280 O.S.T. Free Willy.
    (S)   (7:40)   Epic 45400 Dangerous.

released as by MICHAEL JACKSON & JANET JACKSON:
1995 SCREAM
    (S)   (4:38)   Epic 59000 Michael Jackson - History: Past, Present And Future.
released as by MICHAEL JACKSON:
1995 CHILDHOOD
    (S)   (4:27)   Epic 59000 History - Past, Present And Future.
    (S)   (4:27)   MJJ/550 Music/Epic Soundtrax 67259 O.S.T. Free Willy 2.
1995 YOU ARE NOT ALONE
    (S)   (5:45)   Epic 59000 History - Past, Present And Future.
    (S)   (5:44)   Grammy Recordings/Sony 67565 1996 Grammy Nominees.
1996 THEY DON'T CARE ABOUT US
    (S)   (4:43)   Epic 59000 History - Past, Present And Future.

MILLIE JACKSON
1972 ASK ME WHAT YOU WANT
    (S)   (3:09)   Rhino 72863 Totally Unrestricted! The Millie Jackson Anthology.
1972 MY MAN, A SWEET MAN
    (S)   (2:29)   Ripete 2220 Soul Patrol Vol. 2.
    (M) (2:30)   Rhino 72863 Totally Unrestricted! The Millie Jackson Anthology.
1973 HURTS SO GOOD
    (S)   (3:11)   Rhino 70553 Soul Hits Of The 70's Volume 13.
    (S)   (3:10)   Ripete 2222 Soul Patrol Vol. 4.
    (S)   (3:11)   Priority 53130 Deep Soul Volume Three.
    (S)   (3:27)   Rhino 72863 Totally Unrestricted! The Millie Jackson Anthology.
1977 IF YOU'RE NOT BACK IN LOVE BY MONDAY
    (S)   (4:48)   Time-Life R838-16 Solid Gold Soul 1977.
    (S)   (4:47)   Rhino 72863 Totally Unrestricted! The Millie Jackson Anthology.

REBBIE JACKSON
1985 CENTIPEDE
    (S)   (5:54)   DCC Compact Classics 143 Groove On! Volume 3. *(12" single version)*

STONEWALL JACKSON
1959 WATERLOO
    (S)   (2:27)   Rhino 70680 Billboard's Top Country Hits Of 1959.
    (M) (2:27)   Columbia 46031 Columbia Country Classics Volume 3.
    (S)   (2:26)   Columbia 45070 American Originals.
    (S)   (2:27)   CBS Special Products 8186 The Dynamic.
    (S)   (2:26)   Time-Life CTD-09 Country USA - 1959.
    (S)   (2:27)   K-Tel 225 Country Music Classics Volume I.
    (S)   (2:34)   Scotti Bros. 75483 Country Favorites - The Number One Hits. *(rerecorded)*
    (S)   (2:27)   JCI 3152 1955 - Only Country - 1959.
    (S)   (2:25)   K-Tel 3359 101 Greatest Country Hits Vol. Five: Country Memories. *(rerecording)*
    (S)   (2:26)   Time-Life R808-03 Classic Country 1950-1959.

WANDA JACKSON
1960 LET'S HAVE A PARTY
    (E)   (2:08)   EMI 90614 Non Stop Party Rock.
    (M) (2:08)   Rhino 70742 Rock This Town: Rockabilly Hits Volume 2.
    (M) (2:07)   JCI 3201 Partytime Fifties.
    (E)   (2:07)   Curb 77398 Greatest Hits.
    (M) (2:08)   Rhino 70990 Rockin' In The Country: Best Of.
    (M) (2:03)   Time-Life 2RNR-29 Rock 'N' Roll Era - The 60's Rave On.
    (M) (2:08)   Capitol 36185 Vintage Collections.
    (M) (2:08)   Right Stuff 53316 Hot Rod Rock Volume 1: Rev It Up.
    (M) (2:07)   EMI-Capitol Special Markets 19552 Lost Hits Of The '60s.
1961 RIGHT OR WRONG
    (S)   (2:36)   Curb 77398 Greatest Hits.
    (S)   (2:36)   Rhino 70990 Rockin' In The Country: Best Of.
    (S)   (2:35)   Time-Life CTD-01 Country USA - 1961.
    (S)   (2:35)   Capitol 36185 Vintage Collections.

WANDA JACKSON *(Continued)*

    (S) (2:37) K-Tel 3366 101 Greatest Country Hits Vol. Seven: Country Nights. *(rerecording; truncated fade)*

1961 IN THE MIDDLE OF A HEARTACHE
    (S) (2:32) Curb 77398 Greatest Hits.
    (S) (2:32) Rhino 70990 Rockin' In The Country: Best Of.
    (M) (2:32) Capitol 36185 Vintage Collections.
    (S) (2:33) JCI 3153 1960 - Only Country - 1964.

JACKSON FIVE
1970 I WANT YOU BACK
    (S) (2:58) Rhino 70631 Billboard's Top Rock & Roll Hits Of 1970.
    (S) (2:58) Rhino 72005 Billboard's Top Rock & Roll Hits 1968-1972 Box Set.
    (S) (2:57) Motown 6132 25 #1 Hits From 25 Years.
    (S) (2:58) Motown 0868 and 6194 Anthology.
    (S) (2:58) Motown 9040 and 6070 Compact Command Performances.
    (S) (2:55) Motown 5129 Diana Ross Presents.
    (S) (2:56) Motown 5275 12 #1 Hits From The 70's.
    (S) (2:56) Motown 5312 Great Songs And Performances That Inspired The Motown 25th Anniversary TV Special.
    (S) (2:57) Motown 8019 and 8119 Diana Ross Presents/ABC.
    (S) (2:57) Motown 5201 Greatest Hits.
    (S) (2:56) Motown 0937 20/20 Twenty No. 1 Hits From Twenty Years At Motown.
    (S) (2:50) Motown 9071 Motown Dance Party Volume 1. *(all selections on this cd are segued together)*
    (S) (2:54) Pair 1272 Original Motown Classics.
    (M) (2:58) Motown 6312 Hitsville USA.
    (S) (2:57) Motown 374638506 Motown Legends - Never Can Say Goodbye.
    (S) (2:51) Time-Life RHD-18 Rhythm & Blues - 1970.
    (S) (2:56) Time-Life 2CLR-06 Classic Rock - 1969.
    (S) (2:54) Time-Life R102-34 The Rolling Stone Collection.
    (S) (2:54) Time-Life SOD-11 Sounds Of The Seventies - 1970: Take Two.
    (M) (2:58) Rebound 314520269 Class Reunion 1969.
    (S) (2:58) Motown 314530489 Soulsation! 25th Anniversary Collection.
    (S) (2:57) Motown 314530525 Motown Year By Year - 1969.
    (S) (2:49) Tommy Boy 1136 ESPN Presents Jock Rock Vol. 2. *(all songs on this cd are segued together with crowd sound effects added)*
    (S) (2:58) Motown 314530558 Ultimate Collection.
    (S) (2:56) Columbia 67380 O.S.T. Now And Then.
    (S) (2:56) Time-Life AM1-15 AM Gold - Early '70s Classics.
    (S) (2:51) Time-Life R838-05 Solid Gold Soul - 1970.
    (S) (2:58) Motown 314530852 Greatest Hits. *(remastered edition)*

1970 ABC
(actual 45 and LP time is (2:56) not (2:38) as stated on the record label)
    (S) (2:57) Motown 6132 25 #1 Hits From 25 Years.
    (S) (2:57) Motown 0868 and 6194 Anthology.
    (S) (2:57) Motown 9040 and 6070 Compact Command Performances.
    (S) (2:56) Motown 5275 12 #1 Hits From The 70's.
    (S) (2:56) Motown 5312 Great Songs And Performances That Inspired The Motown 25th Anniversary TV Special.
    (S) (2:56) Motown 8019 and 8119 Diana Ross Presents/ABC.
    (S) (2:54) Motown 5152 ABC. *(truncated fade)*
    (S) (2:57) Motown 5201 Greatest Hits.
    (S) (2:57) Motown 9060 Motown's Biggest Pop Hits.
    (S) (2:53) Motown 9071 Motown Dance Party Volume 1. *(all selections on this cd are segued together)*
    (S) (2:56) Pair 1272 Original Motown Classics.
    (M) (2:56) Motown 6312 Hitsville USA.

    (M) (2:56) Rhino 71195 Kid Rock!
    (S) (2:56) Time-Life SUD-20 Superhits - Early 70's Classics.
    (S) (2:56) Time-Life SOD-01 Sounds Of The Seventies - 1970.
    (S) (2:55) MCA 11036 O.S.T. Crooklyn.
    (S) (2:56) Motown 314530489 Soulsation! 25th Anniversary Collection.
    (S) (3:12) Motown 314530528 Motown Year By Year - 1970. *(:16 longer than the 45 or LP)*
    (S) (2:57) Rhino 72112 Billboard Hot Soul Hits - 1970.
    (S) (2:56) Motown 314530558 Ultimate Collection.
    (S) (2:56) LaserLight 12314 and 15936 The Wonder Years - Party Time.
    (S) (2:56) Motown 314530852 Greatest Hits. *(remastered edition)*
    (S) (2:56) Motown 314530849 Motown 40 Forever.

1970 THE LOVE YOU SAVE
    (S) (3:03) Rhino 70658 Billboard's Top R&B Hits Of 1970.
    (S) (3:03) Motown 0868 and 6194 Anthology.
    (S) (3:02) Motown 9040 and 6070 Compact Command Performances.
    (S) (3:00) Motown 9072 Motown Dance Party Volume 2. *(all selections on this cd are segued together)*
    (S) (3:01) Motown 5312 Great Songs And Performances That Inspired The Motown 25th Anniversary TV Special.
    (S) (3:02) Motown 8019 and 8119 Diana Ross Presents/ABC.
    (S) (2:58) Motown 5152 ABC.
    (S) (3:02) Motown 5201 Greatest Hits.
    (S) (2:58) Pair 1272 Original Motown Classics.
    (M) (3:03) Motown 6312 Hitsville USA.
    (S) (3:02) Time-Life SUD-16 Superhits - The Early 70's.
    (S) (3:02) Motown 314530489 Soulsation! 25th Anniversary Collection.
    (S) (3:03) Motown 314530558 Ultimate Collection.
    (S) (3:02) Time-Life AM1-13 AM Gold - The Early '70s.
    (S) (3:02) Motown 314530852 Greatest Hits. *(remastered edition)*

1970 I'LL BE THERE
(actual 45 time is (3:44) not (3:35) as stated on the record label)
    (S) (3:54) Motown 9110 and 5414 Motown Memories Volume 4. *(LP version)*
    (S) (3:56) Motown 6132 25 #1 Hits From 25 Years. *(LP version)*
    (S) (3:56) Rhino 70658 Billboard's Top R&B Hits Of 1970. *(LP version)*
    (S) (3:56) Motown 0868 and 6194 Anthology. *(LP version)*
    (S) (3:56) Motown 9040 and 6070 Compact Command Performances. *(LP version)*
    (S) (3:57) Motown 5157 Third Album. *(LP version)*
    (S) (3:55) Motown 5402 and 6195 Michael Jackson Anthology. *(LP version)*
    (S) (3:54) Motown 5275 12 #1 Hits From The 70's. *(LP version)*
    (S) (3:54) Motown 5312 Great Songs And Performances That Inspired The Motown 25th Anniversary TV Special. *(LP version)*
    (S) (3:56) Motown 8011 and 8111 Third Album/Maybe Tomorrow. *(LP version)*
    (S) (3:56) Motown 5201 Greatest Hits. *(LP version)*
    (S) (3:55) Motown 9060 Motown's Biggest Pop Hits. *(LP version)*
    (S) (3:55) Motown 0937 20/20 Twenty No. 1 Hits From Twenty Years At Motown. *(LP version)*
    (M) (3:43) Motown 6312 Hitsville USA. *(45 version)*
    (S) (3:55) Motown 6356 Album Inspired By "The Jacksons: An American Dream" Mini Series. *(LP version)*
    (S) (3:51) Time-Life SUD-04 Superhits - 1970. *(LP version)*
    (M) (3:42) Rebound 3145200320 Class Reunion 1970. *(45 version)*
    (S) (3:56) Motown 314530480 Michael Jackson Anthology. *(LP version)*
    (S) (3:55) Motown 314530489 Soulsation! 25th Anniversary Collection. *(LP version)*

(M)	(3:43)	Motown 314530569 Motown Milestones - Motown Love Songs. *(45 version)*
(S)	(3:56)	Motown 314530558 Ultimate Collection. *(LP version)*
(S)	(3:53)	Columbia 67380 O.S.T. Now And Then. *(LP version)*
(S)	(3:51)	Time-Life AM1-02 AM Gold - 1970. *(LP version)*
(S)	(3:55)	Motown 314530852 Greatest Hits. *(remastered edition; LP version)*
(S)	(3:55)	Motown 314530849 Motown 40 Forever. *(LP version)*
(S)	(3:51)	Time-Life R834-13 Body Talk - Just The Two Of Us. *(LP version)*

1971 MAMA'S PEARL

(S)	(3:02)	Motown 0868 and 6194 Anthology. *(:09 shorter than the 45 or LP)*
(S)	(3:12)	Motown 9040 and 6070 Compact Command Performances.
(S)	(3:07)	Motown 5157 Third Album.
(S)	(3:07)	Motown 8011 and 8111 Third Album/Maybe Tomorrow.
(S)	(3:11)	Motown 5201 Greatest Hits.
(S)	(3:12)	Polygram Special Markets 314520300 Motown Legends - Guy Groups.
(S)	(3:10)	Motown 314530489 Soulsation! 25th Anniversary Collection.
(S)	(3:11)	Motown 314530558 Ultimate Collection.
(S)	(3:10)	Motown 314530852 Greatest Hits. *(remastered edition)*

1971 NEVER CAN SAY GOODBYE

(S)	(2:57)	Motown 6137 20 Greatest Songs In Motown History.
(S)	(2:58)	Rhino 70659 Billboard's Top R&B Hits Of 1971.
(S)	(2:57)	Motown 0868 and 6194 Anthology.
(S)	(2:59)	Motown 9040 and 6070 Compact Command Performances.
(S)	(2:59)	Motown 5324 and 9035 Top Ten With A Bullet: Motown Love Songs.
(S)	(2:57)	Motown 5344 Every Great Motown Song: The First 25 Years Volume 2. *(most selections on this cd have noise on the fadeout)*
(S)	(2:57)	Motown 5228 Maybe Tomorrow.
(S)	(2:56)	Motown 5402 and 6195 Michael Jackson Anthology.
(S)	(2:57)	Motown 8034 Every Great Motown Song: The First 25 Years Volumes 1 & 2. *(most selections on this cd have noise on the fadeout)*
(S)	(2:57)	Motown 8011 and 8111 Third Album/Maybe Tomorrow.
(S)	(2:59)	Motown 5201 Greatest Hits.
(S)	(2:57)	Motown 0937 20/20 Twenty No. 1 Hits From Twenty Years At Motown.
(S)	(2:57)	Pair 1272 Original Motown Classics.
(M)	(3:00)	Motown 6312 Hitsville USA.
(S)	(2:59)	Motown 6356 Album Inspired By "The Jacksons: An American Dream" Mini Series.
(S)	(2:56)	Motown 374638506 Motown Legends - Never Can Say Goodbye.
(S)	(2:54)	Time-Life RHD-09 Rhythm & Blues - 1971.
(S)	(2:54)	Time-Life SUD-10 Superhits - 1971.
(S)	(3:00)	Time-Life SOD-02 Sounds Of The Seventies - 1971.
(S)	(2:55)	MCA 11065 O.S.T. Crooklyn Volume II.
(S)	(2:56)	Polygram Special Markets 314520030 Motown Legends - Love Songs.
(S)	(2:59)	Motown 314530480 Michael Jackson Anthology.
(S)	(2:59)	Motown 314530489 Soulsation! 25th Anniversary Collection.
(S)	(2:59)	Motown 314530558 Ultimate Collection.
(S)	(2:54)	Time-Life AM1-06 AM Gold - 1971.
(S)	(2:54)	Time-Life R838-06 Solid Gold Soul - 1971.
(S)	(2:58)	Motown 314530852 Greatest Hits. *(remastered edition)*
(S)	(3:00)	Rhino 72943 VH1 8-Track Flashback: Classic '70s Soul.

1971 MAYBE TOMORROW

(S)	(4:39)	Motown 0868 and 6194 Anthology.
(S)	(4:38)	Motown 9040 and 6070 Compact Command Performances.
(S)	(4:40)	Motown 5228 Maybe Tomorrow.
(S)	(4:37)	Motown 5402 and 6195 Michael Jackson Anthology.
(S)	(4:37)	Motown 5312 Great Songs And Performances That Inspired The Motown 25th Anniversary TV Special.
(S)	(4:39)	Motown 8011 and 8111 Third Album/Maybe Tomorrow.
(S)	(4:38)	Motown 5201 Greatest Hits.
(S)	(4:45)	Motown 314530480 Michael Jackson Anthology.
(S)	(4:44)	Motown 314530489 Soulsation! 25th Anniversary Collection.
(S)	(4:44)	Motown 314530558 Ultimate Collection.
(S)	(4:43)	Motown 314530852 Greatest Hits. *(remastered edition)*

1972 SUGAR DADDY

(S)	(2:30)	Motown 0868 and 6194 Anthology.
(S)	(2:29)	Motown 9040 and 6070 Compact Command Performances.
(S)	(2:29)	Motown 5201 Greatest Hits.
(S)	(2:31)	Motown 314530489 Soulsation! 25th Anniversary Collection.
(S)	(2:31)	Motown 314530558 Ultimate Collection.
(S)	(2:31)	Motown 314530852 Greatest Hits. *(remastered edition)*

1972 LITTLE BITTY PRETTY ONE

(S)	(2:44)	Motown 0868 and 6194 Anthology.
(S)	(2:44)	Motown 374638506 Motown Legends - Never Can Say Goodbye.
(S)	(2:48)	Polygram Special Markets 314520300 Motown Legends - Guy Groups.
(S)	(2:47)	Motown 314530489 Soulsation! 25th Anniversary Collection.

1972 LOOKIN' THROUGH THE WINDOWS

(S)	(3:35)	Motown 0868 and 6194 Anthology.
(S)	(3:31)	Motown 9040 and 6070 Compact Command Performances.
(S)	(3:38)	Motown 314530489 Soulsation! 25th Anniversary Collection.
(S)	(3:37)	Motown 314530558 Ultimate Collection.

1972 CORNER OF THE SKY

(S)	(3:29)	Motown 0868 and 6194 Anthology.
(S)	(3:33)	Motown 5469 Skywriter.
(S)	(3:38)	Motown 314530489 Soulsation! 25th Anniversary Collection.

1973 HALLELUJAH DAY

(S)	(2:45)	Motown 0868 and 6194 Anthology.
(S)	(2:46)	Motown 5469 Skywriter.
(S)	(2:45)	Motown 314530489 Soulsation! 25th Anniversary Collection.

1973 GET IT TOGETHER

(S)	(2:46)	Motown 0868 and 6194 Anthology.
(S)	(2:48)	Motown 9040 and 6070 Compact Command Performances.
(S)	(2:46)	Motown 374638506 Motown Legends - Never Can Say Goodbye.
(S)	(2:47)	Motown 314530510 Motown Year By Year 1973.
(S)	(2:47)	Motown 314530489 Soulsation! 25th Anniversary Collection.
(S)	(2:47)	Motown 314530558 Ultimate Collection.

1974 DANCING MACHINE

(S)	(3:16)	Priority 7976 Mega-Hits Dance Classics Volume 6. *(LP version)*
(S)	(2:35)	Rhino 70635 Billboard's Top Rock & Roll Hits Of 1974. *(45 version)*
(S)	(3:16)	Priority 7059 Mega-Hits Dance Classics Volume 10. *(LP version)*
(S)	(2:34)	Rhino 70274 The Disco Years Volume 3. *(45 version)*
(S)	(3:16)	Motown 5312 Great Songs And Performances That Inspired The Motown 25th Anniversary TV Special. *(LP version)*

JACKSON FIVE (Continued)

- (S) (2:35) Motown 0868 and 6194 Anthology. *(45 version)*
- (S) (3:50) Motown 6250 Original Soul Of Michael Jackson. *(rerecording)*
- (S) (3:16) Motown 5402 and 6195 Michael Jackson Anthology. *(LP version)*
- (S) (3:17) Motown 6070 and 9040 Compact Command Performances. *(LP version)*
- (S) (3:16) Motown 6356 Album Inspired By "The Jacksons: An American Dream" Mini Series. *(LP version)*
- (S) (3:42) Motown 6356 Album Inspired By "The Jacksons: An American Dream" Mini Series. *(remix)*
- (S) (2:40) Motown 6358 Hitsville USA Volume Two. *(includes :06 ending found previously only on the "Get It Together" vinyl LP)*
- (S) (2:34) Razor & Tie 22045 Those Funky 70's. *(45 version)*
- (S) (2:35) Time-Life SOD-15 Sounds Of The Seventies - 1974: Take Two. *(45 version)*
- (S) (3:16) Rebound 314520298 Disco Nights Vol. 9. *(LP version)*
- (S) (2:34) Rebound 314520247 Class Reunion 1974. *(45 version)*
- (S) (3:40) Rebound 314520309 Disco Nights Vol. VII - D.J. Pix. *(remix)*
- (S) (2:40) Motown 314530480 Michael Jackson Anthology. *(includes :06 ending found previously only on the "Get It Together" vinyl LP)*
- (S) (2:35) Motown 314530489 Soulsation! 25th Anniversary Collection. *(45 version; tracks into next selection)*
- (S) (2:40) MCA 11329 Soul Train 25th Anniversary Box Set. *(includes :06 ending found previously only on the "Get It Together" vinyl LP)*
- (S) (2:35) Motown 314530558 Ultimate Collection. *(45 version)*
- (S) (2:34) Time-Life R840-05 Sounds Of The Seventies: '70s Dance Party 1972-1974. *(45 version)*

1975 WHATEVER YOU GOT, I WANT
- (S) (2:49) Motown 0868 and 6194 Anthology.
- (S) (2:55) Motown 314530489 Soulsation! 25th Anniversary Collection.

1975 I AM LOVE
- (S) (7:26) Motown 0868 and 6194 Anthology. *(Parts 1 & 2)*
- (S) (7:28) Motown 314530489 Soulsation! 25th Anniversary Collection. *(Parts 1 & 2)*
- (S) (3:17) Motown 314530531 Motown Year By Year - 1975.
- (S) (7:27) Motown 314530558 Ultimate Collection. *(Parts 1 & 2)*

JACKSONS
1977 ENJOY YOURSELF
- (S) (3:24) Epic 34229 The Jacksons.
- (S) (3:24) Epic/Legacy 64647 The Philly Sound Box Set.
- (S) (3:24) Epic Associated/Legacy 65162 A Postcard From Philly.

1977 SHOW YOU THE WAY TO GO
- (S) (5:29) Epic 34229 The Jacksons. *(LP version)*
- (S) (5:28) Epic/Legacy 64647 The Philly Sound Box Set. *(LP version)*

1979 SHAKE YOUR BODY (DOWN TO THE GROUND)
- (S) (7:59) Epic 35552 Destiny. *(LP version; previous selection tracks over introduction)*

1980 LOVELY ONE
- (S) (4:52) Epic 36424 Triumph. *(tracks into next selection; LP version)*

1981 HEARTBREAK HOTEL
(the LP title of this song is "THIS PLACE HOTEL")
- (S) (5:43) Epic 36424 Triumph. *(LP version)*

1984 STATE OF SHOCK
- (S) (4:29) Epic 38946 Victory. *(LP version)*
- (S) (5:39) Epic 67534 Club Epic Volume 5. *(12" single version)*

1984 TORTURE
- (S) (4:53) Epic 38946 Victory. *(LP version)*

DICK JACOBS
1956 PETTICOATS OF PORTUGAL
1957 FASCINATION
- (S) (2:32) Time-Life R986-07 Instrumental Favorites - Movie Magic. *(rerecording)*

JADE
1992 I WANNA LOVE YOU
- (S) (4:32) Giant 24446 O.S.T. Class Act.
- (S) (4:31) Giant 24466 Jade To The Max.

1993 DON'T WALK AWAY
- (S) (4:43) Giant 24466 Jade To The Max. *(LP version)*
- (S) (4:03) JCI 3132 1990 - Only Rock 'n Roll - 1994. *(45 version)*

1993 ONE WOMAN
- (S) (4:48) Giant 24466 Jade To The Max.

1995 EVERY DAY OF THE WEEK
- (S) (5:14) Giant 24558 Mind, Body & Song.

MICK JAGGER
1985 JUST ANOTHER NIGHT
(dj copies of this 45 ran (4:39) and (5:13); commercial copies were all (5:13))
- (S) (5:14) Columbia 39940 She's The Boss.
- (S) (5:14) Atlantic 82553 She's The Boss.

1985 LUCKY IN LOVE
(dj copies of this 45 ran (3:57) and (4:45); commercial copies were all (4:45))
- (S) (6:12) Columbia 39940 She's The Boss. *(LP version)*
- (S) (6:12) Atlantic 82553 She's The Boss. *(LP version)*

released as by MICK JAGGER/DAVID BOWIE:
1985 DANCING IN THE STREET
- (S) (3:14) Rykodisc 10218/19 David Bowie - The Singles 1969-1993.

released as by MICK JAGGER:
1987 LET'S WORK
- (S) (4:49) Columbia 40919 Primitive Cool. *(LP length)*
- (S) (4:49) Atlantic 82554 Primitive Cool. *(LP length)*

JAGGERZ
1970 THE RAPPER
- (S) (2:42) Rhino 70921 Super Hits Of The 70's Volume 1. *(LP version)*
- (S) (2:42) Rhino 72009 Super Hits Of The 70's Volumes 1-4 Box Set. *(LP version)*
- (S) (2:42) Rhino 70631 Billboard's Top Rock & Roll Hits Of 1970. *(LP version)*
- (S) (2:42) Rhino 72005 Billboard's Top Rock & Roll Hits 1968 - 1972 Box Set. *(LP version)*
- (M) (2:40) Pair 1202 Best Of Buddah. *(45 version)*
- (M) (2:40) Pair 1199 Best Of Bubblegum Music. *(45 version)*
- (M) (2:41) K-Tel 839 Battle Of The Bands Volume 2. *(45 version)*
- (M) (2:40) Priority 7997 Super Songs/70's Greatest Rock Hits Volume 8. *(45 version)*
- (M) (2:40) Special Music 4914 Best Of The Bubblegum Years. *(45 version)*
- (S) (2:42) Rhino 71205 70's Smash Hits Volume 1. *(LP version)*
- (M) (2:40) Essex 7060 The Buddah Box. *(45 version)*
- (S) (2:42) Time-Life SOD-01 Sounds Of The Seventies - 1970. *(LP version)*
- (S) (2:42) Time-Life R968-06 Guitar Rock 1970-1971. *(LP version)*
- (S) (2:42) K-Tel 3386 Best Of Bubblegum Music. *(LP version)*
- (S) (2:42) JCI 3191 1970 - Only Dance - 1974. *(LP version)*
- (S) (2:42) Flashback 72681 '70s Radio Hits Volume 1. *(LP version)*
- (S) (2:42) Flashback 72090 '70s Radio Hits Box Set. *(LP version)*

ETTA JAMES

1960 ALL I COULD DO WAS CRY
- (M) (2:56) Chess 9280 The Sweetest Peaches/Chess Years Volume 1.
- (E) (2:53) Chess 9266 At Last!
- (E) (2:51) Telstar/JCI 3505 Best Of.
- (M) (2:54) Chess 9341 The Essential.
- (E) (2:52) Time-Life 2RNR-48 Rock 'N' Roll Era - R&B Gems II.
- (E) (2:52) Time-Life RHD-15 Rhythm & Blues - 1960.
- (M) (2:52) JCI/Telstar 3516 Sweet Soul Sisters.
- (M) (2:53) Chess 9367 Her Best.
- (E) (2:53) Time-Life R838-20 Solid Gold Soul 1960.

1960 MY DEAREST DARLING
- (S) (3:00) Chess 9266 At Last!
- (S) (2:57) Telstar/JCI 3505 Best Of.
- (S) (2:59) Chess 9341 The Essential.
- (S) (2:58) Chess 9367 Her Best.

1961 AT LAST
- (S) (2:57) Chess 9266 At Last!
- (S) (2:56) Telstar/JCI 3505 Best Of.
- (S) (2:58) Chess 9341 The Essential.
- (S) (2:57) Time-Life RHD-14 Rhythm & Blues - 1961.
- (S) (2:58) Right Stuff 28371 Slow Jams: The 60's Volume Two.
- (S) (2:56) Original Sound 9305 Art Laboe's Dedicated To You Volume 5.
- (S) (2:58) Capitol 91866 O.S.T. Rain Man.
- (S) (2:59) Rhino 71806 The R&B Box: Thirty Years Of Rhythm & Blues.
- (S) (2:58) MCA 10685 Music From The Television Series Northern Exposure.
- (S) (2:56) Original Sound 9305 Art Laboe's Dedicated To You Vol. 5.
- (S) (2:59) Chess 9352 Chess Rhythm & Roll.
- (S) (2:58) MCA 11373 O.S.T. How To Make An American Quilt.
- (S) (2:57) Chess 812 History Of Chess Jazz.
- (S) (2:57) JCI 3164 Eighteen Soulful Ballads.
- (S) (2:58) Hip-O 40029 The Glory Of Love - '60s Sweet & Soulful Love Songs.
- (S) (2:59) Rhino 72618 Smooth Grooves: The '60s Volume 1 Early '60s.
- (S) (2:59) Rhino 72580 Soul Serenade - Intimate R&B.
- (S) (2:58) Chess 9367 Her Best.
- (S) (2:58) Atlantic 82983 Music From And Inspired By The Television Series "Mad About You".
- (S) (2:57) Hollywood 62020 O.S.T. Father Of The Bride II.
- (S) (2:59) Rhino 72514 Sirens Of Song - Classic Torch Singers.
- (S) (2:57) Time-Life R838-19 Solid Gold Soul 1961.

1961 TRUST IN ME
- (S) (2:57) Chess 9266 At Last!
- (S) (2:56) Telstar/JCI 3505 Best Of.
- (S) (2:57) Original Sound 8863 Oldies But Goodies Vol. 13.
- (S) (2:57) Original Sound 2223 Oldies But Goodies Volumes 2,7,9,12 and 13 Box Set. *(Volumes 2, 7 and 12 of this box set use the "Waring - fds" noise reduction process)*
- (S) (2:57) Original Sound 2500 Oldies But Goodies Volumes 1-15 Box Set. *(most volumes in this box set use the "Waring - fds" noise reduction process)*
- (S) (2:57) Chess 9341 The Essential.
- (S) (2:57) Right Stuff 30578 Slow Jams: The 60's Volume 4.
- (S) (2:57) Chess 9367 Her Best.

1962 SOMETHING'S GOT A HOLD ON ME
- (M) (2:46) Chess 31317 Best Of Chess Rhythm & Blues Volume 1.
- (M) (2:46) Chess 9280 The Sweetest Peaches/Chess Years Volume 1.
- (M) (2:45) Telstar/JCI 3505 Best Of.
- (M) (2:46) Chess 9341 The Essential.
- (M) (2:45) Time-Life 2RNR-35 Rock 'N' Roll Era - The 60's Last Dance.
- (M) (2:44) Time-Life RHD-11 Rhythm & Blues - 1962.
- (M) (2:46) Chess 9367 Her Best.

- (M) (2:45) Time-Life R859-05 Living The Blues: 1960-1964 Blues Classics.
- (M) (2:44) Time-Life R838-18 Solid Gold Soul 1962.

1962 STOP THE WEDDING
- (M) (2:40) Chess 9280 The Sweetest Peaches/Chess Years Volume 1.
- (M) (2:30) Telstar/JCI 3505 Best Of. *(missing the first :15 of the song)*
- (M) (2:50) Chess 9341 The Essential.
- (M) (2:50) Chess 9367 Her Best.

1963 PUSHOVER
- (M) (2:54) Chess 9280 The Sweetest Peaches/Chess Years Volume 1.
- (E) (2:54) Telstar/JCI 3505 Best Of.
- (S) (2:51) Ripete 2392192 Beach Music Anthology Box Set.
- (M) (2:53) Chess 9341 The Essential.
- (E) (2:54) JCI/Telstar 3516 Sweet Soul Sisters.
- (M) (2:53) Chess 9367 Her Best.

1968 TELL MAMA
- (S) (2:20) MCA 31205 Vintage Music Volume 8.
- (S) (2:20) MCA 5805 Vintage Music Volumes 7 & 8.
- (S) (2:20) Garland 011 Footstompin' Oldies.
- (S) (2:20) Chess 31318 Best Of Chess Rhythm & Blues Volume 2.
- (M) (2:19) Chess 9269 Tell Mama.
- (S) (2:20) Chess 9281 The Sweetest Peaches/Chess Years Volume 2.
- (M) (2:19) Telstar/JCI 3505 Best Of.
- (S) (2:20) Ripete 2392192 Beach Music Anthology Box Set.
- (S) (2:20) Chess 9341 The Essential.
- (S) (2:20) Rhino 71459 Soul Hits, Volume 1.
- (S) (2:18) Time-Life 2CLR-15 Classic Rock - 1967: Shakin' All Over.
- (S) (2:20) Rhino 71517 The Muscle Shoals Sound.
- (M) (2:19) JCI/Telstar 3516 Sweet Soul Sisters.
- (S) (2:20) Chess 9352 Chess Rhythm & Roll.
- (S) (2:20) MCA 11441 Blues Classics Box Set.
- (S) (2:19) MCA Special Products 20979 Soul Hits Volume 1.
- (S) (2:19) Chess 9367 Her Best.
- (S) (2:19) Flashback 72657 '60s Soul: Try A Little Tenderness.
- (S) (2:19) Flashback 72091 '60s Soul Hits Box Set.
- (M) (2:20) Rhino 72815 Beg, Scream & Shout! The Big Ol' Box Of '60s Soul.
- (S) (2:20) Chess 9389 The Chess Blues-Rock Songbook.
- (S) (2:20) MCA Special Products 21029 The Women Of Soul.

1968 SECURITY
- (M) (2:44) Chess 9269 Tell Mama. *(LP version)*
- (S) (2:27) Chess 9281 The Sweetest Peaches/Chess Years Volume 2. *(edit of the LP version)*
- (M) (2:44) Telstar/JCI 3505 Best Of. *(LP version)*
- (S) (2:27) Chess 9341 The Essential. *(edit of the LP version)*
- (M) (2:44) Time-Life 2CLR-25 Classic Rock - On The Soul Side. *(LP version)*
- (M) (2:45) JCI/Telstar 3516 Sweet Soul Sisters. *(LP version)*
- (M) (2:27) Chess 9367 Her Best. *(edit of the LP version)*

JONI JAMES

1955 HOW IMPORTANT CAN IT BE?
- (M) (2:31) Taragon 3005 Platinum & Gold Hits.

1955 YOU ARE MY LOVE
1956 GIVE US THIS DAY
1958 THERE GOES MY HEART
- (M) (2:32) Taragon 3005 Platinum & Gold Hits.

1959 THERE MUST BE A WAY
1960 LITTLE THINGS MEAN A LOT
- (M) (2:30) Taragon 3005 Platinum & Gold Hits.

RICK JAMES

1978 YOU AND I
- (S) (7:57) Motown 9110 and 5414 Motown Memories Volume 4. *(LP version)*
- (S) (8:04) Motown 5263 Come And Get It. *(LP version)*
- (S) (7:57) Motown 5382 Greatest Hits. *(LP version)*
- (S) (7:58) Motown 6095 Reflections. *(LP version)*

RICK JAMES (Continued)

(S) (3:48) Priority 7044 Rick James And Friends. *(neither the 45 or LP version; slow)*
(S) (3:09) Motown 6358 Hitsville USA Volume Two. *(45 version)*
(S) (3:48) Priority 53729 Mega Hits Dance Classics Vol 11. *(neither the 45 or LP version; slow)*
(S) (8:04) Motown 314530305 Bustin' Out/Best Of. *(LP version)*
(S) (3:08) Motown/Essex 374638516 Motown Legends - Give It To Me Baby. *(45 version)*
(S) (3:09) Rhino 72130 Soul Hits Of The 70's Vol. 20. *(45 version)*
(S) (7:54) Coldfront 3375 Old School Megamix. *(all selections on this cd are sequed together; LP version)*
(S) (3:05) Thump 4060 Old School Volume 6. *(45 version; all selections on this cd are segued together)*
(S) (8:03) Motown 314530559 The Ultimate Collection. *(LP version)*
(S) (3:08) Rebound 314520430 Funk Classics Of The 70's Vol. 2. *(45 version)*
(S) (3:09) JCI 3175 1975 - Only Soul - 1979. *(45 version)*

1981 GIVE IT TO ME BABY
(actual 45 time is (3:53) not (3:48) as stated on the record label; actual LP time is (4:04) not (4:07) as stated on the record label)

(S) (4:16) Motown 6132 25 #1 Hits From 25 Years Volume 2.
(S) (4:15) Priority 7058 Mega-Hits Dance Classics Volume 9.
(S) (4:04) Motown 9100 and 5405 Street Songs.
(S) (4:07) Motown 8012 and 8112 Street Songs/Throwin' Down.
(S) (4:15) Motown 5382 Greatest Hits.
(S) (4:15) Motown 6095 Reflections.
(S) (4:14) Priority 7044 Rick James And Friends.
(S) (4:15) Priority 53703 Hot And Sexy: Passion And Soul.
(S) (3:51) Motown 6358 Hitsville USA Volume Two.
(S) (4:07) Motown 314530305 Bustin' Out/Best Of.
(S) (4:06) Motown/Essex 374638516 Motown Legends - Give It To Me Baby.
(S) (4:06) Rebound 314520034 Funk Classics Of The 70's.
(S) (5:42) Motown 314530572 Funkology Volume Two - Behind The Groove. *(12" single version)*
(S) (4:07) Rhino 72159 Black Entertainment Television - 15th Anniversary.
(S) (3:50) K-Tel 3581 Roller Disco - Boogie From The Skating Rinks.
(S) (4:03) Rebound 314520431 Soul Classics - Best Of The 80's.
(S) (4:06) Motown 314530559 The Ultimate Collection.

1981 SUPER FREAK (PART 1)
(45 length is (3:18); LP length is (3:24))

(S) (3:25) Priority 7983 Mega-Hits Dance Classics Volume 7.
(S) (3:24) Motown 9100 and 5405 Street Songs.
(S) (3:24) Motown 8012 and 8112 Street Songs/Throwin' Down.
(S) (3:25) Motown 5382 Greatest Hits.
(S) (3:24) Motown 6095 Reflections.
(S) (3:25) Priority 7044 Rick James And Friends.
(S) (3:22) Original Sound 9306 Dedicated To You Vol. 6.
(S) (3:18) Motown 6358 Hitsville USA Volume Two.
(S) (3:18) Rhino 71618 Soul Train Hall Of Fame/20th Anniversary.
(S) (3:24) Razor & Tie 22045 Those Funky 70's.
(S) (3:24) Motown 314530305 Bustin' Out/Best Of.
(S) (3:23) Thump 4030 Old School Vol. 3.
(S) (3:18) Time-Life R988-08 Sounds Of The Eighties: 1981.
(S) (3:18) JCI 3149 1980 - Only Dance - 1984.
(S) (3:25) Rebound 314520361 Class Reunion '81.
(S) (3:22) Rebound 314520365 Funk Classics - The 80's.
(S) (3:25) Miramax/Hollywood 62058 O.S.T. The Pallbearer.
(S) (3:23) Motown 314530559 The Ultimate Collection.
(S) (3:25) Robbins 75002 Strip Jointz - Hot Songs For Sexy Dancers.
(S) (3:22) Motown 314530849 Motown 40 Forever.
(S) (3:18) Time-Life R840-09 Sounds Of The Seventies: '70s Dance Party 1979-1981.

1983 COLD BLOODED

(S) (5:56) Motown/Essex 374638516 Motown Legends - Give It To Me Baby. *(LP version)*
(S) (5:56) Motown 314530305 Bustin' Out/Best Of. *(LP version)*
(S) (4:15) Motown 5382 Greatest Hits. *(45 version)*
(S) (4:27) MCA 11329 Soul Train 25th Anniversary Box Set. *(45 version)*
(S) (5:57) Motown 314530559 The Ultimate Collection. *(LP version)*
(S) (5:54) Chronicles 314553403 Cosmic Funk. *(LP version)*

1984 17

(S) (6:39) Motown 314530305 Bustin' Out/Best Of. *(LP version)*
(S) (4:10) Motown 5382 Greatest Hits. *(45 version)*
(S) (6:43) Motown 6095 Reflections. *(LP version)*
(S) (4:10) Priority 7044 Rick James And Friends. *(45 version)*

SONNY JAMES
1957 YOUNG LOVE

(M) (2:29) Curb 77354 50's Hits Volume 1.
(M) (2:29) Curb 77330 50's Hits - Country Volume 1.
(M) (2:30) JCI 3203 Lovin' Fifties.
(M) (2:29) Curb 77359 Greatest Hits.
(M) (2:28) Capitol 91630 Capitol Collector's Series.
(M) (2:29) Curb 77525 Greatest Hits Of Rock 'N' Roll Volume 2.
(M) (2:28) Capitol 95916 Golden Country Jukebox Favorites.
(M) (2:28) Capitol 95917 Opry Legends.
(M) (2:29) Time-Life 2RNR-14 Rock 'N' Roll Era - 1956.
(M) (2:30) Time-Life CTD-02 Country USA - 1957.
(M) (2:28) Time-Life R103-27 Love Me Tender.
(E) (2:29) K-Tel 225 Country Music Classics Volume I.
(M) (2:29) Rhino 71902 Hillbilly Fever! Vol. 3. Legends Of Nashville.
(M) (2:29) Rhino 72442 Heroes Of Country Music Vol. Three.
(M) (2:29) JCI 3183 1955 - Only Love - 1959.
(M) (2:28) JCI 3152 1955 - Only Country - 1959.
(E) (2:29) K-Tel 3367 101 Greatest Country Hits Vol. Eight: Country Romance.
(M) (2:28) Time-Life R857-05 The Heart Of Rock 'n' Roll 1957.
(E) (2:31) Hammer & Lace 697124113 Leading Men: Masters Of Style Volume One.
(E) (2:29) Razor & Tie 2150 Young Love: The Classic Hits Of.
(M) (2:28) Time-Life R808-03 Classic Country 1950-1959.

1957 FIRST DATE, FIRST KISS, FIRST LOVE

(M) (2:26) Capitol 91630 Capitol Collector's Series.
(E) (2:27) Razor & Tie 2150 Young Love: The Classic Hits Of.

TOMMY JAMES and THE SHONDELLS
1966 HANKY PANKY
(no master tape for this song still exists so all cd's that include this song master it from vinyl)

(M) (2:52) Rhino 70627 Billboard's Top Rock & Roll Hits Of 1966.
(M) (2:52) Rhino 72007 Billboard's Top Rock & Roll Hits 1962-1966 Box Set.
(M) (2:51) Priority 7909 Vietnam: Rockin' The Delta.
(M) (2:51) Rhino 70920 Anthology.
(M) (2:51) Rhino 71214 Very Best Of.
(M) (2:51) Era 5025 The Brill Building Sound.
(M) (2:51) Rhino 71026 Best Of/Rhino Special Editions.
(M) (2:51) Time-Life 2CLR-07 Classic Rock - 1966: The Beat Goes On.
(M) (2:51) Rhino 71730 '60s Rock Classics, Vol. 3.
(M) (2:51) Time-Life R968-09 Guitar Rock 1966-1967.
(M) (2:51) JCI 3167 #1 Radio Hits 1965 - Only Rock 'n Roll - 1969.
(M) (2:51) Flashback 72703 '60s Rock: It's A Beautiful Morning.
(M) (2:51) Flashback 72088 '60s Rock Hits Box Set.

(M) (2:51) Flashback 72695 Hanky Panky And Other Hits.
(M) (2:51) Flashback 72087 '60s Rock Legends Box Set.

1966 SAY I AM (WHAT I AM)
(S) (2:29) Rhino 70920 Anthology.
(S) (2:29) Pair 1278 Very Best Of.
(S) (2:29) Rhino 71214 Very Best Of.
(S) (2:29) Time-Life 2CLR-29 Classic Rock - Bubblegum, Garage And Pop Nuggets.
(S) (2:29) Flashback 72695 Hanky Panky And Other Hits.
(S) (2:29) Flashback 72087 '60s Rock Legends Box Set.

1966 IT'S ONLY LOVE
(actual LP time is (2:13) not (2:07) as stated on the LP label)
(S) (2:15) Rhino 70920 Anthology. *(LP length)*
(S) (2:15) Pair 1278 Very Best Of. *(LP length*
(S) (2:15) Rhino 71214 Very Best Of. *(LP length)*
(S) (2:14) Flashback 72696 Crimson And Clover And Other Hits. *(LP length)*

1967 I THINK WE'RE ALONE NOW
(M) (2:07) Rhino 70628 Billboard's Top Rock & Roll Hits Of 1967.
(M) (2:07) Rhino 72007 Billboard's Top Rock & Roll Hits 1962-1966 Box Set.
(M) (2:07) Rhino 70920 Anthology.
(M) (2:08) Rhino 71214 Very Best Of.
(S) (2:21) Rhino 71026 Best Of/Rhino Special Editions. *(:14 longer fade than 45 or LP; missing some overdubs)*
(M) (2:05) Time-Life 2CLR-05 Classic Rock - 1967.
(E) (2:05) Collectables 2510 WCBS-FM History Of Rock - The Rockin' 60's.
(E) (2:05) Collectables 4510 History Of Rock/The Rockin' 60s.
(M) (2:08) Rhino 71728 '60s Rock Classics, Vol. 1.
(S) (2:15) Varese Sarabande 5575 Bubblegum Classics Volume Two. *(:08 longer fade than the 45 or LP; missing some overdubs)*
(M) (2:08) Flashback 72701 '60s Rock: Mony Mony.
(M) (2:08) Flashback 72088 '60s Rock Hits Box Set.
(M) (2:08) Flashback 72695 Hanky Panky And Other Hits.
(M) (2:08) Flashback 72087 '60s Rock Legends Box Set.
(M) (2:08) BMG Special Products 44762 The President's Greatest Hits.

1967 MIRAGE
(S) (2:36) Rhino 70920 Anthology. *(LP version)*
(S) (2:36) Pair 1278 Very Best Of. *(LP version)*
(S) (2:36) Rhino 71214 Very Best Of. *(LP version)*
(S) (2:35) Rhino 71026 Best Of/Rhino Special Editions. *(LP version)*
(S) (2:36) Varese Sarabande 5719 Bubblegum Classics Volume Three. *(LP version)*
(S) (2:36) Flashback 72696 Crimson And Clover And Other Hits. *(LP version)*

1967 I LIKE THE WAY
(S) (2:40) Rhino 70920 Anthology.
(S) (2:40) Pair 1278 Very Best Of.
(S) (2:40) Rhino 71214 Very Best Of.
(S) (2:40) Flashback 72695 Hanky Panky And Other Hits.
(S) (2:40) Flashback 72087 '60s Rock Legends Box Set.

1967 GETTIN' TOGETHER
(S) (2:13) Rhino 70920 Anthology.
(S) (2:13) Pair 1278 Very Best Of.
(S) (2:13) Rhino 71214 Very Best Of.
(S) (2:13) Flashback 72696 Crimson And Clover And Other Hits.

1967 OUT OF THE BLUE
(S) (2:23) Rhino 70920 Anthology.
(S) (2:23) Pair 1278 Very Best Of.
(S) (2:23) Rhino 71214 Very Best Of.
(S) (2:23) Flashback 72695 Hanky Panky And Other Hits.
(S) (2:23) Flashback 72087 '60s Rock Legends Box Set.

1968 GET OUT NOW
(S) (2:10) Rhino 70920 Anthology.
(S) (2:10) Pair 1278 Very Best Of.
(S) (2:10) Flashback 72696 Crimson And Clover And Other Hits.

1968 MONY MONY
(actual 45 time is (2:55) not (2:45) as stated on the record label)
(S) (2:51) Rhino 70629 Billboard's Top Rock & Roll Hits Of 1968.

(S) (2:51) Rhino 72005 Billboard's Top Rock & Roll Hits 1968-1972 Box Set.
(S) (2:50) Original Sound 8894 Dick Clark's 21 All-Time Hits Vol. 3.
(S) (2:51) Rhino 70906 American Bandstand Greatest Hits Collection.
(S) (2:49) DCC Compact Classics 029 Toga Rock. *(remixed)*
(S) (3:17) Rhino 75772 Son Of Frat Rock. *(:26 longer than either the LP or 45 version; remixed)*
(S) (2:50) Warner Special Products 27610 More Party Classics.
(S) (2:52) Rhino 70920 Anthology.
(S) (2:51) Essex 7052 All Time Rock Classics.
(S) (2:52) Rhino 71214 Very Best Of.
(S) (2:50) Rhino 71026 Best Of/Rhino Special Editions.
(S) (2:47) Time-Life 2CLR-11 Classic Rock - 1968: The Beat Goes On.
(S) (2:49) Tommy Boy 1100 ESPN Presents Jock Rock. *(sound effects added to the introduction)*
(S) (2:51) Rhino 71728 '60s Rock Classics, Vol. 1.
(S) (2:47) JCI 3126 1965 - Only Rock 'N Roll - 1969.
(S) (2:51) Rhino 72478 Beverly Hills 90210: Songs From The Peach Pit.
(S) (2:51) Eclipse Music Group 64871 Rock 'n Roll Relix 1968-1969.
(S) (2:51) Eclipse Music Group 64872 Rock 'n Roll Relix 1960-1969.
(S) (2:51) Flashback 72701 '60s Rock: Mony Mony.
(S) (2:51) Flashback 72088 '60s Rock Hits Box Set.
(S) (2:51) Flashback 72711 Sports Rock.
(S) (2:51) Flashback 72696 Crimson And Clover And Other Hits.
(S) (2:51) K-Tel 3913 Superstars Greatest Hits Volume 2.
(S) (2:51) Rhino 75200 Basketball's Greatest Hits.
(S) (3:19) Collectables 1515 and 2515 The Anniversary Album - The 60's. *(:28 longer than either the 45 or LP version; remixed)*

1968 DO SOMETHING TO ME
(S) (2:28) Rhino 70920 Anthology. *(neither the 45 or LP version)*
(S) (3:17) Rhino 70534 Crimson & Clover/Cellophane Symphony. *(LP version running (2:27) + (:50) LP coda)*
(S) (2:28) Pair 1278 Very Best Of. *(neither the 45 or LP version)*
(S) (2:28) Rhino 71214 Very Best Of. *(neither the 45 or LP version)*
(S) (2:28) Flashback 72695 Hanky Panky And Other Hits. *(neither the 45 or LP version)*
(S) (2:28) Flashback 72087 '60s Rock Legends Box Set. *(neither the 45 or LP version)*

1969 CRIMSON AND CLOVER
(S) (3:23) Rhino 70630 Billboard's Top Rock & Roll Hits Of 1969. *(a noble attempt at recreating the 45 version but unfortunately this is not the real 45 version)*
(S) (3:23) Rhino 72005 Billboard's Top Rock & Roll Hits 1968-1972 Box Set. *(a noble attempt at recreating the 45 version but unfortunately this is not the real 45 version)*
(S) (3:26) Original Sound 8895 Dick Clark's 21 All-Time Hits Vol. 4. *(45 version)*
(S) (3:26) K-Tel 686 Battle Of The Bands Volume 4. *(45 version)*
(S) (3:26) Rhino 70920 Anthology. *(45 version)*
(S) (5:30) Rhino 70534 Crimson & Clover/Cellophane Symphony. *(LP version with :07 of studio talk)*
(S) (3:27) Pair 1278 Very Best Of. *(45 version)*
(S) (3:26) Rhino 71214 Very Best Of. *(45 version)*
(S) (3:27) Special Music 5019 At Their Best. *(45 version)*
(S) (3:26) Rhino 71026 Best Of/Rhino Special Editions. *(45 version)*
(S) (5:09) Time-Life 2CLR-04 Classic Rock - 1968. *(LP version faded :14 early)*
(S) (3:21) Time-Life SUD-07 Superhits - 1969. *(a noble attempt at recreating the 45 version but unfortunately this is not the real 45 version)*

(S) (3:26) Collectables 2510 WCBS-FM History Of Rock - The Rockin' 60's. *(45 version)*

(S) (3:26) Collectables 4510 History Of Rock/The Rockin' 60s. *(45 version)*

(S) (3:26) Rhino 71729 '60s Rock Classics, Vol. 2. *(45 version)*

(S) (5:23) K-Tel 3183 Psychedelic Mind Trip. *(LP version)*

(S) (3:23) Eclipse Music Group 64871 Rock 'n Roll Relix 1968-1969. *(a noble attempt at recreating the 45 version but unfortunately this is not the real 45 version)*

(S) (3:23) Eclipse Music Group 64872 Rock 'n Roll Relix 1960-1969. *(a noble attempt at recreating the 45 version but unfortunately this is not the real 45 version)*

(S) (3:21) Time-Life AM1-01 AM Gold - 1969. *(a noble attempt at recreating the 45 version but unfortunately this is not the real 45 version)*

(S) (3:26) Flashback 72702 '60s Rock: The Beat Goes On. *(45 version)*

(S) (3:26) Flashback 72088 '60s Rock Hits Box Set. *(45 version)*

(S) (3:26) Flashback 72696 Crimson And Clover And Other Hits. *(45 version)*

(S) (3:21) K-Tel 3913 Superstars Greatest Hits Volume 2. *(a noble attempt at recreating the 45 version but unfortunately this is not the real 45 version)*

(S) (3:27) Varese Sarabande 5846 On The Radio Volume One. *(45 version)*

1969 SWEET CHERRY WINE
(dj copies of this 45 ran (4:22) not (3:59) as stated on the record label; commercial copies were all (4:14) not (4:25) as stated on the record label; the difference in time between the dj and commercial 45's is due to the fact that the dj copies were :08 slower in pitch)

(S) (4:28) Rhino 70920 Anthology. *(neither the LP or 45 version)*

(S) (4:19) Rhino 70534 Crimson & Clover/Cellophane Symphony. *(LP version)*

(S) (4:28) Pair 1278 Very Best Of. *(neither the 45 or LP version)*

(S) (4:28) Rhino 71214 Very Best Of. *(neither the 45 or LP version)*

(S) (4:28) Special Music 5019 At Their Best. *(neither the 45 or LP version)*

(S) (4:00) Time-Life 2CLR-12 Classic Rock - 1969: The Beat Goes On. *(45 version faded :14 early)*

(S) (4:18) Time-Life SUD-18 Superhits - Late 60's Classics. *(neither the 45 or LP version)*

(S) (4:27) Rhino 71939 Billboard Top Pop Hits, 1969. *(neither the 45 or LP version)*

(S) (4:18) Time-Life AM1-12 AM Gold - Late '60s Classics. *(neither the 45 or LP version)*

(S) (4:27) Flashback 72696 Crimson And Clover And Other Hits. *(neither the 45 or LP version)*

1969 CRYSTAL BLUE PERSUASION
(actual 45 time is (3:52) not (3:45) as stated on the record label)

(S) (4:01) Rhino 70920 Anthology. *(neither the 45 or LP version)*

(S) (4:01) Rhino 70534 Crimson & Clover/Cellophane Symphony. *(LP version)*

(S) (4:01) Pair 1278 Very Best Of. *(neither the 45 or LP version)*

(S) (4:01) Rhino 71214 Very Best Of. *(neither the 45 or LP version)*

(S) (4:01) Special Music 5019 At Their Best. *(neither the 45 or LP version)*

(S) (4:00) Original Sound 8863 Oldies But Goodies Vol. 13. *(neither the 45 or LP version)*

(S) (4:00) Original Sound 2223 Oldies But Goodies Volumes 2,7,9,12 and 13 Box Set. *(Volumes 2, 7 and 12 of this box set use the "Waring - fds" noise reduction process; neither the 45 or LP version)*

(S) (4:00) Original Sound 2500 Oldies But Goodies Volumes 1-15 Box Set. *(most volumes in this box set use the "Waring - fds" noise reduction process; neither the 45 or LP version)*

(S) (4:01) Rhino 71026 Best Of/Rhino Special Editions. *(neither the 45 or LP version)*

(E) (3:58) Time-Life 2CLR-06 Classic Rock - 1969. *(LP version)*

(S) (3:58) Time-Life SUD-14 Superhits - The Late 60's. *(neither the 45 or LP version)*

(S) (4:01) Rhino 71730 '60s Rock Classics, Vol. 3. *(neither the 45 or LP version)*

(S) (4:01) Thump 4730 Old School Love Songs Volume 3. *(neither the 45 or LP version)*

(S) (3:58) Time-Life AM1-14 AM Gold - The Late '60s. *(neither the 45 or LP version)*

(S) (4:01) Flashback 72703 '60s Rock: It's A Beautiful Morning. *(neither the 45 or LP version)*

(S) (4:01) Flashback 72088 '60s Rock Hits Box Set. *(neither the 45 or LP version)*

(S) (4:01) Flashback 72695 Hanky Panky And Other Hits. *(neither the 45 or LP version)*

(S) (4:01) Flashback 72087 '60s Rock Legends Box Set. *(neither the 45 or LP version)*

(S) (4:01) Varese Sarabande 5801 Sunshine Days - Pop Classics Of The '60s Volume 1. *(neither the 45 or LP version)*

1969 BALL OF FIRE
(45 length is (2:55); LP length is (2:47))

(S) (3:04) Rhino 70920 Anthology.

(S) (3:04) Pair 1278 Very Best Of.

(S) (3:04) Rhino 71214 Very Best Of.

(S) (3:03) Rhino 71026 Best Of/Rhino Special Editions.

(S) (3:04) Flashback 72695 Hanky Panky And Other Hits.

(S) (3:04) Flashback 72087 '60s Rock Legends Box Set.

1970 SHE

(S) (2:01) Rhino 70920 Anthology.

(S) (2:01) Pair 1278 Very Best Of.

(S) (2:01) Rhino 71214 Very Best Of.

(S) (1:59) Rhino 71026 Best Of/Rhino Special Editions.

(S) (2:01) Flashback 72696 Crimson And Clover And Other Hits.

1970 GOTTA GET BACK TO YOU

(S) (3:02) Rhino 70920 Anthology.

(S) (3:02) Pair 1278 Very Best Of.

(S) (3:02) Flashback 72695 Hanky Panky And Other Hits.

(S) (3:02) Flashback 72087 '60s Rock Legends Box Set.

1970 COME TO ME
(actual 45 and LP time is (2:35) not (2:56) as the LP label states or (2:31) as the 45 label states)

(S) (3:11) Rhino 70735 The Solo Years (1970 - 1981). *(:36 longer than the 45 or LP)*

(S) (2:35) Pair 1278 Very Best Of.

(S) (3:11) Flashback 72696 Crimson And Clover And Other Hits. *(:36 longer than the 45 or LP)*

released as by TOMMY JAMES:
1971 DRAGGIN' THE LINE
(dj copies of this 45 featured mono and stereo mixes of this song which were different; commercial copies of this 45 were the mono mix)

(S) (2:47) Rhino 70632 Billboard's Top Rock & Roll Hits Of 1971. *(LP mix)*

(S) (2:47) Rhino 72005 Billboard's Top Rock & Roll Hits 1968-1972 Box Set. *(LP mix)*

(S) (2:43) Rhino 70925 Super Hits Of The 70's Volume 5. *(LP mix)*

(S) (2:44) Rhino 70735 The Solo Years (1970 - 1981). *(LP mix)*

(S) (2:43) Rhino 70920 Tommy James & The Shondells Anthology. *(LP mix)*

(S) (2:44) Pair 1278 Very Best Of. *(LP mix)*

(S) (2:44) Rhino 71209 70's Smash Hits Volume 5. *(LP mix)*

(S) (2:44) Rhino 71214 Very Best Of. *(LP mix)*

(S) (2:43) Rhino 71026 Best Of/Rhino Special Editions. *(LP mix)*

(S) (2:45) Time-Life SUD-10 Superhits - 1971. *(LP mix)*

(S)   (2:42)   Time-Life SOD-12 Sounds Of The Seventies - 1971: Take Two. *(LP mix)*

(S)   (2:45)   Madacy Entertainment 1971 Rock On 1971. *(LP mix)*

(S)   (2:45)   Time-Life AM1-06 AM Gold - 1971. *(LP mix)*

(S)   (2:44)   Flashback 72685 '70s Radio Hits Volume 5. *(LP mix)*

(S)   (2:43)   Flashback 72695 Hanky Panky And Other Hits. *(LP mix)*

(S)   (2:43)   Flashback 72087 '60s Rock Legends Box Set. *(LP mix)*

1971 I'M COMIN' HOME

(S)   (2:02)   Rhino 70735 The Solo Years (1970 - 1981).

(S)   (2:03)   Pair 1278 Very Best Of.

1972 NOTHING TO HIDE

(S)   (2:39)   Rhino 70735 The Solo Years (1970 - 1981).

1980 THREE TIMES IN LOVE

(S)   (4:29)   Rhino 70735 The Solo Years (1970 - 1981). *(:20 longer than either the 45 or LP)*

(S)   (4:19)   Aura 20011/12 Discography: Deals & Demos 1974-1992. *(:10 longer than either the 45 or LP)*

(S)   (4:29)   Rhino 71891 Radio Daze: Pop Hits Of The 80's Volume Two. *(:20 longer than either the 45 or LP)*

JAMES GANG

1971 WALK AWAY

(S)   (2:50)   Rhino 70986 Heavy Metal Memories. *(45 version)*

(S)   (3:33)   MCA 31274 Classic Rock Volume 2. *(LP version)*

(S)   (3:31)   MCA 6012 15 Greatest Hits. *(LP version)*

(S)   (3:32)   One Way 22031 Thirds. *(LP version; tracks into next selection)*

(S)   (2:50)   Time-Life R105-24 Guitar Rock Monsters. *(45 version)*

(S)   (3:33)   MCA Special Products 20754 Classic Rock Volume 1. *(LP version)*

(S)   (3:32)   MCA 11233 Joe Walsh - Look What I Did/Anthology. *(LP version)*

(S)   (2:49)   Time-Life R968-11 Guitar Rock - The Early '70s. *(45 version)*

(S)   (3:32)   MCA Special Products 20956 Rockin' Guitars. *(LP version)*

(S)   (3:33)   MCA 11679 Joe Walsh's Greatest Hits. *(LP version)*

(S)   (3:32)   MCA Special Products 20284 Funk #49. *(LP version)*

JAMIES

1958 SUMMERTIME, SUMMERTIME

(S)   (1:59)   Rhino 70087 Summer & Sun.

(M)   (1:59)   Time-Life 2RNR-28 Rock 'N' Roll Era - The 50's Rave On.

(S)   (1:58)   K-Tel 3437 Summer Songs.

(S)   (1:58)   Eric 11502 Hard To Find 45's On CD (Volume I) 1955-60.

(S)   (1:58)   Nick At Nite/550 Music 63435 Beach Blanket Bash.

JAN & ARNIE

1958 JENNIE LEE

(S)   (1:57)   EMI 46885 Best Of Jan & Dean. *(rerecording)*

(M)   (2:01)   Time-Life 2RNR-21 Rock 'N' Roll Era - 1958 Still Rockin'.

(M)   (2:01)   Varese Sarabande 5590 Jan & Dean: Teen Suite 1958-1962.

(M)   (1:59)   One Way 18683 Jan & Dean: Anthology Album. *(pop at very beginning of song)*

(S)   (2:01)   EMI 53730 Jan & Dean: All The Hits - From Surf City To Drag City. *(this song was not originally recorded in stereo - the stereo effect on this cd was derived from synchronizing two different takes of this song)*

JAN & DEAN

1959 BABY TALK

(E)   (2:22)   Curb 77374 All Time Greatest Hits.

(E)   (2:23)   EMI 46885 Best Of Jan & Dean.

(M)   (2:25)   Essex 7053 A Hot Summer Night In '59.

(M)   (2:25)   Collectables 5069 History Of Rock Volume 9.

(M)   (2:24)   Time-Life 2RNR-20 Rock 'N' Roll Era - 1959 Still Rockin'.

(M)   (2:25)   Collectables 2500 WCBS-FM History Of Rock - The 60's Part 1.

(M)   (2:25)   Collectables 4500 History Of Rock/The 60s Part One.

(M)   (2:26)   Collectables 2605 WCBS-FM Jukebox Giants Vol. 3.

(M)   (2:25)   Varese Sarabande 5590 Teen Suite 1958-1962.

(E)   (2:22)   One Way 18838 Golden Hits Volumes 1, 2 & 3.

(M)   (2:24)   Era 5035 Jan & Dean.

(E)   (2:22)   One Way 18839 Drag City/Jan & Dean's Pop Symphony No. 1. *(incorrectly listed on the cd jacket as "SHE'S STILL TALKING BABY TALK")*

(M)   (2:23)   One Way 18683 Anthology Album.

(M)   (2:29)   EMI 53730 All The Hits - From Surf City To Drag City.

1961 HEART AND SOUL

(E)   (2:06)   Curb 77374 All Time Greatest Hits.

(E)   (2:06)   Original Sound 8859 Oldies But Goodies Vol. 9. *(this compact disc uses the "Waring - fds" noise reduction process)*

(E)   (2:06)   EMI 46885 Best Of Jan & Dean.

(M)   (2:07)   Varese Sarabande 5590 Teen Suite 1958-1962.

(E)   (2:06)   One Way 18838 Golden Hits Volumes 1, 2 & 3.

(M)   (2:06)   One Way 18683 Anthology Album.

(S)   (2:03)   EMI 53730 All The Hits - From Surf City To Drag City.

1963 LINDA

(S)   (2:33)   Curb 77374 All Time Greatest Hits.

(S)   (2:46)   EMI 92772 Legendary Masters Series. *(includes :11 of studio talk)*

(S)   (2:34)   One Way 18838 Golden Hits Volumes 1, 2 & 3.

(S)   (2:34)   One Way 18686 Take Linda Surfin'/Ride The Wild Surf.

(S)   (2:27)   One Way 18684 Dead Man's Curve/The New Girl In School/Popsicle.

(S)   (2:32)   One Way 18683 Anthology Album.

(S)   (2:44)   EMI 53730 All The Hits - From Surf City To Drag City. *(includes :09 of studio talk)*

1963 SURF CITY

(S)   (2:26)   Rhino 70624 Billboard's Top Rock & Roll Hits Of 1963.

(S)   (2:26)   Rhino 72007 Billboard's Top Rock & Roll Hits 1962-1966 Box Set.

(S)   (2:26)   JCI 3106 Surfin' Sixties.

(S)   (2:40)   EMI 92772 Legendary Masters Series. *(:14 longer than either the 45 or LP)*

(S)   (2:40)   EMI 96268 24 Greatest Hits Of All Time. *(:14 longer than either the 45 or LP)*

(S)   (2:26)   EMI 90604 Beach Party Blasts.

(S)   (2:26)   Curb 77355 60's Hits Volume 1.

(S)   (2:26)   Rhino 70089 Surfin' Hits.

(S)   (2:26)   Capitol 96861 Monster Summer Hits - Wild Surf.

(M)   (2:28)   Curb 77374 All Time Greatest Hits. *(rerecording)*

(S)   (2:40)   Capitol 98139 Spring Break Volume 2. *(:14 longer than either the 45 or LP)*

(S)   (2:25)   Rhino 71548 Let There Be Drums Volume 2: The 60's.

(S)   (2:25)   Time-Life 2RNR-07 Rock 'N' Roll Era - 1963.

(S)   (2:25)   Time-Life R962-04 History Of Rock 'N' Roll: California Pop 1963-1967.

(S)   (2:25)   JCI 3125 1960 - Only Rock 'N Roll - 1964.

(S)   (2:25)   One Way 18685 Surf City/Folk 'n Roll.

(S)   (2:26)   One Way 18838 Golden Hits Volumes 1, 2 & 3.

(S)   (2:25)   Rhino 72418 Cowabunga! The Surf Box.

(S)   (2:29)   One Way 18683 Anthology Album.

(M)   (2:29)   One Way 18688 Gotta Take That One Last Ride.

(S)   (2:36)   EMI 53730 All The Hits - From Surf City To Drag City. *(:10 longer than either the 45 or LP)*

(S)   (2:48)   EMI 53730 All The Hits - From Surf City To Drag City. *(instrumental track with backing vocals only)*

(E)   (2:27)   K-Tel 6256 Kahuna Classics. *(rerecording)*

(S)   (2:25)   Nick At Nite/550 Music 63435 Beach Blanket Bash.

(S)   (2:26)   I.D. 90072 Jenny McCarthy's Surfin' Safari.

JAN & DEAN *(Continued)*
1963 HONOLULU LULU
- (S) (2:12) Curb 77374 All Time Greatest Hits.
- (S) (2:16) EMI 92772 Legendary Masters Series.
- (S) (2:14) Time-Life 2RNR-46 Rock 'N' Roll Era - 60's Juke Box Memories.
- (S) (2:12) One Way 18685 Surf City/Folk 'n Roll.
- (S) (2:15) One Way 18838 Golden Hits Volumes 1, 2 & 3.
- (S) (2:10) One Way 18448 The Little Old Lady From Pasadena/Filet Of Soul. *(live)*
- (S) (2:15) One Way 18683 Anthology Album.
- (M) (2:15) One Way 18688 Gotta Take That One Last Ride.
- (S) (2:17) EMI 53730 All The Hits - From Surf City To Drag City.

1963 DRAG CITY
- (S) (2:17) EMI 90604 Beach Party Blasts. *(with stereo LP version sound effects)*
- (S) (2:15) Capitol 96862 Monster Summer Hits - Drag City. *(with stereo LP version sound effects)*
- (S) (2:18) Curb 77374 All Time Greatest Hits. *(with stereo LP version sound effects)*
- (S) (2:15) EMI 92772 Legendary Masters Series. *(with stereo LP version sound effects)*
- (S) (2:17) Compose 9927 Car And Driver/Greatest Car Songs. *(with stereo LP version sound effects)*
- (S) (2:13) Time-Life 2RNR-35 Rock 'N' Roll Era - The 60's Last Dance. *(with stereo LP version sound effects)*
- (S) (2:14) Time-Life 2CLR-16 Classic Rock - 1964: Shakin' All Over. *(with stereo LP version sound effects)*
- (S) (2:18) One Way 18839 Drag City/Pop Symphony No. 1. *(with stereo LP version sound effects)*
- (S) (2:14) One Way 18838 Golden Hits Volumes 1, 2 & 3. *(with stereo LP version sound effects)*
- (S) (2:14) One Way 18683 Anthology Album. *(with stereo LP version sound effects)*
- (M) (2:13) One Way 18688 Gotta Take That One Last Ride. *(45 and mono LP version sound effects)*
- (S) (2:34) EMI 53730 All The Hits - From Surf City To Drag City. *(with stereo LP version sound effects; :19 longer than either the 45 or LP)*
- (S) (2:30) EMI 53730 All The Hits - From Surf City To Drag City. *(instrumental track with backing vocals only)*
- (S) (2:27) Right Stuff 53316 Hot Rod Rock Volume 1: Rev It Up. *(with stereo LP version sound effects; :12 longer fade than either the 45 or LP)*

1964 DEAD MAN'S CURVE
(actual 45 time is (2:33) not (2:21) as stated on the record label)
- (S) (2:27) Capitol 96862 Monster Summer Hits - Drag City.
- (S) (2:44) Curb 77374 All Time Greatest Hits. *(noncharting version from the "Drag City" vinyl LP)*
- (S) (2:27) EMI 92772 Legendary Masters Series.
- (S) (2:28) Compose 9923 James Dean/Tribute To A Rebel.
- (S) (2:44) Compose 9927 Car And Driver/Greatest Car Songs. *(noncharting version from the "Drag City" vinyl LP)*
- (S) (2:28) Time-Life 2CLR-03 Classic Rock - 1964.
- (S) (2:27) Original Sound 8883 21 Legendary Superstars.
- (S) (2:27) DCC Compact Classics 078 Best Of Tragedy.
- (S) (2:44) One Way 18839 Drag City/Pop Symphony No. 1. *(noncharting version from the "Drag City" vinyl LP)*
- (S) (2:27) One Way 18838 Golden Hits Volumes 1, 2 & 3.
- (S) (2:50) One Way 18448 The Little Old Lady From Pasadena/Filet Of Soul. *(live)*
- (S) (2:28) One Way 18684 Dead Man's Curve/The New Girl In School/Popsicle.
- (S) (2:27) One Way 18683 Anthology Album.
- (S) (8:02) One Way 18683 Anthology Album. *(live)*
- (M) (2:39) One Way 18688 Gotta Take That One Last Ride.
- (S) (2:57) EMI 53730 All The Hits - From Surf City To Drag City. *(:24 longer than any previously released version)*
- (S) (3:01) EMI 53730 All The Hits - From Surf City To Drag City. *(instrumental track only)*
- (S) (2:27) JCI 3166 #1 Radio Hits 1960 - Only Rock 'n Roll - 1964.

- (S) (2:27) Right Stuff 53316 Hot Rod Rock Volume 1: Rev It Up.
- (E) (2:25) K-Tel 6256 Kahuna Classics. *(rerecording)*

1964 THE NEW GIRL IN SCHOOL
- (S) (3:03) EMI 92772 Legendary Masters Series. *(with :08 of studio talk and :27 longer ending than either the 45 or LP)*
- (S) (2:54) One Way 18838 Golden Hits Volumes 1, 2 & 3. *(:26 longer ending than either the 45 or LP)*
- (S) (2:23) One Way 18684 Dead Man's Curve/The New Girl In School/Popsicle.
- (S) (2:54) One Way 18683 Anthology Album. *(:26 longer ending than either the 45 or LP)*
- (S) (3:00) EMI 53730 All The Hits - From Surf City To Drag City. *(:32 longer ending than either the 45 or LP)*

1964 THE LITTLE OLD LADY (FROM PASADENA)
- (S) (2:22) Rhino 70625 Billboard's Top Rock & Roll Hits Of 1964.
- (S) (2:22) Rhino 72007 Billboard's Top Rock & Roll Hits 1962-1966 Box Set.
- (S) (2:42) Capitol 96862 Monster Summer Hits - Drag City. *(:17 longer than either the LP or 45)*
- (S) (2:22) Curb 77374 All Time Greatest Hits.
- (S) (2:42) EMI 92772 Legendary Masters Series. *(:17 longer ending than either the LP or 45)*
- (S) (2:42) EMI 80055 Ride The Wild Surf/The Little Old Lady From Pasadena. *(:17 longer ending than either the 45 or LP)*
- (S) (2:41) EMI 80055 Ride The Wild Surf/The Little Old Lady From Pasadena. *(:16 longer ending than either the 45 or LP; alternate take with extra verse included)*
- (S) (2:41) Time-Life 2RNR-10 Rock 'N' Roll Era - 1964. *(:16 longer ending than either the 45 or LP)*
- (S) (2:41) One Way 18838 Golden Hits Volumes 1, 2 & 3. *(:16 longer than either the 45 or LP)*
- (S) (2:22) One Way 18448 The Little Old Lady From Pasadena/Filet Of Soul.
- (S) (2:41) One Way 18683 Anthology Album. *(:16 longer than either the 45 or LP)*
- (M) (2:30) One Way 18688 Gotta Take That One Last Ride.
- (S) (2:45) EMI 53730 All The Hits - From Surf City To Drag City. *(:20 longer than either the 45 or LP)*
- (S) (2:40) EMI 53730 All The Hits - From Surf City To Drag City. *(alternate take with extra verse included)*
- (S) (2:23) Priority 50951 I Love Rock & Roll Volume 2: Hits Of The 60's.
- (S) (2:25) K-Tel 6256 Kahuna Classics. *(rerecording)*

1964 RIDE THE WILD SURF
- (S) (2:17) Rhino 70089 Surfin' Hits.
- (M) (2:15) JCI 3106 Surfin' Sixties.
- (S) (2:16) Capitol 96861 Monster Summer Hits - Wild Surf.
- (S) (2:18) Curb 77374 All Time Greatest Hits.
- (S) (2:21) EMI 92772 Legendary Masters Series. *(with :05 countoff)*
- (S) (2:15) EMI 80055 Ride The Wild Surf/The Little Old Lady From Pasadena.
- (S) (2:16) One Way 18838 Golden Hits Volumes 1, 2 & 3.
- (S) (2:17) One Way 18686 Take Linda Surfin'/Ride The Wild Surf.
- (S) (2:16) One Way 18683 Anthology Album.
- (M) (2:16) One Way 18688 Gotta Take That One Last Ride.
- (S) (2:15) EMI 53730 All The Hits - From Surf City To Drag City.
- (S) (2:15) EMI 53730 All The Hits - From Surf City To Drag City. *(instrumental track with backing vocals only)*

1964 SIDEWALK SURFIN'
- (S) (2:15) Capitol 96861 Monster Summer Hits - Wild Surf. *(LP version)*
- (S) (2:34) EMI 92772 Legendary Masters Series. *(45 version but :14 longer)*
- (S) (2:34) EMI 80055 Ride The Wild Surf/The Little Old Lady From Pasadena. *(45 version but :14 longer)*
- (S) (2:33) One Way 18838 Golden Hits Volumes 1, 2 & 3. *(45 version but :13 longer)*

(S) (2:15) One Way 18448 The Little Old Lady From Pasadena/Filet Of Soul. *(LP version)*
(S) (2:15) One Way 18686 Take Linda Surfin'/Ride The Wild Surf. *(LP version)*
(S) (2:33) One Way 18683 Anthology Album. *(45 version but :13 longer)*
(M) (2:18) One Way 18688 Gotta Take That One Last Ride. *(45 version)*
(S) (2:40) EMI 53730 All The Hits - From Surf City To Drag City. *(45 version but :20 longer and missing some skateboard sound effects in the middle of the song)*

1965 YOU REALLY KNOW HOW TO HURT A GUY
(S) (3:18) EMI 92772 Legendary Masters Series.
(S) (3:18) One Way 18838 Golden Hits Volumes 1, 2 & 3.
(S) (3:18) EMI 53730 All The Hits - From Surf City To Drag City.
(S) (3:44) EMI 53730 All The Hits - From Surf City To Drag City. *(alternate take)*

1965 I FOUND A GIRL
(S) (2:31) EMI 92772 Legendary Masters Series.
(S) (2:23) One Way 18685 Surf City/Folk 'n Roll.
(S) (2:37) One Way 18448 The Little Old Lady From Pasadena/Filet Of Soul. *(live)*
(S) (2:37) EMI 53730 All The Hits - From Surf City To Drag City.

1966 POPSICLE
(this song originally appeared on the "Drag City" vinyl LP where it was titled "POPSICLE" on the LP jacket but "POPSICLE TRUCK" on the actual record label)
(S) (2:33) EMI 92772 Legendary Masters Series. *(LP length)*
(S) (2:32) One Way 18839 Drag City/Pop Symphony No. 1. *(LP length; cd title is "POPSICLE TRUCK")*
(S) (2:32) One Way 18684 Dead Man's Curve/The New Girl In School/Popsicle. *(LP length)*
(S) (2:33) One Way 18683 Anthology Album. *(LP length)*
(M) (2:22) One Way 18688 Gotta Take That One Last Ride. *(45 length)*
(S) (2:37) EMI 53730 All The Hits - From Surf City To Drag City. *(LP length)*
(S) (2:39) EMI 53730 All The Hits - From Surf City To Drag City. *(alternate take)*

HORST JANKOWSKI
1965 A WALK IN THE BLACK FOREST
(S) (2:48) Time-Life HPD-34 Your Hit Parade - 60's Instrumentals.
(S) (2:31) Polygram Special Markets 314520273 Great Instrumental Hits. *(rerecording)*
(S) (2:48) Collectors' Choice 003/4 Instrumental Gems Of The 60's.
(S) (2:48) Time-Life R986-22 Instrumental Classics - Pop Classics.

JARMELS
1961 A LITTLE BIT OF SOAP
(S) (2:11) Collectables 5044 14 Golden Classics.
(S) (2:10) Collectables 5067 History Of Rock Volume 7.
(S) (2:09) Ripete 2200 Ocean Drive Volume 3.
(S) (2:10) Time-Life 2RNR-18 Rock 'N' Roll Era - 1961 Still Rockin'.
(M) (2:11) Time-Life R962-08 History Of Rock 'N' Roll: Sound Of The City 1959-1965.
(S) (2:09) Time-Life R102-17 Lost Treasures Of Rock 'N' Roll.
(S) (2:13) Collectables 2505 History Of Rock - The 60's Part 5.
(S) (2:13) Collectables 4505 History Of Rock/The 60s Part Five.
(S) (2:09) Time-Life R857-19 The Heart Of Rock 'n' Roll 1960-1961 Take Three.

AL JARREAU
1981 WE'RE IN THIS LOVE TOGETHER
(S) (3:44) Warner Brothers 3576 Breakin' Away.
(S) (3:44) Warner Brothers 46454 Best Of.
(S) (3:44) Time-Life R834-10 Body Talk - From The Heart.

released as by JARREAU:
1983 MORNIN'
(S) (4:13) Warner Brothers 23801 Jarreau.
(S) (4:13) Warner Brothers 46454 Best Of.
released as by AL JARREAU:
1987 MOONLIGHTING (THEME)
(S) (3:01) MCA 6214 Moonlighting - The Television Soundtrack Album.
(S) (3:01) Warner Brothers 46454 Best Of.

JARS OF CLAY
1996 FLOOD
(S) (3:30) Silvertone 41580 Jars Of Clay.

JAY & THE AMERICANS
1962 SHE CRIED
(S) (2:53) EMI 93448 Come A Little Bit Closer: Best Of. *(time includes :17 of studio talk)*
(S) (2:35) Time-Life 2RNR-02 Rock 'N' Roll Era - 1962.
(S) (2:35) Time-Life SUD-06 Superhits - 1962.
(S) (2:36) Curb 77678 Greatest Hits.
(S) (2:35) Time-Life AM1-18 AM Gold - 1962.
(S) (2:36) Time-Life R857-17 The Heart Of Rock 'n' Roll: The Early '60s.
(S) (2:36) JCI 3184 1960 - Only Love - 1964.

1963 ONLY IN AMERICA
(S) (1:58) EMI 48384 Greatest Hits.
(S) (2:01) EMI 93448 Come A Little Bit Closer: Best Of.
(M) (2:07) Rhino 70593 The Rock 'N' Roll Classics Of Leiber & Stoller. *(slightly slower in pitch than the 45; much slower in pitch than the LP)*
(S) (2:01) Era 5025 The Brill Building Sound.
(S) (2:00) Time-Life 2RNR-42 Rock 'N' Roll Era - The 60's Sock Hop.
(S) (2:00) MCA 11238 God Bless The U.S.A.

1964 COME A LITTLE BIT CLOSER
(E) (2:44) EMI 48384 Greatest Hits.
(M) (2:45) EMI 93448 Come A Little Bit Closer: Best Of.
(M) (2:44) Time-Life 2CLR-03 Classic Rock - 1964.
(M) (2:43) Time-Life SUD-09 Superhits - 1964.
(M) (2:45) Curb 77678 Greatest Hits.
(M) (2:45) Varese Sarabande 5670 Songs Of Tommy Boyce And Bobby Hart.
(M) (2:43) Time-Life AM1-11 AM Gold - 1964.

1965 LET'S LOCK THE DOOR (AND THROW AWAY THE KEY)
(S) (2:29) EMI 93448 Come A Little Bit Closer: Best Of.
(S) (2:25) Time-Life 2RNR-46 Rock 'N' Roll Era - 60's Juke Box Memories.

1965 CARA MIA
(S) (2:30) EMI 48384 Greatest Hits.
(S) (2:32) EMI 93448 Come A Little Bit Closer: Best Of.
(S) (2:31) Time-Life SUD-17 Superhits - Mid 60's Classics.
(S) (2:31) Curb 77678 Greatest Hits.
(S) (2:32) Rhino 72577 Eh, Paisano! Italian-American Classics.
(S) (2:31) Time-Life AM1-16 AM Gold - Mid '60s Classics.
(S) (2:31) Time-Life R857-20 The Heart Of Rock 'n' Roll 1965-1966.
(S) (2:31) Collectables 1515 and 2515 The Anniversary Album - The 60's.

1965 SOME ENCHANTED EVENING
(E) (2:12) EMI 48384 Greatest Hits.
(S) (2:16) EMI 93448 Come A Little Bit Closer: Best Of.
(S) (2:11) Curb 77678 Greatest Hits.

1965 SUNDAY AND ME
(S) (2:55) EMI 93448 Come A Little Bit Closer: Best Of. *(includes :32 of studio talk)*
(S) (2:21) Curb 77678 Greatest Hits.

1966 CRYING
(S) (3:08) EMI 93448 Come A Little Bit Closer: Best Of. *(includes :31 of studio talk and a false start)*

1969 THIS MAGIC MOMENT
(S) (3:02) EMI 96268 24 Greatest Hits Of All Time.
(S) (3:02) EMI 93448 Come A Little Bit Closer: Best Of.
(S) (3:02) Capitol 98139 Spring Break Volume 2. *(truncated fade)*
(S) (3:01) EMI 80244 Sands Of Time/Wax Museum.

JAY & THE AMERICANS *(Continued)*
- (S) (2:56) Time-Life SUD-07 Superhits - 1969.
- (S) (3:02) Curb 77678 Greatest Hits.
- (S) (3:01) Nick At Nite/550 Music/Epic 67768 Fonzie's Make Out Music.
- (S) (2:55) Time-Life AM1-01 AM Gold - 1969.
- (S) (3:01) Time-Life R857-22 The Heart Of Rock 'n' Roll 1967-1969.
- (S) (2:56) Time-Life R814-02 Love Songs.

1970 WALKIN' IN THE RAIN
- (S) (2:46) EMI 93448 Come A Little Bit Closer: Best Of.
- (S) (2:48) EMI 80244 Sands Of Time/Wax Museum.
- (S) (2:47) Varese Sarabande 5534 Rhythm Of The Rain.
- (S) (2:47) Curb 77678 Greatest Hits.

JAY and THE TECHNIQUES
1967 APPLES, PEACHES, PUMPKIN PIE
- (S) (2:24) Mercury 834216 45's On CD Volume 3.
- (S) (2:17) Rhino 71195 Kid Rock! *(rerecording)*
- (S) (2:23) Time-Life 2CLR-15 Classic Rock - 1967: Shakin' All Over.
- (S) (2:25) Collectables 5621 Apples, Peaches, Pumpkin Pie.
- (S) (2:24) Special Music 5026 Let It All Hang Out - 60's Party Hits.
- (S) (2:24) K-Tel 3130 60's Sound Explosion.
- (S) (2:25) Mercury 314526838 Best Of.
- (S) (2:23) JCI 3167 #1 Radio Hits 1965 - Only Rock 'n Roll - 1969.
- (S) (2:24) Time-Life 2CLR-31 Classic Rock - Totally Fantastic '60s.

1967 KEEP THE BALL ROLLIN'
- (S) (3:03) Collectables 5621 Apples, Peaches, Pumpkin Pie.
- (S) (3:03) Mercury 314526838 Best Of.
- (S) (3:06) Varese Sarabande 5718 Soulful Pop.
- (S) (3:06) Varese Sarabande 5890 Bubblegum Classics Volume Four - Soulful Pop.

1968 STRAWBERRY SHORTCAKE
- (S) (2:29) Collectables 5621 Apples, Peaches, Pumpkin Pie.
- (S) (2:41) Mercury 314526838 Best Of. *(:12 longer than the 45 or LP)*

JERRY JAYE
1967 MY GIRL JOSEPHINE
- (M) (1:55) EMI-Capitol Special Markets 19552 Lost Hits Of The '60s.

JAYHAWKS
1956 STRANDED IN THE JUNGLE
- (M) (2:48) Relic 7062 Golden Era Of Doo-Wops: Flash Records.

JAYNETTES
1963 SALLY GO 'ROUND THE ROSES
(actual 45 time is (3:02) not (2:38) as stated on the record label)
- (M) (3:14) Rhino 70988 Best Of The Girl Groups Volume 1. *(neither the LP or 45 version)*
- (S) (3:12) Chess 31320 Best Of Chess Rock 'n' Roll Volume 2. *(missing an organ overdub; :09 longer fade than the 45 or LP)*
- (S) (3:11) Original Sound 8858 Oldies But Goodies Vol. 8. *(this compact disc uses the "Waring - fds" noise reduction process; missing an organ overdub; :09 longer fade than the 45 or LP)*
- (S) (3:11) Original Sound 2222 Oldies But Goodies Volumes 1,4,6,8 and 10 Box Set. *(this box set uses the "Waring - fds" noise reduction process; missing an organ overdub; :09 longer fade than the 45 or LP)*
- (S) (3:11) Original Sound 2500 Oldies But Goodies Volumes 1-15 Box Set. *(this box set uses the "Waring - fds" noise reduction process; missing an organ overdub; L09 longer fade than the 45 or LP)*
- (S) (3:11) Original Sound CDGO-8 Golden Oldies Volume. 8. *(missing an organ overdub; :08 longer fade than the 45 or LP)*

- (S) (3:11) Original Sound 9602 Best Of Oldies But Goodies Vol. 2. *(missing an organ overdub; 08 longer fade than the 45 or LP)*
- (S) (3:12) MCA 31203 Vintage Music Volume 6. *(missing an organ overdub; :09 longer fade than the 45 or LP)*
- (S) (3:12) MCA 5804 Vintage Music Volumes 5 & 6. *(missing an organ overdub; :09 longer fade than the 45 or LP)*
- (M) (3:02) Time-Life 2RNR-07 Rock 'N' Roll Era - 1963.
- (M) (2:58) Time-Life RHD-02 Rhythm & Blues - 1963.
- (M) (2:59) Rhino 71584 Billboard Top Pop Hits, 1963.
- (M) (2:57) Chess 9352 Chess Rhythm & Roll.
- (S) (3:12) MCA Special Products 22172 Vintage Collectibles Volume 10. *(missing an organ overdub; :09 longer fade than the 45 or LP)*
- (M) (3:01) Curb 77773 Hard To Find Hits Of Rock 'N' Roll Volume One.
- (M) (2:58) Time-Life R838-14 Solid Gold Soul - 1963.
- (M) (3:01) K-Tel 3888 Great R&B Female Groups Hits Of The 60's.

JEFFERSON
1970 BABY TAKE ME IN YOUR ARMS
- (S) (2:36) Collectables 0568 Best Of The Rockin' Berries Featuring Jefferson.
- (M) (2:40) Varese Sarabande 5535 Bubblegum Classics Volume One.

JEFFERSON AIRPLANE
1967 SOMEBODY TO LOVE
- (S) (2:57) RCA 8474 Nipper's Greatest Hits Of The 60's Volume 1.
- (S) (2:59) RCA 3766 Surrealistic Pillow.
- (S) (2:58) RCA 5724 2400 Fulton Street.
- (S) (2:55) RCA 4459 Worst Of.
- (S) (2:55) RCA 2078 White Rabbit & Other Hits.
- (S) (2:57) RCA 61110 Loves You.
- (S) (2:58) Elektra 60873 O.S.T. Rude Awakening.
- (S) (2:57) RCA 66197 Best Of.
- (S) (2:57) Time-Life 2CLR-05 Classic Rock - 1967.
- (S) (2:57) RCA 66598 Surrealistic Pillow. *(gold disc)*
- (M) (2:56) RCA 66598 Surrealistic Pillow. *(gold disc)*
- (S) (2:54) MCA 11241 O.S.T. Apollo 13. *(all selections on this cd are segued together; track selection numbers on the cd jacket are incorrect; this cd is a disaster)*
- (S) (2:57) RCA 66862 Hi Octane Hard Drivin' Hits.
- (S) (2:55) Priority 50951 I Love Rock & Roll Volume 2: Hits Of The 60's.
- (S) (2:56) RCA 67420 Worst Of. *(remastered edition)*
- (S) (2:57) Time-Life R13610 Gold And Platinum Box Set - The Ultimate Rock Collection.
- (S) (2:55) Thump 6020 Easyriders Volume 2.

1967 WHITE RABBIT
- (S) (2:30) Atlantic 81742 O.S.T. Platoon.
- (S) (2:32) RCA 3766 Surrealistic Pillow.
- (S) (2:32) RCA 5724 2400 Fulton Street.
- (S) (2:31) RCA 4459 Worst Of.
- (S) (2:31) RCA 2078 White Rabbit & Other Hits.
- (S) (2:32) Pair 1090 Time Machine.
- (S) (2:32) RCA 61110 Loves You.
- (S) (2:22) RCA 61110 Loves You. *(live)*
- (S) (2:32) RCA 66197 Best Of.
- (S) (2:32) RCA 66598 Surrealistic Pillow. *(gold disc)*
- (M) (2:30) RCA 66598 Surrealistic Pillow. *(gold disc)*
- (S) (2:32) Buddah 49507 Psychedelic Pop.
- (S) (2:31) RCA 67420 Worst Of. *(remastered edition)*
- (S) (2:31) London 458556 O.S.T. The Game.
- (S) (3:12) Geffen 25218 O.S.T. Fear And Loathing In Las Vegas. *(time includes :40 of movie dialogue; all songs and the movie dialogue are segued together)*

1967 BALLAD OF YOU & ME & POONEIL
- (S) (4:35) RCA 5724 2400 Fulton Street. *(tracks into next selection)*
- (S) (4:38) RCA 4459 Worst Of.

(S) (4:37) RCA 4545 *After Bathing At Baxter's. (LP version which tracks into "A SMALL PACKAGE OF VALUE WILL COME TO YOU SHORTLY" and "YOUNG GIRL SUNDAY BLUES" for a total time of (9:42))*

(S) (11:38) RCA 61110 *Loves You. (live)*

(S) (4:29) RCA 66798 *After Bathing At Baxter's. (remastered editioin; tracks into next selection; LP version)*

(S) (4:34) RCA 67420 *Worst Of. (remastered edition)*

JEFFERSON STARSHIP (also STARSHIP)
1975 MIRACLES
(S) (6:51) RCA 9684 and 8476 *Nipper's Greatest Hits - The 70's. (LP version)*

(S) (6:53) Rhino 70968 *Marty Balin: Balince. (LP version)*

(S) (3:31) Razor & Tie 4543 *The '70s Preservation Society Presents: Easy '70s. (45 version)*

(S) (3:31) RCA 3247 *Gold. (45 version)*

(S) (6:51) RCA 0999 and 66875 *Red Octopus. (LP version)*

(S) (3:31) RCA 66231 *At Their Best. (45 version)*

(S) (3:30) K-Tel 3639 *Dim The Lights - Soft Rock Hits Of The 70's. (45 version)*

(S) (6:51) Priority 50952 *I Love Rock & Roll Volume 3: Hits Of The 70's. (LP version)*

(S) (3:31) Time-Life R834-07 *Body Talk - Hearts In Motion. (45 version)*

(S) (3:29) K-Tel 4017 *70s Heavy Hitters: Summer Love. (45 version)*

(S) (3:31) Time-Life R13610 *Gold And Platinum Box Set - The Ultimate Rock Collection. (45 version)*

(S) (6:51) RCA 67560 *Gold. (remastered edition; LP version)*

(S) (3:31) Hip-O 40095 *'70s Hit(s) Back. (45 version)*

(S) (3:31) Time-Life R814-05 *Love Songs. (45 version)*

1976 WITH YOUR LOVE
(S) (3:34) RCA 3247 *Gold.*

(S) (3:34) RCA 66876 *Spitfire.*

(S) (3:34) RCA 67560 *Gold. (remastered edition)*

1978 COUNT ON ME
(S) (3:14) RCA 3247 *Gold.*

(S) (3:13) RCA 66231 *At Their Best.*

(S) (3:14) JCI 3131 *1975 - Only Rock 'N Roll - 1979.*

(S) (3:14) RCA 66878 *Earth.*

(S) (3:14) Priority 50991 *The Best Of The 70's - Rock Chart Toppers.*

(S) (3:14) RCA 67560 *Gold. (remastered edition)*

(S) (3:14) Time-Life R834-19 *Body Talk - Always And Forever.*

1978 RUNAWAY
(S) (3:42) RCA 3247 *Gold. (45 version)*

(S) (5:20) RCA 66878 *Earth. (LP version)*

(S) (5:21) RCA 67560 *Gold. (remastered edition; LP version)*

1979 JANE
(dj copies of this 45 ran (3:40) and (4:00); commercial copies were all (4:00))

(S) (4:10) RCA 3452 and 66877 *Freedom At Point Zero. (LP version)*

(S) (4:09) RCA 66231 *At Their Best. (LP version)*

(S) (4:08) RCA 2423 *Starship - Greatest Hits (1979-1991). (LP version)*

1981 FIND YOUR WAY BACK
(S) (4:13) RCA 66231 *At Their Best. (LP version)*

(S) (4:14) RCA 2423 *Starship - Greatest Hits (1979-1991). (LP version)*

(S) (4:13) Rhino 72594 *Billboard Top Album Rock Hits, 1981. (LP version)*

(S) (4:13) Simitar 55502 *The Number One's: Classic Rock. (LP version)*

1983 BE MY LADY
(S) (3:49) RCA 4372 *Winds Of Change.*

1983 WINDS OF CHANGE
(S) (3:50) RCA 4372 *Winds Of Change.*

1984 NO WAY OUT
(S) (4:21) RCA 2423 *Starship - Greatest Hits (1979-1991).*

released as by STARSHIP:
1985 WE BUILT THIS CITY
(dj copies of this 45 ran (4:17) and included some dj rap on one side and excluded the dj rap on the other side; commercial copies were all (4:49) and included the dj rap)

(S) (4:48) Priority 53715 *80's Greatest Rock Hits Volume 3 - Arena Rock.*

(S) (4:48) RCA 9970 *Nipper's Greatest Hits - The 80's.*

(S) (4:54) Rhino 71640 *Billboard Top Hits - 1985.*

(S) (4:54) Grunt/RCA 5488 *Knee Deep In The Hoopla.*

(S) (4:36) RCA 2423 *Starship - Greatest Hits (1979-1991). (previously unreleased version)*

(S) (4:52) Time-Life R988-02 *Sounds Of The Eighties: 1985.*

(S) (4:50) RCA 66862 *Hi Octane Hard Drivin' Hits.*

(S) (4:50) RCA 67474 *Roller Hockey - The Album.*

(S) (4:52) K-Tel 3997 *Arena Rock - The 80's.*

(S) (4:36) Simitar 55142 *80's Rock Classics - Party Town. (previously unreleased version)*

1986 SARA
(S) (4:20) Rhino 71641 *Billboard Top Hits - 1986. (45 version)*

(S) (4:16) Time-Life R105-40 *Rock Dreams. (45 version)*

(S) (4:16) JCI 3119 *18 Rock Classics. (45 version)*

(S) (4:51) Grunt/RCA 5488 *Knee Deep In The Hoopla. (LP version)*

(S) (4:50) RCA 2423 *Starship - Greatest Hits (1979-1991). (LP version)*

(S) (4:48) RCA 66202 *Best Of Starship. (LP version)*

(S) (4:20) Time-Life R988-04 *Sounds Of The Eighties: 1986. (45 version)*

(S) (4:15) JCI 3186 *1985 - Only Love - 1989. (45 version)*

(S) (4:50) Hip-O 40080 *Essential '80s: 1985-1989. (LP version)*

(S) (4:20) Time-Life R834-12 *Body Talk - By Candlelight. (45 version)*

1986 TOMORROW DOESN'T MATTER TONIGHT
(S) (3:41) Grunt/RCA 5488 *Knee Deep In The Hoopla.*

1987 NOTHING'S GONNA STOP US NOW
(S) (4:20) Columbia 44381 *Heart Of Rock.*

(S) (4:31) Rhino 71642 *Billboard Top Hits - 1987.*

(S) (4:27) Grunt/RCA 6413 *No Protection.*

(S) (4:27) RCA 2423 *Starship - Greatest Hits (1979-1991).*

(S) (4:28) RCA 66202 *Best Of Starship.*

(S) (4:30) Time-Life R988-09 *Sounds Of The Eighties: 1987.*

(S) (4:28) RCA 66812 *Do You Love Me? (All-Time Best Love Songs).*

(S) (4:31) Priority 50974 *Premiere The Movie Magazine Presents The Greatest Soundtrack Hits.*

(S) (4:31) Time-Life R834-19 *Body Talk - Always And Forever.*

1987 IT'S NOT OVER ('TIL IT'S OVER)
(S) (4:16) Grunt/RCA 6413 *No Protection.*

(S) (4:13) RCA 2423 *Starship - Greatest Hits (1979-1991).*

(S) (4:14) RCA 66202 *Best Of Starship.*

1989 IT'S NOT ENOUGH
(dj copies of this 45 ran (4:23) and (4:51))

(S) (4:49) RCA 9693 *Love Among The Cannibals.*

(S) (4:43) RCA 2423 *Starship - Greatest Hits (1979-1991).*

(S) (4:48) RCA 66202 *Best Of Starship.*

JOE JEFFREY GROUP
1969 MY PLEDGE OF LOVE
(S) (2:44) Rhino 75774 *Soul Shots. (this song begins in mono but ends in true stereo!)*

(S) (2:40) Capricorn 42003 *The Scepter Records Story. (this song begins in electronic stereo but ends in true stereo!)*

(S) (2:44) Ripete 0001 *Coolin' Out/24 Carolina Classics Volume 1. (this song begins in mono but ends in true stereo!)*

(S) (2:43) Time-Life 2CLR-20 *Classic Rock - 1969: Shakin' All Over. (this song begins in mono but ends in true stereo!)*

(S) (2:44) LaserLight 12318 *Chart Busters. (this song begins in electronic stereo but ends in true stereo!)*

(M) (2:44) Rhino 72815 *Beg, Scream & Shout! The Big Ol' Box Of '60s Soul.*

JELLYBEAN
1986 SIDEWALK TALK
- (S) (3:58) EMI 27674 Living In Oblivion: The 80's Greatest Hits Volume Three.
- (S) (6:06) Chrysalis 21652 and 41652 Rocks The House. *(12" single version)*
- (S) (3:57) Right Stuff 56197 Free To Be Volume 7.
- (S) (3:54) Priority 50940 Shut Up And Dance! The 80's Volume One. *(all selections on this cd are segued together)*

released as by JELLYBEAN/ELISA FIORILLO:
1987 WHO FOUND WHO
- (S) (4:47) Chrysalis 21569 and 41569 Just Visiting This Planet. *(LP version)*
- (S) (6:40) Chrysalis 21652 and 41652 Rocks The House. *(12" single version)*
- (S) (6:15) Priority 53731 80's Greatest Rock Hits Volume 10 - Dance All Night. *(edit of 12" single version)*
- (S) (6:40) Right Stuff 52288 Free To Be Volume 4. *(12" single version)*

JELLY BEANS
1964 I WANNA LOVE HIM SO BAD
- (M) (2:43) Rhino 75891 Wonder Women. *(with handclaps overdubbed)*
- (M) (2:42) Rhino 70988 Best Of The Girl Groups Volume 1. *(with handclaps overdubbed)*
- (M) (2:42) Era 5025 The Brill Building Sound. *(with handclaps overdubbed)*
- (M) (2:41) Time-Life 2CLR-09 Classic Rock - 1964: The Beat Goes On. *(with handclaps overdubbed)*
- (M) (2:41) Time-Life R962-08 History Of Rock 'N' Roll: Sound Of The City 1959-1965. *(with handclaps overdubbed)*
- (M) (2:41) Collectables 2505 History Of Rock - The 60's Part 5. *(with handclaps overdubbed)*
- (M) (2:41) Collectables 4505 History Of Rock/The 60s Part Five. *(with handclaps overdubbed)*
- (E) (2:43) Collectables 5740 Jelly Beans And Friends.
- (S) (2:49) Taragon 1029 Very Best Of Red Bird/Blue Cat Records. *(remix)*

WAYLON JENNINGS
released as by WAYLON & WILLIE (WAYLON JENNINGS & WILLIE NELSON):
1976 GOOD HEARTED WOMAN
- (S) (3:00) RCA 58400 Waylon Jennings: Collector's Series. *(Waylon Jennings solo effort - not the hit version)*
- (S) (2:58) RCA 3378 and 8506 Waylon Jennings Greatest Hits. *(this is the hit duet version)*
- (S) (2:53) Columbia 37542 Willie Nelson - Greatest Hits (And Some That Will Be). *(Willie Nelson solo effort - not the hit version)*
- (S) (2:58) Time-Life CCD-18 Contemporary Country - The Early 70's Hot Hits. *(Waylon Jennings solo effort - not the hit version)*
- (S) (3:00) RCA 66299 Waylon Jennings - Only Daddy That'll Walk The Line. *(Waylon Jennings solo effort - not the hit version)*
- (S) (2:59) RCA 66849 Waylon Jennings - Super Hits. *(Waylon Jennings solo effort - not the hit version)*
- (S) (3:00) RCA 66857 Waylon Jennings - Essential. *(Waylon Jennings solo effort - not the hit version)*
- (S) (2:56) Time-Life R990-10 Willie Nelson - Legendary Country Singers. *(this is the hit duet version)*
- (S) (3:00) Time-Life R990-15 Waylon Jennings - Legendary Country Singers. *(Waylon Jennings solo effort - not the hit version)*
- (S) (3:00) Hip-O 40086 The Class Of Country 1975-1979. *(Waylon Jennings solo effort - not the hit version)*

released as by WAYLON JENNINGS:
1977 LUCKENBACH, TEXAS (BACK TO THE BASICS OF LOVE)
- (S) (3:19) RCA 3378 and 8506 Greatest Hits.
- (S) (3:18) Priority 8671 Country's Greatest Hits: Superstars.
- (S) (3:19) RCA 66080 Texas Collection.

- (S) (3:14) Time-Life CCD-02 Contemporary Country - The Late 70's.
- (S) (3:17) RCA 66299 Only Daddy That'll Walk The Line.
- (S) (3:17) K-Tel 3111 Country Music Classics Vol. XIX.
- (S) (3:15) RCA 66849 Super Hits.
- (S) (3:14) RCA 66945 Super Hits Sampler.
- (S) (3:17) K-Tel 3367 101 Greatest Country Hits Vol. Eight: Country Romance.
- (S) (3:16) Time-Life R990-15 Waylon Jennings - Legendary Country Singers.
- (S) (3:20) DCC Compact Classics 147 Ol' Waylon.

released as by WAYLON:
1980 THEME FROM THE DUKES OF HAZZARD (GOOD OL' BOYS)
- (S) (2:07) RCA 5325 Greatest Hits Volume 2.
- (S) (2:06) Time-Life CCD-15 Contemporary Country - The Early 80's Hot Hits.
- (S) (2:06) RCA 66299 Only Daddy That'll Walk The Line.
- (S) (2:06) Rhino 71893 Radio Daze: Pop Hits Of The 80's Volume Four.
- (S) (2:06) Rhino 71912 Tube Tunes Volume Three - The 80's.
- (S) (2:05) RCA 66849 Super Hits.
- (S) (2:06) RCA 66857 Essential.
- (S) (2:06) Time-Life R990-15 Waylon Jennings - Legendary Country Singers.
- (S) (2:06) Time-Life R988-32 Sounds Of The Eighties: TV Themes Of The '80s.

KRIS JENSEN
1962 TORTURE
- (M) (2:05) Time-Life 2RNR-16 Rock 'N' Roll Era - 1962 Still Rockin'.
- (M) (2:06) Time-Life R102-17 Lost Treasures Of Rock 'N' Roll.
- (M) (2:06) Time-Life R857-12 The Heart Of Rock 'n' Roll 1962-1963.

JESUS JONES
1991 RIGHT HERE, RIGHT NOW
- (S) (3:07) SBK 95715 Doubt.
- (S) (3:07) K-Tel 3849 90s Now Volume 4.
1991 REAL, REAL, REAL
- (S) (3:05) SBK 95715 Doubt.

JETHRO TULL
1973 LIVING IN THE PAST
- (S) (3:19) Warner Special Products 27614 Highs Of The Seventies.
- (S) (4:05) Chrysalis 21655 and 41655 20 Years Of Jethro Tull. *(live)*
- (S) (3:19) Chrysalis 21078 and 41078 M.U. The Best Of.
- (S) (3:18) Chrysalis 21035 and 41035 Living In The Past.
- (S) (3:16) Chrysalis 21515 and 41515 Original Masters.
- (S) (4:05) Chrysalis 21653 and 41653 20 Years Of Tull Box Set. *(live)*
- (S) (3:19) Chrysalis 26015 and 26004 Best Of: 25th Anniversary Collection.
- (S) (3:18) Razor & Tie 22502 Those Rocking 70's.
- (S) (3:19) Time-Life SOD-14 Sounds Of The Seventies - 1973: Take Two.
- (S) (3:22) Rebound 314520507 Class Reunion '73.
1975 BUNGLE IN THE JUNGLE
- (S) (3:36) Priority 7055 Heavy Hitters/70's Greatest Rock Hits Volume 11.
- (S) (3:35) Chrysalis 21078 and 41078 M.U. The Best Of.
- (S) (3:34) Chrysalis 21067 and 41067 Warchild.
- (S) (3:31) Chrysalis 21515 and 41515 Original Masters.
- (S) (3:33) Chrysalis 21653 and 41653 20 Years Of Tull Box Set.
- (S) (3:37) Chrysalis 26015 and 26004 Best Of: 25th Anniversary Collection.
- (S) (3:31) Time-Life SOD-16 Sounds Of The Seventies - 1975: Take Two.

JETS
1986 CRUSH ON YOU
- (S) (4:30) MCA 5667 The Jets. *(LP version)*
- (S) (4:29) MCA 10064 Best Of. *(LP version)*

(S)	(4:29)	Madacy Entertainment 1986 Rock On 1986. *(LP version)*	

(S) (3:41) Time-Life R988-15 Sounds Of The Eighties: The Mid 80's. *(45 version)*

(S) (3:41) Rhino 75217 Heartthrob Hits. *(45 version)*

(S) (4:04) Cold Front 6330 Club Mix: The 80s. *(all selections on this cd are segued together)*

1987 YOU GOT IT ALL

(S) (4:06) Columbia 44382 Heart Of Soul. *(LP version)*

(S) (4:08) MCA 5667 The Jets. *(LP version)*

(S) (4:07) MCA 10064 Best Of. *(LP version)*

(S) (4:06) Priority 53773 80's Greatest Rock Hits Volume II - Teen Idols. *(LP version)*

(S) (4:07) K-Tel 3500 The 80's - Urban Countdown. *(LP version)*

(S) (4:07) Hip-O 40005 The '80s Hit(s) Back....Again! *(LP version)*

(S) (4:08) Hip-O 40031 The Glory Of Love - '80s Sweet & Soulful Love Songs. *(LP version)*

(S) (4:07) Time-Life R988-21 Sounds Of The Eighties: 1986-1989. *(LP version)*

(S) (4:06) Rhino 72977 Smooth Grooves - New Jack Ballads Volume 1. *(LP version)*

(S) (4:07) K-Tel 3864 Slow Dancin'. *(LP version)*

(S) (4:06) Time-Life R834-12 Body Talk - By Candlelight. *(LP version)*

1987 CROSS MY BROKEN HEART

(S) (4:09) MCA 6207 O.S.T. Beverly Hills Cop II.

(S) (4:09) MCA 6330 Soundtrack Smashes - The 80's.

(S) (4:09) MCA 42085 Magic.

(S) (4:06) MCA 10064 Best Of.

(S) (4:07) Madacy Entertainment 1987 Rock On 1987.

1987 I DO YOU

(S) (3:37) EMI 91419 MTV, BET, VH-1 Power Players.

(S) (3:37) MCA 42085 Magic.

1988 ROCKET 2 U

(S) (4:14) MCA 42085 Magic. *(LP version)*

(S) (4:16) MCA 10064 Best Of. *(LP version)*

(S) (4:16) Madacy Entertainment 1988 Rock On 1988. *(LP version)*

(S) (4:09) Priority 50941 Shut Up And Dance! Volume Two - The 80's. *(all songs on this cd are segued together)*

(S) (4:15) Cold Front 6246 Classic Club Mix - R&B Grooves. *(all selections on this cd are segued together)*

1988 MAKE IT REAL

(S) (4:15) MCA 42085 Magic.

(S) (4:16) MCA 10064 Best Of.

(S) (4:15) Hip-O 40000 Thinking About You - A Collection Of Modern Love Songs.

(S) (4:15) Time-Life R834-16 Body Talk - Sweet Nothings.

JOAN JETT & THE BLACKHEARTS

1982 I LOVE ROCK 'N ROLL

(S) (2:54) Reprise 45485 O.S.T. Wayne's World 2. *(LP version)*

(S) (2:54) Blackheart 747 I Love Rock N' Roll. *(LP version)*

(S) (2:54) Blackheart/Mercury 314536440 Fit To Be Tied - Great Hits By. *(LP version)*

1982 CRIMSON AND CLOVER

(S) (3:16) Blackheart 747 I Love Rock N' Roll.

(S) (3:16) Blackheart/Mercury 314536440 Fit To Be Tied - Great Hits By.

1982 DO YOU WANNA TOUCH ME (OH YEAH)

(S) (3:45) Blackheart 707 Bad Reputation.

(S) (3:41) Epic/Legacy 65254 Fizz Pop Modern Rock Volume 1.

(S) (3:43) Blackheart/Mercury 314536440 Fit To Be Tied - Great Hits By.

(S) (3:45) Blackheart/Mercury 483371802 Bad Reputation.

1983 FAKE FRIENDS

(S) (3:17) Blackheart/Mercury 314536440 Fit To Be Tied - Great Hits By. *(tracks into the next selection)*

1983 EVERYDAY PEOPLE

(S) (2:38) Blackheart/Mercury 314536440 Fit To Be Tied - Great Hits By.

released as by THE BARBUSTERS:

1987 LIGHT OF DAY

(S) (3:30) Blackheart 438 Joan Jett And The Blackhearts - Flashback.

(S) (3:29) Blackheart/Mercury 314536440 Fit To Be Tied - Great Hits By. *(tracks into the next selection)*

released as by JOAN JETT & THE BLACKHEARTS:

1988 I HATE MYSELF FOR LOVING YOU

(S) (4:06) Priority 7076 80's Greatest Rock Hits Volume 2 - Leather And Lace.

(S) (4:06) CBS Associated 44146 Up Your Alley.

(S) (4:10) EMI 52498 O.S.T. Striptease.

(S) (4:06) Blackheart/Mercury 314536440 Fit To Be Tied - Great Hits By.

1989 LITTLE LIAR

(S) (3:59) CBS Associated 44146 Up Your Alley.

(S) (4:07) Blackheart/Mercury 314536440 Fit To Be Tied - Great Hits By.

1990 DIRTY DEEDS

(S) (3:17) CBS Associated 45473 The Hit List.

(S) (3:17) Risky Business 53915 Dangerous Women. *(found only on original pressings of this compact disc)*

JEWEL

1996 WHO WILL SAVE YOUR SOUL

(S) (4:00) Atlantic 82700 Pieces Of You.

(S) (3:58) Grammy Recordings/Chronicles 314553292 1997 Grammy Nominees.

(S) (4:00) Atlantic 83088 Atlantic Records: 50 Years - The Gold Anniversary Collection.

1997 YOU WERE MEANT FOR ME

(S) (4:12) Atlantic 82700 Pieces Of You.

1997 FOOLISH GAMES

(S) (5:38) Atlantic 82700 Pieces Of You.

JIGSAW

1975 SKY HIGH

(S) (2:47) Rhino 70670 Billboard Top Hits - 1975.

(S) (2:47) Rhino 70762 Super Hits Of The 70's Volume 15.

(S) (2:51) Original Sound CDGO-7 Golden Oldies Volume. 7.

(S) (2:46) Razor & Tie 22505 More Fabulous 70's Volume 2.

(S) (2:47) Time-Life SOD-31 Sounds Of The Seventies - AM Top Twenty.

(S) (2:51) Hot Productions 71 Best Of.

(S) (5:19) Hot Productions 71 Best Of. *(1995 rerecording)*

(S) (2:51) Eclipse Music Group 64894 Rock 'n Roll Relix 1974-1975.

(S) (2:51) Eclipse Music Group 64897 Rock 'n Roll Relix 1970-1979.

(S) (2:46) Time-Life AM1-22 AM Gold - 1975.

(S) (2:51) Priority 50957 Mega Hits Disco Explosion Volume 4.

1976 LOVE FIRE

(S) (2:41) Rhino 72298 Superhits Of The 70's Volume 24.

JOSE JIMENEZ

1961 THE ASTRONAUT (PARTS 1 & 2)

(S) (5:52) Rhino 70749 Best Of.

JIVE BOMBERS

1957 BAD BOY

(M) (2:50) Time-Life 2RNR-24 Rock 'N' Roll Era - The 50's Keep On Rockin'.

JIVE BUNNY and THE MASTERMIXERS

1990 SWING THE MOOD

(S) (6:07) Atco 91322 The Album. *(LP version)*

JIVE FIVE

1961 MY TRUE STORY

(M) (2:33) Rhino 75763 Best Of Doo Wop Ballads.

(M) (2:33) Rhino 70647 Billboard's Top R&B Hits Of 1961.

(M) (2:31) Original Sound 8854 Oldies But Goodies Vol. 4. *(this compact disc uses the "Waring - fds" noise reduction process)*

JIVE FIVE *(Continued)*

    (M) (2:31)   Original Sound 2221 Oldies But Goodies Volumes 1,4,6,8 and 10 Box Set. *(this box set uses the "Waring - fds" noise reduction process)*

    (M) (2:31)   Original Sound 2500 Oldies But Goodies Volumes 1-15 Box Set. *(this box set uses the "Waring - fds" noise reduction process)*

    (M) (2:30)   Original Sound CDGO-12 Golden Oldies Volume. 12.

    (M) (2:33)   DCC Compact Classics 031 Back Seat Jams.

    (S) (2:23)   Collectables 5022 Their Greatest Hits. *(missing some overdubs)*

    (M) (2:31)   Relic 7007 My True Story.

    (S) (2:47)   Relic 7007 My True Story. *(includes a :17 false start; missing some overdubs)*

    (M) (2:30)   Collectables 5062 History Of Rock Volume 2.

    (M) (2:31)   Rhino 71463 Doo Wop Box.

    (M) (2:31)   Time-Life 2RNR-04 Rock 'N' Roll Era - 1961.

    (M) (2:32)   Time-Life RHD-14 Rhythm & Blues - 1961.

    (M) (2:32)   Time-Life R962-06 History Of Rock 'N' Roll: Doo Wop And Vocal Group Tradition 1955-1962.

    (M) (2:33)   Collectables 2500 WCBS-FM History Of Rock - The 60's Part 1.

    (M) (2:33)   Collectables 4500 History Of Rock/The 60s Part One.

    (M) (2:31)   Collectables 2607 WCBS-FM For Lovers Only Vol. 3.

    (M) (2:30)   Collectables 2603 WCBS-FM Jukebox Giants Vol. 1.

    (M) (2:31)   Collectables 2552 WOGL History Of Rock Vol. 2.

    (M) (2:31)   Time-Life R10513 40 Lovin' Oldies.

    (M) (2:31)   Right Stuff 30578 Slow Jams: The 60's Volume 4.

    (M) (2:31)   Time-Life R857-03 The Heart Of Rock 'n' Roll - 1961.

    (M) (2:31)   Thump 7050 Low Rider Oldies Volume 5.

    (M) (2:31)   JCI 3164 Eighteen Soulful Ballads.

    (M) (2:32)   Time-Life R838-19 Solid Gold Soul 1961.

    (M) (2:30)   K-Tel 3886 Great R&B Male Groups: Hits Of The 60's.

1965 I'M A HAPPY MAN

    (S) (2:36)   EMI 99669 The Complete United Artists Recordings.

    (S) (2:36)   EMI 81128 Rock Is Dead But It Won't Lie Down.

J.J. FAD
1988 SUPERSONIC

    (S) (3:52)   Ruthless 90959 Supersonic. *(tracks into next selection)*

    (S) (3:52)   Priority 7916 Queens Of Rap.

    (S) (3:52)   Priority 50931 Hip Hop Classics Volume Two.

    (S) (3:52)   Elektra 62091 Maximum Rap.

    (S) (3:55)   Ruthless 68766 Ruthless Records Tenth Anniversary Compilation. *(tracks into the next selection)*

DAMITA JO
1960 I'LL SAVE THE LAST DANCE FOR YOU

    (S) (2:10)   Collectors' Choice 5189 I Wish I Were A Princess - The Great Lost Female Teen Idols.

    (S) (2:12)   Collectables 5842 Very Best Of.

1961 I'LL BE THERE

    (S) (2:45)   Collectables 5842 Very Best Of.

SAMI JO
1974 TELL ME A LIE

JoBOXERS
1983 JUST GOT LUCKY

    (S) (4:44)   EMI 89605 Living In Oblivion: The 80's Greatest Hits Volume Two. *(LP version)*

    (S) (3:41)   Rhino 71974 New Wave Hits Of The 80's Vol. 11. *(45 version)*

    (S) (4:44)   Big Ear Music 4002 Only In The 80's Volume Two. *(LP version)*

    (S) (4:42)   K-Tel 3742 The 80's: Hot Rock. *(LP version)*

JODECI
1991 FOREVER MY LADY

    (S) (5:19)   Uptown/MCA 10198 Forever My Lady.

    (S) (5:18)   Uptown 53022 Uptown's Block Party Volume 1.

1992 COME & TALK TO ME

    (S) (6:20)   Tommy Boy 1074 MTV Party To Go Volume 3. *(remix; all tracks on this cd are segued together)*

    (S) (4:35)   Uptown/MCA 10198 Forever My Lady.

    (S) (4:34)   Hip-O 40000 Thinking About You - A Collection Of Modern Love Songs.

    (S) (4:33)   Uptown 53025 Uptown's Block Party Volume 2.

    (S) (4:34)   Beast 53012 Smooth Love Of The 90's Vol. 1.

1993 LATELY

    (S) (6:13)   Uptown/MCA 10858 Uptown MTV Unplugged. *(LP version)*

1993 CRY FOR YOU

    (S) (5:00)   Uptown/MCA 10915 Diary Of A Mad Band.

    (S) (4:26)   Uptown 53025 Uptown's Block Party Volume 2.

1994 FEENIN'

    (S) (5:10)   Uptown/MCA 10915 Diary Of A Mad Band. *(tracks into next selection)*

    (S) (5:08)   Uptown 53025 Uptown's Block Party Volume 2.

1995 FREEK'N YOU

    (S) (6:19)   Uptown/MCA 11258 The Show - The After Party - The Hotel. *(all selections on this cd are segued together)*

    (S) (4:00)   Polygram TV 314553641 Pure Soul 1997.

1995 LOVE U 4 LIFE

    (S) (4:50)   Uptown/MCA 11258 The Show - The After Party - The Hotel. *(all selections on this cd are segued together)*

1996 GET ON UP

    (S) (3:45)   Uptown/MCA 11258 The Show - The After Party - The Hotel. *(all selections on this cd are segued together)*

JOE
1996 ALL THE THINGS (YOUR MAN WON'T DO)

    (S) (6:19)   Island 314524146 and 314524197 O.S.T. Don't Be A Menace.

    (S) (6:18)   Polygram TV 314553641 Pure Soul 1997.

1997 DON'T WANNA BE A PLAYER

    (S) (4:12)   Jive 41604 O.S.T. Booty Call.

    (S) (4:40)   Cold Front 6254 Club Mix '98. *(all selections on this cd are segued together)*

BILLY JOEL
1974 PIANO MAN
(dj copies of this 45 ran (3:16) and (4:30); commercial copies were all (4:30))

    (S) (5:36)   Columbia 40121 Greatest Hits Volume I & II. *(LP version)*

    (S) (5:36)   Columbia 32544 Piano Man. *(LP version)*

    (S) (5:36)   Columbia 68007 The Complete Hits Collection 1973-1997. *(LP version)*

    (S) (6:30)   Columbia 68007 The Complete Hits Collection 1973-1997. *(live)*

1975 THE ENTERTAINER

    (S) (3:38)   Columbia 40121 Greatest Hits Volume I & II. *(LP version)*

    (S) (3:38)   Columbia 33146 Streetlife Serenade. *(LP version)*

    (S) (3:37)   Columbia 68007 The Complete Hits Collection 1973-1997. *(LP version)*

1978 JUST THE WAY YOU ARE

    (S) (3:35)   Columbia 40121 Greatest Hits Volume I & II. *(:08 longer than the 45 version)*

    (S) (4:49)   Columbia 34987 The Stranger. *(LP length)*

    (S) (4:48)   Columbia 68007 The Complete Hits Collection 1973-1997. *(LP length)*

1978 MOVIN' OUT (ANTHONY'S SONG)

    (S) (3:28)   Columbia 40121 Greatest Hits Volume I & II. *(LP version)*

    (S) (3:28)   Columbia 34987 The Stranger. *(LP version)*

    (S) (3:27)   Columbia 68007 The Complete Hits Collection 1973-1997. *(LP version)*

1978 ONLY THE GOOD DIE YOUNG
- (S) (3:52) Columbia 40121 Greatest Hits Volume I & II.
- (S) (3:52) Columbia 34987 The Stranger.
- (S) (3:52) Columbia 68007 The Complete Hits Collection 1973-1997.

1978 SHE'S ALWAYS A WOMAN
- (S) (3:16) Columbia 40121 Greatest Hits Volume I & II.
- (S) (3:19) Columbia 34987 The Stranger.
- (S) (3:19) Columbia 68007 The Complete Hits Collection 1973-1997.

1979 MY LIFE
- (S) (4:42) Columbia 35609 and 52858 and 64412 52nd Street. *(LP version)*
- (S) (3:50) Columbia 40121 Greatest Hits Volume I & II. *(45 version)*
- (S) (4:41) Columbia 68007 The Complete Hits Collection 1973-1997. *(LP version)*

1979 BIG SHOT
(dj copies of this 45 ran (3:39) and (4:01); commercial copies were all (3:39))
- (S) (4:01) Columbia 35609 and 52858 52nd Street. *(LP version)*
- (S) (3:43) Columbia 40121 Greatest Hits Volume I & II. *(45 version)*
- (S) (4:00) Columbia 68007 The Complete Hits Collection 1973-1997. *(LP version)*
- (S) (4:01) Columbia/Legacy 64412 52nd Street. *(gold disc; LP version)*

1979 HONESTY
- (S) (3:52) Columbia 35609 and 52858 52nd Street.
- (S) (3:52) Columbia/Legacy 64412 52nd Street. *(gold disc)*

1980 YOU MAY BE RIGHT
- (S) (4:13) Columbia 36384 Glass Houses. *(LP length)*
- (S) (4:09) Columbia 40121 Greatest Hits Volume I & II. *(LP length)*
- (S) (4:11) Columbia 68007 The Complete Hits Collection 1973-1997. *(LP length)*

1980 IT'S STILL ROCK AND ROLL TO ME
- (S) (2:56) Columbia 36384 Glass Houses.
- (S) (2:54) Columbia 40121 Greatest Hits Volume I & II.
- (S) (2:56) Columbia 68007 The Complete Hits Collection 1973-1997.
- (S) (2:55) Time-Life R13610 Gold And Platinum Box Set - The Ultimate Rock Collection.

1980 DON'T ASK ME WHY
- (S) (2:56) Columbia 36384 Glass Houses.
- (S) (2:56) Columbia 40121 Greatest Hits Volume I & II.
- (S) (2:56) Columbia 68007 The Complete Hits Collection 1973-1997.

1980 SOMETIMES A FANTASY
(LP length is (3:39); dj copies of this 45 ran (3:39) and (4:19); commercial 45's were all (4:19))
- (S) (3:39) Columbia 36384 Glass Houses. *(LP length)*

1981 SAY GOODBYE TO HOLLYWOOD
- (S) (3:54) Columbia 40121 Greatest Hits Volume I & II. *(45 length)*
- (S) (4:24) Columbia 37461 Songs In The Attic. *(LP length)*
- (S) (4:37) Columbia 33848 Turnstiles. *(studio version - not the hit version)*
- (S) (4:24) Columbia 37461 Songs In The Attic. *(LP length)*
- (S) (4:36) Columbia 68007 The Complete Hits Collection 1973-1997. *(studio version - not the hit version)*

1982 SHE'S GOT A WAY
(actual 45 time is (2:58) not (2:44) as stated on the record label)
- (S) (3:00) Columbia 40121 Greatest Hits Volume I & II.
- (S) (3:00) Columbia 37461 Songs In The Attic.
- (S) (3:00) Columbia 68007 The Complete Hits Collection 1973-1997.

1982 PRESSURE
- (S) (3:15) Columbia 40121 Greatest Hits Volume I & II. *(45 version)*
- (S) (4:37) Columbia 38200 Nylon Curtain. *(LP version)*
- (S) (4:37) Columbia 68007 The Complete Hits Collection 1973-1997. *(LP version)*

1983 ALLENTOWN
- (S) (3:48) Columbia 40121 Greatest Hits Volume I & II.

- (S) (3:49) Columbia 38200 Nylon Curtain.
- (S) (3:48) Columbia 68007 The Complete Hits Collection 1973-1997.

1983 TELL HER ABOUT IT
(actual 45 time is (3:47) not (3:35) as stated on the record label)
- (S) (3:35) Columbia 40121 Greatest Hits Volume I & II. *(faded :14 sooner than the 45 or LP)*
- (S) (3:49) Columbia 38837 An Innocent Man.
- (S) (3:48) Columbia 68007 The Complete Hits Collection 1973-1997.

1983 UPTOWN GIRL
- (S) (3:14) Columbia 40121 Greatest Hits Volume I & II.
- (S) (3:15) Columbia 38837 An Innocent Man.
- (S) (3:14) Columbia 68007 The Complete Hits Collection 1973-1997.

1984 AN INNOCENT MAN
- (S) (5:18) Columbia 38837 An Innocent Man.
- (S) (5:17) Columbia 67347 Greatest Hits Volume III.
- (S) (5:18) Columbia 68007 The Complete Hits Collection 1973-1997.

1984 THE LONGEST TIME
- (S) (3:34) Columbia 40121 Greatest Hits Volume I & II.
- (S) (3:37) Columbia 38837 An Innocent Man.
- (S) (3:37) Columbia 68007 The Complete Hits Collection 1973-1997.

1984 LEAVE A TENDER MOMENT ALONE
- (S) (3:52) Columbia 38837 An Innocent Man.

1985 KEEPING THE FAITH
- (S) (4:37) Columbia 38837 An Innocent Man. *(LP version)*
- (S) (4:37) Columbia 67347 Greatest Hits Volume III. *(LP version)*
- (S) (4:37) Columbia 68007 The Complete Hits Collection 1973-1997. *(LP version)*

1985 YOU'RE ONLY HUMAN (SECOND WIND)
- (S) (4:47) Columbia 40121 Greatest Hits Volume I & II. *(LP version)*
- (S) (4:47) Columbia 68007 The Complete Hits Collection 1973-1997. *(LP version)*

1985 THE NIGHT IS STILL YOUNG
- (S) (5:25) Columbia 40121 Greatest Hits Volume I & II. *(LP version)*
- (S) (5:25) Columbia 68007 The Complete Hits Collection 1973-1997. *(LP version)*

1986 MODERN WOMAN
- (S) (3:47) Columbia 44381 Heart Of Rock.
- (S) (3:48) Epic 53439 O.S.T. Peter's Friends.
- (S) (3:48) Epic 40398 O.S.T. Ruthless People.
- (S) (3:48) Columbia 40402 The Bridge.

1986 A MATTER OF TRUST
- (S) (4:08) Columbia 40402 The Bridge.
- (S) (4:08) Columbia 67347 Greatest Hits Volume III.
- (S) (4:08) Columbia 68007 The Complete Hits Collection 1973-1997.

1987 THIS IS THE TIME
- (S) (4:58) Columbia 40402 The Bridge.
- (S) (4:58) Columbia 67347 Greatest Hits Volume III.
- (S) (4:58) Columbia 68007 The Complete Hits Collection 1973-1997.

1989 WE DIDN'T START THE FIRE
- (S) (4:48) Columbia 44366 Storm Front. *(LP length)*
- (S) (4:48) Columbia 67347 Greatest Hits Volume III. *(LP length)*
- (S) (4:48) Columbia 68007 The Complete Hits Collection 1973-1997. *(LP length)*
- (S) (5:10) Columbia 68007 The Complete Hits Collection 1973-1997. *(live; alternate take)*

1990 I GO TO EXTREMES
- (S) (4:21) Columbia 44366 Storm Front.
- (S) (4:21) Columbia 67347 Greatest Hits Volume III.
- (S) (4:20) Columbia 68007 The Complete Hits Collection 1973-1997.

1990 AND SO IT GOES
- (S) (3:37) Columbia 44366 Storm Front.
- (S) (3:36) Columbia 67347 Greatest Hits Volume III.
- (S) (3:36) Columbia 68007 The Complete Hits Collection 1973-1997.

BILLY JOEL *(Continued)*

1993 THE RIVER OF DREAMS
- (S) (4:05) Columbia 53003 River Of Dreams.
- (S) (4:05) Columbia 67347 Greatest Hits Volume III.
- (S) (4:05) Columbia 68007 The Complete Hits Collection 1973-1997.

1993 ALL ABOUT SOUL
- (S) (5:58) Columbia 53003 River Of Dreams.
- (S) (5:57) Columbia 67347 Greatest Hits Volume III. *(remixed)*
- (S) (5:57) Columbia 68007 The Complete Hits Collection 1973-1997. *(remixed)*

JOE PUBLIC

1992 LIVE AND LEARN
- (S) (4:20) Columbia 48628 Joe Public.

ELTON JOHN

1971 YOUR SONG
- (S) (4:00) MCA 31105 Elton John.
- (S) (3:59) MCA 37215 Greatest Hits.
- (S) (3:59) MCA 10110 To Be Continued.
- (S) (3:59) MCA 31016 Your Songs.
- (S) (3:59) JCI 3303 Love Seventies.
- (S) (3:58) Polydor 314512532 Greatest Hits.
- (S) (4:00) Polydor 827689 Elton John.
- (S) (3:57) Original Sound 8909 Best Love Songs Vol 4.
- (S) (3:57) Original Sound 9327 Best Love Songs Vol. 3 & 4.
- (S) (3:57) Original Sound 1236 Best Love Songs Box Set.
- (S) (3:58) Time-Life SUD-04 Superhits - 1970.
- (S) (3:59) Time-Life SOD-02 Sounds Of The Seventies - 1971.
- (S) (3:59) Time-Life R105-26 Our Songs: Singers & Songwriters Encore.
- (S) (3:59) DCC Compact Classics 1071 Greatest Hits. *(gold disc)*
- (S) (4:00) Rocket 314528156 Elton John. *(remastered edition)*
- (S) (3:59) MCA 11481 Love Songs.
- (S) (3:58) Time-Life AM1-02 AM Gold - 1970.
- (S) (3:59) Polygram TV 314555610 The One And Only Love Album.
- (S) (3:59) Time-Life R814-04 Love Songs.

1971 FRIENDS
- (S) (2:22) MCA 10110 To Be Continued.
- (S) (2:21) MCA 31016 Your Songs.
- (S) (2:22) Polydor 314514138 Rare Masters.

1972 LEVON
(actual 45 time is (5:08) not (4:59) as stated on the record label; LP length is (5:20))
- (S) (5:21) MCA 31190 Madman Across The Water.
- (S) (5:20) MCA 37216 Greatest Hits Volume 2.
- (S) (5:21) MCA 10110 To Be Continued.
- (S) (5:20) MFSL 516 Madman Across The Water.
- (S) (5:20) MCA 37216 Greatest Hits Volume 2.
- (S) (5:20) Polydor 314512533 Greatest Hits Volume 2.
- (S) (5:20) Polydor 825487 Madman Across The Water.
- (S) (5:20) Rocket 314528161 Madman Across The Water. *(remastered edition)*

1972 TINY DANCER
(dj copies of this 45 ran (3:45) and (6:12); commercial copies were all (6:12))
- (S) (6:14) MCA 31190 Madman Across The Water.
- (S) (6:13) MCA 10110 To Be Continued.
- (S) (6:12) MCA 31016 Your Songs.
- (S) (6:16) MFSL 516 Madman Across The Water.
- (S) (6:14) Polydor 314512533 Greatest Hits Volume 2.
- (S) (6:14) Polydor 825487 Madman Across The Water.
- (S) (6:13) Epic 57871 O.S.T. My Girl 2.
- (S) (6:14) Rocket 314528161 Madman Across The Water. *(remastered edition)*

1972 ROCKET MAN
- (S) (4:40) MCA 25240 Classic Rock Volume 3.
- (S) (4:38) MCA 31104 Honky Chateau.
- (S) (4:40) MCA 37215 Greatest Hits.
- (S) (4:40) MCA 10110 To Be Continued.
- (S) (4:41) MFSL 536 Honky Chateau. *(gold disc)*

- (S) (4:40) Polydor 314512532 Greatest Hits.
- (S) (4:40) Polydor 829249 Honky Chateau.
- (S) (4:41) Time-Life SOD-03 Sounds Of The Seventies - 1972.
- (S) (4:40) DCC Compact Classics 1071 Greatest Hits. *(gold disc)*
- (S) (4:40) Rocket 314528162 Honky Chateau. *(remastered edition)*

1972 HONKY CAT
- (S) (5:11) MCA 31104 Honky Chateau.
- (S) (5:11) MCA 37215 Greatest Hits. *(glitch at the end of the fade)*
- (S) (5:11) MCA 10110 To Be Continued.
- (S) (5:15) MFSL 536 Honky Chateau. *(gold disc)*
- (S) (5:11) Polydor 314512532 Greatest Hits.
- (S) (5:11) Polydor 829249 Honky Chateau.
- (S) (5:11) DCC Compact Classics 1071 Greatest Hits. *(gold disc)*
- (S) (5:12) Rocket 314528162 Honky Chateau. *(remastered edition)*

1973 CROCODILE ROCK
- (S) (3:54) Rhino 70634 Billboard's Top Rock & Roll Hits Of 1973.
- (S) (3:53) JCI 3301 Rockin' Seventies.
- (S) (3:53) Original Sound 8895 Dick Clark's 21 All-Time Hits Vol. 4.
- (S) (3:55) MCA 31077 Don't Shoot Me I'm Only The Piano Player.
- (S) (3:54) MCA 37215 Greatest Hits.
- (S) (3:54) MCA 10110 To Be Continued.
- (S) (3:54) Polydor 314512532 Greatest Hits.
- (S) (3:54) Polydor 827690 Don't Shoot Me I'm Only The Piano Player.
- (S) (3:52) London 828509 O.S.T. Four Weddings And A Funeral.
- (S) (3:54) DCC Compact Classics 1071 Greatest Hits. *(gold disc)*
- (S) (3:54) Rocket 314528154 Don't Shoot Me I'm Only The Piano Player. *(remastered edition)*
- (S) (3:54) Time-Life R13610 Gold And Platinum Box Set - The Ultimate Rock Collection.

1973 DANIEL
- (S) (3:50) Sandstone 33003 Reelin' In The Years Volume 4. *(unedited version which very closely resembles the U.S. 45 and LP version)*
- (S) (3:53) MCA 31077 Don't Shoot Me I'm Only The Piano Player.
- (S) (3:52) MCA 37215 Greatest Hits.
- (S) (3:52) MCA 10110 To Be Continued.
- (S) (3:52) Polydor 314512532 Greatest Hits.
- (S) (3:52) Polydor 827690 Don't Shoot Me I'm Only The Piano Player.
- (S) (3:50) DCC Compact Classics 065 Rock Of The 70's Volume 4. *(unedited version which very closely resembles the U.S. 45 and LP version)*
- (S) (3:51) Time-Life R102-34 The Rolling Stone Collection.
- (S) (3:51) Time-Life R105-26 Our Songs: Singers & Songwriters Encore.
- (S) (3:52) DCC Compact Classics 1071 Greatest Hits. *(gold disc)*
- (S) (3:53) Rocket 314528154 Don't Shoot Me I'm Only The Piano Player. *(remastered edition)*
- (S) (3:52) MCA 11481 Love Songs.

1973 SATURDAY NIGHT'S ALRIGHT FOR FIGHTING
- (S) (4:52) MCA 31274 Classic Rock Volume 2.
- (S) (4:46) MCA 2-6894 Goodbye Yellow Brick Road.
- (S) (4:52) MCA 37215 Greatest Hits.
- (S) (4:53) MCA 10110 To Be Continued.
- (S) (4:53) MFSL 526 Goodbye Yellow Brick Road. *(gold disc)*
- (S) (4:51) Polydor 314512532 Greatest Hits.
- (S) (4:53) Polydor 821747 Goodbye Yellow Brick Road.
- (S) (4:51) Time-Life R968-05 Guitar Rock 1972-1973.
- (S) (4:51) K-Tel 621 Rock Classics.
- (S) (4:52) DCC Compact Classics 1071 Greatest Hits. *(gold disc)*
- (S) (4:52) Rocket 314528159 Goodbye Yellow Brick Road. *(remastered edition)*

(S) (4:51) Rhino 72893 Hard Rock Cafe: Classic Rock.

1973 GOODBYE YELLOW BRICK ROAD
(S) (3:13) Rhino 70634 Billboard's Top Rock & Roll Hits Of 1973. *(glitch at 3:13)*
(S) (3:12) MCA 2-6894 Goodbye Yellow Brick Road.
(S) (3:13) MCA 37215 Greatest Hits.
(S) (3:13) MCA 10110 To Be Continued.
(S) (3:12) MFSL 526 Goodbye Yellow Brick Road. *(gold disc)*
(S) (3:12) Polydor 314512532 Greatest Hits.
(S) (3:12) Polydor 821747 Goodbye Yellow Brick Road.
(S) (3:13) Time-Life SOD-06 Sounds Of The Seventies - 1973.
(S) (3:13) DCC Compact Classics 1071 Greatest Hits. *(gold disc)*
(S) (3:13) Rocket 314528159 Goodbye Yellow Brick Road. *(remastered edition)*
(S) (3:12) Hollywood 62092 O.S.T. Breaking The Waves.

1974 BENNIE AND THE JETS
(actual 45 time is (5:20) not (5:10) as stated on the record label)
(S) (5:21) MCA 31273 Classic Rock Volume 1.
(S) (5:18) Rhino 70635 Billboard's Top Rock & Roll Hits Of 1974.
(S) (5:21) Sandstone 33004 Reelin' In The Years Volume 5.
(S) (5:21) MCA 2-6894 Goodbye Yellow Brick Road.
(S) (5:20) MCA 37215 Greatest Hits.
(S) (5:21) MFSL 526 Goodbye Yellow Brick Road. *(gold disc)*
(S) (5:10) Polydor 314512532 Greatest Hits. *(:10 shorter than 45 or LP)*
(S) (5:21) Polydor 821747 Goodbye Yellow Brick Road.
(S) (5:19) MCA 10110 To Be Continued.
(S) (5:21) DCC Compact Classics 066 Rock Of The 70's Volume Five.
(S) (5:18) Time-Life SOD-07 Sounds Of The Seventies - 1974.
(S) (5:19) Epic 57871 O.S.T. My Girl 2.
(S) (5:20) DCC Compact Classics 1071 Greatest Hits. *(gold disc)*
(S) (5:21) Rocket 314528159 Goodbye Yellow Brick Road. *(remastered edition)*

1974 DON'T LET THE SUN GO DOWN ON ME
(S) (5:34) Priority 8664 High Times/70's Greatest Rock Hits Volume 3.
(S) (5:35) MCA 37215 Greatest Hits.
(S) (5:35) MCA 31189 Caribou.
(S) (5:34) Polydor 825488 Caribou.
(S) (5:34) Polydor 314512532 Greatest Hits.
(S) (5:37) MCA 10110 To Be Continued. *(live)*
(S) (5:35) DCC Compact Classics 1071 Greatest Hits. *(gold disc)*
(S) (5:35) Rocket 314528158 Caribou. *(remastered edition)*

1974 THE BITCH IS BACK
(S) (3:36) MCA 37216 Greatest Hits Volume 2.
(S) (3:42) MCA 31189 Caribou.
(S) (3:42) Polydor 825488 Caribou.
(S) (3:35) Polydor 314512533 Greatest Hits Volume 2.
(S) (3:42) MCA 10110 To Be Continued.
(S) (3:37) Time-Life SOD-07 Sounds Of The Seventies - 1974.
(S) (3:32) Time-Life OPCD-4521 Guitar Rock.
(S) (3:44) Rocket 314528158 Caribou. *(remastered edition)*

1975 LUCY IN THE SKY WITH DIAMONDS
(S) (5:56) MCA 37216 Greatest Hits Volume 2.
(S) (5:55) Polydor 314512533 Greatest Hits Volume 2.
(S) (6:14) MCA 10110 To Be Continued. *(:18 longer than any previously released version)*
(S) (6:14) Rocket 314528160 Captain Fantastic And The Brown Dirt Cowboy. *(remastered edition; :18 longer than any previously released version)*

1975 PHILADELPHIA FREEDOM
(actual LP length is (5:21) not (5:38) as stated on the record label; 45 length is (5:38))
(S) (5:37) Rhino 70670 Billboard Top Hits - 1975.
(S) (5:20) MCA 37216 Greatest Hits Volume 2.
(S) (5:19) Polydor 314512533 Greatest Hits Volume 2.

(S) (5:37) MCA 10110 To Be Continued.
(S) (5:27) Time-Life SOD-08 Sounds Of The Seventies - 1975.
(S) (5:21) Rocket 314528160 Captain Fantastic And The Brown Dirt Cowboy. *(remastered edition)*

1975 SOMEONE SAVED MY LIFE TONIGHT
(S) (6:42) MCA 37216 Greatest Hits Volume 2.
(S) (6:42) Polydor 314512533 Greatest Hits Volume 2.
(S) (6:43) Polydor 821746 Captain Fantastic And The Brown Dirt Cowboy.
(S) (6:45) MCA 31078 Captain Fantastic And The Brown Dirt Cowboy.
(S) (6:44) Rocket 314528160 Captain Fantastic And The Brown Dirt Cowboy. *(remastered edition)*
(S) (6:44) MCA 10110 To Be Continued.
(S) (6:43) MCA 11481 Love Songs.

1975 ISLAND GIRL
(S) (3:43) Rhino 70670 Billboard Top Hits - 1975.
(S) (3:43) MCA 37216 Greatest Hits Volume 2.
(S) (3:42) MCA 31001 Rock Of The Westies.
(S) (3:42) Polydor 832018 Rock Of The Westies.
(S) (3:43) Polydor 314512533 Greatest Hits Volume 2.
(S) (3:43) MCA 10110 To Be Continued.
(S) (3:43) Time-Life SOD-08 Sounds Of The Seventies - 1975.
(S) (3:41) Rocket 314532432 Rock Of The Westies. *(remastered edition)*

1976 GROW SOME FUNK OF YOUR OWN
(S) (4:16) MCA 37216 Greatest Hits Volume 2. *(fadeout edited)*
(S) (4:43) MCA 31001 Rock Of The Westies.
(S) (4:43) Polydor 832018 Rock Of The Westies.
(S) (4:15) Polydor 314512533 Greatest Hits Volume 2. *(fadeout edited)*
(S) (4:45) Rocket 314532432 Rock Of The Westies. *(remastered edition)*

1976 I FEEL LIKE A BULLET (IN THE GUN OF ROBERT FORD)
(S) (5:27) MCA 37216 Greatest Hits Volume 2.
(S) (5:27) Polydor 832018 Rock Of The Westies.
(S) (5:27) Polydor 314512533 Greatest Hits Volume 2.
(S) (3:33) MCA 10110 To Be Continued. *(live)*
(S) (5:27) Rocket 314532432 Rock Of The Westies. *(remastered edition)*

released as by ELTON JOHN and KIKI DEE:
1976 DON'T GO BREAKING MY HEART
(S) (4:22) Rhino 70671 Billboard Top Hits - 1976.
(S) (4:20) Priority 7059 Mega-Hits Dance Classics Volume 10.
(S) (4:24) MCA 37216 Elton John - Greatest Hits Volume 2.
(S) (4:30) MCA 10693 Elton John - Greatest Hits 1976-1986.
(S) (4:30) MCA 10110 Elton John - To Be Continued.
(S) (4:21) Time-Life SOD-04 Sounds Of The Seventies - 1976.

released as by ELTON JOHN:
1977 SORRY SEEMS TO BE THE HARDEST WORD
(S) (3:44) MCA 37216 Greatest Hits Volume 2.
(S) (3:44) MCA 6011 Blue Moves.
(S) (3:46) MCA 10693 Greatest Hits 1976-1986.
(S) (3:46) MCA 10110 To Be Continued.
(S) (3:47) MCA 11481 Love Songs.
(S) (3:47) MCA 11667 Blue Moves. *(remastered edition)*

1978 EGO
(S) (3:57) MCA 10110 To Be Continued.

1978 PART-TIME LOVE
(S) (3:11) MCA 31181 A Single Man.

1979 MAMA CAN'T BUY YOU LOVE
(S) (4:02) Geffen 24153 Greatest Hits Volume III, 1979-1987.
(S) (4:02) MCA 10693 Greatest Hits 1976-1986.
(S) (4:04) MCA 39115 The Complete Thom Bell Sessions.
(S) (4:03) MCA 10110 To Be Continued.

1979 VICTIM OF LOVE
(S) (4:57) MCA Special Products 22014 Victim Of Love.

1980 LITTLE JEANNIE
(S) (5:10) Rhino 70675 Billboard Top Hits - 1980.
(S) (5:15) Geffen 24153 Greatest Hits Volume III, 1979-1987.

    (S)   (5:16)   MCA 31054 21 At 33.
    (S)   (5:10)   MCA 10693 Greatest Hits 1976-1986.
    (S)   (5:10)   MCA 10110 To Be Continued.
    (S)   (5:10)   Time-Life R988-07 Sounds Of The Eighties: 1980.

1981 NOBODY WINS
    (S)   (3:42)   MCA 10497 The Fox.

1981 CHLOE
    (S)   (4:41)   MCA 10497 The Fox. *(previous selection tracks over the introduction)*
    (S)   (6:19)   MCA 10110 To Be Continued. *(medley of "FANFARE" (1:39) and "CHLOE" (4:40))*

1982 EMPTY GARDEN (HEY HEY JOHNNIE)
(dj copies of this 45 ran (3:59) and (5:09); commercial copies were all (3:59))
    (S)   (5:09)   MCA 10693 Greatest Hits 1976-1986. *(LP version)*
    (S)   (5:10)   Geffen 24153 Greatest Hits Volume III, 1979-1987. *(LP version)*
    (S)   (5:10)   MCA 10499 Jump Up. *(LP version)*
    (S)   (5:09)   MCA 10110 To Be Continued. *(LP version)*
    (S)   (5:08)   Time-Life R988-26 Sounds Of The Eighties: The Rolling Stone Collection 1982-1983. *(LP version)*

1982 BLUE EYES
    (S)   (3:25)   MCA 10693 Greatest Hits 1976-1986.
    (S)   (3:24)   Geffen 24153 Greatest Hits Volume III, 1979-1987.
    (S)   (3:24)   MCA 10499 Jump Up.
    (S)   (3:25)   MCA 10110 To Be Continued.
    (S)   (3:25)   MCA 11481 Love Songs.

1983 I'M STILL STANDING
    (S)   (3:00)   MCA 10693 Greatest Hits 1976-1986.
    (S)   (3:00)   Geffen 4006 Too Low For Zero.
    (S)   (3:01)   Geffen 24153 Greatest Hits Volume III, 1979-1987.
    (S)   (3:00)   MCA 10110 To Be Continued.
    (S)   (3:01)   Pyramid 71830 Earthrise - The Rainforest Album.
    (S)   (3:01)   MCA 10485 Too Low For Zero.

1983 KISS THE BRIDE
    (S)   (4:20)   MCA 10693 Greatest Hits 1976-1986. *(LP version)*
    (S)   (4:20)   Geffen 4006 Too Low For Zero. *(LP version)*
    (S)   (4:21)   Geffen 24153 Greatest Hits Volume III, 1979-1987. *(LP version)*
    (S)   (4:21)   MCA 10485 Too Low For Zero. *(LP version)*

1984 I GUESS THAT'S WHY THEY CALL IT THE BLUES
    (S)   (4:40)   Epic 53439 O.S.T. Peter's Friends.
    (S)   (4:40)   MCA 10693 Greatest Hits 1976-1986.
    (S)   (4:40)   Geffen 4006 Too Low For Zero.
    (S)   (4:41)   Geffen 24153 Greatest Hits Volume III, 1979-1987.
    (S)   (4:40)   MCA 10110 To Be Continued.
    (S)   (4:41)   MCA 10485 Too Low For Zero.
    (S)   (4:41)   Chrysalis 21750 After The Hurricane - Songs For Montserrat.

1984 SAD SONGS (SAY SO MUCH)
    (S)   (4:06)   MCA 10693 Greatest Hits 1976-1986. *(45 version)*
    (S)   (4:47)   Geffen 24153 Greatest Hits Volume III, 1979-1987. *(LP version)*
    (S)   (4:47)   Geffen 24031 Breaking Hearts. *(LP version)*
    (S)   (4:46)   MCA 10501 Breaking Hearts. *(LP version)*
    (S)   (4:07)   MCA 10110 To Be Continued. *(45 version)*

1984 WHO WEARS THESE SHOES?
    (S)   (4:01)   MCA 10693 Greatest Hits 1976-1986. *(LP length)*
    (S)   (4:02)   Geffen 24031 Breaking Hearts. *(LP length)*
    (S)   (4:01)   MCA 10501 Breaking Hearts. *(LP length)*

1985 IN NEON
    (S)   (4:18)   Geffen 24031 Breaking Hearts.
    (S)   (4:17)   MCA 10501 Breaking Hearts.

1985 WRAP HER UP
    (S)   (6:06)   Geffen 24077 Ice On Fire. *(LP version)*
    (S)   (6:06)   MCA 10693 Greatest Hits 1976-1986. *(LP version)*
    (S)   (6:05)   Geffen 24153 Greatest Hits Volume III, 1979-1987. *(LP version)*
    (S)   (6:06)   MCA 10500 Ice On Fire. *(LP version)*

released as by DIONNE and FRIENDS: ELTON JOHN, GLADYS KNIGHT, STEVIE WONDER and DIONNE WARWICK:
1986 THAT'S WHAT FRIENDS ARE FOR
    (S)   (4:15)   Arista 8398 Dionne Warwick - Friends.
    (S)   (4:15)   Arista 8540 Dionne Warwick - Greatest Hits 1979 - 1990.

released as by ELTON JOHN:
1986 NIKITA
(dj copies of this 45 ran (3:59) and (4:54); commercial copies were all (4:54))
    (S)   (5:42)   Geffen 24077 Ice On Fire. *(LP version)*
    (S)   (5:42)   MCA 10693 Greatest Hits 1976-1986. *(LP version)*
    (S)   (5:42)   Geffen 24153 Greatest Hits Volume III, 1979-1987. *(LP version)*
    (S)   (5:42)   MCA 10500 Ice On Fire. *(LP version)*
    (S)   (5:42)   MCA 10110 To Be Continued. *(LP version)*

released as by JENNIFER RUSH with ELTON JOHN:
1987 FLAMES OF PARADISE
(dj copies of this 45 ran (3:58) and (4:42); commercial copies were all (3:58))
    (S)   (4:35)   Epic 40825 Jennifer Rush - Heart Over Mind. *(LP length)*

released as by ELTON JOHN:
1988 CANDLE IN THE WIND
    (S)   (3:59)   MCA 8022 Live In Australia. *(LP length)*
    (S)   (3:57)   MCA 10110 To Be Continued. *(LP length)*
    (S)   (3:47)   Rocket 314528159 Goodbye Yellow Brick Road. *("Goodbye Yellow Brick Road" vinyl LP version)*
    (S)   (3:47)   MCA 6894 Goodbye Yellow Brick Road. *("Goodbye Yellow Brick Road" vinyl LP version)*
    (S)   (3:47)   Rocket 314528159 Goodbye Yellow Brick Road. *("Goodbye Yellow Brick Road" vinyl LP version)*
    (S)   (3:59)   MCA 11481 Love Songs. *(LP length)*

1988 I DON'T WANNA GO ON WITH YOU LIKE THAT
(dj copies of this 45 ran (3:57) and (4:34); commercial copies were all (4:34))
    (S)   (4:32)   MCA 6240 Reg Strikes Back.
    (S)   (7:19)   MCA 10110 To Be Continued. *(12" single version)*

1988 A WORD IN SPANISH
    (S)   (4:37)   MCA 6240 Reg Strikes Back.

released as by ARETHA FRANKLIN and ELTON JOHN:
1989 THROUGH THE STORM
    (S)   (4:20)   Arista 8572 Aretha Franklin - Through The Storm.
    (S)   (4:20)   DCC Compact Classics 104 Duets - A Man & A Woman.

released as by ELTON JOHN:
1989 HEALING HANDS
    (S)   (4:22)   MCA 6321 Sleeping With The Past.

1990 SACRIFICE
    (S)   (5:06)   MCA 10110 To Be Continued.
    (S)   (5:07)   MCA 6321 Sleeping With The Past.
    (S)   (5:06)   MCA 11481 Love Songs.

1990 CLUB AT THE END OF THE STREET
    (S)   (4:49)   MCA 6321 Sleeping With The Past.

1991 YOU GOTTA LOVE SOMEONE
    (S)   (4:56)   MCA 10110 To Be Continued.
    (S)   (4:56)   Geffen 24294 O.S.T. Days Of Thunder.

released as by GEORGE MICHAEL/ELTON JOHN:
1992 DON'T LET THE SUN GO DOWN ON ME
    (S)   (5:45)   Foundation/RCA 66104 Hot #1 Hits.
    (S)   (5:46)   MCA 10926 Elton John - Duets.
    (S)   (5:46)   MCA 11481 Elton John - Love Songs.

released as by ELTON JOHN:
1992 THE ONE
    (S)   (5:52)   Foundation/RCA 66563 Number 1 Hit Mix.
    (S)   (5:51)   MCA 10614 The One.
    (S)   (5:51)   MCA 11481 Love Songs.
    (S)   (5:52)   Time-Life R13610 Gold And Platinum Box Set - The Ultimate Rock Collection.

1992 THE LAST SONG
    (S)   (3:18)   MCA 10614 The One.

1993 SIMPLE LIFE
    (S)   (6:24)   MCA 10614 The One. *(LP version)*

1994 CAN YOU FEEL THE LOVE TONIGHT
- (S) (3:59) Walt Disney 60858 O.S.T. The Lion King.
- (S) (3:59) Grammy Recordings/Sony Music 67043 1995 Grammy Nominees.
- (S) (3:59) MCA 11481 Love Songs.
- (S) (3:58) Rhino 72509 Tim Rice Collection: Stage And Screen Classics.
- (S) (3:59) EMI-Capitol Music Group 54555 Movie Luv.

1994 CIRCLE OF LIFE
- (S) (4:49) Walt Disney 60858 O.S.T. The Lion King.
- (S) (4:49) MCA 11481 Love Songs.

1995 BELIEVE
- (S) (4:54) Rocket 314526915 Made In England.
- (S) (4:41) MCA 11481 Love Songs.

1995 BLESSED
- (S) (4:59) Rocket 314526915 Made In England.
- (S) (4:59) MCA 11481 Love Songs.

1997 CANDLE IN THE WIND
1997 SOMETHING ABOUT THE WAY YOU LOOK TONIGHT
- (S) (5:08) Rocket 314536266 The Big Picture.

LITTLE WILLIE JOHN
1956 FEVER
- (M) (2:39) Atlantic 81769 O.S.T. Big Town.
- (M) (2:40) Rhino 71511 Fever: Best Of.
- (M) (2:39) Time-Life 2RNR-14 Rock 'N' Roll Era - 1956.
- (M) (2:39) Time-Life RHD-05 Rhythm & Blues - 1956.
- (M) (2:40) King 7002 King R&B Box Set.
- (M) (2:44) King 7002 King R&B Box Set. *(with strings overdubbed; personal greeting from Little Willie John overdubbed at the end of the song)*
- (M) (2:40) King 1401 Original Blues.
- (M) (2:40) King 5004 All 15 Of His Chart Hits.
- (M) (2:39) Time-Life R857-13 The Heart Of Rock 'n' Roll 1956-1957.
- (M) (2:40) Hip-O 40083 The King's Record Collection Vol. 2.
- (M) (2:39) Time-Life R838-24 Solid Gold Soul 1956.

1958 TALK TO ME, TALK TO ME
- (M) (2:41) Time-Life 2RNR-21 Rock 'N' Roll Era - 1958: Still Rockin'.
- (M) (2:41) Time-Life RHD-16 Rhythm & Blues - 1958.
- (M) (2:41) Rhino 71511 Fever: Best Of.
- (M) (2:40) King 7002 King R&B Box Set.
- (M) (2:39) King 474 Beale Street Blues.
- (M) (2:41) King 1401 Original Blues.
- (M) (2:40) King 5004 All 15 Of His Chart Hits.
- (M) (2:41) Time-Life R838-22 Solid Gold Soul 1958.

1960 HEARTBREAK (IT'S HURTIN' ME)
- (M) (2:50) Rhino 71511 Fever: Best Of.
- (M) (2:51) King 739 Sure Things.
- (M) (2:48) King 5004 All 15 Of His Chart Hits.

1960 SLEEP
- (M) (2:53) Rhino 71511 Fever: Best Of. *(noisy fadeout)*
- (M) (2:51) King 7002 King R&B Box Set.
- (M) (2:52) King 1401 Original Blues.
- (M) (2:53) King 739 Sure Things.
- (M) (2:52) King 5004 All 15 Of His Chart Hits.

ROBERT JOHN
1968 IF YOU DON'T WANT MY LOVE
- (S) (2:18) CBS Special Products 37915 Endless Beach.
- (S) (2:18) Sony Music Special Products 75066 Endless Beach.

1972 THE LION SLEEPS TONIGHT
- (S) (2:32) Atlantic 81909 Hit Singles 1958 - 1977.
- (S) (3:38) Curb 77532 Your Favorite Songs. *(rerecording)*
- (S) (2:33) Curb 77543 Greatest Hits.
- (S) (2:32) Rhino 71196 Super Hits Of The 70's Volume 16.
- (S) (2:31) Time-Life SOD-32 Sounds Of The Seventies - AM Pop Classics.
- (S) (3:38) Curb 77651 Retro Rock Dance Hits. *(all selections on this cd are remixed with extra instrumentation added)*
- (S) (2:31) K-Tel 3623 Believe In Music.
- (S) (2:31) JCI 3168 #1 Radio Hits 1970 - Only Rock 'n Roll - 1974.

- (S) (2:32) Morgan Creek 20025 O.S.T. Ace Ventura Pet Detective.
- (S) (2:31) Time-Life R840-03 Sounds Of The Seventies - Pop Nuggets: Early '70s.

1979 SAD EYES
(actual LP length is (4:11) not (3:11) as stated on the record label)
- (S) (3:30) Rhino 70674 Billboard Top Hits - 1979. *(45 version)*
- (S) (4:11) Curb 77543 Greatest Hits. *(LP version)*
- (S) (4:13) Razor & Tie 4543 The '70s Preservation Society Presents: Easy '70s. *(LP version)*
- (S) (3:30) Rhino 71202 Super Hits Of The 70's Volume 22. *(45 version)*
- (S) (3:28) Time-Life SOD-34 Sounds Of The Seventies - The Late 70's. *(45 version)*
- (S) (3:30) Time-Life R834-03 Body Talk - Moonlit Nights. *(45 version)*
- (S) (3:29) Time-Life R840-01 Sounds Of The Seventies - Pop Nuggets: Late '70s. *(45 version)*
- (S) (3:29) K-Tel 3907 Starflight Vol. 2. *(45 version)*
- (S) (3:30) Time-Life AM1-26 AM Gold - 1979. *(45 version)*

1980 LONELY EYES
- (S) (3:07) Curb 77543 Greatest Hits.

1980 HEY THERE LONELY GIRL
- (S) (3:04) Curb 77543 Greatest Hits.

JOHNNIE & JOE
1957 OVER THE MOUNTAIN; ACROSS THE SEA
- (M) (2:16) Rhino 70643 Billboard's Top R&B Hits Of 1957.
- (M) (2:15) Chess 31320 Best Of Chess Rock 'n' Roll Volume 2.
- (M) (2:12) Original Sound 8850 Oldies But Goodies Vol. 1. *(this compact disc uses the "Waring - fds" noise reduction process)*
- (M) (2:12) Original Sound 2221 Oldies But Goodies Volumes 1,4,6,8 and 10 Box Set. *(this box set uses the "Waring - fds" noise reduction process)*
- (M) (2:12) Original Sound 2500 Oldies But Goodies Volumes 1-15 Box Set. *(this box set uses the "Waring - fds" noise reduction process)*
- (M) (2:15) Time-Life 2RNR-01 Rock 'N' Roll Era - 1957. *(original pressings of this song on this cd were (E))*
- (M) (2:15) Time-Life RHD-08 Rhythm & Blues - 1957.
- (M) (2:15) Collectables 2509 WCBS-FM For Lovers Only Part 1.
- (M) (2:15) Collectables 2552 WOGL History Of Rock Vol. 2.
- (M) (2:16) Time-Life R103-27 Love Me Tender.
- (M) (2:16) Chess 9352 Chess Rhythm & Roll.
- (M) (2:14) Rhino 72507 Doo Wop Box II.
- (M) (2:15) Time-Life R857-05 The Heart Of Rock 'n' Roll 1957.
- (M) (2:15) Time-Life R838-23 Solid Gold Soul 1957.

JOHNNY and THE HURRICANES
1959 CROSSFIRE
1959 RED RIVER ROCK
- (M) (2:10) Curb 77402 All-Time Great Instrumental Hits Volume 2.
- (M) (2:08) Rhino 71547 Let There Be Drums Volume 1: The 50's.
- (M) (2:10) Rhino 71601 Rock Instrumental Classics Volume 1: The Fifties.
- (M) (2:10) Rhino 72035 Rock Instrumental Classics Vols. 1-5 Box Set.
- (M) (2:10) Time-Life 2RNR-20 Rock 'N' Roll Era - 1959 Still Rockin'.
- (M) (2:10) Capitol Special Markets 57272 Great Instrumental Hits From Rock's Golden Years.

1959 REVEILLE ROCK
- (E) (2:20) K-Tel 3059 Saxy Rock.
- (E) (2:20) K-Tel 3453 Rockin' Instrumentals.

1960 BEATNIK FLY
- (M) (2:08) Rhino 71602 Rock Instrumental Classics Volume 2: The Sixties. *(noise on the introduction)*
- (M) (2:08) Rhino 72035 Rock Instrumental Classics Vols. 1-5 Box Set. *(noise on the introduction)*

1960 DOWN YONDER

JOHNNY HATES JAZZ
1988 SHATTERED DREAMS
     (S)   (3:27)   EMI 27674 Living In Oblivion: The 80's Greatest Hits Volume Three.
     (S)   (3:25)   Priority 53769 Rock Of The 80's Volume 10.
     (S)   (3:28)   Rhino 71643 Billboard Top Hits - 1988.
     (S)   (3:25)   Virgin 90860 and 86032 Turn Back The Clock.
     (S)   (3:27)   Time-Life R988-10 Sounds Of The 80's: 1988.
     (S)   (3:27)   Madacy Entertainment 1988 Rock On 1988.
1988 I DON'T WANT TO BE A HERO
     (S)   (4:29)   Virgin 90860 and 86032 Turn Back The Clock.

SAMMY JOHNS
1975 CHEVY VAN
     (S)   (2:55)   Priority 8670 Hitchin' A Ride/70's Greatest Rock Hits Volume 10. *(45 version)*
     (S)   (2:55)   Rhino 70761 Super Hits Of The 70's Volume 14. *(45 version)*
     (S)   (2:54)   Razor & Tie 22505 More Fabulous 70's Volume 2. *(45 version)*
     (S)   (2:55)   Time-Life SOD-31 Sounds Of The Seventies - AM Top Twenty. *(45 version)*
     (S)   (2:55)   Collectables 5033 Golden Classics. *(45 version)*

BETTY JOHNSON
1957 I DREAMED
1957 LITTLE WHITE LIES
1958 THE LITTLE BLUE MAN
     (M)   (2:39)   Time-Life HPD-40 Your Hit Parade - Golden Goofers.
1958 DREAM

DON JOHNSON
1986 HEARTBEAT
     (S)   (4:17)   Epic 40366 Heartbeat.
     (S)   (4:14)   Time-Life R988-17 Sounds Of The Eighties: The Mid '80s Take Two.
     (S)   (4:18)   Razor & Tie 82168 Heartbeat.
released as by BARBRA STREISAND and DON JOHNSON:
1988 TILL I LOVED YOU
(dj copies of this 45 ran (4:14) and (4:48);
commercial copies were all (4:48))
     (S)   (5:09)   Columbia 40880 Barbra Streisand - Till I Loved You. *(LP version)*

MARV JOHNSON
1959 COME TO ME
     (M)   (2:17)   Collectables 5236 Marvelous Marv/Golden Classics.
     (M)   (2:17)   EMI 98895 Best Of.
1960 YOU GOT WHAT IT TAKES
     (M)   (2:41)   EMI 96268 24 Greatest Hits Of All Time.
     (M)   (2:39)   Rhino 70646 Billboard's Top R&B Hits Of 1960.
     (M)   (2:39)   JCI 3204 Heart & Soul Fifties.
     (M)   (2:39)   Curb 77323 All Time Greatest Hits Of Rock 'N' Roll.
     (M)   (2:40)   Collectables 5236 Marvelous Marv/Golden Classics.
     (M)   (2:40)   EMI 98895 Best Of.
     (M)   (2:36)   Time-Life 2RNR-28 Rock 'N' Roll Era - The 50's Rave On.
     (M)   (2:36)   Time-Life RHD-03 Rhythm & Blues - 1959.
     (M)   (2:39)   Motown 314530436 A Tribute To Berry Gordy.
     (M)   (2:39)   Hip-O 40028 The Glory Of Love - '50s Sweet & Soulful Love Songs.
     (M)   (2:36)   Time-Life R838-21 Solid Gold Soul 1959.
1960 I LOVE THE WAY YOU LOVE
     (M)   (2:36)   Collectables 5236 Marvelous Marv/Golden Classics.
     (M)   (2:37)   EMI 98895 Best Of.
     (M)   (2:36)   Time-Life 2RNR-46 Rock 'N' Roll Era - 60's Juke Box Memories.
     (M)   (2:36)   Time-Life RHD-15 Rhythm & Blues - 1960.
     (M)   (2:36)   Time-Life R838-20 Solid Gold Soul 1960.
1960 (YOU'VE GOT TO) MOVE TWO MOUNTAINS
     (S)   (2:43)   Collectables 5236 Marvelous Marv/Golden Classics.
     (S)   (2:43)   EMI 98895 Best Of. *(alternate take)*
     (S)   (2:42)   EMI-Capitol Special Markets 19552 Lost Hits Of The '60s.

MICHAEL JOHNSON
1978 BLUER THAN BLUE
     (S)   (2:55)   Rhino 71201 Super Hits Of The 70's Volume 21.
     (S)   (2:52)   Time-Life SOD-34 Sounds Of The Seventies - The Late 70's.
     (S)   (2:52)   Madacy Entertainment 1978 Rock On 1978.
     (S)   (2:54)   Time-Life R834-08 Body Talk - On My Mind.
1978 ALMOST LIKE BEING IN LOVE
1979 THIS NIGHT WON'T LAST FOREVER
     (S)   (3:37)   Rhino 71890 Radio Daze: Pop Hits Of The 80's Volume One.
     (S)   (3:37)   Time-Life R834-15 Body Talk - Once In Lifetime.

TOM JOHNSTON
1979 SAVANNAH NIGHTS

JO JO GUNNE
1972 RUN RUN RUN
     (S)   (2:32)   JCI 4510 Masters Of Metal: Crankin' Up 1970-1980.
     (S)   (2:32)   Rhino 70928 Super Hits Of The 70's Volume 8.
     (S)   (2:32)   Time-Life R968-05 Guitar Rock 1972-1973.
     (S)   (2:33)   Time-Life SOD-25 Sounds Of The Seventies - Seventies Generation.

FRANCE JOLI
1979 COME TO ME
(actual 45 time is (4:12) not (4:05) as stated on the record label)
     (S)   (4:12)   Rhino 70493 Billboard Top Dance Hits - 1979. *(45 version)*
     (S)   (4:13)   K-Tel 3251 Disco Fever. *(45 version)*
     (S)   (4:12)   Rhino 72837 Disco Queens: The 70's. *(45 version)*
     (S)   (9:22)   Beast 53202 Disco Divas - A Salute To The Ladies. *(LP version)*

JON & ROBIN and THE IN CROWD
1967 DO IT AGAIN A LITTLE BIT SLOWER
     (S)   (2:30)   Rhino 70995 One Hit Wonders Of The 60's Volume 1.

JON B
released as by JON B featuring BABYFACE:
1995 SOMEONE TO LOVE
     (S)   (4:32)   Yab Yum/550 Music 66436 Bonafide.
     (S)   (4:30)   Work 67009 O.S.T. Bad Boys.
released as by JON B:
1995 PRETTY GIRL
     (S)   (4:16)   Yab Yum/550 Music 66436 Bonafide.

ETTA JONES
1960 DON'T GO TO STRANGERS
     (S)   (3:49)   Prestige 298 Don't Go To Strangers.

HOWARD JONES
1984 NEW SONG
     (S)   (4:14)   Elektra 60346 Human's Lib.
     (S)   (4:13)   Elektra 61540 Best Of.
1984 WHAT IS LOVE?
     (S)   (6:31)   Elektra 60346 Human's Lib. *(LP version)*
     (S)   (3:39)   Elektra 61540 Best Of. *(45 version)*
1985 THINGS CAN ONLY GET BETTER
     (S)   (3:55)   Elektra 60390 Dream Into Action.
     (S)   (3:54)   Elektra 61540 Best Of.
     (S)   (3:54)   JCI 3159 18 Modern Rock Classics From The 80's.
     (S)   (3:54)   JCI 3150 1985 - Only Dance - 1989.
     (S)   (3:54)   Time-Life R988-17 Sounds Of The Eighties: The Mid '80s Take Two.
1985 LIFE IN ONE DAY
     (S)   (3:39)   Elektra 60390 Dream Into Action.
     (S)   (3:37)   Elektra 61540 Best Of.
1986 NO ONE IS TO BLAME
     (S)   (3:28)   Elektra 60390 Dream Into Action. *(this is the "Dream Into Action" LP version and not the hit single version)*

(S)   (4:11)   Elektra 60499   One To One.
(S)   (4:11)   Elektra 61540   Best Of.
(S)   (4:11)   Time-Life R988-04   Sounds Of The Eighties: 1986.
(S)   (4:10)   Madacy Entertainment 1986   Rock On 1986.
(S)   (4:10)   Hollywood 62123   More Music From The Motion Picture "Romy And Michele's High School Reunion".
(S)   (3:28)   Time-Life R834-14   Body Talk - Love And Tenderness.   *(this is the "Dream Into Action" LP version and not the hit single version)*

1986   YOU KNOW I LOVE YOU...DON'T YOU?
(S)   (4:03)   Elektra 60499   One To One.   *(LP length)*
(S)   (4:02)   Elektra 61540   Best Of.   *(LP length)*

1989   EVERLASTING LOVE
(S)   (4:16)   Elektra 60794   Cross That Line.
(S)   (4:18)   Elektra 61540   Best Of.
(S)   (4:16)   Madacy Entertainment 1989   Rock On 1989.
(S)   (4:18)   Time-Life R834-19   Body Talk - Always And Forever.

1989   THE PRISONER
(S)   (4:38)   Elektra 60794   Cross That Line.   *(LP version)*
(S)   (4:40)   Elektra 61540   Best Of.   *(LP version)*

1992   LIFT ME UP
(S)   (3:39)   Elektra 61135   In The Running.
(S)   (3:39)   Elektra 61540   Best Of.

JACK JONES
1963   WIVES AND LOVERS
(S)   (2:28)   Curb 77324   Greatest Hits.
(S)   (2:30)   Time-Life HPD-33   Your Hit Parade - The Early 60's.
(S)   (2:29)   MCA Special Products 22089   The Impossible Dream.
(S)   (2:28)   MCA 11301   Greatest Hits.
(S)   (2:28)   Rhino 72557   Jackpot! The Las Vegas Story.
(S)   (2:28)   K-Tel 3630   Lounge Legends.
(S)   (2:28)   Varese Sarabande 5873   The Burt Bacharach Songbook.

1965   DEAR HEART
(S)   (2:36)   MCA Special Products 22089   The Impossible Dream.
(S)   (2:35)   MCA 11301   Greatest Hits.
(S)   (2:35)   JCI 7022   Those Wonderful Years - It Must Be Him.

1965   THE RACE IS ON
(S)   (1:46)   Curb 77324   Greatest Hits.
(S)   (1:45)   MCA 11301   Greatest Hits.

1966   THE IMPOSSIBLE DREAM
(S)   (2:16)   Curb 77324   Greatest Hits.
(S)   (2:17)   MCA Special Products 22089   The Impossible Dream.   *(noisy fadeout)*
(S)   (2:17)   MCA 11120   Stardust/The Classic Decca Hits & Standards Collection.
(S)   (2:15)   K-Tel 3471   High Hopes - Songs To Lift Your Spirits.
(S)   (2:15)   Time-Life R135-04   Broadway Hit Parade.
(S)   (2:17)   MCA 11301   Greatest Hits.

1967   LADY
(S)   (2:40)   Time-Life R138/05   Look Of Love.
(S)   (2:42)   MCA Special Products 22089   The Impossible Dream.
(S)   (2:41)   MCA 11301   Greatest Hits.

JIMMY JONES
1960   HANDY MAN
(M)   (1:59)   Rhino 70621   Billboard's Top Rock & Roll Hits Of 1960.
(M)   (1:59)   Rhino 72004   Billboard's Top Rock & Roll Hits 1957-1961 Box Set.
(E)   (2:00)   Original Sound 8857   Oldies But Goodies Vol. 7.   *(this compact disc uses the "Waring - fds" noise reduction process)*
(E)   (2:00)   Original Sound 2223   Oldies But Goodies Volumes 2,7,9,12 and 13 Box Set.   *(this box set uses the "Waring - fds" noise reduction process)*
(E)   (2:00)   Original Sound 2500   Oldies But Goodies Volumes 1-15 Box Set.   *(this box set uses the "Waring - fds" noise reduction process)*
(M)   (1:59)   Mercury 832041   45's On CD Volume 1.

(M)   (1:58)   Time-Life 2RNR-11   Rock 'N' Roll Era - 1960.
(M)   (1:55)   Time-Life RHD-15   Rhythm & Blues - 1960.
(M)   (2:03)   Polygram Special Markets 314520264   Soul Hits Of The 60's.
(M)   (1:58)   JCI 3166   #1 Radio Hits 1960 - Only Rock 'n Roll - 1964.
(M)   (2:02)   Eric 11502   Hard To Find 45's On CD (Volume I) 1955-60.
(M)   (1:55)   Time-Life R838-20   Solid Gold Soul 1960.
(M)   (2:02)   Polygram Special Markets 314520478   50's Jukebox Hits.

1960   GOOD TIMIN'
(S)   (2:07)   Mercury 816555   45's On CD Volume 2.   *(reverb is missing)*
(S)   (2:07)   Time-Life 2RNR-11   Rock 'N' Roll Era - 1960.   *(reverb is missing)*
(S)   (2:09)   Eric 11502   Hard To Find 45's On CD (Volume I) 1955-60.
(S)   (2:07)   Eclipse Music Group 64867   Rock 'n Roll Relix 1960-1961.   *(reverb is missing)*
(S)   (2:07)   Eclipse Music Group 64872   Rock 'n Roll Relix 1960-1969.   *(reverb is missing)*

JOE JONES
1960   YOU TALK TOO MUCH
(M)   (2:35)   Collectables 5416   Murray The K - Sing Along With The Golden Greats.
(M)   (2:28)   Rhino 70621   Billboard's Top Rock & Roll Hits Of 1960.   *(found only on the 1993 reissue of this cd)*
(M)   (2:35)   Time-Life 2RNR-11   Rock 'N' Roll Era - 1960.
(M)   (2:35)   Time-Life RHD-15   Rhythm & Blues - 1960.
(M)   (2:34)   JCI 3125   1960 - Only Rock 'N Roll - 1964.
(M)   (2:28)   Rhino 71802   O.S.T. Andre.
(M)   (2:35)   Time-Life R838-20   Solid Gold Soul 1960.

LINDA JONES
1967   HYPNOTIZED
(S)   (2:39)   Rhino 75770   Soul Shots Volume 2.
(S)   (2:39)   Original Sound 8878   Art Laboe's Dedicated To You.
(S)   (2:39)   Original Sound 4001   Art Laboe's 60 Killer Oldies.
(S)   (2:35)   Time-Life RHD-10   Rhythm & Blues - 1967.
(S)   (2:36)   Time-Life 2CLR-28   Classic Rock - On The Soul Side II.
(S)   (2:38)   Collectables 5120   Golden Classics.   *(mastered from a scratchy record)*
(S)   (2:37)   Thump 7020   Low Rider Oldies Volume II.   *(mastered from vinyl)*
(S)   (2:37)   Collectables 5452   20 Golden Classics.   *(mastered from vinyl)*
(S)   (2:39)   Right Stuff 30578   Slow Jams: The 60's Volume 4.
(S)   (2:38)   Warner Brothers 45711   The Best Of Loma Records.
(S)   (2:35)   Collectables 5727   Soul Classics Volume One.
(S)   (2:35)   Time-Life R838-02   Solid Gold Soul - 1967.
(S)   (2:37)   TVT 4010   Rhythm Revue.
(S)   (2:38)   Priority 53108   Slow Grind Volume One.

ORAN "JUICE" JONES
1986   THE RAIN
(dj copies of this 45 ran (3:14) and (5:05); commercial copies were all (5:05))
(S)   (5:08)   Priority 9505   Rap's Greatest Hits Vol. 3.
(S)   (5:08)   Columbia 40367   Oran "Juice" Jones.
(S)   (5:07)   Rhino 72141   Billboard Hot R&B Hits 1986.
(S)   (5:06)   Def Jam 314523848   Def Jam Music Group 10th Year Anniversary.
(S)   (5:07)   Thump 4740   Old School Love Songs Volume 4.

QUINCY JONES
1978   STUFF LIKE THAT
(actual 45 time is (3:08) not (3:00) as stated on the record label)
(S)   (6:16)   A&M 3249   Sounds.....And Stuff Like That.   *(LP version)*
(S)   (3:07)   A&M 6550   Classics Volume 3.   *(45 version)*

QUINCY JONES *(Continued)*

- (S) (3:07) A&M 3200 The Best. *(45 version)*
- (S) (3:06) A&M 314540556 Greatest Hits. *(45 version)*
- (S) (3:05) Hip-O 40041 The Studio Collection Disco 54. *(45 version)*

1981 AI NO CORRIDA
- (S) (6:27) A&M 3248 The Dude. *(LP version)*
- (S) (4:19) A&M 6550 Classics Volume 3. *(45 version but :09 longer)*
- (S) (4:19) A&M 3200 The Best. *(45 version but :09 longer)*
- (S) (4:15) A&M 314540556 Greatest Hits. *(45 version but :05 longer)*

released as by QUINCY JONES featuring JAMES INGRAM:
1981 JUST ONCE
- (S) (4:29) A&M 6550 Quincy Jones - Classics Volume 3.
- (S) (4:32) A&M 3248 Quincy Jones - The Dude.
- (S) (4:29) A&M 3200 Quincy Jones - The Best.
- (S) (4:32) Warner Brothers 26700 James Ingram Greatest Hits.
- (S) (4:30) MCA 11329 Soul Train 25th Anniversary Box Set.
- (S) (4:31) A&M 314540556 Quincy Jones - Greatest Hits.
- (S) (4:32) Time-Life R834-10 Body Talk - From The Heart.

1982 ONE HUNDRED WAYS
- (S) (4:17) Rebound 314520241 Quincy Jones - The Best Volume Two.
- (S) (4:17) A&M 6550 Quincy Jones - Classics Volume 3.
- (S) (4:18) A&M 3248 Quincy Jones - The Dude.
- (S) (4:17) A&M 3278 Quincy Jones - The Best Volume Two.
- (S) (4:18) Warner Brothers 26700 James Ingram Greatest Hits.
- (S) (4:16) A&M 314540556 Quincy Jones - Greatest Hits.
- (S) (4:17) Rebound 314520431 Soul Classics - Best Of The 80's.
- (S) (4:18) Time-Life R834-13 Body Talk - Just The Two Of Us.

released as by QUINCY JONES featuring RAY CHARLES and CHAKA KHAN:
1990 I'LL BE GOOD TO YOU
- (S) (4:54) Qwest/Warner Brothers 26020 Quincy Jones - Back On The Block. *(LP version)*
- (S) (3:55) JCI 3177 1985 - Only Soul - 1989. *(45 version faded :22 early)*

released as by QUINCY JONES featuring AL B. SURE!/ JAMES INGRAM/EL DeBARGE/BARRY WHITE:
1990 THE SECRET GARDEN
- (S) (6:39) Qwest/Warner Brothers 26020 Quincy Jones - Back On The Block.
- (S) (6:45) Mercury 314514143 Barry White - Just For You. *(includes a :06 previously unreleased introduction by Barry White)*

RICKIE LEE JONES
1979 CHUCK E.'s IN LOVE
- (S) (3:27) Warner Brothers 3296 Rickie Lee Jones.
- (S) (3:27) Time-Life SOD-19 Sounds Of The Seventies - 1979: Take Two.

TOM JONES
1965 IT'S NOT UNUSUAL
- (M) (2:00) Rhino 70323 History Of British Rock Volume 5.
- (M) (2:00) Rhino 72022 History Of British Rock Box Set.
- (S) (2:00) London 810192 Golden Hits.
- (S) (1:59) Deram 844322 The Complete Tom Jones.
- (S) (1:58) Rebound 314520243 Tom Jones/Engelbert Humperdinck Back To Back.
- (S) (1:58) Mercury 314528871 O.S.T. Home For The Holidays.
- (S) (1:59) Track Factory 11445 O.S.T. Flipper.
- (S) (1:59) Rebound 422844628 Best Of.

1965 WHAT'S NEW PUSSYCAT?
- (S) (2:04) London 810192 Golden Hits. *(LP version)*
- (S) (2:03) Deram 844322 The Complete Tom Jones. *(LP version)*
- (S) (2:02) Time-Life SUD-03 Superhits - 1965. *(LP version)*
- (M) (2:18) Time-Life HPD-37 Your Hit Parade - The 60's. *(45 version)*

- (S) (2:03) Rebound 314520243 Tom Jones/Engelbert Humperdinck Back To Back. *(LP version)*
- (S) (2:03) Special Music 5039 Great Britons! Volume One. *(LP version)*
- (S) (2:05) London 820523 What's New Pussycat. *(LP version)*
- (S) (2:03) Chronicles 314535875 Bachelor Pad Favorites. *(LP version)*
- (S) (2:02) K-Tel 3630 Lounge Legends. *(LP version)*
- (S) (2:02) Time-Life AM1-10 AM Gold - 1965. *(LP version)*
- (S) (2:03) Polygram Special Markets 314520459 Vocal Treasures. *(LP version)*
- (S) (2:03) Rebound 422844628 Best Of. *(LP version)*

1965 WITH THESE HANDS
- (S) (2:42) London 810192 Golden Hits.
- (S) (2:41) Rebound 314520243 Tom Jones/Engelbert Humperdinck Back To Back.
- (S) (2:41) London 820523 What's New Pussycat.

1966 THUNDERBALL
- (S) (3:00) EMI 46079 James Bond 13 Original Themes.
- (S) (3:00) EMI 90628 O.S.T. Thunderball.
- (S) (3:00) EMI 98560 Best Of James Bond 30th Anniversary.
- (S) (3:00) EMI 98413 Best Of James Bond 30th Anniversary Collection.
- (S) (2:58) Rebound 314520243 Tom Jones/Engelbert Humperdinck Back To Back.

1967 GREEN, GREEN GRASS OF HOME
- (S) (3:10) London 810192 Golden Hits. *(timing index is off by :06)*
- (S) (3:03) London 820182 Green, Green Grass Of Home.
- (S) (3:03) Deram 844322 The Complete Tom Jones.
- (S) (3:02) Time-Life SUD-05 Superhits - 1967.
- (S) (3:02) Rebound 314520243 Tom Jones/Engelbert Humperdinck Back To Back.
- (S) (3:03) Rebound 314520222 Country Memories.
- (S) (3:02) Time-Life AM1-08 AM Gold - 1967.
- (S) (3:02) Rebound 314520450 Tom Jones/Engelbert Humperdinck Sing Country Favorites.
- (S) (3:02) Time-Life R814-01 Love Songs.

1967 DETROIT CITY
- (S) (3:33) London 810192 Golden Hits.
- (S) (3:29) London 820182 Green, Green Grass Of Home.
- (S) (3:32) Deram 844322 The Complete Tom Jones.
- (S) (3:32) Rebound 314520222 Country Memories.
- (S) (3:32) Rebound 422844628 Best Of.

1968 DELILAH
- (S) (3:22) London 810192 Golden Hits. *(LP version)*
- (S) (3:23) London 820486 Delilah. *(LP version)*
- (S) (3:21) Deram 844322 The Complete Tom Jones. *(LP version)*
- (S) (3:20) Time-Life SUD-18 Superhits - Late 60's Classics. *(LP version)*
- (S) (3:24) Rhino 72557 Jackpot! The Las Vegas Story. *(LP version)*
- (S) (3:20) Time-Life AM1-12 AM Gold - Late '60s Classics. *(LP version)*

1968 HELP YOURSELF
- (S) (2:53) London 810192 Golden Hits.
- (S) (2:51) Deram 844322 The Complete Tom Jones.

1969 LOVE ME TONIGHT
- (S) (3:11) London 810192 Golden Hits.
- (S) (3:10) Deram 844322 The Complete Tom Jones.
- (S) (3:10) Rebound 422844628 Best Of.

1969 I'LL NEVER FALL IN LOVE AGAIN
(this 45 was issued in two lengths, (4:18) and (2:55))
- (S) (4:12) London 810192 Golden Hits.
- (S) (4:11) Deram 844322 The Complete Tom Jones.
- (S) (4:11) Time-Life R138/05 Look Of Love.
- (S) (4:10) Hammer & Lace 697124114 Leading Men: Masters Of Style Volume Three.
- (M) (2:53) Rebound 422844628 Best Of.

1970 WITHOUT LOVE (THERE IS NOTHING)
- (S) (3:44) London 810192 Golden Hits.
- (S) (3:43) Deram 844322 The Complete Tom Jones.
- (S) (3:43) Time-Life SUD-20 Superhits - Early 70's Classics.
- (S) (3:43) Time-Life AM1-15 AM Gold - Early '70s Classics.
- (S) (3:43) Rhino 72736 Billboard Top Soft Rock Hits - 1970.

1970 DAUGHTER OF DARKNESS
(S) (3:16) Deram 844322 The Complete Tom Jones.
(S) (3:15) Curb 77716 Greatest Songs.
1970 I (WHO HAVE NOTHING)
(S) (2:56) Rhino 70593 The Rock 'N' Roll Classics Of Leiber & Stoller.
(S) (2:57) Deram 844322 The Complete Tom Jones.
(S) (2:55) Curb 77716 Greatest Songs.
(S) (2:55) Nick At Nite/550 Music 63405 Lounging At The Nick At Niteclub.
(S) (2:56) Simitar 55562 The Number One's: Smooth Love.
1970 CAN'T STOP LOVING YOU
1971 SHE'S A LADY
(S) (2:52) Deram 844322 The Complete Tom Jones.
(S) (2:49) Time-Life SUD-10 Superhits - 1971.
(S) (2:51) Curb 77716 Greatest Songs.
(S) (2:19) MCA 11231 O.S.T. To Wong Foo, Thanks For Everything. *(rerecording)*
(S) (2:52) Rhino 72737 Billboard Top Soft Rock Hits - 1971.
(S) (2:48) Time-Life AM1-06 AM Gold - 1971.
(S) (2:52) Rhino 72516 Behind Closed Doors - '70s Swingers.
(S) (3:14) Geffen 25218 O.S.T. Fear And Loathing In Las Vegas. *(time includes :23 of movie dialogue; all songs and the movie dialogue are segued together)*
1971 PUPPET MAN
(S) (3:22) Curb 77716 Greatest Songs.
1971 RESURRECTION SHUFFLE
(S) (2:54) Curb 77716 Greatest Songs.
1971 TILL
(S) (2:17) Deram 844322 The Complete Tom Jones.
(S) (2:16) Curb 77716 Greatest Songs.
1977 SAY YOU'LL STAY UNTIL TOMORROW
(S) (3:34) Curb 77716 Greatest Songs.
released as by THE ART OF NOISE featuring TOM JONES:
1988 KISS
(S) (3:29) Priority 53721 Rock Of The 80's Volume 5.
(S) (8:09) China/Polydor 837367 Art Of Noise - Best Of. *(remixed)*
(S) (3:29) Discovery 74108 Art Of Noise - Best Of.

JONES GIRLS
1979 YOU GONNA MAKE ME LOVE SOMEBODY ELSE
(S) (4:31) Rhino 71862 Smooth Grooves Volume 4.
(S) (4:30) Hip-O 40041 The Studio Collection Disco 54.
(S) (4:31) Time-Life R838-15 Solid Gold Soul 1979.

JANIS JOPLIN (see also BIG BROTHER and THE HOLDING COMPANY)
1969 KOZMIC BLUES
(S) (4:21) Columbia 9913 I Got Dem Ol' Kozmic Blues Again Mama! *(LP version)*
(S) (4:21) Columbia/Legacy 48845 Janis. *(LP version)*
(S) (4:21) Legacy/Columbia 67005 18 Essential Songs. *(LP version)*
(S) (4:21) Columbia 64804 Cheap Thrills/I Got Dem 'Ol Kozmic Blues Again/Pearl. *(LP version)*
1971 ME AND BOBBY McGEE
(S) (4:29) Columbia 45048 Rock Classics Of The 70's. *(LP version)*
(S) (4:30) Columbia 32168 Greatest Hits. *(LP version)*
(S) (4:29) Columbia 30322 and 53441 and 64413 Pearl. *(LP version)*
(S) (4:28) Sony Music Special Products 48621 Kris Kristofferson: Singer/Songwriter. *(LP version)*
(S) (4:44) Columbia/Legacy 48845 Janis. *(alternate take; includes :49 of studio talk)*
(S) (4:28) Columbia/Legacy 48845 Janis. *(LP version)*
(M) (3:56) Legacy/Columbia 67005 18 Essential Songs. *(acoustic demo)*
(S) (4:29) Columbia 64804 Cheap Thrills/I Got Dem 'Ol Kozmic Blues Again/Pearl. *(LP version)*
(S) (4:28) Eclipse Music Group 64892 Rock 'n Roll Relix 1970-1971. *(LP version)*
(S) (4:28) Eclipse Music Group 64897 Rock 'n Roll Relix 1970-1979. *(LP version)*

(S) (4:27) Time-Life R13610 Gold And Platinum Box Set - The Ultimate Rock Collection. *(LP version)*
1971 CRY BABY
(S) (3:56) Columbia 32168 Greatest Hits.
(S) (3:57) Columbia 30322 and 53441 Pearl.
(S) (4:56) Columbia/Legacy 48845 Janis. *(alternate take)*
(S) (3:57) Columbia 64804 Cheap Thrills/I Got Dem 'Ol Kozmic Blues Again/Pearl.
(S) (3:57) Columbia/Legacy 64413 Pearl. *(gold disc)*

JEREMY JORDAN
1993 THE RIGHT KIND OF LOVE
(S) (4:44) Giant 24465 Beverly Hills, 90210 - The Soundtrack.
(S) (4:31) Giant 24483 Try My Love.
1993 WANNAGIRL
(S) (4:29) Giant 24483 Try My Love.

MONTELL JORDAN
1995 THIS IS HOW WE DO IT
(S) (4:36) PMP/RAL 314527179 This Is How We Do It.
(S) (3:55) Def Jam 314523848 Def Jam Music Group 10th Year Anniversary.
(S) (3:18) Tommy Boy 1163 Jock Jams Volume 2. *(all selections on this cd are segued together)*
(S) (3:55) EMI-Capitol Music Group 54547 Hot Luv.
(S) (3:56) Rebound 314520449 Hip Hop With R&B Flava.
(S) (3:50) Hollywood 62121 Monday Night Football Jamz.
(S) (3:53) Def Jam 314536377 Def Jam's Greatest Hits.
1995 SOMETHIN' 4 DA HONEYZ
(S) (4:34) PMP/RAL 314527179 This Is How We Do It.
(S) (3:57) Def Jam 314523848 Def Jam Music Group 10th Year Anniversary.
released as by MONTELL JORDAN featuring SLICK RICK:
1996 I LIKE
(S) (4:40) Def Jam 314531911 O.S.T. The Nutty Professor.
(S) (4:40) Def Jam 314533191 More....
released as by MONTELL JORDAN:
1996 FALLING
(S) (4:01) Def Jam 314533191 More....
(S) (4:01) Polygram TV 314553641 Pure Soul 1997.
1997 WHAT'S ON TONIGHT
(S) (4:36) Def Jam 314533191 More....

JOURNEY
1979 LOVIN', TOUCHIN', SQUEEZIN'
(S) (3:50) Columbia 35797 and 67726 Evolution. *(tracks into next selection)*
(S) (3:49) Columbia 44493 Greatest Hits.
(S) (4:56) Columbia 48937 and 65159 Time3. *(live)*
(S) (3:49) Razor & Tie 22502 Those Rocking 70's.
1980 ANY WAY YOU WANT IT
(S) (3:22) Columbia 36339 and 67727 Departure.
(S) (3:22) Columbia 44493 Greatest Hits.
(S) (3:21) Columbia 48937 and 65159 Time3.
1980 WALKS LIKE A LADY
(S) (3:14) Columbia 36339 and 67727 Departure.
(S) (7:12) Columbia 48937 and 65159 Time3. *(live)*
(S) (7:08) Columbia 37016 Captured. *(live)*
1981 THE PARTY'S OVER (HOPELESSLY IN LOVE)
(S) (3:39) Columbia 48937 and 65159 Time3.
(S) (3:40) Columbia 37016 Captured.
1981 WHO'S CRYING NOW
(dj copies of this 45 ran (4:20) and (5:01); commercial copies were all (5:01))
(S) (5:01) Columbia 37408 and 67722 Escape.
(S) (5:01) Columbia 44493 Greatest Hits.
(S) (5:00) Columbia 48937 and 65159 Time3.
1981 DON'T STOP BELIEVIN'
(S) (4:11) Columbia 37408 and 67722 Escape.
(S) (4:09) Columbia 44493 Greatest Hits.
(S) (4:10) Columbia 48937 and 65159 Time3.
(S) (4:10) Time-Life R13610 Gold And Platinum Box Set - The Ultimate Rock Collection.
1982 OPEN ARMS
(S) (3:16) CBS Special Products 44363 Rock Of The 80's.
(S) (3:17) Rhino 70677 Billboard Top Hits - 1982.

JOURNEY (Continued)

- (S) (3:18) Full Moon/Elektra 60691 O.S.T. Heavy Metal.
- (S) (3:18) Columbia 44493 Greatest Hits.
- (S) (3:17) Columbia 48937 and 65159 Time3.
- (S) (3:17) Columbia 37408 and 67722 Escape.

1982 STILL THEY RIDE
(dj copies of this 45 ran (2:55) and (3:45);
commercial copies were all (3:45))
- (S) (3:48) Columbia 48937 and 65159 Time3.
- (S) (3:48) Columbia 37408 and 67722 Escape.

1983 SEPARATE WAYS (WORLDS APART)
- (S) (5:24) Columbia 44493 Greatest Hits. *(LP version)*
- (S) (5:24) Columbia 48937 and 65159 Time3. *(LP version)*
- (S) (5:24) Columbia 38504 and 67723 Frontiers. *(LP version)*

1983 FAITHFULLY
- (S) (4:26) Columbia 44493 Greatest Hits.
- (S) (4:26) Columbia 48937 and 65159 Time3.
- (S) (4:26) Columbia 38504 and 67723 Frontiers.

1983 AFTER THE FALL
- (S) (4:58) Columbia 48937 and 65159 Time3.
- (S) (4:59) Columbia 38504 and 67723 Frontiers.

1983 SEND HER MY LOVE
- (S) (3:54) Columbia 44493 Greatest Hits.
- (S) (3:53) Columbia 48937 and 65159 Time3.
- (S) (3:54) Columbia 38504 and 67723 Frontiers.

1985 ONLY THE YOUNG
- (S) (4:05) Geffen 24063 O.S.T. Vision Quest.
- (S) (4:03) Columbia 44493 Greatest Hits.
- (S) (4:04) Columbia 48937 and 65159 Time3.

1986 BE GOOD TO YOURSELF
- (S) (3:50) Columbia 44493 Greatest Hits.
- (S) (3:50) Columbia 48937 and 65159 Time3.
- (S) (3:50) Columbia 39936 and 67724 Raised On Radio.

1986 SUZANNE
- (S) (3:37) Columbia 39936 and 67724 Raised On Radio.

1986 GIRL CAN'T HELP IT
- (S) (3:50) Columbia 44493 Greatest Hits.
- (S) (4:16) Columbia 48937 and 65159 Time3. *(live)*
- (S) (3:50) Columbia 39936 and 67724 Raised On Radio.

1987 I'LL BE ALRIGHT WITHOUT YOU
- (S) (4:33) Columbia 44493 Greatest Hits. *(45 version faded :09 early)*
- (S) (4:50) Columbia 39936 and 67724 Raised On Radio. *(LP version)*
- (S) (4:58) Columbia 48937 and 65159 Time3. *(live)*

1996 WHEN YOU LOVE A WOMAN
- (S) (4:07) Columbia 67514 Trial By Fire.

JUMP 'N THE SADDLE
1984 THE CURLY SHUFFLE
- (S) (2:54) Rhino 72124 Dr. Demento 25th Anniversary Collection.

- (S) (2:54) Time-Life R988-23 Sounds Of The Eighties 1984-1985.

JUNIOR
1982 MAMA USED TO SAY
- (S) (6:40) Rhino 71755 and 72832 Phat Trax - The Best Of Old School, Vol. 4. *(12" single version)*
- (S) (6:36) Mercury 314526972 Best Of. *(12" single version)*
- (S) (3:34) Rhino 72137 Billboard Hot R&B Hits 1982.
- (S) (3:35) Simitar 55542 The Number One's: Soul On Fire.

JUNIOR M.A.F.I.A.
1995 PLAYER'S ANTHEM
- (S) (5:22) Undeas/Big Beat 92614 Conspiracy.

released as by JUNIOR M.A.F.I.A. featuring THE NOTORIOUS B.I.G.:
1996 GET MONEY
- (S) (4:33) Undeas/Big Beat 92614 and 92646 Junior M.A.F.I.A. - Conspiracy.
- (S) (3:46) Arista 18977 Ultimate Hip Hop Party 1998. *(all selections on this cd are segued together; remix)*
- (S) (4:05) Def Jam 314534746 Yo! MTV Raps Compilation. *(clean radio edit)*
- (S) (3:44) Boxtunes 314524387 Big Phat Ones Of Hip-Hop Volume 2. *(all songs on this cd are segued together)*

BILL JUSTIS
1957 RAUNCHY
- (M) (2:21) Rhino 75884 The Sun Story.
- (M) (2:21) Capitol Special Markets 57272 Great Instrumental Hits From Rock's Golden Years.
- (S) (2:24) Mercury 832041 45's On CD Volume 1. *(rerecording)*
- (M) (2:20) RCA 66059 Sun's Greatest Hits.
- (M) (2:20) Rhino 71601 Rock Instrumental Classics Volume 1: The Fifties.
- (M) (2:20) Rhino 72035 Rock Instrumental Classics Vols. 1-5 Box Set.
- (M) (2:20) Time-Life 2RNR-17 Rock 'N' Roll Era - 1957 Still Rockin'.
- (M) (2:20) Rhino 71780 Sun Records Collection.
- (M) (2:21) LaserLight 12316 Rebel Rousers.
- (M) (2:21) K-Tel 3059 Saxy Rock.
- (S) (2:24) Polygram Special Markets 314520273 Great Instrumental Hits. *(rerecording)*
- (S) (2:24) K-Tel 3096 Classic Country Instrumentals. *(rerecording)*
- (M) (2:20) JCI 3188 1955 - Only Dance - 1959.
- (S) (2:24) Polygram Special Markets 314520478 50's Jukebox Hits. *(rerecording)*

JOSHUA KADISON
1994 JESSIE
    (S) (5:18)   SBK 80920 Painted Desert Serenade.
1994 BEAUTIFUL IN MY EYES
    (S) (4:06)   SBK 80920 Painted Desert Serenade.

BERT KAEMPFERT
1961 WONDERLAND BY NIGHT
    (S) (3:13)   Time-Life HPD-34 Your Hit Parade - 60's Instrumentals.
    (S) (3:13)   Time-Life R857-03 The Heart Of Rock 'n' Roll - 1961.
    (S) (3:12)   Time-Life R986-18 Instrumental Favorites - Bert Kaempfert.
    (S) (3:11)   Taragon 1014 Very Best Of.
    (S) (3:11)   Collectors' Choice 5190 More Instrumental Gems Of The 60's.
    (S) (3:12)   Time-Life R814-04 Love Songs.
    (S) (3:13)   Time-Life R986-22 Instrumental Classics - Pop Classics.
1961 TENDERLY
    (S) (3:12)   Taragon 1014 Very Best Of.
1962 AFRIKAAN BEAT
    (S) (2:24)   Taragon 1014 Very Best Of.
    (S) (2:24)   Time-Life R986-18 Instrumental Favorites - Bert Kaempfert.
1965 RED ROSES FOR A BLUE LADY
    (S) (2:19)   MFSL 795 Best Of.
    (S) (2:19)   Taragon 1014 Very Best Of.
    (S) (2:19)   Time-Life R986-18 Instrumental Favorites - Bert Kaempfert.
    (S) (2:19)   Taragon 1043 That Latin Feeling/Blue Midnight.
1965 THREE O'CLOCK IN THE MORNING
    (S) (2:32)   Taragon 1014 Very Best Of.
    (S) (2:32)   Time-Life R986-18 Instrumental Favorites - Bert Kaempfert.
    (S) (2:32)   Taragon 1045 Three O'Clock In The Morning.
    (S) (2:32)   Taragon 1043 That Latin Feeling/Blue Midnight.

KAJAGOOGOO
1983 TOO SHY
    (S) (3:42)   EMI 81417 Living In Oblivion: The 80's Greatest Hits Volume One. *(LP version)*
    (S) (3:42)   Priority 53721 Rock Of The 80's Volume 5. *(LP version)*
    (S) (3:43)   K-Tel 3262 The 80's Video Stars. *(LP version)*
    (S) (3:34)   Rhino 71702 New Wave Hits Of The 80's Vol. 9. *(45 version)*
    (S) (3:43)   Rhino 71834 Classic MTV: Class Of 1983. *(LP version)*
    (S) (3:43)   EMI 27222 Kajagoogoo And Limahl - Too Shy: The Singles And More. *(LP version)*
    (S) (3:41)   Time-Life R988-03 Sounds Of The Eighties: 1983. *(LP version)*
    (S) (3:41)   Madacy Entertainment 1983 Rock On 1983. *(LP version)*
    (S) (3:38)   Simitar 55552 The Number One's: Eighties Rock. *(LP version)*

KALIN TWINS
1958 WHEN
    (M) (2:25)   MCA 31198 Vintage Music Volume 1.
    (M) (2:25)   MCA 5777 Vintage Music Volumes 1 & 2.
    (M) (2:25)   Curb 77354 50's Hits Volume 1.
    (M) (2:25)   Curb 77525 Greatest Hits Of Rock 'N' Roll Volume 2.

    (M) (2:24)   Time-Life 2RNR-24 Rock 'N' Roll Era - The 50's Keep On Rockin'.
    (M) (2:24)   MCA Special Products 20580 Teen Idols.
    (M) (2:25)   MCA 11119 The Decca Rock 'N' Roll Collection.
    (M) (2:25)   MCA 11069 From The Vaults - Decca Country Classics 1934-1973.
1958 FORGET ME NOT

KITTY KALLEN
1959 IF I GIVE MY HEART TO YOU
1963 MY COLORING BOOK
    (S) (3:18)   Time-Life HPD-33 Your Hit Parade - The Early 60's.

INI KAMOZE
1994 HERE COMES THE HOTSTEPPER
    (S) (4:08)   Columbia 57511 Stir It Up.
    (S) (4:09)   Columbia O.S.T. Ready To Wear (Pret-A-Porter).
    (S) (3:54)   Tommy Boy 1138 MTV Party To Go Volume 7. *(all selections on this cd are segued together; remixed)*
    (S) (4:09)   Columbia 67056 Here Comes The Hotstepper.
    (S) (4:09)   EMI-Capitol Music Group 54547 Hot Luv.
    (S) (4:08)   Priority 50946 100% Party Hits Of The 90's Volume One.
    (S) (4:08)   Razor & Tie 4569 '90s Style.

BIG DADDY KANE
1993 VERY SPECIAL
    (S) (5:04)   Cold Chillin'/Reprise 45128 Looks Like A Job For.

KANE GANG
1987 MOTORTOWN
    (S) (4:45)   Capitol 48176 Miracle.

KANSAS
1977 CARRY ON WAYWARD SON
    (S) (5:21)   Foundation/Capitol 96647 Hearts Of Gold - The Classic Rock Collection. *(LP version)*
    (S) (5:20)   Sandstone 33004 Reelin' In The Years Volume 5. *(LP version)*
    (S) (5:21)   Kirshner/Epic 34224 Leftoverture. *(LP version)*
    (S) (5:22)   CBS Associated 39283 Best Of. *(LP version)*
    (S) (5:20)   DCC Compact Classics 066 Rock Of The 70's Volume Five. *(LP version)*
    (S) (5:21)   Time-Life SOD-37 Sounds Of The Seventies - AM Heavy Hits. *(LP version)*
    (S) (5:21)   Epic/Legacy 47364 Kansas. *(LP version)*
    (S) (5:20)   Time-Life R968-17 Guitar Rock - The Late '70s: Take Two. *(LP version)*
    (S) (5:21)   K-Tel 3904 The Rock Album Volume 1. *(LP version)*
1978 POINT OF KNOW RETURN
    (S) (3:11)   Kirshner/Epic 34929 Point Of Know Return.
    (S) (3:11)   CBS Associated 39283 Best Of.
    (S) (3:11)   Epic/Legacy 47364 Kansas.
1978 DUST IN THE WIND
    (S) (3:21)   Priority 8663 The South Rules/70's Greatest Rock Hits Volume 2.
    (S) (3:24)   Sandstone 33003 Reelin' In The Years Volume 4.
    (S) (3:26)   Kirshner/Epic 34929 Point Of Know Return.
    (S) (3:25)   CBS Associated 39283 Best Of.
    (S) (3:25)   DCC Compact Classics 065 Rock Of The 70's Volume 4.

KANSAS *(Continued)*

- (S) (3:24) Time-Life SOD-10 Sounds Of The Seventies - 1978.
- (S) (3:25) Epic/Legacy 47364 Kansas.
- (S) (3:24) JCI 3119 18 Rock Classics.
- (S) (3:24) Time-Life R968-14 Guitar Rock - The Late '70s.

1979 PEOPLE OF THE SOUTH WIND
- (S) (3:38) Kirshner/Epic 36008 Monolith.
- (S) (3:38) Epic/Legacy 47364 Kansas.

1980 HOLD ON
- (S) (3:50) Columbia Special Products 44363 Rock Of The 80's.
- (S) (3:50) CBS Associated 39283 Best Of.
- (S) (3:51) Epic/Legacy 47364 Kansas.
- (S) (3:51) Legacy/Epic Associated 66417 Audio Visions.

1982 PLAY THE GAME TONIGHT
- (S) (3:25) CBS Associated 39283 Best Of.
- (S) (3:25) Legacy/Epic Associated 66418 Vinyl Confessions.

1987 ALL I WANTED
- (S) (3:20) MCA 5838 Power.
- (S) (3:20) Madacy Entertainment 1986 Rock On 1986.

KASENETZ-KATZ SINGING ORCHESTRAL CIRCUS
1968 QUICK JOEY SMALL (RUN JOEY RUN)
- (E) (2:21) Pair 1199 Best Of Bubblegum Music. *(group incorrectly identified on the cd as the "KASENETZ KATZ SUPER CIRCUS")*
- (E) (2:21) Special Music 4914 Best Of The Bubblegum Years.
- (E) (2:23) Essex 7060 The Buddah Box.
- (E) (2:20) Time-Life 2CLR-19 Classic Rock - 1968: Shakin' All Over.
- (M) (2:23) Risky Business 53923 Guilty Pleasures.
- (M) (2:23) K-Tel 3386 Best Of Bubblegum Music.
- (E) (2:23) Buddah 49517 Complete Buddah Chart Singles Volume Two.

KATRINA AND THE WAVES
1985 WALKING ON SUNSHINE
- (S) (3:57) Capitol 98139 Spring Break Volume 2.
- (S) (3:55) EMI 89605 Living In Oblivion: The 80's Greatest Hits Volume Two.
- (S) (3:56) Priority 53768 Rock Of The 80's Volume 14.
- (S) (3:57) Rhino 71978 New Wave Hits Of The 80's Vol. 15.
- (S) (3:57) Capitol 46169 Katrina And The Waves.
- (S) (3:56) Time-Life R988-02 Sounds Of The Eighties: 1985.
- (S) (3:54) Big Ear Music 4003 Only In The 80's Volume Three.
- (S) (3:54) Madacy Entertainment 26927 Sun Splashin'.
- (S) (3:56) Hip-O 40004 The '80s Hit(s) Back!
- (S) (3:51) RCA 66862 Hi Octane Hard Drivin' Hits.
- (S) (3:56) JCI 3150 1985 - Only Dance - 1989.
- (S) (3:57) One Way 18200 Anthology.
- (S) (3:54) K-Tel 3798 The 80's Mega Hits.
- (S) (3:48) Cold Front 6255 Greatest Sports Rock And Jams Volume 2. *(all selections on this cd are segued together)*
- (S) (3:54) Nick At Nite/550 Music 63435 Beach Blanket Bash.
- (S) (3:57) Hip-O 40075 Rock She Said: On The Pop Side.
- (S) (3:48) Mercury 314553774 Bean - The Album.

1985 DO YOU WANT CRYING
- (S) (3:33) Capitol 46169 Katrina And The Waves.
- (S) (3:32) One Way 18200 Anthology.

1989 THAT'S THE WAY
- (S) (3:56) Sandstone 5023 Cosmopolitan Volume 9.
- (S) (3:55) SBK 92649 Break Of Hearts.

SAMMY KAYE
1964 CHARADE
- (S) (2:35) K-Tel 3091 Those Wonderful Instrumentals.

KC and THE SUNSHINE BAND
1975 GET DOWN TONIGHT
(actual 45 time is (3:21) not (3:06) as stated on the record label)
- (S) (3:17) Priority 7973 Mega-Hits Dance Classics Volume 3. *(45 version)*
- (S) (3:11) Rhino 71003 Get Down Tonight: The Best Of T.K. Records. *(45 version)*
- (S) (3:11) Rhino 70670 Billboard Top Hits - 1975. *(45 version)*
- (S) (3:11) Rhino 70274 The Disco Years Volume 3. *(45 version)*
- (S) (3:11) Rhino 71094 Disco Hits Volume 1. *(45 version)*
- (S) (3:11) Rhino 70940 Best Of. *(45 version)*
- (S) (3:10) Rhino 71028 Best Of/Rhino Special Editions. *(45 version)*
- (S) (3:10) Time-Life SOD-16 Sounds Of The Seventies - 1975: Take Two. *(45 version)*
- (S) (5:23) Collectables 5431 Disco Party - The Best Of The T.K. Collection. *(LP version but slowed down considerably)*
- (S) (5:15) Hot Productions 11 Best Of The Sound Of Sunshine. *(LP version)*
- (S) (9:08) Rhino 71854 Part 3.......And More. *(remix)*
- (S) (5:15) Rhino 71890 KC & The Sunshine Band...And More. *(LP version)*
- (S) (7:41) Rhino 71890 KC & The Sunshine Band...And More. *(remix)*
- (S) (5:18) Rebound 314520220 Disco Nights Vol. 4 - Greatest Disco Groups. *(LP version)*
- (S) (3:11) Curb 77780 KC & The Sunshine Band & Silver Convention Greatest Dance Hits. *(rerecording)*
- (S) (3:11) K-Tel 3251 Disco Fever. *(45 version)*
- (S) (3:11) Rhino 72213 Stadium Rock. *(45 version)*
- (S) (3:05) Tommy Boy 1163 Jock Jams Volume 2. *(all selections on this cd are segued together)*
- (S) (3:07) TVT 7010 O.S.T. Last Supper. *(45 version)*
- (S) (3:10) JCI 3148 1975 - Only Dance - 1979. *(45 version)*
- (S) (3:10) JCI 3169 #1 Radio Hits 1975 - Only Rock 'n Roll - 1979. *(45 version)*
- (S) (3:15) Eclipse Music Group 64894 Rock 'n Roll Relix 1974-1975. *(45 version)*
- (S) (3:15) Eclipse Music Group 64897 Rock 'n Roll Relix 1970-1979. *(45 version)*
- (S) (3:17) Time-Life R838-10 Solid Gold Soul - 1975. *(45 version)*
- (S) (3:11) Flashback 72711 Sports Rock. *(45 version)*
- (S) (3:11) Flashback 72688 Disco Hits: Get Down Tonight. *(45 version)*
- (S) (3:11) Flashback 72086 Disco Hits Box Set. *(45 version)*
- (S) (3:11) Flashback 72670 I'm Your Boogie Man And Other Hits. *(45 version)*
- (S) (4:49) Chronicles 314553404 Non-Stop Disco Vol. 1. *(all songs on this cd are segued together)*
- (S) (3:11) Milan 35788 O.S.T. Hotel De Love. *(45 version)*
- (S) (3:11) Rhino 75200 Basketball's Greatest Hits. *(45 version)*
- (S) (3:17) Time-Life R840-06 Sounds Of The Seventies: '70s Dance Party 1975-1976. *(45 version)*
- (S) (3:10) BMG Special Products 44762 The President's Greatest Hits. *(45 version)*

1975 THAT'S THE WAY (I LIKE IT)
- (S) (5:04) Priority 7973 Mega-Hits Dance Classics Volume 3. *(LP version)*
- (S) (3:04) Rhino 70984 The Disco Years Volume 1. *(45 version)*
- (S) (3:03) Rhino 71094 Disco Hits Volume 1. *(45 version)*
- (S) (3:04) Rhino 70940 Best Of. *(45 version)*
- (S) (3:04) Epic 57620 O.S.T. Carlito's Way. *(45 version)*
- (S) (3:00) JCI 3306 Dance Seventies. *(45 version)*
- (S) (3:03) Rhino 71028 Best Of/Rhino Special Editions. *(45 version)*

(S) (4:04) Razor & Tie 22045 Those Funky 70's. *(edit of LP version)*

(S) (3:00) Time-Life SOD-08 Sounds Of The Seventies - 1975. *(45 version)*

(S) (5:06) Hot Productions 11 Best Of The Sound Of Sunshine. *(LP version)*

(S) (5:05) Rhino 71890 KC & The Sunshine Band...And More. *(LP version)*

(S) (5:54) Rhino 71890 KC & The Sunshine Band...And More. *(remix)*

(S) (3:03) JCI 3131 1975 - Only Rock 'N Roll - 1979. *(45 version)*

(S) (3:11) Curb 77780 KC & The Sunshine Band & Silver Convention Greatest Dance Hits. *(rerecording)*

(S) (2:59) Madacy Entertainment 1975 Rock On 1975. *(45 version)*

(S) (3:02) Polydor 314535877 Pure Disco. *(45 version)*

(S) (3:03) Time-Life AM1-22 AM Gold - 1975. *(45 version)*

(S) (3:04) Flashback 72690 Disco Hits: That's The Way I Like It. *(45 version)*

(S) (5:05) Flashback 72671 Shake, Shake, Shake And Other Hits. *(LP version)*

(S) (2:59) Tommy Boy 1214 Jock Jams Volume 3. *(all selections on this cd are segued together; 45 version)*

(S) (3:03) Collectables 1516 and 2516 The Anniversary Album - The 70's. *(45 version)*

1976 (SHAKE, SHAKE, SHAKE) SHAKE YOUR BOOTY

(S) (3:01) Priority 7974 Mega-Hits Dance Classics Volume 4.

(S) (3:05) Rhino 70984 The Disco Years Volume 1.

(S) (3:04) Rhino 71095 Disco Hits Volume 2.

(S) (3:05) Rhino 70940 Best Of.

(S) (3:04) Rhino 71028 Best Of/Rhino Special Editions.

(S) (3:01) Time-Life SOD-18 Sounds Of The Seventies - 1976: Take Two.

(S) (3:04) Pyramid 71888 A Future To This Life - Robocop: The Series Soundtrack.

(S) (3:04) Rhino 71854 Part 3.......And More.

(S) (3:04) K-Tel 3126 Disco Mania.

(S) (3:09) Curb 77780 KC & The Sunshine Band & Silver Convention Greatest Dance Hits. *(rerecording)*

(S) (3:05) Time-Life R138-38 Celebration.

(S) (3:04) Rhino 72275 More Stadium Rock.

(S) (3:04) Madacy Entertainment 1976 Rock On 1976.

(S) (3:04) K-Tel 3796 Music For Your Party.

(S) (3:04) Time-Life AM1-23 AM Gold - 1976.

(S) (3:04) Time-Life R838-11 Solid Gold Soul - 1976.

(S) (3:05) Flashback 72712 Arena Rock.

(S) (3:04) Flashback 72689 Disco Hits: Shake Your Booty.

(S) (3:04) Flashback 72671 Shake, Shake, Shake And Other Hits.

(S) (3:05) Polydor 314555120 Pure Disco 2.

(S) (3:04) Time-Life R840-07 Sounds Of The Seventies: '70s Dance Party 1976-1977.

1977 I'M YOUR BOOGIE MAN

(S) (3:42) Priority 7974 Mega-Hits Dance Classics Volume 4. *(missing the :15 instrumental introduction; sounds like it was mastered from vinyl)*

(S) (4:00) Rhino 71003 Get Down Tonight: The Best Of T.K. Records.

(S) (4:00) Rhino 70672 Billboard Top Hits - 1977.

(S) (4:01) Rhino 71095 Disco Hits Volume 2.

(S) (4:01) Rhino 70940 Best Of.

(S) (4:00) Rhino 71028 Best Of/Rhino Special Editions.

(S) (4:00) Razor & Tie 22496 Disco Fever.

(S) (4:00) Time-Life SOD-17 Sounds Of The Seventies - 1977: Take Two.

(S) (4:01) Rhino 71854 Part 3.......And More. *(tracks into next selection)*

(S) (4:04) Curb 77780 KC & The Sunshine Band & Silver Convention Greatest Dance Hits. *(rerecording)*

(S) (4:01) K-Tel 3371 Hot Nights - Disco Lights.

(S) (4:00) Thump 4099 Old School Boogie.

(S) (4:00) Madacy Entertainment 1977 Rock On 1977.

(S) (4:00) TVT 7010 O.S.T. Last Supper.

(S) (4:00) Time-Life AM1-24 AM Gold - 1977.

(S) (4:00) Flashback 72693 Disco Hits: Good Times.

(S) (4:00) Flashback 72086 Disco Hits Box Set.

(S) (4:00) Flashback 72670 I'm Your Boogie Man And Other Hits.

(S) (4:01) Angel 56344 O.S.T. The People Vs. Larry Flynt.

1977 KEEP IT COMIN' LOVE

(S) (4:20) Priority 7971 Mega-Hits Dance Classics Volume 1. *(LP version)*

(S) (3:52) Rhino 70275 The Disco Years Volume 4. *(45 version)*

(S) (3:52) Rhino 70940 Best Of. *(45 version)*

(S) (3:52) Rhino 71028 Best Of/Rhino Special Editions. *(45 version)*

(S) (3:50) Time-Life SOD-27 Sounds Of The Seventies - Dance Fever. *(45 version)*

(S) (3:52) Rhino 71668 Disco Hits Vol. 5. *(45 version)*

(S) (4:28) Rhino 71854 Part 3.......And More. *(LP version)*

(S) (3:52) K-Tel 3470 Get Up And Disco. *(45 version)*

(S) (3:52) Flashback 72692 Disco Hits: We Are Family. *(45 version)*

(S) (3:52) Flashback 72086 Disco Hits Box Set. *(45 version)*

(S) (4:28) Flashback 72671 Shake, Shake, Shake And Other Hits. *(LP version)*

1978 BOOGIE SHOES
(actual 45 time is (2:09) not (2:15) as stated on the record label; this song was issued in 3 different pitches with the 45 being the fastest, the LP being the slowest and the soundtrack version being in between)

(S) (2:14) Polydor 800068 O.S.T. Saturday Night Fever.

(S) (2:10) Rhino 70940 Best Of.

(S) (2:09) Rhino 71028 Best Of/Rhino Special Editions.

(S) (2:10) Priority 53730 Mega Hits Dance Classics Vol. 13.

(S) (2:09) Rhino 71890 KC & The Sunshine Band...And More.

(S) (2:14) Polydor 422825389 O.S.T. Saturday Night Fever. *(remastered edition)*

(S) (2:09) Flashback 72670 I'm Your Boogie Man And Other Hits.

(S) (2:10) K-Tel 3909 High Energy Volume 2.

(S) (2:09) Capitol 93076 More Music From O.S.T. Boogie Nights.

(S) (2:15) Mobile Fidelity 716 O.S.T. Saturday Night Fever. *(gold disc)*

1978 IT'S THE SAME OLD SONG
(dj copies of this 45 ran (3:18) and (4:23); commercial copies were all (4:23))

(S) (4:24) Flashback 72671 Shake, Shake, Shake And Other Hits.

1979 PLEASE DON'T GO

(S) (3:46) Priority 7983 Mega-Hits Dance Classics Volume 7.

(S) (3:49) Rhino 70675 Billboard Top Hits - 1980.

(S) (3:49) Rhino 71096 Disco Hits Volume 3.

(S) (3:49) Rhino 70940 Best Of.

(S) (3:11) ZYX 20249 Oh Yeah! *(live)*

(S) (3:48) Rhino 71028 Best Of/Rhino Special Editions.

(S) (3:48) JCI 3149 1980 - Only Dance - 1984.

(S) (3:49) Rhino 72478 Beverly Hills 90210: Songs From The Peach Pit.

(S) (3:48) Time-Life R988-14 Sounds Of The Eighties: 1980-1982.

(S) (3:48) Time-Life R834-06 Body Talk - Only You.

(S) (3:49) Rhino 72516 Behind Closed Doors - '70s Swingers.

(S) (3:48) Flashback 72691 Disco Hits: Le Freak.

(S) (3:48) Flashback 72086 Disco Hits Box Set.

(S) (3:48) Flashback 72670 I'm Your Boogie Man And Other Hits.

released as by TERI DeSARIO with KC:
1980 YES I'M READY

(S) (3:15) Casablanca 314516918 Casablanca Records Story.

(S) (3:16) Time-Life R138-18 Body Talk.

KC and THE SUNSHINE BAND (Continued)
- (S) (3:15) Casablanca 314526253 Casablanca Records Greatest Hits.
- (S) (3:15) Time-Life R834-04 Body Talk - Together Forever.
- (S) (3:13) Rebound 314520440 No. 1 Hits Of The 70's.

released as by KC:
1984 GIVE IT UP
- (S) (4:04) Rhino 70940 Best Of.
- (S) (3:30) ZYX 20249 Oh Yeah! *(live)*
- (S) (4:04) Rhino 72122 Disco Years, Vol. 6.

K-CI & JOJO
1997 YOU BRING ME UP
- (S) (4:23) MCA 11613 Love Always.

ERNIE K-DOE
1961 MOTHER-IN-LAW
- (M) (2:34) Rhino 75765 Best Of New Orleans Rhythm & Blues Volume 1.
- (M) (2:35) Rhino 70622 Billboard's Top Rock & Roll Hits Of 1961. *(found only on the original 1988 issue of this cd)*
- (M) (2:35) Rhino 72004 Billboard's Top Rock & Roll Hits 1957-1961 Box Set.
- (E) (2:33) EMI 90614 Non-Stop Party Rock.
- (M) (2:32) Curb 77323 All Time Greatest Hits Of Rock 'N' Roll.
- (M) (2:33) Ripete 2392192 Beach Music Anthology Box Set.
- (M) (2:32) Collectables 5067 History Of Rock Volume 7.
- (M) (2:33) Ripete 0002 Coolin' Out/24 Carolina Classics Vol. 2.
- (M) (3:58) Ripete 2199 Walkin' To New Orleans. *(time includes 1 false start of (1:25) plus countoff)*
- (M) (2:33) Time-Life 2RNR-04 Rock 'N' Roll Era - 1961.
- (M) (2:32) Time-Life RHD-14 Rhythm & Blues - 1961.
- (M) (2:32) Collectables 2502 WCBS-FM History Of Rock - The 60's Part 3.
- (M) (2:32) Collectables 4502 History Of Rock/The 60s Part Three.
- (M) (2:32) Collectables 2603 WCBS-FM Jukebox Giants Vol. 1.
- (M) (2:32) EMI 30879 Minit Records Story.
- (M) (2:33) Rhino 71806 The R&B Box: Thirty Years Of Rhythm & Blues.
- (M) (2:32) EMI 37350 Crescent City Soul: The Sound Of New Orleans 1947-1974.
- (M) (2:32) EMI 37355 Highlights From Crescent City Soul: The Sound Of New Orleans 1947-1974.
- (M) (2:32) JCI 3166 #1 Radio Hits 1960 - Only Rock 'n Roll - 1964.
- (M) (2:33) Time-Life R838-19 Solid Gold Soul 1961.

KEEDY
1991 SAVE SOME LOVE
- (S) (4:11) Arista 8641 Chase The Clouds.

KEITH
1966 AIN'T GONNA LIE
- (S) (2:59) Varese Sarabande 5535 Bubblegum Classics Volume One.
1967 98.6
- (S) (3:02) Mercury 834216 45's On CD Volume 3.
- (S) (3:00) Time-Life 2CLR-15 Classic Rock - 1967: Shakin' All Over.
- (S) (3:00) Time-Life SUD-05 Superhits - 1967.
- (S) (3:05) Polygram Special Markets 314520272 One Hit Wonders.
- (S) (3:02) Special Music/Essex 5035 Prom Night - The 60's.
- (S) (3:04) Buddah 49506 Feelin' Groovy.
- (S) (3:02) Eclipse Music Group 64870 Rock 'n Roll Relix 1966-1967.
- (S) (3:02) Eclipse Music Group 64872 Rock 'n Roll Relix 1960-1969.
- (S) (3:02) Time-Life 2CLR-31 Classic Rock - Totally Fantastic '60s.

- (S) (2:59) Time-Life AM1-08 AM Gold - 1967.
- (M) (3:06) Varese Sarabande 5802 Sunshine Days - Pop Classics Of The '60s Volume 2.
- (S) (3:01) Polygram Special Markets 314520464 60's Rock Hits.
1967 TELL ME TO MY FACE

LISA KEITH
1993 BETTER THAN YOU
- (S) (4:11) Perspective 314549004 Walkin' In The Sun.

JERRY KELLER
1959 HERE COMES SUMMER
- (S) (2:07) MCA 5937 Vintage Music Volumes 13 & 14.
- (S) (2:07) MCA 31211 Vintage Music Volume 14.
- (S) (2:07) Time-Life HPD-38 Your Hit Parade - The 50's Generation.
- (S) (2:07) K-Tel 3437 Summer Songs.
- (S) (2:07) MCA Special Products 20948 Biggest Summer Hits.

MONTY KELLY
1960 SUMMER SET

R. KELLY & PUBLIC ANNOUNCEMENT
1992 HONEY LOVE
- (S) (5:04) Jive 41469 Born Into The 90's.
1993 DEDICATED
- (S) (4:36) Jive 41469 Born Into The 90's.
released as by R. KELLY:
1993 SEX ME (PARTS I & II)
- (S) (11:25) Jive 41527 12 Play.
1994 BUMP N' GRIND
- (S) (4:14) Jive 41527 12 Play.
- (S) (4:12) Boxtunes 162444068 Big Phat Ones Of Hip-Hop Volume 1.
- (S) (4:14) Robbins 75002 Strip Jointz - Hot Songs For Sexy Dancers.
1994 YOUR BODY'S CALLIN'
- (S) (4:36) Jive 41527 12 Play.
- (S) (4:33) Rhino 72159 Black Entertainment Television - 15th Anniversary.
- (S) (4:33) EMI-Capitol Music Group 54548 Smooth Luv.
- (S) (4:34) K-Tel 3850 90s Now Volume 3.
1995 YOU REMIND ME OF SOMETHING
- (S) (4:09) Jive 41579 R. Kelly.
- (S) (4:26) Tommy Boy 1164 MTV Party To Go Volume 9. *(all selections on this cd are segued together)*
released as by R. KELLY featuring RONALD ISLEY:
1996 DOWN LOW (NOBODY HAS TO KNOW)
- (S) (4:48) Jive 41579 R. Kelly.
- (S) (4:25) Arista 18977 Ultimate Hip Hop Party 1998. *(all selections on this cd are segued together; remix)*
released as by R. KELLY:
1996 I CAN'T SLEEP BABY (IF I)
- (S) (5:30) Jive 41579 R. Kelly.
1996 I BELIEVE I CAN FLY
- (S) (5:20) Warner Sunset/Atlantic 82961 O.S.T. Space Jam.
- (S) (4:39) Cold Front 6254 Club Mix '98. *(all selections on this cd are segued together)*
- (S) (5:20) MCA 11752 1998 Grammy Nominees.
1997 GOTHAM CITY
- (S) (4:55) Warner Sunset/Warner Brothers 46620 O.S.T. Batman & Robin.

JOHNNY KEMP
1988 JUST GOT PAID
- (S) (3:29) K-Tel 6102 Funk-Tastic Jams. *(45 version)*
- (S) (5:27) Columbia 40770 Secrets Of Flying. *(LP version)*
- (S) (5:20) Priority 53731 80's Greatest Rock Hits Volume 10 - Dance All Night. *(LP version)*
- (S) (3:31) Rhino 72140 Billboard Hot R&B Hits 1985. *(45 version)*
- (S) (5:24) Rhino 72409 New Jack Hits. *(LP version)*
- (S) (3:22) JCI 3177 1985 - Only Soul - 1989. *(45 version)*

(S) (3:14) Priority 50940 Shut Up And Dance! The 80's Volume One. *(all selections on this cd are segued together)*

1989 BIRTHDAY SUIT
(S) (4:27) Columbia 45086 O.S.T. Sing.

TARA KEMP
1991 HOLD YOU TIGHT
(S) (4:43) Giant 24408 Tara Kemp.
(S) (4:42) Cold Front 3832 Club Mix - Women Of Dance Vol. 1.
(S) (4:43) K-Tel 3848 90s Now Volume 2.
1991 PIECE OF MY HEART
(S) (4:49) Giant 24408 Tara Kemp.

EDDIE KENDRICKS
1973 KEEP ON TRUCKIN' (PART 1)
(actual 45 time is (3:33) not (3:21) as stated on the record label)
(S) (3:33) Rhino 70661 Billboard's Top R&B Hits Of 1973. *(45 version)*
(S) (3:33) Rhino 70551 Soul Hits Of The 70's Volume 11. *(45 version)*
(S) (3:34) Motown 6132 25 #1 Hits From 25 Years. *(45 version)*
(S) (3:32) Priority 7909 Vietnam: Rockin' The Delta. *(45 version)*
(S) (7:58) Motown 5481 At His Best. *(LP version)*
(S) (3:30) Motown 9072 Motown Dance Party Volume 2. *(all selections on this cd are segued together; 45 version)*
(S) (3:33) Motown 9021 and 5309 25 Years Of Grammy Greats. *(45 version)*
(S) (3:28) Motown 5275 12 #1 Hits From The 70's. *(45 version)*
(S) (3:33) Motown 9060 Motown's Biggest Pop Hits. *(45 version)*
(S) (3:28) Motown 0937 20/20 Twenty No. 1 Hits From Twenty Years At Motown. *(45 version)*
(S) (3:33) Rhino 71431 In Yo Face! History Of Funk Volume 1. *(45 version)*
(S) (3:32) Motown 6358 Hitsville USA Volume Two. *(45 version)*
(S) (3:27) Razor & Tie 22045 Those Funky 70's. *(45 version)*
(S) (3:31) Motown 314530510 Motown Year By Year 1973. *(45 version)*
(S) (7:58) Priority 53789 Disco Attack. *(LP version)*
(S) (7:59) Motown 314530615 Temptations - One By One: Best Of Their Solo Years. *(LP version)*
(S) (3:32) Time-Life R838-08 Solid Gold Soul - 1973. *(45 version)*
(S) (3:32) Cold Front 4024 Old School Mega Mix Volume 2. *(45 version)*
(S) (3:31) Motown 314530849 Motown 40 Forever. *(45 version)*
(S) (3:33) Rhino 72943 VH1 8-Track Flashback: Classic '70s Soul. *(45 version)*
(S) (3:33) Time-Life R840-05 Sounds Of The Seventies: '70s Dance Party 1972-1974. *(45 version)*
1974 BOOGIE DOWN
(actual 45 time is (3:46) not (3:30) as stated on the record label; actual LP time is (6:57) not (7:07) as stated on the record label)
(S) (3:48) Rhino 70635 Billboard's Top Rock & Roll Hits Of 1974. *(45 version)*
(S) (3:47) Rhino 70552 Soul Hits Of The 70's Volume 12. *(45 version)*
(S) (3:50) Motown 6110 Motown Grammy Rhythm & Blues Performances Of The 60's & 70's. *(45 version)*
(S) (3:50) Priority 7058 Mega-Hits Dance Classics Volume 9. *(45 version)*
(S) (6:57) Motown 5481 At His Best. *(LP version)*
(S) (3:51) Motown 6358 Hitsville USA Volume Two. *(45 version)*

(S) (3:47) Motown 314530510 Motown Year By Year 1973. *(45 version)*
(S) (7:01) Motown 314530615 Temptations - One By One: Best Of Their Solo Years. *(LP version)*
(S) (6:57) Thump 4099 Old School Boogie. *(LP version)*
(S) (3:50) Polygram Special Markets 314520446 Soul Hits Of The 70's. *(45 version)*
1974 SON OF SAGITTARIUS
1974 TELL HER LOVE HAS FELT THE NEED
(S) (3:10) Motown 9105 and 5410 Motown Memories Volume 2. *(45 version)*
(S) (4:28) Motown 314530615 Temptations - One By One: Best Of Their Solo Years. *(LP version)*
1975 SHOESHINE BOY
(S) (3:10) Motown 9104 and 5409 Motown Memories Volume 1.
(S) (3:11) Motown 5481 At His Best.
(S) (3:09) Rhino 72127 Soul Hits Of The 70's Vol. 17.
(S) (3:15) Motown 314530615 Temptations - One By One: Best Of Their Solo Years.
1976 HE'S A FRIEND
(S) (3:27) Motown 314530513 Motown Year By Year 1976. *(45 version)*
(S) (3:26) Motown 5481 At His Best. *(45 version)*
(S) (4:37) Motown 314530615 Temptations - One By One: Best Of Their Solo Years. *(LP version)*
released as by DARY HALL/JOHN OATES with DAVID RUFFIN and EDDIE KENDRICK:
1985 THE WAY YOU DO THE THINGS YOU DO/MY GIRL
(S) (12:35) RCA 7035 Live At The Apollo. *(LP version which is a medley of a number of different songs)*
(S) (5:42) RCA 66862 Hi Octane Hard Drivin' Hits. *(edit of LP version)*

CHRIS KENNER
1961 I LIKE IT LIKE THAT (PART 1)
(M) (1:55) Warner Brothers 25613 O.S.T. Full Metal Jacket.
(M) (1:55) Rhino 75766 Best Of New Orleans Rhythm & Blues Volume 2.
(M) (1:55) Rhino 70647 Billboard's Top R&B Hits Of 1961.
(E) (2:11) Collectables 5166 I Like It Like That/Golden Classics. *(mastered from vinyl; includes :12 of studio talk)*
(S) (1:56) Rhino 70622 Billboard's Top Rock & Roll Hits Of 1961. *(found only on the 1993 reissue of this cd)*
(S) (1:57) Ripete 0002 Coolin' Out/24 Carolina Classics Vol. 2.
(S) (1:55) Time-Life 2RNR-04 Rock 'N' Roll Era - 1961. *(original pressings of this song on this cd were (M))*
(S) (1:55) Time-Life RHD-14 Rhythm & Blues - 1961.
(S) (1:55) EMI 30879 Minit Records Story.
(M) (1:55) Rhino 71806 The R&B Box: Thirty Years Of Rhythm & Blues.
(S) (1:55) JCI 3125 1960 - Only Rock 'N Roll - 1964.
(S) (1:53) EMI 37350 Crescent City Soul: The Sound Of New Orleans 1947-1974.
(S) (1:55) Time-Life R838-19 Solid Gold Soul 1961.

KENNY G
1987 SONGBIRD
(dj copies of this song ran (3:29) and (5:00); commercial copies were all (5:00))
(S) (5:03) Arista 8496 Duotones.
(S) (5:01) Time-Life R834-02 Body Talk - Just For You.
(S) (3:59) Arista 18991 Greatest Hits. *(this is an extended version of the dj 45 edit)*
1987 DON'T MAKE ME WAIT FOR LOVE
(actual 45 time is (4:02) not (3:55) as stated on the record label)
(S) (4:41) Columbia 44382 Heart Of Soul. *(neither the 45 or LP version)*
(S) (4:04) Arista 8496 Duotones.
(S) (4:04) Arista 18991 Greatest Hits.

KENNY G (Continued)
1988 SILHOUETTE
    (S)   (5:27)   Arista 8457 Silhouette. *(LP version)*
    (S)   (4:46)   JCI 2716 Jazzin II. *(LP version faded :41 early)*
    (S)   (4:30)   Arista 18991 Greatest Hits. *(45 version)*
1993 FOREVER IN LOVE
    (S)   (4:58)   Arista 18646 Breathless.
    (S)   (4:57)   Arista 18991 Greatest Hits.
released as by KENNY G with PEABO BRYSON:
1993 BY THE TIME THIS NIGHT IS OVER
    (S)   (4:44)   Arista 18646 Kenny G - Breathless.
    (S)   (4:17)   Arista 18991 Greatest Hits.

STAN KENTON
1962 MAMA SANG A SONG

KERMIT (real name JIM HENSON)
1979 RAINBOW CONNECTION
    (S)   (3:15)   Jim Henson Records 30019 O.S.T. The Muppet Movie.

CHAKA KHAN (see also RUFUS)
1978 I'M EVERY WOMAN
    (S)   (8:19)   Warner Brothers 25946 Life Is A Dance - The Remix Project. *(remixed)*
    (S)   (3:50)   Rhino 71618 Soul Train Hall Of Fame/20th Anniversary. *(:08 longer than the 45 and :15 shorter than the LP length)*
    (S)   (3:30)   Time-Life SOD-20 Sounds Of The Seventies - 1978: Take Two. *(remixed; extra instrumentation added)*
    (S)   (3:31)   Priority 53728 Mega Hits Dance Classics Vol 12. *(remixed; extra instrumentation added)*
    (S)   (3:29)   Nick At Nite/550 Music 67690 I Am Woman. *(remixed; extra instrumentation added)*
    (S)   (3:30)   JCI 3148 1975 - Only Dance - 1979. *(remixed; extra instrumentation added)*
    (S)   (4:06)   Reprise 45865 Epiphany: The Best Of. *(LP length)*
    (S)   (4:05)   Rebound 314520447 Soul Classics - Best Of The 70's. *(LP length)*
    (S)   (3:48)   Warner Brothers 46479 '70s Soul Revue. *(:06 longer than 45 length)*
    (S)   (3:29)   K-Tel 3909 High Energy Volume 2. *(remixed; extra instrumentation added)*
    (S)   (4:05)   Warner Brothers 3245 Chaka. *(LP length)*
1984 I FEEL FOR YOU
    (S)   (4:03)   JCI 3127 1980 - Only Rock 'N Roll - 1984. *(45 version)*
    (S)   (5:44)   Warner Brothers 25162 I Feel For You. *(LP version)*
    (S)   (8:36)   Warner Brothers 25946 Life Is A Dance - The Remix Project. *(remixed)*
    (S)   (8:37)   K-Tel 3500 The 80's - Urban Countdown. *(remixed)*
    (S)   (4:04)   Time-Life R988-11 Sounds Of The 80's: 1983-1984. *(45 version)*
    (S)   (4:06)   Rhino 72139 Billboard Hot R&B Hits 1984. *(45 version)*
    (S)   (5:44)   Madacy Entertainment 1984 Rock On 1984. *(LP version)*
    (S)   (5:44)   Hip-O 40015 Soulful Ladies Of The 80's. *(LP version)*
    (S)   (5:45)   Reprise 45865 Epiphany: The Best Of. *(LP version)*
    (S)   (3:52)   Cold Front 3865 Club Mix - Women Of Dance Vol. 2. *(remixed)*
    (S)   (3:59)   Cold Front 6330 Club Mix: The 80s. *(all selections on this cd are segued together)*
released as by QUINCY JONES featuring RAY CHARLES and CHAKA KHAN:
1990 I'LL BE GOOD TO YOU
    (S)   (4:54)   Qwest/Warner Brothers 26020 Quincy Jones - Back On The Block. *(LP version)*
    (S)   (3:55)   JCI 3177 1985 - Only Soul - 1989. *(45 version faded :22 early)*

released as by BRANDY, TAMIA, GLADYS KNIGHT and CHAKA KHAN:
1996 MISSING YOU
    (S)   (4:22)   EastWest 61951 O.S.T. Set It Off.

GREG KIHN BAND
1981 THE BREAKUP SONG (THEY DON'T WRITE 'EM)
    (S)   (2:50)   Rhino 70900 Kihnsolidation: The Best Of.
    (S)   (2:49)   Rhino 71697 New Wave Hits Of The 80's Vol. 4.
    (S)   (2:48)   Priority 53798 Best Of 80's Rock Volume 5.
    (S)   (2:49)   Rhino 72491 New Wave Hits, Vol. 2.
    (S)   (2:48)   Time-Life R988-16 Sounds Of The Eighties: The Early '80s.
    (S)   (2:49)   Flashback 72714 Ultimate New Wave Hits.
    (S)   (2:49)   Flashback 72092 New Wave Hits Box Set.
    (S)   (3:10)   Scotti Bros. 75512 New Wave Dance Hits! *(previously unreleased version which is faster than the 45 or LP and ends cold)*
1983 JEOPARDY
    (S)   (3:46)   Rhino 70678 Billboard Top Hits - 1983.
    (S)   (3:46)   Rhino 71701 New Wave Hits Of The 80's Vol. 8.
    (S)   (3:47)   K-Tel 3261 The 80's Rock On.
    (S)   (3:46)   Rhino 70900 Kihnsolidation: The Best Of.
    (S)   (3:47)   Priority 53775 Best Of 80's Rock Volume 1.
    (S)   (3:46)   Time-Life R988-03 Sounds Of The Eighties: 1983.
    (S)   (3:46)   Rhino 72248 O.S.T. Fox Hunt.
    (S)   (3:47)   K-Tel 3904 The Rock Album Volume 2.
released as by GREG KIHN:
1985 LUCKY
    (S)   (3:27)   Rhino 70900 Kihnsolidation: The Best Of.
    (S)   (3:26)   K-Tel 3742 The 80's: Hot Rock.

THEOLA KILGORE
1963 THE LOVE OF MY MAN
    (M)   (3:12)   Time-Life 2RNR-41 Rock 'N' Roll Era - R&B Gems.
    (M)   (3:12)   Time-Life RHD-02 Rhythm & Blues - 1963.
    (M)   (3:12)   Ripete 2222 Soul Patrol Vol. 4.
    (M)   (3:15)   Time-Life R857-08 The Heart Of Rock 'n' Roll 1963.
    (M)   (3:12)   Time-Life R838-14 Solid Gold Soul - 1963.
    (M)   (3:16)   TVT 4010 Rhythm Revue.

ANDY KIM
1968 HOW'D WE EVER GET THIS WAY
1968 SHOOT 'EM UP BABY
1969 BABY, I LOVE YOU
1969 SO GOOD TOGETHER
1970 BE MY BABY
1974 ROCK ME GENTLY
    (S)   (3:28)   EMI 90603 Rock Me Gently.
    (S)   (3:26)   JCI 3303 Love Seventies.
    (S)   (3:27)   Rhino 70760 Super Hits Of The 70's Volume 13.
    (S)   (3:22)   Curb 77356 70's Hits Volume 2.
    (S)   (3:24)   Razor & Tie 22505 More Fabulous 70's Volume 2.
    (S)   (3:25)   Time-Life SOD-31 Sounds Of The Seventies - AM Top Twenty.
    (S)   (3:26)   Capitol 98665 When AM Was King.
    (S)   (3:25)   K-Tel 3211 70's Teen Heart-Throbs.
    (S)   (3:25)   Madacy Entertainment 1974 Rock On 1974.
    (S)   (3:27)   Priority 50952 I Love Rock & Roll Volume 3: Hits Of The 70's.
    (S)   (3:26)   Time-Life AM1-21 AM Gold - 1974.
1974 FIRE, BABY I'M ON FIRE

B.B. KING
1964 ROCK ME BABY
    (M)   (2:58)   MCA 10667 King Of The Blues.
    (S)   (2:47)   K-Tel 3345 Got The Blues. *(rerecording)*
    (M)   (2:58)   Time-Life R859-02 Living The Blues - Blues Masters.
1970 THE THRILL IS GONE
(actual 45 time is (4:05) not (3:55) as stated on the record label)
    (S)   (5:24)   Stax 8551 Superblues Volume 1. *(LP version)*
    (S)   (5:25)   MCA 31040 Best Of. *(LP version)*

(S) (5:24) MCA 31039 Completely Well. *(LP version)*
(S) (5:24) MCA 11207 Completely Well. *(gold disc; LP version)*
(S) (5:24) MCA 10288 Classic Soul. *(LP version)*
(S) (5:05) Virgin 90962 O.S.T. Stormy Monday. *(LP version faded :19 early)*
(S) (5:26) MCA 10667 King Of The Blues. *(LP version)*
(S) (5:23) Rhino 71128 Blues Masters Volume 7: Blues Revival. *(LP version)*
(S) (5:23) Rhino 71132 Blues Masters Volume 9: Postmodern Blues. *(LP version)*
(S) (4:11) MCA 10919 O.S.T. Heart And Souls. *(rerecording)*
(S) (5:23) Rhino 71618 Soul Train Hall Of Fame/20th Anniversary. *(LP version)*
(S) (4:01) Time-Life RHD-18 Rhythm & Blues - 1970. *(45 version)*
(S) (3:50) Time-Life 2CLR-20 Classic Rock - 1969: Shakin' All Over. *(45 version faded :15 early)*
(S) (4:05) Time-Life SOD-11 Sounds Of The Seventies - 1970: Take Two. *(45 version)*
(S) (5:31) MCA Special Products 22020 Best Of The Blues. *(LP version)*
(S) (5:24) MCA Special Products 20256 Why I Sing The Blues. *(LP version)*
(S) (3:30) Ripete 2198 Soul Patrol. *(45 version faded :35 early)*
(S) (5:24) Priority 53736 Three Decades Of Blues. *(LP version)*
(S) (5:23) Rhino 71806 The R&B Box: Thirty Years Of Rhythm & Blues. *(LP version)*
(S) (5:23) Time-Life R859-01 Living The Blues - Blues Legends. *(LP version)*
(S) (4:00) Rhino 72112 Billboard Hot Soul Hits - 1970. *(45 version)*
(S) (5:24) MCA 11389 O.S.T. Casino. *(LP version)*
(S) (5:24) Atlantic 82848 O.S.T. Heaven's Prisoners. *(LP version)*
(S) (5:24) Madacy Entertainment 1970 Rock On 1970. *(LP version)*
(S) (5:24) Hip-O 40009 ABC's Of Soul Volume 1. *(LP version)*
(S) (5:23) MCA 11441 Blues Classics Box Set. *(LP version)*
(S) (4:01) Time-Life R838-05 Solid Gold Soul - 1970. *(45 version)*
(S) (5:25) Platinum Entertainment 514161301 Essential Blues Guitar. *(LP version)*
(S) (5:24) MCA 11768 Completely Well. *(LP version)*

1973 TO KNOW YOU IS TO LOVE YOU
(S) (8:31) MCA 10667 King Of The Blues. *(LP version)*
(S) (8:30) MCA Special Products 22023 Lucille Talks Back. *(LP version)*
(S) (8:29) MCA Special Products 20256 Why I Sing The Blues. *(LP version)*
(S) (8:29) Rhino 72191 Blues Fest: Modern Blues Of The '70s. *(LP version)*
(S) (3:48) Hip-O 40010 ABC's Of Soul Volume 2. *(45 version)*

1974 I LIKE TO LIVE THE LOVE
(S) (3:26) MCA 10667 King Of The Blues. *(45 version but slightly faster and :11 longer than the 45)*
(S) (5:57) MCA Special Products 22023 Lucille Talks Back. *(LP version)*

BEN E. KING
1961 SPANISH HARLEM
(M) (2:53) Atlantic 81296 Atlantic Rhythm & Blues Volume 4.
(M) (2:50) Abkco 7118 Phil Spector/Back To Mono (1958-1969).
(S) (2:57) Atlantic 80213 Ultimate Collection.
(S) (2:56) Atlantic 82305 Atlantic Rhythm And Blues 1947-1974 Box Set.
(M) (2:52) Rhino 71215 Anthology.
(M) (2:52) Era 5025 The Brill Building Sound.

(S) (2:57) Time-Life 2RNR-25 Rock 'N' Roll Era - The 60's Keep On Rockin'.
(S) (2:57) MCA 6232 O.S.T. Salsa. *(rerecording)*
(M) (2:52) Rhino 71806 The R&B Box: Thirty Years Of Rhythm & Blues.
(M) (2:52) Rhino 72417 Rockin' & Driftin' The Drifters Box Set.
(M) (2:52) Time-Life R857-10 The Heart Of Rock 'n' Roll 1960-1961.
(M) (2:52) Flashback 72668 Stand By Me And Other Hits.
(M) (2:52) Flashback 72084 Soul Legends Box Set.
(M) (2:53) Rhino 72970 Very Best Of.

1961 STAND BY ME
(S) (2:58) Rhino 70647 Billboard's Top R&B Hits Of 1961.
(M) (2:54) Atlantic 81296 Atlantic Rhythm & Blues Volume 4.
(M) (2:53) Atlantic 81677 O.S.T. Stand By Me.
(S) (2:58) Atlantic 81911 Golden Age Of Black Music (1960-1970).
(S) (2:58) Warner Brothers 3359 O.S.T. The Wanderers.
(S) (2:58) Warner Special Products 27601 Atlantic Soul Classics.
(M) (2:51) Rhino 70593 The Rock 'N' Roll Classics Of Leiber & Stoller.
(S) (2:58) Atlantic 80213 Ultimate Collection.
(S) (2:58) Atlantic 82305 Atlantic Rhythm And Blues 1947-1974 Box Set.
(S) (2:58) Curb 77594 Best Of.
(M) (2:54) Rhino 71215 Anthology.
(M) (2:54) Era 5025 The Brill Building Sound.
(M) (2:51) Rhino 70622 Billboard's Top Rock & Roll Hits Of 1961. *(found only on the 1993 reissue of this cd)*
(S) (2:56) Time-Life 2RNR-04 Rock 'N' Roll Era - 1961.
(S) (2:57) Time-Life RHD-14 Rhythm & Blues - 1961.
(S) (2:57) Time-Life SUD-15 Superhits - The Early 60's.
(S) (2:57) Time-Life R962-08 History Of Rock 'N' Roll: Sound Of The City 1959-1965.
(S) (2:59) Right Stuff 28371 Slow Jams: The 60's Volume Two.
(S) (2:56) Time-Life OPCD-4517 Tonight's The Night.
(S) (2:57) Original Sound 8859r Oldies But Goodies Vol. 9. *(remastered edition)*
(S) (2:57) Original Sound 2223 Oldies But Goodies Volumes 2,7,9,12 and 13 Box Set. *(Volumes 2, 7 and 12 of this box set use the "Waring - fds" noise reduction process)*
(S) (2:57) Original Sound 2500 Oldies But Goodies Volumes 1-15 Box Set. *(most volumes in this box set use the "Waring - fds" noise reduction process)*
(S) (2:59) Ripete 2183-RE Ocean Drive Volume 1.
(S) (2:58) Time-Life R857-03 The Heart Of Rock 'n' Roll - 1961.
(M) (2:53) Time-Life R138-18 Body Talk.
(M) (2:54) Rhino 72417 Rockin' & Driftin' The Drifters Box Set.
(S) (2:58) JCI 3164 Eighteen Soulful Ballads.
(S) (2:58) JCI 3166 #1 Radio Hits 1960 - Only Rock 'n roll - 1964.
(M) (2:53) Rhino 72618 Smooth Grooves: The '60s Volume 1 Early '60s.
(S) (2:58) Eclipse Music Group 64867 Rock 'n Roll Relix 1960-1961.
(S) (2:58) Eclipse Music Group 64872 Rock 'n Roll Relix 1960-1969.
(S) (2:57) Time-Life AM1-19 AM Gold - The Early '60s.
(S) (2:58) Time-Life R988-31 Sounds Of The Eighties: Cinemax Movie Hits Of The '80s.
(S) (2:58) Time-Life R834-10 Body Talk - From The Heart.
(M) (2:52) Hammer & Lace 697124114 Leading Men: Masters Of Style Volume Three.
(M) (2:54) Flashback 72668 Stand By Me And Other Hits.
(M) (2:54) Flashback 72084 Soul Legends Box Set.
(M) (2:54) Rhino 72815 Beg, Scream & Shout! The Big Ol' Box Of '60s Soul.
(S) (2:57) Repeat/Relativity 1611 A Brand New Bag: #1 Soul Hits Of The 60's Volume 3.

BEN E. KING *(Continued)*
- (S) (2:57) Time-Life R838-19 Solid Gold Soul 1961.
- (M) (2:52) Simitar 55572 The Number One's: Hot In The '60s.
- (M) (2:54) Rhino 72970 Very Best Of.
- (M) (2:53) Atlantic 83088 Atlantic Records: 50 Years - The Gold Anniversary Collection.

1961 AMOR
- (S) (3:04) Atlantic 81296 Atlantic Rhythm & Blues Volume 4.
- (S) (3:04) Atlantic 80213 Ultimate Collection.
- (S) (3:04) Atlantic 82305 Atlantic Rhythm And Blues 1947-1974 Box Set.
- (M) (2:53) Rhino 71215 Anthology.
- (M) (2:53) Flashback 72668 Stand By Me And Other Hits. *(incorrectly identified on the cd jacket as "AMORE")*
- (M) (2:53) Flashback 72084 Soul Legends Box Set. *(incorrectly identified on the cd jacket as "AMORE")*
- (M) (2:54) Rhino 72970 Very Best Of.

1962 DON'T PLAY THAT SONG (YOU LIED)
- (M) (2:50) Atlantic 81296 Atlantic Rhythm & Blues Volume 4. *(45 version)*
- (S) (2:47) Atlantic 80213 Ultimate Collection. *(LP version)*
- (S) (2:47) Atlantic 82305 Atlantic Rhythm And Blues 1947-1974 Box Set. *(LP version)*
- (M) (2:53) Rhino 71215 Anthology. *(45 version)*
- (S) (2:46) Time-Life 2RNR-29 Rock 'N' Roll Era - The 60's Rave On. *(LP version)*
- (S) (2:43) Time-Life RHD-11 Rhythm & Blues - 1962. *(LP version)*
- (M) (2:53) Rhino 72417 Rockin' & Driftin' The Drifters Box Set. *(45 version)*
- (M) (2:53) Flashback 72668 Stand By Me And Other Hits. *(45 version)*
- (M) (2:53) Flashback 72084 Soul Legends Box Set. *(45 version)*
- (S) (2:43) Time-Life R838-18 Solid Gold Soul 1962. *(LP version)*
- (M) (2:53) Rhino 72970 Very Best Of. *(45 version)*
- (M) (2:51) Time-Life R857-18 The Heart Of Rock 'n' Roll 1962-1963 Take Two. *(45 version)*

1963 I (WHO HAVE NOTHING)
- (M) (2:27) Atlantic 81297 Atlantic Rhythm & Blues Volume 5.
- (M) (2:26) Atlantic 80213 Ultimate Collection.
- (M) (2:26) Atlantic 82305 Atlantic Rhythm And Blues 1947-1974 Box Set.
- (M) (2:30) Rhino 71215 Anthology.
- (M) (2:21) Time-Life 2RNR-48 Rock 'N' Roll Era - R&B Gems II.
- (M) (2:29) Rhino 72417 Rockin' & Driftin' The Drifters Box Set.
- (M) (2:30) Flashback 72668 Stand By Me And Other Hits.
- (M) (2:30) Flashback 72084 Soul Legends Box Set.
- (M) (2:30) Rhino 72970 Very Best Of.

1975 SUPERNATURAL THING (PART 1)
(actual 45 time is (3:24) not (3:20) as stated on the record label)
- (S) (3:14) Rhino 70555 Soul Hits Of The 70's Volume 15. *(edit of the LP version in an unsuccessful attempt at reproducing the 45 version)*
- (S) (4:08) Atlantic 80213 Ultimate Collection. *(LP version of Part 1)*
- (S) (4:10) Rhino 71215 Anthology. *(LP version of Part 1)*
- (S) (3:15) Time-Life SOD-36 Sounds Of The Seventies - More AM Nuggets. *(edit of the LP version in an unsuccessful attempt at reproducing the 45 version)*
- (S) (3:14) JCI 3148 1975 - Only Dance - 1979. *(edit of the LP version in an unsuccessful attempt at reproducing the 45 version)*
- (S) (4:11) Time-Life R838-10 Solid Gold Soul - 1975. *(LP version of Part 1)*
- (S) (3:14) Flashback 72668 Stand By Me And Other Hits. *(edit of the LP version in an unsuccessful attempt at reproducing the 45 version)*

- (S) (3:14) Flashback 72084 Soul Legends Box Set. *(edit of the LP version in an unsuccessful attempt at reproducing the 45 version)*
- (S) (3:23) Rhino 72964 Ultimate '70s R&B Smashes! *(45 version)*
- (S) (3:23) Rhino 72970 Very Best Of. *(45 version)*

1986 STAND BY ME
(this song charted in two different years: 1961 & 1986; see 1961 listings)

CAROLE KING
1962 IT MIGHT AS WELL RAIN UNTIL SEPTEMBER
- (M) (2:21) Rhino 70989 Best Of The Girl Groups Volume 2.
- (M) (2:24) Collectables 5414 Carole King Plus.
- (M) (2:21) Era 5025 The Brill Building Sound.
- (M) (2:25) Time-Life 2RNR-35 Rock 'N' Roll Era - The 60's Last Dance.
- (M) (2:22) Rhino 71650 Colpix-Dimension Story.
- (M) (2:22) Varese Sarabande 5534 Rhythm Of The Rain.

1971 IT'S TOO LATE
- (S) (3:52) Epic/Ode 34946 Tapestry.
- (S) (3:53) Epic/Ode 34967 Her Greatest Hits.
- (S) (3:51) Epic/Legacy 48833 and 65426 The Ode Collection.
- (S) (3:52) Epic/Legacy 66226 Tapestry. *(gold disc)*
- (S) (3:51) Time-Life R13610 Gold And Platinum Box Set - The Ultimate Rock Collection.
- (S) (3:51) Time-Life R814-03 Love Songs.

1971 I FEEL THE EARTH MOVE
- (S) (2:56) Epic/Legacy 48833 and 65426 The Ode Collection.
- (S) (2:57) Epic/Ode 34946 Tapestry.
- (S) (2:57) Epic/Ode 34967 Her Greatest Hits.
- (S) (2:57) Epic/Legacy 66226 Tapestry. *(gold disc)*

1971 SO FAR AWAY
- (S) (3:55) Epic/Ode 34946 Tapestry.
- (S) (3:57) Epic/Ode 34967 Her Greatest Hits.
- (S) (3:54) Epic/Legacy 48833 and 65426 The Ode Collection.
- (S) (3:55) Epic/Legacy 66226 Tapestry. *(gold disc)*
- (S) (3:53) Madacy Entertainment 6806 Best Of Love.

1971 SMACKWATER JACK
- (S) (3:41) Epic/Ode 34967 Her Greatest Hits.
- (S) (3:40) Epic/Ode 34946 Tapestry.
- (S) (3:40) Epic/Legacy 48833 and 65426 The Ode Collection.
- (S) (3:40) Epic/Legacy 66226 Tapestry. *(gold disc)*

1972 SWEET SEASONS
- (S) (3:13) Epic/Ode 34949 Music.
- (S) (3:15) Epic/Ode 34967 Her Greatest Hits.
- (S) (3:14) Epic/Legacy 48833 and 65426 The Ode Collection.

1973 BEEN TO CANAAN
- (S) (3:37) Epic/Ode 34950 Rhymes & Reasons.
- (S) (3:39) Epic/Ode 34967 Her Greatest Hits.
- (S) (3:36) Epic/Legacy 48833 and 65426 The Ode Collection.

1973 BELIEVE IN HUMANITY
- (S) (3:19) Epic/Ode 34962 Fantasy. *(all selections on this cd are segued together)*
- (S) (3:19) Epic/Ode 34967 Her Greatest Hits.
- (S) (4:34) Epic/Legacy 48833 and 65426 The Ode Collection. *(live)*

1973 CORAZON
- (S) (4:05) Epic/Ode 34962 Fantasy. *(LP version where previous selection overlaps introduction; tracks into next selection)*
- (S) (3:57) Epic/Ode 34967 Her Greatest Hits. *(45 version)*
- (S) (3:56) Epic/Legacy 48833 and 65426 The Ode Collection. *(45 version)*

1974 JAZZMAN
- (S) (3:42) Epic/Ode 34953 Wrap Around Joy.
- (S) (3:44) Epic/Legacy 48833 and 65426 The Ode Collection.

328

1975 NIGHTINGALE
- (S) (3:35) Epic/Ode 34953 Wrap Around Joy.
- (S) (3:36) Epic/Legacy 48833 and 65426 The Ode Collection.

1976 ONLY LOVE IS REAL
- (S) (3:28) Epic/Ode 34963 Thoroughbred.
- (S) (3:30) Epic/Legacy 48833 and 65426 The Ode Collection.

1977 HARD ROCK CAFE
- (S) (3:41) King's X/Rhythm Safari 53880 Time Gone By.

1980 ONE FINE DAY
- (S) (2:26) Priority 53746 80's Greatest Rock Hits Vol. 12 - Singers/Songwriters.
- (S) (2:26) King's X/Rhythm Safari 53879 Pearls.

CLAUDE KING
1962 WOLVERTON MOUNTAIN
- (S) (2:55) Rhino 70683 Billboard's Top Country Hits Of 1962.
- (S) (2:58) Columbia 46031 Columbia Country Classics Volume 3.
- (S) (2:57) Columbia 45075 American Originals.
- (S) (2:57) Time-Life CTD-03 Country USA - 1962.
- (S) (2:55) K-Tel 320 Country Music Classics Volume II.
- (S) (2:56) Epic 67941 Super Hits Of The 60's.
- (S) (2:48) K-Tel 3368 101 Greatest Country Hits Vol. Nine: Country Classics. *(rerecording)*
- (S) (2:57) Time-Life R808-01 Classic Country 1960-1964.

DIANA KING
1995 SHY GUY
- (S) (4:18) Work 64189 Tougher Than Love.
- (S) (3:40) Work 67009 O.S.T. Bad Boys.

1997 I SAY A LITTLE PRAYER
- (S) (3:34) Work/Sony Music Soundtrax 68166 O.S.T. My Best Friend's Wedding.

EVELYN "CHAMPAGNE" KING
1978 SHAME
- (S) (3:18) Priority 7971 Mega-Hits Dance Classics Volume 1. *(:23 longer than the 45 version)*
- (S) (6:32) RCA 7639 Dance! Dance! Dance! *(LP version)*
- (S) (3:17) RCA 9684 and 8476 Nipper's Greatest Hits - The 70's. *(45 version but :22 longer)*
- (S) (3:16) RCA 61144 The RCA Records Label: The 1st Note In Black Music. *(:21 longer than the 45 version)*
- (S) (2:56) Rhino 70276 The Disco Years Volume 5. *(45 version)*
- (S) (6:32) RCA 61103 Love Come Down: Best Of. *(LP version)*
- (S) (3:17) Razor & Tie 22496 Disco Fever. *(45 version but :22 longer)*
- (S) (2:56) Time-Life SOD-36 Sounds Of The Seventies - More AM Nuggets. *(45 version)*
- (S) (6:30) Rebound 314520217 Disco Nights Vol. 1 - Divas Of Dance. *(LP version)*
- (S) (3:16) K-Tel 3251 Disco Fever. *(45 version but :21 longer)*
- (S) (6:32) Thump 4040 Old School Volume 4. *(LP version)*
- (S) (2:56) Rhino 72414 Dance Floor Divas: The 70's. *(45 version)*
- (S) (2:56) JCI 3163 18 Disco Superhits. *(45 version)*
- (S) (2:56) Scotti Bros. 75504 Club Ladies Night. *(45 version)*
- (S) (3:16) Hip-O 40041 The Studio Collection Disco 54. *(45 version but :21 longer)*
- (S) (3:15) Priority 53142 Mega Hits - Disco Express. *(45 version but :20 longer)*
- (S) (6:32) RCA 66957 Club Cutz 2. *(12" single mix)*
- (S) (6:31) Chronicles 314553404 Non-Stop Disco Vol. 1. *(all songs on this cd are segued together)*
- (S) (5:20) Island 314553411 The Last Party. *(all selections on this cd are segued together)*
- (S) (3:15) Simitar 55602 The Number One's: Silky Soul. *(45 version but :20 longer)*

- (S) (6:32) Beast 53202 Disco Divas - A Salute To The Ladies. *(LP version)*
- (S) (2:56) Time-Life R840-08 Sounds Of The Seventies: '70s Dance Party 1978-1979. *(45 version)*
- (S) (4:15) Rebound 314520520 Body Moves - Non-Stop Disco Workout Vol. 1. *(all selections on this cd are segued together)*

1979 I DON'T KNOW IF IT'S RIGHT
- (S) (4:09) RCA 2357 Dance! Dance! Dance! Volume 2. *(all selections on this cd are segued together; LP length)*
- (S) (3:45) RCA 61103 Love Come Down: Best Of. *(45 length)*
- (S) (3:45) Rhino 72130 Soul Hits Of The 70's Vol. 20. *(45 length)*
- (S) (3:45) Priority 53789 Disco Attack. *(45 length)*

released as by EVELYN KING:
1982 LOVE COME DOWN
- (S) (6:04) Thump 4050 Old School Volume 5. *(LP version)*
- (S) (6:04) RCA 61103 Love Come Down: Best Of. *(LP version)*
- (S) (6:15) RCA 54337 Get Loose. *(LP version)*
- (S) (3:43) Rhino 72159 Black Entertainment Television - 15th Anniversary. *(45 version)*
- (S) (3:45) Rhino 72137 Billboard Hot R&B Hits 1982. *(45 version)*
- (S) (3:45) K-Tel 3673 The 80's - Funky Love. *(45 version)*
- (S) (6:04) Hip-O 40031 The Glory Of Love - '80s Sweet & Soulful Love Songs. *(LP version)*
- (S) (3:44) Rebound 314520431 Soul Classics - Best Of The 80's. *(45 version)*
- (S) (4:09) Thump 4100 Old School Mix. *(all selections on this cd are segued together and remixed)*
- (S) (3:45) Simitar 55542 The Number One's: Soul On Fire. *(45 version)*

FREDDY KING
1961 HIDE AWAY
- (M) (2:34) Time-Life RHD-14 Rhythm & Blues - 1961.
- (M) (2:34) Time-Life 2RNR-36 Rock 'N' Roll Era - Axes & Saxes: The Great Instrumentals.
- (M) (2:34) Rhino 71510 Hide Away: Best Of.
- (M) (2:34) King 7002 King R&B Box Set.
- (M) (2:32) Federal 5012 All His Hits.
- (M) (2:34) King 1408 Original Blues.
- (M) (2:37) King 773 Hide Away Dance Away.
- (M) (2:34) Time-Life R859-05 Living The Blues: 1960-1964 Blues Classics.
- (M) (2:33) Time-Life R838-19 Solid Gold Soul 1961.

JONATHAN KING
1965 EVERYONE'S GONE TO THE MOON
- (S) (2:27) Rhino 70325 History Of British Rock Volume 7.
- (S) (2:27) Rhino 72022 History Of British Rock Box Set.
- (M) (2:31) Varese Sarabande 5846 On The Radio Volume One.

KING CURTIS
1962 SOUL TWIST
- (M) (2:45) Rhino 70648 Billboard's Top R&B Hits Of 1962.
- (S) (2:47) Relic 7009 Raging Harlem Hit Parade.
- (S) (2:35) Capitol 91631 Best Of. *(rerecording)*
- (S) (2:45) Collectables 5119 Soul Twist And Other Golden Classics.
- (S) (2:47) Capricorn 42009 Fire/Fury Records Story.
- (S) (2:47) Rhino 71604 Rock Instrumental Classics Vol. 4: Soul.
- (S) (2:47) Rhino 72035 Rock Instrumental Classics Vols. 1-5 Box Set.
- (S) (2:42) Time-Life 2RNR-44 Rock 'N' Roll Era - Lost Treasures.
- (S) (2:41) Time-Life RHD-11 Rhythm & Blues - 1962.
- (E) (2:46) Collectables 5156 Enjoy...The Best Of. *(mastered from vinyl)*
- (M) (2:45) K-Tel 3241 Let's Twist.
- (M) (2:45) K-Tel 3059 Saxy Rock.

KING CURTIS *(Continued)*
- (M) (2:45) Razor & Tie 2054 Instant Soul: The Legendary.
- (S) (2:47) Hip-O 40008 Soulful Grooves - R&B Instrumental Classics Volume 2.
- (S) (2:40) Capitol 36504 Best Of. *(rerecording)*
- (S) (2:35) Collectables 5687 Best Of. *(rerecording)*
- (M) (2:45) Ripete 2223 Soul Patrol Vol. 5.
- (S) (2:41) Time-Life R838-18 Solid Gold Soul 1962.

1967 MEMPHIS SOUL STEW
- (S) (2:57) Warner Special Products 27609 Memphis Soul Classics.
- (S) (2:56) Atlantic 81298 Atlantic Rhythm & Blues Volume 6.
- (S) (2:54) JCI 3553 Soul Serenade.
- (S) (2:56) Atlantic 82305 Atlantic Rhythm And Blues 1947-1974 Box Set.
- (S) (2:54) Time-Life 2CLR-28 Classic Rock - On The Soul Side II.
- (S) (2:57) Razor & Tie 2054 Instant Soul: The Legendary.
- (S) (2:57) Hip-O 40008 Soulful Grooves - R&B Instrumental Classics Volume 2.
- (M) (2:56) Rhino 72815 Beg, Scream & Shout! The Big Ol' Box Of '60s Soul.
- (S) (2:56) Flashback 72897 25 Years Of R&B - 1967.
- (M) (2:56) Rhino 72963 Ultimate '60s Soul Smashes.

1967 ODE TO BILLIE JOE
- (S) (2:47) JCI 3553 Soul Serenade.
- (M) (2:46) Razor & Tie 2054 Instant Soul: The Legendary.

KING HARVEST
1973 DANCING IN THE MOONLIGHT
- (M) (2:49) Rhino 71197 Super Hits Of The 70's Volume 17. *(neither the 45 or LP version)*
- (M) (2:49) Time-Life SOD-31 Sounds Of The Seventies - AM Top Twenty. *(neither the 45 or LP version)*
- (S) (2:57) Collectables 0528 Dancing In The Moonlight. *(mastered from vinyl)*

KINGSMEN
1964 LOUIE LOUIE
- (E) (2:42) Warner Special Products 27607 Highs Of The 60's.
- (M) (2:42) Original Sound 8861 Oldies But Goodies Vol. 11. *(this compact disc uses the "Waring - fds" noise reduction process)*
- (M) (2:42) Original Sound 2222 Oldies But Goodies Volumes 3,5,11,14 and 15 Box Set. *(this box set uses the "Waring - fds" noise reduction process)*
- (M) (2:42) Original Sound 2500 Oldies But Goodies Volumes 1-15 Box Set. *(this box set uses the "Waring - fds" noise reduction process)*
- (M) (2:42) Original Sound CDGO-4 Golden Oldies Volume. 4.
- (M) (2:42) Original Sound 8895 Dick Clark's 21 All-Time Hits Vol. 4.
- (M) (2:43) Rhino 75778 Frat Rock.
- (M) (2:43) Rhino 70624 Billboard's Top Rock & Roll Hits Of 1963.
- (M) (2:43) Rhino 72007 Billboard's Top Rock & Roll Hits 1962-1966 Box Set.
- (M) (2:43) DCC Compact Classics 029 Toga Rock.
- (M) (2:42) Capitol 48993 Spuds Mackenzie's Party Faves.
- (M) (2:42) Rhino 70605 Best Of Louie Louie.
- (M) (2:43) Rhino 70794 KFOG Presents M. Dung's Idiot Show.
- (M) (2:43) Rhino 70745 Greatest Hits.
- (M) (2:43) Collectables 5073 Louie Louie And Other Golden Classics.
- (M) (2:42) Essex 7052 All Time Rock Classics.
- (M) (2:43) Capricorn 42003 The Scepter Records Story.
- (M) (2:43) Sundazed 6004 In Person. *(no live audience overdub as found on the original vinyl album)*
- (M) (2:43) Jerden 7011 Louie Louie Collection.
- (S) (2:49) Jerden 7011 Louie Louie Collection. *(live)*
- (M) (2:42) Time-Life 2RNR-10 Rock 'N' Roll Era - 1964.
- (M) (2:43) Time-Life 2CLR-09 Classic Rock - 1964: The Beat Goes On.
- (M) (2:42) JCI 3125 1960 - Only Rock 'N Roll - 1964.

- (M) (2:42) Risky Business 66914 Party On.
- (M) (2:44) Ripete 2187-RE Preppy Deluxe.
- (M) (2:41) Tommy Boy 1136 ESPN Presents Jock Rock Vol. 2. *(all songs on this cd are segued together with crowd sound effects added)*
- (M) (2:43) King 1421 Party Time Rock & Roll.
- (M) (2:42) LaserLight 12528 Garage Band Rock.
- (M) (2:43) LaserLight 12424 Best Of.
- (M) (2:42) Cypress 71334 O.S.T. Coupe De Ville.
- (M) (3:38) Cypress 71334 O.S.T. Coupe De Ville. *(remix)*
- (M) (2:43) Priority 50951 I Love Rock & Roll Volume 2: Hits Of The 60's.
- (E) (2:40) Cold Front 6245 Greatest Sports Rock And Jams. *(all selections on this cd are segued together)*
- (M) (2:43) K-Tel 4065 K-Tel's Original Party Music Vol. 1.
- (M) (2:43) K-Tel 4185 Greatest Hits.

1964 MONEY
- (M) (2:29) Rhino 70745 Greatest Hits.
- (M) (2:29) Collectables 5073 Louie Louie And Other Golden Classics.
- (S) (2:24) Sundazed 6004 In Person.
- (S) (2:23) Time-Life 2CLR-17 Classic Rock - Rock Renaissance.
- (S) (2:15) King 499 Classic Rock & Roll. *(ending rudely truncated)*
- (M) (2:30) LaserLight 12424 Best Of.
- (M) (2:29) K-Tel 4185 Greatest Hits.

1964 DEATH OF AN ANGEL
- (M) (2:31) Rhino 70745 Greatest Hits. *(very hissy)*
- (M) (2:33) Collectables 5073 Louie Louie And Other Golden Classics. *(mastered from vinyl)*
- (S) (2:32) Sundazed 6005 Volume 2. *(very hissy)*
- (M) (2:31) LaserLight 12424 Best Of. *(very hissy)*
- (S) (2:31) K-Tel 4185 Greatest Hits. *(very hissy)*

1965 THE JOLLY GREEN GIANT
- (M) (1:57) Rhino 70745 Greatest Hits. *(distorted)*
- (M) (1:57) Collectables 5073 Louie Louie And Other Golden Classics. *(distorted)*
- (M) (1:57) Capricorn 42003 The Scepter Records Story. *(distorted)*
- (S) (1:57) Sundazed 6006 Volume 3. *(distorted)*
- (S) (1:57) K-Tel 3035 Goofy Greats. *(rerecording)*
- (M) (1:57) LaserLight 12424 Best Of. *(distorted)*
- (M) (1:56) K-Tel 4185 Greatest Hits. *(distorted)*

KINGSTON TRIO
1958 TOM DOOLEY
- (E) (3:01) Capitol 90592 Memories Are Made Of This.
- (M) (3:01) Curb 77354 50's Hits Volume 1.
- (M) (3:01) Curb 77385 Greatest Hits.
- (M) (3:01) Capitol 46624 Very Best Of.
- (M) (3:02) Capitol 92710 Capitol Collector's Series.
- (M) (3:01) Capitol 96748 The Kingston Trio/From the Hungry "i".
- (M) (3:02) Rhino 70264 Troubadours Of The Folk Era Volume 3.
- (M) (3:00) Pair 1067 Early American Heroes.
- (M) (3:02) Capitol 98665 When AM Was King.
- (M) (3:01) Time-Life HPD-11 Your Hit Parade 1958.
- (M) (3:02) DCC Compact Classics 078 Best Of Tragedy.
- (M) (3:01) Capitol 28498 The Capitol Years.
- (M) (3:02) Time-Life R132-22 Treasury Of Folk Music Volume One.

1959 THE TIJUANA JAIL
- (S) (2:48) Curb 77385 Greatest Hits.
- (S) (2:46) Capitol 46624 Very Best Of. *(this song appears in mono on cd's that were pressed in Japan)*
- (S) (2:48) Capitol 92710 Capitol Collector's Series.
- (E) (2:48) Pair 1067 Early American Heroes.
- (S) (2:16) Special Music 4803 Greatest Hits. *(live)*
- (S) (2:48) Time-Life HPD-25 Your Hit Parade - The 50's.
- (S) (2:48) Capitol 28498 The Capitol Years.
- (S) (2:48) Time-Life R132-22 Treasury Of Folk Music Volume One.

1959 M.T.A.
- (S) (3:12) Curb 77385 Greatest Hits.

(S) (3:11) Capitol 46624 Very Best Of. *(this song appears in mono on cd's that were pressed in Japan)*
(S) (3:14) Capitol 92710 Capitol Collector's Series.
(S) (3:13) Capitol 96749 At Large/Here We Go Again.
(S) (3:13) Pair 1067 Early American Heroes.
(S) (2:57) Special Music 4803 Greatest Hits. *(live)*
(S) (3:12) Time-Life HPD-13 Your Hit Parade - 1959.
(S) (3:12) Capitol 28498 The Capitol Years.
(S) (3:11) Time-Life R132-22 Treasury Of Folk Music Volume One.

1959 A WORRIED MAN
(S) (2:50) Curb 77385 Greatest Hits.
(S) (2:47) Capitol 46624 Very Best Of. *(this song appears in mono on cd's that were pressed in Japan)*
(S) (3:25) Capitol 92710 Capitol Collector's Series. *(with a :33 false start and studio talk)*
(S) (2:51) Capitol 96749 At Large/Here We Go Again.
(E) (2:50) Pair 1067 Early American Heroes.
(S) (2:50) Time-Life HPD-36 Your Hit Parade - The 50's Pop Revival.
(S) (2:50) Capitol 28498 The Capitol Years.
(S) (2:50) Time-Life R132-22 Treasury Of Folk Music Volume Two.

1962 WHERE HAVE ALL THE FLOWERS GONE
(S) (3:00) Rhino 70734 Songs Of Protest.
(S) (3:01) Curb 77385 Greatest Hits.
(S) (2:58) Capitol 46624 Very Best Of. *(this song appears in mono on cd's that were pressed in Japan)*
(S) (3:01) Capitol 92710 Capitol Collector's Series.
(S) (3:01) Pair 1067 Early American Heroes.
(S) (2:59) Special Music 4803 Greatest Hits. *(live)*
(S) (3:01) JCI 3109 Folk Sixties.
(S) (3:01) Time-Life HPD-33 Your Hit Parade - The Early 60's.
(S) (3:00) Capitol 28498 The Capitol Years.
(S) (3:00) Time-Life R132-22 Treasury Of Folk Music Volume One.

1963 GREENBACK DOLLAR
(S) (2:49) Curb 77385 Greatest Hits. *(uncensored LP version)*
(S) (2:48) Capitol 46624 Very Best Of. *(this song appears in mono on cd's that were pressed in Japan; uncensored LP version)*
(S) (2:49) Capitol 92710 Capitol Collector's Series. *(uncensored LP version)*
(S) (2:49) Pair 1067 Early American Heroes. *(uncensored LP version)*
(S) (2:49) Risky Business 66385 Wall Street's Greatest Hits. *(uncensored LP version)*
(S) (2:49) Capitol 28498 The Capitol Years. *(uncensored LP version)*
(S) (2:49) Time-Life R132-22 Treasury Of Folk Music Volume Two. *(uncensored LP version)*

1963 REVEREND MR. BLACK
(S) (3:01) Curb 77385 Greatest Hits.
(S) (2:58) Capitol 46624 Very Best Of. *(this song appears in mono on cd's that were pressed in Japan)*
(S) (3:12) Capitol 92710 Collector's Series. *(with a countoff and a :13 longer fade than either the 45 or LP)*
(S) (3:01) Pair 1221 Made In The USA.
(S) (2:57) Time-Life SUD-08 Superhits - 1963.
(S) (3:04) Capitol 28498 The Capitol Years.
(S) (2:56) Time-Life R132-22 Treasury Of Folk Music Volume Two.
(S) (2:57) Time-Life AM1-17 AM Gold - 1963.

1963 DESERT PETE
(S) (2:42) Capitol 46624 Very Best Of. *(this song appears in mono on cd's that were pressed in Japan)*
(S) (2:47) Capitol 92710 Capitol Collector's Series.
(S) (2:43) Pair 1221 Made In The USA.
(S) (2:35) Capitol 28498 The Capitol Years. *(alternate take)*

KINKS
1964 YOU REALLY GOT ME
(M) (2:12) Rhino 70906 American Bandstand Greatest Hits Collection.
(M) (2:11) Original Sound 8894 Dick Clark's 21 All-Time Hits Vol. 3.

(M) (2:13) Rhino 70086 Greatest Hits.
(M) (2:12) Rhino 70319 History Of British Rock Volume 1.
(M) (2:12) Rhino 72022 History Of British Rock Box Set.
(M) (2:12) Rhino 72008 History Of British Rock Volumes 1-4 Box Set.
(M) (2:12) Rhino 75772 Son Of Frat Rock.
(M) (2:12) Rhino 70720 Legends Of Guitar - Rock; The 60's.
(M) (2:12) Rhino 70315 You Really Got Me.
(M) (2:11) Time-Life 2CLR-03 Classic Rock - 1964.
(M) (2:12) Time-Life R962-07 History Of Rock 'N' Roll: The British Invasion 1964-1966.
(M) (2:12) Time-Life OPCD-4521 Guitar Rock.
(M) (2:11) JCI 3125 1960 - Only Rock 'N Roll - 1964.
(M) (2:12) Risky Business 66914 Party On.
(M) (2:12) Rhino 71849 Tired Of Waiting For You.
(M) (2:11) MFSL 679 You Really Got Me/Kinda Kinks. *(gold disc)*
(M) (2:12) Rhino 72478 Beverly Hills 90210: Songs From The Peach Pit.
(M) (2:12) Hip-O 40038 Power Chords Volume 1.
(M) (2:11) Rebound 314520435 Classic Rock - 60's.
(M) (2:11) JCI 3189 1960 - Only Dance - 1964.

1965 ALL DAY AND ALL OF THE NIGHT
(M) (2:22) Rhino 70320 History Of British Rock Volume 2.
(M) (2:22) Rhino 72022 History Of British Rock Box Set.
(M) (2:22) Rhino 72008 History Of British Rock Volumes 1-4 Box Set.
(M) (2:21) Rhino 70086 Greatest Hits.
(M) (2:21) Rhino 70316 Kinda Kinks.
(M) (2:20) Time-Life 2CLR-08 Classic Rock - 1965: The Beat Goes On.
(M) (2:21) Time-Life R105-24 Guitar Rock Monsters.
(M) (2:20) JCI 3167 #1 Radio Hits 1965 - Only Rock 'n Roll - 1969.
(M) (2:21) Priority 50951 I Love Rock & Roll Volume 2: Hits Of The 60's.

1965 TIRED OF WAITING FOR YOU
(M) (2:30) Rhino 70321 History Of British Rock Volume 3.
(M) (2:30) Rhino 72022 History Of British Rock Box Set.
(M) (2:30) Rhino 72008 History Of British Rock Volumes 1-4 Box Set.
(M) (2:30) Rhino 70086 Greatest Hits.
(M) (2:29) Rhino 70316 Kinda Kinks.
(M) (2:31) Time-Life 2CLR-01 Classic Rock - 1965.
(M) (2:29) Rhino 71849 Tired Of Waiting For You.
(M) (2:29) MFSL 679 You Really Got Me/Kinda Kinks. *(gold disc)*

1965 SET ME FREE
(M) (2:10) Rhino 70086 Greatest Hits.
(M) (2:10) Rhino 75769 Kink-Size Kinkdom.
(M) (2:09) Time-Life 2CLR-14 Classic Rock - 1965: Shakin' All Over.
(M) (2:10) Rhino 71849 Tired Of Waiting For You.
(M) (2:09) JCI 3160 18 Free & Easy Hits From The 60's.

1965 WHO'LL BE THE NEXT IN LINE
(M) (2:00) Rhino 70086 Greatest Hits.
(M) (2:00) Rhino 75769 Kink-Size Kinkdom.
(M) (2:00) Time-Life 2CLR-23 Classic Rock - 1965: Blowin' Your Mind.
(M) (2:00) Rhino 71849 Tired Of Waiting For You.

1966 A WELL RESPECTED MAN
(M) (2:40) Rhino 70322 History Of British Rock Volume 4.
(M) (2:40) Rhino 72022 History Of British Rock Box Set.
(M) (2:40) Rhino 72008 History Of British Rock Volumes 1-4 Box Set.
(M) (2:41) Rhino 70086 Greatest Hits.
(M) (2:41) Rhino 75769 Kink-Size Kinkdom.
(M) (2:39) Time-Life 2CLR-13 Classic Rock - 1966: Shakin' All Over.

1966 DEDICATED FOLLOWER OF FASHION
(M) (3:00) Island 314518841 O.S.T. In The Name Of The Father.
(M) (2:59) Time-Life 2CLR-21 Classic Rock - Rock Renaissance II.
(M) (3:00) Rhino 70086 Greatest Hits.

(M) (3:00) Rhino 75769 Kink-Size Kinkdom.

1966 SUNNY AFTERNOON
- (M) (3:32) Rhino 70086 Greatest Hits.
- (E) (3:33) Reprise 6454 Kink Kronikles.
- (M) (3:31) Time-Life 2CLR-22 Classic Rock - 1966: Blowin' Your Mind.
- (M) (3:32) Rhino 71849 Tired Of Waiting For You.
- (M) (3:32) Buddah 49506 Feelin' Groovy.

1970 LOLA
- (S) (4:02) Reprise 6423 Lola Versus Powerman And The Moneygoround. ("Coca Cola" version)
- (S) (4:01) Reprise 6454 Kink Kronikles. ("Coca Cola" version)
- (S) (4:42) Priority 7065 70's Greatest Rock Hits Volume 13: Request Line. (live)
- (S) (4:42) Rhino 72131 Frat Rock: The 70's. (live)

1971 APEMAN
- (S) (3:52) Reprise 6423 Lola Versus Powerman And The Moneygoround. (LP version lyrics)
- (S) (3:52) Reprise 6454 Kink Kronikles. (LP version lyrics)

1978 A ROCK 'N' ROLL FANTASY
- (S) (4:59) Warner Special Products 27616 Classic Rock. (LP version)
- (S) (4:58) Arista 8069 Misfits. (LP version)
- (S) (4:58) Priority 7080 70's Greatest Rock Hits Volume 14: Kings Of Rock. (LP version)
- (S) (4:57) Time-Life R102-34 The Rolling Stone Collection. (LP version)
- (S) (4:57) Time-Life SOD-20 Sounds Of The Seventies - 1978: Take Two. (LP version)
- (S) (4:58) Arista 8428 Best Of 1977-1986. (LP version)

1983 COME DANCING
- (S) (3:54) Arista 8428 Best Of 1977-1986.
- (S) (3:54) Arista 8018 State Of Confusion.
- (S) (3:54) Time-Life R988-03 Sounds Of The Eighties: 1983.

1983 DON'T FORGET TO DANCE
- (S) (4:38) Arista 8428 Best Of 1977-1986. (LP version)
- (S) (4:37) Arista 8018 State Of Confusion. (LP version)

KISS

1976 ROCK AND ROLL ALL NITE (live version)
- (S) (3:21) Rhino 70986 Heavy Metal Memories. (45 version)
- (S) (3:59) Casablanca 822780 Alive! (LP version)
- (S) (2:44) Original Sound 8894 Dick Clark's 21 All-Time Hits Vol. 3. (this is the studio version - not the hit version)
- (S) (2:54) Mercury 836427 Smashes, Thrashes & Hits. (this is the studio version - not the hit version)
- (S) (2:43) Casablanca 824155 Double Platinum. (this is the studio version - not the hit version)
- (S) (2:53) Medicine Label 24533 O.S.T. Dazed And Confused. (this is the studio version - not the hit version)
- (S) (4:06) K-Tel 6090 Hit Parader Salutes 20 Years Of Metal. (LP version)
- (S) (3:33) Priority 53745 Back Stage Pass - Live & Rockin' Vol. 1. (this is a live version but not the "hit" live version)
- (S) (2:42) Priority 7963 First Degree Metal. (this is the studio version - not the hit version)
- (S) (3:20) Time-Life R968-10 Guitar Rock Classics. (45 version)
- (S) (2:49) Tommy Boy 1136 ESPN Presents Jock Rock Vol. 2. (all songs on this cd are segued together with crowd sound effects added; studio version)
- (S) (2:43) JCI 4530 Masters Of Metal - Wreaking Havoc 1975-1985 Volume 2. (this is the studio version - not the hit version)
- (S) (2:46) Mercury 314534725 Greatest. (this is the studio version - not the hit version)
- (S) (2:46) Mercury 314532383 Double Platinum. (this is the studio version - not the hit version; remastered edition)

(S) (4:07) Mercury 314532377 Alive! (remastered edition; LP version)

1976 SHOUT IT OUT LOUD (studio version)
- (S) (2:46) Casablanca 824149 Destroyer. (LP version)
- (S) (2:54) Mercury 836427 Smashes, Thrashes & Hits. (neither the 45 or LP version)
- (S) (3:38) Mercury 314534725 Greatest. (this is the live version - not the hit version)
- (S) (2:47) Mercury 314532378 Destroyer. (remastered edition; LP version)

1976 BETH
- (S) (2:43) Casablanca 824149 Destroyer.
- (S) (2:45) Mercury 836427 Smashes, Thrashes & Hits.
- (S) (2:43) Casablanca 824155 Double Platinum.
- (S) (2:43) Time-Life SOD-18 Sounds Of The Seventies - 1976: Take Two.
- (S) (2:43) Priority 7965 Heavy Metal Love.
- (S) (2:43) Elektra 61888 O.S.T. Beautiful Girls.
- (S) (2:44) Mercury 314534725 Greatest.
- (S) (2:45) Mercury 314532383 Double Platinum. (remastered edition)
- (S) (2:44) Mercury 314532378 Destroyer. (remastered edition)

1976 DETROIT ROCK CITY
- (S) (5:19) Casablanca 824149 Destroyer. (LP version; tracks into next selection)
- (S) (3:46) Mercury 836427 Smashes, Thrashes & Hits. (neither the 45 or LP version)
- (S) (3:35) Casablanca 824155 Double Platinum. (neither the 45 or LP version)
- (S) (3:36) Mercury 314534725 Greatest. (neither the 45 or LP version)
- (S) (3:35) Mercury 314532383 Double Platinum. (neither the 45 or LP version; remastered edition)
- (S) (5:17) Mercury 314532378 Destroyer. (remastered edition; LP version; tracks into next selection)

1977 HARD LUCK WOMAN
- (S) (3:26) Casablanca 824150 Rock And Roll Over.
- (S) (3:23) Casablanca 824155 Double Platinum. (missing a bass guitar overdub)
- (S) (3:33) Mercury 314534725 Greatest.
- (S) (3:33) Mercury 314532380 Rock And Roll Over. (remastered edition)
- (S) (3:23) Mercury 314532383 Double Platinum. (remastered edition; missing a bass guitar overdub)

1977 CALLING DR. LOVE
- (S) (3:38) Casablanca 824150 Rock And Roll Over. (LP version)
- (S) (3:39) Mercury 836427 Smashes, Thrashes & Hits. (LP version)
- (S) (3:11) Casablanca 824155 Double Platinum. (neither the 45 or LP version)
- (S) (3:07) Priority 53720 Classic Rock Volume 5 - Glitter Bands. (neither the 45 or LP version)
- (S) (3:29) Time-Life R968-14 Guitar Rock - The Late '70s. (LP version faded :10 early)
- (S) (3:43) Mercury 314534725 Greatest. (LP version)
- (S) (3:43) Mercury 314532380 Rock And Roll Over. (LP version; remastered edition)
- (S) (3:17) Mercury 314532383 Double Platinum. (remastered edition; neither the 45 or LP version)

1977 CHRISTINE SIXTEEN
(actual 45 time is (3:10) not (2:52) as stated on the record label)
- (S) (3:06) Casablanca 824151 Love Gun.
- (S) (3:06) Time-Life R968-15 Guitar Rock - FM Classics.
- (S) (3:12) Mercury 314534725 Greatest.
- (S) (3:12) Mercury 314532381 Love Gun. (remastered edition)

1979 I WAS MADE FOR LOVIN' YOU
- (S) (4:29) Casablanca 812770 Dynasty. (LP version)
- (S) (4:29) Mercury 836427 Smashes, Thrashes & Hits. (LP version)
- (S) (4:29) Mercury 314534725 Greatest. (LP version)

1990 FOREVER
- (S) (3:51) Mercury 838913 Hot In The Shade.

MAC and KATIE KISSOON
1971 CHIRPY CHIRPY CHEEP CHEEP
    (M) (2:54)   Varese Sarabande 5719 Bubblegum Classics Volume Three.

KIX
1989 DON'T CLOSE YOUR EYES
    (S) (4:13)   JCI 4545 Masters Of Metal: Thunder 'N Spice.
    (S) (4:15)   Atlantic 81877 Blow My Fuse.

KLF
1991 3 A.M. ETERNAL
    (S) (3:36)   Arista 18735 House Of Groove.
    (S) (3:13)   Tommy Boy 1053 MTV Party To Go Volume 2. *(all tracks on this cd are segued together)*
    (S) (3:34)   Arista 8657 and 18707 The White Room.
    (S) (5:20)   Beast 53292 Club Hitz Of The 90's Vol. 4. *(all songs on this cd are segued together)*

1992 JUSTIFIED AND ANCIENT
    (S) (5:02)   Arista 8657 and 18707 The White Room. *(this is not the hit version; the hit version is included with this cd as a cd single which runs (3:36) and (5:29) and is titled "STAND BY THE JAMS")*
    (S) (3:35)   Cold Front 6247 Classic Club Mix - Dance Jams. *(all selections on this cd are segued together)*
    (S) (3:36)   Rhino 72839 Disco Queens: The 90's.

KLYMAXX
1986 I MISS YOU
    (S) (4:05)   JCI 3124 Rhythm Of The Night. *(45 version)*
    (S) (4:05)   K-Tel 3263 The 80's Love Jams. *(45 version)*
    (S) (4:07)   MCA 11217 Quiet Storms - 80's Jams Vol. I. *(45 version)*
    (S) (5:31)   MCA 31064 Meeting In The Ladies Room. *(LP version)*
    (S) (5:30)   Rhino 71865 Smooth Grooves Volume 7. *(LP version)*
    (S) (5:30)   MCA 11418 Greatest Hits. *(LP version)*
    (S) (4:05)   K-Tel 3868 Hot Ladies Of Pop. *(45 version)*
    (S) (4:05)   Time-Life R834-12 Body Talk - By Candlelight. *(45 version)*

1986 MAN SIZE LOVE
(actual 45 time is (4:05) not (3:58) as stated on the record label)
    (S) (4:16)   MCA 6330 Soundtrack Smashes - The 80's. *(45 version but :11 longer fade)*
    (S) (4:16)   MCA 6169 O.S.T. Running Scared. *(45 version but :11 longer fade)*
    (S) (5:38)   MCA 5832 Klymaxx. *(LP version)*
    (S) (4:11)   MCA 11418 Greatest Hits. *(45 version but :06 longer fade)*
    (S) (4:16)   Hip-O 40075 Rock She Said: On The Pop Side. *(45 version but :11 longer fade)*

1987 I'D STILL SAY YES
    (S) (4:40)   MCA 5832 Klymaxx. *(LP version)*
    (S) (4:40)   MCA 11431 Quiet Storms 2. *(LP version)*
    (S) (4:40)   MCA 11418 Greatest Hits. *(LP version)*
    (S) (4:39)   Hip-O 40031 The Glory Of Love - '80s Sweet & Soulful Love Songs. *(LP version)*
    (S) (4:40)   Rhino 72757 Smooth Grooves - Wedding Songs. *(LP version)*

KNACK
1979 MY SHARONA
    (S) (4:01)   Rhino 70674 Billboard Top Hits - 1979. *(45 version)*
    (S) (4:53)   Curb 77356 70's Hits Volume 2. *(LP version)*
    (S) (4:52)   Capitol 91848 Get The Knack. *(LP version)*
    (S) (4:52)   Capitol 80537 Retrospective. *(LP version)*
    (S) (4:01)   Rhino 71202 Super Hits Of The 70's Volume 22. *(45 version)*
    (S) (4:52)   Priority 7994 Rock Of The 80's. *(LP version)*
    (S) (4:00)   Razor & Tie 22502 Those Rocking 70's. *(45 version)*
    (S) (3:58)   Time-Life R968-02 Guitar Rock 1978-1979. *(45 version)*

    (S) (3:58)   Time-Life SOD-09 Sounds Of The Seventies - 1979. *(45 version)*
    (S) (4:01)   Rhino 71694 New Wave Hits Of The 80's Vol. 1. *(45 version)*
    (S) (4:52)   JCI 3131 1975 - Only Rock 'N Roll - 1979. *(LP version)*
    (S) (4:01)   Rhino 72131 Frat Rock: The 70's. *(45 version)*
    (S) (4:54)   RCA 66364 O.S.T. Reality Bites. *(LP version; remixed)*
    (S) (4:00)   Madacy Entertainment 1979 Rock On 1979. *(45 version)*
    (S) (4:01)   Rhino 72490 New Wave Hits, Vol. 1. *(45 version)*
    (S) (3:58)   Priority 50952 I Love Rock & Roll Volume 3: Hits Of The 70's. *(45 version)*
    (S) (4:01)   Eclipse Music Group 64896 Rock 'n Roll Relix 1978-1979. *(45 version)*
    (S) (4:01)   Eclipse Music Group 64897 Rock 'n Roll Relix 1970-1979. *(45 version)*
    (S) (4:01)   Flashback 72713 Essential New Wave Hits. *(45 version)*
    (S) (4:01)   Flashback 72092 New Wave Hits Box Set. *(45 version)*
    (S) (4:54)   Scotti Bros. 75518 Big Screen Rock. *(LP version)*
    (S) (4:52)   Rhino 72894 Hard Rock Cafe: New Wave. *(LP version)*
    (S) (4:00)   K-Tel 3904 The Rock Album Volume 2. *(45 version)*
    (S) (4:51)   Simitar 55522 The Number One's: Party Time. *(LP version)*
    (S) (4:52)   Simitar 55582 The Number One's: Rock It Up. *(LP version)*
    (S) (3:58)   Time-Life R840-10 Sounds Of The Seventies: '70s Dance Party 1979. *(45 version)*
    (S) (4:01)   Time-Life AM1-26 AM Gold - 1979. *(45 version)*

1979 GOOD GIRLS DON'T
    (S) (3:07)   Capitol 91848 Get The Knack. *(LP version lyrics)*
    (S) (3:06)   Capitol 80537 Retrospective. *(LP version lyrics)*
    (S) (3:06)   Time-Life SOD-19 Sounds Of The Seventies - 1979: Take Two. *(LP version lyrics)*
    (S) (3:07)   Priority 53754 Rock Of The 80's Volume 15. *(LP version lyrics)*
    (S) (3:06)   Risky Business 57466 Punky But Chic/The American New Wave Scene. *(LP version lyrics)*
    (S) (3:06)   Time-Life R968-14 Guitar Rock - The Late '70s. *(LP version lyrics)*
    (S) (3:07)   Rhino 72728 Poptopia! Power Pop Classics Of The '70s. *(LP version lyrics)*
    (S) (3:06)   EMI-Capitol Music Special Markets 19545 Lost Hits Of The '70s. *(LP version lyrics)*

1980 BABY TALKS DIRTY
    (S) (3:43)   Capitol 80537 Retrospective.
    (S) (3:43)   Razor & Tie 2020......But The Little Girls Understand.

KNICKERBOCKERS
1966 LIES
    (S) (2:40)   K-Tel 713 Battle Of The Bands.
    (S) (2:42)   Rhino 75892 Nuggets.
    (S) (2:42)   JCI 3100 Dance Sixties.
    (S) (2:41)   Warner Special Products 27607 Highs Of The 60's.
    (S) (2:41)   Original Sound 8859 Oldies But Goodies Vol. 9. *(this compact disc uses the "Waring - fds" noise reduction process)*
    (S) (2:40)   Sundazed 11002 The Fabulous Knickerbockers.
    (S) (2:40)   Sundazed 6011 Lies.
    (S) (2:41)   Time-Life 2CLR-07 Classic Rock - 1966: The Beat Goes On.
    (S) (2:40)   Collectables 0531 Golden Classics.
    (M) (2:41)   LaserLight 12528 Garage Band Rock.
    (S) (2:45)   Sundazed 11040 Hits, Rarities, Unissued Cuts And More. *(with cold ending)*
    (M) (2:40)   Columbia 69059 Party Super Hits.

FREDERICK KNIGHT
1972 I'VE BEEN LONELY FOR SO LONG
  - (S) (3:19) Stax 88005 Top Of The Stax.
  - (S) (3:18) Stax 8548 Stax Soul Brothers.
  - (S) (3:18) Rhino 70788 Soul Hits Of The 70's Volume 8.
  - (S) (3:14) Stax 8564 I've Been Lonely For So Long.
  - (S) (3:18) Time-Life RHD-20 Rhythm & Blues - 1972.
  - (S) (3:13) Time-Life SOD-25 Sounds Of The Seventies - Seventies Generation.
  - (S) (3:20) Stax 4415 Complete Stax/Volt Soul Singles Volume 3 1972-1975.
  - (S) (3:18) Time-Life R838-07 Solid Gold Soul - 1972.

GLADYS KNIGHT & THE PIPS (also THE PIPS)
released as by THE PIPS:
1961 EVERY BEAT OF MY HEART
  - (M) (2:00) Rhino 70647 Billboard's Top R&B Hits Of 1961. *(Vee Jay label hit version)*
  - (M) (2:00) Motown 6215 and 9067 Hits From The Legendary Vee-Jay Records. *(Vee Jay label hit version)*
  - (E) (1:59) JCI 3102 Love Sixties. *(Fury label noncharting version; bad dropout at :55)*
  - (M) (2:01) Original Sound 8856 Oldies But Goodies Vol. 6. *(this compact disc uses the "Waring - fds" noise reduction process; Vee Jay label hit version)*
  - (M) (2:01) Original Sound 2221 Oldies But Goodies Volumes 1,4,6,8 and 10 Box Set. *(this box set uses the "Waring - fds" noise reduction process; Vee Jay label hit version)*
  - (M) (2:01) Original Sound 2500 Oldies But Goodies Volumes 1-15 Box Set. *(this box set uses the "Waring - fds" noise reduction process; Vee Jay label hit version)*
  - (M) (2:01) Original Sound 8892 Dick Clark's 21 All-Time Hits Vol. 2. *(Vee Jay label hit version)*
  - (M) (2:04) Arista 8605 16 Original Doo Wop Classics. *(Fury label noncharting version; bad dropout at :58)*
  - (S) (2:03) Relic 7009 Raging Harlem Hit Parade. *(Fury label noncharting version)*
  - (E) (2:00) Curb 77321 Greatest Hits. *(Vee Jay label hit version)*
  - (S) (1:52) Motown 6200 and 0792 Gladys Knight & The Pips Anthology. *(rerecording)*
  - (M) (1:59) Collectables 5062 History Of Rock Volume 2. *(Vee Jay label hit version)*
  - (S) (2:03) Relic 7045 Letter Full Of Tears. *(Fury label noncharting version)*
  - (S) (2:02) Relic 7045 Letter Full Of Tears. *(Fury label alternate take)*
  - (S) (2:03) Capricorn 42009 Fire/Fury Records Story. *(Fury label noncharting version)*
  - (M) (2:00) Vee Jay 709 A Taste Of Doo Wop Volume 1. *(Vee Jay label hit version)*
  - (M) (2:01) Vee Jay 3-400 Celebrating 40 Years Of Classic Hits (1953-1993). *(Vee Jay label hit version)*
  - (S) (2:03) Relic 7063 Golden Era Of Doo-Wops: Fury Records. *(Fury label noncharting version)*
  - (M) (2:00) Time-Life 2RNR-18 Rock 'N' Roll Era - 1961 Still Rockin'. *(Vee Jay label hit version)*
  - (M) (1:59) Time-Life RHD-14 Rhythm & Blues - 1961. *(Vee Jay label hit version)*
  - (M) (2:00) Collectables 2502 WCBS-FM History Of Rock - The 60's Part 3. *(Vee Jay label hit version)*
  - (M) (2:00) Collectables 4502 History Of Rock/The 60s Part Three. *(Vee Jay label hit version)*
  - (M) (2:02) Collectables 5154 Letter Full Of Tears. *(Fury label noncharting version; mastered from vinyl)*
  - (E) (1:59) JCI/Telstar 3516 Sweet Soul Sisters. *(Fury label noncharting version; bad dropout at :55)*
  - (S) (2:03) Ripete 2163-RE Ebb Tide. *(Fury label noncharting version)*
  - (M) (2:01) Rhino 71806 The R&B Box: Thirty Years Of Rhythm & Blues. *(Vee Jay label hit version)*
  - (S) (1:52) Motown 314530483 Anthology. *(rerecording)*

  - (E) (1:59) Rebound 314520369 Soul Classics - Quiet Storm/The 60's. *(Fury label noncharting version; bad dropout at :55)*
  - (S) (2:03) Rhino 72618 Smooth Grooves: The '60s Volume 1 Early '60s. *(Fury label noncharting version)*
  - (M) (2:00) Time-Life R857-10 The Heart Of Rock 'n' Roll 1960-1961. *(Vee Jay label hit version)*
  - (M) (2:00) Time-Life R838-19 Solid Gold Soul 1961. *(Vee Jay label hit version)*

released as by GLADYS KNIGHT & THE PIPS:
1962 LETTER FULL OF TEARS
  - (M) (2:48) Arista 8605 16 Original Doo-Wop Classics.
  - (M) (2:48) Relic 7009 Raging Harlem Hit Parade.
  - (E) (2:42) Curb 77321 Greatest Hits.
  - (S) (3:48) Motown 6200 and 0792 Anthology. *(rerecording)*
  - (M) (2:48) Relic 7045 Letter Full Of Tears.
  - (M) (2:47) Capricorn 42009 Fire/Fury Records Story.
  - (M) (2:44) Time-Life 2RNR-41 Rock 'N' Roll Era - R&B Gems.
  - (M) (2:49) Collectables 5154 Letter Full Of Tears.
  - (S) (3:49) Motown 314530483 Anthology. *(rerecording)*

1968 I HEARD IT THROUGH THE GRAPEVINE
  - (S) (2:46) Rhino 70653 Billboard's Top R&B Hits Of 1967.
  - (S) (2:46) Rhino 72006 Billboard's Top R&B Hits 1965-1969 Box Set.
  - (S) (2:44) Motown 6160 The Good-Feeling Music Of The Big Chill Generation Volume 2.
  - (S) (2:43) Motown 5457 A Collection Of 16 Big Hits Volume 10.
  - (S) (2:46) Curb 77321 Greatest Hits.
  - (S) (2:47) Motown 6109 Compact Command Performances.
  - (S) (2:43) Motown 6200 and 0792 Anthology.
  - (S) (2:44) MCA 10063 Original Television Soundtrack "The Sounds Of Murphy Brown".
  - (S) (2:44) Motown 9097 The Most Played Oldies On America's Jukeboxes.
  - (S) (2:44) Motown 9018 and 5249 16 #1 Hits From The Late 60's.
  - (S) (2:45) Motown 5126 Everybody Needs Love.
  - (S) (2:47) Motown 9086 and 5303 All The Greatest Hits.
  - (S) (2:44) Motown 5343 Every Great Motown Song: The First 25 Years Volume 1. *(most selections on this cd have noise on the fadeout)*
  - (S) (2:44) Motown 8034 and 8134 Every Great Motown Song: The First 25 Years Volumes 1 & 2. *(most selections on this cd have noise on the fadeout)*
  - (S) (2:44) Motown 9095 and 5325 Motown Girl Groups: Top 10 With A Bullet!
  - (S) (2:44) Motown 8031 and 8131 Everybody Needs Love/If I Were Your Woman.
  - (S) (2:43) Motown 9071 Motown Dance Party Volume 1. *(all selections on this cd are segued together)*
  - (M) (2:52) Motown 6312 Hitsville USA.
  - (S) (2:42) Time-Life RHD-10 Rhythm & Blues - 1967.
  - (S) (2:46) Time-Life 2CLR-05 Classic Rock - 1967.
  - (S) (2:44) Polygram Special Markets 314520299 Motown Legends - Girl Groups.
  - (S) (2:44) Polygram Special Markets 314520284 Motown Legends Volume 3.
  - (S) (2:44) Motown 314530483 Anthology.
  - (S) (2:46) Priority 57194 Old School Friday - More Music From The Original Motion Picture.
  - (S) (2:42) Time-Life R838-02 Solid Gold Soul - 1967.
  - (M) (2:53) Motown 314530826 The Ultimate Collection.

1968 THE END OF OUR ROAD
  - (S) (2:18) Motown 6109 Compact Command Performances.
  - (S) (2:15) Motown 6200 and 0792 Anthology.
  - (S) (2:17) Motown 9086 and 5303 All The Greatest Hits.
  - (S) (2:16) Motown 5467 Feelin' Bluesy.
  - (S) (2:17) Motown 314530483 Anthology.
  - (S) (2:16) Motown 314530507 Motown Year By Year 1968.
  - (M) (2:21) Motown 314530826 The Ultimate Collection.

1968 IT SHOULD HAVE BEEN ME
  - (S) (2:47) Motown 6109 Compact Command Performances.
  - (S) (2:58) Motown 6200 and 0792 Anthology.
  - (S) (2:46) Motown 9000 and 5113 Motown Superstar Series.

(S) (2:46) Motown 5467 Feelin' Bluesy.
(S) (2:59) Motown 314530483 Anthology.
(M) (2:58) Motown 314530826 The Ultimate Collection.

1969 THE NITTY GRITTY
(S) (2:59) Motown 9109 and 5413 Motown Memories
Volume 3.
(S) (3:00) Motown 6109 Compact Command Performances.
(S) (2:53) Motown 6200 and 0792 Anthology.
(S) (2:59) Motown 5148 Nitty Gritty.
(S) (2:59) Motown 9086 and 5303 All The Greatest Hits.
(S) (2:59) Motown 314530483 Anthology.
(M) (3:01) Motown 314530826 The Ultimate Collection.

1969 FRIENDSHIP TRAIN
(actual 45 time is (3:45) not (3:30) as stated on the
record label)
(S) (3:46) Curb 77321 Greatest Hits.
(S) (3:47) Motown 6109 Compact Command Performances.
(S) (3:45) Motown 6200 and 0792 Anthology.
(S) (3:47) Motown 9086 and 5303 All The Greatest Hits.
(S) (3:47) Motown 314530483 Anthology.
(S) (3:46) Motown 314530525 Motown Year By Year -
1969.
(S) (3:47) Ichiban 2511 Love, Peace & Understanding.
(M) (3:43) Rhino 72815 Beg, Scream & Shout! The Big Ol'
Box Of '60s Soul.
(M) (3:45) Motown 314530826 The Ultimate Collection.

1970 YOU NEED LOVE LIKE I DO (DON'T YOU)
(S) (3:39) Motown 6109 Compact Command Performances.
(S) (3:38) Motown 6200 and 0792 Anthology.
(S) (3:35) Motown 9072 Motown Dance Party Volume 2.
(all selections on this cd are segued together)
(S) (3:38) Motown 9086 and 5303 All The Greatest Hits.
(S) (3:37) Motown 314530483 Anthology.
(S) (3:37) Motown 314530528 Motown Year By Year -
1970.
(M) (3:34) Motown 314530826 The Ultimate Collection.

1971 IF I WERE YOUR WOMAN
(S) (3:14) Motown 9104 and 5409 Motown Memories
Volume 1.
(S) (3:14) Curb 77321 Greatest Hits.
(S) (3:15) Motown 6109 Compact Command Performances.
(S) (3:12) Motown 6200 and 0792 Anthology.
(S) (3:14) MCA 10063 Original Television Soundtrack "The
Sounds Of Murphy Brown".
(M) (3:11) Motown 5344 Every Great Motown Song: The
First 25 Years Volume 2. *(most selections on this
cd have noise on the fadeout)*
(S) (3:14) Motown 9086 and 5303 All The Greatest Hits.
(S) (3:13) Motown 5388 If I Were Your Woman.
(M) (3:11) Motown 8034 and 8134 Every Great Motown
Song: The First 25 Years Volumes 1 & 2. *(most
selections on this cd have noise on the fadeout)*
(S) (3:14) Motown 8031 and 8131 Everybody Needs Love/If
I Were Your Woman.
(M) (3:11) Motown 6312 Hitsville USA.
(S) (3:09) Time-Life RHD-09 Rhythm & Blues - 1971.
(S) (3:08) Time-Life SUD-10 Superhits - 1971.
(S) (3:13) Motown 314530483 Anthology.
(S) (3:11) Rhino 72113 Billboard Hot Soul Hits - 1971.
(S) (3:14) Motown 314530528 Motown Year By Year -
1970.
(S) (3:13) Motown 314530573 Baddest Love Jams Volume
2 - Fire And Desire.
(S) (3:08) Time-Life AM1-06 AM Gold - 1971.
(S) (3:09) Time-Life R838-06 Solid Gold Soul - 1971.
(M) (3:11) Motown 314530826 The Ultimate Collection.
(M) (3:11) Time-Life R834-11 Body Talk - After Dark.

1971 I DON'T WANT TO DO WRONG
(S) (3:19) Motown 6109 Compact Command Performances.
(S) (3:17) Motown 6200 and 0792 Anthology.
(S) (3:19) Motown 9086 and 5303 All The Greatest Hits.
(S) (3:19) Motown 9000 and 5113 Motown Superstar Series.
(S) (3:18) Motown 5388 If I Were Your Woman.
(S) (3:19) Motown 8031 and 8131 Everybody Needs Love/If
I Were Your Woman.
(M) (3:21) Motown 6312 Hitsville USA.

(S) (3:18) Motown 374638507 Motown Legends - Neither
One Of Us.
(S) (3:19) Ichiban 2507 Cheatin': From A Woman's Point Of
View.
(S) (3:17) Motown 314530483 Anthology.
(M) (3:21) Motown 314530826 The Ultimate Collection.

1972 MAKE ME THE WOMAN THAT YOU GO HOME TO
(S) (3:47) Motown 6109 Compact Command Performances.
(hum noticeable on the fadeout)
(S) (3:44) Motown 6200 and 0792 Anthology.
(S) (3:46) Motown 9086 and 5303 All The Greatest Hits.
(hum noticeable on the fadeout)
(S) (3:45) Motown 314530483 Anthology.
(M) (3:44) Motown 314530826 The Ultimate Collection.

1972 HELP ME MAKE IT THROUGH THE NIGHT
(S) (4:19) Motown 6109 Compact Command Performances.
(hum noticeable on the fadeout)
(S) (4:17) Motown 6200 and 0792 Anthology.
(S) (4:17) Motown 374638507 Motown Legends - Neither
One Of Us.
(S) (4:19) Motown 314530483 Anthology.
(S) (4:19) Motown 314530826 The Ultimate Collection.

1973 NEITHER ONE OF US (WANTS TO BE THE FIRST TO
SAY GOODBYE)
(S) (4:21) Rhino 70661 Billboard's Top R&B Hits Of 1973.
(S) (4:21) Motown 6110 Motown Grammy R&B
Performances Of The 60's & 70's.
(S) (4:21) Curb 77321 Greatest Hits.
(S) (4:21) Motown 6109 Compact Command Performances.
(S) (4:20) Motown 6200 and 0792 Anthology.
(S) (4:21) Motown 8008 and 8108 Neither One Of Us/All I
Need Is Time.
(S) (4:21) Motown 9086 and 5303 All The Greatest Hits.
(S) (4:21) Motown 5193 Neither One Of Us.
(S) (4:20) Motown 374638507 Motown Legends - Neither
One Of Us.
(S) (4:20) Motown 6358 Hitsville USA Volume Two.
(S) (4:20) Time-Life SOD-14 Sounds Of The Seventies -
1973: Take Two.
(S) (4:20) Motown 314530483 Anthology.
(S) (4:20) Motown 314530510 Motown Year By Year 1973.
(S) (4:20) Motown 314530569 Motown Milestones -
Motown Love Songs.
(S) (4:19) MCA 11329 Soul Train 25th Anniversary Box
Set.
(S) (4:19) Rebound 314520447 Soul Classics - Best Of The
70's.
(S) (4:20) Motown 314530826 The Ultimate Collection.
(S) (4:19) Motown 314530849 Motown 40 Forever.
(S) (4:20) Time-Life R834-12 Body Talk - By Candlelight.

1973 DADDY COULD SWEAR, I DECLARE
(S) (3:42) Motown 9109 and 9103 Motown Memories
Volume 3.
(S) (3:43) Motown 6109 Compact Command Performances.
(S) (3:39) Motown 6200 and 0792 Anthology.
(S) (3:42) Motown 8008 and 8108 Neither One Of Us/All I
Need Is Time.
(S) (3:42) Motown 9086 and 5303 All The Greatest Hits.
(S) (3:42) Motown 5193 Neither One Of Us.
(S) (3:40) Motown 314530483 Anthology.
(S) (3:40) Motown 314530510 Motown Year By Year 1973.
(S) (3:42) Motown 314530826 The Ultimate Collection.

1973 WHERE PEACEFUL WATERS FLOW
(S) (4:24) Rhino 70756 Soul Survivors: The Best Of.
(S) (4:25) Pair 1198 Best Of.
(S) (4:23) Pair 3304 Imagination.
(S) (4:26) Special Music 4909 Very Best Of.
(S) (4:24) Buddah 49504 Imagination.
(S) (4:24) K-Tel 3626 Music Power.
(S) (4:24) Right Stuff/Buddah 56441 Imagination.
(S) (4:27) Right Stuff 93403 Best Of.

1973 MIDNIGHT TRAIN TO GEORGIA
(S) (4:38) Rhino 70634 Billboard's Top Rock & Roll Hits Of
1973. *(LP version)*
(S) (4:37) Rhino 70551 Soul Hits Of The 70's Volume 11.
(LP version)

GLADYS KNIGHT & THE PIPS *(Continued)*

- (S) (4:37) Pair 1202 Best Of Buddah. *(LP version)*
- (S) (4:38) Curb 77321 Greatest Hits. *(LP version)*
- (S) (4:37) Rhino 70756 Soul Survivors: The Best Of. *(LP version)*
- (S) (4:37) Pair 1198 Best Of. *(LP version)*
- (S) (4:37) Pair 3304 Imagination. *(LP version)*
- (S) (4:36) Collectables 5064 History Of Rock Volume 4. *(LP version)*
- (S) (4:38) Special Music 4909 Very Best Of. *(LP version)*
- (S) (4:37) Rhino 71618 Soul Train Hall Of Fame/20th Anniversary. *(LP version)*
- (S) (4:36) Essex 7060 The Buddah Box. *(LP version)*
- (S) (4:35) Razor & Tie 22047 Sweet 70's Soul. *(LP version)*
- (S) (4:34) Time-Life SUD-13 Superhits - 1973. *(LP version)*
- (S) (4:37) Time-Life SOD-06 Sounds Of The Seventies - 1973. *(LP version)*
- (S) (4:34) Original Sound 8883 21 Legendary Superstars. *(LP version)*
- (S) (4:37) JCI 3130 1970 - Only Rock 'N Roll - 1974. *(several opening drum beats truncated; LP version)*
- (S) (4:36) Risky Business 67308 Train Trax. *(LP version)*
- (S) (4:36) Buddah 49504 Imagination. *(LP version)*
- (S) (4:37) Madacy Entertainment 1973 Rock On 1973. *(LP version)*
- (S) (4:38) Eclipse Music Group 64893 Rock 'n Roll Relix 1972-1973. *(LP version)*
- (S) (4:38) Eclipse Music Group 64897 Rock 'n Roll Relix 1970-1979. *(LP version)*
- (S) (4:34) Time-Life AM1-03 AM Gold - 1973. *(LP version)*
- (S) (4:37) Time-Life R838-08 Solid Gold Soul - 1973. *(LP version)*
- (S) (4:36) Time-Life R834-10 Body Talk - From The Heart. *(LP version)*
- (S) (4:36) Right Stuff/Buddah 56441 Imagination. *(LP version)*
- (S) (4:35) BMG Special Products 44643 The Best Of Buddah. *(LP version)*
- (S) (4:37) Right Stuff 93403 Best Of. *(LP version)*
- (S) (4:37) Cold Front 4025 Old School Mega Mix Volume 3. *(LP version)*
- (S) (4:37) Rhino 72943 VH1 8-Track Flashback: Classic '70s Soul. *(LP version)*
- (S) (4:36) Collectables 1516 and 2516 The Anniversary Album - The 70's. *(LP version)*

1974 I'VE GOT TO USE MY IMAGINATION
- (S) (3:28) Priority 7974 Mega-Hits Dance Classics Volume 4.
- (S) (3:28) Rhino 70756 Soul Survivors: Best Of.
- (S) (3:28) Pair 1198 Best Of.
- (S) (3:27) Pair 3304 Imagination.
- (S) (3:28) Curb 77321 Greatest Hits.
- (S) (3:28) Special Music 4909 Very Best Of.
- (S) (3:24) Essex 7051 Non-Stop Dance Hits.
- (S) (3:29) Time-Life SOD-15 Sounds Of The Seventies - 1974: Take Two.
- (S) (3:28) Epic 66329 O.S.T. Forrest Gump.
- (S) (3:33) Buddah 49504 Imagination.
- (S) (3:32) Right Stuff/Buddah 56441 Imagination.
- (S) (3:27) K-Tel 3912 Superstars Greatest Hits Volume 1.
- (S) (3:33) BMG Special Products 44644 Best Thing That Ever Happened.
- (S) (3:33) Right Stuff 93403 Best Of.

1974 BEST THING THAT EVER HAPPENED TO ME
- (S) (3:41) JCI 3303 Love Seventies.
- (S) (3:43) Rhino 70662 Billboard's Top R&B Hits Of 1974.
- (S) (3:43) Rhino 70756 Soul Survivors: Best Of.
- (S) (3:44) Pair 1198 Best Of.
- (S) (3:42) Pair 3304 Imagination.
- (S) (3:44) Curb 77321 Greatest Hits.
- (S) (3:44) Special Music 4909 Very Best Of.
- (S) (3:42) Original Sound 8865 Oldies But Goodies Vol. 15. *(this compact disc uses the "Waring - fds" noise reduction process)*

- (S) (3:42) Original Sound 2222 Oldies But Goodies Volumes 3,5,11,14 and 15 Box Set. *(this box set uses the "Waring - fds" noise reduction process)*
- (S) (3:42) Original Sound 2500 Oldies But Goodies Volumes 1-15 Box Set. *(this box set uses the "Waring - fds" noise reduction process)*
- (S) (3:42) Original Sound 8909 Best Love Songs Vol 4.
- (S) (3:42) Original Sound 9327 Best Love Songs Vol. 3 & 4.
- (S) (3:42) Original Sound 1236 Best Love Songs Box Set.
- (S) (3:42) Essex 7060 The Buddah Box.
- (S) (3:42) Original Sound 9305 Art Laboe's Dedicated To You Volume 5.
- (S) (3:43) RCA 66812 Do You Love Me? (All-Time Best Love Songs).
- (S) (3:45) Buddah 49504 Imagination.
- (S) (3:42) Madacy Entertainment 1974 Rock On 1974.
- (S) (3:41) JCI 3145 1970 - Only Love - 1974.
- (S) (3:44) Hip-O 40030 The Glory Of Love - '70s Sweet & Soulful Love Songs.
- (S) (3:42) Time-Life AM1-21 AM Gold - 1974.
- (S) (3:43) Time-Life R838-09 Solid Gold Soul - 1974.
- (S) (3:43) Time-Life R834-02 Body Talk - Just For You.
- (S) (3:44) Right Stuff/Buddah 56441 Imagination.
- (S) (3:43) BMG Special Products 44644 Best Thing That Ever Happened.
- (S) (3:43) Right Stuff 93403 Best Of.
- (S) (3:42) Time-Life R814-05 Love Songs.

1974 ON AND ON
- (S) (3:21) Rhino 70756 Soul Survivors: Best Of. *(45 version)*
- (S) (4:17) Pair 1198 Best Of. *(LP version)*
- (S) (4:17) Curb 77321 Greatest Hits. *(LP version)*
- (S) (4:17) Special Music 4909 Very Best Of. *(LP version)*
- (S) (4:15) Giant 24571 O.S.T. Inkwell. *(LP version)*
- (S) (4:15) K-Tel 3625 Dynamite. *(LP version)*
- (S) (4:16) BMG Special Products 44644 Best Thing That Ever Happened. *(LP version)*
- (S) (4:16) Right Stuff 93403 Best Of. *(LP version)*
- (S) (3:21) Hip-O 40107 Super Bad On Celluloid: Music From '70s Black Cinema. *(45 version)*

1975 I FEEL A SONG (IN MY HEART)
- (S) (3:18) Rhino 70756 Soul Survivors: Best Of.
- (S) (3:19) Pair 1198 Best Of.
- (S) (3:20) Special Music 4909 Very Best Of.
- (S) (3:18) Rhino 72116 Billboard Hot Soul Hits - 1974.
- (S) (3:18) Right Stuff 59939 I Feel A Song.
- (S) (3:16) BMG Special Products 44644 Best Thing That Ever Happened.
- (S) (3:16) Right Stuff 93403 Best Of.

1975 THE WAY WE WERE/TRY TO REMEMBER
- (S) (4:33) Rhino 70756 Soul Survivors: Best Of.
- (S) (4:31) Pair 1198 Best Of.
- (S) (4:32) Special Music 4909 Very Best Of.
- (S) (4:31) Original Sound 8907 Best Love Songs Vol 2.
- (S) (4:31) Original Sound 9326 Best Love Songs Vol. 1 & 2.
- (S) (4:31) Original Sound 1236 Best Love Songs Box Set.
- (S) (4:31) Original Sound 8863 Oldies But Goodies Vol. 13.
- (S) (4:31) Original Sound 2223 Oldies But Goodies Volumes 2,7,9,12 and 13 Box Set. *(Volumes 2, 7 and 12 of this box set use the "Waring - fds" noise reduction process)*
- (S) (4:31) Original Sound 2500 Oldies But Goodies Volumes 1-15 Box Set. *(most volumes in this box set use the "Waring - fds" noise reduction process)*
- (S) (4:57) Right Stuff 59939 I Feel A Song. *(:17 additional ending audience applause than found on the LP; :12 additional ending audience applause than found on the 45)*
- (S) (4:44) Right Stuff 93403 Best Of.
- (S) (4:33) Time-Life R834-13 Body Talk - Just The Two Of Us.

1975 PART TIME LOVE
- (S) (2:30) Rhino 70756 Soul Survivors: Best Of.
- (S) (2:30) Special Music 4924 Very Best Of Volume 2.

336

**released as by DIONNE and FRIENDS: ELTON JOHN,
GLADYS KNIGHT, STEVIE WONDER, and DIONNE WARWICK:**
1986 THAT'S WHAT FRIENDS ARE FOR
- (S) (4:15) Arista 8398 Dionne Warwick - Friends.
- (S) (4:15) Arista 8540 Dionne Warwick - Greatest Hits 1979 - 1990.

released as by GLADYS KNIGHT:
1988 LOVE OVERBOARD
- (S) (5:18) MCA 10288 Classic Soul. *(LP version)*
- (S) (5:18) MCA Special Products 20767 Classic R&B Oldies From The 80's Volume 3. *(LP version)*
- (S) (5:25) MCA 42004 All Our Love. *(LP version)*
- (S) (4:26) Rhino 70756 Soul Survivors: Best Of. *(45 version)*
- (S) (4:24) MCA Special Products Rockin' Country Blues. *(45 version)*
- (S) (4:24) Hip-O 40015 Soulful Ladies Of The 80's. *(45 version)*
- (S) (5:18) MCA Special Products 21032 Soul Legends. *(LP version)*
- (S) (5:17) MCA Special Products 21029 The Women Of Soul. *(LP version)*

**released as by BRANDY, TAMIA, GLADYS KNIGHT and
CHAKA KHAN:**
1996 MISSING YOU
- (S) (4:22) EastWest 61951 O.S.T. Set It Off.

JEAN KNIGHT
1971 MR. BIG STUFF
- (S) (2:44) Stax 88005 Top Of The Stax. *(LP length)*
- (S) (2:43) Stax 8543 Stax Soul Sisters. *(LP length)*
- (S) (2:43) Original Sound 8855 Oldies But Goodies Vol. 5. *(this compact disc uses the "Waring - fds" noise reduction process; ambient background noise throughout the disc; LP length)*
- (S) (2:43) Original Sound 2222 Oldies But Goodies Volumes 3,5,11,14 and 15 Box Set. *(this box set uses the "Waring - fds" noise reduction process; ambient background noise throughout the song; LP length)*
- (S) (2:43) Original Sound 2500 Oldies But Goodies Volumes 1-15 Box Set. *(this box set uses the "Waring - fds" noise reduction process; ambient background noise throughout the song; LP length)*
- (S) (2:42) Original Sound CDGO-11 Golden Oldies Volume. 11. *(LP length)*
- (S) (2:44) Original Sound 8881 Twenty-One #1 Hits. *(this compact disc uses the "Waring - fds" noise reduction process; LP length)*
- (S) (2:27) Rhino 70659 Billboard's Top R&B Hits Of 1971. *(45 length)*
- (S) (2:28) Rhino 70785 Soul Hits Of The 70's Volume 5. *(45 length)*
- (S) (2:28) Rhino 72028 Soul Hits Of The 70's Volumes 1-5 Box Set. *(45 length)*
- (S) (2:44) Stax 8554 Mr. Big Stuff. *(LP length)*
- (S) (2:33) Stax 4411 Complete Stax/Volt Soul Singles 1968 - 1971. *(slightly longer than 45 length)*
- (S) (2:27) Razor & Tie 22047 Sweet 70's Soul. *(45 length)*
- (S) (2:27) Time-Life RHD-09 Rhythm & Blues - 1971. *(45 length)*
- (S) (2:42) Time-Life SOD-12 Sounds Of The Seventies - 1971: Take Two. *(LP length)*
- (S) (2:43) Ripete 2198 Soul Patrol. *(LP length)*
- (S) (2:46) MCA 11036 O.S.T. Crooklyn. *(LP length)*
- (S) (2:42) JCI 3191 1970 - Only Dance - 1974. *(LP length)*
- (S) (2:44) Priority 53129 Deep Soul Volume One. *(LP length)*
- (S) (2:27) Time-Life R838-06 Solid Gold Soul - 1971. *(45 length)*
- (S) (2:27) Hip-O 40096 '70s Hit(s) Back Again. *(45 length)*

ROBERT KNIGHT
1967 EVERLASTING LOVE
- (S) (2:57) Rhino 70996 One Hit Wonders Of The 60's Volume 2.

- (S) (2:55) Ripete 2392192 Beach Music Anthology Box Set.
- (S) (2:56) Time-Life 2CLR-24 Classic Rock - 1967: Blowin' Your Mind.
- (S) (2:56) Ripete 0003 Coolin' Out/24 Carolina Classics Vol. 3.
- (S) (2:58) Sony Music Special Products 66106 The Monument Story.
- (S) (2:58) Collectables 5801 Everlasting Love - A Golden Classics Edition.

SONNY KNIGHT
1956 CONFIDENTIAL
- (M) (2:31) Varese Sarabande 5686 History Of Dot Records Volume One.
- (M) (2:31) Original Sound 8850 Oldies But Goodies Vol. 1. *(this compact disc uses the "Waring - fds" noise reduction process)*
- (M) (2:31) Original Sound 2221 Oldies But Goodies Volumes 1,4,6,8 and 10 Box Set. *(this box set uses the "Waring - fds" noise reduction process)*
- (M) (2:31) Original Sound 2500 Oldies But Goodies Volumes 1-15 Box Set. *(this box set uses the "Waring - fds" noise reduction process)*
- (M) (2:31) Eric 11502 Hard To Find 45's On CD (Volume I) 1955-60.
- (M) (2:31) Time-Life R857-07 The Heart Of Rock 'n' Roll 1956.

FRED KNOBLOCK
1980 WHY NOT ME
- (S) (3:44) Rhino 71892 Radio Daze: Pop Hits Of The 80's Volume Three.
- (S) (3:44) Time-Life R834-15 Body Talk - Once In Lifetime.

released as by FRED KNOBLOCK and SUSAN ANTON:
1981 KILLIN' TIME
- (S) (3:34) Rhino 71893 Radio Daze: Pop Hits Of The 80's Volume Four.

BUDDY KNOX with THE RHYTHM ORCHIDS
1957 PARTY DOLL
- (M) (2:11) Rhino 70741 Rock This Town: Rockabilly Hits Volume 1.
- (M) (2:12) Rhino 70618 Billboard's Top Rock & Roll Hits Of 1957.
- (M) (2:12) Rhino 72004 Billboard's Top Rock & Roll Hits 1957-1961 Box Set.
- (M) (2:11) Rhino 70964 Best Of.
- (M) (2:12) Collectables 5416 Murray The K - Sing Along With The Golden Greats.
- (M) (2:10) MCA 8001 O.S.T. American Graffiti.
- (M) (2:12) Time-Life 2RNR-01 Rock 'N' Roll Era - 1957. *(original pressings of this song on this cd were (E))*
- (M) (2:11) Polygram Special Markets 314520258 No. 1 Hits Of The 50's.
- (M) (2:10) K-Tel 3436 Rockabilly Riot.
- (M) (2:11) Nick At Nite/550 Music 63435 Beach Blanket Bash.

1957 ROCK YOUR LITTLE BABY TO SLEEP
- (M) (2:21) Rhino 70964 Best Of.

1957 HULA LOVE
- (M) (2:19) Rhino 70964 Best Of.
- (M) (2:19) Time-Life 2RNR-17 Rock 'N' Roll Era - 1957 Still Rockin'.

1958 SOMEBODY TOUCHED ME
- (M) (2:15) Rhino 70964 Best Of.

released as by BUDDY KNOX:
1961 LOVEY DOVEY
- (S) (2:10) Rhino 70964 Best Of.
- (S) (2:09) EMI-Capitol Special Markets 19552 Lost Hits Of The '60s.

MOE KOFFMAN QUARTETTE
1958 THE SWINGIN' SHEPHERD BLUES
- (M) (2:11) Time-Life HPD-30 Your Hit Parade - 50's Instrumentals.

KOKOMO
1961 ASIA MINOR
    (S) (1:58) Collectors' Choice 5190 More Instrumental Gems Of The 60's.

KON KAN
1989 I BEG YOUR PARDON
    (S) (3:58) JCI 2702 Hot Moves.
    (S) (3:58) Atlantic 81984 Move To Move.

KOOL & THE GANG
1973 FUNKY STUFF
    (S) (5:02) Mercury 834780 Everything's Kool & The Gang: Greatest Hits. *(remixed)*
    (S) (3:01) Special Music 846494 Celebration.
    (S) (3:01) Mercury 822536 Spin Their Top Hits.
    (S) (3:05) Mercury 314514822 Best Of (1969-1976). *(with countoff)*
    (S) (3:01) K-Tel 30582 Kool & The Gang/Ohio Players.
    (S) (3:00) K-Tel 6011 70's Soul - Super Funky Hits.
    (S) (3:01) Mercury 314514821 Funky Stuff: The Best Of Funk Essentials.
    (S) (3:02) Rhino 71432 In Yo' Face! The History Of Funk, Vol. 2.
    (S) (3:01) MCA 11329 Soul Train 25th Anniversary Box Set.
    (S) (3:00) Mercury 314522082 Wild And Peaceful.
    (S) (3:04) Chronicles 314555137 Funk Of The 70's. *(with countoff)*

1974 JUNGLE BOOGIE
    (S) (3:04) Rhino 70552 Soul Hits Of The 70's Volume 12.
    (S) (3:03) Priority 7057 Mega-Hits Dance Classics Volume 8.
    (S) (3:03) K-Tel 30582 Kool & The Gang/Ohio Players.
    (S) (3:03) Mercury 822536 Spin Their Top Hits.
    (S) (5:50) Mercury 834780 Everything's Kool & The Gang: Greatest Hits. *(remixed)*
    (S) (3:03) Mercury 314514822 Best Of (1969-1976).
    (S) (3:04) Rhino 71433 In Yo Face! History Of Funk Volume 3.
    (S) (3:02) Razor & Tie 22045 Those Funky 70's.
    (S) (3:03) Time-Life SOD-15 Sounds Of The Seventies - 1974: Take Two.
    (S) (3:04) MCA 11103 and 11188 O.S.T. Pulp Fiction.
    (S) (3:03) Rebound 314520218 Disco Nights Vol. 2.
    (S) (3:04) Rhino 72116 Billboard Hot Soul Hits - 1974.
    (S) (3:02) Thump 4099 Old School Boogie.
    (S) (3:03) Mercury 314522082 Wild And Peaceful.
    (S) (3:03) JCI 3173 1970 - Only Soul - 1974.
    (S) (3:03) JCI 3191 1970 - Only Dance - 1974.
    (S) (3:03) Time-Life R838-09 Solid Gold Soul - 1974.
    (S) (3:03) Rebound 314520430 Funk Classics Of The 70's Vol. 2.
    (S) (3:03) K-Tel 3914 Superstars Greatest Hits Volume 3.
    (S) (3:00) Chronicles 314555140 Dance Funk. *(all selections on this cd are segued together)*
    (S) (3:00) Rebound 314520507 Class Reunion '73.

1974 HOLLYWOOD SWINGING
(dj copies of this 45 ran (3:26); commercial copies were all (4:35))
    (S) (4:36) Rhino 70662 Billboard's Top R&B Hits Of 1974.
    (S) (4:36) Rhino 70553 Soul Hits Of The 70's Volume 13.
    (S) (3:26) K-Tel 30582 Kool & The Gang/Ohio Players. *(this is the dj 45 edit)*
    (S) (4:36) Mercury 822536 Spin Their Top Hits.
    (S) (6:16) Mercury 834780 Everything's Kool & The Gang: Greatest Hits. *(remixed)*
    (S) (4:36) Mercury 314514822 Best Of (1969-1976).
    (S) (4:39) Rhino 71434 In Yo Face! History Of Funk Volume 4.
    (S) (4:36) Special Music 846494 Celebration.
    (S) (4:31) Thump 4030 Old School Vol. 3. *(tracks into next selection)*
    (S) (4:36) Rebound 314520034 Funk Classics Of The 70's.
    (S) (4:37) Rebound 314520247 Class Reunion 1974.
    (S) (4:37) Rebound 314520322 Hollywood Swinging.

    (S) (4:36) Mercury 314522082 Wild And Peaceful.
    (S) (4:35) Rebound 314520432 Disco Nights Vol. XI - Disco's Leading Men.
    (S) (3:26) K-Tel 4020 Great R&B Funk Bands Of The 70's. *(this is the dj 45 edit)*
    (S) (3:04) Thump 4100 Old School Mix. *(all selections on this cd are segued together and remixed)*
    (S) (4:37) Time-Life R840-05 Sounds Of The Seventies: '70s Dance Party 1972-1974.

1974 HIGHER PLANE
    (S) (4:58) Special Music 846494 Celebration. *(LP version)*
    (S) (5:00) Rhino 72127 Soul Hits Of The 70's Vol. 17. *(LP version)*
    (S) (4:57) Mercury 314532194 Light Of Worlds. *(LP version)*

1975 SPIRIT OF THE BOOGIE
    (S) (4:51) Mercury 822536 Spin Their Top Hits. *(LP version)*
    (S) (4:51) Mercury 314514822 Best Of (1969-1976). *(LP version)*
    (S) (3:11) Thump 4099 Old School Boogie. *(45 version)*
    (S) (4:51) Mercury 314532934 Spirit Of The Boogie. *(LP version)*

1979 LADIES NIGHT
    (S) (3:27) Priority 7972 Mega-Hits Dance Classics Volume 2. *(45 version)*
    (S) (6:21) Mercury 822537 Ladies Night. *(LP version)*
    (S) (3:31) Priority 7069 Back To Back: Best Of Kool & The Gang/Ohio Players. *(45 version)*
    (S) (6:21) Special Music 846494 Celebration. *(LP version)*
    (S) (3:27) Razor & Tie 22496 Disco Fever. *(45 version)*
    (S) (3:29) Mercury 314522458 Celebration: Best Of 1979-1987. *(45 version)*
    (S) (3:31) Rebound 314520270 Class Reunion 1979. *(45 version)*
    (S) (3:31) Rebound 314520265 Dance Fever. *(45 version)*
    (S) (3:28) JCI 3149 1980 - Only Dance - 1984. *(45 version)*
    (S) (6:21) Rebound 314520334 Ladies Night. *(LP version)*
    (S) (3:26) JCI 3163 18 Disco Superhits. *(45 version)*
    (S) (3:29) Rebound 314520438 No. 1 Hits Of The 80's. *(45 version)*
    (S) (3:29) Time-Life R838-15 Solid Gold Soul 1979. *(45 version)*
    (S) (3:29) Rhino 72943 VH1 8-Track Flashback: Classic '70s Soul. *(45 version)*
    (S) (3:27) Polygram Special Markets 314520446 Soul Hits Of The 70's. *(45 version)*
    (S) (3:28) Time-Life R840-08 Sounds Of The Seventies: '70s Dance Party 1978-1979. *(45 version)*
    (S) (6:22) Priority 50989 70's Greatest Rock Hits Volume 2: Rock & Soul. *(LP version)*

1980 TOO HOT
    (S) (4:55) Mercury 822537 Ladies Night. *(LP version)*
    (S) (4:59) Mercury 834780 Everything's Kool & The Gang: Greatest Hits. *(LP version)*
    (S) (3:48) Priority 7069 Back To Back: Best Of Kool & The Gang/Ohio Players. *(45 version)*
    (S) (4:57) Special Music 846494 Celebration. *(LP version)*
    (S) (5:03) Mercury 314522458 Celebration: Best Of 1979-1987. *(LP version)*
    (S) (5:03) Time-Life R988-07 Sounds Of The Eighties: 1980. *(LP version)*
    (S) (4:54) Rebound 314520334 Ladies Night. *(LP version)*
    (S) (3:47) JCI 3170 #1 Radio Hits 1980 - Only Rock 'n Roll - 1984. *(45 version)*
    (S) (4:54) JCI 3175 1975 - Only Soul - 1979. *(LP version)*
    (S) (5:02) Time-Life R834-13 Body Talk - Just The Two Of Us. *(LP version)*

1981 CELEBRATION
    (S) (4:57) Priority 7983 Mega-Hits Dance Classics Volume 7. *(LP version)*
    (S) (3:41) Rhino 70985 The Disco Years Volume 2. *(45 version)*
    (S) (3:41) Rhino 70494 Billboard Top Dance Hits - 1980. *(45 version)*
    (S) (3:41) Rhino 70676 Billboard Top Hits - 1981. *(45 version)*

(S) (3:41) Original Sound 9307 Dedicated To You Vol. 7. *(45 version)*

(S) (4:57) Mercury 822538 Celebrate. *(LP version)*

(S) (4:57) Mercury 834780 Everything's Kool & The Gang: Greatest Hits. *(LP version)*

(S) (4:57) Special Music 846494 Celebration. *(LP version)*

(S) (3:41) Rhino 71618 Soul Train Hall Of Fame/20th Anniversary. *(45 version)*

(S) (4:58) Mercury 314522458 Celebration: Best Of 1979-1987. *(LP version)*

(S) (4:45) Mercury 314522367 Soccer Rocks The Globe. *(1994 version)*

(S) (3:40) JCI 3127 1980 - Only Rock 'N Roll - 1984. *(45 version)*

(S) (4:56) Rebound 314520218 Disco Nights Vol. 2. *(LP version)*

(S) (4:56) Rebound 314520318 Class Reunion 1980. *(LP version)*

(S) (3:41) Time-Life R988-08 Sounds Of The Eighties: 1981. *(45 version)*

(S) (3:41) Time-Life R138-38 Celebration. *(45 version)*

(S) (3:41) Rhino 72159 Black Entertainment Television - 15th Anniversary. *(45 version)*

(S) (3:42) K-Tel 3575 Hot, Hot Vacation Jams - Week One. *(45 version)*

(S) (3:42) Polygram Special Markets 314520274 Celebration! *(45 version)*

(S) (4:54) Madacy Entertainment 26927 Sun Splashin'. *(LP version)*

(S) (3:41) K-Tel 3796 Music For Your Party. *(45 version)*

(S) (3:40) K-Tel 3795 Music For Your Halloween Party. *(45 version)*

(S) (3:39) Polydor 314535877 Pure Disco. *(45 version)*

(S) (3:40) K-Tel 3795 Spooktacular Party Songs. *(45 version)*

(S) (3:37) Cold Front 6245 Greatest Sports Rock And Jams. *(all selections on this cd are segued together)*

(S) (3:38) Simitar 55522 The Number One's: Party Time. *(45 version)*

(S) (5:23) Curb 77934 Absolute Dance Hits: How Do I Live. *(1998 rerecording)*

(S) (3:41) Time-Life R840-09 Sounds Of The Seventies: '70s Dance Party 1979-1981. *(45 version)*

(S) (3:42) Rebound 314520522 Rockin' Sports Jams. *(45 version)*

1981 JONES Vs. JONES
(S) (4:15) Mercury 822538 Celebrate. *(LP length)*

(S) (4:15) Special Music 846494 Celebration. *(LP length)*

1981 TAKE MY HEART
(S) (4:01) Mercury 822534 Something Special.

(S) (4:04) Mercury 314522458 Celebration: Best Of 1979-1987.

(S) (4:04) Rhino 72123 Disco Years, Vol. 7.

1982 GET DOWN ON IT
(S) (6:07) Mercury 314522460 Funk Funk: Best Of Funk Essentials 2. *(12" single version)*

(S) (3:33) Risky Business 66392 Get Into The Greed: Greatest Hits Of The 80's. *(45 version)*

(S) (4:53) Mercury 314522458 Celebration: Best Of 1979-1987. *(LP version)*

(S) (4:48) Mercury 822534 Something Special. *(LP version)*

(S) (3:33) Rhino 72123 Disco Years, Vol. 7. *(45 version)*

(S) (4:53) Rebound 314520365 Funk Classics - The 80's. *(LP version)*

(S) (4:49) Thump 4060 Old School Volume 6. *(LP version; all selections on this cd are segued together)*

(S) (4:52) Polygram Special Markets 314520445 Soul Hits Of The 80's. *(LP version)*

(S) (3:33) Time-Life R988-22 Sounds Of The Eighties 1980-1983. *(45 version)*

1982 BIG FUN
(S) (5:01) Mercury 822535 As One. *(LP version)*

1983 LET'S GO DANCIN' (OOH LA, LA, LA)
(S) (6:39) Mercury 314522458 Celebration: Best Of 1979-1987. *(LP version)*

(S) (6:39) Mercury 822535 As One. *(LP version)*

1984 JOANNA
(S) (3:57) Rhino 71972 Video Soul - Best Soul Of The 80's Vol. 2. *(45 length)*

(S) (4:21) Mercury 314522458 Celebration: Best Of 1979-1987. *(LP length)*

(S) (4:20) Mercury 834780 Everything's Kool & The Gang: Greatest Hits. *(LP length)*

(S) (4:15) Mercury 814351 In The Heart. *(LP length)*

(S) (3:57) Priority 7069 Back To Back: Best Of Kool & The Gang/Ohio Players. *(45 length)*

(S) (3:58) Time-Life R988-06 Sounds Of The Eighties: 1984. *(45 length)*

(S) (4:00) Rhino 72139 Billboard Hot R&B Hits 1984. *(45 length)*

(S) (4:22) Time-Life R834-05 Body Talk - Sealed With A Kiss. *(LP length)*

(S) (4:22) JCI 3176 1980 - Only Soul - 1984. *(LP length)*

(S) (4:21) Rebound 314520493 Class Reunion '83. *(LP length)*

(S) (4:21) Polygram Special Markets 314520457 #1 Radio Hits Of The 80's. *(LP length)*

1984 TONIGHT
(S) (4:12) Mercury 314522458 Celebration: Best Of 1979-1987. *(12" dj only single version)*

(S) (3:51) Mercury 814351 In The Heart.

(S) (3:54) Rhino 72122 Disco Years, Vol. 6.

(S) (3:54) Rhino 75234 Rupaul's Go-Go Box Classics.

1985 MISLED
(actual 45 time is (4:06) not (3:59) as stated on the record label)

(S) (4:57) Mercury 314522458 Celebration: Best Of 1979-1987. *(LP length)*

(S) (4:57) Mercury 822943 Emergency. *(LP length)*

1985 FRESH
(dj copies of this 45 ran (3:49) and (3:59) (a remix); commercial copies were all (3:49); LP length is (4:21))

(S) (4:04) Rhino 70275 The Disco Years, Vol. 4.

(S) (4:22) Mercury 314522458 Celebration: Best Of 1979-1987.

(S) (4:21) Mercury 822943 Emergency.

(S) (4:20) Priority 7069 Back To Back: Best Of Kool & The Gang/Ohio Players.

1985 CHERISH
(S) (4:16) Rebound 314520033 Quiet Storm: The 70's. *(edit of 12" single version)*

(S) (3:58) K-Tel 3263 The 80's Love Jams. *(45 version)*

(S) (5:39) Mercury 314522458 Celebration: Best Of 1979-1987. *(12" single version)*

(S) (4:47) Mercury 822943 Emergency. *(LP version)*

(S) (4:19) Mercury 834780 Everything's Kool & The Gang: Greatest Hits. *(edit of 12" single version)*

(S) (4:45) Priority 7069 Back To Back: Best Of Kool & The Gang/Ohio Players. *(LP version)*

(S) (4:43) Priority 53796 Hot And Sexy - Love And Romance Volume 3. *(LP version)*

(S) (4:19) Original Sound 9308 Dedicated To You Vol. 8. *(edit of 12" single version)*

(S) (4:19) Time-Life R988-12 Sounds Of The 80's: 1985-1986. *(edit of 12" single version)*

(S) (3:59) Rhino 72140 Billboard Hot R&B Hits 1985. *(45 version)*

(S) (3:59) Time-Life R834-04 Body Talk - Together Forever. *(45 version)*

(S) (5:42) Rhino 72757 Smooth Grooves - Wedding Songs. *(12" single version)*

(S) (3:57) K-Tel 3864 Slow Dancin'. *(45 version)*

(S) (3:58) K-Tel 6257 The Greatest Love Songs - 16 Soft Rock Hits. *(45 version)*

1986 EMERGENCY
(S) (5:17) Mercury 822943 Emergency. *(LP version)*

1987 VICTORY
(S) (4:36) Mercury 830398 Forever. *(LP length)*

1987 STONE LOVE
(S) (4:31) Mercury 834780 Everything's Kool & The Gang: Greatest Hits. *(LP version)*

(S) (4:32) Mercury 830398 Forever. *(LP version)*

(S) (3:54) Mercury 314522458 Celebration: Best Of 1979-1987. *(45 version)*

KORGIS
1980 EVERYBODY'S GOT TO LEARN SOMETIME

KRAFTWERK
1975 AUTOBAHN
    (S) (22:39)   Elektra 25326   Autobahn.   *(LP version)*

BILLY J. KRAMER with THE DAKOTAS
1964 LITTLE CHILDREN
    (M) (2:46)   Rhino 70319   History Of British Rock Volume 1.
    (M) (2:46)   Rhino 72022   History Of British Rock Box Set.
    (M) (2:46)   Rhino 72008   History Of British Rock Volumes 1-4 Box Set.
    (M) (2:45)   EMI 96055   Best Of.
    (M) (2:44)   Time-Life SUD-09   Superhits - 1964.
    (M) (2:45)   Time-Life R962-07   History Of Rock 'N' Roll: The British Invasion 1964-1966.
    (M) (2:44)   Time-Life AM1-11   AM Gold - 1964.
1964 BAD TO ME
    (M) (2:19)   Rhino 70319   History Of British Rock Volume 1.
    (M) (2:19)   Rhino 72022   History Of British Rock Box Set.
    (M) (2:19)   Rhino 72008   History Of British Rock Volumes 1-4 Box Set.
    (S) (2:17)   EMI 96055   Best Of.
    (S) (2:17)   EMI 81128   Rock Is Dead But It Won't Lie Down.
    (M) (2:18)   Time-Life 2CLR-03   Classic Rock - 1964.
1964 I'LL KEEP YOU SATISFIED
    (M) (2:04)   Rhino 70320   History Of British Rock Volume 2.
    (M) (2:04)   Rhino 72022   History Of British Rock Box Set.
    (M) (2:04)   Rhino 72008   History Of British Rock Volumes 1-4 Box Set.
    (S) (2:05)   EMI 96055   Best Of.
1964 FROM A WINDOW
    (S) (1:55)   Rhino 70321   History Of British Rock Volume 3.
    (S) (1:55)   Rhino 72022   History Of British Rock Box Set.
    (S) (1:55)   Rhino 72008   History Of British Rock Volumes 1-4 Box Set.
    (S) (1:53)   EMI 96055   Best Of.

LENNY KRAVITZ
1991 IT AIN'T OVER TIL IT'S OVER
    (S) (4:01)   Virgin 91610 and 86209   Mama Said.
    (S) (4:00)   EMI-Capitol Music Group 54548   Smooth Luv.
    (S) (3:57)   Razor & Tie 4569   '90s Style.

KRIS KROSS
1992 JUMP
    (S) (4:51)   Tommy Boy 1075   MTV Party To Go Volume 4.
    (remix; all tracks on this cd are segued together)
    (S) (3:14)   Ruffhouse/Columbia 48710   Totally Krossed Out.
    (S) (3:51)   Ruffhouse/Columbia 67896   Best Of - Remixed.
    (remixed)
1992 WARM IT UP
    (S) (4:08)   Ruffhouse/Columbia 48710   Totally Krossed Out.
    (S) (3:49)   Ruffhouse/Columbia 67896   Best Of - Remixed.
    (remixed)
released as by KRIS KROSS featuring SUPERCAT:
1993 ALRIGHT
    (S) (4:03)   Ruffhouse/Columbia 57278   Da Bomb.
    (S) (4:06)   Ruffhouse/Columbia 67896   Best Of - Remixed.
    (remixed)
released as by KRIS KROSS:
1996 TONITE'S THA NIGHT
    (S) (3:16)   Ruffhouse/Columbia 67441   Young, Rich & Dangerous.

KRIS KRISTOFFERSON
1971 LOVING HER WAS EASIER (THAN ANYTHING I'LL EVER DO AGAIN)
    (S) (3:46)   CBS Special Products 44352   The Silver Tongued Devil And I.
    (S) (3:46)   CBS Special Products 44350   Songs Of Kristofferson.

    (S) (3:45)   CBS Special Products 46807   Rock Goes To The Movies Volume 4.
    (S) (3:44)   Sony Music Special Products 48621   Singer/Songwriter.
    (S) (3:45)   Sony Music Special Products 66106   The Monument Story.
    (S) (3:43)   Rhino 72516   Behind Closed Doors - '70s Swingers.
1973 WHY ME
    (S) (3:25)   Sony Music Special Products 47064   Jesus Was A Capricorn.
    (S) (3:27)   CBS Special Products 44350   Songs Of Kristofferson.
    (S) (3:26)   Sony Music Special Products 48621   Singer/Songwriter.
    (S) (3:26)   Pair 1078   My Songs.
    (S) (3:25)   Time-Life CCD-06   Contemporary Country - The Early 70's.
    (S) (3:26)   Sony Music Special Products 66106   The Monument Story.
    (S) (3:25)   Rhino 72519   Mellow Rock Hits Of The 70's - Sundown.
    (S) (3:25)   K-Tel 3358   101 Greatest Country Hits Vol. Four: Mellow Country.
    (S) (3:25)   Varese Sarabande 5906   God, Love And Rock & Roll.

K7
1993 COME BABY COME
    (S) (5:17)   Tommy Boy 1097   MTV Party To Go Volume 5.
    (remix; all tracks on this cd are segued together)
    (S) (3:56)   Tommy Boy 1071   Swing Batta Swing.
    (S) (3:56)   Boxtunes 162444068   Big Phat Ones Of Hip-Hop Volume 1.
    (S) (3:56)   Columbia 57761   O.S.T. I Like It Like That.
    (S) (3:56)   Beast 53302   Summer Jammin'.

BOB KUBAN and THE IN-MEN
1966 THE CHEATER
    (S) (2:38)   Rhino 70995   One Hit Wonders Of The 60's Volume 1.
    (S) (2:38)   Ripete 0001   Coolin' Out/24 Carolina Classics Volume 1.
    (S) (2:37)   Time-Life 2CLR-22   Classic Rock - 1966: Blowin' Your Mind.
    (E) (2:35)   Collectables 2502   WCBS-FM History Of Rock - The 60's Part 3.
    (E) (2:35)   Collectables 4502   History Of Rock/The 60s Part Three.
    (S) (2:38)   Collectables 5688   A Golden Classics Edition.
    (truncated fade)
    (M) (2:38)   Rhino 72815   Beg, Scream & Shout! The Big Ol' Box Of '60s Soul.

KUT KLOSE
1995 I LIKE
    (S) (4:23)   Elektra 61668   Surrender.
    (S) (4:23)   Elektra 62090   Maximum Slow Jams.

K.W.S.
1992 PLEASE DON'T GO
    (S) (5:29)   Tommy Boy 1075   MTV Party To Go Volume 4.
    (remix; all tracks on this cd are segued together)
    (S) (4:14)   Next Plateau 828368   Please Don't Go (The Album).

KYPER
1990 TIC-TAC-TOE
    (S) (6:15)   K-Tel 6102   Funk-Tastic Jams.
    (S) (6:19)   Atlantic 82116   Tic Tac Toe.

LaBELLE
1975 LADY MARMALADE

(S) (3:14) Priority 7976 Mega-Hits Dance Classics Volume 6. *(45 version)*

(S) (3:18) Rhino 70554 Soul Hits Of The 70's Volume 14. *(45 version)*

(S) (3:55) Sandstone 33051 and 5019 Cosmopolitan Volume 5. *(LP version)*

(S) (3:55) Epic 33075 Nightbirds. *(LP version)*

(S) (3:55) Epic 36997 Best Of Patti Labelle. *(LP version)*

(S) (3:54) Epic 57620 O.S.T. Carlito's Way. *(LP version)*

(S) (3:13) Razor & Tie 22045 Those Funky 70's. *(45 version)*

(S) (3:16) Time-Life SOD-08 Sounds Of The Seventies - 1975. *(45 version)*

(S) (3:55) Sandstone 33051 and 5019 Cosmopolitan Volume 5. *(LP version)*

(S) (3:55) Risky Business 66663 Sex In The Seventies. *(LP version)*

(S) (3:56) Legacy/Epic 66339 Lady Marmalade: Best Of Patti And Labelle. *(LP version)*

(S) (3:55) Legacy/Epic 66912 Legacy's Rhythm & Soul Revue. *(LP version)*

(S) (3:54) Rebound 314520317 Class Reunion 1975. *(LP version)*

(S) (3:55) DCC Compact Classics 083 Night Moves Volume 3. *(LP version)*

(S) (3:18) MCA 11329 Soul Train 25th Anniversary Box Set. *(45 version)*

(S) (3:18) EMI 37350 Crescent City Soul: The Sound Of New Orleans 1947-1974. *(45 version)*

(S) (3:55) K-Tel 3624 Music Express. *(LP version)*

(S) (3:18) Rhino 72414 Dance Floor Divas: The 70's. *(45 version)*

(S) (3:55) MCA 11526 O.S.T. The Long Kiss Goodnight. *(LP version)*

(S) (3:16) JCI 3148 1975 - Only Dance - 1979. *(45 version)*

(S) (3:55) MCA 11567 Greatest Hits. *(LP version)*

(S) (3:18) Eclipse Music Group 64894 Rock 'n Roll Relix 1974-1975. *(45 version)*

(S) (3:18) Eclipse Music Group 64897 Rock 'n Roll Relix 1970-1979. *(45 version)*

(S) (3:18) Time-Life AM1-22 AM Gold - 1975. *(45 version)*

(S) (3:18) Time-Life R838-10 Solid Gold Soul - 1975. *(45 version)*

(S) (3:55) Warner Brothers 46359 Something Silver. *(LP version)*

(S) (3:55) Robbins 75002 Strip Jointz - Hot Songs For Sexy Dancers. *(LP version)*

(S) (3:54) K-Tel 3889 Great R&B Female Groups: Hits Of The 70s. *(LP version)*

PATTI LaBELLE
1985 NEW ATTITUDE
(actual 45 time is (4:05) not (3:59) as stated on the record label)

(S) (4:35) MCA 10288 Classic Soul. *(LP version)*

(S) (4:37) MCA 6330 Soundtrack Smashes - The 80's. *(LP version)*

(S) (6:12) MCA 6435 Soundtrack Smashes - The 80's And More. *(12" single version)*

(S) (4:37) MCA 5553 O.S.T. Beverly Hills Cop. *(LP version)*

(S) (4:37) Sandstone 33050 and 5018 Cosmopolitan Volume 4. *(LP version)*

(S) (4:37) DCC Compact Classics 089 Night Moves Volume 7. *(LP version)*

(S) (6:13) Big Ear Music 4003 Only In The 80's Volume Three. *(12" single version)*

(S) (4:35) Nick At Nite/550 Music 67690 I Am Woman. *(LP version)*

(S) (4:00) Hip-O 40015 Soulful Ladies Of The 80's. *(45 version)*

(S) (4:07) MCA 11567 Greatest Hits. *(45 version)*

(S) (4:07) Rhino 72838 Disco Queens: The 80's. *(45 version)*

(S) (4:35) MCA Special Products 21032 Soul Legends. *(LP version)*

(S) (4:35) MCA Special Products 21029 The Women Of Soul. *(LP version)*

released as by PATTI LaBELLE and MICHAEL McDONALD:
1986 ON MY OWN

(S) (4:49) MCA 5737 Patti Labelle - Winner In You. *(LP length)*

(S) (4:46) Time-Life R138-18 Body Talk. *(LP length)*

(S) (4:40) MCA 11567 Patti LaBelle - Greatest Hits. *(LP length faded :09 early)*

released as by PATTI LaBELLE:
1986 OH, PEOPLE

(S) (4:19) MCA Special Products 20767 Classic R&B Oldies From The 80's Volume 3. *(45 version)*

(S) (5:16) MCA 5737 Winner In You. *(LP version)*

(S) (4:21) MCA 11567 Greatest Hits. *(45 version)*

PATTI LaBELLE & THE BLUE BELLES
1963 DOWN THE AISLE (WEDDING SONG)

(M) (3:31) Relic 7044 Down The Aisle.

(M) (3:31) Collectables 5090 Golden Classics.

(M) (3:31) Collectables 2608 WCBS-FM For Lovers Only Vol. 4.

(M) (3:31) Columbia 67650 O.S.T. Stonewall.

1964 YOU'LL NEVER WALK ALONE

(S) (3:09) Collectables 5090 Golden Classics.

(S) (3:09) Relic 7044 Down The Aisle.

La BOUCHE
1996 BE MY LOVER

(S) (4:00) RCA 66759 Sweet Dreams.

(S) (7:21) Tommy Boy 1168 MTV Party To Go Volume 10. *(all songs on this cd are segued together; remix)*

(S) (3:48) Arista 18943 Ultimate Dance Party 1997. *(all selections on this cd are segued together)*

(S) (4:00) EMI-Capitol Music Group 54547 Hot Luv.

(S) (4:00) Hollywood 62123 More Music From The Motion Picture "Romy And Michele's High School Reunion".

(S) (3:58) Interhit/Priority 51081 DMA Dance Vol. 2: Eurodance.

1996 SWEET DREAMS

(S) (3:23) RCA 66759 Sweet Dreams.

(S) (4:41) Cold Front 6242 Club Mix '97. *(all selections on this cd are segued together; remix)*

(S) (3:02) Arista 18988 Ultimate Dance Party 1998. *(all selections on this cd are segued together)*

LADY FLASH
1976 STREET SINGIN'

(S) (3:11) Priority 53789 Disco Attack.

L.A. GUNS
1990 THE BALLAD OF JAYNE
- (S) (4:32) Priority 7049 Metal Heat.
- (S) (4:32) Vertigo 838592 Cocked & Loaded.
- (S) (4:32) Priority 50937 Best Of 80's Metal Volume Two: Bang Your Head.
- (S) (4:31) Time-Life R968-25 Guitar Rock - The '90s.
- (S) (4:31) K-Tel 3999 Glam Rock Vol. 2: The 80's And Beyond.

FRANCIS LAI
1971 THEME FROM LOVE STORY
- (S) (3:19) Time-Life R986-22 Instrumental Classics - Pop Classics.

LAID BACK
1984 WHITE HORSE
- (S) (3:49) Priority 7983 Mega-Hits Dance Classics (Volume 7). (45 version)
- (S) (3:48) K-Tel 3343 The 80's Hot Dance Trax. (45 version)
- (S) (5:44) Rhino 71756 and 72833 Phat Trax: The Best Of Old School Vol. 5. (LP version)
- (S) (3:48) Priority 53781 Best Of 80's Rock Volume 2. (45 version)
- (S) (5:44) Original Sound 9306 Dedicated To You Vol. 6. (LP version)
- (S) (5:43) Rhino 71558 Street Jams: Electric Funk Part 4. (LP version)
- (S) (5:43) Rhino 72062 Street Jams: Electric Funk Parts 1-4. (LP version)

FRANKIE LAINE
1955 HUMMING BIRD
1957 MOONLIGHT GAMBLER
- (M) (2:53) Columbia 45029 16 Most Requested Songs.
- (E) (2:54) Columbia 8636 Greatest Hits.
- (M) (2:56) Time-Life HPD-17 Your Hit Parade - 1957.
1957 LOVE IS A GOLDEN RING
- (M) (2:29) Columbia 45029 16 Most Requested Songs.
- (M) (2:28) Time-Life HPD-17 Your Hit Parade - 1957.
1967 I'LL TAKE CARE OF YOUR CARES
- (S) (2:44) Taragon 1017 Very Best Of (ABC Years).
1967 MAKING MEMORIES
- (S) (2:55) Taragon 1017 Very Best Of (ABC Years).
1969 YOU GAVE ME A MOUNTAIN
- (S) (3:55) Taragon 1017 Very Best Of (ABC Years).

GEORGE LAMOND
1990 BAD OF THE HEART
- (S) (4:17) Columbia 45488 Bad Of The Heart.
- (S) (4:01) Priority 51003 Shut Up And Dance! The Best Of Freestyle Volume Two. (all selections on this cd are segued together)

MAJOR LANCE
1963 MONKEY TIME
- (M) (2:46) Rhino 75770 Soul Shots Volume 2.
- (M) (2:45) Rhino 70992 Groove 'n' Grind.
- (M) (2:45) CBS Special Products 37321 Okeh Soul.
- (M) (2:44) Time-Life 2RNR-29 Rock 'N' Roll Era - The 60's Rave On.
- (M) (2:45) Legacy/Epic 66988 Everybody Loves A Good Time - Best Of.
- (M) (2:45) Nick At Nite/Epic 67149 Dick Van Dyke's Dance Party.
- (M) (2:45) Legacy/Epic Associated 64770 Curtis Mayfield's Chicago Soul.
- (M) (2:45) Rhino 72815 Beg, Scream & Shout! The Big Ol' Box Of '60s Soul.
- (M) (2:45) JCI 3189 1960 - Only Dance - 1964.
1963 HEY LITTLE GIRL
- (M) (2:27) CBS Special Products 37321 Okeh Soul.
- (M) (2:24) Time-Life 2RNR-40 Rock 'N' Roll Era - The 60's Teen Time.

- (S) (2:27) Legacy/Epic 66912 Legacy's Rhythm & Soul Revue.
- (S) (2:28) Legacy/Epic 66988 Everybody Loves A Good Time - Best Of.
1964 UM, UM, UM, UM, UM, UM
- (M) (2:19) CBS Special Products 37321 Okeh Soul.
- (S) (2:18) Time-Life RHD-12 Rhythm & Blues - 1964.
- (S) (2:19) Time-Life 2CLR-16 Classic Rock - 1964: Shakin' All Over.
- (S) (2:18) Legacy/Epic 66988 Everybody Loves A Good Time - Best Of.
- (S) (2:18) Time-Life R838-13 Solid Gold Soul - 1964.
1964 THE MATADOR
- (M) (2:23) CBS Special Products 37321 Okeh Soul.
- (S) (2:25) Legacy/Epic 66988 Everybody Loves A Good Time - Best Of.
1964 RHYTHM
- (M) (2:15) CBS Special Products 37321 Okeh Soul.
- (S) (2:20) Legacy/Epic 66988 Everybody Loves A Good Time - Best Of.

MICKEY LEE LANE
1964 SHAGGY DOG
- (M) (2:19) Forevermore 5008 Oldies I Forgot To Buy.

k.d. LANG
1992 CONSTANT CRAVING
- (S) (4:36) Sire 26840 Ingenue.

LARKS
1965 THE JERK
- (S) (2:32) Rhino 70992 Groove 'n' Grind. (alternate vocal take)
- (S) (2:31) Original Sound 8852 Oldies But Goodies Vol. 2. (this compact disc uses the "Waring - fds" noise reduction process; alternate vocal take)
- (S) (2:31) Original Sound 2223 Oldies But Goodies Volumes 2,7,9,12 and 13 Box Set. (this box set uses the "Waring - fds" noise reduction process; alternate vocal take)
- (S) (2:31) Original Sound 2500 Oldies But Goodies Volumes 1-15 Box Set. (this box set uses the "Waring - fds" noise reduction process; alternate vocal take)
- (S) (2:31) Original Sound CDGO-5 Golden Oldies Volume. 5. (alternate vocal take)
- (S) (2:31) Time-Life 2CLR-14 Classic Rock - 1965: Shakin' All Over. (alternate vocal take)
- (S) (2:32) Nick At Nite/550 Music 63407 Dancing At The Nick At Niteclub. (alternate vocal take)

JULIUS LaROSA
1955 DOMANI (TOMORROW)
- (M) (2:31) Collectables 5758 Golden Classics.
1955 SUDDENLY THERE'S A VALLEY
- (M) (2:43) Collectables 5758 Golden Classics.
1956 LIPSTICK AND CANDY AND RUBBERSOLE SHOES
1958 TORERO

LARSEN-FEITEN BAND
1980 WHO'LL BE THE FOOL TONIGHT
- (S) (4:11) Rhino 71892 Radio Daze: Pop Hits Of The 80's Volume Three.

NICOLETTE LARSON
1979 LOTTA LOVE
- (S) (3:07) Rhino 71202 Super Hits Of The 70's Volume 22.
- (S) (3:09) Time-Life SOD-19 Sounds Of The Seventies - 1979: Take Two.
- (S) (3:08) Time-Life R105-26 Our Songs: Singers & Songwriters Encore.
- (S) (3:09) Priority 53724 Country Rock Vol. 2 - Slow Dancin.
- (S) (3:07) Rhino 72445 Listen To The Music: The 70's California Sound.
- (S) (3:08) Madacy Entertainment 1979 Rock On 1979.

(S) (3:07) Time-Life R834-06 Body Talk - Only You.
(S) (3:07) Time-Life AM1-26 AM Gold - 1979.

1980 LET ME GO, LOVE
(S) (3:46) Priority 53746 80's Greatest Rock Hits Vol. 12 - Singers/Songwriters.

DENISE LaSALLE
1971 TRAPPED BY A THING CALLED LOVE
(S) (2:38) Ripete 2220 Soul Patrol Vol. 2.

DAVID LASLEY
1982 IF I HAD MY WISH TONIGHT

JAMES LAST BAND
1980 THE SEDUCTION (LOVE THEME)
(S) (3:37) Polygram Special Markets 314520273 Great Instrumental Hits.

LATIMORE
1974 LET'S STRAIGHTEN IT OUT
(S) (3:25) Rhino 70662 Billboard's Top R&B Hits Of 1974. *(45 version)*
(S) (3:25) Rhino 70554 Soul Hits Of The 70's Volume 14. *(45 version)*
(S) (5:12) Rhino 71132 Blues Masters Volume 9: Postmodern Blues. *(LP version)*
(S) (5:11) Rhino 71994 Straighten It Out: Best Of. *(LP version)*
(S) (3:25) Priority 53131 Deep Soul Volume Two. *(45 version)*
(S) (5:11) TK/Hot Productions 33 Best Of T.K. Soul Singles. *(LP version)*
(S) (5:06) Platinum Entertainment 514161149 Essential Blues. *(LP version)*
(S) (3:24) Cold Front 4024 Old School Mega Mix Volume 2. *(45 version)*
(S) (5:09) Beast 53442 Original Players Of Love. *(LP version)*
(S) (3:25) Time-Life R859-11 Living The Blues - Blues Classics: The '70s. *(45 version)*

LaTOUR
1991 PEOPLE ARE STILL HAVING SEX
(S) (5:15) Smash 848323 LaTour.

KENNY LATTIMORE
1997 FOR YOU
(S) (3:56) Columbia 67125 Kenny Lattimore.
(S) (3:56) Columbia 69145 Songs From The Heart.

STACY LATTISAW
1980 LET ME BE YOUR ANGEL
(S) (4:00) Atlantic 5219 Let Me Be Your Angel.
(S) (3:43) Original Sound 9306 Dedicated To You Vol. 6. *(faded :17 sooner than the 45 or LP)*
(S) (3:59) Rhino 71860 Smooth Grooves Volume 2.
(S) (4:01) Rhino 72945 Very Best Of.

1981 LOVE ON A TWO WAY STREET
(S) (4:08) Atlantic 16049 With You.
(S) (4:08) Rhino 71972 Video Soul - Best Soul Of The 80's Vol. 2.
(S) (4:08) Rhino 71865 Smooth Grooves Volume 7.
(S) (4:08) Rhino 72136 Billboard Hot R&B Hits 1981.
(S) (4:08) Time-Life R834-14 Body Talk - Love And Tenderness.
(S) (4:10) Rhino 72945 Very Best Of.

1983 MIRACLES
(S) (3:31) Rhino 72945 Very Best Of.

CYNDI LAUPER
1984 GIRLS JUST WANT TO HAVE FUN
(S) (3:51) Epic 53439 O.S.T. Peter's Friends.
(S) (3:53) Sandstone 33051 and 5019 Cosmopolitan Volume 5.
(S) (3:53) DCC Compact Classics 083 Night Moves Volume 3.

(S) (3:55) Portrait 38930 She's So Unusual.
(S) (3:54) Epic 66100 Twelve Deadly Cyns.
(S) (3:40) MCA 11231 O.S.T. To Wong Foo, Thanks For Everything. *(rerecording)*
(S) (3:55) Epic/Legacy 65381 She's So Unusual/True Colors/Hat Full Of Stars.
(S) (3:53) Time-Life R13610 Gold And Platinum Box Set - The Ultimate Rock Collection.

1984 TIME AFTER TIME
(S) (3:59) Time-Life R105-40 Rock Dreams.
(S) (3:59) Portrait 38930 She's So Unusual.
(S) (3:58) Epic 66100 Twelve Deadly Cyns.
(S) (3:57) Time-Life R988-27 Sounds Of The Eighties: The Rolling Stone Collection 1983-1985.
(S) (3:58) Time-Life R834-01 Body Talk - Forever Yours.
(S) (3:59) Epic/Legacy 65381 She's So Unusual/True Colors/Hat Full Of Stars.

1984 SHE BOP
(S) (3:42) T.J. Martell Foundation/Columbia 40315 Music For The Miracle. *(45 version)*
(S) (3:45) Time-Life R102-34 The Rolling Stone Collection. *(LP version)*
(S) (3:46) Portrait 38930 She's So Unusual. *(LP version)*
(S) (3:41) Epic 66100 Twelve Deadly Cyns. *(45 version)*
(S) (6:24) Epic 67534 Club Epic Volume 5. *(12" single version)*
(S) (3:46) Epic/Legacy 65381 She's So Unusual/True Colors/Hat Full Of Stars. *(LP version)*

1984 ALL THROUGH THE NIGHT
(S) (4:28) Portrait 38930 She's So Unusual.
(S) (4:27) Epic 66100 Twelve Deadly Cyns.
(S) (4:28) Epic/Legacy 65381 She's So Unusual/True Colors/Hat Full Of Stars.

1985 MONEY CHANGES EVERYTHING
(S) (5:02) Portrait 38930 She's So Unusual. *(LP version)*
(S) (5:01) Epic 66100 Twelve Deadly Cyns. *(LP version)*
(S) (5:02) Epic/Legacy 65381 She's So Unusual/True Colors/Hat Full Of Stars. *(LP version)*

1985 THE GOONIES 'R' GOOD ENOUGH
1986 TRUE COLORS
(S) (3:45) Portrait 40313 True Colors.
(S) (3:45) Epic 66100 Twelve Deadly Cyns.
(S) (3:45) Time-Life R988-28 Sounds Of The Eighties: The Rolling Stone Collection 1986-1987.
(S) (3:45) Epic/Legacy 65381 She's So Unusual/True Colors/Hat Full Of Stars.

1987 CHANGE OF HEART
(S) (4:22) Portrait 40313 True Colors.
(S) (4:22) Epic 66100 Twelve Deadly Cyns.
(S) (7:52) Epic/Legacy 65035 Club Epic Volume 6. *(12" single version)*
(S) (4:16) Time-Life R988-20 Sounds Of The Eighties: The Late '80s Take Two.
(S) (4:22) Epic/Legacy 65381 She's So Unusual/True Colors/Hat Full Of Stars.

1987 WHAT'S GOING ON
(S) (4:38) Portrait 40313 True Colors. *(LP version)*
(S) (3:49) Epic 66100 Twelve Deadly Cyns. *(45 version)*
(S) (4:38) Epic/Legacy 65381 She's So Unusual/True Colors/Hat Full Of Stars. *(LP version)*

1989 I DROVE ALL NIGHT
(S) (4:09) Priority 53732 80's Greatest Rock Hits Volume 8 - Dance Party.
(S) (4:11) Epic 44318 A Night To Remember.
(S) (4:10) Epic 66100 Twelve Deadly Cyns.

ROD LAUREN
1960 IF I HAD A GIRL

EDDIE LAWRENCE
1956 THE OLD PHILOSOPHER
(M) (3:16) Time-Life HPD-40 Your Hit Parade - Golden Goofers.

JOEY LAWRENCE
1993 NOTHIN' MY LOVE CAN'T FIX
(S) (4:03) Impact 10659 Joey Lawrence.

STEVE LAWRENCE
1957 THE BANANA BOAT SONG
    (M) (2:45) Taragon 1008 Songs By.
1957 PARTY DOLL
    (M) (2:10) Taragon 1008 Songs By.
1957 CAN'T WAIT FOR SUMMER
    (M) (2:17) Taragon 1008 Songs By.
1960 PRETTY BLUE EYES
    (S) (1:51) Taragon 1002 Best Of.
1960 FOOTSTEPS
    (S) (2:11) Taragon 1002 Best Of.
1961 PORTRAIT OF MY LOVE
1963 GO AWAY LITTLE GIRL
1963 DON'T BE AFRAID LITTLE DARLIN'
1963 POOR LITTLE RICH GIRL
released as by STEVE and EYDIE (STEVE LAWRENCE and EYDIE GORME):
1963 I WANT TO STAY HERE
released as by STEVE LAWRENCE:
1963 WALKING PROUD

VICKI LAWRENCE
1973 THE NIGHT THE LIGHTS WENT OUT IN GEORGIA
    (S) (3:33) Rhino 70930 Super Hits Of The 70's Volume 10.
    (S) (3:31) Razor & Tie 21640 Those Fabulous 70's.
    (S) (3:33) K-Tel 3885 Story Songs.
    (S) (3:33) K-Tel 3910 Fantastic Volume 1.
    (S) (3:32) K-Tel 3914 Superstars Greatest Hits Volume 3.

JOY LAYNE
1957 YOUR WILD HEART
    (M) (2:44) Collectors' Choice 5189 I Wish I Were A Princess - The Great Lost Female Teen Idols.

LEAVES
1966 HEY JOE
    (M) (2:47) Time-Life 2CLR-17 Classic Rock - Rock Renaissance.
    (M) (2:50) K-Tel 686 Battle Of The Bands Vol. 4.
    (S) (2:46) One Way 29307 Hey Joe!

LeBLANC AND CARR
1978 FALLING
    (S) (3:10) Rhino 72299 Superhits Of The 70's Volume 25.
    (S) (3:09) Time-Life R834-10 Body Talk - From The Heart.

LE CLICK
1997 CALL ME
    (S) (3:43) RCA 67528 Le Click Featuring Kayo.
    (S) (3:42) Beast 54112 Boom!

LED ZEPPELIN
1970 WHOLE LOTTA LOVE
(both commercial and dj 45's were pressed with times of either (3:12) or (5:33))
    (S) (5:33) Atlantic 81908 Classic Rock 1966 - 1988.
    (S) (5:34) Atlantic 19127 Led Zeppelin II.
    (S) (5:33) Atlantic 82144 Led Zeppelin Box.
    (S) (14:23) Swan Song 201 O.S.T. The Song Remains The Same. *(live version)*
    (S) (5:33) Atlantic 82306 Atlantic Rock & Roll Box Set.
    (S) (5:32) Atlantic 82371 Remasters.
    (S) (5:33) Atlantic 82526 Complete Studio Recordings.
    (S) (5:33) Atlantic 82633 Led Zepellin II. *(remastered edition)*
    (S) (5:33) Atlantic 83088 Atlantic Records: 50 Years - The Gold Anniversary Collection.
1971 IMMIGRANT SONG
    (S) (2:24) Atlantic 19128 Led Zeppelin III.
    (S) (2:24) Atlantic 82678 Led Zeppelin III. *(remastered edition)*
    (S) (2:23) Atlantic 82144 Led Zeppelin Box. *(tracks into next selection)*
    (S) (2:23) Atlantic 82371 Remasters. *(tracks into next selection)*

    (S) (2:24) Atlantic 82526 Complete Studio Recordings.
1972 BLACK DOG
(dj copies of this 45 ran (3:50); commercial copies were all (4:55))
    (S) (4:54) Atlantic 19129 and 82638 Led Zeppelin.
    (S) (4:53) Atlantic 82144 Led Zeppelin Box.
    (S) (4:53) Atlantic 82371 Remasters.
    (S) (4:53) Atlantic 82526 Complete Studio Recordings.
1973 D'YER MAK'ER
    (S) (4:23) Atlantic 19130 and 82639 Houses Of The Holy.
    (S) (4:21) Atlantic 82144 Led Zeppelin Box.
    (S) (4:21) Atlantic 82371 Remasters.
    (S) (4:21) Atlantic 82526 Complete Studio Recordings.
1975 TRAMPLED UNDER FOOT
(dj copies of this 45 ran (3:48); commercial copies were all (5:38))
    (S) (5:36) Swan Song 200 Physical Graffiti.
    (S) (5:35) Swan Song 92442 Physical Graffiti. *(remastered edition)*
    (S) (5:35) Atlantic 82371 Remasters.
    (S) (5:34) Atlantic 82144 Led Zeppelin Box.
    (S) (5:34) Atlantic 82526 Complete Studio Recordings.
    (S) (5:32) Time-Life R102-34 The Rolling Stone Collection.
1980 FOOL IN THE RAIN
(dj copies of this 45 ran (3:20) and (6:08); commercial copies were all (6:08))
    (S) (6:09) Swan Song 16002 In Through The Out Door.
    (S) (6:12) Atlantic 82144 Led Zeppelin Box.
    (S) (6:12) Atlantic 82526 Complete Studio Recordings.
    (S) (6:12) Swan Song 92443 In Through The Out Door. *(remastered edition)*

BRENDA LEE
1960 SWEET NOTHIN'S
    (S) (2:21) MCA 31203 Vintage Music Volume 6.
    (S) (2:21) MCA 5804 Vintage Music Volumes 5 & 6.
    (S) (2:22) MCA 10384 Anthology.
    (S) (2:21) MCA 4012 Brenda Lee Story. *(buzz can be heard throughout the song)*
    (S) (2:22) Rhino 70621 Billboard's Top Rock & Roll Hits Of 1960. *(found only on the 1993 reissue of this cd)*
    (S) (2:21) Time-Life 2RNR-11 Rock 'N' Roll Era - 1960.
    (S) (2:21) MCA 11119 The Decca Rock 'N' Roll Collection.
    (S) (2:22) K-Tel 3007 50's Sock Hop.
    (S) (2:21) MCA Special Products 22172 Vintage Collectibles Volume 10.
1960 I'M SORRY
    (S) (2:38) MCA 31202 Vintage Music Volume 5.
    (S) (2:38) MCA 5804 Vintage Music Volumes 5 & 6.
    (S) (2:37) MCA 2-8025 30 Years Of Hits 1958 - 1974.
    (S) (2:37) Original Sound 8864 Oldies But Goodies Vol. 14. *(this compact disc uses the "Waring - fds" noise reduction process)*
    (S) (2:37) Original Sound 2222 Oldies But Goodies Volumes 3,5,11,14 and 15 Box Set. *(this box set uses the "Waring - fds" noise reduction process)*
    (S) (2:37) Original Sound 2500 Oldies But Goodies Volumes 1-15 Box Set. *(this box set uses the "Waring - fds" noise reduction process)*
    (S) (2:39) MCA 10384 Anthology.
    (S) (2:36) MCA 4012 Brenda Lee Story.
    (S) (2:37) Time-Life 2RNR-42 Rock 'N' Roll Era - The 60's Sock Hop.
    (S) (2:38) Time-Life SUD-15 Superhits - The Early 60's.
    (S) (2:37) Time-Life HPD-33 Your Hit Parade - The Early 60's.
    (S) (2:38) Time-Life R962-05 History Of Rock 'N' Roll: The Teenage Years 1957-1964.
    (S) (2:38) Time-Life R103-27 Love Me Tender.
    (S) (2:39) MCA 11069 From The Vaults - Decca Country Classics 1934-1973.
    (S) (2:39) Rhino 71581 Billboard Top Pop Hits, 1960.
    (S) (2:38) Chess 9352 Chess Rhythm & Roll.
    (S) (2:38) MCA Special Products 22179 Vintage Collectibles Volume 9.
    (M) (2:37) K-Tel 3125 Solid Gold Rock N' Roll.
    (S) (2:36) Nouveau 1060 O.S.T. This Boy's Life.

(S) (2:39) Time-Life R857-02 The Heart Of Rock 'n' Roll - 1960.
(S) (2:39) MCA Special Products 20900 Rock Around The Oldies #3.
(S) (2:36) MCA Special Products 20942 Trucker's Jukebox Volume 4.
(S) (2:38) MCA Special Products 20948 Biggest Summer Hits.
(S) (2:36) MCA 11389 O.S.T. Casino.
(S) (2:37) Decca 11330 The Nashville Sound....Owen Bradley.
(S) (2:38) Nick At Nite/550 Music/Epic 67689 Stand By Your Man.
(M) (2:38) JCI 3166 #1 Radio Hits 1960 - Only Rock 'n Roll - 1964.
(S) (2:38) Time-Life AM1-19 AM Gold - The Early '60s.
(S) (2:39) JCI 3184 1960 - Only Love - 1964.
(S) (2:39) Time-Life R857-21 The Heart Of Rock 'n' Roll Slow Dancing Classics.
(S) (2:37) Time-Life R814-05 Love Songs.
(S) (2:39) Time-Life R808-01 Classic Country 1960-1964.

1960 THAT'S ALL YOU GOTTA DO
(S) (2:27) MCA 10384 Anthology.
(S) (2:26) MCA 4012 Brenda Lee Story. *(truncated fade)*

1960 I WANT TO BE WANTED
(M) (3:02) MCA 5939 Vintage Music Volumes 17 & 18.
(M) (3:02) MCA 31215 Vintage Music Volume 18.
(S) (3:03) MCA 10384 Anthology.
(S) (3:02) MCA 4012 Brenda Lee Story.
(M) (3:02) Time-Life 2RNR-47 Rock 'N' Roll Era - Teen Idols II.
(M) (3:02) MCA Special Products 22132 Vintage Collectibles Volume 3.
(S) (3:02) Time-Life R857-10 The Heart Of Rock 'n' Roll 1960-1961.

1961 ROCKIN' AROUND THE CHRISTMAS TREE
(S) (2:03) Rhino 70192 Christmas Classics.
(S) (2:03) Rhino 70636 Billboard's Greatest Christmas Hits.
(S) (2:02) MCA 25991 Christmas Hits.
(S) (2:05) MCA 10384 Anthology.
(S) (2:07) Warner Brothers 26660 A Brenda Lee Christmas. *(rerecording; tracks into next selection)*
(M) (2:04) Curb 77515 Christmas All-Time Greatest Records Volume 2.
(E) (2:03) Time-Life 2RNR-XM Rock 'N' Roll Era - Jingle Bell Rock.
(S) (2:04) MCA 25084 Rockin' Little Christmas.
(M) (2:04) MCA Special Products 20728 Jingle Bell Rock.
(S) (2:03) Collectables 1511 and 2511 and 3511 and 4511 and 9611 and 9711 The Ultimate Christmas Album.
(M) (2:03) MCA Special Products 20629 A Country Christmas To Remember.
(S) (2:04) MCA Special Products 20782 A Christmas Treasury Of Classic Ladies.
(S) (2:02) Oglio 81570 The Coolest Christmas.
(S) (2:05) Warner Brothers 45363 A Christmas Tradition Vol. III. *(rerecording)*
(M) (2:02) LaserLight 12780 A Very Cherry Christmas.
(M) (2:03) Time-Life TCD-107 A Time-Life Treasury Of Christmas.
(S) (2:02) Time-Life R135-12 The Spirit Of Christmas.

1961 EMOTIONS
(M) (2:49) MCA 5937 Vintage Music Volumes 13 & 14.
(M) (2:49) MCA 31210 Vintage Music Volume 13.
(S) (2:48) MCA 10384 Anthology.
(S) (2:47) MCA 4012 Brenda Lee Story.
(S) (2:47) Time-Life R857-14 The Heart Of Rock 'n' Roll 1960-1961 Take Two.

1961 YOU CAN DEPEND ON ME
(S) (3:31) MCA 10384 Anthology.
(S) (3:29) MCA 4012 Brenda Lee Story.
(S) (3:31) Time-Life R974-12 Many Moods Of Romance - You Can Depend On Me.
(S) (3:30) Time-Life R857-19 The Heart Of Rock 'n' Roll 1960-1961 Take Three.

1961 DUM DUM
(S) (2:24) MCA 10384 Anthology.
(S) (2:23) MCA 4012 Brenda Lee Story.
(M) (2:21) Time-Life 2RNR-46 Rock 'N' Roll Era - 60's Juke Box Memories.

1961 FOOL #1
(S) (2:26) MCA 10384 Anthology.
(S) (2:24) MCA 4012 Brenda Lee Story.
(S) (2:25) Time-Life SUD-19 Superhits - Early 60's Classics.
(S) (2:25) Time-Life R857-03 The Heart Of Rock 'n' Roll - 1961.
(S) (2:25) Time-Life AM1-20 AM Gold - Early '60s Classics.

1961 ANYBODY BUT ME
(S) (2:23) MCA 4012 Brenda Lee Story.

1962 BREAK IT TO ME GENTLY
(S) (2:36) MCA 10384 Anthology.
(S) (2:35) MCA 4012 Brenda Lee Story.
(S) (2:36) Time-Life SUD-06 Superhits - 1962.
(S) (2:35) MCA Special Products 20943 Trucker's Jukebox Volume 5.
(S) (2:36) Time-Life R857-12 The Heart Of Rock 'n' Roll 1962-1963.
(S) (2:35) Time-Life AM1-18 AM Gold - 1962.
(S) (2:37) MCA 11539 O.S.T. Trees Lounge.

1962 EVERYBODY LOVES ME BUT YOU
(S) (2:29) MCA 10384 Anthology.
(S) (2:29) Time-Life R857-17 The Heart Of Rock 'n' Roll: The Early '60s.

1962 HEART IN HAND
(S) (2:27) MCA 5939 Vintage Music Volumes 17 & 18.
(S) (2:27) MCA 31214 Vintage Music Volume 17.
(S) (2:26) MCA 10384 Anthology.

1962 IT STARTED ALL OVER AGAIN
1962 ALL ALONE AM I
(M) (2:42) MCA 5936 Vintage Music Volumes 11 & 12.
(M) (2:42) MCA 31708 Vintage Music Volume 11.
(S) (2:42) MCA 10384 Anthology.
(S) (2:41) MCA 4012 Brenda Lee Story.
(S) (2:43) Time-Life SUD-06 Superhits - 1962.
(S) (2:43) Time-Life HPD-37 Your Hit Parade - The 60's.
(M) (2:42) Time-Life R138/05 Look Of Love.
(M) (2:42) MCA Special Products 21742 Vintage Collectibles Volume 12.
(S) (2:42) MCA Special Products 20841 Truckers Jukebox #1.
(M) (2:43) MCA Special Products 20958 Mellow Classics.
(S) (2:42) Time-Life R857-06 The Heart Of Rock 'n' Roll 1962.
(S) (2:43) Time-Life AM1-18 AM Gold - 1962.
(S) (2:43) Time-Life R814-03 Love Songs.

1963 YOUR USED TO BE
1963 LOSING YOU
(S) (2:31) MCA 10384 Anthology.
(S) (2:29) MCA 4012 Brenda Lee Story.
(S) (2:30) Time-Life R857-08 The Heart Of Rock 'n' Roll 1963.
(S) (2:31) Time-Life R857-18 The Heart Of Rock 'n' Roll 1962-1963 Take Two.

1963 MY WHOLE WORLD IS FALLING DOWN
(S) (1:54) MCA 10384 Anthology.
(S) (1:52) MCA 4012 Brenda Lee Story.

1963 I WONDER
(S) (2:57) MCA 10384 Anthology.

1963 THE GRASS IS GREENER
(S) (2:43) MCA 10384 Anthology.

1964 AS USUAL
(S) (2:33) MCA 10384 Anthology.
(S) (2:32) MCA 4012 Brenda Lee Story.

1964 THINK
1964 IS IT TRUE
(S) (2:29) MCA 10384 Anthology. *(includes :04 of studio talk)*
(S) (2:24) MCA Special Products 20957 Solid Gold Rock & Roll.

1965 THANKS A LOT
(S) (2:40) MCA 4012 Brenda Lee Story.

1965 TOO MANY RIVERS
    (S) (2:48) MCA 10384 Anthology.
    (S) (2:47) MCA 4012 Brenda Lee Story.
1965 RUSTY BELLS
1966 COMING ON STRONG
    (S) (2:01) MCA 10384 Anthology.
    (S) (1:59) MCA 4012 Brenda Lee Story.
1969 JOHNNY ONE TIME
    (S) (3:36) MCA 10384 Anthology. *(:21 longer than either the 45 or LP)*
    (S) (3:15) MCA 4012 Brenda Lee Story.

CURTIS LEE
1961 PRETTY LITTLE ANGEL EYES
    (M) (2:44) Abkco 7118 Phil Spector/Back To Mono (1958-1969).
    (M) (2:42) Time-Life 2RNR-18 Rock 'N' Roll Era - 1961 Still Rockin'.
    (M) (2:41) Original Sound 8852 Oldies But Goodies Vol. 2. *(this compact disc uses the "Waring - fds" noise reduction process)*
    (M) (2:41) Original Sound 2223 Oldies But Goodies Volumes 2,7,9,12 and 13 Box Set. *(this box set uses the "Waring - fds" noise reduction process)*
    (M) (2:41) Original Sound 2500 Oldies But Goodies Volumes 1-15 Box Set. *(this box set uses the "Waring - fds" noise reduction process)*
    (M) (2:40) Original Sound CDGO-10 Golden Oldies Volume. 10.
    (M) (2:40) Original Sound 8892 Dick Clark's 21 All-Time Hits Vol. 2.
    (M) (2:41) Collectables 2500 WCBS-FM History Of Rock - The 60's Part 1.
    (M) (2:41) Collectables 4500 History Of Rock/The 60s Part One.
    (M) (2:40) Time-Life R102-17 Lost Treasures Of Rock 'N' Roll.
    (M) (2:42) Varese Sarabande 5670 Songs Of Tommy Boyce And Bobby Hart.
    (M) (2:42) Rhino 72507 Doo Wop Box II.
    (M) (2:42) Collectables 5706 Pretty Little Angel Eyes - A Golden Classics Edition.
    (M) (2:40) Music Club 50015 Love Me Forever - 18 Rock'N' Roll Love Songs.

DICKEY LEE
1962 PATCHES
    (M) (2:57) Era 5025 The Brill Building Sound.
    (E) (2:57) Time-Life SUD-06 Superhits - 1962.
    (M) (2:57) K-Tel 3125 Solid Gold Rock N' Roll.
    (M) (2:56) DCC Compact Classics 078 Best Of Tragedy.
    (M) (2:56) Collectors' Choice 002 Teen Idols....For A Moment.
    (M) (2:56) Mercury 314526691 Fifty Years Of Country Music From Mercury.
    (M) (2:56) Eric 11503 Hard To Find 45's On CD (Volume II) 1961-64.
    (E) (2:57) Time-Life AM1-18 AM Gold - 1962.
    (M) (2:57) K-Tel 3885 Story Songs.
1963 I SAW LINDA YESTERDAY
    (M) (2:02) Mercury 816555 45's On CD Volume 2.
    (M) (1:58) Time-Life 2RNR-42 Rock 'N' Roll Era - The 60's Sock Hop.
    (M) (1:59) Eric 11503 Hard To Find 45's On CD (Volume II) 1961-64.
    (M) (2:00) Eclipse Music Group 64868 Rock 'n Roll Relix 1962-1963.
    (M) (2:00) Eclipse Music Group 64872 Rock 'n Roll Relix 1960-1969.
1965 LAURIE (STRANGE THINGS HAPPEN)
    (S) (3:04) Varese Sarabande 5705 Dick Bartley Presents Collector's Essentials: The 60's. *(mastered from vinyl)*

JACKIE LEE
1966 THE DUCK
    (M) (2:22) DCC Compact Classics 028 Sock Hop.

    (M) (2:13) Collectables 5063 History Of Rock Volume 3. *(mastered from vinyl)*
    (M) (2:19) Curb 77774 Hard To Find Hits Of Rock 'N' Roll Volume Two. *(mastered from vinyl)*
    (M) (2:19) JCI 3190 1965 - Only Dance - 1969. *(mastered from vinyl)*

JOHNNY LEE
1980 LOOKIN' FOR LOVE
    (S) (3:38) Curb 77532 Your Favorite Songs. *(rerecording)*
    (S) (3:37) Warner Brothers 25967 Country Love Songs.
    (S) (3:28) Warner Brothers 23967 Greatest Hits. *(truncated fade; :12 shorter than the 45 or LP)*
    (S) (3:28) Time-Life CCD-03 Contemporary Country - The Early 80's. *(:12 shorter than the 45 or LP)*
    (S) (3:36) Rhino 71893 Radio Daze: Pop Hits Of The 80's Volume Four.
    (S) (3:40) Full Moon/Elektra 60690 O.S.T. Urban Cowboy.
    (S) (3:28) K-Tel 3047 Country Music Classics Volume VI. *(:12 shorter than the 45 or LP)*
    (S) (3:28) JCI 3157 1980 - Only Country - 1984. *(:12 shorter than the 45 or LP)*
    (S) (3:29) Priority 50968 I Love Country Volume Three: Hits Of The 80's. *(:11 shorter than the 45 or LP)*
    (S) (3:29) K-Tel 3367 101 Greatest Country Hits Vol. Eight: Country Romance. *(rerecording)*
    (S) (3:27) Simitar 55082 80's Country 1980-82. *(:13 shorter than the 45 or LP)*

LAURA LEE
1971 WOMEN'S LOVE RIGHTS
    (S) (3:11) Rhino 70786 Soul Hits Of The 70's Volume 6.
    (S) (3:11) HDH 3903 Greatest Hits.
    (S) (3:10) Time-Life RHD-09 Rhythm & Blues - 1971.
    (S) (3:10) Time-Life R838-06 Solid Gold Soul - 1971.
    (S) (3:11) Rhino 72506 Go Girl! Soul Sisters Tellin' It Like It Is.

LEAPY LEE
1968 LITTLE ARROWS
    (M) (2:56) K-Tel 413 Country Music Classics Volume III. *(45 length)*
    (S) (2:40) MCA Special Products 20981 Bubble Gum Classics. *(LP length)*

PEGGY LEE
1958 FEVER
    (S) (3:19) Capitol 90592 Memories Are Made Of This.
    (M) (3:18) Curb 77379 All-Time Greatest Hits.
    (S) (2:59) Capitol 98670 Memories Are Made Of This. *(live)*
    (M) (3:19) Rhino 71252 Sentimental Journey: Pop Vocal Classics Volume 4 (1954-1959).
    (M) (3:19) Rhino 72034 Sentimental Journey Pop Vocal Classics Volumes 1-4 Box Set.
    (M) (3:19) Time-Life HPD-11 Your Hit Parade 1958.
    (S) (3:19) K-Tel 6023 Great Ladies Of Jazz.
    (S) (3:20) Capitol 28533 Spotlight On.
    (S) (3:18) CEMA Special Markets 36258 Fever & Other Hits.
    (M) (3:19) Rhino 72413 Sentimental Favorites.
    (S) (3:18) JCI 7003 Those Wonderful Years - Fever!
    (S) (3:19) Capitol 35972 Ultra Lounge Volume Five: Wild, Cool & Swingin'.
    (M) (3:19) Flashback 72709 Sentimental Favorites.
    (M) (3:19) Capitol 21204 Best Of The Capitol Years.
    (S) (3:19) Capitol 97826 Miss Peggy Lee (Box Set).
    (M) (3:19) Time-Life R132-10 Love Songs Of Your Hit Parade.
1969 IS THAT ALL THERE IS
    (S) (4:19) Curb 77379 All-Time Greatest Hits.
    (S) (4:18) Time-Life R138/05 Look Of Love.
    (S) (4:18) CEMA Special Markets 36258 Fever & Other Hits.
    (S) (4:18) Right Stuff 52289 Free To Be Volume 5.
    (S) (4:18) Capitol 97826 Miss Peggy Lee (Box Set).

RAYMOND LEFEVRE
1958 THE DAY THE RAINS CAME
1968 AME CALINE (SOUL COAXING)

LEFT BANKE
1966 WALK AWAY RENEE
- (S) (2:40) Warner Special Products 27607 Highs Of The 60's.
- (S) (2:41) Mercury 848095 There's Gonna Be A Storm. *(remixed)*
- (S) (2:40) Time-Life 2CLR-07 Classic Rock - 1966: The Beat Goes On.
1967 PRETTY BALLERINA
- (S) (2:34) Mercury 848095 There's Gonna Be A Storm.

LEMON PIPERS
1968 GREEN TAMBOURINE
- (S) (2:24) Rhino 70629 Billboard's Top Rock & Roll Hits Of 1968.
- (S) (2:24) Rhino 72005 Billboard's Top Rock & Roll Hits 1968-1972 Box Set.
- (S) (2:24) Pair 1202 Best Of Buddah.
- (S) (2:24) Pair 1199 Best Of Bubblegum Music.
- (S) (2:24) K-Tel 666 Flower Power.
- (S) (2:24) K-Tel 205 Battle Of The Bands Volume 3.
- (S) (2:24) Special Music 4914 Best Of The Bubblegum Years.
- (S) (2:24) Rhino 70495 Fun Rock!
- (S) (2:23) Collectables 5064 History Of Rock Volume 4.
- (S) (2:24) Collectables 0533 Golden Classics.
- (S) (2:24) Essex 7060 The Buddah Box.
- (S) (2:24) Time-Life 2CLR-11 Classic Rock - 1968: The Beat Goes On.
- (S) (2:23) Time-Life SUD-14 Superhits - The Late 60's.
- (S) (2:24) Buddah 49507 Psychedelic Pop.
- (S) (2:24) Buddah 49516 Complete Buddah Chart Singles Volume One.
- (S) (2:23) Buddah 49514 Green Tambourine.
- (S) (2:24) Time-Life 2CLR-31 Classic Rock - Totally Fantastic '60s.
- (S) (2:23) Time-Life AM1-14 AM Gold - The Late '60s.
- (S) (2:24) BMG Special Products 44643 The Best Of Buddah.

JOHN LENNON (also PLASTIC ONO BAND)
released as by THE PLASTIC ONO BAND:
1969 GIVE PEACE A CHANCE
- (S) (:58) Capitol 46642 Shaved Fish. *(introduction only)*
- (S) (4:51) Capitol 90803 Music From The Original Motion Picture "Imagine". *(with countoff)*
- (S) (4:50) Capitol 91516 Collection. *(with countoff)*
- (S) (4:50) Capitol 95220 Lennon. *(with countoff)*
- (S) (4:50) Parlophone 21954 Lennon Legend. *(with countoff)*
1970 COLD TURKEY
- (S) (5:00) Capitol 46642 Shaved Fish.
- (S) (5:01) Capitol 91516 Collection.
- (S) (5:00) Capitol 95220 Lennon.
- (S) (5:00) Parlophone 21954 Lennon Legend.
released as by JOHN ONO LENNON:
1970 INSTANT KARMA (WE ALL SHINE ON)
- (S) (3:19) Capitol 46642 Shaved Fish.
- (S) (3:19) Capitol 91516 Collection.
- (S) (3:19) Capitol 95220 Lennon.
- (S) (3:18) Parlophone 21954 Lennon Legend.
released as by JOHN LENNON/PLASTIC ONO BAND:
1971 MOTHER
- (S) (5:33) Parlophone 46770 Plastic Ono Band. *(LP version)*
- (S) (5:01) Capitol 46642 Shaved Fish. *(edit of LP version)*
- (S) (4:44) Capitol 90803 Music From The Original Motion Picture "Imagine". *(live version)*
- (S) (5:33) Capitol 95220 Lennon. *(LP version)*
- (S) (3:52) Parlophone 21954 Lennon Legend. *(45 version)*
1971 POWER TO THE PEOPLE
- (S) (3:19) Capitol 46642 Shaved Fish.
- (S) (3:15) Capitol 91516 Collection.

- (S) (3:15) Capitol 95220 Lennon.
- (S) (3:16) Parlophone 21954 Lennon Legend.
1971 IMAGINE
- (S) (3:01) Capitol 46642 Shaved Fish.
- (S) (3:01) Capitol 90803 Music From The Original Motion Picture "Imagine".
- (S) (3:01) Capitol 91516 Collection.
- (S) (3:01) Capitol 95220 Lennon.
- (S) (3:01) Capitol 46641 Imagine.
- (S) (3:00) Polydor 314529508 O.S.T. Mr. Holland's Opus.
- (S) (3:01) Parlophone 21954 Lennon Legend.
released as by JOHN & YOKO with THE HARLEM COMMUNITY CHOIR:
1972 HAPPY XMAS (WAR IS OVER)
- (S) (4:11) Capitol 46642 Shaved Fish. *(with "GIVE PEACE A CHANCE" reprise found on the "Shaved Fish" vinyl LP)*
- (S) (3:31) Capitol 91516 Collection. *(45 version)*
- (S) (3:31) Capitol 95220 Lennon. *(45 version)*
- (S) (3:30) Capitol 35347 Superstars Of Christmas 1995. *(45 version)*
- (S) (3:32) Epic 68750 Superstar Christmas. *(45 version)*
- (S) (3:31) Parlophone 21954 Lennon Legend. *(45 version)*
released as by JOHN LENNON:
1973 MIND GAMES
- (S) (4:11) Parlophone 46769 Mind Games.
- (S) (4:11) Capitol 46642 Shaved Fish.
- (S) (4:11) Capitol 91516 Collection.
- (S) (4:10) Capitol 95220 Lennon.
- (S) (4:09) Parlophone 21954 Lennon Legend.
released as by JOHN LENNON with THE PLASTIC ONO NUCLEAR BAND:
1974 WHATEVER GETS YOU THRU THE NIGHT
(actual 45 time is (3:16) not (3:20) as stated on the record label)
- (S) (3:26) Capitol 95220 Lennon. *(LP length)*
- (S) (3:26) Capitol 46768 Walls And Bridges. *(LP length)*
- (S) (3:01) Capitol 46642 Shaved Fish. *(edited just like the vinyl LP "Shaved Fish")*
- (S) (3:16) Capitol 91516 Collection. *(45 length)*
- (S) (3:17) Parlophone 21954 Lennon Legend. *(45 length)*
released as by JOHN LENNON:
1975 #9 DREAM
(dj copies of this 45 ran (2:58); commercial copies all ran (4:44))
- (S) (4:45) Capitol 95220 Lennon.
- (S) (4:45) Capitol 46768 Walls And Bridges.
- (S) (4:45) Capitol 46642 Shaved Fish.
- (S) (4:45) Capitol 91516 Collection.
- (S) (4:45) Parlophone 21954 Lennon Legend.
1975 STAND BY ME
- (S) (3:25) SBK 93744 China Beach - Music And Memories.
- (S) (3:26) Capitol 95220 Lennon.
- (S) (3:26) Capitol 46707 Rock 'N' Roll.
- (S) (3:25) Capitol 90803 Music From The Original Motion Picture "Imagine".
- (S) (3:24) Capitol 91516 Collection.
- (S) (3:25) Parlophone 21954 Lennon Legend.
1980 (JUST LIKE) STARTING OVER
(dj copies of this song on a 12" single ran (4:17))
- (S) (3:55) Capitol 95220 Lennon.
- (S) (3:54) Geffen 2001 Double Fantasy.
- (S) (3:55) Capitol 91425 Double Fantasy.
- (S) (3:56) Capitol 90803 Music From The Original Motion Picture "Imagine".
- (S) (3:53) Capitol 91516 Collection.
- (S) (3:53) Time-Life R13610 Gold And Platinum Box Set - The Ultimate Rock Collection.
- (S) (3:53) Parlophone 21954 Lennon Legend.
- (S) (3:55) MFSL 600 Double Fantasy. *(gold disc)*
1981 WOMAN
- (S) (3:24) Capitol 95220 Lennon.
- (S) (3:31) Geffen 2001 Double Fantasy.
- (S) (3:32) Capitol 91425 Double Fantasy.
- (S) (3:30) Capitol 90803 Music From The Original Motion Picture "Imagine".
- (S) (3:24) Capitol 91516 Collection.

JOHN LENNON (Continued)
- (S) (3:24) Parlophone 21954 Lennon Legend.
- (S) (3:32) MFSL 600 Double Fantasy. *(gold disc)*

1981 WATCHING THE WHEELS
- (S) (3:30) Capitol 95220 Lennon. *(45 version)*
- (S) (3:30) Geffen 2001 Double Fantasy. *(LP version; ending of this song mistakenly added to the intro of the next selection; tracks into next selection)*
- (S) (3:59) Capitol 91425 Double Fantasy. *(LP version; tracks into the next selection)*
- (S) (3:59) MFSL 600 Double Fantasy. *(LP version; tracks into the next selection)*
- (S) (3:29) Capitol 91516 Collection. *(45 version)*
- (S) (3:29) Parlophone 21954 Lennon Legend. *(45 version)*

1984 NOBODY TOLD ME
- (S) (3:33) Polydor 314515913 Classic Rock Box.
- (S) (3:33) Polydor 817160 Milk And Honey.
- (S) (3:31) Capitol 95220 Lennon.
- (S) (3:31) Parlophone 21954 Lennon Legend.

JULIAN LENNON
1984 VALOTTE
- (S) (4:14) Atlantic 81908 Classic Rock 1966-1988.
- (S) (4:14) Priority 53769 Rock Of The 80's Volume 10.
- (S) (4:15) Atlantic 80184 Valotte.

1985 TOO LATE FOR GOODBYES
- (S) (3:33) Atlantic 80184 Valotte.
- (S) (3:33) Priority 53746 80's Greatest Rock Hits Vol. 12 - Singers/Songwriters.

1985 SAY YOU'RE WRONG
- (S) (3:28) Atlantic 80184 Valotte.

1986 STICK AROUND
- (S) (4:03) Atlantic 81640 Secret Value Of Daydreaming.

LENNON SISTERS (see LAWRENCE WELK)

ANNIE LENNOX
released as by ANNIE LENNOX & AL GREEN:
1989 PUT A LITTLE LOVE IN YOUR HEART
- (S) (3:48) A&M 3921 O.S.T. Scrooged.
released as by ANNIE LENNOX:
1992 WHY
- (S) (4:52) Mercury 314525354 Women For Women.
- (S) (4:52) Arista 18704 Diva.

1992 WALKING ON BROKEN GLASS
- (S) (6:09) Arista 18735 House Of Groove. *(remix)*
- (S) (4:12) Arista 18704 Diva.

1995 NO MORE "I LOVE YOU'S"
- (S) (4:50) Arista 25717 Medusa.
- (S) (3:12) Arista 18943 Ultimate Dance Party 1997. *(all selections on this cd are segued together; remix)*

LE ROUX
1982 NOBODY SAID IT WAS EASY
- (S) (4:05) Razor & Tie 2114 Bayou Degradable: The Best Of.

KETTY LESTER
1962 LOVE LETTERS
- (E) (2:33) Time-Life 2RNR-29 Rock 'N' Roll Era - The 60's Rave On.
- (M) (2:32) Time-Life RHD-11 Rhythm & Blues - 1962.
- (M) (2:39) Time-Life SUD-06 Superhits - 1962.
- (E) (2:33) Time-Life OPCD-4517 Tonight's The Night.
- (E) (2:40) LaserLight 12321 Soulful Love.
- (E) (2:40) K-Tel 539 Great Ladies Of Jazz.
- (E) (2:39) Curb 77775 Hard To Find Original Recordings - Classic Hits.
- (M) (2:39) Time-Life R974-03 Many Moods Of Romance - I Wish You Love.
- (M) (2:42) Hip-O 40029 The Glory Of Love - '60s Sweet & Soulful Love Songs.
- (M) (2:41) Rhino 72618 Smooth Grooves: The '60s Volume 1 Early '60s.
- (M) (2:39) Time-Life R857-06 The Heart Of Rock 'n' Roll 1962.
- (M) (2:39) Time-Life AM1-18 AM Gold - 1962.
- (M) (2:32) Time-Life R838-18 Solid Gold Soul 1962.
- (M) (2:39) Hip-O 40083 The King's Record Collection Vol. 2.

LETTERMEN
1961 THE WAY YOU LOOK TONIGHT
- (S) (2:19) Capitol 46626 All-Time Greatest Hits.
- (S) (2:19) Capitol 48438 Best Of.
- (S) (2:19) Capitol 98537 Capitol Collector's Series.
- (S) (2:19) Curb 77595 Best Of.
- (S) (2:19) Time-Life R857-03 The Heart Of Rock 'n' Roll - 1961.
- (S) (2:19) Time-Life R138-32 Hollywood Hit Parade.
- (S) (2:19) Time-Life R974-02 Many Moods Of Romance - My Heart Reminds Me.
- (S) (2:18) Time-Life R814-02 Love Songs.

1961 WHEN I FALL IN LOVE
- (S) (2:26) Capitol 46626 All-Time Greatest Hits.
- (S) (2:26) Capitol 48438 Best Of.
- (S) (2:21) Capitol 98670 Memories Are Made Of This. *(live)*
- (S) (2:26) Capitol 98537 Capitol Collector's Series.
- (S) (2:25) Curb 77595 Best Of.
- (S) (2:25) Scotti Brothers 75405 There Is Still Love (The Anniversary Songs).
- (S) (2:25) Time-Life SUD-06 Superhits - 1962.
- (S) (2:25) Time-Life HPD-33 Your Hit Parade - The Early 60's.
- (S) (2:25) Time-Life R138/05 Look Of Love.
- (S) (2:26) Time-Life R974-01 Many Moods Of Romance - That's My Desire.
- (S) (2:26) Time-Life R857-06 The Heart Of Rock 'n' Roll 1962.
- (S) (2:25) Time-Life AM1-18 AM Gold - 1962.
- (S) (2:25) Time-Life R814-01 Love Songs.

1962 COME BACK SILLY GIRL
- (S) (2:25) Capitol 98537 Capitol Collector's Series. *(truncated fade)*

1965 THEME FROM "A SUMMER PLACE"
- (M) (2:02) Capitol 46626 All-Time Greatest Hits.
- (S) (2:04) Capitol 48438 Best Of.
- (S) (2:05) Capitol 98537 Capitol Collector's Series.
- (S) (2:05) Curb 77595 Best Of.

1968 GOIN' OUT OF MY HEAD/CAN'T TAKE MY EYES OFF YOU
- (S) (3:10) Capitol 46626 All-Time Greatest Hits.
- (S) (3:04) Capitol 98537 Capitol Collector's Series.
- (S) (3:08) Curb 77595 Best Of.
- (S) (3:02) Time-Life SUD-02 Superhits - 1968.
- (S) (3:02) Time-Life AM1-04 AM Gold - 1968.
- (S) (3:02) Time-Life R814-05 Love Songs.

1969 HURT SO BAD
- (S) (2:17) Capitol 46626 All-Time Greatest Hits.
- (S) (2:17) Capitol 98537 Capitol Collector's Series.

LEVEL 42
1986 SOMETHING ABOUT YOU
- (S) (3:42) Priority 53769 Rock Of The 80's Volume 10. *(45 version)*
- (S) (3:43) Polydor 841399 Level Best. *(45 version)*
- (S) (4:23) Polydor 829627 World Machine. *(LP version)*
- (S) (5:45) Rebound 314520354 World Of Dance: New Wave - The 80's. *(neither the 45, LP or 12" single version)*
- (S) (4:22) Special Music 5041 Great Britons! Volume Three. *(LP version)*
- (S) (3:42) Rebound 314520434 Classic Rock - 80's. *(45 version)*
- (S) (3:42) Time-Life R988-17 Sounds Of The Eighties: The Mid '80s Take Two. *(45 version)*
- (S) (5:45) Rebound 314520442 The Roots Of Rock: 80's New Wave. *(neither the 45, LP or 12" single version)*

1987 LESSONS IN LOVE
- (S) (4:03) Polydor 831593 Running In The Family.
- (S) (4:00) Polydor 841399 Level Best.

LEVERT
1987 CASANOVA
- (S) (4:57) Atlantic 81809 O.S.T. Fatal Beauty. *(soundtrack version)*

(S) (6:12) Atlantic 81913 Golden Age Of Black Music (1977-1988). *(LP version)*

(S) (4:02) JCI 2701 Slow Grooves. *(45 version)*

(S) (6:13) Atlantic 81773 The Big Throwdown. *(LP version)*

(S) (4:03) MCA 11329 Soul Train 25th Anniversary Box Set. *(45 version)*

(S) (6:12) Scotti Bros. 75481 Quiet Storm Memories. *(LP version)*

(S) (4:21) Rhino 72142 Billboard Hot R&B Hits 1987. *(45 version but :19 longer fade)*

(S) (6:13) Elektra 62089 Maximum R&B. *(LP version)*

GERALD LEVERT
1994 I'D GIVE ANYTHING
(S) (4:07) Eastwest 92416 Groove On.

BARBARA LEWIS
1963 HELLO STRANGER
(S) (2:40) Rhino 70649 Billboard's Top R&B Hits Of 1963.

(S) (2:40) Atlantic 81297 Atlantic Rhythm & Blues Volume 5.

(M) (2:36) Original Sound 8865 Oldies But Goodies Vol. 15. *(this compact disc uses the "Waring - fds" noise reduction process)*

(M) (2:36) Original Sound 2222 Oldies But Goodies Volumes 3,5,11,14 and 15 Box Set. *(this box set uses the "Waring - fds" noise reduction process)*

(M) (2:36) Original Sound 2500 Oldies But Goodies Volumes 1-15 Box Set. *(this box set uses the "Waring - fds" noise reduction process)*

(M) (2:34) Original Sound CDGO-11 Golden Oldies Volume. 11.

(S) (2:38) Original Sound 9306 Dedicated To You Vol. 6.

(M) (2:40) Rhino 75891 Wonder Women.

(S) (2:40) Atlantic 82305 Atlantic Rhythm And Blues 1947-1974 Box Set.

(S) (2:38) Collectables 5104 Golden Classics.

(S) (2:39) Ripete 2392192 Beach Music Anthology Box Set.

(S) (2:39) Collectables 5065 History Of Rock Volume 5.

(S) (2:38) Ripete 0001 Coolin' Out/24 Carolina Classics Volume 1.

(S) (2:39) Time-Life 2RNR-07 Rock 'N' Roll Era - 1963.

(S) (2:38) Time-Life RHD-02 Rhythm & Blues - 1963.

(S) (2:39) Time-Life SUD-08 Superhits - 1963.

(S) (2:39) Collectables 2603 WCBS-FM Jukebox Giants Vol. 1.

(S) (2:38) Right Stuff 27306 Slow Jams: The 60's Volume One.

(S) (2:39) Time-Life OPCD-4517 Tonight's The Night.

(M) (2:39) Thump 7010 Low Rider Oldies Volume 1.

(M) (2:40) JCI/Telstar 3516 Sweet Soul Sisters.

(S) (2:43) Rhino 71619 Hello Stranger - Best Of.

(M) (2:36) Collectables 2505 History Of Rock - The 60's Part 5.

(M) (2:36) Collectables 4505 History Of Rock/The 60s Part Five.

(M) (2:34) Collectables 2554 CBS-FM History Of Rock Volume 2.

(M) (2:39) K-Tel 3269 Carolina Beach Music.

(M) (2:40) Rhino 72618 Smooth Grooves: The '60s Volume 1 Early '60s.

(S) (2:39) Time-Life R857-08 The Heart Of Rock 'n' Roll 1963.

(S) (2:39) Time-Life AM1-17 AM Gold - 1963.

(S) (2:38) Time-Life R838-14 Solid Gold Soul - 1963.

(S) (2:42) Repeat/Relativity 1610 Tighten Up: #1 Soul Hits Of The 60's Volume 2.

(M) (2:40) Rhino 72962 Ultimate '60s Soul Sensations.

1964 PUPPY LOVE
(S) (2:19) Rhino 71619 Hello Stranger - Best Of.

(S) (2:17) Collectables 5104 Golden Classics.

(S) (2:17) Ripete 0001 Coolin' Out/24 Carolina Classics Vol. 1.

1965 BABY, I'M YOURS
(S) (2:29) Atlantic 81297 Atlantic Rhythm & Blues Volume 5.

(S) (2:29) Atlantic 82305 Atlantic Rhythm And Blues 1947-1974 Box Set.

(S) (2:27) Collectables 5104 Golden Classics. *(truncated fade)*

(S) (2:29) Ripete 2392192 Beach Music Anthology Box Set.

(S) (2:28) Collectables 5066 History Of Rock Volume 6.

(S) (2:28) Time-Life RHD-07 Rhythm & Blues - 1965.

(S) (2:29) Time-Life 2CLR-01 Classic Rock - 1965.

(S) (2:28) Time-Life OPCD-4517 Tonight's The Night.

(M) (2:27) JCI/Telstar 3516 Sweet Soul Sisters.

(S) (2:30) LaserLight 12321 Soulful Love.

(S) (2:28) Ripete 2163-RE Ebb Tide.

(S) (2:30) Rhino 71619 Hello Stranger - Best Of.

(S) (2:30) Malpaso/Warner Brothers 45949 O.S.T. The Bridges Of Madison County.

(S) (2:28) Right Stuff 30578 Slow Jams: The 60's Volume 4.

(S) (2:30) K-Tel 3518 Sweet Soul Music.

(S) (2:28) Time-Life R838-12 Solid Gold Soul - 1965.

(M) (2:27) Rhino 72815 Beg, Scream & Shout! The Big Ol' Box Of '60s Soul.

(M) (2:27) Flashback 72895 25 Years Of R&B - 1965.

(M) (2:27) Rhino 72963 Ultimate '60s Soul Smashes.

(S) (2:29) Time-Life R857-20 The Heart Of Rock 'n' Roll 1965-1966.

1965 MAKE ME YOUR BABY
(S) (2:29) Warner Special Products 27601 Atlantic Soul Classics.

(S) (2:30) Rhino 75891 Wonder Women.

(E) (2:28) Collectables 5104 Golden Classics.

(S) (2:27) Time-Life 2CLR-14 Classic Rock - 1965: Shakin' All Over.

(S) (2:28) Time-Life SUD-03 Superhits - 1965.

(S) (2:29) JCI/Telstar 3516 Sweet Soul Sisters.

(S) (2:29) Rhino 71619 Hello Stranger - Best Of.

(S) (2:29) Ripete 2148-RE Beach Beat Classics Volume III.

(M) (2:28) Rhino 72619 Smooth Grooves: The '60s Volume 2 Mid '60s.

(S) (2:28) Time-Life AM1-10 AM Gold - 1965.

1966 MAKE ME BELONG TO YOU
(S) (2:27) Ripete 2146-RE Beach Beat Classics Vol. 1.

(S) (2:27) Rhino 71619 Hello Stranger - Best Of.

(S) (2:27) Collectables 5104 Golden Classics.

BOBBY LEWIS
1961 TOSSIN' AND TURNIN'
(actual 45 time is (2:29) not (2:40) as stated on the record label)

(S) (2:33) Rhino 75893 Jukebox Classics Volume 1. *(with a :12 introduction; missing a hi-hat overdub; faded :08 sooner than the 45)*

(S) (2:33) Rhino 70622 Billboard's Top Rock & Roll Hits Of 1961. *(with a :12 introduction; missing a hi-hat overdub; faded :08 sooner than the 45)*

(S) (2:33) Rhino 72004 Billboard's Top Rock & Roll Hits 1957-1961 Box Set. *(with a :12 introduction; missing a hi-hat overdub; faded :08 sooner than the 45)*

(S) (2:33) JCI 3110 Sock Hoppin' Sixties. *(with a :12 introduction; no high end; missing a hi-hat overdub; faded :08 sooner than the 45)*

(S) (2:17) Original Sound 8855 Oldies But Goodies Vol. 5. *(this compact disc uses the "Waring - fds" noise reduction process; ambient background noise throughout the disc; missing a hi-hat overdub; faded :12 sooner than the 45)*

(S) (2:17) Original Sound 2222 Oldies But Goodies Volumes 3,5,11,14 and 15 Box Set. *(this box set uses the "Waring - fds" noise reduction process; ambient background noise throughout the song; missing a hi-hat overdub; faded :12 sooner than the 45)*

BOBBY LEWIS *(Continued)*

> (S) (2:17) Original Sound 2500 Oldies But Goodies Volumes 1-15 Box Set. *(this box set uses the "Waring - fds" noise reduction process; ambient background noise throughout the song; missing a hi-hat overdub; faded :12 sooner than the 45)*
>
> (E) (2:17) Original Sound CDGO-10 Golden Oldies Volume. 10. *(faded :12 sooner than the 45)*
>
> (E) (2:17) Original Sound 8881 Twenty-One #1 Hits. *(this compact disc uses the "Waring - fds" noise reduction process; faded :12 sooner than the 45)*
>
> (E) (2:17) Original Sound 8892 Dick Clark's 21 All-Time Hits Vol. 2. *(faded :12 sooner than the 45)*
>
> (M) (2:14) MCA 31023 O.S.T. Animal House. *(edited; all tracks on this cd are segued together)*
>
> (S) (2:19) Relic 7041 Tossin' N Turnin'. *(missing a hi-hat overdub; faded :10 sooner than the 45)*
>
> (S) (2:18) Collectables 5066 History Of Rock Volume 6. *(missing a hi-hat overdub; faded :11 sooner than the 45)*
>
> (M) (2:15) Time-Life 2RNR-04 Rock 'N' Roll Era - 1961. *(original pressings of this song on this cd were (S) with a :12 introduction and missing a hi-hat overdub; faded :14 sooner than the 45)*
>
> (M) (2:16) Time-Life RHD-14 Rhythm & Blues - 1961. *(faded :13 sooner than the 45)*
>
> (S) (2:16) Collectables 2502 WCBS-FM History Of Rock - The 60's Part 3. *(missing a hi-hat overdub; faded :13 sooner than the 45)*
>
> (S) (2:16) Collectables 4502 History Of Rock/The 60s Part Three. *(missing a hi-hat overdub; faded :13 sooner than the 45)*
>
> (M) (2:15) JCI 3125 1960 - Only Rock 'N Roll - 1964. *(faded :14 sooner than the 45)*
>
> (S) (2:31) Priority 50951 I Love Rock & Roll Volume 2: Hits Of The 60's. *(with :12 introduction; missing a hi-hat overdub; faded :10 sooner than the 45)*
>
> (M) (2:16) Time-Life R838-19 Solid Gold Soul 1961. *(faded :13 sooner than the 45)*

1961 ONE TRACK MIND

> (S) (2:06) Rhino 75894 Jukebox Classics Volume 2.
>
> (S) (2:05) Relic 7041 Tossin' N Turnin'.

DONNA LEWIS

1996 I LOVE YOU ALWAYS FOREVER

> (S) (3:57) Atlantic 82762 Now In A Minute.
>
> (S) (4:39) Atlantic 82762 Now In A Minute. *(remix)*

GARY LEWIS and THE PLAYBOYS

1965 THIS DIAMOND RING
(both the 45 and LP length is (2:01))

> (S) (2:07) Rhino 70626 Billboard's Top Rock & Roll Hits Of 1965.
>
> (S) (2:07) Rhino 72007 Billboard's Top Rock & Roll Hits 1962-1966 Box Set.
>
> (S) (2:13) EMI 96268 24 Greatest Hits Of All Time. *(truncated fade)*
>
> (S) (2:01) EMI 91474 Golden Greats. *(noise on fadeout)*
>
> (S) (2:13) EMI 93449 Legendary Masters Series. *(truncated fade)*
>
> (S) (2:13) Capitol 98139 Spring Break Volume 2. *(truncated fade)*
>
> (S) (2:07) Time-Life 2CLR-01 Classic Rock - 1965.
>
> (S) (2:11) Time-Life SUD-03 Superhits - 1965.
>
> (S) (2:10) Time-Life R962-04 History Of Rock 'N' Roll: California Pop 1963-1967.
>
> (S) (2:07) Curb 77667 Greatest Hits.
>
> (S) (2:11) JCI 3167 #1 Radio Hits 1965 - Only Rock 'n Roll - 1969.
>
> (S) (2:11) Time-Life AM1-10 AM Gold - 1965.

1965 COUNT ME IN

> (S) (2:31) EMI 93449 Legendary Masters Series. *(with countoff)*
>
> (S) (2:22) Time-Life 2CLR-14 Classic Rock - 1965: Shakin' All Over.
>
> (S) (2:22) Curb 77667 Greatest Hits.

1965 SAVE YOUR HEART FOR ME

> (S) (1:54) EMI 91474 Golden Greats.
>
> (S) (2:01) EMI 93449 Legendary Masters Series. *(with countoff)*
>
> (S) (1:54) Time-Life 2CLR-23 Classic Rock - 1965: Blowin' Your Mind.
>
> (S) (1:55) Time-Life SUD-12 Superhits - The Mid 60's.
>
> (S) (1:56) Curb 77667 Greatest Hits.
>
> (S) (1:55) Time-Life AM1-05 AM Gold - The Mid '60s.

1965 EVERYBODY LOVES A CLOWN
(both the 45 and LP length was (2:18))

> (S) (2:23) EMI 91474 Golden Greats.
>
> (S) (2:23) EMI 93449 Legendary Masters Series.
>
> (S) (2:23) EMI 80056 Everybody Loves A Clown/She's Just My Style.
>
> (S) (2:22) Time-Life 2CLR-29 Classic Rock - Bubblegum, Garage And Pop Nuggets.
>
> (S) (2:22) Curb 77667 Greatest Hits.

1966 SHE'S JUST MY STYLE

> (S) (2:51) EMI 91474 Golden Greats.
>
> (S) (3:10) EMI 93449 Legendary Masters Series. *(with countoff; :15 longer than either the 45 or LP)*
>
> (S) (3:12) EMI 80056 Everybody Loves A Clown/She's Just My Style. *(:17 longer than either the 45 or LP)*
>
> (S) (3:00) Time-Life SUD-01 Superhits - 1966.
>
> (S) (2:46) Curb 77667 Greatest Hits.
>
> (M) (2:47) Rhino 71936 Billboard Top Pop Hits, 1966.
>
> (S) (2:59) Time-Life AM1-09 AM Gold - 1966.

1966 SURE GONNA MISS HER

> (S) (2:12) EMI 91474 Golden Greats. *(stereo LP version)*
>
> (S) (2:30) EMI 93449 Legendary Masters Series. *(45 and mono LP version)*
>
> (S) (2:16) Curb 77667 Greatest Hits. *(stereo LP version)*

1966 GREEN GRASS

> (S) (2:13) EMI 93449 Legendary Masters Series.
>
> (S) (2:15) Curb 77667 Greatest Hits.
>
> (S) (2:11) Buddah 49506 Feelin' Groovy.

1966 MY HEART'S SYMPHONY

> (S) (3:01) EMI 93449 Legendary Masters Series. *(with countoff; :20 longer than either the 45 or LP)*
>
> (S) (2:33) Curb 77667 Greatest Hits.

1966 (YOU DON'T HAVE TO) PAINT ME A PICTURE

> (S) (2:32) EMI 93449 Legendary Masters Series. *(includes :10 of studio talk)*
>
> (S) (2:21) Curb 77667 Greatest Hits.

1967 WHERE WILL THE WORDS COME FROM

> (S) (1:59) EMI 93449 Legendary Masters Series.

1967 THE LOSER (WITH A BROKEN HEART)

> (S) (2:17) EMI 93449 Legendary Masters Series.

1967 GIRLS IN LOVE

> (S) (2:24) EMI 93449 Legendary Masters Series.

1968 SEALED WITH A KISS

> (S) (2:25) EMI 93449 Legendary Masters Series.
>
> (S) (2:25) Curb 77667 Greatest Hits.

HUEY LEWIS

1982 DO YOU BELIEVE IN LOVE

> (S) (3:27) Chrysalis 21340 and 41340 Picture This.
>
> (S) (3:26) Elektra 61977 Time Flies....Best Of.
>
> (S) (3:25) Time-Life R988-14 Sounds Of The Eighties: 1980-1982.
>
> (S) (3:27) Simitar 55582 The Number One's: Rock It Up.

1982 HOPE YOU LOVE ME LIKE YOU SAY YOU DO

> (S) (3:43) Chrysalis 21340 and 41340 Picture This.

1983 HEART AND SOUL

> (S) (3:55) T.J. Martell Foundation/Columbia 40315 Music For The Miracle. *(45 length)*
>
> (S) (4:11) Chrysalis 21412 and 41412 Sports. *(LP length)*
>
> (S) (4:10) Elektra 61977 Time Flies....Best Of. *(LP length)*
>
> (S) (4:11) Priority 50953 I Love Rock & Roll Volume 4: Hits Of The 80's. *(LP length)*
>
> (S) (4:10) Time-Life R988-18 Sounds Of The Eighties: The Early '80s Take Two. *(LP length)*

1984 I WANT A NEW DRUG

> (S) (4:43) Chrysalis 21412 and 41412 Sports. *(LP version)*
>
> (S) (4:43) Time-Life R988-11 Sounds Of The 80's: 1983-1984. *(LP version)*

(S) (4:42) Elektra 61977 Time Flies....Best Of. *(LP version)*
(S) (4:43) Time-Life R968-20 Guitar Rock - The '80s. *(LP version)*

1984 THE HEART OF ROCK & ROLL
(actual 45 time is (4:03) not (3:58) as stated
on the record label)
(S) (5:04) Chrysalis 21412 and 41412 Sports. *(LP version)*
(S) (5:03) Time-Life R968-13 Guitar Rock - The Early '80s. *(LP version)*
(S) (5:01) RCA 66862 Hi Octane Hard Drivin' Hits. *(LP version)*
(S) (5:03) Elektra 61977 Time Flies....Best Of. *(LP version)*
(S) (4:03) Time-Life R988-17 Sounds Of The Eighties: The Mid '80s Take Two. *(45 version)*
(S) (4:10) Cold Front 6255 Greatest Sports Rock And Jams Volume 2. *(all selections on this cd are segued together)*

1984 IF THIS IS IT
(S) (3:53) Chrysalis 21412 and 41412 Sports.
(S) (3:50) Elektra 61977 Time Flies....Best Of.
(S) (3:48) Time-Life R834-15 Body Talk - Once In Lifetime.
(S) (3:49) Time-Life R988-23 Sounds Of The Eighties 1984-1985.

1984 WALKING ON A THIN LINE
(S) (5:11) Chrysalis 21412 and 41412 Sports. *(LP version)*

1985 POWER OF LOVE
(S) (3:53) MCA 6144 O.S.T. Back To The Future.
(S) (3:53) Rhino 71640 Billboard Top Hits - 1985.
(S) (3:53) Elektra 61977 Time Flies....Best Of.
(S) (3:52) Time-Life R988-31 Sounds Of The Eighties: Cinemax Movie Hits Of The '80s.
(S) (3:53) Scotti Bros. 75518 Big Screen Rock.
(S) (3:52) Priority 50974 Premiere The Movie Magazine Presents The Greatest Soundtrack Hits.
(S) (3:52) Time-Life R13610 Gold And Platinum Box Set - The Ultimate Rock Collection.

1986 STUCK WITH YOU
(S) (4:26) Rhino 71641 Billboard Top Hits - 1986.
(S) (4:25) Chrysalis 21534 and 41534 Fore!
(S) (4:25) Elektra 61977 Time Flies....Best Of.
(S) (4:25) Time-Life R988-21 Sounds Of The Eighties: 1986-1989.
(S) (4:25) Time-Life R834-11 Body Talk - After Dark.

1986 HIP TO BE SQUARE
(S) (4:03) Chrysalis 21534 and 41534 Fore!

1987 JACOB'S LADDER
(S) (3:30) Chrysalis 21534 and 41534 Fore!
(S) (3:28) Time-Life R988-19 Sounds Of The Eighties: The Late '80s.

1987 I KNOW WHAT I LIKE
(S) (3:56) Chrysalis 21534 and 41534 Fore!

1987 DOING IT ALL FOR MY BABY
(S) (3:36) Chrysalis 21534 and 41534 Fore!
(S) (3:36) Elektra 61977 Time Flies....Best Of.

1988 PERFECT WORLD
(S) (4:05) Chrysalis 21622 and 41622 Small World.
(S) (4:04) Time-Life R988-10 Sounds Of The 80's: 1988.

1988 SMALL WORLD
(S) (4:40) Geffen 24236 Greenpeace - Rainbow Warriors. *(45 version)*
(S) (3:53) Chrysalis 21622 and 41622 Small World. *(LP version)*

1991 COUPLE DAYS OFF
(S) (4:55) EMI 93355 Hard At Play.

1991 IT HIT ME LIKE A HAMMER
(S) (4:00) EMI 93355 Hard At Play.

JERRY LEWIS
1956 ROCK-A-BYE YOUR BABY WITH A DIXIE MELODY
(M) (5:26) Capitol 93196 Capitol Collector's Series. *(includes 2 false starts of (2:53) so the actual song length is (2:33))*
(M) (2:32) Time-Life HPD-23 Your Hit Parade - The Late 50's.

JERRY LEE LEWIS
1957 WHOLE LOTTA SHAKIN' GOING ON
(M) (2:51) Rhino 70618 Billboard's Top Rock & Roll Hits Of 1957.
(M) (2:51) Rhino 72004 Billboard's Top Rock & Roll Hits 1957-1961 Box Set.
(M) (2:49) Original Sound 8854 Oldies But Goodies Vol. 4. *(this compact disc uses the "Waring - fds" noise reduction process)*
(M) (2:49) Original Sound 2221 Oldies But Goodies Volumes 1,4,6,8 and 10 Box Set. *(this box set uses the "Waring - fds" noise reduction process)*
(M) (2:49) Original Sound 2500 Oldies But Goodies Volumes 1-15 Box Set. *(this box set uses the "Waring - fds" noise reduction process)*
(M) (2:49) Original Sound CDGO-10 Golden Oldies Volume. 10.
(M) (2:51) Original Sound 8881 Twenty-One #1 Hits. *(this compact disc uses the "Waring - fds" noise reduction process)*
(M) (2:50) Original Sound 8891 Dick Clark's 21 All-Time Hits Vol. 1.
(M) (2:50) Original Sound 8880 20 Classic Jerry Lee Lewis Hits. *(this cd uses the "Waring - fds" noise reduction process)*
(M) (2:50) Original Sound 1081 All #1 Hits.
(M) (2:51) Rhino 75893 Jukebox Classics Volume 1.
(M) (2:50) Rhino 75884 The Sun Story.
(M) (2:52) Elektra 60107 O.S.T. Diner.
(M) (2:50) DCC Compact Classics 009 Legends.
(M) (2:51) Rhino 70255 and 5255 18 Original Sun Greatest Hits.
(M) (2:50) Rhino 70656 Jerry Lee Lewis.
(S) (2:38) Mercury 826251 Golden Rock Hits. *(all selections on this cd are rerecordings)*
(S) (3:57) Polydor 839516 O.S.T. Great Balls Of Fire. *(rerecording)*
(M) (2:51) RCA 66059 Sun's Greatest Hits.
(M) (2:51) Rhino 71216 Anthology.
(M) (2:50) Time-Life 2RNR-01 Rock 'N' Roll Era - 1957.
(M) (2:51) Time-Life R962-01 History Of Rock 'N' Roll: Rock 'N' Roll Classics 1957-1959.
(M) (2:50) Collectables 2503 WCBS-FM History Of Rock - The 50's Part 2.
(M) (2:47) Collectables 4503 History Of Rock/The 50s Part Two.
(M) (2:50) Rhino 71780 Sun Records Collection.
(M) (2:50) Era 511 Ultimate 50's Party.
(M) (2:51) K-Tel 3511 Jerry Lee Lewis/Mickey Gilley - Back To Back.
(M) (2:50) JCI 3165 #1 Radio Hits 1955 - Only Rock 'n Roll - 1959.
(M) (2:50) Priority 50950 I Love Rock & Roll Volume 1: Hits Of The 50's.
(M) (4:10) Tomato 70392 Rockin' My Life Away. *(all selections on this cd are recorded live)*
(S) (2:38) Polygram Special Markets 314520383 Whole Lotta Shakin'. *(rerecording)*
(S) (2:38) Right Stuff 53319 Hot Rod Rock Volume 4: Hot Rod Rebels. *(rerecording)*
(S) (2:37) Mercury 314534668 The Hits. *(rerecording)*
(S) (5:00) Collectables 5694 The Mercury/Smash Years Recordings. *(live)*
(M) (2:51) Columbia 69075 Great Balls Of Fire Super Hits.

1958 GREAT BALLS OF FIRE
(M) (1:49) Rhino 70243 Greatest Movie Rock Hits.
(M) (1:49) Rhino 70619 Billboard's Top Rock & Roll Hits Of 1958.
(M) (1:49) Rhino 72004 Billboard's Top Rock & Roll Hits 1957-1961 Box Set.
(M) (1:49) Rhino 70906 American Bandstand Greatest Hits Collection.
(M) (1:49) Original Sound 8862 Oldies But Goodies Vol. 12. *(this compact disc uses the "Waring - fds" noise reduction process)*
(M) (1:49) Original Sound 2223 Oldies But Goodies Volumes 2,7,9,12 and 13 Box Set. *(this box set uses the "Waring - fds" noise reduction process)*

JERRY LEE LEWIS (Continued)

(M) (1:49) Original Sound 2500 Oldies But Goodies Volumes 1-15 Box Set. *(this box set uses the "Waring - fds" noise reduction process)*

(M) (1:49) Original Sound 8880 20 Classic Jerry Lee Lewis Hits. *(this cd uses the "Waring - fds" noise reduction process)*

(M) (1:49) Rhino 75884 The Sun Story.

(M) (1:50) Rhino 75894 Jukebox Classics Volume 2.

(M) (1:50) RCA 5463 Rock & Roll - The Early Days.

(M) (1:52) Capitol 48993 Spuds Mackenzie's Party Faves.

(S) (1:47) Mercury 826448 Oldies Golden Million Sellers. *(rerecording)*

(M) (1:48) Atlantic 81677 O.S.T. Stand By Me.

(M) (1:49) JCI 3202 Rockin' Fifties.

(M) (1:50) DCC Compact Classics 009 Legends.

(M) (1:50) Warner Special Products 27602 20 Party Classics.

(M) (1:49) Atlantic 81885 O.S.T. Stealing Home.

(M) (1:49) Rhino 70657 Jerry Lee's Greatest.

(M) (1:50) Rhino 70255 and 5255 18 Original Sun Greatest Hits.

(S) (1:46) Mercury 826251 Golden Rock Hits. *(all selections on this cd are rerecordings)*

(S) (2:31) Polydor 839516 O.S.T. Great Balls Of Fire. *(rerecording)*

(M) (1:50) Polydor 839516 O.S.T. Great Balls Of Fire.

(M) (1:50) RCA 66059 Sun's Greatest Hits.

(M) (1:49) Rhino 71216 Anthology.

(M) (1:50) Time-Life 2RNR-01 Rock 'N' Roll Era - 1957.

(M) (1:49) Collectables 2503 WCBS-FM History Of Rock - The 50's Part 2.

(M) (1:49) Collectables 4503 History Of Rock/The 50s Part Two.

(M) (1:49) Motown 6763 Rites Of Rhythm & Blues Volume 2.

(M) (1:49) Rhino 71780 Sun Records Collection.

(M) (1:49) Original Sound 8883 21 Legendary Superstars.

(M) (1:50) K-Tel 3062 Rockin' Rebels.

(M) (1:50) JCI 3129 1955 - Only Rock 'N Roll - 1959.

(M) (1:50) K-Tel 3125 Solid Gold Rock N' Roll.

(M) (1:49) Tommy Boy 1136 ESPN Presents Jock Rock Vol. 2. *(all songs on this cd are segued together with crowd sound effects added)*

(M) (1:50) K-Tel 3511 Jerry Lee Lewis/Mickey Gilley - Back To Back.

(M) (1:49) Rhino 72275 More Stadium Rock.

(M) (1:49) Nick At Nite/550 Music/Epic 67770 Happy Days Jukebox.

(M) (2:40) Tomato 70392 Rockin' My Life Away. *(all selections on this cd are recorded live)*

(M) (1:49) Flashback 72712 Arena Rock.

(S) (1:45) Mercury 314534668 The Hits. *(rerecording)*

(M) (1:51) K-Tel 4018 Forefathers Of Rock.

(M) (1:50) Flashback 72857 Grease And Other Golden Oldies.

(M) (1:50) Columbia 69075 Great Balls Of Fire Super Hits.

(M) (1:50) K-Tel 4066 K-Tel's Original Party Music Vol. 2.

1958 BREATHLESS

(M) (2:40) Rhino 75884 The Sun Story.

(E) (2:41) Original Sound 8856 Oldies But Goodies Vol. 6. *(this compact disc uses the "Waring - fds" noise reduction process)*

(E) (2:41) Original Sound 2221 Oldies But Goodies Volumes 1,4,6,8 and 10 Box Set. *(this box set uses the "Waring - fds" noise reduction process)*

(E) (2:41) Original Sound 2500 Oldies But Goodies Volumes 1-15 Box Set. *(this box set uses the "Waring - fds" noise reduction process)*

(M) (2:39) Original Sound CDGO-14 Golden Oldies Volume. 14.

(M) (2:39) Original Sound 8880 20 Classic Jerry Lee Lewis Hits. *(this cd uses the "Waring - fds" noise reduction process)*

(M) (2:41) DCC Compact Classics 009 Legends.

(M) (2:41) Rhino 70255 and 5255 18 Original Sun Greatest Hits.

(S) (2:39) Mercury 826251 Golden Rock Hits. *(all selections on this cd are rerecordings)*

(S) (2:49) Polydor 839516 O.S.T. Great Balls Of Fire. *(rerecording)*

(M) (2:41) RCA 66059 Sun's Greatest Hits.

(M) (2:40) Rhino 71216 Anthology.

(M) (2:40) Time-Life 2RNR-05 Rock 'N' Roll Era - 1958.

(M) (2:40) Rhino 71780 Sun Records Collection.

(M) (2:41) K-Tel 3436 Rockabilly Riot.

(M) (2:40) JCI 3188 1955 - Only Dance - 1959.

(S) (2:33) Mercury 314534668 The Hits. *(rerecording)*

1958 HIGH SCHOOL CONFIDENTIAL

(M) (2:27) Rhino 70741 Rock This Town: Rockabilly Hits Volume 1.

(M) (2:28) Rhino 70255 and 5255 18 Original Sun Greatest Hits.

(M) (2:26) Rhino 70656 Jerry Lee Lewis.

(E) (2:27) Original Sound 8859 Oldies But Goodies Vol. 9. *(this compact disc uses the "Waring - fds" noise reduction process)*

(M) (2:27) Original Sound 8880 20 Classic Jerry Lee Lewis Hits. *(this cd uses the "Waring - fds" noise reduction process)*

(S) (2:20) Mercury 826251 Golden Rock Hits. *(all selections on this cd are rerecordings)*

(S) (2:17) Polydor 839516 O.S.T. Great Balls Of Fire. *(rerecording)*

(M) (2:27) Rhino 71216 Anthology.

(M) (2:27) Rhino 71547 Let There Be Drums Volume 1: The 50's.

(M) (2:27) Time-Life 2RNR-21 Rock 'N' Roll Era - 1958 Still Rockin'.

(M) (2:26) Rhino 71780 Sun Records Collection.

(M) (2:28) Columbia 69075 Great Balls Of Fire Super Hits.

1961 WHAT'D I SAY

(M) (2:23) Rhino 70657 Jerry Lee's Greatest.

(E) (2:23) Original Sound 8857 Oldies But Goodies Vol. 7. *(this compact disc uses the "Waring - fds" noise reduction process)*

(E) (2:23) Original Sound 2223 Oldies But Goodies Volumes 2,7,9,12 and 13 Box Set. *(this box set uses the "Waring - fds" noise reduction process)*

(E) (2:23) Original Sound 2500 Oldies But Goodies Volumes 1-15 Box Set. *(this box set uses the "Waring - fds" noise reduction process)*

(M) (2:24) Original Sound 8880 20 Classic Jerry Lee Lewis Hits. *(this cd uses the "Waring - fds" noise reduction process)*

(M) (2:24) Rhino 70255 and 5255 18 Original Sun Greatest Hits.

(M) (4:18) Tomato 70392 Rockin' My Life Away. *(all selections on this cd are recorded live)*

1973 DRINKING WINE SPO-DEE-O'DEE

(S) (3:36) Rhino 71216 Anthology.

(E) (2:33) K-Tel 852 100 Proof Hits. *(earlier recording than the hit version)*

(S) (2:13) Polygram Special Markets 314520383 Whole Lotta Shakin'. *(rerecording)*

(M) (2:32) Original Sound 8880 20 Classic Jerry Lee Lewis Hits. *(this cd uses the "Waring - fds" noise reduction process; earlier recording than the hit version)*

(S) (2:13) Mercury 314534668 The Hits. *(rerecording)*

(S) (3:36) Collectables 5694 The Mercury/Smash Years Recordings.

RAMSEY LEWIS TRIO

1965 THE "IN" CROWD
(actual 45 time is (3:06) not (2:58) as stated on the record label; LP length is (5:50))

(S) (3:18) Rhino 75774 Soul Shots. *(LP audience applause added in an unsuccessful attempt at recreating the 45 version)*

(S) (3:16) Chess 31318 Best Of Chess Rhythm & Blues Volume 2. *(45 version)*

(S) (5:50) Chess 6021 Greatest Hits Of. *(LP version)*

(S) (5:51) Chess 9185 The "In" Crowd. *(LP version)*

(S) (5:50) Telstar/JCI 3605 Best Of. *(LP version)*

(S) (3:15) Rhino 71604 Rock Instrumental Classics Vol. 4: Soul. *(45 version)*

(S) (3:15) Rhino 72035 Rock Instrumental Classics Vols. 1-5 Box Set. *(45 version)*

(S) (3:13) Time-Life RHD-07 Rhythm & Blues - 1965. *(45 version)*

(S) (3:11) Time-Life SUD-03 Superhits - 1965. *(45 version)*

(S) (3:15) Time-Life HPD-39 Your Hit Parade - 60's Instrumentals: Take Two. *(45 version)*

(S) (5:50) MCA 11389 O.S.T. Casino. *(LP version)*

(S) (5:50) Chess 812 History Of Chess Jazz. *(LP version)*

(S) (3:09) Hip-O 40008 Soulful Grooves - R&B Instrumental Classics Volume 2. *(45 version)*

(S) (5:49) Right Stuff 52660 Flick Hits - Old School Tracks. *(LP version)*

(S) (3:15) Rhino 72474 Masters Of Jazz, Vol. 7: Jazz Hit Singles. *(45 version)*

(S) (3:10) Time-Life AM1-10 AM Gold - 1965. *(45 version)*

(S) (3:13) Time-Life R838-12 Solid Gold Soul - 1965. *(45 version)*

(S) (5:46) MCA Special Products 21035 Classic Rock & Roll Instrumental Hits, Volume 2. *(LP version)*

(S) (5:51) MCA Special Products 21025 The Best Of Easy Listening. *(LP version)*

1965 HANG ON SLOOPY
(actual 45 time is (2:57) not (2:50) as stated on the record label)

(S) (3:16) MCA 5940 Vintage Music Volumes 19 & 20. *(LP length)*

(S) (3:16) MCA 31217 Vintage Music Volume 20. *(LP length)*

(S) (3:07) Chess 6021 Greatest Hits Of. *(edit of LP length)*

(S) (3:09) Telstar/JCI 3605 Best Of. *(edit of LP length)*

(S) (3:16) MCA Special Products 22134 Vintage Collectibles Volume 5. *(LP length)*

1966 A HARD DAY'S NIGHT

(S) (4:57) Chess 6021 Greatest Hits Of. *(LP version)*

(S) (4:59) Telstar/JCI 3605 Best Of. *(LP version)*

released as by RAMSEY LEWIS:
1966 WADE IN THE WATER
(actual 45 time is (3:16) not (3:05) as stated on the record label)

(S) (3:46) MCA 5938 Vintage Music Volumes 15 & 16. *(LP version)*

(S) (3:46) MCA 31213 Vintage Music Volume 16. *(LP version)*

(S) (3:48) Chess 6021 Greatest Hits Of. *(LP version)*

(S) (3:49) Chess 6025 Best Of Chess Jazz. *(LP version)*

(S) (3:48) Telstar/JCI 3605 Best Of. *(LP version)*

(S) (3:46) MCA Special Products 22173 Vintage Collectibles Volume 11. *(LP version)*

(S) (3:48) Hip-O 40007 Soulful Grooves - R&B Instrumental Classics Volume 1. *(LP version)*

(S) (3:24) Chess 9388 Chess Soul - A Decade Of Chicago's Finest. *(45 version)*

GORDON LIGHTFOOT
1971 IF YOU COULD READ MY MIND

(S) (3:47) Warner Special Products 27615 Storytellers: Singers & Songwriters.

(S) (3:47) Reprise 2237 Gord's Gold.

(S) (3:47) Reprise 6392 If You Could Read My Mind.

(S) (3:47) Time-Life SOD-02 Sounds Of The Seventies - 1971.

(S) (3:47) Time-Life R103-33 Singers & Songwriters.

1974 SUNDOWN

(S) (3:31) Reprise 2237 Gord's Gold.

(S) (3:32) Reprise 2177 Sundown.

(S) (3:34) Razor & Tie 4543 The '70s Preservation Society Presents: Easy '70s.

(S) (3:32) Time-Life SOD-15 Sounds Of The Seventies - 1974: Take Two.

(S) (3:34) Time-Life R103-33 Singers & Songwriters.

(S) (3:32) Rhino 72519 Mellow Rock Hits Of The 70's - Sundown.

1974 CAREFREE HIGHWAY

(S) (3:38) JCI 3304 Mellow Seventies.

(S) (3:40) Reprise 2237 Gord's Gold.

(S) (3:41) Reprise 2177 Sundown.

(S) (3:39) Time-Life R105-26 Our Songs: Singers & Songwriters Encore.

1975 RAINY DAY PEOPLE

(S) (2:46) Reprise 2237 Gord's Gold.

(S) (2:47) Reprise 45688 Cold On The Shoulder.

1976 THE WRECK OF THE EDMUND FITZGERALD
(dj copies of this 45 ran (5:23); commercial copies were all (5:57))

(S) (6:28) Reprise 2246 Summertime Dream. *(LP version)*

(S) (6:13) Reprise 25784 Gord's Gold Volume II. *(rerecording)*

1978 THE CIRCLE IS SMALL (I CAN SEE IT IN YOUR EYES)

(S) (4:03) Warner Brothers 45685 Endless Wire.

LIGHTHOUSE
1971 ONE FINE MORNING

(S) (5:15) Rhino 70926 Super Hits Of The 70's Volume 6. *(LP version but with alternate bass line)*

(S) (5:14) Time-Life SOD-25 Sounds Of The Seventies - Seventies Generation. *(LP version but with alternate bass line)*

(S) (3:20) Varese Sarabande 5706 Dick Bartley Presents Collector's Essentials: The 70's. *(45 version)*

(S) (5:14) K-Tel 3585 Horn Rock Bands. *(LP version but with alternate bass line)*

1972 SUNNY DAYS

(S) (4:13) K-Tel 3623 Believe In Music.

(S) (4:13) Nick At Nite/550 Music 63436 Patio Pool Party.

LIGHTNING SEEDS
1990 PURE

(S) (3:45) Priority 53740 Cutting Edge Vol. 2 - Best Of Modern Rock Hits.

(S) (3:45) MCA 6404 Cloudcuckooland.

LIL' KIM
1997 NO TIME

(S) (4:59) Undeas/Big Beat/Atlantic 92733 Hard Core.

(S) (4:32) Arista 18977 Ultimate Hip Hop Party 1998. *(all selections on this cd are segued together)*

(S) (4:03) Def Jam 314534746 Yo! MTV Raps Compilation.

1997 NOT TONIGHT

(S) (4:24) Tommy Boy 1169 O.S.T. Nothing To Lose. *(remix)*

(S) (4:24) Tommy Boy 1234 MTV Party To Go '98. *(all songs on this cd are segued together; remix)*

LIMAHL
1985 THE NEVER ENDING STORY
(dj copies of this 45 ran (3:32) and (3:53); commercial copies were all (3:32))

(S) (3:29) EMI 89605 Living In Oblivion: The 80's Greatest Hits Volume Two.

(S) (3:31) EMI 27222 Kajagoogoo And Limahl - Too Shy: The Singles And More.

BOB LIND
1966 ELUSIVE BUTTERFLY

(S) (2:46) EMI 81128 Rock Is Dead But It Won't Lie Down.

(S) (2:48) K-Tel 666 Flower Power.

(S) (2:47) Time-Life 2CLR-22 Classic Rock - 1966: Blowin' Your Mind.

(S) (2:47) Time-Life SUD-01 Superhits - 1966.

(S) (2:47) Time-Life R962-02 History Of Rock 'N' Roll: Folk Rock 1964-1967.

(S) (2:46) EMI 89531 You Might Have Heard My Footsteps - Best Of.

(S) (2:47) Time-Life R132-22 Treasury Of Folk Music Volume Two.

(S) (2:47) Time-Life AM1-09 AM Gold - 1966.

KATHY LINDEN
1958 BILLY
    (M) (1:54)   Collectors' Choice 5189 I Wish I Were A Princess - The Great Lost Female Teen Idols.
1959 GOODBYE JIMMY, GOODBYE
    (M) (2:33)   Collectors' Choice 5189 I Wish I Were A Princess - The Great Lost Female Teen Idols.

LINDISFARNE
1978 RUN FOR HOME

MARK LINDSAY
1970 ARIZONA
    (S) (3:05)   Rhino 70921 Super Hits Of The 70's Volume 1.
    (S) (3:05)   Rhino 72009 Super Hits Of The 70's Volumes 1-4 Box Set.
    (S) (3:05)   Razor & Tie 21640 Those Fabulous 70's.
    (S) (3:05)   Time-Life SUD-20 Superhits - Early 70's Classics.
    (S) (3:05)   Risky Business 66871 Polyester Dreams/Greatest Hits Of The 70's.
    (S) (3:07)   Collectables 5805 A Golden Classics Edition.
    (S) (3:05)   Time-Life AM1-15 AM Gold - Early '70s Classics.
1970 MISS AMERICA
    (S) (3:31)   Collectables 5805 A Golden Classics Edition.
1970 SILVER BIRD
    (S) (3:00)   Rhino 70924 Super Hits Of The 70's Volume 4.
    (S) (3:00)   Rhino 72009 Super Hits Of The 70's Volumes 1-4 Box Set.
    (S) (3:02)   Collectables 5805 A Golden Classics Edition.

LINEAR
1990 SENDING ALL MY LOVE
    (S) (3:50)   Atlantic 82090 Linear.
1992 T.L.C.
    (S) (3:56)   Atlantic 82382 Caught In The Middle.

LIPPS INC.
1980 FUNKYTOWN
(actual 45 time is (4:01) not (3:57) as stated on the record label)
    (S) (3:58)   Priority 7976 Mega-Hits Dance Classics Volume 6. *(45 version)*
    (S) (3:59)   Rhino 70985 The Disco Years Volume 2. *(45 version)*
    (S) (7:49)   Casablanca 838810 Let's Start The Dance (Polygram Dance Classics) Volume 1. *(LP version)*
    (S) (4:04)   Rhino 70494 Billboard Top Dance Hits - 1980. *(45 version)*
    (S) (4:04)   Rhino 70675 Billboard Top Hits - 1980. *(45 version)*
    (S) (7:47)   Casablanca 314512969 Funkyworld: The Best Of. *(LP version)*
    (S) (3:58)   Razor & Tie 22496 Disco Fever. *(45 version)*
    (S) (7:47)   Casablanca 314516918 Casablanca Records Story. *(LP version)*
    (S) (3:58)   Risky Business 53921 Double Knit Dance Hits. *(45 version)*
    (S) (3:58)   JCI 3127 1980 - Only Rock 'N Roll - 1984. *(45 version)*
    (S) (6:02)   Rebound 314520220 Disco Nights Vol. 4 - Greatest Disco Groups. *(neither the 45 or LP version)*
    (S) (3:55)   Rebound 314520318 Class Reunion 1980. *(45 version)*
    (S) (4:00)   K-Tel 3126 Disco Mania. *(45 version)*
    (S) (3:59)   Rhino 71971 Video Soul - Best Soul Of The 80's Vol. 1. *(45 version)*
    (S) (4:04)   Time-Life R988-07 Sounds Of The Eighties: 1980. *(45 version)*
    (S) (4:04)   Time-Life R138-38 Celebration. *(45 version)*
    (S) (3:56)   Casablanca 314526253 Casablanca Records Greatest Hits. *(45 version)*
    (S) (3:55)   Polydor 314535877 Pure Disco. *(45 version)*

    (S) (5:40)   Chronicles 314553404 Non-Stop Disco Vol. 1. *(all songs on this cd are segued together)*
    (S) (4:02)   Island 314553411 The Last Party. *(all selections on this cd are segued together)*
    (S) (4:03)   TVT 8090 O.S.T. My Fellow Americans. *(45 version)*
    (S) (3:55)   Hip-O 40079 Essential '80s: 1980-1984. *(45 version)*
    (S) (3:58)   Thump 3030 TRD - Thump Retro Disco. *(45 version)*
    (S) (3:59)   Time-Life R840-09 Sounds Of The Seventies: '70s Dance Party 1979-1981. *(45 version)*
    (S) (3:39)   Rebound 314520520 Body Moves - Non-Stop Disco Workout Vol. 1. *(all selections on this cd are segued together)*
    (S) (3:58)   Polygram Special Markets 314520457 #1 Radio Hits Of The 80's. *(45 version)*

LISA LISA AND CULT JAM
released as by LISA LISA and CULT JAM with FULL FORCE:
1985 I WONDER IF I TAKE YOU HOME
    (S) (6:43)   Columbia 46088 Club Columbia. *(LP version)*
    (S) (6:44)   Columbia 40135 Lisa Lisa And Cult Jam With Full Force. *(LP version)*
    (S) (6:39)   Rhino 71558 Street Jams: Electric Funk Part 4. *(LP version)*
    (S) (6:39)   Rhino 72062 Street Jams: Electric Funk Parts 1-4. *(LP version)*
    (S) (6:44)   Thump 9949 Past, Present And Future. *(LP version)*
    (S) (6:43)   Columbia/Legacy 65268 Super Hits. *(LP version)*
1986 ALL CRIED OUT
    (S) (4:44)   Columbia 40135 Lisa Lisa And Cult Jam With Full Force.
    (S) (4:42)   Thump 9949 Past, Present And Future.
    (S) (4:42)   Thump 4740 Old School Love Songs Volume 4.
    (S) (4:44)   Columbia/Legacy 65268 Super Hits.
released as by LISA LISA and CULT JAM:
1987 HEAD TO TOE
    (S) (5:02)   Priority 53732 80's Greatest Rock Hits Volume 8 - Dance Party. *(LP version)*
    (S) (3:59)   JCI 3128 1985 - Only Rock 'N Roll - 1989. *(45 version)*
    (S) (5:01)   K-Tel 842 Hot Ladies Of The 80's. *(LP version)*
    (S) (5:02)   Columbia 40477 Spanish Fly. *(LP version)*
    (S) (3:59)   Time-Life R988-09 Sounds Of The Eighties: 1987. *(45 version)*
    (S) (4:01)   Rhino 72142 Billboard Hot R&B Hits 1987. *(45 version)*
    (S) (5:01)   Thump 9949 Past, Present And Future. *(LP version)*
    (S) (3:59)   K-Tel 3868 Hot Ladies Of Pop. *(45 version)*
    (S) (5:01)   Columbia/Legacy 65268 Super Hits. *(LP version)*
1987 LOST IN EMOTION
(actual 45 time is (4:35) not (3:59) as stated on the record label)
    (S) (4:35)   Columbia 44382 The Heart Of Soul. *(45 version)*
    (S) (5:06)   Columbia 40477 Spanish Fly. *(LP version)*
    (S) (5:06)   Priority 53773 80's Greatest Rock Hits Volume II - Teen Idols. *(LP version)*
    (S) (4:34)   JCI 3171 #1 Radio Hits 1985 - Only Rock 'n Roll - 1989. *(45 version)*
    (S) (5:06)   Thump 9949 Past, Present And Future. *(LP version)*
    (S) (4:35)   Time-Life R988-20 Sounds Of The Eighties: The Late '80s Take Two. *(45 version)*
    (S) (5:06)   Columbia/Legacy 65268 Super Hits. *(LP version)*
    (S) (4:35)   Cold Front 3832 Club Mix - Women Of Dance Vol. 1. *(45 version)*
    (S) (4:35)   Time-Life R834-20 Body Talk - Heart And Soul. *(45 version)*
1989 LITTLE JACKIE WANTS TO BE A STAR
    (S) (4:49)   Columbia 44378 Straight To The Sky. *(LP version)*

(S) (4:47) Thump 9949 Past, Present And Future. *(LP version)*
(S) (4:47) Columbia/Legacy 65268 Super Hits. *(LP version)*

1991 LET THE BEAT HIT 'EM
(S) (4:37) Columbia 46035 Straight Outta Hell's Kitchen.
(S) (4:37) Priority 53772 Techno Dance Classics Volume 2 - Feel The Beat.
(S) (4:37) Thump 9949 Past, Present And Future.
(S) (4:31) Priority 50934 Shut Up And Dance! The 90's Volume One. *(all selections on this cd are segued together)*
(S) (4:37) Columbia/Legacy 65268 Super Hits.
(S) (4:37) Rhino 72839 Disco Queens: The 90's.

LITTLE ANTHONY and THE IMPERIALS
1958 TEARS ON MY PILLOW
(M) (2:16) Rhino 70644 Billboard's Top R&B Hits Of 1958.
(M) (2:15) Rhino 70919 Best Of.
(S) (2:12) EMI 91475 Best Of. *(rerecording)*
(S) (2:03) MCA 6171 Good Time Rock 'N' Roll. *(all selections on this cd are recorded live)*
(M) (2:15) Collectables 5422 Imperials Featuring Little Anthony.
(M) (2:15) Collectables 8804 For Collectors Only.
(M) (2:16) Capitol 81475 Rites Of Rhythm & Blues.
(M) (2:15) Special Music 5021 Best Of.
(M) (2:15) Original Sound 9329 Oldies But Goodies Doo Wop Classics.
(M) (2:15) Original Sound 9328 13 Of The Best Doo Wop Love Songs Vol. 2.
(M) (2:15) Rhino 71463 Doo Wop Box.
(M) (2:14) Time-Life 2RNR-05 Rock 'N' Roll Era - 1958.
(M) (2:14) Time-Life RHD-16 Rhythm & Blues - 1958.
(M) (2:16) Collectables 5471 The Spotlight Series - End Records Vol. 2.
(M) (2:15) Collectables 2601 WCBS-FM History Of Rock - The Group Sounds Vol. 2.
(M) (2:14) Collectables 2608 WCBS-FM For Lovers Only Vol. 4.
(M) (2:15) Time-Life R103-27 Love Me Tender.
(M) (2:13) Time-Life R10513 40 Lovin' Oldies.
(M) (2:15) Polygram Special Markets 314520259 Doo Wop Classics.
(M) (2:15) Time-Life R857-04 The Heart Of Rock 'n' Roll - 1958.
(M) (2:15) Rhino 72156 Doo Wop Memories, Vol. 1.
(M) (2:16) Rhino 72158 Shimmy, Shimmy, Ko-Ko-Bop.
(M) (2:14) JCI 3165 #1 Radio Hits 1955 - Only Rock 'n' Roll - 1959.
(S) (2:12) Right Stuff 53320 Hot Rod Rock Volume 5: Back Seat Movers. *(rerecording)*
(M) (2:15) Flashback 72857 Grease And Other Golden Oldies.
(M) (2:14) Time-Life R838-22 Solid Gold Soul 1958.

1960 SHIMMY, SHIMMY, KO-KO-BOP
(S) (2:07) Rhino 70919 Best Of. *(alternate take)*
(S) (2:08) EMI 91475 Best Of. *(alternate take)*
(S) (2:06) Collectables 8804 For Collectors Only.
(S) (2:07) Special Music 5021 Best Of.
(S) (2:06) Rhino 71463 Doo Wop Box.
(S) (2:05) Time-Life 2RNR-22 Rock 'N' Roll Era - 1960 Still Rockin'.
(S) (2:06) Collectables 5471 The Spotlight Series - End Records Vol. 2.
(S) (2:06) Rhino 72158 Shimmy, Shimmy, Ko-Ko-Bop.
(S) (2:07) Nick At Nite/Epic 67149 Dick Van Dyke's Dance Party.
(S) (2:07) JCI 3189 1960 - Only Dance - 1964.

1964 I'M ON THE OUTSIDE (LOOKING IN)
(M) (3:00) Rhino 70919 Best Of.
(S) (3:10) EMI 91475 Best Of.
(S) (3:06) Time-Life 2CLR-16 Classic Rock - 1964: Shakin' All Over.
(M) (3:00) Original Sound 9303 Art Laboe's Dedicated To You Vol. 3.
(M) (3:01) Right Stuff 30578 Slow Jams: The 60's Volume 4.

(S) (3:06) EMI 38208 Best Of.

1964 GOIN' OUT OF MY HEAD
(S) (2:28) EMI 96268 24 Greatest Hits Of All Time.
(S) (2:28) Curb 77355 60's Hits Volume 1.
(S) (2:27) Rhino 70919 Best Of.
(S) (2:29) EMI 91475 Best Of.
(S) (2:18) MCA 6171 Good Time Rock 'N' Roll. *(all selections on this cd are recorded live)*
(S) (2:23) Original Sound 8861 Oldies But Goodies Vol. 11. *(this compact disc uses the "Waring - fds" noise reduction process)*
(S) (2:23) Original Sound 2222 Oldies But Goodies Volumes 3,5,11,14 and 15 Box Set. *(this box set uses the "Waring - fds" noise reduction process)*
(S) (2:23) Original Sound 2500 Oldies But Goodies Volumes 1-15 Box Set. *(this box set uses the "Waring - fds" noise reduction process)*
(S) (2:28) Ripete 2392192 Beach Music Anthology Box Set. *(rerecording)*
(S) (2:27) Capitol 81475 Rites Of Rhythm & Blues.
(S) (2:25) Original Sound 8907 Best Love Songs Vol 2.
(S) (2:25) Original Sound 9326 Best Love Songs Vol. 1 & 2.
(S) (2:25) Original Sound 1236 Best Love Songs Box Set.
(S) (2:27) Time-Life 2RNR-10 Rock 'N' Roll Era - 1964.
(S) (2:26) Time-Life SUD-09 Superhits - 1964.
(S) (2:28) Right Stuff 30577 Slow Jams: The 60's Volume 3.
(S) (2:26) Rhino 72158 Shimmy, Shimmy, Ko-Ko-Bop.
(S) (2:25) EMI 38208 Best Of.
(S) (2:27) Time-Life R857-09 The Heart Of Rock 'n' Roll 1964.
(S) (2:26) Time-Life AM1-11 AM Gold - 1964.
(S) (2:26) Thump 7070 Lowrider Oldies Volume 7.

1965 HURT SO BAD
(S) (2:16) Rhino 70919 Best Of.
(S) (2:19) EMI 91475 Best Of.
(S) (1:48) MCA 6171 Good Time Rock 'N' Roll. *(all selections on this cd are recorded live)*
(S) (2:15) Time-Life RHD-07 Rhythm & Blues - 1965.
(S) (2:15) Time-Life 2CLR-23 Classic Rock - 1965: Blowin' Your Mind.
(S) (2:16) Rhino 71806 The R&B Box: Thirty Years Of Rhythm & Blues.
(S) (2:16) Risky Business 66388 The Big Hurt/Songs To Cry By.
(S) (2:16) Time-Life SUD-17 Superhits - Mid 60's Classics.
(S) (2:17) Right Stuff 28371 Slow Jams: The 60's Volume Two.
(S) (2:16) Time-Life AM1-16 AM Gold - Mid '60s Classics.
(S) (2:16) Varese Sarabande 5670 Songs Of Tommy Boyce And Bobby Hart.
(S) (2:13) EMI 38208 Best Of.
(S) (2:15) JCI 3164 Eighteen Soulful Ballads.
(S) (2:15) Time-Life R838-12 Solid Gold Soul - 1965.
(S) (2:15) Time-Life R857-20 The Heart Of Rock 'n' Roll 1965-1966.

1965 TAKE ME BACK
(M) (2:37) Rhino 70919 Best Of. *(45 version)*
(S) (2:36) EMI 91475 Best Of. *(LP version)*
(M) (2:36) Original Sound 9304 Art Laboe's Dedicated To You Vol. 4. *(45 version)*
(M) (2:36) EMI 38208 Best Of. *(45 version)*

1965 I MISS YOU SO
(S) (2:33) Rhino 70919 Best Of.
(S) (2:36) EMI 91475 Best Of.
(S) (2:32) EMI 38208 Best Of.

LITTLE CAESAR and THE ROMANS
1961 THOSE OLDIES BUT GOODIES (REMIND ME OF YOU) (actual 45 time is (3:22) not (2:58) as stated on the record label)
(M) (3:24) DCC Compact Classics 031 Back Seat Jams.
(M) (3:11) Original Sound 8856 Oldies But Goodies Vol. 6. *(this compact disc uses the "Waring - fds" noise reduction process; sped up slightly and faded :08 earlier than the 45)*

LITTLE CAESAR and THE ROMANS *(Continued)*

(M) (3:11) Original Sound 2221 Oldies But Goodies Volumes 1,4,6,8 and 10 Box Set. *(this box set uses the "Waring - fds" noise reduction process; sped up slightly and faded :08 earlier than the 45)*

(M) (3:11) Original Sound 2500 Oldies But Goodies Volumes 1-15 Box Set. *(this box set uses the "Waring - fds" noise reduction process; sped up slightly and faded :08 earlier than the 45)*

(M) (3:10) Original Sound CDGO-2 Golden Oldies Volume. 2. *(sped up slightly and faded :09 earlier than the 45)*

(M) (3:10) Original Sound 8891 Dick Clark's 21 All-Time Hits Vol. 1. *(sped up slightly and faded :09 earlier than the 45)*

(E) (2:59) Original Sound 8905r 13 Of The Best Doo Wop Love Songs. *(sped up considerably and faded :07 sooner than the 45)*

(E) (2:59) Original Sound 9326 Best Love Songs Vol. 1 & 2. *(sped up considerably and faded :07 sooner than the 45)*

(E) (2:59) Original Sound 4001 Art Laboe's 60 Killer Oldies. *(sped up considerably and faded :07 sooner than the 45)*

(E) (2:59) Original Sound 1236 Best Love Songs Box Set. *(sped up considerably and faded :07 sooner than the 45)*

(M) (3:10) Original Sound 9602 Best Of Oldies But Goodies Vol. 2. *(sped up slightly and faded :09 earlier than the 45)*

(M) (3:26) Time-Life 2RNR-04 Rock 'N' Roll Era - 1961.

(M) (3:36) Del-Fi 71218 Memories Of Those Oldies But Goodies. *(time includes a :09 introduction)*

(M) (3:26) Rhino 72507 Doo Wop Box II.

(M) (3:25) Music Club 50015 Love Me Forever - 18 Rock'N' Roll Love Songs.

(M) (3:26) Time-Life R857-10 The Heart Of Rock 'n' Roll 1960-1961.

(M) (3:26) Time-Life R857-21 The Heart Of Rock 'n' Roll Slow Dancing Classics.

LITTLE DIPPERS
1960 FOREVER

LITTLE EVA
1962 THE LOCO-MOTION
(actual 45 and LP time is (2:20) not (2:12) as stated on the record label)

(M) (2:27) Rhino 70623 Billboard's Top Rock & Roll Hits Of 1962. *(significant dropout at :15; handclaps added that were not on the original 45 or LP)*

(M) (2:27) Rhino 72007 Billboard's Top Rock & Roll Hits 1962-1966 Box Set. *(significant dropout at :15; handclaps added that were not on the original 45 or LP)*

(M) (2:24) Rhino 70989 Best Of The Girl Groups Volume 2.

(M) (2:27) Rhino 70992 Groove 'n' Grind. *(significant dropout at :15; handclaps added that were not on the original 45 or LP)*

(M) (2:26) Rhino 70906 American Bandstand Greatest Hits Collection. *(significant dropout at :15; handclaps added that were not on the original 45 or LP)*

(M) (2:26) Collectables 5414 Carole King Plus. *(truncated fade; handclaps added that were not on the original 45 or LP)*

(M) (2:24) Collectables 5407 Best Of. *(handclaps added that were not on the original 45 or LP)*

(M) (2:24) Era 5025 The Brill Building Sound. *(handclaps added that were not on the original 45 or LP)*

(M) (2:26) Rhino 71195 Kid Rock! *(bad dropout at :15; handclaps added that were not on the original 45 or LP)*

(M) (2:26) Time-Life 2RNR-02 Rock 'N' Roll Era - 1962. *(handclaps added that were not on the original 45 or LP)*

(M) (2:22) Time-Life RHD-11 Rhythm & Blues - 1962. *(handclaps added that were not on the original 45 or LP)*

(M) (2:27) Time-Life R962-08 History Of Rock 'N' Roll: Sound Of The City 1959-1965. *(handclaps added that were not on the original 45 or LP)*

(M) (2:24) Rhino 71650 Colpix-Dimension Story. *(handclaps added that were not on the original 45 or LP)*

(M) (2:24) K-Tel 3331 Do You Wanna Dance. *(handclaps added that were not on the original 45 or LP)*

(M) (2:26) K-Tel 3008 60's Sock Hop. *(significant dropout at :15; handclaps added that were not on the original 45 or LP)*

(M) (2:17) JCI 3125 1960 - Only Rock 'N Roll - 1964.

(M) (2:26) Polygram Special Markets 314520260 Number One Hits Of The Sixties. *(significant dropout at :15; handclaps added that were not on the original 45 or LP)*

(M) (2:24) Nick At Nite/Epic 67149 Dick Van Dyke's Dance Party. *(handclaps added that were not on the original 45 or LP)*

(M) (2:24) Rhino 72273 The Loco-Motion. *(handclaps added that were not on the original 45 or LP)*

(M) (2:24) K-Tel 3796 Music For Your Party. *(handclaps added that were not on the original 45 or LP)*

(M) (2:22) Time-Life R838-18 Solid Gold Soul 1962. *(handclaps added that were not on the original 45 or LP)*

(M) (2:23) Collectables 1515 and 2515 The Anniversary Album - The 60's. *(handclaps added that were not on the original 45 or LP)*

1962 KEEP YOUR HANDS OFF MY BABY
(M) (2:34) Collectables 5414 Carole King Plus.
(M) (2:32) Collectables 5407 Best Of.
(M) (2:32) Era 5025 The Brill Building Sound.
(E) (2:34) Time-Life 2RNR-16 Rock 'N' Roll Era - 1962 Still Rockin'.
(M) (2:33) Rhino 71650 Colpix-Dimension Story.
(M) (2:30) Rhino 72273 The Loco-Motion.

1963 LET'S TURKEY TROT
(M) (2:29) Collectables 5407 Best Of.
(M) (2:29) Rhino 71650 Colpix-Dimension Story.

LITTLE JOE & THE THRILLERS
1957 PEANUTS
(M) (2:27) Collectables 5076 Little Joe & The Thrillers Meet The Schoolboys.
(M) (2:25) CBS Special Products 37649 Okeh Rhythm & Blues.
(M) (2:24) Time-Life 2RNR-44 Rock 'N' Roll Era - Lost Treasures.
(M) (2:25) K-Tel 3409 Funniest Food Songs.
(M) (2:25) Rhino 72507 Doo Wop Box II.

LITTLE JOEY and THE FLIPS
1962 BONGO STOMP
(M) (2:14) Time-Life 2RNR-44 Rock 'N' Roll Era - Lost Treasures.

LITTLE MILTON
1965 WE'RE GONNA MAKE IT
(S) (2:39) Chess 31317 Best Of Chess Rhythm & Blues Volume 1.
(S) (2:39) Chess 5906 We're Gonna Make It/Little Milton Sings The Blues.
(S) (2:35) Time-Life RHD-07 Rhythm & Blues - 1965.
(S) (2:35) Time-Life 2CLR-25 Classic Rock - On The Soul Side.
(S) (2:38) Chess 9350 Welcome To The Club/The Essential Chess Recordings.
(S) (2:37) Rhino 71806 The R&B Box: Thirty Years Of Rhythm & Blues.
(S) (2:37) MCA Special Products 20768 Greatest Blues Legends.
(S) (2:38) Chess 9368 Chess Blues Classics 1957-1967.
(S) (2:37) MCA Special Products 20935 Blues Greatest.
(S) (2:38) Time-Life R859-03 Living The Blues: Blues Greats.
(S) (2:35) Time-Life R838-12 Solid Gold Soul - 1965.
(S) (2:38) MCA Special Products 21010 R&B Crossover Hits Volume 2.

LITTLE RICHARD
1956 TUTTI-FRUTTI

(E)	(2:22)	MCA 6160	O.S.T. Down And Out In Beverly Hills.
(E)	(2:20)	Curb 77739	Greatest Songs. *(rerecording)*
(M)	(2:22)	Rhino 70642	Billboard's Top R&B Hits Of 1956.
(M)	(2:23)	Rhino 75894	Jukebox Classics Volume 2.
(M)	(2:22)	Time-Life 2RNR-08	The Rock 'N' Roll Era 1954-1955.
(M)	(2:23)	Time-Life RHD-17	Rhythm & Blues 1955.
(M)	(2:23)	RCA 5463	Rock & Roll - The Early Days.
(M)	(1:28)	Epic 40389	Greatest Hits. *(all selections on this cd are live with a lot of dialogue preceding each song)*
(M)	(2:23)	Specialty 7012	The Georgia Peach.
(M)	(2:23)	Specialty 2154	Essential.
(E)	(2:22)	Motown 9066	Compact Command Performances. *(rerecorded)*
(M)	(2:23)	Rhino 75899	18 Greatest Hits.
(E)	(2:18)	Special Music 4908	His Greatest Hits. *(rerecorded)*
(M)	(2:23)	Specialty 4412	The Specialty Story.
(M)	(2:22)	Specialty 8508	The Specialty Sessions.
(M)	(2:23)	Elektra 60806	O.S.T. Cocktail.
(M)	(2:21)	Specialty 7063	Little Richard Vol. 2: Shag On Down By The Union Hall. *(alternate take)*
(M)	(2:22)	EMI 37350	Crescent City Soul: The Sound Of New Orleans 1947-1974.
(M)	(2:23)	JCI 3188	1955 - Only Dance - 1959.
(M)	(2:22)	Priority 50950	I Love Rock & Roll Volume 1: Hits Of The 50's.

1956 LONG TALL SALLY

(M)	(2:07)	Rhino 70642	Billboard's Top R&B Hits Of 1956.
(M)	(2:07)	Rhino 75893	Jukebox Classics Volume 1.
(M)	(2:07)	Rhino 75899	18 Greatest Hits.
(M)	(2:07)	Specialty 8508	The Specialty Sessions.
(M)	(2:07)	Specialty 2154	Essential.
(E)	(2:01)	Motown 9066	Compact Command Performances. *(rerecorded)*
(M)	(2:07)	Specialty 7012	The Georgia Peach.
(M)	(2:19)	Epic 40389	Greatest Hits. *(all selections on this cd are live with a lot of dialogue preceding each song)*
(M)	(2:07)	Rhino 71547	Let There Be Drums Volume 1: The 50's.
(E)	(1:57)	Special Music 4908	His Greatest Hits. *(rerecorded)*
(M)	(2:07)	Specialty 4412	The Specialty Story.
(M)	(2:06)	Time-Life 2RNR-14	Rock 'N' Roll Era - 1956.
(M)	(2:07)	Time-Life RHD-05	Rhythm & Blues - 1956.
(M)	(2:07)	Time-Life R962-03	History Of Rock 'N' Roll: Rock 'N' Roll Classics 1954-1956.
(M)	(2:06)	Original Sound 8883	21 Legendary Superstars.
(M)	(2:06)	Era 511	Ultimate 50's Party.
(E)	(2:02)	Curb 77739	Greatest Songs. *(rerecording)*
(M)	(2:08)	Specialty 7063	Little Richard Vol. 2: Shag On Down By The Union Hall. *(original version but not the hit version)*
(M)	(2:07)	Time-Life R838-24	Solid Gold Soul 1956.

1956 RIP IT UP

(M)	(2:21)	Warner Special Products 27602	20 Party Classics.
(M)	(2:20)	Original Sound 8858	Oldies But Goodies Vol. 8. *(this compact disc uses the "Waring - fds" noise reduction process)*
(M)	(2:20)	Original Sound 2221	Oldies But Goodies Volumes 1,4,6,8 and 10 Box Set. *(this box set uses the "Waring - fds" noise reduction process)*
(M)	(2:20)	Original Sound 2500	Oldies But Goodies Volumes 1-15 Box Set. *(this box set uses the "Waring - fds" noise reduction process)*
(M)	(2:21)	Rhino 75899	18 Greatest Hits.
(M)	(2:20)	Specialty 8508	The Specialty Sessions.
(M)	(2:21)	Specialty 2154	Essential.
(E)	(1:58)	Motown 9066	Compact Command Performances. *(rerecorded)*
(M)	(2:21)	Specialty 7012	The Georgia Peach.
(M)	(2:20)	Atlantic 82155	O.S.T. Book Of Love.
(E)	(1:55)	Special Music 4908	His Greatest Hits. *(rerecorded)*

(M)	(2:21)	Specialty 4412	The Specialty Story.
(M)	(2:20)	Time-Life 2RNR-14	Rock 'N' Roll Era - 1956.
(M)	(2:21)	Time-Life RHD-05	Rhythm & Blues - 1956.
(E)	(2:18)	Curb 77739	Greatest Songs. *(rerecording)*
(M)	(2:21)	Specialty 7063	Little Richard Vol. 2: Shag On Down By The Union Hall. *(alternate take)*
(M)	(2:21)	Time-Life R838-24	Solid Gold Soul 1956.

1956 READY TEDDY

(M)	(2:06)	Rhino 75899	18 Greatest Hits.
(M)	(2:06)	Specialty 8508	The Specialty Sessions.
(M)	(2:06)	Specialty 2154	Essential.
(M)	(2:07)	Specialty 7012	The Georgia Peach.
(M)	(2:07)	Specialty 4412	The Specialty Story.
(M)	(2:05)	Time-Life 2RNR-23	Rock 'N' Roll Era - 1956 Still Rockin'.
(E)	(2:09)	Curb 77739	Greatest Songs. *(rerecording)*
(M)	(1:51)	Specialty 7063	Little Richard Vol. 2: Shag On Down By The Union Hall. *(alternate take)*

1957 LUCILLE

(M)	(2:25)	JCI 3204	Heart & Soul Fifties. *(no fidelity)*
(M)	(2:27)	Rhino 70643	Billboard's Top R&B Hits Of 1957.
(M)	(2:27)	Rhino 75899	18 Greatest Hits.
(M)	(2:23)	Specialty 8508	The Specialty Sessions.
(M)	(2:21)	Specialty 2154	Essential.
(E)	(2:14)	Motown 9066	Compact Command Performances. *(rerecorded)*
(M)	(2:23)	Specialty 7012	The Georgia Peach.
(M)	(2:02)	Epic 40389	Greatest Hits. *(all selections on this cd are live with a lot of dialogue preceding each song)*
(E)	(2:11)	Special Music 4908	His Greatest Hits. *(rerecorded)*
(M)	(2:23)	Specialty 4412	The Specialty Story.
(M)	(2:21)	Time-Life RHD-08	Rhythm & Blues - 1957.
(M)	(2:26)	Time-Life 2RNR-17	Rock 'N' Roll Era - 1957 Still Rockin'.
(M)	(2:21)	Time-Life R962-01	History Of Rock 'N' Roll: Rock 'N' Roll Classics 1957-1959.
(E)	(2:25)	Curb 77739	Greatest Songs. *(rerecording)*
(M)	(2:21)	Time-Life R838-23	Solid Gold Soul 1957.

1957 JENNY, JENNY

(M)	(2:01)	Rhino 75899	18 Greatest Hits.
(M)	(2:02)	Specialty 8508	The Specialty Sessions.
(M)	(2:00)	Specialty 2154	Essential.
(E)	(1:57)	Motown 9066	Compact Command Performances. *(rerecorded)*
(M)	(2:01)	Specialty 7012	The Georgia Peach.
(M)	(2:44)	Epic 40389	Greatest Hits. *(all selections on this cd are live with a lot of dialogue preceding each song)*
(M)	(2:01)	Specialty 4412	The Specialty Story.
(M)	(2:01)	Time-Life 2RNR-17	Rock 'N' Roll Era - 1957 Still Rockin'.
(E)	(1:58)	Curb 77739	Greatest Songs. *(rerecording)*

1957 KEEP A KNOCKIN'

(M)	(2:19)	JCI 3202	Rockin' Fifties.
(M)	(2:22)	Rhino 70643	Billboard's Top R&B Hits Of 1957.
(M)	(2:21)	Rhino 75899	18 Greatest Hits.
(M)	(2:17)	Specialty 8508	The Specialty Sessions.
(M)	(2:16)	Specialty 2154	Essential.
(E)	(2:10)	Motown 9066	Compact Command Performances. *(rerecorded)*
(M)	(2:15)	Specialty 7012	The Georgia Peach.
(E)	(2:08)	Special Music 4908	His Greatest Hits. *(rerecorded)*
(M)	(2:15)	Specialty 4412	The Specialty Story.
(M)	(2:15)	Time-Life 2RNR-01	Rock 'N' Roll Era - 1957. *(original pressings of this song on this cd were (E))*
(E)	(2:09)	Curb 77739	Greatest Songs. *(rerecording)*
(M)	(2:15)	Specialty 7063	Little Richard Vol. 2: Shag On Down By The Union Hall. *(alternate take)*

1958 GOOD GOLLY MISS MOLLY

(E)	(2:08)	JCI 3201	Partytime Fifties.
(M)	(2:08)	Rhino 75899	18 Greatest Hits.
(M)	(2:48)	Specialty 8508	The Specialty Sessions. *(includes a :39 false start and studio talk)*
(M)	(2:06)	Specialty 2154	Essential.

LITTLE RICHARD (Continued)

(E)	(2:04)	Motown 9066 Compact Command Performances. *(rerecorded)*
(M)	(2:08)	Specialty 7012 The Georgia Peach.
(M)	(1:43)	Epic 40389 Greatest Hits. *(all selections on this cd are live with a lot of dialogue preceding each song)*
(E)	(2:04)	Special Music 4908 His Greatest Hits. *(rerecorded)*
(M)	(2:08)	Specialty 4412 The Specialty Story.
(M)	(1:59)	Ripete 2199 Walkin' To New Orleans. *(rerecorded)*
(M)	(2:06)	Time-Life 2RNR-05 Rock 'N' Roll Era - 1958.
(M)	(2:06)	Time-Life RHD-16 Rhythm & Blues - 1958.
(E)	(2:05)	Curb 77739 Greatest Songs. *(rerecording)*
(M)	(2:08)	Specialty 7063 Little Richard Vol. 2: Shag On Down By The Union Hall. *(alternate take)*
(M)	(2:06)	Time-Life R838-22 Solid Gold Soul 1958.

LITTLE RIVER BAND
1976 IT'S A LONG WAY THERE

(S)	(4:13)	Capitol 46021 Greatest Hits. *(45 version)*
(S)	(8:35)	Rhino 71745 Reminiscing: Twentieth Anniversary Collection. *(LP version)*
(S)	(8:37)	One Way 19081 Little River Band. *(LP version)*

1977 HELP IS ON ITS WAY

(S)	(3:59)	Priority 8667 FM Hits/70's Greatest Rock Hits Volume 6.
(S)	(4:01)	Capitol 48439 Diamantina Cocktail.
(S)	(4:00)	Capitol 46021 Greatest Hits.
(S)	(4:05)	Rhino 71745 Reminiscing: Twentieth Anniversary Collection.
(S)	(4:00)	Madacy Entertainment 1977 Rock On 1977.
(S)	(4:02)	Capitol 55901 All-Time Greatest Hits.
(S)	(4:00)	Hip-O 40096 '70s Hit(s) Back Again.

1978 HAPPY ANNIVERSARY

(S)	(4:01)	Capitol 48439 Diamantina Cocktail. *(LP version)*
(S)	(3:59)	Capitol 46021 Greatest Hits. *(LP version)*
(S)	(4:04)	Rhino 71745 Reminiscing: Twentieth Anniversary Collection. *(LP version)*
(S)	(3:57)	Capitol 55901 All-Time Greatest Hits. *(LP version)*

1978 REMINISCING

(S)	(4:10)	Priority 8666 Kickin' Back/70's Greatest Rock Hits Volume 5. *(LP version)*
(S)	(3:27)	Rhino 70673 Billboard Top Hits - 1978. *(45 version)*
(S)	(4:11)	Capitol 46021 Greatest Hits. *(LP version)*
(S)	(3:28)	Time-Life SOD-20 Sounds Of The Seventies - 1978: Take Two. *(45 version)*
(S)	(4:13)	Rhino 71745 Reminiscing: Twentieth Anniversary Collection. *(LP version)*
(S)	(4:11)	Madacy Entertainment 1978 Rock On 1978. *(LP version)*
(S)	(4:11)	One Way 19080 Sleeper Catcher. *(LP version)*
(S)	(4:12)	Capitol 55901 All-Time Greatest Hits. *(LP version)*
(S)	(4:11)	Time-Life R834-08 Body Talk - On My Mind. *(LP version)*
(S)	(4:10)	Milan 35788 O.S.T. Hotel De Love. *(LP version)*
(S)	(3:28)	Time-Life AM1-25 AM Gold - 1978. *(45 version)*

1979 LADY

(S)	(4:55)	Capitol 46021 Greatest Hits. *(LP version)*
(S)	(4:56)	Rhino 71745 Reminiscing: Twentieth Anniversary Collection. *(LP version)*
(S)	(4:55)	One Way 19080 Sleeper Catcher. *(LP version)*
(S)	(4:55)	Capitol 55901 All-Time Greatest Hits. *(LP version)*
(S)	(4:55)	Time-Life R834-15 Body Talk - Once In Lifetime. *(LP version)*

1979 LONESOME LOSER

(S)	(3:54)	Capitol 46021 Greatest Hits. *(LP version)*
(S)	(3:57)	Capitol 48440 First Under The Wire. *(LP version)*
(S)	(3:59)	Rhino 71745 Reminiscing: Twentieth Anniversary Collection. *(LP version)*

(S)	(3:52)	JCI 3119 18 Rock Classics. *(LP version)*
(S)	(3:52)	K-Tel 3510 Platinum Rock Volume 2. *(LP version)*
(S)	(3:53)	Madacy Entertainment 1979 Rock On 1979. *(LP version)*
(S)	(3:56)	One Way 19075 First Under The Wire. *(LP version)*
(S)	(3:55)	Hip-O 40022 That Sound From Down Under. *(LP version)*
(S)	(3:53)	Capitol 55901 All-Time Greatest Hits. *(LP version)*
(S)	(3:51)	K-Tel 3907 Starflight Vol. 2. *(LP version)*
(S)	(3:52)	Simitar 55582 The Number One's: Rock It Up.
(S)	(3:52)	Time-Life AM1-26 AM Gold - 1979. *(LP version)*

1980 COOL CHANGE
(actual 45 time is (4:06) not (3:56) as stated on the record label)

(S)	(4:06)	Priority 7066 #1 Groups/70's Greatest Rock Hits Volume 12. *(45 version)*
(S)	(5:07)	Capitol 46021 Greatest Hits. *(LP version)*
(S)	(5:12)	Capitol 48440 First Under The Wire. *(LP version)*
(S)	(5:13)	Rhino 71745 Reminiscing: Twentieth Anniversary Collection. *(LP version)*
(S)	(5:10)	Madacy Entertainment 1980 Rock On 1980. *(LP version)*
(S)	(5:12)	One Way 19075 First Under The Wire. *(LP version)*
(S)	(5:04)	Capitol 55901 All-Time Greatest Hits. *(LP version)*
(S)	(4:06)	Time-Life R988-22 Sounds Of The Eighties 1980-1983. *(45 version)*

1981 THE NIGHT OWLS

(S)	(5:13)	Capitol 46021 Greatest Hits. *(LP version)*
(S)	(5:17)	Rhino 71745 Reminiscing: Twentieth Anniversary Collection. *(LP version)*
(S)	(5:13)	Madacy Entertainment 1981 Rock On 1981. *(LP version)*
(S)	(5:17)	One Way 19078 Time Exposure. *(LP version)*
(S)	(5:13)	Capitol 55901 All-Time Greatest Hits. *(LP version)*

1982 TAKE IT EASY ON ME

(S)	(3:43)	Priority 53699 80's Greatest Rock Hits Volume 7 - Light & Easy.
(S)	(3:44)	Capitol 46021 Greatest Hits.
(S)	(3:45)	One Way 19078 Time Exposure.
(S)	(3:44)	Capitol 55901 All-Time Greatest Hits.

1982 MAN ON YOUR MIND

(S)	(4:05)	Capitol 46021 Greatest Hits.
(S)	(4:15)	One Way 19078 Time Exposure.
(S)	(4:05)	Capitol 55901 All-Time Greatest Hits.

1983 THE OTHER GUY

(S)	(2:48)	Capitol 46021 Greatest Hits.
(S)	(2:46)	Madacy Entertainment 1982 Rock On 1982.
(S)	(2:47)	One Way 19078 Time Exposure.
(S)	(2:47)	Capitol 55901 All-Time Greatest Hits.

1983 WE TWO

(S)	(4:31)	Rhino 71745 Reminiscing: Twentieth Anniversary Collection.

1983 YOU'RE DRIVING ME OUT OF MY MIND

(S)	(5:11)	Rhino 71745 Reminiscing: Twentieth Anniversary Collection. *(LP version)*

LITTLE SISTER
1970 YOU'RE THE ONE (PART 2)
1971 SOMEBODY'S WATCHING YOU

(S)	(2:49)	Rhino 70784 Soul Hits Of The 70's Volume 4.
(S)	(2:49)	Rhino 72028 Soul Hits Of The 70's Volumes 1-5 Box Set.

LIVING COLOUR
1989 CULT OF PERSONALITY

(S)	(4:53)	Priority 53740 Cutting Edge Vol. 2 - Best Of Modern Rock Hits.
(S)	(4:52)	Time-Life R102-34 The Rolling Stone Collection.
(S)	(5:06)	WTG 45140 O.S.T. Say Anything.

(S) (4:53) Epic 44099 Vivid.
(S) (4:52) Epic/Legacy 65276 Super Hits.
(S) (4:52) Razor & Tie 89004 Monsters Of Rock.

1989 GLAMOUR BOYS
(S) (3:39) Epic 44099 Vivid.
(S) (3:39) Epic/Legacy 65276 Super Hits.

LIVING IN A BOX
1987 LIVING IN A BOX
(S) (3:03) EMI 89605 Living In Oblivion: The 80's Greatest Hits Volume Two.
(S) (6:12) SBK 29007 Brilliant! The Global Dance Music Experience Volume 3. *(remix)*
(S) (3:03) Chrysalis 21547 and 41547 Living In A Box.
(S) (6:12) EMI 54097 Retro Dance Club Volume One. *(remix)*

L.L. COOL J
1987 I NEED LOVE
(S) (4:16) EMI 91419 MTV, BET, VH-1 Power Players. *(45 version)*
(S) (5:24) Profile 1268 Mr. Magic's Rap Attack Volume 4. *(LP version)*
(S) (5:21) K-Tel 315 Rap's Biggest Hits. *(LP version)*
(S) (5:22) Def Jam/Columbia 40793 Bigger And Deffer. *(LP version)*
(S) (5:22) Def Jam 314527353 and 314527354 Bigger And Deffer. *(LP version)*
(S) (5:20) Thump 4720 Old School Love Songs Volume 2. *(LP version)*
(S) (5:21) Def Jam 314523848 Def Jam Music Group 10th Year Anniversary. *(LP version)*
(S) (5:21) Def Jam 314534125 All World. *(LP version)*

1988 GOING BACK TO CALI
(S) (4:08) Columbia/Def Jam 44042 O.S.T. Less Than Zero. *(LP length)*
(S) (4:09) Def Jam 314527360 O.S.T. Less Than Zero. *(LP length)*
(S) (4:09) Def Jam/Columbia 45172 Walking With A Panther. *(LP length)*
(S) (4:09) Def Jam 314527355 and 314527356 Walking With A Panther. *(LP length)*
(S) (4:08) Def Jam 314523848 Def Jam Music Group 10th Year Anniversary. *(LP length)*
(S) (4:09) Def Jam 314534125 All World. *(LP length)*
(S) (4:07) Def Jam 314536377 Def Jam's Greatest Hits. *(LP length)*

1989 I'M THAT TYPE OF GUY
(S) (5:16) Def Jam/Columbia 45172 Walking With A Panther. *(LP version)*
(S) (5:16) Def Jam 314527355 and 314527356 Walking With A Panther. *(LP version)*
(S) (5:16) Def Jam 314523848 Def Jam Music Group 10th Year Anniversary. *(LP version)*
(S) (5:00) K-Tel 3751 History Of Rap Volume 3. *(neither the 45 or LP version)*

1991 AROUND THE WAY GIRL
(S) (4:04) Def Jam/Columbia 46888 Mama Said Knock You Out.
(S) (4:04) Def Jam 314523477 Mama Said Knock You Out.
(S) (4:02) Def Jam 314523848 Def Jam Music Group 10th Year Anniversary.
(S) (4:04) Def Jam 314534125 All World.
(S) (3:56) Def Jam 314536377 Def Jam's Greatest Hits.

1991 MAMA SAID KNOCK YOU OUT
(S) (4:48) Def Jam/Columbia 46888 Mama Said Knock You Out.
(S) (4:48) Def Jam 314523477 Mama Said Knock You Out.
(S) (4:47) Def Jam 314523848 Def Jam Music Group 10th Year Anniversary.
(S) (4:47) Def Jam 314534125 All World.
(S) (4:47) Hollywood 62121 Monday Night Football Jamz.

1996 HEY LOVER
(S) (4:43) Def Jam 314523845 Mr. Smith.
(S) (4:59) Tommy Boy 1164 MTV Party To Go Volume 9. *(all selections on this cd are segued together)*

(S) (4:43) Def Jam 314534125 All World.

1996 DOIN IT
(S) (4:53) Def Jam 314523845 Mr. Smith.
(S) (4:52) Def Jam 314534125 All World.

1996 LOUNGIN
(S) (4:11) Def Jam 314523845 Mr. Smith. *(tracks into the next selection)*
(S) (3:44) Def Jam 314534125 All World.
(S) (3:44) Def Jam 314534746 Yo! MTV Raps Compilation.
(S) (3:44) Priority 51021 Hip Hop Coast 2 Coast.

LOBO
1971 ME AND YOU AND A DOG NAMED BOO
(S) (2:50) Rhino 70925 Super Hits Of The 70's Volume 5.
(S) (2:49) Priority 8670 Hitchin A Ride/70's Greatest Rock Hits Volume 10.
(S) (2:53) Curb 77302 Greatest Hits.
(S) (2:50) Rhino 71208 70's Smash Hits Volume 4.
(S) (2:56) Rhino 71254 Best Of.
(S) (2:50) Time-Life SUD-20 Superhits - Early 70's Classics.
(S) (2:50) Time-Life SOD-32 Sounds Of The Seventies - AM Pop Classics.
(S) (2:54) Rhino 72436 I'd Love You To Want Me.
(S) (2:54) Curb 77877 Best Of.
(S) (2:50) Time-Life AM1-15 AM Gold - Early '70s Classics.
(S) (2:54) Rhino 72737 Billboard Top Soft Rock Hits - 1971.
(S) (2:50) Flashback 72684 '70s Radio Hits Volume 4.
(S) (2:50) Flashback 72090 '70s Radio Hits Box Set.
(S) (2:55) Flashback 72676 Me And You And A Dog Named Boo And Other Hits.
(S) (2:56) Walt Disney 60870 Dog Songs.

1972 I'D LOVE YOU TO WANT ME
(S) (4:01) Rhino 70929 Super Hits Of The 70's Volume 9.
(S) (4:03) Curb 77302 Greatest Hits.
(S) (4:01) Rhino 71254 Best Of.
(S) (3:56) Time-Life SUD-11 Superhits - 1972.
(S) (4:01) Rhino 72436 I'd Love You To Want Me.
(S) (3:55) JCI 3145 1970 - Only Love - 1974.
(S) (4:09) Curb 77877 Best Of.
(S) (3:55) Time-Life AM1-07 AM Gold - 1972.
(S) (4:01) Rhino 72738 Billboard Top Soft Rock Hits - 1972.
(S) (4:01) Flashback 72676 Me And You And A Dog Named Boo And Other Hits.
(S) (4:00) Time-Life R834-14 Body Talk - Love And Tenderness.

1973 DON'T EXPECT ME TO BE YOUR FRIEND
(S) (3:34) Curb 77302 Greatest Hits.
(S) (3:31) Rhino 71254 Best Of.
(S) (3:31) Rhino 72436 I'd Love You To Want Me.
(S) (3:34) Curb 77877 Best Of.
(S) (3:31) Flashback 72676 Me And You And A Dog Named Boo And Other Hits.
(S) (3:31) Rhino 72739 Billboard Top Soft Rock Hits - 1973.
(S) (3:31) Time-Life R834-19 Body Talk - Always And Forever.

1973 IT SURE TOOK A LONG, LONG TIME
(S) (3:06) Rhino 71254 Best Of.
(S) (3:06) Rhino 72436 I'd Love You To Want Me.
(S) (3:06) Flashback 72676 Me And You And A Dog Named Boo And Other Hits.
(S) (3:06) K-Tel 3911 Fantastic Volume 2.

1973 HOW CAN I TELL HER
(S) (4:14) Curb 77302 Greatest Hits.
(S) (4:15) Rhino 71254 Best Of.
(S) (4:16) Rhino 72436 I'd Love You To Want Me.
(S) (4:16) Flashback 72676 Me And You And A Dog Named Boo And Other Hits.

1974 STANDING AT THE END OF THE LINE
(S) (3:49) Rhino 71254 Best Of.
(S) (3:50) Rhino 72436 I'd Love You To Want Me.
(S) (3:50) Flashback 72676 Me And You And A Dog Named Boo And Other Hits.

LOBO *(Continued)*
1974 RINGS
- (S) (3:27) Rhino 71254 Best Of.
- (S) (3:27) Rhino 72436 I'd Love You To Want Me.
- (S) (3:27) Flashback 72676 Me And You And A Dog Named Boo And Other Hits.

1975 DON'T TELL ME GOODNIGHT
- (S) (3:04) Rhino 71254 Best Of.
- (S) (3:04) Rhino 72436 I'd Love You To Want Me.
- (S) (3:04) Flashback 72676 Me And You And A Dog Named Boo And Other Hits.

1979 WHERE WERE YOU WHEN I WAS FALLING IN LOVE
- (S) (3:13) Curb 77532 Your Favorite Songs.
- (S) (3:15) Curb 77302 Greatest Hits.
- (S) (3:15) Curb 77877 Best Of.

HANK LOCKLIN
1960 PLEASE HELP ME, I'M FALLING
- (S) (2:21) RCA 8475 Nipper's Greatest Hits Of The 60's Volume 2.
- (S) (2:21) Rhino 70681 Billboard's Top Country Hits Of 1960.
- (S) (2:21) RCA 5802 Best Of The 60's.
- (S) (2:20) Reprise 45516 O.S.T. A Perfect World.
- (S) (2:20) Time-Life CTD-12 Country USA - 1960.
- (S) (2:09) K-Tel 3359 101 Greatest Country Hits Vol. Five: Country Memories. *(rerecording)*
- (S) (2:21) Collectables 5873 Please Help Me I'm Falling.
- (S) (2:20) Time-Life R808-01 Classic Country 1960-1964.

LISA LOEB & NINE STORIES
1994 STAY (I MISSED YOU)
- (S) (3:03) RCA 66364 O.S.T. Reality Bites.
- (S) (3:02) Geffen 24734 Tails.
- (S) (3:03) EMI-Capitol Music Group 54555 Movie Luv.
- (S) (5:24) Geffen 25102 Global Grooves - Remixes. *(remixed)*

1995 DO YOU SLEEP?
- (S) (3:52) Geffen 24734 Tails.

released as by LISA LOEB:
1998 I DO
- (S) (3:39) Geffen 25141 Firecracker.

DAVE LOGGINS
1974 PLEASE COME TO BOSTON
(actual 45 time is (4:07) not (3:57) as stated on the record label)
- (S) (4:06) Columbia/Legacy 46763 Rock Artifacts Volume 2.
- (S) (4:07) Priority 8664 High Times/70's Greatest Rock Hits Volume 3.
- (S) (4:07) Rhino 70760 Super Hits Of The 70's Volume 13.
- (S) (4:06) Time-Life R105-26 Our Songs: Singers & Songwriters Encore.
- (S) (4:06) Risky Business 66871 Polyester Dreams/Greatest Hits Of The 70's.
- (S) (4:06) Time-Life R103-18 Great Love Songs Of The '70s & '80s.
- (S) (4:06) Time-Life AM1-21 AM Gold - 1974.
- (S) (4:06) Time-Life R834-09 Body Talk - Magic Moments.
- (S) (4:07) Rhino 72740 Billboard Top Soft Rock Hits - 1974.

KENNY LOGGINS
1978 WHENEVER I CALL YOU "FRIEND"
- (S) (3:58) Columbia 35387 Nightwatch.
- (S) (3:57) Razor & Tie 4543 The '70s Preservation Society Presents: Easy '70s.
- (S) (4:00) Columbia 67986 Greatest Hits Of.
- (S) (3:57) Time-Life R834-01 Body Talk - Forever Yours.
- (S) (3:58) Columbia/Legacy 65382 Celebrate Me Home/Nightwatch/Keep The Fire.

1980 THIS IS IT
- (S) (3:56) Columbia 36172 Keep The Fire. *(LP length; tracks into next selection)*
- (S) (3:55) Columbia 67986 Greatest Hits Of. *(LP length)*

- (S) (3:56) Columbia/Legacy 65382 Celebrate Me Home/Nightwatch/Keep The Fire. *(LP length; tracks into the next selection)*

1980 I'M ALRIGHT (THEME FROM "CADDYSHACK")
- (S) (3:23) Columbia Special Products 44363 Rock Of The 80's. *(45 length)*
- (S) (3:45) Columbia 67986 Greatest Hits Of. *(LP length)*

released as by KENNY LOGGINS with STEVE PERRY:
1982 DON'T FIGHT IT
- (S) (3:37) Columbia 38127 Kenny Loggins - High Adventure.
- (S) (3:36) Columbia 67986 Kenny Loggins - Greatest Hits Of.

released as by KENNY LOGGINS:
1983 HEART TO HEART
- (S) (5:20) Columbia 38127 High Adventure. *(LP version)*
- (S) (5:19) Columbia 67986 Greatest Hits Of. *(LP version)*

1983 WELCOME TO HEARTLIGHT
- (S) (3:56) Columbia 38127 High Adventure.

1984 FOOTLOOSE
- (S) (3:46) Columbia 39242 O.S.T. Footloose.
- (S) (3:45) Time-Life R988-06 Sounds Of The Eighties: 1984.
- (S) (3:39) Columbia 67986 Greatest Hits Of.

1984 I'M FREE (HEAVEN HELPS THE MAN)
- (S) (3:45) Columbia 39242 O.S.T. Footloose.

1985 VOX HUMANA
- (S) (4:09) Columbia 39174 Vox Humana.

1985 FOREVER
- (S) (4:24) Columbia 39174 Vox Humana.
- (S) (4:22) Columbia 67986 Greatest Hits Of.

1986 DANGER ZONE
- (S) (3:30) Columbia 40323 O.S.T. Top Gun.
- (S) (3:33) Rhino 71641 Billboard Top Hits - 1986.
- (S) (3:33) Columbia 67986 Greatest Hits Of.

1987 MEET ME HALFWAY
- (S) (3:38) Columbia 40655 O.S.T. Over The Top.
- (S) (3:38) Columbia 40535 Back To Avalon.
- (S) (3:38) Columbia 67986 Greatest Hits Of.

1988 NOBODY'S FOOL
- (S) (4:17) Columbia 44317 O.S.T. Caddyshack II.
- (S) (4:17) Columbia 40535 Back To Avalon.

LOGGINS and MESSINA
1973 YOUR MAMA DON'T DANCE
- (S) (2:47) Columbia 45047 Pop Classics Of The 70's.
- (S) (2:46) JCI 3301 Rockin' Seventies.
- (S) (2:47) Columbia 34388 Best Of Friends.
- (S) (2:47) Columbia 31748 Loggins & Messina.
- (S) (2:47) Priority 53725 Country Rock Vol. 1 - Freewheelin'.
- (S) (2:47) Risky Business 66662 Swingin' Singles/Greatest Hits Of The 70's.
- (S) (2:47) Columbia/Legacy 65383 Sittin' In/Loggins & Messina/Full Sail.
- (S) (2:47) Time-Life R13610 Gold And Platinum Box Set - The Ultimate Rock Collection.

1973 THINKING OF YOU
- (S) (2:18) Columbia 34388 Best Of Friends. *(LP version)*
- (S) (2:18) Columbia 31748 Loggins & Messina. *(LP version)*
- (S) (2:18) Columbia/Legacy 65383 Sittin' In/Loggins & Messina/Full Sail. *(LP version)*

1973 MY MUSIC
- (S) (3:02) Columbia 32540 Full Sail.
- (S) (3:03) Columbia 34388 Best Of Friends.
- (S) (3:02) Columbia/Legacy 65383 Sittin' In/Loggins & Messina/Full Sail.

LO-KEY?
1993 I GOTTA THANG 4 YA!
- (S) (5:39) Perspective 1003 Where Dey At?.

LOLITA
1960 SAILOR (YOUR HOME IS THE SEA)
- (S) (2:48) Time-Life HPD-37 Your Hit Parade - The 60's.

JULIE LONDON
1956 CRY ME A RIVER
- (M) (2:55) Scotti Bros. 75402 There Was Love (The Divorce Songs).
- (E) (2:51) CBS Special Products 46850 The Society Of Singers Presents A Gift Of Music Vol. 2.
- (M) (2:56) Time-Life HPD-31 Your Hit Parade - The 50's Forever.
- (M) (2:56) EMI 99804 Julie Is Her Name/Julie Is Her Name Vol. 2.
- (M) (2:56) Rhino 70737 Best Of.
- (M) (2:55) Right Stuff 52289 Free To Be Volume 5.
- (M) (2:56) Rhino 72514 Sirens Of Song - Classic Torch Singers.

LAURIE LONDON
1958 HE'S GOT THE WHOLE WORLD (IN HIS HANDS)
- (M) (2:19) Capitol 98665 When AM Was King.
- (M) (2:19) Time-Life HPD-11 Your Hit Parade 1958.

LONDONBEAT
1991 I'VE BEEN THINKING ABOUT YOU
- (S) (5:16) Radioactive/MCA 10192 In The Blood. (LP version)

1991 A BETTER LOVE
- (S) (3:58) Radioactive/MCA 10192 In The Blood.

LONDON SYMPHONY ORCHESTRA (see also JOHN WILLIAMS)
1977 STAR WARS (MAIN TITLE)
- (S) (5:20) Polydor 800096 O.S.T. Star Wars. (LP version)
- (S) (5:23) 20th Century Fox 11012 Star Wars Trilogy. (LP version)
- (S) (2:17) Rhino 72424 Billboard Top Movie Hits - 1970s. (45 version)
- (S) (2:14) RCA 68746 and 68772 O.S.T. Star Wars - A New Hope. (45 version; there are five alternate takes of this theme buried in track 13 starting at 5:06)

SHORTY LONG
1968 HERE COMES THE JUDGE
- (S) (2:37) Motown 6184 Hard To Find Motown Classics Volume 2.
- (M) (2:35) K-Tel 3036 Silly Songs.
- (S) (2:36) Time-Life 2CLR-27 Classic Rock - 1968: Blowin' Your Mind.

LOOKING GLASS
1972 BRANDY (YOU'RE A FINE GIRL)
- (S) (3:03) Rhino 70929 Super Hits Of The 70's Volume 9. (LP version)
- (S) (3:06) Rhino 70633 Billboard's Top Rock & Roll Hits Of 1972. (LP version)
- (S) (3:06) Rhino 72005 Billboard's Top Rock & Roll Hits Of 1968-1972 Box Set. (LP version)
- (S) (2:55) Columbia/Legacy 46763 Rock Artifacts Volume 2. (45 version)
- (S) (3:05) Razor & Tie 21640 Those Fabulous 70's. (LP version)
- (S) (2:46) Time-Life SUD-11 Superhits - 1972. (45 version)
- (S) (2:55) Time-Life SOD-13 Sounds Of The Seventies - 1972: Take Two. (45 version)
- (S) (3:05) Risky Business 66662 Swingin' Singles/Greatest Hits Of The 70's. (LP version)
- (S) (3:05) K-Tel 3623 Believe In Music. (LP version)
- (S) (3:06) Collectables 5815 Golden Classics. (LP version)
- (S) (3:04) Eclipse Music Group 64893 Rock 'n Roll Relix 1972-1973. (LP version)
- (S) (3:04) Eclipse Music Group 64897 Rock 'n Roll Relix 1970-1979. (LP version)
- (S) (2:54) Time-Life AM1-07 AM Gold - 1972. (45 version)
- (S) (3:03) Rhino 72812 VH1 8-Track Flashback: The One Hit Wonders. (LP version)
- (S) (2:55) Collectables 1516 and 2516 The Anniversary Album - The 70's. (45 version)
- (S) (3:03) K-Tel 3987 70s Heavy Hitters: #1 Pop Hits. (LP version)

1973 JIMMY LOVES MARY-ANNE
- (S) (3:23) Rhino 70930 Super Hits Of The 70's Volume 10.
- (S) (3:24) Columbia/Legacy 46160 Rock Artifacts Volume 1.
- (S) (3:23) Collectables 5815 Golden Classics.

DENISE LOPEZ
1985 SAYIN' SORRY (DON'T MAKE IT RIGHT)
- (S) (4:40) A&M 5226 Truth In Disguise.

TRINI LOPEZ
1963 IF I HAD A HAMMER
- (S) (3:22) WEA Latina 72868 25th Anniversary Album. (live rerecording)
- (S) (2:57) GNP Crescendo 2216 Best Of.
- (S) (2:56) JCI 3109 Folk Sixties.
- (S) (2:56) Time-Life SUD-08 Superhits - 1963.
- (S) (3:00) K-Tel 3455 Folk Hits Around The Campfire.
- (S) (2:56) Time-Life R132-22 Treasury Of Folk Music Volume One.
- (S) (2:56) Time-Life AM1-17 AM Gold - 1963.

1964 KANSAS CITY
- (S) (3:54) WEA Latina 72868 25th Anniversary Album. (live rerecording)
- (S) (3:18) GNP Crescendo 2216 Best Of.
- (E) (3:16) K-Tel 3271 Best Of Kansas City.

1965 LEMON TREE
- (S) (2:44) WEA Latina 72868 25th Anniversary Album. (live rerecording)
- (S) (2:51) GNP Crescendo 2216 Best Of.

1966 I'M COMIN' HOME, CINDY
- (S) (2:19) GNP Crescendo 2216 Best Of.

A'ME LORAIN
1990 WHOLE WIDE WORLD
- (S) (3:51) RCA 9819 O.S.T. True Love.
- (S) (3:51) RCA 2280 Starring In.....Standing In A Monkey Sea.

JEFF LORBER featuring KARYN WHITE
1987 FACTS OF LOVE
- (S) (4:32) Warner Brothers 25492 Jeff Lorber - Private Passion.

TREY LORENZ
1992 SOMEONE TO HOLD
- (S) (4:42) Epic 47840 Trey Lorenz.

GLORIA LORING & CARL ANDERSON
1986 FRIENDS AND LOVERS
- (S) (3:49) Atlantic 81679 Gloria Loring.
- (S) (3:44) K-Tel 3864 Slow Dancin'.
- (S) (3:44) Time-Life R834-16 Body Talk - Sweet Nothings.

LOS BRAVOS
1966 BLACK IS BLACK
- (S) (2:56) Rhino 70325 History Of British Rock Volume 7.
- (S) (2:56) Rhino 72022 History Of British Rock Box Set.
- (S) (2:56) Time-Life 2CLR-07 Classic Rock - 1966: The Beat Goes On.

LOS DEL RIO
1996 MACARENA (BAYSIDE BOYS MIX)
- (S) (3:51) RCA 66745 Club Cutz.
- (S) (3:51) BMG Latin 37587 Macarena Non Stop.

1996 MACARENA
- (S) (4:09) Ariola 18570 A Mi Me Gusta.

LOS INDIOS TABAJARAS
1963 MARIA ELENA
- (S) (3:09) RCA 8474 Nipper's Greatest Hits Of The 60's Volume 1.
- (S) (3:08) Time-Life HPD-34 Your Hit Parade - 60's Instrumentals.
- (S) (3:08) RCA 66881 RCA's Greatest One-Hit Wonders.

LOS INDIOS TABAJARAS *(Continued)*
- (S) (3:08) RCA 3360 Maria Elena - Vol. 1.
- (S) (3:08) Time-Life R986-12 Instrumental Favorites - Latin Rhythms.
- (S) (3:07) Collectables 2705 Maria Elena/Always In My Heart.

LOS LOBOS
1987 LA BAMBA
(dj copies of this 45 ran (2:13) and (2:54); commercial copies were all (2:54))
- (S) (2:53) Slash/Warner Brothers 25605 O.S.T. La Bamba.
- (S) (2:16) JCI 3128 1985 - Only Rock 'N Roll - 1989. *(dj 45 edit)*
- (S) (2:51) Slash/Warner Brothers 45367 Just Another Band From East L.A.: A Collection.
- (S) (2:52) Time-Life R988-01 Sounds Of The Eighties: The Rockin' Eighties.
- (S) (2:51) Madacy Entertainment 6804 More Sun Splashin'.
1987 COME ON, LET'S GO
- (S) (1:59) Slash/Warner Brothers 25605 O.S.T. La Bamba.
- (S) (1:59) Slash/Warner Brothers 45367 Just Another Band From East L.A.: A Collection.

LOST BOYZ
1996 RENEE
- (S) (4:59) Island 31454146 and 314524197 O.S.T. Don't Be A Menace.

LOST GENERATION
1970 THE SLY, SLICK, AND THE WICKED
- (S) (2:56) Rhino 70784 Soul Hits Of The 70's Volume 4.
- (S) (2:56) Rhino 72028 Soul Hits Of The 70's Volumes 1-5 Box Set.

JOHN D. LOUDERMILK
1961 LANGUAGE OF LOVE

LOUIE LOUIE
1990 SITTIN' IN THE LAP OF LUXURY
- (S) (4:03) WTG 45285 The State I'm In.

LOVE
1966 MY LITTLE RED BOOK
- (S) (2:28) JCI 3101 Rockin' Sixties.
- (S) (2:28) Warner Special Products 27610 More Party Classics.
- (S) (2:29) Elektra 74001 Love.
- (S) (2:28) Time-Life 2CLR-21 Classic Rock - Rock Renaissance II.
- (M) (2:29) Rhino 73500 Love Story 1966-1972.
1966 7 AND 7 IS
- (S) (2:13) Warner Special Products 27607 Highs Of The 60's.
- (S) (2:13) Elektra 74005 Da Capo.
- (S) (2:12) Time-Life 2CLR-17 Classic Rock - Rock Renaissance.
- (S) (2:13) K-Tel 3133 Biker Rock.
- (M) (2:23) Rhino 73500 Love Story 1966-1972. *(:10 longer fade than the 45 or LP)*
- (S) (2:13) Time-Life R968-09 Guitar Rock 1966-1967.

DARLENE LOVE
1963 (TODAY I MET) THE BOY I'M GONNA MARRY
- (M) (2:46) Abkco 7118 Phil Spector/Back To Mono (1958-1969).
- (M) (2:46) Abkco 7213 Best Of.
1963 WAIT TIL' MY BOBBY GETS HOME
- (M) (2:21) Abkco 7118 Phil Spector/Back To Mono (1958-1969).
- (M) (2:22) Abkco 7213 Best Of.

MONIE LOVE
1991 IT'S A SHAME (MY SISTER)
- (S) (3:41) Rhino 71916 Whats Up? Rap Hits Of The 90's.
- (S) (3:42) Warner Brothers 26358 Down To Earth.

LOVE AND KISSES
1978 THANK GOD IT'S FRIDAY
- (S) (4:23) Rebound 314520307 Disco Nights Volume VIII. *("Thank God It's Friday" soundtrack version)*
- (S) (4:13) Rebound 314520337 Compiled From O.S.T. Thank God It's Friday. *("Thank God It's Friday" soundtrack version)*
- (S) (4:23) Rebound 314520366 Disco Nights Vol. 10 - Disco's Greatest Movie Hits. *("Thank God It's Friday" soundtrack version)*
- (S) (3:18) Casablanca 314526253 Casablanca Records Greatest Hits. *(45 version)*
- (S) (4:14) Casablanca 314534606 O.S.T. Thank God It's Friday. *("Thank God It's Friday" soundtrack version)*
- (S) (4:22) Thump 4840 Flashback Disco. *(all selections on this cd are segued together; "Thank God It's Friday" soundtrack version)*

LOVE AND ROCKETS
1989 SO ALIVE
- (S) (4:12) RCA 9715 Love And Rockets.
- (S) (4:12) Time-Life R988-13 Sounds Of The Eighties: 1989.
- (S) (4:12) K-Tel 3848 90s Now Volume 2.
- (S) (4:11) Simitar 55612 The Number One's: The '80s.

LOVERBOY
1981 TURN ME LOOSE
(dj copies of this 45 ran (3:28), (3:45) and (5:35); commercial copies were all (3:28))
- (S) (5:36) Columbia 36762 Loverboy. *(LP version)*
- (S) (5:36) Columbia 45411 Big Ones. *(LP version)*
- (S) (5:36) Columbia/Legacy 66648 Classics. *(LP version)*
- (S) (5:36) Epic 67534 Club Epic Volume 5. *(LP version)*
- (S) (5:36) Columbia/Legacy 65272 Super Hits. *(LP version)*
1982 WORKING FOR THE WEEKEND
- (S) (3:38) CBS Special Products 44363 Rock Of The 80's.
- (S) (3:40) Columbia/Legacy 66648 Classics.
- (S) (3:41) Columbia 37638 Get Lucky.
- (S) (3:40) Columbia 45411 Big Ones.
- (S) (3:40) Time-Life R988-18 Sounds Of The Eighties: The Early '80s Take Two.
- (S) (3:40) Time-Life R968-24 Guitar Rock - The '80s Take Two.
- (S) (3:39) Rhino 72595 Billboard Top Album Rock Hits, 1982.
- (S) (3:40) Columbia/Legacy 65272 Super Hits.
1982 WHEN IT'S OVER
- (S) (5:05) Columbia/Legacy 66648 Classics. *(LP version)*
- (S) (5:08) Columbia 37638 Get Lucky. *(LP version)*
- (S) (5:07) Columbia 45411 Big Ones. *(LP version)*
- (S) (5:05) Columbia/Legacy 65272 Super Hits. *(LP version)*
1983 HOT GIRLS IN LOVE
- (S) (3:59) Priority 53702 Hot And Sexy - Rock All Night.
- (S) (3:59) Risky Business 57833 Read The Hits/Best Of The 80's.
- (S) (3:59) Columbia/Legacy 66648 Classics.
- (S) (3:59) Columbia 38703 Keep It Up.
- (S) (3:59) Columbia 45411 Big Ones.
- (S) (3:58) Time-Life R988-16 Sounds Of The Eighties: The Early '80s.
- (S) (3:59) Rhino 72596 Billboard Top Album Rock Hits, 1983.
- (S) (3:59) Columbia/Legacy 65272 Super Hits.
- (S) (3:58) Simitar 55762 Stud Rock - Wild Ride.
1983 QUEEN OF THE BROKEN HEARTS
- (S) (3:49) Columbia 38703 Keep It Up.
- (S) (3:49) Columbia/Legacy 65272 Super Hits.
1985 LOVIN' EVERY MINUTE OF IT
- (S) (3:31) Priority 53715 80's Greatest Rock Hits Volume 3 - Arena Rock.
- (S) (3:31) Time-Life R105-40 Rock Dreams.
- (S) (3:31) Columbia/Legacy 66648 Classics.
- (S) (3:32) Columbia 39953 Lovin' Every Minute Of It.

(S) (3:31) Columbia 45411 Big Ones.

(S) (3:31) Time-Life R988-17 Sounds Of The Eighties: The Mid '80s Take Two.

1986 THIS COULD BE THE NIGHT
(S) (4:57) Sony Music Distribution 57854 For Your Love. *(LP version)*

(S) (4:56) Columbia/Legacy 66648 Classics. *(LP version)*

(S) (4:57) Columbia 39953 Lovin' Every Minute Of It. *(LP version)*

(S) (4:56) Columbia 45411 Big Ones. *(LP version)*

(S) (4:57) Columbia/Legacy 65272 Super Hits. *(LP version)*

1986 HEAVEN IN YOUR EYES
(S) (4:02) Columbia 40323 O.S.T. Top Gun.

(S) (4:02) Columbia/Legacy 66648 Classics.

(S) (4:02) Columbia 45411 Big Ones.

(S) (4:02) Priority 50974 Premiere The Movie Magazine Presents The Greatest Soundtrack Love Songs.

(S) (4:01) Time-Life R834-16 Body Talk - Sweet Nothings.

1987 NOTORIOUS
(S) (4:38) Columbia/Legacy 66648 Classics.

(S) (4:39) Columbia 40893 Wildside.

(S) (4:38) Columbia 45411 Big Ones.

LOVE UNLIMITED
1972 WALKIN' IN THE RAIN WITH THE ONE I LOVE
(dj copies of this 45 ran (3:35); commercial copies were all (4:50))

(S) (4:47) Rhino 70551 Soul Hits Of The 70's Volume 11.

(S) (4:46) Mercury 314514143 Barry White: Just For You.

(S) (4:47) Varese Sarabande 5490 From A Girl's Point Of View.

(S) (4:47) Thump 4730 Old School Love Songs Volume 3.

(S) (4:29) Hip-O 40001 The Glory Of Love - Sweet & Soulful Love Songs. *(faded :18 earlier than the 45 or LP)*

(S) (4:45) Mercury 314532408 Best Of.

(S) (4:42) Time-Life R834-16 Body Talk - Sweet Nothings.

1975 I BELONG TO YOU
(actual 45 time is (3:26) not (3:12) as stated on the record label)

(S) (3:46) Original Sound 8911 Art Laboe's Dedicated To You Vol. 2. *(:20 longer fade than the 45 version)*

(S) (3:46) Original Sound 4001 Art Laboe's 60 Killer Oldies. *(:20 longer fade than the 45 version)*

(S) (5:09) Varese Sarabande 5490 From A Girl's Point Of View. *(LP version)*

(S) (3:44) Mercury 314528091 Love's Train: Best Of Funk Essentials. *(:18 longer fade than the 45 version)*

(S) (5:04) Mercury 314532408 Best Of. *(LP version)*

(S) (3:44) K-Tel 3889 Great R&B Female Groups: Hits Of The 70s. *(:18 longer fade than the 45 version)*

LOVE UNLIMITED ORCHESTRA
1974 LOVE'S THEME
(S) (3:32) Rhino 70553 Soul Hits Of The 70's Volume 13. *(45 version)*

(S) (3:32) Rhino 70799 O.S.T. Spirit Of '76. *(45 version)*

(S) (4:07) Mercury 314514143 Barry White: Just For You. *(LP version)*

(S) (3:32) Razor & Tie 22047 Sweet 70's Soul. *(45 version)*

(S) (4:08) Mercury 314522459 Barry White: All-Time Greatest Hits. *(LP version)*

(S) (4:08) Mercury 314526945 Best Of. *(LP version)*

(S) (4:06) Rebound 314520358 Barry White And The Love Unlimited Orchestra Back To Back: Their Greatest Hits. *(LP version)*

(S) (4:07) K-Tel 3625 Dynamite. *(LP version)*

(S) (3:32) Time-Life R838-09 Solid Gold Soul - 1974. *(45 version)*

(S) (4:08) Polydor 314555120 Pure Disco 2. *(LP version)*

(S) (3:32) K-Tel 6257 The Greatest Love Songs - 16 Soft Rock Hits. *(45 version)*

(S) (3:33) Time-Life R840-05 Sounds Of The Seventies: '70s Dance Party 1972-1974. *(45 version)*

1975 SATIN SOUL
(S) (4:11) Mercury 314514143 Barry White: Just For You. *(LP version)*

(S) (4:11) Mercury 314526945 Best Of. *(LP version)*

LOVIN' SPOONFUL
1965 DO YOU BELIEVE IN MAGIC
(S) (2:04) K-Tel 839 Battle Of The Bands Volume 2. *(LP mix)*

(S) (2:02) Pair 1202 Best Of Buddah. *(LP mix)*

(S) (2:04) Rhino 70944 Anthology. *(LP mix)*

(S) (2:03) Special Music 4916 All The Best. *(LP mix)*

(S) (2:04) Pair 1200 Best Of. *(LP mix)*

(S) (2:03) Buddah 68002 Very Best Of. *(LP mix)*

(S) (2:02) Collectables 5068 History Of Rock Volume 8. *(LP mix)*

(S) (2:04) Rhino 71024 Best Of/Rhino Special Editions. *(LP mix)*

(S) (2:03) Essex 7060 The Buddah Box. *(LP mix)*

(S) (2:02) Time-Life 2CLR-01 Classic Rock - 1965. *(LP mix)*

(S) (2:00) Time-Life SUD-03 Superhits - 1965. *(LP mix)*

(S) (2:03) Time-Life R962-02 History Of Rock 'N' Roll: Folk Rock 1964-1967. *(LP mix)*

(S) (2:04) Time-Life R921-38 Get Together. *(LP mix)*

(S) (2:00) Replay 49500 Do You Believe In Magic/Hums. *(LP mix)*

(S) (2:04) K-Tel 3438 Best Of Folk Rock. *(LP mix)*

(S) (2:00) Buddah 49518 Complete Kama Sutra Singles Volume One. *(LP mix)*

(S) (2:03) Tag 92690 O.S.T. I Shot Andy Warhol. *(LP mix)*

(S) (2:03) JCI 3160 18 Free & Easy Hits From The 60's. *(LP mix)*

(S) (2:00) JCI 3167 #1 Radio Hits 1965 - Only Rock 'n Roll - 1969. *(LP mix)*

(S) (2:03) Eclipse Music Group 64869 Rock 'n Roll Relix 1964-1965. *(LP mix)*

(S) (2:03) Eclipse Music Group 64872 Rock 'n Roll Relix 1960-1969. *(LP mix)*

(S) (2:00) Time-Life AM1-10 AM Gold - 1965. *(LP mix)*

(S) (2:03) Flashback 72694 Do You Believe In Magic And Other Hits. *(LP mix)*

(S) (2:03) Flashback 72087 '60s Rock Legends Box Set. *(LP mix)*

(S) (2:00) BMG Special Products 44643 The Best Of Buddah. *(LP mix)*

(S) (2:03) Simitar 55532 The Number One's: The '60s. *(LP mix)*

1966 YOU DIDN'T HAVE TO BE SO NICE
(S) (2:26) Rhino 70944 Anthology.

(S) (2:26) Special Music 4916 All The Best.

(S) (2:26) Pair 1200 Best Of.

(S) (2:26) K-Tel 666 Flower Power.

(S) (2:25) Buddah 68002 Very Best Of.

(S) (2:25) One Way 22165 Daydream.

(S) (2:26) Rhino 71024 Best Of/Rhino Special Editions.

(S) (2:23) Time-Life 2CLR-13 Classic Rock - 1966: Shakin' All Over.

(S) (2:24) Time-Life SUD-01 Superhits - 1966.

(S) (2:25) Buddah 49508 Daydream.

(S) (2:25) Buddah 49518 Complete Kama Sutra Singles Volume One.

(S) (2:24) Time-Life AM1-09 AM Gold - 1966.

(S) (2:26) Flashback 72694 Do You Believe In Magic And Other Hits.

(S) (2:26) Flashback 72087 '60s Rock Legends Box Set.

1966 DAYDREAM
(S) (2:19) Rhino 70944 Anthology.

(S) (2:18) Special Music 4916 All The Best.

(S) (2:18) Pair 1200 Best Of.

(S) (2:18) Buddah 68002 Very Best Of.

(S) (2:18) One Way 22165 Daydream.

(S) (2:19) Rhino 71093 Better Days.

(S) (2:17) Collectables 5066 History Of Rock Volume 6.

(S) (2:19) Rhino 71024 Best Of/Rhino Special Editions.

(S) (2:18) Essex 7060 The Buddah Box.

LOVIN' SPOONFUL (Continued)

- (S) (2:18) Time-Life 2CLR-07 Classic Rock - 1966: The Beat Goes On.
- (S) (2:18) Time-Life SUD-01 Superhits - 1966.
- (S) (2:18) Rhino 71936 Billboard Top Pop Hits, 1966.
- (S) (2:19) Buddah 49508 Daydream.
- (S) (2:17) Buddah 49506 Feelin' Groovy.
- (S) (2:18) Buddah 49519 Complete Kama Sutra Singles Volume Two.
- (S) (2:17) Time-Life AM1-09 AM Gold - 1966.
- (S) (2:19) Flashback 72687 '60s Rock: Feelin' Groovy.
- (S) (2:19) Flashback 72088 '60s Rock Hits Box Set.
- (S) (2:18) Flashback 72694 Do You Believe In Magic And Other Hits.
- (S) (2:18) Flashback 72087 '60s Rock Legends Box Set.

1966 DID YOU EVER HAVE TO MAKE UP YOUR MIND?

- (S) (1:57) Rhino 70944 Anthology.
- (S) (1:57) JCI 3104 Mellow Sixties.
- (S) (1:57) Special Music 4916 All The Best.
- (S) (1:57) Pair 1200 Best Of.
- (S) (1:57) Buddah 68002 Very Best Of.
- (S) (1:57) Rhino 71024 Best Of/Rhino Special Editions.
- (S) (1:57) Time-Life 2CLR-02 Classic Rock - 1966.
- (S) (1:57) Time-Life SUD-12 Superhits - The Mid 60's.
- (S) (1:57) Replay 49500 Do You Believe In Magic/Hums.
- (S) (1:56) Buddah 49519 Complete Kama Sutra Singles Volume Two.
- (S) (1:57) Time-Life AM1-05 AM Gold - The Mid '60s.
- (S) (1:57) Flashback 72694 Do You Believe In Magic And Other Hits.
- (S) (1:57) Flashback 72087 '60s Rock Legends Box Set.
- (M) (1:56) Varese Sarabande 5803 Sunshine Days - Pop Classics Of The '60s Volume 3.
- (S) (1:57) Play-Tone/Epic 69179 Music From The HBO Miniseries "From The Earth To The Moon". *(hum noticeable at the end of every song on this cd)*

1966 SUMMER IN THE CITY

- (S) (2:38) Rhino 70087 Summer & Sun.
- (S) (2:39) Rhino 70944 Anthology.
- (S) (2:38) Rhino 70627 Billboard's Top Rock & Roll Hits Of 1966.
- (S) (2:38) Rhino 72007 Billboard's Top Rock & Roll Hits 1962-1966 Box Set.
- (S) (2:38) Original Sound CDGO-9 Golden Oldies Volume. 9.
- (S) (2:38) Original Sound 8895 Dick Clark's 21 All-Time Hits Vol. 4.
- (S) (2:35) Pair 1202 Best Of Buddah.
- (S) (2:39) K-Tel 686 Battle Of The Bands Volume 4.
- (S) (2:37) Warner Special Products 27610 More Party Classics.
- (S) (2:39) Special Music 4916 All The Best.
- (S) (2:39) Pair 1200 Best Of.
- (S) (2:38) Pair 3305 Hums Of.
- (S) (2:38) Buddah 68002 Very Best Of.
- (S) (2:37) Collectables 5070 History Of Rock Volume 10.
- (S) (2:38) Rhino 71229 Summer Hits.
- (S) (2:38) JCI 3111 Good Time Sixties.
- (S) (2:39) Rhino 71024 Best Of/Rhino Special Editions.
- (S) (2:39) Essex 7060 The Buddah Box.
- (S) (2:37) Time-Life 2CLR-02 Classic Rock - 1966.
- (S) (2:39) Collectables 2501 WCBS-FM History Of Rock - The 60's Part 2.
- (S) (2:39) Collectables 4501 History Of Rock/The 60s Part Two.
- (S) (2:37) JCI 3126 1965 - Only Rock 'N Roll - 1969.
- (S) (2:39) RCA 68306 O.S.T. Die Hard With A Vengeance.
- (S) (2:39) Replay 49500 Do You Believe In Magic/Hums.
- (S) (2:39) K-Tel 3437 Summer Songs.
- (S) (2:39) Buddah 49519 Complete Kama Sutra Singles Volume Two.
- (S) (2:39) RCA 66862 Hi Octane Hard Drivin' Hits.
- (S) (2:40) Priority 50951 I Love Rock & Roll Volume 2: Hits Of The 60's.
- (S) (2:38) Flashback 72710 Golden Summer.
- (S) (2:39) Flashback 72694 Do You Believe In Magic And Other Hits.
- (S) (2:39) Flashback 72087 '60s Rock Legends Box Set.

- (S) (2:37) Madacy Entertainment 6804 More Sun Splashin'.
- (S) (2:40) Nick At Nite/550 Music 63435 Beach Blanket Bash.

1966 RAIN ON THE ROOF
(the LP title of this song was "YOU AND ME AND RAIN ON THE ROOF")

- (S) (2:12) Rhino 70944 Anthology.
- (S) (2:11) Special Music 4916 All The Best.
- (S) (2:11) Pair 1200 Best Of.
- (S) (2:11) Pair 3305 Hums Of.
- (S) (2:11) Buddah 68002 Very Best Of.
- (S) (2:11) Rhino 71195 Kid Rock!
- (S) (2:11) Rhino 71024 Best Of/Rhino Special Editions.
- (S) (2:11) Time-Life 2CLR-29 Classic Rock - Bubblegum, Garage And Pop Nuggets.
- (S) (2:12) Varese Sarabande 5534 Rhythm Of The Rain.
- (S) (2:11) Replay 49500 Do You Believe In Magic/Hums.
- (S) (2:12) Flashback 72694 Do You Believe In Magic And Other Hits.
- (S) (2:12) Flashback 72087 '60s Rock Legends Box Set.

1967 NASHVILLE CATS

- (S) (2:35) Rhino 70944 Anthology.
- (S) (2:35) Special Music 4916 All The Best.
- (S) (2:34) Pair 1200 Best Of.
- (S) (2:34) Pair 3305 Hums Of.
- (S) (2:33) Buddah 68002 Very Best Of.
- (S) (2:34) Rhino 70495 Fun Rock!
- (S) (2:35) Rhino 71024 Best Of/Rhino Special Editions.
- (S) (2:33) Time-Life 2CLR-10 Classic Rock - 1967: The Beat Goes On.
- (S) (2:34) Time-Life SUD-17 Superhits - Mid 60's Classics.
- (S) (2:35) K-Tel 6137 Peaceful Easy Feeling - The Best Of Country Rock.
- (S) (2:33) K-Tel 3299 Country 'Round The Country.
- (S) (2:35) Replay 49500 Do You Believe In Magic/Hums.
- (S) (2:34) Time-Life AM1-16 AM Gold - Mid '60s Classics.
- (S) (2:35) Flashback 72694 Do You Believe In Magic And Other Hits.
- (S) (2:35) Flashback 72087 '60s Rock Legends Box Set.

1967 DARLING BE HOME SOON

- (S) (3:32) Rhino 70944 Anthology.
- (S) (3:29) Special Music 4916 All The Best.
- (S) (3:32) Pair 1200 Best Of.
- (S) (3:30) Buddah 68002 Very Best Of. *(sounds like it was mastered from vinyl)*
- (S) (3:32) Rhino 71024 Best Of/Rhino Special Editions.
- (S) (3:29) JCI 3114 Easy Sixties.
- (S) (3:32) Time-Life 2CLR-24 Classic Rock - 1967: Blowin' Your Mind.
- (S) (3:32) Time-Life SUD-14 Superhits - The Late 60's.
- (S) (3:32) JCI 3185 1965 - Only Love - 1969.
- (S) (3:32) Time-Life AM1-14 AM Gold - The Late '60s.
- (S) (3:32) Flashback 72694 Do You Believe In Magic And Other Hits.
- (S) (3:32) Flashback 72087 '60s Rock Legends Box Set.

1967 SIX O'CLOCK

- (S) (2:41) Rhino 70944 Anthology.
- (S) (2:40) Special Music 4916 All The Best.
- (S) (2:41) Pair 1200 Best Of.
- (S) (2:41) Buddah 68002 Very Best Of.
- (S) (2:41) Rhino 71066 Summer Of Love Volume 2.
- (S) (2:41) Rhino 71024 Best Of/Rhino Special Editions.
- (S) (2:41) Risky Business 66387 Rock Around The Clock.
- (S) (2:40) Flashback 72694 Do You Believe In Magic And Other Hits.
- (S) (2:40) Flashback 72087 '60s Rock Legends Box Set.

1967 SHE IS STILL A MYSTERY

- (S) (3:00) Rhino 70944 Anthology.
- (S) (2:57) Special Music 4916 All The Best.
- (S) (2:58) Pair 1200 Best Of.
- (S) (2:58) Buddah 68002 Very Best Of. *(poor sound quality; sounds like it was mastered from vinyl)*
- (S) (2:59) Rhino 71024 Best Of/Rhino Special Editions.
- (S) (2:59) Flashback 72694 Do You Believe In Magic And Other Hits.
- (S) (2:59) Flashback 72087 '60s Rock Legends Box Set.

JIM LOWE
1956 THE GREEN DOOR
    (M) (2:11)   Rhino 70599 Billboard's Top Rock & Roll Hits Of 1956.
    (M) (2:11)   Time-Life HPD-15 Your Hit Parade - 1956.
    (M) (2:11)   Varese Sarabande 5687 History Of Dot Records Volume Two.
    (M) (2:12)   JCI 3165 #1 Radio Hits 1955 - Only Rock 'n Roll - 1959.
1957 FOUR WALLS
1957 TALKIN' TO THE BLUES

NICK LOWE
1979 CRUEL TO BE KIND
    (S) (3:27)   Sandstone 33051 and 5019 Cosmopolitan Volume 5.
    (S) (3:26)   Columbia 45313 Basher: Best Of.
    (S) (3:26)   Columbia 36087 Labour Of Lust.
    (S) (3:26)   Time-Life SOD-21 Sounds Of The Seventies - Rock 'N' Soul Seventies.
    (S) (3:26)   Rhino 71694 New Wave Hits Of The 80's Vol. 1.
    (S) (3:27)   DCC Compact Classics 083 Night Moves Volume 3.
    (S) (3:26)   Time-Life R968-14 Guitar Rock - The Late '70s.
    (S) (3:26)   Rhino 72728 Poptopia! Power Pop Classics Of The '70s.

LSG
1997 MY BODY
    (S) (4:06)   EastWest 62125 Levert-Sweat-Gill.

L.T.D.
1976 LOVE BALLAD
(actual 45 time is (3:41) not (3:31) as stated on the record label)
    (S) (4:34)   A&M 2525 Classics Volume 27. *(LP length)*
    (S) (4:33)   Rebound 314520367 Soul Classics - Quiet Storm/The 70's. *(LP length)*
    (S) (4:32)   A&M 750213146 Love To The World. *(LP length)*
    (S) (4:32)   A&M 314540520 Greatest Hits. *(LP length)*
    (S) (3:41)   Time-Life R838-11 Solid Gold Soul - 1976. *(45 length)*
    (S) (4:34)   Time-Life R834-11 Body Talk - After Dark. *(LP length)*
1978 (EVERY TIME I TURN AROUND) BACK IN LOVE AGAIN
    (S) (3:34)   Priority 7975 Mega-Hits Dance Classics Volume 5. *(45 version)*
    (S) (4:43)   A&M 2525 Classics Volume 27. *(LP version)*
    (S) (3:37)   Rhino 71618 Soul Train Hall Of Fame/20th Anniversary. *(45 version)*
    (S) (3:40)   Time-Life SOD-17 Sounds Of The Seventies - 1977: Take Two. *(45 version)*
    (S) (3:39)   Rhino 72129 Soul Hits Of The 70's Vol. 19. *(45 version)*
    (S) (4:38)   A&M 750213148 Something To Love. *(LP version)*
    (S) (4:38)   A&M 314540520 Greatest Hits. *(LP version)*
    (S) (4:37)   Chronicles 314555137 Funk Of The 70's. *(LP version)*
    (S) (3:41)   Rhino 72943 VH1 8-Track Flashback: Classic '70s Soul. *(45 version)*
1981 SHINE ON
    (S) (3:57)   A&M 2525 Classics Volume 27.
    (S) (3:57)   A&M 750214819 Shine On.
    (S) (3:57)   A&M 314540520 Greatest Hits.

LUCAS
1994 LUCAS WITH THE LID OFF
    (S) (4:00)   Big Beat/Atlantic 92467 <<Lunacentric>>.
    (S) (3:58)   Razor & Tie 4569 '90s Style.

LUKE featuring 2 LIVE CREW (see also 2 LIVE CREW)
1990 BANNED IN THE U.S.A.
    (S) (4:23)   Luke/Atlantic 91427 and 91424 Banned In The U.S.A.

    (S) (4:23)   Luke 114 and 115 Banned In The U.S.A.

ROBIN LUKE
1958 SUSIE DARLIN'
    (M) (2:36)   MCA 31202 Vintage Music Volume 5.
    (M) (2:36)   MCA 5804 Vintage Music Volumes 5 & 6.
    (M) (2:31)   Original Sound CDGO-10 Golden Oldies Volume. 10. *(alternate take)*
    (M) (2:36)   Curb 77354 50's Hits Volume 1.
    (M) (2:36)   Curb 77525 Greatest Hits Of Rock 'N' Roll Volume 2.
    (M) (2:36)   Time-Life 2RNR-24 Rock 'N' Roll Era - The 50's Keep On Rockin'.
    (M) (2:36)   Time-Life R962-05 History Of Rock 'N' Roll: The Teenage Years 1957-1964.
    (M) (2:36)   K-Tel 478 More 50's Jukebox Favorites.
    (M) (2:36)   MCA Special Products 22179 Vintage Collectibles Volume 9.
    (M) (2:36)   Time-Life R857-04 The Heart Of Rock 'n' Roll - 1958.
    (M) (2:36)   Varese Sarabande 5686 History Of Dot Records Volume One.

LULU
1967 TO SIR WITH LOVE
    (S) (2:44)   Columbia 44373 Hollywood Magic - The 1960's.
    (S) (2:44)   Columbia/Legacy 46983 Rock Artifacts Volume 3.
    (S) (2:41)   Rhino 70324 History Of British Rock Volume 6. *(noise on fadeout)*
    (S) (2:41)   Rhino 72022 History Of British Rock Box Set. *(noise on fadeout)*
    (S) (2:43)   Time-Life SUD-18 Superhits - Late 60's Classics.
    (M) (2:42)   Rhino 71815 From Crayons To Perfume: Best Of.
    (M) (2:42)   Rhino 71937 Billboard Top Pop Hits, 1967.
    (S) (2:45)   Nick At Nite/550 Music/Epic 67689 Stand By Your Man.
    (S) (2:43)   Time-Life AM1-12 AM Gold - Late '60s Classics.
    (S) (2:43)   Time-Life R814-03 Love Songs.
    (S) (2:43)   Collectables 1515 and 2515 The Anniversary Album - The 60's.
1968 BEST OF BOTH WORLDS
    (S) (3:00)   Columbia/Legacy 46984 Rock Artifacts Volume 4.
    (M) (3:00)   Rhino 71815 From Crayons To Perfume: Best Of.
1970 OH ME OH MY (I'M A FOOL FOR YOU BABY)
    (S) (2:41)   Rhino 70926 Super Hits Of The 70's Volume 6.
    (S) (2:41)   Rhino 71815 From Crayons To Perfume: Best Of.
1981 I COULD NEVER MISS YOU (MORE THAN I DO)
    (S) (3:08)   Rhino 71815 From Crayons To Perfume: Best Of.

BOB LUMAN
1960 LET'S THINK ABOUT LIVING
    (S) (2:02)   Time-Life CTD-12 Country USA - 1960.
    (S) (2:01)   Time-Life SUD-19 Superhits - Early 60's Classics.
    (S) (2:19)   Columbia 45078 American Originals. *(rerecording)*
    (S) (1:56)   K-Tel 3366 101 Greatest Country Hits Vol. Seven: Country Nights. *(rerecording)*
    (S) (2:01)   Time-Life AM1-20 AM Gold - Early '60s Classics.

VICTOR LUNDBERG
1967 AN OPEN LETTER TO MY TEENAGE SON

LUNIZ
1995 I GOT 5 ON IT
    (S) (4:12)   Noo Trybe 40523 Operation Stackola.
    (S) (4:13)   Priority 51021 Hip Hop Coast 2 Coast.

LUSCIOUS JACKSON
1997 NAKED EYE
    (S) (4:39)   Grand Royal/Capitol 35534 Fever In Fever Out.

ARTHUR LYMAN GROUP
1961 YELLOW BIRD
- (S) (2:43) DCC Compact Classics 613 Exotic Sound Of.
- (S) (2:43) Time-Life HPD-34 Your Hit Parade - 60's Instrumentals.
- (S) (2:42) K-Tel 3091 Those Wonderful Instrumentals.
- (S) (2:43) DCC Compact Classics 079 Music For A Bachelor's Den.
- (S) (2:42) Collectors' Choice 003/4 Instrumental Gems Of The 60's.
- (S) (2:43) DCC Compact Classics 096 More Of The Best Of.
- (S) (2:42) Time-Life R986-19 Instrumental Favorites - Exotic Moods.

FRANKIE LYMON and THE TEENAGERS
released as by THE TEENAGERS featuring FRANKIE LYMON:
1956 WHY DO FOOLS FALL IN LOVE
- (M) (2:17) Rhino 70642 Billboard's Top R&B Hits Of 1956.
- (M) (2:16) Rhino 70599 Billboard's Top Rock & Roll Hits Of 1956.
- (M) (2:15) Rhino 70906 American Bandstand Greatest Hits Collection.
- (M) (2:16) Rhino 75764 Best Of Doo Wop Uptempo.
- (M) (2:16) Rhino 70918 Best Of.
- (M) (2:17) MCA 10063 Original Television Soundtrack "The Sounds Of Murphy Brown".
- (M) (2:16) Atlantic 82155 O.S.T. Book Of Love.
- (M) (2:16) Collectables 5416 Murray The K - Sing Along With The Golden Greats.
- (M) (2:17) Pair 1279 Goody Goody.
- (M) (2:17) Special Music 5020 Singing Their Hits.
- (M) (2:17) MCA 8001 O.S.T. American Graffiti.
- (M) (2:16) Rhino 71463 Doo Wop Box.
- (M) (2:16) Time-Life 2RNR-14 Rock 'N' Roll Era - 1956.
- (M) (2:16) Time-Life RHD-05 Rhythm & Blues - 1956.
- (M) (2:07) Time-Life R962-03 History Of Rock 'N' Roll: Rock 'N' Roll Classics 1954-1956.
- (M) (2:13) Collectables 5462 The Spotlight Series - Gee Records Vol. 1.
- (M) (2:17) Collectables 2600 WCBS-FM History Of Rock - The Group Sounds Volume 1.
- (M) (2:15) Time-Life R10513 40 Lovin' Oldies.
- (M) (2:17) K-Tel 3007 50's Sock Hop.
- (M) (2:15) Collectables 8817 For Collectors Only.
- (M) (2:16) JCI 3129 1955 - Only Rock 'N Roll - 1959.
- (M) (2:17) Polygram Special Markets 314520259 Doo Wop Classics.
- (M) (2:16) Rhino 72157 Doo Wop Memories, Vol. 2.
- (M) (2:16) Flashback 72716 Doo Wop - Sh-Boom.
- (M) (2:17) Rhino 72874 Let's Dance! The Best Of Ballroom: Swing, Lindy, Jitterbug And Jive.
- (M) (2:16) Time-Life R838-24 Solid Gold Soul 1956.

released as by FRANKIE LYMON and THE TEENAGERS:
1956 I WANT YOU TO BE MY GIRL
- (M) (2:55) Rhino 71806 The R&B Box: Thirty Years Of Rhythm & Blues.
- (M) (2:53) Rhino 71463 Doo Wop Box.
- (M) (2:41) Collectables 8817 For Collectors Only. *(alternate take with :03 of studio talk)*
- (M) (2:36) Collectables 8817 For Collectors Only. *(alternate take)*
- (M) (2:53) Collectables 8817 For Collectors Only.
- (M) (2:53) Collectables 2601 WCBS-FM History Of Rock - The Group Sounds Volume 2.
- (E) (2:56) Time-Life 2RNR-23 Rock 'N' Roll Era - 1956: Still Rockin'.
- (M) (2:56) JCI 3165 #1 Radio Hits 1955 - Only Rock 'n Roll - 1959.

1957 GOODY GOODY
- (M) (2:09) Rhino 70918 Best Of.
- (M) (2:09) Pair 1279 Goody Goody.
- (M) (2:09) Special Music 5020 Singing Their Hits.
- (M) (2:10) Collectables 7005 Harlem N.Y. - The Doo Wop Era Part 2.
- (M) (2:10) Collectables 8817 For Collectors Only.
- (M) (2:16) Collectables 8817 For Collectors Only. *(alternate take)*

- (M) (2:09) Collectables 5483 Spotlite On Gee Records Volume 4.

BARBARA LYNN
1962 YOU'LL LOSE A GOOD THING
- (M) (2:20) Rhino 70648 Billboard's Top R&B Hits Of 1962. *(sounds like it was mastered from vinyl)*
- (M) (2:17) MCA 6228 O.S.T. Hairspray. *(sounds like it was mastered from vinyl)*
- (M) (2:19) Capitol 91184 O.S.T. Everybody's All-American. *(sounds like it was mastered from vinyl)*
- (M) (2:18) Collectables 5065 History Of Rock Volume 5. *(sounds like it was mastered from vinyl)*
- (M) (2:18) Time-Life 2RNR-02 Rock 'N' Roll Era - 1962.
- (M) (2:18) Time-Life RHD-11 Rhythm & Blues - 1962.
- (M) (2:18) Original Sound 8911 Art Laboe's Dedicated To You Vol. 2. *(sounds like it was mastered from vinyl)*
- (M) (2:18) Original Sound 4001 Art Laboe's 60 Killer Oldies. *(sounds like it was mastered from vinyl)*
- (M) (2:16) Time-Life OPCD-4517 Tonight's The Night.
- (M) (2:20) Thump 7010 Low Rider Oldies Volume 1. *(sounds like it was mastered from vinyl)*
- (S) (3:01) Ichiban 2505 Best Of - The Atlantic Years. *(rerecorded)*
- (S) (2:22) Rhino 72618 Smooth Grooves: The '60s Volume 1 Early '60s.
- (M) (2:37) Time-Life R857-06 The Heart Of Rock 'n' Roll 1962. *(:15 longer than the 45 or LP)*
- (S) (2:21) TVT 4010 Rhythm Revue.
- (S) (2:21) Repeat/Relativity 1611 A Brand New Bag: #1 Soul Hits Of The 60's Volume 3.
- (M) (2:18) Time-Life R838-18 Solid Gold Soul 1962.
- (S) (2:29) JCI 3184 1960 - Only Love - 1964.

CHERYL LYNN
1979 GOT TO BE REAL
- (S) (5:06) Columbia 40517 Let's Dance. *(LP version)*
- (S) (3:41) Epic 46940 O.S.T. Queens Logic. *(45 version)*
- (S) (3:42) Priority 7972 Mega-Hits Dance Classics Volume 2. *(45 version)*
- (S) (3:42) Rhino 70985 The Disco Years Volume 2. *(45 version)*
- (S) (5:05) Columbia 35486 Cheryl Lynn. *(LP version)*
- (S) (5:05) Epic 57620 O.S.T. Carlito's Way. *(LP version)*
- (S) (3:42) Razor & Tie 22496 Disco Fever. *(45 version)*
- (S) (3:42) Time-Life SOD-36 Sounds Of The Seventies - More AM Nuggets. *(45 version)*
- (S) (5:06) Rhino 71756 and 72833 Phat Trax: The Best Of Old School Volume 5. *(LP version)*
- (S) (5:06) Thump 4020 Old School Vol. 2. *(LP version)*
- (S) (5:06) Risky Business 53921 Double Knit Dance Hits. *(LP version)*
- (S) (5:05) Rebound 314520217 Disco Nights Vol. 1 - Divas Of Dance. *(LP version)*
- (S) (5:05) Rhino 72130 Soul Hits Of The 70's Vol. 20. *(LP version)*
- (S) (5:06) K-Tel 3251 Disco Fever. *(LP version)*
- (S) (3:48) Columbia/Legacy 64856 Best Of: Got To Be Real. *(45 version; includes :05 countoff)*
- (S) (3:42) Rhino 72414 Dance Floor Divas: The 70's. *(45 version)*
- (S) (3:42) K-Tel 3581 Roller Disco - Boogie From The Skating Rinks. *(45 version)*
- (S) (5:03) Coldfront 3375 Old School Megamix. *(all selections on this cd are sequed together; LP version)*
- (S) (3:42) Scotti Bros. 75504 Club Ladies Night. *(45 version)*
- (S) (5:06) Priority 50957 Mega Hits Disco Explosion Volume 4. *(LP version)*
- (S) (3:19) Popular 12011 Disco Dance Hits. *(rerecorded)*
- (S) (3:42) Time-Life R838-17 Solid Gold Soul 1978. *(45 version)*
- (S) (3:42) Time-Life R840-09 Sounds Of The Seventies: '70s Dance Party 1979-1981. *(45 version)*

GLORIA LYNNE
1964 I WISH YOU LOVE
(actual 45 time is (3:39) not (2:52) as stated on the record label)
- (S) (3:39) Collectables 5138 Golden Classics. *(truncated fade)*
- (S) (3:38) LaserLight 12321 Soulful Love.
- (S) (3:38) K-Tel 539 Great Ladies Of Jazz.
- (S) (3:38) Time-Life R974-03 Many Moods Of Romance - I Wish You Love.
- (S) (3:41) Rhino 72618 Smooth Grooves: The '60s Volume 1 Early '60s.
- (S) (3:38) Epic 68778 O.S.T. U Turn.
- (S) (3:37) Collectables 5855 I Wish You Love/Go! Go! Go!

LYNYRD SKYNYRD
1974 SWEET HOME ALABAMA
(dj copies of the 45 ran (3:20) and (4:42); commercial copies were all (4:42))
- (S) (4:43) MCA 31274 Classic Rock Volume 2.
- (S) (4:42) Priority 7995 Country's Greatest Hits: Southern Country Rock Volume 2.
- (S) (4:42) Priority 8663 The South Rules/70's Greatest Rock Hits Volume 2.
- (S) (3:37) Rhino 70635 Billboard's Top Rock & Roll Hits Of 1974. *(:17 longer than the 45 dj edit)*
- (S) (4:41) Sandstone 33001 Reelin' In The Years Volume 2.
- (S) (4:43) MCA 42293 Skynyrd's Innyrds/Their Greatest Hits.
- (S) (4:43) MCA 1686 Second Helping. *(tracks into next selection)*
- (S) (4:42) MCA 6898 Gold & Platinum.
- (S) (4:44) MCA 10390 Lynyrd Skynyrd Box.
- (S) (4:41) DCC Compact Classics 063 Rock Of The 70's Volume 2.
- (S) (4:43) MFSL 556 Second Helping. *(tracks into next selection; gold disc)*
- (S) (4:42) Razor & Tie 22502 Those Rocking 70's.
- (S) (4:40) Time-Life R968-01 Guitar Rock 1974-1975.
- (S) (4:40) Time-Life SOD-07 Sounds Of The Seventies - 1974.
- (S) (4:39) Time-Life OPCD-4521 Guitar Rock.
- (S) (4:43) K-Tel 6045 Southern Fried Rock.
- (S) (4:41) Epic 66329 O.S.T. Forrest Gump.
- (S) (4:41) Varese Sarabande 5503 and 5504 and 5505 and 5506 and 5507 and 5508 and 5509 and 5513 and 5571 Arrow: All Rock & Roll Oldies Volume One.
- (S) (4:42) Rebound 314520256 Best Of Southern Rock.
- (S) (4:43) MCA Special Products 20893 Greatest Tour Bands Ever Recorded.
- (S) (4:43) MCA Special Products 20910 Rockin' 70's.
- (S) (4:42) K-Tel 3463 Platinum Rock.
- (S) (4:40) Madacy Entertainment 1974 Rock On 1974.
- (S) (4:43) MCA Special Products 20401 What's Your Name.
- (S) (4:41) K-Tel 3972 Southern Rockin' Rebels: The South's Gone And Done It.
- (S) (4:59) Critique 15467 Fast Cars And Southern Stars. *(time includes a :15 introduction by Kyle Petty)*
- (S) (4:43) MCA 11648 Second Helping. *(remastered edition; tracks into next selection)*
- (S) (3:27) Varese Sarabande 5847 On The Radio Volume Two. *(dj 45 version)*
- (S) (4:40) Madacy Entertainment 6805 The Power Of Rock.

1975 FREE BIRD (studio version)
- (S) (9:04) MCA 31273 Classic Rock Volume 1. *(LP version)*
- (S) (4:40) Original Sound 8894 Dick Clark's 21 All-Time Hits Vol. 3. *(45 version)*
- (S) (4:41) Priority 7055 Heavy Hitters/70's Greatest Rock Hits Volume 11. *(45 version)*
- (S) (4:40) Priority 7942 Hard Rockin' 70's. *(45 version)*
- (S) (9:08) Warner Special Products 27616 Classic Rock. *(LP version)*
- (S) (9:06) Foundation/Capitol 96647 Hearts Of Gold - The Classic Rock Collection. *(LP version)*

- (S) (10:06) MCA 42293 Skynyrd's Innyrds/Their Greatest Hits. *(alternate take)*
- (S) (9:05) MCA 1685 Prounounced Leh-Nerd Skin-Nerd. *(LP version)*
- (S) (9:09) MCA 10390 Lynyrd Skynyrd Box. *(LP version)*
- (S) (9:04) Time-Life R968-01 Guitar Rock 1974-1975. *(LP version)*
- (S) (4:41) Time-Life SOD-08 Sounds Of The Seventies - 1975. *(45 version)*
- (S) (4:40) Time-Life OPCD-4521 Guitar Rock. *(45 version)*
- (S) (4:41) Priority 53713 Classic Rock Volume 1 - Highway Rockers. *(45 version)*
- (S) (9:06) Rhino 72131 Frat Rock: The 70's. *(LP version)*
- (S) (9:05) Cabin Fever Music 973 Harley Davidson: The American Motorcycle Soundtrack. *(LP version)*
- (S) (9:05) MCA Special Products 20903 The 70's Come Alive Again. *(LP version)*
- (S) (9:08) MCA Special Products 20949 Rockin' 70's Volume 2. *(LP version)*
- (S) (4:40) Epic/Legacy 65020 Ultimate Rock 'n' Roll Collection. *(45 version)*
- (S) (9:06) MCA 11534 Pronounced Leh-Nerd Skin-Nerd. *(LP version; remastered edition)*
- (S) (9:04) MCA Special Products 20956 Rockin' Guitars. *(LP version)*
- (S) (4:06) Rebound 314520406 The Roots Of Rock: Southern Rock. *(rerecording)*
- (S) (4:06) MCA Special Products 21011 70's Biggest Hits. *(rerecording)*
- (S) (9:07) Rhino 72893 Hard Rock Cafe: Classic Rock. *(LP version)*
- (S) (10:07) Critique 15467 Fast Cars And Southern Stars. *(alternate take)*
- (S) (10:07) Thump 6020 Easyriders Volume 2. *(alternate take)*
- (S) (4:06) Rebound 314520475 The Roots Of Rock: Southern Rock. *(rerecording)*

1975 SATURDAY NIGHT SPECIAL
- (S) (5:08) MCA 25240 Classic Rock Volume Three. *(LP version with countoff)*
- (S) (5:03) Time-Life SOD-23 Sounds Of The Seventies - Guitar Power. *(LP version)*
- (S) (5:07) Time-Life R105-24 Guitar Rock Monsters. *(LP version with countoff)*
- (S) (5:03) Rhino 70721 Legends Of Guitar - The 70's Vol. 1. *(LP version)*
- (S) (5:08) MCA 10390 Lynyrd Skynyrd Box. *(LP version with countoff)*
- (S) (5:05) MCA 6898 Gold & Platinum. *(LP version with countoff)*
- (S) (5:08) MCA 42293 Skynyrd's Innyrds/Their Greatest Hits. *(LP version with countoff)*
- (S) (5:07) Time-Life R968-08 Guitar Rock - The Mid '70s. *(LP version with countoff)*
- (S) (5:04) K-Tel 3510 Platinum Rock Volume 2. *(LP version with countoff)*
- (S) (4:59) JCI 3140 18 Screamers From The 70's. *(LP version)*
- (S) (5:07) Hip-O 40039 Power Chords Volume 2. *(LP version with countoff)*
- (S) (5:07) Hip-O 40095 '70s Hit(s) Back. *(LP version with countoff)*
- (S) (5:08) Priority 50962 70's Greatest Rock Hits Volume 7: Southern Rock. *(LP version with countoff; hum noticeable on the introduction)*

1977 FREE BIRD (live version)
- (S) (14:13) JCI 3402 Live Volume 2. *(LP version)*
- (S) (13:28) Rhino 70586 Rebel Rousers: Southern Rock Classics. *(LP version but missing the spoken introduction)*
- (S) (13:35) MCA 6897 One More From The Road. *(LP version but missing the spoken introduction which was placed at the end of the preceding track)*
- (S) (14:07) MCA 6898 Gold & Platinum. *(LP version)*
- (S) (4:57) K-Tel 3221 Axe Gods. *(45 version)*
- (S) (4:57) K-Tel 6083 Southern Fried Rock - Second Helping. *(45 version)*

LYNYRD SKYNYRD *(Continued)*

    (S) (13:39)   MCA 11533 One More From The Road. *(remastered edition; LP version but missing the spoken introduction which was placed at the end of the preceding track)*

    (S) (13:50)   MCA Special Products 22142 Classic Live Performances. *(LP version with :08 of the introduction edited out)*

    (S) (14:05)   Time-Life R968-23 Guitar Rock - Live! *(LP version)*

1978 WHAT'S YOUR NAME

    (S) (3:32)   Priority 8668 Rough And Rowdy/70's Greatest Rock Hits Volume 7. *(LP version)*

    (S) (3:30)   MCA 42293 Skynyrd's Innyrds/Their Greatest Hits. *(LP version)*

    (S) (3:30)   MCA 1687 and 11171 Street Survivors. *(LP version)*

    (S) (3:31)   MCA 6898 Gold & Platinum. *(LP version)*

    (S) (3:35)   MCA 10390 Lynyrd Skynyrd Box. *(previously unreleased alternate mix)*

    (S) (3:30)   MCA 10390 Lynyrd Skynyrd Box. *(LP version)*

    (S) (3:30)   Time-Life R968-03 Guitar Rock 1976-1977. *(LP version)*

    (S) (3:30)   Time-Life SOD-20 Sounds Of The Seventies - 1978: Take Two. *(LP version)*

    (S) (3:30)   Time-Life R105-24 Guitar Rock Monsters. *(LP version)*

    (S) (3:30)   JCI 3119 18 Rock Classics. *(LP version)*

    (S) (3:32)   MCA Special Products 20754 Classic Rock Volume 1. *(LP version)*

    (S) (3:31)   MCA Special Products 20949 Rockin' 70's Volume 2. *(LP version)*

    (S) (3:31)   DCC Compact Classics 139 Rock The First Volume 9. *(LP version)*

    (S) (3:31)   MCA Special Products 20401 What's Your Name. *(LP version)*

    (S) (3:30)   Priority 50952 I Love Rock & Roll Volume 3: Hits Of The 70's. *(LP version)*

    (S) (3:32)   K-Tel 3904 The Rock Album Volume 2. *(LP version)*

    (S) (3:32)   K-Tel 3986 70's Heavy Hitters: Arena Rockers 1975-79. *(LP version)*

    (S) (3:29)   Simitar 55762 Stud Rock - Wild Ride. *(LP version)*

M
1979 POP MUZIK
    (dj copies of this 45 ran (3:20) and (4:58);
    commercial copies were all (3:20))
- (S) (3:19) Priority 7059 Mega-Hits Dance Classics Volume 10. *(45 version)*
- (S) (3:18) Sire 26954 Just Say Yesterday. *(45 version)*
- (S) (3:20) Rhino 71695 New Wave Hits Of The 80's Vol. 2. *(45 version)*
- (S) (3:19) Rhino 72490 New Wave Hits, Vol. 1. *(45 version)*
- (S) (3:19) Time-Life R840-01 Sounds Of The Seventies - Pop Nuggets: Late '70s. *(45 version)*
- (S) (3:20) Flashback 72713 Essential New Wave Hits. *(45 version)*
- (S) (3:20) Flashback 72092 New Wave Hits Box Set. *(45 version)*
- (S) (4:53) Collectables 5885 Pop Muzik. *(LP version)*

BYRON MacGREGOR
1974 AMERICANS

MARY MacGREGOR
1977 TORN BETWEEN TWO LOVERS
    (actual LP time is (3:51) not (3:46) as stated
    on the record label; actual 45 time is (3:44)
    not (3:40) as stated on the record label)
- (S) (3:51) Priority 8669 Hits/70's Greatest Rock Hits Volume 9.
- (S) (3:44) Rhino 71199 Super Hits Of The 70's Volume 19.
- (S) (3:40) Time-Life SOD-35 Sounds Of The Seventies - AM Nuggets.
- (S) (3:40) RCA 66812 Do You Love Me? (All-Time Best Love Songs).
- (S) (3:40) Madacy Entertainment 1977 Rock On 1977.
- (S) (3:51) Priority 53140 Best Of The 70's: Legendary Ladies.
- (S) (3:43) Simitar 55512 The Number One's: Lovin' Feelings.
- (S) (3:44) Rhino 75233 '70s Party (Killers) Classics.
- (S) (3:43) Time-Life R834-12 Body Talk - By Candlelight.
- (S) (3:42) Time-Life R814-04 Love Songs.

CRAIG MACK
1994 FLAVA IN YA EAR
- (S) (3:37) Bad Boy/Arista 73001 Project: Funk Da World.
- (S) (3:37) Boxtunes 162444068 Big Phat Ones Of Hip-Hop Volume 1.

1995 GET DOWN
- (S) (4:26) Bad Boy/Arista 73001 Project: Funk Da World.

LONNIE MACK
1963 MEMPHIS
- (M) (2:30) Warner Special Products 27610 More Party Classics.
- (M) (2:29) Capitol Special Markets 57272 Great Instrumental Hits From Rock's Golden Years.
- (M) (2:29) Curb 77402 All-Time Great Instrumental Hits Volume 2.
- (S) (2:31) Rhino 71602 Rock Instrumental Classics Volume 2: The Sixties.
- (S) (2:31) Rhino 72035 Rock Instrumental Classics Vols. 1-5 Box Set.
- (M) (2:28) Time-Life 2RNR-07 Rock 'N' Roll Era - 1963.
- (E) (2:24) Era 840 Rock N' Roll Guitar Classics.
- (S) (2:26) LaserLight 12316 Rebel Rousers.

- (E) (2:24) K-Tel 3125 Solid Gold Rock N' Roll.
- (M) (2:41) Hip-O 40076 Chuck B. Covered: A Tribute To Chuck Berry. *(:10 longer than any previously issued version)*

1963 WHAM!
- (M) (2:10) Rhino 71602 Rock Instrumental Classics Volume 2: The Sixties.
- (M) (2:10) Rhino 72035 Rock Instrumental Classics Vols. 1-5 Box Set.
- (M) (2:08) Time-Life 2RNR-36 Rock 'N' Roll Era - Axes & Saxes/The Great Instrumentals.
- (E) (2:08) Era 840 Rock N' Roll Guitar Classics.

MACK 10 & THA DOGG POUND
1997 NOTHIN' BUT THE CAVI HIT
- (S) (4:03) Priority 50635 O.S.T. Rhyme & Reason.
released as by MACK 10:
1997 BACKYARD BOOGIE
- (S) (4:18) Priority 50675 Based On A True Story.

GISELE MacKENZIE
1955 HARD TO GET
- (M) (2:59) Time-Life HPD-09 Your Hit Parade 1955.
- (M) (2:59) Collectors' Choice 021 Hard To Get/Best Of.
- (M) (2:59) Time-Life R132-10 Love Songs Of Your Hit Parade.

GORDON MacRAE
1958 THE SECRET
- (M) (2:38) Time-Life HPD-28 Your Hit Parade - The Fabulous 50's.

MAD COBRA
1993 FLEX
- (S) (3:59) Columbia 52751 Hard To Wet, Easy To Dry.

JOHNNY MADDOX
1955 THE CRAZY OTTO
- (M) (3:01) Time-Life HPD-30 Your Hit Parade - 50's Instrumentals.

BETTY MADIGAN
1958 DANCE EVERYONE DANCE
- (M) (2:23) Time-Life HPD-35 Your Hit Parade - The Fun-Times 50's & 60's.

MADNESS
1983 OUR HOUSE
- (S) (3:20) Rhino 71703 New Wave Hits Of The 80's Vol. 10.
- (S) (3:20) Rhino 71834 Classic MTV: Class Of 1983.
- (S) (4:57) Right Stuff 29671 Sedated In The Eighties No. 3. *(12" single version)*
- (S) (3:19) Priority 53781 Best Of 80's Rock Volume 2.
- (S) (3:20) Rhino 72133 Frat Rock: The 80's.
- (S) (3:21) Time-Life R988-03 Sounds Of The Eighties: 1983.
- (S) (3:19) Geffen 24805 Geffen Vintage 80's Volume 1.
- (S) (3:18) Geffen 4003 Madness.
- (S) (3:18) JCI 3159 18 Modern Rock Classics From The 80's.
- (S) (3:17) Hip-O 40023 Smash Alternatives - 14 Classic New Wave Hits.
- (S) (3:16) Arista 18985 Ultimate New Wave Party 1998. *(all selections on this cd are segued together)*

MADNESS (Continued)
- (S) (3:19) Geffen 25145 Total Madness...The Very Best Of.
- (S) (3:19) Intersound 9521 Retro Lunch Box - Squeeze The Cheese.

1983 IT MUST BE LOVE
- (S) (3:25) Rhino 71975 New Wave Hits Of The 80's Vol. 12.
- (S) (3:21) Priority 53795 Best Of 80's Rock Volume 3.
- (S) (3:22) Geffen 4003 Madness.
- (S) (3:23) Geffen 25151 Geffen Vintage 80s Vol. II.
- (S) (3:23) Geffen 25145 Total Madness...The Very Best Of.

MADONNA
1984 HOLIDAY
- (S) (4:03) Sire/Warner Brothers 26440 The Immaculate Collection. *(neither the 45 or LP version; remixed in "Q" sound)*
- (S) (6:32) Sire 25535 You Can Dance. *(remixed)*
- (S) (6:56) Sire 25535 You Can Dance. *(dub version)*
- (S) (6:06) Sire/Warner Brothers 23867 Madonna. *(LP version)*
- (S) (4:03) Sire/Warner Brothers 26464 The Royal Box. *(neither the 45 or LP version)*

1984 BORDERLINE
- (S) (3:54) Time-Life R102-34 The Rolling Stone Collection. *(45 version)*
- (S) (3:58) Sire/Warner Brothers 26440 The Immaculate Collection. *(45 version remixed in "Q" sound)*
- (S) (5:15) Sire/Warner Brothers 23867 Madonna. *(LP version)*
- (S) (3:58) Sire/Warner Brothers 26464 The Royal Box. *(45 version remixed in "Q" sound)*

1984 LUCKY STAR
- (S) (3:36) Sire/Warner Brothers 26440 The Immaculate Collection. *(45 version faded :09 early; remixed in "Q" sound)*
- (S) (5:34) Sire/Warner Brothers 23867 Madonna. *(LP version)*
- (S) (3:36) Sire/Warner Brothers 26464 The Royal Box. *(45 version faded :09 early; remixed in "Q" sound)*

1985 LIKE A VIRGIN
- (S) (3:09) Sire/Warner Brothers 26440 The Immaculate Collection. *(faded :29 earlier than the 45 or LP; remixed in "Q" sound)*
- (S) (3:38) Sire 25157 Like A Virgin.
- (S) (3:09) Sire/Warner Brothers 26464 The Royal Box. *(faded :29 earlier than the 45 or LP; remixed in "Q" sound)*

1985 MATERIAL GIRL
- (S) (3:50) Sire/Warner Brothers 26440 The Immaculate Collection. *(remixed in "Q" sound)*
- (S) (4:00) Sire 25157 Like A Virgin.
- (S) (3:50) Sire/Warner Brothers 26464 The Royal Box. *(remixed in "Q" sound)*

1985 CRAZY FOR YOU
(actual 45 time is (3:58) not (4:08) as stated on the record label)
- (S) (4:11) Geffen 24063 O.S.T. Vision Quest.
- (S) (3:44) Sire/Warner Brothers 26440 The Immaculate Collection. *(faded :14 earlier than the 45 and :27 earlier than the LP; remixed in "Q" sound)*
- (S) (3:44) Sire/Warner Brothers 26464 The Royal Box. *(faded :14 earlier than the 45 and :27 earlier than the LP; remixed in "Q" sound)*
- (S) (4:01) Maverick/Sire/Warner Brothers 46100 Something To Remember.

1985 ANGEL
- (S) (3:55) Sire 25157 Like A Virgin. *(LP length)*

1985 DRESS YOU UP
(dj copies of this 45 ran (3:45) and (3:58); commercial copies were all (3:58))
- (S) (4:01) Sire 25157 Like A Virgin.

1986 LIVE TO TELL
- (S) (5:15) Sire/Warner Brothers 26440 The Immaculate Collection. *(neither the 45 or LP version; remixed in "Q" sound)*
- (S) (5:49) Sire 25442 True Blue. *(LP version)*

- (S) (5:15) Sire/Warner Brothers 26464 The Royal Box. *(neither the 45 or LP version)*
- (S) (5:49) Maverick/Sire/Warner Brothers 46100 Something To Remember. *(LP version)*

1986 PAPA DON'T PREACH
(dj copies of this 45 ran (3:47) and (4:27); commercial copies were all (3:47))
- (S) (4:06) Sire/Warner Brothers 26440 The Immaculate Collection. *(remixed in "Q" sound)*
- (S) (4:28) Sire 25442 True Blue. *(LP length)*
- (S) (4:06) Sire/Warner Brothers 26464 The Royal Box. *(remixed in "Q" sound)*

1986 TRUE BLUE
(dj copies of this 45 ran (3:59) and (4:16); commercial copies were all (3:59))
- (S) (4:16) Sire 25442 True Blue.

1987 OPEN YOUR HEART
(dj copies of this 45 ran (3:59) and (4:12); commercial copies were all (4:12))
- (S) (3:48) Sire/Warner Brothers 26440 The Immaculate Collection. *(faded :23 sooner than the 45 or LP; remixed in "Q" sound)*
- (S) (4:11) Sire 25442 True Blue.
- (S) (3:48) Sire/Warner Brothers 26464 The Royal Box. *(faded :23 sooner than the 45 or LP; remixed in "Q" sound)*

1987 LA ISLA BONITA
(dj copies of this 45 ran (3:58) (a remix) and (4:01); commercial copies were all (4:01))
- (S) (3:45) Sire/Warner Brothers 26440 The Immaculate Collection. *(previously unreleased version)*
- (S) (4:00) Sire 25442 True Blue.
- (S) (3:45) Sire/Warner Brothers 26464 The Royal Box. *(previously unreleased version)*

1987 WHO'S THAT GIRL
- (S) (3:57) Sire 25611 O.S.T. Who's That Girl.

1987 CAUSING A COMMOTION
(dj copies of this 45 ran (4:00) and (4:10); commercial copies were all (4:00))
- (S) (4:18) Sire 25611 O.S.T. Who's That Girl. *(LP length)*

1989 LIKE A PRAYER
- (S) (5:49) Sire/Warner Brothers 26440 The Immaculate Collection. *(previously unreleased version)*
- (S) (5:39) Sire 25844 Like A Prayer. *(LP version)*
- (S) (5:49) Sire/Warner Brothers 26464 The Royal Box. *(previously unreleased version)*
- (S) (5:48) Time-Life R13610 Gold And Platinum Box Set - The Ultimate Rock Collection. *(previously unreleased version)*

1989 EXPRESS YOURSELF
(actual 45 time is (4:35) not (4:30) as stated on the record label)
- (S) (4:01) Sire/Warner Brothers 26440 The Immaculate Collection. *(previously unreleased version)*
- (S) (4:37) Sire 25844 Like A Prayer.
- (S) (4:01) Sire/Warner Brothers 26464 The Royal Box. *(previously unreleased version)*

1989 CHERISH
- (S) (3:49) Sire/Warner Brothers 26440 The Immaculate Collection. *(previously unreleased version)*
- (S) (5:03) Sire 25844 Like A Prayer. *(LP version)*
- (S) (3:49) Sire/Warner Brothers 26464 The Royal Box. *(previously unreleased version)*

1989 OH FATHER
- (S) (4:57) Sire 25844 Like A Prayer.
- (S) (4:57) Maverick/Sire/Warner Brothers 46100 Something To Remember.

1990 KEEP IT TOGETHER
- (S) (5:02) Sire 25844 Like A Prayer. *(LP version)*

1990 VOGUE
- (S) (4:49) Sire/Warner Brothers 26209 I'm Breathless. *(LP version)*
- (S) (5:16) Sire/Warner Brothers 26440 The Immaculate Collection. *(previously unreleased version)*
- (S) (5:16) Sire/Warner Brothers 26464 The Royal Box. *(previously unreleased version)*

1990 HANKY PANKY
    (S)   (3:57)   Sire/Warner Brothers 26209 I'm Breathless.

1991 JUSTIFY MY LOVE
    (S)   (4:58)   Sire/Warner Brothers 26440 The Immaculate Collection. *(remixed in "Q" sound)*
    (S)   (4:58)   Sire/Warner Brothers 26464 The Royal Box.

1991 RESCUE ME
    (S)   (5:30)   Sire/Warner Brothers 26440 The Immaculate Collection. *(remixed in "Q" sound)*
    (S)   (5:30)   Sire/Warner Brothers 26464 The Royal Box.

1992 THIS USED TO BE MY PLAYGROUND
    (S)   (4:41)   Warner Brothers 26974 Barcelona Gold.
    (S)   (5:06)   Maverick/Sire/Warner Brothers 46100 Something To Remember.

1992 EROTICA
    (S)   (5:18)   Maverick/Sire 45031 and 45154 Erotica.

1993 DEEPER AND DEEPER
    (S)   (4:55)   Tommy Boy 1074 MTV Party To Go Volume 3. *(remix; all tracks on this cd are segued together)*
    (S)   (5:33)   Maverick/Sire 45031 and 45154 Erotica.

1993 BAD GIRL
    (S)   (5:23)   Maverick/Sire 45031 and 45154 Erotica.

1993 RAIN
    (S)   (5:24)   Maverick/Sire 45031 and 45154 Erotica.
    (S)   (5:25)   Maverick/Sire/Warner Brothers 46100 Something To Remember.

1994 I'LL REMEMBER
    (S)   (4:19)   Maverick/Sire/Warner Brothers 45549 O.S.T. With Honors.
    (S)   (4:21)   Maverick/Sire/Warner Brothers 46100 Something To Remember.

1994 SECRET
    (S)   (5:02)   Maverick/Sire/Warner Brothers 45767 Bedtime Stories.

1995 TAKE A BOW
    (S)   (5:18)   Maverick/Sire/Warner Brothers 45767 Bedtime Stories.
    (S)   (5:18)   Maverick/Sire/Warner Brothers 46100 Something To Remember.

1995 YOU'LL SEE
    (S)   (4:38)   Maverick/Sire/Warner Brothers 46100 Something To Remember.

1997 YOU MUST LOVE ME
    (S)   (2:49)   Warner Brothers 46346 The Complete Motion Picture Soundtrack "Evita".
    (S)   (2:49)   Warner Brothers 46692 Music From The Motion Picture "Evita".

1997 DON'T CRY FOR ME ARGENTINA
    (S)   (5:31)   Warner Brothers 46346 The Complete Motion Picture Soundtrack "Evita".
    (S)   (5:34)   Warner Brothers 46692 Music From The Motion Picture "Evita".

JOHNNY MAESTRO
1961 MODEL GIRL
    (S)   (2:16)   Rhino 70948 Best Of The Crests.
    (S)   (2:21)   Collectables 8812 Johnny Maestro & The Crests For Collectors Only.

CLEDUS MAGGARD and THE CITIZEN'S BAND
1976 THE WHITE KNIGHT
    (S)   (4:04)   Risky Business 66395 Jokers & Wildcards.

MAGIC LANTERNS
1968 SHAME, SHAME
    (S)   (3:01)   Rhino 70277 Rare Soul: Beach Music Classics Volume 1.

GEORGE MAHARIS
1962 TEACH ME TONIGHT
    (S)   (2:51)   K-Tel 3388 TV Stars Sing.

MAIN INGREDIENT
1972 EVERYBODY PLAYS THE FOOL
    (S)   (3:18)   RCA 8476 and 9684 Nipper's Greatest Hits Of The 70's.

    (S)   (3:19)   Rhino 70789 Soul Hits Of The 70's Volume 9.
    (S)   (3:22)   RCA 9591 All Time Greatest Hits.
    (S)   (3:22)   RCA 61144 The RCA Records Label: The First Note In Black Music.
    (S)   (3:21)   Collectables 5101 Golden Classics.
    (S)   (3:17)   Razor & Tie 22047 Sweet 70's Soul.
    (S)   (3:18)   Time-Life RHD-20 Rhythm & Blues - 1972.
    (S)   (3:16)   Time-Life SUD-11 Superhits - 1972.
    (S)   (3:21)   Time-Life SOD-13 Sounds Of The Seventies - 1972: Take Two. *(introduction is partially clipped)*
    (S)   (3:21)   JCI 3130 1970 - Only Rock 'N Roll - 1974.
    (S)   (3:18)   RCA 66812 Do You Love Me? (All-Time Best Love Songs).
    (S)   (3:17)   DCC Compact Classics 142 Groove On! Volume 2.
    (S)   (3:16)   Time-Life AM1-07 AM Gold - 1972.
    (S)   (3:17)   Time-Life R838-07 Solid Gold Soul - 1972.
    (S)   (3:18)   Time-Life R834-11 Body Talk - After Dark.
    (S)   (3:20)   RCA 66860 A Quiet Storm.
    (S)   (3:18)   K-Tel 3900 Great R&B Male Groups: Hits Of The 70's.

1974 JUST DON'T WANT TO BE LONELY
    (S)   (3:37)   Rhino 70552 Soul Hits Of The 70's Volume 12.
    (S)   (3:30)   Collectables 5101 Golden Classics.
    (S)   (3:31)   RCA 9591 All Time Greatest Hits.
    (S)   (3:37)   RCA 66860 A Quiet Storm.
    (S)   (3:36)   Time-Life SOD-33 Sounds Of The Seventies - AM Pop Classics II.
    (S)   (3:36)   Time-Life R834-18 Body Talk - Romantic Moments.

1974 HAPPINESS IS JUST AROUND THE BEND
    (S)   (6:20)   RCA 7639 Dance! Dance! Dance! *(LP version)*
    (S)   (6:19)   Collectables 5101 Golden Classics. *(LP version)*

MAJORS
1962 A WONDERFUL DREAM
    (M)   (2:00)   Collectables 5249 A Golden Classics Edition.
    (M)   (2:01)   Time-Life 2RNR-16 Rock 'N' Roll Era - 1962 Still Rockin'.
    (M)   (2:01)   EMI-Capitol Special Markets 19552 Lost Hits Of The '60s.

MIRIAM MAKEBA
1967 PATA PATA
    (M)   (3:07)   Time-Life 2CLR-24 Classic Rock - 1967: Blowin' Your Mind.

MALO
1972 SUAVECITO
    (S)   (3:23)   Rhino 70787 Soul Hits Of The 70's Volume 7. *(45 version)*
    (S)   (6:32)   GNP Crescendo 2205 Best Of. *(LP version)*
    (S)   (3:24)   GNP Crescendo 2205 Best Of. *(45 version)*
    (S)   (3:24)   Rhino 71210 70's Smash Hits Volume 6. *(45 version)*
    (S)   (3:23)   Time-Life SOD-36 Sounds Of The Seventies - More AM Nuggets. *(45 version)*
    (S)   (6:31)   Thump 4710 Old School Love Songs. *(LP version)*
    (S)   (6:33)   Warner Brothers 45889 Malo. *(LP version)*
    (S)   (3:23)   Flashback 72686 '70s Radio Hits Volume 6. *(45 version)*
    (S)   (3:25)   Rhino 72920 Raza Rock Of The '70s & '80s. *(45 version)*

MAMA CASS
1968 DREAM A LITTLE DREAM OF ME
    (S)   (3:12)   MCA 31147 Mama's Big Ones.
    (S)   (3:12)   MCA 10195 Creeque Alley/History Of The Mama's & Papa's.
    (S)   (3:13)   MCA 31335 The Papa's & The Mama's.
    (S)   (3:12)   MCA 5701 16 Of Their Greatest Hits. *(missing the MC introduction)*
    (S)   (3:10)   Time-Life SUD-02 Superhits - 1968.
    (S)   (3:10)   Rhino 72265 Lullabies For Little Dreamers. *(missing the MC introduction)*

MAMA CASS (Continued)

(S)	(3:12)	MCA 11552 O.S.T. Beautiful Thing.
(S)	(3:11)	Nick At Nite/550 Music/Epic 67689 Stand By Your Man.
(S)	(3:13)	MCA 11523 Dream A Little Dream: The Cass Elliot Collection.
(S)	(3:10)	Time-Life AM1-04 AM Gold - 1968.
(S)	(3:13)	MCA 11740 Mama's & Papa's Greatest Hits.
(S)	(3:13)	Time-Life R814-04 Love Songs.

1969 IT'S GETTING BETTER

(S)	(2:57)	MCA 31147 Mama's Big Ones.
(S)	(3:00)	MCA 10195 Creeque Alley/History Of The Mama's & Papa's.
(S)	(2:57)	MCA 11552 O.S.T. Beautiful Thing.
(S)	(2:59)	MCA 11523 Dream A Little Dream: The Cass Elliot Collection.
(S)	(3:00)	Varese Sarabande 5801 Sunshine Days - Pop Classics Of The '60s Volume 1.

released as by MAMA CASS ELLIOT:

1969 MAKE YOUR OWN KIND OF MUSIC

(S)	(2:18)	MCA 31147 Mama's Big Ones.
(S)	(2:23)	MCA 10195 Creeque Alley/History Of The Mama's & Papa's.
(S)	(2:19)	MCA 11552 O.S.T. Beautiful Thing.
(S)	(2:23)	MCA 11523 Dream A Little Dream: The Cass Elliot Collection.

1970 NEW WORLD COMING

(S)	(2:09)	MCA 31147 Mama's Big Ones.
(S)	(2:09)	MCA 11523 Dream A Little Dream: The Cass Elliot Collection.

MAMA'S & PAPA'S

1966 CALIFORNIA DREAMIN'

(S)	(2:37)	MCA 31207 Vintage Music Volume 10.
(S)	(2:37)	MCA 5806 Vintage Music Volumes 9 & 10.
(S)	(2:37)	MCA 25240 Classic Rock Volume 3.
(S)	(2:37)	K-Tel 666 Flower Power.
(S)	(2:37)	JCI 3104 Mellow Sixties.
(S)	(2:39)	Motown 6159 The Good-Feeling Music Of The Big Chill Generation Volume 1.
(S)	(2:38)	MCA 10195 Creeque Alley/History Of.
(S)	(2:37)	MCA 31042 If You Can Believe Your Eyes And Ears.
(S)	(2:39)	MCA 5701 16 Of Their Greatest Hits.
(S)	(2:37)	MCA 6467 O.S.T. Air America.
(S)	(2:37)	Time-Life 2CLR-07 Classic Rock - 1966: The Beat Goes On.
(S)	(2:36)	Time-Life SUD-01 Superhits - 1966.
(S)	(2:38)	Time-Life R962-04 History Of Rock 'N' Roll: California Pop 1963-1967.
(S)	(2:37)	Collectables 2504 WCBS-FM History Of Rock - The 60's Part 4.
(S)	(2:37)	Collectables 4504 History Of Rock/The 60s Part Four.
(S)	(2:37)	MCA Special Products 20783 Rock Around The Oldies #1.
(S)	(2:37)	MCA Special Products 22130 Vintage Collectibles Volume 1.
(S)	(2:37)	Epic 66329 O.S.T. Forrest Gump.
(S)	(2:37)	JCI 3126 1965 - Only Rock 'N Roll - 1969.
(S)	(2:38)	MCA Special Products 20754 Classic Rock Volume 1.
(S)	(2:38)	MCA Special Products 22113 California Dreamin'.
(S)	(2:38)	K-Tel 3130 60's Sound Explosion.
(S)	(2:37)	K-Tel 3438 Best Of Folk Rock.
(S)	(2:37)	K-Tel 3455 Folk Hits Around The Campfire.
(S)	(2:38)	MCA Special Products 20903 The 70's Come Alive Again.
(S)	(2:38)	MCA 11552 O.S.T. Beautiful Thing.
(S)	(2:36)	Time-Life AM1-09 AM Gold - 1966.
(S)	(2:38)	MCA 11739 If You Can Believe Your Eyes And Ears. *(remastered edition)*
(S)	(2:38)	MCA 11740 Greatest Hits.

1966 MONDAY, MONDAY

(S)	(3:22)	Rhino 70627 Billboard's Top Rock & Roll Hits Of 1966.
(S)	(3:22)	Rhino 72007 Billboard's Top Rock & Roll Hits 1962-1966 Box Set.
(S)	(3:25)	Motown 6159 The Good-Feeling Music Of The Big Chill Generation Volume 1.
(S)	(3:23)	MCA 31206 Vintage Music Volume 9.
(S)	(3:23)	MCA 5806 Vintage Music Volumes 9 & 10.
(S)	(3:25)	MCA 10195 Creeque Alley/History Of.
(S)	(3:24)	MCA 31042 If You Can Believe Your Eyes And Ears.
(S)	(3:24)	MCA 5701 16 Of Their Greatest Hits.
(S)	(3:25)	Pair 1322 Words Of Love.
(S)	(3:18)	Time-Life 2CLR-02 Classic Rock - 1966.
(S)	(3:16)	Time-Life SUD-12 Superhits - The Mid 60's.
(S)	(3:16)	Time-Life R962-02 History Of Rock 'N' Roll: Folk Rock 1964-1967.
(S)	(3:22)	Collectables 2504 WCBS-FM History Of Rock - The 60's Part 4.
(S)	(3:22)	Collectables 4504 History Of Rock/The 60s Part Four.
(S)	(3:22)	MCA Special Products 22019 Summer Hits Of The 50's And 60's.
(S)	(3:25)	MCA Special Products 22105 Greatest Classic Rock Hits.
(S)	(3:23)	MCA Special Products 22131 Vintage Collectibles Volume 2.
(S)	(3:25)	MCA Special Products 22113 California Dreamin'.
(S)	(3:23)	MCA Special Products 20899 Rock Around The Oldies #4.
(S)	(3:23)	MCA Special Products 20958 Mellow Classics.
(S)	(3:25)	MCA 11552 O.S.T. Beautiful Thing.
(S)	(3:16)	JCI 3160 18 Free & Easy Hits From The 60's.
(S)	(3:25)	Priority 50951 I Love Rock & Roll Volume 2: Hits Of The 60's.
(S)	(3:25)	MCA Special Products 21017 The Rockin' Sixties.
(S)	(3:16)	Time-Life AM1-05 AM Gold - The Mid '60s.
(S)	(3:24)	Varese Sarabande 5803 Sunshine Days - Pop Classics Of The '60s Volume 3.
(S)	(3:23)	MCA Special Products 21046 Top Singles Of The Sixties.
(S)	(3:24)	MCA 11739 If You Can Believe Your Eyes And Ears. *(remastered edition)*
(S)	(3:25)	MCA 11740 Greatest Hits.

1966 I SAW HER AGAIN

(S)	(3:11)	MCA 10195 Creeque Alley/History Of. *(LP version)*
(S)	(3:12)	MCA 5701 16 Of Their Greatest Hits. *(LP version)*
(S)	(3:11)	MCA 31043 The Mama's & Papa's. *(LP version)*
(S)	(3:11)	Time-Life 2CLR-22 Classic Rock - 1966: Blowin' Your Mind. *(LP version)*
(S)	(3:12)	MCA Special Products 20948 Biggest Summer Hits. *(LP version)*
(S)	(3:11)	MCA 11552 O.S.T. Beautiful Thing. *(LP version)*
(S)	(3:11)	Rhino 72819 16 Magazine - Who's Your Fave Rave. *(LP version)*
(S)	(2:52)	Varese Sarabande 5846 On The Radio Volume One. *(45 version)*
(S)	(3:11)	MCA 11740 Greatest Hits. *(LP version)*

1966 LOOK THROUGH MY WINDOW

(S)	(3:05)	MCA 5938 Vintage Music Volumes 15 & 16. *(LP version)*
(S)	(3:05)	MCA 31212 Vintage Music Volume 15. *(LP version)*
(S)	(3:03)	MCA 10195 Creeque Alley/History Of. *(LP version)*
(S)	(3:06)	MCA 31044 Deliver. *(LP version)*
(S)	(3:20)	MCA 5701 16 Of Their Greatest Hits. *(LP version; :15 longer than any previously issued version of this song)*
(S)	(3:03)	Pair 1322 Words Of Love. *(LP version)*
(S)	(3:03)	MCA 11552 O.S.T. Beautiful Thing. *(LP version)*
(S)	(3:05)	MCA 11740 Greatest Hits. *(LP version)*

1967 WORDS OF LOVE
- (S) (2:12) MCA 5939 Vintage Music Volumes 17 & 18. *(LP version)*
- (S) (2:12) MCA 31215 Vintage Music Volume 18. *(LP version)*
- (S) (2:12) MCA 10195 Creeque Alley/History Of. *(LP version)*
- (S) (2:12) MCA 31147 Mama's Big Ones. *(LP version)*
- (S) (2:15) MCA 5701 16 Of Their Greatest Hits. *(LP version)*
- (S) (2:13) MCA 31043 The Mama's & Papa's. *(LP version)*
- (S) (2:12) Pair 1322 Words Of Love. *(LP version)*
- (S) (2:12) Time-Life 2CLR-24 Classic Rock - 1967: Blowin' Your Mind. *(LP version)*
- (S) (2:12) MCA Special Products 22132 Vintage Collectibles Volume 3. *(LP version)*
- (S) (2:12) MCA Special Products 22113 California Dreamin'. *(LP version)*
- (S) (2:11) MCA 11552 O.S.T. Beautiful Thing. *(LP version)*
- (S) (2:12) JCI 3185 1965 - Only Love - 1969. *(LP version)*
- (S) (2:13) MCA 11740 Greatest Hits. *(LP version)*

1967 DEDICATED TO THE ONE I LOVE
- (S) (2:56) MCA 5937 Vintage Music Volumes 13 & 14.
- (S) (2:56) MCA 31210 Vintage Music Volume 13.
- (S) (2:56) MCA 10195 Creeque Alley/History Of.
- (S) (2:58) MCA 31044 Deliver.
- (S) (2:59) MCA 5701 16 Of Their Greatest Hits. *(the first :34 of this song are remixed with almost no audible instrumentation and Michelle Phillips' voice is not double tracked)*
- (S) (2:57) Time-Life 2CLR-05 Classic Rock - 1967.
- (S) (2:57) Time-Life SUD-05 Superhits - 1967.
- (S) (2:56) Rhino 71937 Billboard Top Pop Hits, 1967.
- (S) (2:56) MCA Special Products 20900 Rock Around The Oldies #3.
- (S) (2:56) MCA 11552 O.S.T. Beautiful Thing.
- (S) (2:56) Time-Life AM1-08 AM Gold - 1967.
- (S) (2:57) Varese Sarabande 5802 Sunshine Days - Pop Classics Of The '60s Volume 2.
- (S) (2:56) MCA 11740 Greatest Hits.
- (S) (2:56) Time-Life R857-22 The Heart Of Rock 'n' Roll 1967-1969.

1967 CREEQUE ALLEY
- (S) (3:46) MCA 10195 Creeque Alley/History Of. *(stereo LP version)*
- (S) (3:47) MCA 31044 Deliver. *(stereo LP version)*
- (S) (3:48) MCA 5701 16 Of Their Greatest Hits. *(stereo LP version; out of phase)*
- (S) (3:46) Time-Life 2CLR-15 Classic Rock - 1967: Shakin' All Over. *(stereo LP version)*
- (S) (3:45) Time-Life SUD-14 Superhits - The Late 60's. *(stereo LP version)*
- (S) (3:46) MCA 11552 O.S.T. Beautiful Thing. *(stereo LP version)*
- (S) (3:45) Time-Life AM1-14 AM Gold - The Late '60s. *(stereo LP version)*
- (S) (3:46) MCA 11740 Greatest Hits. *(stereo LP version)*

1967 TWELVE THIRTY (YOUNG GIRLS ARE COMING TO THE CANYON)
- (S) (3:23) MCA 10195 Creeque Alley/History Of.
- (S) (3:23) MCA 31335 The Papa's & The Mama's.
- (S) (3:23) MCA 5701 16 Of Their Greatest Hits.
- (S) (3:20) Rhino 71066 Summer Of Love Volume 2.
- (S) (3:23) Pair 1322 Words Of Love.
- (S) (3:23) Risky Business 66387 Rock Around The Clock.
- (S) (3:23) MCA Special Products 22113 California Dreamin'.
- (S) (3:23) MCA 11740 Greatest Hits.

1967 GLAD TO BE UNHAPPY
- (S) (1:41) MCA 5940 Vintage Music Volumes 19 & 20.
- (S) (1:41) MCA 31216 Vintage Music Volume 19.
- (S) (1:41) MCA 10195 Creeque Alley/History Of.
- (S) (1:42) MCA 5701 16 Of Their Greatest Hits.
- (S) (1:41) MCA Special Products 22133 Vintage Collectibles Volume 4.
- (S) (1:41) MCA Special Products 22113 California Dreamin'.
- (S) (1:40) MCA 11740 Greatest Hits.

MELISSA MANCHESTER
1975 MIDNIGHT BLUE
- (S) (3:55) Priority 8664 High Times/70's Greatest Rock Hits Volume 3. *(LP length)*
- (S) (3:55) Arista 8004 Greatest Hits. *(LP length)*
- (S) (3:30) Razor & Tie 4543 The '70s Preservation Society Presents: Easy '70s. *(45 length)*
- (S) (3:30) Time-Life R834-02 Body Talk - Just For You. *(45 length)*
- (S) (3:53) Arista 18967 The Essence Of. *(LP length)*
- (S) (3:53) Simitar 55512 The Number One's: Lovin' Feelings. *(LP length)*
- (S) (3:30) Time-Life R814-05 Love Songs. *(45 length)*

1975 JUST TOO MANY PEOPLE
- (S) (3:33) Arista 8004 Greatest Hits.
- (S) (3:36) Arista 18967 The Essence Of.

1976 JUST YOU AND I
- (S) (4:20) Arista 8004 Greatest Hits. *(much slower than the 45 or LP)*
- (S) (4:04) Arista 18967 The Essence Of. *(LP length)*

1979 DON'T CRY OUT LOUD
- (S) (3:50) Arista 8004 Greatest Hits.
- (S) (3:49) Priority 53140 Best Of The 70's: Legendary Ladies.
- (S) (3:46) Arista 18967 The Essence Of.

1980 PRETTY GIRLS
- (S) (3:58) Rhino 71890 Radio Daze: Pop Hits Of The 80's Volume One.

1980 FIRE IN THE MORNING
- (S) (3:52) Rhino 71892 Radio Daze: Pop Hits Of The 80's Volume Three.
- (S) (3:51) Arista 18967 The Essence Of.

1982 YOU SHOULD HEAR HOW SHE TALKS ABOUT YOU
- (S) (4:15) Arista 8268 Arista's Perfect 10.
- (S) (4:14) Priority 53746 80's Greatest Rock Hits Vol. 12 - Singers/Songwriters.
- (S) (4:12) Arista 18967 The Essence Of.

HENRY MANCINI
1960 MR. LUCKY
- (S) (2:12) RCA 8321 All Time Greatest Hits Volume 1.
- (S) (2:12) RCA 3667 Pure Gold.
- (S) (2:13) RCA 2198 Music From "Mr. Lucky".
- (S) (2:11) RCA 53822 Best Of.
- (S) (2:10) RCA 51843 A Legendary Performer.
- (S) (2:11) Time-Life HPD-39 Your Hit Parade - 60's Instrumentals: Take Two.
- (S) (2:12) Time-Life R986-01 Henry Mancini - Instrumental Favorites.
- (S) (2:11) RCA 66603 The Days Of Wine And Roses Box Set.

1961 MOON RIVER
- (S) (2:39) RCA 8321 All Time Greatest Hits Volume 1.
- (S) (2:43) RCA 5938 Mancini's Classic Movie Scores.
- (S) (2:40) RCA 3667 Pure Gold.
- (S) (2:39) RCA 2077 Moon River, The Pink Panther & Other Hits.
- (S) (2:40) RCA 2362 Breakfast At Tiffany's.
- (S) (2:39) MCA 6340 O.S.T. Born On The Fourth Of July.
- (S) (2:41) RCA 55938 Pink Panther And Other Hits.
- (S) (2:40) Pair 1092 Collection.
- (S) (2:41) Pair 1213 Academy Award Collection.
- (S) (2:39) RCA 53822 Best Of.
- (S) (2:42) RCA 60966 Themes From Academy Award Winners.
- (S) (2:39) RCA 66099 Hooray For Hollywood.
- (S) (2:39) Time-Life HPD-37 Your Hit Parade - The 60's.
- (S) (2:40) Time-Life R986-01 Henry Mancini - Instrumental Favorites.
- (S) (2:39) Rhino 71868 Academy Award Winning Songs.
- (S) (2:39) Rhino 72278 Academy Award Winning Songs Volume 3.
- (S) (2:39) Rhino 72423 Billboard Top Movie Hits - 1960s.
- (S) (2:41) RCA 66603 The Days Of Wine And Roses Box Set.
- (S) (2:40) Time-Life R857-10 The Heart Of Rock 'n' Roll 1960-1961.

HENRY MANCINI (Continued)

    (S) (2:39) Time-Life R857-21 The Heart Of Rock 'n' Roll Slow Dancing Classics.

1963 DAYS OF WINE AND ROSES
    (S) (2:05) RCA 8321 All Time Greatest Hits Volume 1.
    (S) (2:06) RCA 3667 Pure Gold.
    (S) (2:06) Pair 1092 Collection.
    (S) (2:08) Pair 1213 Academy Award Collection.
    (S) (2:05) RCA 53822 Best Of.
    (S) (2:06) Time-Life R986-01 Henry Mancini - Instrumental Favorites.
    (M) (2:05) Rhino 71868 Academy Award Winning Songs.
    (S) (2:06) Time-Life R974-03 Many Moods Of Romance - I Wish You Love.
    (M) (2:05) Rhino 72278 Academy Award Winning Songs Volume 3.
    (S) (2:05) RCA 66603 The Days Of Wine And Roses Box Set.

1964 CHARADE
    (S) (2:34) RCA 3667 Pure Gold.
    (S) (2:35) RCA 5938 Mancini's Classic Movie Scores.
    (S) (2:34) RCA 2755 O.S.T. Charade.
    (S) (2:05) Pair 1092 Collection. *(main title version from the soundtrack - not the hit version)*
    (S) (3:41) RCA 60974 As Time Goes By And Other Classic Movie Love Songs. *(instrumental rerecording)*
    (S) (2:35) RCA 55938 The Pink Panther And Other Hits.
    (S) (2:07) RCA 8321 All Time Greatest Hits Volume 1. *(main title version from the soundtrack - not the hit version)*
    (S) (2:34) RCA 53822 Best Of.
    (S) (2:35) Time-Life R986-01 Henry Mancini - Instrumental Favorites.
    (S) (2:34) RCA 66603 The Days Of Wine And Roses Box Set.

1964 THE PINK PANTHER THEME
    (S) (2:35) Time-Life HPD-34 Your Hit Parade - 60's Instrumentals.
    (S) (2:34) RCA 3667 Pure Gold.
    (S) (2:36) RCA 5938 Mancini's Classic Movie Scores.
    (S) (2:36) Pair 1092 Collection.
    (S) (2:36) RCA 2077 Moon River, The Pink Panther & Other Hits.
    (S) (2:36) RCA 55938 The Pink Panther And Other Hits.
    (S) (2:32) RCA 51843 A Legendary Performer.
    (S) (2:35) RCA 8321 All Time Greatest Hits Volume 1.
    (S) (2:36) RCA 2795 O.S.T. The Pink Panther.
    (S) (2:36) Time-Life R986-01 Henry Mancini - Instrumental Favorites.
    (S) (2:35) RCA 66603 The Days Of Wine And Roses Box Set.

1969 LOVE THEME FROM ROMEO & JULIET
    (S) (2:31) RCA 8474 Nipper's Greatest Hits Of The 60's Volume 1.
    (S) (2:31) RCA 8321 All Time Greatest Hits Volume 1.
    (S) (2:31) RCA 3667 Pure Gold.
    (S) (2:31) Pair 1187 Mancini Magic.
    (S) (2:32) Pair 1092 Collection.
    (S) (2:31) RCA 51843 A Legendary Performer.
    (S) (2:31) Time-Life R138/05 Look Of Love.
    (S) (2:32) Time-Life R986-01 Henry Mancini - Instrumental Favorites.
    (S) (2:31) Rhino 71939 Billboard Top Pop Hits, 1969.
    (S) (2:31) Time-Life R974-01 Many Moods Of Romance - That's My Desire.
    (S) (2:31) Rhino 72423 Billboard Top Movie Hits - 1960s.
    (S) (2:31) RCA 66603 The Days Of Wine And Roses Box Set.
    (S) (2:31) RCA 66859 To Mom With Love.
    (S) (2:30) Time-Life R834-14 Body Talk - Love And Tenderness.
    (S) (2:32) Time-Life R814-01 Love Songs.

1971 THEME FROM LOVE STORY
    (S) (2:49) RCA 8321 All Time Greatest Hits Volume 1.
    (S) (2:50) Pair 1296 Love Story.
    (S) (2:49) Time-Life R986-01 Henry Mancini - Instrumental Favorites.

    (S) (2:50) RCA 66603 The Days Of Wine And Roses Box Set.
    (S) (2:50) RCA 66859 To Mom With Love.
    (S) (2:49) Priority 50974 Premiere The Movie Magazine Presents The Greatest Soundtrack Love Songs.
    (S) (2:49) Time-Life R834-17 Body Talk - Heart To Heart.

BARBARA MANDRELL
1979 (IF LOVING YOU IS WRONG) I DON'T WANT TO BE RIGHT
    (S) (3:04) MCA 8025 30 Years Of Hits (1975-1988).
    (S) (3:04) MCA 6422 16 Top Country Hits Volume 2.
    (S) (3:04) MCA 31302 Greatest Hits.
    (S) (3:05) K-Tel 3163 Behind Closed Doors.
    (S) (3:04) JCI 3156 1975 - Only Country - 1979.

MANFRED MANN
1964 DO WAH DIDDY DIDDY
    (S) (2:21) Rhino 70320 History Of British Rock Volume 2.
    (S) (2:21) Rhino 72022 History Of British Rock Box Set.
    (S) (2:21) Rhino 72008 History Of British Rock Volumes 1-4 Box Set.
    (S) (2:21) Rhino 70625 Billboard's Top Rock & Roll Hits Of 1964.
    (S) (2:21) Rhino 72007 Billboard's Top Rock & Roll Hits 1962-1966 Box Set.
    (M) (2:21) Curb 77355 60's Hits Volume 1.
    (M) (2:21) Epic 48732 O.S.T. My Girl.
    (M) (2:21) EMI 48397 Best Of.
    (M) (2:21) Capitol 98138 Spring Break Volume 1.
    (M) (2:31) EMI 96096 Best Of. *(includes :09 of studio talk; original unedited version which was not the hit version)*
    (S) (2:21) EMI 96096 Best Of.
    (S) (2:21) EMI 81128 Rock Is Dead But It Won't Lie Down.
    (M) (2:21) Era 5025 The Brill Building Sound.
    (E) (2:21) JCI 3107 British Sixties.
    (S) (2:21) Time-Life 2CLR-03 Classic Rock - 1964.
    (S) (2:20) Time-Life R962-07 History Of Rock 'N' Roll: The British Invasion 1964-1966.
    (S) (2:21) Risky Business 66914 Party On.
    (S) (2:21) EMI 37067 Manfred Mann Album/Five Faces Of.

1965 SHA LA LA
    (M) (2:29) Rhino 70321 History Of British Rock Volume 3.
    (M) (2:29) Rhino 72022 History Of British Rock Box Set.
    (M) (2:29) Rhino 72008 History Of British Rock Volumes 1-4 Box Set.
    (M) (2:30) EMI 48397 Best Of.
    (M) (2:29) EMI 96096 Best Of.
    (M) (2:29) EMI 37067 Manfred Mann Album/Five Faces Of.

1966 PRETTY FLAMINGO
    (S) (2:32) Rhino 70322 History Of British Rock Volume 4.
    (S) (2:32) Rhino 72022 History Of British Rock Box Set.
    (S) (2:32) Rhino 72008 History Of British Rock Volumes 1-4 Box Set.
    (M) (2:33) EMI 48397 Best Of.
    (S) (2:29) EMI 96096 Best Of.

1968 MIGHTY QUINN (QUINN THE ESKIMO)
    (M) (2:50) Fontana 314522665 Best Of The Fontana Years.
    (S) (6:14) Warner Brothers 46231 Best Of Manfred Mann's Earth Band. *(rerecording)*
    (M) (2:54) Eclipse Music Group 64871 Rock 'n Roll Relix 1968-1969.
    (M) (2:54) Eclipse Music Group 64872 Rock 'n Roll Relix 1960-1969.
    (M) (2:49) Rebound 314520435 Classic Rock - 60's.

released as by MANFRED MANN'S EARTH BAND:
1977 BLINDED BY THE LIGHT
    (S) (3:48) JCI 3302 Electric Seventies. *(45 version)*
    (S) (7:07) Warner Special Products 27614 Highs Of The Seventies. *(LP version)*
    (S) (3:47) Time-Life SOD-05 Sounds Of The Seventies - 1977. *(45 version)*
    (S) (7:04) Warner Brothers 46231 Best Of Manfred Mann's Earth Band. *(LP version)*

1984 RUNNER

CHUCK MANGIONE
1978 FEELS SO GOOD
- (S) (9:39) A&M 3219 Feels So Good. *(LP version)*
- (S) (3:29) A&M 3282 Best Of. *(45 version)*
- (S) (9:40) A&M 2502 Classics Volume 6. *(LP version)*
- (S) (9:39) Verve 314521007 Playboy's 40th Anniversary: Four Decades Of Jazz (1953-1993). *(LP version)*
- (S) (3:36) Rhino 72298 Superhits Of The 70's Volume 24. *(45 version)*
- (S) (9:32) A&M 314540514 Greatest Hits. *(LP version)*
- (S) (3:29) Time-Life R840-04 Sounds Of The Seventies: A Loss For Words. *(45 version)*
- (S) (3:29) Time-Life AM1-25 AM Gold - 1978. *(45 version)*
- (S) (3:29) Time-Life R986-22 Instrumental Classics - Pop Classics. *(45 version)*
- (S) (3:29) Rebound 314520492 Class Reunion '78. *(45 version)*

1980 GIVE IT ALL YOU GOT
- (S) (6:09) A&M 3193 Fun And Games. *(LP version)*
- (S) (3:55) A&M 3282 Best Of. *(45 version)*
- (S) (6:10) A&M 2502 Classics Volume 6. *(LP version)*
- (S) (6:09) Rebound 314520242 Fun And Games. *(LP version)*
- (S) (6:06) A&M 314540514 Greatest Hits. *(LP version)*

MANHATTANS
1973 THERE'S NO ME WITHOUT YOU
- (S) (3:37) Columbia 36861 Greatest Hits.
- (S) (3:37) Right Stuff 28372 Slow Jams: The 70's Volume Two.
- (S) (3:37) Priority 53130 Deep Soul Volume Three.
- (S) (3:37) Legacy/Columbia 64662 Best Of: Kiss And Say Goodbye.
- (*) (*:**) Time-Life R838-08 Solid Gold Soul - 1973. *(this song is listed on the cd jacket as "THERE'S NO ME WITHOUT YOU" but in reality it is the song "DON'T TAKE YOUR LOVE")*

1975 DON'T TAKE YOUR LOVE
- (S) (3:05) Columbia 36861 Greatest Hits. *(45 version)*
- (S) (3:26) Legacy/Columbia 64662 Best Of: Kiss And Say Goodbye. *(LP version)*
- (S) (3:36) Time-Life R838-08 Solid Gold Soul - 1973. *(this song is listed on the cd jacket as "THERE'S NO ME WITHOUT YOU" but in reality it is the LP version of "DON'T TAKE YOUR LOVE")*

1976 KISS AND SAY GOODBYE
(dj copies of this 45 ran (2:32) and (3:29); commercial copies were all (3:29))
- (S) (4:25) Columbia 36861 Greatest Hits. *(LP version)*
- (S) (3:30) Razor & Tie 22047 Sweet 70's Soul. *(45 version)*
- (S) (3:31) Time-Life SOD-34 Sounds Of The Seventies - The Late 70's. *(45 version)*
- (S) (4:25) Original Sound 9305 Art Laboe's Dedicated To You Volume 5. *(LP version)*
- (S) (4:26) Right Stuff 29138 Slow Jams: The 70's Vol. 3. *(LP version)*
- (S) (4:25) Legacy/Epic 66912 Legacy's Rhythm & Soul Revue. *(LP version)*
- (S) (3:30) Rhino 72128 Hot Soul Hits Of The 70's Vol. 18. *(45 version)*
- (S) (3:29) K-Tel 3535 Slow Groove Love Jams Of The 70's. *(45 version)*
- (S) (4:25) Legacy/Columbia 64662 Best Of: Kiss And Say Goodbye. *(LP version)*
- (S) (4:25) Eclipse Music Group 64895 Rock 'n Roll Relix 1976-1977. *(LP version)*
- (S) (4:25) Eclipse Music Group 64897 Rock 'n Roll Relix 1970-1979. *(LP version)*
- (S) (3:31) Time-Life AM1-23 AM Gold - 1976. *(45 version)*
- (S) (3:30) Time-Life R838-11 Solid Gold Soul - 1976. *(45 version)*
- (S) (4:25) Time-Life R834-01 Body Talk - Forever Yours. *(LP version)*
- (S) (4:24) Simitar 55512 The Number One's: Lovin' Feelings. *(LP version)*
- (S) (3:30) JCI 3175 1975 - Only Soul - 1979. *(45 version)*

- (S) (3:30) Collectables 1516 and 2516 The Anniversary Album - The 70's. *(45 veersion)*

1980 SHINING STAR
- (S) (4:38) Columbia 36861 Greatest Hits. *(LP length; truncated fade)*
- (S) (4:40) Rhino 71859 Smooth Grooves Volume 1. *(LP length)*
- (S) (3:46) Rhino 71971 Video Soul - Best Soul Of The 80's Vol. 1. *(45 length)*
- (S) (3:47) Rhino 72135 Billboard Hot R&B Hits 1980. *(45 length)*
- (S) (3:47) Hip-O 40001 The Glory Of Love - Sweet & Soulful Love Songs. *(45 length)*
- (S) (4:39) Legacy/Columbia 64662 Best Of: Kiss And Say Goodbye. *(LP length)*
- (S) (4:39) JCI 3170 #1 Radio Hits 1980 - Only Rock 'n Roll - 1984. *(LP length)*
- (S) (3:45) K-Tel 3673 The 80's - Funky Love. *(45 length)*
- (S) (3:47) Time-Life R988-14 Sounds Of The Eighties: 1980-1982. *(45 length)*
- (S) (4:39) Time-Life R834-09 Body Talk - Magic Moments. *(LP length)*
- (S) (4:47) Original Sound 9306 Dedicated To You Vol. 6. *(LP length)*

MANHATTAN TRANSFER
1975 OPERATOR
- (S) (3:09) Rhino 71053 Anthology.
- (S) (3:10) Atlantic 18133 Manhattan Transfer.
- (S) (3:07) Atlantic 19319 Best Of.
- (S) (3:09) Rhino 71560 Very Best Of.

1980 TWILIGHT ZONE/TWILIGHT TONE
- (S) (3:55) Rhino 71096 Disco Hits Volume 3. *(45 version)*
- (S) (6:28) Turnstyle/Atlantic 14215 Atlantic Dance Classics. *(12" single version)*
- (S) (6:03) Rhino 71053 Anthology. *(LP version)*
- (S) (6:02) Atlantic 81565 Extensions. *(LP version)*
- (S) (6:02) MFSL 578 Extensions. *(gold disc)*
- (S) (3:53) Atlantic 19319 Best Of. *(45 version)*
- (S) (6:04) Rhino 71560 Very Best Of. *(LP version)*
- (S) (3:55) Flashback 72691 Disco Hits: Le Freak. *(45 version)*
- (S) (3:55) Flashback 72086 Disco Hits Box Set. *(45 version)*
- (S) (6:04) Flashback 72884 Boy From New York City And Other Hits. *(LP version)*

1981 BOY FROM NEW YORK CITY
- (S) (3:39) Rhino 71053 Anthology.
- (S) (3:39) Atlantic 16036 Mecca For Moderns.
- (S) (3:38) Atlantic 19319 Best Of.
- (S) (3:39) Rhino 71560 Very Best Of.
- (S) (3:38) Time-Life R988-16 Sounds Of The Eighties: The Early '80s.
- (S) (3:38) Flashback 72884 Boy From New York City And Other Hits.

BARRY MANILOW
1975 MANDY
(actual 45 time is (3:20) not (3:15) as stated on the record label; LP length is (3:33))
- (S) (3:22) Arista 8039 Greatest Hits.
- (S) (3:19) Arista 8598 Greatest Hits Volume 1.
- (S) (3:33) Arista 8560 Barry Manilow II.
- (S) (3:44) Arista 18714 Complete Collection And Then Some. *(alternate take with studio talk on intro and outro)*
- (S) (3:33) Arista 18944 Barry Manilow II.

1975 IT'S A MIRACLE
- (S) (3:43) Arista 8039 Greatest Hits. *(edit of LP version)*
- (S) (3:53) Arista 8598 Greatest Hits Volume 1. *(alternate take)*
- (S) (3:59) Arista 8560 Barry Manilow II. *(LP version)*
- (S) (3:59) Arista 18714 Complete Collection And Then Some. *(LP version)*
- (S) (3:59) Arista 18944 Barry Manilow II. *(LP version)*

1975 COULD IT BE MAGIC
- (S) (6:47) Arista 8039 Greatest Hits. *(LP version)*

BARRY MANILOW *(Continued)*

    (S) (6:47)   Arista 8599 Greatest Hits Volume II. *(LP version)*
    (S) (6:47)   Arista 8559 Barry Manilow I. *(LP version)*
    (E) (2:31)   Arista 18714 Complete Collection And Then Some. *(1971 recording - not the hit version)*
    (S) (6:47)   Arista 18714 Complete Collection And Then Some. *(LP version)*
    (S) (3:10)   Priority 50960 Work It! Dance = Life. *(remix; all selections on this cd are segued together)*
    (S) (6:47)   Time-Life R834-17 Body Talk - Heart To Heart. *(LP version)*

1976 I WRITE THE SONGS
    (S) (3:53)   Arista 8039 Greatest Hits. *(LP length)*
    (S) (3:53)   Arista 8599 Greatest Hits Volume II. *(LP length)*
    (S) (3:54)   Arista 8070 Trying To Get The Feeling Again. *(LP length)*
    (S) (3:53)   Arista 18714 Complete Collection And Then Some. *(LP length)*

1976 TRYIN' TO GET THE FEELING AGAIN
    (S) (3:49)   Arista 8039 Greatest Hits.
    (S) (3:49)   Arista 8598 Greatest Hits Volume 1.
    (S) (3:49)   Arista 8070 Trying To Get The Feeling Again.
    (S) (4:42)   Arista 18714 Complete Collection And Then Some. *(alternate take)*

1976 THIS ONE'S FOR YOU
    (S) (3:28)   Arista 8039 Greatest Hits.
    (S) (3:27)   Arista 8599 Greatest Hits Volume II.
    (S) (3:28)   Arista 8331 This One's For You.
    (S) (3:06)   Arista 18714 Complete Collection And Then Some. *(demo version)*

1977 WEEKEND IN NEW ENGLAND
    (S) (3:44)   Arista 8039 Greatest Hits.
    (S) (3:43)   Arista 8599 Greatest Hits Volume II.
    (S) (3:44)   Arista 8331 This One's For You.
    (S) (3:44)   Arista 18714 Complete Collection And Then Some.

1977 LOOKS LIKE WE MADE IT
    (S) (3:33)   Arista 8039 Greatest Hits.
    (S) (3:32)   Arista 8598 Greatest Hits Volume 1.
    (S) (3:33)   Arista 8331 This One's For You.

1977 DAYBREAK
(actual 45 time is (3:42) not (3:36) as stated on the record label)
    (S) (3:38)   Arista 8039 Greatest Hits. *(some pressings of this cd feature the studio version of this song which is (S) and runs (3:06))*
    (S) (3:06)   Arista 8598 Greatest Hits Volume 1. *(studio recording which was not the hit version)*
    (S) (3:06)   Arista 8331 This One's For You. *(studio recording which was not the hit version)*
    (S) (3:48)   Arista 18714 Complete Collection And Then Some.
    (S) (3:38)   Arista 8049 Live.

1978 CAN'T SMILE WITHOUT YOU
    (S) (3:12)   Arista 8039 Greatest Hits.
    (S) (3:10)   Arista 8598 Greatest Hits Volume 1.
    (S) (3:11)   Arista 8230 Even Now.
    (S) (3:05)   Arista 18714 Complete Collection And Then Some. *(alternate take)*
    (S) (3:11)   Arista 18946 Even Now.

1978 EVEN NOW
    (S) (3:30)   Arista 8039 Greatest Hits.
    (S) (3:28)   Arista 8598 Greatest Hits Volume 1.
    (S) (3:28)   Arista 8230 Even Now.
    (S) (3:34)   Arista 18714 Complete Collection And Then Some. *(live)*
    (S) (3:28)   Time-Life R834-02 Body Talk - Just For You.
    (S) (3:28)   Arista 18946 Even Now.

1978 COPACABANA (AT THE COPA)
(dj and commercial copies of this 45 ran (3:57) on one side and (5:46) on the other; actual 45 time is (3:57) not (3:48) as stated on the record label)
    (S) (3:58)   Arista 8039 Greatest Hits. *(edited 45 version)*
    (S) (5:43)   Arista 8599 Greatest Hits Volume II.
    (S) (5:43)   Arista 8230 Even Now.
    (S) (1:32)   Arista 18714 Complete Collection And Then Some. *(demo; tracks into next selection)*

    (S) (4:04)   Arista 18714 Complete Collection And Then Some. *(edited 45 version; previous selection tracks over :06 of the introduction)*
    (S) (5:43)   Arista 18946 Even Now.

1978 READY TO TAKE A CHANCE AGAIN
    (S) (3:01)   Arista 8039 Greatest Hits.
    (S) (3:01)   Arista 8600 Greatest Hits Volume III.
    (S) (2:59)   Arista 18714 Complete Collection And Then Some.

1979 SOMEWHERE IN THE NIGHT
    (S) (3:27)   Arista 8039 Greatest Hits.
    (S) (3:26)   Arista 8599 Greatest Hits Volume II.
    (S) (3:24)   Arista 8230 Even Now.
    (S) (3:26)   Arista 18714 Complete Collection And Then Some.
    (S) (3:24)   Arista 18946 Even Now.

1979 SHIPS
    (S) (3:59)   Arista 8102 Greatest Hits Volume II.
    (S) (3:59)   Arista 8600 Greatest Hits Volume III.
    (S) (3:58)   Arista 18714 Complete Collection And Then Some. *(live)*

1980 WHEN I WANTED YOU
1981 I MADE IT THROUGH THE RAIN
(actual 45 time is (4:23) not (3:57) as stated on the record label)
    (S) (4:24)   Arista 8102 Greatest Hits Volume II.
    (S) (4:23)   Arista 8600 Greatest Hits Volume III.
    (S) (4:18)   Arista 18714 Complete Collection And Then Some. *(alternate take)*

1981 THE OLD SONGS
(actual 45 time is (4:18) not (3:58) as stated on the record label; actual LP time is (4:34) not (4:42) as stated on the record label)
    (S) (4:34)   Arista 8102 Greatest Hits Volume II. *(LP length)*
    (S) (4:39)   Arista 8600 Greatest Hits Volume III. *(slightly longer than LP length)*
    (S) (4:51)   Arista 18714 Complete Collection And Then Some. *(alternate take)*

1982 SOMEWHERE DOWN THE ROAD
    (S) (3:57)   Arista 8102 Greatest Hits Volume II.
    (S) (3:56)   Arista 8600 Greatest Hits Volume III.
    (S) (4:04)   Arista 18714 Complete Collection And Then Some. *(demo version)*

1982 LET'S HANG ON
    (S) (3:07)   Arista 8102 Greatest Hits Volume II.
    (S) (3:07)   Arista 8600 Greatest Hits Volume III.

1982 OH JULIE
1983 MEMORY
(actual 45 time is (4:57) not (4:34) as stated on the record label)
    (S) (4:57)   Arista 8102 Greatest Hits Volume II.
    (S) (4:55)   Arista 8600 Greatest Hits Volume III.
    (S) (4:25)   Arista 18714 Complete Collection And Then Some. *(live)*

1983 SOME KIND OF FRIEND
(actual 45 time is (3:53) not (3:44) as stated on the record label)
    (S) (4:02)   Arista 8102 Greatest Hits Volume II. *(LP length)*
    (S) (4:01)   Arista 8598 Greatest Hits Volume I. *(LP length)*

1984 READ 'EM AND WEEP
(dj copies of this 45 ran (4:54) and (5:26); commercial copies were all (5:26))
    (S) (5:25)   Arista 8102 Greatest Hits Volume II.
    (S) (5:25)   Arista 8600 Greatest Hits Volume III.
    (S) (5:09)   Arista 18714 Complete Collection And Then Some. *(edited)*

BARRY MANN
1961 WHO PUT THE BOMP (IN THE BOMP, BOMP, BOMP)
    (S) (2:43)   MCA 31202 Vintage Music Volume 5.
    (S) (2:43)   MCA 5804 Vintage Music Volumes 5 & 6.
    (S) (2:43)   Era 5025 The Brill Building Sound.
    (S) (2:43)   Time-Life 2RNR-18 Rock 'N' Roll Era - 1961 Still Rockin'.
    (S) (2:43)   Collectables 2504 WCBS-FM History Of Rock - The 60's Part 4.

(S) (2:43) Collectables 4504 History Of Rock/The 60s Part Four.
(S) (2:42) MCA Special Products 22028 Cra-a-zy Hits.
(S) (2:43) MCA Special Products 22179 Vintage Collectibles Volume 9.
(S) (2:43) K-Tel 3035 Goofy Greats.

CARL MANN
1959 MONA LISA
(M) (2:26) Rhino 75884 The Sun Story.
(M) (2:26) RCA 66059 Sun's Greatest Hits.
(M) (2:26) Time-Life 2RNR-33 Rock 'N' Roll Era - The 50's Last Dance.
(M) (2:26) Rhino 71780 Sun Records Collection.

GLORIA MANN
1955 EARTH ANGEL (WILL YOU BE MINE)
1956 TEEN AGE PRAYER
(E) (2:26) Original Sound 8854 Oldies But Goodies Vol. 4. *(this compact disc uses the "Waring - fds" noise reduction process)*
(E) (2:26) Original Sound 2221 Oldies But Goodies Volumes 1,4,6,8 and 10 Box Set. *(this box set uses the "Waring - fds" noise reduction process)*
(E) (2:26) Original Sound 2500 Oldies But Goodies Volumes 1-15 Box Set. *(this box set uses the "Waring - fds" noise reduction process)*

HERBIE MANN
1975 HIJACK
(S) (5:13) Turnstyle/Atlantic 14215 Atlantic Dance Classics. *(LP version)*
(S) (5:14) Rhino 71549 Let There Be Drums Vol. 3: The 70's. *(LP version)*
(S) (5:13) Rhino 71634 Evolution Of Mann/Anthology. *(LP version)*
1979 SUPERMAN

MANTOVANI
1957 AROUND THE WORLD
(S) (2:03) London 800085 Golden Hits.
(S) (2:03) Time-Life R986-05 Instrumental Favorites.
(S) (2:03) Time-Life R986-22 Instrumental Classics - Pop Classics.
1960 MAIN THEME FROM EXODUS (ARI'S THEME)
(S) (3:10) Polygram Special Markets 314520273 Great Instrumental Hits.

MARATHONS
1961 PEANUT BUTTER
(M) (2:00) Rhino 75772 Son Of Frat Rock.
(M) (1:57) Chess 9283 Best Of Chess Vocal Groups Volume 2.
(M) (2:01) DCC Compact Classics 057 Olympics All-Time Greatest Hits.
(E) (2:01) Collectables 5081 The Olympics Meet The Marathons.
(M) (2:01) Sandstone 33078 Olympics All-Time Greatest Hits.
(M) (2:00) Time-Life 2RNR-25 Rock 'N' Roll Era - The 60's Keep On Rockin'.
(M) (1:57) Chess 9352 Chess Rhythm & Roll.
(E) (2:00) K-Tel 3409 Funniest Food Songs.

MARCELS
1961 BLUE MOON
(S) (2:13) Rhino 75764 Best Of Doo Wop Uptempo.
(S) (2:13) Rhino 70622 Billboard's Top Rock & Roll Hits Of 1961.
(S) (2:13) Rhino 72004 Billboard's Top Rock & Roll Hits 1957-1961 Box Set.
(S) (2:14) Rhino 70953 Best Of.
(S) (2:14) Rhino 71463 Doo Wop Box.
(S) (2:13) Time-Life 2RNR-04 Rock 'N' Roll Era - 1961.
(S) (2:13) Time-Life RHD-14 Rhythm & Blues - 1961.
(S) (2:14) Time-Life R962-06 History Of Rock 'N' Roll: Doo Wop And Vocal Group Tradition 1955-1962.

(S) (2:14) Collectables 2601 WCBS-FM History Of Rock - The Group Sounds Vol. 2.
(S) (2:14) Rhino 71650 Colpix-Dimension Story.
(S) (2:12) Time-Life R10513 40 Lovin' Oldies.
(S) (2:14) MCA Special Products 20753 Classic R&B Oldies From The 60's.
(S) (2:14) Rhino 71806 The R&B Box: Thirty Years Of Rhythm & Blues.
(S) (2:14) K-Tel 3008 60's Sock Hop.
(S) (2:14) Polygram Special Markets 314520259 Doo Wop Classics.
(S) (2:15) Collectables 5626 Spotlite On Colpix Records Volume 1.
(S) (2:14) Rhino 72156 Doo Wop Memories, Vol. 1.
(S) (2:13) Eclipse Music Group 64867 Rock 'n Roll Relix 1960-1961.
(S) (2:13) Eclipse Music Group 64872 Rock 'n Roll Relix 1960-1969.
(S) (2:14) Flashback 72717 Doo Wop - Blue Moon.
(S) (2:13) Time-Life R838-19 Solid Gold Soul 1961.
(S) (2:14) Flashback 72857 Grease And Other Golden Oldies.
1961 HEARTACHES
(S) (2:31) Rhino 70953 Best Of.
(S) (2:30) Time-Life 2RNR-25 Rock 'N' Roll Era - The 60's Keep On Rockin'.
(S) (2:31) Rhino 71650 Colpix-Dimension Story.
(S) (2:29) Collectables 5626 Spotlite On Colpix Records Volume 1.
(S) (2:30) Rhino 72507 Doo Wop Box II.

LITTLE PEGGY MARCH
1963 I WILL FOLLOW HIM
(S) (2:27) RCA 8474 Nipper's Greatest Hits Of The 60's Volume 1.
(S) (2:25) RCA 9902 Nipper's #1 Hits 1956 - 1986.
(S) (2:24) Time-Life 2RNR-29 Rock 'N' Roll Era - The 60's Rave On.
(S) (2:26) Nick At Nite/550 Music/Epic 67689 Stand By Your Man.
(S) (2:25) Eric 11503 Hard To Find 45's On CD (Volume II) 1961-64.
(S) (2:26) Collectables 5830 I Will Follow Him - A Golden Classics Edition.
(S) (2:42) Taragon 1027 Very Best Of. *(time includes :09 of studio talk)*
(S) (2:26) Collectables 1515 and 2515 The Anniversary Album - The 60's.
1963 I WISH I WERE A PRINCESS
(M) (2:12) MCA 6228 O.S.T. Hairspray.
(S) (2:11) Collectors' Choice 5189 I Wish I Were A Princess - The Great Lost Female Teen Idols.
(S) (2:11) Collectables 5830 I Will Follow Him - A Golden Classics Edition.
(S) (2:16) Taragon 1027 Very Best Of.
1963 HELLO HEARTACHE, GOODBYE LOVE
(S) (2:26) RCA 8475 Nipper's Greatest Hits Of The 60's Volume 2.
(M) (2:23) Collectables 5830 I Will Follow Him - A Golden Classics Edition.
(S) (2:25) Taragon 1027 Very Best Of.

BOBBY MARCHAN
1960 THERE'S SOMETHING ON YOUR MIND (PART 2)
(M) (2:45) Rhino 70646 Billboard's Top R&B Hits Of 1960.
(M) (4:50) Relic 7009 Raging Harlem Hit Parade. *(Parts 1 & 2)*
(M) (4:49) Capricorn 42009 Fire/Fury Records Story. *(Parts 1 & 2)*
(M) (4:46) Time-Life 2RNR-22 Rock 'N' Roll Era - 1960 Still Rockin'. *(Parts 1 & 2)*
(M) (4:45) Time-Life RHD-15 Rhythm & Blues - 1960. *(Parts 1 & 2)*
(M) (2:49) Collectables 5113 Golden Classics.
(M) (4:49) Ripete 2223 Soul Patrol Vol. 5. *(Parts 1 & 2)*

BOBBY MARCHAN (Continued)
(M) (4:45) Time-Life R838-20 Solid Gold Soul 1960. (Parts 1 & 2)
(M) (2:49) Relic 7072 Something On Your Mind.

BENNY MARDONES
1980 INTO THE NIGHT
(dj copies of this 45 ran (3:43) and (4:29);
commercial copies were all (4:29))
(S) (4:18) Curb 77532 Your Favorite Songs. (rerecording)
(S) (4:29) Polydor 839582 Never Run Never Hide.
(S) (4:21) Curb 77292 Benny Mardones. (rerecording)
(S) (4:29) Rebound 314520318 Class Reunion 1980.
(S) (4:31) Rhino 71892 Radio Daze: Pop Hits Of The 80's Volume Three.
(S) (4:29) Rebound 314520438 No. 1 Hits Of The 80's.
(S) (4:30) Time-Life R834-13 Body Talk - Just The Two Of Us.
1989 INTO THE NIGHT
(this song charted in 1980 and 1989; see 1980 listings)

ERNIE MARESCA
1962 SHOUT! SHOUT! (KNOCK YOURSELF OUT)
(S) (2:09) Rhino 75772 Son Of Frat Rock.
(M) (2:10) JCI 3110 Sock Hoppin' Sixties.
(S) (2:06) Collectables 5070 History Of Rock Volume 10.
(S) (2:07) Time-Life 2RNR-29 Rock 'N' Roll Era - The 60's Rave On.

TEENA MARIE
1981 I NEED YOUR LOVIN'
(S) (3:48) Motown 314530516 Motown Year By Year 1980. (45 version but :12 longer fade)
(S) (7:30) Motown 314530309 I Need Your Lovin'. (LP version)
(S) (3:40) Gordy 8003 Irons In The Fire/It Must Be Magic. (45 version)
(S) (3:34) Motown 5370 Greatest Hits. (45 version)
(S) (3:51) Motown 314530409 Motown Milestones - Motown's Leading Ladies. (45 version but :15 longer fade)
(S) (3:50) Motown 314530607 Best Of - Motown Milestones. (45 version but :14 longer fade)
(S) (3:34) Polydor 314535877 Pure Disco. (45 version)
(S) (3:47) Simitar 55602 The Number One's: Silky Soul. (45 version but :11 longer fade)
1985 LOVERGIRL
(S) (5:46) Epic 46087 Club Epic. (remix)
(S) (4:42) Priority 53703 Hot And Sexy - Passion And Soul. (LP version faded :10 early)
(S) (4:41) Rebound 314520357 World Of Dance - The 80's. (LP version faded :11 early)
(S) (4:50) Epic/Legacy 65070 Lovergirl: The Teena Marie Story. (LP version)
(S) (5:46) Epic/Legacy 65504 Disco Super Hits. (remix)

MARK IV
1959 I GOT A WIFE
(M) (2:02) Time-Life HPD-40 Your Hit Parade - Golden Goofers.

MARKETTS
1962 SURFER'S STOMP
(S) (1:56) Rhino 70089 Surfin' Hits.
(S) (1:56) Capitol Special Markets 57272 Great Instrumental Hits From Rock's Golden Years.
(S) (1:56) EMI 90604 Beach Party Blasts.
(S) (1:56) Curb 77402 All-Time Great Instrumental Hits Volume 2.
(S) (1:56) Capitol 96861 Monster Summer Hits - Wild Surf.
(S) (1:56) K-Tel 3059 Saxy Rock.
(S) (1:56) Rhino 72418 Cowabunga! The Surf Box.
(S) (1:56) K-Tel 6256 Kahuna Classics.
1964 OUT OF LIMITS
(S) (2:04) Rhino 70089 Surfin' Hits.

(S) (2:05) Rhino 71492 Elvira Presents Haunted Hits.
(S) (2:04) Rhino 70625 Billboard's Top Rock & Roll Hits Of 1964.
(S) (2:04) Rhino 72007 Billboard's Top Rock & Roll Hits 1962-1966 Box Set.
(S) (2:04) Warner Special Products 27607 Highs Of The 60's.
(S) (2:04) JCI 3106 Surfin' Sixties.
(S) (2:04) Rhino 71602 Rock Instrumental Classics Volume 2: The Sixties.
(S) (2:04) Rhino 72035 Rock Instrumental Classics Vols. 1-5 Box Set.
(S) (2:03) Time-Life 2CLR-03 Classic Rock - 1964.
(S) (2:04) Sundazed 6085 Out Of Limits.
(S) (2:06) K-Tel 6256 Kahuna Classics. (rerecording)
1966 BATMAN THEME
(S) (2:39) Warner Special Products 27610 More Party Classics.

MAR-KEYS
1961 LAST NIGHT
(M) (2:36) Atlantic Group 88218 Complete Stax/Volt Singles.
(M) (2:34) Warner Special Products 27609 Memphis Soul Classics.
(M) (2:34) Atlantic 81296 Atlantic Rhythm & Blues Volume 4.
(M) (2:36) Stax 88008 Top Of The Stax Volume 2.
(M) (2:36) Atlantic 82305 Atlantic Rhythm And Blues 1947-1974 Box Set.
(M) (2:36) Rhino 71604 Rock Instrumental Classics Vol. 4: Soul.
(M) (2:36) Rhino 72035 Rock Instrumental Classics Vols. 1-5 Box Set.
(M) (2:34) Time-Life 2RNR-18 Rock 'N' Roll Era - 1961 Still Rockin'.
(M) (2:37) Rhino 72815 Beg, Scream & Shout! The Big Ol' Box Of '60s Soul.
(M) (2:36) Rhino 72963 Ultimate '60s Soul Smashes.

PIGMEAT MARKHAM
1968 HERE COMES THE JUDGE
(*) (*:**) Priority 53747 Wild & Crazy Tunes. (this is not the song "HERE COMES THE JUDGE" as the label states but another song titled "THE TRIAL")
(M) (2:40) MCA Special Products 22028 Cra-a-zy Hits.

MARKY MARK & THE FUNKY BUNCH
released as by MARKY MARK & THE FUNKY BUNCH featuring LOLEATTA HOLLOWAY:
1991 GOOD VIBRATIONS
(S) (4:29) Foundation/RCA 66104 Hot #1 Hits.
(S) (4:28) JCI 2717 Shake It Up.
(S) (4:29) Sandstone 33055 and 5014 Rock The First Volume Eight.
(S) (5:49) Tommy Boy 1053 MTV Party To Go Volume 2. (remix; all tracks on this cd are segued together)
(S) (4:28) Interscope 91737 Music For The People.
(S) (4:28) Cold Front 6255 Greatest Sports Rock And Jams Volume 2. (all selections on this cd are segued together)
released as by MARKY MARK & THE FUNKY BUNCH:
1992 WILDSIDE
(S) (5:06) Rhino 71916 Whats Up? Rap Hits Of The 90's.
(S) (5:06) Interscope 91737 Music For The People.

ZIGGY MARLEY
1988 TOMORROW PEOPLE
(S) (3:36) Rebound 314520313 Caribbean Nights I.
(S) (3:36) Virgin 90878 and 86038 Conscious Party.
(S) (3:35) Priority 53797 Best Of 80's Rock Volume 4.
(S) (3:35) K-Tel 6067 Best Of Reggae.
(S) (3:36) Virgin 44098 Best Of (1988-1993).
(S) (3:36) Rebound 314520313 Reggae Dance Party I.

378

MARMALADE
1970 REFLECTIONS OF MY LIFE
(dj copies of this 45 ran (3:18) even though the
label stated (3:12); commercial copies were all (4:18))
    (S) (4:14) Rhino 70922 Super Hits Of The 70's Volume 2.
    (S) (4:14) Rhino 72009 Super Hits Of The 70's Volumes 1-4 Box Set.
    (S) (4:14) Rhino 70327 History Of British Rock Volume 9.
    (S) (4:14) Rhino 72022 History Of British Rock Box Set.
    (S) (3:47) Polygram Special Markets 314520272 One Hit Wonders. *(:29 longer than the dj edit; much slower than the 45 or LP)*

M/A/R/R/S
1988 PUMP UP THE VOLUME
    (S) (4:06) Polydor 837798 O.S.T. My Stepmother Is An Alien.
    (S) (7:09) Priority 9753 Rap The Beat. *(12" single version)*
    (S) (4:05) Warner Brothers 25688 O.S.T. Bright Lights, Big City.
    (S) (3:57) Tommy Boy 1137 ESPN Presents Jock Jams. *(all songs on this cd are segued together with crowd sound effects added)*
    (S) (4:01) Cold Front 6245 Greatest Sports Rock And Jams. *(all selections on this cd are segued together)*
    (S) (3:51) Cold Front 6284 More Of! Club Mix's Biggest Jams. *(all selections on this cd are segued together)*
    (S) (7:09) 4th & B'way 162440452 Pump Up The Volume. *(12" single version)*
    (S) (4:06) 4th & B'way 162440452 Pump Up The Volume.

MARSHALL HAIN
1979 DANCING IN THE CITY

MARSHALL TUCKER BAND
1977 HEARD IT IN A LOVE SONG
    (S) (4:52) Rhino 70586 Rebel Rousers: Southern Rock Classics. *(LP version)*
    (S) (4:54) AJK 799 Greatest Hits. *(LP version)*
    (S) (4:54) AJK 780 Carolina Dreams. *(LP version)*
    (S) (4:52) K-Tel 3099 Charlie Daniels Band/Marshall Tucker Band. *(LP version)*
    (S) (3:27) Time-Life R968-03 Guitar Rock 1976-1977. *(45 version)*
    (S) (3:27) Time-Life SOD-05 Sounds Of The Seventies - 1977. *(45 version)*
    (S) (4:52) K-Tel 6083 Southern Fried Rock - Second Helping. *(LP version)*
    (S) (3:29) Era 5027 Best Of - The Capricorn Years. *(45 version)*
    (S) (4:52) DCC Compact Classics 139 Rock The First Volume 9. *(LP version)*
    (S) (4:53) Era 5036 Country Tucker. *(LP version)*
    (S) (3:28) Rebound 314520422 Greatest Hits. *(45 version)*
    (S) (3:28) K-Tel 3972 Southern Rockin' Rebels: The South's Gone And Done It. *(45 version)*
    (S) (4:55) Critique 15467 Fast Cars And Southern Stars. *(LP version)*
    (S) (3:28) K-Tel 3904 The Rock Album Volume 2. *(45 version)*
    (S) (3:28) Rebound 314520505 Keeping The Love Alive. *(45 version)*

RALPH MARTERIE
1957 TRICKY
    (S) (2:33) Mercury 314532874 Best Of.
1957 SHISH-KEBAB
    (S) (2:31) Mercury 314532874 Best Of.
    (S) (2:30) Time-Life R986-19 Instrumental Favorites - Exotic Moods.

MARTHA & THE VANDELLAS
1963 COME AND GET THESE MEMORIES
    (S) (2:26) Motown 9105 and 5410 Motown Memories Volume 2.

    (S) (2:26) Motown 5448 A Package Of 16 Original Big Hits.
    (S) (2:27) Motown 9057 and 6170 Compact Command Performances.
    (S) (2:27) Motown 9011 and 5204 Greatest Hits.
    (S) (2:26) Pair 1275 Original Motown Classics.
    (M) (2:23) Motown 6312 Hitsville USA.
    (M) (2:23) Motown 6313 Live Wire! The Singles 1962-1972.
    (S) (2:26) Time-Life 2RNR-25 Rock 'N' Roll Era - The 60's Keep On Rockin'.
    (M) (2:23) Motown 314530403 Motown Classic Hits Vol. 1.
    (M) (2:22) Motown 314530366 Come And Get These Memories.
    (M) (2:23) Motown 314530405 Motown Milestones - Best Of.
    (M) (2:25) Motown 314530858 Ultimate Collection.

1963 HEAT WAVE
    (E) (2:43) Motown 6159 The Good-Feeling Music Of The Big Chill Generation Volume 1.
    (E) (2:44) Motown 6138 The Composer Series: Holland/Dozier/Holland.
    (S) (2:41) Motown 5449 A Collection Of 16 Big Hits Volume 2. *(neither the 45 or LP version)*
    (E) (2:43) Motown 6110 Motown Grammy R&B Performances Of The 60's & 70's.
    (E) (2:44) Rhino 70649 Billboard's Top R&B Hits Of 1963.
    (E) (2:43) Motown 9057 and 6170 Compact Command Performances.
    (E) (2:45) Motown 8049 and 8149 Heat Wave/Dance Party.
    (E) (2:43) Motown 9017 and 5248 16 #1 Hits From The Early 60's.
    (E) (2:43) Motown 9021 and 5309 25 Years Of Grammy Greats.
    (E) (2:43) Motown 9011 and 5204 Greatest Hits.
    (E) (2:43) Motown 5343 Every Great Motown Song: The First 25 Years Volume 1. *(most selections on this cd have noise on the fadeout)*
    (E) (2:43) Motown 8034 and 8134 Every Great Motown Song: The First 25 Years Volumes 1 & 2. *(most selections on this cd have noise on the fadeout)*
    (E) (2:43) Motown 9098 Radio's #1 Hits.
    (E) (2:43) Motown 9095 and 5325 Motown Girl Groups: Top 10 With A Bullet!
    (E) (2:44) Motown 5145 Heat Wave.
    (E) (2:41) Motown 9071 Motown Dance Party Volume 1. *(all selections on this cd are segued together)*
    (E) (2:43) Pair 1275 Original Motown Classics.
    (M) (2:45) Motown 6312 Hitsville USA.
    (M) (2:45) Motown 6313 Live Wire! The Singles 1962-1972.
    (E) (2:43) Motown 374638508 Motown Legends - Jimmy Mack.
    (E) (2:42) Time-Life 2RNR-19 Rock 'N' Roll Era - 1963 Still Rockin'.
    (S) (2:40) Time-Life RHD-02 Rhythm & Blues - 1963. *(neither the 45 or LP version)*
    (E) (2:43) Polygram Special Markets 314520299 Motown Legends - Girl Groups.
    (E) (2:43) Polygram Special Markets 314520282 Motown Legends - Volume 1.
    (M) (2:42) Motown 314530419 Motown Classic Hits Vol. II.
    (M) (2:45) Motown 314530405 Motown Milestones - Best Of.
    (M) (2:45) Motown 314530647 O.S.T. Nothing But A Man.
    (E) (2:43) Priority 50951 I Love Rock & Roll Volume 2: Hits Of The 60's.
    (S) (2:40) Time-Life R838-14 Solid Gold Soul - 1963. *(neither the 45 or LP version)*
    (E) (2:44) Nick At Nite/550 Music 63435 Beach Blanket Bash.
    (M) (2:44) Motown 314530858 Ultimate Collection.
    (E) (2:41) Motown 314530849 Motown 40 Forever.
    (M) (2:44) Collectables 1515 and 2515 The Anniversary Album - The 60's.

1964 QUICKSAND
    (S) (2:42) Motown 5450 A Collection Of 16 Big Hits Volume 3. *(LP version)*

MARTHA & THE VANDELLAS *(Continued)*

- (S) (2:33) Motown 9057 and 6170 Compact Command Performances. *(45 version)*
- (S) (2:33) Motown 9011 and 5204 Greatest Hits. *(45 version)*
- (M) (2:36) Motown 6313 Live Wire! The Singles 1962-1972. *(45 version)*
- (S) (2:32) Time-Life 2CLR-16 Classic Rock - 1964: Shakin' All Over. *(45 version)*
- (M) (2:37) Rhino 71806 The R&B Box: Thirty Years Of Rhythm & Blues. *(45 version)*
- (M) (2:33) Motown 314530421 Motown Classics Vol. IV. *(45 version)*
- (M) (2:37) Motown 314530405 Motown Milestones - Best Of. *(45 version)*
- (M) (2:36) Motown 314530858 Ultimate Collection. *(45 version)*

1964 LIVE WIRE
- (S) (2:35) Motown 9057 and 6170 Compact Command Performances.
- (S) (2:34) Motown 9011 and 5204 Greatest Hits.
- (M) (2:30) Motown 6313 Live Wire! The Singles 1962-1972.
- (M) (2:30) Motown 314530405 Motown Milestones - Best Of.
- (M) (2:37) Motown 314530858 Ultimate Collection.

1964 DANCING IN THE STREET
- (S) (2:37) Motown 6137 20 Greatest Songs In Motown History.
- (S) (2:39) Motown 5450 A Collection Of 16 Big Hits Volume 3. *(reverb missing)*
- (S) (2:37) Original Sound 8864 Oldies But Goodies Vol. 14. *(this compact disc uses the "Waring - fds" noise reduction process)*
- (S) (2:37) Original Sound 2222 Oldies But Goodies Volumes 3,5,11,14 and 15 Box Set. *(this box set uses the "Waring - fds" noise reduction process)*
- (S) (2:37) Original Sound 2500 Oldies But Goodies Volumes 1-15 Box Set. *(this box set uses the "Waring - fds" noise reduction process)*
- (S) (2:37) Motown 6120 and 6062 O.S.T. The Big Chill.
- (S) (2:39) Rhino 70650 Billboard's Top R&B Hits Of 1964.
- (S) (2:37) Motown 9057 and 6170 Compact Command Performances.
- (S) (2:37) Motown 8049 and 8149 Heat Wave/Dance Party.
- (S) (2:36) Motown 9072 Motown Dance Party Volume 2. *(all selections on this cd are segued together)*
- (S) (2:37) Motown 9011 and 5204 Greatest Hits.
- (S) (2:37) Motown 5433 Dance Party.
- (S) (2:37) Motown 5343 Every Great Motown Song: The First 25 Years Volume 1. *(most selections on this cd have noise on the fadeout)*
- (S) (2:37) Motown 8034 and 8134 Every Great Motown Song: The First 25 Years Volumes 1 & 2. *(most selections on this cd have noise on the fadeout)*
- (S) (2:37) Motown 9098 Radio's #1 Hits.
- (S) (2:36) Motown 6094 More Songs From The Original Soundtrack Of The "Big Chill".
- (S) (2:38) Motown 9095 and 5325 Motown Girl Groups: Top 10 With A Bullet!
- (S) (2:39) Motown 5322 and 9087 Girl Groups: The Story Of A Sound. *(highly distorted)*
- (S) (2:37) Pair 1275 Original Motown Classics.
- (M) (2:37) Motown 6312 Hitsville USA.
- (S) (2:39) Capitol 81475 Rites Of Rhythm & Blues.
- (M) (2:37) Motown 6313 Live Wire! The Singles 1962-1972.
- (S) (2:39) Time-Life 2RNR-10 Rock 'N' Roll Era - 1964.
- (S) (2:36) Time-Life RHD-12 Rhythm & Blues - 1964.
- (S) (2:37) Polygram Special Markets 314520299 Motown Legends - Girl Groups.
- (S) (2:37) Rebound 314520298 Disco Nights Vol. 9.
- (M) (2:38) Motown 314530421 Motown Classics Vol. IV.
- (S) (2:38) Motown 314530504 Motown Year By Year 1964. *(reverb missing)*

- (M) (2:38) Motown 314530405 Motown Milestones - Best Of.
- (M) (2:38) Rhino 72275 More Stadium Rock.
- (S) (2:36) Time-Life R838-13 Solid Gold Soul - 1964.
- (M) (2:38) Flashback 72712 Arena Rock.
- (M) (2:38) Motown 314530858 Ultimate Collection.
- (S) (2:37) Simitar 55572 The Number One's: Hot In The '60s.
- (S) (2:37) Motown 314530849 Motown 40 Forever.
- (S) (2:37) JCI 3189 1960 - Only Dance - 1964.

1965 WILD ONE
- (S) (2:42) Motown 9057 and 6170 Compact Command Performances.
- (S) (2:43) Motown 8049 and 8149 Heat Wave/Dance Party.
- (S) (2:42) Motown 9011 and 5204 Greatest Hits.
- (S) (2:43) Motown 5433 Dance Party.
- (M) (2:42) Motown 6313 Live Wire! The Singles 1962-1972.
- (S) (2:42) Motown 314530504 Motown Year By Year 1964.
- (M) (2:42) Motown 314530405 Motown Milestones - Best Of.
- (M) (2:41) Motown 314530858 Ultimate Collection.

1965 NOWHERE TO RUN
- (S) (2:54) A&M 3913 and 3340 O.S.T. Good Morning Vietnam.
- (S) (2:55) Motown 5452 A Collection Of 16 Big Hits Volume 5.
- (S) (2:53) Priority 7909 Vietnam: Rockin' The Delta. *(truncated fade)*
- (S) (2:55) Motown 9057 and 6170 Compact Command Performances.
- (S) (2:55) MCA 10063 Original Television Soundtrack "The Sounds Of Murphy Brown".
- (S) (2:56) Motown 8049 and 8149 Heat Wave/Dance Party.
- (S) (2:53) Motown 9072 Motown Dance Party Volume 2. *(all selections on this cd are segued together)*
- (S) (2:55) Motown 9011 and 5204 Greatest Hits.
- (S) (2:55) Motown 5433 Dance Party.
- (M) (2:55) Motown 6312 Hitsville USA.
- (S) (2:53) Capitol 81475 Rites Of Rhythm & Blues.
- (M) (2:55) Motown 6313 Live Wire! The Singles 1962-1972.
- (S) (2:53) Time-Life RHD-07 Rhythm & Blues - 1965.
- (S) (2:55) Time-Life 2CLR-08 Classic Rock - 1965: The Beat Goes On.
- (M) (2:55) Motown 314530405 Motown Milestones - Best Of.
- (S) (2:53) Time-Life R838-12 Solid Gold Soul - 1965.
- (M) (2:49) Motown 314530858 Ultimate Collection.
- (M) (2:49) Rebound 314520522 Rockin' Sports Jams.

1966 MY BABY LOVES ME
- (S) (3:01) Motown 9109 and 5413 Motown Memories Volume 3.
- (S) (3:01) Motown 5453 A Collection Of 16 Big Hits Volume 6.
- (S) (3:01) Motown 9057 and 6170 Compact Command Performances.
- (S) (3:02) Motown 9011 and 5204 Greatest Hits. *(noise on fadeout)*
- (S) (3:01) Motown 5111 Superstar Series Volume 11.
- (M) (3:07) Motown 6313 Live Wire! The Singles 1962-1972.
- (M) (3:07) Motown 314530405 Motown Milestones - Best Of.
- (M) (3:07) Thump 9947 Cruizin' To Motown.
- (M) (3:05) Motown 314530858 Ultimate Collection.

1966 I'M READY FOR LOVE
- (S) (2:49) Motown 5454 A Collection Of 16 Big Hits Volume 7.
- (S) (2:54) Motown 9057 and 6170 Compact Command Performances.
- (S) (2:51) Motown 6767 Watchout.
- (M) (2:53) Motown 6313 Live Wire! The Singles 1962-1972.
- (S) (2:50) Motown 314530522 Motown Year By Year - 1966.
- (M) (2:53) Motown 314530405 Motown Milestones - Best Of.
- (M) (2:52) Motown 314530858 Ultimate Collection.

1967 JIMMY MACK
- (S) (2:41) Motown 9104 and 5409 Motown Memories Volume 1. *(LP version)*
- (S) (2:48) Motown 5455 A Collection Of 16 Big Hits Volume 8. *(alternate take)*
- (S) (2:41) Motown 6161 The Good-Feeling Music Of The Big Chill Generation Volume 3. *(LP version)*
- (M) (2:48) Rhino 70653 Billboard's Top R&B Hits Of 1967. *(45 version)*
- (M) (2:48) Rhino 72006 Billboard's Top R&B Hits 1965-1969 Box Set. *(45 version)*
- (S) (2:41) Motown 9057 and 6170 Compact Command Performances. *(LP version)*
- (S) (2:42) Motown 6767 Watchout. *(LP version)*
- (S) (2:41) Motown 9095 and 5325 Motown Girl Groups: Top 10 With A Bullet! *(LP version)*
- (M) (2:50) Motown 9071 Motown Dance Party Volume 1. *(45 version; all selections on this cd are segued together)*
- (M) (2:48) Ripete 392183 Ocean Drive. *(45 version)*
- (M) (2:51) Motown 6312 Hitsville USA. *(45 version)*
- (M) (2:51) Motown 6313 Live Wire! The Singles 1962-1972. *(45 version)*
- (S) (2:42) Motown 374638508 Motown Legends - Jimmy Mack. *(LP version)*
- (M) (2:47) Time-Life RHD-10 Rhythm & Blues - 1967. *(45 version)*
- (S) (2:41) Time-Life 2CLR-10 Classic Rock - 1967: The Beat Goes On. *(LP version)*
- (S) (2:42) Polygram Special Markets 314520299 Motown Legends - Girl Groups. *(LP version)*
- (M) (2:51) Motown 314530405 Motown Milestones - Best Of. *(45 version)*
- (S) (2:41) Polygram Special Markets 314520292 Motown Legends - Volume 4. *(LP version)*
- (M) (2:47) Time-Life R838-02 Solid Gold Soul - 1967. *(45 version)*
- (M) (2:51) Motown 314530858 Ultimate Collection. *(45 version)*

1967 LOVE BUG LEAVE MY HEART ALONE
- (S) (2:03) Motown 5457 A Collection Of 16 Big Hits Volume 10.
- (S) (2:07) Motown 9057 and 6170 Compact Command Performances.
- (M) (2:10) Motown 6313 Live Wire! The Singles 1962-1972.
- (M) (2:10) Motown 314530405 Motown Milestones - Best Of.
- (M) (2:08) Motown 314530858 Ultimate Collection.

released as by MARTHA REEVES & THE VANDELLAS:
1967 HONEY CHILE
- (S) (2:56) Motown 5456 A Collection Of 16 Big Hits Volume 9.
- (S) (2:57) Motown 9057 and 6170 Compact Command Performances.
- (S) (2:54) Motown 5111 Superstar Series Volume 11.
- (M) (2:56) Motown 6313 Live Wire! The Singles 1962-1972.
- (S) (2:55) Time-Life 2CLR-24 Classic Rock - 1967: Blowin' Your Mind.
- (M) (2:56) Motown 314530405 Motown Milestones - Best Of.
- (M) (2:55) Motown 314530858 Ultimate Collection.

MARTIKA
1989 MORE THAN YOU KNOW
- (S) (4:05) Columbia 44290 Martika.
1989 TOY SOLDIERS
- (S) (4:36) Rhino 71644 Billboard Top Hits - 1989. *(45 version)*
- (S) (4:47) Columbia 44290 Martika. *(LP version)*
- (S) (4:36) Time-Life R988-13 Sounds Of The Eighties: 1989. *(45 version)*
- (S) (4:36) K-Tel 3868 Hot Ladies Of Pop. *(45 version)*
1989 I FEEL THE EARTH MOVE
(actual 45 time is (4:04) not (3:58) as stated on the record label)
- (S) (4:12) Columbia 44290 Martika. *(LP version)*
1991 LOVE...THY WILL BE DONE
- (S) (5:01) Columbia 46827 Martika's Kitchen.

BOBBI MARTIN
1965 DON'T FORGET I STILL LOVE YOU
- (S) (2:41) Time-Life HPD-37 Your Hit Parade - The 60's.
1970 FOR THE LOVE OF HIM
- (S) (2:35) Rhino 70922 Super Hits Of The 70's Volume 2.
- (S) (2:35) Rhino 72009 Super Hits Of The 70's Volumes 1-4 Box Set.
- (S) (2:35) Rhino 72736 Billboard Top Soft Rock Hits - 1970.

DEAN MARTIN
1956 MEMORIES ARE MADE OF THIS
- (E) (2:17) Capitol 90592 Memories Are Made Of This.
- (M) (2:16) Curb 77354 50's Hits Volume 1.
- (M) (2:14) Capitol 46627 Best Of.
- (M) (2:15) Capitol 91633 Capitol Collector's Series.
- (E) (2:15) Pair 1029 Dreams And Memories.
- (M) (2:14) Capitol 98670 Memories Are Made Of This.
- (M) (2:15) Rhino 71252 Sentimental Journey: Pop Vocal Classics Volume 4 (1954-1959).
- (M) (2:15) Rhino 72034 Sentimental Journey Pop Vocal Classics Volumes 1-4 Box Set.
- (M) (2:15) Time-Life HPD-15 Your Hit Parade - 1956.
- (M) (2:15) Rhino 71580 Billboard Pop Memories 1955-1959.
- (E) (2:15) JCI 7007 Those Wonderful Years - Because Of You.
- (M) (2:15) Capitol 37571 That's Amore: Best Of.
- (M) (2:23) Capitol 98409 The Capitol Years. *(includes a :07 spoken introduction)*
- (M) (2:15) Capitol 55915 Best Of.
- (M) (2:15) Time-Life R132-12 Your Hit Parade - #1 Hits Of The '50s.
1958 RETURN TO ME
- (S) (2:41) Capitol 46627 Best Of. *(rerecording)*
- (M) (2:23) Capitol 91633 Capitol Collector's Series.
- (E) (2:22) Pair 1029 Dreams And Memories.
- (M) (2:23) Time-Life HPD-11 Your Hit Parade 1958.
- (M) (2:23) Capitol 37571 That's Amore: Best Of.
- (M) (2:23) EMI 52498 O.S.T. Striptease.
- (M) (2:22) Capitol 98409 The Capitol Years.
- (M) (2:22) Capitol 55915 Best Of.
- (M) (2:22) Time-Life R132-10 Love Songs Of Your Hit Parade.
1958 ANGEL BABY
- (M) (2:44) Capitol 91633 Capitol Collector's Series.
- (M) (2:43) Capitol 55915 Best Of.
1958 VOLARE (NEL BLU DIPINTO DI BLU)
- (M) (2:57) Capitol 46627 Best Of.
- (M) (2:58) Capitol 91633 Capitol Collector's Series.
- (E) (2:58) Pair 1029 Dreams And Memories.
- (M) (2:58) Compose 9928 Now That's Italian.
- (M) (2:58) Capitol 37571 That's Amore: Best Of.
- (M) (2:58) Capitol 98409 The Capitol Years.
- (M) (2:58) Capitol 35972 Ultra Lounge Volume Five: Wild, Cool & Swingin'.
- (M) (2:58) Capitol 55915 Best Of.
1964 EVERYBODY LOVES SOMEBODY
1964 THE DOOR IS STILL OPEN TO MY HEART
1965 YOU'RE NOBODY TILL SOMEBODY LOVES YOU
- (S) (2:11) Capitol 46627 Best Of. *(Capitol recording - not the hit Reprise version)*
- (S) (2:11) Pair 1029 Dreams And Memories. *(Capitol recording - not the hit Reprise version)*
- (S) (2:11) Capitol 29389 Spotlight On. *(Capitol Recording - not the hit Reprise version)*
- (S) (2:11) MCA 11389 O.S.T. Casino. *(Capitol Recording - not the hit Reprise version)*
- (S) (2:11) A&M 314540424 O.S.T. Things To Do In Denver When You're Dead. *(Capitol recording - not the hit Reprise version)*
- (S) (2:11) Capitol 37571 That's Amore: Best Of. *(Capitol recording - not the hit Reprise version)*
- (S) (2:11) Miramax/Hollywood 206162091 O.S.T. Swingers. *(Capitol recording - not the hit Reprise version)*
1965 SEND ME THE PILLOW YOU DREAM ON

DEAN MARTIN *(Continued)*
1965 (REMEMBER ME) I'M THE ONE WHO LOVES YOU
1965 HOUSTON
1965 I WILL
1966 SOMEWHERE THERE'S A SOMEONE
1966 COME RUNNING BACK
1967 IN THE CHAPEL IN THE MOONLIGHT

MARILYN MARTIN
released as by PHIL COLLINS and MARILYN MARTIN:
1985 SEPARATE LIVES (LOVE THEME FROM WHITE
NIGHTS)
    (S) (4:05)   Atlantic 81273 O.S.T. White Knights.
    (S) (4:06)   Madacy Entertainment 6806 Best Of Love.
released as by MARILYN MARTIN:
1986 NIGHT MOVES

MOON MARTIN
1979 ROLENE
    (S) (3:34)   Rhino 71890 Radio Daze: Pop Hits Of The 80's
                Volume One.
    (S) (3:34)   Time-Life R968-17 Guitar Rock - The Late '70s:
                Take Two.
    (S) (3:34)   EMI-Capitol Music Special Markets 19545 Lost
                Hits Of The '70s.

STEVE MARTIN and THE TOOT UNCOMMONS
1978 KING TUT
    (S) (2:10)   Rhino 75768 Dr. Demento Presents The Greatest
                Novelty CD Of All Time.
    (S) (2:10)   Rhino 70743 Dr. Demento 20th Anniversary
                Collection.
    (S) (2:10)   Time-Life SOD-35 Sounds Of The Seventies -
                AM Nuggets.
    (S) (2:10)   Time-Life R830-02 The Dr. Demento Collection -
                The Late 70's.

TRADE MARTIN
1962 THAT STRANGER USED TO BE MY GIRL
    (S) (2:47)   Collectors' Choice 002 Teen Idols....For A
                Moment.

VINCE MARTIN (see THE TARRIERS)

WINK MARTINDALE
1959 DECK OF CARDS
    (S) (3:51)   Varese Sarabande 5906 God, Love And Rock &
                Roll.

NANCY MARTINEZ
1986 FOR TONIGHT
    (S) (7:05)   Atlantic 81746 Dance Traxx Volume 2. *(remix)*
    (S) (4:07)   Atlantic 81720 Not Just The Girl Next Door.

AL MARTINO
1963 I LOVE YOU BECAUSE
    (S) (2:41)   Capitol 91145 Best Of.
    (S) (2:40)   Curb 77401 Greatest Hits.
    (S) (2:41)   Capitol 96430 Capitol Collector's Series.
    (S) (2:40)   Capitol 98670 Memories Are Made Of This.
    (S) (2:40)   Time-Life HPD-33 Your Hit Parade - The Early 60's.
    (S) (2:40)   Time-Life R138/05 Look Of Love.
    (S) (2:40)   Time-Life R974-17 Many Moods Of Romance -
                Till The End Of Time.
    (S) (2:41)   Collectables 5644 Best Of.
    (S) (2:41)   JCI 7022 Those Wonderful Years - It Must Be
                Him.
1963 PAINTED, TAINTED ROSE
    (M) (2:46)   Capitol 91145 Best Of.
    (M) (2:46)   Capitol 96430 Capitol Collector's Series.
    (M) (2:46)   Collectables 5644 Best Of.
1963 LIVING A LIE
    (S) (2:29)   Capitol 91145 Best Of.
    (S) (2:28)   Capitol 96430 Capitol Collector's Series.
    (S) (2:29)   Collectables 5644 Best Of.

1964 I LOVE YOU MORE AND MORE EVERY DAY
    (S) (2:13)   Capitol 91145 Best Of.
    (S) (2:13)   Curb 77401 Greatest Hits.
    (S) (2:13)   Capitol 96430 Capitol Collector's Series.
    (S) (2:12)   Time-Life HPD-37 Your Hit Parade - The 60's.
    (S) (2:13)   Collectables 5644 Best Of.
1964 TEARS AND ROSES
    (S) (2:17)   Capitol 96430 Capitol Collector's Series.
1966 SPANISH EYES
    (S) (2:44)   Curb 77355 60's Hits Volume 1.
    (S) (2:45)   Capitol 91145 Best Of.
    (S) (2:44)   Curb 77401 Greatest Hits.
    (S) (3:52)   Capitol 96430 Capitol Collector's Series. *(time
                includes 2 false starts of (1:06) total time)*
    (S) (2:46)   Capitol 91231 Spanish Eyes.
    (S) (2:45)   Time-Life R138/05 Look Of Love.
    (S) (2:45)   Collectables 5644 Best Of.
    (S) (2:44)   Rhino 72557 Jackpot! The Las Vegas Story.
    (S) (2:44)   Rhino 72577 Eh, Paisano! Italian-American
                Classics.
    (S) (2:44)   Hammer & Lace 697124114 Leading Men:
                Masters Of Style Volume Two.
    (S) (2:44)   Time-Life R814-02 Love Songs.
1966 THINK I'LL GO SOMEWHERE AND CRY MYSELF TO
SLEEP
    (S) (2:45)   Capitol 96430 Capitol Collector's Series.
    (S) (2:44)   Capitol 91231 Spanish Eyes.
1967 MARY IN THE MORNING
    (S) (2:49)   Capitol 91145 Best Of. *(LP version)*
    (S) (2:49)   Curb 77401 Greatest Hits. *(LP version)*
    (S) (2:54)   Capitol 96430 Capitol Collector's Series. *(LP
                version)*
    (S) (2:50)   Collectables 5644 Best Of. *(LP version)*
1975 TO THE DOOR OF THE SUN (ALLE PORTE DEL SOLE)
    (S) (3:22)   Capitol 96430 Capitol Collector's Series.
    (S) (3:20)   Curb 77401 Greatest Hits.

MARVELETTES
1961 PLEASE MR. POSTMAN
    (M) (2:26)   Rhino 70622 Billboard's Top Rock & Roll Hits Of
                1961. *(found only on the original 1988 issue of
                this cd)*
    (M) (2:26)   Rhino 72004 Billboard's Top Rock & Roll Hits
                1957-1961 Box Set.
    (M) (2:27)   Motown 6132 25 #1 Hits From 25 Years.
    (M) (2:26)   Motown 6159 The Good-Feeling Music Of The
                Big Chill Generation Volume 1.
    (S) (2:20)   Motown 5448 A Package Of 16 Big Hits.
                *(missing the "deliver de letter" line near the end of
                the song)*
    (M) (2:26)   Motown 9056 and 6169 Compact Command
                Performances.
    (M) (2:26)   Motown 9017 and 5248 16 #1 Hits From The
                Early 60's.
    (M) (2:26)   Motown 9097 Most Played Oldies On America's
                Jukeboxes.
    (M) (2:26)   Motown 5180 Greatest Hits. *(noise on fadeout)*
    (M) (2:26)   Motown 5343 Every Great Motown Song: The
                First 25 Years Volume 1. *(most selections on this
                cd have noise on the fadeout)*
    (M) (2:26)   Motown 8034 and 8134 Every Great Motown
                Song: The First 25 Years Volumes 1 & 2. *(most
                selections on this cd have noise on the fadeout)*
    (M) (2:25)   Motown 9098 Radio's #1 Hits.
    (M) (2:27)   Motown 5266 Please Mr. Postman.
    (M) (2:26)   Motown 5322 and 9087 Girl Groups: The Story
                Of A Sound.
    (M) (2:28)   Motown 6312 Hitsville USA.
    (M) (2:27)   Motown 6253 Looking Back 1961-1964.
    (M) (2:25)   Time-Life 2RNR-04 Rock 'N' Roll Era - 1961.
    (M) (2:24)   Time-Life RHD-14 Rhythm & Blues - 1961.
    (M) (2:27)   Motown 314530403 Motown Classic Hits Vol. 1.
    (M) (2:26)   Polygram Special Markets 314520283 Motown
                Legends Volume 2.
    (M) (2:27)   Motown 314530408 Motown Milestones - Best Of.
    (M) (2:27)   Motown 374636259 Deliver: The Singles 1961-
                1971.

(M) (2:25) Repeat/Relativity 1609 Tell It Like It Is: #1 Soul Hits Of The 60's Volume 1.
(M) (2:24) Time-Life R838-19 Solid Gold Soul 1961.
(M) (2:25) K-Tel 3888 Great R&B Female Groups Hits Of The 60's.
(M) (2:27) Motown 314530856 Ultimate Collection.
(M) (2:25) Motown 314530849 Motown 40 Forever.

1962 TWISTIN' POSTMAN
(S) (2:29) Motown 9056 and 6169 Compact Command Performances.
(S) (2:29) Motown 5180 Greatest Hits.
(M) (2:27) Motown 6253 Looking Back 1961-1964.
(M) (2:27) K-Tel 3241 Let's Twist.
(M) (2:27) Motown 314530408 Motown Milestones - Best Of.
(M) (2:27) Motown 374636259 Deliver: The Singles 1961-1971.
(M) (2:28) Motown 314530856 Ultimate Collection.

1962 PLAYBOY
(S) (2:46) Motown 5449 A Collection Of 16 Big Hits Volume 2.
(E) (2:45) Motown 9056 and 6169 Compact Command Performances.
(S) (2:43) Motown 5473 Playboy.
(E) (2:45) Motown 5180 Greatest Hits.
(M) (2:46) Motown 6253 Looking Back 1961-1964.
(E) (2:44) Time-Life 2RNR-25 Rock 'N' Roll Era - The 60's Keep On Rockin'.
(M) (2:46) Motown/Essex 374638517 Motown Legends - Beechwood 4-5789.
(M) (2:46) Motown 314530420 Motown Classic Hits Vol. III.
(M) (2:46) Motown 314530408 Motown Milestones - Best Of.
(M) (2:46) Motown 374636259 Deliver: The Singles 1961-1971. *(this song is not listed on the cardboard packaging surrounding the jewel box but it is listed on the packaging included inside the jewel box)*
(M) (2:46) Motown 314530856 Ultimate Collection.

1962 BEECHWOOD 4-5789
(S) (2:08) Motown 5448 A Package Of 16 Big Hits.
(E) (2:10) Motown 9056 and 6169 Compact Command Performances.
(S) (2:09) Motown 5473 Playboy.
(E) (2:10) Motown 5180 Greatest Hits.
(M) (2:11) Motown 6312 Hitsville USA.
(M) (2:11) Motown 6253 Looking Back 1961-1964.
(E) (2:09) Time-Life 2RNR-16 Rock 'N' Roll Era - 1962 Still Rockin'.
(M) (2:11) Motown 314530403 Motown Classic Hits Vol. 1.
(M) (2:11) Motown/Essex 374638517 Motown Legends - Beechwood 4-5789.
(M) (2:11) Motown 314530408 Motown Milestones - Best Of.
(S) (2:08) Eclipse Music Group 64868 Rock 'n Roll Relix 1962-1963.
(S) (2:08) Eclipse Music Group 64872 Rock 'n Roll Relix 1960-1969.
(M) (2:11) Motown 374636259 Deliver: The Singles 1961-1971.
(M) (2:11) Motown 314530856 Ultimate Collection.

1965 TOO MANY FISH IN THE SEA
(S) (2:19) Motown 5451 A Collection Of 16 Big Hits Volume 4.
(S) (2:27) Motown 6120 and 6062 O.S.T. The Big Chill.
(S) (2:27) Motown 9056 and 6169 Compact Command Performances.
(S) (2:28) Motown 5180 Greatest Hits.
(S) (2:26) Motown 6094 More Songs From The Original Soundtrack Of The "Big Chill".
(S) (2:26) Motown 9071 Motown Dance Party Volume 1. *(all selections on this cd are segued together)*
(M) (2:26) Motown 6253 Looking Back 1961-1964.
(S) (2:26) Time-Life 2CLR-16 Classic Rock - 1964: Shakin' All Over.
(M) (2:24) Motown 314530422 Motown Classics Vol. V.
(M) (2:26) Motown 314530408 Motown Milestones - Best Of.

(M) (2:26) Motown 374636259 Deliver: The Singles 1961-1971.
(M) (2:25) Motown 314530856 Ultimate Collection.

1965 I'LL KEEP HOLDING ON
(E) (2:25) Motown 5452 A Collection Of 16 Big Hits Volume 5.
(E) (2:25) Motown 9056 and 6169 Compact Command Performances.
(M) (2:25) Motown 6253 Looking Back 1961-1964.
(M) (2:25) Motown 314530408 Motown Milestones - Best Of.
(M) (2:25) Motown 374636259 Deliver: The Singles 1961-1971.
(M) (2:25) Motown 314530856 Ultimate Collection.

1966 DON'T MESS WITH BILL
(S) (2:48) Motown 9104 and 5409 Motown Memories Volume 1.
(S) (2:49) Motown 5453 A Collection Of 16 Big Hits Volume 6.
(S) (2:48) Motown 9056 and 6169 Compact Command Performances.
(S) (2:49) Motown 5180 Greatest Hits.
(S) (2:48) Motown 9095 and 5325 Motown Girl Groups: Top 10 With A Bullet!
(M) (2:48) Motown 6312 Hitsville USA.
(M) (2:48) Motown 6253 Looking Back 1961-1964.
(S) (2:48) Time-Life 2CLR-13 Classic Rock - 1966: Shakin' All Over. *(noisy introduction)*
(S) (2:49) Polygram Special Markets 314520299 Motown Legends - Girl Groups. *(noisy introduction)*
(M) (2:48) Motown 314530408 Motown Milestones - Best Of.
(M) (2:48) Motown 374636259 Deliver: The Singles 1961-1971.
(M) (2:48) Motown 314530856 Ultimate Collection.

1967 THE HUNTER GETS CAPTURED BY THE GAME
(S) (2:46) Motown 5454 A Collection Of 16 Big Hits Volume 7.
(S) (2:47) Motown 9056 and 6169 Compact Command Performances.
(S) (2:47) Motown 5421 The Marvelettes.
(S) (2:47) Motown 8055 and 8155 Sophisticated Soul/Marvelettes.
(M) (2:47) Motown 6312 Hitsville USA.
(M) (2:47) Motown 6253 Looking Back 1961-1964.
(S) (2:46) Time-Life RHD-10 Rhythm & Blues - 1967.
(S) (2:47) Time-Life 2CLR-24 Classic Rock - 1967: Blowin' Your Mind.
(M) (2:47) Motown 314530408 Motown Milestones - Best Of.
(S) (2:47) Time-Life R838-02 Solid Gold Soul - 1967.
(M) (2:47) Motown 374636259 Deliver: The Singles 1961-1971.
(M) (2:46) Motown 314530856 Ultimate Collection.

1967 WHEN YOU'RE YOUNG AND IN LOVE
(S) (2:35) Motown 9056 and 6169 Compact Command Performances.
(S) (2:34) Motown 5421 The Marvelettes.
(S) (2:34) Motown 8055 and 8155 Sophisticated Soul/Marvelettes.
(M) (2:38) Motown 6253 Looking Back 1961-1964.
(M) (2:38) Motown 314530408 Motown Milestones - Best Of.
(M) (2:38) Motown 374636259 Deliver: The Singles 1961-1971.
(M) (2:37) Motown 314530856 Ultimate Collection.

1968 MY BABY MUST BE A MAGICIAN
(S) (2:32) Motown 5456 A Collection Of 16 Big Hits Volume 9.
(S) (2:33) Motown 9056 and 6169 Compact Command Performances.
(S) (2:34) Motown 5430 Sophisticated Soul.
(S) (2:33) Motown 8055 and 8155 Sophisticated Soul/Marvelettes.
(M) (2:32) Motown 6253 Looking Back 1961-1964.

MARVELETTES *(Continued)*

- (S) (2:33) Time-Life 2CLR-27 Classic Rock - 1968: Blowin' Your Mind.
- (M) (2:32) Motown 314530408 Motown Milestones - Best Of.
- (M) (2:32) Motown 374636259 Deliver: The Singles 1961-1971.
- (M) (2:31) Motown 314530856 Ultimate Collection.

MARVELOWS
1965 I DO
- (M) (2:25) Rhino 75757 Soul Shots Volume 3.
- (E) (2:25) MCA 5937 Vintage Music Volumes 13 & 14.
- (E) (2:25) MCA 31210 Vintage Music Volume 13.
- (M) (2:25) Rhino 71463 Doo Wop Box.
- (M) (2:24) Time-Life 2CLR-25 Classic Rock - On The Soul Side.
- (E) (2:25) Collectables 2504 WCBS-FM History Of Rock - The 60's Part 4.
- (E) (2:25) Collectables 4504 History Of Rock/The 60s Part Four.
- (M) (2:25) Hip-O 40009 ABC's Of Soul Volume 1.
- (E) (2:26) Collectables 5685 A Golden Classics Edition.
- (E) (2:25) MCA Special Products 21030 Beach Music Hits.
- (M) (2:25) Rhino 72815 Beg, Scream & Shout! The Big Ol' Box Of '60s Soul.

RICHARD MARX
1987 DON'T MEAN NOTHING
- (S) (4:40) Manhattan 46760 Richard Marx.
- (S) (4:40) Capitol 21914 Greatest Hits.
1987 SHOULD'VE KNOWN BETTER
- (S) (4:05) Foundation/Capitol 96427 Hearts Of Gold: The Pop Collection. *(LP version)*
- (S) (3:37) EMI 91419 MTV, BET, VH-1 Power Players. *(45 version)*
- (S) (4:04) Columbia 44381 Heart Of Rock. *(LP version)*
- (S) (4:10) Manhattan 46760 Richard Marx. *(LP version)*
- (S) (4:10) Big Ear Music 4003 Only In The 80's Volume Three. *(LP version)*
- (S) (4:07) Priority 50953 I Love Rock & Roll Volume 4: Hits Of The 80's. *(LP version)*
- (S) (3:31) Capitol 21914 Greatest Hits. *(45 version)*
1988 ENDLESS SUMMER NIGHTS
- (S) (4:30) Manhattan 46760 Richard Marx. *(LP version)*
- (S) (4:29) Time-Life R834-07 Body Talk - Hearts In Motion. *(LP version)*
- (S) (4:30) Capitol 21914 Greatest Hits. *(LP version)*
1988 HOLD ON TO THE NIGHTS
(dj copies of this 45 ran (4:20) and (4:34); commercial copies were all (4:34))
- (S) (4:34) Rhino 71643 Billboard Top Hits - 1988. *(45 version)*
- (S) (5:11) Sandstone 33045 and 5011 Rock The First Volume Five. *(LP version)*
- (S) (5:15) Manhattan 46760 Richard Marx. *(LP version)*
- (S) (4:32) Time-Life R988-10 Sounds Of The 80's: 1988. *(45 version)*
- (S) (4:24) Time-Life R834-03 Body Talk - Moonlit Nights. *(45 version)*
- (S) (5:12) Capitol 21914 Greatest Hits. *(LP version)*
1989 SATISFIED
(actual 45 time is (4:10) not (3:58) as stated on the record label)
- (S) (4:13) EMI 90380 Repeat Offender.
- (S) (4:13) Capitol 21914 Greatest Hits.
1989 RIGHT HERE WAITING
- (S) (4:23) Rhino 71644 Billboard Top Hits - 1989.
- (S) (4:21) Time-Life R105-40 Rock Dreams.
- (S) (4:22) EMI 90380 Repeat Offender.
- (S) (4:23) Time-Life R988-13 Sounds Of The Eighties: 1989.
- (S) (4:22) Time-Life R834-08 Body Talk - On My Mind.
- (S) (4:22) Capitol 21914 Greatest Hits.
1989 ANGELIA
- (S) (5:17) EMI 90380 Repeat Offender. *(LP version)*
- (S) (5:16) Capitol 21914 Greatest Hits. *(LP version)*

1990 TOO LATE TO SAY GOODBYE
- (S) (4:52) EMI 90380 Repeat Offender. *(LP version)*
1990 CHILDREN OF THE NIGHT
- (S) (4:43) EMI 90380 Repeat Offender.
- (S) (4:43) Capitol 21914 Greatest Hits.
1991 KEEP COMING BACK
- (S) (6:49) Capitol 95874 Rush Street.
- (S) (6:48) Capitol 21914 Greatest Hits.
1992 HAZARD
- (S) (5:16) Capitol 95874 Rush Street.
- (S) (5:15) Capitol 21914 Greatest Hits.
1992 TAKE THIS HEART
- (S) (4:09) Capitol 95874 Rush Street.
- (S) (3:54) JCI 3132 1990 - Only Rock 'n Roll - 1994. *(faded :15 earlier than the LP)*
- (S) (4:08) Capitol 21914 Greatest Hits.
1992 CHAINS AROUND MY HEART
- (S) (5:40) Capitol 95874 Rush Street.
1994 NOW AND FOREVER
- (S) (3:31) Capitol 81232 Paid Vacation.
- (S) (3:31) Capitol 21914 Greatest Hits.
1994 THE WAY SHE LOVES ME
- (S) (4:14) Capitol 81232 Paid Vacation.
- (S) (4:14) Capitol 21914 Greatest Hits.

MARY JANE GIRLS
1985 IN MY HOUSE
- (S) (3:55) Motown 314530519 Motown Year By Year 1985. *(45 version)*
- (S) (4:28) Priority 7044 Rick James And Friends. *(LP version)*
- (S) (5:00) Motown 314530310 In My House. *(12" single version)*
- (S) (5:00) Motown 5406 Only For You. *(12" single version)*
- (S) (3:55) Motown 6358 Hitsville USA Volume Two. *(45 version)*
- (S) (4:58) Rebound 314520357 World Of Dance - The 80's. *(12" single version)*
- (S) (3:56) Time-Life R988-23 Sounds Of The Eighties 1984-1985. *(45 version)*

MASE
released as by PUFF DADDY featuring MASE:
1997 CAN'T NOBODY HOLD ME DOWN
- (S) (3:50) Bad Boy 73012 and 73014 Puff Daddy: No Way Out.
- (S) (5:05) Polygram TV 314536204 The Source Presents Hip Hop Hits Volume 1.
released as by THE NOTORIOUS B.I.G. featuring PUFF DADDY & MASE:
1997 MO MONEY MO PROBLEMS
- (S) (4:17) Bad Boy 73011 and 73019 Notorious B.I.G.: Life After Death.
- (S) (3:49) Arista 18988 Ultimate Dance Party 1998. *(all selections on this cd are segued together)*
released as by BRIAN McKNIGHT featuring MASE:
1997 YOU SHOULD BE MINE (DON'T WASTE YOUR TIME)
- (S) (4:47) Mercury 314536215 Brian McKnight: Anytime.
released as by MASE:
1997 FEEL SO GOOD
- (S) (4:00) Arista18975 Money Talks - The Album.
released as by PUFF DADDY & THE FAMILY featuring THE NOTORIOUS B.I.G. & MASE:
1998 BEEN AROUND THE WORLD
- (S) (5:25) Bad Boy 73012 and 73014 Puff Daddy - No Way Out.

HUGH MASEKELA
1968 GRAZING IN THE GRASS
- (S) (2:37) Rhino 70629 Billboard's Top Rock & Roll Hits Of 1968.
- (S) (2:37) Rhino 72005 Billboard's Top Rock & Roll Hits 1968-1972 Box Set.
- (S) (2:35) MCA 5940 Vintage Music Volumes 19 & 20.
- (S) (2:35) MCA 31216 Vintage Music Volume 19.

(S)	(2:36)	MCA 10288 Classic Soul.	

(S) (2:36) MCA 10288   Classic Soul.
(S) (2:37) One Way 22077   The Promise Of A Future.
(S) (2:36) Rhino 71604   Rock Instrumental Classics Vol. 4: Soul.
(S) (2:36) Rhino 72035   Rock Instrumental Classics Vols. 1-5 Box Set.
(S) (2:33) Time-Life RHD-04   Rhythm & Blues - 1968.
(S) (2:34) Time-Life SUD-02   Superhits - 1968.
(S) (2:34) MCA Special Products 20753   Classic R&B Oldies From The 60's.
(S) (2:35) MCA Special Products 22133   Vintage Collectibles Volume 4.
(S) (2:35) MCA Special Products 20902   Classic Rock & Roll Instrumental Hits, Volume 1.
(S) (2:35) Hip-O 40007   Soulful Grooves - R&B Instrumental Classics Volume 1.
(S) (2:34) JCI 3160   18 Free & Easy Hits From The 60's.
(S) (2:34) Time-Life AM1-04   AM Gold - 1968.
(S) (2:33) Time-Life R838-03   Solid Gold Soul - 1968.
(S) (2:36) Repeat/Relativity 1610   Tighten Up: #1 Soul Hits Of The 60's Volume 2.
(S) (2:36) MCA Special Products 21025   The Best Of Easy Listening.
(S) (2:35) MCA Special Products 21046   Top Singles Of The Sixties.

MASHMAKHAN
1970   AS THE YEARS GO BY
(S) (3:44) Columbia/Legacy 46160   Rock Artifacts Volume 1. *(neither the LP or 45 version)*

BARBARA MASON
1965   YES, I'M READY
(S) (3:02) Time-Life 2CLR-14   Classic Rock - 1965: Shakin' All Over. *(dropout on the introduction)*
(S) (3:03) Time-Life SUD-17   Superhits - Mid 60's Classics. *(dropout on the introduction)*
(M) (4:45) Right Stuff 27306   Slow Jams: The 60's Volume One. *(rerecording)*
(S) (3:10) Time-Life OPCD-4517   Tonight's The Night. *(rerecording)*
(S) (3:02) Thump 7010   Low Rider Oldies Volume 1. *(dropout on the introduction)*
(S) (3:02) JCI 3185   1965 - Only Love - 1969. *(dropout on the introduction)*
(S) (4:24) WMOT/Hot Productions 38   Best Of WMOT Records. *(rerecording)*
(S) (3:03) Time-Life AM1-16   AM Gold - Mid '60s Classics. *(dropout on the introduction)*
(M) (3:03) Rhino 72815   Beg, Scream & Shout! The Big Ol' Box Of '60s Soul.
(S) (3:00) TVT 4010   Rhythm Revue.
(S) (3:01) Time-Life R857-20   The Heart Of Rock 'n' Roll 1965-1966.

1965   SAD, SAD GIRL
1973   GIVE ME YOUR LOVE
1975   FROM HIS WOMAN TO YOU
(S) (4:56) Essex 7060   The Buddah Box. *(LP version)*
(S) (3:28) Right Stuff 29140   Slow Jams: The Timeless Collection Volume 2. *(45 version)*
(S) (3:28) Ichiban 2507   Cheatin': From A Woman's Point Of View. *(45 version)*

DAVE MASON
1970   ONLY YOU KNOW AND I KNOW
(S) (4:05) MCA 31273   Classic Rock Volume 1.
(S) (4:06) MCA 31170   Alone Together.
(S) (4:06) MFSL 573   Alone Together. *(gold disc)*
(S) (4:02) MCA 31169   Very Best Of.
(S) (4:20) Columbia 37089   Best Of. *(live)*
(S) (4:05) Time-Life SOD-26   Sounds Of The Seventies - FM Rock II.
(S) (4:05) MCA Special Products 20754   Classic Rock Volume 1.
(S) (4:04) Blue Thumb 7002   All Day Thumbsucker Revisited.
(S) (4:05) Time-Life R968-06   Guitar Rock 1970-1971.

(S) (4:06) MCA Special Products 20949   Rockin' 70's Volume 2.
(S) (4:20) Legacy/Columbia 57165   Best Of. *(live)*
(S) (4:05) MCA Special Products 20956   Rockin' Guitars.
(S) (4:05) MCA Special Products 21011   70's Biggest Hits.

1977   WE JUST DISAGREE
(S) (2:59) Columbia 37089   Best Of. *(LP version)*
(S) (3:00) Columbia 34680   Let It Flow. *(LP version)*
(S) (2:59) Time-Life SOD-34   Sounds Of The Seventies - The Late 70's. *(LP version)*
(S) (2:59) Time-Life R105-26   Our Songs: Singers & Songwriters Encore. *(LP version)*
(S) (2:59) Legacy/Columbia 57165   Best Of. *(LP version)*
(S) (2:59) Rhino 72446   Listen To The Music: 70's Male Singer/Songwriters. *(LP version)*
(S) (2:59) Eclipse Music Group 64895   Rock 'n Roll Relix 1976-1977. *(LP version)*
(S) (2:59) Eclipse Music Group 64897   Rock 'n Roll Relix 1970-1979. *(LP version)*
(S) (2:59) Time-Life AM1-24   AM Gold - 1977. *(LP version)*

1978   WILL YOU STILL LOVE ME TOMORROW
(S) (5:02) Columbia 37089   Best Of. *(LP version)*
(S) (3:50) Legacy/Columbia 57165   Best Of. *(45 version)*

MASS PRODUCTION
1979   FIRECRACKER
(S) (6:14) Rhino 71752 and 72829   Phat Trax: The Best Of Old School Volume 1. *(LP version)*
(S) (6:14) Rhino 72487   Street Jams - Back 2 The Old Skool, Part 1. *(LP version)*
(S) (6:15) JCI 3121   Monster Funk. *(LP version)*
(S) (6:15) Rhino 72522   Firecrackers: Best Of. *(LP version)*
(S) (4:58) K-Tel 4020   Great R&B Funk Bands Of The 70's. *(45 version)*
(S) (5:00) Rhino 72964   Ultimate '70s R&B Smashes! *(45 version)*
(S) (6:30) Hip-O 40091   Disco 54: Funkin' On The Floor. *(LP version)*

MASTA ACE INCORPORATED
1994   BORN TO ROLL
(S) (4:13) Delicious Vinyl 32873 and 71811   Sittin' On Chrome.
(S) (4:13) Priority 53777   Rap G Style.
(S) (4:11) Coldfront 6146   Phat Rap Flava '95. *(remix; all selections on this cd are segued together)*

MASTER P featuring PIMP C AND THE SHOCKER
1997   I MISS MY HOMIES
(S) (5:22) No Limit/Priority 50659   Ghetto D.

TOBIN MATHEWS & CO.
1960   RUBY DUBY DU

JOHNNY MATHIS
1957   WONDERFUL! WONDERFUL!
(M) (2:45) Columbia 34667   Johnny's Greatest Hits.
(M) (2:46) Columbia 40217   16 Most Requested Songs.
(M) (2:47) Columbia/Legacy 48932   A Personal Collection.
(M) (2:46) Time-Life HPD-31   Your Hit Parade - The 50's Forever.
(M) (2:45) Columbia 64810   Heavenly/Johnny's Greatest Hits/Live.
(M) (2:47) Columbia/Legacy 65540   The Ultimate Collection.

1957   IT'S NOT FOR ME TO SAY
(M) (3:03) Columbia 45111   16 Most Requested Songs Of The 50's Volume 2.
(M) (3:02) Columbia 34667   Johnny's Greatest Hits.
(M) (3:02) Columbia 40217   16 Most Requested Songs.
(M) (3:03) Columbia/Legacy 48932   A Personal Collection.
(M) (3:02) Time-Life HPD-23   Your Hit Parade - The Late 50's.
(M) (3:02) Columbia 64810   Heavenly/Johnny's Greatest Hits/Live.

JOHNNY MATHIS (Continued)

(M) (3:03) Rhino 72422 Billboard Top Movie Hits 1955-1959.

(M) (3:02) Columbia/Legacy 65540 The Ultimate Collection.

1957 CHANCES ARE

(S) (3:00) Columbia 45110 16 Most Requested Songs Of The 50's Volume 1.

(S) (3:00) Columbia 45017 Radio Classics Of The 50's.

(M) (3:00) Columbia 34667 Johnny's Greatest Hits.

(M) (3:01) Columbia 40217 16 Most Requested Songs.

(M) (3:00) Rhino 71252 Sentimental Journey: Pop Vocal Classics Volume 4 (1954-1959).

(M) (3:00) Rhino 72034 Sentimental Journey Pop Vocal Classics Volumes 1-4 Box Set.

(M) (3:00) Columbia/Legacy 48932 A Personal Collection.

(E) (3:02) Original Sound 8907 Best Love Songs Vol 2.

(E) (3:02) Original Sound 9326 Best Love Songs Vol. 1 & 2.

(E) (3:02) Original Sound 1236 Best Love Songs Box Set.

(M) (3:00) Time-Life HPD-23 Your Hit Parade - The Late 50's.

(S) (3:00) Time-Life R103-27 Love Me Tender.

(M) (3:00) Columbia 64810 Heavenly/Johnny's Greatest Hits/Live.

(S) (3:00) Nick At Nite/Epic 67148 Donna Reed's Dinner Party.

(M) (3:01) JCI 7021 Those Wonderful Years - April Love.

(S) (3:00) Time-Life R857-05 The Heart Of Rock 'n' Roll 1957.

(S) (3:01) Columbia/Legacy 64861 Martinis And A Broken Heart To Go.

(S) (3:00) Collectables 1514 and 2514 The Anniversary Album - The 50's.

(M) (3:00) Columbia/Legacy 65540 The Ultimate Collection.

1957 THE TWELFTH OF NEVER

(M) (2:27) Columbia 34667 Johnny's Greatest Hits.

(M) (2:27) Columbia 40217 16 Most Requested Songs.

(M) (2:25) Columbia/Legacy 48932 A Personal Collection.

(M) (2:27) Columbia 64810 Heavenly/Johnny's Greatest Hits/Live.

(M) (2:25) Columbia/Legacy 65540 The Ultimate Collection.

1957 WILD IS THE WIND

(M) (2:25) Columbia 44374 Hollywood Magic - The 50's.

(M) (2:25) Columbia 34667 Johnny's Greatest Hits.

(M) (2:25) Columbia 40217 16 Most Requested Songs.

(M) (2:23) Columbia/Legacy 48932 A Personal Collection.

(M) (2:25) Columbia 64810 Heavenly/Johnny's Greatest Hits/Live.

(M) (2:23) Columbia/Legacy 65540 The Ultimate Collection.

1957 NO LOVE (BUT YOUR LOVE)

(M) (2:17) Columbia 34667 Johnny's Greatest Hits.

(M) (2:16) Columbia/Legacy 57899 Encore!: 16 Most Requested Songs.

(M) (2:17) Columbia 64810 Heavenly/Johnny's Greatest Hits/Live.

1958 COME TO ME

(M) (3:02) Columbia 34667 Johnny's Greatest Hits.

(S) (3:00) Columbia/Legacy 57899 Encore!: 16 Most Requested Songs.

(M) (3:02) Columbia 64810 Heavenly/Johnny's Greatest Hits/Live.

1958 ALL THE TIME

(M) (2:42) Columbia 34667 Johnny's Greatest Hits.

(M) (2:42) Columbia 64810 Heavenly/Johnny's Greatest Hits/Live.

1958 TEACHER, TEACHER

(S) (2:38) Columbia 8150 More Johnny's Greatest Hits.

(S) (2:37) Columbia/Legacy 57899 Encore!: 16 Most Requested Songs.

1958 A CERTAIN SMILE

(M) (2:48) Columbia 44374 Hollywood Magic - The 50's.

(S) (2:46) Columbia 8150 More Johnny's Greatest Hits.

(S) (2:45) Columbia 40217 16 Most Requested Songs.

(S) (2:46) Columbia/Legacy 48932 A Personal Collection.

(S) (2:45) Columbia/Legacy 65540 The Ultimate Collection.

1958 CALL ME

(S) (2:45) Columbia 8150 More Johnny's Greatest Hits.

(S) (2:44) Columbia/Legacy 57899 Encore!: 16 Most Requested Songs.

1959 LET'S LOVE

(S) (2:43) Columbia 8150 More Johnny's Greatest Hits.

(S) (2:41) Columbia/Legacy 57899 Encore!: 16 Most Requested Songs.

1959 SOMEONE

(S) (2:55) Columbia 8150 More Johnny's Greatest Hits.

(S) (2:56) Columbia/Legacy 48932 A Personal Collection.

(S) (2:55) Columbia/Legacy 57899 Encore!: 16 Most Requested Songs.

1959 SMALL WORLD

(S) (3:18) Columbia 8150 More Johnny's Greatest Hits.

(S) (3:16) Columbia 40217 16 Most Requested Songs.

(S) (3:17) Columbia/Legacy 48932 A Personal Collection.

1959 MISTY

(S) (3:32) Columbia 40217 16 Most Requested Songs.

(S) (3:33) Columbia/Legacy 48932 A Personal Collection.

(S) (3:33) Time-Life HPD-13 Your Hit Parade - 1959.

(S) (3:32) Time-Life R974-05 Many Moods Of Romance - You Belong To Me.

(S) (3:33) Time-Life R814-03 Love Songs.

(S) (3:32) Time-Life R132-10 Love Songs Of Your Hit Parade.

(S) (3:32) Columbia/Legacy 65540 The Ultimate Collection.

1960 STARBRIGHT

(S) (2:43) Columbia/Legacy 57899 Encore!: 16 Most Requested Songs.

1962 GINA

(S) (2:45) Columbia 40217 16 Most Requested Songs.

(S) (2:47) Columbia/Legacy 48932 A Personal Collection.

(S) (2:43) Time-Life HPD-32 Your Hit Parade - Into The 60's.

(S) (2:47) Time-Life R857-06 The Heart Of Rock 'n' Roll 1962.

1963 WHAT WILL MY MARY SAY

(S) (3:08) Columbia 40217 16 Most Requested Songs.

(S) (3:08) Columbia/Legacy 48932 A Personal Collection.

1963 EVERY STEP OF THE WAY

released as by JOHNNY MATHIS/DENIECE WILLIAMS:

1978 TOO MUCH, TOO LITTLE, TOO LATE

(S) (2:54) Columbia 47982 Johnny Mathis - Better Together: The Duet Album.

(S) (3:00) Columbia 36871 Johnny Mathis - Best Of 1975-1980.

(S) (2:55) Columbia 35259 Johnny Mathis - You Light Up My Life.

(S) (2:57) Razor & Tie 4543 The '70s Preservation Society Presents: Easy '70s.

(S) (2:58) Columbia/Legacy 57899 Johnny Mathis - Encore! 16 Most Requested Songs.

(S) (2:54) DCC Compact Classics 104 Duets - A Man & A Woman.

(S) (2:58) Columbia/Legacy 64839 Gonna Take A Miracle: Best Of Deniece Williams.

(S) (2:56) Eclipse Music Group 64896 Rock 'n Roll Relix 1978-1979.

(S) (2:56) Eclipse Music Group 64897 Rock 'n Roll Relix 1970-1979.

(S) (2:57) Time-Life R834-01 Body Talk - Forever Yours.

(S) (2:57) Time-Life R838-17 Solid Gold Soul 1978.

(S) (2:54) Columbia/Legacy 65384 Johnny Mathis - That's What Friends Are For/You Light Up My Life/Better Together: The Duet Album.

(S) (2:58) Columbia/Legacy 65540 The Ultimate Collection.

released as by DIONNE WARWICK and JOHNNY MATHIS:

1982 FRIENDS IN LOVE

(S) (3:57) Arista 8540 Dionne Warwick - Greatest Hits 1979-1990.

IAN MATTHEWS
1979 SHAKE IT
- (S) (3:09) Rhino 72299 Superhits Of The 70's Volume 25. *(45 length)*
- (S) (3:21) Varese Sarabande 5706 Dick Bartley Presents Collector's Essentials: The 70's. *(LP length)*
- (S) (3:19) Varese Sarabande 5738 The Seattle Years 1978-1984. *(LP length)*

MATTHEWS' SOUTHERN COMFORT
1971 WOODSTOCK
(dj copies of this 45 ran (3:18); commercial copies were all (4:26))
- (S) (4:27) Rhino 70924 Super Hits Of The 70's Volume 4.
- (S) (4:27) Rhino 72009 Super Hits Of The 70's Volumes 1-4 Box Set.
- (S) (4:27) MCA 10519 Best Of.
- (S) (4:26) Time-Life SOD-12 Sounds Of The Seventies - 1971: Take Two.
- (S) (4:26) Madacy Entertainment 1971 Rock On 1971.
- (S) (4:27) MCA Special Products 21011 70's Biggest Hits.
- (S) (3:22) Varese Sarabande 5847 On The Radio Volume Two. *(dj 45 version but missing a bass guitar overdub on the introduction)*

PAUL MAURIAT
1968 LOVE IS BLUE
- (S) (2:36) Philips 830769 Love Is Blue. *(rerecording)*
- (S) (2:35) Philips 834259 Love Is Blue/20th Anniversary Collection. *(rerecording)*
- (S) (2:32) Time-Life R138/05 Look Of Love.
- (S) (2:33) Rhino 71938 Billboard Top Pop Hits, 1968.
- (S) (2:32) Collectors' Choice 003/4 Instrumental Gems Of The 60's.
- (M) (2:32) LaserLight 12311 and 15936 The Wonder Years - First Love.
- (S) (2:32) Time-Life R814-01 Love Songs.
- (S) (2:32) Time-Life R986-22 Instrumental Classics - Pop Classics.

MAXWELL
1996 ASCENSION (DON'T EVER WONDER)
- (S) (5:45) Columbia 66434 Maxwell's Urban Hang Suite.

ROBERT MAXWELL
1964 SHANGRI-LA
- (S) (2:03) Collectors' Choice 003/4 Instrumental Gems Of The 60's.
- (S) (2:02) Hip-O 40034 Cigar Classics Volume 4 - Smokin' Lounge.
- (S) (2:02) MCA Special Products 21035 Classic Rock & Roll Instrumental Hits, Volume 2.
- (S) (2:02) MCA Special Products 21025 The Best Of Easy Listening.

NATHANIEL MAYER and THE FABULOUS TWILIGHTS
1962 VILLAGE OF LOVE

CURTIS MAYFIELD
1971 (DON'T WORRY) IF THERE'S A HELL BELOW WE'RE ALL GOING TO GO
- (S) (7:03) Curtom 2902 Of All Time/Classic Collection. *(edit of LP version)*
- (S) (7:49) MCA 10664 Curtis Mayfield & The Impressions Anthology 1961-1977. *(LP version)*
- (S) (7:42) Capitol 32438 O.S.T. Dead Presidents. *(LP version)*
- (S) (7:49) Rhino 72262 The Curtis Mayfield Story. *(LP version)*
- (S) (7:46) Curtom 9504 Curtis. *(LP version)*
- (S) (7:50) Rhino 72584 Very Best Of. *(LP version)*

1972 FREDDIE'S DEAD (THEME FROM "SUPERFLY")
- (S) (3:46) Rhino 70660 Billboard's Top R&B Hits Of 1972. *(neither the 45 or LP version)*
- (S) (3:46) Rhino 70789 Soul Hits Of The 70's Volume 9. *(neither the 45 or LP version)*
- (S) (5:26) Curtom 2002 and 9503 Superfly. *(LP version)*
- (S) (5:25) MCA 10664 Curtis Mayfield & The Impressions Anthology 1961-1977. *(LP version)*
- (S) (3:47) Rhino 71431 In Yo Face! History Of Funk Volume 1. *(neither the 45 or LP version)*
- (S) (5:25) Essex 7060 The Buddah Box. *(LP version)*
- (S) (3:43) Razor & Tie 22047 Sweet 70's Soul. *(neither the 45 or LP version)*
- (S) (3:19) Time-Life RHD-20 Rhythm & Blues - 1972. *(neither the 45 or LP version)*
- (S) (3:19) Time-Life SOD-13 Sounds Of The Seventies - 1972: Take Two. *(neither the 45 or LP version)*
- (S) (5:24) Priority 57194 Old School Friday - More Music From The Original Motion Picture. *(LP version)*
- (S) (5:25) Rhino 72262 The Curtis Mayfield Story. *(LP version)*
- (S) (3:19) Time-Life R838-07 Solid Gold Soul - 1972. *(neither the 45 or LP version)*
- (M) (3:15) Rhino 72584 Very Best Of. *(45 version)*
- (S) (5:25) Rhino 72836 Superfly - Deluxe 25th Anniversary Edition. *(LP version)*
- (M) (3:16) Rhino 72836 Superfly - Deluxe 25th Anniversary Edition. *(45 version)*
- (M) (4:46) Rhino 72836 Superfly - Deluxe 25th Anniversary Edition. *(instrumental version)*
- (S) (5:26) Hip-O 40107 Super Bad On Celluloid: Music From '70s Black Cinema. *(LP version)*

1973 SUPERFLY
- (S) (3:12) Rhino 70790 Soul Hits Of The 70's Volume 10. *(45 length)*
- (S) (3:53) Curtom 2002 and 9503 Superfly. *(LP length)*
- (S) (3:51) MCA 10664 Curtis Mayfield & The Impressions Anthology 1961-1977. *(LP length)*
- (S) (3:51) Essex 7060 The Buddah Box. *(LP length)*
- (S) (3:52) Time-Life SOD-06 Sounds Of The Seventies - 1973. *(LP length)*
- (S) (3:51) K-Tel 6011 70's Soul: Super Funky Hits. *(LP length)*
- (S) (3:52) Rhino 72262 The Curtis Mayfield Story. *(LP length)*
- (S) (3:51) Coldfront 3517 Players & Hustlers Of The 70's - Can You Dig It?. *(LP length)*
- (S) (3:52) JCI 3173 1970 - Only Soul - 1974. *(LP length)*
- (S) (3:51) Priority 53129 Deep Soul Volume One. *(LP length)*
- (S) (3:12) Time-Life R838-08 Solid Gold Soul - 1973. *(45 length)*
- (S) (3:52) Rhino 72584 Very Best Of. *(LP length)*
- (S) (3:52) Rhino 72836 Superfly - Deluxe 25th Anniversary Edition. *(LP length)*
- (M) (3:07) Rhino 72836 Superfly - Deluxe 25th Anniversary Edition. *(45 length)*

1973 FUTURE SHOCK
- (S) (3:33) Rhino 71432 In Yo Face! History Of Funk Volume 2. *(45 version)*
- (S) (3:35) Rhino 72262 The Curtis Mayfield Story. *(45 version)*
- (S) (5:11) Priority 53131 Deep Soul Volume Two. *(LP version)*
- (S) (3:35) Rhino 72584 Very Best Of. *(45 version)*

1974 KUNG FU
- (S) (3:47) Rhino 72262 The Curtis Mayfield Story. *(45 version)*
- (S) (6:11) Curtom 9502 Living Legend. *(LP version)*
- (S) (3:47) Rhino 72584 Very Best Of. *(45 version)*

MAC McANALLY
1977 IT'S A CRAZY WORLD
1983 MINIMUM LOVE

MC BRAINS
1992 OOCHIE COOCHIE
- (S) (3:43) Rhino 71916 Whats Up? Rap Hits Of The 90's.
- (S) (3:40) Motown 6342 Lovers Lane.

C.W. McCALL
1976 CONVOY
- (S) (3:46) Rhino 70762 Super Hits Of The 70's Volume 15.
- (S) (3:51) American Gramophone 890 The Real McCall. *(rerecording)*
- (S) (3:47) Polydor 825793 Greatest Hits.

    (S)   (3:46)   Time-Life CCD-08 Contemporary Country - The Mid 70's Pure Gold.

    (S)   (3:46)   Rhino 71750 Spy Magazine Presents: White Men Can't Wrap.

    (S)   (3:46)   Rhino 71671 Country Shots: Gear-Jammin' Greats.

    (S)   (3:47)   K-Tel 3095 Country Comedy Classics.

    (S)   (3:46)   Priority 50967 I Love Country Volume Two: Hits Of The 70's.

    (S)   (3:47)   K-Tel 3369 101 Greatest Country Hits Vol. Ten: Country Roads.

    (S)   (3:47)   Polygram Special Markets 314520394 Best Of.

    (S)   (3:46)   Time-Life R830-01 The Dr. Demento Collection - The Mid 70's.

    (S)   (3:47)   Hip-O 40086 The Class Of Country 1975-1979.

PETER McCANN
1977 DO YOU WANNA MAKE LOVE

    (S)   (3:29)   Rhino 71200 Super Hits Of The 70's Volume 20.

    (S)   (3:29)   Time-Life R834-18 Body Talk - Romantic Moments.

PAUL McCARTNEY (also WINGS)
1971 ANOTHER DAY

    (S)   (3:40)   Capitol 48287 Paul McCartney: All The Best.

    (S)   (3:41)   Capitol 46056 Wings Greatest.

released as by PAUL & LINDA McCARTNEY:
1971 UNCLE ALBERT/ADMIRAL HALSEY

    (S)   (4:54)   Capitol 46612 Ram. *(LP length; tracks into next selection just like the "Ram" vinyl LP)*

    (S)   (4:39)   Capitol 48287 Paul McCartney: All The Best. *(:08 shorter than the 45 length)*

    (S)   (4:40)   Capitol 46056 Wings Greatest. *(:07 shorter than 45 length)*

    (S)   (4:54)   DCC Compact Classics 1037 Ram. *(LP length; tracks into next selection just like the "Ram" vinyl LP; gold disc)*

released as by WINGS:
1972 GIVE IRELAND BACK TO THE IRISH
1972 MARY HAD A LITTLE LAMB

    (S)   (3:32)   Capitol 52017 Wings Wild Life. *A*

1973 HI HI HI

    (S)   (3:07)   Capitol 46056 Wings Greatest. *B*

released as by PAUL McCARTNEY & WINGS:
1973 MY LOVE

    (S)   (4:07)   Capitol 52026 Red Rose Speedway.

    (S)   (4:07)   Capitol 48287 Paul McCartney: All The Best.

    (S)   (4:07)   Capitol 46056 Wings Greatest.

    (S)   (4:07)   DCC Compact Classics 1091 Red Rose Speedway. *(gold disc)*

released as by WINGS:
1973 LIVE AND LET DIE

    (S)   (3:10)   EMI 46079 James Bond 13 Original Themes.

    (S)   (3:11)   EMI 90629 O.S.T. Live And Let Die.

    (S)   (3:10)   Capitol 48287 Paul McCartney: All The Best.

    (S)   (3:10)   Capitol 46056 Wings Greatest.

    (S)   (3:11)   EMI 98560 Best Of James Bond 30th Anniversary.

    (S)   (3:11)   EMI 98413 Best Of James Bond 30th Anniversary Collection.

released as by PAUL McCARTNEY & WINGS:
1974 HELEN WHEELS

    (S)   (3:42)   Capitol 46675 Band On The Run. *C*

    (S)   (3:42)   DCC Compact Classics 1030 Band On The Run. *(gold disc)*

1974 JET
(dj copies of this 45 ran (2:49) and (4:08); commercial copies were all (4:08))

    (S)   (4:06)   Capitol 46056 Wings Greatest.

    (S)   (4:06)   Capitol 48287 Paul McCartney: All The Best.

    (S)   (4:05)   Capitol 46675 Band On The Run.

    (S)   (4:05)   DCC Compact Classics 1030 Band On The Run. *(gold disc)*

1974 BAND ON THE RUN
(dj copies of this 45 ran (3:50) and (5:09); commercial copies were all (5:09))

    (S)   (5:10)   Capitol 46056 Wings Greatest.

    (S)   (5:10)   Capitol 48287 Paul McCartney: All The Best.

    (S)   (5:11)   Capitol 46675 Band On The Run.

    (S)   (5:11)   DCC Compact Classics 1030 Band On The Run. *(gold disc)*

    (S)   (5:10)   Time-Life R13610 Gold And Platinum Box Set - The Ultimate Rock Collection.

1975 JUNIOR'S FARM
(dj copies of this 45 ran (3:03) and (4:20); commercial copies were all (4:20))

    (S)   (4:20)   Capitol 46056 Wings Greatest.

    (S)   (4:20)   Capitol 48287 Paul McCartney: All The Best.

1975 SALLY G

    (S)   (3:38)   Capitol 48199 Wings At The Speed Of Sound. *D*

released as by WINGS:
1975 LISTEN TO WHAT THE MAN SAID

    (S)   (3:53)   Capitol 48287 Paul McCartney: All The Best. *(45 version)*

    (S)   (4:00)   Capitol 46984 Wings: Venus And Mars. *(LP version; tracks into next selection)*

    (S)   (4:00)   DCC Compact Classics 1067 Wings: Venus And Mars. *(gold disc; LP version; tracks into next selection)*

1975 VENUS AND MARS ROCK SHOW
(the LP version of this song is a medley of "VENUS AND MARS" (1:19) and "ROCK SHOW" (5:31) with a combined time of (6:50))

    (S)   (6:50)   Capitol 46984 Wings: Venus And Mars. *(LP version; tracks into next selection)* *E*

    (S)   (6:50)   DCC Compact Classics 1067 Wings: Venus And Mars. *(gold disc; LP version; tracks into next selection)*

    (S)   (5:33)   Foundation/RCA 66109 Ultimate Rock Album. *(this is the "Rock Show" portion of the LP version)*

1976 SILLY LOVE SONGS
(dj copies of this 45 ran (3:28) and (5:54); commercial copies were all (5:54))

    (S)   (5:52)   Capitol 46056 Wings Greatest.

    (S)   (5:52)   Capitol 48287 Paul McCartney: All The Best.

    (S)   (5:52)   Capitol 48199 Wings At The Speed Of Sound.

1976 LET 'EM IN
(dj copies of this 45 ran (3:43) and (5:08); commercial copies were all (5:08))

    (S)   (5:07)   Capitol 46056 Wings Greatest.

    (S)   (5:08)   Capitol 48287 Paul McCartney: All The Best.

    (S)   (5:08)   Capitol 48199 Wings At The Speed Of Sound.

1977 MAYBE I'M AMAZED (live version)
(dj copies of this 45 ran (3:43); commercial copies were all (5:11))

    (S)   (3:50)   Capitol 46611 McCartney. *(studio version which was not the hit version)*

    (S)   (5:20)   Capitol 46715 Wings Over America. *F*

    (S)   (5:17)   Time-Life R102-34 The Rolling Stone Collection.

1977 GIRL'S SCHOOL
(dj copies of this 45 ran (3:19); commercial copies were all (4:34))

    (S)   (4:33)   Capitol 48198 Wings: London Town. *G*

1978 WITH A LITLE LUCK
(dj copies of this 45 ran (3:13); commercial copies were all (5:45))

    (S)   (5:44)   Capitol 46056 Wings Greatest.

    (S)   (3:11)   Capitol 48287 Paul McCartney: All The Best.

    (S)   (5:44)   Capitol 48198 Wings: London Town.

1978 I'VE HAD ENOUGH

    (S)   (3:01)   Capitol 48198 Wings: London Town. *G*

1978 GOODNIGHT TONIGHT

    (S)   (4:17)   Capitol 48287 Paul McCartney: All The Best.

1979 GETTING CLOSER

    (S)   (3:21)   Capitol 48200 Wings: Back To The Egg. *H*

1979 ARROW THROUGH ME

    (S)   (3:35)   Capitol 48200 Wings: Back To The Egg. *H*

released as by PAUL McCARTNEY & WINGS:
1980 COMING UP (LIVE AT GLASGOW)

    (S)   (3:28)   Capitol 48287 Paul McCartney: All The Best. *(:20 of audience applause and crowd noise edited from the ending)*

    (S)   (3:52)   Capitol 52024 McCartney II. *(studio version which was not the hit version)*

released as by PAUL McCARTNEY with STEVIE WONDER:
1982 EBONY AND IVORY
- (S) (3:42) Capitol 46057 Paul McCartney: Tug Of War.
- (S) (3:40) Capitol 48287 Paul McCartney: All The Best.
- (S) (3:41) Chrysalis 21750 After The Hurricane - Songs For Montserrat.
- (S) (3:40) Motown 314530767 Stevie Wonder: Song Review - A Greatest Hits Collection. *(all songs on this cd are segued together)*

released as by PAUL McCARTNEY:
1982 TAKE IT AWAY
- (S) (4:14) Capitol 46057 Tug Of War. *(LP version)*

released as by MICHAEL JACKSON/PAUL McCARTNEY:
1983 THE GIRL IS MINE
(dj copies of this 45 ran (3:32) and (3:41);
commercial copies were all (3:41))
- (S) (3:41) Epic 38112 Michael Jackson: Thriller.
- (S) (3:40) Epic 59000 Michael Jackson: History - Past, Present And Future.

released as by PAUL McCARTNEY and MICHAEL JACKSON:
1983 SAY SAY SAY
- (S) (3:54) Capitol 46018 Paul McCartney - Pipes Of Peace.
- (S) (3:54) Columbia 39149 Paul McCartney - Pipes Of Peace.
- (S) (3:53) Capitol 48287 Paul McCartney: All The Best.

released as by PAUL McCARTNEY:
1984 SO BAD
- (S) (3:24) Capitol 46043 Give My Regards To Broad Street.
- (S) (3:17) Columbia 39613 Give My Regards To Broad Street.

1984 NO MORE LONELY NIGHTS
- (S) (5:12) Capitol 46043 Give My Regards To Broad Street. *(LP ballad version)*
- (S) (5:02) Capitol 46043 Give My Regards To Broad Street. *(LP playout version)*
- (S) (4:57) Columbia 39613 Give My Regards To Broad Street. *(LP ballad version)*
- (S) (5:11) Columbia 39613 Give My Regards To Broad Street. *(LP playout version)*
- (S) (4:38) Capitol 48287 Paul McCartney: All The Best. *(45 ballad version)*

1986 SPIES LIKE US
(dj copies of this 45 ran (3:46) and (4:40);
commercial copies were all (4:42))

1986 PRESS
(dj copies of this 45 ran (3:35) and (4:07);
commercial copies were all (3:35))
- (S) (4:42) Capitol 46269 Press To Play. *(LP version)*

1989 MY BRAVE FACE
- (S) (3:17) Capitol 91653 Flowers In The Dirt.

ALTON McCLAIN & DESTINY
1979 IT MUST BE LOVE
- (S) (2:58) Rebound 314520309 Disco Nights Vol. VII - D.J. Pix.

DELBERT McCLINTON
1981 GIVING IT UP FOR YOUR LOVE
- (S) (3:44) Curb 77415 Best Of. *(LP length)*
- (S) (3:45) Curb 77664 Classics Volume One. *(LP length)*

MARILYN McCOO & BILLY DAVIS JR.
1977 YOU DON'T HAVE TO BE A STAR (TO BE IN MY SHOW)
- (S) (3:50) Time-Life SOD-34 Sounds Of The Seventies - The Late 70's. *(45 version but :10 longer fade than the 45)*
- (S) (4:36) Razor & Tie 2098 I Hope We Get To Love In Time. *(LP version)*
- (S) (3:57) Razor & Tie 4543 The '70s Preservation Society Presents: Easy '70s. *(45 version but :17 longer fade than the 45)*
- (S) (3:50) Time-Life AM1-24 AM Gold - 1977. *(45 version but :10 longer fade than the 45)*
- (S) (3:50) Time-Life R838-11 Solid Gold Soul - 1976. *(45 version but :10 longer fade than the 45)*

- (S) (3:50) Time-Life R834-05 Body Talk - Sealed With A Kiss. *(45 version but :10 longer fade than the 45)*
- (S) (3:57) Time-Life R840-01 Sounds Of The Seventies - Pop Nuggets: Late '70s. *(45 version but :17 longer fade than the 45)*
- (S) (3:49) K-Tel 3887 Soul Brothers & Sisters Of The 70's. *(45 version but :09 longer fade than the 45)*

1977 YOUR LOVE
- (S) (3:49) Razor & Tie 2098 I Hope We Get To Love In Time. *(LP version)*

VAN McCOY
1975 THE HUSTLE
(45 length is (3:27); LP length is (4:03))
- (S) (3:44) Rhino 70984 The Disco Years Volume 1.
- (S) (3:32) Rhino 70799 O.S.T. Spirit Of '76.
- (S) (3:26) Priority 7059 Mega-Hits Dance Classics Volume 10.
- (S) (3:44) Rhino 71094 Disco Hits Volume 1.
- (S) (3:44) Rhino 71603 Rock Instrumental Classics Volume 3: The Seventies.
- (S) (3:44) Rhino 72035 Rock Instrumental Classics Vols. 1-5 Box Set.
- (S) (3:26) Essex 7051 Non-Stop Dance Hits.
- (S) (3:26) Original Sound 8881 Twenty-One #1 Hits. *(this compact disc uses the "Waring - fds" noise reduction process)*
- (S) (3:44) Razor & Tie 22496 Disco Fever.
- (S) (3:26) Time-Life SOD-08 Sounds Of The Seventies - 1975.
- (S) (3:44) Risky Business 53921 Double Knit Dance Hits.
- (S) (3:42) JCI 3131 1975 - Only Rock 'N Roll - 1979.
- (S) (4:06) K-Tel 3126 Disco Mania.
- (S) (3:45) Priority 53141 Mega Hits Disco Locomotion Volume 2.
- (S) (3:43) Rebound 314520432 Disco Nights Vol. XI - Disco's Leading Men.
- (S) (3:44) Flashback 72688 Disco Hits: Get Down Tonight.
- (S) (3:44) Flashback 72086 Disco Hits Box Set.
- (S) (3:28) Chronicles 314553404 Non-Stop Disco Vol. 1. *(all songs on this cd are segued together)*
- (S) (3:26) Polydor 314555120 Pure Disco 2.
- (S) (4:06) Cold Front 4025 Old School Mega Mix Volume 3.
- (S) (3:26) Time-Life R840-06 Sounds Of The Seventies: '70s Dance Party 1975-1976.

McCOYS
1965 HANG ON SLOOPY
(the original 45 and LP time was (3:02) even though the record label stated (2:57); the (3:52) version first appeared on the "Bang And Shout Superhits" various artist compilation LP in 1970)
- (M) (3:02) Rhino 70626 Billboard's Top Rock & Roll Hits Of 1965. *(found only on the first pressings of this cd)*
- (M) (3:02) Rhino 72007 Billboard's Top Rock & Roll Hits 1962-1966 Box Set.
- (M) (3:52) Rhino 70996 One Hit Wonders Of The 60's Volume 2.
- (M) (3:52) Rhino 70732 Grandson Of Frat Rock.
- (E) (2:59) Original Sound 8864 Oldies But Goodies Vol. 14. *(this compact disc uses the "Waring - fds" noise reduction process)*
- (E) (2:59) Original Sound 2222 Oldies But Goodies Volumes 3,5,11,14 and 15 Box Set. *(this box set uses the "Waring - fds" noise reduction process)*
- (E) (2:59) Original Sound 2500 Oldies But Goodies Volumes 1-15 Box Set. *(this box set uses the "Waring - fds" noise reduction process)*
- (E) (2:59) Original Sound CDGO-4 Golden Oldies Volume. 4.
- (E) (3:00) Original Sound 8881 Twenty-One #1 Hits. *(this compact disc uses the "Waring - fds" noise reduction process)*
- (E) (3:00) Original Sound 8895 Dick Clark's 21 All-Time Hits Vol. 4.

McCOYS *(Continued)*

- (E) (2:59) Original Sound 1081 All #1 Hits.
- (E) (2:59) SBK 93744 China Beach - Music & Memories.
- (M) (3:02) K-Tel 713 Battle Of The Bands.
- (E) (3:01) Sony Music Special Products 46994 The Immediate Singles Collection Volume 2. *(numerous droupouts)*
- (M) (3:01) Time-Life 2CLR-01 Classic Rock - 1965.
- (E) (3:00) Collectables 2510 WCBS-FM History Of Rock - The Rockin' 60's.
- (E) (3:00) Collectables 4510 History Of Rock/The Rockin' 60s.
- (M) (3:52) Hollywood 62032 O.S.T. Operation Dumbo Drop.
- (S) (3:51) Legacy/Epic Associated 47074 Hang On Sloopy: The Best Of.
- (S) (3:50) Eclipse Music Group 64869 Rock 'n Roll Relix 1964-1965.
- (S) (3:50) Eclipse Music Group 64872 Rock 'n Roll Relix 1960-1969.
- (S) (3:51) Angel 56344 O.S.T. The People Vs. Larry Flynt.
- (S) (3:01) Varese Sarabande 5846 On The Radio Volume One.
- (M) (3:01) Simitar 55532 The Number One's: The '60s. *(dropout on the first drumbeat)*

1965 FEVER

- (E) (2:50) Sony Music Special Products 46994 The Immediate Singles Collection Volume 2.
- (S) (2:47) Legacy/Epic Associated 47074 Hang On Sloopy: The Best Of.

1966 COME ON LET'S GO

- (M) (2:37) Sony Music Special Products 47351 The Immediate Singles Collection Volume 1.
- (S) (2:38) Legacy/Epic Associated 47074 Hang On Sloopy: The Best Of.

JIMMY McCRACKLIN
1958 THE WALK

- (M) (2:44) Rhino 70992 Groove 'n' Grind. *(some vocal distortion)*
- (M) (2:44) Chess 31317 Best Of Chess Rhythm & Blues Volume 1. *(some vocal distortion)*
- (E) (2:44) Time-Life 2RNR-21 Rock 'N' Roll Era - 1958 Still Rockin'. *(some vocal distortion)*
- (M) (2:44) Razor & Tie 2124 The Walk: Jimmy McCracklin At His Best. *(some vocal distortion)*
- (M) (2:44) Time-Life R859-04 Living The Blues: 1957-1959 Blues Classics. *(some vocal distortion)*

GEORGE McCRAE
1974 ROCK YOUR BABY

- (S) (3:12) Priority 7972 Mega-Hits Dance Classics Volume 2. *(45 version)*
- (S) (3:17) Rhino 70662 Billboard's Top R&B Hits Of 1974. *(LP version faded to simulate the 45 version)*
- (S) (3:18) Rhino 71003 Get Down Tonight: The Best Of T.K. Records. *(LP version faded to simulate the 45 version)*
- (S) (3:18) Rhino 70553 Soul Hits Of The 70's Volume 13. *(LP version faded to simulate the 45 version)*
- (S) (3:18) Rhino 71094 Disco Hits Volume 1. *(LP version faded to simulate the 45 version)*
- (S) (6:22) Collectables 5430 George & Gwen McCrae: Golden Classics. *(LP version)*
- (S) (3:17) JCI 3306 Dance Seventies. *(LP version faded to simulate the 45 version)*
- (S) (3:17) Rhino 71549 Let There Be Drums Vol. 3: The 70's. *(LP version faded to simulate the 45 version)*
- (S) (3:18) Razor & Tie 22047 Sweet 70's Soul. *(LP version faded to simulate the 45 version)*
- (S) (3:17) Time-Life SOD-15 Sounds Of The Seventies - 1974: Take Two. *(LP version faded to simulate the 45 version)*
- (S) (4:20) Collectables 5431 Disco Party - The Best Of The T.K. Collection. *(neither the 45 or LP version; tracks into the next selection)*
- (S) (6:22) Hot Productions 11 Best Of The Sound Of Sunshine. *(LP version)*

- (S) (6:21) Rebound 314520245 Disco Nights Vol. 6 - #1 Disco Hits. *(LP version)*
- (S) (6:22) Hot Productions 30 Best Of. *(LP version)*
- (S) (3:17) Madacy Entertainment 1974 Rock On 1974. *(LP version faded to simulate the 45 version)*
- (S) (3:17) JCI 3163 18 Disco Superhits. *(LP version faded to simulate the 45 version)*
- (S) (3:17) JCI 3191 1970 - Only Dance - 1974. *(LP version faded to simulate the 45 version)*
- (S) (3:17) Rebound 314520432 Disco Nights Vol. XI - Disco's Leading Men. *(LP version faded to simulate the 45 version)*
- (S) (3:18) Time-Life R838-09 Solid Gold Soul - 1974. *(LP version faded to simulate the 45 version)*
- (S) (3:18) Flashback 72688 Disco Hits: Get Down Tonight. *(LP version faded to simulate the 45 version)*
- (S) (3:18) Flashback 72086 Disco Hits Box Set. *(LP version faded to simulate the 45 version)*
- (S) (5:20) Chronicles 314553405 Non-Stop Disco Vol. 2. *(all songs on this cd are segued together)*
- (S) (3:18) Rhino 72812 VH1 8-Track Flashback: The One Hit Wonders. *(LP version faded to simulate the 45 version)*
- (S) (3:18) Hip-O 40096 '70s Hit(s) Back Again. *(LP version faded to simulate the 45 version)*
- (S) (3:18) Time-Life R840-05 Sounds Of The Seventies: '70s Dance Party 1972-1974. *(LP version faded to simulate the 45 version)*

GWEN McCRAE
1975 ROCKIN' CHAIR

- (S) (3:18) Rhino 71003 Get Down Tonight: The Best Of T.K. Records.
- (S) (3:17) Rhino 70555 Soul Hits Of The 70's Volume 15.
- (S) (3:18) Rhino 71094 Disco Hits Volume 1.
- (S) (3:18) Collectables 5430 George & Gwen McCrae: Golden Classics.
- (S) (3:16) Time-Life SOD-33 Sounds Of The Seventies - AM Pop Classics II.
- (S) (3:17) Rhino 72414 Dance Floor Divas: The 70's.
- (S) (3:18) TK/Hot Productions 33 Best Of T.K. Soul Singles.
- (S) (3:17) Time-Life R838-10 Solid Gold Soul - 1975.
- (S) (3:18) Flashback 72688 Disco Hits: Get Down Tonight.
- (S) (3:18) Flashback 72086 Disco Hits Box Set.
- (S) (3:17) Time-Life R840-06 Sounds Of The Seventies: '70s Dance Party 1975-1976.

GENE McDANIELS
1961 A HUNDRED POUNDS OF CLAY

- (S) (2:18) EMI 91681 Golden Greats.
- (S) (2:20) EMI 99998 Best Of/A Hundred Pounds Of Clay.
- (S) (2:20) EMI 81128 Rock Is Dead But It Won't Lie Down.
- (S) (2:18) Time-Life 2RNR-18 Rock 'N' Roll Era - 1961 Still Rockin'.
- (S) (2:16) Time-Life SUD-15 Superhits - The Early 60's.
- (S) (2:20) Collectables 5646 Best Of/A Hundred Pounds Of Clay.
- (S) (2:17) Time-Life AM1-19 AM Gold - The Early '60s.
- (S) (2:18) Time-Life R857-19 The Heart Of Rock 'n' Roll 1960-1961 Take Three.

1961 A TEAR

- (S) (2:07) EMI 91681 Golden Greats.
- (S) (2:07) EMI 99998 Best Of/A Hundred Pounds Of Clay.
- (S) (2:06) Collectables 5646 Best Of/A Hundred Pounds Of Clay.

1961 TOWER OF STRENGTH

- (S) (2:15) EMI 91681 Golden Greats.
- (S) (2:31) EMI 99998 Best Of/A Hundred Pounds Of Clay. *(time includes :10 of studio talk)*
- (S) (2:13) Time-Life 2RNR-42 Rock 'N' Roll Era - The 60's Sock Hop.
- (S) (2:13) Time-Life SUD-19 Superhits - Early 60's Classics.
- (S) (2:30) Collectables 5646 Best Of/A Hundred Pounds Of Clay. *(time includes :10 of studio talk)*
- (S) (2:13) Time-Life AM1-20 AM Gold - Early '60s Classics.

1962 CHIP CHIP
- (S) (2:17) EMI 91681 Golden Greats.
- (S) (2:27) EMI 99998 Best Of/A Hundred Pounds Of Clay. *(:10 longer than any previously released version)*
- (S) (2:16) Time-Life 2RNR-46 Rock 'N' Roll Era - 60's Juke Box Memories.
- (S) (2:26) Collectables 5646 Best Of/A Hundred Pounds Of Clay. *(:09 longer than any previously released version)*

1962 POINT OF NO RETURN
- (S) (2:13) EMI 91681 Golden Greats.
- (S) (2:16) EMI 99998 Best Of/A Hundred Pounds Of Clay.
- (S) (2:14) Collectables 5646 Best Of/A Hundred Pounds Of Clay.

1962 SPANISH LACE
- (S) (2:21) EMI 91681 Golden Greats.
- (S) (2:24) EMI 99998 Best Of/A Hundred Pounds Of Clay.
- (S) (2:24) Collectables 5646 Best Of/A Hundred Pounds Of Clay.

CHAS. McDEVITT SKIFFLE GROUP
1957 FREIGHT TRAIN

MICHAEL McDONALD
1982 I KEEP FORGETTIN'
- (S) (3:40) Sandstone 33047 and 5015 Cosmopolitan Volume 1.
- (S) (3:40) Warner Brothers 23703 If That's What It Takes.
- (S) (3:40) Priority 53746 80's Greatest Rock Hits Vol. 12 - Singers/Songwriters.
- (S) (3:39) Time-Life R988-05 Sounds Of The Eighties: 1982.
- (S) (3:39) Time-Life R138-18 Body Talk.
- (S) (3:39) JCI 3170 #1 Radio Hits 1980 - Only Rock 'n Roll - 1984.
- (S) (3:38) Time-Life R834-03 Body Talk - Moonlit Nights.

1983 I GOTTA TRY
- (S) (3:50) Warner Brothers 23703 If That's What It Takes.

released as by JAMES INGRAM with MICHAEL McDONALD:
1984 YAH MO B THERE
- (S) (4:39) Qwest 23970 James Ingram - It's Your Night. *(LP version)*
- (S) (4:29) Warner Brothers 26700 James Ingram Greatest Hits. *(LP version)*
- (S) (4:29) Time-Life R834-20 Body Talk - Heart And Soul. *(LP version)*
- (S) (4:29) Time-Life R988-23 Sounds Of The Eighties 1984-1985. *(LP version)*

released as by MICHAEL McDONALD:
1985 NO LOOKIN' BACK
- (S) (3:54) Warner Brothers 25291 No Lookin' Back.

released as by PATTI LaBELLE and MICHAEL McDONALD:
1986 ON MY OWN
- (S) (4:49) MCA 5737 Patti LaBelle - Winner In You. *(LP length)*
- (S) (4:46) Time-Life R138-18 Body Talk. *(LP length)*
- (S) (4:40) MCA 11567 Patti LaBelle - Greatest Hits. *(LP length faded :09 early)*

released as by MICHAEL McDONALD:
1986 SWEET FREEDOM
(dj copies of this 45 ran (3:58), (4:10) and (6:48); commercial copies were all (3:58))
- (S) (7:39) MCA 6169 O.S.T. Running Scared. *(soundtrack LP version)*
- (S) (4:02) MCA 6435 Soundtrack Smashes - The 80's And More. *(45 version)*

RONNIE McDOWELL
1977 THE KING IS GONE
- (S) (3:15) Risky Business 66394 Gone But Not Forgotten.
- (S) (3:13) Rhino 72298 Superhits Of The 70's Volume 24.

McFADDEN & WHITEHEAD
1979 AIN'T NO STOPPIN' US NOW
- (S) (7:01) Philadelphia International 39307 Ten Years Of Hits. *(LP version)*
- (S) (3:36) Priority 7976 Mega-Hits Dance Classics Volume 6. *(45 version)*
- (S) (3:37) Rhino 70985 The Disco Years Volume 2. *(45 version)*
- (S) (7:00) Epic/Legacy 52402 Club Epic - A Collection Of Classic Dance Mixes Volume 2. *(LP version)*
- (S) (7:01) Right Stuff 66692 McFadden & Whitehead. *(LP version)*
- (S) (3:37) Razor & Tie 22496 Disco Fever. *(45 version)*
- (S) (7:01) Right Stuff 29669 Movin' On Up Vol. 2. *(LP version)*
- (S) (3:40) Rhino 72130 Soul Hits Of The 70's Vol. 20. *(45 version)*
- (S) (3:35) K-Tel 3371 Hot Nights - Disco Lights. *(45 version)*
- (S) (3:37) MCA 11329 Soul Train 25th Anniversary Box Set. *(45 version)*
- (S) (3:28) Coldfront 3375 Old School Megamix. *(all selections on this cd are sequed together)*
- (S) (10:43) Rhino 72588 Phat Trax: The Best Of Old School, Vol. 7. *(12" single version)*
- (S) (3:37) Time-Life R838-15 Solid Gold Soul 1979. *(45 version)*
- (S) (3:39) Capitol 56312 O.S.T. Boogie Nights. *(45 version)*
- (S) (3:40) Rhino 75200 Basketball's Greatest Hits. *(45 version)*
- (S) (3:37) Time-Life R840-08 Sounds Of The Seventies: '70s Dance Party 1978-1979. *(45 version)*

BOBBY McFERRIN
1988 DON'T WORRY BE HAPPY
- (S) (4:48) Elektra 60806 O.S.T. Cocktail. *(LP version)*
- (S) (3:53) Foundation/WEA 26097 Super Sessions Volume Two. *(45 version)*
- (S) (3:53) Rhino 71643 Billboard Top Hits - 1988. *(45 version)*
- (S) (4:48) Sandstone 33046 and 5012 Rock The First Volume Six. *(LP version)*
- (S) (4:48) Rebound 314520314 Caribbean Nights II. *(LP version)*
- (S) (4:49) EMI-Manhattan 48059 Simple Pleasures. *(LP version)*
- (S) (3:52) Time-Life R988-10 Sounds Of The 80's: 1988. *(45 version)*
- (S) (4:49) K-Tel 3575 Hot, Hot Vacation Jams - Week One. *(LP version)*
- (S) (4:48) Madacy Entertainment 1988 Rock On 1988. *(LP version)*
- (S) (3:53) Madacy Entertainment 26927 Sun Splashin'. *(45 version)*
- (S) (4:49) Blue Note 53329 Best Of. *(LP version)*
- (S) (3:53) Time-Life R988-31 Sounds Of The Eighties: Cinemax Movie Hits Of The '80s. *(45 version)*
- (S) (3:52) Matador/Capitol 23544 O.S.T. Welcome To Sarajevo. *(45 version)*
- (S) (4:48) Rebound 314520314 Reggae Dance Party II. *(LP version)*

MAUREEN McGOVERN
1973 THE MORNING AFTER
- (S) (2:20) Rhino 70758 Super Hits Of The 70's Volume 11.
- (S) (2:19) Curb 77337 Greatest Hits.
- (S) (2:20) Razor & Tie 22505 More Fabulous 70's Volume 2.
- (S) (2:17) Time-Life SUD-13 Superhits - 1973.
- (S) (2:20) Rhino 71868 Academy Award Winning Songs.
- (S) (2:18) Polygram Special Markets 314520271 Hits Of The 70's.
- (S) (2:18) Special Music/Essex 5036 Prom Night - The 70's.
- (S) (2:20) Rhino 72279 Academy Award Winning Songs Volume 4.

MAUREEN McGOVERN *(Continued)*

    (S)   (2:18)   LaserLight 12315 and 15936 The Wonder Years - Movin' On.
    (S)   (2:17)   Time-Life AM1-03 AM Gold - 1973.
    (S)   (2:20)   K-Tel 3911 Fantastic Volume 2.
    (S)   (2:20)   K-Tel 3914 Superstars Greatest Hits Volume 3.
    (S)   (2:18)   Time-Life R814-05 Love Songs.
    (S)   (2:18)   Rebound 314520519 Love At The Movies.
    (S)   (2:17)   Polygram Special Markets 314520456 #1 Radio Hits Of The 70's.

1979 DIFFERENT WORLDS

    (S)   (2:14)   Curb 77317 70's Hits Volume 1.
    (S)   (2:14)   Curb 77337 Greatest Hits.
    (S)   (2:15)   Rhino 71911 Tube Tunes Volume Two - The 70's & 80's.
    (S)   (2:14)   Madacy Entertainment 1979 Rock On 1979.

TIM McGRAW
1994 INDIAN OUTLAW

    (S)   (3:00)   Curb 77659 Not A Moment Too Soon.

1994 DON'T TAKE THE GIRL

    (S)   (4:09)   Curb 77659 Not A Moment Too Soon.

1995 I LIKE IT, I LOVE IT

    (S)   (3:23)   Curb 77800 All I Want.

released as by TIM McGRAW with FAITH HILL:
1997 IT'S YOUR LOVE

    (S)   (3:44)   Curb 77886 Everywhere.

JIMMY McGRIFF
1962 I'VE GOT A WOMAN (PART 1)

    (M)   (2:26)   Collectables 5123 Best Of Sue Records.
    (E)   (4:35)   Collectables 5125 Golden Classics. *(mastered from a scratchy record; Parts 1 & 2)*
    (M)   (2:32)   EMI 80932 Sue Records Story.
    (E)   (2:23)   Hip-O 40008 Soulful Grooves - R&B Instrumental Classics Volume 2.
    (M)   (4:30)   Collectables 5752 I've Got A Woman. *(Parts 1 & 2)*

McGUINN, CLARK & HILLMAN
1979 DON'T YOU WRITE HER OFF

    (S)   (3:16)   Capitol 96355 McGuinn, Clark & Hillman.

McGUINNESS FLINT
1971 WHEN I'M DEAD AND GONE

    (S)   (3:38)   EMI-Capitol Music Special Markets 19545 Lost Hits Of The '70s.

BARRY McGUIRE
1965 EVE OF DESTRUCTION

    (S)   (3:35)   Rhino 70734 Songs Of Protest. *(lots of tape hiss; noisy introduction)*
    (S)   (3:35)   Rhino 70626 Billboard's Top Rock & Roll Hits Of 1965. *(noisy introduction)*
    (S)   (3:35)   Rhino 72007 Billboard's Top Rock & Roll Hits 1962-1966 Box Set. *(noisy introduction)*
    (S)   (3:35)   Motown 6161 The Good-Feeling Music Of The Big Chill Generation Volume 3. *(noisy introduction)*
    (S)   (3:32)   MCA 31206 Vintage Music Volume 9. *(noisy introduction)*
    (S)   (3:32)   MCA 5806 Vintage Music Volumes 9 & 10. *(noisy introduction)*
    (S)   (3:33)   Priority 53701 Best Of The 60's & 70's Rock: Protest Rock. *(noisy introduction)*
    (S)   (3:35)   One Way 22094 Anthology. *(lots of tape hiss; noisy introduction)*
    (S)   (3:32)   Time-Life 2CLR-08 Classic Rock - 1965: The Beat Goes On. *(noisy introduction)*
    (S)   (3:33)   Time-Life R962-02 History Of Rock 'N' Roll: Folk Rock 1964-1967. *(lots of tape hiss; noisy introduction)*
    (S)   (3:33)   Risky Business 53919 Songs Of Peacemakers, Protesters And Potheads. *(noisy introduction)*
    (S)   (3:32)   MCA Special Products 22131 Vintage Collectibles Volume 2. *(noisy introduction)*

    (S)   (3:32)   K-Tel 3438 Best Of Folk Rock. *(noisy introduction)*
    (S)   (3:33)   MCA Special Products 20948 Biggest Summer Hits. *(noisy introduction)*
    (S)   (3:32)   MCA Special Products 20958 Mellow Classics. *(noisy introduction)*
    (S)   (3:33)   JCI 3167 #1 Radio Hits 1965 - Only Rock 'n Roll - 1969. *(noisy introduction)*
    (S)   (3:32)   MCA Special Products 21017 The Rockin' Sixties. *(noisy introduction)*
    (S)   (3:32)   MCA Special Products 21046 Top Singles Of The Sixties. *(very noisy introduction)*

McGUIRE SISTERS
1955 SINCERELY

    (M)   (2:58)   MCA 31341 Greatest Hits.
    (M)   (2:57)   Time-Life HPD-09 Your Hit Parade 1955.
    (M)   (2:57)   Rhino 71580 Billboard Pop Memories 1955-1959.
    (M)   (2:57)   JCI 7014 Those Wonderful Years - Mr. Sandman.
    (M)   (2:57)   Time-Life R132-12 Your Hit Parade - #1 Hits Of The '50s.
    (E)   (2:57)   MCA Special Products 21022 McGuire Sisters/Andrews Sisters Back To Back.

1955 SOMETHING'S GOTTA GIVE

    (M)   (2:51)   MCA 31341 Greatest Hits.

1955 HE

    (M)   (2:34)   MCA 31341 Greatest Hits.

1956 PICNIC

    (M)   (2:43)   MCA 31341 Greatest Hits.

1956 EV'RY DAY OF MY LIFE

    (M)   (2:37)   MCA 31341 Greatest Hits.

1957 GOODNIGHT MY LOVE, PLEASANT DREAMS

    (M)   (2:55)   Nick At Nite/550 Music/Epic 67768 Fonzie's Make Out Music.

1958 SUGARTIME

    (M)   (2:31)   MCA 31200 Vintage Music Volume 3. *(numerous dropouts)*
    (M)   (2:31)   MCA 5778 Vintage Music Volumes 3 & 4. *(numerous dropouts)*
    (M)   (2:31)   MCA 31341 Greatest Hits. *(numerous dropouts)*
    (M)   (2:32)   Time-Life HPD-11 Your Hit Parade 1958.
    (M)   (2:31)   JCI 7021 Those Wonderful Years - April Love. *(numerous dropouts)*
    (E)   (2:31)   MCA Special Products 21022 McGuire Sisters/Andrews Sisters Back To Back. *(numerous dropouts)*
    (M)   (2:31)   Time-Life R132-14 Golden Groups Of Your Hit Parade.

1958 DING DONG
1959 MAY YOU ALWAYS

    (S)   (2:56)   MCA 31341 Greatest Hits.
    (M)   (2:56)   Time-Life HPD-23 Your Hit Parade - The Late 50's.
    (S)   (2:56)   MCA Special Products 21022 McGuire Sisters/Andrews Sisters Back To Back.

1961 JUST FOR OLD TIME'S SAKE

    (S)   (2:48)   MCA 31341 Greatest Hits. *(hum noticeable on fadeout)*
    (S)   (2:48)   Time-Life HPD-37 Your Hit Parade - The 60's.

M.C. HAMMER
1990 YOU CAN'T TOUCH THIS

    (S)   (4:16)   Foundation/Capitol 96426 Hearts Of Gold: The Rap Collection.
    (S)   (4:16)   Capitol 92857 Please Hammer Don't Hurt 'Em.
    (S)   (4:14)   Capitol 54074 Greatest Hits.
    (S)   (4:16)   Street Life 75510 West Coast Collection, Volume 1.
    (S)   (4:15)   K-Tel 3847 90s Now Volume 1.
    (S)   (4:13)   K-Tel 4046 More Music For Your Party.

1990 HAVE YOU SEEN HER

    (S)   (4:41)   Capitol 92857 Please Hammer Don't Hurt 'Em.
    (S)   (4:41)   Capitol 54074 Greatest Hits.
    (S)   (4:41)   K-Tel 3849 90s Now Volume 4.

1990 PRAY

    (S)   (5:12)   Capitol 92857 Please Hammer Don't Hurt 'Em.
    (S)   (4:07)   JCI 3132 1990 - Only Rock 'n Roll - 1994. *(radio station edit)*
    (S)   (5:11)   Capitol 54074 Greatest Hits.

released as by HAMMER:
1992 2 LEGIT 2 QUIT
    (S) (5:33) Capitol 98151 Too Legit To Quit.
    (S) (5:34) Capitol 54074 Greatest Hits.
    (S) (5:01) Razor & Tie 4569 '90s Style.
1992 ADDAMS GROOVE
    (S) (3:56) Capitol 54074 Greatest Hits.
1994 PUMPS AND A BUMP
    (S) (5:05) Giant 24545 The Funky Headhunter.

BOB & DOUG McKENZIE
1982 TAKE OFF
    (S) (2:43) Priority 53747 Wild & Crazy Tunes. *(45 version)*
    (S) (4:43) Mercury 314534010 Best Of. *(LP version)*

SCOTT McKENZIE
1967 SAN FRANCISCO (BE SURE TO WEAR FLOWERS IN
     YOUR HAIR)
     (the commercial 45's were pressed in two completely
     different mixes)
    (S) (2:57) Columbia/Legacy 46983 Rock Artifacts Volume 3.
    (M) (2:58) Rhino 71065 Summer Of Love Volume 1. *(hum*
                 noticeable on fadeout)
    (S) (2:56) Time-Life 2CLR-05 Classic Rock - 1967.
    (S) (2:56) Time-Life R962-04 History Of Rock 'N' Roll:
                 California Pop 1963-1967.
    (M) (2:57) Epic 66329 O.S.T. Forrest Gump.
    (S) (2:56) Risky Business 53919 Songs Of Peacemakers,
                 Protesters And Potheads.
    (S) (2:58) Rhino 71937 Billboard Top Pop Hits, 1967.
    (S) (2:56) JCI 3160 18 Free & Easy Hits From The 60's.
    (S) (2:56) Simitar 55532 The Number One's: The '60s.
1967 LIKE AN OLD TIME MOVIE
    (S) (3:14) Columbia/Legacy 46983 Rock Artifacts Volume 3.

BRIAN McKNIGHT
released as by VANESSA WILLIAMS & BRIAN McKNIGHT:
1993 LOVE IS
    (S) (4:44) Giant 24465 Beverly Hills, 90210 - The
                 Soundtrack.
    (S) (4:44) Foundation/RCA 66563 Number 1 Hit Mix.
released as by BRIAN McKNIGHT:
1993 ONE LAST CRY
    (S) (4:54) Mercury 848605 Brian McKnight.
    (S) (4:54) Rebound 314520439 Soul Classics - Best Of The 90's.
    (S) (4:55) Beast 53012 Smooth Love Of The 90's Vol. 1.
released as by BRIAN McKNIGHT featuring MASE:
1997 YOU SHOULD BE MINE (DON'T WASTE YOUR TIME)
    (S) (4:47) Mercury 314536215 Brian McKnight - Anythime.

SARAH McLACHLAN
1997 BUILDING A MYSTERY
    (S) (4:05) Arista 18970 Surfacing.

TOMMY McLAIN
1966 SWEET DREAMS
    (M) (3:19) LaserLight 12318 Chart Busters.
    (M) (3:22) Time-Life R857-20 The Heart Of Rock 'n' Roll
                 1965-1966.

DON McLEAN
1972 AMERICAN PIE (PARTS 1 & 2)
     (dj copies of this 45 ran (4:21); commercial copies were
     split into side 1 (4:11) and side 2 (4:31); the dj 45 was
     not the same as the commercial 45)
    (S) (8:23) MCA 6340 O.S.T. Born On The Fourth Of July.
                 (LP version)
    (S) (8:33) EMI 46555 American Pie. *(LP version)*
    (S) (8:33) EMI 91476 Best Of. *(LP version)*
    (S) (8:31) EMI 46586 Greatest Hits: Then & Now. *(LP version)*
    (S) (8:33) Curb 77547 Classics. *(LP version)*
    (S) (8:56) Curb 77547 Classics. *(rerecording)*
    (S) (8:31) EMI 81128 Rock Is Dead But It Won't Lie Down.
                 (LP version)

    (S) (8:32) EMI 98603 Favorites And Rarities. *(LP version)*
    (S) (4:05) JCI 3130 1970 - Only Rock 'N Roll - 1974. *(Part*
                 1 of the commercial 45)
    (S) (4:07) EMI 35974 American Pie & Other Hits. *(Part 1*
                 of the commercial 45)
    (S) (8:31) Collectables 1516 and 2516 The Anniversary
                 Album - The 70's. *(LP version)*
    (S) (4:07) K-Tel 4065 K-Tel's Original Party Music Vol. 1.
                 (Part 1 of the commercial 45)
1972 VINCENT
    (S) (3:58) EMI 46555 American Pie.
    (S) (3:58) EMI 91476 Best Of.
    (S) (3:58) EMI 46586 Greatest Hits: Then & Now.
    (S) (5:16) Curb 77547 Classics. *(rerecording)*
    (S) (3:58) Priority 53706 Singers/Songwriters/70's Greatest
                 Rock Hits Volume 15.
    (S) (3:58) EMI 98603 Favorites And Rarities.
    (S) (3:57) Time-Life SUD-16 Superhits - The Early 70's.
    (S) (3:57) Time-Life R105-26 Our Songs: Singers &
                 Songwriters Encore.
    (S) (4:01) Rhino 71843 Troubadours Of The Folk Era Vol. 4.
    (S) (3:58) EMI 35974 American Pie & Other Hits.
    (S) (3:57) JCI 3145 1970 - Only Love - 1974.
    (S) (3:57) Rhino 72519 Mellow Rock Hits Of The 70's -
                 Sundown.
    (S) (3:57) Time-Life AM1-13 AM Gold - The Early '70s.
1973 DREIDEL
    (S) (3:44) EMI 91476 Best Of.
    (S) (3:44) EMI 98603 Favorites And Rarities.
    (S) (3:43) EMI 35974 American Pie & Other Hits.
1981 CRYING
    (S) (3:39) EMI 46586 Greatest Hits: Then & Now.
    (S) (3:39) EMI 98603 Favorites And Rarities.
    (S) (3:39) EMI 91476 Best Of.
    (S) (3:47) Curb 77547 Classics. *(much slower than the 45*
                 or LP)
    (S) (3:39) Risky Business 66388 The Big Hurt/Songs To Cry
                 By.
    (S) (3:39) Priority 53746 80's Greatest Rock Hits Vol. 12 -
                 Singers/Songwriters.
    (S) (3:39) Time-Life R988-08 Sounds Of The Eighties: 1981.
    (S) (3:47) JCI 3147 1980 - Only Love - 1984. *(much slower*
                 than the 45 or LP)
    (S) (3:47) Hip-O 40061 Chain Lightning. *(much slower*
                 than the 45 or LP)
    (S) (3:39) Time-Life R834-11 Body Talk - After Dark.
1981 SINCE I DON'T HAVE YOU
    (S) (2:32) EMI 98603 Favorites And Rarities.
    (S) (2:32) Curb 77547 Classics.
    (S) (2:33) Hip-O 40061 Chain Lightning.
1981 CASTLES IN THE AIR
    (S) (3:40) EMI 46586 Greatest Hits: Then & Now.
    (S) (3:40) EMI 98603 Favorites And Rarities.
    (S) (2:52) EMI 98603 Favorites And Rarities. *(original*
                 recording which was not the hit version)
    (S) (3:40) EMI 91476 Best Of.
    (S) (3:40) Curb 77547 Classics.
    (S) (2:53) EMI 35974 American Pie & Other Hits. *(original*
                 recording which was not the hit version)

PHIL McLEAN
1962 SMALL SAD SAM

MC LYTE
1993 RUFFNECK
    (S) (3:56) First Priority 92230 Ain't No Other.
    (S) (3:48) Elektra 62091 Maximum Rap.
1996 KEEP ON, KEEPIN' ON
    (S) (4:31) EastWest 61781 and 61952 Bad As I Wanna B.
    (S) (4:32) Flavor Unit/EastWest 61904 O.S.T. Sunset Park.
1997 COLD ROCK A PARTY
    (S) (4:17) EastWest 61781 and 61952 Bad As I Wanna B.
                 (LP version)
    (M) (3:29) Elektra 62088 Party Over Here '98. *(all tracks on*
                 this cd are segued together)

ROBIN McNAMARA
1970 LAY A LITTLE LOVIN' ON ME
    (S) (3:00) Rhino 70922 Super Hits Of The 70's Volume 2.
    (S) (3:00) Rhino 72009 Super Hits Of The 70's Volumes 1-4 Box Set.
    (S) (3:00) Time-Life SOD-32 Sounds Of The Seventies - AM Pop Classics.
    (S) (3:01) Varese Sarabande 5719 Bubblegum Classics Volume Three.

CLYDE McPHATTER
1956 TREASURE OF LOVE
    (M) (2:07) Rhino 70642 Billboard's Top R&B Hits Of 1956.
    (M) (2:07) Atlantic 81295 Atlantic Rhythm & Blues Volume 3.
    (M) (2:08) Curb 77417 Greatest Hits.
    (M) (2:08) Atlantic 82314 Deep Sea Ball.
    (M) (2:08) Atlantic 82305 Atlantic Rhythm And Blues 1947-1974 Box Set.
    (M) (2:07) Time-Life 2RNR-14 Rock 'N' Roll Era - 1956.
    (M) (2:07) Time-Life RHD-05 Rhythm & Blues - 1956.
    (M) (2:07) Rhino 72417 Rockin' & Driftin' The Drifters Box Set.
    (M) (2:07) JCI 3165 #1 Radio Hits 1955 - Only Rock 'n Roll - 1959.
    (M) (2:07) Time-Life R857-13 The Heart Of Rock 'n' Roll 1956-1957.
    (M) (2:07) Time-Life R857-07 The Heart Of Rock 'n' Roll 1956.
    (M) (2:08) Flashback 72708 Treasure Of Love And Other Hits.
    (M) (2:08) Flashback 72085 '50s R&B Golden Archives Box Set.
    (M) (2:07) Time-Life R838-24 Solid Gold Soul 1956.
1957 WITHOUT LOVE (THERE IS NOTHING)
    (M) (2:55) Atlantic 82305 Atlantic Rhythm And Blues 1947-1974 Box Set. *(dropout on the opening)*
    (M) (2:55) Time-Life 2RNR-17 The Rock 'N' Roll Era - 1957: Still Rockin'. *(dropout on the opening)*
    (M) (2:55) Atlantic 81295 Atlantic Rhythm & Blues Volume 3. *(dropout on the opening)*
    (M) (2:55) Atlantic 82314 Deep Sea Ball. *(dropout on the opening)*
    (M) (2:55) Curb 77417 Greatest Hits. *(dropout on the opening)*
    (M) (2:54) Rhino 72417 Rockin' & Driftin' The Drifters Box Set.
    (M) (2:55) Flashback 72708 Treasure Of Love And Other Hits. *(dropout on the opening)*
    (M) (2:55) Flashback 72085 '50s R&B Golden Archives Box Set. *(dropout on the opening)*
    (S) (4:06) Collectables 5692 The Mercury Sessions. *(live)*
    (M) (2:54) Rhino 72961 Ultimate '50s R&B Smashes!
    (M) (2:55) Time-Life R857-16 The Heart Of Rock 'n' Roll The Late '50s. *(dropout on the opening)*
1957 JUST TO HOLD MY HAND
    (M) (2:21) Atlantic 82314 Deep Sea Ball.
1957 LONG LONELY NIGHTS
    (M) (2:22) Atlantic 82314 Deep Sea Ball.
    (M) (2:22) Atlantic 82305 Atlantic Rhythm And Blues 1947-1974 Box Set.
    (M) (2:24) Rhino 72417 Rockin' & Driftin' The Drifters Box Set.
    (M) (2:22) Flashback 72708 Treasure Of Love And Other Hits.
    (M) (2:22) Flashback 72085 '50s R&B Golden Archives Box Set.
1959 A LOVER'S QUESTION
    (M) (2:32) Atlantic 81295 Atlantic Rhythm & Blues Volume 3.
    (M) (2:32) Curb 77417 Greatest Hits.
    (M) (2:33) Atlantic 82314 Deep Sea Ball.
    (M) (2:33) Atlantic 82305 Atlantic Rhythm And Blues 1947-1974 Box Set.
    (M) (2:32) Time-Life 2RNR-13 Rock 'N' Roll Era - 1959.
    (S) (2:29) Time-Life RHD-16 Rhythm & Blues - 1958.
    (M) (2:32) Rhino 71806 The R&B Box: Thirty Years Of Rhythm & Blues.

    (M) (2:32) Rhino 72157 Doo Wop Memories, Vol. 2.
    (M) (2:32) Rhino 72417 Rockin' & Driftin' The Drifters Box Set.
    (M) (2:32) JCI 3183 1955 - Only Love - 1959.
    (M) (2:32) Time-Life R857-11 The Heart Of Rock 'n' Roll 1958-1959.
    (M) (2:32) Flashback 72717 Doo Wop - Blue Moon.
    (M) (2:33) Flashback 72708 Treasure Of Love And Other Hits.
    (M) (2:33) Flashback 72085 '50s R&B Golden Archives Box Set.
    (S) (2:56) Collectables 5692 The Mercury Sessions. *(live)*
    (S) (2:29) Time-Life R838-22 Solid Gold Soul 1958.
1959 SINCE YOU'VE BEEN GONE
    (M) (2:25) Atlantic 82314 Deep Sea Ball.
    (M) (2:25) Flashback 72708 Treasure Of Love And Other Hits.
    (M) (2:25) Flashback 72085 '50s R&B Golden Archives Box Set.
1960 TA TA
    (S) (2:13) Mercury 838243 Mercury R&B '46 - '62.
    (M) (2:12) Curb 77417 Greatest Hits.
    (S) (2:13) Time-Life 2RNR-40 Rock 'N' Roll Era - The 60's Teen Time.
    (M) (2:12) Polygram Special Markets 314520264 Soul Hits Of The 60's.
    (S) (2:11) Eric 11502 Hard To Find 45's On CD (Volume I) 1955-60.
    (S) (1:57) Collectables 5692 The Mercury Sessions. *(live)*
1962 LOVER PLEASE
    (S) (1:54) Mercury 838243 Mercury R&B '46 - '62. *(missing the echo on the handclaps)*
    (S) (1:54) JCI 3204 Heart & Soul Fifties. *(missing the echo on the handclaps; no high end)*
    (M) (1:45) Curb 77417 Greatest Hits.
    (S) (1:54) Time-Life 2RNR-02 Rock 'N' Roll Era - 1962. *(missing the echo on the handclaps)*
    (M) (1:52) Rhino 72417 Rockin' & Driftin' The Drifters Box Set.
    (S) (1:54) Eric 11503 Hard To Find 45's On CD (Volume II) 1961-64. *(missing the echo on the handclaps)*
    (S) (1:54) Eclipse Music Group 64868 Rock 'n Roll Relix 1962-1963. *(missing the echo on the handclaps)*
    (S) (1:54) Eclipse Music Group 64872 Rock 'n Roll Relix 1960-1969. *(missing the echo on the handclaps)*
    (S) (1:55) Polygram Special Markets 314520454 Soul Hits Of The 60's. *(missing the echo on the handclaps)*
1962 LITTLE BITTY PRETTY ONE
    (S) (2:14) Mercury 838243 Mercury R&B '46 - '62.
    (M) (2:10) Curb 77417 Greatest Hits.
    (S) (2:15) Special Music/Essex 5035 Prom Night - The 60's.

CHRISTINE McVIE
1984 GOT A HOLD ON ME
    (S) (3:43) JCI 2720 Rockin' Ladies Of The 80's. *(faded :08 sooner than the 45 or LP)*
    (S) (3:51) Warner Brothers 25059 Christine McVie.
    (S) (3:48) JCI 3193 18 Rock Classics Volume 3.
1984 LOVE WILL SHOW US HOW
    (S) (4:12) Warner Brothers 25059 Christine McVie.

SISTER JANET MEAD
1974 THE LORD'S PRAYER
    (S) (2:53) Rhino 70759 Super Hits Of The 70's Volume 12.

MEATLOAF
1978 TWO OUT OF THREE AIN'T BAD
(dj copies of this 45 ran (3:50) and (4:26); commercial copies ran (3:50) and (5:23); the actual time is (3:58) not (3:50) as stated on the record label)
    (S) (5:23) Epic 34974 and 57443 Bat Out Of Hell.
    (S) (5:23) Razor & Tie 22502 Those Rocking 70's.
    (S) (5:22) Time-Life SOD-10 Sounds Of The Seventies - 1978.
    (S) (5:22) Time-Life R105-40 Rock Dreams.
    (S) (5:23) Risky Business 66662 Swingin' Singles/Greatest Hits Of The 70's.

(S) (5:23) Cleveland International/Epic 57615 Hits Out Of Hell.
(S) (5:23) Epic/Legacy 64404 Bat Out Of Hell. *(gold disc)*
(S) (3:57) Madacy Entertainment 6806 Best Of Love.
(S) (5:22) Time-Life R834-16 Body Talk - Sweet Nothings.

1978 PARADISE BY THE DASHBOARD LIGHT
(S) (8:27) Epic 34974 and 57443 Bat Out Of Hell. *(LP version)*
(S) (8:28) Rhino 71549 Let There Be Drums Vol. 3: The 70's. *(LP version)*
(S) (8:22) MCA 10671 Leap Of Faith. *(LP version)*
(S) (8:28) Cleveland International/Epic 57615 Hits Out Of Hell. *(LP version)*
(S) (8:27) Epic/Legacy 65020 Ultimate Rock 'n' Roll Collection. *(LP version)*
(S) (8:27) Eclipse Music Group 64896 Rock 'n Roll Relix 1978-1979. *(LP version)*
(S) (8:27) Eclipse Music Group 64897 Rock 'n Roll Relix 1970-1979. *(LP version)*
(S) (8:27) Epic/Legacy 64404 Bat Out Of Hell. *(gold disc; LP version)*
(S) (5:29) Sony Music Special Products 26069 Rock Hits Of The 70's. *(highly edited)*

1993 I'D DO ANYTHING FOR LOVE (BUT I WON'T DO THAT)
(S) (11:58) MCA 10699 and 10971 Bat Out Of Hell II. *(LP version)*
(S) (5:13) Time-Life R13610 Gold And Platinum Box Set - The Ultimate Rock Collection. *(45 version)*

1994 ROCK AND ROLL DREAMS COME THROUGH
(S) (5:49) MCA 10699 and 10971 Bat Out Of Hell II.

1994 OBJECTS IN THE REAR VIEW MIRROR MAY APPEAR CLOSER THAN THEY ARE
(S) (10:14) MCA 10699 and 10971 Bat Out Of Hell II. *(LP version)*

1995 I'D LIE FOR YOU (AND THAT'S THE TRUTH)
(S) (6:40) MCA 11341 Welcome To The Neighborhood.

MECO
1977 STAR WARS THEME/CANTINA BAND
(S) (3:33) Rhino 71201 Super Hits Of The 70's Volume 21. *(dropouts at 1:37, 2:18 and 3:24)*
(S) (7:34) Casablanca 314516918 Casablanca Records Story. *(promotional only 12" single version)*
(S) (6:22) Rebound 314520219 Disco Nights Vol. 3 - Best Of Eurodisco.
(S) (6:22) Rebound 314520366 Disco Nights Vol. 10 - Disco's Greatest Movie Hits.
(S) (3:31) Casablanca 314526253 Casablanca Records Greatest Hits. *(dropouts at 2:18 and 3:24)*
(S) (3:44) Casablanca 314553255 Best Of. *(45 version with LP introduction)*
(S) (3:33) Time-Life AM1-24 AM Gold - 1977. *(dropouts at 1:37; 2:18 and 3:24)*
(S) (3:43) Thump 4840 Flashback Disco. *(all selections on this cd are segued together; 45 version with LP introduction)*
(S) (3:33) Time-Life R840-07 Sounds Of The Seventies: '70s Dance Party 1976-1977. *(dropouts at 1:37, 2:18 and 3:24)*

1978 THEME FROM CLOSE ENCOUNTERS
(S) (3:00) Casablanca 314553255 Best Of.

1978 THEMES FROM THE WIZARD OF OZ
(S) (2:55) Casablanca 314553255 Best Of.

1980 EMPIRE STRIKES BACK
(S) (3:02) Rebound 314520318 Class Reunion 1980. *(45 version)*
(S) (3:01) Rhino 71893 Radio Daze: Pop Hits Of The 80's Volume Four. *(45 version)*
(S) (4:02) Casablanca 314553255 Best Of. *(EP version)*

1982 POP GOES THE MOVIES (PART 1)

GLENN MEDEIROS
1987 NOTHING'S GONNA CHANGE MY LOVE FOR YOU
(S) (3:49) Amherst 94401 Nothing's Gonna Change My Love For You.
(S) (3:48) Priority 53773 80's Greatest Rock Hits Volume II - Teen Idols.
(S) (3:47) Rhino 75217 Heartthrob Hits.
(S) (3:48) Time-Life R834-16 Body Talk - Sweet Nothings.

released as by GLENN MEDEIROS featuring BOBBY BROWN:
1990 SHE AIN'T WORTH IT
(S) (3:35) MCA 6399 Glenn Medeiros.
(S) (3:25) Priority 50934 Shut Up And Dance! The 90's Volume One. *(all selections on this cd are segued together)*

released as by GLENN MEDEIROS featuring RAY PARKER JR.:
1990 ALL I'M MISSING IS YOU
(S) (4:17) MCA 6399 Glenn Medeiros.

BILL MEDLEY
1968 BROWN EYED WOMAN
(S) (3:43) Rhino 71488 Righteous Brothers Anthology.
(S) (4:15) Curb 77522 Best Of The Righteous Brothers. *(rerecorded)*
(S) (4:15) Curb 77307 Best Of. *(rerecorded)*
(S) (4:15) MCA/Curb 42257 Best Of. *(rerecorded)*

released as by BILL MEDLEY and JENNIFER WARNES:
1987 (I'VE HAD) THE TIME OF MY LIFE
(S) (4:49) RCA 6408 O.S.T. Dirty Dancing.
(S) (4:44) Rhino 71868 Academy Award Winning Songs.
(S) (4:46) Curb 77307 and 42257 Best Of Bill Medley.
(S) (4:44) Rhino 72280 Academy Award Winning Songs Volume 5.
(S) (4:45) EMI-Capitol Music Group 54555 Movie Luv.

RANDY MEISNER
1980 DEEP INSIDE MY HEART
(actual 45 time is (3:24) not (3:34) as stated on the record label)
(S) (3:24) Epic 36748 One More Song.

1981 HEARTS ON FIRE
(S) (2:44) Epic 36748 One More Song.
(S) (2:44) Risky Business 66392 Get Into The Greed: Greatest Hits Of The 80's.
(S) (2:43) Rhino 71894 Radio Daze: Pop Hits Of The 80's Volume Five.

1982 NEVER BEEN IN LOVE

MEL and TIM
1969 BACKFIELD IN MOTION
(S) (2:30) Ripete 2392192 Beach Music Anthology Box Set.
(S) (2:30) Original Sound 8852 Oldies But Goodies Vol. 2. *(this compact disc uses the "Waring - fds" noise reduction process)*
(S) (2:30) Original Sound 2223 Oldies But Goodies Volumes 2,7,9,12 and 13 Box Set. *(this box set uses the "Waring - fds" noise reduction process)*
(S) (2:30) Original Sound 2500 Oldies But Goodies Volumes 1-15 Box Set. *(this box set uses the "Waring - fds" noise reduction process)*
(S) (2:29) Original Sound CDGO-8 Golden Oldies Volume. 8.
(S) (2:30) Collectables 5064 History Of Rock Volume 4.
(S) (2:29) Ripete 0001 Coolin' Out/24 Carolina Classics Volume 1.
(S) (2:30) Time-Life RHD-13 Rhythm & Blues - 1969.
(S) (2:30) Time-Life 2CLR-12 Classic Rock - 1969: The Beat Goes On.
(S) (2:30) JCI 3167 #1 Radio Hits 1965 - Only Rock 'n Roll - 1969.
(S) (2:32) Sundazed 6078 Good Guys Only Win In The Movies.
(S) (2:30) Time-Life R838-04 Solid Gold Soul - 1969.
(M) (2:29) Rhino 72815 Beg, Scream & Shout! The Big Ol' Box Of '60s Soul.
(M) (2:29) Flashback 72899 25 Years Of Soul - 1969.
(S) (2:32) Simitar 55522 The Number One's: Party Time.

1972 STARTING ALL OVER AGAIN
(dj copies of this 45 ran (3:20) and (3:55); actual commercial and dj 45 time is (3:51) not (3:55) as stated on the record label)
(S) (3:29) Stax 88005 Top Of The Stax. *(:09 longer fade than the dj 45 edit)*
(S) (3:32) Rhino 70789 Soul Hits Of The 70's Volume 9. *(:12 longer fade than the dj 45 edit)*

(S) (4:05) Stax 8574 Starting All Over Again. *(LP length)*

(S) (3:32) Time-Life RHD-20 Rhythm & Blues - 1972. *(:12 longer fade than the dj 45 edit)*

(S) (3:26) Time-Life SOD-22 Sounds Of The Seventies - Seventies Top Forty. *(:06 longer fade than the dj 45 edit)*

(S) (4:03) Rhino 71517 The Muscle Shoals Sound. *(LP length)*

(M) (3:48) Stax 4415 Complete Stax/Volt Soul Singles Volume 3 1972-1975.

(S) (3:36) Time-Life R103-18 Great Love Songs Of The '70s & '80s. *(:16 longer fade than the dj 45 edit)*

(S) (3:32) Time-Life R838-07 Solid Gold Soul - 1972. *(:12 longer fade than the dj 45 edit)*

MELANIE
released as by MELANIE with THE EDWIN HAWKINS SINGERS:
1970 LAY DOWN (CANDLES IN THE RAIN)

(S) (3:59) Rhino 70923 Super Hits Of The 70's Volume 3. *(:13 longer than the 45 and "Candles In The Rain" LP)*

(S) (3:59) Rhino 72009 Super Hits Of The 70's Volumes 1-4 Box Set. *(:13 longer than the 45 and "Candles In The Rain" LP)*

(S) (3:47) Pair 1202 Best Of Buddah.

(S) (3:45) Rhino 70991 Melanie - Best Of.

(S) (3:47) Pair 1203 Melanie - Best Of.

(S) (3:46) Pair 3302 Melanie -Candles In The Rain. *(truncated fade)*

(S) (3:45) Rhino 71206 70's Smash Hits Volume 2.

(S) (3:47) Pair 4915 Melanie - Best Of.

(S) (3:46) Essex 7060 The Buddah Box.

(S) (3:52) Time-Life SUD-04 Superhits - 1970.

(S) (3:47) Time-Life R103-33 Singers & Songwriters.

(S) (3:45) Time-Life R921-38 Get Together.

(S) (3:46) JCI 3130 1970 - Only Rock 'N Roll - 1974.

(S) (3:45) Buddah 49509 Melanie - Candles In The Rain.

(S) (3:47) Eclipse Music Group 64892 Rock 'n Roll Relix 1970-1971.

(S) (3:47) Eclipse Music Group 64897 Rock 'n Roll Relix 1970-1979.

(S) (3:52) Time-Life AM1-02 AM Gold - 1970.

(S) (3:45) Flashback 72682 '70s Radio Hits Volume 2.

(S) (3:45) Flashback 72090 '70s Radio Hits Box Set.

released as by MELANIE:
1970 PEACE WILL COME (ACCORDING TO PLAN)

(M) (3:18) Rhino 70991 Best Of. *(45 version)*

(E) (3:20) Pair 1203 Best Of. *(45 version)*

(S) (4:46) One Way 27648 Leftover Wine. *(LP version)*

1971 RUBY TUESDAY

(S) (4:34) Rhino 70991 Best Of.

(S) (4:35) Pair 1203 Best Of.

(S) (4:35) Pair 4915 Best Of.

(S) (4:36) Buddah 49509 Candles In The Rain.

1971 BRAND NEW KEY

(S) (2:23) Rhino 70991 Best Of.

(S) (2:22) Rhino 70927 Super Hits Of The 70's Volume 7.

(S) (2:23) Rhino 71210 70's Smash Hits Volume 6.

(S) (2:22) Razor & Tie 22505 More Fabulous 70's Volume 2.

(S) (2:23) K-Tel 3454 70s Folk Rock Hits.

(S) (2:22) Time-Life AM1-06 AM Gold - 1971.

(S) (2:22) Time-Life R840-03 Sounds Of The Seventies - Pop Nuggets: Early '70s.

(S) (2:23) Flashback 72686 '70s Radio Hits Volume 6.

(S) (2:23) Capitol 56312 O.S.T. Boogie Nights.

(S) (2:23) BMG Special Products 44643 The Best Of Buddah.

1972 RING THE LIVING BELL

(S) (5:01) Rhino 70991 Best Of. *(LP version)*

1972 THE NICKEL SONG

(S) (3:43) Rhino 70991 Best Of.

(S) (3:48) Pair 1203 Best Of.

(S) (3:48) Pair 4915 Best Of.

1973 BITTER BAD

(S) (2:29) Rhino 70991 Best Of.

JOHN COUGAR MELLENCAMP
released as by JOHN COUGAR:
1979 I NEED A LOVER
(dj copies of this 45 ran (3:40) and (5:35); commercial copies were all (3:40))

(S) (5:35) Riva 7401 and 814995 John Cougar. *(LP version)*

(S) (5:35) Mercury 314536738 The Best That I Could Do 1978-1988. *(LP version)*

1980 THIS TIME
(dj copies of this 45 ran (3:56) and (4:18); commercial copies were all (4:18))

(S) (4:17) Riva 7403 and 814994 Nothin' Matters And What If It Did.

1981 AIN'T EVEN DONE WITH THE NIGHT

(S) (4:35) Riva 7403 and 814994 Nothin' Matters And What If It Did. *(LP version)*

(S) (4:35) Mercury 314536738 The Best That I Could Do 1978-1988. *(LP version)*

1982 HURTS SO GOOD

(S) (3:38) Riva 7501 and 814993 American Fool.

(S) (3:36) Time-Life R13610 Gold And Platinum Box Set - The Ultimate Rock Collection.

(S) (3:38) Mercury 314536738 The Best That I Could Do 1978-1988.

1982 JACK & DIANE

(S) (4:14) Riva 7501 and 814993 American Fool.

(S) (4:13) Time-Life R988-26 Sounds Of The Eighties: The Rolling Stone Collection 1982-1983.

(S) (4:13) Mercury 314536738 The Best That I Could Do 1978-1988.

1983 HAND TO HOLD ON TO

(S) (3:23) Riva 7501 and 814993 American Fool.

released as by JOHN COUGAR MELLENCAMP:
1983 CRUMBLIN' DOWN

(S) (3:34) Riva 7504 and 814450 Uh-Huh.

(S) (3:33) Mercury 314536738 The Best That I Could Do 1978-1988.

1984 PINK HOUSES
(dj copies of this 45 ran (3:59) and (4:43); commercial copies were all (4:43))

(S) (5:03) Polydor 314515913 Classic Rock Box. *(live)*

(S) (4:43) Riva 7504 and 814450 Uh-Huh.

(S) (4:42) Mercury 314536738 The Best That I Could Do 1978-1988.

1984 AUTHORITY SONG

(S) (3:48) Riva 7504 and 814450 Uh-Huh.

(S) (3:47) Mercury 314536738 The Best That I Could Do 1978-1988.

1985 LONELY OL' NIGHT

(S) (3:43) Riva 824865 Scarecrow.

(S) (3:43) MFSL 604 Scarecrow. *(gold disc)*

(S) (3:44) Mercury 314536738 The Best That I Could Do 1978-1988.

1986 SMALL TOWN

(S) (3:40) Riva 824865 Scarecrow.

(S) (3:40) MFSL 604 Scarecrow. *(gold disc)*

(S) (3:40) Mercury 314536738 The Best That I Could Do 1978-1988.

1986 R.O.C.K. IN THE U.S.A.

(S) (2:54) Foundation/RCA 66109 The Ultimate Rock Album. *(LP version)*

(S) (2:53) Riva 824865 Scarecrow. *(LP version)*

(S) (2:53) MFSL 604 Scarecrow. *(LP version; gold disc)*

(S) (2:53) Mercury 314536738 The Best That I Could Do 1978-1988.

1986 RAIN ON THE SCARECROW

(S) (3:41) Time-Life R102-34 The Rolling Stone Collection.

(S) (3:44) Riva 824865 Scarecrow.

(S) (3:44) MFSL 604 Scarecrow. *(gold disc)*

1986 RUMBLESEAT

(S) (2:56) Riva 824865 Scarecrow.

(S) (2:56) MFSL 604 Scarecrow. *(gold disc)*

1987 PAPER IN FIRE

(S) (3:48) Mercury 832465 The Lonesome Jubilee.

(S) (3:48) MFSL 634 The Lonesome Jubilee. *(gold disc)*

(S) (3:48) Time-Life R988-29 Sounds Of The Eighties: The Rolling Stone Collection 1987-1988.

(S) (3:49) Mercury 314536738 The Best That I Could Do 1978-1988.

1987 CHERRY BOMB
(S) (4:46) Mercury 832465 The Lonesome Jubilee.

(S) (4:46) MFSL 634 The Lonesome Jubilee. *(gold disc)*

(S) (4:46) Mercury 314536738 The Best That I Could Do 1978-1988.

1988 CHECK IT OUT
(S) (4:19) Mercury 832465 The Lonesome Jubilee.

(S) (4:19) MFSL 634 The Lonesome Jubilee. *(gold disc)*

(S) (4:19) Mercury 314536738 The Best That I Could Do 1978-1988.

1989 POP SINGER
(S) (2:47) Mercury 838220 Big Daddy.

released as by JOHN MELLENCAMP:
1991 GET A LEG UP
(S) (3:47) Mercury 314501151 Whenever We Wanted.

1992 AGAIN TONIGHT
(S) (3:16) Mercury 314501151 Whenever We Wanted.

1993 HUMAN WHEELS
(S) (5:33) Mercury 314518088 Human Wheels.

released as by JOHN MELLENCAMP with ME'SHELL NDEGEOCELLO:
1994 WILD NIGHT
(S) (3:27) Mercury 314522428 and 314522664 Dance Naked.

released as by JOHN MELLENCAMP:
1996 KEY WEST INTERMEZZO (I SAW YOU FIRST)
(S) (4:54) Mercury 3145328962 and 314534169 Mr. Happy Go Lucky.

MELLO-TONES
1957 ROSIE LEE
(M) (2:50) Collectables 5463 The Spotlight Series - Gee Records Vol. 2.

MELLOW MAN ACE
1990 MENTIROSA
(S) (4:16) Priority 8657 Yo Rap Hits. *(very narrow stereo separation)*

(S) (4:16) Rebound 314520245 Disco Nights Vol. 6 - Disco Hits. *(very narrow stereo separation)*

(S) (4:16) Capitol 91295 Escape From Havana. *(very narrow stereo separation)*

(S) (4:16) Rhino 71923 Latin Lingo: Hip-Hop From The Raza. *(very narrow stereo separation)*

(S) (4:16) Coldfront 3501 Rap's Biggest Hits Volume II. *(very narrow stereo separation)*

(S) (4:15) Thump 9951 Power 106 10th Anniversary Collection. *(all songs on this cd are segued together; very narrow stereo separation)*

(S) (4:15) Priority 50921 Latin Hip Hop Flava. *(very narrow stereo separation)*

HAROLD MELVIN and THE BLUE NOTES
1972 IF YOU DON'T KNOW ME BY NOW
(S) (3:25) Rhino 70789 Soul Hits Of The 70's Volume 9.

(S) (3:25) Rhino 70660 Billboard's Top R&B Hits Of 1972.

(S) (3:25) Philadelphia International 39255 Philly Ballads Volume 1.

(S) (3:25) Epic 48732 O.S.T. My Girl.

(S) (3:25) Philadelphia International 34232 Collectors' Item.

(S) (3:25) Original Sound 8908 Best Love Songs Vol 3.

(S) (3:25) Original Sound 9327 Best Love Songs Vol. 3 & 4.

(S) (3:25) Original Sound 1236 Best Love Songs Box Set.

(S) (3:25) Rhino 71618 Soul Train Hall Of Fame/20th Anniversary.

(S) (3:24) Razor & Tie 22047 Sweet 70's Soul.

(S) (3:25) Time-Life SUD-16 Superhits - The Early 70's.

(S) (3:25) Time-Life SOD-13 Sounds Of The Seventies - 1972: Take Two.

(S) (3:25) Right Stuff 28372 Slow Jams: The 70's Volume Two.

(S) (3:25) Legacy/Epic 66338 Best Of.

(S) (3:21) K-Tel 3535 Slow Groove Love Jams Of The 70's.

(S) (3:25) Rhino 72114 Billboard Hot Soul Hits - 1972.

(S) (3:31) Scotti Bros. 75481 Quiet Storm Memories. *(rerecording)*

(S) (3:25) Thump 4730 Old School Love Songs Volume 3.

(S) (3:24) JCI 3145 1970 - Only Love - 1974.

(S) (3:25) Eclipse Music Group 64893 Rock 'n Roll Relix 1972-1973.

(S) (3:25) Eclipse Music Group 64897 Rock 'n Roll Relix 1970-1979.

(S) (3:25) Time-Life AM1-13 AM Gold - The Early '70s.

(S) (3:25) Time-Life R834-01 Body Talk - Forever Yours.

(S) (3:24) Epic/Legacy 64647 The Philly Sound Box Set.

(S) (4:06) Epic Associated/Legacy 65162 A Postcard From Philly. *(live)*

(S) (3:25) Epic Associated/Legacy 65365 Blue Notes & Ballads.

1973 THE LOVE I LOST (PART 1)
(S) (3:41) Rhino 70661 Billboard's Top R&B Hits Of 1973. *(45 version)*

(S) (3:37) Rhino 70552 Soul Hits Of The 70's Volume 12. *(45 version)*

(S) (6:22) Philadelphia International 34232 Collectors' Item. *(LP version; Parts 1 & 2)*

(S) (3:41) Time-Life SOD-27 Sounds Of The Seventies - Dance Fever. *(45 version)*

(S) (6:18) Epic 66155 Club Epic Volume 3. *(LP version; Parts 1 & 2; tracks into next selection)*

(S) (6:23) Legacy/Epic 66338 Best Of. *(LP version; Parts 1 & 2)*

(S) (3:37) Rhino 72115 Billboard Hot Soul Hits - 1973. *(45 version)*

(S) (3:41) Time-Life R838-08 Solid Gold Soul - 1973. *(45 version)*

(S) (6:22) Epic/Legacy 64647 The Philly Sound Box Set. *(LP version; Parts 1 & 2)*

(S) (6:22) Simitar 55602 The Number One's: Silky Soul. *(LP version; Parts 1 & 2)*

(S) (3:37) Time-Life R840-05 Sounds Of The Seventies: '70s Dance Party 1972-1974. *(45 version)*

1975 BAD LUCK (PART 1)
(S) (8:00) Philadelphia International 34940 Philadelphia Classics. *(this version first appeared on the "Philadelphia Classics" vinyl LP in 1977)*

(S) (3:15) Razor & Tie 22496 Disco Fever. *(45 version)*

(S) (6:23) Legacy/Epic 66338 Best Of. *(LP version)*

(S) (3:06) Rhino 72127 Soul Hits Of The 70's Vol. 17. *(45 version)*

(S) (3:13) Time-Life R838-10 Solid Gold Soul - 1975. *(45 version)*

(S) (6:24) Epic/Legacy 64647 The Philly Sound Box Set. *(LP version)*

1976 WAKE UP EVERYBODY (PART 1)
(dj copies of this 45 ran (3:09); commercial copies were all (3:39))
(S) (7:31) Philadelphia International 33808 Wake Up Everybody. *(LP version)*

(S) (7:30) Philadelphia International 34232 Collectors' Item. *(LP version)*

(S) (7:32) Legacy/Epic 66912 Legacy's Rhythm & Soul Revue. *(LP version)*

(S) (7:31) Legacy/Epic 66338 Best Of. *(LP version)*

(S) (7:29) Right Stuff 29669 Movin' On Up Vol. 2. *(LP version)*

(S) (3:39) Rhino 72128 Hot Soul Hits Of The 70's Vol. 18. *(45 version)*

(S) (7:31) DCC Compact Classics 143 Groove On! Volume 3. *(LP version)*

(S) (3:39) Time-Life R838-11 Solid Gold Soul - 1976. *(45 version)*

(S) (7:32) Epic/Legacy 64647 The Philly Sound Box Set. *(LP version)*

MEN AT LARGE
1993 SO ALONE
(S) (7:25) EastWest 92159 Men At Large.

MEN AT WORK
1982 WHO CAN IT BE NOW?
- (S) (3:21) Priority 53684 Rock Of The 80's Volume 4.
- (S) (3:20) Rhino 71699 New Wave Hits Of The 80's Vol. 6.
- (S) (3:20) Rhino 70677 Billboard Top Hits - 1982.
- (S) (3:20) Rhino 71590 O.S.T. Valley Girl.
- (S) (3:21) Columbia 37978 Business As Usual.
- (S) (3:20) Time-Life R988-05 Sounds Of The Eighties: 1982.
- (S) (3:20) Rhino 72491 New Wave Hits, Vol. 2.
- (S) (3:20) Columbia/Legacy 64791 Contraband: The Best Of.
- (S) (3:20) Flashback 72714 Ultimate New Wave Hits.
- (S) (3:20) Flashback 72092 New Wave Hits Box Set.

1983 DOWN UNDER
- (S) (3:35) Priority 53748 Rock Of The 80's Volume 8.
- (S) (3:41) Rhino 70678 Billboard Top Hits - 1983.
- (S) (3:41) Sandstone 33046 and 5012 Rock The First Volume Six.
- (S) (3:41) Columbia 37978 Business As Usual.
- (S) (3:41) Time-Life R988-01 Sounds Of The Eighties: The Rockin' Eighties.
- (S) (3:40) Columbia/Legacy 64791 Contraband: The Best Of.
- (S) (3:41) Rhino 72894 Hard Rock Cafe: New Wave.
- (S) (3:41) K-Tel 3866 The 80's: Number One Pop Hits.

1983 OVERKILL
- (S) (3:44) Priority 53749 Rock Of The 80's Volume 6.
- (S) (3:44) Columbia 38660 Cargo.
- (S) (3:43) Columbia/Legacy 64791 Contraband: The Best Of.
- (S) (3:44) Time-Life R988-16 Sounds Of The Eighties: The Early '80s.

1983 IT'S A MISTAKE
- (S) (4:30) Priority 53751 Rock Of The 80's Volume 13.
- (S) (4:32) Rhino 71978 New Wave Hits Of The 80's Vol. 15.
- (S) (4:32) Columbia 38660 Cargo.
- (S) (4:31) Columbia/Legacy 64791 Contraband: The Best Of.
- (S) (4:30) Risky Business 66396 Oldies But 80's: Best Of The 80's.
- (S) (4:30) Time-Life R988-18 Sounds Of The Eighties: The Early '80s Take Two.

1983 DR. HECKYLL & MR. JIVE
- (S) (4:38) Columbia 38660 Cargo. *(LP version)*
- (S) (4:35) Risky Business 67307 Wave Goodbye To The 80's. *(LP version)*
- (S) (4:36) Columbia/Legacy 64791 Contraband: The Best Of. *(LP version)*

SERGIO MENDES & BRASIL '66
1968 THE LOOK OF LOVE
- (S) (2:41) A&M 6012 Four Sider.
- (S) (2:39) A&M 2516 Classics Volume 18.
- (S) (2:41) A&M 3258 Greatest Hits.
- (S) (2:38) Time-Life SUD-02 Superhits - 1968.
- (S) (2:40) Chronicles 314535882 Lounge Music Goes Latin.
- (S) (2:38) Time-Life AM1-04 AM Gold - 1968.
- (S) (2:38) Time-Life R814-04 Love Songs.

1968 THE FOOL ON THE HILL
- (S) (3:09) A&M 6012 Four Sider.
- (S) (3:10) A&M 2516 Classics Volume 18.
- (S) (3:13) A&M 3258 Greatest Hits.
- (S) (3:13) A&M 3108 Fool On The Hill.
- (S) (3:12) Rebound 314520296 Fool On The Hill.
- (S) (3:07) Chronicles 314535875 Bachelor Pad Favorites.

1968 SCARBOROUGH FAIR
- (S) (3:17) A&M 2516 Classics Volume 18.
- (S) (3:18) A&M 3258 Greatest Hits.
- (S) (3:17) A&M 3108 Fool On The Hill.
- (S) (3:17) Rebound 314520296 Fool On The Hill.

released as by SERGIO MENDES:
1983 NEVER GONNA LET YOU GO
- (S) (4:14) A&M 2516 Classics Volume 18.
- (S) (4:14) A&M 4937 Sergio Mendes.

- (S) (4:13) Madacy Entertainment 6803 Power Of Love.
- (S) (4:14) Time-Life R834-04 Body Talk - Together Forever.

1984 ALIBIS
- (S) (4:01) A&M 2516 Classics Volume 18.
- (S) (4:03) A&M 4984 Confetti.

MEN WITHOUT HATS
1983 THE SAFETY DANCE
(dj copies of this 45 ran (4:32) and (2:44); commercial copies were all (2:44))
- (S) (4:32) Sandstone 33043 and 5009 Rock The First Volume Three. *(LP version)*
- (S) (4:31) MCA Special Products 20897 Greatest Rock Hits Of The 80's. *(LP version)*
- (S) (2:43) Oglio 81587 Collection. *(45 version)*
- (S) (4:30) Oglio 81584 Hit That Perfect Beat Volume 2. *(12" single version; all songs on this cd are segued together)*
- (S) (2:43) Rhino 72771 The Big 80's. *(45 version)*
- (S) (4:33) Priority 50552 O.S.T. Bio-Dome. *(remix)*
- (S) (2:43) Hip-O 40004 The '80s Hit(s) Back! *(45 version)*

1988 POP GOES THE WORLD
- (S) (3:39) Priority 53767 Rock Of The 80's Volume 11.
- (S) (3:41) Mercury 832730 Pop Goes The World.
- (S) (3:43) Oglio 81587 Collection.
- (S) (3:44) Rebound 314520442 The Roots Of Rock: 80's New Wave.

NATALIE MERCHANT
1995 CARNIVAL
- (S) (5:57) Elektra 61745 Tigerlily.
1996 WONDER
- (S) (4:25) Elektra 61745 Tigerlily.
1996 JEALOUSY
- (S) (2:40) Elektra 61745 Tigerlily. *(LP version)*

MERCY
1969 LOVE (CAN MAKE YOU HAPPY)
- (S) (3:12) Rhino 70996 One Hit Wonders Of The 60's Volume 2. *(sounds like it was mastered from vinyl; Sundi version)*
- (S) (3:12) Time-Life SUD-07 Superhits - 1969. *(sounds like it was mastered from vinyl; Sundi version)*
- (M) (3:17) Collectables 2501 WCBS-FM History Of Rock - The 60's Part 2. *(mastered from vinyl; no fidelity; Sundi version)*
- (M) (3:17) Collectables 4501 History Of Rock/The 60s Part Two. *(mastered from vinyl; no fidelity; Sundi version)*
- (S) (3:12) Time-Life R921-38 Get Together. *(sounds like it was mastered from vinyl; Sundi version)*
- (S) (3:12) LaserLight 12318 Chart Busters. *(sounds like it was mastered from vinyl; Sundi version)*
- (S) (3:12) Time-Life AM1-01 AM Gold - 1969. *(sounds like it was mastered from vinyl; Sundi version)*
- (S) (3:12) MCA Special Products 20997 Mellow Rock. *(sounds like it was mastered from vinyl; Sundi version)*
- (S) (3:11) Varese Sarabande 5801 Sunshine Days - Pop Classics Of The '60s Volume 1. *(Sundi version)*
- (S) (3:12) Time-Life R814-03 Love Songs. *(sounds like it was mastered from vinyl; Sundi Version)*

METALLICA
1989 ONE
- (S) (7:23) Elektra 60812 ...And Justice For All. *(LP version)*
1991 ENTER SANDMAN
- (S) (5:30) Elektra 61113 Metallica.
1992 THE UNFORGIVEN
- (S) (6:24) Elektra 61113 Metallica.
1992 NOTHING ELSE MATTERS
- (S) (6:27) Elektra 61113 Metallica.
1996 UNTIL IT SLEEPS
- (S) (4:29) Elektra 61923 Load.
1997 THE MEMORY REMAINS
- (S) (4:37) Elektra 62126 Reload.

METERS
1969 SOPHISTICATED CISSY
- (S) (2:53) Rhino 71869 Anthology.
- (S) (2:53) Rhino 72642 Very Best Of.

1969 CISSY STRUT
- (S) (2:59) Rhino 75766 Best Of New Orleans Rhythm & Blues Volume 2.
- (S) (3:00) Ripete 2199 Walkin' To New Orleans.
- (S) (2:57) Time-Life RHD-13 Rhythm & Blues - 1969.
- (S) (2:59) Rhino 71615 In Yo Face! The Roots Of Funk Vol. 1/2.
- (S) (2:59) Rhino 71753 and 72830 Phat Trax: The Best Of Old School Volume 2.
- (S) (3:03) Rhino 71869 Anthology.
- (S) (3:01) EMI 37350 Crescent City Soul: The Sound Of New Orleans 1947-1974.
- (S) (2:57) Time-Life R838-04 Solid Gold Soul - 1969.
- (S) (3:03) Rhino 72642 Very Best Of.
- (M) (3:00) Rhino 72815 Beg, Scream & Shout! The Big Ol' Box Of '60s Soul.
- (S) (2:59) Flashback 72899 25 Years Of Soul - 1969.

METHOD MAN
released as by METHOD MAN/MARY J BLIGE:
1995 I'LL BE THERE FOR YOU/YOU'RE ALL I NEED TO GET BY
- (S) (5:06) Def Jam 314523848 Def Jam Music Group 10th Year Anniversary.
- (S) (4:48) Tommy Boy 1139 MTV Party To Go Volume 8. (all selections on this cd are segued together; remix)
- (S) (3:56) Rebound 314520449 Hip Hop With R&B Flava.

released as by REDMAN/METHOD MAN:
1995 HOW HIGH
- (M) (4:39) Def Jam 314529021 and 314529068 O.S.T. The Show.
- (M) (3:58) Def Jam 314523848 Def Jam Music Group 10th Year Anniversary.
- (M) (4:00) Rebound 314520449 Hip Hop With R&B Flava.
- (M) (3:56) Def Jam 314536377 Def Jam's Greatest Hits.

MFSB featuring THE THREE DEGREES
1974 TSOP (THE SOUND OF PHILADELPHIA)
- (S) (5:45) Philadelphia International 34940 Philadelphia Classics. (this version first appeared on the "Philadelphia Classics" vinyl LP released in 1977)
- (S) (3:40) Philadelphia International 39307 Ten Years Of Hits.
- (S) (3:34) Rhino 70552 Soul Hits Of The 70's Volume 12.
- (S) (3:34) Epic 57620 O.S.T. Carlito's Way.
- (S) (3:34) Rhino 71603 Rock Instrumental Classics Volume 3: The Seventies.
- (S) (3:34) Rhino 72035 Rock Instrumental Classics Vols. 1-5 Box Set.
- (S) (3:34) Rhino 71618 Soul Train Hall Of Fame/20th Anniversary.
- (S) (3:34) Rhino 71549 Let There Be Drums Vol. 3: The 70's.
- (S) (3:40) Razor & Tie 22496 Disco Fever.
- (S) (3:32) Time-Life SOD-27 Sounds Of The Seventies - Dance Fever.
- (S) (3:34) Rhino 71910 Tube Tunes Volume One - The 70's.
- (S) (3:34) MCA 11329 Soul Train 25th Anniversary Box Set.
- (S) (3:34) Rhino 72116 Billboard Hot Soul Hits - 1974.
- (S) (3:40) Priority 53790 Disco Nice And Nasty.
- (S) (5:47) Epic Associated/Legacy 64915 Best Of The Three Degrees: When Will I See You Again. (this version first appeared on the "Philadelphia Classics" vinyl LP released in 1977)
- (S) (5:47) Legacy/Epic Associated 66689 Best Of MFSB: Love Is The Message. (this version first appeared on the "Philadelphia Classics" vinyl LP released in 1977)
- (S) (3:33) Eclipse Music Group 64894 Rock 'n Roll Relix 1974-1975.

- (S) (3:33) Eclipse Music Group 64897 Rock 'n Roll Relix 1970-1979.
- (S) (3:34) Time-Life R840-04 Sounds Of The Seventies: A Loss For Words.
- (S) (3:33) Time-Life AM1-21 AM Gold - 1974.
- (S) (3:34) Time-Life R838-09 Solid Gold Soul - 1974.
- (S) (5:47) Epic/Legacy 64647 The Philly Sound Box Set. (this version first appeared on the "Philadelphia Classics" vinyl LP released in 1977)
- (S) (5:47) Epic Associated/Legacy 65162 A Postcard From Philly. (this version first appeared on the "Philadelphia Classics" vinyl LP released in 1977)
- (S) (3:34) Time-Life R840-05 Sounds Of The Seventies: '70s Dance Party 1972-1974.

MIAMI SOUND MACHINE (see GLORIA ESTEFAN)

GEORGE MICHAEL (also WHAM!)
released as by WHAM!:
1984 WAKE ME UP BEFORE YOU GO-GO
- (S) (3:50) Priority 7054 80's Greatest Rock Hits Volume 4 - Party On.
- (S) (3:50) Rhino 70679 Billboard Top Hits - 1984.
- (S) (3:51) Columbia 39595 Make It Big.
- (S) (3:50) Time-Life R13610 Gold And Platinum Box Set - The Ultimate Rock Collection.

released as by WHAM! featuring GEORGE MICHAEL:
1985 CARELESS WHISPER
- (S) (4:59) T.J. Martell Foundation/Columbia 40315 Music For The Miracle. (45 version)
- (S) (6:28) Columbia 39595 Make It Big. (LP version)

released as by WHAM!:
1985 EVERYTHING SHE WANTS
- (S) (5:02) Priority 53714 80's Greatest Rock Hits Volume 1 - Passion & Power. (LP version)
- (S) (5:02) Columbia 39595 Make It Big. (LP version)

1985 FREEDOM
- (S) (5:02) Columbia 39595 Make It Big.

1986 I'M YOUR MAN
- (S) (6:04) Columbia 40285 Wham! - Music From The Edge Of Heaven. (LP version)
- (S) (6:51) Epic/Legacy 65035 Club Epic Volume 6. (12" single version)

released as by GEORGE MICHAEL:
1986 A DIFFERENT CORNER
- (S) (4:29) Columbia 40285 Wham! - Music From The Edge Of Heaven. (LP version)

released as by WHAM!:
1986 THE EDGE OF HEAVEN
- (S) (4:30) Columbia 40285 Wham! - Music From The Edge Of Heaven.

released as by ARETHA FRANKLIN and GEORGE MICHAEL:
1987 I KNEW YOU WERE WAITING (FOR ME)
- (S) (3:58) Rhino 71642 Billboard Top Hits - 1987.
- (S) (3:59) Arista 8442 Aretha.
- (S) (3:59) Arista 18722 Aretha Franklin - Greatest Hits (1980-1994).
- (S) (3:59) Time-Life R103-18 Great Love Songs Of The '70s & '80s.
- (S) (3:59) Time-Life R988-19 Sounds Of The Eighties: The Late '80s.
- (S) (3:59) Time-Life R834-02 Body Talk - Just For You.
- (S) (3:57) K-Tel 3868 Hot Ladies Of Pop.

released as by GEORGE MICHAEL:
1987 I WANT YOUR SEX
- (S) (4:44) MCA 6207 O.S.T. Beverly Hills Cop II. (45 version)
- (S) (9:13) Columbia 40867 Faith. (LP version)
- (S) (4:44) Time-Life R988-28 Sounds Of The Eighties: The Rolling Stone Collection 1986-1987. (45 version)

1987 FAITH
- (S) (3:15) Columbia 40867 Faith.
- (S) (3:12) Time-Life R13610 Gold And Platinum Box Set - The Ultimate Rock Collection.

1988 FATHER FIGURE
- (S) (5:36) Columbia 40867 Faith.

GEORGE MICHAEL (Continued)
- (S) (5:36) Time-Life R988-28 Sounds Of The Eighties: The Rolling Stone Collection 1986-1987.

1988 ONE MORE TRY
- (S) (5:48) Foundation/WEA 26097 Super Sessions Volume Two.
- (S) (5:49) Columbia 40867 Faith.

1988 MONKEY
- (S) (5:04) Columbia 40867 Faith. *(LP version)*

1988 KISSING A FOOL
- (S) (4:33) Columbia 40867 Faith.

released as by DEON ESTUS with GEORGE MICHAEL:
1989 HEAVEN HELP ME
- (S) (4:38) Mika/Polydor 835713 Deon Estus - Spell.
- (S) (4:37) Polydor 314535195 The Power Of Love - Best Of The "Soul Essentials" Ballads.

released as by GEORGE MICHAEL:
1990 PRAYING FOR TIME
- (S) (4:39) Foundation/Capitol 96427 Hearts Of Gold: The Pop Collection.
- (S) (4:40) Columbia 46898 Listen Without Prejudice Vol. 1.

1990 FREEDOM
- (S) (6:29) Columbia 46898 Listen Without Prejudice Vol. 1.

1991 WAITING FOR THAT DAY
- (S) (4:48) Columbia 46898 Listen Without Prejudice Vol. 1.

released as by GEORGE MICHAEL/ELTON JOHN:
1992 DON'T LET THE SUN GO DOWN ON ME
- (S) (5:45) Foundation/RCA 66104 Hot #1 Hits.
- (S) (5:46) MCA 10926 Elton John - Duets.
- (S) (5:46) MCA 11481 Elton John - Love Songs.

released as by GEORGE MICHAEL:
1992 TOO FUNKY
- (S) (5:36) Columbia 52826 Red Hot + Dance. *(LP version)*

released as by GEORGE MICHAEL and QUEEN:
1993 SOMEBODY TO LOVE
- (S) (5:16) Hollywood 61479 George Michael And Queen - Five Live.

released as by GEORGE MICHAEL:
1996 JESUS TO A CHILD
- (S) (6:50) DreamWorks 50000 Older.

1996 FASTLOVE
- (S) (5:24) DreamWorks 50000 Older.

LEE MICHAELS
1971 DO YOU KNOW WHAT I MEAN
- (S) (3:12) Rhino 70927 Super Hits Of The 70's Volume 7.
- (S) (3:12) DCC Compact Classics 045 Golden Age Of Underground Radio.
- (S) (3:12) Warner Special Products 27616 Classic Rock.
- (S) (3:12) Rhino 70374 Collection.
- (S) (3:12) Rhino 71209 70's Smash Hits Volume 5.
- (S) (3:11) Razor & Tie 22502 Those Rocking 70's.
- (S) (3:12) Time-Life SOD-02 Sounds Of The Seventies - 1971.
- (S) (3:12) Varese 5635 and 5654 and 5655 and 5657 Arrow: All Rock & Roll Oldies Volume Two.
- (S) (3:12) Varese Sarabande 5708 All Rock & Roll Hits Vol. One.
- (S) (3:12) One Way 33644 5th.
- (S) (3:11) JCI 3168 #1 Radio Hits 1970 - Only Rock 'n Roll - 1974.
- (S) (3:12) Flashback 72685 '70s Radio Hits Volume 5.
- (S) (3:12) Hip-O 40095 '70s Hit(s) Back.
- (S) (3:11) JCI 3192 18 Rock Classics Volume 2.
- (S) (3:11) Simitar 55752 Stud Rock - Heart Breakers.
- (S) (3:12) Thump 6010 Easyriders Volume 1.

1971 CAN I GET A WITNESS
- (S) (3:03) Rhino 70374 Collection.
- (S) (3:03) One Way 33644 5th.

MICHEL'LE
1990 NO MORE LIES
- (S) (3:42) Ruthless/Atco 91282 Michel'le.
- (S) (3:42) K-Tel 6101 Hot Ladies Of The 90's - Dazzling Divas.
- (S) (3:42) Elektra 62089 Maximum R&B.

1990 NICETY
- (S) (3:25) Ruthless/Atco 91282 Michel'le.
- (S) (3:23) Ruthless 68766 Ruthless Records Tenth Anniversary Compilation.

1991 SOMETHING IN MY HEART
- (S) (5:49) Ruthless/Atco 91282 Michel'le.
- (S) (5:48) Elektra 62090 Maximum Slow Jams.
- (S) (5:48) Ruthless 68766 Ruthless Records Tenth Anniversary Compilation.

MICKEY and SYLVIA
1957 LOVE IS STRANGE
- (M) (2:54) Rhino 70643 Billboard's Top R&B Hits Of 1957. *(contains some female background overdubs that were not on the original hit)*
- (M) (2:54) Original Sound 8854 Oldies But Goodies Vol. 4. *(this compact disc uses the "Waring - fds" noise reduction process)*
- (M) (2:54) Original Sound 2221 Oldies But Goodies Volumes 1,4,6,8 and 10 Box Set. *(this box set uses the "Waring - fds" noise reduction process)*
- (M) (2:54) Original Sound 2500 Oldies But Goodies Volumes 1-15 Box Set. *(this box set uses the "Waring - fds" noise reduction process)*
- (M) (2:53) RCA 6408 O.S.T. Dirty Dancing.
- (M) (2:55) RCA 8467 Nipper's Greatest Hits Of The 50's Volume 2. *(contains some female background overdubs that were not on the original hit)*
- (M) (2:55) Geffen 24310 O.S.T. Mermaids.
- (M) (2:54) Rhino 70561 Legends Of Guitar - Rock: The 50's Volume 2.
- (M) (2:55) RCA 9900 Love Is Strange & Other Hits.
- (M) (2:54) RCA 61144 The RCA Records Label: The First Note In Black Music.
- (M) (2:52) Time-Life RHD-08 Rhythm & Blues - 1957.
- (M) (2:53) Time-Life 2RNR-14 Rock 'N' Roll Era - 1956. *(contains some female background overdubs that were not on the original hit)*
- (M) (2:53) Time-Life R962-03 History Of Rock 'N' Roll: Rock 'N' Roll Classics 1954-1956.
- (M) (2:52) MCA 11389 O.S.T. Casino.
- (M) (2:52) RCA 66881 RCA's Greatest One-Hit Wonders. *(contains some female background overdubs that were not on the original hit)*
- (M) (2:54) Time-Life R857-13 The Heart Of Rock 'n' Roll 1956-1957.
- (M) (2:53) Collectables 5833 Love Is Strange - A Golden Classics Edition.
- (M) (2:52) Time-Life R838-23 Solid Gold Soul 1957.

BETTE MIDLER
1973 DO YOU WANT TO DANCE?
- (S) (2:42) Atlantic 7238 The Divine Miss M.
- (S) (2:42) Atlantic 82497 Experience The Divine: Best Of.
- (S) (2:42) Atlantic 82785 The Divine Miss M. *(remastered edition)*

1973 BOOGIE WOOGIE BUGLE BOY
(actual 45 time is (2:16) not (2:32) as stated on the record label)
- (M) (2:22) Atlantic 7238 The Divine Miss M. *(LP version)*
- (S) (2:15) Atlantic 82497 Experience The Divine: Best Of. *(45 version)*
- (S) (2:23) Atlantic 82785 The Divine Miss M. *(LP version; remastered edition)*

1973 FRIENDS
- (S) (2:53) Atlantic 7238 The Divine Miss M.
- (S) (2:53) Atlantic 82497 Experience The Divine: Best Of.
- (S) (2:48) Atlantic 82785 The Divine Miss M. *(remastered edition)*

1974 IN THE MOOD
- (S) (2:37) Atlantic 7270 Bette Midler.
- (S) (2:37) Atlantic 82779 Bette Midler. *(remastered edition)*

1980 WHEN A MAN LOVES A WOMAN
- (S) (4:59) Atlantic 16010 O.S.T. The Rose. *(LP version)*
- (S) (4:53) Atlantic 82497 Experience The Divine: Best Of. *(LP version)*

(S) (4:59) Atlantic 82778 O.S.T. The Rose. *(remastered edition; LP version)*

1980 THE ROSE

(S) (3:32) Atlantic 81910 Hit Singles 1980-1988. *(45 version)*

(S) (3:40) Atlantic 16010 O.S.T. The Rose. *(LP version with audience applause overdubbed)*

(S) (3:32) Atlantic 82497 Experience The Divine: Best Of. *(45 version)*

(S) (3:40) Atlantic 82778 O.S.T. The Rose. *(LP version with audience applause overdubbed; remastered edition)*

1989 WIND BENEATH MY WINGS
(dj copies of this 45 ran (4:19) and (4:54);
commercial copies were all (4:54))

(S) (4:51) Atlantic 82497 Experience The Divine: Best Of.

(S) (4:52) Atlantic 81933 O.S.T. Beaches.

(S) (4:18) Atlantic 83088 Atlantic Records: 50 Years - The Gold Anniversary Collection.

1990 FROM A DISTANCE

(S) (4:37) Atlantic 82497 Experience The Divine: Best Of.

(S) (4:37) Atlantic 82129 Some People's Lives.

MIDNIGHT OIL
1988 BEDS ARE BURNING

(S) (4:14) Foundation/WEA 26096 Super Sessions Volume One.

(S) (4:14) Columbia 40967 Diesel And Dust.

(S) (4:14) Time-Life R988-28 Sounds Of The Eighties: The Rolling Stone Collection 1986-1987.

(S) (4:14) Columbia 68848 20,000 Watt R.S.L..

1990 BLUE SKY MINE

(S) (4:15) Columbia 45398 Blue Sky Mining.

(S) (4:20) Columbia 68848 20,000 Watt R.S.L..

MIDNIGHT STAR
1985 OPERATOR

(S) (7:27) Solar 60384 Planetary Invasion. *(LP version)*

(S) (7:28) Right Stuff/Solar 53074 Planetary Invasion. *(LP version)*

(S) (4:58) Thump 9956 Old School Funk. *(all selections on this cd are segued together; edit of LP version)*

MIKE + THE MECHANICS
1986 SILENT RUNNING

(S) (6:11) Chrysalis 41663 and 21663 The Carrack Collection. *(LP version)*

(S) (6:12) Atlantic 81287 Mike + The Mechanics. *(LP version)*

(S) (4:10) Chrysalis 27221 The Paul Carrack Collection. *(45 version)*

1986 ALL I NEED IS A MIRACLE

(S) (4:09) Atlantic 81908 Classic Rock 1966-1988. *(LP length)*

(S) (6:29) JCI 3122 Lost Mixes. *(remixed)*

(S) (4:10) Atlantic 81287 Mike + The Mechanics. *(LP length)*

(S) (3:41) Time-Life R988-12 Sounds Of The 80's: 1985-1986. *(45 length)*

1986 TAKEN IN

(S) (4:16) Atlantic 81287 Mike + The Mechanics.

1989 THE LIVING YEARS
(dj copies of this 45 ran (4:25) and (5:30);
commercial copies were all (5:30))

(S) (5:30) Chrysalis 27221 The Paul Carrack Collection.

(S) (5:30) Atlantic 81923 Living Years.

(S) (5:30) Time-Life R988-13 Sounds Of The Eighties: 1989.

GARRY MILES
1960 LOOK FOR A STAR

(M) (2:23) EMI-Capitol Special Markets 19552 Lost Hits Of The '60s.

(M) (2:24) Time-Life R857-19 The Heart Of Rock 'n' Roll 1960-1961 Take Three.

JOHN MILES
1977 SLOWDOWN
(actual LP time is (4:18) not (4:46) as
stated on the LP)

(S) (4:17) Rhino 70491 Billboard Top Dance Hits - 1977.

(S) (4:49) Special Music 5041 Great Britons! Volume Three. *(:32 longer than either the 45 or LP)*

ROBERT MILES
1996 CHILDREN

(S) (7:05) Arista 18930 Dreamland.

(S) (3:58) Arista 18943 Ultimate Dance Party 1997. *(all selections on this cd are segued together)*

1997 I CARE 'BOUT YOU

(S) (4:34) LaFace 26041 O.S.T. Soul Food.

CHUCK MILLER
1955 THE HOUSE OF BLUE LIGHTS

(M) (2:24) Eric 11502 Hard To Find 45's On CD (Volume I) 1955-60.

JODY MILLER
1965 QUEEN OF THE HOUSE

(S) (2:16) Time-Life CTD-21 Country USA - 1966.

(S) (2:16) K-Tel 413 Country Music Classics Volume III.

(S) (2:15) Nick At Nite/550 Music/Epic 67689 Stand By Your Man.

(S) (2:37) K-Tel 3369 101 Greatest Country Hits Vol. Ten: Country Roads. *(rerecording)*

1965 HOME OF THE BRAVE

MITCH MILLER
1955 YELLOW ROSE OF TEXAS

(M) (3:00) Columbia 45110 16 Most Requested Songs Of The 50's Volume 1.

(M) (3:01) Columbia 44374 Hollywood Magic - The 1950's.

(M) (3:00) Columbia 1544 Mitch's Greatest Hits.

(M) (3:00) Columbia 44406 16 Most Requested Songs.

(M) (3:03) Time-Life HPD-09 Your Hit Parade 1955.

1956 LISBON ANTIGUA
1956 THEME SONG FROM "SONG FOR A SUMMER NIGHT"

(M) (3:09) Columbia 1544 Mitch's Greatest Hits.

(M) (3:08) Time-Life HPD-30 Your Hit Parade - 50's Instrumentals.

1958 MARCH FROM THE RIVER KWAI AND COLONEL BOGEY

(M) (2:24) Columbia 44374 Hollywood Magic - The 1950's.

(M) (2:25) Columbia 1544 Mitch's Greatest Hits.

(M) (2:24) Columbia 44406 16 Most Requested Songs.

(M) (2:26) Time-Life HPD-11 Your Hit Parade 1958.

(M) (2:25) Legacy/Columbia 66131 O.S.T. Bridge On The River Kwai.

1959 THE CHILDREN'S MARCHING SONG

(M) (2:48) Columbia 1544 Mitch's Greatest Hits.

(M) (2:46) Columbia 44406 16 Most Requested Songs.

NED MILLER
1963 FROM A JACK TO A KING

(M) (2:09) Rhino 70684 Billboard's Top Country Hits Of 1963. *(alternate take)*

(E) (2:05) Time-Life CTD-11 Country USA - 1963. *(alternate take)*

(M) (2:08) K-Tel 320 Country Music Classics Volume II.

(M) (2:06) JCI 3153 1960 - Only Country - 1964. *(mastered from vinyl)*

(S) (2:08) K-Tel 3368 101 Greatest Country Hits Vol. Nine: Country Classics. *(rerecording)*

(M) (2:08) Time-Life R808-01 Classic Country 1960-1964.

ROGER MILLER
1964 DANG ME

(S) (1:48) Mercury 826261 Golden Hits.

(S) (1:41) Curb 77511 Best Of. *(all tracks on this cd are rerecordings)*

(S) (1:48) Mercury 314512646 Best Of Volume Two.

(S) (1:48) Time-Life CTD-14 Country USA - 1964.

ROGER MILLER *(Continued)*
- (S) (1:48) Time-Life SUD-12 Superhits - The Mid 60's.
- (S) (1:41) Epic 53017 King Of The Road. *(all tracks on this cd are rerecorded)*
- (S) (1:48) K-Tel 3037 Wacky Weirdos.
- (S) (1:48) K-Tel 3109 Country Music Classics Volume XVII.
- (M) (1:46) Mercury 314526993 King Of The Road: Genius Of.
- (S) (1:48) Varese Sarabande 5606 Through The Years - Country Hits Of The 60's.
- (S) (1:48) Polygram Special Markets 314520280 At His Best.
- (S) (1:41) Epic 67537 Super Hits. *(all selections on this cd are rerecorded)*
- (S) (1:48) Time-Life AM1-05 AM Gold - The Mid '60s.
- (M) (1:46) Mercury 314534670 The Hits.
- (M) (1:46) Polygram Special Markets 314520441 #1 Country Hits Of The 60's.
- (S) (1:48) Time-Life R808-01 Classic Country 1960-1964.

1964 CHUG-A-LUG
- (S) (2:02) Rhino 70732 Grandson Of Frat Rock.
- (S) (2:02) Mercury 826261 Golden Hits.
- (S) (1:58) Curb 77511 Best Of. *(all tracks on this cd are rerecordings)*
- (S) (2:02) Mercury 314512646 Best Of Volume Two.
- (S) (2:01) Time-Life CTD-14 Country USA - 1964.
- (S) (1:58) Epic 53017 King Of The Road. *(all tracks on this cd are rerecorded)*
- (S) (2:02) K-Tel 852 100 Proof Hits.
- (M) (2:00) Mercury 314526993 King Of The Road: Genius Of.
- (S) (2:02) K-Tel 3629 Madcap Melodies.
- (S) (2:02) K-Tel 3640 Corny Country.
- (S) (1:58) Epic 67537 Super Hits. *(all selections on this cd are rerecorded)*
- (M) (2:00) Mercury 314534670 The Hits.
- (S) (1:59) Columbia 69059 Party Super Hits. *(rerecording)*

1965 DO-WACKA-DO
- (S) (1:44) Mercury 826261 Golden Hits.
- (S) (1:44) Curb 77511 Best Of. *(all tracks on this cd are rerecordings)*
- (S) (1:44) Mercury 314512646 Best Of Volume Two.
- (S) (1:44) K-Tel 3150 Dumb Ditties.
- (M) (1:43) Mercury 314526993 King Of The Road: Genius Of.
- (M) (1:43) Mercury 314534670 The Hits.

1965 KING OF THE ROAD
- (S) (2:26) Mercury 826261 Golden Hits.
- (S) (2:21) Curb 77511 Best Of. *(all tracks on this cd are rerecordings)*
- (S) (2:25) Mercury 314512646 Best Of Volume Two.
- (S) (2:24) Time-Life CTD-10 Country USA - 1965. *(timing index is off by :01 on all tracks of this cd)*
- (S) (2:26) Time-Life SUD-03 Superhits - 1965.
- (S) (2:25) Epic 53017 King Of The Road. *(all tracks on this cd are rerecorded)*
- (S) (2:26) K-Tel 3243 Kooky Kountry.
- (S) (2:25) Epic 66632 Music From The Motion Picture "Love & A .45".
- (S) (2:26) Polygram Special Markets 314520261 Number One Country Hits 50's Through The 80's.
- (S) (2:25) K-Tel 413 Country Music Classics Volume III.
- (S) (2:25) Scotti Bros. 75483 Country Favorites - The Number One Hits. *(rerecorded)*
- (M) (2:24) Mercury 314526993 King Of The Road: Genius Of.
- (S) (2:26) K-Tel 3187 Country's Greatest Singer/Songwriters.
- (M) (2:24) Mercury 314526691 Fifty Years Of Country Music From Mercury.
- (S) (2:25) Polygram Special Markets 314520280 At His Best.
- (S) (2:24) Epic 67537 Super Hits. *(all selections on this cd are rerecorded)*
- (S) (2:26) Priority 50966 I Love Country Volume One: Hits Of The 60's.

- (S) (2:25) K-Tel 3369 101 Greatest Country Hits Vol. Ten: Country Roads.
- (S) (2:26) Time-Life AM1-10 AM Gold - 1965.
- (S) (2:26) Hammer & Lace 697124114 Leading Men: Masters Of Style Volume Three.
- (S) (2:25) Right Stuff 53317 Hot Rod Rock Volume 2: Hot Rod Cowboys.
- (M) (2:24) Mercury 314534670 The Hits.
- (S) (2:26) Miramax/Hollywood 206162091 O.S.T. Swingers. *(rerecording)*
- (S) (2:26) Polygram Special Markets 314520459 Vocal Treasures.
- (S) (2:24) Time-Life R808-02 Classic Country 1965-1969.
- (M) (2:24) Polygram Special Markets 314520495 45's On CD Volume 2.

1965 ENGINE ENGINE #9
- (S) (2:16) Mercury 826261 Golden Hits.
- (S) (1:58) Curb 77511 Best Of. *(all tracks on this cd are rerecordings)*
- (S) (2:16) Mercury 314512646 Best Of Volume Two.
- (S) (2:16) K-Tel 3110 Country Music Classics Volume XVIII.
- (M) (2:16) Mercury 314526993 King Of The Road: Genius Of.
- (S) (2:14) Risky Business 67308 Train Trax. *(rerecording)*
- (S) (2:16) Polygram Special Markets 314520280 At His Best.
- (M) (2:16) Mercury 314534670 The Hits.

1965 ONE DYIN' AND A BURYIN'
- (S) (2:00) Mercury 826261 Golden Hits.
- (M) (2:00) Mercury 314526993 King Of The Road: Genius Of.

1965 KANSAS CITY STAR
- (S) (2:15) Mercury 826261 Golden Hits.
- (S) (2:17) Curb 77511 Best Of. *(all tracks on this cd are rerecordings)*
- (S) (2:15) Mercury 314512646 Best Of Volume Two.
- (S) (2:14) Time-Life CTD-10 Country USA - 1965. *(timing index is off by :01 on all tracks of this cd)*
- (S) (2:15) K-Tel 3299 Country 'Round The Country.
- (M) (2:16) Mercury 314526993 King Of The Road: Genius Of.

1966 ENGLAND SWINGS
- (S) (1:52) Mercury 826261 Golden Hits.
- (S) (1:50) Curb 77511 Best Of. *(all tracks on this cd are rerecordings)*
- (S) (1:51) Mercury 314512646 Best Of Volume Two.
- (S) (1:52) Time-Life CTD-21 Country USA - 1966.
- (S) (1:53) Epic 53017 King Of The Road. *(all tracks on this cd are rerecorded)*
- (M) (1:52) Mercury 314526993 King Of The Road: Genius Of.
- (S) (1:53) Epic 67537 Super Hits. *(all selections on this cd are rerecorded)*
- (M) (1:51) Mercury 314534670 The Hits.

1966 HUSBANDS AND WIVES
- (S) (2:21) Mercury 848977 Best Of.
- (S) (2:22) Curb 77511 Best Of. *(all tracks on this cd are rerecordings)*
- (S) (2:24) Epic 53017 King Of The Road. *(all tracks on this cd are rerecorded)*
- (M) (2:21) Mercury 314526993 King Of The Road: Genius Of.
- (S) (2:21) Polygram Special Markets 314520280 At His Best.
- (S) (2:24) Epic 67537 Super Hits. *(all selections on this cd are rerecorded)*
- (M) (2:21) Mercury 314534670 The Hits.

1966 YOU CAN'T ROLLER SKATE IN A BUFFALO HERD
- (S) (1:53) Rhino 72125 Dr. Demento's Country Corn.
- (S) (1:53) Mercury 314512646 Best Of Volume Two.
- (S) (1:50) Epic 53017 King Of The Road. *(all tracks on this cd are rerecorded)*
- (S) (1:50) Curb 77511 Best Of. *(all tracks on this cd are rerecordings)*
- (S) (1:53) Smash 826261 Golden Hits.
- (M) (1:52) Mercury 314526993 King Of The Road: Genius Of.

(S) (1:52) K-Tel 3411 Tacky Tunes.

(S) (1:53) Polygram Special Markets 314520280 At His Best.

(S) (1:50) Epic 67537 Super Hits. *(all selections on this cd are rerecorded)*

(M) (1:52) Mercury 314534670 The Hits.

1967 WALKIN' IN THE SUNSHINE

(M) (2:37) Mercury 314526993 King Of The Road: Genius Of.

(M) (2:36) Mercury 314534670 The Hits.

STEVE MILLER BAND
1974 THE JOKER

(S) (3:36) Rhino 70635 Billboard's Top Rock & Roll Hits Of 1974. *(45 version)*

(S) (3:35) Capitol 46101 Greatest Hits 1974-78. *(45 version)*

(S) (4:24) Capitol 95271 Best Of 1968-1973. *(LP version)*

(S) (4:24) Capitol 94445 The Joker. *(LP version)*

(S) (3:34) Time-Life SOD-15 Sounds Of The Seventies - 1974: Take Two. *(45 version)*

(S) (4:24) Capitol 89826 Steve Miller Band Box Set. *(LP version)*

(S) (4:23) Time-Life R968-16 Guitar Rock - The Mid '70s: Take Two. *(LP version)*

(S) (4:23) Rhino 72518 Mellow Rock Hits Of The 70's - Summer Breeze. *(LP version)*

(S) (3:34) Time-Life R13610 Gold And Platinum Box Set - The Ultimate Rock Collection. *(45 version)*

1974 LIVING IN THE U.S.A.

(S) (4:01) Sandstone 33000 Reelin' In The Years Volume 1.

(S) (4:03) Capitol 95271 Best Of 1968-1973.

(S) (4:03) Capitol 94488 Anthology.

(S) (4:01) Capitol 94449 Sailor.

(S) (4:01) DCC Compact Classics 062 Rock Of The 70's Volume 1.

(S) (4:01) Capitol 89826 Steve Miller Band Box Set.

(S) (4:03) Medicine Label 24588 Even More Dazed And Confused.

(S) (4:03) Time-Life R968-07 Guitar Rock 1968-1969.

released as by STEVE MILLER:
1976 TAKE THE MONEY AND RUN

(S) (2:49) Capitol 46101 Greatest Hits 1974-78.

(S) (2:47) Capitol 46475 Fly Like An Eagle.

(S) (2:47) DCC Compact Classics 1033 Fly Like An Eagle. *(gold disc)*

(S) (2:48) Time-Life SOD-18 Sounds Of The Seventies - 1976: Take Two.

(S) (2:47) Capitol 89826 Steve Miller Band Box Set.

(S) (2:47) Priority 50952 I Love Rock & Roll Volume 3: Hits Of The 70's.

1976 ROCK 'N ME

(S) (3:06) Capitol 46101 Greatest Hits 1974-78.

(S) (3:04) Capitol 46475 Fly Like An Eagle.

(S) (3:04) DCC Compact Classics 1033 Fly Like An Eagle. *(gold disc)*

(S) (3:06) Time-Life SOD-04 Sounds Of The Seventies - 1976.

(S) (3:04) Capitol 89826 Steve Miller Band Box Set.

(S) (3:06) Rhino 72893 Hard Rock Cafe: Classic Rock.

(S) (3:03) K-Tel 3904 The Rock Album Volume 2.

1977 FLY LIKE AN EAGLE

(S) (3:00) Capitol 46101 Greatest Hits 1974-78. *(45 version)*

(S) (4:42) Capitol 46475 Fly Like An Eagle. *(LP version)*

(S) (4:42) DCC Compact Classics 1033 Fly Like An Eagle. *(LP version; gold disc)*

(S) (3:00) Time-Life SOD-05 Sounds Of The Seventies - 1977. *(45 version)*

(S) (4:42) Capitol 89826 Steve Miller Band Box Set. *(LP version)*

(S) (3:00) Time-Life R968-17 Guitar Rock - The Late '70s: Take Two. *(45 version)*

(S) (4:42) Rhino 72517 Mellow Rock Hits Of The 70's - Ventura Highway. *(LP version)*

(S) (3:01) Eclipse Music Group 64895 Rock 'n Roll Relix 1976-1977. *(45 version)*

(S) (3:01) Eclipse Music Group 64897 Rock 'n Roll Relix 1970-1979. *(45 version)*

released as by THE STEVE MILLER BAND:
1977 JET AIRLINER

(S) (3:34) Capitol 46101 Greatest Hits 1974-78. *(:14 longer fade than the 45; LP sound effects on intro but otherwise the 45 version)*

(S) (4:23) Capitol 46476 Book Of Dreams. *(LP version)*

(S) (4:23) DCC Compact Classics 1077 Book Of Dreams. *(LP version; gold disc)*

(S) (3:32) Time-Life SOD-17 Sounds Of The Seventies - 1977: Take Two. *(missing the opening drum beats; :12 longer fade than the 45 but otherwise the 45 version)*

(S) (4:22) Capitol 89826 Steve Miller Band Box Set. *(LP version)*

1977 JUNGLE LOVE

(S) (3:08) Capitol 46101 Greatest Hits 1974-78.

(S) (3:06) Capitol 46476 Book Of Dreams.

(S) (3:06) Capitol 89826 Steve Miller Band Box Set.

(S) (3:06) DCC Compact Classics 1077 Book Of Dreams. *(gold disc)*

1978 SWINGTOWN

(S) (3:28) Capitol 46101 Greatest Hits 1974-78. *(45 version)*

(S) (3:54) Capitol 46476 Book Of Dreams. *(LP version)*

(S) (3:54) Capitol 89826 Steve Miller Band Box Set. *(LP version)*

(S) (3:26) Epic 57871 O.S.T. My Girl 2. *(45 version)*

(S) (3:54) DCC Compact Classics 1077 Book Of Dreams. *(gold disc; LP version)*

1981 HEART LIKE A WHEEL

(S) (3:59) Capitol 94446 Circle Of Love. *(LP version)*

(S) (3:59) Time-Life R968-13 Guitar Rock - The Early '80s. *(LP version)*

1982 ABRACADABRA

(S) (5:05) Capitol 46102 Abracadabra. *(LP version)*

(S) (5:05) Capitol 89826 Steve Miller Band Box Set. *(LP version)*

(S) (3:35) Rhino 72771 The Big 80's. *(45 version)*

(S) (5:06) Priority 50953 I Love Rock & Roll Volume 4: Hits Of The 80's. *(LP version)*

(S) (3:38) Time-Life R988-14 Sounds Of The Eighties: 1980-1982. *(45 version)*

MILLI VANILLI
1989 GIRL YOU KNOW IT'S TRUE

(S) (4:11) Arista 8592 Girl You Know It's True. *(LP version)*

(S) (6:27) Arista 8592 Girl You Know It's True. *(remix)*

(S) (5:31) Arista 8622 The Remix Album. *(remix)*

1989 BABY DON'T FORGET MY NUMBER

(S) (4:15) Arista 8592 Girl You Know It's True. *(LP version)*

(S) (5:34) Arista 8622 The Remix Album. *(remix)*

1989 GIRL I'M GONNA MISS YOU

(S) (3:57) Arista 8592 Girl You Know It's True. *(LP version which is titled "I'M GONNA MISS YOU")*

(S) (5:15) Arista 8622 The Remix Album. *(remix)*

1989 BLAME IT ON THE RAIN

(S) (4:18) Arista 8592 Girl You Know It's True. *(LP version)*

(S) (5:49) Arista 8622 The Remix Album. *(remix)*

1990 ALL OR NOTHING

(S) (3:15) Arista 8592 Girl You Know It's True.

(S) (5:38) Arista 8622 The Remix Album. *(remix)*

FRANK MILLS
1979 MUSIC BOX DANCER

(S) (3:15) Time-Life SOD-36 Sounds Of The Seventies - More AM Nuggets.

(S) (3:15) Time-Life R986-22 Instrumental Classics - Pop Classics.

GARRY MILLS
1960 LOOK FOR A STAR

HAYLEY MILLS
1961 LET'S GET TOGETHER
- (M) (1:28) Walt Disney 60865 Classic Disney Volume 1.
- (S) (1:28) Collectors' Choice 5189 I Wish I Were A Princess - The Great Lost Female Teen Idols.
- (M) (1:28) Walt Disney 60407 Let's Get Together With Hayley Mills.

1962 JOHNNY JINGO
- (M) (1:39) Collectors' Choice 5189 I Wish I Were A Princess - The Great Lost Female Teen Idols.
- (M) (1:39) Walt Disney 60407 Let's Get Together With Hayley Mills.

STEPHANIE MILLS
1979 WHAT CHA GONNA DO WITH MY LOVIN'
- (S) (4:01) Casablanca 832519 In My Life: Greatest Hits. *(LP version)*
- (S) (4:36) Rebound 314520270 Class Reunion 1979. *(neither the 45 or LP version)*
- (S) (8:01) Casablanca 314526720 Best Of. *(12" single version)*
- (S) (4:01) Thump 4040 Old School Volume 4. *(LP version)*
- (S) (4:36) Polygram Special Markets 314520397 Best Of. *(neither the 45 or LP version)*

1980 NEVER KNEW LOVE LIKE THIS BEFORE
- (S) (5:00) Priority 7983 Mega-Hits Dance Classics Volume 7. *(truncated fade; :27 shorter than the LP version)*
- (S) (5:24) Casablanca 832519 In My Life: Greatest Hits. *(LP version)*
- (S) (5:24) Sandstone 33052 and 5020 Cosmopolitan Volume 6. *(LP version)*
- (S) (3:31) Rhino 71618 Soul Train Hall Of Fame/20th Anniversary. *(45 version)*
- (S) (5:00) Razor & Tie 22496 Disco Fever. *(:27 shorter than the LP version)*
- (S) (5:24) Sandstone 33052 and 5020 Cosmopolitan Volume 6. *(LP version)*
- (S) (4:37) Rebound 314520217 Disco Nights Vol. 1 - Divas Of Dance. *(neither the 45 or LP version)*
- (S) (5:23) Rebound 314520318 Class Reunion 1980. *(LP version)*
- (S) (5:24) DCC Compact Classics 084 Night Moves Volume 4. *(LP version)*
- (S) (5:24) Casablanca 314526720 Best Of. *(LP version)*
- (S) (3:51) Polygram Special Markets 314520397 Best Of. *(45 version but with a :20 longer fade)*
- (S) (5:24) Time-Life R834-07 Body Talk - Hearts In Motion. *(LP version)*
- (S) (5:24) Simitar 55602 The Number One's: Silky Soul. *(LP version)*
- (S) (5:22) Polygram TV 314555610 The One And Only Love Album. *(LP version)*
- (S) (3:51) JCI 3176 1980 - Only Soul - 1984. *(45 version but with a :20 longer fade)*
- (S) (3:31) Time-Life R840-09 Sounds Of The Seventies: '70s Dance Party 1979-1981. *(45 version)*

MILLS BROTHERS
1958 GET A JOB
1968 CAB DRIVER
- (M) (2:55) Ranwood 7035 22 Great Hits. *(rerecorded)*
- (S) (2:53) MCA 11279 Anthology 1931-1968.
- (S) (2:53) Varese Sarabande 5686 History Of Dot Records Volume One.
- (S) (2:53) MCA 11569 All Time Greatest Hits.

RONNIE MILSAP
1977 IT WAS ALMOST LIKE A SONG
- (S) (3:35) RCA 5986 and 66402 It Was Almost Like A Song.
- (S) (3:37) RCA 3772 and 8504 Greatest Hits.
- (S) (3:35) Time-Life CCD-02 Contemporary Country - The Late 70's.
- (S) (3:37) Priority 53716 Branson USA Vol. 3 - Country Legends.
- (S) (3:36) K-Tel 3355 101 Greatest Country Hits Vol. One: Forever Country.

1981 SMOKY MOUNTAIN RAIN
- (S) (3:44) RCA 3772 and 8504 Greatest Hits.
1981 (THERE'S) NO GETTIN' OVER ME
- (S) (3:13) RCA 7004 14 Country Hits.
- (S) (3:13) RCA 5425 Greatest Hits Volume 2.
- (S) (3:14) RCA 4060 There's No Gettin' Over Me.
- (S) (3:11) Time-Life CCD-03 Contemporary Country - The Early 80's.
- (S) (3:13) RCA 66534 Essential.
- (S) (3:13) RCA 66851 Super Hits.
- (S) (3:13) K-Tel 4004 Country Favorites Of The 80s.

1982 I WOULDN'T HAVE MISSED IT FOR THE WORLD
- (S) (3:32) RCA 4060 There's No Gettin' Over Me.
- (S) (3:27) RCA 5425 Greatest Hits Volume 2.
- (S) (3:32) RCA 66534 Essential.
- (S) (3:32) K-Tel 3047 Country Music Classics Volume VI.

1982 ANY DAY NOW
- (S) (3:40) RCA 4311 Inside.
- (S) (3:39) RCA 5425 Greatest Hits Volume 2.
- (S) (3:40) RCA 66534 Essential.
- (S) (3:38) RCA 66851 Super Hits.
- (S) (3:38) RCA 66818 The Essential Series Sampler.
- (S) (3:38) RCA 66945 Super Hits Sampler.
- (S) (3:38) Simitar 55092 80's Country 1982-94.

1983 STRANGER IN MY HOUSE
(actual 45 time is (4:08) not (3:42) as stated on the record label)
- (S) (4:10) RCA 5993 Keyed Up.
- (S) (4:06) RCA 5425 Greatest Hits Volume 2.
- (S) (4:09) RCA 66534 Essential.
- (S) (4:08) RCA 66818 The Essential Series Sampler.

GARNET MIMMS & THE ENCHANTERS
1963 CRY BABY
- (S) (3:25) Rhino 70649 Billboard's Top R&B Hits Of 1963.
- (S) (3:24) Collectables 5248 Garnett Mimms & The Enchanters.
- (M) (3:24) Original Sound 9307 Dedicated To You Vol. 7.
- (S) (3:23) EMI 81128 Rock Is Dead But It Won't Lie Down.
- (S) (3:23) EMI 80183 Best Of: Cry Baby.
- (M) (3:23) Time-Life 2RNR-07 Rock 'N' Roll Era - 1963.
- (S) (3:23) Time-Life RHD-02 Rhythm & Blues - 1963.
- (M) (3:23) JCI 3164 Eighteen Soulful Ballads.
- (S) (3:25) Time-Life R857-12 The Heart Of Rock 'n' Roll 1962-1963.
- (S) (3:23) Time-Life R838-14 Solid Gold Soul - 1963.
- (M) (3:23) Rhino 72815 Beg, Scream & Shout! The Big Ol' Box Of '60s Soul.
- (S) (3:22) Repeat/Relativity 1611 A Brand New Bag: #1 Soul Hits Of The 60's Volume 3.

1963 BABY DON'T YOU WEEP
- (S) (3:27) Collectables 5248 Garnett Mimms & The Enchanters.
- (S) (3:26) EMI 80183 Best Of: Cry Baby.

1964 FOR YOUR PRECIOUS LOVE
- (S) (3:02) Collectables 5248 Garnett Mimms & The Enchanters.
- (S) (3:01) Virgin 92153 and 86289 O.S.T. American Me.
- (S) (3:01) EMI 80183 Best Of: Cry Baby.
- (S) (3:00) Right Stuff 30577 Slow Jams: The 60's Volume 3.

released as by GARNET MIMMS:
1966 I'LL TAKE GOOD CARE OF YOU
- (S) (3:17) Collectables 5248 Garnett Mimms & The Enchanters.
- (S) (3:26) EMI 80183 Best Of: Cry Baby.

MINDBENDERS (also WAYNE FONTANA & THE MINDBENDERS)
released as by WAYNE FONTANA & THE MINDBENDERS:
1965 GAME OF LOVE
- (M) (2:06) Mercury 816555 45's On CD Volume 2.
- (M) (2:04) A&M 3913 and 3340 O.S.T. Good Morning Vietnam. *(the preceding dialogue overlaps the first music note)*
- (M) (2:06) Rhino 70323 History Of British Rock Volume 5.
- (M) (2:06) Rhino 72022 History Of British Rock Box Set.
- (M) (2:04) Time-Life 2CLR-23 Classic Rock - 1965: Blowin' Your Mind.

(M) (2:04) Time-Life SUD-03 Superhits - 1965.
(M) (2:06) Time-Life R962-07 History Of Rock 'N' Roll: The British Invasion 1964-1966.
(M) (2:03) Collectables 2510 WCBS-FM History Of Rock - The Rockin' 60's.
(M) (2:03) Collectables 4510 History Of Rock/The Rockin' 60s.
(M) (2:05) Fontana 314522666 Best Of.
(M) (2:06) Rhino 71935 Billboard Top Pop Hits, 1965.
(M) (2:05) Special Music 5040 Great Britons! Volume Two.
(M) (2:05) Eclipse Music Group 64869 Rock 'n Roll Relix 1964-1965.
(M) (2:05) Eclipse Music Group 64872 Rock 'n Roll Relix 1960-1969.
(M) (2:04) Time-Life AM1-10 AM Gold - 1965.
(M) (2:05) Polygram Special Markets 314520495 45's On CD Volume 2.

released as by THE MINDBENDERS:
1966 A GROOVY KIND OF LOVE
(M) (1:57) Mercury 816555 45's On CD Volume 2.
(M) (1:59) Rhino 70324 History Of British Rock Volume 6.
(M) (1:59) Rhino 72022 History Of British Rock Box Set.
(M) (1:56) Time-Life 2CLR-22 Classic Rock - 1966: Blowin' Your Mind.
(M) (1:56) Time-Life SUD-01 Superhits - 1966.
(M) (1:57) Collectables 2510 WCBS-FM History Of Rock - The Rockin' 60's.
(M) (1:57) Collectables 4510 History Of Rock/The Rockin' 60s.
(M) (1:59) Fontana 314522666 Best Of.
(M) (1:57) LaserLight 12311 and 15936 The Wonder Years - First Love.
(M) (1:57) Special Music 5039 Great Britons! Volume One.
(M) (1:57) Eclipse Music Group 64870 Rock 'n Roll Relix 1966-1967.
(M) (1:57) Eclipse Music Group 64872 Rock 'n Roll Relix 1960-1969.
(M) (1:56) Time-Life AM1-09 AM Gold - 1966.
(M) (1:58) Time-Life R857-20 The Heart Of Rock 'n' Roll 1965-1966.

SAL MINEO
1957 START MOVIN' (IN MY DIRECTION)
(M) (2:30) Collectors' Choice 002 Teen Idols....For A Moment.
1957 LASTING LOVE

KYLIE MINOGUE
1988 I SHOULD BE SO LUCKY
(S) (3:22) Geffen 24195 Kylie.
1988 THE LOCO-MOTION
(S) (3:12) A&M 3916 O.S.T. Arthur 2 On The Rocks.
(S) (3:12) Foundation/WEA 26097 Super Sessions Volume Two.
(S) (3:12) K-Tel 3343 The 80's Hot Dance Trax.
(S) (3:12) Sandstone 33050 and 5018 Cosmopolitan Volume 4.
(S) (3:12) DCC Compact Classics 089 Night Moves Volume 7.
(S) (3:12) Geffen 24195 Kylie.
(S) (3:12) Time-Life R988-10 Sounds Of The 80's: 1988.
(S) (3:11) Hip-O 40022 That Sound From Down Under.
(S) (3:12) Rhino 75217 Heartthrob Hits.
1989 IT'S NO SECRET
(S) (3:56) Geffen 24195 Kylie.

MINT CONDITION
1992 BREAKIN' MY HEART
(S) (5:55) Perspective 1001 Meant To Be Mint.
1994 U SEND ME SWINGIN'
(S) (5:14) Perspective 314549005 From The Mint Factory.
1996 WHAT KIND OF MAN WOULD I BE
(S) (4:24) Perspective 314549028 Definition Of A Band.
(S) (4:24) Polygram TV 314553641 Pure Soul 1997.

1997 YOU DON'T HAVE TO HURT NO MORE
(S) (5:21) Perspective 314549028 Definition Of A Band.

MIRACLES (also SMOKEY ROBINSON & THE MIRACLES)
released as by THE MIRACLES:
1961 SHOP AROUND
(M) (2:44) Motown 9041 and 6071 Compact Command Performances.
(M) (2:47) Rhino 70647 Billboard's Top R&B Hits Of 1961.
(M) (2:43) Motown 6159 The Good-Feeling Music Of The Big Chill Generation Volume 1.
(M) (2:44) Motown 6139 The Composer Series: Smokey Robinson.
(M) (2:44) Motown 5448 A Package Of 16 Big Hits. (cd jacket mistakenly credits this song to the CONTOURS)
(M) (2:44) Motown 6196 and 0793 Anthology.
(M) (2:43) Motown 9017 and 5248 16 #1 Hits From The Early 60's.
(M) (2:44) Motown 5316 Great Songs And Performances That Inspired The Motown 25th Anniversary TV Special.
(M) (2:43) Motown 5343 Every Great Motown Song: The First 25 Years Volume 1. (most selections on this cd have noise on the fadeout)
(M) (2:43) Motown 8034 and 8134 Every Great Motown Song: The First 25 Years Volumes 1 & 2. (most selections on this cd have noise on the fadeout)
(M) (2:47) Motown 5160 Hi We're The Miracles.
(M) (2:49) Motown 6312 Hitsville USA.
(M) (2:43) Motown 374638509 Motown Legends - I Second That Emotion.
(M) (3:00) Motown 6334 35th Anniversary Collection. (original version but not the hit version)
(M) (2:48) Motown 6334 35th Anniversary Collection.
(M) (2:44) Time-Life 2RNR-04 Rock 'N' Roll Era - 1961.
(M) (2:44) Time-Life RHD-14 Rhythm & Blues - 1961.
(M) (2:47) Motown 314530403 Motown Classic Hits Vol. 1.
(M) (2:43) Polygram Special Markets 314520282 Motown Legends - Volume 1.
(M) (2:48) Motown 314530472 Anthology.
(M) (2:45) Time-Life R838-19 Solid Gold Soul 1961.
(M) (2:47) Motown 314530857 Ultimate Collection.
(M) (2:42) Motown 314530849 Motown 40 Forever.
1962 WHAT'S SO GOOD ABOUT GOOD-BY
(S) (2:59) Motown 9105 and 5410 Motown Memories Volume 2. (LP version)
(S) (3:04) Motown 5450 A Collection Of 16 Big Hits Volume 3. (LP version)
(S) (2:59) Motown 6202 Compact Command Performances Volume 2. (LP version)
(S) (3:00) Motown 6196 and 0793 Anthology. (LP version)
(M) (2:20) Motown 6334 35th Anniversary Collection. (45 version)
(M) (2:20) Motown 314530420 Motown Classic Hits Vol. III. (45 version)
(M) (2:20) Motown 314530472 Anthology. (45 version)
1962 I'LL TRY SOMETHING NEW
(E) (2:35) Motown 9041 and 6071 Compact Command Performances.
(E) (2:38) Motown 6196 and 0793 Anthology.
(M) (2:35) Motown 6334 35th Anniversary Collection.
(M) (2:33) Time-Life 2RNR-42 Rock 'N' Roll Era - The 60's Sock Hop.
(M) (2:35) Motown 314530472 Anthology.
(M) (2:37) Motown 314530647 O.S.T. Nothing But A Man.
(M) (2:34) Eclipse Music Group 64868 Rock 'n Roll Relix 1962-1963.
(M) (2:34) Eclipse Music Group 64872 Rock 'n Roll Relix 1960-1969.
(M) (2:35) Motown 314530857 Ultimate Collection.
1963 YOU'VE REALLY GOT A HOLD ON ME (actual 45 time is (2:56) not (2:49) as stated on the record label)
(E) (2:56) Motown 6160 The Good-Feeling Music Of The Big Chill Generation Volume 2.

MIRACLES (Continued)

- (E) (2:57) Motown 6139 The Composer Series: Smokey Robinson.
- (M) (2:57) Geffen 24310 O.S.T. Mermaids.
- (S) (2:50) Motown 5448 A Package Of 16 Big Hits.
- (M) (2:56) Rhino 70649 Billboard's Top R&B Hits Of 1963.
- (E) (2:56) Motown 9041 and 6071 Compact Command Performances.
- (S) (2:49) Motown 6196 and 0793 Anthology.
- (E) (2:56) Motown 9017 and 5248 16 #1 Hits From The Early 60's.
- (S) (2:56) Motown 5316 Great Songs And Performances That Inspired The Motown 25th Anniversary TV Special.
- (M) (2:56) Motown 6312 Hitsville USA.
- (S) (2:49) K-Tel 3063 Marvin Gaye/Smokey Robinson & The Miracles.
- (M) (2:56) Motown 6334 35th Anniversary Collection.
- (E) (2:55) Time-Life 2RNR-16 Rock 'N' Roll Era - 1962 Still Rockin'.
- (S) (2:50) Time-Life RHD-02 Rhythm & Blues - 1963.
- (S) (2:50) Time-Life SUD-06 Superhits - 1962.
- (M) (2:57) Motown 314530419 Motown Classic Hits Vol. II.
- (M) (2:56) Motown 314530472 Anthology.
- (E) (2:56) Polygram Special Markets 314520292 Motown Legends - Volume 4.
- (M) (2:56) EMI 52498 O.S.T. Striptease.
- (M) (4:51) Motown 314530647 O.S.T. Nothing But A Man. *(live)*
- (M) (2:56) Time-Life R857-08 The Heart Of Rock 'n' Roll 1963.
- (S) (2:50) Time-Life AM1-18 AM Gold - 1962.
- (S) (2:50) Time-Life R838-14 Solid Gold Soul - 1963.
- (M) (2:55) Motown 314530857 Ultimate Collection.
- (M) (2:56) Polygram Special Markets 314520454 Soul Hits Of The 60's.

1963 MICKEY'S MONKEY

- (S) (2:47) Rhino 70992 Groove 'N' Grind.
- (S) (2:45) Motown 5450 A Collection Of 16 Big Hits Volume 3.
- (S) (2:45) Motown 9041 and 6071 Compact Command Performances.
- (S) (2:47) Motown 6196 and 0793 Anthology.
- (S) (2:45) Motown 5316 Great Songs And Performances That Inspired The Motown 25th Anniversary TV Special.
- (S) (2:44) Motown 5439 Doin' Mickey's Monkey.
- (S) (2:45) Motown 8050 and 8150 Doin' Mickey's Monkey/Away We A Go-Go.
- (S) (2:42) Motown 9071 Motown Dance Party Volume 1. *(all selections on this cd are segued together)*
- (S) (2:47) Rhino 70291 Bo Diddley Beats.
- (M) (2:44) Motown 6312 Hitsville USA.
- (M) (2:44) Motown 6334 35th Anniversary Collection.
- (S) (2:44) Time-Life 2RNR-19 Rock 'N' Roll Era - 1963 Still Rockin'.
- (M) (2:44) Rhino 71806 The R&B Box: Thirty Years Of Rhythm & Blues.
- (S) (2:44) K-Tel 3331 Do You Wanna Dance.
- (M) (2:44) Motown 314530420 Motown Classic Hits Vol. III.
- (M) (2:44) Motown 314530472 Anthology.
- (M) (2:46) Motown 314530647 O.S.T. Nothing But A Man.
- (M) (2:44) Motown 314530857 Ultimate Collection.

1964 I LIKE IT LIKE THAT

- (S) (2:41) Motown 6202 Compact Command Performances Volume 2.
- (S) (2:42) Motown 6196 and 0793 Anthology.
- (M) (2:34) Motown 6334 35th Anniversary Collection.
- (M) (2:34) Motown 314530472 Anthology.
- (M) (2:33) Motown 314530857 Ultimate Collection.

1964 THAT'S WHAT LOVE IS MADE OF

- (S) (2:53) Motown 5451 A Collection Of 16 Big Hits Volume 4.
- (S) (2:47) Motown 6202 Compact Command Performances Volume 2.
- (S) (2:49) Motown 6196 and 0793 Anthology.
- (M) (2:55) Motown 6334 35th Anniversary Collection.

- (M) (2:54) Motown 314530422 Motown Classics Vol. V.
- (M) (2:55) Motown 314530472 Anthology.

1965 OOO BABY BABY

- (S) (2:44) Motown 6161 The Good-Feeling Music Of The Big Chill Generation Volume 3.
- (S) (2:45) Motown 6139 The Composer Series: Smokey Robinson.
- (S) (2:44) Motown 6202 Compact Command Performances Volume 2.
- (S) (2:44) Motown 6196 and 0793 Anthology.
- (S) (2:43) Original Sound 8863 Oldies But Goodies Vol. 13.
- (S) (2:43) Original Sound 2223 Oldies But Goodies Volumes 2,7,9,12 and 13 Box Set. *(Volumes 2, 7 and 12 of this box set use the "Waring - fds" noise reduction process)*
- (S) (2:43) Original Sound 2500 Oldies But Goodies Volumes 1-15 Box Set. *(most volumes in this box set use the "Waring - fds" noise reduction process)*
- (S) (2:44) Motown 9097 The Most Played Oldies On America's Jukeboxes.
- (S) (2:44) Motown 5316 Great Songs And Performances That Inspired The Motown 25th Anniversary TV Special.
- (S) (2:45) Motown 5210 Greatest Hits Volume 2.
- (S) (2:44) Motown 5269 Going To A Go-Go.
- (S) (2:44) Motown 5343 Every Great Motown Song: The First 25 Years Volume 1. *(most selections on this cd have noise on the fadeout)*
- (S) (2:44) Motown 8034 and 8134 Every Great Motown Song: The First 25 Years Volumes 1 & 2. *(most selections on this cd have noise on the fadeout)*
- (S) (2:43) Motown 8004 and 8104 Going To A Go-Go/Tears Of A Clown.
- (M) (2:42) Motown 6312 Hitsville USA.
- (M) (2:42) Motown 6334 35th Anniversary Collection.
- (S) (2:44) Time-Life 2CLR-08 Classic Rock - 1965: The Beat Goes On.
- (S) (2:44) Time-Life SUD-12 Superhits - The Mid 60's.
- (S) (2:45) Right Stuff 28371 Slow Jams: The 60's Volume Two.
- (S) (2:44) Time-Life OPCD-4517 Tonight's The Night.
- (S) (2:44) Thump 7030 Low Rider Oldies Volume III.
- (S) (2:44) Motown/Essex 374638529 Motown Legends - The Ballad Album.
- (S) (2:44) Rebound 314520033 Quiet Storm: The 70's.
- (S) (2:44) Polygram Special Markets 314520300 Motown Legends - Guy Groups.
- (M) (2:42) Motown 314530472 Anthology.
- (M) (2:43) Motown 314530569 Motown Milestones - Motown Love Songs.
- (M) (2:42) Motown 314530478 O.S.T. The Walking Dead.
- (S) (2:44) Polygram Special Markets 314520293 Motown Legends - Volume 5.
- (S) (2:45) Rebound 314520369 Soul Classics - Quiet Storm/The 60's.
- (S) (2:44) Time-Life AM1-05 AM Gold - The Mid '60s.
- (M) (2:41) Motown 314530857 Ultimate Collection.
- (M) (2:42) Time-Life R834-14 Body Talk - Love And Tenderness.
- (M) (2:41) Time-Life R857-20 The Heart Of Rock 'n' Roll 1965-1966.

1965 THE TRACKS OF MY TEARS

- (S) (2:53) Motown 6137 20 Greatest Songs In Motown History.
- (S) (2:53) Atlantic 81742 O.S.T. Platoon.
- (S) (2:54) Motown 6120 and 6062 O.S.T. The Big Chill.
- (S) (2:52) Motown 5452 A Collection Of 16 Big Hits Volume 5.
- (S) (2:53) Motown 6139 The Composer Series: Smokey Robinson.
- (S) (2:53) Rhino 70651 Billboard's Top R&B Hits Of 1965.
- (S) (2:53) Rhino 72006 Billboard's Top R&B Hits 1965-1969 Box Set.
- (S) (2:53) MCA 10063 Original Television Soundtrack "The Sounds Of Murphy Brown".
- (S) (2:53) Motown 9041 and 6071 Compact Command Performances.

(S) (2:53) Motown 6196 and 0793 Anthology.
(S) (2:53) Motown 9097 The Most Played Oldies On America's Jukeboxes.
(S) (2:53) Motown 5316 Great Songs And Performances That Inspired The Motown 25th Anniversary TV Special.
(S) (2:54) Motown 5210 Greatest Hits Volume 2.
(S) (2:53) Motown 5269 Going To A Go-Go.
(S) (2:56) Motown 5275 12 #1 Hits From The 70's.
(S) (2:53) Motown 8004 and 8104 Going To A Go-Go/Tears Of A Clown.
(M) (3:00) Motown 6312 Hitsville USA.
(M) (3:00) Motown 6334 35th Anniversary Collection.
(S) (2:51) Time-Life RHD-07 Rhythm & Blues - 1965.
(S) (2:52) Time-Life 2CLR-01 Classic Rock - 1965.
(S) (2:51) Time-Life SUD-03 Superhits - 1965.
(S) (2:52) Time-Life OPCD-4517 Tonight's The Night.
(S) (2:52) Original Sound 8883 21 Legendary Superstars.
(S) (2:53) Motown/Essex 374638529 Motown Legends - The Ballad Album.
(M) (3:00) Motown 314530472 Anthology.
(M) (3:00) Right Stuff 30577 Slow Jams: The 60's Volume 3.
(M) (2:59) Motown 314530478 O.S.T. The Walking Dead.
(M) (3:00) LaserLight 12315 and 15936 The Wonder Years - Movin' On.
(S) (2:51) Time-Life AM1-10 AM Gold - 1965.
(S) (2:51) Time-Life R838-12 Solid Gold Soul - 1965.
(M) (2:59) Motown 314530857 Ultimate Collection.

1965 MY GIRL HAS GONE
(S) (2:52) Motown 5454 A Collection Of 16 Big Hits Volume 7.
(S) (2:49) Motown 6202 Compact Command Performances Volume 2.
(S) (2:49) Motown 6196 and 0793 Anthology.
(S) (2:50) Motown 5210 Greatest Hits Volume 2.
(S) (2:49) Motown 5269 Going To A Go-Go.
(S) (2:49) Motown 8004 and 8104 Going To A Go-Go/Tears Of A Clown.
(M) (2:52) Motown 6334 35th Anniversary Collection.
(M) (2:52) Motown 314530472 Anthology.
(M) (2:51) Motown 314530857 Ultimate Collection.

1966 GOING TO A GO-GO
(S) (2:45) Rhino 70652 Billboard's Top R&B Hits Of 1966.
(S) (2:45) Rhino 72006 Billboard's Top R&B Hits 1965-1969 Box Set.
(S) (2:46) Motown 6139 The Composer Series: Smokey Robinson.
(S) (2:44) Motown 5453 A Collection Of 16 Big Hits Volume 6.
(S) (2:45) Motown 9041 and 6071 Compact Command Performances.
(S) (2:44) Motown 6196 and 0793 Anthology.
(S) (2:43) Motown 9072 Motown Dance Party Volume 2. *(all selections on this cd are segued together)*
(S) (2:45) Motown 5316 Great Songs And Performances That Inspired The Motown 25th Anniversary TV Special.
(S) (2:46) Motown 5210 Greatest Hits Volume 2.
(S) (2:45) Motown 5269 Going To A Go-Go.
(S) (2:45) Motown 8004 and 8104 Going To A Go-Go/Tears Of A Clown.
(S) (2:44) K-Tel 3063 Marvin Gaye/Smokey Robinson & The Miracles.
(M) (2:49) Motown 6334 35th Anniversary Collection.
(S) (2:43) Time-Life RHD-01 Rhythm & Blues - 1966.
(S) (2:44) Time-Life 2CLR-07 Classic Rock - 1966: The Beat Goes On.
(S) (2:45) Rebound 314520298 Disco Nights Vol. 9.
(M) (2:49) Motown 314530472 Anthology.
(S) (2:44) Motown 314530522 Motown Year By Year - 1966.
(S) (2:43) Time-Life R838-01 Solid Gold Soul - 1966.
(M) (2:48) Motown 314530857 Ultimate Collection.

1966 (COME 'ROUND HERE) I'M THE ONE YOU NEED
(S) (2:29) Motown 5455 A Collection Of 16 Big Hits Volume 8.

(S) (2:28) Motown 6202 Compact Command Performances Volume 2.
(S) (2:30) Motown 6196 and 0793 Anthology.
(S) (2:30) Motown 5210 Greatest Hits Volume 2.
(S) (2:28) Motown 5136 Away We A Go Go.
(S) (2:30) Motown 8050 and 8150 Doin' Mickey's Monkey/Away We A Go-Go.
(M) (2:29) Motown 6334 35th Anniversary Collection.
(M) (2:29) Motown 314530472 Anthology.
(M) (2:28) Motown 314530857 Ultimate Collection.

released as by SMOKEY ROBINSON & THE MIRACLES:
1967 THE LOVE I SAW IN YOU WAS JUST A MIRAGE
(M) (2:59) Motown 6334 35th Anniversary Collection.
(M) (2:59) Motown 314530472 Anthology.
(S) (2:56) Motown 5210 Greatest Hits Volume 2.
(S) (2:56) Motown 6196 and 0793 Anthology.
(S) (2:57) Motown 6202 Compact Command Performances Volume 2.
(S) (2:57) Motown 8004 and 8104 Going To A Go-Go/Tears Of A Clown.
(S) (2:57) Motown 9092 and 5156 Tears Of A Clown.
(M) (2:59) Eclipse Music Group 64870 Rock 'n Roll Relix 1966-1967.
(M) (2:59) Eclipse Music Group 64872 Rock 'n Roll Relix 1960-1969.
(M) (2:59) Rhino 72815 Beg, Scream & Shout! The Big Ol' Box Of '60s Soul.
(M) (2:56) Motown 314530857 Ultimate Collection.

1967 MORE LOVE
(S) (2:45) Motown 5456 A Collection Of 16 Big Hits Volume 9.
(S) (2:46) Motown 6139 The Composer Series: Smokey Robinson.
(S) (2:43) Motown 6202 Compact Command Performances Volume 2.
(S) (2:44) Motown 6196 and 0793 Anthology.
(S) (2:44) Motown 5210 Greatest Hits Volume 2.
(S) (2:46) Motown 9092 and 5156 Tears Of A Clown.
(S) (2:46) Motown 8004 and 8104 Going To A Go-Go/Tears Of A Clown.
(M) (2:47) Motown 6312 Hitsville USA.
(S) (2:44) K-Tel 3063 Marvin Gaye/Smokey Robinson & The Miracles.
(M) (2:47) Motown 6334 35th Anniversary Collection.
(S) (2:44) Motown/Essex 374638529 Motown Legends - The Ballad Album.
(M) (2:47) Motown 314530472 Anthology.
(M) (2:47) Motown 314530857 Ultimate Collection.

1967 I SECOND THAT EMOTION
(S) (2:45) Motown 6160 The Good-Feeling Music Of The Big Chill Generation Volume 2.
(S) (2:46) Motown 6139 The Composer Series: Smokey Robinson.
(S) (2:46) Motown 6110 Motown Grammy R&B Performances Of The 60's & 70's.
(S) (2:43) Motown 5456 A Collection Of 16 Big Hits Volume 9.
(S) (2:46) Motown 6120 and 6062 O.S.T. The Big Chill.
(S) (2:44) Rhino 70654 Billboard's Top R&B Hits Of 1968.
(S) (2:44) Rhino 72006 Billboard's Top R&B Hits 1965-1969 Box Set.
(S) (2:46) Motown 9041 and 6071 Compact Command Performances.
(S) (2:43) Motown 6196 and 0793 Anthology.
(S) (2:45) Motown 9018 and 5249 16 #1 Hits From The Late 60's.
(S) (2:45) Motown 9021 and 5309 25 Years Of Grammy Greats.
(S) (2:45) Motown 5316 Great Songs And Performances That Inspired The Motown 25th Anniversary TV Special.
(S) (2:45) Motown 5210 Greatest Hits Volume 2.
(M) (2:40) Motown 6312 Hitsville USA.
(S) (2:43) Motown 374638509 Motown Legends - I Second That Emotion.
(M) (2:40) Motown 6334 35th Anniversary Collection.
(S) (2:43) Time-Life RHD-04 Rhythm & Blues - 1968.

MIRACLES (Continued)

(S) (2:44) Time-Life 2CLR-05 Classic Rock - 1967.
(S) (2:42) Time-Life SUD-05 Superhits - 1967.
(S) (2:45) Polygram Special Markets 314520284 Motown Legends Volume 3.
(M) (2:40) Motown 314530472 Anthology.
(S) (2:42) Time-Life AM1-08 AM Gold - 1967.
(S) (2:43) Time-Life R838-03 Solid Gold Soul - 1968.
(M) (2:40) Motown 314530857 Ultimate Collection.

1968 IF YOU CAN WANT

(S) (2:42) Motown 9041 and 6071 Compact Command Performances. *(LP length)*
(S) (2:41) Motown 6196 and 0793 Anthology. *(LP length)*
(S) (2:42) Motown 8043 and 8143 Time Out For/Special Occasion. *(LP length)*
(S) (2:42) Motown 5418 Special Occasion. *(LP length)*
(S) (2:41) Motown 374638509 Motown Legends - I Second That Emotion. *(LP length)*
(M) (2:25) Motown 6334 35th Anniversary Collection. *(45 length)*
(M) (2:25) Motown 314530472 Anthology. *(45 length)*
(M) (2:24) Motown 314530857 Ultimate Collection. *(45 length)*

1968 YESTER LOVE

(S) (2:17) Motown 6202 Compact Command Performances Volume 2.
(S) (2:13) Motown 6196 and 0793 Anthology.
(S) (2:17) Motown 8043 and 8143 Time Out For/Special Occasion.
(S) (2:17) Motown 5418 Special Occasion.
(M) (2:17) Motown 6334 35th Anniversary Collection.
(M) (2:17) Motown 314530472 Anthology.
(S) (2:15) Motown 314530507 Motown Year By Year 1968.
(M) (2:17) Motown 314530857 Ultimate Collection.

1968 SPECIAL OCCASION

(S) (2:19) Motown 6202 Compact Command Performances Volume 2.
(S) (2:19) Motown 6196 and 0793 Anthology.
(S) (2:20) Motown 8043 and 8143 Time Out For/Special Occasion.
(S) (2:20) Motown 5418 Special Occasion.
(M) (2:17) Motown 6334 35th Anniversary Collection.
(M) (2:17) Motown 314530472 Anthology.
(M) (2:16) Motown 314530857 Ultimate Collection.

1969 BABY, BABY DON'T CRY
(actual 45 time is (3:54) not (3:29) as stated on the record label; actual LP time is (3:58) not (3:29) as stated on the record label)

(S) (4:01) Motown 9041 and 6071 Compact Command Performances.
(S) (4:01) Motown 6196 and 0793 Anthology.
(S) (3:55) Motown 8043 and 8143 Time Out For/Special Occasion.
(S) (4:01) Motown 5437 Time Out For.
(M) (3:56) Motown 6312 Hitsville USA.
(M) (3:56) Motown 6334 35th Anniversary Collection.
(S) (4:01) Time-Life RHD-13 Rhythm & Blues - 1969.
(S) (4:01) Time-Life 2CLR-06 Classic Rock - 1969.
(S) (4:01) Motown/Essex 374638529 Motown Legends - The Ballad Album.
(S) (4:01) Polygram Special Markets 314520300 Motown Legends - Guy Groups.
(M) (3:56) Motown 314530472 Anthology.
(M) (3:55) Motown 314530525 Motown Year By Year - 1969.
(M) (3:56) Motown 314530569 Motown Milestones - Motown Love Songs.
(M) (3:56) Thump 9947 Cruizin' To Motown.
(S) (4:01) Time-Life R838-04 Solid Gold Soul - 1969.
(M) (3:56) Motown 314530857 Ultimate Collection.
(M) (3:55) Time-Life R834-12 Body Talk - By Candlelight.

1969 DOGGONE RIGHT

(S) (2:56) Motown 9041 and 6071 Compact Command Performances.
(S) (2:56) Motown 6196 and 0793 Anthology.
(S) (2:56) Motown 8043 and 8143 Time Out For/Special Occasion.

(S) (2:56) Motown 5437 Time Out For.
(M) (2:57) Motown 6334 35th Anniversary Collection.
(M) (2:57) Motown 314530472 Anthology.

1970 TEARS OF A CLOWN

(S) (2:58) Rhino 70631 Billboard's Top Rock & Roll Hits Of 1970. *(LP version)*
(S) (2:58) Rhino 72005 Billboard's Top Rock & Roll Hits 1968-1972 Box Set. *(LP version)*
(S) (2:59) Motown 6132 25 #1 Hits From 25 Years. *(LP version)*
(S) (2:58) Motown 6177 Endless Love. *(LP version)*
(S) (2:59) Motown 6139 The Composer Series: Smokey Robinson. *(LP version)*
(S) (2:56) Motown 5275 12 #1 Hits From The 70's. *(LP version)*
(S) (2:59) Motown 9041 and 6071 Compact Command Performances. *(LP version)*
(S) (2:58) Motown 6196 and 0793 Anthology. *(LP version)*
(S) (2:58) Motown 9097 The Most Played Oldies On America's Jukeboxes. *(LP version)*
(S) (2:58) Motown 5316 Great Songs And Performances That Inspired The Motown 25th Anniversary TV Special. *(LP version)*
(S) (3:00) Motown 9092 and 5156 Tears Of A Clown. *(LP version)*
(S) (3:01) Motown 8004 and 8104 Going To A Go-Go/Tears Of A Clown. *(LP version)*
(S) (2:58) Motown 9060 Motown's Biggest Pop Hits. *(LP version)*
(S) (2:58) Motown 0937 20/20 Twenty No. 1 Hits From Twenty Years At Motown. *(LP version)*
(S) (2:54) Motown 9071 Motown Dance Party Volume 1. *(all selections on this cd are segued together; LP version)*
(M) (3:03) Motown 6312 Hitsville USA. *(45 version)*
(S) (2:58) K-Tel 3063 Marvin Gaye/Smokey Robinson & The Miracles. *(LP version)*
(M) (3:03) Motown 6334 35th Anniversary Collection. *(45 version)*
(S) (2:56) Time-Life RHD-18 Rhythm & Blues - 1970. *(LP version)*
(S) (2:56) Time-Life SUD-16 Superhits - The Early 70's. *(LP version)*
(S) (2:58) Time-Life SOD-01 Sounds Of The Seventies - 1970. *(LP version)*
(M) (3:03) MCA 11065 O.S.T. Crooklyn Volume II. *(45 version)*
(M) (3:03) Motown 314530472 Anthology. *(45 version)*
(M) (3:03) LaserLight 12315 and 15936 The Wonder Years - Movin' On. *(45 version)*
(S) (2:56) Time-Life AM1-13 AM Gold - The Early '70s. *(LP version)*
(S) (2:56) Time-Life R838-05 Solid Gold Soul - 1970. *(LP version)*
(M) (3:02) Motown 314530857 Ultimate Collection. *(45 version)*
(S) (2:58) Motown 314530849 Motown 40 Forever. *(LP version)*
(S) (2:58) Collectables 1516 and 2516 The Anniversary Album - The 70's. *(LP version; truncated fade)*

1971 I DON'T BLAME YOU AT ALL

(S) (3:09) Motown 9041 and 6071 Compact Command Performances.
(S) (3:08) Motown 6196 and 0793 Anthology.
(M) (3:05) Motown 6334 35th Anniversary Collection.
(M) (3:05) Motown 314530472 Anthology.

released as by THE MIRACLES:
1974 DO IT BABY

(S) (2:53) Motown 9104 and 5409 Motown Memories Volume 1.
(S) (3:02) Rhino 70554 Soul Hits Of The 70's Volume 14.
(S) (2:57) Motown 6196 and 0793 Anthology.
(S) (2:53) Motown 6202 Compact Command Performances Volume 2.
(S) (3:01) Motown 6358 Hitsville USA Volume Two.
(S) (3:02) Motown 6334 35th Anniversary Collection.

1976 LOVE MACHINE (PART 1)

    (S)   (2:51)   Priority 7975 Mega-Hits Dance Classics Volume 5. *(45 version)*

    (S)   (2:59)   Rhino 70671 Billboard Top Hits - 1976. *(45 version)*

    (S)   (2:54)   Motown 0937 20/20 Twenty No. 1 Hits From Twenty Years At Motown. *(45 version)*

    (S)   (2:54)   Motown 5275 12 #1 Hits From The 70's. *(45 version)*

    (S)   (2:54)   Rhino 70274 The Disco Years Volume 3. *(45 version)*

    (S)   (6:47)   Motown 6196 and 0793 Anthology. *(LP version)*

    (S)   (6:49)   Motown 6202 Compact Command Performances Volume 2. *(LP version)*

    (S)   (2:58)   Motown 6358 Hitsville USA Volume Two. *(45 version)*

    (S)   (2:58)   Motown 6334 35th Anniversary Collection. *(45 version)*

    (S)   (6:49)   Rebound 314520298 Disco Nights Vol. 9. *(LP version)*

    (S)   (2:59)   Rebound 314520317 Class Reunion 1975. *(45 version)*

    (S)   (6:52)   Motown 314530531 Motown Year By Year - 1975. *(12" dj only single version)*

    (S)   (2:53)   Motown 314530531 Motown Year By Year - 1975. *(45 version)*

    (S)   (2:59)   Time-Life R838-11 Solid Gold Soul - 1976. *(45 version)*

    (S)   (2:59)   K-Tel 3908 High Energy Volume 1. *(45 version)*

    (S)   (2:58)   JCI 3175 1975 - Only Soul - 1979. *(45 version)*

    (S)   (2:54)   Time-Life R840-06 Sounds Of The Seventies: '70s Dance Party 1975-1976. *(45 version)*

MISSING PERSONS
1982 WORDS

    (S)   (4:25)   Priority 7994 Rock Of The 80's.

    (S)   (4:26)   Capitol 46628 Best Of.

    (S)   (4:23)   Rhino 72820 VH1 - More Of The Big 80's.

1982 DESTINATION UNKNOWN

    (S)   (3:33)   EMI 89605 Living In Oblivion: The 80's Greatest Hits Volume Two.

    (S)   (3:32)   Priority 53749 Rock Of The 80's Volume 6.

    (S)   (3:31)   K-Tel 3262 The 80's Video Stars.

    (S)   (3:33)   Capitol 46628 Best Of.

    (S)   (3:29)   Simitar 55612 The Number One's: The '80s.

MR. BIG
1992 TO BE WITH YOU

    (S)   (3:25)   JCI 3135 14 Original Metal Ballads.

    (S)   (3:25)   Atlantic 82209 Lean Into It.

    (S)   (3:25)   Time-Life R968-25 Guitar Rock - The '90s.

    (S)   (3:25)   K-Tel 3850 90s Now Volume 3.

    (S)   (3:25)   Time-Life R834-19 Body Talk - Always And Forever.

1992 JUST TAKE MY HEART

    (S)   (4:22)   Atlantic 82209 Lean Into It.

1993 WILD WORLD

    (S)   (3:27)   Atlantic 82495 Bump Ahead.

MR. MISTER
1985 BROKEN WINGS

    (S)   (5:23)   RCA 9970 Nipper's Greatest Hits - The 80's. *(faded :20 earlier than the LP version)*

    (S)   (4:43)   Rhino 71640 Billboard Top Hits - 1985. *(45 version)*

    (S)   (4:36)   JCI 3128 1985 - Only Rock 'N Roll - 1989. *(45 version)*

    (S)   (5:43)   RCA 8045 Welcome To The Real World. *(LP version)*

    (S)   (4:41)   Time-Life R988-02 Sounds Of The Eighties: 1985. *(45 version)*

    (S)   (5:34)   K-Tel 3473 The 80s: New Wave. *(LP version faded :09 early)*

    (S)   (4:40)   RCA 66812 Do You Love Me? (All-Time Best Love Songs). *(45 version)*

    (S)   (4:43)   Time-Life R834-04 Body Talk - Together Forever. *(45 version)*

    (S)   (4:43)   Hip-O 40080 Essential '80s: 1985-1989. *(45 version)*

1986 KYRIE

    (S)   (4:28)   RCA 9902 Nipper's #1 Hits 1956-1986. *(LP version)*

    (S)   (4:13)   Rhino 71641 Billboard Top Hits - 1986. *(45 version)*

    (S)   (4:23)   RCA 8045 Welcome To The Real World. *(LP version)*

    (S)   (4:29)   Priority 53798 Best Of 80's Rock Volume 5. *(LP version)*

    (S)   (4:13)   Time-Life R988-04 Sounds Of The Eighties: 1986. *(45 version)*

    (S)   (4:23)   RCA 66862 Hi Octane Hard Drivin' Hits. *(LP version)*

    (S)   (4:13)   JCI 3171 #1 Radio Hits 1985 - Only Rock 'n Roll - 1989. *(45 version)*

    (S)   (4:28)   Simitar 55612 The Number One's: The '80s. *(LP version)*

1986 IS IT LOVE

    (S)   (3:33)   RCA 8045 Welcome To The Real World.

    (S)   (3:23)   JCI 3186 1985 - Only Love - 1989.

1987 SOMETHING REAL (INSIDE ME/INSIDE YOU)

    (S)   (4:20)   RCA 6276 Go On.

MR. PRESIDENT
1997 COCO JAMBOO

    (S)   (3:37)   Warner Brothers 46655 Mr. President.

GUY MITCHELL
1956 NINETY NINE YEARS (DEAD OR ALIVE)
1956 SINGING THE BLUES

    (M)   (2:24)   Columbia 45110 16 Most Requested Songs Of The 50's Volume 1.

    (M)   (2:24)   Columbia 45017 Radio Classics Of The 50's.

    (M)   (2:24)   Columbia 46096 16 Most Requested Songs.

    (M)   (2:25)   Rhino 71252 Sentimental Journey: Pop Vocal Classics Volume 4 (1954-1959).

    (M)   (2:25)   Rhino 72034 Sentimental Journey Pop Vocal Classics Volumes 1-4 Box Set.

    (M)   (2:25)   Time-Life HPD-15 Your Hit Parade - 1956.

    (M)   (2:24)   JCI 3129 1955 - Only Rock 'N Roll - 1959.

    (M)   (2:24)   JCI 7021 Those Wonderful Years - April Love.

    (M)   (2:25)   Time-Life R132-12 Your Hit Parade - #1 Hits Of The '50s.

1957 KNEE DEEP IN THE BLUES

    (M)   (2:10)   Columbia 46096 16 Most Requested Songs.

1957 ROCK-A-BILLY

    (M)   (2:11)   Time-Life HPD-38 Your Hit Parade - The 50's Generation.

1959 HEARTACHES BY THE NUMBER

    (S)   (2:37)   Time-Life HPD-13 Your Hit Parade - 1959.

JONI MITCHELL
1973 YOU TURN ME ON, I'M A RADIO

    (S)   (2:38)   Asylum 5057 For The Roses.

    (S)   (4:08)   Asylum 202 Miles Of Aisles. *(live)*

    (S)   (2:36)   Time-Life R105-26 Our Songs: Singers & Songwriters Encore.

    (S)   (2:38)   Reprise 46326 Hits.

1974 HELP ME

    (S)   (3:28)   Warner Special Products 27615 Storytellers: Singers & Songwriters.

    (S)   (3:22)   Asylum 1001 Court And Spark. *(tracks into next selection)*

    (S)   (3:22)   DCC Compact Classics 1025 Court And Spark. *(tracks into next selection; gold disc)*

    (S)   (3:20)   Time-Life SOD-07 Sounds Of The Seventies - 1974.

    (S)   (3:19)   Time-Life R105-26 Our Songs: Singers & Songwriters Encore.

    (S)   (3:21)   Reprise 46326 Hits.

1974 FREE MAN IN PARIS

    (S)   (3:01)   Asylum 1001 Court And Spark.

    (S)   (3:01)   DCC Compact Classics 1025 Court And Spark. *(gold disc)*

    (S)   (3:01)   Reprise 46326 Hits.

JONI MITCHELL *(Continued)*
1975 BIG YELLOW TAX (live version)
- (S) (3:08) Asylum 202 Miles Of Aisles.
- (S) (2:14) Reprise 46326 Hits. *(studio version)*

WILLIE MITCHELL
1964 20-75
- (S) (2:12) MCA 25226 History Of Hi Records Rhythm & Blues Volume 1.
- (S) (2:11) Time-Life 2RNR-36 Rock 'N' Roll Era - Axes & Saxes/The Great Instrumentals.
- (M) (2:13) Right Stuff 30584 Hi Times - The Hi Records R&B Years.

1968 SOUL SERENADE
- (S) (2:17) MCA 25226 History Of Hi Records Rhythm & Blues Volume 1.
- (S) (2:17) Rhino 70562 Legends Of Guitar - Rock: The 60's Volume 2.
- (S) (2:17) Time-Life 2CLR-27 Classic Rock - 1968: Blowin' Your Mind.
- (S) (2:18) Right Stuff 30584 Hi Times - The Hi Records R&B Years.
- (*) (*:**) Right Stuff 53318 Hot Rod Rock Volume 3: Big Boss Instrumentals. *(this is not the song "SOUL SERENADE" as claimed on the cd jacket but another song titled "SOUL FINGER")*

MOCEDADES
1974 ERES TU (TOUCH THE WIND)
(actual 45 time is (3:30) not (3:12) as stated on the record label)
- (S) (3:31) Rhino 70759 Super Hits Of The 70's Volume 12.
- (S) (3:30) Warner Brothers 45904 O.S.T. Tommy Boy (The Movie).

MODELS
1986 OUT OF MIND, OUT OF SIGHT
- (S) (3:34) Hip-O 40022 That Sound From Down Under.
- (S) (3:34) Geffen 25151 Geffen Vintage 80s Vol. II.

DOMENICO MODUGNO
1958 NEL BLU DIPINTO DI BLUE (VOLARE)
- (M) (3:30) Time-Life HPD-31 Your Hit Parade - The 50's Forever.
- (M) (3:33) K-Tel 3209 Italian Love Songs.
- (M) (3:34) Rhino 72577 Eh, Paisano! Italian-American Classics.

MOJO MEN
1967 SIT DOWN, I THINK I LOVE YOU
- (M) (2:20) Warner Special Products 27610 More Party Classics.
- (M) (2:19) Rhino 70536 San Francisco Nights.
- (M) (2:19) JCI 3114 Easy Sixties.
- (M) (2:18) Time-Life 2CLR-29 Classic Rock - Bubblegum, Garage And Pop Nuggets.
- (M) (2:19) Sundazed 11032 Sit Down...It's The Mojo Men.
- (M) (2:18) JCI 3160 18 Free & Easy Hits From The 60's.
- (M) (2:18) JCI 3185 1965 - Only Love - 1969.

MOKENSTEF
1995 HE'S MINE
- (S) (4:13) OutBurst 314527364 Azz Izz.
- (S) (3:57) Def Jam 314523848 Def Jam Music Group 10th Year Anniversary. *(remix)*
- (S) (4:12) Loud/RCA 67423 All That - The Album.
- (S) (4:12) Polygram TV 314553641 Pure Soul 1997.

MOMENTS
1970 LOVE ON A TWO-WAY STREET
(actual LP length is (3:43) not (3:50) as stated on the record label; actual 45 length is (3:25) not (3:05) as stated on the record label)
- (S) (3:26) Rhino 70658 Billboard's Top R&B Hits Of 1970.
- (S) (3:26) Rhino 70782 Soul Hits Of The 70's Volume 2.
- (S) (3:26) Rhino 72028 Soul Hits Of The 70's Volumes 1-5 Box Set.
- (S) (3:26) Rhino 71206 70's Smash Hits Volume 2.
- (S) (3:42) Time-Life SOD-01 Sounds Of The Seventies - 1970.
- (S) (3:43) Thump 7040 Low Rider Oldies Volume 4.
- (S) (3:26) Ripete 2163-RE Ebb Tide.
- (S) (3:26) Ripete 2220 Soul Patrol Vol. 2.
- (S) (3:43) Rhino 72112 Billboard Hot Soul Hits - 1970.
- (S) (3:43) Priority 53130 Deep Soul Volume Three.
- (S) (3:33) Rhino 72415 Best Of: Love On A Two Way Street.
- (S) (3:42) JCI 3173 1970 - Only Soul - 1974.
- (S) (3:26) Flashback 72682 '70s Radio Hits Volume 2.
- (S) (3:26) Flashback 72090 '70s Radio Hits Box Set.
- (S) (3:33) Flashback 72900 25 Years Of Soul - 1970.
- (S) (3:26) K-Tel 3900 Great R&B Male Groups: Hits Of The 70's.

1974 SEXY MAMA
- (S) (6:36) Thump 7040 Low Rider Oldies Volume 4. *(edit of LP version)*
- (S) (3:08) K-Tel 6013 70's Soul - Sexy Ballads. *(45 version)*
- (S) (3:08) Rhino 72126 Soul Hits Of The 70's Vol. 16. *(45 version)*
- (S) (8:50) Rhino 72415 Best Of: Love On A Two Way Street. *(LP version)*
- (S) (8:50) Rhino 72511 Smooth Grooves: A Sensual Collection Volume 9. *(LP version)*

1975 LOOK AT ME (I'M IN LOVE)
- (S) (3:15) Rhino 72415 Best Of: Love On A Two Way Street.
- (S) (3:07) Priority 53146 Slow Grind Volume Two.

EDDIE MONEY
1978 BABY HOLD ON
- (S) (3:29) Epic 46940 O.S.T. Queens Logic. *(LP version)*
- (S) (3:30) Columbia 34909 and 66228 Eddie Money. *(LP version)*
- (S) (3:30) Columbia 45381 Greatest Hits: Sound Of Money. *(LP version)*
- (S) (3:30) Razor & Tie 22502 Those Rocking 70's. *(LP version)*
- (S) (3:30) Time-Life SOD-10 Sounds Of The Seventies - 1978. *(LP version)*
- (S) (3:29) Time-Life R968-17 Guitar Rock - The Late 70s: Take Two. *(LP version)*
- (S) (3:30) Columbia/Legacy 65385 Eddie Money/Life For The Taking/No Control. *(LP version)*
- (S) (3:30) Columbia/Legacy 65274 Super Hits. *(LP version)*

1978 TWO TICKETS TO PARADISE
- (S) (3:57) Columbia 34909 and 66228 Eddie Money. *(LP version)*
- (S) (3:56) Columbia 45381 Greatest Hits: Sound Of Money. *(LP version)*
- (S) (3:56) Time-Life SOD-37 Sounds Of The Seventies - AM Heavy Hits. *(LP version)*
- (S) (3:56) Time-Life R968-14 Guitar Rock - The Late '70s. *(LP version)*
- (S) (3:56) Epic/Legacy 65020 Ultimate Rock 'n' Roll Collection. *(LP version)*
- (S) (3:56) Priority 50991 The Best Of The 70's - Rock Chart Toppers. *(LP version)*
- (S) (3:57) Columbia/Legacy 65385 Eddie Money/Life For The Taking/No Control. *(LP version)*
- (S) (3:56) Columbia/Legacy 65274 Super Hits. *(LP version)*
- (S) (3:56) K-Tel 3904 The Rock Album Volume 1. *(LP version)*
- (S) (3:57) CMC International 86234 Rockin' The 80's. *(live)*
- (S) (3:56) Sony Music Special Products 26069 Rock Hits Of The 70's. *(LP version)*
- (S) (3:56) Simitar 55582 The Number One's: Rock It Up. *(LP version)*
- (S) (3:56) JCI 3193 18 Rock Classics Volume 3. *(LP version)*
- (S) (3:56) Thump 6010 Easyriders Volume 1. *(LP version)*

1979 MAYBE I'M A FOOL
(S) (3:03) Columbia 35598 Life For The Taking.
(S) (3:03) Columbia/Legacy 65385 Eddie Money/Life For The Taking/No Control.

1982 THINK I'M IN LOVE
(S) (3:08) Columbia 37960 No Control.
(S) (3:07) Columbia 45381 Greatest Hits: Sound Of Money.
(S) (3:07) Rhino 72595 Billboard Top Album Rock Hits, 1982.
(S) (3:08) Columbia/Legacy 65385 Eddie Money/Life For The Taking/No Control.
(S) (3:07) Columbia/Legacy 65274 Super Hits.

1986 TAKE ME HOME TONIGHT
(S) (3:28) Priority 53702 Hot And Sexy - Rock All Night.
(S) (3:31) Rhino 71641 Billboard Top Hits - 1986.
(S) (3:27) Time-Life R105-40 Rock Dreams.
(S) (3:30) Columbia 40096 Can't Hold Back.
(S) (3:28) Columbia 45381 Greatest Hits: Sound Of Money.
(S) (3:31) Time-Life R988-12 Sounds Of The 80's: 1985-1986.
(S) (3:30) Columbia/Legacy 65274 Super Hits.
(S) (4:11) CMC International 86234 Rockin' The 80's. *(live)*

1986 I WANNA GO BACK
(S) (3:54) Columbia 40096 Can't Hold Back.
(S) (3:52) Columbia 45381 Greatest Hits: Sound Of Money.
(S) (3:55) Columbia/Legacy 65274 Super Hits.

1987 ENDLESS NIGHTS
(S) (3:22) Columbia 40096 Can't Hold Back.

1988 WALK ON WATER
(actual 45 time is (4:11) not (4:20) as stated on the record label)
(S) (4:38) Risky Business 57833 Read The Hits/Best Of The 80's. *(LP length)*
(S) (4:37) Columbia 44302 Nothing To Lose. *(LP length)*
(S) (4:37) Columbia 45381 Greatest Hits: Sound Of Money. *(LP length)*
(S) (4:37) Columbia/Legacy 65274 Super Hits. *(LP length)*

1989 THE LOVE IN YOUR EYES
(S) (4:05) Columbia 44302 Nothing To Lose.

1989 PEACE IN OUR TIME
(S) (4:59) Columbia 45381 Greatest Hits: Sound Of Money. *(LP version)*

1992 I'LL GET BY
(S) (3:31) Sandstone 33053 and 5021 Cosmopolitan Volume 7.
(S) (3:31) DCC Compact Classics 081 Night Moves Volume 1.
(S) (3:31) Columbia 46756 Right Here.
(S) (3:31) Time-Life R834-20 Body Talk - Heart And Soul.

MONICA
1995 DON'T TAKE IT PERSONAL (JUST ONE OF DEM DAYS)
(S) (4:17) Rowdy 37006 Miss Thang.
(S) (3:49) Rowdy 37006 Miss Thang. *(remix)*
(S) (3:39) Arista 18977 Ultimate Hip Hop Party 1998. *(all selections on this cd are segued together)*

1995 BEFORE YOU WALK OUT OF MY LIFE
(S) (4:52) Rowdy 37006 Miss Thang.

1995 LIKE THIS AND LIKE THAT
(S) (4:41) Rowdy 37006 Miss Thang.

1996 WHY I LOVE YOU SO MUCH
(S) (4:29) Rowdy 37006 Miss Thang.

1997 FOR YOU I WILL
(S) (4:54) Warner Sunset/Atlantic 82961 O.S.T. Space Jam.

MONIFAH
1996 YOU
(S) (4:22) Uptown/Universal 30042 Moods...Moments.

MONKEES
1966 LAST TRAIN TO CLARKSVILLE
(S) (2:44) Arista 8313 Greatest Hits. *(truncated fade)*
(S) (2:44) Arista 8524 The Monkees. *(truncated fade)*
(M) (2:41) Arista 8432 Then & Now...The Best Of.
(S) (2:43) Rhino 70566 Listen To The Band.

(M) (2:41) Time-Life 2CLR-07 Classic Rock - 1966: The Beat Goes On.
(S) (2:43) Rhino 71790 The Monkees.
(S) (2:43) Rhino 71936 Billboard Top Pop Hits, 1966.
(S) (2:43) Varese Sarabande 5670 Songs Of Tommy Boyce And Bobby Hart.
(S) (2:43) Rhino 72190 Greatest Hits.
(S) (2:43) Rhino 75269 Anthology.

1966 I'M A BELIEVER
(S) (2:45) Rhino 70627 Billboard's Top Rock & Roll Hits Of 1966.
(S) (2:45) Rhino 72007 Billboard's Top Rock & Roll Hits 1962-1966 Box Set.
(S) (2:42) Original Sound 8853 Oldies But Goodies Vol. 3. *(this compact disc uses the "Waring - fds" noise reduction process)*
(S) (2:42) Original Sound 2222 Oldies But Goodies Volumes 3,5,11,14 and 15 Box Set. *(this box set uses the "Waring - fds" noise reduction process)*
(S) (2:42) Original Sound 2500 Oldies But Goodies Volumes 1-15 Box Set. *(this box set uses the "Waring - fds" noise reduction process)*
(S) (2:44) Arista 8313 Greatest Hits.
(S) (2:44) Arista 8525 More Of The Monkees.
(S) (2:44) Arista 8432 Then & Now...The Best Of.
(S) (2:43) Rhino 70566 Listen To The Band.
(S) (2:44) Time-Life 2CLR-02 Classic Rock - 1966.
(S) (2:43) Time-Life SUD-01 Superhits - 1966.
(S) (2:42) Original Sound 8883 21 Legendary Superstars.
(S) (2:43) Rhino 71791 More Of The Monkees.
(M) (2:51) Rhino 71791 More Of The Monkees. *(demo version)*
(S) (2:44) Varese Sarabande 5575 Bubblegum Classics Volume Two.
(M) (2:44) Rhino 72190 Greatest Hits.
(S) (2:43) JCI 3167 #1 Radio Hits 1965 - Only Rock 'n Roll - 1969.
(S) (2:43) Time-Life AM1-09 AM Gold - 1966.
(S) (2:44) Flashback 72883 I'm A Believer And Other Hits.
(S) (2:44) Rhino 75269 Anthology.

1966 (I'M NOT YOUR) STEPPIN' STONE
(S) (2:21) Arista 8313 Greatest Hits. *(LP version)*
(S) (2:21) Arista 8525 More Of The Monkees. *(LP version)*
(S) (2:22) Arista 8432 Then & Now...The Best Of. *(LP version)*
(S) (2:20) Rhino 70566 Listen To The Band. *(45 version)*
(S) (2:21) JCI 3111 Good Time Sixties. *(LP version)*
(S) (2:21) Time-Life 2CLR-15 Classic Rock - 1967: Shakin' All Over. *(LP version)*
(S) (2:21) Rhino 71791 More Of The Monkees. *(LP version)*
(M) (2:19) Rhino 72190 Greatest Hits. *(45 version)*
(M) (2:19) Flashback 72883 I'm A Believer And Other Hits. *(45 version)*
(M) (2:19) Rhino 75269 Anthology. *(45 version)*

1967 A LITTLE BIT ME, A LITTLE BIT YOU
(S) (2:48) K-Tel 839 Battle Of The Bands Volume 2. *(LP version)*
(S) (2:49) Arista 8313 Greatest Hits. *(LP version)*
(S) (2:49) Arista 8432 Then & Now...The Best Of. *(LP Version)*
(M) (2:47) Rhino 70566 Listen To The Band. *(45 version)*
(S) (2:45) Time-Life 2CLR-10 Classic Rock - 1967: The Beat Goes On. *(LP version)*
(M) (2:46) Rhino 71937 Billboard Top Pop Hits, 1967. *(45 version)*
(M) (2:47) Rhino 72190 Greatest Hits. *(45 version)*
(M) (2:47) Varese Sarabande 5719 Bubblegum Classics Volume Three. *(45 version)*
(S) (2:47) Flashback 72883 I'm A Believer And Other Hits. *(LP version)*
(M) (2:47) Rhino 75269 Anthology. *(45 version)*

1967 PLEASANT VALLEY SUNDAY
(S) (3:13) Rhino 75892 Nuggets. *(LP version without "PET PIG PORKY" introduction)*
(S) (3:13) Arista 8313 Greatest Hits. *(LP version without "PET PIG PORKY" introduction)*

MONKEES *(Continued)*

(S) (3:13) Arista 8432 Then & Now...The Best Of. *(LP version without "PET PIG PORKY" introduction)*
(S) (3:40) Arista 8603 Pices, Aquarius, Capricorn & Jones Ltd. *(LP version with :27 "PET PIG PORKY" introduction)*
(S) (3:16) Rhino 70566 Listen To The Band. *(neither the LP or 45 version; remixed; slightly longer fade than the 45 or LP version)*
(S) (3:12) Time-Life 2CLR-10 Classic Rock - 1967: The Beat Goes On. *(LP version without "PET PIG PORKY" introduction)*
(S) (3:12) Rhino 71793 Pisces, Aquarius, Capricorn & Jones Ltd. *(LP version with "PET PIG PORKY" introduction listed as a separate track)*
(M) (3:07) Rhino 72190 Greatest Hits. *(45 version)*
(S) (3:12) Time-Life 2CLR-31 Classic Rock - Totally Fantastic '60s. *(LP version without "PET PIG PORKY" introduction)*
(M) (3:06) Rhino 75269 Anthology. *(45 version)*

1967 WORDS

(S) (2:52) Arista 8432 Then & Now...The Best Of. *(LP version)*
(S) (2:50) Arista 8334 More Greatest Hits. *(LP version)*
(S) (2:51) Arista 8603 Pisces, Aquarius, Capricorn & Jones Ltd. *(previous selection tracks over introduction; LP version)*
(S) (2:53) Rhino 70566 Listen To The Band. *(LP version)*
(S) (2:48) Rhino 71793 Pisces, Aquarius, Capricorn & Jones Ltd. *(previous selection tracks into introduction; LP version)*
(M) (2:48) Rhino 72190 Greatest Hits. *(45 version)*
(M) (2:48) Rhino 75269 Anthology. *(45 version)*

1967 DAYDREAM BELIEVER
(45 and LP length is (2:56))

(S) (3:05) Rhino 70628 Billboard's Top Rock & Roll Hits Of 1967.
(S) (3:04) Arista 8313 Greatest Hits.
(S) (3:05) Arista 8432 Then & Now...The Best Of.
(S) (3:08) Rhino 70566 Listen To The Band.
(S) (2:56) Time-Life 2CLR-05 Classic Rock - 1967. *(missing the :07 spoken introduction)*
(S) (2:53) Time-Life SUD-05 Superhits - 1967. *(missing the :07 spoken introduction)*
(S) (2:56) Rhino 71794 The Birds, The Bees & The Monkees.
(S) (2:57) Rhino 72190 Greatest Hits.
(S) (2:56) JCI 3160 18 Free & Easy Hits From The 60's. *(missing the :07 spoken introduction)*
(S) (2:48) Columbia 67380 O.S.T. Now And Then. *(missing the :07 introduction)*
(S) (2:53) Time-Life AM1-08 AM Gold - 1967. *(missing the :07 spoken introduction)*
(S) (2:57) Varese Sarabande 5802 Sunshine Days - Pop Classics Of The '60s Volume 2.
(S) (2:56) Rhino 72819 16 Magazine - Who's Your Fave Rave.
(S) (2:56) Rhino 75269 Anthology.
(S) (2:48) Collectables 1515 and 2515 The Anniversary Album - The 60's. *(missing the :07 spoken introduction)*

1968 VALLERI

(S) (2:12) Warner Special Products 27602 20 Party Classics.
(S) (2:18) Arista 8432 Then & Now...The Best Of. *(cold ending unlike the 45 and LP and slightly longer because of the different ending)*
(S) (2:18) Rhino 75892 Nuggets. *(same comments as for Arista 8432)*
(S) (2:16) Arista 8334 More Greatest Hits. *(same comments as for Arista 8432)*
(S) (2:19) Rhino 70566 Listen To The Band. *(same comments as for Arista 8432)*
(S) (2:18) Time-Life 2CLR-04 Classic Rock - 1968. *(same comments as for Arista 8432)*
(S) (2:12) Rhino 71794 The Birds, The Bees & The Monkees.
(S) (2:30) Varese Sarabande 5670 Songs Of Tommy Boyce And Bobby Hart. *(TV series version)*

(S) (2:18) Rhino 72190 Greatest Hits. *(same comments as for Arista 8432)*
(S) (2:18) JCI 3190 1965 - Only Dance - 1969. *(same comments as for Arista 8432)*
(S) (2:18) Rhino 75269 Anthology. *(same comments as for Arista 8432)*

1968 D.W. WASHBURN

(S) (2:47) Arista 8432 Then & Now...The Best Of.
(S) (2:47) Rhino 70566 Listen To The Band.
(S) (2:47) Rhino 72190 Greatest Hits.

released as by MICKEY DOLENZ and PETER TORK of THE MONKEES:
1986 THAT WAS THEN, THIS IS NOW

(S) (4:00) Arista 8432 Then & Now...The Best Of The Monkees.
(S) (4:00) Rhino 70566 Monkees - Listen To The Band.
(S) (4:00) Rhino 72190 Monkees - Greatest Hits.
(S) (4:01) Rhino 75269 Anthology.

MONOTONES
1958 BOOK OF LOVE

(M) (2:18) Rhino 75764 Best Of Doo Wop Uptempo.
(M) (2:18) Rhino 70644 Billboard's Top R&B Hits Of 1958.
(M) (2:19) MCA 31198 Vintage Music Volume 1.
(M) (2:19) MCA 5777 Vintage Music Volumes 1 & 2.
(M) (2:17) Chess 31320 Best Of Chess Rock 'n' Roll Volume 2.
(E) (2:17) Collectables 2508 History Of Rock - The Doo Wop Era Part 2.
(E) (2:17) Collectables 4508 History Of Rock/The Doo Wop Era Part Two.
(M) (2:18) Collectables 5427 Who Wrote The Book Of Love.
(M) (2:23) Collectables 5427 Who Wrote The Book Of Love. *(alternate take)*
(M) (2:18) MCA 8001 O.S.T. American Graffiti. *(Wolfman Jack talks over the introduction)*
(M) (2:18) Rhino 71463 Doo Wop Box.
(M) (2:18) Time-Life 2RNR-05 Rock 'N' Roll Era - 1958.
(M) (2:17) Time-Life RHD-16 Rhythm & Blues - 1958.
(M) (2:18) Time-Life R962-01 History Of Rock 'N' Roll: Rock 'N' Roll Classics 1957-1959.
(M) (2:18) Collectables 2503 WCBS-FM History Of Rock - The 50's Part 2.
(M) (2:17) Collectables 4503 History Of Rock/The 50s Part Two.
(M) (2:18) Collectables 2552 WOGL History Of Rock Vol. 2.
(M) (2:18) Time-Life R10513 40 Lovin' Oldies.
(M) (2:19) Chess 9352 Chess Rhythm & Roll.
(M) (2:19) Polygram Special Markets 314520259 Doo Wop Classics.
(M) (2:18) Rhino 72157 Doo Wop Memories, Vol. 2.
(M) (2:18) JCI 3188 1955 - Only Dance - 1959.
(M) (2:19) Nick At Nite/550 Music 63456 Double Date With Joanie And Chachi.
(M) (2:17) Time-Life R838-22 Solid Gold Soul 1958.

MATT MONRO
1961 MY KIND OF GIRL

(S) (2:54) Enigma 73531 O.S.T. Scandal. *(rerecording)*
(E) (2:53) Time-Life HPD-33 Your Hit Parade - The Early 60's.
(S) (2:53) Capitol 29394 Spotlight On.
(S) (2:53) Collectables 5581 My Kind Of Girl.

1965 WALK AWAY

(S) (3:03) Time-Life R974-07 Many Moods Of Romance - The Glory Of Love.

VAUGHN MONROE
1956 IN THE MIDDLE OF THE HOUSE

LOU MONTE
1958 LAZY MARY

(S) (2:38) RCA 8466 Nipper's Greatest Hits Of The 50's Volume 1.
(S) (2:38) Time-Life HPD-38 Your Hit Parade - The 50's Generation.
(S) (2:38) Taragon 1030 Very Best Of.

1963 PEPINO THE ITALIAN MOUSE
- (S) (2:36) Compose 9928 Now That's Italian.
- (S) (2:35) Time-Life HPD-40 Your Hit Parade - Golden Goofers.
- (S) (2:38) Rhino 72577 Eh, Paisano! Italian-American Classics.
- (S) (2:37) Taragon 1030 Very Best Of.

HUGO MONTENEGRO
1968 THE GOOD, THE BAD AND THE UGLY
- (S) (2:43) RCA 8475 Nipper's Greatest Hits Of The 60's Volume 2.
- (S) (2:44) RCA 66019 The Good, The Band And The Ugly.
- (S) (2:44) RCA 66099 Hooray For Hollywood.
- (S) (2:44) Rhino 71263 and 71451 Songs Of The West.
- (S) (2:41) Time-Life SUD-18 Superhits - Late 60's Classics.
- (S) (2:41) Time-Life HPD-39 Your Hit Parade - 60's Instrumentals: Take Two.
- (S) (2:44) Rhino 71684 Songs Of The West Vol. Four: Movie And Television Themes.
- (S) (2:44) RCA 53927 Music From "The Good, The Bad And The Ugly" & "A Fistfull Of Dollars" & "For A Few Dollars More".
- (S) (2:38) Rhino 71858 The Ennio Morricone Anthology - A Fistful Of Film Music. *(soundtrack version not performed by HUGO MONTENEGRO)*
- (S) (2:43) RCA 66881 RCA's Greatest One-Hit Wonders.
- (S) (2:41) Time-Life AM1-12 AM Gold - Late '60s Classics.

CHRIS MONTEZ
1962 LET'S DANCE
- (M) (2:15) MCA 31023 O.S.T. Animal House. *(no countoff; all selections on this cd are segued together)*
- (S) (2:27) DCC Compact Classics 056 All-Time Greatest Hits. *(time includes a :03 countoff)*
- (S) (2:27) Sandstone 33082 All-Time Greatest Hits. *(time includes a :03 countoff)*
- (M) (2:15) Time-Life 2RNR-16 Rock 'N' Roll Era - 1962 Still Rockin'. *(time includes a :02 countoff)*
- (M) (2:23) Rhino 71583 Billboard Top Pop Hits, 1962. *(time includes a :03 countoff)*
- (M) (2:15) JCI 3166 #1 Radio Hits 1960 - Only Rock 'n Roll - 1964. *(time includes a :03 countoff)*
- (M) (2:23) JCI 3189 1960 - Only Dance - 1964. *(time includes a :03 countoff)*

1966 CALL ME
- (S) (2:46) DCC Compact Classics 056 All-Time Greatest Hits.
- (S) (2:46) Sandstone 33082 All-Time Greatest Hits.

1966 THE MORE I SEE YOU
- (S) (2:54) DCC Compact Classics 056 All-Time Greatest Hits.
- (S) (2:54) Sandstone 33082 All-Time Greatest Hits.
- (S) (2:40) Chronicles 314535875 Bachelor Pad Favorites.

1966 THERE WILL NEVER BE ANOTHER YOU
- (S) (2:52) DCC Compact Classics 056 All-Time Greatest Hits.
- (S) (2:52) Sandstone 33082 All-Time Greatest Hits.

1966 TIME AFTER TIME
- (S) (2:29) DCC Compact Classics 056 All-Time Greatest Hits.
- (S) (2:29) Sandstone 33082 All-Time Greatest Hits.

MOODY BLUES
1965 GO NOW!
- (M) (3:10) Rhino 70323 History Of British Rock Volume 5.
- (M) (3:10) Rhino 72022 History Of British Rock Box Set.
- (M) (3:10) London 820758 Magnificent Moodies.
- (M) (3:10) Time-Life 2CLR-23 Classic Rock - 1965: Blowin' Your Mind.
- (M) (3:10) Time-Life R962-07 History Of Rock 'N' Roll: The British Invasion 1964-1966.
- (M) (3:10) Special Music 5040 Great Britons! Volume Two.
- (M) (3:10) Polydor 314535800 Best Of.

1968 TUESDAY AFTERNOON (FOREVER AFTERNOON)
- (S) (5:05) Polygram 837362 O.S.T. 1969. *(edit of the LP version)*
- (S) (8:23) Deram 820006 Days Of Future Passed. *(complete LP version which according to the cd jacket is a medley of "FOREVER AFTERNOON (TUESDAY)" and "(EVENING) TIME TO GET AWAY"; the vinyl LP jacket simply called the track "FOREVER AFTERNOON (TUESDAY)"; missing some vocal harmony overdubs in the "(EVENING) TIME TO GET AWAY" portion)*
- (S) (4:50) Threshold/Polydor 840659 Greatest Hits. *(edit of the LP version)*
- (S) (4:01) Threshold 820007 This Is The Moody Blues. *(edit of the LP version; all selections on this cd are segued together)*
- (S) (8:22) MFSL 512 Days Of Future Passed. *(complete LP version which according to the cd jacket is a medley of "FOREVER AFTERNOON (TUESDAY)" and "(EVENING) TIME TO GET AWAY"; the vinyl LP jacket simply called the track "FOREVER AFTERNOON (TUESDAY)"; gold disc; missing some vocal harmony overdubs in the "(EVENING) TIME TO GET AWAY" portion)*
- (S) (4:48) Time-Life 2CLR-30 Classic Rock - Rock Renaissance IV. *(edit of the LP version)*
- (S) (4:47) Polydor 314516436 and 314535223 Time Traveller. *(edit of the LP version)*
- (S) (4:47) LaserLight 12315 and 15936 The Wonder Years - Movin' On. *(edit of the LP version)*
- (S) (4:09) Polydor 314535800 Best Of. *(edit of the LP version)*
- (S) (8:23) Deram 422844767 Days Of Future Passed. *(remastered edition; complete LP version which according to the cd jacket is a medley of "FOREVER AFTERNOON (TUESDAY)" AND "(EVENING) TIME TO GET AWAY"; the vinyl LP jacket simply called the track "FOREVER AFTERNOON (TUESDAY)"; missing some vocal harmony overdubs in the "(EVENING) TIME TO GET AWAY" portion)*
- (S) (4:48) Polygram Special Markets 314520464 60's Rock Hits. *(edit of the LP version)*

1970 QUESTION
- (S) (5:42) Warner Special Products 27614 Highs Of The 70's. *(LP version)*
- (S) (5:43) Threshold/Polydor 840659 Greatest Hits. *(rerecording)*
- (S) (5:39) Threshold 820007 This Is The Moody Blues. *(neither the 45 or LP version; all selections on this cd are segued together)*
- (S) (5:48) Threshold 820211 Question Of Balance. *(timing index is off by :04; LP version; all selections on this cd are segued together)*
- (S) (4:54) Time-Life SOD-11 Sounds Of The Seventies - 1970: Take Two. *(45 version)*
- (S) (5:39) Polydor 314516436 and 314535223 Time Traveller. *(neither the 45 or LP version; tracks into the next selection)*
- (S) (4:54) Threshold 820155 Voices In The Sky/Best Of. *(45 version)*
- (S) (5:38) Rebound 3145200320 Class Reunion 1970. *(neither the 45 or LP version)*
- (S) (5:42) Time-Life R968-15 Guitar Rock - FM Classics. *(rerecording)*
- (S) (5:43) Polydor 314535800 Best Of. *(LP version)*
- (S) (5:38) Rebound 314520440 No. 1 Hits Of The 70's. *(neither the 45 or LP version)*
- (S) (5:43) Threshold 422844771 Question Of Balance. *(remastered edition; LP version; all selections on this cd are segued together)*

1971 THE STORY IN YOUR EYES
(45 length is (3:03); LP length is (2:56))
- (S) (3:03) Threshold/Polydor 840659 Greatest Hits.
- (S) (2:44) Threshold 820007 This Is The Moody Blues. *(all selections on this cd are segued together)*

MOODY BLUES *(Continued)*

(S) (2:56) Threshold 820160 Every Good Boy Deserves Favour. *(all selections on this cd are segued together)*

(S) (2:55) Time-Life SOD-24 Sounds Of The Seventies - FM Rock.

(S) (2:52) Polydor 314516436 and 314535223 Time Traveller. *(previous selection tracks into introduction; tracks into the following selection)*

(S) (2:45) Rebound 314520278 Hard Rock Essentials - The 70's. *(sounds like it was edited from the "Every Good Boy Deserves Favour" LP because of the introduction which fails to have a clean beginning)*

(S) (2:56) MFSL 643 Every Good Boy Deserves Favour. *(all selections on this cd are segued together; gold disc)*

(S) (3:03) Time-Life R968-19 Guitar Rock - The Early '70s: Take Two.

(S) (2:45) Rebound 314520364 Class Reunion '71. *(sounds like it was edited from the "Every Good Boy Deserves Favour" LP because of the introduction which fails to have a clean beginning)*

(S) (3:03) Rebound 314520437 Classic Rock - 70's.

(S) (2:51) Polydor 314535800 Best Of.

(S) (2:56) Threshold 422844772 *(remastered edition; all selections on this cd are segued together)*

1972 ISN'T LIFE STRANGE

(S) (6:37) Threshold/Polydor 840659 Greatest Hits. *(rerecording)*

(S) (5:59) Threshold 820155 Voices In The Sky/Best Of.

(S) (5:32) Threshold 820007 This Is The Moody Blues. *(:28 shorter than either the 45 or LP; all selections on this cd are segued together)*

(S) (6:00) Threshold 820159 Seventh Sojourn. *(all selections on this cd are segued together)*

(S) (6:07) Polydor 314516436 and 314535223 Time Traveller.

(S) (6:04) Polydor 314535800 Best Of.

(S) (6:06) Threshold 422844773 Seventh Sojourn. *(remastered edition; all selections on this cd are segued together)*

(S) (6:06) MFSL 718 Seventh Sojourn. *(gold disc; all selections on this cd are segued together)*

1972 NIGHTS IN WHITE SATIN
(at least some of the 45 dj copies had a printed label time of (4:20) when the actual time was (3:13); commercial copies were all (4:26))

(S) (5:50) Rhino 70633 Billboard's Top Rock & Roll Hits Of 1972. *(neither the 45 or LP version)*

(S) (5:50) Rhino 72005 Billboard's Top Rock & Roll Hits 1968-1972 Box Set. *(neither the 45 or LP version)*

(S) (4:24) Original Sound 8895 Dick Clark's 21 All-Time Hits Vol. 4. *(45 version)*

(M) (4:26) Rhino 70326 History Of British Rock Volume 8. *(45 version)*

(M) (4:26) Rhino 72022 History Of British Rock Box Set. *(45 version)*

(S) (4:25) Threshold 820155 Voices In The Sky/Best Of. *(45 version)*

(S) (7:24) Deram 820006 Days Of Future Passed. *(LP version)*

(S) (7:23) Sandstone 33003 Reelin' In The Years Volume 4. *(LP version)*

(S) (7:22) Milan 35609 O.S.T. Shattered. *(LP version)*

(S) (7:38) Threshold/Polydor 840659 Greatest Hits. *(slightly longer than the LP version)*

(S) (4:32) Threshold 820007 This Is The Moody Blues. *(this song segues into the next track which is given the title "LATE LAMENT" but in reality this is a portion of the full album length version of "NIGHTS IN WHITE SATIN")*

(S) (7:23) MFSL 512 Days Of Future Passed. *(LP version; gold disc)*

(S) (7:38) Priority 7065 70's Greatest Rock Hits Volume 13: Request Line. *(slightly longer than the LP version)*

(S) (7:23) DCC Compact Classics 065 Rock Of The 70's Volume 4. *(LP version)*

(M) (4:26) Epic 57560 O.S.T. A Bronx Tale. *(45 version)*

(S) (4:23) Time-Life SUD-11 Superhits - 1972. *(45 version)*

(S) (5:50) Time-Life SOD-03 Sounds Of The Seventies - 1972. *(neither the 45 or LP version)*

(S) (7:39) Polydor 314516436 and 314535223 Time Traveller. *(slightly longer than the LP version)*

(M) (4:25) MCA 11389 O.S.T. Casino. *(45 version)*

(S) (5:50) MCA Special Products 20893 Greatest Tour Bands Ever Recorded. *(neither the 45 or LP version)*

(M) (4:26) Rebound 314520372 The Roots Of Rock: Soft Rock. *(45 version)*

(S) (4:23) Polydor 314535800 Best Of. *(45 version)*

(S) (4:23) Time-Life AM1-07 AM Gold - 1972. *(45 version)*

(S) (7:22) Deram 422844767 Days Of Future Passed. *(remastered edition; LP version)*

(S) (4:23) Polygram TV 314555610 The One And Only Love Album. *(45 version)*

1973 I'M JUST A SINGER (IN A ROCK AND ROLL BAND)

(S) (4:16) Threshold/Polydor 840659 Greatest Hits. *(LP version)*

(S) (4:14) Threshold 820155 Voices In The Sky/Best Of. *(45 version)*

(S) (4:10) Threshold 820007 This Is The Moody Blues. *(all selections on this cd are segued together; 45 version)*

(S) (4:16) Threshold 820159 Seventh Sojourn. *(all selections on this cd are segued together; LP version)*

(S) (4:16) Foundation/RCA 66109 Ultimate Rock Album. *(LP version)*

(S) (4:14) Time-Life R968-05 Guitar Rock 1972-1973. *(45 version)*

(S) (4:14) Time-Life SOD-14 Sounds Of The Seventies - 1973: Take Two. *(45 version)*

(S) (4:13) Time-Life OPCD-4521 Guitar Rock. *(45 version)*

(S) (4:16) Polydor 314516436 and 314535223 Time Traveller. *(45 version)*

(S) (4:15) Polydor 314535800 Best Of. *(45 version; song switches to (M) for one second at :47)*

(S) (4:16) Threshold 422844773 Seventh Sojourn. *(remastered edition; all selections on this cd are segued together; LP version)*

(S) (4:16) MFSL 718 Seventh Sojourn. *(gold disc; LP version; all selections on this cd are segued together)*

(S) (4:15) Rebound 314520507 Class Reunion '73. *(LP version)*

1981 GEMINI DREAM

(S) (4:06) Threshold 820105 Long Distance Voyager. *(LP version)*

(S) (4:05) Threshold 840659 Greatest Hits. *(LP version)*

(S) (3:47) Threshold 820155 Voices In The Sky. *(45 version)*

(S) (4:04) Polydor 3145164367 and 314535223 Time Traveller. *(LP version)*

(S) (3:47) Time-Life R988-08 Sounds Of The Eighties: 1981. *(45 version)*

(S) (4:05) Rebound 314520361 Class Reunion '81. *(LP version)*

(S) (4:05) Rebound 314520434 Classic Rock - 80's. *(LP version)*

(S) (4:04) Polydor 314535800 Best Of. *(LP version)*

(S) (4:06) MFSL 700 Long Distance Voyager. *(gold disc; LP version)*

1981 THE VOICE
(actual 45 time is (4:13) not (4:08) as stated on the record label)

(S) (5:20) Threshold 820105 Long Distance Voyager. *(LP version)*

(S) (5:14) Threshold 840659 Greatest Hits. *(LP version)*

(S) (4:12) Threshold 820155 Voices In The Sky. *(45 version)*
(S) (5:16) Polydor 314516436 and 314535223 Time Traveller. *(LP version)*
(S) (4:12) JCI 3119 18 Rock Classics. *(45 version)*
(S) (5:13) Polydor 314535800 Best Of. *(LP version)*
(S) (5:13) Rhino 72594 Billboard Top Album Rock Hits, 1981. *(LP version)*
(S) (5:20) MFSL 700 Long Distance Voyager. *(gold disc; LP version)*

1983 SITTING AT THE WHEEL
(S) (5:37) Threshold 810119 The Present. *(previous selection tracks over introduction; LP version)*
(S) (5:34) Polydor 314516436 and 314535223 Time Traveller. *(LP version; previous selection tracks over introduction)*
(S) (5:35) Rebound 314520521 Highway Rockin'. *(LP version)*
(S) (3:27) Rebound 314520493 Class Reunion '83. *(45 version)*

1986 YOUR WILDEST DREAMS
(S) (3:48) Time-Life R105-40 Rock Dreams. *(45 version)*
(S) (4:50) Threshold 829179 The Other Side Of Life. *(LP version)*
(S) (4:50) Threshold 840659 Greatest Hits. *(LP version)*
(S) (4:50) Polydor 314516436 and 314535223 Time Traveller. *(LP version)*
(S) (4:51) Time-Life R988-12 Sounds Of The 80's: 1985-1986. *(LP version)*
(S) (4:49) Time-Life R103-18 Great Love Songs Of The '70s & '80s. *(LP version)*
(S) (4:49) Polydor 314535800 Best Of. *(LP version)*

1988 I KNOW YOU'RE OUT THERE SOMEWHERE
(S) (6:36) Polydor 314515913 Classic Rock Box. *(LP version)*
(S) (6:36) Polydor 314516436 and 314535223 Time Traveller. *(LP version)*
(S) (6:36) Threshold 840659 Greatest Hits. *(LP version)*
(S) (6:36) Polydor 835756 Sur La Mer. *(LP version)*
(S) (6:35) Polydor 314535800 Best Of. *(LP version)*

ART MOONEY
1955 HONEY-BABE
(M) (2:52) Time-Life HPD-31 Your Hit Parade - The 50's Forever.

1956 NUTTIN' FOR CHRISTMAS

MOONGLOWS (also HARVEY and THE MOONGLOWS)
1955 SINCERELY
(M) (3:09) Rhino 75763 Best Of Doo-Wop Ballads.
(M) (3:09) Original Sound 8905r 13 Of The Best Doo Wop Love Songs.
(M) (3:09) Original Sound 8850 Oldies But Goodies Vol. 1. *(this compact disc uses the "Waring - fds" noise reduction process)*
(M) (3:09) Original Sound 2221 Oldies But Goodies Volumes 1,4,6,8 and 10 Box Set. *(this box set uses the "Waring - fds" noise reduction process)*
(M) (3:09) Original Sound 2500 Oldies But Goodies Volumes 1-15 Box Set. *(this box set uses the "Waring - fds" noise reduction process)*
(M) (3:09) Original Sound 9326 Best Love Songs.
(M) (3:09) Rhino 70598 Billboard Top Rock 'N' Roll Hits - 1955.
(M) (3:09) Chess 31319 Best Of Chess Rock 'N' Roll Volume One.
(M) (3:09) Collectables 2509 For Lovers Only Part 1.
(M) (3:09) Collectables 2552 WOGL History Of Rock Vol. 2.
(M) (3:09) MCA 5777 Vintage Music Volumes 1 & 2.
(M) (3:09) MCA 31199 Vintage Music Volume 2.
(M) (3:09) Time-Life 2RNR-08 The Rock 'N' Roll Era - 1954-1955.
(M) (3:09) Time-Life RHD-19 Rhythm & Blues - 1954.
(M) (3:09) Rhino 71463 Doo Wop Box.
(M) (3:09) Chess 9345 Blue Velvet/Ultimate Collection.
(E) (3:04) Atlantic 82152 O.S.T. Goodfellas. *(mastered from vinyl)*

(M) (3:08) Atlantic 82155 O.S.T. Book Of Love.
(M) (3:08) Chess 31270 From The Motion Picture "Rock, Rock, Rock".
(M) (3:09) MCA Special Products 22165 Vintage Collectibles Volume 7.
(M) (3:10) Chess 9379 Their Greatest Hits.
(M) (3:08) Time-Life R857-15 The Heart Of Rock 'n' Roll 1953-1955.

1956 SEE SAW
(M) (2:24) MCA 5937 Vintage Music Volumes 13 & 14.
(M) (2:24) MCA 31210 Vintage Music Volume 13.
(M) (2:24) Chess 9283 Best Of Chess Vocal Groups Volume 2.
(M) (2:23) Chess 31270 From The Motion Picture "Rock, Rock, Rock".
(M) (2:25) Chess 9345 Blue Velvet/Ultimate Collection.
(M) (2:24) Time-Life 2RNR-28 Rock 'N' Roll Era - The 50's Rave On.
(M) (2:24) Chess 9352 Chess Rhythm & Roll.
(M) (2:25) Chess 9379 Their Greatest Hits.

released as by HARVEY and THE MOONGLOWS:
1958 TEN COMMANDMENTS OF LOVE
(actual 45 time is (3:03) not (2:43) as stated on the record label)
(M) (3:40) Rhino 75763 Best Of Doo Wop Ballads. *(LP version)*
(M) (4:02) MCA 31198 Vintage Music Volume 1. *(complete recording session but with overdubbed drums)*
(M) (4:02) MCA 5777 Vintage Music Volumes 1 & 2. *(complete recording session but with overdubbed drums)*
(M) (4:01) Chess 31320 Best Of Chess Rock 'n' Roll Volume 2. *(complete recording session but with overdubbed drums)*
(M) (3:38) Original Sound 8861 Oldies But Goodies Vol. 11. *(this compact disc uses the "Waring - fds" noise reduction process; LP version)*
(M) (3:38) Original Sound 2222 Oldies But Goodies Volumes 3,5,11,14 and 15 Box Set. *(this box set uses the "Waring - fds" noise reduction process; LP version)*
(M) (3:38) Original Sound 2500 Oldies But Goodies Volumes 1-15 Box Set. *(this box set uses the "Waring - fds" noise reduction process; LP version)*
(M) (3:38) Chess 31267 Look, It's The Moonglows. *(LP version)*
(M) (3:57) Rhino 71463 Doo Wop Box. *(complete recording session)*
(M) (4:06) Chess 9345 Blue Velvet/Ultimate Collection. *(includes :02 studio talk; complete recording session)*
(M) (4:01) Epic 57560 O.S.T. A Bronx Tale. *(complete recording session but with overdubbed drums)*
(E) (3:37) Time-Life 2RNR-21 Rock 'N' Roll Era - 1958 Still Rockin'. *(LP version)*
(M) (4:02) Time-Life R962-06 History Of Rock 'N' Roll: Doo Wop And Vocal Group Tradition 1955-1962. *(complete recording session but with overdubbed drums)*
(M) (3:34) Collectables 2506 WCBS-FM History Of Rock - The 50's Part 1. *(mastered from vinyl)*
(M) (3:34) Collectables 4506 History Of Rock/The 50s Part One. *(mastered from vinyl)*
(M) (3:39) Original Sound 8911 Art Laboe's Dedicated To You Vol. 2. *(LP version but with overdubbed drums)*
(M) (3:39) Original Sound 4001 Art Laboe's 60 Killer Oldies. *(LP version but with overdubbed drums)*
(M) (3:37) Time-Life R10513 40 Lovin' Oldies. *(LP version)*
(M) (3:56) Time-Life R857-04 The Heart Of Rock 'n' Roll - 1958. *(complete recording session)*
(M) (4:03) Chess 9379 Their Greatest Hits. *(complete recording session)*

BOB MOORE
1961 MEXICO
- (S) (2:36) Time-Life HPD-34 Your Hit Parade - 60's Instrumentals.
- (S) (2:34) Sony Music Special Products 66106 The Monument Story.
- (S) (2:35) K-Tel 3583 Those Wonderful Instrumentals Volume 3.
- (S) (2:35) Time-Life R986-12 Instrumental Favorites - Latin Rhythms.
- (S) (2:34) Collectors' Choice 5190 More Instrumental Gems Of The 60's.
- (S) (2:36) Collectables 5844 Mexico.

BOBBY MOORE & THE RHYTHM ACES
1966 SEARCHING FOR MY BABY
- (M) (2:30) Rhino 75770 Soul Shots Volume 2.
- (M) (2:29) MCA 31204 Vintage Music Volume 7.
- (M) (2:29) MCA 5805 Vintage Music Volumes 7 & 8.
- (M) (2:29) Chess 31317 Best Of Chess Rhythm & Blues Volume 1.
- (M) (2:30) Original Sound 9307 Dedicated To You Vol. 7.
- (M) (2:29) Ripete 2392192 Beach Music Anthology Box Set.
- (M) (2:29) Time-Life 2CLR-28 Classic Rock - On The Soul Side II.
- (M) (2:29) MCA Special Products 22135 Vintage Collectibles Volume 6.
- (M) (2:29) Chess 9352 Chess Rhythm & Roll.
- (M) (2:29) Rhino 72815 Beg, Scream & Shout! The Big Ol' Box Of '60s Soul.
- (M) (2:29) Chess 9388 Chess Soul - A Decade Of Chicago's Finest.

DOROTHY MOORE
1976 MISTY BLUE
- (S) (3:35) JCI 3303 Love Seventies.
- (S) (3:35) Time-Life SOD-18 Sounds Of The Seventies - 1976: Take Two.
- (S) (3:38) Right Stuff 28372 Slow Jams: The 70's Volume Two.
- (S) (3:37) K-Tel 6013 70's Soul - Sexy Ballads.
- (S) (3:36) K-Tel 3535 Slow Groove Love Jams Of The 70's.
- (S) (3:37) Scotti Bros. 75481 Quiet Storm Memories.
- (S) (3:38) Rebound 314520367 Soul Classics - Quiet Storm/The 70's.
- (S) (3:34) Madacy Entertainment 1976 Rock On 1976.
- (S) (3:36) Reprise 46360 O.S.T. Phenomenon.
- (S) (3:37) Malaco 7481 Misty Blue And Other Greatest Hits.
- (S) (3:38) Right Stuff 52660 Flick Hits - Old School Tracks.
- (S) (3:35) Time-Life R838-11 Solid Gold Soul - 1976.
- (S) (3:37) Time-Life R834-09 Body Talk - Magic Moments.
1977 I BELIEVE YOU
- (S) (3:39) Malaco 7481 Misty Blue And Other Greatest Hits.

JACKIE MOORE
1971 PRECIOUS PRECIOUS
- (S) (3:26) Atlantic 81912 Golden Age Of Black Music (1970-1975).
- (S) (3:23) Rhino 70784 Soul Hits Of The 70's Volume 4.
- (S) (3:23) Rhino 72028 Soul Hits Of The 70's Volumes 1-5 Box Set.
- (S) (3:25) Atlantic 82305 Atlantic Rhythm And Blues 1947-1974 Box Set.
- (S) (3:23) Rhino 71208 70's Smash Hits Volume 4.
- (S) (3:25) Ripete 2198 Soul Patrol.
- (S) (3:24) Ichiban 2502 Precious Precious/Best Of.
- (S) (3:23) Flashback 72684 '70s Radio Hits Volume 4.
- (S) (3:23) Flashback 72090 '70s Radio Hits Box Set.
1973 SWEET CHARLIE BABE
- (S) (2:35) Ichiban 2502 Precious Precious/Best Of.

MICHAEL MORALES
1989 WHO DO YOU GIVE YOUR LOVE TO?
- (S) (4:04) Wing 835810 Michael Morales.
1989 WHAT I LIKE ABOUT YOU
- (S) (3:04) Wing 835810 Michael Morales.

JANE MORGAN
1957 FASCINATION
- (S) (2:20) Elektra 60107 O.S.T. Diner. *(rerecording)*
- (E) (2:21) Curb 77405 Greatest Hits.
- (M) (2:21) Rhino 71252 Sentimental Journey: Pop Vocal Classics Volume 4 (1954-1959).
- (M) (2:21) Rhino 72034 Sentimental Journey Pop Vocal Classics Volumes 1-4 Box Set.
- (M) (2:21) Time-Life HPD-17 Your Hit Parade - 1957.
- (M) (2:21) Time-Life R974-09 Many Moods Of Romance - True Love.
- (M) (2:21) Rhino 72422 Billboard Top Movie Hits 1955-1959.
- (S) (2:19) Varese Sarabande 5783 The '50s Remembered: Arden, Kallen, Morgan & Syms. *(rerecording)*
- (S) (2:19) Varese Sarabande 5822 The Jane Morgan Collection. *(rerecording)*
- (M) (2:21) Time-Life R132-10 Love Songs Of Your Hit Parade.
1958 THE DAY THE RAINS CAME
- (S) (2:57) Curb 77405 Greatest Hits.
- (M) (2:58) Time-Life HPD-31 Your Hit Parade - The 50's Forever.
- (S) (2:56) Varese Sarabande 5783 The '50s Remembered: Arden, Kallen, Morgan & Syms.
- (S) (2:57) Varese Sarabande 5822 The Jane Morgan Collection.

JAYE P. MORGAN
1955 THAT'S ALL I WANT FROM YOU
- (M) (2:39) Time-Life HPD-09 Your Hit Parade 1955.
- (E) (2:38) JCI 7021 Those Wonderful Years - April Love.
- (M) (2:37) Collectors' Choice 030 Jaye P. Morgan On RCA.
- (E) (2:36) Simitar 55372 Her Greatest Hits.
- (M) (2:39) Time-Life R132-10 Love Songs Of Your Hit Parade.
1955 DANGER! HEARTBREAK AHEAD
- (M) (3:00) Collectors' Choice 030 Jaye P. Morgan On RCA.
- (M) (2:59) Simitar 55372 Her Greatest Hits.
1955 CHEE-CHEE-OO CHEE (SANG THE LITTLE BIRD)
- (M) (2:24) Collectors' Choice 030 Jaye P. Morgan On RCA.
- (M) (2:23) Simitar 55372 Her Greatest Hits.
1955 THE LONGEST WALK
- (M) (2:13) Time-Life HPD-36 Your Hit Parade - The 50's Pop Revival.
- (M) (2:13) Collectors' Choice 030 Jaye P. Morgan On RCA.
- (M) (2:13) Simitar 55372 Her Greatest Hits.
1955 IF YOU DON'T WANT MY LOVE
- (M) (2:40) Collectors' Choice 030 Jaye P. Morgan On RCA.
- (M) (2:39) Simitar 55372 Her Greatest Hits.

RUSS MORGAN
1956 THE POOR PEOPLE OF PARIS
- (M) (2:24) MCA 4036 Music In The Morgan Manner/Best Of.

ALANIS MORISSETTE
1996 IRONIC
- (S) (3:47) Maverick/Reprise 45901 Jagged Little Pill.
- (S) (3:46) Grammy Recordings/Chronicles 314553292 1997 Grammy Nominees.
1996 YOU LEARN
- (S) (3:57) Maverick/Reprise 45901 Jagged Little Pill.
1996 YOU OUGHTA KNOW
- (S) (4:06) Maverick/Reprise 45901 Jagged Little Pill.

MORMON TABERNACLE CHOIR
1959 BATTLE HYMN OF THE REPUBLIC
- (S) (4:47) Columbia 48297 Songs Of The Civil War.
- (S) (4:46) Columbia 48295 God Bless America.

GIORGIO MORODER
1979 CHASE
- (S) (8:22) Casablanca 314516918 Casablanca Records Story. *(LP version from the vinyl album "O.S.T. Midnight Express")*

(S) (4:18) Rebound 314520366 Disco Nights Vol. 10 - Disco's Greatest Movie Hits.
(S) (3:38) Casablanca 314526253 Casablanca Records Greatest Hits. *(45 version)*

MARK MORRISON
1997 RETURN OF THE MACK
(S) (7:19) Atlantic 82963 Return Of The Mack.
(S) (5:24) Strictly Rhythm 6313 Strictly Rhythm Superjams. *(all selections on this cd are segued together)*
(S) (3:29) Arista 18988 Ultimate Dance Party 1998. *(all selections on this cd are segued together)*
(S) (5:04) Tommy Boy 1234 MTV Party To Go '98. *(all songs on this cd are segued together; remix)*
(S) (7:05) Elektra 62088 Party Over Here '98. *(all tracks on this cd are segued together)*

VAN MORRISON
1967 BROWN EYED GIRL
(S) (3:06) JCI 3104 Mellow Sixties. *(with "making love" lyric)*
(S) (3:06) Atlantic 82032 The Wonder Years. *(with "making love" lyric)*
(S) (3:05) MCA 6340 O.S.T. Born On The Fourth Of July. *(with "making love" lyric)*
(M) (3:02) Mercury 841970 Best Of. *(with "laughin' and runnin'" lyric)*
(S) (3:03) Epic/Legacy 47041 Bang Masters. *(with "making love" lyric)*
(S) (3:39) Epic/Legacy 47041 Bang Masters. *(alternate take; includes :12 of studio talk and countoff)*
(M) (3:00) Columbia 46093 T.B. Sheets. *(with "laughin' and runnin'" lyric)*
(S) (3:02) Columbia 47380 O.S.T. Sleeping With The Enemy. *(with "making love" lyric)*
(S) (3:05) Time-Life 2CLR-10 Classic Rock - 1967: The Beat Goes On. *(with "making love" lyric)*
(S) (3:03) Time-Life SUD-14 Superhits - The Late 60's. *(with "making love" lyric)*
(S) (3:05) Time-Life R105-26 Our Songs: Singers & Songwriters Encore. *(with "making love" lyric)*
(S) (3:01) Madacy Entertainment 26927 Sun Splashin'. *(with "making love" lyric)*
(S) (3:03) Time-Life AM1-14 AM Gold - The Late '60s. *(with "making love" lyric)*
(S) (3:03) Time-Life R13610 Gold And Platinum Box Set - The Ultimate Rock Collection. *(with "making love" lyric)*
(S) (3:03) Thump 6010 Easyriders Volume 1. *(with "making love" lyric)*
1970 COME RUNNING
(S) (2:30) Warner Brothers 3103 Moondance.
1971 DOMINO
(S) (3:06) Warner Brothers 1884 His Band And The Street Choir. *(LP version)*
(S) (3:03) Mercury 841970 Best Of. *(LP version)*
(S) (3:07) Time-Life SOD-01 Sounds Of The Seventies - 1970. *(LP version)*
(S) (3:06) Time-Life R103-33 Singers & Songwriters. *(LP version)*
1971 BLUE MONEY
(S) (3:43) Warner Brothers 1884 His Band And The Street Choir.
(S) (3:41) Time-Life SOD-12 Sounds Of The Seventies - 1971: Take Two.
1971 WILD NIGHT
(S) (3:31) Warner Brothers 1950 Tupelo Honey.
(S) (3:31) Mercury 841970 Best Of.
(S) (3:31) Time-Life SOD-02 Sounds Of The Seventies - 1971.
(S) (3:32) Polydor 314537450 Tupelo Honey.

MOTELS
1982 ONLY THE LONELY
(S) (3:14) EMI 89605 Living In Oblivion: The 80's Greatest Hits Volume Two.

(S) (3:14) Priority 7076 80's Greatest Rock Hits Volume 2 - Leather And Lace.
(S) (3:14) Sandstone 33052 and 5020 Cosmopolitan Volume 6.
(S) (3:14) DCC Compact Classics 084 Night Moves Volume 4.
(S) (3:14) Capitol 90930 Best Of.
(S) (3:14) Time-Life R988-05 Sounds Of The Eighties: 1982.
(S) (3:13) Madacy Entertainment 1982 Rock On 1982.
(S) (3:12) JCI 3147 1980 - Only Love - 1984.
(S) (3:14) Hip-O 40047 The '80s Hit(s) Back 3.
(S) (3:14) Time-Life R834-11 Body Talk - After Dark.
1983 SUDDENLY LAST SUMMER
(S) (3:37) Priority 53768 Rock Of The 80's Volume 14.
(S) (3:37) Sandstone 33045 and 5011 Rock The First Volume Five.
(S) (3:37) K-Tel 3261 The 80's Rock On.
(S) (3:37) Capitol 90930 Best Of.
(S) (3:37) Time-Life R988-11 Sounds Of The 80's: 1983-1984.
(S) (3:37) Madacy Entertainment 1983 Rock On 1983.
(S) (3:35) Priority 50953 I Love Rock & Roll Volume 4: Hits Of The 80's.
1984 REMEMBER THE NIGHTS
(S) (3:03) Capitol 90930 Best Of.
1985 SHAME
(S) (4:10) Capitol 46165 Shock.
(S) (4:09) Capitol 90930 Best Of.

MOTHERLODE
1969 WHEN I DIE
(S) (3:20) Pair 1202 Best Of Buddah.
(S) (3:20) Essex 7060 The Buddah Box.
(S) (3:20) Varese Sarabande 5803 Sunshine Days - Pop Classics Of The '60s Volume 3.

MOTLEY CRUE
1985 SMOKIN' IN THE BOYS ROOM
(S) (3:26) Elektra 60418 Theatre Of Pain.
(S) (3:25) Elektra 61204 Decade Of Decadence.
1987 GIRLS, GIRLS, GIRLS
(S) (4:29) Elektra 60725 Girls, Girls, Girls.
(S) (4:28) Elektra 61204 Decade Of Decadence.
1989 DR. FEELGOOD
(S) (4:50) Elektra 60829 Dr. Feelgood.
(S) (4:47) Elektra 61204 Decade Of Decadence.
1990 KICKSTART MY HEART
(S) (4:41) Elektra 60829 Dr. Feelgood.
(S) (4:57) Elektra 61204 Decade Of Decadence. *(live)*
(S) (4:41) Time-Life R968-25 Guitar Rock - The '90s.
1990 WITHOUT YOU
(S) (4:28) Elektra 60829 Dr. Feelgood.
1990 DON'T GO AWAY MAD (JUST GO AWAY)
(S) (4:38) Elektra 60829 Dr. Feelgood.
1991 HOME SWEET HOME '91
(S) (3:52) JCI 3135 Hard Love - 14 Original Metal Ballads. *(1985 version)*
(S) (4:00) Elektra 61204 Decade Of Decadence. *(1991 version)*
(S) (3:55) Elektra 60418 Theatre Of Pain. *(1985 version)*

MOTT THE HOOPLE
1972 ALL THE YOUNG DUDES
(S) (3:29) JCI 3302 Electric Seventies. *("Marks & Sparks" version)*
(S) (3:29) Columbia 45048 Rock Classics Of The 70's. *("Marks & Sparks" version)*
(S) (3:28) Epic 46490 O.S.T. Queens Logic. *("Marks & Sparks" version)*
(S) (3:30) Columbia 34368 Greatest Hits. *("Marks & Sparks" version)*
(S) (3:29) Columbia 31750 All The Young Dudes. *("Marks & Sparks" version; previous song tracks over the introduction)*
(S) (3:29) Priority 7055 Heavy Hitters/70's Greatest Rock Hits Volume 11. *("Marks & Sparks" version)*

MOTT THE HOOPLE (Continued)

(S) (3:30) Columbia/Legacy 46973 Ballad Of Mott: A Retrospective. *("Marks & Sparks" version)*

(S) (3:29) Atlantic 82530 O.S.T. Amongst Friends. *("Marks & Sparks" version)*

(S) (3:29) Razor & Tie 22502 Those Rocking 70's. *("Marks & Sparks" version)*

(S) (3:27) Time-Life R102-34 The Rolling Stone Collection. *("Marks & Sparks" version)*

(S) (3:29) Time-Life R968-05 Guitar Rock 1972-1973. *("Marks & Sparks" version)*

(S) (3:31) Time-Life SOD-13 Sounds Of The Seventies - 1972: Take Two. *("Marks & Sparks" version)*

(S) (3:27) Time-Life OPCD-4521 Guitar Rock. *("Marks & Sparks" version)*

(S) (3:30) Risky Business 57470 Wham Bam, Thank You Glam! *("Marks & Sparks" version; glitch on introduction)*

(S) (3:28) Atlantic 82530 O.S.T. Amongst Friends. *("Marks & Sparks" version)*

(S) (3:29) Eclipse Music Group 64893 Rock 'n Roll Relix 1972-1973. *("Marks & Sparks" version)*

(S) (3:29) Eclipse Music Group 64897 Rock 'n Roll Relix 1970-1979. *("Marks & Sparks" version)*

(S) (3:29) Columbia/Legacy 65273 Super Hits. *("Marks & Sparks" version)*

MOUNTAIN
1970 MISSISSIPPI QUEEN

(S) (2:28) Columbia 45048 Rock Classics Of The 70's.

(S) (2:29) Priority 7942 Hard Rockin' 70's.

(S) (2:29) Priority 8662 Hard 'N Heavy/70's Greatest Rock Hits Volume 1.

(S) (2:30) Rhino 70921 Super Hits Of The 70's Volume 1. *(hum noticeable on the introduction)*

(S) (2:30) Rhino 72009 Super Hits Of The 70's Volumes 1-4 Box Set. *(hum noticeable on the introduction)*

(S) (2:29) Rhino 70986 Heavy Metal Memories. *(hum noticeable on the introduction)*

(S) (2:29) JCI 3302 Electric Seventies. *(hum noticeable on the introduction)*

(S) (2:29) CBS Special Products 46806 Rock Goes To The Movies Volume 1.

(S) (2:29) Columbia 32079 Best Of.

(S) (2:29) Priority 53680 Spring Break.

(S) (4:27) Columbia 44491 Metal Giants. *(live)*

(S) (2:29) Razor & Tie 22502 Those Rocking 70's.

(S) (2:29) Time-Life SOD-11 Sounds Of The Seventies - 1970: Take Two. *(hum noticeable on the introduction)*

(S) (2:29) Time-Life OPCD-4521 Guitar Rock.

(S) (2:29) K-Tel 6090 Hit Parader Salutes 20 Years Of Metal.

(S) (2:28) Columbia/Legacy 47361 Mountain Climbing. *(hum noticeable on the introduction)*

(S) (2:29) K-Tel 621 Rock Classics. *(hum noticeable on the introduction)*

(S) (2:30) Legacy/Columbia 57167 Over The Top. *(hum noticeable on the introduction)*

(S) (2:29) Time-Life R968-06 Guitar Rock 1970-1971.

(S) (2:29) Hip-O 40039 Power Chords Volume 2.

(S) (2:29) Madacy Entertainment 6805 The Power Of Rock.

(S) (2:29) K-Tel 3985 70s Heavy Hitters: Arena Rockers 1970-74.

(S) (2:29) Thump 6010 Easyriders Volume 1. *(hum noticeable on the introduction)*

MOUTH & MACNEAL
1972 HOW DO YOU DO?

(S) (3:13) Rhino 70928 Super Hits Of The 70's Volume 8. *(45 version but :15 longer)*

(S) (3:13) Rhino 71210 70's Smash Hits Volume 6. *(45 version but :15 longer)*

(S) (3:12) Time-Life SOD-31 Sounds Of The Seventies - AM Top Twenty. *(45 version but :14 longer)*

(S) (2:58) K-Tel 3623 Believe In Music. *(45 version)*

(S) (4:03) Popular/Critique 12009 Dutch Treats. *(LP version)*

(S) (3:13) Flashback 72686 '70s Radio Hits Volume 6. *(45 version but :15 longer)*

MOVING PICTURES
1982 WHAT ABOUT ME

ALISON MOYET
1985 INVISIBLE

(S) (3:57) Columbia 39956 Alf.

MICKEY MOZART QUINTET
1959 LITTLE DIPPER

M PEOPLE
1994 MOVING ON UP

(S) (5:28) Epic 64209 Elegant Slumming.

(S) (5:28) RCA 68904 O.S.T. The Full Monty.

(S) (3:30) Beast 53022 Club Hitz Of The 90's Vol. 1. *(all songs on this cd are segued together)*

MARIA MULDAUR
1974 MIDNIGHT AT THE OASIS

(S) (3:40) JCI 3303 Love Seventies.

(S) (3:44) Rhino 70760 Super Hits Of The 70's Volume 13.

(S) (3:46) Warner Special Products 27615 Storytellers: Singers & Songwriters.

(S) (3:43) Razor & Tie 22505 More Fabulous 70's Volume 2.

(S) (3:36) Time-Life SOD-07 Sounds Of The Seventies - 1974.

(S) (3:46) Time-Life R103-33 Singers & Songwriters.

(S) (3:47) Reprise 2148 Maria Muldaur.

(S) (3:43) JCI 3145 1970 - Only Love - 1974.

(S) (3:44) Time-Life AM1-21 AM Gold - 1974.

(S) (3:45) Time-Life R834-19 Body Talk - Always And Forever.

1975 I'M A WOMAN

(S) (4:05) Reprise 2194 Waitress In The Donut Shop. *(LP version)*

MUNGO JERRY
1970 IN THE SUMMERTIME

(S) (3:30) Rhino 70923 Super Hits Of The 70's Volume 3.

(S) (3:30) Rhino 72009 Super Hits Of The 70's Volumes 1-4 Box Set.

(S) (3:30) Rhino 70087 Summer & Sun.

(S) (3:29) Collectables 5067 History Of Rock Volume 7.

(S) (3:30) Rhino 71207 70's Smash Hits Volume 3.

(S) (3:30) Rhino 71229 Summer Hits.

(S) (3:29) Razor & Tie 22505 More Fabulous 70's Volume 2.

(S) (3:28) Time-Life SUD-04 Superhits - 1970.

(M) (3:28) Time-Life SOD-11 Sounds Of The Seventies - 1970: Take Two.

(S) (3:28) JCI 3130 1970 - Only Rock 'N Roll - 1974.

(S) (3:31) Ripete 2187-RE Preppy Deluxe.

(S) (3:30) K-Tel 3437 Summer Songs.

(S) (3:28) Time-Life AM1-02 AM Gold - 1970.

(S) (3:30) Flashback 72710 Golden Summer.

(S) (3:30) Flashback 72683 '70s Radio Hits Volume 3.

(S) (3:30) Flashback 72090 '70s Radio Hits Box Set.

(S) (2:33) Inner-State/London 314540735 O.S.T. Twin Town. *(faded :57 early)*

(S) (3:30) Rhino 72812 VH1 8-Track Flashback: The One Hit Wonders.

SHIRLEY MURDOCK
1987 AS WE LAY

(S) (5:55) Ichiban 2507 Cheatin': From A Woman's Point Of View. *(LP version)*

(S) (5:55) Rhino 71860 Smooth Grooves Volume 2. *(LP version)*

(S) (5:54) Right Stuff 31973 Slow Jams: The Timeless Collection Volume 3. *(LP version)*

(S)	(5:27)	Elektra 60443 Shirley Murdock! *(alternate mix)*
(S)	(5:55)	Elektra 60443 Shirley Murdock! *(LP version)*
(S)	(5:27)	Madacy Entertainment 1987 Rock On 1987. *(alternate mix)*
(S)	(3:54)	JCI 3177 1985 - Only Soul - 1989. *(45 version)*

MURMAIDS
1964 POPSICLES AND ICICLES
(M)	(2:31)	Rhino 70989 Best Of The Girl Groups Volume 2.
(M)	(2:30)	Time-Life 2CLR-09 Classic Rock - 1964: The Beat Goes On.
(M)	(2:30)	Time-Life SUD-08 Superhits - 1963.
(M)	(2:31)	Original Sound 8852 Oldies But Goodies Vol. 2. *(this compact disc uses the "Waring - fds" noise reduction process)*
(M)	(2:31)	Original Sound 2223 Oldies But Goodies Volumes 2,7,9,12 and 13 Box Set. *(this box set uses the "Waring - fds" noise reduction process)*
(M)	(2:31)	Original Sound 2500 Oldies But Goodies Volumes 1-15 Box Set. *(this box set uses the "Waring - fds" noise reduction process)*
(M)	(2:30)	Rhino 71585 Billboard Top Pop Hits, 1964.
(E)	(2:30)	Collectables 5538 Popsicles And Icicles.
(M)	(2:30)	Eric 11503 Hard To Find 45's On CD (Volume II) 1961-64.
(M)	(2:30)	Time-Life R857-09 The Heart Of Rock 'n' Roll 1964.
(M)	(2:30)	Time-Life AM1-17 AM Gold - 1963.

MICHAEL MURPHEY
1975 WILDFIRE
(S)	(4:46)	Columbia/Legacy 46763 Rock Artifacts Volume 2. *(LP version)*
(S)	(3:16)	Priority 8664 High Times/70's Greatest Rock Hits Volume 3. *(45 version)*
(S)	(3:16)	Rhino 70761 Super Hits Of The 70's Volume 14. *(45 version)*
(S)	(4:46)	Epic 33290 Blue Sky/Night Thunder. *(LP version)*
(S)	(5:05)	EMI 92736 Best Of. *(rerecording)*
(S)	(3:16)	Razor & Tie 22505 More Fabulous 70's Volume 2. *(45 version)*
(S)	(3:13)	Time-Life SOD-32 Sounds Of The Seventies - AM Pop Classics. *(45 version)*
(S)	(3:12)	Time-Life R105-26 Our Songs: Singers & Songwriters Encore. *(45 version)*
(S)	(3:16)	Risky Business 66871 Polyester Dreams/Greatest Hits Of The 70's. *(45 version)*
(S)	(3:16)	K-Tel 3624 Music Express. *(45 version)*
(S)	(3:14)	Eclipse Music Group 64894 Rock 'n Roll Relix 1974-1975. *(45 version)*
(S)	(3:14)	Eclipse Music Group 64897 Rock 'n Roll Relix 1970-1979. *(45 version)*
(S)	(3:16)	Time-Life AM1-22 AM Gold - 1975. *(45 version)*
(S)	(3:16)	Time-Life R840-01 Sounds Of The Seventies - Pop Nuggets: Late '70s. *(45 version)*
(S)	(3:16)	K-Tel 3885 Story Songs. *(45 version)*
(S)	(4:46)	Time-Life R834-20 Body Talk - Heart And Soul. *(LP version)*

1975 CAROLINA IN THE PINES
(S)	(3:55)	Epic 33290 Blue Sky/Night Thunder. *(LP version)*
(S)	(4:08)	EMI 92736 Best Of. *(rerecording)*

1982 WHAT'S FOREVER FOR
(S)	(2:49)	EMI 92736 Best Of.
(S)	(2:49)	K-Tel 3289 The Ties That Bind - Country Love Songs.

EDDIE MURPHY
1986 PARTY ALL THE TIME
(S)	(4:13)	Columbia 39952 How Could It Be.
(S)	(4:09)	Time-Life R988-12 Sounds Of The 80's: 1985-1986.

1989 PUT YOUR MOUTH ON ME
(S)	(4:03)	Columbia 40970 So Happy.

WALTER MURPHY & THE BIG APPLE BAND
1976 A FIFTH OF BEETHOVEN
(S)	(3:01)	Rhino 70799 O.S.T. Spirit Of '76.
(S)	(3:01)	Polydor 800068 O.S.T. Saturday Night Fever.
(S)	(3:01)	Rhino 71603 Rock Instrumental Classics Volume 3: The Seventies.
(S)	(3:01)	Rhino 72035 Rock Instrumental Classics Vols. 1-5 Box Set.
(S)	(3:01)	Razor & Tie 22496 Disco Fever.
(S)	(3:01)	K-Tel 3126 Disco Mania.
(S)	(3:01)	K-Tel 3470 Get Up And Disco.
(S)	(3:01)	Polydor 422825389 O.S.T. Saturday Night Fever. *(remastered edition)*
(S)	(3:01)	Priority 50956 Mega Hits - Disco Heat.
(S)	(3:01)	Time-Life R840-04 Sounds Of The Seventies: A Loss For Words.
(S)	(3:02)	Mobile Fidelity 716 O.S.T. Saturday Night Fever. *(gold disc)*
(S)	(3:01)	Time-Life R840-07 Sounds Of The Seventies: '70s Dance Party 1976-1977.

ANNE MURRAY
1970 SNOWBIRD
(S)	(2:09)	Capitol 46058 Greatest Hits.
(S)	(2:08)	Capitol 95954 Fifteen Of The Best.
(S)	(2:09)	Time-Life CTD-04 Country USA - 1970.
(S)	(2:07)	Time-Life SUD-04 Superhits - 1970.
(S)	(2:09)	Capitol 31158 The Best....So Far.
(S)	(2:08)	Capitol 36387 Now & Forever.
(S)	(1:59)	Capitol 36387 Now & Forever. *(live)*
(S)	(2:07)	Time-Life AM1-02 AM Gold - 1970.

1973 DANNY'S SONG
(S)	(3:04)	Capitol 48446 Danny's Song.
(S)	(3:03)	Capitol 46058 Greatest Hits.
(S)	(3:04)	Capitol 95954 Fifteen Of The Best.
(S)	(3:04)	Capitol 31158 The Best....So Far.
(S)	(3:03)	Capitol 36387 Now & Forever.

1974 LOVE SONG
(S)	(2:46)	Capitol 46058 Greatest Hits.
(S)	(2:46)	Capitol 31158 The Best....So Far.
(S)	(2:46)	Capitol 36387 Now & Forever.

1974 YOU WON'T SEE ME
(S)	(4:06)	Capitol 46058 Greatest Hits. *(LP version)*
(S)	(4:02)	Capitol 31158 The Best....So Far. *(LP version)*
(S)	(3:41)	Capitol 36387 Now & Forever. *(live)*

1978 YOU NEEDED ME
(S)	(3:35)	Capitol 95954 Fifteen Of The Best.
(S)	(3:35)	Capitol 46058 Greatest Hits.
(S)	(3:35)	Priority 8671 Country's Greatest Hits: Superstars.
(S)	(3:34)	Time-Life CCD-10 Contemporary Country - The Late 70's Pure Gold.
(S)	(3:38)	Capitol 31158 The Best....So Far.
(S)	(3:36)	K-Tel 605 Country Music Classics Volume V.
(S)	(3:56)	Capitol 36387 Now & Forever. *(includes :17 introduction)*

1979 I JUST FALL IN LOVE AGAIN
(S)	(2:46)	Capitol 95954 Fifteen Of The Best.
(S)	(2:47)	Capitol 46058 Greatest Hits.
(S)	(2:46)	Priority 9305 Country Gold.
(S)	(2:48)	Capitol 31158 The Best....So Far.
(S)	(2:48)	Capitol 36387 Now & Forever.

1979 SHADOWS IN THE MOONLIGHT
(S)	(3:21)	Capitol 95954 Fifteen Of The Best.
(S)	(3:21)	Capitol 46058 Greatest Hits.
(S)	(3:28)	Capitol 31158 The Best....So Far.
(S)	(3:24)	Capitol 36387 Now & Forever.

1979 BROKEN HEARTED ME
(actual LP length is (3:55) not (3:43) as stated on the record label)
(S)	(3:55)	Capitol 95954 Fifteen Of The Best. *(LP length)*
(S)	(3:55)	Capitol 46058 Greatest Hits. *(LP length)*
(S)	(3:57)	Capitol 31158 The Best....So Far. *(LP length)*
(S)	(3:43)	Capitol 36387 Now & Forever. *(Spanish version)*

1980 DAYDREAM BELIEVER
(S)	(2:24)	Capitol 46058 Greatest Hits.
(S)	(2:27)	Capitol 31158 The Best....So Far.
(S)	(2:26)	Capitol 36387 Now & Forever.

ANNE MURRAY *(Continued)*
1980 COULD I HAVE THIS DANCE
- (S) (3:14) Full Moon/Elektra 60690 O.S.T. Urban Cowboy.
- (S) (3:13) Liberty 95954 Fifteen Of The Best.
- (S) (3:13) Capitol 46058 Greatest Hits.
- (S) (3:14) Capitol 31158 The Best....So Far.
- (S) (3:12) Time-Life CCD-03 Contemporary Country - The Early 80's.
- (S) (3:14) Capitol 36387 Now & Forever.
- (S) (3:12) Time-Life R814-02 Love Songs.

1981 BLESSED ARE THE BELIEVERS
- (S) (2:38) Capitol 95954 Fifteen Of The Best.
- (S) (2:39) Capitol 46487 Country Hits.
- (S) (2:39) Capitol 92072 Greatest Hits Volume 2.
- (S) (2:40) Capitol 31158 The Best....So Far.
- (S) (2:38) Capitol 36387 Now & Forever.

MUSICAL YOUTH
1983 PASS THE DUTCHIE
- (S) (3:24) Rhino 71700 New Wave Hits Of The 80's Vol. 7.
- (S) (3:23) One Way 22123 Anthology.
- (S) (3:24) Priority 53765 Rock Of The 80's Volume 9.
- (S) (3:22) MCA Special Products 20897 Greatest Rock Hits Of The 80's.
- (S) (3:23) Time-Life R988-16 Sounds Of The Eighties: The Early '80s.
- (S) (3:23) Hip-O 40047 The '80s Hit(s) Back 3.
- (S) (3:23) Intersound 9521 Retro Lunch Box - Squeeze The Cheese.
- (S) (3:23) Maverick/Warner Brothers 46840 O.S.T. The Wedding Singer.
- (S) (3:22) Simitar 55112 Great Reggae.

MUSIC EXPLOSION
1967 LITTLE BIT O' SOUL
- (M) (2:20) Warner Special Products 27602 20 Party Classics.
- (S) (2:19) Rhino 75772 Son Of Frat Rock.
- (S) (2:19) Rhino 70628 Billboard Top Rock & Roll Hits Of 1967.
- (S) (2:19) Original Sound 8862 Oldies But Goodies Vol. 12. *(this compact disc uses the "Waring - fds" noise reduction process)*
- (S) (2:19) Original Sound 2223 Oldies But Goodies Volumes 2,7,9,12 and 13 Box Set. *(this box set uses the "Waring - fds" noise reduction process)*
- (S) (2:19) Original Sound 2500 Oldies But Goodies Volumes 1-15 Box Set. *(this box set uses the "Waring - fds" noise reduction process)*
- (S) (2:18) Original Sound CDGO-4 Golden Oldies Volume. 4.
- (E) (2:18) Pair 1199 Best Of Bubblegum Music.
- (S) (2:19) DCC Compact Classics 029 Toga Rock.
- (S) (2:19) K-Tel 713 Battle Of The Bands.
- (E) (2:18) Special Music 4914 Best Of The Bubblegum Years.
- (S) (2:17) Collectables 5061 History Of Rock Volume 1.
- (S) (2:18) JCI 3111 Good Time Sixties.
- (M) (2:17) Time-Life 2CLR-05 Classic Rock - 1967.
- (S) (2:14) Collectables 2510 WCBS-FM History Of Rock - The Rockin' 60's.
- (S) (2:14) Collectables 4510 History Of Rock/The Rockin' 60s.
- (S) (2:18) Collectables 2501 WCBS-FM History Of Rock - The 60's Part 2.

- (S) (2:18) Collectables 4501 History Of Rock/The 60s Part Two.
- (S) (2:19) Risky Business 66914 Party On.
- (S) (2:19) One Way 18260 Anthology. *(remixed)*
- (M) (2:17) JCI 3190 1965 - Only Dance - 1969.
- (M) (2:18) MCA Special Products 20981 Bubble Gum Classics.

MUSIC MACHINE
1966 TALK TALK
- (S) (1:55) Rhino 75777 More Nuggets.
- (S) (1:54) Original Sound 8894 Dick Clark's 21 All-Time Hits Vol. 3.
- (M) (1:55) K-Tel 713 Battle Of The Bands.
- (S) (1:54) Original Sound CDGO-7 Golden Oldies Volume. 7.
- (S) (1:55) JCI 3111 Good Time Sixties.
- (S) (1:55) Time-Life 2CLR-15 Classic Rock - 1967: Shakin' All Over.
- (S) (1:55) Performance 397 (Turn On) The Music Machine.
- (S) (1:55) K-Tel 3133 Biker Rock.
- (S) (1:55) Time-Life R968-12 Guitar Rock - The Late '60s.
- (S) (1:54) LaserLight 12528 Garage Band Rock.
- (S) (1:54) JCI 3167 #1 Radio Hits 1965 - Only Rock 'n Roll - 1969.
- (S) (1:54) Hip-O 40038 Power Chords Volume 1.
- (S) (1:55) Simitar 55362 Garage Band Classics.

ALANNAH MYLES
1990 BLACK VELVET
- (S) (4:43) JCI 3123 Harvest.
- (S) (4:46) Atlantic 81956 Alannah Myles.
- (S) (4:45) Razor & Tie 4569 '90s Style.

1990 LOVE IS
- (S) (3:37) Atlantic 81956 Alannah Myles.

BILLY MYLES
1957 THE JOKER (THAT'S WHAT THEY CALL ME)
- (M) (2:35) Time-Life 2RNR-44 Rock 'N' Roll Era - Lost Treasures.

MYSTICS
1959 HUSHABYE
- (S) (2:30) Rhino 75764 Best Of Doo Wop Uptempo.
- (S) (2:32) Collectables 2507 History Of Rock - The Doo Wop Era Part 1.
- (S) (2:32) Collectables 4507 History Of Rock/The Doo Wop Era Part One.
- (S) (2:31) Essex 7053 A Hot Summer Night In '59.
- (S) (2:31) Collectables 5043 16 Golden Classics. *(sounds like it was mastered from vinyl)*
- (S) (2:30) Collectables 5066 History Of Rock Volume 6.
- (S) (2:28) Era 5025 The Brill Building Sound.
- (S) (2:29) Rhino 71463 Doo Wop Box.
- (S) (2:28) Time-Life 2RNR-20 Rock 'N' Roll Era - 1959 Still Rockin'.
- (S) (2:32) Collectables 2503 WCBS-FM History Of Rock - The 50's Part 2.
- (S) (2:31) Collectables 4503 History Of Rock/The 50s Part Two.
- (S) (2:28) Time-Life R10513 40 Lovin' Oldies.
- (S) (2:32) K-Tel 478 More 50's Jukebox Favorites.
- (S) (2:29) Time-Life R857-01 The Heart Of Rock 'n' Roll - 1959.
- (S) (2:33) Right Stuff 53320 Hot Rod Rock Volume 5: Back Seat Movers.

NAKED EYES
1983 ALWAYS SOMETHING THERE TO REMIND ME
(dj copies of this 45 were issued in two different mixes - one is the same mix as the commercial LP and 45 and the other one which starts without drums has yet to appear on compact disc)
- (S) (3:39) EMI 81417 Living In Oblivion: The 80's Greatest Hits Volume One.
- (S) (3:40) Priority 53705 Rock Of The 80's Volume 2.
- (S) (3:38) Rhino 71834 Classic MTV: Class Of 1983.
- (S) (3:40) EMI 95843 Best Of.
- (S) (3:40) EMI 27226 Very Best Of.
- (S) (3:38) Time-Life R988-03 Sounds Of The Eighties: 1983.
- (S) (3:38) Madacy Entertainment 1983 Rock On 1983.
- (S) (3:39) Hollywood 62098 O.S.T. Romy And Michele's High School Reunion.

1983 PROMISES, PROMISES
- (S) (3:46) Priority 53749 Rock Of The 80's Volume 6.
- (S) (3:45) Rhino 71703 New Wave Hits Of The 80's Vol. 10.
- (S) (3:58) EMI 32694 Living In Oblivion - The 80's Greatest Hits Volume Five.
- (S) (3:48) EMI 95843 Best Of.
- (S) (3:43) EMI 27226 Very Best Of.
- (S) (3:45) Time-Life R988-11 Sounds Of The 80's: 1983-1984.
- (S) (3:44) Simitar 55552 The Number One's: Eighties Rock.

1983 WHEN THE LIGHTS GO OUT
- (S) (3:01) Priority 53748 Rock Of The 80's Volume 8.
- (S) (3:00) EMI 27226 Very Best Of.

1984 (WHAT) IN THE NAME OF LOVE
- (S) (4:24) EMI 27226 Very Best Of.
- (S) (4:24) Priority 53765 Rock Of The 80's Volume 9.

NAPOLEON XIV
1966 THEY'RE COMING TO TAKE ME AWAY, HA-HAAA!
- (S) (2:10) Rhino 75768 Dr. Demento Presents.
- (S) (2:09) Rhino 70743 Dr. Demento 20th Anniversary Collection.
- (S) (2:07) K-Tel 3036 Silly Songs.
- (S) (2:07) Time-Life 2RNR-37 Rock 'N' Roll Era - Weird, Wild & Wacky.
- (S) (2:09) Rhino 71750 Spy Magazine Presents: White Men Can't Wrap.
- (S) (2:09) Rhino 72402 The Second Coming.
- (S) (2:09) Rhino 72258 Dumb And Dumber: Get Down, Get Dumb.

NAS
1997 STREET DREAMS
- (S) (4:39) Columbia 67015 and 67745 It Was Written.
released as by ALLURE featuring NAS:
1997 HEAD OVER HEELS
- (S) (4:11) Crave/Track Masters 67848 Allure. *(tracks into next selection)*

GRAHAM NASH
1971 CHICAGO
- (S) (2:51) Atlantic 7204 Songs For Beginners. *(45 version)*
- (S) (3:57) Atlantic 82319 Crosby, Stills & Nash Box Set. *(LP version which is a medley with "WE CAN CHANGE THE WORLD")*
released as by GRAHAM NASH & DAVID CROSBY:
1972 IMMIGRATION MAN
- (S) (2:57) Atlantic 82319 Crosby, Stills & Nash Box Set.

JOHNNY NASH
1958 A VERY SPECIAL LOVE
released as by PAUL ANKA-GEORGE HAMILTON IV-JOHNNY NASH:
1959 THE TEEN COMMANDMENTS
- (M) (1:41) Rhino 71489 Paul Anka - 30th Anniversary Collection.
released as by JOHNNY NASH:
1968 HOLD ME TIGHT
- (S) (2:42) Epic/Legacy 52770 Reggae Collection.
- (S) (2:41) Time-Life 2CLR-27 Classic Rock - 1968: Blowin' Your Mind.

1970 CUPID
- (S) (3:24) Epic/Legacy 52770 Reggae Collection.

1972 I CAN SEE CLEARLY NOW
- (S) (2:46) Rhino 70633 Billboard's Top Rock & Roll Hits Of 1972.
- (S) (2:46) Rhino 72005 Billboard's Top Rock & Roll Hits 1969-1972 Box Set.
- (S) (2:42) Columbia/Legacy 46763 Rock Artifacts Volume 2.
- (S) (2:45) Rhino 70789 Soul Hits Of The 70's Volume 9.
- (S) (2:38) Columbia/Legacy 47966 Rhythm Come Forward Volume 2. *(tracks into next selection)*
- (S) (2:44) JCI 3304 Mellow Seventies.
- (S) (2:44) Epic 31067 I Can See Clearly Now.
- (S) (2:54) Epic/Legacy 52770 Reggae Collection. *(alternate take)*
- (S) (2:41) Time-Life SUD-11 Superhits - 1972.
- (S) (2:46) Time-Life SOD-03 Sounds Of The Seventies - 1972.
- (S) (2:44) Risky Business 66871 Polyester Dreams/Greatest Hits Of The 70's.
- (S) (2:42) MCA 11065 O.S.T. Crooklyn Volume II.
- (S) (2:43) Rebound 314520313 Caribbean Nights I.
- (S) (2:42) Madacy Entertainment 26927 Sun Splashin'.
- (S) (2:46) Eclipse Music Group 64893 Rock 'n Roll Relix 1972-1973.
- (S) (2:46) Eclipse Music Group 64897 Rock 'n Roll Relix 1970-1979.
- (S) (2:41) Time-Life AM1-07 AM Gold - 1972.
- (S) (2:41) K-Tel 3912 Superstars Greatest Hits Volume 1.
- (S) (2:42) London 422828867 O.S.T. Grosse Pointe Blank.
- (S) (2:43) Rebound 314520313 Reggae Dance Party I.

1973 STIR IT UP
- (S) (3:02) Epic 46490 O.S.T. Queens Logic.
- (S) (3:01) Columbia/Legacy 46763 Rock Artifacts Volume 2.
- (S) (2:58) Rhino 70790 Soul Hits Of The 70's Volume 10.
- (S) (3:02) Epic 31067 I Can See Clearly Now.
- (S) (3:01) Columbia/Legacy 52726 Rhythm Come Forward Volume 3.
- (S) (3:03) Epic/Legacy 52770 Reggae Collection.
- (S) (3:01) Time-Life SOD-14 Sounds Of The Seventies - 1973: Take Two.
- (S) (3:02) MCA 11077 More Music From Northern Exposure.
- (S) (3:00) Rebound 314520314 Caribbean Nights II.
- (S) (3:02) K-Tel 6067 Best Of Reggae.
- (S) (3:04) Simitar 55112 Great Reggae.
- (S) (3:00) Rebound 314520314 Reggae Dance Party II.

NASHVILLE TEENS
1964 TOBACCO ROAD
- (M) (2:25) Time-Life 2CLR-26 Classic Rock - Rock Renaissance III.
- (M) (2:24) One Way 19099 Tobacco Road.

NATE DOGG
released as by WARREN G & NATE DOGG:
1994 REGULATE
- (S) (4:08) Death Row/Interscope 92359 and 92403 and 50606 O.S.T. Above The Rim. *(very poor stereo separation*
- (S) (4:08) Violator/RAL 314523335 and 314523364 Regulate...G Funk Era. *(very poor stereo separation)*
- (S) (4:08) Boxtunes 162444068 Big Phat Ones Of Hip-Hop Volume 1. *(very poor stereo separation)*
- (S) (4:08) Def Jam 314523848 Def Jam Music Group 10th Year Anniversary. *(very poor stereo separation)*
- (S) (4:06) Rebound 314520449 Hip Hop With R&B Flava. *(very poor stereo separation)*
- (S) (4:07) Def Jam 314536377 Def Jam's Greatest Hits. *(very poor stereo separation)*

released as by NATE DOGG featuring SNOOP DOGGY DOGG:
1996 NEVER LEAVE ME ALONE

NATURAL FOUR
1974 CAN THIS BE REAL
- (S) (3:29) K-Tel 3535 Slow Groove Love Jams Of The 70's.

NATURAL SELECTION
1991 DO ANYTHING
- (S) (3:56) EastWest 91787 Natural Selection.
- (S) (6:05) EastWest 91787 Natural Selection. *(remix)*
1992 HEARTS DON'T THINK (THEY FEEL)
- (S) (4:15) EastWest 91787 Natural Selection.

DAVID NAUGHTON
1979 MAKIN' IT
- (S) (3:11) Rebound 314520307 Disco Nights Volume VIII.
- (S) (3:08) Rhino 71911 Tube Tunes Volume Two - The 70's & 80's.
- (S) (3:08) Rhino 72298 Superhits Of The 70's Volume 24.
- (S) (3:08) Time-Life R840-02 Sounds Of The Seventies - TV Themes.
- (S) (3:10) Rebound 314520440 No. 1 Hits Of The 70's.
- (S) (3:08) Time-Life R840-09 Sounds Of The Seventies: '70s Dance Party 1979-1981.
- ↱ (S) (3:08) Time-Life AM1-26 AM Gold - 1979.
- (S) (2:24) Rebound 314520520 Body Moves - Non-Stop Disco Workout Vol. 1. *(all selections on this cd are segued together)*

NAUGHTY BY NATURE
1991 O.P.P.
- (S) (6:06) Tommy Boy 1053 MTV Party To Go Volume 2. *(remix; all tracks on this cd are segued together)*
- (S) (4:29) Tommy Boy 1044 Naughty By Nature.
- (S) (4:29) Rebound 314520360 Major Flavas Rap Classics.
1993 HIP HOP HOORAY
- (S) (3:47) Tommy Boy 1075 MTV Party To Go Volume 4. *(remix; all tracks on this cd are segued together)*
- (S) (4:24) Tommy Boy 1069 19 Naughty III.
- (S) (3:51) Tommy Boy 1137 ESPN Presents Jock Jams. *(all songs on this cd are segued together with crowd sound effects added)*
- (S) (4:24) MCA 11329 Soul Train 25th Anniversary Box Set.
- (S) (4:21) Razor & Tie 4569 '90s Style.
- (S) (4:02) Priority 50935 100% Party Hits Of The 90's Volume Two. *(all selections on this cd are segued together)*
1995 FEEL ME FLOW
- (S) (3:32) Tommy Boy 1111 Poverty's Paradise.

NAZARETH
1976 LOVE HURTS
- (S) (3:52) A&M 3225 Hair Of The Dog. *(LP version)*
- (S) (3:51) A&M 3226 Hot Tracks. *(LP version)*
- (S) (3:50) A&M 2514 Classics Volume 14. *(LP version)*
- (S) (3:50) Polydor 314515913 Classic Rock Box. *(LP version)*
- (S) (3:00) Priority 7080 70's Greatest Rock Hits Volume 14: Kings Of Rock. *(45 version)*

- (S) (3:01) Rhino 71197 Super Hits Of The 70's Volume 17. *(45 version)*
- (S) (3:50) Medicine Label 24533 O.S.T. Dazed And Confused. *(LP version)*
- (S) (3:00) Time-Life R968-01 Guitar Rock 1974-1975. *(45 version)*
- (S) (3:51) Varese 5635 and 5654 and 5655 and 5657 Arrow: All Rock & Roll Oldies Volume Two. *(LP version)*
- (S) (3:50) Rebound 314520368 Class Reunion '76. *(LP version)*
- (S) (3:52) A&M 314540513 Greatest Hits. *(LP version)*
- (S) (3:51) Varese Sarabande 5708 All Rock & Roll Hits Vol. One. *(LP version)*
- (S) (3:51) A&M 314540513 Greatest Hits. *(LP version)*
- (S) (3:51) Rebound 314520437 Classic Rock - 70's. *(LP version)*
- (S) (3:00) Time-Life R834-18 Body Talk - Romantic Moments. *(45 version)*

SAM NEELY
1972 LOVING YOU JUST CROSSED MY MIND
- (S) (3:16) EMI 90603 Rock Me Gently.
1974 YOU CAN HAVE HER

NEIGHBORHOOD
1970 BIG YELLOW TAXI

NELSON
1990 (CAN'T LIVE WITHOUT YOUR) LOVE AND AFFECTION
- (S) (3:56) Priority 7049 Metal Heat.
- (S) (3:54) DGC 24290 After The Rain.
- (S) (3:54) K-Tel 3848 90s Now Volume 2.
- (S) (3:50) Rhino 75217 Heartthrob Hits.
1991 AFTER THE RAIN
- (S) (4:03) DGC 24290 After The Rain.
- (S) (4:03) MCA Special Products 21028 The Best Of Hard Rock.
1991 MORE THAN EVER
- (S) (3:28) DGC 24290 After The Rain.
1991 ONLY TIME WILL TELL
- (S) (5:17) DGC 24290 After The Rain. *(LP version which includes a (1:02) instrumental introduction titled "TRACY'S SONG")*

RICK NELSON
released as by RICKY NELSON:
1957 I'M WALKING
- ✓ (M) (1:56) Mercury 832041 45's On CD Volume 1.
- (M) (1:56) Curb 77372 All-Time Greatest Hits.
- (S) (1:40) MCA 6163 All My Best. *(all tracks on this cd are rerecordings)*
- (M) (1:57) Time-Life 2RNR-31 Rock 'N' Roll Era - Rick Nelson 1957-1972.
- (M) (1:57) Special Music/Essex 5034 Prom Night - The 50's.
1957 A TEENAGER'S ROMANCE
- (M) (2:16) Curb 77372 All-Time Greatest Hits.
- (M) (2:17) Time-Life 2RNR-31 Rock 'N' Roll Era - Rick Nelson 1957-1972.
- (M) (2:17) Time-Life R962-05 History Of Rock 'N' Roll: The Teenage Years 1957-1964.
- ✓ (M) (2:17) Eric 11502 Hard To Find 45's On CD (Volume I) 1955-60.
- (M) (2:17) Time-Life R857-05 The Heart Of Rock 'n' Roll 1957.
1957 YOU'RE MY ONE AND ONLY LOVE
- (M) (2:04) Curb 77372 All-Time Greatest Hits.
- (M) (2:04) Eric 11502 Hard To Find 45's On CD (Volume I) 1955-60.
- (M) (2:04) Hammer & Lace 697124114 Leading Men: Masters Of Style Volume Three.
1957 BE-BOP BABY
- (M) (2:02) EMI 46588 Best Of.
- (M) (2:22) EMI 92771 Legendary Masters Volume 1. *(includes :21 of studio talk and a false start)*
- (M) (2:02) Time-Life 2RNR-31 Rock 'N' Roll Era - Rick Nelson 1957-1972.

1957 HAVE I TOLD YOU LATELY THAT I LOVE YOU?
(M) (1:56)   EMI 92771   Legendary Masters Volume 1.

1958 STOOD UP
(M) (1:51)   EMI 46588   Best Of.
(M) (1:50)   EMI 92771   Legendary Masters Volume 1.
(M) (1:50)   Curb 77372   All-Time Greatest Hits.
(S) (1:40)   MCA 6163   All My Best. *(all tracks on this cd are rerecordings)*
(E) (1:51)   EMI 92707   Souvenirs.
(M) (1:51)   Time-Life 2RNR-31   Rock 'N' Roll Era - Rick Nelson 1957-1972.

1958 WAITIN' IN SCHOOL
(M) (2:00)   Rhino 70561   Legends Of Guitar - Rock: The 50's Volume 2.
(M) (2:01)   EMI 46588   Best Of.
(M) (2:01)   EMI 92771   Legendary Masters Volume 1.
(E) (2:01)   EMI 92707   Souvenirs.
(M) (2:01)   Time-Life 2RNR-31   Rock 'N' Roll Era - Rick Nelson 1957-1972.

1958 BELIEVE WHAT YOU SAY
(M) (2:03)   Rhino 70741   Rock This Town: Rockabilly Hits Volume 1. *(45 version)*
(M) (2:02)   Rhino 70561   Legends Of Guitar - Rock: The 50's Volume 2. *(45 version)*
(M) (2:02)   EMI 46588   Best Of. *(LP version)*
(M) (2:03)   EMI 92771   Legendary Masters Volume 1. *(45 version)*
(M) (2:02)   Curb 77372   All-Time Greatest Hits. *(LP version)*
(S) (2:09)   MCA 6163   All My Best. *(all tracks on this cd are rerecordings)*
(M) (2:03)   Time-Life 2RNR-31   Rock 'N' Roll Era - Rick Nelson 1957-1972. *(LP version)*
(M) (2:03)   JCI 3188   1955 - Only Dance - 1959. *(45 version)*

1958 MY BUCKET'S GOT A HOLE IN IT
(M) (2:01)   EMI 92771   Legendary Masters Volume 1.

1958 POOR LITTLE FOOL
(E) (2:30)   EMI 96268   24 Greatest Hits Of All Time.
(M) (2:30)   Curb 77354   50's Hits Volume 1.
(M) (2:30)   EMI 46588   Best Of.
(M) (2:30)   EMI 92771   Legendary Masters Volume 1.
(S) (2:32)   MCA 6163   All My Best. *(all tracks on this cd are rerecordings)*
(M) (2:30)   Curb 77525   Greatest Hits Of Rock 'N' Roll Volume 2.
(E) (2:29)   EMI 92707   Souvenirs.
(M) (2:31)   Time-Life 2RNR-31   Rock 'N' Roll Era - Rick Nelson 1957-1972.
(M) (2:30)   Time-Life R857-11   The Heart Of Rock 'n' Roll 1958-1959.

1958 LONESOME TOWN
(M) (2:13)   EMI 46588   Best Of.
(M) (2:12)   EMI 92771   Legendary Masters Volume 1.
(M) (2:13)   Curb 77372   All-Time Greatest Hits.
(S) (2:14)   MCA 6163   All My Best. *(all tracks on this cd are rerecordings)*
(M) (2:14)   Time-Life 2RNR-31   Rock 'N' Roll Era - Rick Nelson 1957-1972.
(M) (2:13)   MCA 11103 and 11188   O.S.T. Pulp Fiction.
(M) (2:12)   Time-Life R857-04   The Heart Of Rock 'n' Roll - 1958.
(M) (2:13)   Epic 68778   O.S.T. U Turn.

1958 I GOT A FEELING
(M) (2:03)   EMI 92771   Legendary Masters Volume 1.
(S) (1:57)   MCA 6163   All My Best. *(all tracks on this cd are rerecordings)*

1959 NEVER BE ANYONE ELSE BUT YOU
(M) (2:13)   EMI 46588   Best Of.
(S) (2:16)   EMI 92771   Legendary Masters Volume 1. *(alternate take)*
(M) (2:13)   Curb 77372   All-Time Greatest Hits.
(S) (2:15)   MCA 6163   All My Best. *(all tracks on this cd are rerecordings)*
(S) (2:16)   Time-Life 2RNR-31   Rock 'N' Roll Era - Rick Nelson 1957-1972.
(S) (2:16)   Time-Life R857-16   The Heart Of Rock 'n' Roll The Late '50s.

1959 IT'S LATE
(M) (1:56)   EMI 46588   Best Of.

(M) (2:27)   EMI 92771   Legendary Masters Volume 1. *(includes a :31 false start and countoff)*
(S) (2:00)   MCA 6163   All My Best. *(all tracks on this cd are rerecordings)*
(M) (1:57)   Time-Life 2RNR-31   Rock 'N' Roll Era - Rick Nelson 1957-1972.

1959 JUST A LITTLE TOO MUCH
(M) (2:10)   EMI 46588   Best Of.
(S) (2:09)   EMI 92771   Legendary Masters Volume 1.
(S) (2:03)   MCA 6163   All My Best. *(all tracks on this cd are rerecordings)*
(E) (2:09)   EMI 92707   Souvenirs.
(M) (2:09)   Time-Life 2RNR-31   Rock 'N' Roll Era - Rick Nelson 1957-1972.

1959 SWEETER THAN YOU
(S) (2:09)   EMI 92771   Legendary Masters Volume 1. *(alternate take)*

1960 I WANNA BE LOVED
(M) (2:43)   EMI 92771   Legendary Masters Volume 1. *(background hum noticeable)*

1960 YOUNG EMOTIONS
(M) (2:32)   EMI 46588   Best Of.
(M) (2:32)   EMI 92771   Legendary Masters Volume 1.
(E) (2:30)   EMI 92707   Souvenirs.
(M) (2:31)   Time-Life R857-02   The Heart Of Rock 'n' Roll - 1960.

1960 I'M NOT AFRAID
(M) (2:36)   EMI 92771   Legendary Masters Volume 1.

1961 YOU ARE THE ONLY ONE
(S) (2:39)   EMI 95219   Best Of Volume 2.

1961 TRAVELIN' MAN
(S) (2:20)   EMI 46588   Best Of. *(ends cold)*
(S) (2:20)   EMI 95219   Best Of Volume 2. *(ends cold)*
(S) (2:23)   MCA 6163   All My Best. *(all tracks on this cd are rerecordings)*
(S) (2:20)   EMI 81128   Rock Is Dead But It Won't Lie Down. *(ends cold)*
(E) (2:18)   EMI 92707   Souvenirs. *(ending fades out)*
(S) (2:21)   Curb 77637   All Time Greatest Hits Of Rock 'N' Roll Volume 3. *(ends cold)*
(S) (2:20)   Time-Life 2RNR-31   Rock 'N' Roll Era - Rick Nelson 1957-1972. *(ends cold)*
(S) (2:20)   Time-Life R857-03   The Heart Of Rock 'n' Roll - 1961. *(ends cold)*
(S) (2:20)   Rhino 72819   16 Magazine - Who's Your Fave Rave. *(ends cold)*
(S) (2:20)   Collectables 1515 and 2515   The Anniversary Album - The 60's. *(ends cold)*

1961 HELLO MARY LOU
(S) (2:17)   Curb 77532   Your Favorite Songs.
(S) (2:17)   EMI 46588   Best Of.
(S) (2:41)   EMI 95219   Best Of Volume 2. *(includes a :24 false start and countoff)*
(S) (2:18)   MCA 6163   All My Best. *(all tracks on this cd are rerecordings)*
(E) (2:16)   EMI 92707   Souvenirs.
(S) (2:17)   Time-Life 2RNR-31   Rock 'N' Roll Era - Rick Nelson 1957-1972.
(S) (2:17)   K-Tel 3388   TV Stars Sing.

released as by RICK NELSON:
1961 A WONDER LIKE YOU
(M) (2:34)   EMI 95219   Best Of Volume 2.

1961 EVERLOVIN'
(M) (2:06)   EMI 95219   Best Of Volume 2.

1962 YOUNG WORLD
(M) (2:23)   EMI 46588   Best Of.
(M) (2:24)   EMI 95219   Best Of Volume 2.
(S) (2:20)   MCA 6163   All My Best. *(all tracks on this cd are rerecordings)*
(M) (2:24)   Time-Life 2RNR-31   Rock 'N' Roll Era - Rick Nelson 1957-1972.
(M) (2:24)   Time-Life R857-06   The Heart Of Rock 'n' Roll 1962.

1962 TEEN AGE IDOL
(M) (2:26)   EMI 46588   Best Of.
(M) (2:26)   EMI 95219   Best Of Volume 2.

RICK NELSON (Continued)

- (S) (2:30) MCA 6163 All My Best. *(all tracks on this cd are rerecordings)*
- (M) (2:26) Time-Life 2RNR-31 Rock 'N' Roll Era - Rick Nelson 1957-1972.
- (M) (2:26) Time-Life R857-12 The Heart Of Rock 'n' Roll 1962-1963.

1963 IT'S UP TO YOU
- (S) (2:44) EMI 46588 Best Of.
- (S) (2:56) EMI 95219 Best Of Volume 2. *(:13 longer than the 45)*
- (S) (2:49) MCA 6163 All My Best. *(all tracks on this cd are rerecordings)*
- (S) (2:51) Time-Life 2RNR-31 Rock 'N' Roll Era - Rick Nelson 1957-1972.
- (S) (2:55) Time-Life R857-08 The Heart Of Rock 'n' Roll 1963. *(:12 longer than the 45)*

1963 STRING ALONG
(actual 45 time is (2:19) not (2:14) as stated on the record label)
- (S) (2:18) MCA 10098 Best Of (1963-1975).
- (S) (2:23) Time-Life 2RNR-31 Rock 'N' Roll Era - Rick Nelson 1957-1972. *(slightly longer than the 45 and LP; includes cold ending)*

1963 FOOLS RUSH IN
- (S) (2:30) MCA 10098 Best Of (1963-1975).
- (S) (2:30) MCA 31363 Sings "For You".
- (S) (2:31) Curb 77372 All-Time Greatest Hits.
- (S) (2:39) MCA 6163 All My Best. *(all tracks on this cd are rerecordings)*
- (S) (2:31) Time-Life 2RNR-31 Rock 'N' Roll Era - Rick Nelson 1957-1972.

1964 FOR YOU
- (S) (2:14) MCA 10098 Best Of (1963-1975).
- (S) (2:15) MCA 31363 Sings "For You".
- (S) (2:15) Curb 77372 All-Time Greatest Hits.
- (S) (2:19) Time-Life 2RNR-31 Rock 'N' Roll Era - Rick Nelson 1957-1972. *(slightly longer than the 45 and LP; includes cold ending)*

1964 THE VERY THOUGHT OF YOU
- (S) (1:54) MCA 10098 Best Of (1963-1975).

1970 SHE BELONGS TO ME
- (S) (3:01) MCA 10098 Best Of (1963-1975).
- (S) (3:01) Time-Life 2RNR-31 Rock 'N' Roll Era - Rick Nelson 1957-1972.

released as by RICK NELSON & THE STONE CANYON BAND:
1972 GARDEN PARTY
- (S) (3:45) MCA 10098 Best Of (1963-1975).
- (S) (3:45) MCA 31364 Garden Party.
- (S) (3:45) Curb 77372 All-Time Greatest Hits.
- (S) (4:02) MCA 6163 All My Best. *(all tracks on this cd are rerecordings)*
- (S) (3:45) Time-Life 2RNR-31 Rock 'N' Roll Era - Rick Nelson 1957-1972.
- (S) (3:45) Time-Life SUD-11 Superhits - 1972.
- (S) (3:45) Time-Life AM1-07 AM Gold - 1972.

SANDY NELSON
1959 TEEN BEAT
- (M) (2:22) Rhino 71547 Let There Be Drums Volume 1: The 50's.
- (M) (2:23) Rhino 71601 Rock Instrumental Classics Volume 1: The Fifties.
- (M) (2:23) Rhino 72035 Rock Instrumental Classics Vols. 1-5 Box Set.
- (E) (2:22) Original Sound 8854 Oldies But Goodies Vol. 4. *(this compact disc uses the "Waring - fds" noise reduction process)*
- (E) (2:22) Original Sound 2221 Oldies But Goodies Volumes 1,4,6,8 and 10 Box Set. *(this box set uses the "Waring - fds" noise reduction process)*
- (E) (2:22) Original Sound 2500 Oldies But Goodies Volumes 1-15 Box Set. *(this box set uses the "Waring - fds" noise reduction process)*
- (E) (2:21) Original Sound CDGO-6 Golden Oldies Volume. 6.
- (E) (3:06) Original Sound 9602 Best Of Oldies But Goodies Vol. 2. *(extended version)*

- (M) (2:23) Time-Life 2RNR-24 Rock 'N' Roll Era - The 50's Keep On Rockin'.
- (M) (2:22) LaserLight 12316 Rebel Rousers.
- (M) (2:22) Collectables 5887 Let There Be Drums/Drums Are My Beat.

1961 LET THERE BE DRUMS
- (M) (2:18) Curb 77402 All-Time Great Instrumental Hits Volume 2.
- (M) (2:21) Rhino 71547 Let There Be Drums Volume 1: The 50's.
- (M) (2:20) Time-Life 2RNR-36 Rock 'N' Roll Era - Axes & Saxes/The Great Instrumentals.
- (M) (2:17) K-Tel 3453 Rockin' Instrumentals.
- (M) (2:17) Capitol Special Markets 57272 Great Instrumental Hits From Rock's Golden Years.
- (M) (2:16) Collectables 5887 Let There Be Drums/Drums Are My Beat.

1962 DRUMS ARE MY BEAT
- (M) (2:12) Collectables 5887 Let There Be Drums/Drums Are My Beat.

1964 TEEN BEAT '65
- (M) (2:30) Collectables 5887 Let There Be Drums/Drums Are My Beat.

WILLIE NELSON
1975 BLUE EYES CRYING IN THE RAIN
- (S) (2:18) Columbia 46033 Columbia Country Classics Volume 5.
- (S) (2:18) Columbia 33482 Red Headed Stranger.
- (S) (2:18) Columbia 37542 Greatest Hits (And Some That Will Be).
- (S) (2:17) Time-Life CCD-04 Contemporary Country - The Mid 70's.
- (S) (2:17) Priority 53762 Three Decades Of Country.
- (S) (2:17) Columbia 64184 Super Hits.
- (S) (2:18) K-Tel 605 Country Music Classics Volume V.
- (S) (2:48) Columbia 36752 Honeysuckle Rose. *(live)*
- (S) (2:45) Epic 67942 Super Hits Of The '70s. *(live)*
- (S) (2:17) Time-Life R990-10 Willie Nelson - Legendary Country Singers.
- (S) (2:18) Columbia/Legacy 65386 To Lefty From Willie/Always On My Mind/Red Headed Stranger.
- (S) (2:17) Columbia 69071 Cryin' Time Super Hits.

released as by WAYLON & WILLIE (WAYLON JENNINGS & WILLIE NELSON):
1976 GOOD HEARTED WOMAN
- (S) (3:00) RCA 58400 Waylon Jennings - Collector's Series. *(Waylon solo effort - not the hit version)*
- (S) (2:58) RCA 3378 and 8506 Waylon Jennings - Greatest Hits. *(this is the hit duet version)*
- (S) (2:53) Columbia 37542 Willie Nelson: Greatest Hits (And Some That Will Be). *(Willie Nelson solo effort - not the hit version)*
- (S) (2:58) Time-Life CCD-18 Contemporary Country - The Early 70's Hot Hits. *(Waylon Jennings solo effort - not the hit version)*
- (S) (3:00) RCA 66299 Waylon Jennings - Only Daddy That'll Walk The Line. *(Waylon Jennings solo effort - not the hit version)*
- (S) (2:59) RCA 66849 Waylon Jennings - Super Hits. *(Waylon Jennings solo effort - not the hit version)*
- (S) (3:00) RCA 66857 Waylon Jennings - Essential. *(Waylon Jennings solo effort - not the hit version)*
- (S) (2:56) Time-Life R990-10 Willie Nelson - Legendary Country Singers. *(this is the hit duet version)*
- (S) (3:00) Time-Life R990-15 Waylon Jennings - Legendary Country Singers. *(Waylon Jennings solo effort - not the hit version)*
- (S) (3:00) Hip-O 40086 The Class Of Country 1975-1979. *(Waylon Jennings solo effort - not the hit version)*

released as by WILLIE NELSON:
1980 ON THE ROAD AGAIN
- (S) (2:31) Epic 40248 Hot Country Rock Volume 1.
- (S) (2:31) Epic 46214 Truckers Jukebox - Top Radio Requests.
- (S) (2:31) Columbia 44281 Greatest Country Hits Of The 80's - 1980.

(S) (2:25) Columbia 36752 Honeysuckle Rose.
(S) (2:31) Columbia 37542 Greatest Hits (And Some That Will Be).
(S) (2:34) Columbia 53060 30 Years Of Hits Volume 15.
(S) (2:29) Time-Life CCD-03 Contemporary Country - The Early 80's.
(S) (2:31) Priority 53725 Country Rock Vol. 1 - Freewheelin'.
(S) (2:31) Columbia 64185 Country Super Hits.
(S) (2:28) Epic 66329 O.S.T. Forrest Gump.
(S) (2:29) K-Tel 3111 Country Music Classics Vol. XIX.
(S) (2:32) Columbia 64184 Super Hits.
(S) (2:31) Risky Business 57473 Country Goes To The Movies.
(S) (2:32) Right Stuff 36476 Harley Davidson Country Road Songs.
(S) (2:29) K-Tel 3369 101 Greatest Country Hits Vol. Ten: Country Roads.
(S) (2:30) Time-Life R990-10 Willie Nelson - Legendary Country Singers.
(S) (2:31) Epic/Legacy 65396 Trucker's Jukebox/Trucker's Jukebox - Top Radio Requests/Trucker's Jukebox Volume 2.

1982 ALWAYS ON MY MIND
(S) (3:31) Columbia 44430 Greatest Country Hits Of The 80's, 1982.
(S) (3:30) Time-Life CCD-15 Contemporary Country - The Early 80's Hot Hits.
(S) (3:31) Columbia 64184 Super Hits.
(S) (3:31) K-Tel 3047 Country Music Classics Volume VI.
(S) (3:29) JCI 3157 1980 - Only Country - 1984.
(S) (3:31) Time-Life R990-10 Willie Nelson - Legendary Country Singers.
(S) (3:31) Columbia 37951 Always On My Mind.
(S) (3:31) Columbia/Legacy 65386 To Lefty From Willie/Always On My Mind/Red Headed Stranger.
(S) (3:31) Time-Life R814-03 Love Songs.

released as by JULIO IGLESIAS & WILLIE NELSON:
1984 TO ALL THE GIRLS I'VE LOVED BEFORE
(S) (3:32) Columbia 44428 Greatest Country Hits Of The 80's, 1984.
(S) (3:31) Columbia 39157 Julio Iglesias - 1100 Bel Air Place.
(S) (3:31) Columbia 39990 Willie Nelson - Half Nelson.

NENA
1984 99 LUFTBALLONS
(S) (3:50) Priority 53704 Rock Of The 80's Volume 3. *(German lyrics)*
(S) (3:50) Risky Business 57468 This Ain't No Disco/New Wave Dance Hits. *(English lyrics)*
(S) (3:50) Risky Business 57833 Read The Hits/Best Of The 80's. *(English lyrics)*
(S) (3:52) Rhino 71974 New Wave Hits Of The 80's Vol. 11. *(German lyrics)*
(S) (4:44) Epic 39294 99 Luftballons. *(English lyrics; neither the 45 or LP version)*
(S) (3:51) Epic 39294 99 Luftballons. *(German lyrics)*
(S) (3:51) Time-Life R988-06 Sounds Of The Eighties: 1984. *(German lyrics)*
(S) (3:51) Rhino 72771 The Big 80's. *(English lyrics)*
(S) (3:49) Epic 67534 Club Epic Volume 5. *(English lyrics)*
(S) (3:49) Rebound 314520442 The Roots Of Rock: 80's New Wave. *(English lyrics)*
(S) (3:49) Epic/Legacy 65254 Fizz Pop Modern Rock Volume 1. *(English lyrics)*

NEON PHILHARMONIC
1969 MORNING GIRL
(S) (2:11) Rhino 70996 One Hit Wonders Of The 60's Volume 2.
(S) (2:12) Sundazed 6084 The Moth Confesses.
(S) (2:11) JCI 3185 1965 - Only Love - 1969.

PETER NERO
1972 THEME FROM "SUMMER OF '42"
(S) (2:51) Columbia 31105 Summer Of '42.
(S) (2:50) Columbia 33136 Greatest Hits.

(S) (2:52) Time-Life R986-07 Instrumental Favorites - Movie Magic.

NERVOUS NORVUS
1956 TRANSFUSION
(M) (2:23) Rhino 75768 Dr. Demento Presents.
(M) (2:24) Rhino 70743 Dr. Demento 20th Anniversary Collection.
(M) (2:24) MCA 31200 Vintage Music Volume 3.
(M) (2:24) MCA 5778 Vintage Music Volumes 3 & 4.
(M) (2:23) Time-Life 2RNR-37 Rock 'N' Roll Era - Weird, Wild & Wacky.
(M) (2:23) K-Tel 3037 Wacky Weirdos.
(M) (2:23) MCA Special Products 22028 Cra-a-zy Hits.
(M) (2:23) Cypress 71334 O.S.T. Coupe De Ville.

1956 APE CALL
(M) (2:35) Time-Life HPD-40 Your Hit Parade - Golden Goofers.

MICHAEL NESMITH & THE FIRST NATIONAL BAND
1970 JOANNE
(S) (3:10) Rhino 70763 The Older Stuff/Best Of The Early Years.
(S) (3:10) Pacific Arts Audio 5066 Complete.
(S) (3:10) Time-Life SOD-36 Sounds Of The Seventies - More AM Nuggets.

1971 SILVER MOON
(S) (3:10) Rhino 70763 The Older Stuff/Best Of The Early Years.
(S) (3:10) Pacific Arts Audio 5066 Complete.

ROBBIE NEVIL
1987 C'EST LA VIE
(S) (3:29) EMI 91419 MTV, BET, VH-1 Power Players. *(45 version)*
(S) (3:47) Columbia 44381 Heart Of Rock. *(edit of LP version)*
(S) (3:24) Rhino 71642 Billboard Top Hits - 1987. *(45 version)*
(S) (4:28) Sandstone 33041 and 5007 Rock The First Volume 1. *(LP version)*
(S) (4:29) Sandstone 33052 and 5020 Cosmopolitan Volume 6. *(LP version)*
(S) (4:29) DCC Compact Classics 084 Night Moves Volume 4. *(LP version)*
(S) (4:28) Manhattan 46390 Robbie Nevil. *(LP version)*
(S) (4:28) Priority 53746 80's Greatest Rock Hits Vol. 12 - Singers/Songwriters. *(LP version)*
(S) (3:23) Time-Life R988-09 Sounds Of The Eighties: 1987. *(45 version)*
(S) (4:28) Madacy Entertainment 1986 Rock On 1986. *(LP version)*
(S) (3:28) Hip-O 40047 The '80s Hit(s) Back 3. *(45 version)*

1987 DOMINOES
(S) (4:45) Manhattan 46390 Robbie Nevil. *(LP version)*

1987 WOT'S IT TO YA?
(S) (3:47) Manhattan 46390 Robbie Nevil.

1988 BACK ON HOLIDAY
(S) (3:58) EMI Manhattan 48359 A Place Like This.
(S) (7:40) EMI 54099 Retro Dance Club Volume Two. *(remix)*

1991 JUST LIKE YOU
(S) (4:05) EMI 91067 Day 1.

AARON NEVILLE
1967 TELL IT LIKE IT IS
(M) (2:40) Rhino 70653 Billboard's Top R&B Hits Of 1967.
(M) (2:40) Rhino 72006 Billboard's Top R&B Hits 1965-1969 Box Set.
(S) (3:04) Original Sound CDGO-11 Golden Oldies Volume. 11. *(rerecording)*
(S) (4:15) Mango 539909 O.S.T. The Big Easy. *(live)*
(M) (2:38) Curb 77303 Greatest Hits.
(E) (2:40) Curb 77491 Tell It Like It Is.
(M) (2:39) Collectables 5067 History Of Rock Volume 7.
(M) (2:39) Original Sound 8908 Best Love Songs Vol 3.

AARON NEVILLE *(Continued)*

(M)	(2:39)	Original Sound 9327 Best Love Songs Vol. 3 & 4.
(M)	(2:39)	Original Sound 1236 Best Love Songs Box Set.
(M)	(2:39)	Original Sound 8859r Oldies But Goodies Vol. 9. *(remastered edition)*
(M)	(2:39)	Original Sound 2223 Oldies But Goodies Volumes 2,7,9,12 and 13 Box Set. *(Volumes 2, 7 and 12 of this box set use the "Waring - fds" noise reduction process)*
(M)	(2:39)	Original Sound 2500 Oldies But Goodies Volumes 1-15 Box Set. *(most volumes in this box set use the "Waring - fds" noise reduction process)*
(M)	(2:37)	Epic 57560 O.S.T. A Bronx Tale.
(M)	(2:38)	Time-Life RHD-10 Rhythm & Blues - 1967.
(M)	(2:39)	Time-Life 2CLR-02 Classic Rock - 1966.
(M)	(2:39)	Time-Life SUD-05 Superhits - 1967.
(M)	(2:40)	Collectables 5132 Tell It Like It Is.
(M)	(2:40)	Collectables 2501 WCBS-FM History Of Rock - The 60's Part 2.
(M)	(2:40)	Collectables 4501 History Of Rock/The 60s Part Two.
(M)	(2:36)	Right Stuff 27306 Slow Jams: The 60's Volume One.
(M)	(2:39)	Time-Life OPCD-4517 Tonight's The Night.
(M)	(2:39)	Thump 7010 Low Rider Oldies Volume 1.
(M)	(2:38)	LaserLight 12318 Chart Busters.
(S)	(2:38)	Ripete 2163-RE Ebb Tide. *(mastered from vinyl)*
(M)	(2:39)	Rhino 71806 The R&B Box: Thirty Years Of Rhythm & Blues.
(S)	(3:06)	Scotti Bros. 75481 Quiet Storm Memories. *(rerecording)*
(M)	(2:40)	Collectables 2554 CBS-FM History Of Rock Volume 2.
(M)	(2:39)	EMI 37350 Crescent City Soul: The Sound Of New Orleans 1947-1974.
(S)	(2:40)	Varese Sarabande 5705 Dick Bartley Presents Collector's Essentials: The 60's. *(mastered from vinyl)*
(M)	(2:38)	MCA Special Products Rockin' Country Blues.
(M)	(2:39)	JCI 3164 Eighteen Soulful Ballads.
(M)	(2:38)	LaserLight 12751 Tell It Like It Is - Best Of.
(S)	(2:40)	Rhino 72626 Very Best Of The Neville Brothers. *(mastered from vinyl)*
(S)	(2:40)	Rhino 72620 Smooth Grooves: The '60s Volume 3 Late '60s. *(mastered from vinyl)*
(M)	(2:35)	K-Tel 3680 Mardi Gras Party Time!
(M)	(2:39)	Time-Life AM1-08 AM Gold - 1967.
(M)	(2:38)	Time-Life R838-02 Solid Gold Soul - 1967.
(M)	(2:39)	Time-Life R834-01 Body Talk - Forever Yours.
(M)	(2:38)	Repeat/Relativity 1609 Tighten Up: #1 Soul Hits Of The 60's Volume 1.
(M)	(2:40)	Time-Life R857-22 The Heart Of Rock 'n' Roll 1967-1969.

released as by LINDA RONSTADT featuring AARON NEVILLE:
1989 DON'T KNOW MUCH

(S)	(3:32)	Foundation/Capitol 96427 Hearts Of Gold: The Pop Collection.
(S)	(3:32)	Sandstone 33049 and 5017 Cosmopolitan Volume 3.
(S)	(3:32)	DCC Compact Classics 088 Night Moves Volume 6.
(S)	(3:32)	Elektra 60872 Linda Ronstadt: Cry Like A Rainstorm - Howl Like The Wind.
(S)	(3:32)	Time-Life R138-18 Body Talk.
(S)	(3:30)	Madacy Entertainment 6803 Power Of Love.
(S)	(3:31)	Time-Life R103-18 Great Love Songs Of The '70s & '80s.
(S)	(3:32)	Time-Life R834-03 Body Talk - Moonlit Nights.
(S)	(3:32)	K-Tel 6257 The Greatest Love Songs - 16 Soft Rock Hits.

1990 ALL MY LIFE

(S)	(3:30)	Elektra 60872 Linda Ronstadt: Cry Like A Rainstorm - Howl Like The Wind.
(S)	(3:26)	Time-Life R834-06 Body Talk - Only You.

released as by AARON NEVILLE:
1991 EVERYBODY PLAYS THE FOOL

(S)	(4:24)	A&M 5354 Warm Your Heart.
(S)	(4:24)	K-Tel 3864 Slow Dancin'.

IVAN NEVILLE
1988 NOT JUST ANOTHER GIRL

(S)	(4:06)	Polydor 837798 O.S.T. My Stepmother Is An Alien.
(S)	(4:05)	Polydor 834896 If My Ancestors Could See Me Now.

NEWBEATS
1964 BREAD AND BUTTER

(S)	(1:57)	Rhino 70625 Billboard's Top Rock & Roll Hits Of 1964.
(S)	(1:57)	Rhino 72007 Billboard's Top Rock & Roll Hits 1962-1966 Box Set.
(S)	(1:55)	Original Sound 8852 Oldies But Goodies Vol. 2. *(this compact disc uses the "Waring - fds" noise reduction process)*
(S)	(1:55)	Original Sound 2223 Oldies But Goodies Volumes 2,7,9,12 and 13 Box Set. *(this box set uses the "Waring - fds" noise reduction process)*
(S)	(1:55)	Original Sound 2500 Oldies But Goodies Volumes 1-15 Box Set. *(this box set uses the "Waring - fds" noise reduction process)*
(S)	(1:55)	Original Sound CDGO-9 Golden Oldies Volume. 9.
(S)	(1:56)	Rhino 70732 Grandson Of Frat Rock.
(S)	(1:55)	Collectables 5069 History Of Rock Volume 9.
(S)	(1:55)	Time-Life 2CLR-03 Classic Rock - 1964.
(S)	(1:56)	Collectables 2510 WCBS-FM History Of Rock - The Rockin' 60's.
(S)	(1:56)	Collectables 4510 History Of Rock/The Rockin' 60s.
(S)	(1:56)	Collectables 2505 History Of Rock - The 60's Part 5.
(S)	(1:56)	Collectables 4505 History Of Rock/The 60s Part Five.
(S)	(1:51)	K-Tel 3035 Goofy Greats. *(rerecording)*
(S)	(1:51)	K-Tel 3409 Funniest Food Songs. *(rerecording)*
(S)	(1:56)	Collectables 5660 A Golden Classics Edition.

1964 EVERYTHING'S ALRIGHT

(S)	(2:10)	Collectables 5660 A Golden Classics Edition.

1965 BREAK AWAY (FROM THAT BOY)

(S)	(2:24)	Collectables 5660 A Golden Classics Edition.

1965 RUN, BABY RUN (BACK INTO MY ARMS)

(S)	(2:56)	Collectables 5070 History Of Rock Volume 10.
(S)	(2:56)	Original Sound 8858 Oldies But Goodies Vol. 8. *(this compact disc uses the "Waring - fds" noise reduction process)*
(S)	(2:56)	Original Sound 2221 Oldies But Goodies Volumes 1,4,6,8 and 10 Box Set. *(this box set uses the "Waring - fds" noise reduction process)*
(S)	(2:56)	Original Sound 2500 Oldies But Goodies Volumes 1-15 Box Set. *(this box set uses the "Waring - fds" noise reduction process)*
(S)	(2:56)	Time-Life 2CLR-23 Classic Rock - 1965: Blowin' Your Mind.
(S)	(2:57)	Original Sound CDGO-7 Golden Oldies Volume. 7.
(S)	(2:54)	Collectables 5660 A Golden Classics Edition.

NEW BIRTH
1973 I CAN UNDERSTAND IT

(S)	(6:20)	Collectables 5100 Golden Classics.
(S)	(4:20)	RCA 7639 Dance! Dance! Dance!
(S)	(6:21)	RCA 66732 Very Best Of New Birth.

1975 DREAM MERCHANT

(S)	(4:36)	Essex 7060 The Buddah Box. *(LP version)*
(S)	(4:24)	K-Tel 3887 Soul Brothers & Sisters Of The 70's. *(LP version)*
(S)	(4:24)	Chronicles 314555138 Funk Ballads. *(LP version)*
(S)	(4:24)	Priority 53108 Slow Grind Volume One. *(LP version)*

NEW CHRISTY MINSTRELS
1963 GREEN, GREEN

(S)	(2:07)	Columbia 9279 Greatest Hits.
(S)	(2:07)	Rhino 70264 Troubadours Of The Folk Era Volume 3. *(truncated fade)*

(S)   (2:07)   Columbia 8855   Ramblin'.
(S)   (2:06)   JCI 3109   Folk Sixties.
(S)   (2:06)   Time-Life HPD-33   Your Hit Parade - The Early 60's.
(S)   (2:06)   Vanguard 26789   Very Best Of.
(S)   (2:07)   Time-Life R132-22   Treasury Of Folk Music Volume One.
(S)   (2:06)   Collectables 5837   Today/Ramblin'.
(S)   (2:06)   Collectors' Choice Music 044   The Definitive.

1963   SATURDAY NIGHT
(S)   (2:19)   Vanguard 26789   Very Best Of.
(S)   (2:19)   Collectors' Choice Music 044   The Definitive.

1964   TODAY
(S)   (2:43)   Columbia 9279   Greatest Hits.
(S)   (2:43)   Vanguard 26789   Very Best Of.
(S)   (2:43)   Time-Life R132-22   Treasury Of Folk Music Volume Two.
(S)   (2:43)   Collectables 5837   Today/Ramblin'.
(S)   (2:43)   Collectors' Choice Music 044   The Definitive.

NEW COLONY SIX
1968   I WILL ALWAYS THINK ABOUT YOU
(S)   (2:22)   Mercury 834216   45's On CD Volume 3.
(S)   (2:22)   Rhino 71188   Colonized! Best Of.

1969   THINGS I'D LIKE TO SAY
(S)   (2:19)   Rhino 71188   Colonized! Best Of. *(noise on fadeout)*
(S)   (2:18)   Eclipse Music Group 64871 and 64872   Rock 'n Roll Relix 1968-1969.
(S)   (2:18)   Eclipse Music Group 64872   Rock 'n Roll Relix 1960-1969.

NEW EDITION
1984   COOL IT NOW
(S)   (6:04)   MCA 10288   Classic Soul. *(12" single version)*
(S)   (5:46)   MCA 31028   New Edition. *(LP version)*
(S)   (5:43)   MCA 10434   Greatest Hits. *(LP version)*
(S)   (5:43)   K-Tel 3500   The 80's - Urban Countdown. *(LP version)*
(S)   (5:45)   Madacy Entertainment 1985   Rock On 1985. *(LP version)*
(S)   (4:09)   Time-Life R988-15   Sounds Of The Eighties: The Mid 80's. *(45 version)*

1985   MR. TELEPHONE MAN
(S)   (3:57)   MCA Special Products 20767   Classic R&B Oldies From The 80's Volume 3.
(S)   (3:59)   MCA 31028   New Edition.
(S)   (3:58)   MCA 10434   Greatest Hits.

1985   LOST IN LOVE
(actual 45 time is (4:02) not (3:50) as stated on the record label)
(S)   (4:12)   MCA 31028   New Edition. *(LP length)*
(S)   (4:10)   MCA 10434   Greatest Hits. *(LP length)*

1986   A LITTLE BIT OF LOVE (IS ALL IT TAKES)
(S)   (4:07)   MCA 5679   All For Love.
(S)   (4:03)   MCA 10434   Greatest Hits.

1986   EARTH ANGEL
(S)   (4:01)   MCA 5912   Under The Blue Moon.

1988   IF IT ISN'T LOVE
(S)   (5:09)   MCA 42207   Heart Break. *(LP version)*
(S)   (5:09)   MCA 10434   Greatest Hits. *(LP version)*

1996   HIT ME OFF
(S)   (4:21)   MCA 11480   Home Again.

1997   I'M STILL IN LOVE WITH YOU
(S)   (4:38)   MCA 11480   Home Again.

NEW ENGLAND
1979   DON'T EVER WANNA LOSE YA
(dj copies of this 45 ran (3:15), (3:28) and (5:22); commercial copies were all (3:28))

NEW KIDS ON THE BLOCK
1988   PLEASE DON'T GO GIRL
(actual 45 time is (4:08) not (3:59) as stated on the record label)
(S)   (4:28)   Columbia 40985   Hangin' Tough. *(LP length)*
(S)   (5:02)   Columbia 46959   No More Games/The Remix Album. *(remix)*

1989   YOU GOT IT (THE RIGHT STUFF)
(dj copies of this 45 ran (3:32) and (4:09))
(S)   (4:09)   Columbia 40985   Hangin' Tough.
(S)   (5:35)   Columbia 46959   No More Games/The Remix Album. *(remix)*
(S)   (4:08)   Rhino 75217   Heartthrob Hits.

1989   I'LL BE LOVING YOU (FOREVER)
(S)   (4:23)   Columbia 40985   Hangin' Tough. *(LP version)*
(S)   (4:23)   Time-Life R988-13   Sounds Of The Eighties: 1989. *(LP version)*
(S)   (4:23)   Time-Life R834-20   Body Talk - Heart And Soul. *(LP version)*

1989   HANGIN' TOUGH
(S)   (3:51)   Rhino 71644   Billboard Top Hits - 1989. *(45 version)*
(S)   (4:16)   Columbia 40985   Hangin' Tough. *(LP version)*
(S)   (4:58)   Columbia 46959   No More Games/The Remix Album. *(remix)*
(S)   (3:51)   Time-Life R988-20   Sounds Of The Eighties: The Late '80s Take Two. *(45 version)*

1989   COVER GIRL
(S)   (4:01)   Columbia 40985   Hangin' Tough.
(S)   (5:46)   Columbia 46959   No More Games/The Remix Album. *(live)*

1989   DIDN'T I (BLOW YOUR MIND)
(S)   (4:24)   Columbia 40475   New Kids On The Block.

1989   THIS ONE'S FOR THE CHILDREN
(S)   (3:55)   Columbia 45280   Merry, Merry Christmas.

1990   STEP BY STEP
(S)   (4:26)   Foundation/RCA 66104   Hot #1 Hits.
(S)   (4:26)   Columbia 45129   Step By Step.
(S)   (6:06)   Columbia 46959   No More Games/The Remix Album. *(remix)*
(S)   (4:25)   Priority 50946   100% Party Hits Of The 90's Volume One.

1990   TONIGHT
(S)   (3:26)   Columbia 45129   Step By Step.

released as by NKOTB:
1992   IF YOU GO AWAY
(S)   (5:28)   Columbia 52969   Face The Music.

JIMMY NEWMAN
1957   A FALLEN STAR
(S)   (2:11)   K-Tel 3108   Country Music Classics Volume XVI.

RANDY NEWMAN
1978   SHORT PEOPLE
(S)   (2:54)   Priority 53706   Singers/Songwriters/70's Greatest Rock Hits Volume 15.
(S)   (2:53)   Warner Brothers 3079   Little Criminals.
(S)   (2:53)   Time-Life SOD-10   Sounds Of The Seventies - 1978.
(S)   (2:53)   Time-Life R103-33   Singers & Songwriters.

TED NEWMAN
1957   PLAYTHING

NEW ORDER
1988   TRUE FAITH
(dj copies of this 45 ran (4:02) and (4:12))
(S)   (5:48)   JCI 2703   Cutting Edge. *(LP version)*
(S)   (5:51)   Warner Brothers 25688   O.S.T. Bright Lights, Big City. *(LP version)*
(S)   (5:51)   Qwest 25621   Substance. *(LP version)*
(S)   (4:27)   Qwest 45794   Best Of. *(rerecording titled "TRUE FAITH 94")*
(S)   (5:51)   Rhino 72501   Modern Rock 1987 - Hang The DJ. *(LP version)*
(S)   (4:05)   JCI 3159   18 Modern Rock Classics From The 80's. *(45 version)*

1993   REGRET
(S)   (4:07)   Qwest 45250   Republic.
(S)   (4:07)   Qwest 45794   Best Of.

NEW SEEKERS
1970 LOOK WHAT THEY'VE DONE TO MY SONG MA
1972 I'D LIKE TO TEACH THE WORLD TO SING (IN PERFECT HARMONY)
- (S) (2:22) Rhino 71196 Super Hits Of The 70's Volume 16.
- (S) (2:21) Time-Life SOD-32 Sounds Of The Seventies - AM Pop Classics.
- (S) (2:21) Time-Life R921-38 Get Together.
- (S) (2:30) K-Tel 3455 Folk Hits Around The Campfire. *(rerecording)*

1973 PINBALL WIZARD/SEE ME, FEEL ME

JUICE NEWTON
1981 ANGEL OF THE MORNING
(actual 45 time is (3:59) not (3:49) as stated on the record label)
- (S) (4:11) Capitol 95956 All Time Country Classics Volume 2. *(LP length)*
- (S) (4:10) Capitol 46489 Greatest Hits (And More). *(LP length)*
- (S) (4:10) Curb 77367 Greatest Country Hits. *(LP length)*
- (S) (4:05) Priority 7999 Country's Greatest Hits: Country Crossroads. *(LP length)*
- (S) (4:09) Priority 53699 80's Greatest Rock Hits Volume 7 - Light & Easy. *(LP length)*
- (S) (3:55) Time-Life R988-18 Sounds Of The Eighties: The Early '80s Take Two. *(45 length)*
- (S) (3:56) Varese Sarabande 5847 On The Radio Volume Two. *(45 length)*
- (S) (4:12) DCC Compact Classics 152 Juice. *(LP length)*
- (S) (3:55) Time-Life R834-16 Body Talk - Sweet Nothings. *(45 length)*
- (S) (3:55) Time-Life R814-02 Love Songs. *(45 length)*
- (S) (4:08) K-Tel 4041 Kim Carnes/Juice Newton Back To Back. *(LP length)*
- (S) (4:12) River North 514161361 The Trouble With Angels. *(rerecording)*

1981 QUEEN OF HEARTS
- (S) (3:26) Capitol 95956 All Time Country Classics Volume 2.
- (S) (3:26) Rhino 70676 Billboard Top Hits - 1981.
- (S) (3:23) Capitol 46489 Greatest Hits (And More).
- (S) (3:23) Curb 77367 Greatest Country Hits.
- (S) (3:21) Time-Life R105-26 Our Songs: Singers & Songwriters Encore.
- (S) (3:22) Priority 53746 80's Greatest Rock Hits Vol. 12 - Singers/Songwriters.
- (S) (3:26) Time-Life R988-08 Sounds Of The Eighties: 1981.
- (S) (3:22) Madacy Entertainment 1981 Rock On 1981.
- (S) (3:28) DCC Compact Classics 152 Juice.
- (S) (3:22) K-Tel 4041 Kim Carnes/Juice Newton Back To Back.
- (S) (3:25) River North 514161361 The Trouble With Angels. *(rerecording)*

1982 THE SWEETEST THING (I'VE EVER KNOWN)
(actual 45 time is (4:05) not (3:58) as stated on the record label)
- (S) (4:04) Time-Life CCD-15 Contemporary Country - The Early 80's Hot Hits. *(45 version)*
- (S) (4:04) K-Tel 3253 Old-Fashioned Love: Country Style. *(45 version)*
- (S) (4:04) K-Tel 3113 Country Music Classics Volume XXI. *(45 version)*
- (S) (4:04) Capitol 46489 Greatest Hits (And More). *(45 version)*
- (S) (4:04) JCI 3147 1980 - Only Love - 1984. *(45 version)*
- (S) (4:04) JCI 3157 1980 - Only Country - 1984. *(45 version)*
- (S) (4:05) Priority 50968 I Love Country Volume Three: Hits Of The 80's. *(45 version)*
- (S) (4:04) K-Tel 3367 101 Greatest Country Hits Vol. Eight: Country Romance. *(45 version)*
- (S) (4:05) K-Tel 4004 Country Favorites Of The 80s. *(45 version)*
- (S) (4:06) DCC Compact Classics 152 Juice. *(45 version)*

- (S) (4:04) Simitar 55082 80's Country 1980-82. *(45 version)*
- (S) (4:04) Time-Life R834-11 Body Talk - After Dark. *(45 version)*
- (S) (4:04) Time-Life R988-22 Sounds Of The Eighties 1980-1983. *(45 version)*
- (S) (4:03) K-Tel 4041 Kim Carnes/Juice Newton Back To Back. *(45 version)*
- (S) (4:12) River North 514161361 The Trouble With Angels. *(rerecording)*

1982 LOVE'S BEEN A LITTLE BIT HARD ON ME
- (S) (3:12) Capitol 46489 Greatest Hits (And More).
- (S) (3:11) Madacy Entertainment 1982 Rock On 1982.
- (S) (3:12) Time-Life R834-18 Body Talk - Romantic Moments.
- (S) (3:07) River North 514161361 The Trouble With Angels. *(rerecording)*

1982 BREAK IT TO ME GENTLY
- (S) (4:00) Capitol 46489 Greatest Hits (And More).
- (S) (4:00) K-Tel 3233 More Great Ladies Of Country.
- (S) (4:00) Simitar 55092 80's Country 1982-94.
- (S) (4:00) Time-Life R834-15 Body Talk - Once In Lifetime.
- (S) (4:00) K-Tel 4041 Kim Carnes/Juice Newton Back To Back.
- (S) (4:02) River North 514161361 The Trouble With Angels. *(rerecording)*

1983 HEART OF THE NIGHT
- (S) (4:06) Capitol 46489 Greatest Hits (And More). *(LP version)*
- (S) (4:06) K-Tel 4041 Kim Carnes/Juice Newton Back To Back. *(LP version)*

1983 TELL HER NO
- (S) (3:32) Capitol 46489 Greatest Hits (And More).

WAYNE NEWTON
1963 DANKE SHOEN
- (S) (2:34) Curb 77355 60's Hits Volume 1.
- (S) (2:34) Curb 77270 Best Of Now. *(rerecording)*
- (S) (2:34) Capitol 91634 Capitol Collector's Series.
- (S) (2:34) Capitol 98670 Memories Are Made Of This.
- (S) (2:33) Curb 77605 Greatest Hits.
- (S) (2:34) Time-Life HPD-32 Your Hit Parade - Into The 60's.
- (S) (2:33) Rhino 72557 Jackpot! The Las Vegas Story.
- (S) (2:33) Capitol 35972 Ultra Lounge Volume Five: Wild, Cool & Swingin'.

1965 RED ROSES FOR A BLUE LADY
- (S) (2:50) Curb 77270 Best Of Now. *(rerecording)*
- (S) (2:21) Capitol 91634 Capitol Collector's Series.
- (S) (2:20) Curb 77605 Greatest Hits.

1972 DADDY DON'T YOU WALK SO FAST
- (S) (3:24) Curb 77317 70's Hits Volume 1.
- (S) (3:17) Curb 77270 Best Of Now. *(rerecording)*
- (S) (3:23) Curb 77605 Greatest Hits.
- (S) (3:22) Rhino 71196 Super Hits Of The 70's Volume 16. *(background rumble noticeable on the introduction)*

1980 YEARS
- (S) (3:53) Curb 77270 Best Of Now. *(rerecording)*

OLIVIA NEWTON-JOHN
1971 IF NOT FOR YOU
- (S) (2:51) MCA 5226 Greatest Hits.
- (S) (2:48) MCA 31017 Let Me Be There.

1974 LET ME BE THERE
- (S) (2:56) MCA 5226 Greatest Hits.
- (S) (2:58) MCA 31017 Let Me Be There.

1974 IF YOU LOVE ME (LET ME KNOW)
- (S) (3:11) Geffen 24470 Back To Basics.
- (S) (3:10) MCA 5226 Greatest Hits.
- (S) (3:12) MCA 31018 If You Love Me, Let Me Know.
- (S) (3:12) Time-Life R808-04 Classic Country 1970-1974.

1974 I HONESTLY LOVE YOU
- (S) (3:36) Geffen 24470 Back To Basics.
- (S) (3:36) MCA 5226 Greatest Hits.
- (S) (3:36) MCA 31018 If You Love Me, Let Me Know.
- (S) (3:36) Time-Life R834-03 Body Talk - Moonlit Nights.

(S) (3:36) Milan 35788 O.S.T. Hotel De Love.
(S) (3:36) Time-Life R814-01 Love Songs.

1975 HAVE YOU NEVER BEEN MELLOW
(S) (3:29) MCA 1676 Have You Never Been Mellow.
(S) (3:29) Geffen 24470 Back To Basics.
(S) (3:29) Razor & Tie 4543 The '70s Preservation Society Presents: Easy '70s.
(S) (3:28) MCA 5226 Greatest Hits.
(S) (3:29) JCI 3146 1975 - Only Love - 1979.

1975 PLEASE MR. PLEASE
(S) (3:21) MCA 1676 Have You Never Been Mellow.
(S) (3:21) Geffen 24470 Back To Basics.
(S) (3:21) MCA 5226 Greatest Hits.

1975 SOMETHING BETTER TO DO
(S) (3:15) MCA 5882 Come On Over/Clearly Love.
(S) (3:14) MCA 31111 Clearly Love.
(S) (3:14) MCA 5226 Greatest Hits.

1976 LET IT SHINE
(S) (2:25) MCA 5882 Come On Over/Clearly Love.
(S) (2:25) MCA 31111 Clearly Love.
(S) (2:24) MCA 5226 Greatest Hits.

1976 COME ON OVER
(S) (3:39) MCA 8025 30 Years Of Hits (1975-1988).
(S) (3:40) MCA 5882 Come On Over/Clearly Love.
(S) (3:39) MCA 31082 Come On Over.
(S) (3:38) MCA 5226 Greatest Hits.

1976 DON'T STOP BELIEVIN'
(S) (3:36) MCA 5878 Don't Stop Believin'/Totally Hot.
(S) (3:37) MCA 5226 Greatest Hits.

1977 SAM
(S) (3:41) MCA 5878 Don't Stop Believin'/Totally Hot.
(S) (3:41) Geffen 24470 Back To Basics.
(S) (3:40) MCA 5226 Greatest Hits.

released as by JOHN TRAVOLTA and OLIVIA NEWTON-JOHN:
1978 YOU'RE THE ONE THAT I WANT
(S) (2:48) Polydor 825095 O.S.T. Grease.
(S) (2:46) Geffen 24470 Olivia Newton-John: Back To Basics.
(S) (2:47) MCA 5347 Olivia Newton-John: Greatest Hits Volume 2.

released as by OLIVIA NEWTON-JOHN:
1978 HOPELESSLY DEVOTED TO YOU
(S) (3:03) Polydor 825095 O.S.T. Grease.
(S) (3:04) Geffen 24470 Back To Basics.
(S) (3:05) MCA 5347 Greatest Hits Volume 2.

released as by JOHN TRAVOLTA and OLIVIA NEWTON-JOHN:
1978 SUMMER NIGHTS
(S) (3:36) Polydor 825095 O.S.T. Grease.
(S) (3:35) Geffen 24470 Olivia Newton-John: Back To Basics.

released as by OLIVIA NEWTON-JOHN:
1979 A LITTLE MORE LOVE
(S) (3:27) Geffen 24470 Back To Basics.
(S) (3:29) MCA 5347 Greatest Hits Volume 2.

1979 DEEPER THAN THE NIGHT
(S) (3:37) Geffen 24470 Back To Basics.

released as by ANDY GIBB and OLIVIA NEWTON-JOHN:
1980 I CAN'T HELP IT
(actual 45 time is (4:06) not (3:54) as stated on the record label)
(S) (4:06) Polydor 511585 Andy Gibb.
(S) (4:06) Polydor 314539922 Andy Gibb - After Dark.
(S) (4:06) Time-Life R834-20 Body Talk - Heart And Soul.

released as by OLIVIA NEWTON-JOHN:
1980 MAGIC
(S) (4:29) Geffen 24470 Back To Basics.
(S) (4:29) MCA 5347 Greatest Hits Volume 2.
(S) (4:28) Time-Life R988-07 Sounds Of The Eighties: 1980.

released as by OLIVIA NEWTON-JOHN/ELECTRIC LIGHT ORCHESTRA:
1980 XANADU
(S) (3:28) MCA 5347 Olivia Newton-John: Greatest Hits Volume 2.

released as by OLIVIA NEWTON-JOHN and CLIFF RICHARD:
1980 SUDDENLY
(S) (3:59) MCA 5347 Olivia Newton-John: Greatest Hits Volume 2.

(S) (3:58) Razor & Tie 2039 Cliff Richard: Collection 1970-1994.

released as by OLIVIA NEWTON-JOHN:
1981 PHYSICAL
(S) (3:42) Rhino 70676 Billboard Top Hits - 1981.
(S) (3:42) MCA 31110 Physical.
(S) (3:41) Geffen 24470 Back To Basics.
(S) (3:43) MCA 5347 Greatest Hits Volume 2.
(S) (3:42) Time-Life R138-38 Celebration.
(S) (3:42) Time-Life R840-09 Sounds Of The Seventies: '70s Dance Party 1979-1981.

1982 MAKE A MOVE ON ME
(S) (3:17) MCA 5347 Greatest Hits Volume 2.
(S) (3:14) MCA 31110 Physical.

1982 HEART ATTACK
(S) (3:07) MCA 5347 Greatest Hits Volume 2.

1984 TWIST OF FATE
(S) (3:39) Geffen 24470 Back To Basics.
(S) (3:41) MCA 11738 O.S.T. Twist Of Fate.

1984 LIVIN' IN DESPERATE TIMES
(S) (4:02) MCA 11738 O.S.T. Twist Of Fate.

1985 SOUL KISS
(S) (4:30) MCA 6151 and 31083 Soul Kiss. *(LP version)*

NEW VAUDEVILLE BAND
1966 WINCHESTER CATHEDRAL
(M) (2:23) Rhino 70325 History Of British Rock Volume 7.
(M) (2:23) Rhino 72022 History Of British Rock Box Set.
(M) (2:23) Time-Life SUD-01 Superhits - 1966.
(M) (2:23) Collectables 0562 Winchester Cathedral.
(M) (2:23) Rhino 71936 Billboard Top Pop Hits, 1966.
(E) (2:23) LaserLight 12313 and 15936 The Wonder Years - Summer Time. *(numerous dropouts; first note partially truncated)*
(M) (2:23) Time-Life AM1-09 AM Gold - 1966.

NEW YORK CITY
1973 I'M DOIN' FINE NOW
(S) (2:51) Rhino 70790 Soul Hits Of The 70's Volume 10.
(E) (2:46) Collectables 5272 I'm Doin' Fine Now.
(S) (2:48) Time-Life SOD-31 Sounds Of The Seventies - AM Top Twenty.
(S) (2:48) Madacy Entertainment 1973 Rock On 1973.
(S) (2:44) K-Tel 3911 Fantastic Volume 2.
(S) (2:45) K-Tel 3914 Superstars Greatest Hits Volume 3.
(S) (2:43) K-Tel 3900 Great R&B Male Groups: Hits Of The 70's.

NEXT
1997 BUTTA LOVE
(S) (4:55) Arista 18973 Rated Next.

PAUL NICHOLAS
1977 HEAVEN ON THE 7TH FLOOR
(S) (2:46) Rhino 72298 Superhits Of The 70's Volume 24.
(S) (2:47) Special Music 5041 Great Britons! Volume Three.
(S) (2:46) Polygram Special Markets 314520456 #1 Radio Hits Of The 70's.

STEVIE NICKS
released as by STEVIE NICKS with TOM PETTY and THE HEARTBREAKERS:
1981 STOP DRAGGIN' MY HEART AROUND
(S) (4:01) Atlantic 82306 Atlantic Rock & Roll Box Set.
(S) (4:01) Atlantic 81908 Classic Rock 1966-1988.
(S) (4:01) Modern 38139 Stevie Nicks - Bella Donna.
(S) (4:03) Modern 91711 Stevie Nicks - Timespace: Best Of.
(S) (4:00) Time-Life R988-25 Sounds Of The Eighties: The Rolling Stone Collection 1980-1981.
(S) (4:11) MCA 11375 Tom Petty: Playback. *(demo)*
(S) (4:00) Time-Life R13610 Gold And Platinum Box Set - The Ultimate Rock Collection.
(S) (4:01) Atlantic 83088 Atlantic Records: 50 Years - The Gold Anniversary Collection.
(S) (4:02) Atlantic 83093 Enchanted (Box Set).

STEVIE NICKS *(Continued)*

released as by STEVIE NICKS with DON HENLEY:
1982 LEATHER AND LACE
- (S) (3:41) Modern 38139 Stevie Nicks - Bella Donna. *(LP version)*
- (S) (3:46) Modern 91711 Stevie Nicks - Timespace: Best Of. *(remixed LP version)*
- (S) (3:54) Atlantic 83093 Stevie Nicks - Enchanted (Box Set). *(LP version but with a :13 longer fade)*

released as by STEVIE NICKS:
1982 EDGE OF SEVENTEEN
(dj copies of this 45 ran (4:10) and (5:57); commercial copies were all (4:10); actual 45 time is (4:30) not (4:10) as stated on both the dj and commercial copies)
- (S) (5:25) Modern 90427 Bella Donna. *(LP version)*
- (S) (5:26) Modern 91711 Timespace: Best Of. *(LP version)*
- (S) (5:25) Time-Life R968-13 Guitar Rock - The Early '80s. *(LP version)*
- (S) (4:30) JCI 3147 1980 - Only Love - 1984. *(45 version)*
- (S) (8:04) Atlantic 83093 Enchanted (Box Set). *(live)*

1982 AFTER THE GLITTER FADES
- (S) (3:26) Modern 90427 Bella Donna.
- (S) (3:28) Atlantic 83093 Enchanted (Box Set).

1983 STAND BACK
- (S) (4:48) Modern 90084 The Wild Heart. *(LP version)*
- (S) (4:55) Modern 91711 Timespace: Best Of. *(LP version)*
- (S) (4:20) Time-Life R988-03 Sounds Of The Eighties: 1983. *(45 version)*
- (S) (4:48) Atlantic 83093 Enchanted (Box Set). *(LP version)*

1983 IF ANYONE FALLS
- (S) (4:06) Modern 90084 The Wild Heart.
- (S) (4:06) Modern 91711 Timespace: Best Of.
- (S) (4:06) Atlantic 83093 Enchanted (Box Set).

released as by STEVIE NICKS with SANDY STEWART:
1984 NIGHTBIRD
- (S) (4:57) Modern 90084 Stevie Nicks - The Wild Heart. *(LP version)*
- (S) (4:58) Atlantic 83093 Enchanted (Box Set). *(LP version)*

released as by STEVIE NICKS:
1986 TALK TO ME
- (S) (4:09) Modern 90479 Rock A Little.
- (S) (4:09) Modern 91711 Timespace: Best Of.
- (S) (4:11) Time-Life R988-04 Sounds Of The Eighties: 1986.
- (S) (4:10) JCI 3171 #1 Radio Hits 1985 - Only Rock 'n Roll - 1989.
- (S) (4:09) Atlantic 83093 Enchanted (Box Set).

released as by TOM PETTY and THE HEARTBREAKERS with STEVIE NICKS:
1986 NEEDLES AND PINS
- (S) (2:25) MCA 8021 Tom Petty: Pack Up The Plantation - Live.

released as by STEVIE NICKS:
1986 I CAN'T WAIT
(dj copies of this 45 ran (4:01) and (4:14); commercial copies were all (4:01))
- (S) (4:35) Modern 90479 Rock A Little. *(LP version)*
- (S) (4:35) Modern 91711 Timespace: Best Of. *(LP version)*
- (S) (5:57) Atlantic 83093 Enchanted (Box Set). *(remixed)*

1989 ROOMS ON FIRE
- (S) (4:34) Modern 91245 The Other Side Of The Mirror.
- (S) (4:37) Modern 91711 Timespace: Best Of.
- (S) (4:32) Atlantic 83093 Enchanted (Box Set).

NIELSEN-PEARSON
1980 IF YOU SHOULD SAIL
- (S) (3:28) Rhino 71894 Radio Daze: Pop Hits Of The 80's Volume Five.
- (S) (3:28) EMI-Capitol Music Special Markets 19460 Lost Hits Of The '80s.

NIGHT
1979 HOT SUMMER NIGHTS
released as by CHRIS THOMPSON & NIGHT:
1979 IF YOU REMEMBER ME

MAXINE NIGHTINGALE
1976 RIGHT BACK WHERE WE STARTED FROM
- (S) (3:14) Priority 7059 Mega-Hits Dance Classics Volume 10.
- (S) (3:14) Rhino 71198 Super Hits Of The 70's Volume 18.
- (S) (3:13) Razor & Tie 22496 Disco Fever.
- (S) (3:14) Time-Life SOD-18 Sounds Of The Seventies - 1976: Take Two.
- (S) (3:14) Time-Life R138-38 Celebration.
- (S) (3:14) Varese Sarabande 5718 Soulful Pop.
- (S) (3:13) Time-Life AM1-23 AM Gold - 1976.
- (S) (3:14) Varese Sarabande 5890 Bubblegum Classics Volume Four - Soulful Pop.
- (S) (3:13) Hip-O 40092 Disco 54: Where We Started From.
- (S) (3:13) Time-Life R840-07 Sounds Of The Seventies: '70s Dance Party 1976-1977.

1979 LEAD ME ON
- (S) (2:46) Rhino 72299 Superhits Of The 70's Volume 25.
- (S) (2:47) Time-Life R834-06 Body Talk - Only You.
- (S) (2:44) K-Tel 3907 Starflight Vol. 2.
- (S) (2:44) Simitar 55512 The Number One's: Lovin' Feelings.

NIGHT RANGER
1984 SISTER CHRISTIAN
(dj copies of this 45 ran (3:55) and (4:04); commercial copies were all (4:04); actual 45 time is (4:14) not (4:04) as stated on the commercial and dj copies)
- (S) (4:56) JCI 4545 Masters Of Metal: Thunder 'N Spice. *(LP version)*
- (S) (4:59) Priority 53735 Monsters Of Rock Vol. 1 - Heaven And Hell. *(LP version)*
- (S) (4:59) Priority 7077 80's Greatest Rock Hits Volume 5 - From The Heart. *(LP version)*
- (S) (5:00) MCA 31160 Midnight Madness. *(LP version)*
- (S) (5:00) MCA 42307 Greatest Hits. *(LP version)*
- (S) (4:56) Time-Life R968-18 Guitar Rock - The Heavy '80s. *(LP version)*
- (S) (4:59) MCA Special Products 20893 Greatest Tour Bands Ever Recorded. *(LP version)*
- (S) (4:15) Rhino 72771 The Big 80's. *(45 version)*
- (S) (4:59) Hip-O 40005 The '80s Hit(s) Back....Again! *(LP version)*
- (S) (5:00) Priority 50937 Best Of 80's Metal Volume Two: Bang Your Head. *(LP version)*
- (S) (4:14) Time-Life R988-15 Sounds Of The Eighties: The Mid 80's. *(45 version)*
- (S) (5:01) Rhino 72597 Billboard Top Album Rock Hits, 1984. *(LP version)*
- (S) (4:49) K-Tel 3883 The 80's: Glam Rock. *(LP version)*
- (S) (4:59) Capitol 56312 O.S.T. Boogie Nights. *(LP version)*
- (S) (4:55) Razor & Tie 89004 Monsters Of Rock. *(LP version)*

1984 WHEN YOU CLOSE YOUR EYES
(actual 45 time is (4:08) not (4:02) as stated on the record label)
- (S) (4:07) Time-Life R105-40 Rock Dreams. *(45 length)*
- (S) (4:14) MCA 31160 Midnight Madness. *(LP length)*
- (S) (4:16) MCA 42307 Greatest Hits. *(LP length)*

1985 SENTIMENTAL STREET
(dj copies of this 45 ran (3:50) and (4:10); commercial copies were all (4:10))
- (S) (4:10) JCI 3119 18 Rock Classics.
- (S) (4:11) MCA 5593 7 Wishes.
- (S) (4:10) MCA 42307 Greatest Hits.
- (S) (4:09) Madacy Entertainment 1985 Rock On 1985.
- (S) (4:09) Simitar 55142 80's Rock Classics - Party Town.

1985 FOUR IN THE MORNING
(dj copies of this 45 ran (3:32) and (3:51); commercial copies were all (3:32))
- (S) (3:52) MCA 5593 7 Wishes. *(LP version)*

(S) (3:51) MCA 42307 Greatest Hits. *(LP version)*

1986 GOODBYE
(dj copies of this 45 ran (3:52) and (4:20);
commercial copies were all (4:20))
(S) (4:17) MCA 5593 7 Wishes.
(S) (4:17) MCA 42307 Greatest Hits.
(S) (4:17) Madacy Entertainment 1986 Rock On 1986.

NIKKI
1990 NOTICE ME
(S) (5:07) Geffen 24223 Nikki.

NILSSON
1969 EVERYBODY'S TALKIN'
(S) (2:30) EMI 48409 O.S.T. Midnight Cowboy. *(alternate take)*
(S) (2:43) RCA 8475 Nipper's Greatest Hits Of The 60's Volume 2.
(S) (2:43) RCA 9670 All Time Greatest Hits.
(S) (2:43) Pair 1214 Best Of. *(truncated fade)*
(S) (2:41) Time-Life 2CLR-12 Classic Rock - 1969: The Beat Goes On.
(S) (2:40) Time-Life SUD-07 Superhits - 1969.
(S) (2:42) Time-Life R103-33 Singers & Songwriters.
(S) (2:42) Epic 66329 O.S.T. Forrest Gump.
(S) (2:49) RCA 66354 Personal Best - Anthology.
(S) (2:40) Time-Life AM1-01 AM Gold - 1969.
(S) (2:42) Time-Life R132-22 Treasury Of Folk Music Volume Two.

1969 I GUESS THE LORD MUST BE IN NEW YORK CITY
(S) (2:42) RCA 9670 All Time Greatest Hits.
(S) (2:42) Pair 1214 Best Of. *(truncated fade)*
(S) (2:42) RCA 61138 and 61155 Songwriter.
(S) (2:42) RCA 66354 Personal Best - Anthology.
(S) (2:42) DCC Compact Classics 155 Harry.

1971 ME AND MY ARROW
(S) (2:10) RCA 9670 All Time Greatest Hits. *(includes a :05 introductory narration)*
(S) (2:04) RCA 2593 The Point. *(all selections on this cd are segued together)*
(S) (2:10) RCA 61138 and 61155 Songwriter. *(includes a :05 introductory narration)*
(S) (2:04) RCA 66354 Personal Best - Anthology.
(S) (2:10) Walt Disney 60870 Dog Songs. *(includes a :05 introductory narration)*
(S) (2:05) DCC Compact Classics 158 The Point. *(all selections on this cd are segued together)*

1972 WITHOUT YOU
(S) (3:13) RCA 9902 Nipper's #1 Hits 1956-1986.
(S) (3:16) RCA 8476 and 9684 Nipper's Greatest Hits Of The 70's.
(S) (3:17) RCA 9670 All Time Greatest Hits.
(S) (3:20) RCA 4515 Nilsson Schmilsson.
(S) (3:20) MFSL 541 Nilsson Schmilsson.
(S) (3:18) Pair 1214 Best Of.
(S) (3:17) Time-Life SUD-11 Superhits - 1972.
(S) (3:19) Time-Life SOD-03 Sounds Of The Seventies - 1972.
(S) (3:19) Time-Life R105-26 Our Songs: Singers & Songwriters Encore.
(S) (3:19) RCA 66354 Personal Best - Anthology.
(S) (3:20) RCA 66599 Nilsson Schmilsson. *(gold disc)*
(S) (3:18) MCA 11389 O.S.T. Casino.
(S) (3:20) RCA 66812 Do You Love Me? (All-Time Best Love Songs).
(S) (3:20) JCI 3168 #1 Radio Hits 1970 - Only Rock 'n Roll - 1974.
(S) (3:16) Eclipse Music Group 64892 Rock 'n Roll Relix 1970-1971.
(S) (3:16) Eclipse Music Group 64897 Rock 'n Roll Relix 1970-1979.
(S) (3:17) Time-Life AM1-07 AM Gold - 1972.
(S) (3:15) Time-Life R834-02 Body Talk - Just For You.
(S) (3:19) Rhino 72738 Billboard Top Soft Rock Hits - 1972.

(S) (3:18) Priority 50974 Premiere The Movie Magazine Presents The Greatest Soundtrack Love Songs.
(S) (3:15) Simitar 55512 The Number One's: Lovin' Feelings.
(S) (3:20) Polygram TV 314555610 The One And Only Love Album.
(S) (3:17) Time-Life R814-01 Love Songs.
(S) (3:14) Collectables 1516 and 2516 The Anniversary Album - The 70's. *(truncated fade)*

1972 JUMP INTO THE FIRE
(dj copies of this 45 ran (3:32) and (6:54);
commercial copies were all (3:32))
(S) (2:54) RCA 9670 All Time Greatest Hits. *(edited)*
(S) (7:01) RCA 4515 Nilsson Schmilsson. *(LP version)*
(S) (7:05) MFSL 541 Nilsson Schmilsson. *(LP version)*
(M) (3:32) Pair 1214 Best Of. *(45 version)*
(S) (2:54) RCA 61138 and 61155 Songwriter. *(edited)*
(S) (3:32) Time-Life SOD-36 Sounds Of The Seventies - More AM Nuggets. *(45 version)*
(S) (3:31) RCA 66354 Personal Best - Anthology. *(45 version)*
(S) (6:52) RCA 66599 Nilsson Schmilsson. *(gold disc; LP version)*
(S) (3:31) JCI 3140 18 Screamers From The 70's. *(45 version)*

1972 COCONUT
(S) (3:49) RCA 9670 All Time Greatest Hits.
(S) (3:51) RCA 4515 Nilsson Schmilsson.
(S) (3:50) MFSL 541 Nilsson Schmilsson.
(S) (3:50) RCA 61138 and 61155 Songwriter.
(S) (3:49) Time-Life SUD-20 Superhits - Early 70's Classics.
(S) (3:49) MCA 10541 and 11188 O.S.T. Reservoir Dogs.
(S) (3:46) RCA 66354 Personal Best - Anthology.
(S) (3:50) RCA 66599 Nilsson Schmilsson. *(gold disc)*
(S) (3:48) Madacy Entertainment 26927 Sun Splashin'.
(S) (3:49) Time-Life AM1-15 AM Gold - Early '70s Classics.
(S) (3:49) Time-Life R840-03 Sounds Of The Seventies - Pop Nuggets: Early '70s.
(S) (3:49) Velvel/Reel Sounds 79713 O.S.T. The Ice Storm.

1972 SPACEMAN
(S) (3:30) RCA 9670 All Time Greatest Hits.
(S) (3:34) RCA 3812 Son Of Schmilsson.
(S) (3:30) RCA 61138 and 61155 Songwriter.
(S) (3:32) RCA 66354 Personal Best - Anthology.
(S) (3:32) Varese Sarabande 5882 They Came From Outer Space.

1974 DAYBREAK
(S) (2:42) RCA 9670 All Time Greatest Hits. *(LP version)*

1910 FRUITGUM COMPANY
1968 SIMON SAYS
(S) (2:14) Pair 1202 Best Of Buddah. *(LP version)*
(S) (2:14) Pair 1199 Best Of Bubblegum Music. *(LP version)*
(S) (2:14) Special Music 4914 Best Of The Bubblegum Years. *(LP version)*
(S) (2:14) Rhino 70495 Fun Rock! *(LP version)*
(S) (2:13) Collectables 5068 History Of Rock Volume 8. *(LP version)*
(S) (2:14) Collectables 0534 Golden Classics. *(LP version)*
(S) (2:14) Essex 7060 The Buddah Box. *(LP version)*
(S) (2:13) Time-Life 2CLR-27 Classic Rock - 1968: Blowin' Your Mind. *(LP version)*
(S) (2:15) Varese Sarabande 5575 Bubblegum Classics Volume Two. *(LP version)*
(S) (2:40) Rhino 71919 Dr. Demento Gooses Mother. *(includes :28 of banter by Dr. Demento at the end of the song; LP version)*
(M) (2:17) Buddah 49516 Complete Buddah Chart Singles Volume One. *(45 version)*
(S) (2:14) BMG Special Products 44643 The Best Of Buddah. *(LP version)*

1968 1,2,3 RED LIGHT
(S) (2:06) Pair 1199 Best Of Bubblegum Music. *(the group is incorrectly identified as the "OHIO EXPRESS" on the cd jacket)*

1910 FRUITGUM COMPANY (Continued)
- (S) (2:06) Special Music 4914 Best Of The Bubblegum Years.
- (S) (2:07) Collectables 0534 Golden Classics.
- (S) (2:08) Essex 7060 The Buddah Box.
- (S) (2:07) K-Tel 3386 Best Of Bubblegum Music.
- (S) (2:07) Buddah 49516 Complete Buddah Chart Singles Volume One.

1968 GOODY GOODY GUMDROPS
- (S) (2:15) Pair 1199 Best Of Bubblegum Music.
- (S) (2:15) Special Music 4914 Best Of The Bubblegum Years.
- (S) (2:15) Collectables 0534 Golden Classics.
- (S) (2:15) Buddah 49517 Complete Buddah Chart Singles Volume Two.

1969 INDIAN GIVER
- (S) (2:40) Pair 1199 Best Of Bubblegum Music.
- (S) (2:40) K-Tel 205 Battle Of The Bands Volume 3.
- (S) (2:40) Special Music 4914 Best Of The Bubblegum Years.
- (S) (2:41) Collectables 0534 Golden Classics.
- (S) (2:39) Time-Life 2CLR-29 Classic Rock - Bubblegum, Garage And Pop Nuggets.
- (S) (2:40) Varese Sarabande 5535 Bubblegum Classics Volume One.
- (S) (2:41) Buddah 49517 Complete Buddah Chart Singles Volume Two.

1969 SPECIAL DELIVERY
- (S) (2:36) Pair 1199 Best Of Bubblegum Music. (LP version)
- (S) (2:36) Special Music 4914 Best Of The Bubblegum Years. (LP version)
- (S) (2:38) Collectables 0534 Golden Classics. (LP version)

98 DEGREES
1997 INVISIBLE MAN
- (S) (4:41) Motown 314530796 98 Degrees.

95 SOUTH
1993 WHOOT, THERE IT IS
- (S) (3:03) Wrap 8117 Quad City Knock.
- (S) (4:27) Quality 5008 Dance Box Set. (all selections on this cd are segued together; remix)
- (S) (3:04) Priority 50961 Booty And The Beat - Bass Jams Vol.1.

NIRVANA
1992 SMELLS LIKE TEEN SPIRIT
- (S) (5:00) DGC 24425 Nevermind.
- (S) (5:00) MFSL 666 Nevermind. (gold disc)
1992 COME AS YOU ARE
- (S) (3:38) DGC 24425 Nevermind.
- (S) (3:39) Pointblank 42088 Fender 50th Anniversary Guitar Legends.
- (S) (3:39) MFSL 666 Nevermind. (gold disc)

NITE-LITERS
1971 K-JEE
- (S) (3:59) Collectables 5214 K-Jee/Golden Classics.
- (S) (4:01) Rhino 71603 Rock Instrumental Classics Volume 3: The Seventies.
- (S) (4:01) Rhino 72035 Rock Instrumental Classics Vols. 1-5 Box Set.
- (S) (4:00) RCA 66732 Very Best Of New Birth.

NITTY GRITTY DIRT BAND (also DIRT BAND)
1971 MR. BOJANGLES
- (S) (3:34) Rhino 70924 Super Hits Of The 70's Volume 4. (45 version)
- (S) (3:34) Rhino 72009 Super Hits Of The 70's Volumes 1-4 Box Set. (45 version)
- (S) (3:33) Priority 8665 Southern Comfort/70's Greatest Rock Hits Volume 4. (45 version)
- (S) (3:24) EMI 90603 Rock Me Gently. (alternate take)
- (S) (3:34) Curb 77356 70's Hits Volume 2. (45 version)

- (S) (5:13) EMI 46591 Best Of. (LP version with prologue)
- (S) (3:33) Curb 77357 Greatest Hits. (45 version)
- (S) (5:02) Warner Brothers 25382 Twenty Years Of Dirt. (LP version with prologue)
- (S) (3:34) Time-Life R103-33 Singers & Songwriters. (45 version)
- (S) (3:36) Liberty 90430 Uncle Charlie And His Dog Teddy. (prologue is given a separate track number on this cd; LP version)
- (S) (3:32) JCI 3130 1970 - Only Rock 'N Roll - 1974. (45 version)
- (S) (3:34) Rhino 71904 Hillbilly Fever Vol. 5. - Legends Of Country Rock. (45 version)
- (S) (3:34) Rhino 71843 Troubadours Of The Folk Era Vol. 4. (45 version)
- (S) (3:33) K-Tel 3454 70s Folk Rock Hits. (45 version)
- (S) (3:23) Madacy Entertainment 1971 Rock On 1971. (alternate take)
- (S) (3:34) Rhino 72444 Heroes Of Country Music Vol. Five. (45 version)
- (S) (3:34) Time-Life AM1-06 AM Gold - 1971. (45 version)
- (S) (3:33) K-Tel 3885 Story Songs. (45 version)

released as by THE DIRT BAND:
1980 AN AMERICAN DREAM
- (S) (3:28) EMI 46591 Best Of. (45 length)
- (S) (3:48) Warner Brothers 25382 Best Of/Twenty Years Of Dirt. (LP length)
- (S) (3:28) Curb 77357 Greatest Hits. (45 length)
- (S) (3:28) Priority 7041 Country's Greatest Hits: American Pride. (45 length)
- (S) (3:32) Rhino 71890 Radio Daze: Pop Hits Of The 80's Volume One. (45 length)
- (S) (3:28) Madacy Entertainment 1979 Rock On 1979. (45 length)
- (S) (3:31) Rhino 72518 Mellow Rock Hits Of The 70's - Summer Breeze. (45 length)
- (S) (3:32) Time-Life R988-22 Sounds Of The Eighties 1980-1983. (45 length)

1980 MAKE A LITTLE MAGIC
(actual 45 time is (3:33) not (3:40) as stated on the record label; LP time is (3:55))
- (S) (3:55) EMI 46591 Best Of.
- (S) (3:45) Warner Brothers 25382 Best Of/Twenty Years Of Dirt.
- (S) (3:53) Curb 77357 Greatest Hits.
- (S) (3:55) K-Tel 3697 Best Of Country Rock.

JACK NITZSCHE
1963 THE LONELY SURFER
- (S) (2:33) Rhino 70089 Surfin' Hits.
- (S) (2:33) JCI 3106 Surfin' Sixties.
- (S) (2:34) Rhino 71605 Rock Instrumental Classics Volume 5: Surf.
- (S) (2:34) Rhino 72035 Rock Instrumental Classics Vols. 1-5 Box Set.
- (S) (2:32) Time-Life 2RNR-36 Rock 'N' Roll Era - Axes & Saxes/The Great Instrumentals.
- (S) (2:33) Rhino 72418 Cowabunga! The Surf Box.

NKOTB (see NEW KIDS ON THE BLOCK)

NICK NOBLE
1955 THE BIBLE TELLS ME SO
1956 TO YOU MY LOVE
1957 A FALLEN STAR

CLIFF NOBLES & CO.
1968 THE HORSE
(the actual 45 and LP time is (2:44))
- (S) (2:39) Rhino 70629 Billboard's Top Rock & Roll Hits Of 1968.
- (S) (2:39) Rhino 72005 Billboard's Top Rock & Roll Hits 1966-1972 Box Set.
- (S) (2:37) Time-Life RHD-04 Rhythm & Blues - 1968.
- (S) (2:37) Time-Life 2CLR-19 Classic Rock - 1968: Shakin' All Over.

(S)   (2:37)   Time-Life R838-03   Solid Gold Soul - 1968.
(M)   (2:52)   Rhino 72815   Beg, Scream & Shout! The Big Ol' Box Of '60s Soul.

NO DOUBT
1996   JUST A GIRL
(S)   (3:27)   Trauma/Interscope 92580   Tragic Kingdom.

JACKY NOGUEZ
1959   CIAO, CIAO BAMBINA

KENNY NOLAN
1977   I LIKE DREAMIN'
(S)   (3:27)   Rhino 71199   Super Hits Of The 70's Volume 19.
(S)   (3:27)   Razor & Tie 4543   The '70s Preservation Society Presents: Easy '70s.
(S)   (3:27)   Time-Life AM1-24   AM Gold - 1977.
(S)   (3:27)   Time-Life R834-05   Body Talk - Sealed With A Kiss.
(S)   (3:28)   K-Tel 3908   High Energy Volume 1.
1977   LOVE'S GROWN DEEP
(S)   (3:50)   K-Tel 3906   Starflight Vol. 1.

NO MERCY
1996   WHERE DO YOU GO
(S)   (4:31)   Arista 18941   No Mercy.
(S)   (4:23)   Arista 18943   Ultimate Dance Party 1997. *(all selections on this cd are segued together)*
(S)   (4:42)   Cold Front 6254   Club Mix '98. *(all selections on this cd are segued together)*
1997   PLEASE DON'T GO
(S)   (3:59)   Arista 18941   No Mercy.
(S)   (3:58)   Beast 54112   Boom!

NONCHALANT
1996   5 O'CLOCK
(S)   (4:44)   MCA 11265   Until The Day.
(S)   (4:27)   Boxtunes 314524387   Big Phat Ones Of Hip-Hop Volume 2. *(all songs on this cd are segued together)*

FREDDIE NORTH
1971   SHE'S ALL I GOT
(S)   (2:36)   Ripete 2220   Soul Patrol Vol. 2.

NOTORIOUS B.I.G.
1994   JUICY
(S)   (5:02)   Bad Boy/Arista 73000   Ready To Die.
(S)   (4:13)   Boxtunes 162444068   Big Phat Ones Of Hip-Hop Volume 1.
1994   UNBELIEVABLE
(S)   (3:43)   Bad Boy/Arista 73000   Ready To Die.
1995   BIG POPPA
(S)   (4:12)   Bad Boy/Arista 73000   Ready To Die.
(S)   (4:05)   Tommy Boy 1139   MTV Party To Go Volume 8. *(all selections on this cd are segued together)*
1995   WARNING
(S)   (3:40)   Bad Boy/Arista 73000   Ready To Die.
1995   ONE MORE CHANCE
(S)   (4:42)   Bad Boy/Arista 73000   Ready To Die.
(S)   (5:12)   Tommy Boy 1164   MTV Party To Go Volume 9. *(all selections on this cd are segued together)*
(S)   (4:04)   Arista 18977   Ultimate Hip Hop Party 1998. *(all selections on this cd are segued together; remix)*
1995   THE WHAT
(S)   (3:57)   Bad Boy/Arista 73000   Ready To Die.
released as by TOTAL featuring THE NOTORIOUS B.I.G.:
1995   CAN'T YOU SEE
(S)   (4:41)   Bad Boy 73006   Total.
(S)   (4:50)   Tommy Boy 1114   O.S.T. New Jersey Drive.
released as by JUNIOR M.A.F.I.A. featuring THE NOTORIOUS B.I.G.:
1996   GET MONEY
(S)   (4:33)   Undeas/Big Beat 92614   Junior M.A.F.I.A - Conspiracy.

(S)   (3:46)   Arista 18977   Ultimate Hip Hop Party 1998. *(all selections on this cd are segued together; remix)*
(S)   (4:05)   Def Jam 314534746   Yo! MTV Raps Compilation. *(clean radio edit)*
(S)   (3:44)   Boxtunes 314524387   Big Phat Ones Of Hip-Hop Volume 2. *(all songs on this cd are segued together)*
released as by 112 featuring THE NOTORIOUS B.I.G.:
1996   ONLY YOU
(S)   (4:20)   Bad Boy 73009   112.
(S)   (4:49)   Bad Boy 73009   112. *(remix)*
(S)   (4:31)   Arista 18977   Ultimate Hip Hop Party 1998. *(all selections on this cd are segued together; remix)*
released as by THE NOTORIOUS B.I.G.:
1997   HYPNOTIZE
(S)   (3:49)   Bad Boy 73011 and 73019   Life After Death. *(tracks into the next selection)*
(S)   (4:02)   Polygram TV 314536204   The Source Presents Hip Hop Hits Volume 1.
released as by THE NOTORIOUS B.I.G. featuring PUFF DADDY & MASE:
1997   MO MONEY MO PROBLEMS
(S)   (4:17)   Bad Boy 73011 and 73019   Life After Death.
(S)   (3:49)   Arista 18988   Ultimate Dance Party 1998. *(all selections on this cd are segued together)*
released as by THE NOTORIOUS B.I.G.:
1998   GOING BACK TO CALI
(S)   (5:07)   Bad Boy 73011 and 73019   Life After Death.
released as by PUFF DADDY & THE FAMILY featuring THE NOTORIOUS B.I.G. & MASE:
1998   BEEN AROUND THE WORLD
(S)   (5:25)   Bad Boy 73012 and 73014   Puff Daddy - No Way Out.

ALDO NOVA
1982   FANTASY
(S)   (5:02)   Priority 7961   Three Decades Of Rock. *(LP version)*
(S)   (3:58)   Risky Business 66392   Get Into The Greed: Greatest Hits Of The 80's. *(neither the 45 or LP version)*
(S)   (5:04)   Portrait 37498   Aldo Nova. *(LP version)*
(S)   (5:02)   Epic/Legacy 48522   A Portrait Of. *(LP version)*
(S)   (5:03)   Hip-O 40040   Power Chords Volume 3. *(LP version)*
(S)   (5:02)   Time-Life R988-22   Sounds Of The Eighties 1980-1983. *(LP version)*

N2DEEP
1992   BACK TO THE HOTEL
(S)   (3:52)   Tommy Boy 1075   MTV Party To Go Volume 4. *(remix; all tracks on this cd are segued together)*
(S)   (5:04)   Profile 1427   Back To The Hotel.

N II U
1995   I MISS YOU
(S)   (3:59)   Arista 18751   N II U.

NU FLAVOR
1998   HEAVEN
(S)   (4:54)   Reprise 46408   Nu Flavor.

TED NUGENT
1977   CAT SCRATCH FEVER
(S)   (3:03)   Priority 7942   Hard Rockin' 70's. *(45 length)*
(S)   (3:38)   Epic 34700   Cat Scratch Fever. *(LP length)*
(S)   (3:38)   Epic 37667   Great Gonzos/Best Of. *(LP length)*
(S)   (3:38)   Epic/Legacy 47039   Out Of Control. *(LP length)*
(S)   (3:36)   Razor & Tie 22502   Those Rocking 70's. *(LP length)*
(S)   (3:02)   Time-Life R968-03   Guitar Rock 1976-1977. *(45 length)*
(S)   (3:04)   Time-Life SOD-23   Sounds Of The Seventies - Guitar Power. *(45 length)*
(S)   (3:04)   Time-Life R105-24   Guitar Rock Monsters. *(45 length)*
(S)   (3:04)   JCI 4520   Masters Of Metal: Wrecking Havoc 1975-1985 Volume 1. *(45 length)*

TED NUGENT *(Continued)*

- (S) (3:38) K-Tel 3221   Axe Gods. *(LP length)*
- (S) (3:38) Right Stuff 31324 and 31327   Harley-Davidson Road Songs. *(LP length)*
- (S) (3:38) Epic/Legacy 65020   Ultimate Rock 'n' Roll Collection. *(LP length)*
- (S) (3:36) Warner Brothers 46477   Howard Stern Private Parts: The Album. *(LP length)*
- (S) (3:37) Hip-O 40070   Rock For The Ages. *(LP length)*
- (S) (3:38) Epic/Legacy 65387   Ted Nugent/Cat Scratch Fever/Free-For All. *(LP length)*
- (S) (3:37) Epic/Legacy 65400   Super Hits. *(LP length)*
- (S) (3:37) K-Tel 3986   70's Heavy Hitters: Arena Rockers 1975-79. *(LP length)*

GARY NUMAN
1980 CARS

- (S) (3:48) Priority 53705   Rock Of The 80's Volume 2. *(:09 shorter than the 45 or LP)*
- (S) (3:56) Rhino 71696   New Wave Hits Of The 80's Vol. 3.
- (S) (3:52) K-Tel 3262   The 80's Video Stars.
- (S) (3:56) Time-Life R988-07   Sounds Of The Eighties: 1980.
- (S) (3:56) Rhino 72771   The Big 80's.
- (S) (3:56) Rhino 72490   New Wave Hits, Vol. 1.
- (S) (3:56) JCI 3159   18 Modern Rock Classics From The 80's.
- (S) (3:55) JCI 3170   #1 Radio Hits 1980 - Only Rock 'n Roll - 1984.
- (S) (3:56) Flashback 72713   Essential New Wave Hits.
- (S) (3:56) Flashback 72092   New Wave Hits Box Set.
- (S) (3:56) Rhino 72894   Hard Rock Cafe: New Wave.

NU SHOOZ
1986 I CAN'T WAIT

- (S) (6:15) Atlantic 81746   Dance Traxx Volume 2. *(12" single version)*
- (S) (5:24) Atlantic 81910   Hit Singles 1980-1988. *(LP version)*

- (S) (3:40) Priority 53732   80's Greatest Rock Hits Volume 8 - Dance Party. *(45 version)*
- (S) (5:24) K-Tel 3343   The 80's Hot Dance Trax. *(LP version)*
- (S) (3:38) Rhino 70276   The Disco Years, Vol. 5. *(45 version)*
- (S) (5:24) Atlantic 81647   Poolside. *(LP version)*
- (S) (3:39) Rhino 72141   Billboard Hot R&B Hits 1986. *(45 version)*
- (S) (5:24) Madacy Entertainment 1986   Rock On 1986. *(LP version)*
- (S) (3:39) JCI 3150   1985 - Only Dance - 1989. *(45 version)*
- (S) (3:39) Time-Life R988-17   Sounds Of The Eighties: The Mid '80s Take Two. *(45 version)*
- (S) (3:39) Rhino 72838   Disco Queens: The 80's. *(45 version)*

1986 POINT OF NO RETURN

- (S) (6:31) Atlantic 81746   Dance Traxx Volume 2. *(neither the 45, LP or 12" single version)*
- (S) (4:23) Atlantic 81647   Poolside. *(LP version)*
- (S) (3:47) Rhino 72122   Disco Years, Vol. 6. *(45 version)*

NU TORNADOS
1958 PHILADELPHIA, U.S.A.

NUTTY SQUIRRELS
1959 UH! OH! (PART 2)

- (E) (2:22) Sony Music Special Products 22210   Fun Rock. *(the cd jacket says that this is Part 1 but this is really Part 2)*

NYLONS
1987 KISS HIM GOODBYE

- (S) (3:30) Open Air 10308   Best Of.
- (S) (3:33) Open Air 0306   Happy Together.
- (S) (3:30) Windham Hill 11222   Perfect Fit.

OAK RIDGE BOYS
1981 ELVIRA
- (S) (2:37) MCA 8025 30 Years Of Hits (1975-1988). *(45 version)*
- (S) (3:39) MCA 5209 Fancy Free. *(LP version)*
- (S) (2:37) MCA 10581 Collection. *(45 version)*
- (S) (2:37) Time-Life CCD-09 Contemporary Country - The Early 80's Pure Gold. *(45 version)*
- (S) (2:38) K-Tel 3113 Country Music Classics Volume XXI. *(45 version)*
- (S) (3:39) MCA Special Products 20845 Truckers Jukebox #3. *(LP version)*
- (S) (2:37) MCA Special Products 20846 Greatest Country Classics Volume One. *(45 version)*
- (S) (3:40) JCI 3157 1980 - Only Country - 1984. *(LP version)*
- (S) (3:39) MCA Special Products 20878 Country Stars Of Branson, Missouri. *(LP version)*
- (S) (2:37) Time-Life R990-20 Oak Ridge Boys - Legendary Country Singers. *(45 version)*
- (S) (3:39) Hip-O 40042 The Class Of Country 1980-1984. *(LP version)*
- (S) (2:38) K-Tel 4004 Country Favorites Of The 80s. *(45 version)*
- (S) (3:39) Simitar 55082 80's Country 1980-82. *(LP version)*

1982 BOBBIE SUE
- (S) (2:50) Time-Life CCD-15 Contemporary Country - The Early 80's Hot Hits.
- (S) (2:51) MCA 5922 Bobbie Sue/Step On Out.
- (S) (2:50) MCA 5294 Bobbie Sue.
- (S) (2:50) MCA 42294 Greatest Hits Volume Three.
- (S) (2:50) MCA Special Products 20969 Country Classics Volume 9.
- (S) (2:50) Time-Life R990-20 Oak Ridge Boys - Legendary Country Singers.
- (S) (2:50) MCA Special Products 21036 Legends Of Country Music.

OASIS
1996 WONDERWALL
- (S) (4:18) Epic 67351 (What's The Story) Morning Glory?.

JOHN O'BANION
1981 LOVE YOU LIKE I NEVER LOVED BEFORE
- (S) (3:21) Rhino 71894 Radio Daze: Pop Hits Of The 80's Volume Five.

RIC OCASEK
1986 EMOTION IN MOTION
- (S) (4:40) Geffen 24098 This Side Of Paradise. *(LP version)*
- (S) (4:40) Geffen 24805 Geffen Vintage 80's Volume 1. *(LP version)*

OCEAN
1971 PUT YOUR HAND IN THE HAND
- (S) (2:55) Rhino 70924 Super Hits Of The 70's Volume 4.
- (S) (2:55) Rhino 72009 Super Hits Of The 70's Volumes 1-4 Box Set.
- (S) (2:20) Pair 1202 Best Of Buddah. *(edited)*
- (S) (2:55) Rhino 71208 70's Smash Hits Volume 4.
- (S) (2:52) Essex 7060 The Buddah Box.
- (S) (2:51) Time-Life SUD-10 Superhits - 1971.
- (S) (2:51) Time-Life AM1-06 AM Gold - 1971.
- (S) (2:55) Rhino 72737 Billboard Top Soft Rock Hits - 1971.
- (S) (2:55) Flashback 72684 '70s Radio Hits Volume 4.

- (S) (2:55) Flashback 72090 '70s Radio Hits Box Set.
- (S) (2:55) Rhino 72812 VH1 8-Track Flashback: The One Hit Wonders.
- (S) (2:55) Varese Sarabande 5906 God, Love And Rock & Roll.

BILLY OCEAN
1976 LOVE REALLY HURTS WITHOUT YOU
- (S) (2:59) Rhino 72297 Superhits Of The 70's Volume 23.

1984 CARIBBEAN QUEEN (NO MORE LOVE ON THE RUN) (actual 45 time is (3:39) not (3:32) as stated on the record label)
- (S) (7:55) Arista 8416 Perfect 10 III. *(LP version)*
- (S) (3:41) Rhino 70679 Billboard Top Hits - 1984. *(45 version)*
- (S) (4:05) Rebound 314520313 Caribbean Nights I. *(45 version but with a :26 longer fade and additional background vocals at the very end)*
- (S) (7:55) Jive 8213 and 1222 Suddenly. *(LP version)*
- (S) (4:06) Jive 1271 Greatest Hits. *(45 version but with a :27 longer fade and additional background vocals at the very end)*
- (S) (3:40) K-Tel 3500 The 80's - Urban Countdown. *(45 version)*
- (S) (3:40) Time-Life R988-06 Sounds Of The Eighties: 1984. *(45 version)*
- (S) (3:40) JCI 3149 1980 - Only Dance - 1984. *(45 version)*
- (S) (4:04) MCA 11329 Soul Train 25th Anniversary Box Set. *(45 version but with a :25 longer fade and additional background vocals at the very end)*
- (S) (4:05) K-Tel 3575 Hot, Hot Vacation Jams - Week One. *(45 version but with a :26 longer fade and additional background vocals at the very end)*
- (S) (3:40) K-Tel 3866 The 80's: Number One Pop Hits. *(45 version)*
- (S) (4:05) Rebound 314520313 Reggae Dance Party I. *(45 version but with a :26 longer fade and additional background vocals at the very end)*

1985 LOVERBOY (actual 45 time is (4:12) not (3:58) as stated on the record label)
- (S) (5:15) Arista 8308 Arista's Perfect 10 Rides Again. *(LP version)*
- (S) (4:09) Rhino 71640 Billboard Top Hits - 1985. *(45 version)*
- (S) (5:15) Jive 8213 and 1222 Suddenly. *(LP version)*
- (S) (4:09) Jive 1271 Greatest Hits. *(45 version)*
- (S) (4:09) Priority 53700 80's Greatest Rock Hits Volume 13 - Soft Sounds. *(45 version)*
- (S) (4:09) JCI 3171 #1 Radio Hits 1985 - Only Rock 'n Roll - 1989. *(45 version)*
- (S) (4:08) Time-Life R988-17 Sounds Of The Eighties: The Mid '80s Take Two. *(45 version)*

1985 SUDDENLY
- (S) (3:49) Original Sound 8909 Best Love Songs Vol. 4.
- (S) (3:49) Original Sound 9322 Best Love Songs Vol. 3 & 4.
- (S) (3:49) Original Sound 1236 Best Love Songs Box Set.
- (S) (3:50) Scotti Brothers 75419 Fabio After Dark.
- (S) (3:54) Jive 8213 and 1222 Suddenly.
- (S) (3:51) Jive 1271 Greatest Hits.
- (S) (3:49) JCI 3177 1985 - Only Soul - 1989.
- (S) (3:51) Hip-O 40031 The Glory Of Love - '80s Sweet & Soulful Love Songs.
- (S) (3:50) K-Tel 3798 The 80's Mega Hits.
- (S) (3:50) Time-Life R834-02 Body Talk - Just For You.
- (S) (3:49) Simitar 55562 The Number One's: Smooth Love.

BILLY OCEAN (Continued)

1985 MYSTERY LADY
(actual 45 time is (3:56) not (3:46) as stated on the record label)
- (S) (5:00) Jive 8213 and 1222 Suddenly. *(LP version)*
- (S) (3:55) Jive 1271 Greatest Hits. *(45 version)*

1986 WHEN THE GOING GETS TOUGH, THE TOUGH GET GOING
(actual 45 time is (4:05) not (3:53) as stated on the record label)
- (S) (5:40) Jive 8406 O.S.T. Jewel Of The Nile. *(LP version)*
- (S) (4:07) Rhino 71641 Billboard Top Hits - 1986. *(45 version)*
- (S) (4:07) Rebound 314520314 Caribbean Nights II. *(45 version)*
- (S) (5:42) Jive 8409 and 1223 Love Zone. *(LP version)*
- (S) (4:07) Jive 1271 Greatest Hits. *(45 version)*
- (S) (4:07) Time-Life R988-31 Sounds Of The Eighties: Cinemax Movie Hits Of The '80s. *(45 version)*
- (S) (4:07) Priority 50974 Premiere The Movie Magazine Presents The Greatest Soundtrack Hits. *(45 version)*
- (S) (4:04) Cold Front 6255 Greatest Sports Rock And Jams Volume 2. *(all selections on this cd are segued together)*
- (S) (4:07) Rebound 314520314 Reggae Dance Party II. *(45 version)*

1986 THERE'LL BE SAD SONGS (TO MAKE YOU CRY)
(actual 45 time is (4:13) not (4:02) as stated on the record label)
- (S) (4:50) Priority 53699 80's Greatest Rock Hits Volume 7 - Light & Easy. *(LP version)*
- (S) (4:50) K-Tel 3263 The 80's Love Jams. *(LP version)*
- (S) (4:51) Jive 8409 and 1223 Love Zone. *(LP version)*
- (S) (4:50) Jive 1271 Greatest Hits. *(LP version)*
- (S) (4:50) Time-Life R988-12 Sounds Of The 80's: 1985-1986. *(LP version)*
- (S) (4:13) Rhino 72141 Billboard Hot R&B Hits 1986. *(45 version)*
- (S) (4:50) Time-Life R834-05 Body Talk - Sealed With A Kiss. *(LP version)*

1986 LOVE ZONE
(actual 45 time is (4:11) not (3:58) as stated on the record label)
- (S) (5:34) Jive 8409 and 1223 Love Zone. *(LP version)*
- (S) (4:12) Jive 1271 Greatest Hits. *(45 version)*
- (S) (5:34) K-Tel 6257 The Greatest Love Songs - 16 Soft Rock Hits. *(LP version)*
- (S) (4:12) Time-Life R834-11 Body Talk - After Dark. *(45 version)*

1986 LOVE IS FOREVER
(actual 45 time is (4:16) not (3:58) as stated on the record label)
- (S) (4:13) Jive 8409 and 1223 Love Zone.
- (S) (4:12) Time-Life R834-07 Body Talk - Hearts In Motion.

1988 GET OUTTA MY DREAMS, GET INTO MY CAR
- (S) (4:43) MCA 6241 O.S.T. License To Drive. *(45 version)*
- (S) (4:44) Rhino 71643 Billboard Top Hits - 1988. *(45 version)*
- (S) (4:43) Jive 1271 Greatest Hits. *(45 version)*
- (S) (5:34) Jive 8495 and 1224 Tear Down These Walls. *(LP version)*
- (S) (4:44) Priority 53731 80's Greatest Rock Hits Volume 10 - Dance All Night. *(45 version)*
- (S) (5:32) EMI 52498 O.S.T. Striptease. *(LP version)*
- (S) (4:43) Time-Life R988-21 Sounds Of The Eighties: 1986-1989. *(45 version)*

1988 THE COLOUR OF LOVE
- (S) (4:22) Jive 1271 Greatest Hits.
- (S) (4:24) Jive 8495 and 1224 Tear Down These Walls.
- (S) (4:23) Scotti Bros. 75481 Quiet Storm Memories.
- (S) (4:21) Time-Life R834-18 Body Talk - Romantic Moments.

1989 LICENCE TO CHILL
- (S) (4:52) Jive 1271 Greatest Hits.

SINEAD O'CONNOR
1990 NOTHING COMPARES 2 U
- (S) (5:07) Foundation/Capitol 96427 Hearts Of Gold: The Pop Collection.
- (S) (5:08) Ensign/Chrysalis 21759 I Do Not Want What I Haven't Got.
- (S) (5:08) EMI-Capitol 23685 So Far...The Best Of.

ALAN O'DAY
1977 UNDERCOVER ANGEL
- (S) (3:30) Rhino 70672 Billboard Top Hits - 1977. *(45 length)*
- (S) (3:25) Rhino 71199 Super Hits Of The 70's Volume 19. *(45 length)*
- (S) (3:24) Time-Life SOD-34 Sounds Of The Seventies - The Late 70's. *(45 length)*
- (S) (3:38) Scotti Bros. 75465 Angel Hits. *(rerecording)*
- (S) (3:29) Time-Life AM1-24 AM Gold - 1977. *(45 length)*
- (S) (3:25) Time-Life R840-01 Sounds Of The Seventies - Pop Nuggets: Late '70s. *(45 length)*

KENNY O'DELL
1967 BEAUTIFUL PEOPLE
- (S) (2:21) Varese Sarabande 5803 Sunshine Days - Pop Classics Of The '60s Volume 3.

ODYSSEY
1978 NATIVE NEW YORKER
- (S) (5:33) RCA 7639 Dance! Dance! Dance! *(12" single version)*
- (S) (6:15) RCA 2357 Dance! Dance! Dance! Volume 2. *(previously unreleased version; all selections on this cd are segued together)*
- (S) (5:32) RCA 9684 Nipper's Greatest Hits - The 70's. *(12" single version)*
- (S) (5:31) RCA 61144 The RCA Records Label: The First Note In Black Music. *(12" single version)*
- (S) (5:30) Collectables 8500 Native New Yorker. *(12" single version)*
- (S) (4:21) Priority 53730 Mega Hits Dance Classics Vol. 13. *(LP version but sped up)*
- (S) (5:27) Rebound 314520220 Disco Nights Vol. 4 - Greatest Disco Groups. *(12" single version)*
- (S) (5:31) Hip-O 40041 The Studio Collection Disco 54. *(12" single version)*
- (S) (5:30) RCA 66957 Club Cutz 2. *(12" single version)*
- (S) (4:54) Chronicles 314553405 Non-Stop Disco Vol. 2. *(all songs on this cd are segued together)*
- (S) (4:21) Priority 50957 Mega Hits Disco Explosion Volume 4. *(LP version but sped up)*
- (S) (5:29) Rhino 72837 Disco Queens: The 70's. *(12" single version)*
- (S) (5:31) Simitar 55542 The Number One's: Soul On Fire. *(12" single version)*

OHIO EXPRESS
1967 BEG, BORROW AND STEAL
- (S) (2:31) Collectables 0580 Rare Breed - The Super K Collection. *(this is the orignal version, not the hit version, recorded by the RARE BREED who later changed their name to the OHIO EXPRESS)*
- (S) (2:24) Varese Sarabande 5575 Bubblegum Classics Volume Two. *(hit version credited on the cd to the RARE BREED)*

1968 YUMMY YUMMY YUMMY
- (S) (2:20) Rhino 70629 Billboard's Top Rock & Roll Hits Of 1968.
- (S) (2:20) Rhino 72005 Billboard's Top Rock & Roll Hits 1968-1972 Box Set.
- (S) (2:18) Pair 1202 Best Of Buddah.
- (S) (2:18) Pair 1199 Best Of Bubblegum Music.
- (S) (2:18) Special Music 4914 Best Of The Bubblegum Years.

(M)	(2:18)	Collectables 5067 History Of Rock Volume 7.
(S)	(2:19)	Collectables 0535 Golden Classics.
(S)	(2:19)	Essex 7060 The Buddah Box.
(S)	(2:18)	Time-Life 2CLR-27 Classic Rock - 1968: Blowin' Your Mind.
(S)	(2:20)	Varese Sarabande 5535 Bubblegum Classics Volume One.
(S)	(2:19)	K-Tel 3386 Best Of Bubblegum Music.
(M)	(2:18)	Buddah 49516 Complete Buddah Chart Singles Volume One.
(S)	(2:19)	Eclipse Music Group 64871 Rock 'n Roll Relix 1968-1969.
(S)	(2:19)	Eclipse Music Group 64872 Rock 'n Roll Relix 1960-1969.
(S)	(2:19)	Time-Life 2CLR-31 Classic Rock - Totally Fantastic '60s.

1968 DOWN AT LULU'S

(S)	(1:53)	Pair 1199 Best Of Bubblegum Music.
(S)	(1:53)	Special Music 4914 Best Of The Bubblegum Years.
(S)	(1:53)	Collectables 0535 Golden Classics.
(M)	(1:56)	Buddah 49517 Complete Buddah Chart Singles Volume Two.

1968 CHEWY CHEWY

(S)	(2:36)	Pair 1199 Best Of Bubblegum Music.
(S)	(2:36)	Special Music 4914 Best Of The Bubblegum Years.
(S)	(2:36)	Collectables 0535 Golden Classics.
(S)	(2:36)	Essex 7060 The Buddah Box.
(M)	(2:37)	Buddah 49517 Complete Buddah Chart Singles Volume Two.
(M)	(2:35)	Varese Sarabande 5719 Bubblegum Classics Volume Three.

1969 MERCY

(S)	(2:21)	Pair 1199 Best Of Bubblegum Music.
(S)	(2:21)	Special Music 4914 Best Of The Bubblegum Years.
(S)	(2:23)	Collectables 0535 Golden Classics.

OHIO PLAYERS
1973 FUNKY WORM
1973 ECSTASY
1974 SKIN TIGHT

(S)	(2:50)	K-Tel 30582 Kool & The Gang/Ohio Players. (45 version)
(S)	(7:51)	Mercury 824461 Gold. (LP version)
(S)	(7:51)	Mercury 848345 Skin Tight. (LP version)
(S)	(7:51)	Priority 7069 Back To Back: Best Of Kool & The Gang/Ohio Players. (LP version)
(S)	(2:49)	Time-Life SOD-21 Sounds Of The Seventies - Rock 'N' Soul Seventies. (45 version)
(S)	(7:51)	Risky Business 66663 Sex In The Seventies. (LP version)
(S)	(2:53)	Rhino 72126 Soul Hits Of The 70's Vol. 16. (45 version)
(S)	(7:51)	Mercury 314528102 Funk On Fire: The Mercury Anthology. (LP version)
(S)	(2:49)	MCA 11329 Soul Train 25th Anniversary Box Set. (45 version)
(S)	(2:58)	Priority 50929 Rare Grooves Volume 2. (45 version)
(S)	(2:48)	Polygram Special Markets 314520384 Best Of. (45 version)
(S)	(2:52)	Time-Life R838-09 Solid Gold Soul - 1974. (45 version)

1975 FIRE

(S)	(3:15)	Rhino 70554 Soul Hits Of The 70's Volume 14. (45 version)
(S)	(4:33)	Priority 7059 Mega-Hits Dance Classics Volume 10. (LP version)
(S)	(4:31)	K-Tel 30582 Kool & The Gang/Ohio Players. (LP version)
(S)	(4:24)	Mercury 824461 Gold. (LP version)
(S)	(4:33)	Mercury 848346 Fire. (LP version)
(S)	(4:23)	Priority 7069 Back To Back: Best Of Kool & The Gang/Ohio Players. (LP version)
(S)	(3:12)	Time-Life SOD-22 Sounds Of The Seventies - Seventies Top Forty. (45 version)
(S)	(4:20)	Thump 4030 Old School Vol. 3. (tracks into next selection; LP version)

(S)	(4:29)	Rebound 314520265 Dance Fever. (LP version)
(S)	(4:33)	Mercury 314528102 Funk On Fire: The Mercury Anthology. (LP version)
(S)	(3:14)	Giant 24571 O.S.T. Inkwell. (45 version)
(S)	(3:12)	JCI 3173 1970 - Only Soul - 1974. (45 version)
(S)	(3:14)	Time-Life R838-10 Solid Gold Soul - 1975. (45 version)
(S)	(4:29)	K-Tel 4020 Great R&B Funk Bands Of The 70's. (LP version)
(S)	(4:31)	Chronicles 314555137 Funk Of The 70's. (LP version)
(S)	(4:21)	Cold Front 4025 Old School Mega Mix Volume 3. (LP version)
(S)	(3:15)	Rhino 72943 VH1 8-Track Flashback: Classic '70s Soul. (45 version)
(S)	(3:14)	Time-Life R840-05 Sounds Of The Seventies: '70s Dance Party 1972-1974. (45 version)

1975 I WANT TO BE FREE

(S)	(3:13)	K-Tel 30582 Kool & The Gang/Ohio Players. (45 version)
(S)	(6:48)	Mercury 824461 Gold. (LP version)
(S)	(6:51)	Mercury 848346 Fire. (LP version)
(S)	(6:49)	Mercury 314528102 Funk On Fire: The Mercury Anthology. (LP version)

1975 SWEET STICKY THING

(S)	(6:11)	Mercury 824461 Gold. (LP version)
(S)	(6:10)	Mercury 848347 Honey. (LP version)
(S)	(6:11)	Priority 7069 Back To Back: Best Of Kool & The Gang/Ohio Players. (LP version)
(S)	(6:14)	Mercury 314528102 Funk On Fire: The Mercury Anthology. (LP version)
(S)	(6:10)	Thump 4720 Old School Love Songs Volume 2. (LP version)
(S)	(3:25)	Beast 53442 Original Players Of Love. (45 version)

1976 LOVE ROLLERCOASTER

(S)	(2:50)	Priority 7975 Mega-Hits Dance Classics Volume 5. (45 version)
(M)	(4:45)	K-Tel 30582 Kool & The Gang/Ohio Players. (LP version)
(S)	(4:43)	Mercury 824461 Gold. (LP version)
(S)	(4:47)	Mercury 848347 Honey. (LP version)
(S)	(4:44)	Priority 7069 Back To Back: Best Of Kool & The Gang/Ohio Players. (LP version)
(S)	(4:45)	Razor & Tie 22047 Sweet 70's Soul. (LP version)
(S)	(2:51)	Time-Life SOD-25 Sounds Of The Seventies - Seventies Generation. (45 version)
(S)	(2:50)	Thump 4020 Old School Vol. 2. (45 version)
(S)	(2:50)	Rebound 314520317 Class Reunion 1975. (45 version)
(S)	(2:53)	Rhino 72127 Soul Hits Of The 70's Vol. 17. (45 version)
(S)	(4:47)	Mercury 314528102 Funk On Fire: The Mercury Anthology. (LP version)
(S)	(2:51)	Time-Life R838-11 Solid Gold Soul - 1976. (45 version)
(S)	(2:50)	Time-Life R840-01 Sounds Of The Seventies - Pop Nuggets: Late '70s. (45 version)
(S)	(4:46)	Rebound 314520430 Funk Classics Of The 70's Vol. 2. (LP version)
(S)	(2:28)	Thump 4100 Old School Mix. (all selections on this cd are segued together and remixed)
(S)	(4:14)	Chronicles 314555140 Dance Funk. (all selections on this cd are segued together)
(S)	(2:52)	Polydor 314555120 Pure Disco 2. (45 version)
(S)	(4:47)	JCI 3175 1975 - Only Soul - 1979. (LP version)
(S)	(2:52)	Time-Life R840-06 Sounds Of The Seventies: '70s Dance Party 1975-1976. (45 version)

1976 FOPP

(S)	(3:48)	Mercury 824461 Gold.
(S)	(3:51)	Mercury 848347 Honey.
(S)	(3:51)	Mercury 314528102 Funk On Fire: The Mercury Anthology.
(S)	(3:46)	K-Tel 6011 70's Soul - Super Funky Hits.
(S)	(3:47)	Priority 50928 Rare Grooves Volume 1.
(S)	(3:51)	Thump 4740 Old School Love Songs Volume 4.

1976 WHO'D SHE COO?

(M)	(4:27)	K-Tel 30582 Kool & The Gang/Ohio Players. (LP version)

OHIO PLAYERS (Continued)

- (S) (4:28)   Mercury 824461   Gold. *(LP version)*
- (S) (4:30)   Mercury 848348   Contradiction. *(LP version)*
- (S) (4:26)   Priority 7069   Back To Back: Best Of Kool & The Gang/Ohio Players. *(LP version)*
- (S) (3:21)   Rhino 72128   Hot Soul Hits Of The 70's Vol. 18. *(45 version)*
- (S) (4:30)   Mercury 314528102   Funk On Fire: The Mercury Anthology. *(LP version)*
- (S) (3:19)   Polygram Special Markets 314520384   Best Of. *(45 version)*

O'JAYS
1972   BACK STABBERS

- (S) (3:06)   Rhino 70633   Billboard's Top Rock & Roll Hits Of 1972.
- (S) (3:06)   Rhino 72005   Billboard's Top Rock & Roll Hits 1968-1972 Box Set.
- (S) (3:05)   Rhino 70788   Soul Hits Of The 70's Volume 8.
- (S) (3:06)   Philadelphia International 35024   Collectors' Items.
- (S) (3:06)   Philadelphia International 39251   Greatest Hits.
- (S) (3:06)   Epic 57620   O.S.T. Carlito's Way.
- (S) (3:04)   Razor & Tie 22047   Sweet 70's Soul.
- (S) (3:06)   Time-Life SOD-03   Sounds Of The Seventies - 1972.
- (S) (3:05)   Epic/Legacy 66114   Love Train: Best Of.
- (S) (3:05)   Legacy/Epic 66912   Legacy's Rhythm & Soul Revue.
- (S) (3:04)   Priority 53790   Disco Nice And Nasty.
- (S) (3:05)   Epic Associated/Legacy 66113   Back Stabbers.
- (S) (3:06)   JCI 3191   1970 - Only Dance - 1974.
- (S) (3:06)   Eclipse Music Group 64893   Rock 'n Roll Relix 1972-1973.
- (S) (3:06)   Eclipse Music Group 64897   Rock 'n Roll Relix 1970-1979.
- (S) (3:05)   Epic/Legacy 64647   The Philly Sound Box Set.
- (S) (3:06)   K-Tel 3913   Superstars Greatest Hits Volume 2.
- (S) (3:05)   Epic Associated/Legacy 65445   Super Hits.

1973   LOVE TRAIN
(the original 45 and LP length was (2:58); a (6:15) version first surfaced on the "Philadelphia Classics" vinyl LP in 1977)

- (S) (2:58)   Rhino 70634   Billboard's Top Rock & Roll Hits Of 1973.
- (S) (2:58)   Rhino 70552   Soul Hits Of The 70's Volume 12.
- (S) (6:15)   Philadelphia International 34940   Philadelphia Classics.
- (S) (2:57)   Philadelphia International 35024   Collectors' Items.
- (S) (2:57)   Philadelphia International 39251   Greatest Hits.
- (S) (2:55)   Priority 7976   Mega-Hits Dance Classics Volume 6.
- (S) (2:58)   Rhino 71618   Soul Train Hall Of Fame/20th Anniversary.
- (S) (2:55)   Time-Life SUD-16   Superhits - The Early 70's.
- (S) (2:57)   Time-Life SOD-06   Sounds Of The Seventies - 1973.
- (S) (2:58)   Time-Life R921-38   Get Together.
- (S) (6:14)   Epic 66155   Club Epic Volume 3. *(tracks into the next selection)*
- (S) (2:58)   Epic/Legacy 66114   Love Train: Best Of.
- (S) (2:56)   Capitol 32438   O.S.T. Dead Presidents.
- (S) (2:58)   Ichiban 2511   Love, Peace & Understanding.
- (S) (2:56)   Risky Business 67308   Train Trax.
- (S) (2:57)   Epic Associated/Legacy 66113   Back Stabbers.
- (S) (2:56)   Right Stuff 52660   Flick Hits - Old School Tracks.
- (S) (2:57)   JCI 3173   1970 - Only Soul - 1974.
- (S) (2:58)   Priority 50956   Mega Hits - Disco Heat.
- (S) (2:55)   Time-Life AM1-13   AM Gold - The Early '70s.
- (S) (2:58)   Time-Life R838-08   Solid Gold Soul - 1973.
- (S) (2:58)   Epic/Legacy 64647   The Philly Sound Box Set.
- (S) (2:58)   Epic Associated/Legacy 65162   A Postcard From Philly.
- (S) (2:58)   Epic Associated/Legacy 65445   Super Hits.
- (S) (6:14)   Epic/Legacy 65504   Disco Super Hits.
- (S) (2:58)   Time-Life R840-05   Sounds Of The Seventies: '70s Dance Party 1972-1974.
- (S) (2:58)   Collectables 1516 and 2516   The Anniversary Album - The 70's.

1973   TIME TO GET DOWN

- (S) (2:51)   Epic/Legacy 66114   Love Train: Best Of.
- (S) (2:51)   Epic Associated/Legacy 66113   Back Stabbers.
- (S) (2:51)   Epic Associated/Legacy 65445   Super Hits.

1974   PUT YOUR HANDS TOGETHER

- (S) (4:05)   Philadelphia International 32408   Ship Ahoy. *(LP version)*
- (S) (4:05)   Epic/Legacy 66114   Love Train: Best Of. *(LP version)*
- (S) (4:05)   Rhino 72126   Soul Hits Of The 70's Vol. 16. *(LP version)*
- (S) (4:05)   Epic Associated/Legacy 65445   Super Hits. *(LP version)*

1974   FOR THE LOVE OF MONEY

- (S) (3:46)   Rhino 70554   Soul Hits Of The 70's Volume 14. *(45 version)*
- (S) (3:42)   Priority 7057   Mega-Hits Dance Classics Volume 8. *(45 version)*
- (S) (3:46)   Philadelphia International 39251   Greatest Hits. *(45 version)*
- (S) (7:17)   Philadelphia International 32408   Ship Ahoy. *(LP version)*
- (S) (7:17)   Philadelphia International 35024   Collectors' Items. *(LP version)*
- (S) (3:44)   Rhino 71432   In Yo Face! History Of Funk Volume 2. *(45 version)*
- (S) (3:42)   Priority 53730   Mega Hits Dance Classics Vol. 13. *(45 version)*
- (S) (7:20)   Epic/Legacy 66114   Love Train: Best Of. *(LP version)*
- (S) (7:19)   Risky Business 66385   Wall Street's Greatest Hits. *(LP version)*
- (S) (3:45)   Eclipse Music Group 64894   Rock 'n Roll Relix 1974-1975. *(45 version)*
- (S) (3:45)   Eclipse Music Group 64897   Rock 'n Roll Relix 1970-1979. *(45 version)*
- (S) (7:18)   Epic/Legacy 64647   The Philly Sound Box Set. *(LP version)*
- (S) (6:06)   Thump 9960   Old School Funk II. *(neither the 45 or LP version)*

1975   GIVE THE PEOPLE WHAT THEY WANT

- (S) (4:09)   Philadelphia International 35024   Collectors' Items. *(LP version)*
- (S) (3:13)   Rhino 71433   In Yo Face! History Of Funk Volume 3. *(45 version)*
- (S) (4:11)   Legacy/Epic 66112   Give The People What They Want. *(LP version)*
- (S) (3:13)   Right Stuff 29669   Movin' On Up Vol. 2. *(45 version)*

1976   I LOVE MUSIC (PART 1)

- (S) (9:46)   Philadelphia International 34940   Philadelphia Classics. *(this version first appeared on the "Philadelphia Classics" vinyl LP in 1977)*
- (S) (6:53)   Philadelphia International 39307   Ten Years Of Hits. *(LP version)*
- (S) (3:43)   Priority 7983   Mega-Hits Dance Classics Volume 7. *(45 version)*
- (S) (6:05)   Epic/Legacy 52402   Club Epic - A Collection Of Classic Dance Mixes Volume 2. *(remixed)*
- (S) (3:42)   Philadelphia International 39251   Greatest Hits. *(45 version)*
- (S) (6:50)   Philadelphia International 35024   Collectors' Items. *(LP version)*
- (S) (6:50)   Philadelphia International 33807   Family Reunion. *(LP version)*
- (S) (6:51)   Epic/Legacy 66114   Love Train: Best Of. *(LP version)*
- (S) (3:33)   Rhino 72127   Soul Hits Of The 70's Vol. 17. *(45 version)*
- (S) (3:33)   MCA 11329   Soul Train 25th Anniversary Box Set. *(45 version)*
- (S) (6:31)   Rhino 72183   Give Your Body Up - Club Classics & House Foundations Volume One. *(LP version faded :20 early)*
- (S) (3:42)   Time-Life R838-10   Solid Gold Soul - 1975. *(45 version)*
- (S) (6:50)   Epic/Legacy 64647   The Philly Sound Box Set. *(LP version)*

(S)	(6:50)	Epic Associated/Legacy 65445 Super Hits. *(LP version)*
(S)	(3:33)	Time-Life R840-06 Sounds Of The Seventies: '70s Dance Party 1975-1976. *(45 version)*

1976 LIVIN' FOR THE WEEKEND

(S)	(6:33)	Philadelphia International 35024 Collectors' Items. *(LP version)*
(S)	(6:32)	Philadelphia International 33807 Family Reunion. *(LP version)*
(S)	(6:35)	Epic/Legacy 66114 Love Train: Best Of. *(LP version)*
(S)	(6:35)	Epic/Legacy 65035 Club Epic Volume 6. *(LP version)*
(S)	(2:51)	Time-Life R838-11 Solid Gold Soul - 1976. *(45 version)*
(S)	(6:35)	Epic/Legacy 64647 The Philly Sound Box Set. *(LP version)*

1978 USE TA BE MY GIRL

(S)	(4:00)	Philadelphia International 39307 Ten Years Of Hits. *(LP version)*
(S)	(3:22)	Philadelphia International 39251 Greatest Hits. *(45 version)*
(S)	(3:19)	Time-Life SOD-10 Sounds Of The Seventies - 1978. *(45 version)*
(S)	(4:01)	Ripete 2219 Beach Fever. *(LP version)*
(S)	(3:24)	Rhino 72130 Soul Hits Of The 70's Vol. 20. *(45 version)*
(S)	(3:19)	EMI 38306 In Bed With The O'Jays: Their Greatest Love Songs. *(45 version)*
(S)	(3:18)	JCI 3146 1975 - Only Love - 1979. *(45 version)*
(S)	(3:23)	Time-Life R838-17 Solid Gold Soul 1978. *(45 version)*
(S)	(3:23)	Time-Life R840-08 Sounds Of The Seventies: '70s Dance Party 1978-1979. *(45 version)*
(S)	(3:24)	Time-Life AM1-25 AM Gold - 1978. *(45 version)*

1980 FOREVER MINE

(S)	(3:45)	Philadelphia International 39251 Greatest Hits.
(S)	(3:36)	Original Sound 9304 Art Laboe's Dedicated To You Vol. 4.
(S)	(6:08)	Rhino 71859 Smooth Grooves Volume 1.
(S)	(3:42)	Thump 4740 Old School Love Songs Volume 4.

O'KAYSIONS

1968 GIRL WATCHER

(M)	(2:32)	Ripete 2392192 Beach Music Anthology Box Set.
(M)	(2:30)	Collectables 5067 History Of Rock Volume 7. *(no low end)*
(E)	(2:31)	Original Sound 8858 Oldies But Goodies Vol. 8. *(this compact disc uses the "Waring - fds" noise reduction process)*
(E)	(2:31)	Original Sound 2221 Oldies But Goodies Volumes 1,4,6,8 and 10 Box Set. *(this box set uses the "Waring - fds" noise reduction process)*
(E)	(2:31)	Original Sound 2500 Oldies But Goodies Volumes 1-15 Box Set. *(this box set uses the "Waring - fds" noise reduction process)*
(E)	(2:31)	Original Sound CDGO-8 Golden Oldies Volume. 8.
(E)	(2:31)	Original Sound 8892 Dick Clark's 21 All-Time Hits Vol. 2.
(M)	(2:32)	Ripete 0002 Coolin' Out/24 Carolina Classics Vol. 2.
(M)	(2:32)	Time-Life RHD-04 Rhythm & Blues - 1968.
(E)	(2:33)	Time-Life 2CLR-11 Classic Rock - 1968: The Beat Goes On.
(E)	(2:30)	Collectables 2502 WCBS-FM History Of Rock - The 60's Part 3.
(E)	(2:30)	Collectables 4502 History Of Rock/The 60s Part Three.
(M)	(2:34)	MCA Special Products 20753 Classic R&B Oldies From The 60's.
(E)	(2:34)	MCA Special Products 20948 Biggest Summer Hits.
(M)	(2:29)	K-Tel 3269 Carolina Beach Music.
(M)	(2:32)	Time-Life R838-03 Solid Gold Soul - 1968.
(M)	(2:34)	MCA Special Products 21030 Beach Music Hits.

(M)	(2:34)	Rhino 72815 Beg, Scream & Shout! The Big Ol' Box Of '60s Soul.

DANNY O'KEEFE

1972 GOOD TIME CHARLIE'S GOT THE BLUES

(S)	(2:38)	JCI 3304 Mellow Seventies. *(rerecording)*
(S)	(3:00)	Rhino 71197 Super Hits Of The 70's Volume 17.
(S)	(2:58)	Atlantic 81427 Breezy Stories. *(rerecording)*
(S)	(2:58)	Time-Life SUD-11 Superhits - 1972.
(S)	(2:59)	Time-Life R103-33 Singers & Songwriters.
(S)	(2:58)	Time-Life AM1-07 AM Gold - 1972.
(S)	(2:59)	Rhino 72738 Billboard Top Soft Rock Hits - 1972.

MIKE OLDFIELD

1974 TUBULAR BELLS

(S)	(25:28)	Virgin 90589 and 86007 Tubular Bells. *(LP version)*
(S)	(4:15)	Virgin 39069 Best Of/Elements. *(neither the 45 or LP version)*
(S)	(3:17)	Rhino 72297 Superhits Of The 70's Volume 23. *(neither the 45 or LP version)*
(S)	(4:14)	Madacy Entertainment 1974 Rock On 1974. *(neither the 45 or LP version)*
(S)	(4:15)	Time-Life R840-04 Sounds Of The Seventies: A Loss For Words. *(neither the 45 or LP version)*
(S)	(4:56)	Virgin 42186 Pure Moods. *(neither the 45 or LP version)*
(S)	(4:15)	Hip-O 40013 Synth Me Up - 14 Classic Electronic Hits. *(neither the 45 or LP version)*

OLIVER

1969 GOOD MORNING STARSHINE

(S)	(3:35)	JCI 3104 Mellow Sixties.
(M)	(3:39)	Rhino 71093 Better Days.
(S)	(3:35)	Time-Life SUD-07 Superhits - 1969.
(S)	(3:35)	Time-Life R921-38 Get Together.
(M)	(3:37)	Rhino 71730 '60s Rock Classics, Vol. 3.
(S)	(3:35)	Time-Life AM1-01 AM Gold - 1969.
(M)	(3:39)	Flashback 72687 '60s Rock: Feelin' Groovy.
(M)	(3:39)	Flashback 72088 '60s Rock Hits Box Set.
(M)	(3:37)	Flashback 72703 '60s Rock: It's A Beautiful Morning.
(M)	(3:37)	Flashback 72088 '60s Rock Hits Box Set.

1969 JEAN

(S)	(3:16)	Time-Life SUD-18 Superhits - Late 60's Classics.
(S)	(3:17)	Rhino 71939 Billboard Top Pop Hits, 1969.
(S)	(3:17)	Rhino 72423 Billboard Top Movie Hits - 1960s.
(S)	(3:16)	Time-Life AM1-12 AM Gold - Late '60s Classics.
(S)	(3:16)	Time-Life R814-04 Love Songs.

1969 SUNDAY MORNIN'

OLLIE & JERRY

1984 BREAKIN'...THERE'S NO STOPPING US

(S)	(3:40)	Rebound 314520309 Disco Nights Vol. VII - D.J. Pix. *(45 length)*
(S)	(4:31)	Rebound 314520366 Disco Nights Vol. 10 - Disco's Greatest Movie Hits. *("Breakin'" soundtrack LP length)*
(S)	(4:21)	Cold Front 6284 More Of! Club Mix's Biggest Jams. *(all selections on this cd are segued together)*
(S)	(4:29)	Simitar 55602 The Number One's: Silky Soul. *("Breakin'" soundtrack LP length)*

NIGEL OLSSON

1979 DANCIN' SHOES

(actual 45 time is (3:55) not (3:45) as stated on the record label)

(S)	(4:01)	Rhino 71202 Super Hits Of The 70's Volume 22.
(S)	(4:02)	Collectables 5836 A Golden Classics Edition.

1979 LITTLE BIT OF SOAP

(S)	(3:25)	Collectables 5836 A Golden Classics Edition.

OLYMPICS

1958 WESTERN MOVIES

(M)	(2:19)	Curb 77323 All Time Greatest Hits Of Rock 'N' Roll.

439

  (M) (2:19) Original Sound CDGO-3 Golden Oldies Volume. 3.

  (M) (2:19) Original Sound 8891 Dick Clark's 21 All-Time Hits Vol. 1.

  (M) (2:19) DCC Compact Classics 057 All-Time Greatest Hits.

  (M) (2:19) Sandstone 33078 Olympics All-Time Greatest Hits.

  (E) (2:19) Time-Life 2RNR-21 Rock 'N' Roll Era - 1958 Still Rockin'.

  (M) (2:19) Time-Life RHD-16 Rhythm & Blues - 1958.

  (M) (2:20) Collectables 2605 WCBS-FM Jukebox Giants Vol. 3.

  (M) (2:19) Time-Life R838-22 Solid Gold Soul 1958.

1960 BIG BOY PETE
(actual 45 time is (2:25) not (2:15) as stated on the record label)

  (M) (2:26) DCC Compact Classics 057 All-Time Greatest Hits.

  (M) (2:08) Collectables 5081 The Olympics Meet The Marathons. *(:18 edited off the ending)*

  (M) (2:26) Sandstone 33078 Olympics All-Time Greatest Hits.

  (M) (2:25) Time-Life RHD-15 Rhythm & Blues - 1960.

  (M) (2:07) Collectables 2502 WCBS-FM History Of Rock - The 60's Part 3. *(:19 edited off the ending)*

  (M) (2:07) Collectables 4502 History Of Rock/The 60s Part Three. *(:19 edited off the ending)*

  (M) (2:25) Time-Life R838-20 Solid Gold Soul 1960.

1960 SHIMMY LIKE KATE

  (M) (2:20) DCC Compact Classics 057 All-Time Greatest Hits.

  (M) (2:21) Collectables 5081 The Olympics Meet The Marathons.

  (M) (2:20) Sandstone 33078 Olympics All-Time Greatest Hits.

1961 DANCE BY THE LIGHT OF THE MOON

  (M) (2:12) DCC Compact Classics 057 All-Time Greatest Hits.

  (M) (2:12) Collectables 5081 The Olympics Meet The Marathons.

  (M) (2:12) Sandstone 33078 Olympics All-Time Greatest Hits.

  (M) (2:11) Time-Life 2RNR-49 Rock 'N' Roll Era - Lost Treasures II.

ALEXANDER O'NEAL
released as by CHERRELLE with ALEXANDER O'NEAL:
1986 SATURDAY LOVE

  (S) (8:41) Epic 46087 Club Epic. *(remix)*

  (S) (6:28) Tabu 40094 Cherrelle - High Priority. *(LP version)*

  (S) (4:56) Tabu 314530592 Cherrelle - Best Of. *(LP version but missing the introduction)*

released as by ALEXANDER O'NEAL:
1987 FAKE

  (S) (3:55) Tabu 40320 Alexander O'Neal - Hearsay.

  (S) (3:49) Tabu 53833 Alexander O'Neal - Greatest Hits. *(1988 remix)*

  (S) (3:56) Tabu 314530591 Alexander O'Neal - Best Of.

released as by ALEXANDER O'NEAL featuring CHERRELLE:
1988 NEVER KNEW LOVE LIKE THIS

  (S) (5:08) Tabu 40320 Alexander O'Neal - Hearsay. *(LP version)*

  (S) (3:28) Tabu 53833 Alexander O'Neal - Greatest Hits. *(45 version)*

  (S) (5:09) Tabu 314530591 Alexander O'Neal - Best Of. *(LP version)*

SHAQUILLE O'NEAL
released as by FU-SCHNICKENS with SHAQUILLE O'NEAL:
1993 WHAT'S UP DOC? (CAN WE ROCK)

  (S) (3:52) Jive 41529 Shaquille O'Neal - Shaq Diesel.

  (S) (3:56) Jive 41519 Fu-Schnickens - Nervous Breakdown.

  (S) (3:51) Jive 41582 Fu-Schnickens - Greatest Hits.

  (S) (3:52) Jive 41599 Shaquille O'Neal - Best Of.

released as by SHAQUILLE O'NEAL:
1993 (I KNOW I GOT) SKILLZ

  (S) (4:22) Jive 41529 Shaquille O'Neal - Shaq Diesel.

  (S) (4:04) Coldfront 6146 Phat Rap Flava '95. *(all selections on this cd are segued together)*

  (S) (4:22) Jive 41599 Shaquille O'Neal - Best Of.

100 PROOF AGED IN SOUL
1970 SOMEBODY'S BEEN SLEEPING

  (S) (2:45) Rhino 70783 Soul Hits Of The 70's Volume 3. *(45 version)*

  (S) (2:45) Rhino 72028 Soul Hits Of The 70's Volumes 1-5 Box Set. *(45 version)*

  (S) (4:09) HDH 3904 Greatest Hits. *(LP version)*

  (S) (4:09) Essex 7060 The Buddah Box. *(LP version)*

  (S) (2:45) Time-Life SOD-25 Sounds Of The Seventies - Seventies Generation. *(45 version)*

  (S) (2:44) JCI 3173 1970 - Only Soul - 1974. *(45 version)*

  (S) (2:45) Flashback 72900 25 Years Of Soul - 1970. *(45 version)*

112
released as by 112 featuring THE NOTORIOUS B.I.G.:
1996 ONLY YOU

  (S) (4:20) Bad Boy 73009 112.

  (S) (4:49) Bad Boy 73009 112. *(remix)*

  (S) (4:31) Arista 18977 Ultimate Hip Hop Party 1998. *(all selections on this cd are segued together; remix)*

released as by 112:
1997 COME SEE ME

  (S) (4:25) Bad Boy 73009 112.

1997 CUPID

  (S) (4:11) Bad Boy 73009 112.

released as by PUFF DADDY & FAITH EVANS featuring 112:
1997 I'LL BE MISSING YOU

  (S) (5:42) Bad Boy 73012 and 73014 No Way Out.

released as by ALLURE featuring 112:
1997 ALL CRIED OUT

  (S) (4:35) Crave/Track Masters 67848 Allure. *(tracks into the next selection)*

  (S) (4:36) Beast 54112 Boom! *(remix)*

ONE 2 MANY
1989 DOWNTOWN

  (S) (4:26) A&M 5237 Mirror.

ONYX
1993 SLAM

  (S) (5:28) Tommy Boy 1097 MTV Party To Go Volume 5. *(remix; all tracks on this cd are segued together)*

  (S) (3:38) JMJ/RAL/Chaos/Columbia 53302 Bacdafucup.

  (S) (3:36) Def Jam 314536377 Def Jam's Greatest Hits.

  (S) (3:38) JMJ/RAL 314523447 Bacdafucup.

OPUS
1986 LIVE IS LIFE

ROY ORBISON
1960 ONLY THE LONELY (KNOW HOW I FEEL)

  (S) (2:25) Rhino 71493 For The Lonely: 18 Greatest Hits.

  (S) (2:26) CBS Special Products 44348 All-Time Greatest Hits Volume 1.

  (S) (2:25) CBS Special Products 45116 All-Time Greatest Hits.

  (S) (2:25) CBS Special Products 46809 Legendary.

  (S) (2:26) Virgin 90604 In Dreams: The Greatest Hits. *(all selections on this cd are rerecorded)*

  (S) (2:23) CBS Special Products 21427 Sings Lonely And Blue.

  (S) (2:24) Time-Life 2RNR-11 Rock 'N' Roll Era - 1960.

  (S) (2:24) Time-Life 2RNR-34 Rock 'N' Roll Era - Roy Orbison 1960-1965.

  (S) (2:24) Sony Music Special Products 66106 The Monument Story.

  (S) (2:25) Time-Life R857-02 The Heart Of Rock 'n' Roll - 1960.

  (S) (2:25) Columbia 67297 Super Hits.

  (S) (2:24) Monument/Legacy 66219 Sings Lonely And Blue. *(gold disc)*

  (S) (2:26) Virgin 42350 Very Best Of. *(rerecording)*

  (S) (2:25) Eclipse Music Group 64867 Rock 'n Roll Relix 1960-1961.

  (S) (2:25) Eclipse Music Group 64872 Rock 'n Roll Relix 1960-1969.

(S) (2:25) DCC Compact Classics 1118 All-Time Greatest Hits. *(gold disc)*
(S) (2:26) Orbison Records 1000 In Dreams - Greatest Hits. *(all songs on this cd are rerecorded)*

1960 BLUE ANGEL
(S) (2:49) Rhino 71493 For The Lonely: 18 Greatest Hits.
(S) (2:49) CBS Special Products 44348 All-Time Greatest Hits Volume 1.
(S) (2:49) CBS Special Products 45116 All-Time Greatest Hits.
(S) (2:49) CBS Special Products 46809 Legendary.
(S) (2:46) Virgin 90604 In Dreams: The Greatest Hits. *(all selections on this cd are rerecorded)*
(S) (2:50) CBS Special Products 21427 Sings Lonely And Blue.
(S) (2:49) Time-Life 2RNR-34 Rock 'N' Roll Era - Roy Orbison 1960-1965.
(S) (2:49) Columbia 67297 Super Hits.
(S) (2:50) Monument/Legacy 66219 Sings Lonely And Blue. *(gold disc)*
(S) (2:46) Virgin 42350 Very Best Of. *(rerecording)*
(S) (2:49) Time-Life R857-14 The Heart Of Rock 'n' Roll 1960-1961 Take Two.
(S) (2:51) DCC Compact Classics 1118 All-Time Greatest Hits. *(gold disc)*
(S) (2:46) Orbison Records 1000 In Dreams - Greatest Hits. *(all songs on this cd are rerecorded)*

1961 I'M HURTIN'
(S) (2:42) CBS Special Products 44349 All-Time Greatest Hits Volume 2.
(S) (2:42) Rhino 71493 For The Lonely: 18 Greatest Hits.
(S) (2:42) CBS Special Products 45116 All-Time Greatest Hits.
(S) (2:41) CBS Special Products 46809 Legendary.
(S) (2:46) Virgin 90604 In Dreams: The Greatest Hits. *(all selections on this cd are rerecorded)*
(S) (2:41) CBS Special Products 21427 Sings Lonely And Blue.
(S) (2:41) Time-Life 2RNR-34 Rock 'N' Roll Era - Roy Orbison 1960-1965.
(S) (2:42) Risky Business 66388 The Big Hurt/Songs To Cry By.
(S) (2:42) Columbia 67297 Super Hits.
(S) (2:41) Monument/Legacy 66219 Sings Lonely And Blue. *(gold disc)*
(S) (2:43) DCC Compact Classics 1118 All-Time Greatest Hits. *(gold disc)*
(S) (2:46) Orbison Records 1000 In Dreams - Greatest Hits. *(all songs on this cd are rerecorded)*

1961 RUNNING SCARED
(S) (2:11) CBS Special Products 44349 All-Time Greatest Hits Volume 2.
(S) (2:10) Rhino 71493 For The Lonely: 18 Greatest Hits.
(S) (2:10) CBS Special Products 45116 All-Time Greatest Hits.
(S) (2:10) CBS Special Products 46809 Legendary.
(S) (2:12) Virgin 90604 In Dreams: The Greatest Hits. *(all selections on this cd are rerecorded)*
(S) (2:10) CBS Special Products 21428 Crying.
(S) (2:10) Rhino 71548 Let There Be Drums Volume 2: The 60's.
(S) (2:09) Time-Life 2RNR-34 Rock 'N' Roll Era - Roy Orbison 1960-1965.
(S) (2:10) Time-Life HPD-32 Your Hit Parade - Into The 60's.
(S) (2:10) Columbia 67297 Super Hits.
(S) (2:27) Virgin 42350 Very Best Of. *(live)*
(S) (2:10) Time-Life R857-10 The Heart Of Rock 'n' Roll 1960-1961.
(S) (2:11) DCC Compact Classics 1118 All-Time Greatest Hits. *(gold disc)*
(S) (2:12) Orbison Records 1000 In Dreams - Greatest Hits. *(all songs on this cd are rerecorded)*

1961 CRYING
(S) (2:44) Rhino 71493 For The Lonely: 18 Greatest Hits.
(S) (2:44) CBS Special Products 44348 All-Time Greatest Hits Volume 1.
(S) (2:44) CBS Special Products 45116 All-Time Greatest Hits.
(S) (2:44) CBS Special Products 46809 Legendary.

(S) (2:45) Virgin 90604 In Dreams: The Greatest Hits. *(all selections on this cd are rerecorded)*
(S) (2:44) CBS Special Products 21428 Crying.
(S) (2:44) Time-Life 2RNR-34 Rock 'N' Roll Era - Roy Orbison 1960-1965.
(S) (2:44) Time-Life R857-03 The Heart Of Rock 'n' Roll - 1961.
(S) (2:44) Columbia 67297 Super Hits.
(S) (3:46) Virgin 42350 Very Best Of. *(duet with k.d. Lang)*
(S) (2:46) DCC Compact Classics 1118 All-Time Greatest Hits. *(gold disc)*
(S) (2:46) Orbison Records 1000 In Dreams - Greatest Hits. *(all songs on this cd are rerecorded)*
(S) (2:45) Time-Life R814-03 Love Songs.

1961 CANDY MAN
(S) (2:43) Rhino 71493 For The Lonely: 18 Greatest Hits.
(S) (2:43) CBS Special Products 44348 All-Time Greatest Hits Volume 1.
(S) (2:43) CBS Special Products 45116 All-Time Greatest Hits.
(S) (2:43) CBS Special Products 46809 Legendary.
(S) (2:57) Virgin 90604 In Dreams: The Greatest Hits. *(all selections on this cd are rerecorded)*
(S) (2:42) Time-Life 2RNR-34 Rock 'N' Roll Era - Roy Orbison 1960-1965.
(S) (2:44) DCC Compact Classics 1118 All-Time Greatest Hits. *(gold disc)*
(S) (2:57) Orbison Records 1000 In Dreams - Greatest Hits. *(all songs on this cd are rerecorded)*

1962 DREAM BABY (HOW LONG MUST I DREAM)
(S) (2:30) Rhino 71493 For The Lonely: 18 Greatest Hits.
(S) (2:31) CBS Special Products 44348 All-Time Greatest Hits Volume 1.
(S) (2:31) CBS Special Products 45116 All-Time Greatest Hits.
(S) (2:31) CBS Special Products 46809 Legendary.
(S) (2:48) Virgin 90604 In Dreams: The Greatest Hits. *(all selections on this cd are rerecorded)*
(S) (2:30) Time-Life 2RNR-34 Rock 'N' Roll Era - Roy Orbison 1960-1965.
(S) (3:52) Virgin 42350 Very Best Of. *(live)*
(S) (2:31) Time-Life R857-06 The Heart Of Rock 'n' Roll 1962.
(S) (2:32) DCC Compact Classics 1118 All-Time Greatest Hits. *(gold disc)*
(S) (2:49) Orbison Records 1000 In Dreams - Greatest Hits. *(all songs on this cd are rerecorded)*

1962 THE CROWD
(S) (2:21) CBS Special Products 44349 All-Time Greatest Hits Volume 2.
(S) (2:21) CBS Special Products 45116 All-Time Greatest Hits.
(S) (2:21) CBS Special Products 46809 Legendary.
(S) (2:20) Time-Life 2RNR-34 Rock 'N' Roll Era - Roy Orbison 1960-1965.
(S) (2:21) DCC Compact Classics 1118 All-Time Greatest Hits. *(gold disc)*

1962 LEAH
(S) (2:38) Rhino 71493 For The Lonely: 18 Greatest Hits.
(S) (2:38) CBS Special Products 44348 All-Time Greatest Hits Volume 1.
(S) (2:38) CBS Special Products 45116 All-Time Greatest Hits.
(S) (2:38) CBS Special Products 46809 Legendary.
(S) (2:42) Virgin 90604 In Dreams: The Greatest Hits. *(all selections on this cd are rerecorded)*
(S) (2:37) Time-Life 2RNR-34 Rock 'N' Roll Era - Roy Orbison 1960-1965.
(S) (2:41) DCC Compact Classics 1118 All-Time Greatest Hits. *(gold disc)*
(S) (2:42) Orbison Records 1000 In Dreams - Greatest Hits. *(all songs on this cd are rerecorded)*

1962 WORKIN' FOR THE MAN
(S) (2:25) Rhino 71493 For The Lonely: 18 Greatest Hits.
(S) (2:25) CBS Special Products 44348 All-Time Greatest Hits Volume 1.
(S) (2:24) CBS Special Products 45116 All-Time Greatest Hits.

ROY ORBISON (Continued)

(S) (2:24) CBS Special Products 46809 Legendary.
(S) (2:43) Virgin 90604 In Dreams: The Greatest Hits. (all selections on this cd are rerecorded)
(S) (2:24) Time-Life 2RNR-34 Rock 'N' Roll Era - Roy Orbison 1960-1965.
(S) (2:24) Columbia 67297 Super Hits.
(S) (2:27) DCC Compact Classics 1118 All-Time Greatest Hits. (gold disc)
(S) (2:43) Orbison Records 1000 In Dreams - Greatest Hits. (all songs on this cd are rerecorded)

1963 IN DREAMS

(S) (2:47) Rhino 71493 For The Lonely: 18 Greatest Hits.
(S) (2:47) CBS Special Products 44348 All-Time Greatest Hits Volume 1.
(S) (2:47) CBS Special Products 45116 All-Time Greatest Hits.
(S) (2:47) CBS Special Products 46809 Legendary.
(S) (2:48) Virgin 90604 In Dreams: The Greatest Hits. (all selections on this cd are rerecorded)
(S) (2:47) CBS Special Products 21429 In Dreams.
(S) (2:47) Time-Life 2RNR-34 Rock 'N' Roll Era - Roy Orbison 1960-1965.
(S) (2:47) Columbia 67297 Super Hits.
(S) (2:49) Virgin 42350 Very Best Of. (rerecording)
(S) (2:49) DCC Compact Classics 1118 All-Time Greatest Hits. (gold disc)
(S) (2:48) Orbison Records 1000 In Dreams - Greatest Hits. (all songs on this cd are rerecorded)

1963 FALLING

(S) (2:21) CBS Special Products 44349 All-Time Greatest Hits Volume 2.
(S) (2:20) CBS Special Products 45116 All-Time Greatest Hits.
(S) (2:21) CBS Special Products 46809 Legendary.
(S) (2:24) Virgin 90604 In Dreams: The Greatest Hits. (all selections on this cd are rerecorded)
(S) (2:20) Time-Life 2RNR-34 Rock 'N' Roll Era - Roy Orbison 1960-1965.
(S) (2:24) Virgin 42350 Very Best Of. (rerecording)
(S) (2:21) DCC Compact Classics 1118 All-Time Greatest Hits. (gold disc)
(S) (2:23) Orbison Records 1000 In Dreams - Greatest Hits. (all songs on this cd are rerecorded)

1963 MEAN WOMAN BLUES

(S) (2:24) CBS Special Products 44349 All-Time Greatest Hits Volume 2.
(S) (2:23) Rhino 71493 For The Lonely: 18 Greatest Hits.
(S) (2:23) CBS Special Products 45116 All-Time Greatest Hits.
(S) (2:23) CBS Special Products 46809 Legendary.
(S) (2:24) Virgin 90604 In Dreams: The Greatest Hits. (all selections on this cd are rerecorded)
(S) (2:23) Time-Life 2RNR-34 Rock 'N' Roll Era - Roy Orbison 1960-1965.
(S) (2:23) Sony Music Special Products 66106 The Monument Story.
(S) (3:02) Virgin 42350 Very Best Of. (live)
(S) (2:25) DCC Compact Classics 1118 All-Time Greatest Hits. (gold disc)
(S) (2:24) Orbison Records 1000 In Dreams - Greatest Hits. (all songs on this cd are rerecorded)

1963 BLUE BAYOU

(S) (2:27) CBS Special Products 44349 All-Time Greatest Hits Volume 2.
(S) (2:28) Rhino 71493 For The Lonely: 18 Greatest Hits.
(S) (2:27) CBS Special Products 45116 All-Time Greatest Hits.
(S) (2:25) CBS Special Products 46809 Legendary.
(S) (2:48) Virgin 90604 In Dreams: The Greatest Hits. (all selections on this cd are rerecorded)
(S) (2:25) CBS Special Products 21429 In Dreams.
(S) (2:26) Time-Life 2RNR-34 Rock 'N' Roll Era - Roy Orbison 1960-1965.
(S) (2:27) Columbia 67297 Super Hits.
(S) (2:49) Virgin 42350 Very Best Of. (rerecording)
(S) (2:27) Time-Life R857-12 The Heart Of Rock 'n' Roll 1962-1963.
(S) (2:30) DCC Compact Classics 1118 All-Time Greatest Hits. (gold disc)

(S) (2:48) Orbison Records 1000 In Dreams - Greatest Hits. (all songs on this cd are rerecorded)

1964 PRETTY PAPER

(S) (2:45) Rhino 70192 Christmas Classics.
(S) (2:44) CBS Special Products 44349 All-Time Greatest Hits Volume 2.
(S) (2:45) Rhino 71493 For The Lonely: 18 Greatest Hits.
(S) (2:44) CBS Special Products 45116 All-Time Greatest Hits.
(S) (2:45) CBS Special Products 46809 Legendary.
(S) (2:43) Time-Life 2RNR-34 Rock 'N' Roll Era - Roy Orbison 1960-1965.
(S) (2:44) Collectables 1512 and 2512 and 3512 and 4512 and 9612 Ultimate Christmas Album Vol. II.
(S) (2:43) Oglio 81570 The Coolest Christmas.
(M) (2:41) Virgin 42350 Very Best Of. (live)
(S) (2:43) Time-Life TCD-109B Country Christmas.
(S) (2:43) Time-Life R135-12 The Spirit Of Christmas.
(S) (2:46) DCC Compact Classics 1118 All-Time Greatest Hits. (gold disc)

1964 IT'S OVER

(S) (2:46) Rhino 71493 For The Lonely: 18 Greatest Hits.
(S) (2:46) CBS Special Products 44348 All-Time Greatest Hits Volume 1.
(S) (2:46) CBS Special Products 45116 All-Time Greatest Hits.
(S) (2:46) CBS Special Products 46809 Legendary.
(S) (2:50) Virgin 90604 In Dreams: The Greatest Hits. (all selections on this cd are rerecorded)
(S) (2:45) Time-Life 2RNR-34 Rock 'N' Roll Era - Roy Orbison 1960-1965.
(S) (2:46) Time-Life 2CLR-09 Classic Rock - 1964: The Beat Goes On.
(S) (2:46) Columbia 67297 Super Hits.
(S) (3:12) Virgin 42350 Very Best Of. (live)
(S) (2:45) Time-Life R857-09 The Heart Of Rock 'n' Roll 1964.
(S) (2:47) DCC Compact Classics 1118 All-Time Greatest Hits. (gold disc)
(S) (2:50) Orbison Records 1000 In Dreams - Greatest Hits. (all songs on this cd are rerecorded)

released as by ROY ORBISON and THE CANDY MEN:
1964 OH, PRETTY WOMAN

(S) (2:56) EMI 93492 O.S.T. Pretty Woman. (LP version)
(S) (2:56) CBS Special Products 46808 Rock Goes To The Movies Volume 5. (LP version)
(S) (2:56) CBS Special Products 44349 All-Time Greatest Hits Volume 2. (LP version)
(S) (2:55) Rhino 71493 For The Lonely: 18 Greatest Hits. (LP version)
(S) (2:55) CBS Special Products 45116 All-Time Greatest Hits. (LP version)
(M) (2:55) CBS Special Products 46809 Legendary. (45 version)
(S) (3:01) Virgin 90604 In Dreams: The Greatest Hits. (all selections on this cd are rerecorded)
(S) (2:56) JCI 3112 Pop Sixties. (LP version)
(S) (2:54) Time-Life 2RNR-10 Rock 'N' Roll Era - 1964. (LP version)
(S) (2:55) Time-Life 2RNR-34 Rock 'N' Roll Era - Roy Orbison 1960-1965. (LP version)
(S) (2:55) Time-Life 2CLR-16 Classic Rock - 1964: Shakin' All Over. (LP version)
(M) (2:55) Sony Music Special Products 66106 The Monument Story. (45 version)
(S) (2:55) Columbia 67297 Super Hits. (LP version)
(S) (3:00) Virgin 42350 Very Best Of. (rerecording)
(S) (2:55) Eclipse Music Group 64869 Rock 'n Roll Relix 1964-1965. (LP version)
(S) (2:55) Eclipse Music Group 64872 Rock 'n Roll Relix 1960-1969. (LP version)
(S) (2:56) DCC Compact Classics 1118 All-Time Greatest Hits. (gold disc; LP version)
(S) (3:01) Orbison Records 1000 In Dreams - Greatest Hits. (all songs on this cd are rerecorded)
(M) (2:55) Collectables 1515 and 2515 The Anniversary Album - The 60's. (45 version)

released as by ROY ORBISON:
1965 GOODNIGHT
- (S) (2:27) CBS Special Products 45113 Our Love Song.
- (S) (2:27) CBS Special Products 46809 Legendary.
- (S) (2:27) Time-Life 2RNR-34 Rock 'N' Roll Era - Roy Orbison 1960-1965.
- (S) (2:27) Risky Business 57472 Have A Nice Life/More Great Breakup Songs Of The 60's.

1965 RIDE AWAY
- (S) (3:27) Mercury 816555 45's On CD Volume 2.
- (S) (3:27) Polydor 839234 Singles Collection (1965-1973).
- (S) (3:27) Rhino 70711 Classic Roy Orbison (1965-1968).
- (S) (3:27) CBS Special Products 46809 Legendary.
- (S) (3:27) Special Music 847983 Ride Away.

1966 BREAKIN' UP IS BREAKIN' MY HEART
- (S) (2:06) Polydor 839234 Singles Collection (1965-1973).
- (S) (2:06) Rhino 70711 Classic Roy Orbison (1965-1968).
- (S) (2:06) CBS Special Products 46809 Legendary.
- (S) (2:06) Special Music 847983 Ride Away.

1966 TWINKLE TOES
- (S) (2:34) Polydor 839234 Singles Collection (1965-1973).
- (S) (2:34) Rhino 70711 Classic Roy Orbison (1965-1968).

1989 YOU GOT IT
- (S) (3:29) Virgin 91058 and 86103 Mystery Girl.
- (S) (3:28) Time-Life R988-30 Sounds Of The Eighties: The Rolling Stone Collection 1988-1989.
- (S) (3:29) Virgin 42350 Very Best Of.

ORCHESTRAL MANOEUVRES IN THE DARK
1985 SO IN LOVE
- (S) (3:28) Rhino 71978 New Wave Hits Of The 80's Vol. 15.
- (S) (3:27) A&M 5186 In The Dark: Best Of.
- (S) (3:28) A&M 3336 Crush.

1986 IF YOU LEAVE
- (S) (4:25) A&M 3293 O.S.T. Pretty In Pink.
- (S) (4:27) A&M 5186 In The Dark: Best Of.
- (S) (4:24) Rhino 72500 Modern Rock 1986 - Hang The DJ.
- (S) (4:25) JCI 3159 18 Modern Rock Classics From The 80's.
- (S) (4:26) Time-Life R988-15 Sounds Of The Eighties: The Mid 80's.

1986 (FOREVER) LIVE AND DIE
- (S) (3:34) A&M 5186 In The Dark: Best Of.
- (S) (3:36) A&M 5144 The Pacific Age.

1988 DREAMING
- (S) (3:53) A&M 5186 In The Dark: Best Of.

ORIGINAL CASTE
1970 ONE TIN SOLDIER

ORIGINAL CASUALS
1958 SO TOUGH
- (M) (2:14) MCA 31202 Vintage Music Volume 5.
- (M) (2:14) MCA 5804 Vintage Music Volumes 5 & 6.
- (M) (2:18) MCA 10666 Duke-Peacock's Greatest Hits.
- (M) (2:14) Time-Life 2RNR-33 Rock 'N' Roll Era - The 50's Last Dance.
- (M) (2:14) MCA Special Products 22179 Vintage Collectibles Volume 9.

ORIGINALS
1969 BABY, I'M FOR REAL
- (S) (3:16) Motown 6183 Hard To Find Motown Classics Volume 1.
- (S) (3:17) Rhino 70655 Billboard's Top R&B Hits Of 1969.
- (S) (3:17) Rhino 72006 Billboard's Top R&B Hits 1965-1969 Box Set.
- (S) (3:17) Motown 5462 Baby I'm For Real.
- (S) (3:18) Motown 5110 Motown Superstar Series Volume 10.
- (M) (3:17) Motown 6312 Hitsville USA.
- (S) (3:14) Time-Life RHD-13 Rhythm & Blues - 1969.
- (S) (3:12) Time-Life 2CLR-25 Classic Rock - On The Soul Side.
- (S) (3:17) Original Sound 8911 Art Laboe's Dedicated To You Vol. 2.
- (S) (3:17) Original Sound 4001 Art Laboe's 60 Killer Oldies.

- (S) (3:16) Right Stuff 27306 Slow Jams: The 60's Volume One.
- (S) (3:17) Thump 7010 Low Rider Oldies Volume 1.
- (S) (3:18) Polygram Special Markets 314520300 Motown Legends - Guy Groups.
- (S) (3:19) Motown 314530525 Motown Year By Year - 1969.
- (M) (3:17) Motown 314530569 Motown Milestones - Motown Love Songs.
- (M) (3:17) Thump 9947 Cruizin' To Motown.
- (S) (3:18) Motown 314530573 Baddest Love Jams Volume 2 - Fire And Desire.
- (S) (3:14) Time-Life R838-04 Solid Gold Soul - 1969.
- (S) (3:14) Repeat/Relativity 1609 Tell It Like It Is: #1 Soul Hits Of The 60's Volume 1.
- (S) (3:16) Motown 314530849 Motown 40 Forever.

1970 THE BELLS
- (S) (3:00) Motown 9105 and 5410 Motown Memories Volume 2.
- (S) (3:02) Motown 6183 Hard To Find Motown Classics Volume 1.
- (S) (3:04) Rhino 70782 Soul Hits Of The 70's Volume 2.
- (S) (3:04) Rhino 72028 Soul Hits Of The 70's Volumes 1-5 Box Set.
- (S) (2:58) Motown 5461 Portrait Of.
- (S) (3:01) Original Sound 9306 Dedicated To You Vol. 6.
- (S) (3:03) Motown 5110 Motown Superstar Series Volume 10.
- (M) (2:54) Motown 6312 Hitsville USA.
- (S) (3:00) Time-Life RHD-18 Rhythm & Blues - 1970.
- (S) (3:03) Thump 7020 Low Rider Oldies Volume II.
- (S) (3:02) Motown 314530544 Baddest Love Jams Volume 3: After The Dance.
- (S) (3:00) Time-Life R838-05 Solid Gold Soul - 1970.
- (S) (3:03) Time-Life R834-07 Body Talk - Hearts In Motion.

TONY ORLANDO (see also DAWN)
1961 HALFWAY TO PARADISE
- (M) (2:37) Era 5025 The Brill Building Sound.
- (S) (2:34) Collectables 5827 Bless You And Seventeen Other Great Hits.

1961 BLESS YOU
- (M) (2:16) Era 5025 The Brill Building Sound.
- (S) (2:07) Collectors' Choice 002 Teen Idols....For A Moment.
- (S) (2:07) Collectables 5827 Bless You And Seventeen Other Great Hits.

ORLEANS
1975 DANCE WITH ME
- (S) (3:19) Priority 8666 Kickin' Back/70's Greatest Rock Hits Volume 5. *(LP version)*
- (S) (3:19) Elektra 60909 Still The One. *(LP version)*
- (S) (2:59) Razor & Tie 4543 The '70s Preservation Society Presents: Easy '70s. *(45 version)*
- (S) (2:59) Rhino 71197 Super Hits Of The 70's Volume 17. *(45 version)*
- (S) (2:59) Time-Life SOD-08 Sounds Of The Seventies - 1975. *(45 version)*
- (S) (2:59) JCI 3146 1975 - Only Love - 1979. *(45 version)*
- (S) (2:59) Time-Life AM1-22 AM Gold - 1975. *(45 version)*
- (S) (2:58) Time-Life R834-10 Body Talk - From The Heart. *(45 version)*
- (S) (2:59) Rhino 72848 Dance With Me: Best Of. *(45 version)*

1976 STILL THE ONE
- (S) (3:52) Priority 7066 #1 Groups/70's Greatest Rock Hits Volume 12.
- (S) (3:53) Elektra 60909 Still The One.
- (S) (3:52) Rhino 71199 Super Hits Of The 70's Volume 19.
- (S) (3:53) Time-Life SOD-04 Sounds Of The Seventies - 1976.
- (S) (3:51) JCI 3131 1975 - Only Rock 'N Roll - 1979.
- (S) (3:52) Madacy Entertainment 1976 Rock On 1976.
- (S) (3:52) Rhino 72517 Mellow Rock Hits Of The 70's - Ventura Highway.
- (S) (3:52) Priority 50952 I Love Rock & Roll Volume 3: Hits Of The 70's.
- (S) (3:52) Eclipse Music Group 64895 Rock 'n Roll Relix 1976-1977.
- (S) (3:52) Eclipse Music Group 64897 Rock 'n Roll Relix 1970-1979.

ORLEANS (Continued)
- (S) (3:51) Time-Life AM1-23 AM Gold - 1976.
- (S) (3:49) Rhino 72848 Dance With Me: Best Of.
- (S) (3:52) Hip-O 40096 '70s Hit(s) Back Again.

1979 LOVE TAKES TIME
(45 length is (3:57); LP length is (4:02))
- (S) (3:58) Rhino 72299 Superhits Of The 70's Volume 25.
- (S) (3:58) Varese Sarabande 5706 Dick Bartley Presents Collector's Essentials: The 70's.
- (S) (4:16) Rhino 72848 Dance With Me: Best Of. *(neither the 45 or LP version)*
- (S) (3:56) K-Tel 3909 High Energy Volume 2.

ORLONS
1962 THE WAH WATUSI
1962 DON'T HANG UP
1963 SOUTH STREET
1963 NOT ME
1963 CROSS FIRE!

BENJAMIN ORR
1987 STAY THE NIGHT
- (S) (4:26) Elektra 60460 The Lace.
- (S) (4:25) Priority 53797 Best Of 80's Rock Volume 4.

ROBERT ELLIS ORRALL with CARLENE CARTER
1983 I COULDN'T SAY NO

JEFFREY OSBORNE
1983 ON THE WINGS OF LOVE
- (S) (4:01) A&M 3272 Jeffrey Osborne.
1983 DON'T YOU GET SO MAD
- (S) (3:51) A&M 3337 Stay With Me Tonight.
1984 STAY WITH ME TONIGHT
- (S) (4:58) A&M 3337 Stay With Me Tonight. *(LP version)*
1985 THE BORDERLINES
- (S) (5:27) A&M 5017 Don't Stop. *(LP version)*
1986 YOU SHOULD BE MINE (THE WOO WOO SONG)
(actual 45 time is (4:17) not (4:11) as stated on the record label)
- (S) (4:26) Sandstone 33052 and 5020 Cosmopolitan Volume 6. *(LP length)*
- (S) (4:26) DCC Compact Classics 084 Night Moves Volume 4. *(LP length)*
- (S) (4:25) A&M 5103 Emotional. *(LP length)*
released as by DIONNE WARWICK & JEFFREY OSBORNE:
1987 LOVE POWER
- (S) (4:31) JCI 2701 Slow Grooves.
- (S) (4:32) Arista 8446 Dionne Warwick - Reservations For Two.
- (S) (4:32) Arista 8540 Dionne Warwick - Greatest Hits 1979-1990.

JOAN OSBORNE
1996 ONE OF US
- (S) (5:20) Mercury 314526699 Relish.
- (S) (5:19) Grammy Recordings/Sony 67565 1996 Grammy Nominees.

OZZY OSBOURNE
released as by LITA FORD with OZZY OSBOURNE:
1989 CLOSE MY EYES FOREVER
- (S) (4:41) RCA 6397 Lita Ford.
- (S) (4:40) RCA 66037 Lita Ford - Best Of.
released as by OZZY OSBOURNE:
1992 MAMA, I'M COMING HOME
- (S) (4:11) Epic Associated 46795 and 67243 No More Tears.

DONNY OSMOND
1971 SWEET AND INNOCENT
- (M) (2:52) Curb 77510 Greatest Hits. *(45 version)*
- (M) (3:02) Curb 77787 Donny Osmond - 25 Hits. *(45 version)*
1971 GO AWAY LITTLE GIRL
- (S) (2:30) Curb 77510 Greatest Hits.
- (S) (2:29) Curb 77787 Donny Osmond - 25 Hits.

1972 HEY GIRL
- (S) (3:10) Curb 77510 Greatest Hits.
- (S) (3:10) Curb 77787 Donny Osmond - 25 Hits.
1972 PUPPY LOVE
- (S) (3:03) Curb 77510 Greatest Hits.
- (S) (3:02) Curb 77787 Donny Osmond - 25 Hits.
1972 TOO YOUNG
- (E) (3:05) Curb 77510 Greatest Hits.
- (E) (3:05) Curb 77787 Donny Osmond - 25 Hits.
1972 WHY
- (S) (2:42) Curb 77510 Greatest Hits.
- (S) (2:42) Curb 77787 Donny Osmond - 25 Hits.
1973 THE TWELFTH OF NEVER
- (S) (2:40) Curb 77510 Greatest Hits.
- (S) (2:40) Curb 77787 Donny Osmond - 25 Hits.
1973 A MILLION TO ONE
- (E) (2:58) Curb 77510 Greatest Hits.
- (S) (2:57) Curb 77787 Donny Osmond - 25 Hits.
1973 YOUNG LOVE
- (S) (2:29) Curb 77510 Greatest Hits.
- (S) (2:29) Curb 77787 Donny Osmond - 25 Hits.
1974 ARE YOU LONESOME TONIGHT
- (S) (3:07) Curb 77510 Greatest Hits.
- (S) (3:06) Curb 77787 Donny Osmond - 25 Hits.
1989 SOLDIER OF LOVE
- (S) (3:48) Curb 77651 Retro Rock Dance Hits. *(all selections on this cd are remixed with extra instrumentation added)*
- (S) (3:48) Rhino 71644 Billboard Top Hits - 1989.
- (S) (3:49) Capitol 92354 Donny Osmond.
- (S) (3:48) Curb 77674 Best Of.
- (S) (3:48) Priority 53795 Best Of 80's Rock Volume 3.
- (S) (3:48) Curb 77787 Donny Osmond - 25 Hits.
- (S) (3:49) Time-Life R988-13 Sounds Of The Eighties: 1989.
1989 SACRED EMOTION
- (S) (5:11) Capitol 92354 Donny Osmond. *(LP version)*
- (S) (5:08) Curb 77674 Best Of. *(LP version)*
- (S) (5:08) Curb 77787 Donny Osmond - 25 Hits. *(LP version)*
- (S) (5:08) Madacy Entertainment 1989 Rock On 1989. *(LP version)*
1990 MY LOVE IS A FIRE
- (S) (4:27) Capitol 94051 Eyes Don't Lie.
- (S) (4:26) Curb 77674 Best Of.

DONNY and MARIE OSMOND
1974 I'M LEAVING IT (ALL) UP TO YOU
- (S) (2:49) Curb 77610 Greatest Hits.
- (S) (2:51) Curb 77787 Donny Osmond - 25 Hits.
1975 MORNING SIDE OF THE MOUNTAIN
- (S) (3:01) Curb 77610 Greatest Hits.
- (S) (3:01) Curb 77787 Donny Osmond - 25 Hits.
1976 DEEP PURPLE
- (S) (2:45) Curb 77610 Greatest Hits.
- (S) (2:44) Curb 77787 Donny Osmond - 25 Hits.
released as by DONNY & MARIE:
1977 AIN'T NOTHING LIKE THE REAL THING
- (S) (2:19) Curb 77610 Greatest Hits.
1978 (YOU'RE MY) SOUL AND INSPIRATION
1978 ON THE SHELF
- (S) (3:39) Curb 77610 Greatest Hits.

LITTLE JIMMY OSMOND
1972 LONG HAIRED LOVER FROM LIVERPOOL
- (M) (2:12) Rhino 71228 Yesterday's Heroes: '70's Teen Idols.

MARIE OSMOND
1973 PAPER ROSES
- (S) (2:36) Curb 77263 Best Of. *(rerecording)*
- (M) (2:37) Curb 77793 Marie Osmond - 25 Hits.
- (M) (2:38) Time-Life R808-04 Classic Country 1970-1974.
1975 WHO'S SORRY NOW

OSMONDS
1971 ONE BAD APPLE
    (S)   (2:43)   Rhino 70632 Billboard's Top Rock & Roll Hits Of 1971.
    (S)   (2:43)   Rhino 72005 Billboard's Top Rock & Roll Hits 1968-1972 Box Set.
    (S)   (2:43)   Curb 77529 Osmond Brothers Greatest Hits.
    (S)   (2:42)   Razor & Tie 22505 More Fabulous 70's Volume 2.
    (S)   (2:43)   Curb 77788 Osmonds - 21 Hits.
1971 DOUBLE LOVIN'
    (S)   (2:32)   Curb 77529 Osmond Brothers Greatest Hits.
    (S)   (2:32)   Curb 77788 Osmonds - 21 Hits.
1971 YO-YO
    (S)   (3:12)   Curb 77529 Osmond Brothers Greatest Hits. *(LP version)*
    (S)   (3:12)   Curb 77788 Osmonds - 21 Hits. *(LP version)*
1972 DOWN BY THE LAZY RIVER
    (S)   (2:41)   Curb 77529 Osmond Brothers Greatest Hits.
    (S)   (2:41)   Curb 77788 Osmonds - 21 Hits.
1972 HOLD HER TIGHT
    (S)   (3:13)   Curb 77529 Osmond Brothers Greatest Hits.
    (S)   (3:13)   Curb 77788 Osmonds - 21 Hits.
1972 CRAZY HORSES
    (S)   (2:28)   Curb 77529 Osmond Brothers Greatest Hits.
    (S)   (2:27)   Curb 77788 Osmonds - 21 Hits.
    (S)   (3:03)   Curb 77934 Absolute Dance Hits: How Do I Live. *(all songs on this cd are remixed)*
1973 GOIN' HOME
    (S)   (2:27)   Curb 77529 Osmond Brothers Greatest Hits.
    (S)   (2:27)   Curb 77788 Osmonds - 21 Hits.
1973 LET ME IN
    (S)   (3:38)   Curb 77529 Osmond Brothers Greatest Hits.
    (S)   (3:37)   Curb 77788 Osmonds - 21 Hits.
1974 LOVE ME FOR A REASON
    (S)   (4:00)   Curb 77529 Osmond Brothers Greatest Hits. *(LP length)*
    (S)   (3:59)   Curb 77788 Osmonds - 21 Hits. *(LP length)*
1975 THE PROUD ONE
    (S)   (3:02)   Curb 77529 Osmond Brothers Greatest Hits.
    (S)   (3:02)   Curb 77788 Osmonds - 21 Hits.

GILBERT O'SULLIVAN
1972 ALONE AGAIN (NATURALLY)
    (S)   (3:37)   Rhino 70928 Super Hits Of The 70's Volume 8.
    (S)   (3:38)   Rhino 70633 Billboard's Top Rock & Roll Hits Of 1972.
    (S)   (3:38)   Rhino 72005 Billboard's Top Rock & Roll Hits 1968-1972 Box Set.
    (S)   (3:36)   Priority 8669 Hits/70's Greatest Rock Hits Volume 9.
    (S)   (3:36)   Rhino 70560 Best Of.
    (S)   (3:36)   Rhino 71209 70's Smash Hits Volume 5.
    (S)   (3:37)   Razor & Tie 22505 More Fabulous 70's Volume 2.
    (S)   (3:36)   Time-Life SUD-11 Superhits - 1972.
    (S)   (3:36)   Time-Life AM1-07 AM Gold - 1972.
    (S)   (3:36)   Flashback 72686 '70s Radio Hits Volume 6.
    (S)   (3:36)   Time-Life R814-03 Love Songs.
1972 CLAIR
    (S)   (2:59)   Rhino 70929 Super Hits Of The 70's Volume 9.
    (S)   (3:00)   Rhino 70560 Best Of.
    (S)   (3:00)   Hollywood 62134 O.S.T. Air Bud.
1973 OUT OF THE QUESTION
    (S)   (2:56)   Rhino 70560 Best Of.
1973 GET DOWN
    (S)   (2:39)   Rhino 70758 Super Hits Of The 70's Volume 11.
    (S)   (2:39)   Rhino 70560 Best Of.
1973 OOH BABY
    (S)   (3:13)   Rhino 70560 Best Of.

OTHER ONES
1987 HOLIDAY
    (S)   (3:42)   Priority 53768 Rock Of The 80's Volume 14.

JOHNNY OTIS SHOW
1958 WILLIE AND THE HAND JIVE
    (M)   (2:34)   Rhino 70644 Billboard's Top R&B Hits Of 1958.

    (M)   (2:35)   Rhino 70719 Legends Of Guitar - Rock; The 50's.
    (E)   (2:34)   EMI 90614 Non Stop Party Rock.
    (M)   (2:34)   Capitol 48993 Spuds Mackenzie's Party Faves.
    (E)   (2:32)   Curb 77323 All Time Greatest Hits Of Rock 'N' Roll.
    (M)   (2:34)   Capitol 92858 The Capitol Years.
    (M)   (2:33)   Capitol 98138 Spring Break Volume 1.
    (M)   (2:34)   Rhino 70291 Bo Diddley Beats.
    (E)   (2:34)   Time-Life 2RNR-21 Rock 'N' Roll Era - 1958 Still Rockin'.
    (M)   (2:32)   Time-Life RHD-16 Rhythm & Blues - 1958.
    (M)   (2:33)   Time-Life R962-01 History Of Rock 'N' Roll: Rock 'N' Roll Classics 1957-1959.
    (M)   (2:34)   Motown 6763 Rites Of Rhythm & Blues Volume 2.
    (M)   (2:33)   Music For Little People 42581 A Child's Celebration Of Rock 'N' Roll.
    (S)   (2:36)   Cold Front 6245 Greatest Sports Rock And Jams. *(all selections on this cd are segued together; rerecording)*
    (M)   (2:33)   Nick At Nite/550 Music 63407 Dancing At The Nick At Niteclub.
    (M)   (2:32)   Time-Life R838-22 Solid Gold Soul 1958.
    (S)   (2:37)   K-Tel 4066 K-Tel's Original Party Music Vol. 2. *(rerecording)*

OTIS & CARLA (OTIS REDDING & CARLA THOMAS)
1967 TRAMP
    (M)   (2:59)   Atlantic Group 88218 Complete Stax/Volt Singles.
    (S)   (2:59)   Atlantic 81762 The Otis Redding Story.
    (S)   (2:59)   Atco 80254 Otis Redding - The Dock Of The Bay.
    (S)   (2:59)   Atlantic 82256 Otis Redding & Carla Thomas: King & Queen.
    (S)   (2:57)   Warner Special Products 27608 Ultimate Otis Redding.
    (S)   (2:59)   Atlantic 82305 Atlantic Rhythm And Blues 1947-1974 Box Set.
    (M)   (2:58)   Rhino 71147 Otis Redding - Very Best Of.
    (M)   (2:59)   Rhino 71439 The Definitive Otis Redding.
    (M)   (2:50)   Time-Life RHD-10 Rhythm & Blues - 1967.
    (S)   (2:56)   Time-Life 2CLR-15 Classic Rock - 1967: Shakin' All Over.
    (M)   (2:59)   Rhino 71754 and 72831 Phat Trax: The Best Of Old School Volume 3.
    (M)   (2:59)   Rhino 71633 Gee Whiz - Best Of Carla Thomas.
    (M)   (2:50)   Time-Life R838-02 Solid Gold Soul - 1967.
    (M)   (3:00)   Flashback 72669 Carla Thomas - Gee Whiz And Other Hits.
    (M)   (3:00)   Flashback 72083 Kings And Queens Of Soul Box Set.
    (M)   (2:59)   Flashback 72897 25 Years Of R&B - 1967.
    (M)   (2:59)   Rhino 72962 Ultimate '60s Soul Sensations.
1967 KNOCK ON WOOD
    (M)   (2:49)   Atlantic Group 88218 Complete Stax/Volt Singles.
    (S)   (2:50)   Atlantic 82256 Otis Redding & Carla Thomas: King & Queen.
    (S)   (2:50)   Atlantic 81762 The Otis Redding Story.
    (M)   (2:49)   Flashback 72669 Carla Thomas - Gee Whiz And Other Hits.
    (M)   (2:49)   Flashback 72083 Kings And Queens Of Soul Box Set.
    (M)   (2:49)   Rhino 71930 Otis Redding - Very Best Of Vol. 2.

OUTFIELD
1986 YOUR LOVE
    (S)   (3:35)   Priority 53768 Rock Of The 80's Volume 14.
    (S)   (3:36)   Risky Business 57833 Read The Hits/Best Of The 80's.
    (S)   (3:36)   Columbia 40027 Play Deep.
    (S)   (3:42)   Legacy 64943 Big Innings: Best Of.
    (S)   (3:38)   Time-Life R988-21 Sounds Of The Eighties: 1986-1989.
1986 ALL THE LOVE IN THE WORLD
    (S)   (3:31)   Columbia 40027 Play Deep.
    (S)   (3:30)   Legacy 64943 Big Innings: Best Of.
1987 SINCE YOU'VE BEEN GONE
(actual 45 time is (4:10) not (3:58) as stated on the record label)
    (S)   (4:43)   Columbia 40619 Bangin'. *(LP length)*
    (S)   (4:40)   Risky Business 66390 Hazy Shade Of 80's. *(LP length)*
    (S)   (4:42)   Legacy 64943 Big Innings: Best Of. *(LP length)*

OUTFIELD (Continued)
1989 THE VOICES OF BABYLON
- (S) (3:30) Columbia 44449 Voices Of Babylon.
- (S) (3:30) Legacy 64943 Big Innings: Best Of.

1991 FOR YOU
- (S) (4:26) MCA 10111 Diamond Days.
- (S) (4:26) Legacy 64943 Big Innings: Best Of.

1992 CLOSER TO ME
- (S) (3:16) MCA 10476 Rockeye.
- (S) (3:15) Legacy 64943 Big Innings: Best Of.

OUTKAST
1994 PLAYER'S BALL
- (S) (4:21) LaFace 26010 Southernplayalisticadillacmuzik.

1996 ELEVATORS (ME & YOU)
- (S) (4:24) LaFace 26029 and 26032 Atliens.
- (S) (4:19) Def Jam 314534746 Yo! MTV Raps Compilation.
- (S) (4:00) Polygram TV 314536204 The Source Presents Hip Hop Hits Volume 1.

1997 ATLIENS
- (S) (3:50) LaFace 26029 and 26032 Atliens.

OUTLAWS
1975 THERE GOES ANOTHER LOVE SONG
- (S) (3:02) Priority 8665 Southern Comfort/70's Greatest Rock Hits Volume 4.
- (S) (3:03) Arista 8319 Greatest Hits.
- (S) (3:04) Time-Life SOD-22 Sounds Of The Seventies - Seventies Top Forty.
- (S) (3:03) K-Tel 6045 Southern Fried Rock.
- (S) (3:03) Arista 18936 Best Of.....Green Grass & High Tides.

1981 (GHOST) RIDERS IN THE SKY
- (S) (3:35) Priority 8663 The South Rules/70's Greatest Rock Hits Volume 2. *(45 version)*
- (S) (7:01) Arista 8319 Greatest Hits. *(live)*
- (S) (3:36) Time-Life R968-04 Guitar Rock 1980-1981. *(45 version)*
- (S) (5:50) Rebound 314520256 Best Of Southern Rock. *(LP version)*
- (S) (4:08) K-Tel 3510 Platinum Rock Volume 2. *(:32 longer than the 45 version)*
- (S) (4:10) DCC Compact Classics 139 Rock The First Volume 9. *(:34 longer than the 45 version)*
- (S) (5:51) Arista 18936 Best Of.....Green Grass & High Tides. *(LP version)*
- (S) (4:06) K-Tel 3972 Southern Rockin' Rebels: The South's Gone And Done It. *(:30 longer than the 45 version)*
- (S) (4:08) K-Tel 3997 Arena Rock - The 80's. *(:32 longer than the 45 version)*

OUTSIDERS
1966 TIME WON'T LET ME
- (S) (2:48) EMI 90614 Non-Stop Party Rock.
- (S) (2:48) Capitol 48993 Spuds Mackenzie's Party Faves.
- (M) (2:48) K-Tel 839 Battle Of The Bands Volume 2. *(truncated fade)*
- (S) (3:01) Capitol 94076 Capitol Collector's Series. *(includes a :02 countoff; :10 longer than the 45 or LP)*
- (S) (3:01) Capitol 98138 Spring Break Volume 1. *(includes a :02 countoff; :10 longer than the 45 or LP)*
- (S) (2:59) Capitol 98665 When AM Was King. *(:10 longer than the 45 or LP)*
- (S) (2:45) Time-Life 2CLR-07 Classic Rock - 1966: The Beat Goes On. *(drum introduction missing)*
- (S) (2:58) JCI 3167 #1 Radio Hits 1965 - Only Rock 'n Roll - 1969. *(:09 longer than the 45 or LP)*
- (S) (2:47) Right Stuff 53319 Hot Rod Rock Volume 4: Hot Rod Rebels.
- (S) (3:01) Collectables 5686 Collectors Series. *(includes a :02 countoff; :10 longer than the 45 or LP)*

1966 GIRL IN LOVE
- (S) (3:18) Capitol 94076 Capitol Collector's Series.
- (S) (3:18) Collectables 5686 Collectors Series.

1966 RESPECTABLE
- (S) (2:00) Capitol 94076 Capitol Collector's Series.
- (S) (2:00) Capitol 98139 Spring Break Volume 2.
- (S) (2:00) Collectables 5686 Collectors Series.

1966 HELP ME GIRL
- (S) (2:45) Capitol 94076 Capitol Collector's Series.
- (S) (2:45) Collectables 5686 Collectors Series.

REG OWEN
1959 MANHATTAN SPIRITUAL

BUCK OWENS
1965 I'VE GOT A TIGER BY THE TAIL
- (S) (2:09) Rhino 70686 Billboard's Top Country Hits Of 1965.
- (S) (2:09) Curb 77342 All-Time Greatest Hits.
- (S) (2:11) Rhino 71016 The Buck Owens Collection.
- (S) (2:08) Time-Life CTD-10 Country USA - 1965. *(timing index is off by :01 on all tracks of this cd)*
- (S) (2:11) Rhino 71816 Very Best Of Volume 1.
- (S) (2:09) K-Tel 3110 Country Music Classics Volume XVIII.
- (S) (2:10) Sundazed 6047 I've Got A Tiger By The Tail.
- (S) (2:10) JCI 3154 1965 - Only Country - 1969.
- (S) (2:09) Time-Life R990-18 Buck Owens - Legendary Country Singers.

DONNIE OWENS
1958 NEED YOU
- (M) (2:15) Time-Life R857-16 The Heart Of Rock 'n' Roll The Late '50s.

OXO
1983 WHIRLY GIRL
- (S) (2:55) K-Tel 3262 The 80's Video Stars.
- (S) (2:56) Rhino 71701 New Wave Hits Of The 80's Vol. 8.
- (S) (2:56) Priority 53797 Best Of 80's Rock Volume 4.
- (S) (2:56) Geffen 25151 Geffen Vintage 80s Vol. II.
- (S) (2:56) Intersound 9521 Retro Lunch Box - Squeeze The Cheese.
- (S) (2:56) Simitar 55612 The Number One's: The '80s.

OZARK MOUNTAIN DAREDEVILS
1974 IF YOU WANNA GET TO HEAVEN
- (S) (3:02) Priority 7995 Country's Greatest Hits: Southern Country Rock Volume 2.
- (S) (3:03) A&M 3110 Ozark Mountain Daredevils.
- (S) (3:02) Priority 8663 The South Rules/70's Greatest Rock Hits Volume 2.
- (S) (3:04) A&M 3202 The Best.
- (S) (3:04) K-Tel 6045 Southern Fried Rock.
- (S) (3:02) K-Tel 6137 Peaceful Easy Feeling - The Best Of Country Rock.
- (S) (3:03) Rebound 314520256 Best Of Southern Rock.
- (S) (3:04) Rebound 314520247 Class Reunion 1974.
- (S) (3:03) K-Tel 3972 Southern Rockin' Rebels: The South's Gone And Done It.

1975 JACKIE BLUE
- (S) (4:07) Priority 8665 Southern Comfort/70's Greatest Rock Hits Volume 4. *(LP version)*
- (S) (3:34) Rhino 70670 Billboard Top Hits - 1975. *(:18 longer than the 45 version)*
- (S) (3:34) Rhino 70761 Super Hits Of The 70's Volume 14. *(:18 longer than the 45 version)*
- (S) (3:34) Rhino 70586 Rebel Rousers: Southern Rock Classics. *(:18 longer than the 45 version)*
- (S) (4:08) A&M 3202 The Best. *(LP version)*
- (S) (3:33) Razor & Tie 22505 More Fabulous 70's Volume 2. *(:18 longer than the 45 version)*
- (S) (3:34) Time-Life SOD-08 Sounds Of The Seventies - 1975. *(:19 longer than the 45 version)*
- (S) (4:08) Rebound 314520406 The Roots Of Rock: Southern Rock. *(LP version)*
- (S) (3:34) Time-Life AM1-22 AM Gold - 1975. *(:19 longer than the 45 version)*
- (S) (4:03) TVT 8110 O.S.T. All Over Me. *(LP version)*
- (S) (4:08) Critique 15467 Fast Cars And Southern Stars. *(LP version)*
- (S) (4:09) Rebound 314520475 The Roots Of Rock: Southern Rock. *(LP version)*

PABLO CRUISE
1977 WHATCHA GONNA DO?
- (S) (4:18) Priority 8667 FM Hits/70's Greatest Rock Hits Volume 6. *(LP version)*
- (S) (4:16) A&M 3236 A Place In The Sun. *(LP version)*
- (S) (4:19) A&M 2524 Classics Volume 26. *(LP version)*
- (S) (4:15) Time-Life SOD-17 Sounds Of The Seventies - 1977: Take Two. *(LP version)*

1978 LOVE WILL FIND A WAY
- (S) (4:10) Priority 8666 Kickin' Back/70's Greatest Rock Hits Volume 5. *(LP version)*
- (S) (4:10) A&M 3198 Worlds Away. *(LP version)*
- (S) (4:11) A&M 2524 Classics Volume 26. *(LP version)*
- (S) (3:57) Time-Life SOD-35 Sounds Of The Seventies - AM Nuggets. *(edit of the LP version)*
- (S) (4:09) Rebound 314520372 The Roots Of Rock: Soft Rock. *(LP version)*
- (S) (4:12) Rhino 72517 Mellow Rock Hits Of The 70's - Ventura Highway. *(LP version)*
- (S) (4:12) Time-Life R834-20 Body Talk - Heart And Soul. *(LP version)*
- (S) (3:57) Time-Life AM1-25 AM Gold - 1978. *(edit of the LP version)*

1978 DON'T WANT TO LIVE WITHOUT IT
- (S) (4:35) A&M 3198 Worlds Away. *(LP version)*
- (S) (4:36) A&M 2524 Classics Volume 26. *(LP version)*

1979 I WANT YOU TONIGHT
1981 COOL LOVE
- (S) (3:52) A&M 2524 Classics Volume 26.
- (S) (3:51) Rebound 314520361 Class Reunion '81.

PACIFIC GAS & ELECTRIC
1970 ARE YOU READY?
(dj copies of this 45 ran (2:40) and (5:47); commercial copies were all (5:47))
- (S) (5:47) Rhino 70782 Soul Hits Of The 70's Volume 2.
- (S) (5:47) Rhino 72028 Soul Hits Of The 70's Volumes 1-5 Box Set.
- (S) (5:46) Columbia/Legacy 46160 Rock Artifacts Volume 1.
- (S) (5:45) Sandstone 33002 Reelin' In The Years Volume 3.
- (S) (5:45) DCC Compact Classics 064 Rock Of The 70's Volume Three.
- (S) (5:48) Time-Life SOD-37 Sounds Of The Seventies - AM Heavy Hits.
- (S) (5:45) Time-Life R968-11 Guitar Rock - The Early '70s.
- (S) (2:42) Varese Sarabande 5706 Dick Bartley Presents Collector's Essentials: The 70's. *(this is the dj 45 edit)*
- (S) (5:22) Collectables 5860 Are You Ready/Pacific Gas And Electric. *(:25 edited off the ending)*

PACKERS
1965 HOLE IN THE WALL
- (M) (2:49) Hip-O 40008 Soulful Grooves - R&B Instrumental Classics Volume 2. *(sounds like it was mastered from vinyl)*

MARTIN PAGE
1995 IN THE HOUSE OF STONE AND LIGHT
- (S) (4:58) Mercury 314522104 In The House Of Stone And Light.

PATTI PAGE
1956 ALLEGHENY MOON
- (M) (2:50) Mercury 510434 The Mercury Years Volume 2.
- (S) (2:56) Columbia 9326 Greatest Hits. *(rerecording)*

- (M) (2:51) Time-Life HPD-15 Your Hit Parade - 1956.
- (M) (2:50) Polygram Special Markets 314520267 Hits To Remember.
- (M) (2:50) Mercury 826255 Golden Hits.
- (S) (2:46) Curb 77749 Greatest Songs. *(all selections on this cd are rerecorded)*
- (M) (2:50) JCI 7021 Those Wonderful Years - April Love.
- (M) (2:50) Polygram Special Markets 314520404 Golden Greats.
- (M) (2:50) Mercury 314534720 A Golden Celebration.

1956 MAMA FROM THE TRAIN
- (M) (2:50) Mercury 510434 The Mercury Years Volume 2.
- (M) (2:51) Time-Life HPD-25 Your Hit Parade - The 50's.
- (M) (2:50) Polygram Special Markets 314520404 Golden Greats.
- (M) (2:50) Mercury 314534720 A Golden Celebration.

1957 A POOR MAN'S ROSES (OR A RICH MAN'S GOLD)
- (M) (2:28) Mercury 510434 The Mercury Years Volume 2.
- (M) (2:28) Polygram Special Markets 314520404 Golden Greats.

1957 OLD CAPE COD
- (M) (2:34) Mercury 510434 The Mercury Years Volume 2.
- (S) (3:08) Columbia 9326 Greatest Hits. *(rerecording)*
- (S) (3:06) Columbia 44401 16 Most Requested Songs. *(rerecording)*
- (M) (2:34) Rhino 71252 Sentimental Journey: Pop Vocal Classics Volume 4 (1954-1959).
- (M) (2:34) Rhino 72034 Sentimental Journey Pop Vocal Classics Volumes 1-4 Box Set.
- (M) (2:34) Time-Life HPD-17 Your Hit Parade - 1957.
- (M) (2:34) Mercury 826255 Golden Hits.
- (S) (2:47) Curb 77749 Greatest Songs. *(all selections on this cd are rerecorded)*
- (M) (2:34) Polygram Special Markets 314520404 Golden Greats.
- (M) (2:34) Mercury 314534720 A Golden Celebration.

1957 I'LL REMEMBER TODAY
- (M) (2:39) Mercury 510434 The Mercury Years Volume 2.
- (M) (2:40) Polygram Special Markets 314520404 Golden Greats.
- (M) (2:39) Mercury 314534720 A Golden Celebration.

1958 BELONGING TO SOMEONE
- (M) (2:06) Time-Life R974-09 Many Moods Of Romance - True Love.

1958 ANOTHER TIME, ANOTHER PLACE
- (M) (2:27) Polygram Special Markets 314520404 Golden Greats.

1958 LEFT RIGHT OUT OF YOUR HEART
- (S) (2:18) Mercury 510434 The Mercury Years Volume 2.
- (M) (2:18) Time-Life HPD-23 Your Hit Parade - The Late 50's.
- (M) (2:13) Curb 77749 Greatest Songs. *(all selections on this cd are rerecorded)*
- (S) (2:18) Polygram Special Markets 314520404 Golden Greats.
- (S) (2:17) Mercury 314534720 A Golden Celebration.

1958 FIBBIN'
1959 TRUST IN ME
1960 ONE OF US (WILL WEEP TONIGHT)
- (S) (2:31) Mercury 510434 The Mercury Years Volume 2.
- (S) (2:30) Mercury 314534720 A Golden Celebration.

1962 GO ON HOME
- (S) (2:29) Mercury 314534720 A Golden Celebration.

1962 MOST PEOPLE GET MARRIED
- (S) (2:03) Mercury 510434 The Mercury Years Volume 2.

1965 HUSH, HUSH, SWEET CHARLOTTE
- (S) (2:31) Columbia 44401 16 Most Requested Songs.
- (S) (2:30) Time-Life HPD-32 Your Hit Parade - Into The 60's.
- (S) (2:30) Curb 77749 Greatest Songs. *(all selections on this cd are rerecorded)*
- (S) (2:30) Rhino 72423 Billboard Top Movie Hits - 1960s.
- (S) (2:31) Polygram Special Markets 314520404 Golden Greats.

TOMMY PAGE
1989 A SHOULDER TO CRY ON
    (S) (3:22) Sire 25740 Tommy Page.
1990 I'LL BE YOUR EVERYTHING
    (S) (4:06) Sire 26148 Paintings In My Mind.
1990 WHEN I DREAM OF YOU
    (S) (4:06) Sire 26148 Paintings In My Mind.

KEVIN PAIGE
1989 DON'T SHUT ME OUT
    (S) (3:51) Chrysalis 21683 Kevin Paige.
1990 ANYTHING I WANT
    (S) (4:45) Chrysalis 21683 Kevin Paige.

ROBERT PALMER
1978 EVERY KINDA PEOPLE
    (S) (3:46) Island 314510345 Addictions Volume 2. *(rerecording)*
    (S) (3:15) Island 90494 and 422842592 Double Fun.
    (S) (3:23) Island 91318 and 422842301 Addictions Volume 1. *(remixed)*
    (S) (3:19) Guardian 55312 Very Best Of. *(remixed)*
    (S) (3:22) Rebound 314520437 Classic Rock - 70's. *(remixed)*
    (S) (4:45) Rebound 314520492 Class Reunion '78. *(remixed)*
1979 BAD CASE OF LOVING YOU (DOCTOR, DOCTOR)
    (S) (3:11) Island 90089 and 422842354 Secrets.
    (S) (3:10) Island 91318 and 422842301 Addictions Volume 1. *(remixed)*
    (S) (3:11) Time-Life R968-02 Guitar Rock 1978-1979.
    (S) (3:09) Guardian 55312 Very Best Of. *(remixed)*
    (S) (3:10) Hollywood 62123 More Music From The Motion Picture "Romy And Michele's High School Reunion". *(remixed)*
    (S) (3:11) K-Tel 3904 The Rock Album Volume 1.
    (S) (3:10) Simitar 55582 The Number One's: Rock It Up. *(remixed)*
    (S) (3:10) Priority 53139 The Best Of 70's: Rock Chart Toppers. *(remixed)*
1986 ADDICTED TO LOVE
    (S) (3:54) Time-Life R105-40 Rock Dreams. *(neither the 45 or LP version)*
    (S) (4:24) Island 91318 and 422842301 Addictions Volume I. *(neither the 45 or LP version)*
    (S) (6:02) Island 90471 and 422826463 Riptide. *(LP version)*
    (S) (3:54) Island 90684 and 842901 The Island Story. *(neither the 45 or LP version)*
    (S) (6:02) Rhino 72133 Frat Rock: The 80's. *(LP version)*
    (S) (4:01) Time-Life R988-04 Sounds Of The Eighties: 1986. *(45 version)*
    (S) (5:17) Guardian 55312 Very Best Of. *(1997 rerecording)*
    (S) (4:23) Guardian 55312 Very Best Of. *(neither the 45 or LP version)*
    (S) (4:24) Rebound 314520434 Classic Rock - 80's. *(neither the 45 or LP version)*
    (S) (4:23) Hip-O 40080 Essential '80s: 1985-1989. *(neither the 45 or LP version)*
1986 HYPERACTIVE
    (S) (5:09) Island 90471 and 422826463 Riptide. *(LP version)*
1986 I DIDN'T MEAN TO TURN YOU ON
    (S) (3:43) EMI 91419 MTV, BET, VH-1 Power Players.
    (S) (3:42) Columbia 44381 Heart Of Rock.
    (S) (3:35) Island 314510345 Addictions Volume 2.
    (S) (3:43) Island 90471 and 422826463 Riptide.
    (S) (3:35) Time-Life R988-01 Sounds Of The Eighties: The Rockin' Eighties.
    (S) (3:35) Guardian 55312 Very Best Of.
1988 SIMPLY IRRESISTIBLE
    (S) (4:13) Island 91318 and 422842301 Addictions Volume I.
    (S) (4:14) EMI Manhattan 48057 Heavy Nova.
    (S) (4:14) Time-Life R988-10 Sounds Of The 80's: 1988.
    (S) (4:14) Madacy Entertainment 1988 Rock On 1988.
    (S) (4:11) Guardian 55312 Very Best Of.
    (S) (4:13) Priority 50953 I Love Rock & Roll Volume 4: Hits Of The 80's.

1988 EARLY IN THE MORNING
    (S) (4:40) EMI Manhattan 48057 Heavy Nova. *(LP version)*
1991 YOU'RE AMAZING
    (S) (3:48) EMI 93935 Don't Explain.
1991 MERCY MERCY ME (THE ECOLOGY)/I WANT YOU
    (S) (5:56) Sandstone 33052 and 5020 Cosmopolitan Volume 6.
    (S) (5:56) DCC Compact Classics 084 Night Moves Volume 4.
    (S) (5:57) EMI 93935 Don't Explain.
    (S) (5:50) Guardian 55312 Very Best Of.

PAPERBOY
1993 DITTY
    (S) (4:01) Next Plateau 162351012 The Nine Yards.
    (S) (3:59) Rebound 314520360 Major Flavas Rap Classics.
    (S) (3:57) Thump 9951 Power 106 10th Anniversary Collection. *(all songs on this cd are segued together)*
    (S) (4:01) Rhino 72734 Latin Lingo: Hip-Hop From La Raza, Vol. 2.

PAPER LACE
1974 THE NIGHT CHICAGO DIED
    (S) (3:29) Rhino 70760 Super Hits Of The 70's Volume 13.
    (S) (3:28) Razor & Tie 21640 Those Fabulous 70's.
    (S) (3:29) Time-Life SOD-31 Sounds Of The Seventies - AM Top Twenty.
    (S) (3:29) Rebound 314520247 Class Reunion 1974.
    (S) (3:28) Special Music/Essex 5036 Prom Night - The 70's.
    (S) (3:28) Special Music 5039 Great Britons! Volume One.
    (S) (3:29) Time-Life AM1-21 AM Gold - 1974.
    (S) (3:29) Rhino 75233 '70s Party (Killers) Classics.

PARADE
1967 SUNSHINE GIRL
    (S) (2:43) Rhino 75777 More Nuggets.
    (M) (2:43) Rhino 71065 Summer Of Love Volume 1.
    (S) (2:38) Time-Life 2CLR-29 Classic Rock - Bubblegum, Garage And Pop Nuggets.

PARADONS
1960 DIAMONDS AND PEARLS
    (M) (2:14) DCC Compact Classics 031 Back Seat Jams.
    (E) (2:16) Original Sound 8855 Oldies But Goodies Vol. 5. *(this compact disc uses the "Waring - fds" noise reduction process; ambient background noise throughout the disc)*
    (E) (2:16) Original Sound 2222 Oldies But Goodies Volumes 3,5,11,14 and 15 Box Set. *(this box set uses the "Waring - fds" noise reduction process; ambient background noise throughout the song)*
    (E) (2:16) Original Sound 2500 Oldies But Goodies Volumes 1-15 Box Set. *(this box set uses the "Waring - fds" noise reduction process; ambient background noise throughout the song)*
    (E) (2:15) Original Sound CDGO-12 Golden Oldies Volume 12.
    (S) (2:15) Collectables 5068 History Of Rock Volume 8.
    (S) (2:15) Time-Life 2RNR-22 Rock 'N' Roll Era - 1960 Still Rockin'.
    (S) (2:14) Collectables 2607 WCBS-FM For Lovers Only Vol. 3.
    (S) (2:15) Collectables 2603 WCBS-FM Jukebox Giants Vol. 1.
    (S) (2:15) Collectables 2501 WCBS-FM History Of Rock - The 60's Part 2.
    (S) (2:15) Collectables 4501 History Of Rock/The 60s Part Two.
    (S) (2:14) Rhino 72507 Doo Wop Box II.
    (M) (2:14) Time-Life R857-14 The Heart Of Rock 'n' Roll 1960-1961 Take Two.
    (S) (2:13) Rhino 72869 Brown Eyed Soul Vol. 2.

PARIS SISTERS
1961 I LOVE HOW YOU LOVE ME
    (M) (2:05)   Rhino 70989 Best Of The Girl Groups Volume 2.
    (M) (2:04)   Abkco 7118 Phil Spector/Back To Mono (1958-1969).
    (E) (2:04)   Original Sound 8857 Oldies But Goodies Vol. 7. *(this compact disc uses the "Waring - fds" noise reduction process)*
    (E) (2:04)   Original Sound 2223 Oldies But Goodies Volumes 2,7,9,12 and 13 Box Set. *(this box set uses the "Waring - fds" noise reduction process)*
    (E) (2:04)   Original Sound 2500 Oldies But Goodies Volumes 1-15 Box Set. *(this box set uses the "Waring - fds" noise reduction process)*
    (M) (2:04)   Era 5025 The Brill Building Sound.
    (M) (2:05)   Time-Life 2RNR-18 Rock 'N' Roll Era - 1961 Still Rockin'.
    (M) (2:05)   Time-Life R962-08 History Of Rock 'N' Roll: Sound Of The City 1959-1965.
    (M) (2:03)   LaserLight 12320 Love Songs.
    (M) (2:05)   Time-Life R857-10 The Heart Of Rock 'n' Roll 1960-1961.
    (M) (2:05)   Time-Life R857-21 The Heart Of Rock 'n' Roll Slow Dancing Classics.

1962 HE KNOWS I LOVE HIM TOO MUCH

FESS PARKER
1955 BALLAD OF DAVY CROCKETT
    (M) (1:39)   Columbia 46031 Columbia Country Classics Vol. 3.
    (M) (1:39)   Columbia 45110 16 Most Requested Songs Of The 1950's Vol. 1.
    (M) (1:39)   Columbia 44374 Hollywood Magic - The 1950's.
    (M) (1:39)   Columbia 53609 Television Themes: 16 Most Requested Songs.
    (M) (2:54)   Rhino 70403 The Cowboy Album. *(rerecording)*
    (M) (1:39)   Risky Business 57474 Small Screen Cowboy Heroes.

1957 WRINGLE WRANGLE

RAY PARKER JR. (also RAYDIO)
released as by RAYDIO:
1978 JACK AND JILL
    (S) (4:33)   Arista 18737 Greatest Hits. *(LP length)*
    (S) (3:32)   Time-Life SOD-20 Sounds Of The Seventies - 1978: Take Two. *(45 length)*
    (S) (4:33)   Rhino 72129 Soul Hits Of The 70's Vol. 19. *(LP length)*
    (S) (3:32)   Time-Life R838-17 Solid Gold Soul 1978. *(45 length)*
    (S) (4:33)   Time-Life R834-17 Body Talk - Heart To Heart. *(LP length)*

1979 YOU CAN'T CHANGE THAT
    (S) (3:22)   Arista 18737 Greatest Hits.
    (S) (3:21)   Razor & Tie 22047 Sweet 70's Soul.
    (S) (3:21)   Time-Life SOD-19 Sounds Of The Seventies - 1979: Take Two.
    (S) (3:22)   Rhino 72130 Soul Hits Of The 70's Vol. 20.
    (S) (3:22)   Hip-O 40030 The Glory Of Love - '70s Sweet & Soulful Love Songs.
    (S) (3:21)   Time-Life R838-15 Solid Gold Soul 1979.
    (S) (3:21)   Hip-O 40096 '70s Hit(s) Back Again.
    (S) (3:21)   Time-Life R834-15 Body Talk - Once In Lifetime.

released as by RAY PARKER JR. & RAYDIO:
1980 TWO PLACES AT THE SAME TIME
    (S) (3:52)   Arista 18737 Greatest Hits.

1981 A WOMAN NEEDS LOVE (JUST LIKE YOU DO)
(actual 45 time is (3:58) not (3:46) as stated on the record label)
    (S) (4:03)   Arista 18737 Greatest Hits.
    (S) (4:03)   Rhino 71971 Video Soul - Best Soul Of The 80's Vol. 1.
    (S) (4:03)   Priority 53700 80's Greatest Rock Hits Volume 13 - Soft Sounds.
    (S) (3:38)   Time-Life R988-08 Sounds Of The Eighties: 1981. *(faded :20 sooner than the 45 or LP)*
    (S) (4:03)   Rhino 72136 Billboard Hot R&B Hits 1981.
    (S) (4:00)   Time-Life R834-02 Body Talk - Just For You.
    (S) (4:02)   JCI 3176 1980 - Only Soul - 1984.

    (S) (4:01)   K-Tel 6257 The Greatest Love Songs - 16 Soft Rock Hits.

1981 THAT OLD SONG
(actual 45 time is (4:06) not (3:54) as stated on the record label)
    (S) (4:18)   Arista 18737 Greatest Hits. *(LP length)*

released as by RAY PARKER JR.:
1982 THE OTHER WOMAN
(actual 45 time is (4:02) not (3:46) as stated on the record label)
    (S) (4:02)   Rhino 71972 Video Soul - Best Soul Of The 80's Vol. 2.
    (S) (4:02)   Arista 18732 Greatest Hits.
    (S) (3:46)   Time-Life R988-05 Sounds Of The Eighties: 1982. *(faded :16 earlier than the 45 or LP)*
    (S) (3:46)   JCI 3149 1980 - Only Dance - 1984. *(faded :16 earlier than the 45 or LP)*
    (S) (4:02)   Rhino 72137 Billboard Hot R&B Hits 1982.
    (S) (4:02)   Madacy Entertainment 1982 Rock On 1982.

1983 BAD BOY
    (S) (4:11)   Arista 18732 Greatest Hits.

1984 I STILL CAN'T GET OVER LOVING YOU
(actual 45 time is (4:05) not (3:50) as stated on the record label)
    (S) (4:04)   Arista 18732 Greatest Hits.

1984 GHOSTBUSTERS
(actual 45 time is (4:04) not (3:46) as stated on the record label)
    (S) (4:04)   Arista 8308 Arista's Perfect 10 Rides Again.
    (S) (4:04)   Arista 8246 O.S.T. Ghostbusters.
    (S) (4:04)   Rhino 70679 Billboard Top Hits - 1984.
    (S) (4:05)   Rhino 70243 Greatest Movie Rock Hits.
    (S) (4:05)   Rhino 71492 Elvira Presents Haunted Hits.
    (S) (4:05)   Rhino 70535 Halloween Hits.
    (S) (4:03)   Risky Business 66391 Ghastly Grooves.
    (S) (4:03)   JCI 3127 1980 - Only Rock 'N Roll - 1984.
    (S) (3:57)   Arista 18732 Greatest Hits.
    (S) (4:03)   K-Tel 3500 The 80's - Urban Countdown.
    (S) (4:04)   Time-Life R988-06 Sounds Of The Eighties: 1984.
    (S) (4:04)   K-Tel 3795 Music For Your Halloween Party.
    (S) (4:02)   K-Tel 3795 Spooktacular Party Songs.
    (S) (4:03)   Time-Life R988-31 Sounds Of The Eighties: Cinemax Movie Hits Of The '80s.
    (S) (3:58)   Priority 50974 Premiere The Movie Magazine Presents The Greatest Soundtrack Hits.
    (S) (4:03)   Rhino 72481 Haunted Hits.
    (S) (4:03)   K-Tel 4033 Ghasty Grooves.

1985 JAMIE
(actual 45 time is (4:13) not (3:58) as stated on the record label)
    (S) (4:14)   Arista 18732 Greatest Hits.
    (S) (4:12)   JCI 3177 1985 - Only Soul - 1989.

1985 GIRLS ARE MORE FUN
(actual 45 time is (4:20) not (3:46) as stated on the record label)
    (S) (4:22)   Arista 18732 Greatest Hits.

released as by GLENN MEDEIROS featuring RAY PARKER JR.:
1990 ALL I'M MISSING IS YOU
    (S) (4:17)   MCA 6399 Glenn Medeiros.

ROBERT PARKER
1966 BAREFOOTIN'
    (M) (2:33)   Rhino 70652 Billboard's Top R&B Hits Of 1966.
    (M) (2:33)   Rhino 72006 Billboard's Top R&B Hits 1965-1969 Box Set.
    (M) (2:29)   Garland 011 Footstompin' Oldies.
    (M) (2:33)   Ripete 2392192 Beach Music Anthology Box Set.
    (M) (2:33)   Ripete 2199 Walkin' To New Orleans.
    (M) (2:33)   Time-Life RHD-01 Rhythm & Blues - 1966.
    (M) (2:33)   Time-Life 2CLR-13 Classic Rock - 1966: Shakin' All Over.
    (E) (2:32)   Collectables 5163 Barefootin'.
    (M) (2:32)   JCI 3161 18 Soul Hits From The 60's.
    (M) (2:32)   Time-Life R838-01 Solid Gold Soul - 1966.
    (M) (2:25)   Compose 131 Unforgettable - Gold For The Road.
    (M) (2:33)   Island 314524394 Island Records 40th Anniversary Volume 2 1964-1969: Rhythm & Blues.

ROBERT PARKER (Continued)

    (M) (2:30)   Rhino 72815 Beg, Scream & Shout! The Big Ol' Box Of '60s Soul.

    (M) (2:32)   Jewel 5057 Rockin' 50's & 60's. *(mastered from vinyl; track lineup on the cd jacket is incorrect)*

MICHAEL PARKS
1970 LONG LONESOME HIGHWAY
    (M) (2:05)   Time-Life R840-02 Sounds Of The Seventies - TV Themes.

PARLIAMENT
1976 TEAR THE ROOF OFF THE SUCKER (GIVE UP THE FUNK)
    (S) (5:42)   Casablanca 822637 Greatest Hits. *(LP version)*

    (S) (5:45)   Casablanca 824502 Mothership Connection. *(LP version)*

    (S) (5:45)   Casablanca 314514417 Tear The Roof Off. *(LP version)*

    (S) (3:43)   Rhino 71434 In Yo Face! History Of Funk Volume 4. *(45 version)*

    (S) (5:45)   Mercury 314514821 Funky Stuff: The Best Of Funk Essentials. *(LP version)*

    (S) (3:43)   Rhino 71618 Soul Train Hall Of Fame/20th Anniversary. *(45 version)*

    (S) (5:41)   Razor & Tie 22045 Those Funky 70's. *(LP version)*

    (S) (3:38)   Time-Life SOD-18 Sounds Of The Seventies - 1976: Take Two. *(45 version)*

    (S) (5:43)   Thump 4030 Old School Vol. 3. *(tracks into next selection; LP version)*

    (S) (5:44)   Priority 8658 All Star Funk. *(LP version)*

    (S) (5:45)   Casablanca 314516918 Casablanca Records Story. *(LP version)*

    (S) (5:45)   Casablanca 314526995 Best Of: Give Up The Funk. *(LP version)*

    (S) (3:41)   Casablanca 314526253 Casablanca Records Greatest Hits. *(45 version)*

    (S) (3:36)   JCI 3148 1975 - Only Dance - 1979. *(45 version)*

    (S) (3:43)   Rhino 72943 VH1 8-Track Flashback: Classic '70s Soul. *(45 version)*

1978 FLASH LIGHT
    (S) (10:42)   Casablanca 838810 Let's Start The Dance (Polygram Dance Classics) Volume 1. *(12" single version)*

    (S) (4:27)   Casablanca 822637 Greatest Hits. *(45 version)*

    (S) (5:46)   Casablanca 824501 Funkentelechy Vs. The Placebo Syndrome. *(LP version)*

    (S) (10:41)   Casablanca 314514417 Tear The Roof Off. *(12" single version)*

    (S) (4:29)   Rhino 71435 In Yo Face! History Of Funk Volume 5. *(45 version)*

    (S) (10:42)   Mercury 314514821 Funky Stuff: The Best Of Funk Essentials. *(12" single version)*

    (S) (4:24)   Time-Life SOD-20 Sounds Of The Seventies - 1978: Take Two. *(45 version)*

    (S) (5:30)   Thump 4010 Old School. *(LP version faded :16 early)*

    (S) (5:31)   Priority 8658 All Star Funk. *(LP version faded :15 early)*

    (S) (5:46)   Casablanca 314516918 Casablanca Records Story. *(LP version)*

    (S) (5:46)   Rebound 314520218 Disco Nights Vol. 2. *(LP version)*

    (S) (4:26)   Rebound 314520265 Dance Fever. *(45 version)*

    (S) (5:46)   Casablanca 314526995 Best Of: Give Up The Funk. *(LP version)*

    (S) (4:26)   Coldfront 3638 Funk Nation - Free Your Mind And Your @#s Will Follow. *(45 version)*

    (S) (4:29)   Time-Life R838-17 Solid Gold Soul 1978. *(45 version)*

    (S) (4:42)   Chronicles 314555140 Dance Funk. *(all selections on this cd are segued together)*

    (S) (5:30)   Scotti Bros. 75512 Slammin' Ol' Skool Trax. *(LP version faded :16 early)*

    (S) (5:46)   Simitar 55542 The Number One's: Soul On Fire. *(LP version)*

    (S) (5:47)   Hip-O 40091 Disco 54: Funkin' On The Floor. *(LP version)*

PARLIAMENTS
1967 (I WANNA) TESTIFY
    (M) (3:09)   Ripete 2223 Soul Patrol Vol. 5.

JOHN PARR
1985 NAUGHTY, NAUGHTY
    (S) (3:39)   JCI 3143 18 Screamers From The 80's.

    (S) (3:38)   Simitar 55142 80's Rock Classics - Party Town.

1985 ST. ELMO'S FIRE (MAN IN MOTION)
    (S) (4:09)   Atlantic 81910 Hit Singles 1980-1988.

    (S) (4:09)   Atlantic 81261 O.S.T. St. Elmo's Fire.

    (S) (4:09)   K-Tel 898 Romantic Hits Of The 80's.

    (S) (4:08)   Rhino 71640 Billboard Top Hits - 1985.

    (S) (4:08)   JCI 3128 1985 - Only Rock 'N Roll - 1989.

    (S) (4:09)   Priority 53775 Best Of 80's Rock Volume 1.

    (S) (4:08)   Time-Life R988-02 Sounds Of The Eighties: 1985.

    (S) (4:09)   Time-Life R988-31 Sounds Of The Eighties: Cinemax Movie Hits Of The '80s.

    (S) (4:09)   Scotti Bros. 75518 Big Screen Rock.

ALAN PARSONS PROJECT
released as by ALAN PARSONS:
1977 I WOULDN'T WANT TO BE LIKE YOU
    (S) (3:20)   Warner Special Products 27614 Highs Of The Seventies. *(LP version)*

    (S) (3:11)   Arista 8193 Best Of. *(neither the 45 or LP version)*

    (S) (3:21)   Arista 8040 I Robot. *(previous selection tracks over introduction; LP version)*

    (S) (3:16)   JCI 3305 Progressive Seventies. *(neither the 45 or LP version)*

    (S) (3:21)   K-Tel 3510 Platinum Rock Volume 2. *(LP version)*

    (S) (3:21)   Arista 18962 Definitive Collection. *(LP version)*

released as by THE ALAN PARSONS PROJECT:
1979 DAMNED IF I DO
    (S) (4:48)   Arista 8062 Eve. *(LP version)*

    (S) (3:33)   Arista 8193 Best Of. *(45 version)*

    (S) (4:49)   Arista 18962 Definitive Collection. *(LP version)*

1981 GAMES PEOPLE PLAY
    (S) (4:19)   Arista 8268 Arista's Perfect 10. *(LP version)*

    (S) (4:18)   Priority 8667 FM Hits/70's Greatest Rock Hits Volume 6. *(LP version)*

    (S) (4:20)   Arista 8226 Turn Of A Friendly Card. *(LP version)*

    (S) (4:20)   Arista 8193 Best Of. *(LP version)*

    (S) (4:17)   Priority 53752 Rock Of The 80's Volume 12. *(LP version)*

    (S) (4:18)   K-Tel 3798 The 80's Mega Hits. *(LP version)*

    (S) (4:22)   Arista 18962 Definitive Collection. *(LP version)*

    (S) (4:19)   Simitar 55142 80's Rock Classics - Party Town. *(LP version)*

    (S) (4:17)   Time-Life R988-22 Sounds Of The Eighties 1980-1983. *(LP version)*

1981 TIME
(actual 45 time is (4:25) not (4:11) as stated on the record label)
    (S) (5:04)   Arista 8226 Turn Of A Friendly Card. *(LP length; tracks into next selection)*

    (S) (4:59)   Arista 8193 Best Of. *(LP length)*

    (S) (4:59)   Priority 53795 Best Of 80's Rock Volume 3. *(LP length)*

    (S) (5:02)   Arista 18962 Definitive Collection. *(LP length)*

    (S) (4:58)   JCI 3193 18 Rock Classics Volume 3. *(LP length)*

1982 EYE IN THE SKY
(actual 45 time is (3:55) not (3:46) as stated on the record label)
    (S) (4:33)   Arista 8268 Arista's Perfect 10. *(LP version)*

    (S) (4:29)   Priority 53750 Rock Of The 80's Volume 7. *(LP version)*

    (S) (3:55)   Rhino 70677 Billboard Top Hits - 1982. *(45 version)*

    (S) (6:29)   Sandstone 33003 Reelin' In The Years Volume 4. *(neither the 45 or LP version)*

    (S) (3:44)   JCI 3119 18 Rock Classics. *(45 version faded :11 early)*

(S) (4:34) Arista 8033 Eye In The Sky. *(LP version)*
(S) (4:36) Arista 8193 Best Of. *(LP version)*
(S) (3:55) Time-Life R988-05 Sounds Of The Eighties: 1982. *(45 version)*
(S) (3:55) K-Tel 3742 The 80's: Hot Rock. *(45 version)*
(S) (4:35) Arista 18962 Definitive Collection. *(LP version)*
(S) (4:33) Time-Life R834-17 Body Talk - Heart To Heart. *(LP version)*

1984 DON'T ANSWER ME
(actual 45 time is (4:09) not (3:58) as stated on the record label)
(S) (4:11) Arista 8204 Ammonia Avenue.
(S) (4:10) Arista 8486 Best Of Volume 2.
(S) (4:11) Arista 18962 Definitive Collection.

1984 PRIME TIME
(S) (5:03) Arista 8204 Ammonia Avenue. *(LP version)*
(S) (3:48) Arista 8486 Best Of Volume 2. *(45 version)*
(S) (5:02) Arista 18962 Definitive Collection. *(LP version)*

BILL PARSONS (see BOBBY BARE)

PARTLAND BROTHERS
1987 SOUL CITY
(S) (3:49) Capitol 46655 Electric Honey.

PARTNERS IN KRYME
1990 TURTLE POWER!
(S) (4:17) SBK 91066 O.S.T. Teenage Mutant Ninja Turtles.
(S) (4:21) SBK 89016 O.S.T. Teenage Mutant Ninja Turtles III.

DOLLY PARTON
1978 HERE YOU COME AGAIN
(S) (2:52) RCA 9684 and 8476 Nipper's Greatest Hits - The 70's.
(S) (2:56) RCA 4422 and 8505 Greatest Hits.
(S) (2:55) RCA 66127 The RCA Years 1967-1986.
(S) (2:54) Time-Life CCD-02 Contemporary Country - The Late 70's.
(S) (2:54) Priority 7078 Country's Greatest Hits - Superstars II.
(S) (2:56) K-Tel 3111 Country Music Classics Vol. XIX.
(S) (2:54) RCA 66852 Super Hits.
(S) (2:54) Priority 53140 Best Of The 70's: Legendary Ladies.
(S) (2:56) Time-Life R990-13 Dolly Parton - Legendary Country Singers.
(S) (2:54) RCA 66933 Essential Vol. 2.
(S) (2:54) Hip-O 40086 The Class Of Country 1975-1979.
(S) (2:55) Time-Life AM1-25 AM Gold - 1978.
(S) (2:55) DCC Compact Classics 162 Here You Come Again.

1978 TWO DOORS DOWN
(S) (3:01) RCA 4422 and 8505 Greatest Hits.
(S) (3:00) RCA 66533 Essential Dolly Parton One.
(S) (3:00) Time-Life R990-13 Dolly Parton - Legendary Country Singers.
(S) (3:04) DCC Compact Classics 162 Here You Come Again.

1979 BABY I'M BURNIN'
(S) (2:35) RCA 66127 The RCA Years 1967-1986.

1981 9 TO 5
(S) (2:39) RCA 9902 Nipper's #1 Hits 1956-1986.
(S) (2:44) RCA 9970 Nipper's Greatest Hits - The 80's.
(S) (2:44) RCA 7004 14 Country Hits.
(S) (2:44) Rhino 70676 Billboard Top Hits - 1981.
(S) (2:44) RCA 4422 and 8505 Greatest Hits.
(S) (2:43) RCA 66127 The RCA Years 1967-1986.
(S) (2:43) Time-Life CCD-15 Contemporary Country - The Early 80's Hot Hits.
(S) (2:42) RCA 56337 "9 To 5" And Odd Jobs.
(S) (2:39) K-Tel 3085 Great Ladies Of Country.
(S) (2:43) Nick At Nite/550 Music 67690 I Am Woman.
(S) (2:42) RCA 66852 Super Hits.
(S) (2:43) RCA 66818 The Essential Series Sampler.
(S) (2:41) RCA 66945 Super Hits Sampler.
(S) (2:44) RCA 66533 Essential Dolly Parton One.
(S) (2:44) Time-Life R990-13 Dolly Parton - Legendary Country Singers.
(S) (2:44) Time-Life R988-31 Sounds Of The Eighties: Cinemax Movie Hits Of The '80s.
(S) (2:44) Simitar 55082 80's Country 1980-82.

released as by KENNY ROGERS with DOLLY PARTON:
1983 ISLANDS IN THE STREAM
(S) (4:07) Time-Life CCD-03 Contemporary Country - The Early 80's.
(S) (4:08) RCA 4697 Kenny Rogers - Eyes That See In The Dark.
(S) (4:09) RCA 8731 Kenny Rogers - Greatest Hits.
(S) (4:09) RCA 4422 and 8505 Dolly Parton - Greatest Hits.
(S) (4:08) RCA 66533 Essential Dolly Parton One.
(S) (4:07) RCA 66948 The Essential Series Sampler Volume II.
(S) (4:08) Time-Life R990-13 Dolly Parton - Legendary Country Singers.
(S) (4:08) Reprise 46571 Kenny Rogers - A Decade Of Hits.
(S) (4:08) Time-Life R834-14 Body Talk - Love And Tenderness.

PARTRIDGE FAMILY
1970 I THINK I LOVE YOU
(actual 45 time is (2:50) not (2:28) as stated on the record label)
(S) (2:50) Rhino 70923 Super Hits Of The 70's Volume 3.
(S) (2:50) Rhino 72009 Super Hits Of The 70's Volumes 1-4 Box Set.
(S) (2:50) Rhino 70631 Billboard's Top Rock & Roll Hits Of 1970.
(S) (2:50) Rhino 72005 Billboard's Top Rock & Roll Hits 1968-1972 Box Set.
(S) (2:51) Priority 8669 Hits/70's Greatest Rock Hits Volume 9.
(S) (2:51) Arista 8604 Greatest Hits.
(S) (2:51) Rhino 71208 70's Smash Hits Volume 4.
(S) (2:51) Razor & Tie 2012 Partridge Family Album.
(S) (2:50) Razor & Tie 21640 Those Fabulous 70's.
(S) (2:48) Time-Life SUD-04 Superhits - 1970.
(S) (2:51) Varese Sarabande 5535 Bubblegum Classics Volume One.
(S) (2:50) K-Tel 3211 70's Teen Heart-Throbs.
(S) (2:48) Eclipse Music Group 64892 Rock 'n Roll Relix 1970-1971.
(S) (2:48) Eclipse Music Group 64897 Rock 'n Roll Relix 1970-1979.
(S) (2:48) Time-Life AM1-02 AM Gold - 1970.
(S) (2:51) Flashback 72684 '70s Radio Hits Volume 4.
(S) (2:51) Flashback 72090 '70s Radio Hits Box Set.

1971 DOESN'T SOMEBODY WANT TO BE WANTED
(S) (2:45) Arista 8604 Greatest Hits.
(S) (2:46) Razor & Tie 2013 Up To Date.
(S) (2:46) Time-Life SOD-36 Sounds Of The Seventies - More AM Nuggets.

1971 I'LL MEET YOU HALFWAY
(S) (3:47) Arista 8604 Greatest Hits. *(LP length)*
(S) (3:48) Razor & Tie 2013 Up To Date. *(LP length)*
(S) (3:44) Time-Life SOD-33 Sounds Of The Seventies - AM Pop Classics II. *(LP length)*

1971 I WOKE UP IN LOVE THIS MORNING
(S) (2:37) Arista 8604 Greatest Hits.
(S) (2:40) Razor & Tie 2021 Sound Magazine.
(S) (2:35) Time-Life SUD-16 Superhits - The Early 70's.
(S) (2:35) Time-Life AM1-13 AM Gold - The Early '70s.

1972 IT'S ONE OF THOSE NIGHTS (YES LOVE)
(S) (3:33) Arista 8604 Greatest Hits.
(S) (3:33) Razor & Tie 2022 Shopping Bag.

1972 BREAKING UP IS HARD TO DO
1973 LOOKING THROUGH THE EYES OF LOVE
(S) (3:04) Arista 8604 Greatest Hits.

PARTY
1992 IN MY DREAMS
(S) (3:36) Hollywood 61225 In The Meantime, In Between Time.
(S) (3:36) Hollywood 62122 Greatest Hits.

PASTELS
1958 BEEN SO LONG
(M) (2:40) MCA 5778 Vintage Music Volumes 3 & 4.
(M) (2:40) MCA 31201 Vintage Music Volume 4.
(M) (2:39) Time-Life 2RNR-41 The Rock 'N' Roll Era - R&B Gems.

PASTELS (Continued)

    (M) (2:39)   Chess 9283 Best Of Chess Vocal Groups Vol. 2.
    (M) (2:40)   Rhino 75763 Best Of Doo Wop Ballads.
    (M) (2:40)   Rhino 71463 Doo Wop Box.
    (M) (2:40)   MCA Special Products 22166 Vintage Collectibles Volume 8.
    (M) (2:39)   Rhino 72156 Doo Wop Memories, Vol. 1.
    (M) (2:39)   MCA Special Products 20941 R&B Crossover Oldies Vol. 1.
    (M) (2:40)   Time-Life R857-16 The Heart Of Rock 'n' Roll The Late '50s.

PASTEL SIX
1963 THE CINNAMON CINDER (IT'S A VERY NICE DANCE)

    (E) (1:58)   JCI 3189 1960 - Only Dance - 1964. *(no fidelity)*

JOHNNY PATE QUINTET
1958 SWINGING SHEPHERD BLUES

PATIENCE & PRUDENCE
1956 TONIGHT YOU BELONG TO ME

    (M) (1:51)   Time-Life HPD-21 Your Hit Parade - The Mid 50's.

1956 GONNA GET ALONG WITHOUT YA NOW

    (M) (1:53)   Time-Life HPD-36 Your Hit Parade - The 50's Pop Revival.
    (M) (1:53)   EMI-Capitol Music Special Markets 19446 Lost Hits Of The '50s.

ROBBIE PATTON
1981 DON'T GIVE IT UP

PATTY & THE EMBLEMS
1964 MIXED-UP, SHOOK-UP, GIRL

    (M) (2:03)   Ripete 2392192 Beach Music Anthology Box Set.
    (M) (2:03)   Time-Life 2RNR-40 Rock 'N' Roll Era - The 60's Teen Time.
    (M) (2:01)   Collectables 5657 Spotlite On Herald Records Volume 2.
    (M) (2:03)   Ripete 2184-RE Ocean Drive Vol. 2.
    (M) (2:02)   Collectables 5765 Golden Classics.

BILLY PAUL
1972 ME AND MRS. JONES
    (dj copies of this 45 ran (4:42) and (3:41);
    commercial copies were all (4:42))

    (S) (4:46)   Rhino 70660 Billboard's Top R&B Hits Of 1972.
    (S) (4:45)   Rhino 70789 Soul Hits Of The 70's Volume 9.
    (S) (4:46)   Philadelphia International 39307 Ten Years Of Hits.
    (S) (4:40)   Razor & Tie 22047 Sweet 70's Soul.
    (S) (4:44)   Time-Life RHD-20 Rhythm & Blues - 1972.
    (S) (4:44)   Time-Life SUD-11 Superhits - 1972.
    (S) (4:46)   Time-Life SOD-21 Sounds Of The Seventies - Rock 'N' Soul Seventies.
    (S) (4:40)   Ichiban 2508 Cheatin': From A Man's Point Of View.
    (S) (4:40)   Risky Business 66663 Sex In The Seventies.
    (S) (4:44)   Legacy/Epic 66913 From Philly With Love.
    (S) (4:47)   Legacy/Epic 66912 Legacy's Rhythm & Soul Revue.
    (S) (4:40)   Right Stuff 30576 Slow Jams: The 70's Volume 4.
    (S) (4:44)   Elektra 61888 O.S.T. Beautiful Girls.
    (S) (4:44)   JCI 3173 1970 - Only Soul - 1974.
    (S) (4:44)   Time-Life AM1-07 AM Gold - 1972.
    (S) (4:44)   Time-Life R838-07 Solid Gold Soul - 1972.
    (S) (4:44)   Time-Life R834-01 Body Talk - Forever Yours.
    (S) (4:44)   Epic/Legacy 64647 The Philly Sound Box Set.
    (S) (4:44)   K-Tel 3912 Superstars Greatest Hits Volume 1.
    (S) (4:44)   Thump 4740 Old School Love Songs Volume 4.
    (S) (4:44)   Epic Associated/Legacy 65162 A Postcard From Philly.
    (S) (4:38)   BMG Special Products 44762 The President's Greatest Hits.

LES PAUL & MARY FORD
1955 HUMMINGBIRD

    (M) (2:37)   Capitol 97654 The Legend And The Legacy.

    (M) (2:37)   Capitol 99617 Best Of The Capitol Masters.
    (M) (2:37)   Time-Life HPD-23 Your Hit Parade - The Late 50's.

1957 CINCO ROBLES (FIVE OAKS)

    (M) (3:04)   Capitol 97654 The Legend And The Legacy.

1958 PUT A RING ON MY FINGER

PAUL & PAULA
1963 HEY PAULA

    (M) (2:29)   Mercury 826448 Oldies Golden Million Sellers.
    (E) (2:36)   MCA 31023 O.S.T. Animal House. *(sound effects added to the introduction; all tracks on this cd are segued together)*
    (M) (2:28)   Rhino 70588 Rockin' & Rollin' Wedding Songs Volume 1.
    (M) (2:28)   Time-Life 2RNR-19 Rock 'N' Roll Era - 1963 Still Rockin'.
    (M) (2:27)   Time-Life SUD-08 Superhits - 1963.
    (M) (2:28)   Time-Life R962-05 History Of Rock 'N' Roll: The Teenage Years 1957-1964.
    (M) (2:28)   Collectables 2500 WCBS-FM History Of Rock - The 60's Part 1. *(mastered from vinyl)*
    (M) (2:28)   Collectables 4500 History Of Rock/The 60s Part One. *(mastered from vinyl)*
    (M) (2:27)   Collectables 2604 WCBS-FM Jukebox Giants Vol. 2.
    (M) (2:29)   Rhino 71584 Billboard Top Pop Hits, 1963.
    (M) (2:29)   Scotti Brothers 75434 Romantic Duets.
    (M) (2:29)   K-Tel 3523 Best Of.
    (M) (2:29)   Eclipse Music Group 64868 Rock 'n Roll Relix 1962-1963.
    (M) (2:29)   Eclipse Music Group 64872 Rock 'n Roll Relix 1960-1969.
    (M) (2:28)   Time-Life R857-08 The Heart Of Rock 'n' Roll 1963.
    (M) (2:27)   Time-Life AM1-17 AM Gold - 1963.
    (M) (2:29)   Time-Life R857-21 The Heart Of Rock 'n' Roll Slow Dancing Classics.
    (M) (2:28)   Polygram Special Markets 314520460 #1 Radio Hits Of The 60's.
    (M) (2:28)   Polygram Special Markets 314520516 45's On CD Volume 1.
    (M) (2:28)   BMG Special Products 44762 The President's Greatest Hits.

1963 YOUNG LOVERS

    (M) (2:29)   Time-Life 2RNR-47 Rock 'N' Roll Era - Teen Idols II.
    (S) (2:31)   Special Music/Essex 5035 Prom Night - The 60's.
    (M) (2:31)   K-Tel 3523 Best Of.
    (S) (2:32)   Eric 11503 Hard To Find 45's On CD (Volume II) 1961-64.
    (M) (2:29)   Time-Life R857-18 The Heart Of Rock 'n' Roll 1962-1963 Take Two.

1963 FIRST QUARREL

    (M) (2:34)   K-Tel 3523 Best Of.

RITA PAVONE
1964 REMEMBER ME

    (S) (2:07)   Collectors' Choice 5189 I Wish I Were A Princess - The Great Lost Female Teen Idols.

FREDA PAYNE
1970 BAND OF GOLD

    (S) (2:51)   DCC Compact Classics 033 Beachbeat Shaggin'.
    (S) (2:53)   Rhino 70782 Soul Hits Of The 70's Volume 2.
    (S) (2:53)   Rhino 72028 Soul Hits Of The 70's Volumes 1-5 Box Set.
    (S) (2:53)   HDH 3905 Greatest Hits.
    (S) (2:52)   Ripete 2392156 Grand Stand Gold.
    (S) (2:52)   Time-Life RHD-18 Rhythm & Blues - 1970.
    (S) (2:52)   Time-Life SOD-22 Sounds Of The Seventies - Seventies Top Forty.
    (S) (2:53)   Ripete 2156-RE Grand Stand Gold Vol. 1.
    (S) (2:52)   Columbia 67380 O.S.T. Now And Then.
    (S) (2:53)   Priority 53140 Best Of The 70's: Legendary Ladies.
    (S) (2:52)   Time-Life R838-05 Solid Gold Soul - 1970.

1970 DEEPER & DEEPER
    (S)   (3:01)   Rhino 70784   Soul Hits Of The 70's Volume 4. *(LP version)*
    (S)   (3:01)   Rhino 72028   Soul Hits Of The 70's Volumes 1-5 Box Set. *(LP version)*
    (S)   (3:00)   HDH 3905   Greatest Hits. *(LP version)*

1971 CHERISH WHAT IS DEAR TO YOU (WHILE IT'S NEAR TO YOU)
    (S)   (3:55)   HDH 3905   Greatest Hits. *(LP version)*

1971 BRING THE BOYS HOME
    (S)   (3:28)   Rhino 70785   Soul Hits Of The 70's Volume 5. *(LP version)*
    (S)   (3:28)   Rhino 72028   Soul Hits Of The 70's Volumes 1-5 Box Set. *(LP version)*
    (S)   (3:28)   HDH 3905   Greatest Hits. *(LP version)*

PEACH UNION
1997 ON MY OWN
    (S)   (4:54)   Mute/Epic 68553   Audiopeach.
    (S)   (3:18)   Beast 54112   Boom! *(radio edit)*

PEACHES & HERB
1967 LET'S FALL IN LOVE
    (S)   (2:38)   Original Sound 9402   Sweethearts Of Soul.
    (S)   (2:38)   Ichiban 2512   Soulful Love - Duets Vol. 1.
    (S)   (2:36)   Epic/Legacy 64842   Love Is Strange: Best Of.

1967 CLOSE YOUR EYES
    (S)   (2:33)   Time-Life RHD-10   Rhythm & Blues - 1967.
    (S)   (2:33)   Time-Life 2CLR-24   Classic Rock - 1967: Blowin' Your Mind.
    (S)   (2:34)   Time-Life OPCD-4517   Tonight's The Night.
    (S)   (2:33)   Original Sound 9402   Sweethearts Of Soul.
    (S)   (2:34)   Thump 4720   Old School Love Songs Volume 2.
    (S)   (2:33)   Hip-O 40001   The Glory Of Love - Sweet & Soulful Love Songs.
    (S)   (2:33)   Epic/Legacy 64842   Love Is Strange: Best Of.
    (S)   (2:33)   Rhino 72619   Smooth Grooves: The '60s Volume 2 Mid '60s.
    (S)   (2:33)   Time-Life R838-02   Solid Gold Soul - 1967.
    (S)   (2:33)   Rhino 72870   Brown Eyed Soul Vol. 3.
    (S)   (2:33)   Time-Life R834-17   Body Talk - Heart To Heart.
    (S)   (2:33)   Time-Life R857-22   The Heart Of Rock 'n' Roll 1967-1969.

1967 FOR YOUR LOVE
    (S)   (2:36)   Original Sound 9402   Sweethearts Of Soul.
    (S)   (2:34)   Epic/Legacy 64842   Love Is Strange: Best Of.
    (S)   (2:34)   Hip-O 40029   The Glory Of Love - '60s Sweet & Soulful Love Songs.

1967 LOVE IS STRANGE
    (S)   (3:00)   Original Sound 9402   Sweethearts Of Soul.
    (S)   (2:59)   Epic/Legacy 64842   Love Is Strange: Best Of.

1968 TWO LITTLE KIDS
    (S)   (2:49)   Original Sound 9402   Sweethearts Of Soul.
    (S)   (2:47)   Epic/Legacy 64842   Love Is Strange: Best Of.

1968 UNITED
    (S)   (2:47)   Original Sound 9402   Sweethearts Of Soul.
    (M)   (2:45)   Epic/Legacy 64842   Love Is Strange: Best Of.

1979 SHAKE YOUR GROOVE THING
(both dj and commercial copies of this 45 were pressed with times of either (3:25) or (3:39))
    (S)   (3:24)   Priority 7972   Mega-Hits Dance Classics Volume 2. *(45 version)*
    (S)   (3:24)   Rhino 70984   The Disco Years Volume 1. *(45 version)*
    (S)   (3:24)   Rhino 70492   Billboard Top Dance Hits - 1978. *(45 version)*
    (S)   (3:25)   Special Music 839785   Reunited. *(45 version)*
    (S)   (3:25)   Time-Life SOD-19   Sounds Of The Seventies - 1979: Take Two. *(45 version)*
    (S)   (6:37)   Rebound 314520218   Disco Nights Vol. 2. *(12" single version)*
    (S)   (6:37)   Rebound 314520220   Disco Nights Vol. 4 - Greatest Disco Groups. *(12" single version)*
    (S)   (3:24)   Rebound 314520265   Dance Fever. *(45 version)*
    (S)   (6:36)   Mother 314516937   O.S.T. The Adventures Of Priscilla - Queen Of The Desert. *(12" single version)*

    (S)   (5:31)   Mother 314516937   O.S.T. The Adventures Of Priscilla - Queen Of The Desert. *(LP version)*
    (S)   (3:24)   Time-Life R138-38   Celebration. *(45 version)*
    (S)   (5:30)   Polydor 314529650   Best Of. *(LP version)*
    (S)   (6:35)   Polydor 314529650   Best Of. *(12" single version)*
    (S)   (3:24)   Time-Life R838-17   Solid Gold Soul 1978. *(45 version)*
    (S)   (3:58)   JCI 3175   1975 - Only Soul - 1979. *(neither the 45 or LP version)*
    (S)   (3:24)   Time-Life R840-08   Sounds Of The Seventies: '70s Dance Party 1978-1979. *(45 version)*
    (S)   (4:17)   Rebound 314520520   Body Moves - Non-Stop Disco Workout Vol. 1. *(all selections on this cd are segued together)*

1979 REUNITED
    (S)   (5:44)   Special Music 839785   Reunited. *(LP version)*
    (S)   (5:41)   Original Sound 8862   Oldies But Goodies Vol. 12. *(this compact disc uses the "Waring - fds" noise reduction process; LP version)*
    (S)   (5:41)   Original Sound 2223   Oldies But Goodies Volumes 2,7,9,12 and 13 Box Set. *(this box set uses the "Waring - fds" noise reduction process; LP version)*
    (S)   (5:41)   Original Sound 2500   Oldies But Goodies Volumes 1-15 Box Set. *(this box set uses the "Waring - fds" noise reduction process; LP version)*
    (S)   (3:57)   Time-Life SOD-09   Sounds Of The Seventies - 1979. *(45 version)*
    (S)   (5:41)   Original Sound 9402   Sweethearts Of Soul. *(LP version)*
    (S)   (5:44)   Rebound 314520033   Quiet Storm: The 70's. *(LP version)*
    (S)   (5:44)   Polygram Special Markets 314520302   At Their Best. *(LP version)*
    (S)   (5:42)   Polygram Special Markets 314520271   Hits Of The 70's. *(LP version)*
    (S)   (3:59)   Rhino 72130   Soul Hits Of The 70's Vol. 20. *(45 version)*
    (S)   (3:57)   Time-Life R138-18   Body Talk. *(45 version)*
    (S)   (3:58)   Rebound 314520367   Soul Classics - Quiet Storm/The 70's. *(45 version)*
    (S)   (5:40)   Polydor 314529650   Best Of. *(LP version)*
    (S)   (3:56)   JCI 3146   1975 - Only Love - 1979. *(45 version)*
    (S)   (3:57)   Time-Life R834-04   Body Talk - Together Forever. *(45 version)*
    (S)   (5:41)   Angel 56580   Men Are From Mars, Women Are From Venus - Songs For Loving Couples. *(LP version)*
    (S)   (3:59)   K-Tel 3887   Soul Brothers & Sisters Of The 70's. *(45 version)*
    (S)   (5:44)   Thump 4740   Old School Love Songs Volume 4. *(LP version)*
    (S)   (3:57)   Time-Life R838-15   Solid Gold Soul 1979. *(45 version)*
    (S)   (3:58)   K-Tel 3906   Starflight Vol. 1. *(45 version)*
    (S)   (5:40)   Polygram TV 314555610   The One And Only Love Album. *(LP version)*
    (S)   (3:57)   Time-Life R840-10   Sounds Of The Seventies: '70s Dance Party 1979. *(45 version)*
    (S)   (3:57)   Time-Life R814-04   Love Songs. *(45 version)*

1980 I PLEDGE MY LOVE
    (S)   (4:11)   Special Music 839785   Reunited.
    (S)   (4:11)   Polygram Special Markets 314520302   At Their Best.
    (S)   (4:12)   Rhino 71891   Radio Daze: Pop Hits Of The 80's Volume Two.
    (S)   (4:10)   Polydor 314529650   Best Of.
    (S)   (4:10)   Polydor 314535195   The Power Of Love - Best Of The "Soul Essentials" Ballads.
    (S)   (4:17)   Hip-O 40031   The Glory Of Love - '80s Sweet & Soulful Love Songs.
    (S)   (4:12)   Time-Life R834-07   Body Talk - Hearts In Motion.
    (S)   (4:12)   Rhino 72757   Smooth Grooves - Wedding Songs.
    (S)   (4:10)   Polygram Special Markets 314520445   Soul Hits Of The 80's.

LESLIE PEARL
1982 IF THE LOVE FITS WEAR IT

PEARL JAM
1994 TREMOR CHRIST
- (S) (4:09) Epic 66900 Vitalogy.

1994 SPIN THE BLACK CIRCLE
- (S) (2:47) Epic 66900 Vitalogy.

1995 I GOT ID
1995 LONG ROAD
1996 WHO YOU ARE
- (S) (3:48) Epic 67500 No Code.

PEBBLES
1988 GIRLFRIEND
- (S) (6:40) MCA 42094 Pebbles. *(LP version)*
- (S) (4:15) Rhino 72140 Billboard Hot R&B Hits 1985. *(45 version)*
- (S) (4:12) Time-Life R988-20 Sounds Of The Eighties: The Late '80s Take Two. *(45 version)*

1988 MERCEDES BOY
- (S) (4:53) JCI 2702 Hot Moves. *(LP version)*
- (S) (5:07) K-Tel 842 Hot Ladies Of The 80's. *(remixed)*
- (S) (4:55) MCA 42094 Pebbles. *(LP version)*
- (S) (5:07) K-Tel 3500 The 80's - Urban Countdown. *(remixed)*
- (S) (3:54) MCA 11329 Soul Train 25th Anniversary Box Set. *(45 version)*
- (S) (4:55) Madacy Entertainment 1988 Rock On 1988. *(LP version)*
- (S) (4:54) Priority 50941 Shut Up And Dance! Volume Two - The 80's. *(all songs on this cd are segued together)*
- (S) (3:55) Rhino 72838 Disco Queens: The 80's. *(45 version)*
- (S) (5:07) Cold Front 6284 More Of! Club Mix's Biggest Jams. *(all selections on this cd are segued together; remixed)*
- (S) (4:29) Cold Front 6330 Club Mix: The 80s. *(all selections on this cd are segued together)*

1990 GIVING YOU THE BENEFIT
- (S) (5:40) MCA 10025 Always. *(LP version)*
- (S) (5:38) Rhino 72159 Black Entertainment Television - 15th Anniversary. *(LP version)*
- (S) (4:26) Cold Front 3832 Club Mix - Women Of Dance Vol. 1. *(45 version)*

1991 LOVE MAKES THINGS HAPPEN
- (S) (5:08) MCA 10025 Always.

ANN PEEBLES
1970 PART TIME LOVE
- (S) (2:50) Hi 25226 History Of Hi R&B Volume 1.
- (S) (2:50) MCA 25225 Greatest Hits.
- (S) (2:51) Right Stuff/Hi 28539 Part Time Love.
- (S) (2:51) Ichiban 2507 Cheatin': From A Woman's Point Of View.
- (M) (2:53) Right Stuff/Hi 30584 Hi Times - The Hi Records R&B Years.
- (S) (2:51) Right Stuff/Hi 52659 Best Of.

NIA PEEPLES
1988 TROUBLE
- (S) (6:28) Mercury 834303 Nothin' But Trouble. *(LP version)*
- (S) (3:47) Priority 50941 Shut Up And Dance! Volume Two - The 80's. *(all songs on this cd are segued together)*
- (S) (4:16) Cold Front 3865 Club Mix - Women Of Dance Vol. 2. *(45 version)*

1991 STREET OF DREAMS
- (S) (4:22) Charisma 91768 and 86249 Nia Peeples.
- (S) (4:22) K-Tel 6101 Hot Ladies Of The 90's - Dazzling Divas.

TEDDY PENDERGRASS
1978 CLOSE THE DOOR
- (S) (5:25) Philadelphia International 39307 Ten Years Of Hits. *(LP version)*
- (S) (5:23) Original Sound 8908 Best Love Songs Vol 3. *(LP version)*
- (S) (5:23) Original Sound 9327 Best Love Songs Vol. 3 & 4. *(LP version)*
- (S) (5:23) Original Sound 1236 Best Love Songs Box Set. *(LP version)*
- (S) (5:25) Right Stuff 27118 Life Is A Song Worth Singing. *(LP version)*
- (S) (5:25) Right Stuff 27307 Slow Jams: The 70's Volume One. *(LP version)*
- (S) (5:25) Right Stuff 52660 Flick Hits - Old School Tracks. *(LP version)*
- (S) (5:24) Hip-O 40030 The Glory Of Love - '70s Sweet & Soulful Love Songs. *(LP version)*
- (S) (5:24) Time-Life R834-09 Body Talk - Magic Moments. *(LP version)*
- (S) (3:33) Time-Life R838-17 Solid Gold Soul 1978. *(45 version)*
- (S) (5:26) Right Stuff 36994 Greatest Hits. *(LP version)*

PENGUINS
1955 EARTH ANGEL (WILL YOU BE MINE)
- (M) (2:55) Rhino 75763 Best Of Doo Wop Ballads.
- (M) (2:55) Rhino 70598 Billboard's Top Rock & Roll Hits Of 1955.
- (M) (2:55) Original Sound 8850 Oldies But Goodies Vol. 1. *(this compact disc uses the "Waring - fds" noise reduction process)*
- (M) (2:55) Original Sound 2221 Oldies But Goodies Volumes 1,4,6,8 and 10 Box Set. *(this box set uses the "Waring - fds" noise reduction process)*
- (M) (2:55) Original Sound 2500 Oldies But Goodies Volumes 1-15 Box Set. *(this box set uses the "Waring - fds" noise reduction process)*
- (M) (2:48) Original Sound 1960 Memories Of El Monte. *(previous song tracks into the introduction)*
- (M) (2:48) Original Sound 4001 Art Laboe's 60 Killer Oldies. *(previous song tracks into the introduction; this song appears twice on this box set)*
- (M) (2:54) Original Sound 8891 Dick Clark's 21 All-Time Hits Vol. 1.
- (M) (2:54) Collectables 5045 Golden Classics. *(truncated fade)*
- (M) (2:54) Collectables 5048 Dootone Rhythm And Blues. *(truncated fade)*
- (S) (6:46) Special Music 4913 Rock & Roll Revival. *(live)*
- (M) (2:52) Rhino 71463 Doo Wop Box.
- (M) (2:49) Juke Box Treasures 6009 Authentic Golden Hits. *(missing the first :05 of the song)*
- (M) (2:54) Original Sound 8905r 13 Of The Best Doo Wop Love Songs.
- (M) (2:54) Original Sound 9326 Best Love Songs Vol. 1 & 2.
- (M) (2:54) Original Sound 4001 Art Laboe's 60 Killer Oldies. *(this song appears twice on this box set)*
- (M) (2:54) Original Sound 1236 Best Love Songs Box Set.
- (M) (2:55) Time-Life 2RNR-08 Rock 'N' Roll Era - 1954-1955.
- (M) (2:55) Time-Life RHD-17 Rhythm & Blues - 1955.
- (M) (2:55) Time-Life R962-06 History Of Rock 'N' Roll: Doo Wop And Vocal Group Tradition 1955-1962.
- (M) (2:55) Collectables 2509 WCBS-FM For Lovers Only Part 1.
- (M) (2:55) Time-Life R103-27 Love Me Tender.
- (M) (2:55) Time-Life R10513 40 Lovin' Oldies.
- (M) (2:55) LaserLight 12323 American Dreams.
- (M) (2:57) Special Music/Essex 5034 Prom Night - The 50's.
- (S) (2:49) Scotti Bros. 75465 Angel Hits. *(rerecording)*
- (M) (2:55) Thump 7060 Low Rider Oldies Volume 6.
- (M) (2:54) JCI 3165 #1 Radio Hits 1955 - Only Rock 'n Roll - 1959.
- (M) (2:53) K-Tel 3812 Doo Wop's Greatest Hits.
- (M) (2:57) Right Stuff 53320 Hot Rod Rock Volume 5: Back Seat Movers.
- (M) (2:55) Time-Life R857-21 The Heart Of Rock 'n' Roll Slow Dancing Classics.
- (M) (2:52) Time-Life R857-15 The Heart Of Rock 'n' Roll 1953-1955.

CE CE PENISTON
1992 FINALLY
- (S) (6:44) Tommy Boy 1074 MTV Party To Go Volume 3. *(remix; all tracks on this cd are segued together)*

(S) (6:23) Rebound 314520246 Disco Nights Vol. 5 - Best Of Housemusic. *(remix)*
(S) (4:03) A&M 5381 Finally.
(S) (4:07) Mother 314516937 O.S.T. The Adventures Of Priscilla - Queen Of The Desert.
(S) (3:59) Mercury 314532494 100% Pure Dance. *(all songs on this cd are segued together)*
(S) (4:37) Priority 50954 Power Workout High NRG Megamix Volume 1. *(remixed; all selections on this cd are segued together)*
(S) (4:02) Rebound 314520439 Soul Classics - Best Of The 90's.

1992 WE GOT A LOVE THANG
(S) (5:27) A&M 5381 Finally.
(S) (3:51) Tommy Boy 1163 Jock Jams Volume 2. *(all selections on this cd are segued together)*

1992 KEEP ON WALKIN'
(S) (4:30) A&M 5381 Finally.
(S) (3:59) MCA 11329 Soul Train 25th Anniversary Box Set.

1994 I'M IN THE MOOD
(S) (4:10) A&M 314540138 Thought 'Ya Knew.

MICHAEL PENN
1990 NO MYTH
(S) (4:09) Priority 53741 Cutting Edge Vol. 1 - Best Of Modern Rock Hits.
(S) (4:09) RCA 9692 March.
(S) (4:08) Priority 50947 A Bunch O' Hits: The Best Rock Of The 90's Volume 1.

PEOPLE
1968 I LOVE YOU
(dj copies of this 45 ran (4:31) and (2:43); commercial copies were all (4:31) even though the time on the record label stated (4:37))
(E) (4:29) K-Tel 686 Battle Of The Bands Volume 4.
(S) (4:31) Time-Life 2CLR-19 Classic Rock - 1968: Shakin' All Over.
(S) (4:31) Capitol 29797 I Love You.
(S) (4:31) EMI-Capitol Special Markets 19552 Lost Hits Of The '60s.

PEOPLE'S CHOICE
1975 DO IT ANY WAY YOU WANNA
(S) (3:16) Rhino 71756 and 72833 Phat Trax: The Best Of Old School Volume 5.
(S) (3:11) Epic 66155 Club Epic Volume 3. *(tracks into next selection)*
(S) (3:14) Rhino 72127 Soul Hits Of The 70's Vol. 17.
(S) (3:13) Time-Life R840-04 Sounds Of The Seventies: A Loss For Words.
(S) (3:13) Time-Life R838-10 Solid Gold Soul - 1975.
(S) (3:16) Epic/Legacy 64647 The Philly Sound Box Set.
(S) (3:12) Epic/Legacy 65504 Disco Super Hits.

PEPPERMINT RAINBOW
1969 WILL YOU BE STAYING AFTER SUNDAY
(S) (2:29) Varese Sarabande 5535 Bubblegum Classics Volume One.
(S) (2:28) MCA Special Products 20981 Bubble Gum Classics.

PERFECT GENTLEMEN
1990 OOH LA LA (I CAN'T GET OVER YOU)
(S) (4:45) Columbia 46070 Rated PG.

EMILIO PERICOLI
1962 AL DI LA'
(M) (2:03) Time-Life HPD-32 Your Hit Parade - Into The 60's.
(M) (2:03) Rhino 72577 Eh, Paisano! Italian-American Classics.
(M) (2:03) Time-Life R814-05 Love Songs.

CARL PERKINS
1956 BLUE SUEDE SHOES
(M) (2:13) Rhino 70599 Billboard's Top Rock & Roll Hits Of 1956.

(M) (2:13) RCA 5463 Rock & Roll - The Early Days. *(echo added)*
(M) (2:11) Original Sound 8854 Oldies But Goodies Vol. 4. *(this compact disc uses the "Waring - fds" noise reduction process)*
(M) (2:11) Original Sound 2221 Oldies But Goodies Volumes 1,4,6,8 and 10 Box Set. *(this box set uses the "Waring - fds" noise reduction process)*
(M) (2:11) Original Sound 2500 Oldies But Goodies Volumes 1-15 Box Set. *(this box set uses the "Waring - fds" noise reduction process)*
(M) (2:10) Original Sound CDGO-10 Golden Oldies Volume. 10.
(M) (2:11) Original Sound 8891 Dick Clark's 21 All-Time Hits Vol. 1.
(M) (2:13) Rhino 75884 The Sun Story.
(M) (2:13) DCC Compact Classics 009 Legends.
(M) (2:13) Rhino 75893 Jukebox Classics Volume 1. *(echo added)*
(M) (2:13) Rhino 70741 Rock This Town: Rockabilly Hits Volume 1.
(M) (2:12) JCI 3202 Rockin' Fifties.
(M) (2:13) Rhino 75890 Original Sun Greatest Hits.
(M) (2:14) RCA 66059 Sun's Greatest Hits.
(M) (2:13) Curb 77598 Best Of.
(M) (2:14) Curb 77637 All Time Greatest Hits Of Rock 'N' Roll Volume 3.
(M) (2:12) Time-Life 2RNR-14 Rock 'N' Roll Era - 1956. *(truncated fade)*
(M) (2:13) Time-Life CTD-13 Country USA - 1956.
(M) (2:14) Time-Life R962-03 History Of Rock 'N' Roll: Rock 'N' Roll Classics 1954-1956.
(M) (2:13) Collectables 2503 WCBS-FM History Of Rock - The 50's Part 2.
(M) (2:14) Collectables 4503 History Of Rock/The 50s Part Two.
(M) (2:12) Rhino 71780 Sun Records Collection.
(M) (2:10) Original Sound 8883 21 Legendary Superstars.
(M) (2:13) K-Tel 3062 Rockin' Rebels.
(M) (2:13) JCI 3129 1955 - Only Rock 'N Roll - 1959.
(M) (2:13) Varese Sarabande 5605 Through The Years - Country Hits Of The 50's.
(M) (2:14) K-Tel 3436 Rockabilly Riot.
(M) (2:12) Nick At Nite/550 Music/Epic 67770 Happy Days Jukebox.
(M) (2:14) JCI 3152 1955 - Only Country - 1959.
(M) (2:12) Priority 50950 I Love Rock & Roll Volume 1: Hits Of The 50's.
(M) (2:13) K-Tel 4018 Forefathers Of Rock.
(M) (2:13) Flashback 72857 Grease And Other Golden Oldies.
(M) (2:13) Columbia 69075 Great Balls Of Fire Super Hits.
(M) (2:13) Hip-O 40082 The King's Record Collection Vol. 1.

TONY PERKINS
1957 MOON-LIGHT SWIM
(M) (2:18) RCA 66881 RCA's Greatest One-Hit Wonders.

STEVE PERRY
released as by KENNY LOGGINS with STEVE PERRY:
1982 DON'T FIGHT IT
(S) (3:37) Columbia 38127 Kenny Loggins - High Adventure.
(S) (3:36) Columbia 67986 Kenny Loggins - Greatest Hits Of.
released as by STEVE PERRY:
1984 OH SHERRIE
(S) (3:48) Columbia 39344 and 67849 Street Talk.
1984 SHE'S MINE
(S) (4:26) Columbia 39344 and 67849 Street Talk. *(LP version)*
1984 STRUNG OUT
(S) (3:51) Columbia 39344 and 67849 Street Talk.
1985 FOOLISH HEART
(S) (3:38) Columbia 39344 and 67849 Street Talk.
1994 YOU BETTER WAIT
(S) (4:50) Columbia 44287 For The Love Of Strange Medicine.

PERSUADERS
1971 THIN LINE BETWEEN LOVE & HATE
- (S) (3:21) Rhino 70786 Soul Hits Of The 70's Volume 6.
- (S) (3:21) Rhino 70659 Billboard's Top R&B Hits Of 1971.
- (S) (3:23) Atlantic 81299 Atlantic Rhythm & Blues Volume 7.
- (S) (3:22) Atlantic 82305 Atlantic Rhythm And Blues 1947-1974 Box Set.
- (S) (3:21) Rhino 71209 70's Smash Hits Volume 5.
- (S) (3:20) Time-Life RHD-09 Rhythm & Blues - 1971.
- (M) (3:17) Time-Life SOD-22 Sounds Of The Seventies - Seventies Top Forty.
- (S) (3:23) Collectables 5139 Thin Line Between Love & Hate.
- (M) (3:17) Original Sound 9303 Art Laboe's Dedicated To You Vol. 3.
- (S) (3:24) MCA 11036 O.S.T. Crooklyn.
- (S) (3:21) Thump 7010 Low Rider Oldies Volume 1.
- (S) (3:21) Rhino 72113 Billboard Hot Soul Hits - 1971.
- (M) (3:17) JCI 3173 1970 - Only Soul - 1974.
- (S) (3:20) Time-Life R838-06 Solid Gold Soul - 1971.
- (S) (3:21) Time-Life R834-10 Body Talk - From The Heart.
- (S) (3:21) Flashback 72685 '70s Radio Hits Volume 5.
- (S) (3:21) K-Tel 3900 Great R&B Male Groups: Hits Of The 70's.

1973 SOME GUYS HAVE ALL THE LUCK

PETER and GORDON
1964 A WORLD WITHOUT LOVE
- (S) (2:39) Rhino 70319 History Of British Rock Volume 1.
- (S) (2:39) Rhino 72022 History Of British Rock Box Set.
- (S) (2:39) Rhino 72008 History Of British Rock Volumes 1-4 Box Set.
- (S) (2:38) Rhino 70748 Best Of.
- (S) (2:37) Capitol 98665 When AM Was King.
- (S) (2:38) JCI 3107 British Sixties.
- (S) (2:38) Time-Life 2CLR-03 Classic Rock - 1964.
- (S) (2:37) Time-Life SUD-09 Superhits - 1964.
- (S) (2:38) Time-Life R962-07 History Of Rock 'N' Roll: The British Invasion 1964-1966.
- (S) (2:38) Rhino 71585 Billboard Top Pop Hits, 1964.
- (S) (2:37) Time-Life AM1-11 AM Gold - 1964.
- (S) (2:38) Collectables 2717 A World Without Love/I Don't Want To See You Again.

1964 NOBODY I KNOW
- (S) (2:28) Rhino 70319 History Of British Rock Volume 1.
- (S) (2:28) Rhino 72022 History Of British Rock Box Set.
- (S) (2:28) Rhino 72008 History Of British Rock Volumes 1-4 Box Set.
- (S) (2:27) Rhino 70748 Best Of.
- (S) (2:26) Time-Life 2CLR-03 Classic Rock - 1964.
- (S) (2:27) Collectables 2717 A World Without Love/I Don't Want To See You Again.

1964 I DON'T WANT TO SEE YOU AGAIN
- (S) (1:59) Rhino 70320 History Of British Rock Volume 2.
- (S) (1:59) Rhino 72022 History Of British Rock Box Set.
- (S) (1:59) Rhino 72008 History Of British Rock Volumes 1-4 Box Set.
- (S) (1:59) Rhino 70748 Best Of.
- (S) (1:58) Time-Life 2CLR-16 Classic Rock - 1964: Shakin' All Over.
- (S) (1:59) Collectables 2717 A World Without Love/I Don't Want To See You Again.

1965 I GO TO PIECES
- (S) (2:21) Rhino 70321 History Of British Rock Volume 3.
- (S) (2:21) Rhino 72022 History Of British Rock Box Set.
- (S) (2:21) Rhino 72008 History Of British Rock Volumes 1-4 Box Set.
- (S) (2:20) Rhino 70748 Best Of.
- (S) (2:20) Time-Life 2CLR-14 Classic Rock - 1965: Shakin' All Over.
- (S) (2:19) Time-Life SUD-03 Superhits - 1965.
- (S) (2:19) Time-Life AM1-10 AM Gold - 1965.
- (S) (2:21) Collectables 2715 I Go To Pieces/True Love Ways.

1965 TRUE LOVE WAYS
- (S) (2:37) Rhino 70321 History Of British Rock Volume 3.
- (S) (2:37) Rhino 72022 History Of British Rock Box Set.

- (S) (2:37) Rhino 72008 History Of British Rock Volumes 1-4 Box Set.
- (S) (2:39) Collectables 2715 I Go To Pieces/True Love Ways.
- (S) (2:37) Rhino 70748 Best Of.

1965 TO KNOW YOU IS TO LOVE YOU
- (S) (2:35) Rhino 70320 History Of British Rock Volume 2.
- (S) (2:35) Rhino 72022 History Of British Rock Box Set.
- (S) (2:35) Rhino 72008 History Of British Rock Volumes 1-4 Box Set.
- (S) (2:34) Rhino 70748 Best Of.
- (S) (2:34) Collectables 2715 I Go To Pieces/True Love Ways.

1966 WOMAN
- (M) (2:27) Rhino 70322 History Of British Rock Volume 4.
- (M) (2:27) Rhino 72022 History Of British Rock Box Set.
- (M) (2:27) Rhino 72008 History Of British Rock Volumes 1-4 Box Set.
- (M) (2:25) Rhino 70748 Best Of.
- (E) (2:26) Collectables 2716 Woman/Lady Godiva. *(noisy fadeout)*

1966 LADY GODIVA
- (S) (2:24) Rhino 70322 History Of British Rock Volume 4.
- (S) (2:24) Rhino 72022 History Of British Rock Box Set.
- (S) (2:24) Rhino 72008 History Of British Rock Volumes 1-4 Box Set.
- (S) (2:24) Rhino 70748 Best Of.
- (S) (2:23) Time-Life SUD-12 Superhits - The Mid 60's.
- (S) (2:23) Time-Life AM1-05 AM Gold - The Mid '60s.
- (S) (2:24) Collectables 2716 Woman/Lady Godiva.

1967 KNIGHT IN RUSTY ARMOUR
- (M) (2:36) Rhino 70326 History Of British Rock Volume 8. *(45 version)*
- (M) (2:36) Rhino 72022 History Of British Rock Box Set. *(45 version)*
- (S) (2:36) Rhino 70748 Best Of. *(LP version)*
- (S) (2:36) Collectables 2716 Woman/Lady Godiva. *(LP version)*

1967 SUNDAY FOR TEA
- (S) (2:19) Rhino 70748 Best Of.
- (S) (2:19) Collectables 2715 I Go To Pieces/True Love Ways.

PETER, PAUL & MARY
1962 LEMON TREE
- (S) (2:55) Warner Brothers 1449 Peter, Paul & Mary.
- (S) (2:55) Warner Brothers 3105 Best Of/Ten Years Together.

1962 IF I HAD A HAMMER (THE HAMMER SONG)
- (S) (2:09) Warner Brothers 1449 Peter, Paul & Mary. *(LP version)*
- (S) (2:09) Warner Brothers 3105 Best Of/Ten Years Together. *(LP version)*
- (S) (2:09) Warner Brothers 46873 Around The Campfire. *(LP version)*

1963 PUFF (THE MAGIC DRAGON)
- (S) (3:36) Warner Brothers 1785 Peter, Paul And Mommy. *(rerecording)*
- (S) (3:26) Warner Brothers 1473 Moving.
- (S) (3:26) Warner Brothers 3105 Best Of/Ten Years Together.
- (S) (4:17) Warner Brothers 46873 Around The Campfire. *(live)*

1963 BLOWIN' IN THE WIND
- (S) (2:55) Warner Brothers 26224 In The Wind.
- (S) (2:55) Warner Brothers 3105 Best Of/Ten Years Together.
- (S) (2:55) Warner Brothers 46873 Around The Campfire.

1963 DON'T THINK TWICE, IT'S ALL RIGHT
- (S) (3:12) Warner Brothers 26224 In The Wind.
- (S) (3:12) Warner Brothers 3105 Best Of/Ten Years Together.

1964 STEWBALL
- (S) (3:08) Warner Brothers 26224 In The Wind.
- (S) (3:08) Warner Brothers 3105 Best Of/Ten Years Together.
- (S) (3:09) Warner Brothers 46873 Around The Campfire.

1964 TELL IT ON THE MOUNTAIN
- (S) (2:54) Warner Brothers 26224 In The Wind.

1965 FOR LOVIN' ME
- (S) (2:07) Warner Brothers 26225 A Song Will Rise.
- (S) (2:07) Warner Brothers 3105 Best Of/Ten Years Together.

1967 I DIG ROCK AND ROLL MUSIC
- (S) (2:29) Warner Brothers 1700 Album 1700.
- (S) (2:30) Warner Brothers 3105 Best Of/Ten Years Together.

1967 TOO MUCH OF NOTHING
    (S)   (2:28)   Warner Brothers 26666 Late Again.
    (S)   (2:27)   Warner Brothers 3105 Best Of/Ten Years Together.

1969 DAY IS DONE
    (S)   (3:12)   Warner Brothers 1785 Peter, Paul And Mommy.
    (LP version)
    (S)   (3:20)   Warner Brothers 3105 Best Of/Ten Years Together. *(45 version)*
    (S)   (3:27)   Warner Brothers 46873 Around The Campfire. *(neither the 45 or LP version)*

1969 LEAVING ON A JET PLANE
    (S)   (3:26)   Warner Brothers 1700 Album 1700.
    (S)   (3:26)   Warner Brothers 3105 Best Of/Ten Years Together.
    (S)   (3:25)   Warner Brothers 46873 Around The Campfire.

BERNADETTE PETERS
1980 GEE WHIZ
    (S)   (2:34)   MCA 10612 Bernadette.
    (S)   (2:33)   Rhino 71890 Radio Daze: Pop Hits Of The 80's Volume One.

PAUL PETERSEN
1962 SHE CAN'T FIND HER KEYS
    (M)   (2:32)   Time-Life 2RNR-47 Rock 'N' Roll Era - Teen Idols II.
    (S)   (2:31)   Rhino 71650 Colpix-Dimension Story.
    (S)   (2:31)   AVI 5014 Best Of.

1963 MY DAD
    (M)   (2:26)   Era 5025 The Brill Building Sound. *(bad dropout at :12)*
    (S)   (2:26)   Rhino 71650 Colpix-Dimension Story.
    (S)   (2:25)   Nick At Nite/Epic 67148 Donna Reed's Dinner Party.
    (S)   (2:25)   AVI 5014 Best Of.
    (S)   (2:25)   K-Tel 3388 TV Stars Sing.

RAY PETERSON
1959 THE WONDER OF YOU
    (M)   (2:34)   RCA 8467 Nipper's Greatest Hits Of The 50's Volume 2.
    (E)   (2:34)   Collectables 5876 Tell Laura I Love Her.
    (M)   (2:33)   Hip-O 40083 The King's Record Collection Vol. 2.

1960 TELL LAURA I LOVE HER
    (S)   (2:54)   RCA 8474 Nipper's Greatest Hits Of The 60's Volume 1.
    (S)   (2:54)   Time-Life 2RNR-27 Rock 'N' Roll Era - Teen Idols.
    (S)   (2:54)   DCC Compact Classics 078 Best Of Tragedy.
    (S)   (2:54)   Time-Life R857-14 The Heart Of Rock 'n' Roll 1960-1961 Take Two.
    (S)   (2:54)   Collectables 5876 Tell Laura I Love Her.

1961 CORINNA, CORINNA
    (M)   (2:39)   Abkco 7118 Phil Spector/Back To Mono (1958-1969).
    (S)   (2:42)   Eric 11502 Hard To Find 45's On CD (Volume I) 1955-60.
    (S)   (2:42)   Collectables 5876 Tell Laura I Love Her.

1961 MISSING YOU
    (S)   (2:45)   Collectables 5876 Tell Laura I Love Her.

PETS
1958 CHA-HUA-HUA

PET SHOP BOYS
1986 WEST END GIRLS
    (S)   (4:49)   Hot Productions 2 Best Of 'O' Records. *(mistakenly identified on both the cd and jacket as track 12 when it is actually track 13; alternate take)*
    (S)   (4:45)   EMI 46271 Please. *(LP length)*
    (S)   (3:58)   EMI 97097 Discography. *(45 length)*
    (S)   (7:48)   Oglio 81584 Hit That Perfect Beat Volume 2. *(12" single version; all songs on this cd are segued together)*
    (S)   (6:28)   EMI-Capitol Entertainment Properties 93688 Essential. *(remix)*

1986 OPPORTUNITIES (LET'S MAKE LOTS OF MONEY)
    (S)   (3:43)   EMI 46271 Please.
    (S)   (3:35)   EMI 97097 Discography.
    (S)   (3:46)   EMI-Capitol Entertainment Properties 93688 Essential. *(buzz noticeable on fadeout)*

1987 IT'S A SIN
    (S)   (4:58)   EMI Manhattan 46972 Actually.
    (S)   (4:58)   EMI 97097 Discography.

released as by THE PET SHOP BOYS and DUSTY SPRINGFIELD:
1988 WHAT HAVE I DONE TO DESERVE THIS?
    (S)   (4:16)   EMI Manhattan 46972 Pet Shop Boys - Actually.
    (S)   (4:18)   EMI 97097 Pet Shop Boys - Discography.
    (S)   (4:10)   Mercury 314553501 Dusty Springfield Anthology.

released as by THE PET SHOP BOYS:
1988 ALWAYS ON MY MIND
    (S)   (9:02)   EMI Manhattan 90868 Introspective. *(LP version)*
    (S)   (3:52)   EMI 97097 Discography. *(45 version)*

1988 DOMINO DANCING
    (S)   (7:41)   EMI Manhattan 90868 Introspective. *(LP version)*
    (S)   (4:16)   EMI 97097 Discography. *(45 version)*
    (S)   (4:40)   EMI-Capitol Entertainment Properties 93688 Essential. *(rerecording)*

TOM PETTY and THE HEARTBREAKERS
1978 BREAKDOWN
    (S)   (2:40)   Rhino 70721 Legends Of Guitar: The 70's Volume 1.
    (S)   (2:41)   MCA 10135 Tom Petty And The Heartbreakers.
    (S)   (2:40)   MCA 10813 Greatest Hits.
    (S)   (2:41)   MCA 11375 Playback.

1980 DON'T DO ME LIKE THAT
    (S)   (2:43)   MCA 31161 Damn The Torpedos.
    (S)   (2:43)   MFSL 551 Damn The Torpedoes. *(gold disc)*
    (S)   (2:41)   MCA 10813 Greatest Hits.
    (S)   (2:41)   MCA 11375 Playback.
    (S)   (2:40)   Time-Life R13610 Gold And Platinum Box Set - The Ultimate Rock Collection.

1980 REFUGEE
    (S)   (3:22)   MCA 31161 Damn The Torpedos.
    (S)   (3:22)   MFSL 551 Damn The Torpedoes. *(gold disc)*
    (S)   (3:18)   Time-Life R102-34 The Rolling Stone Collection.
    (S)   (3:20)   MCA 10813 Greatest Hits.
    (S)   (3:20)   MCA 11375 Playback.

1981 THE WAITING
    (S)   (3:55)   MCA 31066 Hard Promises.
    (S)   (3:55)   MFSL 565 Hard Promises. *(gold disc)*
    (S)   (3:57)   MCA 10813 Greatest Hits.
    (S)   (3:58)   MCA 11375 Playback.

released as by STEVIE NICKS with TOM PETTY and THE HEARTBREAKERS:
1981 STOP DRAGGIN' MY HEART AROUND
    (S)   (4:01)   Atlantic 82306 Atlantic Rock & Roll Box Set.
    (S)   (4:01)   Atlantic 81908 Classic Rock 1966-1988.
    (S)   (4:01)   Modern 38139 Stevie Nicks: Bella Donna.
    (S)   (4:03)   Modern 91711 Stevie Nicks: Timespace: Best Of.
    (S)   (4:00)   Time-Life R988-25 Sounds Of The Eighties: The Rolling Stone Collection 1980-1981.
    (S)   (4:11)   MCA 11375 Tom Petty: Playback. *(demo)*
    (S)   (4:00)   Time-Life R13610 Gold And Platinum Box Set - The Ultimate Rock Collection.
    (S)   (4:01)   Atlantic 83088 Atlantic Records: 50 Years - The Gold Anniversary Collection.
    (S)   (4:02)   Atlantic 83093 Stevie Nicks: Enchanted (Box Set).

released as by TOM PETTY and THE HEARTBREAKERS:
1983 YOU GOT LUCKY
    (S)   (3:31)   MCA 31027 Long After Dark.
    (S)   (3:34)   MCA 10813 Greatest Hits.
    (S)   (3:35)   MCA 11375 Playback.

1983 CHANGE OF HEART
    (S)   (3:17)   MCA 31027 Long After Dark.
    (S)   (3:17)   MCA 11375 Playback.

1985 DON'T COME AROUND HERE NO MORE
    (S)   (5:04)   MCA 5486 Southern Accents. *(LP version)*
    (S)   (5:02)   MCA 10813 Greatest Hits. *(LP version)*

TOM PETTY and THE HEARTBREAKERS (Continued)

    (S)   (5:02)   Time-Life R988-27 Sounds Of The Eighties: The Rolling Stone Collection 1983-1985. *(LP version)*

    (S)   (5:03)   MCA 11375 Playback. *(LP version)*

released as by TOM PETTY and THE HEARTBREAKERS with STEVIE NICKS:
1986 NEEDLES AND PINS

    (S)   (2:25)   MCA 8021 Tom Petty: Pack Up The Plantation - Live.

released as by TOM PETTY and THE HEARTBREAKERS:
1987 JAMMIN' ME

    (S)   (4:08)   MCA 5836 Let Me Up (I've Had Enough).

    (S)   (4:07)   MCA 11375 Playback. *(LP version)*

released as by TOM PETTY:
1989 I WON'T BACK DOWN

    (S)   (2:54)   MCA 6253 Full Moon Fever.

    (S)   (2:54)   MCA 10813 Greatest Hits.

    (S)   (2:55)   MCA 11375 Playback.

1989 RUNNIN' DOWN A DREAM
(dj copies of this 45 ran (4:08) and (4:23); commercial copies were all (4:23))

    (S)   (4:22)   MCA 6253 Full Moon Fever.

    (S)   (4:21)   MCA 10813 Greatest Hits.

    (S)   (4:22)   MCA 11375 Playback.

1990 FREE FALLIN'

    (S)   (4:14)   MCA 6253 Full Moon Fever.

    (S)   (4:14)   MCA 10813 Greatest Hits.

    (S)   (4:13)   Time-Life R988-30 Sounds Of The Eighties: The Rolling Stone Collection 1988-1989.

    (S)   (4:15)   MCA 11375 Playback.

released as by TOM PETTY and THE HEARTBREAKERS:
1991 LEARNING TO FLY

    (S)   (4:01)   MCA 10317 Into The Great Wide Open.

    (S)   (4:00)   MCA 10813 Greatest Hits.

    (S)   (4:00)   MCA 11375 Playback.

1994 MARY JANE'S LAST DANCE

    (S)   (4:31)   MCA 10813 Greatest Hits.

    (S)   (4:31)   MCA 11375 Playback.

1995 YOU DON'T KNOW HOW IT FEELS

    (S)   (4:48)   Warner Brothers 45759 Wildflowers.

ESTHER PHILLIPS
1962 RELEASE ME

    (S)   (3:16)   Rhino 70648 Billboard's Top R&B Hits Of 1962.

    (M)   (3:16)   Atlantic 81297 Atlantic Rhythm & Blues Volume 5.

    (S)   (3:16)   Atlantic 82305 Atlantic Rhythm And Blues 1947-1974 Box Set.

    (S)   (3:15)   Time-Life 2RNR-41 Rock 'N' Roll Era - R&B Gems.

    (S)   (3:16)   Time-Life RHD-11 Rhythm & Blues - 1962.

    (S)   (3:15)   Time-Life HPD-33 Your Hit Parade - The Early 60's.

    (S)   (3:16)   Rhino 71806 The R&B Box: Thirty Years Of Rhythm & Blues.

    (S)   (3:16)   Ripete 2223 Soul Patrol Vol. 5.

    (S)   (3:17)   Rhino 72624 Best Of.

    (M)   (3:15)   Rhino 72815 Beg, Scream & Shout! The Big Ol' Box Of '60s Soul.

    (S)   (3:16)   Repeat/Relativity 1611 A Brand New Bag: #1 Soul Hits Of The 60's Volume 3.

    (S)   (3:16)   Time-Life R838-18 Solid Gold Soul 1962.

1975 WHAT A DIFF'RENCE A DAY MAKES
(dj copies of this 45 ran (3:12) and (4:28); commercial copies were all (3:12))

    (S)   (4:29)   CBS Associated 40710 What A Difference A Day Makes. *(LP version)*

    (S)   (4:21)   Epic/Legacy 45483 Best Of. *(LP version)*

    (S)   (4:29)   Ripete 2219 Beach Fever. *(LP version)*

JOHN PHILLIPS
1970 MISSISSIPPI

    (S)   (3:33)   MCA 10195 Creeque Alley/History Of The Mama's & Papa's.

PHIL PHILLIPS with THE TWILIGHTS
1959 SEA OF LOVE

    (M)   (2:20)   Mercury 842170 O.S.T. Sea Of Love.

    (M)   (2:20)   Rhino 70645 Billboard's Top R&B Hits Of 1959.

    (M)   (2:20)   Mercury 832041 45's On CD Volume 1.

    (M)   (2:20)   Garland 012 Remember When.

    (M)   (2:19)   Essex 7053 A Hot Summer Night In '59.

    (M)   (2:20)   Collectables 5070 History Of Rock Volume 10.

    (M)   (2:20)   Time-Life 2RNR-13 Rock 'N' Roll Era - 1959.

    (M)   (2:20)   Time-Life RHD-03 Rhythm & Blues - 1959.

    (M)   (2:20)   Time-Life R103-27 Love Me Tender.

    (M)   (2:20)   Time-Life R857-01 The Heart Of Rock 'n' Roll - 1959.

    (M)   (2:20)   JCI 3183 1955 - Only Love - 1959.

    (M)   (2:20)   Hip-O 40028 The Glory Of Love - '50s Sweet & Soulful Love Songs.

    (M)   (2:20)   Right Stuff 53320 Hot Rod Rock Volume 5: Back Seat Movers.

    (M)   (2:20)   Time-Life R838-21 Solid Gold Soul 1959.

    (M)   (2:20)   Collectables 1514 and 2514 The Anniversary Album - The 50's.

JIM PHOTOGLO
released as by PHOTOGLO:
1980 WE WERE MEANT TO BE LOVERS

    (S)   (3:34)   Rhino 71891 Radio Daze: Pop Hits Of The 80's Volume Two.

released as by JIM PHOTOGLO:
1981 FOOL IN LOVE WITH YOU

BOBBY "BORIS" PICKETT and THE CRYPT-KICKERS
1962 MONSTER MASH

    (S)   (3:10)   Rhino 71492 Elvira Presents Haunted Hits.

    (S)   (3:10)   Rhino 75768 Dr. Demento Presents.

    (S)   (3:10)   DCC Compact Classics 050 Monster Rock 'N Roll Show.

    (S)   (3:10)   Rhino 70743 Dr. Demento 20th Anniversary Collection.

    (S)   (3:09)   Rhino 70535 Halloween Hits.

    (S)   (3:11)   Deram 844147 The Original Monster Mash.

    (S)   (3:08)   Time-Life 2RNR-37 Rock 'N' Roll Era - Weird, Wild & Wacky.

    (S)   (3:22)   K-Tel 3037 Wacky Weirdos. *(rerecording)*

    (S)   (3:12)   Priority 53747 Wild & Crazy Tunes.

    (S)   (3:09)   Collectables 2505 History Of Rock - The 60's Part 5.

    (S)   (3:09)   Collectables 4505 History Of Rock/The 60s Part Five.

    (M)   (3:02)   Rhino 71778 Elvira Presents Monster Hits. *(rerecording)*

    (S)   (3:11)   Polygram Special Markets 314520272 One Hit Wonders.

    (S)   (3:07)   Risky Business 67311 The Ultimate Party Survival Kit.

    (M)   (3:08)   Music For Little People 42581 A Child's Celebration Of Rock 'N' Roll. *(rerecording)*

    (S)   (3:21)   K-Tel 3795 Music For Your Halloween Party. *(rerecording)*

    (S)   (3:21)   K-Tel 3795 Spooktacular Party Songs. *(rerecording)*

    (S)   (3:10)   Eclipse Music Group 64868 Rock 'n Roll Relix 1962-1963.

    (S)   (3:10)   Eclipse Music Group 64872 Rock 'n Roll Relix 1960-1969.

    (S)   (3:09)   Rhino 72481 Haunted Hits.

    (S)   (3:10)   Polygram Special Markets 314520456 #1 Radio Hits Of The 70's.

1962 MONSTER'S HOLIDAY

    (M)   (3:07)   Rhino 70192 Christmas Classics.

    (M)   (3:08)   Deram 844147 The Original Monster Mash.

    (M)   (3:07)   Rhino 72179 Elvira Presents: Revenge Of The Monster Hits.

1973 MONSTER MASH
(this song was a hit in 1962 and 1973; see 1962 listings)

WILSON PICKETT
1965 IN THE MIDNIGHT HOUR

    (S)   (2:29)   JCI 3100 Dance Sixties. *(no fidelity)*

    (S)   (2:26)   Atlantic 81297 Atlantic Rhythm & Blues Volume 5.

(S) (2:29) Warner Special Products 27601 Atlantic Soul Classics.
(M) (2:32) Atco 91813 Classic Recordings.
(M) (2:35) Atlantic 81737 Greatest Hits. *(missing the opening drum roll; :06 longer than the 45 or LP)*
(S) (2:26) Atlantic 81283 Best Of.
(M) (2:36) Atlantic 82305 Atlantic Rhythm And Blues 1947-1974 Box Set. *(:07 longer than the 45 or LP)*
(M) (2:31) Rhino 70287 A Man And A Half.
(S) (8:09) Rhino 70287 A Man And A Half. *(live)*
(M) (2:31) Rhino 71212 Very Best Of.
(M) (2:31) Rhino 71276 The Exciting.
(M) (2:30) Rhino 71275 In The Midnight Hour.
(M) (2:31) Rhino 71459 Soul Hits, Volume 1.
(M) (2:31) Rhino 71548 Let There Be Drums Volume 2: The 60's.
(M) (2:29) Time-Life RHD-07 Rhythm & Blues - 1965. *(missing the opening drum roll)*
(S) (2:25) Time-Life 2CLR-01 Classic Rock - 1965.
(M) (2:31) Rhino 71729 '60s Rock Classics, Vol. 2.
(S) (2:25) JCI 3126 1965 - Only Rock 'N Roll - 1969.
(S) (2:25) Eclipse Music Group 64869 Rock 'n Roll Relix 1964-1965.
(S) (2:25) Eclipse Music Group 64872 Rock 'n Roll Relix 1960-1969.
(M) (2:29) Time-Life R838-12 Solid Gold Soul - 1965. *(missing the opening drum roll)*
(M) (2:31) Flashback 72702 '60s Rock: The Beat Goes On.
(M) (2:31) Flashback 72088 '60s Rock Hits Box Set.
(M) (2:31) Flashback 72657 '60s Soul: Try A Little Tenderness.
(M) (2:31) Flashback 72091 '60s Soul Hits Box Set.
(M) (2:31) Flashback 72667 In The Midnight Hour And Other Hits.
(M) (2:31) Flashback 72083 Kings And Queens Of Soul Box Set.
(M) (2:31) TVT 8090 O.S.T. My Fellow Americans.
(M) (2:30) TVT 4010 Rhythm Revue.
(M) (2:31) Flashback 72895 25 Years Of R&B - 1965.
(M) (2:31) Rhino 72962 Ultimate '60s Soul Sensations.
(M) (2:37) Atlantic 83088 Atlantic Records: 50 Years - The Gold Anniversary Collection.

1966 634-5789 (SOULSVILLE U.S.A.)
(M) (2:54) Rhino 70652 Billboard's Top R&B Hits Of 1966.
(M) (2:54) Rhino 72006 Billboard's Top R&B Hits 1965-1969 Box Set.
(M) (2:55) Warner Special Products 27609 Memphis Soul Classics.
(M) (2:55) Atlantic 81737 Greatest Hits.
(M) (2:55) Atlantic 81283 Best Of.
(M) (2:55) Atlantic 82305 Atlantic Rhythm And Blues 1947-1974 Box Set.
(M) (2:56) Rhino 70287 A Man And A Half.
(M) (2:56) Rhino 71212 Very Best Of.
(M) (2:56) Rhino 71276 The Exciting.
(M) (2:56) Rhino 71460 Soul Hits, Volume 2.
(M) (2:51) Time-Life RHD-01 Rhythm & Blues - 1966.
(M) (2:53) Time-Life 2CLR-13 Classic Rock - 1966: Shakin' All Over.
(M) (2:56) Rhino 71806 The R&B Box: Thirty Years Of Rhythm & Blues.
(M) (2:51) Time-Life R838-01 Solid Gold Soul - 1966.
(M) (2:56) Flashback 72658 '60s Soul: Baby I Love You.
(M) (2:56) Flashback 72091 '60s Soul Hits Box Set.
(M) (2:55) Flashback 72667 In The Midnight Hour And Other Hits.
(M) (2:55) Flashback 72083 Kings And Queens Of Soul Box Set.
(M) (2:56) Flashback 72896 25 Years Of R&B - 1966.

1966 LAND OF 1000 DANCES
(M) (2:25) Atlantic 81298 Atlantic Rhythm & Blues Volume 6.
(M) (2:25) Warner Special Products 27602 20 Party Classics.
(M) (2:23) Atlantic 81737 Greatest Hits.
(M) (2:23) Atlantic 81283 Best Of.
(M) (2:23) Atlantic 82305 Atlantic Rhythm And Blues 1947-1974 Box Set.
(M) (2:24) Rhino 70287 A Man And A Half.
(M) (2:23) Capitol 81475 Rites Of Rhythm & Blues.
(M) (2:24) Rhino 71212 Very Best Of.

(M) (2:24) Rhino 71276 The Exciting.
(M) (2:24) Rhino 71460 Soul Hits, Volume 2.
(M) (2:24) Time-Life 2CLR-07 Classic Rock - 1966: The Beat Goes On.
(M) (2:23) Epic 66329 O.S.T. Forrest Gump.
(M) (2:24) Rhino 72213 Stadium Rock.
(M) (2:24) JCI 3161 18 Soul Hits From The 60's.
(M) (2:24) Flashback 72711 Sports Rock.
(M) (2:24) Flashback 72658 '60s Soul: Baby I Love You.
(M) (2:24) Flashback 72091 '60s Soul Hits Box Set.
(M) (2:24) Flashback 72667 In The Midnight Hour And Other Hits.
(M) (2:24) Flashback 72083 Kings And Queens Of Soul Box Set.
(M) (2:23) RCA 68904 O.S.T. The Full Monty.
(M) (2:24) Flashback 72896 25 Years Of R&B - 1966.
(M) (2:24) Rhino 72963 Ultimate '60s Soul Smashes.

1966 MUSTANG SALLY
(M) (3:04) Atlantic 81298 Atlantic Rhythm & Blues Volume 6.
(E) (3:04) JCI 3105 Soul Sixties. *(no fidelity)*
(M) (3:05) Atco 91813 Classic Recordings.
(M) (3:04) Atlantic 81737 Greatest Hits.
(M) (3:04) Atlantic 81283 Best Of.
(M) (3:04) Atlantic 82305 Atlantic Rhythm And Blues 1947-1974 Box Set.
(M) (3:05) Rhino 70287 A Man And A Half.
(M) (3:03) Capitol 81475 Rites Of Rhythm & Blues.
(M) (3:05) Rhino 71212 Very Best Of.
(M) (3:02) Time-Life 2CLR-25 Classic Rock - On The Soul Side.
(M) (3:04) Rhino 71517 The Muscle Shoals Sound.
(M) (3:02) JCI 3167 #1 Radio Hits 1965 - Only Rock 'n Roll - 1969.
(M) (3:05) Flashback 72667 In The Midnight Hour And Other Hits.
(M) (3:05) Flashback 72083 Kings And Queens Of Soul Box Set.
(M) (3:05) Right Stuff 53316 Hot Rod Rock Volume 1: Rev It Up.
(M) (3:04) Play-Tone/Epic 69179 Music From The HBO Miniseries "From The Earth To The Moon". *(hum noticeable at the end of every song on this cd)*

1967 EVERYBODY NEEDS SOMEBODY TO LOVE
(M) (2:16) Atlantic 81737 Greatest Hits.
(M) (2:16) Atlantic 81283 Best Of.
(M) (2:17) Rhino 70287 A Man And A Half.
(M) (2:17) Rhino 71212 Very Best Of.

1967 I FOUND A LOVE (PART 1)
(M) (2:54) Atlantic 81283 Best Of. *(mastered from vinyl; not the solo hit recording but the version released in 1963 when Wilson Pickett sang with the Falcons)*
(M) (2:54) Atlantic 81737 Greatest Hits. *(same comments as for Atlantic 81283)*
(M) (2:55) Rhino 71212 Very Best Of. *(same comments as for Atlantic 81283)*

1967 FUNKY BROADWAY
(M) (2:31) Atlantic 81298 Atlantic Rhythm & Blues Volume 6.
(S) (2:33) Atlantic 81737 Greatest Hits.
(S) (2:30) Original Sound 8864 Oldies But Goodies Vol. 14. *(this compact disc uses the "Waring - fds" noise reduction process)*
(S) (2:30) Original Sound 2222 Oldies But Goodies Volumes 3,5,11,14 and 15 Box Set. *(this box set uses the "Waring - fds" noise reduction process)*
(S) (2:30) Original Sound 2500 Oldies But Goodies Volumes 1-15 Box Set. *(this box set uses the "Waring - fds" noise reduction process)*
(S) (2:33) Atlantic 81283 Best Of.
(S) (2:33) Atlantic 82305 Atlantic Rhythm And Blues 1947-1974 Box Set.
(M) (2:35) Rhino 70287 A Man And A Half.
(M) (2:36) Rhino 71212 Very Best Of.
(M) (2:36) Rhino 71460 Soul Hits, Volume 2.
(M) (2:30) Time-Life RHD-10 Rhythm & Blues - 1967.
(M) (2:31) Time-Life 2CLR-05 Classic Rock - 1967.
(M) (2:30) JCI 3190 1965 - Only Dance - 1969.
(M) (2:30) Time-Life R838-02 Solid Gold Soul - 1967.

WILSON PICKETT (Continued)
- (M) (2:35) Flashback 72658 '60s Soul: Baby I Love You.
- (M) (2:35) Flashback 72091 '60s Soul Hits Box Set.
- (M) (2:35) Flashback 72667 In The Midnight Hour And Other Hits.
- (M) (2:35) Flashback 72083 Kings And Queens Of Soul Box Set.
- (M) (2:36) Flashback 72897 25 Years Of R&B - 1967.

1967 STAG-O-LEE
(LP title of this song was "STAGGER LEE")
- (S) (2:20) Rhino 70287 A Man And A Half.
- (M) (2:19) Rhino 72219 In Philadelphia.
- (M) (2:19) Flashback 72667 In The Midnight Hour And Other Hits.
- (M) (2:19) Flashback 72083 Kings And Queens Of Soul Box Set.

1968 SHE'S LOOKIN' GOOD
- (M) (2:19) Atlantic 81737 Greatest Hits.
- (S) (2:26) Rhino 70287 A Man And A Half.
- (S) (2:26) Rhino 71212 Very Best Of.
- (M) (2:21) Rhino 72219 In Philadelphia.

1968 I'M A MIDNIGHT MOVER
- (S) (2:23) Atlantic 81737 Greatest Hits.
- (S) (2:23) Atlantic 81283 Best Of.
- (S) (2:23) Rhino 70287 A Man And A Half.
- (S) (2:23) Rhino 71212 Very Best Of.
- (S) (2:20) Time-Life 2CLR-27 Classic Rock - 1968: Blowin' Your Mind.
- (S) (2:23) Flashback 72667 In The Midnight Hour And Other Hits.
- (S) (2:23) Flashback 72083 Kings And Queens Of Soul Box Set.
- (S) (2:23) Flashback 72898 25 Years Of R&B - 1968.

1969 HEY JUDE
- (S) (4:03) Atlantic 81737 Greatest Hits.
- (S) (4:05) Rhino 70287 A Man And A Half.
- (S) (4:05) Rhino 71212 Very Best Of.
- (S) (4:02) Rhino 71517 The Muscle Shoals Sound.
- (S) (4:03) Risky Business 53918 Rubber Souled.
- (S) (4:02) Flashback 72667 In The Midnight Hour And Other Hits.
- (S) (4:02) Flashback 72083 Kings And Queens Of Soul Box Set.
- (S) (4:05) Hip-O 40064 Meet The Covers.

1970 SUGAR SUGAR
- (S) (2:55) Atlantic 81737 Greatest Hits.
- (S) (2:55) Rhino 70287 A Man And A Half.
- (S) (2:55) Rhino 71212 Very Best Of.
- (S) (2:55) Flashback 72667 In The Midnight Hour And Other Hits.
- (S) (2:55) Flashback 72083 Kings And Queens Of Soul Box Set.
- (S) (2:56) Flashback 72900 25 Years Of Soul - 1970.

1970 ENGINE NUMBER 9
(LP title is "GET ME BACK ON TIME, ENGINE NUMBER 9")
- (S) (6:24) Rhino 70287 A Man And A Half. *(LP version)*
- (S) (6:24) Rhino 71212 Very Best Of. *(LP version)*
- (S) (6:23) Rhino 72219 In Philadelphia. *(LP version)*
- (M) (2:47) Rhino 72219 In Philadelphia. *(45 version)*
- (M) (2:47) Flashback 72900 25 Years Of Soul - 1970. *(45 version)*

1971 DON'T LET THE GREEN GRASS FOOL YOU
- (S) (2:45) Atlantic 81912 Golden Age Of Black Music (1970-1975).
- (S) (2:45) Atlantic 81737 Greatest Hits.
- (S) (3:03) Rhino 70287 A Man And A Half. *(includes :16 of studio talk)*
- (S) (3:03) Rhino 71212 Very Best Of. *(includes :16 of studio talk)*
- (S) (2:45) Rhino 72219 In Philadelphia.
- (M) (2:44) Rhino 72219 In Philadelphia.
- (S) (2:46) Epic/Legacy 64647 The Philly Sound Box Set.

1971 DON'T KNOCK MY LOVE (PART 1)
- (S) (2:21) Atlantic 81912 Golden Age Of Black Music (1970-1975). *(introduction fades in; taken from the LP version)*
- (S) (2:20) Atlantic 81737 Greatest Hits. *(introduction fades in; taken from the LP version)*

- (S) (2:20) Atlantic 82305 Atlantic Rhythm And Blues 1947-1974 Box Set. *(introduction fades in; taken from the LP version)*
- (S) (2:15) Rhino 70287 A Man And A Half.
- (S) (2:15) Rhino 71212 Very Best Of.
- (S) (2:12) Rhino 72113 Billboard Hot Soul Hits - 1971.
- (S) (2:12) Rhino 72964 Ultimate '70s R&B Smashes!

1972 FIRE AND WATER
- (S) (3:29) Rhino 70287 A Man And A Half. *(tracks into the next selection, "(YOUR LOVE HAS BROUGHT ME) A MIGHTY LONG WAY," just like the original vinyl LP)*
- (S) (3:15) Rhino 71212 Very Best Of.

WEBB PIERCE
1959 I AIN'T NEVER
- (S) (1:52) MCA 5939 Vintage Music Volumes 17 & 18.
- (S) (1:52) MCA 31215 Vintage Music Volume 18.
- (S) (1:53) Rhino 70680 Billboard Top Country Hits Of 1959.
- (S) (1:53) MCA 2-8025 30 Years Of Hits 1958 - 1974.
- (S) (1:53) Time-Life CTD-09 Country USA - 1959.
- (S) (1:53) MCA 11069 From The Vaults - Decca Country Classics 1934-1973.
- (S) (1:52) MCA Special Products 22132 Vintage Collectibles Volume 3.
- (S) (1:53) Decca 11330 The Nashville Sound....Owen Bradley.
- (S) (1:53) MCA Special Products 21036 Legends Of Country Music.

PILOT
1975 MAGIC
- (S) (3:02) Rhino 70761 Super Hits Of The 70's Volume 14.
- (S) (3:02) Razor & Tie 22505 More Fabulous 70's Volume 2.
- (S) (3:02) Time-Life SOD-21 Sounds Of The Seventies - Rock 'N' Soul Seventies.
- (S) (3:03) Risky Business 53923 Guilty Pleasures.
- (S) (3:01) Madacy Entertainment 1975 Rock On 1975.
- (S) (3:02) Time-Life AM1-22 AM Gold - 1975.
- (S) (3:02) Collectables 5868 Magic.
- (S) (3:02) Hip-O 40096 '70s Hit(s) Back Again.
- (S) (3:02) Collectables 1516 and 2516 The Anniversary Album - The 70's.

RICK PINETTE and OAK
1980 KING OF THE HILL
- (S) (3:17) Rhino 71893 Radio Daze: Pop Hits Of The 80's Volume Four.

PINK FLOYD
1973 MONEY
(mono dj copies of this 45 edited out the word "shit")
- (S) (6:24) Capitol 46001 Dark Side Of The Moon. *(LP version; tracks into next selection)*
- (S) (6:22) Foundation/Capitol 96647 Hearts Of Gold - The Classic Rock Collection. *(LP version)*
- (S) (6:22) MFSL 517 Dark Side Of The Moon. *(LP version; tracks into next selection; gold disc)*
- (S) (6:22) Columbia 53180 Shine On. *(LP version)*

1980 ANOTHER BRICK IN THE WALL (PART 2)
- (S) (3:52) Columbia 53180 Shine On. *(LP version)*
- (S) (4:01) Columbia 36183 and 68519 The Wall. *(LP version)*

PIPKINS
1970 GIMME DAT DING
- (S) (2:10) Rhino 70926 Super Hits Of The 70's Volume 6.
- (S) (2:10) Time-Life SOD-33 Sounds Of The Seventies - AM Pop Classics II.
- (S) (2:11) Varese Sarabande 5725 Love Grows (Where My Rosemary Goes) - The Voice Of Tony Burrows.
- (S) (2:11) Capitol Special Markets 57272 Great Instrumental Hits From Rock's Golden Years.

PIPS (see GLADYS KNIGHT & THE PIPS)

GENE PITNEY

1961 (I WANNA) LOVE MY LIFE AWAY
    (M) (1:52)   Rhino 75896 Anthology.
    (M) (1:52)   Collectables 5084 His Golden Classics.
    (M) (1:51)   Time-Life 2RNR-42 Rock 'N' Roll Era - The 60's
                          Sock Hop.
    (M) (1:52)   K-Tel 3028 Best Of.
    (M) (1:49)   One Way 31368 Anthology.
    (M) (1:48)   Tomato 71732 The Great Recordings.
    (M) (1:52)   Curb 77758 Greatest Hits.

1961 EVERY BREATH I TAKE
    (M) (2:39)   Garland 012 Remember When.
    (M) (2:44)   Rhino 75896 Anthology.
    (M) (2:42)   Abkco 7118 Phil Spector/Back To Mono (1958-
                          1969).
    (M) (2:44)   Collectables 5084 His Golden Classics.
    (M) (2:44)   Era 5025 The Brill Building Sound.
    (M) (2:42)   Time-Life 2RNR-35 Rock 'N' Roll Era - The 60's
                          Last Dance.
    (M) (2:42)   One Way 31368 Anthology.
    (M) (2:39)   Tomato 71732 The Great Recordings.
    (M) (2:44)   Curb 77758 Greatest Hits.
    (M) (2:45)   King 494 Today's Teardrops.
    (M) (2:43)   Time-Life R857-19 The Heart Of Rock 'n' Roll
                          1960-1961 Take Three.

1962 TOWN WITHOUT PITY
    (M) (2:51)   MCA 6228 O.S.T. Hairspray.
    (M) (2:53)   Rhino 75896 Anthology.
    (M) (2:52)   Collectables 5084 His Golden Classics.
    (M) (2:52)   Time-Life SUD-15 Superhits - The Early 60's.
    (M) (2:52)   K-Tel 3125 Solid Gold Rock N' Roll.
    (M) (2:52)   K-Tel 3028 Best Of.
    (M) (2:51)   One Way 31368 Anthology.
    (M) (2:51)   Tomato 71732 The Great Recordings.
    (M) (2:51)   Curb 77758 Greatest Hits.
    (M) (2:52)   LaserLight 12421 Best Of.
    (M) (2:52)   Time-Life AM1-19 AM Gold - The Early '60s.

1962 (THE MAN WHO SHOT) LIBERTY VALANCE
    (S) (2:55)   Rhino 75896 Anthology.
    (S) (2:55)   Collectables 5084 His Golden Classics.
    (S) (2:54)   Time-Life 2RNR-16 Rock 'N' Roll Era - 1962 Still
                          Rockin'.
    (S) (2:53)   Time-Life SUD-19 Superhits - Early 60's Classics.
    (S) (2:56)   LaserLight 12318 Chart Busters.
    (S) (2:55)   K-Tel 3028 Best Of.
    (S) (2:53)   One Way 31368 Anthology.
    (S) (2:53)   Tomato 71732 The Great Recordings.
    (S) (2:54)   K-Tel 3323 Gunfighter Ballads.
    (S) (2:56)   Curb 77758 Greatest Hits.
    (S) (2:53)   Time-Life AM1-20 AM Gold - Early '60s
                          Classics.

1962 ONLY LOVE CAN BREAK A HEART
    (S) (2:48)   JCI 3102 Love Sixties.
    (S) (2:49)   Rhino 75896 Anthology.
    (S) (2:49)   Collectables 5084 His Golden Classics.
    (S) (2:49)   Time-Life 2RNR-02 Rock 'N' Roll Era - 1962.
    (S) (2:48)   Time-Life SUD-06 Superhits - 1962.
    (S) (2:49)   Time-Life R103-27 Love Me Tender.
    (S) (2:47)   Time-Life R138/05 Look Of Love.
    (S) (2:47)   Rhino 71583 Billboard Top Pop Hits, 1962.
    (S) (2:49)   LaserLight 12323 American Dreams.
    (S) (2:49)   K-Tel 3028 Best Of.
    (S) (2:47)   One Way 31368 Anthology.
    (S) (2:47)   Tomato 71732 The Great Recordings.
    (M) (2:51)   Curb 77758 Greatest Hits.
    (M) (2:51)   LaserLight 12421 Best Of.
    (S) (2:49)   Time-Life R857-06 The Heart Of Rock 'n' Roll
                          1962.
    (S) (2:48)   Time-Life AM1-18 AM Gold - 1962.
    (S) (2:50)   Varese Sarabande 5873 The Burt Bacharach
                          Songbook.
    (S) (2:47)   Time-Life R814-04 Love Songs.

1963 HALF HEAVEN - HALF HEARTACHE
    (S) (2:42)   Rhino 75896 Anthology.
    (S) (2:42)   Collectables 5084 His Golden Classics.
    (S) (2:42)   K-Tel 3028 Best Of.
    (S) (2:41)   One Way 31368 Anthology.

    (S) (2:45)   Tomato 71732 The Great Recordings.
    (M) (2:45)   Curb 77758 Greatest Hits.
    (M) (2:46)   LaserLight 12421 Best Of.
    (S) (2:42)   Time-Life R857-17 The Heart Of Rock 'n' Roll:
                          The Early '60s.

1963 MECCA
    (S) (2:19)   Rhino 75896 Anthology.
    (S) (2:19)   Collectables 5084 His Golden Classics.
    (S) (2:17)   One Way 31368 Anthology.
    (S) (2:14)   Tomato 71732 The Great Recordings.
    (S) (2:18)   Curb 77758 Greatest Hits.
    (S) (2:18)   King 494 Today's Teardrops.
    (S) (2:18)   LaserLight 12421 Best Of.

1963 TRUE LOVE NEVER RUNS SMOOTH
    (S) (2:24)   Rhino 75896 Anthology.
    (S) (2:24)   Collectables 5084 His Golden Classics.
    (S) (2:23)   One Way 31368 Anthology.
    (S) (2:20)   Tomato 71732 The Great Recordings.

1963 TWENTY FOUR HOURS FROM TULSA
    (S) (2:57)   Rhino 75896 Anthology.
    (S) (2:57)   Collectables 5084 His Golden Classics.
    (S) (2:57)   Time-Life 2RNR-19 Rock 'N' Roll Era - 1963 Still
                          Rockin'.
    (S) (2:57)   K-Tel 3028 Best Of.
    (S) (2:55)   One Way 31368 Anthology.
    (S) (2:56)   Tomato 71732 The Great Recordings.
    (S) (2:56)   Curb 77758 Greatest Hits.
    (S) (2:56)   LaserLight 12421 Best Of.

1964 IT HURTS TO BE IN LOVE
    (M) (2:31)   Garland 012 Remember When.
    (M) (2:31)   Rhino 75896 Anthology. *(truncated fade)*
    (M) (2:31)   Collectables 5084 His Golden Classics.
    (M) (2:31)   Era 5025 The Brill Building Sound.
    (M) (2:31)   Time-Life 2RNR-10 Rock 'N' Roll Era - 1964.
    (M) (2:31)   Time-Life SUD-17 Superhits - Mid 60's Classics.
    (M) (2:31)   K-Tel 3028 Best Of.
    (M) (2:29)   One Way 31368 Anthology.
    (E) (2:29)   Tomato 71732 The Great Recordings.
    (M) (2:32)   Curb 77758 Greatest Hits.
    (M) (2:30)   JCI 3166 #1 Radio Hits 1960 - Only Rock 'n Roll -
                          1964.
    (M) (2:32)   LaserLight 12421 Best Of.
    (M) (2:31)   Time-Life AM1-16 AM Gold - Mid '60s Classics.
    (M) (2:32)   Simitar 55572 The Number One's: Hot In The '60s.

1964 I'M GONNA BE STRONG
    (S) (2:12)   Rhino 75896 Anthology.
    (S) (2:12)   Collectables 5084 His Golden Classics.
    (S) (2:11)   Era 5025 The Brill Building Sound.
    (S) (2:12)   Time-Life 2CLR-09 Classic Rock - 1964: The
                          Beat Goes On.
    (S) (2:11)   Time-Life SUD-09 Superhits - 1964.
    (S) (2:11)   Time-Life R962-08 History Of Rock 'N' Roll:
                          Sound Of The City 1959-1965.
    (S) (2:12)   K-Tel 3028 Best Of.
    (S) (2:09)   One Way 31368 Anthology.
    (S) (2:12)   Tomato 71732 The Great Recordings.
    (S) (2:12)   Curb 77758 Greatest Hits.
    (S) (2:12)   LaserLight 12421 Best Of.
    (S) (2:11)   Time-Life R857-09 The Heart Of Rock 'n' Roll
                          1964.
    (S) (2:11)   Time-Life AM1-11 AM Gold - 1964.

1965 I MUST BE SEEING THINGS
    (S) (2:27)   Varese Sarabande 5569 More Greatest Hits.
    (S) (2:23)   One Way 31368 Anthology.
    (S) (2:25)   Tomato 71732 The Great Recordings.

1965 LAST CHANCE TO TURN AROUND
    (S) (3:04)   Rhino 75896 Anthology.
    (S) (3:04)   K-Tel 3028 Best Of.
    (S) (3:02)   One Way 31368 Anthology.
    (S) (3:04)   Tomato 71732 The Great Recordings.
    (S) (3:03)   LaserLight 12421 Best Of.

1965 LOOKING THROUGH THE EYES OF LOVE
    (S) (3:14)   Rhino 75896 Anthology. *(truncated fade)*
    (S) (3:11)   One Way 31368 Anthology. *(truncated fade)*
    (S) (3:11)   Tomato 71732 The Great Recordings.

1965 PRINCESS IN RAGS
    (S) (2:37)   Varese Sarabande 5569 More Greatest Hits.
    (S) (2:37)   One Way 31368 Anthology.

GENE PITNEY (Continued)
    (S) (2:35) Tomato 71732 The Great Recordings.
1966 BACKSTAGE
    (S) (2:36) Varese Sarabande 5569 More Greatest Hits.
    (M) (2:33) One Way 31368 Anthology.
    (S) (2:36) Tomato 71732 The Great Recordings.
    (S) (2:34) LaserLight 12421 Best Of.
1968 SHE'S A HEARTBREAKER
    (S) (3:15) Rhino 75896 Anthology.
    (S) (3:15) Collectables 5084 His Golden Classics.
    (S) (3:13) Time-Life 2CLR-27 Classic Rock - 1968: Blowin' Your Mind.
    (S) (3:15) K-Tel 3028 Best Of.
    (S) (3:13) One Way 31368 Anthology.
    (S) (3:14) Tomato 71732 The Great Recordings.
    (S) (3:14) LaserLight 12421 Best Of.

PLANET SOUL
1996 SET U FREE
    (S) (4:14) Strictly Rhythm 325 Energy And Harmony.
    (S) (3:38) Tommy Boy 1164 MTV Party To Go Volume 9. *(remix; all selections on this cd are segued together)*
    (S) (4:11) Quality 5008 Dance Box Set. *(all selections on this cd are segued together)*
    (S) (4:11) Strictly Rhythm 6313 Strictly Rhythm Superjams. *(all selections on this cd are segued together)*
    (S) (3:51) Rhino 72839 Disco Queens: The 90's.
    (S) (3:56) Boxtunes 162531071 Big Ones Of Dance Volume 1. *(all selections on this cd are segued together)*
    (S) (4:08) Columbia 68602 Total Dance Explosion. *(all songs on this cd are segued together)*
    (S) (4:42) Priority 53110 Dance Mix '96. *(all selections on this cd are segued together; remix)*

ROBERT PLANT
1983 BIG LOG
(dj copies of this 45 ran (3:45) and (5:03); commercial copies were all (5:03))
    (S) (5:02) Es Paranza 90101 The Principle Of Moments.
1984 IN THE MOOD
(dj copies of this 45 ran (3:44) and (5:19); commercial copies were all (5:19))
    (S) (5:18) Es Paranza 90101 The Principle Of Moments.
1985 LITTLE BY LITTLE
(dj copies of this 45 ran (4:09) and (4:43); commercial copies were all (4:43))
    (S) (4:43) Es Paranza 90265 Shaken 'N Stirred.
1988 TALL COOL ONE
    (S) (4:37) Atlantic 81908 Classic Rock 1966-1988. *(LP version)*
    (S) (4:37) Es Paranza 90863 Now And Zen. *(LP version)*
    (S) (4:37) Time-Life R988-29 Sounds Of The Eighties: The Rolling Stone Collection 1987-1988. *(LP version)*
    (S) (4:37) Time-Life R968-18 Guitar Rock - The Heavy '80s. *(LP version)*

PLASTIC ONO BAND (see JOHN LENNON)

EDDIE PLATT
1958 TEQUILA

PLATTERS
1955 ONLY YOU (AND YOU ALONE)
    (M) (2:36) Rhino 70598 Billboard's Top Rock & Roll Hits Of 1955.
    (M) (2:36) Mercury 826448 Oldies Golden Million Sellers.
    (M) (2:34) JCI 3203 Lovin' Fifties.
    (M) (2:36) Mercury 826447 Golden Hits.
    (M) (2:36) Mercury 510317 Very Best Of.
    (M) (2:36) Mercury 510314 The Magic Touch: An Anthology.
    (M) (2:38) MCA 8001 O.S.T. American Graffiti. *(Wolfman Jack talks over the introduction)*
    (M) (2:36) Rhino 71463 Doo Wop Box.

    (M) (2:34) Original Sound 8860 Oldies But Goodies Vol. 10. *(this compact disc uses the "Waring - fds" noise reduction process)*
    (M) (2:34) Original Sound 2221 Oldies But Goodies Volumes 1,4,6,8 and 10 Box Set. *(this box set uses the "Waring - fds" noise reduction process)*
    (M) (2:34) Original Sound 2500 Oldies But Goodies Volumes 1-15 Box Set. *(this box set uses the "Waring - fds" noise reduction process)*
    (M) (2:33) Original Sound 8907 Best Love Songs Vol 2.
    (M) (2:33) Original Sound 9326 Best Love Songs Vol. 1 & 2.
    (M) (2:33) Original Sound 1236 Best Love Songs Box Set.
    (M) (2:34) Time-Life 2RNR-24 Rock 'N' Roll Era - The 50's Keep On Rockin'.
    (M) (2:35) Time-Life RHD-17 Rhythm & Blues - 1955.
    (M) (2:36) Time-Life HPD-09 Your Hit Parade 1955.
    (M) (2:35) Time-Life R962-03 History Of Rock 'N' Roll: Rock 'N' Roll Classics 1954-1956.
    (M) (2:36) Special Music/Essex 5034 Prom Night - The 50's.
    (M) (3:02) King 7002 King R&B Box Set. *(originsl recording but not the hit version)*
    (M) (2:34) Nick At Nite/550 Music/Epic 67768 Fonzie's Make Out Music.
    (M) (2:34) JCI 3164 Eighteen Soulful Ballads.
    (M) (2:35) JCI 3165 #1 Radio Hits 1955 - Only Rock 'n Roll - 1959.
    (M) (2:35) Rhino 72580 Soul Serenade - Intimate R&B.
    (M) (2:36) Rebound 314520420 Soul Classics - Best Of The 60's.
    (M) (2:35) Polygram Special Markets 314520462 50's Soul.
    (M) (2:35) Time-Life R857-21 The Heart Of Rock 'n' Roll Slow Dancing Classics.
    (M) (2:35) Time-Life R857-15 The Heart Of Rock 'n' Roll 1953-1955.
1956 THE GREAT PRETENDER
    (M) (2:37) Rhino 70642 Billboard's Top R&B Hits Of 1956.
    (M) (2:36) Mercury 826447 Golden Hits.
    (M) (2:37) Mercury 510317 Very Best Of.
    (M) (2:37) Mercury 510314 The Magic Touch: An Anthology.
    (M) (2:37) Atlantic 82155 O.S.T. Book Of Love.
    (M) (2:37) Rhino 71463 Doo Wop Box.
    (M) (2:37) Time-Life 2RNR-08 Rock 'N' Roll Era - 1954-1955.
    (M) (2:37) Time-Life RHD-05 Rhythm & Blues - 1956.
    (M) (2:37) Time-Life HPD-25 Your Hit Parade - The 50's.
    (M) (2:37) JCI 3129 1955 - Only Rock 'N Roll - 1959.
    (M) (2:38) Ripete 5151 Ocean Drive 4.
    (M) (2:37) Time-Life R857-13 The Heart Of Rock 'n' Roll 1956-1957.
    (M) (2:37) Nick At Nite/550 Music 63456 Double Date With Joanie And Chachi.
    (M) (2:37) Time-Life R838-24 Solid Gold Soul 1956.
    (M) (2:37) Time-Life R132-14 Golden Groups Of Your Hit Parade.
1956 (YOU'VE GOT) THE MAGIC TOUCH
    (M) (2:25) Mercury 826447 Golden Hits.
    (M) (2:27) Mercury 510317 Very Best Of.
    (M) (2:27) Mercury 510314 The Magic Touch: An Anthology.
    (E) (2:25) Time-Life 2RNR-23 Rock 'N' Roll Era - 1956 Still Rockin'.
    (M) (2:27) Time-Life HPD-21 Your Hit Parade - The Mid 50's.
    (M) (2:27) Polygram Special Markets 314520386 Very Best Of.
    (M) (2:27) Time-Life R857-07 The Heart Of Rock 'n' Roll 1956.
1956 MY PRAYER
    (M) (2:44) Mercury 832041 45's On CD Volume 1.
    (M) (2:42) Mercury 826447 Golden Hits.
    (M) (2:42) Original Sound 8853 Oldies But Goodies Vol. 3. *(this compact disc uses the "Waring - fds" noise reduction process)*
    (M) (2:42) Original Sound 2222 Oldies But Goodies Volumes 3,5,11,14 and 15 Box Set. *(this box set uses the "Waring - fds" noise reduction process)*
    (M) (2:42) Original Sound 2500 Oldies But Goodies Volumes 1-15 Box Set. *(this box set uses the "Waring - fds" noise reduction process)*

(M) (2:44) Mercury 510317 Very Best Of.
(M) (2:44) Mercury 510314 The Magic Touch: An Anthology.
(M) (2:44) Time-Life 2RNR-14 Rock 'N' Roll Era - 1956.
(M) (2:45) Time-Life HPD-15 Your Hit Parade - 1956.
(M) (2:44) Time-Life R962-06 History Of Rock 'N' Roll: Doo Wop And Vocal Group Tradition 1955-1962.
(M) (2:44) Time-Life R10513 40 Lovin' Oldies.
(M) (2:44) Rhino 72507 Doo Wop Box II.
(M) (2:44) JCI 7021 Those Wonderful Years - April Love.
(M) (2:44) Polygram Special Markets 314520386 Very Best Of.
(M) (2:45) Time-Life R857-07 The Heart Of Rock 'n' Roll 1956.
(M) (2:45) Time-Life R132-12 Your Hit Parade - #1 Hits Of The '50s.
(M) (2:45) Time-Life R132-14 Golden Groups Of Your Hit Parade.

1956 YOU'LL NEVER NEVER KNOW
(S) (1:54) Mercury 830773 More Golden Hits. *(this is not the song "YOU'LL NEVER NEVER KNOW" as the cd jacket states but a similarly titled song, "YOU'LL NEVER KNOW")*
(M) (2:37) Mercury 826447 Golden Hits.
(M) (2:37) Mercury 510317 Very Best Of.
(M) (2:37) Mercury 510314 The Magic Touch: An Anthology.
(M) (2:37) Polygram Special Markets 314520386 Very Best Of.
(M) (2:36) Time-Life R857-13 The Heart Of Rock 'n' Roll 1956-1957.

1956 IT ISN'T RIGHT
(M) (2:24) Mercury 830773 More Golden Hits.
(M) (2:24) Mercury 510314 The Magic Touch: An Anthology.

1957 ON MY WORD OF HONOR
(M) (2:41) Mercury 510317 Very Best Of.
(M) (2:41) Mercury 510314 The Magic Touch: An Anthology.

1957 ONE IN A MILLION
(M) (2:52) Mercury 830773 More Golden Hits.
(M) (2:52) Mercury 510314 The Magic Touch: An Anthology.
(M) (2:52) Time-Life R857-16 The Heart Of Rock 'n' Roll The Late '50s.

1957 I'M SORRY
(E) (2:52) Mercury 830773 More Golden Hits.
(M) (2:51) Mercury 510317 Very Best Of.
(M) (2:51) Mercury 510314 The Magic Touch: An Anthology.
(M) (2:52) Time-Life 2RNR-17 Rock 'N' Roll Era - 1957 Still Rockin'.
(M) (2:53) Time-Life RHD-08 Rhythm & Blues - 1957.
(M) (2:53) Time-Life R857-05 The Heart Of Rock 'n' Roll 1957.
(M) (2:53) Time-Life R838-23 Solid Gold Soul 1957.

1957 HE'S MINE
(M) (2:21) Mercury 510314 The Magic Touch: An Anthology.

1957 MY DREAM
(E) (2:37) Mercury 830773 More Golden Hits.
(M) (2:36) Mercury 510314 The Magic Touch: An Anthology.

1958 TWILIGHT TIME
(M) (2:43) Mercury 826447 Golden Hits. *(45 version)*
(S) (2:44) Mercury 510317 Very Best Of. *(stereo LP version)*
(S) (2:44) Mercury 510314 The Magic Touch: An Anthology. *(stereo LP version)*
(E) (2:43) Time-Life 2RNR-21 Rock 'N' Roll Era - 1958 Still Rockin'. *(45 version)*
(S) (2:44) Time-Life RHD-16 Rhythm & Blues - 1958. *(stereo LP version)*
(S) (2:45) Time-Life HPD-11 Your Hit Parade 1958. *(stereo LP version)*
(E) (2:43) Time-Life R103-27 Love Me Tender. *(45 version)*
(S) (2:44) Time-Life R857-04 The Heart Of Rock 'n' Roll - 1958. *(stereo LP version)*
(S) (2:44) JCI 3183 1955 - Only Love - 1959. *(stereo LP version)*
(S) (2:44) Polygram Special Markets 314520386 Very Best Of. *(stereo LP version)*
(S) (2:44) Polygram Special Markets 314520462 50's Soul. *(stereo LP version)*
(S) (2:44) Time-Life R838-22 Solid Gold Soul 1958. *(stereo LP version)*

1958 I WISH
(S) (2:44) Mercury 830773 More Golden Hits.
(S) (2:41) Mercury 510314 The Magic Touch: An Anthology.

1959 SMOKE GETS IN YOUR EYES
(M) (2:38) Mercury 826448 Oldies Golden Million Sellers.
(M) (2:38) Mercury 826447 Golden Hits.
(S) (2:37) Mercury 510317 Very Best Of. *(very poor stereo separation)*
(S) (2:36) Mercury 510314 The Magic Touch: An Anthology. *(very poor stereo separation)*
(S) (2:37) MCA 8001 O.S.T. American Graffiti.
(E) (2:38) Original Sound 8864 Oldies But Goodies Vol. 14. *(this compact disc uses the "Waring - fds" noise reduction process)*
(E) (2:38) Original Sound 2222 Oldies But Goodies Volumes 3,5,11,14 and 15 Box Set. *(this box set uses the "Waring - fds" noise reduction process)*
(E) (2:38) Original Sound 2500 Oldies But Goodies Volumes 1-15 Box Set. *(this box set uses the "Waring - fds" noise reduction process)*
(E) (2:37) Original Sound 8905r 13 Of The Best Doo Wop Love Songs.
(E) (2:37) Original Sound 9326 Best Love Songs Vol. 1 & 2.
(E) (2:37) Original Sound 8891 Dick Clark's 21 All-Time Hits Vol. 1.
(E) (2:37) Original Sound 4001 Art Laboe's 60 Killer Oldies.
(E) (2:37) Original Sound 1236 Best Love Songs Box Set.
(M) (2:38) Time-Life 2RNR-20 Rock 'N' Roll Era - 1959 Still Rockin'.
(S) (2:37) Time-Life RHD-03 Rhythm & Blues - 1959. *(very poor stereo separation)*
(S) (2:37) Time-Life HPD-13 Your Hit Parade - 1959. *(very poor stereo separation)*
(S) (2:37) Time-Life R103-27 Love Me Tender.
(M) (2:38) Polygram Special Markets 314520258 No. 1 Hits Of The 50's.
(S) (2:37) Time-Life R857-01 The Heart Of Rock 'n' Roll - 1959.
(S) (2:37) Time-Life R974-03 Many Moods Of Romance - I Wish You Love.
(M) (2:38) LaserLight 12314 and 15936 The Wonder Years - Party Time.
(M) (2:37) Priority 50950 I Love Rock & Roll Volume 1: Hits Of The 50's.
(S) (2:37) Right Stuff 53320 Hot Rod Rock Volume 5: Back Seat Movers.
(S) (2:38) Time-Life R838-21 Solid Gold Soul 1959. *(very poor stereo separation)*
(S) (2:36) Time-Life R814-04 Love Songs.
(S) (2:37) Time-Life R132-10 Love Songs Of Your Hit Parade.
(S) (2:37) Time-Life R132-14 Golden Groups Of Your Hit Parade.
(S) (2:36) Collectables 1514 and 2514 The Anniversary Album - The 50's.

1959 ENCHANTED
(E) (2:52) Mercury 830773 More Golden Hits.
(S) (2:51) Mercury 510317 Very Best Of. *(very poor stereo separation)*
(S) (2:51) Mercury 510314 The Magic Touch: An Anthology. *(very poor stereo separation)*
(S) (2:51) Time-Life R857-11 The Heart Of Rock 'n' Roll 1958-1959. *(very poor stereo separation)*

1959 REMEMBER WHEN
(S) (2:47) Mercury 830773 More Golden Hits.
(M) (2:47) Mercury 510314 The Magic Touch: An Anthology.

1960 HARBOR LIGHTS
(E) (3:06) Mercury 826447 Golden Hits. *(LP version)*
(S) (3:09) Mercury 510317 Very Best Of. *(LP version)*
(S) (3:09) Mercury 510314 The Magic Touch: An Anthology. *(LP version)*
(S) (2:44) Time-Life SUD-19 Superhits - Early 60's Classics. *(45 version)*
(S) (2:44) Time-Life HPD-32 Your Hit Parade - Into The 60's. *(45 version)*
(S) (3:09) Polygram Special Markets 314520264 Soul Hits Of The 60's. *(LP version)*
(S) (2:43) Time-Life R857-02 The Heart Of Rock 'n' Roll - 1960. *(45 version)*

(S) (2:43) Time-Life R974-16 Many Moods Of Romance - The Look Of Love. *(45 version)*

(S) (3:09) Rebound 314520369 Soul Classics - Quiet Storm/The 60's. *(LP version)*

(S) (2:44) Time-Life AM1-20 AM Gold - Early '60s Classics. *(45 version)*

(S) (3:09) JCI 3184 1960 - Only Love - 1964. *(LP version)*

1960 RED SAILS IN THE SUNSET

(E) (2:23) Mercury 826447 Golden Hits.

(S) (2:20) Mercury 510314 The Magic Touch: An Anthology. *(very poor stereo separation)*

(S) (2:20) Special Music/Essex 5035 Prom Night - The 60's. *(very poor stereo separation)*

1960 TO EACH HIS OWN

(S) (2:48) Mercury 830773 More Golden Hits.

(S) (2:47) Mercury 510314 The Magic Touch: An Anthology. *(very poor stereo separation)*

(S) (2:48) Time-Life R857-19 The Heart Of Rock 'n' Roll 1960-1961 Take Three. *(very poor stereo separation)*

1961 IF I DIDN'T CARE

(S) (3:06) Mercury 830773 More Golden Hits.

(S) (3:07) Mercury 510317 Very Best Of.

(S) (3:06) Mercury 510314 The Magic Touch: An Anthology.

1961 I'LL NEVER SMILE AGAIN

(S) (2:51) Mercury 830773 More Golden Hits.

(S) (2:51) Mercury 510314 The Magic Touch: An Anthology. *(very poor stereo separation)*

(S) (2:51) Time-Life R857-17 The Heart Of Rock 'n' Roll: The Early '60s. *(very poor stereo separation)*

(S) (2:51) Polygram Special Markets 314520454 Soul Hits Of The 60's.

1966 I LOVE YOU 1000 TIMES

(S) (2:41) Ripete 2392192 Beach Music Anthology Box Set.

(S) (2:40) Ripete 2163-RE Ebb Tide.

(S) (2:42) Collectables 5577 The Musicor Years.

(S) (2:40) Ripete 2184-RE Ocean Drive Vol. 2.

(S) (2:39) Curb 77825 Greatest Hits Volume 2.

(S) (2:42) Varese Sarabande 5774 Very Best Of 1966-1969.

(S) (2:39) TVT 4010 Rhythm Revue.

1967 WITH THIS RING

(S) (2:41) Rhino 70589 Rockin' & Rollin' Wedding Songs Volume 2.

(S) (2:41) Ripete 2392192 Beach Music Anthology Box Set.

(S) (2:42) Ripete 2187-RE Preppy Deluxe.

(S) (2:40) Collectables 5577 The Musicor Years.

(S) (2:41) Ripete 2184-RE Ocean Drive Vol. 2.

(S) (2:40) K-Tel 3269 Carolina Beach Music.

(S) (2:40) Curb 77825 Greatest Hits Volume 2.

(S) (2:39) Varese Sarabande 5774 Very Best Of 1966-1969.

(S) (2:40) K-Tel 3901 Soul Brothers & Sisters Of The 60's.

PLAYER

1978 BABY COME BACK

(S) (3:23) Priority 7066 #1 Groups/70's Greatest Rock Hits Volume 12. *(45 version faded :08 early)*

(S) (3:33) Rhino 70673 Billboard Top Hits - 1978. *(45 version)*

(S) (3:29) Razor & Tie 4543 The '70s Preservation Society Presents: Easy '70s. *(45 version)*

(S) (3:34) Rhino 71201 Super Hits Of The 70's Volume 21. *(45 version)*

(S) (3:29) Time-Life SOD-20 Sounds Of The Seventies - 1978: Take Two. *(45 version)*

(S) (3:33) Polygram Special Markets 314520271 Hits Of The 70's. *(45 version)*

(S) (3:32) Rebound 314520372 The Roots Of Rock: Soft Rock. *(45 version)*

(S) (4:09) Rhino 72517 Mellow Rock Hits Of The 70's - Ventura Highway. *(LP version)*

(S) (3:34) Time-Life R834-04 Body Talk - Together Forever. *(45 version)*

(S) (3:33) Hip-O 40096 '70s Hit(s) Back Again. *(45 version)*

(S) (3:34) Time-Life AM1-25 AM Gold - 1978. *(45 version)*

(S) (3:33) Collectables 1516 and 2516 The Anniversary Album - The 70's. *(45 version)*

(S) (3:28) K-Tel 3987 70s Heavy Hitters: #1 Pop Hits. *(45 version)*

1978 THIS TIME I'M IN IT FOR LOVE

(S) (3:28) Special Music/Essex 5036 Prom Night - The 70's. *(45 version)*

(S) (3:43) Rhino 72297 Superhits Of The 70's Volume 23. *(45 version but :17 longer fade than the 45)*

(S) (3:42) Time-Life R834-20 Body Talk - Heart And Soul. *(45 version but :16 longer fade than the 45)*

1978 PRISONER OF YOUR LOVE

(S) (6:26) Special Music 5040 Great Britons! Volume Two. *(LP version)*

PLAYMATES

1958 JO-ANN

(M) (2:34) Collectables 5418 Golden Classics.

1958 DON'T GO HOME

(M) (2:33) Collectables 5418 Golden Classics.

1958 BEEP BEEP

(actual 45 time is (2:29) not (2:20) as stated on the record label)

(S) (2:42) Rhino 70743 Dr. Demento 20th Anniversary Collection. *(LP version edited in an unsuccessful attempt at recreating the 45 version; much slower than the 45)*

(S) (3:04) Collectables 5416 Murray The K - Sing Along With The Golden Gassers. *(LP version)*

(S) (3:04) Collectables 5418 Golden Classics. *(LP version)*

(E) (2:27) K-Tel 3036 Silly Songs. *(45 version but slightly faster)*

(M) (2:27) Time-Life 2RNR-37 Rock 'N' Roll Era - Weird, Wild & Wacky. *(45 version but slightly faster)*

1959 WHAT IS LOVE?

(S) (2:16) Collectables 5418 Golden Classics.

(M) (2:11) Essex 7053 A Hot Summer Night In '59.

1960 WAIT FOR ME

(S) (2:49) Collectables 5418 Golden Classics.

P.M. DAWN

1991 SET ADRIFT ON MEMORY BLISS

(S) (5:16) Columbia 52826 Red Hot + Dance. *(remixed)*

(S) (5:12) Tommy Boy 1053 MTV Party To Go Volume 2. *(remix; all tracks on this cd are segued together)*

(S) (4:10) Foundation/RCA 66563 Number 1 Hit Mix.

(S) (4:10) Gee Street 314510276 and 32509 Of The Heart, Of The Soul And Of The Cross: The Utopian Experience.

(S) (4:09) Razor & Tie 4569 '90s Style.

1992 PAPER DOLL

(S) (4:50) Gee Street 314510276 and 32509 Of The Heart, Of The Soul And Of The Cross: The Utopian Experience.

1992 I'D DIE WITHOUT YOU

(S) (4:10) LaFace 26006 O.S.T. Boomerang.

(S) (4:10) Gee Street 314514517 and 32510 The Bliss Album.

(S) (4:10) EMI-Capitol Music Group 54555 Movie Luv.

(S) (4:10) Priority 50974 Premiere The Movie Magazine Presents The Greatest Soundtrack Love Songs.

1993 LOOKING THROUGH PATIENT EYES

(S) (4:06) Gee Street 314514517 and 32510 The Bliss Album.

POCO

1979 CRAZY LOVE

(S) (2:54) MCA 31019 Legend.

(S) (2:54) MCA 11206 Legend. *(gold disc)*

(S) (2:54) MCA 45323 Crazy Loving/Best Of 1975-82.

(S) (2:54) MCA Special Products 20910 Rockin' 70's.

(S) (2:54) MCA Special Products 20958 Mellow Classics.

(S) (2:53) JCI 3146 1975 - Only Love - 1979.

(S) (2:54) Time-Life R834-05 Body Talk - Sealed With A Kiss.

(S) (2:53) K-Tel 4017 70s Heavy Hitters: Summer Love.

1979 HEART OF THE NIGHT

(S) (4:50) MCA 31019 Legend.

(S) (4:50) MCA 11206 Legend. *(gold disc)*

(S) (4:50) MCA 45323 Crazy Loving/Best Of 1975-82.
(S) (4:50) K-Tel 3697 Best Of Country Rock.
(S) (4:48) Rhino 72518 Mellow Rock Hits Of The 70's - Summer Breeze.
(S) (4:50) JCI 3193 18 Rock Classics Volume 3.
(S) (4:51) Priority 50962 70's Greatest Rock Hits Volume 7: Southern Rock.

1989 CALL IT LOVE
(S) (4:16) K-Tel 6006 Lite Rock. *(LP version)*
(S) (4:16) RCA 9694 Legacy. *(LP version)*

POINT BLANK
1981 NICOLE
(S) (3:58) K-Tel 6083 Southern Fried Rock - Second Helping.

BONNIE POINTER
1979 HEAVEN MUST HAVE SENT YOU
(actual LP time is (7:12) not (6:59) as stated on the record label)
(S) (3:33) Motown 9110 and 5414 Motown Memories Volume 4. *(45 version)*
(S) (3:33) Priority 7973 Mega-Hits Dance Classics Volume 3. *(45 version)*
(S) (3:33) Motown 6358 Hitsville USA Volume Two. *(45 version)*
(S) (3:31) Time-Life SOD-19 Sounds Of The Seventies - 1979: Take Two. *(45 version)*
(S) (7:11) Rebound 314520298 Disco Nights Vol. 9. *(LP version)*
(S) (3:20) Rhino 71890 Radio Daze: Pop Hits Of The 80's Volume One. *(previously unreleased version)*
(S) (3:20) K-Tel 3906 Starflight Vol. 1. *(previously unreleased version)*
(S) (5:58) Robbins Entertainment 75008 Dance Party (Like It's 1998). *(LP version faded :14 early; all songs on this cd are segued together)*
(S) (3:33) Time-Life R840-09 Sounds Of The Seventies: '70s Dance Party 1979-1981. *(45 version)*
(S) (2:34) Rebound 314520520 Body Moves - Non-Stop Disco Workout Vol. 1. *(all selections on this cd are segued together)*

POINTER SISTERS
1973 YES WE CAN CAN
(dj copies of this 45 ran (2:40); commercial copies were all (3:55))
(S) (3:05) Rhino 70551 Soul Hits Of The 70's Volume 11. *(previously unreleased version)*
(S) (5:59) MCA 31377 The Pointer Sisters. *(LP version)*
(S) (3:05) Rhino 71618 Soul Train Hall Of Fame/20th Anniversary. *(previously unreleased version)*
(S) (3:51) Razor & Tie 22045 Those Funky 70's. *(45 version)*
(S) (4:14) Time-Life SOD-14 Sounds Of The Seventies - 1973: Take Two. *(45 version but :19 longer)*
(S) (5:59) Blue Thumb 7002 All Day Thumbsucker Revisited. *(LP version)*
(S) (3:05) Ichiban 2511 Love, Peace & Understanding. *(previously unreleased version)*
(S) (3:04) RCA 66863 Fire - Very Best Of. *(previously unreleased version)*
(S) (4:13) K-Tel 3625 Dynamite. *(45 version but :18 longer)*
(S) (6:00) Hip-O 40010 ABC's Of Soul Volume 2. *(LP version)*
(S) (6:00) Hip-O 40035 Cigar Classics Volume 2 - Urban Fire. *(LP version)*
(S) (6:00) Hip-O 40052 Yes We Can Can: Best Of The Blue Thumb Recordings. *(LP version)*
(S) (3:05) Rhino 72837 Disco Queens: The 70's. *(previously unreleased version)*

1974 FAIRYTALE
(S) (5:02) RCA 66863 Fire - Very Best Of. *(LP version)*
(S) (3:01) Hip-O 40052 Yes We Can Can: Best Of The Blue Thumb Recordings. *(45 version)*

1975 HOW LONG (BETCHA' GOT A CHICK ON THE SIDE)
(S) (7:20) MCA 10288 Classic Soul. *(LP version)*
(S) (3:25) RCA 66863 Fire - Very Best Of. *(45 version)*

(S) (7:20) Hip-O 40011 ABC's Of Soul Volume 3. *(LP version)*
(S) (7:20) Hip-O 40052 Yes We Can Can: Best Of The Blue Thumb Recordings. *(LP version)*
(S) (3:29) JCI 3175 1975 - Only Soul - 1979. *(45 version)*
(S) (7:19) K-Tel 3889 Great R&B Female Groups: Hits Of The 70s. *(LP version)*

1979 FIRE
(actual 45 and LP time is (3:27) not (3:41) as stated on the record label)
(S) (3:27) Rhino 70674 Billboard Top Hits - 1979.
(S) (3:27) RCA 9816 Greatest Hits.
(S) (3:29) Rhino 71227 Black On White: Great R&B Covers Of Rock Classics.
(S) (3:25) RCA 66198 Best Of 1978-1981.
(S) (3:26) Time-Life SOD-09 Sounds Of The Seventies - 1979.
(S) (3:27) RCA 66863 Fire - Very Best Of.
(S) (3:25) Nick At Nite/550 Music 67690 I Am Woman.
(S) (3:27) Priority 53140 Best Of The 70's: Legendary Ladies.
(S) (3:27) Time-Life R834-09 Body Talk - Magic Moments.
(S) (3:27) K-Tel 3908 High Energy Volume 1.
(S) (3:26) Hip-O 40096 '70s Hit(s) Back Again.
(S) (3:26) Time-Life R840-10 Sounds Of The Seventies: '70s Dance Party 1979.

1979 HAPPINESS
(S) (3:56) RCA 66198 Best Of 1978-1981.
(S) (3:57) RCA 66863 Fire - Very Best Of.

1980 HE'S SO SHY
(S) (3:36) Rhino 70675 Billboard Top Hits - 1980.
(S) (3:37) RCA 9816 Greatest Hits.
(S) (3:35) RCA 66198 Best Of 1978-1981.
(S) (3:35) Priority 53730 Mega Hits Dance Classics Vol. 13.
(S) (3:36) Rhino 71971 Video Soul - Best Soul Of The 80's Vol. 1.
(S) (3:36) Time-Life R988-07 Sounds Of The Eighties: 1980.
(S) (3:37) RCA 66863 Fire - Very Best Of.
(S) (3:37) Hip-O 40075 Rock She Said: On The Pop Side.
(S) (3:36) Time-Life R834-18 Body Talk - Romantic Moments.

1981 SLOW HAND
(S) (3:49) RCA 61153 and 61135 Sweet & Soulful.
(S) (3:51) RCA 9816 Greatest Hits.
(S) (3:50) RCA 66198 Best Of 1978-1981.
(S) (3:54) RCA 55092 Black & White.
(S) (3:50) Time-Life R988-08 Sounds Of The Eighties: 1981.
(S) (3:50) Time-Life R138-18 Body Talk.
(S) (3:53) RCA 66812 Do You Love Me? (All-Time Best Love Songs).
(S) (3:48) Rebound 314520361 Class Reunion '81.
(S) (3:50) RCA 66863 Fire - Very Best Of.
(S) (3:50) JCI 3170 #1 Radio Hits 1980 - Only Rock 'n Roll - 1984.
(S) (3:50) Madacy Entertainment 6803 Power Of Love.
(S) (3:50) Time-Life R834-02 Body Talk - Just For You.
(S) (3:53) JCI 3176 1980 - Only Soul - 1984.
(S) (3:53) BMG Special Products 44762 The President's Greatest Hits.

1982 SHOULD I DO IT
(S) (3:53) RCA 55092 Black & White.
(S) (3:49) RCA 66198 Best Of 1978-1981.
(S) (3:49) RCA 61153 and 61135 Sweet & Soulful.
(S) (3:50) RCA 66863 Fire - Very Best Of.

1982 AMERICAN MUSIC
(S) (3:58) RCA 9816 Greatest Hits. *(LP length)*
(S) (3:58) MCA 11238 God Bless The U.S.A. *(LP length)*
(S) (3:58) RCA 66863 Fire - Very Best Of. *(LP length)*

1982 I'M SO EXCITED
(this song appeared on two different POINTER SISTERS albums in two different versions; the 1982 version appeared on the "So Excited!" vinyl LP while the 1984 version appeared on the second pressing of the "Break Out" vinyl LP)
(S) (5:37) Arista 8593 O.S.T. Working Girl. *(12" single version)*
(S) (4:51) T.J. Martell Foundation/Columbia 40315 Music For The Miracle. *("Break Out" LP version)*
(S) (5:38) RCA 61144 The RCA Records Label: The 1st Note In Black Music. *(12" single version)*

POINTER SISTERS *(Continued)*

(S)   (4:53)   RCA 4705   Break Out. *("Break Out" LP version)*
(S)   (5:38)   RCA 9816   Greatest Hits. *(12" single version)*
(S)   (4:22)   Time-Life R988-11   Sounds Of The 80's: 1983-1984. *("Break Out" LP version faded :31 early)*
(S)   (4:22)   Time-Life R138-38   Celebration. *("Break Out" LP version faded :31 early)*
(S)   (4:51)   Big Ear Music 4002   Only In The 80's Volume Two. *("Break Out" LP version)*
(S)   (3:52)   RCA 66863   Fire - Very Best Of. *(1984 45 version)*
(S)   (5:35)   RCA 67474   Roller Hockey - The Album. *(12" single version)*
(S)   (4:44)   Cold Front 6255   Greatest Sports Rock And Jams Volume 2. *(all selections on this cd are segued together; "Break Out" LP version)*
(S)   (4:44)   K-Tel 4065   K-Tel's Original Party Music Vol. 1. *("Break Out" LP version)*

1984   AUTOMATIC
(dj copies of this 45 ran (3:59) and (4:48);
commercial copies were all (3:59))

(S)   (6:04)   RCA 2357   Dance, Dance, Dance Volume II. *(12" single version)*
(S)   (4:46)   RCA 4705   Break Out. *(LP version)*
(S)   (6:05)   RCA 9816   Greatest Hits. *(12" single version)*
(S)   (4:47)   Rhino 72139   Billboard Hot R&B Hits 1984. *(LP version)*
(S)   (4:46)   RCA 66863   Fire - Very Best Of. *(LP version)*
(S)   (4:47)   JCI 3163   18 Disco Superhits. *(LP version)*
(S)   (4:46)   Time-Life R988-17   Sounds Of The Eighties: The Mid '80s Take Two. *(LP version)*

1984   JUMP (FOR MY LOVE)
(this song can be found on the POINTER SISTERS "Break Out" album which appeared in two different incarnations with different track lineups and mixes)

(S)   (6:23)   RCA 2357   Dance, Dance, Dance Volume II. *(12" single version)*
(S)   (3:58)   Rhino 70679   Billboard Top Hits - 1984. *(45 version)*
(S)   (3:57)   JCI 3127   1980 - Only Rock 'N Roll - 1984. *(45 version)*
(S)   (6:24)   Rebound 314520309   Disco Nights Vol. VII - D.J. Pix. *(12" single version)*
(S)   (3:58)   Rhino 71972   Video Soul - Best Soul Of The 80's Vol. 2. *(45 version)*
(S)   (4:26)   RCA 4705   Break Out. *(second "Break Out" LP version)*
(S)   (6:24)   RCA 9816   Greatest Hits. *(12" single version)*
(S)   (4:26)   K-Tel 3500   The 80's - Urban Countdown. *(second "Break Out"LP version)*
(S)   (3:58)   Time-Life R988-06   Sounds Of The Eighties: 1984. *(45 version)*
(S)   (3:58)   MCA 11329   Soul Train 25th Anniversary Box Set. *(45 version)*
(S)   (4:22)   RCA 66863   Fire - Very Best Of. *(first "Break Out" LP version)*
(S)   (3:59)   Hip-O 40015   Soulful Ladies Of The 80's. *(45 version)*
(S)   (3:58)   Rhino 72838   Disco Queens: The 80's. *(45 version)*
(S)   (3:56)   K-Tel 4046   More Music For Your Party. *(45 version)*
(S)   (3:56)   K-Tel 4066   K-Tel's Original Party Music Vol. 2. *(45 version)*

1984   I'M SO EXCITED
(this song charted in two different years: 1982 & 1984; see 1982 listings)

1985   NEUTRON DANCE

(S)   (4:14)   MCA 5553   O.S.T. Beverly Hills Cop. *(LP version)*
(S)   (4:12)   RCA 4705   Break Out. *(LP version)*
(S)   (5:33)   RCA 9816   Greatest Hits.
(S)   (4:11)   Big Ear Music 4003   Only In The 80's Volume Three. *(LP version)*
(S)   (4:13)   RCA 66863   Fire - Very Best Of. *(LP version)*
(S)   (4:10)   JCI 3150   1985 - Only Dance - 1989. *(LP version)*
(S)   (4:12)   Time-Life R988-15   Sounds Of The Eighties: The Mid 80's. *(LP version)*
(S)   (4:09)   Chronicles 314553404   Non-Stop Disco Vol. 1. *(all songs on this cd are segued together)*

(S)   (5:32)   Priority 50974   Premiere The Movie Magazine Presents The Greatest Soundtrack Hits.
(S)   (4:12)   Cold Front 3865   Club Mix - Women Of Dance Vol. 2. *(LP version)*

1985   DARE ME
(dj copies of this 45 ran (3:41) and (4:05);
commercial copies were all (3:41))

(S)   (4:16)   RCA 9970   Nipper's Greatest Hits - The 80's. *(LP version)*
(S)   (4:17)   RCA 5487   Contact. *(LP version)*
(S)   (4:17)   RCA 61153   Sweet & Soulful. *(LP version)*
(S)   (6:17)   RCA 9816   Greatest Hits. *(remixed)*
(S)   (3:41)   RCA 66863   Fire - Very Best Of.

1986   GOLDMINE

(S)   (3:50)   RCA 5609   Hot Together.
(S)   (3:50)   RCA 66863   Fire - Very Best Of.
(S)   (3:50)   Rhino 75234   Rupaul's Go-Go Box Classics.

POISON

1987   TALK DIRTY TO ME

(S)   (3:43)   Capitol 46735   Look What The Cat Dragged In.
(S)   (3:43)   Time-Life R988-09   Sounds Of The Eighties: 1987.
(S)   (3:43)   Time-Life R968-18   Guitar Rock - The Heavy '80s.
(S)   (3:43)   Rhino 72291   Heavy Metal Hits Of The 80's Volume 1.
(S)   (3:43)   Capitol 53375   Greatest Hits 1986-1996.
(S)   (3:43)   Simitar 55762   Stud Rock - Wild Ride.

1987   I WON'T FORGET YOU

(S)   (3:34)   Capitol 46735   Look What The Cat Dragged In.
(S)   (3:34)   Capitol 53375   Greatest Hits 1986-1996.

1988   NOTHIN' BUT A GOOD TIME

(S)   (3:43)   Enigma 48493   Open Up And Say...Ahh!
(S)   (3:43)   Rhino 72133   Frat Rock: The 80's.
(S)   (3:42)   Capitol 53375   Greatest Hits 1986-1996.
(S)   (3:44)   Priority 50936   Best Of 80's Metal Volume One: Bang Your Head.
(S)   (3:41)   Time-Life R988-20   Sounds Of The Eighties: The Late '80s Take Two.
(S)   (3:41)   Time-Life R968-20   Guitar Rock - The '80s.

1988   FALLEN ANGEL

(S)   (3:55)   Enigma 48493   Open Up And Say...Ahh!
(S)   (3:54)   Capitol 53375   Greatest Hits 1986-1996.

1988   EVERY ROSE HAS ITS THORN

(S)   (4:18)   Sandstone 33045 and 5011   Rock The First Volume Five.
(S)   (4:18)   Enigma 48493   Open Up And Say...Ahh!
(S)   (4:17)   Time-Life R988-10   Sounds Of The 80's: 1988.
(S)   (4:17)   Capitol 53375   Greatest Hits 1986-1996.
(S)   (4:19)   K-Tel 3866   The 80's: Number One Pop Hits.
(S)   (4:18)   Razor & Tie 89004   Monsters Of Rock.

1989   YOUR MAMA DON'T DANCE

(S)   (2:59)   Enigma 48493   Open Up And Say...Ahh!
(S)   (2:58)   Capitol 53375   Greatest Hits 1986-1996.
(S)   (3:00)   Priority 50953   I Love Rock & Roll Volume 4: Hits Of The 80's.

1990   UNSKINNY BOP

(S)   (3:47)   Enigma 91813   Flesh & Blood.
(S)   (3:46)   Capitol 53375   Greatest Hits 1986-1996.

1990   SOMETHING TO BELIEVE IN

(S)   (5:27)   JCI 3135   14 Original Metal Ballads.
(S)   (5:27)   Enigma 91813   Flesh & Blood.
(S)   (5:27)   Capitol 53375   Greatest Hits 1986-1996.

1991   RIDE THE WIND

(S)   (3:50)   Enigma 91813   Flesh & Blood.
(S)   (3:50)   Capitol 53375   Greatest Hits 1986-1996.

1991   LIFE GOES ON

(S)   (4:45)   Enigma 91813   Flesh & Blood.
(S)   (4:46)   Capitol 53375   Greatest Hits 1986-1996.

POLICE

1979   ROXANNE

(S)   (3:10)   A&M 3902   Every Breath You Take/The Singles.
(S)   (3:11)   A&M 3311   Outlandos d'Amour.
(S)   (3:10)   A&M 314540150   Message In A Box: The Complete Recordings.

(S) (3:10) A&M 314540380 Every Breath You Take - The Classics.

(S) (3:11) A&M 314540834 Very Best Of Sting & The Police.

1981 DE DO DO DO, DE DA DA DA
(dj copies of this 45 ran (3:12); commercial copies were all (4:09))

(S) (4:07) A&M 3720 Zenyatta Mondatta.

(S) (4:05) A&M 3902 Every Breath You Take/The Singles.

(S) (4:04) A&M 314540150 Message In A Box: The Complete Recordings.

(S) (4:04) A&M 314540380 Every Breath You Take - The Classics.

1981 DON'T STAND SO CLOSE TO ME

(S) (3:59) A&M 3720 Zenyatta Mondatta.

(S) (3:58) A&M 314540150 Message In A Box: The Complete Recordings.

(S) (3:58) A&M 314540380 Every Breath You Take - The Classics.

(S) (3:58) Rhino 72894 Hard Rock Cafe: New Wave.

(S) (3:59) A&M 314540834 Very Best Of Sting & The Police.

1981 EVERY LITTLE THING SHE DOES IS MAGIC

(S) (4:19) A&M 3902 Every Breath You Take/The Singles. *(LP length)*

(S) (4:19) A&M 3730 Ghosts In The Machine. *(LP length)*

(S) (4:18) A&M 314540150 Message In A Box: The Complete Recordings. *(LP length)*

(S) (4:18) A&M 314540380 Every Breath You Take - The Classics. *(LP length)*

(S) (4:19) A&M 314540834 Very Best Of Sting & The Police. *(LP length)*

(S) (4:18) Maverick/Warner Brothers 46840 O.S.T. The Wedding Singer. *(LP length)*

1982 SPIRITS IN THE MATERIAL WORLD

(S) (2:57) A&M 314540150 Message In A Box: The Complete Recordings.

(S) (2:57) A&M 3730 Ghosts In The Machine.

(S) (2:56) A&M 3902 Every Breath You Take/The Singles.

(S) (2:56) A&M 314540380 Every Breath You Take - The Classics.

1983 EVERY BREATH YOU TAKE

(S) (4:13) A&M 314540150 Message In A Box: The Complete Recordings.

(S) (4:12) A&M 3902 Every Breath You Take/The Singles.

(S) (4:13) A&M 3735 Synchronicity.

(S) (4:13) MFSL 511 Synchronicity. *(gold disc)*

(S) (4:12) A&M 314540380 Every Breath You Take - The Classics.

(S) (4:11) Time-Life R13610 Gold And Platinum Box Set - The Ultimate Rock Collection.

(S) (4:10) A&M 314540834 Very Best Of Sting & The Police.

1983 KING OF PAIN

(S) (4:57) A&M 314540150 Message In A Box: The Complete Recordings.

(S) (4:56) A&M 3902 Every Breath You Take/The Singles.

(S) (4:56) A&M 3735 Synchronicity.

(S) (4:56) MFSL 511 Synchronicity. *(gold disc)*

(S) (4:57) A&M 314540380 Every Breath You Take - The Classics.

1983 SYNCHRONICITY II

(S) (5:00) A&M 314540150 Message In A Box: The Complete Recordings.

(S) (4:59) A&M 3735 Synchronicity.

1984 WRAPPED AROUND YOUR FINGER

(S) (5:13) A&M 314540150 Message In A Box: The Complete Recordings.

(S) (5:12) A&M 3902 Every Breath You Take/The Singles.

(S) (5:13) A&M 3735 Synchronicity.

(S) (5:12) A&M 314540380 Every Breath You Take - The Classics.

PONI-TAILS
1958 BORN TOO LATE

(S) (2:17) MCA 31201 Vintage Music Volume 4.

(S) (2:17) MCA 5778 Vintage Music Volumes 3 & 4.

(S) (2:17) Curb 77354 50's Hits Volume 1.

(S) (2:16) Curb 77525 Greatest Hits Of Rock 'N' Roll Volume 2.

(S) (2:16) MCA Special Products 20783 Rock Around The Oldies #1.

(S) (2:16) K-Tel 478 More 50's Jukebox Favorites.

(S) (2:17) MCA Special Products 22166 Vintage Collectibles Volume 8.

(S) (2:16) Eric 11502 Hard To Find 45's On CD (Volume I) 1955-60.

IGGY POP with KATE PIERSON
1991 CANDY

(S) (4:13) Virgin 91381 and 86173 Brick By Brick.

(S) (4:14) Virgin 42351 Nude & Rude: The Best Of.

POPPY FAMILY featuring SUSAN JACKS
1970 WHICH WAY YOU GOIN' BILLY?
(actual 45 time is (3:25) not (3:10) as stated on the record label)

(S) (3:20) Rhino 70922 Super Hits Of The 70's Volume 2. *(LP length)*

(S) (3:20) Rhino 72009 Super Hits Of The 70's Volumes 1-4 Box Set. *(LP length)*

(S) (3:22) March 60017 A Good Thing Lost: 1968-1973. *(LP length)*

(S) (3:20) Time-Life R840-03 Sounds Of The Seventies - Pop Nuggets: Early '70s. *(LP length)*

1970 THAT'S WHERE I WENT WRONG

(S) (2:32) March 60017 A Good Thing Lost: 1968-1973. *(Canadian version)*

(M) (2:32) March 60017 A Good Thing Lost: 1968-1973. *(U.S. version)*

PORTRAIT
1993 HERE WE GO AGAIN!

(S) (4:20) Capitol 93496 Portrait.

SANDY POSEY
1966 BORN A WOMAN
(actual LP time is (1:51) not (2:06) as stated on the record label)

(S) (1:49) Collectables 5665 Best Of. *(LP length; very poor stereo separation)*

1967 SINGLE GIRL

(S) (2:31) Collectables 5665 Best Of. *(very poor stereo separation)*

1967 WHAT A WOMAN IN LOVE WON'T DO

(M) (2:10) Collectables 5665 Best Of.

1967 I TAKE IT BACK

(S) (2:23) Collectables 5665 Best Of. *(very poor stereo separation)*

POSITIVE K
1993 I GOT A MAN

(S) (6:23) Tommy Boy 1074 MTV Party To Go Volume 3. *(remix; all tracks on this cd are segued together)*

(S) (3:52) Island 314514057 The Skills Dat Pay Da Bills.

(S) (3:48) Rebound 314520360 Major Flavas Rap Classics.

MIKE POST
1975 THE ROCKFORD FILES

(S) (3:11) Rhino 71197 Super Hits Of The 70's Volume 17.

(S) (3:12) Rebound 314520317 Class Reunion 1975.

(S) (3:11) Rhino 71910 Tube Tunes Volume One - The 70's.

(S) (3:11) K-Tel 3624 Music Express.

(S) (3:11) Time-Life R840-02 Sounds Of The Seventies - TV Themes.

(S) (3:12) Hip-O 40013 Synth Me Up - 14 Classic Electronic Hits.

1981 THE THEME FROM HILL STREET BLUES

(S) (3:10) Rhino 71912 Tube Tunes Volume Three - The 80's.

(S) (3:11) Hip-O 40017 Mission Accomplished: Themes For Spies & Cops.

(S) (3:10) JCI 3170 #1 Radio Hits 1980 - Only Rock 'n Roll - 1984.

(S) (3:10) Time-Life R988-32 Sounds Of The Eighties: TV Themes Of The '80s.

MIKE POST (Continued)
1982 THEME FROM MAGNUM P.I.
- (S) (3:23) Rhino 71911 Tube Tunes Volume Two - The 70's & 80's.
- (S) (3:22) Time-Life R988-32 Sounds Of The Eighties: TV Themes Of The '80s.

FRANCK POURCEL
1959 ONLY YOU
- (M) (2:29) Capitol 98670 Memories Are Made Of This.

JANE POWELL
1956 TRUE LOVE

JOEY POWERS
1964 MIDNIGHT MARY
- (M) (2:24) Rhino 70995 One Hit Wonders Of The 60's Volume 1. (alternate take)
- (M) (2:22) Collectors' Choice 002 Teen Idols....For A Moment.

POWER STATION
1985 SOME LIKE IT HOT
- (S) (3:42) Time-Life R105-40 Rock Dreams. (45 version)
- (S) (5:05) Capitol 46127 The Power Station CD. (LP version)
- (S) (5:05) Priority 53775 Best Of 80's Rock Volume 1. (LP version)
- (S) (3:42) Time-Life R988-02 Sounds Of The Eighties: 1985. (45 version)
- (S) (3:42) Time-Life R968-20 Guitar Rock - The '80s. (45 version)
- (S) (4:55) Cold Front 6255 Greatest Sports Rock And Jams Volume 2. (all selections on this cd are segued together; LP version)

1985 GET IT ON (BANG A GONG)
- (S) (3:43) EMI 89605 Living In Oblivion: The 80's Greatest Hits Volume Two. (45 version)
- (S) (3:44) Priority 53702 Hot And Sexy - Rock All Night. (45 version)
- (S) (5:29) Sandstone 33041 and 5007 Rock The First Volume 1. (LP version)
- (S) (5:29) Capitol 46127 The Power Station CD. (LP version)
- (S) (3:43) Time-Life R988-23 Sounds Of The Eighties 1984-1985. (45 version)

1985 COMMUNICTION
- (S) (3:35) Capitol 46127 The Power Station CD.

POZO-SECO SINGERS
1966 I CAN MAKE IT WITH YOU
- (S) (2:15) Columbia/Legacy 46983 Rock Artifacts Volume 3.
- (S) (2:16) Collector's Choice 016 Time/I Can Make It With You.

1967 LOOK WHAT YOU'VE DONE
- (S) (2:48) Collector's Choice 016 Time/I Can Make It With You.

PEREZ PRADO
1955 CHERRY PINK AND APPLE BLOSSOM WHITE
- (M) (3:01) RCA 8466 Nipper's Greatest Hits Of The 50's Volume 1.
- (M) (3:00) Time-Life HPD-09 Your Hit Parade 1955.
- (M) (2:59) Rhino 71580 Billboard Pop Memories 1955-1959.
- (M) (2:59) Rhino 71889 Mondo Mambo: Best Of.
- (M) (3:01) K-Tel 3472 Those Wonderful Instrumentals Volume 2.
- (M) (2:59) Rhino 72422 Billboard Top Movie Hits 1955-1959.
- (M) (2:58) Time-Life R132-12 Your Hit Parade - #1 Hits Of The '50s.
- (M) (3:01) Time-Life R986-20 Instrumental Favorites - Whimsical Interludes.

1958 PATRICIA
- (S) (2:19) RCA 8467 Nipper's Greatest Hits Of The 50's Volume 2.
- (S) (2:19) Time-Life HPD-11 Your Hit Parade 1958.
- (S) (2:19) Rhino 71889 Mondo Mambo: Best Of.

- (M) (2:26) Time-Life R986-12 Instrumental Favorites - Latin Rhythms. (alternate take)

PRATT & McCLAIN
1976 HAPPY DAYS
- (S) (2:34) Rhino 71198 Super Hits Of The 70's Volume 18.
- (S) (2:34) Time-Life SOD-34 Sounds Of The Seventies - The Late 70's.
- (S) (2:34) Rhino 71910 Tube Tunes Volume One - The 70's.
- (S) (2:34) Time-Life AM1-23 AM Gold - 1976.
- (S) (2:34) Time-Life R840-02 Sounds Of The Seventies - TV Themes.
- (S) (2:34) Time-Life R830-01 The Dr. Demento Collection - The Mid 70's.
- (S) (2:41) Nick At Nite/550 Music 63456 Double Date With Joanie And Chachi.

PRELUDE
1974 AFTER THE GOLDRUSH
- (S) (2:07) Atlas 314523070 O.S.T. Jimmy Hollywood.
- (S) (2:06) K-Tel 3627 Out Of Sight.
- (S) (2:08) One Way 34432 After The Gold Rush.

PREMIERS
1964 FARMER JOHN
- (S) (2:32) Warner Special Products 27610 More Party Classics. (LP version which includes a :20 introduction)
- (M) (2:15) Original Sound CDGO-10 Golden Oldies Volume. 10. (45 version)
- (M) (2:12) Rhino 75772 Son Of Frat Rock. (45 version)
- (M) (2:11) Time-Life 2CLR-03 Classic Rock - 1964. (45 version)
- (M) (2:26) Rhino 72869 Brown Eyed Soul Vol. 2. (LP version which includes a :20 introduction)

PRESIDENTS
1970 5-10-15-20 (25-30 YEARS OF LOVE)
- (S) (3:07) Rhino 70783 Soul Hits Of The 70's Volume 3. (sounds like it is mastered from vinyl)
- (S) (3:07) Rhino 72028 Soul Hits Of The 70's Volumes 1-5 Box Set. (sounds like it is mastered from vinyl)
- (S) (3:06) Ripete 2223 Soul Patrol Vol. 5. (sounds like it is mastered from vinyl)

PRESIDENTS OF THE UNITED STATES
1996 PEACHES
- (S) (2:49) Columbia 67291 The Presidents Of The United States.

ELVIS PRESLEY
1956 HEARTBREAK HOTEL
- (M) (2:06) RCA 8466 Nipper's Greatest Hits Of The 50's Volume 1.
- (M) (2:06) RCA 8533 O.S.T. Heartbreak Hotel.
- (M) (2:06) RCA 6383 and 56383 The Top Ten Hits.
- (M) (2:05) RCA 6382 The Number One Hits.
- (M) (2:06) RCA 6401 and 56401 50 Worldwide Gold Award Hits.
- (E) (2:08) RCA 2227 The Great Performances.
- (S) (1:57) RCA 3114 Collectors Gold. (live)
- (M) (2:06) RCA 5196 Elvis' Golden Records.
- (M) (2:05) RCA 2079 Heartbreak Hotel, Hound Dog & Other Top Ten Hits.
- (M) (2:05) Pair 1251 Great Performances.
- (M) (2:05) Special Music 2705 A Legendary Performer Volume 1.
- (M) (2:07) RCA 66050 The Complete 50's Masters.
- (M) (2:33) RCA 66050 The Complete 50's Masters. (live; includes a :35 introduction)
- (M) (2:07) Time-Life 2RNR-06 Rock 'N' Roll Era - Elvis Presley 1954-1961.
- (M) (2:06) Time-Life CTD-13 Country USA - 1956.
- (M) (2:08) RCA 66817 and 66856 Elvis 56.
- (M) (2:12) RCA 66817 and 66856 Elvis 56. (includes :03 of studio talk; alternate take)

(M) (2:01) RCA 67458 O.S.T. Blue Suede Shoes. *(most songs on this cd are segued together; this cd is a disaster)*
(M) (2:14) RCA 67469 Platinum - A Life In Music. *(alternate take with studio talk)*
(M) (2:07) RCA 67462 Elvis' Golden Records.
(M) (2:07) DCC Compact Classics 1117 24 Karat Hits. *(gold disc)*
(M) (2:07) RCA 67565 Elvis' Greatest Jukebox Hits.
(M) (2:14) RCA 67592 A Touch Of Platinum - A Life In Music. *(alternate take with studio talk)*
(M) (2:07) Time-Life R806-02 The Elvis Presley Collection - Rock 'N' Roll.
(M) (2:07) Time-Life R808-03 Classic Country 1950-1959.
(M) (2:08) Collectables 1514 and 2514 The Anniversary Album - The 50's.

1956 I WAS THE ONE
(M) (2:34) RCA 6401 and 56401 50 Worldwide Gold Award Hits.
(M) (2:32) RCA 1990 For LP Fans Only.
(M) (2:35) RCA 5353 A Valentine Gift For You.
(M) (2:33) RCA 66050 The Complete 50's Masters.
(M) (2:33) RCA 66817 and 66856 Elvis 56.
(M) (2:32) Time-Life R857-13 The Heart Of Rock 'n' Roll 1956-1957.
(S) (1:01) RCA 67469 Platinum - A Life In Music. *(live)*
(M) (2:32) RCA 67462 Elvis' Golden Records.
(M) (2:32) Time-Life R806-01 The Elvis Presley Collection - Love Songs.

1956 BLUE SUEDE SHOES
(M) (1:58) RCA 66050 The Complete 50's Masters.
(M) (1:59) RCA 5182 Rocker.
(M) (1:59) RCA 5198 Elvis Presley.
(M) (1:39) Pair 1251 Great Performances. *(live)*
(M) (1:59) A&M 3930 O.S.T. Heart Of Dixie.
(M) (1:59) Time-Life 2RNR-26 Rock 'N' Roll Era - Elvis, The King: 1954-1965.
(M) (1:58) RCA 66659 Elvis Presley. *(gold disc)*
(M) (1:58) RCA 2227 The Great Performances.
(M) (1:58) RCA 66817 and 66856 Elvis 56.
(M) (2:00) RCA 67458 O.S.T. Blue Suede Shoes. *(most songs on this cd are segued together; this cd is a disaster)*
(S) (2:42) RCA 67458 O.S.T. Blue Suede Shoes. *(instrumental rerecording; most songs on this cd are segued together; this cd is a disaster)*
(S) (2:05) RCA 66960 and 67460 O.S.T. G.I. Blues. *(1960 rerecording)*
(M) (1:58) RCA 67462 Elvis' Golden Records.
(M) (1:58) Time-Life R806-02 The Elvis Presley Collection - Rock 'N' Roll.

1956 I WANT YOU, I NEED YOU, I LOVE YOU
(M) (2:36) RCA 6383 and 56383 The Top Ten Hits.
(M) (2:36) RCA 6382 The Number One Hits.
(M) (2:36) RCA 6401 and 56401 50 Worldwide Gold Award Hits.
(M) (2:38) RCA 5196 Elvis' Golden Records.
(M) (2:40) Pair 1251 Great Performances. *(alternate take)*
(M) (2:40) Special Music 2706 A Legendary Performer Volume 2. *(alternate take)*
(M) (2:39) RCA 66050 The Complete 50's Masters.
(M) (2:39) RCA 66050 The Complete 50's Masters. *(alternate take)*
(M) (2:37) A&M 3930 O.S.T. Heart Of Dixie.
(M) (2:38) Time-Life 2RNR-06 Rock 'N' Roll Era - Elvis Presley 1954-1961.
(M) (2:37) Time-Life CTD-13 Country USA - 1956.
(M) (2:37) RCA 66532 Heart And Soul.
(M) (2:39) RCA 66817 and 66856 Elvis 56.
(M) (2:37) Time-Life R857-07 The Heart Of Rock 'n' Roll 1956.
(M) (2:32) RCA 67458 O.S.T. Blue Suede Shoes. *(most songs on this cd are segued together; this cd is a disaster)*
(M) (2:45) RCA 67469 Platinum - A Life In Music. *(alternate take)*
(M) (2:38) RCA 67462 Elvis' Golden Records.
(M) (2:45) RCA 67592 A Touch Of Platinum - A Life In Music. *(alternate take)*
(M) (2:39) Time-Life R806-01 The Elvis Presley Collection - Love Songs.

1956 MY BABY LEFT ME
(M) (2:11) RCA 66050 The Complete 50's Masters.

(M) (2:09) RCA 5418 Reconsider Baby.
(M) (2:10) RCA 1990 For LP Fans Only.
(M) (2:09) Time-Life 2RNR-26 Rock 'N' Roll Era - Elvis, The King: 1954-1965.
(M) (2:11) RCA 66817 and 66856 Elvis 56.
(M) (2:11) RCA 66921 The Other Sides - Worldwide Gold Award Hits Volume 2.
(M) (2:10) RCA 67462 Elvis' Golden Records.

1956 DON'T BE CRUEL
(M) (2:01) Rhino 70599 Billboard's Top Rock & Roll Hits Of 1956.
(E) (2:03) Elektra 60107 O.S.T. Diner.
(M) (2:01) RCA 8467 Nipper's Greatest Hits Of The 50's Volume 2.
(M) (2:01) RCA 6383 and 56383 The Top Ten Hits.
(M) (2:00) RCA 6382 The Number One Hits.
(M) (2:01) RCA 6401 and 56401 50 Worldwide Gold Award Hits.
(M) (2:02) RCA 2227 The Great Performances.
(M) (2:02) RCA 5196 Elvis' Golden Records.
(M) (2:00) RCA 2079 Heartbreak Hotel, Hound Dog & Other Top Ten Hits.
(M) (2:00) Pair 1251 Great Performances.
(M) (2:00) Special Music 2705 A Legendary Performer Volume 1.
(M) (2:00) RCA 66050 The Complete 50's Masters.
(M) (2:02) RCA 53732 Pure Gold.
(M) (2:01) Time-Life 2RNR-06 Rock 'N' Roll Era - Elvis Presley 1954-1961.
(M) (2:01) Time-Life R962-03 History Of Rock 'N' Roll: Rock 'N' Roll Classics 1954-1956.
(M) (2:01) RCA 66817 and 66856 Elvis 56.
(M) (1:27) RCA 67458 O.S.T. Blue Suede Shoes. *(most songs on this cd are segued together; this cd is a disaster)*
(M) (2:00) RCA 67469 Platinum - A Life In Music.
(M) (2:00) RCA 67462 Elvis' Golden Records.
(M) (2:01) DCC Compact Classics 1117 24 Karat Hits. *(gold disc)*
(M) (2:00) RCA 67565 Elvis' Greatest Jukebox Hits.
(M) (2:00) RCA 67592 A Touch Of Platinum - A Life In Music.
(M) (2:01) Time-Life R806-02 The Elvis Presley Collection - Rock 'N' Roll.
(M) (2:01) Time-Life R808-03 Classic Country 1950-1959.

1956 HOUND DOG
(M) (2:16) Rhino 70599 Billboard's Top Rock & Roll Hits Of 1956.
(M) (2:14) RCA 6383 and 56383 The Top Ten Hits.
(M) (2:14) RCA 6382 The Number One Hits.
(M) (2:14) RCA 6401 and 56401 50 Worldwide Gold Award Hits.
(M) (2:14) RCA 5182 Rocker.
(S) (0:58) RCA 6985 The Alternate Aloha. *(all selections on this cd are live)*
(M) (2:14) RCA 5196 Elvis' Golden Records.
(M) (2:13) RCA 3026 Sings Leiber & Stoller.
(M) (2:14) RCA 2079 Heartbreak Hotel, Hound Dog & Other Top Ten Hits.
(M) (2:14) RCA 66050 The Complete 50's Masters.
(M) (2:14) Time-Life 2RNR-06 Rock 'N' Roll Era - Elvis Presley 1954-1961.
(M) (2:14) Epic 66329 O.S.T. Forrest Gump.
(M) (2:14) RCA 66817 and 66856 Elvis 56.
(S) (2:42) RCA 67458 O.S.T. Blue Suede Shoes. *(instrumental rerecording; most songs on this cd are segued together; this cd is a disaster)*
(M) (2:34) RCA 67469 Platinum - A Life In Music. *(live)*
(M) (2:15) RCA 67462 Elvis' Golden Records.
(M) (2:14) DCC Compact Classics 1117 24 Karat Hits. *(gold disc)*
(M) (2:14) RCA 67565 Elvis' Greatest Jukebox Hits.
(M) (2:34) RCA 67592 A Touch Of Platinum - A Life In Music. *(live)*
(M) (2:14) Time-Life R806-02 The Elvis Presley Collection - Rock 'N' Roll.
(M) (2:12) Collectables 1514 and 2514 The Anniversary Album - The 50's.

1956 LOVE ME TENDER
(M) (2:44) RCA 6383 and 56383 The Top Ten Hits.
(M) (2:43) RCA 6382 The Number One Hits.

ELVIS PRESLEY (Continued)

(M) (2:43) RCA 6401 and 56401 50 Worldwide Gold Award Hits.
(M) (2:40) RCA 6738 Essential Elvis.
(M) (1:11) RCA 6738 Essential Elvis. *(alternate take)*
(S) (3:14) RCA 3114 Collectors Gold. *(live)*
(M) (2:44) RCA 5196 Elvis' Golden Records.
(M) (2:43) RCA 2079 Heartbreak Hotel, Hound Dog & Other Top Ten Hits.
(M) (2:43) Pair 1251 Great Performances.
(M) (2:43) Special Music 2705 A Legendary Performer Volume 1.
(M) (2:40) RCA 66050 The Complete 50's Masters.
(M) (2:40) RCA 53732 Pure Gold.
(M) (2:44) Time-Life 2RNR-06 Rock 'N' Roll Era - Elvis Presley 1954-1961.
(M) (2:39) Time-Life HPD-15 Your Hit Parade - 1956.
(M) (2:40) Time-Life R103-27 Love Me Tender.
(S) (2:41) RCA 66532 Heart And Soul.
(M) (2:40) Time-Life R857-07 The Heart Of Rock 'n' Roll 1956.
(M) (2:47) RCA 67458 O.S.T. Blue Suede Shoes. *(alternate take; most songs on this cd are segued together; this cd is a disaster)*
(M) (2:40) RCA 67453 O.S.T. Jailhouse Rock.
(M) (1:07) RCA 67453 O.S.T. Jailhouse Rock. *(soundtrack end title version)*
(S) (2:41) RCA 67453 O.S.T. Jailhouse Rock.
(M) (3:16) RCA 67469 Platinum - A Life In Music. *(live with :41 introduction)*
(M) (2:40) RCA 67462 Elvis' Golden Records.
(S) (2:41) DCC Compact Classics 1117 24 Karat Hits. *(gold disc)*
(S) (2:41) RCA 67595 Love Songs.
(M) (3:16) RCA 67592 A Touch Of Platinum - A Life In Music. *(live with a :41 introduction)*
(M) (2:40) Time-Life R806-01 The Elvis Presley Collection - Love Songs.

1956 ANYWAY YOU WANT ME (THAT'S HOW I WILL BE)
(M) (2:12) RCA 6401 and 56401 50 Worldwide Gold Award Hits.
(M) (2:13) RCA 5196 Elvis' Golden Records.
(M) (2:12) RCA 2079 Heartbreak Hotel, Hound Dog & Other Top Ten Hits.
(M) (2:13) RCA 66050 The Complete 50's Masters.
(M) (2:12) Time-Life 2RNR-26 Rock 'N' Roll Era - Elvis, The King: 1954-1965.
(M) (2:13) RCA 66817 and 66856 Elvis 56.
(M) (2:13) RCA 67462 Elvis' Golden Records.
(M) (2:13) Time-Life R806-01 The Elvis Presley Collection - Love Songs.

1956 LOVE ME
(M) (2:41) Rhino 70593 The Rock 'N' Roll Classics Of Leiber & Stoller.
(M) (2:41) RCA 6383 and 56383 The Top Ten Hits.
(M) (2:42) RCA 5199 Elvis.
(S) (1:42) RCA 6985 The Alternate Aloha. *(all selections on this cd are live)*
(M) (2:42) RCA 5196 Elvis' Golden Records.
(M) (2:41) RCA 3026 Sings Leiber & Stoller.
(M) (2:42) RCA 66050 The Complete 50's Masters.
(M) (2:43) Time-Life 2RNR-06 Rock 'N' Roll Era - Elvis Presley 1954-1961.
(M) (2:42) RCA 66532 Heart And Soul.
(M) (2:43) RCA 66817 and 66856 Elvis 56.
(M) (2:43) RCA 66921 The Other Sides - Worldwide Gold Award Hits Volume 2.
(M) (2:42) Time-Life R857-13 The Heart Of Rock 'n' Roll 1956-1957.
(M) (2:42) RCA 67462 Elvis' Golden Records.
(M) (2:43) DCC Compact Classics 1117 24 Karat Hits. *(gold disc)*
(M) (2:43) Time-Life R806-01 The Elvis Presley Collection - Love Songs.

1957 WHEN MY BLUE MOON TURNS TO GOLD AGAIN
(M) (2:20) RCA 66050 The Complete 50's Masters.
(M) (2:20) RCA 5199 Elvis.
(M) (2:20) RCA 66921 The Other Sides - Worldwide Gold Award Hits Volume 2.
(M) (:35) RCA 67469 Platinum - A Life In Music. *(live)*

1957 POOR BOY
(M) (2:14) RCA 1990 For LP Fans Only.
(M) (2:13) RCA 66050 The Complete 50's Masters.
(M) (2:13) RCA 6738 Essential Elvis.
(M) (2:13) RCA 66921 The Other Sides - Worldwide Gold Award Hits Volume 2.
(M) (2:13) RCA 67453 O.S.T. Jailhouse Rock.
(S) (1:39) RCA 67453 O.S.T. Jailhouse Rock. *(alternate take)*

1957 TOO MUCH
(M) (2:30) RCA 6383 and 56383 The Top Ten Hits.
(M) (2:30) RCA 6382 The Number One Hits.
(M) (2:30) RCA 6401 and 56401 50 Worldwide Gold Award Hits.
(M) (2:31) RCA 5196 Elvis' Golden Records.
(M) (2:30) RCA 66050 The Complete 50's Masters.
(M) (2:33) Time-Life 2RNR-06 Rock 'N' Roll Era - Elvis Presley 1954-1961.
(M) (2:30) RCA 66817 and 66856 Elvis 56.
(M) (2:30) RCA 67462 Elvis' Golden Records.
(M) (2:30) RCA 67565 Elvis' Greatest Jukebox Hits.
(M) (2:30) Time-Life R806-02 The Elvis Presley Collection - Rock 'N' Roll.

1957 PLAYING FOR KEEPS
(M) (2:48) RCA 6401 and 56401 50 Worldwide Gold Award Hits.
(M) (2:51) RCA 1990 For LP Fans Only.
(M) (2:49) RCA 5353 A Valentine Gift For You.
(M) (2:49) RCA 66050 The Complete 50's Masters.
(M) (2:49) RCA 67463 50,000,000 Elvis Fans Can't Be Wrong: Elvis' Gold Records Volume 2.

1957 ALL SHOOK UP
(M) (1:56) Rhino 70618 Billboard's Top Rock & Roll Hits Of 1957.
(M) (1:56) Rhino 72004 Billboard's Top Rock & Roll Hits 1957-1961 Box Set.
(M) (1:56) RCA 6383 and 56383 The Top Ten Hits.
(M) (1:56) RCA 6382 The Number One Hits.
(M) (1:56) RCA 6401 and 56401 50 Worldwide Gold Award Hits.
(M) (1:57) RCA 5196 Elvis' Golden Records.
(M) (1:56) RCA 9589 Stereo '57/Essential Elvis Volume 2.
(M) (1:57) RCA 61144 The RCA Records Label: The First Note In Black Music.
(M) (1:56) RCA 66050 The Complete 50's Masters.
(M) (1:56) RCA 53732 Pure Gold.
(M) (1:58) Time-Life 2RNR-06 Rock 'N' Roll Era - Elvis Presley 1954-1961.
(M) (1:56) RCA 67469 Platinum - A Life In Music.
(M) (1:56) RCA 67462 Elvis' Golden Records.
(M) (1:56) DCC Compact Classics 1117 24 Karat Hits. *(gold disc)*
(M) (1:56) RCA 67565 Elvis' Greatest Jukebox Hits.
(M) (1:56) RCA 67592 A Touch Of Platinum - A Life In Music.
(M) (1:56) Time-Life R806-02 The Elvis Presley Collection - Rock 'N' Roll.

1957 (THERE'LL BE) PEACE IN THE VALLEY (FOR ME)
(M) (1:40) RCA 9586 Elvis Gospel 1957-1971. *(mastered from vinyl; live)*
(M) (3:20) RCA 3758 How Great Thou Art.
(M) (3:20) Pair 1251 Great Performances.
(M) (3:19) Special Music 2472 You'll Never Walk Alone.
(M) (3:20) Special Music 2705 A Legendary Performer Volume 1.
(M) (3:22) Pair 1010 Double Dynamite.
(M) (3:19) RCA 66050 The Complete 50's Masters.
(M) (3:19) RCA 66421 Amazing Grace: His Greatest Sacred Performances.
(M) (3:21) RCA 5486 Elvis' Christmas Album.
(M) (3:22) RCA 67469 Platinum - A Life In Music. *(alternate take)*
(M) (3:19) RCA 67463 50,000,000 Elvis Fans Can't Be Wrong: Elvis' Gold Records Volume 2.
(M) (3:22) RCA 67592 A Touch Of Platinum - A Life In Music. *(alternate take)*

1957 (LET ME BE YOUR) TEDDY BEAR
(M) (1:47) RCA 6383 and 56383 The Top Ten Hits.
(M) (1:46) RCA 6382 The Number One Hits.
(M) (1:47) RCA 6401 and 56401 50 Worldwide Gold Award Hits.
(M) (1:46) RCA 2227 The Great Performances.

(M) (1:46) RCA 6738 Essential Elvis.
(M) (1:46) RCA 1515 Loving You.
(M) (1:47) RCA 5196 Elvis' Golden Records.
(M) (1:46) RCA 2079 Heartbreak Hotel, Hound Dog & Other Top Ten Hits.
(M) (1:45) Special Music 2704 Sings For Children.
(M) (1:45) RCA 66050 The Complete 50's Masters.
(M) (1:47) Time-Life 2RNR-06 Rock 'N' Roll Era - Elvis Presley 1954-1961.
(M) (1:45) Time-Life R962-05 History Of Rock 'N' Roll: The Teenage Years 1957-1964.
(M) (1:44) RCA 67458 O.S.T. Blue Suede Shoes. *(most songs on this cd are segued together; this cd is a disaster)*
(M) (1:45) RCA 67452 O.S.T. Loving You.
(M) (1:45) RCA 67469 Platinum - A Life In Music.
(M) (1:45) RCA 67462 Elvis' Golden Records.
(M) (1:46) DCC Compact Classics 1117 24 Karat Hits. *(gold disc)*
(M) (1:45) RCA 67565 Elvis' Greatest Jukebox Hits.
(M) (1:45) RCA 67592 A Touch Of Platinum - A Life In Music.
(M) (1:45) Time-Life R806-02 The Elvis Presley Collection - Rock 'N' Roll.

1957 LOVING YOU

(M) (2:14) RCA 6401 and 56401 50 Worldwide Gold Award Hits.
(M) (2:12) RCA 6738 Essential Elvis. *(with :22 of studio talk; alternate take)*
(M) (2:07) RCA 6738 Essential Elvis. *(with :42 of studio talk; alternate take)*
(M) (1:45) RCA 6738 Essential Elvis. *(with :06 of studio talk; alternate take)*
(M) (1:51) RCA 6738 Essential Elvis. *(alternate take)*
(M) (1:26) RCA 6738 Essential Elvis. *(alternate take)*
(M) (2:14) RCA 1515 Loving You.
(M) (2:15) RCA 5196 Elvis' Golden Records.
(M) (2:13) RCA 3026 Sings Leiber & Stoller.
(M) (2:15) Pair 1185 Forever.
(M) (2:11) RCA 66050 The Complete 50's Masters.
(M) (1:47) RCA 66050 The Complete 50's Masters. *(alternate take)*
(M) (1:24) RCA 66050 The Complete 50's Masters. *(alternate take)*
(M) (2:11) RCA 53732 Pure Gold.
(M) (2:14) Time-Life 2RNR-26 Rock 'N' Roll Era - Elvis, The King 1954-1965.
(M) (2:11) RCA 66532 Heart And Soul.
(M) (2:11) RCA 67452 O.S.T. Loving You.
(M) (1:24) RCA 67452 O.S.T. Loving You. *(alternate uptempo version)*
(M) (2:11) RCA 67462 Elvis' Golden Records.
(M) (2:11) Time-Life R806-01 The Elvis Presley Collection - Love Songs.
(M) (1:24) Time-Life R806-05 The Elvis Presley Collection - Movie Magic. *(rerecording)*
(M) (2:11) Time-Life R857-16 The Heart Of Rock 'n' Roll The Late '50s.

1957 JAILHOUSE ROCK

(M) (2:25) Rhino 70618 Billboard's Top Rock & Roll Hits Of 1957.
(M) (2:25) Rhino 72004 Billboard's Top Rock & Roll Hits 1957-1961 Box Set.
(M) (2:26) Rhino 70593 The Rock 'N' Roll Classics Of Leiber & Stoller.
(M) (2:27) RCA 6383 and 56383 The Top Ten Hits.
(M) (2:25) RCA 6382 The Number One Hits.
(M) (2:26) RCA 6401 and 56401 50 Worldwide Gold Award Hits.
(M) (2:25) RCA 5182 Rocker.
(M) (2:25) RCA 2227 The Great Performances.
(M) (2:35) RCA 6738 Essential Elvis. *(alternate take)*
(M) (1:56) RCA 6738 Essential Elvis. *(alternate take)*
(M) (2:25) RCA 5196 Elvis' Golden Records.
(M) (2:29) RCA 3026 Sings Leiber & Stoller.
(M) (2:23) RCA 2079 Heartbreak Hotel, Hound Dog & Other Top Ten Hits.
(M) (2:22) Pair 1251 Great Performances.
(M) (2:22) Special Music 2706 A Legendary Performer Volume 2.
(M) (2:26) RCA 66050 The Complete 50's Masters.

(M) (2:26) RCA 53732 Pure Gold.
(M) (2:25) Time-Life 2RNR-06 Rock 'N' Roll Era - Elvis Presley 1954-1961.
(M) (2:17) RCA 67458 O.S.T. Blue Suede Shoes. *(alternate take; most songs on this cd are segued together; this cd is a disaster)*
(M) (2:27) RCA 67453 O.S.T. Jailhouse Rock.
(M) (2:31) RCA 67453 O.S.T. Jailhouse Rock. *(soundtrack version)*
(M) (2:26) RCA 67469 Platinum - A Life In Music.
(M) (2:26) RCA 67462 Elvis' Golden Records.
(M) (2:26) DCC Compact Classics 1117 24 Karat Hits. *(gold disc)*
(M) (2:26) RCA 67565 Elvis' Greatest Jukebox Hits.
(M) (2:26) RCA 67592 A Touch Of Platinum - A Life In Music.
(M) (2:26) Time-Life R806-02 The Elvis Presley Collection - Rock 'N' Roll.
(M) (2:32) Time-Life R806-05 The Elvis Presley Collection - Movie Magic. *(alternate take)*
(M) (2:25) Collectables 1514 and 2514 The Anniversary Album - The 50's.

1957 TREAT ME NICE

(M) (2:09) RCA 66050 The Complete 50's Masters.
(S) (1:59) RCA 2227 The Great Performances. *(alternate take)*
(M) (2:11) RCA 6401 and 56401 50 Worldwide Gold Award Hits.
(M) (2:12) RCA 5196 Elvis' Golden Records.
(M) (2:07) RCA 6738 Essential Elvis. *(alternate take; includes countoff and :09 of studio talk)*
(M) (2:09) RCA 6738 Essential Elvis.
(M) (2:11) RCA 3026 Sings Leiber & Stoller.
(M) (2:11) Time-Life 2RNR-26 Rock 'N' Roll Era - Elvis, The King: 1954-1965.
(M) (2:10) RCA 67453 O.S.T. Jailhouse Rock.
(M) (1:58) RCA 67453 O.S.T. Jailhouse Rock. *(soundtrack version)*
(M) (2:09) RCA 67462 Elvis' Golden Records.
(M) (2:11) TVT 8090 O.S.T. My Fellow Americans.
(M) (2:10) Time-Life R806-05 The Elvis Presley Collection - Movie Magic.

1958 DON'T

(M) (2:47) RCA 6383 and 56383 The Top Ten Hits.
(M) (2:47) RCA 6382 The Number One Hits.
(M) (2:48) RCA 6401 and 56401 50 Worldwide Gold Award Hits.
(M) (2:49) RCA 5197 50,000,000 Elvis Fans Can't Be Wrong.
(M) (2:52) RCA 3026 Sings Leiber & Stoller. *(includes :05 of studio talk)*
(M) (2:47) RCA 66050 The Complete 50's Masters.
(M) (2:48) Time-Life 2RNR-06 Rock 'N' Roll Era - Elvis Presley 1954-1961.
(M) (2:47) Time-Life CTD-07 Country USA - 1958.
(M) (2:47) Time-Life HPD-36 Your Hit Parade - The 50's Pop Revival.
(M) (2:47) RCA 66532 Heart And Soul.
(M) (2:47) Time-Life R974-02 Many Moods Of Romance - My Heart Reminds Me.
(M) (2:47) Time-Life R857-11 The Heart Of Rock 'n' Roll 1958-1959.
(S) (1:55) RCA 67469 Platinum - A Life In Music. *(live)*
(M) (2:47) RCA 67463 50,000,000 Elvis Fans Can't Be Wrong: Elvis' Gold Records Volume 2.
(M) (2:47) Time-Life R806-01 The Elvis Presley Collection - Love Songs.
(M) (2:47) Time-Life R857-21 The Heart Of Rock 'n' Roll Slow Dancing Classics.

1958 I BEG OF YOU

(M) (1:52) RCA 6383 and 56383 The Top Ten Hits.
(M) (1:52) RCA 6401 and 56401 50 Worldwide Gold Award Hits.
(M) (1:53) RCA 5197 50,000,000 Elvis Fans Can't Be Wrong.
(S) (2:08) RCA 9589 Stereo '57/Essential Elvis Volume 2. *(alternate take)*
(S) (2:46) RCA 9589 Stereo '57/Essential Elvis Volume 2. *(alternate take)*
(S) (1:59) RCA 9589 Stereo '57/Essential Elvis Volume 2. *(alternate take)*
(M) (1:50) RCA 66050 The Complete 50's Masters.

ELVIS PRESLEY *(Continued)*

    (M) (1:51) RCA 66050 The Complete 50's Masters. *(alternate take)*

    (M) (1:50) RCA 67452 O.S.T. Loving You. *(alternate take)*

    (M) (1:50) RCA 67463 50,000,000 Elvis Fans Can't Be Wrong: Elvis' Gold Records Volume 2.

    (M) (1:50) Time-Life R806-06 The Elvis Presley Collection - The Rocker.

1958 WEAR MY RING AROUND YOUR NECK

    (M) (2:13) RCA 6383 and 56383 The Top Ten Hits. *(missing some overdubs)*

    (M) (2:13) RCA 6401 and 56401 50 Worldwide Gold Award Hits. *(missing some overdubs)*

    (M) (2:14) RCA 5197 50,000,000 Elvis Fans Can't Be Wrong. *(missing some overdubs)*

    (M) (2:13) RCA 2229 Hits Like Never Before/Essential Elvis Volume 3. *(missing some overdubs)*

    (M) (2:13) RCA 2229 Hits Like Never Before/Essential Elvis Volume 3.

    (M) (2:13) RCA 66050 The Complete 50's Masters.

    (M) (2:14) Time-Life 2RNR-06 Rock 'N' Roll Era - Elvis Presley 1954-1961.

    (M) (2:11) RCA 67458 O.S.T. Blue Suede Shoes. *(most songs on this cd are segued together; this cd is a disaster)*

    (M) (2:13) RCA 67463 50,000,000 Elvis Fans Can't Be Wrong: Elvis' Gold Records Volume 2.

    (M) (2:12) DCC Compact Classics 1117 24 Karat Hits. *(gold disc)*

    (M) (2:13) Time-Life R806-02 The Elvis Presley Collection - Rock 'N' Roll.

1958 DONCHA' THINK IT'S TIME

    (M) (1:56) RCA 66050 The Complete 50's Masters. *(45 version)*

    (M) (1:55) RCA 2229 Hits Like Never Before/Essential Elvis Volume 3. *(LP version)*

    (M) (1:56) RCA 2229 Hits Like Never Before/Essential Elvis Volume 3. *(45 version)*

    (M) (1:56) RCA 5197 50,000,000 Elvis Fans Can't Be Wrong. *(LP version)*

    (M) (1:56) RCA 66921 The Other Sides - Worldwide Gold Award Hits Volume 2. *(45 version)*

    (M) (1:56) RCA 67463 50,000,000 Elvis Fans Can't Be Wrong: Elvis' Gold Records Volume 2. *(45 version)*

    (M) (1:56) Time-Life R806-06 The Elvis Presley Collection - The Rocker. *(45 version)*

1958 HARD HEADED WOMAN

    (M) (1:52) Rhino 70619 Billboard's Top Rock & Roll Hits Of 1958.

    (M) (1:52) Rhino 72004 Billboard's Top Rock & Roll Hits 1957-1961 Box Set.

    (M) (1:52) RCA 9902 Nipper's #1 Hits 1956-1986.

    (M) (1:52) RCA 6383 and 56383 The Top Ten Hits.

    (M) (1:52) RCA 6382 The Number One Hits.

    (M) (1:52) RCA 6401 and 56401 50 Worldwide Gold Award Hits.

    (M) (1:52) RCA 3733 and 67454 King Creole.

    (M) (1:52) RCA 66050 The Complete 50's Masters.

    (M) (1:52) Time-Life 2RNR-06 Rock 'N' Roll Era - Elvis Presley 1954-1961.

    (E) (1:53) RCA 67458 O.S.T. Blue Suede Shoes. *(most songs on this cd are segued together; this cd is a disaster)*

    (M) (1:52) RCA 67463 50,000,000 Elvis Fans Can't Be Wrong: Elvis' Gold Records Volume 2.

    (M) (1:52) RCA 67565 Elvis' Greatest Jukebox Hits.

    (M) (1:52) Time-Life R806-02 The Elvis Presley Collection - Rock 'N' Roll.

1958 DON'T ASK ME WHY

    (M) (2:07) RCA 66050 The Complete 50's Masters.

    (M) (2:04) RCA 3733 and 67454 King Creole.

    (M) (2:04) RCA 66921 The Other Sides - Worldwide Gold Award Hits Volume 2.

1958 ONE NIGHT

    (M) (2:30) RCA 8533 O.S.T. Heartbreak Hotel.

    (M) (2:30) RCA 6383 and 56383 The Top Ten Hits.

    (M) (2:31) RCA 5197 50,000,000 Elvis Fans Can't Be Wrong.

    (M) (2:42) RCA 5418 Reconsider Baby. *(alternate take; includes :07 of studio talk)*

    (M) (2:32) RCA 9965 Great American Vocalists.

    (M) (2:29) RCA 66050 The Complete 50's Masters.

    (E) (2:31) Time-Life 2RNR-06 Rock 'N' Roll Era - Elvis Presley 1954-1961.

    (M) (2:29) RCA 66921 The Other Sides - Worldwide Gold Award Hits Volume 2.

    (M) (1:41) RCA 67458 O.S.T. Blue Suede Shoes. *("one night of sin" alternate lyric version; most songs on this cd are segued together; this cd is a disaster)*

    (M) (2:35) RCA 67452 O.S.T. Loving You. *("one night of sin" alternate lyric)*

    (M) (2:29) RCA 67463 50,000,000 Elvis Fans Can't Be Wrong: Elvis' Gold Records Volume 2.

    (M) (2:29) Time-Life R806-02 The Elvis Presley Collection - Rock 'N' Roll.

1958 I GOT STUNG

    (M) (1:48) RCA 6383 and 56383 The Top Ten Hits.

    (M) (1:49) RCA 6401 and 56401 50 Worldwide Gold Award Hits.

    (M) (1:50) RCA 5197 50,000,000 Elvis Fans Can't Be Wrong.

    (M) (1:30) RCA 2229 Hits Like Never Before/Essential Elvis Volume 3. *(time includes :06 of studio talk; alternate take)*

    (M) (2:00) RCA 2229 Hits Like Never Before/Essential Elvis Volume 3. *(time includes a :09 false start; alternate take)*

    (M) (1:49) RCA 2229 Hits Like Never Before/Essential Elvis Volume 3. *(alternate take)*

    (M) (1:49) RCA 66050 The Complete 50's Masters.

    (M) (1:49) Time-Life 2RNR-26 Rock 'N' Roll Era - Elvis, The King 1954-1965.

    (M) (1:49) RCA 67463 50,000,000 Elvis Fans Can't Be Wrong: Elvis' Gold Records Volume 2.

    (M) (1:49) RCA 67565 Elvis' Greatest Jukebox Hits.

    (M) (1:49) Time-Life R806-06 The Elvis Presley Collection - The Rocker.

1959 (NOW AND THEN THERE'S) A FOOL SUCH AS I

    (M) (2:28) RCA 6383 and 56383 The Top Ten Hits.

    (M) (2:29) RCA 6401 and 56401 50 Worldwide Gold Award Hits.

    (M) (2:30) RCA 5197 50,000,000 Elvis Fans Can't Be Wrong.

    (M) (2:38) RCA 2229 Hits Like Never Before/Essential Elvis Volume 3. *(alternate take)*

    (M) (2:36) RCA 66050 The Complete 50's Masters.

    (M) (2:33) Time-Life 2RNR-06 Rock 'N' Roll Era - Elvis Presley 1954-1961.

    (M) (2:36) RCA 66880 Great Country Songs.

    (M) (2:35) Time-Life R857-11 The Heart Of Rock 'n' Roll 1958-1959.

    (M) (2:36) RCA 67463 50,000,000 Elvis Fans Can't Be Wrong: Elvis' Gold Records Volume 2.

    (M) (2:36) Time-Life R806-04 The Elvis Presley Collection - Country.

1959 I NEED YOUR LOVE TONIGHT

    (M) (2:02) RCA 6383 and 56383 The Top Ten Hits.

    (M) (2:03) RCA 5197 50,000,000 Elvis Fans Can't Be Wrong.

    (M) (2:07) RCA 2229 Hits Like Never Before/Essential Elvis Volume 3. *(includes an :08 false start; alternate take)*

    (M) (1:57) RCA 2229 Hits Like Never Before/Essential Elvis Volume 3. *(alternate take)*

    (M) (2:03) RCA 66050 The Complete 50's Masters.

    (M) (2:02) Time-Life 2RNR-26 Rock 'N' Roll Era - Elvis, The King 1954-1965.

    (M) (2:03) RCA 66921 The Other Sides - Worldwide Gold Award Hits Volume 2.

    (M) (2:00) RCA 67469 Platinum - A Life In Music. *(alternate take)*

    (M) (2:03) RCA 67463 50,000,000 Elvis Fans Can't Be Wrong: Elvis' Gold Records Volume 2.

    (M) (2:00) RCA 67592 A Touch Of Platinum - A Life In Music. *(alternate take)*

    (M) (2:03) Time-Life R806-02 The Elvis Presley Collection - Rock 'N' Roll.

1959 A BIG HUNK O' LOVE

    (M) (2:03) Rhino 70620 Billboard's Top Rock & Roll Hits Of 1959.

    (M) (2:03) Rhino 72004 Billboard's Top Rock & Roll Hits 1957-1961 Box Set.

(M) (2:10) RCA 6382 The Number One Hits.
(M) (2:07) RCA 6401 and 56401 50 Worldwide Gold Award Hits.
(S) (2:34) RCA 6985 The Alternate Aloha. *(all selections on this cd are live)*
(M) (2:05) RCA 5197 50,000,000 Elvis Fans Can't Be Wrong.
(M) (2:16) RCA 2229 Hits Like Never Before/Essential Elvis Volume 3. *(alternate take)*
(M) (2:11) RCA 8468 Elvis In Nashvillle.
(M) (2:12) RCA 66050 The Complete 50's Masters.
(M) (2:12) Time-Life 2RNR-06 Rock 'N' Roll Era - Elvis Presley 1954-1961.
(M) (2:13) RCA 6383 and 56383 The Top Ten Hits.
(M) (1:43) RCA 67458 O.S.T. Blue Suede Shoes. *(edited; most songs on this cd are segued together; this cd is a disaster)*
(M) (2:12) RCA 67469 Platinum - A Life In Music. *(alternate take)*
(M) (2:13) RCA 67463 50,000,000 Elvis Fans Can't Be Wrong: Elvis' Gold Records Volume 2.
(M) (2:14) DCC Compact Classics 1117 24 Karat Hits. *(gold disc)*
(M) (2:12) RCA 67565 Elvis' Greatest Jukebox Hits.
(M) (2:12) RCA 67592 A Touch Of Platinum - A Life In Music. *(alternate take)*
(M) (2:12) Time-Life R806-02 The Elvis Presley Collection - Rock 'N' Roll.

1959 MY WISH CAME TRUE
(M) (2:35) RCA 5197 50,000,000 Elvis Fans Can't Be Wrong.
(M) (2:33) RCA 66050 The Complete 50's Masters.
(M) (2:33) RCA 66921 The Other Sides - Worldwide Gold Award Hits Volume 2.
(M) (2:33) RCA 67463 50,000,000 Elvis Fans Can't Be Wrong: Elvis' Gold Records Volume 2.

1960 STUCK ON YOU
(S) (2:14) Rhino 70621 Billboard's Top Rock & Roll Hits Of 1960. *(found only on the original 1988 pressings of this cd)*
(S) (2:14) Rhino 72004 Billboard's Top Rock & Roll Hits 1957-1961 Box Set.
(S) (2:15) RCA 6383 and 56383 The Top Ten Hits.
(S) (2:14) RCA 6382 The Number One Hits.
(S) (2:18) RCA 6401 and 56401 50 Worldwide Gold Award Hits.
(S) (2:17) RCA 5600 Return Of The Rocker.
(S) (2:17) RCA 2765 Elvis' Golden Records Volume 3.
(S) (2:18) RCA 66160 From Nashville To Memphis: The Essential 60's Masters I.
(S) (2:18) Time-Life 2RNR-06 Rock 'N' Roll Era - Elvis Presley 1954-1961.
(S) (1:39) RCA 67458 O.S.T. Blue Suede Shoes. *(most songs on this cd are segued together; this cd is a disaster)*
(E) (2:25) RCA 67469 Platinum - A Life In Music. *(live)*
(S) (2:18) RCA 67464 Golden Records Volume 3.
(S) (2:18) DCC Compact Classics 1117 24 Karat Hits. *(gold disc)*
(S) (2:17) RCA 67565 Elvis' Greatest Jukebox Hits.
(E) (2:25) RCA 67592 A Touch Of Platinum - A Life In Music. *(live)*
(S) (2:17) Time-Life R806-02 The Elvis Presley Collection - Rock 'N' Roll.

1960 FAME AND FORTUNE
(S) (2:30) RCA 2227 The Great Performances.
(S) (2:32) RCA 5353 A Valentine Gift For You.
(S) (2:31) RCA 2765 Elvis' Golden Records Volume 3.
(S) (2:28) RCA 66160 From Nashville To Memphis: The Essential 60's Masters I.
(S) (2:28) RCA 66532 Heart And Soul.
(S) (2:28) RCA 66921 The Other Sides - Worldwide Gold Award Hits Volume 2.
(E) (2:24) RCA 67469 Platinum - A Life In Music. *(live)*
(S) (2:29) RCA 67464 Golden Records Volume 3.
(S) (2:29) Time-Life R857-17 The Heart Of Rock 'n' Roll: The Early '60s.
(E) (2:24) RCA 67592 A Touch Of Platinum - A Life In Music. *(live)*

1960 IT'S NOW OR NEVER
(S) (3:13) Rhino 70621 Billboard's Top Rock & Roll Hits Of 1960. *(found only on the original 1988 pressings of this cd)*
(S) (3:13) Rhino 72004 Billboard's Top Rock & Roll Hits 1957-1961 Box Set.
(S) (3:15) RCA 8474 Nipper's Greatest Hits Of The 60's Volume 1.
(S) (3:13) RCA 6383 and 56383 The Top Ten Hits.
(S) (3:13) RCA 6382 The Number One Hits.
(S) (3:13) RCA 6401 and 56401 50 Worldwide Gold Award Hits.
(S) (3:16) RCA 2765 Elvis' Golden Records Volume 3.
(M) (3:12) Pair 1251 Great Performances.
(M) (3:12) Special Music 2706 A Legendary Performer Volume2.
(S) (3:14) RCA 66160 From Nashville To Memphis: The Essential 60's Masters I.
(S) (3:14) RCA 66160 From Nashville To Memphis: The Essential 60's Masters I. *(missing some overdubs)*
(S) (3:15) Time-Life 2RNR-06 Rock 'N' Roll Era - Elvis Presley 1954-1961.
(S) (3:13) RCA 66532 Heart And Soul.
(S) (3:14) Time-Life R857-14 The Heart Of Rock 'n' Roll 1960-1961 Take Two.
(S) (3:13) RCA 67469 Platinum - A Life In Music.
(S) (3:14) RCA 67464 Golden Records Volume 3.
(S) (3:15) DCC Compact Classics 1117 24 Karat Hits. *(gold disc)*
(S) (3:13) RCA 67565 Elvis' Greatest Jukebox Hits.
(S) (3:14) RCA 67595 Love Songs.
(S) (3:13) RCA 67592 A Touch Of Platinum - A Life In Music.
(S) (3:14) Time-Life R806-01 The Elvis Presley Collection - Love Songs.

1960 A MESS OF BLUES
(S) (2:39) RCA 66160 From Nashville To Memphis: The Essential 60's Masters I.
(S) (2:39) RCA 6401 and 56401 50 Worldwide Gold Award Hits.
(S) (2:39) RCA 5600 Return Of The Rocker.
(S) (2:39) RCA 1297 Elvis' Gold Records Volume 4.
(S) (2:39) Time-Life 2RNR-26 Rock 'N' Roll Era - Elvis, The King: 1954-1965.
(S) (2:43) RCA 67469 Platinum - A Life In Music. *(alternate take)*
(S) (2:39) RCA 67465 Elvis' Gold Records Volume 4.
(S) (2:43) RCA 67592 A Touch Of Platinum - A Life In Music. *(alternate take)*

1960 ARE YOU LONESOME TONIGHT?
(S) (3:05) RCA 6383 and 56383 The Top Ten Hits.
(S) (3:05) RCA 6382 The Number One Hits.
(S) (3:06) RCA 6401 and 56401 50 Worldwide Gold Award Hits.
(S) (3:07) RCA 5353 A Valentine Gift For You.
(S) (3:03) RCA 2765 Elvis' Golden Records Volume 3.
(S) (3:05) RCA 66160 From Nashville To Memphis: The Essential 60's Masters I.
(S) (3:05) Time-Life 2RNR-06 Rock 'N' Roll Era - Elvis Presley 1954-1961.
(S) (3:03) Time-Life R103-27 Love Me Tender.
(S) (3:05) RCA 66532 Heart And Soul.
(S) (3:05) Time-Life R857-10 The Heart Of Rock 'n' Roll 1960-1961.
(S) (3:05) RCA 67458 O.S.T. Blue Suede Shoes. *(most songs on this cd are segued together; this cd is a disaster)*
(S) (3:05) RCA 67469 Platinum - A Life In Music.
(S) (3:05) RCA 67464 Golden Records Volume 3.
(S) (3:05) DCC Compact Classics 1117 24 Karat Hits. *(gold disc)*
(S) (3:05) RCA 67595 Love Songs.
(S) (3:05) RCA 67592 A Touch Of Platinum - A Life In Music.
(S) (3:05) Time-Life R806-01 The Elvis Presley Collection - Love Songs.
(S) (3:05) Time-Life R857-21 The Heart Of Rock 'n' Roll Slow Dancing Classics.
(S) (3:06) Time-Life R814-05 Love Songs.

1960 I GOTTA KNOW
(S) (2:14) RCA 66160 From Nashville To Memphis: The Essential 60's Masters I.
(S) (2:13) RCA 6401 and 56401 50 Worldwide Gold Award Hits.
(S) (2:13) RCA 2765 Elvis' Golden Records Volume 3.
(S) (2:14) RCA 67464 Golden Records Volume 3.
(S) (2:14) Time-Life R806-06 The Elvis Presley Collection - The Rocker.

ELVIS PRESLEY (Continued)

1961 SURRENDER
- (S) (1:50)   RCA 6383 and 56383   The Top Ten Hits.
- (S) (1:51)   RCA 6382   The Number One Hits.
- (S) (1:50)   RCA 6401 and 56401   50 Worldwide Gold Award Hits.
- (S) (1:53)   RCA 2765   Elvis' Golden Records Volume 3.
- (S) (1:51)   RCA 66160   From Nashville To Memphis: The Essential 60's Masters I.
- (S) (1:50)   RCA 66160   From Nashville To Memphis: The Essential 60's Masters I.   *(alternate take)*
- (S) (1:51)   Time-Life R857-14   The Heart Of Rock 'n' Roll 1960-1961 Take Two.
- (S) (1:51)   RCA 67464   Golden Records Volume 3.
- (S) (1:53)   DCC Compact Classics 1117   24 Karat Hits.   *(gold disc)*
- (S) (1:51)   RCA 67595   Love Songs.
- (S) (1:51)   Time-Life R806-01   The Elvis Presley Collection - Love Songs.

1961 LONELY MAN
- (S) (2:42)   RCA 66601   Command Performances - The Essential 60's Masters II.
- (S) (2:42)   RCA 66557   Flaming Star/Wild In The Country/Follow That Dream.
- (S) (2:01)   RCA 3114   Collectors Gold.   *(alternate take)*
- (S) (2:44)   RCA 1297   Elvis' Gold Records Volume 4.
- (S) (2:42)   RCA 66921   The Other Sides - Worldwide Gold Award Hits Volume 2.
- (S) (2:42)   RCA 67465   Elvis' Gold Records Volume 4.

1961 FLAMING STAR
- (S) (2:24)   RCA 66557   Flaming Star/Wild In The Country/Follow That Dream.
- (S) (2:24)   RCA 66601   Command Performances - The Essential 60's Masters II.
- (S) (2:24)   Time-Life R806-05   The Elvis Presley Collection - Movie Magic.

1961 I FEEL SO BAD
- (S) (2:50)   RCA 6383 and 56383   The Top Ten Hits.
- (S) (2:50)   RCA 6401 and 56401   50 Worldwide Gold Award Hits.
- (S) (2:51)   RCA 5418   Reconsider Baby.
- (S) (2:51)   RCA 2765   Elvis' Golden Records Volume 3.
- (S) (2:52)   RCA 66160   From Nashville To Memphis: The Essential 60's Masters I.
- (S) (2:51)   Time-Life 2RNR-26   Rock 'N' Roll Era - Elvis, The King 1954-1965.
- (S) (2:55)   RCA 67469   Platinum - A Life In Music.   *(alternate take)*
- (S) (2:52)   RCA 67464   Golden Records Volume 3.
- (S) (2:55)   RCA 67592   A Touch Of Platinum - A Life In Music.   *(alternate take)*

1961 WILD IN THE COUNTRY
- (S) (1:51)   RCA 66557   Flaming Star/Wild In The Country/Follow That Dream.
- (S) (1:51)   RCA 66601   Command Performances - The Essential 60's Masters II.
- (S) (1:51)   RCA 66921   The Other Sides - Worldwide Gold Award Hits Volume 2.
- (S) (1:51)   RCA 67464   Golden Records Volume 3.

1961 LITTLE SISTER
- (S) (2:28)   RCA 6383 and 56383   The Top Ten Hits.
- (S) (2:29)   RCA 6401 and 56401   50 Worldwide Gold Award Hits.
- (S) (2:29)   RCA 5600   Return Of The Rocker.
- (S) (2:28)   RCA 2765   Elvis' Golden Records Volume 3.
- (S) (2:30)   RCA 66160   From Nashville To Memphis: The Essential 60's Masters I.
- (S) (2:31)   Time-Life 2RNR-06   Rock 'N' Roll Era - Elvis Presley 1954-1961.
- (S) (2:30)   RCA 67464   Golden Records Volume 3.
- (S) (2:30)   DCC Compact Classics 1117   24 Karat Hits.   *(gold disc)*
- (S) (2:30)   RCA 67565   Elvis' Greatest Jukebox Hits.
- (S) (2:30)   Time-Life R806-02   The Elvis Presley Collection - Rock 'N' Roll.

1961 (MARIE'S THE NAME) HIS LATEST FLAME
- (S) (2:03)   RCA 6383 and 56383   The Top Ten Hits.
- (S) (2:04)   RCA 5600   Return Of The Rocker.

- (S) (2:04)   RCA 2765   Elvis' Golden Records Volume 3.
- (S) (2:06)   RCA 66160   From Nashville To Memphis: The Essential 60's Masters I.
- (S) (1:59)   RCA 66160   From Nashville To Memphis: The Essential 60's Masters I.   *(alternate take)*
- (S) (2:04)   Time-Life 2RNR-26   Rock 'N' Roll Era - Elvis, The King 1954-1965.
- (S) (2:06)   RCA 66921   The Other Sides - Worldwide Gold Award Hits Volume 2.
- (S) (2:06)   RCA 67464   Golden Records Volume 3.
- (S) (2:06)   DCC Compact Classics 1117   24 Karat Hits.   *(gold disc)*
- (S) (2:06)   Time-Life R806-02   The Elvis Presley Collection - Rock 'N' Roll.

1962 CAN'T HELP FALLING IN LOVE
- (S) (3:00)   RCA 6383 and 56383   The Top Ten Hits.
- (S) (3:00)   RCA 6401 and 56401   50 Worldwide Gold Award Hits.
- (S) (3:04)   RCA 6985   The Alternate Aloha.   *(all selections on this cd are live)*
- (S) (3:00)   RCA 5353   A Valentine Gift For You.
- (S) (2:59)   RCA 3683   O.S.T. Blue Hawaii.
- (S) (2:59)   Pair 1251   Great Performances.
- (S) (2:58)   Special Music 2705   A Legendary Performer Volume 1.
- (E) (2:59)   Time-Life 2RNR-06   Rock 'N' Roll Era - Elvis Presley 1954-1961.
- (S) (2:58)   Time-Life R103-27   Love Me Tender.
- (S) (2:58)   RCA 66532   Heart And Soul.
- (S) (2:58)   RCA 66601   Command Performances - The Essential 60's Masters II.
- (S) (2:58)   Time-Life R974-04   Many Moods Of Romance - As Time Goes By.
- (S) (2:58)   Time-Life R857-10   The Heart Of Rock 'n' Roll 1960-1961.
- (S) (2:59)   RCA 66959 and 67459   O.S.T. Blue Hawaii.   *(remastered edition)*
- (S) (1:52)   RCA 66959 and 67459   O.S.T. Blue Hawaii.   *(soundtrack version)*
- (S) (2:58)   RCA 67469   Platinum - A Life In Music.
- (S) (2:58)   RCA 67464   Golden Records Volume 3.
- (S) (2:58)   DCC Compact Classics 1117   24 Karat Hits.   *(gold disc)*
- (S) (2:58)   RCA 67595   Love Songs.
- (S) (2:58)   RCA 67592   A Touch Of Platinum - A Life In Music.
- (S) (2:58)   Time-Life R806-01   The Elvis Presley Collection - Love Songs.
- (S) (1:52)   Time-Life R806-05   The Elvis Presley Collection - Movie Magic.   *(rerecording)*
- (S) (2:58)   Time-Life R814-05   Love Songs.

1962 ROCK-A-HULA BABY
- (S) (1:58)   RCA 6401 and 56401   50 Worldwide Gold Award Hits.
- (S) (1:58)   RCA 3683   O.S.T. Blue Hawaii.
- (S) (1:57)   RCA 66601   Command Performances - The Essential 60's Masters II.
- (S) (1:57)   RCA 66959 and 67459   O.S.T. Blue Hawaii.   *(remastered edition)*
- (S) (2:13)   RCA 66959 and 67459   O.S.T. Blue Hawaii.   *(alternate take with :22 of studio talk)*
- (S) (1:57)   RCA 67465   Elvis' Gold Records Volume 4.
- (S) (1:57)   Time-Life R806-06   The Elvis Presley Collection - The Rocker.

1962 GOOD LUCK CHARM
- (S) (2:23)   RCA 6383 and 56383   The Top Ten Hits.
- (S) (2:23)   RCA 6382   The Number One Hits.
- (S) (2:21)   RCA 6401 and 56401   50 Worldwide Gold Award Hits.
- (S) (2:20)   RCA 2765   Elvis' Golden Records Volume 3.
- (S) (2:23)   RCA 66160   From Nashville To Memphis: The Essential 60's Masters I.
- (S) (2:22)   Time-Life 2RNR-26   Rock 'N' Roll Era - Elvis, The King 1954-1965.
- (S) (2:23)   RCA 67464   Golden Records Volume 3.
- (S) (2:24)   DCC Compact Classics 1117   24 Karat Hits.   *(gold disc)*
- (S) (2:23)   RCA 67565   Elvis' Greatest Jukebox Hits.
- (S) (2:24)   RCA 67595   Love Songs.

474

(S) (2:23) Time-Life R806-02 The Elvis Presley Collection - Rock 'N' Roll.

1962 ANYTHING THAT'S PART OF YOU
(S) (2:05) RCA 6401 and 56401 50 Worldwide Gold Award Hits.
(S) (2:04) RCA 66160 From Nashville To Memphis: The Essential 60's Masters I.
(S) (2:04) RCA 66532 Heart And Soul.
(S) (2:01) RCA 2765 Elvis' Golden Records Volume 3.
(S) (2:06) RCA 6383 and 56383 Elvis In Nashville.
(S) (2:04) RCA 67464 Golden Records Volume 3.
(S) (2:04) Time-Life R806-01 The Elvis Presley Collection - Love Songs.

1962 FOLLOW THAT DREAM
(E) (1:35) RCA 5600 Return Of The Rocker.
(M) (1:37) Pair 1010 Double Dynamite.
(M) (1:36) RCA 66557 Flaming Star/Wild In The Country/Follow That Dream.
(S) (1:36) RCA 66601 Command Performances - The Essential 60's Masters II. *(alternate take)*
(S) (1:36) RCA 67464 Golden Records Volume 3. *(alternate take)*
(M) (1:36) Time-Life R806-05 The Elvis Presley Collection - Movie Magic.

1962 SHE'S NOT YOU
(S) (2:07) RCA 6383 and 56383 The Top Ten Hits.
(S) (2:07) RCA 6401 and 56401 50 Worldwide Gold Award Hits.
(S) (2:06) RCA 2765 Elvis' Golden Records Volume 3.
(S) (2:08) RCA 66160 From Nashville To Memphis: The Essential 60's Masters I.
(S) (2:07) RCA 66532 Heart And Soul.
(S) (2:07) DCC Compact Classics 1117 24 Karat Hits. *(gold disc)*
(S) (2:08) Time-Life R857-17 The Heart Of Rock 'n' Roll: The Early '60s.
(S) (2:07) RCA 67565 Elvis' Greatest Jukebox Hits.
(S) (2:08) RCA 67595 Love Songs.
(S) (2:08) Time-Life R806-01 The Elvis Presley Collection - Love Songs.

1962 KING OF THE WHOLE WIDE WORLD
(S) (2:40) RCA 66130 Kid Galahad and Girls! Girls! Girls! *(complete unedited version which was first released in 1986)*
(S) (2:05) RCA 66601 Command Performances - The Essential 60's Masters II.
(S) (2:05) RCA 67464 Golden Records Volume 3.
(S) (2:06) Time-Life R806-05 The Elvis Presley Collection - Movie Magic.

1962 RETURN TO SENDER
(S) (2:06) RCA 6383 and 56383 The Top Ten Hits. *(very poor stereo separation)*
(S) (2:04) RCA 6401 and 56401 50 Worldwide Gold Award Hits. *(very poor stereo separation)*
(S) (2:06) RCA 2227 The Great Performances.
(S) (2:08) RCA 5600 Return Of The Rocker. *(very poor stereo separation)*
(S) (2:06) RCA 66130 Kid Galahad/Girls! Girls! Girls!
(S) (2:08) Time-Life 2RNR-26 Rock 'N' Roll Era - Elvis, The King 1954-1965.
(S) (2:06) RCA 66601 Command Performances - The Essential 60's Masters II.
(S) (2:05) RCA 67469 Platinum - A Life In Music.
(S) (2:06) DCC Compact Classics 1117 24 Karat Hits. *(gold disc)*
(S) (2:05) RCA 67565 Elvis' Greatest Jukebox Hits.
(S) (2:06) RCA 67465 Elvis' Gold Records Volume 4.
(S) (2:05) RCA 67592 A Touch Of Platinum - A Life In Music.
(S) (2:05) Time-Life R806-02 The Elvis Presley Collection - Rock 'N' Roll.

1963 ONE BROKEN HEART FOR SALE
(E) (1:34) RCA 6401 and 56401 50 Worldwide Gold Award Hits.
(S) (2:20) RCA 3114 Collectors Gold. *(alternate take)*
(S) (1:45) RCA 66131 It Happened At The World's Fair/Fun In Acapulco.
(S) (2:22) RCA 66131 It Happened At The World's Fair/Fun In Acapulco. *(alternate take)*

(S) (1:45) RCA 66601 Command Performances - The Essential 60's Masters II.
(S) (1:45) Time-Life R806-05 The Elvis Presley Collection - Movie Magic.

1963 (YOU'RE THE) DEVIL IN DISGUISE
(S) (2:16) RCA 6383 and 56383 The Top Ten Hits.
(S) (2:19) RCA 1297 Elvis' Gold Records Volume 4.
(S) (2:16) RCA 6401 and 56401 50 Worldwide Gold Award Hits.
(S) (2:19) RCA 61024 The Lost Album.
(S) (2:16) Mercury 841583 O.S.T. She-Devil.
(S) (2:19) RCA 66160 From Nashville To Memphis: The Essential 60's Masters I.
(S) (2:16) Time-Life 2RNR-26 Rock 'N' Roll Era - Elvis, The King 1954-1965.
(E) (2:06) RCA 67458 O.S.T. Blue Suede Shoes. *(edited; most songs on this cd are segued together; this cd is a disaster)*
(S) (2:20) DCC Compact Classics 1117 24 Karat Hits. *(gold disc)*
(S) (2:19) RCA 67565 Elvis' Greatest Jukebox Hits.
(S) (2:19) RCA 67465 Elvis' Gold Records Volume 4.
(S) (2:20) Time-Life R806-02 The Elvis Presley Collection - Rock 'N' Roll.

1963 BOSSA NOVA BABY
(S) (1:59) RCA 6383 and 56383 The Top Ten Hits.
(S) (1:59) RCA 6401 and 56401 50 Worldwide Gold Award Hits.
(S) (2:01) RCA 3026 Sings Leiber & Stoller.
(S) (2:01) RCA 66131 It Happened At The World's Fair/Fun In Acapulco.
(S) (2:01) RCA 66601 Command Performances - The Essential 60's Masters II.
(S) (1:54) RCA 67458 O.S.T. Blue Suede Shoes. *(alternate take; most songs on this cd are segued together; this cd is a disaster)*
(S) (2:13) RCA 67469 Platinum - A Life In Music. *(alternate take)*
(S) (2:01) RCA 67465 Elvis' Gold Records Volume 4.
(S) (2:13) RCA 67592 A Touch Of Platinum - A Life In Music. *(alternate take)*
(S) (2:01) Time-Life R806-05 The Elvis Presley Collection - Movie Magic.

1963 WITCHCRAFT
(S) (2:21) RCA 1297 Elvis' Gold Records Volume 4.
(S) (2:18) RCA 61024 The Lost Album.
(S) (2:30) RCA 3114 Collectors Gold. *(alternate take)*
(S) (2:27) RCA 5600 Return Of The Rocker.
(S) (2:18) RCA 66160 From Nashville To Memphis: The Essential 60's Masters I.
(S) (2:18) RCA 66921 The Other Sides - Worldwide Gold Award Hits Volume 2.
(S) (2:18) RCA 67465 Elvis' Gold Records Volume 4.
(S) (2:17) Time-Life R806-06 The Elvis Presley Collection - The Rocker.

1964 KISSIN' COUSINS
(S) (2:11) RCA 6401 and 56401 50 Worldwide Gold Award Hits.
(S) (1:14) RCA 66362 Kissin' Cousins/Clambake/Stay Away, Joe. *(not the hit song but another song titled "KISSIN' COUSINS (NUMBER 2)")*
(S) (2:11) RCA 66362 Kissin' Cousins/Clambake/Stay Away, Joe.
(S) (2:11) RCA 66601 Command Performances - The Essential 60's Masters II.
(S) (2:11) RCA 67465 Elvis' Gold Records Volume 4.
(S) (2:11) Time-Life R806-06 The Elvis Presley Collection - The Rocker.

1964 IT HURTS ME
(S) (2:26) RCA 61024 The Lost Album.
(S) (2:27) RCA 66160 From Nashville To Memphis: The Essential 60's Masters I.
(S) (2:27) RCA 1297 Elvis' Gold Records Volume 4.
(S) (2:27) RCA 66532 Heart And Soul.
(S) (2:26) RCA 66921 The Other Sides - Worldwide Gold Award Hits Volume 2.
(S) (2:27) RCA 67465 Elvis' Gold Records Volume 4.

ELVIS PRESLEY *(Continued)*

1964 KISS ME QUICK
- (S) (2:44) RCA 2523 Pot Luck With Elvis.
- (S) (2:46) Pair 1037 Remembering.
- (S) (2:46) RCA 66160 From Nashville To Memphis: The Essential 60's Masters I.

1964 WHAT'D I SAY
- (S) (3:03) RCA 1297 Elvis' Gold Records Volume 4.
- (S) (5:43) RCA 3114 Collectors Gold. *(live)*
- (S) (3:01) RCA 66129 Viva Las Vegas/Roustabout.
- (S) (3:01) RCA 66601 Command Performances - The Essential 60's Masters II.
- (S) (4:45) RCA 67469 Platinum - A Life In Music. *(live)*
- (S) (3:01) RCA 67465 Elvis' Gold Records Volume 4.

1964 VIVA LAS VEGAS
- (M) (2:10) RCA 6401 and 56401 50 Worldwide Gold Award Hits.
- (S) (2:19) RCA 66129 Viva Las Vegas/Roustabout.
- (S) (2:19) RCA 66601 Command Performances - The Essential 60's Masters II.
- (S) (2:19) RCA 67565 Elvis' Greatest Jukebox Hits.
- (S) (2:19) RCA 67465 Elvis' Gold Records Volume 4.
- (S) (2:19) Time-Life R806-05 The Elvis Presley Collection - Movie Magic.

1964 SUCH A NIGHT
- (S) (2:59) RCA 2231 Elvis Is Back.
- (S) (3:47) Pair 1251 Great Performances. *(includes 2 false starts of :50)*
- (S) (3:48) Special Music 2706 A Legendary Performer Volume 2. *(includes 2 false starts of :50)*
- (S) (2:58) Time-Life 2RNR-26 Rock 'N' Roll Era - Elvis, The King 1954-1965.
- (S) (2:58) RCA 67595 Love Songs.

1964 ASK ME
- (S) (2:05) RCA 1297 Elvis' Gold Records Volume 4.
- (S) (2:05) RCA 61024 The Lost Album.
- (S) (2:06) RCA 3114 Collectors Gold. *(alternate take)*
- (S) (2:06) RCA 66160 From Nashville To Memphis: The Essential 60's Masters I.
- (S) (2:05) RCA 66921 The Other Sides - Worldwide Gold Award Hits Volume 2.
- (S) (2:06) RCA 67465 Elvis' Gold Records Volume 4.

1964 AIN'T THAT LOVING YOU BABY
- (M) (2:22) RCA 1297 Elvis' Gold Records Volume 4.
- (M) (2:21) RCA 6401 and 56401 50 Worldwide Gold Award Hits.
- (M) (2:33) RCA 5418 Reconsider Baby. *(alternate take)*
- (M) (2:23) RCA 2229 Hits Like Never Before/Essential Elvis Volume 3. *(alternate take)*
- (M) (2:06) RCA 2229 Hits Like Never Before/Essential Elvis Volume 3. *(time includes :18 of studio talk and a false start; alternate take)*
- (M) (2:22) RCA 66050 The Complete 50's Masters.
- (M) (2:22) RCA 67465 Elvis' Gold Records Volume 4.
- (M) (2:22) Time-Life R806-06 The Elvis Presley Collection - The Rocker.

1965 DO THE CLAM
- (S) (3:19) RCA 66128 Harum Scarum/Girl Happy.
- (S) (3:19) RCA 66601 Command Performances - The Essential 60's Masters II.

1965 CRYING IN THE CHAPEL
- (M) (2:22) RCA 6383 and 56383 The Top Ten Hits.
- (M) (2:22) RCA 6401 and 56401 50 Worldwide Gold Award Hits.
- (M) (2:22) RCA 3758 How Great Thou Art.
- (M) (2:23) Time-Life 2RNR-26 Rock 'N' Roll Era - Elvis, The King 1954-1965.
- (S) (2:23) RCA 66421 Amazing Grace: His Greatest Sacred Performances.
- (S) (2:24) DCC Compact Classics 1117 24 Karat Hits. *(gold disc)*
- (S) (2:24) RCA 67465 Elvis' Gold Records Volume 4.
- (S) (2:24) Time-Life R808-02 Classic Country 1965-1969.

1965 (SUCH AN) EASY QUESTION
- (S) (2:16) RCA 2523 Pot Luck With Elvis.
- (S) (2:19) Pair 1037 Remembering.
- (S) (2:18) RCA 66160 From Nashville To Memphis: The Essential 60's Masters I.

1965 I'M YOURS
- (S) (2:20) RCA 2523 Pot Luck With Elvis. *(LP version)*
- (S) (2:19) RCA 66160 From Nashville To Memphis: The Essential 60's Masters I. *(LP version)*
- (S) (2:19) Time-Life R806-01 The Elvis Presley Collection - Love Songs. *(LP version)*

1965 PUPPET ON A STRING
- (S) (2:38) Special Music 2704 Sings For Children.
- (S) (2:39) RCA 66128 Harum Scarum/Girl Happy.
- (S) (2:39) RCA 66601 Command Performances - The Essential 60's Masters II.
- (S) (2:39) RCA 66921 The Other Sides - Worldwide Gold Award Hits Volume 2.
- (S) (2:39) RCA 67595 Love Songs.
- (S) (2:39) Time-Life R806-01 The Elvis Presley Collection - Love Songs.

1966 TELL ME WHY
- (M) (2:08) RCA 5353 A Valentine Gift For You.
- (M) (2:08) RCA 9589 Stereo '57/Essential Elvis Volume 2.
- (M) (2:05) RCA 66050 The Complete 50's Masters.
- (M) (2:05) RCA 66921 The Other Sides - Worldwide Gold Award Hits Volume 2.
- (M) (2:06) RCA 67452 O.S.T. Loving You.

1966 FRANKIE AND JOHNNY
- (S) (2:32) Pair 1010 Double Dynamite.
- (S) (2:33) RCA 66360 Frankie And Johnny/Paradise, Hawaiian Style.
- (S) (2:32) RCA 66601 Command Performances - The Essential 60's Masters II.

1966 LOVE LETTERS
- (S) (2:49) RCA 1297 Elvis' Gold Records Volume 4.
- (S) (3:38) RCA 3114 Collectors Gold. *(alternate take; includes :46 of false starts)*
- (S) (2:51) RCA 5353 A Valentine Gift For You.
- (S) (2:50) RCA 54350 Love Letters From Elvis. *(rerecording)*
- (S) (2:50) RCA 66160 From Nashville To Memphis: The Essential 60's Masters I.
- (S) (2:49) RCA 66532 Heart And Soul.
- (S) (2:50) RCA 67465 Elvis' Gold Records Volume 4.
- (S) (2:49) Time-Life R806-01 The Elvis Presley Collection - Love Songs.

1966 SPINOUT
- (S) (2:32) RCA 66361 Spinout/Double Trouble.
- (S) (2:32) RCA 66601 Command Performances - The Essential 60's Masters II.

1966 ALL THAT I AM
- (S) (2:15) RCA 66361 Spinout/Double Trouble.
- (S) (2:15) RCA 66601 Command Performances - The Essential 60's Masters II.

1967 INDESCRIBABLY BLUE
- (S) (2:47) RCA 1297 Elvis' Gold Records Volume 4.
- (S) (2:46) RCA 66160 From Nashville To Memphis: The Essential 60's Masters I.
- (S) (2:46) RCA 67465 Elvis' Gold Records Volume 4.

1967 LONG LEGGED GIRL (WITH THE SHORT DRESS ON)
- (S) (1:26) RCA 66361 Spinout/Double Trouble.
- (S) (1:26) RCA 66601 Command Performances - The Essential 60's Masters II.

1967 BIG BOSS MAN
- (S) (2:50) RCA 66160 From Nashville To Memphis: The Essential 60's Masters I.
- (S) (2:50) Pair 1010 Elvis! Double Dynamite.
- (S) (3:36) RCA 66160 From Nashville To Memphis: The Essential 60's Masters I. *(alternate take; includes :11 of studio talk)*
- (S) (2:32) RCA 67458 O.S.T. Blue Suede Shoes. *(edited; most songs on this cd are segued together; this cd is a disaster)*
- (S) (2:50) RCA 67466 Elvis' Gold Records Volume 5.

1967 YOU DON'T KNOW ME
- (S) (2:27) RCA 66160 From Nashville To Memphis: The Essential 60's Masters I.
- (S) (2:11) RCA 66362 Kissin' Cousins/Clambake/Stay Away, Joe. *("Clambake" soundtrack version)*
- (S) (2:11) RCA 66601 Command Performances - The Essential 60's Masters II. *("Clambake" soundtrack version)*

476

(S)　(2:27)　Time-Life R806-04　The Elvis Presley Collection -
　　　　　　　Country.

1968　GUITAR MAN
**(this song charted in different versions for Elvis
in 1968 and 1981; see 1981 listings also)**
(M)　(2:14)　RCA 8468　Elvis In Nashville.
(S)　(2:17)　Pair 1250　Double Feature: Speedway/Clambake.
(M)　(2:13)　RCA 9970　Nipper's Greatest Hits - The 80's. *(this
　　　　　　　is the 1968 version mistaken for the 1981 version
　　　　　　　which should have been included on this cd)*
(S)　(2:55)　RCA 66160　From Nashville To Memphis: The
　　　　　　　Essential 60's Masters I. *(this is the complete
　　　　　　　original unedited version)*
(S)　(2:54)　RCA 67458　O.S.T. Blue Suede Shoes. *(most songs
　　　　　　　on this cd are segued together; this cd is a disaster)*
(S)　(2:25)　RCA 67469　Platinum - A Life In Music.
　　　　　　　(alternate take)
(S)　(2:15)　RCA 67466　Elvis' Gold Records Volume 5.
(S)　(2:25)　RCA 67592　A Touch Of Platinum - A Life In
　　　　　　　Music. *(alternate take)*
(S)　(2:54)　Time-Life R806-02　The Elvis Presley Collection -
　　　　　　　Rock 'N' Roll. *(this is the complete original
　　　　　　　unedited version)*

1968　U.S. MALE
(S)　(2:41)　Pair 1010　Double Dynamite.
(S)　(2:41)　RCA 66160　From Nashville To Memphis: The
　　　　　　　Essential 60's Masters I.
(S)　(2:41)　RCA 67466　Elvis' Gold Records Volume 5.
(S)　(2:41)　Time-Life R806-02　The Elvis Presley Collection -
　　　　　　　Rock 'N' Roll.

1969　IF I CAN DREAM
(E)　(3:07)　RCA 8533　O.S.T. Heartbreak Hotel. *(45 version)*
(E)　(3:07)　RCA 6401 and 56401　50 Worldwide Gold Award
　　　　　　　Hits. *(45 version)*
(S)　(3:09)　RCA 2227　The Great Performances. *(45 version)*
(E)　(3:19)　RCA 61021　NBC-TV Special. *(LP version which
　　　　　　　features ending audience applause)*
(S)　(3:10)　RCA 4941　Gold Records Volume 5. *(45 version)*
(E)　(3:15)　Pair 1251　Great Performances. *(LP version
　　　　　　　which features ending audience applause)*
(E)　(3:15)　Special Music 2706　A Legendary Performer
　　　　　　　Volume 2. *(LP version which features ending
　　　　　　　audience applause)*
(S)　(3:07)　RCA 67469　Platinum - A Life In Music.
　　　　　　　(alternate take)
(E)　(3:11)　RCA 67466　Elvis' Gold Records Volume 5. *(LP
　　　　　　　version which features ending audience applause)*

1969　MEMORIES
(S)　(2:19)　RCA 2227　The Great Performances. *(highly edited)*
(S)　(2:43)　RCA 3114　Collectors Gold. *(live; rerecording)*
(E)　(3:16)　RCA 61021　NBC-TV Special. *(LP version which
　　　　　　　features audience applause on introduction and
　　　　　　　ending)*
(E)　(3:05)　RCA 67466　Elvis' Gold Records Volume 5. *(LP
　　　　　　　version faded :11 early)*

1969　IN THE GHETTO
(S)　(2:43)　RCA 6383 and 56383　The Top Ten Hits.
(S)　(2:45)　RCA 6401 and 56401　50 Worldwide Gold Award Hits.
(S)　(2:45)　RCA 6221　The Memphis Record.
(S)　(2:46)　RCA 51456　From Elvis In Memphis.
(S)　(2:46)　RCA 4941　Gold Records Volume 5.
(S)　(2:46)　RCA 53732　Pure Gold.
(S)　(2:45)　RCA 66160　From Nashville To Memphis: The
　　　　　　　Essential 60's Masters I.
(S)　(2:46)　RCA 66160　From Nashville To Memphis: The
　　　　　　　Essential 60's Masters I. *(alternate take)*
(S)　(2:48)　RCA 67458　O.S.T. Blue Suede Shoes. *(alternate
　　　　　　　take; most songs on this cd are segued together;
　　　　　　　this cd is a disaster)*
(S)　(2:39)　RCA 67469　Platinum - A Life In Music.
　　　　　　　(alternate take)
(S)　(2:43)　DCC Compact Classics 1117　24 Karat Hits.
　　　　　　　(gold disc)
(S)　(2:44)　RCA 67466　Elvis' Gold Records Volume 5.

1969　CLEAN UP YOUR OWN BACK YARD
(S)　(3:09)　RCA 4941　Gold Records Volume 5.
(S)　(3:07)　RCA 66559　Live A Little, Love A Little/Charro!/
　　　　　　　The Trouble With Girls/Change Of Habit.

(S)　(3:07)　RCA 66559　Live A Little, Love A Little/Charro!/The
　　　　　　　Trouble With Girls/Change Of Habit. *(missing
　　　　　　　some overdubs)*
(S)　(3:07)　RCA 66601　Command Performances - The
　　　　　　　Essential 60's Masters II.
(S)　(3:06)　RCA 67466　Elvis' Gold Records Volume 5.

1969　SUSPICIOUS MINDS
(S)　(4:16)　RCA 9902　Nipper's #1 Hits 1956-1986.
(S)　(4:18)　RCA 8475　Nipper's Greatest Hits Of The 60's
　　　　　　　Volume 2.
(S)　(3:21)　RCA 6383 and 56383　The Top Ten Hits. *(edited)*
(S)　(3:38)　RCA 6382　The Number One Hits. *(edited)*
(S)　(4:26)　RCA 6401 and 56401　50 Worldwide Gold Award
　　　　　　　Hits.
(S)　(3:24)　RCA 6221　The Memphis Record. *(edited)*
(S)　(3:59)　RCA 6985　The Alternate Aloha. *(all selections
　　　　　　　on this cd are live)*
(S)　(4:20)　RCA 4941　Gold Records Volume 5.
(S)　(4:28)　RCA 66160　From Nashville To Memphis: The
　　　　　　　Essential 60's Masters I.
(S)　(3:14)　RCA 66160　From Nashville To Memphis: The
　　　　　　　Essential 60's Masters I. *(alternate take)*
(S)　(4:20)　Time-Life CTD-08　Country USA - 1969.
(S)　(4:28)　RCA 66532　Heart And Soul.
(S)　(3:17)　RCA 67469　Platinum - A Life In Music.
　　　　　　　(alternate take)
(S)　(4:28)　DCC Compact Classics 1117　24 Karat Hits.
　　　　　　　(gold disc)
(S)　(4:28)　RCA 67565　Elvis' Greatest Jukebox Hits.
(S)　(4:29)　RCA 67466　Elvis' Gold Records Volume 5.
(S)　(4:28)　Time-Life R13610　Gold And Platinum Box Set -
　　　　　　　The Ultimate Rock Collection.
(S)　(4:27)　Simitar 55532　The Number One's: The '60s.
(S)　(4:28)　RCA 67595　Love Songs.
(S)　(4:28)　Time-Life R806-01　The Elvis Presley Collection -
　　　　　　　Love Songs.
(S)　(4:20)　Time-Life R808-02　Classic Country 1965-1969.

1970　DON'T CRY DADDY
(S)　(2:48)　RCA 6383 and 56383　The Top Ten Hits.
(E)　(2:45)　RCA 6401 and 56401　50 Worldwide Gold Award
　　　　　　　Hits.
(S)　(2:48)　RCA 6221　The Memphis Record.
(E)　(2:46)　RCA 5430　Always On My Mind.
(S)　(2:46)　RCA 66160　From Nashville To Memphis: The
　　　　　　　Essential 60's Masters I.

1970　RUBBERNECKIN'
(S)　(2:08)　RCA 66559　Live A Little, Love A Little/
　　　　　　　Charro/The Trouble With Girls/Change Of Habit.
(S)　(2:09)　RCA 66160　From Nashville To Memphis: The
　　　　　　　Essential 60's Masters I.
(S)　(2:07)　RCA 6221　The Memphis Record.
(S)　(2:12)　Pair 1010　Elvis! Double Dynamite.

1970　KENTUCKY RAIN
(S)　(3:12)　RCA 6401 and 56401　50 Worldwide Gold Award
　　　　　　　Hits.
(S)　(3:15)　RCA 6221　The Memphis Record.
(S)　(3:23)　RCA 4941　Gold Records Volume 5.
(E)　(3:22)　RCA 53732　Pure Gold.
(S)　(3:14)　RCA 66160　From Nashville To Memphis: The
　　　　　　　Essential 60's Masters I.
(S)　(3:10)　RCA 66160　From Nashville To Memphis: The
　　　　　　　Essential 60's Masters I. *(alternate take)*
(S)　(3:13)　RCA 66880　Great Country Songs.
(S)　(3:13)　RCA 67466　Elvis' Gold Records Volume 5.
(S)　(3:13)　RCA 67595　Love Songs.
(S)　(3:13)　Time-Life R806-04　The Elvis Presley Collection -
　　　　　　　Country.

1970　THE WONDER OF YOU
(S)　(2:36)　RCA 6383 and 56383　The Top Ten Hits.
(S)　(2:38)　RCA 54362　Elvis On Stage.
(S)　(2:35)　RCA 66670　Walk A Mile In My Shoes - The
　　　　　　　Essential 70's Masters.
(S)　(2:34)　RCA 66921　The Other Sides - Worldwide Gold
　　　　　　　Award Hits Volume 2.
(S)　(2:36)　RCA 67469　Platinum - A Life In Music.
(S)　(2:34)　RCA 67595　Love Songs.
(S)　(2:34)　Time-Life R806-01　The Elvis Presley Collection -
　　　　　　　Love Songs.

1970 MAMA LIKED THE ROSES
- (S) (2:46) RCA 66160 From Nashville To Memphis: The Essential 60's Masters I. *(:15 longer than the 45 or LP)*
- (S) (2:31) RCA 6221 The Memphis Record.
- (S) (2:46) RCA 67458 O.S.T. Blue Suede Shoes. *(most songs on this cd are segued together; this cd is a disaster)*

1970 I'VE LOST YOU
- (S) (3:39) RCA 5430 Always On My Mind. *(live LP version)*
- (S) (3:40) MFSL 560 That's The Way It Is. *(live LP version; gold disc)*
- (S) (3:40) RCA 54114 That's The Way It Is. *(live LP version)*
- (S) (3:54) RCA 66532 Heart And Soul. *(:33 longer than the 45)*
- (S) (3:29) RCA 66670 Walk A Mile In My Shoes - The Essential 70's Masters. *(45 version)*
- (S) (4:22) RCA 66866 A Hundred Years From Now. *(alternate take)*
- (S) (3:29) RCA 66921 The Other Sides - Worldwide Gold Award Hits Volume 2. *(45 version)*

1970 THE NEXT STEP IS LOVE
- (S) (3:31) MFSL 560 That's The Way It Is. *(gold disc)*
- (S) (3:31) RCA 54114 That's The Way It Is.
- (S) (3:31) RCA 66670 Walk A Mile In My Shoes - The Essential 70's Masters.
- (S) (3:30) RCA 66921 The Other Sides - Worldwide Gold Award Hits Volume 2.

1970 YOU DON'T HAVE TO SAY YOU LOVE ME
- (S) (2:29) MFSL 560 That's The Way It Is. *(gold disc)*
- (S) (2:29) RCA 54114 That's The Way It Is.
- (S) (2:29) RCA 66532 Heart And Soul.
- (S) (2:29) RCA 66670 Walk A Mile In My Shoes - The Essential 70's Masters.
- (S) (2:29) RCA 66866 A Hundred Years From Now. *(alternate take)*
- (S) (2:29) RCA 66921 The Other Sides - Worldwide Gold Award Hits Volume 2.
- (S) (2:29) RCA 67469 Platinum - A Life In Music.
- (S) (2:29) RCA 67466 Elvis' Gold Records Volume 5.

1970 PATCH IT UP
- (S) (4:00) MFSL 560 That's The Way It Is. *(gold disc; "That's The Way It Is" vinyl LP version which was not the hit version)*
- (S) (4:00) RCA 54114 That's The Way It Is. *("That's The Way It Is" vinyl LP version which was not the hit version)*
- (S) (3:08) RCA 66670 Walk A Mile In My Shoes - The Essential 70's Masters. *(45 version)*
- (S) (3:19) RCA 66866 A Hundred Years From Now. *(alternate take)*
- (S) (3:08) RCA 66921 The Other Sides - Worldwide Gold Award Hits Volume 2. *(45 version)*
- (S) (3:08) Time-Life R806-06 The Elvis Presley Collection - The Rocker. *(45 version)*

1971 I REALLY DON'T WANT TO KNOW
- (S) (2:44) RCA 52274 Welcome To My World. *(45 version but missing the final drum beat)*
- (S) (2:50) RCA 66279 I'm 10,000 Years Old/Elvis Country. *(LP version; tracks into next selection)*
- (S) (2:43) RCA 66670 Walk A Mile In My Shoes - The Essential 70's Masters. *(45 version but missing the final drum beat)*
- (S) (2:43) RCA 66880 Great Country Songs. *(45 version but missing the final drum beat)*
- (S) (2:43) RCA 66921 The Other Sides - Worldwide Gold Award Hits Volume 2. *(45 version but missing the final drum beat)*
- (S) (2:43) Time-Life R806-04 The Elvis Presley Collection - Country. *(45 version but missing the final drum beat)*

1971 THERE GOES MY EVERYTHING
- (S) (3:10) RCA 66279 I'm 10,000 Years Old/Elvis Country. *(LP version which tracks into next selection)*
- (S) (2:57) RCA 66670 Walk A Mile In My Shoes - The Essential 70's Masters. *(45 version)*
- (S) (2:45) RCA 66880 Great Country Songs. *(alternate take)*
- (S) (2:57) RCA 66921 The Other Sides - Worldwide Gold Award Hits Volume 2. *(45 version)*

- (S) (2:57) Time-Life R806-04 The Elvis Presley Collection - Country. *(45 version)*

1971 WHERE DID THEY GO, LORD
- (S) (2:26) RCA 66670 Walk A Mile In My Shoes - The Essential 70's Masters.
- (S) (2:19) RCA 66866 A Hundred Years From Now. *(alternate take)*

1971 RAGS TO RICHES
- (S) (1:53) RCA 66670 Walk A Mile In My Shoes - The Essential 70's Masters.
- (S) (1:50) RCA 66866 A Hundred Years From Now. *(alternate take)*

1971 I'M LEAVIN'
- (S) (3:50) RCA 66670 Walk A Mile In My Shoes - The Essential 70's Masters.
- (S) (3:50) RCA 67595 Love Songs.

1972 UNTIL IT'S TIME FOR YOU TO GO
- (S) (3:56) RCA 54671 Elvis Now.
- (S) (3:57) RCA 66670 Walk A Mile In My Shoes - The Essential 70's Masters.
- (S) (3:31) RCA 66866 A Hundred Years From Now. *(alternate take)*
- (S) (3:58) Time-Life R806-01 The Elvis Presley Collection - Love Songs.

1972 BURNING LOVE
- (S) (2:53) RCA 8476 and 9684 Nipper's Greatest Hits Of The 70's.
- (S) (2:51) RCA 8533 O.S.T. Heartbreak Hotel.
- (S) (2:52) RCA 6383 and 56383 The Top Ten Hits.
- (S) (2:55) RCA 6985 The Alternate Aloha. *(all selections on this cd are live)*
- (S) (2:53) RCA 4941 Gold Records Volume 5.
- (S) (2:50) Pair 1010 Double Dynamite.
- (S) (2:51) Special Music 2595 Burning Love - Hits From His Movies Volume 2.
- (S) (2:49) RCA 66670 Walk A Mile In My Shoes - The Essential 70's Masters.
- (S) (3:03) RCA 67469 Platinum - A Life In Music. *(alternate take)*
- (S) (2:48) RCA 67565 Elvis' Greatest Jukebox Hits.
- (S) (2:49) RCA 67466 Elvis' Gold Records Volume 5.
- (S) (2:49) Time-Life R806-02 The Elvis Presley Collection - Rock 'N' Roll.
- (M) (3:00) Time-Life R806-06 The Elvis Presley Collection - The Rocker. *(alternate take)*

1973 SEPARATE WAYS
- (S) (2:33) RCA 5430 Always On My Mind.
- (S) (2:35) Pair 1010 Double Dynamite.
- (S) (2:35) RCA 66670 Walk A Mile In My Shoes - The Essential 70's Masters.
- (S) (2:36) RCA 67469 Platinum - A Life In Music. *(alternate take)*
- (S) (2:35) RCA 67595 Love Songs.

1973 STEAMROLLER BLUES
- (S) (3:15) RCA 6985 The Alternate Aloha. *(all selections on this cd are live; alternate take)*
- (S) (3:03) RCA 66670 Walk A Mile In My Shoes - The Essential 70's Masters. *(missing :03 of the introduction found on the 45)*
- (S) (3:00) RCA 52642 Aloha From Hawaii Via Satellite. *(:03 of the introduction found on the 45 is missing but can be found at the end of the preceding track)*
- (S) (2:50) RCA 67469 Platinum - A Life In Music. *(live)*
- (S) (3:09) RCA 67609 Aloha From Hawaii Via Satellite. *(remastered edition)*

1973 FOOL
- (S) (2:40) RCA 50283 Elvis.
- (S) (2:41) RCA 66670 Walk A Mile In My Shoes - The Essential 70's Masters.
- (S) (2:30) RCA 66866 A Hundred Years From Now. *(alternate take)*

1973 RAISED ON ROCK
- (S) (2:39) RCA 50388 Raised On Rock.
- (S) (2:38) RCA 66670 Walk A Mile In My Shoes - The Essential 70's Masters.

1974 I'VE GOT A THING ABOUT YOU BABY
- (S) (2:20) RCA 50475 Good Times.
- (S) (2:19) RCA 66670 Walk A Mile In My Shoes - The Essential 70's Masters.
- (S) (2:19) RCA 67469 Platinum - A Life In Music.
- (S) (2:19) Time-Life R806-04 The Elvis Presley Collection - Country.

1974 TAKE GOOD CARE OF HER
- (S) (2:51) RCA 50475 Good Times.
- (S) (2:50) RCA 66670 Walk A Mile In My Shoes - The Essential 70's Masters.
- (S) (2:52) RCA 67469 Platinum - A Life In Music. *(alternate take)*
- (S) (2:50) Time-Life R806-04 The Elvis Presley Collection - Country.

1974 IF YOU TALK IN YOUR SLEEP
- (S) (2:28) RCA 4941 Gold Records Volume 5.
- (S) (2:25) RCA 0873 Promised Land.
- (S) (2:33) RCA 66670 Walk A Mile In My Shoes - The Essential 70's Masters.
- (S) (2:33) RCA 67466 Elvis' Gold Records Volume 5.

1975 PROMISED LAND
- (S) (2:51) RCA 0873 Promised Land.
- (S) (2:54) RCA 66670 Walk A Mile In My Shoes - The Essential 70's Masters.
- (S) (3:21) RCA 67469 Platinum - A Life In Music. *(alternate take)*
- (S) (2:55) Time-Life R806-02 The Elvis Presley Collection - Rock 'N' Roll.

1975 MY BOY
- (S) (3:10) RCA 5430 Always On My Mind.
- (S) (3:18) RCA 66670 Walk A Mile In My Shoes - The Essential 70's Masters.
- (S) (3:18) RCA 50475 Good Times.

1975 T-R-O-U-B-L-E
- (S) (3:02) Pair 1185 Forever.
- (S) (3:02) RCA 51039 Today.
- (S) (3:01) RCA 66670 Walk A Mile In My Shoes - The Essential 70's Masters.
- (S) (3:01) RCA 67469 Platinum - A Life In Music.
- (S) (3:01) Time-Life R806-02 The Elvis Presley Collection - Rock 'N' Roll.

1976 HURT
- (S) (2:06) RCA 5430 Always On My Mind.
- (S) (2:07) RCA 1506 From Elvis Presley Boulevard, Memphis, Tennessee.
- (S) (2:06) RCA 66670 Walk A Mile In My Shoes - The Essential 70's Masters.
- (S) (2:08) RCA 67469 Platinum - A Life In Music. *(alternate take)*

1976 FOR THE HEART
- (S) (3:20) RCA 1506 From Elvis Presley Boulevard, Memphis, Tennessee.
- (S) (3:21) RCA 66670 Walk A Mile In My Shoes - The Essential 70's Masters.
- (S) (3:28) RCA 4941 Gold Records Volume 5.
- (S) (3:46) RCA 67469 Platinum - A Life In Music. *(alternate take)*
- (S) (3:21) RCA 67466 Elvis' Gold Records Volume 5.

1977 MOODY BLUE
- (S) (2:55) RCA 4941 Gold Records Volume 5.
- (S) (2:49) RCA 2428 Moody Blue.
- (S) (2:52) Time-Life CCD-02 Contemporary Country - The Late 70's.
- (S) (2:49) RCA 66670 Walk A Mile In My Shoes - The Essential 70's Masters.
- (S) (2:48) RCA 67469 Platinum - A Life In Music.
- (S) (2:49) RCA 67466 Elvis' Gold Records Volume 5.
- (S) (2:49) Time-Life R806-04 The Elvis Presley Collection - Country.

1977 SHE THINKS I STILL CARE
- (S) (3:47) RCA 2428 Moody Blue.
- (S) (3:49) RCA 66670 Walk A Mile In My Shoes - The Essential 70's Masters.
- (S) (3:25) RCA 66670 Walk A Mile In My Shoes - The Essential 70's Masters. *(alternate take)*

- (S) (3:49) Time-Life R806-04 The Elvis Presley Collection - Country.

1977 WAY DOWN
- (S) (2:36) RCA 4941 Gold Records Volume 5.
- (S) (2:37) RCA 2428 Moody Blue.
- (S) (2:37) Time-Life CCD-14 Contemporary Country - The Late 70's Hot Hits.
- (S) (2:36) RCA 66670 Walk A Mile In My Shoes - The Essential 70's Masters.
- (S) (3:04) RCA 67469 Platinum - A Life In Music. *(alternate take)*
- (S) (2:36) RCA 67565 Elvis' Greatest Jukebox Hits.
- (S) (2:36) RCA 67466 Elvis' Gold Records Volume 5.
- (S) (2:37) Time-Life R806-06 The Elvis Presley Collection - The Rocker.

1977 MY WAY (live)
- (S) (4:08) RCA 52587 Elvis In Concert. *(LP version)*
- (S) (3:58) RCA 52642 Aloha From Hawaii Via Satellite. *(live version but not the "hit" live version)*
- (S) (3:54) RCA 6985 The Alternate Aloha. *(live version but not the "hit" live version)*
- (S) (4:31) RCA 66670 Walk A Mile In My Shoes - The Essential 70's Masters. *(studio version)*
- (S) (3:48) RCA 67469 Platinum - A Life In Music. *(live version but not the "hit" live version)*

1981 GUITAR MAN
(this song charted in different versions for Elvis in 1968 and 1981; see 1968 listings also)
- (M) (2:13) RCA 9970 Nipper's Greatest Hits - The 80's. *(this is mistakenly the 1968 version included on this 80's compilation)*
- (S) (2:49) RCA 7004 14 Country Hits.
- (S) (2:46) Time-Life CCD-15 Contemporary Country - The Early 80's Hot Hits.
- (S) (2:49) RCA 66880 Great Country Songs.
- (S) (2:25) RCA 67469 Platinum - A Life In Music. *(alternate take)*
- (S) (2:25) RCA 67592 A Touch Of Platinum - A Life In Music. *(alternate take)*

BILLY PRESTON
1972 OUTA-SPACE
- (S) (4:08) A&M 3205 Best Of.
- (S) (4:08) Rhino 71603 Rock Instrumental Classics Volume 3: The Seventies.
- (S) (4:08) Rhino 72035 Rock Instrumental Classics Vols. 1-5 Box Set.
- (S) (4:07) Rebound 314520034 Funk Classics Of The 70's.
- (S) (4:08) Rhino 72114 Billboard Hot Soul Hits - 1972.
- (S) (4:08) Time-Life R840-04 Sounds Of The Seventies: A Loss For Words.
- (S) (4:08) Rebound 314520447 Soul Classics - Best Of The 70's.
- (S) (4:08) Hip-O 40013 Synth Me Up - 14 Classic Electronic Hits.

1973 WILL IT GO ROUND IN CIRCLES
- (S) (3:43) Rhino 70634 Billboard's Top Rock & Roll Hits Of 1973.
- (S) (3:47) Rhino 70551 Soul Hits Of The 70's Volume 11.
- (S) (3:43) A&M 3205 Best Of.
- (S) (3:41) Razor & Tie 22045 Those Funky 70's.
- (S) (3:42) Time-Life SOD-14 Sounds Of The Seventies - 1973: Take Two.
- (S) (3:46) Time-Life R840-03 Sounds Of The Seventies - Pop Nuggets: Early '70s.
- (S) (3:43) Rebound 314520440 No. 1 Hits Of The 70's.

1973 SPACE RACE
- (S) (3:26) A&M 3205 Best Of.
- (S) (3:27) Rhino 72115 Billboard Hot Soul Hits - 1973.

1974 NOTHING FROM NOTHING
- (S) (2:34) Rhino 70635 Billboard's Top Rock & Roll Hits Of 1974.
- (S) (2:35) Rhino 70553 Soul Hits Of The 70's Volume 13.
- (S) (2:36) A&M 3205 Best Of.
- (S) (2:36) Time-Life SOD-15 Sounds Of The Seventies - 1974: Take Two.
- (S) (2:35) Rebound 314520247 Class Reunion 1974.

BILLY PRESTON (Continued)
1975 STRUTTIN'
    (S)   (2:33)   A&M 3205 Best Of.

released as by BILLY PRESTON & SYREETA:
1980 WITH YOU I'M BORN AGAIN
    (S)   (3:37)   Motown 6177 Endless Love: 15 Of Motown's Greatest Love Songs.
    (S)   (3:37)   Motown 6184 20 Hard To Find Motown Classics Volume 2.
    (S)   (3:38)   Motown 9082 and 5385 Great Motown Love Songs.
    (S)   (3:38)   Motown 6358 Hitsville USA Volume Two.
    (S)   (3:38)   Motown 314530516 Motown Year By Year 1980.
    (S)   (3:38)   Rhino 71891 Radio Daze: Pop Hits Of The 80's Volume Two.
    (S)   (3:38)   Ichiban 2513 Soulful Love - Duets Vol. 2.
    (S)   (3:38)   Time-Life R834-04 Body Talk - Together Forever.
    (S)   (3:38)   JCI 3175 1975 - Only Soul - 1979.

JOHNNY PRESTON
1960 RUNNING BEAR
    (M)   (2:36)   Rhino 70621 Billboard's Top Rock & Roll Hits Of 1960.
    (M)   (2:36)   Rhino 72004 Billboard's Top Rock & Roll Hits 1957-1961 Box Set.
    (M)   (2:35)   Mercury 832041 45's On CD Volume 1.
    (M)   (2:36)   Mercury 826448 Oldies Golden Million Sellers.
    (E)   (2:35)   Time-Life 2RNR-22 Rock 'N' Roll Era - 1960 Still Rockin'.
    (M)   (2:35)   Polygram Special Markets 314520258 No. 1 Hits Of The 50's.
    (M)   (2:34)   DCC Compact Classics 078 Best Of Tragedy.
    (M)   (2:34)   Mercury 314526691 Fifty Years Of Country Music From Mercury.
    (M)   (2:36)   Collectables 5558 Running Bear.
    (M)   (2:34)   Polygram Special Markets 314520478 50's Jukebox Hits.
1960 CRADLE OF LOVE
    (M)   (2:17)   Time-Life 2RNR-35 Rock 'N' Roll Era - The 60's Last Dance.
    (M)   (2:18)   Collectables 5558 Running Bear.
    (M)   (2:19)   Eric 11502 Hard To Find 45's On CD (Volume I) 1955-60.
1960 FEEL SO FINE
    (M)   (2:05)   Time-Life 2RNR-25 Rock 'N' Roll Era - The 60's Keep On Rockin'.
    (M)   (2:07)   Collectables 5558 Running Bear.

PRETENDERS
1980 BRASS IN POCKET (I'M SPECIAL)
    (S)   (3:02)   Sire 6083 Pretenders.
    (S)   (3:03)   Sire 25664 The Singles.
    (S)   (3:00)   Time-Life R102-34 The Rolling Stone Collection.
    (S)   (3:02)   Time-Life R988-07 Sounds Of The Eighties: 1980.
    (S)   (3:03)   Time-Life R968-13 Guitar Rock - The Early '80s.
    (S)   (3:03)   Rhino 72856 Just Can't Get Enough: New Wave Women.
1983 BACK ON THE CHAIN GANG
    (S)   (3:49)   Rhino 71834 Classic MTV: Class Of 1983.
    (S)   (3:50)   Sire 23980 Learning To Crawl.
    (S)   (3:49)   Sire 25664 The Singles.
    (S)   (3:49)   Time-Life R988-26 Sounds Of The Eighties: The Rolling Stone Collection 1982-1983.
    (S)   (3:50)   JCI 3149 1980 - Only Dance - 1984.
    (S)   (3:50)   Rhino 72596 Billboard Top Album Rock Hits, 1983.
    (S)   (3:49)   Time-Life R13610 Gold And Platinum Box Set - The Ultimate Rock Collection.
1984 MIDDLE OF THE ROAD
    (S)   (4:12)   Geffen 24236 Greenpeace - Rainbow Warriors.
    (S)   (4:11)   Time-Life R105-24 Guitar Rock Monsters.
    (S)   (4:13)   Sire 23980 Learning To Crawl.
    (S)   (4:12)   Sire 25664 The Singles.
    (S)   (4:12)   Time-Life R988-01 Sounds Of The Eighties: The Rockin' Eighties.
    (S)   (4:12)   Time-Life R968-20 Guitar Rock - The '80s.
    (S)   (4:14)   Rhino 72597 Billboard Top Album Rock Hits, 1984.

1984 SHOW ME
    (S)   (4:06)   Sire 23980 Learning To Crawl.
    (S)   (4:06)   Sire 25664 The Singles.
1986 DON'T GET ME WRONG
    (S)   (3:47)   Epic 53439 O.S.T. Peter's Friends.
    (S)   (3:47)   Sire 25664 The Singles.
    (S)   (3:45)   Sire 25488 Get Close.
    (S)   (3:47)   Time-Life R988-04 Sounds Of The Eighties: 1986.
    (S)   (3:45)   Rhino 72500 Modern Rock 1986 - Hang The DJ.
    (S)   (3:46)   JCI 3150 1985 - Only Dance - 1989.
1994 I'LL STAND BY YOU
    (S)   (3:58)   Sire/Warner Brothers 45572 Last Of The Independents.
    (S)   (3:57)   Polygram TV 314555610 The One And Only Love Album.

PRETTY POISON
1987 (CATCH ME) I'M FALLING
    (S)   (4:24)   Virgin 90661 O.S.T. Hiding Out. *(45 version)*
    (S)   (4:54)   Virgin 90885 Catch Me I'm Falling. *(LP version)*
    (S)   (4:53)   Right Stuff 52288 Free To Be Volume 4. *(LP version)*
    (S)   (4:53)   Svengali 9610 Greatest Hits Vol. 1. *(LP version)*
    (S)   (4:26)   Cold Front 6247 Classic Club Mix - Dance Jams. *(all selections on this cd are segued together; 45 version)*
    (S)   (4:25)   Rhino 72838 Disco Queens: The 80's. *(45 version)*
    (S)   (4:03)   Cold Front 6330 Club Mix: The 80s. *(all selections on this cd are segued together)*
1988 NIGHTIME
    (S)   (4:16)   Virgin 90885 Catch Me I'm Falling.
    (S)   (5:22)   Svengali 9610 Greatest Hits Vol. 1. *(remix)*

LLOYD PRICE
1957 JUST BECAUSE
    (M)   (2:45)   Rhino 75766 Best Of New Orleans Rhythm & Blues Volume 2.
    (E)   (2:45)   Original Sound 8864 Oldies But Goodies Vol. 14. *(this compact disc uses the "Waring - fds" noise reduction process)*
    (E)   (2:45)   Original Sound 2222 Oldies But Goodies Volumes 3,5,11,14 and 15 Box Set. *(this box set uses the "Waring - fds" noise reduction process)*
    (E)   (2:45)   Original Sound 2500 Oldies But Goodies Volumes 1-15 Box Set. *(this box set uses the "Waring - fds" noise reduction process)*
    (M)   (2:44)   Sire 26617 Music From The Film A Rage In Harlem.
    (S)   (2:43)   Capitol 91184 O.S.T. Everybody's All-American. *(rerecording)*
    (S)   (2:42)   Time-Life 2RNR-17 Rock 'N' Roll Era - 1957 Still Rockin'. *(rerecording)*
    (M)   (2:45)   Time-Life RHD-08 Rhythm & Blues - 1957.
    (E)   (2:43)   Curb 77654 Sings His Big Ten.
    (M)   (2:45)   MCA 11184 Greatest Hits.
    (M)   (2:45)   Time-Life R857-13 The Heart Of Rock 'n' Roll 1956-1957.
    (M)   (2:45)   Time-Life R838-23 Solid Gold Soul 1957.
1959 STAGGER LEE
    (S)   (2:20)   Rhino 70620 Billboard's Top Rock & Roll Hits Of 1959.
    (S)   (2:20)   Rhino 72004 Billboard's Top Rock & Roll Hits 1957-1961 Box Set.
    (S)   (2:20)   MCA 31199 Vintage Music Volume 2.
    (S)   (2:20)   MCA 5777 Vintage Music Volumes 1 & 2.
    (S)   (2:20)   Original Sound 8850 Oldies But Goodies Vol. 1. *(this compact disc uses the "Waring - fds" noise reduction process)*
    (S)   (2:20)   Original Sound 2221 Oldies But Goodies Volumes 1,4,6,8 and 10 Box Set. *(this box set uses the "Waring - fds" noise reduction process)*
    (S)   (2:20)   Original Sound 2500 Oldies But Goodies Volumes 1-15 Box Set. *(this box set uses the "Waring - fds" noise reduction process)*
    (S)   (2:20)   Garland 011 Footstompin' Oldies
    (S)   (2:17)   JCI 3204 Heart & Soul Fifties.
    (S)   (2:20)   Curb 77525 Greatest Hits Of Rock 'N' Roll Volume 2.
    (S)   (2:20)   Curb 77305 Greatest Hits.

(S) (2:20) Pair 1257 Greatest Hits.
(S) (2:20) Ripete 2392192 Beach Music Anthology Box Set.
(S) (2:19) Collectables 5065 History Of Rock Volume 5.
(S) (2:20) Time-Life 2RNR-13 Rock 'N' Roll Era - 1959.
(S) (2:20) Time-Life RHD-03 Rhythm & Blues - 1959.
(S) (2:20) Curb 77654 Sings His Big Ten.
(S) (2:21) MCA 11184 Greatest Hits.
(M) (2:09) MCA 11184 Greatest Hits. *(rerecording with sanitized lyrics)*
(M) (2:20) MCA Special Products 22165 Vintage Collectibles Volume 7.
(S) (2:19) K-Tel 3885 Story Songs.
(S) (2:20) Time-Life R838-21 Solid Gold Soul 1959.

1959 WHERE WERE YOU (ON OUR WEDDING DAY)?
(E) (2:36) Curb 77654 Sings His Big Ten.
(S) (2:39) MCA 11184 Greatest Hits.

1959 PERSONALITY
(S) (2:33) Rhino 70645 Billboard's Top R&B Hits Of 1959.
(S) (2:33) Garland 012 Remember When.
(S) (2:33) MCA 31201 Vintage Music Volume 4.
(S) (2:33) MCA 5778 Vintage Music Volumes 3 & 4.
(S) (2:33) Curb 77305 Greatest Hits.
(S) (2:33) Pair 1257 Greatest Hits.
(S) (2:33) Collectables 5067 History Of Rock Volume 7.
(S) (2:33) Time-Life 2RNR-13 Rock 'N' Roll Era - 1959.
(S) (2:33) Curb 77654 Sings His Big Ten.
(S) (2:35) MCA 11184 Greatest Hits.
(S) (2:33) MCA Special Products 22166 Vintage Collectibles Volume 8.

1959 I'M GONNA GET MARRIED
(E) (2:18) MCA 5938 Vintage Music Volumes 15 & 16.
(E) (2:18) MCA 31212 Vintage Music Volume 15.
(S) (2:18) Rhino 70589 Rockin' & Rollin' Wedding Songs Volume 2.
(E) (2:18) Curb 77305 Greatest Hits.
(M) (2:18) Time-Life 2RNR-20 Rock 'N' Roll Era - 1959 Still Rockin'.
(E) (2:18) Curb 77654 Sings His Big Ten.
(S) (2:19) MCA 11184 Greatest Hits.

1959 COME INTO MY HEART
(M) (2:04) MCA 11184 Greatest Hits.

1960 LADY LUCK
(E) (2:14) Curb 77654 Sings His Big Ten.
(E) (2:12) MCA Special Products 20783 Rock Around The Oldies .
(M) (2:14) MCA 11184 Greatest Hits.

1960 NO IF'S - NO AND'S
(M) (2:19) MCA 11184 Greatest Hits.

1960 QUESTION
(S) (2:29) MCA 11184 Greatest Hits.

1963 MISTY
(S) (2:53) Ripete 2199 Walkin' To New Orleans.

RAY PRICE
1971 FOR THE GOOD TIMES
(S) (3:47) Rhino 70924 Super Hits Of The 70's Volume 4.
(S) (3:47) Rhino 72009 Super Hits Of The 70's Volumes 1-4 Box Set.
(M) (3:46) Columbia 46032 Columbia Country Classics Volume 4.
(S) (3:47) Columbia 45068 American Originals.
(S) (3:47) Sony Music Special Products 48621 Kris Kristofferson: Singer/Songwriter.
(S) (3:46) Pair 1044 Happens To Be The Best.
(S) (3:47) Time-Life CTD-04 Country USA - 1970.
(S) (3:46) Time-Life CCD-06 Contemporary Country - The Early 70's.
(S) (3:46) K-Tel 567 Country Music Classics Volume IV.
(S) (3:46) JCI 3155 1970 - Only Country - 1974.
(S) (3:47) Priority 50967 I Love Country Volume Two: Hits Of The 70's.
(S) (3:47) Epic 67942 Super Hits Of The '70s.
(S) (3:45) K-Tel 3357 101 Greatest Country Hits Vol. Three: Easy Country.
(S) (3:47) Time-Life R990-17 Ray Price - Legendary Country Singers.

(S) (3:47) Columbia 68198 Super Hits.
(S) (3:47) Time-Life R808-04 Classic Country 1970-1974.

CHARLEY PRIDE
1972 KISS AN ANGEL GOOD MORNIN'
(S) (2:02) Priority 8671 Country's Greatest Hits: Superstars.
(S) (2:02) Time-Life CTD-05 Country USA - 1971.
(S) (2:01) Time-Life CCD-06 Contemporary Country - The Early 70's.
(S) (2:01) K-Tel 3111 Country Music Classics Vol. XIX.
(S) (2:00) RCA 58448 Best Of Volume II.
(S) (2:00) K-Tel 3356 101 Greatest Country Hits Vol. Two: Country Sunshine.
(S) (2:00) Time-Life R990-14 Charley Pride - Legendary Country Singers.
(S) (2:00) RCA 67428 Essential.
(S) (2:00) Hip-O 40085 The Class Of Country 1970-1974.
(S) (2:00) Time-Life R808-04 Classic Country 1970-1974.

MAXI PRIEST
1988 WILD WORLD
(S) (3:32) Virgin 86075 Maxi Priest.
(S) (3:35) Charisma 91804 and 86259 Best Of Me.
(S) (3:31) Madacy Entertainment 26927 Sun Splashin'.

1990 CLOSE TO YOU
(S) (5:27) Sandstone 33047 and 5015 Cosmopolitan Volume 1. *(LP version)*
(S) (5:25) Charisma 91384 and 86176 Bonafide. *(LP version)*
(S) (5:28) Charisma 91804 and 86259 Best Of Me. *(LP version)*
(S) (4:00) Hip-O 40000 Thinking About You - A Collection Of Modern Love Songs. *(45 version)*
(S) (5:28) K-Tel 3848 90s Now Volume 2. *(LP version)*

released as by ROBERTA FLACK with MAXI PRIEST:
1991 SET THE NIGHT TO MUSIC
(S) (5:21) Atlantic 82498 Roberta Flack - Softly With These Songs: Best Of. *(LP version)*
(S) (5:20) Atlantic 82321 Roberta Flack - Set The Night To Music. *(LP version)*

released as by MAXI PRIEST featuring SHAGGY:
1996 THAT GIRL
(S) (3:57) Virgin 41612 Maxi Priest - Man With The Fun.
(S) (3:54) Cold Front 6254 Club Mix '98. *(all selections on this cd are segued together)*

LOUIS PRIMA & KEELY SMITH
1958 THAT OLD BLACK MAGIC
(M) (2:55) Rhino 70225 Best Of.
(M) (2:55) Capitol 94072 Capitol Collectors Series.
(M) (2:54) Capitol 98670 Memories Are Made Of This.
(M) (2:54) Time-Life HPD-11 Your Hit Parade 1958.
(M) (2:55) Rhino 72557 Jackpot! The Las Vegas Story.
(M) (2:54) Capitol 35972 Ultra Lounge Volume Five: Wild, Cool & Swingin'.
(M) (2:54) Hammer & Lace 697124113 Leading Men: Masters Of Style Volume One.
(M) (2:54) Rhino 72239 Cocktail Mix, Vol. 3: Swingin' Singles.

released as by LOUIS PRIMA:
1960 WONDERLAND BY NIGHT

PRINCE
1980 I WANNA BE YOUR LOVER
(S) (5:46) Warner Brothers 3366 Prince. *(LP version)*
(S) (2:56) Paisley Park 45440 The Hits/The B-Sides. *(45 version)*
(S) (2:56) Paisley Park 45435 The Hits 2. *(45 version)*
(S) (2:56) Rhino 71618 Soul Train Hall Of Fame/20th Anniversary. *(45 version)*

1983 LITTLE RED CORVETTE
(dj copies of this 45 ran (3:08) and (4:32); commercial copies were all (3:08))
(S) (5:00) Time-Life R102-34 The Rolling Stone Collection. *(LP version)*
(S) (5:03) Warner Brothers 23720 1999. *(LP version)*
(S) (4:55) Paisley Park 45435 The Hits 2. *(LP version)*
(S) (4:55) Paisley Park 45440 The Hits/The B-Sides. *(LP version)*

PRINCE (Continued)

1983 1999
- (S) (6:14) Warner Brothers 23720 1999. *(LP version)*
- (S) (3:36) Paisley Park 45431 The Hits 1. *(45 version)*
- (S) (3:36) Paisley Park 45440 The Hits/The B-Sides. *(45 version)*

1983 DELIRIOUS
(actual 45 time is (2:37) not (3:56) as stated on the record label)
- (S) (3:57) Warner Brothers 23720 1999. *(LP version)*
- (S) (2:37) Paisley Park 45435 The Hits 2. *(45 version)*
- (S) (2:37) Paisley Park 45440 The Hits/The B-Sides. *(45 version)*

1984 WHEN DOVES CRY
(dj copies of this 45 ran (3:59) and (5:52);
commercial copies were all (3:59))
- (S) (5:51) Time-Life R102-34 The Rolling Stone Collection. *(LP version)*
- (S) (5:51) Warner Brothers 25110 Music From Purple Rain. *(LP version)*
- (S) (3:47) Paisley Park 45431 The Hits 1. *(45 version)*

released as by PRINCE and THE REVOLUTION:
1984 LET'S GO CRAZY
- (S) (4:39) Warner Brothers 25110 Music From Purple Rain. *(LP version)*
- (S) (4:39) Paisley Park 45431 The Hits 1. *(LP version)*
- (S) (4:39) Paisley Park 45440 The Hits/The B-Sides. *(LP version)*

1984 PURPLE RAIN
- (S) (8:40) Warner Brothers 25110 Music From Purple Rain. *(LP version)*
- (S) (8:40) Paisley Park 45435 The Hits 2. *(LP version)*
- (S) (8:39) Paisley Park 45440 The Hits/The B-Sides. *(LP version)*

1985 I WOULD DIE 4 U
- (S) (2:49) Warner Brothers 25110 Music From Purple Rain. *(LP version)*
- (S) (2:56) Paisley Park 45435 The Hits 2. *(45 version)*
- (S) (2:56) Paisley Park 45440 The Hits/The B-Sides. *(45 version)*

1985 TAKE ME WITH U
- (S) (3:53) Warner Brothers 25110 Music From Purple Rain.

1985 RASPBERRY BERET
- (S) (3:32) Paisley Park 25286 Around The World In A Day.
- (S) (3:31) Paisley Park 45435 The Hits 2.
- (S) (3:31) Paisley Park 45440 The Hits/The B-Sides.

1985 POP LIFE
- (S) (3:43) Paisley Park 25286 Around The World In A Day.
- (S) (3:41) Paisley Park 45431 The Hits 1.
- (S) (3:41) Paisley Park 45440 The Hits/The B-Sides.

1986 KISS
- (S) (3:37) Paisley Park 25395 Parade. *(LP version)*
- (S) (3:45) Paisley Park 45435 The Hits 2. *(45 version)*
- (S) (3:45) Paisley Park 45440 The Hits/The B-Sides. *(45 version)*

1986 MOUNTAINS
- (S) (3:57) Paisley Park 25395 Parade.

released as by PRINCE:
1987 SIGN 'O' THE TIMES
- (S) (4:56) Paisley Park 25577 Sign 'O' The Times. *(LP version)*
- (S) (3:42) Paisley Park 45431 The Hits 1. *(45 version)*
- (S) (3:42) Paisley Park 45440 The Hits/The B-Sides. *(45 version)*

1987 U GOT THE LOOK
(actual 45 time is (3:45) not (3:58) as stated on the record label)
- (S) (3:46) Paisley Park 25577 Sign 'O' The Times.
- (S) (3:46) Paisley Park 45435 The Hits 2.
- (S) (3:46) Paisley Park 45440 The Hits/The B-Sides.

1988 I COULD NEVER TAKE THE PLACE OF YOUR MAN
- (S) (6:28) Paisley Park 25577 Sign 'O' The Times. *(LP version)*
- (S) (3:38) Paisley Park 45431 The Hits 1. *(45 version)*
- (S) (3:38) Paisley Park 45440 The Hits/The B-Sides. *(45 version)*

1988 ALPHABET ST.
- (S) (5:38) Paisley Park 25720 Lovesexy. *(LP version)*
- (S) (5:38) Paisley Park 45431 The Hits 1. *(LP version)*
- (S) (5:38) Paisley Park 45440 The Hits/The B-Sides. *(LP version)*

1989 BATDANCE
- (S) (6:13) Warner Brothers 25936 and 25978 O.S.T. Batman. *(LP version)*

1989 PARTYMAN
- (S) (3:11) Warner Brothers 25936 and 25978 O.S.T. Batman.

released as by PRINCE with SHEENA EASTON:
1989 THE ARMS OF ORION
- (S) (5:02) Warner Brothers 25936 and 25978 O.S.T. Batman.

released as by PRINCE:
1990 THIEVES IN THE TEMPLE
- (S) (3:19) Paisley Park 27493 Music From Graffiti Bridge.
- (S) (3:19) Paisley Park 45431 The Hits 1.
- (S) (3:19) Paisley Park 45440 The Hits/The B-Sides.

released as by PRINCE and THE N.P.G.:
1991 GETT OFF
- (S) (4:31) Paisley Park 25379 Diamonds And Pearls.
- (S) (4:29) Paisley Park 45435 The Hits 2.
- (S) (4:29) Paisley Park 45440 The Hits/The B-Sides.

1991 CREAM
- (S) (4:13) Paisley Park 25379 Diamonds And Pearls.
- (S) (4:12) Paisley Park 45435 The Hits 2.
- (S) (4:12) Paisley Park 45440 The Hits/The B-Sides.

1992 DIAMONDS AND PEARLS
- (S) (4:45) Paisley Park 25379 Diamonds And Pearls.
- (S) (4:19) Paisley Park 45431 The Hits 1.
- (S) (4:19) Paisley Park 45440 The Hits/The B-Sides.

1992 MONEY DON'T MATTER 2 NIGHT
- (S) (4:46) Paisley Park 25379 Diamonds And Pearls.

1992 MY NAME IS PRINCE
- (S) (6:38) Paisley Park 45037 Prince & The New Power Generation. *(uncensored version)*
- (S) (6:37) Paisley Park 45123 Prince & The New Power Generation. *(censored version)*

1993 7
- (S) (5:13) Paisley Park 45037 Prince & The New Power Generation.
- (S) (5:13) Paisley Park 45123 Prince & The New Power Generation.
- (S) (5:08) Paisley Park 45431 The Hits 1.
- (S) (5:08) Paisley Park 45440 The Hits/The B-Sides.

released as by PRINCE:
1994 THE MOST BEAUTIFUL GIRL IN THE WORLD
- (S) (4:36) NPG 71003 The Beautiful Experience.
- (S) (4:24) Warner Brothers/NPG 45999 The Gold Experience. *(tracks into the next selection)*

1994 LETITGO
- (S) (5:32) Warner Brothers 45700 1958-1993 Come. *(tracks into the next selection)*

1995 I HATE U
- (S) (5:53) Warner Brothers/NPG 45999 The Gold Experience. *(tracks into the next selection)*

PRISM
1982 DON'T LET HIM KNOW
- (S) (3:10) Renaissance 0113 Best Of.

P.J. PROBY
1967 NIKI HOEKY
- (S) (2:29) Ripete 2200 Ocean Drive Volume 3.
- (S) (2:29) EMI-Capitol Special Markets 19552 Lost Hits Of The '60s.

PROCLAIMERS
1993 I'M GONNA BE (500 MILES)
- (S) (3:34) Milan 35644 O.S.T. Benny & Joon.
- (S) (3:35) Chrysalis 21668 and 41668 Sunshine On Leith.
- (S) (3:33) EMI-Capitol Music Group 54555 Movie Luv.
- (S) (3:33) Scotti Bros. 75518 Big Screen Rock.

PROCOL HARUM
1967 A WHITER SHADE OF PALE
- (E) (4:03) Motown 6120 and 6062 O.S.T. The Big Chill.
- (E) (4:02) Original Sound 8894 Dick Clark's 21 All-Time Hits Vol. 3.
- (M) (3:57) Rhino 70326 History Of British Rock Volume 8.
- (M) (3:57) Rhino 72022 History Of British Rock Box Set.
- (E) (4:03) A&M 2515 Classics Volume 17.
- (M) (3:57) Rhino 71066 Summer Of Love Volume 2.
- (E) (4:02) JCI 3114 Easy Sixties.
- (E) (3:59) Time-Life 2CLR-05 Classic Rock - 1967.
- (M) (3:57) Rhino 71937 Billboard Top Pop Hits, 1967.
- (M) (3:57) A&M 314540523 Greatest Hits.
- (M) (4:03) Hollywood 62092 O.S.T. Breaking The Waves.

1967 HOMBURG
- (M) (3:55) A&M 2515 Classics Volume 17.
- (S) (3:46) Time-Life 2CLR-17 Classic Rock - Rock Renaissance.
- (M) (3:55) A&M 314540523 Greatest Hits.

1972 CONQUISTADOR
(actual LP time is (5:06) not (4:16) as stated on the record label; 45 length is (4:14))
- (S) (4:11) JCI 3402 Live Volume 2.
- (S) (4:09) Rhino 70326 History Of British Rock Volume 8.
- (S) (4:09) Rhino 72022 History Of British Rock Box Set.
- (S) (4:13) A&M 2515 Classics Volume 17.
- (S) (5:07) MFSL 788 Live. (includes :03 silent lead into selection)
- (S) (4:13) Razor & Tie 22502 Those Rocking 70's.
- (S) (4:13) A&M 314540523 Greatest Hits.

PRODIGY
1997 FIRESTARTER
- (S) (4:39) Maverick/Warner Brothers 46606 The Fat Of The Land.

JEANNE PRUETT
1973 SATIN SHEETS
- (S) (3:20) MCA 2-8025 30 Years Of Hits 1958-1974.
- (S) (3:20) MCA 6421 16 Top Country Hits Volume 1.
- (S) (3:15) Time-Life CCD-04 Contemporary Country - The Mid 70's.
- (S) (3:20) MCA Special Products 20846 Greatest Country Classics Volume One.
- (S) (3:13) JCI 3155 1970 - Only Country - 1974.
- (S) (2:41) K-Tel 3366 101 Greatest Country Hits Vol. Seven: Country Nights. (rerecording)
- (S) (3:20) Hip-O 40085 The Class Of Country 1970-1974.
- (S) (3:14) Time-Life R808-04 Classic Country 1970-1974.

PSEUDO ECHO
1987 FUNKY TOWN
- (S) (3:41) Priority 53767 Rock Of The 80's Volume 11. (45 version)
- (S) (4:52) RCA 9970 Nipper's Greatest Hits - The 80's. (LP version)
- (S) (4:50) RCA 2357 Dance, Dance, Dance Volume II. (LP version)
- (S) (4:52) RCA 5730 Love An Adventure. (LP version)
- (S) (3:41) Time-Life R988-19 Sounds Of The Eighties: The Late '80s. (45 version)

PSYCHEDELIC FURS
1987 HEARTBREAK BEAT
- (S) (5:09) Priority 53748 Rock Of The 80's Volume 8. (LP version)
- (S) (5:09) Columbia 40466 Midnight To Midnight. (LP version)
- (S) (5:09) Columbia 44377 All Of This And Nothing. (LP version)
- (S) (5:08) Rhino 72501 Modern Rock 1987 - Hang The DJ. (LP version)
- (S) (5:08) Risky Business 66396 Oldies But 80's: Best Of The 80's. (LP version)
- (S) (5:12) Columbia/Legacy 65152 Should God Forget: A Retrospective. (LP version)

PUBLIC ENEMY
1994 GIVE IT UP
- (S) (4:31) Def Jam/RAL 314523362 and 314523399 Muse Sick-N-Hour Mess Age. (tracks into next selection)
- (S) (4:41) Def Jam 314523848 Def Jam Music Group 10th Year Anniversary.

GARY PUCKETT and THE UNION GAP (also UNION GAP)
released as by THE UNION GAP featuring GARY PUCKETT:
1968 WOMAN, WOMAN
- (S) (3:33) Columbia/Legacy 46984 Rock Artifacts Volume 4. (:20 longer than either the LP or 45)
- (S) (3:14) Columbia 1042 Greatest Hits.
- (S) (3:33) Columbia/Legacy 48959 Looking Glass. (:20 longer than either the 45 or LP)
- (S) (3:09) Time-Life SUD-18 Superhits - Late 60's Classics.
- (S) (3:09) Time-Life AM1-12 AM Gold - Late '60s Classics.
- (S) (3:13) Collectables 5826 A Golden Classics Edition.

1968 YOUNG GIRL
(actual 45 time is (3:07) not (3:12) as stated on the record label; LP length is (3:12))
- (S) (3:03) Columbia 45019 Pop Classics Of The 60's.
- (S) (3:11) Columbia 1042 Greatest Hits.
- (S) (3:11) Columbia/Legacy 48959 Looking Glass.
- (S) (3:01) Time-Life 2CLR-19 Classic Rock - 1968: Shakin' All Over.
- (S) (3:03) Time-Life SUD-14 Superhits - The Late 60's.
- (S) (3:12) Rhino 71938 Billboard Top Pop Hits, 1968.
- (S) (3:12) Priority 50951 I Love Rock & Roll Volume 2: Hits Of The 60's.
- (S) (3:03) Time-Life AM1-14 AM Gold - The Late '60s.
- (S) (3:09) Collectables 5826 A Golden Classics Edition.
- (S) (3:03) Collectables 1515 and 2515 The Anniversary Album - The 60's.
- (S) (3:01) BMG Special Products 44762 The President's Greatest Hits.

released as by GARY PUCKETT and THE UNION GAP:
1968 LADY WILLPOWER
- (S) (2:36) Columbia 1042 Greatest Hits.
- (S) (2:45) Columbia/Legacy 48959 Looking Glass. (:07 longer than the 45 or LP)
- (S) (2:35) Collectables 5826 A Golden Classics Edition.

1968 OVER YOU
- (S) (2:21) Columbia 1042 Greatest Hits.
- (S) (2:23) Columbia/Legacy 48959 Looking Glass.
- (S) (2:19) Collectables 5826 A Golden Classics Edition.
- (M) (2:21) Varese Sarabande 5803 Sunshine Days - Pop Classics Of The '60s Volume 3.

1969 DON'T GIVE IN TO HIM
(actual 45 time is (2:21) not (2:25) as stated on the record label; LP length is (2:18))
- (S) (2:11) Columbia 1042 Greatest Hits.
- (S) (2:29) Columbia/Legacy 48959 Looking Glass.
- (S) (2:15) Collectables 5826 A Golden Classics Edition.

1969 THIS GIRL IS A WOMAN NOW
- (S) (3:06) Columbia 1042 Greatest Hits.
- (S) (3:07) Columbia/Legacy 48959 Looking Glass.
- (S) (3:07) Collectables 5826 A Golden Classics Edition.

1970 LET'S GIVE ADAM AND EVE ANOTHER CHANCE
- (S) (2:46) Columbia 1042 Greatest Hits.
- (S) (2:44) Columbia/Legacy 48959 Looking Glass.
- (S) (2:42) Collectables 5826 A Golden Classics Edition.

PUFF DADDY
released as by PUFF DADDY featuring MASE:
1997 CAN'T NOBODY HOLD ME DOWN
- (S) (3:50) Bad Boy 73012 and 73014 No Way Out.
- (S) (5:05) Polygram TV 314536204 The Source Presents Hip Hop Hits Volume 1.

released as by SWV featuring PUFF DADDY:
1997 SOMEONE
- (S) (4:06) RCA 67525 SWV - Release Some Tension.

released as by PUFF DADDY & FAITH EVANS featuring 112:
1997 I'LL BE MISSING YOU
- (S) (5:42) Bad Boy 73012 and 73014 No Way Out.

PUFF DADDY *(Continued)*
released as by THE NOTORIOUS B.I.G. featuring PUFF DADDY & MASE:
1997 MO MONEY MO PROBLEMS
- (S) (4:17) Bad Boy 73011 and 73019 Notorious B.I.G. - Life After Death.
- (S) (3:49) Arista 18988 Ultimate Dance Party 1998. *(all selections on this cd are segued together)*

released as by PUFF DADDY & THE FAMILY:
1998 IT'S ALL ABOUT THE BENJAMINS
- (S) (4:38) Bad Boy 73012 and 73014 No Way Out.

released as by PUFF DADDY & THE FAMILY featuring THE NOTORIOUS B.I.G. & MASE:
1998 BEEN AROUND THE WORLD
- (S) (5:25) Bad Boy 73012 and 73014 Puff Daddy - No Way Out.

PURE PRAIRIE LEAGUE
1975 AMIE
- (S) (4:05) Priority 8665 Southern Comfort/70's Greatest Rock Hits Volume 4. *(neither the 45 or LP version)*
- (S) (4:18) RCA 52163 Amie & Other Hits. *(LP version)*
- (S) (4:18) RCA 4656 Bustin' Out. *(LP version)*
- (S) (3:14) Time-Life SOD-35 Sounds Of The Seventies - AM Nuggets. *(neither the 45 or LP version)*
- (S) (4:19) K-Tel 6137 Peaceful Easy Feeling - The Best Of Country Rock. *(LP version)*
- (S) (4:19) Rhino 71904 Hillbilly Fever Vol. 5. - Legends Of Country Rock. *(LP version)*
- (S) (4:17) Mercury 314528236 Best Of. *(LP version)*
- (S) (2:37) Rhino 72297 Superhits Of The 70's Volume 23. *(45 version)*
- (S) (4:19) Rhino 72444 Heroes Of Country Music Vol. Five. *(LP version)*
- (S) (4:18) K-Tel 3639 Dim The Lights - Soft Rock Hits Of The 70's. *(LP version)*
- (S) (4:18) K-Tel 3697 Best Of Country Rock. *(LP version)*
- (S) (4:18) Rhino 72517 Mellow Rock Hits Of The 70's - Ventura Highway. *(LP version)*
- (S) (4:18) Time-Life R840-01 Sounds Of The Seventies - Pop Nuggets: Late '70s. *(LP version)*
- (S) (2:37) Varese Sarabande 5847 On The Radio Volume Two. *(45 version)*

1980 LET ME LOVE YOU TONIGHT
- (S) (2:43) Mercury 314514686 Firin' Up.
- (S) (2:43) Rebound 314520256 Best Of Southern Rock.
- (S) (2:42) Rebound 314520318 Class Reunion 1980.
- (S) (2:43) Rhino 71892 Radio Daze: Pop Hits Of The 80's Volume Three.
- (S) (2:42) Mercury 314528236 Best Of.
- (S) (2:42) Time-Life R834-07 Body Talk - Hearts In Motion.
- (S) (2:42) Critique 15467 Fast Cars And Southern Stars.
- (S) (2:42) Polygram Special Markets 314520457 #1 Radio Hits Of The 80's.

1980 I'M ALMOST READY
- (S) (3:38) Mercury 314514686 Firin' Up.
- (S) (3:39) Mercury 314528236 Best Of.
- (S) (3:39) Rebound 314520475 The Roots Of Rock: Southern Rock.

1981 STILL RIGHT HERE IN MY HEART
- (S) (2:56) Mercury 314514684 Something In The Night.
- (S) (2:56) Mercury 314528236 Best Of.
- (S) (2:56) Time-Life R834-13 Body Talk - Just The Two Of Us.

JAMES & BOBBY PURIFY
1966 I'M YOUR PUPPET
- (M) (2:59) Rhino 75774 Soul Shots.
- (M) (2:59) JCI 3102 Love Sixties.
- (M) (2:58) Original Sound 8862 Oldies But Goodies Vol. 12. *(this compact disc uses the "Waring - fds" noise reduction process)*
- (M) (2:58) Original Sound 2223 Oldies But Goodies Volumes 2,7,9,12 and 13 Box Set. *(this box set uses the "Waring - fds" noise reduction process)*
- (M) (2:58) Original Sound 2500 Oldies But Goodies Volumes 1-15 Box Set. *(this box set uses the "Waring - fds" noise reduction process)*
- (M) (2:58) Original Sound CDGO-12 Golden Oldies Volume. 12.
- (M) (2:58) Original Sound 8878 Art Laboe's Dedicated To You.
- (M) (2:58) Original Sound 4001 Art Laboe's 60 Killer Oldies.
- (M) (2:58) Time-Life RHD-01 Rhythm & Blues - 1966.
- (M) (2:58) Time-Life 2CLR-13 Classic Rock - 1966: Shakin' All Over.
- (M) (2:58) Rhino 71517 The Muscle Shoals Sound.
- (M) (2:58) Right Stuff 27306 Slow Jams: The 60's Volume One.
- (M) (2:58) Thump 7020 Low Rider Oldies Volume II.
- (M) (2:58) Hip-O 40001 The Glory Of Love - Sweet & Soulful Love Songs.
- (M) (2:58) JCI 3185 1965 - Only Love - 1969.
- (M) (2:58) EastWest 61748 O.S.T. My Family.
- (M) (2:58) Time-Life R838-01 Solid Gold Soul - 1966.
- (M) (2:58) Rhino 72815 Beg, Scream & Shout! The Big Ol' Box Of '60s Soul.
- (M) (2:58) Time-Life R857-20 The Heart Of Rock 'n' Roll 1965-1966.

1967 WISH YOU DIDN'T HAVE TO GO
- (M) (2:15) Ripete 2183-RE Ocean Drive Volume 1.

1967 SHAKE A TAIL FEATHER
- (M) (2:08) JCI 3105 Soul Sixties.
- (S) (2:07) Rhino 70732 Grandson Of Frat Rock.
- (S) (2:06) Time-Life 2CLR-24 Classic Rock - 1967: Blowin' Your Mind.
- (S) (2:08) Ripete 2219 Beach Fever.
- (S) (2:06) JCI 3161 18 Soul Hits From The 60's.

1967 LET LOVE COME BETWEEN US
- (S) (2:24) Rhino 75757 Soul Shots Volume 3.
- (S) (2:22) Time-Life 2CLR-25 Classic Rock - On The Soul Side.
- (S) (2:24) Ripete 2219 Beach Fever.
- (S) (2:25) Varese Sarabande 5718 Soulful Pop.
- (S) (2:25) Varese Sarabande 5890 Bubblegum Classics Volume Four - Soulful Pop.

BILL PURSELL
1963 OUR WINTER LOVE
- (S) (2:21) Time-Life HPD-34 Your Hit Parade - 60's Instrumentals.
- (S) (2:22) K-Tel 3091 Those Wonderful Instrumentals.
- (S) (2:20) Collectors' Choice 003/4 Instrumental Gems Of The 60's.
- (S) (2:22) Nick At Nite/Epic 67148 Donna Reed's Dinner Party.
- (S) (2:21) Time-Life R986-16 Instrumental Favorites - Romantic Moments.
- (S) (2:22) Collectables 5850 Our Winter Love.
- (S) (2:22) Columbia 64937 Instrumental Themes For Young Lovers.

PYRAMIDS
1964 PENETRATION
- (M) (2:00) Rhino 70089 Surfin' Hits.
- (M) (1:57) DCC Compact Classics 030 Beach Classics.
- (M) (2:00) Rhino 71605 Rock Instrumental Classics Volume 5: Surf.
- (M) (2:00) Rhino 72035 Rock Instrumental Classics Vols. 1-5 Box Set.
- (M) (1:57) Time-Life 2RNR-36 Rock 'N' Roll Era - Axes & Saxes/The Great Instrumentals. *(tape splice noticeable at :03)*
- (M) (1:56) Time-Life 2CLR-09 Classic Rock - 1964: The Beat Goes On. *(tape splice noticeable at :03)*
- (M) (1:59) Sundazed 11023 Penetration! - Best Of.
- (M) (1:59) Rhino 72418 Cowabunga! The Surf Box.
- (M) (1:59) K-Tel 6256 Kahuna Classics.

Q
1977 DANCIN' MAN
    (S)   (2:36)   Priority 53729 Mega Hits Dance Classics Vol. 11.
    (S)   (2:35)   Epic 66155 Club Epic Volume 3.

QUAD CITY DJ's
1996 C'MON N' RIDE IT (THE TRAIN)
    (S)   (7:31)   Atlantic/Big Beat 82905 Get On Up And Dance.
    (S)   (8:04)   Atlantic/Big Beat 82905 Get On Up And Dance. *(remix)*
    (S)   (3:53)   Big Beat/Atlantic 92709 O.S.T. High School High. *(remix)*
    (S)   (3:52)   Arista 18943 Ultimate Dance Party 1997. *(all selections on this cd are segued together; remix)*
    (S)   (4:28)   Cold Front 6242 Club Mix '97. *(all selections on this cd are segued together; remix)*
    (S)   (4:03)   Tommy Boy 1214 Jock Jams Volume 3. *(all selections on this cd are segued together)*
1997 SPACE JAM
    (S)   (5:05)   Warner Sunset/Atlantic 82961 O.S.T. Space Jam.

QUAKER CITY BOYS
1959 TEASIN'

QUARTERFLASH
1982 HARDEN MY HEART
    (45 length is (3:33); LP length is (3:50))
    (S)   (3:33)   Rhino 70677 Billboard Top Hits - 1982.
    (S)   (3:50)   Sandstone 33050 and 5018 Cosmopolitan Volume 4.
    (S)   (3:31)   Scotti Brothers 75402 There Was Love (The Divorce Songs).
    (S)   (3:32)   Time-Life R105-40 Rock Dreams.
    (S)   (3:49)   JCI 3127 1980 - Only Rock 'N Roll - 1984.
    (S)   (3:49)   MCA Special Products 20754 Classic Rock Volume 1.
    (S)   (3:50)   DCC Compact Classics 089 Night Moves Volume 7.
    (S)   (3:50)   Geffen 2003 Quarterflash.
    (S)   (3:33)   Time-Life R988-05 Sounds Of The Eighties: 1982.
    (S)   (3:31)   Geffen 24805 Geffen Vintage 80's Volume 1.
    (S)   (3:49)   Madacy Entertainment 1982 Rock On 1982.
    (S)   (3:50)   Hip-O 40005 The '80s Hit(s) Back....Again!
    (S)   (3:50)   Geffen 25123 Harden My Heart....Best Of.
    (S)   (3:49)   Geffen 25151 Geffen Vintage 80s Vol. II.
    (S)   (3:50)   Simitar 55502 The Number One's: Classic Rock.
    (S)   (3:32)   JCI 3193 18 Rock Classics Volume 3.
1982 FIND ANOTHER FOOL
    (S)   (4:32)   Geffen 2003 Quarterflash. *(LP version)*
    (S)   (4:34)   Geffen 25123 Harden My Heart....Best Of. *(LP version)*
1983 TAKE ME TO HEART
    (S)   (3:32)   Geffen 4011 Take Another Picture.
    (S)   (3:31)   Geffen 25123 Harden My Heart....Best Of.

SUZI QUATRO and CHRIS NORMAN
1979 STUMBLIN' IN
    (S)   (3:28)   Rhino 71202 Super Hits Of The 70's Volume 22.
    (S)   (3:57)   Razor & Tie 2102 The Wild One: Classic Quatro. *(neither the 45 or LP version)*
    (S)   (3:28)   Time-Life AM1-26 AM Gold - 1979.

QUEEN
1975 KILLER QUEEN
    (S)   (2:59)   Elektra 564 Greatest Hits.

    (S)   (2:59)   Hollywood 61036 Sheer Heart Attack.
    (S)   (2:59)   Hollywood 61265 Greatest Hits.
    (S)   (2:59)   Hollywood 61407 The Queen Collection.
    (S)   (2:59)   Hollywood 62042 Greatest Hits I & II.
    (S)   (2:59)   Hip-O 40039 Power Chords Volume 2.
1976 BOHEMIAN RHAPSODY
    (S)   (5:55)   Reprise 26805 Music From The Motion Picture "Wayne's World".
    (S)   (5:55)   Elektra 564 Greatest Hits.
    (S)   (5:54)   Hollywood 61065 A Night At The Opera. *(tracks into next selection)*
    (S)   (5:54)   Hollywood 61311 Classic Queen.
    (S)   (5:54)   Hollywood 61407 The Queen Collection.
    (S)   (5:55)   Hollywood 62042 Greatest Hits I & II.
    (S)   (5:54)   MFSL 568 A Night At The Opera. *(tracks into next selection; gold disc)*
1976 YOU'RE MY BEST FRIEND
    (S)   (2:50)   Elektra 564 Greatest Hits.
    (S)   (2:50)   Hollywood 61065 A Night At The Opera.
    (S)   (2:50)   Hollywood 61265 Greatest Hits.
    (S)   (2:50)   Hollywood 61407 The Queen Collection.
    (S)   (2:50)   MFSL 568 A Night At The Opera. *(gold disc)*
    (S)   (2:50)   Epic 53439 O.S.T. Peter's Friends.
    (S)   (2:50)   Hollywood 62042 Greatest Hits I & II.
1977 SOMEBODY TO LOVE
    (S)   (4:54)   Elektra 564 Greatest Hits.
    (S)   (4:54)   Hollywood 61035 A Day At The Races.
    (S)   (4:59)   Hollywood 61035 A Day At The Races. *(1991 remix)*
    (S)   (4:54)   Hollywood 61265 Greatest Hits.
    (S)   (4:54)   Hollywood 61407 The Queen Collection.
    (S)   (4:56)   Hollywood 62042 Greatest Hits I & II.
    (S)   (4:54)   MFSL 668 A Day At The Races. *(gold disc)*
1978 WE ARE THE CHAMPIONS
    (S)   (2:59)   Rhino 70673 Billboard Top Hits - 1978.
    (S)   (4:59)   Original Sound 8894 Dick Clark's 21 All-Time Hits Vol. 3. *(this is a medley of "WE WILL ROCK YOU" (2:00) and "WE ARE THE CHAMPIONS" (2:59))*
    (S)   (2:58)   Elektra 564 Greatest Hits.
    (S)   (2:59)   Hollywood 61037 News Of The World.
    (S)   (2:59)   MFSL 588 News Of The World. *(gold disc)*
    (S)   (2:59)   Hollywood 61265 Greatest Hits.
    (S)   (2:59)   Hollywood 61407 The Queen Collection.
    (S)   (2:58)   Time-Life SOD-10 Sounds Of The Seventies - 1978.
    (S)   (2:59)   Mercury 314522367 Soccer Rocks The Globe.
    (S)   (2:59)   Tommy Boy 1136 ESPN Presents Jock Rock Vol. 2. *(all songs on this cd are segued together with crowd sound effects added)*
    (S)   (2:59)   Hollywood 62042 Greatest Hits I & II.
1978 BICYCLE RACE
    (S)   (3:00)   Elektra 564 Greatest Hits.
    (S)   (3:01)   Hollywood 61062 Jazz.
    (S)   (4:56)   Hollywood 61062 Jazz. *(1991 remix)*
    (S)   (3:01)   Hollywood 61265 Greatest Hits.
    (S)   (3:01)   Hollywood 61407 The Queen Collection.
    (S)   (3:01)   Hollywood 62042 Greatest Hits I & II.
1978 FAT BOTTOMED GIRLS
    (S)   (3:22)   Elektra 564 Greatest Hits. *(45 version)*
    (S)   (4:14)   Hollywood 61062 Jazz. *(LP version)*
    (S)   (4:22)   Hollywood 61062 Jazz. *(1991 remix)*
    (S)   (4:15)   Hollywood 61265 Greatest Hits. *(LP version)*
    (S)   (4:15)   Hollywood 61407 The Queen Collection. *(LP version)*
    (S)   (3:21)   Hollywood 62042 Greatest Hits I & II. *(45 version)*

QUEEN (Continued)

(S) (4:15) Hollywood 62132 Queen Rocks. *(LP version)*

1980 CRAZY LITTLE THING CALLED LOVE
(S) (2:42) Elektra 564 Greatest Hits.
(S) (2:41) Hollywood 61063 The Game.
(S) (2:42) Hollywood 61265 Greatest Hits.
(S) (2:42) Hollywood 61407 The Queen Collection.
(S) (2:42) MFSL 610 The Game. *(gold disc)*
(S) (2:41) Time-Life R988-07 Sounds Of The Eighties: 1980.
(S) (2:42) Hollywood 62041 O.S.T. Mr. Wrong.
(S) (2:42) Hollywood 62042 Greatest Hits I & II.
(S) (2:41) Priority 50991 The Best Of The 70's - Rock Chart Toppers.

1980 PLAY THE GAME
(S) (3:27) Elektra 564 Greatest Hits.
(S) (3:29) Hollywood 61063 The Game.
(S) (3:30) Hollywood 61265 Greatest Hits.
(S) (3:30) Hollywood 61407 The Queen Collection.
(S) (3:30) MFSL 610 The Game. *(gold disc)*
(S) (3:30) Hollywood 62042 Greatest Hits I & II.

1980 ANOTHER ONE BITES THE DUST
(S) (3:34) Elektra 564 Greatest Hits.
(S) (3:34) Hollywood 61063 The Game.
(S) (3:34) Hollywood 61265 Greatest Hits.
(S) (3:34) Hollywood 61407 The Queen Collection.
(S) (3:34) MFSL 610 The Game. *(gold disc)*
(S) (3:34) Time-Life R988-01 Sounds Of The Eighties: The Rockin' Eighties.
(S) (3:34) Time-Life R988-25 Sounds Of The Eighties: The Rolling Stone Collection 1980-1981.
(S) (3:34) Hollywood 62042 Greatest Hits I & II.
(S) (3:34) Hollywood 62077 Official Party Album - ABC's Monday Night Football.
(S) (3:33) Hip-O 40047 The '80s Hit(s) Back 3.

1981 FLASH'S THEME aka FLASH
(S) (2:45) Elektra 564 Greatest Hits. *(45 version)*
(S) (3:30) Hollywood 61203 Flash Gordon. *(LP version)*
(S) (2:46) Hollywood 62042 Greatest Hits I & II. *(45 version)*

released as by QUEEN & DAVID BOWIE:
1982 UNDER PRESSURE
(S) (4:01) Hollywood 61407 Queen Collection.
(S) (4:01) Hollywood 61311 Classic Queen.
(S) (4:02) Elektra 564 Queen - Greatest Hits.
(S) (4:03) Hollywood 61038 Queen - Hot Space.
(S) (4:01) Rykodisc 10218/19 David Bowie - The Singles 1969-1993.
(S) (4:03) Virgin 40982 David Bowie - Let's Dance.
(S) (3:55) Hollywood 62042 Queen - Greatest Hits I & II.
(S) (4:01) London 422828867 O.S.T. Grosse Pointe Blank.

released as by QUEEN:
1982 BODY LANGUAGE
(S) (4:32) Hollywood 61407 Queen Collection.
(S) (4:32) Hollywood 61265 Greatest Hits.
(S) (4:32) Hollywood 61038 Hot Space.

1984 RADIO GA GA
(S) (5:47) Hollywood 61407 Queen Collection. *(LP version)*
(S) (5:47) Hollywood 61311 Classic Queen. *(LP version)*
(S) (5:47) Hollywood 61233 The Works. *(LP version)*
(S) (5:42) Hollywood 62042 Greatest Hits I & II. *(LP version)*

1992 BOHEMIAN RHAPSODY
(this song charted in two different years: 1976 & 1992; see 1976 listings)

released as by GEORGE MICHAEL and QUEEN:
1993 SOMEBODY TO LOVE
(S) (5:16) Hollywood 61479 George Michael And Queen - Five Live.

QUEEN LATIFAH
1994 U.N.I.T.Y.
(S) (4:10) Motown 374636370 Black Reign.
(S) (4:10) MCA 11329 Soul Train 25th Anniversary Box Set.
(S) (4:10) Mercury 314535649 O.S.T. Girls Town.

QUEENSRYCHE
1991 SILENT LUCIDITY
(S) (5:46) EMI 92806 Empire.

? & THE MYSTERIANS
1966 96 TEARS
1966 I NEED SOMEBODY

QUIET RIOT
1983 CUM ON FEEL THE NOIZE
(S) (3:26) CBS Special Products 44363 Rock Of The 80's. *(45 version)*
(S) (4:49) K-Tel 6090 Hit Parader Salutes 20 Years Of Metal. *(LP version)*
(S) (4:49) Priority 7963 First Degree Metal. *(LP version)*
(S) (4:40) Priority 53702 Hot And Sexy - Rock All Night. *(LP version)*
(S) (4:49) Risky Business 57833 Read The Hits/Best Of The 80's. *(LP version)*
(S) (4:49) Pasha 38443 Metal Health. *(LP version)*
(S) (4:50) Time-Life R988-03 Sounds Of The Eighties: 1983. *(LP version)*
(S) (4:49) Time-Life R968-13 Guitar Rock - The Early '80s. *(LP version)*
(S) (4:49) Rhino 72291 Heavy Metal Hits Of The 80's Volume 1. *(LP version)*
(S) (4:48) Rhino 72275 More Stadium Rock. *(LP version)*
(S) (4:46) Epic 64233 Greatest Hits. *(LP version)*
(S) (4:50) Epic/Legacy 65020 Ultimate Rock 'n' Roll Collection. *(LP version)*
(S) (4:48) Hip-O 40040 Power Chords Volume 3. *(LP version)*
(S) (4:48) Flashback 72712 Arena Rock. *(LP version)*
(S) (4:47) K-Tel 3883 The 80's: Glam Rock. *(LP version)*
(S) (4:49) Razor & Tie 89004 Monsters Of Rock. *(LP version)*

1984 BANG YOUR HEAD (METAL HEALTH)
(LP title of this song is "METAL HEALTH")
(S) (5:16) Priority 7962 Head Banging Metal. *(LP version)*
(S) (5:17) Pasha 38443 Metal Health. *(LP version)*
(S) (5:16) Epic 64233 Greatest Hits. *(LP version)*
(S) (3:54) JCI 3144 18 Headbangers From The 80's. *(45 version)*
(S) (5:17) Priority 50936 Best Of 80's Metal Volume One: Bang Your Head. *(LP version)*

QUIN-TONES
1958 DOWN THE AISLE OF LOVE
(M) (2:48) Rhino 70589 Rockin' & Rollin' Wedding Songs Volume 2.
(M) (2:50) Vee Jay 708 The Unavailable 16/The Original Nitty Gritty.
(E) (2:48) Time-Life 2RNR-33 Rock 'N' Roll Era - The 50's Last Dance.
(E) (2:48) Time-Life R102-17 Lost Treasures Of Rock 'N' Roll.
(M) (2:48) Time-Life R857-16 The Heart Of Rock 'n' Roll The Late '50s.

R

EDDIE RABBITT
1979 EVERY WHICH WAY BUT LOOSE
- (S) (2:48) Risky Business 57473 Country Goes To The Movies.
- (S) (2:48) Rhino 72424 Billboard Top Movie Hits - 1970s.
- (S) (2:49) Priority 50967 I Love Country Volume Two: Hits Of The 70's.

1979 SUSPICIONS
- (S) (4:19) Capitol 94346 Ten Years Of Greatest Hits. *(rerecording)*
- (S) (4:19) Warner Brothers 26467 All Time Greatest Hits.
- (S) (4:19) Priority 8671 Country's Greatest Hits: Superstars.

1980 DRIVIN' MY LIFE AWAY
- (S) (3:11) Capitol 94346 Ten Years Of Greatest Hits. *(rerecording)*
- (S) (3:13) Warner Brothers 26467 All Time Greatest Hits.
- (S) (3:14) Warner Brothers 45706 Greatest Country Hits Of The 80's Volume III.
- (S) (3:12) JCI 3157 1980 - Only Country - 1984.

1981 I LOVE A RAINY NIGHT
- (S) (3:11) Capitol 94346 Ten Years Of Greatest Hits. *(rerecording)*
- (S) (3:08) Warner Brothers 26467 All Time Greatest Hits.
- (S) (3:07) Time-Life CCD-03 Contemporary Country - The Early 80's.
- (S) (3:08) Varese Sarabande 5534 Rhythm Of The Rain.
- (S) (3:09) Warner Brothers 45664 Greatest Country Hits Of The 80's Vol. I.
- (S) (3:08) K-Tel 3047 Country Music Classics Volume VI.
- (S) (3:07) JCI 3170 #1 Radio Hits 1980 - Only Rock 'n Roll - 1984.
- (S) (3:07) K-Tel 3367 101 Greatest Country Hits Vol. Eight: Country Romance.
- (S) (3:07) Time-Life R103-18 Great Love Songs Of The '70s & '80s.
- (S) (3:02) Simitar 55082 80's Country 1980-82.

1981 STEP BY STEP
- (S) (3:39) Capitol 90531 Step By Step.
- (S) (3:39) Capitol 95373 Classics Collection.

1982 SOMEONE COULD LOSE A HEART TONIGHT
- (S) (3:25) Capitol 90531 Step By Step.
- (S) (3:25) Capitol 95373 Classics Collection.

released as by EDDIE RABBITT with CRYSTAL GAYLE:
1983 YOU AND I
- (S) (3:53) Priority 8674 Country's Greatest Hits - 80's Country Duets.
- (S) (3:57) Warner Brothers 45512 Great Wedding Songs.
- (S) (3:57) Warner Brothers 45668 Greatest Country Hits Of The 80's Volume II.
- (S) (3:57) Capitol 94652 Radio Romance.
- (S) (3:52) Priority 50968 I Love Country Volume Three: Hits Of The 80's.
- (S) (3:52) K-Tel 3358 101 Greatest Country Hits Vol. Four: Mellow Country.
- (S) (3:57) Time-Life R834-15 Body Talk - Once In Lifetime.

RADIOHEAD
1993 CREEP
- (S) (3:55) EMI 32393 Loaded Volume 1.
- (S) (3:55) Capitol 81409 Pablo Honey.
- (S) (3:55) Mammoth 92672 and 354980125 MTV Buzz Bin Volume 1.

GERRY RAFFERTY
1978 BAKER STREET
(dj copies of this 45 ran (3:47), (4:08) and (5:56); commercial copies were all (4:08); the dj 45's were all pressed at different pitches with the (3:47) version being the fastest and the (5:56) version being the slowest)
- (S) (6:26) EMI 93264 Right Down The Line: Best Of. *(much slower and slightly longer than the LP version)*
- (S) (5:57) EMI 46049 City To City. *(LP version)*
- (S) (6:06) DCC Compact Classics 1075 City To City. *(gold disc; LP version)*
- (S) (4:06) Capitol 23338 O.S.T. Good Will Hunting. *(45 version)*

1978 RIGHT DOWN THE LINE
(dj copies of this 45 ran (3:33) and (4:17); commercial copies were all (3:33))
- (S) (4:26) EMI 93264 Right Down The Line: Best Of. *(LP version)*
- (S) (4:17) EMI 46049 City To City. *(LP version)*
- (S) (4:26) DCC Compact Classics 1075 City To City. *(gold disc; LP version)*

1979 HOME AND DRY
- (S) (4:48) EMI 46049 City To City. *(LP version)*
- (S) (4:55) DCC Compact Classics 1075 City To City. *(gold disc; LP version)*

1979 DAYS GONE DOWN (STILL GOT THE LIGHT IN YOUR EYES)
1979 GET IT RIGHT NEXT TIME
- (S) (4:40) EMI 93264 Right Down The Line: Best Of. *(LP version)*

RAIDERS (see PAUL REVERE & THE RAIDERS)

RAINBOW
1982 STONE COLD
- (S) (5:14) JCI 4541 Masters Of Metal: Strikeforce Volume 2. *(LP version)*
- (S) (5:17) Priority 7962 Head Banging Metal. *(LP version)*
- (S) (5:14) Time-Life R968-24 Guitar Rock - The '80s Take Two. *(LP version)*

RAINDROPS
1963 WHAT A GUY
- (M) (2:17) Time-Life 2RNR-44 Rock 'N' Roll Era - Lost Treasures.

1963 THE KIND OF BOY YOU CAN'T FORGET
- (S) (2:08) Rhino 70989 Best Of The Girl Groups Volume 2.
- (S) (2:08) Era 5025 The Brill Building Sound.
- (M) (2:08) Time-Life 2RNR-19 Rock 'N' Roll Era - 1963 Still Rockin'.

MARVIN RAINWATER
1957 GONNA FIND ME A BLUEBIRD

BONNIE RAITT
1991 SOMETHING TO TALK ABOUT
- (S) (3:47) Capitol 96111 Luck Of The Draw.
- (S) (3:45) Pointblank 42088 Fender 50th Anniversary Guitar Legends.
- (S) (3:46) Time-Life R13610 Gold And Platinum Box Set - The Ultimate Rock Collection.

BONNIE RAITT *(Continued)*
1992 I CAN'T MAKE YOU LOVE ME
    (S) (5:32) Capitol 96111 Luck Of The Draw.
1992 NOT THE ONLY ONE
    (S) (5:02) Capitol 96111 Luck Of The Draw.
1994 LOVE SNEAKIN' UP ON YOU
    (S) (3:39) Capitol 81427 Longing In Their Hearts.
    (S) (3:38) Grammy Recordings/Sony Music 67043 1995 Grammy Nominees.
1995 YOU GOT IT
    (S) (3:25) Arista 18748 O.S.T. Boys On The Side.

EDDIE RAMBEAU
1965 CONCRETE AND CLAY

RAM JAM
1977 BLACK BETTY
    (S) (5:27) Epic 46087 Club Epic. *(remix)*
    (S) (3:56) Priority 8662 Hard N' Heavy/70's Greatest Rock Hits Volume 1. *(LP version)*
    (S) (2:29) Rhino 71201 Super Hits Of The 70's Volume 21. *(45 version)*
    (S) (2:29) Time-Life R968-03 Guitar Rock 1976-1977. *(45 version)*
    (S) (2:29) Time-Life SOD-17 Sounds Of The Seventies - 1977: Take Two. *(45 version)*
    (S) (3:56) Priority 87963 First Degree Metal. *(LP version)*
    (S) (3:57) Risky Business 57471 Godfathers Of Grunge. *(LP version)*
    (S) (3:57) Epic/Legacy 65020 Ultimate Rock 'n' Roll Collection. *(LP version)*
    (S) (3:56) Collectables 5812 Golden Classics. *(LP version)*
    (S) (5:27) Epic/Legacy 65504 Disco Super Hits. *(remix)*
    (S) (2:29) K-Tel 4065 K-Tel's Original Party Music Vol. 1. *(45 version)*
    (S) (3:57) K-Tel 4030 Rock Anthems. *(LP version)*

RAMPAGE featuring BILLY LAWRENCE
1997 TAKE IT TO THE STREETS
    (S) (3:59) Elektra 62022 Scouts Honor...By Way Of Blood.
    (S) (3:58) Elektra 62088 Party Over Here '98. *(all tracks on this cd are segued together)*

RAMRODS
1961 (GHOST) RIDERS IN THE SKY
    (M) (2:38) Rhino 71602 Rock Instrumental Classics Volume 2: The Sixties. *(mastered from vinyl)*
    (M) (2:38) Rhino 72035 Rock Instrumental Classics Vols. 1-5 Box Set. *(mastered from vinyl)*
    (M) (2:37) Time-Life 2RNR-36 Rock 'N' Roll Era - Axes & Saxes/The Great Instrumentals.

RAN-DELLS
1963 MARTIAN HOP
    (M) (2:10) Rhino 70535 Halloween Hits.
    (M) (2:10) Varese Sarabande 5882 They Came From Outer Space.

BOOTS RANDOLPH
1963 YAKETY SAX
    (S) (2:01) CBS Special Products 44356 Yakety Sax.
    (S) (2:01) CBS Special Products 44355 Greatest Hits.
    (E) (2:01) Special Music 825 Yakin' Sax Man. *(rerecording)*
    (E) (2:00) Special Music 2523 Chet, Floyd & Boots. *(rerecording)*
    (S) (2:01) Time-Life HPD-34 Your Hit Parade - 60's Instrumentals.
    (S) (2:01) Sony Music Special Products 66106 The Monument Story.
    (S) (2:01) Collectors' Choice 5190 More Instrumental Gems Of The 60's.
    (S) (2:01) Columbia 69059 Party Super Hits.
    (S) (2:18) Curb 77880 Best Of. *(rerecording)*

RANDY & THE RAINBOWS
1963 DENISE
    (M) (1:59) Rhino 75764 Best Of Doo Wop Uptempo.
    (M) (1:55) Collectables 2508 History Of Rock - The Doo Wop Era Part 2.
    (M) (1:55) Collectables 4508 History Of Rock/The Doo Wop Era Part Two.
    (M) (1:55) Collectables 5068 History Of Rock Volume 8.
    (M) (1:55) Rhino 71463 Doo Wop Box.
    (M) (1:59) Rainbeaux 1947 Silver And Gold.
    (M) (1:59) Time-Life 2RNR-07 Rock 'N' Roll Era - 1963.
    (M) (1:59) Collectables 2500 WCBS-FM History Of Rock - The 60's Part 1.
    (M) (1:59) Collectables 4500 History Of Rock/The 60s Part One.
    (M) (1:58) Time-Life R10513 40 Lovin' Oldies.
    (M) (1:55) Time-Life R102-17 Lost Treasures Of Rock 'N' Roll.
    (M) (1:55) JCI 3184 1960 - Only Love - 1964.

SHABBA RANKS featuring JOHNNY GILL
1993 SLOW AND SEXY
    (S) (5:19) Epic 52464 Shabba Ranks - X-Tra Naked.

RAPPIN' 4-TAY
1994 PLAYAZ CLUB
    (S) (4:24) Chrysalis/EMI/Rag Top 30889 Don't Fight The Feelin'.
    (S) (4:20) Boxtunes 162444068 Big Phat Ones Of Hip-Hop Volume 1.
released as by RAPPIN' 4-TAY featuring THE SPINNERS:
1995 I'LL BE AROUND
    (S) (5:14) Rag Top Records 30889 Rappin' 4-Tay : Don't Fight The Feelin'.

RARE EARTH
1970 GET READY
    (E) (2:46) Motown 6183 Hard To Find Motown Classics Volume 1. *(45 version)*
    (E) (2:47) JCI 3100 Dance Sixties. *(45 version)*
    (E) (2:45) Original Sound 8894 Dick Clark's 21 All-Time Hits Vol. 3. *(45 version)*
    (E) (2:45) Priority 8662 Hard 'N Heavy/70's Greatest Rock Hits Volume 1. *(45 version)*
    (S) (2:57) DCC Compact Classics 043 Toga Rock II. *(:11 longer fade than the 45; missing the fake crowd noise overdub on the introduction.)*
    (S) (20:04) Motown 8033 and 8133 Get Ready/Ecology. *(edit of LP version)*
    (S) (21:27) Motown 5229 Get Ready. *(LP version)*
    (E) (2:46) Motown 5482 Greatest Hits And Rare Classics. *(45 version)*
    (E) (2:45) Motown 9071 Motown Dance Party Volume 1. *(all selections on this cd are segued together; 45 version)*
    (M) (2:46) Motown 6312 Hitsville USA. *(45 version)*
    (E) (2:46) Time-Life SOD-11 Sounds Of The Seventies - 1970: Take Two. *(45 version)*
    (S) (21:32) Motown 314530357 Earth Tones: The Essential. *(LP version)*
    (M) (2:45) Rebound 3145200320 Class Reunion 1970. *(45 version)*
    (S) (2:51) Motown 314530486 Anthology. *(45 version)*
    (S) (2:51) Motown 314530528 Motown Year By Year - 1970. *(45 version)*
    (M) (2:46) Motown 314530478 O.S.T. The Walking Dead. *(45 version)*
    (S) (2:53) Tommy Boy 1136 ESPN Presents Jock Rock Vol. 2. *(all songs on this cd are segued together with crowd sound effects added)*
    (S) (2:51) Rebound 314520440 No. 1 Hits Of The 70's. *(45 version)*
1970 (I KNOW) I'M LOSING YOU
    (M) (3:35) Motown 6183 Hard To Find Motown Classics Volume 1. *(45 version)*
    (E) (3:35) Motown 8033 and 8133 Get Ready/Ecology. *(45 version)*

(S) (10:54) Motown 5202 Ecology. *(LP version)*
(E) (3:35) Motown 5482 Greatest Hits And Rare Classics. *(45 version)*
(S) (10:56) Motown 314530357 Earth Tones: The Essential. *(LP version)*
(M) (3:38) Motown 314530486 Anthology. *(45 version)*

1971 BORN TO WANDER
(45 length is (2:56); LP length is (3:18))
(S) (2:56) Motown 6184 Hard To Find Motown Classics Volume 2.
(S) (3:09) Motown 8033 and 8133 Get Ready/Ecology.
(S) (3:20) Motown 5202 Ecology. *(truncated fade)*
(S) (3:18) Motown 5482 Greatest Hits And Rare Classics.
(S) (2:59) Motown 314530486 Anthology.

1971 I JUST WANT TO CELEBRATE
(S) (3:33) Motown 6184 Hard To Find Motown Classics Volume 2. *(LP version)*
(S) (3:33) MCA 25240 Classic Rock Volume 3. *(LP version)*
(S) (3:35) Motown 5482 Greatest Hits And Rare Classics. *(LP version)*
(S) (3:35) Priority 7055 Heavy Hitters/70's Greatest Rock Hits Volume 11. *(LP version)*
(M) (2:51) Motown 6312 Hitsville USA. *(45 version)*
(S) (3:33) Razor & Tie 22502 Those Rocking 70's. *(LP version)*
(S) (2:52) Time-Life SOD-12 Sounds Of The Seventies - 1971: Take Two. *(edit of LP version in an unsuccessful attempt at recreating the 45 version)*
(S) (3:36) Motown 314530357 Earth Tones: The Essential. *(LP version)*
(M) (2:52) Motown 314530486 Anthology. *(45 version)*
(S) (3:35) Rebound 314520364 Class Reunion '71. *(LP version)*

1972 HEY BIG BROTHER
(dj copies of this 45 ran (2:48) and (4:45);
commercial copies were all (2:59))
(S) (4:43) Motown 5482 Greatest Hits And Rare Classics.
(S) (5:42) Motown 314530357 Earth Tones: The Essential. *(live)*
(S) (4:45) Motown 314530486 Anthology.

RASCALS (also YOUNG RASCALS)
released as by THE YOUNG RASCALS:
1966 GOOD LOVIN'
(S) (2:28) JCI 3101 Rockin' Sixties.
(S) (2:28) Atlantic 81909 Hit Singles 1958-1977.
(S) (2:28) Motown 6120 and 6062 O.S.T. The Big Chill.
(S) (2:28) Warner Special Products 27602 20 Party Classics.
(S) (2:28) Epic 48732 O.S.T. My Girl.
(S) (2:27) Warner Special Products 27605 Ultimate.
(S) (2:27) Atlantic 8190 Greatest Hits/Time Peace.
(S) (2:27) Warner Special Products 27617 The Young Rascals.
(M) (2:30) Rhino 71031 Anthology (1965-1972).
(M) (2:29) Rhino 71277 Very Best Of.
(M) (2:30) Rhino 71436 Good Lovin'.
(M) (2:28) Time-Life 2CLR-02 Classic Rock - 1966.
(M) (2:29) Rhino 71728 '60s Rock Classics, Vol. 1.
(M) (2:29) Rhino 72275 More Stadium Rock.
(M) (2:29) JCI 3190 1965 - Only Dance - 1969.
(S) (2:27) Eclipse Music Group 64870 Rock 'n Roll Relix 1966-1967.
(S) (2:27) Eclipse Music Group 64872 Rock 'n Roll Relix 1960-1969.
(M) (2:29) Flashback 72701 '60s Rock: Mony Mony.
(M) (2:29) Flashback 72088 '60s Rock Hits Box Set.
(M) (2:29) Flashback 72712 Arena Rock.
(M) (2:30) Flashback 72697 Good Lovin' And Other Hits.
(M) (2:30) Flashback 72087 '60s Rock Legends Box Set.
(M) (2:30) Rhino 75200 Basketball's Greatest Hits.

1966 YOU BETTER RUN
(S) (2:25) Warner Special Products 27605 Ultimate.
(S) (2:25) Atlantic 8190 Greatest Hits/Time Peace.
(S) (2:24) Warner Special Products 27619 Groovin'.
(M) (2:26) Rhino 71031 Anthology (1965-1972).
(M) (2:27) Rhino 71277 Very Best Of.
(M) (2:25) Rhino 71436 Good Lovin'.
(M) (2:26) Flashback 72698 Groovin' And Other Hits.

1967 I'VE BEEN LONELY TOO LONG
(LP title was simply "LONELY TOO LONG")
(S) (2:58) SBK 93744 China Beach - Music & Memories. *(LP version)*
(S) (2:59) Warner Special Products 27605 Ultimate. *(LP version)*
(S) (2:58) Atlantic 8190 Greatest Hits/Time Peace. *(LP version)*
(S) (2:59) Warner Special Products 27618 Collections. *(LP version)*
(M) (2:04) Rhino 71031 Anthology (1965-1972). *(45 version)*
(M) (2:04) Rhino 71277 Very Best Of. *(45 version)*
(M) (2:04) Rhino 71436 Good Lovin'. *(45 version)*
(S) (2:58) Time-Life 2CLR-15 Classic Rock - 1967: Shakin' All Over. *(LP version)*
(M) (2:04) Rhino 71728 '60s Rock Classics, Vol. 1. *(45 version)*
(S) (2:57) JCI 3167 #1 Radio Hits 1965 - Only Rock 'n Roll - 1969. *(LP version)*
(M) (2:04) Atlantic 82983 Music From And Inspired By The Television Series "Mad About You". *(45 version)*
(M) (2:04) Flashback 72701 '60s Rock: Mony Mony. *(45 version)*
(M) (2:04) Flashback 72088 '60s Rock Hits Box Set. *(45 version)*
(M) (2:04) Flashback 72698 Groovin' And Other Hits. *(45 version)*

1967 GROOVIN'
(E) (2:27) Atlantic 81742 O.S.T. Platoon. *(45 version)*
(S) (2:29) Atlantic 81909 Hit Singles 1958-1977. *(LP version)*
(S) (2:29) Warner Special Products 27605 Ultimate. *(LP version)*
(S) (2:28) Atlantic 8190 Greatest Hits/Time Peace. *(LP version)*
(S) (2:29) Warner Special Products 27619 Groovin'. *(LP version)*
(M) (2:28) Rhino 71031 Anthology (1965-1972). *(45 version)*
(M) (2:27) Rhino 71065 Summer Of Love Volume 1. *(45 version)*
(M) (2:27) Rhino 71277 Very Best Of. *(45 version)*
(S) (2:29) Time-Life 2CLR-05 Classic Rock - 1967. *(LP version)*
(S) (2:28) Time-Life SUD-14 Superhits - The Late 60's. *(LP version)*
(M) (2:28) Rhino 71730 '60s Rock Classics, Vol. 3. *(45 version)*
(S) (2:28) JCI 3126 1965 - Only Rock 'N Roll - 1969. *(LP version)*
(M) (2:26) MCA 11241 O.S.T. Apollo 13. *(all selections on this cd are segued together; track selection numbers on the cd jacket are incorrect; this cd is a disaster; 45 version)*
(S) (2:28) JCI 3160 18 Free & Easy Hits From The 60's. *(LP version)*
(S) (2:28) Time-Life AM1-14 AM Gold - The Late '60s. *(LP version)*
(M) (2:28) Flashback 72703 '60s Rock: It's A Beautiful Morning. *(45 version)*
(M) (2:28) Flashback 72088 '60s Rock Hits Box Set. *(45 version)*
(M) (2:28) Flashback 72698 Groovin' And Other Hits. *(45 version)*
(S) (2:28) Madacy Entertainment 6804 More Sun Splashin'. *(LP version)*

1967 A GIRL LIKE YOU
(S) (2:47) Warner Special Products 27605 Ultimate.
(S) (2:46) Atlantic 8190 Greatest Hits/Time Peace.
(S) (2:48) Warner Special Products 27619 Groovin'.
(M) (2:46) Rhino 71031 Anthology (1965-1972).
(M) (2:45) Rhino 71277 Very Best Of.
(S) (2:48) JCI 3185 1965 - Only Love - 1969.
(M) (2:46) Flashback 72697 Good Lovin' And Other Hits.
(M) (2:46) Flashback 72087 '60s Rock Legends Box Set.

1967 HOW CAN I BE SURE
(S) (2:50) Warner Special Products 27605 Ultimate.
(S) (2:50) Atlantic 8190 Greatest Hits/Time Peace.

489

RASCALS *(Continued)*
- (S) (2:51) Warner Special Products 27619 Groovin'.
- (M) (2:52) Rhino 71031 Anthology (1965-1972).
- (M) (2:52) Rhino 71277 Very Best Of.
- (S) (2:51) Time-Life 2CLR-24 Classic Rock - 1967: Blowin' Your Mind.
- (S) (2:51) Time-Life SUD-05 Superhits - 1967. *(noisy introduction)*
- (S) (2:51) Time-Life OPCD-4517 Tonight's The Night. *(noisy introduction)*
- (M) (2:52) Rhino 72478 Beverly Hills 90210: Songs From The Peach Pit.
- (S) (2:51) Time-Life AM1-08 AM Gold - 1967. *(noisy introduction)*
- (M) (2:52) Flashback 72697 Good Lovin' And Other Hits.
- (M) (2:52) Flashback 72087 '60s Rock Legends Box Set.
- (S) (2:51) Time-Life R834-14 Body Talk - Love And Tenderness. *(noisy introduction)*
- (M) (2:52) Time-Life R857-22 The Heart Of Rock 'n' Roll 1967-1969.

1968 IT'S WONDERFUL
(actual 45 time is (3:20) not (2:30) as stated on the record label)
- (S) (2:16) Warner Special Products 27605 Ultimate. *(neither the LP or 45 version; LP speed but missing the intro and outro sound effects; this version can be found on the original pressings of this cd which did not feature a group photo on the cover)*
- (S) (2:14) Atlantic 8190 Greatest Hits/Time Peace. *(neither the LP or 45 version; LP speed but missing the intro and outro sound effects)*
- (M) (3:21) Rhino 71031 Anthology (1965-1972). *(commercial 45 version)*
- (M) (3:21) Rhino 71277 Very Best Of. *(commercial 45 version)*
- (S) (3:09) Warner Special Products 27605 Ultimate. *(LP introductory sound effects with 45 version concluding sound effects; LP speed; this version can be found only on the remastered cd which features a group photo on the cover)*
- (M) (3:21) Flashback 72697 Good Lovin' And Other Hits. *(commercial 45 version)*
- (M) (3:21) Flashback 72087 '60s Rock Legends Box Set. *(commercial 45 version)*

released as by THE RASCALS:
1968 A BEAUTIFUL MORNING
- (S) (2:32) JCI 3104 Mellow Sixties.
- (S) (2:32) Warner Special Products 27605 Ultimate.
- (S) (2:31) Atlantic 8190 Greatest Hits/Time Peace.
- (S) (2:33) Rhino 71031 Anthology (1965-1972).
- (S) (2:33) Rhino 71093 Better Days.
- (S) (2:33) Rhino 71277 Very Best Of.
- (S) (2:31) Epic 57560 O.S.T. A Bronx Tale.
- (S) (2:30) Time-Life 2CLR-04 Classic Rock - 1968.
- (S) (2:31) Time-Life SUD-02 Superhits - 1968.
- (S) (2:33) Time-Life R921-38 Get Together.
- (S) (2:33) Rhino 71730 '60s Rock Classics, Vol. 3.
- (S) (2:33) Rhino 71938 Billboard Top Pop Hits, 1968.
- (S) (2:31) Work 67814 O.S.T. First Wives Club.
- (S) (2:31) Time-Life AM1-04 AM Gold - 1968.
- (S) (2:33) Flashback 72687 '60s Rock: Feelin' Groovy.
- (S) (2:33) Flashback 72088 '60s Rock Hits Box Set.
- (S) (2:33) Flashback 72703 '60s Rock: It's A Beautiful Morning.
- (S) (2:33) Flashback 72088 '60s Rock Hits Box Set.
- (S) (2:33) Flashback 72697 Good Lovin' And Other Hits.
- (S) (2:33) Flashback 72087 '60s Rock Legends Box Set.

1968 PEOPLE GOT TO BE FREE
- (S) (2:58) Atlantic 81909 Hit Singles 1958-1977.
- (M) (2:59) Rhino 70734 Songs Of Protest.
- (S) (2:57) Warner Special Products 27610 More Party Classics.
- (S) (2:57) Priority 7909 Vietnam: Rockin' The Delta.
- (S) (2:57) Warner Special Products 27605 Ultimate.
- (S) (2:58) Rhino 71031 Anthology (1965-1972).
- (S) (2:58) Priority 53701 Best Of The 60's & 70's Rock: Protest Rock.

- (S) (2:57) Rhino 71277 Very Best Of.
- (S) (2:58) Rhino 71548 Let There Be Drums Volume 2: The 60's.
- (S) (2:55) Time-Life 2CLR-11 Classic Rock - 1968: The Beat Goes On.
- (S) (2:58) Time-Life SUD-18 Superhits - Late 60's Classics.
- (S) (2:58) Time-Life R921-38 Get Together.
- (S) (2:58) Rhino 71729 '60s Rock Classics, Vol. 2.
- (S) (2:57) Eclipse Music Group 64871 Rock 'n Roll Relix 1968-1969.
- (S) (2:57) Eclipse Music Group 64872 Rock 'n Roll Relix 1960-1969.
- (S) (2:58) Time-Life AM1-12 AM Gold - Late '60s Classics.
- (S) (2:58) Flashback 72702 '60s Rock: The Beat Goes On.
- (S) (2:58) Flashback 72088 '60s Rock Hits Box Set.
- (S) (2:58) Flashback 72698 Groovin' And Other Hits.

1968 A RAY OF HOPE
- (S) (3:39) Warner Special Products 27605 Ultimate.
- (S) (3:41) Rhino 71031 Anthology (1965-1972).
- (S) (3:40) Rhino 71277 Very Best Of.
- (S) (3:40) Flashback 72698 Groovin' And Other Hits.

1969 HEAVEN
- (S) (3:21) Warner Special Products 27605 Ultimate.
- (S) (3:21) Rhino 71031 Anthology (1965-1972).
- (S) (3:21) Rhino 71277 Very Best Of.
- (S) (3:22) Flashback 72697 Good Lovin' And Other Hits.
- (S) (3:22) Flashback 72087 '60s Rock Legends Box Set.

1969 SEE
- (S) (5:01) Warner Special Products 27605 Ultimate. *(LP length)*
- (S) (4:44) Rhino 71031 Anthology (1965-1972). *(:10 longer than the 45)*
- (S) (4:40) Rhino 71277 Very Best Of. *(:06 longer than the 45)*
- (S) (4:40) Flashback 72698 Groovin' And Other Hits. *(:06 longer than the 45)*

1969 CARRY ME BACK
- (S) (2:49) Warner Special Products 27605 Ultimate.
- (S) (2:49) Rhino 71031 Anthology (1965-1972).
- (S) (2:49) Rhino 71277 Very Best Of.
- (S) (2:49) Flashback 72697 Good Lovin' And Other Hits.
- (S) (2:49) Flashback 72087 '60s Rock Legends Box Set.

RASPBERRIES
1972 GO ALL THE WAY
- (S) (3:17) JCI 3301 Rockin' Seventies. *(poor stereo separation)*
- (S) (3:19) Capitol 92126 Capitol Collectors Series. *(poor stereo separation)*
- (S) (3:19) Capitol 98139 Spring Break Volume 2. *(poor stereo separation)*
- (S) (3:19) Capitol 98665 When AM Was King. *(poor stereo separation)*
- (S) (3:19) Time-Life SOD-03 Sounds Of The Seventies - 1972. *(poor stereo separation)*
- (S) (3:19) Varese Sarabande 5503 and 5504 and 5505 and 5506 and 5507 and 5508 and 5509 and 5513 and 5571 Arrow: All Rock & Roll Oldies Volume One. *(poor stereo separation)*
- (S) (3:19) Capitol 33669 Greatest Hits. *(poor stereo separation)*
- (S) (3:18) Time-Life R968-11 Guitar Rock - The Early '70s. *(poor stereo separation)*
- (S) (3:19) Priority 50952 I Love Rock & Roll Volume 3: Hits Of The 70's. *(poor stereo separation)*
- (S) (3:19) Eclipse Music Group 64893 Rock 'n Roll Relix 1972-1973. *(poor stereo separation)*
- (S) (3:19) Eclipse Music Group 64897 Rock 'n Roll Relix 1970-1979. *(poor stereo separation)*
- (S) (3:18) Arista 18963 Eric Carmen -- The Definitive Collection. *(poor stereo separation)*
- (S) (3:19) Rhino 72728 Poptopia! Power Pop Classics Of The '70s. *(poor stereo separation)*
- (S) (3:19) BMG Special Products 44762 The President's Greatest Hits. *(poor stereo separation)*

1973 I WANNA BE WITH YOU
- (S) (3:04) Capitol 92126 Capitol Collectors Series.

(S) (3:03) Time-Life SOD-22 Sounds Of The Seventies -
Seventies Top Forty.
(S) (3:03) Capitol 33669 Greatest Hits.
(S) (3:03) Time-Life R968-16 Guitar Rock - The Mid '70s:
Take Two.
(S) (3:00) Oglio 81573 Straight Outta Cleveland.
(S) (3:01) Arista 18963 Eric Carmen -- The Definitive Collection.
(S) (3:02) K-Tel 3910 Fantastic Volume 1.

1973 LET'S PRETEND
(S) (3:39) Capitol 92126 Capitol Collectors Series. *(LP length and speed)*
(S) (3:39) Capitol 33669 Greatest Hits. *(LP length and speed)*
(S) (3:37) Arista 18963 Eric Carmen -- The Definitive Collection. *(LP length and speed)*
(S) (3:36) EMI-Capitol Music Special Markets 19545 Lost Hits Of The '70s. *(LP length and speed)*

1974 OVERNIGHT SENSATION (HIT RECORD)
(actual 45 and LP time is (5:24) not (5:34) as stated on the record label; dj copies of this 45 ran (3:38) and (5:24))
(S) (5:22) Capitol 92126 Capitol Collector's Series.
(S) (5:22) Rhino 71549 Let There Be Drums Vol. 3: The 70's.
(S) (5:22) Time-Life SOD-37 Sounds Of The Seventies - AM Heavy Hits.
(S) (5:22) Capitol 33669 Greatest Hits.
(S) (5:20) Arista 18963 Eric Carmen -- The Definitive Collection.

RATT
1984 ROUND AND ROUND
(S) (4:22) Atlantic 81908 Classic Rock 1966-1988. *(LP version)*
(S) (4:23) Atlantic 80143 Out Of The Cellar. *(LP version)*
(S) (4:23) Atlantic 82260 Ratt & Roll 8191. *(LP version)*
(S) (4:23) Time-Life R968-18 Guitar Rock - The Heavy '80s. *(LP version)*
(S) (4:23) Epic/Legacy 65020 Ultimate Rock 'n' Roll Collection. *(LP version)*
(S) (4:23) JCI 3144 18 Headbangers From The 80's. *(LP version)*
(S) (4:23) Priority 50936 Best Of 80's Metal Volume One: Bang Your Head. *(LP version)*
(S) (4:23) Time-Life R988-17 Sounds Of The Eighties: The Mid '80s Take Two. *(LP version)*
(S) (4:23) K-Tel 3883 The 80's: Glam Rock. *(LP version)*
(S) (4:23) Hip-O 40070 Rock For The Ages. *(LP version)*
(S) (4:23) Razor & Tie 89004 Monsters Of Rock. *(LP version)*

LOU RAWLS
1966 LOVE IS A HURTIN' THING
(S) (2:11) Rhino 75774 Soul Shots.
(S) (2:16) Curb 77355 60's Hits Volume 1.
(S) (2:15) Capitol 91147 Best Of.
(S) (2:16) Curb 77380 Greatest Hits.
(S) (2:12) Capitol 98306 The Legendary Lou Rawls. *(truncated fade)*
(S) (2:10) Time-Life RHD-01 Rhythm & Blues - 1966.
(S) (2:10) Time-Life 2CLR-28 Classic Rock - On The Soul Side II.
(S) (2:12) Rhino 71806 The R&B Box: Thirty Years Of Rhythm & Blues.
(S) (2:15) CEMA Special Markets 35958 Greatest Hits.
(S) (2:10) Time-Life R838-01 Solid Gold Soul - 1966.
(S) (2:19) EMI 57181 Love Is A Hurtin' Thing: The Silk & Soul Of Lou Rawls.
(S) (2:11) Repeat/Relativity 1609 Tell It Like It Is: #1 Soul Hits Of The 60's Volume 1.

1967 DEAD END STREET
(S) (3:57) Capitol 91147 Best Of. *(this cd splits this song into two separate tracks: track 5 is the "DEAD END STREET MONOLOGUE" (1:37) and track 6 which is "DEAD END STREET" (2:20); LP version)*
(*) (****) Curb 77380 Greatest Hits. *(cd jacket claims this song is included on the cd but it is not)*

(S) (3:57) Capitol 98306 The Legendary Lou Rawls. *(LP version)*
(S) (3:57) CEMA Special Markets 35958 Greatest Hits. *(LP version)*
(S) (4:00) EMI 57181 Love Is A Hurtin' Thing: The Silk & Soul Of Lou Rawls. *(LP version)*
(M) (3:46) Rhino 72815 Beg, Scream & Shout! The Big Ol' Box Of '60s Soul. *(LP version)*

1969 YOUR GOOD THING (IS ABOUT TO END)
(S) (4:24) Curb 77380 Greatest Hits. *(LP version)*
(S) (2:51) Capitol 98306 The Legendary Lou Rawls. *(45 version)*
(S) (2:51) Right Stuff 28371 Slow Jams: The 60's Volume Two. *(45 version)*
(S) (4:24) CEMA Special Markets 35958 Greatest Hits. *(LP version)*
(S) (4:41) EMI 57181 Love Is A Hurtin' Thing: The Silk & Soul Of Lou Rawls. *(LP version but :16 longer)*

1971 A NATURAL MAN
(S) (3:34) Rhino 70786 Soul Hits Of The 70's Volume 6.
(S) (3:38) Curb 77443 Mike Curb Congregation Greatest Hits.
(S) (3:39) Curb 77380 Greatest Hits.
(S) (3:34) Rhino 71209 70's Smash Hits Volume 5.
(S) (3:41) Rebound 314520364 Class Reunion '71.
(S) (3:34) Flashback 72685 '70s Radio Hits Volume 5.
(S) (3:40) Polygram Special Markets 314520446 Soul Hits Of The 70's.
(S) (3:39) Polygram Special Markets 314520456 #1 Radio Hits Of The 70's.

1976 YOU'LL NEVER FIND ANOTHER LOVE LIKE MINE
(actual 45 time is (3:31) not (3:36) as stated on the record label)
(S) (4:25) JCI 3303 Love Seventies. *(LP version)*
(S) (4:28) Philadelphia International 39307 Ten Years Of Hits. *(LP version)*
(S) (4:26) Philadelphia International 39255 Philly Ballads Volume 1. *(LP version)*
(S) (4:26) Priority 7972 Mega-Hits Dance Classics Volume 2. *(LP version)*
(S) (4:25) Right Stuff 66689 All Things In Time. *(LP version)*
(S) (3:30) Original Sound 8909 Best Love Songs Vol 4. *(45 version)*
(S) (3:30) Original Sound 9327 Best Love Songs Vol. 3 & 4. *(45 version)*
(S) (3:30) Original Sound 1236 Best Love Songs Box Set. *(45 version)*
(S) (3:30) Rhino 71618 Soul Train Hall Of Fame/20th Anniversary. *(45 version)*
(S) (4:28) Razor & Tie 22496 Disco Fever. *(LP version)*
(S) (3:30) Rhino 72128 Hot Soul Hits Of The 70's Vol. 18. *(45 version)*
(S) (4:25) CEMA Special Markets 35958 Greatest Hits. *(LP version)*
(S) (3:30) Time-Life AM1-23 AM Gold - 1976. *(45 version)*
(S) (3:30) Time-Life R838-11 Solid Gold Soul - 1976. *(45 version)*
(S) (4:26) Time-Life R834-01 Body Talk - Forever Yours. *(LP version)*
(S) (3:30) Rhino 72516 Behind Closed Doors - '70s Swingers. *(45 version)*
(S) (4:16) JCI 3175 1975 - Only Soul - 1979. *(LP version faded early)*
(S) (3:30) Time-Life R840-06 Sounds Of The Seventies: '70s Dance Party 1975-1976. *(45 version)*

1978 LADY LOVE
(S) (4:01) Right Stuff 27628 When You Hear Lou, You've Heard It All. *(LP version)*
(S) (3:39) Legacy/Epic 66913 From Philly With Love. *(live)*
(S) (3:40) Rhino 72129 Soul Hits Of The 70's Vol. 19. *(45 version)*

DIANE RAY
1963 PLEASE DON'T TALK TO THE LIFEGUARD
   (S) (1:43)   Mercury 314528171 Growin' Up Too Fast - The Girl Group Anthology.
   (S) (1:43)   Collectors' Choice 5189 I Wish I Were A Princess - The Great Lost Female Teen Idols.

JAMES RAY
1962 IF YOU GOTTA MAKE A FOOL OF SOMEBODY
   (S) (1:57)   Collectables 5066 History Of Rock Volume 6.
   (S) (1:55)   Time-Life 2RNR-25 Rock 'N' Roll Era - The 60's Keep On Rockin'.
   (S) (1:59)   Collectables 5199 If You Gotta Make A Fool Of Somebody. *(mastered from vinyl)*
   (S) (1:55)   Time-Life R857-18 The Heart Of Rock 'n' Roll 1962-1963 Take Two.

JOHNNIE RAY
1956 JUST WALKING IN THE RAIN
   (M) (2:36)   Columbia 45110 16 Most Requested Songs Of The 50's Volume 1.
   (M) (2:37)   Columbia 30609 Best Of.
   (M) (2:37)   Columbia/Legacy 46095 16 Most Requested Songs.
   (M) (2:39)   Time-Life HPD-15 Your Hit Parade - 1956.
   (S) (2:47)   Curb 77750 Greatest Songs. *(rerecording)*
   (M) (2:39)   Time-Life R857-07 The Heart Of Rock 'n' Roll 1956.
1957 YOU DON'T OWE ME A THING
   (M) (2:25)   Curb 77750 Greatest Songs. *(rerecording)*
1957 YES TONIGHT, JOSEPHINE

RAYBON BROTHERS
1997 BUTTERFLY KISSES
   (S) (4:44)   MCA 70014 Raybon Brothers.

MARGIE RAYBURN
1957 I'M AVAILABLE
   (M) (1:49)   Collectors' Choice 5189 I Wish I Were A Princess - The Great Lost Female Teen Idols.

RAYDIO (see RAY PARKER JR.)

RAY, GOODMAN & BROWN
1980 SPECIAL LADY
(actual LP time is (4:14) not (4:38) as stated on the record label; dj copies of this 45 were issued with and without rap in the introduction; commercial copies all featured the rap in the introduction)
   (S) (4:15)   Rhino 71861 Smooth Grooves Volume 3. *(LP version)*
   (S) (3:38)   Rebound 314520318 Class Reunion 1980. *(commercial 45 version)*
   (S) (4:13)   Rhino 71971 Video Soul - Best Soul Of The 80's Vol. 1. *(LP version)*
   (S) (3:39)   Priority 53796 Hot And Sexy - Love And Romance Volume 3. *(commercial 45 version)*
   (S) (3:38)   Thump 4720 Old School Love Songs Volume 2. *(commercial 45 version)*
   (S) (3:39)   Rhino 72135 Billboard Hot R&B Hits 1980. *(commercial 45 version)*
   (S) (4:12)   Polydor 314529665 Best Of. *(LP version)*
   (S) (3:37)   Rebound 314520370 Soul Classics - Quiet Storm/The 80's. *(commercial 45 version)*
   (S) (3:38)   Rhino 72580 Soul Serenade - Intimate R&B. *(commercial 45 version)*
   (S) (3:41)   Time-Life R103-18 Great Love Songs Of The '70s & '80s. *(dj 45 version without rap in the introduction)*
   (S) (4:14)   Time-Life R834-08 Body Talk - On My Mind. *(LP version)*
   (S) (3:37)   Beast 53442 Original Players Of Love. *(commercial 45 version)*
   (S) (4:02)   Priority 53108 Slow Grind Volume One. *(live)*

RAY J
1997 LET IT GO
   (S) (4:52)   EastWest 61951 O.S.T. Set It Off.

RAYS
1957 SILHOUETTES
   (M) (2:41)   Original Sound 8854 Oldies But Goodies Vol. 4. *(this compact disc uses the "Waring - fds" noise reduction process)*
   (M) (2:41)   Original Sound 2221 Oldies But Goodies Volumes 1,4,6,8 and 10 Box Set. *(this box set uses the "Waring - fds" noise reduction process)*
   (M) (2:41)   Original Sound 2500 Oldies But Goodies Volumes 1-15 Box Set. *(this box set uses the "Waring - fds" noise reduction process)*
   (M) (2:40)   Original Sound 8905r 13 Of The Best Doo Wop Love Songs.
   (M) (2:40)   Original Sound 9326 Best Love Songs Vol. 1 & 2.
   (M) (2:40)   Original Sound 4001 Art Laboe's 60 Killer Oldies.
   (M) (2:40)   Original Sound 1236 Best Love Songs Box Set.

CHRIS REA
1978 FOOL (IF YOU THINK IT'S OVER)
   (S) (4:03)   Atco 91732 Best Of/New Light Through Old Windows. *(rerecording)*
   (S) (4:03)   EastWest 61758 Best Of. *(rerecording)*

READY FOR THE WORLD
1985 OH SHEILA
   (S) (3:59)   MCA Special Products 20767 Classic R&B Oldies From The 80's Volume 3. *(LP version)*
   (S) (3:37)   Rhino 71640 Billboard Top Hits - 1985. *(45 version)*
   (S) (3:59)   Thump 4020 Old School Volume 2. *(LP version)*
   (S) (3:59)   MCA 11218 On The Beat - 80's Jams Vol. II. *(LP version)*
   (S) (4:00)   MCA 5594 Ready For The World. *(LP version)*
   (S) (4:00)   MCA 10905 Greatest Hits. *(LP version)*
   (S) (3:38)   Time-Life R988-12 Sounds Of The 80's: 1985-1986. *(45 version)*
   (S) (3:37)   Madacy Entertainment 1985 Rock On 1985. *(45 version)*
   (S) (4:00)   MCA Special Products 21034 Club Disco Dance Hits. *(LP version)*
   (S) (4:00)   K-Tel 3866 The 80's: Number One Pop Hits. *(LP version)*
   (S) (4:00)   Hip-O 40080 Essential '80s: 1985-1989. *(LP version)*
   (S) (3:52)   Cold Front 6330 Club Mix: The 80s. *(all selections on this cd are segued together)*
   (S) (3:59)   Priority 50940 Shut Up And Dance! The 80's Volume One. *(all selections on this cd are segued together)*
1986 DIGITAL DISPLAY
   (S) (5:35)   MCA 5594 Ready For The World. *(LP version)*
   (S) (5:35)   MCA 10905 Greatest Hits. *(LP version)*
   (S) (5:32)   Thump 4060 Old School Volume 6. *(LP version; all selections on this cd are segued together)*
1987 LOVE YOU DOWN
   (S) (6:30)   MCA 11217 Quiet Storms - 80's Jams Vol. I. *(LP version)*
   (S) (6:29)   MCA 5829 Long Time Coming. *(LP version)*
   (S) (6:29)   MCA 10905 Greatest Hits. *(LP version)*
   (S) (6:28)   Thump 4720 Old School Love Songs Volume 2. *(LP version)*
   (S) (6:28)   Rhino 71865 Smooth Grooves Volume 7. *(LP version)*
   (S) (4:00)   Rhino 72141 Billboard Hot R&B Hits 1986. *(45 version)*
   (S) (6:29)   Madacy Entertainment 1987 Rock On 1987. *(LP version)*
   (S) (4:01)   K-Tel 3673 The 80's - Funky Love. *(45 version)*
   (S) (4:03)   Hip-O 40031 The Glory Of Love - '80s Sweet & Soulful Love Songs. *(45 version)*

(S) (6:29) Rhino 72977 Smooth Grooves - New Jack Ballads
            Volume 1. *(LP version)*
(S) (3:59) Time-Life R834-12 Body Talk - By Candlelight.
            (45 version)

REAL LIFE
1984 SEND ME AN ANGEL
(S) (6:12) Curb 77651 Retro Rock Dance Hits. *(all
            selections on this cd are remixed with extra
            instrumentation added)*
(S) (3:53) Rhino 71974 New Wave Hits Of The 80's Vol. 11.
(S) (3:53) Hip-O 40022 That Sound From Down Under.
1989 SEND ME AN ANGEL '89
(S) (3:49) Curb 77532 Your Favorite Songs.
(S) (3:49) Curb 10614 Send Me An Angel '89.
(S) (6:13) Curb 10614 Send Me An Angel '89. *(remix)*
(S) (6:12) K-Tel 3473 The 80s: New Wave. *(remix)*
(S) (6:12) Curb 77934 Absolute Dance Hits: How Do I Live.
            (all songs on this cd are remixed)

REAL McCOY
1994 ANOTHER NIGHT
(S) (3:56) Arista 18778 Another Night. *(tracks into next
            selection)*
(S) (3:50) Arista 18943 Ultimate Dance Party 1997. *(all
            selections on this cd are segued together)*
1995 RUN AWAY
(S) (4:03) Arista 18778 Another Night.
(S) (3:48) Tommy Boy 1164 MTV Party To Go Volume 9.
            (remix; all selections on this cd are segued together)
(S) (4:03) EMI-Capitol Music Group 54547 Hot Luv.
1995 COME AND GET YOUR LOVE
(S) (3:13) Arista 19778 Another Night.
(S) (3:47) Cold Front 6242 Club Mix '97. *(all selections on
            this cd are segued together; remix)*
1997 ONE MORE TIME
(S) (3:58) Arista 18965 One More Time.
(S) (3:50) Arista 18988 Ultimate Dance Party 1998. *(all
            selections on this cd are segued together)*

REBELS
1963 WILD WEEKEND
(M) (2:16) Forevermore 5001 Wild Weekend.
(M) (2:14) Rhino 71602 Rock Instrumental Classics Volume
            2: The Sixties.
(M) (2:14) Rhino 72035 Rock Instrumental Classics Vols. 1-
            5 Box Set.
(M) (2:13) Time-Life 2RNR-19 Rock 'N' Roll Era - 1963 Still
            Rockin'.
(M) (2:13) Time-Life R102-17 Lost Treasures Of Rock 'N' Roll.

REDBONE
1972 THE WITCH QUEEN OF NEW ORLEANS
(S) (2:45) Rhino 70927 Super Hits Of The 70's Volume 7.
(S) (2:55) Columbia/Legacy 46160 Rock Artifacts Volume
            1. *(neither the LP or 45 version.)*
(S) (2:42) DCC Compact Classics 050 Monster Rock 'n' Roll
            Show. *(tracks into next selection)*
(M) (2:43) Time-Life SOD-32 Sounds Of The Seventies -
            AM Pop Classics.
(S) (2:55) Risky Business 66391 Ghastly Grooves. *(neither
            the 45 or LP version)*
(S) (3:34) Curb 77746 Greatest Songs. *(rerecording)*
(S) (2:43) Collectables 5802 Golden Classics.
(S) (2:55) K-Tel 4033 Ghasty Grooves. *(neither the 45 or
            LP version)*
1974 COME AND GET YOUR LOVE
(S) (4:57) Columbia/Legacy 46763 Rock Artifacts Volume
            2. *(LP version)*
(S) (3:30) Rhino 70635 Billboard's Top Rock & Roll Hits Of
            1974. *(45 version)*
(S) (3:31) Rhino 70759 Super Hits Of The 70's Volume 12.
            (45 version)
(S) (4:57) Sandstone 33002 Reelin' In The Years Volume 3.
            (LP version)

(S) (4:57) Epic 32462 Wovoka. *(LP version)*
(S) (4:57) DCC Compact Classics 064 Rock Of The 70's
            Volume Three. *(LP version)*
(S) (3:30) Time-Life SOD-07 Sounds Of The Seventies -
            1974. *(45 version)*
(S) (3:29) Curb 77746 Greatest Songs. *(rerecording)*
(S) (3:30) Collectables 5802 Golden Classics. *(45 version)*
(S) (3:31) Time-Life AM1-21 AM Gold - 1974. *(45 version)*
(S) (3:31) Time-Life R840-03 Sounds Of The Seventies -
            Pop Nuggets: Early '70s. *(45 version)*
(S) (3:30) Collectables 1516 and 2516 The Anniversary
            Album - The 70's. *(45 version)*

GENE REDDING
1974 THIS HEART

OTIS REDDING
1965 I'VE BEEN LOVING YOU TOO LONG (TO STOP NOW)
(M) (2:52) Atlantic Group 88218 Complete Stax/Volt
            Singles. *(45 version)*
(M) (3:11) Atlantic 81297 Atlantic Rhythm & Blues Volume
            5. *(LP version)*
(S) (3:11) Warner Special Products 27615 Atlantic Soul
            Classics. *(LP version)*
(M) (2:53) Atco 80318 Otis Blue. *(45 version)*
(S) (3:11) Atlantic 81762 Otis Redding Story. *(LP version)*
(S) (3:12) Warner Special Products 27608 Ultimate. *(LP
            version)*
(S) (3:11) Atlantic 82305 Atlantic Rhythm And Blues 1947-
            1974 Box Set. *(LP version)*
(M) (2:53) Rhino 71147 Very Best Of. *(45 version)*
(M) (2:52) Rhino 71430 Respect. *(45 version)*
(M) (2:53) Rhino 71439 The Definitive. *(45 version)*
(S) (4:08) Rhino 71439 The Definitive. *(live)*
(S) (3:10) Time-Life RHD-07 Rhythm & Blues - 1965. *(LP
            version)*
(S) (3:10) Time-Life 2CLR-08 Classic Rock - 1965: The
            Beat Goes On. *(LP version)*
(S) (3:12) Right Stuff 27306 Slow Jams: The 60's Volume
            One. *(LP version)*
(S) (3:10) Ripete 2198 Soul Patrol. *(LP version)*
(S) (3:10) Time-Life R838-12 Solid Gold Soul - 1965. *(LP
            version)*
(M) (2:53) Flashback 72662 I've Been Loving You Too Long
            And Other Hits. *(45 version)*
(M) (2:53) Flashback 72083 Kings And Queens Of Soul Box
            Set. *(45 version)*
(M) (2:53) Rhino 72815 Beg, Scream & Shout! The Big Ol'
            Box Of '60s Soul. *(45 version)*
(M) (2:53) Flashback 72895 25 Years Of R&B - 1965. *(45
            version)*
(M) (2:53) Rhino 72955 Love Songs. *(45 version)*
(M) (2:52) Time-Life R857-20 The Heart Of Rock 'n' Roll
            1965-1966. *(45 version)*
1965 RESPECT
(M) (2:06) Atlantic Group 88218 Complete Stax/Volt
            Singles. *(45 version)*
(S) (2:05) JCI 3100 Dance Sixties. *(several dropouts on the
            introduction; LP version)*
(M) (2:04) Atlantic 81297 Atlantic Rhythm & Blues Volume
            5. *(45 version)*
(M) (2:04) Stax 88008 Top Of The Stax Volume 2. *(45
            version)*
(M) (2:04) Atco 80318 Otis Blue. *(45 version)*
(S) (2:05) Atlantic 81762 Otis Redding Story. *(LP version)*
(S) (2:06) Warner Special Products 27608 Ultimate. *(LP
            version)*
(M) (2:04) Atlantic 82305 Atlantic Rhythm And Blues 1947-
            1974 Box Set. *(45 version)*
(M) (1:53) Stax 8572 Remember Me. *(alternate take)*
(M) (2:07) Rhino 71147 Very Best Of. *(45 version)*
(M) (2:06) Rhino 71430 Respect. *(45 version)*
(M) (2:08) Rhino 71439 The Definitive. *(45 version)*
(S) (3:04) Rhino 71439 The Definitive. *(live)*
(S) (2:04) Time-Life 2CLR-23 Classic Rock - 1965: Blowin'
            Your Mind. *(LP version)*

OTIS REDDING (Continued)

(M) (2:07) Rhino 71728 '60s Rock Classics, Vol. 1. (45 version)

(M) (2:07) Flashback 72701 '60s Rock: Mony Mony. (45 version)

(M) (2:07) Flashback 72088 '60s Rock Hits Box Set. (45 version)

(M) (2:08) Flashback 72662 I've Been Loving You Too Long And Other Hits. (45 version)

(M) (2:08) Flashback 72083 Kings And Queens Of Soul Box Set. (45 version)

(M) (2:08) Flashback 72895 25 Years Of R&B - 1965. (45 version)

1966 SATISFACTION

(M) (2:43) Atlantic Group 88218 Complete Stax/Volt Singles.

(M) (2:43) Atco 80318 Otis Blue.

(S) (2:43) Atlantic 81762 Otis Redding Story.

(S) (2:45) Warner Special Products 27608 Ultimate.

(M) (2:43) Rhino 71147 Very Best Of.

(M) (2:43) Rhino 71430 Respect.

(M) (2:43) Rhino 71439 The Definitive.

(S) (2:56) Rhino 71439 The Definitive. (live)

(M) (2:52) Rhino 72478 Beverly Hills 90210: Songs From The Peach Pit.

(M) (2:52) Flashback 72662 I've Been Loving You Too Long And Other Hits.

(M) (2:52) Flashback 72083 Kings And Queens Of Soul Box Set.

(M) (2:43) Hip-O 40078 Cover You: A Tribute To The Rolling Stones.

1966 FA-FA-FA-FA-FA (SAD SONG)

(M) (2:40) Atlantic Group 88218 Complete Stax/Volt Singles. (truncated fade)

(S) (2:38) Atlantic 81762 Otis Redding Story.

(M) (2:39) Atco 91707 Dictionary Of Soul.

(M) (2:39) Warner Special Products 27608 Ultimate.

(M) (2:39) Rhino 71147 Very Best Of. (truncated fade)

(M) (2:39) Rhino 71439 The Definitive.

(S) (4:08) Rhino 71439 The Definitive. (live)

(S) (2:38) Time-Life 2CLR-25 Classic Rock - On The Soul Side.

(M) (2:39) MCA 11389 O.S.T. Casino.

1967 TRY A LITTLE TENDERNESS
(45 length is (3:17); LP length is (3:46))

(M) (3:17) Atlantic Group 88218 Complete Stax/Volt Singles.

(S) (3:46) JCI 3105 Soul Sixties.

(S) (3:47) Atlantic 81298 Atlantic Rhythm & Blues Volume 6.

(S) (3:46) Warner Special Products 27609 Memphis Soul Classics.

(M) (3:46) Atco 91813 Classic Recordings.

(S) (3:46) Atlantic 81762 Otis Redding Story.

(M) (3:46) Atco 91707 Dictionary Of Soul.

(S) (3:48) Warner Special Products 27608 Ultimate.

(S) (3:47) Atlantic 82305 Atlantic Rhythm And Blues 1947-1974 Box Set.

(S) (3:59) Stax 8572 Remember Me. (alternate take; 2 severe dropouts on the introduction)

(M) (3:17) Rhino 71147 Very Best Of.

(M) (3:17) Rhino 71459 Soul Hits, Volume 1.

(M) (3:46) Rhino 71439 The Definitive.

(S) (5:14) Rhino 71439 The Definitive. (live)

(S) (3:42) Time-Life RHD-01 Rhythm & Blues - 1966.

(S) (3:44) Time-Life 2CLR-24 Classic Rock - 1967: Blowin' Your Mind.

(M) (3:18) Right Stuff 28371 Slow Jams: The 60's Volume Two.

(M) (3:17) Rhino 71806 The R&B Box: Thirty Years Of Rhythm & Blues.

(S) (3:44) JCI 3161 18 Soul Hits From The 60's.

(S) (3:42) JCI 3164 Eighteen Soulful Ballads.

(S) (3:42) Time-Life R838-01 Solid Gold Soul - 1966.

(M) (3:17) Flashback 72657 '60s Soul: Try A Little Tenderness.

(M) (3:17) Flashback 72091 '60s Soul Hits Box Set.

(M) (3:17) Flashback 72896 25 Years Of R&B - 1966.

(M) (3:46) Rhino 72955 Love Songs.

(M) (3:17) Rhino 72963 Ultimate '60s Soul Smashes.

(M) (3:46) Time-Life R857-22 The Heart Of Rock 'n' Roll 1967-1969.

released as by OTIS & CARLA (OTIS REDDING & CARLA THOMAS):
1967 TRAMP

(M) (2:59) Atlantic Group 88218 Complete Stax/Volt Singles.

(S) (2:59) Atlantic 81762 Otis Redding Story.

(S) (2:59) Atco 80254 Otis Redding - The Dock Of The Bay.

(S) (2:59) Atlantic 82256 Otis Redding & Carla Thomas: King & Queen.

(S) (2:57) Warner Special Products 27608 Ultimate Otis Redding.

(S) (2:59) Atlantic 82305 Atlantic Rhythm And Blues 1947-1974 Box Set.

(M) (2:58) Rhino 71147 Otis Redding - Very Best Of.

(M) (2:59) Rhino 71439 The Definitive Otis Redding.

(M) (2:50) Time-Life RHD-10 Rhythm & Blues - 1967.

(S) (2:56) Time-Life 2CLR-15 Classic Rock - 1967: Shakin' All Over.

(M) (2:59) Rhino 71754 and 72831 Phat Trax: The Best Of Old School Volume 3.

(M) (2:59) Rhino 71633 Gee Whiz - Best Of Carla Thomas.

(M) (2:50) Time-Life R838-02 Solid Gold Soul - 1967.

(M) (3:00) Flashback 72669 Carla Thomas - Gee Whiz And Other Hits.

(M) (3:00) Flashback 72083 Kings And Queens Of Soul Box Set.

(M) (2:59) Flashback 72897 25 Years Of R&B - 1967.

(M) (2:59) Rhino 72962 Ultimate '60s Soul Sensations.

1967 KNOCK ON WOOD

(M) (2:49) Atlantic Group 88218 Complete Stax/Volt Singles.

(S) (2:50) Atlantic 82256 Otis Redding & Carla Thomas: King & Queen.

(S) (2:50) Atlantic 81762 The Otis Redding Story.

(M) (2:49) Flashback 72669 Carla Thomas - Gee Whiz And Other Hits.

(M) (2:49) Flashback 72083 Kings And Queens Of Soul Box Set.

(M) (2:49) Rhino 71930 Otis Redding - Very Best Of Vol. 2.

released as by OTIS REDDING:
1968 (SITTIN' ON) THE DOCK OF THE BAY

(M) (2:38) Atlantic Group 88218 Complete Stax/Volt Singles.

(M) (2:41) Atlantic 81298 Atlantic Rhythm & Blues Volume 6.

(E) (2:41) Atlantic 81742 O.S.T. Platoon.

(S) (2:41) Atlantic 81911 Golden Age Of Black Music (1960-1970).

(S) (2:39) Stax 88005 Top Of The Stax.

(S) (2:40) Atlantic 81762 Otis Redding Story.

(S) (2:41) Atco 80254 The Dock Of The Bay.

(S) (2:40) Warner Special Products 27608 Ultimate.

(S) (2:40) Atlantic 82305 Atlantic Rhythm And Blues 1947-1974 Box Set.

(S) (2:58) Stax 8572 Remember Me. (includes :07 of studio talk; alternate take)

(S) (2:42) Stax 8572 Remember Me. (includes a :02 countoff; alternate take)

(M) (2:38) Rhino 71147 Very Best Of.

(M) (2:39) Rhino 71460 Soul Hits, Volume 2.

(M) (2:37) Rhino 71439 The Definitive.

(S) (2:39) Time-Life RHD-04 Rhythm & Blues - 1968.

(M) (2:41) Time-Life 2CLR-04 Classic Rock - 1968.

(S) (2:40) Time-Life SUD-02 Superhits - 1968.

(S) (2:39) JCI 3126 1965 - Only Rock 'N Roll - 1969.

(S) (2:40) Time-Life AM1-04 AM Gold - 1968.

(S) (2:39) Time-Life R838-03 Solid Gold Soul - 1968.

(M) (2:38) Flashback 72658 '60s Soul: Baby I Love You.

(M) (2:38) Flashback 72091 '60s Soul Hits Box Set.

(M) (2:38) Flashback 72898 25 Years Of R&B - 1968.

(M) (2:44) Rhino 72962 Ultimate '60s Soul Sensations.

(S) (2:40) Simitar 55572 The Number One's: Hot In The '60s.

(S) (2:41) Atlantic 83088 Atlantic Records: 50 Years - The Gold Anniversary Collection.

1968 THE HAPPY SONG (DUM-DUM)

(M) (2:41) Atlantic Group 88218 Complete Stax/Volt Singles.

(S) (2:37) Atlantic 81762 Otis Redding Story.
(S) (2:40) Atco 80270 The Immortal Otis Redding.
(M) (2:41) Rhino 71147 Very Best Of.
(M) (2:40) Rhino 71439 The Definitive.
(S) (2:35) Time-Life 2CLR-27 Classic Rock - 1968: Blowin' Your Mind.

1968 AMEN
(S) (3:01) Atlantic 81762 Otis Redding Story.
(S) (3:02) Atco 80270 The Immortal Otis Redding.
(M) (3:03) Rhino 71439 The Definitive.
(M) (3:03) Rhino 71930 Very Best Of Vol. 2.

1968 I'VE GOT DREAMS TO REMEMBER
(S) (3:13) Atco 91813 Classic Recordings.
(S) (3:11) Atlantic 81762 Otis Redding Story.
(S) (3:14) Atco 80270 The Immortal Otis Redding.
(M) (3:12) Rhino 71147 Very Best Of.
(M) (3:12) Rhino 71439 The Definitive.

1968 PAPA'S GOT A BRAND NEW BAG
(M) (2:29) Atlantic 81762 Otis Redding Story. *(45 version)*
(M) (4:57) Rhino 71439 The Definitive. *(LP version)*
(M) (2:30) Rhino 71930 Very Best Of Vol. 2. *(45 version)*
(M) (2:30) Flashback 72899 25 Years Of Soul - 1969. *(45 version)*

HELEN REDDY
1971 I DON'T KNOW HOW TO LOVE HIM
(S) (3:15) Capitol 46490 Greatest Hits (And More).
(S) (3:15) Pair 1066 Lust For Life.
(S) (3:15) Capitol 55903 All-Time Greatest Hits.

1972 I AM WOMAN
(S) (3:22) Capitol 46490 Greatest Hits (And More).
(S) (3:19) Pair 1066 Lust For Life.
(S) (3:20) Razor & Tie 21640 Those Fabulous 70's.
(S) (3:22) Nick At Nite/550 Music 67690 I Am Woman.
(S) (3:20) Capitol 55903 All-Time Greatest Hits.

1973 PEACEFUL
(S) (2:49) Capitol 46490 Greatest Hits (And More).
(S) (2:49) Capitol 55903 All-Time Greatest Hits.

1973 DELTA DAWN
(S) (3:06) Capitol 46490 Greatest Hits (And More).
(S) (3:06) Pair 1066 Lust For Life.
(S) (3:06) Capitol 98665 When AM Was King.
(S) (3:05) Time-Life SUD-13 Superhits - 1973.
(S) (3:06) Capitol 55903 All-Time Greatest Hits.
(S) (3:05) Time-Life AM1-03 AM Gold - 1973.

1974 LEAVE ME ALONE (RUBY RED DRESS)
(S) (3:24) Pair 1066 Lust For Life.
(S) (3:24) Capitol 46490 Greatest Hits (And More).
(S) (3:24) Capitol 55903 All-Time Greatest Hits.
(S) (3:22) Rhino 72739 Billboard Top Soft Rock Hits - 1973.

1974 KEEP ON SINGING
(S) (3:02) Capitol 46490 Greatest Hits (And More).

1974 YOU AND ME AGAINST THE WORLD
(S) (3:09) Capitol 46490 Greatest Hits (And More).
(S) (3:09) Capitol 55903 All-Time Greatest Hits.

1974 ANGIE BABY
(S) (3:26) Pair 1066 Lust For Life.
(S) (3:27) Capitol 46490 Greatest Hits (And More).
(S) (3:27) Capitol 55903 All-Time Greatest Hits.
(S) (3:26) Time-Life AM1-21 AM Gold - 1974.
(S) (3:25) Rhino 72740 Billboard Top Soft Rock Hits - 1974.

1975 EMOTION
(S) (4:08) Pair 1066 Lust For Life. *(LP version)*
(S) (2:51) Capitol 46490 Greatest Hits (And More). *(45 version)*

1975 BLUEBIRD
1975 AIN'T NO WAY TO TREAT A LADY
(S) (3:25) Pair 1066 Lust For Life.
(S) (3:25) Capitol 46490 Greatest Hits (And More).
(S) (3:24) Capitol 55903 All-Time Greatest Hits.
(S) (3:25) Priority 53140 Best Of The 70's: Legendary Ladies.

1976 SOMEWHERE IN THE NIGHT
(S) (3:26) Pair 1066 Lust For Life.

(S) (3:26) Capitol 46490 Greatest Hits (And More).
(S) (3:26) Capitol 55903 All-Time Greatest Hits.

1976 I CAN'T HEAR YOU NO MORE
(S) (2:46) Capitol 46490 Greatest Hits (And More).

1977 YOU'RE MY WORLD
(S) (2:41) Pair 1066 Lust For Life.
(S) (2:42) Capitol 46490 Greatest Hits (And More).
(S) (2:42) Capitol 55903 All-Time Greatest Hits.

REDEYE
1971 GAMES
(S) (3:00) Rhino 70925 Super Hits Of The 70's Volume 5. *(LP version)*

RED HOT CHILI PEPPERS
1992 UNDER THE BRIDGE
(S) (4:24) Warner Brothers 26681 Blood, Sugar, Sex, Magik.

1993 SOUL TO SQUEEZE
(S) (4:50) Warner Brothers 45345 O.S.T. Coneheads.

REDMAN/METHOD MAN
1995 HOW HIGH
(M) (4:39) Def Jam 314529021 and 314529068 O.S.T. The Show.
(M) (3:58) Def Jam 314523848 Def Jam Music Group 10th Year Anniversary.
(M) (4:00) Rebound 314520449 Hip Hop With R&B Flava.
(M) (3:56) Def Jam 314536377 Def Jam's Greatest Hits.

REDNEX
1995 COTTON EYE JOE
(S) (3:10) Battery 46000 Sex & Violins.
(S) (3:09) Quality 5008 Dance Box Set. *(all selections on this cd are segued together)*
(S) (2:54) Tommy Boy 1214 Jock Jams Volume 3. *(all selections on this cd are segued together)*
(S) (4:39) Beast 53022 Club Hitz Of The 90's Vol. 1. *(all songs on this cd are segued together)*
(S) (3:10) K-Tel 4065 K-Tel's Original Party Music Vol. 1.
(S) (3:10) Rebound 314520522 Rockin' Sports Jams.
(S) (3:08) Priority 50935 100% Party Hits Of The 90's Volume Two. *(all selections on this cd are segued together)*

JERRY REED
1971 AMOS MOSES
(S) (2:19) Rhino 70923 Super Hits Of The 70's Volume 3.
(S) (2:19) Rhino 72009 Super Hits Of The 70's Volumes 1-4 Box Set.
(S) (2:17) RCA 8476 and 9684 Nipper's Greatest Hits Of The 70's.
(S) (2:15) RCA 54109 Best Of.
(S) (2:18) RCA 66592 Essential.
(S) (2:17) RCA 66818 The Essential Series Sampler.
(S) (2:17) RCA 67406 Super Hits.
(S) (2:17) Collectables 2702 When You're Hot, You're Hot/Ko-Ko-Joe.

1971 WHEN YOU'RE HOT, YOU'RE HOT
(S) (2:18) Rhino 70925 Super Hits Of The 70's Volume 5.
(S) (2:16) RCA 54109 Best Of.
(S) (2:18) Time-Life CTD-05 Country USA - 1971.
(S) (2:18) Time-Life CCD-06 Contemporary Country - The Early 70's.
(S) (2:16) K-Tel 3111 Country Music Classics Vol. XIX.
(S) (2:18) Rhino 72125 Dr. Demento's Country Corn.
(S) (2:18) RCA 66592 Essential.
(S) (2:16) Hollywood 62077 Official Party Album - ABC's Monday Night Football.
(S) (2:17) RCA 67406 Super Hits.
(S) (2:14) Collectables 2702 When You're Hot, You're Hot/Ko-Ko-Joe.
(S) (2:17) Time-Life R830-03 The Dr. Demento Collection: The Early '70s.
(S) (2:18) Hip-O 40085 The Class Of Country 1970-1974.
(S) (2:18) Time-Life R808-04 Classic Country 1970-1974.

JIMMY REED
1957 HONEST I DO
- (M) (2:39) Time-Life RHD-08 Rhythm & Blues - 1957.
- (M) (2:44) Tel-Star 3502 Best Of.
- (M) (2:41) Sire 26617 O.S.T. A Rage In Harlem.
- (E) (2:43) Stax 8551 Superblues Vol. 1.
- (M) (2:43) DCC Compact Classics 026 The Real Blues Brothers.
- (M) (2:44) Vee-Jay 705 Speak The Lyrics To Me, Mama Reed.
- (M) (2:44) K-Tel 3345 Got The Blues.
- (M) (2:42) Collectables 5129 Collectables Blues Collection Vol. 3. *(no fidelity)*
- (M) (2:43) Time-Life R859-04 Living The Blues: 1957-1959 Blues Classics.
- (M) (2:39) Time-Life R838-23 Solid Gold Soul 1957.

1960 BABY WHAT YOU WANT ME TO DO
- (M) (2:17) Time-Life 2RNR-41 The Rock 'N' Roll Era - R&B Gems.
- (S) (2:25) Tel-Star 3502 Best Of.
- (S) (2:26) DCC Compact Classics 026 The Real Blues Brothers.
- (M) (2:22) Rhino 71128 Blues Masters Volume 7.
- (S) (2:23) Original Sound 8861 Oldies But Goodies Vol. 11. *(this compact disc uses the "Waring - fds" noise reduction process)*
- (S) (2:23) Original Sound 2222 Oldies But Goodies Volumes 3,5,11,14 and 15 Box Set. *(this box set uses the "Waring - fds" noise reduction process)*
- (S) (2:23) Original Sound 2500 Oldies But Goodies Volumes 1-15 Box Set. *(this box set uses the "Waring - fds" noise reduction process)*
- (M) (2:21) Tomato 71660 The Classic Recordings.
- (M) (2:22) Vee-Jay 705 Speak The Lyrics To Me, Mama Reed.
- (M) (2:22) Time-Life R859-02 Living The Blues - Blues Masters.
- (M) (2:22) K-Tel 528 Blues Classics.
- (M) (2:22) Collectables 5128 Collectables Blues Collection Volume 2.
- (M) (2:21) Platinum Entertainment 514161183 Essential Blues 2.

LOU REED
1973 WALK ON THE WILD SIDE
- (S) (4:09) Priority 7997 Super Songs/70's Greatest Rock Hits Volume 8. *(LP version)*
- (S) (4:11) RCA 3753 Walk On The Wild Side: The Best Of. *(LP version)*
- (S) (4:09) RCA 52162 Walk On The Wild Side & Other Hits. *(LP version)*
- (S) (4:12) RCA 2356 Between Thought And Expression. *(LP version)*
- (S) (4:11) Polydor 314515913 Classic Rock Box. *(LP version)*
- (S) (4:55) Special Music 1024 Wild Child. *(live)*
- (S) (4:10) Razor & Tie 22502 Those Rocking 70's. *(LP version)*
- (S) (4:08) Time-Life R102-34 The Rolling Stone Collection. *(LP version)*
- (S) (4:11) Time-Life SOD-06 Sounds Of The Seventies - 1973. *(LP version)*
- (S) (4:10) Epic/Legacy 65020 Ultimate Rock 'n' Roll Collection. *(LP version)*
- (S) (4:11) RCA 66864 Different Times: Lou Reed In The 70's. *(LP version)*
- (S) (4:10) Simitar 55582 The Number One's: Rock It Up. *(LP version)*

DELLA REESE
1957 AND THAT REMINDS ME
- (M) (2:27) Time-Life HPD-38 Your Hit Parade - The 50's Generation.
- (M) (2:28) Collector's Choice 7190 And That Reminds Me.
- (S) (2:30) Varese Sarabande 5907 The Della Reese Collection. *(rerecording)*

1959 DON'T YOU KNOW
- (S) (2:31) RCA 8467 Nipper's Greatest Hits Of The 50's Volume 2.
- (S) (2:31) Epic 57560 O.S.T. A Bronx Tale.
- (S) (2:30) Time-Life RHD-03 Rhythm & Blues - 1959.
- (S) (2:32) Time-Life HPD-13 Your Hit Parade - 1959.
- (S) (2:31) Time-Life R974-11 Many Moods Of Romance - With A Song In My Heart.
- (S) (2:32) RCA 66917 Voice Of An Angel.
- (S) (2:30) Time-Life R857-11 The Heart Of Rock 'n' Roll 1958-1959.
- (S) (2:30) Time-Life R838-21 Solid Gold Soul 1959.
- (S) (2:31) Time-Life R857-21 The Heart Of Rock 'n' Roll Slow Dancing Classics.

1960 NOT ONE MINUTE MORE
- (M) (2:36) Time-Life HPD-37 Your Hit Parade - The 60's.

JIM REEVES
1957 FOUR WALLS
- (M) (2:49) RCA 8467 Nipper's Greatest Hits Of The 50's Volume 2.
- (M) (2:49) RCA 2493 Four Walls - The Legend Begins.
- (M) (2:49) RCA 3936 Pure Gold Volume 1.
- (M) (2:49) RCA 58451 Best Of.
- (M) (2:49) RCA 52301 He'll Have To Go And Other Favorites.
- (M) (2:50) RCA 66125 Welcome To My World: The Essential Collection.
- (M) (2:49) Special Music 2652 I Guess I'm Crazy.
- (E) (2:49) Time-Life CTD-02 Country USA - 1957.
- (M) (2:50) Time-Life HPD-23 Your Hit Parade - The Late 50's.
- (M) (2:49) RCA 58404 Pure Gold, Volume 1.
- (M) (2:48) RCA 66589 Essential.
- (M) (2:47) RCA 66818 The Essential Series Sampler.
- (M) (2:49) Time-Life R990-11 Jim Reeves - Legendary Country Singers.
- (M) (2:49) Time-Life R857-05 The Heart Of Rock 'n' Roll 1957.
- (M) (2:49) Time-Life R808-03 Classic Country 1950-1959.

1960 HE'LL HAVE TO GO
- (S) (2:19) RCA 8466 Nipper's Greatest Hits Of The 50's Volume 1.
- (S) (2:19) RCA 58451 Best Of.
- (S) (2:19) RCA 52301 He'll Have To Go And Other Favorites.
- (S) (2:19) RCA 66125 Welcome To My World: The Essential Collection.
- (S) (2:18) Time-Life CTD-09 Country USA - 1959.
- (S) (2:18) Time-Life HPD-13 Your Hit Parade - 1959.
- (S) (2:17) Time-Life R103-27 Love Me Tender.
- (S) (2:19) K-Tel 3108 Country Music Classics Volume XVI.
- (S) (2:17) Varese Sarabande 5606 Through The Years - Country Hits Of The 60's.
- (S) (2:17) RCA 66589 Essential.
- (S) (2:18) Time-Life R857-02 The Heart Of Rock 'n' Roll - 1960.
- (S) (2:18) K-Tel 3358 101 Greatest Country Hits Vol. Four: Mellow Country.
- (S) (2:17) Time-Life R990-11 Jim Reeves - Legendary Country Singers.
- (S) (2:17) Time-Life R814-05 Love Songs.
- (S) (2:17) Time-Life R808-01 Classic Country 1960-1964.

1960 AM I LOSING YOU
- (M) (2:43) RCA 2493 Four Walls - The Legend Begins. *(1957 country & western chart hit version)*
- (S) (2:15) RCA 58451 Best Of. *(1960 pop chart hit version)*
- (S) (2:15) RCA 52301 He'll Have To Go And Other Favorites. *(1960 pop chart hit version)*
- (S) (2:15) RCA 66125 Welcome To My World: The Essential Collection. *(1960 pop chart hit version)*
- (E) (2:16) Special Music 2652 I Guess I'm Crazy. *(1960 pop chart hit version)*
- (S) (2:16) Time-Life CTD-02 Country USA - 1957. *(1960 pop chart hit version)*
- (S) (2:31) RCA 66589 Essential. *(rerecording)*
- (M) (2:42) Time-Life R990-11 Jim Reeves - Legendary Country Singers. *(1957 country & western chart hit version)*

REFLECTIONS
1964 (JUST LIKE) ROMEO & JULIET
    (M) (2:18) Time-Life 2CLR-09 Classic Rock - 1964: The Beat Goes On.
    (S) (2:18) Varese Sarabande 5847 On The Radio Volume Two.
    (M) (2:16) Collectables 1515 and 2515 The Anniversary Album - The 60's.

RE-FLEX
1984 THE POLITICS OF DANCING
    (S) (3:54) EMI 81417 Living In Oblivion: The 80's Greatest Hits Volume One. *(45 version)*
    (S) (3:54) Priority 53684 Rock Of The 80's Volume 4. *(45 version)*
    (S) (6:34) K-Tel 3262 The 80's Video Stars. *(LP version)*
    (S) (3:55) Rhino 71975 New Wave Hits Of The 80's Vol. 12. *(45 version)*
    (S) (6:32) Rebound 314520354 World Of Dance: New Wave - The 80's. *(LP version)*
    (S) (3:54) Time-Life R988-17 Sounds Of The Eighties: The Mid '80s Take Two. *(45 version)*
    (S) (6:32) Simitar 55552 The Number One's: Eighties Rock. *(LP version)*

REFUGEE CAMP ALL STARS featuring PRAS with KY-MANI
1997 AVENUES
    (S) (4:18) Arista 18975 Money Talks - The Album.

REGENTS
1961 BARBARA ANN
    (M) (2:13) Rhino 70906 American Bandstand Greatest Hits Collection.
    (M) (2:13) Collectables 5403 Barbara-Ann.
    (M) (2:13) Essex 7052 All Time Rock Classics.
    (M) (2:11) MCA 8001 O.S.T. American Graffiti. *(Wolfman Jack talks over the fadeout)*
    (M) (2:12) Rhino 71463 Doo Wop Box.
    (M) (2:16) Time-Life 2RNR-18 Rock 'N' Roll Era - 1961 Still Rockin'.
    (M) (2:16) Collectables 2601 WCBS-FM History Of Rock - The Group Sounds Vol. 2.
    (M) (2:12) Time-Life R102-17 Lost Treasures Of Rock 'N' Roll.
    (M) (2:13) Rhino 72156 Doo Wop Memories, Vol. 1.
    (M) (2:12) Collectables 5483 Spotlite On Gee Records Volume 4.
    (M) (2:13) Flashback 72857 Grease And Other Golden Oldies.
1961 RUNAROUND
    (S) (2:19) Collectables 5403 Barbara-Ann. *(truncated fade)*
    (S) (2:19) Collectables 5462 The Spotlight Series - Gee Records Vol. 1.
    (S) (2:16) Rhino 72507 Doo Wop Box II.

REGINA
1986 BABY LOVE
    (S) (6:29) Atlantic 81746 Dance Traxx Volume 2. *(12" single version)*
    (S) (4:07) Atlantic 81671 Curiosity.
    (S) (3:55) Cold Front 6330 Club Mix: The 80s. *(all selections on this cd are segued together)*

CLARENCE REID
1969 NOBODY BUT YOU BABE
    (M) (2:45) Rhino 71615 In Yo' Face! The Roots Of Funk Vol. 1/2.

R.E.M.
1987 THE ONE I LOVE
    (S) (3:15) IRS 29695 On The Charts: IRS Records 1979-1994.
    (S) (3:15) Sandstone 33042 and 5008 Rock The First Volume 2.
    (S) (3:15) IRS 42059 Document.

    (S) (3:14) Time-Life R988-29 Sounds Of The Eighties: The Rolling Stone Collection 1987-1988.
1989 STAND
    (S) (3:07) JCI 2703 Cutting Edge.
    (S) (3:09) Warner Brothers 25795 Green.
1991 LOSING MY RELIGION
    (S) (4:25) Time-Life R102-34 The Rolling Stone Collection.
    (S) (4:25) Warner Brothers 26496 Out Of Time.
    (S) (4:25) Time-Life R13610 Gold And Platinum Box Set - The Ultimate Rock Collection.
1991 SHINY HAPPY PEOPLE
    (S) (3:43) Warner Brothers 26496 Out Of Time.
1992 DRIVE
    (S) (4:29) Warner Brothers 45055 Automatic For The People.
1993 MAN ON THE MOON
    (S) (5:12) Warner Brothers 45055 Automatic For The People.
1993 EVERYBODY HURTS
    (S) (5:15) Warner Brothers 45055 Automatic For The People.
    (S) (4:56) Columbia 69012 Diana Princess Of Wales Tribute.
1994 WHAT'S THE FREQUENCY, KENNETH?
    (S) (3:58) Warner Brothers 45740 Monster.
1995 BANG AND BLAME
    (S) (5:29) Warner Brothers 45740 Monster.

REMBRANDTS
1991 JUST THE WAY IT IS BABY
    (S) (4:05) JCI 3123 Harvest.
    (S) (4:06) Atco 91412 The Rembrandts.
1995 THIS HOUSE IS NOT A HOME
    (S) (3:16) EastWest 61752 LP.
1995 I'LL BE THERE FOR YOU
    (S) (3:06) EastWest 61752 LP. *(this is track 15 on this cd even though the cd jacket does not list this song as being on this cd at all)*

DIANE RENAY
1964 NAVY BLUE
    (M) (2:25) Time-Life 2RNR-47 Rock 'N' Roll Era - Teen Idols II.
    (M) (2:25) Time-Life SUD-09 Superhits - 1964.
    (M) (2:28) Mercury 314528171 Growin' Up Too Fast - The Girl Group Anthology.
    (M) (2:27) Eric 11503 Hard To Find 45's On CD (Volume II) 1961-64.
    (M) (2:28) Eclipse Music Group 64868 Rock 'n Roll Relix 1962-1963.
    (M) (2:28) Eclipse Music Group 64872 Rock 'n Roll Relix 1960-1969.
    (M) (2:25) Time-Life R857-09 The Heart Of Rock 'n' Roll 1964.
    (M) (2:25) Time-Life AM1-11 AM Gold - 1964.
    (M) (2:26) Collectors' Choice 5189 I Wish I Were A Princess - The Great Lost Female Teen Idols.
    (M) (2:28) Collectables 5877 Navy Blue.
    (M) (2:27) Polygram Special Markets 314520516 45's On CD Volume 1.
1964 KISS ME SAILOR
    (M) (2:48) Mercury 314528171 Growin' Up Too Fast - The Girl Group Anthology.
    (M) (2:48) Collectors' Choice 5189 I Wish I Were A Princess - The Great Lost Female Teen Idols.
    (M) (2:48) Collectables 5877 Navy Blue.

RENE & RENE
1969 LO MUCHO QUE TE QUIERO (THE MORE I LOVE YOU)
    (M) (2:58) Original Sound 1960 Memories Of El Monte.
    (M) (2:58) Original Sound 4001 Art Laboe's 60 Killer Oldies.
    (E) (2:45) Thump 7100 Latin Oldies. *(rerecording)*

MIKE RENO and ANN WILSON
1984 ALMOST PARADISE...LOVE THEME FROM "FOOTLOOSE"
    (S) (3:48) Columbia 39242 O.S.T. Footloose.
    (S) (3:49) Priority 53681 80's Greatest Rock Hits - Agony & Ecstasy.
    (S) (3:38) Madacy Entertainment 6806 Best Of Love.

REO SPEEDWAGON
1981 KEEP ON LOVING YOU
    (S)   (3:19)   Priority 7961 Three Decades Of Rock.
    (S)   (3:20)   Epic 36844 Hi Infidelity.
    (S)   (3:20)   Epic 44202 The Hits.
    (S)   (3:19)   Priority 53714 80's Greatest Rock Hits Volume 1: Passion & Power.
    (S)   (3:19)   Time-Life R968-04 Guitar Rock 1980-1981.
    (S)   (3:19)   Time-Life R105-40 Rock Dreams.
    (S)   (3:19)   CBS Special Products 44363 Rock Of The 80's.
    (S)   (3:19)   Risky Business 57833 Read The Hits/Best Of The 80's.
    (S)   (3:19)   JCI 3119 18 Rock Classics.
    (S)   (3:39)   Epic 48527 The Second Decade Of Rock And Roll 1981-1991. *(live)*
    (S)   (3:19)   Time-Life R988-08 Sounds Of The Eighties: 1981.
    (S)   (3:19)   Epic/Legacy 65020 Ultimate Rock 'n' Roll Collection.
    (S)   (3:19)   JCI 3147 1980 - Only Love - 1984.
    (S)   (3:20)   Time-Life R834-01 Body Talk - Forever Yours.
    (S)   (3:20)   Epic/Legacy 66233 Hi-Infidelity. *(gold disc)*
    (S)   (3:19)   K-Tel 3904 The Rock Album Volume 1.
    (S)   (3:19)   Madacy Entertainment 6806 Best Of Love.
    (S)   (3:20)   Simitar 55502 The Number One's: Classic Rock.
1981 TAKE IT ON THE RUN
    (S)   (3:59)   Epic 36844 Hi Infidelity. *(LP version)*
    (S)   (3:59)   Epic 44202 The Hits. *(LP version)*
    (S)   (3:58)   Time-Life R968-04 Guitar Rock 1980-1981. *(LP version)*
    (S)   (3:35)   JCI 3127 1980 - Only Rock 'N Roll - 1984. *(45 version)*
    (S)   (4:16)   Epic 48527 The Second Decade Of Rock And Roll 1981-1991. *(live)*
    (S)   (3:59)   Time-Life R988-16 Sounds Of The Eighties: The Early '80s. *(LP version)*
    (S)   (3:59)   Epic/Legacy 66233 Hi-Infidelity. *(gold disc; LP version)*
    (S)   (3:35)   Time-Life R13610 Gold And Platinum Box Set - The Ultimate Rock Collection. *(45 version)*
    (S)   (3:34)   Sony Music Special Products 26069 Rock Hits Of The 70's. *(45 version)*
    (S)   (3:58)   JCI 3193 18 Rock Classics Volume 3. *(LP version)*
1981 DON'T LET HIM GO
    (S)   (3:45)   Epic 36844 Hi Infidelity. *(LP length)*
    (S)   (3:45)   Epic 44202 The Hits. *(LP length)*
    (S)   (4:15)   Epic 48527 The Second Decade Of Rock And Roll 1981-1991. *(live)*
    (S)   (3:44)   JCI 3143 18 Screamers From The 80's. *(LP length)*
    (S)   (3:45)   Epic/Legacy 66233 Hi-Infidelity. *(gold disc; LP length)*
1981 IN YOUR LETTER
    (S)   (3:15)   Epic 36844 Hi Infidelity.
    (S)   (3:15)   Epic/Legacy 66233 Hi-Infidelity. *(gold disc)*
1982 KEEP THE FIRE BURNIN'
    (S)   (3:55)   Epic 38100 Good Trouble.
    (S)   (4:38)   Epic 48527 The Second Decade Of Rock And Roll 1981-1991. *(live)*
    (S)   (3:54)   Time-Life R988-05 Sounds Of The Eighties: 1982.
    (S)   (3:54)   Time-Life R968-13 Guitar Rock - The Early '80s.
    (S)   (3:54)   Rhino 72595 Billboard Top Album Rock Hits, 1982.
    (S)   (3:54)   Time-Life R834-20 Body Talk - Heart And Soul.
1982 SWEET TIME
    (S)   (3:06)   Epic 38100 Good Trouble.
1984 I DO'WANNA KNOW
(dj copies of this 45 ran (3:14) and (4:10); commercial copies all ran (4:10))
    (S)   (4:12)   Epic 39593 Wheels Are Turnin'.
    (S)   (4:14)   Epic 48527 The Second Decade Of Rock And Roll 1981-1991. *(live)*
1985 CAN'T FIGHT THIS FEELING
(actual 45 time is (4:47) not (4:54) as stated on the record label)
    (S)   (4:47)   T.J. Martell Foundation/Columbia 40315 Music For The Miracle.

    (S)   (4:49)   Priority 7077 80's Greatest Rock Hits Volume 5 - From The Heart.
    (S)   (4:53)   Rhino 71640 Billboard Top Hits - 1985.
    (S)   (4:54)   Sony Music Distribution 57854 For Your Love.
    (S)   (4:54)   Epic 39593 Wheels Are Turnin'.
    (S)   (4:50)   Epic 44202 The Hits.
    (S)   (4:55)   Epic 48527 The Second Decade Of Rock And Roll 1981-1991. *(live)*
    (S)   (4:54)   Time-Life R988-01 Sounds Of The Eighties: The Rockin' Eighties.
    (S)   (4:51)   JCI 3171 #1 Radio Hits 1985 - Only Rock 'n Roll - 1989.
    (S)   (4:43)   Rhino 72579 Feel Like Makin' Love - Romantic Power Ballads. *(faster than the 45 and LP)*
    (S)   (4:49)   Time-Life R834-09 Body Talk - Magic Moments.
1985 ONE LONELY NIGHT
    (S)   (3:20)   Epic 39593 Wheels Are Turnin'.
    (S)   (3:20)   Epic 44202 The Hits.
1985 LIVE EVERY MOMENT
    (S)   (4:59)   Epic 39593 Wheels Are Turnin'.
    (S)   (4:58)   Epic 48527 The Second Decade Of Rock And Roll 1981-1991.
1987 THAT AIN'T LOVE
    (S)   (3:59)   Epic 40444 Life As We Know It.
    (S)   (4:00)   Epic 44202 The Hits.
    (S)   (4:18)   Epic 48527 The Second Decade Of Rock And Roll 1981-1991. *(live)*
1987 IN MY DREAMS
    (S)   (4:30)   Epic 40444 Life As We Know It. *(LP length)*
    (S)   (4:22)   Epic 44202 The Hits. *(45 length)*
1988 HERE WITH ME
(dj copies of this 45 ran (4:29) and (4:53); commercial copies were all (4:53))
    (S)   (5:03)   Epic 44202 The Hits.

RESTLESS HEART
1987 I'LL STILL BE LOVING YOU
    (S)   (4:16)   RCA 5648 Wheels.
    (S)   (4:15)   RCA 61041 Best Of.
    (S)   (4:11)   K-Tel 3048 Country Music Classics Volume VII.
1993 WHEN SHE CRIES
    (S)   (3:43)   RCA 66049 Big Iron Horses.

REUNION
1974 LIFE IS A ROCK (BUT THE RADIO ROLLED ME)
(a (3:30) extended version has appeared previously on several various artist compilation vinyl albums but there never was a REUNION LP)
    (S)   (3:29)   RCA 9684 and 8476 Nipper's Greatest Hits - The 70's. *(:35 longer than the 45 version)*
    (S)   (3:30)   Rhino 70760 Super Hits Of The 70's Volume 13. *(:36 longer than the 45 version)*
    (S)   (3:30)   Time-Life SOD-32 Sounds Of The Seventies - AM Pop Classics. *(:36 longer than the 45 version)*
    (S)   (3:28)   K-Tel 3627 Out Of Sight. *(:34 longer than the 45 version)*
    (S)   (3:28)   Time-Life R840-03 Sounds Of The Seventies - Pop Nuggets: Early '70s. *(:34 longer than the 45 version)*
    (S)   (3:30)   Time-Life R830-01 The Dr. Demento Collection - The Mid 70's. *(:36 longer than the 45 version)*

REVELS
1959 MIDNIGHT STROLL
    (M)   (2:33)   DCC Compact Classics 050 Monster Rock 'n Roll Show.
    (M)   (2:29)   Time-Life 2RNR-48 Rock 'N' Roll Era - R&B Gems II.

PAUL REVERE and THE RAIDERS (also RAIDERS)
1961 LIKE, LONG HAIR
    (M)   (1:55)   Columbia 45311 The Legend Of Paul Revere. *(mastered from vinyl)*
1966 JUST LIKE ME
    (M)   (2:21)   Columbia 45019 Pop Classics Of The 60's.
    (M)   (2:21)   Rhino 75778 Frat Rock.

(E) (2:21) Columbia 35593 Greatest Hits.
(S) (2:23) Columbia 45311 The Legend Of Paul Revere. *(remixed)*
(M) (2:20) Time-Life 2CLR-13 Classic Rock - 1966: Shakin' All Over.
(S) (2:32) Columbia 48949 The Essential Ride '63 - '67.

1966 KICKS
(E) (2:21) Columbia 45018 Rock Classics Of The 60's.
(E) (2:21) Columbia 35593 Greatest Hits.
(S) (2:26) Columbia 45311 The Legend Of Paul Revere. *(remixed)*
(S) (2:25) Columbia 9308 Midnight Ride. *(remixed)*
(E) (2:21) Era 5025 The Brill Building Sound.
(E) (2:21) Time-Life 2CLR-02 Classic Rock - 1966.
(M) (2:21) Time-Life R962-04 History Of Rock 'N' Roll: California Pop 1963-1967.
(S) (2:25) Risky Business 66914 Party On.
(E) (2:21) Time-Life R968-09 Guitar Rock 1966-1967.
(S) (2:25) Columbia 48949 The Essential Ride '63 - '67.

1966 HUNGRY
(M) (2:58) Rhino 75778 Frat Rock.
(S) (2:54) Columbia 35593 Greatest Hits.
(S) (2:54) Columbia 45311 The Legend Of Paul Revere. *(remixed)*
(S) (2:54) Era 5025 The Brill Building Sound.
(M) (2:58) Time-Life 2CLR-07 Classic Rock - 1966: The Beat Goes On.
(S) (3:31) Columbia 48949 The Essential Ride '63 - '67. *(alternate take)*
(S) (2:55) Sundazed 6095 Spirit Of '67.
(S) (3:30) Sundazed 6095 Spirit Of '67. *(alternate take)*

1966 THE GREAT AIRPLANE STRIKE
(S) (3:06) Columbia 35593 Greatest Hits. *(LP version)*
(S) (2:54) Columbia 45311 The Legend Of Paul Revere. *(remixed 45 version)*
(S) (5:41) Columbia 48949 The Essential Ride '63 - '67. *(neither the 45 or LP version)*
(S) (3:06) Sundazed 6095 Spirit Of '67. *(LP version)*
(M) (2:57) Sundazed 6095 Spirit Of '67. *(45 version)*

1967 GOOD THING
(M) (3:02) Rhino 70628 Billboard's Top Rock & Roll Hits Of 1967.
(E) (3:00) Columbia 35593 Greatest Hits.
(S) (3:01) Columbia 45311 The Legend Of Paul Revere. *(remixed)*
(E) (2:59) JCI 3111 Good Time Sixties.
(M) (3:00) Time-Life 2CLR-05 Classic Rock - 1967.
(M) (3:01) Time-Life R968-12 Guitar Rock - The Late '60s.
(S) (3:02) Columbia 48949 The Essential Ride '63 - '67.
(S) (3:02) Sundazed 6095 Spirit Of '67.

1967 UPS AND DOWNS
(E) (2:44) Columbia 35593 Greatest Hits.
(M) (2:48) Columbia 45311 The Legend Of Paul Revere.
(M) (2:49) Columbia 48949 The Essential Ride '63 - '67.
(M) (2:48) Sundazed 6096 Revolution.

1967 HIM OR ME - WHAT'S IT GONNA BE?
(M) (2:38) Columbia 45311 The Legend Of Paul Revere.
(M) (2:38) Time-Life 2CLR-10 Classic Rock - 1967: The Beat Goes On.
(S) (2:50) Columbia 48949 The Essential Ride '63 - '67. *(:11 longer than the 45 or LP; this song ends with :15 of silence followed by a (1:02) "Spirit Of '67" vinyl LP radio commercial, all on track 20)*
(S) (2:50) Sundazed 6096 Revolution. *(:11 longer than the 45 or LP)*

1967 I HAD A DREAM
(S) (2:17) Columbia 45311 The Legend Of Paul Revere.
(S) (2:19) Sundazed 6096 Revolution.

1967 PEACE OF MIND
(M) (2:25) Columbia 45311 The Legend Of Paul Revere.

1968 TOO MUCH TALK
(M) (2:13) Columbia 45311 The Legend Of Paul Revere. *(with a :15 introduction hidden with a negative index preceding track 5; 45 version)*
(S) (3:48) Sundazed 6097 Something Happening. *(time includes a :13 "Happening" introduction; LP version)*

(M) (2:11) Sundazed 6097 Something Happening. *(45 version)*

1968 DON'T TAKE IT SO HARD
(S) (2:23) Columbia 45311 The Legend Of Paul Revere.
(S) (2:22) Sundazed 6097 Something Happening.

1969 MR. SUN, MR. MOON
(S) (2:43) Columbia 45311 The Legend Of Paul Revere.

1969 LET ME
(S) (2:39) Columbia 45311 The Legend Of Paul Revere. *(45 version except for the word "let" which is mixed out at 2:16; :10 longer fade than the 45)*

1969 WE GOTTA ALL GET TOGETHER
(S) (2:58) Columbia 45311 The Legend Of Paul Revere. *(45 version)*

released as by THE RAIDERS:
1971 INDIAN RESERVATION
(S) (2:52) Rhino 70632 Billboard's Top Rock & Roll Hits Of 1971.
(S) (2:52) Rhino 72005 Billboard's Top Rock & Roll Hits 1968-1972 Box Set.
(S) (2:53) Rhino 70925 Super Hits Of The 70's Volume 5.
(S) (2:51) Columbia 45047 Pop Classics Of The 70's.
(S) (2:51) Columbia 45311 The Legend Of Paul Revere.
(S) (2:51) Razor & Tie 21640 Those Fabulous 70's.
(S) (2:52) Time-Life SUD-10 Superhits - 1971.
(S) (2:51) Time-Life SOD-12 Sounds Of The Seventies - 1971: Take Two.
(S) (2:51) Risky Business 53919 Songs Of Peacemakers, Protesters And Potheads.
(S) (2:52) Eclipse Music Group 64892 Rock 'n Roll Relix 1970-1971.
(S) (2:52) Eclipse Music Group 64897 Rock 'n Roll Relix 1970-1979.
(S) (2:52) Time-Life AM1-06 AM Gold - 1971.

1971 BIRDS OF A FEATHER
(S) (2:36) Columbia 45311 The Legend Of Paul Revere.

DEBBIE REYNOLDS
1957 TAMMY
(M) (3:04) Curb 77435 Best Of.
(M) (3:04) Rhino 71252 Sentimental Journey: Pop Vocal Classics Volume 4 (1954-1959).
(M) (3:04) Rhino 72034 Sentimental Journey Pop Vocal Classics Volumes 1-4 Box Set.
(M) (3:04) Time-Life HPD-17 Your Hit Parade - 1957.
(M) (3:00) MCA Special Products 20751 Rock Around The Oldies #2. *(song slowly fades out instead of ending cold)*
(M) (3:04) Rhino 72422 Billboard Top Movie Hits 1955-1959.
(S) (2:42) Nick At Nite/550 Music/Epic 67689 Stand By Your Man. *(rerecording)*
(M) (3:03) JCI 7011 Those Wonderful Years - That's Hollywood.
(S) (2:42) MCA Special Products 20936 Legends Of Stage And Screen. *(rerecording)*
(M) (3:04) Time-Life R132-10 Love Songs Of Your Hit Parade.
(M) (3:03) Geffen 25218 O.S.T. Fear And Loathing In Las Vegas. *(all songs on this cd are segued together)*

1958 A VERY SPECIAL LOVE
(M) (2:36) Curb 77435 Best Of.

1960 AM I THAT EASY TO FORGET
(S) (2:18) Curb 77435 Best Of.
(S) (2:17) Varese Sarabande 5686 History Of Dot Records Volume One.

JODY REYNOLDS
1958 ENDLESS SLEEP
(M) (2:20) Time-Life 2RNR-05 Rock 'N' Roll Era - 1958.
(E) (2:21) Time-Life R102-17 Lost Treasures Of Rock 'N' Roll.
(E) (2:21) Original Sound CDGO-14 Golden Oldies Volume. 14.
(M) (2:25) DCC Compact Classics 078 Best Of Tragedy.
(M) (2:19) Time-Life R857-11 The Heart Of Rock 'n' Roll 1958-1959.

LAWRENCE REYNOLDS
1969 JESUS IS A SOUL MAN

RHYTHM HERITAGE
1976 THEME FROM S.W.A.T.
- (S) (2:49) Rhino 70671 Billboard Top Hits - 1976. *(45 version)*
- (S) (2:49) Rhino 71911 Tube Tunes Volume Two - The 70's & 80's. *(45 version)*
- (S) (3:20) Hip-O 40017 Mission Accomplished: Themes For Spies & Cops. *(LP version)*
- (M) (2:48) Time-Life R840-02 Sounds Of The Seventies - TV Themes. *(45 version)*
- (S) (4:07) Rhino 72851 Kurtis Blow Presents The History Of Rap Vol. 1. *(previously unreleased extended version)*

1976 BARETTA'S THEME ("KEEP YOUR EYE ON THE SPARROW")
- (S) (3:13) Madacy Entertainment 1976 Rock On 1976. *(45 version)*
- (S) (5:07) Hip-O 40017 Mission Accomplished: Themes For Spies & Cops. *(LP version)*
- (S) (3:11) Time-Life R840-02 Sounds Of The Seventies - TV Themes. *(45 version)*

CHARLIE RICH
1960 LONELY WEEKENDS
- (M) (2:07) Rhino 75884 The Sun Story.
- (M) (2:07) DCC Compact Classics 009 Legends.
- (M) (2:07) RCA 66059 Sun's Greatest Hits.
- (M) (2:03) Mercury 314512643 The Complete "Smash" Sessions. *(rerecording)*
- (M) (2:07) Time-Life 2RNR-22 Rock 'N' Roll Era - 1960 Still Rockin'.
- (M) (2:07) Rhino 71780 Sun Records Collection. *(missing the choral overdubs)*
- (M) (2:08) Varese Sarabande 5695 Sun Sessions.
- (S) (2:04) AVI 5016 Lonely Weekends: Best Of The Sun Years.
- (M) (2:09) Epic/Legacy 64762 Feel Like Going Home: The Essential.
- (M) (2:08) Columbia 69075 Great Balls Of Fire Super Hits.

1965 MOHAIR SAM
- (S) (2:07) Mercury 314512643 The Complete "Smash" Sessions.
- (S) (2:07) Ripete 5151 Ocean Drive 4.
- (S) (2:07) Mercury 314526691 Fifty Years Of Country Music From Mercury.
- (S) (2:06) Epic/Legacy 64762 Feel Like Going Home: The Essential.

1973 BEHIND CLOSED DOORS
- (S) (2:55) Columbia 46032 Columbia Country Classics Volume 4.
- (S) (2:52) JCI 3304 Mellow Seventies.
- (S) (2:54) Epic 34240 Greatest Hits.
- (S) (2:54) Epic 32247 Behind Closed Doors.
- (S) (2:53) Columbia 45073 American Originals.
- (S) (2:55) Time-Life CCD-06 Contemporary Country - The Early 70's.
- (S) (2:53) K-Tel 567 Country Music Classics Volume IV.
- (S) (2:54) K-Tel 3163 Behind Closed Doors.
- (S) (2:53) Epic 67126 Super Hits.
- (S) (2:54) JCI 3155 1970 - Only Country - 1974.
- (S) (2:53) Risky Business 67309 Sexy Country.
- (S) (2:53) Epic/Legacy 64762 Feel Like Going Home: The Essential.
- (S) (2:53) Epic 67942 Super Hits Of The '70s.
- (S) (2:53) K-Tel 3367 101 Greatest Country Hits Vol. Eight: Country Romance.
- (S) (2:53) Rhino 72516 Behind Closed Doors - '70s Swingers.
- (S) (2:55) Time-Life R814-03 Love Songs.
- (S) (2:55) Time-Life R808-04 Classic Country 1970-1974.

1973 THE MOST BEAUTIFUL GIRL
- (S) (2:41) Columbia 46032 Columbia Country Classics Volume 4.
- (S) (2:43) Epic 34240 Greatest Hits.
- (S) (2:42) Epic 32247 Behind Closed Doors.
- (S) (2:41) Columbia 45073 American Originals.
- (S) (2:41) Time-Life CCD-04 Contemporary Country - The Mid 70's.
- (S) (2:40) K-Tel 3111 Country Music Classics Vol. XIX.
- (S) (2:42) Risky Business 66662 Swingin' Singles/Greatest Hits Of The 70's.
- (S) (2:42) Epic 67126 Super Hits.
- (S) (2:41) Epic/Legacy 64762 Feel Like Going Home: The Essential.
- (S) (2:42) Rhino 72739 Billboard Top Soft Rock Hits - 1973.
- (S) (2:40) Time-Life R814-01 Love Songs.
- (S) (2:41) Time-Life R808-04 Classic Country 1970-1974.

1974 THERE WON'T BE ANYMORE
- (S) (2:23) Epic/Legacy 64762 Feel Like Going Home: The Essential.

1974 A VERY SPECIAL LOVE SONG
- (S) (2:44) Epic 34240 Greatest Hits.
- (S) (2:43) Time-Life CCD-08 Contemporary Country - The Mid 70's Pure Gold.
- (S) (2:43) K-Tel 816 Country Music Classics Volume XII.
- (S) (2:43) Epic 67126 Super Hits.
- (S) (2:42) Rhino 72740 Billboard Top Soft Rock Hits - 1974.

1974 I LOVE MY FRIEND
- (S) (2:24) Epic 34240 Greatest Hits.

1975 EVERY TIME YOU TOUCH ME (I GET HIGH)
- (S) (3:00) Epic 34240 Greatest Hits.

TONY RICH PROJECT
1996 NOBODY KNOWS
- (S) (5:06) LaFace 26022 Words.
- (S) (5:06) Grammy Recordings/Chronicles 314553292 1997 Grammy Nominees.

CLIFF RICHARD
1959 LIVING DOLL
1964 IT'S ALL IN THE GAME
1976 DEVIL WOMAN
- (S) (3:35) Rhino 71200 Super Hits Of The 70's Volume 20. *(LP version)*
- (S) (3:36) Time-Life SOD-22 Sounds Of The Seventies - Seventies Top Forty. *(LP version)*
- (S) (3:33) Razor & Tie 2039 Collection 1970-1994. *(LP version)*

1980 WE DON'T TALK ANYMORE
- (S) (4:12) Razor & Tie 2039 Collection 1970-1994. *(LP version)*
- (S) (4:12) Madacy Entertainment 1979 Rock On 1979. *(LP version)*

1980 CARRIE
- (S) (3:38) Razor & Tie 2039 Collection 1970-1994.

1980 DREAMING
- (S) (3:36) Razor & Tie 2039 Collection 1970-1994.

released as by OLIVIA NEWTON-JOHN and CLIFF RICHARD:
1980 SUDDENLY
- (S) (3:59) MCA 5347 Olivia Newton-John: Greatest Hits Volume 2.
- (S) (3:58) Razor & Tie 2039 Cliff Richard: Collection 1970-1994.

released as by CLIFF RICHARD:
1981 A LITTLE IN LOVE
- (S) (3:21) Razor & Tie 2039 Collection 1970-1994.

1981 GIVE A LITTLE BIT MORE
1982 DADDY'S HOME
- (S) (2:57) Razor & Tie 2039 Collection 1970-1994.

LIONEL RICHIE
released as by DIANA ROSS & LIONEL RICHIE:
1981 ENDLESS LOVE
- (S) (4:26) Motown 6177 Endless Love: 15 Of Motown's Greatest Love Songs.
- (S) (4:26) Motown 6143 and 5386 The Composer Series: Lionel Richie.
- (S) (4:26) Motown 9021 and 5309 25 Years Of Grammy Greats.

(S) (4:26) Motown 9082 and 5385 Great Motown Love Songs.
(S) (4:26) Motown 9035 and 5324 Top Ten With A Bullet!
(S) (4:26) Motown 6192 You Can't Hurry Love: All The
            Great Love Songs Of The Past 25 Years.
(S) (4:26) Motown 6132 25 #1 Hits From 25 Years Volume 2.
(S) (4:24) Motown 6197 and 6049 Diana Ross Anthology.
(S) (4:45) RCA 61154 and 61136 Diana Ross: Endless Love.
            (rerecording with Diana Ross solo)
(S) (4:25) Motown 0960 Diana Ross: All The Great Hits.
(S) (4:26) Motown 6072 Diana Ross: Compact Command
            Performances.
(S) (4:26) Motown 6105 All The Great Love Songs.
(S) (4:26) Motown 6357 Diana Ross Forever: Musical
            Memories.
(S) (4:26) Polygram Special Markets 314520030 Motown
            Legends - Love Songs.
(S) (4:26) Motown 314530428 Diana Ross Ultimate
            Collection.
(S) (4:26) Rhino 72159 Black Entertainment Television -
            15th Anniversary.
(S) (4:26) Rebound 314520361 Class Reunion '81.
(S) (4:25) Rebound 314520370 Soul Classics - Quiet
            Storm/The 80's.
(S) (4:26) Polygram Special Markets 314520031 Motown
            Legends - Duets.
(S) (4:26) Time-Life R834-04 Body Talk - Together
            Forever.
(S) (4:26) Angel 56580 Men Are From Mars, Women Are
            From Venus - Songs For Loving Couples.
(S) (4:54) RCA 67410 Diana Ross - Greatest Hits - The
            RCA Years. *(rerecording with Diana Ross solo)*
(S) (4:23) Motown 314530846 Lionel Richie: Truly - The
            Love Songs.
(S) (3:03) Madacy Entertainment 6806 Best Of Love.
            (edited)
(S) (4:26) Polygram TV 314555610 The One And Only
            Love Album.
(S) (4:26) Time-Life R814-02 Love Songs.
(S) (4:25) Rebound 314520519 Love At The Movies.

released as by LIONEL RICHIE:
1982 TRULY
(S) (3:20) Motown 6007 Lionel Richie.
(S) (3:18) Motown 314530534 Motown Year By Year - 1982.
(S) (3:19) MCA 11329 Soul Train 25th Anniversary Box Set.
(S) (3:20) Time-Life R834-09 Body Talk - Magic Moments.
(S) (3:19) Motown 314530846 Truly - The Love Songs.
(S) (3:19) Time-Life R814-04 Love Songs.
1983 YOU ARE
(S) (5:00) Motown 6007 Lionel Richie. *(LP length)*
1983 MY LOVE
(S) (4:04) Motown 6007 Lionel Richie.
1983 ALL NIGHT LONG
(S) (6:19) Motown 6059 Can't Slow Down. *(LP version)*
(S) (4:16) Motown 6358 Hitsville USA Volume Two. *(45
            version)*
(S) (4:16) Rhino 72159 Black Entertainment Television -
            15th Anniversary. *(45 version)*
(S) (4:12) Motown 314530849 Motown 40 Forever. *(45
            version)*
1984 RUNNING WITH THE NIGHT
(S) (4:09) T.J. Martell Foundation/Columbia 40315 Music
            For The Miracle. *(45 version)*
(S) (5:58) Motown 6059 Can't Slow Down. *(LP version)*
1984 HELLO
(S) (4:07) Motown 6059 Can't Slow Down.
(S) (4:06) Motown 314530846 Truly - The Love Songs.
1984 STUCK ON YOU
(S) (3:10) Motown 6059 Can't Slow Down.
(S) (3:08) Motown 314530846 Truly - The Love Songs.
1984 PENNY LOVER
(S) (5:30) Motown 6059 Can't Slow Down. *(LP version)*
(S) (3:44) Motown 314530846 Truly - The Love Songs.
            (45 version)
(S) (3:45) Time-Life R834-16 Body Talk - Sweet Nothings.
            (45 version)

1985 SAY YOU, SAY ME
(S) (4:00) Rhino 71868 Academy Award Winning Songs.
(S) (3:58) Motown 314530519 Motown Year By Year 1985.
(S) (4:00) Motown 6158 Dancing On The Ceiling.
(S) (4:00) Rhino 72280 Academy Award Winning Songs
            Volume 5.
(S) (3:59) Motown 314530846 Truly - The Love Songs.
(S) (3:59) Time-Life R834-18 Body Talk - Romantic
            Moments.
1986 DANCING ON THE CEILING
(S) (4:31) Motown 6158 Dancing On The Ceiling.
1986 LOVE WILL CONQUER ALL
(S) (5:40) Motown 6158 Dancing On The Ceiling. *(LP
            version)*
(S) (5:37) Rebound 314520431 Soul Classics - Best Of The
            80's. *(LP version)*
(S) (4:15) Motown 314530846 Truly - The Love Songs.
            (45 version)
1986 BALLERINA GIRL
(S) (3:36) Motown 6158 Dancing On The Ceiling.
1987 SE LA
(S) (5:49) Motown 6158 Dancing On The Ceiling. *(LP
            version)*
(S) (4:27) Motown 314530557 Motown Year By Year -
            1987. *(45 version)*
(S) (8:15) Motown 314530557 Motown Year By Year -
            1987. *(12" dj only single version)*
1992 DO IT TO ME
(S) (6:03) Motown 6338 Back To Front.
(S) (6:00) Motown 314530846 Truly - The Love Songs.

NELSON RIDDLE
1956 LISBON ANTIGUA
(M) (2:33) Capitol 90592 Memories Are Made Of This.
(M) (2:34) Curb 77403 All-Time Great Instrumental Hits
            Volume 1.
(M) (2:34) Capitol 91228 Best Of.
(M) (2:33) Capitol 98670 Memories Are Made Of This.
(M) (2:33) Time-Life HPD-15 Your Hit Parade - 1956.
(M) (2:33) JCI 7010 Those Wonderful Years - Melodies Of
            Love.
(M) (2:34) Time-Life R986-10 Nelson Riddle - Instrumental
            Favorites.
(E) (2:32) Curb 77872 Best Of.
1956 PORT AU PRINCE
(M) (2:21) Time-Life R986-10 Nelson Riddle - Instrumental
            Favorites.
1956 THEME FROM "THE PROUD ONES"
(M) (2:45) Time-Life R986-10 Nelson Riddle - Instrumental
            Favorites.
1962 ROUTE 66 THEME
(S) (2:08) Capitol 91228 Best Of.
(S) (2:07) Pair 1173 The Riddle Touch.
(S) (2:06) Rhino 70281 The Beat Generation.
(S) (2:07) Time-Life HPD-34 Your Hit Parade - 60's
            Instrumentals.
(S) (2:07) K-Tel 3091 Those Wonderful Instrumentals.
(S) (2:07) DCC Compact Classics 079 Music For A
            Bachelor's Den.
(S) (2:07) Collectors' Choice 003/4 Instrumental Gems Of
            The 60's.
(S) (2:07) Time-Life R986-10 Nelson Riddle - Instrumental
            Favorites.
(S) (2:07) Capitol 35177 Ultra Lounge Volume Four:
            Bachelor Pad Romance.
(S) (2:07) Right Stuff 53318 Hot Rod Rock Volume 3: Big
            Boss Instrumentals.
(S) (2:07) Curb 77872 Best Of.
(S) (2:07) Time-Life AM1-27 AM Gold 60's TV Themes.
(S) (2:08) Capitol 38376 Ultra Lounge Sampler.

RIFF
1991 MY HEART IS FAILING ME
(S) (4:19) SBK 95828 Riff.

RIGHTEOUS BROTHERS
1965 YOU'VE LOST THAT LOVIN' FEELIN'

    (S) (3:43) Rhino 70626 Billboard's Top Rock & Roll Hits Of 1965.

    (S) (3:43) Rhino 72007 Billboard's Top Rock & Roll Hits 1962-1966 Box Set.

    (S) (3:38) Original Sound 8860 Oldies But Goodies Vol. 10. *(this compact disc uses the "Waring - fds" noise reduction process)*

    (S) (3:38) Original Sound 2221 Oldies But Goodies Volumes 1,4,6,8 and 10 Box Set. *(this box set uses the "Waring - fds" noise reduction process)*

    (S) (3:38) Original Sound 2500 Oldies But Goodies Volumes 1-15 Box Set. *(this box set uses the "Waring - fds" noise reduction process)*

    (M) (3:45) Abkco 7118 Phil Spector/Back To Mono (1958-1969).

    (S) (4:27) MCA/Curb 42257 Best Of Bill Medley. *(rerecorded)*

    (S) (3:43) Verve 847248 Very Best Of.

    (S) (3:43) Rhino 71488 Anthology.

    (S) (3:49) Curb 77423 Reunion. *(rerecorded)*

    (S) (3:40) Curb 77381 Best Of.

    (S) (3:43) Special Music 511078 You've Lost That Lovin' Feelin'.

    (S) (3:39) Time-Life 2CLR-01 Classic Rock - 1965.

    (S) (3:40) Time-Life SUD-03 Superhits - 1965.

    (S) (3:43) K-Tel 3008 60's Sock Hop.

    (S) (3:39) Polygram Special Markets 314520260 Number One Hits Of The Sixties.

    (S) (3:40) Time-Life AM1-10 AM Gold - 1965.

    (S) (3:43) Time-Life R834-07 Body Talk - Hearts In Motion. *(noisy fadeout)*

    (S) (3:49) Madacy Entertainment 6806 Best Of Love. *(rerecording)*

1965 JUST ONCE IN MY LIFE

    (M) (3:52) Abkco 7118 Phil Spector/Back To Mono (1958-1969).

    (S) (3:47) Verve 847248 Very Best Of.

    (S) (3:47) Rhino 71488 Anthology.

    (S) (4:02) Curb 77423 Reunion. *(rerecorded)*

    (S) (4:04) Curb 77381 Best Of. *(rerecorded)*

    (S) (3:47) Special Music 511078 You've Lost That Lovin' Feelin'.

1965 UNCHAINED MELODY

    (M) (3:35) Abkco 7118 Phil Spector/Back To Mono (1958-1969).

    (S) (3:36) Curb 77532 Your Favorite Songs. *(rerecorded)*

    (S) (3:35) Verve 847248 Very Best Of.

    (S) (3:35) Rhino 71488 Anthology.

    (S) (3:35) Curb 77423 Reunion. *(rerecording which charted in 1990)*

    (S) (6:33) Curb 77423 Reunion. *(remix of the rerecording which charted in 1990)*

    (S) (3:37) Curb 77381 Best Of. *(rerecording which charted in 1990)*

    (S) (3:34) Original Sound 8863 Oldies But Goodies Vol. 13. *(rerecording which charted in 1990)*

    (S) (3:34) Original Sound 2223 Oldies But Goodies Volumes 2,7,9,12 and 13 Box Set. *(Volumes 2, 7 and 12 of this box set use the "Waring - fds" noise reduction process; rerecording which charted in 1990)*

    (S) (3:34) Original Sound 2500 Oldies But Goodies Volumes 1-15 Box Set. *(most volumes in this box set use the "Waring - fds" noise reduction process; rerecording which charted in 1990)*

    (S) (3:35) Special Music 511078 You've Lost That Lovin' Feelin'.

    (S) (3:35) Time-Life 2CLR-14 Classic Rock - 1965: Shakin' All Over.

    (S) (3:34) Time-Life SUD-12 Superhits - The Mid 60's.

    (S) (6:30) Curb 77651 Retro Rock Dance Hits. *(all selections on this cd are remixed with extra instrumentation added)*

    (S) (6:32) Curb 77934 Absolute Dance Hits: How Do I Live. *(all songs on this cd are remixed)*

    (S) (3:34) Time-Life OPCD-4517 Tonight's The Night.

    (S) (3:35) Time-Life R974-01 Many Moods Of Romance - That's My Desire.

    (S) (3:35) Milan 35733 O.S.T. Ghost.

    (S) (3:35) Varese Sarabande 5276 O.S.T. Ghost.

    (S) (3:34) Madacy Entertainment 6803 Power Of Love. *(rerecording which charted in 1990)*

    (S) (3:35) EMI-Capitol Music Group 54555 Movie Luv.

    (S) (3:34) Time-Life AM1-05 AM Gold - The Mid '60s.

    (S) (3:35) Time-Life R988-31 Sounds Of The Eighties: Cinemax Movie Hits Of The '80s.

    (S) (3:35) Time-Life R834-04 Body Talk - Together Forever.

    (S) (3:34) Time-Life R814-01 Love Songs.

1966 EBB TIDE

    (M) (2:48) Abkco 7118 Phil Spector/Back To Mono (1958-1969). *(with 45 version reverb)*

    (S) (2:47) Verve 847248 Very Best Of. *(LP version)*

    (S) (2:47) Rhino 71488 Anthology. *(LP version)*

    (S) (2:49) Curb 77423 Reunion. *(rerecorded)*

    (S) (2:50) Curb 77381 Best Of. *(rerecorded)*

    (S) (2:47) Special Music 511078 You've Lost That Lovin' Feelin'. *(LP version)*

    (S) (2:47) Time-Life R138/05 Look Of Love. *(LP version)*

    (S) (2:47) Time-Life R834-13 Body Talk - Just The Two Of Us. *(LP version)*

    (S) (2:47) Time-Life R814-02 Love Songs. *(LP version)*

1966 (YOU'RE MY) SOUL AND INSPIRATION

    (S) (3:04) Rhino 70627 Billboard's Top Rock & Roll Hits Of 1966.

    (S) (3:04) Rhino 72007 Billboard's Top Rock & Roll Hits 1962-1966 Box Set.

    (S) (3:19) Verve 847248 Very Best Of. *(:15 longer than either the 45 or LP)*

    (S) (3:03) Original Sound 8861 Oldies But Goodies Vol. 11. *(this compact disc uses the "Waring - fds" noise reduction process)*

    (S) (3:03) Original Sound 2222 Oldies But Goodies Volumes 3,5,11,14 and 15 Box Set. *(this box set uses the "Waring - fds" noise reduction process)*

    (S) (3:03) Original Sound 2500 Oldies But Goodies Volumes 1-15 Box Set. *(this box set uses the "Waring - fds" noise reduction process)*

    (S) (3:19) Rhino 71488 Anthology. *(:15 longer than either the 45 or LP)*

    (S) (3:22) Curb 77423 Reunion. *(rerecorded)*

    (S) (3:19) Curb 77381 Best Of. *(:15 longer than either the 45 or LP)*

    (S) (3:19) Special Music 511078 You've Lost That Lovin' Feelin'. *(:15 longer than either the 45 or LP)*

    (S) (3:19) Era 5025 The Brill Building Sound. *(:15 longer than either the 45 or LP)*

    (S) (2:59) Time-Life 2CLR-13 Classic Rock - 1966: Shakin' All Over.

    (S) (3:18) Time-Life SUD-01 Superhits - 1966. *(:14 longer than either the 45 or LP)*

    (S) (3:21) Scotti Brothers 75434 Romantic Duets. *(rerecorded)*

    (S) (3:19) Polygram Special Markets 314520264 Soul Hits Of The 60's. *(:15 longer than either the 45 or LP)*

    (S) (3:18) Time-Life AM1-09 AM Gold - 1966. *(:14 longer than either the 45 or LP)*

    (S) (3:04) Time-Life R834-18 Body Talk - Romantic Moments.

    (S) (3:03) Time-Life R857-20 The Heart Of Rock 'n' Roll 1965-1966.

    (S) (3:19) Polygram Special Markets 314520460 #1 Radio Hits Of The 60's. *(:15 longer than either the 45 or LP)*

    (S) (3:19) Rebound 314520504 Soul And Inspiration. *(:15 longer than either the 45 or LP)*

1966 HE

    (S) (3:00) Verve 847248 Very Best Of.

    (S) (2:59) Rhino 71488 Anthology.

    (S) (3:00) Rebound 314520504 Soul And Inspiration.

1966 GO AHEAD AND CRY

    (S) (2:35) Verve 847248 Very Best Of.

    (S) (2:34) Rhino 71488 Anthology. *(truncated fade)*

    (S) (2:35) Rebound 314520504 Soul And Inspiration.

1974 ROCK AND ROLL HEAVEN
- (S) (3:32) Rhino 71488 Anthology.
- (S) (3:32) Curb 77522 Best Of.
- (S) (3:22) Curb 77522 Best Of. *(1992 rerecording)*
- (S) (3:22) Curb 77423 Reunion. *(1992 rerecording)*
- (S) (3:28) Razor & Tie 22505 More Fabulous 70's Volume 2.
- (S) (3:30) Time-Life SOD-33 Sounds Of The Seventies - AM Pop Classics II.
- (S) (3:32) Risky Business 66394 Gone But Not Forgotten.
- (S) (3:32) Time-Life R840-03 Sounds Of The Seventies - Pop Nuggets: Early '70s.

1974 GIVE IT TO THE PEOPLE
- (S) (3:25) Rhino 71488 Anthology.
- (S) (3:20) Curb 77522 Best Of. *(truncated fade)*

1974 DREAM ON
- (S) (3:31) Rhino 71488 Anthology. *(LP version)*
- (S) (2:59) Curb 77522 Best Of. *(45 version)*

1990 UNCHAINED MELODY
(this song charted in two different years: 1965 & 1990; see 1965 listings)

1990 UNCHAINED MELODY
(this is the rerecorded version of this song which charted simultaneously with the original hit version in 1990)
- (S) (3:35) Curb 77423 Reunion.
- (S) (6:33) Curb 77423 Reunion. *(remix)*
- (S) (3:37) Curb 77381 Best Of.
- (S) (3:34) Madacy Entertainment 6803 Power Of Love.

RIGHT SAID FRED
1992 I'M TOO SEXY
- (S) (2:50) Sandstone 5022 Cosmopolitan Volume 8.
- (S) (5:41) Tommy Boy 1074 MTV Party To Go Volume 3. *(remix; all tracks on this cd are segued together)*
- (S) (2:49) Foundation/RCA 66563 Number 1 Hit Mix.
- (S) (2:49) DCC Compact Classics 082 Night Moves Volume 2.
- (S) (2:50) Priority 53770 Techno Dance Classics Volume 1 - Pump Up The Jam.
- (S) (2:49) Charisma 92107 Up.
- (S) (2:49) JCI 3132 1990 - Only Rock 'n Roll - 1994.
- (S) (2:50) EMI 55204 O.S.T. Beverly Hills Ninja.
- (S) (2:49) K-Tel 3847 90s Now Volume 1.

CHERYL "PEPSII" RILEY
1988 THANKS FOR MY CHILD
- (S) (5:16) Columbia 44409 Me, Myself And I. *(LP version)*
- (S) (5:15) Rhino 71865 Smooth Grooves Volume 7. *(LP version)*

JEANNIE C. RILEY
1968 HARPER VALLEY P.T.A.
- (S) (3:09) Rhino 70689 Billboard's Top Country Hits Of 1968.
- (S) (3:13) Time-Life CTD-06 Country USA - 1968.
- (S) (3:10) Original Sound 8854 Oldies But Goodies Vol. 4. *(this compact disc uses the "Waring - fds" noise reduction process)*
- (S) (3:10) Original Sound 2221 Oldies But Goodies Volumes 1,4,6,8 and 10 Box Set. *(this box set uses the "Waring - fds" noise reduction process)*
- (S) (3:10) Original Sound 2500 Oldies But Goodies Volumes 1-15 Box Set. *(this box set uses the "Waring - fds" noise reduction process)*
- (S) (3:05) K-Tel 3085 Great Ladies Of Country.
- (S) (3:05) K-Tel 413 Country Music Classics Volume III.
- (S) (3:10) Rhino 71938 Billboard Top Pop Hits, 1968.
- (S) (3:10) Varese Sarabande 5606 Through The Years - Country Hits Of The 60's.
- (S) (3:19) MCA Special Products 20900 Rock Around The Oldies #3. *(rerecording)*
- (S) (3:20) MCA Special Products 20846 Greatest Country Classics Volume One. *(rerecording)*
- (S) (3:11) Varese Sarabande 5748 Best Of.
- (S) (3:05) K-Tel 3368 101 Greatest Country Hits Vol. Nine: Country Classics. *(rerecording)*
- (S) (3:13) Time-Life R808-02 Classic Country 1965-1969.

LEANN RIMES
1996 BLUE
- (S) (2:47) Curb 77821 Blue.

1997 HOW DO I LIVE
- (S) (4:55) Curb 77885 You Light Up My Life.
- (S) (3:53) Curb 77934 Absolute Dance Hits: How Do I Live. *(all songs on this cd are remixed)*

1997 YOU LIGHT UP MY LIFE
- (S) (3:35) Curb 77885 You Light Up My Life.

RINKY DINKS
1958 EARLY IN THE MORNING
- (M) (2:14) Warner Special Products 27606 Ultimate Bobby Darin.

MIGUEL RIOS
1970 A SONG OF JOY

RIP CHORDS
1964 HEY LITTLE COBRA
- (M) (2:00) DCC Compact Classics 030 Beach Classics.
- (S) (1:57) Columbia 45018 Rock Classics Of The 60's.
- (S) (2:00) Compose 9923 James Dean/Tribute To A Rebel.
- (M) (1:59) Time-Life 2CLR-09 Classic Rock - 1964: The Beat Goes On.
- (S) (1:57) Time-Life R962-04 History Of Rock 'N' Roll: California Pop 1963-1967.
- (S) (2:00) Rhino 71585 Billboard Top Pop Hits, 1964.
- (S) (2:00) Sony Music Special Products 37412 California U.S.A.
- (S) (1:59) Sundazed 6098 Hey Little Cobra.
- (S) (1:57) Right Stuff 53316 Hot Rod Rock Volume 1: Rev It Up.

1964 THREE WINDOW COUPE
- (S) (1:57) Columbia/Legacy 46984 Rock Artifacts Volume 4.
- (S) (1:58) Sundazed 6099 Three Window Coupe.

MINNIE RIPERTON
1975 LOVIN' YOU
- (S) (3:22) Rhino 70555 Soul Hits Of The 70's Volume 15. *(45 version)*
- (S) (3:21) Capitol 91784 Best Of. *(45 version)*
- (S) (3:21) Capitol 80516 Capitol Gold: The Best Of. *(45 version)*
- (S) (3:58) Razor & Tie 4543 The '70s Preservation Society Presents: Easy '70s. *(LP version)*
- (S) (3:22) Time-Life SOD-34 Sounds Of The Seventies - The Late 70's. *(45 version)*
- (S) (3:21) Right Stuff 30576 Slow Jams: The 70's Volume 4. *(45 version)*
- (S) (3:22) Madacy Entertainment 1975 Rock On 1975. *(45 version)*
- (S) (3:21) K-Tel 3624 Music Express. *(45 version)*
- (S) (3:21) Right Stuff 52660 Flick Hits - Old School Tracks. *(45 version)*
- (S) (3:58) JCI 3146 1975 - Only Love - 1979. *(LP version)*
- (S) (3:22) Hip-O 40030 The Glory Of Love - '70s Sweet & Soulful Love Songs. *(45 version)*
- (S) (3:21) Priority 53129 Deep Soul Volume One. *(45 version)*
- (S) (3:22) Time-Life AM1-22 AM Gold - 1975. *(45 version)*
- (S) (3:22) Time-Life R834-01 Body Talk - Forever Yours. *(45 version)*
- (S) (3:21) K-Tel 4017 70s Heavy Hitters: Summer Love. *(45 version)*
- (S) (3:59) Simitar 55512 The Number One's: Lovin' Feelings. *(LP version)*

RITCHIE FAMILY
1975 BRAZIL
- (S) (5:08) Rebound 314520307 Disco Nights Volume VIII. *(LP version)*
- (S) (5:07) Hot Productions 41 Best Of. *(LP version)*
- (S) (3:55) K-Tel 3470 Get Up And Disco. *(45 version but :44 longer)*

RITCHIE FAMILY *(Continued)*
- (S) (5:07) Time-Life R840-06 Sounds Of The Seventies: '70s Dance Party 1975-1976. *(LP version)*

1976 THE BEST DISCO IN TOWN
- (S) (6:16) Collectables 5431 Disco Party - The Best Of The T.K. Collection. *(previous selection tracks over introduction; LP version)*
- (S) (6:33) Hot Productions 41 Best Of. *(LP version)*
- (S) (2:41) Rhino 72123 Disco Years, Vol. 7. *(45 version)*
- (S) (2:40) K-Tel 3371 Hot Nights - Disco Lights. *(45 version)*
- (S) (3:12) Polydor 314535877 Pure Disco. *(edit of the LP version in an unsuccessful attempt at recreating the 45 version)*
- (S) (2:41) Rhino 72837 Disco Queens: The 70's. *(45 version)*
- (S) (6:16) Thump 4840 Flashback Disco. *(all selections on this cd are segued together)*

LEE RITENOUR
1981 IS IT YOU
- (S) (4:23) GRP 9645 Collection. *(LP version)*
- (S) (4:25) Discovery 71013 Rit. *(LP version)*

TEX RITTER
1961 I DREAMED OF A HILL-BILLY HEAVEN
- (S) (3:07) Curb 77397 Greatest Hits.
- (S) (3:08) Capitol 95036 Capitol Collector's Series.
- (M) (3:08) Capitol 95917 Opry Legends.
- (S) (3:08) Time-Life CTD-01 Country USA - 1961.
- (S) (3:08) K-Tel 320 Country Music Classics Volume II.
- (S) (3:07) Capitol 36903 Vintage Collections.
- (S) (3:07) K-Tel 3365 101 Greatest Country Hits Vol. Six: Timeless Country.

JOHNNY RIVERS
1964 MEMPHIS
- (S) (2:30) Rhino 70793 Anthology 1964-1977. *(no audience applause at the end; 45 version)*
- (S) (2:31) EMI 90727 Very Best Of. *(audience applause at the end; LP version)*
- (S) (2:33) EMI 46594 Best Of. *(audience applause at the end; LP version)*
- (S) (2:44) EMI 32819 Totally Live At The Whisky A Go Go. *(audience applause at the end; LP version)*
- (S) (2:33) EMI 35976 Greatest Hits. *(audience applause at the end; LP version)*
- (S) (2:29) Soul City 2008 The Memphis Sun Recordings. *(rerecording)*
- (S) (2:35) Soul City 1007 Greatest Hits. *(rerecording)*

1964 MAYBELLINE
- (S) (2:13) Rhino 70793 Anthology 1964-1977. *(ends with :03 of different audience applause than found on the LP version)*
- (S) (2:14) EMI 90727 Very Best Of. *(LP version which has ending audience applause)*
- (S) (2:16) EMI 46594 Best Of. *(LP version which has ending audience applause)*
- (S) (2:17) Pair 1195 Good Rockin'. *(LP version which has ending audience applause)*
- (S) (2:17) EMI 32819 Totally Live At The Whisky A Go Go. *(LP version which has ending audience applause)*
- (S) (2:15) EMI 35976 Greatest Hits. *(LP version which has ending audience applause)*
- (S) (1:55) Soul City 1007 Greatest Hits. *(rerecording)*

1964 MOUNTAIN OF LOVE
- (S) (2:39) Rhino 70793 Anthology 1964-1977.
- (S) (2:38) EMI 46594 Best Of.
- (S) (3:29) Soul City 2008 The Memphis Sun Recordings. *(rerecording)*
- (S) (2:44) Soul City 1007 Greatest Hits. *(rerecording)*

1965 MIDNIGHT SPECIAL
- (S) (2:29) Rhino 70793 Anthology 1964-1977. *(LP version which has audience applause at the end)*
- (S) (2:29) EMI 90727 Very Best Of. *(LP version which has audience applause at the end)*

- (S) (2:29) EMI 46594 Best Of. *(LP version which has audience applause at the end)*
- (S) (2:34) Pair 1195 Good Rockin'. *(LP version which has audience applause at the end)*
- (S) (2:30) EMI 32819 Totally Live At The Whisky A Go Go. *(LP version which has audience applause at the end)*
- (S) (2:29) EMI 35976 Greatest Hits. *(LP version which has audience applause at the end)*
- (S) (2:31) Soul City 1007 Greatest Hits. *(rerecording)*

1965 SEVENTH SON
- (S) (2:47) Rhino 70793 Anthology 1964-1977.
- (S) (2:49) EMI 90727 Very Best Of.
- (S) (2:47) EMI 46594 Best Of.
- (S) (2:46) EMI 35976 Greatest Hits.
- (S) (2:16) Soul City 1007 Greatest Hits. *(rerecording)*

1965 WHERE HAVE ALL THE FLOWERS GONE
- (S) (3:16) Rhino 70793 Anthology 1964-1977. *(45 version but :14 longer fade)*
- (S) (3:45) EMI 46594 Best Of. *(LP version)*
- (S) (3:44) EMI 35976 Greatest Hits. *(LP version)*

1966 UNDER YOUR SPELL AGAIN
(actual 45 time is (3:15) not (3:02) as stated on the record label)
- (M) (3:28) Pair 1195 Good Rockin'. *(:13 longer than the 45)*
- (S) (3:13) Rhino 70793 Anthology 1964-1977.

1966 SECRET AGENT MAN
- (S) (3:04) Rhino 70793 Anthology 1964-1977.
- (S) (3:04) EMI 90727 Very Best Of.
- (S) (3:04) EMI 46594 Best Of.
- (S) (3:04) Rhino 71749 Spy Magazine Presents: Spy Music.
- (S) (3:03) EMI 35976 Greatest Hits.
- (S) (3:05) Soul City 1007 Greatest Hits. *(rerecording)*

1966 (I WASHED MY HANDS IN) MUDDY WATER
- (S) (3:00) Rhino 70793 Anthology 1964-1977.
- (S) (3:04) EMI 46594 Best Of.

1966 POOR SIDE OF TOWN
- (S) (3:45) Rhino 70793 Anthology 1964-1977. *(:10 longer than LP length)*
- (S) (3:05) EMI 90727 Very Best Of. *(45 length)*
- (S) (3:35) EMI 46594 Best Of. *(LP length)*
- (S) (3:44) EMI 99900 Changes/Rewind. *(:09 longer than LP length)*
- (S) (3:34) EMI 35976 Greatest Hits. *(LP length)*
- (S) (4:26) Soul City 2008 The Memphis Sun Recordings. *(rerecording)*
- (S) (3:04) Soul City 1007 Greatest Hits. *(rerecording)*

1967 BABY I NEED YOUR LOVIN'
- (S) (3:17) Rhino 70793 Anthology 1964-1977. *(45 version but :10 longer)*
- (S) (3:05) EMI 90727 Very Best Of. *(LP version)*
- (S) (3:07) EMI 46594 Best Of. *(LP version)*
- (S) (3:24) EMI 99900 Changes/Rewind. *(LP version but :18 longer than the 45 or LP)*
- (S) (3:05) EMI 35976 Greatest Hits. *(LP version)*
- (S) (3:07) Soul City 1007 Greatest Hits. *(rerecording)*

1967 THE TRACKS OF MY TEARS
- (S) (2:56) Rhino 70793 Anthology 1964-1977.
- (S) (2:54) EMI 90727 Very Best Of.
- (S) (2:54) EMI 46594 Best Of.
- (S) (2:52) Pair 1195 Good Rockin'.
- (S) (2:59) EMI 99900 Changes/Rewind.
- (S) (2:53) EMI 35976 Greatest Hits.
- (S) (2:46) Soul City 1007 Greatest Hits. *(rerecording)*

1968 SUMMER RAIN
- (S) (3:49) Rhino 70793 Anthology 1964-1977. *(45 version but :12 longer)*
- (S) (3:37) EMI 46594 Best Of. *(LP version faded before ending sound effects)*
- (S) (3:52) Pair 1195 Good Rockin'. *(LP version with ending sound effects)*
- (S) (3:34) Soul City 1007 Greatest Hits. *(rerecording)*

1968 LOOK TO YOUR SOUL
- (S) (3:30) Rhino 70793 Anthology 1964-1977. *(:30 longer than 45 the version)*
- (S) (3:12) EMI 46594 Best Of. *(sound effects on introduction and ending; LP version)*

1969 MUDDY RIVER
    (S) (3:14) Rhino 70793 Anthology 1964-1977.

1973 ROCKIN' PNEUMONIA - BOOGIE WOOGIE FLU
    (S) (3:11) Rhino 70793 Anthology 1964-1977. *(edited; :15 shorter than either the LP or 45)*
    (S) (3:25) EMI 90727 Very Best Of.
    (S) (3:26) EMI 46594 Best Of.
    (S) (3:10) Epic 57871 O.S.T. My Girl 2. *(edited; :16 shorter than either the 45 or LP)*
    (S) (3:24) EMI 35976 Greatest Hits.
    (S) (2:31) Soul City 1007 Greatest Hits. *(rerecording)*

1973 BLUE SUEDE SHOES
    (S) (2:46) Rhino 70793 Anthology 1964-1977.
    (S) (2:49) EMI 90727 Very Best Of.
    (S) (2:45) EMI 46594 Best Of.
    (S) (2:48) Capitol 98139 Spring Break Volume 2.

1975 HELP ME RHONDA
    (S) (2:54) Rhino 70793 Anthology 1964-1977.
    (S) (2:52) Risky Business 67312 Got You Covered! Songs Of The Beach Boys.
    (S) (2:51) Eclipse Music Group 64894 Rock 'n Roll Relix 1974-1975.
    (S) (2:51) Eclipse Music Group 64897 Rock 'n Roll Relix 1970-1979.
    (S) (2:51) Soul City 1007 Greatest Hits. *(rerecording)*

1977 SWAYIN' TO THE MUSIC (SLOW DANCIN')
(dj copies of this 45 ran (3:25) and (3:58); commercial copies were all (3:58))
    (S) (4:01) Rhino 70793 Anthology 1964-1977.
    (S) (4:00) Soul City 1007 Greatest Hits. *(no fidelity)*

1978 CURIOUS MIND (UM, UM, UM, UM, UM, UM)

RIVIERAS
1964 CALIFORNIA SUN
    (M) (2:22) Rhino 70087 Summer & Sun.
    (M) (2:22) Rhino 75772 Son Of Frat Rock.
    (M) (2:21) JCI 3106 Surfin' Sixties.
    (M) (2:22) DCC Compact Classics 030 Beach Classics.
    (M) (2:22) A&M 3913 and 3340 O.S.T. Good Morning Vietnam.
    (M) (2:22) Rhino 71229 Summer Hits.
    (M) (2:22) Time-Life 2RNR-10 Rock 'N' Roll Era - 1964.
    (M) (2:22) Collectables 2510 WCBS-FM History Of Rock - The Rockin' 60's.
    (M) (2:22) Collectables 4510 History Of Rock/The Rockin' 60s.
    (E) (2:22) LaserLight 12322 Greatest Hit Singles Collection.
    (M) (2:22) Flashback 72710 Golden Summer.

RIVINGTONS
1962 PAPA-OOM-MOW-MOW
    (S) (2:21) EMI 90614 Non-Stop Party Rock.
    (S) (2:21) EMI 96268 24 Greatest Hits Of All Time.
    (S) (2:22) Capitol 48993 Spuds Mackenzie's Party Faves.
    (S) (2:22) Capitol 96861 Monster Summer Hits - Wild Surf.
    (S) (2:23) DCC Compact Classics 043 Toga Rock II.
    (S) (2:20) EMI 95204 The Liberty Years.
    (S) (2:22) Capitol 98138 Spring Break Volume 1.
    (S) (2:21) Time-Life 2RNR-29 Rock 'N' Roll Era - The 60's Rave On.
    (E) (2:15) K-Tel 6256 Kahuna Classics. *(rerecording)*

ROACHFORD
1989 CUDDLY TOY (FEEL FOR ME)
    (S) (3:47) Epic 45097 Roachford.
    (S) (3:47) Epic/Legacy 65255 Fizz Pop Modern Rock Volume 2.

ROB BASE & D.J. E-Z ROCK
1988 IT TAKES TWO
    (S) (5:00) Profile 1268 Mr. Magic's Rap Attack Volume 4.
    (S) (5:00) Priority 7990 Rapmasters 14 - The Best Of Hype.
    (S) (4:58) K-Tel 315 Rap's Biggest Hits.
    (S) (4:57) Thump 4010 Old School.
    (S) (4:58) Profile 1267 It Takes Two.

    (S) (4:32) Tommy Boy 1137 ESPN Presents Jock Jams. *(all songs on this cd are segued together with crowd sound effects added)*
    (S) (4:55) Thump 9951 Power 106 10th Anniversary Collection. *(all songs on this cd are segued together)*
    (S) (4:58) Rhino 72853 Kurtis Blow Presents The History Of Rap Vol. 3.

MARTY ROBBINS
1956 SINGING THE BLUES
    (M) (2:24) Columbia 46032 Columbia Country Classics Volume 4.
    (M) (2:25) Columbia 38870 A Lifetime Of Song.
    (M) (2:25) Columbia 45069 American Originals.
    (M) (2:25) Columbia 48537 Essential Marty Robbins.
    (M) (2:26) Time-Life CTD-13 Country USA - 1956.
    (M) (2:24) K-Tel 3108 Country Music Classics Volume XVI.
    (M) (2:24) K-Tel 794 Marty Robbins/Johnny Horton.
    (M) (2:24) Rhino 71902 Hillbilly Fever! Vol. 3. Legends Of Nashville.
    (M) (2:23) Time-Life R990-06 Marty Robbins - Legendary Country Singers.
    (M) (2:25) Columbia/Legacy 64763 The Story Of My Life: Best Of.
    (M) (2:24) Time-Life R808-03 Classic Country 1950-1959.

1957 A WHITE SPORT COAT (AND A PINK CARNATION)
    (M) (2:27) Columbia 45111 16 Most Requested Songs Of The 50's Volume 2.
    (M) (2:28) Columbia 38870 A Lifetime Of Song.
    (M) (2:28) Columbia 48537 Essential Marty Robbins.
    (M) (2:29) Time-Life CTD-02 Country USA - 1957.
    (M) (2:28) Time-Life HPD-36 Your Hit Parade - The 50's Pop Revival.
    (M) (2:29) K-Tel 794 Marty Robbins/Johnny Horton.
    (M) (2:28) Time-Life R990-06 Marty Robbins - Legendary Country Singers.
    (M) (2:28) Columbia/Legacy 64763 The Story Of My Life: Best Of.
    (M) (2:28) Time-Life R857-05 The Heart Of Rock 'n' Roll 1957.
    (M) (2:28) Verve 314537908 O.S.T. Going All The Way.
    (M) (2:28) Time-Life R808-03 Classic Country 1950-1959.

1958 THE STORY OF MY LIFE
    (M) (2:30) Columbia 38870 A Lifetime Of Song.
    (M) (2:31) Columbia 48537 Essential Marty Robbins.
    (M) (2:31) Time-Life CTD-02 Country U.S.A. - 1957.
    (S) (2:28) Time-Life R990-06 Marty Robbins - Legendary Country Singers.
    (M) (2:31) Columbia/Legacy 64763 The Story Of My Life: Best Of.

1958 JUST MARRIED
    (M) (2:06) Columbia 48537 Essential Marty Robbins.
    (M) (2:07) Time-Life CTD-07 Country U.S.A. - 1958.
    (S) (2:05) Time-Life R990-06 Marty Robbins - Legendary Country Singers.
    (S) (2:05) Columbia/Legacy 64763 The Story Of My Life: Best Of.

1958 SHE WAS ONLY SEVENTEEN (HE WAS ONE YEAR MORE)
    (S) (2:20) Columbia 48537 Essential Marty Robbins.
    (M) (2:22) Columbia 45069 American Originals.

1959 THE HANGING TREE
    (S) (2:50) Columbia 48537 Essential Marty Robbins.
    (M) (2:52) Columbia 38870 A Lifetime Of Song.
    (S) (2:50) Columbia 31361 All-Time Greatest Hits.
    (M) (2:49) Columbia 44374 Hollywood Magic - The 1950's.

1960 EL PASO
(stereo versions of El Paso omit several lines that are found on the mono or 45 version of this song; those lines start 1:28 into the mono version with "just for a moment....." and go to 1:43 ".....and that was to run"; dj copies of this 45 ran (4:37) and (2:58); commercial copies were all (4:37))
    (S) (4:19) Columbia 45017 Radio Classics Of The 50's.
    (M) (4:39) Rhino 70681 Billboard's Top Country Hits Of 1960.
    (M) (4:39) Rhino 70718 Legends Of Guitar - Country Volume 1.

MARTY ROBBINS *(Continued)*

(S)	(4:19)	Columbia 46031	Columbia Country Classics Volume 3.
(S)	(4:22)	Columbia 08435	More Greatest Hits.
(S)	(4:20)	Columbia 38309	Biggest Hits.
(S)	(4:20)	Columbia 00116	Gunfighter Ballads.
(M)	(4:39)	Columbia 38870	A Lifetime Of Song.
(S)	(4:20)	Columbia 31361	All Time Greatest.
(M)	(4:38)	Columbia 48537	Essential Marty Robbins.
(M)	(4:39)	Time-Life CTD-09	Country USA - 1959.
(M)	(4:38)	Time-Life SUD-15	Superhits - The Early 60's.
(M)	(4:39)	Time-Life HPD-13	Your Hit Parade - 1959.
(S)	(4:21)	Legacy 66796	Texas.
(M)	(4:38)	Columbia/Legacy 53817	All-Time Legends Of Country Music.
(S)	(4:22)	K-Tel 794	Marty Robbins/Johnny Horton.
(S)	(4:21)	K-Tel 225	Country Music Classics Volume I.
(M)	(4:39)	DCC Compact Classics 078	Best Of Tragedy.
(M)	(4:37)	Time-Life R990-06	Marty Robbins - Legendary Country Singers.
(S)	(4:21)	K-Tel 3323	Gunfighter Ballads.
(S)	(4:20)	Columbia 67131	Super Hits.
(S)	(4:21)	Columbia/Legacy 64763	The Story Of My Life: Best Of.
(S)	(4:19)	JCI 3152	1955 - Only Country - 1959.
(S)	(4:21)	K-Tel 3355	101 Greatest Country Hits Vol. One: Forever Country.
(M)	(4:39)	Time-Life AM1-19	AM Gold - The Early '60s.
(S)	(4:20)	Columbia 67737	Texas Super Hits.
(M)	(4:38)	Time-Life R808-01	Classic Country 1960-1964.

1960 BIG IRON

(S)	(3:57)	Columbia 46031	Columbia Country Classics Volume 3.
(S)	(3:57)	Columbia 08435	More Greatest Hits.
(S)	(3:57)	Columbia 00116	Gunfighter Ballads.
(M)	(3:54)	Columbia 38870	A Lifetime Of Song.
(S)	(3:56)	Columbia 31361	All Time Greatest.
(M)	(3:52)	Columbia 48537	Essential Marty Robbins.
(S)	(3:56)	Rhino 71263 and 71451	Songs Of The West.
(S)	(3:57)	Time-Life CTD-12	Country USA - 1960.
(S)	(3:56)	Rhino 71681	Songs Of The West Vol. One: Cowboy Classics.
(S)	(3:57)	K-Tel 3329	The Singing Cowboys.
(S)	(3:57)	Time-Life R990-06	Marty Robbins - Legendary Country Singers.
(S)	(3:57)	K-Tel 3323	Gunfighter Ballads.
(S)	(3:55)	Columbia/Legacy 64763	The Story Of My Life: Best Of.

1960 IS THERE ANY CHANCE

(S)	(2:09)	Columbia 08435	More Greatest Hits.

1960 BALLAD OF THE ALAMO

(S)	(3:39)	Columbia 08435	More Greatest Hits.
(S)	(3:39)	Rhino 71263 and 71451	Songs Of The West.
(S)	(3:39)	Rhino 71684	Songs Of The West Vol. Four: Movie And Television Themes.
(S)	(3:38)	Legacy 66796	Texas.
(S)	(3:38)	Legacy/Columbia 66138	O.S.T. The Alamo.
(S)	(3:39)	Rhino 72423	Billboard Top Movie Hits - 1960s.

1961 DON'T WORRY

(S)	(3:13)	Columbia 08435	More Greatest Hits.
(M)	(3:09)	Columbia 38870	A Lifetime Of Song.
(S)	(3:12)	Columbia 31361	All Time Greatest.
(M)	(3:08)	Columbia 48537	Essential Marty Robbins.
(M)	(3:08)	Reprise 45516	O.S.T. A Perfect World.
(M)	(3:09)	Time-Life CTD-01	Country USA - 1961.
(M)	(3:10)	K-Tel 763	Country Music Classics Volume VIII.
(S)	(3:13)	Time-Life R990-06	Marty Robbins - Legendary Country Singers.
(S)	(3:13)	Columbia/Legacy 64763	The Story Of My Life: Best Of.
(S)	(3:13)	JCI 3153	1960 - Only Country - 1964.

1962 DEVIL WOMAN

(S)	(2:50)	Columbia 46032	Columbia Country Classics Volume 4.
(M)	(2:51)	Columbia 38870	A Lifetime Of Song.
(S)	(2:51)	Columbia 31361	All Time Greatest.
(S)	(2:50)	Columbia 48537	Essential Marty Robbins.

(S)	(2:51)	Time-Life CTD-03	Country USA - 1962.
(S)	(2:51)	K-Tel 794	Marty Robbins/Johnny Horton.
(S)	(2:50)	Time-Life R990-06	Marty Robbins - Legendary Country Singers.
(S)	(2:51)	Columbia 67131	Super Hits.
(S)	(2:51)	Columbia/Legacy 64763	The Story Of My Life: Best Of.
(S)	(2:50)	Epic 67941	Super Hits Of The 60's.

1962 RUBY ANN

(M)	(1:58)	Columbia 38870	A Lifetime Of Song.
(M)	(1:58)	Columbia 45069	American Originals.
(M)	(1:59)	Columbia 48537	Essential Marty Robbins.
(M)	(1:58)	Time-Life CTD-03	Country USA - 1962.
(S)	(1:58)	Time-Life R990-06	Marty Robbins - Legendary Country Singers.
(S)	(1:58)	Columbia/Legacy 64763	The Story Of My Life: Best Of.
(S)	(1:59)	Koch 7932	Rock'n Roll'n Robbins.

1970 MY WOMAN, MY WOMAN, MY WIFE

(S)	(3:31)	Columbia 38870	A Lifetime Of Song.
(S)	(3:30)	Columbia 31361	All Time Greatest.
(S)	(3:31)	Columbia 48537	Essential Marty Robbins.
(S)	(3:29)	Time-Life CTD-04	Country USA - 1970.
(S)	(3:31)	K-Tel 794	Marty Robbins/Johnny Horton.
(S)	(3:30)	Time-Life R990-06	Marty Robbins - Legendary Country Singers.
(S)	(3:30)	Columbia 67131	Super Hits.
(S)	(3:30)	Time-Life R808-04	Classic Country 1970-1974.

ROBERT & JOHNNY
1958 WE BELONG TOGETHER

(M)	(2:43)	Sire 26617	O.S.T. A Rage In Harlem.
(M)	(2:44)	Time-Life 2RNR-21	The Rock 'N' Roll Era - 1958: Still Rockin'.
(M)	(2:46)	Rhino 72507	Doo Wop Box II.
(M)	(2:44)	K-Tel 3812	Doo Wop's Greatest Hits.
(M)	(2:46)	Time-Life R857-16	The Heart Of Rock 'n' Roll The Late '50s.

AUSTIN ROBERTS
1972 SOMETHING'S WRONG WITH ME

(S)	(3:07)	Rhino 70929	Super Hits Of The 70's Volume 9.
(S)	(3:07)	Varese Sarabande 5670	Songs Of Tommy Boyce And Bobby Hart.
(S)	(3:06)	K-Tel 3623	Believe In Music.

1975 ROCKY

(S)	(3:35)	Rhino 70762	Super Hits Of The 70's Volume 15.
(S)	(3:35)	K-Tel 3624	Music Express.

KANE ROBERTS
1991 DOES ANYBODY REALLY FALL IN LOVE ANYMORE?

(S)	(4:24)	DGC 24320	Saints And Sinners.

DON ROBERTSON
1956 THE HAPPY WHISTLER

(M)	(2:23)	Time-Life HPD-28	Your Hit Parade - The Fabulous 50's.
(M)	(2:24)	EMI-Capitol Music Special Markets 19446	Lost Hits Of The '50s.

IVO ROBIC
1959 MORGEN

ROBIN S
1993 SHOW ME LOVE

(S)	(4:27)	Big Beat 92425	Start The Party Volume 1. *(remix)*
(S)	(4:27)	Atlantic 82509	Show Me Love.
(S)	(7:42)	Atlantic 82509	Show Me Love. *(remix)*
(S)	(4:27)	JCI 3132	1990 - Only Rock 'n Roll - 1994.
(S)	(4:27)	Razor & Tie 4569	'90s Style.

FLOYD ROBINSON
1959 MAKIN' LOVE

(S)	(1:54)	RCA 8466	Nipper's Greatest Hits Of The 50's Volume 1.
(S)	(1:53)	RCA 66881	RCA's Greatest One-Hit Wonders.

SMOKEY ROBINSON
1974 BABY COME CLOSE
- (S) (3:26) Motown 6071 Smokey Robinson & The Miracles Compact Command Performances. *(45 version)*
- (S) (3:24) Motown 5118 Superstar Series Volume 18. *(45 version)*
- (S) (4:58) Motown 5134 Smokey. *(LP version)*
- (S) (3:46) Motown 8028 and 8128 Smokey/A Quiet Storm. *(edit of LP version)*
- (S) (3:26) Motown 5401 Blame It On Love And All The Great Hits. *(45 version)*
- (S) (3:27) Motown 314530510 Motown Year By Year 1973. *(45 version)*
- (S) (4:57) Right Stuff 31973 Slow Jams: The Timeless Collection Volume 3. *(LP version)*
- (S) (3:27) MCA 11329 Soul Train 25th Anniversary Box Set. *(45 version)*
- (S) (4:57) Motown 314530775 The Ultimate Collection. *(LP version)*

1975 BABY THAT'S BACKATCHA
- (S) (3:39) Motown 6071 Smokey Robinson & The Miracles Compact Command Performances. *(45 version)*
- (S) (3:48) Motown 5197 A Quiet Storm. *(LP version sound effects; tracks into next selection)*
- (S) (3:38) Motown 5118 Superstar Series Volume 18. *(45 version)*
- (S) (3:48) Motown 8028 and 8128 Smokey/A Quiet Storm. *(LP version sound effects; tracks into next selection)*
- (S) (3:38) Motown 314530531 Motown Year By Year - 1975. *(45 version)*
- (S) (3:48) Thump 9947 Cruizin' To Motown. *(LP version sound effects)*
- (S) (3:48) Motown 314530775 The Ultimate Collection. *(LP version sound effects; tracks into next selection)*

1975 THE AGONY AND THE ECSTASY
(actual 45 time is (3:13) not (4:15) as stated on the record label)
- (S) (4:46) Original Sound 9303 Art Laboe's Dedicated To You Vol. 3. *(LP version)*
- (S) (3:13) Motown 5118 Superstar Series Volume 18. *(45 version)*
- (S) (3:23) Motown 8028 and 8128 Smokey/A Quiet Storm. *(edit of LP version)*
- (S) (4:49) Motown 5197 A Quiet Storm. *(LP version)*
- (S) (4:48) Motown 314530573 Baddest Love Jams Volume 2 - Fire And Desire. *(LP version)*
- (S) (4:42) Right Stuff 54485 Slow Jams: The Timeless Collection Volume 7. *(LP version faded :07 early)*
- (S) (4:47) Motown 314530775 The Ultimate Collection. *(LP version)*

1980 CRUISIN'
(actual 45 time is (4:26) not (4:11) as stated on the record label)
- (S) (4:27) Motown 6139 The Composer Series: Smokey Robinson. *(45 version)*
- (S) (4:26) Motown 6177 Endless Love: 15 Of Motown's Greatest Love Songs. *(45 version)*
- (S) (4:25) Motown 6110 Motown Grammy Rhythm & Blues Performances Of The 60's & 70's. *(45 version)*
- (S) (4:26) Motown 9035 and 5324 Top Ten With A Bullet! *(45 version)*
- (S) (4:26) Motown 6071 Smokey Robinson & The Miracles Compact Command Performances. *(45 version)*
- (S) (5:53) Motown 5267 Where There's Smoke. *(LP version)*
- (S) (5:53) Motown 8001 and 8101 Being With You/Where There's Smoke. *(LP version)*
- (S) (4:19) Motown 5401 Blame It On Love And All The Great Hits. *(45 version faded :07 early)*
- (S) (4:28) Motown 6358 Hitsville USA Volume Two. *(45 version)*
- (S) (4:28) Motown 6334 Smokey Robinson & The Miracles 35th Anniversary Collection. *(45 version)*
- (S) (4:28) Rhino 71618 Soul Train Hall Of Fame/20th Anniversary. *(45 version)*

- (S) (4:19) Time-Life SOD-19 Sounds Of The Seventies - 1979: Take Two. *(45 version faded :07 early)*
- (S) (4:18) Motown/Essex 374638529 Motown Legends - The Ballad Album. *(45 version faded :06 early)*
- (S) (4:24) Original Sound 8859r Oldies But Goodies Vol. 9. *(remastered edition)*
- (S) (4:24) Original Sound 2223 Oldies But Goodies Volumes 2,7,9,12 and 13 Box Set. *(Volumes 2, 7 and 12 of this box set use the "Waring - fds" noise reduction process)*
- (S) (4:24) Original Sound 2500 Oldies But Goodies Volumes 1-15 Box Set. *(most volumes in this box set use the "Waring - fds" noise reduction process)*
- (S) (4:25) Polygram Special Markets 314520030 Motown Legends - Love Songs. *(45 version)*
- (S) (4:26) Time-Life R988-07 Sounds Of The Eighties: 1980. *(45 version)*
- (S) (4:25) Time-Life R138-18 Body Talk. *(45 version)*
- (S) (4:27) Thump 9947 Cruizin' To Motown. *(45 version)*
- (S) (5:53) Motown 314530544 Baddest Love Jams Volume 3: After The Dance. *(LP version)*
- (S) (4:18) JCI 3147 1980 - Only Love - 1984. *(45 version faded :06 early)*
- (S) (4:26) Motown/Essex 374638519 Motown Legends - Cruisin'/Being With You. *(45 version)*
- (S) (4:26) Priority 50928 Rare Grooves Volume 1. *(45 version)*
- (S) (4:27) Time-Life R834-04 Body Talk - Together Forever. *(45 version)*
- (S) (5:53) Motown 314530775 The Ultimate Collection. *(LP version)*
- (S) (4:27) JCI 3175 1975 - Only Soul - 1979. *(45 version)*

1980 LET ME BE THE CLOCK
- (S) (3:38) Motown 5401 Blame It On Love And All The Great Hits. *(45 version)*
- (S) (3:42) Motown 314530516 Motown Year By Year 1980. *(45 version)*
- (S) (5:14) Motown 314530775 The Ultimate Collection. *(LP version)*

1981 BEING WITH YOU
(45 length is (3:57); LP length is (4:05))
- (S) (4:06) Motown 6139 The Composer Series: Smokey Robinson.
- (S) (4:05) Motown 6177 Endless Love: 15 Of Motown's Greatest Love Songs.
- (S) (4:05) Motown 9082 and 5385 Great Motown Love Songs.
- (S) (4:05) Motown 9035 and 5324 Top Ten With A Bullet!
- (S) (3:57) Rhino 70676 Billboard Top Hits - 1981.
- (S) (4:05) Motown 6071 Smokey Robinson & The Miracles Compact Command Performances.
- (S) (4:07) Motown 8001 and 8101 Being With You/Where There's Smoke.
- (S) (4:07) Motown 5349 Being With You.
- (S) (3:58) Motown 5401 Blame It On Love And All The Great Hits.
- (S) (3:59) Motown 6358 Hitsville USA Volume Two.
- (S) (3:59) Motown 6334 Smokey Robinson & The Miracles 35th Anniversary Collection.
- (S) (4:05) Polygram Special Markets 314520030 Motown Legends - Love Songs.
- (S) (4:05) K-Tel 3263 The 80's Love Jams.
- (S) (3:57) Time-Life R988-08 Sounds Of The Eighties: 1981.
- (S) (3:59) Rhino 72159 Black Entertainment Television - 15th Anniversary.
- (S) (3:57) Rebound 314520361 Class Reunion '81.
- (S) (3:58) Motown/Essex 374638519 Motown Legends - Cruisin'/Being With You.
- (S) (4:05) Time-Life R834-05 Body Talk - Sealed With A Kiss.
- (S) (4:00) Motown 314530775 The Ultimate Collection.
- (S) (3:57) Beast 53442 Original Players Of Love.

1982 TELL ME TOMORROW (PART 1)
- (S) (5:06) Motown 5401 Blame It On Love And All The Great Hits. *(neither the 45 or LP version)*
- (S) (3:47) Motown 314530534 Motown Year By Year - 1982.
- (S) (3:47) Motown 314530775 The Ultimate Collection.

1987 JUST TO SEE HER
- (S) (4:02) Sandstone 33049 and 5017 Cosmopolitan Volume 3.

SMOKEY ROBINSON *(Continued)*

- (S) (4:02) DCC Compact Classics 088 Night Moves Volume 6.
- (S) (4:02) Motown 6358 Hitsville USA Volume Two.
- (S) (4:02) Motown 6226 One Heartbeat.
- (S) (4:01) Motown 314530557 Motown Year By Year - 1987.
- (S) (4:01) Time-Life R834-10 Body Talk - From The Heart.
- (S) (4:01) Motown 314530775 The Ultimate Collection.
- (S) (4:00) Polygram Special Markets 314520445 Soul Hits Of The 80's.

1987 ONE HEARTBEAT
(actual 45 time is (4:05) not (3:38) as stated on the record label)

- (S) (4:03) Motown 6358 Hitsville USA Volume Two.
- (S) (4:04) Motown 6226 One Heartbeat.
- (S) (4:04) Motown 314530557 Motown Year By Year - 1987.
- (S) (4:01) Time-Life R834-07 Body Talk - Hearts In Motion.
- (S) (4:03) Motown 314530775 The Ultimate Collection.

SMOKEY ROBINSON & THE MIRACLES (see MIRACLES)

VICKI SUE ROBINSON
1976 TURN THE BEAT AROUND

- (S) (5:31) RCA 7639 Dance! Dance! Dance! *(LP version)*
- (S) (4:07) RCA 9684 and 8476 Nipper's Greatest Hits - The 70's. *(neither the LP or 45 length)*
- (S) (3:23) Rhino 70984 The Disco Years Volume 1. *(45 version)*
- (S) (3:23) Rhino 70799 O.S.T. Spirit Of '76. *(45 version)*
- (S) (3:22) Razor & Tie 22496 Disco Fever. *(45 version)*
- (S) (3:23) Time-Life SOD-27 Sounds Of The Seventies - Dance Fever. *(45 version)*
- (S) (5:32) Priority 53728 Mega Hits Dance Classics Vol 12. *(LP version)*
- (S) (5:29) Rebound 314520217 Disco Nights Vol. 1 - Divas Of Dance. *(LP version)*
- (S) (3:23) Rhino 72414 Dance Floor Divas: The 70's. *(45 version)*
- (S) (3:22) JCI 3148 1975 - Only Dance - 1979. *(45 version)*
- (S) (3:23) JCI 3163 18 Disco Superhits. *(45 version)*
- (S) (3:22) Scotti Bros. 75504 Club Ladies Night. *(45 version)*
- (S) (4:07) Eclipse Music Group 64895 Rock 'n Roll Relix 1976-1977. *(neither the 45 or LP length)*
- (S) (4:07) Eclipse Music Group 64897 Rock 'n Roll Relix 1970-1979. *(neither the 45 or LP length)*
- (S) (3:23) Rhino 72812 VH1 8-Track Flashback: The One Hit Wonders. *(45 version)*
- (S) (3:23) Polydor 314555120 Pure Disco 2. *(45 version)*
- (S) (5:30) Beast 53202 Disco Divas - A Salute To The Ladies. *(LP version)*
- (S) (3:23) Time-Life R840-07 Sounds Of The Seventies: '70s Dance Party 1976-1977. *(45 version)*
- (S) (3:22) Collectables 1516 and 2516 The Anniversary Album - The 70's. *(45 version)*
- (S) (4:05) K-Tel 4066 K-Tel's Original Party Music Vol. 2. *(neither the 45 or LP length)*

ROBYN
1997 DO YOU KNOW (WHAT IT TAKES)

- (S) (3:40) RCA 67477 Robyn Is Here.

1997 SHOW ME LOVE

- (S) (3:48) RCA 67477 Robyn Is Here.

ROCHELL and THE CANDLES
1961 ONCE UPON A TIME

- (M) (2:38) Collectables 5062 History Of Rock Volume 2. *(mastered from vinyl)*
- (M) (2:39) Collectables 2502 WCBS-FM History Of Rock - The 60's Part 3. *(mastered from vinyl)*
- (M) (2:39) Collectables 4502 History Of Rock/The 60s Part Three. *(mastered from vinyl)*

ROCK-A-TEENS
1959 WOO-HOO

- (M) (2:05) Rhino 70742 Rock This Town: Rockabilly Hits Volume 2. *(sounds like it was mastered from vinyl)*
- (M) (2:03) Rhino 71601 Rock Instrumental Classics Volume 1: The Fifties. *(sounds like it was mastered from vinyl)*
- (M) (2:03) Rhino 72035 Rock Instrumental Classics Vols. 1-5 Box Set. *(sounds like it was mastered from vinyl)*
- (M) (2:03) Time-Life 2RNR-33 Rock 'N' Roll Era - The 50's Last Dance. *(sounds like it was mastered from vinyl)*
- (M) (2:05) MCA Special Products 20902 Classic Rock & Roll Instrumental Hits, Volume 1. *(sounds like it was mastered from vinyl)*
- (M) (2:02) JCI 3188 1955 - Only Dance - 1959. *(sounds like it was mastered from vinyl)*
- (M) (2:02) Sony Music Special Products 22210 Fun Rock. *(sounds like it was mastered from vinyl)*

ROCKETS
1979 OH WELL

- (S) (3:09) Rhino 72132 Frat Rock: More Of The 70's.
- (S) (3:08) Rhino 72299 Superhits Of The 70's Volume 25.

ROCKWELL
1984 SOMEBODY'S WATCHING ME

- (S) (4:57) Motown 9110 Motown Memories Vol. 4 - Where Were You When. *(LP version)*
- (S) (4:54) Rebound 314520307 Disco Nights Volume VIII. *(LP version)*
- (S) (3:57) Motown 6358 Hitsville USA Volume Two. *(45 version)*
- (S) (3:56) Time-Life R988-06 Sounds Of The Eighties. 1984. *(45 version)*
- (S) (3:57) Rhino 72159 Black Entertainment Television - 15th Anniversary. *(45 version)*
- (S) (3:54) Motown 314530849 Motown 40 Forever. *(45 version)*
- (S) (3:57) JCI 3176 1980 - Only Soul - 1984. *(45 version)*

1984 OBSCENE PHONE CALLER

- (S) (3:25) Priority 53703 Hot And Sexy - Passion And Soul.

ROCKY FELLERS
1963 KILLER JOE

- (M) (2:18) Garland 011 Footstompin' Oldies.
- (M) (2:19) Capricorn 42003 The Scepter Records Story.
- (E) (2:18) Time-Life 2RNR-29 Rock 'N' Roll Era - The 60's Rave On.
- (S) (2:18) Ripete 2187-RE Preppy Deluxe. *(mastered from vinyl)*
- (M) (2:19) King 1421 Party Time Rock & Roll.

EILEEN RODGERS
1956 MIRACLE OF LOVE
1958 TREASURE OF YOUR LOVE

JIMMIE RODGERS
1957 HONEYCOMB

- (M) (2:14) Rhino 70942 Best Of.
- (M) (2:14) Collectables 5416 Murray The K - Sing Along With The Golden Gassers. *(truncated fade)*
- (S) (2:11) MCA 31086 Best Of. *(rerecording)*
- (S) (2:11) Curb 77442 Best Of. *(rerecording)*
- (M) (2:13) Time-Life 2RNR-33 Rock 'N' Roll Era - The 50's Last Dance.
- (E) (2:14) Time-Life CTD-02 Country USA - 1957.
- (M) (2:14) Time-Life HPD-17 Your Hit Parade - 1957.
- (M) (2:14) Polygram Special Markets 314520258 No. 1 Hits Of The 50's.
- (M) (2:13) JCI 7021 Those Wonderful Years - April Love.
- (M) (2:15) Time-Life R808-03 Classic Country 1950-1959.

1957 KISSES SWEETER THAN WINE

- (M) (2:19) Rhino 70942 Best Of.
- (S) (2:16) MCA 31086 Best Of. *(rerecording)*
- (S) (2:16) Curb 77442 Best Of. *(rerecording)*

(M) (2:19)   Time-Life HPD-17   Your Hit Parade - 1957.
(M) (2:20)   JCI 3152   1955 - Only Country - 1959.

1958 OH-OH, I'M FALLING IN LOVE AGAIN
(M) (2:12)   Rhino 70942   Best Of.
(S) (2:15)   MCA 31086   Best Of. *(rerecording)*
(S) (2:15)   Curb 77442   Best Of. *(rerecording)*
(M) (2:10)   Time-Life HPD-11   Your Hit Parade 1958.

1958 SECRETLY
(M) (2:34)   Rhino 70942   Best Of.
(M) (2:34)   Curb 77442   Best Of.
(M) (2:34)   Time-Life HPD-11   Your Hit Parade 1958.
(M) (2:34)   Time-Life R857-04   The Heart Of Rock 'n' Roll - 1958.
(M) (2:34)   JCI 3183   1955 - Only Love - 1959.

1958 MAKE ME A MIRACLE
(M) (2:00)   Rhino 70942   Best Of.
(M) (2:00)   Curb 77442   Best Of.

1958 ARE YOU REALLY MINE
(S) (2:25)   Rhino 70942   Best Of.
(S) (2:15)   MCA 31086   Best Of. *(rerecording)*
(S) (2:15)   Curb 77442   Best Of. *(rerecording)*

1958 BIMBOMBEY
(M) (2:14)   Rhino 70942   Best Of.
(S) (2:10)   MCA 31086   Best Of. *(rerecording)*
(S) (2:10)   Curb 77442   Best Of. *(rerecording)*

1959 I'M NEVER GONNA TELL
(M) (1:50)   Rhino 70942   Best Of.

1959 RING-A-LING-A-LARIO
(S) (2:20)   Rhino 70942   Best Of.

1959 TUCUMCARI
(S) (2:12)   Rhino 70942   Best Of.
(S) (2:12)   Curb 77442   Best Of.

1960 T.L.C. TENDER LOVE AND CARE
(S) (2:14)   Rhino 70942   Best Of.

1966 IT'S OVER
(S) (2:37)   Rhino 70942   Best Of.
(S) (2:37)   MCA 31086   Best Of.
(S) (2:37)   Curb 77442   Best Of.

1967 CHILD OF CLAY
(S) (4:07)   Rhino 70942   Best Of.

TOMMY ROE
1962 SHEILA
(S) (1:59)   Rhino 70623   Billboard's Top Rock & Roll Hits Of 1962. *(LP mix)*
(S) (1:59)   Rhino 72007   Billboard's Top Rock & Roll Hits 1962-1966 Box Set. *(LP mix)*
(S) (2:02)   MCA 31203   Vintage Music Volume 6. *(LP mix)*
(S) (2:02)   MCA 5804   Vintage Music Volumes 5 & 6. *(LP mix)*
(S) (2:02)   Curb 77525   Greatest Hits Of Rock 'N' Roll Volume 2. *(LP mix)*
(S) (2:03)   Curb 77299   Best Of. *(LP mix)*
(M) (2:01)   MCA 10884   Greatest Hits. *(45 mix)*
(S) (1:59)   Time-Life 2RNR-02   Rock 'N' Roll Era - 1962. *(LP mix)*
(S) (1:58)   Time-Life R962-05   History Of Rock 'N' Roll: The Teenage Years 1957-1964. *(LP mix)*
(S) (2:02)   Collectables 2504   WCBS-FM History Of Rock - The 60's Part 4. *(LP mix)*
(S) (2:02)   Collectables 4504   History Of Rock/The 60s Part Four. *(LP mix)*
(S) (2:03)   Curb 77652   Greatest Hits. *(LP mix)*
(S) (2:02)   MCA Special Products 22019   Summer Hits Of The 50's And 60's. *(LP mix)*
(S) (2:02)   MCA Special Products 22172   Vintage Collectibles Volume 10. *(LP mix)*
(S) (2:02)   MCA Special Products 20899   Rock Around The Oldies #4. *(LP mix)*
(M) (2:01)   MCA Special Products 21023   Tommy Roe/Brian Hyland Sing The Big Hits. *(45 mix)*

1962 SUSIE DARLIN'
1963 EVERYBODY
(E) (1:49)   MCA 5938   Vintage Music Volumes 15 & 16.
(E) (1:49)   MCA 31212   Vintage Music Volume 15.
(S) (3:11)   Curb 77299   Best Of. *(rerecording)*
(M) (1:55)   MCA 10884   Greatest Hits.

(M) (1:48)   Time-Life 2RNR-19   Rock 'N' Roll Era - 1963 Still Rockin'.
(M) (1:55)   Curb 77652   Greatest Hits.
(S) (4:23)   Curb 77651   Retro Rock Dance Hits. *(all selections on this cd are remixed with extra instrumentation added)*
(M) (1:54)   MCA Special Products 21023   Tommy Roe/Brian Hyland Sing The Big Hits.

1964 COME ON
(M) (2:04)   MCA 10884   Greatest Hits.

1966 SWEET PEA
(S) (2:08)   MCA 5939   Vintage Music Volumes 17 & 18.
(S) (2:08)   MCA 31215   Vintage Music Volume 18.
(S) (2:08)   Curb 77299   Best Of.
(S) (2:10)   MCA 10884   Greatest Hits.
(S) (2:08)   Curb 77652   Greatest Hits.
(S) (2:08)   MCA Special Products 22132   Vintage Collectibles Volume 3.
(S) (2:09)   MCA Special Products 20948   Biggest Summer Hits.
(S) (2:09)   MCA Special Products 21023   Tommy Roe/Brian Hyland Sing The Big Hits.

1966 HOORAY FOR HAZEL
(S) (2:27)   MCA 10884   Greatest Hits.
(S) (2:25)   Curb 77652   Greatest Hits.
(S) (2:25)   MCA Special Products 20981   Bubble Gum Classics.

1967 IT'S NOW WINTERS DAY
(S) (3:21)   MCA 10884   Greatest Hits.
(S) (3:22)   Risky Business 53922   Whole Lotta Lava.
(S) (3:21)   Varese Sarabande 5801   Sunshine Days - Pop Classics Of The '60s Volume 1.

1969 DIZZY
(S) (2:57)   Rhino 70630   Billboard's Top Rock & Roll Hits Of 1969. *(LP speed)*
(S) (2:57)   Rhino 72005   Billboard's Top Rock & Roll Hits 1968-1972 Box Set. *(LP speed)*
(S) (2:57)   MCA 31207   Vintage Music Volume 10. *(LP speed)*
(S) (2:57)   MCA 5806   Vintage Music Volumes 9 & 10. *(LP speed)*
(S) (2:56)   Curb 77299   Best Of. *(LP speed)*
(S) (2:52)   MCA 10884   Greatest Hits. *(45 speed)*
(S) (2:56)   Time-Life 2CLR-06   Classic Rock - 1969. *(LP speed)*
(S) (2:56)   Curb 77652   Greatest Hits. *(LP speed)*
(S) (2:56)   MCA Special Products 20580   Teen Idols. *(LP speed)*
(S) (2:56)   MCA Special Products 20783   Rock Around The Oldies #1. *(LP speed)*
(S) (2:57)   MCA Special Products 22130   Vintage Collectibles Volume 1. *(LP speed)*
(S) (2:52)   Varese Sarabande 5575   Bubblegum Classics Volume Two. *(45 speed)*
(S) (2:52)   K-Tel 3386   Best Of Bubblegum Music. *(45 speed)*
(S) (2:56)   MCA Special Products 20900   Rock Around The Oldies #3. *(LP speed)*
(S) (2:52)   MCA Special Products 20981   Bubble Gum Classics. *(45 speed)*
(S) (2:56)   MCA Special Products 21017   The Rockin' Sixties. *(LP speed)*
(S) (2:52)   MCA Special Products 21023   Tommy Roe/Brian Hyland Sing The Big Hits. *(45 speed)*
(S) (2:52)   MCA Special Products 21046   Top Singles Of The Sixties. *(45 speed)*

1969 HEATHER HONEY
(S) (2:51)   MCA 10884   Greatest Hits.

1970 JAM UP JELLY TIGHT
(S) (2:18)   MCA 10884   Greatest Hits.
(S) (2:18)   Time-Life 2CLR-12   Classic Rock - 1969: The Beat Goes On.
(S) (2:18)   Curb 77652   Greatest Hits.
(S) (2:18)   Varese Sarabande 5535   Bubblegum Classics Volume One.
(S) (2:18)   MCA Special Products 21023   Tommy Roe/Brian Hyland Sing The Big Hits.

1971 STAGGER LEE
- (S) (3:20) MCA 10884 Greatest Hits. *(faster pitch than either the 45 or LP; neither the LP version which faded in or the 45 version which faded :28 sooner)*
- (S) (3:20) Madacy Entertainment 1971 Rock On 1971. *(faster pitch than either the 45 or LP; neither the LP version which faded in or the 45 version which faded :28 sooner)*

ROGER
1988 I WANT TO BE YOUR MAN
- (S) (4:10) Reprise 25496 Unlimited!
- (S) (4:08) Reprise 45143 Zapp & Roger - All The Greatest Hits.
- (S) (4:01) Rhino 72142 Billboard Hot R&B Hits 1987.
- (S) (4:08) Thump 4730 Old School Love Songs Volume 3.
- (S) (3:46) JCI 3177 1985 - Only Soul - 1989. *(neither the 45 or LP version)*
- (S) (4:01) Warner Brothers 46130 Love Jams Volume Two.
- (S) (4:01) Time-Life R834-10 Body Talk - From The Heart.
- (S) (3:59) K-Tel 6257 The Greatest Love Songs - 16 Soft Rock Hits.

released as by ZAPP & ROGER:
1994 SLOW AND EASY
- (S) (5:10) Reprise 45143 Zapp & Roger - All The Greatest Hits.

JULIE ROGERS
1965 THE WEDDING
- (S) (2:25) Eric 11503 Hard To Find 45's On CD (Volume II) 1961-64.

KENNY ROGERS
1977 LUCILLE
- (S) (3:37) Liberty 46004 Greatest Hits.
- (S) (3:34) EMI 46106 Twenty Greatest Hits.
- (S) (3:36) EMI 48047 Ten Years Of Gold.
- (S) (3:38) EMI 48402 Kenny Rogers.
- (S) (3:34) EMI 46673 25 Greatest Hits.
- (S) (3:34) Curb 77358 Greatest Country Hits.
- (S) (3:31) Reprise 26711 20 Great Years. *(all selections on this cd are rerecorded)*
- (S) (3:34) Capitol 35779 Best Of.

1977 DAYTIME FRIENDS
- (S) (3:08) EMI 46106 Twenty Greatest Hits.
- (S) (3:08) EMI 48047 Ten Years Of Gold.
- (S) (3:10) EMI 46673 25 Greatest Hits.
- (S) (3:10) Curb 77358 Greatest Country Hits.
- (S) (3:22) Reprise 26711 20 Great Years. *(all selections on this cd are rerecorded)*

1978 LOVE OR SOMETHING LIKE IT
- (S) (2:50) EMI 46106 Twenty Greatest Hits.
- (S) (2:50) EMI 46673 25 Greatest Hits.

1979 THE GAMBLER
- (S) (3:28) Liberty 46004 Greatest Hits.
- (S) (3:31) EMI 46106 Twenty Greatest Hits.
- (S) (3:32) EMI 48404 The Gambler.
- (S) (3:31) EMI 46673 25 Greatest Hits.
- (S) (3:31) Curb 77358 Greatest Country Hits.
- (S) (3:28) Reprise 26711 20 Great Years. *(all selections on this cd are rerecorded)*
- (S) (3:31) Capitol 35779 Best Of.

1979 SHE BELIEVES IN ME
- (S) (4:09) Liberty 46004 Greatest Hits.
- (S) (4:11) EMI 46106 Twenty Greatest Hits.
- (S) (4:13) EMI 48404 The Gambler.
- (S) (4:11) EMI 46673 25 Greatest Hits.
- (S) (4:11) Curb 77358 Greatest Country Hits.
- (S) (4:14) Reprise 26711 20 Great Years. *(all selections on this cd are rerecorded)*
- (S) (4:12) Capitol 35779 Best Of.
- (S) (4:11) Time-Life R814-02 Love Songs.

1979 YOU DECORATED MY LIFE
- (S) (3:36) Liberty 46004 Greatest Hits.
- (S) (3:37) EMI 46106 Twenty Greatest Hits.

- (S) (3:38) EMI 46673 25 Greatest Hits.
- (S) (3:37) Reprise 26711 20 Great Years. *(all selections on this cd are rerecorded)*
- (S) (3:36) Razor & Tie 2041 Kenny.
- (S) (3:37) Capitol 35779 Best Of.

1980 COWARD OF THE COUNTY
- (S) (4:16) Liberty 46004 Greatest Hits.
- (S) (4:19) EMI 46106 Twenty Greatest Hits.
- (S) (4:19) EMI 46673 25 Greatest Hits.
- (S) (4:19) Curb 77358 Greatest Country Hits.
- (S) (4:30) Reprise 26711 20 Great Years. *(all selections on this cd are rerecorded)*
- (S) (4:17) Razor & Tie 2041 Kenny.
- (S) (4:19) Capitol 35779 Best Of.

released as by KENNY ROGERS with KIM CARNES:
1980 DON'T FALL IN LOVE WITH A DREAMER
- (S) (3:38) EMI 98223 Gypsy Honeymoon: Best Of Kim Carnes.
- (S) (3:37) Liberty 46004 Kenny Rogers - Greatest Hits.
- (S) (3:38) EMI 46106 Kenny Rogers - Twenty Greatest Hits.
- (S) (3:39) EMI 46595 Kenny Rogers - Duets.
- (S) (3:38) EMI 46673 Kenny Rogers - 25 Greatest Hits.
- (S) (3:42) Reprise 26711 Kenny Rogers - 20 Great Years. *(all selections on this cd are rerecorded)*
- (S) (3:38) Razor & Tie 2042 Kenny Rogers - Gideon.
- (S) (3:38) Capitol 35779 Kenny Rogers - Best Of.
- (S) (3:38) K-Tel 4041 Kim Carnes/Juice Newton Back To Back.

released as by KENNY ROGERS:
1980 LOVE THE WORLD AWAY
- (S) (3:09) Liberty 46004 Greatest Hits.
- (S) (3:09) Full Moon/Elektra 60690 O.S.T. Urban Cowboy.

1980 LADY
- (S) (3:50) Liberty 46004 Greatest Hits.
- (S) (3:51) EMI 46106 Twenty Greatest Hits.
- (S) (3:51) EMI 46673 25 Greatest Hits.
- (S) (3:51) Curb 77358 Greatest Country Hits.
- (S) (3:44) Reprise 26711 20 Great Years. *(all selections on this cd are rerecorded)*
- (S) (3:50) Capitol 35779 Best Of.
- (S) (3:45) Time-Life R814-01 Love Songs.

released as by DOTTIE WEST with KENNY ROGERS:
1981 WHAT ARE WE DOIN' IN LOVE
- (S) (2:59) Priority 9305 Country Gold.
- (S) (3:00) Razor & Tie 2160 Are You Happy Baby? The Dottie West Collection (1976-1984).

released as by KENNY ROGERS:
1981 I DON'T NEED YOU
- (S) (3:26) EMI 46106 Twenty Greatest Hits.
- (S) (3:26) EMI 46673 25 Greatest Hits.
- (S) (3:26) Curb 77358 Greatest Country Hits.
- (S) (3:26) Razor & Tie 2049 Share Your Love.
- (S) (3:26) Capitol 35779 Best Of.

1981 SHARE YOUR LOVE WITH ME
- (S) (3:16) Razor & Tie 2049 Share Your Love.

1982 THROUGH THE YEARS
- (S) (4:42) Razor & Tie 2049 Share Your Love. *(LP version)*
- (S) (4:20) EMI 46106 Twenty Greatest Hits. *(45 version)*
- (S) (4:21) EMI 46673 Kenny Rogers - 25 Greatest Hits. *(45 version)*

1982 LOVE WILL TURN YOU AROUND
- (S) (3:40) EMI Manhattan 48407 Love Will Turn You Around.
- (S) (3:36) EMI 46106 Twenty Greatest Hits.
- (S) (3:38) EMI 46673 Kenny Rogers - 25 Greatest Hits.
- (S) (3:37) Curb 77358 Greatest Country Hits.

released as by KENNY ROGERS and SHEENA EASTON:
1983 WE'VE GOT TONIGHT
- (S) (3:49) EMI 91754 Sheena Easton - Best Of.
- (S) (3:49) EMI 81491 Sheena Easton - World Of: The Singles Collection.
- (S) (3:49) Razor & Tie 2050 Kenny Rogers - We've Got Tonight.
- (S) (3:49) EMI 48405 Kenny Rogers - We've Got Tonight.
- (S) (3:48) Curb 77358 Kenny Rogers - Greatest Country Hits.

(S) (3:48) EMI 46106 Kenny Rogers - 20 Greatest Hits.
(S) (3:50) EMI 46595 Kenny Rogers - Duets.
(S) (3:48) EMI 46673 Kenny Rogers - 25 Greatest Hits.
(S) (3:48) Capitol 35779 Kenny Rogers - Best Of.

released as by KENNY ROGERS:
1983 ALL MY LIFE
(S) (3:51) Razor & Tie 2050 We've Got Tonight.
(S) (3:51) EMI 48405 We've Got Tonight.

released as by KENNY ROGERS with DOLLY PARTON:
1983 ISLANDS IN THE STREAM
(S) (4:07) Time-Life CCD-03 Contemporary Country - The Early 80's.
(S) (4:08) RCA 4697 Kenny Rogers - Eyes That See In The Dark.
(S) (4:09) RCA 8731 Kenny Rogers - Greatest Hits.
(S) (4:09) RCA 4422 and 8505 Dolly Parton - Greatest Hits.
(S) (4:08) RCA 66533 Essential Dolly Parton One.
(S) (4:07) RCA 66948 The Essential Series Sampler Volume II.
(S) (4:08) Time-Life R990-13 Dolly Parton - Legendary Country Singers.
(S) (4:08) Reprise 46571 Kenny Rogers - A Decade Of Hits.
(S) (4:08) Time-Life R834-14 Body Talk - Love And Tenderness.

released as by KENNY ROGERS:
1984 THIS WOMAN
(S) (3:41) RCA 4697 Eyes That See In The Dark.

released as by KENNY ROGERS with KIM CARNES and JAMES INGRAM:
1984 WHAT ABOUT ME
(S) (4:22) RCA 5335 Kenny Rogers - What About Me?.
(S) (4:20) Reprise 46571 Kenny Rogers - A Decade Of Hits.

KENNY ROGERS and THE FIRST EDITION (also FIRST EDITION)
released as by THE FIRST EDITION:
1968 JUST DROPPED IN (TO SEE WHAT CONDITION MY CONDITION WAS IN)
(S) (3:19) Rhino 75754 Even More Nuggets.
(S) (3:18) MCA 5895 15 Greatest Hits.
(S) (3:18) MCA 31311 Greatest Hits.
(S) (3:19) EMI 48047 Kenny Rogers: Ten Years Of Gold. *(rerecorded)*
(S) (3:18) Pair 1238 Breakout.
(S) (3:19) Special Music 4801 Early Years.
(S) (3:18) Time-Life 2CLR-11 Classic Rock - 1968: The Beat Goes On.
(S) (3:19) MCA Special Products 22055 Kenny Rogers & The First Edition Greatest Hits Vol. 1.
(S) (3:18) MCA Special Products 22011 Featuring The Songs Of Kenny Rogers & The First Edition.
(S) (3:18) Hip-O 40016 Kenny Rogers & The First Edition Greatest Hits.
(S) (3:18) K-Tel 3610 Psychedelic Mind Trip Vol. 2: Another Flashback.

1969 BUT YOU KNOW I LOVE YOU
(S) (3:01) MCA 5895 15 Greatest Hits.
(S) (3:12) EMI 48047 Kenny Rogers: Ten Years Of Gold. *(rerecorded)*
(S) (3:01) Curb 77358 Greatest Country Hits.
(S) (3:04) MCA Special Products 22055 Kenny Rogers & The First Edition Greatest Hits Vol. 1.
(S) (3:04) MCA Special Products 22039 Kenny Rogers & The First Edition: Love Songs.
(S) (3:03) Hip-O 40016 Kenny Rogers & The First Edition Greatest Hits.

released as by KENNY ROGERS and THE FIRST EDITION:
1969 RUBY, DON'T TAKE YOUR LOVE TO TOWN
(S) (2:56) MCA 5895 15 Greatest Hits.
(S) (2:56) MCA 31311 Greatest Hits.
(S) (2:50) Reprise 26711 Kenny Rogers 20 Great Years. *(all selections on this cd are rerecorded)*
(S) (2:49) EMI 46106 Kenny Rogers Twenty Greatest Hits. *(rerecorded)*
(S) (2:49) EMI 48047 Kenny Rogers: Ten Years Of Gold. *(rerecorded)*
(S) (2:53) Pair 1238 Breakout.

(S) (2:48) Liberty 46004 Kenny Rogers Greatest Hits. *(rerecorded)*
(S) (2:49) EMI 46673 Kenny Rogers 25 Greatest Hits. *(rerecorded)*
(S) (2:54) Special Music 4801 Early Years.
(S) (2:53) Time-Life CTD-08 Country USA - 1969.
(S) (2:53) Time-Life SUD-18 Superhits - Late 60's Classics.
(S) (2:58) MCA Special Products 22056 Kenny Rogers & The First Edition Greatest Hits Vol. 2.
(S) (2:58) Hip-O 40016 Kenny Rogers & The First Edition Greatest Hits.
(S) (2:56) MCA Special Products 20878 Country Stars Of Branson, Missouri.
(S) (2:53) Time-Life AM1-12 AM Gold - Late '60s Classics.
(S) (2:53) Time-Life R808-02 Classic Country 1965-1969.

1969 RUBEN JAMES
(S) (2:45) MCA 5895 15 Greatest Hits.
(S) (2:45) MCA 31311 Greatest Hits.
(S) (2:37) EMI 46106 Kenny Rogers Twenty Greatest Hits. *(rerecorded)*
(S) (2:37) EMI 48047 Kenny Rogers: Ten Years Of Gold. *(rerecorded)*
(S) (2:44) Pair 1238 Breakout.
(S) (2:37) Liberty 46004 Kenny Rogers Greatest Hits. *(rerecorded)*
(S) (2:37) EMI 46673 Kenny Rogers 25 Greatest Hits. *(rerecorded)*
(S) (2:45) Curb 77358 Greatest Country Hits.
(S) (2:43) Special Music 4801 Early Years.
(S) (2:46) MCA Special Products 22056 Kenny Rogers & The First Edition Greatest Hits Vol. 2.
(S) (2:45) Hip-O 40016 Kenny Rogers & The First Edition Greatest Hits.

1970 SOMETHING'S BURNING
(S) (3:55) MCA 5895 15 Greatest Hits.
(S) (3:55) MCA 31311 Greatest Hits.
(S) (4:02) Reprise 26711 Kenny Rogers 20 Great Years. *(all selections on this cd are rerecorded)*
(S) (4:17) EMI 46106 Kenny Rogers Twenty Greatest Hits. *(rerecorded)*
(S) (4:16) EMI 48047 Kenny Rogers: Ten Years Of Gold. *(rerecorded)*
(S) (3:48) Pair 1238 Breakout.
(S) (4:17) EMI 46673 Kenny Rogers 25 Greatest Hits. *(rerecorded)*
(S) (3:48) Special Music 4801 Early Years.
(S) (3:57) MCA Special Products 22055 Kenny Rogers & The First Edition Greatest Hits Vol. 1.
(S) (3:56) MCA Special Products 22011 Featuring The Songs Of Kenny Rogers & The First Edition.
(S) (3:56) Hip-O 40016 Kenny Rogers & The First Edition Greatest Hits.

1970 TELL IT ALL BROTHER
(S) (3:20) MCA 5895 15 Greatest Hits.
(S) (3:20) MCA 31311 Greatest Hits.
(S) (3:22) Pair 1238 Breakout.
(S) (3:22) Special Music 4801 Early Years.
(S) (3:21) MCA Special Products 22055 Kenny Rogers & The First Edition Greatest Hits Vol. 1.
(S) (3:20) MCA Special Products 22011 Featuring The Songs Of Kenny Rogers & The First Edition.
(S) (3:20) Hip-O 40016 Kenny Rogers & The First Edition Greatest Hits.

1970 HEED THE CALL
(S) (3:17) MCA 5895 15 Greatest Hits.
(S) (3:17) MCA 31311 Greatest Hits.
(S) (3:18) Pair 1238 Breakout.
(S) (3:18) Hip-O 40016 Kenny Rogers & The First Edition Greatest Hits.

TIMMIE "OH YEAH" ROGERS
1957 BACK TO SCHOOL AGAIN

ROLLING STONES
1964 TELL ME (YOU'RE COMING BACK)
(M) (2:45) Abkco 1218 and 1231 Singles Collection: The London Years. *(45 version)*

ROLLING STONES *(Continued)*

(M) (3:46) Abkco 8001 Big Hits (High Tide And Green Grass). *(LP version)*

(M) (3:46) Abkco 7375 England's Newest Hitmakers. *(LP version)*

(M) (3:46) Abkco 6267 More Hot Rocks. *(LP version)*

1964 IT'S ALL OVER NOW

(M) (3:26) Abkco 1218 and 1231 Singles Collection: The London Years.

(M) (3:26) Abkco 8001 Big Hits (High Tide And Green Grass).

(M) (3:25) Abkco 7402 12 x 5.

(M) (3:26) Abkco 6267 More Hot Rocks.

1964 TIME IS ON MY SIDE

(M) (2:57) Abkco 1218 and 1231 Singles Collection: The London Years. *(neither the U.S. 45 or LP version; this version first appeared up on the vinyl LP "Big Hits (High Tide And Green Grass)")*

(M) (2:49) Abkco 8001 Big Hits (High Tide And Green Grass). *(45 and "12 x 5" LP version; not the version that appeared on the vinyl LP "Big Hits (High Tide And Green Grass)")*

(M) (2:51) Abkco 7402 12 x 5.

(M) (2:57) Abkco 6667 Hot Rocks 1964-1971. *(neither the U.S. 45 or LP version; this version first appeared on the vinyl LP "Big Hits (High Tide And Green Grass)")*

1965 HEART OF STONE

(M) (2:42) Abkco 1218 and 1231 Singles Collection: The London Years. *(the first :01 is stereo, the rest of the song is mono)*

(S) (2:45) Abkco 8001 Big Hits (High Tide And Green Grass).

(S) (2:45) Abkco 7420 Now!

(M) (2:42) Abkco 6667 Hot Rocks 1964-1971. *(the first :01 is stereo, the rest of the song is mono)*

1965 THE LAST TIME

(M) (3:38) Abkco 1218 and 1231 Singles Collection: The London Years.

(M) (3:39) Abkco 7429 Out Of Our Heads.

(M) (3:39) Abkco 8001 Big Hits (High Tide And Green Grass).

(M) (3:39) Abkco 6267 More Hot Rocks.

1965 (I CAN'T GET NO) SATISFACTION

(M) (3:44) Abkco 1218 and 1231 Singles Collection: The London Years.

(M) (3:42) Abkco 7429 Out Of Our Heads.

(M) (3:42) Abkco 8001 Big Hits (High Tide And Green Grass).

(M) (3:44) Abkco 6667 Hot Rocks 1964-1971.

1965 GET OFF MY CLOUD

(M) (2:54) Abkco 1218 and 1231 Singles Collection: The London Years.

(M) (2:56) Abkco 7451 December's Children.

(M) (2:56) Abkco 8001 Big Hits (High Tide And Green Grass).

(M) (2:54) Abkco 6667 Hot Rocks 1964-1971.

1966 AS TEARS GO BY

(M) (2:42) Abkco 1218 and 1231 Singles Collection: The London Years.

(M) (2:43) Abkco 7451 December's Children.

(M) (2:42) Abkco 8001 Big Hits (High Tide And Green Grass).

(M) (2:43) Abkco 6667 Hot Rocks 1964-1971.

1966 19TH NERVOUS BREAKDOWN

(M) (3:56) Abkco 1218 and 1231 Singles Collection: The London Years.

(M) (3:56) Abkco 8001 Big Hits (High Tide And Green Grass).

(M) (3:56) Abkco 6667 Hot Rocks 1964-1971.

1966 PAINT IT, BLACK

(M) (3:44) Abkco 1218 and 1231 Singles Collection: The London Years. *(:23 longer than the 45 and LP)*

(M) (3:45) Abkco 8003 Through The Past Darkly (Big Hits Vol. 2). *(:24 longer than the 45 and LP)*

(M) (3:44) Abkco 6667 Hot Rocks 1964-1971. *(:23 longer than the 45 and LP)*

(M) (3:46) Abkco 7476 Aftermath. *(:25 longer than the 45 and LP)*

1966 MOTHERS LITTLE HELPER

(M) (2:45) Abkco 1218 and 1231 Singles Collection: The London Years.

(E) (2:45) Abkco 8003 Through The Past Darkly (Big Hits Vol. 2).

(E) (2:45) Abkco 6667 Hot Rocks 1964-1971.

(E) (2:45) Abkco 7509 Flowers.

1966 LADY JANE

(S) (3:06) Abkco 1218 and 1231 Singles Collection: The London Years.

(S) (3:09) Abkco 6267 More Hot Rocks.

(S) (3:09) Abkco 7509 Flowers.

1966 HAVE YOU SEEN YOUR MOTHER, BABY, STANDING IN THE SHADOW?

(E) (2:33) Abkco 1218 and 1231 Singles Collection: The London Years.

(E) (2:33) Abkco 8003 Through The Past Darkly (Big Hits Vol. 2).

(E) (2:33) Abkco 6267 More Hot Rocks.

(E) (2:33) Abkco 7509 Flowers.

1967 RUBY TUESDAY

(M) (3:11) Abkco 1218 and 1231 Singles Collection: The London Years.

(S) (3:15) Abkco 8003 Through The Past Darkly (Big Hits Vol. 2).

(S) (3:15) Abkco 7499 Between The Buttons.

(S) (3:15) Abkco 6667 Hot Rocks 1964-1971.

(S) (3:15) Abkco 7509 Flowers.

1967 LET'S SPEND THE NIGHT TOGETHER
(actual LP time is (3:36) not (3:29) as stated on the record label; actual 45 time is (3:25) not (3:29) as stated on the record label)

(M) (3:24) Abkco 1218 and 1231 Singles Collection: The London Years.

(S) (3:37) Abkco 8003 Through The Past Darkly (Big Hits Vol. 2).

(E) (3:36) Abkco 7499 Between The Buttons.

(S) (3:36) Abkco 6667 Hot Rocks 1964-1971.

(S) (3:36) Abkco 7509 Flowers.

1967 DANDELION
(actual LP time is (3:30) not (3:56) as stated on the record label; actual 45 time is (3:50) not (3:56) as stated on the record label)

(M) (3:47) Abkco 1218 and 1231 Singles Collection: The London Years. *(45 version)*

(S) (3:30) Abkco 8003 Through The Past Darkly (Big Hits Vol. 2). *(LP version)*

(S) (3:30) Abkco 6267 More Hot Rocks. *(LP version)*

1968 SHE'S A RAINBOW

(M) (4:08) Abkco 1218 and 1231 Singles Collection: The London Years. *(45 version)*

(S) (4:35) Abkco 8003 Through The Past Darkly (Big Hits Vol. 2). *(LP version)*

(S) (4:35) Abkco 6267 More Hot Rocks. *(LP version)*

(S) (5:18) Abkco 8002 Their Satanic Majesties Request. *(LP version; mistakenly includes :42 outro from the selection "SING ALL THIS TOGETHER (SEE WHAT HAPPENS)")*

1968 JUMPIN' JACK FLASH

(S) (3:39) Abkco 1218 and 1231 Singles Collection: The London Years.

(M) (3:40) Abkco 8003 Through The Past Darkly (Big Hits Vol. 2).

(S) (3:39) Abkco 6667 Hot Rocks 1964-1971.

1968 STREET FIGHTING MAN

(S) (3:15) Abkco 1218 and 1231 Singles Collection: The London Years. *(very poor stereo separation)*

(S) (3:16) Abkco 8003 Through The Past Darkly (Big Hits Vol. 2). *(very poor stereo separation)*

(S) (3:15) Abkco 7539 Beggar's Banquet. *(very poor stereo separation)*

(S) (3:14) Abkco 6667 Hot Rocks 1964-1971. *(very poor stereo separation)*

1969 HONKY TONK WOMEN

(M) (2:59) Abkco 1218 and 1231 Singles Collection: The London Years.

(M) (3:00) Abkco 8003 Through The Past Darkly (Big Hits Vol. 2). *(noise on the introduction)*

(M) (2:59) Abkco 6667 Hot Rocks 1964-1971.

1971 BROWN SUGAR
(S) (3:47) Atlantic 81908 Classic Rock 1966-1988. *(LP version)*
(S) (3:47) Atlantic 82306 Atlantic Rock & Roll Box Set. *(LP version)*
(S) (3:47) Abkco 1218 and 1231 Singles Collection: The London Years. *(LP version)*
(S) (3:47) Abkco 6667 Hot Rocks 1964-1971. *(LP version)*
(S) (3:48) Rolling Stones 40488 Sticky Fingers. *(LP version)*
(S) (3:47) Rolling Stones 40505 Rewind. *(LP version)*
(S) (3:49) Rolling Stones 40494 Made In The Shade. *(LP version)*
(S) (3:48) Virgin 39504 and 39525 Sticky Fingers. *(LP version)*
(S) (3:48) Atlantic 83088 Atlantic Records: 50 Years - The Gold Anniversary Collection.

1971 WILD HORSES
(dj copies of this 45 ran (5:38) and (3:25); commercial copies were all (5:38))
(S) (5:39) Abkco 1218 and 1231 Singles Collection: The London Years.
(S) (5:39) Abkco 6667 Hot Rocks 1964-1971.
(S) (5:40) Rolling Stones 40488 Sticky Fingers.
(S) (5:41) Rolling Stones 40494 Made In The Shade.
(S) (5:41) Virgin 39504 and 39525 Sticky Fingers.

1972 TUMBLING DICE
(S) (3:42) Rolling Stones 40489 Exile On Main Street.
(S) (3:37) Rolling Stones 40505 Rewind.
(S) (3:44) Rolling Stones 40494 Made In The Shade.
(S) (3:45) Virgin 39503 and 39524 Exile On Main Street.

1972 HAPPY
(S) (3:01) Rolling Stones 40489 Exile On Main Street.
(S) (3:03) Rolling Stones 40494 Made In The Shade.
(S) (3:04) Virgin 39503 and 39524 Exile On Main Street.

1973 YOU CAN'T ALWAYS GET WHAT YOU WANT
(S) (4:49) Abkco 1218 and 1231 Singles Collection: The London Years. *(45 version)*
(S) (7:27) Abkco 8004 Let It Bleed. *(LP version)*
(S) (7:29) Abkco 6667 Hot Rocks 1964-1971. *(LP version)*

1973 ANGIE
(S) (4:30) Rolling Stones 40492 Goats Head Soup.
(S) (4:30) Rolling Stones 40505 Rewind.
(S) (4:29) Rolling Stones 40494 Made In The Shade.
(S) (4:31) Virgin 39498 and 39519 Goats Head Soup.

1974 DOO DOO DOO DOO DOO (HEARTBREAKER)
(S) (3:25) Rolling Stones 40492 Goats Head Soup.
(S) (3:25) Rolling Stones 40494 Made In The Shade.
(S) (3:25) Rolling Stones 40505 Rewind.
(S) (3:26) Virgin 39498 and 39519 Goats Head Soup.

1974 IT'S ONLY ROCK 'N ROLL (BUT I LIKE IT)
(dj copies of this 45 ran (4:46); commercial copies were all (5:03))
(S) (5:05) Rolling Stones 40494 Made In The Shade.
(S) (5:06) Rolling Stones 40493 It's Only Rock 'N Roll.
(S) (5:06) Rolling Stones 40505 Rewind.
(S) (5:06) Virgin 39500 and 39522 It's Only Rock 'N Roll.

1974 AIN'T TOO PROUD TO BEG
(S) (3:30) Rolling Stones 40493 It's Only Rock 'N Roll.
(S) (3:30) Virgin 39500 and 39522 It's Only Rock 'N Roll.

1975 I DON'T KNOW WHY
(S) (3:00) Abkco 1218 Singles Collection: The London Years.

1976 FOOL TO CRY
(dj copies of this 45 ran (4:06) not (3:58) as stated on the record label; commercial copies were all (5:03))
(S) (4:06) Rolling Stones 40501 Sucking In The Seventies.
(S) (5:02) Rolling Stones 40495 Black And Blue.
(S) (5:03) Rolling Stones 40505 Rewind.
(S) (5:03) Virgin 39499 and 39520 Black And Blue.

1978 MISS YOU
(S) (4:48) Atlantic 82306 Atlantic Rock & Roll Box Set. *(LP version)*
(S) (4:48) Atlantic 81908 Classic Rock 1966-1988. *(LP version)*
(S) (4:48) Rolling Stones 40449 Some Girls. *(LP version)*
(S) (4:46) Rolling Stones 40505 Rewind. *(LP version)*

(S) (4:48) Virgin 39505 and 39526 Some Girls. *(LP version)*

1978 BEAST OF BURDEN
(dj copies of this 45 ran (3:20) and (4:24); commercial copies were all (4:24))
(S) (3:26) Rolling Stones 40501 Sucking In The Seventies.
(S) (4:24) Rolling Stones 40449 Some Girls.
(S) (4:24) Rolling Stones 40505 Rewind.
(S) (4:24) Virgin 39505 and 39526 Some Girls.

1979 SHATTERED
(dj copies of this 45 ran (2:44) and (3:46); commercial copies were all (3:46))
(S) (3:45) Rolling Stones 40501 Sucking In The Seventies.
(S) (3:46) Rolling Stones 40449 Some Girls.
(S) (3:46) Virgin 39505 and 39526 Some Girls.

1980 EMOTIONAL RESCUE
(dj copies of this 45 ran (4:18) and (5:38); commercial copies were all (5:38))
(S) (5:38) Rolling Stones 40500 Emotional Rescue.
(S) (5:36) Rolling Stones 40505 Rewind.
(S) (5:38) Virgin 39501 and 39523 Emotional Rescue.

1980 SHE'S SO COLD
(some dj copies of this 45 featured a censored version with the words "God damn" removed)
(S) (4:12) Rolling Stones 40500 Emotional Rescue. *(uncensored)*
(S) (4:12) Virgin 39501 and 39523 Emotional Rescue. *(uncensored)*

1981 START ME UP
(S) (3:31) Rolling Stones 40502 Tattoo You.
(S) (3:32) Rolling Stones 40505 Rewind.
(S) (3:32) Virgin 39502 and 39521 Tattoo You.

1982 WAITING ON A FRIEND
(S) (4:33) Virgin 39502 and 39521 Tattoo You. *(LP version)*
(S) (4:33) Rolling Stones 40502 Tattoo You. *(LP version)*
(S) (4:35) Rolling Stones 40505 Rewind. *(LP version)*

1982 HANG FIRE
(S) (2:20) Virgin 39502 and 39521 Tattoo You.
(S) (2:20) Rolling Stones 40502 Tattoo You.
(S) (2:21) Rolling Stones 40505 Rewind.

1982 GOING TO A GO GO
(S) (3:19) Rolling Stones 40503 Still Life.

1983 UNDERCOVER OF THE NIGHT
(S) (4:31) Rolling Stones 40504 Undercover. *(LP length)*
(S) (4:31) Virgin 39649 Undercover. *(LP length)*
(S) (4:31) Rolling Stones 40505 Rewind. *(LP length)*

1986 HARLEM SHUFFLE
(S) (3:23) Rolling Stones 40250 Dirty Work.
(S) (3:23) Virgin 39648 Dirty Work.

1986 ONE HIT (TO THE BODY)
(S) (4:43) Rolling Stones 40250 Dirty Work. *(LP version)*
(S) (4:43) Virgin 39648 Dirty Work. *(LP version)*

1989 MIXED EMOTIONS
(S) (4:37) Rolling Stones 45333 Steel Wheels. *(LP length)*
(S) (4:37) Virgin 39647 Steel Wheels. *(LP length)*

1989 ROCK AND A HARD PLACE
(S) (5:24) Rolling Stones 45333 Steel Wheels. *(LP version)*
(S) (5:24) Virgin 39647 Steel Wheels. *(LP version)*

ROMANTICS
1980 WHAT I LIKE ABOUT YOU
(S) (2:55) Time-Life R968-04 Guitar Rock 1980-81.
(S) (2:55) Priority 53712 Classic Rock Volume 3 - Wild Weekend.
(S) (2:55) Priority 7054 80's Greatest Rock Hits Volume 4 - Party On.
(S) (2:55) Rhino 71696 New Wave Hits Of The 80's Vol. 3.
(S) (2:55) Right Stuff 27754 Sedated In The Eighties.
(S) (2:54) Rhino 71178 DIY: Shake It Up! - American Power Pop II.
(S) (2:55) Sandstone 5023 Cosmopolitan Volume 9.
(S) (2:54) Tommy Boy 1100 ESPN Presents Jock Rock Vol. 1. *(sound effects added to the introduction)*
(S) (2:55) Epic Associated 47043 What I Like About You (And Other Romantic Hits).

ROMANTICS *(Continued)*
- (S) (2:55) Time-Life R988-07 Sounds Of The Eighties: 1980.
- (S) (2:55) Big Ear Music 4001 Only In The 80's Volume One.
- (S) (2:55) Oglio 24353 Richard Blade's Flashback Favorites Volume 3.
- (S) (2:55) Epic 67534 Club Epic Volume 5.
- (S) (2:55) Rhino 72490 New Wave Hits, Vol. 1.
- (S) (2:55) Eclipse Music Group 64896 Rock 'n Roll Relix 1978-1979.
- (S) (2:55) Eclipse Music Group 64897 Rock 'n Roll Relix 1970-1979.
- (S) (2:55) Flashback 72713 Essential New Wave Hits.
- (S) (2:55) Flashback 72092 New Wave Hits Box Set.
- (S) (2:54) Rhino 72820 VH1 - More Of The Big 80's.
- (S) (2:55) Rhino 72729 Poptopia! Power Pop Classics Of The '80s.
- (S) (2:54) Cold Front 6255 Greatest Sports Rock And Jams Volume 2. *(all selections on this cd are segued together)*
- (S) (2:53) Arista 18985 Ultimate New Wave Party 1998. *(all selections on this cd are segued together)*
- (S) (2:55) Epic/Legacy 65254 Fizz Pop Modern Rock Volume 1.
- (S) (2:55) Epic Associated/Legacy 65441 Super Hits.
- (S) (2:55) K-Tel 4066 K-Tel's Original Party Music Vol. 2.

1984 TALKING IN YOUR SLEEP
- (S) (3:52) CBS Special Products 44363 Rock Of The 80's.
- (S) (3:54) Priority 53704 Rock Of The 80's Volume 3.
- (S) (3:55) Rhino 70679 Billboard Top Hits - 1984.
- (S) (3:53) Time-Life R105-40 Rock Dreams.
- (S) (3:55) Risky Business 57833 Read The Hits/Best Of The 80's.
- (S) (3:55) Rhino 71834 Classic MTV: Class Of 1983.
- (S) (3:54) K-Tel 3261 The 80's Rock On.
- (S) (3:54) Rhino 71974 New Wave Hits Of The 80's Vol. 11.
- (S) (3:54) Epic Associated 47043 What I Like About You (And Other Romantic Hits).
- (S) (3:55) Nemperor 38880 In Heat.
- (S) (3:54) Time-Life R988-06 Sounds Of The Eighties: 1984.
- (S) (3:54) Big Ear Music 4003 Only In The 80's Volume Three.
- (S) (3:56) Epic/Legacy 65255 Fizz Pop Modern Rock Volume 2.
- (S) (3:53) Epic Associated/Legacy 65441 Super Hits.

1984 ONE IN A MILLION
- (S) (3:40) Epic Associated 47043 What I Like About You (And Other Romantic Hits).
- (S) (3:40) Nemperor 38880 In Heat.
- (S) (3:39) Epic Associated/Legacy 65441 Super Hits.

ROME
1997 I BELONG TO YOU (EVERY TIME I SEE YOUR FACE)
- (S) (4:32) RCA 67441 Rome.
1997 DO YOU LIKE THIS
- (S) (4:52) RCA 67441 Rome.

ROMEO VOID
1984 A GIRL IN TROUBLE (IS A TEMPORARY THING)
- (S) (6:11) Columbia/415/Legacy 47965 Best Of 415 Records. *(12" single version)*
- (S) (4:15) Priority 53750 Rock Of The 80's Volume 7.
- (S) (4:16) Right Stuff 28996 Sedated In The Eighties No. 2.
- (S) (4:17) Risky Business 57468 This Ain't No Disco/New Wave Dance Hits.
- (S) (6:11) Epic 67534 Club Epic Volume 5. *(12" single version)*
- (S) (4:15) Epic/Legacy 65255 Fizz Pop Modern Rock Volume 2.

RONALD and RUBY
1958 LOLLIPOP

DON RONDO
1956 TWO DIFFERENT WORLDS
- (M) (3:00) Time-Life HPD-27 Your Hit Parade - The Unforgettable 50's.

514

1957 WHITE SILVER SANDS
- (M) (2:38) Time-Life HPD-17 Your Hit Parade - 1957.

RONETTES
1963 BE MY BABY
- (M) (2:38) RCA 6408 O.S.T. Dirty Dancing.
- (M) (2:39) Abkco 7118 Phil Spector/Back To Mono (1958-1969).
- (M) (2:39) Abkco 7212 Best Of.
1964 BABY, I LOVE YOU
- (M) (2:48) Abkco 7118 Phil Spector/Back To Mono (1958-1969).
- (M) (2:49) Abkco 7212 Best Of.
1964 (THE BEST PART OF) BREAKIN' UP
- (M) (3:00) Abkco 7118 Phil Spector/Back To Mono (1958-1969).
- (M) (3:00) Abkco 7212 Best Of.
1964 DO I LOVE YOU?
- (M) (2:49) Abkco 7118 Phil Spector/Back To Mono (1958-1969).
- (M) (2:49) Abkco 7212 Best Of.
1964 WALKING IN THE RAIN
- (M) (3:14) Abkco 7118 Phil Spector/Back To Mono (1958-1969).
- (M) (3:14) Abkco 7212 Best Of.

RONNIE and THE HI-LITES
1962 I WISH THAT WE WERE MARRIED
- (M) (2:50) Rhino 70589 Rockin' & Rollin' Wedding Songs Volume 2.
- (M) (2:49) Time-Life 2RNR-45 Rock 'N' Roll Era - Street Corner Serenade.
- (M) (2:48) Eric 11503 Hard To Find 45's On CD (Volume II) 1961-64.
- (M) (2:50) Time-Life R857-12 The Heart Of Rock 'n' Roll 1962-1963.

RONNY & THE DAYTONAS
1964 G.T.O.
- (M) (2:26) JCI 3106 Surfin' Sixties.
- (M) (2:27) DCC Compact Classics 030 Beach Classics.
- (M) (2:25) Compose 9927 Car And Driver/Greatest Car Songs.
- (M) (2:26) Time-Life 2RNR-10 Rock 'N' Roll Era - 1964.
- (M) (2:28) Rhino 71585 Billboard Top Pop Hits, 1964.
- (M) (2:28) Sundazed 11046 G.T.O./Best Of The Mala Recordings.
- (M) (2:28) Right Stuff 53316 Hot Rod Rock Volume 1: Rev It Up.
- (M) (2:27) Simitar 55532 The Number One's: The '60s.
1965 SANDY
- (M) (2:45) Sundazed 11046 G.T.O./Best Of The Mala Recordings.
- (M) (2:45) Varese Sarabande 5802 Sunshine Days - Pop Classics Of The '60s Volume 2.

LINDA RONSTADT
1970 LONG LONG TIME
- (S) (4:21) Asylum 106 Greatest Hits. *(LP version)*
- (S) (4:21) DCC Compact Classics 1040 Greatest Hits. *(LP version; gold disc)*
- (S) (4:19) Capitol 80126 Silk Purse. *(LP version)*
1975 YOU'RE NO GOOD
- (S) (3:39) JCI 3304 Mellow Seventies.
- (S) (3:40) Sandstone 33000 Reelin' In The Years Volume 1.
- (S) (3:44) Asylum 106 Greatest Hits.
- (S) (3:41) Capitol 46073 Heart Like A Wheel.
- (S) (3:40) DCC Compact Classics 062 Rock Of The 70's Volume 1.
- (S) (3:44) DCC Compact Classics 1040 Greatest Hits. *(gold disc)*
- (S) (3:40) Time-Life SOD-08 Sounds Of The Seventies - 1975.
- (S) (3:40) Time-Life R105-26 Our Songs: Singers & Songwriters Encore.
- (S) (3:39) JCI 3169 #1 Radio Hits 1975 - Only Rock 'n Roll - 1979.
- (S) (3:38) Time-Life AM1-22 AM Gold - 1975.

1975 WHEN WILL I BE LOVED
(actual 45 and LP time is (2:06) not (2:52) as
stated on the record label)
- (S) (2:08) Rhino 70670 Billboard Top Hits - 1975.
- (S) (2:08) Asylum 106 Greatest Hits.
- (S) (2:04) Capitol 46073 Heart Like A Wheel. *(tracks into the next selection)*
- (S) (2:08) DCC Compact Classics 1040 Greatest Hits. *(gold disc)*
- (S) (2:04) Time-Life SOD-16 Sounds Of The Seventies - 1975: Take Two.
- (S) (2:08) Rhino 72445 Listen To The Music: The 70's California Sound.

1975 HEAT WAVE
- (S) (2:44) Asylum 106 Greatest Hits.
- (S) (2:44) Asylum 1045 Prisoner In Disguise.
- (S) (2:44) DCC Compact Classics 1040 Greatest Hits. *(gold disc)*

1976 TRACKS OF MY TEARS
- (S) (3:12) Asylum 106 Greatest Hits.
- (S) (3:12) Asylum 1045 Prisoner In Disguise.
- (S) (3:12) DCC Compact Classics 1040 Greatest Hits. *(gold disc)*
- (S) (3:12) Time-Life R834-19 Body Talk - Always And Forever.

1976 THAT'LL BE THE DAY
- (S) (2:30) Asylum 106 Greatest Hits.
- (S) (2:31) Asylum 1072 Hasten Down The Wind.
- (S) (2:31) DCC Compact Classics 1040 Greatest Hits. *(gold disc)*
- (S) (2:30) Time-Life SOD-04 Sounds Of The Seventies - 1976.

1977 BLUE BAYOU
- (S) (3:51) Sandstone 33049 and 5017 Cosmopolitan Volume 3.
- (S) (3:51) Asylum 516 Greatest Hits Volume 2.
- (S) (3:55) Asylum 104 Simple Dreams.
- (S) (3:51) Razor & Tie 4543 The '70s Preservation Society Presents: Easy '70s.
- (S) (3:51) Time-Life CCD-10 Contemporary Country - The Late 70's Pure Gold.
- (S) (3:51) Time-Life SOD-05 Sounds Of The Seventies - 1977.
- (S) (3:51) Time-Life R103-33 Singers & Songwriters.
- (S) (3:53) Priority 53724 Country Rock Vol. 2 - Slow Dancin.
- (S) (3:51) DCC Compact Classics 088 Night Moves Volume 6.
- (S) (3:53) JCI 3137 Rock Your Boots Off.
- (S) (3:51) JCI 3146 1975 - Only Love - 1979.
- (S) (3:53) Rhino 72518 Mellow Rock Hits Of The 70's - Summer Breeze.
- (S) (3:51) Time-Life R834-06 Body Talk - Only You.
- (S) (3:52) Time-Life R814-05 Love Songs.

1977 IT'S SO EASY
- (S) (2:26) Asylum 516 Greatest Hits Volume 2.
- (S) (2:26) Asylum 104 Simple Dreams.
- (S) (2:25) JCI 3307 Easy Seventies.
- (S) (2:26) Time-Life SOD-05 Sounds Of The Seventies - 1977.
- (S) (2:25) Priority 50952 I Love Rock & Roll Volume 3: Hits Of The 70's.
- (S) (2:25) Hip-O 40024 Country Wildflowers.
- (S) (2:25) Time-Life AM1-24 AM Gold - 1977.

1978 POOR POOR PITIFUL ME
- (S) (3:37) Asylum 516 Greatest Hits Volume 2.
- (S) (3:40) Asylum 104 Simple Dreams.

1978 TUMBLING DICE
- (S) (3:02) Asylum 516 Greatest Hits Volume 2.
- (S) (3:05) Asylum 104 Simple Dreams.
- (S) (3:00) Time-Life SOD-25 Sounds Of The Seventies - Seventies Generation.
- (S) (3:04) Hip-O 40078 Cover You: A Tribute To The Rolling Stones.

1978 BACK IN THE U.S.A.
- (S) (2:55) Asylum 516 Greatest Hits Volume 2.
- (S) (3:00) Asylum 155 Living In The U.S.A.

- (S) (2:55) Time-Life SOD-20 Sounds Of The Seventies - 1978: Take Two.
- (S) (2:56) Hip-O 40076 Chuck B. Covered: A Tribute To Chuck Berry.

1979 OOH BABY BABY
- (S) (3:15) Asylum 516 Greatest Hits Volume 2.
- (S) (3:16) Asylum 155 Living In The U.S.A.
- (S) (3:14) Time-Life SOD-10 Sounds Of The Seventies - 1978.
- (S) (3:14) Time-Life R138-18 Body Talk.
- (S) (3:14) Time-Life R103-18 Great Love Songs Of The '70s & '80s.
- (S) (3:15) Time-Life R834-03 Body Talk - Moonlit Nights.

1980 HOW DO I MAKE YOU
- (S) (2:20) JCI 2720 Rockin' Ladies Of The 80's.
- (S) (2:16) Asylum 516 Greatest Hits Volume 2.
- (S) (2:21) Asylum 510 Mad Love.
- (S) (2:16) Time-Life R988-16 Sounds Of The Eighties: The Early '80s.

1980 HURT SO BAD
- (S) (3:09) Asylum 516 Greatest Hits Volume 2.
- (S) (3:13) Asylum 510 Mad Love.
- (S) (3:12) Priority 53746 80's Greatest Rock Hits Vol. 12 - Singers/Songwriters.
- (S) (3:11) JCI 3147 1980 - Only Love - 1984.
- (S) (3:12) Time-Life R988-14 Sounds Of The Eighties: 1980-1982.

1980 I CAN'T LET GO
- (S) (2:40) Asylum 516 Greatest Hits Volume 2.
- (S) (2:42) Asylum 510 Mad Love.

1982 GET CLOSER
- (S) (2:28) Asylum 60185 Get Closer.

1983 I KNEW YOU WHEN
- (S) (2:53) Asylum 60185 Get Closer.

released as by LINDA RONSTADT and JAMES INGRAM:
1987 SOMEWHERE OUT THERE
- (S) (3:57) MCA 39096 O.S.T. An American Tail.
- (S) (3:57) Warner Brothers 26700 James Ingram Greatest Hits.

released as by LINDA RONSTADT featuring AARON NEVILLE:
1989 DON'T KNOW MUCH
- (S) (3:32) Foundation/Capitol 96427 Hearts Of Gold: The Pop Collection.
- (S) (3:32) Sandstone 33049 and 5017 Cosmopolitan Volume 3.
- (S) (3:32) DCC Compact Classics 088 Night Moves Volume 6.
- (S) (3:32) Elektra 60872 Linda Ronstadt: Cry Like A Rainstorm - Howl Like The Wind.
- (S) (3:32) Time-Life R138-18 Body Talk.
- (S) (3:30) Madacy Entertainment 6803 Power Of Love.
- (S) (3:31) Time-Life R103-18 Great Love Songs Of The '70s & '80s.
- (S) (3:32) Time-Life R834-03 Body Talk - Moonlit Nights.
- (S) (3:32) K-Tel 6257 The Greatest Love Songs - 16 Soft Rock Hits.

1990 ALL MY LIFE
- (S) (3:30) Elektra 60872 Linda Ronstadt: Cry Like A Rainstorm - Howl Like The Wind.
- (S) (3:26) Time-Life R834-06 Body Talk - Only You.

ROOFTOP SINGERS
✓**1963 WALK RIGHT IN**
- (S) (2:32) Vanguard 17/18 Greatest Folksingers Of The 60's.
- (S) (2:33) Rhino 70995 One Hit Wonders Of The 60's Volume 1.
- (S) (2:33) Rhino 70264 Troubadours Of The Folk Era Volume 3.
- (M) (2:33) Vanguard 79457 Best Of.
- (S) (2:34) JCI 3109 Folk Sixties.
- (S) (2:32) Time-Life SUD-08 Superhits - 1963.
- ✓(S) (2:32) Time-Life HPD-32 Your Hit Parade - Into The 60's.
- (S) (2:33) Rhino 71584 Billboard Top Pop Hits, 1963.
- (S) (2:32) Epic 66329 O.S.T. Forrest Gump.

ROOFTOP SINGERS *(Continued)*

(S) (2:31) Rebound 314520371 The Roots Of Rock: 60's Folk.
(S) (2:32) Time-Life R132-22 Treasury Of Folk Music Volume One.
(S) (2:32) Time-Life AM1-17 AM Gold - 1963.
(M) (2:33) Vanguard 163/66 Vanguard Collector's Edition Box Set.

1963 TOM CAT
(M) (2:25) Vanguard 79457 Best Of.

ROOTS
1997 WHAT THEY DO
(S) (5:56) DGC 24972 Illadelph Halflife.

DAVID ROSE
1962 THE STRIPPER
(S) (1:54) Rhino 70995 One Hit Wonders Of The 60's Volume 1.
✓(S) (1:54) Time-Life HPD-34 Your Hit Parade - 60's Instrumentals.
(S) (1:55) Rhino 71583 Billboard Top Pop Hits, 1962.
(S) (1:54) Polygram Special Markets 314520273 Great Instrumental Hits.
✓(S) (1:53) Collectors' Choice 003/4 Instrumental Gems Of The 60's.
(S) (1:54) Taragon 1015 Very Best Of.
(S) (1:55) K-Tel 3583 Those Wonderful Instrumentals Volume 3.
(S) (1:54) Chronicles 314535875 Bachelor Pad Favorites.
(S) (1:54) Rhino 72724 Striptease Classics.

ROSE GARDEN
1967 NEXT PLANE TO LONDON
(M) (2:29) JCI 3185 1965 - Only Love - 1969.

ROSE ROYCE
1977 CAR WASH
(dj copies of this 45 state times of (3:18) and (5:06) even though the actual running times are (3:12) and (4:49))
(S) (4:58) Priority 7974 Mega-Hits Dance Classics Volume 4. *(:07 shorter than the LP version)*
(S) (3:14) Rhino 70984 The Disco Years Volume 1. *(45 version)*
(S) (3:30) Rhino 70672 Billboard Top Hits - 1977. *(:18 longer than the 45 version)*
(S) (3:17) Whitfield 3457 Greatest Hits. *(45 version)*
(S) (3:13) Razor & Tie 22496 Disco Fever. *(45 version)*
(S) (3:13) Time-Life SOD-17 Sounds Of The Seventies - 1977: Take Two. *(45 version)*
(S) (5:06) MCA Special Products 22092 Best Of From "Car Wash". *(LP version)*
(S) (5:04) JCI 3131 1975 - Only Rock 'N Roll - 1979. *(LP version)*
(S) (5:05) MCA Special Products 20949 Rockin' 70's Volume 2. *(LP version)*
(S) (5:07) Priority 53141 Mega Hits Disco Locomotion Volume 2. *(LP version)*
(S) (5:05) K-Tel 3581 Roller Disco - Boogie From The Skating Rinks. *(LP version)*
(S) (5:05) MCA 11502 O.S.T. Car Wash. *(LP version)*
(S) (5:05) Hip-O 40041 The Studio Collection Disco 54. *(LP version)*
(S) (5:05) Hip-O 40035 Cigar Classics Volume 2 - Urban Fire. *(LP version)*
✓(S) (3:13) Time-Life AM1-24 AM Gold - 1977. *(45 version)*
(S) (3:14) Rhino 72837 Disco Queens: The 70's. *(45 version)*
(S) (5:05) K-Tel 3887 Soul Brothers & Sisters Of The 70's. *(LP version)*
(S) (3:14) Time-Life R838-16 Solid Gold Soul 1977. *(45 version)*
(S) (5:00) Cold Front 4025 Old School Mega Mix Volume 3. *(LP version)*
(S) (3:13) Right Stuff 52274 Flick Hits Take 2. *(45 version)*

(S) (5:03) Simitar 55542 The Number One's: Soul On Fire. *(LP version)*
(S) (3:14) Time-Life R840-07 Sounds Of The Seventies: '70s Dance Party 1976-1977. *(45 version)*

✓1977 I WANNA GET NEXT TO YOU
(45 length is (3:31); LP length is (3:55))
(S) (3:54) Whitfield 3457 Greatest Hits.
✓(S) (3:53) Time-Life SOD-35 Sounds Of The Seventies - AM Nuggets.
(S) (3:56) MCA Special Products 20752 Classic R&B Oldies From The 70's Vol. 2.
(S) (3:57) MCA Special Products 22092 Best Of From "Car Wash".
(S) (3:54) Priority 57194 Old School Friday - More Music From The Original Motion Picture.
(S) (3:54) Original Sound 9308 Dedicated To You Vol. 8.
(S) (3:56) Rhino 72128 Hot Soul Hits Of The 70's Vol. 18.
(S) (3:54) Thump 4720 Old School Love Songs Volume 2.
(S) (3:56) Madacy Entertainment 1977 Rock On 1977.
(S) (3:54) Priority 53959 O.S.T. Friday.
(S) (3:56) Hip-O 40001 The Glory Of Love - Sweet & Soulful Love Songs.
(S) (3:57) MCA 11502 O.S.T. Car Wash.
(S) (3:58) MCA Special Products 20958 Mellow Classics.
(S) (3:55) Right Stuff 52660 Flick Hits - Old School Tracks.
(S) (3:58) MCA Special Products 20997 Mellow Rock.
(S) (3:53) Time-Life R834-12 Body Talk - By Candlelight.
(S) (3:56) Hip-O 40107 Super Bad On Celluloid: Music From '70s Black Cinema.

1977 DO YOUR DANCE (PART 1)
(S) (5:21) Whitfield 3457 Greatest Hits. *(neither the 45 or LP version)*
(S) (9:16) Warner Brothers 3074 In Full Bloom. *(LP version)*

1979 LOVE DON'T LIVE HERE ANYMORE
(S) (3:55) Whitfield 3457 Greatest Hits.
(S) (3:56) Warner Brothers 46130 Love Jams Volume Two.
(S) (3:55) Chronicles 314555138 Funk Ballads.

ROSIE and THE ORIGINALS
1961 ANGEL BABY
(actual 45 time is (3:42) not (2:45) as stated on the record label)
(M) (3:31) Original Sound 8878 Art Laboe's Dedicated To You. *(faded :11 early)*
(M) (3:31) Original Sound 4001 Art Laboe's 60 Killer Oldies. *(faded :11 early)*
(M) (3:33) Original Sound 8855 Oldies But Goodies Vol. 5. *(this compact disc uses the "Waring - fds" noise reduction process; ambient background noise throughout the disc; faded :09 early)*
(M) (3:33) Original Sound 2222 Oldies But Goodies Volumes 3,5,11,14 and 15 Box Set. *(this box set uses the "Waring - fds" noise reduction process; ambient background noise throughout the song; faded 09 early)*
(M) (3:33) Original Sound 2500 Oldies But Goodies Volumes 1-15 Box Set. *(this box set uses the "Waring - fds" noise reduction process; ambient background noise throughout the song; faded :09 early)*
(M) (3:32) Original Sound CDGO-2 Golden Oldies Volume. 2. *(faded :10 early)*
(M) (3:31) Original Sound 9603 Best Of Oldies But Goodies Vol. 3. *(faded :11 early)*
(M) (3:42) Vee Jay 708 The Unavailable 16/The Original Nitty Gritty. *(sounds like it was mastered from vinyl; poor quality)*
(M) (3:28) Time-Life 2RNR-11 Rock 'N' Roll Era - 1960. *(faded :14 early)*
(M) (2:46) Time-Life R962-05 History Of Rock 'N' Roll: The Teenage Years 1957-1964. *(highly edited)*
(M) (3:14) Collectables 2500 WCBS-FM History Of Rock - The 60's Part 1. *(mastered from vinyl; faded :28 early)*
(M) (3:14) Collectables 4500 History Of Rock/The 60s Part One. *(mastered from vinyl; faded :28 early)*
(M) (3:14) Collectables 2509 WCBS-FM For Lovers Only Part 1. *(mastered from vinyl; faded :28 early)*

(M) (2:46) Thump 7010 Low Rider Oldies Volume 1.
(highly edited)
(M) (3:31) Scotti Bros. 75465 Angel Hits. *(faded :11 early)*
(M) (2:46) Time-Life R857-03 The Heart Of Rock 'n' Roll - 1961. *(highly edited)*
✓(M) (3:43) Eclipse Music Group 64867 Rock 'n Roll Relix 1960-1961.
(M) (3:43) Eclipse Music Group 64872 Rock 'n Roll Relix 1960-1969.
✓(M) (3:43) Collectors' Choice 5189 I Wish I Were A Princess - The Great Lost Female Teen Idols.
(M) (2:46) Thump 7100 Latin Oldies. *(highly edited)*

DIANA ROSS
1970 REACH OUT AND TOUCH (SOMEBODY'S HAND)
(S) (3:04) Motown 6140 The Composer Series: Ashford & Simpson.
(S) (3:03) Motown 9097 The Most Played Oldies On America's Jukeboxes.
(S) (2:58) Motown 6197 and 6049 Anthology.
(S) (3:03) Motown 6072 Compact Command Performances.
(S) (2:58) Motown 0869 Greatest Hits. *(truncated fade)*
(S) (2:58) Motown 0960 All The Great Hits.
(S) (3:03) Motown 8042 and 8142 Ain't No Mountain High Enough/Surrender.
(S) (3:02) Motown 5135 Ain't No Mountain High Enough.
(M) (2:56) Motown 6357 Forever: Musical Memories.
(M) (2:58) Motown 314530428 Diana Ross Ultimate Collection.
(S) (2:58) Ichiban 2511 Love, Peace & Understanding.

1970 AIN'T NO MOUNTAIN HIGH ENOUGH
(actual 45 time is (3:28) not (3:15) as stated on the record label)
(S) (3:29) Motown 6132 25 #1 Hits From 25 Years. *(neither the 45 or LP version)*
(S) (3:29) Motown 6140 The Composer Series: Ashford & Simpson. *(neither the 45 or LP version)*
(S) (3:55) Rhino 70658 Billboard's Top R&B Hits Of 1970. *(neither the 45 or LP version)*
(S) (3:28) Motown 5344 Every Great Motown Song: The First 25 Years Volume 2. *(most selections on this cd have noise on the fadeout; neither the 45 or LP version)*
(S) (3:28) Motown 8034 and 8134 Every Great Motown Song: The First 25 Years Volumes 1 & 2. *(most selections on this cd have noise on the fadeout; neither the 45 or LP version)*
(S) (3:28) Motown 9060 Motown's Biggest Pop Hits. *(neither the 45 or LP version)*
(S) (6:15) Motown 0937 20/20 Twenty No. 1 Hits From Twenty Years At Motown. *(LP version)*
(S) (3:40) Motown 6197 and 6049 Anthology. *(neither the 45 or LP version)*
(S) (6:16) Motown 6072 Compact Command Performances. *(LP version)*
(S) (6:16) Motown 0869 Greatest Hits. *(LP version)*
(S) (6:16) Motown 0960 All The Great Hits. *(LP version)*
(S) (6:14) Motown 8042 and 8142 Ain't No Mountain High Enough/Surrender. *(LP version)*
(S) (6:15) Motown 5135 Ain't No Mountain High Enough. *(LP version)*
(M) (3:29) Motown 6312 Hitsville USA. *(45 version)*
(M) (3:27) Motown 6357 Forever: Musical Memories. *(45 version)*
(S) (3:52) Time-Life RHD-18 Rhythm & Blues - 1970. *(neither the 45 or LP version)*
(S) (3:46) Time-Life SUD-04 Superhits - 1970. *(neither the 45 or LP version)*
(S) (3:28) Time-Life SOD-21 Sounds Of The Seventies - Rock 'N' Soul Seventies. *(neither the 45 or LP version)*
(M) (3:28) Rebound 3145200320 Class Reunion 1970. *(45 version)*
(M) (3:27) Motown 314530428 Diana Ross Ultimate Collection. *(45 version)*
(S) (3:35) Motown 314530528 Motown Year By Year - 1970. *(neither the 45 or LP version)*

(M) (3:29) Motown 314530409 Motown Milestones - Motown's Leading Ladies. *(45 version)*
(M) (3:28) LaserLight 12314 and 15936 The Wonder Years - Party Time. *(45 version)*
(S) (3:46) Time-Life AM1-02 AM Gold - 1970. *(neither the 45 or LP version)*
(S) (3:51) Time-Life R838-05 Solid Gold Soul - 1970. *(neither the 45 or LP version)*

1971 REMEMBER ME
(actual 45 time is (3:16) not (3:09) as stated on the record label; actual LP time is (3:29) not (3:16) as stated on the record label)
(S) (3:28) Motown 9109 and 5413 Motown Memories Volume 3.
(S) (3:30) Motown 6140 The Composer Series: Ashford & Simpson.
(S) (3:16) Motown 6197 and 6049 Anthology.
(S) (3:29) Motown 6072 Compact Command Performances.
(S) (3:17) Motown 0869 Greatest Hits.
(S) (3:16) Motown 0960 All The Great Hits.
(S) (3:29) Motown 8042 and 8142 Ain't No Mountain High Enough/Surrender.
(S) (3:26) Motown 5423 Surrender.
(S) (3:26) Motown 6357 Forever: Musical Memories.

1971 REACH OUT I'LL BE THERE
(actual LP time is (5:29) not (4:50) as stated on the record label)
(S) (5:34) Motown 6197 and 6049 Anthology. *(LP version)*
(S) (4:01) Motown 6072 Compact Command Performances. *(neither 45 or LP version)*
(S) (5:27) Motown 8042 and 8142 Ain't No Mountain High Enough/Surrender. *(LP version)*
(S) (5:25) Motown 5423 Surrender. *(LP version)*
(S) (5:21) Motown 6357 Forever: Musical Memories. *(LP version)*

1973 GOOD MORNING HEARTACHE
(S) (2:19) Motown 6197 and 6049 Anthology.
(S) (2:20) Motown 6072 Compact Command Performances.
(S) (2:19) Motown 0869 Greatest Hits.
(S) (2:19) Motown 6357 Forever: Musical Memories.

1973 TOUCH ME IN THE MORNING
(45 length is (3:54); LP length is (3:25))
(S) (3:26) Motown 6137 20 Greatest Songs In Motown History.
(S) (3:25) Motown 6177 Endless Love.
(S) (3:25) Motown 5385 Three Times A Lady: Great Motown Love Songs.
(S) (3:25) Motown 9021 and 5309 25 Years Of Grammy Greats.
(S) (3:25) Motown 5344 Every Great Motown Song: The First 25 Years Volume 2. *(most selections on this cd have noise on the fadeout)*
(S) (3:25) Motown 5275 12 #1 Hits From The 70's.
(S) (3:26) Motown 8034 and 8134 Every Great Motown Song: The First 25 Years Volumes 1 & 2. *(most selections on this cd have noise on the fadeout)*
(S) (3:47) Motown 6197 and 6049 Anthology.
(S) (3:25) Motown 6072 Compact Command Performances.
(S) (3:51) Motown 0869 Greatest Hits.
(S) (3:51) Motown 0960 All The Great Hits.
(S) (3:25) Motown 6105 All The Great Love Songs.
(S) (3:51) Motown 5163 Touch Me In The Morning.
(S) (3:26) Motown 8026 and 8126 Touch Me In The Morning/Baby It's Me.
(S) (3:25) Motown 6357 Forever: Musical Memories. *(hissy)*
(S) (3:26) Motown 6358 Hitsville USA Volume Two.
(S) (3:25) Time-Life SUD-13 Superhits - 1973.
(S) (3:25) Motown 314530428 Diana Ross Ultimate Collection. *(hissy)*
(S) (3:26) Motown 314530510 Motown Year By Year 1973.
(S) (3:25) Time-Life AM1-03 AM Gold - 1973.
(S) (3:25) Time-Life R834-04 Body Talk - Together Forever.
(S) (3:25) Time-Life R814-03 Love Songs.

DIANA ROSS (Continued)
released as by DIANA ROSS & MARVIN GAYE:
**1973 YOU'RE A SPECIAL PART OF ME
(actual 45 time is (3:37) not (3:15) as stated on the
record label)**

(S)	(3:36)	Motown 9109 and 5413 Motown Memories Volume 3.
(S)	(3:37)	Motown 6153 and 9053 Marvin Gaye & His Women.
(S)	(3:36)	Motown 8015 and 8115 Marvin Gaye & Tami Terrell's Greatest Hits/Diana & Marvin.
(S)	(4:36)	Motown 6311 The Marvin Gaye Collection. *(previously unreleased extended version)*
(S)	(3:36)	Motown 6197 and 6049 Diana Ross Anthology.
(S)	(3:36)	Motown 9090 and 5124 Diana & Marvin.
(S)	(4:31)	Motown 314530510 Motown Year By Year 1973. *(with countoff; previously unreleased extended version)*

released as by DIANA ROSS:
1974 LAST TIME I SAW HIM

(S)	(2:36)	Motown 6197 and 6049 Diana Ross Anthology. *(:12 shorter than either the 45 or LP)*
(S)	(2:40)	Motown 6072 Compact Command Performances. *(:08 shorter than either the 45 or LP)*
(S)	(2:48)	Motown 0869 Greatest Hits.
(S)	(2:47)	Motown 6357 Forever: Musical Memories.

released as by DIANA ROSS & MARVIN GAYE:
1974 MY MISTAKE (WAS TO LOVE YOU)

(S)	(2:54)	Motown 6153 and 9053 Marvin Gaye & His Women.
(S)	(3:02)	Motown 6311 Marvin Gaye Collection. *(:07 longer than either the 45 or LP)*
(S)	(2:54)	Motown 9090 and 5124 Diana & Marvin.
(S)	(2:52)	Motown 9031 and 5214 Diana's Duets.
(S)	(2:53)	Motown 6197 and 6049 Diana Ross Anthology.
(S)	(2:54)	Motown 8015 and 8115 Marvin Gaye & Tami Terrell's Greatest Hits/Diana & Marvin.
(S)	(2:53)	Motown 6357 Diana Ross Forever: Musical Memories.
(S)	(2:54)	Motown 314530492 Marvin Gaye The Master 1961 - 1984.
(S)	(2:54)	Motown 314530529 Marvin Gaye - Anthology.

released as by DIANA ROSS:
**1976 THEME FROM MAHOGANY (DO YOU KNOW WHERE
YOU'RE GOING TO)**

(S)	(3:21)	Motown 6177 Endless Love: 15 Of Motown's Greatest Love Songs.
(S)	(3:21)	Motown 0937 20/20 Twenty No. 1 Hits From Twenty Years At Motown.
(S)	(3:21)	Motown 5344 Every Great Motown Song: The First 25 Years Volume 2.
(S)	(3:21)	Motown 5275 12 #1 Hits From The 70's.
(S)	(3:21)	Motown 6197 and 6049 Diana Ross Anthology.
(S)	(3:21)	Motown 0960 All The Great Hits.
(S)	(3:21)	Motown 6072 Compact Command Performances.
(S)	(3:21)	Motown 0869 Greatest Hits.
(S)	(3:21)	Motown 6105 All The Great Love Songs.
(S)	(3:21)	Motown 5294 Diana Ross.
(S)	(3:21)	Motown 6357 Forever: Musical Memories.
(S)	(3:21)	Motown 314530428 Diana Ross Ultimate Collection.
(S)	(3:22)	Time-Life R103-18 Great Love Songs Of The '70s & '80s.
(S)	(3:21)	Time-Life R834-07 Body Talk - Hearts In Motion.

**1976 LOVE HANGOVER
(actual 45 time is (3:46) not (3:40) as stated on the
record label)**

(S)	(3:46)	Motown 6137 20 Greatest Songs In Motown History. *(45 version)*
(S)	(3:46)	Priority 7972 Mega-Hits Dance Classics Volume 2. *(45 version)*
(S)	(3:47)	Rhino 70984 The Disco Years Volume 1. *(45 version)*
(S)	(3:46)	Motown 0937 20/20 Twenty No. 1 Hits From Twenty Years At Motown. *(45 version)*
(S)	(3:46)	Motown 6110 Motown Grammy Rhythm & Blues Performances Of The 60's & 70's. *(45 version)*
(S)	(3:46)	Motown 8034 and 8134 Every Great Motown Song: The First 25 Years Volumes 1 & 2. *(45 version)*
(S)	(3:46)	Motown 5344 Every Great Motown Song: The First 25 Years Volume 2. *(45 version)*
(S)	(3:42)	Motown 6192 You Can't Hurry Love: All The Great Love Songs Of The Past 25 Years. *(45 version)*
(S)	(3:46)	Motown 5275 12 #1 Hits From The 70's. *(45 version)*
(S)	(3:47)	Rhino 70490 Billboard Top Dance Hits - 1976. *(45 version)*
(S)	(3:44)	Motown 6197 and 6049 Diana Ross Anthology. *(45 version)*
(S)	(3:46)	Motown 0960 All The Great Hits. *(45 version)*
(S)	(7:47)	Motown 6072 Compact Command Performances. *(LP version)*
(S)	(7:47)	Motown 0869 Greatest Hits. *(LP version)*
(S)	(7:47)	Motown 5294 Diana Ross. *(LP version)*
(S)	(3:44)	Motown 6357 Forever: Musical Memories. *(45 version)*
(S)	(3:47)	Motown 6358 Hitsville USA Volume Two. *(45 version)*
(S)	(3:46)	Razor & Tie 22496 Disco Fever. *(45 version)*
(S)	(3:46)	Time-Life SOD-18 Sounds Of The Seventies - 1976: Take Two. *(45 version)*
(S)	(8:21)	Motown 6377 Diana Extended/The Remixes. *(all selections on this cd are remixed with extra instrumentation added)*
(S)	(7:47)	Rebound 314520298 Disco Nights Vol. 9. *(LP version)*
(S)	(3:43)	Motown 314530428 Diana Ross Ultimate Collection. *(45 version)*
(S)	(7:45)	Motown 314530513 Motown Year By Year 1976. *(12" single version)*
(S)	(3:47)	Motown 314530513 Motown Year By Year 1976. *(45 version)*
(S)	(3:46)	Rebound 314520368 Class Reunion '76. *(45 version)*
(S)	(3:44)	Polydor 314535877 Pure Disco. *(45 version)*
(S)	(3:47)	JCI 3175 1975 - Only Soul - 1979. *(45 version)*
(S)	(3:47)	Time-Life R840-06 Sounds Of The Seventies: '70s Dance Party 1975-1976. *(45 version)*

**1976 ONE LOVE IN MY LIFETIME
(actual 45 time is (3:56) not (3:48) as stated on the
record label)**

(S)	(3:56)	Motown 6197 and 6049 Diana Ross Anthology. *(45 length)*
(S)	(3:56)	Motown 0869 Greatest Hits. *(45 length)*
(S)	(3:35)	Motown 5294 Diana Ross. *(LP length)*

1978 GETTIN' READY FOR LOVE

(S)	(2:44)	Motown 6197 and 6049 Diana Ross Anthology. *(LP length)*
(S)	(2:44)	Motown 8026 and 8126 Touch Me In The Morning/Baby It's Me. *(LP length)*
(S)	(2:44)	Motown 5434 Baby It's Me. *(LP length)*
(S)	(2:45)	Motown 6357 Forever: Musical Memories. *(LP length)*

**1979 THE BOSS
(actual 45 time is (3:56) not (3:34) as stated on the
record label)**

(S)	(3:56)	Motown 6140 The Composer Series: Ashford & Simpson.
(S)	(6:38)	Rhino 70493 Billboard Top Dance Hits - 1979. *(medley of "NO ONE GETS THE PRIZE/THE BOSS")*
(S)	(3:47)	Motown 6197 and 6049 Diana Ross Anthology.
(S)	(3:53)	Motown 0960 All The Great Hits.
(S)	(3:56)	Motown 6072 Compact Command Performances.
(S)	(3:58)	Motown 8002 and 8102 Diana/The Boss.
(S)	(3:58)	Motown 5198 The Boss.
(S)	(3:56)	Motown 6357 Forever: Musical Memories.
(S)	(6:26)	Motown 6377 Diana Extended/The Remixes. *(all selections on this cd are remixed with extra instrumentation added)*

(S) (6:27) Motown 314530608 Funkology Volume Three: Dance Divas. *(remixed with extra instrumentation added)*

1980 UPSIDE DOWN
(45 length is (3:38); LP length is (4:04))
(S) (4:04) Motown 9060 Motown's Biggest Pop Hits.
(S) (3:38) Rhino 70276 The Disco Years Volume 5.
(S) (3:38) Rhino 70675 Billboard Top Hits - 1980.
(S) (3:37) Motown 6197 and 6049 Diana Ross Anthology.
(S) (4:04) Motown 0960 All The Great Hits.
(S) (4:04) Motown 6072 Compact Command Performances.
(S) (4:06) Motown 8002 and 8102 Diana/The Boss.
(S) (4:05) Motown 5383 Diana.
(S) (4:04) Motown 6357 Forever: Musical Memories.
(S) (3:38) Motown 6358 Hitsville USA Volume Two.
(S) (3:38) Rhino 71618 Soul Train Hall Of Fame/20th Anniversary.
(S) (8:03) Motown 6377 Diana Extended/The Remixes. *(all selections on this cd are remixed with extra instrumentation added)*
(S) (4:05) Priority 53728 Mega Hits Dance Classics Vol 12.
(S) (8:02) SBK 29007 Brilliant! The Global Dance Music Experience Volume 3. *(remix)*
(S) (4:04) Rebound 314520298 Disco Nights Vol. 9.
(S) (4:04) Motown 314530428 Diana Ross Ultimate Collection.
(S) (3:37) Motown 314530516 Motown Year By Year 1980.
(S) (3:38) Time-Life R138-38 Celebration.
(S) (4:04) Motown 314530572 Funkology Volume Two - Behind The Groove.
(S) (3:38) Time-Life R988-14 Sounds Of The Eighties: 1980-1982.
(S) (4:05) Polydor 314555120 Pure Disco 2.
(S) (3:38) Time-Life R840-09 Sounds Of The Seventies: '70s Dance Party 1979-1981.

1980 I'M COMING OUT
(S) (3:55) Rhino 70275 The Disco Years Volume 4. *(45 version)*
(S) (3:55) Motown 6197 and 6049 Diana Ross Anthology. *(45 version)*
(S) (5:22) Motown 0960 All The Great Hits. *(LP version)*
(S) (5:23) Motown 6072 Compact Command Performances. *(LP version)*
(S) (5:23) Motown 8002 and 8102 Diana/The Boss. *(LP version)*
(S) (5:23) Motown 5383 Diana. *(LP version)*
(S) (5:23) Motown 6357 Forever: Musical Memories. *(LP version)*
(S) (8:06) Motown 6377 Diana Extended/The Remixes. *(all selections on this cd are remixed with extra instrumentation added)*
(S) (3:53) Motown 314530516 Motown Year By Year 1980. *(45 version)*
(S) (3:55) Motown 314530516 Motown Year By Year 1980. *(12" single version)*
(S) (3:54) MCA 11329 Soul Train 25th Anniversary Box Set. *(45 version)*
(S) (3:53) Motown 314530849 Motown 40 Forever. *(45 version)*
(S) (3:56) Time-Life R988-22 Sounds Of The Eighties 1980-1983. *(45 version)*

1981 IT'S MY TURN
(S) (3:55) Motown 6177 Endless Love: 15 Of Motown's Greatest Love Songs.
(S) (3:55) Motown 9082 and 5385 Great Motown Love Songs.
(S) (3:52) Motown 6197 and 6049 Diana Ross Anthology.
(S) (3:55) Motown 6072 Compact Command Performances.
(S) (3:55) Motown 6105 All The Great Love Songs.
(S) (3:55) Motown 6357 Forever: Musical Memories.
(S) (3:56) Rebound 314520318 Class Reunion 1980.
(S) (3:54) Motown 314530516 Motown Year By Year 1980.
(S) (3:52) Polygram Special Markets 314520445 Soul Hits Of The 80's.
(S) (3:54) Rebound 314520519 Love At The Movies.

released as by DIANA ROSS & LIONEL RICHIE:
1981 ENDLESS LOVE
(S) (4:26) Motown 6177 Endless Love: 15 Of Motown's Greatest Love Songs.

(S) (4:26) Motown 6143 and 5386 The Composer Series: Lionel Richie.
(S) (4:26) Motown 9021 and 5309 25 Years Of Grammy Greats.
(S) (4:26) Motown 9082 and 5385 Great Motown Love Songs.
(S) (4:26) Motown 9035 and 5324 Top Ten With A Bullet!
(S) (4:26) Motown 6192 You Can't Hurry Love: All The Great Love Songs Of The Past 25 Years.
(S) (4:26) Motown 6132 25 #1 Hits From 25 Years Volume 2.
(S) (4:24) Motown 6197 and 6049 Diana Ross Anthology.
(S) (4:45) RCA 61154 and 61136 Endless Love. *(rerecording with Diana Ross solo)*
(S) (4:25) Motown 0960 All The Great Hits.
(S) (4:26) Motown 6072 Compact Command Performances.
(S) (4:26) Motown 6105 All The Great Love Songs.
(S) (4:26) Motown 6357 Diana Ross Forever: Musical Memories.
(S) (4:26) Polygram Special Markets 314520030 Motown Legends - Love Songs.
(S) (4:26) Motown 314530428 Diana Ross Ultimate Collection.
(S) (4:26) Rhino 72159 Black Entertainment Television - 15th Anniversary.
(S) (4:26) Rebound 314520361 Class Reunion '81.
(S) (4:25) Rebound 314520370 Soul Classics - Quiet Storm/The 80's.
(S) (4:26) Polygram Special Markets 314520031 Motown Legends - Duets.
(S) (4:26) Time-Life R834-04 Body Talk - Together Forever.
(S) (4:26) Angel 56580 Men Are From Mars, Women Are From Venus - Songs For Loving Couples.
(S) (4:54) RCA 67410 Diana Ross - Greatest Hits - The RCA Years. *(rerecording with Diana Ross solo)*
(S) (4:23) Motown 314530846 Lionel Richie: Truly - The Love Songs.
(S) (3:03) Madacy Entertainment 6806 Best Of Love. *(edited)*
(S) (4:26) Polygram TV 314555610 The One And Only Love Album.
(S) (4:26) Time-Life R814-02 Love Songs.
(S) (4:25) Rebound 314520519 Love At The Movies.

released as by DIANA ROSS:
1981 WHY DO FOOLS FALL IN LOVE
(S) (2:53) Motown 6357 Forever: Musical Memories.
(S) (2:52) Motown 314530428 Diana Ross Ultimate Collection.
(S) (2:52) RCA 67410 Greatest Hits - The RCA Years.

1982 MIRROR, MIRROR
(S) (6:08) Motown 6357 Forever: Musical Memories. *(LP version)*
(S) (4:04) RCA 67410 Greatest Hits - The RCA Years. *(45 version)*

1982 MUSCLES
(dj copies of this 45 ran (3:59) and (4:36); commercial copies were all (3:59))
(S) (4:37) Motown 6357 Forever: Musical Memories. *(LP version)*
(S) (4:36) RCA 61154 and 61136 Endless Love. *(LP version)*
(S) (4:37) RCA 4384 Silk Electric. *(LP version)*
(S) (4:02) RCA 67410 Greatest Hits - The RCA Years. *(45 version)*

1983 SO CLOSE
(S) (4:12) RCA 4384 Silk Electric.

1983 PIECES OF ICE

released as by JULIO IGLESIAS & DIANA ROSS:
1984 ALL OF YOU
(S) (4:01) Columbia 39157 Julio Iglesias - 1100 Bel Air Place.
(S) (3:59) RCA 5009 Diana Ross - Swept Away.

released as by DIANA ROSS:
1984 SWEPT AWAY
(S) (5:22) Motown 6357 Forever: Musical Memories. *(LP version)*
(S) (5:21) RCA 61154 and 61136 Endless Love. *(LP version)*
(S) (5:23) RCA 5009 Swept Away. *(LP version)*
(S) (4:02) RCA 67410 Greatest Hits - The RCA Years. *(45 version)*

DIANA ROSS *(Continued)*
1985 MISSING YOU
    (actual 45 time is (4:02) not (4:16) as stated on
    the record label; LP length is (4:15))
    (S) (4:14)   Motown 314530428 Diana Ross Ultimate
                  Collection.
    (S) (4:14)   Motown 6357 Forever: Musical Memories.
    (S) (4:15)   RCA 5009 Swept Away.
    (S) (4:01)   RCA 67410 Greatest Hits - The RCA Years.
    (S) (4:14)   Columbia 69012 Diana Princess Of Wales Tribute.

JACK ROSS
1962 CINDERELLA

JACKIE ROSS
1964 SELFISH ONE
    (S) (3:15)   MCA 31205 Vintage Music Volume 8.
    (S) (3:15)   MCA 5805 Vintage Music Volumes 7 & 8.
    (S) (3:15)   Chess 31318 Best Of Chess Rhythm & Blues
                  Volume 2.
    (S) (3:03)   Time-Life RHD-12 Rhythm & Blues - 1964.
                  (faded :12 sooner than the 45 or LP)
    (S) (3:15)   Time-Life 2CLR-25 Classic Rock - On The Soul Side.
    (S) (3:03)   Time-Life R838-13 Solid Gold Soul - 1964.
                  (faded :12 sooner than the 45 or LP)
    (S) (3:17)   Rhino 72815 Beg, Scream & Shout! The Big Ol'
                  Box Of '60s Soul. *(noisy fadeout)*
    (S) (3:16)   Chess 9388 Chess Soul - A Decade Of Chicago's
                  Finest.

SPENCER ROSS
1960 TRACY'S THEME
    (S) (2:49)   Time-Life HPD-39 Your Hit Parade - 60's
                  Instrumentals: Take Two.

DAVID LEE ROTH
1985 CALIFORNIA GIRLS
    (S) (2:48)   MCA 6160 O.S.T. Down And Out In Beverly Hills.
    (S) (2:48)   Priority 7054 80's Greatest Rock Hits Volume 4 -
                  Party On.
    (S) (2:46)   Sandstone 33047 and 5015 Cosmopolitan Volume
                  1.
    (S) (2:45)   JCI 3128 1985 - Only Rock 'N Roll - 1989.
    (S) (2:47)   Warner Brothers 25222 Crazy From The Heat.
    (S) (2:44)   Time-Life R988-02 Sounds Of The Eighties: 1985.
    (S) (2:44)   Time-Life R988-31 Sounds Of The Eighties:
                  Cinemax Movie Hits Of The '80s.
    (S) (2:42)   Madacy Entertainment 6804 More Sun Splashin'.
    (S) (2:48)   Rhino 72941 and 72988 The Best.
1985 JUST A GIGOLO/I AIN'T GOT NOBODY
    (S) (4:39)   Sandstone 33041 and 5007 Rock The First
                  Volume 1. *(LP version)*
    (S) (4:39)   Warner Brothers 25222 Crazy From The Heat.
                  (LP version)
    (S) (4:17)   Time-Life R988-12 Sounds Of The 80's: 1985-
                  1986. *(45 version)*
    (S) (4:40)   Rhino 72941 and 72988 The Best. *(LP version)*
1986 YANKEE ROSE
    (S) (3:49)   Warner Brothers 25470 Eat 'Em And Smile.
    (S) (3:49)   JCI 3143 18 Screamers From The 80's.
    (S) (3:49)   Rhino 72941 and 72988 The Best.
1988 JUST LIKE PARADISE
    (S) (4:02)   Warner Brothers 25671 Skyscraper.
    (S) (4:02)   Time-Life R988-21 Sounds Of The Eighties:
                  1986-1989.
    (S) (4:04)   Rhino 72941 and 72988 The Best.

ROUTERS
1962 LET'S GO (PONY)
    (S) (2:16)   Warner Special Products 27610 More Party Classics.
    (S) (2:16)   JCI 3106 Surfin' Sixties.
    (S) (2:17)   Rhino 71602 Rock Instrumental Classics Volume
                  2: The Sixties.
    (S) (2:17)   Rhino 72035 Rock Instrumental Classics Vols. 1-
                  5 Box Set.

    (S) (2:16)   Time-Life 2RNR-46 Rock 'N' Roll Era - 60's Juke
                  Box Memories.
    (S) (2:17)   K-Tel 3453 Rockin' Instrumentals.

ROVER BOYS
1956 GRADUATION DAY

ROVERS (see IRISH ROVERS)

ROXETTE
1989 THE LOOK
    (S) (3:54)   Sandstone 33043 and 5009 Rock The First
                  Volume Three.
    (S) (3:54)   Time-Life R105-40 Rock Dreams.
    (S) (3:56)   EMI 91098 Look Sharp!
    (S) (3:54)   Time-Life R988-13 Sounds Of The Eighties: 1989.
1989 DRESSED FOR SUCCESS
    (S) (4:09)   EMI 91098 Look Sharp!
1989 LISTEN TO YOUR HEART
    (S) (5:12)   SBK 31181 Moments In Love.
    (S) (5:27)   EMI 91098 Look Sharp!
1990 DANGEROUS
    (S) (3:48)   Foundation/Capitol 96427 Hearts Of Gold: The
                  Pop Collection.
    (S) (3:48)   Sandstone 33046 and 5012 Rock The First
                  Volume Six.
    (S) (3:49)   EMI 91098 Look Sharp!
1990 IT MUST HAVE BEEN LOVE
    (S) (4:19)   EMI 93492 O.S.T. Pretty Woman. *(LP version)*
    (S) (4:17)   EMI-Capitol Music Group 54555 Movie Luv.
                  (LP version)
1991 JOYRIDE
    (S) (4:23)   Foundation/RCA 66104 Hot #1 Hits.
    (S) (4:23)   EMI 94435 Joyride.
1991 FADING LIKE A FLOWER (EVERY TIME YOU LEAVE)
    (S) (3:49)   EMI 94435 Joyride.
1991 SPENDING MY TIME
    (S) (4:34)   EMI 94435 Joyride.
1992 CHURCH OF YOUR HEART
    (S) (3:15)   EMI 94435 Joyride.

ROXY MUSIC
1976 LOVE IS THE DRUG
    (S) (4:06)   Reprise 26043 Siren. *(LP version)*
    (S) (4:04)   Reprise 25857 Street Life. *(LP version)*
    (S) (3:56)   Time-Life SOD-18 Sounds Of The Seventies -
                  1976: Take Two. *(45 version)*
    (S) (4:06)   MCA 11389 O.S.T. Casino. *(LP version)*

BILLY JOE ROYAL
1965 DOWN IN THE BOONDOCKS
    (S) (2:32)   Columbia 45018 Rock Classics Of The 60's.
    (S) (2:32)   Columbia 45063 Greatest Hits.
    (S) (2:37)   Special Music 4815 Greatest Hits. *(rerecording)*
    (S) (2:39)   Pair 1262 Best Of. *(rerecording)*
    (S) (2:32)   JCI 3112 Pop Sixties.
    (S) (2:32)   Time-Life 2CLR-01 Classic Rock - 1965.
    (S) (2:32)   Collectables 5859 Down In The Boondocks/Cherry
                  Hill Park.
1965 I KNEW YOU WHEN
    (S) (2:30)   Columbia 45063 Greatest Hits.
    (S) (2:31)   Collectables 5859 Down In The
                  Boondocks/Cherry Hill Park.
1966 I'VE GOT TO BE SOMEBODY
    (S) (3:01)   Columbia 45063 Greatest Hits.
    (S) (3:00)   Collectables 5859 Down In The Boondocks/Cherry
                  Hill Park.
1969 CHERRY HILL PARK
    (S) (2:59)   Columbia 45063 Greatest Hits. *(includes
                  additional background vocals not found on the 45
                  or LP; :13 longer than the 45 or LP)*
    (S) (2:46)   Rhino 70921 Super Hits Of The 70's Volume 1.
    (S) (2:46)   Rhino 72009 Super Hits Of The 70's Volumes 1-4
                  Box Set.
    (S) (2:52)   Special Music 4815 Greatest Hits. *(rerecording)*

520

(S) (2:51) Pair 1262 Best Of. *(rerecording)*
(S) (2:47) Collectables 5859 Down In The Boondocks/Cherry Hill Park.

ROYALETTES
1965 IT'S GONNA TAKE A MIRACLE
(E) (3:10) Ripete 5151 Ocean Drive 4.
(M) (3:10) Ichiban 2110 It's Gonna Take A Miracle - The MGM Sides.
(M) (3:11) Mercury 314528171 Growin' Up Too Fast - The Girl Group Anthology.
(M) (3:12) Varese Sarabande 5705 Dick Bartley Presents Collector's Essentials: The 60's.

ROYAL GUARDSMEN
1967 SNOOPY VS. THE RED BARON
(M) (2:42) Collectables 5069 History Of Rock Volume 9.
(M) (2:44) One Way 18147 Anthology.
1967 RETURN OF THE RED BARON
(M) (2:51) One Way 18147 Anthology. *(missing some sound effects)*
1967 SNOOPY'S CHRISTMAS
(M) (3:08) One Way 18147 Anthology.
1969 BABY LET'S WAIT
(M) (2:35) K-Tel 205 Battle Of The Bands Volume 3.
(M) (2:34) Collectables 5065 History Of Rock Volume 5.
(M) (2:35) One Way 18147 Anthology.

ROYAL PHILHARMONIC ORCHESTRA
1982 HOOKED ON CLASSICS
(S) (5:04) RCA 9970 Nipper's Greatest Hits - The 80's.

ROYAL SCOTS DRAGOON GUARDS
1972 AMAZING GRACE
(S) (3:18) RCA 52008 Amazing Grace.
(S) (3:19) RCA 66881 RCA's Greatest One-Hit Wonders.
(S) (3:18) Time-Life R840-04 Sounds Of The Seventies: A Loss For Words.
(S) (3:18) Varese Sarabande 5906 God, Love And Rock & Roll.

ROYAL TEENS
1958 SHORT SHORTS
(M) (2:36) MCA 31201 Vintage Music Volume 4. *(complete recording session length; background hum noticeable on the introduction)*
(M) (2:36) MCA 5778 Vintage Music Volumes 3 & 4. *(complete recording session length; background hum noticeable on the introduction)*
(M) (2:33) Time-Life 2RNR-37 Rock 'N' Roll Era - Weird, Wild & Wacky. *(complete recording session length; background hum noticeable on the introduction)*
(M) (2:34) Collectables 2503 WCBS-FM History Of Rock - The 50's Part 2. *(complete recording session length; background hum noticeable on the introduction)*
(M) (2:35) Collectables 4503 History Of Rock/The 50s Part Two. *(complete recording session length; background hum noticeable on the introduction)*
(M) (2:11) Collectables 5094 Short Shorts And Other Golden Classics. *(45 length; distorted)*
(M) (2:33) MCA Special Products 22028 Cra-a-zy Hits. *(complete recording session length; background hum noticeable on the introduction)*
(M) (2:34) MCA Special Products 22166 Vintage Collectibles Volume 8. *(complete recording session length; background hum noticeable on the introduction)*
(M) (2:33) K-Tel 3035 Goofy Greats. *(complete recording session length; background hum noticeable on the introduction)*
(M) (2:34) DCC Compact Classics 077 Too Cute! *(complete recording session length; background hum noticeable on the introduction)*

1959 BELIEVE ME
(M) (2:25) Collectables 5094 Short Shorts And More Golden Classics. *(mastered from a scratchy record)*
(M) (2:29) Rhino 72507 Doo Wop Box II.

ROYALTONES
1958 POOR BOY
(M) (2:17) Rhino 71601 Rock Instrumental Classics Volume 1: The Fifties.
(M) (2:17) Rhino 72035 Rock Instrumental Classics Vols. 1-5 Box Set.
(M) (2:15) Time-Life 2RNR-49 Rock 'N' Roll Era - Lost Treasures II.

ROZALLA
1992 EVERYBODY'S FREE (TO FEEL GOOD)
(S) (3:31) Sandstone 33055 and 5014 Rock The First Volume Eight.
(S) (3:31) Epic 52897 Everybody's Free.
(S) (3:28) Thump 9951 Power 106 10th Anniversary Collection. *(all songs on this cd are segued together)*
(S) (3:19) Cold Front 6284 More Of! Club Mix's Biggest Jams. *(all selections on this cd are segued together)*
(S) (4:58) Beast 53022 Club Hitz Of The 90's Vol. 1. *(all songs on this cd are segued together)*

RTZ
1992 UNTIL YOUR LOVE COMES BACK AROUND
(S) (5:52) Giant 24422 Return To Zero.

RUBETTES
1974 SUGAR BABY LOVE
(S) (3:30) Time-Life SOD-35 Sounds Of The Seventies - AM Nuggets.
(S) (3:27) Polydor 314527493 O.S.T. Muriel's Wedding.

RUBICON
1978 I'M GONNA TAKE CARE OF EVERYTHING

RUBY and THE ROMANTICS
1963 OUR DAY WILL COME
(S) (2:31) Rhino 70649 Billboard's Top R&B Hits Of 1963.
(S) (2:31) MCA 31206 Vintage Music Volume 9.
(S) (2:31) MCA 5806 Vintage Music Volumes 9 & 10.
(S) (2:29) Original Sound 8862 Oldies But Goodies Vol. 12. *(this compact disc uses the "Waring - fds" noise reduction process)*
(S) (2:29) Original Sound 2223 Oldies But Goodies Volumes 2,7,9,12 and 13 Box Set. *(this box set uses the "Waring - fds" noise reduction process)*
(S) (2:29) Original Sound 2500 Oldies But Goodies Volumes 1-15 Box Set. *(this box set uses the "Waring - fds" noise reduction process)*
(S) (2:30) Target 1000 Very Best Of.
(S) (2:30) Time-Life 2RNR-07 Rock 'N' Roll Era - 1963.
(S) (2:27) Time-Life RHD-02 Rhythm & Blues - 1963.
(S) (2:29) Time-Life SUD-08 Superhits - 1963.
(S) (2:29) Time-Life OPCD-4517 Tonight's The Night.
(S) (2:30) MCA Special Products 20753 Classic R&B Oldies From The 60's.
(S) (2:31) MCA Special Products 22131 Vintage Collectibles Volume 2.
(S) (2:30) Hip-O 40029 The Glory Of Love - '60s Sweet & Soulful Love Songs.
(S) (2:30) Time-Life R857-08 The Heart Of Rock 'n' Roll 1963.
(S) (2:29) Time-Life AM1-17 AM Gold - 1963.
(S) (2:27) Time-Life R838-14 Solid Gold Soul - 1963.
(S) (2:30) K-Tel 3901 Soul Brothers & Sisters Of The 60's.
(S) (2:29) Repeat/Relativity 1609 Tell It Like It Is: #1 Soul Hits Of The 60's Volume 1.
(S) (2:30) MCA Special Products 21046 Top Singles Of The Sixties.
(S) (2:30) JCI 3184 1960 - Only Love - 1964.

RUBY and THE ROMANTICS _(Continued)_
1963 MY SUMMER LOVE
(S) (2:55) Target 1000 Very Best Of. *(time includes :13 of studio talk)*
(S) (2:42) Time-Life R857-18 The Heart Of Rock 'n' Roll 1962-1963 Take Two.
1963 HEY THERE LONELY BOY
(S) (2:50) Target 1000 Very Best Of.

RUDE BOYS
1991 WRITTEN ALL OVER YOUR FACE
(S) (6:20) Atlantic 82121 Rude Awakening.

DAVID RUFFIN
1969 MY WHOLE WORLD ENDED (THE MOMENT YOU LEFT ME)
(S) (3:26) Motown 6183 Hard To Find Motown Classics Volume 1.
(S) (3:26) Motown 5211 At His Best.
(S) (3:26) Motown 5108 Jimmy & David Ruffin Superstar Series Volume 8.
(M) (3:26) Motown 6312 Hitsville USA.
(S) (3:26) Time-Life RHD-13 Rhythm & Blues - 1969.
(S) (3:26) Time-Life 2CLR-12 Classic Rock - 1969: The Beat Goes On.
(S) (3:27) Motown/Essex 374638521 Motown Legends - I've Lost Everything I've Ever Loved.
(S) (3:25) Motown 314530525 Motown Year By Year - 1969.
(M) (3:26) Motown 314530615 Temptations - One By One: Best Of Their Solo Years.
(S) (3:26) Rebound 314520369 Soul Classics - Quiet Storm/The 60's.
(S) (3:26) Time-Life R838-04 Solid Gold Soul - 1969.
(M) (3:25) Rhino 72815 Beg, Scream & Shout! The Big Ol' Box Of '60s Soul.

1976 WALK AWAY FROM LOVE
(S) (3:13) Motown 9105 and 5410 Motown Memories Volume 2. *(45 version)*
(S) (3:17) Motown 5211 At His Best. *(45 version)*
(S) (3:17) Motown 6358 Hitsville USA Volume Two. *(45 version)*
(S) (3:16) Motown/Essex 374638521 Motown Legends - I've Lost Everything I've Ever Loved. *(45 version)*
(S) (3:16) Motown 314530531 Motown Year By Year - 1975. *(45 version)*
(S) (5:28) Motown 314530615 Temptations - One By One: Best Of Their Solo Years. *(LP version)*
(S) (3:17) JCI 3175 1975 - Only Soul - 1979. *(45 version)*

released as by DARY HALL/JOHN OATES with DAVID RUFFIN and EDDIE KENDRICK:
1985 THE WAY YOU DO THE THINGS YOU DO/MY GIRL
(S) (12:35) RCA 7035 Live At The Apollo. *(LP version which is a medley of a number of different songs)*
(S) (5:42) RCA 66862 Hi Octane Hard Drivin' Hits. *(edit of LP version)*

JIMMY RUFFIN
1966 WHAT BECOMES OF THE BROKEN HEARTED
(S) (2:57) Motown 6183 Hard To Find Motown Classics Volume 1. *(LP mix)*
(S) (2:56) Motown 5454 A Collection Of 16 Big Hits Volume 7. *(LP mix)*
(S) (2:57) Motown 5445 Sings Top Ten. *(LP mix)*
(S) (2:57) Motown 5108 Jimmy & David Ruffin Superstar Series Volume 8. *(LP mix)*
(M) (3:00) Motown 6312 Hitsville USA. *(45 mix)*
(S) (2:55) Time-Life RHD-01 Rhythm & Blues - 1966. *(LP mix)*
(S) (2:57) Time-Life 2CLR-13 Classic Rock - 1966: Shakin' All Over. *(LP mix)*
(S) (2:58) Right Stuff 30577 Slow Jams: The 60's Volume 3. *(LP mix)*
(M) (3:00) Motown 314530569 Motown Milestones - Motown Love Songs. *(45 mix)*
(S) (2:57) Rebound 314520369 Soul Classics - Quiet Storm/The 60's. *(LP mix)*

(S) (2:55) Time-Life R838-01 Solid Gold Soul - 1966. *(LP mix)*
(S) (2:57) Simitar 55572 The Number One's: Hot In The '60s. *(LP mix)*
(S) (2:56) Motown 314530849 Motown 40 Forever. *(LP mix)*
(M) (3:00) Time-Life R857-20 The Heart Of Rock 'n' Roll 1965-1966. *(45 mix)*
1967 I'VE PASSED THIS WAY BEFORE
(S) (2:41) Motown 6183 Hard To Find Motown Classics Volume 1. *(LP version)*
(S) (2:41) Motown 5445 Sings Top Ten. *(LP version)*
(S) (2:41) Motown 5108 Jimmy & David Ruffin Superstar Series Volume 8. *(LP version)*
(S) (2:41) Motown 314530522 Motown Year By Year - 1966. *(LP version)*
1967 GONNA GIVE HER ALL THE LOVE I'VE GOT
(S) (2:33) Motown 5455 A Collection Of 16 Big Hits Vol. 8.
(S) (2:35) Motown 9109 Motown Memories Vol. 3.
(S) (2:35) Motown 5445 Sings Top Ten.
1980 HOLD ON TO MY LOVE
(S) (3:03) Ripete 5151 Ocean Drive 4.

RUFUS
1974 TELL ME SOMETHING GOOD
(S) (4:37) MCA 10288 Classic Soul. *(LP version)*
(S) (3:30) Rhino 70553 Soul Hits Of The 70's Volume 13. *(45 version)*
(S) (4:36) MCA 31365 Rags To Rufus. *(LP version)*
(S) (3:34) Rhino 71432 In Yo Face! History Of Funk Volume 2. *(45 version)*
(S) (3:30) Rhino 71549 Let There Be Drums Vol. 3: The 70's. *(45 version)*
(S) (3:29) Razor & Tie 22045 Those Funky 70's. *(45 version)*
(S) (3:31) Time-Life SOD-25 Sounds Of The Seventies - Seventies Generation. *(45 version)*
(S) (4:36) K-Tel 6011 70's Soul: Super Funky Hits. *(LP version)*
(S) (3:29) MCA 11329 Soul Train 25th Anniversary Box Set. *(45 version)*
(S) (3:30) Madacy Entertainment 1974 Rock On 1974. *(45 version)*
(S) (4:38) Hip-O 40010 ABC's Of Soul Volume 2. *(LP version)*
(S) (3:29) JCI 3168 #1 Radio Hits 1970 - Only Rock 'n Roll - 1974. *(45 version)*
(S) (4:38) MCA 11543 Very Best Of Featuring Chaka Khan. *(LP version)*
(S) (4:35) Thump 4060 Old School Volume 6. *(LP version; all selections on this cd are segued together)*
(S) (4:36) MCA Special Products 20979 Soul Hits Volume 1. *(LP version)*
(S) (4:39) Hip-O 40035 Cigar Classics Volume 2 - Urban Fire. *(LP version)*
(S) (3:30) Time-Life R838-09 Solid Gold Soul - 1974. *(45 version)*
(S) (4:37) MCA Special Products 21032 Soul Legends. *(LP version)*
(S) (4:37) MCA Special Products 21029 The Women Of Soul. *(LP version)*
(S) (4:38) Hip-O 40095 '70s Hit(s) Back. *(LP version)*
(S) (3:30) Time-Life R840-05 Sounds Of The Seventies: '70s Dance Party 1972-1974. *(45 version)*

released as by RUFUS featuring CHAKA KHAN:
1974 YOU GOT THE LOVE
(S) (4:38) MCA 31365 Rags To Rufus. *(LP version)*
(S) (4:38) MCA Special Products 20752 Classic R&B Oldies From The 70's Vol. 2. *(LP version)*
(S) (4:41) Hip-O 40010 ABC's Of Soul Volume 2. *(LP version)*
(S) (4:38) JCI 3173 1970 - Only Soul - 1974. *(LP version)*
(S) (4:42) MCA 11543 Very Best Of Featuring Chaka Khan. *(LP version)*
(S) (4:38) Priority 53129 Deep Soul Volume One. *(LP version)*
(S) (4:38) K-Tel 4020 Great R&B Funk Bands Of The 70's. *(LP version)*

522

1975 ONCE YOU GET STARTED
    (S)   (3:25)   Rhino 70555 Soul Hits Of The 70's Volume 15.
                      (45 version)
    (S)   (4:28)   MCA 10236 Rufusized. *(LP version)*
    (S)   (3:24)   Rhino 72414 Dance Floor Divas: The 70's. *(45 version)*
    (S)   (4:18)   MCA 11543 Very Best Of Featuring Chaka Khan. *(neither the 45 or LP version; bad edit at :17 on original pressings of this cd)*

1976 SWEET THING
    (S)   (3:18)   MCA 31373 Rufus Featuring Chaka Khan.
    (S)   (3:16)   Rhino 71618 Soul Train Hall Of Fame/20th Anniversary.
    (S)   (3:19)   Time-Life SOD-18 Sounds Of The Seventies - 1976: Take Two.
    (S)   (3:19)   Rhino 72128 Hot Soul Hits Of The 70's Vol. 18.
    (S)   (3:17)   K-Tel 3535 Slow Groove Love Jams Of The 70's.
    (S)   (3:18)   Madacy Entertainment 1976 Rock On 1976.
    (S)   (3:19)   Hip-O 40011 ABC's Of Soul Volume 3.
    (S)   (3:18)   MCA 11543 Very Best Of Featuring Chaka Khan.
    (S)   (3:19)   Hip-O 40030 The Glory Of Love - '70s Sweet & Soulful Love Songs.
    (S)   (3:18)   Priority 50928 Rare Grooves Volume 1.
    (S)   (3:19)   Time-Life R838-11 Solid Gold Soul - 1976.
    (S)   (3:19)   Time-Life R834-05 Body Talk - Sealed With A Kiss.

1976 DANCE WIT ME
    (S)   (3:57)   MCA 31373 Rufus Featuring Chaka Khan.
    (S)   (3:58)   Rhino 71433 In Yo Face! History Of Funk Volume 3.
    (S)   (3:59)   Priority 53786 Planet Funk Volume 3.
    (S)   (3:57)   MCA 11543 Very Best Of Featuring Chaka Khan.
    (S)   (3:58)   Hip-O 40091 Disco 54: Funkin' On The Floor.

1977 AT MIDNIGHT (MY LOVE WILL LIFT YOU UP)
    (S)   (4:20)   MCA 10449 Ask Rufus. *(LP version)*
    (S)   (4:18)   MCA 11543 Very Best Of Featuring Chaka Khan. *(LP version)*
    (S)   (4:18)   Time-Life R838-16 Solid Gold Soul 1977. *(LP version)*
    (S)   (4:17)   Simitar 55602 The Number One's: Silky Soul. *(LP version)*

1977 HOLLYWOOD
    (S)   (4:09)   MCA 10449 Ask Rufus.
    (S)   (4:07)   Rhino 71862 Smooth Grooves Volume 4.
    (S)   (4:08)   MCA 11543 Very Best Of Featuring Chaka Khan.

released as by RUFUS and CHAKA:
1980 DO YOU LOVE WHAT YOU FEEL
    (S)   (4:29)   MCA 10763 Masterjam. *(LP length)*
    (S)   (4:28)   Rhino 71755 and 72832 Phat Trax: The Best Of Old School Volume 4. *(LP length)*
    (S)   (4:28)   Thump 4050 Old School Volume 5. *(LP length)*
    (S)   (4:28)   Madacy Entertainment 1980 Rock On 1980. *(LP length)*
    (S)   (4:26)   MCA 11543 Very Best Of Featuring Chaka Khan. *(LP length)*
    (S)   (4:28)   Hip-O 40041 The Studio Collection Disco 54. *(LP length)*
    (S)   (4:28)   Time-Life R838-15 Solid Gold Soul 1979. *(LP length)*

released as by RUFUS and CHAKA KHAN:
1983 AIN'T NOBODY
    (S)   (4:01)   Rhino 71972 Video Soul - Best Soul Of The 80's Vol. 2. *(45 version)*
    (S)   (4:41)   Warner Brothers 23679 Live - Stompin' At The Savoy. *(LP version)*
    (S)   (4:01)   Rhino 72138 Billboard Hot R&B Hits 1983. *(45 version)*

RUGBYS
1969 YOU, I
    (S)   (2:54)   Collectables 0686 Rugbys Meet Lazarus. *(noisy fadeout)*

TODD RUNDGREN (also RUNT)
released as by RUNT:
1971 WE GOTTA GET YOU A WOMAN
    (S)   (3:06)   Rhino 71491 Anthology (1968-1985).

    (S)   (3:06)   Rhino 70862 Runt.
    (S)   (3:05)   Time-Life SUD-20 Superhits - Early 70's Classics.
    (S)   (3:05)   Time-Life SOD-12 Sounds Of The Seventies - 1971: Take Two.
    (S)   (3:06)   Rhino 71029 Best Of.
    (S)   (3:06)   Pyramid 71888 A Future To This Life - Robocop: The Series Soundtrack.
    (S)   (3:05)   JCI 3139 18 Free And Easy Hits From The 70's.
    (S)   (3:06)   Time-Life AM1-15 AM Gold - Early '70s Classics.
    (S)   (3:06)   Flashback 72677 I Saw The Light And Other Hits.
    (S)   (3:06)   Flashback 72089 '70s Rock Legends Box Set.
    (S)   (3:06)   Rhino 72811 Very Best Of.

released as by TODD RUNDGREN:
1972 I SAW THE LIGHT
    (S)   (2:57)   Sandstone 33000 Reelin' In The Years Volume 1.
    (S)   (2:57)   Epic 48732 O.S.T. My Girl.
    (S)   (2:57)   Rhino 71491 Anthology (1968-1985).
    (S)   (2:59)   Rhino 71107 Something/Anything.
    (S)   (2:57)   DCC Compact Classics 062 Rock Of The 70's Volume 1.
    (S)   (2:58)   Time-Life SOD-03 Sounds Of The Seventies - 1972.
    (S)   (2:57)   Rhino 71029 Best Of.
    (S)   (2:56)   Priority 53720 Classic Rock Volume 5 - Glitter Bands.
    (S)   (2:57)   Madacy Entertainment 1972 Rock On 1972.
    (S)   (2:56)   A&M 314540563 O.S.T. Kingpin.
    (S)   (2:57)   Flashback 72677 I Saw The Light And Other Hits.
    (S)   (2:57)   Flashback 72089 '70s Rock Legends Box Set.
    (S)   (2:58)   Rhino 72811 Very Best Of.
    (S)   (2:59)   MFSL 591 Something/Anything. *(gold disc)*

1973 HELLO IT'S ME
    (S)   (3:47)   Priority 7997 Super Songs/70's Greatest Rock Hits Volume 8. *(:17 longer than the 45 version)*
    (S)   (3:49)   Sandstone 33003 Reelin' In The Years Volume 4. *(:19 longer than the 45 version)*
    (S)   (3:49)   Rhino 71491 Anthology (1968-1985). *(:19 longer than the 45 version)*
    (S)   (4:37)   Rhino 71107 Something/Anything. *(time includes :19 of studio talk; LP version)*
    (S)   (3:49)   DCC Compact Classics 065 Rock Of The 70's Volume 4. *(:19 longer than the 45 version)*
    (S)   (4:01)   JCI 3114 Easy Sixties. *(this is the Nazz version mistakenly credited to Todd Rundgren)*
    (S)   (3:48)   Razor & Tie 22502 Those Rocking 70's. *(:18 longer than the 45 version)*
    (S)   (3:37)   Time-Life SUD-13 Superhits - 1973. *(:07 longer than the 45 version)*
    (S)   (3:37)   Time-Life SOD-06 Sounds Of The Seventies - 1973. *(:07 longer than the 45 version)*
    (S)   (3:37)   Time-Life R105-26 Our Songs: Singers & Songwriters Encore. *(:07 longer than the 45 version)*
    (S)   (3:49)   Rhino 71029 Best Of. *(:19 longer than the 45 version)*
    (S)   (4:18)   Rhino 72446 Listen To The Music: 70's Male Singer/Songwriters. *(LP version)*
    (S)   (3:37)   Time-Life AM1-03 AM Gold - 1973. *(:07 longer than the 45 version)*
    (S)   (3:37)   Time-Life R834-10 Body Talk - From The Heart. *(:07 longer than the 45 version)*
    (S)   (3:49)   Flashback 72677 I Saw The Light And Other Hits. *(:19 longer than the 45 version)*
    (S)   (3:49)   Flashback 72089 '70s Rock Legends Box Set. *(:19 longer than the 45 version)*
    (S)   (3:37)   K-Tel 4017 70s Heavy Hitters: Summer Love. *(:07 longer than the 45 version)*
    (S)   (4:20)   Rhino 72811 Very Best Of. *(LP version)*

1976 GOOD VIBRATIONS
    (S)   (3:42)   Rhino 70868 Faithful.
    (S)   (3:42)   Flashback 72677 I Saw The Light And Other Hits.
    (S)   (3:42)   Flashback 72089 '70s Rock Legends Box Set.

1978 CAN WE STILL BE FRIENDS
    (S)   (3:34)   Rhino 70871 Hermit Of Mink Hollow. *(LP version)*

TODD RUNDGREN (Continued)
- (S) (3:35) Rhino 71491 Anthology (1968-1985). *(LP version)*
- (S) (3:08) Time-Life SOD-20 Sounds Of The Seventies - 1978: Take Two. *(45 version)*
- (S) (3:35) Rhino 71029 Best Of. *(LP version)*
- (S) (3:35) Flashback 72677 I Saw The Light And Other Hits. *(LP version)*
- (S) (3:35) Flashback 72089 '70s Rock Legends Box Set. *(LP version)*
- (S) (3:35) Rhino 72811 Very Best Of. *(LP version)*

RUN-D.M.C.
1986 WALK THIS WAY
- (S) (5:09) Priority 7989 Rapmasters 13 - The Best Of The Bass. *(LP version)*
- (S) (5:09) K-Tel 315 Rap's Biggest Hits. *(LP version)*
- (S) (3:39) Rhino 71227 Black On White: Great R&B Covers Of Rock Classics. *(45 version)*
- (S) (5:10) Sandstone 33041 and 5007 Rock The First Volume 1. *(LP version)*
- (S) (5:09) Time-Life R102-34 The Rolling Stone Collection. *(LP version)*
- (S) (5:09) Profile 1217 Raising Hell. *(LP version)*
- (S) (5:09) Time-Life R988-04 Sounds Of The Eighties: 1986. *(LP version)*
- (S) (5:09) Cold Front 3309 Rap: 10 Years Of Gold 1985-1994. *(LP version)*
- (S) (5:10) Time-Life R968-20 Guitar Rock - The '80s. *(LP version)*
- (S) (5:09) Profile 1419 Greatest Hits. *(LP version)*
1986 YOU BE ILLIN'
- (S) (3:26) Priority 7956 Rapmasters 6 - The Best Of The Beat.
- (S) (3:25) Profile 1217 Raising Hell.
- (S) (3:25) Profile 1419 Greatest Hits.
- (S) (5:22) Scotti Bros. 75512 Slammin' Ol' Skool Trax.
1993 DOWN WITH THE KING
- (S) (5:02) Profile 1440 Down With The King.

RUNT (see TODD RUNDGREN)

RUSH
1982 NEW WORLD MAN
- (S) (3:39) Priority 7961 Three Decades Of Rock.
- (S) (3:40) Priority 7992 Killer Metal.
- (S) (3:40) Mercury 810002 Signals.
- (S) (3:40) Mercury 838936 Chronicles.
- (S) (3:40) MFSL 614 Signals. *(gold disc)*
- (S) (3:39) Time-Life R968-13 Guitar Rock - The Early '80s.
- (S) (3:41) Mercury 314534910 Retrospective II 1981-1987.
- (S) (3:40) Mercury 314534633 Signals. *(remastered edition)*

JENNIFER RUSH with ELTON JOHN
1987 FLAMES OF PARADISE
(dj copies of this 45 ran (3:58) and (4:42); commercial copies were all (3:58))
- (S) (4:35) Epic 40825 Jennifer Rush - Heart Over Mind. *(LP length)*

MERRILEE RUSH and THE TURNABOUTS
1968 ANGEL OF THE MORNING
- (M) (3:09) Rhino 70996 One Hit Wonders Of The 60's Volume 2.
- (E) (3:06) K-Tel 666 Flower Power.
- (M) (3:08) Time-Life 2CLR-27 Classic Rock - 1968: Blowin' Your Mind.
- (M) (3:08) Time-Life SUD-02 Superhits - 1968.
- (M) (3:08) Eclipse Music Group 64871 Rock 'n Roll Relix 1968-1969.
- (M) (3:08) Eclipse Music Group 64872 Rock 'n Roll Relix 1960-1969.
- (M) (3:08) Time-Life AM1-04 AM Gold - 1968.

PATRICE RUSHEN
1982 FORGET ME NOTS
(actual 45 time is (4:04) not (3:38) as stated on the record label)
- (S) (4:40) Priority 7975 Mega-Hits Dance Classics (Volume 5). *(noise at the end of the fadeout; LP version)*
- (S) (4:04) Rhino 70985 The Disco Years, Vol. 2. *(45 version)*
- (S) (4:40) Rhino 71862 Smooth Grooves Volume 4. *(LP version)*
- (S) (4:37) Thump 4040 Old School Volume 4. *(LP version)*
- (S) (4:40) Madacy Entertainment 1982 Rock On 1982. *(LP version)*
- (S) (4:04) Rhino 72414 Dance Floor Divas: The 70's. *(45 version)*
- (S) (4:43) Rhino 73508 Straight From The Heart. *(LP version)*
- (S) (4:42) Rhino 73513 Haven't You Heard: The Best Of. *(LP version)*
- (S) (4:41) Elektra 62089 Maximum R&B. *(LP version)*
- (S) (4:40) Time-Life R834-19 Body Talk - Always And Forever. *(LP version)*

BOBBY RUSSELL
1968 1432 FRANKLIN PIKE CIRCLE HERO
1971 SATURDAY MORNING CONFUSION
- (S) (3:04) Rhino 70926 Super Hits Of The 70's Volume 6.
- (S) (3:04) Rhino 72125 Dr. Demento's Country Corn.

BRENDA RUSSELL
1979 SO GOOD, SO RIGHT
- (S) (3:21) A&M 5396 Greatest Hits.
- (S) (3:20) A&M 3174 Brenda Russell.
1988 PIANO IN THE DARK
- (S) (4:22) Priority 7040 Making Love. *(faded :56 sooner than the 45 or LP)*
- (S) (5:18) A&M 5178 Get Here.
- (S) (5:18) A&M 5396 Greatest Hits.
- (S) (5:18) Rebound 314520370 Soul Classics - Quiet Storm/The 80's.
- (S) (5:18) Time-Life R834-07 Body Talk - Hearts In Motion

LEON RUSSELL
1972 TIGHT ROPE
- (S) (2:57) Priority 7997 Super Songs/70's Greatest Rock Hit Volume 8.
- (S) (2:59) Shelter/DCC Compact Classics 8006 Carney.
- (S) (2:58) Shelter/DCC Compact Classics 8017 Best Of. *(noise on fadeout)*
- (S) (2:58) Time-Life SOD-13 Sounds Of The Seventies - 1972: Take Two.
- (S) (2:59) Right Stuff/Shelter 35538 Carney.
- (S) (2:53) EMI 52644 Gimme Shelter! Best Of.
- (S) (2:59) Right Stuff 59785 Retrospective.
1975 LADY BLUE
- (S) (3:30) Priority 8665 Southern Comfort/70's Greatest Rock Hits Volume 4.
- (S) (3:30) Sandstone 33003 Reelin' In The Years Volume 4
- (S) (3:30) Shelter/DCC Compact Classics 8007 Will O' The Wisp.
- (S) (3:30) Shelter/DCC Compact Classics 8017 Best Of.
- (S) (3:30) DCC Compact Classics 065 Rock Of The 70's Volume 4.
- (S) (3:30) Time-Life SOD-25 Sounds Of The Seventies - Seventies Generation.
- (S) (3:29) Time-Life R105-26 Our Songs: Singers & Songwriters Encore.
- (S) (3:29) Time-Life R138-18 Body Talk.
- (S) (3:30) Right Stuff/Shelter 35539 Will O' The Wisp.
- (S) (3:29) EMI 52644 Gimme Shelter! Best Of.
- (S) (3:32) Right Stuff 59785 Retrospective.
- (S) (3:30) Time-Life R834-14 Body Talk - Love And Tenderness.

CHARLIE RYAN and THE TIMBERLINE RIDERS
1960 HOT ROD LINCOLN
    (E)   (2:30)   Time-Life CTD-12 Country USA - 1960.
    (E)   (2:32)   K-Tel 3640 Corny Country.

BOBBY RYDELL
1959 KISSIN' TIME
1959 WE GOT LOVE
1960 WILD ONE
1960 SWINGIN' SCHOOL
1960 DING-A-LING
1960 VOLARE
1960 SWAY
1961 GOOD TIME BABY
1961 THAT OLD BLACK MAGIC
1961 THE FISH
1961 I WANNA THANK YOU
released as by BOBBY RYDELL/CHUBBY CHECKER:
1962 JINGLE BELL ROCK
released as by BOBBY RYDELL:
1962 I'VE GOT BONNIE
1962 I'LL NEVER DANCE AGAIN
1962 THE CHA-CHA-CHA
1963 BUTTERFLY BABY
1963 WILDWOOD DAYS
1964 FORGET HIM

MITCH RYDER and THE DETROIT WHEELS
1966 JENNY TAKE A RIDE!
    (S)   (3:20)   DCC Compact Classics 029 Toga Rock.
    (E)   (3:20)   JCI 3101 Rockin' Sixties.
    (S)   (3:21)   K-Tel 686 Battle Of The Bands Volume 4.
    (S)   (3:21)   Rhino 70941 Rev Up: The Best Of.
    (S)   (3:22)   Sundazed 6007 Take A Ride.
    (S)   (3:21)   Rhino 71548 Let There Be Drums Volume 2: The
                     60's.
    (S)   (3:19)   Time-Life 2CLR-08 Classic Rock - 1965: The
                     Beat Goes On.
    (S)   (3:21)   Rhino 71729 '60s Rock Classics, Vol. 2.
    (S)   (3:21)   K-Tel 3133 Biker Rock.
    (M) (3:20)   Sundazed 6033 All Hits.
    (S)   (3:21)   Flashback 72702 '60s Rock: The Beat Goes On.
    (S)   (3:21)   Flashback 72088 '60s Rock Hits Box Set.
    (S)   (3:21)   Flashback 72700 Devil With A Blue Dress On
                     And Other Hits.
    (S)   (3:21)   Flashback 72087 '60s Rock Legends Box Set.
1966 LITTLE LATIN LUPE LU
    (S)   (3:06)   Rhino 70941 Rev Up: The Best Of.
    (S)   (3:06)   Pair 1277 Big Wheels.
    (S)   (3:06)   Special Music 5022 Rockin' Hits Of.
    (S)   (3:08)   Sundazed 6033 Breakout!!!
    (M) (3:07)   Sundazed 6033 All Hits.
    (S)   (3:06)   Rhino 71872 Devil With The Blue Dress On.
    (S)   (3:07)   Flashback 72700 Devil With A Blue Dress On
                     And Other Hits.
    (S)   (3:07)   Flashback 72087 '60s Rock Legends Box Set.
1966 DEVIL WITH A BLUE DRESS ON & GOOD GOLLY MISS
MOLLY
(actual 45 time is (3:14) not (3:01) as stated on the
record label)
    (S)   (3:04)   Rhino 70906 American Bandstand Greatest Hits
                     Collection. *(LP version)*
    (S)   (3:04)   Rhino 75772 Son Of Frat Rock. *(LP version)*
    (S)   (3:03)   JCI 3100 Dance Sixties. *(LP version)*
    (S)   (3:04)   DCC Compact Classics 029 Toga Rock. *(LP*
                     version)
    (S)   (3:28)   Rhino 70941 Rev Up: The Best Of Mitch Ryder.
                     (very similar to the 45 version but includes some
                     extra background vocals near the end and a :14
                     longer fade)
    (S)   (3:28)   Pair 1277 Big Wheels. *(same comments as for*
                     Rhino 70941)
    (S)   (3:28)   Special Music 5022 Rockin' Hits Of. *(same*
                     comments as for Rhino 70941)
    (S)   (3:04)   Sundazed 6008 Breakout!!! *(LP version)*

    (S)   (3:02)   Time-Life 2CLR-07 Classic Rock - 1966: The
                     Beat Goes On. *(LP version)*
    (S)   (3:03)   Collectables 2510 WCBS-FM History Of Rock -
                     The Rockin' 60's. *(LP version)*
    (S)   (3:03)   Collectables 4510 History Of Rock/The Rockin'
                     60s. *(LP version)*
    (S)   (3:28)   Rhino 71730 '60s Rock Classics, Vol. 3. *(same*
                     comments as for Rhino 70941)
    (M) (3:12)   Sundazed 6033 All Hits. *(45 version but faster*
                     pitch)
    (S)   (3:02)   JCI 3126 1965 - Only Rock 'N Roll - 1969. *(LP*
                     version)
    (S)   (3:28)   Rhino 71872 Devil With The Blue Dress On.
                     (same comments as for Rhino 70941)
    (S)   (3:01)   Tommy Boy 1136 ESPN Presents Jock Rock Vol.
                     2. *(all songs on this cd are segued together with*
                     crowd sound effects added)
    (S)   (3:28)   Rhino 72478 Beverly Hills 90210: Songs From
                     The Peach Pit. *(same comments as for Rhino*
                     70941)
    (S)   (3:28)   Eclipse Music Group 64870 Rock 'n Roll Relix
                     1966-1967. *(same comments as for Rhino 70941)*
    (S)   (3:28)   Eclipse Music Group 64872 Rock 'n Roll Relix
                     1960-1969. *(same comments as for Rhino 70941)*
    (S)   (3:28)   Flashback 72703 '60s Rock: It's A Beautiful
                     Morning. *(same comments as for Rhino 70941)*
    (S)   (3:28)   Flashback 72088 '60s Rock Hits Box Set. *(same*
                     comments as for Rhino 70941)
    (S)   (3:28)   Flashback 72700 Devil With A Blue Dress On
                     And Other Hits. *(same comments as for Rhino*
                     70941)
    (S)   (3:28)   Flashback 72087 '60s Rock Legends Box Set.
                     (same comments as for Rhino 70941)
1967 SOCK IT TO ME BABY!
    (S)   (3:10)   Rhino 70941 Rev Up: The Best Of. *(LP version)*
    (S)   (3:10)   Rhino 70794 KFOG Presents M. Dung's Idiot
                     Show. *(LP version)*
    (S)   (3:03)   Sundazed 6009 Sock It To Me. *(LP version)*
    (E)   (2:56)   Time-Life 2CLR-10 Classic Rock - 1967: The
                     Beat Goes On. *(45 version)*
    (S)   (3:09)   Rhino 71730 '60s Rock Classics, Vol. 3. *(LP*
                     version)
    (M) (2:58)   Sundazed 6033 All Hits. *(45 version)*
    (S)   (3:10)   Risky Business 66914 Party On. *(LP version)*
    (S)   (3:10)   Rhino 71872 Devil With The Blue Dress On.
                     (LP version)
    (S)   (3:02)   Rhino 71937 Billboard Top Pop Hits, 1967. *(LP*
                     version)
    (S)   (3:10)   Time-Life R968-09 Guitar Rock 1966-1967. *(LP*
                     version)
    (S)   (3:09)   JCI 3190 1965 - Only Dance - 1969. *(LP*
                     version)
    (S)   (3:09)   Flashback 72703 '60s Rock: It's A Beautiful
                     Morning. *(LP version)*
    (S)   (3:09)   Flashback 72088 '60s Rock Hits Box Set. *(LP*
                     version)
    (S)   (3:09)   Flashback 72700 Devil With A Blue Dress On
                     And Other Hits. *(LP version)*
    (S)   (3:09)   Flashback 72087 '60s Rock Legends Box Set.
                     (LP version)
1967 TOO MANY FISH IN THE SEA & THREE LITTLE FISHES
    (S)   (2:59)   Rhino 70941 Rev Up: The Best Of.
    (S)   (2:59)   Pair 1277 Big Wheels.
    (S)   (2:59)   Special Music 5022 Rockin' Hits Of.
    (S)   (2:57)   Sundazed 6009 Sock It To Me.
    (M) (2:56)   Sundazed 6033 All Hits.
    (S)   (2:59)   Rhino 71872 Devil With The Blue Dress On.
    (S)   (2:59)   Flashback 72700 Devil With A Blue Dress On
                     And Other Hits.
    (S)   (2:59)   Flashback 72087 '60s Rock Legends Box Set.
released as by MITCH RYDER:
1967 JOY
    (S)   (3:07)   Rhino 70941 Rev Up: The Best Of.
    (S)   (3:07)   Pair 1277 Big Wheels.
    (S)   (3:07)   Special Music 5022 Rockin' Hits Of.
    (S)   (3:09)   Sundazed 6007 Take A Ride.
    (M) (3:10)   Sundazed 6033 All Hits.

MITCH RYDER and THE DETROIT WHEELS (Continued)
1967   **WHAT NOW MY LOVE**
        (actual LP time is (4:14) not (4:22) as stated
        on the record label)
        (S)   (3:58)   Pair 1277 Big Wheels. *(faded :16 sooner than*
                                    the 45 or LP)
        (S)   (3:58)   Special Music 5022 Rockin' Hits Of. *(faded :16*
                                    sooner than the 45 or LP)

RYTHM SYNDICATE
1991   **P.A.S.S.I.O.N.**
        (S)   (4:12)   Impact 10225 Rythm Syndicate. *(LP version)*
        (S)   (3:39)   K-Tel 3850 90s Now Volume 3. *(45 version)*
1991   **HEY DONNA**
        (S)   (4:37)   Impact 10225 Rythm Syndicate.

RAPHAEL SAADIQ
1995 ASK OF YOU
    (S) (6:00)   550 Music/Epic Soundtrax 66944 O.S.T. Higher Learning.

SADE
1985 SMOOTH OPERATOR
    (dj copies of this 45 ran (3:46) and (4:54);
    commercial copies all ran (4:54))
    (S) (3:45)   T.J. Martell Foundation/Columbia 40315 Music For The Miracle. *(this is the dj 45 edit)*
    (S) (4:56)   Sandstone 33053 and 5021 Cosmopolitan Volume 7.
    (S) (4:15)   Epic 66686 Best Of. *(neither the 45 or LP version)*
    (S) (4:56)   DCC Compact Classics 081 Night Moves Volume 1.
    (S) (4:57)   Portrait 39581 Diamond Life.
1986 THE SWEETEST TABOO
    (S) (4:24)   Epic 66686 Best Of. *(45 length)*
    (S) (4:36)   Portrait 40263 Promise. *(LP length)*
1986 NEVER AS GOOD AS THE FIRST TIME
    (S) (3:57)   Epic 66686 Best Of. *(45 version)*
    (S) (4:58)   Portrait 40263 Promise. *(LP version)*
1988 PARADISE
    (S) (3:36)   Epic 66686 Best Of. *(45 version)*
    (S) (4:01)   Epic 44210 Stronger Than Pride. *(LP version)*
1993 NO ORDINARY LOVE
    (S) (7:18)   Epic 66686 Best Of.
    (S) (7:18)   Epic 53178 Love Deluxe.
    (S) (7:17)   EMI-Capitol Music Group 54548 Smooth Luv.

SSgt. BARRY SADLER
1966 THE BALLAD OF THE GREEN BERETS
    (S) (2:27)   RCA 8475 Nipper's Greatest Hits Of The 60's Volume 2.
    (S) (2:27)   RCA 9902 Nipper's #1 Hits 1956-1986.
    (S) (2:27)   RCA 5802 Best Of The 60's.
    (S) (2:27)   Rhino 71936 Billboard Top Pop Hits, 1966.
    (S) (2:26)   Collectors' Choice 037 Ballads Of The Green Berets.
1966 THE "A" TEAM
    (M) (2:06)   Collectors' Choice 037 Ballads Of The Green Berets.

SAFARIS
1960 IMAGE OF A GIRL
    (M) (2:35)   Time-Life 2RNR-11 Rock 'N' Roll Era - 1960.
    (M) (2:29)   Collectables 2509 WCBS-FM For Lovers Only Part 1.
    (M) (2:37)   LaserLight 12320 Love Songs.
    (M) (2:36)   Time-Life R857-02 The Heart Of Rock 'n' Roll - 1960.
    (M) (2:36)   Eric 11502 Hard To Find 45's On CD (Volume I) 1955-60.
    (M) (2:36)   Rhino 72870 Brown Eyed Soul Vol. 3.

SA-FIRE
1989 THINKING OF YOU
    (S) (4:47)   K-Tel 898 Romantic Hits Of The 80's.
    (S) (4:49)   Cutting/Mercury 834922 Sa-Fire.

SAGA
1983 ON THE LOOSE
    (S) (4:11)   Portrait 38246 Worlds Apart.

CAROLE BAYER SAGER
1981 STRONGER THAN BEFORE

SAIGON KICK
1992 LOVE IS ON THE WAY
    (S) (4:22)   JCI 3135 14 Original Metal Ballads.
    (S) (4:23)   Third Stone/Atlantic 92158 The Lizard.

SAILCAT
1972 MOTORCYCLE MAMA
    (S) (2:04)   Rhino 70928 Super Hits Of The 70's Volume 8.
    (S) (2:03)   Time-Life SUD-20 Superhits - Early 70's Classics.
    (M) (2:04)   K-Tel 3133 Biker Rock.
    (S) (2:03)   Time-Life AM1-15 AM Gold - Early '70s Classics.

BUFFY SAINTE-MARIE
1972 MISTER CAN'T YOU SEE

CRISPIAN ST. PETERS
1966 THE PIED PIPER
    (M) (2:31)   Collectables 5615 Follow Me.
    (M) (2:31)   One Way 31379 The Pied Piper.
    (M) (2:31)   Varese Sarabande 5705 Dick Bartley Presents Collector's Essentials: The 60's.
    (M) (2:31)   Time-Life 2CLR-31 Classic Rock - Totally Fantastic '60s.
1967 YOU WERE ON MY MIND
    (M) (2:40)   Collectables 5615 Follow Me.
    (M) (2:41)   One Way 31379 The Pied Piper.

KYU SAKAMOTO
1963 SUKIYAKI
    (M) (3:03)   Capitol 98665 When AM Was King. *(sounds like it was mastered from vinyl)*
    (M) (3:03)   Rhino 71584 Billboard Top Pop Hits, 1963.

SALSOUL ORCHESTRA
1976 TANGERINE
    (S) (4:37)   Salsoul 2008 Anthology. *(LP version)*
    (S) (4:36)   Salsoul 20112 Salsoul Classics 2. *(LP version)*
    (S) (4:32)   Right Stuff/Salsoul 53321 Disco Boogie Volume One. *(edit of LP version; all songs on this cd are segued together)*
    (S) (4:36)   Salsoul/Right Stuff 53849 Anthology. *(LP version)*
1976 NICE 'N' NAASTY
    (S) (4:46)   Salsoul 2008 Anthology. *(LP version)*
    (S) (4:46)   Priority 53790 Disco Nice And Nasty. *(LP version)*
    (S) (4:32)   Right Stuff/Salsoul 53321 Disco Boogie Volume One. *(LP version; all songs on this cd are segued together)*
    (S) (4:46)   Salsoul/Right Stuff 53849 Anthology. *(LP version)*

SALT-N-PEPA
1988 PUSH IT
    (S) (4:28)   JCI 2702 Hot Moves.
    (S) (4:27)   Profile 1268 Mr. Magic's Rap Attack Volume 4. *(remixed)*
    (S) (4:28)   Priority 7990 Rapmasters 14 - The Best Of Hype. *(remixed)*
    (S) (4:28)   Thump 4020 Old School Volume 2.
    (S) (5:05)   Next Plateau 1025 and 828365 A Blitz Of Salt-N-Pepa Hits. *(remixed)*
    (S) (4:28)   Rebound 314520365 Funk Classics - The 80's.
    (S) (4:28)   JCI 3177 1985 - Only Soul - 1989.
    (S) (4:28)   K-Tel 3750 History Of Rap Volume 2. *(remixed)*
    (S) (4:28)   Priority 50931 Hip Hop Classics Volume Two. *(remixed)*

SALT-N-PEPA *(Continued)*
1990 EXPRESSION
- (S) (3:53) Jive 1420 Yo! MTV Raps Vol. 2.
- (S) (3:54) Priority 8657 Yo Rap Hits.
- (S) (3:53) Next Plateau 1019 and 828362 Black's Magic.
- (S) (4:45) Next Plateau 1025 and 828365 A Blitz Of Salt-N-Pepa Hits. *(remixed)*

1991 DO YOU WANT ME
- (S) (3:49) K-Tel 6102 Funk-Tastic Jams.
- (S) (3:49) Rhino 71916 Whats Up? Rap Hits Of The 90's.
- (S) (3:29) Next Plateau 1019 and 828362 Black's Magic.
- (S) (5:58) Next Plateau 1025 and 828365 A Blitz Of Salt-N-Pepa Hits. *(remixed)*

1991 LET'S TALK ABOUT SEX
- (S) (5:42) Tommy Boy 1053 MTV Party To Go Volume 2. *(remixed; all tracks on this cd are segued together)*
- (S) (3:30) Priority 53711 Rap Hitz.
- (S) (3:29) Next Plateau 1019 and 828362 Black's Magic.
- (S) (4:42) Next Plateau 1025 and 828365 A Blitz Of Salt-N-Pepa Hits. *(remixed)*
- (S) (3:29) Razor & Tie 4569 '90s Style.

1993 SHOOP
- (S) (4:21) Tommy Boy 1109 MTV Party To Go Volume 6. *(remix; all tracks on this cd are segued together)*
- (S) (4:06) Next Plateau 828392 Very Necessary.
- (S) (4:06) Boxtunes 162444068 Big Phat Ones Of Hip-Hop Volume 1.
- (S) (4:06) Rebound 314520439 Soul Classics - Best Of The 90's.
- (S) (4:06) Rebound 314520449 Hip Hop With R&B Flava.

released as by SALT-N-PEPA featuring EN VOGUE:
1994 WHATTA MAN
- (S) (5:07) Next Plateau 828392 Salt-N-Pepa - Very Necessary.
- (S) (4:53) Eastwest 92296 En Vogue - Runaway Love.

released as by SALT-N-PEPA:
1994 NONE OF YOUR BUSINESS
- (S) (3:32) Next Plateau 828392 Very Necessary.

SAM & DAVE
1966 HOLD ON! I'M COMIN'
- (M) (2:34) Atlantic Group 88218 Complete Stax/Volt Singles.
- (M) (2:32) Atlantic 81297 Atlantic Rhythm & Blues Volume 5.
- (S) (2:28) JCI 3105 Soul Sixties.
- (S) (2:26) Stax 88005 Top Of The Stax.
- (M) (2:34) Warner Special Products 27602 20 Party Classics.
- (S) (2:29) Atlantic 82305 Atlantic Rhythm And Blues 1947-1974 Box Set.
- (S) (2:29) Atlantic 81279 Best Of.
- (S) (2:30) Atlantic 80255 Hold On I'm Comin'.
- (M) (2:34) Rhino 71253 Anthology.
- (M) (2:34) Rhino 71459 Soul Hits, Volume 1.
- (M) (2:34) Rhino 71232 Soothe Me.
- (S) (2:26) Time-Life RHD-01 Rhythm & Blues - 1966.
- (S) (2:29) Time-Life 2CLR-07 Classic Rock - 1966: The Beat Goes On.
- (M) (2:34) Rhino 71730 '60s Rock Classics, Vol. 3.
- (M) (2:34) Rhino 71871 Very Best Of.
- (M) (2:39) Curb 77740 Greatest Songs. *(all songs on this cd are rerecorded)*
- (M) (2:28) Tommy Boy 1136 ESPN Presents Jock Rock Vol. 2. *(all songs on this cd are segued together with crowd sound effects added)*
- (M) (2:33) JCI 3161 18 Soul Hits From The 60's.
- (M) (2:34) JCI 3190 1965 - Only Dance - 1969.
- (S) (2:26) Time-Life R838-01 Solid Gold Soul - 1966.
- (M) (2:34) Flashback 72703 '60s Rock: It's A Beautiful Morning.
- (M) (2:34) Flashback 72088 '60s Rock Hits Box Set.
- (M) (2:34) Flashback 72657 '60s Soul: Try A Little Tenderness.
- (M) (2:34) Flashback 72091 '60s Soul Hits Box Set.
- (M) (2:34) Flashback 72664 Soul Man And Other Hits.
- (S) (2:29) Repeat/Relativity 1611 A Brand New Bag: #1 Soul Hits Of The 60's Volume 3.
- (M) (2:34) Flashback 72896 25 Years Of R&B - 1966.
- (M) (2:34) Rhino 72962 Ultimate '60s Soul Sensations.

1967 SOUL MAN
- (M) (2:37) Atlantic Group 88218 Complete Stax/Volt Singles. *(45 version)*
- (M) (2:34) Atlantic 81298 Atlantic Rhythm & Blues Volume 6. *(LP version)*
- (M) (2:34) Atlantic 81911 Golden Age Of Black Music (1960-1970). *(LP version)*
- (S) (2:35) Warner Special Products 27601 Atlantic Soul Classics. *(LP version)*
- (M) (2:36) Atlantic 82305 Atlantic Rhythm And Blues 1947-1974 Box Set. *(45 version)*
- (M) (2:36) Atlantic 81279 Best Of. *(45 version)*
- (S) (2:36) Rhino 70296 Soul Men. *(LP version)*
- (M) (2:37) Rhino 71253 Anthology. *(45 version)*
- (M) (2:37) Rhino 71461 Soul Hits, Volume 3. *(45 version)*
- (M) (2:37) Rhino 71548 Let There Be Drums Volume 2: The 60's. *(45 version)*
- (M) (2:34) Time-Life RHD-10 Rhythm & Blues - 1967. *(45 version)*
- (M) (2:34) Time-Life 2CLR-10 Classic Rock - 1967: The Beat Goes On. *(LP version)*
- (M) (2:34) JCI 3126 1965 - Only Rock 'N Roll - 1969. *(LP version)*
- (M) (2:37) Rhino 71871 Very Best Of. *(45 version)*
- (M) (2:35) Curb 77740 Greatest Songs. *(all songs on this cd are rerecorded)*
- (M) (2:36) Hollywood 62077 Official Party Album - ABC's Monday Night Football. *(45 version)*
- (M) (2:34) Time-Life R838-02 Solid Gold Soul - 1967. *(45 version)*
- (M) (2:37) Flashback 72659 '60s Soul: When A Man Loves A Woman. *(45 version)*
- (M) (2:37) Flashback 72091 '60s Soul Hits Box Set. *(45 version)*
- (M) (2:37) Flashback 72664 Soul Man And Other Hits. *(45 version)*
- (M) (2:37) Flashback 72897 25 Years Of R&B - 1967. *(45 version)*
- (M) (2:37) Rhino 72963 Ultimate '60s Soul Smashes. *(45 version)*
- (M) (2:37) Atlantic 83088 Atlantic Records: 50 Years - The Gold Anniversary Collection. *(45 version)*

1968 I THANK YOU
- (M) (2:43) Atlantic Group 88218 Complete Stax/Volt Singles.
- (S) (2:52) Warner Special Products 27609 Memphis Soul Classics.
- (S) (2:51) Atlantic 81279 Best Of.
- (S) (2:53) Rhino 71012 I Thank You.
- (M) (2:43) Rhino 71253 Anthology.
- (S) (2:49) Time-Life RHD-04 Rhythm & Blues - 1968.
- (S) (2:50) Time-Life 2CLR-04 Classic Rock - 1968.
- (M) (2:43) Rhino 71806 The R&B Box: Thirty Years Of Rhythm & Blues.
- (M) (2:43) Rhino 71871 Very Best Of.
- (M) (2:41) Curb 77740 Greatest Songs. *(all songs on this cd are rerecorded)*
- (S) (2:49) Time-Life R838-03 Solid Gold Soul - 1968.
- (M) (2:43) Flashback 72664 Soul Man And Other Hits.
- (M) (2:43) Flashback 72898 25 Years Of R&B - 1968.

SAM THE SHAM and THE PHARAOHS
1965 WOOLY BULLY
- (S) (2:18) Warner Brothers 25613 O.S.T. Full Metal Jacket.
- (M) (2:18) Rhino 70626 Billboard's Top Rock & Roll Hits Of 1965.
- (M) (2:18) Rhino 72007 Billboard's Top Rock & Roll Hits 1962-1966 Box Set.
- (M) (2:18) Rhino 75778 Frat Rock.
- (S) (2:19) Original Sound 8860 Oldies But Goodies Vol. 10. *(this compact disc uses the "Waring - fds" noise reduction process)*
- (S) (2:19) Original Sound 2221 Oldies But Goodies Volumes 1,4,6,8 and 10 Box Set. *(this box set uses the "Waring - fds" noise reduction process)*
- (S) (2:19) Original Sound 2500 Oldies But Goodies Volumes 1-15 Box Set. *(this box set uses the "Waring - fds" noise reduction process)*

(S) (2:18) Mercury 816555 45's On CD Volume 2.
(S) (2:18) DCC Compact Classics 029 Toga Rock.
(S) (2:19) K-Tel 205 Battle Of The Bands Volume 3.
(S) (2:19) Warner Special Products 27607 Highs Of The 60's.
(S) (2:17) Priority 7909 Vietnam: Rockin' The Delta.
(S) (2:19) Polydor 827917 Best Of.
(S) (2:18) Time-Life 2CLR-01 Classic Rock - 1965.
(S) (2:19) Collectables 2505 History Of Rock - The 60's Part 5.
(S) (2:19) Collectables 4505 History Of Rock/The 60s Part Five.
(S) (2:18) Special Music 5026 Let It All Hang Out - 60's Party Hits.
(S) (2:18) K-Tel 3411 Tacky Tunes.
(M) (2:17) Tommy Boy 1136 ESPN Presents Jock Rock Vol. 2. *(all songs on this cd are segued together with crowd sound effects added)*
(S) (2:18) JCI 3190 1965 - Only Dance - 1969.
(S) (2:18) Eclipse Music Group 64869 Rock 'n Roll Relix 1964-1965.
(S) (2:18) Eclipse Music Group 64872 Rock 'n Roll Relix 1960-1969.
(S) (2:19) Thump 7200 Latin Oldies Volume Two.
(S) (2:18) Rebound 314520522 Rockin' Sports Jams.
(S) (2:18) Polygram Special Markets 314520495 45's On CD Volume 2.

1965 JU JU HAND
(M) (2:07) Polydor 827917 Best Of.
(M) (2:06) Rhino 71783 Texas Music Volume 3: Garage Bands & Psychedelia.

1965 RING DANG DOO
(M) (2:21) Rhino 70794 KFOG Presents M. Dung's Idiot Show.
(S) (2:24) Polydor 827917 Best Of.

1966 LIL' RED RIDING HOOD
(M) (2:38) DCC Compact Classics 050 Monster Rock 'n' Roll Show.
(M) (2:39) Polydor 827917 Best Of.
(S) (2:42) K-Tel 3150 Dumb Ditties. *(rerecording)*
(M) (2:38) Time-Life 2CLR-13 Classic Rock - 1966: Shakin' All Over.
(M) (2:39) Special Music 5025 Rebel Rousers! Best Of Southern Rock.
(M) (2:41) Eclipse Music Group 64870 Rock 'n Roll Relix 1966-1967.
(M) (2:41) Eclipse Music Group 64872 Rock 'n Roll Relix 1960-1969.
(M) (2:40) Polygram Special Markets 314520460 #1 Radio Hits Of The 60's.

1966 THE HAIR ON MY CHINNY CHIN CHIN
(M) (2:35) Polydor 827917 Best Of.

1967 HOW DO YOU CATCH A GIRL

SANDPEBBLES
1968 LOVE POWER
(S) (2:24) AVI 5015 Soul Of The 60's Volume 1: Calla Records.
(S) (2:24) K-Tel 3901 Soul Brothers & Sisters Of The 60's.

SANDPIPERS
1966 GUANTANAMERA
(S) (3:10) Priority 9461 Mellow 60's.
(S) (3:10) JCI 3109 Folk Sixties.
(S) (3:10) Chronicles 314535882 Lounge Music Goes Latin.

1966 LOUIE LOUIE
(S) (2:47) Rhino 70605 Best Of Louie Louie. *(sounds like it was mastered from vinyl)*

1970 COME SATURDAY MORNING
(S) (2:59) Rhino 70921 Super Hits Of The 70's Volume 1.
(S) (2:59) Rhino 72009 Super Hits Of The 70's Volumes 1-4 Box Set.

JODIE SANDS
1957 WITH ALL MY HEART
(M) (2:41) Time-Life HPD-38 Your Hit Parade - The 50's Generation.

(M) (2:39) K-Tel 478 More 50's Jukebox Favorites.
(M) (2:42) Curb 77775 Hard To Find Original Recordings - Classic Hits.
(M) (2:41) Taragon 1018 Chancellor Records Story, Volume 1.

TOMMY SANDS
1957 TEEN-AGE CRUSH
(M) (2:21) Time-Life 2RNR-27 Rock 'N' Roll Era - Teen Idols.
(M) (2:21) Collectors' Choice 002 Teen Idols....For A Moment.
(M) (2:22) Right Stuff 53320 Hot Rod Rock Volume 5: Back Seat Movers.
(M) (2:20) Collectables 5869 Steady Date With.

1957 GOIN' STEADY
(M) (2:32) Collectables 5869 Steady Date With.

1958 SING BOY SING
(M) (2:22) Collectables 5869 Steady Date With.

SANFORD/TOWNSEND BAND
1977 SMOKE FROM A DISTANT FIRE
(S) (3:30) Rhino 71200 Super Hits Of The 70's Volume 20.
(S) (3:31) Time-Life SOD-17 Sounds Of The Seventies - 1977: Take Two.
(S) (3:31) Madacy Entertainment 1977 Rock On 1977.
(S) (3:30) JCI 3139 18 Free And Easy Hits From The 70's.

SAMANTHA SANG
1978 EMOTION
(S) (3:55) Rhino 72298 Superhits Of The 70's Volume 24.
(S) (3:52) Madacy Entertainment 1978 Rock On 1978.
(S) (3:55) Right Stuff 35600 Soul Of The Bee Gees.
(S) (3:52) Original Sound 9308 Dedicated To You Vol. 8.
(S) (3:52) JCI 3163 18 Disco Superhits.
(S) (3:52) Simitar 55562 The Number One's: Smooth Love.
(S) (3:55) Time-Life R834-12 Body Talk - By Candlelight.

SAN REMO GOLDEN STRINGS
1965 HUNGRY FOR LOVE
(S) (2:57) Collectors' Choice 5190 More Instrumental Gems Of The 60's.

SANTA ESMERALDA
1978 DON'T LET ME BE MISUNDERSTOOD
(dj copies of this 45 ran (3:48) and (5:25);
commercial copies were all (3:48))
(S) (16:09) Philips 830766 Best Of. *(includes the full length LP version of "DON'T LET ME BE MISUNDERSTOOD" - (7:59) which segues into "ESMERALDA SUITE" - (8:10); both songs are considered 1 track on this cd)*
(S) (3:54) Razor & Tie 22496 Disco Fever. *(edit of LP version in an unsuccessful attempt at recreating the 45 version)*
(S) (13:37) Hot Productions 43 Best Of. *(this is the complete "DON'T LET ME BE MISUNDERSTOOD" which segues into an edited version of "ESMERALDA SUITE"; both songs are considered 1 track on this cd)*
(S) (7:57) Hot Productions 6634 Don't Let Me Be Misunderstood. *(this is the true LP version of this song which segues into the next track "ESMERALDA SUITE" but it is given its own individual track number on this cd)*
(S) (3:38) Island 314553411 The Last Party. *(all selections on this cd are segued together)*
(S) (6:36) Priority 50957 Mega Hits Disco Explosion Volume 4. *(edit of the LP version)*
(S) (16:03) Thump 4840 Flashback Disco. *(all selections on this cd are segued together; this is the full length LP version of "DON'T LET ME BE MISUNDERSTOOD" - (7:49) which segues into "ESMERALDA SUITE" - (8:14); both songs are considered 1 track on this cd)*

MONGO SANTAMARIA
1963 WATERMELON MAN
    (S) (3:12) Columbia 1060 Greatest Hits. *(rerecording)*
    (S) (2:24) Rhino 71604 Rock Instrumental Classics Vol. 4: Soul.
    (S) (2:24) Rhino 72035 Rock Instrumental Classics Vols. 1-5 Box Set.
    (S) (2:25) Time-Life HPD-34 Your Hit Parade - 60's Instrumentals.
    (S) (2:25) Nick At Nite/Epic 67149 Dick Van Dyke's Dance Party.
    (S) (2:24) Hip-O 40007 Soulful Grooves - R&B Instrumental Classics Volume 1.
    (M) (2:26) Rhino 72474 Masters Of Jazz, Vol. 7: Jazz Hit Singles.

1969 CLOUD NINE
    (S) (4:17) Columbia 1060 Greatest Hits.

SANTANA
1970 EVIL WAYS
    (actual 45 time is (2:59) not (2:35) as stated on the record label)
    (S) (3:51) Columbia 45018 Rock Classics Of The 60's. *(LP version)*
    (S) (3:55) Columbia 9781 Santana. *(LP version)*
    (S) (3:49) Time-Life 2CLR-21 Classic Rock - Rock Renaissance II. *(LP version)*
    (S) (3:13) Time-Life SOD-11 Sounds Of The Seventies - 1970: Take Two. *(neither the 45 or LP version)*
    (S) (3:00) Columbia 33050 Greatest Hits. *(neither the 45 or LP version)*
    (S) (3:53) Columbia 44344 Viva Santana! *(LP version)*
    (S) (3:51) Time-Life R968-07 Guitar Rock 1968-1969. *(LP version)*
    (S) (3:55) Legacy/Columbia 64605 and 65411 Dance Of The Rainbow Serpent. *(LP version)*
    (S) (3:55) K-Tel 3463 Platinum Rock. *(LP version)*
    (S) (3:55) Columbia/Legacy 65389 Santana/Abraxas/Santana. *(LP version)*
    (S) (3:55) Columbia/Legacy 64212 Santana. *(gold disc; LP version)*
    (S) (3:55) Columbia/Legacy 65489 Santana. *(remastered edition; LP version)*
    (S) (3:54) Columbia/Legacy 65561 Best Of. *(LP version)*

1971 BLACK MAGIC WOMAN
    (the LP version is a medley of "BLACK MAGIC WOMAN" and "GYPSY QUEEN")
    (S) (3:17) Rhino 70632 Billboard's Top Rock & Roll Hits Of 1971. *(remixed 45 version)*
    (S) (3:17) JCI 3302 Electric 70's. *(45 version)*
    (S) (5:20) Columbia 45048 Rock Classics Of The 70's. *(LP version)*
    (S) (5:16) Columbia 30130 Abraxas. *(LP version; previous selection tracks over introduction)*
    (S) (5:19) MFSL 552 Abraxas. *(LP version; previous selection tracks over introduction; gold disc)*
    (S) (3:15) Time-Life SOD-01 Sounds Of The Seventies - 1970. *(remixed 45 version)*
    (S) (3:15) Columbia 33050 Greatest Hits. *(45 version)*
    (S) (3:14) K-Tel 3221 Axe Gods. *(45 version)*
    (S) (3:13) K-Tel 621 Rock Classics. *(45 version)*
    (S) (5:20) Columbia 44344 Viva Santana! *(remixed LP version)*
    (S) (6:23) Columbia 44344 Viva Santana! *(live)*
    (S) (5:17) Risky Business 66391 Ghastly Grooves. *(LP version)*
    (S) (5:19) Time-Life R968-06 Guitar Rock 1970-1971. *(LP version)*
    (S) (5:17) Legacy/Columbia 64605 and 65411 Dance Of The Rainbow Serpent. *(LP version)*
    (S) (3:14) Epic/Legacy 65020 Ultimate Rock 'n' Roll Collection. *(45 version)*
    (S) (3:18) Eclipse Music Group 64892 Rock 'n Roll Relix 1970-1971. *(45 version)*
    (S) (3:18) Eclipse Music Group 64897 Rock 'n Roll Relix 1970-1979. *(45 version)*

    (S) (5:17) Rhino 72893 Hard Rock Cafe: Classic Rock. *(LP version)*
    (S) (5:17) K-Tel 4033 Ghasty Grooves. *(LP version)*
    (S) (5:16) Columbia/Legacy 65389 Santana/Abraxas/Santana. *(LP version; previous selection tracks over the introduction)*
    (S) (3:15) Time-Life R13610 Gold And Platinum Box Set - The Ultimate Rock Collection. *(45 version)*
    (S) (5:19) Columbia/Legacy 65490 Abraxas. *(remastered edition; LP version; previous selection tracks over the introduction)*
    (S) (5:19) Columbia/Legacy 65561 Best Of. *(LP version)*

1971 OYE COMO VA
    (S) (4:15) Columbia 30130 Abraxas. *(LP version)*
    (S) (4:16) MFSL 552 Abraxas. *(LP version; gold disc)*
    (S) (4:15) Virgin 92153 and 86289 O.S.T. American Me. *(LP version)*
    (S) (4:14) Epic 57620 O.S.T. Carlito's Way. *(LP version)*
    (S) (4:15) Time-Life SOD-02 Sounds Of The Seventies - 1971. *(LP version)*
    (S) (4:16) Columbia 33050 Greatest Hits. *(LP version)*
    (S) (4:17) Columbia 44344 Viva Santana! *(live)*
    (S) (4:15) Time-Life R968-10 Guitar Rock Classics. *(LP version)*
    (S) (4:15) Legacy/Columbia 64605 and 65411 Dance Of The Rainbow Serpent. *(LP version)*
    (S) (4:15) Thump 7100 Latin Oldies. *(LP version)*
    (S) (4:15) Columbia/Legacy 65389 Santana/Abraxas/Santana. *(LP version)*
    (S) (4:16) Rhino 72920 Raza Rock Of The '70s & '80s. *(LP version)*
    (S) (4:16) Columbia/Legacy 65490 Abraxas. *(remastered edition; LP version)*
    (S) (4:16) Columbia/Legacy 65561 Best Of. *(LP version)*

1971 EVERYBODY'S EVERYTHING
    (S) (3:27) Columbia 30595 Santana.
    (S) (3:25) Time-Life R102-34 The Rolling Stone Collection.
    (S) (3:26) Time-Life SOD-26 Sounds Of The Seventies - FM Rock II.
    (S) (3:30) Columbia 33050 Greatest Hits.
    (S) (3:30) Columbia 44344 Viva Santana! *(studio recording with fake audience applause added to the intro)*
    (S) (3:25) Time-Life R968-11 Guitar Rock - The Early '70s.
    (S) (3:29) Legacy/Columbia 64605 and 65411 Dance Of The Rainbow Serpent.
    (S) (3:27) Columbia/Legacy 65389 Santana/Abraxas/Santana.
    (S) (3:29) Columbia/Legacy 65491 Santana. *(remastered edition)*
    (S) (3:29) Columbia/Legacy 65561 Best Of.

1972 NO ONE TO DEPEND ON
    (S) (5:30) Columbia 30595 Santana. *(LP version; this song, the preceding song and the following song are all segued together)*
    (S) (5:27) Time-Life R968-19 Guitar Rock - The Early '70s: Take Two. *(LP version)*
    (S) (5:30) Columbia/Legacy 65389 Santana/Abraxas/Santana. *(LP version; this song the preceding song and the following song are all segued together)*
    (S) (5:31) Columbia/Legacy 65491 Santana. *(remastered edition; LP version; this song, the preceding song and the following song are all segued together)*
    (S) (5:32) Columbia/Legacy 65561 Best Of. *(LP version; tracks into the next selection)*

1977 SHE'S NOT THERE
    (S) (4:08) Columbia 34914 Moonflower. *(LP version)*
    (S) (4:21) Columbia 44344 Viva Santana! *(live; tracks into next selection)*
    (S) (4:07) Time-Life R968-14 Guitar Rock - The Late '70s. *(LP version)*
    (S) (4:07) MCA 11526 O.S.T. The Long Kiss Goodnight. *(LP version)*
    (S) (4:08) Columbia/Legacy 65561 Best Of. *(LP version)*

1979 STORMY
    (S) (4:45) Columbia 35600 Inner Secrets. *(LP version)*

1980 YOU KNOW THAT I LOVE YOU
    (S) (4:23) Columbia 36154 Marathon. *(LP version)*

1981 WINNING
    (S) (3:29)   Columbia 37158 Zebop.
    (S) (3:27)   Time-Life R968-04 Guitar Rock 1980-1981.
    (S) (3:27)   Columbia/Legacy 65561 Best Of.
1982 HOLD ON
    (S) (4:19)   Columbia 38122 Shango. *(LP version)*
    (S) (4:21)   Columbia/Legacy 65561 Best Of. *(LP version)*

LINA SANTIAGO
1996 FEELS SO GOOD (SHOW ME YOUR LOVE)
    (S) (3:34)   Universal 53008 Feels So Good.
    (S) (3:34)   MCA 11487 Ultimate House Nrg (Way Cool Dance Hits).
    (S) (4:33)   Priority 50955 Power Workout High NRG Megamix Volume 2. *(all selections on this cd are segued together; remixed)*
    (S) (4:09)   Cold Front 6242 Club Mix '97. *(all selections on this cd are segued together; remixed)*

SANTO & JOHNNY
1959 SLEEP WALK
    (M) (2:20)   Rhino 70620 Billboard's Top Rock & Roll Hits Of 1959.
    (M) (2:20)   Rhino 72004 Billboard's Top Rock & Roll Hits 1957-1961 Box Set.
    (M) (2:20)   Geffen 24310 O.S.T. Mermaids.
    (M) (2:20)   Rhino 70561 Legends Of Guitar - Rock: The 50's Volume 2.
    (M) (2:20)   Original Sound 8850 Oldies But Goodies Vol. 1. *(this compact disc uses the "Waring - fds" noise reduction process)*
    (M) (2:20)   Original Sound 2221 Oldies But Goodies Volumes 1,4,6,8 and 10 Box Set. *(this box set uses the "Waring - fds" noise reduction process)*
    (M) (2:20)   Original Sound 2500 Oldies But Goodies Volumes 1-15 Box Set. *(this box set uses the "Waring - fds" noise reduction process)*
    (M) (2:20)   Original Sound 8907 Best Love Songs Vol 2.
    (M) (2:20)   Original Sound 9326 Best Love Songs Vol. 1 & 2.
    (M) (2:20)   Original Sound 1236 Best Love Songs Box Set.
    (M) (2:20)   Original Sound 9306 Dedicated To You Vol. 6.
    (M) (2:20)   Rhino 71601 Rock Instrumental Classics Volume 1: The Fifties.
    (M) (2:20)   Rhino 72035 Rock Instrumental Classics Vols. 1-5 Box Set.
    (M) (2:20)   Time-Life 2RNR-13 Rock 'N' Roll Era - 1959.
    (M) (2:21)   Time-Life R103-27 Love Me Tender.
    (M) (2:20)   Era 840 Rock N' Roll Guitar Classics.
    (M) (2:20)   Thump 7040 Low Rider Oldies Volume 4.
    (M) (2:20)   Rhino 71580 Billboard Pop Memories 1955-1959.
    (M) (2:21)   LaserLight 12316 Rebel Rousers.
    (M) (2:20)   Time-Life R857-01 The Heart Of Rock 'n' Roll - 1959.
    (M) (2:20)   Right Stuff 53320 Hot Rod Rock Volume 5: Back Seat Movers.
    (M) (2:20)   Elektra 62093 O.S.T. A Smile Like Yours.
    (M) (2:20)   Collectables 1514 and 2514 The Anniversary Album - The 50's.
1960 TEAR DROP

SAPPHIRES
1964 WHO DO YOU LOVE
    (M) (2:35)   Time-Life 2RNR-48 Rock 'N' Roll Era - R&B Gems II.
    (M) (2:40)   Time-Life RHD-12 Rhythm & Blues - 1964.
    (M) (2:35)   Original Sound 9307 Dedicated To You Vol. 7.
    (M) (2:40)   Collectables 5007 Who Do You Love/Golden Classics.
    (M) (2:40)   Time-Life R838-13 Solid Gold Soul - 1964.

CHANTAY SAVAGE
1996 I WILL SURVIVE
    (S) (6:12)   RCA 66775 I Will Survive (Doin' It My Way).
    (S) (6:11)   Work 67814 O.S.T. First Wives Club.

SAVAGE GARDEN
1997 I WANT YOU
    (S) (3:51)   Columbia 67954 Savage Garden.
1997 TO THE MOON AND BACK
    (S) (5:40)   Columbia 67954 Savage Garden.
1998 TRULY MADLY DEEPLY
    (S) (4:36)   Columbia 67954 Savage Garden.

LEO SAYER
1975 LONG TALL GLASSES (I CAN DANCE)
    (S) (3:03)   Rhino 70761 Super Hits Of The 70's Volume 14.
    (S) (3:00)   Chrysalis 26010 All The Best.
    (S) (3:02)   Rhino 71985 Anthology.
    (S) (2:59)   Time-Life AM1-22 AM Gold - 1975.
1976 YOU MAKE ME FEEL LIKE DANCING
    (S) (2:50)   Priority 7973 Mega-Hits Dance Classics Volume 3. *(45 version)*
    (S) (2:50)   Rhino 70672 Billboard Top Hits - 1977. *(hiss on the fadeout; 45 version)*
    (S) (3:40)   Chrysalis 41125 Endless Flight. *(LP version)*
    (S) (3:36)   Chrysalis 26010 All The Best. *(LP version)*
    (S) (2:49)   Time-Life SOD-17 Sounds Of The Seventies - 1977: Take Two. *(45 version)*
    (S) (2:50)   Rhino 71985 Anthology. *(45 version)*
    (S) (2:49)   Time-Life R840-07 Sounds Of The Seventies: '70s Dance Party 1976-1977. *(45 version)*
1977 WHEN I NEED YOU
    (S) (4:11)   Priority 8666 Kickin' Back/70's Greatest Rock Hits Volume 5.
    (S) (4:09)   Chrysalis 41125 Endless Flight.
    (S) (4:07)   Chrysalis 26010 All The Best.
    (S) (4:09)   Rhino 71985 Anthology.
    (S) (4:06)   Time-Life R834-08 Body Talk - On My Mind.
    (S) (4:10)   Rhino 72516 Behind Closed Doors - '70s Swingers.
    (S) (4:06)   Time-Life R814-05 Love Songs.
1977 HOW MUCH LOVE
    (S) (3:37)   Chrysalis 41125 Endless Flight.
    (S) (3:27)   Chrysalis 26010 All The Best.
    (S) (3:30)   Rhino 71985 Anthology.
1977 THUNDER IN MY HEART
    (S) (3:32)   Chrysalis 26010 All The Best.
    (S) (3:34)   Rhino 71985 Anthology.
1977 EASY TO LOVE
    (S) (3:37)   Chrysalis 26010 All The Best.
    (S) (3:40)   Rhino 71985 Anthology.
1980 MORE THAN I CAN SAY
    (S) (3:36)   Chrysalis 26010 All The Best.
    (S) (3:39)   Rhino 71985 Anthology.
    (S) (3:35)   Time-Life R834-11 Body Talk - After Dark.
    (S) (3:36)   Time-Life R988-22 Sounds Of The Eighties 1980-1983.
1981 LIVING IN A FANTASY
    (S) (4:19)   Chrysalis 26010 All The Best.
    (S) (4:21)   Rhino 71985 Anthology.

BOZ SCAGGS
1976 LOWDOWN
    (S) (5:16)   Columbia 33920 and 57205 Silk Degrees. *(LP version)*
    (S) (4:25)   Columbia 36841 Hits! *(edit of LP version)*
    (S) (5:16)   MFSL 535 Silk Degrees. *(LP version)*
    (S) (5:16)   Columbia/Legacy 65390 Slow Dance/Silk Degrees/Down Two Then Left. *(LP version)*
    (S) (5:16)   Columbia/Legacy 64420 Silk Degrees. *(gold disc; LP version)*
    (S) (5:15)   Columbia/Legacy 65208 My Time: A Boz Scaggs Anthology (1969-1997). *(LP version)*
1977 LIDO SHUFFLE
    (S) (3:42)   Columbia 33920 and 57205 Silk Degrees.
    (S) (3:38)   Columbia 36841 Hits!
    (S) (3:42)   MFSL 535 Silk Degrees.
    (S) (3:42)   Columbia/Legacy 65390 Slow Dance/Silk Degrees/Down Two Then Left.
    (S) (3:42)   Columbia/Legacy 64420 Silk Degrees. *(gold disc)*
    (S) (3:41)   Columbia/Legacy 65208 My Time: A Boz Scaggs Anthology (1969-1997).

BOZ SCAGGS *(Continued)*

    (S) (3:38) Time-Life R13610 Gold And Platinum Box Set - The Ultimate Rock Collection.

1980 BREAKDOWN DEAD AHEAD
(actual 45 time is (4:00) not (4:06) as stated on the record label)

    (S) (4:33) Columbia 36106 Middle Man. *(LP version)*
    (S) (4:00) Columbia 36841 Hits! *(45 version)*
    (S) (4:33) Columbia/Legacy 65208 My Time: A Boz Scaggs Anthology (1969-1997). *(LP version)*

1980 JO JO

    (S) (4:07) Sandstone 33051 and 5019 Cosmopolitan Volume 5. *(45 version)*
    (S) (5:50) Columbia 36106 Middle Man. *(LP version)*
    (S) (4:06) Columbia 36841 Hits! *(45 version)*
    (S) (4:06) Sandstone 33051 and 5019 Cosmopolitan Volume 5. *(45 version)*
    (S) (4:06) DCC Compact Classics 083 Night Moves Volume 3. *(45 version)*
    (S) (5:50) Columbia/Legacy 65208 My Time: A Boz Scaggs Anthology (1969-1997). *(LP version)*

1980 LOOK WHAT YOU'VE DONE TO ME

    (S) (5:14) Columbia 36841 Hits! *(LP version)*
    (S) (5:27) Full Moon/Elektra 60690 O.S.T. Urban Cowboy. *(LP version)*
    (S) (5:16) Columbia/Legacy 65208 My Time: A Boz Scaggs Anthology (1969-1997). *(LP version)*

1981 MISS SUN

    (S) (5:28) Columbia 36841 Hits! *(LP version)*
    (S) (5:30) Columbia/Legacy 65208 My Time: A Boz Scaggs Anthology (1969-1997). *(LP version)*

1988 HEART OF MINE

    (S) (4:11) Columbia 40463 Other Roads.
    (S) (4:11) Columbia/Legacy 65208 My Time: A Boz Scaggs Anthology (1969-1997).

SCANDAL featuring PATTY SMYTH (also PATTY SMYTH)
1984 THE WARRIOR

    (S) (3:55) Priority 53768 Rock Of The 80's Volume 14.
    (S) (3:57) Priority 7076 80's Greatest Rock Hits Volume 2 - Leather And Lace.
    (S) (3:56) Risky Business 53915 Dangerous Women. *(found only on 2nd pressings of this compact disc)*
    (S) (3:59) Columbia 39173 Warrior.
    (S) (3:56) Time-Life R988-06 Sounds Of The Eighties: 1984.
    (S) (3:56) Time-Life R968-18 Guitar Rock - The Heavy '80s.
    (S) (3:50) JCI 3143 18 Screamers From The 80's.
    (S) (3:56) Rhino 72597 Billboard Top Album Rock Hits, 1984.
    (S) (3:56) K-Tel 3868 Hot Ladies Of Pop.

released as by PATTY SMYTH:
1992 SOMETIMES LOVE JUST AIN'T ENOUGH

    (S) (4:25) MCA 10633 Patty Smyth.
    (S) (4:25) JCI 3132 1990 - Only Rock 'n Roll - 1994.

1993 NO MISTAKES

    (S) (5:22) MCA 10633 Patty Smyth.

JOEY SCARBURY
1981 THEME FROM "GREATEST AMERICAN HERO"
(BELIEVE IT OR NOT)

    (S) (3:12) Rhino 71912 Tube Tunes Volume Three - The 80's.
    (S) (3:12) Time-Life R988-32 Sounds Of The Eighties: TV Themes Of The '80s.

SCARFACE
1995 I NEVER SEEN A MAN CRY
(LP title is "I SEEN A MAN DIE")

    (S) (4:32) Rap-A-Lot 39946 The Diary.

released as by SCARFACE featuring 2PAC & JOHNNY P:
1997 SMILE

    (S) (5:00) Rap-A-Lot 42799 The Untouchable.

SCARLETT & BLACK
1988 YOU DON'T KNOW

    (S) (3:47) Virgin 90661 O.S.T. Hiding Out.

    (S) (3:38) EMI 28339 Living In Oblivion: The 80's Greatest Hits - Volume Four.
    (S) (3:39) Virgin 90647 Scarlett & Black.

LALO SCHIFRIN
1968 MISSION-IMPOSSIBLE

    (S) (2:31) One Way 22122 Mission:Anthology.
    (S) (2:30) Time-Life HPD-39 Your Hit Parade - 60's Instrumentals: Take Two.
    (S) (2:29) Rhino 71749 Spy Magazine Presents: Spy Music.
    (S) (2:29) Collectors' Choice 003/4 Instrumental Gems Of The 60's.
    (S) (2:30) Hip-O 40017 Mission Accomplished: Themes For Spies & Cops.
    (S) (2:31) Hip-O 40021 Music From "Mission: Impossible".
    (S) (0:51) Morgan Creek 20025 O.S.T. Ace Ventura Pet Detective. *(alternate version)*
    (S) (2:30) Time-Life AM1-27 AM Gold 60's TV Themes.

PETER SCHILLING
1983 MAJOR TOM (COMING HOME)

    (S) (4:57) EMI 32694 Living In Oblivion - The 80's Greatest Hits Volume Five. *(LP version)*
    (S) (4:09) Rhino 72820 VH1 - More Of The Big 80's. *(45 version but :10 longer)*

TIMOTHY B. SCHMIT
1987 BOY'S NIGHT OUT

JOHN SCHNEIDER
1981 IT'S NOW OR NEVER

    (S) (3:22) K-Tel 3163 Behind Closed Doors.

EDDIE SCHWARTZ
1982 ALL OUR TOMORROWS

SCORPIONS
1984 ROCK YOU LIKE A HURRICANE

    (S) (4:10) JCI 4541 Masters Of Metal: Strikeforce Volume 2.
    (S) (4:11) K-Tel 6090 Hit Parader Salutes 20 Years Of Metal.
    (S) (4:11) Priority 53753 Monsters Of Rock Vol. 2 - Metal Masters.
    (S) (4:11) Priority 7992 Killer Metal.
    (S) (4:10) Time-Life R105-24 Guitar Rock Monsters.
    (S) (4:11) Mercury 814981 Love At First Sting.
    (S) (4:11) Mercury 842002 Best Of Rockers 'N' Ballads.
    (S) (4:10) Time-Life R968-10 Guitar Rock Classics.
    (S) (4:10) Rhino 72291 Heavy Metal Hits Of The 80's Volume 1.
    (S) (4:11) Special Music 5038 Guitar Heroes.
    (S) (4:11) Mercury 314534787 Love At First Sting. *(remastered edition)*
    (S) (4:11) Mercury 314534344 and 314536285 Deadly Sting: The Mercury Years.
    (S) (4:10) K-Tel 3997 Arena Rock - The 80's.
    (S) (4:11) Rebound 314520522 Rockin' Sports Jams.
    (S) (4:17) Rebound 314520511 Big City Nights. *(live)*

1991 WIND OF CHANGE

    (S) (5:10) Mercury 846908 Crazy World.
    (S) (5:10) Time-Life R968-25 Guitar Rock - The '90s.
    (S) (5:09) Razor & Tie 4569 '90s Style.
    (S) (5:10) Mercury 314534344 and 314536285 Deadly Sting: The Mercury Years.
    (S) (5:46) Rebound 314520511 Big City Nights. *(live)*

1992 SEND ME AN ANGEL

    (S) (4:31) Mercury 846908 Crazy World.
    (S) (4:31) Mercury 314534344 and 314536285 Deadly Sting: The Mercury Years.
    (S) (4:31) Rebound 314520511 Big City Nights.

BOBBY SCOTT
1956 CHAIN GANG

    (M) (2:51) Time-Life HPD-28 Your Hit Parade - The Fabulous 50's.

FREDDIE SCOTT
1963 HEY, GIRL
- (S) (3:06) Collectables 5413 Sings And Sings And Sings. *(truncated fade)*
- (M) (3:07) Era 5025 The Brill Building Sound.
- (S) (3:04) Time-Life 2RNR-19 Rock 'N' Roll Era - 1963 Still Rockin'.
- (S) (3:04) Time-Life SUD-08 Superhits - 1963.
- (S) (3:06) Time-Life R962-08 History Of Rock 'N' Roll: Sound Of The City 1959-1965.
- (S) (3:07) Rhino 71650 Colpix-Dimension Story.
- (S) (3:05) Time-Life R102-17 Lost Treasures Of Rock 'N' Roll.
- (S) (3:07) Time-Life R857-08 The Heart Of Rock 'n' Roll 1963.
- (S) (3:04) Time-Life AM1-17 AM Gold - 1963.

1967 ARE YOU LONELY FOR ME
- (M) (3:09) Time-Life RHD-10 Rhythm & Blues - 1967.
- (S) (3:20) Ripete 2198 Soul Patrol.
- (S) (3:17) Legacy 66179 Lost Soul.
- (M) (3:09) Time-Life R838-02 Solid Gold Soul - 1967.
- (M) (3:12) Rhino 72815 Beg, Scream & Shout! The Big Ol' Box Of '60s Soul.
- (M) (3:16) TVT 4010 Rhythm Revue.
- (S) (3:17) Repeat/Relativity 1610 Tighten Up: #1 Soul Hits Of The 60's Volume 2.
- (S) (3:15) Columbia/Legacy 65241 Cry To Me - Best Of.

JACK SCOTT
1958 LEROY
- (M) (2:07) Curb 77255 Greatest Hits.
- (M) (2:07) Time-Life 2RNR-32 Rock 'N' Roll Era - Red Hot Rockabilly.
- (M) (2:07) K-Tel 4018 Forefathers Of Rock.

1958 MY TRUE LOVE
- (M) (2:45) Curb 77354 50's Hits Volume 1.
- (M) (2:44) Curb 77525 Greatest Hits Of Rock 'N' Roll Volume 2.
- (M) (2:44) Curb 77255 Greatest Hits.
- (M) (2:43) Time-Life 2RNR-28 Rock 'N' Roll Era - The 50's Rave On.
- (M) (2:43) Time-Life R962-05 History Of Rock 'N' Roll: The Teenage Years 1957-1964.
- (M) (2:43) Time-Life R102-17 Lost Treasures Of Rock 'N' Roll.
- (M) (2:44) LaserLight 12323 American Dreams.
- (M) (2:43) Time-Life R857-04 The Heart Of Rock 'n' Roll - 1958.

1958 WITH YOUR LOVE
- (M) (2:01) Curb 77255 Greatest Hits.

1959 GOODBYE BABY
- (M) (2:07) Elektra 60107 O.S.T. Diner.
- (M) (2:07) Curb 77255 Greatest Hits.
- (M) (2:06) Time-Life 2RNR-28 Rock 'N' Roll Era - The 50's Rave On.
- (M) (2:07) Curb 77775 Hard To Find Original Recordings - Classic Hits.
- (M) (2:07) Time-Life R857-01 The Heart Of Rock 'n' Roll - 1959.

1959 THE WAY I WALK
- (M) (2:40) Rhino 70742 Rock This Town: Rockabilly Hits Volume 2.
- (M) (2:40) Curb 77255 Greatest Hits.
- (M) (2:40) Time-Life 2RNR-32 Rock 'N' Roll Era - Red Hot Rockabilly.

1960 WHAT IN THE WORLD'S COME OVER YOU
- (S) (2:42) Curb 77355 60's Hits Volume 1.
- (S) (2:51) Capitol 93192 Capitol Collector's Series. *(time includes :08 of studio talk)*
- (S) (2:42) Curb 77255 Greatest Hits.
- (S) (2:41) Time-Life 2RNR-29 Rock 'N' Roll Era - The 60's Rave On.
- (S) (2:41) Time-Life SUD-15 Superhits - The Early 60's.
- (S) (2:41) Time-Life R103-27 Love Me Tender.
- (S) (2:41) Time-Life R857-02 The Heart Of Rock 'n' Roll - 1960.
- (S) (2:41) Time-Life AM1-19 AM Gold - The Early '60s.

1960 BURNING BRIDGES
- (S) (2:41) Capitol 93192 Capitol Collector's Series.
- (S) (2:39) Curb 77255 Greatest Hits.
- (S) (2:36) Time-Life 2RNR-42 Rock 'N' Roll Era - The 60's Sock Hop.

- (S) (2:36) Time-Life SUD-19 Superhits - Early 60's Classics.
- (S) (2:37) Time-Life R857-10 The Heart Of Rock 'n' Roll 1960-1961.
- (S) (2:36) Time-Life AM1-20 AM Gold - Early '60s Classics.

1960 IT ONLY HAPPENED YESTERDAY
- (S) (2:44) Capitol 93192 Capitol Collector's Series.

LINDA SCOTT
1961 I'VE TOLD EVERY LITTLE STAR
- (S) (2:13) Time-Life 2RNR-42 Rock 'N' Roll Era - The 60's Sock Hop.
- (S) (2:13) Time-Life SUD-15 Superhits - The Early 60's.
- (S) (2:13) Time-Life R102-17 Lost Treasures Of Rock 'N' Roll.
- (S) (2:14) Rhino 71582 Billboard Top Pop Hits, 1961.
- (S) (2:16) Nick At Nite/Epic 67148 Donna Reed's Dinner Party.
- (S) (2:16) Time-Life R857-14 The Heart Of Rock 'n' Roll 1960-1961 Take Two.
- (S) (2:13) Time-Life AM1-19 AM Gold - The Early '60s.
- (S) (2:13) Collectors' Choice 5189 I Wish I Were A Princess - The Great Lost Female Teen Idols.

1961 DON'T BET MONEY HONEY
- (S) (2:25) Time-Life 2RNR-46 Rock 'N' Roll Era - 60's Juke Box Memories.
- (S) (2:25) Time-Life R857-19 The Heart Of Rock 'n' Roll 1960-1961 Take Three.

1961 I DON'T KNOW WHY

PEGGY SCOTT & JO JO BENSON
1968 LOVER'S HOLIDAY
- (S) (2:38) Ripete 2392192 Beach Music Anthology Box Set.
- (S) (2:36) Ripete 0001 Coolin' Out/24 Carolina Classics Volume 1.
- (S) (2:37) Time-Life RHD-04 Rhythm & Blues - 1968.
- (S) (2:46) Ichiban 2103 Best Of.
- (S) (2:44) Ichiban 2512 Soulful Love - Duets Vol. 1.
- (S) (2:37) Time-Life R838-03 Solid Gold Soul - 1968.

1968 PICKIN' WILD MOUNTAIN BERRIES
- (M) (2:38) Ripete 0002 Coolin' Out/24 Carolina Classics Vol. 2.
- (M) (2:49) Ichiban 2103 Best Of.
- (E) (2:45) K-Tel 3901 Soul Brothers & Sisters Of The 60's.

1969 SOUL SHAKE
- (S) (2:21) Ripete 0003 Coolin' Out/24 Carolina Classics Vol. 3.
- (S) (2:24) Ichiban 2103 Best Of.

SCRITTI POLITTI
1985 PERFECT WAY
(actual 45 time is (4:02) not (4:31) as stated on the record label)
- (S) (4:00) EMI 27674 Living In Oblivion: The 80's Greatest Hits Volume Three. *(45 version)*
- (S) (4:30) Priority 53752 Rock Of The 80's Volume 12. *(LP version)*
- (S) (5:26) JCI 3117 Lost Mixes - Extended Ecstasy. *(remix)*
- (S) (4:02) Rhino 71978 New Wave Hits Of The 80's Vol. 15. *(45 version)*
- (S) (4:30) Warner Brothers 25302 Cupid & Psyche 85. *(LP version)*
- (S) (4:00) Time-Life R988-12 Sounds Of The 80's: 1985-1986. *(45 version)*
- (S) (4:28) K-Tel 3473 The 80s: New Wave. *(LP version)*
- (S) (4:02) JCI 3159 18 Modern Rock Classics From The 80's. *(45 version)*
- (S) (4:02) Intersound 9521 Retro Lunch Box - Squeeze The Cheese. *(45 version)*

JOHNNY SEA
1966 DAY FOR DECISION

SEAL
1991 CRAZY
- (S) (5:43) Columbia 52826 Red Hot + Dance. *(remix)*
- (S) (5:55) Sandstone 33048 and 5016 Cosmopolitan Volume 2. *(LP version)*

- (S) (6:44) JCI 3117 Lost Mixes - Extended Ecstasy. *(remix)*
- (S) (5:55) DCC Compact Classics 087 Night Moves Volume 5. *(LP version)*
- (S) (5:55) Warner Brothers 26627 Seal. *(LP version)*
- (S) (4:28) Pyramid 71830 Earthrise - The Rainforest Album. *(45 version)*
- (S) (4:28) Sire/Reprise 45565 O.S.T. Naked In New York. *(45 version)*

1994 PRAYER FOR THE DYING
- (S) (5:29) Warner Brothers 45415 Seal.
- (S) (5:30) Grammy Recordings/Sony Music 67043 1995 Grammy Nominees.
- (S) (4:14) Columbia 69012 Diana Princess Of Wales Tribute.

1995 KISS FROM A ROSE
- (S) (4:47) Warner Brothers 45415 Seal.
- (S) (3:36) Atlantic 82759 Batman Forever.
- (S) (4:46) Grammy Recordings/Sony 67565 1996 Grammy Nominees.

1996 DON'T CRY
- (S) (6:17) Warner Brothers 45415 Seal.

1997 FLY LIKE AN EAGLE
- (S) (4:13) Warner Sunset/Atlantic 82961 O.S.T. Space Jam.

SEALS & CROFTS
1972 SUMMER BREEZE
- (S) (3:24) Warner Brothers 3109 Greatest Hits.
- (S) (3:22) Time-Life SUD-11 Superhits - 1972.
- (S) (3:23) Time-Life SOD-13 Sounds Of The Seventies - 1972: Take Two.
- (S) (3:21) Time-Life R103-33 Singers & Songwriters.
- (S) (3:23) Time-Life R921-38 Get Together.
- (S) (3:21) Razor & Tie 4543 The '70s Preservation Society Presents: Easy '70s.
- (S) (3:22) Medicine Label 24588 Even More Dazed And Confused.
- (S) (3:23) Warner Brothers 2629 Summer Breeze.
- (S) (3:21) K-Tel 3437 Summer Songs.
- (S) (3:22) Madacy Entertainment 26927 Sun Splashin'.
- (S) (3:23) JCI 3168 #1 Radio Hits 1970 - Only Rock 'n Roll - 1974.
- (S) (3:22) Rhino 72518 Mellow Rock Hits Of The 70's - Summer Breeze.
- (S) (3:22) Time-Life AM1-07 AM Gold - 1972.
- (S) (3:23) Time-Life R834-10 Body Talk - From The Heart.

1973 HUMMINGBIRD
(dj copies of this 45 ran (3:30) and (4:35); commercial copies were all (4:35))
- (S) (4:36) Warner Brothers 3109 Greatest Hits.
- (S) (4:34) Warner Brothers 2629 Summer Breeze.

1973 DIAMOND GIRL
- (S) (4:12) Warner Brothers 3109 Greatest Hits. *(LP version)*
- (S) (3:50) Time-Life SUD-13 Superhits - 1973. *(edit of LP version)*
- (S) (3:53) Time-Life SOD-06 Sounds Of The Seventies - 1973. *(edit of LP version)*
- (S) (3:52) Time-Life R105-26 Our Songs: Singers & Songwriters Encore. *(edit of LP version)*
- (S) (4:07) JCI 3130 1970 - Only Rock 'N Roll - 1974. *(LP version)*
- (S) (3:52) Madacy Entertainment 1973 Rock On 1973. *(edit of LP version)*
- (S) (3:53) K-Tel 3625 Dynamite. *(edit of LP version)*
- (S) (4:10) Rhino 72517 Mellow Rock Hits Of The 70's - Ventura Highway. *(LP version)*
- (S) (3:50) Time-Life AM1-03 AM Gold - 1973. *(edit of LP version)*
- (S) (4:09) Time-Life R834-14 Body Talk - Love And Tenderness. *(LP version)*

1973 WE MAY NEVER PASS THIS WAY (AGAIN)
- (S) (4:15) Warner Brothers 3109 Greatest Hits.
- (S) (4:13) Rhino 72739 Billboard Top Soft Rock Hits - 1973.

1975 I'LL PLAY FOR YOU
- (S) (4:04) Warner Brothers 3109 Greatest Hits.

1976 GET CLOSER
(actual 45 time is (3:54) not (3:45) as stated on the record label)
- (S) (3:54) Priority 53706 Singers/Songwriters/70's Greatest Rock Hits Volume 15.
- (S) (3:55) Rhino 71200 Super Hits Of The 70's Volume 20.
- (S) (3:53) JCI 3307 Easy Seventies.
- (S) (3:54) Time-Life SOD-04 Sounds Of The Seventies - 1976.
- (S) (3:54) JCI 3146 1975 - Only Love - 1979.
- (S) (3:54) Time-Life AM1-23 AM Gold - 1976.
- (S) (3:55) Time-Life R834-05 Body Talk - Sealed With A Kiss.
- (S) (3:53) K-Tel 4017 70s Heavy Hitters: Summer Love.

1977 MY FAIR SHARE
1978 YOU'RE THE LOVE
- (S) (3:17) Time-Life R834-17 Body Talk - Heart To Heart.

SEARCHERS
1964 NEEDLES AND PINS
- (S) (2:11) Rhino 70319 History Of British Rock Volume 1.
- (S) (2:11) Rhino 70319 History Of British Rock Box Set.
- (S) (2:11) Rhino 72008 History Of British Rock Volumes 1-4 Box Set.
- (S) (2:11) Rhino 75773 Greatest Hits.
- (S) (2:10) Time-Life 2CLR-03 Classic Rock - 1964.
- (S) (2:10) Time-Life SUD-17 Superhits - Mid 60's Classics.
- (S) (2:11) Time-Life R962-07 History Of Rock 'N' Roll: The British Invasion 1964-1966.
- (M) (2:11) Collectables 0564 "Some Other Guys" 32 Merseybeat Nuggets 1963-1966.
- (S) (2:10) Collectables 8815 30th Anniversary Collection.
- (S) (2:11) MFSL 667 It's The Searchers/Take Me For What I'm Worth. *(gold disc)*
- (S) (2:11) LaserLight 12317 The British Invasion.
- (S) (2:10) Time-Life AM1-16 AM Gold - Mid '60s Classics.

1964 DON'T THROW YOUR LOVE AWAY
- (S) (2:15) Rhino 70320 History Of British Rock Volume 2.
- (S) (2:15) Rhino 70319 History Of British Rock Box Set.
- (S) (2:15) Rhino 72008 History Of British Rock Volumes 1-4 Box Set.
- (S) (2:15) Rhino 75773 Greatest Hits.
- (S) (2:14) Time-Life 2CLR-16 Classic Rock - 1964: Shakin' All Over.
- (S) (2:14) Collectables 8815 30th Anniversary Collection.
- (M) (2:14) MFSL 667 It's The Searchers/Take Me For What I'm Worth. *(gold disc)*

1964 SOME DAY WE'RE GONNA LOVE AGAIN
- (S) (1:57) Rhino 75773 Greatest Hits.
- (M) (1:57) Collectables 8815 30th Anniversary Collection.

1964 WHEN YOU WALK INTO THE ROOM
- (S) (2:20) Rhino 75773 Greatest Hits.
- (S) (2:19) Time-Life 2CLR-26 Classic Rock - Rock Renaissance III.
- (S) (2:20) Time-Life R962-02 History Of Rock 'N' Roll: Folk Rock 1964-1967.
- (M) (2:19) Collectables 8815 30th Anniversary Collection.

1965 LOVE POTION NUMBER NINE
- (S) (2:04) Rhino 70321 History Of British Rock Volume 3.
- (S) (2:04) Rhino 70319 History Of British Rock Box Set.
- (S) (2:04) Rhino 72008 History Of British Rock Volumes 1-4 Box Set.
- (S) (2:04) Rhino 75773 Greatest Hits.
- (M) (2:02) JCI 3107 British Sixties.
- (S) (2:04) Time-Life 2CLR-09 Classic Rock - 1964: The Beat Goes On.
- (S) (2:03) Time-Life SUD-12 Superhits - The Mid 60's.
- (M) (2:03) Collectables 8815 30th Anniversary Collection.
- (S) (2:04) Rhino 71935 Billboard Top Pop Hits, 1965.
- (S) (2:04) LaserLight 12317 The British Invasion.
- (M) (2:03) MFSL 693 Meet The Searchers/Sounds Like The Searchers. *(gold disc)*
- (S) (2:03) Time-Life AM1-05 AM Gold - The Mid '60s.

1965 WHAT HAVE THEY DONE TO THE RAIN
- (S) (2:33) Rhino 75773 Greatest Hits.
- (M) (2:31) Collectables 8815 30th Anniversary Collection.

1965 BUMBLE BEE
- (S) (2:14) Rhino 75773 Greatest Hits.
- (S) (2:14) Time-Life 2CLR-21 Classic Rock - Rock Renaissance II.
- (M) (2:12) Collectables 8815 30th Anniversary Collection.
- (M) (2:12) MFSL 693 Meet The Searchers/Sounds Like The Searchers. *(gold disc)*

JOHN SEBASTIAN
1976 WELCOME BACK KOTTER
- (S) (2:49) Rhino 70170 Best Of.
- (S) (2:49) Razor & Tie 22505 More Fabulous 70's Volume 2.
- (S) (2:49) Time-Life SOD-04 Sounds Of The Seventies - 1976.
- (S) (2:49) Time-Life R103-33 Singers & Songwriters.
- (S) (2:49) JCI 3131 1975 - Only Rock 'N Roll - 1979.
- (S) (2:50) Rhino 71911 Tube Tunes Volume Two - The 70's & 80's.
- (S) (2:49) Time-Life AM1-23 AM Gold - 1976.
- (S) (2:50) Time-Life R840-02 Sounds Of The Seventies - TV Themes.

JON SECADA
1992 JUST ANOTHER DAY
- (S) (6:32) SBK 28403 Brilliant! The Global Dance Music Experience Volume 1. *(remix)*
- (S) (5:26) Foundation/RCA 66563 Number 1 Hit Mix.
- (S) (4:15) SBK 31181 Moments In Love.
- (S) (5:26) SBK 98845 Jon Secada.
- (S) (6:32) EMI 54097 Retro Dance Club Volume One. *(remix)*

1992 DO YOU BELIEVE IN US
- (S) (3:58) SBK 98845 Jon Secada.

1993 ANGEL
- (S) (4:34) SBK 98845 Jon Secada.

1993 I'M FREE
- (S) (3:59) SBK 98845 Jon Secada.

1994 IF YOU GO
- (S) (4:33) SBK 29272 Heart, Soul & A Voice.

1995 MENTAL PICTURE
- (S) (4:18) SBK 29272 Heart, Soul & A Voice.

SECRETS
1963 THE BOY NEXT DOOR
- (M) (1:58) Special Music/Essex 5035 Prom Night - The 60's.
- (M) (1:58) Mercury 314528171 Growin' Up Too Fast - The Girl Group Anthology.
- (M) (1:58) Eclipse Music Group 64868 Rock 'n Roll Relix 1962-1963.
- (M) (1:58) Eclipse Music Group 64872 Rock 'n Roll Relix 1960-1969.

NEIL SEDAKA
1959 THE DIARY
- (S) (2:12) RCA 8467 Nipper's Greatest Hits Of The 50's Volume 2.
- (S) (2:14) RCA 6876 All Time Greatest Hits.
- (S) (2:51) RCA 2406 All Time Greatest Hits Volume 2. *(alternate take; includes :06 of studio talk)*
- (S) (2:15) Pair 1283 Neil Sedaka's Diary.
- (M) (2:14) RCA 53465 Sings His Greatest Hits.
- (S) (2:14) Time-Life 2RNR-33 Rock 'N' Roll Era - The 50's Last Dance.

1959 I GO APE
- (S) (2:31) RCA 2406 All Time Greatest Hits Volume 2.
- (S) (2:31) Pair 1283 Neil Sedaka's Diary.

1959 OH! CAROL
- (S) (2:14) RCA 8466 Nipper's Greatest Hits Of The 50's Volume 1.
- (S) (2:15) RCA 6876 All Time Greatest Hits.
- (S) (2:14) Special Music 2701 Oh! Carol And Other Hits.
- (S) (2:14) Pair 1283 Neil Sedaka's Diary.
- (S) (2:13) RCA 53465 Sings His Greatest Hits.
- (S) (2:14) Era 5025 The Brill Building Sound.
- (S) (2:13) Time-Life 2RNR-27 Rock 'N' Roll Era - Teen Idols.
- (S) (2:15) Varese Sarabande 5549 Tuneweaver. *(rerecorded)*

- (S) (2:15) Priority 50950 I Love Rock & Roll Volume 1: Hits Of The 50's.

1960 STAIRWAY TO HEAVEN
- (S) (2:40) RCA 6876 All Time Greatest Hits.
- (E) (2:41) RCA 53465 Sings His Greatest Hits.
- (S) (2:39) Era 5025 The Brill Building Sound.
- (S) (2:36) Time-Life 2RNR-35 Rock 'N' Roll Era - The 60's Last Dance.
- (S) (2:40) Varese Sarabande 5549 Tuneweaver. *(rerecorded)*

1960 YOU MEAN EVERYTHING TO ME
- (S) (2:37) RCA 6876 All Time Greatest Hits.
- (S) (2:36) Pair 1283 Neil Sedaka's Diary.
- (S) (2:35) RCA 53465 Sings His Greatest Hits.

1960 RUN SAMSON RUN
- (S) (2:51) RCA 6876 All Time Greatest Hits.
- (S) (2:49) RCA 53465 Sings His Greatest Hits.
- (S) (2:55) Varese Sarabande 5549 Tuneweaver. *(rerecorded)*

1961 CALENDAR GIRL
- (S) (2:37) RCA 6876 All Time Greatest Hits
- (S) (2:36) Special Music 2701 Oh! Carol And Other Hits.
- (S) (2:35) Pair 1283 Neil Sedaka's Diary.
- (S) (2:36) RCA 53465 Sings His Greatest Hits.
- (S) (2:35) Era 5025 The Brill Building Sound.
- (S) (2:36) Time-Life 2RNR-11 Rock 'N' Roll Era - 1960. *(original pressings of this song on this cd were (M))*
- (S) (2:36) Time-Life SUD-15 Superhits - The Early 60's.
- (S) (2:36) Columbia 57317 O.S.T. Calendar Girl.
- (S) (2:38) Varese Sarabande 5549 Tuneweaver. *(rerecorded)*
- (S) (2:36) Eclipse Music Group 64867 Rock 'n Roll Relix 1960-1961.
- (S) (2:36) Eclipse Music Group 64872 Rock 'n Roll Relix 1960-1969.
- (S) (2:35) Time-Life AM1-19 AM Gold - The Early '60s.

1961 LITTLE DEVIL
- (S) (2:42) RCA 6876 All Time Greatest Hits.
- (S) (2:41) Special Music 2701 Oh! Carol And Other Hits.
- (S) (2:41) Pair 1283 Neil Sedaka's Diary.
- (S) (2:41) RCA 53465 Sings His Greatest Hits.
- (S) (2:39) Varese Sarabande 5549 Tuneweaver. *(rerecorded)*

1961 HAPPY BIRTHDAY, SWEET SIXTEEN
- (S) (2:34) RCA 6876 All Time Greatest Hits.
- (S) (2:41) RCA 53465 Sings His Greatest Hits.
- (S) (2:36) Era 5025 The Brill Building Sound.
- (S) (2:33) Time-Life 2RNR-27 Rock 'N' Roll Era - Teen Idols.
- (S) (2:38) Varese Sarabande 5549 Tuneweaver. *(rerecorded)*

1962 BREAKING UP IS HARD TO DO
- (S) (2:14) Rhino 70623 Billboard's Top Rock & Roll Hits Of 1962.
- (S) (2:14) Rhino 72007 Billboard's Top Rock & Roll Hits Of 1962-1966 Box Set.
- (S) (2:17) RCA 9902 Nipper's #1 Hits 1956-1986.
- (S) (2:20) RCA 8474 Nipper's Greatest Hits Of The 60's Volume 1.
- (S) (2:15) RCA 6876 All Time Greatest Hits.
- (S) (2:15) Special Music 2701 Oh! Carol And Other Hits.
- (S) (2:16) RCA 53465 Sings His Greatest Hits.
- (S) (2:17) Era 5025 The Brill Building Sound.
- (S) (2:13) Time-Life 2RNR-16 Rock 'N' Roll Era - 1962 Still Rockin'.
- (S) (2:18) Time-Life SUD-06 Superhits - 1962.
- (S) (2:14) Time-Life R962-08 History Of Rock 'N' Roll: Sound Of The City 1959-1965.
- (S) (2:16) Varese Sarabande 5549 Tuneweaver. *(rerecorded)*
- (S) (2:15) Eclipse Music Group 64868 Rock 'n Roll Relix 1962-1963.
- (S) (2:15) Eclipse Music Group 64872 Rock 'n Roll Relix 1960-1969.
- (S) (2:18) Time-Life AM1-18 AM Gold - 1962.
- (S) (2:17) JCI 3184 1960 - Only Love - 1964.
- (S) (2:19) Collectables 1515 and 2515 The Anniversary Album - The 60's.

1962 NEXT DOOR TO AN ANGEL
- (S) (2:24) RCA 6876 All Time Greatest Hits.
- (S) (2:24) RCA 53465 Sings His Greatest Hits.
- (S) (2:22) Time-Life 2RNR-47 Rock 'N' Roll Era - Teen Idols II.

NEIL SEDAKA *(Continued)*
- (S) (2:36) Varese Sarabande 5549 Tuneweaver. *(rerecorded)*
- (S) (2:22) JCI 3166 #1 Radio Hits 1960 - Only Rock 'n Roll - 1964.

1963 ALICE IN WONDERLAND
- (S) (2:32) RCA 6876 All Time Greatest Hits.

1963 LET'S GO STEADY AGAIN
- (S) (2:34) RCA 6876 All Time Greatest Hits.

1963 BAD GIRL
- (S) (2:38) RCA 2406 All-Time Greatest Hits, Volume 2.

1975 LAUGHTER IN THE RAIN
- (S) (2:49) Polydor 831235 My Friend.
- (S) (2:43) Time-Life SOD-33 Sounds Of The Seventies - AM Pop Classics II.
- (S) (2:46) Razor & Tie 4543 The '70s Preservation Society Presents: Easy '70s.
- (S) (2:48) Varese Sarabande 5534 Rhythm Of The Rain.
- (S) (2:49) Varese Sarabande 5539 Best Of 1974-1980.
- (S) (4:43) Varese Sarabande 5549 Tuneweaver. *(rerecorded)*
- (S) (2:43) JCI 3146 1975 - Only Love - 1979.
- (S) (2:46) Time-Life R103-18 Great Love Songs Of The '70s & '80s.
- (S) (2:49) Rhino 72740 Billboard Top Soft Rock Hits - 1974.
- (S) (2:43) Time-Life R814-02 Love Songs.
- (S) (2:48) Collectables 1516 and 2516 The Anniversary Album - The 70's. *(truncated fade)*

1975 THE IMMIGRANT
- (S) (4:22) Polydor 831235 My Friend. *(LP version)*
- (S) (4:23) Varese Sarabande 5539 Best Of 1974-1980. *(LP version)*

1975 THAT'S WHEN THE MUSIC TAKES ME
- (S) (3:34) Polydor 831235 My Friend.
- (S) (3:34) Varese Sarabande 5539 Best Of 1974-1980.

1975 BAD BLOOD
- (S) (3:06) Rhino 70670 Billboard Top Hits - 1975.
- (S) (3:06) Polydor 831235 My Friend.
- (S) (3:06) Varese Sarabande 5539 Best Of 1974-1980.

1976 BREAKING UP IS HARD TO DO
- (S) (3:14) Polydor 831235 My Friend.
- (S) (3:15) Varese Sarabande 5539 Best Of 1974-1980.

1976 LOVE IN THE SHADOWS
- (S) (3:20) Polydor 831235 My Friend.
- (S) (3:19) Varese Sarabande 5539 Best Of 1974-1980.

released as by NEIL SEDAKA and DARA SEDAKA:
1980 SHOULD'VE NEVER LET YOU GO
- (S) (4:16) Polydor 831235 Neil Sedaks - My Friend.
- (S) (4:16) Varese Sarabande 5539 Neil Sedaka - Best Of 1974-1980.

SEDUCTION
1989 (YOU'RE MY ONE AND ONLY) TRUE LOVE
- (S) (3:50) Vendetta/A&M 5280 Nothing Matters Without Love.

1990 TWO TO MAKE IT RIGHT
- (S) (5:58) Columbia 48840 Clivilles & Cole's Greatest Remixes Volume 1. *(remixed)*
- (S) (4:41) Vendetta/A&M 5280 Nothing Matters Without Love.
- (S) (6:18) Rebound 314520359 World Of Dance - The 90's. *(remix)*
- (S) (4:39) Mercury 314532494 100% Pure Dance. *(all songs on this cd are segued together)*

1990 HEARTBEAT
- (S) (7:02) Vendetta/A&M 5280 Nothing Matters Without Love.

1990 COULD THIS BE LOVE
- (S) (6:19) Vendetta/A&M 5280 Nothing Matters Without Love.
- (S) (6:18) Vendetta/A&M 5280 Nothing Matters Without Love. *(remix)*

SEEDS
1967 PUSHIN' TOO HARD
- (E) (2:37) Warner Special Products 27607 Highs Of The 60's.
- (E) (2:35) Rhino 75892 Nuggets.
- (E) (2:37) DCC Compact Classics 029 Toga Rock.
- (E) (2:34) K-Tel 713 Battle Of The Bands.
- (E) (2:34) MCA 6467 O.S.T. Air America.
- (E) (2:35) GNP Crescendo 2023 The Seeds.
- (E) (2:33) JCI 3116 Psychedelic Sixties.
- (E) (2:33) Time-Life 2CLR-21 Classic Rock - Rock Renaissance II.
- (E) (2:37) K-Tel 3133 Biker Rock.
- (E) (2:33) Time-Life R968-09 Guitar Rock 1966-1967.
- (E) (2:33) LaserLight 12528 Garage Band Rock.
- (E) (2:36) K-Tel 3610 Psychedelic Mind Trip Vol. 2: Another Flashback.
- (E) (2:33) Hip-O 40038 Power Chords Volume 1.
- (E) (2:35) Simitar 55362 Garage Band Classics.
- (E) (2:33) Thump 6020 Easyriders Volume 2.

SEEKERS
1965 I'LL NEVER FIND ANOTHER YOU
- (M) (2:41) Rhino 70321 History Of British Rock Volume 3.
- (M) (2:41) Rhino 70319 History Of British Rock Box Set.
- (M) (2:41) Rhino 72008 History Of British Rock Volumes 1-4 Box Set.
- (S) (2:39) Curb 77485 Best Of Today. *(rerecording)*
- (M) (2:41) Capitol 91846 Capitol Collectors Series.
- (M) (2:41) Scotti Brothers 75402 There Was Love (The Divorce Songs).
- (M) (2:41) Time-Life SUD-03 Superhits - 1965.
- (M) (2:41) Time-Life R962-02 History Of Rock 'N' Roll: Folk Rock 1964-1967.
- (M) (2:40) Time-Life AM1-10 AM Gold - 1965.
- (M) (2:41) Time-Life R132-22 Treasury Of Folk Music Volume Two.
- (M) (2:41) Collectables 2719 Very Best Of.

1965 A WORLD OF OUR OWN
- (S) (2:42) Curb 77485 Best Of Today. *(rerecording)*
- (S) (2:57) Capitol 91846 Capitol Collectors Series. *(time includes :15 of studio talk)*
- (S) (2:40) Collectables 2719 Very Best Of.

1967 GEORGY GIRL
- (S) (2:19) Rhino 70322 History Of British Rock Volume 4.
- (S) (2:19) Rhino 70319 History Of British Rock Box Set.
- (S) (2:19) Rhino 72008 History Of British Rock Volumes 1-4 Box Set.
- (S) (2:28) Curb 77485 Best Of Today. *(rerecording)*
- (S) (2:18) Capitol 91846 Capitol Collectors Series.
- (S) (2:18) Capitol 98665 When AM Was King.
- (E) (2:18) JCI 3112 Pop Sixties.
- (S) (2:15) Time-Life SUD-01 Superhits - 1966.
- (S) (2:15) Time-Life AM1-09 AM Gold - 1966.
- (S) (2:13) Collectables 2719 Very Best Of.

BOB SEGER
released as by THE BOB SEGER SYSTEM:
1969 RAMBLIN' GAMBLIN' MAN
- (E) (2:20) Capitol 96261 Ramblin' Gamblin' Man.

released as by BOB SEGER:
1977 NIGHT MOVES
(dj copies of this 45 ran (3:20) and (5:25); commercial copies were all (3:20))
- (S) (5:23) Capitol 46075 Night Moves. *(LP version)*
- (S) (5:23) DCC Compact Classics 1028 Night Moves. *(LP version; gold disc)*
- (S) (5:23) Capitol 30334 Greatest Hits. *(LP version)*

1977 MAINSTREET
- (S) (3:39) Capitol 46075 Night Moves.
- (S) (3:39) DCC Compact Classics 1028 Night Moves. *(gold disc)*
- (S) (3:39) Capitol 30334 Greatest Hits.

1977 ROCK AND ROLL NEVER FORGETS
- (S) (3:48) Capitol 46075 Night Moves. *(LP length)*
- (S) (3:48) DCC Compact Classics 1028 Night Moves. *(LP length; gold disc)*

released as by BOB SEGER & THE SILVER BULLET BAND:
1978 STILL THE SAME
- (S) (3:17) Capitol 46074 Stranger In Town.
- (S) (3:18) Capitol 30334 Greatest Hits.

1978 HOLLYWOOD NIGHTS
(dj copies of this 45 ran (3:16); commercial copies
were all (5:00))
    (S) (4:58)   Capitol 46074 Stranger In Town.
    (S) (4:59)   Capitol 30334 Greatest Hits.
1979 WE'VE GOT TONITE
    (S) (4:37)   Capitol 46074 Stranger In Town. *(LP version)*
    (S) (4:37)   Capitol 30334 Greatest Hits. *(LP version)*
1979 OLD TIME ROCK & ROLL
    (S) (3:12)   Capitol 46074 Stranger In Town.
    (S) (3:12)   Capitol 30334 Greatest Hits.
released as by BOB SEGER:
1980 FIRE LAKE
    (S) (3:30)   Capitol 46060 Against The Wind.
1980 AGAINST THE WIND
    (S) (5:30)   Capitol 46060 Against The Wind. *(LP version)*
    (S) (5:31)   Capitol 30334 Greatest Hits. *(LP version)*
    (S) (5:31)   Epic 66329 O.S.T. Forrest Gump. *(LP version)*
    (S) (5:30)   Right Stuff 31324 and 31327 Harley-Davidson
                  Road Songs. *(LP version)*
1980 YOU'LL ACCOMP'NY ME
    (S) (3:57)   Capitol 46060 Against The Wind. *(LP version)*
    (S) (3:58)   Capitol 30334 Greatest Hits. *(LP version)*
1981 TRYIN' TO LIVE MY LIFE WITHOUT YOU
    (S) (4:03)   Capitol 46086 Nine Tonight. *(LP length)*
released as by BOB SEGER & THE SILVER BULLET BAND:
1983 SHAME ON THE MOON
(dj copies of this 45 ran (4:22) and (4:55);
commercial copies were all (4:55))
    (S) (4:53)   Capitol 46005 The Distance.
1983 EVEN NOW
(dj copies of this 45 ran (4:04) and (4:31);
commercial copies were all (4:31))
    (S) (4:32)   Capitol 46005 The Distance.
1983 ROLL ME AWAY
    (S) (4:38)   Capitol 46005 The Distance.
    (S) (4:37)   Capitol 30334 Greatest Hits.
1984 UNDERSTANDING
    (S) (3:51)   Capitol 46062 O.S.T. Teachers.
1986 AMERICAN STORM
    (S) (4:15)   Capitol 46195 Like A Rock. *(LP version)*
1986 LIKE A ROCK
(dj copies of this 45 ran (4:36) and (5:53);
commercial copies were all (5:53))
    (S) (5:53)   Capitol 30334 Greatest Hits.
    (S) (5:53)   Capitol 46195 Like A Rock.
released as by BOB SEGER:
1987 SHAKEDOWN
    (S) (4:02)   MCA 6207 O.S.T. Beverly Hills Cop II.
released as by BOB SEGER & THE SILVER BULLET BAND:
1991 THE REAL LOVE
    (S) (4:38)   Capitol 91134 The Fire Inside.

SELENA
1995 DREAMING OF YOU
    (S) (5:14)   EMI Latin 34123 Dreaming Of You.
    (S) (5:12)   EMI Latin 55535 O.S.T. Selena.

MICHAEL SEMBELLO
1983 MANIAC
    (S) (4:01)   Casablanca 811492 O.S.T. Flashdance. *(faded
                  :08 earlier than the vinyl LP version)*
    (S) (5:53)   Casablanca 314516917 The Casablanca Records
                  Story. *(12" dj single version)*
    (S) (4:01)   Priority 7971 Mega-Hits Dance Classics (Volume
                  1). *(faded :08 earlier than the vinyl LP version)*
    (S) (4:09)   Rhino 70678 Billboard Top Hits - 1983.
    (S) (4:16)   Rebound 314520307 Disco Nights Volume VIII.
    (S) (4:09)   Time-Life R988-03 Sounds Of The Eighties: 1983.
    (S) (4:09)   Time-Life R138-38 Celebration.
    (S) (4:16)   Rebound 314520366 Disco Nights Vol. 10 -
                  Disco's Greatest Movie Hits.
    (S) (4:16)   Casablanca 314526253 Casablanca Records
                  Greatest Hits.
    (S) (4:17)   Rebound 314520438 No. 1 Hits Of The 80's.

    (S) (4:09)   Time-Life R988-31 Sounds Of The Eighties:
                  Cinemax Movie Hits Of The '80s.
    (S) (7:26)   Chronicles 314553404 Non-Stop Disco Vol. 1.
                  *(all songs on this cd are segued together; megamix
                  medley with Irene Cara's "FLASHDANCE")*
    (S) (4:10)   Priority 50974 Premiere The Movie Magazine
                  Presents The Greatest Soundtrack Hits.
    (S) (4:16)   Hip-O 40079 Essential '80s: 1980-1984.
    (S) (4:17)   Rebound 314520493 Class Reunion '83.
    (S) (4:16)   Rebound 314520520 Body Moves - Non-Stop
                  Disco Workout Vol. 1. *(all selections on this cd
                  are segued together)*
1983 AUTOMATIC MAN

SENATOR BOBBY
1967 WILD THING

SENSATIONS
1962 LET ME IN
    (M) (3:05)   Rhino 70648 Billboard's Top R&B Hits Of 1962.
    (M) (3:04)   MCA 31203 Vintage Music Volume 6.
    (M) (3:04)   MCA 5804 Vintage Music Volumes 5 & 6.
    (M) (3:02)   JCI 3110 Sock Hoppin' Sixties.
    (M) (3:01)   Garland 011 Footstompin' Oldies.
    (M) (3:02)   Chess 31320 Best Of Chess Rock 'n' Roll Volume 2.
    (M) (3:04)   Time-Life 2RNR-02 Rock 'N' Roll Era - 1962.
    (M) (3:01)   Time-Life RHD-11 Rhythm & Blues - 1962.
    (M) (3:03)   Chess 9352 Chess Rhythm & Roll.
    (M) (3:03)   MCA Special Products 22172 Vintage
                  Collectibles Volume 10.
    (M) (3:01)   Time-Life R838-18 Solid Gold Soul 1962.

SERENDIPITY SINGERS
1964 DON'T LET THE RAIN COME DOWN (CROOKED LITTLE
MAN)
    (S) (2:42)   JCI 3109 Folk Sixties.
    (S) (2:43)   Time-Life SUD-17 Superhits - Mid 60's Classics.
    (S) (2:43)   Time-Life AM1-16 AM Gold - Mid '60s Classics.
    (S) (2:43)   Time-Life R132-22 Treasury Of Folk Music
                  Volume One.
    (S) (2:43)   Mercury 314534401 Don't Let The Rain Come
                  Down: Best Of.
    (S) (2:42)   Polygram Special Markets 314520516 45's On CD
                  Volume 1.
1964 BEANS IN MY EARS
    (S) (2:08)   Time-Life HPD-35 Your Hit Parade - The Fun-
                  Times 50's & 60's.
    (S) (2:05)   K-Tel 3411 Tacky Tunes. *(rerecording)*
    (S) (2:08)   Mercury 314534401 Don't Let The Rain Come
                  Down: Best Of. *(noisy fadeout)*

702
released as by SUBWAY featuring 702:
1995 THIS LIL' GAME WE PLAY
    (S) (4:52)   BIV 10 Records 314530354 Good Times.
released as by 702:
1996 STEELO
    (S) (4:16)   Biv Ten 314530738 No Doubt.
    (S) (4:16)   Polygram TV 314553641 Pure Soul 1997.
    (S) (3:59)   Tommy Boy 1234 MTV Party To Go '98. *(all
                  songs on this cd are segued together)*
    (M) (4:07)   Elektra 62088 Party Over Here '98. *(all tracks on
                  this cd are segued together)*
1997 GET IT TOGETHER
    (S) (4:50)   Biv Ten 314530738 No Doubt.
1997 ALL I WANT
    (S) (3:58)   Capitol 57955 O.S.T. Good Burger.

SEVEN MARY THREE
1996 CUMBERSOME
    (S) (3:56)   Mammoth/Atlantic 92633 American Standard.

DAVID SEVILLE (see also THE CHIPMUNKS)
1956 ARMEN'S THEME

DAVID SEVILLE *(Continued)*
1958 WITCH DOCTOR
    (M) (2:18) Rhino 70743 Dr. Demento 20th Anniversary
                  Collection.
    (S) (2:00) EMI 91684 Very Best Of The Chipmunks.
                  (rerecording)
    (M) (2:18) Time-Life 2RNR-37 Rock 'N' Roll Era - Weird,
                  Wild & Wacky.
    (M) (2:18) K-Tel 3037 Wacky Weirdos.
    (M) (1:39) Priority 53747 Wild & Crazy Tunes. *(rerecording)*
    (M) (2:20) DCC Compact Classics 077 Too Cute!
    (M) (2:18) K-Tel 3795 Music For Your Halloween Party.
    (M) (2:18) K-Tel 3795 Spooktacular Party Songs.
1958 THE BIRD ON MY HEAD

CHARLIE SEXTON
1986 BEAT'S SO LONELY
    (S) (5:14) Rhino 71978 New Wave Hits Of The 80's Vol. 15.
    (S) (5:14) MCA 5629 Pictures For Pleasure.

PHIL SEYMOUR
1981 PRECIOUS TO ME
    (S) (2:49) Rhino 71894 Radio Daze: Pop Hits Of The 80's
                  Volume Five.
    (S) (2:50) Right Stuff 37519 Precious To Me.

SHADES OF BLUE
1966 OH HOW HAPPY
    (M) (2:08) Time-Life 2CLR-22 Classic Rock - 1966: Blowin'
                  Your Mind.
    (M) (2:09) LaserLight 12318 Chart Busters.
    (M) (2:09) Original Sound 8852 Oldies But Goodies Vol. 2.
                  *(this compact disc uses the "Waring - fds" noise
                  reduction process)*
    (M) (2:09) Original Sound 2223 Oldies But Goodies
                  Volumes 2,7,9,12 and 13 Box Set. *(this box set
                  uses the "Waring - fds" noise reduction process)*
    (M) (2:09) Original Sound 2500 Oldies But Goodies
                  Volumes 1-15 Box Set. *(this box set uses the
                  "Waring - fds" noise reduction process)*
    (M) (2:09) Original Sound CDGO-10 Golden Oldies Volume.
                  10.
    (S) (2:13) Ripete 2184-RE Ocean Drive Vol. 2.
    (S) (2:16) Varese Sarabande 5705 Dick Bartley Presents
                  Collector's Essentials: The 60's.
    (M) (2:08) MCA Special Products 20957 Solid Gold Rock &
                  Roll.
    (S) (2:15) Hip-O 40029 The Glory Of Love - '60s Sweet &
                  Soulful Love Songs.
    (E) (2:15) Collectables 5751 A Golden Classics Edition.

SHADOWS OF KNIGHT
1966 GLORIA
    (M) (2:34) Warner Special Products 27607 Highs Of The 60's.
    (M) (2:34) JCI 3101 Rockin' Sixties.
    (S) (2:34) Rhino 75754 Even More Nuggets.
    (M) (2:34) Time-Life 2CLR-02 Classic Rock - 1966.
    (S) (2:33) Rhino 71723 Dark Sides - Best Of.
    (M) (2:34) JCI 3126 1965 - Only Rock 'N Roll - 1969.
    (S) (2:33) Time-Life R968-09 Guitar Rock 1966-1967.

SHAGGY
1995 BOOMBASTIC
    (S) (4:06) Virgin 40158 Boombastic.
    (S) (4:34) Tommy Boy 1139 MTV Party To Go Volume 8.
                  (all selections on this cd are segued together)
    (S) (3:51) EMI-Capitol Music Group 54547 Hot Luv.
1995 IN THE SUMMERTIME
    (S) (3:55) Virgin 40158 Boombastic.
    (S) (3:55) Beast 53302 Summer Jammin'.
released as by MAXI PRIEST featuring SHAGGY:
1996 THAT GIRL
    (S) (3:57) Virgin 41612 Maxi Priest - Man With The Fun.
    (S) (3:54) Cold Front 6254 Club Mix '98. *(all selections on
                  this cd are segued together)*

SHAI
1992 IF I EVER FALL IN LOVE
    (S) (4:48) Gasoline Alley 10762 ...If I Ever Fall In Love.
                  (remix)
    (S) (3:08) Gasoline Alley 10762 ...If I Ever Fall In Love. *(a
                  cappella version)*
    (S) (3:08) MCA 11431 Quiet Storms 2. *(a cappella version)*
    (S) (3:08) Razor & Tie 4569 '90s Style. *(a cappella version)*
    (S) (4:47) Beast 53012 Smooth Love Of The 90's Vol. 1.
                  (remix)
    (S) (3:08) Time-Life R834-17 Body Talk - Heart To Heart.
                  (a cappella version)
1993 COMFORTER
    (S) (4:09) Gasoline Alley 10762 ...If I Ever Fall In Love.
1993 BABY I'M YOURS
    (S) (4:33) Gasoline Alley 10762 ...If I Ever Fall In Love.
1994 THE PLACE WHERE YOU BELONG
    (S) (4:22) MCA 11021 O.S.T. Beverly Hills Cop III.

SHAKESPEAR'S SISTER
1992 STAY
    (S) (3:46) London 828266 Hormonally Yours.

SHALAMAR
1977 UPTOWN FESTIVAL
    (S) (4:19) Priority 7976 Mega-Hits Dance Classics (Volume
                  6). *(:22 longer fade than the 45 version)*
    (S) (3:57) Solar/Epic 75308 Greatest Hits. *(45 version)*
    (S) (8:49) Epic/Legacy 52402 Club Epic Volume 2. *(LP
                  version)*
    (S) (8:51) Solar/Right Stuff 38361 Uptown Festival. *(LP
                  version)*
1980 THE SECOND TIME AROUND
    (S) (7:15) Epic 46087 Club Epic. *(12" single version but
                  slower)*
    (S) (3:41) Priority 7972 Mega-Hits Dance Classics Volume
                  2. *(45 version; buzz noticeable on fadeout)*
    (S) (4:28) Solar/Epic 75308 Greatest Hits. *(remixed with
                  additional instrumentation added)*
    (S) (4:27) Rhino 71618 Soul Train Hall Of Fame/20th
                  Anniversary. *(remixed with additional
                  instrumentation added)*
    (S) (7:13) Right Stuff/Solar 53038 Big Fun. *(12" single
                  version but slower)*
    (S) (6:30) Thump 9960 Old School Funk II. *(neither the 45,
                  LP or 12" single version)*
1982 A NIGHT TO REMEMBER
    (S) (5:01) Solar/Epic 75308 Greatest Hits. *(LP version)*
    (S) (5:11) Right Stuff/Solar 53039 Friends. *(LP version)*
1983 DEAD GIVEAWAY
    (S) (3:43) Priority 7972 Mega-Hits Dance Classics (Volume
                  2). *(45 version)*
    (S) (5:02) Solar/Right Stuff 57535 The Look. *(LP version)*
1984 DANCING IN THE SHEETS
    (dj copies of this 45 ran (3:44) and (4:01);
    commercial copies were all (4:01))
    (S) (4:00) Columbia 39242 O.S.T. Footloose.
    (S) (3:44) Priority 53703 Hot And Sexy - Passion And Soul.
                  (this is the dj 45 edit)
    (S) (3:43) Solar/Epic 75308 Greatest Hits. *(this is the dj 45
                  edit)*
    (S) (4:01) Solar 60385 Heart Break.
    (S) (4:02) Solar/Right Stuff 57536 Heart Break.

SHAMEN
1992 MOVE ANY MOUNTAIN
    (S) (3:25) Epic 48722 En-Tact.
    (S) (4:45) Beast 53022 Club Hitz Of The 90's Vol. 1. *(all
                  songs on this cd are segued together)*

SHANGRI-LAS
1964 REMEMBER (WALKIN' IN THE SAND)
    (M) (2:16) Rhino 70988 Best Of The Girl Groups Volume 1.
    (M) (2:14) Atlantic 82152 O.S.T. Goodfellas. *(buzz
                  noticeable on fadeout)*

(M) (2:16) Original Sound 8856 Oldies But Goodies Vol. 6. *(this compact disc uses the "Waring - fds" noise reduction process)*

(M) (2:16) Original Sound 2221 Oldies But Goodies Volumes 1,4,6,8 and 10 Box Set. *(this box set uses the "Waring - fds" noise reduction process)*

(M) (2:16) Original Sound 2500 Oldies But Goodies Volumes 1-15 Box Set. *(this box set uses the "Waring - fds" noise reduction process)*

(E) (2:16) Motown 5322 and 9087 Girl Groups: The Story Of A Sound.

(M) (2:15) Time-Life 2CLR-03 Classic Rock - 1964.

(M) (2:15) Time-Life SUD-17 Superhits - Mid 60's Classics.

(M) (2:15) Collectables 2500 WCBS-FM History Of Rock - The 60's Part 1.

(M) (2:15) Collectables 4500 History Of Rock/The 60s Part One.

(M) (2:16) Collectables 2604 WCBS-FM Jukebox Giants Vol. 2.

(M) (2:15) JCI 3125 1960 - Only Rock 'N Roll - 1964.

(M) (2:17) Mercury 314532371 Best Of.

(M) (2:19) Mercury 314528171 Growin' Up Too Fast - The Girl Group Anthology.

(M) (2:17) Columbia 67650 O.S.T. Stonewall.

(M) (2:15) Time-Life AM1-16 AM Gold - Mid '60s Classics.

(M) (2:16) Time-Life R857-17 The Heart Of Rock 'n' Roll: The Early '60s.

(S) (2:39) Taragon 1029 Very Best Of Red Bird/Blue Cat Records. *(:22 longer than the 45 or LP; missing echo throughout)*

1964 LEADER OF THE PACK
(actual 45 time is (2:59) not (2:48) as stated
on the record label)

(M) (2:51) Warner Special Products 27602 20 Party Classics.

(M) (2:51) Rhino 70625 Billboard's Top Rock & Roll Hits Of 1964.

(M) (2:51) Rhino 72007 Billboard's Top Rock & Roll Hits Of 1962-1966 Box Set.

(E) (2:48) Original Sound 8865 Oldies But Goodies Vol. 15. *(this compact disc uses the "Waring - fds" noise reduction process)*

(E) (2:48) Original Sound 2222 Oldies But Goodies Volumes 3,5,11,14 and 15 Box Set. *(this box set uses the "Waring - fds" noise reduction process)*

(E) (2:48) Original Sound 2500 Oldies But Goodies Volumes 1-15 Box Set. *(this box set uses the "Waring - fds" noise reduction process)*

(E) (2:47) Original Sound CDGO-9 Golden Oldies Volume. 9.

(E) (2:49) Original Sound 8881 Twenty-One #1 Hits. *(this compact disc uses the "Waring - fds" noise reduction process)*

(E) (2:48) Original Sound 8892 Dick Clark's 21 All-Time Hits Vol. 2.

(M) (2:51) Rhino 70988 Best Of The Girl Groups Volume 1.

(E) (2:48) Pair 1202 Best Of Buddah. *(mastered from vinyl)*

(M) (2:50) JCI 3110 Sock Hoppin' Sixties.

(E) (2:49) Motown 5322 and 9087 Girl Groups: The Story Of A Sound.

(S) (2:49) Era 5025 The Brill Building Sound. *(missing the line "one day my dad said find someone new")*

(E) (2:49) Compose 9923 James Dean/Tribute To A Rebel.

(M) (2:52) Time-Life 2RNR-10 Rock 'N' Roll Era - 1964.

(M) (2:48) Time-Life R962-08 History Of Rock 'N' Roll: Sound Of The City 1959-1965.

(M) (2:47) Collectables 2502 WCBS-FM History Of Rock - The 60's Part 3.

(M) (2:47) Collectables 4502 History Of Rock/The 60s Part Three.

(M) (2:50) Collectables 2510 WCBS-FM History Of Rock - The Rockin' 60's.

(M) (2:50) Collectables 4510 History Of Rock/The Rockin' 60s.

(M) (2:48) Collectables 2605 WCBS-FM Jukebox Giants Vol. 3.

(E) (2:51) MCA Special Products 20751 Rock Around The Oldies #2.

(M) (2:50) Polygram Special Markets 314520260 Number One Hits Of The Sixties.

(M) (2:57) DCC Compact Classics 078 Best Of Tragedy.

(M) (2:47) Collectables 2554 CBS-FM History Of Rock Volume 2. *(no fidelity)*

(S) (2:49) K-Tel 3035 Goofy Greats. *(missing the line "one day my dad said find someone new")*

(M) (2:50) Mercury 314532371 Best Of.

(M) (2:51) Mercury 314528171 Growin' Up Too Fast - The Girl Group Anthology.

(S) (2:58) Taragon 1029 Very Best Of Red Bird/Blue Cat Records.

(M) (2:51) Polygram Special Markets 314520516 45's On CD Volume 1.

(M) (2:50) Rebound 314520502 Leader Of The Pack.

1965 GIVE HIM A GREAT BIG KISS

(M) (2:10) Rhino 70988 Best Of The Girl Groups Volume 1.

(M) (2:09) Motown 5322 and 9087 Girl Groups: The Story Of A Sound.

(M) (2:04) Time-Life 2CLR-09 Classic Rock - 1964: The Beat Goes On.

(M) (2:04) Collectables 2501 WCBS-FM History Of Rock - The 60's Part 2.

(M) (2:04) Collectables 4501 History Of Rock/The 60s Part Two.

(M) (2:11) Special Music/Essex 5035 Prom Night - The 60's.

(M) (2:11) Mercury 314532371 Best Of.

(M) (2:11) Columbia 67650 O.S.T. Stonewall.

(S) (7:40) Columbia 67650 O.S.T. Stonewall. *(remix)*

(S) (2:12) Taragon 1029 Very Best Of Red Bird/Blue Cat Records. *(remix)*

(M) (2:10) Rebound 314520502 Leader Of The Pack.

1965 GIVE US YOUR BLESSINGS

(M) (3:13) Mercury 314532371 Best Of.

1965 I CAN NEVER GO HOME ANYMORE

(M) (3:12) Time-Life 2CLR-08 Classic Rock - 1965: The Beat Goes On.

(M) (3:11) Collectables 2501 WCBS-FM History Of Rock - The 60's Part 2.

(M) (3:11) Collectables 4501 History Of Rock/The 60s Part Two.

(M) (3:11) Mercury 314532371 Best Of.

(M) (3:12) Mercury 314528171 Growin' Up Too Fast - The Girl Group Anthology.

(M) (3:12) Simitar 55572 The Number One's: Hot In The '60s.

(S) (3:12) Taragon 1029 Very Best Of Red Bird/Blue Cat Records. *(includes an extra line at 2:30 that goes "listen, I'm not finished" which was not on the original 45 or LP)*

(M) (3:12) Polygram Special Markets 314520495 45's On CD Volume 2.

1966 LONG LIVE OUR LOVE

(M) (2:53) Mercury 314532371 Best Of.

SHANICE
1992 I LOVE YOUR SMILE

(S) (4:17) Motown 6319 Inner Child.

(S) (4:22) Motown 6358 Hitsville USA Volume Two.

(S) (4:16) Priority 50946 100% Party Hits Of The 90's Volume One.

(S) (4:17) Rebound 314520439 Soul Classics - Best Of The 90's.

(S) (4:17) Cold Front 6247 Classic Club Mix - Dance Jams. *(all selections on this cd are segued together)*

(S) (4:21) Motown 314530849 Motown 40 Forever.

released as by SHANICE featuring JOHNNY GILL:
1992 SILENT PRAYER

(S) (5:03) Motown 6319 Shanice - Inner Child.

released as by SHANICE:
1993 SAVING FOREVER FOR YOU

(S) (4:27) Giant 24465 Beverly Hills, 90210 - The Soundtrack.

SHANNON
1984 LET THE MUSIC PLAY
(dj copies of this 45 ran (3:48) and (4:38);
commercial copies were all (4:38))

(S) (5:30) Rhino 70576 Street Jams: Electric Funk - Part 2. *(remix)*

(S) (4:36) JCI 3149 1980 - Only Dance - 1984. *(45 version)*

SHANNON (Continued)

(S) (4:35) Rhino 72139 Billboard Hot R&B Hits 1984. *(45 version)*

(S) (5:30) Rhino 72062 Street Jams: Electric Funk Parts 1-4. *(remix)*

(S) (6:05) Epic 67506 Club Epic Volume 4. *(remix)*

(S) (4:36) Time-Life R988-17 Sounds Of The Eighties: The Mid '80s Take Two. *(45 version)*

DEL SHANNON
1961 RUNAWAY

(M) (2:19) Rhino 70622 Billboard's Top Rock & Roll Hits Of 1961.

(M) (2:19) Rhino 72007 Billboard's Top Rock & Roll Hits Of 1962-1966 Box Set.

(E) (2:17) JCI 3110 Sock Hoppin' Sixties.

(E) (2:18) Original Sound 8859 Oldies But Goodies Vol. 9. *(this compact disc uses the "Waring - fds" noise reduction process)*

(M) (2:17) Original Sound 8859r Oldies But Goodies Vol. 9. *(remastered edition)*

(M) (2:17) Original Sound 2223 Oldies But Goodies Volumes 2,7,9,12 and 13 Box Set. *(Volumes 2, 7 and 12 of this box set use the "Waring - fds" noise reduction process)*

(M) (2:17) Original Sound 2500 Oldies But Goodies Volumes 1-15 Box Set. *(most volumes in this box set use the "Waring - fds" noise reduction process)*

(E) (2:17) Original Sound 8881 Twenty-One #1 Hits. *(this compact disc uses the "Waring - fds" noise reduction process)*

(E) (2:16) Original Sound 8892 Dick Clark's 21 All-Time Hits Vol. 2.

(E) (2:17) Original Sound 1081 All #1 Hits.

(M) (2:18) Rhino 70977 Greatest Hits.

(S) (2:17) Rhino 70983 Little Town Flirt. *(alternate take)*

(M) (2:20) Pair 1293 Runaway.

(M) (2:17) MCA 8001 O.S.T. American Graffiti.

(M) (2:16) Time-Life 2RNR-04 Rock 'N' Roll Era - 1961. *(original pressings of this song on this cd were (E))*

(M) (2:15) Collectables 2510 WCBS-FM History Of Rock - The Rockin' 60's.

(M) (2:15) Collectables 4510 History Of Rock/The Rockin' 60s.

(M) (2:18) K-Tel 3062 Rockin' Rebels.

(M) (2:18) K-Tel 3008 60's Sock Hop.

(M) (2:18) Risky Business 66388 The Big Hurt/Songs To Cry By.

(M) (2:16) JCI 3125 1960 - Only Rock 'N Roll - 1964.

(M) (2:18) K-Tel 3125 Solid Gold Rock N' Roll.

(M) (2:18) Curb 77756 Greatest Hits.

(S) (2:18) Taragon 1022 Runaway/One Thousand Six Hundred Sixty One Seconds. *(alternate take; mastered from vinyl)*

(M) (2:17) Eclipse Music Group 64867 Rock 'n Roll Relix 1960-1961.

(M) (2:17) Eclipse Music Group 64872 Rock 'n Roll Relix 1960-1969.

(M) (2:18) Right Stuff 53319 Hot Rod Rock Volume 4: Hot Rod Rebels.

(M) (2:18) Music Club 50044 This Is - 16 Great Original Hit Recordings.

(M) (2:17) Simitar 55532 The Number One's: The '60s.

1961 HATS OFF TO LARRY

(M) (1:59) Rhino 70977 Greatest Hits.

(S) (2:00) Rhino 70983 Little Town Flirt.

(S) (2:00) Pair 1293 Runaway.

(S) (2:00) Special Music 4823 At His Best.

(S) (1:59) Time-Life 2RNR-04 Rock 'N' Roll Era - 1961. *(original pressings of this song on this cd were (E))*

(M) (1:55) Collectables 2510 WCBS-FM History Of Rock - The Rockin' 60's. *(mastered from vinyl)*

(M) (1:55) Collectables 4510 History Of Rock/The Rockin' 60s. *(mastered from vinyl)*

(M) (1:59) Curb 77756 Greatest Hits.

(S) (1:59) JCI 3166 #1 Radio Hits 1960 - Only Rock 'n Roll - 1964.

(M) (1:58) Music Club 50044 This Is - 16 Great Original Hit Recordings.

1961 SO LONG BABY

(M) (1:58) Rhino 70977 Greatest Hits.

(M) (1:59) Pair 1293 Runaway.

(M) (1:59) Special Music 4823 At His Best.

(M) (1:58) Curb 77756 Greatest Hits.

(M) (1:58) Music Club 50044 This Is - 16 Great Original Hit Recordings.

1963 LITTLE TOWN FLIRT

(M) (2:47) Rhino 70977 Greatest Hits.

(S) (2:47) Rhino 70983 Little Town Flirt.

(S) (2:47) Pair 1293 Runaway.

(S) (2:47) Special Music 4823 At His Best.

(S) (2:46) Time-Life 2RNR-02 Rock 'N' Roll Era - 1962.

(M) (2:47) Curb 77756 Greatest Hits.

(S) (2:46) Music Club 50044 This Is - 16 Great Original Hit Recordings.

1964 HANDY MAN

(M) (2:11) Rhino 70977 Greatest Hits.

(M) (2:08) Pair 1293 Runaway. *(truncated fade)*

(M) (2:08) Special Music 4823 At His Best. *(truncated fade)*

(M) (2:11) Curb 77756 Greatest Hits.

(M) (2:11) Music Club 50044 This Is - 16 Great Original Hit Recordings.

1965 KEEP SEARCHIN' (WE'LL FOLLOW THE SUN)

(M) (2:10) Rhino 70977 Greatest Hits.

(M) (2:08) Pair 1293 Runaway.

(M) (2:08) Special Music 4823 At His Best.

(M) (2:10) Time-Life 2RNR-10 Rock 'N' Roll Era - 1964.

(M) (2:06) Collectables 2500 WCBS-FM History Of Rock - The 60's Part 1.

(M) (2:06) Collectables 4500 History Of Rock/The 60s Part One.

(M) (2:10) Curb 77756 Greatest Hits.

(S) (2:06) Taragon 1022 Runaway/One Thousand Six Hundred Sixty One Seconds. *(mastered from vinyl)*

(M) (2:10) Music Club 50044 This Is - 16 Great Original Hit Recordings.

1965 STRANGER IN TOWN

(M) (2:30) Rhino 70977 Greatest Hits.

(M) (2:30) Pair 1293 Runaway.

(M) (2:30) Special Music 4823 At His Best.

(M) (2:30) Curb 77756 Greatest Hits.

(S) (2:29) Taragon 1022 Runaway/One Thousand Six Hundred Sixty One Seconds. *(mastered from vinyl)*

(M) (2:29) Music Club 50044 This Is - 16 Great Original Hit Recordings.

1982 SEA OF LOVE

(S) (2:33) Varese Sarabande 5927 Drop Down And Get Me.

DEE DEE SHARP
1962 MASHED POTATO TIME

(M) (2:26) Original Sound CDGO-5 Golden Oldies Volume. 5.

(M) (2:26) Original Sound 8856 Oldies But Goodies Vol. 6. *(this compact disc uses the "Waring - fds" noise reduction process)*

(M) (2:26) Original Sound 2221 Oldies But Goodies Volumes 1,4,6,8 and 10 Box Set. *(this box set uses the "Waring - fds" noise reduction process)*

(M) (2:26) Original Sound 2500 Oldies But Goodies Volumes 1-15 Box Set. *(this box set uses the "Waring - fds" noise reduction process)*

(E) (2:26) Original Sound 1081 All #1 Hits.

(E) (2:27) Original Sound 8881 Twenty-One #1 Hits. *(this compact disc uses the "Waring - fds" noise reduction process)*

(E) (2:26) Original Sound 9601 Best Of Oldies But Goodies Vol. 1.

1962 GRAVY (FOR MY MASHED POTATOES)

(S) (2:10) Hollywood 61334 O.S.T. Sister Act. *(rerecorded)*

(S) (2:10) Hollywood 62080 O.S.T. Sister Act & Sister Act 2: Back In The Habit. *(rerecorded)*

(S) (2:10)   K-Tel 3409   Funniest Food Songs. *(rerecorded)*

1962 RIDE!
1963 DO THE BIRD
1963 WILD!

SANDIE SHAW
1965 GIRL DON'T COME
    (E) (2:12)   Time-Life R962-07   History Of Rock 'N' Roll: The British Invasion 1964-1966.

TOMMY SHAW
1984 GIRLS WITH GUNS

DUNCAN SHEIK
1997 BARELY BREATHING
    (S) (4:14)   Atlantic 82879   Duncan Sheik.

SHEILA E.
1984 THE GLAMOROUS LIFE
    (S) (9:00)   Sandstone 33047 and 5015   Cosmopolitan Volume 1. *(LP version)*
    (S) (3:41)   JCI 3127   1980 - Only Rock 'N Roll - 1984. *(45 version)*
    (S) (9:00)   Warner Brothers 25107   The Glamorous Life. *(LP version)*
    (S) (6:33)   Warner Brothers 25107   The Glamorous Life. *(12" single version)*
    (S) (3:40)   Time-Life R988-06   Sounds Of The Eighties: 1984. *(45 version)*
    (S) (6:34)   Rebound 314520357   World Of Dance - The 80's. *(12" single version)*
    (S) (3:43)   Rhino 72838   Disco Queens: The 80's. *(45 version)*
1984 THE BELLE OF ST. MARK
    (S) (5:09)   Warner Brothers 25107   The Glamorous Life. *(LP version)*
1986 A LOVE BIZARRE
    (S) (12:16)   Warner Brothers 25317 Romance 1600. *(LP version)*
    (S) (3:46)   JCI 3186   1985 - Only Love - 1989. *(45 version)*
    (S) (3:45)   Chronicles 314553403   Cosmic Funk. *(45 version)*
    (S) (3:46)   K-Tel 3868   Hot Ladies Of Pop. *(45 version)*

SHELLS
1961 BABY OH BABY
    (M) (2:27)   Collectables 2507   History Of Rock - The Doo Wop Era Part 1.
    (M) (2:27)   Collectables 4507   History Of Rock/The Doo Wop Era Part One.
    (M) (2:27)   Rhino 71463   Doo Wop Box.
    (M) (2:24)   Time-Life 2RNR-45   Rock 'N' Roll Era - Street Corner Serenade.
    (M) (2:28)   Collectables 2607   WCBS-FM For Lovers Only Vol. 3.
    (M) (2:28)   Collectables 5173   Memories Of Times Square Record Shop Volume 2.
    (M) (2:27)   Collectables 5077   Golden Classics.
    (M) (2:27)   Time-Life R857-19   The Heart Of Rock 'n' Roll 1960-1961 Take Three.

SHE MOVES
1997 BREAKING ALL THE RULES
    (S) (3:27)   Geffen 25161   Breaking All The Rules.
    (S) (3:29)   Beast 54112   Boom! *(remix)*

SHEP and THE LIMELITES
1961 DADDY'S HOME
    (M) (2:48)   Rhino 75763   Best Of Doo Wop Ballads.
    (M) (2:50)   Rhino 70952   Best Of The Heartbeats.
    (E) (2:44)   Original Sound 8855   Oldies But Goodies Vol. 5. *(this compact disc uses the "Waring - fds" noise reduction process; ambient background noise throughout the disc)*
    (E) (2:44)   Original Sound 2222   Oldies But Goodies Volumes 3,5,11,14 and 15 Box Set. *(this box set uses the "Waring - fds" noise reduction process; ambient background noise throughout the song)*

    (E) (2:44)   Original Sound 2500   Oldies But Goodies Volumes 1-15 Box Set. *(this box set uses the "Waring - fds" noise reduction process; ambient background noise throughout the song)*
    (E) (2:43)   Original Sound CDGO-12   Golden Oldies Volume. 12.
    (M) (2:50)   Collectables 8805   Heartbeats/Shep & The Limelites For Collectors Only.
    (S) (2:41)   Special Music 4913   Rock & Roll Revival. *(live)*
    (M) (2:51)   Rhino 71463   Doo Wop Box.
    (M) (2:50)   Rhino 70622   Billboard's Top Rock & Roll Hits Of 1961. *(found only on the 1993 reissue of this cd)*
    (E) (2:44)   Original Sound 8905r   13 Of The Best Doo Wop Love Songs.
    (M) (2:44)   Original Sound 9326   Best Love Songs Vol. 1 & 2.
    (E) (2:44)   Original Sound 4001   Art Laboe's 60 Killer Oldies.
    (E) (2:44)   Original Sound 1236   Best Love Songs Box Set.
    (M) (2:50)   Time-Life 2RNR-04   Rock 'N' Roll Era - 1961.
    (M) (2:50)   Time-Life RHD-14   Rhythm & Blues - 1961.
    (M) (2:50)   Collectables 2601   WCBS-FM History Of Rock - The Group Sounds Vol. 2.
    (M) (2:48)   Time-Life R103-27   Love Me Tender.
    (M) (2:50)   Time-Life R10513   40 Lovin' Oldies.
    (M) (2:50)   Polygram Special Markets 314520259   Doo Wop Classics.
    (M) (2:50)   Right Stuff 30578   Slow Jams: The 60's Volume 4.
    (M) (2:51)   Time-Life R857-03   The Heart Of Rock 'n' Roll - 1961.
    (M) (2:51)   Thump 7050   Low Rider Oldies Volume 5.
    (M) (2:51)   Rhino 72157   Doo Wop Memories, Vol. 2.
    (M) (2:51)   Flashback 72716   Doo Wop - Sh-Boom.
    (M) (2:50)   Time-Life R838-19   Solid Gold Soul 1961.

SHEPHERD SISTERS
1957 ALONE (WHY MUST I BE ALONE)
    (M) (2:31)   Time-Life 2RNR-49   Rock 'N' Roll Era - Lost Treasures II.

T.G. SHEPPARD
1981 I LOVED 'EM EVERY ONE
    (S) (3:37)   Warner Brothers 26468   All Time Greatest Hits.
    (S) (3:36)   Curb 77545   Best Of.
    (S) (3:35)   K-Tel 3113   Country Music Classics Volume XXI.
    (S) (3:35)   K-Tel 3356   101 Greatest Country Hits Vol. Two: Country Sunshine.

SHERIFF
1989 WHEN I'M WITH YOU
    (S) (3:53)   K-Tel 898   Romantic Hits Of The 80's.
    (S) (3:53)   Priority 7077   80's Greatest Rock Hits Volume 5 - From The Heart.
    (S) (3:52)   Sandstone 33045 and 5011   Rock The First Volume Five.
    (S) (3:46)   Priority 53798   Best Of 80's Rock Volume 5.
    (S) (3:51)   Capitol 91216   Sheriff.
    (S) (3:52)   Madacy Entertainment 1988   Rock On 1988.
    (S) (3:53)   Time-Life R988-13   Sounds Of The Eighties: 1989.
    (S) (3:52)   K-Tel 3866   The 80's: Number One Pop Hits.
    (S) (3:53)   Time-Life R834-11   Body Talk - After Dark.

ALLAN SHERMAN
1963 HELLO MUDDAH, HELLO FADDUH! (A LETTER FROM CAMP)
    (S) (2:47)   Rhino 75768   Dr. Demento Presents.
    (S) (2:44)   Rhino 70743   Dr. Demento 20th Anniversary Collection.
    (S) (2:50)   Rhino 75771   My Son, The Greatest: Best Of.
    (S) (2:41)   Time-Life HPD-40   Your Hit Parade - Golden Goofers.
    (S) (2:43)   K-Tel 3411   Tacky Tunes.
1965 CRAZY DOWNTOWN
    (S) (2:56)   Rhino 75771   My Son, The Greatest: Best Of.

BOBBY SHERMAN
1969 LITTLE WOMAN
    (S) (2:19)   Restless 2520   Very Best Of.
    (S) (2:26)   K-Tel 3427   Bobby Sherman.

BOBBY SHERMAN (Continued)

  (S) (2:26) K-Tel 3432 Greatest Hits.
  (S) (2:20) Varese Sarabande 5719 Bubblegum Classics Volume Three.

1970 LA LA LA (IF I HAD YOU)

  (S) (2:40) Restless 2520 Very Best Of.
  (S) (2:46) K-Tel 3428 Here Comes Bobby.
  (S) (2:47) K-Tel 3386 Best Of Bubblegum Music.
  (S) (2:46) K-Tel 3432 Greatest Hits.

1970 EASY COME, EASY GO

  (S) (2:38) Restless 2520 Very Best Of.
  (S) (2:38) Rhino 71228 Yesterday's Heroes: 70's Teen Idols.
  (S) (2:39) Varese Sarabande 5575 Bubblegum Classics Volume Two.
  (S) (2:41) K-Tel 3428 Here Comes Bobby.
  (S) (2:41) K-Tel 3432 Greatest Hits.

1970 HEY, MISTER SUN

  (S) (2:29) Restless 2520 Very Best Of.
  (S) (2:37) K-Tel 3429 With Love, Bobby.
  (S) (2:37) K-Tel 3432 Greatest Hits.

1970 JULIE, DO YOU LOVE ME

  (S) (2:53) Rhino 70923 Super Hits Of The 70's Volume 3.
  (S) (2:53) Rhino 72009 Super Hits Of The 70's Volumes 1-4 Box Set.
  (S) (2:52) Restless 2520 Very Best Of.
  (S) (2:53) Rhino 71207 70's Smash Hits Volume 3.
  (S) (2:52) Rhino 71228 Yesterday's Heroes: 70's Teen Idols.
  (S) (2:52) Varese Sarabande 5535 Bubblegum Classics Volume One.
  (S) (2:52) K-Tel 3211 70's Teen Heart-Throbs.
  (S) (2:52) K-Tel 3429 With Love, Bobby.
  (S) (2:52) K-Tel 3432 Greatest Hits.
  (S) (2:53) Flashback 72683 '70s Radio Hits Volume 3.
  (S) (2:53) Flashback 72090 '70s Radio Hits Box Set.
  (S) (2:52) Rhino 72819 16 Magazine - Who's Your Fave Rave.

1971 CRIED LIKE A BABY

  (S) (3:17) Restless 2520 Very Best Of.
  (S) (3:17) K-Tel 3430 Portrait Of Bobby.
  (S) (3:17) K-Tel 3432 Greatest Hits.

1971 THE DRUM

  (S) (2:16) Restless 2520 Very Best Of.
  (S) (2:17) K-Tel 3430 Portrait Of Bobby.
  (S) (2:17) K-Tel 3432 Greatest Hits.

SHERRYS
1962 POP POP POP-PIE

SHIELDS
1958 YOU CHEATED

  (M) (2:25) MCA 5936 Vintage Music Volumes 11 & 12.
  (M) (2:25) MCA 31209 Vintage Music Volume 12.
  (M) (2:25) Original Sound 8853 Oldies But Goodies Vol. 3. *(this compact disc uses the "Waring - fds" noise reduction process)*
  (M) (2:25) Original Sound 2222 Oldies But Goodies Volumes 3,5,11,14 and 15 Box Set. *(this box set uses the "Waring - fds" noise reduction process)*
  (M) (2:25) Original Sound 2500 Oldies But Goodies Volumes 1-15 Box Set. *(this box set uses the "Waring - fds" noise reduction process)*
  (M) (2:18) Original Sound 1960 Memories Of El Monte.
  (M) (2:18) Original Sound 4001 Art Laboe's 60 Killer Oldies.
  (M) (2:25) Rhino 71463 Doo Wop Box.
  (M) (2:25) Time-Life 2RNR-21 Rock 'N' Roll Era - 1958 Still Rockin'.
  (M) (2:25) Collectables 2503 WCBS-FM History Of Rock - The 50's Part 2.
  (M) (2:24) Collectables 4503 History Of Rock/The 50s Part Two.
  (M) (2:25) Time-Life R102-17 Lost Treasures Of Rock 'N' Roll.
  (M) (2:25) Time-Life R857-04 The Heart Of Rock 'n' Roll - 1958.
  (M) (2:25) Thump 7060 Low Rider Oldies Volume 6.
  (M) (2:24) Varese Sarabande 5687 History Of Dot Records Volume Two.

SHIRELLES
1958 I MET HIM ON A SUNDAY (RONDE-RONDE)

  (M) (2:13) Rhino 70989 Best Of The Girl Groups Volume 2.
  (M) (2:12) MCA 5937 Vintage Music Volumes 13 & 14.
  (M) (2:12) MCA 31211 Vintage Music Volume 14.
  (E) (2:01) Special Music 4805 Greatest Hits. *(rerecording)*
  (E) (2:40) Pair 1241 Dedicated To You. *(rerecording)*
  (M) (2:12) Time-Life 2RNR-33 Rock 'N' Roll Era - The 50's Last Dance.
  (M) (2:12) MCA 11119 The Decca Rock 'N' Roll Collection.
  (M) (2:13) Rhino 71807 Very Best Of.
  (S) (1:58) Tomato 71731 World's Greatest Girls Group. *(rerecording)*
  (M) (2:12) MCA Special Products 20900 Rock Around The Oldies #3.
  (E) (2:12) MCA Special Products 20948 Biggest Summer Hits.
  (S) (1:59) Curb 77782 Greatest Hits. *(rerecording)*
  (M) (2:12) MCA Special Products 20957 Solid Gold Rock & Roll.

1960 TONIGHT'S THE NIGHT

  (S) (1:59) Rhino 75891 Wonder Women.
  (S) (2:00) Rhino 75897 Anthology.
  (S) (1:59) Collectables 5247 Golden Classics.
  (S) (1:55) Special Music 4805 Greatest Hits.
  (S) (1:56) Pair 1241 Dedicated To You.
  (S) (1:58) Capricorn 42003 The Scepter Records Story. *(includes :05 of studio talk)*
  (S) (1:57) Time-Life 2RNR-22 Rock 'N' Roll Era - 1960 Still Rockin'.
  (S) (1:59) Ripete 0003 Coolin' Out/24 Carolina Classics Vol. 3.
  (S) (1:56) Time-Life OPCD-4517 Tonight's The Night.
  (S) (1:59) Rhino 71807 Very Best Of.
  (S) (1:55) Collectables 8821 For Collectors Only.
  (S) (1:58) Tomato 71731 World's Greatest Girls Group.
  (S) (1:57) Curb 77782 Greatest Hits.
  (S) (1:55) Time-Life R857-19 The Heart Of Rock 'n' Roll 1960-1961 Take Three.

1961 WILL YOU LOVE ME TOMORROW

  (S) (2:41) Rhino 70622 Billboard's Top Rock & Roll Hits Of 1961.
  (S) (2:41) Rhino 72007 Billboard's Top Rock & Roll Hits Of 1962-1966 Box Set.
  (S) (2:40) Original Sound 8864 Oldies But Goodies Vol. 14. *(this compact disc uses the "Waring - fds" noise reduction process)*
  (S) (2:40) Original Sound 2222 Oldies But Goodies Volumes 3,5,11,14 and 15 Box Set. *(this box set uses the "Waring - fds" noise reduction process)*
  (S) (2:40) Original Sound 2500 Oldies But Goodies Volumes 1-15 Box Set. *(this box set uses the "Waring - fds" noise reduction process)*
  (S) (2:34) Original Sound CDGO-6 Golden Oldies Volume. 6.
  (S) (2:35) Original Sound 8881 Twenty-One #1 Hits. *(this compact disc uses the "Waring - fds" noise reduction process)*
  (S) (2:35) Original Sound 1081 All #1 Hits.
  (S) (2:40) Rhino 70988 Best Of The Girl Groups Volume 1.
  (S) (2:33) JCI 3102 Love Sixties.
  (S) (2:40) RCA 6965 More Dirty Dancing.
  (S) (2:36) Motown 5322 and 9087 Girl Groups: The Story Of A Sound.
  (S) (2:40) Rhino 75897 Anthology.
  (S) (2:41) Collectables 5247 Golden Classics.
  (S) (2:39) Special Music 4805 Greatest Hits.
  (S) (2:40) Pair 1241 Dedicated To You.
  (M) (2:40) Capricorn 42003 The Scepter Records Story.
  (S) (2:41) Era 5025 The Brill Building Sound.
  (S) (2:41) Ripete 0001 Coolin' Out/24 Carolina Classics Volume 1.
  (S) (2:41) Time-Life 2RNR-04 Rock 'N' Roll Era - 1961.
  (S) (2:40) Time-Life RHD-14 Rhythm & Blues - 1961.
  (S) (2:40) Time-Life SUD-15 Superhits - The Early 60's.
  (S) (2:40) Time-Life R962-08 History Of Rock 'N' Roll: Sound Of The City 1959-1965.

(S) (2:40) Motown 6763 Rites Of Rhythm & Blues Volume 2.
(S) (2:40) Time-Life R10513 40 Lovin' Oldies.
(S) (2:40) Rhino 71807 Very Best Of.
(S) (2:39) Collectables 8821 For Collectors Only.
(S) (2:40) JCI 3125 1960 - Only Rock 'N Roll - 1964.
(S) (2:39) Tomato 71731 World's Greatest Girls Group.
(S) (2:41) Curb 77782 Greatest Hits.
(S) (2:40) Collectables 2554 CBS-FM History Of Rock Volume 2.
(S) (2:33) Nick At Nite/550 Music/Epic 67768 Fonzie's Make Out Music.
(S) (2:41) LaserLight 12423 Best Of.
(S) (2:40) Eclipse Music Group 64867 Rock 'n Roll Relix 1960-1961.
(S) (2:40) Eclipse Music Group 64872 Rock 'n Roll Relix 1960-1969.
(S) (2:40) Time-Life R857-10 The Heart Of Rock 'n' Roll 1960-1961.
(S) (2:40) Time-Life AM1-19 AM Gold - The Early '60s.
(S) (2:40) Right Stuff 53320 Hot Rod Rock Volume 5: Back Seat Movers.
(S) (2:40) Time-Life R838-19 Solid Gold Soul 1961.
(M) (2:39) K-Tel 3888 Great R&B Female Groups Hits Of The 60's.
(S) (2:40) Thump 7070 Lowrider Oldies Volume 7.

1961 DEDICATED TO THE ONE I LOVE
(M) (2:04) DCC Compact Classics 031 Back Seat Jams.
(M) (2:02) Original Sound 8860 Oldies But Goodies Vol. 10. *(this compact disc uses the "Waring - fds" noise reduction process)*
(M) (2:02) Original Sound 2221 Oldies But Goodies Volumes 1,4,6,8 and 10 Box Set. *(this box set uses the "Waring - fds" noise reduction process)*
(M) (2:02) Original Sound 2500 Oldies But Goodies Volumes 1-15 Box Set. *(this box set uses the "Waring - fds" noise reduction process)*
(M) (2:02) Original Sound CDGO-1 Golden Oldies Volume. 1.
(M) (2:03) Rhino 75897 Anthology.
(M) (2:03) Collectables 5247 Golden Classics.
(M) (2:01) Special Music 4805 Greatest Hits.
(M) (2:01) Pair 1241 Dedicated To You.
(M) (2:03) Capricorn 42003 The Scepter Records Story.
(M) (2:02) Original Sound 8878 Art Laboe's Dedicated To You.
(M) (2:02) Original Sound 4001 Art Laboe's 60 Killer Oldies.
(E) (2:01) Original Sound 8905r 13 Of The Best Doo Wop Love Songs.
(E) (2:01) Original Sound 9326 Best Love Songs Vol. 1 & 2.
(E) (2:01) Original Sound 4001 Art Laboe's 60 Killer Oldies.
(E) (2:01) Original Sound 1236 Best Love Songs Box Set.
(M) (2:03) Time-Life 2RNR-04 Rock 'N' Roll Era - 1961.
(M) (2:00) Collectables 2606 WCBS-FM For Lovers Only Vol. 2.
(M) (2:01) Thump 7010 Low Rider Oldies Volume 1.
(M) (2:01) Rhino 71582 Billboard Top Pop Hits, 1961.
(M) (2:03) Ripete 2163-RE Ebb Tide.
(M) (2:03) Rhino 71807 Very Best Of.
(M) (2:01) Collectables 8821 For Collectors Only.
(M) (2:02) Tomato 71731 World's Greatest Girls Group.
(M) (2:03) Right Stuff 30578 Slow Jams: The 60's Volume 4.
(M) (2:01) Time-Life R857-03 The Heart Of Rock 'n' Roll - 1961.
(M) (2:03) Curb 77782 Greatest Hits.
(M) (2:01) Rhino 72507 Doo Wop Box II.
(M) (2:03) Nick At Nite/550 Music/Epic 67689 Stand By Your Man.
(M) (2:03) LaserLight 12423 Best Of.
(M) (2:03) Eclipse Music Group 64867 Rock 'n Roll Relix 1960-1961.
(M) (2:03) Eclipse Music Group 64872 Rock 'n Roll Relix 1960-1969.

1961 MAMA SAID
(S) (2:09) Rhino 75891 Wonder Women.

(E) (2:09) Original Sound 8855 Oldies But Goodies Vol. 5. *(this compact disc uses the "Waring - fds" noise reduction process; ambient background noise throughout the disc)*
(E) (2:09) Original Sound 2222 Oldies But Goodies Volumes 3,5,11,14 and 15 Box Set. *(this box set uses the "Waring - fds" noise reduction process; ambient background noise throughout the song)*
(E) (2:09) Original Sound 2500 Oldies But Goodies Volumes 1-15 Box Set. *(this box set uses the "Waring - fds" noise reduction process; ambient background noise throughout the song)*
(E) (2:08) Original Sound CDGO-3 Golden Oldies Volume. 3.
(S) (2:07) Garland 011 Footstompin' Oldies.
(S) (2:09) Rhino 75897 Anthology.
(S) (2:09) Collectables 5247 Golden Classics.
(S) (2:04) Special Music 4805 Greatest Hits.
(S) (2:05) Pair 1241 Dedicated To You.
(S) (2:21) Capricorn 42003 The Scepter Records Story. *(alternate take)*
(S) (2:05) Time-Life 2RNR-18 Rock 'N' Roll Era - 1961 Still Rockin'.
(S) (3:01) Ripete 0003 Coolin' Out/24 Carolina Classics Vol. 3. *(time includes a :53 fake introduction which overlaps the true introduction to the song)*
(M) (2:09) Sundazed 6016 Sing To Trumpets And Strings.
(S) (2:09) Rhino 71807 Very Best Of.
(S) (2:04) Collectables 8821 For Collectors Only.
(S) (2:06) Tomato 71731 World's Greatest Girls Group.
(S) (2:09) Curb 77782 Greatest Hits.4
(S) (2:10) King 1421 Party Time Rock & Roll.
(S) (2:09) LaserLight 12423 Best Of.
(S) (2:06) Columbia 67916 O.S.T. One Fine Day.

1961 A THING OF THE PAST
(S) (2:36) Rhino 75897 Anthology.
(S) (2:36) Collectables 5247 Golden Classics.
(S) (2:35) Pair 1241 Dedicated To You.
(S) (2:35) Time-Life 2RNR-42 Rock 'N' Roll Era - The 60's Sock Hop.
(S) (2:36) Rhino 71807 Very Best Of.
(S) (2:36) Collectables 8821 For Collectors Only.
(S) (2:35) Tomato 71731 World's Greatest Girls Group.

1961 BIG JOHN
(S) (2:20) Rhino 75897 Anthology.
(*) (*:**) Special Music 4805 Greatest Hits. *(the cd jacket states that "BIG JOHN" is track 11, when in reality track 11 is "THANK YOU BABY")*
(M) (2:24) Capricorn 42003 The Scepter Records Story. *(includes :05 of studio talk)*
(S) (2:17) Sundazed 6012 Baby It's You.
(S) (2:20) Rhino 71807 Very Best Of.
(S) (2:17) Collectables 8821 For Collectors Only.
(S) (2:17) Tomato 71731 World's Greatest Girls Group.
(S) (2:16) LaserLight 12423 Best Of.

1962 BABY IT'S YOU
(S) (2:37) Rhino 70988 Best Of The Girl Groups Volume 1. *(LP lyrics)*
(S) (2:38) Atlantic 81885 O.S.T. Stealing Home. *(LP lyrics)*
(M) (2:40) Warner Brothers 3359 O.S.T. The Wanderers. *(45 lyrics)*
(S) (2:38) Rhino 75897 Anthology. *(LP lyrics)*
(S) (2:37) Collectables 5247 Golden Classics. *(LP lyrics)*
(S) (2:36) Special Music 4805 Greatest Hits. *(LP lyrics)*
(S) (2:36) Pair 1241 Dedicated To You. *(LP lyrics)*
(M) (2:41) Capricorn 42003 The Scepter Records Story. *(45 lyrics)*
(M) (2:40) Sundazed 6012 Baby It's You. *(45 lyrics)*
(M) (2:39) Time-Life 2RNR-02 Rock 'N' Roll Era - 1962. *(45 lyrics)*
(S) (2:34) Time-Life RHD-11 Rhythm & Blues - 1962. *(LP lyrics)*
(S) (2:36) Time-Life OPCD-4517 Tonight's The Night. *(LP lyrics)*
(S) (2:39) LaserLight 12320 Love Songs. *(LP lyrics)*

(M) (2:41) Rhino 71807 Very Best Of. *(45 lyrics)*
(M) (2:40) Collectables 8821 For Collectors Only. *(45 lyrics)*
(S) (2:35) Tomato 71731 World's Greatest Girls Group. *(LP lyrics)*
(S) (2:39) Curb 77782 Greatest Hits. *(LP lyrics)*
(S) (2:37) Hip-O 40029 The Glory Of Love - '60s Sweet & Soulful Love Songs. *(LP lyrics)*
(M) (2:40) Time-Life R857-06 The Heart Of Rock 'n' Roll 1962. *(45 lyrics)*
(S) (2:34) Time-Life R838-18 Solid Gold Soul 1962. *(LP lyrics)*

1962 SOLDIER BOY
(S) (2:39) Rhino 70623 Billboard's Top Rock & Roll Hits Of 1962.
(S) (2:39) Rhino 72007 Billboard's Top Rock & Roll Hits Of 1962-1966 Box Set.
(S) (2:40) Original Sound 8854 Oldies But Goodies Vol. 4. *(this compact disc uses the "Waring - fds" noise reduction process)*
(S) (2:40) Original Sound 2221 Oldies But Goodies Volumes 1,4,6,8 and 10 Box Set. *(this box set uses the "Waring - fds" noise reduction process)*
(S) (2:40) Original Sound 2500 Oldies But Goodies Volumes 1-15 Box Set. *(this box set uses the "Waring - fds" noise reduction process)*
(S) (2:39) Original Sound CDGO-2 Golden Oldies Volume. 2.
(S) (2:40) Original Sound 8892 Dick Clark's 21 All-Time Hits Vol. 2.
(S) (2:39) Rhino 75891 Wonder Women.
(S) (2:39) Garland 012 Remember When.
(M) (2:39) Warner Brothers 3359 O.S.T. The Wanderers.
(S) (2:41) MCA 6340 O.S.T. Born On The Fourth Of July.
(S) (2:39) Rhino 75897 Anthology.
(M) (2:39) Collectables 5247 Golden Classics.
(S) (2:38) Special Music 4805 Greatest Hits.
(S) (2:38) Pair 1241 Dedicated To You.
(S) (2:44) Capricorn 42003 The Scepter Records Story. *(includes a :04 countoff)*
(S) (2:39) Sundazed 6012 Baby It's You.
(S) (2:39) JCI 3112 Pop Sixties.
(S) (2:39) Time-Life 2RNR-02 Rock 'N' Roll Era - 1962.
(S) (2:38) Time-Life SUD-06 Superhits - 1962.
(S) (2:39) Rhino 71807 Very Best Of.
(S) (2:39) Collectables 8821 For Collectors Only.
(S) (2:38) Tomato 71731 World's Greatest Girls Group.
(S) (2:39) Curb 77782 Greatest Hits.
(S) (2:38) Collectables 2554 CBS-FM History Of Rock Volume 2.
(S) (2:39) LaserLight 12423 Best Of.
(S) (2:39) Eclipse Music Group 64868 Rock 'n Roll Relix 1962-1963.
(S) (2:39) Eclipse Music Group 64872 Rock 'n Roll Relix 1960-1969.
(S) (2:38) Time-Life R857-12 The Heart Of Rock 'n' Roll 1962-1963.
(S) (2:39) Time-Life AM1-18 AM Gold - 1962.
(S) (2:37) Compose 131 Unforgettable - Gold For The Road.
(S) (2:38) Time-Life R857-21 The Heart Of Rock 'n' Roll Slow Dancing Classics.

1962 WELCOME HOME BABY
(S) (2:31) Pair 1241 Dedicated To You.
(M) (2:31) Capricorn 42003 The Scepter Records Story.
(S) (2:30) Sundazed 6013 Shirelles & King Curtis Give A Twist Party.
(S) (2:31) Rhino 71807 Very Best Of.
(M) (2:31) Collectables 8821 For Collectors Only.
(S) (2:30) Tomato 71731 World's Greatest Girls Group.
(M) (2:31) Curb 77782 Greatest Hits.
(M) (2:31) LaserLight 12423 Best Of.

1963 EVERYBODY LOVES A LOVER
(S) (2:40) Rhino 75897 Anthology.
(S) (2:39) Collectables 5247 Golden Classics.
(S) (2:39) Special Music 4805 Greatest Hits.
(S) (2:38) Pair 1241 Dedicated To You.
(S) (2:39) Time-Life 2RNR-25 Rock 'N' Roll Era - The 60's Keep On Rockin'.

(S) (2:40) Rhino 71807 Very Best Of.
(S) (2:38) Collectables 8821 For Collectors Only.
(S) (2:38) Tomato 71731 World's Greatest Girls Group.
(S) (2:40) Curb 77782 Greatest Hits.
(S) (2:40) LaserLight 12423 Best Of.

1963 FOOLISH LITTLE GIRL
(S) (2:18) Rhino 75897 Anthology.
(S) (2:17) Collectables 5247 Golden Classics.
(S) (2:14) Special Music 4805 Greatest Hits.
(S) (2:15) Pair 1241 Dedicated To You.
(S) (2:15) Capricorn 42003 The Scepter Records Story.
(S) (2:18) Era 5025 The Brill Building Sound.
(S) (2:17) Time-Life 2RNR-19 Rock 'N' Roll Era - 1963 Still Rockin'.
(M) (2:18) Sundazed 6017 Foolish Little Girl.
(E) (2:14) Thump 7040 Low Rider Oldies Volume 4.
(S) (2:17) Rhino 71807 Very Best Of.
(S) (2:15) Collectables 8821 For Collectors Only.
(S) (2:16) Tomato 71731 World's Greatest Girls Group.
(S) (2:18) Curb 77782 Greatest Hits.
(S) (2:18) LaserLight 12423 Best Of.
(S) (2:15) Time-Life R857-18 The Heart Of Rock 'n' Roll 1962-1963 Take Two.

1963 DON'T SAY GOODNIGHT AND MEAN GOODBYE
(S) (2:41) Rhino 75897 Anthology.
(S) (2:40) Collectables 5247 Golden Classics.
(S) (2:40) Pair 1241 Dedicated To You.
(M) (2:49) Sundazed 6017 Foolish Little Girl.
(S) (2:41) Rhino 71807 Very Best Of.
(S) (2:39) Collectables 8821 For Collectors Only.
(S) (2:40) Tomato 71731 World's Greatest Girls Group.
(S) (2:40) LaserLight 12423 Best Of.

DON SHIRLEY TRIO
1961 WATER BOY
(S) (2:32) Collectors' Choice 003/4 Instrumental Gems Of The 60's. *(alternate take)*
(M) (2:54) Varese Sarabande 5579 History Of Cadence Records Volume 2. *(45 version)*
(M) (4:44) Collectables 5746 Golden Classics. *(LP version)*

SHIRLEY and COMPANY
1975 SHAME, SHAME, SHAME
(S) (3:56) Rhino 70984 The Disco Years Volume 1. *(poor stereo separation)*
(S) (3:51) Rhino 70554 Soul Hits Of The 70's Volume 14. *(poor stereo separation)*
(S) (3:48) Priority 7057 Mega-Hits Dance Classics Volume 8. *(poor stereo separation)*
(S) (3:51) Rhino 70291 Bo Diddley Beats. *(poor stereo separation)*
(S) (3:59) Time-Life SOD-16 Sounds Of The Seventies - 1975: Take Two. *(poor stereo separation)*
(S) (3:56) Rhino 71667 Disco Hits Vol. 4. *(poor stereo separation)*
(S) (3:48) JCI/Telstar 3516 Sweet Soul Sisters. *(poor stereo separation)*
(S) (3:58) K-Tel 3251 Disco Fever. *(poor stereo separation)*
(S) (3:51) Rhino 72248 O.S.T. Fox Hunt. *(poor stereo separation)*
(S) (3:51) Rhino 72414 Dance Floor Divas: The 70's. *(poor stereo separation)*
(S) (3:52) Time-Life R838-10 Solid Gold Soul - 1975. *(poor stereo separation)*
(S) (3:55) Flashback 72690 Disco Hits: That's The Way I Like It. *(poor stereo separation)*
(M) (3:51) Hip-O 40092 Disco 54: Where We Started From.
(S) (3:52) Time-Life R840-06 Sounds Of The Seventies: '70s Dance Party 1975-1976. *(poor stereo separation)*

SHIRLEY & LEE
1956 LET THE GOOD TIMES ROLL
(M) (2:22) Rhino 75766 Best Of New Orleans Rhythm & Blues Volume 2.
(M) (2:22) Rhino 70642 Billboard's Top R&B Hits Of 1956.
(E) (2:22) EMI 90614 Non-Stop Party Rock.

(M) (2:22) Original Sound 8850 Oldies But Goodies Vol. 1. *(this compact disc uses the "Waring - fds" noise reduction process)*

(M) (2:22) Original Sound 2221 Oldies But Goodies Volumes 1,4,6,8 and 10 Box Set. *(this box set uses the "Waring - fds" noise reduction process)*

(M) (2:22) Original Sound 2500 Oldies But Goodies Volumes 1-15 Box Set. *(this box set uses the "Waring - fds" noise reduction process)*

(M) (2:22) Sire 26617 Music From The Film A Rage In Harlem.

(M) (2:21) Atlantic 81677 O.S.T. Stand By Me.

(M) (2:22) EMI 96268 24 Greatest Hits Of All Time.

(M) (2:20) Curb 77323 All Time Greatest Hits Of Rock 'N' Roll.

(M) (2:21) Atlantic 82155 O.S.T. Book Of Love.

(M) (2:22) EMI 92775 Legendary Masters Series.

(M) (2:22) Virgin 92153 and 86289 O.S.T. American Me.

(M) (2:20) Time-Life 2RNR-14 Rock 'N' Roll Era - 1956.

(M) (2:22) Time-Life RHD-05 Rhythm & Blues - 1956.

(M) (2:22) Time-Life R962-03 History Of Rock 'N' Roll: Rock 'N' Roll Classics 1954-1956.

(M) (2:22) Motown 6763 Rites Of Rhythm & Blues Volume 2.

(M) (2:22) EMI 30882 Aladdin Records Story.

(M) (2:21) Collectables 5637 Legendary Masters Series.

(M) (2:21) EMI 37350 Crescent City Soul: The Sound Of New Orleans 1947-1974.

(M) (2:21) EMI 37355 Highlights From Crescent City Soul: The Sound Of New Orleans 1947-1974.

(M) (2:22) Time-Life R838-24 Solid Gold Soul 1956.

1956 I FEEL GOOD

(M) (2:17) EMI 92775 Legendary Masters Series.

(M) (2:17) Collectables 5637 Legendary Masters Series.

(M) (2:16) EMI 37350 Crescent City Soul: The Sound Of New Orleans 1947-1974.

SHOCKING BLUE
1970 VENUS

(M) (3:03) Rhino 70921 Super Hits Of The 70's Volume 1.

(M) (3:03) Rhino 72009 Super Hits Of The 70's Volumes 1-4 Box Set.

(E) (2:59) Original Sound 8865 Oldies But Goodies Vol. 15. *(this compact disc uses the "Waring - fds" noise reduction process)*

(E) (2:59) Original Sound 2222 Oldies But Goodies Volumes 3,5,11,14 and 15 Box Set. *(this box set uses the "Waring - fds" noise reduction process)*

(E) (2:59) Original Sound 2500 Oldies But Goodies Volumes 1-15 Box Set. *(this box set uses the "Waring - fds" noise reduction process)*

(E) (2:58) Original Sound CDGO-7 Golden Oldies Volume. 7.

(M) (3:03) Rhino 70631 Billboard's Top Rock & Roll Hits Of 1970.

(M) (3:03) Rhino 72005 Billboard's Top Rock & Roll Hits 1968-1972 Box Set.

(M) (3:03) JCI 3101 Rockin' Sixties.

(M) (2:59) JCI 3115 Groovin' Sixties.

(M) (3:03) Rhino 71205 70's Smash Hits Volume 1.

(E) (2:58) Time-Life 2CLR-06 Classic Rock - 1969.

(M) (2:57) Time-Life SOD-11 Sounds Of The Seventies - 1970: Take Two.

(E) (3:00) Milan 35698 O.S.T. Brady Bunch Movie.

(E) (3:00) JCI 3130 1970 - Only Rock 'N Roll - 1974.

(E) (2:58) TVT 6810 O.S.T. Grumpier Old Men.

(M) (2:57) Madacy Entertainment 1970 Rock On 1970.

(E) (3:01) LaserLight 12528 Garage Band Rock.

(M) (2:57) JCI 3191 1970 - Only Dance - 1974.

(E) (2:59) Popular/Critique 12009 Dutch Treats.

(M) (3:03) Eclipse Music Group 64871 Rock 'n Roll Relix 1968-1969.

(M) (3:03) Eclipse Music Group 64872 Rock 'n Roll Relix 1960-1969.

(M) (3:03) Flashback 72681 '70s Radio Hits Volume 1. *(buzz noticeable on fadeout)*

(M) (3:03) Flashback 72090 '70s Radio Hits Box Set. *(buzz noticeable on fadeout)*

(M) (3:03) Rhino 72812 VH1 8-Track Flashback: The One Hit Wonders. *(buzz noticeable on fadeout)*

(M) (2:58) Hip-O 40095 '70s Hit(s) Back.

(E) (2:57) K-Tel 3987 70s Heavy Hitters: #1 Pop Hits.

1970 MIGHTY JOE

(E) (2:59) JCI 3115 Groovin' Sixties.

TROY SHONDELL
1961 THIS TIME

(M) (2:34) Collectables 5068 History Of Rock Volume 8.

(M) (2:35) Time-Life 2RNR-18 Rock 'N' Roll Era - 1961 Still Rockin'. *(no fidelity)*

(M) (2:35) Collectables 2504 WCBS-FM History Of Rock - The 60's Part 4.

(M) (2:35) Collectables 4504 History Of Rock/The 60s Part Four.

(M) (2:34) Collectables 2604 WCBS-FM Jukebox Giants Vol. 2.

(M) (2:35) Time-Life R102-17 Lost Treasures Of Rock 'N' Roll.

(E) (2:35) LaserLight 12322 Greatest Hit Singles Collection.

(M) (2:35) Time-Life R857-03 The Heart Of Rock 'n' Roll - 1961.

(M) (2:35) EMI-Capitol Special Markets 19552 Lost Hits Of The '60s.

(E) (2:34) Columbia 69059 Party Super Hits.

DINAH SHORE
1957 CHANTEZ-CHANTEZ

(S) (1:55) Curb 77459 Best Of. *(rerecorded)*

1957 FASCINATION

BUNNY SIGLER
1967 LET THE GOOD TIMES ROLL & FEEL SO GOOD

SILHOUETTES
1958 GET A JOB

(M) (2:44) Rhino 75764 Best Of Doo Wop Uptempo.

(M) (2:44) Rhino 70619 Billboard's Top Rock & Roll Hits Of 1958.

(M) (2:44) Rhino 72004 Billboard's Top Rock & Roll Hits 1957-1961 Box Set.

(M) (2:45) JCI 3204 Heart & Soul Fifties.

(M) (2:44) Atlantic 81677 O.S.T. Stand By Me. *(sounds like it was mastered from vinyl)*

(M) (2:45) Arista 8605 16 Original Doo-Wop Classics.

(M) (2:45) Collectables 2508 History Of Rock - The Doo Wop Era Part 2.

(M) (2:45) Collectables 4508 History Of Rock/The Doo Wop Era Part Two.

(M) (2:44) Collectables 5062 History Of Rock Volume 2.

(M) (2:45) MCA 8001 O.S.T. American Graffiti.

(M) (2:44) Rhino 71463 Doo Wop Box.

(M) (2:45) Time-Life 2RNR-05 Rock 'N' Roll Era - 1958.

(M) (2:44) Time-Life RHD-16 Rhythm & Blues - 1958.

(M) (2:45) Time-Life R962-01 History Of Rock 'N' Roll: Rock 'N' Roll Classics 1957-1959.

(M) (2:44) Collectables 2506 WCBS-FM History Of Rock - The 50's Part 1.

(M) (2:44) Collectables 4506 History Of Rock/The 50s Part One.

(M) (2:44) Collectables 5057 Harlem Holiday - N.Y. Rhythm & Blues Vol. 7.

(M) (2:44) Collectables 5038 Great Groups Of The Fifties Volume II.

(M) (2:44) Collectables 2605 WCBS-FM Jukebox Giants Vol. 3. *(truncated fade)*

(M) (2:45) Time-Life R10513 40 Lovin' Oldies.

(M) (2:44) Collectables 5653 Spotlite On Ember Records Volume 1.

(M) (2:42) Music For Little People 42581 A Child's Celebration Of Rock 'N' Roll.

(M) (2:45) JCI 3165 #1 Radio Hits 1955 - Only Rock 'n Roll - 1959.

(M) (2:44) K-Tel 3812 Doo Wop's Greatest Hits.

(M) (2:46) Collectables 5748 Get A Job - A Golden Classics Edition. *(truncated fade)*

(M) (2:45) Nick At Nite/550 Music 63456 Double Date With Joanie And Chachi.

(M) (2:45) Relic 7060 The Golden Era Of Doo Wops: Ember Records.

(M) (2:44) Time-Life R838-22 Solid Gold Soul 1958.

SILK
1993 FREAK ME
- (S) (4:34) Elektra 61394 Lose Control.
- (S) (4:33) Elektra 62090 Maximum Slow Jams.

1993 GIRL U FOR ME
- (S) (4:30) Elektra 61394 Lose Control.

SILKIE
1965 YOU'VE GOT TO HIDE YOUR LOVE AWAY
- (M) (2:11) Rhino 70324 History Of British Rock Volume 6.
- (M) (2:11) Rhino 70319 History Of British Rock Box Set.
- (M) (2:10) Time-Life SUD-17 Superhits - Mid 60's Classics.
- (M) (2:11) Time-Life R962-02 History Of Rock 'N' Roll: Folk Rock 1964-1967.
- (M) (2:10) One Way 31441 You've Got To Hide Your Love Away.
- (E) (2:11) Special Music 5039 Great Britons! Volume One. *(mastered from vinyl; distorted)*
- (M) (2:10) Time-Life AM1-16 AM Gold - Mid '60s Classics.

SILVER
1976 WHAM BAM SHANG-A-LANG
- (S) (3:31) Rhino 71199 Super Hits Of The 70's Volume 19.
- (S) (3:31) Time-Life SOD-33 Sounds Of The Seventies - AM Pop Classics II.

SILVER CONDOR
1981 YOU COULD TAKE MY HEART AWAY

SILVER CONVENTION
1975 FLY, ROBIN, FLY
- (S) (5:00) Priority 7983 Mega-Hits Dance Classics Volume 7. *(:31 shorter than the LP version)*
- (S) (5:20) Rhino 71094 Disco Hits Volume 1. *(:11 shorter than the LP version)*
- (S) (4:59) Razor & Tie 22496 Disco Fever. *(:32 shorter than the LP version)*
- (S) (3:17) Time-Life SOD-27 Sounds Of The Seventies - Dance Fever. *(edit of the LP version in an unsuccessful attempt at recreating the 45 version)*
- (S) (3:16) K-Tel 3126 Disco Mania. *(edit of the LP version in an unsuccessful attempt at recreating the 45 version)*
- (S) (7:44) Curb 77780 KC & The Sunshine Band & Silver Convention Greatest Dance Hits. *(remix)*
- (S) (3:47) Rhino 72123 Disco Years, Vol. 7. *(neither the 45 or LP version)*
- (S) (3:16) Madacy Entertainment 1975 Rock On 1975. *(edit of the LP version in an unsuccessful attempt at recreating the 45 version)*
- (S) (3:16) K-Tel 3624 Music Express. *(edit of LP version in an unsuccessful attempt at recreating the 45 version)*
- (S) (3:47) Rhino 72414 Dance Floor Divas: The 70's. *(neither the 45 or LP version)*
- (S) (3:46) Priority 53142 Mega Hits - Disco Express. *(neither the 45 or LP version)*
- (S) (7:43) Hot Productions 23 Best Of. *(remix)*
- (S) (3:47) Time-Life R838-10 Solid Gold Soul - 1975. *(neither the 45 or LP version)*
- (S) (3:17) Time-Life R840-01 Sounds Of The Seventies - Pop Nuggets: Late '70s. *(edit of the LP version in an unsuccessful attempt at recreating the 45 version)*
- (S) (5:20) Flashback 72688 Disco Hits: Get Down Tonight. *(:11 shorter than the LP version)*
- (S) (5:20) Flashback 72086 Disco Hits Box Set. *(:11 shorter than the LP version)*
- (S) (3:16) Cold Front 4024 Old School Mega Mix Volume 2. *(edit of the LP version in an unsuccessful attempt at recreating the 45 version)*
- (S) (5:00) Polydor 314555120 Pure Disco 2. *(:31 shorter than the LP version)*
- (S) (5:00) Time-Life R840-06 Sounds Of The Seventies: '70s Dance Party 1975-1976. *(:31 shorter than the LP version)*

1976 GET UP AND BOOGIE (THAT'S RIGHT)
- (S) (7:51) Curb 77780 KC & The Sunshine Band & Silver Convention Greatest Dance Hits. *(remix)*
- (S) (2:45) Rhino 72122 Disco Years, Vol. 6. *(45 version)*
- (S) (3:59) K-Tel 3470 Get Up And Disco. *(neither the 45, LP or 12" single version)*
- (S) (3:58) Time-Life R138-38 Celebration. *(neither the 45, LP or 12" single version)*
- (S) (7:51) Thump 4099 Old School Boogie. *(remix)*
- (S) (2:44) Madacy Entertainment 1976 Rock On 1976. *(45 version)*
- (S) (2:45) Priority 53141 Mega Hits Disco Locomotion Volume 2. *(45 version)*
- (S) (3:59) JCI 3163 18 Disco Superhits. *(neither the 45, LP or 12" single version)*
- (S) (7:49) Hot Productions 23 Best Of. *(remix)*
- (S) (3:59) Time-Life R840-07 Sounds Of The Seventies: '70s Dance Party 1976-1977. *(neither the 45, LP or 12" single version)*

HARRY SIMEONE CHORALE
1959 THE LITTLE DRUMMER BOY
- (S) (3:18) Rhino 70636 Billboard's Greatest Christmas Hits. *(rerecording)*
- (S) (3:18) MCA 25988 Traditional Christmas Classics. *(rerecording)*
- (M) (3:02) Casablanca 822744 The Little Drummer Boy.
- (S) (3:09) Special Music 4601 The Little Drummer Boy. *(rerecording)*
- (S) (3:19) MCA Special Products 22080 Little Drummer Boy. *(rerecording)*
- (S) (3:17) Collectables 1511 and 2511 and 3511 and 4511 and 9611 and 9711 The Ultimate Christmas Album. *(rerecording)*
- (S) (3:10) Special Music 4623 Wonderful World Of Christmas Vol. 1. *(rerecording)*
- (M) (3:17) Rhino 72175 Santamental Christmas. *(noisy fadeout; rerecording)*
- (S) (3:19) Time-Life TCD-107 A Time-Life Treasury Of Christmas. *(rerecording)*

1960 THE LITTLE DRUMMER BOY
(see 1959 listings above)

1961 THE LITTLE DRUMMER BOY
(see 1959 listings above)

1962 THE LITTLE DRUMMER BOY
(see 1959 listings above)

JUMPIN GENE SIMMONS
1964 HAUNTED HOUSE
- (M) (2:32) Rhino 71492 Elvira Presents Haunted Hits.
- (M) (2:32) Rhino 70535 Halloween Hits.
- (M) (2:31) Time-Life 2RNR-37 Rock 'N' Roll Era - Weird, Wild & Wacky.
- (M) (2:32) Time-Life 2CLR-16 Classic Rock - 1964: Shakin' All Over.
- (E) (2:32) Risky Business 66391 Ghastly Grooves.
- (S) (2:27) K-Tel 3411 Tacky Tunes. *(rerecording)*
- (S) (2:26) K-Tel 3795 Music For Your Halloween Party. *(rerecording)*
- (S) (2:26) K-Tel 3795 Spooktacular Party Songs. *(rerecording)*
- (M) (2:31) Rhino 72481 Haunted Hits.
- (E) (2:32) K-Tel 4033 Ghasty Grooves.
- (M) (2:31) EMI-Capitol Special Markets 19552 Lost Hits Of The '60s.

PATRICK SIMMONS
1983 SO WRONG

CARLY SIMON
1971 THAT'S THE WAY I'VE ALWAYS HEARD IT SHOULD BE
- (S) (4:15) Elektra 109 Best Of.
- (S) (4:15) Elektra 74082 Carly Simon.
- (S) (4:13) Time-Life SUD-10 Superhits - 1971.
- (S) (4:15) Time-Life SOD-22 Sounds Of The Seventies - Seventies Top Forty.

(S) (4:14) Time-Life R103-33 Singers & Songwriters.
(S) (4:15) Arista 18798 Clouds In My Coffee 1965-1995.
(S) (4:13) JCI 3145 1970 - Only Love - 1974.
(S) (4:13) Time-Life AM1-06 AM Gold - 1971.
(S) (4:14) Time-Life R834-10 Body Talk - From The Heart.

1972 ANTICIPATION
(S) (3:18) JCI 3304 Mellow Seventies.
(S) (3:18) Elektra 109 Best Of.
(S) (3:18) Elektra 75016 Anticipation.
(S) (3:18) Time-Life SOD-21 Sounds Of The Seventies - Rock 'N' Soul Seventies.
(S) (3:18) Time-Life R105-26 Our Songs: Singers & Songwriters Encore.
(S) (3:19) Arista 18798 Clouds In My Coffee 1965-1995.
(S) (3:19) Rhino 72738 Billboard Top Soft Rock Hits - 1972.

1973 YOU'RE SO VAIN
(S) (4:17) Priority 8664 High Times/70's Greatest Rock Hits Volume 3.
(S) (4:16) Elektra 109 Best Of.
(S) (4:17) Elektra 75049 No Secrets.
(S) (4:15) Time-Life SUD-13 Superhits - 1973.
(S) (4:15) Time-Life SOD-25 Sounds Of The Seventies - Seventies Generation.
(S) (4:16) Time-Life R103-33 Singers & Songwriters.
(S) (4:15) JCI 3130 1970 - Only Rock 'N Roll - 1974.
(S) (4:17) Arista 18798 Clouds In My Coffee 1965-1995.
(S) (4:15) Time-Life AM1-03 AM Gold - 1973.
(S) (4:17) Rhino 72739 Billboard Top Soft Rock Hits - 1973.

1973 THE RIGHT THING TO DO
(S) (2:57) Elektra 109 Best Of.
(S) (2:58) Elektra 75049 No Secrets.
(S) (2:57) Arista 18798 Clouds In My Coffee 1965-1995.
(S) (2:58) Priority 53140 Best Of The 70's: Legendary Ladies.
(S) (2:57) Time-Life R834-14 Body Talk - Love And Tenderness.

released as by CARLY SIMON and JAMES TAYLOR:
1974 MOCKINGBIRD
(S) (3:48) Elektra 109 Carly Simon - Best Of. *(45 length)*
(S) (4:11) Elektra 1002 Carly Simon - Hotcakes. *(LP length)*
(S) (3:48) Epic 57682 More Songs For Sleepless Nights. *(45 length)*
(S) (4:09) Time-Life SOD-15 Sounds Of The Seventies - 1974: Take Two. *(LP length)*
(S) (4:10) Arista 18798 Carly Simon - Clouds In My Coffee 1965-1995. *(LP length)*
(S) (3:48) Rhino 72494 For Our Children Too! *(45 length)*
(S) (3:48) Time-Life AM1-21 AM Gold - 1974. *(45 length)*

released as by CARLY SIMON:
1974 HAVEN'T GOT TIME FOR THE PAIN
(actual 45 time is (3:37) not (3:50) as stated on the record label)
(S) (3:35) Elektra 109 Best Of. *(45 length)*
(S) (3:52) Elektra 1002 Hotcakes. *(LP length)*
(S) (3:49) Time-Life SOD-15 Sounds Of The Seventies - 1974: Take Two. *(LP length)*
(S) (3:54) Arista 18798 Clouds In My Coffee 1965-1995. *(LP length)*
(S) (3:36) Rhino 72740 Billboard Top Soft Rock Hits - 1974. *(45 length)*
(S) (3:36) Time-Life R834-19 Body Talk - Always And Forever. *(45 length)*

1975 ATTITUDE DANCING
(S) (3:52) Elektra 109 Best Of.
(S) (3:51) Elektra 1033 Playing Possum.

1977 NOBODY DOES IT BETTER
(S) (3:29) EMI 46079 James Bond 13 Original Themes.
(S) (3:29) EMI 98560 Best Of James Bond 30th Anniversary.
(S) (3:29) EMI 96211 O.S.T. The Spy Who Loved Me.
(S) (3:27) EMI 98413 Best Of James Bond 30th Anniversary Collection.
(S) (3:41) Arista 18798 Clouds In My Coffee 1965-1995. *(:12 longer than the 45 or LP)*

1978 YOU BELONG TO ME
(S) (3:50) Sandstone 33049 and 5017 Cosmopolitan Volume 3. *(LP length)*
(S) (3:50) Elektra 128 Boys In The Trees. *(LP length)*

(S) (3:12) Time-Life SOD-20 Sounds Of The Seventies - 1978: Take Two. *(45 length)*
(S) (3:12) Time-Life R105-26 Our Songs: Singers & Songwriters Encore. *(45 length)*
(S) (3:50) DCC Compact Classics 088 Night Moves Volume 6. *(LP length)*
(S) (3:48) Arista 18798 Clouds In My Coffee 1965-1995. *(LP length)*
(S) (3:50) Time-Life R834-06 Body Talk - Only You. *(LP length)*

1980 JESSE
(S) (4:16) Rhino 71893 Radio Daze: Pop Hits Of The 80's Volume Four.
(S) (4:13) Arista 18798 Clouds In My Coffee 1965-1995.
(S) (4:16) JCI 3170 #1 Radio Hits 1980 - Only Rock 'n Roll - 1984.
(S) (4:16) Time-Life R988-16 Sounds Of The Eighties: The Early '80s.

1987 COMING AROUND AGAIN
(S) (6:29) Mercury 314525354 Women For Women. *(live)*
(S) (3:37) Arista 8443 Coming Around Again.
(S) (3:38) Arista 18798 Clouds In My Coffee 1965-1995.

JOE SIMON
1968 (YOU KEEP ME) HANGIN' ON
(S) (2:43) Ripete 2392175 Lookin' Back.
(S) (2:43) Collectables 5114 Golden Classics.
(S) (2:44) Ripete 2222 Soul Patrol Vol. 4.
(S) (2:45) Rhino 72865 Music In My Bones: Best Of.

1969 THE CHOKIN' KIND
(S) (2:39) Ripete 2392175 Lookin' Back.
(S) (2:39) Collectables 5114 Golden Classics.
(S) (2:39) Sony Music Special Products 66106 The Monument Story.
(M) (2:40) Rhino 72815 Beg, Scream & Shout! The Big Ol' Box Of '60s Soul.
(S) (2:39) Repeat/Relativity 1609 Tell It Like It Is: #1 Soul Hits Of The 60's Volume 1.
(S) (2:40) Rhino 72865 Music In My Bones: Best Of.

1971 YOUR TIME TO CRY
(S) (2:56) Rhino 72865 Music In My Bones: Best Of.

1972 DROWNING IN THE SEA OF LOVE
(S) (3:20) Rhino 70787 Soul Hits Of The 70's Volume 7.
(S) (3:20) Ripete 2222 Soul Patrol Vol. 4.
(S) (3:21) Priority 53130 Deep Soul Volume Three.
(S) (3:19) Epic/Legacy 64647 The Philly Sound Box Set.
(S) (3:26) Rhino 72865 Music In My Bones: Best Of.
(S) (3:25) Beast 53442 Original Players Of Love.

1972 POWER OF LOVE
(S) (2:55) Rhino 70660 Billboard's Top R&B Hits Of 1972.
(S) (2:55) Rhino 70788 Soul Hits Of The 70's Volume 8.
(S) (2:55) JCI 3173 1970 - Only Soul - 1974.
(S) (2:55) Rhino 72865 Music In My Bones: Best Of.

1973 STEP BY STEP
(S) (3:21) Rhino 72865 Music In My Bones: Best Of.

1973 THEME FROM CLEOPATRA JONES
(S) (3:45) Rhino 70552 Soul Hits Of The 70's Volume 12.
(S) (3:48) Rhino 72865 Music In My Bones: Best Of.
(S) (3:45) Hip-O 40107 Super Bad On Celluloid: Music From '70s Black Cinema.

1975 GET DOWN, GET DOWN (GET ON THE FLOOR)
(S) (3:55) Rhino 70555 Soul Hits Of The 70's Volume 15.
(S) (3:56) Rhino 72865 Music In My Bones: Best Of.

PAUL SIMON
1972 MOTHER AND CHILD REUNION
(S) (3:03) Warner Brothers 25588 Paul Simon.
(S) (2:48) Warner Brothers 25789 Negotiations And Love Songs (1971 - 1986). *(:15 shorter than either the 45 or LP)*
(S) (2:50) Columbia 35042 Greatest Hits, Etc. *(:13 shorter than either the 45 or LP)*
(S) (2:57) Warner Brothers 45394 Paul Simon 1964/1993.
(S) (3:02) Time-Life R102-34 The Rolling Stone Collection.
(S) (3:03) Time-Life SOD-13 Sounds Of The Seventies - 1972: Take Two.

PAUL SIMON (Continued)

(S) (3:03) Time-Life R103-33 Singers & Songwriters.

1972 ME AND JULIO DOWN BY THE SCHOOLYARD

(S) (2:41) Warner Brothers 25588 Paul Simon.

(S) (2:41) Warner Brothers 25789 Negotiations And Love Songs (1971 - 1986).

(S) (2:42) Columbia 35042 Greatest Hits, Etc.

(S) (2:42) Warner Brothers 45394 Paul Simon 1964/1993.

1973 KODACHROME

(dj copies of this 45 were pressed with a mono mix (3:24) and a stereo mix (3:29); commercial copies were all the stereo mix)

(S) (3:32) Warner Brothers 25589 There Goes Rhymin' Simon.

(S) (3:30) Warner Brothers 25789 Negotiations And Love Songs (1971 - 1986).

(S) (3:32) Columbia 35042 Greatest Hits, Etc.

(S) (3:27) Warner Brothers 45345 O.S.T. Coneheads.

(S) (3:30) Warner Brothers 45394 Paul Simon 1964/1993.

(S) (3:31) Time-Life SOD-14 Sounds Of The Seventies - 1973: Take Two.

(S) (3:32) Time-Life R13610 Gold And Platinum Box Set - The Ultimate Rock Collection.

released as by PAUL SIMON with THE DIXIE HUMMINGBIRDS:

1973 LOVES ME LIKE A ROCK

(actual 45 time is (3:28) not (3:32) as stated on the record label)

(S) (3:32) Warner Brothers 25589 There Goes Rhymin' Simon. *(LP version which includes a :04 intro)*

(S) (3:17) Warner Brothers 25789 Negotiations And Love Songs (1971 - 1986). *(45 version which does not include an intro but :11 shorter than the 45)*

(S) (3:27) Columbia 35042 Greatest Hits, Etc. *(45 version)*

(S) (3:19) Warner Brothers 45394 Paul Simon 1964/1993. *(includes the :04 LP intro but faded :12 earlier than the LP)*

(S) (3:27) Time-Life SOD-06 Sounds Of The Seventies - 1973. *(45 version)*

released as by PAUL SIMON:

1974 AMERICAN TUNE

(S) (4:04) Columbia 35032 Greatest Hits. *(live)*

(S) (3:43) Warner Brothers 25589 There Goes Rhymin' Simon.

(S) (3:43) Warner Brothers 45394 Paul Simon 1964/1993.

released as by PAUL SIMON/PHOEBE SNOW with THE JESSY DIXON SINGERS:

1975 GONE AT LAST

(S) (3:38) Warner Brothers 25591 Paul Simon - Still Crazy After All These Years.

(S) (3:28) Warner Brothers 45394 Paul Simon 1964/1993.

released as by PAUL SIMON:

1976 50 WAYS TO LEAVE YOUR LOVER

(S) (3:31) Warner Brothers 25789 Negotiations And Love Songs (1971 - 1986). *(LP version)*

(S) (3:27) Columbia 35032 Greatest Hits. *(45 version)*

(S) (3:36) Warner Brothers 25591 Still Crazy After All These Years. *(LP version)*

(S) (3:06) Warner Brothers 45394 Paul Simon 1964/1993. *(neither the 45 or LP version; missing a good portion of the introduction)*

(S) (3:35) Time-Life SOD-04 Sounds Of The Seventies - 1976. *(LP version)*

(S) (3:31) Time-Life R103-33 Singers & Songwriters. *(LP version)*

1978 SLIP SLIDIN' AWAY

(S) (4:43) Warner Brothers 25789 Negotiations And Love Songs (1971 - 1986).

(S) (4:45) Columbia 35032 Greatest Hits.

(S) (4:43) Warner Brothers 45394 Paul Simon 1964/1993.

(S) (4:42) Time-Life SOD-05 Sounds Of The Seventies - 1977.

released as by ART GARFUNKEL with JAMES TAYLOR & PAUL SIMON:

1978 (WHAT A) WONDERFUL WORLD

(S) (3:29) Columbia 34975 Art Garfunkel: Watermark.

(S) (3:28) Columbia 45008 Art Garfunkel: Garfunkel.

released as by PAUL SIMON:

1980 LATE IN THE EVENING

(S) (4:02) Warner Brothers 27407 One-Trick Pony.

(S) (3:53) Warner Brothers 25789 Negotiations And Love Songs (1971 - 1986).

(S) (3:55) Warner Brothers 45394 Paul Simon 1964/1993.

1987 YOU CAN CALL ME AL

(S) (4:40) Warner Brothers 45394 Paul Simon 1964/1993.

(S) (4:39) Warner Brothers 25447 Graceland.

(S) (4:39) Warner Brothers 25789 Negotiations And Love Songs (1971 - 1986).

(S) (4:38) Warner Brothers 46430 Graceland. *(remastered edition)*

SIMON & GARFUNKEL

1966 THE SOUNDS OF SILENCE

(S) (3:03) Columbia 3180 O.S.T. The Graduate.

(S) (3:07) Columbia 3180 O.S.T. The Graduate. *(acoustic version peculiar to this soundtrack)*

(S) (3:03) Columbia 9049 Wednesday Morning 3 A.M. *(original acoustic version but not the hit version)*

(S) (3:04) Columbia 9269 Sounds Of Silence.

(S) (3:03) Columbia 31350 Greatest Hits. *(applause from preceding selection tracks over introduction)*

(S) (3:03) Columbia 45322 Collected Works. *(original acoustic version but not the hit version)*

(S) (3:04) Columbia 45322 Collected Works.

(S) (3:04) Columbia 47113 Up 'Til Now. *(original acoustic version but not the hit version)*

(S) (3:04) Warner Brothers 45394 Paul Simon 1964/1993.

(S) (5:39) Warner Brothers 45394 Paul Simon 1964/1993. *(live)*

(S) (3:05) Columbia/Legacy 64780 Old Friends. *(original acoustic version but not the hit version)*

(S) (3:04) Columbia/Legacy 64780 Old Friends.

(S) (3:04) Time-Life R13610 Gold And Platinum Box Set - The Ultimate Rock Collection.

1966 HOMEWARD BOUND

(S) (2:26) Columbia 9363 Parsley, Sage, Rosemary & Tyme.

(S) (2:42) Columbia 31350 Greatest Hits. *(live)*

(S) (2:26) Columbia 45322 Collected Works.

(S) (2:28) Columbia/Legacy 64780 Old Friends.

1966 I AM A ROCK

(S) (2:49) Columbia 9269 Sounds Of Silence. *(LP version)*

(S) (2:50) Columbia 31350 Greatest Hits. *(LP version)*

(S) (2:49) Columbia 45322 Collected Works. *(LP version)*

(S) (2:49) Columbia/Legacy 64780 Old Friends. *(LP version)*

1966 THE DANGLING CONVERSATION

(S) (2:35) Columbia 9363 Parsley, Sage, Rosemary & Tyme.

(S) (2:35) Columbia 45322 Collected Works.

(S) (2:36) Columbia/Legacy 64780 Old Friends.

1966 A HAZY SHADE OF WINTER

(S) (2:17) Columbia 9529 Bookends. *(tracks into the next selection)*

(S) (2:17) Columbia 45322 Collected Works. *(tracks into the next selection)*

(S) (2:17) Columbia/Legacy 64780 Old Friends.

1967 AT THE ZOO

(S) (2:21) Columbia 9529 Bookends.

(S) (2:21) Columbia 45322 Collected Works.

(S) (2:21) Columbia/Legacy 64780 Old Friends.

1967 FAKIN' IT

(S) (3:14) Columbia 9529 Bookends.

(S) (3:14) Columbia 45322 Collected Works.

(S) (3:16) Columbia/Legacy 64780 Old Friends.

1968 SCARBOROUGH FAIR

(S) (6:19) Columbia 3180 O.S.T. The Graduate. *(soundtrack version)*

(S) (3:07) Columbia 9363 Parsley, Sage, Rosemary & Tyme.

(S) (3:08) Columbia 31350 Greatest Hits.

(S) (3:07) Columbia 45322 Collected Works.

(S) (3:09) Columbia/Legacy 64780 Old Friends.

1968 MRS. ROBINSON

(S) (1:12) Columbia 3180 O.S.T. The Graduate. *(soundtrack version 1)*

(S) (1:09) Columbia 3180 O.S.T. The Graduate. *(soundtrack version 2)*

(S) (3:59) Columbia 9529   Bookends.
(S) (3:50) Columbia 31350   Greatest Hits.
(S) (3:59) Columbia 45322   Collected Works.
(S) (3:54) Warner Brothers 45394   Paul Simon 1964/1993.
(S) (3:49) Epic 66329   O.S.T. Forrest Gump.
(S) (4:02) Columbia/Legacy 64780   Old Friends.

1969 THE BOXER
(S) (5:08) Columbia 9914 and 53444   Bridge Over Troubled Water.
(S) (5:08) Columbia 31350   Greatest Hits.
(S) (5:07) Columbia 45322   Collected Works.
(S) (5:08) Warner Brothers 45394   Paul Simon 1964/1993.
(S) (5:07) Columbia/Legacy 64780   Old Friends.
(S) (5:08) Columbia/Legacy 64421   Bridge Over Troubled Water. *(gold disc)*

1970 BRIDGE OVER TROUBLED WATER
(S) (4:51) Columbia 9914 and 53444   Bridge Over Troubled Water.
(S) (4:51) Columbia 31350   Greatest Hits. *(applause from previous selection tracks over introduction)*
(S) (4:51) Columbia 45322   Collected Works.
(S) (2:33) Warner Brothers 45394   Paul Simon 1964/1993. *(demo version; tracks into hit version)*
(S) (4:49) Warner Brothers 45394   Paul Simon 1964/1993.
(S) (4:52) Columbia/Legacy 64780   Old Friends.
(S) (4:51) Columbia/Legacy 64421   Bridge Over Troubled Water. *(gold disc)*

1970 CECILIA
(S) (2:54) Columbia 9914 and 53444   Bridge Over Troubled Water. *(tracks into next selection)*
(S) (2:52) Columbia 31350   Greatest Hits.
(S) (2:54) Columbia 45322   Collected Works. *(tracks into next selection)*
(S) (2:54) Warner Brothers 45394   Paul Simon 1964/1993. *(tracks into next selection)*
(S) (2:54) Columbia/Legacy 64780   Old Friends.
(S) (2:54) Columbia/Legacy 64421   Bridge Over Troubled Water. *(gold disc; tracks into the next selection)*

1970 EL CONDOR PASA
(S) (3:06) Columbia 9914 and 53444   Bridge Over Troubled Water.
(S) (3:05) Columbia 31350   Greatest Hits.
(S) (3:05) Columbia 45322   Collected Works.
(S) (3:05) Warner Brothers 45394   Paul Simon 1964/1993.
(S) (3:05) Columbia/Legacy 64780   Old Friends.
(S) (3:06) Columbia/Legacy 64421   Bridge Over Troubled Water. *(gold disc)*

1975 MY LITTLE TOWN
(S) (3:50) Columbia 33700   Art Garfunkel: Breakaway.
(S) (3:49) Warner Brothers 25591   Paul Simon: Still Crazy After All These Years.
(S) (3:49) Warner Brothers 45394   Paul Simon 1964/1993.
(S) (3:50) Columbia/Legacy 64780   Old Friends.

1982 WAKE UP LITTLE SUSIE
(S) (2:18) Warner Brothers 3654   The Concert In Central Park.

NINA SIMONE
1959 I LOVES YOU, PORGY
(S) (2:29) Verve 314521007   Playboy's 40th Anniversary: Four Decades Of Jazz (1953-1993). *(live)*
(S) (2:29) Philips 822846   Best Of. *(live)*
(M) (4:06) Time-Life HPD-27   Your Hit Parade - The Unforgettable 50's.
(S) (4:07) Bethlehem Jazz 30042   Little Girl Blue. *(truncated fade)*
(S) (2:29) Rebound 314520429   The Great Ladies Sing Gershwin. *(live)*

SIMPLE MINDS
1985 DON'T YOU (FORGET ABOUT ME)
(S) (4:20) A&M 3294   O.S.T. Breakfast Club.
(S) (4:18) A&M 314540052   Glittering Prize.
(S) (4:20) Rhino 72894   Hard Rock Cafe: New Wave.
(S) (4:18) Time-Life R13610   Gold And Platinum Box Set - The Ultimate Rock Collection.

1986 ALIVE & KICKING
(S) (5:23) A&M 5092   Once Upon A Time. *(LP version)*
(S) (4:45) A&M 314540052   Glittering Prize. *(45 version)*

1986 SANCTIFY YOURSELF
(S) (5:00) A&M 5092   Once Upon A Time. *(LP version)*
(S) (3:54) A&M 314540052   Glittering Prize. *(neither the 45 or LP version)*

1986 ALL THE THINGS SHE SAID
(S) (4:16) A&M 5092   Once Upon A Time. *(LP version)*
(S) (4:15) A&M 314540052   Glittering Prize. *(LP version)*

SIMPLY RED
1986 HOLDING BACK THE YEARS
(S) (4:28) Elektra 60452   Picture Book. *(LP version)*
(S) (4:28) EastWest 61993   Greatest Hits. *(LP version)*

1986 MONEY$ TOO TIGHT (TO MENTION)
(S) (4:12) Elektra 60452   Picture Book. *(LP length)*
(S) (4:27) EastWest 61993   Greatest Hits. *(:15 longer than LP length)*

1987 THE RIGHT THING
(S) (4:18) Elektra 60727   Men And Women.
(S) (4:21) EastWest 61993   Greatest Hits.

1989 IF YOU DON'T KNOW ME BY NOW
(S) (3:23) Elektra 60828   A New Flame.
(S) (3:25) EastWest 61993   Greatest Hits.
(S) (3:25) Elektra 62090   Maximum Slow Jams.

1991 SOMETHING GOT ME STARTED
(S) (3:59) EastWest 91773   Stars.
(S) (3:59) EastWest 61993   Greatest Hits.

1992 STARS
(S) (4:07) EastWest 91773   Stars.
(S) (4:07) EastWest 61993   Greatest Hits.
(S) (4:08) Columbia 69012   Diana Princess Of Wales Tribute.

FRANK SINATRA
1955 SAME OLD SATURDAY NIGHT
(M) (2:27) Capitol 92160   Capitol Collector's Series.
(M) (2:27) Capitol 35952   Sinatra 80th: All The Best.
(M) (2:27) Capitol 38089   The Complete Capitol Singles Collection.

1955 LEARNIN' THE BLUES
(M) (2:59) Capitol 94317   The Capitol Years.
(M) (2:59) Capitol 92160   Capitol Collector's Series.
(S) (2:29) Reprise 1016   A Man And His Music. *(rerecording; includes a :04 introduction)*
(M) (2:59) Capitol 35952   Sinatra 80th: All The Best.
(M) (2:59) Capitol 99225   The Best Of The Capitol Years.
(M) (2:59) Capitol 38089   The Complete Capitol Singles Collection.

1955 LOVE AND MARRIAGE
(M) (2:36) Capitol 94317   The Capitol Years.
(M) (2:36) Capitol 92160   Capitol Collector's Series.
(S) (2:12) Reprise 26501   Sinatra Reprise: The Very Good Years. *(rerecording)*
(S) (1:29) Reprise 1016   A Man And His Music. *(rerecording)*
(S) (2:12) Reprise 26340   The Reprise Collection. *(rerecording)*
(M) (2:36) Capitol 99225   The Best Of The Capitol Years.
(M) (2:36) Capitol 99374   At The Movies.
(M) (2:36) Capitol 35952   Sinatra 80th: All The Best.
(M) (2:36) Capitol 38089   The Complete Capitol Singles Collection.
(S) (2:12) Reprise 46589   Very Best Of. *(rerecording)*

1956 (LOVE IS) THE TENDER TRAP
(M) (2:55) Capitol 92160   Capitol Collector's Series.
(M) (2:55) Capitol 94317   The Capitol Years.
(M) (2:55) Capitol 99374   At The Movies.
(M) (2:55) Capitol 99225   The Best Of The Capitol Years.
(M) (2:55) Capitol 35952   Sinatra 80th: All The Best.
(M) (2:55) Capitol 38089   The Complete Capitol Singles Collection.

1956 FLOWERS MEAN FORGIVENESS
(M) (3:04) Capitol 38089   The Complete Capitol Singles Collection.

1956 (HOW LITTLE IT MATTERS) HOW LITTLE WE KNOW
(M) (2:37) Capitol 94317   The Capitol Years.

    (M) (3:22) Capitol 92160 Capitol Collector's Series. *(time includes a :43 false start)*
    (M) (2:37) Capitol 99225 The Best Of The Capitol Years.
    (M) (2:37) Capitol 35952 Sinatra 80th: All The Best.
    (M) (2:37) Capitol 38089 The Complete Capitol Singles Collection.

1956 HEY! JEALOUS LOVER

    (M) (2:20) Capitol 94317 The Capitol Years.
    (M) (2:39) Capitol 92160 Capitol Collector's Series. *(time includes :19 of studio talk)*
    (M) (2:19) Capitol 35952 Sinatra 80th: All The Best.
    (M) (2:19) Capitol 38089 The Complete Capitol Singles Collection.

1957 CAN I STEAL A LITTLE LOVE

    (M) (2:30) Capitol 92160 Capitol Collector's Series.
    (M) (2:29) Capitol 38089 The Complete Capitol Singles Collection.

1958 ALL THE WAY

    (M) (2:51) Capitol 94317 The Capitol Years.
    (M) (2:53) Capitol 91150 All The Way.
    (M) (2:53) Capitol 92160 Capitol Collector's Series.
    (S) (3:28) Reprise 1011 Academy Award Winners. *(rerecording)*
    (S) (3:54) Reprise 1016 A Man And His Music. *(rerecording; with spoken introduction)*
    (M) (2:50) Capitol 99225 The Best Of The Capitol Years.
    (M) (2:51) Reprise 45091 Soundtrack To The Mini Series "Sinatra".
    (M) (2:51) Capitol 99374 At The Movies.
    (M) (2:50) Capitol 35952 Sinatra 80th: All The Best.
    (M) (2:50) Capitol 38089 The Complete Capitol Singles Collection.
    (S) (3:28) Reprise 46589 Very Best Of. *(rerecording)*

1958 WITCHCRAFT

    (M) (2:51) Capitol 94317 The Capitol Years.
    (M) (2:51) Capitol 91150 All The Way.
    (M) (2:51) Capitol 92160 Capitol Collector's Series.
    (S) (2:42) Reprise 1016 A Man And His Music. *(rerecording; includes spoken introduction)*
    (M) (2:51) Capitol 99225 The Best Of The Capitol Years.
    (M) (2:50) Capitol 35952 Sinatra 80th: All The Best.
    (M) (2:50) Capitol 38089 The Complete Capitol Singles Collection.
    (S) (2:36) Reprise 46589 Very Best Of. *(rerecording)*

1958 MR. SUCCESS

    (S) (2:40) Capitol 38089 The Complete Capitol Singles Collection.

1959 HIGH HOPES

    (S) (2:40) Capitol 94317 The Capitol Years.
    (S) (2:41) Capitol 91150 All The Way.
    (S) (2:51) Capitol 92160 Capitol Collector's Series. *(time includes :09 of studio talk)*
    (S) (2:40) Capitol 99225 The Best Of The Capitol Years.
    (S) (2:40) Reprise 45091 Soundtrack To The Mini Series "Sinatra".
    (S) (2:41) Capitol 99374 At The Movies.
    (S) (2:40) Capitol 35952 Sinatra 80th: All The Best.
    (S) (2:40) Capitol 38089 The Complete Capitol Singles Collection.

1959 TALK TO ME

    (S) (2:59) Capitol 91150 All The Way.
    (S) (2:58) Capitol 38089 The Complete Capitol Singles Collection.

1960 OL' MacDONALD

    (S) (2:39) Capitol 91150 All The Way.
    (S) (2:40) Capitol 99956 Concepts.
    (S) (2:40) Capitol 46573 Sinatra's Swingin' Session And More.
    (S) (2:39) Capitol 38089 The Complete Capitol Singles Collection.

1962 POCKETFUL OF MIRACLES

    (S) (2:38) Reprise 1010 Sinatra's Sinatra.
    (S) (2:38) Reprise 46013 The Complete Reprise Studio Recordings.
    (S) (2:38) Reprise 46589 Very Best Of.

1964 SOFTLY, AS I LEAVE YOU

    (S) (3:00) Reprise 1016 A Man And His Music. *(a (1:02) spoken introduction precedes music; talk extends over the music introduction; edited)*
    (S) (2:51) Reprise 1013 Softly As I Leave You.
    (S) (2:50) Reprise 2274 Greatest Hits.
    (S) (2:50) Reprise 46013 The Complete Reprise Studio Recordings.
    (S) (2:51) Reprise 46589 Very Best Of.

1965 SOMEWHERE IN YOUR HEART

    (S) (2:27) Reprise 2274 Greatest Hits.
    (S) (2:28) Reprise 46013 The Complete Reprise Studio Recordings.

1966 IT WAS A VERY GOOD YEAR

    (S) (4:25) Reprise 26501 Sinatra Reprise: The Very Good Years.
    (S) (4:25) Reprise 1014 September Of My Years.
    (S) (4:25) Reprise 2274 Greatest Hits.
    (S) (4:25) Reprise 26340 The Reprise Collection.
    (S) (4:26) Reprise 45091 Soundtrack To The Mini Series "Sinatra".
    (S) (4:25) Reprise 46013 The Complete Reprise Studio Recordings.
    (S) (4:26) Reprise 46589 Very Best Of.

1966 STRANGERS IN THE NIGHT

    (S) (2:35) Reprise 26501 Sinatra Reprise: The Very Good Years.
    (S) (2:35) Reprise 1017 Strangers In The Night.
    (S) (2:35) Reprise 2274 Greatest Hits.
    (S) (2:35) Reprise 26340 The Reprise Collection.
    (S) (2:35) Reprise 46013 The Complete Reprise Studio Recordings.
    (S) (2:35) Reprise 46589 Very Best Of.

1966 SUMMER WIND

    (S) (2:54) Reprise 26501 Sinatra Reprise: The Very Good Years.
    (S) (2:54) Reprise 1017 Strangers In The Night.
    (S) (2:54) Reprise 2274 Greatest Hits.
    (S) (2:54) Reprise 46013 The Complete Reprise Studio Recordings.
    (S) (2:54) Reprise 46116 Everything Happens To Me.
    (S) (2:54) Reprise 46589 Very Best Of.

1966 THAT'S LIFE

    (S) (3:06) Reprise 26501 Sinatra Reprise: The Very Good Years.
    (S) (3:06) Reprise 1020 That's Life.
    (S) (3:06) Reprise 2274 Greatest Hits.
    (S) (3:06) Reprise 26340 The Reprise Collection.
    (S) (3:06) Reprise 45091 Soundtrack To The Mini Series "Sinatra".
    (S) (3:06) Reprise 46013 The Complete Reprise Studio Recordings.
    (S) (3:06) Reprise 46589 Very Best Of.

1967 THE WORLD WE KNEW (OVER AND OVER)

    (S) (2:46) Reprise 1022 The World We Knew.
    (S) (2:46) Reprise 2274 Greatest Hits.
    (S) (2:46) Reprise 46013 The Complete Reprise Studio Recordings.

1968 CYCLES

    (S) (3:09) Reprise 1027 Cycles.
    (S) (3:09) Reprise 2275 Greatest Hits Volume 2.
    (S) (3:09) Reprise 46013 The Complete Reprise Studio Recordings.

1969 MY WAY

    (S) (4:35) Reprise 26501 Sinatra Reprise: The Very Good Years.
    (S) (4:35) Reprise 1029 My Way.
    (S) (4:31) Reprise 2275 Greatest Hits Volume 2.
    (S) (4:35) Reprise 26340 The Reprise Collection.
    (S) (4:35) Reprise 45091 Soundtrack To The Mini Series "Sinatra".
    (S) (4:35) Reprise 46013 The Complete Reprise Studio Recordings.
    (S) (4:35) Reprise 46589 Very Best Of.

1980 THEME FROM NEW YORK, NEW YORK
- (S) (3:25) Reprise 45091 Soundtrack To The Mini Series "Sinatra".
- (S) (3:25) Reprise 26340 The Reprise Collection.
- (S) (3:25) Reprise 26501 Sinatra Reprise: The Very Good Years.
- (S) (3:25) Reprise 2300 Trilogy: Past, Present & Future.
- (S) (3:26) Reprise 46013 The Complete Reprise Studio Recordings.
- (S) (3:26) Reprise 46589 Very Best Of.

NANCY SINATRA
1966 THESE BOOTS ARE MADE FOR WALKIN'
- (S) (2:39) Warner Brothers 25613 O.S.T. Full Metal Jacket.
- (S) (2:43) Rhino 70627 Billboard's Top Rock & Roll Hits Of 1966.
- (S) (2:43) Rhino 72007 Billboard's Top Rock & Roll Hits 1962-1966 Box Set.
- (S) (2:40) Priority 7909 Vietnam: Rockin' The Delta.
- (S) (2:43) Rhino 75885 The Hit Years.
- (S) (2:41) Time-Life 2CLR-13 Classic Rock - 1966: Shakin' All Over.
- (S) (2:41) Sundazed 6052 Boots.
- (M) (2:42) Sundazed 6052 Boots. *(45 mix)*

1966 HOW DOES THAT GRAB YOU DARLIN'?
- (S) (2:32) Rhino 75885 The Hit Years.
- (S) (2:29) Sundazed 6053 How Does That Grab You?.
- (S) (2:32) Atlantic 82865 O.S.T. Feeling Minnesota.

1967 SUGAR TOWN
- (S) (2:23) Rhino 75885 The Hit Years.
- (S) (2:22) Sundazed 6055 Sugar.

1967 LOVE EYES
- (S) (2:33) Rhino 75885 The Hit Years.
- (S) (2:34) Sundazed 6055 Sugar.

1967 LIGHTNING'S GIRL
- (S) (2:53) Rhino 75885 The Hit Years.
- (S) (2:52) Sundazed 6053 How Does That Grab You?.

NANCY SINATRA & LEE HAZLEWOOD
1967 JACKSON
- (S) (2:45) Rhino 75885 Nancy Sinatra - The Hit Years.
- (S) (2:47) Rhino 70166 Nancy Sinatra & Lee Hazlewood - Fairytales And Fantasies: The Best Of.
- (S) (2:45) Sundazed 6057 Nancy Sinatra - Movin' With Nancy.
- (S) (2:44) Sundazed 6056 Nancy Sinatra - Country, My Way.

1967 LADY BIRD
- (S) (3:00) Rhino 75885 Nancy Sinatra - The Hit Years.
- (S) (3:01) Rhino 70166 Nancy Sinatra & Lee Hazlewood - Fairytales And Fantasies: The Best Of.

1968 SOME VELVET MORNING
- (S) (3:37) Rhino 75885 Nancy Sinatra - The Hit Years.
- (S) (3:40) Rhino 70166 Nancy Sinatra & Lee Hazlewood - Fairytales And Fantasies: The Best Of.
- (S) (3:36) Sundazed 6057 Nancy Sinatra - Movin' With Nancy.

NANCY SINATRA & FRANK SINATRA
1967 SOMETHIN' STUPID
- (S) (2:43) Reprise 1022 Frank Sinatra: The World We Knew.
- (S) (2:43) Reprise 2274 Frank Sinatra's Greatest Hits.
- (S) (2:40) Reprise 26340 Frank Sinatra: The Reprise Collection.
- (S) (2:39) Rhino 75885 Nancy Sinatra - The Hit Years.
- (S) (2:38) Sundazed 6055 Nancy Sinatra - Sugar.
- (S) (2:38) Reprise 46589 Very Best Of Frank Sinatra.

GORDON SINCLAIR
1974 THE AMERICANS (A CANADIAN'S OPINION)
- (S) (4:49) K-Tel 3626 Music Power.

SINGING NUN
1963 DOMINIQUE
- (M) (2:53) Time-Life SUD-15 Superhits - The Early 60's.
- (M) (2:55) Rhino 71584 Billboard Top Pop Hits, 1963.

- (M) (2:53) Polygram Special Markets 314520272 One Hit Wonders.
- (M) (2:53) Eric 11503 Hard To Find 45's On CD (Volume II) 1961-64.
- (M) (2:54) Time-Life AM1-19 AM Gold - The Early '60s.
- (M) (2:55) Varese Sarabande 5906 God, Love And Rock & Roll.
- (M) (2:53) Polygram Special Markets 314520460 #1 Radio Hits Of The 60's.
- (M) (2:52) Polygram Special Markets 314520516 45's On CD Volume 1.

SIOUXSIE and THE BANSHEES
1991 KISS THEM FOR ME
- (S) (4:35) Geffen 24387 Superstition.
- (S) (4:34) DCC Compact Classics 140 Rock The First Volume 10.

SIR DOUGLAS QUINTET
1965 SHE'S ABOUT A MOVER
- (M) (2:19) Time-Life 2CLR-08 Classic Rock - 1965: The Beat Goes On.
- (M) (3:13) Rhino 71783 Texas Music Volume 3: Garage Bands & Psychedelia. *(rerecording)*

1966 THE RAINS CAME
- (M) (2:13) Time-Life 2CLR-21 Classic Rock - Rock Renaissance II.

1969 MENDOCINO
- (S) (2:38) Mercury 834216 45's On CD Volume 3.
- (S) (2:38) Mercury 846586 Best Of Doug Sahm & The Sir Douglas Quintet.
- (S) (2:38) Time-Life 2CLR-06 Classic Rock - 1969.
- (S) (2:38) Rebound 314520269 Class Reunion 1969.
- (S) (2:38) Special Music 5026 Let It All Hang Out - 60's Party Hits.
- (S) (2:38) Polygram Special Markets 314520464 60's Rock Hits.

SIR MIX-A-LOT
1992 BABY GOT BACK
- (S) (6:23) Tommy Boy 1074 MTV Party To Go Volume 3. *(all tracks on this cd are segued together)*
- (S) (4:20) Foundation/RCA 66563 Number 1 Hit Mix.
- (S) (4:21) Def American 26765 Mack Daddy.

SISTER HAZEL
1997 ALL FOR YOU
- (S) (3:38) Universal 53030 ...Somewhere More Familiar.

SISTER SLEDGE
1979 HE'S THE GREATEST DANCER
- (S) (3:33) Rhino 70275 The Disco Years Volume 4. *(45 version)*
- (S) (3:33) Rhino 71096 Disco Hits Volume 3. *(45 version)*
- (S) (6:02) Turnstyle/Atlantic 14215 Atlantic Dance Classics. *(LP version)*
- (S) (6:13) Rhino 71060 Best Of (1973-1985). *(LP version)*
- (S) (3:33) Time-Life SOD-27 Sounds Of The Seventies - Dance Fever. *(45 version)*
- (S) (6:11) Rebound 314520245 Disco Nights Vol. 6 - #1 Disco Hits. *(LP version)*
- (S) (6:13) Rhino 71587 We Are Family. *(LP version)*
- (S) (3:33) Flashback 72691 Disco Hits: Le Freak. *(45 version)*
- (S) (3:33) Flashback 72086 Disco Hits Box Set. *(45 version)*
- (S) (5:51) Chronicles 314553405 Non-Stop Disco Vol. 2. *(all songs on this cd are segued together)*
- (S) (3:33) Rhino 72837 Disco Queens: The 70's. *(45 version)*
- (S) (3:33) Time-Life R840-09 Sounds Of The Seventies: '70s Dance Party 1979-1981. *(45 version)*

1979 WE ARE FAMILY
- (S) (3:35) Atlantic 81913 Golden Age Of Black Music (1977-1988). *(45 version)*
- (S) (3:34) Priority 7974 Mega-Hits Dance Classics Volume 4. *(45 version)*

SISTER SLEDGE (Continued)

- (S) (3:34) Rhino 70274 The Disco Years Volume 3. *(45 version)*
- (S) (3:34) Rhino 71096 Disco Hits Volume 3. *(45 version)*
- (S) (8:19) Rhino 71060 Best Of (1973-1985). *(LP version)*
- (S) (8:19) JCI 3306 Dance Seventies. *(LP version)*
- (S) (3:34) Original Sound 9306 Dedicated To You Vol. 6. *(45 version)*
- (S) (3:34) Rhino 71618 Soul Train Hall Of Fame/20th Anniversary. *(45 version)*
- (S) (3:34) Time-Life SOD-09 Sounds Of The Seventies - 1979. *(45 version)*
- (S) (8:20) Rhino 71587 We Are Family. *(LP version)*
- (S) (8:01) Rhino 71587 We Are Family. *(remix)*
- (S) (8:09) Rhino 71587 We Are Family. *(remix)*
- (S) (3:34) Rhino 72275 More Stadium Rock. *(45 version)*
- (S) (3:34) Rhino 72414 Dance Floor Divas: The 70's. *(45 version)*
- (S) (3:34) JCI 3148 1975 - Only Dance - 1979. *(45 version)*
- (S) (3:34) Flashback 72692 Disco Hits: We Are Family. *(45 version)*
- (S) (3:34) Flashback 72086 Disco Hits Box Set. *(45 version)*
- (S) (3:34) Flashback 72712 Arena Rock. *(45 version)*
- (S) (3:34) RCA 68904 O.S.T. The Full Monty. *(45 version)*
- (S) (3:34) Time-Life R838-15 Solid Gold Soul 1979. *(45 version)*
- (S) (3:34) K-Tel 3909 High Energy Volume 2. *(45 version)*
- (S) (3:34) Flashback 72803 We Are Family And Other Hits. *(45 version)*
- (S) (3:34) Polydor 314555120 Pure Disco 2. *(45 version)*
- (S) (3:36) Rhino 75200 Basketball's Greatest Hits. *(45 version)*
- (S) (3:36) Rhino 72964 Ultimate '70s R&B Smashes! *(45 version)*
- (S) (3:34) Atlantic 83088 Atlantic Records: 50 Years - The Gold Anniversary Collection. *(45 version)*
- (S) (3:34) Time-Life R840-10 Sounds Of The Seventies: '70s Dance Party 1979. *(45 version)*

1982 MY GUY

- (S) (3:43) Rhino 71971 Video Soul - Best Soul Of The 80's Vol. 1.
- (S) (3:43) Rhino 71060 Best Of (1973-1985).
- (S) (3:43) Flashback 72803 We Are Family And Other Hits.

SIX TEENS
1956 A CASUAL LOOK

69 BOYZ
1995 TOOTSEE ROLL

- (S) (4:14) Rip It 6901 199Quad. *(tracks into next selection)*
- (S) (4:02) Tommy Boy 1137 ESPN Presents Jock Jams. *(all songs on this cd are segued together with crowd sound effects added)*
- (S) (4:19) Boxtunes 162444068 Big Phat Ones Of Hip-Hop Volume 1.
- (S) (4:21) Coldfront 6146 Phat Rap Flava '95. *(remix; all selections on this cd are segued together)*
- (S) (4:17) Quality 5008 Dance Box Set. *(all selections on this cd are segued together)*
- (S) (6:03) Priority 50961 Booty And The Beat - Bass Jams Vol.1. *(remixed)*
- (S) (4:22) Cold Front 6246 Classic Club Mix - R&B Grooves. *(all selections on this cd are segued together; remix)*

SKEE-LO
1995 I WISH

- (S) (4:09) Sunshine/Scotti Bros. 75486 I Wish.
- (S) (4:31) Tommy Boy 1139 MTV Party To Go Volume 8. *(all selections on this cd are segued together)*
- (S) (4:10) Street Life 75510 West Coast Collection, Volume 1.
- (S) (4:08) Beast 53302 Summer Jammin'.
- (S) (4:02) Priority 50935 100% Party Hits Of The 90's Volume Two. *(all selections on this cd are segued together)*

SKID ROW
1989 18 AND LIFE

- (S) (3:49) Atlantic 81936 Skid Row.

1990 I REMEMBER YOU

- (S) (5:13) Atlantic 81936 Skid Row.
- (S) (5:13) Rhino 72579 Feel Like Makin' Love - Romantic Power Ballads.
- (S) (5:13) Time-Life R968-25 Guitar Rock - The '90s.
- (S) (5:12) Razor & Tie 4569 '90s Style.

SKIP & FLIP
1959 IT WAS I

- (M) (2:18) Time-Life 2RNR-24 Rock 'N' Roll Era - The 50's Keep On Rockin'.
- (M) (2:17) Time-Life R857-11 The Heart Of Rock 'n' Roll 1958-1959.

1960 CHERRY PIE

- (M) (2:04) Time-Life 2RNR-22 Rock 'N' Roll Era - 1960 Still Rockin'. *(mastered from vinyl)*
- (M) (2:12) Time-Life R102-17 Lost Treasures Of Rock 'N' Roll.
- (M) (2:12) LaserLight 12322 Greatest Hit Singles Collection.
- (M) (2:12) K-Tel 3409 Funniest Food Songs.
- (M) (2:12) Time-Life R857-10 The Heart Of Rock 'n' Roll 1960-1961.

SKYLARK
1973 WILDFLOWER
(dj copies of this 45 were issued in lengths of (4:07) and (3:08); commercial copies were all (4:07))

- (S) (4:07) Rhino 70930 Super Hits Of The 70's Volume 10.
- (S) (4:06) EMI 90603 Rock Me Gently.
- (S) (4:07) Time-Life SUD-13 Superhits - 1973.
- (S) (4:06) Time-Life SOD-32 Sounds Of The Seventies - AM Pop Classics.
- (S) (4:04) Madacy Entertainment 1973 Rock On 1973.
- (S) (4:06) Collectables 5800 Wildflower - A Golden Classics Edition.
- (S) (4:06) Time-Life AM1-03 AM Gold - 1973.
- (S) (4:07) Time-Life R834-08 Body Talk - On My Mind.
- (S) (4:06) EMI-Capitol Music Special Markets 19545 Lost Hits Of The '70s.

SKYLINERS
1959 SINCE I DON'T HAVE YOU

- (M) (2:38) Rhino 75763 Best Of Doo Wop Ballads.
- (M) (2:35) DCC Compact Classics 031 Back Seat Jams.
- (E) (2:35) Original Sound 8855 Oldies But Goodies Vol. 5. *(this compact disc uses the "Waring - fds" noise reduction process; ambient background noise throughout the disc)*
- (E) (2:35) Original Sound 2222 Oldies But Goodies Volumes 3,5,11,14 and 15 Box Set. *(this box set uses the "Waring - fds" noise reduction process; ambient background noise throughout the song)*
- (E) (2:35) Original Sound 2500 Oldies But Goodies Volumes 1-15 Box Set. *(this box set uses the "Waring - fds" noise reduction process; ambient background noise throughout the song)*
- (E) (2:34) Original Sound CDGO-12 Golden Oldies Volume. 12.
- (E) (2:34) Original Sound 8878 Art Laboe's Dedicated To You.
- (E) (2:34) Original Sound 4001 Art Laboe's 60 Killer Oldies.
- (E) (2:34) Original Sound 8891 Dick Clark's 21 All-Time Hits Vol. 1.
- (E) (3:28) Original Sound 9601 Best Of Oldies But Goodies Vol. 1. *(extended version)*
- (M) (2:35) MCA 8001 O.S.T. American Graffiti.
- (M) (2:39) Rhino 71463 Doo Wop Box.
- (M) (2:35) Time-Life 2RNR-20 Rock 'N' Roll Era - 1959 Still Rockin'.
- (E) (2:35) Original Sound 8873 Greatest Hits.
- (M) (2:37) Time-Life R103-27 Love Me Tender.
- (M) (2:35) Time-Life R10513 40 Lovin' Oldies.
- (M) (2:37) Time-Life R857-01 The Heart Of Rock 'n' Roll - 1959.

(M) (2:35) Nick At Nite/550 Music/Epic 67768 Fonzie's Make Out Music.

(M) (2:38) Collectables 1514 and 2514 The Anniversary Album - The 50's.

1959 THIS I SWEAR

(E) (2:30) Original Sound 8905r 13 Of The Best Doo Wop Love Songs.

(E) (2:30) Original Sound 9326 Best Love Songs Vol. 1 & 2.

(M) (2:31) Original Sound 8856 Oldies But Goodies Vol. 6. *(this compact disc uses the "Waring - fds" noise reduction process)*

(M) (2:31) Original Sound 2221 Oldies But Goodies Volumes 1,4,6,8 and 10 Box Set. *(this box set uses the "Waring - fds" noise reduction process)*

(M) (2:31) Original Sound 2500 Oldies But Goodies Volumes 1-15 Box Set. *(this box set uses the "Waring - fds" noise reduction process)*

(M) (2:30) Original Sound CDGO-2 Golden Oldies Volume 2.

(E) (2:30) Original Sound 4001 Art Laboe's 60 Killer Oldies.

(E) (2:30) Original Sound 1236 Best Love Songs Box Set.

(M) (2:31) Original Sound 9603 Best Of Oldies But Goodies Vol. 3.

(M) (2:34) Time-Life 2RNR-45 Rock 'N' Roll Era - Street Corner Serenade.

(E) (2:30) Original Sound 8873 Greatest Hits.

(E) (2:31) LaserLight 12320 Love Songs.

(E) (2:36) K-Tel 478 More 50's Jukebox Favorites.

(M) (2:38) Rhino 72507 Doo Wop Box II.

(M) (2:29) Music Club 50015 Love Me Forever - 18 Rock'N' Roll Love Songs.

(M) (2:34) Time-Life R857-11 The Heart Of Rock 'n' Roll 1958-1959.

(M) (2:38) Collectables 1514 and 2514 The Anniversary Album - The 50's.

1960 PENNIES FROM HEAVEN

(S) (2:07) Original Sound 8873 Greatest Hits.

(S) (2:06) Original Sound CDGO-6 Golden Oldies Volume. 6.

SKYY
1982 CALL ME

(S) (6:21) Thump 4050 Old School Volume 5. *(LP version)*

(S) (6:21) Salsoul 1000 and 1027 Original Salsoul Classics. *(LP version)*

(S) (6:21) Salsoul 8002 Original Salsoul Classics Volume Two. *(LP version)*

(S) (4:06) Rebound 314520365 Funk Classics - The 80's. Greatest Movie Hits. *(neither the 45, 12" single or LP version)*

(S) (6:21) Salsoul 1015 and 1029 Skyy Line. *(LP version)*

(S) (4:47) Right Stuff/Salsoul 52193 Greatest Hits. *(edit of LP version)*

(S) (4:54) Right Stuff 56197 Free To Be Volume 7. *(edit of LP version)*

(S) (6:20) K-Tel 3908 High Energy Volume 1. *(LP version)*

SLADE
1984 RUN RUNAWAY

(S) (5:00) Risky Business 57833 Read The Hits/Best Of The 80's. *(LP version)*

(S) (5:00) CBS Associated 39336 Keep Your Hands To Yourself. *(LP version)*

1984 MY OH MY

(S) (4:11) Risky Business 57469 Don't Touch My 45's/Great Lost Singles Of The 80's.

(S) (4:12) CBS Associated 39336 Keep Your Hands To Yourself.

SLAUGHTER
1990 UP ALL NIGHT

(S) (4:17) Chrysalis 21702 Stick It To Ya. *(LP version)*

(S) (3:44) K-Tel 3999 Glam Rock Vol. 2: The 80's And Beyond. *(45 version)*

1990 FLY TO THE ANGELS

(S) (5:06) Chrysalis 21702 Stick It To Ya.

1991 SPEND MY LIFE

(S) (3:20) Chrysalis 21702 Stick It To Ya.

SLAVE
1977 SLIDE

(S) (3:19) Rhino 71434 In Yo Face! History Of Funk Volume 4. *(45 version)*

(S) (6:49) Priority 53766 All Star Funk Vol. 2. *(LP version)*

(S) (6:49) Rhino 71592 Best Of. *(LP version)*

(S) (6:46) Rhino 72487 Street Jams - Back 2 The Old Skool, Part 1. *(LP version)*

(S) (6:48) JCI 3121 Monster Funk. *(LP version)*

(S) (6:34) Coldfront 3375 Old School Megamix. *(all selections on this cd are sequed together; remixed)*

(S) (6:49) Rhino 72564 Slave. *(LP version)*

(S) (6:39) Thump 4060 Old School Volume 6. *(LP version; all selections on this cd are segued together)*

(S) (3:18) K-Tel 4020 Great R&B Funk Bands Of The 70's. *(45 version)*

(S) (4:49) Thump 4100 Old School Mix. *(all selections on this cd are segued together and remixed)*

(S) (3:18) Time-Life R838-16 Solid Gold Soul 1977. *(45 version)*

(S) (3:18) Cold Front 4025 Old School Mega Mix Volume 3. *(45 version)*

(S) (3:21) Rhino 72964 Ultimate '70s R&B Smashes! *(45 version)*

PERCY SLEDGE
1966 WHEN A MAN LOVES A WOMAN

(M) (2:49) Atlantic 81911 Golden Age Of Black Music (1960-1970).

(M) (2:49) Atlantic 81742 O.S.T. Platoon.

(M) (2:50) Atlantic 81297 Atlantic Rhythm & Blues Volume 5.

(S) (2:52) JCI 3509 Masters Of The Blues: Soul x Four. *(rerecording)*

(E) (2:50) Warner Special Products 27601 Atlantic Soul Classics.

(M) (2:50) MCA 6214 Moonlighting - TV Soundtrack.

(E) (2:49) Priority 7909 Vietnam: Rockin' The Delta.

(M) (2:49) Motown 6094 More Songs From The Original Soundtrack Of The "Big Chill".

(M) (2:49) Atlantic 82305 Atlantic Rhythm And Blues 1947-1974 Box Set.

(E) (2:49) Atlantic 8210 Best Of.

(M) (2:50) Atlantic 80212 Ultimate Collection.

(M) (2:50) Rhino 70285 It Tears Me Up.

(M) (2:49) Ripete 2392192 Beach Music Anthology Box Set.

(E) (2:49) SBK 89024 O.S.T. The Crying Game.

(M) (2:54) Rhino 71461 Soul Hits, Volume 3.

(M) (2:54) Rhino 71517 The Muscle Shoals Sound.

(M) (2:54) Rhino 71548 Let There Be Drums Volume 2: The 60's.

(M) (2:48) Original Sound 8908 Best Love Songs Vol 3.

(M) (2:48) Original Sound 9327 Best Love Songs Vol. 3 & 4.

(M) (2:48) Original Sound 1236 Best Love Songs Box Set.

(M) (2:48) Original Sound 8859r Oldies But Goodies Vol. 9. *(remastered edition)*

(M) (2:48) Original Sound 2223 Oldies But Goodies Volumes 2,7,9,12 and 13 Box Set. *(Volumes 2, 7 and 12 of this box set use the "Waring - fds" noise reduction process)*

(M) (2:48) Original Sound 2500 Oldies But Goodies Volumes 1-15 Box Set. *(most volumes in this box set use the "Waring - fds" noise reduction process)*

(M) (2:49) Time-Life RHD-02 Rhythm & Blues - 1966.

(M) (2:50) Time-Life 2CLR-02 Classic Rock - 1966.

(M) (2:49) Time-Life SUD-01 Superhits - 1966.

(M) (2:49) Right Stuff 27306 Slow Jams: The 60's Volume One.

(M) (2:49) Time-Life OPCD-4517 Tonight's The Night.

(M) (2:49) Ripete 2163-RE Ebb Tide.

(M) (2:54) Rhino 71806 The R&B Box: Thirty Years Of Rhythm & Blues.

(M) (2:54) Hollywood 61606 O.S.T. When A Man Loves A Woman.

(M) (2:50) Time-Life R138-18 Body Talk.

(E) (2:49) Collectables 2554 CBS-FM History Of Rock Volume 2.

(M) (2:49) Curb 77778 Best Of.

PERCY SLEDGE *(Continued)*

(M) (2:49) JCI 3164 Eighteen Soulful Ballads.
(M) (2:55) Rhino 72619 Smooth Grooves: The '60s Volume 2 Mid '60s.
(M) (2:54) Rhino 72580 Soul Serenade - Intimate R&B.
(M) (2:49) Time-Life AM1-09 AM Gold - 1966.
(M) (2:49) Time-Life R838-01 Solid Gold Soul - 1966.
(M) (2:50) Time-Life R834-03 Body Talk - Moonlit Nights.
(M) (2:48) Hammer & Lace 697124114 Leading Men: Masters Of Style Volume Three.
(M) (2:54) Flashback 72659 '60s Soul: When A Man Loves A Woman.
(M) (2:54) Flashback 72091 '60s Soul Hits Box Set.
(M) (2:50) Priority 50974 Premiere The Movie Magazine Presents The Greatest Soundtrack Love Songs.
(M) (2:54) Repeat/Relativity 1610 Tighten Up: #1 Soul Hits Of The 60's Volume 2.
(M) (2:54) Flashback 72896 25 Years Of R&B - 1966.
(M) (2:54) Rhino 72969 Very Best Of.
(M) (2:55) Rhino 72963 Ultimate '60s Soul Smashes.
(M) (2:49) Simitar 55572 The Number One's: Hot In The '60s.
(M) (2:49) Atlantic 83088 Atlantic Records: 50 Years - The Gold Anniversary Collection.
(M) (2:50) Time-Life R857-20 The Heart Of Rock 'n' Roll 1965-1966.

1966 WARM AND TENDER LOVE

(E) (3:12) Atlantic 8210 Best Of.
(M) (3:18) Atlantic 80212 Ultimate Collection.
(M) (3:17) Rhino 70285 It Tears Me Up. *(truncated fade)*
(M) (3:15) Time-Life 2CLR-22 Classic Rock - 1966: Blowin' Your Mind.
(M) (3:16) Time-Life OPCD-4517 Tonight's The Night.
(M) (3:18) Ripete 2163-RE Ebb Tide.
(M) (3:15) JCI 3161 18 Soul Hits From The 60's.
(M) (3:18) Rhino 72969 Very Best Of.

1966 IT TEARS ME UP

(E) (2:45) Atlantic 8210 Best Of.
(M) (2:46) Atlantic 80212 Ultimate Collection.
(M) (2:46) Rhino 70285 It Tears Me Up.
(M) (2:47) Time-Life 2CLR-28 Classic Rock - On The Soul Side II.
(M) (2:46) Curb 77778 Best Of.
(M) (2:47) Rhino 72815 Beg, Scream & Shout! The Big Ol' Box Of '60s Soul.
(M) (2:47) Rhino 72969 Very Best Of.

1968 TAKE TIME TO KNOW HER
(actual LP time is (3:01) not (2:55) as stated
on the record label; actual 45 time is (2:52)
not (2:55) as stated on the record label)

(S) (3:01) Atlantic 8210 Best Of.
(S) (3:01) Atlantic 80212 Ultimate Collection.
(S) (2:55) JCI 3509 Masters Of The Blues: Soul x Four. *(rerecording)*
(S) (3:01) Rhino 70285 It Tears Me Up.
(S) (2:57) Time-Life RHD-04 Rhythm & Blues - 1968.
(S) (2:57) Time-Life 2CLR-19 Classic Rock - 1968: Shakin' All Over.
(M) (2:52) Rhino 71517 The Muscle Shoals Sound.
(S) (3:00) Ripete 2198 Soul Patrol.
(S) (3:01) Right Stuff 30577 Slow Jams: The 60's Volume 3.
(S) (3:01) Curb 77778 Best Of.
(S) (2:57) Time-Life R838-03 Solid Gold Soul - 1968.
(M) (2:53) Rhino 72969 Very Best Of.

SLY & THE FAMILY STONE
1968 DANCE TO THE MUSIC

(M) (2:56) Rhino 75778 Frat Rock.
(S) (2:58) DCC Compact Classics 043 Toga Rock II.
(M) (2:57) Rhino 70536 San Francisco Nights.
(S) (2:58) Epic 30325 Greatest Hits.
(S) (2:58) Epic 37071 Anthology.
(S) (2:58) Columbia/Legacy 52454 A Tribute To Black Entertainers.
(M) (2:56) Time-Life 2CLR-11 Classic Rock - 1968: The Beat Goes On.

(S) (2:54) Tommy Boy 1100 ESPN Presents Jock Rock. *(sound effects added to the introduction)*
(S) (6:35) Epic 66155 Club Epic Volume 3. *(remixed version originally released on the 1979 vinyl LP "Ten Years Too Soon")*
(S) (2:56) Legacy/Epic 66427 Dance To The Music.

1969 EVERYDAY PEOPLE

(S) (2:19) Rhino 70655 Billboard's Top R&B Hits Of 1969.
(S) (2:19) Rhino 72006 Billboard's Top R&B Hits 1965-1969 Box Set.
(S) (2:20) Epic 30325 Greatest Hits.
(S) (2:20) Epic 37071 Anthology.
(S) (2:18) Epic 26456 and 53410 Stand!
(S) (2:19) Time-Life RHD-13 Rhythm & Blues - 1969.
(S) (2:19) Time-Life 2CLR-04 Classic Rock - 1968.
(S) (2:20) Time-Life R921-38 Get Together.
(S) (2:19) MCA 11036 O.S.T. Crooklyn.
(S) (2:19) Time-Life R838-04 Solid Gold Soul - 1969.
(S) (2:19) Repeat/Relativity 1609 Tell It Like It Is: #1 Soul Hits Of The 60's Volume 1.

1969 STAND!

(S) (3:05) Epic 30325 Greatest Hits.
(S) (3:05) Epic 37071 Anthology.
(S) (3:05) Epic 26456 and 53410 Stand!
(S) (3:05) Right Stuff 28373 Movin' On Up.
(S) (3:05) JCI 3111 Good Time Sixties.
(S) (3:02) Time-Life 2CLR-20 Classic Rock - 1969: Shakin' All Over.

1969 HOT FUN IN THE SUMMERTIME

(S) (3:02) Columbia/Legacy 46160 Rock Artifacts Volume 1. *(:25 longer than either the 45 or LP; "Greatest Hits" quadraphonic vinyl LP version)*
(M) (2:37) Rhino 70655 Billboard's Top R&B Hits Of 1969.
(M) (2:37) Rhino 72006 Billboard's Top R&B Hits 1965-1969 Box Set.
(M) (2:37) Rhino 70087 Summer & Sun.
(E) (2:36) Epic 48732 O.S.T. My Girl.
(E) (2:37) Epic 30325 Greatest Hits.
(E) (2:37) Epic 37071 Anthology.
(M) (2:36) Time-Life RHD-13 Rhythm & Blues - 1969.
(E) (2:36) Time-Life 2CLR-06 Classic Rock - 1969.
(E) (2:36) K-Tel 3437 Summer Songs.
(S) (3:01) Madacy Entertainment 26927 Sun Splashin'. *(rerecording)*
(M) (2:36) Time-Life R838-04 Solid Gold Soul - 1969.
(M) (2:37) Nick At Nite/550 Music 63436 Patio Pool Party.

1970 THANK YOU (FALETTINME BE MICE ELF AGIN)

(E) (4:38) Epic 46940 O.S.T. Queenslogic.
(E) (4:48) Epic 30325 Greatest Hits.
(E) (4:48) Epic 37071 Anthology.
(M) (4:44) Rhino 71431 In Yo Face! History Of Funk Volume 1.
(M) (4:46) Razor & Tie 22045 Those Funky 70's.
(S) (4:48) Time-Life RHD-18 Rhythm & Blues - 1970.
(S) (4:49) Time-Life R102-34 The Rolling Stone Collection.
(S) (4:49) Time-Life SOD-01 Sounds Of The Seventies - 1970.
(E) (4:44) K-Tel 6011 70's Soul: Super Funky Hits.
(S) (4:18) Columbia 52826 Red Hot + Dance. *(remixed)*
(S) (4:50) Rhino 72112 Billboard Hot Soul Hits - 1970.
(S) (4:50) Time-Life R838-05 Solid Gold Soul - 1970.

1970 EVERYBODY IS A STAR

(E) (3:00) Epic 30325 Greatest Hits.
(E) (3:00) Epic 37071 Anthology.
(E) (2:58) MCA 11065 O.S.T. Crooklyn Volume II.

1970 I WANT TO TAKE YOU HIGHER

(S) (5:22) Epic 30325 Greatest Hits. *(LP version)*
(S) (5:22) Epic 37071 Anthology. *(LP version)*
(S) (5:19) Epic 26456 and 53410 Stand! *(LP version)*
(S) (2:57) Time-Life 2CLR-12 Classic Rock - 1969: The Beat Goes On. *(45 version)*

1971 FAMILY AFFAIR

(S) (3:03) Rhino 70632 Billboard's Top Rock & Roll Hits Of 1971.
(S) (3:03) Rhino 72005 Billboard's Top Rock & Roll Hits 1968-1972 Box Set.
(S) (3:01) JCI 3304 Mellow Seventies.

(S) (3:03) Epic 37071 Anthology.
(S) (3:02) Epic 30986 There's A Riot Goin' On.
(S) (3:48) Epic/Legacy 52402 Club Epic - A Collection Of Classic Dance Mixes Volume 2. *(neither the 45 or LP version)*
(S) (3:04) Rhino 71432 In Yo Face! History Of Funk Volume 2.
(S) (2:59) Razor & Tie 22047 Sweet 70's Soul.
(S) (3:04) Time-Life SOD-02 Sounds Of The Seventies - 1971.
(S) (3:03) Eclipse Music Group 64892 Rock 'n Roll Relix 1970-1971.
(S) (3:03) Eclipse Music Group 64897 Rock 'n Roll Relix 1970-1979.

1972 RUNNIN' AWAY
(S) (2:53) Epic 37071 Anthology.
(S) (2:53) Epic 30986 There's A Riot Goin' On.

1972 SMILIN'
(S) (2:51) Epic 37071 Anthology.
(S) (2:51) Epic 30986 There's A Riot Goin' On.

1973 IF YOU WANT ME TO STAY
(S) (2:56) Epic 37071 Anthology.
(S) (2:57) Epic 32134 Fresh.
(S) (2:59) Rhino 71434 In Yo Face! History Of Funk Volume 4.
(S) (2:55) Capitol 32438 O.S.T. Dead Presidents.

1974 TIME FOR LIVIN'

SLY FOX
1986 LET'S GO ALL THE WAY
(S) (5:06) Madacy Entertainment 1985 Rock On 1985. *(LP version)*
(S) (3:55) JCI 3177 1985 - Only Soul - 1989. *(45 version)*
(S) (5:06) Time-Life R988-21 Sounds Of The Eighties: 1986-1989. *(LP version)*
(S) (4:48) Priority 50940 Shut Up And Dance! The 80's Volume One. *(all selections on this cd are segued together)*

MILLIE SMALL
1964 MY BOY LOLLIPOP
(M) (1:59) Island 90684 and 842901 The Island Story. *(cd jacket identifies the singer only as "MILLIE")*
(M) (1:55) Time-Life SUD-12 Superhits - The Mid 60's.
(M) (2:00) Mango 162539935 Story Of Jamaican Music. *(cd jacket identifies the singer only as "MILLIE")*
(M) (1:55) Time-Life AM1-05 AM Gold - The Mid '60s.
(M) (1:59) Island 314524393 Island Records 40th Anniversary Volume 1 1959-1964: Ska's The Limit.

1964 SWEET WILLIAM

SMALL FACES
1968 ITCHYCOO PARK
(M) (2:44) Sony Music Special Products 47351 The Immediate Singles Collection Volume 1.
(S) (2:48) Sony Music Special Products 47895 There Are But Four Small Faces.
(S) (2:47) Pair 1287 Original British Rock Classics.
(S) (2:47) Special Music 4941 More Of The Best Of British Rock.
(M) (2:43) JCI 3107 British Sixties.
(S) (2:45) Time-Life 2CLR-11 Classic Rock - 1968: The Beat Goes On.
(E) (2:42) Risky Business 53919 Songs Of Peacemakers, Protesters And Potheads.

SMASHING PUMPKINS
1995 BULLET WITH BUTTERFLY WINGS
(S) (4:16) Virgin 40861 Mellon Collie And The Infinite Sadness.

1996 1979
(S) (4:24) Virgin 40861 Mellon Collie And The Infinite Sadness.
(S) (4:22) Grammy Recordings/Chronicles 314553292 1997 Grammy Nominees.
(S) (4:22) Time-Life R13610 Gold And Platinum Box Set - The Ultimate Rock Collection.

1996 TONIGHT, TONIGHT
(S) (4:14) Virgin 40861 Mellon Collie And The Infinite Sadness.
1997 THIRTY-THREE
(S) (4:10) Virgin 40861 Mellon Collie And The Infinite Sadness.

SMITH
1969 BABY IT'S YOU
(S) (3:21) Rhino 70921 Super Hits Of The 70's Volume 1. *(LP version)*
(S) (3:21) Rhino 72009 Super Hits Of The 70's Volumes 1-4 Box Set. *(LP version)*
(S) (3:25) MCA 31274 Classic Rock Volume 2. *(LP version)*
(S) (3:20) JCI 3101 Rockin' Sixties. *(LP version)*
(S) (3:22) Rhino 71205 70's Smash Hits Volume 1. *(LP version)*
(S) (3:09) Time-Life SUD-07 Superhits - 1969. *(LP version faded :16 early)*
(S) (3:25) Varese Sarabande 5489 A Group Called Smith. *(LP version)*
(S) (3:23) Hip-O 40038 Power Chords Volume 1. *(LP version)*
(S) (3:09) Time-Life AM1-01 AM Gold - 1969. *(LP version faded :16 early)*
(S) (3:22) Flashback 72681 '70s Radio Hits Volume 1. *(LP version)*
(S) (3:22) Flashback 72090 '70s Radio Hits Box Set. *(LP version)*
(S) (2:33) Varese Sarabande 5846 On The Radio Volume One. *(45 version)*

1970 TAKE A LOOK AROUND
(S) (2:51) Varese Sarabande 5489 A Group Called Smith.

FRANKIE SMITH
1981 DOUBLE DUTCH BUS
(S) (5:20) Thump 4010 Old School. *(LP version)*
(S) (4:18) K-Tel 3581 Roller Disco - Boogie From The Skating Rinks. *(neither the 45, 12" single or LP version)*
(S) (5:14) WMOT/Hot Productions 38 Best Of WMOT Records. *(LP version)*

HUEY "PIANO" SMITH and THE CLOWNS
1958 DON'T YOU JUST KNOW IT
(M) (2:27) Rhino 70794 KFOG Presents M. Dung's Idiot Show.
(M) (2:27) Original Sound 8853 Oldies But Goodies Vol. 3. *(this compact disc uses the "Waring - fds" noise reduction process)*
(M) (2:27) Original Sound 2222 Oldies But Goodies Volumes 3,5,11,14 and 15 Box Set. *(this box set uses the "Waring - fds" noise reduction process)*
(M) (2:27) Original Sound 2500 Oldies But Goodies Volumes 1-15 Box Set. *(this box set uses the "Waring - fds" noise reduction process)*
(M) (2:26) Original Sound CDGO-3 Golden Oldies Volume. 3.
(M) (2:27) Original Sound 9603 Best Of Oldies But Goodies Vol. 3.
(M) (2:30) Rhino 70587 New Orleans Party Classics.
(M) (2:30) Ace 2021 Rock 'N Roll Revival.
(M) (2:29) Rock 'n' Roll 75406 Best Of Ace Records: The R&B Hits.
(M) (2:28) Time-Life 2RNR-05 Rock 'N' Roll Era - 1958.
(M) (2:29) Time-Life RHD-16 Rhythm & Blues - 1958.
(M) (2:29) Rhino 71806 The R&B Box: Thirty Years Of Rhythm & Blues.
(M) (2:30) Era 511 Ultimate 50's Party.
(M) (2:28) EMI 37350 Crescent City Soul: The Sound Of New Orleans 1947-1974.
(M) (2:30) K-Tel 3680 Mardi Gras Party Time!
(M) (2:29) Time-Life R838-22 Solid Gold Soul 1958.

HURRICANE SMITH
1973 OH BABE, WHAT WOULD YOU SAY?
(S) (3:26) Rhino 70930 Super Hits Of The 70's Volume 10.
(S) (3:26) EMI 90603 Rock Me Gently.
(S) (3:25) Capitol 98665 When AM Was King.
(S) (3:25) Time-Life SUD-20 Superhits - Early 70's Classics.

HURRICANE SMITH *(Continued)*

- (S) (3:25) Time-Life AM1-15 AM Gold - Early '70s Classics.
- (S) (3:25) Time-Life R840-03 Sounds Of The Seventies - Pop Nuggets: Early '70s.

JIMMY SMITH
1962 WALK ON THE WILD SIDE (PART 1)

- (S) (5:53) Verve 831374 Jimmy Smith: Compact Jazz. *(Parts 1 & 2)*
- (S) (5:53) Verve 314521007 Playboy's 40th Anniversary: Four Decades Of Jazz (1953-1993). *(Parts 1 & 2)*
- (S) (5:53) Verve 314521737 The Verve Story 1944-1994. *(Parts 1 & 2)*
- (S) (5:53) Time-Life HPD-39 Your Hit Parade - 60's Instrumentals: Take Two. *(Parts 1 & 2)*
- (S) (2:33) Polygram Special Markets 314520273 Great Instrumental Hits. *(Part 1)*
- (S) (5:53) Collectors' Choice 003/4 Instrumental Gems Of The 60's. *(Parts 1 & 2)*
- (S) (5:53) MCA 11389 O.S.T. Casino. *(Parts 1 & 2)*
- (S) (5:53) Verve 314527950 Walk On The Wild Side - Best Of The Verve Years. *(Parts 1 & 2)*
- (S) (5:53) Verve 314521855 Jazz Masters 29. *(Parts 1 & 2)*
- (S) (5:56) Rhino 72474 Masters Of Jazz, Vol. 7: Jazz Hit Singles. *(Parts 1 & 2)*

MICHAEL W. SMITH
1991 PLACE IN THIS WORLD

- (S) (3:58) RCA/Reunion 66271 and 49230 Crossfire/A Contemporary Christian Collection.
- (S) (3:57) Reunion 66314 and 49231 The First Decade 1983-1993.
- (S) (3:57) Reunion 66348 The Wonder Years.
- (S) (3:59) Reunion 24325 and 66164 and 49203 Go West Young Man.

1992 I WILL BE HERE FOR YOU

- (S) (4:32) Foundation/RCA 66563 Number 1 Hit Mix.
- (S) (4:33) Reunion 66314 and 49231 The First Decade 1983-1993.
- (S) (4:33) Reunion 66348 The Wonder Years.
- (S) (4:32) Reunion 24491 and 66163 and 49202 Change Your World.

O.C. SMITH
1968 THE SON OF HICKORY HOLLER'S TRAMP

- (S) (3:48) Sony Music Special Products 22094 Me And You.
- (S) (3:47) K-Tel 3885 Story Songs.

1968 LITTLE GREEN APPLES

- (S) (3:54) Columbia 45019 Pop Classics Of The 60's.
- (S) (3:56) Sony Music Special Products 22094 Me And You.
- (S) (3:52) Time-Life SUD-18 Superhits - Late 60's Classics.
- (S) (3:52) Time-Life AM1-12 AM Gold - Late '60s Classics.
- (S) (3:54) Hammer & Lace 697124114 Leading Men: Masters Of Style Volume Two.
- (S) (3:53) Time-Life R814-01 Love Songs.

1969 DADDY'S LITTLE MAN

PATTI SMITH GROUP
1978 BECAUSE THE NIGHT

- (S) (3:19) Sandstone 33000 Reelin' In The Years Volume 1.
- (S) (3:20) Arista 8166 and 18826 Easter.
- (S) (3:19) Polydor 314515913 Classic Rock Box.
- (S) (3:19) DCC Compact Classics 062 Rock Of The 70's Volume 1.
- (S) (3:19) Razor & Tie 22502 Those Rocking 70's.
- (S) (3:19) Time-Life SOD-10 Sounds Of The Seventies - 1978.
- (S) (3:19) Right Stuff 28996 Sedated In The Eighties No. 2.

RAY SMITH
1960 ROCKIN' LITTLE ANGEL

- (M) (2:12) Vee Jay 708 The Unavailable 16/The Original Nitty Gritty.
- (M) (2:13) Time-Life 2RNR-44 Rock 'N' Roll Era - Lost Treasures.

REX SMITH
1979 YOU TAKE MY BREATH AWAY

- (S) (3:11) Rhino 71202 Super Hits Of The 70's Volume 22.
- (S) (3:17) Risky Business 66662 Swingin' Singles/Greatest Hits Of The 70's.
- (S) (3:11) Time-Life R834-20 Body Talk - Heart And Soul.
- (S) (3:10) Time-Life AM1-26 AM Gold - 1979.

released as by REX SMITH/RACHEL SWEET:
1981 EVERLASTING LOVE

- (S) (3:43) Sony Music Distribution 57854 For Your Love.

SAMMI SMITH
1971 HELP ME MAKE IT THROUGH THE NIGHT

- (S) (2:31) Rhino 70924 Super Hits Of The 70's Volume 4.
- (S) (2:31) Rhino 72009 Super Hits Of The 70's Volumes 1-4 Box Set.
- (S) (2:31) Sony Music Special Products 48621 Kris Kristofferson: Singer/Songwriter.
- (S) (2:31) Time-Life CTD-05 Country USA - 1971.
- (S) (2:30) Time-Life CCD-06 Contemporary Country - The Early 70's.
- (S) (2:31) K-Tel 567 Country Music Classics Volume IV.
- (S) (2:31) Varese Sarabande 5607 Through The Years - Country Hits Of The 70's.
- (S) (2:31) K-Tel 3163 Behind Closed Doors.
- (S) (2:31) Madacy Entertainment 1971 Rock On 1971.
- (S) (2:31) Varese Sarabande 5574 Best Of.
- (S) (2:30) JCI 3155 1970 - Only Country - 1974.
- (S) (2:31) Priority 53140 Best Of The 70's: Legendary Ladies.
- (S) (2:31) K-Tel 3367 101 Greatest Country Hits Vol. Eight: Country Romance.
- (S) (2:31) Velvel/Reel Sounds 79713 O.S.T. The Ice Storm.
- (S) (2:31) Epic 68778 O.S.T. U Turn.
- (S) (2:30) Time-Life R814-05 Love Songs.
- (S) (2:30) Time-Life R808-04 Classic Country 1970-1974.

SOMETHIN' SMITH & THE REDHEADS
1955 IT'S A SIN TO TELL A LIE

- (M) (2:55) Time-Life HPD-23 Your Hit Parade - The Late 50's.
- (M) (2:55) Collectors' Choice Music 044 Ain't That Somethin' - Best Of.

1956 IN A SHANTY IN OLD SHANTY TOWN

- (M) (2:51) Collectors' Choice Music 044 Ain't That Somethin' - Best Of.

VERDELLE SMITH
1966 TAR AND CEMENT

WHISTLING JACK SMITH
1967 I WAS KAISER BILL'S BATMAN

- (S) (2:18) Collectors' Choice 003/4 Instrumental Gems Of The 60's.

SMITHEREENS
1990 A GIRL LIKE YOU

- (S) (4:41) Capitol 91194 11.
- (S) (4:39) Capitol 31481 Blown To Smithereens - Best Of.
- (S) (4:39) Priority 50953 I Love Rock & Roll Volume 4: Hits Of The 80's.

1992 TOO MUCH PASSION

- (S) (4:34) Capitol 94963 Blow Up.
- (S) (4:29) Capitol 31481 Blown To Smithereens - Best Of.

SMOKIE
1977 LIVING NEXT DOOR TO ALICE

- (S) (3:28) Rhino 71200 Super Hits Of The 70's Volume 20.

PATTY SMYTH (see SCANDAL)

SNAP
1990 THE POWER

- (S) (5:54) Luke 91663 O.S.T. Hangin' With The Homeboys. *(remix)*
- (S) (3:38) Arista 18735 House Of Groove. *(45 version)*
- (S) (5:40) JCI 2717 Shake It Up. *(LP version)*

556

(S) (5:41) Priority 7053 Best Of Hip Hop. *(LP version)*
(S) (5:40) Priority 8657 Yo Rap Hits. *(LP version)*
(S) (5:39) Rebound 314520246 Disco Nights Vol. 5 - Best Of Housemusic. *(LP version)*
(S) (5:40) Arista 8536 World Power. *(LP version)*
(S) (4:12) Tommy Boy 1137 ESPN Presents Jock Jams. *(all songs on this cd are segued together with crowd sound effects added)*
(S) (5:40) Fox/Atlantic 82777 O.S.T. Mighty Morphin Power Rangers. *(LP version)*
(S) (3:38) Risky Business 67310 We Came To Play. *(45 version)*
(S) .(8:13) Arista 18964 Best Of Snap! Remixes & All. *(remix)*
(S) (6:39) Arista 18964 Best Of Snap! Remixes & All. *(1997 rerecording)*
(S) (5:31) Cold Front 6245 Greatest Sports Rock And Jams. *(all selections on this cd are segued together)*
(S) (4:12) Hollywood 62121 Monday Night Football Jamz. *(neither the 45 or LP version)*
(S) (5:34) Cold Front 6254 Club Mix '98. *(all selections on this cd are segued together)*
(S) (5:40) K-Tel 3848 90s Now Volume 2. *(LP version)*
(S) (5:12) Beast 53292 Club Hitz Of The 90's Vol. 4. *(all songs on this cd are segued together)*
(S) (5:33) Priority 50935 100% Party Hits Of The 90's Volume Two. *(all selections on this cd are segued together)*

1990 OOOPS UP
(S) (6:41) DCC Compact Classics 082 Night Moves Volume 2.
(S) (6:40) Arista 8536 World Power.
(S) (5:52) Arista 18964 Best Of Snap! Remixes & All. *(live)*
(S) (4:53) Beast 53232 Club Hitz Of The 90's Vol. 3. *(all songs on this cd are segued together)*

1992 RHYTHM IS A DANCER
(S) (5:11) Arista 18735 House Of Groove. *(12" single version)*
(S) (5:28) Sandstone 33055 and 5014 Rock The First Volume Eight. *(LP version)*
(S) (6:51) Tommy Boy 1075 MTV Party To Go Volume 4. *(remix; all tracks on this cd are segued together)*
(S) (5:28) Rhino 71916 Whats Up? Rap Hits Of The 90's. *(LP version)*
(S) (5:28) Arista 18693 The Madman's Return. *(LP version)*
(S) (5:28) Original Sound 9308 Dedicated To You Vol. 8. *(LP version)*
(S) (5:11) Rebound 314520359 World Of Dance - The 90's. *(12" single version)*
(S) (5:12) Arista 18964 Best Of Snap! Remixes & All. *(12" single version)*
(S) (10:17) Arista 18964 Best Of Snap! Remixes & All. *(remix)*
(S) (2:57) Priority 50954 Power Workout High NRG Megamix Volume 1. *(all selections on this cd are segued together)*
(S) (3:48) Cold Front 6247 Classic Club Mix - Dance Jams. *(all selections on this cd are segued together; 45 version)*
(S) (3:47) Cold Front 6255 Greatest Sports Rock And Jams Volume 2. *(all selections on this cd are segued together; 45 version)*
(S) (5:11) Rhino 72839 Disco Queens: The 90's. *(12" single version)*
(S) (5:09) Beast 53032 Club Hitz Of The 90's Vol. 2. *(all songs on this cd are segued together)*
(S) (5:11) Interhit/Priority 51080 DMA Dance Vol. 1: Eurodance. *(12" single version)*

SNEAKER
1982 MORE THAN JUST THE TWO OF US

SNIFF 'N THE TEARS
1979 DRIVER'S SEAT
(S) (3:59) Rhino 71202 Super Hits Of The 70's Volume 22. *(LP length)*
(S) (3:44) Time-Life SOD-37 Sounds Of The Seventies - AM Heavy Hits. *(45 length)*

(S) (3:58) Capitol 93076 More Music From O.S.T. Boogie Nights. *(LP length)*

SNOOP DOGGY DOGG
1994 WHAT'S MY NAME?
(S) (4:06) Death Row/Interscope 92279 and 50605 Doggystyle.
1994 GIN AND JUICE
(S) (3:31) Death Row/Interscope 92279 and 50605 Doggystyle. *(tracks into next selection)*
(S) (3:31) Death Row/Interscope 50677 Death Row Greatest Hits. *(all songs on this cd are segued together)*
(S) (5:01) Death Row/Interscope 50677 Death Row Greatest Hits. *(all songs on this cd are segued together; remixed)*

released as by NATE DOGG featuring SNOOP DOGGY DOGG:
1996 NEVER LEAVE ME ALONE

SNOW
1993 INFORMER
(S) (4:58) Tommy Boy 1097 MTV Party To Go Volume 5. *(remix; all tracks on this cd are segued together)*
(S) (4:27) EastWest 92207 12 Inches Of Snow.
(S) (4:27) Razor & Tie 4569 '90s Style.
(S) (4:27) Elektra 62089 Maximum R&B.
(S) (4:28) EastWest 62075 Greatest Hits Of.
1993 GIRL, I'VE BEEN HURT
(S) (4:11) EastWest 92207 12 Inches Of Snow.

PHOEBE SNOW
1975 POETRY MAN
(S) (4:35) Sandstone 33003 Reelin' In The Years Volume 4. *(LP version)*
(S) (4:36) Columbia 37091 Best Of. *(LP version)*
(S) (4:36) Shelter/DCC Compact Classics 8004 Phoebe Snow. *(LP version)*
(S) (4:36) DCC Compact Classics 065 Rock Of The 70's Volume 4. *(LP version)*
(S) (4:36) DCC Compact Classics 1051 Phoebe Snow. *(LP version; gold disc)*
(S) (4:34) Time-Life SOD-16 Sounds Of The Seventies - 1975: Take Two. *(LP version)*
(S) (4:34) Time-Life R103-33 Singers & Songwriters. *(LP version)*
(S) (4:35) Rhino 71843 Troubadours Of The Folk Era Vol. 4. *(LP version)*
(S) (4:36) Right Stuff/Shelter 31972 Phoebe Snow. *(LP version)*
(S) (4:36) Rhino 72447 Listen To The Music: 70's Female Singer/Songwriters. *(LP version)*
(S) (4:34) Time-Life R103-18 Great Love Songs Of The '70s & '80s. *(LP version)*
(S) (4:35) Time-Life AM1-22 AM Gold - 1975. *(LP version)*
(S) (4:36) Time-Life R834-07 Body Talk - Hearts In Motion. *(LP version)*

released as by PAUL SIMON/PHOEBE SNOW with THE JESSY DIXON SINGERS:
1975 GONE AT LAST
(S) (3:38) Warner Brothers 25591 Paul Simon: Still Crazy After All These Years.
(S) (3:28) Warner Brothers 45394 Paul Simon 1964/1993.

SOFT CELL
1982 TAINTED LOVE
(S) (2:38) Priority 53705 Rock Of The 80's Volume 2.
(S) (2:40) Rhino 71697 New Wave Hits Of The 80's Vol. 4.
(S) (2:40) Warner Brothers 45345 O.S.T. Coneheads.
(S) (5:50) Rebound 314520324 Alterno-Daze: Survival Of 80's The Fittest. *(neither the 45, LP or 12" single version; remixed)*
(S) (2:40) Time-Life R988-05 Sounds Of The Eighties: 1982.
(S) (2:38) K-Tel 3473 The 80s: New Wave.

SOFT CELL (Continued)

- (S) (5:50) Rebound 314520354 World Of Dance: New Wave - The 80's. *(neither the 45, LP or 12" single version; remixed)*
- (S) (5:50) Mercury 314510178 Memorabilia. *(neither the 45, LP or 12" single version; remixed)*
- (S) (8:54) Oglio 24353 Richard Blade's Flashback Favorites Volume 3. *(12" single version)*
- (S) (2:34) Hip-O 40023 Smash Alternatives - 14 Classic New Wave Hits.
- (S) (4:11) Rhino 72894 Hard Rock Cafe: New Wave. *(neither the 45, LP or 12" single version)*
- (S) (2:32) Arista 18985 Ultimate New Wave Party 1998. *(all selections on this cd are segued together)*

SOHO
1990 HIPPY CHICK
- (S) (3:12) Atco 91585 Goddess. *(tracks into the next selection)*
- (S) (3:14) Elektra 62161 Maximum Dance Hits Vol. 1.
- (S) (3:12) Intersound 9521 Retro Lunch Box - Squeeze The Cheese.

SOMETHIN' FOR THE PEOPLE featuring TRINA & TAMARA
1997 MY LOVE IS THE SHHH!
- (S) (4:31) Warner Brothers 46753 This Time It's Personal.

JOANIE SOMMERS
1962 JOHNNY GET ANGRY
- (S) (2:31) Rhino 70989 Best Of The Girl Groups Volume 2.
- (S) (2:28) Time-Life 2RNR-35 Rock 'N' Roll Era - The 60's Last Dance.
- (S) (2:30) Time-Life R102-17 Lost Treasures Of Rock 'N' Roll.

SONNY
1965 LAUGH AT ME
- (M) (2:54) Rhino 70734 Songs Of Protest.
- (M) (2:51) Atco 91796 Sonny & Cher: The Beat Goes On.
- (M) (2:50) Rhino 71233 Sonny & Cher: I Got You Babe.
- (M) (2:50) Time-Life 2CLR-23 Classic Rock - 1965: Blowin' Your Mind.
- (M) (2:54) Time-Life R962-02 History Of Rock 'N' Roll: Folk Rock 1964-1967.
- (M) (2:53) Sundazed 6140 The Wondrous World Of Sonny & Cher.

SONNY & CHER
1965 I GOT YOU BABE
- (S) (3:08) Atlantic 81905 O.S.T. Buster. *(segues together with the preceding selection)*
- (M) (3:10) Atco 91796 The Beat Goes On.
- (M) (2:15) Atco 91796 The Beat Goes On. *(this version is from the "Good Times" soundtrack and is not the hit version)*
- (M) (3:10) Rhino 70626 Billboard's Top Rock & Roll Hits Of 1965. *(found only on the 2nd pressings of this compact disc)*
- (M) (3:09) Epic 53760 O.S.T. Groundhog Day.
- (M) (3:10) Rhino 71233 I Got You Babe.
- (M) (3:09) Time-Life 2CLR-01 Classic Rock - 1965.
- (M) (3:08) Time-Life SUD-03 Superhits - 1965.
- (M) (3:09) Time-Life R962-04 History Of Rock 'N' Roll: California Pop 1963-1967.
- (S) (3:14) MCA Special Products 22025 All I Ever Need Is You. *(live)*
- (M) (3:09) Rhino 71728 '60s Rock Classics, Vol. 1.
- (M) (3:09) JCI 3126 1965 - Only Rock 'N Roll - 1969.
- (M) (3:08) JCI 3160 18 Free & Easy Hits From The 60's.
- (S) (3:06) Eclipse Music Group 64869 Rock 'n Roll Relix 1964-1965.
- (S) (3:06) Eclipse Music Group 64872 Rock 'n Roll Relix 1960-1969.
- (M) (3:08) Time-Life AM1-10 AM Gold - 1965.
- (M) (3:09) Flashback 72701 '60s Rock: Mony Mony.

- (M) (3:09) Flashback 72088 '60s Rock Hits Box Set.
- (M) (3:10) Rhino 72819 16 Magazine - Who's Your Fave Rave.
- (M) (3:10) Time-Life R13610 Gold And Platinum Box Set - The Ultimate Rock Collection.
- (M) (3:11) Flashback 72806 I Got You Babe And Other Hits.
- (S) (4:34) MCA 11745 Cher And Sonny & Cher - Greatest Hits. *(live)*
- (M) (3:10) Sundazed 6139 Look At Us.
- (M) (3:10) Atlantic 83088 Atlantic Records: 50 Years - The Gold Anniversary Collection.

1965 BABY DON'T GO
- (E) (3:08) Warner Special Products 27610 More Party Classics.
- (E) (3:08) JCI 3110 Sock Hoppin' Sixties.
- (M) (3:09) Atco 91796 The Beat Goes On.
- (E) (3:02) Time-Life 2CLR-23 Classic Rock - 1965: Blowin' Your Mind.

1965 JUST YOU
- (M) (4:04) Atco 91796 The Beat Goes On. *(LP version lyrics but :34 longer than the vinyl LP version)*
- (M) (4:04) Rhino 71233 I Got You Babe. *(LP version lyrics but :34 longer than the vinyl LP version)*
- (M) (4:04) Flashback 72806 I Got You Babe And Other Hits. *(LP version lyrics but :34 longer than the vinyl LP version)*
- (M) (3:28) Sundazed 6139 Look At Us.

1965 BUT YOU'RE MINE
- (M) (3:02) Atco 91796 The Beat Goes On.
- (M) (3:02) Rhino 71233 I Got You Babe.
- (M) (3:01) JCI 3185 1965 - Only Love - 1969.
- (M) (3:02) Flashback 72806 I Got You Babe And Other Hits.
- (M) (3:01) Sundazed 6140 The Wondrous World Of.

1966 WHAT NOW MY LOVE
- (M) (3:36) Atco 91796 The Beat Goes On.
- (M) (3:35) Rhino 71233 I Got You Babe.
- (M) (3:36) Flashback 72806 I Got You Babe And Other Hits.
- (M) (3:39) Sundazed 6140 The Wondrous World Of.

1966 LITTLE MAN
- (M) (3:19) Atco 91796 The Beat Goes On.
- (M) (3:19) Flashback 72806 I Got You Babe And Other Hits.
- (M) (3:19) Sundazed 6141 In Case You're In Love.

1967 THE BEAT GOES ON
- (S) (3:26) Warner Special Products 27602 20 Party Classics.
- (S) (3:26) Atlantic 81909 Hit Singles 1958-1977.
- (S) (3:26) Atco 91796 The Beat Goes On.
- (M) (3:23) Rhino 71066 Summer Of Love Volume 2. *(noisy fadeout)*
- (M) (3:23) Rhino 71233 I Got You Babe. *(noisy fadeout)*
- (S) (3:19) Time-Life 2CLR-15 Classic Rock - 1967: Shakin' All Over.
- (S) (9:10) MCA Special Products 22025 All I Ever Need Is You. *(live)*
- (S) (3:26) Rhino 71729 '60s Rock Classics, Vol. 2.
- (S) (3:18) JCI 3167 #1 Radio Hits 1965 - Only Rock 'n Roll - 1969.
- (M) (3:23) Rhino 72478 Beverly Hills 90210: Songs From The Peach Pit. *(noisy fadeout)*
- (S) (3:26) Flashback 72702 '60s Rock: The Beat Goes On.
- (S) (3:26) Flashback 72088 '60s Rock Hits Box Set.
- (S) (3:26) Flashback 72806 I Got You Babe And Other Hits.
- (S) (3:25) Sundazed 6141 In Case You're In Love.

1972 ALL I EVER NEED IS YOU
- (S) (2:33) MCA Special Products 22025 All I Ever Need Is You.
- (S) (2:37) MCA 11300 All I Ever Need - The Kapp/MCA Anthology.
- (S) (2:37) MCA 11745 Cher And Sonny & Cher - Greatest Hits.

1972 A COWBOYS WORK IS NEVER DONE
- (S) (3:14) MCA Special Products 22025 All I Ever Need Is You.
- (S) (3:14) MCA 11300 All I Ever Need - The Kapp/MCA Anthology.
- (S) (3:14) MCA 11745 Cher And Sonny & Cher - Greatest Hits.

1972 WHEN YOU SAY LOVE
- (S) (2:26) MCA Special Products 22025 All I Ever Need Is You.
- (S) (2:26) MCA 11300 All I Ever Need - The Kapp/MCA Anthology.
- (S) (2:26) MCA 11745 Cher And Sonny & Cher - Greatest Hits.

SOPWITH "CAMEL"
1967 HELLO HELLO
- (S) (2:24) Pair 1202 Best Of Buddah.
- (M) (2:23) Rhino 70536 San Francisco Nights.
- (M) (2:23) K-Tel 666 Flower Power.
- (S) (2:24) One Way 29311 Sopwith Camel.
- (S) (2:23) Essex 7060 The Buddah Box.
- (S) (2:24) Time-Life 2CLR-29 Classic Rock - Bubblegum, Garage And Pop Nuggets.
- (S) (2:23) Buddah 49506 Feelin' Groovy.

S.O.S. BAND
1980 TAKE YOUR TIME (DO IT RIGHT) PART 1
- (S) (7:46) Epic 46087 Club Epic. *(remix)*
- (S) (7:35) Priority 7983 Mega-Hits Dance Classics Volume 7. *(LP version)*
- (S) (3:30) Rhino 70276 The Disco Years Volume 5. *(neither the 45 or LP version)*
- (S) (3:29) Rhino 70675 Billboard Top Hits - 1980. *(neither the 45 or LP version)*
- (S) (7:40) Tabu 36332 S.O.S. *(LP version)*
- (S) (3:56) Razor & Tie 22496 Disco Fever. *(edit of the LP version in an unsuccessful attempt at recreating the 45 version)*
- (S) (7:38) Tabu 314530594 Best Of. *(LP version)*

DAVID SOUL
1977 DON'T GIVE UP ON US
- (S) (3:35) Rhino 71199 Super Hits Of The 70's Volume 19. *(dropout at :04)*
- (S) (3:34) Razor & Tie 4543 The '70s Preservation Society Presents: Easy '70s.
- (S) (3:35) Rhino 71228 Yesterday's Heroes: 70's Teen Idols. *(dropout at :04)*
- (S) (3:35) Madacy Entertainment 1977 Rock On 1977.
- (S) (3:35) Time-Life AM1-24 AM Gold - 1977. *(dropout at :04)*
- (S) (3:35) Time-Life R834-05 Body Talk - Sealed With A Kiss. *(dropout at :04)*
- (S) (3:35) Rhino 72516 Behind Closed Doors - '70s Swingers. *(dropout at :04)*
- (S) (3:34) Simitar 55512 The Number One's: Lovin' Feelings.

JIMMY SOUL
1962 TWISTIN' MATILDA
- (M) (2:52) Rhino 70527 Best Of Jimmy Soul.

1963 IF YOU WANNA BE HAPPY
(45 time is (2:08); LP time is (2:14))
- (M) (2:09) Rhino 75772 Son Of Frat Rock.
- (S) (2:10) Rhino 70995 One Hit Wonders Of The 60's Volume 1.
- (S) (2:09) Original Sound CDGO-10 Golden Oldies Volume. 10.
- (S) (2:10) Geffen 24310 O.S.T. Mermaids.
- (S) (2:19) Rhino 70527 Best Of Jimmy Soul.
- (S) (2:19) Rhino 70589 Rockin' & Rollin' Wedding Songs Volume 2.
- (S) (2:19) Rhino 70624 Billboard's Top Rock & Roll Hits Of 1963. *(found only on the 1993 reissue of this cd)*
- (M) (2:11) Time-Life 2RNR-07 Rock 'N' Roll Era - 1963. *(truncated fade)*
- (M) (2:19) Work 68166 O.S.T. My Best Friend's Wedding.

SOUL ASYLUM
1993 RUNAWAY TRAIN
- (S) (4:24) Columbia 48898 Grave Dancers Union.

1995 MISERY
- (S) (4:24) Columbia 57616 Let Your Dim Light Shine.

SOUL CHILDREN
1972 HEARSAY
- (S) (3:32) Rhino 70789 Soul Hits Of The 70's Volume 9.
- (S) (3:30) Stax 88008 Top Of The Stax Volume 2.
- (S) (3:34) Stax 4120 Chronicle.
- (S) (3:32) Time-Life RHD-20 Rhythm & Blues - 1972.
- (S) (3:28) Stax 4415 Complete Stax/Volt Soul Singles Volume 3 1972-1975.
- (S) (3:32) Time-Life R838-07 Solid Gold Soul - 1972.

1974 I'LL BE THE OTHER WOMAN
- (S) (3:32) Stax 88005 Top Of The Stax.
- (S) (3:34) Stax 4415 Complete Stax/Volt Soul Singles Volume 3 1972-1975.
- (S) (3:32) Stax 4120 Chronicle.

SOUL FOR REAL
1995 CANDY RAIN
- (S) (4:34) Uptown/MCA 11125 Candy Rain.
- (S) (4:27) Loud/RCA 67423 All That - The Album.
- (S) (4:24) Uptown 53025 Uptown's Block Party Volume 2.

1995 EVERY LITTLE THING I DO
- (S) (4:17) Uptown/MCA 11125 Candy Rain.
- (S) (3:37) Priority 50935 100% Party Hits Of The 90's Volume Two. *(all selections on this cd are segued together)*

SOUL SURVIVORS
1967 EXPRESSWAY TO YOUR HEART
- (M) (2:20) DCC Compact Classics 029 Toga Rock.
- (M) (2:18) Rhino 70996 One Hit Wonders Of The 60's Volume 2.
- (M) (2:14) Original Sound 8861 Oldies But Goodies Vol. 11. *(this compact disc uses the "Waring - fds" noise reduction process)*
- (M) (2:14) Original Sound 2222 Oldies But Goodies Volumes 3,5,11,14 and 15 Box Set. *(this box set uses the "Waring - fds" noise reduction process)*
- (M) (2:14) Original Sound 2500 Oldies But Goodies Volumes 1-15 Box Set. *(this box set uses the "Waring - fds" noise reduction process)*
- (M) (2:14) Original Sound CDGO-4 Golden Oldies Volume. 4.
- (E) (2:18) K-Tel 686 Battle Of The Bands Volume 4.
- (M) (2:17) Collectables 5070 History Of Rock Volume 10.
- (M) (2:18) Rhino 71460 Soul Hits, Volume 2.
- (M) (2:19) Time-Life 2CLR-10 Classic Rock - 1967: The Beat Goes On.
- (E) (2:19) Collectables 2501 WCBS-FM History Of Rock - The 60's Part 2.
- (E) (2:19) Collectables 4501 History Of Rock/The 60s Part Two.
- (E) (2:20) Collectables 0502 When The Whistle Blows.
- (M) (2:16) Collectables 2604 WCBS-FM Jukebox Giants Vol. 2.
- (M) (2:20) Curb 77774 Hard To Find Hits Of Rock 'N' Roll Volume Two.
- (E) (2:19) Collectables 2554 CBS-FM History Of Rock Volume 2.
- (M) (2:14) EMI 52498 O.S.T. Striptease.
- (M) (2:19) JCI 3190 1965 - Only Dance - 1969.
- (M) (2:18) Flashback 72658 '60s Soul: Baby I Love You.
- (M) (2:18) Flashback 72091 '60s Soul Hits Box Set.
- (E) (2:18) Collectables 0502 Expressway To Your Heart.
- (M) (2:18) Epic/Legacy 64647 The Philly Sound Box Set.
- (M) (2:19) Rhino 72815 Beg, Scream & Shout! The Big Ol' Box Of '60s Soul.
- (E) (2:18) Right Stuff 52274 Flick Hits Take 2.
- (E) (2:18) Simitar 55152 Blue Eyed Soul.

1968 EXPLOSION (IN YOUR SOUL)
- (M) (2:35) Varese Sarabande 5705 Dick Bartley Presents Collector's Essentials: The 60's.
- (M) (2:32) Collectables 0502 Expressway To Your Heart.

S.O.U.L. SYSTEM
1993 IT'S GONNA BE A LOVELY DAY
- (S) (4:15) Arista 18735 House Of Groove. *(remix)*
- (S) (4:49) Arista 18699 O.S.T. The Bodyguard.

S.O.U.L. SYSTEM (Continued)
- (S) (4:49) Priority 53771 Ultimate Dance Classics.
- (S) (4:15) Rebound 314520359 World Of Dance - The 90's. *(remix)*

SOUL II SOUL
1989 KEEP ON MOVIN'
- (S) (5:58) Virgin 91267 and 86122 Keep On Movin'. *(LP version)*
- (S) (5:58) MCA 11329 Soul Train 25th Anniversary Box Set. *(LP version)*
- (S) (3:35) Rhino 72144 Billboard Hot R&B Hits 1989. *(45 version)*

1989 BACK TO LIFE (HOWEVER DO YOU WANT ME)
- (S) (3:47) Priority 53732 80's Greatest Rock Hits Volume 8 - Dance Party.
- (S) (5:07) Virgin 91292 O.S.T. Black Rain. *(remix)*
- (S) (3:46) Rebound 314520246 Disco Nights Vol. 5 - Best Of Housemusic.
- (S) (3:46) Virgin 91267 and 86122 Keep On Movin'.
- (S) (3:45) Cold Front 6247 Classic Club Mix - Dance Jams. *(all selections on this cd are segued together)*
- (S) (3:46) Rhino 72839 Disco Queens: The 90's.

SOUNDS OF SUNSHINE
1971 LOVE MEANS (YOU NEVER HAVE TO SAY YOU'RE SORRY)

SOUNDS ORCHESTRAL
1965 CAST YOUR FATE TO THE WIND
- (S) (3:11) Rhino 70995 One Hit Wonders Of The 60's Volume 1.
- (S) (3:05) K-Tel 3472 Those Wonderful Instrumentals Volume 2.

SOUP DRAGONS
1992 DIVINE THING
- (S) (3:50) Big Life/Mercury 314513178 Hotwired.

JOE SOUTH
1969 GAMES PEOPLE PLAY
- (S) (3:32) EMI 90603 Rock Me Gently.
- (S) (3:29) Rhino 70994 Best Of.
- (S) (3:31) Capitol 98665 When AM Was King.
- (S) (3:32) Time-Life 2CLR-12 Classic Rock - 1969: The Beat Goes On.

released as by JOE SOUTH and THE BELIEVERS:
1970 WALK A MILE IN MY SHOES
- (S) (3:42) Rhino 70994 Best Of. *(out of phase)*
- (S) (3:41) Time-Life SUD-20 Superhits - Early 70's Classics. *(out of phase)*
- (S) (3:41) Time-Life SOD-11 Sounds Of The Seventies - 1970: Take Two. *(out of phase)*
- (S) (3:41) Time-Life AM1-15 AM Gold - Early '70s Classics. *(out of phase)*

J.D. SOUTHER
1979 YOU'RE ONLY LONELY
- (S) (3:41) Epic 46940 O.S.T. Queens Logic.
- (S) (3:44) Priority 8663 The South Rules/70's Greatest Rock Hits Volume 2.
- (S) (3:43) Priority 53706 Singers/Songwriters/70's Greatest Rock Hits Volume 15.
- (S) (3:46) Columbia 36093 You're Only Lonely.
- (S) (3:44) Time-Life SOD-09 Sounds Of The Seventies - 1979.
- (S) (3:43) Time-Life R105-26 Our Songs: Singers & Songwriters Encore.
- (S) (3:46) Risky Business 66388 The Big Hurt/Songs To Cry By.
- (S) (3:45) Rhino 71890 Radio Daze: Pop Hits Of The 80's Volume One.
- (S) (3:43) Time-Life R834-01 Body Talk - Forever Yours.
- (S) (3:46) Sony Music Special Products 26069 Rock Hits Of The 70's.

released as by JAMES TAYLOR and J.D. SOUTHER:
1981 HER TOWN TOO
- (S) (4:33) Columbia 37009 James Taylor: Dad Loves His Work.
- (S) (4:33) Columbia 64807 James Taylor - JT/Flag/Dad Loves His Work.
- (S) (4:24) Madacy Entertainment 6803 Power Of Love.
- (S) (4:19) Time-Life R988-16 Sounds Of The Eighties: The Early '80s.
- (S) (4:23) Time-Life R834-09 Body Talk - Magic Moments.

SOUTHER, HILLMAN, FURAY BAND
1974 FALLIN' IN LOVE
- (S) (3:29) JCI 3303 Love Seventies.
- (S) (3:29) Time-Life SOD-25 Sounds Of The Seventies - Seventies Generation.
- (S) (3:29) JCI 3145 1970 - Only Love - 1974.
- (S) (3:28) K-Tel 3697 Best Of Country Rock.
- (S) (3:29) Rhino 72518 Mellow Rock Hits Of The 70's - Summer Breeze.

RED SOVINE
1976 TEDDY BEAR
- (S) (5:08) Deluxe 1013 16 Greatest Hits.
- (S) (5:07) Time-Life CCD-16 Contemporary Country - The Mid 70's Hot Hits.
- (S) (5:07) JCI 3156 1975 - Only Country - 1979.

SPACEHOG
1996 IN THE MEANTIME
- (S) (4:57) Sire 61834 Resident Alien. *(tracks into next selection)*

SPACEMEN
1959 THE CLOUDS

SPANDAU BALLET
1983 TRUE
(dj copies of this 45 ran (4:58) and (5:40); commercial copies all ran (5:40))
- (S) (5:40) Rhino 70678 Billboard Top Hits - 1983. *(45 version)*
- (S) (5:39) Rhino 71834 Classic MTV: Class Of 1983. *(45 version)*
- (S) (5:30) SBK 31181 Moments In Love. *(45 version)*
- (S) (5:33) EMI 28339 Living In Oblivion: The 80's Greatest Hits - Volume Four. *(45 version)*
- (S) (5:33) Rhino 71974 New Wave Hits Of The 80's Vol. 11. *(45 version)*
- (S) (6:26) Chrysalis 21403 and 41403 True. *(LP version)*
- (S) (5:35) Chrysalis 21498 and 41498 Singles Collection. *(45 version)*
- (S) (5:39) Time-Life R988-03 Sounds Of The Eighties: 1983. *(45 version)*
- (S) (5:34) Chrysalis 35978 Greatest Hits. *(45 version)*
- (S) (5:40) Time-Life R834-08 Body Talk - On My Mind. *(45 version)*
- (S) (5:31) Polygram TV 314555610 The One And Only Love Album. *(45 version)*

1984 GOLD
- (S) (3:53) Priority 53750 Rock Of The 80's Volume 7. *(45 version)*
- (S) (3:51) Rhino 71975 New Wave Hits Of The 80's Vol. 2. *(45 version)*
- (S) (4:48) Chrysalis 21403 and 41403 True. *(LP version)*
- (S) (3:54) Chrysalis 21498 and 41498 Singles Collection. *(45 version)*
- (S) (3:53) Chrysalis 35978 Greatest Hits. *(45 version)*
- (S) (3:51) Simitar 55552 The Number One's: Eighties Rock. *(45 version)*

1984 ONLY WHEN YOU LEAVE
- (S) (4:46) Priority 53798 Best Of 80's Rock Volume 5. *(45 length)*
- (S) (5:08) Chrysalis 21473 and 41473 Parade. *(LP length)*

(S) (4:47) Chrysalis 21498 and 41498 Singles Collection. *(45 length)*

(S) (4:45) Chrysalis 35978 Greatest Hits. *(45 length)*

SPANKY and OUR GANG
1967 SUNDAY WILL NEVER BE THE SAME
(S) (2:55) Mercury 834216 45's On CD Volume 3.

(S) (2:56) Mercury 832584 Greatest Hits.

(S) (2:55) K-Tel 666 Flower Power.

(S) (2:55) Time-Life SUD-05 Superhits - 1967.

(S) (2:55) Special Music 5026 Let It All Hang Out - 60's Party Hits.

(S) (2:56) Rebound 314520371 The Roots Of Rock: 60's Folk.

(S) (2:55) JCI 3160 18 Free & Easy Hits From The 60's.

(S) (2:56) Eclipse Music Group 64870 Rock 'n Roll Relix 1966-1967.

(S) (2:56) Eclipse Music Group 64872 Rock 'n Roll Relix 1960-1969.

(S) (2:55) Time-Life AM1-08 AM Gold - 1967.

(M) (2:56) Varese Sarabande 5801 Sunshine Days - Pop Classics Of The '60s Volume 1.

1967 MAKING EVERY MINUTE COUNT
(S) (2:32) Mercury 832584 Greatest Hits.

(S) (2:31) Polygram Special Markets 314520464 60's Rock Hits.

1967 LAZY DAY
(S) (3:04) Mercury 832584 Greatest Hits.

(M) (3:04) Rhino 71065 Summer Of Love Volume 1.

(S) (3:05) Rhino 71093 Better Days.

(S) (3:04) Buddah 49506 Feelin' Groovy.

(S) (3:05) Flashback 72687 '60s Rock: Feelin' Groovy.

(S) (3:05) Flashback 72088 '60s Rock Hits Box Set.

1968 SUNDAY MORNIN'
(S) (6:11) Mercury 832584 Greatest Hits. *(this version first appeared on the vinyl LP "Spanky's Greatest Hits")*

(S) (3:41) JCI 3114 Easy Sixties. *(LP version faded :12 early)*

1968 LIKE TO GET TO KNOW YOU
(S) (3:17) Mercury 832584 Greatest Hits.

(S) (3:08) Time-Life 2CLR-04 Classic Rock - 1968.

(S) (3:08) Time-Life SUD-02 Superhits - 1968.

(S) (3:16) Time-Life R921-38 Get Together.

(S) (3:16) LaserLight 12311 and 15936 The Wonder Years - First Love.

(S) (3:16) Eclipse Music Group 64871 Rock 'n Roll Relix 1968-1969.

(S) (3:16) Eclipse Music Group 64872 Rock 'n Roll Relix 1960-1969.

(S) (3:08) Time-Life AM1-04 AM Gold - 1968.

1968 GIVE A DAMN
(S) (3:34) Mercury 832584 Greatest Hits.

JUDSON SPENCE
1988 YEAH, YEAH, YEAH
(dj copies of this 45 ran (4:00) and (4:36); commercial copies were all (4:36))
(S) (4:32) Atlantic 81902 Judson Spence.

TRACIE SPENCER
1988 SYMPTOMS OF TRUE LOVE
(S) (5:02) Capitol 48186 Tracie Spencer. *(LP version)*

1991 THIS HOUSE
(S) (5:05) Capitol 92153 Make The Difference.

SPICE GIRLS
1997 WANNABE
(S) (2:52) Virgin 42174 Spice.

(S) (3:25) Tommy Boy 1207 MTV Grind Volume One. *(remix; all selections on this cd are segued together)*

1997 SAY YOU'LL BE THERE
(S) (3:55) Virgin 42174 Spice.

1997 2 BECOME 1
(S) (4:00) Virgin 42174 Spice.

1997 SPICE UP YOUR LIFE
(S) (2:53) Virgin 45111 Spiceworld.

SPIDER
1980 NEW ROMANCE (IT'S A MYSTERY)

SPIN DOCTORS
1992 LITTLE MISS CAN'T BE WRONG
(S) (3:51) Time-Life R102-34 The Rolling Stone Collection.

(S) (3:52) Epic 47461 Pocket Full Of Kryptonite.

1993 TWO PRINCES
(S) (4:15) Chaos/Columbia 57303 O.S.T. So I Married An Axe Murderer.

(S) (4:15) Priority 53740 Cutting Edge Vol. 2 - Best Of Modern Rock Hits.

(S) (4:15) Epic 47461 Pocket Full Of Kryptonite.

SPINNERS
1961 THAT'S WHAT GIRLS ARE MADE FOR
(E) (3:07) Motown 5450 A Collection Of 16 Big Hits Volume 3.

(M) (3:06) Atlantic 82332 A One Of A Kind Love Affair.

(M) (3:07) Time-Life 2RNR-48 Rock 'N' Roll Era - R&B Gems II.

1965 I'LL ALWAYS LOVE YOU
(S) (2:43) Motown 9109 Motown Memories Vol. 3.

(S) (2:43) Motown 6183 Hard To Find Motown Classics Volume 1.

(S) (2:43) Motown 5199 and 9008 Best Of.

(S) (2:43) Atlantic 82332 A One Of A Kind Love Affair.

1970 IT'S A SHAME
(S) (3:11) Motown 6183 Hard To Find Motown Classics Volume 1.

(S) (3:10) Rhino 70783 Soul Hits Of The 70's Volume 3.

(S) (3:10) Rhino 72028 Soul Hits Of The 70's Volumes 1-5 Box Set.

(S) (3:10) Motown 5199 and 9008 Best Of.

(S) (3:10) Atlantic 82332 A One Of A Kind Love Affair.

(S) (3:10) Ripete 392183 Ocean Drive.

(M) (3:06) Motown 6312 Hitsville USA.

(S) (3:10) Rhino 71207 70's Smash Hits Volume 3.

(M) (3:07) Rhino 71213 Very Best Of.

(S) (3:09) Time-Life RHD-18 Rhythm & Blues - 1970.

(S) (3:10) Rebound 314520232 Very Best Of.

(S) (3:10) Motown 314530528 Motown Year By Year - 1970.

(S) (3:09) Time-Life R838-05 Solid Gold Soul - 1970.

(S) (3:11) Flashback 72683 '70s Radio Hits Volume 3.

(S) (3:11) Flashback 72090 '70s Radio Hits Box Set.

1972 I'LL BE AROUND
(S) (3:08) Atlantic 81299 Atlantic Rhythm & Blues Volume 7.

(S) (3:09) Atlantic 81912 Golden Age Of Black Music (1970-1975).

(S) (3:08) Atlantic 82305 Atlantic Rhythm And Blues 1947-1974 Box Set.

(S) (3:08) Atlantic 81547 Best Of.

(S) (3:09) Atlantic 82332 A One Of A Kind Love Affair.

(S) (3:09) Rhino 71213 Very Best Of.

(S) (3:10) Time-Life RHD-20 Rhythm & Blues - 1972.

(S) (3:10) Time-Life SOD-22 Sounds Of The Seventies - Seventies Top Forty.

(S) (3:09) Rhino 71806 The R&B Box: Thirty Years Of Rhythm & Blues.

(S) (3:08) Rebound 314520232 Very Best Of.

(S) (3:09) Rhino 71882 Spinners.

(S) (3:08) Capitol 32438 O.S.T. Dead Presidents.

(S) (3:09) Rhino 72114 Billboard Hot Soul Hits - 1972.

(S) (3:10) Time-Life R838-07 Solid Gold Soul - 1972.

(S) (3:09) Time-Life R834-10 Body Talk - From The Heart.

(S) (3:09) Flashback 72672 I'll Be Around And Other Hits.

(S) (3:09) Rhino 72943 Ultimate '70s R&B Smashes!

(S) (3:09) Rhino 72943 VH1 8-Track Flashback: Classic '70s Soul.

1973 COULD IT BE I'M FALLING IN LOVE
(S) (4:09) Atlantic 81299 Atlantic Rhythm & Blues Volume 7.

561

SPINNERS *(Continued)*

(S) (4:10) Rhino 70906 American Bandstand Greatest Hits Collection.
(S) (4:10) Atlantic 81912 Golden Age Of Black Music (1970-1975).
(S) (4:09) Atlantic 82305 Atlantic Rhythm And Blues 1947-1974 Box Set. *(truncated fade)*
(S) (4:09) Atlantic 81547 Best Of.
(S) (4:31) Atlantic 82332 A One Of A Kind Love Affair. *(includes previously unreleased :20 a cappella coda)*
(S) (4:11) Rhino 71213 Very Best Of.
(S) (4:09) Time-Life SUD-13 Superhits - 1973.
(S) (4:10) Time-Life SOD-06 Sounds Of The Seventies - 1973.
(S) (4:11) Rebound 314520232 Very Best Of.
(S) (4:11) Rhino 71882 Spinners.
(S) (4:10) Thump 4730 Old School Love Songs Volume 3.
(S) (4:09) Elektra 61888 O.S.T. Beautiful Girls.
(S) (4:11) Hip-O 40001 The Glory Of Love - Sweet & Soulful Love Songs.
(S) (4:10) JCI 3145 1970 - Only Love - 1974.
(S) (4:09) Time-Life AM1-03 AM Gold - 1973.
(S) (4:12) Flashback 72673 Could It Be I'm Falling In Love And Other Hits.
(S) (4:11) Time-Life R834-14 Body Talk - Love And Tenderness.

1973 ONE OF A KIND (LOVE AFFAIR)

(S) (3:20) Atlantic 82305 Atlantic Rhythm And Blues 1947-1974 Box Set. *(censored version)*
(S) (3:19) Atlantic 81547 Best Of. *(censored version)*
(S) (3:30) Atlantic 82332 A One Of A Kind Love Affair. *(uncensored version)*
(S) (3:30) Rhino 71213 Very Best Of. *(uncensored version)*
(S) (3:17) Time-Life SOD-14 Sounds Of The Seventies - 1973: Take Two. *(censored version)*
(S) (3:30) Rhino 71882 Spinners. *(uncensored version)*
(S) (3:19) Rhino 72115 Billboard Hot Soul Hits - 1973. *(censored version)*
(S) (3:17) Time-Life R838-08 Solid Gold Soul - 1973. *(censored version)*
(S) (3:19) Flashback 72672 I'll Be Around And Other Hits. *(censored version)*
(S) (3:17) Time-Life R834-18 Body Talk - Romantic Moments. *(censored version)*

1973 GHETTO CHILD

(S) (3:43) Atlantic 81547 Best Of.
(S) (3:46) Atlantic 82332 A One Of A Kind Love Affair. *(tracks into next selection)*
(S) (3:46) Rhino 71213 Very Best Of.
(S) (3:47) Rhino 71882 Spinners.
(S) (3:46) Flashback 72672 I'll Be Around And Other Hits.

1974 MIGHTY LOVE (PART 1)

(S) (4:55) Atlantic 81299 Atlantic Rhythm & Blues Volume 7. *(LP version)*
(S) (4:55) Atlantic 82305 Atlantic Rhythm And Blues (1947-1974) Box Set. *(LP version)*
(S) (4:56) Atlantic 19179 Best Of. *(LP version)*
(S) (4:55) Atlantic 82332 A One Of A Kind Love Affair. *(LP version; tracks into next selection; preceded by a :05 hidden countoff)*
(S) (3:14) Rhino 71213 Very Best Of. *(45 version)*
(S) (3:18) Time-Life SOD-36 Sounds Of The Seventies - More AM Nuggets. *(45 version)*
(S) (4:57) MCA 11036 O.S.T. Crooklyn. *(LP version)*
(S) (4:57) Rhino 71586 Mighty Love. *(LP version)*
(S) (3:14) Rhino 72116 Billboard Hot Soul Hits - 1974. *(45 version)*
(S) (3:18) Time-Life R838-09 Solid Gold Soul - 1974. *(45 version)*
(S) (3:14) Flashback 72672 I'll Be Around And Other Hits. *(45 version)*
(S) (4:54) Beast 53442 Original Players Of Love. *(LP version)*

1974 I'M COMING HOME

(S) (4:09) Atlantic 82332 A One Of A Kind Love Affair. *(LP version)*
(S) (3:21) Rhino 71213 Very Best Of. *(45 version)*

(S) (4:09) Rhino 71586 Mighty Love. *(LP version)*

released as by DIONNE WARWICKE and THE SPINNERS:

1974 THEN CAME YOU

(S) (3:56) Atlantic 81912 Golden Age Of Black Music (1970-1975).
(S) (3:56) Atlantic 19179 Best Of The Spinners.
(S) (3:56) Atlantic 82332 Spinners - A One Of A Kind Love Affair.
(S) (3:57) Rhino 71213 Very Best Of The Spinners.
(S) (3:55) Razor & Tie 22047 Sweet 70's Soul.
(S) (3:54) Time-Life SOD-07 Sounds Of The Seventies - 1974.
(S) (3:57) JCI 3130 1970 - Only Rock 'N Roll - 1974.
(S) (3:57) Rhino 71883 Spinners - New And Improved.
(S) (3:57) Rhino 72116 Billboard Hot Soul Hits - 1974.
(S) (3:57) DCC Compact Classics 141 Groove On! Volume 1.
(S) (3:54) JCI 3173 1970 - Only Soul - 1974.
(S) (3:57) Rhino 72580 Soul Serenade - Intimate R&B.
(S) (3:54) Time-Life R103-18 Great Love Songs Of The '70s & '80s.
(S) (3:54) Time-Life AM1-21 AM Gold - 1974.
(S) (3:54) Time-Life R838-09 Solid Gold Soul - 1974.
(S) (3:57) Flashback 72673 Spinners - Could It Be I'm Falling In Love And Other Hits.

released as by THE SPINNERS:

1974 LOVE DON'T LOVE NOBODY (PART 1)

(S) (7:10) Atlantic 82332 A One Of A Kind Love Affair. *(LP version)*
(S) (3:33) Rhino 71213 Very Best Of. *(45 version)*
(S) (3:33) Rhino 71618 Soul Train Hall Of Fame/20th Anniversary. *(45 version)*
(S) (7:12) Rhino 71586 Mighty Love. *(LP version)*
(S) (7:11) Rhino 71863 Smooth Grooves Volume 5. *(LP version)*
(S) (3:33) Flashback 72673 Could It Be I'm Falling In Love And Other Hits. *(45 version)*
(S) (7:11) Time-Life R834-19 Body Talk - Always And Forever. *(LP version)*

1975 LIVING A LITTLE, LAUGHING A LITTLE

(S) (5:01) Atlantic 82332 A One Of A Kind Love Affair. *(LP version)*
(S) (3:14) Rhino 71213 Very Best Of. *(45 version)*
(S) (5:02) Rhino 71883 New And Improved. *(LP version)*
(S) (3:14) Flashback 72672 I'll Be Around And Other Hits. *(45 version)*

1975 THEY JUST CAN'T STOP IT THE (GAMES PEOPLE PLAY)

(S) (3:26) Atlantic 81912 Golden Age Of Black Music (1970-1975). *(45 version)*
(S) (3:25) Atlantic 19179 Best Of. *(45 version)*
(S) (4:40) Atlantic 82332 A One Of A Kind Love Affair. *(LP version)*
(S) (3:28) Rhino 71213 Very Best Of. *(45 version)*
(S) (3:25) Time-Life SOD-16 Sounds Of The Seventies - 1975: Take Two. *(45 version)*
(S) (4:40) Rhino 71884 Pick Of The Litter. *(LP version)*
(S) (4:39) JCI 3169 #1 Radio Hits 1975 - Only Rock 'n Roll - 1979. *(LP version)*
(S) (3:28) Flashback 72673 Could It Be I'm Falling In Love And Other Hits. *(45 version)*

1976 LOVE OR LEAVE

(S) (4:57) Atlantic 82332 A One Of A Kind Love Affair. *(LP version)*
(S) (4:57) Rhino 71884 Pick Of The Litter. *(LP version)*
(S) (4:55) Flashback 72673 Could It Be I'm Falling In Love And Other Hits. *(LP version)*
(S) (3:29) Rhino 72756 Very Best Of, Vol. 2. *(45 version)*

1976 THE RUBBERBAND MAN

(S) (3:32) Priority 7058 Mega-Hits Dance Classics Volume 9. *(45 version)*
(S) (3:32) Atlantic 19179 Best Of. *(45 version)*
(S) (7:20) Atlantic 82332 A One Of A Kind Love Affair. *(LP version)*
(S) (3:44) Rhino 71213 Very Best Of. *(initial pressings of this cd mistakenly used Part 2 of the LP version instead of the single version)*
(S) (3:31) JCI 3306 Dance Seventies. *(45 version)*

(S)	(3:32)	Time-Life SOD-04 Sounds Of The Seventies - 1976. *(45 version)*	
(S)	(3:32)	JCI 3148 1975 - Only Dance - 1979. *(45 version)*	
(S)	(3:32)	Time-Life R838-11 Solid Gold Soul - 1976. *(45 version)*	
(S)	(3:32)	Flashback 72672 I'll Be Around And Other Hits. *(45 version)*	

1980 WORKING MY WAY BACK TO YOU/FORGIVE ME, GIRL

(S)	(4:00)	Rhino 70675 Billboard Top Hits - 1980. *(45 version)*
(S)	(6:01)	Rhino 71115 Dancin' And Lovin'. *(LP version)*
(S)	(6:00)	Atlantic 82332 A One Of A Kind Love Affair. *(LP version)*
(S)	(4:01)	Rhino 71213 Very Best Of. *(45 version)*
(S)	(4:00)	Time-Life SOD-27 Sounds Of The Seventies - Dance Fever. *(45 version)*
(S)	(4:00)	Rhino 71971 Video Soul - Best Soul Of The 80's Vol. 1. *(45 version)*
(S)	(4:00)	Madacy Entertainment 1980 Rock On 1980. *(45 version)*
(S)	(4:00)	Time-Life R988-14 Sounds Of The Eighties: 1980-1982. *(45 version)*
(S)	(4:01)	Flashback 72673 Could It Be I'm Falling In Love And Other Hits. *(45 version)*
(S)	(4:01)	Time-Life R840-09 Sounds Of The Seventies: '70s Dance Party 1979-1981. *(45 version)*

1980 CUPID/I'VE LOVED YOU FOR A LONG TIME

(S)	(3:54)	Rhino 71213 Very Best Of.
(S)	(3:53)	Rhino 71971 Video Soul - Best Soul Of The 80's Vol. 1.
(S)	(3:50)	Priority 53796 Hot And Sexy - Love And Romance Volume 3.

released as by RAPPIN' 4-TAY featuring THE SPINNERS:
1995 I'LL BE AROUND

(S)	(5:14)	Rag Top Records 30889 Rappin' 4-Tay: Don't Fight The Feelin'.

SPIRAL STARECASE
1969 MORE TODAY THAN YESTERDAY
(45 length is (2:48); LP length is (2:54))

(S)	(2:55)	Rhino 70921 Super Hits Of The 70's Volume 1.
(S)	(2:55)	Rhino 72009 Super Hits Of The 70's Volumes 1-4 Box Set.
(S)	(2:48)	Columbia 45019 Pop Classics Of The 60's.
(S)	(2:54)	Columbia/Legacy 46160 Rock Artifacts Volume 1.
(S)	(2:54)	Epic 48732 O.S.T. My Girl.
(S)	(3:12)	Taragon 1007 Very Best Of. *(time includes :05 of studio talk)*
(S)	(2:54)	Ripete 2219 Beach Fever.
(S)	(2:51)	Collectables 1515 and 2515 The Anniversary Album - The 60's.

SPIRIT
1969 I GOT A LINE ON YOU

(S)	(2:39)	JCI 3103 Electric Sixties.
(S)	(2:39)	Epic 32271 Best Of.
(S)	(2:46)	Epic/Legacy 47363 Time Circle. *(:07 longer than the 45 or LP)*
(S)	(2:38)	Time-Life 2CLR-12 Classic Rock - 1969: The Beat Goes On.
(S)	(2:38)	K-Tel 621 Rock Classics.
(S)	(2:46)	Time-Life R968-07 Guitar Rock 1968-1969. *(:07 longer than the 45 or LP)*
(S)	(2:38)	Ode/Epic/Legacy 65001 The Family That Plays Together. *(tracks into the next selection)*
(S)	(2:46)	Simitar 55772 Stud Rock - Rock Me. *(:07 longer than the 45 or LP)*
(S)	(2:46)	Thump 6010 Easyriders Volume 1. *(:07 longer than the 45 or LP)*

SPOKESMEN
1965 DAWN OF CORRECTION

(S)	(3:23)	MCA 31206 Vintage Music Volume 9. *(dreadful sounding stereo with reverb added)*
(S)	(3:23)	MCA 5806 Vintage Music Volumes 9 & 10. *(dreadful sounding stereo with reverb added)*

(S)	(3:23)	MCA Special Products 22131 Vintage Collectibles Volume 2. *(dreadful sounding stereo with reverb added)*

DUSTY SPRINGFIELD
1964 I ONLY WANT TO BE WITH YOU

(M)	(2:35)	Rhino 70323 History Of British Rock Volume 5.
(M)	(2:35)	Rhino 70319 History Of British Rock Box Set.
(M)	(2:34)	Time-Life SUD-17 Superhits - Mid 60's Classics.
(M)	(2:35)	Mercury 314528171 Growin' Up Too Fast - The Girl Group Anthology.
(M)	(2:34)	Time-Life AM1-16 AM Gold - Mid '60s Classics.
(S)	(2:34)	Taragon 1025 Stay Awhile/Dusty. *(this song was not originally recorded in stereo - the stereo effect on this cd was derived by synchronizing the original mono track with a recently discovered alternate backing vocal track)*
(E)	(2:35)	Mercury 314553501 Anthology.
(M)	(2:34)	Mercury 314558208 Very Best Of.

1964 STAY AWHILE

(M)	(1:55)	Mercury 314528171 Growin' Up Too Fast - The Girl Group Anthology.
(M)	(1:55)	Special Music 5039 Great Britons! Volume One.
(S)	(1:55)	Taragon 1025 Stay Awhile/Dusty.
(M)	(1:55)	Mercury 314553501 Anthology.
(M)	(1:55)	Mercury 314558208 Very Best Of.

1964 WISHIN' AND HOPIN'

(S)	(2:52)	Rhino 70324 History Of British Rock Volume 6.
(S)	(2:52)	Rhino 70319 History Of British Rock Box Set.
(M)	(2:52)	Time-Life SUD-09 Superhits - 1964.
(M)	(2:52)	Time-Life AM1-11 AM Gold - 1964.
(S)	(2:52)	Taragon 1025 Stay Awhile/Dusty.
(E)	(2:52)	Mercury 314553501 Anthology.
(E)	(2:52)	Polygram Special Markets 314520460 #1 Radio Hits Of The 60's.
(E)	(2:52)	Polygram Special Markets 314520516 45's On CD Volume 1.
(S)	(2:53)	Mercury 314558208 Very Best Of.

1964 ALL CRIED OUT

(S)	(3:02)	Taragon 1025 Stay Awhile/Dusty.
(E)	(3:01)	Mercury 314553501 Anthology.
(M)	(3:01)	Mercury 314558208 Very Best Of.

1966 YOU DON'T HAVE TO SAY YOU LOVE ME

(S)	(2:47)	Rhino 70325 History Of British Rock Volume 7.
(S)	(2:47)	Rhino 70319 History Of British Rock Box Set.
(S)	(2:46)	Time-Life SUD-01 Superhits - 1966.
(S)	(2:47)	Time-Life R962-07 History Of Rock 'N' Roll: The British Invasion 1964-1966.
(S)	(2:46)	Time-Life AM1-09 AM Gold - 1966.
(S)	(2:47)	Mercury 314553501 Anthology.
(S)	(2:46)	Simitar 55572 The Number One's: Hot In The '60s.
(E)	(2:48)	Polygram Special Markets 314520459 Vocal Treasures.
(S)	(2:47)	Time-Life R857-20 The Heart Of Rock 'n' Roll 1965-1966.
(S)	(2:47)	Time-Life R814-01 Love Songs.
(S)	(2:47)	Mercury 314558208 Very Best Of.

1966 ALL I SEE IS YOU

(S)	(3:20)	Mercury 314553501 Anthology.
(S)	(3:20)	Mercury 314558208 Very Best Of.

1967 I'LL TRY ANYTHING

(M)	(2:31)	Mercury 314553501 Anthology.
(M)	(2:31)	Mercury 314558208 Very Best Of.

1967 THE LOOK OF LOVE

(S)	(4:06)	Varese 5265 O.S.T. Casino Royale. *(rerecording)*
(S)	(3:29)	Time-Life R138/05 Look Of Love.
(S)	(3:29)	Time-Life R974-16 Many Moods Of Romance - The Look Of Love.
(S)	(3:32)	Mercury 314553501 Anthology.
(S)	(3:32)	Rebound 314520519 Love At The Movies.
(S)	(3:32)	Mercury 314558208 Very Best Of.

1969 SON-OF-A PREACHER MAN

(S)	(2:26)	Atlantic 81909 Hit Singles 1958-1977.
(S)	(2:25)	Rhino 71035 Dusty In Memphis.
(S)	(2:25)	Time-Life 2CLR-27 Classic Rock - 1968: Blowin' Your Mind.

DUSTY SPRINGFIELD (Continued)
- (S) (2:25) MCA 11103 and 11188 O.S.T. Pulp Fiction.
- (S) (2:24) JCI 3190 1965 - Only Dance - 1969.
- (S) (2:25) Mercury 314553501 Anthology.
- (S) (2:25) Mercury 314558208 Very Best Of.

1969 THE WINDMILLS OF YOUR MIND
- (S) (3:49) Rhino 71035 Dusty In Memphis.
- (S) (3:49) Rhino 71868 Academy Award Winning Songs.
- (S) (3:49) Rhino 72278 Academy Award Winning Songs Volume 3.
- (S) (3:47) Mercury 314553501 Anthology.

1970 A BRAND NEW ME
- (S) (2:26) Rhino 71036 A Brand New Me.
- (S) (2:25) JCI 3185 1965 - Only Love - 1969.
- (S) (2:24) Mercury 314553501 Anthology.
- (S) (2:23) Mercury 314558208 Very Best Of.

released as by THE PET SHOP BOYS and DUSTY SPRINGFIELD:
1988 WHAT HAVE I DONE TO DESERVE THIS?
- (S) (4:16) EMI Manhattan 46972 Pet Shop Boys - Actually.
- (S) (4:18) EMI 97097 Pet Shop Boys - Discography.
- (S) (4:10) Mercury 314553501 Dusty Springfield Anthology.

RICK SPRINGFIELD
1972 SPEAK TO THE SKY
- (S) (2:40) Rhino 70929 Super Hits Of The 70's Volume 9.
- (S) (2:40) Rhino 71228 Yesterday's Heroes: 70's Teen Idols.
- (S) (2:40) Time-Life SUD-16 Superhits - The Early 70's.
- (S) (2:40) K-Tel 3211 70's Teen Heart-Throbs.
- (S) (2:40) K-Tel 3623 Believe In Music.
- (S) (2:40) Time-Life AM1-13 AM Gold - The Early '70s.
- (S) (2:40) EMI-Capitol Music Special Markets 19545 Lost Hits Of The '70s.

1981 JESSIE'S GIRL
- (S) (3:12) RCA 9902 Nipper's #1 Hits 1956-1986.
- (S) (3:12) RCA 9970 Nipper's Greatest Hits - The 80's.
- (S) (3:13) Rhino 70676 Billboard Top Hits - 1981.
- (S) (3:12) RCA 9817 Greatest Hits.
- (S) (3:14) RCA 3697 Working Class Dog.
- (S) (3:11) Time-Life R105-40 Rock Dreams.
- (S) (3:12) Time-Life R988-08 Sounds Of The Eighties: 1981.
- (S) (3:12) RCA 66862 Hi Octane Hard Drivin' Hits.
- (S) (3:12) K-Tel 3742 The 80's: Hot Rock.
- (S) (3:11) Hip-O 40022 That Sound From Down Under.
- (S) (3:11) Capitol 93076 More Music From O.S.T. Boogie Nights.
- (S) (3:12) Hip-O 40079 Essential '80s: 1980-1984.

1981 I'VE DONE EVERYTHING FOR YOU
(dj copies of this 45 ran (2:42) and (3:16);
commercial copies were all (2:42))
- (S) (2:42) RCA 9817 Greatest Hits. *(45 version)*
- (S) (3:16) RCA 3697 Working Class Dog. *(LP version)*
- (S) (2:43) Big Ear Music 4001 Only In The 80's Volume One. *(45 version)*
- (S) (3:16) Rhino 72819 16 Magazine - Who's Your Fave Rave. *(LP version)*

1982 LOVE IS ALRIGHT TONITE
- (S) (3:27) RCA 3697 Working Class Dog.
- (S) (3:19) RCA 9817 Greatest Hits.

1982 DON'T TALK TO STRANGERS
- (S) (2:58) Rhino 70677 Billboard Top Hits - 1982.
- (S) (2:58) RCA 54125 Success Hasn't Spoiled Me Yet.
- (S) (2:56) RCA 9817 Greatest Hits.
- (S) (2:57) Time-Life R988-14 Sounds Of The Eighties: 1980-1982.
- (S) (2:56) Simitar 55142 80's Rock Classics - Party Town.

1982 WHAT KIND OF FOOL AM I
- (S) (3:18) RCA 54125 Success Hasn't Spoiled Me Yet.
- (S) (3:17) RCA 9817 Greatest Hits.

1982 I GET EXCITED
- (S) (2:32) RCA 54125 Success Hasn't Spoiled Me Yet.

1983 AFFAIR OF THE HEART
- (S) (4:33) RCA 4660 Living In Oz. *(LP version)*
- (S) (3:34) RCA 9817 Greatest Hits. *(45 version)*

1983 HUMAN TOUCH
- (S) (3:53) Priority 53798 Best Of 80's Rock Volume 5. *(45 version)*

- (S) (5:07) RCA 4660 Living In Oz. *(LP version)*
- (S) (3:54) RCA 9817 Greatest Hits. *(45 version)*

1983 SOULS
- (S) (4:14) RCA 4660 Living In Oz. *(LP version)*

1984 LOVE SOMEBODY
- (S) (3:33) Razor & Tie 2056 Hard To Hold Soundtrack Recording.
- (S) (3:33) RCA 9817 Greatest Hits.
- (S) (3:33) Scotti Bros. 75518 Big Screen Rock.

1984 DON'T WALK AWAY
- (S) (4:03) Razor & Tie 2056 Hard To Hold Soundtrack Recording.

1984 BOP 'TIL YOU DROP
- (S) (4:17) Razor & Tie 2056 Hard To Hold Soundtrack Recording. *(LP version)*
- (S) (4:00) RCA 9817 Greatest Hits. *(45 version)*

1985 BRUCE
1985 CELEBRATE YOUTH
- (S) (3:52) RCA 5370 Tao.
- (S) (3:53) RCA 9817 Greatest Hits.

1985 STATE OF THE HEART
- (S) (4:01) RCA 5370 Tao. *(LP version)*
- (S) (4:01) RCA 9817 Greatest Hits. *(LP version)*

1988 ROCK OF LIFE
- (S) (3:51) RCA 6620 Rock Of Life. *(LP version)*
- (S) (3:27) RCA 9817 Greatest Hits. *(45 version)*

SPRINGFIELDS
1962 SILVER THREADS AND GOLDEN NEEDLES
- (M) (2:12) Rhino 70264 Troubadours Of The Folk Era Volume 3.
- (M) (2:11) Time-Life SUD-19 Superhits - Early 60's Classics.
- (M) (2:11) Time-Life AM1-20 AM Gold - Early '60s Classics.
- (M) (2:12) Time-Life R132-22 Treasury Of Folk Music Volume Two.
- (E) (2:11) Mercury 314553501 Dusty Springfield Anthology.

BRUCE SPRINGSTEEN
1975 BORN TO RUN
- (S) (4:28) Columbia 33795 and 52859 Born To Run.
- (S) (4:27) Time-Life R102-34 The Rolling Stone Collection.
- (S) (4:29) Columbia 67060 Greatest Hits.
- (S) (4:28) Columbia/Legacy 64406 Born To Run. *(gold disc)*
- (S) (4:28) Time-Life R13610 Gold And Platinum Box Set - The Ultimate Rock Collection.

1978 PROVE IT ALL NIGHT
- (S) (3:56) Columbia 35318 Darkness On The Edge Of Town.

1981 HUNGRY HEART
- (S) (3:18) Columbia 36854 The River.
- (S) (3:17) Epic 53439 O.S.T. Peter's Friends.
- (S) (3:17) Columbia 67060 Greatest Hits.

1981 FADE AWAY
- (S) (4:40) Columbia 36854 The River.

1984 DANCING IN THE DARK
- (S) (4:01) Columbia 67060 Greatest Hits.
- (S) (4:01) Columbia 38653 Born In The U.S.A.
- (S) (4:01) Time-Life R13610 Gold And Platinum Box Set - The Ultimate Rock Collection.

1984 COVER ME
- (S) (3:25) T.J. Martell Foundation/Columbia 40315 Music For The Miracle.
- (S) (3:26) Columbia 38653 Born In The U.S.A.

1985 BORN IN THE U.S.A.
- (S) (4:34) Time-Life R102-34 The Rolling Stone Collection.
- (S) (4:38) Columbia 67060 Greatest Hits.
- (S) (4:38) Columbia 38653 Born In The U.S.A.

1985 I'M ON FIRE
- (S) (2:36) Columbia 38653 Born In The U.S.A.

1985 GLORY DAYS
- (S) (3:47) Columbia 67060 Greatest Hits. *(faded :27 sooner than either the 45 or LP)*
- (S) (4:14) Columbia 38653 Born In The U.S.A.

1985 I'M GOIN' DOWN
- (S) (3:29) Columbia 38653 Born In The U.S.A.

1986 MY HOMETOWN
- (S) (4:08) Columbia 67060 Greatest Hits. *(faded :27 sooner than the 45 or LP)*
- (S) (4:35) Columbia 38653 Born In The U.S.A.

released as by BRUCE SPRINGSTEEN & THE E STREET BAND:
1986 WAR
- **(dj copies of this 45 ran (3:15) and (5:10); commercial copies all ran (5:10))**
- (S) (4:51) Columbia 40558 and 65328 Live 1975-1985.

released as by BRUCE SPRINGSTEEN:
1987 BRILLIANT DISGUISE
- (S) (4:12) Columbia 44381 Heart Of Rock.
- (S) (4:14) Columbia 67060 Greatest Hits.
- (S) (4:14) Columbia 40999 Tunnel Of Love.

1988 TUNNEL OF LOVE
- (S) (5:09) Columbia 40999 Tunnel Of Love.

1988 ONE STEP UP
- (S) (4:20) Columbia 40999 Tunnel Of Love.

1992 HUMAN TOUCH
- (S) (5:08) Columbia 67060 Greatest Hits. *(radio edit)*
- (S) (6:28) Columbia 53000 Human Touch. *(LP version)*

1994 STREETS OF PHILADELPHIA
- (S) (4:13) Epic 57624 O.S.T. Philadelphia.
- (S) (3:14) Columbia 67060 Greatest Hits.
- (S) (3:51) Grammy Recordings/Sony Music 67043 1995 Grammy Nominees.
- (S) (3:14) Columbia 69012 Diana Princess Of Wales Tribute.

1997 SECRET GARDEN
- (S) (4:26) Columbia 67060 Greatest Hits.

SPYRO GYRA
1979 MORNING DANCE
- (S) (3:57) MCA 37148 Morning Dance.
- (S) (3:58) GRP 9642 Collection.

SQUEEZE
1987 HOURGLASS
- (S) (3:16) A&M 5161 Babylon And On.
- (S) (3:15) A&M 314540425 The Piccadilly Collection.

1988 853-5937
- (S) (3:16) A&M 5161 Babylon And On.

BILLY SQUIER
1981 THE STROKE
- (S) (3:37) Capitol 46479 Don't Say No.
- (S) (3:36) Sandstone 33042 and 5008 Rock The First Volume 2.
- (S) (3:36) Capitol 31831 Best Of.
- (S) (3:36) Time-Life R968-13 Guitar Rock - The Early '80s.
- (S) (3:36) Madacy Entertainment 1981 Rock On 1981.
- (S) (3:36) Chronicles 314529296 Reach For The Sky - Anthology.
- (S) (3:36) RCA 66862 Hi Octane Hard Drivin' Hits.
- (S) (3:36) JCI 3143 18 Screamers From The 80's.
- (S) (3:37) Priority 50938 Best Of 80's Metal Volume Three: Bang Your Head.
- (S) (3:36) Time-Life R988-18 Sounds Of The Eighties: The Early '80s Take Two.
- (S) (3:36) Scotti Bros. 75518 Big Screen Rock.
- (S) (3:36) Rhino 72594 Billboard Top Album Rock Hits, 1981.
- (S) (3:36) Simitar 55582 The Number One's: Rock It Up.

1981 IN THE DARK
- (S) (4:08) Capitol 31831 Best Of.
- (S) (4:09) Capitol 46479 Don't Say No.
- (S) (4:08) Chronicles 314529296 Reach For The Sky - Anthology.

1982 EVERYBODY WANTS YOU
- (S) (3:45) Priority 7054 80's Greatest Rock Hits Volume 4 - Party On.
- (S) (3:45) Capitol 31831 Best Of.
- (S) (3:47) Capitol 46480 Emotions In Motion.
- (S) (3:45) Time-Life R968-18 Guitar Rock - The Heavy '80s.

- (S) (3:45) Chronicles 314529296 Reach For The Sky - Anthology.
- (S) (3:45) Hip-O 40040 Power Chords Volume 3.
- (S) (3:46) Rhino 72595 Billboard Top Album Rock Hits, 1982.

1984 ROCK ME TONITE
(this 45 label listed a time of (3:67) which translates to (4:07))
- (S) (4:54) Priority 53680 Spring Break. *(LP length)*
- (S) (4:54) Capitol 31831 Best Of. *(LP length)*
- (S) (4:54) Time-Life R988-11 Sounds Of The 80's: 1983-1984. *(LP length)*
- (S) (4:54) Madacy Entertainment 1984 Rock On 1984. *(LP length)*
- (S) (4:54) Chronicles 314529296 Reach For The Sky - Anthology. *(LP length)*
- (S) (4:54) Time-Life R968-20 Guitar Rock - The '80s. *(LP length)*
- (S) (4:54) Rhino 72597 Billboard Top Album Rock Hits, 1984. *(LP length)*

STACEY Q
1986 TWO OF HEARTS
- (S) (7:47) Atlantic 81746 Dance Traxx Volume 2. *(remix)*
- (S) (3:58) K-Tel 3343 The 80's Hot Dance Trax. *(45 version)*
- (S) (3:59) Priority 53731 80's Greatest Rock Hits Volume 10 - Dance All Night. *(45 version)*
- (S) (7:12) Atlantic 81676 Better Than Heaven. *(LP version)*
- (S) (4:54) Thump 9945 Greatest Hits. *(neither the 45, LP or 12" single version)*
- (S) (6:03) DCC Compact Classics 131 HI-NRG Dance Classics Volume 1. *(European mix)*
- (S) (3:57) JCI 3150 1985 - Only Dance - 1989. *(45 version)*
- (S) (3:56) Time-Life R988-15 Sounds Of The Eighties: The Mid 80's. *(45 version)*
- (S) (3:58) Rhino 72838 Disco Queens: The 80's. *(45 version)*
- (S) (3:57) K-Tel 3868 Hot Ladies Of Pop. *(45 version)*
- (S) (2:52) Thump 4830 Thump'n Disco Quick Mixx II. *(all selections on this cd are segued together)*

1987 WE CONNECT
- (S) (4:13) Atlantic 81676 Better Than Heaven.
- (S) (7:32) DCC Compact Classics 132 HI-NRG Dance Classics Volume 2. *(European mix)*

JIM STAFFORD
1973 SWAMP WITCH
- (S) (3:46) Polydor 833073 Jim Stafford.
- (S) (3:45) Polygram Special Markets 314520399 Best Of.

1974 SPIDERS & SNAKES
- (S) (3:05) Polydor 833073 Jim Stafford.
- (S) (3:04) Rhino 70759 Super Hits Of The 70's Volume 12.
- (S) (3:04) K-Tel 3050 Ray Stevens/Jim Stafford.
- (S) (3:04) K-Tel 3036 Silly Songs.
- (S) (3:04) Razor & Tie 22505 More Fabulous 70's Volume 2.
- (S) (3:03) Time-Life SOD-22 Sounds Of The Seventies - Seventies Top Forty.
- (S) (3:04) Priority 53716 Branson USA Vol. 3 - Country Legends.
- (S) (3:05) Special Music/Essex 5036 Prom Night - The 70's.
- (S) (3:04) Curb 77736 Greatest Hits.
- (S) (3:04) K-Tel 3626 Music Power.
- (S) (3:05) Priority 50952 I Love Rock & Roll Volume 3: Hits Of The 70's.
- (S) (3:05) Polygram Special Markets 314520399 Best Of.
- (S) (3:04) Rebound 314520507 Class Reunion '73.

1974 MY GIRL BILL
- (S) (3:11) Rhino 70760 Super Hits Of The 70's Volume 13.
- (S) (3:11) K-Tel 3050 Ray Stevens/Jim Stafford.
- (S) (3:11) Polydor 833073 Jim Stafford.
- (S) (3:11) K-Tel 3095 Country Comedy Classics.
- (S) (3:11) Curb 77736 Greatest Hits.

1974 WILDWOOD WEED
- (S) (2:39) K-Tel 3050 Ray Stevens/Jim Stafford.
- (S) (2:39) Polydor 833073 Jim Stafford.
- (S) (2:39) Curb 77736 Greatest Hits.

JIM STAFFORD *(Continued)*
- (S) (2:38) Rhino 72125 Dr. Demento's Country Corn.
- (S) (2:38) Time-Life R830-01 The Dr. Demento Collection - The Mid 70's.

1975 YOUR BULLDOG DRINKS CHAMPAGNE
- (S) (3:11) K-Tel 3050 Ray Stevens/Jim Stafford.
- (S) (3:11) Polygram Special Markets 314520399 Best Of.

1975 I GOT STONED AND I MISSED IT
- (S) (3:32) K-Tel 3050 Ray Stevens/Jim Stafford.

JO STAFFORD
1955 SUDDENLY THERE'S A VALLEY
1956 IT'S ALMOST TOMORROW
1956 ON LONDON BRIDGE

TERRY STAFFORD
1964 SUSPICION
- (M) (2:28) Rhino 70625 Billboard's Top Rock & Roll Hits Of 1964.
- (M) (2:28) Rhino 72007 Billboard's Top Rock & Roll Hits 1962-1966 Box Set.
- (M) (2:27) Original Sound 8861 Oldies But Goodies Vol. 11. *(this compact disc uses the "Waring - fds" noise reduction process)*
- (M) (2:27) Original Sound 2222 Oldies But Goodies Volumes 3,5,11,14 and 15 Box Set. *(this box set uses the "Waring - fds" noise reduction process)*
- (M) (2:27) Original Sound 2500 Oldies But Goodies Volumes 1-15 Box Set. *(this box set uses the "Waring - fds" noise reduction process)*
- (M) (2:27) Original Sound CDGO-10 Golden Oldies Volume. 10.
- (M) (2:27) Original Sound 8892 Dick Clark's 21 All-Time Hits Vol. 2.
- (M) (2:28) Garland 012 Remember When.
- (M) (2:28) Time-Life 2RNR-10 Rock 'N' Roll Era - 1964.
- (M) (2:28) Time-Life SUD-09 Superhits - 1964.
- (E) (2:29) Collectables 5024 Suspicion.
- (M) (2:28) Time-Life R102-17 Lost Treasures Of Rock 'N' Roll.
- (M) (2:27) LaserLight 12322 Greatest Hit Singles Collection.
- (M) (2:28) Risky Business 66388 The Big Hurt/Songs To Cry By.
- (E) (2:29) Curb 77867 Best Of.
- (M) (2:28) Time-Life R857-09 The Heart Of Rock 'n' Roll 1964.
- (M) (2:28) Time-Life AM1-11 AM Gold - 1964.

1964 I'LL TOUCH A STAR
- (S) (2:21) Collectables 5024 Suspicion.
- (S) (2:21) Curb 77867 Best Of.

STALLION
1977 OLD FASHIONED BOY (YOU'RE THE ONE)

FRANK STALLONE
1983 FAR FROM OVER
- (S) (3:53) Polydor 813269 O.S.T. Staying Alive.

STAMPEDERS
1971 SWEET CITY WOMAN
- (S) (3:25) Rhino 70926 Super Hits Of The 70's Volume 6. *(LP length)*
- (S) (3:25) Rhino 71209 70's Smash Hits Volume 5. *(LP length)*
- (S) (3:23) Razor & Tie 22505 More Fabulous 70's Volume 2. *(LP length)*
- (S) (3:22) Time-Life SUD-10 Superhits - 1971. *(LP length)*
- (S) (3:24) Collectables 0660 Sweet City Woman. *(LP length)*
- (S) (3:25) Flashback 72685 '70s Radio Hits Volume 5. *(LP length)*

JOE STAMPLEY
1973 SOUL SONG
- (S) (2:28) Varese Sarabande 5568 Best Of.

STANDELLS
1966 DIRTY WATER
- (M) (2:46) Rhino 75892 Nuggets.
- (M) (2:46) DCC Compact Classics 029 Toga Rock.
- (M) (2:44) Original Sound CDGO-7 Golden Oldies Volume. 7.
- (M) (2:44) Original Sound 8895 Dick Clark's 21 All-Time Hits Vol. 4.
- (M) (2:57) Rhino 70732 Grandson Of Frat Rock. *(:10 longer than the 45 or LP)*
- (M) (2:47) K-Tel 713 Battle Of The Bands.
- (M) (2:57) Rhino 70176 Best Of. *(:10 longer than the 45 or LP)*
- (M) (2:45) JCI 3111 Good Time Sixties.
- (M) (2:40) Time-Life 2CLR-02 Classic Rock - 1966.
- (M) (2:46) Sundazed 6019 Dirty Water.
- (M) (2:41) Time-Life R968-09 Guitar Rock 1966-1967.
- (M) (2:45) LaserLight 12528 Garage Band Rock.
- (M) (2:40) Hip-O 40038 Power Chords Volume 1.
- (M) (2:45) Simitar 55362 Garage Band Classics.
- (S) (3:04) Hip-O 40109 Very Best Of. *(:18 longer than the 45 or LP)*
- (M) (2:46) Hip-O 40109 Very Best Of.

MICHAEL STANLEY BAND
1981 HE CAN'T LOVE YOU
- (S) (3:33) Razor & Tie 1991 Right Back At Ya.
- (S) (3:33) Razor & Tie 2002 Heartland.
- (S) (3:32) Time-Life R968-20 Guitar Rock - The '80s.

LISA STANSFIELD
1990 ALL AROUND THE WORLD
- (S) (4:26) Sandstone 33048 and 5016 Cosmopolitan Volume 2.
- (S) (4:26) DCC Compact Classics 087 Night Moves Volume 5.
- (S) (4:26) Arista 8554 Affection.
- (S) (4:26) Razor & Tie 4569 '90s Style.
- (S) (4:26) Cold Front 3832 Club Mix - Women Of Dance Vol. 1.
- (S) (4:26) Time-Life R834-17 Body Talk - Heart To Heart.

1990 YOU CAN'T DENY IT
- (S) (4:31) Arista 8554 Affection.
- (S) (4:31) K-Tel 3867 The 80's: Hot Ladies.

1990 THIS IS THE RIGHT TIME
- (S) (4:29) Arista 8554 Affection.

1991 CHANGE
- (S) (5:15) Columbia 52826 Red Hot + Dance. *(remixed)*
- (S) (5:36) Arista 18679 Real Love.

STAPLE SINGERS
1971 HEAVY MAKES YOU HAPPY (SHA-NA-BOOM BOOM)
- (S) (3:05) Rhino 70784 Soul Hits Of The 70's Volume 4.
- (S) (3:05) Rhino 72028 Soul Hits Of The 70's Volumes 1-5 Box Set.
- (S) (3:05) Stax 60-007 Best Of.
- (S) (3:06) Stax 8573 The Staple Singers.
- (S) (3:04) Stax 4411 Complete Stax/Volt Soul Singles 1968 - 1971.

1971 RESPECT YOURSELF
- (S) (4:51) Stax 88005 Top Of The Stax. *(LP version)*
- (S) (3:30) Rhino 70786 Soul Hits Of The 70's Volume 6. *(45 version)*
- (S) (3:31) Warner Special Products 27609 Memphis Soul Classics. *(45 version)*
- (S) (4:53) Stax 60-007 Best Of. *(LP version)*
- (S) (4:52) Stax 4116 Be Altitude: Respect Yourself. *(LP version)*
- (S) (3:29) Stax 4411 Complete Stax/Volt Soul Singles 1968 - 1971. *(45 version)*
- (S) (4:51) Right Stuff 28373 Movin' On Up. *(LP version)*
- (S) (3:28) Time-Life RHD-09 Rhythm & Blues - 1971. *(45 version)*
- (S) (3:31) Time-Life SOD-12 Sounds Of The Seventies - 1971: Take Two. *(45 version)*
- (S) (4:52) MCA 11036 O.S.T. Crooklyn. *(LP version)*

(S) (3:30) MCA 11329 Soul Train 25th Anniversary Box Set. *(45 version)*
(S) (3:30) JCI 3191 1970 - Only Dance - 1974. *(45 version)*
(S) (3:28) Time-Life R838-06 Solid Gold Soul - 1971. *(45 version)*

1972 I'LL TAKE YOU THERE
(S) (3:14) Rhino 70660 Billboard's Top R&B Hits Of 1972. *(45 version)*
(S) (3:14) Rhino 70788 Soul Hits Of The 70's Volume 8. *(45 version)*
(S) (4:37) Stax 88005 Top Of The Stax. *(LP version)*
(S) (4:44) Stax 60-007 Best Of. *(LP version)*
(S) (4:44) Stax 4116 Be Altitude: Respect Yourself. *(LP version)*
(S) (3:14) Rhino 71431 In Yo Face! History Of Funk Volume 1. *(45 version)*
(S) (4:24) Rhino 71517 The Muscle Shoals Sound. *(LP version)*
(S) (3:14) Rhino 71618 Soul Train Hall Of Fame/20th Anniversary. *(45 version)*
(S) (3:14) Rhino 71549 Let There Be Drums Vol. 3: The 70's. *(45 version)*
(S) (3:13) Razor & Tie 22045 Those Funky 70's. *(45 version)*
(S) (3:14) Time-Life RHD-20 Rhythm & Blues - 1972. *(45 version)*
(S) (3:14) Time-Life SOD-03 Sounds Of The Seventies - 1972. *(45 version)*
(S) (3:14) Time-Life R921-38 Get Together. *(45 version)*
(S) (3:05) Ripete 2198 Soul Patrol. *(45 version faded :09 early)*
(S) (3:12) Stax 4415 Complete Stax/Volt Soul Singles Volume 3 1972-1975. *(45 version)*
(S) (4:32) MCA 11065 O.S.T. Crooklyn Volume II. *(LP version faded :10 early)*
(S) (4:37) Right Stuff 29669 Movin' On Up Vol. 2. *(LP version)*
(S) (4:27) MCA 11389 O.S.T. Casino. *(LP version faded :15 early)*
(S) (3:13) Nick At Nite/550 Music 67690 I Am Woman. *(45 version)*
(S) (4:28) Right Stuff 52660 Flick Hits - Old School Tracks. *(LP version faded :14 early)*
(S) (3:14) JCI 3173 1970 - Only Soul - 1974. *(45 version)*
(S) (3:14) Time-Life R838-07 Solid Gold Soul - 1972. *(45 version)*

1972 THIS WORLD
(S) (3:32) Stax 60-007 Best Of.
(S) (3:37) Stax 4116 Be Altitude: Respect Yourself.
(S) (3:33) Stax 4415 Complete Stax/Volt Soul Singles Volume 3 1972-1975.

1973 OH LA DE DA
(S) (3:34) Stax 60-007 Best Of.
(S) (3:33) Stax 4415 Complete Stax/Volt Soul Singles Volume 3 1972-1975.

1973 IF YOU'RE READY (COME GO WITH ME)
(S) (3:22) Rhino 70551 Soul Hits Of The 70's Volume 11. *(45 version)*
(S) (3:21) Rhino 70661 Billboard's Top R&B Hits Of 1973. *(45 version)*
(S) (3:20) Stax 88008 Top Of The Stax Volume 2. *(45 version)*
(S) (4:27) Stax 60-007 Best Of. *(LP version)*
(S) (4:26) Stax 4116 Be What You Are. *(LP version)*
(S) (3:19) Stax 4415 Complete Stax/Volt Soul Single Volume 3 1972-1975. *(45 version)*

1974 TOUCH A HAND, MAKE A FRIEND
(S) (3:28) Stax 88008 Top Of The Stax Volume 2. *(45 length)*
(S) (4:01) Stax 8553 Be What You Are. *(LP length)*
(S) (4:02) Stax 60-007 Best Of. *(LP length)*
(S) (3:25) Stax 4415 Complete Stax/Volt Soul Single Volume 3 1972-1975. *(45 length)*
(S) (3:28) Rhino 72126 Soul Hits Of The 70's Vol. 16. *(45 length)*

1975 LET'S DO IT AGAIN
(dj copies of this 45 ran (3:28) and (4:52); commercial copies were all (3:28))
(S) (3:27) Rhino 70555 Soul Hits Of The 70's Volume 15.
(S) (3:26) Essex 7060 The Buddah Box.

(S) (3:27) Time-Life SOD-08 Sounds Of The Seventies - 1975.
(S) (3:27) JCI 3148 1975 - Only Dance - 1979.
(S) (3:26) JCI 3169 #1 Radio Hits 1975 - Only Rock 'n Roll - 1979.
(S) (3:27) Priority 53129 Deep Soul Volume One.
(S) (3:27) K-Tel 3887 Soul Brothers & Sisters Of The 70's.
(S) (3:24) Cold Front 4025 Old School Mega Mix Volume 3.

CYRIL STAPLETON
1956 THE ITALIAN THEME
1959 THE CHILDREN'S MARCHING SONG

STARBUCK
1976 MOONLIGHT FEELS RIGHT
(S) (3:35) Rhino 71198 Super Hits Of The 70's Volume 18.
(S) (3:34) Time-Life SOD-31 Sounds Of The Seventies - AM Top Twenty.
(S) (3:33) Madacy Entertainment 1976 Rock On 1976.
(S) (3:34) Time-Life AM1-23 AM Gold - 1976.

BUDDY STARCHER
1966 HISTORY REPEATS ITSELF
(E) (2:27) One Way 22035 Sixties Rule - Chapter Two.

STARGARD
1978 THEME SONG FROM "WHICH WAY IS UP"
(S) (3:05) Time-Life R838-17 Solid Gold Soul 1978.
(S) (3:08) Hip-O 40091 Disco 54: Funkin' On The Floor.
(S) (3:09) K-Tel 3889 Great R&B Female Groups: Hits Of The 70s.

STARLAND VOCAL BAND
1976 AFTERNOON DELIGHT
(S) (3:12) Rhino 71198 Super Hits Of The 70's Volume 18. *(mastered from vinyl)*
(S) (3:09) Razor & Tie 21640 Those Fabulous 70's. *(mastered from vinyl)*
(S) (3:12) Time-Life SOD-31 Sounds Of The Seventies - AM Top Twenty.
(S) (3:11) K-Tel 3278 Afternoon Delight: Best Of.
(S) (3:12) Collectables 0586 Afternoon Delight.
(S) (3:08) Eclipse Music Group 64895 Rock 'n Roll Relix 1976-1977.
(S) (3:08) Eclipse Music Group 64897 Rock 'n Roll Relix 1970-1979.
(S) (3:11) Time-Life AM1-23 AM Gold - 1976.
(S) (3:12) Rhino 72812 VH1 8-Track Flashback: The One Hit Wonders.
(S) (3:11) Nick At Nite/550 Music 63436 Patio Pool Party.
(S) (3:07) Simitar 55512 The Number One's: Lovin' Feelings.
(S) (3:12) Rhino 75233 '70s Party (Killers) Classics.
(S) (3:11) Time-Life R834-16 Body Talk - Sweet Nothings.
(S) (3:12) BMG Special Products 44762 The President's Greatest Hits.

STARPOINT
1986 OBJECT OF MY DESIRE
(S) (5:03) Elektra 60424 Restless. *(LP version)*

BRENDA K. STARR
1988 I STILL BELIEVE
(S) (3:49) MCA 42088 Brenda K Starr.
1988 WHAT YOU SEE IS WHAT YOU GET
(dj copies of this 45 ran (3:23) and (3:46); commercial copies were all (3:23))
(S) (5:17) MCA 42088 Brenda K Starr. *(LP version)*

EDWIN STARR
1965 AGENT DOUBLE-O-SOUL
(M) (2:39) Rhino 75757 Soul Shots Volume 3.
(E) (2:38) Motown 6219 Hard To Find Motown Classics Volume 3.
(M) (2:38) Time-Life 2CLR-23 Classic Rock - 1965: Blowin' Your Mind.
(M) (2:39) Rhino 71749 Spy Magazine Presents: Spy Music.

EDWIN STARR (Continued)

(M) (2:39) Eclipse Music Group 64869 Rock 'n Roll Relix 1964-1965.

(M) (2:39) Eclipse Music Group 64872 Rock 'n Roll Relix 1960-1969.

(M) (2:43) Rhino 72815 Beg, Scream & Shout! The Big Ol' Box Of '60s Soul.

1969 TWENTY-FIVE MILES

(S) (3:17) Motown 6183 Hard To Find Motown Classics Volume 1.

(S) (3:18) Motown 8120 and 8020 25 Miles/War And Peace.

(S) (3:18) Motown 5426 25 Miles.

(S) (3:16) Motown 9071 Motown Dance Party Volume 1. *(all selections on this cd are segued together)*

(S) (3:16) Motown 5103 Superstar Series Volume 3.

(M) (3:19) Motown 6312 Hitsville USA.

(S) (3:17) Time-Life RHD-13 Rhythm & Blues - 1969.

(S) (3:17) Time-Life 2CLR-20 Classic Rock - 1969: Shakin' All Over.

(S) (3:18) Motown/Essex 374638522 Motown Legends - War.

(S) (3:16) Motown 314530525 Motown Year By Year - 1969.

(S) (3:17) Time-Life R838-04 Solid Gold Soul - 1969.

1970 WAR

(S) (3:21) Rhino 70734 Songs Of Protest.

(S) (3:22) Rhino 70631 Billboard's Top Rock & Roll Hits Of 1970.

(S) (3:22) Rhino 72005 Billboard's Top Rock & Roll Hits 1968-1972 Box Set.

(S) (3:21) DCC Compact Classics 043 Toga Rock II.

(S) (3:21) Motown 6183 Hard To Find Classics Volume 1.

(S) (3:21) Rhino 70783 Soul Hits Of The 70's Volume 3.

(S) (3:21) Rhino 72028 Soul Hits Of The 70's Volumes 1-5 Box Set.

(S) (3:17) Priority 7909 Vietnam: Rockin' The Delta.

(S) (3:19) Motown 9072 Motown Dance Party Volume 2. *(all selections on this cd are segued together)*

(S) (3:18) Motown 5275 12 #1 Hits From The 70's.

(S) (3:21) Motown 9060 Motown's Biggest Pop Hits.

(S) (3:19) Motown 8120 and 8020 25 Miles/War And Peace.

(S) (3:19) Motown 5170 War And Peace.

(S) (3:20) Motown 5103 Superstar Series Volume 3.

(S) (3:21) Priority 53706 Singers/Songwriters/70's Greatest Rock Hits Volume 15.

(M) (3:26) Motown 6312 Hitsville USA.

(S) (3:21) Rhino 71207 70's Smash Hits Volume 3. *(defective transfer to compact disc -- at least on initial pressings)*

(S) (3:20) Time-Life RHD-18 Rhythm & Blues - 1970.

(S) (3:21) Time-Life SOD-01 Sounds Of The Seventies - 1970.

(M) (3:26) Motown/Essex 374638522 Motown Legends - War.

(M) (3:25) Rebound 3145200320 Class Reunion 1970.

(S) (3:20) Motown 314530528 Motown Year By Year - 1970.

(M) (3:25) Motown 314530478 O.S.T. The Walking Dead.

(S) (3:20) LaserLight 12313 and 15936 The Wonder Years - Summer Time.

(S) (3:20) Time-Life R838-05 Solid Gold Soul - 1970.

(S) (3:22) Flashback 72683 '70s Radio Hits Volume 3.

(S) (3:22) Flashback 72090 '70s Radio Hits Box Set.

(S) (3:20) Motown 314530849 Motown 40 Forever.

1971 STOP THE WAR NOW

KAY STARR
1956 ROCK AND ROLL WALTZ

(M) (2:56) RCA 8466 Nipper's Greatest Hits Of The 50's Volume 1.

(M) (2:55) RCA 9902 Nipper's Hits 1956-1986.

(S) (2:44) Capitol 94080 Capitol Collector's Series. *(rerecording)*

(M) (2:55) Time-Life HPD-15 Your Hit Parade - 1956.

1957 MY HEART REMINDS ME

(M) (2:56) Time-Life HPD-17 Your Hit Parade - 1957.

(M) (2:55) Time-Life R132-10 Love Songs Of Your Hit Parade.

RANDY STARR
1957 AFTER SCHOOL

RINGO STARR
1971 IT DON'T COME EASY

(S) (3:01) Capitol 46663 Blast From Your Past.

(S) (3:00) Capitol 95637 Ringo.

(S) (3:02) DCC Compact Classics 1066 Ringo. *(gold disc)*

(S) (2:59) Time-Life R13610 Gold And Platinum Box Set - The Ultimate Rock Collection.

1972 BACK OFF BOOGALOO

(S) (3:16) Capitol 46663 Blast From Your Past.

1973 PHOTOGRAPH

(S) (3:53) Capitol 46663 Blast From Your Past.

(S) (3:55) Capitol 95637 Ringo.

(S) (3:58) DCC Compact Classics 1066 Ringo. *(gold disc)*

1974 YOU'RE SIXTEEN

(S) (2:46) Capitol 95637 Ringo.

(S) (2:45) Capitol 46663 Blast From Your Past.

(S) (2:49) DCC Compact Classics 1066 Ringo. *(gold disc)*

1974 OH MY MY

(S) (4:15) Capitol 95637 Ringo. *(LP length)*

(S) (4:13) Capitol 46663 Blast From Your Past. *(LP length)*

(S) (4:18) DCC Compact Classics 1066 Ringo. *(gold disc; LP length)*

1975 ONLY YOU

(S) (3:22) Capitol 46663 Blast From Your Past.

(S) (3:24) Capitol 80378 Goodnight Vienna.

1975 NO NO SONG

(S) (2:27) Capitol 46663 Blast From Your Past.

(S) (2:31) Capitol 80378 Goodnight Vienna.

1975 IT'S ALL DOWN TO GOODNIGHT VIENNA
(LP title was simply "GOODNIGHT VIENNA")

(S) (2:34) Capitol 80378 Goodnight Vienna.

1976 A DOSE OF ROCK 'N' ROLL
(dj copies of this 45 ran (3:17) and (3:24); commercial copies were all (3:24))

(S) (3:23) Rhino 70135 Starr Struck: Best Of Volume 2.

1981 WRACK MY BRAIN

(S) (2:20) Rhino 70135 Starr Struck: Best Of Volume 2.

STARSHIP (see JEFFERSON STARSHIP)

STARS ON 45
1981 MEDLEY
(dj copies of this 45 ran (3:21) and (4:05); commercial copies were all (4:05))
1982 STARS ON 45 III

STARZ
1977 CHERRY BABY

(S) (3:46) Metal Blade 26559 Violation. *(LP version)*

(S) (3:46) Time-Life R968-17 Guitar Rock - The Late '70s: Take Two. *(LP version)*

STATLER BROTHERS
1966 FLOWERS ON THE WALL

(S) (2:18) Rhino 70687 Billboard's Top Country Hits Of 1966.

(S) (2:18) Columbia 45019 Pop Classics Of The 60's.

(S) (2:18) Columbia 46031 Columbia Country Classics Volume 3.

(S) (2:18) Columbia 31557 World Of.

(S) (2:17) Time-Life CTD-10 Country USA - 1965. *(timing index is off by :01 on all tracks of this cd)*

(S) (2:23) MCA 11103 and 11188 O.S.T. Pulp Fiction. *(rerecording)*

(S) (2:18) Columbia/Legacy 53817 All-Time Legends Of Country Music.

(S) (2:18) K-Tel 771 Country Music Classics Volume IX.

(S) (2:18) K-Tel 3039 Statler Brothers/Jordanaires.

(S) (2:23) Mercury 314518945 30th Anniversary Collection. *(rerecording)*

(S) (2:18) Columbia/Legacy 64764 Flowers On The Wall: Essential Statler Brothers 1964-1969.

(S) (2:18) JCI 3154 1965 - Only Country - 1969.

(S) (2:18) K-Tel 3355 101 Greatest Country Hits Vol. One: Forever Country.

(S) (2:18) Time-Life R990-12 Statler Brothers - Legendary Country Singers.
(S) (2:18) Time-Life R808-02 Classic Country 1965-1969.

CANDI STATON
1970 STAND BY YOUR MAN
(S) (2:51) Ripete 2198 Soul Patrol.
1976 YOUNG HEARTS RUN FREE
(S) (4:06) Rhino 70274 The Disco Years Volume 3. *(LP length)*
(S) (4:05) Rhino 70279 Rare Soul: Beach Music Classics Volume 3. *(LP length)*
(S) (4:08) Warner Brothers 45730 Best Of. *(LP length)*
(S) (4:06) Rhino 72414 Dance Floor Divas: The 70's. *(LP length)*
(S) (4:06) Time-Life R838-11 Solid Gold Soul - 1976. *(LP length)*

STATUS QUO
1968 PICTURES OF MATCHSTICK MEN
(M) (3:08) Rhino 70326 History Of British Rock Volume 8.
(M) (3:08) Rhino 70319 History Of British Rock Box Set.
(M) (3:07) Time-Life 2CLR-04 Classic Rock - 1968.
(M) (3:08) Time-Life R968-07 Guitar Rock 1968-1969.
(E) (3:08) K-Tel 3183 Psychedelic Mind Trip.
(M) (3:08) Buddah 49507 Psychedelic Pop.
(S) (3:14) LaserLight 12317 The British Invasion. *(missing a guitar overdub and the phasing effect)*

STEALERS WHEEL
1973 STUCK IN THE MIDDLE WITH YOU
(S) (3:23) Rhino 70930 Super Hits Of The 70's Volume 10.
(S) (3:23) Time-Life SUD-13 Superhits - 1973.
(S) (3:23) Time-Life SOD-06 Sounds Of The Seventies - 1973.
(S) (3:22) MCA 10541 and 11188 O.S.T. Reservoir Dogs.
(S) (3:23) Priority 50552 O.S.T. Bio-Dome.
(S) (3:23) Time-Life AM1-03 AM Gold - 1973.
(S) (3:23) Rebound 314520507 Class Reunion '73.
1974 STAR
(S) (2:58) Rhino 70759 Super Hits Of The 70's Volume 12.
(S) (2:58) Time-Life SOD-36 Sounds Of The Seventies - More AM Nuggets.

STEAM
1969 NA NA HEY HEY KISS HIM GOODBYE
(S) (4:08) Rhino 70921 Super Hits Of The 70's Volume 1. *(LP version)*
(S) (4:08) Rhino 72009 Super Hits Of The 70's Volumes 1-4 Box Set. *(LP version)*
(S) (4:03) Rhino 70630 Billboard's Top Rock & Roll Hits Of 1969. *(LP version)*
(S) (4:03) Rhino 72005 Billboard's Top Rock & Roll Hits 1968-1972 Box Set. *(LP version)*
(S) (4:05) Mercury 834216 45's On CD Volume 3. *(LP version)*
(S) (4:03) Original Sound 8895 Dick Clark's 21 All-Time Hits Vol. 4. *(LP version)*
(S) (4:05) DCC Compact Classics 029 Toga Rock. *(LP version)*
(S) (4:09) K-Tel 205 Battle Of The Bands Volume 3. *(LP version)*
(S) (4:08) Scotti Brothers 75402 There Was Love (The Divorce Songs). *(LP version)*
(S) (4:09) Rhino 71205 70's Smash Hits Volume 1. *(LP version)*
(S) (4:01) Time-Life 2CLR-20 Classic Rock - 1969: Shakin' All Over. *(LP version)*
(S) (3:59) Tommy Boy 1100 ESPN Presents Jock Rock. *(sound effects added to the ending)*
(S) (4:04) Collectables 2505 History Of Rock - The 60's Part 5. *(LP version)*
(S) (4:04) Collectables 4505 History Of Rock/The 60s Part Five. *(LP version)*
(S) (4:04) Rebound 314520269 Class Reunion 1969. *(LP version)*

(S) (4:04) Polygram Special Markets 314520260 Number One Hits Of The Sixties. *(LP version)*
(S) (3:54) Risky Business 67310 We Came To Play. *(LP version)*
(S) (4:08) Rhino 72213 Stadium Rock. *(LP version)*
(S) (4:09) LaserLight 12313 and 15936 The Wonder Years - Summer Time. *(LP version)*
(S) (4:04) Eclipse Music Group 64871 Rock 'n Roll Relix 1968-1969. *(LP version)*
(S) (4:04) Eclipse Music Group 64872 Rock 'n Roll Relix 1960-1969. *(LP version)*
(S) (4:00) Cold Front 6245 Greatest Sports Rock And Jams. *(all selections on this cd are segued together)*
(S) (4:09) Time-Life 2CLR-31 Classic Rock - Totally Fantastic '60s. *(LP version)*
(S) (4:09) Flashback 72681 '70s Radio Hits Volume 1. *(LP version)*
(S) (4:09) Flashback 72090 '70s Radio Hits Box Set. *(LP version)*
(S) (4:08) Flashback 72711 Sports Rock. *(LP version)*
(S) (4:09) Rebound 314520522 Rockin' Sports Jams. *(LP version)*

STEEL BREEZE
1982 YOU DON'T WANT ME ANYMORE
(S) (3:24) Renaissance 0209 Steel Breeze.
1983 DREAMIN' IS EASY
(S) (3:36) Renaissance 0209 Steel Breeze.

STEELHEART
1991 I'LL NEVER LET YOU GO
(S) (5:04) Priority 53753 Monsters Of Rock Vol. 2 - Metal Masters.
(S) (5:04) MCA 6368 Steelheart.
(S) (5:04) MCA Special Products 21028 The Best Of Hard Rock.

STEELY DAN
1973 DO IT AGAIN
(actual 45 time is (4:08) not (3:57) as stated on the record label)
(S) (5:53) MCA 31273 Classic Rock Volume 1. *(LP version)*
(S) (5:00) MCA 6467 O.S.T. Air America. *(neither the LP or 45 version)*
(S) (5:53) MCA 31192 Can't Buy A Thrill. *(LP version)*
(S) (5:55) MCA 5570 A Decade Of. *(LP version)*
(S) (5:54) MCA 11214 A Decade Of. *(gold disc; LP version)*
(S) (5:55) MCA 10981 Citizen Steely Dan 1972-1980. *(LP version)*
(M) (4:10) Time-Life SOD-14 Sounds Of The Seventies - 1973: Take Two. *(45 version)*
(S) (5:54) MCA 11553 A Decade Of. *(remastered edition; LP version)*
(M) (4:10) Time-Life R13610 Gold And Platinum Box Set - The Ultimate Rock Collection. *(45 version)*
1973 REELING IN THE YEARS
(S) (4:32) MCA 25240 Classic Rock Volume 3.
(S) (4:33) MCA 31192 Can't Buy A Thrill.
(S) (4:36) MCA 5570 A Decade Of.
(S) (4:34) MCA 11214 A Decade Of. *(gold disc)*
(S) (4:34) MCA 10981 Citizen Steely Dan 1972-1980.
(S) (4:30) Time-Life R968-05 Guitar Rock 1972-1973.
(S) (4:31) Time-Life SOD-14 Sounds Of The Seventies - 1973: Take Two.
(S) (4:34) MCA 11553 A Decade Of. *(remastered edition)*
1974 RIKKI DON'T LOSE THAT NUMBER
(S) (4:31) MCA 31274 Classic Rock Volume 2. *(LP version)*
(S) (4:32) MCA 5570 A Decade Of. *(LP version)*
(S) (4:30) MCA 11214 A Decade Of. *(gold disc; LP version)*
(S) (4:30) MCA 31165 Pretzel Logic. *(LP version)*
(S) (4:06) MCA 10981 Citizen Steely Dan 1972-1980. *(45 version and LP speed on original pressings but LP version and LP speed on subsequent pressings)*
(S) (3:56) Time-Life SOD-07 Sounds Of The Seventies - 1974. *(45 version)*

STEELY DAN *(Continued)*
- (S) (4:30) MCA Special Products 20754 Classic Rock Volume 1. *(LP version)*
- (S) (4:30) MCA 11553 A Decade Of. *(remastered edition; LP version)*

1975 BLACK FRIDAY
- (S) (3:38) MCA 5570 A Decade Of.
- (S) (3:38) MCA 11214 A Decade Of. *(gold disc)*
- (S) (3:40) MCA 31194 Katy Lied.
- (S) (3:38) MCA 10981 Citizen Steely Dan 1972-1980.
- (S) (3:37) MCA 11553 A Decade Of. *(remastered edition)*

1978 PEG
- (S) (3:56) MCA 5570 A Decade Of.
- (S) (3:54) MCA 11214 A Decade Of. *(gold disc)*
- (S) (3:56) MCA 37214 Aja.
- (S) (3:56) MFSL 515 Aja. *(gold disc)*
- (S) (3:55) MCA 10981 Citizen Steely Dan 1972-1980.
- (S) (3:55) Time-Life SOD-10 Sounds Of The Seventies - 1978.
- (S) (3:54) MCA 11553 A Decade Of. *(remastered edition)*

1978 DEACON BLUES
- (S) (7:33) MCA 5570 A Decade Of. *(LP version)*
- (S) (7:32) MCA 11214 A Decade Of. *(gold disc; LP version)*
- (S) (7:33) MCA 37214 Aja. *(LP version)*
- (S) (7:33) MFSL 515 Aja. *(LP version; gold disc)*
- (S) (7:30) MCA 10387 Gold. *(LP version)*
- (S) (7:33) MCA 10981 Citizen Steely Dan 1972-1980. *(LP version)*
- (S) (7:32) MCA 11553 A Decade Of. *(remastered edition; LP version)*

1978 FM (NO STATIC AT ALL)
(actual 45 time is (3:51) not (3:40) as stated on the record label)
- (S) (4:50) MCA 5570 A Decade Of. *(LP length)*
- (S) (4:48) MCA 11214 A Decade Of. *(gold disc; LP length)*
- (S) (5:03) MCA 10387 Gold. *(LP length)*
- (S) (5:03) MCA 10981 Citizen Steely Dan 1972-1980. *(LP length)*
- (S) (4:46) MCA 11553 A Decade Of. *(remastered edition; LP length)*

1978 JOSIE
- (S) (4:31) MCA 37214 Aja.
- (S) (4:31) MFSL 515 Aja. *(gold disc)*
- (S) (4:29) MCA 10981 Citizen Steely Dan 1972-1980.

1981 HEY NINETEEN
(actual 45 time is (4:44) not (4:31) as stated on the record label)
- (S) (5:06) MCA 5570 A Decade Of. *(LP length)*
- (S) (5:04) MCA 11214 A Decade Of. *(gold disc; LP length)*
- (S) (5:03) MCA 10387 Gold. *(LP length)*
- (S) (5:06) MCA 37220 Gaucho. *(LP length)*
- (S) (5:06) MFSL 545 Gaucho. *(LP length; gold disc)*
- (S) (5:04) MCA 10981 Citizen Steely Dan 1972-1980. *(LP length)*
- (S) (5:04) MCA 11553 A Decade Of. *(remastered edition; LP length)*

1981 TIME OUT OF MIND
- (S) (4:10) MCA 37220 Gaucho.
- (S) (4:10) MFSL 545 Gaucho. *(gold disc)*
- (S) (4:09) MCA 10981 Citizen Steely Dan 1972-1980.

LOU STEIN
1957 ALMOST PARADISE

JIM STEINMAN
1981 ROCK AND ROLL DREAMS COME THROUGH
- (S) (6:25) Epic 36531 Bad For Good. *(LP version)*

VAN STEPHENSON
1984 MODERN DAY DELILAH

STEPPENWOLF
1968 BORN TO BE WILD
(actual 45 time is (3:03) not (2:55) as stated on the record label)
- (S) (3:28) Rhino 70629 Billboard's Top Rock & Roll Hits Of 1968. *(LP version)*

- (S) (3:28) Rhino 72005 Billboard's Top Rock & Roll Hits 1968-1972 Box Set. *(LP version)*
- (S) (3:37) MCA 31206 Vintage Music Volume 9. *(long version that has a cold ending and is missing a guitar overdub that should start at 3:12)*
- (S) (3:37) MCA 5806 Vintage Music Volumes 9 & 10. *(long version that has a cold ending and is missing a guitar overdub that should start at 3:12)*
- (S) (3:28) MCA 31273 Classic Rock Volume 1. *(LP version)*
- (S) (3:28) MCA 37049 16 Greatest Hits. *(LP version)*
- (S) (3:27) MCA 10389 Born To Be Wild/A Retrospective. *(LP version)*
- (S) (3:28) MCA 31020 Steppenwolf. *(LP version)*
- (S) (3:27) WTG 46042 O.S.T. Flashback. *(LP version)*
- (S) (3:28) Rhino 71548 Let There Be Drums Volume 2: The 60's. *(LP version)*
- (S) (3:27) Time-Life 2CLR-04 Classic Rock - 1968. *(LP version)*
- (S) (3:28) Time-Life R105-24 Guitar Rock Monsters. *(LP version)*
- (S) (3:27) K-Tel 6090 Hit Parader Salutes 20 Years Of Metal. *(LP version)*
- (S) (3:25) Tommy Boy 1100 ESPN Presents Jock Rock. *(LP version with sound effects added to the ending)*
- (S) (3:38) K-Tel 3133 Biker Rock. *(long version that has a cold ending and is missing a guitar overdub that should start at 3:12)*
- (S) (3:24) K-Tel 621 Rock Classics. *(LP version)*
- (S) (3:28) Right Stuff 31324 and 31327 Harley-Davidson Road Songs. *(LP version)*
- (S) (3:37) MCA Special Products 22131 Vintage Collectibles Volume 2. *(long version that has a cold ending and is missing a guitar overdub that should start at 3:12)*
- (S) (3:27) Cabin Fever Music 973 Harley Davidson: The American Motorcycle Soundtrack. *(LP version)*
- (S) (3:28) Time-Life R968-07 Guitar Rock 1968-1969. *(LP version)*
- (S) (3:28) MCA Special Products 20903 The 70's Come Alive Again. *(LP version)*
- (S) (3:27) Rhino 72275 More Stadium Rock. *(LP version)*
- (S) (3:28) JCI 3167 #1 Radio Hits 1965 - Only Rock 'n Roll - 1969. *(LP version)*
- (S) (3:28) Priority 50951 I Love Rock & Roll Volume 2: Hits Of The 60's. *(LP version)*
- (S) (3:36) Cold Front 6245 Greatest Sports Rock And Jams. *(all selections on this cd are segued together; this is the long version that has a cold ending and is missing a guitar overdub that should start at 3:12)*
- (S) (3:27) Flashback 72712 Arena Rock. *(LP version)*
- (S) (3:29) Rhino 72893 Hard Rock Cafe: Classic Rock. *(LP version)*
- (S) (3:35) Hip-O 40062 Under My Wheels: 12 Road Trippin' Tracks. *(LP version but missing a guitar overdub that should start at 3:12)*
- (S) (3:38) K-Tel 3996 Rockin' Down The Highway. *(long version that has a cold ending and is missing a guitar overdub that should start at 3:12)*
- (S) (3:34) Simitar 55522 The Number One's: Party Time. *(LP version but missing a guitar overdub that should start at 3:12)*
- (S) (3:28) Rebound 314520521 Highway Rockin'. *(LP version)*

1968 MAGIC CARPET RIDE
- (S) (4:26) MCA 25240 Classic Rock Volume 3. *(LP version)*
- (S) (4:24) JCI 3103 Electric Sixties. *(LP version)*
- (S) (4:28) MCA 31207 Vintage Music Volume 10. *(LP version)*
- (S) (4:28) MCA 5806 Vintage Music Volumes 9 & 10. *(LP version)*
- (S) (4:26) MCA 37049 16 Greatest Hits. *(LP version)*
- (S) (4:19) MCA 10389 Born To Be Wild/A Retrospective. *(LP version)*
- (S) (4:27) MCA 31021 The Second. *(LP version)*
- (S) (4:23) Time-Life 2CLR-11 Classic Rock - 1968: The Beat Goes On. *(LP version)*
- (S) (4:28) MCA Special Products 22130 Vintage Collectibles Volume 1. *(LP version)*

(S) (4:21) JCI 3126 1965 - Only Rock 'N Roll - 1969. *(LP version)*

(S) (4:24) Time-Life R968-12 Guitar Rock - The Late '60s. *(LP version)*

(S) (4:26) K-Tel 3183 Psychedelic Mind Trip. *(LP version)*

(S) (4:19) MCA Special Products 20893 Greatest Tour Bands Ever Recorded. *(LP version)*

(S) (4:19) Varese 5635 and 5654 and 5655 and 5657 Arrow: All Rock & Roll Oldies Volume Two. *(LP version)*

(S) (4:25) K-Tel 3510 Platinum Rock Volume 2. *(LP version)*

(S) (4:19) Varese Sarabande 5708 All Rock & Roll Hits Vol. One. *(LP version)*

(S) (4:25) Hollywood 62077 Official Party Album - ABC's Monday Night Football. *(LP version)*

(S) (4:19) Epic/Legacy 65020 Ultimate Rock 'n' Roll Collection. *(LP version)*

(M) (2:53) Varese Sarabande 5846 On The Radio Volume One. *(45 version)*

(S) (4:21) Madacy Entertainment 6805 The Power Of Rock. *(LP version)*

(S) (4:18) Simitar 55762 Stud Rock - Wild Ride. *(LP version)*

(S) (4:22) Thump 6020 Easyriders Volume 2. *(LP version)*

1969 ROCK ME
(S) (3:35) MCA 5937 Vintage Music Volumes 13 & 14.
(S) (3:35) MCA 31210 Vintage Music Volume 13.
(S) (3:39) MCA 37049 16 Greatest Hits.
(S) (3:40) MCA 10389 Born To Be Wild/A Retrospective.
(S) (3:38) MCA 1668 At Your Birthday Party.
(S) (3:34) Time-Life 2CLR-12 Classic Rock - 1969: The Beat Goes On.
(S) (3:38) Time-Life R968-22 Guitar Rock - The Late '60s Take Two.

1969 IT'S NEVER TOO LATE
(S) (3:00) MCA 37049 16 Greatest Hits. *(45 version)*
(S) (4:02) MCA 10389 Born To Be Wild/A Retrospective. *(LP version)*
(S) (4:02) MCA 1668 At Your Birthday Party. *(LP version)*

1969 MOVE OVER
(S) (2:52) MCA 37049 16 Greatest Hits.
(S) (2:51) MCA 10389 Born To Be Wild/A Retrospective.
(S) (2:52) MCA 31328 Monster.

1970 MONSTER
(the LP version of this song is a medley of "MONSTER", "SUICIDE" and "AMERICA")
(S) (3:55) MCA 37049 16 Greatest Hits. *(45 version)*
(S) (9:12) MCA 10389 Born To Be Wild/A Retrospective. *(LP version)*
(S) (9:17) MCA 31328 Monster. *(LP version)*

1970 HEY LAWDY MAMA
(S) (2:54) MCA 37049 16 Greatest Hits.
(S) (2:53) MCA 10389 Born To Be Wild/A Retrospective.
(S) (2:52) Time-Life SOD-21 Sounds Of The Seventies - Rock 'N' Soul Seventies.
(S) (2:53) Time-Life R968-11 Guitar Rock - The Early '70s.
(S) (2:53) MCA Special Products 20949 Rockin' 70's Volume 2.
(S) (2:53) Madacy Entertainment 1970 Rock On 1970.

1974 STRAIGHT SHOOTIN' WOMAN
(S) (4:01) MCA 10389 Born To Be Wild/A Retrospective. *(LP version)*

STEREO MC'S
1993 CONNECTED
(S) (5:09) Rebound 314520325 Alterno-Daze: 90's Natural Selection. *(LP version)*
(S) (5:10) Gee Street 314514061 Connected. *(LP version)*
(S) (4:46) Boxtunes 162531071 Big Ones Of Dance Volume 1. *(all selections on this cd are segued together)*

STEREOS
1961 I REALLY LOVE YOU
(S) (2:16) Rhino 75764 Best Of Doo Wop Uptempo.
(S) (2:14) Time-Life 2RNR-40 Rock 'N' Roll Era - The 60's Teen Time.

(S) (2:16) Rhino 72507 Doo Wop Box II.
(S) (2:16) Eric 11503 Hard To Find 45's On CD (Volume II) 1961-64.

STEVE and EYDIE (see STEVE LAWRENCE and EYDIE GORME)

CAT STEVENS
1971 WILD WORLD
(S) (3:18) A&M 4519 Greatest Hits.
(S) (3:17) A&M 4280 Tea For The Tillerman.
(S) (3:18) MFSL 519 Tea For The Tillerman. *(gold disc)*
(S) (3:17) Rebound 314520364 Class Reunion '71.

1971 MOON SHADOW
(S) (2:47) A&M 2522 Classics Volume 24.
(S) (2:48) A&M 4519 Greatest Hits.
(S) (2:48) A&M 4313 Teaser And The Firecat.
(S) (2:48) MFSL 649 Teaser And The Firecat. *(gold disc)*

1971 PEACE TRAIN
(S) (4:00) A&M 2522 Classics Volume 24. *(LP length)*
(S) (4:11) A&M 4519 Greatest Hits. *(:10 longer than LP length)*
(S) (4:01) A&M 4313 Teaser And The Firecat. *(LP length)*
(S) (4:05) Rebound 314520372 The Roots Of Rock: Soft Rock. *(LP length)*
(S) (4:03) MFSL 649 Teaser And The Firecat. *(gold disc; LP length)*
(S) (4:00) Time-Life R13610 Gold And Platinum Box Set - The Ultimate Rock Collection. *(LP length)*

1972 MORNING HAS BROKEN
(S) (3:15) A&M 2522 Classics Volume 24.
(S) (3:17) A&M 4519 Greatest Hits.
(S) (3:16) A&M 4313 Teaser And The Firecat.
(S) (3:17) MFSL 649 Teaser And The Firecat. *(gold disc)*
(S) (3:14) Rhino 72738 Billboard Top Soft Rock Hits - 1972.

1973 SITTING
(S) (3:10) A&M 2522 Classics Volume 24.
(S) (3:11) A&M 4519 Greatest Hits.
(S) (3:10) A&M 4365 Catch Bull At Four.
(S) (3:09) Rebound 314520507 Class Reunion '73.

1973 THE HURT
(S) (4:16) A&M 3285 Footsteps In The Dark/Greatest Hits Volume 2.
(S) (4:17) A&M 4391 Foreigner.

1974 OH VERY YOUNG
(S) (2:34) A&M 3623 Buddah And The Chocolate Box.
(S) (2:34) A&M 2522 Classics Volume 24.
(S) (2:33) A&M 4519 Greatest Hits.

1974 ANOTHER SATURDAY NIGHT
(S) (2:28) A&M 4519 Greatest Hits.

1975 READY
(S) (3:14) A&M 4519 Greatest Hits.

1975 TWO FINE PEOPLE
(S) (3:31) A&M 4519 Greatest Hits.

1977 (REMEMBER THE DAYS OF THE) OLD SCHOOLYARD
(S) (2:42) A&M 4702 Izitso.
(S) (2:42) A&M 2522 Classics Volume 24.
(S) (2:42) MFSL 661 Numbers, Izitso And Back To Earth. *(gold disc)*

CONNIE STEVENS
released as by EDWARD BYRNES and CONNIE STEVENS:
1959 KOOKIE, KOOKIE (LEND ME YOUR COMB)
(S) (2:03) Time-Life 2RNR-47 Rock 'N' Roll Era - Teen Idols II.
(S) (2:03) K-Tel 3037 Wacky Weirdos.
(S) (2:04) DCC Compact Classics 077 Too Cute!
(S) (2:04) Collectors' Choice 002 Teen Idols....For A Moment.
(S) (2:03) K-Tel 3388 TV Stars Sing.

released as by CONNIE STEVENS:
1960 SIXTEEN REASONS
(M) (1:55) Time-Life 2RNR-27 Rock 'N' Roll Era - Teen Idols.
(M) (1:55) Time-Life R857-02 The Heart Of Rock 'n' Roll - 1960.
(S) (1:54) K-Tel 3388 TV Stars Sing.

CONNIE STEVENS (Continued)

(S) (1:54) JCI 3166 #1 Radio Hits 1960 - Only Rock 'n Roll - 1964.

(S) (1:54) Collectors' Choice 5189 I Wish I Were A Princess - The Great Lost Female Teen Idols.

DODIE STEVENS
1959 PINK SHOE LACES

(S) (2:22) MCA 5939 Vintage Music Volumes 17 & 18. *(rerecording)*

(S) (2:22) MCA 31215 Vintage Music Volume 18. *(rerecording)*

(M) (2:25) Time-Life 2RNR-47 Rock 'N' Roll Era - Teen Idols II.

(S) (2:22) MCA Special Products 22132 Vintage Collectibles Volume 3. *(rerecording)*

(M) (2:26) DCC Compact Classics 077 Too Cute!

(M) (2:26) Varese Sarabande 5687 History Of Dot Records Volume Two.

RAY STEVENS
1961 JEREMIAH PEABODY'S POLY UNSATURATED QUICK DISSOLVING FAST ACTING PLEASANT TASTING GREEN AND PURPLE PILLS

(S) (2:22) MCA 42062 Greatest Hits Volume 2.

(S) (2:21) Special Music 838169 Ahab The Arab.

(M) (2:22) K-Tel 30502 Ray Stevens/Jim Stafford.

(S) (2:22) Mercury 422832770 Best Of.

(S) (2:22) Polygram Special Markets 314520288 All-Time Hits.

(M) (2:22) Rhino 72867 Best Of.

1962 AHAB, THE ARAB

(S) (3:48) Mercury 826448 Oldies Golden Million Sellers. *(LP version)*

(S) (3:32) RCA 5153 Greatest Hits. *(live)*

(S) (3:47) MCA 5918 Greatest Hits. *(live)*

(S) (3:45) Curb 77312 His All-Time Greatest Comic Hits. *(live)*

(S) (3:47) Special Music 838169 Ahab The Arab. *(LP version)*

(M) (3:44) K-Tel 30502 Ray Stevens/Jim Stafford. *(LP version)*

(S) (3:47) MCA 10776 Collection. *(live)*

(S) (3:47) Rhino 70495 Fun Rock! *(LP version)*

(S) (3:53) Mercury 422832770 Best Of. *(live)*

(S) (3:45) Time-Life 2RNR-37 Rock 'N' Roll Era - Weird, Wild & Wacky. *(LP version)*

(S) (3:45) K-Tel 3037 Wacky Weirdos. *(LP version)*

(S) (3:35) Curb 77753 20 Comedy Hits. *(live)*

(M) (3:44) Polygram Special Markets 314520288 All-Time Hits. *(LP version)*

(S) (4:08) Varese Sarabande 5685 Gitarzan. *(rerecording)*

(S) (3:46) Rhino 72867 Best Of. *(LP version)*

1963 SANTA CLAUS IS WATCHING YOU

(M) (3:16) Rhino 70192 Christmas Classics. *(LP version)*

(S) (3:21) MCA 10776 Collection. *(LP version)*

(S) (2:17) Mercury 422832770 Best Of. *(45 version)*

(M) (3:15) Rhino 72176 Dr. Demento: Holiday In Dementia. *(LP version)*

(E) (2:16) Polygram Special Markets 314520288 All-Time Hits. *(45 version)*

(M) (3:17) Rhino 72867 Best Of. *(LP version)*

(E) (2:16) Time-Life R135-14 Havin' A Fun Christmas. *(45 version)*

(S) (3:15) MCA 70004 Christmas Through A Different Window. *(LP version)*

1963 HARRY THE HAIRY APE

(S) (2:49) Special Music 838169 Ahab The Arab.

(M) (2:47) K-Tel 30502 Ray Stevens/Jim Stafford.

(S) (2:49) Mercury 422832770 Best Of.

(S) (3:08) K-Tel 3150 Dumb Ditties. *(live)*

(S) (2:49) Polygram Special Markets 314520288 All-Time Hits.

(S) (3:12) Varese Sarabande 5685 Gitarzan. *(rerecording)*

(M) (2:48) Rhino 72867 Best Of.

1968 MR. BUSINESSMAN

(S) (3:22) RCA 5153 Greatest Hits. *(45 version)*

(S) (3:21) MCA 42062 Greatest Hits Volume 2. *(45 version)*

(S) (3:21) Curb 77464 Greatest Hits. *(45 version)*

(S) (3:21) RCA 52161 Everything Is Beautiful & Other Hits. *(45 version)*

(S) (3:40) Varese Sarabande 5684 Even Stevens. *(LP version but :19 longer than the LP or 45)*

(S) (3:21) Varese Sarabande 5684 Even Stevens. *(45 version)*

(S) (3:39) Rhino 72867 Best Of. *(LP version but :18 longer than the 45 or LP)*

1969 GITARZAN

(S) (3:10) Rhino 70743 Dr. Demento 20th Anniversary Collection. *(LP version)*

(S) (3:10) Rhino 70794 KFOG Presents M. Dung's Idiot Show. *(LP version)*

(S) (3:11) RCA 5153 Greatest Hits. *(LP version)*

(S) (3:13) MCA 5918 Greatest Hits. *(LP version)*

(S) (3:13) Curb 77312 His All-Time Greatest Comic Hits. *(LP version)*

(S) (3:13) MCA 10776 Collection. *(LP version)*

(S) (3:13) RCA 52161 Everything Is Beautiful & Other Hits. *(LP version)*

(S) (3:08) Sony Music Special Products 66106 The Monument Story. *(LP version)*

(S) (3:10) K-Tel 3035 Goofy Greats. *(LP version)*

(S) (3:13) Curb 77753 20 Comedy Hits. *(LP version)*

(S) (3:06) Varese Sarabande 5685 Gitarzan. *(LP version)*

(S) (3:09) K-Tel 3640 Corny Country. *(LP version)*

(S) (3:08) Rhino 72867 Best Of. *(LP version)*

1969 ALONG CAME JONES

(S) (3:45) Rhino 70593 The Rock 'N' Roll Classics Of Leiber & Stoller.

(S) (3:45) MCA 5918 Greatest Hits.

(S) (3:45) Curb 77464 Greatest Hits.

(S) (3:44) K-Tel 3243 Kooky Kountry.

(S) (3:44) K-Tel 3095 Country Comedy Classics.

(S) (3:47) Varese Sarabande 5685 Gitarzan.

(S) (3:45) Rhino 72867 Best Of.

(S) (3:44) LaserLight 12820 The Streak.

1970 EVERYTHING IS BEAUTIFUL

(S) (3:29) Rhino 70922 Super Hits Of The 70's Volume 2.

(S) (3:29) Rhino 72009 Super Hits Of The 70's Volumes 1-4 Box Set.

(S) (3:26) Original Sound 8853 Oldies But Goodies Vol. 3. *(this compact disc uses the "Waring - fds" noise reduction process)*

(S) (3:26) Original Sound 2222 Oldies But Goodies Volumes 3,5,11,14 and 15 Box Set. *(this box set uses the "Waring - fds" noise reduction process)*

(S) (3:26) Original Sound 2500 Oldies But Goodies Volumes 1-15 Box Set. *(this box set uses the "Waring - fds" noise reduction process)*

(S) (3:31) RCA 5153 Greatest Hits.

(S) (3:32) MCA 5918 Greatest Hits.

(S) (3:32) Curb 77464 Greatest Hits.

(S) (3:32) MCA 10776 Collection.

(S) (3:27) Time-Life SUD-04 Superhits - 1970.

(S) (3:31) RCA 52161 Everything Is Beautiful & Other Hits.

(S) (3:29) Priority 53716 Branson USA Vol. 3 - Country Legends.

(S) (3:27) Rhino 72272 Everything Is Beautiful.

(S) (3:26) Madacy Entertainment 1970 Rock On 1970.

(S) (3:27) JCI 3145 1970 - Only Love - 1974.

(S) (3:27) Time-Life AM1-02 AM Gold - 1970.

(S) (3:30) Rhino 72867 Best Of.

(S) (3:28) Time-Life R814-04 Love Songs.

1974 THE STREAK

(S) (3:15) Rhino 70759 Super Hits Of The 70's Volume 12.

(S) (3:15) K-Tel 30502 Ray Stevens/Jim Stafford.

(S) (3:15) MCA 10776 Collection.

(S) (3:15) MCA 5918 Greatest Hits.

(S) (3:15) RCA 5153 Greatest Hits.

(S) (3:15) Curb 77312 His All-Time Greatest Comic Hits.

(S) (3:15) RCA 52161 Everything Is Beautiful & Other Hits.

(S) (3:15) Priority 53747 Wild & Crazy Tunes.

(S) (3:14) Rhino 72125 Dr. Demento's Country Corn.

(S)   (3:15)   Curb 77753   20 Comedy Hits.
(S)   (3:14)   Rhino 72272   Everything Is Beautiful.
(S)   (3:15)   Varese Sarabande 5685   Gitarzan.
(S)   (3:14)   K-Tel 3629   Madcap Melodies.
(S)   (3:14)   K-Tel 3627   Out Of Sight.
(S)   (3:14)   Time-Life R830-01   The Dr. Demento Collection - The Mid 70's.
(S)   (3:15)   Rhino 72867   Best Of.
(S)   (3:13)   LaserLight 12820   The Streak.

1975   MISTY
(S)   (2:53)   MCA 5918   Greatest Hits.
(S)   (2:53)   Curb 74464   Greatest Hits.
(S)   (2:52)   RCA 5153   Greatest Hits.
(S)   (2:51)   RCA 52161   Everything Is Beautiful & Other Hits.
(S)   (2:52)   K-Tel 605   Country Music Classics Volume V.
(S)   (2:53)   Varese Sarabande 5607   Through The Years - Country Hits Of The 70's.
(S)   (2:52)   Rhino 72272   Everything Is Beautiful.
(S)   (2:51)   K-Tel 3624   Music Express.
(S)   (2:51)   K-Tel 3356   101 Greatest Country Hits Vol. Two: Country Sunshine.
(S)   (2:53)   Rhino 72867   Best Of.
(S)   (2:48)   LaserLight 12820   The Streak.
(S)   (2:53)   Varese Sarabande 5844   The Country Hits Collection.

B.W. STEVENSON
1973   MY MARIA
(S)   (2:24)   RCA 8476 and 9684   Nipper's Greatest Hits Of The 70's.
(S)   (2:29)   Rhino 70758   Super Hits Of The 70's Volume 11.
(S)   (2:22)   Time-Life SUD-13   Superhits - 1973.
(S)   (2:24)   Eclipse Music Group 64893   Rock 'n Roll Relix 1972-1973.
(S)   (2:24)   Eclipse Music Group 64897   Rock 'n Roll Relix 1970-1979.
(S)   (2:22)   Time-Life AM1-03   AM Gold - 1973.
(S)   (2:29)   Rhino 72739   Billboard Top Soft Rock Hits - 1973.

STEVIE B
1989   I WANNA BE THE ONE
(S)   (5:01)   LMR/RCA 2334   In My Eyes.
(S)   (4:57)   LMR/RCA 61030   Best Of.
1989   IN MY EYES
(S)   (5:16)   LMR/RCA 2334   In My Eyes.
(S)   (5:15)   LMR/RCA 61030   Best Of.
1990   LOVE ME FOR LIFE
(S)   (5:17)   LMR/RCA 61159   Because I Love You.
(S)   (5:15)   LMR/RCA 61030   Best Of.
1990   LOVE AND EMOTION
(S)   (3:42)   LMR/RCA 61159   Because I Love You.
(S)   (3:42)   LMR/RCA 2307   Love & Emotion.
(S)   (3:42)   LMR/RCA 61030   Best Of.
1990   BECAUSE I LOVE YOU (THE POSTMAN SONG)
(S)   (4:20)   Foundation/Capitol 96427   Hearts Of Gold: The Pop Collection.   *(45 length)*
(S)   (3:44)   JCI 3124   Rhythm Of The Night.   *(neither the 45 or LP version)*
(S)   (4:59)   LMR/RCA 61159   Because I Love You.   *(LP length)*
(S)   (4:59)   LMR/RCA 2307   Love & Emotion.   *(LP length)*
(S)   (4:59)   LMR/RCA 61030   Best Of.   *(LP length)*
(S)   (4:59)   Priority 50946   100% Party Hits Of The 90's Volume One.   *(LP length)*
(S)   (4:59)   K-Tel 3848   90s Now Volume 2.   *(LP length)*
(S)   (4:59)   Time-Life R834-15   Body Talk - Once In Lifetime.   *(LP length)*
1991   I'LL BE BY YOU SIDE
(S)   (4:58)   LMR/RCA 2307   Love & Emotion.
(S)   (4:59)   LMR/RCA 61030   Best Of.
1995   DREAM ABOUT YOU
(S)   (4:03)   Thump 9934   Funky Melody.
1995   FUNKY MELODY
(S)   (4:53)   Thump 9934   Funky Melody.

AL STEWART
1977   YEAR OF THE CAT
(S)   (6:30)   Arista 8308   Arista's Perfect 10 Rides Again.   *(LP version)*
(S)   (6:37)   Priority 8666   Kickin' Back/70's Greatest Rock Hits Volume 5.   *(LP version)*
(S)   (4:34)   Warner Special Products 27614   Highs Of The Seventies.   *(45 version)*
(S)   (6:39)   Arista 8433   Best Of.   *(LP version)*
(S)   (6:36)   Arista 8229   Year Of The Cat.   *(LP version)*
(S)   (4:34)   JCI 3307   Easy Seventies.   *(45 version)*
(S)   (4:34)   Razor & Tie 22502   Those Rocking 70's.   *(45 version)*
(S)   (4:34)   Time-Life SOD-05   Sounds Of The Seventies - 1977.   *(45 version)*
(S)   (4:34)   Time-Life R103-33   Singers & Songwriters.   *(45 version)*
(S)   (4:34)   Madacy Entertainment 1977   Rock On 1977.   *(45 version)*
(S)   (4:34)   Time-Life AM1-24   AM Gold - 1977.   *(45 version)*
(S)   (4:36)   Varese Sarabande 5847   On The Radio Volume Two.   *(45 version)*
(S)   (4:35)   Time-Life R834-17   Body Talk - Heart To Heart.   *(45 version)*
1977   ON THE BORDER
(S)   (4:32)   Arista 8433   Best Of.   *(live)*
(S)   (3:19)   Arista 8229   Year Of The Cat.
1978   TIME PASSAGES
(S)   (6:38)   Priority 8667   FM Hits/70's Greatest Rock Hits Volume 6.   *(LP version)*
(S)   (6:35)   Sandstone 33003   Reelin' In The Years Volume 4.   *(LP version)*
(S)   (6:41)   Arista 8433   Best Of.   *(LP version)*
(S)   (6:37)   Arista 8342   Time Passages.   *(LP version)*
(S)   (6:35)   DCC Compact Classics 065   Rock Of The 70's Volume 4.   *(LP version)*
(S)   (4:36)   Time-Life R105-26   Our Songs: Singers & Songwriters Encore.   *(45 version)*
(S)   (6:36)   K-Tel 3454   70s Folk Rock Hits.   *(LP version)*
(S)   (4:36)   Time-Life AM1-25   AM Gold - 1978.   *(45 version)*
1979   SONG ON THE RADIO
(S)   (6:22)   Arista 8433   Best Of.   *(LP version)*
(S)   (6:20)   Arista 8342   Time Passages.   *(LP version)*
1980   MIDNIGHT ROCKS
(S)   (3:54)   Arista 8433   Best Of.
(S)   (3:55)   Razor & Tie 2008   24 Carrots.
(S)   (3:53)   Rhino 71892   Radio Daze: Pop Hits Of The 80's Volume Three.

AMII STEWART
1979   KNOCK ON WOOD
(S)   (4:49)   Priority 7058   Mega-Hits Dance Classics Volume 10.   *(edit of LP version; sped up considerably)*
(S)   (3:51)   Rhino 70274   The Disco Years Volume 3.   *(neither the 45, LP or 12" single version)*
(S)   (4:49)   Razor & Tie 22496   Disco Fever.   *(edit of LP version; sped up considerably)*
(S)   (3:49)   K-Tel 3371   Hot Nights - Disco Lights.   *(neither the 45, LP or 12" single version)*
(S)   (3:49)   Rhino 72414   Dance Floor Divas: The 70's.   *(neither the 45, LP or 12" single version)*
(S)   (3:43)   Polydor 314535877   Pure Disco.   *(neither the 45, LP or 12" single version)*
(S)   (3:49)   Priority 50956   Mega Hits - Disco Heat.   *(neither the 45, LP or 12" single version)*
(S)   (3:50)   Rhino 72812   VH1 8-Track Flashback: The One Hit Wonders.   *(neither the 45, LP or 12" single version)*
(S)   (3:49)   K-Tel 3908   High Energy Volume 1.   *(neither the 45, LP or 12" single version)*
(S)   (3:49)   Time-Life R840-08   Sounds Of The Seventies: '70s Dance Party 1978-1979.   *(neither the 45, LP or 12" single version)*

BILLY STEWART
1965 I DO LOVE YOU
- (S) (2:58) Garland 012 Remember When. *(LP version)*
- (S) (2:58) Chess 31317 Best Of Chess Rhythm & Blues Volume 1. *(LP version)*
- (S) (2:58) MCA 31207 Vintage Music Volume 10. *(LP version)*
- (S) (2:58) MCA 5806 Vintage Music Volumes 9 & 10. *(LP version)*
- (M) (3:00) Chess 6027 One More Time. *(45 version)*
- (S) (2:57) MCA 10288 Classic Soul. *(LP version)*
- (S) (2:56) Original Sound 8878 Art Laboe's Dedicated To You. *(LP version)*
- (S) (2:56) Original Sound 4001 Art Laboe's 60 Killer Oldies. *(LP version)*
- (S) (2:57) Ripete 2392192 Beach Music Anthology Box Set. *(LP version)*
- (M) (2:59) Time-Life RHD-07 Rhythm & Blues - 1965. *(45 version)*
- (M) (2:58) Time-Life 2CLR-25 Classic Rock - On The Soul Side. *(45 version)*
- (S) (2:58) MCA Special Products 22130 Vintage Collectibles Volume 1. *(LP version)*
- (S) (2:57) Right Stuff 30577 Slow Jams: The 60's Volume 3. *(LP version)*
- (S) (2:57) Hip-O 40001 The Glory Of Love - Sweet & Soulful Love Songs. *(LP version)*
- (M) (3:02) Rhino 72619 Smooth Grooves: The '60s Volume 2 Mid '60s. *(45 version)*
- (M) (2:59) Time-Life R838-12 Solid Gold Soul - 1965. *(45 version)*
- (M) (3:00) MCA Special Products 21009 I Do Love You. *(45 version)*
- (M) (3:02) Rhino 72815 Beg, Scream & Shout! The Big Ol' Box Of '60s Soul. *(45 version)*
- (S) (2:58) Chess 9388 Chess Soul - A Decade Of Chicago's Finest. *(LP version)*
- (M) (2:59) TVT 4010 Rhythm Revue. *(45 version)*

1965 SITTING IN THE PARK
- (S) (3:15) Chess 6027 One More Time.
- (S) (3:15) Original Sound 1960 Memories Of El Monte.
- (S) (3:15) Original Sound 4001 Art Laboe's 60 Killer Oldies.
- (S) (3:15) Ripete 2392192 Beach Music Anthology Box Set.
- (S) (3:14) Time-Life 2CLR-28 Classic Rock - On The Soul Side II.
- (S) (3:14) Thump 7040 Low Rider Oldies Volume 4.
- (S) (3:15) MCA Special Products 21009 I Do Love You.
- (M) (3:34) Rhino 72869 Brown Eyed Soul Vol. 2. *(:19 longer than any previously issued version)*

1966 SUMMERTIME
- (S) (2:40) Rhino 70087 Summer & Sun. *(45 version)*
- (S) (2:40) Rhino 75774 Soul Shots. *(45 version)*
- (S) (4:54) Chess 6027 One More Time. *(LP version with a :40 introduction)*
- (S) (4:55) MCA 31205 Vintage Music Volume 8. *(LP version with a :40 introduction)*
- (S) (4:55) MCA 5805 Vintage Music Volumes 7 & 8. *(LP version with a :40 introduction)*
- (S) (4:55) Chess 31318 Best Of Chess Rhythm & Blues Volume 2. *(LP version with a :40 introduction)*
- (S) (4:55) Ripete 2392192 Beach Music Anthology Box Set. *(LP version with a :40 introduction)*
- (S) (2:39) Rhino 71229 Summer Hits. *(45 version)*
- (S) (4:54) Time-Life 2CLR-22 Classic Rock - 1966: Blowin' Your Mind. *(LP version with a :40 introduction)*
- (S) (4:55) MCA Special Products 22019 Summer Hits Of The 50's And 60's. *(LP version with a :40 introduction)*
- (S) (2:39) Rhino 71806 The R&B Box: Thirty Years Of Rhythm & Blues. *(45 version)*
- (S) (4:55) K-Tel 3437 Summer Songs. *(LP version with a :40 introduction)*
- (S) (2:39) Flashback 72710 Golden Summer. *(45 version)*
- (S) (4:50) Nick At Nite/550 Music 63436 Patio Pool Party. *(LP version with a :37 introduction)*

1966 SECRET LOVE
- (S) (2:58) Chess 6027 One More Time.
- (S) (2:58) Ripete 2392156 Grand Stand Gold.

DAVID A. STEWART introducing CANDY DULFER
1991 LILY WAS HERE
- (S) (4:19) Arista 8670 O.S.T. Lily Was Here.
- (S) (4:18) Arista 8674 Candy Dulfer - Saxuality.
- (S) (4:25) Arista 8674 Candy Dulfer - Saxuality. *(remix)*

JERMAINE STEWART
1986 WE DON'T HAVE TO TAKE OUR CLOTHES OFF
- (S) (4:51) Arista 8395 Frantic Romantic. *(LP version)*
1988 SAY IT AGAIN
- (S) (4:08) Arista 8455 Say It Again.

JOHN STEWART
1979 GOLD
(dj copies of this 45 ran (3:35); commercial copies were all (4:21))
- (S) (4:22) Rhino 71202 Super Hits Of The 70's Volume 22. *(truncated fade)*
- (S) (4:20) Time-Life SOD-34 Sounds Of The Seventies - The Late 70's.
- (S) (4:21) Rebound 314520270 Class Reunion 1979.
- (S) (4:23) Razor & Tie 2034 Bombs Away Dream Babies.
- (S) (4:23) Priority 50991 The Best Of The 70's - Rock Chart Toppers.
- (S) (4:22) Time-Life AM1-26 AM Gold - 1979.
1979 MIDNIGHT WIND
- (S) (2:32) Razor & Tie 2034 Bombs Away Dream Babies.
1980 LOST HER IN THE SUN
- (S) (3:46) Razor & Tie 2034 Bombs Away Dream Babies.
- (S) (3:28) Rhino 71891 Radio Daze: Pop Hits Of The 80's Volume Two.

ROD STEWART
1971 MAGGIE MAY
(actual 45 time is (5:11) not (5:15) as stated on the record label)
- (S) (5:12) Rhino 70632 Billboard's Top Rock & Roll Hits Of 1971. *(45 version)*
- (S) (5:12) Rhino 72005 Billboard's Top Rock & Roll Hits 1968-1972 Box Set. *(45 version)*
- (S) (5:12) Warner Special Products 27614 Highs Of The 70's. *(45 version)*
- (S) (5:10) Original Sound 8894 Dick Clark's 21 All-Time Hits Vol. 3. *(45 version)*
- (S) (3:43) Priority 7997 Super Songs/70's Greatest Rock Hits Volume 8. *(highly edited)*
- (S) (5:13) Sandstone 33001 Reelin' In The Years Volume 2. *(45 version)*
- (S) (5:12) Mercury 824882 Sing It Again Rod. *(45 version)*
- (S) (5:43) Mercury 822385 Every Picture Tells A Story. *(LP version)*
- (S) (4:57) Warner Brothers 3373 Greatest Hits. *(:14 shorter than the 45 version)*
- (S) (5:44) Warner Brothers 25987 Storyteller. *(LP version)*
- (S) (5:45) MFSL 532 Every Picture Tells A Story. *(LP version)*
- (S) (5:43) Special Music 836739 You Wear It Well. *(LP version)*
- (S) (5:44) Mercury 314512805 Mercury Anthology. *(LP version)*
- (S) (5:12) Special Music 846495 Stay With Me. *(45 version)*
- (S) (5:13) DCC Compact Classics 063 Rock Of The 70's Volume 2. *(45 version)*
- (S) (5:13) Mercury 314518097 Vintage. *(45 version)*
- (S) (5:12) Razor & Tie 22502 Those Rocking 70's. *(45 version)*
- (S) (5:11) Time-Life SUD-16 Superhits - The Early 70's. *(45 version)*
- (S) (5:10) Time-Life R102-34 The Rolling Stone Collection. *(45 version)*
- (S) (5:12) Time-Life SOD-02 Sounds Of The Seventies - 1971. *(45 version)*
- (S) (5:12) Time-Life R103-33 Singers & Songwriters. *(45 version)*

(S) (5:10) Time-Life OPCD-4521 Guitar Rock. *(45 version)*
(S) (5:44) Rebound 314520231 Best Of. *(LP version)*
(S) (5:12) Polygram Special Markets 314520271 Hits Of The 70's. *(45 version)*
(S) (5:44) Time-Life R968-19 Guitar Rock - The Early '70s: Take Two. *(LP version)*
(S) (5:13) MCA Special Products 20903 The 70's Come Alive Again. *(45 version)*
(S) (5:12) MCA Special Products 20893 Greatest Tour Bands Ever Recorded. *(45 version)*
(S) (5:44) Rebound 314520364 Class Reunion '71. *(LP version)*
(S) (5:13) Special Music 5039 Great Britons! Volume One. *(45 version)*
(S) (3:41) Rebound 314520390 Legendary Hits. *(highly edited)*
(S) (5:11) Time-Life AM1-13 AM Gold - The Early '70s. *(45 version)*
(S) (5:12) Rhino 72893 Hard Rock Cafe: Classic Rock. *(45 version)*
(S) (5:12) Time-Life R13610 Gold And Platinum Box Set - The Ultimate Rock Collection. *(45 version)*
(S) (5:10) Madacy Entertainment 6806 Best Of Love. *(45 version)*
(S) (5:45) Mercury 314558060 Every Picture Tells A Story. *(LP version; remastered edition)*
(S) (5:13) Mercury 314558062 Sing It Again Rod. *(remastered edition; previous selection tracks into the introduction; 45 version)*
(S) (5:11) Collectables 1516 and 2516 The Anniversary Album - The 70's. *(45 version; truncated fade)*
(S) (3:39) Polygram Special Markets 314520479 70's Rock Hits. *(highly edited)*
(S) (5:13) Rebound 314520498 The Rock Album. *(45 version)*

released as by ROD STEWART with FACES:
1972 (I KNOW) I'M LOSING YOU
(S) (3:40) Rhino 70327 History Of British Rock Volume 9. *(45 version)*
(S) (3:40) Rhino 70319 History Of British Rock Box Set. *(45 version)*
(S) (5:03) Mercury 824882 Rod Stewart - Sing It Again Rod. *(edit of LP version; preceding selection, this song, and the following selection are all segued together)*
(S) (5:20) Mercury 822385 Rod Stewart - Every Picture Tells A Story. *(LP version)*
(S) (5:19) Warner Brothers 25987 Rod Stewart - Storyteller. *(LP version)*
(S) (5:20) MFSL 532 Rod Stewart - Every Picture Tells A Story. *(LP version)*
(S) (5:20) Special Music 836739 Rod Stewart - You Wear It Well. *(LP version)*
(S) (3:38) Time-Life R968-10 Guitar Rock Classics. *(45 version)*
(S) (5:19) Mercury 314512805 Rod Stewart - Mercury Anthology. *(LP version)*
(S) (3:41) Priority 7065 70's Greatest Rock Hits Volume 12: Request Line. *(45 version)*
(S) (4:48) Special Music 846495 Rod Stewart - Stay With Me. *(edit of LP version)*
(S) (3:38) Time-Life SOD-02 Sounds Of The Seventies - 1971. *(45 version)*
(S) (3:38) Time-Life OPCD-4521 Guitar Rock. *(45 version)*
(S) (5:19) Rebound 314520278 Hard Rock Essentials - The 70's. *(LP version)*
(S) (3:39) Rebound 314520231 Rod Stewart - Best Of. *(45 version)*
(S) (5:19) Varese 5635 and 5654 and 5655 and 5657 Arrow: All Rock & Roll Oldies Volume Two. *(LP version)*
(S) (3:39) Special Music 5041 Great Britons! Volume Three. *(45 version)*
(S) (5:20) Varese Sarabande 5708 All Rock & Roll Hits Vol. One. *(LP version)*
(S) (3:39) Rebound 314520390 Rod Stewart - Legendary Hits. *(45 version)*
(S) (3:39) Rebound 314520440 No. 1 Hits Of The 70's. *(45 version)*

(S) (5:20) Mercury 314558060 Every Picture Tells A Story. *(LP version; remastered edition)*
(S) (5:04) Mercury 314558062 Sing It Again Rod. *(remastered edition; previous selection tracks into the introduction; edit of the LP version)*

released as by ROD STEWART:
1972 HANDBAGS AND GLADRAGS
(S) (4:21) Mercury 824882 Sing It Again Rod.
(S) (4:21) Warner Brothers 25987 Storyteller.
(S) (4:21) Mercury 830572 The Rod Stewart album.
(S) (4:21) Mercury 314512805 Mercury Anthology.
(S) (4:21) Mercury 314518097 Vintage.
(S) (4:21) Rebound 314520231 Best Of.
(S) (4:23) Rebound 314520497 The Ballad Album.
(S) (4:23) Mercury 314558058 The Rod Stewart Album. *(remastered edition)*

1972 YOU WEAR IT WELL
(actual 45 time is (4:07) not (4:21) as stated on the record label)
(S) (4:17) Warner Special Products 27616 Classic Rock.
(S) (4:20) Mercury 826263 Never A Dull Moment.
(S) (4:10) Mercury 824882 Sing It Again Rod. *(tracks into next selection)*
(S) (5:01) Warner Brothers 25987 Storyteller. *(includes a :39 introduction)*
(S) (4:22) Special Music 836739 You Wear It Well.
(S) (4:20) Mercury 314512805 Mercury Anthology.
(S) (4:20) Priority 7080 70's Greatest Rock Hits Volume 14: Kings Of Rock.
(S) (4:19) Mercury 314518097 Vintage. *(truncated fade)*
(S) (4:20) Time-Life SOD-13 Sounds Of The Seventies - 1972: Take Two.
(S) (4:19) Time-Life R105-26 Our Songs: Singers & Songwriters Encore.
(S) (4:20) Rebound 314520231 Best Of.
(S) (4:07) Polygram Special Markets 314520271 Hits Of The 70's.
(S) (4:21) Mercury 314558061 Never A Dull Moment. *(remastered edition)*
(S) (4:11) Mercury 314558062 Sing It Again Rod. *(remastered edition; previous selection tracks into the introduction; tracks into the next selection)*

1972 ANGEL
(S) (4:02) Mercury 826263 Never A Dull Moment.
(S) (4:03) Warner Brothers 25987 Storyteller.
(S) (4:02) Mercury 314512805 Mercury Anthology.
(S) (4:31) Special Music 846495 Stay With Me. *(live)*
(S) (4:03) Mercury 314558061 Never A Dull Moment. *(remastered edition)*
(S) (4:03) Rebound 314520497 The Ballad Album.

1976 TONIGHT'S THE NIGHT (GONNA BE ALRIGHT)
(S) (3:54) Warner Brothers 25987 Storyteller.
(S) (3:34) Warner Brothers 3373 Greatest Hits. *(tracks into next selection; edited; missing closing female overdubs)*
(S) (3:54) Warner Brothers 26158 Downtown Train.
(S) (3:53) Warner Brothers 3116 A Night On The Town.
(S) (3:52) Time-Life SOD-04 Sounds Of The Seventies - 1976.
(S) (3:32) Warner Brothers 46452 If We Fall In Love Tonight. *(edited; missing the closing female overdubs)*

1977 THE FIRST CUT IS THE DEEPEST
(S) (4:26) Warner Brothers 25987 Storyteller. *(LP version)*
(S) (3:51) Warner Brothers 3373 Greatest Hits. *(neither the 45 or LP version)*
(S) (4:26) Warner Brothers 3116 A Night On The Town. *(LP version)*
(S) (3:49) Warner Brothers 46452 If We Fall In Love Tonight. *(neither the 45 or LP version)*

1977 THE KILLING OF GEORGIE (PART 1 & 2)
(S) (6:26) Warner Brothers 25987 Storyteller.
(S) (6:28) Warner Brothers 3373 Greatest Hits.
(S) (6:26) Warner Brothers 26158 Downtown Train.
(S) (6:26) Warner Brothers 3116 A Night On The Town.

1978 YOU'RE IN MY HEART (THE FINAL ACCLAIM)
(S) (4:28) Warner Brothers 25987 Storyteller.

ROD STEWART (Continued)

    (S)   (4:28)   Warner Brothers 3373   Greatest Hits.
    (S)   (4:29)   Warner Brothers 3092   Foot Loose & Fancy Free.
    (S)   (4:27)   Time-Life SOD-10   Sounds Of The Seventies - 1978.
    (S)   (4:27)   Warner Brothers 46452   If We Fall In Love Tonight.

1978 HOT LEGS

    (S)   (5:14)   Warner Brothers 25987   Storyteller. *(LP version)*
    (S)   (4:13)   Warner Brothers 3373   Greatest Hits. *(edit of LP version; tracks into next selection)*
    (S)   (5:14)   Warner Brothers 3092   Foot Loose & Fancy Free. *(LP version)*

1978 I WAS ONLY JOKING

    (S)   (6:06)   Warner Brothers 25987   Storyteller. *(LP version)*
    (S)   (6:06)   Warner Brothers 3092   Foot Loose & Fancy Free. *(LP version)*

1979 DO YA THINK I'M SEXY?
(dj copies of this 45 ran (4:16) and (5:21); commercial copies were all (5:21))

    (S)   (5:28)   Warner Brothers 25987   Storyteller.
    (S)   (5:27)   Warner Brothers 3373   Greatest Hits. *(tracks into next selection)*
    (S)   (5:28)   Warner Brothers 3261   Blondes Have More Fun.
    (S)   (5:23)   Time-Life SOD-09   Sounds Of The Seventies - 1979.
    (S)   (5:23)   Time-Life R840-10   Sounds Of The Seventies: '70s Dance Party 1979.

1979 AIN'T LOVE A BITCH

    (S)   (4:38)   Warner Brothers 3261   Blondes Have More Fun. *(LP length)*

1981 PASSION
(dj copies of this 45 ran (4:45) and (5:29); commercial copies were all (5:29))

    (S)   (5:30)   Warner Brothers 25987   Storyteller.
    (S)   (5:30)   Warner Brothers 26158   Downtown Train.

1981 YOUNG TURKS

    (S)   (5:02)   Warner Brothers 3602   Tonight I'm Yours. *(LP version)*
    (S)   (5:01)   Warner Brothers 25987   Storyteller. *(LP version)*
    (S)   (5:01)   Warner Brothers 26158   Downtown Train. *(LP version)*

1982 TONIGHT I'M YOURS (DON'T HURT ME)

    (S)   (4:10)   Warner Brothers 25987   Storyteller. *(LP version)*
    (S)   (4:10)   Warner Brothers 23602   Tonight I'm Yours. *(LP version)*

1983 BABY JANE

    (S)   (4:42)   Warner Brothers 25987   Storyteller.

1983 WHAT AM I GONNA DO (I'M SO IN LOVE WITH YOU)

    (S)   (4:17)   Warner Brothers 25987   Storyteller. *(LP length)*

1984 INFATUATION

    (S)   (5:12)   Warner Brothers 26158   Downtown Train. *(LP version)*
    (S)   (5:12)   Warner Brothers 25987   Storyteller. *(LP version)*
    (S)   (5:13)   Warner Brothers 25095   Camouflage. *(LP version)*

1984 SOME GUYS HAVE ALL THE LUCK

    (S)   (4:31)   Warner Brothers 25987   Storyteller. *(LP version)*
    (S)   (4:32)   Warner Brothers 25095   Camouflage. *(LP version)*
    (S)   (4:31)   Time-Life R988-27   Sounds Of The Eighties: The Rolling Stone Collection 1983-1985. *(LP version)*

1986 LOVE TOUCH (THEME FROM LEGAL EAGLES)

    (S)   (4:02)   Warner Brothers 25446   Rod Stewart.
    (S)   (4:02)   Warner Brothers 25987   Storyteller.

1988 LOST IN YOU

    (S)   (4:56)   Warner Brothers 25987   Storyteller. *(LP length)*
    (S)   (4:57)   Warner Brothers 25684   Out Of Order. *(LP length)*

1988 FOREVER YOUNG

    (S)   (4:03)   Foundation/Capitol 96427   Hearts Of Gold: The Pop Collection.
    (S)   (4:03)   Warner Brothers 26158   Downtown Train.
    (S)   (4:03)   Warner Brothers 25987   Storyteller.
    (S)   (4:03)   Warner Brothers 25684   Out Of Order.
    (S)   (4:02)   Time-Life R988-29   Sounds Of The Eighties: The Rolling Stone Collection 1987-1988.
    (S)   (4:52)   Warner Brothers 46452   If We Fall In Love Tonight. *(1996 rerecording)*

1989 MY HEART CAN'T TELL YOU NO

    (S)   (5:11)   Warner Brothers 26158   Downtown Train.

    (S)   (5:11)   Warner Brothers 25987   Storyteller.
    (S)   (5:10)   Warner Brothers 25684   Out Of Order.
    (S)   (5:09)   Warner Brothers 46452   If We Fall In Love Tonight.

1989 CRAZY ABOUT HER

    (S)   (4:53)   Warner Brothers 25987   Storyteller. *(LP version)*
    (S)   (4:53)   Warner Brothers 25684   Out Of Order. *(LP version)*

1990 DOWNTOWN TRAIN

    (S)   (4:39)   Warner Brothers 26158   Downtown Train.
    (S)   (4:39)   Warner Brothers 25987   Storyteller.
    (S)   (4:37)   Warner Brothers 46452   If We Fall In Love Tonight.
    (S)   (4:38)   Time-Life R13610   Gold And Platinum Box Set - The Ultimate Rock Collection.

released as by ROD STEWART with RONALD ISLEY:
1990 THIS OLD HEART OF MINE

    (S)   (4:10)   Warner Brothers 26158   Downtown Train.
    (S)   (4:10)   Warner Brothers 25987   Storyteller.

released as by ROD STEWART:
1991 RHYTHM OF MY HEART

    (S)   (4:12)   Warner Brothers 26300   Vagabond Heart.

1991 THE MOTOWN SONG

    (S)   (3:57)   Warner Brothers 26300   Vagabond Heart.

1991 BROKEN ARROW

    (S)   (4:22)   Warner Brothers 26300   Vagabond Heart.
    (S)   (4:20)   Warner Brothers 46452   If We Fall In Love Tonight.

1993 HAVE I TOLD YOU LATELY

    (S)   (4:08)   Warner Brothers 45289   Unplugged.
    (S)   (3:57)   Warner Brothers 46452   If We Fall In Love Tonight. *(studio version - not the hit version)*

1993 REASON TO BELIEVE

    (S)   (4:07)   Warner Brothers 45289   Unplugged.

released as by BRYAN ADAMS/ROD STEWART/STING:
1994 ALL FOR LOVE

    (S)   (4:43)   Hollywood 61581   O.S.T. The Three Musketeers.
    (S)   (4:40)   Warner Brothers 46452   Rod Stewart - If We Fall In Love Tonight.

released as by ROD STEWART:
1994 HAVING A PARTY

    (S)   (4:43)   Warner Brothers 45289   Unplugged.

SANDY STEWART
1963 MY COLORING BOOK

    (S)   (3:25)   Rhino 71650   Colpix-Dimension Story.

CURTIS STIGERS
1991 I WONDER WHY

    (S)   (4:25)   Sandstone 33052 and 5020   Cosmopolitan Volume 6.
    (S)   (4:24)   JCI 3123   Harvest.
    (S)   (4:25)   DCC Compact Classics 084   Night Moves Volume 4.
    (S)   (4:25)   Arista 8660   Curtis Stigers.
    (S)   (4:25)   Time-Life R834-14   Body Talk - Love And Tenderness.

STEPHEN STILLS
1971 LOVE THE ONE YOU'RE WITH

    (S)   (3:03)   Atlantic 81909   Hit Singles 1958-1977.
    (S)   (3:03)   Priority 8664   High Times/70's Greatest Rock Hits Volume 3.
    (S)   (3:04)   Atlantic 82319   Crosby, Stills & Nash Box Set.
    (S)   (3:04)   Atlantic 7202   Stephen Stills.
    (S)   (3:04)   Foundation/Capitol 96647   Hearts Of Gold - The Classic Rock Collection.
    (S)   (3:03)   Time-Life SOD-02   Sounds Of The Seventies - 1971.
    (S)   (3:03)   Time-Life R103-33   Singers & Songwriters.
    (S)   (3:03)   Time-Life OPCD-4521   Guitar Rock.
    (S)   (3:04)   Atlantic 82809   Stephen Stills. *(remastered edition)*
    (S)   (3:03)   JCI 3168   #1 Radio Hits 1970 - Only Rock 'n Roll - 1974.
    (S)   (3:03)   Simitar 55752   Stud Rock - Heart Breakers.

1971 SIT YOURSELF DOWN

    (S)   (3:04)   Atlantic 7202   Stephen Stills.

1971 CHANGE PARTNERS

    (S)   (3:13)   Atlantic 82319   Crosby, Stills & Nash Box Set. *(tracks into next selection)*

(S) (3:14) Atlantic 7206 Stephen Stills 2.
1971 MARIANNE
    (S) (2:27) Atlantic 7206 Stephen Stills 2.

STING
1985 IF YOU LOVE SOMEBODY SET THEM FREE
    (S) (4:10) Time-Life R102-34 The Rolling Stone Collection.
    (S) (4:11) A&M 3750 The Dream Of The Blue Turtles.
    (S) (4:11) MFSL 528 The Dream Of The Blue Turtles. *(gold disc)*
    (S) (4:13) A&M 314540269 Fields Of Gold - Best Of.
    (S) (4:13) Time-Life R13610 Gold And Platinum Box Set - The Ultimate Rock Collection.
    (S) (4:12) A&M 314540834 Very Best Of Sting & The Police.
1985 FORTRESS AROUND YOUR HEART
    (S) (4:37) A&M 3750 The Dream Of The Blue Turtles.
    (S) (4:37) MFSL 528 The Dream Of The Blue Turtles. *(gold disc)*
    (S) (4:35) A&M 314540269 Fields Of Gold - Best Of.
1986 LOVE IS THE SEVENTH WAVE
    (S) (3:28) Geffen 24236 Greenpeace - Rainbow Warriors.
    (S) (3:28) A&M 3750 The Dream Of The Blue Turtles.
    (S) (3:28) MFSL 528 The Dream Of The Blue Turtles. *(gold disc)*
1986 RUSSIANS
    (S) (3:55) A&M 3750 The Dream Of The Blue Turtles.
    (S) (3:55) MFSL 528 The Dream Of The Blue Turtles. *(gold disc)*
    (S) (3:55) A&M 314540269 Fields Of Gold - Best Of.
    (S) (3:55) A&M 314540834 Very Best Of Sting & The Police.
1987 WE'LL BE TOGETHER
    (S) (4:51) A&M 6402 ...Nothing Like The Sun.
    (S) (4:51) MFSL 546 ...Nothing Like The Sun. *(gold disc)*
    (S) (4:49) A&M 314540269 Fields Of Gold - Best Of.
1988 BE STILL MY BEATING HEART
    (S) (5:31) A&M 6402 ...Nothing Like The Sun. *(LP version)*
    (S) (5:31) MFSL 546 ...Nothing Like The Sun. *(LP version; gold disc)*
    (S) (5:31) A&M 314540269 Fields Of Gold - Best Of. *(LP version)*
1991 ALL THIS TIME
    (S) (4:54) A&M 6405 The Soul Cages.
    (S) (4:53) A&M 314540269 Fields Of Gold - Best Of.
1993 IF I EVER LOSE MY FAITH IN YOU
    (S) (4:28) A&M 314540070 Ten Summoner's Tales.
    (S) (4:30) A&M 314540269 Fields Of Gold - Best Of.
    (S) (4:29) A&M 314540834 Very Best Of Sting & The Police.
1993 FIELDS OF GOLD
    (S) (3:37) A&M 314540070 Ten Summoner's Tales.
    (S) (3:37) A&M 314540269 Fields Of Gold - Best Of.
    (S) (3:36) A&M 314540834 Very Best Of Sting & The Police.
released as by BRYAN ADAMS/ROD STEWART/STING:
1994 ALL FOR LOVE
    (S) (4:43) Hollywood 61581 O.S.T. The Three Musketeers.
    (S) (4:40) Warner Brothers 46452 Rod Stewart - If We Fall In Love Tonight.
released as by STING:
1994 WHEN WE DANCE
    (S) (5:57) A&M 314540269 Fields Of Gold - Best Of.

GARY STITES
1959 LONELY FOR YOU

MORRIS STOLOFF
1956 MOONGLOW AND THEME FROM "PICNIC"
    (M) (2:48) MCA 5936 Vintage Music Volumes 11 & 12. *(45 version)*
    (M) (2:48) MCA 31209 Vintage Music Volume 12. *(45 version)*
    (M) (2:49) Time-Life HPD-15 Your Hit Parade - 1956. *(45 version)*
    (M) (2:49) Rhino 71580 Billboard Pop Memories 1955-1959. *(45 version)*

    (M) (2:49) JCI 7010 Those Wonderful Years - Melodies Of Love. *(45 version)*
    (S) (3:45) DCC Compact Classics 079 Music For A Bachelor's Den. *("Picnic" soundtrack LP version)*
    (S) (3:46) Time-Life R986-07 Instrumental Favorites - Movie Magic. *("Picnic" soundtrack LP version)*
    (M) (2:49) Time-Life R138-32 Hollywood Hit Parade. *(45 version)*
    (M) (2:49) Time-Life R974-02 Many Moods Of Romance - My Heart Reminds Me. *(45 version)*
    (E) (3:45) MCA 31357 O.S.T. Picnic. *("Picnic" soundtrack LP version)*
    (M) (2:49) Rhino 72422 Billboard Top Movie Hits 1955-1959. *(45 version)*
    (M) (2:49) Time-Life R132-12 Your Hit Parade - #1 Hits Of The '50s. *(45 version)*
    (M) (2:49) Time-Life R986-22 Instrumental Classics - Pop Classics. *(45 version)*

KIRBY STONE FOUR
1958 BAUBLES, BANGLES AND BEADS
    (S) (2:11) Collectables 5473 Baubles, Bangles And Beads.

STONEBOLT
1978 I WILL STILL LOVE YOU

STONE PONEYS
1968 DIFFERENT DRUM
    (S) (2:35) JCI 3104 Mellow Sixties. *(45 version)*
    (S) (2:36) Asylum 106 Linda Ronstadt's Greatest Hits. *(45 version)*
    (S) (2:34) Time-Life 2CLR-19 Classic Rock - 1968: Shakin' All Over. *(45 version)*
    (S) (2:33) Time-Life SUD-05 Superhits - 1967. *(45 version)*
    (S) (2:36) Capitol 80131 Linda Ronstadt - Different Drum. *(45 version)*
    (S) (2:35) Capitol 80129 Evergreen Vol. 2. *(45 version)*
    (S) (2:33) JCI 3160 18 Free & Easy Hits From The 60's. *(45 version)*
    (S) (2:33) Time-Life AM1-08 AM Gold - 1967. *(45 version)*

PAUL STOOKEY
1971 WEDDING SONG (THERE IS LOVE)

STORIES
1973 BROTHER LOUIE
    (S) (3:54) Rhino 70930 Super Hits Of The 70's Volume 10.
    (S) (3:54) Rhino 70634 Billboard's Top Rock & Roll Hits Of 1973.
    (S) (3:54) Original Sound 8895 Dick Clark's 21 All-Time Hits Vol. 4.
    (S) (3:54) Pair 1202 Best Of Buddah.
    (S) (3:53) Priority 7942 Hard Rockin' 70's.
    (S) (3:53) Pair 3303 About Us.
    (S) (3:55) Essex 7060 The Buddah Box.
    (S) (3:53) Razor & Tie 21640 Those Fabulous 70's.
    (S) (3:54) Time-Life SOD-06 Sounds Of The Seventies - 1973.
    (S) (3:54) Buddah 49513 About Us.
    (S) (3:53) JCI 3191 1970 - Only Dance - 1974.
    (S) (3:52) Eclipse Music Group 64893 Rock 'n Roll Relix 1972-1973.
    (S) (3:52) Eclipse Music Group 64897 Rock 'n Roll Relix 1970-1979.
    (S) (3:53) Thump 7200 Latin Oldies Volume Two.
    (S) (3:54) K-Tel 3913 Superstars Greatest Hits Volume 2.
    (S) (3:54) BMG Special Products 44643 The Best Of Buddah.
    (S) (3:53) Hip-O 40095 '70s Hit(s) Back.
    (S) (3:54) Simitar 55152 Blue Eyed Soul.
    (S) (3:53) K-Tel 3987 70s Heavy Hitters: #1 Pop Hits.
    (S) (3:53) Rebound 314520507 Class Reunion '73.
    (S) (3:54) Priority 50989 70's Greatest Rock Hits Volume 2: Rock & Soul.

STORM
1992 I'VE GOT A LOT TO LEARN ABOUT LOVE
    (S)   (4:25)   Interscope 91741 The Storm.

BILLY STORM
1959 I'VE COME OF AGE

GALE STORM
1956 I HEAR YOU KNOCKING
    (M)   (2:19)   Time-Life HPD-21 Your Hit Parade - The Mid 50's.
    (M)   (2:21)   Varese Sarabande 5523 Dark Moon: Best Of.
1956 MEMORIES ARE MADE OF THIS
    (M)   (2:17)   Varese Sarabande 5523 Dark Moon: Best Of.
1956 TEEN AGE PRAYER
    (M)   (2:13)   Varese Sarabande 5523 Dark Moon: Best Of.
1956 WHY DO FOOLS FALL IN LOVE
    (M)   (2:17)   Varese Sarabande 5523 Dark Moon: Best Of.
1956 IVORY TOWER
    (M)   (2:43)   Varese Sarabande 5523 Dark Moon: Best Of.
    (M)   (2:42)   Varese Sarabande 5686 History Of Dot Records Volume One.
1957 DARK MOON
    (M)   (2:26)   Time-Life HPD-17 Your Hit Parade - 1957.
    (M)   (2:26)   Varese Sarabande 5523 Dark Moon: Best Of.
    (M)   (2:26)   Time-Life R857-05 The Heart Of Rock 'n' Roll 1957.
    (M)   (2:26)   Time-Life R132-10 Love Songs Of Your Hit Parade.

STRANGELOVES
1965 I WANT CANDY
    (M)   (2:33)   DCC Compact Classics 043 Toga Rock II. *(mastered from vinyl)*
    (M)   (2:33)   Rhino 70732 Grandson Of Frat Rock.
    (M)   (2:33)   Rhino 70291 Bo Diddley Beats.
    (M)   (2:33)   Rhino 71548 Let There Be Drums Volume 2: The 60's.
    (M)   (2:33)   Time-Life 2CLR-14 Classic Rock - 1965: Shakin' All Over.
    (S)   (2:56)   Legacy/Epic Associated 47075 I Want Candy: The Best Of. *(neither the 45 or LP version)*
    (S)   (2:56)   Nick At Nite/Epic 67149 Dick Van Dyke's Dance Party. *(neither the 45 or LP version)*
    (S)   (2:56)   Varese Sarabande 5705 Dick Bartley Presents Collector's Essentials: The 60's. *(neither the 45 or LP version)*
1965 CARA-LIN
    (S)   (2:42)   Legacy/Epic Associated 47075 I Want Candy: The Best Of.
1966 NIGHT TIME
    (S)   (3:23)   Legacy/Epic Associated 47075 I Want Candy: The Best Of. *(LP version but :15 longer)*

STRAWBERRY ALARM CLOCK
1967 INCENSE AND PEPPERMINTS
    (M)   (2:46)   MCA 5940 Vintage Music Volumes 19 & 20.
    (M)   (2:46)   MCA 31217 Vintage Music Volume 20.
    (M)   (2:46)   MCA 31206 Vintage Music Volume 9.
    (M)   (2:46)   MCA 5806 Vintage Music Volumes 9 & 10.
    (M)   (2:46)   K-Tel 666 Flower Power.
    (M)   (2:48)   Rhino 75754 Even More Nuggets.
    (M)   (2:47)   Rhino 70628 Billboard's Top Rock & Roll Hits Of 1967.
    (M)   (2:45)   Priority 7909 Vietnam: Rockin' The Delta.
    (M)   (2:46)   Rhino 71066 Summer Of Love Volume 2.
    (M)   (2:47)   One Way 22083 Anthology.
    (M)   (2:45)   Time-Life 2CLR-05 Classic Rock - 1967.
    (M)   (2:46)   MCA Special Products 22134 Vintage Collectibles Volume 5.
    (M)   (2:46)   MCA Special Products 22131 Vintage Collectibles Volume 2.
    (M)   (2:45)   Time-Life R968-12 Guitar Rock - The Late '60s.
    (M)   (2:46)   K-Tel 3183 Psychedelic Mind Trip.
    (M)   (2:47)   MCA Special Products 20900 Rock Around The Oldies #3.
    (M)   (2:46)   Buddah 49507 Psychedelic Pop.

    (M)   (2:45)   Hollywood 62112 O.S.T. Austin Roberts.
    (M)   (2:46)   MCA Special Products 21046 Top Singles Of The Sixties.
1968 TOMORROW
    (S)   (2:13)   One Way 22083 Anthology.
    (S)   (2:13)   Varese Sarabande 5803 Sunshine Days - Pop Classics Of The '60s Volume 3.

STRAY CATS
1982 ROCK THIS TOWN
    (M)   (2:38)   EMI 27674 Living In Oblivion: The 80's Greatest Hits Volume Three. *(45 version)*
    (M)   (3:23)   Priority 53712 Classic Rock Volume 3 - Wild Weekend. *(LP version)*
    (M)   (3:23)   Priority 7054 80's Greatest Rock Hits Volume 4 - Party On. *(LP version)*
    (M)   (2:38)   Rhino 70742 Rock This Town: Rockabilly Hits Vol. 2. *(45 version)*
    (M)   (3:23)   Sandstone 33000 Reelin' In The Years Volume 1. *(LP version)*
    (M)   (2:37)   Rhino 71834 Classic MTV: Class Of 1983. *(45 version)*
    (M)   (3:23)   K-Tel 3261 The 80's Rock On. *(LP version)*
    (M)   (3:23)   Curb 77592 Greatest Hits. *(LP version)*
    (M)   (3:23)   EMI 94975 Best Of - Rock This Town. *(LP version)*
    (M)   (3:24)   EMI Manhattan 46103 Built For Speed. *(LP version)*
    (M)   (2:38)   Rhino 72133 Frat Rock: The 80's. *(45 version)*
    (M)   (2:37)   Time-Life R988-26 Sounds Of The Eighties: The Rolling Stone Collection 1982-1983. *(45 version)*
    (M)   (3:23)   Time-Life R968-13 Guitar Rock - The Early '80s. *(LP version)*
    (M)   (3:22)   JCI 3149 1980 - Only Dance - 1984. *(LP version)*
    (M)   (3:23)   Madacy Entertainment 1982 Rock On 1982. *(LP version)*
    (M)   (3:23)   EMI 53728 Runaway Boys: A Retrospective '81 - '92. *(LP version)*
    (M)   (2:36)   Tommy Boy 1194 ESPN Presents Slam Jams Vol. 1. *(45 version; all selections on this cd are segued together)*
    (M)   (2:37)   Priority 50953 I Love Rock & Roll Volume 4: Hits Of The 80's. *(45 version)*
    (M)   (3:22)   Cold Front 6255 Greatest Sports Rock And Jams Volume 2. *(all selections on this cd are segued together; LP version)*
    (M)   (3:23)   Simitar 55612 The Number One's: The '80s. *(LP version)*
1983 STRAY CAT STRUT
    (S)   (3:14)   Priority 53737 Classic Rock Volume 4 - American Music.
    (S)   (3:14)   Rhino 70678 Billboard Top Hits - 1983.
    (S)   (3:14)   Sandstone 33044 and 5010 Rock The First Volume Four.
    (S)   (3:14)   Curb 77592 Greatest Hits.
    (S)   (3:14)   EMI 94975 Best Of - Rock This Town.
    (S)   (3:14)   EMI Manhattan 46103 Built For Speed.
    (S)   (3:15)   Time-Life R988-01 Sounds Of The Eighties: The Rockin' Eighties.
    (S)   (3:14)   Madacy Entertainment 1983 Rock On 1983.
    (S)   (3:14)   JCI 3170 #1 Radio Hits 1980 - Only Rock 'n Roll - 1984.
    (S)   (3:14)   EMI 53728 Runaway Boys: A Retrospective '81 - '92.
    (S)   (3:15)   Time-Life R968-20 Guitar Rock - The '80s.
    (S)   (3:14)   Rhino 72820 VH1 - More Of The Big 80's.
1983 (SHE'S) SEXY + 17
    (S)   (3:28)   EMI 81417 Living In Oblivion: The 80's Greatest Hits Volume One. *(LP version)*
    (S)   (3:12)   Rhino 71975 New Wave Hits Of The 80's Vol. 12. *(45 version)*
    (S)   (3:28)   Curb 77592 Greatest Hits. *(LP version)*
    (S)   (3:28)   EMI 94975 Best Of - Rock This Town. *(LP version)*
    (S)   (3:28)   Time-Life R988-03 Sounds Of The Eighties: 1983. *(LP version)*
    (S)   (3:28)   EMI 53728 Runaway Boys: A Retrospective '81 - '92. *(LP version)*
    (S)   (3:28)   Simitar 55552 The Number One's: Eighties Rock. *(LP version)*

1983 I WON'T STAND IN YOUR WAY
- (S) (3:54) Curb 77592 Greatest Hits.
- (S) (3:55) EMI 94975 Best Of - Rock This Town.

STREET PEOPLE
1970 JENNIFER TOMKINS
- (S) (1:53) Varese Sarabande 5535 Bubblegum Classics Volume One.

BARBRA STREISAND
1964 PEOPLE
- (S) (3:39) Columbia 9968 Greatest Hits.
- (S) (5:00) Columbia 3220 O.S.T. Funny Girl. *(soundtrack version - not the hit version)*
- (S) (3:40) Columbia 9015 People.
- (S) (3:38) Columbia 44111 Just For The Record.
- (S) (3:38) Columbia 52849 Highlights From Just For The Record.

1966 SECOND HAND ROSE
- (S) (2:08) Columbia 9968 Greatest Hits.
- (S) (2:09) Columbia 9209 My Name Is Barbra, Two.

1971 STONEY END
- (S) (2:58) Columbia 35679 Greatest Hits Volume 2.
- (S) (2:57) Columbia 30378 Stoney End.
- (S) (2:57) Columbia 44111 Just For The Record.

1971 WHERE YOU LEAD
- (S) (2:58) Columbia 30792 Barbra Joan Streisand.

1974 THE WAY WE WERE
- (S) (3:29) Columbia 35679 Greatest Hits Volume 2.
- (S) (3:28) Columbia 37678 Memories.
- (S) (3:29) Columbia 32801 The Way We Were.
- (S) (3:50) Columbia 44111 Just For The Record. *(soundtrack version)*
- (S) (4:50) Columbia 44111 Just For The Record. *(includes a :54 spoken introduction, 1:56 of an alternate lyric version and 2:00 of the hit version)*
- (S) (3:50) Columbia 57381 O.S.T. The Way We Were. *(soundtrack version)*

1977 LOVE THEME FROM "A STAR IS BORN" (EVERGREEN)
- (S) (3:04) Columbia 35679 Greatest Hits Volume 2.
- (S) (3:03) Columbia 37678 Memories.
- (S) (3:12) Columbia 44111 Just For The Record. *(includes :57 of a demo version which tracks into an abridged version of the hit)*
- (S) (3:12) Columbia 52849 Highlights From Just For The Record. *(includes :57 of a demo version which tracks into an abridged version of the hit)*
- (S) (3:04) Columbia 57375 A Star Is Born.
- (S) (3:04) Columbia 69012 Diana Princess Of Wales Tribute.

1977 MY HEART BELONGS TO ME
- (S) (3:20) Columbia 35679 Greatest Hits Volume 2.
- (S) (3:20) Columbia 37678 Memories.
- (S) (3:20) Columbia 34380 Superman.

1978 SONGBIRD
- (S) (3:43) Columbia 35375 Songbird.
- (S) (3:43) Columbia 35679 Greatest Hits Volume 2.

1978 LOVE THEME FROM "EYES OF LAURA MARS" (PRISONER)
- (S) (3:53) Columbia 35679 Greatest Hits Volume 2.

released as by BARBRA & NEIL (BARBRA STREISAND & NEIL DIAMOND):
1978 YOU DON'T BRING ME FLOWERS
- (S) (3:56) Columbia 35375 Barbra Streisand: Songbird. *(Barbra Streisand solo)*
- (S) (3:23) Columbia 35679 Barbra Streisand: Greatest Hits Volume 2. *(LP length)*
- (S) (3:22) Columbia 37678 Barbra Streisand: Memories. *(LP length)*
- (S) (3:36) Columbia 44111 Barbra Streisand: Just For The Record. *(live)*
- (S) (3:35) Columbia 52849 Barbra Streisand: Highlights From Just For The Record. *(live)*
- (S) (3:14) Columbia 35625 Neil Diamond: You Don't Bring Me Flowers. *(45 length)*
- (S) (3:07) Columbia 34990 Neil Diamond: I'm Glad You're Here With Me Tonight. *(Neil Diamond solo)*
- (S) (3:22) Columbia 52703 Neil Diamond: Greatest Hits 1966-1992. *(LP length)*
- (S) (3:23) Columbia 38068 Neil Diamond: 12 Greatest Hits Volume II. *(LP length)*
- (S) (3:13) Columbia 65013 Neil Diamond: In My Lifetime Box Set. *(45 length)*

released as by BARBRA STREISAND:
1979 THE MAIN EVENT/FIGHT
(dj copies of this 45 ran (3:59) and (4:51); commercial copies were all (4:51))
- (S) (4:51) Columbia 45369 A Collection/Greatest Hits And More.
- (S) (4:52) Columbia 57376 O.S.T. The Main Event.

released as by BARBRA STREISAND/DONNA SUMMER:
1979 NO MORE TEARS (ENOUGH IS ENOUGH)
- (S) (4:42) Columbia 37678 Barbra Streisand: Memories. *(45 version)*
- (S) (8:19) Columbia 36258 Barbra Streisand: Wet. *("Wet" LP version)*
- (S) (11:42) Casablanca 822558 Donna Summer: On The Radio/Greatest Hits Volume I & II. *(12" single version as well as the "On The Radio" LP version; tracks into next selection)*
- (S) (11:41) Casablanca 830534 Donna Summer: The Dance Collection. *(12" single version as well as the "On The Radio" LP version)*
- (S) (4:47) Mercury 826144 Donna Summer: The Summer Collection. *(alternate take)*
- (S) (4:41) Casablanca 314518144 Donna Summer Anthology. *(45 version)*
- (S) (4:47) Casablanca 314526178 Donna Summer - Endless Summer. *(alternate take)*

released as by BARBRA STREISAND:
1980 KISS ME IN THE RAIN
- (S) (4:16) Columbia 36258 Wet.

1980 WOMAN IN LOVE
- (S) (3:49) Columbia 36750 Guilty.
- (S) (3:50) Columbia 45369 A Collection/Greatest Hits And More.

released as by BARBRA STREISAND & BARRY GIBB:
1981 GUILTY
- (S) (4:22) Columbia 36750 Barbra Streisand: Guilty.
- (S) (4:22) Columbia 45369 Barbra Streisand: A Collection/Greatest Hits And More.
- (S) (4:26) Columbia 44111 Barbra Streisand: Just For The Record. *(with countoff and studio talk on the ending)*

1981 WHAT KIND OF FOOL
- (S) (4:03) Columbia 36750 Barbra Streisand: Guilty.
- (S) (4:03) Columbia 45369 Barbra Streisand: A Collection/Greatest Hits And More.

released as by BARBRA STREISAND:
1982 COMIN' IN AND OUT OF YOUR LIFE
- (S) (4:08) Columbia 45369 Barbra Streisand: A Collection/Greatest Hits And More.
- (S) (4:07) Columbia 37678 Memories.

1983 THE WAY HE MAKES ME FEEL
- (S) (4:09) Columbia 45369 Barbra Streisand: A Collection/Greatest Hits And More.
- (S) (3:44) Columbia 39152 O.S.T. Yentl. *(soundtrack version)*
- (S) (4:09) Columbia 39152 O.S.T. Yentl.

released as by BARBRA STREISAND and DON JOHNSON:
1988 TILL I LOVED YOU
(dj copies of this 45 ran (4:14) and (4:48); commercial copies were all (4:48))
- (S) (5:09) Columbia 40880 Barbra Streisand - Till I Loved You. *(LP version)*

released as by BARBRA STREISAND and BRYAN ADAMS:
1997 I FINALLY FOUND SOMEONE
- (S) (3:41) Columbia 67887 O.S.T. The Mirror Has Two Faces.

STRING-A-LONGS
1961 WHEELS
- (S) (1:55) Rhino 71602 Rock Instrumental Classics Volume 2: The Sixties.

(S) (1:55) Rhino 72035 Rock Instrumental Classics Vols. 1-5 Box Set.

(S) (1:54) Time-Life 2RNR-18 Rock 'N' Roll Era - 1961 Still Rockin'.

(S) (1:54) Collectors' Choice 003/4 Instrumental Gems Of The 60's.

1961 BRASS BUTTONS

BARRETT STRONG
1960 MONEY (THAT'S WHAT I WANT)

(E) (2:34) Motown 5448 A Package Of 16 Big Hits.

(M) (2:33) Rhino 75778 Frat Rock.

(M) (2:35) Rhino 70646 Billboard's Top R&B Hits Of 1960.

(M) (2:33) Motown 6184 Hard To Find Motown Classics Volume 2.

(M) (2:33) Garland 011 Footstompin' Oldies.

(M) (2:33) DCC Compact Classics 043 Toga Rock II.

(M) (2:34) Motown 5448 A Package Of 16 Big Hits.

(M) (2:35) Motown 6312 Hitsville USA.

(M) (2:33) Time-Life 2RNR-22 Rock 'N' Roll Era - 1960 Still Rockin'.

(M) (2:33) Private Music 82119 O.S.T. Getting Even With Dad.

(M) (2:34) Motown 314530403 Motown Classic Hits Vol. 1.

(M) (2:35) Motown 314530436 A Tribute To Berry Gordy.

(M) (2:34) Polygram Special Markets 314520454 Soul Hits Of The 60's.

JUD STRUNK
1973 DAISY A DAY

(S) (2:47) Rhino 70758 Super Hits Of The 70's Volume 11.

(S) (2:46) Curb 77443 Mike Curb Congregation Greatest Hits.

STRYPER
1988 HONESTLY

(S) (4:06) Enigma 73237 To Hell With The Devil.

(S) (4:06) Hollywood 61185 To Hell With The Devil.

STYLE COUNCIL
1984 MY EVER CHANGING MOODS

(S) (5:41) Priority 53781 Best Of 80's Rock Volume 2. *(LP version)*

(S) (5:42) Polydor 837896 The Singular Adventures Of The Style Council. *(LP version)*

STYLISTICS
1971 STOP, LOOK, LISTEN (TO YOUR HEART)

(S) (2:52) Amherst 748 Stylistics.

(S) (2:52) Priority 53146 Slow Grind Volume Two.

1972 YOU ARE EVERYTHING

(S) (2:54) Amherst 9743 Best Of.

(S) (2:53) Right Stuff 27307 Slow Jams: The 70's Volume One.

(S) (2:54) Amherst 748 Stylistics.

(S) (2:53) K-Tel 3535 Slow Groove Love Jams Of The 70's.

(S) (2:53) Time-Life R834-06 Body Talk - Only You.

1972 BETCHA BY GOLLY, WOW

(S) (3:15) Amherst 9743 Best Of. *(45 version)*

(S) (3:15) Scotti Brothers 75405 There Is Still Love (The Anniversary Songs). *(45 version)*

(S) (3:17) Thump 7030 Low Rider Oldies Volume III. *(45 version)*

(S) (3:15) LaserLight 12321 Soulful Love. *(45 version)*

(S) (3:15) Right Stuff 29138 Slow Jams: The 70's Vol. 3. *(45 version)*

(S) (3:45) Amherst 748 Stylistics. *(LP version)*

(S) (3:15) Rhino 72126 Soul Hits Of The 70's Vol. 16. *(45 version)*

(S) (3:15) Rhino 72114 Billboard Hot Soul Hits - 1972. *(45 version)*

(S) (3:15) Hip-O 40030 The Glory Of Love - '70s Sweet & Soulful Love Songs. *(45 version)*

(S) (3:15) Time-Life R834-09 Body Talk - Magic Moments. *(45 version)*

(S) (3:15) Rhino 72943 VH1 8-Track Flashback: Classic '70s Soul. *(45 version)*

(S) (3:15) Collectables 1516 and 2516 The Anniversary Album - The 70's. *(45 version)*

1972 PEOPLE MAKE THE WORLD GO ROUND

(S) (3:28) Amherst 9743 Best Of. *(45 version)*

(S) (6:24) Amherst 748 Stylistics. *(LP version)*

(S) (6:21) MCA 11065 O.S.T. Crooklyn Volume II. *(LP version)*

1972 I'M STONE IN LOVE WITH YOU

(S) (3:17) Amherst 9743 Best Of.

(S) (3:16) Original Sound 8863 Oldies But Goodies Vol. 13.

(S) (3:16) Original Sound 2223 Oldies But Goodies Volumes 2,7,9,12 and 13 Box Set. *(Volumes 2, 7 and 12 of this box set use the "Waring - fds" noise reduction process)*

(S) (3:16) Original Sound 2500 Oldies But Goodies Volumes 1-15 Box Set. *(most volumes in this box set use the "Waring - fds" noise reduction process)*

(S) (3:17) MCA 11065 O.S.T. Crooklyn Volume II.

1973 BREAK UP TO MAKE UP

(S) (3:57) Amherst 9743 Best Of.

(S) (3:58) Thump 7040 Low Rider Oldies Volume 4.

(S) (3:56) Original Sound 9304 Art Laboe's Dedicated To You Vol. 4.

(S) (3:54) Rhino 71861 Smooth Grooves Volume 3.

(S) (3:56) Madacy Entertainment 1973 Rock On 1973.

(S) (3:55) Time-Life R834-03 Body Talk - Moonlit Nights.

1973 YOU'LL NEVER GET TO HEAVEN (IF YOU BREAK MY HEART)

(S) (3:36) Amherst 9745 Best Of Volume 2.

(S) (3:36) Varese Sarabande 5873 The Burt Bacharach Songbook.

1973 ROCKIN' ROLL BABY

(S) (3:14) Amherst 9743 Best Of.

1974 YOU MAKE ME FEEL BRAND NEW

(S) (4:43) Amherst 9746 Greatest Love Hits.

(S) (4:45) Amherst 9743 Best Of.

(M) (4:43) Original Sound 8908 Best Love Songs Vol 3.

(M) (4:43) Original Sound 9327 Best Love Songs Vol. 3 & 4.

(M) (4:43) Original Sound 1236 Best Love Songs Box Set.

1974 LET'S PUT IT ALL TOGETHER

(S) (2:56) Amherst 9743 Best Of.

1974 HEAVY FALLIN' OUT

(S) (5:15) Amherst 9743 Best Of. *(LP version)*

STYX
1975 LADY

(S) (2:58) RCA 9684 and 8476 Nipper's Greatest Hits - The 70's.

(S) (2:55) RCA 3597 Best Of.

1976 LORELEI

(S) (3:19) A&M 3217 Equinox.

(S) (3:21) A&M 314540387 Greatest Hits.

1976 MADEMOISELLE

(S) (3:56) A&M 3218 Crystal Ball.

(S) (3:57) A&M 314540550 Greatest Hits Part 2.

1978 COME SAIL AWAY

(S) (3:10) Priority 7066 #1 Groups/70's Greatest Rock Hits Volume 12. *(45 version)*

(S) (5:29) A&M 2513 Classics Volume 15. *(edit of LP version)*

(S) (6:05) A&M 3223 Grand Illusion. *(LP version)*

(S) (6:03) A&M 314540387 Greatest Hits. *(LP version)*

(S) (8:33) CMC International 86233 Superstar Hits. *(live)*

(S) (5:59) Simitar 55502 The Number One's: Classic Rock. *(LP version)*

1978 FOOLING YOURSELF (THE ANGRY YOUNG MAN) (dj copies of this 45 ran (3:35) and (5:29); commercial copies were all labeled (5:29) but the actual 45 running time is (5:22) not (5:29) as stated on both the commercial and dj 45's)

(S) (5:07) A&M 2513 Classics Volume 15. *(edit of both the LP and 45)*

(S) (5:27) A&M 3223 Grand Illusion.

(S) (5:27) A&M 314540387 Greatest Hits.

1978 BLUE COLLAR MAN (LONG NIGHTS) (dj copies of this 45 ran (3:37); commercial copies were all (4:04))

(S) (4:04) A&M 2513 Classics Volume 15.

(S) (4:04)   A&M 3224   Pieces Of Eight.
(S) (4:04)   A&M 314540387   Greatest Hits.
1979 RENEGADE
(S) (4:11)   A&M 2513   Classics Volume 15.
(S) (4:12)   A&M 3224   Pieces Of Eight.
(S) (4:12)   Rebound 314520278   Hard Rock Essentials - The 70's.
(S) (4:12)   A&M 314540387   Greatest Hits.
(S) (4:08)   K-Tel 3908   High Energy Volume 1.
(S) (4:10)   K-Tel 3904   The Rock Album Volume 2.
1979 BABE
(both dj and commercial copies of this 45 state (4:26) on the label but the actual running time is (4:02))
(S) (4:24)   A&M 2513   Classics Volume 15. *(LP version)*
(S) (4:24)   A&M 3239   Cornerstone. *(LP version)*
(S) (4:24)   A&M 314540387   Greatest Hits. *(LP version)*
1980 WHY ME
(S) (3:53)   A&M 3239   Cornerstone.
1981 THE BEST OF TIMES
(S) (4:16)   A&M 2513   Classics Volume 15.
(S) (4:17)   A&M 3240   Paradise Theatre.
(S) (4:16)   Priority 53714   80's Greatest Rock Hits Volume 1: Passion & Power.
(S) (4:17)   A&M 314540387   Greatest Hits.
1981 TOO MUCH TIME ON MY HANDS
(dj copies of this 45 featured a :07 introduction on one side with no introduction on the other; commercial copies all had a :07 introduction)
(S) (4:30)   A&M 2513   Classics Volume 15.
(S) (4:31)   A&M 3240   Paradise Theatre.
(S) (4:31)   Priority 53715   80's Greatest Rock Hits Volume 3: Arena Rock.
(S) (4:31)   A&M 314540387   Greatest Hits.
1983 MR. ROBOTO
(S) (5:28)   A&M 3734   Kilroy Was Here. *(LP version)*
(S) (5:27)   A&M 314540387   Greatest Hits. *(LP version)*
(S) (5:27)   Rebound 314520434   Classic Rock - 80's. *(LP version)*
(S) (5:28)   Rebound 314520493   Class Reunion '83. *(LP version)*
1983 DON'T LET IT END
(S) (4:53)   A&M 3734   Kilroy Was Here.
(S) (4:53)   A&M 314540387   Greatest Hits.
1991 SHOW ME THE WAY
(S) (4:34)   A&M 5327   Edge Of The Century.
(S) (4:33)   A&M 314540387   Greatest Hits.
1991 LOVE AT FIRST SIGHT
(S) (4:33)   A&M 5327   Edge Of The Century.

SUAVE
1988 MY GIRL
(S) (5:36)   Capitol 48686   I'm Your Playmate.

SUBWAY featuring 702
1995 THIS LIL' GAME WE PLAY
(S) (4:52)   BIV 10 Records 314530354   Good Times.

SUGARHILL GANG
1980 RAPPER'S DELIGHT
(S) (6:32)   Rhino 70957   Hip Hop Greats: Classic Raps. *(neither the 45, LP or 12" single version)*
(S) (14:25) Rhino 70577 and 72063   Street Jams: Hip Hop From The Top Part 1. *(edit of 12" single extended version)*
(S) (5:01)   Priority 7960   Rapmasters 10: Best Of Scratchin'. *(45 short version)*
(S) (14:15) Thump 4510   Old School Rap Volume 1. *(edit of 12" single extended version)*
(S) (5:02)   Rhino 72248   O.S.T. Fox Hunt. *(45 short version)*
(S) (14:34) Rhino 71986   Best Of. *(edit of 12" single extended version)*
(S) (14:34) Rhino 72449   Sugar Hill Records Story. *(edit of 12" single extended version)*
(S) (6:05)   Hot Productions 26   Best Of Sugar Hill Records. *(neither the 45, LP or 12" single version)*
(S) (7:10)   Rhino 72852   Kurtis Blow Presents The History Of Rap Vol. 2. *(neither the 45, LP or 12" single version)*

SUGARLOAF
1970 GREEN-EYED LADY
(dj copies of this 45 ran (2:58) and (3:33); commercial 45's ran (3:37) and (5:58))
(S) (3:37)   Rhino 70923   Super Hits Of The 70's Volume 3. *(45 version)*
(S) (3:37)   Rhino 72009   Super Hits Of The 70's Volumes 1-4 Box Set. *(45 version)*
(S) (3:38)   Rhino 70631   Billboard's Top Rock & Roll Hits Of 1970. *(45 version)*
(S) (3:38)   Rhino 72005   Billboard's Top Rock & Roll Hits 1968-1972 Box Set. *(45 version)*
(S) (3:38)   EMI 90603   Rock Me Gently. *(45 version)*
(S) (3:38)   Curb 77356   70's Hits Volume 2. *(45 version)*
(S) (3:38)   Priority 7066   #1 Groups/70's Greatest Rock Hits Volume 12. *(45 version)*
(S) (3:38)   Rhino 71207   70's Smash Hits Volume 3. *(45 version)*
(S) (6:48)   Curb 77597   Best Of. *(LP version)*
(S) (3:36)   Time-Life SUD-04   Superhits - 1970. *(45 version)*
(S) (3:38)   Time-Life SOD-01   Sounds Of The Seventies - 1970. *(45 version)*
(S) (6:48)   Varese Sarabande 5503 and 5504 and 5505 and 5506 and 5507 and 5508 and 5509 and 5513 and 5571   Arrow: All Rock & Roll Oldies Volume One. *(LP version)*
(S) (3:37)   Time-Life R968-06   Guitar Rock 1970-1971. *(45 version)*
(S) (3:36)   Madacy Entertainment 1970   Rock On 1970. *(45 version)*
(S) (3:37)   JCI 3168   #1 Radio Hits 1970 - Only Rock 'n Roll - 1974. *(45 version)*
(S) (3:38)   Priority 50952   I Love Rock & Roll Volume 3: Hits Of The 70's. *(45 version)*
(S) (3:36)   Time-Life AM1-02   AM Gold - 1970. *(45 version)*
(S) (3:38)   Flashback 72683   '70s Radio Hits Volume 3. *(45 version)*
(S) (3:38)   Flashback 72090   '70s Radio Hits Box Set. *(45 version)*
(S) (6:48)   Rhino 72893   Hard Rock Cafe: Classic Rock. *(LP version)*
(S) (6:48)   Collectables 5871   Sugarloaf/Spaceship Earth. *(LP version)*
(S) (3:38)   Hollywood 62138   O.S.T. Home Alone 3. *(45 version)*
released as by SUGARLOAF/JERRY CORBETTA:
1975 DON'T CALL US, WE'LL CALL YOU
(S) (3:19)   Rhino 70761   Super Hits Of The 70's Volume 14.
(S) (3:22)   Curb 77597   Best Of.
(S) (3:19)   Time-Life SOD-32   Sounds Of The Seventies - AM Pop Classics.
(S) (3:19)   Varese Sarabande 5706   Dick Bartley Presents Collector's Essentials: The 70's.
(S) (3:22)   Collectables 5871   Sugarloaf/Spaceship Earth.

DONNA SUMMER
1976 LOVE TO LOVE YOU BABY
(dj copies ran (3:27) and (4:57); commercial copies were all (4:57))
(S) (4:14)   Casablanca 822558   On The Radio/Greatest Hits Volumes I & II. *(most selections on this cd are segued together; this is neither the commercial 45 version, the dj 45 version or the LP version)*
(S) (16:47) Casablanca 822792   Love To Love You Baby. *(LP version)*
(S) (3:21)   Casablanca 314518144   Anthology. *(this is not the dj 45 edit as it is missing some overdubs)*
(S) (4:53)   Time-Life SOD-04   Sounds Of The Seventies - 1976. *(45 version)*
(S) (16:47) Casablanca 314516918   Casablanca Records Story. *(LP version)*
(S) (3:21)   Casablanca 314526178   Endless Summer. *(this is not the dj 45 edit as it is missing some overdubs)*
(S) (5:40)   Rebound 314520219   Disco Nights Vol. 3 - Best Of Eurodisco. *(neither the 45, LP or 12" single version)*

DONNA SUMMER *(Continued)*

(S) (3:20) Rebound 314520368 Class Reunion '76. *(this is not the dj edit as it is missing some overdubs)*

1977 I FEEL LOVE
(dj copies of this 45 ran (3:42); commercial copies were all (5:53))

(S) (5:53) Rhino 70276 The Disco Years Volume 5.

(S) (5:53) Rhino 70491 Billboard Top Dance Hits - 1977.

(S) (8:13) Casablanca 830534 The Dance Collection. *(12" single version)*

(S) (3:21) Casablanca 822558 On The Radio/Greatest Hits Volumes I & II. *(most selections on this cd are segued together; edited version of the dj edit)*

(S) (5:52) Casablanca 826237 I Remember Yesterday.

(S) (5:38) Casablanca 810011 Walk Away. *(edited)*

(S) (5:51) Casablanca 314518144 Anthology.

(S) (5:53) Time-Life SOD-35 Sounds Of The Seventies - AM Nuggets.

(S) (8:12) Casablanca 314516918 Casablanca Records Story. *(12" single version)*

(S) (3:45) Casablanca 314526178 Endless Summer. *(this is the dj 45 edit)*

(S) (3:45) Casablanca 314526253 Casablanca Records Greatest Hits. *(this is the dj 45 edit)*

(S) (6:20) Mercury 314532494 100% Pure Dance. *(all songs on this cd are segued together; remix)*

(S) (3:54) Polydor 314535877 Pure Disco. *(previously unreleased version)*

(S) (5:53) Time-Life R840-07 Sounds Of The Seventies: '70s Dance Party 1976-1977.

(S) (9:32) Priority 51041 Disco In The House. *(all selections on this cd are segued together; remix)*

1978 I LOVE YOU

(S) (3:11) Casablanca 822558 On The Radio/Greatest Hits Volumes I & II. *(most selections on this cd are segued together; 45 version)*

(S) (3:12) Mercury 826144 The Summer Collection. *(45 version)*

(S) (4:40) Casablanca 314518144 Anthology. *(LP version)*

1978 LAST DANCE

(S) (3:18) Rhino 70492 Billboard Top Dance Hits - 1978. *(45 version)*

(S) (8:09) Casablanca 830534 The Dance Collection. *(12" single version)*

(S) (4:56) Casablanca 822558 On The Radio/Greatest Hits Volumes I & II. *(most selections on this cd are segued together; neither the 45 or LP version)*

(S) (3:18) Mercury 826144 The Summer Collection. *(45 version)*

(S) (3:17) Casablanca 810011 Walk Away. *(45 version)*

(S) (4:56) Casablanca 314518144 Anthology. *(neither the 45 or LP version)*

(S) (3:18) Time-Life SOD-34 Sounds Of The Seventies - The Late 70's. *(45 version)*

(S) (8:09) Casablanca 314516918 Casablanca Records Story. *(12" single version)*

(S) (3:17) Casablanca 314526178 Endless Summer. *(45 version)*

(S) (3:18) Rhino 71868 Academy Award Winning Songs. *(45 version)*

(S) (5:49) Rebound 314520217 Disco Nights Vol. 1 - Divas Of Dance. *(neither the 45, LP or 12" single version)*

(S) (3:18) Time-Life R138-38 Celebration. *(45 version)*

(S) (3:17) MCA 11329 Soul Train 25th Anniversary Box Set. *(45 version)*

(S) (3:18) Rhino 72279 Academy Award Winning Songs Volume 4. *(45 version)*

(S) (8:09) Rebound 314520337 Compiled From O.S.T. Thank God It's Friday. *(12" single version)*

(S) (5:49) Rebound 314520366 Disco Nights Vol. 10 - Disco's Greatest Movie Hits. *(neither the 45, LP or 12" single version)*

(S) (3:17) Casablanca 314526253 Casablanca Records Greatest Hits. *(45 version)*

(S) (8:08) Casablanca 314534606 O.S.T. Thank God It's Friday. *(12" single version)*

(S) (3:16) Casablanca 314534606 O.S.T. Thank God It's Friday. *(this is not the single version - this is the "LAST DANCE" reprise)*

(S) (3:34) Island 314553411 The Last Party. *(all selections on this cd are segued together)*

(S) (3:18) Polydor 314555120 Pure Disco 2. *(45 version)*

(S) (3:17) Thump 4840 Flashback Disco. *(all selections on this cd are segued together; 45 version)*

(S) (3:17) Time-Life R840-08 Sounds Of The Seventies: '70s Dance Party 1978-1979. *(45 version)*

(S) (3:17) Rebound 314520519 Love At The Movies. *(45 version)*

1978 MacARTHUR PARK
(dj copies of this 45 ran (3:53) and (6:24); commercial copies were all (3:59))

(S) (17:46) Rhino 70492 Billboard Top Dance Hits - 1978. *(LP version titled "Mac ARTHUR PARK SUITE")*

(S) (17:45) Casablanca 830534 The Dance Collection. *(LP version titled "Mac ARTHUR PARK SUITE")*

(S) (3:54) Casablanca 822558 On The Radio/Greatest Hits Volumes I & II. *(most selections on this cd are segued together; 45 version)*

(S) (3:55) Mercury 826144 The Summer Collection. *(45 version)*

(S) (3:53) Casablanca 810011 Walk Away. *(45 version)*

(S) (6:24) Casablanca 314518144 Anthology. *(this is the long dj 45 version)*

(S) (17:32) Casablanca 314516918 Casablanca Records Story. *(LP version titled "Mac ARTHUR PARK SUITE")*

(S) (3:55) Casablanca 314526178 Endless Summer. *(45 version)*

released as by DONNA SUMMER with BROOKLYN DREAMS:
1979 HEAVEN KNOWS

(S) (3:22) Mercury 826144 The Summer Collection. *(neither the 45 or LP version)*

(S) (3:51) Casablanca 314518144 Anthology. *(:14 longer fade than the 45 version)*

(S) (3:21) Casablanca 314526178 Endless Summer. *(neither the 45 or LP version)*

(S) (5:54) Rebound 314520217 Disco Nights Vol. 1 - Divas Of Dance. *(neither the 45 or LP version)*

(S) (6:41) Rebound 314520309 Disco Nights Vol. VII - D.J. Pix. *(neither the 45 or LP version)*

released as by DONNA SUMMER:
1979 HOT STUFF
(there were 2 different 12" single versions of this song: one tracked into BAD GIRLS and ran (11:40), the other was simply HOT STUFF which ran (6:46))

(S) (4:28) Rhino 70275 The Disco Years Volume 4. *(edit of LP version)*

(S) (11:40) Rhino 70493 Billboard Top Dance Hits - 1979. *(12" single version which is a medley of "HOT STUFF"/"BAD GIRLS")*

(S) (6:40) Casablanca 830534 The Dance Collection. *(all selections on this cd are the 12" single version)*

(S) (2:54) Casablanca 822558 On The Radio/Greatest Hits Volumes I & II. *(most selections on this cd are segued together; neither the LP or 45 version)*

(S) (5:14) Casablanca 822557 Bad Girls. *(LP version which tracks into "BAD GIRLS" (4:54))*

(S) (3:42) Casablanca 810011 Walk Away. *(45 version)*

(S) (6:46) Casablanca 314518144 Anthology. *(12" single version which tracks into "BAD GIRLS")*

(S) (6:40) JCI 3306 Dance Seventies. *(12" single version)*

(S) (4:26) Time-Life SOD-27 Sounds Of The Seventies - Dance Fever. *(edit of the LP version)*

(S) (6:46) Casablanca 314516918 Casablanca Records Story. *(12" single version which tracks into "BAD GIRLS")*

(S) (3:49) Casablanca 314526178 Endless Summer. *(45 version)*

(S) (6:38) Rebound 314520307 Disco Nights Volume VIII. *(12" single version)*

(S) (3:48) Rebound 314520270 Class Reunion 1979. *(45 version)*

(S) (5:14) Casablanca 314526253 Casablanca Records Greatest Hits. *(LP version which tracks into "BAD GIRLS" (4:54))*
(S) (3:48) Polydor 314535877 Pure Disco. *(45 version)*
(S) (3:48) RCA 68904 O.S.T. The Full Monty. *(45 version)*
(S) (3:48) Time-Life R840-09 Sounds Of The Seventies: '70s Dance Party 1979-1981. *(45 version)*

1979 BAD GIRLS
(S) (3:58) Rhino 70274 The Disco Years Volume 3. *(45 version)*
(S) (11:40) Rhino 70493 Billboard Top Dance Hits - 1979. *(12" single version which is a medley of "HOT STUFF"/"BAD GIRLS")*
(S) (3:05) Casablanca 822558 On The Radio/Greatest Hits Volumes I & II. *(most selections on this cd are segued together; neither the 45 or LP version)*
(S) (3:54) Mercury 826144 The Summer Collection. *(45 version)*
(S) (4:54) Casablanca 822557 Bad Girls. *(LP version which was originally a medley with "HOT STUFF" (5:13) but is given separate track identification on this cd)*
(S) (3:52) Casablanca 810011 Walk Away. *(45 version)*
(S) (4:54) Casablanca 314518144 Anthology. *(12" single version which was originally a medley with "HOT STUFF" (6:46) but it is given separate track identification on this cd)*
(S) (3:59) Rhino 71618 Soul Train Hall Of Fame/20th Anniversary. *(45 version)*
(S) (3:51) Time-Life SOD-09 Sounds Of The Seventies - 1979. *(45 version)*
(S) (4:54) Casablanca 314516918 Casablanca Records Story. *(12" single version which was originally a medley with "HOT STUFF" (6:46) but it is given separate track identification on this cd)*
(S) (3:53) Casablanca 314526178 Endless Summer. *(45 version)*
(S) (4:55) Rebound 314520245 Disco Nights Vol. 6 - #1 Disco Hits. *(12" single version which was originally a medley with "HOT STUFF" but it is given a separate track identification on this cd)*
(S) (4:54) Casablanca 314526253 Casablanca Records Greatest Hits. *(LP version which is a medley with "HOT STUFF" (5:14) but is given a separate track identification on this cd)*
(S) (3:54) Rebound 314520447 Soul Classics - Best Of The 70's. *(45 version)*
(S) (5:02) Chronicles 314553404 Non-Stop Disco Vol. 1. *(all songs on this cd are segued together)*
(S) (3:58) Time-Life R838-15 Solid Gold Soul 1979. *(45 version)*
(S) (3:50) Time-Life R840-10 Sounds Of The Seventies: '70s Dance Party 1979. *(45 version)*
(S) (4:49) Rebound 314520520 Body Moves - Non-Stop Disco Workout Vol. 1. *(all selections on this cd are segued together)*

1979 DIM ALL THE LIGHTS
(S) (7:14) Casablanca 830534 The Dance Collection. *(all selections on this cd are the 12" single version)*
(S) (4:10) Casablanca 822558 On The Radio/Greatest Hits Volumes I & II. *(most selections on this cd are segued together; :15 longer than the 45 version)*
(S) (4:40) Casablanca 822557 Bad Girls. *(LP version)*
(S) (4:23) Casablanca 314518144 Anthology. *(LP version faded early)*
(S) (4:12) Priority 53728 Mega Hits Dance Classics Vol 12. *(:17 longer than the 45 version)*
(S) (4:04) Casablanca 314526178 Endless Summer. *(:09 longer fade than the 45 version)*
(S) (4:03) Casablanca 314526253 Casablanca Records Greatest Hits. *(:08 longer fade that the 45 version)*
(S) (4:23) JCI 3175 1975 - Only Soul - 1979. *(LP version faded early)*
(S) (4:03) Time-Life R840-09 Sounds Of The Seventies: '70s Dance Party 1979-1981. *(:08 longer fade than the 45 version)*

released as by BARBRA STREISAND/DONNA SUMMER:
1979 NO MORE TEARS (ENOUGH IS ENOUGH)
(S) (4:42) Columbia 37678 Barbra Streisand: Memories. *(45 version)*
(S) (8:19) Columbia 36258 Barbra Streisand: Wet. *("Wet" LP version)*
(S) (11:42) Casablanca 822558 Donna Summer: On The Radio/Greatest Hits Volume I & II. *(12" single version as well as the "On The Radio" LP version; tracks into next selection)*
(S) (11:41) Casablanca 830534 Donna Summer: The Dance Collection. *(12" single version as well as the "On The Radio" LP version)*
(S) (4:47) Mercury 826144 Donna Summer: The Summer Collection. *(alternate take)*
(S) (4:41) Casablanca 314518144 Donna Summer - Anthology. *(45 version)*
(S) (4:47) Casablanca 314526178 Donna Summer - Endless Summer. *(alternate take)*

released as by DONNA SUMMER:
1980 ON THE RADIO
(actual 45 time is (4:04) not (3:59) as stated on the record label; there are two versions of this song on the vinyl LP titled ON THE RADIO, one ran (5:50) and the other (4:01))
(S) (4:01) Casablanca 822558 On The Radio/Greatest Hits Volumes I & II. *(most selections on this cd are segued together)*
(S) (5:50) Casablanca 822558 On The Radio/Greatest Hits Volumes I & II. *(most selections on this cd are segued together)*
(S) (4:03) Mercury 826144 The Summer Collection. *(45 version)*
(S) (4:02) Casablanca 810011 Walk Away. *(45 version)*
(S) (5:49) Casablanca 314518144 Anthology. *(LP version)*
(S) (7:33) Casablanca 314516918 Casablanca Records Story. *(LP version from the vinyl album "O.S.T. Foxes")*
(S) (4:03) Casablanca 314526178 Endless Summer. *(45 version)*
(S) (4:03) Casablanca 314526253 Casablanca Records Greatest Hits. *(45 version)*
(S) (4:03) Time-Life R988-14 Sounds Of The Eighties: 1980-1982. *(45 version)*

1980 THE WANDERER
(S) (3:45) Casablanca 314518144 Anthology.
(S) (3:45) Priority 53730 Mega Hits Dance Classics Vol. 13.
(S) (3:45) Casablanca 314526178 Endless Summer.
(S) (3:42) Rebound 314520318 Class Reunion 1980.
(S) (3:46) Casablanca 314522942 The Wanderer.
(S) (3:44) Time-Life R988-07 Sounds Of The Eighties: 1980.

1981 COLD LOVE
(S) (3:37) Casablanca 314522942 The Wanderer.
(S) (3:38) Casablanca 314518144 Anthology.

1981 WHO DO YOU THINK YOU'RE FOOLIN'
(S) (4:17) Casablanca 314522942 The Wanderer.

1982 LOVE IS IN CONTROL (FINGER ON THE TRIGGER)
(S) (4:19) Casablanca 314522943 Donna Summer. *(LP length)*
(S) (4:18) Casablanca 314518144 Anthology. *(LP length)*
(S) (4:18) Casablanca 314526178 Endless Summer. *(LP length)*
(S) (4:19) Priority 53789 Disco Attack. *(LP length)*

1983 THE WOMAN IN ME
(S) (3:54) Casablanca 314522943 Donna Summer. *(LP version)*

1983 SHE WORKS HARD FOR THE MONEY
(S) (5:17) Rebound 314520307 Disco Nights Volume VIII *(LP version)*
(S) (5:18) Casablanca 314518144 Anthology. *(LP version)*
(S) (5:18) Mercury 812265 She Works Hard For The Money. *(LP version)*
(S) (4:32) Mercury 826144 Donna Summer: The Summer Collection. *(:23 longer than the 45 version)*
(S) (4:32) Casablanca 314526178 Endless Summer. *(:23 longer than the 45 version)*
(S) (4:08) Time-Life R988-11 Sounds Of The 80's: 1983-1984. *(45 version)*

DONNA SUMMER *(Continued)*

- (S) (4:09) Rhino 72138 Billboard Hot R&B Hits 1983. *(45 version)*
- (S) (4:13) Nick At Nite/550 Music 67690 I Am Woman. *(45 version)*
- (S) (4:31) Hip-O 40015 Soulful Ladies Of The 80's. *(:22 longer than the 45 version)*
- (S) (3:52) Edel America 29782 O.S.T. The Birdcage. *(45 version faded :17 early)*
- (S) (5:06) Chronicles 314553405 Non-Stop Disco Vol. 2. *(all songs on this cd are segued together)*
- (S) (4:32) JCI 3176 1980 - Only Soul - 1984. *(:23 longer than the 45 version)*

1984 THERE GOES MY BABY
- (S) (4:06) Casablanca 314518144 Anthology.
- (S) (4:05) Geffen 24040 Cats Without Claws.
- (S) (4:06) Casablanca 314522944 Cats Without Claws.

1989 THIS TIME I KNOW IT'S FOR REAL
- (S) (3:36) Casablanca 314518144 Anthology.
- (S) (3:36) Atlantic 81987 Another Place And Time.
- (S) (3:36) Casablanca 314526178 Endless Summer.
- (S) (3:36) Casablanca 314528685 Another Place And Time.

HENRY LEE SUMMER
1988 I WISH I HAD A GIRL
- (S) (3:59) Foundation/WEA 26097 Super Sessions Volume Two. *(45 length)*
- (S) (4:23) K-Tel 3261 The 80's Rock On. *(LP length)*
- (S) (4:24) CBS Associated 40895 Henry Lee Summer. *(LP length)*

1989 HEY BABY
- (S) (3:51) CBS Associated 45124 I've Got Everything.
- (S) (3:49) Time-Life R968-24 Guitar Rock - The '80s Take Two.

SUNNY & THE SUNGLOWS
1963 TALK TO ME
- (M) (2:43) Collectables 5533 Talk To Me.
- (M) (2:44) Ripete 2184-RE Ocean Drive Vol. 2.
- (M) (2:44) Thump 7070 Lowrider Oldies Volume 7.
- (M) (2:44) Time-Life R857-18 The Heart Of Rock 'n' Roll 1962-1963 Take Two.

SUNNYSIDERS
1955 HEY, MR. BANJO

SUNSCREAM
1993 LOVE U MORE
- (S) (4:11) Columbia 53449 O3. *(timing index is off on this selection which tracks for 1:00 into the following selection)*

SUNSHINE COMPANY
1967 HAPPY
1967 BACK ON THE STREET AGAIN
- (S) (2:27) Rhino 75754 Even More Nuggets.
- (S) (2:25) K-Tel 666 Flower Power.
- (S) (2:26) Time-Life 2CLR-29 Classic Rock - Bubblegum, Garage And Pop Nuggets.
- (M) (2:26) Rhino 71066 Summer Of Love Volume 2.
- (S) (2:27) Time-Life R962-04 California Pop 1963-1967.
- (S) (2:25) EMI-Capitol Special Markets 19552 Lost Hits Of The '60s.

SUPERTRAMP
1975 BLOODY WELL RIGHT
(dj copies of this 45 ran (3:00); commercial copies were all (4:31))
- (S) (4:31) A&M 3647 Crime Of The Century.
- (S) (4:31) MFSL 505 Crime Of The Century. *(gold disc)*
- (S) (4:15) A&M 2507 Classics Volume 9. *(faded :16 earlier than the 45 or LP)*

1977 GIVE A LITTLE BIT
(dj copies of this 45 ran (3:32) and (4:07); commercial copies were all (4:07))
- (S) (4:07) A&M 3297 Even In The Quietest Moments.

- (S) (4:06) A&M 2507 Classics Volume 9.

1979 THE LOGICAL SONG
(actual 45 time is (3:39) not (3:45) as stated on the record label)
- (S) (4:07) A&M 3708 Breakfast In America. *(LP length)*
- (S) (4:07) MFSL 534 Breakfast In America. *(LP length; gold disc)*
- (S) (3:46) A&M 2507 Classics Volume 9. *(45 length)*
- (S) (3:46) Time-Life R13610 Gold And Platinum Box Set - The Ultimate Rock Collection. *(45 length)*

1979 GOODBYE STRANGER
(dj copies of this 45 ran (4:25) and (5:49); commercial copies were all (5:49))
- (S) (5:47) A&M 3708 Breakfast In America.
- (S) (5:47) MFSL 534 Breakfast In America. *(gold disc)*
- (S) (4:27) A&M 2507 Classics Volume 9.

1979 TAKE THE LONG WAY HOME
(actual 45 and LP time is (5:07) not (5:02) as the record labels state; dj copies of this 45 ran (4:03) and (5:07); commercial copies were all (5:07))
- (S) (5:08) A&M 3708 Breakfast In America.
- (S) (4:04) A&M 2507 Classics Volume 9.
- (S) (5:08) MFSL 534 Breakfast In America. *(gold disc)*

1980 DREAMER
- (S) (3:28) A&M 3647 Crime Of The Century. *(tracks into the next selection)*
- (S) (3:29) A&M 2507 Classics Volume 9.

1983 IT'S RAINING AGAIN
- (S) (4:20) A&M 2507 Classics Volume 9.
- (S) (4:25) A&M 3284 Famous Last Words.

1983 MY KIND OF LADY
- (S) (5:13) A&M 3284 Famous Last Words. *(LP version)*

1985 CANNONBALL
- (S) (4:47) A&M 2507 Classics Volume 9. *(45 version)*
- (S) (7:38) A&M 5014 Brother Where You Bound. *(LP version)*

SUPREMES
1964 WHEN THE LOVELIGHT STARTS SHINING THROUGH HIS EYES
- (S) (2:35) Motown 5449 A Collection Of 16 Big Hits Volume 2. *(45 version)*
- (S) (3:03) Motown 5270 Where Did Our Love Go. *(LP version)*
- (S) (2:38) Motown 6198 and 0794 Anthology. *(45 version)*
- (S) (3:02) Motown 6193 25th Anniversary. *(LP version)*
- (S) (2:36) Motown 8029 and 8129 and 0237 Greatest Hits Volume 1/Greatest Hits Volume 2. *(45 version)*
- (S) (2:36) Motown 5357 Greatest Hits Volume 1. *(45 version)*
- (S) (3:02) Motown 8005 and 8105 Where Did Our Love Go/I Hear A Symphony. *(LP version)*
- (S) (3:02) Motown 6073 Compact Command Performances. *(LP version)*
- (S) (2:37) Motown 5101 Superstar Series Volume 1. *(45 version)*
- (M) (2:37) Motown 6357 Diana Ross Forever: Musical Memories. *(45 version)*
- (S) (3:02) Time-Life 2RNR-12 Rock 'N' Roll Era - The Supremes 1963-1969. *(LP version)*
- (E) (3:01) Motown/Essex 374638520 Motown Legends - My World Is Empty Without You. *(LP version)*
- (M) (2:35) Motown 314530419 Motown Classic Hits Vol. II. *(45 version)*
- (M) (3:04) Motown 314530511 Anthology. *(LP version)*
- (M) (3:02) Motown 314530827 The Ultimate Collection. *(LP version)*

1964 WHERE DID OUR LOVE GO
- (S) (2:31) Motown 6159 The Good-Feeling Music Of The Big Chill Generation Volume 1. *(noisy intro)*
- (S) (2:31) Motown 6137 20 Greatest Songs In Motown History.
- (S) (2:31) Original Sound 8858 Oldies But Goodies Vol. 8. *(this compact disc uses the "Waring - fds" noise reduction process)*
- (S) (2:31) Original Sound 2221 Oldies But Goodies Volumes 1,4,6,8 and 10 Box Set. *(this box set uses the "Waring - fds" noise reduction process)*

(S) (2:31) Original Sound 2500 Oldies But Goodies Volumes 1-15 Box Set. *(this box set uses the "Waring - fds" noise reduction process)*

(S) (2:32) Motown 6138 The Composer Series: Holland/Dozier/Holland.

(S) (2:29) Motown 5452 A Collection Of 16 Big Hits Volume 5. *(pop noticeable at 2:26)*

(S) (2:31) Rhino 70650 Billboard's Top R&B Hits Of 1964.

(S) (2:31) Motown 9017 and 5248 16 #1 Hits From The Early 60's.

(S) (2:31) Motown 9097 The Most Played Oldies On America's Jukeboxes.

(S) (2:31) Motown 5343 Every Great Motown Song: The First 25 Years Volume 1. *(most selections on this cd have noise on the fadeout)*

(S) (2:31) Motown 8034 and 8134 Every Great Motown Song: The First 25 Years Volumes 1 & 2. *(most selections on this cd have noise on the fadeout)*

(S) (2:31) Motown 9098 Radio's #1 Hits.

(S) (2:31) Motown 9060 Motown's Biggest Pop Hits.

(S) (2:31) Motown 5270 Where Did Our Love Go.

(S) (2:30) Motown 5313 Great Songs And Performances That Inspired The Motown 25th Anniversary TV Special.

(S) (2:29) Motown 6198 and 0794 Anthology.

(S) (2:30) Motown 8005 and 8105 Where Did Our Love Go/I Hear A Symphony.

(S) (2:31) Motown 6193 25th Anniversary.

(S) (2:30) Motown 8029 and 8129 and 0237 Greatest Hits Volume 1/Greatest Hits Volume 2.

(M) (2:31) Motown 9038 and 5498 Every Great #1 Hit.

(S) (2:30) Motown 5357 Greatest Hits Volume 1.

(S) (2:31) Motown 6073 Compact Command Performances.

(S) (2:31) Motown 6192 You Can't Hurry Love: All The Great Love Songs Of The Past 25 Years.

(S) (2:29) Motown 9071 Motown Dance Party Volume 1. *(all selections on this cd are segued together)*

(M) (2:33) Motown 6357 Diana Ross Forever: Musical Memories. *(pop noticeable at 2:28)*

(S) (2:30) Time-Life 2RNR-10 Rock 'N' Roll Era - 1964.

(S) (2:31) Time-Life 2CLR-09 Classic Rock - 1964: The Beat Goes On.

(S) (2:30) Time-Life SUD-12 Superhits - The Mid 60's.

(S) (2:30) Original Sound 8883 21 Legendary Superstars.

(S) (2:31) Polygram Special Markets 314520283 Motown Legends Volume 2.

(M) (2:33) Motown 314530428 Diana Ross Ultimate Collection. *(pop noticeable at 2:28)*

(S) (2:31) Motown 314530504 Motown Year By Year 1964.

(S) (2:31) Thump 9947 Cruizin' To Motown.

(M) (2:32) Motown 314530511 Anthology.

(S) (2:30) Time-Life AM1-05 AM Gold - The Mid '60s.

(M) (2:32) Elektra 62093 O.S.T. A Smile Like Yours.

(M) (2:31) Motown 314530827 The Ultimate Collection.

1964 BABY LOVE

(S) (2:36) Motown 6132 25 #1 Hits From 25 Years.

(S) (2:35) Motown 6161 The Good-Feeling Music Of The Big Chill Generation Volume 3.

(S) (2:36) Motown 6138 The Composer Series: Holland/Dozier/Holland.

(S) (2:32) Motown 5451 A Collection Of 16 Big Hits Volume 4.

(S) (2:35) Motown 6110 Motown Grammy R&B Performances Of The 60's & 70's.

(S) (2:40) Rhino 70650 Billboard's Top R&B Hits Of 1964.

(S) (2:35) Motown 9017 and 5248 16 #1 Hits From The Early 60's.

(S) (2:35) Motown 9097 The Most Played Oldies On America's Jukeboxes.

(S) (2:35) Motown 5343 Every Great Motown Song: The First 25 Years Volume 1. *(most selections on this cd have noise on the fadeout)*

(S) (2:35) Motown 8034 and 8134 Every Great Motown Song: The First 25 Years Volumes 1 & 2. *(most selections on this cd have noise on the fadeout)*

(S) (2:35) Motown 9060 Motown's Biggest Pop Hits.

(S) (2:35) Motown 5322 and 9087 Girl Groups: The Story Of A Sound.

(S) (2:35) Motown 5270 Where Did Our Love Go.

(S) (2:34) Motown 5313 Great Songs And Performances That Inspired The Motown 25th Anniversary TV Special.

(S) (2:33) Motown 6198 and 0794 Anthology.

(S) (2:35) Motown 8005 and 8105 Where Did Our Love Go/I Hear A Symphony.

(S) (2:35) Motown 6193 25th Anniversary.

(S) (2:34) Motown 8029 and 8129 and 0237 Greatest Hits Volume 1/Greatest Hits Volume 2.

(M) (2:33) Motown 9038 and 5498 Every Great #1 Hit.

(S) (2:34) Motown 5357 Greatest Hits Volume 1.

(S) (2:35) Motown 6073 Compact Command Performances.

(S) (2:35) Motown 6192 You Can't Hurry Love: All The Great Love Songs Of The Past 25 Years.

(M) (2:35) Motown 6312 Hitsville USA. *(noisy fadeout)*

(M) (2:34) Motown 6357 Diana Ross Forever: Musical Memories. *(noisy fadeout)*

(S) (2:35) Time-Life 2RNR-12 Rock 'N' Roll Era - The Supremes 1963-1969.

(S) (2:38) Time-Life RHD-12 Rhythm & Blues - 1964.

(S) (2:35) Time-Life 2CLR-16 Classic Rock - 1964: Shakin' All Over.

(S) (2:37) Time-Life SUD-09 Superhits - 1964.

(M) (2:34) Epic 57871 O.S.T. My Girl 2.

(M) (2:34) Motown 314530422 Motown Classics Vol. V.

(M) (2:34) Motown 314530428 Diana Ross Ultimate Collection.

(S) (2:34) Motown 314530504 Motown Year By Year 1964.

(M) (2:35) Motown 314530511 Anthology.

(S) (2:35) Polygram Special Markets 314520293 Motown Legends - Volume 5.

(S) (2:40) Time-Life R857-09 The Heart Of Rock 'n' Roll 1964.

(S) (2:37) Time-Life AM1-11 AM Gold - 1964.

(S) (2:38) Time-Life R838-13 Solid Gold Soul - 1964.

(M) (2:34) Motown 314530827 The Ultimate Collection.

(S) (2:33) Polygram Special Markets 314520454 Soul Hits Of The 60's.

1964 COME SEE ABOUT ME

(S) (2:41) Motown 6159 The Good-Feeling Music Of The Big Chill Generation Volume 1.

(S) (2:42) Motown 6138 The Composer Series: Holland/Dozier/Holland. *(truncated fade)*

(S) (2:35) Motown 5452 A Collection Of 16 Big Hits Volume 5.

(S) (2:40) Motown 9072 Motown Dance Party Volume 2. *(all selections on this cd are segued together)*

(S) (2:41) Motown 9017 and 5248 16 #1 Hits From The Early 60's.

(S) (2:41) Motown 9060 Motown's Biggest Pop Hits.

(S) (2:41) Motown 5322 and 9087 Girl Groups: The Story Of A Sound.

(S) (2:41) Motown 5270 Where Did Our Love Go.

(S) (2:41) Motown 5313 Great Songs And Performances That Inspired The Motown 25th Anniversary TV Special.

(S) (2:35) Motown 6198 and 0794 Anthology. *(hum noticeable on both the introduction and the fadeout)*

(S) (2:41) Motown 8005 and 8105 Where Did Our Love Go/I Hear A Symphony.

(S) (2:41) Motown 6193 25th Anniversary.

(S) (2:35) Motown 8029 and 8129 and 0237 Greatest Hits Volume 1/Greatest Hits Volume 2.

(M) (2:38) Motown 9038 and 5498 Every Great #1 Hit.

(S) (2:34) Motown 5357 Greatest Hits Volume 1.

(S) (2:42) Motown 6073 Compact Command Performances.

(M) (2:39) Motown 6312 Hitsville USA.

(S) (2:35) Motown 374638510 Motown Legends - Come See About Me. *(hum noticeable on both the introduction and fadeout)*

(M) (2:39) Motown 6357 Diana Ross Forever: Musical Memories. *(noisy throughout)*

(S) (2:41) Time-Life 2RNR-12 Rock 'N' Roll Era - The Supremes 1963-1969.

SUPREMES (Continued)

(S) (2:41) Time-Life 2CLR-03 Classic Rock - 1964.
(M) (2:39) Rhino 71585 Billboard Top Pop Hits, 1964.
(S) (2:41) Polygram Special Markets 314520282 Motown Legends - Volume 1.
(M) (2:39) Motown 314530511 Anthology.
(S) (2:34) MCA 11021 O.S.T. Beverly Hills Cop III.
(M) (2:39) Motown 314530827 The Ultimate Collection.

1965 STOP! IN THE NAME OF LOVE

(S) (2:51) Motown 6160 The Good-Feeling Music Of The Big Chill Generation Volume 2.
(S) (2:51) Motown 6137 20 Greatest Songs In Motown History.
(S) (2:52) Motown 6138 The Composer Series: Holland/Dozier/Holland.
(S) (2:51) Motown 5453 A Collection Of 16 Big Hits Volume 6.
(S) (2:51) Rhino 70651 Billboard's Top R&B Hits Of 1965.
(S) (2:51) Rhino 72006 Billboard's Top R&B Hits 1965-1969 Box Set.
(S) (2:49) Motown 9072 Motown Dance Party Volume 2. *(all selections on this cd are segued together)*
(S) (2:51) Motown 9017 and 5248 16 #1 Hits From The Early 60's.
(S) (2:51) Motown 9097 The Most Played Oldies On America's Jukeboxes.
(S) (2:51) Motown 9098 Radio's #1 Hits.
(S) (2:51) Motown 5322 and 9087 Girl Groups: The Story Of A Sound.
(S) (2:53) Motown 8051 and 8151 More Hits By The Supremes/Sing Holland-Dozier-Holland.
(S) (2:51) Motown 5313 Great Songs And Performances That Inspired The Motown 25th Anniversary TV Special.
(S) (2:52) Motown 5440 More Hits By The Supremes.
(S) (2:49) Motown 6198 and 0794 Anthology.
(S) (2:51) Motown 6193 25th Anniversary.
(S) (2:50) Motown 8029 and 8129 and 0237 Greatest Hits Volume 1/Greatest Hits Volume 2.
(M) (2:49) Motown 9038 and 5498 Every Great #1 Hit.
(S) (2:50) Motown 5357 Greatest Hits Volume 1.
(S) (2:52) Motown 6073 Compact Command Performances.
(S) (2:50) Motown 6192 You Can't Hurry Love: All The Great Love Songs Of The Past 25 Years.
(S) (2:48) Motown 374638510 Motown Legends - Come See About Me.
(M) (2:50) Motown 6357 Diana Ross Forever: Musical Memories.
(S) (2:50) Time-Life 2RNR-12 Rock 'N' Roll Era - The Supremes 1963-1969.
(S) (2:50) Time-Life RHD-07 Rhythm & Blues - 1965.
(S) (2:50) Time-Life 2CLR-14 Classic Rock - 1965: Shakin' All Over.
(S) (2:51) Polygram Special Markets 314520284 Motown Legends Volume 3.
(M) (2:50) Motown 314530428 Diana Ross Ultimate Collection.
(S) (2:50) Rhino 71935 Billboard Top Pop Hits, 1965.
(M) (2:50) Motown 314530511 Anthology.
(S) (2:50) Time-Life R838-12 Solid Gold Soul - 1965.
(M) (2:51) Motown 314530827 The Ultimate Collection.
(S) (2:51) Motown 314530849 Motown 40 Forever.
(S) (2:51) Collectables 1515 and 2515 The Anniversary Album - The 60's.

1965 BACK IN MY ARMS AGAIN
(the vocals start differently on the stereo
version of this song compared to the mono version)

(S) (2:51) Motown 6161 The Good-Feeling Music Of The Big Chill Generation Volume 3.
(S) (2:49) Motown 5454 A Collection Of 16 Big Hits Volume 7.
(S) (2:51) Motown 9017 and 5248 16 #1 Hits From The Early 60's.
(S) (2:51) Motown 5322 and 9087 Girl Groups: The Story Of A Sound.
(S) (2:51) Motown 8051 and 8151 More Hits By The Supremes/Sing Holland-Dozier-Holland.

(S) (2:50) Motown 5313 Great Songs And Performances That Inspired The Motown 25th Anniversary TV Special.
(S) (2:51) Motown 5440 More Hits By The Supremes.
(S) (2:51) Motown 6198 and 0794 Anthology.
(S) (2:51) Motown 6193 25th Anniversary.
(S) (2:50) Motown 8029 and 8129 and 0237 Greatest Hits Volume 1/Greatest Hits Volume 2.
(M) (2:53) Motown 9038 and 5498 Every Great #1 Hit.
(S) (2:50) Motown 5357 Greatest Hits Volume 1.
(S) (2:52) Motown 6073 Compact Command Performances.
(M) (2:54) Motown 6357 Diana Ross Forever: Musical Memories.
(S) (2:51) Time-Life 2RNR-12 Rock 'N' Roll Era - The Supremes 1963-1969.
(S) (2:50) Time-Life 2CLR-01 Classic Rock - 1965.
(S) (2:49) Time-Life SUD-03 Superhits - 1965.
(M) (2:52) Motown 314530511 Anthology.
(S) (2:51) Polygram Special Markets 314520293 Motown Legends - Volume 5.
(S) (2:53) Nick At Nite/550 Music/Epic 67689 Stand By Your Man.
(S) (2:49) Time-Life AM1-10 AM Gold - 1965.
(M) (2:54) Motown 314530827 The Ultimate Collection.

1965 NOTHING BUT HEARTACHES

(S) (2:57) Motown 8051 and 8151 More Hits By The Supremes/Sing Holland-Dozier-Holland. *(LP length)*
(S) (2:55) Motown 5440 More Hits By The Supremes. *(LP length)*
(S) (2:54) Motown 6198 and 0794 Anthology. *(LP length)*
(S) (2:56) Motown 6193 25th Anniversary. *(LP length)*
(S) (2:55) Motown 8029 and 8129 and 0237 Greatest Hits Volume 1/Greatest Hits Volume 2. *(LP length)*
(S) (2:55) Motown 5357 Greatest Hits Volume 1. *(LP length)*
(S) (2:54) Motown 5101 Superstar Series Volume 1. *(LP length)*
(M) (2:42) Motown 6357 Diana Ross Forever: Musical Memories. *(45 length)*
(S) (2:56) Time-Life 2RNR-12 Rock 'N' Roll Era - The Supremes 1963-1969. *(LP length)*
(S) (2:55) Time-Life 2CLR-23 Classic Rock - 1965: Blowin' Your Mind. *(LP length)*
(M) (2:41) Motown 314530511 Anthology. *(45 length)*
(M) (2:40) Motown 314530827 The Ultimate Collection. *(45 length)*

1965 I HEAR A SYMPHONY

(E) (2:41) Motown 6160 The Good-Feeling Music Of The Big Chill Generation Volume 2.
(S) (2:36) Motown 5454 A Collection Of 16 Big Hits Volume 7.
(M) (2:42) Motown 6138 The Composer Series: Holland/Dozier/Holland.
(E) (2:41) Motown 9017 and 5248 16 #1 Hits From The Early 60's.
(E) (2:41) Motown 5313 Great Songs And Performances That Inspired The Motown 25th Anniversary TV Special.
(S) (2:38) Motown 6198 and 0794 Anthology. *(hum noticeable on fadeout)*
(E) (2:41) Motown 6193 25th Anniversary.
(S) (2:37) Motown 8029 and 8129 and 0237 Greatest Hits Volume 1/Greatest Hits Volume 2.
(M) (2:41) Motown 9038 and 5498 Every Great #1 Hit.
(S) (2:37) Motown 5358 Greatest Hits Volume 2.
(E) (2:41) Motown 9027 and 5147 I Hear A Symphony.
(E) (2:41) Motown 8005 and 8105 Where Did Our Love Go/I Hear A Symphony.
(E) (2:42) Motown 6073 Compact Command Performances.
(M) (2:42) Motown 6357 Diana Ross Forever: Musical Memories. *(noisy throughout)*
(E) (2:41) Time-Life 2RNR-12 Rock 'N' Roll Era - The Supremes 1963-1969.
(E) (2:41) Time-Life 2CLR-08 Classic Rock - 1965: The Beat Goes On.
(M) (2:40) Motown/Essex 374638520 Motown Legends - My World Is Empty Without You.

(M) (2:41) Motown 314530511 *Anthology.*
(E) (2:41) Polygram Special Markets 314520292 Motown Legends - Volume 4.
(M) (2:41) Motown 314530827 *The Ultimate Collection.*

1966 MY WORLD IS EMPTY WITHOUT YOU
(S) (2:33) Motown 6138 The Composer Series: Holland/Dozier/Holland.
(S) (2:30) Motown 5455 A Collection Of 16 Big Hits Volume 8.
(S) (2:32) Motown 9095 and 5325 Motown Girl Groups: Top 10 With A Bullet!
(S) (2:32) Motown 6198 and 0794 *Anthology. (hum noticeable on fadeout)*
(S) (2:33) Motown 6193 25th Anniversary.
(S) (2:31) Motown 8029 and 8129 and 0237 Greatest Hits Volume 1/Greatest Hits Volume 2.
(S) (2:31) Motown 5358 Greatest Hits Volume 2.
(S) (2:33) Motown 9027 and 5147 I Hear A Symphony.
(E) (2:33) Motown 8005 and 8105 Where Did Our Love Go/I Hear A Symphony.
(S) (2:33) Motown 6073 Compact Command Performances.
(M) (2:34) Motown 6357 Diana Ross Forever: Musical Memories. *(includes the 45 version reverb)*
(S) (2:32) Time-Life 2RNR-12 Rock 'N' Roll Era - The Supremes 1963-1969.
(S) (2:33) Time-Life 2CLR-07 Classic Rock - 1966: The Beat Goes On.
(M) (2:34) Motown/Essex 374638520 Motown Legends - My World Is Empty Without You. *(includes the 45 version reverb)*
(S) (2:33) Polygram Special Markets 314520299 Motown Legends - Girl Groups.
(M) (2:32) Motown 314530511 *Anthology. (includes the 45 version reverb)*
(M) (2:31) Motown 314530827 *The Ultimate Collection. (includes the 45 version reverb)*

1966 LOVE IS LIKE AN ITCHING IN MY HEART
(S) (2:54) Motown 9072 *Motown Dance Party Volume 2. (all selections on this cd are segued together)*
(S) (2:55) Motown 6198 and 0794 *Anthology.*
(S) (2:53) Motown 8021 and 8121 Love Child/Supremes A Go Go.
(S) (2:51) Motown 6193 25th Anniversary.
(S) (2:54) Motown 8029 and 8129 and 0237 Greatest Hits Volume 1/Greatest Hits Volume 2.
(S) (2:54) Motown 5358 Greatest Hits Volume 2.
(S) (2:53) Motown 5138 Supremes A Go Go.
(S) (2:52) Motown 6073 Compact Command Performances.
(M) (2:52) Motown 6357 Diana Ross Forever: Musical Memories.
(S) (2:51) Time-Life 2RNR-12 Rock 'N' Roll Era - The Supremes 1963-1969.
(S) (2:54) Motown 314530522 Motown Year By Year - 1966.
(M) (2:53) Motown 314530511 *Anthology.*
(M) (2:53) Rhino 72815 Beg, Scream & Shout! The Big Ol' Box Of '60s Soul.
(M) (2:52) Motown 314530827 *The Ultimate Collection.*

1966 YOU CAN'T HURRY LOVE
(the stereo and mono mixes of this song
are substantially different)
(S) (2:45) Rhino 70627 Billboard's Top Rock & Roll Hits Of 1966.
(S) (2:45) Rhino 72007 Billboard's Top Rock & Roll Hits 1962-1966 Box Set.
(S) (2:46) Motown 6132 25 #1 Hits From 25 Years.
(S) (2:45) Motown 6161 The Good-Feeling Music Of The Big Chill Generation Volume 3.
(S) (2:44) Motown 6137 20 Greatest Songs In Motown History.
(S) (2:43) Motown 5455 A Collection Of 16 Big Hits Volume 8.
(S) (2:46) Motown 6138 The Composer Series: Holland/Dozier/Holland.
(S) (2:44) Motown 9018 and 5249 16 #1 Hits From The Late 60's.

(S) (2:44) Motown 9098 Radio's #1 Hits.
(S) (2:44) Motown 5313 Great Songs And Performances That Inspired The Motown 25th Anniversary TV Special.
(S) (2:44) Motown 6198 and 0794 *Anthology. (hum noticeable on fadeout)*
(S) (2:45) Motown 8021 and 8121 Love Child/Supremes A Go Go.
(S) (2:44) Motown 6193 25th Anniversary.
(S) (2:44) Motown 8029 and 8129 and 0237 Greatest Hits Volume 1/Greatest Hits Volume 2.
(M) (2:44) Motown 9038 and 5498 Every Great #1 Hit.
(S) (2:44) Motown 5358 Greatest Hits Volume 2.
(S) (2:44) Motown 5138 Supremes A Go Go.
(S) (2:45) Motown 6073 Compact Command Performances.
(S) (2:44) Motown 6192 You Can't Hurry Love: All The Great Love Songs Of The Past 25 Years.
(S) (2:42) Motown 9071 *Motown Dance Party Volume 1. (all selections on this cd are segued together)*
(M) (2:50) Motown 6312 Hitsville USA.
(M) (2:51) Motown 6357 Diana Ross Forever: Musical Memories.
(S) (2:43) Time-Life 2RNR-12 Rock 'N' Roll Era - The Supremes 1963-1969.
(S) (2:43) Time-Life RHD-01 Rhythm & Blues - 1966.
(S) (2:43) Time-Life 2CLR-22 Classic Rock - 1966: Blowin' Your Mind.
(S) (2:43) Time-Life SUD-01 Superhits - 1966.
(M) (2:52) Motown 314530428 Diana Ross Ultimate Collection.
(M) (2:50) Motown 314530511 *Anthology.*
(S) (2:45) Polygram Special Markets 314520293 Motown Legends - Volume 5.
(S) (2:43) Time-Life AM1-09 AM Gold - 1966.
(S) (2:43) Time-Life R838-01 Solid Gold Soul - 1966.
(M) (2:52) Motown 314530827 *The Ultimate Collection.*

1966 YOU KEEP ME HANGIN' ON
(S) (2:41) Motown 6159 The Good-Feeling Music Of The Big Chill Generation Volume 1.
(S) (2:41) Motown 6137 20 Greatest Songs In Motown History.
(S) (2:39) Motown 5456 A Collection Of 16 Big Hits Volume 9.
(S) (2:42) Motown 6138 The Composer Series: Holland/Dozier/Holland.
(S) (2:45) Rhino 70652 Billboard's Top R&B Hits Of 1966. *(includes extra background vocals)*
(S) (2:45) Rhino 72006 Billboard's Top R&B Hits 1965-1969 Box Set. *(includes extra background vocals)*
(S) (2:41) Motown 9018 and 5249 16 #1 Hits From The Late 60's.
(S) (2:41) Motown 5343 Every Great Motown Song: The First 25 Years Volume 1. *(most selections on this cd have noise on the fadeout)*
(S) (2:41) Motown 8034 and 8134 Every Great Motown Song: The First 25 Years Volumes 1 & 2. *(most selections on this cd have noise on the fadeout)*
(S) (2:40) Motown 8051 and 8151 More Hits By The Supremes/Sing Holland-Dozier-Holland.
(S) (2:40) Motown 6198 and 0794 *Anthology. (hum noticeable on fadeout)*
(S) (2:41) Motown 6193 25th Anniversary. *(noisy fadeout)*
(S) (2:39) Motown 8029 and 8129 and 0237 Greatest Hits Volume 1/Greatest Hits Volume 2.
(M) (2:44) Motown 9038 and 5498 Every Great #1 Hit.
(S) (2:39) Motown 5358 Greatest Hits Volume 2.
(S) (2:41) Motown 5182 Sing Holland-Dozier-Holland.
(S) (2:41) Motown 6073 Compact Command Performances.
(S) (2:38) Motown 9071 *Motown Dance Party Volume 1. (all selections on this cd are segued together)*
(M) (2:43) Motown 6357 Diana Ross Forever: Musical Memories.
(S) (2:40) Time-Life 2RNR-12 Rock 'N' Roll Era - The Supremes 1963-1969.
(S) (2:40) Time-Life 2CLR-02 Classic Rock - 1966.
(S) (2:41) Polygram Special Markets 314520282 Motown Legends - Volume 1.

SUPREMES (Continued)

- (S) (2:39) Motown 314530522 Motown Year By Year - 1966.
- (M) (2:45) Motown 314530511 Anthology.
- (M) (2:43) Motown 314530827 The Ultimate Collection.

1967 LOVE IS HERE AND NOW YOU'RE GONE
(all stereo versions of this song feature a
splicing glitch at 1:25)

- (S) (2:45) Motown 6160 The Good-Feeling Music Of The Big Chill Generation Volume 2.
- (S) (2:44) Motown 5456 A Collection Of 16 Big Hits Volume 9.
- (S) (2:45) Rhino 70653 Billboard's Top R&B Hits Of 1967.
- (S) (2:45) Rhino 72006 Billboard's Top R&B Hits 1965-1969 Box Set.
- (S) (2:45) Motown 9018 and 5249 16 #1 Hits From The Late 60's.
- (S) (2:46) Motown 8051 and 8151 More Hits By The Supremes/Sing Holland-Dozier-Holland.
- (S) (2:44) Motown 6198 and 0794 Anthology.
- (S) (2:45) Motown 6193 25th Anniversary.
- (S) (2:45) Motown 8029 and 8129 and 0237 Greatest Hits Volume 1/Greatest Hits Volume 2.
- (S) (2:45) Motown 5203 Greatest Hits Volume 3. *(truncated fade)*
- (M) (2:46) Motown 9038 and 5498 Every Great #1 Hit.
- (S) (2:45) Motown 5358 Greatest Hits Volume 2.
- (S) (2:46) Motown 5182 Sing Holland-Dozier-Holland.
- (S) (2:45) Motown 6073 Compact Command Performances.
- (S) (2:45) Motown 6192 You Can't Hurry Love: All The Great Love Songs Of The Past 25 Years.
- (M) (2:46) Motown 6357 Diana Ross Forever: Musical Memories.
- (S) (2:45) Time-Life 2RNR-12 Rock 'N' Roll Era - The Supremes 1963-1969.
- (S) (2:43) Time-Life RHD-10 Rhythm & Blues - 1967.
- (S) (2:45) Time-Life 2CLR-05 Classic Rock - 1967.
- (S) (2:43) Time-Life SUD-05 Superhits - 1967.
- (S) (2:45) Polygram Special Markets 314520283 Motown Legends Volume 2.
- (M) (2:46) Motown 314530511 Anthology.
- (S) (2:43) Time-Life AM1-08 AM Gold - 1967.
- (S) (2:43) Time-Life R838-02 Solid Gold Soul - 1967.
- (M) (2:46) Motown 314530827 The Ultimate Collection.

1967 THE HAPPENING

- (S) (2:47) Motown 6161 The Good-Feeling Music Of The Big Chill Generation Volume 3.
- (S) (2:45) Motown 5457 A Collection Of 16 Big Hits Volume 10.
- (S) (2:47) Motown 9018 and 5249 16 #1 Hits From The Late 60's.
- (S) (2:48) Motown 6198 and 0794 Anthology. *(hum noticeable on fadeout)*
- (S) (2:47) Motown 6193 25th Anniversary.
- (S) (2:48) Motown 8029 and 8129 and 0237 Greatest Hits Volume 1/Greatest Hits Volume 2.
- (S) (2:48) Motown 5203 Greatest Hits Volume 3.
- (M) (2:49) Motown 9038 and 5498 Every Great #1 Hit.
- (S) (2:48) Motown 5358 Greatest Hits Volume 2.
- (S) (2:46) Motown 5101 Superstar Series Volume 1. *(numerous dropouts)*
- (S) (2:47) Motown 374638510 Motown Legends - Come See About Me.
- (M) (2:48) Motown 6357 Diana Ross Forever: Musical Memories.
- (S) (2:47) Time-Life 2RNR-12 Rock 'N' Roll Era - The Supremes 1963-1969.
- (S) (2:47) Time-Life 2CLR-10 Classic Rock - 1967: The Beat Goes On.
- (M) (2:49) Motown 314530511 Anthology.
- (S) (2:47) Polygram Special Markets 314520292 Motown Legends - Volume 4.
- (M) (2:49) Motown 314530827 The Ultimate Collection.

released as by DIANA ROSS and THE SUPREMES:
1967 REFLECTIONS

- (S) (2:50) Motown 6138 The Composer Series: Holland/Dozier/Holland.

- (S) (2:13) SBK 93744 China Beach - Music & Memories. *(sound effects can be heard over the intro; edited)*
- (S) (2:49) Motown 9095 and 5325 Motown Girl Groups: Top 10 With A Bullet!
- (S) (2:49) Motown 5494 Reflections.
- (S) (2:48) Motown 6198 and 0794 Anthology.
- (S) (2:50) Motown 6193 25th Anniversary.
- (S) (2:50) Motown 5203 Greatest Hits Volume 3.
- (S) (2:49) Motown 6073 Compact Command Performances.
- (E) (2:50) Motown 6357 Diana Ross Forever: Musical Memories.
- (S) (2:49) Time-Life 2RNR-12 Rock 'N' Roll Era - The Supremes 1963-1969.
- (S) (2:49) Time-Life 2CLR-15 Classic Rock - 1967: Shakin' All Over.
- (S) (2:49) Polygram Special Markets 314520299 Motown Legends - Girl Groups.
- (E) (2:50) Motown 314530428 Diana Ross Ultimate Collection.
- (M) (2:50) Motown 314530511 Anthology.
- (M) (2:50) Motown 314530827 The Ultimate Collection.

1967 IN AND OUT OF LOVE

- (S) (2:38) Motown 5494 Reflections.
- (S) (2:37) Motown 6198 and 0794 Anthology.
- (S) (2:38) Motown 6193 25th Anniversary.
- (S) (2:39) Motown 5203 Greatest Hits Volume 3.
- (M) (2:37) Motown 6357 Diana Ross Forever: Musical Memories.
- (S) (2:38) Time-Life 2RNR-12 Rock 'N' Roll Era - The Supremes 1963-1969.
- (M) (2:37) Motown 314530511 Anthology.
- (M) (2:37) Motown 314530827 The Ultimate Collection.

1968 FOREVER CAME TODAY

- (S) (3:12) Motown 5494 Reflections.
- (S) (3:12) Motown 6198 and 0794 Anthology.
- (S) (3:11) Motown 6193 25th Anniversary.
- (S) (3:12) Motown 5203 Greatest Hits Volume 3.
- (M) (3:17) Motown 6357 Diana Ross Forever: Musical Memories.
- (S) (3:11) Time-Life 2RNR-12 Rock 'N' Roll Era - The Supremes 1963-1969.
- (M) (3:17) Motown 314530511 Anthology.
- (M) (3:17) Motown 314530827 The Ultimate Collection.

1968 SOME THINGS YOU NEVER GET USED TO

- (S) (2:24) Motown 6140 The Composer Series: Ashford & Simpson.
- (S) (2:22) Motown 6198 and 0794 Anthology.
- (S) (2:23) Motown 8021 and 8121 Love Child/Supremes A Go Go.
- (S) (2:23) Motown 6193 25th Anniversary.
- (S) (2:22) Motown 5245 Love Child.
- (S) (2:22) Motown 5203 Greatest Hits Volume 3.
- (S) (2:23) Time-Life 2RNR-12 Rock 'N' Roll Era - The Supremes 1963-1969.
- (M) (2:23) Motown 314530511 Anthology.
- (M) (2:23) Motown 314530827 The Ultimate Collection.

1968 LOVE CHILD

- (S) (2:55) Motown 6159 The Good-Feeling Music Of The Big Chill Generation Volume 1.
- (S) (2:55) Motown 6177 Endless Love.
- (S) (2:54) Rhino 70629 Billboard's Top Rock & Roll Hits Of 1968.
- (S) (2:54) Rhino 72005 Billboard's Top Rock & Roll Hits 1968-1972 Box Set.
- (S) (2:54) MCA 10063 Original Television Soundtrack "The Sounds Of Murphy Brown".
- (S) (2:56) Motown 5385 Three Times A Lady: Great Motown Love Songs.
- (S) (2:55) Motown 9018 and 5249 16 #1 Hits From The Late 60's.
- (S) (2:55) Motown 9060 Motown's Biggest Pop Hits.
- (S) (2:54) Motown 5313 Great Songs And Performances That Inspired The Motown 25th Anniversary TV Special.
- (S) (2:54) Motown 6198 and 0794 Anthology.
- (S) (2:54) Motown 8021 and 8121 Love Child/Supremes A Go Go.
- (S) (2:55) Motown 6193 25th Anniversary.

(S) (2:54) Motown 5245 Love Child.
(S) (2:54) Motown 5203 Greatest Hits Volume 3.
(M) (2:54) Motown 9038 and 5498 Every Great #1 Hit.
(S) (2:55) Motown 6073 Compact Command Performances.
(S) (2:51) Motown 6192 You Can't Hurry Love: All The
           Great Love Songs Of The Past 25 Years.
(S) (2:53) Motown 5101 Superstar Series Volume 1.
(M) (3:00) Motown 6312 Hitsville USA.
(M) (2:56) Motown 6357 Diana Ross Forever: Musical
           Memories.
(S) (2:55) Time-Life 2RNR-12 Rock 'N' Roll Era - The
           Supremes 1963-1969.
(S) (2:55) Time-Life 2CLR-04 Classic Rock - 1968.
(S) (2:55) Polygram Special Markets 314520282 Motown
           Legends - Volume 1.
(S) (2:53) Motown 314530507 Motown Year By Year 1968.
(M) (3:00) Motown 314530511 Anthology.
(M) (3:00) Motown 314530827 The Ultimate Collection.

released as by DIANA ROSS and THE SUPREMES &
THE TEMPTATIONS:
1969 I'M GONNA MAKE YOU LOVE ME
(S) (3:05) Motown 6160 The Good-Feeling Music Of The
           Big Chill Generation Volume 2.
(S) (3:05) Motown 9031 and 5214 Diana's Duets.
(S) (3:05) Motown 6198 and 0794 Supremes Anthology.
(S) (3:05) Motown 6193 Diana Ross & The Supremes 25th
           Anniversary.
(S) (3:05) Motown 5139 Diana Ross And The Supremes
           Join The Temptations.
(S) (3:05) Motown 8038 and 8138 Diana Ross And The
           Supremes Join The Temptations/Diana Ross & The
           Supremes & The Temptations Together.
(S) (3:06) Motown 6073 Supremes Compact Command
           Performances.
(S) (3:05) Motown 0782 and 6189 Temptations Anthology.
(S) (3:05) Motown 6204 and 5389 Temptations 25th
           Anniversary.
(S) (2:56) Motown 6357 Diana Ross Forever: Musical
           Memories.
(S) (3:05) Time-Life 2CLR-06 Classic Rock - 1969.
(S) (3:05) Time-Life SUD-07 Superhits - 1969.
(S) (3:05) Motown 314530338 Temptations - Emperors Of
           Soul.
(S) (3:05) Polygram Special Markets 314520284 Motown
           Legends Volume 3.
(S) (3:05) Motown 314530524 Temptations Anthology.
(S) (3:05) Motown 314530507 Motown Year By Year 1968.
(S) (3:06) Polygram Special Markets 314520031 Motown
           Legends - Duets.
(S) (3:05) Columbia 67380 O.S.T. Now And Then.
(S) (3:05) Time-Life AM1-01 AM Gold - 1969.
(S) (3:05) Rebound 314520420 Soul Classics - Best Of The
           60's.
(M) (3:05) Motown 314530827 The Ultimate Collection.

released as by DIANA ROSS and THE SUPREMES:
1969 I'M LIVING IN SHAME
(S) (2:58) Motown 9095 and 5325 Motown Girl Groups:
           Top 10 With A Bullet!
(S) (2:55) Motown 6198 and 0794 Anthology.
(S) (2:58) Motown 6193 25th Anniversary.
(S) (2:57) Motown 5203 Greatest Hits Volume 3.
(S) (2:58) Motown 5305 Let The Sunshine In.
(S) (2:58) Motown 8032 and 8132 Let The Sunshine
           In/Cream Of The Crop.
(S) (2:56) Motown 5101 Superstar Series Volume 1.
(M) (2:58) Motown 6357 Diana Ross Forever: Musical
           Memories.
(S) (2:58) Time-Life 2RNR-12 Rock 'N' Roll Era - The
           Supremes 1963-1969.
(S) (2:57) Polygram Special Markets 314520299 Motown
           Legends - Girl Groups.
(M) (3:06) Motown 314530511 Anthology. *(:08 longer than*
           the 45 or LP)
(M) (3:06) Motown 314530827 The Ultimate Collection.
           (:08 longer than the 45 or LP)

released as by DIANA ROSS and THE SUPREMES &
THE TEMPTATIONS:
1969 I'LL TRY SOMETHING NEW
(S) (2:19) Motown 9031 and 5214 Diana's Duets.
(S) (2:19) Motown 5313 Diana Ross & The Supremes: Great
           Songs And Performances That Inspired The
           Motown 25th Anniversary TV Special.
(S) (2:17) Motown 6198 and 0794 Supremes Anthology.
(S) (2:19) Motown 5139 Diana Ross And The Supremes
           Join The Temptations.
(S) (2:19) Motown 8038 and 8138 Diana Ross And The
           Supremes Join The Temptations/Diana Ross & The
           Supremes & The Temptations Together.
(S) (2:19) Motown 6073 Supremes Compact Command
           Performances.
(M) (2:24) Motown 314530511 Diana Ross & The Supremes -
           Anthology.
(M) (2:22) Motown 314530338 Temptations - Emperors Of
           Soul.
(M) (2:23) Motown 314530827 The Ultimate Collection.

released as by DIANA ROSS and THE SUPREMES:
1969 THE COMPOSER
(S) (2:57) Motown 6198 and 0794 Anthology.
(S) (2:56) Motown 6193 25th Anniversary.
(S) (2:59) Motown 5203 Greatest Hits Volume 3.
(S) (2:59) Motown 5305 Let The Sunshine In.
(S) (2:56) Time-Life 2RNR-12 Rock 'N' Roll Era - The
           Supremes 1963-1969.
(M) (2:55) Motown 314530511 Anthology.
(M) (2:51) Motown 314530827 The Ultimate Collection.

1969 NO MATTER WHAT SIGN YOU ARE
(E) (2:46) Motown 6198 and 0794 Anthology.
(E) (2:45) Motown 6193 25th Anniversary.
(E) (2:52) Motown 5203 Greatest Hits Volume 3.
(E) (2:52) Motown 5305 Let The Sunshine In.
(E) (2:52) Motown 8032 and 8132 Let The Sunshine
           In/Cream Of The Crop.
(E) (2:45) Time-Life 2RNR-12 Rock 'N' Roll Era - The
           Supremes 1963-1969.
(M) (2:55) Motown 314530511 Anthology.
(M) (2:53) Motown 314530827 The Ultimate Collection.

released as by DIANA ROSS and THE SUPREMES &
THE TEMPTATIONS:
1969 THE WEIGHT
(S) (3:00) Motown 8038 and 8138 Diana Ross & The
           Supremes Join The Temptations/Diana Ross & The
           Supremes & The Temptations Together.
(S) (3:00) Motown 5436 Diana Ross & The Supremes & The
           Temptations Together.

released as by DIANA ROSS and THE SUPREMES:
1969 SOMEDAY WE'LL BE TOGETHER
(actual 45 time is (3:30) not (3:14) as stated on the
record label)
(S) (3:28) Motown 6160 The Good-Feeling Music Of The
           Big Chill Generation Volume 2. *(LP version)*
(S) (3:28) Motown 6177 Endless Love. *(LP version)*
(S) (3:29) Rhino 70655 Billboard's Top R&B Hits Of 1969.
           (LP version)
(S) (3:29) Rhino 72006 Billboard's Top R&B Hits 1965-
           1969 Box Set. *(LP version)*
(S) (3:28) Motown 9097 The Most Played Oldies On
           America's Jukeboxes. *(LP version)*
(S) (3:27) Motown 9018 and 5249 16 #1 Hits From The Late
           60's. *(LP version)*
(S) (3:28) Motown 9098 Radio's #1 Hits. *(LP version;*
           noisy fadeout)
(S) (3:28) Motown 5322 and 9087 Girl Groups: The Story
           Of A Sound. *(LP version)*
(S) (3:28) Motown 0937 20/20 Twenty No. 1 Hits From
           Twenty Years At Motown. *(LP version)*
(S) (3:28) Motown 5313 Great Songs And Performances
           That Inspired The Motown 25th Anniversary TV
           Special. *(LP version)*
(S) (3:25) Motown 6198 and 0794 Anthology. *(LP version)*
(S) (3:27) Motown 6193 25th Anniversary. *(LP version)*

SUPREMES *(Continued)*

(S) (3:30) Motown 5203 Greatest Hits Volume 3. *(LP version)*

(M) (3:19) Motown 9038 and 5498 Every Great #1 Hit. *(:10 shorter than either the 45 or LP; 45 version))*

(S) (3:31) Motown 5435 Cream Of The Crop. *(LP version)*

(S) (3:31) Motown 8032 and 8132 Let The Sunshine In/Cream Of The Crop. *(LP version)*

(S) (3:29) Motown 6073 Compact Command Performances. *(LP version)*

(S) (3:27) Motown 5101 Superstar Series Volume 1. *(LP version)*

(M) (3:23) Motown 6357 Diana Ross Forever: Musical Memories. *(45 version)*

(S) (3:25) Time-Life 2RNR-12 Rock 'N' Roll Era - The Supremes 1963-1969. *(LP version)*

(S) (3:27) Time-Life RHD-13 Rhythm & Blues - 1969. *(LP version)*

(S) (3:26) Time-Life 2CLR-20 Classic Rock - 1969: Shakin' All Over. *(LP version)*

(S) (3:25) Time-Life SUD-07 Superhits - 1969. *(LP version)*

(S) (8:42) Motown 6377 Diana Extended/The Remixes. *(all selections on this cd are remixed with extra instrumentation added)*

(S) (3:28) Time-Life R921-38 Get Together. *(LP version)*

(S) (8:42) SBK 30048 Brilliant! The Global Dance Music Experience Volume 4. *(remix)*

(S) (3:28) Polygram Special Markets 314520284 Motown Legends Volume 3. *(LP version)*

(S) (3:02) Motown 314530428 Diana Ross Ultimate Collection. *(remixed)*

(S) (3:30) Motown 314530525 Motown Year By Year - 1969. *(LP version)*

(M) (3:32) Motown 314530511 Anthology. *(45 version)*

(S) (3:25) LaserLight 12311 and 15936 The Wonder Years - First Love. *(LP version)*

(S) (3:25) Time-Life AM1-01 AM Gold - 1969. *(LP version)*

(S) (3:26) Time-Life R838-04 Solid Gold Soul - 1969. *(LP version)*

(M) (3:24) Motown 314530827 The Ultimate Collection. *(45 version)*

(S) (3:27) Motown 314530849 Motown 40 Forever. *(LP version)*

released as by THE SUPREMES:
1970 UP THE LADDER TO THE ROOF

(S) (3:10) Motown 9110 and 5414 Motown Memories Volume 4. *(alternate take)*

(M) (3:15) Motown 5487 Greatest Hits And Rare Classics.

(S) (3:09) Motown 6198 and 0794 Anthology.

(S) (3:10) Motown 5442 Right On.

(S) (3:11) Motown 6073 Compact Command Performances.

(M) (3:15) Motown 6312 Hitsville USA.

(M) (3:15) Motown 314530511 Anthology.

1970 EVERYBODY'S GOT THE RIGHT TO LOVE

(M) (2:33) Motown 5487 Greatest Hits And Rare Classics.

(S) (2:35) Motown 6198 and 0794 Anthology.

(S) (2:36) Motown 5442 Right On.

(M) (2:38) Motown 314530511 Anthology.

1970 STONED LOVE
(actual 45 time is (2:57) not (2:49) as stated on the record label)

(S) (4:06) Motown 9109 and 5413 Motown Memories Volume 3. *(LP version)*

(S) (3:43) Rhino 70658 Billboard's Top R&B Hits Of 1970. *(45 lyrics with LP introduction)*

(S) (3:16) Motown 9072 Motown Dance Party Volume 2. *(all selections on this cd are segued together; LP lyrics but missing the spoken introduction)*

(M) (2:57) Motown 5487 Greatest Hits And Rare Classics. *(45 version)*

(S) (4:06) Motown 6198 and 0794 Anthology. *(LP version)*

(S) (4:07) Motown 6073 Compact Command Performances. *(LP version)*

(S) (4:06) Motown 6192 You Can't Hurry Love: All The Great Love Songs Of The Past 25 Years. *(LP version)*

(S) (4:07) Motown 5497 New Ways But Love Stays. *(LP version)*

(M) (2:58) Motown 6312 Hitsville USA. *(45 version)*

(S) (3:42) Time-Life RHD-18 Rhythm & Blues - 1970. *(45 lyrics with LP introduction)*

(M) (2:58) Epic 66329 O.S.T. Forrest Gump. *(45 version)*

(S) (2:57) Motown 314530528 Motown Year By Year - 1970. *(45 version)*

(M) (2:58) Motown 314530511 Anthology. *(45 version)*

(M) (2:57) Motown/Essex 374638523 Motown Legends - Stoned Love/Nathan Jones. *(45 version)*

(S) (3:42) Time-Life R838-05 Solid Gold Soul - 1970. *(45 lyrics with LP introduction)*

released as by SUPREMES & FOUR TOPS:
1971 RIVER DEEP - MOUNTAIN HIGH
(actual 45 time is (3:13) not (3:05) as stated on the record label)

(S) (4:47) Motown 6184 20 Hard To Find Motown Classics Volume 2. *(LP version)*

(M) (3:13) Motown 5491 Best Of The Supremes & Four Tops. *(45 version)*

(S) (4:50) Motown 5123 Magnificent 7. *(LP version)*

(E) (4:29) Motown 0809 and 6188 Four Tops Anthology. *(edit of the LP version)*

(M) (3:13) Motown 314530511 Diana Ross & The Supremes Anthology. *(45 version)*

released as by THE SUPREMES:
1971 NATHAN JONES

(S) (3:00) Motown 9095 and 5325 Motown Girl Groups: Top 10 With A Bullet!

(M) (3:02) Motown 5487 Greatest Hits And Rare Classics.

(S) (2:57) Motown 6198 and 0794 Anthology.

(S) (3:00) Motown 5447 Touch.

(S) (3:00) Motown 6073 Compact Command Performances.

(M) (3:02) Motown 6312 Hitsville USA.

(S) (3:00) Polygram Special Markets 314520299 Motown Legends - Girl Groups.

(M) (3:02) Motown 314530511 Anthology.

(S) (3:00) Motown/Essex 374638523 Motown Legends - Stoned Love/Nathan Jones.

1972 FLOY JOY

(S) (2:30) Motown 9104 and 5409 Motown Memories Volume 1. *(45 length)*

(M) (2:45) Motown 5487 Greatest Hits And Rare Classics. *(LP length)*

(M) (2:30) Motown 6198 and 0794 Anthology. *(45 length)*

(S) (2:49) Motown 5441 Floy Joy. *(LP length)*

(M) (2:31) Motown 6358 Hitsville USA Volume Two. *(45 length)*

(M) (2:32) Motown 314530511 Anthology. *(45 length)*

1972 AUTOMATICALLY SUNSHINE

(M) (3:02) Motown 5487 Greatest Hits And Rare Classics. *(previously unreleased extended version; truncated fade)*

(S) (2:35) Motown 6198 and 0794 Anthology.

(S) (2:37) Motown 5441 Floy Joy.

(S) (2:40) Motown 314530511 Anthology.

(S) (2:38) Nick At Nite/550 Music 63435 Beach Blanket Bash.

SURFACE
1987 HAPPY

(S) (3:54) Columbia 48649 Best Of.

(S) (3:57) Columbia 40374 Surface.

1989 SHOWER ME WITH YOUR LOVE

(S) (4:53) Sony Music Distribution 57854 For Your Love. *(LP version)*

(S) (4:53) K-Tel 6006 Lite Rock. *(LP version)*

(S) (4:53) Columbia 48649 Best Of. *(LP version)*

(S) (4:53) Columbia 44284 2nd Wave. *(LP version)*

(S) (4:50) Rhino 72144 Billboard Hot R&B Hits 1989. *(LP version)*

(S) (4:53) Time-Life R834-13 Body Talk - Just The Two Of Us. *(LP version)*

1991 THE FIRST TIME

(S) (4:14) JCI 3124 Rhythm Of The Night.

(S) (4:14) Columbia 48649 Best Of.

(S) (4:15) Columbia 46772 3 Deep.

(S) (4:14) Priority 50946 100% Party Hits Of The 90's Volume One.

(S) (4:15) Time-Life R834-16 Body Talk - Sweet Nothings.

1991 NEVER GONNA LET YOU DOWN

(S) (3:46) Columbia 48649 Best Of.

(S) (4:01) Columbia 46772 3 Deep.

SURFARIS

1963 WIPE OUT

(M) (2:36) Rhino 70089 Surfin' Hits. *(:19 longer than the 45 or LP)*

(M) (2:37) Rhino 75778 Frat Rock. *(:20 longer than the 45 or LP)*

(E) (2:37) RCA 6965 More Dirty Dancing. *(:20 longer than the 45 or LP)*

(M) (2:37) MCA 31205 Vintage Music Volume 8. *(:20 longer than the 45 or LP)*

(M) (2:37) MCA 5805 Vintage Music Volumes 7 & 8. *(:20 longer than the 45 or LP)*

(M) (2:37) JCI 3106 Surfin' Sixties. *(:20 longer than the 45 or LP)*

(M) (2:28) Original Sound 8858 Oldies But Goodies Vol. 8. *(this compact disc uses the "Waring - fds" noise reduction process; :11 longer than the 45 or LP)*

(M) (2:28) Original Sound 2221 Oldies But Goodies Volumes 1,4,6,8 and 10 Box Set. *(this box set uses the "Waring - fds" noise reduction process; :11 longer than the 45 or LP)*

(M) (2:28) Original Sound 2500 Oldies But Goodies Volumes 1-15 Box Set. *(this box set uses the "Waring - fds" noise reduction process; :11 longer than the 45 or LP)*

(M) (2:36) Rhino 70794 KFOG Presents M. Dung's Idiot Show. *(:19 longer than the 45 or LP)*

(M) (2:36) Rhino 71229 Summer Hits. *(:19 longer than the 45 or LP)*

(M) (2:36) Rhino 71548 Let There Be Drums Volume 2: The 60's. *(:19 longer than the 45 or LP)*

(M) (2:37) Rhino 71605 Rock Instrumental Classics Volume 5: Surf. *(:20 longer than the 45 or LP)*

(M) (2:37) Rhino 72035 Rock Instrumental Classics Vols. 1-5 Box Set. *(:20 longer than the 45 or LP)*

(M) (2:38) Time-Life 2RNR-07 Rock 'N' Roll Era - 1963. *(:21 longer than the 45 or LP)*

(M) (2:37) Collectables 2504 WCBS-FM History Of Rock - The 60's Part 4. *(:20 longer than the 45 or LP)*

(M) (2:37) Collectables 4504 History Of Rock/The 60s Part Four. *(:20 longer than the 45 or LP)*

(M) (2:37) MCA Special Products 22019 Summer Hits Of The 50's And 60's. *(:20 longer than the 45 or LP)*

(M) (2:37) MCA Special Products 22028 Cra-a-zy Hits. *(:20 longer than the 45 or LP)*

(M) (2:37) MCA Special Products 20783 Rock Around The Oldies #1. *(:20 longer than the 45 or LP)*

(M) (2:37) Varese Sarabande 5478 Wipe Out! Best Of. *(:20 longer than the 45 or LP)*

(M) (2:37) Rhino 71584 Billboard Top Pop Hits, 1963. *(:20 longer than the 45 or LP)*

(M) (2:36) MCA 11234 Revenge Of The Surf Instrumentals. *(:19 longer than the 45 or LP)*

(M) (2:37) MCA Special Products 20902 Classic Rock & Roll Instrumental Hits, Volume 1. *(:20 longer than the 45 or LP)*

(M) (2:37) Rhino 72418 Cowabunga! The Surf Box. *(:20 longer than the 45 or LP)*

(M) (2:37) LaserLight 12312 and 15936 The Wonder Years - Good Times, Good Friends. *(:20 longer than the 45 or LP)*

(M) (2:36) Flashback 72710 Golden Summer. *(:19 longer than the 45 or LP)*

(E) (2:12) K-Tel 6256 Kahuna Classics. *(rerecording)*

(M) (2:34) Cold Front 6255 Greatest Sports Rock And Jams Volume 2. *(all selections on this cd are segued together)*

(M) (2:32) K-Tel 4046 More Music For Your Party. *(:15 longer than the 45 or LP)*

(M) (2:37) Simitar 55522 The Number One's: Party Time. *(:20 longer than the 45 or LP)*

(M) (2:37) I.D. 90072 Jenny McCarthy's Surfin' Safari. *(:20 longer than the 45 or LP)*

1966 WIPE OUT

(this song was a hit in 1963 and 1966; see 1963 listings)

SURVIVOR

1981 POOR MAN'S SON

(S) (3:24) Scotti Bros. 75408 Greatest Hits.

(S) (3:19) Scotti Brothers 45433 Greatest Hits.

1982 EYE OF THE TIGER

(S) (3:45) CBS Special Products 44363 Rock Of The 80's. *(45 length)*

(S) (3:46) Scotti Brothers 40203 and 75420 O.S.T. Rocky IV. *(45 length)*

(S) (3:45) Scotti Brothers 5201 The Rocky Story. *(45 length)*

(S) (4:06) Scotti Brothers 38062 Eye Of The Tiger. *(LP length)*

(S) (4:03) Scotti Bros. 5216 Eye Of The Tiger. *(LP length)*

(S) (4:05) Scotti Bros. 75408 Greatest Hits. *(LP length)*

(S) (4:04) Scotti Brothers 45433 Greatest Hits. *(LP length)*

(S) (4:04) Scotti Bros. 75518 Big Screen Rock. *(LP length)*

1982 AMERICAN HEARTBEAT

(S) (4:10) Scotti Brothers 38062 Eye Of The Tiger. *(LP length)*

(S) (4:09) Scotti Bros. 5216 Eye Of The Tiger. *(LP length)*

(S) (4:09) Scotti Bros. 75408 Greatest Hits. *(LP length)*

1984 I CAN'T HOLD BACK

(S) (3:58) Scotti Bros. 39578 Vital Signs.

(S) (3:57) Scotti Bros. 5215 Vital Signs.

(S) (3:57) Scotti Bros. 75408 Greatest Hits.

(S) (3:57) Scotti Brothers 45433 Greatest Hits.

(S) (3:57) Scotti Bros. 75436 Jim Jamison/Survivor Collection Volume 2.

(S) (3:57) JCI 3193 18 Rock Classics Volume 3.

1985 HIGH ON YOU

(S) (4:07) Priority 53715 80's Greatest Rock Hits Volume 3 - Arena Rock.

(S) (4:08) Scotti Brothers 39578 Vital Signs.

(S) (4:07) Scotti Bros. 5215 Vital Signs.

(S) (4:06) Scotti Bros. 75408 Greatest Hits.

(S) (4:07) Scotti Brothers 45433 Greatest Hits.

(S) (4:06) Time-Life R968-20 Guitar Rock - The '80s.

(S) (4:06) Time-Life R988-23 Sounds Of The Eighties 1984-1985.

1985 THE SEARCH IS OVER

(S) (4:10) Priority 7077 80's Greatest Rock Hits Volume 5 - From The Heart.

(S) (4:12) Scotti Brothers 39578 Vital Signs.

(S) (4:11) Scotti Bros. 5215 Vital Signs.

(S) (4:10) Scotti Bros. 75408 Greatest Hits.

(S) (4:12) Scotti Brothers 45433 Greatest Hits.

(S) (4:11) Time-Life R988-12 Sounds Of The 80's: 1985-1986.

(S) (4:10) Time-Life R834-12 Body Talk - By Candlelight.

1986 BURNING HEART

(S) (3:50) Rhino 71641 Billboard Top Hits - 1986.

(S) (3:51) Scotti Brothers 40203 and 75420 O.S.T. Rocky IV.

(S) (3:51) Scotti Brothers 5201 The Rocky Story.

(S) (3:51) Time-Life R105-40 Rock Dreams.

(S) (3:49) Priority 53797 Best Of 80's Rock Volume 4.

(S) (3:50) Scotti Bros. 75408 Greatest Hits.

(S) (3:50) Scotti Bros. 75436 Jim Jamison/Survivor Collection Volume 2.

(S) (3:50) Time-Life R988-04 Sounds Of The Eighties: 1986.

(S) (3:51) Madacy Entertainment 1986 Rock On 1986.

(S) (3:49) Priority 50974 Premiere The Movie Magazine Presents The Greatest Soundtrack Hits.

(S) (3:49) K-Tel 3997 Arena Rock - The 80's.

(S) (3:48) Simitar 55142 80's Rock Classics - Party Town.

1987 IS THIS LOVE

(S) (3:38) Scotti Brothers 40457 When Seconds Count.

(S) (3:42) Scotti Bros. 75236 When Seconds Count.

(S) (3:40) Scotti Bros. 75408 Greatest Hits.

(S) (3:41) Scotti Brothers 45433 Greatest Hits.

SURVIVOR *(Continued)*
- (S) (3:40) Madacy Entertainment 1987 Rock On 1987.
- (S) (3:39) Time-Life R988-21 Sounds Of The Eighties: 1986-1989.

SUTHERLAND BROTHERS & QUIVER
1973 (I DON'T WANT TO LOVE YOU BUT) YOU GOT ME ANYWAY
- (S) (3:03) Rhino 71197 Super Hits Of The 70's Volume 17. *(hissy)*

BILLY SWAN
1974 I CAN HELP
- (S) (2:55) Rhino 70635 Billboard's Top Rock & Roll Hits Of 1974. *(45 version)*
- (S) (2:55) Rhino 70760 Super Hits Of The 70's Volume 13. *(45 version)*
- (S) (2:55) Rhino 70742 Rock This Town: Rockabilly Hits Volume 2. *(45 version)*
- (S) (4:00) Sony Music Special Products 57913 Best. *(LP version)*
- (S) (2:55) Time-Life CCD-08 Contemporary Country - The Mid 70's Pure Gold. *(45 version)*
- (S) (2:55) Time-Life SOD-07 Sounds Of The Seventies - 1974. *(45 version)*
- (S) (2:55) Time-Life R921-38 Get Together. *(45 version)*
- (S) (2:55) Risky Business 66871 Polyester Dreams/Greatest Hits Of The 70's. *(45 version)*
- (S) (2:55) Sony Music Special Products 66106 The Monument Story. *(45 version)*
- (S) (3:59) K-Tel 816 Country Music Classics Volume XII *(LP version)*
- (S) (2:55) K-Tel 3625 Dynamite. *(45 version)*
- (S) (2:54) JCI 3155 1970 - Only Country - 1974. *(45 version)*
- (S) (3:59) Epic 67942 Super Hits Of The '70s. *(LP version)*
- (S) (2:54) Eclipse Music Group 64894 Rock 'n Roll Relix 1974-1975. *(45 version)*
- (S) (2:54) Eclipse Music Group 64897 Rock 'n Roll Relix 1970-1979. *(45 version)*
- (S) (2:56) K-Tel 3358 101 Greatest Country Hits Vol. Four: Mellow Country. *(45 version)*
- (S) (2:55) Time-Life AM1-21 AM Gold - 1974. *(45 version)*
- (S) (3:59) Collectables 5828 Golden Classics. *(LP version)*
- (S) (3:57) Epic/Legacy 65218 Best Of. *(LP version)*
- (S) (2:55) Time-Life R808-04 Classic Country 1970-1974. *(45 version)*

BETTYE SWANN
1967 MAKE ME YOURS
- (E) (2:56) Collectables 5177 Make Me Yours. *(sounds like it was mastered from vinyl)*
- (M) (2:56) Rhino 72815 Beg, Scream & Shout! The Big Ol' Box Of '60s Soul.
1969 DON'T TOUCH ME
- (S) (2:31) Ripete 2200 Ocean Drive Volume 3.

PATRICK SWAYZE
1988 SHE'S LIKE THE WIND
- (S) (3:52) RCA 6408 O.S.T. Dirty Dancing.

KEITH SWEAT
1988 I WANT HER
- (S) (5:58) Elektra 60763 Make It Last Forever. *(LP version)*
- (S) (5:57) Elektra 62089 Maximum R&B. *(LP version)*
1990 MAKE YOU SWEAT
- (S) (5:18) Elektra 60861 I'll Give All My Love To You.
1991 I'LL GIVE ALL MY LOVE TO YOU
- (S) (6:31) Elektra 60861 I'll Give All My Love To You.
1992 KEEP IT COMIN'
- (S) (4:35) Warner Brothers 26974 Barcelona Gold.
- (S) (4:09) Elektra 61216 Keep It Comin'.
- (S) (5:21) Elektra 61216 Keep It Comin'.
1996 TWISTED
- (S) (4:29) Elektra 61707 Keith Sweat.

- (M) (3:40) Elektra 62088 Party Over Here '98. *(all tracks on this cd are segued together)*

released as by KEITH SWEAT featuring ATHENA CAGE:
1996 NOBODY
- (S) (4:24) Elektra 61707 Keith Sweat.

SWEATHOG
1971 HALLELUJAH
- (S) (2:57) Rhino 70927 Super Hits Of The 70's Volume 7.
- (S) (2:56) Columbia/Legacy 46160 Rock Artifacts Volume 1.

SWEET
1973 LITTLE WILLY
- (S) (3:12) Capitol 80324 Best Of.
- (S) (3:10) Razor & Tie 22505 More Fabulous 70's Volume 2.
- (S) (3:12) Time-Life SOD-22 Sounds Of The Seventies - Seventies Top Forty.
- (S) (3:12) Madacy Entertainment 1973 Rock On 1973.
- (S) (3:13) Varese Sarabande 5719 Bubblegum Classics Volume Three.
1975 BALLROOM BLITZ
- (S) (4:02) Capitol 48452 Desolation Boulevard.
- (S) (4:00) Capitol 80324 Best Of.
- (S) (4:00) Time-Life R968-16 Guitar Rock - The Mid '70s: Take Two.
- (S) (3:54) Tommy Boy 1194 ESPN Presents Slam Jams Vol. 1. *(all selections on this cd are segued together)*
- (S) (4:00) Priority 50952 I Love Rock & Roll Volume 3: Hits Of The 70's.
- (S) (4:00) Hip-O 40039 Power Chords Volume 2.
- (S) (4:00) Time-Life AM1-22 AM Gold - 1975.
- (S) (4:01) Mercury 314535648 O.S.T. Bordello Of Blood.
1976 FOX ON THE RUN
- (S) (3:23) Capitol 48452 Desolation Boulevard.
- (S) (3:22) Capitol 80324 Best Of.
- (S) (3:23) Medicine Label 24533 O.S.T. Dazed And Confused.
- (S) (3:23) Rhino 72297 Superhits Of The 70's Volume 23.
- (S) (3:21) Simitar 55582 The Number One's: Rock It Up.
1976 ACTION
- (S) (3:17) Capitol 80324 Best Of. *(neither the 45 or LP version)*
- (S) (3:43) JCI 4510 Masters Of Metal: Crankin' Up 1970-1980. *(LP version)*
1978 LOVE IS LIKE OXYGEN
- (S) (3:44) Capitol 80324 Best Of. *(45 version)*
- (S) (3:45) Rhino 72299 Superhits Of The 70's Volume 25. *(45 version)*
- (S) (3:43) Madacy Entertainment 1978 Rock On 1978. *(45 version)*
- (S) (3:44) Time-Life AM1-25 AM Gold - 1978. *(45 version)*

SWEET INSPIRATIONS
1968 SWEET INSPIRATION
- (S) (2:52) Rhino 75757 Soul Shots Volume 3.
- (S) (2:52) Stax 8565 Estelle, Myrna And Sylvia.
- (M) (2:52) Rhino 70278 Rare Soul: Beach Music Classics Volume 2.
- (S) (2:52) Ichiban 2506 Best Of. *(mistakenly identified as track 8 on the cd jacket when it is really track 7)*
- (S) (2:51) JCI 3167 #1 Radio Hits 1965 - Only Rock 'n Roll - 1969.
- (M) (2:52) Rhino 72815 Beg, Scream & Shout! The Big Ol' Box Of '60s Soul.
- (M) (2:52) K-Tel 3888 Great R&B Female Groups Hits Of The 60's.

SWEET SENSATION (group from Manchester, England)
1975 SAD SWEET DREAMER
- (S) (3:18) Time-Life SOD-33 Sounds Of The Seventies - AM Pop Classics II.
- (S) (3:18) Madacy Entertainment 1975 Rock On 1975.

SWEET SENSATION (group from New York City)
1989 SINCERELY YOURS
- (S) (4:51) Atco 90917 Take It While It's Hot. *(LP version)*

(S) (6:24) Atco 91722 Time To Jam! *(remix)*
1989 HOOKED ON YOU
(dj copies of this 45 ran (4:06) and (4:26) (a remix);
commercial 45's were all (4:06))
    (S) (5:06) Atco 90917 Take It While It's Hot. *(LP version)*
    (S) (4:26) Atco 91722 Time To Jam! *(radio remix)*
1990 LOVE CHILD
    (S) (4:11) Atco 91307 Love Child.
    (S) (4:59) Atco 91722 Time To Jam! *(remix)*
1990 IF WISHES CAME TRUE
    (S) (4:46) JCI 3124 Rhythm Of The Night.
    (S) (5:14) Atco 91307 Love Child.

SWINGING BLUE JEANS
1964 HIPPY HIPPY SHAKE
    (S) (1:44) Rhino 70319 History Of British Rock Volume 1.
    (S) (1:44) Rhino 70319 History Of British Rock Box Set.
    (S) (1:44) Rhino 72008 History Of British Rock Volumes 1-4 Box Set.
    (S) (1:42) EMI 81128 Rock Is Dead But It Won't Lie Down. *(includes complete countoff)*
    (S) (2:36) EMI 80256 Hippy Hippy Shake: The Definitive Collection. *(time includes a :55 false start)*
    (S) (1:43) Time-Life 2CLR-03 Classic Rock - 1964.
    (S) (1:43) Time-Life R962-07 History Of Rock 'N' Roll: The British Invasion 1964-1966.
    (S) (1:42) Cold Front 6255 Greatest Sports Rock And Jams Volume 2. *(all selections on this cd are segued together)*

SWINGIN' MEDALLIONS
1966 DOUBLE SHOT (OF MY BABY'S LOVE)
(both the 45 and some album pressings changed
the lyric from "worst hangover" to "worst morning
after")
    (S) (2:18) Warner Special Products 27607 Highs Of The 60's. *("worst hangover" lyric)*
    (M) (2:12) Rhino 75778 Frat Rock. *("worst hangover" lyric)*
    (S) (2:18) Mercury 816555 45's On CD Volume 2. *("worst hangover" lyric)*
    (S) (2:18) DCC Compact Classics 029 Toga Rock. *("worst hangover" lyric)*
    (S) (2:18) Ripete 2392192 Beach Music Anthology Box Set. *("worst hangover" lyric)*
    (S) (2:17) Collectables 5068 History Of Rock Volume 8. *("worst hangover" lyric)*
    (M) (2:17) Time-Life 2CLR-13 Classic Rock - 1966: Shakin' All Over. *("worst hangover" lyric)*
    (S) (2:18) Collectables 2501 WCBS-FM History Of Rock - The 60's Part 2. *("worst hangover" lyric)*
    (S) (2:18) Collectables 4501 History Of Rock/The 60s Part Two. *("worst hangover" lyric)*
    (S) (2:17) Collectables 2604 WCBS-FM Jukebox Giants Vol. 2. *("worst hangover" lyric)*
    (S) (2:18) Special Music 5026 Let It All Hang Out - 60's Party Hits. *("worst hangover" lyric)*
    (S) (2:19) Ripete 2187-RE Preppy Deluxe. *("worst hangover" lyric)*
    (E) (2:14) Curb 77774 Hard To Find Hits Of Rock 'N' Roll Volume Two. *("worst hangover" lyric)*
    (S) (2:18) Ripete 5145 Anthology. *("worst hangover" lyric)*
    (S) (2:17) Collectables 2554 CBS-FM History Of Rock Volume 2. *("worst hangover" lyric)*
    (S) (2:18) Eclipse Music Group 64870 Rock 'n Roll Relix 1966-1967. *("worst hangover" lyric)*
    (S) (2:18) Eclipse Music Group 64872 Rock 'n Roll Relix 1960-1969. *("worst hangover" lyric)*

SWING OUT SISTER
1987 BREAKOUT
    (S) (3:46) Priority 53769 Rock Of The 80's Volume 10.
    (S) (3:42) K-Tel 3343 The 80's Hot Dance Trax.
    (S) (3:46) Mercury 823213 It's Better To Travel.
1988 TWILIGHT WORLD
    (S) (6:28) Mercury 823213 It's Better To Travel. *(LP version)*

1992 AM I THE SAME GIRL
    (S) (4:06) Fontana 314512241 Get In Touch With Yourself.

SWV
1993 I'M SO INTO YOU
    (S) (4:37) RCA 66074 It's About Time.
    (S) (5:47) RCA 66401 The Remix EP. *(remix)*
1993 WEAK
    (S) (5:54) Tommy Boy 1097 MTV Party To Go Volume 5. *(remix; all tracks on this cd are segued together)*
    (S) (4:51) RCA 66074 It's About Time.
    (S) (5:01) RCA 66401 The Remix EP. *(remix)*
    (S) (4:50) EMI-Capitol Music Group 54548 Smooth Luv.
1993 RIGHT HERE (HUMAN NATURE)
    (S) (3:49) MJJ/Epic 57280 O.S.T. Free Willy. *(remixed)*
    (S) (4:37) RCA 66074 It's About Time.
    (S) (4:57) RCA 66401 The Remix EP. *(remix)*
1993 DOWNTOWN
    (S) (5:11) RCA 66074 It's About Time.
    (S) (4:33) RCA 66401 The Remix EP. *(remix)*
    (S) (5:10) Rhino 72159 Black Entertainment Television - 15th Anniversary.
1994 ANYTHING
    (S) (4:07) Death Row/Interscope 92403 and 92359 and 50606 O.S.T. Above The Rim.
    (S) (4:55) RCA 66401 The Remix EP. *(remix)*
1996 YOU'RE THE ONE
    (S) (4:42) RCA 66487 New Beginning.
    (S) (4:32) Tommy Boy 1168 MTV Party To Go Volume 10. *(all songs on this cd are segued together)*
1996 USE YOUR HEART
    (S) (4:48) RCA 66487 New Beginning.
released as by SWV featuring PUFF DADDY:
1997 SOMEONE
    (S) (4:06) RCA 67525 SWV - Release Some Tension.

SYBIL
1989 DON'T MAKE ME OVER
    (S) (3:58) JCI 3124 Rhythm Of The Night.
    (S) (3:58) K-Tel 6102 Funk-Tastic Jams.
    (S) (3:58) Next Plateau 1018 Sybil.

SYLVERS
1976 BOOGIE FEVER
    (S) (3:27) Priority 7974 Mega-Hits Dance Classics Volume 4.
    (S) (3:27) Rhino 70799 O.S.T. Spirit Of '76.
    (S) (3:27) Curb 77356 70's Hits Volume 2.
    (S) (3:27) Rhino 70274 The Disco Years Volume 3.
    (S) (3:26) Razor & Tie 22496 Disco Fever.
    (S) (3:25) Time-Life SOD-27 Sounds Of The Seventies - Dance Fever.
    (S) (3:28) Rhino 71668 Disco Hits Vol. 5.
    (S) (3:24) Curb 77683 Greatest Hits.
    (S) (3:24) JCI 3131 1975 - Only Rock 'N Roll - 1979.
    (S) (3:22) Razor & Tie 2058 Boogie Fever: Best Of.
    (S) (3:25) Thump 4099 Old School Boogie.
    (S) (3:24) Madacy Entertainment 1976 Rock On 1976.
    (S) (3:25) K-Tel 3581 Roller Disco - Boogie From The Skating Rinks.
    (S) (3:24) JCI 3163 18 Disco Superhits.
    (S) (3:24) Priority 53142 Mega Hits - Disco Express.
    (S) (3:27) Time-Life R838-11 Solid Gold Soul - 1976.
    (S) (3:27) Time-Life R840-01 Sounds Of The Seventies - Pop Nuggets: Late '70s.
    (S) (3:27) Flashback 72692 Disco Hits: We Are Family.
    (S) (3:27) Flashback 72086 Disco Hits Box Set.
    (S) (3:23) Cold Front 4024 Old School Mega Mix Volume 2.
    (S) (3:27) Time-Life R840-06 Sounds Of The Seventies: '70s Dance Party 1975-1976.

1977 HOT LINE
    (S) (3:00) Priority 7974 Mega-Hits Dance Classics Volume 4. *(45 version)*
    (S) (4:31) Curb 77683 Greatest Hits. *(LP version)*
    (S) (4:33) Razor & Tie 2058 Boogie Fever: Best Of. *(LP version)*

SYLVERS *(Continued)*
- (S) (4:34) Priority 53141 Mega Hits Disco Locomotion Volume 2. *(LP version)*
- (S) (3:00) Time-Life R838-16 Solid Gold Soul 1977. *(45 version)*
- (S) (3:00) Time-Life R840-07 Sounds Of The Seventies: '70s Dance Party 1976-1977. *(45 version)*

1977 HIGH SCHOOL DANCE
- (S) (3:45) Curb 77683 Greatest Hits.
- (S) (3:49) Razor & Tie 2058 Boogie Fever: Best Of.

FOSTER SYLVERS
1973 MISDEMEANOR
- (S) (2:31) Razor & Tie 2058 Boogie Fever: Best Of The Sylvers.
- (S) (2:38) Rhino 72126 Soul Hits Of The 70's Vol. 16.
- (S) (2:30) K-Tel 3911 Fantastic Volume 2.

SYLVESTER
1978 DANCE (DISCO HEAT)
- (S) (4:05) Priority 7976 Mega-Hits Dance Classics Volume 6. *(45 version)*
- (S) (4:04) Rhino 70274 The Disco Years Volume 3. *(45 version)*
- (S) (5:50) Fantasy 7710 The Original Hits. *(LP version)*
- (S) (11:06) Fantasy 79010 Living Proof. *(live)*
- (S) (5:46) Priority 53142 Mega Hits - Disco Express. *(LP version)*
- (S) (4:04) Rhino 72837 Disco Queens: The 70's. *(45 version)*

1979 YOU MAKE ME FEEL (MIGHTY REAL)
- (S) (5:26) Rebound 314520245 Disco Nights Vol. 6 - #1 Disco Hits. *(neither the 45, LP or 12" single version)*
- (S) (6:34) Fantasy 7710 The Original Hits. *(LP version)*
- (S) (10:34) Fantasy 79010 Living Proof. *(live)*
- (S) (4:50) Priority 53729 Mega Hits Dance Classics Vol. 11. *(rerecording)*
- (S) (3:45) Rhino 70492 Billboard Top Dance Hits - 1978. *(45 version)*
- (S) (3:45) Rhino 70984 The Disco Years, Vol. 1. *(45 version)*
- (S) (6:34) Priority 50956 Mega Hits - Disco Heat. *(LP version)*

SYLVIA (Sylvia Robinson, r&b singer)
1973 PILLOW TALK
(actual 45 time is (4:04) not (3:41) as stated on the record label)
- (M) (4:05) Rhino 70790 Soul Hits Of The 70's Volume 10. *(45 length)*
- (M) (4:18) Thump 7040 Low Rider Oldies Volume 4. *(LP length)*
- (M) (3:43) JCI/Telstar 3516 Sweet Soul Sisters. *(mastered from vinyl; :21 shorter than the 45 length)*
- (M) (4:05) Right Stuff 29138 Slow Jams: The 70's Vol. 3. *(45 length)*

- (M) (4:20) Risky Business 66663 Sex In The Seventies. *(LP length)*
- (M) (4:20) K-Tel 6013 70's Soul - Sexy Ballads. *(LP length)*
- (M) (4:06) Ripete 2222 Soul Patrol Vol. 4. *(45 length)*
- (S) (4:22) Rhino 71987 Pillow Talk: The Sensuous Sound Of Sylvia. *(LP length)*
- (M) (4:04) Time-Life R838-08 Solid Gold Soul - 1973. *(45 length)*
- (M) (4:04) Time-Life R834-12 Body Talk - By Candlelight. *(45 length)*

SYLVIA (Sylvia Allen, c&w singer)
1982 NOBODY
- (S) (3:16) RCA 9970 Nipper's Greatest Hits - The 80's.
- (S) (3:18) RCA 7004 14 Hits.
- (S) (3:17) RCA 5766 Country Love Songs.
- (S) (3:16) K-Tel 3113 Country Music Classics Volume XXI.
- (S) (3:16) K-Tel 4004 Country Favorites Of The 80s.
- (S) (3:16) K-Tel 3944 The 80's: Country's Number One Ladies.
- (S) (3:16) K-Tel 3233 More Great Ladies Of Country.
- (S) (3:17) JCI 3176 1980 - Only Soul - 1984.
- (S) (3:17) Renaissance 0210 Anthology.

SYNCH (see JIMMY HARNEN)

SYNDICATE OF SOUND
1966 LITTLE GIRL
- (S) (2:27) Warner Special Products 27602 20 Party Classics.
- (S) (2:25) Rhino 75892 Nuggets.
- (S) (2:25) K-Tel 839 Battle Of The Bands Volume 2.
- (M) (2:25) JCI 3111 Good Time Sixties.
- (S) (2:25) Time-Life 2CLR-13 Classic Rock - 1966: Shakin' All Over.
- (S) (2:26) Performance 399 Little Girl: History Of.
- (S) (2:25) Time-Life R968-09 Guitar Rock 1966-1967.
- (S) (2:26) Sundazed 6120 Little Girl.

SYSTEM
1987 DON'T DISTURB THIS GROOVE
- (S) (3:48) Priority 53732 80's Greatest Rock Hits Volume 8 - Dance Party. *(45 version)*
- (S) (5:17) Atlantic 81691 Don't Disturb This Groove. *(LP version)*
- (S) (3:43) JCI 3150 1985 - Only Dance - 1989. *(45 version)*
- (S) (3:48) Time-Life R988-20 Sounds Of The Eighties: The Late '80s Take Two. *(45 version)*
- (S) (5:13) Cold Front 6247 Classic Club Mix - Dance Jams. *(all selections on this cd are segued together; LP version)*
- (S) (5:23) Rhino 72977 Smooth Grooves - New Jack Ballads Volume 1. *(LP version)*

T

TACO
1983 PUTTIN' ON THE RITZ
- (S) (4:37) Priority 53767 Rock Of The 80's Volume 11. *(LP version)*
- (S) (4:35) RCA 9970 Nipper's Greatest Hits - The 80's. *(LP version)*
- (S) (3:24) Rhino 71703 New Wave Hits Of The 80's Vol. 10. *(45 version)*
- (S) (3:23) Time-Life R988-11 Sounds Of The 80's: 1983-1984. *(45 version)*
- (S) (3:24) Rhino 72491 New Wave Hits, Vol. 2. *(45 version)*
- (S) (4:35) RCA 66881 RCA's Greatest One-Hit Wonders. *(LP version)*
- (S) (3:24) Flashback 72714 Ultimate New Wave Hits. *(45 version)*
- (S) (3:24) Flashback 72092 New Wave Hits Box Set. *(45 version)*

TAG TEAM
1993 WHOOMP! (THERE IT IS)
- (S) (4:55) Tommy Boy 1097 MTV Party To Go Volume 5. *(remix; all tracks on this cd are segued together)*
- (S) (3:54) Life/Bellmark 78000 Whoomp! (There It Is).
- (S) (3:42) Tommy Boy 1137 ESPN Presents Jock Jams. *(all songs on this cd are segued together with crowd sound effects added)*
- (S) (3:35) MCA 11329 Soul Train 25th Anniversary Box Set.
- (S) (3:35) Cold Front 6245 Greatest Sports Rock And Jams. *(all selections on this cd are segued together)*
- (S) (3:34) Cold Front 6246 Classic Club Mix - R&B Grooves. *(all selections on this cd are segued together)*
- (S) (3:54) Razor & Tie 4569 '90s Style.
- (S) (3:36) Cold Front 6285 Bass Mix USA.
- (S) (3:43) Hollywood 62121 Monday Night Football Jamz. *(includes live audience overdubs)*
- (S) (3:54) Simitar 55522 The Number One's: Party Time.
- (S) (3:35) K-Tel 4065 K-Tel's Original Party Music Vol. 1.

TAKE THAT
1995 BACK FOR GOOD
- (S) (4:00) Arista 18800 Nobody Else.

TALKING HEADS
1979 TAKE ME TO THE RIVER
- (S) (5:00) Sire 26760 Sand In The Vaseline. *(LP version)*
- (S) (5:01) Sire 6058 More Songs About Buildings And Food. *(LP version)*
- (S) (5:59) Sire 25186 Stop Making Sense. *(live)*
1983 BURNING DOWN THE HOUSE
- (S) (4:00) Rhino 71834 Classic MTV: Class Of 1983.
- (S) (4:00) Sire 26760 Sand In The Vaseline.
- (S) (4:13) Sire 25186 Stop Making Sense. *(live)*
- (S) (4:02) Sire 23883 Speaking In Tongues.
- (S) (4:01) Time-Life R988-26 Sounds Of The Eighties: The Rolling Stone Collection 1982-1983.
- (S) (4:02) JCI 3149 1980 - Only Dance - 1984.
1986 WILD WILD LIFE
- (S) (3:39) Sire 25512 True Stories.
- (S) (5:29) Sire 25512 True Stories. *(remixed)*
- (S) (3:39) Sire 26760 Sand In The Vaseline.
- (S) (3:39) JCI 3150 1985 - Only Dance - 1989.

TALK TALK
1984 IT'S MY LIFE
- (S) (3:52) EMI 27674 Living In Oblivion: The 80's Greatest Hits Volume Three.
- (S) (3:52) Priority 53767 Rock Of The 80's Volume 11.
- (S) (5:57) EMI 95965 History Revisited - The Remixes. *(remix)*
- (S) (3:51) EMI 93976 Very Best Of - Natural History.
- (S) (3:52) EMI Manhattan 46063 It's My Life.
- (S) (3:51) Simitar 55552 The Number One's: Eighties Rock.

TA MARA & THE SEEN
1986 EVERYBODY DANCE
- (S) (5:40) Rebound 314520357 World Of Dance - The 80's. *(LP version)*

TAMIA
released as by BRANDY, TAMIA, GLADYS KNIGHT and CHAKA KHAN:
1996 MISSING YOU
- (S) (4:22) EastWest 61951 O.S.T. Set It Off.

TAMI SHOW
1991 THE TRUTH
- (S) (4:07) Dreamland/RCA 2289 Wanderlust.

TAMS
1964 WHAT KIND OF FOOL (DO YOU THINK I AM)
- (M) (1:59) MCA 31207 Vintage Music Volume 10.
- (M) (1:59) MCA 5806 Vintage Music Volumes 9 & 10.
- (E) (1:59) Ripete 35190 15 Greatest Hits.
- (M) (1:59) Ripete 392183 Ocean Drive.
- (M) (1:58) Time-Life RHD-12 Rhythm & Blues - 1964.
- (M) (1:59) Time-Life 2CLR-03 Classic Rock - 1964.
- (M) (1:59) MCA Special Products 22130 Vintage Collectibles Volume 1.
- (M) (1:59) MCA Special Products 20838 Tams & Impressions Greatest Hits.
- (M) (1:59) K-Tel 3269 Carolina Beach Music.
- (M) (1:59) Hip-O 40009 ABC's Of Soul Volume 1.
- (M) (1:59) MCA Special Products 20958 Mellow Classics.
- (M) (1:58) Time-Life R838-13 Solid Gold Soul - 1964.
- (M) (1:59) MCA Special Products 21030 Beach Music Hits.

NORMA TANEGA
1966 WALKIN' MY CAT NAMED DOG
- (S) (2:15) Varese Sarabande 5847 On The Radio Volume Two.

TARRIERS
released as by VINCE MARTIN with THE TARRIERS:
1956 CINDY, OH CINDY
released as by THE TARRIERS:
1957 THE BANANA BOAT SONG
- (M) (2:58) Rhino 70264 Troubadours Of The Folk Era Volume 3. *(mastered from a very scratchy record)*

TASTE OF HONEY
1978 BOOGIE OOGIE OOGIE
- (S) (4:04) Priority 7972 Mega-Hits Dance Classics Volume 2. *(:19 longer than the 45 version)*
- (S) (3:37) Rhino 70984 The Disco Years Volume 1. *(45 version)*

595

TASTE OF HONEY *(Continued)*

(S) (3:37) Rhino 70492 Billboard Top Dance Hits - 1978. *(45 version)*

(S) (7:19) Capitol 91639 Golden Honey. *(remixed)*

(S) (4:03) Razor & Tie 22496 Disco Fever. *(:18 longer than the 45 version)*

(S) (3:36) Time-Life SOD-27 Sounds Of The Seventies - Dance Fever. *(45 version)*

(S) (3:37) Rhino 71669 Disco Hits Vol. 6. *(45 version)*

(S) (4:03) Risky Business 53921 Double Knit Dance Hits. *(:18 longer than the 45 version)*

(S) (3:36) JCI 3131 1975 - Only Rock 'N Roll - 1979. *(45 version)*

(S) (6:21) Rebound 314520220 Disco Nights Vol. 4 - Greatest Disco Groups. *(neither the 45 or LP version)*

(S) (3:41) K-Tel 3126 Disco Mania. *(45 version)*

(S) (5:30) One Way 18501 Anthology. *(LP version)*

(S) (3:41) Thump 4099 Old School Boogie. *(45 version)*

(S) (3:36) Madacy Entertainment 1978 Rock On 1978. *(45 version)*

(S) (3:37) Rhino 72414 Dance Floor Divas: The 70's. *(45 version)*

(S) (3:41) K-Tel 3581 Roller Disco - Boogie From The Skating Rinks. *(45 version)*

(S) (4:04) Hip-O 40041 The Studio Collection Disco 54. *(:19 longer than the 45 version)*

(S) (4:02) Priority 53142 Mega Hits - Disco Express. *(:17 longer than the 45 version)*

(S) (4:03) Eclipse Music Group 64896 Rock 'n Roll Relix 1978-1979. *(:18 longer than the 45 version)*

(S) (4:03) Eclipse Music Group 64897 Rock 'n Roll Relix 1970-1979. *(:18 longer than the 45 version)*

(S) (3:37) Flashback 72693 Disco Hits: Good Times. *(45 version)*

(S) (3:37) Flashback 72086 Disco Hits Box Set. *(45 version)*

(S) (6:45) Chronicles 314553405 Non-Stop Disco Vol. 2. *(all songs on this cd are segued together)*

(S) (3:37) Time-Life R838-17 Solid Gold Soul 1978. *(45 version)*

(S) (5:30) EMI 57179 Beauty And The Boogie. *(LP version)*

(S) (5:29) Simitar 55522 The Number One's: Party Time. *(LP version)*

(S) (5:29) Beast 53202 Disco Divas - A Salute To The Ladies. *(LP version)*

(S) (3:37) Time-Life R840-08 Sounds Of The Seventies: '70s Dance Party 1978-1979. *(45 version)*

1981 SUKIYAKI

(S) (3:39) Capitol 91639 Golden Honey.

(S) (3:39) One Way 18501 Anthology.

(S) (3:41) Rhino 71865 Smooth Grooves Volume 7.

(S) (3:39) Madacy Entertainment 1981 Rock On 1981.

(S) (3:40) Time-Life R988-18 Sounds Of The Eighties: The Early '80s Take Two.

(S) (3:41) Time-Life R834-09 Body Talk - Magic Moments.

(S) (3:41) EMI 57179 Beauty And The Boogie.

TAVARES

1973 CHECK IT OUT

(S) (3:17) Capitol 91640 Best Of.

(S) (3:25) Capitol 89380 Capitol Gold: The Best Of.

(S) (3:15) Priority 53131 Deep Soul Volume Two.

1975 REMEMBER WHAT I TOLD YOU TO FORGET

(S) (4:10) Capitol 91640 Best Of. *(LP version)*

(S) (4:10) Capitol 89380 Capitol Gold: The Best Of. *(LP version)*

(S) (4:10) Right Stuff 30576 Slow Jams: The 70's Volume 4. *(LP version)*

(S) (4:10) EMI 55345 It Only Takes A Minute: A Lifetime With Tavares. *(LP version)*

1975 IT ONLY TAKES A MINUTE
(dj copies of this 45 ran (3:19) and (4:46);
commercial copies were all (3:19))

(S) (3:11) Priority 7983 Mega-Hits Dance Classics Volume 7. *(45 version)*

(S) (3:13) Rhino 70555 Soul Hits Of The 70's Volume 15. *(45 version)*

(S) (3:59) Capitol 91640 Best Of. *(LP version)*

(S) (3:57) Capitol 89380 Capitol Gold: The Best Of. *(LP version)*

(S) (3:13) Madacy Entertainment 1975 Rock On 1975. *(45 version)*

(S) (3:57) DCC Compact Classics 141 Groove On! Volume 1. *(LP version)*

(S) (3:58) EMI 55345 It Only Takes A Minute: A Lifetime With Tavares. *(LP version)*

(S) (3:13) Time-Life R838-10 Solid Gold Soul - 1975. *(45 version)*

(S) (3:47) Chronicles 314553404 Non-Stop Disco Vol. 1. *(all songs on this cd are segued together)*

(S) (3:55) Hip-O 40092 Disco 54: Where We Started From. *(LP version)*

1976 HEAVEN MUST BE MISSING AN ANGEL (PART 1)

(S) (3:32) Priority 7974 Mega-Hits Dance Classics Volume 4. *(45 version)*

(S) (6:32) Capitol 91640 Best Of. *(LP version)*

(S) (6:32) Capitol 89380 Capitol Gold: The Best Of. *(LP version)*

(S) (3:29) Time-Life SOD-27 Sounds Of The Seventies - Dance Fever. *(45 version)*

(S) (6:31) Rebound 314520220 Disco Nights Vol. 4 - Greatest Disco Groups. *(LP version)*

(S) (6:32) K-Tel 3470 Get Up And Disco. *(LP version)*

(S) (3:32) Priority 53141 Mega Hits Disco Locomotion Volume 2. *(45 version)*

(S) (6:29) EMI 55345 It Only Takes A Minute: A Lifetime With Tavares. *(LP version)*

(S) (5:01) Thump 9956 Old School Funk. *(all selections on this cd are segued together; edit of LP version)*

(S) (3:31) Simitar 55602 The Number One's: Silky Soul. *(45 version)*

(S) (3:32) Time-Life R840-07 Sounds Of The Seventies: '70s Dance Party 1976-1977. *(45 version)*

1976 DON'T TAKE AWAY THE MUSIC

(S) (3:34) Priority 7975 Mega-Hits Dance Classics Volume 5. *(45 version)*

(S) (6:14) Capitol 91640 Best Of. *(LP version)*

(S) (6:12) Capitol 89380 Capitol Gold: The Best Of. *(LP version)*

(S) (6:12) Priority 50956 Mega Hits - Disco Heat. *(LP version)*

1977 WHODUNIT

(S) (3:33) Capitol 89380 Capitol Gold: The Best Of.

(S) (3:34) Time-Life R838-16 Solid Gold Soul 1977.

1978 MORE THAN A WOMAN

(S) (3:29) Priority 7058 Mega-Hits Dance Classics Volume 9. *(:14 longer than the 45 or LP)*

(S) (3:27) Capitol 89380 Capitol Gold: The Best Of. *(:12 longer than the 45 or LP)*

(S) (3:15) Razor & Tie 22496 Disco Fever.

(S) (3:15) Polydor 800068 O.S.T. Saturday Night Fever.

(S) (3:15) Rebound 314520366 Disco Nights Vol. 10 - Disco's Greatest Movie Hits.

(S) (3:14) Polydor 422825389 O.S.T. Saturday Night Fever. *(remastered edition)*

(S) (3:15) Right Stuff 35600 Soul Of The Bee Gees.

(S) (3:15) Priority 50957 Mega Hits Disco Explosion Volume 4.

(S) (3:15) Mobile Fidelity 716 O.S.T. Saturday Night Fever. *(gold disc)*

(S) (3:15) Right Stuff 52274 Flick Hits Take 2.

1982 A PENNY FOR YOUR THOUGHTS

(S) (3:49) Right Stuff 31973 Slow Jams: The Timeless Collection Volume 3. *(45 length)*

(S) (4:24) Original Sound 9308 Dedicated To You Vol. 8. *(LP length)*

(S) (4:24) Rhino 72511 Smooth Grooves: A Sensual Collection Volume 9. *(LP length)*

ANDY TAYLOR
1986 TAKE IT EASY

BOBBY TAYLOR & THE VANCOUVERS
1968 DOES YOUR MAMA KNOW ABOUT ME

(M) (2:45) Motown 314530507 Motown Year By Year 1968.

(M) (2:46) Motown 6312 Hitsville USA.

(S) (2:50) Motown 6183 20 Hard To Find Motown Classics Volume One.

(S) (2:50) Motown 314530363 Bobby Taylor & The Vancouvers.

(M) (2:46) Motown 314530569 Motown Milestones - Motown Love Songs.

(S) (2:50) Motown 314530573 Baddest Love Jams Volume 2 - Fire And Desire.

JAMES TAYLOR
1970 FIRE AND RAIN

(S) (3:19) Warner Special Products 27615 Storytellers: Singers & Songwriters.

(S) (3:21) Priority 8664 High Times/70's Greatest Rock Hits Volume 3.

(S) (3:20) Warner Brothers 1843 Sweet Baby James.

(S) (3:22) Warner Brothers 3113 Greatest Hits.

(S) (3:15) JCI 3307 Easy Seventies.

(S) (3:20) Razor & Tie 4543 The '70s Preservation Society Presents: Easy '70s.

(S) (3:20) Rhino 71549 Let There Be Drums Vol. 3: The 70's.

(S) (3:16) Time-Life SUD-16 Superhits - The Early 70's.

(S) (3:20) Time-Life SOD-01 Sounds Of The Seventies - 1970.

(S) (3:21) Time-Life R103-33 Singers & Songwriters.

(S) (3:20) JCI 3130 1970 - Only Rock 'N Roll - 1974.

(S) (3:22) K-Tel 3455 Folk Hits Around The Campfire.

(S) (3:21) Rhino 72446 Listen To The Music: 70's Male Singer/Songwriters.

(S) (3:19) Eclipse Music Group 64892 Rock 'n Roll Relix 1970-1971.

(S) (3:19) Eclipse Music Group 64897 Rock 'n Roll Relix 1970-1979.

(S) (3:16) Time-Life AM1-13 AM Gold - The Early '70s.

1971 COUNTRY ROAD

(S) (3:20) Warner Brothers 1843 Sweet Baby James.

(S) (3:21) Warner Brothers 3113 Greatest Hits.

(S) (3:20) Rhino 71843 Troubadours Of The Folk Era Vol. 4.

1971 YOU'VE GOT A FRIEND

(S) (4:20) Warner Brothers 2561 Mud Slide Slim And The Blue Horizon.

(S) (4:27) Warner Brothers 3113 Greatest Hits.

(S) (4:27) Time-Life SUD-20 Superhits - Early 70's Classics.

(S) (4:27) Time-Life SOD-02 Sounds Of The Seventies - 1971.

(S) (4:27) Time-Life R103-33 Singers & Songwriters.

(S) (4:27) Time-Life R921-38 Get Together.

(S) (4:27) Time-Life AM1-15 AM Gold - Early '70s Classics.

1971 LONG AGO AND FAR AWAY

(S) (2:19) Warner Brothers 2561 Mud Slide Slim And The Blue Horizon.

1973 DON'T LET ME BE LONELY TONIGHT

(S) (2:34) Warner Brothers 3113 Greatest Hits.

(S) (2:33) Warner Brothers 25933 One Man Dog.

(S) (2:33) Sandstone 33048 and 5016 Cosmopolitan Volume 2.

(S) (2:33) Time-Life SUD-13 Superhits - 1973.

(S) (2:33) Time-Life SOD-14 Sounds Of The Seventies - 1973: Take Two.

(S) (2:33) Time-Life R105-26 Our Songs: Singers & Songwriters Encore.

(S) (2:33) Time-Life R921-38 Get Together.

(S) (2:33) DCC Compact Classics 087 Night Moves Volume 5.

(S) (2:33) Time-Life R834-02 Body Talk - Just For You.

released as by CARLY SIMON and JAMES TAYLOR:
1974 MOCKINGBIRD

(S) (3:48) Elektra 109 Best Of Carly Simon. *(45 length)*

(S) (4:11) Elektra 1002 Carly Simon - Hotcakes. *(LP length)*

(S) (3:48) Epic 57682 More Songs For Sleepless Nights. *(45 length)*

(S) (4:09) Time-Life SOD-15 Sounds Of The Seventies - 1974: Take Two. *(LP length)*

(S) (4:10) Arista 18798 Carly Simon - Clouds In My Coffee 1965-1995. *(LP length)*

(S) (3:48) Rhino 72494 For Our Children Too! *(45 length)*

(S) (3:48) Time-Life AM1-21 AM Gold - 1974. *(45 length)*

released as by JAMES TAYLOR:
1975 HOW SWEET IT IS (TO BE LOVED BY YOU)

(S) (3:33) Warner Brothers 3113 Greatest Hits.

(S) (3:33) Warner Brothers 2866 Gorilla.

1976 SHOWER THE PEOPLE

(S) (4:29) Warner Brothers 2912 In The Pocket. *(LP version)*

(S) (3:56) Warner Brothers 3113 Greatest Hits. *(45 version)*

(S) (3:55) Time-Life SOD-25 Sounds Of The Seventies - Seventies Generation. *(45 version)*

(S) (3:57) K-Tel 3454 70s Folk Rock Hits. *(45 version)*

(S) (3:56) K-Tel 4017 70s Heavy Hitters: Summer Love. *(45 version)*

(S) (3:53) Time-Life R834-15 Body Talk - Once In Lifetime. *(45 version)*

1977 HANDY MAN

(S) (3:15) Columbia 34811 and 53787 JT.

(S) (3:15) Time-Life SOD-05 Sounds Of The Seventies - 1977.

(S) (3:15) Columbia 64807 JT/Flag/Dad Loves His Work.

(S) (3:15) Columbia/Legacy 64415 JT. *(gold disc)*

1977 YOUR SMILING FACE

(S) (2:43) Priority 53706 Singers/Songwriters/70's Greatest Rock Hits Volume 15.

(S) (2:44) Columbia 34811 and 53787 JT.

(S) (2:44) Columbia 64807 JT/Flag/Dad Loves His Work.

(S) (2:44) Columbia/Legacy 64415 JT. *(gold disc)*

released as by ART GARFUNKEL with JAMES TAYLOR & PAUL SIMON:
1978 (WHAT A) WONDERFUL WORLD

(S) (3:29) Columbia 34975 Art Garfunkel: Watermark.

(S) (3:28) Columbia 45008 Art Garfunkel: Garfunkel.

released as by JAMES TAYLOR:
1979 UP ON THE ROOF

(S) (4:19) Columbia 36058 Flag.

(S) (4:19) Columbia 64807 JT/Flag/Dad Loves His Work.

released as by JAMES TAYLOR and J.D. SOUTHER:
1981 HER TOWN TOO
(actual 45 time is (4:28) not (4:35) as stated on the record label)

(S) (4:33) Columbia 37009 James Taylor - Dad Loves His Work.

(S) (4:33) Columbia 64807 James Taylor - JT/Flag/Dad Loves His Work.

(S) (4:24) Madacy Entertainment 6803 Power Of Love.

(S) (4:19) Time-Life R988-16 Sounds Of The Eighties: The Early '80s.

(S) (4:23) Time-Life R834-09 Body Talk - Magic Moments.

JOHN TAYLOR
1986 I DO WHAT I DO

(S) (3:43) Capitol 46722 O.S.T. 9 1/2 Weeks.

JOHNNIE TAYLOR
1968 WHO'S MAKING LOVE

(S) (2:47) Rhino 75770 Soul Shots Volume 2.

(S) (2:46) JCI 3105 Soul Sixties.

(S) (2:45) Original Sound 8855 Oldies But Goodies Vol. 5. *(this compact disc uses the "Waring - fds" noise reduction process; ambient background noise throughout the disc)*

(S) (2:45) Original Sound 2222 Oldies But Goodies Volumes 3,5,11,14 and 15 Box Set. *(this box set uses the "Waring - fds" noise reduction process; ambient background noise throughout the song)*

(S) (2:45) Original Sound 2500 Oldies But Goodies Volumes 1-15 Box Set. *(this box set uses the "Waring - fds" noise reduction process; ambient background noise throughout the song)*

(S) (2:44) Original Sound CDGO-11 Golden Oldies Volume 11.

JOHNNIE TAYLOR *(Continued)*

- (S) (2:46) Original Sound 8881 Twenty-One #1 Hits. *(this compact disc uses the "Waring - fds" noise reduction process)*
- (S) (2:47) Rhino 70654 Billboard's Top R&B Hits Of 1968.
- (S) (2:47) Rhino 72006 Billboard's Top R&B Hits 1965-1969 Box Set.
- (S) (2:46) Stax 88005 Top Of The Stax.
- (S) (2:46) Warner Special Products 27609 Memphis Soul Classics.
- (S) (2:46) Stax 60-006 Chronicle: The 20 Greatest Hits.
- (S) (2:45) Stax 4115 Who's Making Love.
- (S) (2:46) Ripete 2200 Ocean Drive Volume 3.
- (S) (2:46) Stax 4411 Complete Stax/Volt Soul Singles 1968 - 1971.
- (S) (2:46) Time-Life RHD-04 Rhythm & Blues - 1968.
- (S) (2:46) Time-Life 2CLR-04 Classic Rock - 1968.
- (S) (2:46) Rhino 71806 The R&B Box: Thirty Years Of Rhythm & Blues.
- (S) (2:46) JCI 3161 18 Soul Hits From The 60's.
- (S) (2:46) Time-Life R838-03 Solid Gold Soul - 1968.
- (M) (2:49) Rhino 72815 Beg, Scream & Shout! The Big Ol' Box Of '60s Soul.
- (S) (2:46) Repeat/Relativity 1611 A Brand New Bag: #1 Soul Hits Of The 60's Volume 3.

1969 TAKE CARE OF YOUR HOMEWORK
- (S) (2:38) Stax 60-006 Chronicle: The 20 Greatest Hits. *(noise on fadeout)*
- (S) (2:37) Stax 4115 Who's Making Love. *(noise on fadeout)*
- (S) (2:35) Stax 4411 Complete Stax/Volt Soul Singles 1968 - 1971.

1969 TESTIFY (I WONNA)
- (S) (4:03) Stax 88008 Top Of The Stax Volume 2.
- (S) (4:03) Stax 60-006 Chronicle: The 20 Greatest Hits.
- (S) (4:03) Stax 8563 Johnnie Taylor Philosophy Continues.
- (M) (4:00) Stax 4411 Complete Stax/Volt Soul Singles 1968 - 1971.

1970 LOVE BONES
- (S) (4:03) Stax 60-006 Chronicle: The 20 Greatest Hits. *(LP version)*
- (S) (4:04) Stax 8563 Johnnie Taylor Philosophy Continues. *(LP version)*
- (S) (3:19) Stax 4411 Complete Stax/Volt Soul Singles 1968 - 1971. *(45 version)*

1970 STEAL AWAY
- (S) (3:26) Stax 8547 Stax Blues Brothers.
- (S) (3:27) Stax 8559 Superblues Volume 2.
- (S) (3:27) Stax 60-006 Chronicle: The 20 Greatest Hits.
- (S) (7:48) Stax 8558 Little Bluebird. *(live)*
- (S) (3:26) Stax 4411 Complete Stax/Volt Soul Singles 1968 - 1971.

1970 I AM SOMEBODY (PART 2)
- (S) (3:22) Stax 60-006 Chronicle: The 20 Greatest Hits.
- (S) (3:23) Stax 4411 Complete Stax/Volt Soul Singles 1968 - 1971.

1971 JODY'S GOT YOUR GIRL AND GONE
- (S) (2:59) Stax 60-006 Chronicle: The 20 Greatest Hits.
- (S) (5:47) Stax 8558 Little Bluebird. *(live)*
- (S) (3:00) Stax 4411 Complete Stax/Volt Soul Singles 1968 - 1971.
- (S) (2:59) Rhino 72113 Billboard Hot Soul Hits - 1971.

1973 I BELIEVE IN YOU (YOU BELIEVE IN ME)
(actual 45 time is (4:32); some 45 labels read (4:37) and others (3:58))
- (S) (4:31) Stax 88008 Top Of The Stax Volume 2. *(45 version)*
- (S) (5:06) Stax 60-006 Chronicle: The 20 Greatest Hits. *(LP version)*
- (S) (4:31) Stax 4415 Complete Stax/Volt Soul Singles Volume 3 1972-1975. *(45 version)*
- (S) (4:31) Rhino 72115 Billboard Hot Soul Hits - 1973. *(45 version)*
- (S) (5:06) Stax 8588 Taylored In Silk. *(LP version)*
- (S) (4:29) JCI 3173 1970 - Only Soul - 1974. *(45 version)*

1973 CHEAPER TO KEEP HER
- (S) (2:46) Stax 88005 Top Of The Stax. *(edited)*
- (S) (3:25) Stax 60-006 Chronicle: The 20 Greatest Hits. *(truncated fade)*

- (S) (3:27) Stax 4415 Complete Stax/Volt Soul Singles Volume 3 1972-1975.
- (S) (3:27) Rhino 72126 Soul Hits Of The 70's Vol. 16.
- (S) (3:26) Stax 8588 Taylored In Silk.
- (S) (3:22) Priority 53131 Deep Soul Volume Two.
- (S) (3:26) Time-Life R859-11 Living The Blues - Blues Classics: The '70s.

1976 DISCO LADY
(dj copies of this 45 ran (3:50); commercial copies were all (4:20))
- (S) (4:27) Priority 7975 Mega-Hits Dance Classics Volume 5.
- (S) (3:49) Essex 7051 Non-Stop Dance Hits. *(edit of the LP length - this is not the dj 45 edit)*
- (S) (4:28) Razor & Tie 22496 Disco Fever.
- (S) (4:27) Time-Life SOD-18 Sounds Of The Seventies - 1976: Take Two.
- (S) (4:24) Risky Business 53921 Double Knit Dance Hits.
- (S) (4:25) K-Tel 3251 Disco Fever.
- (S) (4:27) Columbia/Legacy 64818 Rated X-Traordinaire: Best Of.
- (S) (4:27) JCI 3148 1975 - Only Dance - 1979.
- (S) (4:26) Time-Life R838-11 Solid Gold Soul - 1976.
- (S) (4:27) Priority 50957 Mega Hits Disco Explosion Volume 4.
- (S) (4:27) Rhino 72943 VH1 8-Track Flashback: Classic '70s Soul.
- (S) (4:24) Time-Life R840-07 Sounds Of The Seventies: '70s Dance Party 1976-1977.

LITTLE JOHNNY TAYLOR
1963 PART TIME LOVE
- (S) (3:47) Stax 8551 Superblues Volume 1.
- (S) (3:50) Fantasy 4510 Greatest Hits.
- (S) (3:51) Rhino 71121 Blues Masters Volume 1: Urban Blues.
- (S) (3:51) Rhino 72027 Blues Masters Vols. 1-5 Box Set.
- (S) (3:45) Time-Life RHD-02 Rhythm & Blues - 1963.
- (S) (3:50) Time-Life R859-05 Living The Blues: 1960-1964 Blues Classics.
- (S) (3:45) Time-Life R838-14 Solid Gold Soul - 1963.
- (S) (3:46) Repeat/Relativity 1611 A Brand New Bag: #1 Soul Hits Of The 60's Volume 3.

LIVINGSTON TAYLOR
1978 I WILL BE IN LOVE WITH YOU
- (S) (3:30) Rhino 72445 Listen To The Music: The 70's California Sound.
- (S) (3:29) Epic/Legacy 57312 3-Way Mirror.
- (S) (3:29) Razor & Tie 2161 Carolina Day: The Livingston Taylor Collection.

R. DEAN TAYLOR
1970 INDIANA WANTS ME
(there are two 45 versions of this song; one runs (3:01) and has no sirens on the intro, the other runs (3:35) and has sirens on the intro; the real LP time is (3:43) not (3:15) as stated on the record label)
- (S) (3:39) Rhino 70923 Super Hits Of The 70's Volume 3. *(LP version; stereo sound effects but the rest of the song is (E))*
- (S) (3:39) Rhino 72009 Super Hits Of The 70's Volumes 1-4 Box Set. *(LP version; stereo sound effects but the rest of the song is (E))*
- (E) (3:45) Motown 6184 Hard To Find Motown Classics Volume 2. *(LP version)*
- (S) (3:39) Rhino 71207 70's Smash Hits Volume 3. *(LP version; stereo sound effects but the rest of the song is (E))*
- (S) (3:37) Razor & Tie 22505 More Fabulous 70's Volume 2. *(LP version; stereo sound effects but the rest of the song is (E))*
- (S) (3:31) Time-Life SUD-04 Superhits - 1970. *(LP version faded :12 early; stereo sound effects but the rest of the song is (E))*
- (S) (3:31) Time-Life AM1-02 AM Gold - 1970. *(LP version faded :12 early; stereo sound effects but the rest of the song is (E))*

(E) (3:44) Rebound 314520440 No. 1 Hits Of The 70's. *(LP version)*

(S) (3:39) Flashback 72683 '70s Radio Hits Volume 3. *(LP version; stereo sound effects but the rest of the song is (E))*

(S) (3:39) Flashback 72090 '70s Radio Hits Box Set. *(LP version; stereo sound effects but the rest of the song is (E))*

T-BONES
1966 NO MATTER WHAT SHAPE (YOUR STOMACH'S IN)
(S) (2:15) Curb 77402 All-Time Great Instrumental Hits Volume 2.

(S) (2:15) Capitol Special Markets 57272 Great Instrumental Hits From Rock's Golden Years.

(S) (2:16) Rhino 71602 Rock Instrumental Classics Volume 2: The Sixties.

(S) (2:16) Rhino 72035 Rock Instrumental Classics Vols. 1-5 Box Set.

(S) (2:14) Time-Life SUD-17 Superhits - Mid 60's Classics.

(S) (2:14) Time-Life HPD-39 Your Hit Parade - 60's Instrumentals: Take Two.

(S) (2:16) Rhino 71936 Billboard Top Pop Hits, 1966.

(S) (2:27) Collectors' Choice 003/4 Instrumental Gems Of The 60's. *(:12 longer than the 45 or LP)*

(S) (2:15) Collectables 5691 No Matter What Shape (Your Stomach's In).

(S) (2:14) Time-Life AM1-16 AM Gold - Mid '60s Classics.

T-BOZ
1996 TOUCH MYSELF
(S) (4:09) Rowdy 37012 O.S.T. Fled.
released as by DA BRAT featuring T-BOZ:
1997 GHETTO LOVE
(S) (3:21) So So Def/Columbia 67813 Anuthatantrum.

TEARS FOR FEARS
1985 EVERYBODY WANTS TO RULE THE WORLD
(S) (4:11) T.J. Martell Foundation/Columbia 40315 Music For The Miracle.

(S) (4:07) Epic 53439 O.S.T. Peter's Friends.

(S) (4:07) Priority 53750 Rock Of The 80's Volume 7.

(S) (4:10) Mercury 824300 Songs From The Big Chair.

(S) (4:07) Fontana 314510939 Tears Roll Down (Greatest Hits 82-92).

(S) (4:08) Time-Life R988-02 Sounds Of The Eighties: 1985.

(S) (4:10) Rebound 314520434 Classic Rock - 80's.

(S) (4:07) Rebound 314520442 The Roots Of Rock: 80's New Wave.

(S) (4:10) Hollywood 62098 O.S.T. Romy And Michele's High School Reunion.

(S) (4:06) Simitar 55612 The Number One's: The '80s.
1985 SHOUT
(S) (6:32) Priority 53684 Rock Of The 80's Volume 4. *(LP version)*

(S) (4:03) Rhino 71640 Billboard Top Hits - 1985. *(45 version)*

(S) (6:32) Mercury 824300 Songs From The Big Chair. *(LP version)*

(S) (6:30) Fontana 314510939 Tears Roll Down (Greatest Hits 82-92). *(LP version)*

(S) (4:03) Time-Life R988-01 Sounds Of The Eighties: The Rockin' Eighties. *(45 version)*

(S) (5:56) Rebound 314520354 World Of Dance: New Wave - The 80's. *(12" single version)*

(S) (4:04) Rhino 72894 Hard Rock Cafe: New Wave. *(45 version)*

(S) (4:02) Hip-O 40080 Essential '80s: 1985-1989. *(45 version)*
1985 HEAD OVER HEELS
(S) (4:14) Priority 53752 Rock Of The 80's Volume 12. *(45 version)*

(S) (4:17) Rhino 71978 New Wave Hits Of The 80's Vol. 15. *(45 version)*

(S) (5:01) Mercury 824300 Songs From The Big Chair. *(LP version)*

(S) (4:14) Fontana 314510939 Tears Roll Down (Greatest Hits 82-92). *(45 version)*

(S) (4:14) Time-Life R988-12 Sounds Of The 80's: 1985-1986. *(45 version)*
1986 MOTHERS TALK
(S) (5:07) Mercury 824300 Songs From The Big Chair.

(S) (4:59) Fontana 314510939 Tears Roll Down (Greatest Hits 82-92).
1989 SOWING THE SEEDS OF LOVE
(S) (5:43) Rhino 71644 Billboard Top Hits - 1989. *(45 length)*

(S) (5:41) Priority 53775 Best Of 80's Rock Volume 1. *(45 length)*

(S) (6:15) Fontana 838730 The Seeds Of Love. *(LP length)*

(S) (6:15) Fontana 314510939 Tears Roll Down (Greatest Hits 82-92). *(LP length)*

(S) (5:42) Time-Life R988-13 Sounds Of The Eighties: 1989. *(45 length)*

(S) (5:42) Time-Life R13610 Gold And Platinum Box Set - The Ultimate Rock Collection. *(45 length)*
1990 WOMAN IN CHAINS
(S) (6:29) Fontana 838730 The Seeds Of Love.

(S) (6:28) Fontana 314510939 Tears Roll Down (Greatest Hits 82-92).
1993 BREAK IT DOWN AGAIN
(S) (4:30) Mercury 314514875 Elemental.

TECHNOTRONIC
released as by TECHNOTRONIC featuring FELLY:
1990 PUMP UP THE JAM
(S) (5:21) JCI 2717 Shake It Up. *(LP version)*

(S) (3:35) Priority 7053 Best Of Hip Hop. *(45 version)*

(S) (3:34) Priority 8657 Yo Rap Hits. *(45 version)*

(S) (5:19) Sandstone 33043 and 5009 Rock The First Volume Three. *(LP version)*

(S) (5:19) Sandstone 33055 and 5014 Rock The First Volume Eight. *(LP version)*

(S) (3:35) Rebound 314520246 Disco Nights Vol. 5 - Best Of Housemusic. *(45 version)*

(S) (5:17) Priority 53770 Techno Dance Classics Volume 1 - Pump Up The Jam. *(LP version)*

(S) (5:21) SBK 93422 Pump Up The Jam. *(LP version)*

(S) (5:24) SBK 95028 Trip On This - The Remixes. *(remix)*

(S) (3:58) Tommy Boy 1137 ESPN Presents Jock Jams. *(all songs on this cd are segued together with crowd sound effects added)*

(S) (5:18) Madacy Entertainment 1989 Rock On 1989. *(LP version)*

(S) (4:55) Cold Front 6255 Greatest Sports Rock And Jams Volume 2. *(all selections on this cd are segued together; LP version)*

(S) (3:35) Rhino 75200 Basketball's Greatest Hits. *(45 version)*

(S) (5:19) K-Tel 3847 90s Now Volume 1. *(LP version)*

(S) (5:00) Priority 50935 100% Party Hits Of The 90's Volume Two. *(all selections on this cd are segued together)*
released as by TECHNOTRONIC:
1990 GET UP! (BEFORE THE NIGHT IS OVER)
(S) (5:36) Priority 53772 Techno Dance Classics Volume 2 - Feel The Beat. *(LP version)*

(S) (5:36) SBK 93422 Pump Up The Jam. *(LP version)*

(S) (7:15) SBK 95028 Trip On This - The Remixes. *(remix)*

(S) (5:34) Beast 53022 Club Hitz Of The 90's Vol. 1. *(all songs on this cd are segued together)*
1990 MOVE THIS
(S) (5:19) SBK 28403 Brilliant! The Global Dance Music Experience Volume 1. *(remix)*

(S) (5:20) Sandstone 5022 Cosmopolitan Volume 8. *(LP version)*

(S) (5:20) DCC Compact Classics 082 Night Moves Volume 2. *(LP version)*

(S) (5:20) SBK 93422 Pump Up The Jam. *(LP version)*

(S) (3:37) JCI 3132 1990 - Only Rock 'n Roll - 1994. *(45 version)*

(S) (5:18) EMI 54097 Retro Dance Club Volume One. *(remix)*

(S) (3:44) Priority 50934 Shut Up And Dance! The 90's Volume One. *(all selections on this cd are segued together)*

(S) (3:38) Right Stuff 56198 Free To Be Volume 8. *(45 version)*

TECHNOTRONIC *(Continued)*

    (S)   (5:20)   Rhino 72839 Disco Queens: The 90's. *(LP version)*

TEDDY BEARS
1958 TO KNOW HIM, IS TO LOVE HIM

    (M)   (2:22)   Rhino 70619 Billboard's Top Rock & Roll Hits Of 1958.

    (M)   (2:22)   Rhino 72004 Billboard's Top Rock & Roll Hits 1957-1961 Box Set.

    (E)   (2:22)   Original Sound 8852 Oldies But Goodies Vol. 2. *(this compact disc uses the "Waring - fds" noise reduction process)*

    (E)   (2:22)   Original Sound 2223 Oldies But Goodies Volumes 2,7,9,12 and 13 Box Set. *(this box set uses the "Waring - fds" noise reduction process)*

    (E)   (2:22)   Original Sound 2500 Oldies But Goodies Volumes 1-15 Box Set. *(this box set uses the "Waring - fds" noise reduction process)*

    (E)   (2:22)   Original Sound 8891 Dick Clark's 21 All-Time Hits Vol. 1.

    (M)   (2:22)   Abkco 7118 Phil Spector/Back To Mono (1958-1969).

    (M)   (2:21)   Time-Life 2RNR-05 Rock 'N' Roll Era - 1958. *(this song appears only on original pressings of this cd)*

    (M)   (2:22)   K-Tel 3007 50's Sock Hop.

    (M)   (2:22)   K-Tel 3125 Solid Gold Rock N' Roll.

TEEGARDEN & VAN WINKLE
1970 GOD, LOVE AND ROCK & ROLL

    (S)   (3:00)   Varese Sarabande 5906 God, Love And Rock & Roll.

TEENAGERS (see FRANKIE LYMON & THE TEENAGERS)

TEEN QUEENS
1956 EDDIE MY LOVE

    (M)   (3:12)   Time-Life 2RNR-14 The Rock 'N' Roll Era - 1956.

    (M)   (3:11)   Time-Life RHD-05 Rhythm & Blues - 1956.

    (M)   (3:11)   Original Sound 8850 Oldies But Goodies Vol. 1. *(this compact disc uses the "Waring - fds" noise reduction process)*

    (M)   (3:11)   Original Sound 2221 Oldies But Goodies Volumes 1,4,6,8 and 10 Box Set. *(this box set uses the "Waring - fds" noise reduction process)*

    (M)   (3:11)   Original Sound 2500 Oldies But Goodies Volumes 1-15 Box Set. *(this box set uses the "Waring - fds" noise reduction process)*

    (M)   (3:11)   Rhino 70642 Billboard Top R&B Hits - 1956.

    (M)   (3:12)   DCC Compact Classics 031 Back Seat Jams.

    (E)   (3:11)   Collectables 2506 WCBS-FM History Of Rock - The 50's Part 1.

    (E)   (3:11)   Collectables 4506 History Of Rock/The 50s Part One.

    (E)   (3:12)   Collectables 2509 WCBS-FM For Lovers Only Part 1.

    (M)   (3:10)   Rhino 72507 Doo Wop Box II.

    (M)   (3:11)   Time-Life R857-07 The Heart Of Rock 'n' Roll 1956.

    (M)   (3:11)   Time-Life R838-24 Solid Gold Soul 1956.

TEE SET
1970 MA BELLE AMIE

    (S)   (3:12)   Rhino 70922 Super Hits Of The 70's Volume 2.

    (S)   (3:12)   Rhino 72009 Super Hits Of The 70's Volumes 1-4 Box Set.

    (S)   (3:13)   Original Sound CDGO-7 Golden Oldies Volume. 7.

    (S)   (3:12)   JCI 3115 Groovin' Sixties.

    (S)   (3:12)   Time-Life SUD-04 Superhits - 1970.

    (S)   (3:08)   Collectables 0548 Golden Classics.

    (S)   (3:12)   JCI 3191 1970 - Only Dance - 1974.

    (S)   (3:15)   Popular/Critique 12009 Dutch Treats.

    (S)   (3:11)   Time-Life AM1-02 AM Gold - 1970.

    (S)   (3:12)   Time-Life R840-03 Sounds Of The Seventies - Pop Nuggets: Early '70s.

NINO TEMPO & APRIL STEVENS
1963 DEEP PURPLE

    (S)   (2:40)   Atlantic 81909 Hit Singles 1958-1977.

    (S)   (2:40)   Rhino 70624 Billboard's Top Rock & Roll Hits Of 1963. *(found only on the 1993 reissue of this cd)*

    (S)   (2:39)   Time-Life 2RNR-42 Rock 'N' Roll Era - The 60's Sock Hop.

    (S)   (2:39)   Time-Life SUD-08 Superhits - 1963.

    (S)   (2:39)   Time-Life HPD-33 Your Hit Parade - The Early 60's.

    (S)   (2:40)   Time-Life R103-27 Love Me Tender.

    (S)   (2:39)   Time-Life OPCD-4517 Tonight's The Night.

    (M)   (2:39)   Varese Sarabande 5592 Sweet And Lovely: Best Of.

    (S)   (2:40)   Time-Life R857-08 The Heart Of Rock 'n' Roll 1963.

    (S)   (2:39)   Time-Life AM1-17 AM Gold - 1963.

1964 WHISPERING

    (M)   (2:26)   Varese Sarabande 5592 Sweet And Lovely: Best Of.

1964 STARDUST

    (S)   (2:57)   Varese Sarabande 5592 Sweet And Lovely: Best Of.

1966 ALL STRUNG OUT

    (S)   (2:59)   Varese Sarabande 5592 Sweet And Lovely: Best Of.

TEMPOS
1959 SEE YOU IN SEPTEMBER

    (M)   (2:06)   Essex 7053 A Hot Summer Night In '59.

    (S)   (2:07)   MCA 8001 O.S.T. American Graffiti.

    (S)   (2:07)   Time-Life HPD-38 Your Hit Parade - The 50's Generation.

    (S)   (2:07)   Time-Life R857-01 The Heart Of Rock 'n' Roll - 1959.

    (S)   (2:07)   Time-Life R132-14 Golden Groups Of Your Hit Parade.

TEMPTATIONS (New York group)
1960 BARBARA

    (S)   (2:50)   Collectables 5479 Spotlite Series - Goldisc Records Volume 1.

    (S)   (2:50)   Rhino 72507 Doo Wop Box II.

TEMPTATIONS (Detroit group)
1964 THE WAY YOU DO THE THINGS YOU DO
(45 length is (2:36); LP length is (2:42))

    (S)   (2:44)   Motown 6139 The Composer Series: Smokey Robinson.

    (S)   (2:35)   Motown 5450 A Collection Of 16 Big Hits Volume 3.

    (S)   (2:44)   Rhino 70650 Billboard's Top R&B Hits Of 1964. *(excessive noise at 2:44)*

    (S)   (2:42)   Motown 0782 and 6189 Anthology.

    (S)   (2:42)   Motown 5411 Greatest Hits.

    (S)   (2:42)   Motown 8060 and 8160 Meet The Temptations Temptations Sing Smokey.

    (S)   (2:44)   Motown 5205 Temptations Sing Smokey.

    (S)   (2:44)   Motown 5140 Meet The Temptations.

    (S)   (2:42)   Motown 9071 Motown Dance Party Volume 1. *(all selections on this cd are segued together)*

    (M)   (2:39)   Motown 6312 Hitsville USA.

    (S)   (2:35)   Time-Life RHD-12 Rhythm & Blues - 1964.

    (S)   (2:42)   Time-Life 2CLR-03 Classic Rock - 1964.

    (M)   (2:38)   Motown 314530338 Emperors Of Soul.

    (M)   (2:37)   Motown 314530420 Motown Classic Hits Vol. III.

    (M)   (2:36)   Motown 314530524 Anthology.

    (S)   (2:37)   Motown 314530504 Motown Year By Year 1964.

    (M)   (2:36)   Priority 57194 Old School Friday - More Music From The Original Motion Picture.

    (S)   (2:35)   Time-Life R838-13 Solid Gold Soul - 1964.

    (M)   (2:38)   Motown 314530562 The Ultimate Collection.

    (S)   (2:38)   Motown 314530853 Greatest Hits. *(remastered edition)*

1964 I'LL BE IN TROUBLE

    (S)   (2:51)   Motown 5451 A Collection Of 16 Big Hits Volume 4.

(S) (2:54) Motown 0782 and 6189 Anthology.
(S) (2:54) Motown 5411 Greatest Hits.
(M) (3:16) Motown 314530338 Emperors Of Soul. *(:23 longer than the 45 or LP)*
(M) (2:51) Motown 314530422 Motown Classics Vol. V.
(M) (2:51) Motown 314530524 Anthology.

1964 GIRL (WHY YOU WANNA MAKE ME BLUE)
(45 length is (2:10); LP length is (2:16))
(S) (2:16) Motown 0782 and 6189 Anthology.
(S) (2:17) Motown 6125 Compact Command Performances.
(S) (2:16) Motown 5411 Greatest Hits.
(S) (2:16) Motown 5374 The Temptin' Temptations.
(M) (2:11) Motown 314530338 Emperors Of Soul.
(S) (2:16) Motown/Essex 374638525 Motown Legends - My Girl.
(M) (2:11) Motown 314530524 Anthology.
(S) (2:16) Motown 314530853 Greatest Hits. *(remastered edition)*

1965 MY GIRL
(the mono mix of this song is far superior to the stereo mixes which have problems with phase cancellation, thus wiping out portions of the background harmony)
(S) (2:42) Motown 6132 25 #1 Hits From 25 Years. *(noisy intro)*
(M) (2:55) Motown 6120 and 6062 O.S.T. The Big Chill. *(:14 longer than either the LP or 45)*
(E) (2:55) Motown 5452 A Collection Of 16 Big Hits Volume 5. *(:14 longer than either the 45 or LP)*
(S) (2:42) Motown 6137 20 Greatest Songs In Motown History. *(noisy intro)*
(S) (2:42) Motown 6159 The Good-Feeling Music Of The Big Chill Generation Volume 1.
(S) (2:43) Motown 6139 The Composer Series: Smokey Robinson.
(S) (2:42) Rhino 70651 Billboard's Top R&B Hits Of 1965.
(S) (2:42) Rhino 72006 Billboard's Top R&B Hits 1965-1969 Box Set.
(S) (2:41) Epic 48732 O.S.T. My Girl.
(S) (2:41) MCA 6340 O.S.T. Born On The Fourth Of July.
(S) (2:41) Motown 9017 and 5248 16 #1 Hits From The Early 60's.
(S) (2:42) Motown 9097 The Most Played Oldies On America's Jukeboxes.
(S) (2:42) Motown 5343 Every Great Motown Song: The First 25 Years Volume 1. *(most selections on this cd have noise on the fadeout)*
(S) (2:42) Motown 8034 and 8134 Every Great Motown Song: The First 25 Years Volumes 1 & 2. *(most selections on this cd have noise on the fadeout)*
(S) (2:41) Motown 0782 and 6189 Anthology.
(S) (2:43) Motown 6125 Compact Command Performances.
(S) (2:42) Motown 6204 and 5389 25th Anniversary.
(S) (2:42) Motown 9033 and 5315 Great Songs And Performances That Inspired The Motown 25th Anniversary TV Special.
(E) (2:55) Motown 5212 All The Million Sellers. *(:15 longer than either the 45 or LP)*
(S) (2:42) Motown 5411 Greatest Hits.
(S) (2:41) Motown 8060 and 8160 Meet The Temptations/Temptations Sing Smokey.
(S) (2:41) Motown 5205 Temptations Sing Smokey.
(S) (2:40) Original Sound 8859r Oldies But Goodies Vol. 9. *(remastered edition)*
(S) (2:40) Original Sound 2223 Oldies But Goodies Volumes 2,7,9,12 and 13 Box Set. *(Volumes 2, 7 and 12 of this box set use the "Waring - fds" noise reduction process)*
(S) (2:40) Original Sound 2500 Oldies But Goodies Volumes 1-15 Box Set. *(most volumes in this box set use the "Waring - fds" noise reduction process)*
(S) (2:41) Ripete 392183 Ocean Drive. *(truncated fade; noise on the introduction)*
(M) (2:54) Motown 6312 Hitsville USA. *(:14 longer than either the 45 or LP)*
(E) (2:55) Motown 5211 David Ruffin At His Best. *(:15 longer than either the 45 or LP)*

(S) (2:41) K-Tel 3065 Temptations/Four Tops.
(S) (2:41) Time-Life RHD-07 Rhythm & Blues - 1965.
(S) (2:41) Time-Life 2CLR-01 Classic Rock - 1965.
(E) (2:39) Time-Life SUD-03 Superhits - 1965.
(S) (2:41) Time-Life OPCD-4517 Tonight's The Night.
(S) (2:41) Epic 57871 O.S.T. My Girl 2. *(noisy intro)*
(M) (2:55) Motown 314530338 Emperors Of Soul. *(:15 longer fade than either the 45 or LP)*
(S) (2:41) Ripete 2183-RE Ocean Drive Volume 1.
(S) (2:42) Motown/Essex 374638525 Motown Legends - My Girl.
(S) (2:42) Polygram Special Markets 314520283 Motown Legends Volume 2. *(noisy intro)*
(M) (2:54) Motown 314530524 Anthology. *(:14 longer fade than either the 45 or LP)*
(M) (2:54) Rhino 71935 Billboard Top Pop Hits, 1965. *(:14 longer fade than either the 45 or LP)*
(M) (2:54) Thump 9947 Cruizin' To Motown. *(:14 longer fade than either the 45 or LP)*
(S) (2:41) LaserLight 12311 and 15936 The Wonder Years - First Love.
(S) (2:39) Time-Life AM1-10 AM Gold - 1965.
(S) (2:41) Time-Life R838-12 Solid Gold Soul - 1965.
(M) (2:54) Motown 314530562 The Ultimate Collection. *(:14 longer fade than either the 45 or LP)*
(M) (1:20) Motown 314530562 The Ultimate Collection. *(a cappella excerpt)*
(S) (2:41) Elektra 62093 O.S.T. A Smile Like Yours.
(S) (2:42) Motown 314530853 Greatest Hits. *(remastered edition)*
(S) (2:41) Motown 314530849 Motown 40 Forever.
(M) (2:54) Time-Life R857-20 The Heart Of Rock 'n' Roll 1965-1966. *(:14 longer fade than either the 45 or LP)*

1965 IT'S GROWING
(S) (2:55) Motown 5452 A Collection Of 16 Big Hits Volume 5.
(S) (2:56) Motown 0782 and 6189 Anthology.
(S) (2:56) Motown 5411 Greatest Hits.
(S) (2:55) Motown 8060 and 8160 Meet The Temptations/Temptations Sing Smokey.
(S) (2:55) Motown 5205 Temptations Sing Smokey.
(S) (2:55) Time-Life 2CLR-14 Classic Rock - 1965: Shakin' All Over.
(M) (2:56) Motown 314530338 Emperors Of Soul.
(S) (2:56) Motown/Essex 374638524 Motown Legends - Just My Imagination.
(M) (2:56) Motown 314530524 Anthology.
(S) (2:56) Motown 314530562 The Ultimate Collection.
(S) (2:55) Motown 314530853 Greatest Hits. *(remastered edition)*

1965 SINCE I LOST MY BABY
(E) (2:50) Motown 9105 and 5410 Motown Memories Volume 2.
(E) (2:50) Motown 0782 and 6189 Anthology.
(E) (2:51) Motown 6125 Compact Command Performances.
(E) (2:50) Motown 6204 and 5389 25th Anniversary. *(noisy fadeout)*
(E) (2:50) Motown 5411 Greatest Hits.
(E) (2:50) Motown 5374 The Temptin' Temptations.
(E) (2:50) K-Tel 3065 Temptations/Four Tops.
(M) (2:50) Time-Life 2CLR-23 Classic Rock - 1965: Blowin' Your Mind.
(E) (2:51) Right Stuff 28371 Slow Jams: The 60's Volume Two.
(M) (2:48) Motown 314530338 Emperors Of Soul.
(M) (2:48) Motown 314530524 Anthology.
(E) (2:50) Rebound 314520369 Soul Classics - Quiet Storm/The 60's.
(E) (2:50) Cypress 71334 O.S.T. Coupe De Ville.
(M) (2:48) Motown 314530562 The Ultimate Collection.
(S) (2:49) Motown 314530853 Greatest Hits. *(remastered edition)*

1965 MY BABY
(S) (3:00) Motown 5453 A Collection Of 16 Big Hits Volume 6.
(S) (3:00) Motown 0782 and 6189 Anthology.
(S) (3:00) Motown 5411 Greatest Hits.

TEMPTATIONS *(Continued)*

(S) (3:00) Motown 5374 The Temptin' Temptations.
(M) (2:56) Motown 314530338 Emperors Of Soul.
(S) (3:00) Motown/Essex 374638525 Motown Legends - My Girl.
(M) (2:56) Motown 314530524 Anthology.
(S) (2:58) Motown 314530853 Greatest Hits. *(remastered edition)*

1966 GET READY

(S) (2:37) Motown 6160 The Good-Feeling Music Of The Big Chill Generation Volume 2.
(S) (2:38) Motown 6139 The Composer Series: Smokey Robinson.
(S) (2:35) MCA 10063 Original Television Soundtrack "The Sounds Of Murphy Brown".
(S) (2:36) MCA 6467 O.S.T. Air America.
(S) (2:36) Motown 9072 Motown Dance Party Volume 2. *(all selections on this cd are segued together)*
(S) (2:38) Motown 9097 The Most Played Oldies On America's Jukeboxes.
(S) (2:37) Motown 9018 and 5249 16 #1 Hits From The Late 60's.
(S) (2:37) Motown 0782 and 6189 Anthology.
(S) (2:37) Motown 6204 and 5389 25th Anniversary.
(S) (2:38) Motown 9033 and 5315 Great Songs And Performances That Inspired The Motown 25th Anniversary TV Special.
(S) (2:37) Motown 5411 Greatest Hits.
(S) (2:37) Motown 5373 Gettin' Ready.
(S) (2:36) K-Tel 3065 Temptations/Four Tops.
(S) (2:36) Time-Life 2CLR-22 Classic Rock - 1966: Blowin' Your Mind.
(M) (2:36) Motown 314530338 Emperors Of Soul.
(S) (2:37) Polygram Special Markets 314520283 Motown Legends Volume 2.
(M) (2:35) Motown 314530524 Anthology.
(S) (2:38) Motown 314530522 Motown Year By Year - 1966.
(M) (2:35) Motown 314530562 The Ultimate Collection.
(S) (2:37) Motown 314530853 Greatest Hits. *(remastered edition)*

1966 AIN'T TOO PROUD TO BEG

(S) (2:31) Motown 6160 The Good-Feeling Music Of The Big Chill Generation Volume 2. *(noisy intro)*
(S) (2:31) Motown 6120 and 6062 O.S.T. The Big Chill.
(S) (2:32) Motown 5454 A Collection Of 16 Big Hits Volume 7.
(S) (2:32) Rhino 70652 Billboard's Top R&B Hits Of 1966.
(S) (2:32) Rhino 72006 Billboard's Top R&B Hits 1965-1969 Box Set.
(S) (2:31) Motown 9018 and 5249 16 #1 Hits From The Late 60's.
(S) (2:31) Motown 0782 and 6189 Anthology.
(S) (2:32) Motown 6125 Compact Command Performances.
(S) (2:31) Motown 6204 and 5389 25th Anniversary.
(S) (2:31) Motown 9033 and 5315 Great Songs And Performances That Inspired The Motown 25th Anniversary TV Special.
(S) (2:31) Motown 5212 All The Million Sellers.
(S) (2:31) Motown 5411 Greatest Hits.
(S) (2:31) Motown 5373 Gettin' Ready.
(S) (2:29) Motown 9071 Motown Dance Party Volume 1. *(all selections on this cd are segued together)*
(S) (2:31) Ripete 392183 Ocean Drive.
(M) (2:31) Motown 6312 Hitsville USA.
(S) (2:29) Motown 5211 David Ruffin At His Best.
(S) (2:30) Time-Life RHD-01 Rhythm & Blues - 1966.
(S) (2:31) Time-Life 2CLR-13 Classic Rock - 1966: Shakin' All Over.
(M) (2:31) Motown 314530338 Emperors Of Soul.
(M) (2:32) Rhino 71806 The R&B Box: Thirty Years Of Rhythm & Blues.
(S) (2:31) Polygram Special Markets 314520284 Motown Legends Volume 3.
(M) (2:31) Motown 314530524 Anthology.
(S) (2:30) Time-Life R838-01 Solid Gold Soul - 1966.

(M) (2:31) Motown 314530562 The Ultimate Collection.
(M) (2:31) Rebound 314520420 Soul Classics - Best Of The 60's.
(S) (2:31) Motown 314530853 Greatest Hits. *(remastered edition)*

1966 BEAUTY IS ONLY SKIN DEEP

(S) (2:21) Motown 6159 The Good-Feeling Music Of The Big Chill Generation Volume 1. *(noisy intro)*
(S) (2:20) Motown 5455 A Collection Of 16 Big Hits Volume 8.
(S) (2:21) Rhino 70652 Billboard's Top R&B Hits Of 1966.
(S) (2:21) Rhino 72006 Billboard's Top R&B Hits 1965-1969 Box Set.
(S) (2:21) Motown 0782 and 6189 Anthology.
(S) (2:21) Motown 5411 Greatest Hits.
(M) (2:21) Motown 6312 Hitsville USA.
(S) (2:19) Time-Life RHD-01 Rhythm & Blues - 1966.
(S) (2:21) Time-Life 2CLR-02 Classic Rock - 1966.
(S) (2:20) Time-Life SUD-17 Superhits - Mid 60's Classics.
(M) (2:20) Motown 314530338 Emperors Of Soul.
(S) (2:20) Motown/Essex 374638524 Motown Legends - Just My Imagination.
(S) (2:21) Polygram Special Markets 314520282 Motown Legends - Volume 1.
(M) (2:20) Motown 314530524 Anthology.
(S) (2:21) Motown 314530522 Motown Year By Year - 1966.
(S) (2:20) Time-Life AM1-16 AM Gold - Mid '60s Classics.
(S) (2:19) Time-Life R838-01 Solid Gold Soul - 1966.
(S) (2:21) Motown 314530853 Greatest Hits. *(remastered edition)*
(S) (2:20) Polygram Special Markets 314520454 Soul Hits Of The 60's.

1966 (I KNOW) I'M LOSING YOU

(S) (2:25) Motown 6161 The Good-Feeling Music Of The Big Chill Generation Volume 3.
(S) (2:25) Motown 5455 A Collection Of 16 Big Hits Volume 8.
(S) (2:26) Motown 9018 and 5249 16 #1 Hits From The Late 60's.
(S) (2:25) Motown 0782 and 6189 Anthology.
(S) (2:26) Motown 6125 Compact Command Performances.
(S) (2:26) Motown 9033 and 5315 Great Songs And Performances That Inspired The Motown 25th Anniversary TV Special.
(S) (2:24) Motown 5412 Greatest Hits Volume 2.
(S) (2:24) Motown 8137 and 8037 Live At The Copa/With A Lot O' Soul.
(S) (2:25) Motown 5299 With A Lot O' Soul.
(M) (2:25) Motown 6312 Hitsville USA.
(S) (2:23) Motown 5211 David Ruffin At His Best.
(S) (2:25) Time-Life 2CLR-02 Classic Rock - 1966.
(M) (2:26) Motown 314530338 Emperors Of Soul.
(M) (2:26) Motown/Essex 374638525 Motown Legends - My Girl.
(M) (2:25) Motown 314530524 Anthology.
(S) (2:26) Polygram Special Markets 314520292 Motown Legends - Volume 4.
(M) (2:25) Motown 314530562 The Ultimate Collection.
(M) (2:26) Rhino 72815 Beg, Scream & Shout! The Big Ol' Box Of '60s Soul.
(S) (2:26) Motown 314530854 Greatest Hits Volume 2. *(remastered edition)*

1967 ALL I NEED
(actual 45 time is (3:14) not (2:59) as stated on the record label; the LP time is (3:07) not (2:59) as stated on the record label)

(S) (3:05) Motown 5456 A Collection Of 16 Big Hits Volume 9. *(LP length)*
(S) (3:05) Motown 0782 and 6189 Anthology. *(LP length)*
(S) (3:06) Motown 8137 and 8037 Live At The Copa/With A Lot O' Soul. *(LP length)*
(S) (3:07) Motown 5299 With A Lot O' Soul. *(LP length)*
(M) (3:16) Motown 314530338 Emperors Of Soul. *(45 length)*
(M) (3:15) Motown 314530524 Anthology. *(45 length)*
(M) (3:15) Motown 314530562 The Ultimate Collection. *(45 length)*

**1967 YOU'RE MY EVERYTHING
(actual 45 time is (3:09) not (2:59) as stated on the
record label)**

(S) (2:57) Motown 0782 and 6189 Anthology. *(LP length)*
(S) (2:57) Motown 6125 Compact Command Performances. *(LP length)*
(S) (2:57) Motown 5412 Greatest Hits Volume 2. *(LP length)*
(S) (2:56) Motown 8137 and 8037 Live At The Copa/With A Lot O' Soul. *(LP length)*
(S) (2:56) Motown 5299 With A Lot O' Soul. *(LP length)*
(S) (2:56) Time-Life RHD-10 Rhythm & Blues - 1967. *(LP length)*
(S) (2:56) Time-Life 2CLR-10 Classic Rock - 1967: The Beat Goes On. *(LP length)*
(S) (2:57) Time-Life SUD-14 Superhits - The Late 60's. *(LP length)*
(M) (3:09) Motown 314530338 Emperors Of Soul. *(45 length)*
(M) (3:09) Motown 314530524 Anthology. *(45 length)*
(S) (2:56) Time-Life AM1-14 AM Gold - The Late '60s. *(LP length)*
(S) (2:56) Time-Life R838-02 Solid Gold Soul - 1967. *(LP length)*
(M) (3:11) Motown 314530562 The Ultimate Collection. *(45 length; with countoff)*
(S) (2:55) Motown 314530854 Greatest Hits Volume 2. *(remastered edition; LP length)*

1967 (LONELINESS MADE ME REALIZE) IT'S YOU THAT I NEED

(S) (2:34) Motown 5456 A Collection Of 16 Big Hits Volume 9.
(S) (2:35) Motown 0782 and 6189 Anthology.
(S) (2:34) Motown 5412 Greatest Hits Volume 2.
(S) (2:33) Motown 8137 and 8037 Live At The Copa/With A Lot O' Soul.
(S) (2:33) Motown 5299 With A Lot O' Soul.
(M) (2:35) Motown 314530338 Emperors Of Soul.
(M) (2:35) Motown 314530524 Anthology.
(S) (2:34) Motown 314530854 Greatest Hits Volume 2. *(remastered edition)*

1968 I WISH IT WOULD RAIN

(S) (2:45) Motown 6160 The Good-Feeling Music Of The Big Chill Generation Volume 2.
(S) (2:45) Motown 5457 A Collection Of 16 Big Hits Volume 10.
(S) (2:45) Rhino 70654 Billboard's Top R&B Hits Of 1968.
(S) (2:45) Rhino 72006 Billboard's Top R&B Hits 1965-1969 Box Set.
(S) (2:45) Motown 9018 and 5249 16 #1 Hits From The Late 60's.
(S) (2:44) Motown 0782 and 6189 Anthology.
(S) (2:47) Motown 6125 Compact Command Performances.
(S) (2:47) Motown 9033 and 5315 Great Songs And Performances That Inspired The Motown 25th Anniversary TV Special.
(S) (2:48) Motown 5212 All The Million Sellers.
(S) (2:45) Motown 5412 Greatest Hits Volume 2.
(S) (2:41) Motown 5276 I Wish It Would Rain.
(M) (2:50) Motown 6312 Hitsville USA.
(S) (2:46) Motown 5211 David Ruffin At His Best.
(S) (2:44) Motown/Essex 374638511 Motown Legends - Cloud Nine.
(S) (2:45) Time-Life RHD-04 Rhythm & Blues - 1968.
(S) (2:44) Time-Life 2CLR-11 Classic Rock - 1968: The Beat Goes On.
(S) (2:44) Time-Life SUD-02 Superhits - 1968.
(S) (2:45) Time-Life OPCD-4517 Tonight's The Night.
(S) (2:50) Varese Sarabande 5534 Rhythm Of The Rain.
(M) (2:51) Motown 314530338 Emperors Of Soul.
(S) (2:45) Polygram Special Markets 314520284 Motown Legends Volume 3.
(S) (2:45) Polygram Special Markets 314520300 Motown Legends - Guy Groups.
(M) (2:50) Motown 314530524 Anthology.
(S) (2:46) Motown 314530507 Motown Year By Year 1968.
(S) (2:45) Thump 9947 Cruizin' To Motown.
(S) (2:44) Time-Life AM1-04 AM Gold - 1968.
(S) (2:44) Time-Life R838-03 Solid Gold Soul - 1968.

(S) (2:45) Time-Life R834-07 Body Talk - Hearts In Motion.
(M) (2:50) Motown 314530562 The Ultimate Collection.
(S) (2:46) Motown 314530854 Greatest Hits Volume 2. *(remastered edition)*
(S) (2:45) Time-Life R857-22 The Heart Of Rock 'n' Roll 1967-1969.

**1968 I COULD NEVER LOVE ANOTHER (AFTER LOVING YOU)
(actual 45 time is (3:34) not (3:15) as stated on the
record label)**

(S) (3:32) Motown 9109 and 5413 Motown Memories Volume 3.
(S) (3:32) Motown 6161 The Good-Time Feeling Of The Big Chill Generation Volume 3.
(S) (3:32) Motown 0782 and 6189 Anthology.
(S) (3:33) Motown 6125 Compact Command Performances.
(S) (3:29) Motown 6192 You Can't Hurry Love: All The Great Love Songs Of The Past 25 Years.
(S) (3:32) Motown 9033 and 5315 Great Songs And Performances That Inspired The Motown 25th Anniversary TV Special.
(S) (3:32) Motown 5412 Greatest Hits Volume 2.
(S) (3:34) Motown 5276 I Wish It Would Rain.
(S) (3:32) K-Tel 3065 Temptations/Four Tops.
(M) (3:36) Motown 314530338 Emperors Of Soul.
(M) (3:35) Motown 314530524 Anthology.
(S) (3:32) Polygram Special Markets 314520293 Motown Legends - Volume 5.
(S) (3:31) Motown 314530854 Greatest Hits Volume 2. *(remastered edition)*

1968 PLEASE RETURN YOUR LOVE TO ME

(S) (2:19) Motown 9105 and 5410 Motown Memories Volume 2.
(S) (2:21) Motown 0782 and 6189 Anthology.
(S) (2:21) Motown 5412 Greatest Hits Volume 2.
(S) (2:22) Motown 5276 I Wish It Would Rain.
(M) (2:21) Motown 314530338 Emperors Of Soul.
(M) (2:20) Motown 314530524 Anthology.
(S) (2:21) Motown 314530854 Greatest Hits Volume 2. *(remastered edition)*

**1969 CLOUD NINE
(actual 45 time is (3:33) not (3:15) as stated on the
record label)**

(S) (3:30) Motown 6110 Motown Grammy R&B Performances Of The 60's & 70's.
(S) (3:29) Rhino 70654 Billboard's Top R&B Hits Of 1968.
(S) (3:29) Rhino 72006 Billboard's Top R&B Hits 1965-1969 Box Set.
(S) (3:29) Motown 9021 and 5309 25 Years Of Grammy Greats.
(S) (3:29) Motown 0782 and 6189 Anthology.
(S) (3:30) Motown 6125 Compact Command Performances.
(S) (4:15) Motown 6204 and 5389 25th Anniversary. *(live)*
(S) (3:29) Motown 9033 and 5315 Great Songs And Performances That Inspired The Motown 25th Anniversary TV Special.
(S) (3:28) Motown 5212 All The Million Sellers.
(S) (3:29) Motown 5412 Greatest Hits Volume 2.
(S) (3:29) Motown 9096 and 5159 Cloud Nine.
(S) (3:29) Motown 8016 and 8116 Cloud Nine/Puzzle People.
(M) (3:35) Motown 6312 Hitsville USA.
(S) (3:29) Motown/Essex 374638511 Motown Legends - Cloud Nine.
(S) (3:29) Time-Life 2CLR-04 Classic Rock - 1968.
(M) (3:34) Motown 314530338 Emperors Of Soul.
(S) (3:29) Polygram Special Markets 314520300 Motown Legends - Guy Groups.
(S) (3:27) Motown 314530524 Anthology.
(S) (3:28) Motown 314530507 Motown Year By Year 1968.
(M) (3:34) Motown 314530478 O.S.T. The Walking Dead.
(M) (3:34) Motown 314530562 The Ultimate Collection.
(S) (3:27) Motown 314530854 Greatest Hits Volume 2. *(remastered edition)*

**released as by DIANA ROSS and THE SUPREMES &
THE TEMPTATIONS:**
1969 I'M GONNA MAKE YOU LOVE ME

(S) (3:05) Motown 6160 The Good-Feeling Music Of The Big Chill Generation Volume 2.

(S) (3:05) Motown 9031 and 5214 Diana's Duets.

(S) (3:05) Motown 6198 and 0794 Supremes Anthology.

(S) (3:05) Motown 6193 Diana Ross & The Supremes 25th Anniversary.

(S) (3:05) Motown 5139 Diana Ross And The Supremes Join The Temptations.

(S) (3:05) Motown 8038 and 8138 Diana Ross And The Supremes Join The Temptations/Diana Ross & The Supremes & The Temptations Together.

(S) (3:06) Motown 6073 Supremes Compact Command Performances.

(S) (3:05) Motown 0782 and 6189 Temptations Anthology.

(S) (3:05) Motown 6204 and 5389 Temptations 25th Anniversary.

(S) (2:56) Motown 6357 Diana Ross Forever: Musical Memories.

(S) (3:05) Time-Life 2CLR-06 Classic Rock - 1969.

(S) (3:05) Time-Life SUD-07 Superhits - 1969.

(S) (3:05) Motown 314530338 Temptations - Emperors Of Soul.

(S) (3:05) Polygram Special Markets 314520284 Motown Legends Volume 3.

(S) (3:05) Motown 314530524 Temptations - Anthology.

(S) (3:05) Motown 314530507 Motown Year By Year 1968.

(S) (3:06) Polygram Special Markets 314520031 Motown Legends - Duets.

(S) (3:05) Columbia 67380 O.S.T. Now And Then.

(S) (3:05) Time-Life AM1-01 AM Gold - 1969.

(S) (3:05) Rebound 314520420 Soul Classics - Best Of The 60's.

(M) (3:05) Motown 314530827 The Ultimate Collection.

released as by THE TEMPTATIONS:
1969 RUN AWAY CHILD, RUNNING WILD
(actual 45 time is (4:46) not (4:30) as stated on the record label)

(S) (4:52) Motown 6161 The Good-Feeling Music Of The Big Chill Generation Volume 3. *(45 version)*

(S) (4:36) Motown 0782 and 6189 Anthology. *(45 version but faded :10 early)*

(S) (4:52) Motown 6125 Compact Command Performances. *(45 version)*

(S) (4:52) Motown 9033 and 5315 Great Songs And Performances That Inspired The Motown 25th Anniversary TV Special. *(45 version)*

(S) (4:49) Motown 5212 All The Million Sellers. *(45 version)*

(S) (4:52) Motown 5412 Greatest Hits Volume 2. *(45 version)*

(S) (9:33) Motown 9096 and 5159 Cloud Nine. *(LP version)*

(S) (4:36) Motown 8016 and 8116 Cloud Nine/Puzzle People. *(45 version but faded :10 early)*

(S) (4:48) Time-Life 2CLR-12 Classic Rock - 1969: The Beat Goes On. *(45 version)*

(M) (4:45) Motown 314530338 Emperors Of Soul. *(45 version)*

(S) (4:47) Motown 314530524 Anthology. *(45 version)*

(S) (4:41) Motown 314530525 Motown Year By Year - 1969. *(45 version)*

(S) (4:52) Polygram Special Markets 314520293 Motown Legends - Volume 5. *(45 version)*

(S) (4:45) Motown 314530854 Greatest Hits Volume 2. *(remastered edition; 45 version)*

released as by DIANA ROSS and THE SUPREMES &
THE TEMPTATIONS:
1969 I'LL TRY SOMETHING NEW

(S) (2:19) Motown 9031 and 5214 Diana's Duets.

(S) (2:19) Motown 5313 Diana Ross & The Supremes: Great Songs And Performances That Inspired The Motown 25th Anniversary TV Special.

(S) (2:17) Motown 6198 and 0794 Supremes - Anthology.

(S) (2:19) Motown 5139 Diana Ross And The Supremes Join The Temptations.

(S) (2:19) Motown 8038 and 8138 Diana Ross And The Supremes Join The Temptations/Diana Ross & The Supremes & The Temptations Together.

(S) (2:19) Motown 6073 Supremes - Compact Command Performances.

(M) (2:24) Motown 314530511 Diana Ross & The Supremes - Anthology.

(M) (2:22) Motown 314530338 Temptations - Emperors Of Soul.

(M) (2:23) Motown 314530827 The Ultimate Collection.

released as by THE TEMPTATIONS:
1969 DON'T LET THE JONESES GET YOU DOWN
(actual 45 time is (4:37) not (4:15) as stated on the record label)

(S) (4:43) Motown 0782 and 6189 Anthology.

(S) (4:43) Motown 5412 Greatest Hits Volume 2.

(S) (4:43) Motown 8016 and 8116 Cloud Nine/Puzzle People.

(S) (4:43) Motown 5172 Puzzle People.

(M) (4:38) Motown 314530338 Emperors Of Soul.

(S) (4:43) Motown 314530524 Anthology.

(S) (4:41) Motown 314530854 Greatest Hits Volume 2. *(remastered edition)*

1969 I CAN'T GET TO YOU

(S) (2:52) Rhino 70630 Billboard's Top Rock & Roll Hits Of 1969.

(S) (2:52) Rhino 72005 Billboard's Top Rock & Roll Hits 1968-1972 Box Set.

(S) (2:51) Motown 6161 The Good-Feeling Music Of The Big Chill Generation Volume 3.

(S) (2:50) Motown 9072 Motown Dance Party Volume 2. *(all selections on this cd are segued together)*

(S) (2:51) Motown 9018 and 5249 16 #1 Hits From The Late 60's.

(S) (2:52) Motown 9060 Motown's Biggest Pop Hits.

(S) (2:51) Motown 0782 and 6189 Anthology.

(S) (2:52) Motown 6125 Compact Command Performances.

(S) (2:12) Motown 6204 and 5389 25th Anniversary. *(live)*

(S) (2:51) Motown 9033 and 5315 Great Songs And Performances That Inspired The Motown 25th Anniversary TV Special.

(S) (2:51) Motown 5212 All The Million Sellers.

(S) (2:51) Motown 5412 Greatest Hits Volume 2.

(S) (2:51) Motown 8016 and 8116 Cloud Nine/Puzzle People.

(S) (2:51) Motown 5172 Puzzle People.

(M) (2:53) Motown 6312 Hitsville USA.

(S) (2:51) Time-Life RHD-13 Rhythm & Blues - 1969.

(S) (2:51) Time-Life 2CLR-06 Classic Rock - 1969.

(M) (2:52) Motown 314530338 Emperors Of Soul.

(M) (2:53) Rebound 314520269 Class Reunion 1969.

(S) (2:52) Motown 314530524 Anthology.

(S) (2:50) Motown 314530525 Motown Year By Year - 1969.

(S) (2:51) Polygram Special Markets 314520292 Motown Legends - Volume 4.

(S) (2:51) Time-Life R838-04 Solid Gold Soul - 1969.

(M) (2:51) Motown 314530562 The Ultimate Collection.

(S) (2:51) Motown 314530854 Greatest Hits Volume 2. *(remastered edition)*

released as by DIANA ROSS and THE SUPREMES &
THE TEMPTATIONS:
1969 THE WEIGHT

(S) (3:00) Motown 8038 and 8138 Diana Ross & The Supremes Join The Temptations/Diana Ross & The Supremes & The Temptations Together.

(S) (3:00) Motown 5436 Diana Ross & The Supremes & The Temptations Together.

released as by THE TEMPTATIONS:
1970 PSYCHEDELIC SHACK

(S) (3:50) Motown 0782 and 6189 Anthology. *(LP version)*

(S) (3:50) Motown 6125 Compact Command Performances. *(LP version)*

(E) (3:48) Motown 5212 All The Million Sellers. *(45 version)*

(S) (3:50) Motown 5412 Greatest Hits Volume 2. *(LP version)*

(S) (3:50) Motown 8022 and 8122 All Directions/Psychedelic Shack. *(LP version)*

(S) (3:49) Motown 5164 Psychedelic Shack. *(LP version)*

(M) (4:15) Motown 314530338 Emperors Of Soul. *(45 version with the :22 LP introduction, which is stereo)*

(S) (3:50) Motown 314530524 Anthology. *(LP version)*
(S) (3:51) Motown 314530854 Greatest Hits Volume 2.
(remastered edition; LP version)

1970 BALL OF CONFUSION (THAT'S WHAT THE WORLD IS TODAY)
(S) (4:04) Rhino 70734 Songs Of Protest.
(S) (4:04) Rhino 70658 Billboard's Top R&B Hits Of 1970.
(S) (4:04) Motown 0782 and 6189 Anthology.
(S) (4:04) Motown 6125 Compact Command Performances.
(S) (4:04) Motown 9033 and 5315 Great Songs And Performances That Inspired The Motown 25th Anniversary TV Special.
(S) (4:04) Motown 5212 All The Million Sellers.
(S) (4:03) Motown 5412 Greatest Hits Volume 2.
(M) (4:02) Motown 6312 Hitsville USA.
(S) (4:04) Time-Life RHD-18 Rhythm & Blues - 1970.
(S) (4:03) Time-Life SOD-11 Sounds Of The Seventies - 1970: Take Two.
(M) (4:01) Motown 314530338 Emperors Of Soul.
(S) (4:05) Polygram Special Markets 314520300 Motown Legends - Guy Groups.
(S) (4:04) Motown 314530524 Anthology.
(S) (4:03) Motown 314530528 Motown Year By Year - 1970.
(S) (4:04) Time-Life R838-05 Solid Gold Soul - 1970.
(M) (4:00) Motown 314530562 The Ultimate Collection.
(S) (4:03) Motown 314530854 Greatest Hits Volume 2.
(remastered edition)

1970 UNGENA ZA ULIMWENGU (UNITE THE WORLD) (actual 45 time is (4:14) not (3:45) as stated on the record label)
(S) (4:28) Motown 5474 Sky's The Limit. *(LP length)*
(M) (4:11) Rhino 71180 Hum Along And Dance: More Of The Best. *(45 length)*
(M) (4:11) Motown 314530338 Emperors Of Soul. *(45 length)*

1971 JUST MY IMAGINATION (RUNNING AWAY WITH ME)
(S) (3:48) Motown 6132 25 #1 Hits From 25 Years.
(S) (3:47) Motown 6137 20 Greatest Songs In Motown History.
(S) (3:52) Rhino 70659 Billboard's Top R&B Hits Of 1971.
(S) (3:46) Motown 5344 Every Great Motown Song: The First 25 Years Volume 2. *(most selections on this cd have noise on the fadeout)*
(S) (3:46) Motown 5275 12 #1 Hits From The 70's.
(S) (3:47) Motown 8034 and 8134 Every Great Motown Song: The First 25 Years Volumes 1 & 2. *(most selections on this cd have noise on the fadeout)*
(S) (3:46) Motown 9060 Motown's Biggest Pop Hits. *(buzz noticeable on fadeout)*
(S) (3:46) Motown 0782 and 6189 Anthology.
(S) (3:47) Motown 6125 Compact Command Performances.
(S) (3:46) Motown 6204 and 5389 25th Anniversary.
(S) (3:45) Motown 5212 All The Million Sellers.
(S) (3:46) Motown 5474 Sky's The Limit.
(M) (3:51) Motown 6312 Hitsville USA.
(S) (3:45) Razor & Tie 22047 Sweet 70's Soul.
(S) (3:44) Time-Life RHD-09 Rhythm & Blues - 1971.
(S) (3:44) Time-Life SUD-10 Superhits - 1971.
(S) (3:46) Time-Life SOD-02 Sounds Of The Seventies - 1971.
(S) (3:46) Thump 7030 Low Rider Oldies Volume III.
(S) (3:51) Motown 314530338 Emperors Of Soul.
(M) (3:50) Motown/Essex 374638524 Motown Legends - Just My Imagination.
(S) (3:46) Motown 314530524 Anthology.
(M) (3:51) Motown 314530569 Motown Milestones - Motown Love Songs.
(S) (3:46) Rebound 314520364 Class Reunion '71.
(M) (3:51) Rebound 314520367 Soul Classics - Quiet Storm/The 70's.
(M) (3:51) Capitol 35818 O.S.T. Dead Presidents Volume II.
(S) (3:45) Time-Life R103-18 Great Love Songs Of The '70s & '80s.
(S) (3:43) Time-Life AM1-06 AM Gold - 1971.
(S) (3:44) Time-Life R838-06 Solid Gold Soul - 1971.
(S) (3:46) Time-Life R834-04 Body Talk - Together Forever.

(M) (3:50) Motown 314530562 The Ultimate Collection.
(S) (3:46) Motown 314530849 Motown 40 Forever.

1971 SUPERSTAR (REMEMBER HOW YOU GOT WHERE YOU ARE)
(S) (2:50) Motown 0782 and 6189 Anthology.
(S) (2:51) Motown 6125 Compact Command Performances.
(S) (2:52) Motown 5480 Solid Rock.
(S) (2:53) Motown 314530338 Emperors Of Soul.
(S) (2:53) Motown 314530524 Anthology.

1972 TAKE A LOOK AROUND (actual 45 time is (3:10) not (2:59) as stated on the record label)
(S) (2:42) Motown 5480 Solid Rock. *(LP version)*
(M) (3:08) Rhino 71180 Hum Along And Dance: More Of The Best. *(45 version)*
(S) (3:09) Motown 314530338 Emperors Of Soul. *(45 version)*

1972 PAPA WAS A ROLLIN' STONE
(M) (6:52) Rhino 70633 Billboard's Top Rock & Roll Hits Of 1972. *(45 version)*
(M) (6:52) Rhino 72005 Billboard's Top Rock & Roll Hits 1968-1972 Box Set. *(45 version)*
(E) (6:54) Motown 6110 Motown Grammy R&B Performances Of The 60's & 70's. *(45 version)*
(E) (6:53) Motown 6132 25 #1 Hits From 25 Years. *(45 version)*
(E) (6:52) Motown 9021 and 5309 25 Years Of Grammy Greats. *(45 version)*
(E) (6:52) Motown 0937 20/20 Twenty No. 1 Hits From Twenty Years At Motown. *(45 version)*
(E) (6:51) Motown 0782 and 6189 Anthology. *(45 version)*
(E) (6:53) Motown 6125 Compact Command Performances. *(tracks into next selection; 45 version)*
(S) (7:23) Motown 6204 and 5389 25th Anniversary. *(live)*
(E) (6:54) Motown 9033 and 5315 Great Songs And Performances That Inspired The Motown 25th Anniversary TV Special. *(45 version)*
(E) (6:55) Motown 5212 All The Million Sellers. *(45 version)*
(S) (11:43) Motown 8022 and 8122 All Directions/Psychedelic Shack. *(LP version)*
(S) (11:44) Motown 5172 All Directions. *(LP version)*
(M) (6:56) Motown 6358 Hitsville USA Volume Two. *(45 version)*
(S) (6:56) Time-Life SOD-13 Sounds Of The Seventies - 1972: Take Two. *(45 version)*
(S) (6:57) Motown 314530338 Emperors Of Soul. *(45 version)*
(S) (6:57) Motown 314530524 Anthology. *(45 version)*
(S) (3:41) Motown 314530557 Motown Year By Year - 1987. *(remix)*
(S) (6:57) MCA 11329 Soul Train 25th Anniversary Box Set. *(45 version)*
(S) (6:56) Motown 314530562 The Ultimate Collection. *(45 version)*
(M) (6:54) Rebound 314520447 Soul Classics - Best Of The 70's. *(45 version)*
(S) (6:40) Chronicles 314555140 Dance Funk. *(all selections on this cd are segued together)*
(S) (6:56) Motown 314530849 Motown 40 Forever. *(45 version)*
(M) (6:57) Rhino 72943 VH1 8-Track Flashback: Classic '70s Soul. *(45 version)*

1973 MASTERPIECE (actual 45 time is (4:26) not (5:30) as stated on the record label)
(S) (4:22) Rhino 70661 Billboard's Top R&B Hits Of 1973. *(45 version)*
(S) (4:19) Motown 0782 and 6189 Anthology. *(45 version)*
(S) (13:48) Motown 5144 Masterpiece. *(LP version)*
(S) (13:35) Motown 8035 and 8135 A Song For You/Masterpiece. *(:13 shorter than the LP version)*
(S) (4:20) Motown 314530338 Emperors Of Soul. *(45 version)*
(S) (4:20) Motown 314530524 Anthology. *(45 version)*
(S) (4:21) Motown 314530510 Motown Year By Year 1973. *(45 version)*

TEMPTATIONS *(Continued)*

1973 THE PLASTIC MAN
(dj copies of this 45 ran (3:38) and (4:45);
commercial copies were all (4:45))
- (S) (5:52) Motown 5144 Masterpiece. *(LP version)*
- (S) (3:23) Motown 8035 and 8135 A Song For You/Masterpiece. *(this is the dj 45 edit faded :15 early)*
- (S) (3:36) Rhino 71180 Hum Along And Dance: More Of The Best. *(this is the dj 45 edit)*
- (S) (4:14) Motown 314530338 Emperors Of Soul. *(neither the 45 or LP version)*

1973 HEY GIRL (I LIKE YOUR STYLE)
- (S) (2:38) Motown 6125 Compact Command Performances. *(this is not "HEY GIRL (I LIKE YOUR STYLE)" as the jacket indicates but an earlier song simply titled "HEY GIRL")*
- (S) (3:05) Motown 6204 and 5389 25th Anniversary. *(this is not "HEY GIRL (I LIKE YOUR STYLE)" as the jacket indicates but an earlier song simply titled "HEY GIRL")*
- (S) (4:35) Motown 5144 Masterpiece. *(LP version)*
- (S) (4:37) Motown 9104 and 5409 Motown Memories Volume 1. *(LP version)*
- (S) (3:19) Motown 8035 and 8135 A Song For You/Masterpiece. *(45 version)*
- (S) (4:36) Motown 314530338 Emperors Of Soul. *(LP version)*
- (S) (3:27) Motown 314530524 Anthology. *(45 version)*
- (S) (4:36) Motown 314530573 Baddest Love Jams Volume 2 - Fire And Desire. *(LP version)*

1974 LET YOUR HAIR DOWN
- (S) (2:39) Motown 314530338 Emperors Of Soul.
- (S) (2:37) Motown 314530524 Anthology.

1975 SHAKEY GROUND
- (S) (3:59) Motown 5272 A Song For You. *(LP version)*
- (S) (3:15) Motown 8035 and 8135 A Song For You/Masterpiece. *(45 version)*
- (S) (3:15) Motown 0782 and 6189 Anthology. *(45 version)*
- (S) (3:18) Rhino 71432 In Yo Face! History Of Funk Volume 2. *(45 version)*
- (S) (4:01) Motown 314530338 Emperors Of Soul. *(LP version)*
- (S) (4:01) Motown 314530524 Anthology. *(LP version)*
- (S) (4:00) Motown 314530531 Motown Year By Year - 1975. *(LP version)*
- (S) (3:59) Atlantic 82865 O.S.T. Feeling Minnesota. *(LP version)*
- (S) (4:00) Motown 314530562 The Ultimate Collection. *(LP version)*

10cc

1975 I'M NOT IN LOVE
(actual 45 time is (3:46) not (3:40) as stated on the record label)
- (S) (3:58) Rhino 70761 Super Hits Of The 70's Volume 14. *(:12 longer than the 45 version)*
- (S) (6:00) Mercury 830776 The Original Soundtrack. *(LP version)*
- (S) (6:00) Polydor 314515913 Classic Rock Box. *(LP version)*
- (S) (6:03) Mercury 800562 Greatest Hits 1972-1978. *(LP version)*
- (S) (3:43) Razor & Tie 4543 The '70s Preservation Society Presents: Easy '70s. *(45 version)*
- (S) (3:46) Time-Life SOD-16 Sounds Of The Seventies - 1975: Take Two. *(45 version)*
- (S) (6:03) Rebound 314520317 Class Reunion 1975. *(LP version)*
- (S) (3:44) Time-Life R138-18 Body Talk. *(45 version)*
- (S) (6:02) Special Music 5041 Great Britons! Volume Three. *(LP version)*
- (S) (3:43) Eclipse Music Group 64894 Rock 'n Roll Relix 1974-1975. *(45 version)*
- (S) (3:43) Eclipse Music Group 64897 Rock 'n Roll Relix 1970-1979. *(45 version)*
- (S) (3:44) Time-Life AM1-22 AM Gold - 1975. *(45 version)*

- (S) (3:56) Time-Life R834-07 Body Talk - Hearts In Motion. *(:10 longer than the 45 version)*
- (S) (6:03) Milan 35788 O.S.T. Hotel De Love. *(LP version)*
- (S) (6:02) Mercury 314536007 Very Best Of. *(LP version)*
- (S) (5:57) Polygram TV 314555610 The One And Only Love Album. *(LP version)*

1977 THE THINGS WE DO FOR LOVE
- (S) (3:29) Mercury 836948 Deceptive Bends.
- (S) (3:28) Rhino 71199 Super Hits Of The 70's Volume 19.
- (S) (3:19) Mercury 800562 Greatest Hits 1972-1978.
- (S) (3:30) Time-Life SOD-05 Sounds Of The Seventies - 1977.
- (S) (3:29) Rebound 314520437 Classic Rock - 70's.
- (S) (3:28) Time-Life AM1-24 AM Gold - 1977.
- (S) (3:29) Mercury 314536007 Very Best Of.
- (S) (3:29) Simitar 55512 The Number One's: Lovin' Feelings.
- (S) (3:28) Priority 53139 The Best Of 70's: Rock Chart Toppers.

10,000 MANIACS
1994 BECAUSE THE NIGHT
- (S) (3:43) Elektra 61569 MTV Unplugged.
1997 MORE THAN THIS
- (S) (4:25) Geffen 25009 Love Among The Ruins.

TEN YEARS AFTER
1971 I'D LOVE TO CHANGE THE WORLD
- (S) (3:42) DCC Compact Classics 045 Golden Age Of Underground Radio. *(LP version)*
- (S) (3:41) Priority 7942 Hard Rockin' 70's. *(LP version)*
- (S) (3:43) Rhino 70272 Metal Age: The Roots Of Metal. *(LP version)*
- (S) (3:43) Rhino 71196 Super Hits Of The 70's Volume 16. *(LP version)*
- (S) (3:42) Chrysalis 21857 Essential Ten Years After Collection. *(LP version)*
- (S) (3:42) Time-Life SOD-22 Sounds Of The Seventies - Seventies Top Forty. *(LP version)*
- (S) (3:42) Time-Life R921-38 Get Together. *(LP version)*
- (S) (3:42) Time-Life R105-24 Guitar Rock Monsters. *(LP version)*
- (S) (3:42) Time-Life R968-06 Guitar Rock 1970-1971. *(LP version)*
- (S) (3:42) TVT 7010 O.S.T. Last Supper. *(LP version)*
- (S) (3:42) K-Tel 3985 70s Heavy Hitters: Arena Rockers 1970-74. *(LP version)*

ROBERT TEPPER
1986 NO EASY WAY OUT
- (S) (4:20) Scotti Brothers 40203 and 75420 O.S.T. Rocky IV.
- (S) (4:18) Scotti Brothers 5201 The Rocky Story.
- (S) (4:21) Scotti Brothers 40128 No Easy Way Out.

TONY TERRY
1991 WITH YOU
- (S) (5:04) Epic 45015 Tony Terry.

TESLA
1990 LOVE SONG
- (S) (5:21) Geffen 24224 The Great Radio Controversy. *(LP version)*
- (S) (5:21) Geffen 24833 Time's Makin' Changes: Best Of. *(LP version)*
- (S) (5:20) Rhino 72579 Feel Like Makin' Love - Romantic Power Ballads. *(LP version)*
1991 SIGNS
- (S) (3:14) Geffen 24311 Five Man Acoustical Jam. *(LP version lyrics)*
- (S) (3:13) Geffen 24833 Time's Makin' Changes: Best Of. *(LP version lyrics)*

JOE TEX
1965 HOLD WHAT YOU'VE GOT
- (M) (3:04) Atlantic 81297 Atlantic Rhythm & Blues Volume 5.
- (M) (3:04) Atlantic 82305 Atlantic Rhythm And Blues 1947-1974 Box Set.

(M) (3:07) Rhino 70191 Best Of.

(M) (3:07) Curb 77520 Greatest Hits.

(M) (3:07) Time-Life RHD-07 Rhythm & Blues - 1965.

(M) (3:02) Time-Life 2CLR-08 Classic Rock - 1965: The Beat Goes On.

(M) (3:07) Collectables 5451 Golden Classics.

(M) (3:07) Rhino 71806 The R&B Box: Thirty Years Of Rhythm & Blues.

(M) (3:07) K-Tel 3518 Sweet Soul Music.

(M) (3:07) Rhino 72565 Very Best Of.

(M) (3:08) Ripete 2223 Soul Patrol Vol. 5.

(M) (3:08) Rhino 72619 Smooth Grooves: The '60s Volume 2 Mid '60s.

(M) (3:07) Time-Life R838-12 Solid Gold Soul - 1965.

(M) (3:04) K-Tel 4014 His Best.

(M) (3:05) Rhino 72963 Ultimate '60s Soul Smashes.

1965 I WANT TO (DO EVERYTHING FOR YOU)

(M) (2:08) Atlantic 82305 Atlantic Rhythm And Blues 1947-1974 Box Set.

(M) (2:08) Rhino 70191 Best Of.

(M) (2:07) Curb 77520 Greatest Hits.

(M) (2:08) Collectables 5451 Golden Classics.

(M) (2:08) Rhino 72565 Very Best Of.

(M) (2:07) K-Tel 4014 His Best.

(M) (2:08) Repeat/Relativity 1609 Tell It Like It Is: #1 Soul Hits Of The 60's Volume 1.

(M) (2:09) Flashback 72895 25 Years Of R&B - 1965.

1966 A SWEET WOMAN LIKE YOU

(M) (2:36) Rhino 70652 Billboard's Top R&B Hits Of 1966.

(M) (2:36) Rhino 72006 Billboard's Top R&B Hits 1965-1969 Box Set.

(M) (2:35) Atlantic 82305 Atlantic Rhythm And Blues 1947-1974 Box Set.

(M) (2:36) Rhino 70191 Best Of.

(M) (2:35) Curb 77520 Greatest Hits.

(M) (2:36) Collectables 5451 Golden Classics.

(M) (2:36) Rhino 72565 Very Best Of.

(M) (2:34) K-Tel 4014 His Best.

(M) (2:35) Repeat/Relativity 1610 Tighten Up: #1 Soul Hits Of The 60's Volume 2.

(M) (2:36) Flashback 72896 25 Years Of R&B - 1966.

1967 PAPA WAS TOO

(S) (2:56) Rhino 70191 Best Of.

(S) (2:54) Curb 77520 Greatest Hits.

(S) (2:56) Collectables 5451 Golden Classics.

(S) (2:56) Rhino 72565 Very Best Of.

1967 SHOW ME

(S) (2:53) Atlantic 82305 Atlantic Rhythm And Blues 1947-1974 Box Set.

(S) (2:54) Atlantic 81298 Atlantic Rhythm & Blues Volume 6.

(S) (2:54) Rhino 71461 Soul Hits, Vol. 3.

(S) (2:54) Rhino 70191 Best Of.

(S) (2:53) Curb 77520 Greatest Hits.

(S) (2:54) Collectables 5451 Golden Classics.

(S) (2:53) Atco 91813 Classic Recordings.

(S) (2:53) JCI 3161 18 Soul Hits From The 60's.

(S) (2:54) Rhino 72565 Very Best Of.

(S) (2:54) Flashback 72659 '60s Soul: When A Man Loves A Woman.

(S) (2:54) Flashback 72091 '60s Soul Hits Box Set.

(M) (2:53) K-Tel 4014 His Best.

(M) (2:54) Rhino 72815 Beg, Scream & Shout! The Big Ol' Box Of '60s Soul.

(M) (2:54) Rhino 72962 Ultimate '60s Soul Sensations.

1968 SKINNY LEGS AND ALL

(M) (3:09) Atlantic 81298 Atlantic Rhythm & Blues Volume 6. (45 introduction)

(S) (3:05) Rhino 70653 Billboard's Top R&B Hits Of 1967. (45 introduction)

(S) (3:05) Rhino 72006 Billboard's Top R&B Hits 1965-1969 Box Set. (45 introduction)

(S) (3:09) Atlantic 82305 Atlantic Rhythm And Blues 1947-1974 Box Set. (45 introduction)

(S) (3:04) Rhino 70191 Best Of. (45 introduction)

(S) (3:04) Curb 77520 Greatest Hits. (45 introduction)

(S) (3:05) Rhino 71460 Soul Hits, Volume 2. (45 introduction)

(S) (3:03) Time-Life 2CLR-24 Classic Rock - 1967: Blowin' Your Mind. (45 introduction)

(S) (3:05) Collectables 5451 Golden Classics. (45 introduction)

(S) (3:04) Rhino 72565 Very Best Of. (45 introduction)

(S) (3:05) Flashback 72658 '60s Soul: Baby I Love You. (45 introduction)

(S) (3:05) Flashback 72091 '60s Soul Hits Box Set. (45 introduction)

(M) (3:11) K-Tel 4014 His Best. (45 introduction)

(S) (3:04) Flashback 72897 25 Years Of R&B - 1967. (45 introduction)

1968 MEN ARE GETTIN' SCARCE

(M) (3:13) Collectables 5451 Golden Classics.

(M) (3:07) Rhino 72565 Very Best Of.

(M) (3:12) K-Tel 4014 His Best.

(M) (3:07) Flashback 72898 25 Years Of R&B - 1968.

1972 I GOTCHA

(S) (2:27) Rhino 70788 Soul Hits Of The 70's Volume 8.

(S) (2:26) Rhino 70660 Billboard's Top R&B Hits Of 1972.

(S) (2:27) Rhino 70191 Best Of.

(S) (2:26) Curb 77520 Greatest Hits.

(S) (2:27) Rhino 71210 70's Smash Hits Volume 6.

(S) (2:25) Razor & Tie 22047 Sweet 70's Soul.

(S) (2:27) Time-Life RHD-20 Rhythm & Blues - 1972.

(S) (2:26) Time-Life SOD-22 Sounds Of The Seventies - Seventies Top Forty.

(S) (2:27) Collectables 5451 Golden Classics.

(S) (2:26) MCA 10541 and 11188 O.S.T. Reservoir Dogs.

(S) (2:25) Madacy Entertainment 1972 Rock On 1972.

(S) (2:26) JCI 3173 1970 - Only Soul - 1974.

(S) (2:27) Rhino 72565 Very Best Of.

(S) (2:26) Hip-O 40035 Cigar Classics Volume 2 - Urban Fire.

(S) (2:26) Time-Life R838-07 Solid Gold Soul - 1972.

(S) (2:27) Flashback 72686 '70s Radio Hits Volume 6.

(S) (2:37) K-Tel 4014 His Best. (with alternate introduction)

(S) (2:25) Columbia 69059 Party Super Hits.

1972 YOU SAID A BAD WORD

(M) (2:32) Collectables 5451 Golden Classics.

(M) (2:30) Rhino 72565 Very Best Of.

1977 AIN'T GONNA BUMP NO MORE (WITH NO BIG FAT WOMAN)

(S) (6:43) Collectables 5451 Golden Classics. (LP version)

(S) (3:28) Epic 66155 Club Epic Volume 3. (45 version)

(S) (3:28) Risky Business 53921 Double Knit Dance Hits. (45 version)

(S) (3:28) Rhino 72129 Soul Hits Of The 70's Vol. 19. (45 version)

(S) (6:37) K-Tel 3371 Hot Nights - Disco Lights. (LP version)

(S) (6:37) Priority 53141 Mega Hits Disco Locomotion Volume 2. (LP version)

(S) (3:28) Rhino 72565 Very Best Of. (45 version)

(S) (6:34) K-Tel 4014 His Best. (LP version)

(S) (3:28) Time-Life R838-16 Solid Gold Soul 1977. (45 version)

(S) (6:42) Columbia 69059 Party Super Hits. (LP version)

(S) (3:28) Time-Life R840-07 Sounds Of The Seventies: '70s Dance Party 1976-1977. (45 version)

THEM

1965 HERE COMES THE NIGHT

(S) (2:46) Rhino 70324 History Of British Rock Volume 6.

(S) (2:46) Rhino 70319 History Of British Rock Box Set.

(S) (2:45) Mercury 841970 Best Of Van Morrison.

(S) (2:46) London 810165 Them Featuring Van Morrison.

(S) (2:44) Time-Life 2CLR-23 Classic Rock - 1965: Blowin' Your Mind.

(S) (2:45) Deram 422844833 The Story Of Them Featuring Van Morrison.

1965 MYSTIC EYES

(S) (2:41) Rhino 70324 History Of British Rock Volume 6.

(S) (2:41) Rhino 70319 History Of British Rock Box Set.

(S) (2:41) London 810165 Them Featuring Van Morrison.

(S) (2:40) London 820563 Them.

(S) (2:39) Time-Life 2CLR-21 Classic Rock - Rock Renaissance II.

(S) (2:41) Deram 422844833 The Story Of Them Featuring Van Morrison.

THINK
1972 ONCE YOU UNDERSTAND

THIN LIZZY
1976 THE BOYS ARE BACK IN TOWN
(actual LP time is (4:27) not (5:00) as stated on the
record label; dj copies of this 45 ran (3:11) not
(3:26) as stated on the record label)

(S)	(4:27)	Sandstone 33000 Reelin' In The Years Volume 1. *(LP version)*
(S)	(4:26)	Mercury 848530 Dedication. *(LP version)*
(S)	(4:26)	Vertigo 822785 Jailbreak. *(LP version)*
(S)	(4:26)	Polydor 314515913 Classic Rock Box. *(LP version)*
(S)	(4:26)	Priority 7080 70's Greatest Rock Hits Volume 14: Kings Of Rock. *(LP version)*
(S)	(4:27)	DCC Compact Classics 062 Rock Of The 70's Volume 1. *(LP version)*
(S)	(3:34)	Time-Life SOD-18 Sounds Of The Seventies - 1976: Take Two. *(45 version)*

3RD BASS
1991 POP GOES THE WEASEL

(S)	(3:53)	Def Jam/Columbia 47369 Derelicts Of Dialect.
(S)	(3:53)	Def Jam 314523502 Derelicts Of Dialect.
(S)	(3:53)	Def Jam 314523848 Def Jam Music Group 10th Year Anniversary.

THIRD EYE BLIND
1997 SEMI-CHARMED LIFE

(S)	(4:26)	Elektra 62012 Third Eye Blind.

1998 HOW'S IT GOING TO BE

(S)	(4:11)	Elektra 62012 Third Eye Blind.

38 SPECIAL
1981 HOLD ON LOOSELY

(S)	(4:35)	A&M 3910 Flashback. *(LP length)*
(S)	(4:38)	A&M 3298 Wild-Eyed Southern Boys. *(LP length)*
(S)	(3:49)	Time-Life R968-04 Guitar Rock 1980-1981. *(45 length)*
(S)	(3:49)	Time-Life R105-24 Guitar Rock Monsters. *(45 length)*
(S)	(3:53)	K-Tel 6045 Southern Fried Rock. *(45 length)*
(S)	(4:36)	Rebound 314520256 Best Of Southern Rock. *(LP length)*
(S)	(4:38)	Rebound 314520257 Hard Rock Essentials - The 80's. *(LP length)*
(S)	(4:36)	Rebound 314520361 Class Reunion '81. *(LP length)*
(S)	(4:36)	Rhino 72594 Billboard Top Album Rock Hits, 1981. *(LP length)*
(S)	(4:34)	Razor & Tie 89004 Monsters Of Rock. *(LP length)*

1982 CAUGHT UP IN YOU
(dj copies of this 45 ran (3:55) and (4:37);
commercial copies were all (4:37))

(S)	(3:56)	Priority 7995 Country's Greatest Hits - Southern Country Rock.
(S)	(4:36)	Rhino 70586 Rebel Rousers - Southern Rock Classics.
(S)	(4:36)	K-Tel 6083 Southern Fried Rock - Second Helping.
(S)	(4:37)	A&M 3299 Special Forces.
(S)	(4:34)	A&M 3910 Flashback.
(S)	(4:34)	Time-Life R968-13 Guitar Rock - The Early '80s.
(S)	(4:33)	Time-Life R988-14 Sounds Of The Eighties: 1980-1982.
(S)	(4:36)	Rhino 72595 Billboard Top Album Rock Hits, 1982.
(S)	(4:35)	K-Tel 3972 Southern Rockin' Rebels: The South's Gone And Done It.
(S)	(4:35)	K-Tel 3997 Arena Rock - The 80's.

1982 YOU KEEP RUNNIN' AWAY

(S)	(3:56)	A&M 3299 Special Forces.
(S)	(3:55)	Rebound 314520434 Classic Rock - 80's.

1984 IF I'D BEEN THE ONE

(S)	(3:51)	Rebound 314520256 Best Of Southern Rock.
(S)	(3:51)	A&M 3910 Flashback.
(S)	(3:54)	A&M 3310 Tour De Force.
(S)	(3:53)	Rhino 72596 Billboard Top Album Rock Hits, 1983.

1984 BACK WHERE YOU BELONG

(S)	(4:26)	A&M 3910 Flashback. *(LP version)*
(S)	(4:28)	A&M 3310 Tour De Force. *(LP version)*

1984 TEACHER TEACHER

(S)	(3:15)	Capitol 46062 O.S.T. Teachers.
(S)	(3:12)	A&M 3910 Flashback.
(S)	(3:12)	Time-Life R968-20 Guitar Rock - The '80s.

1986 LIKE NO OTHER NIGHT

(S)	(3:57)	A&M 5115 Strength In Numbers.
(S)	(3:55)	A&M 3910 Flashback.

1989 SECOND CHANCE

(S)	(4:33)	Priority 7077 80's Greatest Rock Hits Volume 5 - From The Heart. *(45 length)*
(S)	(5:01)	A&M 5218 Rock & Roll Strategy. *(LP length)*
(S)	(4:33)	Time-Life R834-14 Body Talk - Love And Tenderness. *(45 length)*

1991 THE SOUND OF YOUR VOICE

(S)	(4:56)	Charisma 91640 and 86345 Bone Against Steel.

B.J. THOMAS
released as by B.J. THOMAS and THE TRIUMPHS:
1966 I'M SO LONESOME I COULD CRY

(M)	(3:08)	Rhino 70752 Greatest Hits.
(E)	(3:11)	Original Sound 8854 Oldies But Goodies Vol. 4. *(this compact disc uses the "Waring - fds" noise reduction process; alternate take)*
(E)	(3:11)	Original Sound 2221 Oldies But Goodies Volumes 1,4,6,8 and 10 Box Set. *(this box set uses the "Waring - fds" noise reduction process; alternate take)*
(E)	(3:11)	Original Sound 2500 Oldies But Goodies Volumes 1-15 Box Set. *(this box set uses the "Waring - fds" noise reduction process; alternate take)*
(M)	(3:06)	Deluxe 1014 16 Greatest Hits.
(M)	(3:08)	Collectables 5099 His Golden Classics.
(M)	(3:07)	Curb 77452 Greatest Hits.
(M)	(3:07)	Capricorn 42003 The Scepter Records Story.
(M)	(3:06)	Time-Life SUD-01 Superhits - 1966.
(M)	(3:03)	Deluxe 7902 16 Greatest Hits.
(S)	(2:42)	K-Tel 3451 Hank Williams You Wrote My Life - A Tribute To Hank Williams. *(rerecording)*
(M)	(3:03)	LaserLight 12422 Best Of.
(M)	(3:06)	Time-Life AM1-09 AM Gold - 1966.
(M)	(3:08)	Time-Life R857-20 The Heart Of Rock 'n' Roll 1965-1966.
(M)	(3:07)	Time-Life R814-05 Love Songs.

released as by B.J. THOMAS:
1966 MAMA
(actual LP time is (2:56) not (2:47) as stated on the
record label)

(S)	(2:55)	Rhino 70752 Greatest Hits. *(LP length)*
(S)	(2:53)	Deluxe 1014 16 Greatest Hits. *(LP length)*
(S)	(2:55)	Collectables 5099 His Golden Classics. *(LP length)*
(S)	(2:45)	Capricorn 42003 The Scepter Records Story. *(45 length)*
(S)	(2:52)	Deluxe 7902 16 Greatest Hits. *(LP length)*
(S)	(2:52)	LaserLight 12422 Best Of. *(LP length)*

released as by B.J. THOMAS and THE TRIUMPHS:
1966 BILLY AND SUE

(S)	(3:11)	Rhino 70752 Greatest Hits.
(S)	(3:11)	Curb 77452 Greatest Hits.
(S)	(3:01)	Deluxe 7902 16 Greatest Hits. *(rerecording)*

released as by B.J. THOMAS:
1968 THE EYES OF A NEW YORK WOMAN

(S)	(3:00)	Rhino 70752 Greatest Hits.
(S)	(3:00)	Deluxe 1014 16 Greatest Hits.
(S)	(3:00)	Collectables 5099 His Golden Classics.
(S)	(3:01)	Curb 77452 Greatest Hits.
(S)	(2:59)	Capricorn 42003 The Scepter Records Story.
(S)	(2:59)	Deluxe 7902 16 Greatest Hits.
(S)	(2:59)	LaserLight 12422 Best Of.

1969 HOOKED ON A FEELING

(S)	(2:44)	Rhino 70752 Greatest Hits. *(LP version)*
(S)	(2:44)	Deluxe 1014 16 Greatest Hits. *(LP version)*
(S)	(2:44)	Collectables 5099 His Golden Classics. *(LP version)*
(S)	(2:44)	Curb 77452 Greatest Hits. *(LP version)*

(S) (2:45) Capricorn 42003 The Scepter Records Story. *(LP version)*
(S) (2:44) Time-Life SUD-02 Superhits - 1968. *(LP version)*
(S) (2:44) Deluxe 7902 16 Greatest Hits. *(LP version)*
(S) (2:44) LaserLight 12422 Best Of. *(LP version)*
(M) (2:43) Priority 50951 I Love Rock & Roll Volume 2: Hits Of The 60's. *(45 version)*
(S) (2:44) Time-Life AM1-04 AM Gold - 1968. *(LP version)*
(S) (2:45) Varese Sarabande 5813 Very Best Of. *(LP version)*

1969 IT'S ONLY LOVE
(S) (2:53) Collectables 5099 His Golden Classics.
(S) (2:54) Deluxe 7902 16 Greatest Hits.

1970 RAINDROPS KEEP FALLIN' ON MY HEAD
(S) (2:57) Priority 8669 Hits/70's Greatest Rock Hits Volume 9.
(S) (2:59) Rhino 70752 Greatest Hits.
(S) (3:01) Deluxe 1014 16 Greatest Hits.
(S) (2:59) Collectables 5099 His Golden Classics.
(S) (3:00) Curb 77452 Greatest Hits.
(S) (3:00) Capricorn 42003 The Scepter Records Story.
(S) (2:57) A&M 3159 O.S.T. Butch Cassidy & The Sundance Kid.
(S) (2:59) Rhino 71093 Better Days.
(S) (2:55) Time-Life SUD-07 Superhits - 1969.
(S) (2:59) Time-Life R921-38 Get Together.
(S) (2:59) Time-Life R138/05 Look Of Love.
(S) (3:14) Varese Sarabande 5534 Rhythm Of The Rain. *(alternate take)*
(S) (2:59) Epic 66329 O.S.T. Forrest Gump.
(S) (3:14) Rhino 71868 Academy Award Winning Songs. *(alternate take)*
(S) (3:14) Rhino 72278 Academy Award Winning Songs Volume 3. *(alternate take)*
(S) (3:01) Deluxe 7902 16 Greatest Hits.
(S) (3:14) Rhino 72423 Billboard Top Movie Hits - 1960s. *(alternate take)*
(S) (2:55) Madacy Entertainment 1970 Rock On 1970.
(S) (3:00) LaserLight 12422 Best Of.
(S) (2:55) Time-Life R103-18 Great Love Songs Of The '70s & '80s.
(S) (2:55) Time-Life AM1-01 AM Gold - 1969.
(S) (2:59) Flashback 72687 '60s Rock: Feelin' Groovy.
(S) (2:59) Flashback 72088 '60s Rock Hits Box Set.
(S) (2:57) Priority 50974 Premiere The Movie Magazine Presents The Greatest Soundtrack Hits.
(S) (3:14) Varese Sarabande 5813 Very Best Of. *(alternate take)*
(S) (2:58) Time-Life R814-01 Love Songs.

1970 EVERYBODY'S OUT OF TOWN
(S) (2:40) Rhino 70752 Greatest Hits.
(S) (2:40) Collectables 5099 His Golden Classics.
(S) (2:42) Capricorn 42003 The Scepter Records Story.
(S) (2:40) Deluxe 7902 16 Greatest Hits.
(S) (2:40) LaserLight 12422 Best Of.
(S) (2:40) Varese Sarabande 5813 Very Best Of.

1970 I JUST CAN'T HELP BELIEVING
(S) (2:54) Rhino 70752 Greatest Hits.
(S) (2:56) Deluxe 1014 16 Greatest Hits.
(S) (2:54) Collectables 5099 His Golden Classics.
(S) (2:56) Curb 77452 Greatest Hits.
(S) (2:55) Capricorn 42003 The Scepter Records Story.
(S) (2:54) Deluxe 7902 16 Greatest Hits.
(S) (2:53) LaserLight 12422 Best Of.
(S) (2:54) Rhino 72736 Billboard Top Soft Rock Hits - 1970.
(S) (2:54) Rhino 72516 Behind Closed Doors - '70s Swingers.
(S) (2:55) Varese Sarabande 5803 Sunshine Days - Pop Classics Of The '60s Volume 3.
(S) (2:54) Varese Sarabande 5813 Very Best Of.

1971 MOST OF ALL
(S) (2:51) Rhino 70752 Greatest Hits.
(S) (2:52) Deluxe 1014 16 Greatest Hits.
(S) (2:52) Collectables 5099 His Golden Classics.
(S) (2:50) Deluxe 7902 16 Greatest Hits.
(S) (2:52) Varese Sarabande 5813 Very Best Of.

1971 NO LOVE AT ALL
(S) (2:51) Rhino 70752 Greatest Hits.
(S) (2:52) Deluxe 1014 16 Greatest Hits.
(S) (2:51) Collectables 5099 His Golden Classics.
(S) (2:52) Capricorn 42003 The Scepter Records Story. *(truncated fade)*
(S) (2:51) Deluxe 7902 16 Greatest Hits.
(S) (2:51) Madacy Entertainment 1971 Rock On 1971.
(S) (2:51) LaserLight 12422 Best Of.
(S) (2:51) Varese Sarabande 5813 Very Best Of.

1971 MIGHTY CLOUDS OF JOY
(S) (3:13) Rhino 70752 Greatest Hits.
(S) (3:14) Deluxe 1014 16 Greatest Hits.
(S) (3:13) Collectables 5099 His Golden Classics.
(S) (3:12) Deluxe 7902 16 Greatest Hits.
(S) (3:13) LaserLight 12422 Best Of.
(S) (3:13) Varese Sarabande 5813 Very Best Of.
(S) (3:13) Varese Sarabande 5906 God, Love And Rock & Roll.

1972 ROCK AND ROLL LULLABY
(commercial 45's were all (4:30); dj copies ran (4:30) and (4:08); LP length is (4:08))
(S) (4:11) Rhino 70752 Greatest Hits. *(LP version)*
(S) (4:08) Deluxe 1014 16 Greatest Hits. *(LP version)*
(S) (4:11) Collectables 5099 His Golden Classics. *(LP version)*
(S) (4:08) Curb 77452 Greatest Hits. *(LP version)*
(S) (4:10) Capricorn 42003 The Scepter Records Story. *(LP version)*
(S) (4:10) Time-Life SUD-20 Superhits - Early 70's Classics. *(LP version)*
(S) (4:08) Deluxe 7902 16 Greatest Hits. *(LP version)*
(S) (4:08) LaserLight 12422 Best Of. *(LP version)*
(S) (4:10) Time-Life AM1-15 AM Gold - Early '70s Classics. *(LP version)*
(S) (4:11) Varese Sarabande 5813 Very Best Of. *(LP version)*

1975 (HEY WON'T YOU PLAY) ANOTHER SOMEBODY DONE SOMEBODY WRONG SONG
(S) (3:22) Curb 77452 Greatest Hits.
(S) (3:21) Rhino 70752 Greatest Hits.
(S) (3:18) Time-Life CCD-04 Contemporary Country - The Mid 70's.
(S) (3:24) K-Tel 3111 Country Music Classics Vol. XIX.
(S) (3:22) Varese Sarabande 5609 More Greatest Hits.
(S) (3:22) K-Tel 3356 101 Greatest Country Hits Vol. Two: Country Sunshine.
(S) (3:21) Time-Life AM1-22 AM Gold - 1975.
(S) (3:23) Hip-O 40086 The Class Of Country 1975-1979.

1977 DON'T WORRY BABY
(S) (3:01) Curb 77452 Greatest Hits.
(S) (2:56) Varese Sarabande 5609 More Greatest Hits.
(S) (3:00) MCA Special Products 20997 Mellow Rock.

CARLA THOMAS
1961 GEE WHIZ (LOOK AT HIS EYES)
(M) (2:18) Atlantic Group 88218 Complete Stax/Volt Singles.
(M) (2:17) Atlantic 81296 Atlantic Rhythm & Blues Volume 4. *(some vocal distortion)*
(M) (2:18) Atlantic 82305 Atlantic Rhythm And Blues 1947-1974 Box Set.
(M) (2:18) Capitol 81475 Rites Of Rhythm & Blues.
(M) (2:18) Time-Life 2RNR-18 Rock 'N' Roll Era - 1961 Still Rockin'.
(M) (2:18) Time-Life RHD-14 Rhythm & Blues - 1961.
(M) (2:18) Rhino 71806 The R&B Box: Thirty Years Of Rhythm & Blues.
(M) (2:18) Rhino 71633 Gee Whiz - Best Of.
(M) (2:18) Time-Life R857-03 The Heart Of Rock 'n' Roll - 1961.
(M) (2:18) JCI 3164 Eighteen Soulful Ballads.
(M) (2:19) Rhino 72618 Smooth Grooves: The '60s Volume 1 Early '60s.
(M) (2:19) Flashback 72669 Gee Whiz And Other Hits.
(M) (2:19) Flashback 72083 Kings And Queens Of Soul Box Set.
(M) (2:18) Time-Life R838-19 Solid Gold Soul 1961.

CARLA THOMAS (Continued)
1966 B-A-B-Y
- (M) (2:53) Atlantic Group 88218 Complete Stax/Volt Singles.
- (E) (2:46) Stax 88005 Top Of The Stax.
- (E) (2:47) Warner Special Products 27609 Memphis Soul Classics.
- (E) (2:46) JCI 3105 Soul Sixties.
- (M) (2:52) Atlantic 82340 Carla.
- (M) (2:46) Capitol 81475 Rites Of Rhythm & Blues.
- (M) (2:46) Time-Life RHD-01 Rhythm & Blues - 1966.
- (M) (2:46) Time-Life 2CLR-25 Classic Rock - On The Soul Side.
- (M) (2:53) Rhino 71633 Gee Whiz - Best Of.
- (M) (2:46) JCI 3161 18 Soul Hits From The 60's.
- (M) (2:53) Rhino 72478 Beverly Hills 90210: Songs From The Peach Pit.
- (M) (2:46) Time-Life R838-01 Solid Gold Soul - 1966.
- (M) (2:54) Flashback 72669 Gee Whiz And Other Hits.
- (M) (2:54) Flashback 72083 Kings And Queens Of Soul Box Set.
- (M) (2:53) Rhino 72815 Beg, Scream & Shout! The Big Ol' Box Of '60s Soul.
- (M) (2:54) Flashback 72896 25 Years Of R&B - 1966.
- (M) (2:53) Rhino 72963 Ultimate '60s Soul Smashes.

released as by OTIS & CARLA (OTIS REDDING & CARLA THOMAS):
1967 TRAMP
- (M) (2:59) Atlantic Group 88218 Complete Stax/Volt Singles.
- (S) (2:59) Atlantic 81762 Otis Redding Story.
- (S) (2:59) Atco 80254 Otis Redding - The Dock Of The Bay.
- (S) (2:59) Atlantic 82256 Otis Redding & Carla Thomas: King & Queen.
- (S) (2:57) Warner Special Products 27608 Ultimate Otis Redding.
- (S) (2:59) Atlantic 82305 Atlantic Rhythm And Blues 1947-1974 Box Set.
- (M) (2:58) Rhino 71147 Very Best Of Otis Redding.
- (M) (2:59) Rhino 71439 The Definitive Otis Redding.
- (M) (2:50) Time-Life RHD-10 Rhythm & Blues - 1967.
- (S) (2:56) Time-Life 2CLR-15 Classic Rock - 1967: Shakin' All Over.
- (M) (2:59) Rhino 71754 and 72831 Phat Trax: The Best Of Old School Volume 3.
- (M) (2:59) Rhino 71633 Gee Whiz - Best Of Carla Thomas.
- (M) (2:50) Time-Life R838-02 Solid Gold Soul - 1967.
- (M) (3:00) Flashback 72669 Carla Thomas - Gee Whiz And Other Hits.
- (M) (3:00) Flashback 72083 Kings And Queens Of Soul Box Set.
- (M) (2:59) Flashback 72897 25 Years Of R&B - 1967.
- (M) (2:59) Rhino 72962 Ultimate '60s Soul Sensations.

1967 KNOCK ON WOOD
- (M) (2:49) Atlantic Group 88218 Complete Stax/Volt Singles.
- (S) (2:50) Atlantic 82256 Otis Redding & Carla Thomas: King & Queen.
- (S) (2:50) Atlantic 81762 The Otis Redding Story.
- (M) (2:49) Flashback 72669 Carla Thomas - Gee Whiz And Other Hits.
- (M) (2:49) Flashback 72083 Kings And Queens Of Soul Box Set.
- (M) (2:49) Rhino 71930 Otis Redding - Very Best Of Vol. 2.

IAN THOMAS
1973 PAINTED LADIES
- (S) (3:30) Rhino 71197 Super Hits Of The 70's Volume 17.

IRMA THOMAS
1964 WISH SOMEONE WOULD CARE
- (M) (2:19) Rhino 75765 Best Of New Orleans Rhythm & Blues Volume 1.
- (S) (2:18) Stax 8551 Superblues Volume 1.
- (S) (2:27) EMI 97988 Time Is On My Side - The Best Of.
- (M) (2:17) Time-Life 2RNR-39 Rock 'N' Roll Era - The New Orleans Sound.
- (M) (2:19) Motown 6763 Rites Of Rhythm & Blues Volume 2.
- (S) (2:18) Razor & Tie 2097 Collection.
- (M) (2:19) Rhino 72815 Beg, Scream & Shout! The Big Ol' Box Of '60s Soul.

RUFUS THOMAS
1963 WALKING THE DOG
- (M) (2:33) Atlantic Group 88218 Complete Stax/Volt Singles.
- (M) (2:29) Warner Special Products 27602 20 Party Classics.
- (M) (2:28) Warner Special Products 27609 Memphis Soul Classics.
- (M) (2:28) Atlantic 81297 Atlantic Rhythm & Blues Volume 5.
- (M) (2:33) Atlantic 82305 Atlantic Rhythm And Blues 1947-1974 Box Set.
- (M) (2:31) Atlantic 82254 Walking The Dog.
- (M) (2:24) Stax 8569 Can't Get Away From The Dog. *(alternate take)*
- (M) (2:34) Rhino 71461 Soul Hits, Volume 3.
- (M) (2:28) Time-Life 2RNR-07 Rock 'N' Roll Era - 1963.
- (M) (2:27) Time-Life RHD-02 Rhythm & Blues - 1963.
- (M) (2:34) Rhino 72410 Best Of.
- (M) (2:27) Time-Life R838-14 Solid Gold Soul - 1963.
- (M) (2:33) Flashback 72659 '60s Soul: When A Man Loves A Woman.
- (M) (2:33) Flashback 72091 '60s Soul Hits Box Set.
- (M) (2:30) Walt Disney 60870 Dog Songs.
- (M) (2:34) Rhino 72962 Ultimate '60s Soul Sensations.
- (M) (2:32) JCI 3189 1960 - Only Dance - 1964.

1964 CAN YOUR MONKEY DO THE DOG
- (M) (1:53) Atlantic 82254 Walking The Dog. *(LP version)*
- (M) (2:25) Atlantic Group 88218 Complete Stax/Volt Singles. *(45 version)*
- (M) (2:02) Stax 8569 Can't Get Away From The Dog. *(alternate take)*
- (M) (2:25) Rhino 72410 Best Of. *(45 version)*

1970 DO THE FUNKY CHICKEN
- (M) (3:15) Stax 4411 Complete Stax/Volt Soul Singles 1968 - 1971.
- (S) (3:14) Stax 4124 Rufus & Carla Thomas Chronicle.
- (S) (3:16) Rhino 72410 Best Of.

1971 (DO THE) PUSH AND PULL (PART 1)
- (S) (3:17) Stax 88005 Top Of The Stax.
- (S) (2:17) Stax 4124 Rufus & Carla Thomas Chronicle. *(edited)*
- (M) (3:16) Stax 4411 Complete Stax/Volt Soul Singles 1968 - 1971.
- (S) (3:16) Razor & Tie 22045 Those Funky 70's.
- (S) (3:16) Time-Life RHD-09 Rhythm & Blues - 1971.
- (S) (3:19) Rhino 72113 Billboard Hot Soul Hits - 1971.
- (S) (4:42) Stax 88026 Did You Heard Me?/Crown Prince Of Dance. *(Parts 1 and 2)*
- (S) (3:19) Rhino 72410 Best Of.
- (S) (3:16) Time-Life R838-06 Solid Gold Soul - 1971.

1971 THE BREAKDOWN (PART 1)
- (S) (3:17) Stax 88008 Top Of The Stax Volume 2.
- (S) (3:17) Stax 4124 Rufus & Carla Thomas Chronicle.
- (S) (3:12) Stax 4411 Complete Stax/Volt Soul Singles 1968 - 1971.
- (S) (3:18) Stax 88026 Did You Heard Me?/Crown Prince Of Dance.
- (S) (3:18) Rhino 72410 Best Of.

TIMMY THOMAS
1973 WHY CAN'T WE LIVE TOGETHER
- (M) (3:53) Rhino 70661 Billboard's Top R&B Hits Of 1973. *(:25 longer fade than the 45 version)*
- (M) (3:53) Rhino 71003 Best Of TK Records. *(:25 longer fade than the 45 version)*
- (M) (3:53) Rhino 70790 Soul Hits Of The 70's Volume 10 . *(:25 longer fade than the 45 version)*
- (M) (4:37) Collectables 5433 Why Can't We Live Together. *(LP version)*
- (M) (3:52) Time-Life SOD-14 Sounds Of The Seventies - 1973: Take Two. *(:24 longer fade than the 45 version)*
- (M) (3:53) Rhino 72115 Billboard Hot Soul Hits - 1973. *(:25 longer fade than the 45 version)*
- (M) (3:53) Ichiban 2511 Love, Peace & Understanding. *(:25 longer fade than the 45 version)*
- (M) (4:35) TK/Hot Productions 33 Best Of T.K. Soul Singles. *(LP version)*
- (M) (3:30) Time-Life R838-08 Solid Gold Soul - 1973. *(45 version)*

(M) (3:50) K-Tel 3913 Superstars Greatest Hits Volume 2.
(:22 longer than the 45 version)

CHRIS THOMPSON & NIGHT (see NIGHT)

SUE THOMPSON
1961 SAD MOVIES (MAKE ME CRY)
(S) (3:15) Curb 77462 Greatest Hits.
(S) (3:14) Collectables 5070 History Of Rock Volume 10.
(S) (3:14) Time-Life 2RNR-46 Rock 'N' Roll Era - 60's Juke
Box Memories.
(S) (3:14) Time-Life SUD-15 Superhits - The Early 60's.
(S) (3:14) Collectables 5661 Golden Classics.
(S) (3:14) Time-Life AM1-19 AM Gold - The Early '60s.
(S) (3:13) Time-Life R857-17 The Heart Of Rock 'n' Roll:
The Early '60s.

1962 NORMAN
(S) (2:17) Curb 77462 Greatest Hits.
(S) (2:16) Collectables 5063 History Of Rock Volume 3.
(S) (2:16) Time-Life 2RNR-47 Rock 'N' Roll Era - Teen
Idols II.
(S) (2:15) Collectables 2502 WCBS-FM History Of Rock -
The 60's Part 3.
(S) (2:15) Collectables 4502 History Of Rock/The 60s Part
Three.
(S) (2:17) Rhino 71583 Billboard Top Pop Hits, 1962.
(S) (2:17) Collectables 5661 Golden Classics.

1962 TWO OF A KIND
(S) (2:47) Curb 77462 Greatest Hits.
(S) (2:47) Collectables 5661 Golden Classics.

1962 HAVE A GOOD TIME
(S) (3:12) Curb 77462 Greatest Hits.
(S) (3:03) Collectables 5661 Golden Classics. *(truncated
fade)*

1962 JAMES (HOLD THE LADDER STEADY)
(S) (2:12) Curb 77462 Greatest Hits.
(S) (2:11) Collectables 5661 Golden Classics.

1965 PAPER TIGER
(S) (2:25) Curb 77462 Greatest Hits.
(S) (2:24) Collectables 5064 History Of Rock Volume 4.
(S) (2:24) Collectables 5661 Golden Classics.

THOMPSON TWINS
1983 LIES
(S) (3:11) Rhino 71701 New Wave Hits Of The 80's Vol. 8.
(S) (5:20) Risky Business 57468 This Ain't No Disco/New
Wave Dance Hits. *("Best Of/Greatest Mixes" LP
version)*
(S) (3:11) Rhino 71834 Classic MTV: Class Of 1983.
(S) (5:20) Priority 53795 Best Of 80's Rock Volume 3.
("Best Of/Greatest Mixes" LP version)
(S) (3:12) Arista 8002 Side Kicks.
(S) (5:20) Arista 8542 Best Of/Greatest Mixes. *("Best
Of/Greatest Mixes" LP version)*
(S) (3:11) Rhino 72491 New Wave Hits, Vol. 2.
(S) (3:11) Arista 18940 Greatest Hits.
(S) (3:11) Flashback 72714 Ultimate New Wave Hits.
(S) (3:11) Flashback 72092 New Wave Hits Box Set.
(S) (3:11) Time-Life R988-22 Sounds Of The Eighties 1980-
1983.

1984 HOLD ME NOW
(S) (4:44) Arista 8268 Arista's Perfect 10.
(S) (4:44) Priority 53705 Rock Of The 80's Volume 2.
(S) (4:45) K-Tel 3262 The 80's Video Stars.
(S) (4:44) Rhino 70679 Billboard Top Hits - 1984.
(S) (4:44) Rhino 71976 New Wave Hits Of The 80's Vol. 13.
(S) (4:45) Arista 8200 Thompson Twins.
(S) (7:06) Arista 8542 Best Of/Greatest Mixes. *("Best
Of/Greatest Mixes" LP version)*
(S) (4:44) Time-Life R988-06 Sounds Of The Eighties: 1984.
(S) (4:10) Madacy Entertainment 1984 Rock On 1984. *(:34
shorter than the 45 or LP)*
(S) (4:44) Arista 18940 Greatest Hits.
(S) (4:12) JCI 3159 18 Modern Rock Classics From The
80's. *(:32 shorter than the 45 or LP)*

(S) (7:05) Risky Business 66396 Oldies But 80's: Best Of
The 80's. *("Best Of/Greatest Mixes" LP version)*
(S) (4:44) Rhino 72894 Hard Rock Cafe: New Wave.
(S) (4:43) Maverick/Warner Brothers 46840 O.S.T. The
Wedding Singer.
(S) (4:43) Simitar 55562 The Number One's: Smooth Love.
(S) (4:44) Time-Life R834-17 Body Talk - Heart To Heart.

1984 DOCTOR! DOCTOR!
(S) (4:36) Priority 53751 Rock Of The 80's Volume 13.
(S) (4:38) Arista 8200 Thompson Twins.
(S) (5:46) Arista 8542 Best Of/Greatest Mixes. *("Best
Of/Greatest Mixes" LP version)*
(S) (5:44) K-Tel 3473 The 80s: New Wave. *("Best
Of/Greatest Mixes" LP version)*
(S) (4:37) Arista 18940 Greatest Hits.
(S) (4:36) Rhino 72820 VH1 - More Of The Big 80's.
(S) (4:36) Simitar 55612 The Number One's: The '80s.
(S) (4:35) Time-Life R988-23 Sounds Of The Eighties 1984-
1985.

1985 LAY YOUR HANDS ON ME
(S) (4:08) Arista 8278 O.S.T. Perfect. *(neither the 45 or LP
version)*
(S) (4:08) EMI 89605 Living In Oblivion: The 80's Greatest
Hits Volume Two. *(neither the 45 or LP version)*
(S) (4:21) Geffen 24236 Greenpeace - Rainbow Warriors.
(LP version)
(S) (4:21) Arista 8276 Here's To Future Days. *(LP version)*
(S) (4:59) Priority 53749 Rock Of The 80's Volume 6.
("Best Of/Greatest Mixes" LP version)
(S) (5:11) Arista 8542 Best Of/Greatest Mixes. *("Best
Of/Greatest Mixes" LP version)*
(S) (4:59) Time-Life R988-12 Sounds Of The 80's: 1985-
1986. *("Best Of/Greatest Mixes" LP version)*
(S) (4:03) Arista 18940 Greatest Hits. *(neither the 45 or LP
version)*

1986 KING FOR A DAY
**(actual 45 time is (4:08) not (3:58) as stated
on the record label)**
(S) (5:57) Priority 53748 Rock Of The 80's Volume 8.
("Best Of/Greatest Mixes" LP version)
(S) (5:20) Arista 8276 Here's To Future Days. *(LP version)*
(S) (5:57) Arista 8542 Best Of/Greatest Mixes. *("Best
Of/Greatest Mixes" LP version)*
(S) (5:57) Risky Business 67307 Wave Goodbye To The
80's. *("Best Of/Greatest Mixes" LP version)*
(S) (5:57) Madacy Entertainment 1986 Rock On 1986.
("Best Of/Greatest Mixes" LP version)
(S) (5:19) Arista 18940 Greatest Hits. *(LP version)*
(S) (4:08) Time-Life R988-15 Sounds Of The Eighties: The
Mid 80's. *(45 version)*

1987 GET THAT LOVE
**(actual 45 time is (3:58) not (3:46) as stated on the
record label)**
(S) (3:59) Arista 8449 Close To The Bone.
(S) (4:55) Arista 8542 Best Of/Greatest Mixes. *("Best
Of/Greatest Mixes" LP version)*
(S) (3:54) Arista 18940 Greatest Hits.

1989 SUGAR DADDY
(S) (3:31) Warner Brothers 25291 Big Trash.

ALI THOMSON
1980 TAKE A LITTLE RHYTHM
(S) (3:25) Rhino 71892 Radio Daze: Pop Hits Of The 80's
Volume Three.

THREE DEGREES
1970 MAYBE
(S) (3:37) Rhino 70782 Soul Hits Of The 70's Volume 2.
(S) (3:37) Rhino 72028 Soul Hits Of The 70's Volumes 1-5
Box Set.
(S) (3:37) Original Sound 9306 Dedicated To You Vol. 6.
released as by MFSB featuring THE THREE DEGREES:
1974 TSOP (THE SOUND OF PHILADELPHIA)
(S) (5:45) Philadelphia International 34940 Philadelphia
Classics. *(this version first appeared on the
"Philadelphia Classics" vinyl LP in 1977)*

THREE DEGREES (Continued)

(S) (3:40) Philadelphia International 39307 Ten Years Of Hits.
(S) (3:34) Rhino 70552 Soul Hits Of The 70's Volume 12.
(S) (3:34) Epic 57620 O.S.T. Carlito's Way.
(S) (3:34) Rhino 71603 Rock Instrumental Classics Volume 3: The Seventies.
(S) (3:34) Rhino 72035 Rock Instrumental Classics Vols. 1-5 Box Set.
(S) (3:34) Rhino 71618 Soul Train Hall Of Fame/20th Anniversary.
(S) (3:34) Rhino 71549 Let There Be Drums Vol. 3: The 70's.
(S) (3:40) Razor & Tie 22496 Disco Fever.
(S) (3:32) Time-Life SOD-27 Sounds Of The Seventies - Dance Fever.
(S) (3:34) Rhino 71910 Tube Tunes Volume One - The 70's.
(S) (3:34) MCA 11329 Soul Train 25th Anniversary Box Set.
(S) (3:34) Rhino 72116 Billboard Hot Soul Hits - 1974.
(S) (3:40) Priority 53790 Disco Nice And Nasty.
(S) (5:47) Epic Associated/Legacy 64915 Best Of The Three Degrees: When Will I See You Again. *(this version first appeared on the "Philadelphia Classics" vinyl LP in 1977)*
(S) (5:47) Legacy/Epic Associated 66689 Best Of MFSB: Love Is The Message. *(this version first appeared on the "Philadelphia Classics" vinyl LP released in 1977)*
(S) (3:33) Eclipse Music Group 64894 Rock 'n Roll Relix 1974-1975.
(S) (3:33) Eclipse Music Group 64897 Rock 'n Roll Relix 1970-1979.
(S) (3:34) Time-Life R840-04 Sounds Of The Seventies: A Loss For Words.
(S) (3:33) Time-Life AM1-21 AM Gold - 1974.
(S) (3:34) Time-Life R838-09 Solid Gold Soul - 1974.
(S) (5:47) Epic/Legacy 64647 The Philly Sound Box Set. *(this version first appeared on the "Philadelphia Classics" vinyl LP released in 1977)*
(S) (5:47) Epic Associated/Legacy 65162 A Postcard From Philly. *(this version first appeared on the "Philadelphia Classics" vinyl LP released in 1977)*
(S) (3:34) Time-Life R840-05 Sounds Of The Seventies: '70s Dance Party 1972-1974.

released as by THE THREE DEGREES:
1974 WHEN WILL I SEE YOU AGAIN

(S) (2:36) Priority 7972 Mega-Hits Dance Classics Volume 2. *(:22 shorter than the 45 or LP)*
(S) (2:58) Rhino 70554 Soul Hits Of The 70's Volume 14.
(S) (2:57) Razor & Tie 22047 Sweet 70's Soul.
(S) (2:58) Original Sound 8911 Art Laboe's Dedicated To You Vol. 2.
(S) (2:58) Original Sound 4001 Art Laboe's 60 Killer Oldies.
(S) (2:58) Sony Music Distribution 57854 For Your Love.
(S) (2:58) Legacy/Epic 66913 From Philly With Love.
(S) (2:58) Epic Associated/Legacy 64915 Best Of: When Will I See You Again.
(S) (2:58) DCC Compact Classics 143 Groove On! Volume 3.
(S) (2:58) Rhino 72414 Dance Floor Divas: The 70's.
(S) (2:57) Eclipse Music Group 64894 Rock 'n Roll Relix 1974-1975.
(S) (2:57) Eclipse Music Group 64897 Rock 'n Roll Relix 1970-1979.
(S) (2:57) Time-Life AM1-21 AM Gold - 1974.
(S) (2:58) Time-Life R838-09 Solid Gold Soul - 1974.
(S) (2:58) Time-Life R834-09 Body Talk - Magic Moments.
(S) (2:57) Epic/Legacy 64647 The Philly Sound Box Set.
(S) (2:58) Time-Life R840-05 Sounds Of The Seventies: '70s Dance Party 1972-1974.
(S) (2:57) K-Tel 3889 Great R&B Female Groups: Hits Of The 70s.

THREE DOG NIGHT
1969 TRY A LITTLE TENDERNESS

(S) (4:09) MCA 6018 Best Of. *(LP version)*
(S) (4:05) MCA 31045 Three Dog Night. *(LP version)*
(M) (4:23) MCA 10956 Celebrate: Three Dog Night Story. *(45 version)*

(S) (4:05) Original Sound 8908 Best Love Songs Vol 3. *(LP version)*
(S) (4:05) Original Sound 9327 Best Love Songs Vol. 3 & 4. *(LP version)*
(S) (4:05) Original Sound 1236 Best Love Songs Box Set. *(LP version)*

1969 ONE

(S) (3:00) MCA 31206 Vintage Music Volume 9.
(S) (3:00) MCA 5806 Vintage Music Volumes 9 & 10.
(S) (3:03) MCA 6018 Best Of.
(S) (3:02) MCA 1466 Joy To The World: Their Greatest Hits.
(S) (3:04) MCA 31045 Three Dog Night.
(S) (3:03) MCA 10956 Celebrate: Three Dog Night Story.
(S) (3:00) Time-Life 2CLR-06 Classic Rock - 1969.
(S) (3:00) Time-Life SUD-18 Superhits - Late 60's Classics.
(S) (3:00) Time-Life OPCD-4517 Tonight's The Night.
(S) (3:00) MCA Special Products 20783 Rock Around The Oldies #1.
(S) (3:00) MCA Special Products 22131 Vintage Collectibles Volume 2.
(S) (3:00) Time-Life AM1-12 AM Gold - Late '60s Classics.
(S) (3:00) Time-Life R857-22 The Heart Of Rock 'n' Roll 1967-1969.

1969 EASY TO BE HARD

(S) (3:11) MCA 5936 Vintage Music Volumes 11 & 12.
(S) (3:11) MCA 31209 Vintage Music Volume 12.
(S) (3:10) MCA 6018 Best Of.
(S) (3:11) MCA 31046 Suitable For Framing.
(S) (3:11) MCA 10956 Celebrate: Three Dog Night Story.
(S) (3:11) JCI 3114 Easy Sixties.
(S) (3:10) Time-Life SUD-07 Superhits - 1969.
(S) (3:09) MCA Special Products 20903 The 70's Come Alive Again.
(S) (3:09) JCI 3185 1965 - Only Love - 1969.
(S) (3:09) Time-Life AM1-01 AM Gold - 1969.

1969 ELI'S COMING

(S) (2:40) MCA 31207 Vintage Music Volume 10. *(LP version)*
(S) (2:40) MCA 5806 Vintage Music Volumes 9 & 10. *(LP version)*
(S) (2:40) MCA 6018 Best Of. *(LP version)*
(S) (2:40) MCA 31046 Suitable For Framing. *(LP version)*
(S) (2:46) MCA 10956 Celebrate: Three Dog Night Story. *(45 version but missing a guitar overdub)*
(S) (2:39) Time-Life 2CLR-20 Classic Rock - 1969: Shakin' All Over. *(LP version)*
(S) (2:40) MCA Special Products 22130 Vintage Collectibles Volume 1. *(LP version)*
(S) (2:39) JCI 3126 1965 - Only Rock 'N Roll - 1969. *(LP version)*
(S) (2:46) MCA Special Products 20893 Greatest Tour Bands Ever Recorded. *(45 version but missing a guitar overdub)*

1970 CELEBRATE

(S) (3:13) MCA 6018 Best Of. *(LP version)*
(S) (3:13) MCA 31046 Suitable For Framing. *(LP version)*
(M) (3:00) MCA 10956 Celebrate: Three Dog Night Story. *(45 version)*
(S) (3:12) JCI 3160 18 Free & Easy Hits From The 60's. *(LP version)*
(S) (3:13) JCI 3190 1965 - Only Dance - 1969. *(LP version)*

1970 MAMA TOLD ME (NOT TO COME)

(S) (3:17) Rhino 70631 Billboard's Top Rock & Roll Hits Of 1970.
(S) (3:17) Rhino 72005 Billboard's Top Rock & Roll Hits 1968-1972 Box Set.
(S) (3:17) Motown 6161 The Good-Feeling Music Of The Big Chill Generation Volume 3.
(S) (3:17) DCC Compact Classics 043 Toga Rock II.
(S) (3:17) MCA 31274 Classic Rock Volume 2.
(S) (3:17) MCA 5940 Vintage Music Volumes 19 & 20.
(S) (3:17) MCA 31216 Vintage Music Volume 19.
(S) (3:16) MCA 6018 Best Of.
(S) (3:17) MCA 31047 It Ain't Easy.
(S) (3:16) Priority 7066 #1 Groups/70's Greatest Rock Hits Volume 12.

612

(S) (3:18) MCA 10956 Celebrate: Three Dog Night Story.
(S) (3:17) Razor & Tie 22502 Those Rocking 70's. *(hissy)*
(S) (3:17) Time-Life SOD-01 Sounds Of The Seventies - 1970.
(S) (3:17) MCA Special Products 22133 Vintage Collectibles Volume 4.
(S) (3:16) JCI 3130 1970 - Only Rock 'N Roll - 1974.
(S) (3:16) Madacy Entertainment 1970 Rock On 1970.
(S) (3:16) Hollywood 62109 O.S.T. G.I. Jane.
(S) (3:15) Capitol 93076 More Music From O.S.T. Boogie Nights.
(S) (3:17) Hip-O 40096 '70s Hit(s) Back Again.
(S) (3:16) K-Tel 3987 70s Heavy Hitters: #1 Pop Hits.
(S) (3:49) Geffen 25218 O.S.T. Fear And Loathing In Las Vegas. *(time includes :33 of movie dialogue; all songs and the movie dialogue are segued together)*

1970 OUT IN THE COUNTRY
(S) (3:07) MCA 6018 Best Of.
(S) (3:07) MCA 31047 It Ain't Easy.
(S) (3:07) MCA 10956 Celebrate: Three Dog Night Story.

1970 ONE MAN BAND
(S) (2:49) MCA 6018 Best Of.
(S) (2:50) MCA 1466 Joy To The World: Their Greatest Hits.
(S) (2:51) MCA 31355 Naturally.
(S) (2:50) MCA 10956 Celebrate: Three Dog Night Story.

1971 JOY TO THE WORLD
(M) (3:16) Rhino 70632 Billboard's Top Rock & Roll Hits Of 1971. *(45 version)*
(M) (3:16) Rhino 72005 Billboard's Top Rock & Roll Hits 1968-1972 Box Set. *(45 version)*
(S) (3:36) Motown 6160 The Good-Feeling Music Of The Big Chill Generation Volume 2. *(LP version)*
(S) (3:34) Motown 6120 and 6062 O.S.T. The Big Chill. *(LP version)*
(S) (3:33) MCA 6018 Best Of. *(LP version)*
(S) (3:36) MCA 1466 Joy To The World: Their Greatest Hits. *(LP version)*
(S) (3:39) MCA 31355 Naturally. *(LP version)*
(M) (3:14) MCA 10956 Celebrate: Three Dog Night Story. *(45 version)*
(M) (3:14) Razor & Tie 22505 More Fabulous 70's Volume 2. *(45 version)*
(M) (3:16) Time-Life SOD-02 Sounds Of The Seventies - 1971. *(45 version)*
(M) (3:16) Time-Life R921-38 Get Together. *(45 version)*
(M) (3:16) Epic 66329 O.S.T. Forrest Gump. *(45 version)*
(M) (3:13) JCI 3130 1970 - Only Rock 'N Roll - 1974. *(45 version)*
(S) (3:39) Rhino 72131 Frat Rock: The 70's. *(LP version)*
(S) (3:40) MCA Special Products 20910 Rockin' 70's. *(LP version)*
(S) (3:31) K-Tel 3796 Music For Your Party. *(LP version)*
(M) (3:15) Time-Life R840-03 Sounds Of The Seventies - Pop Nuggets: Early '70s. *(45 version)*
(M) (3:16) Collectables 1516 and 2516 The Anniversary Album - The 70's. *(45 version; truncated fade)*
(S) (3:50) K-Tel 4066 K-Tel's Original Party Music Vol. 2. *(LP version but much slower)*

1971 LIAR
(S) (3:02) MCA 6018 Best Of. *(45 version but :16 shorter than the 45)*
(S) (3:02) MCA 1466 Joy To The World: Their Greatest Hits. *(45 version but :16 shorter than the 45)*
(S) (3:52) MCA 31355 Naturally. *(LP version)*
(M) (3:18) MCA 10956 Celebrate: Three Dog Night Story. *(45 version)*
(S) (3:37) Time-Life SOD-12 Sounds Of The Seventies - 1971: Take Two. *(neither the 45 or LP version)*
(S) (3:02) Time-Life R968-11 Guitar Rock - The Early '70s. *(45 version but :16 shorter than the 45)*

1971 AN OLD FASHIONED LOVE SONG
(actual 45 time is (3:42) not (3:21) as stated on the record label)
(S) (3:23) MCA 6018 Best Of. *(LP version)*
(S) (3:22) MCA 1466 Joy To The World: Their Greatest Hits. *(LP version)*
(S) (3:23) MCA 31329 Harmony. *(LP version)*

(S) (3:48) MCA 10956 Celebrate: Three Dog Night Story. *(45 version with slightly longer fade)*
(S) (3:16) Time-Life SUD-10 Superhits - 1971. *(LP version)*
(S) (3:22) MCA Special Products 20949 Rockin' 70's Volume 2. *(LP version)*
(S) (3:45) Madacy Entertainment 1971 Rock On 1971. *(45 version)*
(S) (3:19) K-Tel 3639 Dim The Lights - Soft Rock Hits Of The 70's. *(LP version)*
(S) (3:16) Time-Life AM1-06 AM Gold - 1971. *(LP version)*
(S) (3:46) Rhino 72738 Billboard Top Soft Rock Hits - 1972. *(45 version)*

1972 NEVER BEEN TO SPAIN
(S) (3:42) MCA 6018 Best Of.
(S) (3:43) MCA 1466 Joy To The World: Their Greatest Hits.
(S) (3:44) MCA 31329 Harmony.
(S) (3:43) MCA 10956 Celebrate: Three Dog Night Story.
(S) (3:41) Time-Life SOD-33 Sounds Of The Seventies - AM Pop Classics II.
(S) (3:43) Madacy Entertainment 1972 Rock On 1972.
(S) (3:40) JCI 3168 #1 Radio Hits 1970 - Only Rock 'n Roll - 1974.
(S) (3:43) Priority 50952 I Love Rock & Roll Volume 3: Hits Of The 70's.

1972 THE FAMILY OF MAN
(S) (3:08) MCA 6018 Best Of. *(LP version faded in an unsuccessful attempt at recreating the 45 version)*
(S) (3:09) MCA 1466 Joy To The World: Their Greatest Hits. *(LP version faded in an unsuccessful attempt at recreating the 45 version)*
(S) (3:33) MCA 31329 Harmony. *(LP version)*
(M) (3:25) MCA 10956 Celebrate: Three Dog Night Story. *(45 version but :13 longer fade than the 45)*

1972 BLACK & WHITE
(S) (3:47) Rhino 70633 Billboard's Top Rock & Roll Hits Of 1972. *(LP version)*
(S) (3:47) Rhino 72005 Billboard's Top Rock & Roll Hits 1968-1972 Box Set. *(LP version)*
(S) (3:44) MCA 6018 Best Of. *(LP version)*
(S) (3:47) MCA 1466 Joy To The World: Their Greatest Hits. *(LP version)*
(S) (3:49) MCA 31399 Seven Separate Fools. *(LP version)*
(S) (3:24) MCA 10956 Celebrate: Three Dog Night Story. *(45 version)*
(S) (3:44) Time-Life SUD-11 Superhits - 1972. *(LP version)*
(S) (3:47) Time-Life SOD-03 Sounds Of The Seventies - 1972. *(LP version)*
(S) (3:44) Time-Life AM1-07 AM Gold - 1972. *(LP version)*

1973 PIECES OF APRIL
(S) (4:10) MCA 6018 Best Of.
(S) (4:10) MCA 31399 Seven Separate Fools.
(M) (4:10) MCA 10956 Celebrate: Three Dog Night Story.

1973 SHAMBALA
(E) (3:22) MCA 6018 Best Of.
(E) (3:23) MCA 1466 Joy To The World: Their Greatest Hits.
(E) (3:23) MCA 31366 Cyan.
(M) (3:25) MCA 10956 Celebrate: Three Dog Night Story.
(E) (3:19) Time-Life SUD-13 Superhits - 1973.
(E) (3:17) Time-Life SOD-14 Sounds Of The Seventies - 1973: Take Two.
(M) (3:23) Madacy Entertainment 1973 Rock On 1973.
(E) (3:21) K-Tel 3625 Dynamite.
(M) (3:25) Rhino 72739 Billboard Top Soft Rock Hits - 1973.

1973 LET ME SERENADE YOU
(S) (3:02) MCA 6018 Best Of. *(:08 shorter than the 45)*
(S) (3:03) MCA 1466 Joy To The World: Their Greatest Hits. *(:07 shorter than the 45)*
(S) (3:15) MCA 31366 Cyan. *(LP length)*
(S) (3:15) MCA 10956 Celebrate: Three Dog Night Story. *(LP length)*

1974 THE SHOW MUST GO ON
(S) (3:26) MCA 6018 Best Of. *(45 version faded :10 early)*
(S) (3:34) MCA 1466 Joy To The World: Their Greatest Hits. *(45 version)*
(S) (4:24) MCA 31362 Hard Labor. *(LP version)*
(S) (3:44) MCA 10956 Celebrate: Three Dog Night Story. *(45 version but :08 longer fade)*

THREE DOG NIGHT *(Continued)*
- (S) (3:34) Time-Life AM1-21 AM Gold - 1974. *(45 version)*

1974 SURE AS I'M SITTIN' HERE
- (S) (4:46) MCA 31362 Hard Labor. *(LP version)*
- (S) (4:46) MCA 10956 Celebrate: Three Dog Night Story. *(LP version)*

1974 PLAY SOMETHING SWEET (BRICKYARD BLUES)
- (S) (4:48) MCA 6018 Best Of. *(LP version)*
- (S) (4:47) MCA 31362 Hard Labor. *(LP version)*
- (S) (4:48) MCA 10956 Celebrate: Three Dog Night Story. *(LP version)*

1975 TIL THE WORLD ENDS
- (S) (3:31) MCA 10956 Celebrate: Three Dog Night Story.

3T
1996 ANYTHING
- (S) (5:21) MJJ Music/550 Music 57450 Brotherhood.

JOHNNY THUNDER
1963 LOOP DE LOOP
- (M) (2:16) Time-Life R962-08 History Of Rock 'N' Roll: Sound Of The City 1959-1965. *(intro fades in unlike the original hit version)*
- (S) (2:21) Ripete 0003 Coolin' Out/24 Carolina Classics Vol. 3.

THUNDERCLAP NEWMAN
1969 SOMETHING IN THE AIR
(this 45 was reissued in 1973 and dj copies ran (2:45) and (3:55))
- (S) (3:53) Rebound 314520269 Class Reunion 1969. *(LP mix)*
- (S) (3:53) Rebound 314520277 Hard Rock Essentials - The 60's. *(LP mix)*
- (S) (3:53) Polydor 833794 Hollywood Dream. *(LP mix)*
- (S) (3:54) Polydor 833794 Hollywood Dream. *(45 mix)*
- (S) (3:52) CBS Special Products 46807 Rock Goes To The Movies 4. *(LP mix)*
- (S) (3:53) MCA 25240 Classic Rock Volume Three. *(LP mix)*
- (M) (3:50) Rhino 70327 History Of British Rock Volume 9. *(45 mix)*
- (M) (3:50) Rhino 72022 History Of British Rock Box Set. *(45mix)*
- (S) (3:52) Time-Life 2CLR-20 Classic Rock - 1969: Shakin' All Over. *(LP mix)*
- (S) (3:54) Special Music 5040 Great Britons! Volume Two. *(LP mix)*
- (S) (3:53) Touchwood 2013 Hollywood Dream. *(LP mix)*
- (S) (3:54) Touchwood 2013 Hollywood Dream. *(45 mix)*

TIERRA
1981 TOGETHER
(actual LP time is (4:24) not (4:15) as stated on the record label)
- (S) (4:13) Original Sound 8878 Art Laboe's Dedicated To You.
- (S) (4:20) Original Sound 8865 Oldies But Goodies Vol. 15. *(this compact disc uses the "Waring - fds" noise reduction process)*
- (S) (4:20) Original Sound 2222 Oldies But Goodies Volumes 3,5,11,14 and 15 Box Set. *(this box set uses the "Waring - fds" noise reduction process)*
- (S) (4:20) Original Sound 2500 Oldies But Goodies Volumes 1-15 Box Set. *(this box set uses the "Waring - fds" noise reduction process)*
- (S) (4:13) Original Sound 4001 Art Laboe's 60 Killer Oldies.
- (S) (4:18) Original Sound CDGO-11 Golden Oldies Volume. 11.
- (S) (4:16) Thump 9910 Tonight. *(1993 rerecording)*
- (S) (4:23) Rhino 72868 Brown Eyed Soul Vol. 1.
- (S) (4:18) Thump 7100 Latin Oldies. *(rerecording)*
- (S) (4:22) Rhino 72920 Raza Rock Of The '70s & '80s.

TIFFANY
1987 I THINK WE'RE ALONE NOW
- (S) (3:46) MCA 5793 Tiffany.
- (S) (3:45) Time-Life R988-09 Sounds Of The Eighties: 1987.

- (S) (3:46) Big Ear Music 4003 Only In The 80's Volume Three.
- (S) (3:46) MCA Special Products 20897 Greatest Rock Hits Of The 80's.
- (S) (3:45) Madacy Entertainment 1987 Rock On 1987.
- (S) (3:47) Hip-O 40018 Greatest Hits.
- (S) (3:46) JCI 3171 #1 Radio Hits 1985 - Only Rock 'n Roll - 1989.
- (S) (3:46) Hollywood 62123 More Music From The Motion Picture "Romy And Michele's High School Reunion".
- (S) (3:47) Hip-O 40075 Rock She Said: On The Pop Side.
- (S) (3:47) Hip-O 40080 Essential '80s: 1985-1989.
- (S) (3:47) Rhino 75217 Heartthrob Hits.

1988 COULD'VE BEEN
- (S) (3:32) MCA 5793 Tiffany.
- (S) (3:32) Hip-O 40018 Greatest Hits.
- (S) (3:32) Time-Life R988-19 Sounds Of The Eighties: The Late '80s.
- (S) (3:32) Time-Life R834-12 Body Talk - By Candlelight.

1988 I SAW HIM STANDING THERE
- (S) (4:11) MCA 5793 Tiffany. *(LP length)*
- (S) (4:10) Hip-O 40018 Greatest Hits. *(LP length)*

1989 ALL THIS TIME
- (S) (4:20) MCA 6267 Hold An Old Friend's Hand.
- (S) (4:20) Hip-O 40018 Greatest Hits.

1989 RADIO ROMANCE
- (S) (4:04) MCA 6267 Hold An Old Friend's Hand.
- (S) (4:04) Hip-O 40018 Greatest Hits.

JOHNNY TILLOTSON
1960 WHY DO I LOVE YOU SO
- (S) (2:04) Varese Sarabande 5570 Poetry In Motion - Best Of.
- (S) (2:02) Collectables 5251 Golden Classics.

1960 POETRY IN MOTION
- (S) (2:30) Rhino 75893 Jukebox Classics Volume 1.
- (S) (2:29) Original Sound 8892 Dick Clark's 21 All-Time Hits Vol. 2.
- (S) (2:28) Time-Life 2RNR-27 Rock 'N' Roll Era - Teen Idols.
- (S) (2:31) Varese Sarabande 5570 Poetry In Motion - Best Of.
- (S) (2:28) Time-Life R857-02 The Heart Of Rock 'n' Roll - 1960.
- (S) (2:31) Varese Sarabande 5579 History Of Cadence Records Volume 2.
- (S) (2:30) Collectables 5251 Golden Classics.
- (S) (2:28) Music Club 50015 Love Me Forever - 18 Rock'N' Roll Love Songs. *(alternate take)*

1961 JIMMY'S GIRL
- (S) (2:41) Varese Sarabande 5570 Poetry In Motion - Best Of.
- (M) (2:41) Collectables 5251 Golden Classics.

1961 WITHOUT YOU
- (M) (2:07) Time-Life HPD-37 Your Hit Parade - The 60's.
- (M) (2:05) Varese Sarabande 5570 Poetry In Motion - Best Of.
- (M) (2:06) Varese Sarabande 5579 History Of Cadence Records Volume 2.
- (M) (2:06) Collectables 5251 Golden Classics.
- (M) (2:07) Time-Life R857-14 The Heart Of Rock 'n' Roll 1960-1961 Take Two.

1962 DREAMY EYES
- (M) (2:21) Varese Sarabande 5570 Poetry In Motion - Best Of.
- (E) (2:20) K-Tel 478 More 50's Jukebox Favorites.
- (M) (2:21) LaserLight 12323 American Dreams.
- (M) (2:20) Collectables 5251 Golden Classics.

1962 IT KEEPS RIGHT ON A-HURTIN'
- (S) (2:51) Rhino 75894 Jukebox Classics Volume 2.
- (S) (2:47) Time-Life 2RNR-47 Rock 'N' Roll Era - Teen Idols II.
- (S) (2:49) Time-Life SUD-06 Superhits - 1962.
- (S) (2:47) Risky Business 66388 The Big Hurt/Songs To Cry By.
- (S) (2:46) Varese Sarabande 5570 Poetry In Motion - Best Of.
- (S) (2:46) Varese Sarabande 5578 History Of Cadence Records Volume 1.
- (S) (2:49) Time-Life AM1-18 AM Gold - 1962.
- (S) (2:47) Collectables 5251 Golden Classics.
- (S) (2:47) JCI 3184 1960 - Only Love - 1964.
- (S) (2:49) Varese Sarabande 5845 The Country Hits Collection. *(rerecording)*

1962 SEND ME THE PILLOW YOU DREAM ON
- (S) (2:50) Varese Sarabande 5570 Poetry In Motion - Best Of.
- (S) (2:50) Collectables 5251 Golden Classics.
- (S) (2:52) Music Club 50015 Love Me Forever - 18 Rock'N' Roll Love Songs.
- (S) (2:18) Varese Sarabande 5845 The Country Hits Collection. *(rerecording)*

1962 I CAN'T HELP IT (IF I'M STILL IN LOVE WITH YOU)
- (S) (2:23) Varese Sarabande 5570 Poetry In Motion - Best Of.
- (S) (2:23) Collectables 5251 Golden Classics.

1963 OUT OF MY MIND
- (M) (2:37) Varese Sarabande 5570 Poetry In Motion - Best Of.
- (M) (2:37) Collectables 5251 Golden Classics.

1963 YOU CAN NEVER STOP ME LOVING YOU
- (M) (2:41) Varese Sarabande 5570 Poetry In Motion - Best Of.
- (M) (2:41) Collectables 5251 Golden Classics.

1964 TALK BACK TREMBLING LIPS
- (S) (2:36) Varese Sarabande 5570 Poetry In Motion - Best Of.
- (S) (2:36) Collectables 5251 Golden Classics.
- (S) (2:36) Varese Sarabande 5845 The Country Hits Collection.
- (S) (2:35) Polygram Special Markets 314520460 #1 Radio Hits Of The 60's.

1964 WORRIED GUY

1964 I RISE, I FALL
- (S) (2:15) Varese Sarabande 5845 The Country Hits Collection.

1964 SHE UNDERSTANDS ME
- (S) (1:57) Varese Sarabande 5570 Poetry In Motion - Best Of.

1965 HEARTACHES BY THE NUMBER
- (S) (2:35) Varese Sarabande 5570 Poetry In Motion - Best Of.
- (S) (2:34) Varese Sarabande 5845 The Country Hits Collection.

'TIL TUESDAY
1985 VOICES CARRY
- (S) (4:17) JCI 2720 Rockin' Ladies Of The 80's.
- (S) (4:20) Priority 53721 Rock Of The 80's Volume 5.
- (S) (4:20) Risky Business 57833 Read The Hits/Best Of The 80's.
- (S) (4:20) K-Tel 3261 The 80's Rock On.
- (S) (4:21) Rhino 71977 New Wave Hits Of The 80's Vol. 14.
- (S) (4:20) Epic 39458 Voices Carry.
- (S) (4:20) Time-Life R988-02 Sounds Of The Eighties: 1985.
- (S) (4:19) Epic 67534 Club Epic Volume 5.
- (S) (4:20) Epic/Legacy 64944 Coming Up Close: A Retrospective.
- (S) (4:19) Priority 50953 I Love Rock & Roll Volume 4: Hits Of The 80's.
- (S) (4:20) Right Stuff 57092 Free To Be Volume 9.
- (S) (4:20) Time-Life R834-20 Body Talk - Heart And Soul.

1986 WHAT ABOUT LOVE
- (S) (3:56) Priority 53749 Rock Of The 80's Volume 6.
- (S) (3:56) Risky Business 66392 Get Into The Greed: Greatest Hits Of The 80's.
- (S) (3:56) Epic 40314 Welcome Home.
- (S) (3:56) Epic/Legacy 64944 Coming Up Close: A Retrospective.

TIMBALAND AND MAGOO
1997 UP JUMPS DA BOOGIE
- (S) (5:00) Blackground/Atlantic 92772 Welcome To Our World. *(tracks into the next selection)*

TIMBUK 3
1986 THE FUTURE'S SO BRIGHT I GOTTA WEAR SHADES
- (S) (3:21) EMI 27674 Living In Oblivion: The 80's Greatest Hits Volume Three.
- (S) (3:20) IRS 82010 These People Are Nuts.
- (S) (3:20) IRS 29695 On The Charts: IRS Records 1979-1994.
- (S) (3:21) Priority 53721 Rock Of The 80's Volume 5.
- (S) (3:21) Sandstone 33050 and 5018 Cosmopolitan Volume 4.
- (S) (3:21) K-Tel 3261 The 80's Rock On.
- (S) (3:21) DCC Compact Classics 089 Night Moves Volume 7.
- (S) (3:22) IRS 5739 Greetings From Timbuk3.
- (S) (3:22) IRS 13162 Some Of The Best Of/Field Guide.

- (S) (3:21) Time-Life R988-04 Sounds Of The Eighties: 1986.
- (S) (3:21) Big Ear Music 4003 Only In The 80's Volume Three.
- (S) (3:21) Hip-O 40004 The '80s Hit(s) Back!
- (S) (3:21) JCI 3150 1985 - Only Dance - 1989.

TIME
1985 JUNGLE LOVE
- (S) (5:28) Rhino 71972 Video Soul - Best Soul Of The 80's Vol. 2. *(LP version)*
- (S) (5:30) Warner Brothers 25109 Ice Cream Castle. *(LP version)*

1985 THE BIRD
- (S) (7:42) Warner Brothers 25109 Ice Cream Castle. *(LP version)*

1990 JERK OUT
- (S) (6:49) Paisley Park/Reprise 27490 Pandemonium. *(LP version)*
- (S) (4:22) Cold Front 6284 More Of! Club Mix's Biggest Jams. *(all selections on this cd are segued together; remix)*

TIMES TWO
1988 STRANGE BUT TRUE
- (S) (4:07) Reprise 25624 X2.

TIMEX SOCIAL CLUB
1986 RUMORS
- (S) (4:50) Priority 7954 Rapmasters 4 - The Best Of Hip Hop. *(LP version)*
- (S) (4:41) Priority 9466 Rap's Greatest Hits. *(LP version)*
- (S) (4:45) Rhino 70590 West Coast Rap: The First Dynasty, Vol. 1. *(LP version)*
- (S) (4:45) Rhino 72141 Billboard Hot R&B Hits 1986. *(LP version)*
- (S) (5:44) Rhino 72409 New Jack Hits. *(remixed)*
- (S) (4:29) Priority 50941 Shut Up And Dance! Volume Two - The 80's. *(all songs on this cd are segued together)*
- (S) (4:29) Cold Front 6247 Classic Club Mix - Dance Jams. *(all songs on this cd are segued together)*

TIMMY -T-
1991 ONE MORE TRY
- (S) (3:28) Quality 15103 Time After Time.
- (S) (3:13) Time-Life R834-18 Body Talk - Romantic Moments.

TIN TIN
1971 TOAST AND MARMALADE FOR TEA
- (M) (2:23) Rhino 71196 Super Hits Of The 70's Volume 16.
- (M) (2:21) Time-Life SOD-33 Sounds Of The Seventies - AM Pop Classics II.

TINY TIM
1968 TIP-TOE THRU' THE TULIPS WITH ME
- (S) (1:43) K-Tel 3036 Silly Songs. *(rerecorded)*
- (S) (1:50) Time-Life HPD-40 Your Hit Parade - Golden Goofers.
- (S) (1:49) Rhino 72124 Dr. Demento 25th Anniversary Collection.

TLC
1992 AIN'T 2 PROUD 2 BEG
- (S) (6:21) Arista 18735 House Of Groove. *(remix)*
- (S) (4:07) Rhino 71916 Whats Up? Rap Hits Of The 90's. *(45 version)*
- (S) (5:36) LaFace 26003 Ooooooohhh...On The TLC Tip. *(LP version)*

1992 BABY-BABY-BABY
- (S) (4:56) Tommy Boy 1075 MTV Party To Go Volume 4. *(remix; all tracks on this cd are segued together)*
- (S) (5:14) LaFace 26003 Ooooooohhh...On The TLC Tip.
- (S) (5:12) K-Tel 6101 Hot Ladies Of The 90's - Dazzling Divas.

1992 WHAT ABOUT YOUR FRIENDS
- (S) (4:53) LaFace 26003 Ooooooohhh...On The TLC Tip.

1993 HAT 2 DA BACK
- (S) (4:13) K-Tel 6102 Funk-Tastic Jams.
- (S) (4:16) LaFace 26003 Ooooooohhh...On The TLC Tip.

TLC *(Continued)*
1993 GET IT UP
   (S) (4:23)   Epic 57131 O.S.T. Poetic Justice.
1995 CREEP
   (S) (4:28)   LaFace 26009 Crazy Sexy Cool.
1995 RED LIGHT SPECIAL
   (S) (5:02)   LaFace 26009 Crazy Sexy Cool.
1995 WATERFALLS
   (S) (4:39)   LaFace 26009 Crazy Sexy Cool.
   (S) (4:39)   Grammy Recordings/Sony 67565 1996 Grammy Nominees.
1996 DIGGIN' ON YOU
   (S) (4:14)   LaFace 26009 Crazy Sexy Cool.

TOAD THE WET SPROCKET
1992 ALL I WANT
   (S) (3:16)   Columbia 47309 Fear.
1993 WALK ON THE OCEAN
   (S) (2:59)   Columbia 47309 Fear. *(LP version)*
1994 FALL DOWN
   (S) (3:22)   Columbia 57744 Dulcinea.

TOBY BEAU
1978 MY ANGEL BABY
   (S) (3:36)   Scotti Bros. 75465 Angel Hits.
   (S) (3:35)   RCA 66812 Do You Love Me? (All-Time Best Love Songs).
   (S) (3:29)   Rhino 72299 Superhits Of The 70's Volume 25.
   (S) (3:29)   Varese Sarabande 5706 Dick Bartley Presents Collector's Essentials: The 70's.
   (S) (3:30)   Simitar 55562 The Number One's: Smooth Love.
   (S) (3:35)   Time-Life R834-11 Body Talk - After Dark.

ART and DOTTY TODD
1958 CHANSON d'AMOUR (SONG OF LOVE)
   (M) (2:50)   Time-Life HPD-23 Your Hit Parade - The Late 50's.
   (M) (2:52)   K-Tel 478 More 50's Jukebox Favorites. *(no fidelity)*
   (E) (2:52)   Curb 77775 Hard To Find Original Recordings - Classic Hits. *(no fidelity)*

NICK TODD
1957 PLAYTHING
   (M) (2:03)   Varese Sarabande 5687 History Of Dot Records Volume Two.
1958 AT THE HOP

TOKENS
1961 TONIGHT I FELL IN LOVE
   (M) (1:44)   Rhino 71463 Doo Wop Box.
   (S) (1:45)   Warlock 8702 Silver Anniversary/Greatest Hits. *(rerecording)*
   (S) (1:48)   B.T. Puppy 0519 Oldies Are Now. *(rerecording)*
   (M) (1:44)   Time-Life 2RNR-45 Rock 'N' Roll Era - Street Corner Serenade.
1961 THE LION SLEEPS TONIGHT
   (S) (2:39)   Rhino 70622 Billboard's Top Rock & Roll Hits Of 1961. *(found only on the original 1988 issue of this cd)*
   (S) (2:39)   Rhino 72004 Billboard's Top Rock & Roll Hits 1957-1961 Box Set.
   (S) (2:39)   RCA 8474 Nipper's Greatest Hits Of The 60's Volume 1.
   (S) (2:39)   RCA 9902 Nipper's #1 Hits 1956-1986.
   (S) (2:38)   Rhino 70495 Fun Rock!
   (S) (2:45)   Warlock 8702 Silver Anniversary/Greatest Hits. *(rerecording)*
   (S) (2:36)   B.T. Puppy 0519 Oldies Are Now. *(rerecording)*
   (S) (2:38)   Time-Life 2RNR-04 Rock 'N' Roll Era - 1961.
   (S) (2:38)   Time-Life R962-06 History Of Rock 'N' Roll: Doo Wop And Vocal Group Tradition 1955-1962.
   (S) (2:38)   Time-Life R10513 40 Lovin' Oldies.
   (S) (2:40)   RCA 66474 Wimoweh!!! The Best Of.
   (S) (2:40)   RCA 66510 The Lion Sleeps Tonight.
   (M) (2:36)   Priority 50951 I Love Rock & Roll Volume 2: Hits Of The 60's.

   (S) (2:38)   Eclipse Music Group 64867 Rock 'n Roll Relix 1960-1961.
   (S) (2:38)   Eclipse Music Group 64872 Rock 'n Roll Relix 1960-1969.
   (S) (2:37)   Collectables 1515 and 2515 The Anniversary Album - The 60's.
1966 I HEAR TRUMPETS BLOW
   (S) (2:39)   Warlock 8702 Silver Anniversary/Greatest Hits. *(rerecording)*
   (S) (2:51)   B.T. Puppy 0519 Oldies Are Now. *(rerecording)*
1967 PORTRAIT OF MY LOVE
   (S) (2:24)   Warlock 8702 Silver Anniversary/Greatest Hits. *(rerecording)*

TOMMY TUTONE
1980 ANGEL SAY NO
   (S) (3:10)   Rhino 71892 Radio Daze: Pop Hits Of The 80's Volume Three.
   (S) (3:11)   Priority 53775 Best Of 80's Rock Volume 1.
   (S) (3:08)   Collectables 5845 Tommy Tutone/Tommy Tutone-2.
1982 867-5309/JENNY
   (S) (3:45)   Rhino 71698 New Wave Hits Of The 80's Vol. 5.
   (S) (3:43)   Time-Life R105-40 Rock Dreams.
   (S) (3:44)   Risky Business 57833 Read The Hits/Best Of The 80's.
   (S) (3:45)   Rhino 72133 Frat Rock: The 80's.
   (S) (3:44)   Time-Life R988-05 Sounds Of The Eighties: 1982.
   (S) (3:45)   Rhino 72771 The Big 80's.
   (S) (3:43)   JCI 3143 18 Screamers From The 80's.
   (S) (3:45)   Priority 50953 I Love Rock & Roll Volume 4: Hits Of The 80's.
   (S) (3:45)   Rhino 72595 Billboard Top Album Rock Hits, 1982.
   (S) (3:44)   Collectables 5845 Tommy Tutone/Tommy Tutone-2.
   (S) (3:43)   Simitar 55142 80's Rock Classics - Party Town.

TOM TOM CLUB
1982 GENIUS OF LOVE
   (S) (5:34)   Original Sound 9303 Art Laboe's Dedicated To You Vol. 3. *(LP version)*
   (S) (5:34)   Sire 3628 Tom Tom Club. *(LP version)*

TONE LOC
1989 WILD THING
   (S) (4:22)   JCI 2713 Bust It.
   (S) (4:22)   K-Tel 315 Rap's Biggest Hits.
   (S) (4:24)   Sandstone 33046 and 5012 Rock The First Volume Six.
   (S) (4:23)   Delicious Vinyl 3000 and 71813 Loc-ed After Dark.
   (S) (4:23)   Time-Life R988-30 Sounds Of The Eighties: The Rolling Stone Collection 1988-1989.
   (S) (4:20)   Atlantic 82530 O.S.T. Amongst Friends. *(missing the opening line)*
   (S) (4:08)   Thump 4530 Old School Rap Volume 3. *(all songs on this cd are segued together)*
   (S) (4:23)   Priority 50982 Rap's Greatest Hits Volume Two.
   (S) (4:22)   Cold Front 6245 Greatest Sports Rock And Jams. *(all selections on this cd are segued together)*
   (S) (4:23)   Street Life 75510 West Coast Collection, Volume 1.
   (S) (4:22)   Robbins 75002 Strip Jointz - Hot Songs For Sexy Dancers.
1989 FUNKY COLD MEDINA
   (S) (4:12)   Priority 7940 On The Rap Tip.
   (S) (4:11)   Priority 53732 80's Greatest Rock Hits Volume 8 - Dance Party.
   (S) (4:07)   Delicious Vinyl 3000 and 71813 Loc-ed After Dark.
   (S) (4:07)   K-Tel 3750 History Of Rap Volume 2.
   (S) (4:11)   Time-Life R988-13 Sounds Of The Eighties: 1989.
   (S) (4:07)   Cold Front 6246 Classic Club Mix - R&B Grooves. *(all selections on this cd are segued together)*

OSCAR TONEY JR.
1967 FOR YOUR PRECIOUS LOVE

TONY and JOE
1958 THE FREEZE

TONY! TONI! TONE!
1990 FEELS GOOD
    (S) (4:53) Priority 7053 Best Of Hip Hop.
    (S) (6:43) Tommy Boy 1037 MTV Party To Go Volume 1.
              (remix; all tracks on this cd are segued together)
    (S) (4:57) Wing 841902 The Revival.
    (S) (4:57) Mercury 314536368 Hits.
1991 IT NEVER RAINS (IN SOUTHERN CALIFORNIA)
    (S) (5:02) Wing 841902 The Revival.
    (S) (4:56) Mercury 314536368 Hits.
1993 IF I HAD NO LOOT
    (S) (4:01) Wing 314514933 Sons Of Soul.
    (S) (4:01) Mercury 314536368 Hits.
1993 ANNIVERSARY
    (S) (6:21) Tommy Boy 1097 MTV Party To Go Volume 5.
              (remix; all tracks on this cd are segued together)
    (S) (9:23) Wing 314514933 Sons Of Soul.
    (S) (4:29) Mercury 314536368 Hits.
1994 (LAY YOUR HEAD ON MY) PILLOW
    (S) (6:10) Wing 314514933 Sons Of Soul.
    (S) (6:05) Mercury 314536368 Hits.
1997 THINKING OF YOU
    (S) (3:57) Mercury 314534250 House Of Music.
    (S) (3:54) Mercury 314536368 Hits.

TORNADOES
1962 TELSTAR
    (M) (3:17) Rhino 70323 History Of British Rock Volume 5.
    (M) (3:17) Rhino 70319 History Of British Rock Box Set.
    (M) (3:17) Rhino 71602 Rock Instrumental Classics Volume 2: The Sixties.
    (M) (3:17) Rhino 72035 Rock Instrumental Classics Vols. 1-5 Box Set.
    (M) (3:17) Razor & Tie 2080 It's Hard To Believe It: The Amazing World Of Joe Meek.
    (S) (3:14) K-Tel 6256 Kahuna Classics. *(rerecording)*
    (E) (3:20) Music Club 50029 Very Best Of.

MITCHELL TOROK
1957 PLEDGE OF LOVE
1959 CARIBBEAN

TOTAL
released as by TOTAL featuring THE NOTORIOUS B.I.G.:
1995 CAN'T YOU SEE
    (S) (4:41) Bad Boy 73006 Total.
    (S) (4:50) Tommy Boy 1114 O.S.T. New Jersey Drive.
released as by TOTAL featuring DA BRAT:
1996 NO ONE ELSE
    (S) (4:20) Bad Boy 73006 Total.
    (S) (4:13) Arista 18977 Ultimate Hip Hop Party 1998. *(all selections on this cd are segued together; remix)*
released as by TOTAL:
1996 KISSIN' YOU
    (S) (4:40) Bad Boy 73006 Total.
1997 WHAT ABOUT US
    (S) (4:22) LaFace 26041 O.S.T. Soul Food.

TOTO
1979 HOLD THE LINE
    (S) (3:55) Columbia 45368 Past To Present (1977-1990). *(LP version)*
    (S) (3:55) Columbia 35317 Toto. *(LP version)*
    (S) (3:55) Time-Life R968-02 Guitar Rock 1978-1979. *(LP version)*
    (S) (3:30) Time-Life SOD-21 Sounds Of The Seventies - Rock 'N' Soul Seventies. *(45 version)*
    (S) (3:29) Time-Life R105-24 Guitar Rock Monsters. *(45 version)*
    (S) (3:55) MCA Special Products 20754 Classic Rock Volume 1. *(LP version)*
    (S) (3:55) Eclipse Music Group 64896 Rock 'n Roll Relix 1978-1979. *(LP version)*
    (S) (3:55) Eclipse Music Group 64897 Rock 'n Roll Relix 1970-1979. *(LP version)*
    (S) (3:55) Columbia/Legacy 65394 Toto/Hydra/Toto IV. *(LP version)*
    (S) (3:55) K-Tel 3904 The Rock Album Volume 1. *(LP version)*
    (S) (3:55) Time-Life AM1-26 AM Gold - 1979. *(LP version)*
    (S) (3:55) Priority 53139 The Best Of 70's: Rock Chart Toppers. *(LP version)*
1980 99
    (S) (5:12) Columbia 45368 Past To Present (1977-1990). *(LP version)*
    (S) (5:12) Columbia 36229 Hydra. *(LP version)*
    (S) (5:12) Columbia/Legacy 65394 Toto/Hydra/Toto IV. *(LP version)*
1982 ROSANNA
    (S) (4:00) CBS Special Products 44363 Rock Of The 80's. *(45 version)*
    (S) (4:01) Priority 53714 80's Greatest Rock Hits Volume 1 - Passion & Power. *(45 version)*
    (S) (4:01) Rhino 70677 Billboard Top Hits - 1982. *(45 version)*
    (S) (5:31) Risky Business 57833 Read The Hits/Best Of The 80's. *(LP version)*
    (S) (5:32) Columbia 37728 Toto IV. *(LP version)*
    (S) (5:29) Columbia 45368 Past To Present (1977-1990). *(LP version)*
    (S) (4:01) Time-Life R988-05 Sounds Of The Eighties: 1982. *(45 version)*
    (S) (4:00) K-Tel 3798 The 80's Mega Hits. *(45 version)*
    (S) (4:01) Time-Life R834-01 Body Talk - Forever Yours. *(45 version)*
    (S) (5:32) Columbia/Legacy 65394 Toto/Hydra/Toto IV. *(LP version)*
    (S) (5:32) Columbia/Legacy 64423 Toto IV. *(gold disc; LP version)*
1982 MAKE BELIEVE
    (S) (3:45) Columbia 37728 Toto IV.
    (S) (3:45) Columbia/Legacy 65394 Toto/Hydra/Toto IV.
    (S) (3:45) Columbia/Legacy 64423 Toto IV. *(gold disc)*
1983 AFRICA
    (S) (4:18) Rhino 70678 Billboard Top Hits - 1983. *(45 version)*
    (S) (4:56) JCI 3119 18 Rock Classics. *(LP version)*
    (S) (4:57) Columbia 37728 Toto IV. *(LP version)*
    (S) (4:56) Columbia 45368 Past To Present (1977-1990). *(LP version)*
    (S) (4:17) Time-Life R988-03 Sounds Of The Eighties: 1983. *(45 version)*
    (S) (4:57) Columbia/Legacy 65394 Toto/Hydra/Toto IV. *(LP version)*
    (S) (4:57) Columbia/Legacy 64423 Toto IV. *(gold disc; LP version)*
    (S) (4:56) Time-Life R834-13 Body Talk - Just The Two Of Us. *(LP version)*
1983 I WON'T HOLD YOU BACK
    (S) (4:55) Columbia 37728 Toto IV. *(LP version)*
    (S) (4:55) Columbia 45368 Past To Present (1977-1990). *(LP version)*
    (S) (4:55) Columbia/Legacy 65394 Toto/Hydra/Toto IV. *(LP version)*
    (S) (4:55) Columbia/Legacy 64423 Toto IV. *(gold disc; LP version)*
    (S) (4:54) Time-Life R834-16 Body Talk - Sweet Nothings. *(LP version)*
1984 STRANGER IN TOWN
    (S) (4:49) Columbia 38962 Isolation. *(LP version)*
1986 I'LL BE OVER YOU
    (S) (3:49) Columbia 40273 Fahrenheit.
    (S) (3:49) Columbia 45368 Past To Present (1977-1990).
    (S) (3:48) Time-Life R834-17 Body Talk - Heart To Heart.
1987 WITHOUT YOUR LOVE
    (S) (4:32) Columbia 40273 Fahrenheit.
1988 PAMELA
    (S) (5:09) Columbia 40873 The Seventh One. *(LP length)*
    (S) (5:09) Columbia 45368 Past To Present (1977-1990). *(LP length)*

TOWER OF POWER
1972 YOU'RE STILL A YOUNG MAN
    (S) (3:36) Original Sound 1960 Memories Of El Monte. *(45 version)*

TOWER OF POWER (Continued)

- (S) (3:36) Original Sound 4001   Art Laboe's 60 Killer Oldies. *(45 version)*
- (S) (5:34) Warner Brothers 2616   Bump City. *(LP version)*
- (S) (5:34) Thump 4710   Old School Love Songs. *(LP version)*
- (S) (3:36) Rhino 72126   Soul Hits Of The 70's Vol. 16. *(45 version)*
- (S) (5:17) Priority 53131   Deep Soul Volume Two. *(live)*
- (S) (3:36) Warner Brothers 46479   '70s Soul Revue. *(45 version)*
- (S) (5:34) Rhino 72920   Raza Rock Of The '70s & '80s. *(LP version)*
- (S) (5:34) Priority 50989   70's Greatest Rock Hits Volume 2: Rock & Soul. *(LP version)*

1973   SO VERY HARD TO GO

- (S) (3:38) Warner Brothers 2681   Tower Of Power.
- (S) (3:38) Razor & Tie 22047   Sweet 70's Soul.
- (S) (3:38) Time-Life SOD-21   Sounds Of The Seventies - Rock 'N' Soul Seventies.
- (S) (3:38) Right Stuff 29138   Slow Jams: The 70's Vol. 3.
- (S) (3:38) K-Tel 6013   70's Soul - Sexy Ballads.
- (S) (3:38) Rhino 72127   Soul Hits Of The 70's Vol. 17.
- (S) (3:38) Chronicles 314555138   Funk Ballads.

1974   DON'T CHANGE HORSES (IN THE MIDDLE OF A STREAM)

- (S) (4:41) Warner Brothers 2749   Back To Oakland.

LIDELL TOWNSELL
1992   NU NU

- (S) (5:02) Rebound 314520246   Disco Nights Vol. 5 - Best Of Housemusic.
- (S) (3:19) Mercury 314512328   Harmony.

ED TOWNSEND
1958   FOR YOUR LOVE

- (M) (2:48) Capitol 98138   Spring Break Volume 1.
- (M) (2:50) Time-Life 2RNR-28   Rock 'N' Roll Era - The 50's Rave On.
- (M) (2:50) Time-Life R102-17   Lost Treasures Of Rock 'N' Roll.
- (M) (2:49) Collectables 5509   For Your Love.
- (M) (2:49) Time-Life R857-04   The Heart Of Rock 'n' Roll - 1958.
- (M) (2:49) Hip-O 40028   The Glory Of Love - '50s Sweet & Soulful Love Songs.
- (M) (2:48) Collectables 1514 and 2514   The Anniversary Album - The 50's.

PETE TOWNSHEND
1980   LET MY LOVE OPEN THE DOOR

- (S) (2:41) Atco 32100   Empty Glass.
- (S) (2:42) Atlantic 82544   Empty Glass. *(gold disc)*
- (S) (2:42) Atlantic 82811   Empty Glass. *(remastered edition)*
- (S) (2:41) Atlantic 82712   Best Of.
- (S) (4:55) Atlantic 82712   Best Of. *(remix)*
- (S) (4:55) London 422828867   O.S.T. Grosse Pointe Blank. *(remix)*

1986   FACE THE FACE
(actual 45 time is (3:58) not (4:28) as stated on the record label)

- (S) (5:50) Atco 90473   White City. *(LP version)*
- (S) (5:51) Atlantic 82712   Best Of. *(LP version)*

TOYS
1965   A LOVER'S CONCERTO

- (M) (2:34) JCI 3102   Love Sixties.
- (M) (2:38) Rhino 70626   Billboard's Top Rock & Roll Hits Of 1965. *(found only on the 2nd pressings of this compact disc)*
- (M) (2:39) Rhino 70989   Best Of The Girl Groups Volume 2.
- (E) (2:34) Time-Life 2CLR-01   Classic Rock - 1965.
- (M) (2:34) Sundazed 6034   A Lover's Concerto/Attack.
- (M) (2:38) Rhino 71802   O.S.T. Andre.
- (M) (2:37) Polydor 314529508   O.S.T. Mr. Holland's Opus.
- (M) (2:32) TVT 7010   O.S.T. Last Supper. *(song fades in)*
- (M) (2:39) Varese Sarabande 5847   On The Radio Volume Two.
- (E) (2:34) K-Tel 3888   Great R&B Female Groups Hits Of The 60's.

- (M) (2:34) Collectables 1515 and 2515   The Anniversary Album - The 60's.

1966   ATTACK

- (M) (3:03) Sundazed 6034   A Lover's Concerto/Attack.

T'PAU
1987   HEART AND SOUL

- (S) (4:14) EMI 89605   Living In Oblivion: The 80's Greatest Hits Volume Two. *(LP version)*
- (S) (3:37) Priority 53754   Rock Of The 80's Volume 15. *(45 version)*
- (S) (4:14) K-Tel 3343   The 80's Hot Dance Trax. *(LP version)*
- (S) (4:14) Virgin 90595 and 86010   T'Pau. *(LP version)*
- (S) (4:13) K-Tel 3867   The 80's: Hot Ladies. *(LP version)*
- (S) (4:11) Renaissance 0164   Heart And Soul: The Best Of. *(LP version)*

TRADEWINDS
1965   NEW YORK'S A LONELY TOWN

- (M) (2:16) Rhino 70089   Surfin' Hits.
- (M) (2:13) DCC Compact Classics 030   Beach Classics.
- (E) (2:15) Era 5025   The Brill Building Sound.
- (M) (2:11) Time-Life 2RNR-42   Rock 'N' Roll Era - The 60's Sock Hop.
- (M) (2:14) Rhino 72418   Cowabunga! The Surf Box.
- (E) (2:16) K-Tel 6256   Kahuna Classics.
- (M) (2:10) Taragon 1029   Very Best Of Red Bird/Blue Cat Records.

TRAMMPS
1976   HOLD BACK THE NIGHT

- (S) (3:49) Priority 7972   Mega-Hits Dance Classics (Volume 2). *(LP length)*
- (S) (3:43) Ripete 2392192   Beach Music Anthology Box Set. *(LP length)*
- (S) (3:18) Rhino 71724   Best Of. *(45 length)*
- (S) (3:46) Essex 7051   Non-Stop Dance Hits - Greatest Disco Hits. *(LP length)*
- (S) (3:17) Ripete 2187-RE   Preppy Deluxe. *(45 length)*
- (S) (3:50) Ripete 2392187   Preppy Deluxe. *(LP length)*
- (S) (3:53) Collectables 5117   Golden Classics. *(LP length)*
- (S) (3:00) K-Tel 3269   Carolina Beach Music. *(:17 shorter than the 45)*
- (S) (3:17) Robbins Entertainment 75005   Super Rare Disco. *(45 length)*

1976   THAT'S WHERE THE HAPPY PEOPLE GO

- (S) (3:15) Rhino 71094   Disco Hits, Vol. 1.
- (S) (3:14) Rhino 71724   Best Of.
- (S) (3:14) K-Tel 3470   Get Up And Disco.
- (S) (3:15) Flashback 72688   Disco Hits: Get Down Tonight.
- (S) (3:15) Flashback 72086   Disco Hits Box Set.

1978   DISCO INFERNO

- (S) (3:33) Rhino 70984   The Disco Years Volume 1. *(45 version)*
- (S) (3:33) Rhino 70799   O.S.T. Spirit Of '76. *(45 version)*
- (S) (10:50) Polydor 800068 O.S.T. Saturday Night Fever. *(LP version)*
- (S) (3:33) Rhino 71095   Disco Hits Volume 2. *(45 version)*
- (S) (10:55) Atlantic 18211   Disco Inferno. *(LP version)*
- (S) (10:53) JCI 3306   Dance Seventies. *(LP version)*
- (S) (3:33) Razor & Tie 22496   Disco Fever. *(45 version)*
- (S) (3:32) Time-Life SOD-20   Sounds Of The Seventies - 1978: Take Two. *(45 version)*
- (S) (10:54) Rhino 71724 Best Of. *(LP version)*
- (S) (6:25) Rebound 314520220   Disco Nights Vol. 4 - Greatest Disco Groups. *(neither the 45, LP or 12" single version)*
- (S) (6:25) Rebound 314520366   Disco Nights Vol. 10 - Disco's Greatest Movie Hits. *(neither the 45, LP or 12" single version)*
- (S) (10:49) Polydor 422825389   O.S.T. Saturday Night Fever. *(remastered edition; LP version)*
- (S) (3:32) JCI 3148   1975 - Only Dance - 1979. *(45 version)*
- (S) (3:33) A&M 314540563   O.S.T. Kingpin. *(45 version)*

(S) (3:33) Flashback 72689 Disco Hits: Shake Your Booty.
(45 version)

(S) (10:51) Mobile Fidelity 716 O.S.T. Saturday Night Fever.
(gold disc; LP version)

(S) (3:33) Rhino 72964 Ultimate '70s R&B Smashes! *(45 version)*

(S) (8:44) Elektra 62218 Maximum Club Classics Vol. 2.
(neither the 45 or LP version)

(S) (3:33) Time-Life R840-08 Sounds Of The Seventies: '70s Dance Party 1978-1979. *(45 version)*

TRASHMEN
1964 SURFIN' BIRD
(M) (2:21) Rhino 70089 Surfin' Hits.
(M) (2:20) DCC Compact Classics 030 Beach Classics.
(M) (2:21) Rhino 70732 Grandson Of Frat Rock.
(M) (2:21) Rhino 70743 Dr. Demento 20th Anniversary Collection.
(E) (2:14) Warner Brothers 25613 O.S.T. Full Metal Jacket.
(M) (2:19) Rhino 70794 KFOG Presents M. Dung's Idiot Show.
(M) (2:20) Curb 77356 70's Hits Volume 2.
(M) (2:20) Capitol 96861 Monster Summer Hits - Wild Surf.
(M) (2:20) Sundazed 11011 Tube City! The Best Of.
(M) (2:20) Rhino 70495 Fun Rock!
(M) (2:19) Collectables 5061 History Of Rock Volume 1.
(M) (2:19) Time-Life 2RNR-10 Rock 'N' Roll Era - 1964.
(M) (2:20) Rhino 71585 Billboard Top Pop Hits, 1964.
(M) (2:20) K-Tel 3035 Goofy Greats.
(M) (2:20) Sundazed 6064 Surfin' Bird.
(M) (2:18) Sundazed 6064 Surfin' Bird. *(demo version)*
(M) (2:20) Rhino 72418 Cowabunga! The Surf Box.
(M) (2:20) K-Tel 3629 Madcap Melodies.
(M) (2:20) K-Tel 3796 Music For Your Party.
(M) (2:18) Tommy Boy 1194 ESPN Presents Slam Jams Vol. 1. *(all selections on this cd are segued together)*
(E) (2:14) Cold Front 6245 Greatest Sports Rock And Jams. *(all selections on this cd are segued together)*
(M) (2:20) Hip-O 40058 O.S.T. Pink Flamingos.
(E) (2:15) K-Tel 6256 Kahuna Classics.
(M) (2:24) Sundazed 11022 Bird Call.
(E) (2:14) Simitar 55522 The Number One's: Party Time.
(E) (2:15) JCI 3189 1960 - Only Dance - 1964.
(M) (2:21) I.D. 90072 Jenny McCarthy's Surfin' Safari.
(E) (2:15) K-Tel 4065 K-Tel's Original Party Music Vol. 1.
1964 BIRD DANCE BEAT
(M) (2:07) Sundazed 11011 Tube City! The Best Of.
(M) (2:05) Sundazed 6064 Surfin' Bird. *(demo version)*
(M) (2:12) Sundazed 11022 Bird Call.

TRAVIS & BOB
1959 TELL HIM NO
(M) (2:08) Varese Sarabande 5687 History Of Dot Records Volume Two.

JOHN TRAVOLTA
1976 LET HER IN
(S) (3:02) K-Tel 3211 70's Teen Heart-Throbs.
(S) (3:01) Varese Sarabande 5682 Sings.
(S) (2:58) Rhino 72297 Superhits Of The 70's Volume 23. *(sounds like it was mastered from vinyl)*
(S) (2:58) Hot 93 Best Of.
(S) (3:00) K-Tel 3757 Best Of: Let Her In.
(S) (2:56) MCA Special Products 20981 Bubble Gum Classics.
(S) (3:00) Rhino 72516 Behind Closed Doors - '70s Swingers.
(S) (3:00) Rhino 72819 16 Magazine - Who's Your Fave Rave.
(S) (2:55) Simitar 55512 The Number One's: Lovin' Feelings.
1976 WHENEVER I'M AWAY FROM YOU
(S) (3:12) Varese Sarabande 5682 Sings.
(S) (3:10) K-Tel 3757 Best Of: Let Her In.
1977 ALL STRUNG OUT ON YOU
(S) (3:30) Varese Sarabande 5682 Sings.
(S) (3:30) K-Tel 3757 Best Of: Let Her In.

released as by JOHN TRAVOLTA and OLIVIA NEWTON-JOHN:
1978 YOU'RE THE ONE THAT I WANT
(S) (2:48) Polydor 825095 O.S.T. Grease.
(S) (2:46) Geffen 24470 Olivia Newton-John: Back To Basics.
(S) (2:47) MCA 5347 Olivia Newton-John: Greatest Hits Volume 2.
1978 SUMMER NIGHTS
(S) (3:36) Polydor 825095 O.S.T. Grease.
(S) (3:35) Geffen 24470 Olivia Newton-John: Back To Basics.

TREMELOES
1967 HERE COMES MY BABY
(M) (2:45) Rhino 70324 History Of British Rock Volume 6. *(45 version)*
(M) (2:45) Rhino 70319 History Of British Rock Box Set. *(45 version)*
(M) (2:45) Rhino 70528 Best Of. *(45 version)*
(M) (3:01) Time-Life 2CLR-24 Classic Rock - 1967: Blowin' Your Mind. *(LP version)*
1967 SILENCE IS GOLDEN
(M) (3:07) Columbia/Legacy 46984 Rock Artifacts Volume 4.
(M) (3:06) Rhino 70325 History Of British Rock Volume 7.
(M) (3:06) Rhino 70319 History Of British Rock Box Set.
(M) (3:07) Rhino 70528 Best Of.
(M) (3:06) Time-Life 2CLR-29 Classic Rock - Bubblegum, Garage And Pop Nuggets.
(M) (3:06) Time-Life SUD-18 Superhits - Late 60's Classics.
(M) (3:06) Time-Life 2CLR-31 Classic Rock - Totally Fantastic '60s.
(M) (3:06) Time-Life AM1-12 AM Gold - Late '60s Classics.
1967 EVEN THE BAD TIMES ARE GOOD
(M) (2:35) Rhino 70528 Best Of. *(45 version)*
1968 SUDDENLY YOU LOVE ME
(M) (2:44) Rhino 70528 Best Of.

RALPH TRESVANT
1991 SENSITIVITY
(S) (4:40) MCA 10116 Ralph Tresvant.
(S) (4:58) MCA 10116 Ralph Tresvant. *(with Ralph's rap)*
(S) (4:37) MCA 11570 New Edition Solo Hits.
(S) (4:37) Beast 53012 Smooth Love Of The 90's Vol. 1.
1991 STONE COLD GENTLEMAN
(S) (5:02) MCA 10116 Ralph Tresvant.
(S) (5:01) MCA 11570 New Edition Solo Hits.
released as by LUTHER VANDROSS and JANET JACKSON with BBD and RALPH TRESVANT:
1992 THE BEST THINGS IN LIFE ARE FREE
(S) (4:35) Perspective 1004 O.S.T. Mo' Money.
(S) (4:01) LV Records/Epic 68220 Luther Vandross - One Night With You: The Best Of Love Volume 2.

T. REX
1972 BANG A GONG (GET IT ON)
(S) (4:23) Reprise 6466 Electric Warrior.
(S) (4:24) JCI 4510 Masters Of Metal: Crankin' Up 1970-1980.
(S) (4:24) Time-Life R968-05 Guitar Rock 1972-1973.
(S) (4:24) Time-Life SOD-13 Sounds Of The Seventies - 1972: Take Two.
(S) (4:23) Time-Life OPCD-4521 Guitar Rock.

TRIPLETS
1991 YOU DON'T HAVE TO GO HOME TONIGHT
(S) (3:56) Mercury 848290 Thicker Than Water.

TRIUMPH
1979 HOLD ON
(S) (6:01) JCI 4520 Masters Of Metal: Wrecking Havoc 1975-1985 Volume 1. *(LP version)*
1986 SOMEBODY'S OUT THERE
(S) (4:00) Priority 7961 Three Decades Of Rock.
(S) (4:04) MCA 5786 The Sport Of Kings.
(S) (4:03) Simitar 55142 80's Rock Classics - Party Town.

KATHY TROCCOLI
1992 EVERYTHING CHANGES
- (S) (4:21) RCA/Reunion 66271 and 49230 Crossfire/A Contemporary Christian Collection.
- (S) (4:20) Sandstone 33050 and 5018 Cosmopolitan Volume 4.
- (S) (4:20) DCC Compact Classics 089 Night Moves Volume 7.
- (S) (4:21) Reunion 24453 and 66193 and 49225 Pure Attraction.

TROGGS
1966 WILD THING
- (M) (2:34) Warner Special Products 27610 More Party Classics.
- (M) (2:33) Original Sound 8862 Oldies But Goodies Vol. 12. *(this compact disc uses the "Waring - fds" noise reduction process)*
- (M) (2:33) Original Sound 2223 Oldies But Goodies Volumes 2,7,9,12 and 13 Box Set. *(this box set uses the "Waring - fds" noise reduction process)*
- (M) (2:33) Original Sound 2500 Oldies But Goodies Volumes 1-15 Box Set. *(this box set uses the "Waring - fds" noise reduction process)*
- (M) (2:33) Original Sound 8894 Dick Clark's 21 All-Time Hits Vol. 3.
- (M) (2:34) Rhino 70321 History Of British Rock Volume 3.
- (M) (2:34) Rhino 70319 History Of British Rock Box Set.
- (M) (2:34) Rhino 72008 History Of British Rock Volumes 1-4 Box Set.
- (M) (2:34) Rhino 75892 Nuggets.
- (M) (2:33) Rhino 75778 Frat Rock.
- (M) (2:34) Rhino 70627 Billboard's Top Rock & Roll Hits Of 1966.
- (M) (2:34) Rhino 72007 Billboard's Top Rock & Roll Hits 1962-1966 Box Set.
- (M) (2:34) Rhino 70243 Greatest Movie Rock Hits.
- (M) (2:33) Mercury 816555 45's On CD Volume 2.
- (M) (2:33) Rhino 70794 KFOG Presents M. Dung's Idiot Show.
- (M) (2:34) Fontana 314512936 Archeology.
- (M) (2:33) Time-Life 2CLR-02 Classic Rock - 1966.
- (M) (2:33) Time-Life R962-07 History Of Rock 'N' Roll: The British Invasion 1964-1966.
- (M) (2:33) Collectables 2510 WCBS-FM History Of Rock - The Rockin' 60's.
- (M) (2:33) Collectables 4510 History Of Rock/The Rockin' 60s.
- (M) (2:34) Fontana 314522841 Best Of.
- (M) (2:34) Rebound 314520277 Hard Rock Essentials - The 60's.
- (M) (2:34) Rebound 314520323 Alterno-Daze: Origin Of The Species.
- (M) (2:35) Ripete 2187-RE Preppy Deluxe.
- (M) (2:33) Time-Life R968-09 Guitar Rock 1966-1967.
- (M) (2:33) Collectables 2554 CBS-FM History Of Rock Volume 2.
- (M) (2:34) Hollywood 62077 Official Party Album - ABC's Monday Night Football.
- (M) (2:34) Special Music 5040 Great Britons! Volume Two.
- (M) (2:34) Eclipse Music Group 64870 Rock 'n Roll Relix 1966-1967.
- (M) (2:34) Eclipse Music Group 64872 Rock 'n Roll Relix 1960-1969.
- (M) (2:33) Hip-O 40038 Power Chords Volume 1.
- (M) (2:34) Rebound 314520522 Rockin' Sports Jams.
- (M) (2:33) Polygram Special Markets 314520464 60's Rock Hits.

1966 WITH A GIRL LIKE YOU
- (M) (2:05) Time-Life 2CLR-26 Classic Rock - Rock Renaissance III.
- (M) (2:07) Rhino 70322 History Of British Rock Volume 4.
- (M) (2:07) Fontana 314522841 Best Of.
- (M) (2:07) Fontana 314512936 Archeology.

1966 I CAN'T CONTROL MYSELF
- (M) (3:03) Fontana 314512936 Archeology.
- (M) (3:02) Time-Life 2CLR-21 Classic Rock - Rock Renaissance II.

- (M) (3:03) Fontana 314522841 Best Of.

1968 LOVE IS ALL AROUND
- (M) (2:54) Mercury 834216 45's On CD Volume 3.
- (M) (2:59) Rhino 70326 History Of British Rock Volume 8.
- (M) (2:59) Rhino 70319 History Of British Rock Box Set.
- (M) (2:58) Rhino 71065 Summer Of Love Volume 1.
- (M) (2:58) Fontana 314512936 Archeology.
- (M) (2:56) Time-Life 2CLR-04 Classic Rock - 1968.
- (M) (2:56) Collectables 2510 WCBS-FM History Of Rock - The Rockin' 60's.
- (M) (2:56) Collectables 4510 History Of Rock/The Rockin' 60s.
- (M) (2:54) Time-Life R921-38 Get Together.
- (M) (2:58) Fontana 314522841 Best Of.
- (M) (2:54) Special Music 5039 Great Britons! Volume One.
- (M) (2:54) Eclipse Music Group 64871 Rock 'n Roll Relix 1968-1969.
- (M) (2:54) Eclipse Music Group 64872 Rock 'n Roll Relix 1960-1969.
- (M) (2:57) Simitar 55532 The Number One's: The '60s.

DORIS TROY
1963 JUST ONE LOOK
- (E) (2:22) Warner Special Prouducts 27601 Atlantic Soul Classics.
- (E) (2:27) JCI 3105 Soul Sixties.
- (M) (2:28) Atlantic 81297 Atlantic Rhythm & Blues Volume 5.
- (M) (2:26) Geffen 24310 O.S.T. Mermaids.
- (M) (2:28) Atlantic 82305 Atlantic Rhythm And Blues 1947-1974 Box Set.
- (M) (2:22) Time-Life 2RNR-19 Rock 'N' Roll Era - 1963 Still Rockin'.
- (M) (2:27) Time-Life RHD-02 Rhythm & Blues - 1963.
- (M) (2:27) Right Stuff 28371 Slow Jams: The 60's Volume Two.
- (E) (2:27) JCI/Telstar 3516 Sweet Soul Sisters.
- (M) (2:28) Ichiban 2504 Just One Look/Best Of.
- (M) (2:28) Rhino 71806 The R&B Box: Thirty Years Of Rhythm & Blues.
- (M) (2:28) Time-Life R857-08 The Heart Of Rock 'n' Roll 1963.
- (M) (2:27) Time-Life R838-14 Solid Gold Soul - 1963.
- (M) (2:28) Rhino 72815 Beg, Scream & Shout! The Big Ol' Box Of '60s Soul.
- (M) (2:28) Thump 7070 Lowrider Oldies Volume 7.

ANDREA TRUE CONNECTION
1976 MORE, MORE, MORE (PART 1)
- (S) (3:02) Priority 7971 Mega-Hits Dance Classics Volume 1. *(45 version)*
- (S) (3:00) Rhino 70984 The Disco Years Volume 1. *(45 version)*
- (S) (3:00) Rhino 70490 Billboard Top Dance Hits - 1976. *(45 version)*
- (S) (3:00) Rhino 71094 Disco Hits Volume 1. *(45 version)*
- (S) (6:09) Essex 7051 Non-Stop Dance Hits. *(LP version)*
- (S) (3:01) Essex 7060 The Buddah Box. *(45 version)*
- (S) (3:00) Razor & Tie 22496 Disco Fever. *(45 version)*
- (S) (3:00) Time-Life R138-38 Celebration. *(45 version)*
- (S) (3:02) K-Tel 3251 Disco Fever. *(45 version)*
- (S) (3:01) Priority 53142 Mega Hits - Disco Express. *(45 version)*
- (S) (3:00) Flashback 72688 Disco Hits: Get Down Tonight. *(45 version)*
- (S) (3:00) Flashback 72086 Disco Hits Box Set. *(45 version)*
- (S) (3:00) Rhino 72837 Disco Queens: The 70's. *(45 version)*
- (S) (6:15) Right Stuff 59783 More, More More - The Best Of. *(LP version)*
- (S) (3:10) Right Stuff 59783 More, More More - The Best Of. *(45 version)*
- (S) (2:58) BMG Special Products 44643 The Best Of Buddah. *(45 version but a few seconds of the introduction are truncated)*
- (S) (3:00) Time-Life R840-06 Sounds Of The Seventies: '70s Dance Party 1975-1976. *(45 version)*

(S)   (2:58)   BMG Special Products 44762 The President's Greatest Hits. *(45 version but a few seconds of the introduction are truncated)*

1977 N.Y., YOU GOT ME DANCING
(S)   (3:39)   Priority 7983 Mega-Hits Dance Classics (Volume 7). *(45 version)*

(S)   (6:08)   Priority 53141 Mega Hits Disco Locomotion Volume 2. *(LP version)*

(S)   (6:23)   Right Stuff 59783 More, More More - The Best Of. *(12" single version)*

(S)   (3:37)   Right Stuff 59783 More, More More - The Best Of. *(45 version)*

TUBES
1981 DON'T WANT TO WAIT ANYMORE
(S)   (4:15)   Capitol 48454 Completion Backwards Principle. *(LP version)*

(S)   (4:13)   Capitol 98359 Best Of. *(LP version)*

(S)   (4:14)   Priority 53797 Best Of 80's Rock Volume 4. *(LP version)*

1983 SHE'S A BEAUTY
(S)   (3:57)   Priority 53704 Rock Of The 80's Volume 3. *(LP version)*

(S)   (3:28)   Rhino 71701 New Wave Hits Of The 80's Vol. 8. *(45 version)*

(S)   (3:55)   K-Tel 3261 The 80's Rock On. *(LP version)*

(S)   (3:56)   Capitol 98359 Best Of. *(LP version)*

(S)   (3:57)   Capitol 48453 Outside Inside. *(LP version)*

(S)   (3:57)   Time-Life R988-11 Sounds Of The 80's: 1983-1984. *(LP version)*

(S)   (3:57)   Madacy Entertainment 1983 Rock On 1983. *(LP version)*

(S)   (3:55)   Priority 50953 I Love Rock & Roll Volume 4: Hits Of The 80's. *(LP version)*

(S)   (3:28)   Rhino 72820 VH1 - More Of The Big 80's. *(45 version)*

(S)   (3:28)   Rhino 72596 Billboard Top Album Rock Hits, 1983. *(45 version)*

(S)   (3:28)   Simitar 55552 The Number One's: Eighties Rock. *(45 version)*

TANYA TUCKER
1975 LIZZIE AND THE RAINMAN
(S)   (3:01)   MCA 31153 Greatest Hits.

(S)   (3:02)   MCA Special Products 20219 Lizzie & The Rain Man.

(S)   (3:00)   MCA Special Products 20770 Today's Hot Country.

(S)   (3:01)   MCA Special Products 20846 Greatest Country Classics Volume One.

TOMMY TUCKER
1964 HI-HEEL SNEAKERS
(M)   (2:49)   Rhino 75758 Soul Shots Volume 4.

(M)   (2:48)   MCA 31204 Vintage Music Volume 7.

(M)   (2:48)   MCA 5805 Vintage Music Volumes 7 & 8.

(M)   (2:48)   Garland 011 Footstompin' Oldies.

(M)   (2:48)   Chess 31320 Best Of Chess Rock 'n' Roll Volume 2.

(M)   (2:48)   Time-Life 2RNR-10 Rock 'N' Roll Era - 1964.

(M)   (2:47)   Time-Life RHD-12 Rhythm & Blues - 1964.

(M)   (2:48)   MCA Special Products 22135 Vintage Collectibles Volume 6.

(M)   (2:49)   Chess 9352 Chess Rhythm & Roll.

(M)   (2:47)   Time-Life R838-13 Solid Gold Soul - 1964.

(M)   (2:48)   Chess 9389 The Chess Blues-Rock Songbook.

(M)   (2:49)   Hip-O 40083 The King's Record Collection Vol. 2.

(M)   (2:48)   JCI 3189 1960 - Only Dance - 1964.

TUNE WEAVERS
1957 HAPPY, HAPPY BIRTHDAY BABY
(M)   (2:17)   MCA 31200 Vintage Music Volume 3.

(M)   (2:17)   MCA 5778 Vintage Music Volumes 3 & 4.

(M)   (2:16)   Garland 012 Remember When.

(M)   (2:16)   Original Sound 8860 Oldies But Goodies Vol. 10. *(this compact disc uses the "Waring - fds" noise reduction process)*

(M)   (2:16)   Original Sound 2221 Oldies But Goodies Volumes 1,4,6,8 and 10 Box Set. *(this box set uses the "Waring - fds" noise reduction process)*

(M)   (2:16)   Original Sound 2500 Oldies But Goodies Volumes 1-15 Box Set. *(this box set uses the "Waring - fds" noise reduction process)*

(M)   (2:16)   Chess 31320 Best Of Chess Rock 'n' Roll Volume 2.

(M)   (2:16)   Time-Life 2RNR-01 Rock 'N' Roll Era - 1957.

(M)   (2:16)   Time-Life RHD-08 Rhythm & Blues - 1957.

(M)   (2:16)   Time-Life R103-27 Love Me Tender.

(M)   (2:17)   Chess 9352 Chess Rhythm & Roll.

(M)   (2:16)   Time-Life R857-05 The Heart Of Rock 'n' Roll 1957.

(M)   (2:17)   Hip-O 40058 O.S.T. Pink Flamingos.

(M)   (2:16)   Time-Life R838-23 Solid Gold Soul 1957.

TURBANS
1956 WHEN YOU DANCE
(M)   (2:52)   Rhino 70641 Billboard Top R&B Hits - 1955.

(M)   (2:54)   Rhino 71463 The Doo Wop Box.

(M)   (2:52)   Arista 8605 16 Original Doo-Wop Classics.

(M)   (2:51)   Time-Life RHD-17 Rhythm & Blues - 1955.

(M)   (2:51)   Time-Life 2RNR-23 The Rock 'N' Roll Era - 1956 Still Rockin'.

(M)   (2:55)   Collectables 2508 History Of The Doo-Wop Era Part 2.

(M)   (2:55)   Collectables 4508 History Of Rock/The Doo Wop Era Part Two.

(M)   (2:54)   Collectables 5063 History Of Rock Volume Three.

(M)   (2:54)   Collectables 5055 Harlem Holiday - N.Y. Rhythm Blues Vol. 5.

(E)   (2:56)   Collectables 2506 WCBS-FM History Of Rock - The 50's Part 1.

(E)   (2:56)   Collectables 4506 History Of Rock/The 50s Part One.

(M)   (2:54)   Relic 7039 When You Dance.

(M)   (2:52)   Angel Herald 55531 The Herald-Ember Groups - Vol. 1.

(M)   (2:54)   Collectables 5019 Best Of.

(M)   (2:55)   Collectables 5656 Spotlite On Herald Records Volume 1.

(M)   (2:54)   Time-Life R857-15 The Heart Of Rock 'n' Roll 1953-1955.

IKE & TINA TURNER
1960 A FOOL IN LOVE
(M)   (2:50)   EMI 95846 Proud Mary/Best Of.

(M)   (2:49)   Curb 77332 Greatest Hits.

(M)   (2:49)   EMI 46599 Best Of.

(S)   (2:54)   Virgin 88189 Tina Turner: What's Love Got To Do With It. *(rerecording)*

(M)   (2:49)   Original Sound 9323 Legendary Superstars.

(M)   (3:00)   Ripete 0002 Coolin' Out/24 Carolina Classics Vol. 2. *(no high end)*

(M)   (2:49)   Time-Life 2RNR-22 Rock 'N' Roll Era - 1960 Still Rockin'.

(M)   (2:49)   Time-Life RHD-15 Rhythm & Blues - 1960.

(M)   (2:50)   Collectables 5123 Best Of Sue Records.

(M)   (2:48)   Ripete 0003 Coolin' Out/24 Carolina Classics Vol. 3.

(M)   (2:51)   EMI 80932 Sue Records Story.

(M)   (2:50)   Capitol 29724 Tina Turner - Collected Recordings Sixties To Nineties.

(M)   (2:49)   Collectables 5107 Golden Classics. *(this cd was originally issued in 1988 but was remastered in 1994)*

(M)   (2:50)   Collectables 5297 The Soul Of.

(M)   (2:51)   Rhino 72815 Beg, Scream & Shout! The Big Ol' Box Of '60s Soul.

(M)   (2:49)   Time-Life R838-20 Solid Gold Soul 1960.

1961 IT'S GONNA WORK OUT FINE
(actual 45 time is (2:38) not (2:20) as stated on the record label)
(M)   (3:02)   Garland 011 Footstompin' Oldies.

(M)   (3:00)   EMI 95846 Proud Mary/Best Of.

(M)   (3:01)   Curb 77323 All Time Greatest Hits Of Rock 'N' Roll.

IKE & TINA TURNER *(Continued)*

- (M) (3:02) Stax 8551 Superblues Volume 1.
- (M) (3:02) Curb 77332 Greatest Hits.
- (M) (3:02) EMI 46599 Best Of.
- (M) (2:52) Original Sound 9323 Legendary Superstars.
- (M) (3:03) Special Music 4826 So Fine!
- (M) (3:03) Pair 1292 Workin' It Out.
- (S) (2:26) Saja 91228 Greatest Hits Volume 3. *(rerecording)*
- (S) (2:48) Virgin 88189 Tina Turner: What's Love Got To Do With It. *(rerecording)*
- (M) (3:01) Time-Life 2RNR-25 Rock 'N' Roll Era - The 60's Keep On Rockin'.
- (M) (3:01) Time-Life RHD-14 Rhythm & Blues - 1961.
- (M) (2:57) Collectables 5123 Best Of Sue Records.
- (M) (3:01) Collectables 5137 It's Gonna Work Out Fine. *(mastered from vinyl)*
- (M) (3:01) EMI 80932 Sue Records Story.
- (M) (3:01) Capitol 29724 Tina Turner - Collected Recordings Sixties To Nineties.
- (M) (3:00) Collectables 5107 Golden Classics. *(this cd was originally issued in 1988 but was remastered in 1994)*
- (M) (3:01) Ichiban 2512 Soulful Love - Duets Vol. 1.
- (M) (3:01) Time-Life R838-19 Solid Gold Soul 1961.

1962 POOR FOOL
- (M) (2:31) EMI 95846 Proud Mary/Best Of.
- (E) (2:32) Curb 77332 Greatest Hits.
- (M) (2:32) Special Music 4826 So Fine!
- (M) (2:32) Pair 1292 Workin' It Out.
- (M) (2:30) Collectables 5123 Best Of Sue Records.
- (M) (2:32) Collectables 5137 It's Gonna Work Out Fine. *(mastered from vinyl)*
- (M) (2:34) Collectables 5107 Golden Classics. *(mastered from vinyl)*
- (M) (2:32) EMI 80932 Sue Records Story.
- (M) (2:31) Capitol 29724 Tina Turner - Collected Recordings Sixties To Nineties.
- (M) (2:28) Collectables 5107 Golden Classics. *(this cd was originally issued in 1988 but was remastered in 1994)*

1970 I WANT TO TAKE YOU HIGHER
- (S) (2:51) EMI 95846 Proud Mary/Best Of. *(45 version)*
- (S) (3:43) Curb 77332 Greatest Hits. *(LP version)*
- (S) (2:50) Original Sound 9323 Legendary Superstars. *(45 version)*
- (S) (2:52) Rhino 71207 70's Smash Hits Vol. 3. *(45 version)*
- (S) (2:52) Rhino 70783 Soul Hits Of The 70's Volume 3. *(45 version)*
- (S) (2:52) Virgin 92153 and 86289 O.S.T. American Me. *(45 version)*
- (S) (2:52) Flashback 72683 '70s Radio Hits Volume 3. *(45 version)*
- (S) (2:52) Flashback 72090 '70s Radio Hits Box Set. *(45 version)*
- (S) (2:50) Priority 50989 70's Greatest Rock Hits Volume 2: Rock & Soul. *(45 version)*

1971 PROUD MARY
- (S) (3:27) Rhino 70784 Soul Hits Of The 70's Volume 4. *(:12 longer than 45 version)*
- (S) (3:27) Rhino 72028 Soul Hits Of The 70's Volumes 1-5 Box Set. *(:12 longer than 45 version)*
- (S) (4:55) EMI 95846 Proud Mary/Best Of. *(LP version)*
- (S) (4:54) EMI 96268 24 Greatest Hits Of All Time. *(LP version)*
- (S) (4:53) Original Sound 9323 Legendary Superstars. *(LP version)*
- (S) (3:15) JCI 3100 Dance Sixties. *(45 version)*
- (S) (4:55) Curb 77356 70's Hits Volume 2. *(LP version)*
- (S) (4:55) Curb 77332 Greatest Hits. *(LP version)*
- (S) (4:55) EMI 46599 Best Of. *(LP version)*
- (S) (2:38) Saja 91223 Greatest Hits Volume 1. *(rerecording)*
- (S) (3:21) Rhino 71227 Black On White: Great R&B Covers Of Rock Classics. *(45 version)*
- (S) (5:24) Virgin 88189 Tina Turner: What's Love Got To Do With It. *(rerecording)*
- (S) (4:53) Razor & Tie 22047 Sweet 70's Soul. *(LP version)*

- (S) (3:19) Time-Life RHD-09 Rhythm & Blues - 1971. *(45 version)*
- (S) (3:20) Time-Life SOD-02 Sounds Of The Seventies - 1971. *(45 version)*
- (S) (3:28) Rhino 71806 The R&B Box: Thirty Years Of Rhythm & Blues. *(:13 longer than the 45 version)*
- (S) (3:28) Capitol 29724 Tina Turner - Collected Recordings Sixties To Nineties. *(:13 longer than the 45 version)*
- (S) (4:52) JCI 3130 1970 - Only Rock 'N Roll - 1974. *(LP version)*
- (S) (3:27) Priority 50952 I Love Rock & Roll Volume 3: Hits Of The 70's. *(:12 longer than the 45 version)*
- (S) (3:19) Time-Life R838-06 Solid Gold Soul - 1971. *(45 version)*
- (S) (4:55) Hip-O 40095 '70s Hit(s) Back. *(LP version)*

1973 NUTBUSH CITY LIMITS
- (S) (2:56) EMI 95846 Proud Mary/Best Of.
- (S) (2:55) Curb 77332 Greatest Hits.
- (S) (2:56) EMI 46599 Best Of.
- (S) (3:18) Virgin 88189 Tina Turner: What's Love Got To Do With It. *(rerecording)*
- (S) (2:57) Capitol 29724 Tina Turner - Collected Recordings Sixties To Nineties.

JESSE LEE TURNER
1959 THE LITTLE SPACE GIRL

SAMMY TURNER
1959 LAVENDER-BLUE
- (M) (2:14) Time-Life 2RNR-24 Rock 'N' Roll Era - The 50's Keep On Rockin'.
- (M) (2:14) Time-Life R103-27 Love Me Tender.
- (M) (2:14) Time-Life R102-17 Lost Treasures Of Rock 'N' Roll.
- (M) (2:14) Time-Life R857-01 The Heart Of Rock 'n' Roll - 1959.

1959 ALWAYS

SPYDER TURNER
1967 STAND BY ME
- (S) (5:37) Ripete 5151 Ocean Drive 4.
- (S) (5:35) Eclipse Music Group 64870 Rock 'n Roll Relix 1966-1967.
- (S) (5:35) Eclipse Music Group 64872 Rock 'n Roll Relix 1960-1969.
- (S) (5:35) Collectables 5695 Golden Classics.

TINA TURNER
1984 LET'S STAY TOGETHER
- (S) (5:16) Capitol 29724 Collected Recordings Sixties To Nineties. *(LP version)*
- (S) (5:15) Capitol 46041 Private Dancer. *(LP version)*
- (S) (3:37) Capitol 97152 Simply The Best. *(45 version)*

1984 WHAT'S LOVE GOT TO DO WITH IT
- (S) (3:47) Epic 53439 O.S.T. Peter's Friends.
- (S) (3:45) Priority 7076 80's Greatest Rock Hits Volume 2 - Leather And Lace.
- (S) (3:47) Rhino 70679 Billboard Top Hits - 1984.
- (S) (3:45) Sandstone 33045 and 5011 Rock The First Volume Five.
- (S) (3:47) Time-Life R105-40 Rock Dreams.
- (S) (3:46) Capitol 29724 Collected Recordings Sixties To Nineties.
- (S) (3:48) Capitol 46041 Private Dancer.
- (S) (3:48) Virgin 88189 What's Love Got To Do With It.
- (S) (3:48) Capitol 97152 Simply The Best.
- (S) (3:47) Time-Life R988-27 Sounds Of The Eighties: The Rolling Stone Collection 1983-1985.
- (S) (3:47) Hip-O 40015 Soulful Ladies Of The 80's.

1984 BETTER BE GOOD TO ME
- (S) (5:08) MCA 6150 Music From The Television Series Miami Vice. *(LP version)*
- (S) (5:09) Capitol 29724 Collected Recordings Sixties To Nineties. *(LP version)*

(S) (5:09)   Capitol 46041   Private Dancer. *(LP version)*
(S) (3:38)   Capitol 97152   Simply The Best. *(45 version)*
(S) (3:35)   Time-Life R13610   Gold And Platinum Box Set -
            The Ultimate Rock Collection. *(45 version)*

1985 PRIVATE DANCER
(S) (7:11)   Capitol 29724   Collected Recordings Sixties To
            Nineties. *(LP version)*
(S) (7:11)   Capitol 46041   Private Dancer. *(LP version)*
(S) (4:00)   Capitol 97152   Simply The Best. *(45 version)*

1985 SHOW SOME RESPECT
(S) (3:18)   Capitol 46041   Private Dancer.

1985 WE DON'T NEED ANOTHER HERO
(S) (4:14)   Capitol 29724   Collected Recordings Sixties To
            Nineties.
(S) (4:14)   Capitol 97152   Simply The Best.
(S) (4:13)   Time-Life R988-31   Sounds Of The Eighties:
            Cinemax Movie Hits Of The '80s.

1985 ONE OF THE LIVING
released as by BRYAN ADAMS/TINA TURNER:
1986 IT'S ONLY LOVE
(S) (3:15)   Capitol 29724   Tina Turner - Collected Recordings
            Sixties To Nineties.
(S) (3:14)   A&M 5013   Bryan Adams - Reckless.
(S) (3:14)   MFSL 544   Bryan Adams - Reckless. *(gold disc)*
(S) (3:14)   A&M 314540157   Bryan Adams - So Far So Good.

released as by TINA TURNER:
1986 TYPICAL MALE
(S) (4:15)   Capitol 29724   Collected Recordings Sixties To
            Nineties.
(S) (4:14)   K-Tel 842   Hot Ladies Of The 80's.
(S) (4:15)   Capitol 46323   Break Every Rule.
(S) (4:14)   Capitol 97152   Simply The Best.

1987 TWO PEOPLE
(S) (4:08)   Capitol 46323   Break Every Rule.

1987 WHAT YOU GET IS WHAT YOU SEE
(S) (4:25)   Capitol 29724   Collected Recordings Sixties To
            Nineties. *(LP version)*
(S) (4:26)   Capitol 46323   Break Every Rule. *(LP version)*
(S) (4:25)   Capitol 97152   Simply The Best. *(LP version)*

1989 THE BEST
(S) (5:27)   Mercury 314522367   Soccer Rocks The Globe.
            (LP version)
(S) (5:28)   Capitol 29724   Collected Recordings Sixties To
            Nineties. *(LP version)*
(S) (5:28)   Mercury 314525354   Women For Women. *(live)*
(S) (5:28)   Capitol 91873   Foreign Affair. *(LP version)*
(S) (4:08)   Capitol 97152   Simply The Best. *(45 version)*

1990 STEAMY WINDOWS
(S) (4:02)   Capitol 29724   Collected Recordings Sixties To
            Nineties.
(S) (4:03)   Capitol 91873   Foreign Affair.
(S) (4:02)   Capitol 97152   Simply The Best.

1993 I DON'T WANNA FIGHT
(S) (6:05)   Capitol 29724   Collected Recordings Sixties To
            Nineties.
(S) (6:05)   Virgin 88189   What's Love Got To Do With It.
(S) (6:04)   EMI-Capitol Music Group 54555   Movie Luv.

TURTLES
1965 IT AIN'T ME BABE
(S) (2:06)   Rhino 5160   20 Greatest Hits.
(S) (2:02)   Collectables 5067   History Of Rock Volume 7.
(S) (2:04)   Original Sound 8854   Oldies But Goodies Vol. 4.
            *(this compact disc uses the "Waring - fds" noise
            reduction process)*
(S) (2:04)   Original Sound 2221   Oldies But Goodies
            Volumes 1,4,6,8 and 10 Box Set. *(this box set uses
            the "Waring - fds" noise reduction process)*
(S) (2:04)   Original Sound 2500   Oldies But Goodies
            Volumes 1-15 Box Set. *(this box set uses the
            "Waring - fds" noise reduction process)*
(S) (2:03)   Original Sound CDGO-9   Golden Oldies Volume. 9.
(S) (2:06)   Time-Life 2CLR-08   Classic Rock - 1965: The
            Beat Goes On.
(S) (2:04)   Time-Life R962-02   History Of Rock 'N' Roll:
            Folk Rock 1964-1967.

(S) (2:08)   Sundazed 6035   It Ain't Me Babe.
(S) (2:05)   K-Tel 3438   Best Of Folk Rock.
(S) (2:06)   LaserLight 15-969   30 Years Of Rock N' Roll Box.
(S) (2:06)   JCI 3160   18 Free & Easy Hits From The 60's.
(S) (2:05)   Rhino 71027   Best Of.
(S) (2:09)   LaserLight 12380   California Gold. *(all songs on
            this cd are live recordings)*

1965 LET ME BE
(M) (2:21)   Rhino 70734   Songs Of Protest.
(S) (2:22)   Rhino 5160   20 Greatest Hits.
(S) (2:21)   Sundazed 6036   You Baby.
(S) (2:22)   LaserLight 15-969   30 Years Of Rock N' Roll Box.
(S) (2:22)   Rhino 71027   Best Of.
(S) (2:46)   LaserLight 12380   California Gold. *(all songs on
            this cd are live recordings)*

1966 YOU BABY
(S) (2:15)   K-Tel 839   Battle Of The Bands Volume 2.
(S) (2:16)   Rhino 5160   20 Greatest Hits.
(S) (2:15)   Collectables 5062   History Of Rock Volume 2.
(S) (2:16)   Rhino 71195   Kid Rock!
(S) (2:15)   Time-Life 2CLR-22   Classic Rock - 1966: Blowin'
            Your Mind.
(S) (2:15)   Sundazed 6036   You Baby.
(S) (2:16)   LaserLight 15-969   30 Years Of Rock N' Roll Box.
(S) (2:16)   Rhino 71027   Best Of.
(S) (2:32)   LaserLight 12380   California Gold. *(all songs on
            this cd are live recordings)*
(M) (2:14)   LaserLight 12380   California Gold. *(all songs on
            this cd are live recordings)*

1967 HAPPY TOGETHER
(S) (2:53)   Rhino 70628   Billboard's Top Rock & Roll Hits Of
            1967.
(S) (2:53)   Rhino 5160   20 Greatest Hits.
(S) (2:53)   Original Sound 8865   Oldies But Goodies Vol. 15.
            *(this compact disc uses the "Waring - fds" noise
            reduction process)*
(S) (2:53)   Original Sound 2222   Oldies But Goodies
            Volumes 3,5,11,14 and 15 Box Set. *(this box set
            uses the "Waring - fds" noise reduction process)*
(S) (2:53)   Original Sound 2500   Oldies But Goodies
            Volumes 1-15 Box Set. *(this box set uses the
            "Waring - fds" noise reduction process)*
(S) (2:52)   Rhino 71093   Better Days.
(S) (2:52)   K-Tel 666   Flower Power.
(S) (2:52)   Collectables 5070   History Of Rock Volume 10.
(S) (2:53)   JCI 3114   Easy Sixties.
(S) (2:52)   Time-Life 2CLR-05   Classic Rock - 1967.
(S) (2:51)   Time-Life SUD-05   Superhits - 1967.
(S) (2:52)   Time-Life R962-04   History Of Rock 'N' Roll:
            California Pop 1963-1967.
(S) (2:51)   Collectables 2603   WCBS-FM Jukebox Giants
            Vol. 1.
(S) (2:52)   Collectables 2501   WCBS-FM History Of Rock -
            The 60's Part 2.
(S) (2:52)   Collectables 4501   History Of Rock/The 60s Part
            Two.
(S) (2:53)   Sundazed 6037   Happy Together.
(S) (2:52)   JCI 3126   1965 - Only Rock 'N Roll - 1969.
(S) (2:53)   Rhino 71873   Love Songs.
(S) (2:52)   Curb 77774   Hard To Find Hits Of Rock 'N' Roll
            Volume Two.
(S) (2:53)   LaserLight 15-969   30 Years Of Rock N' Roll Box.
(S) (2:52)   Collectables 2554   CBS-FM History Of Rock
            Volume 2.
(S) (2:52)   Polydor 314527493   O.S.T. Muriel's Wedding.
(S) (2:51)   LaserLight 12315 and 15936   The Wonder Years -
            Movin' On.
(S) (2:52)   Rhino 71027   Best Of.
(S) (2:52)   Eclipse Music Group 64870   Rock 'n Roll Relix
            1966-1967.
(S) (2:52)   Eclipse Music Group 64872   Rock 'n Roll Relix
            1960-1969.
(S) (2:51)   Time-Life AM1-08   AM Gold - 1967.
(S) (2:52)   Flashback 72687   '60s Rock: Feelin' Groovy.
(S) (2:52)   Flashback 72088   '60s Rock Hits Box Set.

    (S) (4:18) LaserLight 12380 California Gold. *(all songs on this cd are live recordings)*

    (M) (2:49) LaserLight 12380 California Gold. *(all songs on this cd are live recordings)*

1967 SHE'D RATHER BE WITH ME

    (S) (2:14) JCI 3104 Mellow Sixties.

    (S) (2:17) Original Sound 8853 Oldies But Goodies Vol. 3. *(this compact disc uses the "Waring - fds" noise reduction process)*

    (S) (2:17) Original Sound 2222 Oldies But Goodies Volumes 3,5,11,14 and 15 Box Set. *(this box set uses the "Waring - fds" noise reduction process)*

    (S) (2:17) Original Sound 2500 Oldies But Goodies Volumes 1-15 Box Set. *(this box set uses the "Waring - fds" noise reduction process)*

    (S) (2:16) Original Sound CDGO-7 Golden Oldies Volume. 7.

    (S) (2:19) K-Tel 205 Battle Of The Bands Volume 3.

    (S) (2:18) Rhino 5160 20 Greatest Hits.

    (S) (2:16) Collectables 5068 History Of Rock Volume 8.

    (S) (2:16) Time-Life 2CLR-15 Classic Rock - 1967: Shakin' All Over.

    (S) (2:17) Time-Life SUD-18 Superhits - Late 60's Classics.

    (S) (2:17) Collectables 2502 WCBS-FM History Of Rock - The 60's Part 3.

    (S) (2:17) Collectables 4502 History Of Rock/The 60s Part Three.

    (S) (2:18) Sundazed 6037 Happy Together.

    (S) (2:18) LaserLight 15-969 30 Years Of Rock N' Roll Box.

    (S) (2:18) Buddah 49506 Feelin' Groovy.

    (S) (2:18) Collectables 2554 CBS-FM History Of Rock Volume 2.

    (S) (2:18) Rhino 71027 Best Of.

    (S) (2:16) Time-Life AM1-12 AM Gold - Late '60s Classics.

    (S) (2:34) LaserLight 12380 California Gold. *(all songs on this cd are live recordings)*

    (M) (2:17) LaserLight 12380 California Gold. *(all songs on this cd are live recordings)*

1967 YOU KNOW WHAT I MEAN

    (S) (1:59) Rhino 5160 20 Greatest Hits.

    (S) (1:59) Sundazed 6037 Happy Together.

    (S) (1:59) LaserLight 15-969 30 Years Of Rock N' Roll Box.

    (S) (1:58) Rhino 71027 Best Of.

1967 SHE'S MY GIRL

    (E) (2:31) Rhino 5160 20 Greatest Hits.

    (M) (2:30) Time-Life 2CLR-24 Classic Rock - 1967: Blowin' Your Mind.

    (S) (2:34) Sundazed 6037 Happy Together.

    (M) (2:31) K-Tel 3130 60's Sound Explosion.

    (S) (2:34) LaserLight 15-969 30 Years Of Rock N' Roll Box.

    (S) (2:34) Varese Sarabande 5705 Dick Bartley Presents Collector's Essentials: The 60's. *(splice noticeable at 2:17)*

    (M) (2:30) Rhino 71027 Best Of.

    (S) (3:26) LaserLight 12380 California Gold. *(all songs on this cd are live recordings)*

1968 ELENORE

    (S) (2:29) Rhino 5160 20 Greatest Hits.

    (S) (2:28) Original Sound 8857 Oldies But Goodies Vol. 7. *(this compact disc uses the "Waring - fds" noise reduction process)*

    (S) (2:28) Original Sound 2223 Oldies But Goodies Volumes 2,7,9,12 and 13 Box Set. *(this box set uses the "Waring - fds" noise reduction process)*

    (S) (2:28) Original Sound 2500 Oldies But Goodies Volumes 1-15 Box Set. *(this box set uses the "Waring - fds" noise reduction process)*

    (S) (2:27) Original Sound CDGO-3 Golden Oldies Volume. 3.

    (S) (2:29) Essex 7052 All Time Rock Classics.

    (S) (2:28) Collectables 5065 History Of Rock Volume 5.

    (S) (2:28) Time-Life 2CLR-11 Classic Rock - 1968: The Beat Goes On.

    (S) (2:28) Time-Life SUD-14 Superhits - The Late 60's.

    (S) (2:29) Collectables 2501 WCBS-FM History Of Rock - The 60's Part 2.

    (S) (2:29) Collectables 4501 History Of Rock/The 60s Part Two.

    (S) (2:29) Sundazed 6038 The Battle Of The Bands.

    (M) (2:31) Rhino 71873 Love Songs.

    (S) (2:29) LaserLight 15-969 30 Years Of Rock N' Roll Box.

    (S) (2:29) Rhino 71027 Best Of.

    (S) (2:28) Time-Life AM1-14 AM Gold - The Late '60s.

    (S) (3:00) LaserLight 12380 California Gold. *(all songs on this cd are live recordings)*

1969 YOU SHOWED ME

    (S) (3:13) Rhino 5160 20 Greatest Hits.

    (S) (3:11) Time-Life 2CLR-06 Classic Rock - 1969.

    (S) (3:05) Time-Life SUD-07 Superhits - 1969.

    (S) (3:13) Sundazed 6038 The Battle Of The Bands.

    (M) (3:01) Rhino 71873 Love Songs.

    (S) (3:13) LaserLight 15-969 30 Years Of Rock N' Roll Box.

    (S) (3:10) Rhino 71027 Best Of.

    (S) (3:05) Time-Life AM1-01 AM Gold - 1969.

    (M) (3:02) Varese Sarabande 5801 Sunshine Days - Pop Classics Of The '60s Volume 1.

    (S) (2:44) LaserLight 12380 California Gold. *(all songs on this cd are live recordings)*

TUXEDO JUNCTION
1978 CHATTANOOGA CHOO CHOO

    (S) (5:01) Hot Productions 9 Best Of Butterfly Records. *(edit of LP version)*

    (S) (6:52) Hot Productions 91 Best Of Tuxedo Junction. *(remix; edit of LP version)*

    (S) (7:07) Flashback 72689 Disco Hits: Shake Your Booty. *(LP version)*

SHANIA TWAIN
1995 ANY MAN OF MINE

    (S) (4:06) Mercury 314522886 The Woman In Me.

1995 WHOSE BED HAVE YOUR BOOTS BEEN UNDER?

    (S) (4:24) Mercury 314522886 The Woman In Me.

1997 LOVE GETS ME EVERY TIME

    (S) (3:32) Mercury 314536003 Come On Over.

12 GAUGE
1994 DUNKIE BUTT

    (M) (4:17) Street Life/Scotti Bros. 75439 12 Gauge.

    (M) (4:17) Cold Front 6299 Da Booty - 17 Smash Bass Hits.

20 FINGERS
1995 SHORT DICK MAN
(the compact disc title of this song is "SHORT, SHORT MAN")

    (M) (3:17) Zoo 11102 and 31102 and 11105 and 31105 Gillette - On The Attack.

    (M) (4:52) Tommy Boy 1138 MTV Party To Go Volume 7. *(all selections on this cd are segued together; remixed)*

    (M) (3:17) Zoo 11113 and 31113 20 Fingers Compilation.

    (M) (3:16) Quality 5008 Dance Box Set. *(all selections on this cd are segued together)*

    (M) (3:14) Beast 53032 Club Hitz Of The 90's Vol. 2. *(all songs on this cd are segued together)*

DWIGHT TWILLEY BAND
1975 I'M ON FIRE

    (S) (3:15) Priority 8665 Southern Comfort/70's Greatest Rock Hits Volume 4.

    (S) (3:14) Rhino 70762 Super Hits Of The 70's Volume 15.

    (S) (3:09) Warner Special Products 27616 Classic Rock.

    (S) (3:15) Shelter/DCC Compact Classics 8002 Sincerely.

    (S) (3:14) Time-Life R968-01 Guitar Rock 1974-1975.

    (S) (3:14) Time-Life SOD-16 Sounds Of The Seventies - 1975: Take Two.

    (S) (3:15) Rhino 72728 Poptopia! Power Pop Classics Of The '70s.

    (S) (3:16) Right Stuff 56976 Sincerely.

    (S) (3:13) EMI-Capitol Music Special Markets 19545 Lost Hits Of The '70s.

1984 GIRLS

    (S) (3:28) Rhino 71976 New Wave Hits Of The 80's Vol. 13.

(S) (3:28) Rhino 72597 Billboard Top Album Rock Hits, 1984.
(S) (3:28) Time-Life R988-23 Sounds Of The Eighties 1984-1985.

TWISTED SISTER
1984 WE'RE NOT GONNA TAKE IT
(S) (3:38) Atlantic 80156 Stay Hungry.
(S) (3:37) K-Tel 6090 Hit Parader Salutes 20 Years Of Metal.
(S) (3:38) Atlantic 82380 Big Hits And Nasty Cuts.
(S) (3:37) Time-Life R968-18 Guitar Rock - The Heavy '80s.
(S) (3:38) Rhino 72291 Heavy Metal Hits Of The 80's Volume 1.
(S) (3:37) JCI 3143 18 Screamers From The 80's.
(S) (3:38) Priority 50936 Best Of 80's Metal Volume One: Bang Your Head.
(S) (3:37) K-Tel 3883 The 80's: Glam Rock.
(S) (3:38) Time-Life R988-23 Sounds Of The Eighties 1984-1985.
(S) (3:37) Razor & Tie 89004 Monsters Of Rock.

CONWAY TWITTY
1958 IT'S ONLY MAKE BELIEVE
(S) (2:11) Rhino 70619 Billboard's Top Rock & Roll Hits Of 1958.
(S) (2:11) Rhino 72004 Billboard's Top Rock & Roll Hits 1957-1961 Box Set.
(S) (2:11) JCI 3203 Lovin' Fifties.
(S) (2:11) Mercury 849574 Best Of Volume 1: Rockin' Years.
(S) (2:19) Curb 77365 Greatest Hits. *(rerecording)*
(S) (2:11) Special Music 837668 It's Only Make Believe.
(S) (2:19) MCA 31240 Greatest Hits Volume 2. *(rerecording)*
(S) (2:11) Time-Life 2RNR-05 Rock 'N' Roll Era - 1958.
(S) (2:11) Time-Life CTD-07 Country USA - 1958.
(S) (2:11) Time-Life R103-27 Love Me Tender.
(S) (2:11) MCA 11095 Collection.
(S) (2:11) Polygram Special Markets 314520258 No. 1 Hits Of The 50's.
(S) (2:11) Mercury 314519958 Rockin' Conway.
(S) (2:12) Time-Life R990-04 Conway Twitty - Legendary Country Singers.
(S) (2:11) Time-Life R857-04 The Heart Of Rock 'n' Roll - 1958.
(S) (2:11) K-Tel 3436 Rockabilly Riot.
(S) (2:11) Polygram Special Markets 314520389 Best Of The Early Years.
(S) (2:11) Mercury 314536218 The Hits.
(S) (2:26) Simitar 55032 The Late Great. *(rerecording; the printed track lineup does not match the actual track lineup)*
(S) (2:11) Time-Life R808-03 Classic Country 1950-1959.
(S) (2:11) Collectables 1514 and 2514 The Anniversary Album - The 50's.
1959 THE STORY OF MY LOVE
(S) (2:15) Special Music 837668 It's Only Make Believe.
(S) (2:15) MCA 11095 Collection.
(S) (2:15) Polygram Special Markets 314520389 Best Of The Early Years.
(S) (2:15) Mercury 314536218 The Hits.
1959 MONA LISA
(S) (2:24) Mercury 849574 Best Of Volume 1: Rockin' Years.
(S) (2:23) Mercury 314536218 The Hits.
1959 DANNY BOY
(M) (2:44) Rhino 70742 Rock This Town: Rockabilly Hits Volume 2.
(S) (2:44) Mercury 849574 Best Of Volume 1: Rockin' Years.
(S) (2:43) Special Music 837668 It's Only Make Believe.
(S) (2:44) Mercury 314519958 Rockin' Conway.
(S) (2:44) Polygram Special Markets 314520389 Best Of The Early Years.
(S) (2:44) Mercury 314536218 The Hits.
1960 LONELY BLUE BOY
(S) (2:13) Mercury 832041 45's On CD Volume 1.
(S) (2:12) Mercury 849574 Best Of Volume 1: Rockin' Years.

(S) (2:12) Curb 77365 Greatest Hits.
(S) (2:12) Special Music 837668 It's Only Make Believe.
(S) (2:12) Time-Life 2RNR-11 Rock 'N' Roll Era - 1960.
(S) (2:12) MCA 11095 Collection.
(S) (2:12) Mercury 314519958 Rockin' Conway.
(S) (2:12) Eric 11502 Hard To Find 45's On CD (Volume I) 1955-60.
(S) (2:12) Time-Life R857-14 The Heart Of Rock 'n' Roll 1960-1961 Take Two.
(S) (2:12) Mercury 314536218 The Hits.
1960 WHAT AM I LIVING FOR
(S) (2:35) Mercury 849574 Best Of Volume 1: Rockin' Years.
(S) (2:33) Curb 77365 Greatest Hits.
(S) (2:35) MCA 11095 Collection.
(S) (2:35) Mercury 314536218 The Hits.
1960 IS A BLUE BIRD BLUE
(S) (2:34) Mercury 849574 Best Of Volume 1: Rockin' Years.
(S) (2:34) Time-Life 2RNR-40 Rock 'N' Roll Era - The 60's Teen Time.
(S) (2:35) Mercury 314519958 Rockin' Conway.
(S) (2:35) Mercury 314536218 The Hits.
1961 C'EST SI BON (IT'S SO GOOD)
(S) (2:15) Mercury 849574 Best Of Volume 1: Rockin' Years.
(S) (2:12) Mercury 314536218 The Hits.
1973 YOU'VE NEVER BEEN THIS FAR BEFORE
(S) (2:59) Curb 77365 Greatest Hits.
(S) (2:58) MCA 31240 Greatest Hits Volume 2.
(S) (2:58) MCA 5976 20 Greatest Hits.
(S) (2:58) MCA 31238 Very Best Of.
(S) (2:58) MCA 8035 Silver Anniversary Collection.
(S) (2:59) Time-Life CCD-04 Contemporary Country - The Mid 70's.
(S) (2:59) MCA 11095 Collection.
(S) (2:59) Priority 53716 Branson USA Vol. 3 - Country Legends.
(S) (2:59) K-Tel 567 Country Music Classics Volume IV.
(S) (2:59) Time-Life R990-04 Conway Twitty - Legendary Country Singers.
(S) (3:06) Risky Business 67309 Sexy Country. *(much slower than the 45 or LP)*
(S) (2:59) K-Tel 3366 101 Greatest Country Hits Vol. Seven: Country Nights.
(S) (3:05) Simitar 55032 The Late Great. *(rerecording; the printed track lineup does not match the actual track lineup)*

2 IN A ROOM
1990 WIGGLE IT
(S) (4:04) K-Tel 6102 Funk-Tastic Jams.
(S) (4:04) Priority 53772 Techno Dance Classics Volume 2 - Feel The Beat.
(S) (4:04) Cutting/Charisma 91594 and 86347 Wiggle It.
(S) (3:55) Cutting/Charisma 91594 and 86347 Wiggle It. *(remix)*
(S) (5:41) Priority 50934 Shut Up And Dance! The 90's Volume One. *(remix; all selections on this cd are segued together)*
(S) (4:03) Cold Front 6245 Greatest Sports Rock And Jams. *(all selections on this cd are segued together)*
(S) (4:03) Robbins 75002 Strip Jointz - Hot Songs For Sexy Dancers.

2 LIVE CREW (see also LUKE)
1989 ME SO HORNY
(S) (4:36) Luke/Atlantic 91598 Bass Waves Volume Three. *(explicit lyrics)*
(S) (4:36) Priority 7993 Explicit Rap. *(explicit lyrics)*
(S) (4:25) Luke/Atlantic 91652 As Clean As They Wanna Be. *(censored lyrics)*
(S) (4:36) Luke/Atlantic 91651 As Nasty As They Wanna Be. *(explicit lyrics)*
(S) (4:36) Luke 107 As Nasty As They Wanna Be. *(explicit lyrics)*
(S) (4:36) Luke 122 Greatest Hits. *(explicit lyrics)*
(S) (4:25) Luke 123 Greatest Hits. *(censored lyrics)*

2 LIVE CREW *(Continued)*

- (S) (4:25) Coldfront 3501 Rap's Biggest Hits Volume II. *(censored lyrics)*
- (S) (4:25) Priority 50961 Booty And The Beat - Bass Jams Vol.1. *(censored lyrics)*
- (S) (4:24) Robbins 75002 Strip Jointz - Hot Songs For Sexy Dancers. *(censored lyrics)*

released as by LUKE featuring 2 LIVE CREW:
1990 BANNED IN THE U.S.A.

- (S) (4:23) Luke/Atlantic 91427 and 91424 Banned In The U.S.A.
- (S) (4:23) Luke 114 and 115 Banned In The U.S.A.

2PAC
1993 I GET AROUND

- (S) (4:18) Tommy Boy 1097 MTV Party To Go Volume 5. *(remix; all tracks on this cd are segued together)*
- (S) (4:18) Interscope 92209 Strictly 4 My N.I.G.G.A.Z..
- (M) (4:00) Death Row/Interscope 50677 Death Row Greatest Hits. *(all songs on this cd are segued together; remix)*
- (S) (4:17) Def Jam 314534746 Yo! MTV Raps Compilation.
- (S) (3:54) Boxtunes 314524387 Big Phat Ones Of Hip-Hop Volume 2. *(all songs on this cd are segued together)*
- (S) (4:18) Amaru/Jive 41634 Strictly 4 My N.I.G.G.A.Z..

1993 KEEP YA HEAD UP

- (S) (4:22) Interscope 92209 Strictly 4 My N.I.G.G.A.Z..
- (M) (4:22) Death Row/Interscope 50677 Death Row Greatest Hits. *(all songs on this cd are segued together)*
- (S) (4:22) Amaru/Jive 41634 Strictly 4 My N.I.G.G.A.Z..

1995 DEAR MAMA

- (S) (4:38) Interscope 92399 Me Against The World.
- (S) (4:38) Amaru/Jive 41636 Me Against The World.

1996 HOW DO U WANT IT

- (S) (4:47) Death Row/Interscope 314524204 All Eyez On Me.

1996 CALIFORNIA LOVE

- (S) (6:25) Death Row/Interscope 314524204 All Eyez On Me.
- (S) (4:32) Tommy Boy 1168 MTV Party To Go Volume 10. *(all songs on this cd are segued together; radio edit)*

released as by SCARFACE featuring 2PAC & JOHNNY P:
1997 SMILE

- (S) (5:00) Rap-A-Lot 42799 The Untouchable.

2 UNLIMITED
1995 GET READY FOR THIS

- (S) (3:42) Critique 15407 Get Ready.
- (S) (5:25) Critique 15407 Get Ready. *(instrumental version)*
- (S) (3:41) Critique 15446 Hits Unlimited.
- (S) (3:25) Tommy Boy 1137 ESPN Presents Jock Jams. *(crowd sound effects added to intro and outro; edited)*
- (S) (3:41) EMI-Capitol Music Group 54547 Hot Luv.

- (S) (3:39) Cold Front 6245 Greatest Sports Rock And Jams. *(all selections on this cd are segued together)*
- (S) (3:41) Hollywood 62121 Monday Night Football Jamz. *(includes live audience overdubs)*
- (S) (5:21) Beast 53292 Club Hitz Of The 90's Vol. 4. *(all songs on this cd are segued together)*

TYCOON
1979 SUCH A WOMAN

- (S) (4:20) Renaissance 0163 Tycoon/Turn Out The Lights. *(LP version)*

BONNIE TYLER
1978 IT'S A HEARTACHE

- (S) (3:30) RCA 8476 Nipper's Greatest Hits - The 70's.
- (S) (3:30) Rhino 70673 Billboard Top Hits - 1978.
- (S) (3:30) Rhino 71201 Super Hits Of The 70's Volume 21.
- (S) (3:31) Time-Life SOD-20 Sounds Of The Seventies - 1978: Take Two.
- (S) (3:28) JCI 3131 1975 - Only Rock 'N Roll - 1979.
- (S) (3:30) Rhino 72132 Frat Rock: More Of The 70's.
- (S) (3:29) LaserLight 12317 The British Invasion.
- (S) (3:28) Priority 53139 The Best Of 70's: Rock Chart Toppers.

1983 TOTAL ECLIPSE OF THE HEART
(actual 45 time is (5:31) not (4:29) as stated on the record label)

- (S) (4:43) CBS Special Products 44363 Rock Of The 80's. *(neither the 45 or LP version)*
- (S) (5:33) Rhino 70678 Billboard Top Hits - 1983. *(45 version)*
- (S) (6:56) Risky Business 57833 Read The Hits/Best Of The 80's. *(LP version)*
- (S) (6:56) Columbia 38710 Faster Than The Speed Of Light. *(LP version)*
- (S) (4:41) Time-Life R988-16 Sounds Of The Eighties: The Early '80s. *(neither the 45 or LP version)*
- (S) (5:33) Time-Life R834-01 Body Talk - Forever Yours. *(45 version)*

1984 HOLDING OUT FOR A HERO

- (S) (5:48) Columbia 39242 O.S.T. Footloose.
- (S) (6:19) Epic 67506 Club Epic Volume 4. *(remix)*

TYMES
1963 SO MUCH IN LOVE
1963 WONDERFUL! WONDERFUL!
1964 SOMEWHERE
1974 YOU LITTLE TRUSTMAKER

- (S) (2:48) RCA 9684 and 8476 Nipper's Greatest Hits - The 70's.
- (S) (2:48) Rhino 70554 Soul Hits Of The 70's Volume 14.
- (S) (2:48) Time-Life SOD-36 Sounds Of The Seventies - More AM Nuggets.
- (S) (2:46) Eclipse Music Group 64894 Rock 'n Roll Relix 1974-1975.
- (S) (2:46) Eclipse Music Group 64897 Rock 'n Roll Relix 1970-1979.
- (S) (2:48) Robbins Entertainment 75005 Super Rare Disco.
- (S) (2:48) Koch 7983 Great Soul Hits.

UB40
1984 RED RED WINE
    (S)   (5:18)   A&M 4980 Labour Of Love. *(1988 45 version and LP version)*
    (S)   (3:01)   Virgin 41009 Best Of Volume One. *(1984 45 version)*
    (S)   (5:18)   Virgin 86412 Labour Of Love. *(1988 45 version and LP version)*
1985 I GOT YOU BABE
    (S)   (3:09)   A&M 5090 Little Baggariddim.
    (S)   (3:06)   Virgin 41009 Best Of Volume One.
    (S)   (3:09)   Virgin 86387 Little Baggariddim.
1988 RED RED WINE
(this song charted in two different years: 1984 & 1988; see 1984 listings)
1990 THE WAY YOU DO THE THINGS YOU DO
    (S)   (3:15)   Virgin 91292 O.S.T. Black Rain.
    (S)   (3:01)   Virgin 91324 and 86146 Labour Of Love II.
    (S)   (3:01)   Virgin 41010 Best Of Volume Two.
1991 HERE I AM (COME AND TAKE ME)
    (S)   (4:00)   Virgin 91324 and 86146 Labour Of Love II.
    (S)   (4:00)   Virgin 41010 Best Of Volume Two.
1993 CAN'T HELP FALLING IN LOVE
    (S)   (3:23)   Virgin 88064 O.S.T. Sliver.
    (S)   (3:26)   Virgin 88229 Promises And Lies.
    (S)   (3:25)   Virgin 41010 Best Of Volume Two.

UGLY KID JOE
1992 EVERYTHING ABOUT YOU
    (S)   (4:13)   Stardog 868823 As Ugly As They Wanna Be.
1993 CAT'S IN THE CRADLE
    (S)   (4:01)   Stardog/Mercury 314512571 and 314512784 America's Least Wanted.

U-KREW
1990 IF U WERE MINE
    (S)   (4:12)   Enigma 773524 The U-Krew.

TRACY ULLMAN
1984 THEY DON'T KNOW
    (S)   (2:59)   Rhino 71975 New Wave Hits Of The 80's Vol. 12.
    (S)   (2:59)   Rhino 70292 Best Of.
    (S)   (2:59)   Rhino 72820 VH1 - More Of The Big 80's.
    (S)   (2:58)   Hip-O 40075 Rock She Said: On The Pop Side.

UNCLE SAM
1998 I DON'T EVER WANT TO SEE YOU AGAIN
    (S)   (5:42)   Stonecreek/Epic 67731 Uncle Sam.

UNDERGROUND SUNSHINE
1969 BIRTHDAY

UNDISPUTED TRUTH
1971 SMILING FACES SOMETIMES
    (S)   (3:14)   Motown 6184 Hard To Find Motown Classics Volume 2.
    (S)   (3:14)   Rhino 70785 Soul Hits Of The 70's Volume 5.
    (S)   (3:14)   Rhino 72028 Soul Hits Of The 70's Volumes 1-5 Box Set.
    (M) (3:17)   Motown 5489 Best Of.
    (M) (3:15)   Motown 6312 Hitsville USA.
    (S)   (3:14)   Rhino 71209 70's Smash Hits Volume 5.
    (S)   (3:13)   Razor & Tie 22047 Sweet 70's Soul.
    (S)   (3:11)   Time-Life RHD-09 Rhythm & Blues - 1971.

    (S)   (3:13)   Time-Life SOD-12 Sounds Of The Seventies - 1971: Take Two.
    (S)   (3:15)   Rhino 72113 Billboard Hot Soul Hits - 1971.
    (S)   (3:15)   Motown 314530570 Motown Milestones - Best Of.
    (M) (3:12)   Motown 314530478 O.S.T. The Walking Dead.
    (S)   (3:14)   Capitol 35818 O.S.T. Dead Presidents Volume II.
    (S)   (3:11)   Time-Life R838-06 Solid Gold Soul - 1971.
    (S)   (3:14)   Flashback 72685 '70s Radio Hits Volume 5.

UNIFICS
1968 COURT OF LOVE
    (S)   (2:49)   Rhino 72620 Smooth Grooves: The '60s Volume 3 Late '60s.
1969 THE BEGINNING OF MY END
    (S)   (3:16)   Right Stuff 29140 Slow Jams - The Timeless Collection Volume 2.

UNION GAP (see GARY PUCKETT & THE UNION GAP)

UNIT FOUR PLUS TWO
1965 CONCRETE AND CLAY
    (M) (2:16)   Rhino 70324 History Of British Rock Volume 6.
    (M) (2:16)   Rhino 70319 History Of British Rock Box Set.
    (E)   (2:16)   Simitar 55532 The Number One's: The '60s.

UNV
1993 SOMETHING'S GOIN' ON
    (S)   (5:35)   Maverick/Sire 45287 Something's Goin' On.

PHILIP UPCHURCH COMBO
1961 YOU CAN'T SIT DOWN (PART 2)
    (M) (2:13)   Time-Life 2RNR-36 Rock 'N' Roll Era - Axes & Saxes/The Great Instrumentals.

URBAN DANCE SQUAD
1991 DEEPER SHADE OF SOUL
    (S)   (4:32)   Arista 8640 Mental Floss For The Globe.

URIAH HEEP
1972 EASY LIVIN
    (S)   (2:35)   Rhino 70986 Heavy Metal Memories.
    (S)   (2:35)   JCI 3302 Electric Seventies.
    (S)   (2:35)   Mercury 822476 Best Of.
    (S)   (2:35)   Mercury 812297 Demons And Wizards.
    (S)   (2:35)   Time-Life SOD-25 Sounds Of The Seventies - Seventies Generation.
    (S)   (2:35)   Rebound 314520278 Hard Rock Essentials - The 70's.
    (S)   (2:35)   Time-Life R968-10 Guitar Rock Classics.
    (S)   (2:35)   Special Music 5040 Great Britons! Volume Two.
    (S)   (2:35)   K-Tel 3985 70s Heavy Hitters: Arena Rockers 1970-74.
    (S)   (2:35)   Thump 6020 Easyriders Volume 2.
    (S)   (2:36)   Rebound 314520521 Highway Rockin'.

U.S.A. FOR AFRICA
1985 WE ARE THE WORLD
    (S)   (7:03)   Polygram 824822 We Are The World.

USHER
1997 YOU MAKE ME WANNA...
    (S)   (3:39)   LaFace 26043 and 26046 My Way.

US3
1994 CANTALOOP (FLIP FANTASIA)
>   (S) (4:28) Capitol 89117 O.S.T. Super Mario Brothers.
>   (S) (4:27) Giant 24565 Beverly Hills, 90210 - The College Years.
>   (S) (3:43) Tommy Boy 1109 MTV Party To Go Volume 6.
>   *(remix; all tracks on this cd are segued together)*
>   (S) (4:37) Blue Note 80883 Hand On The Torch.
>   (S) (4:36) Mammoth 92672 and 354980125 MTV Buzz Bin Volume 1.
>   (S) (3:40) JCI 3132 1990 - Only Rock 'n Roll - 1994. *(edited)*
>   (S) (4:37) Priority 53066 Hip Hop Jazz.

UTOPIA
1980 SET ME FREE
>   (S) (3:06) Rhino 70892 Anthology (1974-1985).
>   (S) (3:06) Rhino 70872 Adventures In Utopia.
>   (S) (3:06) Rhino 71890 Radio Daze: Pop Hits Of The 80's Volume One.

U2
1984 PRIDE (IN THE NAME OF LOVE)
>   (S) (4:32) Geffen 24236 Greenpeace - Rainbow Warriors. *(live)*
>   (S) (3:45) Time-Life R102-34 The Rolling Stone Collection.
>   (S) (3:07) Island 91003 and 422842299 Rattle And Hum. *(live)*
>   (S) (3:36) Island 90231 and 422822898 The Unforgettable Fire.
>   (S) (3:44) MFSL 624 The Unforgettable Fire. *(gold disc)*
1987 WITH OR WITHOUT YOU
>   (S) (4:56) Rhino 71642 Billboard Top Hits - 1987.
>   (S) (4:55) Island 90581 and 422842298 The Joshua Tree.
>   (S) (4:55) MFSL 650 Joshua Tree. *(gold disc)*
>   (S) (4:54) 550 Music/Epic 66145 O.S.T. Blown Away.
>   (S) (4:50) Island 90684 and 842901 The Island Story.
>   (S) (4:55) Time-Life R13610 Gold And Platinum Box Set - The Ultimate Rock Collection.

1987 I STILL HAVEN'T FOUND WHAT I'M LOOKING FOR
>   (S) (5:53) Island 91003 and 422842299 Rattle And Hum. *(live)*
>   (S) (4:37) Island 90581 and 422842298 The Joshua Tree.
>   (S) (4:36) Time-Life R988-28 Sounds Of The Eighties: The Rolling Stone Collection 1986-1987.
>   (S) (4:36) Pyramid 71830 Earthrise - The Rainforest Album.
>   (S) (4:37) MFSL 650 Joshua Tree. *(gold disc)*
1987 WHERE THE STREETS HAVE NO NAME
>   (S) (5:35) Island 90581 and 422842298 The Joshua Tree.
>   (S) (5:34) Time-Life R988-28 Sounds Of The Eighties: The Rolling Stone Collection 1986-1987.
>   (S) (5:35) MFSL 650 Joshua Tree. *(gold disc)*
1988 DESIRE
>   (S) (2:59) Foundation/WEA 26096 Super Sessions Volume One.
>   (S) (2:57) Island 91003 and 422842299 Rattle And Hum.
1989 ANGEL OF HARLEM
>   (S) (3:49) Island 91003 and 422842299 Rattle And Hum.
1992 MYSTERIOUS WAYS
>   (S) (4:01) Island 314510347 Achtung Baby.
1992 ONE
>   (S) (4:34) Island 314510347 Achtung Baby.
1992 EVEN BETTER THAN THE REAL THING
>   (S) (3:40) Island 314510347 Achtung Baby.
1992 WHO'S GONNA RIDE YOUR WILD HORSES
>   (S) (5:13) Island 314510347 Achtung Baby.
1995 HOLD ME, THRILL ME, KISS ME, KILL ME
>   (S) (4:45) Atlantic 82759 O.S.T. Batman Forever.
1997 DISCOTHEQUE
>   (S) (5:19) Island 314524334 Pop.
>   (S) (3:57) Polygram TV 314553847 Pure Dance 1998. *(all songs on this cd are segued together)*
1997 STARING AT THE SUN
>   (S) (4:36) Island 314524334 Pop.

JERRY VALE
1956 INNAMORATA
   (M) (2:52)   Columbia 40216 17 Most Requested Songs.
   (M) (2:51)   Rhino 72577 Eh, Paisano! Italian-American
                    Classics.
1956 YOU DON'T KNOW ME
   (M) (2:31)   Columbia 40216 17 Most Requested Songs.
   (M) (2:32)   Time-Life HPD-15 Your Hit Parade - 1956.
   (M) (2:31)   Hammer & Lace 697124113 Leading Men:
                    Masters Of Style Volume One.
1957 PRETEND YOU DON'T SEE HER
   (E) (2:41)   Columbia 40216 17 Most Requested Songs.
1965 HAVE YOU LOOKED INTO YOUR HEART
   (S) (2:21)   Columbia 40216 17 Most Requested Songs.
   (S) (2:20)   Time-Life R974-07 Many Moods Of Romance -
                    The Glory Of Love.

RITCHIE VALENS
1959 DONNA
   (actual 45 time is (2:26) not (2:20) as stated on the
   record label)
   (M) (2:23)   DCC Compact Classics 031 Back Seat Jams.
                    (faded :03 sooner than the 45)
   (M) (2:20)   Original Sound 8857 Oldies But Goodies Vol. 7.
                    (this compact disc uses the "Waring - fds" noise
                    reduction process; faded :06 sooner than the 45)
   (M) (2:20)   Original Sound 2223 Oldies But Goodies
                    Volumes 2,7,9,12 and 13 Box Set. *(this box set*
                    uses the "Waring - fds" noise reduction process;
                    faded :06 sooner than the 45)
   (M) (2:20)   Original Sound 2500 Oldies But Goodies
                    Volumes 1-15 Box Set. *(this box set uses the*
                    "Waring - fds" noise reduction process; faded :06
                    sooner than the 45)
   (M) (2:20)   Original Sound CDGO-1 Golden Oldies Volume.
                    1. *(faded :06 sooner than the 45)*
   (M) (2:20)   Original Sound 8891 Dick Clark's 21 All-Time
                    Hits Vol. 1. *(faded :06 sooner than the 45)*
   (M) (2:20)   Rhino 70178 Best Of. *(faded :06 sooner than the*
                    45)
   (M) (2:20)   Del Fi 71012 Best Of. *(faded :06 sooner than the*
                    45)
   (M) (2:20)   Time-Life 2RNR-13 Rock 'N' Roll Era - 1959.
                    (faded :06 sooner than the 45)
   (M) (2:28)   Time-Life R962-05 History Of Rock 'N' Roll: The
                    Teenage Years 1957-1964.
   (M) (2:21)   LaserLight 12323 American Dreams. *(faded :05*
                    sooner than the 45)
   (M) (2:28)   LaserLight 12319 Frankie Avalon/Fabian/Ritchie
                    Valens - Their Greatest Hits.
   (M) (2:24)   Del-Fi 71219 A Barrel Of Oldies. *(truncated fade)*
   (M) (2:25)   Del-Fi 9001 Rockin' All Night: Very Best Of.
   (M) (2:20)   JCI 3129 1955 - Only Rock 'N Roll - 1959. *(faded*
                    :06 earlier than the 45)
   (M) (2:28)   Time-Life R857-01 The Heart Of Rock 'n' Roll - 1959.
   (M) (2:27)   Thump 7200 Latin Oldies Volume Two.
1959 LA BAMBA
   (M) (2:02)   Rhino 70243 Greatest Movie Rock Hits. *(faded*
                    :03 sooner than the 45)
   (M) (2:02)   Rhino 75772 Son Of Frat Rock. *(faded :03*
                    sooner than the 45)
   (M) (2:04)   Rhino 70617 Best Of La Bamba.
   (M) (2:03)   Original Sound 8858 Oldies But Goodies Vol. 8.
                    (this compact disc uses the "Waring - fds" noise
                    reduction process; faded :02 sooner than the 45)

   (M) (2:03)   Original Sound 2221 Oldies But Goodies
                    Volumes 1,4,6,8 and 10 Box Set. *(this box set uses*
                    the "Waring - fds" noise reduction process; faded
                    :02 sooner than the 45)
   (M) (2:03)   Original Sound 2500 Oldies But Goodies
                    Volumes 1-15 Box Set. *(this box set uses the*
                    "Waring - fds" noise reduction process; faded :02
                    sooner than the 45)
   (M) (2:03)   Original Sound CDGO-5 Golden Oldies Volume.
                    5. *(faded :02 sooner than the 45)*
   (M) (2:03)   Original Sound 9601 Best Of Oldies But Goodies
                    Vol. 1. *(faded :02 sooner than the 45)*
   (M) (2:02)   Capitol 48993 Spuds Mackenzie's Party Faves.
                    (faded :03 sooner than the 45)
   (M) (2:01)   Rhino 70178 Best Of. *(faded :04 sooner than the*
                    45)
   (M) (2:01)   Del Fi 71012 Best Of. *(faded :04 sooner than the 45)*
   (M) (2:01)   Essex 7052 All Time Rock Classics. *(faded :04*
                    sooner than the 45)
   (M) (2:02)   Time-Life 2RNR-20 Rock 'N' Roll Era - 1959 Still
                    Rockin'. *(faded :03 sooner than the 45)*
   (M) (2:05)   Time-Life R962-01 History Of Rock 'N' Roll:
                    Rock 'N' Roll Classics 1957-1959.
   (M) (2:03)   Original Sound 8883 21 Legendary Superstars.
                    (faded :02 sooner than the 45)
   (M) (2:06)   LaserLight 12319 Frankie Avalon/Fabian/Ritchie
                    Valens - Their Greatest Hits.
   (M) (2:02)   Del-Fi 71210 Del-Fi Record Hop. *(faded :03*
                    sooner than the 45)
   (M) (2:05)   Del-Fi 71219 A Barrel Of Oldies.
   (S) (2:05)   Del-Fi 9001 Rockin' All Night: Very Best Of.
                    (this song was never originally released in stereo --
                    the stereo effect on this song is a result of
                    overdubbing and editing an instrumental track
                    recorded at a previous recording session)
   (M) (2:06)   Del-Fi 70008 The Del-Fi & Donna Story.
   (M) (2:05)   Music For Little People 42581 A Child's
                    Celebration Of Rock 'N' Roll.
   (M) (2:05)   Priority 50950 I Love Rock & Roll Volume 1:
                    Hits Of The 50's.
   (M) (2:04)   Flashback 72857 Grease And Other Golden Oldies.
   (M) (2:02)   K-Tel 4046 More Music For Your Party. *(faded*
                    :03 sooner than the 45)
   (M) (2:06)   Simitar 55522 The Number One's: Party Time.
   (M) (2:02)   Collectables 1514 and 2514 The Anniversary
                    Album - The 50's. *(sped up slightly)*

CATERINA VALENTE
1955 THE BREEZE AND I (ANDALUCIA)
   (M) (3:26)   Time-Life HPD-28 Your Hit Parade - The
                    Fabulous 50's.
   (M) (3:26)   Varese Sarabande 5823 The Caterina Valente
                    Collection.

MARK VALENTINO
1962 THE PUSH AND KICK
   (M) (2:24)   Forevermore 5008 Oldies I Forgot To Buy.

JOE VALINO
1956 GARDEN OF EDEN
   (M) (2:41)   Time-Life HPD-23 Your Hit Parade - The Late 50's.

VALJEAN
1962 THEME FROM BEN CASEY

FRANKIE VALLI (see also FOUR SEASONS)
1966 (YOU'RE GONNA) HURT YOURSELF
- (S) (2:30) Rhino 72998 Four Seasons 25th Anniversary Collection.
- (S) (2:30) Curb 77714 Greatest Hits.

1967 CAN'T TAKE MY EYES OFF YOU
- (S) (3:20) Rhino 72998 Four Seasons 25th Anniversary Collection.
- (S) (3:20) Rhino 71490 Four Seasons Anthology.
- (S) (3:20) Rhino 70595 Four Seasons Greatest Hits Volume 2.
- (S) (3:19) Time-Life SUD-14 Superhits - The Late 60's.
- (S) (3:19) Time-Life R138/05 Look Of Love.
- (S) (3:20) Capitol 89098 O.S.T. Wild Palms.
- (S) (3:19) Warner Special Products 1625 Four Seasons Sing For You.
- (S) (3:20) Curb 77714 Greatest Hits.
- (S) (3:19) Time-Life AM1-14 AM Gold - The Late '60s.
- (S) (3:19) Hammer & Lace 697124113 Leading Men: Masters Of Style Volume One.
- (S) (3:20) Time-Life R857-22 The Heart Of Rock 'n' Roll 1967-1969.
- (S) (3:19) Time-Life R814-01 Love Songs.

1967 I MAKE A FOOL OF MYSELF
- (M) (3:38) Rhino 72998 Four Seasons 25th Anniversary Collection.

1968 TO GIVE (THE REASON I LIVE)
- (S) (3:21) Rhino 72998 Four Seasons 25th Anniversary Collection.
- (S) (3:21) Curb 77714 Greatest Hits.

1969 THE GIRL I'LL NEVER KNOW (ANGELS NEVER FLY THIS LOW)
- (S) (3:39) Rhino 72998 Four Seasons 25th Anniversary Collection.

1975 MY EYES ADORED YOU
- (S) (3:31) Rhino 70595 Four Seasons Greatest Hits Volume 2.
- (S) (3:31) Rhino 72998 Four Seasons 25th Anniversary Collection.
- (S) (3:29) Original Sound 8907 Best Love Songs Vol 2.
- (S) (3:29) Original Sound 9326 Best Love Songs Vol. 1 & 2.
- (S) (3:29) Original Sound 1236 Best Love Songs Box Set.
- (S) (3:29) Razor & Tie 4543 The '70s Preservation Society Presents: Easy '70s.
- (S) (3:25) Time-Life SOD-33 Sounds Of The Seventies - AM Pop Classics II.
- (S) (3:30) Time-Life R138-18 Body Talk.
- (S) (3:31) Curb 77714 Greatest Hits.
- (S) (3:29) JCI 3169 #1 Radio Hits 1975 - Only Rock 'n Roll - 1979.
- (S) (3:29) Time-Life AM1-22 AM Gold - 1975.
- (S) (3:31) Time-Life R834-03 Body Talk - Moonlit Nights.
- (S) (3:29) Time-Life R840-03 Sounds Of The Seventies - Pop Nuggets: Early '70s.
- (S) (3:31) Rhino 72740 Billboard Top Soft Rock Hits - 1974.
- (S) (3:31) Time-Life R814-02 Love Songs.

1975 SWEARIN' TO GOD
- (S) (3:59) Rhino 70595 Four Seasons Greatest Hits Volume 2.
- (S) (4:00) Rhino 72998 Four Seasons 25th Anniversary Collection.
- (S) (3:59) Rebound 314520245 Disco Nights Vol. 6 - #1 Disco Hits.
- (S) (3:59) Curb 77714 Greatest Hits.
- (S) (3:58) Rebound 314520432 Disco Nights Vol. XI - Disco's Leading Men.
- (S) (3:59) Rhino 72516 Behind Closed Doors - '70s Swingers.
- (S) (4:00) Time-Life R840-06 Sounds Of The Seventies: '70s Dance Party 1975-1976.

1975 OUR DAY WILL COME
- (S) (4:03) Rhino 72998 Four Seasons 25th Anniversary Collection.
- (S) (4:03) Curb 77714 Greatest Hits.

1976 FALLEN ANGEL
1978 GREASE
- (S) (3:23) Polydor 825095 O.S.T. Grease.
- (S) (3:22) Rhino 72998 Four Seasons 25th Anniversary Collection.
- (S) (3:22) Rhino 70595 Four Seasons Greatest Hits Volume 2.
- (S) (3:20) JCI 3306 Dance Seventies.
- (S) (3:20) Time-Life SOD-20 Sounds Of The Seventies - 1978: Take Two.
- (S) (3:22) Curb 77714 Greatest Hits.
- (S) (3:22) JCI 3148 1975 - Only Dance - 1979.
- (S) (3:22) Flashback 72857 Grease And Other Golden Oldies.

JUNE VALLI
1959 THE WEDDING
1960 APPLE GREEN

LUTHER VANDROSS
1981 NEVER TOO MUCH
- (S) (3:49) Epic 37451 and 53443 Never Too Much.
- (S) (3:50) Epic 45320 Best Of Love.
- (S) (3:49) Epic 64803 Never Too Much/Forever, For Always, For Love/Busy Body.
- (S) (3:49) Simitar 55602 The Number One's: Silky Soul.

released as by DIONNE WARWICK and LUTHER VANDROSS:
1983 HOW MANY TIMES CAN WE SAY GOODBYE
- (S) (3:26) Arista 8540 Dionne Warwick - Greatest Hits 1979-1990.

released as by LUTHER VANDROSS:
1985 'TIL MY BABY COMES HOME
- (S) (5:31) Epic 39882 The Night I Fell In Love. *(LP version)*
- (S) (5:32) Epic 45320 Best Of Love. *(LP version)*

1987 STOP TO LOVE
- (S) (5:08) Epic 40415 Give Me The Reason. *(LP version)*
- (S) (5:09) Epic 45320 Best Of Love. *(LP version)*

1989 SHE WON'T TALK TO ME
- (S) (4:34) Epic 44308 Any Love. *(LP version)*

1990 HERE AND NOW
- (S) (5:22) K-Tel 6006 Lite Rock.
- (S) (5:21) Epic 45320 Best Of Love.
- (S) (5:21) Rhino 72159 Black Entertainment Television - 15th Anniversary.
- (S) (5:21) Time-Life R834-16 Body Talk - Sweet Nothings.

1991 POWER OF LOVE/LOVE POWER
- (S) (6:41) Epic 46789 Power Of Love. *(LP version)*
- (S) (6:37) Madacy Entertainment 6803 Power Of Love. *(LP version)*
- (S) (10:27) Epic 67505 If You Love Dance. *(remix)*
- (S) (6:41) LV Records/Epic 68220 One Night With You - The Best Of Love Volume 2. *(LP version)*
- (S) (6:41) Time-Life R834-20 Body Talk - Heart And Soul. *(LP version)*

1991 DON'T WANT TO BE A FOOL
- (S) (4:34) Epic 46789 Power Of Love.
- (S) (4:34) LV Records/Epic 68220 One Night With You - The Best Of Love Volume 2.

released as by LUTHER VANDROSS and JANET JACKSON with BBD and RALPH TRESVANT:
1992 THE BEST THINGS IN LIFE ARE FREE
- (S) (4:35) Perspective 1004 O.S.T. Mo' Money.
- (S) (4:01) LV Records/Epic 68220 One Night With You - The Best Of Love Volume 2.

released as by LUTHER VANDROSS:
1993 LITTLE MIRACLES (HAPPEN EVERY DAY)
- (S) (4:41) Epic 53231 Never Let Me Go. *(LP version)*
- (S) (4:41) LV Records/Epic 68220 One Night With You - The Best Of Love Volume 2. *(LP version)*

released as by LUTHER VANDROSS & MARIAH CAREY:
1994 ENDLESS LOVE
- (S) (4:18) Epic/LV 57775 Luther Vandross - Songs.
- (S) (4:18) LV Records/Epic 68220 One Night With You - The Best Of Love Volume 2.

LEROY VAN DYKE
1956 THE AUCTIONEER
- (M) (2:52) Time-Life HPD-35 Your Hit Parade - The Fun-Times 50's & 60's.
- (S) (2:27) K-Tel 3108 Country Music Classics Volume XVI. *(rerecording)*
- (S) (2:56) Mercury 314526541 Walk On By. *(rerecording)*
- (S) (2:27) K-Tel 3640 Corny Country. *(rerecording)*

1961 WALK ON BY
  (S) (2:19) Rhino 70682 Billboard's Top Country Hits Of 1961.
  (S) (2:19) Time-Life CTD-01 Country USA - 1961.
  (S) (2:19) Polygram Special Markets 314520261 Number One Country Hits 50's Through The 80's.
  (S) (2:20) K-Tel 320 Country Music Classics Volume II.
  (S) (2:20) Mercury 314526541 Walk On By.
  (S) (2:20) Mercury 314526691 Fifty Years Of Country Music From Mercury.
  (S) (2:20) K-Tel 3355 101 Greatest Country Hits Vol. One: Forever Country.
  (S) (2:19) Time-Life R857-10 The Heart Of Rock 'n' Roll 1960-1961.
  (S) (2:19) Time-Life R808-01 Classic Country 1960-1964.
1962 IF A WOMAN ANSWERS (HANG UP THE PHONE)
  (S) (2:20) Mercury 314526541 Walk On By.

VANGELIS
1982 CHARIOTS OF FIRE -- TITLES
  (S) (20:39) Polydor 800020 Chariots Of Fire. *(LP version)*
  (S) (3:22) Polydor 314531151 Portraits. *(this is not the 45 version; segues into the next selection)*
  (S) (20:39) MFSL 622 Chariots Of Fire. *(gold disc)*
  (S) (3:28) Time-Life R814-04 Love Songs. *(neither the 45 or LP version)*

VAN HALEN
1978 YOU REALLY GOT ME
  (S) (2:36) Warner Brothers 3075 Van Halen.
1979 DANCE THE NIGHT AWAY
  (S) (3:08) Warner Brothers 3312 Van Halen II.
  (S) (3:04) Warner Brothers 46332 Best Of Volume 1.
1982 (OH) PRETTY WOMAN
  (S) (2:53) Warner Brothers 3677 Diver Down.
1982 DANCING IN THE STREET
  (S) (3:44) Warner Brothers 3677 Diver Down.
1984 JUMP
  (S) (4:00) Warner Brothers 23985 1984.
  (S) (4:00) Time-Life R988-27 Sounds Of The Eighties: The Rolling Stone Collection 1983-1985.
  (S) (4:00) Warner Brothers 46332 Best Of Volume 1.
1984 I'LL WAIT
  (S) (4:40) Warner Brothers 23985 1984. *(LP version)*
1984 PANAMA
  (S) (3:30) Warner Brothers 23985 1984.
  (S) (3:30) Warner Brothers 46332 Best Of Volume 1.
1986 WHY CAN'T THIS BE LOVE
  (S) (3:47) Warner Brothers 25394 5150.
  (S) (3:45) Warner Brothers 46332 Best Of Volume 1.
  (S) (3:45) Time-Life R13610 Gold And Platinum Box Set - The Ultimate Rock Collection.
1986 DREAMS
  (S) (4:53) Warner Brothers 25394 5150. *(LP version)*
  (S) (4:50) Fox/Atlantic 82777 O.S.T. Mighty Morphin Power Rangers. *(LP version)*
  (S) (4:50) Warner Brothers 46332 Best Of Volume 1. *(LP version)*
1986 LOVE WALKS IN
  (S) (5:09) Warner Brothers 25394 5150. *(LP version)*
1988 BLACK AND BLUE
  (S) (5:25) Warner Brothers 25732 OU812. *(LP length)*
1988 WHEN IT'S LOVE
  (dj copies of this 45 ran (4:32) and (5:36))
  (S) (5:36) Warner Brothers 25732 OU812.
  (S) (5:37) Warner Brothers 46332 Best Of Volume 1.
1988 FINISH WHAT YA STARTED
  (S) (4:22) Warner Brothers 25732 OU812.
1989 FEELS SO GOOD
  (S) (4:30) Warner Brothers 25732 OU812. *(LP version)*
1991 TOP OF THE WORLD
  (S) (3:52) Warner Brothers 26594 For Unlawful Carnal Knowledge.
1995 CAN'T STOP LOVIN' YOU
  (S) (4:07) Warner Brothers 45760 Balance.

VANILLA FUDGE
1968 YOU KEEP ME HANGIN' ON
  (the true LP version of this song is a medley of "ILLUSIONS OF MY CHILDHOOD PART 1", "YOU KEEP ME HANGIN' ON" and "ILLUSIONS OF MY CHILDHOOD PART 2")
  (M) (2:57) Warner Special Products 27607 Highs Of The 60's. *(45 version)*
  (M) (7:24) JCI 3103 Electric Sixties. *(LP version)*
  (M) (7:25) Atlantic 81908 Classic Rock 1966-1988. *(LP version)*
  (M) (7:25) Atlantic 82306 Atlantic Rock & Roll Box Set. *(LP version)*
  (M) (7:25) Atco 33224 Vanilla Fudge. *(LP version)*
  (M) (7:23) Atco 90006 Best Of. *(this cd breaks down the medley into three distinct tracks which are still segued together just like the vinyl LP)*
  (M) (2:58) Rhino 71154 Psychedelic Sundae: Best Of. *(45 version)*
  (M) (2:57) Time-Life 2CLR-04 Classic Rock - 1968. *(45 version)*
  (M) (2:57) Rhino 71729 '60s Rock Classics, Vol. 2. *(45 version)*
  (M) (6:40) Time-Life R968-09 Guitar Rock 1966-1967. *(this is just the "YOU KEEP ME HANGING ON" portion of the LP version minus the "ILLUSIONS OF MY CHILDHOOD" segments)*
  (M) (2:57) Buddah 49507 Psychedelic Pop. *(45 version)*
  (M) (2:57) JCI 3160 18 Free & Easy Hits From The 60's. *(45 version)*
  (M) (2:58) Flashback 72702 '60s Rock: The Beat Goes On. *(45 version)*
  (M) (2:58) Flashback 72088 '60s Rock Hits Box Set. *(45 version)*
  (M) (2:58) Flashback 72802 Vanilla Fudge & Iron Butterfly Hits. *(45 version)*

VANILLA ICE
1990 ICE ICE BABY
  (S) (4:29) Foundation/Capitol 96426 Hearts Of Gold: The Rap Collection.
  (S) (4:29) SBK 95325 To The Extreme.
  (S) (4:29) K-Tel 3847 90s Now Volume 1.
  (S) (4:28) Rhino 75217 Heartthrob Hits.
1991 PLAY THAT FUNKY MUSIC
  (S) (4:23) Tommy Boy 1037 MTV Party To Go Volume 1. *(remix; all tracks on this cd are segued together)*
  (S) (4:44) Rhino 71916 Whats Up? Rap Hits Of The 90's.
  (S) (4:43) SBK 95325 To The Extreme.

VANITY FARE
1970 EARLY IN THE MORNING
  (LP length is (2:42); 45 length is (2:48))
  (S) (2:42) Rhino 70921 Super Hits Of The 70's Volume 1. *(LP mix)*
  (S) (2:42) Rhino 72009 Super Hits Of The 70's Volumes 1-4 Box Set. *(LP mix)*
  (S) (2:43) Collectables 5066 History Of Rock Volume 6. *(LP mix)*
  (S) (2:44) Collectables 5614 The Sun The Wind And Other Things. *(LP mix)*
1970 HITCHIN' A RIDE
  (M) (3:04) Rhino 70922 Super Hits Of The 70's Volume 2. *(with LP ending)*
  (M) (3:04) Rhino 72009 Super Hits Of The 70's Volumes 1-4 Box Set. *(with LP ending)*
  (M) (3:01) Collectables 5061 History Of Rock Volume 1. *(with LP ending)*
  (M) (3:04) Rhino 71205 70's Smash Hits Volume 1. *(with LP ending)*
  (M) (3:04) Time-Life SUD-20 Superhits - Early 70's Classics. *(with LP ending)*
  (M) (3:01) Time-Life SOD-31 Sounds Of The Seventies - AM Top Twenty. *(with LP ending)*
  (S) (2:55) Collectables 5614 The Sun The Wind And Other Things. *(with LP ending; stereo LP mix)*

VANITY FARE *(Continued)*

- (S) (2:55) Columbia 67380 O.S.T. Now And Then. *(with LP ending; stereo LP mix)*
- (M) (3:04) Time-Life AM1-15 AM Gold - Early '70s Classics. *(with LP ending)*
- (M) (3:04) Flashback 72682 '70s Radio Hits Volume 2. *(with LP ending)*
- (M) (3:04) Flashback 72090 '70s Radio Hits Box Set. *(with LP ending)*
- (S) (2:41) Varese Sarabande 5846 On The Radio Volume One. *(45 mix and ending)*

GINO VANNELLI
1974 PEOPLE GOTTA MOVE
- (S) (3:17) A&M 2505 Classics Volume 7.
- (S) (3:18) A&M 3260 Best Of.
- (S) (3:18) A&M 3120 Powerful People.
- (S) (4:25) Sin-Drome 2093 Sin-Drome Collection Vol. 2. *(live)*
- (S) (3:18) Rebound 314520440 No. 1 Hits Of The 70's.

1978 I JUST WANNA STOP
- (S) (3:35) Priority 7997 Super Songs/70's Greatest Rock Hits Volume 8.
- (S) (3:37) A&M 2505 Classics Volume 7.
- (S) (3:35) A&M 3260 Best Of.
- (S) (3:35) A&M 3170 Brother To Brother.
- (S) (3:36) Rhino 72299 Superhits Of The 70's Volume 25.
- (S) (3:33) K-Tel 3639 Dim The Lights - Soft Rock Hits Of The 70's.
- (S) (3:34) Time-Life R834-04 Body Talk - Together Forever.
- (S) (3:36) Rhino 72516 Behind Closed Doors - '70s Swingers.
- (S) (3:33) K-Tel 3906 Starflight Vol. 1.
- (S) (3:34) K-Tel 3908 High Energy Volume 1.
- (S) (3:34) Time-Life AM1-25 AM Gold - 1978.

1981 LIVING INSIDE MYSELF
(actual 45 time is (4:00) not (3:48) as stated on the record label)
- (S) (4:19) Arista 8268 Arista's Perfect 10. *(LP length)*
- (S) (4:22) Arista 8186 Nightwalker. *(LP length)*
- (S) (4:22) Priority 53714 80's Greatest Rock Hits Volume 1: Passion & Power. *(LP length)*
- (S) (4:19) Arista 8268 Arista's Perfect 10. *(LP length)*
- (S) (3:59) Rhino 71894 Radio Daze: Pop Hits Of The 80's Volume Five. *(45 length)*
- (S) (4:22) Time-Life R138-18 Body Talk. *(LP length)*
- (S) (3:59) Madacy Entertainment 1981 Rock On 1981. *(45 length)*
- (S) (4:21) K-Tel 3798 The 80's Mega Hits. *(LP length)*
- (S) (4:22) Time-Life R834-02 Body Talk - Just For You. *(LP length)*
- (S) (4:23) Simitar 55562 The Number One's: Smooth Love. *(LP length)*

RANDY VANWARMER
1979 JUST WHEN I NEEDED YOU MOST
- (S) (3:58) JCI 3303 Love Seventies.
- (S) (3:59) Rhino 70674 Billboard Top Hits - 1979.
- (S) (3:58) Time-Life SOD-35 Sounds Of The Seventies - AM Nuggets.
- (S) (3:59) Time-Life R834-06 Body Talk - Only You.
- (S) (3:59) Time-Life R840-01 Sounds Of The Seventies - Pop Nuggets: Late '70s.
- (S) (3:59) K-Tel 3907 Starflight Vol. 2.
- (S) (3:59) Time-Life AM1-26 AM Gold - 1979.

VAPORS
1980 TURNING JAPANESE
- (S) (3:42) Priority 53704 Rock Of The 80's Volume 3. *(LP version)*
- (S) (3:43) Rhino 71695 New Wave Hits Of The 80's Vol. 2. *(LP version)*
- (S) (3:41) EMI 81417 Living In Oblivion: The 80's Greatest Hits Volume One. *(LP version)*
- (S) (3:42) One Way 18332 Anthology. *(LP version)*
- (S) (3:41) Hip-O 40023 Smash Alternatives - 14 Classic New Wave Hits. *(LP version)*

- (S) (3:43) Hollywood 62098 O.S.T. Romy And Michele's High School Reunion. *(LP version)*
- (S) (3:43) Time-Life R988-22 Sounds Of The Eighties 1980-1983. *(LP version)*

VARIOUS ARTISTS
1997 ESPN PRESENTS THE JOCK JAM
- (S) (3:13) Tommy Boy 1214 Jock Jams Volume 3. *(all selections on this cd are segued together)*

FRANKIE VAUGHAN
1958 JUDY

SARAH VAUGHAN
1955 MAKE YOURSELF COMFORTABLE
- (M) (2:38) Mercury 824891 Golden Hits.
- (M) (2:38) Mercury 826320 Complete On Mercury Volume 1.
- (M) (2:38) Verve 314512904 Essential: The Great Songs.
- (M) (2:38) Time-Life HPD-21 Your Hit Parade - The Mid 50's.
- (M) (2:38) Polygram Special Markets 314520267 Hits To Remember.

1955 HOW IMPORTANT CAN IT BE?
- (M) (2:26) Mercury 824891 Golden Hits.
- (M) (2:27) Mercury 826320 Complete On Mercury Volume 1.

1955 WHATEVER LOLA WANTS
- (M) (2:35) Mercury 824891 Golden Hits.
- (M) (2:35) Mercury 826320 Complete On Mercury Volume 1.
- (M) (2:35) Time-Life HPD-09 Your Hit Parade 1955.
- (M) (2:35) Time-Life R135-04 Broadway Hit Parade.

1955 EXPERIENCE UNNECESSARY
- (M) (2:49) Mercury 824891 Golden Hits.
- (M) (2:49) Mercury 826320 Complete On Mercury Volume 1.

1955 C'EST LA VIE
- (M) (2:32) Mercury 824891 Golden Hits.
- (M) (2:32) Mercury 826320 Complete On Mercury Volume 1.
- (M) (2:29) Mercury 826320 Complete On Mercury Volume 1. *(alternate take)*
- (M) (2:31) Time-Life HPD-31 Your Hit Parade - The 50's Forever.

1956 MR. WONDERFUL
- (M) (2:47) Mercury 826320 Complete On Mercury Volume 1.

1956 FABULOUS CHARACTER
- (M) (2:40) Mercury 826320 Complete On Mercury Volume 1.

1956 THE BANANA BOAT SONG
- (M) (2:20) Mercury 824891 Golden Hits.
- (M) (2:20) Mercury 826327 Complete On Mercury Volume 2.

1959 BROKEN-HEARTED MELODY
- (S) (2:22) Mercury 824891 Golden Hits.
- (S) (2:23) Mercury 826333 Complete On Mercury Volume 3.
- (S) (2:21) Essex 7053 A Hot Summer Night In '59.
- (M) (2:22) Verve 314512904 Essential: The Great Songs.
- (S) (2:22) Time-Life HPD-13 Your Hit Parade - 1959.
- (S) (2:22) Eric 11502 Hard To Find 45's On CD (Volume I) 1955-60.

1959 SMOOTH OPERATOR
- (S) (2:18) Rhino 75757 Soul Shots Volume 3.
- (S) (2:19) Mercury 824891 Golden Hits. *(truncated fade)*
- (S) (2:19) Mercury 826333 Complete On Mercury Volume 3.

BILLY VAUGHN
1955 MELODY OF LOVE
- (E) (2:59) Curb 77345 Greatest Hits.
- (M) (2:59) Time-Life HPD-09 Your Hit Parade 1955.
- (M) (2:59) Varese Sarabande 5525 Melody Of Love: Best Of.
- (M) (2:59) Varese Sarabande 5686 History Of Dot Records Volume One.
- (M) (2:59) Time-Life R986-15 Instrumental Favorites - Billy Vaughn.

1955 THE SHIFTING WHISPERING SANDS (PARTS 1 & 2)
- (S) (2:57) Curb 77345 Greatest Hits. *(Part 1; extra instrumentation and background vocals added to the original mono recording to get stereo)*
- (S) (2:52) Curb 77345 Greatest Hits. *(Part 2; extra instrumentation and background vocals added to the original mono recording to get stereo)*

(M) (5:53) Varese Sarabande 5525 Melody Of Love: Best Of.
            (Parts 1 & 2)
(M) (2:59) Time-Life R986-15 Instrumental Favorites - Billy
            Vaughn. *(Part 1)*
(M) (2:53) Time-Life R986-15 Instrumental Favorites - Billy
            Vaughn. *(Part 2)*

1956 WHEN THE WHITE LILACS BLOOM AGAIN
(*) (*:**) Curb 77345 Greatest Hits. *(this is not the song
            "WHEN THE WHITE LILACS BLOOM AGAIN"
            as the cd jacket states)*
(M) (2:32) Varese Sarabande 5525 Melody Of Love: Best Of.
(M) (2:32) Time-Life R986-15 Instrumental Favorites - Billy
            Vaughn.

1957 RAUNCHY
(M) (2:12) Curb 77345 Greatest Hits. *(truncated fade)*
(M) (2:12) MCA Special Products 21035 Classic Rock &
            Roll Instrumental Hits, Volume 2.

1958 SAIL ALONG SILVERY MOON
(E) (2:07) Curb 77345 Greatest Hits.
(S) (1:59) Ranwood 7025 22 Of His Greatest Hits.
            (rerecording)
(M) (2:07) Time-Life HPD-11 Your Hit Parade 1958.
(M) (2:07) Varese Sarabande 5525 Melody Of Love: Best Of.
(E) (2:05) Time-Life R986-15 Instrumental Favorites - Billy
            Vaughn.
(M) (2:07) Time-Life R986-22 Instrumental Classics - Pop
            Classics.

1958 TUMBLING TUMBLEWEEDS
(M) (1:59) Curb 77345 Greatest Hits.
(M) (2:05) Varese Sarabande 5525 Melody Of Love: Best Of.

1958 LA PALOMA
(S) (2:29) Varese Sarabande 5525 Melody Of Love: Best Of.
(S) (2:28) Time-Life R986-12 Instrumental Favorites - Latin
            Rhythms.
(S) (2:32) Varese Sarabande 5784 La Paloma.

1959 BLUE HAWAII
(S) (2:01) Curb 77345 Greatest Hits.
(S) (1:51) Ranwood 7025 22 Of His Greatest Hits.
            (rerecording)
(S) (2:00) Varese Sarabande 5525 Melody Of Love: Best Of.

1960 LOOK FOR A STAR
(S) (2:11) Time-Life HPD-39 Your Hit Parade - 60's
            Instrumentals: Take Two.
(S) (2:10) Varese Sarabande 5525 Melody Of Love: Best Of.
(S) (2:11) Time-Life R986-15 Instrumental Favorites - Billy
            Vaughn.

1961 WHEELS
(S) (2:04) Varese Sarabande 5525 Melody Of Love: Best Of.
(S) (2:03) Curb 77345 Greatest Hits.
(S) (2:03) Time-Life R986-15 Instrumental Favorites - Billy
            Vaughn.

1962 A SWINGIN' SAFARI
(M) (2:14) MCA 5937 Vintage Music Volumes 13 & 14.
(M) (2:14) MCA 31211 Vintage Music Volume 14.
(S) (2:12) Curb 77345 Greatest Hits.
(S) (2:13) Time-Life HPD-34 Your Hit Parade - 60's
            Instrumentals.
(S) (2:15) Varese Sarabande 5525 Melody Of Love: Best Of.
(S) (2:13) Collectors' Choice 003/4 Instrumental Gems Of
            The 60's.
(M) (2:14) MCA Special Products 20902 Classic Rock &
            Roll Instrumental Hits, Volume 1.
(M) (2:14) K-Tel 3583 Those Wonderful Instrumentals
            Volume 3.
(M) (2:40) Time-Life R986-15 Instrumental Favorites - Billy
            Vaughn.
(S) (2:13) Time-Life AM1-27 AM Gold 60's TV Themes.
(M) (2:14) MCA Special Products 21025 The Best Of Easy
            Listening.

BOBBY VEE
1960 DEVIL OR ANGEL
(S) (2:17) EMI 48412 Best Of.
(S) (2:18) EMI 92774 Legendary Masters Series.
(S) (2:17) Time-Life 2RNR-29 Rock 'N' Roll Era - The 60's
            Rave On.

(S) (2:17) Curb 77666 Greatest Hits.
(S) (2:17) Time-Life R857-02 The Heart Of Rock 'n' Roll -
            1960.
(S) (2:17) JCI 3184 1960 - Only Love - 1964.

1961 RUBBER BALL
(both the 45 and LP length is (2:17))
(S) (2:17) EMI 48412 Best Of.
(S) (2:30) EMI 92774 Legendary Masters Series.
(S) (2:16) Time-Life 2RNR-27 Rock 'N' Roll Era - Teen
            Idols.
(S) (2:26) Time-Life SUD-15 Superhits - The Early 60's.
(S) (2:24) Curb 77666 Greatest Hits.
(S) (2:26) Time-Life AM1-19 AM Gold - The Early '60s.

1961 STAYIN' IN
(S) (2:02) EMI 92774 Legendary Masters Series.
(S) (2:01) Curb 77666 Greatest Hits.

1961 TAKE GOOD CARE OF MY BABY
(S) (2:27) EMI 96268 24 Greatest Hits Of All Time.
(S) (2:36) Rhino 70622 Billboard's Top Rock & Roll Hits Of
            1961. *(:10 longer than the 45 length; found only
            on the original 1988 issue of this cd)*
(S) (2:36) Rhino 72004 Billboard's Top Rock & Roll Hits
            1957 - 1961 Box Set. *(:10 longer than the 45 length)*
(S) (2:27) EMI 48412 Best Of.
(S) (2:38) EMI 92774 Legendary Masters Series. *(:12
            longer than the 45 length)*
(S) (2:26) Era 5025 The Brill Building Sound.
(S) (2:26) JCI 3112 Pop Sixties.
(S) (2:26) Time-Life 2RNR-18 Rock 'N' Roll Era - 1961 Still
            Rockin'.
(S) (2:30) Time-Life R962-05 History Of Rock 'N' Roll: The
            Teenage Years 1957-1964.
(S) (2:27) Curb 77666 Greatest Hits.
(S) (2:37) Time-Life R857-14 The Heart Of Rock 'n' Roll
            1960-1961 Take Two. *(:11 longer than the 45
            length)*

1961 RUN TO HIM
(S) (2:13) EMI 92774 Legendary Masters Series. *(includes
            a :04 countoff)*
(S) (2:07) Era 5025 The Brill Building Sound.
(S) (2:06) Time-Life 2RNR-42 Rock 'N' Roll Era - The 60's
            Sock Hop.
(S) (2:07) Rhino 71582 Billboard Top Pop Hits, 1961.
(S) (2:07) Curb 77666 Greatest Hits.
(S) (2:07) Time-Life R857-03 The Heart Of Rock 'n' Roll -
            1961.

1962 PLEASE DON'T ASK ABOUT BARBARA
(S) (2:01) EMI 48412 Best Of.
(S) (2:03) EMI 92774 Legendary Masters Series.

1962 SHARING YOU
(S) (2:01) EMI 92774 Legendary Masters Series.
(S) (2:00) Time-Life 2RNR-47 Rock 'N' Roll Era - Teen
            Idols II.
(S) (1:59) Curb 77666 Greatest Hits.

1962 PUNISH HER
(S) (1:52) EMI 48412 Best Of.
(S) (1:59) EMI 92774 Legendary Masters Series.

1963 THE NIGHT HAS A THOUSAND EYES
(S) (2:33) Curb 77355 60's Hits Volume 1.
(S) (2:34) EMI 48412 Best Of.
(S) (2:40) EMI 92774 Legendary Masters Series. *(includes
            a :06 countoff)*
(S) (2:32) Time-Life 2RNR-27 Rock 'N' Roll Era - Teen Idols.
(S) (2:32) Time-Life SUD-08 Superhits - 1963.
(S) (2:33) Curb 77666 Greatest Hits.
(S) (2:33) Time-Life R857-08 The Heart Of Rock 'n' Roll
            1963.
(S) (2:32) Time-Life AM1-17 AM Gold - 1963.
(S) (2:33) Hammer & Lace 697124114 Leading Men:
            Masters Of Style Volume Two.

1963 CHARMS
(S) (2:21) EMI 92774 Legendary Masters Series.

1963 BE TRUE TO YOURSELF
(S) (2:03) EMI 92774 Legendary Masters Series.
            (truncated fade)
(S) (2:01) Curb 77666 Greatest Hits.

BOBBY VEE (Continued)
released as by BOBBY VEE and THE STRANGERS:
1967 COME BACK WHEN YOU GROW UP
- (S) (2:14) EMI 48412 Best Of.
- (S) (2:52) EMI 92774 Legendary Masters Series. *(includes a :04 countoff and a previously unreleased :07 introduction; :24 longer fade than either the 45 or LP)*
- (S) (2:39) Time-Life SUD-05 Superhits - 1967. *(previously unreleased :06 introduction; :19 longer fade than either the 45 or LP)*
- (S) (2:13) Curb 77666 Greatest Hits.
- (S) (2:39) Time-Life AM1-08 AM Gold - 1967. *(previously unreleased :06 introduction; :19 longer fade than either the 45 or LP)*

1967 BEAUTIFUL PEOPLE
- (S) (2:16) EMI 48412 Best Of.
- (S) (2:18) EMI 92774 Legendary Masters Series.
- (S) (2:16) Curb 77666 Greatest Hits.

released as by BOBBY VEE:
1968 MY GIRL/HEY GIRL (medley)
- (S) (2:32) EMI 92774 Legendary Masters Series. *(truncated fade)*

SUZANNE VEGA
1987 LUKA
- (S) (3:51) A&M 5136 Solitude Standing.
- (S) (3:50) Time-Life R988-29 Sounds Of The Eighties: The Rolling Stone Collection 1987-1988.
- (S) (3:51) K-Tel 6143 New Folk Generation.

released as by D.N.A. featuring SUZANNE VEGA:
1990 TOM'S DINER
- (S) (3:47) Foundation/Capitol 96427 Hearts Of Gold: The Pop Collection.
- (S) (5:27) A&M 5339 The A&M Underground Dance Compilation. *(remix)*
- (S) (5:07) Tommy Boy 1037 MTV Party To Go Volume 1. *(remix; all tracks on this cd are segued together)*
- (S) (3:47) A&M 5363 Tom's Album.
- (M) (2:08) A&M 5136 Suzanne Vega - Solitude Standing. *(a cappella version)*
- (M) (2:05) A&M 5363 Tom's Album. *(a cappella version)*
- (S) (3:47) Razor & Tie 4569 '90s Style.

VELVETS
1961 TONIGHT (COULD BE THE NIGHT)
- (S) (2:04) Rhino 71463 Doo Wop Box.
- (S) (2:04) Time-Life 2RNR-45 Rock 'N' Roll Era - Street Corner Serenade.
- (S) (2:04) Sony Music Special Products 66106 The Monument Story.
- (S) (2:05) Sony Music Special Products 75052 Tonight (Could Be The Night).

VENTURES
1960 WALK--DON'T RUN
- (S) (2:03) Rhino 70621 Billboard's Top Rock & Roll Hits Of 1960.
- (S) (2:03) Rhino 72004 Billboard's Top Rock & Roll Hits 1957-1961 Box Set.
- (M) (2:04) Capitol Special Markets 57272 Great Instrumental Hits From Rock's Golden Years.
- (M) (2:04) Curb 77402 All-Time Great Instrumental Hits Volume 2.
- (S) (2:02) EMI 96268 24 Greatest Hits Of All Time.
- (E) (2:04) EMI 90614 Non Stop Party Rock.
- (S) (2:02) EMI 93451 Walk Don't Run - The Best Of.
- (E) (2:03) Curb 77376 Greatest Hits.
- (E) (2:03) EMI 46600 Best Of.
- (S) (2:03) Rhino 71548 Let There Be Drums Volume 2: The 60's.
- (S) (2:02) Rhino 71602 Rock Instrumental Classics Volume 2: The Sixties.
- (S) (2:02) Rhino 72035 Rock Instrumental Classics Vols. 1-5 Box Set.
- (S) (2:02) Time-Life 2RNR-11 Rock 'N' Roll Era - 1960. *(original pressings of this song on this cd were (M))*

- (E) (2:03) Era 840 Rock N' Roll Guitar Classics.
- (S) (2:02) MCA 11234 Revenge Of The Surf Instrumentals.
- (M) (2:02) JCI 3125 1960 - Only Rock 'N Roll - 1964.
- (S) (2:02) K-Tel 3453 Rockin' Instrumentals.
- (S) (2:02) One Way 18932 Walk Don't Run/Walk Don't Run Vol. 2.
- (M) (2:04) EMI 55906 Walk - Don't Run/All-Time Greatest Hits.
- (S) (2:02) Right Stuff 53318 Hot Rod Rock Volume 3: Big Boss Instrumentals.
- (S) (2:02) I.D. 90072 Jenny McCarthy's Surfin' Safari.

1960 PERFIDIA
- (S) (2:03) EMI 93451 Walk Don't Run - The Best Of.
- (S) (2:03) Curb 77376 Greatest Hits.
- (S) (2:03) EMI 46600 Best Of.
- (S) (2:02) Time-Life 2RNR-25 Rock 'N' Roll Era - The 60's Keep On Rockin'.
- (S) (2:02) MCA 11234 Revenge Of The Surf Instrumentals.
- (S) (2:02) Nouveau 1060 O.S.T. This Boy's Life.
- (S) (2:02) One Way 18925 Another Smash/The Ventures.
- (S) (2:03) EMI 55906 Walk - Don't Run/All-Time Greatest Hits.

1961 RAM-BUNK-SHUSH
- (S) (1:43) EMI 93451 Walk Don't Run - The Best Of.
- (S) (1:42) Curb 77376 Greatest Hits.
- (S) (1:42) EMI 46600 Best Of.
- (S) (1:42) One Way 18925 Another Smash/The Ventures.
- (S) (1:42) EMI 55906 Walk - Don't Run/All-Time Greatest Hits.

1964 WALK--DON'T RUN '64
- (S) (2:28) EMI 93451 Walk Don't Run - The Best Of. *(includes a :03 countoff; 3 extra drum beats at (2:21)- (2:22) not found on either the 45 or LP)*
- (S) (2:22) Time-Life 2CLR-16 Classic Rock - 1964: Shakin' All Over.
- (S) (2:22) Time-Life R962-04 History Of Rock 'N' Roll: California Pop 1963-1967.
- (S) (2:21) Rhino 72418 Cowabunga! The Surf Box.
- (S) (2:20) One Way 18932 Walk Don't Run/Walk Don't Run Vol. 2.

1964 SLAUGHTER ON TENTH AVENUE
- (S) (2:14) EMI 46600 Best Of. *(live)*
- (S) (2:14) Curb 77376 Greatest Hits. *(live)*
- (S) (2:19) EMI 93451 Walk Don't Run - The Best Of. *(with countoff)*
- (S) (2:14) Time-Life 2RNR-36 The Rock 'N' Roll Era - Axes & Saxes: The Great Instrumentals.
- (S) (2:13) One Way 18930 Where The Action Is/Knock Me Out.
- (S) (2:14) EMI 55906 Walk - Don't Run/All-Time Greatest Hits. *(live)*
- (S) (2:13) K-Tel 6256 Kahuna Classics. *(live)*

1969 HAWAII FIVE-O
- (S) (1:50) Curb 77402 All-Time Great Instrumental Hits Volume 2.
- (S) (1:51) Capitol Special Markets 57272 Great Instrumental Hits From Rock's Golden Years.
- (S) (1:51) EMI 90604 Beach Party Blasts.
- (S) (1:51) Capitol 96861 Monster Summer Hits - Wild Surf.
- (S) (1:51) EMI 93451 Walk Don't Run - The Best Of.
- (S) (1:50) Curb 77376 Greatest Hits.
- (S) (1:50) EMI 46600 Best Of.
- (S) (1:50) Time-Life 2CLR-06 Classic Rock - 1969.
- (S) (1:50) Rhino 71939 Billboard Top Pop Hits, 1969.
- (S) (1:50) Time-Life R968-12 Guitar Rock - The Late '60s.
- (S) (1:49) One Way 18924 Hawaii Five-O/Swamp Rock.
- (S) (1:50) EMI 53738 Tele-Ventures.
- (S) (1:50) EMI 55906 Walk - Don't Run/All-Time Greatest Hits.
- (S) (1:49) Collectors' Choice 5190 More Instrumental Gems Of The 60's.
- (S) (1:49) One Way 19390 T.V. Themes/Bobby Vee Meets The Ventures.
- (S) (1:50) Nick At Nite/550 Music 63435 Beach Blanket Bash.
- (S) (1:51) I.D. 90072 Jenny McCarthy's Surfin' Safari.

VIK VENUS
1969 MOONFLIGHT
    (M) (2:57)   Essex 7060 The Buddah Box.

BILLY VERA
1968 COUNTRY GIRL - CITY MAN
    (S) (2:31)   Ichiban 2101 Billy Vera & Judy Clay.
1968 WITH PEN IN HAND
released as by BILLY & THE BEATERS:
1987 AT THIS MOMENT
    (S) (4:16)   K-Tel 898 Romantic Hits Of The 80's.
    (S) (4:13)   Rhino 71642 Billboard Top Hits - 1987.
    (S) (4:13)   Rhino 71759 Tales From The Rhino: The Rhino
                  Records Story.
    (S) (3:29)   JCI 3171 #1 Radio Hits 1985 - Only Rock 'n Roll -
                  1989. *(1981 Alfa Records version which did not*
                  chart in the Top 40)
    (S) (4:14)   Madacy Entertainment 6803 Power Of Love.
    (S) (4:12)   Time-Life R988-19 Sounds Of The Eighties: The
                  Late '80s.
    (S) (4:13)   Time-Life R834-03 Body Talk - Moonlit Nights.
    (S) (4:13)   Hip-O 40080 Essential '80s: 1985-1989.

LARRY VERNE
1960 MR. CUSTER
    (M) (3:02)   Rhino 70495 Fun Rock!
    (E) (3:03)   Collectables 5070 History Of Rock Volume 10.
                  (rerecording)
    (M) (3:03)   Time-Life 2RNR-37 Rock 'N' Roll Era - Weird,
                  Wild & Wacky.
    (M) (3:02)   Time-Life SUD-19 Superhits - Early 60's Classics.
    (E) (3:05)   Collectables 2500 WCBS-FM History Of Rock -
                  The 60's Part 1. *(rerecording)*
    (E) (3:05)   Collectables 4500 History Of Rock/The 60s Part
                  One. *(rerecording)*
    (E) (3:05)   K-Tel 3037 Wacky Weirdos. *(rerecording)*
    (E) (3:05)   K-Tel 3243 Kooky Kountry. *(rerecording)*
    (M) (3:03)   Rhino 71581 Billboard Top Pop Hits, 1960.
    (E) (3:05)   Curb 77773 Hard To Find Hits Of Rock 'N' Roll
                  Volume One. *(rerecording)*
    (M) (3:02)   Rhino 72124 Dr. Demento 25th Anniversary
                  Collection.
    (M) (3:02)   Time-Life AM1-20 AM Gold - Early '60s Classics.

VERVE PIPE
1997 THE FRESHMEN
    (S) (5:07)   RCA 66809 Villains.

VIBRATIONS
1961 THE WATUSI
    (M) (2:34)   MCA 5939 Vintage Music Volumes 17 & 18.
    (M) (2:34)   MCA 31215 Vintage Music Volume 18.
    (M) (2:37)   Chess 31317 Best Of Chess Rhythm & Blues
                  Volume 1.
    (M) (2:33)   Time-Life 2RNR-29 Rock 'N' Roll Era - The 60's
                  Rave On.
    (M) (2:35)   K-Tel 3331 Do You Wanna Dance.
    (M) (2:33)   Nick At Nite/550 Music 63407 Dancing At The
                  Nick At Niteclub.
1964 MY GIRL SLOOPY
    (M) (2:51)   Time-Life 2RNR-38 Rock 'N' Roll Era - Rock
                  Classics/The Originals.

VILLAGE PEOPLE
1978 MACHO MAN
    (S) (4:59)   Priority 7974 Mega-Hits Dance Classics Volume
                  4. *(:13 shorter than LP version)*
    (S) (3:26)   Rhino 70274 The Disco Years Volume 3. *(45
                  version)*
    (S) (5:14)   Rhino 70167 Greatest Hits. *(LP version)*
    (S) (5:12)   Casablanca 314522039 Best Of. *(LP version)*
    (S) (5:12)   Casablanca 314516918 Casablanca Records Story.
                  (LP version)

    (S) (5:11)   Rebound 314520245 Disco Nights Vol. 6 - #1
                  Disco Hits. *(LP version)*
    (S) (3:27)   Casablanca 314526253 Casablanca Records
                  Greatest Hits. *(45 version)*
    (S) (5:14)   Casablanca 314532170 Macho Man. *(LP
                  version; tracks into the next selection)*
    (S) (3:25)   Tommy Boy 1163 Jock Jams Volume 2. *(all
                  selections on this cd are segued together)*
    (S) (4:51)   Chronicles 314553404 Non-Stop Disco Vol. 1.
                  (all songs on this cd are segued together)
    (S) (3:26)   Polydor 314555120 Pure Disco 2. *(45 version)*
    (S) (5:11)   Motown 314530841 O.S.T. In & Out. *(LP
                  version; previous selection tracks into the*
                  introduction)
    (S) (3:26)   Time-Life R840-08 Sounds Of The Seventies: '70s
                  Dance Party 1978-1979. *(45 version)*

1979 Y.M.C.A.
(actual 45 time is (3:42) not (3:30) as stated on the
record label)
    (S) (4:46)   Priority 7973 Mega-Hits Dance Classics Volume
                  3. *(LP version)*
    (S) (3:42)   Rhino 70985 The Disco Years Volume 2. *(45
                  version)*
    (S) (3:42)   Rhino 70674 Billboard Top Hits - 1979. *(45
                  version)*
    (S) (4:00)   Rhino 70492 Billboard Top Dance Hits - 1978.
                  (45 version but :18 longer fade)
    (S) (3:42)   Rhino 70167 Greatest Hits. *(45 version)*
    (S) (3:42)   Reprise 45485 O.S.T. Wayne's World 2. *(45
                  version)*
    (S) (4:46)   Casablanca 314522039 Best Of. *(LP version)*
    (S) (6:46)   Casablanca 314522039 Best Of. *(12" single
                  version)*
    (S) (3:42)   Razor & Tie 22496 Disco Fever. *(45 version)*
    (S) (4:00)   Time-Life SOD-19 Sounds Of The Seventies -
                  1979: Take Two. *(45 version but :18 longer fade)*
    (S) (4:42)   Casablanca 314516918 Casablanca Records Story.
                  (LP version)
    (S) (4:45)   Rebound 314520220 Disco Nights Vol. 4 -
                  Greatest Disco Groups. *(LP version)*
    (S) (4:46)   Rebound 314520265 Dance Fever. *(LP version)*
    (S) (4:02)   K-Tel 3126 Disco Mania. *(45 version but :20
                  longer fade)*
    (S) (4:40)   Tommy Boy 1137 ESPN Presents Jock Jams. *(all
                  songs on this cd are segued together with crowd*
                  sound effects added)
    (S) (3:45)   Casablanca 314526253 Casablanca Records
                  Greatest Hits. *(45 version)*
    (S) (4:45)   Casablanca 314532171 Cruisin'. *(LP version)*
    (S) (3:44)   Polydor 314535877 Pure Disco. *(45 version)*
    (S) (2:35)   Popular 12011 Disco Dance Hits. *(edited)*
    (S) (3:42)   Time-Life R840-09 Sounds Of The Seventies: '70s
                  Dance Party 1979-1981. *(45 version)*

1979 IN THE NAVY
(actual 45 time is (3:45) not (3:35) as stated on the
record label; actual LP time is (5:39) not (6:05) as
stated on the record label)
    (S) (3:43)   Priority 7971 Mega-Hits Dance Classics Volume
                  1. *(45 version)*
    (S) (5:39)   Rhino 70167 Greatest Hits. *(LP version)*
    (S) (3:43)   Rhino 70167 Greatest Hits. *(45 version)*
    (S) (3:43)   Casablanca 314522039 Best Of. *(45 version)*
    (S) (6:21)   Casablanca 314522039 Best Of. *(12" single
                  version)*
    (S) (3:42)   Time-Life SOD-34 Sounds Of The Seventies -
                  The Late 70's. *(45 version)*
    (S) (3:42)   Casablanca 314516918 Casablanca Records Story.
                  (45 version)
    (S) (3:44)   Rebound 314520270 Class Reunion 1979. *(45
                  version)*
    (S) (6:18)   Rebound 314520309 Disco Nights Vol. VII - D.J.
                  Pix. *(12" single version)*
    (S) (3:43)   Time-Life R138-38 Celebration. *(45 version)*
    (S) (3:42)   Casablanca 314526253 Casablanca Records
                  Greatest Hits. *(45 version)*
    (S) (5:39)   Casablanca 314532172 Go West. *(LP version)*

VILLAGE STOMPERS
1963 WASHINGTON SQUARE
- (S) (2:02) JCI 3109 Folk Sixties. *(at least on initial pressings, the timing index is off :04 and the song was mastered from a 33 1/3 rpm vinyl album played at 45 rpm)*
- (S) (2:38) Time-Life SUD-08 Superhits - 1963.
- (S) (2:38) Time-Life HPD-34 Your Hit Parade - 60's Instrumentals.
- (S) (2:03) Risky Business 53923 Guilty Pleasures. *(the timing index is off :04 and the song was mastered from a 33 1/3 rpm vinyl album played at 45 rpm; this company has stated it will not spend the money to remaster this track)*
- (S) (2:37) Collectors' Choice 003/4 Instrumental Gems Of The 60's.
- (S) (2:38) Time-Life AM1-17 AM Gold - 1963.
- (S) (2:41) Collectables 5840 Washington Square/More Sounds Of Washington Square.

GENE VINCENT and HIS BLUE CAPS
1956 BE-BOP-A-LULA
- (M) (2:34) Rhino 70599 Billboard's Top Rock & Roll Hits Of 1956.
- (M) (2:33) Rhino 70906 American Bandstand Greatest Hits Collection.
- (M) (2:34) JCI 3202 Rockin' Fifties.
- (E) (2:34) EMI 90614 Non Stop Party Rock.
- (M) (2:33) Curb 77323 All Time Greatest Hits Of Rock 'N' Roll.
- (M) (2:34) Capitol 98138 Spring Break Volume 1.
- (M) (2:33) Capitol 94074 Capitol Collector's Series.
- (M) (2:34) Capitol 91151 Greatest.
- (M) (2:34) Curb 77623 Greatest Hits.
- (M) (2:33) Rhino 71547 Let There Be Drums Volume 1: The 50's.
- (M) (2:34) Time-Life 2RNR-14 Rock 'N' Roll Era - 1956.
- (M) (2:34) Time-Life R962-03 History Of Rock 'N' Roll: Rock 'N' Roll Classics 1954-1956.
- (M) (2:33) K-Tel 3062 Rockin' Rebels.
- (M) (2:33) JCI 3129 1955 - Only Rock 'N Roll - 1959.
- (M) (2:34) Razor & Tie 2123 The Screaming End - Best Of.
- (M) (2:34) Priority 50950 I Love Rock & Roll Volume 1: Hits Of The 50's.
- (M) (2:34) Right Stuff 53319 Hot Rod Rock Volume 4: Hot Rod Rebels.
- (M) (2:33) K-Tel 4018 Forefathers Of Rock.
- (M) (2:34) Collectables 2714 Gene Vincent Rocks & The Bluecaps Roll/A Gene Vincent Record Date.

1957 LOTTA LOVIN'
- (M) (2:09) Rhino 70741 Rock This Town: Rockabilly Hits Volume 1.
- (M) (2:09) Capitol 98139 Spring Break Volume 2.
- (M) (2:09) Capitol 94074 Capitol Collector's Series.
- (M) (2:09) Capitol 91151 Greatest.
- (M) (2:09) Curb 77623 Greatest Hits.
- (M) (2:09) Time-Life 2RNR-17 Rock 'N' Roll Era - 1957 Still Rockin'.
- (M) (2:09) Razor & Tie 2123 The Screaming End - Best Of.
- (M) (2:09) Collectables 2720 Sounds Like Gene Vincent/Crazy Times.

1957 DANCE TO THE BOP
- (M) (2:13) Capitol 94074 Capitol Collector's Series.
- (M) (2:13) Curb 77623 Greatest Hits.
- (M) (2:13) Time-Life 2RNR-32 Rock 'N' Roll Era - Red Hot Rockabilly.
- (M) (2:14) Razor & Tie 2123 The Screaming End - Best Of.

BOBBY VINTON
1962 ROSES ARE RED (MY LOVE)
- (S) (2:36) Epic 26098 Greatest Hits.
- (S) (2:35) Curb 77253 Greatest Hits.
- (S) (2:37) Epic/Legacy 47855 16 Most Requested Songs.
- (S) (3:45) Curb 77412 His Greatest Songs Today. *(rerecorded)*
- (S) (2:37) Epic/Legacy 53570 The Essence Of.

- (S) (2:37) Time-Life HPD-32 Your Hit Parade - Into The 60's.
- (S) (2:37) Time-Life R138/05 Look Of Love.
- (S) (2:38) Rhino 71583 Billboard Top Pop Hits, 1962.
- (S) (2:37) Time-Life R857-06 The Heart Of Rock 'n' Roll 1962.
- (S) (2:38) JCI 3184 1960 - Only Love - 1964.

1962 I LOVE YOU THE WAY YOU ARE
- (S) (2:53) Epic 26098 Greatest Hits.

1962 RAIN RAIN GO AWAY
- (S) (2:54) Epic 26098 Greatest Hits.

1963 TROUBLE IS MY MIDDLE NAME
- (S) (2:25) Epic 26098 Greatest Hits.

1963 LET'S KISS AND MAKE UP
- (S) (2:26) Epic 26098 Greatest Hits.
- (S) (2:26) Time-Life R974-10 Many Moods Of Romance - Dream Along With Me.

1963 OVER THE MOUNTAIN (ACROSS THE SEA)
- (S) (2:25) Epic 26098 Greatest Hits.
- (S) (2:24) Epic/Legacy 47855 16 Most Requested Songs.

1963 BLUE ON BLUE
- (S) (2:21) Epic 26098 Greatest Hits.
- (S) (3:09) Curb 77253 Greatest Hits. *(rerecorded)*
- (S) (2:29) Epic/Legacy 47855 16 Most Requested Songs.
- (S) (3:09) Curb 77412 His Greatest Songs Today. *(rerecorded)*
- (S) (2:29) Epic/Legacy 53570 The Essence Of.
- (S) (2:21) Time-Life SUD-19 Superhits - Early 60's Classics.
- (S) (2:21) Time-Life HPD-33 Your Hit Parade - The Early 60's.
- (S) (2:21) Time-Life R857-12 The Heart Of Rock 'n' Roll 1962-1963.
- (S) (2:21) Time-Life AM1-20 AM Gold - Early '60s Classics.

1963 BLUE VELVET
- (S) (2:45) Curb 77532 Your Favorite Songs.
- (S) (2:47) Epic 26098 Greatest Hits.
- (S) (2:46) Curb 77253 Greatest Hits.
- (S) (2:47) Epic/Legacy 47855 16 Most Requested Songs.
- (S) (4:25) Curb 77412 His Greatest Songs Today. *(rerecorded)*
- (S) (2:47) Epic/Legacy 53570 The Essence Of.
- (S) (2:47) Time-Life SUD-08 Superhits - 1963.
- (S) (2:47) Time-Life OPCD-4517 Tonight's The Night.
- (S) (2:48) Rhino 71584 Billboard Top Pop Hits, 1963.
- (S) (2:47) Risky Business 53923 Guilty Pleasures.
- (S) (2:47) Nick At Nite/Epic 67148 Donna Reed's Dinner Party.
- (S) (2:46) Nick At Nite/550 Music/Epic 67768 Fonzie's Make Out Music.
- (S) (2:47) Time-Life R857-08 The Heart Of Rock 'n' Roll 1963.
- (S) (2:46) Time-Life AM1-17 AM Gold - 1963.
- (S) (2:47) Columbia/Legacy 64861 Martinis And A Broken Heart To Go.
- (S) (2:46) Time-Life R814-01 Love Songs.

1964 THERE! I'VE SAID IT AGAIN
- (S) (2:19) Epic 26098 Greatest Hits.
- (S) (2:20) Epic/Legacy 47855 16 Most Requested Songs.
- (S) (2:18) Time-Life SUD-12 Superhits - The Mid 60's.
- (S) (2:20) Rhino 71585 Billboard Top Pop Hits, 1964.
- (S) (2:18) Time-Life AM1-05 AM Gold - The Mid '60s.
- (S) (2:19) Time-Life R974-18 The Many Moods Of Romance - Prelude To A Kiss.
- (S) (2:19) Time-Life R814-03 Love Songs.

1964 MY HEART BELONGS TO ONLY YOU
- (S) (2:40) Epic 26098 Greatest Hits.
- (S) (2:41) Epic/Legacy 47855 16 Most Requested Songs.
- (S) (2:40) Time-Life R974-15 Many Moods Of Romance - Cheek To Cheek.

1964 TELL ME WHY
- (S) (2:36) Epic 26098 Greatest Hits.
- (S) (2:35) Epic/Legacy 47855 16 Most Requested Songs.

1964 CLINGING VINE
- (S) (2:27) Epic 26187 More Of Bobby's Greatest Hits.

1964 MR. LONELY
- (S) (2:39) Epic 26098 Greatest Hits.
- (S) (2:38) Curb 77253 Greatest Hits.
- (S) (2:39) Epic/Legacy 47855 16 Most Requested Songs.
- (S) (2:41) Curb 77412 His Greatest Songs Today. *(rerecorded)*

(S) (2:39) Epic/Legacy 53570 The Essence Of.
(S) (2:38) Time-Life 2CLR-16 Classic Rock - 1964: Shakin'
All Over.
(S) (2:39) Time-Life SUD-09 Superhits - 1964.
(S) (2:39) Time-Life R103-27 Love Me Tender.
(S) (2:39) Risky Business 66388 The Big Hurt/Songs To Cry
By.
(S) (2:39) DCC Compact Classics 078 Best Of Tragedy.
(S) (2:39) Time-Life R857-09 The Heart Of Rock 'n' Roll
1964.
(S) (2:38) Time-Life AM1-11 AM Gold - 1964.

1965 LONG LONELY NIGHTS
(S) (2:26) Epic 26187 More Of Bobby's Greatest Hits.
(S) (2:26) Epic/Legacy 53570 The Essence Of.

1965 L-O-N-E-L-Y
(S) (2:23) Epic 26187 More Of Bobby's Greatest Hits.
(S) (2:23) Epic/Legacy 47855 16 Most Requested Songs.

1965 WHAT COLOR (IS A MAN)
(S) (1:55) Epic 26187 More Of Bobby's Greatest Hits.

1966 SATIN PILLOWS
(S) (2:25) Epic 26187 More Of Bobby's Greatest Hits.
(S) (2:25) Epic/Legacy 53570 The Essence Of.

1966 DUM-DE-DA
(S) (2:05) Epic 26187 More Of Bobby's Greatest Hits.

1967 COMING HOME SOLDIER
(S) (2:28) Epic/Legacy 47855 16 Most Requested Songs.

1967 PLEASE LOVE ME FOREVER
(S) (2:34) Epic/Legacy 47855 16 Most Requested Songs.

1968 JUST AS MUCH AS EVER
(S) (2:20) Epic/Legacy 47855 16 Most Requested Songs.

1968 TAKE GOOD CARE OF MY BABY
(S) (2:45) Epic/Legacy 47855 16 Most Requested Songs.

1968 HALFWAY TO PARADISE
(S) (2:39) Epic/Legacy 47855 16 Most Requested Songs.

1969 I LOVE HOW YOU LOVE ME
(S) (2:29) Epic/Legacy 47855 16 Most Requested Songs.
(S) (2:27) Hammer & Lace 697124113 Leading Men:
Masters Of Style Volume One.

1969 TO KNOW YOU IS TO LOVE YOU
(S) (2:20) Epic/Legacy 47855 16 Most Requested Songs.

1969 THE DAYS OF SAND AND SHOVELS
1970 MY ELUSIVE DREAMS
1972 EVERY DAY OF MY LIFE
1972 SEALED WITH A KISS
(S) (2:42) Curb 77253 Greatest Hits. *(rerecording)*
(S) (5:50) Curb 77651 Retro Rock Dance Hits. *(all
selections on this cd are remixed with extra
instrumentation added)*

1974 MY MELODY OF LOVE
(S) (3:08) Curb 77317 70's Hits Volume 1.
(S) (3:11) Curb 77412 His Greatest Songs Today.
(rerecorded)
(S) (3:08) Curb 77253 Greatest Hits.

1975 BEER BARRELL POLKA
(S) (2:41) Curb 77499 Greatest Polka Hits Of All Time.
(rerecorded)

VIRTUES
1959 GUITAR BOOGIE SHUFFLE
(E) (2:32) Rhino 70719 Legends Of Guitar - Rock; The 50's.
(E) (2:31) Virtue 1991 Frank Virtue & The Virtues.
(M) (2:35) Rhino 71601 Rock Instrumental Classics Volume
1: The Fifties.
(M) (2:35) Rhino 72035 Rock Instrumental Classics Vols. 1-
5 Box Set.
(M) (2:25) Time-Life 2RNR-24 Rock 'N' Roll Era - The 50's
Keep On Rockin'.
(E) (2:32) Collectables 0536 Guitar In Orbit.
(M) (2:23) Era 840 Rock N' Roll Guitar Classics.
(M) (2:23) LaserLight 12316 Rebel Rousers.
(M) (2:35) Priority 50950 I Love Rock & Roll Volume 1:
Hits Of The 50's.
(M) (3:36) MCA Special Products 21035 Classic Rock &
Roll Instrumental Hits, Volume 2.

VISCOUNTS
1960 HARLEM NOCTURNE
(M) (2:20) Rhino 71601 Rock Instrumental Classics Volume
1: The Fifties. *(sounds like it was mastered from
vinyl)*
(M) (2:20) Rhino 72035 Rock Instrumental Classics Vols. 1-
5 Box Set. *(sounds like it was mastered from vinyl)*
(M) (2:20) Time-Life 2RNR-36 Rock 'N' Roll Era - Axes &
Saxes/The Great Instrumentals.
(M) (2:20) K-Tel 3059 Saxy Rock.

1965 HARLEM NOCTURNE
(this song was a hit in 1960 and 1965; see 1960 listings)

VIXEN
1988 EDGE OF A BROKEN HEART
(S) (4:21) Priority 7965 Heavy Metal Love. *(LP version)*
(S) (4:22) Priority 53753 Monsters Of Rock Vol. 2 - Metal
Masters. *(LP version)*
(S) (3:32) Priority 8676 Metal Mania. *(45 version)*
(S) (4:21) Sandstone 33044 and 5010 Rock The First
Volume Four. *(LP version)*
(S) (4:22) EMI Manhattan 46991 Vixen. *(LP version)*
(S) (4:21) Rhino 72292 Heavy Metal Hits Of The 80's
Volume 2. *(LP version)*
(S) (4:21) Time-Life R968-24 Guitar Rock - The '80s Take
Two. *(LP version)*
(S) (3:31) EMI-Capitol Music Special Markets 19460 Lost
Hits Of The '80s. *(45 version)*
(S) (4:21) K-Tel 3999 Glam Rock Vol. 2: The 80's And
Beyond. *(LP version)*
(S) (4:20) Hip-O 40077 Rock She Said: Guitars + Attitudes.
(LP version)

1989 CRYIN'
(S) (3:31) EMI Manhattan 46991 Vixen.

VOGUES
1965 YOU'RE THE ONE
(E) (2:21) Rhino 70245 Greatest Hits.
(E) (2:16) Time-Life 2CLR-14 Classic Rock - 1965: Shakin'
All Over.
(E) (2:18) Time-Life SUD-03 Superhits - 1965.
(M) (2:20) Collectables 2604 WCBS-FM Jukebox Giants
Vol. 2.
(E) (2:21) Rhino 71730 '60s Rock Classics, Vol. 3.
(M) (2:21) LaserLight 12318 Chart Busters.
(M) (2:21) Collectables 2505 History Of Rock - The 60's Part
5.
(M) (2:21) Collectables 4505 History Of Rock/The 60s Part
Five.
(M) (2:22) Varese Sarabande 5680 You're The One: Best Of.
(M) (2:21) Time-Life 2CLR-31 Classic Rock - Totally
Fantastic '60s.
(E) (2:18) Time-Life AM1-10 AM Gold - 1965.
(E) (2:21) Flashback 72703 '60s Rock: It's A Beautiful
Morning.
(E) (2:21) Flashback 72088 '60s Rock Hits Box Set.

1966 FIVE O'CLOCK WORLD
(S) (2:18) Warner Special Products 27610 More Party
Classics. *(additional instrumentation added to
obtain stereo effect)*
(S) (2:18) A&M 3913 and 3340 O.S.T. Good Morning
Vietnam. *(additional instrumentation added to
obtain stereo effect)*
(E) (2:06) Rhino 70243 Greatest Movie Rock Hits.
(E) (2:06) Rhino 70245 Greatest Hits.
(M) (2:06) Collectables 5062 History Of Rock Volume 2.
(E) (2:05) Time-Life 2CLR-13 Classic Rock - 1966: Shakin'
All Over.
(E) (2:06) Time-Life SUD-12 Superhits - The Mid 60's.
(E) (2:06) Collectables 2504 WCBS-FM History Of Rock -
The 60's Part 4.
(E) (2:06) Collectables 4504 History Of Rock/The 60s Part
Four.
(E) (2:06) Collectables 2510 WCBS-FM History Of Rock -
The Rockin' 60's.

VOGUES *(Continued)*

    (E) (2:06) Collectables 4510 History Of Rock/The Rockin' 60s.

    (E) (2:06) Rhino 71728 '60s Rock Classics, Vol. 1.

    (M) (2:06) Collectables 2554 CBS-FM History Of Rock Volume 2.

    (M) (2:07) Varese Sarabande 5680 You're The One: Best Of.

    (M) (2:07) Priority 50951 I Love Rock & Roll Volume 2: Hits Of The 60's.

    (E) (2:06) Time-Life AM1-05 AM Gold - The Mid '60s.

    (E) (2:06) Flashback 72701 '60s Rock: Mony Mony.

    (E) (2:06) Flashback 72088 '60s Rock Hits Box Set.

    (E) (2:06) Simitar 55572 The Number One's: Hot In The '60s.

1966 MAGIC TOWN

    (E) (3:10) Rhino 70245 Greatest Hits.

    (M) (3:09) Collectables 5066 History Of Rock Volume 6.

    (E) (3:10) Era 5025 The Brill Building Sound.

    (M) (3:09) Varese Sarabande 5680 You're The One: Best Of.

1966 THE LAND OF MILK AND HONEY

    (E) (2:43) Rhino 70245 Greatest Hits.

    (S) (2:43) Varese Sarabande 5680 You're The One: Best Of.

1968 TURN AROUND, LOOK AT ME

    (S) (2:44) Rhino 70245 Greatest Hits.

    (S) (2:43) Time-Life SUD-02 Superhits - 1968.

    (S) (2:43) Time-Life AM1-04 AM Gold - 1968.

1968 MY SPECIAL ANGEL

    (S) (2:57) Rhino 70245 Greatest Hits.

    (S) (2:57) Time-Life SUD-14 Superhits - The Late 60's.

    (S) (2:58) Time-Life R138/05 Look Of Love.

    (S) (2:57) Time-Life AM1-14 AM Gold - The Late '60s.

    (S) (2:58) Milan 35786 O.S.T. Angel Baby.

    (S) (2:58) Time-Life R857-22 The Heart Of Rock 'n' Roll 1967-1969.

    (S) (2:57) Time-Life R814-01 Love Songs.

1968 TILL

    (S) (2:19) Rhino 70245 Greatest Hits.

1969 WOMAN HELPING MAN

    (S) (3:10) Rhino 70245 Greatest Hits.

1969 NO, NOT MUCH

    (S) (3:22) Rhino 70245 Greatest Hits.

1969 EARTH ANGEL (WILL YOU BE MINE)

    (S) (2:33) Rhino 70245 Greatest Hits.

VOICES THAT CARE
1991 VOICES THAT CARE

    (S) (4:58) Giant 40054 Voices That Care. *(available only on this compact disc maxi-single)*

VOLUMES
1962 I LOVE YOU

    (M) (2:35) Rhino 75764 Best Of Doo Wop Uptempo.

    (M) (2:34) Collectables 5032 I Love You/Golden Classics. *(truncated fade)*

    (M) (2:35) Collectables 5067 History Of Rock Volume 7.

    (M) (2:34) Time-Life 2RNR-16 Rock 'N' Roll Era - 1962 Still Rockin'.

    (M) (2:35) Time-Life R962-06 History Of Rock 'N' Roll: Doo Wop And Vocal Group Tradition 1955-1962.

    (M) (2:34) Collectables 2502 WCBS-FM History Of Rock - The 60's Part 3. *(truncated fade)*

    (M) (2:34) Collectables 4502 History Of Rock/The 60s Part Three. *(truncated fade)*

    (M) (2:34) Collectables 2552 WOGL History Of Rock Vol. 2. *(truncated fade)*

    (M) (2:35) Rhino 72507 Doo Wop Box II.

    (M) (2:35) Flashback 72717 Doo Wop - Blue Moon.

ROGER VOUDOURIS
1979 GET USED TO IT

    (S) (2:59) Rhino 72299 Superhits Of The 70's Volume 25.

VOXPOPPERS
1958 WISHING FOR YOUR LOVE

    (M) (1:58) Eric 11502 Hard To Find 45's On CD (Volume I) 1955-60.

ADAM WADE
1961 TAKE GOOD CARE OF HER
    (S) (2:32) Collectables 5455 Greatest Hits. *(rerecording)*
    (S) (2:32) Time-Life HPD-32 Your Hit Parade - Into The 60's. *(rerecording)*
1961 THE WRITING ON THE WALL
    (S) (2:28) Collectables 5455 Greatest Hits. *(rerecording)*
1961 AS IF I DIDN'T KNOW
    (S) (2:57) Time-Life HPD-37 Your Hit Parade - The 60's. *(rerecording)*
    (S) (2:58) Collectables 5455 Greatest Hits. *(rerecording)*

WADSWORTH MANSION
1971 SWEET MARY
    (M) (2:39) Rhino 70924 Super Hits Of The 70's Volume 4. *(45 version)*
    (M) (2:39) Rhino 72009 Super Hits Of The 70's Volumes 1-4 Box Set. *(45 version)*
    (M) (2:39) Rhino 71207 70's Smash Hits Volume 3. *(45 version)*
    (M) (2:39) Time-Life SUD-20 Superhits - Early 70's Classics. *(45 version)*
    (M) (2:38) Time-Life AM1-15 AM Gold - Early '70s Classics. *(45 version)*
    (M) (2:38) Time-Life R840-03 Sounds Of The Seventies - Pop Nuggets: Early '70s. *(45 version)*
    (M) (2:39) Flashback 72684 '70s Radio Hits Volume 4. *(45 version)*
    (M) (2:39) Flashback 72090 '70s Radio Hits Box Set. *(45 version)*

JACK WAGNER
1985 ALL I NEED
    (S) (3:25) JCI 3186 1985 - Only Love - 1989.
    (S) (3:27) Time-Life R988-15 Sounds Of The Eighties: The Mid 80's.
    (S) (3:27) Time-Life R834-06 Body Talk - Only You.
    (S) (3:27) Rhino 75217 Heartthrob Hits.

WAIKIKIS
1965 HAWAII TATTOO

WAILERS
1959 TALL COOL ONE
    (E) (2:34) Collectables 0573 Tall Cool On/Golden Classics.
    (E) (2:34) Right Stuff 53318 Hot Rod Rock Volume 3: Big Boss Instrumentals.
    (M) (2:32) Hollywood 62138 O.S.T. Home Alone 3.

LOUDON WAINWRIGHT III
1973 DEAD SKUNK
    (S) (3:05) Rhino 70930 Super Hits Of The 70's Volume 10. *(numerous dropouts from 2:23 to the end of the song)*
    (S) (3:03) Priority 8670 Hitchin' A Ride/70's Greatest Rock Hits Volume 10.
    (S) (3:06) Columbia 31462 Album III.
    (S) (3:05) Time-Life R830-03 The Dr. Demento Collection: The Early '70s. *(numerous dropouts from 2:23 to the end of song)*

JOHN WAITE
1984 MISSING YOU
    (S) (4:26) Priority 7961 Three Decades Of Rock. *(LP length)*
    (S) (4:27) Priority 53714 80's Greatest Rock Hits Volume 1 - Passion & Power. *(LP length)*

    (S) (4:27) Sandstone 33045 and 5011 Rock The First Volume Five. *(LP length)*
    (S) (4:26) Sandstone 33052 and 5020 Cosmopolitan Volume 6. *(LP length)*
    (S) (4:00) Time-Life R105-40 Rock Dreams. *(45 length)*
    (S) (4:26) DCC Compact Classics 084 Night Moves Volume 4. *(LP length)*
    (S) (4:27) Priority 53681 80's Greatest Rock Hits - Agony & Ecstasy. *(LP length)*
    (S) (4:27) EMI 46078 No Brakes. *(LP length)*
    (S) (4:24) Chrysalis 21864 Essential 1976-1986. *(LP length)*
    (S) (4:26) Time-Life R988-06 Sounds Of The Eighties: 1984. *(LP length)*
    (S) (4:26) Time-Life R138-18 Body Talk. *(LP length)*
    (S) (4:26) Madacy Entertainment 1984 Rock On 1984. *(LP length)*
    (S) (4:29) EMI 54241 The Complete John Waite, Volume One: Falling Backwards. *(LP length)*
    (S) (4:24) Priority 50953 I Love Rock & Roll Volume 4: Hits Of The 80's. *(LP length)*
    (S) (4:26) Time-Life R834-08 Body Talk - On My Mind. *(LP length)*
    (S) (4:00) Hip-O 40079 Essential '80s: 1980-1984. *(45 length)*
    (S) (4:00) Simitar 55562 The Number One's: Smooth Love. *(45 length)*
1984 TEARS
    (S) (3:57) EMI 46078 No Brakes. *(LP length)*
1985 EVERY STEP OF THE WAY

JOHNNY WAKELIN & THE KINSHASA BAND
1975 BLACK SUPERMAN - "MUHAMMAD ALI"
    (S) (3:34) Rhino 70762 Super Hits Of The 70's Volume 15.
    (S) (3:34) Razor & Tie 22505 More Fabulous 70's Volume 2.
    (S) (3:33) K-Tel 3624 Music Express.

CHRIS WALKER
1992 TAKE TIME
    (S) (4:19) Pendulum 61136 First Time.

JR. WALKER & THE ALL STARS
1965 SHOTGUN
    (S) (3:01) Motown 6160 The Good-Feeling Music Of The Big Chill Generation Volume 2. *(LP version)*
    (S) (3:00) Motown 5452 A Collection Of 16 Big Hits Volume 5. *(LP version)*
    (S) (3:01) Rhino 70651 Billboard's Top R&B Hits Of 1965. *(LP version)*
    (S) (3:01) Rhino 72006 Billboard's Top R&B Hits 1965-1969 Box Set. *(LP version)*
    (S) (3:01) Motown 9017 and 5248 16 #1 Hits From The Early 60's. *(LP version)*
    (S) (3:00) Motown 9012 and 5208 Greatest Hits. *(LP version)*
    (S) (3:00) Motown 6203 Compact Command Performances. *(LP version)*
    (S) (3:00) Motown 5297 All The Great Hits. *(LP version)*
    (S) (3:00) Motown 5141 Shotgun. *(LP version)*
    (S) (3:00) Motown 8023 and 8123 Shotgun/Road Runner. *(LP version)*
    (S) (2:59) Motown 9071 Motown Dance Party Volume 1. *(all selections on this cd are segued together; LP version)*
    (M) (2:57) Motown 6312 Hitsville USA. *(45 version)*
    (S) (3:00) Motown 374638512 Motown Legends - What Does It Take (To Win Your Love). *(LP version)*
    (M) (2:57) Motown 6270 Nothin' But Soul. *(45 version)*

JR. WALKER & THE ALL STARS (Continued)

- (S) (3:01) Time-Life RHD-07 Rhythm & Blues - 1965. *(LP version)*
- (S) (3:00) Time-Life 2CLR-01 Classic Rock - 1965. *(LP version)*
- (S) (3:00) Thump 7030 Low Rider Oldies Volume III. *(LP version)*
- (S) (2:57) Tommy Boy 1100 ESPN Presents Jock Rock. *(sound effects added to the ending; LP version)*
- (M) (2:57) Polygram Special Markets 314520284 Motown Legends Volume 3. *(45 version)*
- (S) (3:02) Polygram Special Markets 314520300 Motown Legends - Guy Groups. *(LP version)*
- (S) (2:59) Risky Business 66914 Party On. *(LP version)*
- (S) (3:01) Qwest/Reprise 45130 O.S.T. Malcolm X. *(LP version)*
- (S) (3:01) Time-Life R838-12 Solid Gold Soul - 1965. *(LP version)*
- (S) (2:56) Nick At Nite/550 Music 63407 Dancing At The Nick At Niteclub. *(45 version opening sound effect with an alternate stereo LP mix)*
- (M) (2:56) Motown 314530828 The Ultimate Collection. *(45 version)*

1965 DO THE BOOMERANG

- (S) (2:20) Motown 6203 Compact Command Performances.
- (S) (2:20) Motown 5141 Shotgun.
- (S) (2:20) Motown 8023 and 8123 Shotgun/Road Runner.
- (M) (2:20) Motown 6270 Nothin' But Soul.
- (M) (2:19) Motown 314530828 The Ultimate Collection.

1965 SHAKE AND FINGERPOP

- (S) (2:41) Motown 5453 A Collection Of 16 Big Hits Volume 6.
- (S) (2:40) Motown 9012 and 5208 Greatest Hits.
- (S) (2:40) Motown 6203 Compact Command Performances.
- (S) (2:40) Motown 5297 All The Great Hits.
- (S) (2:42) Motown 5141 Shotgun.
- (S) (2:42) Motown 8023 and 8123 Shotgun/Road Runner.
- (M) (2:42) Motown 6270 Nothin' But Soul.
- (M) (2:43) Rhino 72815 Beg, Scream & Shout! The Big Ol' Box Of '60s Soul.
- (M) (2:41) Motown 314530828 The Ultimate Collection.

1965 CLEO'S BACK

- (S) (2:30) Motown 5141 Shotgun.
- (S) (2:30) Motown 8023 and 8123 Shotgun/Road Runner.
- (M) (2:30) Motown 6270 Nothin' But Soul.
- (M) (2:29) Motown 314530828 The Ultimate Collection.

✕1966 (I'M A) ROAD RUNNER

- (S) (2:40) Motown 5455 A Collection Of 16 Big Hits Volume 8. *(:07 shorter than the 45 or LP)*
- (S) (2:39) Motown 9072 Motown Dance Party Volume 2. *(all selections on this cd are segued together; :08 shorter than the 45 or LP)*
- (S) (2:47) Motown 5427 Road Runner.
- (S) (2:41) Motown 9012 and 5208 Greatest Hits. *(:06 shorter than the 45 or LP)*
- (S) (2:41) Motown 6203 Compact Command Performances. *(:06 shorter than the 45 or LP)*
- (S) (2:46) Motown 8023 and 8123 Shotgun/Road Runner.
- (M) (2:46) Motown 6312 Hitsville USA.
- (M) (2:48) Motown 6270 Nothin' But Soul.
- (S) (2:40) Time-Life RHD-01 Rhythm & Blues - 1966. *(:07 shorter than the 45 or LP)*
- (S) (2:40) Time-Life 2CLR-22 Classic Rock - 1966: Blowin' Your Mind. *(:07 shorter than the 45 or LP)*
- (S) (2:41) Motown 314530522 Motown Year By Year - 1966. *(:06 shorter than the 45 or LP)*
- (S) (2:40) Time-Life R838-01 Solid Gold Soul - 1966. *(:07 shorter than the 45 or LP)*
- (M) (2:46) Motown 314530828 The Ultimate Collection.

1966 HOW SWEET IT IS (TO BE LOVED BY YOU)

- (S) (2:57) Motown 5454 A Collection Of 16 Big Hits Volume 7.
- (S) (2:57) Motown 9098 Radio's #1 Hits.
- (S) (2:58) Motown 5460 Gotta Hold On To This Feeling.
- (S) (3:01) Motown 5427 Road Runner.
- (S) (2:57) Motown 9012 and 5208 Greatest Hits.
- (S) (2:58) Motown 6203 Compact Command Performances.
- (S) (2:57) Motown 5297 All The Great Hits.
- (S) (3:01) Motown 8023 and 8123 Shotgun/Road Runner.
- (S) (2:58) Ripete 392183 Ocean Drive.
- (M) (3:01) Motown 6312 Hitsville USA.
- (M) (3:00) Motown 6270 Nothin' But Soul.
- (M) (2:59) Motown 314530828 The Ultimate Collection.

1967 PUCKER UP BUTTERCUP

- (S) (3:13) Motown 5454 A Collection Of 16 Big Hits Volume 7.
- (S) (3:13) Motown 5427 Road Runner.
- (S) (3:17) Motown 9012 and 5208 Greatest Hits.
- (S) (3:17) Motown 6203 Compact Command Performances.
- (S) (3:13) Motown 8023 and 8123 Shotgun/Road Runner.
- (M) (3:13) Motown 6270 Nothin' But Soul.
- (S) (3:16) Time-Life 2CLR-28 Classic Rock - On The Soul Side II.
- (M) (3:13) Motown 314530828 The Ultimate Collection.

1968 COME SEE ABOUT ME

- (S) (2:59) Motown 5456 A Collection Of 16 Big Hits Volume 9.
- (S) (2:58) Motown 9012 and 5208 Greatest Hits.
- (S) (2:58) Motown 6203 Compact Command Performances.
- (M) (3:04) Motown 6270 Nothin' But Soul.
- (S) (2:59) Motown 314530402 Home Cookin.
- (M) (3:04) Motown 314530828 The Ultimate Collection.

1968 HIP CITY (PART 2)
(actual 45 time is (3:12) not (2:57) as stated on the record label; LP length is (2:55))

- (S) (2:55) Motown 9012 and 5208 Greatest Hits.
- (S) (2:55) Motown 6203 Compact Command Performances.
- (S) (2:48) Motown 5297 All The Great Hits.
- (M) (3:11) Motown 6270 Nothin' But Soul.
- (S) (2:57) Motown 314530402 Home Cookin.
- (S) (2:54) Motown 314530507 Motown Year By Year 1968.
- (M) (3:10) Motown 314530828 The Ultimate Collection.

1969 WHAT DOES IT TAKE (TO WIN YOUR LOVE)

- (S) (2:23) Motown 9104 and 5409 Motown Memories Volume 1.
- (S) (2:26) Motown 6160 The Good-Feeling Music Of The Big Chill Generation Volume 2.
- (S) (2:26) Motown 6110 Motown Grammy R&B Performances Of The 60's & 70's.
- (S) (2:23) Original Sound 8863 Oldies But Goodies Vol. 13.
- (S) (2:23) Original Sound 2223 Oldies But Goodies Volumes 2,7,9,12 and 13 Box Set. *(Volumes 2, 7 and 12 of this box set use the "Waring - fds" noise reduction process)*
- (S) (2:23) Original Sound 2500 Oldies But Goodies Volumes 1-15 Box Set. *(most volumes in this box set use the "Waring - fds" noise reduction process)*
- (S) (2:26) Rhino 70655 Billboard's Top R&B Hits Of 1969.
- (S) (2:26) Rhino 72006 Billboard's Top R&B Hits 1965-1969 Box Set.
- (S) (2:26) Motown 5460 Gotta Hold On To This Feeling.
- (S) (2:23) Motown 9012 and 5208 Greatest Hits.
- (S) (2:23) Motown 6203 Compact Command Performances.
- (S) (2:23) Motown 5297 All The Great Hits.
- (S) (2:25) Ripete 392183 Ocean Drive.
- (M) (2:28) Motown 6312 Hitsville USA.
- (S) (2:23) Motown 374638512 Motown Legends - What Does It Take (To Win Your Love).
- (S) (2:28) Motown 6270 Nothin' But Soul.
- (S) (2:26) Time-Life RHD-13 Rhythm & Blues - 1969.
- (S) (2:23) Time-Life 2CLR-06 Classic Rock - 1969.
- (S) (2:23) Time-Life SUD-07 Superhits - 1969.
- (S) (2:27) Motown 314530402 Home Cookin.
- (M) (2:28) Rebound 314520269 Class Reunion 1969.
- (S) (2:26) Polygram Special Markets 314520283 Motown Legends Volume 2.
- (S) (2:27) Motown 314530525 Motown Year By Year - 1969.
- (M) (2:28) Thump 9947 Cruizin' To Motown.
- (S) (2:23) Time-Life AM1-01 AM Gold - 1969.
- (S) (2:26) Time-Life R838-04 Solid Gold Soul - 1969.
- (S) (2:27) Motown 314530828 The Ultimate Collection.
- (S) (2:27) Repeat/Relativity 1611 A Brand New Bag: #1 Soul Hits Of The 60's Volume 3.

(S) (2:26)   Time-Life R857-22   The Heart Of Rock 'n' Roll 1967-1969.

1969 THESE EYES
(S) (3:33)   Motown 9105 and 5410   Motown Memories Volume 2.
(S) (3:34)   Motown 5460   Gotta Hold On To This Feeling.
(S) (3:33)   Motown 6203   Compact Command Performances.
(S) (3:33)   Motown 5297   All The Great Hits.
(M) (3:36)   Rhino 71227   Black On White: Great R&B Covers Of Rock Classics.
(M) (3:36)   Motown 6270   Nothin' But Soul.
(M) (3:35)   Motown 314530828   The Ultimate Collection.

1970 GOTTA HOLD ON TO THIS FEELING
(S) (3:35)   Rhino 70658   Billboard's Top R&B Hits Of 1970.
(S) (3:32)   Motown 5460   Gotta Hold On To This Feeling.
(S) (3:31)   Motown 6203   Compact Command Performances.
(S) (3:30)   Motown 5297   All The Great Hits.
(S) (3:34)   Motown 6270   Nothin' But Soul.
(S) (3:32)   Motown 314530528   Motown Year By Year - 1970.
(S) (3:32)   Motown 314530828   The Ultimate Collection.

1970 DO YOU SEE MY LOVE (FOR YOU GROWING)
(S) (3:25)   Motown 6203   Compact Command Performances.
(S) (3:25)   Motown 5297   All The Great Hits.
(M) (3:29)   Motown 6270   Nothin' But Soul.
(M) (3:28)   Motown 314530828   The Ultimate Collection.

WALKER BROTHERS
1965 MAKE IT EASY ON YOURSELF
(S) (3:11)   Rhino 70324   History Of British Rock Volume 6.
(S) (3:11)   Rhino 70319   History Of British Rock Box Set.
(S) (3:10)   One Way 31440   Anthology.

1966 THE SUN AIN'T GONNA SHINE (ANYMORE)
(S) (3:00)   Mercury 816555   45's On CD Volume 2.
(M) (3:04)   JCI 3102   Love Sixties.
(S) (3:00)   Rhino 70325   History Of British Rock Volume 7.
(S) (3:00)   Rhino 70319   History Of British Rock Box Set.
(S) (3:01)   One Way 31440   Anthology.
(S) (3:00)   Eclipse Music Group 64870   Rock 'n Roll Relix 1966-1967.
(S) (3:00)   Eclipse Music Group 64872   Rock 'n Roll Relix 1960-1969.
(S) (2:59)   Simitar 55532   The Number One's: The '60s.
(S) (3:01)   Simitar 55152   Blue Eyed Soul.
(S) (2:59)   Polygram Special Markets 314520459   Vocal Treasures.

JERRY WALLACE
1958 HOW THE TIME FLIES
(M) (2:25)   Curb 77262   Greatest Hits.
(M) (2:26)   Collectables 5080   Golden Classics.

1959 PRIMROSE LANE
(E) (2:16)   Curb 77262   Greatest Hits. *(much faster than the original recording speed)*
(M) (2:25)   Collectables 5080   Golden Classics. *(truncated fade)*
(M) (2:25)   Time-Life HPD-13   Your Hit Parade - 1959.
(M) (2:16)   Curb 77775   Hard To Find Original Recordings - Classic Hits. *(much faster than the original recording speed)*

1960 LITTLE COCO PALM
(M) (2:19)   Curb 77262   Greatest Hits.
(M) (2:20)   Collectables 5080   Golden Classics.

1961 THERE SHE GOES
(S) (2:29)   Curb 77262   Greatest Hits. *(rerecording)*
(S) (2:38)   Collectables 5080   Golden Classics. *(rerecording)*

1963 SHUTTERS AND BOARDS
(S) (2:43)   Curb 77262   Greatest Hits. *(much faster than the original recording speed)*
(M) (2:52)   Collectables 5080   Golden Classics.

1964 IN THE MISTY MOONLIGHT
(S) (2:48)   Curb 77262   Greatest Hits. *(much faster than the original recording speed)*
(M) (3:00)   Collectables 5080   Golden Classics. *(a fraction of the introduction is chopped off)*
(S) (2:59)   Time-Life HPD-33   Your Hit Parade - The Early 60's.

(S) (2:48)   K-Tel 3366   101 Greatest Country Hits Vol. Seven: Country Nights. *(rerecording; truncated fade)*

1972 IF YOU LEAVE ME TONIGHT I'LL CRY
(S) (2:33)   Curb 77262   Greatest Hits. *(much faster than the original recording speed)*
(M) (2:41)   Collectables 5080   Golden Classics.

JOE WALSH
1973 ROCKY MOUNTAIN WAY
(S) (3:48)   Rhino 70986   Heavy Metal Memories. *(neither the 45 or LP version)*
(S) (5:15)   MCA 31273   Classic Rock Volume 1. *(LP version)*
(S) (3:39)   Warner Special Products 27616   Classic Rock. *(45 version)*
(S) (5:12)   Priority 8662   Hard 'N Heavy/70's Greatest Rock Hits Volume 1. *(LP version)*
(S) (5:13)   Sandstone 33002   Reelin' In The Years Volume 3. *(LP version)*
(S) (5:14)   MCA 1601   Best Of. *(LP version)*
(S) (5:14)   MCA 31121 and 11170   The Smoker You Drink, The Player You Get. *(LP version)*
(S) (5:13)   DCC Compact Classics 064   Rock Of The 70's Volume Three. *(LP version)*
(S) (5:13)   Time-Life R968-05   Guitar Rock 1972-1973. *(LP version)*
(S) (5:10)   Time-Life SOD-23   Sounds Of The Seventies - Guitar Power. *(LP version)*
(S) (5:09)   Time-Life OPCD-4521   Guitar Rock. *(LP version)*
(S) (5:13)   Varese Sarabande 5503 and 5504 and 5505 and 5506 and 5507 and 5508 and 5509 and 5513 and 5571   Arrow: All Rock & Roll Oldies Volume One. *(LP version)*
(S) (5:13)   MCA Special Products 20754   Classic Rock Volume 1. *(LP version)*
(S) (5:14)   MCA 11233   Look What I Did/Anthology. *(LP version)*
(S) (5:15)   MCA Special Products 20903   The 70's Come Alive Again. *(LP version)*
(S) (5:15)   MCA Special Products 20910   Rockin' 70's. *(LP version)*
(S) (5:13)   Madacy Entertainment 1973   Rock On 1973. *(LP version)*
(S) (3:39)   JCI 3140   18 Screamers From The 70's. *(45 version)*
(S) (5:14)   MCA Special Products 20956   Rockin' Guitars. *(LP version)*
(S) (5:14)   MCA Special Products 20255   Rocky Mountain Way. *(LP version)*
(S) (5:14)   Hip-O 40039   Power Chords Volume 2. *(LP version)*
(S) (5:13)   MCA Special Products 21011   70's Biggest Hits. *(LP version)*
(S) (5:14)   Hip-O 40070   Rock For The Ages. *(LP version)*
(S) (5:14)   MCA 11679   Greatest Hits. *(LP version)*
(S) (5:14)   Hip-O 40095   '70s Hit(s) Back. *(LP version)*
(S) (3:39)   Simitar 55772   Stud Rock - Rock Me. *(45 version)*

1978 LIFE'S BEEN GOOD
(S) (8:55)   Elektra 141   But Seriously Folks. *(LP version)*
(S) (4:38)   Razor & Tie 22502   Those Rocking 70's. *(45 version)*
(S) (4:37)   Time-Life R968-02   Guitar Rock 1978-1979. *(45 version)*
(S) (4:38)   Time-Life SOD-10   Sounds Of The Seventies - 1978. *(45 version)*
(S) (4:38)   Time-Life R105-24   Guitar Rock Monsters. *(45 version)*
(S) (8:02)   K-Tel 3221   Axe Gods. *(edit of LP version)*
(S) (8:02)   MCA 11233   Look What I Did/Anthology. *(edit of LP version)*
(S) (8:01)   Rhino 72132   Frat Rock: More Of The 70's. *(edit of LP version)*
(S) (8:02)   MCA 11679   Greatest Hits. *(edit of LP version)*

1980 ALL NIGHT LONG
(S) (3:34)   Time-Life R968-04   Guitar Rock 1980-1981. *(45 version)*

JOE WALSH *(Continued)*

    (S)   (3:31)   MCA 11233 Look What I Did/Anthology. *(45 version)*

    (S)   (3:50)   Full Moon/Elektra 60690 O.S.T. Urban Cowboy. *(LP version)*

    (S)   (3:34)   JCI 3143 18 Screamers From The 80's. *(45 version)*

    (S)   (3:32)   MCA 11679 Greatest Hits. *(45 version)*

1981 A LIFE OF ILLUSION

    (S)   (3:30)   Elektra 523 There Goes The Neighborhood.

    (S)   (3:29)   MCA 11233 Look What I Did/Anthology.

    (S)   (3:31)   Rhino 72594 Billboard Top Album Rock Hits, 1981.

    (S)   (3:29)   MCA 11679 Greatest Hits.

JAMIE WALTERS

1995 HOLD ON

    (S)   (4:24)   Atlantic 82600 Jamie Walters.

WALTER WANDERLY

1966 SUMMER SAMBA (SO NICE)

    (S)   (3:03)   Verve 833289 Best Of Bossa Nova.

    (S)   (3:03)   Time-Life HPD-39 Your Hit Parade - 60's Instrumentals: Take Two.

    (S)   (3:03)   K-Tel 3472 Those Wonderful Instrumentals Volume 2.

    (S)   (3:03)   Time-Life R986-12 Instrumental Favorites - Latin Rhythms.

    (S)   (3:03)   Collectors' Choice 5190 More Instrumental Gems Of The 60's.

WANG CHUNG

1984 DON'T LET GO

    (S)   (4:19)   Geffen 4004 Points On The Curve. *(LP version)*

    (S)   (4:20)   Geffen 25122 Everybody Wang Chung Tonight....Greatest Hits. *(LP version)*

1984 DANCE HALL DAYS

    (S)   (3:57)   Priority 53752 Rock Of The 80's Volume 12.

    (S)   (3:56)   EMI 28339 Living In Oblivion: The 80's Greatest Hits - Volume Four.

    (S)   (3:58)   Rhino 71976 New Wave Hits Of The 80's Vol. 13.

    (S)   (3:58)   Geffen 4004 Points On The Curve.

    (S)   (3:58)   Geffen 24805 Geffen Vintage 80's Volume 1.

    (S)   (3:57)   Time-Life R988-17 Sounds Of The Eighties: The Mid '80s Take Two.

    (S)   (3:58)   Geffen 25122 Everybody Wang Chung Tonight....Greatest Hits.

    (S)   (3:55)   Hollywood 62098 O.S.T. Romy And Michele's High School Reunion.

    (S)   (3:58)   Rhino 72894 Hard Rock Cafe: New Wave.

    (S)   (3:54)   Cold Front 6254 Club Mix '98. *(all selections on this cd are segued together)*

    (S)   (3:57)   Simitar 55552 The Number One's: Eighties Rock.

1985 TO LIVE AND DIE IN L.A.

    (S)   (4:52)   Geffen 24081 Music From The Original Motion Picture "To Live And Die In L.A.". *(LP version)*

    (S)   (4:51)   Geffen 25122 Everybody Wang Chung Tonight....Greatest Hits. *(LP version)*

1986 EVERYBODY HAVE FUN TONIGHT
(actual 45 time is (4:14) not (3:59) as stated on the record label)

    (S)   (4:46)   Priority 53684 Rock Of The 80's Volume 4. *(LP version)*

    (S)   (4:45)   K-Tel 3342 The 80's Pop Explosion. *(LP version)*

    (S)   (4:46)   Geffen 24115 Mosaic. *(LP version)*

    (S)   (4:14)   Time-Life R988-04 Sounds Of The Eighties: 1986. *(45 version)*

    (S)   (4:46)   Geffen 24805 Geffen Vintage 80's Volume 1. *(LP version)*

    (S)   (4:46)   MCA Special Products 20897 Greatest Rock Hits Of The 80's. *(LP version)*

    (S)   (4:46)   Hip-O 40004 The '80s Hit(s) Back! *(LP version)*

    (S)   (4:46)   Hollywood 62077 Official Party Album - ABC's Monday Night Football. *(LP version)*

    (S)   (4:12)   JCI 3150 1985 - Only Dance - 1989. *(45 version)*

    (S)   (4:46)   Geffen 25122 Everybody Wang Chung Tonight....Greatest Hits. *(LP version)*

    (S)   (4:45)   Rhino 72820 VH1 - More Of The Big 80's. *(LP version)*

    (S)   (4:44)   Hollywood 62123 More Music From The Motion Picture "Romy And Michele's High School Reunion". *(LP version)*

    (S)   (4:35)   Cold Front 6255 Greatest Sports Rock And Jams Volume 2. *(all selections on this cd are segued together; LP version)*

    (S)   (4:46)   Intersound 9521 Retro Lunch Box - Squeeze The Cheese. *(LP version)*

    (S)   (4:44)   Simitar 55522 The Number One's: Party Time. *(LP version)*

1987 LET'S GO

    (S)   (4:28)   Priority 53781 Best Of 80's Rock Volume 2. *(LP version)*

    (S)   (4:29)   Geffen 24115 Mosaic. *(LP version)*

    (S)   (4:29)   Time-Life R988-09 Sounds Of The Eighties: 1987. *(LP version)*

    (S)   (4:29)   Madacy Entertainment 1987 Rock On 1987. *(LP version)*

    (S)   (4:27)   Geffen 25122 Everybody Wang Chung Tonight....Greatest Hits. *(LP version)*

    (S)   (4:28)   Geffen 25151 Geffen Vintage 80s Vol. II. *(LP version)*

    (S)   (4:30)   MCA Special Products 21028 The Best Of Hard Rock. *(LP version)*

1987 HYPNOTIZE ME

    (S)   (4:38)   Geffen 24115 Mosaic. *(LP version)*

    (S)   (4:38)   Geffen 25122 Everybody Wang Chung Tonight....Greatest Hits. *(LP version)*

WAR (also ERIC BURDON & WAR)
released as by ERIC BURDON & WAR:
1970 SPILL THE WINE
(dj copies of this 45 ran (4:03) and (4:51); commercial copies were all (4:51))

    (M)   (4:03)   Priority 9467 Best Of War. *(dj 45 edit)*

    (M)   (4:03)   Rhino 70072 Best Of. *(dj 45 edit)*

    (S)   (4:52)   Rhino 71050 Eric Burdon Declares "War".

    (S)   (4:51)   Time-Life SOD-11 Sounds Of The Seventies - 1970: Take Two.

    (S)   (4:03)   Avenue 71774 Anthology 1970-1994. *(dj 45 edit)*

    (S)   (4:03)   Avenue 71954 Best Of Eric Burdon & War. *(dj 45 edit)*

    (S)   (4:06)   Avenue 72526 Best Of War And More...Vol. 2. *(remix)*

    (S)   (4:51)   Thump 7200 Latin Oldies Volume Two.

    (S)   (4:01)   Capitol 56312 O.S.T. Boogie Nights. *(dj 45 edit)*

    (S)   (4:51)   Avenue 10604 Eric Burdon Declares "War". *(gold disc)*

    (S)   (4:00)   Right Stuff 52274 Flick Hits Take 2. *(dj 45 edit)*

released as by WAR:
1971 ALL DAY MUSIC
(dj copies of this song ran (2:34) and (3:50); commercial copies were all (3:59))

    (S)   (2:34)   Priority 9467 Best Of. *(dj 45 edit)*

    (S)   (2:34)   Rhino 70072 Best Of. *(dj 45 edit)*

    (S)   (4:03)   Rhino 71042 All Day Music. *(tracks into the next selection)*

    (S)   (3:57)   Avenue 71774 Anthology 1970-1994.

    (S)   (4:03)   Rhino 72868 Brown Eyed Soul Vol. 1.

    (S)   (3:57)   Avenue 72866 Coleccion Latina.

    (S)   (5:10)   Avenue 10605 All Day Music. *(gold disc; contains a (1:05) instrumental introduction not found on the vinyl LP "All Day Music"; tracks into the next selection)*

1972 SLIPPIN' INTO DARKNESS
(actual time of the commercial 45 was (4:15) not (3:59) as stated on the record label; dj copies ran (3:45))

    (S)   (3:45)   Priority 9467 Best Of. *(dj 45 edit)*

    (S)   (3:45)   Rhino 70072 Best Of. *(dj 45 edit)*

    (S)   (6:59)   Rhino 71042 All Day Music. *(tracks into the next selection; LP version)*

    (S)   (3:44)   Virgin 92153 and 86289 O.S.T. American Me. *(dj 45 edit)*

    (S)   (3:45)   K-Tel 6011 70's Soul: Super Funky Hits. *(dj 45 edit)*

(S)	(6:57)	Avenue 71774 Anthology 1970-1994. *(LP version)*	
(S)	(7:02)	Avenue 10605 All Day Music. *(gold disc; LP version; tracks into the next selection)*	

1973 THE WORLD IS A GHETTO

(S)	(4:05)	Rhino 70790 Soul Hits Of The 70's Volume 10. *(45 version)*
(S)	(10:13)	Rhino 71043 The World Is A Ghetto. *(LP version)*
(S)	(4:02)	Time-Life SOD-14 Sounds Of The Seventies - 1973: Take Two. *(45 version)*
(S)	(4:02)	Avenue 71774 Anthology 1970-1994. *(45 version)*
(S)	(4:05)	Right Stuff 29669 Movin' On Up Vol. 2. *(45 version)*
(S)	(4:04)	MCA 11329 Soul Train 25th Anniversary Box Set. *(45 version)*
(S)	(4:02)	Avenue 72526 Best Of War And More...Vol. 2. *(45 version)*
(S)	(4:03)	Time-Life R838-08 Solid Gold Soul - 1973. *(45 version)*
(S)	(10:08)	Avenue 10603 The World Is A Ghetto. *(gold disc; LP version)*

1973 THE CISCO KID
(dj copies of this 45 ran (3:50); commercial copies were all (4:35))

(S)	(3:51)	Priority 9467 Best Of. *(dj 45 edit)*
(S)	(3:50)	Rhino 70072 Best Of. *(dj 45 edit)*
(S)	(4:32)	Rhino 71043 The World Is A Ghetto.
(S)	(3:47)	Razor & Tie 22045 Those Funky 70's. *(dj 45 edit)*
(S)	(3:50)	Time-Life SOD-06 Sounds Of The Seventies - 1973. *(dj 45 edit)*
(S)	(4:26)	Avenue 71774 Anthology 1970-1994.
(S)	(3:49)	Rebound 314520430 Funk Classics Of The 70's Vol. 2. *(dj 45 edit)*
(S)	(4:25)	Avenue 72866 Colleccion Latina.
(S)	(4:29)	Thump 7100 Latin Oldies. *(with countoff)*
(S)	(4:29)	Avenue 10603 The World Is A Ghetto. *(gold disc)*
(S)	(3:42)	Cold Front 4025 Old School Mega Mix Volume 3. *(dj 45 edit)*

1973 GYPSY MAN
(dj copies of this 45 ran (3:50) and (5:22); commercial copies were all (5:22))

(S)	(11:34)	Rhino 71044 Deliver The Word. *(LP version)*
(S)	(5:21)	Avenue 71774 Anthology 1970-1994. *(45 version)*
(S)	(5:21)	Avenue 72526 Best Of War And More...Vol. 2. *(45 version)*
(S)	(5:21)	Avenue 72866 Colleccion Latina. *(45 version)*
(S)	(11:34)	Avenue 10607 Deliver The Word. *(LP version; gold disc)*

1974 ME AND BABY BROTHER

(S)	(3:30)	Rhino 71044 Deliver The Word.
(S)	(3:28)	Priority 9467 Best Of.
(S)	(3:28)	Rhino 70072 Best Of.
(S)	(3:30)	Rhino 71431 In Yo Face! History Of Funk Volume 1.
(S)	(3:25)	Avenue 71774 Anthology 1970-1994.
(S)	(3:25)	Avenue 72866 Colleccion Latina.
(S)	(3:30)	Avenue 10607 Deliver The Word. *(gold disc)*

1974 BALLERO

(S)	(8:29)	Rhino 71052 Live. *(LP version)*
(S)	(3:20)	Avenue 71774 Anthology 1970-1994. *(45 version)*
(S)	(3:21)	Avenue 72526 Best Of War And More...Vol. 2. *(45 version)*
(S)	(3:20)	Avenue 72866 Colleccion Latina. *(45 version)*

1975 WHY CAN'T WE BE FRIENDS?

(S)	(3:48)	Rhino 71051 Why Can't We Be Friends.
(S)	(3:51)	Priority 9467 Best Of.
(S)	(3:50)	Rhino 70072 Best Of.
(S)	(3:50)	Time-Life SOD-08 Sounds Of The Seventies - 1975.
(S)	(3:51)	Time-Life R921-38 Get Together.
(S)	(3:46)	Avenue 71774 Anthology 1970-1994.
(S)	(3:48)	Medicine Label 24588 Even More Dazed And Confused.

(S)	(3:48)	Rhino 72127 Soul Hits Of The 70's Vol. 17.
(S)	(3:47)	Time-Life AM1-22 AM Gold - 1975.
(S)	(3:50)	Time-Life R838-10 Solid Gold Soul - 1975.
(S)	(3:48)	Rhino 72869 Brown Eyed Soul Vol. 2.
(S)	(3:47)	Avenue 10602 Why Can't We Be Friends. *(gold disc)*

1975 LOW RIDER

(S)	(3:00)	Original Sound 8878 Art Laboe's Dedicated To You. *(:10 edited from the end of the song)*
(S)	(3:02)	Original Sound 8865 Oldies But Goodies Vol. 15. *(this compact disc uses the "Waring - fds" noise reduction process; :08 edited from the end of the song)*
(S)	(3:02)	Original Sound 2222 Oldies But Goodies Volumes 3,5,11,14 and 15 Box Set. *(this box set uses the "Waring - fds" noise reduction process; :08 edited from the end of the song)*
(S)	(3:02)	Original Sound 2500 Oldies But Goodies Volumes 1-15 Box Set. *(this box set uses the "Waring - fds" noise reduction process; :08 edited from the end of the song)*
(S)	(3:00)	Original Sound 4001 Art Laboe's 60 Killer Oldies. *(:10 edited from the end of the song)*
(S)	(3:10)	Rhino 71051 Why Can't We Be Friends.
(S)	(3:13)	Priority 9467 Best Of.
(S)	(3:12)	Rhino 70072 Best Of.
(S)	(3:08)	Original Sound CDGO-9 Golden Oldies Volume. 9.
(S)	(3:10)	Medicine Label 24533 O.S.T. Dazed And Confused.
(S)	(3:01)	Time-Life SOD-16 Sounds Of The Seventies - 1975: Take Two. *(:09 edited from the end of the song)*
(S)	(3:09)	Avenue 71774 Anthology 1970-1994.
(S)	(3:10)	Priority 57194 Old School Friday - More Music From The Original Motion Picture.
(S)	(3:01)	Tommy Boy 1136 ESPN Presents Jock Rock Vol. 2. *(all songs on this cd are segued together with crowd sound effects added)*
(S)	(3:09)	EMI 55204 O.S.T. Beverly Hills Ninja.
(S)	(3:17)	Avenue 72866 Colleccion Latina. *(Spanish version)*
(S)	(8:59)	Avenue 72866 Colleccion Latina. *(remix)*
(S)	(3:09)	Avenue 10602 Why Can't We Be Friends. *(gold disc)*
(S)	(3:10)	Rhino 72920 Raza Rock Of The '70s & '80s.

1976 SUMMER

(S)	(3:59)	Priority 9467 Best Of. *(45 version)*
(S)	(3:58)	Rhino 70072 Best Of. *(45 version)*
(S)	(3:59)	Time-Life SOD-36 Sounds Of The Seventies - More AM Nuggets. *(45 version)*
(S)	(6:34)	Avenue 71774 Anthology 1970-1994. *(LP version)*
(S)	(3:58)	Time-Life R838-11 Solid Gold Soul - 1976. *(45 version)*

1978 GALAXY

(S)	(8:10)	Avenue 71192 Galaxy. *(LP version)*
(S)	(5:16)	Avenue 71774 Anthology 1970-1994. *(neither the 45 or LP version)*

ANITA WARD
1979 RING MY BELL

(S)	(3:16)	Priority 7971 Mega-Hits Dance Classics Volume 1. *(:14 shorter than the 45 version)*
(S)	(3:32)	Rhino 70985 The Disco Years Volume 2. *(45 version)*
(S)	(3:31)	Rhino 71003 Get Down Tonight: The Best Of T.K. Records. *(45 version)*
(S)	(3:34)	Rhino 70674 Billboard Top Hits - 1979. *(correct vocal take but the instrumentation is completely different from the 45 and LP versions)*
(S)	(3:31)	Rhino 70493 Billboard Top Dance Hits - 1979. *(45 version)*
(S)	(3:31)	Rhino 71096 Disco Hits Volume 3. *(45 version)*
(S)	(3:31)	Razor & Tie 22496 Disco Fever. *(45 version)*
(S)	(3:29)	Time-Life SOD-09 Sounds Of The Seventies - 1979. *(45 version)*
(S)	(6:13)	Hot Productions 11 Best Of The Sound Of Sunshine. *(neither the 45, 12" single or LP version)*

ANITA WARD *(Continued)*
- (M) (6:12) Rebound 314520217 Disco Nights Vol. 1 - Divas Of Dance. *(neither the 45, LP or 12" single version)*
- (S) (3:32) K-Tel 3126 Disco Mania. *(45 version)*
- (S) (3:29) Madacy Entertainment 1979 Rock On 1979. *(45 version)*
- (S) (3:32) Priority 53141 Mega Hits Disco Locomotion Volume 2. *(45 version)*
- (S) (3:30) JCI 3163 18 Disco Superhits. *(45 version)*
- (S) (3:30) Coldfront 3375 Old School Megamix. *(all selections on this cd are sequed together)*
- (S) (3:31) Flashback 72691 Disco Hits: Le Freak. *(45 version)*
- (S) (3:31) Flashback 72086 Disco Hits Box Set. *(45 version)*
- (S) (3:32) Rhino 72812 VH1 8-Track Flashback: The One Hit Wonders. *(45 version)*
- (S) (3:31) Rhino 72837 Disco Queens: The 70's. *(45 version)*
- (S) (3:31) Polydor 314555120 Pure Disco 2. *(45 version)*
- (S) (3:14) Simitar 55522 The Number One's: Party Time. *(:16 shorter than the 45 version)*
- (S) (3:31) Beast 53202 Disco Divas - A Salute To The Ladies. *(45 version)*
- (S) (3:29) Time-Life R840-10 Sounds Of The Seventies: '70s Dance Party 1979. *(45 version)*

BILLY WARD and HIS DOMINOES
1956 ST. THERESE OF THE ROSES
- (M) (3:07) Rhino 70775 Jackie Wilson - Mr. Excitement.
1957 STAR DUST
- (M) (3:10) Atlantic 82152 O.S.T. Goodfellas.
- (M) (3:10) Rhino 71509 Sixty Minute Men: Best Of.
- (M) (3:10) Time-Life R857-05 The Heart Of Rock 'n' Roll 1957.
1957 DEEP PURPLE
- (M) (2:12) Time-Life R857-13 The Heart Of Rock 'n' Roll 1956-1957.

DALE WARD
1964 LETTER FROM SHERRY
- (M) (2:19) MCA 5940 Vintage Music Volumes 19 & 20.
- (M) (2:19) MCA 31216 Vintage Music Volume 19.
- (M) (2:19) MCA Special Products 22133 Vintage Collectibles Volume 4.
- (M) (2:19) Collectors' Choice 002 Teen Idols....For A Moment.
- (M) (2:19) Varese Sarabande 5686 History Of Dot Records Volume One.
- (M) (2:19) Time-Life R857-18 The Heart Of Rock 'n' Roll 1962-1963 Take Two.

ROBIN WARD
1963 WONDERFUL SUMMER
- (S) (2:25) MCA 5936 Vintage Music Volumes 11 & 12.
- (S) (2:25) MCA 31208 Vintage Music Volume 11.
- (S) (2:25) Rhino 70989 Best Of The Girl Groups Volume 2.
- (S) (2:25) Rhino 71229 Summer Hits.
- (S) (2:25) Time-Life HPD-37 Your Hit Parade - The 60's.
- (S) (2:25) MCA Special Products 22019 Summer Hits Of The 50's And 60's.
- (S) (2:25) K-Tel 3437 Summer Songs.
- (S) (2:25) MCA Special Products 21742 Vintage Collectibles Volume 12.
- (S) (2:26) Varese Sarabande 5686 History Of Dot Records Volume One.
- (S) (2:26) Time-Life R857-12 The Heart Of Rock 'n' Roll 1962-1963.
- (S) (2:25) Flashback 72710 Golden Summer.

JENNIFER WARNES
1977 RIGHT TIME OF THE NIGHT
- (S) (2:53) Arista 8348 Best Of.
- (S) (2:51) Time-Life SOD-34 Sounds Of The Seventies - The Late 70's.
- (S) (2:51) Time-Life R105-26 Our Songs: Singers & Songwriters Encore.
- (S) (2:52) JCI 3131 1975 - Only Rock 'N Roll - 1979.
- (S) (2:49) Madacy Entertainment 1977 Rock On 1977.
- (S) (2:50) Time-Life R840-01 Sounds Of The Seventies - Pop Nuggets: Late '70s.
1979 I KNOW A HEARTACHE WHEN I SEE ONE
- (S) (3:27) Arista 8348 Best Of.
released as by JOE COCKER and JENNIFER WARNES:
1982 UP WHERE WE BELONG
- (S) (3:51) Island 90017 and 422842715 O.S.T. An Officer And A Gentleman.
- (S) (3:55) Island 90684 and 842901 The Island Story.
- (S) (3:57) Rhino 70677 Billboard Top Hits - 1982.
- (S) (3:53) Sandstone 33048 and 5016 Cosmopolitan Volume 2.
- (S) (3:56) Rhino 71868 Academy Award Winning Songs.
- (S) (3:53) DCC Compact Classics 087 Night Moves Volume 5.
- (S) (3:52) Capitol 81243 Joe Cocker - Best Of.
- (S) (3:56) Time-Life R988-05 Sounds Of The Eighties: 1982.
- (S) (3:56) Time-Life R138-18 Body Talk.
- (S) (3:54) A&M 314540236 Joe Cocker - The Long Voyage Home - Silver Anniversary Collection.
- (S) (3:56) Rhino 72280 Academy Award Winning Songs Volume 5.
- (S) (3:52) Rebound 314520372 The Roots Of Rock: Soft Rock.
- (S) (3:51) Rebound 314520438 No. 1 Hits Of The 80's.
- (S) (3:56) Time-Life R988-31 Sounds Of The Eighties: Cinemax Movie Hits Of The '80s.
- (S) (3:56) Time-Life R834-04 Body Talk - Together Forever.
- (S) (3:50) Priority 50974 Premiere The Movie Magazine Presents The Greatest Soundtrack Love Songs.
- (S) (3:55) Hip-O 40079 Essential '80s: 1980-1984.
- (S) (3:54) Polygram TV 314555610 The One And Only Love Album.
- (S) (3:51) Rebound 314520519 Love At The Movies.
released as by BILL MEDLEY and JENNIFER WARNES:
1987 (I'VE HAD) THE TIME OF MY LIFE
- (S) (4:49) RCA 6408 O.S.T. Dirty Dancing.
- (S) (4:44) Rhino 71868 Academy Award Winning Songs.
- (S) (4:46) Curb 77307 and 42257 Best Of Bill Medley.
- (S) (4:44) Rhino 72280 Academy Award Winning Songs Volume 5.
- (S) (4:45) EMI-Capitol Music Group 54555 Movie Luv.

WARRANT
1989 DOWN BOYS
- (S) (4:01) K-Tel 6090 Hit Parader Salutes 20 Years Of Metal.
- (S) (4:02) Priority 53733 80's Greatest Rock Hits Vol. 9.
- (S) (4:02) Columbia 44383 Dirty Rotten Filthy Stinking Rich.
- (S) (4:03) Legacy 64775 Best Of.
- (S) (4:02) Time-Life R968-24 Guitar Rock - The '80s Take Two.
- (S) (3:50) CMC International 86234 Rockin' The 80's. *(live)*
1989 HEAVEN
- (S) (3:55) Priority 53735 Monsters Of Rock Vol. 1 - Heaven And Hell. *(LP version)*
- (S) (4:04) Rhino 71644 Billboard Top Hits - 1989. *(45 version)*
- (S) (3:55) Columbia 44383 Dirty Rotten Filthy Stinking Rich. *(LP version)*
- (S) (3:55) Legacy 64775 Best Of. *(LP version)*
- (S) (3:55) Rhino 72579 Feel Like Makin' Love - Romantic Power Ballads. *(LP version)*
- (S) (3:55) K-Tel 3883 The 80's: Glam Rock. *(LP version)*
- (S) (2:37) CMC International 86233 Superstar Hits. *(live)*
1990 SOMETIMES SHE CRIES
- (S) (4:41) Columbia 44383 Dirty Rotten Filthy Stinking Rich.
- (S) (4:42) Legacy 64775 Best Of.
1990 CHERRY PIE
- (S) (3:20) Columbia 45487 Cherry Pie.
- (S) (3:20) Legacy 64775 Best Of.

(S) (7:16) CMC International 86234 Rockin' The 80's. *(live)*
(S) (3:19) Razor & Tie 89004 Monsters Of Rock.
1991 I SAW RED
(S) (3:46) JCI 3135 14 Original Metal Ballads.
(S) (3:46) Columbia 45487 Cherry Pie.
(S) (3:44) Legacy 64775 Best Of. *(acoustic version)*
(S) (3:46) Time-Life R968-25 Guitar Rock - The '90s.

WARREN G
released as by WARREN G & NATE DOGG:
1994 REGULATE
(S) (4:08) Death Row/Interscope 92359 and 92403 and 50606 O.S.T. Above The Rim. *(very poor stereo separation*
(S) (4:08) Violator/RAL 314523335 and 314523364 Regulate...G Funk Era. *(very poor stereo separation)*
(S) (4:08) Boxtunes 162444068 Big Phat Ones Of Hip-Hop Volume 1. *(very poor stereo separation)*
(S) (4:08) Def Jam 314523848 Def Jam Music Group 10th Year Anniversary. *(very poor stereo separation)*
(S) (4:06) Rebound 314520449 Hip Hop With R&B Flava. *(very poor stereo separation)*
(S) (4:07) Def Jam 314536377 Def Jam's Greatest Hits. *(very poor stereo separation)*
released as by WARREN G:
1994 THIS D.J.
(M) (3:22) Violator/RAL 314523335 and 314523364 Regulate...G Funk Era.
released as by WARREN G featuring ADINA HOWARD:
1996 WHAT'S LOVE GOT TO DO WITH IT
(S) (4:16) Interscope 90088 O.S.T. Supercop.
released as by WARREN G:
1997 I SHOT THE SHERIFF
(S) (4:06) Def Jam 314537234 and 314537254 Take A Look Over Your Shoulder (Reality).
(S) (3:25) Def Jam 314537234 and 314537254 Take A Look Over Your Shoulder (Reality). *(remix)*
released as by WARREN G featuring RONALD ISLEY:
1997 SMOKIN' ME OUT
(S) (3:40) Def Jam 314537234 and 314537254 Take A Look Over Your Shoulder (Reality).

DIONNE WARWICK
1963 DON'T MAKE ME OVER
(S) (2:45) Rhino 75891 Wonder Women.
(S) (2:45) Rhino 75898 Anthology 1962 - 1969.
(S) (3:21) Rhino 71100 Collection - Her Greatest Hits. *(previously unreleased version)*
(S) (2:44) Pair 1243 At Her Very Best.
(S) (2:41) Original Sound 8864 Oldies But Goodies Vol. 14. *(this compact disc uses the "Waring - fds" noise reduction process)*
(S) (2:41) Original Sound 2222 Oldies But Goodies Volumes 3,5,11,14 and 15 Box Set. *(this box set uses the "Waring - fds" noise reduction process)*
(S) (2:41) Original Sound 2500 Oldies But Goodies Volumes 1-15 Box Set. *(this box set uses the "Waring - fds" noise reduction process)*
(S) (2:53) Capricorn 42003 The Scepter Records Story. *(includes :08 of studio talk)*
(S) (2:44) Pair 4929 Her Greatest Hits.
(S) (3:19) Time-Life 2RNR-42 Rock 'N' Roll Era - The 60's Sock Hop. *(previously unreleased version)*
(S) (3:19) Time-Life RHD-02 Rhythm & Blues - 1963. *(previously unreleased version)*
(S) (3:21) Time-Life R857-12 The Heart Of Rock 'n' Roll 1962-1963. *(previously unreleased version)*
(S) (3:19) Time-Life R838-14 Solid Gold Soul - 1963. *(previously unreleased version)*
(M) (2:47) Rhino 72815 Beg, Scream & Shout! The Big Ol' Box Of '60s Soul.
1964 ANYONE WHO HAD A HEART
(actual 45 time is (3:08) not (2:58) as stated on the record label)
(S) (2:59) Rhino 75898 Anthology 1962 - 1969. *(mastered from vinyl; LP length*

(S) (3:07) Rhino 71100 Collection - Her Greatest Hits. *(45 length)*
(S) (2:58) Pair 1243 At Her Very Best. *(LP length)*
(S) (2:58) Capricorn 42003 The Scepter Records Story. *(LP length)*
(S) (2:58) Pair 4929 Her Greatest Hits. *(LP length)*
(S) (3:02) Time-Life SUD-08 Superhits - 1963. *(LP length)*
(S) (3:02) Time-Life AM1-17 AM Gold - 1963. *(LP length)*
(S) (3:07) Curb 77874 Her Classic Songs Volume 1. *(45 length)*
(S) (2:58) Time-Life R857-17 The Heart Of Rock 'n' Roll: The Early '60s. *(LP length)*
1964 WALK ON BY
(S) (2:51) JCI 3102 Love Sixties.
(S) (2:51) Rhino 75898 Anthology 1962 - 1969.
(S) (2:54) Rhino 71100 Collection - Her Greatest Hits.
(S) (2:51) Pair 1243 At Her Very Best.
(S) (3:00) Capricorn 42003 The Scepter Records Story. *(includes :05 countoff)*
(S) (2:52) Pair 4929 Her Greatest Hits.
(S) (2:50) Time-Life RHD-12 Rhythm & Blues - 1964.
(S) (2:50) Time-Life 2CLR-16 Classic Rock - 1964: Shakin' All Over.
(S) (2:50) Time-Life SUD-09 Superhits - 1964.
(S) (2:53) Time-Life HPD-37 Your Hit Parade - The 60's.
(S) (2:51) Time-Life R962-08 History Of Rock 'N' Roll: Sound Of The City 1959-1965.
(S) (2:51) Right Stuff 28371 Slow Jams: The 60's Volume Two.
(S) (2:45) Original Sound 8865 Oldies But Goodies Vol. 15. *(this compact disc uses the "Waring - fds" noise reduction process)*
(S) (2:45) Original Sound 2222 Oldies But Goodies Volumes 3,5,14 and 15 Box Set. *(this box set uses the "Waring - fds" noise reduction process)*
(S) (2:45) Original Sound 2500 Oldies But Goodies Volumes 1-15 Box Set. *(this box set uses the "Waring - fds" noise reduction process)*
(S) (2:45) Original Sound 8883 21 Legendary Superstars.
(S) (2:53) JCI 3125 1960 - Only Rock 'N Roll - 1964.
(S) (2:53) Nick At Nite/550 Music 67690 I Am Woman.
(S) (2:53) Time-Life R857-09 The Heart Of Rock 'n' Roll 1964.
(S) (2:49) Time-Life AM1-11 AM Gold - 1964.
(S) (2:50) Time-Life R838-13 Solid Gold Soul - 1964.
(S) (2:50) Curb 77874 Her Classic Songs Volume 1.
(S) (2:54) Time-Life R857-21 The Heart Of Rock 'n' Roll Slow Dancing Classics.
(S) (2:52) Time-Life R814-02 Love Songs.
1964 YOU'LL NEVER GET TO HEAVEN (IF YOU BREAK MY HEART)
(S) (3:06) Rhino 75898 Anthology 1962 - 1969.
(S) (3:07) Rhino 71100 Collection - Her Greatest Hits.
(S) (3:05) Pair 1243 At Her Very Best.
(S) (3:05) Pair 4929 Her Greatest Hits.
1964 REACH OUT FOR ME
(S) (2:47) Rhino 75898 Anthology 1962 - 1969.
(S) (2:50) Rhino 71100 Collection - Her Greatest Hits.
(S) (2:46) Pair 1243 At Her Very Best.
(S) (2:48) Curb 77894 I Say A Little Prayer.
1966 ARE YOU THERE (WITH ANOTHER GIRL)
(S) (2:49) Rhino 75898 Anthology 1962 - 1969.
(S) (2:48) Rhino 71100 Collection - Her Greatest Hits.
(S) (2:49) Pair 1243 At Her Very Best.
1966 MESSAGE TO MICHAEL
(M) (3:04) Rhino 75898 Anthology 1962 - 1969.
(S) (3:05) Rhino 71100 Collection - Her Greatest Hits.
(M) (3:04) Pair 1243 At Her Very Best.
(M) (3:04) Pair 4929 Her Greatest Hits.
(S) (3:04) Time-Life SUD-01 Superhits - 1966.
(S) (3:04) Time-Life AM1-09 AM Gold - 1966.
(S) (3:04) Curb 77874 Her Classic Songs Volume 1.
1966 TRAINS AND BOATS AND PLANES
(S) (2:46) Rhino 75898 Anthology 1962 - 1969. *(truncated fade)*
(S) (2:46) Rhino 71100 Collection - Her Greatest Hits.
(S) (2:43) Pair 1243 At Her Very Best.

DIONNE WARWICK *(Continued)*

    (S)   (2:44)   Curb 77874 Her Classic Songs Volume 1.

1966 I JUST DON'T KNOW WHAT TO DO WITH MYSELF

    (S)   (2:44)   Rhino 71100 Collection - Her Greatest Hits.

    (S)   (2:43)   Pair 1243 At Her Very Best.

1967 ALFIE

    (S)   (2:43)   Rhino 75898 Anthology 1962 - 1969.

    (S)   (2:43)   Rhino 71100 Collection - Her Greatest Hits.

    (S)   (2:43)   Pair 1243 At Her Very Best.

    (S)   (2:43)   Pair 4929 Her Greatest Hits.

    (S)   (2:43)   Time-Life SUD-14 Superhits - The Late 60's.

    (S)   (2:43)   CBS Special Products 46850 Society Of Singers Presents A Gift Of Music Vol. 2.

    (S)   (2:43)   JCI 7022 Those Wonderful Years - It Must Be Him.

    (S)   (2:43)   Time-Life AM1-14 AM Gold - The Late '60s.

    (S)   (2:43)   Curb 77874 Her Classic Songs Volume 1.

    (S)   (2:43)   Time-Life R834-19 Body Talk - Always And Forever.

1967 THE WINDOWS OF THE WORLD

    (S)   (3:16)   Rhino 75898 Anthology 1962 - 1969.

    (S)   (3:16)   Rhino 71100 Collection - Her Greatest Hits.

    (S)   (3:16)   Pair 1243 At Her Very Best.

1967 I SAY A LITTLE PRAYER

    (S)   (3:06)   Rhino 75898 Anthology 1962 - 1969.

    (S)   (3:04)   Rhino 71100 Collection - Her Greatest Hits.

    (S)   (3:06)   Pair 1243 At Her Very Best.

    (S)   (3:17)   Capricorn 42003 The Scepter Records Story. *(includes :15 of studio talk)*

    (S)   (3:05)   Pair 4929 Her Greatest Hits.

    (S)   (3:00)   Time-Life SUD-05 Superhits - 1967.

    (S)   (3:00)   JCI 3185 1965 - Only Love - 1969.

    (S)   (3:00)   Time-Life AM1-08 AM Gold - 1967.

    (S)   (3:03)   Curb 77894 I Say A Little Prayer.

1968 (THEME FROM) VALLEY OF THE DOLLS

    (S)   (3:36)   Rhino 75898 Anthology 1962 - 1969.

    (S)   (3:36)   Rhino 71100 Collection - Her Greatest Hits.

    (S)   (3:32)   Capricorn 42003 The Scepter Records Story.

    (S)   (3:30)   Time-Life SUD-02 Superhits - 1968.

    (S)   (3:34)   Time-Life OPCD-4517 Tonight's The Night.

    (S)   (3:33)   Time-Life R138/05 Look Of Love.

    (S)   (3:36)   Rhino 72423 Billboard Top Movie Hits - 1960s.

    (S)   (3:30)   Time-Life AM1-04 AM Gold - 1968.

    (S)   (3:35)   Curb 77874 Her Classic Songs Volume 1. *(truncated fade)*

    (S)   (3:35)   Time-Life R834-14 Body Talk - Love And Tenderness.

    (S)   (3:36)   Time-Life R857-22 The Heart Of Rock 'n' Roll 1967-1969.

1968 DO YOU KNOW THE WAY TO SAN JOSE

    (S)   (2:56)   Rhino 75898 Anthology 1962 - 1969.

    (S)   (2:55)   Rhino 71100 Collection - Her Greatest Hits.

    (S)   (2:55)   Pair 1243 At Her Very Best.

    (S)   (2:55)   Pair 4929 Her Greatest Hits.

    (S)   (2:52)   Time-Life SUD-02 Superhits - 1968.

    (S)   (2:52)   Time-Life AM1-04 AM Gold - 1968.

    (S)   (2:53)   Curb 77894 I Say A Little Prayer.

1968 WHO IS GONNA LOVE ME?

    (S)   (3:10)   Rhino 70329 Hidden Gems.

    (M)   (3:07)   Pair 1243 At Her Very Best.

1968 PROMISES, PROMISES

    (S)   (2:58)   Rhino 75898 Anthology 1962 - 1969.

    (S)   (2:56)   Rhino 71100 Collection - Her Greatest Hits.

    (S)   (2:55)   Curb 77874 Her Classic Songs Volume 1. *(truncated fade)*

1969 THIS GIRL'S IN LOVE WITH YOU

    (S)   (5:20)   Rhino 70329 Hidden Gems. *(previously unreleased version)*

    (M)   (4:12)   Pair 1243 At Her Very Best.

    (M)   (4:12)   Pair 4929 Her Greatest Hits.

    (S)   (4:07)   Time-Life SUD-07 Superhits - 1969.

    (S)   (4:06)   Time-Life R974-01 Many Moods Of Romance - That's My Desire.

    (S)   (4:06)   Time-Life AM1-01 AM Gold - 1969.

    (S)   (4:09)   Curb 77894 I Say A Little Prayer.

    (S)   (4:06)   Time-Life R834-14 Body Talk - Love And Tenderness.

1969 THE APRIL FOOLS

    (S)   (3:15)   Rhino 71100 Collection - Her Greatest Hits.

1969 YOU'VE LOST THAT LOVIN' FEELING

    (S)   (4:14)   Pair 1243 At Her Very Best.

    (S)   (4:14)   Pair 4929 Her Greatest Hits.

1970 I'LL NEVER FALL IN LOVE AGAIN

    (S)   (2:52)   Rhino 75898 Anthology 1962 - 1969.

    (S)   (3:00)   Rhino 71100 Collection - Her Greatest Hits.

    (S)   (2:51)   Pair 1243 At Her Very Best.

    (S)   (2:52)   Capricorn 42003 The Scepter Records Story.

    (S)   (2:52)   Pair 4929 Her Greatest Hits.

    (S)   (2:55)   Time-Life SUD-04 Superhits - 1970.

    (S)   (2:59)   Rebound 3145200320 Class Reunion 1970.

    (S)   (2:59)   JCI 3145 1970 - Only Love - 1974.

    (S)   (2:55)   Time-Life AM1-02 AM Gold - 1970.

    (S)   (3:00)   Rhino 72736 Billboard Top Soft Rock Hits - 1970.

    (S)   (2:59)   Curb 77874 Her Classic Songs Volume 1. *(truncated fade)*

    (S)   (3:00)   Time-Life R834-16 Body Talk - Sweet Nothings.

    (S)   (2:55)   Time-Life R814-04 Love Songs.

1970 LET ME GO TO HIM

    (S)   (3:50)   Rhino 70329 Hidden Gems.

1970 PAPER MACHE

1970 MAKE IT EASY ON YOURSELF

    (M)   (2:40)   Rhino 70329 Hidden Gems. *(studio recording - the hit version was live)*

    (S)   (2:58)   Pair 1243 At Her Very Best. *(studio recording - the hit version was live)*

released as by DIONNE WARWICKE and THE SPINNERS:

1974 THEN CAME YOU

    (S)   (3:56)   Atlantic 81912 Golden Age Of Black Music (1970-1975).

    (S)   (3:56)   Atlantic 19179 Best Of The Spinners.

    (S)   (3:56)   Atlantic 82332 Spinners: A One Of A Kind Love Affair.

    (S)   (3:57)   Rhino 71213 Very Best Of The Spinners.

    (S)   (3:55)   Razor & Tie 22047 Sweet 70's Soul.

    (S)   (3:54)   Time-Life SOD-07 Sounds Of The Seventies - 1974.

    (S)   (3:57)   JCI 3130 1970 - Only Rock 'N Roll - 1974.

    (S)   (3:57)   Rhino 71883 Spinners - New And Improved.

    (S)   (3:57)   Rhino 72116 Billboard Hot Soul Hits - 1974.

    (S)   (3:57)   DCC Compact Classics 141 Groove On! Volume 1.

    (S)   (3:54)   JCI 3173 1970 - Only Soul - 1974.

    (S)   (3:57)   Rhino 72580 Soul Serenade - Intimate R&B.

    (S)   (3:54)   Time-Life R103-18 Great Love Songs Of The '70s & '80s.

    (S)   (3:54)   Time-Life AM1-21 AM Gold - 1974.

    (S)   (3:54)   Time-Life R838-09 Solid Gold Soul - 1974.

    (S)   (3:57)   Flashback 72673 Spinners - Could It Be I'm Falling In Love And Other Hits.

released as by DIONNE WARWICK:

1979 I'LL NEVER LOVE THIS WAY AGAIN

    (S)   (3:28)   Arista 8540 Greatest Hits 1979-1990.

    (S)   (3:31)   Razor & Tie 4543 The '70s Preservation Society Presents: Easy '70s.

    (S)   (3:27)   Priority 53796 Hot And Sexy - Love And Romance Volume 3.

    (S)   (3:31)   Time-Life R834-02 Body Talk - Just For You.

    (S)   (3:28)   Simitar 55562 The Number One's: Smooth Love.

    (S)   (3:26)   Time-Life AM1-26 AM Gold - 1979.

1980 DEJA VU

    (S)   (5:06)   Arista 8416 Perfect 10 III. *(LP version)*

    (S)   (3:47)   Arista 8540 Greatest Hits 1979-1990. *(45 version)*

    (S)   (3:47)   Right Stuff 54245 Slow Jams: The 70's Volume 5. *(45 version)*

1980 NO NIGHT SO LONG

    (S)   (3:24)   Arista 8540 Greatest Hits 1979-1990.

    (S)   (3:24)   Time-Life R834-17 Body Talk - Heart To Heart.

released as by DIONNE WARWICK and JOHNNY MATHIS:

1982 FRIENDS IN LOVE

    (S)   (3:57)   Arista 8540 Dionne Warwick - Greatest Hits 1979-1990.

released as by DIONNE WARWICK:

1982 HEARTBREAKER

    (S)   (4:17)   Arista 8268 Arista's Perfect 10.

    (S)   (4:16)   Arista 8540 Greatest Hits 1979-1990.

(S)　(4:17)　Arista 8006　Heartbreaker.
(S)　(4:14)　Hip-O 40015　Soulful Ladies Of The 80's.
(S)　(4:15)　Right Stuff 35600　Soul Of The Bee Gees.
(S)　(4:15)　Time-Life R834-15　Body Talk - Once In Lifetime.

released as by DIONNE WARWICK and LUTHER VANDROSS:
1983　HOW MANY TIMES CAN WE SAY GOODBYE
(S)　(3:26)　Arista 8540　Dionne Warwick - Greatest Hits 1979-1990.

released as by DIONNE and FRIENDS: DIONNE WARWICK,
ELTON JOHN, GLADYS KNIGHT and STEVIE WONDER:
1986　THAT'S WHAT FRIENDS ARE FOR
(S)　(4:15)　Arista 8398　Dionne Warwick - Friends.
(S)　(4:15)　Arista 8540　Dionne Warwick - Greatest Hits 1979 - 1990.

released as by DIONNE WARWICK & JEFFREY OSBORNE:
1987　LOVE POWER
(S)　(4:31)　JCI 2701　Slow Grooves.
(S)　(4:32)　Arista 8446　Dionne Warwick - Reservations For Two.
(S)　(4:32)　Arista 8540　Dionne Warwick - Greatest Hits 1979-1990.

DINAH WASHINGTON
1959　WHAT A DIFF'RENCE A DAY MAKES
(S)　(2:28)　Mercury 818815　What A Difference A Day Makes.
(S)　(2:27)　Mercury 838956　Complete Dinah Washington On Mercury Volume 6.
(S)　(2:28)　Mercury 830700　Compact Jazz.
(S)　(2:27)　Verve 314512905　Essential: The Great Songs.
(S)　(2:27)　Mercury 314514841　First Issue: The Dinah Washington Story.
(S)　(2:26)　Rhino 71252　Sentimental Journey: Pop Vocal Classics Volume 4 (1954-1959).
(S)　(2:26)　Rhino 72034　Sentimental Journey Pop Vocal Classics Volumes 1-4 Box Set.
(S)　(2:27)　Verve 314521007　Playboy's 40th Anniversary: Four Decades Of Jazz (1953-1993).
(S)　(2:28)　Time-Life RHD-03　Rhythm & Blues - 1959.
(S)　(2:26)　Time-Life HPD-13　Your Hit Parade - 1959.
(S)　(2:30)　Collectables 5200　Golden Classics. *(mastered from a scratchy record)*
(S)　(2:27)　RCA 66443　O.S.T. Corrina, Corrina.
(S)　(2:27)　Verve 314517176　The Essential American Singers.
(S)　(2:27)　Rebound 314520312　Great Ladies Of Jazz.
(S)　(2:28)　Time-Life R974-01　Many Moods Of Romance - That's My Desire.
(S)　(2:27)　MCA 11389　O.S.T. Casino.
(S)　(2:26)　Rhino 72413　Sentimental Favorites.
(M)　(2:27)　Rhino 72514　Sirens Of Song - Classic Torch Singers.
(S)　(2:26)　Flashback 72709　Sentimental Favorites.
(S)　(2:28)　Time-Life R838-21　Solid Gold Soul 1959.
(S)　(2:28)　MFSL 698　What A Diff'rence A Day Makes! *(gold disc)*
(S)　(2:27)　Polygram Special Markets 314520462　50's Soul.
1959　UNFORGETTABLE
(S)　(2:41)　Mercury 838956　Complete Dinah Washington On Mercury Volume 6.
(S)　(2:43)　Original Sound 8864　Oldies But Goodies Vol. 14. *(this compact disc uses the "Waring - fds" noise reduction process)*
(S)　(2:43)　Original Sound 2222　Oldies But Goodies Volumes 3,5,11,14 and 15 Box Set. *(this box set uses the "Waring - fds" noise reduction process)*
(S)　(2:43)　Original Sound 2500　Oldies But Goodies Volumes 1-15 Box Set. *(this box set uses the "Waring - fds" noise reduction process)*
(S)　(2:41)　Mercury 510602　Unforgettable.
(S)　(2:40)　Mercury 830700　Compact Jazz.
(S)　(2:41)　Mercury 314514841　First Issue: The Dinah Washington Story.
(S)　(2:43)　Time-Life HPD-13　Your Hit Parade - 1959.
released as by DINAH WASHINGTON & BROOK BENTON:
1960　BABY (YOU'VE GOT WHAT IT TAKES)
(S)　(2:44)　Mercury 816555　45's On CD Volume 2.

(S)　(2:44)　Mercury 836755　Brook Benton: Forty Greatest Hits.
(S)　(2:43)　Rhino 70646　Billboard's Top R&B Hits Of 1960.
(S)　(2:44)　Mercury 838956　Complete Dinah Washington On Mercury Volume 6.
(S)　(2:44)　Verve 314512905　Essential Dinah Washington: The Great Songs.
(S)　(2:44)　Mercury 314514841　First Issue: The Dinah Washington Story.
(S)　(2:41)　Time-Life RHD-15　Rhythm & Blues - 1960.
(S)　(2:42)　Time-Life SUD-15　Superhits - The Early 60's.
(S)　(2:42)　Verve/Mercury 314526467　The Two Of Us.
(S)　(2:53)　Curb 77741　Brook Benton - Greatest Songs. *(rerecording)*
(S)　(2:43)　Ripete 5151　Ocean Drive 4.
(S)　(2:44)　Ichiban 2512　Soulful Love - Duets Vol. 1.
(S)　(2:44)　Polygram Special Markets 314520405　Brook Benton - Greatest Hits.
(S)　(2:42)　Time-Life AM1-19　AM Gold - The Early '60s.
(S)　(2:43)　Rebound 314520420　Soul Classics - Best Of The 60's.
(S)　(2:41)　Time-Life R838-20　Solid Gold Soul 1960.
(S)　(2:44)　Polygram Special Markets 314520454　Soul Hits Of The 60's.

1960　A ROCKIN' GOOD WAY (TO MESS AROUND AND FALL IN LOVE)
(S)　(2:25)　Rhino 70646　Billboard's Top R&B Hits Of 1960.
(S)　(2:25)　Mercury 836755　Brook Benton: Forty Greatest Hits.
(S)　(2:25)　Curb 77445　Best Of Brook Benton.
(S)　(2:25)　Mercury 838956　Complete Dinah Washington On Mercury Volume 6.
(S)　(2:25)　Mercury 314514841　First Issue: The Dinah Washington Story.
(S)　(2:25)　Polygram Special Markets 314520264　Soul Hits Of The 60's.
(S)　(2:24)　Verve/Mercury 314526467　The Two Of Us.
(S)　(2:25)　Curb 77741　Brook Benton - Greatest Songs. *(rerecording)*
(S)　(2:25)　Ripete 5151　Ocean Drive 4.
released as by DINAH WASHINGTON:
1960　THIS BITTER EARTH
(S)　(2:25)　Mercury 838956　Complete Dinah Washington On Mercury Volume 6.
(S)　(2:26)　Mercury 510602　Unforgettable.
(S)　(2:25)　Mercury 830700　Compact Jazz.
(S)　(2:25)　Verve 314512905　Essential: The Great Songs.
(S)　(2:25)　Mercury 314514841　First Issue: The Dinah Washington Story.
1960　LOVE WALKED IN
(S)　(2:08)　Mercury 838956　Complete Dinah Washington On Mercury Volume 6.
1961　SEPTEMBER IN THE RAIN
(S)　(2:06)　Mercury 838956　Complete Dinah Washington On Mercury Volume 6.
(S)　(2:04)　Mercury 314514841　First Issue: The Dinah Washington Story.
(S)　(2:05)　K-Tel 539　Great Ladies Of Jazz.
1962　WHERE ARE YOU

GROVER WASHINGTON JR. with BILL WITHERS
1981　JUST THE TWO OF US
(actual 45 time is (3:56) not (3:40) as stated on the record label)
(S)　(7:23)　Elektra 305　Grover Washington Jr. - Winelight. *(LP version)*
(S)　(7:19)　Elektra 60415　Grover Washington Jr. - Anthology. *(LP version)*
(S)　(3:56)　Columbia 37199　Bill Withers Greatest Hits. *(45 version)*
(S)　(3:57)　Columbia/Legacy 52924　Bill Withers: Lean On Me/Best Of. *(45 version)*
(S)　(3:56)　Rhino 71894　Radio Daze: Pop Hits Of The 80's Volume Five. *(45 version)*
(S)　(3:55)　Rhino 71971　Video Soul - Best Soul Of The 80's Vol. 1. *(45 version)*
(S)　(3:29)　Time-Life R138-18　Body Talk. *(45 version faded :27 early)*

GROVER WASHINGTON JR. with BILL WITHERS *(Continued)*

- (S) (3:56)   Rhino 72136 Billboard Hot R&B Hits 1981. *(45 version)*
- (S) (7:22)   MCA 11431 Quiet Storms 2. *(LP version)*
- (S) (3:29)   JCI 3170 #1 Radio Hits 1980 - Only Rock 'n Roll - 1984. *(45 version faded :27 early)*
- (S) (3:57)   Time-Life R834-03 Body Talk - Moonlit Nights. *(45 version)*
- (S) (3:29)   K-Tel 6257 The Greatest Love Songs - 16 Soft Rock Hits. *(45 version faded :27 early)*
- (S) (3:57)   Time-Life R988-22 Sounds Of The Eighties 1980-1983. *(45 version)*

WAS (NOT WAS)
1988 SPY IN THE HOUSE OF LOVE
- (S) (4:16)   Chrysalis 21664 What Up, Dog?.
- (S) (4:15)   Time-Life R988-29 Sounds Of The Eighties: The Rolling Stone Collection 1987-1988.

1989 WALK THE DINOSAUR
- (S) (4:21)   MCA 10452 O.S.T. The Flintstones. *(LP version)*
- (S) (4:21)   Chrysalis 21664 What Up, Dog?. *(LP version)*
- (S) (4:21)   Madacy Entertainment 1989 Rock On 1989. *(LP version)*
- (S) (3:36)   Hip-O 40004 The '80s Hit(s) Back! *(45 version)*
- (S) (4:21)   Time-Life R988-13 Sounds Of The Eighties: 1989. *(LP version)*
- (S) (4:22)   Scotti Bros. 75512 New Wave Dance Hits! *(LP version)*

WATERFRONT
1989 CRY
- (S) (3:54)   Polydor 837970 Waterfront.

CRYSTAL WATERS
1991 GYPSY WOMAN (SHE'S HOMELESS)
- (S) (5:19)   Columbia 52826 Red Hot + Dance. *(remixed)*
- (S) (3:49)   Sandstone 5022 Cosmopolitan Volume 8.
- (S) (3:48)   Rebound 314520246 Disco Nights Vol. 5 - Best Of Housemusic.
- (S) (3:49)   DCC Compact Classics 082 Night Moves Volume 2.
- (S) (3:49)   Priority 53772 Techno Dance Classics Volume 2 - Feel The Beat.
- (S) (3:48)   Mercury 848894 Surprise.
- (S) (3:46)   Rebound 314520359 World Of Dance - The 90's.
- (S) (5:43)   Priority 50955 Power Workout High NRG Megamix Volume 2. *(all selections on this cd are segued together; remixed)*
- (S) (3:46)   Rhino 72839 Disco Queens: The 90's.
- (S) (3:48)   Cold Front 3832 Club Mix - Women Of Dance Vol. 1.
- (S) (5:07)   Cold Front 6284 More Of! Club Mix's Biggest Jams. *(all selections on this cd are segued together; remix)*

1994 100% PURE LOVE
- (S) (4:38)   Mercury 314522105 Storyteller.
- (S) (3:01)   Mercury 314532494 100% Pure Dance. *(radio edit; all songs on this cd are segued together)*
- (S) (4:38)   EMI-Capitol Music Group 54547 Hot Luv.
- (S) (4:03)   Arista 18988 Ultimate Dance Party 1998. *(all selections on this cd are segued together)*
- (S) (4:15)   Boxtunes 162531071 Big Ones Of Dance Volume 1. *(all selections on this cd are segued together)*

1997 SAY...IF YOU FEEL ALRIGHT
- (S) (3:55)   Mercury 314536014 Crystal Waters.
- (S) (4:20)   Cold Front 6254 Club Mix '98. *(all selections on this cd are segued together)*
- (S) (3:29)   Polygram TV 314553847 Pure Dance 1998. *(all songs on this cd are segued together)*

JODY WATLEY
1987 LOOKING FOR A NEW LOVE
- (S) (5:06)   MCA 11218 On The Beat - 80's Jams Vol. II. *(LP version)*
- (S) (5:07)   MCA 5898 Jody Watley. *(LP version)*

- (S) (7:29)   MCA 5898 Jody Watley. *(12" single version)*
- (S) (5:20)   MCA 6343 You Wanna Dance With Me? *(remix)*
- (S) (3:58)   Time-Life R988-09 Sounds Of The Eighties: 1987. *(45 version)*
- (S) (3:58)   Rhino 72159 Black Entertainment Television - 15th Anniversary. *(45 version)*
- (S) (3:58)   Rhino 72142 Billboard Hot R&B Hits 1987. *(45 version)*
- (S) (5:06)   MCA 11400 Greatest Hits. *(LP version)*
- (S) (3:58)   Hip-O 40015 Soulful Ladies Of The 80's. *(45 version)*
- (S) (5:06)   Right Stuff 52288 Free To Be Volume 4. *(LP version)*
- (S) (3:58)   JCI 3171 #1 Radio Hits 1985 - Only Rock 'n Roll - 1989. *(45 version)*
- (S) (3:58)   K-Tel 3673 The 80's - Funky Love. *(45 version)*
- (S) (5:23)   MCA Special Products 21034 Club Disco Dance Hits. *(remix)*
- (S) (4:00)   Rhino 72838 Disco Queens: The 80's. *(45 version)*
- (S) (3:58)   Cold Front 3832 Club Mix - Women Of Dance Vol. 1. *(45 version)*
- (S) (5:05)   Priority 50940 Shut Up And Dance! The 80's Volume One. *(all selections on this cd are segued together)*

1987 DON'T YOU WANT ME
- (S) (4:10)   EMI 91419 MTV, BET, VH-1 Power Players.
- (S) (4:11)   MCA 5898 Jody Watley.
- (S) (5:22)   MCA 6343 You Wanna Dance With Me?. *(remix)*
- (S) (4:10)   MCA 11400 Greatest Hits. *(remix)*
- (S) (5:31)   Rebound 314520357 World Of Dance - The 80's. *(remix)*
- (S) (4:11)   Madacy Entertainment 1987 Rock On 1987.
- (S) (4:03)   Thump 9951 Power 106 10th Anniversary Collection. *(all songs on this cd are segued together)*
- (S) (4:09)   Cold Front 6246 Classic Club Mix - R&B Grooves. *(all selections on this cd are segued together; remix)*

1988 SOME KIND OF LOVER
- (S) (4:06)   Sandstone 33043 and 5009 Rock The First Volume Three.
- (S) (4:06)   MCA 5898 Jody Watley.
- (S) (6:57)   MCA 6343 You Wanna Dance With Me? *(remix)*
- (S) (4:33)   MCA 11400 Greatest Hits. *(remix)*
- (S) (4:06)   Madacy Entertainment 1988 Rock On 1988.

1989 REAL LOVE
- (S) (4:21)   JCI 3124 Rhythm Of The Night.
- (S) (4:21)   MCA 6276 Larger Than Life.
- (S) (5:44)   MCA 6343 You Wanna Dance With Me? *(remix)*
- (S) (4:19)   Rhino 72144 Billboard Hot R&B Hits 1989.
- (S) (4:22)   MCA 11400 Greatest Hits.
- (S) (4:21)   Madacy Entertainment 1989 Rock On 1989.
- (S) (4:21)   MCA Special Products 21029 The Women Of Soul.
- (S) (4:21)   Cold Front 3865 Club Mix - Women Of Dance Vol. 2.

1989 FRIENDS
- (S) (4:28)   MCA 6276 Larger Than Life.
- (S) (5:51)   MCA 6343 You Wanna Dance With Me? *(remix)*
- (S) (4:29)   MCA 11400 Greatest Hits.
- (S) (4:26)   K-Tel 3867 The 80's: Hot Ladies.

1989 EVERYTHING
- (S) (4:15)   MCA 11217 Quiet Storms - 80's Jams Vol. I.
- (S) (4:15)   MCA 6276 Larger Than Life.
- (S) (4:14)   MCA 11400 Greatest Hits.
- (S) (4:14)   Hip-O 40000 Thinking About You - A Collection Of Modern Love Songs.
- (S) (4:14)   Hip-O 40031 The Glory Of Love - '80s Sweet & Soulful Love Songs.

1992 I'M THE ONE YOU NEED
- (S) (4:20)   MCA 10355 Affairs Of The Heart.

WATTS 103rd STREET RHYTHM BAND (see CHARLES WRIGHT & THE WATTS 103rd STREET BAND)

WA WA NEE
1987 SUGAR FREE
(S) (4:28) Epic 40858 Wa Wa Nee. *(LP length)*

THOMAS WAYNE with THE DeLONS
1959 TRAGEDY
(M) (2:08) Time-Life 2RNR-24 Rock 'N' Roll Era - The 50's Keep On Rockin'.
(M) (2:07) Time-Life R102-17 Lost Treasures Of Rock 'N' Roll.
(M) (2:07) LaserLight 12322 Greatest Hit Singles Collection.
(M) (2:07) Time-Life R857-01 The Heart Of Rock 'n' Roll - 1959.

JIM WEATHERLY
1974 THE NEED TO BE

JOAN WEBER
1955 LET ME GO LOVER
(M) (2:22) Columbia 45110 16 Most Requested Songs Of The 50's Volume 1.
(M) (2:22) Columbia 45017 Radio Classics Of The 50's.
(M) (2:21) Rhino 71252 Sentimental Journey: Pop Vocal Classics Volume 4 (1954-1959).
(M) (2:21) Rhino 72034 Sentimental Journey Pop Vocal Classics Volumes 1-4 Box Set.
(M) (2:21) Time-Life HPD-09 Your Hit Parade 1955.
(M) (2:21) Time-Life R132-10 Love Songs Of Your Hit Parade.

WEDNESDAY
1974 LAST KISS

WE FIVE
1965 YOU WERE ON MY MIND
(E) (2:34) Priority 9461 Mellow 60's.
(M) (2:36) Rhino 70536 San Francisco Nights.
(S) (2:32) Rhino 70995 One Hit Wonders Of The 60's Volume 1. *(missing some overdubs)*
(E) (2:35) JCI 3109 Folk Sixties.
(E) (2:35) Time-Life 2CLR-14 Classic Rock - 1965: Shakin' All Over.
(M) (2:34) Time-Life SUD-03 Superhits - 1965.
(M) (2:36) Rhino 71935 Billboard Top Pop Hits, 1965.
(E) (2:35) K-Tel 3438 Best Of Folk Rock.
(E) (2:35) Rebound 314520371 The Roots Of Rock: 60's Folk.
(M) (2:35) Collectors' Choice Music 5172 You Were On My Mind/Make Someone Happy.
(M) (2:33) Time-Life AM1-10 AM Gold - 1965.
(M) (2:34) Time-Life R132-22 Treasury Of Folk Music Volume One.
(E) (2:35) Polygram Special Markets 314520495 45's On CD Volume 2.
1965 LET'S GET TOGETHER
(S) (2:56) Collectors' Choice Music 5172 You Were On My Mind/Make Someone Happy.

ERIC WEISSBERG & STEVE MANDELL
1973 DUELING BANJOS
(S) (2:16) Rhino 70758 Super Hits Of The 70's Volume 11. *(neither the LP or 45 version; hiss on introduction)*
(S) (3:14) Warner Brothers 2683 O.S.T. Deliverance. *(LP version)*
(S) (2:16) Time-Life SUD-20 Superhits - Early 70's Classics. *(neither the 45 or LP version; hiss on introduction)*
(S) (3:14) Priority 53718 Branson USA Vol. 1 - Pickers & Fiddlers. *(LP version)*
(M) (2:12) K-Tel 3111 Country Music Classics Vol. XIX. *(45 version)*
(S) (2:16) Rhino 72424 Billboard Top Movie Hits - 1970s. *(neither the 45 or LP version; hiss on introduction)*
(S) (2:16) Time-Life AM1-15 AM Gold - Early '70s Classics. *(neither the 45 or LP version)*
(S) (3:14) Time-Life R840-04 Sounds Of The Seventies: A Loss For Words. *(LP version)*

(S) (2:17) Rhino 72739 Billboard Top Soft Rock Hits - 1973. *(neither the 45 or LP version)*

BOB WELCH
1977 SENTIMENTAL LADY
(actual LP and 45 time is (2:56) not (2:51) as stated on the record label)
(S) (2:57) Sandstone 33003 Reelin' In The Years Volume 4.
(S) (3:08) Rhino 70597 Best Of. *(:11 longer than any previously released version)*
(S) (2:57) Capitol 91850 French Kiss.
(S) (2:57) DCC Compact Classics 065 Rock Of The 70's Volume 4.
(S) (2:53) Time-Life SOD-35 Sounds Of The Seventies - AM Nuggets.
(S) (2:52) Curb 77684 Greatest Hits.
(S) (2:53) JCI 3119 18 Rock Classics.
(S) (3:08) Varese 5635 and 5654 and 5655 and 5657 Arrow: All Rock & Roll Oldies Volume Two. *(:11 longer than any previously released version)*
(S) (3:08) Rhino 72445 Listen To The Music: The 70's California Sound. *(:11 longer than any previously released version)*
(S) (2:56) Madacy Entertainment 1977 Rock On 1977.
(S) (3:08) Varese Sarabande 5708 All Rock & Roll Hits Vol. One. *(:11 longer than any previously released version)*
(S) (2:53) Time-Life R834-08 Body Talk - On My Mind.
(S) (2:53) Time-Life AM1-25 AM Gold - 1978.
(S) (2:52) Rebound 314520492 Class Reunion '78.
1978 EBONY EYES
(S) (3:33) Rhino 70597 Best Of. *(LP length)*
(S) (3:31) Capitol 91850 French Kiss. *(LP length)*
(S) (3:31) Time-Life SOD-34 Sounds Of The Seventies - The Late 70's. *(LP length)*
(S) (3:29) Curb 77684 Greatest Hits. *(LP length)*
(S) (3:31) Madacy Entertainment 1978 Rock On 1978. *(LP length)*
(S) (3:31) JCI 3140 18 Screamers From The 70's. *(LP length)*
(S) (3:33) Priority 50989 70's Greatest Rock Hits Volume 2: Rock & Soul. *(LP length)*
1978 HOT LOVE, COLD WORLD
(S) (3:39) Capitol 91850 French Kiss.
(S) (3:34) Rhino 70597 Best Of.
(S) (3:39) Curb 77684 Greatest Hits.
1979 PRECIOUS LOVE
(S) (3:13) Rhino 70597 Best Of.
(S) (3:13) Curb 77684 Greatest Hits.
(S) (3:12) Capitol 38247 Three Hearts.

LENNY WELCH
1963 SINCE I FELL FOR YOU
(S) (2:53) Rhino 75893 Jukebox Classics Volume 1.
(M) (2:51) Original Sound 8862 Oldies But Goodies Vol. 12. *(this compact disc uses the "Waring - fds" noise reduction process)*
(M) (2:51) Original Sound 2223 Oldies But Goodies Volumes 2,7,9,12 and 13 Box Set. *(this box set uses the "Waring - fds" noise reduction process)*
(M) (2:51) Original Sound 2500 Oldies But Goodies Volumes 1-15 Box Set. *(this box set uses the "Waring - fds" noise reduction process)*
(M) (2:50) Original Sound CDGO-2 Golden Oldies Volume. 2.
(S) (2:51) Columbia 45019 Pop Classics Of The 60's.
(E) (2:51) Original Sound 8907 Best Love Songs Vol 2.
(E) (2:51) Original Sound 9326 Best Love Songs Vol. 1 & 2.
(E) (2:51) Original Sound 1236 Best Love Songs Box Set.
(E) (2:51) Original Sound 9603 Best Of Oldies But Goodies Vol. 3.
(S) (2:52) Time-Life 2RNR-46 Rock 'N' Roll Era - 60's Juke Box Memories.
(S) (2:51) Time-Life SUD-08 Superhits - 1963.
(S) (2:52) Time-Life R103-27 Love Me Tender.
(S) (2:52) Time-Life OPCD-4517 Tonight's The Night.
(S) (2:52) Time-Life R138/05 Look Of Love.
(S) (2:52) LaserLight 12321 Soulful Love.

LENNY WELCH (Continued)

- (S) (2:52) Collectables 5252 Since I Fell For You.
- (S) (2:53) Varese Sarabande 5579 History Of Cadence Records Volume 2.
- (S) (3:04) Taragon 1013 Anthology. *(time includes :05 of studio talk preceding the song and :06 of studio talk following the song)*
- (S) (2:51) Nick At Nite/550 Music/Epic 67768 Fonzie's Make Out Music.
- (S) (2:53) Music Club 50015 Love Me Forever - 18 Rock'N' Roll Love Songs.
- (S) (2:52) K-Tel 3630 Lounge Legends.
- (S) (2:51) Time-Life R857-08 The Heart Of Rock 'n' Roll 1963.
- (S) (2:51) Time-Life AM1-17 AM Gold - 1963.
- (S) (2:52) Time-Life R814-03 Love Songs.
- (S) (2:51) Collectables 1515 and 2515 The Anniversary Album - The 60's.

1964 EBB TIDE
- (M) (2:30) LaserLight 12321 Soulful Love. *(sounds like it was mastered from vinyl)*
- (M) (2:30) Collectables 5252 Since I Fell For You.
- (S) (2:36) Taragon 1013 Anthology.
- (S) (2:36) Hip-O 40029 The Glory Of Love - '60s Sweet & Soulful Love Songs.

1970 BREAKING UP IS HARD TO DO

LAWRENCE WELK and HIS ORCHESTRA
1956 MORITAT (A THEME FROM "THE THREE PENNY OPERA")
1956 THE POOR PEOPLE OF PARIS
released as by LAWRENCE WELK and HIS SPARKLING STRINGS
(with THE LENNON SISTERS and THE SPARKLERS):
1956 TONIGHT YOU BELONG TO ME
- (M) (2:00) Time-Life R132-14 Golden Groups Of Your Hit Parade.

released as by LAWRENCE WELK and HIS ORCHESTRA:
1960 LAST DATE
- (S) (2:17) Ranwood 8226 Best Of - 18 Great Hits.
1961 CALCUTTA
- (S) (2:13) Ranwood 8226 Best Of - 18 Great Hits.
- (S) (2:12) Ranwood 1004 A Musical Anthology.
- (S) (2:13) Time-Life HPD-34 Your Hit Parade - 60's Instrumentals.
- (S) (2:13) K-Tel 3091 Those Wonderful Instrumentals.
- (S) (2:12) Collectors' Choice 003/4 Instrumental Gems Of The 60's.
- (M) (2:12) Time-Life R986-14 Instrumental Favorites - Lawrence Welk.
- (S) (2:12) MCA Special Products 21035 Classic Rock & Roll Instrumental Hits, Volume 2.

MARY WELLS
1962 THE ONE WHO REALLY LOVES YOU
- (S) (2:26) Motown 9105 and 5410 Motown Memories Volume 2.
- (S) (2:28) Motown 5448 A Package Of 16 Big Hits.
- (S) (2:26) Motown 9095 and 5325 Motown Girl Groups: Top 10 With A Bullet! *(buzz noticeable on fadeout)*
- (S) (2:27) Motown 6171 Compact Command Performances.
- (S) (2:27) Motown 9016 and 5233 Greatest Hits.
- (S) (2:26) Motown 5420 The One Who Really Loves You.
- (M) (2:26) Motown 6312 Hitsville USA.
- (M) (2:27) Motown 6253 Looking Back 1961-1964.
- (S) (2:26) Time-Life 2RNR-25 Rock 'N' Roll Era - The 60's Keep On Rockin'.
- (S) (2:26) Thump 7010 Low Rider Oldies Volume 1.
- (M) (2:26) Motown 314530403 Motown Classic Hits Vol. 1.
- (M) (2:27) Rhino 71806 The R&B Box: Thirty Years Of Rhythm & Blues.
- (S) (2:27) Polygram Special Markets 314520299 Motown Legends - Girl Groups.
- (M) (2:27) Time-Life R857-12 The Heart Of Rock 'n' Roll 1962-1963.
- (M) (2:24) Motown 314530859 Ultimate Collection.

1962 YOU BEAT ME TO THE PUNCH
- (S) (2:43) Motown 6160 The Good-Feeling Music Of The Big Chill Generation Volume 2.
- (S) (2:46) Motown 5448 A Package Of 16 Big Hits.
- (S) (2:44) Rhino 70648 Billboard's Top R&B Hits Of 1962.
- (S) (2:43) Motown 6171 Compact Command Performances.
- (S) (2:43) Motown 9016 and 5233 Greatest Hits.
- (S) (2:43) Motown 5420 The One Who Really Loves You.
- (S) (2:43) Pair 1270 Original Motown Classics.
- (M) (2:42) Motown 6312 Hitsville USA.
- (M) (2:42) Motown 6253 Looking Back 1961-1964.
- (S) (2:43) Time-Life 2RNR-16 Rock 'N' Roll Era - 1962 Still Rockin'.
- (S) (2:42) Time-Life RHD-11 Rhythm & Blues - 1962.
- (M) (2:40) Motown 314530403 Motown Classic Hits Vol 1.
- (M) (2:42) Motown/Essex 374638526 Motown Legends - You Beat Me To The Punch.
- (S) (2:43) Polygram Special Markets 314520292 Motown Legends - Volume 4.
- (M) (2:44) Motown 314530647 O.S.T. Nothing But A Man.
- (S) (2:43) Repeat/Relativity 1610 Tighten Up: #1 Soul Hits Of The 60's Volume 2.
- (S) (2:42) Time-Life R838-18 Solid Gold Soul 1962.
- (M) (2:39) Motown 314530859 Ultimate Collection.
- (S) (2:43) Time-Life R857-18 The Heart Of Rock 'n' Roll 1962-1963 Take Two.

1963 TWO LOVERS
- (S) (2:45) Motown 6161 The Good-Feeling Music Of The Big Chill Generation Volume 3.
- (S) (2:41) Motown 5451 A Collection Of 16 Big Hits Volume 4.
- (S) (2:45) Rhino 70649 Billboard's Top R&B Hits Of 1963.
- (S) (2:45) Motown 9095 and 5325 Motown Girl Groups: Top 10 With A Bullet!
- (S) (2:45) Motown 6171 Compact Command Performances.
- (S) (2:45) Motown 9016 and 5233 Greatest Hits.
- (S) (2:46) Motown 5221 Two Lovers.
- (S) (2:45) Motown 8024 and 8124 Two Lovers/My Guy.
- (M) (2:45) Motown 6312 Hitsville USA.
- (M) (2:45) Motown 6253 Looking Back 1961-1964.
- (S) (2:44) Time-Life 2RNR-16 Rock 'N' Roll Era - 1962 Still Rockin'.
- (S) (2:43) Time-Life RHD-02 Rhythm & Blues - 1963.
- (S) (2:44) Time-Life SUD-06 Superhits - 1962.
- (M) (2:45) Motown/Essex 374638526 Motown Legends - You Beat Me To The Punch.
- (S) (2:45) Polygram Special Markets 314520299 Motown Legends - Girl Groups.
- (M) (2:45) Motown 314530422 Motown Classics Vol. V.
- (M) (2:45) Motown 314530409 Motown Milestones - Motown's Leading Ladies.
- (S) (2:45) Polygram Special Markets 314520293 Motown Legends - Volume 5.
- (S) (2:45) Time-Life R857-08 The Heart Of Rock 'n' Roll 1963.
- (S) (2:44) Time-Life AM1-18 AM Gold - 1962.
- (S) (2:43) Time-Life R838-14 Solid Gold Soul - 1963.
- (S) (2:44) Thump 7200 Latin Oldies Volume Two.
- (M) (2:44) Motown 314530859 Ultimate Collection.

1963 LAUGHING BOY
- (S) (2:48) Motown 6171 Compact Command Performances.
- (S) (2:48) Motown 9016 and 5233 Greatest Hits.
- (S) (2:49) Motown 5221 Two Lovers.
- (S) (2:48) Motown 8024 and 8124 Two Lovers/My Guy.
- (S) (2:49) Pair 1270 Original Motown Classics.
- (M) (2:55) Motown 6253 Looking Back 1961-1964.
- (M) (2:55) Motown/Essex 374638526 Motown Legends - You Beat Me To The Punch.
- (M) (2:52) Motown 314530859 Ultimate Collection.

1963 YOU LOST THE SWEETEST BOY
- (S) (2:26) Motown 5449 A Collection Of 16 Big Hits Volume 2.
- (S) (2:26) Motown 6171 Compact Command Performances.
- (S) (2:26) Motown 9016 and 5233 Greatest Hits.
- (S) (2:26) Pair 1270 Original Motown Classics.

(M) (2:31)   Motown 6253   Looking Back 1961-1964.
(M) (2:30)   Motown 314530419   Motown Classic Hits Vol. II.
(M) (2:29)   Motown 314530859   Ultimate Collection.
1964   WHAT'S EASY FOR TWO IS SO HARD FOR ONE
(S) (2:58)   Motown 5450   A Collection Of 16 Big Hits Volume 3.
(S) (2:50)   Motown 6171   Compact Command Performances.
(S) (2:50)   Motown 9016 and 5233   Greatest Hits.
(M) (2:52)   Motown 6253   Looking Back 1961-1964.
(M) (2:51)   Motown 314530421   Motown Classic Hits Vol. IV.
(M) (2:50)   Motown 314530859   Ultimate Collection.
1964   MY GUY
(45 time is (2:45); LP time is (2:52))
(S) (2:51)   Motown 6159   The Good-Feeling Music Of The Big Chill Generation Volume 1.
(S) (2:49)   Motown 5451   A Collection Of 16 Big Hits Volume 4.
(S) (2:51)   Motown 6139   The Composer Series: Smokey Robinson.
(S) (2:43)   Rhino 70650   Billboard's Top R&B Hits Of 1964.
(S) (2:48)   Motown 9072   Motown Dance Party Volume 2. *(all selections on this cd are segued together)*
(S) (2:50)   Motown 9017 and 5248   16 #1 Hits From The Early 60's.
(S) (2:50)   Motown 9097   The Most Played Oldies On America's Jukeboxes.
(S) (2:50)   Motown 5322 and 9087   Girl Groups: The Story Of A Sound.
(S) (2:51)   Motown 6171   Compact Command Performances.
(S) (2:51)   Motown 9016 and 5233   Greatest Hits.
(S) (2:51)   Motown 8024 and 8124   Two Lovers/My Guy.
(S) (2:51)   Motown 5167   My Guy.
(S) (2:51)   Ripete 392183   Ocean Drive.
(S) (2:51)   Pair 1270   Original Motown Classics.
(M) (2:47)   Motown 6312   Hitsville USA.
(M) (2:47)   Motown 6253   Looking Back 1961-1964.
(S) (2:48)   Time-Life 2RNR-10   Rock 'N' Roll Era - 1964.
(S) (2:47)   Time-Life RHD-12   Rhythm & Blues - 1964.
(S) (2:47)   Time-Life SUD-09   Superhits - 1964.
(S) (2:49)   Time-Life OPCD-4517   Tonight's The Night.
(S) (2:50)   Thump 7020   Low Rider Oldies Volume II.
(M) (2:44)   Motown/Essex 374638526   Motown Legends - You Beat Me To The Punch.
(S) (2:50)   Polygram Special Markets 314520282   Motown Legends - Volume 1.
(S) (2:44)   Motown 314530504   Motown Year By Year 1964.
(S) (2:51)   Ripete 2219   Beach Fever.
(M) (2:47)   Thump 9947   Cruizin' To Motown.
(M) (2:47)   Nick At Nite/550 Music/Epic 67689   Stand By Your Man.
(S) (2:43)   Time-Life R857-09   The Heart Of Rock 'n' Roll 1964.
(S) (2:47)   Time-Life AM1-11   AM Gold - 1964.
(S) (2:47)   Time-Life R838-13   Solid Gold Soul - 1964.
(M) (2:46)   Motown 314530859   Ultimate Collection.
(S) (2:50)   Motown 314530849   Motown 40 Forever.
released as by MARVIN GAYE & MARY WELLS:
1964   ONCE UPON A TIME
(S) (2:29)   Motown 0791 and 6199   Marvin Gaye Anthology.
(S) (2:29)   Motown 6153 and 9053   Marvin Gaye & His Women.
(M) (2:29)   Motown 6311   The Marvin Gaye Collection.
(S) (2:27)   Motown 5451   A Collection Of 16 Big Hits Volume 4.
(S) (2:30)   Motown 5246   Marvin Gaye And His Girls.
(S) (2:28)   Motown 5260   Marvin Gaye & Mary Wells Together.
(M) (2:30)   Motown 6253   Mary Wells - Looking Back 1961-1964.
(M) (2:29)   Motown 314530422   Motown Classics Vol. V.
(M) (2:30)   Motown 314530492   Marvin Gaye The Master 1961 - 1984.
(M) (2:26)   Motown 314530859   Mary Wells Ultimate Collection.
1964   WHAT'S THE MATTER WITH YOU BABY
(S) (2:21)   Motown 5451   A Collection Of 16 Big Hits Volume 4.

(S) (2:25)   Motown 0791 and 6199   Marvin Gaye Anthology.
(S) (2:26)   Motown 6153 and 9053   Marvin Gaye & His Women.
(M) (2:21)   Motown 6311   The Marvin Gaye Collection.
(S) (2:24)   Motown 5246   Marvin Gaye And His Girls.
(S) (2:21)   Motown 5260   Marvin Gaye & Mary Wells Together.
(M) (2:21)   Motown 6253   Mary Wells - Looking Back 1961-1964.
(M) (2:19)   Motown 314530422   Motown Classics Vol. V.
(M) (2:21)   Motown 314530492   Marvin Gaye The Master 1961 - 1984.
(M) (2:21)   Motown 314530529   Marvin Gaye - Anthology.
(M) (2:21)   Motown 314530859   Mary Wells Ultimate Collection.
released as by MARY WELLS:
1965   USE YOUR HEAD
(M) (2:07)   Varese Sarabande 5514   Ain't It The Truth - Best Of.
(M) (2:07)   Ichiban 2109   Never, Never Leave Me/The 20th Century Sides.
(M) (2:06)   Motown 314530859   Ultimate Collection.

FRED WESLEY & THE JB'S (see also JAMES BROWN)
1973   DOING IT TO DEATH
(M) (5:07)   Rhino 70661   Billboard's Top R&B Hits 1973.
(E) (5:07)   Rhino 70551   Soul Hits Of The 70's Volume 11.
(M) (5:21)   Polydor 825714   CD Of JB. *(includes :24 introduction)*
(M) (5:14)   Polydor 849109   Star Time.
(E) (5:08)   Rhino 71431   In Yo Face! History Of Funk Volume 1.
(M) (5:04)   Rebound 314520034   Funk Classics Of The 70's.
(M) (5:07)   Time-Life R838-08   Solid Gold Soul - 1973.

DOTTIE WEST with KENNY ROGERS
1981   WHAT ARE WE DOIN' IN LOVE
(S) (2:59)   Priority 9305   Country Gold.
(S) (3:00)   Razor & Tie 2160   Are You Happy Baby? The Dottie West Collection (1976-1984).

WEST COAST RAP ALL-STARS
1990   WE'RE ALL IN THE SAME GANG
(S) (7:24)   Warner Brothers 26241   We're All In The Same Gang.
(S) (8:17)   Warner Brothers 26241   We're All In The Same Gang. *(remix)*

WESTSIDE CONNECTION
1996   BOW DOWN
(S) (3:26)   Priority 50583   Bow Down.
(S) (3:37)   Polygram TV 314536204   The Source Presents Hip Hop Hits Volume 1.
(S) (3:28)   Priority 50978   Hip Hop's Most Wanted 2.
1997   GANGSTAS MAKE THE WORLD GO ROUND
(S) (4:32)   Priority 50583   Bow Down. *(tracks into the next selection)*

WET WILLIE
1974   KEEP ON SMILIN'
(S) (3:23)   Priority 7995   Country's Greatest Hits: Southern Country Rock Volume 2. *(45 version)*
(S) (3:23)   Priority 8663   The South Rules/70's Greatest Rock Hits Volume 2. *(45 version)*
(S) (3:31)   Rhino 70760   Super Hits Of The 70's Volume 13. *(:08 longer fade than the 45 version)*
(S) (3:31)   Rhino 70586   Rebel Rousers: Southern Rock Classics. *(:08 longer fade than the 45 version)*
(S) (3:53)   K-Tel 30522   Elvin Bishop/Wet Willie. *(LP version)*
(S) (3:52)   Polydor 835116   Greatest Hits. *(LP version)*
(S) (3:23)   Time-Life SOD-07   Sounds Of The Seventies - 1974. *(45 version)*
(S) (3:55)   Polydor 314519606   Best Of. *(LP version)*
(S) (3:54)   Rebound 314520256   Best Of Southern Rock. *(LP version)*
(S) (3:54)   Rebound 314520247   Class Reunion 1974. *(LP version)*

WET WILLIE *(Continued)*

(S) (3:54) Rebound 314520202 Greatest Hits. *(LP version)*
(S) (3:56) K-Tel 6083 Southern Fried Rock - Second Helping. *(LP version)*
(S) (3:54) Rebound 314520290 Allman Brothers/Wet Willie Back To Back. *(LP version)*
(S) (3:54) Capricorn 314536134 Keep On Smilin'. *(LP version)*
(S) (3:55) Critique 15467 Fast Cars And Southern Stars. *(LP version)*
(S) (3:54) Simitar 55152 Blue Eyed Soul. *(LP version)*

1978 STREET CORNER SERENADE
(S) (3:42) Rhino 72298 Superhits Of The 70's Volume 24.

1979 WEEKEND
(S) (6:03) Ripete 2183-RE Ocean Drive Volume 1. *(LP version)*

WHAM! (see GEORGE MICHAEL)

WHEN IN ROME
1988 THE PROMISE
(S) (3:39) K-Tel 3343 The 80's Hot Dance Trax.
(S) (3:38) EMI 32694 Living In Oblivion - The 80's Greatest Hits Volume Five.
(S) (3:39) Priority 53765 Rock Of The 80's Volume 9.
(S) (3:38) Virgin 90994 and 86084 When In Rome.

WHISPERS
1980 AND THE BEAT GOES ON
(S) (7:36) Epic 46087 Club Epic. *(remix)*
(S) (3:55) Priority 7976 Mega-Hits Dance Classics Volume 6. *(edit of LP version in an unsuccessful attempt to recreate the 45 version)*
(S) (5:54) Thump 9956 Old School Funk. *(all selections on this cd are segued together; edit of LP version)*
(S) (4:51) Solar/Right Stuff 57604 Greatest Hits. *(neither the 45 or LP version)*

1980 LADY
(dj copies of this 45 ran (3:29) and (5:05); commercial copies were all (5:05))
(S) (5:03) Rhino 71618 Soul Train Hall Of Fame/20th Anniversary.
(S) (5:03) Right Stuff/Solar 52273 Greatest Slow Jams.
(S) (3:40) Solar/Right Stuff 57604 Greatest Hits. *(neither the 45 or LP version)*

1981 IT'S A LOVE THING
(S) (3:45) Solar/Right Stuff 57604 Greatest Hits. *(45 version)*
(S) (5:09) Solar/Right Stuff 57534 Imagination. *(LP version)*
(S) (3:43) Thump 9960 Old School Funk II. *(45 version)*

1987 ROCK STEADY
(S) (4:47) Solar/Epic 75303 Just Gets Better With Time. *(LP version)*
(S) (4:47) Right Stuff/Solar 53040 Just Gets Better With Time. *(LP version)*
(S) (4:40) Thump 9956 Old School Funk. *(all selections on this cd are segued together; LP version)*
(S) (4:46) Solar/Right Stuff 57604 Greatest Hits. *(LP version)*

WHISTLE
1990 ALWAYS AND FOREVER

IAN WHITCOMB
1965 YOU TURN ME ON (TURN ON SONG)
(M) (2:42) Rhino 70322 History Of British Rock Volume 4.
(M) (2:42) Rhino 70319 History Of British Rock Box Set.
(M) (2:42) Rhino 72008 History Of British Rock Volumes 1-4 Box Set.
(M) (2:37) Original Sound CDGO-4 Golden Oldies Volume. 4.
(M) (2:40) Time-Life 2CLR-23 Classic Rock - 1965: Blowin' Your Mind.
(M) (2:37) K-Tel 3629 Madcap Melodies.
(M) (2:41) Sundazed 11044 You Turn Me On/Ian Whitcomb's Mod, Mod Music Hall.
(M) (2:42) Varese Sarabande 5897 Very Best Of.

BARRY WHITE
1973 I'M GONNA LOVE YOU JUST A LITTLE MORE BABY
(actual LP time is (7:07) not (7:20) as stated on the record label; actual 45 time is (4:08) not (3:58) as stated on the record label)
(S) (4:08) Rhino 70551 Soul Hits Of The 70's Volume 11. *(45 version)*
(S) (4:10) Casablanca 822782 Greatest Hits. *(45 version)*
(S) (3:55) K-Tel 30572 Barry White/Isaac Hayes. *(45 version)*
(S) (7:07) Mercury 314514143 Just For You. *(LP version)*
(S) (3:59) Mercury 314522459 All-Time Greatest Hits. *(45 version)*
(S) (7:09) Mercury 814836 I've Got So Much To Give. *(LP version)*
(S) (4:06) K-Tel 6013 70's Soul - Sexy Ballads. *(45 version)*
(S) (4:08) Rhino 72115 Billboard Hot Soul Hits - 1973. *(45 version)*
(S) (4:07) Time-Life R838-08 Solid Gold Soul - 1973. *(45 version)*
(S) (4:08) Time-Life R834-04 Body Talk - Together Forever. *(45 version)*
(S) (3:58) Rebound 314520447 Soul Classics - Best Of The 70's. *(45 version faded :10 early)*
(S) (3:52) K-Tel 3911 Fantastic Volume 2. *(45 version faded :16 early)*

1973 I'VE GOT SO MUCH TO GIVE
(dj copies of this 45 were issued in two lengths - one ran (3:37) not (3:27) as stated on the record label and the other ran (5:17) not (5:02) as stated on the record label; commercial 45's were all (5:15) not (5:02) as stated on the record label)
(S) (3:06) Casablanca 822782 Greatest Hits. *(neither the 45 or LP version)*
(S) (8:10) Mercury 314514143 Just For You. *(LP version)*
(S) (5:17) Mercury 314522459 All-Time Greatest Hits. *(45 version)*
(S) (8:13) Mercury 814836 I've Got So Much To Give. *(LP version)*
(S) (5:16) Rebound 314520033 Quiet Storm: The 70's. *(45 version)*
(S) (3:31) Rebound 314520367 Soul Classics - Quiet Storm/The 70's. *(this is the dj 45 edit)*
(S) (5:16) Rebound 314520358 Barry White And The Love Unlimited Orchestra Back To Back: Their Greatest Hits. *(45 version)*

1974 NEVER, NEVER GONNA GIVE YOU UP
(dj copies of this 45 ran (3:58) and (4:44); commercial copies were all (3:58))
(S) (4:00) K-Tel 30572 Barry White/Isaac Hayes. *(45 version)*
(S) (4:47) Casablanca 822782 Greatest Hits. *(dj 45 edit)*
(S) (7:58) Mercury 314514143 Just For You. *(LP version)*
(S) (4:07) Mercury 314522459 All-Time Greatest Hits. *(:09 longer than the commercial 45 version)*
(S) (4:46) Right Stuff 29138 Slow Jams: The 70's Vol. 3. *(dj 45 edit)*
(S) (7:53) Mercury 836516 Stone Gon'. *(LP version)*
(S) (7:56) Capitol 32438 O.S.T. Dead Presidents. *(LP version)*
(S) (4:06) Rebound 314520432 Disco Nights Vol. XI - Disco's Leading Men. *(:08 longer than the commercial 45 version)*
(S) (4:46) Time-Life R834-12 Body Talk - By Candlelight. *(dj 45 edit)*
(S) (4:46) Time-Life R840-05 Sounds Of The Seventies: '70s Dance Party 1972-1974. *(dj 45 edit)*

1974 HONEY PLEASE, CAN'T YA SEE
(S) (3:11) Casablanca 822782 Greatest Hits. *(45 version)*
(S) (5:09) Mercury 314514143 Just For You. *(LP version)*
(S) (3:13) Mercury 314522459 All-Time Greatest Hits. *(45 version)*
(S) (5:10) Mercury 836516 Stone Gon'. *(LP version)*

1974 CAN'T GET ENOUGH OF YOUR LOVE, BABE
(actual 45 time is (3:24) not (3:15) as stated on the record label)
(S) (3:21) K-Tel 30572 Barry White/Isaac Hayes. *(45 version)*

(S) (4:28) Casablanca 822782 Greatest Hits. *(LP version)*
(S) (4:29) Mercury 314514143 Just For You. *(LP version)*
(S) (4:02) Razor & Tie 22047 Sweet 70's Soul. *(neither the 45 or LP version)*
(S) (3:44) Time-Life SOD-15 Sounds Of The Seventies - 1974: Take Two. *(neither the 45 or LP version)*
(S) (3:51) Mercury 314522459 All-Time Greatest Hits. *(:27 longer than the 45 version)*
(S) (4:28) Rebound 314520307 Disco Nights Volume VIII. *(LP version)*
(S) (4:28) Polygram Special Markets 314520271 Hits Of The 70's. *(LP version)*
(S) (3:42) Rhino 72116 Billboard Hot Soul Hits - 1974. *(neither the 45 or LP version)*
(S) (3:21) Rebound 314520358 Barry White And The Love Unlimited Orchestra Back To Back: Their Greatest Hits. *(45 version)*
(S) (4:29) Mercury 314532165 Can't Get Enough. *(LP version)*
(S) (3:43) Time-Life SOD-09 Solid Gold Soul - 1974. *(neither the 45 or LP version)*
(S) (4:28) Time-Life R834-07 Body Talk - Hearts In Motion. *(LP version)*
(S) (4:04) Chronicles 314553405 Non-Stop Disco Vol. 2. *(all songs on this cd are segued together)*
(S) (3:52) Polydor 314555120 Pure Disco 2. *(:28 longer than the 45 version)*
(S) (3:21) Beast 53442 Original Players Of Love. *(45 version)*
(S) (3:42) Rhino 72943 VH1 8-Track Flashback: Classic '70s Soul. *(neither the 45 or LP version)*

1975 YOU'RE THE FIRST, THE LAST, MY EVERYTHING (actual 45 time is (3:30) not (3:25) as stated on the record label)
(S) (3:31) K-Tel 30572 Barry White/Isaac Hayes. *(45 version)*
(S) (4:33) Casablanca 822782 Greatest Hits. *(LP version)*
(S) (4:53) Mercury 314514143 Just For You. *(LP version;time includes :19 of studio talk)*
(S) (4:33) Scotti Brothers 75405 There Is Still Love (The Anniversary Songs). *(LP version)*
(S) (3:31) Time-Life SOD-16 Sounds Of The Seventies - 1975: Take Two. *(45 version)*
(S) (3:24) Mercury 314522459 All-Time Greatest Hits. *(edit of the LP version)*
(S) (4:32) Rebound 314520265 Dance Fever. *(LP version)*
(S) (3:31) Ripete 5151 Ocean Drive 4. *(45 version)*
(S) (3:31) MCA 11329 Soul Train 25th Anniversary Box Set. *(45 version)*
(S) (4:32) Mercury 314532165 Can't Get Enough. *(LP version)*
(S) (3:23) Polydor 314535877 Pure Disco. *(edit of the LP version)*
(S) (4:33) Time-Life R840-06 Sounds Of The Seventies: '70s Dance Party 1975-1976. *(LP version)*

1975 WHAT AM I GONNA DO WITH YOU
(S) (3:32) Casablanca 822782 Greatest Hits.
(S) (3:35) Mercury 314514143 Just For You.
(S) (3:33) Mercury 314522459 All-Time Greatest Hits.
(S) (3:36) Mercury 314532166 Just Another Way To Say I Love You.

1975 I'LL DO FOR YOU ANYTHING YOU WANT ME TO
(S) (4:09) Mercury 314514143 Just For You. *(45 version)*
(S) (4:09) Mercury 314522459 All-Time Greatest Hits. *(45 version)*
(S) (6:07) Mercury 314532166 Just Another Way To Say I Love You. *(LP version)*

1976 LET THE MUSIC PLAY
(S) (3:33) Casablanca 822783 Greatest Hits Volume 2. *(45 version)*
(S) (6:15) Mercury 314514143 Just For You. *(LP version)*
(S) (3:30) Mercury 314522459 All-Time Greatest Hits. *(45 version)*
(S) (3:30) Rebound 314520317 Class Reunion 1975. *(45 version)*
(S) (3:30) Rebound 314520368 Class Reunion '76. *(45 version)*
(S) (6:14) Mercury 314532167 Let The Music Play. *(LP version)*

(S) (3:30) Polygram Special Markets 314520446 Soul Hits Of The 70's. *(45 version)*

1977 IT'S ECSTASY WHEN YOU LAY DOWN NEXT TO ME
(S) (3:22) K-Tel 30572 Barry White/Isaac Hayes. *(45 version)*
(S) (6:54) Casablanca 822783 Greatest Hits Volume 2. *(LP version)*
(S) (6:57) Mercury 314514143 Just For You. *(LP version)*
(S) (3:33) Time-Life SOD-17 Sounds Of The Seventies - 1977: Take Two. *(45 version)*
(S) (3:25) Mercury 314522459 All-Time Greatest Hits. *(45 version)*
(S) (6:54) Mercury 314532935 Sings For Someone You Love. *(LP version)*
(S) (3:32) Time-Life R838-16 Solid Gold Soul 1977. *(45 version)*
(S) (3:32) Time-Life R834-13 Body Talk - Just The Two Of Us. *(45 version)*

1978 OH WHAT A NIGHT FOR DANCING
(S) (3:14) Casablanca 822783 Greatest Hits Volume 2. *(45 version)*
(S) (3:54) Mercury 314514143 Just For You. *(LP version)*
(S) (3:15) Mercury 314522459 All-Time Greatest Hits. *(45 version)*
(S) (3:14) Rebound 314520358 Barry White And The Love Unlimited Orchestra Back To Back: Their Greatest Hits. *(45 version)*
(S) (3:55) Mercury 314532935 Sings For Someone You Love. *(LP version)*

released as by QUINCY JONES featuring AL B. SURE!/ JAMES INGRAM/EL DeBARGE/BARRY WHITE:
1990 THE SECRET GARDEN
(S) (6:39) Qwest/Warner Brothers 26020 Quincy Jones - Back On The Block.
(S) (6:45) Mercury 314514143 Barry White - Just For You. *(includes a :06 previously unreleased introduction by Barry White)*

released as by BARRY WHITE:
1994 PRACTICE WHAT YOU PREACH
(S) (5:57) A&M 314540115 The Icon Is Love.
(S) (5:56) EMI-Capitol Music Group 54548 Smooth Luv.
(S) (4:00) Polygram TV 314553641 Pure Soul 1997.

KARYN WHITE
released as by JEFF LORBER featuring KARYN WHITE:
1987 FACTS OF LOVE
(S) (4:32) Warner Brothers 25492 Jeff Lorber - Private Passion.

released as by KARYN WHITE:
1989 THE WAY YOU LOVE ME
(S) (3:48) JCI 3124 Rhythm Of The Night. *(45 version)*
(S) (4:54) K-Tel 842 Hot Ladies Of The 80's. *(LP version)*
(S) (4:54) Warner Brothers 25637 Karyn White. *(LP version)*
(S) (3:43) JCI 3186 1985 - Only Love - 1989. *(45 version)*
(S) (4:54) Cold Front 3832 Club Mix - Women Of Dance Vol. 1. *(LP version)*

1989 SUPERWOMAN
(S) (5:47) Warner Brothers 25637 Karyn White. *(LP version)*
(S) (4:31) Rhino 72159 Black Entertainment Television - 15th Anniversary. *(45 version)*
(S) (4:12) JCI 3177 1985 - Only Soul - 1989. *(neither the 45 or LP version)*
(S) (4:31) Warner Brothers 46130 Love Jams Volume Two. *(45 version)*
(S) (4:30) Razor & Tie 4569 '90s Style. *(45 version)*

1989 SECRET RENDEZVOUS (actual 45 time is (4:06) not (3:58) as stated on the record label)
(S) (5:36) Warner Brothers 25637 Karyn White. *(LP version)*
(S) (4:09) JCI 3150 1985 - Only Dance - 1989. *(45 version)*

1991 ROMANTIC
(S) (4:05) Warner Brothers 26320 Ritual Of Love.

1992 THE WAY I FEEL ABOUT YOU
(S) (4:33) Warner Brothers 26320 Ritual Of Love.

TONY JOE WHITE
1969 POLK SALAD ANNIE
- (S) (3:42) JCI 3101 Rockin' Sixties. *(missing the "4" countoff on the introduction)*
- (S) (3:41) Warner Brothers 25966 Swingin' Country Favorites. *(missing the "4" countoff on the introduction)*
- (S) (3:40) Warner Brothers 45305 Best Of. *(missing the "4" countoff on the introduction)*
- (S) (3:42) Time-Life 2CLR-12 Classic Rock - 1969: The Beat Goes On. *(missing the "4" countoff on the introduction)*
- (S) (3:40) Sony Music Special Products 66106 The Monument Story. *(missing the "4" countoff on introduction)*

WHITE LION
1988 WAIT
- (S) (4:00) Atlantic 81908 Classic Rock 1966-1988.
- (S) (4:01) Foundation/WEA 26096 Super Sessions Volume One.
- (S) (4:00) Time-Life R105-40 Rock Dreams.
- (S) (4:00) Atlantic 81768 Pride.
- (S) (4:00) Atlantic 82425 Best Of.
- (S) (4:01) Time-Life R968-18 Guitar Rock - The Heavy '80s.
- (S) (4:00) Rhino 72293 Heavy Metal Hits Of The 80's Volume 3.
- (S) (4:00) Madacy Entertainment 1988 Rock On 1988.
- (S) (3:59) JCI 3144 18 Headbangers From The 80's.
- (S) (4:01) Time-Life R988-19 Sounds Of The Eighties: The Late '80s.
- (S) (3:59) K-Tel 3883 The 80's: Glam Rock.
- (S) (3:59) Simitar 55762 Stud Rock - Wild Ride.

1989 WHEN THE CHILDREN CRY
(actual 45 time is (4:03) not (4:20) as stated on the record label)
- (S) (4:16) JCI 4545 Masters Of Metal: Thunder 'N Spice. *(LP version)*
- (S) (4:03) JCI 3128 1985 - Only Rock 'N Roll - 1989. *(45 version)*
- (S) (4:18) Atlantic 81768 Pride. *(LP version)*
- (S) (4:18) Atlantic 82425 Best Of. *(LP version)*
- (S) (4:18) Priority 50938 Best Of 80's Metal Volume Three: Bang Your Head. *(LP version)*
- (S) (4:04) Time-Life R988-13 Sounds Of The Eighties: 1989. *(45 version)*

WHITE PLAINS
1970 MY BABY LOVES LOVIN'
(actual 45 time is (2:49) not (2:28) as stated on the record label; the LP time is (3:04))
- (S) (2:57) Rhino 70922 Super Hits Of The 70's Volume 2.
- (S) (2:57) Rhino 72009 Super Hits Of The 70's Volumes 1-4 Box Set.
- (S) (2:57) Rhino 71205 70's Smash Hits Volume 1.
- (S) (2:55) Time-Life SOD-31 Sounds Of The Seventies - AM Top Twenty.
- (S) (2:57) Varese Sarabande 5575 Bubblegum Classics Volume Two.
- (S) (2:56) Ripete 2187-RE Preppy Deluxe.
- (S) (2:45) Mother 314516937 O.S.T. The Adventures Of Priscilla - Queen Of The Desert.
- (S) (2:56) Varese Sarabande 5725 Love Grows (Where My Rosemary Goes) - The Voice Of Tony Burrows.
- (S) (2:44) Special Music 5041 Great Britons! Volume Three.
- (S) (2:57) Flashback 72682 '70s Radio Hits Volume 2.
- (S) (2:57) Flashback 72090 '70s Radio Hits Box Set.

WHITESNAKE
1987 HERE I GO AGAIN
- (S) (4:33) Rebound 314520257 Hard Rock Essentials - The 80's. *(LP version)*
- (S) (4:34) Geffen 24099 Whitesnake. *(LP version)*
- (S) (4:33) Time-Life R988-09 Sounds Of The Eighties: 1987. *(LP version)*
- (S) (4:34) Time-Life R968-18 Guitar Rock - The Heavy '80s. *(LP version*
- (S) (3:53) Geffen 24833 Time's Makin' Changes: Best Of. *(45 version)*
- (S) (5:08) Geffen 24173 Saints & Sinners. *(original LP version but not the "hit" LP version)*
- (S) (4:34) Priority 50937 Best Of 80's Metal Volume Two: Bang Your Head. *(LP version)*
- (S) (3:53) K-Tel 3883 The 80's: Glam Rock. *(45 version)*
- (S) (3:52) K-Tel 3866 The 80's: Number One Pop Hits. *(45 version)*
- (S) (4:34) Hip-O 40080 Essential '80s: 1985-1989. *(LP version)*
- (S) (4:34) JCI 3193 18 Rock Classics Volume 3. *(LP version)*
- (S) (4:33) Razor & Tie 89004 Monsters Of Rock. *(LP version)*

1987 IS THIS LOVE
- (S) (4:40) Time-Life R105-40 Rock Dreams. *(LP version)*
- (S) (4:42) JCI 3135 14 Original Metal Ballads. *(LP version)*
- (S) (4:42) Geffen 24099 Whitesnake. *(LP version)*
- (S) (4:43) Geffen 24833 Time's Makin' Changes: Best Of. *(LP version)*
- (S) (4:40) Rhino 72579 Feel Like Makin' Love - Romantic Power Ballads. *(LP version)*
- (S) (4:43) Time-Life R988-19 Sounds Of The Eighties: The Late '80s. *(LP version)*
- (S) (4:43) Geffen 25151 Geffen Vintage 80s Vol. II. *(LP version)*
- (S) (4:44) MCA Special Products 21028 The Best Of Hard Rock. *(LP version)*
- (S) (4:43) Simitar 55762 Stud Rock - Wild Ride. *(LP version)*
- (S) (4:39) Time-Life R834-18 Body Talk - Romantic Moments. *(LP version)*

1989 FOOL FOR YOUR LOVING
- (S) (4:10) Geffen 24249 Slip Of The Tongue.
- (S) (4:09) Geffen 24833 Time's Makin' Changes: Best Of.
- (S) (4:10) Simitar 55772 Stud Rock - Rock Me.

1990 THE DEEPER THE LOVE
- (S) (4:22) Geffen 24249 Slip Of The Tongue.
- (S) (4:22) Geffen 24833 Time's Makin' Changes: Best Of.
- (S) (4:19) Time-Life R968-25 Guitar Rock - The '90s.

WHITE TOWN
1997 YOUR WOMAN
- (S) (4:17) Chrysalis/EMI 56129 Women In Technology.
- (S) (3:12) Tommy Boy 1207 MTV Grind Volume One. *(all selections on this cd are segued together)*

MARGARET WHITING
1966 THE WHEEL OF HURT

ROGER WHITTAKER
1975 THE LAST FAREWELL
- (S) (3:38) RCA 5166 Best Of.
- (S) (3:40) RCA 0855 The Last Farewell.
- (S) (3:57) RCA 61986 Greatest Hits. *(alternate take)*
- (S) (3:40) Time-Life R974-02 Many Moods Of Romance - My Heart Reminds Me.
- (S) (3:40) Time-Life R814-05 Love Songs.

WHO
1967 HAPPY JACK
- (E) (2:11) MCA 31331 A Quick One (Happy Jack).
- (M) (2:12) MCA 37001 Meaty Beaty Big And Bouncy.
- (M) (2:08) MCA 1496 Greatest Hits.
- (M) (2:11) MCA 8031 Who's Better, Who's Best.
- (S) (2:11) MCA 6899 The Kids Are Alright. *(live)*
- (M) (2:11) MCA 11020 Thirty Years Of Maximum R&B.
- (M) (2:51) MCA 11267 A Quick One. *(acoustic version)*
- (M) (2:11) MCA 11462 My Generation - Very Best Of.

1967 I CAN SEE FOR MILES
- (M) (4:01) MCA 12001 Hooligans.
- (S) (4:05) MCA 31332 Sell Out. *(most selections on this cd are segued together)*
- (S) (4:05) MCA 37001 Meaty Beaty Big And Bouncy.
- (S) (4:06) MCA 8031 Who's Better, Who's Best.

(S) (4:16) MCA 6899 The Kids Are Alright.
(S) (4:03) Time-Life R102-34 The Rolling Stone Collection.
(S) (4:14) MCA 11020 Thirty Years Of Maximum R&B. *(tracks into next selection)*
(S) (4:18) MCA 11268 Who Sell Out. *(previous selection tracks over introduction)*
(S) (4:09) MCA 11241 O.S.T. Apollo 13. *(all selections on this cd are segued together; track selection numbers on the cd jacket are incorrect; this cd is a disaster)*
(S) (4:21) MCA 11462 My Generation - Very Best Of.

1968 CALL ME LIGHTNING
(E) (2:23) MCA 31333 Magic Bus.
(M) (2:19) MCA 11020 Thirty Years Of Maximum R&B.

1968 MAGIC BUS
(S) (3:17) MCA 31333 Magic Bus.
(S) (3:19) MCA 37001 Meaty Beaty Big And Bouncy.
(M) (3:20) MCA 1496 Greatest Hits.
(S) (3:17) MCA 8031 Who's Better, Who's Best.
(E) (3:21) MCA 6899 The Kids Are Alright.
(M) (3:15) MCA 11020 Thirty Years Of Maximum R&B.
(M) (3:15) MCA 11462 My Generation - Very Best Of.
(S) (7:34) Epic 67910 O.S.T. Jerry Maguire. *(live)*
(E) (3:15) Play-Tone/Epic 69179 Music From The HBO Miniseries "From The Earth To The Moon". *(hum noticeable at the end of every song on this cd)*

1969 PINBALL WIZARD
(S) (2:59) MCA 12001 Hooligans.
(S) (2:58) MCA 37001 Meaty Beaty Big And Bouncy.
(M) (2:59) MCA 1496 Greatest Hits.
(S) (3:00) MCA 2-10005 Tommy.
(S) (2:59) MCA 8031 Who's Better, Who's Best.
(S) (2:47) MCA 6899 The Kids Are Alright. *(live)*
(S) (3:00) MFSL 533 Tommy. *(gold disc)*
(S) (3:00) MCA 10801 Tommy.
(S) (2:59) MCA 11020 Thirty Years Of Maximum R&B. *(previous selection tracks over the introduction)*
(S) (3:00) MCA 11417 Tommy. *(remastered edition; different guitar bridge from 2:14-2:28 than appeared on the original 45 or LP)*
(S) (3:00) MCA 11462 My Generation - Very Best Of. *(different guitar bridge from 2:14- 2:28 than appeared on the original 45 or LP)*
(S) (3:00) Time-Life R13610 Gold And Platinum Box Set - The Ultimate Rock Collection.

1969 I'M FREE
(S) (2:38) MCA 2-10005 Tommy.
(S) (2:38) MCA 8031 Who's Better, Who's Best.
(S) (2:38) MFSL 533 Tommy. *(gold disc)*
(S) (2:38) MCA 10801 Tommy.
(S) (2:36) MCA 11020 Thirty Years Of Maximum R&B. *(tracks into the next selection)*
(S) (2:40) MCA 11417 Tommy. *(remastered edition)*

1970 THE SEEKER
(S) (3:11) MCA 37001 Meaty Beaty Big And Bouncy.
(S) (3:10) MCA 1496 Greatest Hits.
(S) (3:21) MCA 11020 Thirty Years Of Maximum R&B. *(previously unreleased version)*
(S) (3:23) MCA 11462 My Generation - Very Best Of. *(previously unreleased version)*

1970 SUMMERTIME BLUES
(S) (3:22) MCA 12001 Hooligans. *(45 version)*
(S) (3:29) MCA 37000 Live At Leeds. *(LP version)*
(S) (3:33) MCA 11020 Thirty Years Of Maximum R&B. *(LP version)*
(S) (3:21) MCA 11215 and 11230 Live At Leeds. *(remastered edition; LP version)*
(M) (3:13) MCA 11718 Odds & Sods. *(remastered edition; studio version)*

1970 SEE ME, FEEL ME
(S) (3:30) MCA 8031 Who's Better, Who's Best. *(:10 longer than the 45 version)*
(S) (7:00) MCA 2-10005 Tommy. *(this track is only part of the selection known as "WE'RE NOT GONNA TAKE IT"; starts at 3:28 and ends at 7:00, about :12 longer than the 45 version)*

(S) (7:04) MFSL 533 Tommy. *(this track is only part of the selection known as "WE'RE NOT GONNA TAKE IT"; starts at 3:28 and ends at 7:04, about :16 longer than the 45 version; gold disc)*
(S) (5:25) MCA 6899 The Kids Are Alright. *(live)*
(S) (7:03) MCA 10801 Tommy. *(this track is only part of the selection known as "WE'RE NOT GONNA TAKE IT"; starts at 3:28 and ends at 7:03, about :15 longer than the 45 version)*
(S) (3:31) MCA 11020 Thirty Years Of Maximum R&B. *(live)*
(S) (7:06) MCA 11417 Tommy. *(remastered edition; this track is only part of the selection known as "WE'RE NOT GONNA TAKE IT"; starts at 3:29 and ends at 7:06; about :17 longer than the 45 version)*

1971 WON'T GET FOOLED AGAIN
(S) (8:30) MCA 1496 Greatest Hits. *(LP version)*
(S) (8:29) MCA 37217 Who's Next. *(LP version)*
(S) (3:36) MCA 8031 Who's Better, Who's Best. *(45 version)*
(S) (9:48) MCA 6899 The Kids Are Alright. *(live)*
(S) (8:27) Time-Life R102-34 The Rolling Stone Collection. *(LP version)*
(S) (8:31) MCA 11020 Thirty Years Of Maximum R&B. *(LP version)*
(S) (8:32) MCA 11312 Who's Next. *(gold disc; LP version)*
(S) (8:31) MCA 11269 Who's Next. *(remastered edition)*
(S) (8:32) MCA 11462 My Generation - Very Best Of. *(LP version)*
(S) (8:32) Time-Life R13610 Gold And Platinum Box Set - The Ultimate Rock Collection. *(LP version)*

1971 BEHIND BLUE EYES
(S) (3:38) MCA 12001 Hooligans.
(S) (3:40) MCA 37217 Who's Next.
(S) (3:36) MCA 11020 Thirty Years Of Maximum R&B. *(tracks into next selection)*
(S) (3:41) MCA 11312 Who's Next. *(gold disc)*
(S) (3:40) MCA 11269 Who's Next. *(remastered edition; contains some additional background vocals not found on any previous vinyl or cd release)*
(S) (3:25) MCA 11269 Who's Next. *(remastered edition; alternate take)*

1972 JOIN TOGETHER
(S) (4:20) MCA 12001 Hooligans.
(S) (4:18) MCA 8031 Who's Better, Who's Best.
(S) (4:17) MCA 11020 Thirty Years Of Maximum R&B. *(tracks into next selection; contains an extra flute overdub on the ending not on the original 45 or LP version)*
(S) (4:22) MCA 11462 My Generation - Very Best Of. *(contains an extra flute overdub on the ending not found on the original 45 or LP version)*

1973 THE RELAY
(S) (3:27) MCA 12001 Hooligans. *("Hooligans" vinyl LP version which is :25 shorter than the 45)*
(S) (3:44) MCA 1496 Greatest Hits. *(:08 shorter than the 45)*
(S) (4:00) MCA 11020 Thirty Years Of Maximum R&B. *(previous selection tracks over introduction; :08 longer fade than the 45)*

1976 SQUEEZE BOX
(S) (2:40) MCA 1496 Greatest Hits.
(S) (2:40) MCA 37002 The Who By Numbers.
(S) (2:40) MCA 12001 Hooligans.
(S) (2:39) MCA 8031 Who's Better, Who's Best.
(S) (2:38) MCA 11020 Thirty Years Of Maximum R&B. *(tracks into next selection)*
(S) (2:40) MCA 11462 My Generation - Very Best Of.
(S) (2:40) MCA 11493 By The Numbers. *(remastered edition)*

1978 WHO ARE YOU
(S) (6:22) MCA 37003 Who Are You. *(LP version)*
(S) (5:02) MCA 1496 Greatest Hits. *(edit of LP version)*
(S) (6:20) MCA 12001 Hooligans. *(LP version)*
(S) (5:02) MCA 8031 Who's Better, Who's Best. *(edit of LP version)*
(S) (6:22) MFSL 561 Who Are You. *(LP version; gold disc)*
(S) (4:58) MCA 11020 Thirty Years Of Maximum R&B. *(edit of LP version)*

WHO (Continued)

- (S) (4:58) MCA 11462 My Generation - Very Best Of. *(edit of LP version)*
- (S) (6:16) MCA 11492 Who Are You. *(remastered edition; LP version)*
- (S) (6:19) MCA 11492 Who Are You. *(remastered edition; previously unreleased version)*

1981 YOU BETTER YOU BET
- (S) (5:37) MCA 25987 Face Dances. *(LP version)*
- (S) (5:36) MCA 8031 Who's Better, Who's Best. *(LP version)*
- (S) (5:34) Sandstone 33044 and 5010 Rock The First Volume 4. *(LP version)*
- (S) (5:30) MCA 11020 Thirty Years Of Maximum R&B. *(tracks into next selection; LP version)*
- (S) (5:37) MCA 11462 My Generation - Very Best Of. *(LP version)*
- (S) (5:35) MCA 11634 Face Dances. *(remastered edition; LP version)*

1982 ATHENA
- (S) (3:46) MCA 25986 It's Hard.
- (S) (3:46) MCA 11635 It's Hard. *(remastered edition)*

JANE WIEDLIN
1988 RUSH HOUR
- (S) (4:01) EMI Manhattan 48683 Fur.

HARLOW WILCOX and THE OAKIES
1969 GROOVY GRUBWORM
- (E) (2:10) K-Tel 3096 Classic Country Instrumentals. *(sounds like it was mastered from vinyl)*

WILD CHERRY
1976 PLAY THAT FUNKY MUSIC
(dj copies of this 45 were issued in both a censored version which eliminated the words "white boy" and an uncensored version which left those words intact; commercial copies were all uncensored)
- (S) (4:55) Epic 46940 O.S.T. Queens Logic. *(LP version)*
- (S) (3:12) Priority 7975 Mega-Hits Dance Classics Volume 5. *(censored dj 45 version)*
- (S) (3:15) Rhino 70671 Billboard Top Hits - 1976. *(uncensored lyrics but this is an improper edit of the LP version in an attempt to recreate the 45 version)*
- (S) (4:59) Epic 34195 Wild Cherry. *(LP version)*
- (S) (3:15) Rhino 71433 In Yo Face! History Of Funk Volume 3. *(uncensored 45 lyrics but this is an improper edit of the LP version in an attempt to recreate the 45 version)*
- (S) (4:56) Razor & Tie 21640 Those Fabulous 70's. *(LP version)*
- (S) (3:15) Time-Life SOD-04 Sounds Of The Seventies - 1976. *(uncensored 45 lyrics but this is an improper edit of the LP version in an attempt to recreate the 45 version)*
- (S) (4:53) JCI 3131 1975 - Only Rock 'N Roll - 1979. *(LP version)*
- (S) (4:56) Risky Business 66914 Party On. *(LP version)*
- (S) (4:58) Thump 4040 Old School Volume 4. *(LP version)*
- (S) (4:58) Epic 67506 Club Epic Volume 4. *(LP version)*
- (S) (4:58) Priority 50956 Mega Hits - Disco Heat. *(LP version)*
- (S) (4:55) Eclipse Music Group 64895 Rock 'n Roll Relix 1976-1977. *(LP version)*
- (S) (4:55) Eclipse Music Group 64897 Rock 'n Roll Relix 1970-1979. *(LP version)*
- (S) (3:15) Rhino 72812 VH1 8-Track Flashback: The One Hit Wonders. *(uncensored 45 lyrics but this is an improper edit of the LP version in an attempt to recreate the 45 version)*
- (S) (3:14) Polydor 314555120 Pure Disco 2. *(uncensored 45 lyrics but this is an improper edit of the LP version in an attempt to recreate the 45 version)*
- (S) (4:59) Epic/Legacy 65504 Disco Super Hits. *(LP version)*
- (S) (3:14) Time-Life R840-06 Sounds Of The Seventies: '70s Dance Party 1975-1976. *(uncensored 45 lyrics but this is an improper edit of the LP version in an attempt to recreate the 45 version)*

- (S) (3:14) K-Tel 4065 K-Tel's Original Party Music Vol. 1. *(uncensored 45 lyrics but this is an improper edit of the LP version in an attempt to recreate the 45 version)*

KIM WILDE
1982 KIDS IN AMERICA
- (S) (3:22) EMI 81417 Living In Oblivion: The 80's Greatest Hits Volume One.
- (S) (3:26) Rhino 71698 New Wave Hits Of The 80's Vol. 5.
- (S) (3:26) EMI 90994 Kim Wilde.
- (S) (3:24) MCA 10972 The Singles Collection 1981-1993.
- (S) (3:25) MCA 11239 You Can Still Rock In America.
- (S) (3:25) Simitar 55552 The Number One's: Eighties Rock.
- (S) (3:25) Time-Life R988-22 Sounds Of The Eighties 1980-1983.

1987 YOU KEEP ME HANGIN' ON
- (S) (4:14) K-Tel 3343 The 80's Hot Dance Trax.
- (S) (4:14) Rhino 71642 Billboard Top Hits - 1987.
- (S) (4:10) Sandstone 33046 and 5012 Rock The First Volume Six.
- (S) (4:13) Time-Life R105-40 Rock Dreams.
- (S) (4:13) Priority 53765 Rock Of The 80's Volume 9.
- (S) (4:14) MCA 5903 Another Step.
- (S) (4:14) MCA 10972 The Singles Collection 1981-1993.
- (S) (4:14) Time-Life R988-09 Sounds Of The Eighties: 1987.
- (S) (4:14) MCA Special Products 20897 Greatest Rock Hits Of The 80's.
- (S) (4:09) Rebound 314520357 World Of Dance - The 80's.
- (S) (4:10) Madacy Entertainment 1987 Rock On 1987.
- (S) (4:14) Hip-O 40004 The '80s Hit(s) Back!
- (S) (4:14) MCA Special Products 21034 Club Disco Dance Hits.
- (S) (4:14) Rhino 72838 Disco Queens: The 80's.
- (S) (4:14) Hollywood 62123 More Music From The Motion Picture "Romy And Michele's High School Reunion".
- (S) (4:13) Cold Front 3865 Club Mix - Women Of Dance Vol. 2.
- (S) (4:14) Hip-O 40075 Rock She Said: On The Pop Side.
- (S) (4:14) Hip-O 40080 Essential '80s: 1985-1989.

MATTHEW WILDER
1983 BREAK MY STRIDE
- (S) (3:02) Risky Business 57469 Don't Touch My 45's/Great Lost Singles Of The 80's.
- (S) (3:01) Priority 53775 Best Of 80's Rock Volume 1.
- (S) (3:05) Private I 39112 I Don't Speak The Language.
- (S) (2:59) Time-Life R988-17 Sounds Of The Eighties: The Mid '80s Take Two.

1984 THE KID'S AMERICAN
- (S) (4:36) Private I 39112 I Don't Speak The Language.

ANDY WILLIAMS
1956 CANADIAN SUNSET
- (M) (2:36) Columbia 40213 16 Most Requested Songs.
- (M) (2:35) Curb 77439 Best Of.
- (M) (2:35) Time-Life HPD-15 Your Hit Parade - 1956.
- (M) (2:35) Varese Sarabande 5578 History Of Cadence Records Volume 1.
- (M) (2:35) Varese Sarabande 5644 Best Of The Cadence Years.

1956 BABY DOLL
- (M) (2:01) Varese Sarabande 5644 Best Of The Cadence Years.

1957 BUTTERFLY
- (M) (2:19) Curb 77439 Best Of.
- (M) (2:21) Time-Life HPD-17 Your Hit Parade - 1957.
- (M) (2:22) Legacy/Columbia 66143 Encore: 16 Most Requested Songs.
- (M) (2:20) Varese Sarabande 5579 History Of Cadence Records Volume 2.
- (M) (2:20) Varese Sarabande 5644 Best Of The Cadence Years.

1957 I LIKE YOUR KIND OF LOVE
- (M) (2:27) Curb 77439 Best Of.
- (M) (2:29) Time-Life HPD-23 Your Hit Parade - The Late 50's.
- (M) (2:28) Varese Sarabande 5644 Best Of The Cadence Years.

1957 LIPS OF WINE
- (M) (2:21) Varese Sarabande 5644 Best Of The Cadence Years.

1958 ARE YOU SINCERE
- (S) (2:44) Curb 77439 Best Of.
- (S) (2:38) Time-Life HPD-11 Your Hit Parade 1958.
- (M) (2:37) Legacy/Columbia 66143 Encore: 16 Most Requested Songs.
- (M) (2:38) Varese Sarabande 5644 Best Of The Cadence Years.

1958 PROMISE ME, LOVE
- (M) (2:21) Varese Sarabande 5644 Best Of The Cadence Years.

1959 THE HAWAIIAN WEDDING SONG
- (E) (2:26) Curb 77532 Your Favorite Songs.
- (S) (2:24) Columbia 40213 16 Most Requested Songs.
- (S) (2:25) Columbia 9979 Greatest Hits.
- (M) (2:26) Curb 77439 Best Of.
- (S) (2:25) Time-Life HPD-13 Your Hit Parade - 1959.
- (S) (2:26) Varese Sarabande 5644 Best Of The Cadence Years.
- (S) (2:25) Columbia/Legacy 65398 Greatest Hits/Greatest Hits Volume 2/Love Story.

1959 LONELY STREET
- (S) (2:44) Columbia 32384 Greatest Hits Volume 2. *(LP version)*
- (E) (2:42) Curb 77439 Best Of. *(LP version)*
- (S) (2:43) Time-Life HPD-13 Your Hit Parade - 1959. *(LP version)*
- (S) (2:41) Legacy/Columbia 66143 Encore: 16 Most Requested Songs. *(LP version)*
- (M) (2:42) Varese Sarabande 5644 Best Of The Cadence Years. *(45 version)*
- (S) (2:44) Columbia/Legacy 65398 Greatest Hits/Greatest Hits Volume 2/Love Story. *(LP version)*
- (S) (2:42) Time-Life R132-10 Love Songs Of Your Hit Parade. *(LP version)*

1960 THE VILLAGE OF ST. BERNADETTE
- (S) (3:19) Columbia 32384 Greatest Hits Volume 2.
- (S) (3:19) Curb 77439 Best Of.
- (S) (3:18) Legacy/Columbia 66143 Encore: 16 Most Requested Songs.
- (S) (3:18) Varese Sarabande 5644 Best Of The Cadence Years.
- (S) (3:19) Columbia/Legacy 65398 Greatest Hits/Greatest Hits Volume 2/Love Story.

1961 THE BILBAO SONG
- (M) (2:11) Curb 77439 Best Of. *(45 version)*
- (S) (2:14) Varese Sarabande 5644 Best Of The Cadence Years. *(LP version)*

1962 STRANGER ON THE SHORE
1963 CAN'T GET USED TO LOSING YOU
- (S) (2:20) Columbia 40213 16 Most Requested Songs.
- (S) (2:20) Columbia 9979 Greatest Hits.
- (S) (2:20) Columbia/Legacy 53572 The Essence Of.
- (S) (2:19) Time-Life HPD-32 Your Hit Parade - Into The 60's.
- (S) (2:20) Time-Life R136-38 Very Best Of.
- (S) (2:20) Nick At Nite/Epic 67148 Donna Reed's Dinner Party.
- (S) (2:20) Hammer & Lace 697124114 Leading Men: Masters Of Style Volume Three.
- (S) (2:20) Columbia/Legacy 65398 Greatest Hits/Greatest Hits Volume 2/Love Story.

1963 DAYS OF WINE AND ROSES
- (S) (2:44) Columbia 40213 16 Most Requested Songs.
- (S) (2:44) Columbia 9979 Greatest Hits.
- (S) (2:43) Columbia/Legacy 57741 Academy Award Winners: 16 Most Requested Songs.
- (S) (2:44) Time-Life R136-38 Very Best Of.
- (S) (2:44) Columbia/Legacy 65398 Greatest Hits/Greatest Hits Volume 2/Love Story.

1963 HOPELESS
1964 A FOOL NEVER LEARNS
- (S) (2:38) Columbia/Legacy 53572 The Essence Of. *(neither the 45 or LP version)*
- (S) (1:55) Time-Life HPD-37 Your Hit Parade - The 60's.

1964 WRONG FOR EACH OTHER
1964 ON THE STREET WHERE YOU LIVE
- (S) (3:08) Legacy/Columbia 66143 Encore: 16 Most Requested Songs.

1965 DEAR HEART
- (S) (2:53) Columbia 40213 16 Most Requested Songs.
- (S) (2:52) Columbia 9979 Greatest Hits.
- (S) (2:53) Columbia/Legacy 53572 The Essence Of.
- (S) (2:53) Time-Life R136-38 Very Best Of.
- (S) (2:52) Time-Life R138-32 Hollywood Hit Parade.
- (S) (2:52) Time-Life R974-01 Many Moods Of Romance - That's My Desire.
- (S) (2:52) Columbia/Legacy 65398 Greatest Hits/Greatest Hits Volume 2/Love Story.

1965 AND ROSES AND ROSES
- (S) (2:22) Time-Life R136-38 Very Best Of.

1965 AIN'T IT TRUE
1967 MUSIC TO WATCH GIRLS BY
- (S) (2:32) Columbia/Legacy 53572 The Essence Of.
- (S) (2:34) Columbia 32384 Greatest Hits Volume 2.
- (S) (2:34) Columbia/Legacy 65398 Greatest Hits/Greatest Hits Volume 2/Love Story.
- (S) (2:34) Legacy/Columbia 66143 Encore: 16 Most Requested Songs.

1968 BATTLE HYMN OF THE REPUBLIC
1969 HAPPY HEART
- (S) (3:11) Columbia 9979 Greatest Hits.
- (S) (3:12) Time-Life R136-38 Very Best Of.
- (S) (3:11) Legacy/Columbia 66143 Encore: 16 Most Requested Songs.
- (S) (3:11) Columbia/Legacy 65398 Greatest Hits/Greatest Hits Volume 2/Love Story.

1971 (WHERE DO I BEGIN) LOVE STORY
- (S) (3:08) Columbia 30497 Love Story.
- (S) (3:11) Columbia 32384 Greatest Hits Volume 2.
- (S) (3:09) Columbia/Legacy 53572 The Essence Of.
- (S) (3:11) Risky Business 66871 Polyester Dreams/Greatest Hits Of The 70's.
- (S) (3:09) Time-Life R136-38 Very Best Of.
- (S) (3:09) Legacy/Columbia 66143 Encore: 16 Most Requested Songs.
- (S) (3:11) K-Tel 3630 Lounge Legends.
- (S) (3:11) Columbia/Legacy 65398 Greatest Hits/Greatest Hits Volume 2/Love Story.
- (S) (3:09) Time-Life R814-03 Love Songs.

1972 LOVE THEME FROM "THE GODFATHER" (SPEAK SOFTLY LOVE)
- (S) (3:00) Columbia 32384 Greatest Hits Volume 2.
- (S) (2:59) Time-Life R136-38 Very Best Of.
- (S) (2:59) Legacy/Columbia 66143 Encore: 16 Most Requested Songs.
- (S) (3:00) Columbia/Legacy 65398 Greatest Hits/Greatest Hits Vol. 2/Love Story.

BILLY WILLIAMS
1957 I'M GONNA SIT RIGHT DOWN AND WRITE MYSELF A LETTER
- (M) (2:07) Time-Life HPD-23 Your Hit Parade - The Late 50's.
- (M) (2:06) MCA 11120 Stardust/The Classic Decca Hits & Standards Collection.
- (M) (2:07) K-Tel 478 More 50's Jukebox Favorites.

1959 NOLA

DANNY WILLIAMS
1964 WHITE ON WHITE
- (S) (2:16) Time-Life HPD-37 Your Hit Parade - The 60's.

DENIECE WILLIAMS
1977 FREE
- (S) (5:57) Columbia 34242 This Is Niecy. *(LP version)*
- (S) (5:59) Thump 4730 Old School Love Songs Volume 3. *(LP version)*
- (S) (5:56) DCC Compact Classics 142 Groove On! Volume 2. *(LP version)*
- (S) (5:56) Columbia/Legacy 64839 Gonna Take A Miracle: Best Of. *(LP version)*
- (S) (5:56) Time-Life R834-20 Body Talk - Heart And Soul. *(LP version)*

released as by JOHNNY MATHIS/DENIECE WILLIAMS:
1978 TOO MUCH, TOO LITTLE, TOO LATE
- (S) (2:54) Columbia 47982 Johnny Mathis - Better Together: The Duet Album.
- (S) (3:00) Columbia 36871 Best Of Johnny Mathis 1975-1980.

(S) (2:55) Columbia 35259 Johnny Mathis: You Light Up My Life.
(S) (2:58) Columbia/Legacy 57899 Johnny Mathis Encore!: 16 Most Requested Songs.
(S) (2:57) Razor & Tie 4543 The '70s Preservation Society Presents: Easy '70s.
(S) (2:54) DCC Compact Classics 104 Duets - A Man & A Woman.
(S) (2:58) Columbia/Legacy 64839 Gonna Take A Miracle: Best Of Deneice Williams.
(S) (2:56) Eclipse Music Group 64896 Rock 'n Roll Relix 1978-1979.
(S) (2:56) Eclipse Music Group 64897 Rock 'n Roll Relix 1970-1979.
(S) (2:57) Time-Life R834-01 Body Talk - Forever Yours.
(S) (2:57) Time-Life R838-17 Solid Gold Soul 1978.
(S) (2:54) Columbia/Legacy 65384 Johnny Mathis - That's What Friends Are For/You Light Up My Life/Better Together: The Duet Album.
(S) (2:58) Columbia/Legacy 65540 The Ultimate Collection.

released as by DENIECE WILLIAMS:
1982 IT'S GONNA TAKE A MIRACLE
(S) (4:08) Original Sound 9304 Art Laboe's Dedicated To You Vol. 4.
(S) (4:09) K-Tel 3263 The 80's Love Jams.
(S) (4:09) Rhino 72137 Billboard Hot R&B Hits 1982.
(S) (4:09) Columbia/Legacy 64839 Gonna Take A Miracle: Best Of.
(S) (4:08) Time-Life R834-09 Body Talk - Magic Moments.
1984 LET'S HEAR IT FOR THE BOY
(S) (4:19) Columbia 39242 O.S.T. Footloose.
(S) (6:00) Columbia 46088 Club Columbia. (12" single version)
(S) (4:16) Priority 53728 Mega-Hits Dance Classics (Volume 12).
(S) (4:17) Rhino 70679 Billboard Top Hits - 1984.
(S) (4:19) Sandstone 33051 and 5019 Cosmopolitan Volume 5.
(S) (4:19) DCC Compact Classics 083 Night Moves Volume 3.
(S) (4:20) Columbia 39366 Let's Hear It For The Boy.
(S) (4:17) Time-Life R988-06 Sounds Of The Eighties: 1984.
(S) (4:17) JCI 3149 1980 - Only Dance - 1984.
(S) (4:19) Columbia/Legacy 64839 Gonna Take A Miracle: Best Of.
(S) (4:20) Priority 50974 Premiere The Movie Magazine Presents The Greatest Soundtrack Hits.
(S) (4:17) Rhino 72838 Disco Queens: The 80's.
(S) (4:15) Cold Front 6255 Greatest Sports Rock And Jams Volume 2. (all selections on this cd are segued together)

DON WILLIAMS
1980 I BELIEVE IN YOU
(S) (4:04) MCA 5944 20 Greatest Hits.
(S) (4:05) MCA 31247 Best Of Volume III.
(S) (4:03) MCA 31122 I Believe In You.
(S) (4:03) MCA 5870 I Believe In You/Especially For You.
(S) (4:04) Priority 9305 Country Gold.
(S) (4:03) Time-Life CCD-03 Contemporary Country - The Early 80's.
(S) (4:05) MCA Special Products 20727 Country's Greatest Legends.
(S) (4:03) K-Tel 3111 Country Music Classics Vol. XIX.
(S) (4:04) MCA 31167 Legends.
(S) (4:04) Rhino 71893 Radio Daze: Pop Hits Of The 80's Volume Four.
(S) (4:04) MCA Special Products 20365 Country's Greatest Hits Volume 2.
(S) (4:03) MCA Special Products 20842 Truckers Jukebox #2.
(S) (4:03) K-Tel 3358 101 Greatest Country Hits Vol. Four: Mellow Country.
(S) (4:04) Hip-O 40042 The Class Of Country 1980-1984.
(S) (4:05) Simitar 55082 80's Country 1980-82.

JOHN WILLIAMS (see also LONDON SYMPHONY ORCHESTRA)
1975 MAIN TITLE (THEME FROM "JAWS")
(S) (2:16) MCA 1660 O.S.T. Jaws.
(S) (2:16) MCA 6330 Soundtrack Smashes - The 80's.
1978 THEME FROM "CLOSE ENCOUNTERS OF THE THIRD KIND"
(S) (3:08) Rhino 72424 Billboard Top Movie Hits - 1970s.
(S) (3:08) Varese Sarabande 5275 O.S.T. Close Encounters Of The Third Kind.
(S) (3:09) Hip-O 40049 Alien Encounters.

LARRY WILLIAMS
1957 SHORT FAT FANNIE
(M) (2:23) Specialty 2109 Here's Larry Williams.
(M) (2:23) Specialty 7002 Bad Boy. (echo added)
(M) (2:22) Specialty 4412 The Specialty Story.
(M) (2:23) Time-Life 2RNR-01 Rock 'N' Roll Era - 1957.
(M) (2:22) Time-Life RHD-08 Rhythm & Blues - 1957. (echo added)
(M) (2:22) Era 511 Ultimate 50's Party.
(M) (2:22) JCI 3188 1955 - Only Dance - 1959.
(M) (2:22) Time-Life R838-23 Solid Gold Soul 1957. (echo added)
1957 BONY MORONIE
(M) (3:05) Rhino 75894 Jukebox Classics Volume 2.
(M) (3:01) JCI 3202 Rockin' Fifties.
(M) (3:04) Specialty 2109 Here's Larry Williams.
(M) (3:06) Specialty 7002 Bad Boy.
(M) (3:06) Specialty 4412 The Specialty Story.
(M) (3:03) Time-Life 2RNR-17 Rock 'N' Roll Era - 1957 Still Rockin'.

MASON WILLIAMS
1968 CLASSICAL GAS
(S) (3:02) Warner Brothers 1729 Phonograph Record.
(S) (2:36) Vanguard 137/38 Music 1968-1971. (rerecording)
(S) (3:02) Rhino 71602 Rock Instrumental Classics Volume 2: The Sixties.
(S) (3:02) Rhino 72035 Rock Instrumental Classics Vols. 1-5 Box Set.
(S) (3:01) Time-Life SUD-02 Superhits - 1968.
(S) (3:01) Time-Life HPD-39 Your Hit Parade - 60's Instrumentals: Take Two.
(S) (3:02) Capitol 89098 O.S.T. Wild Palms.
(S) (3:02) Rhino 71938 Billboard Top Pop Hits, 1968.
(S) (3:01) Collectors' Choice 003/4 Instrumental Gems Of The 60's.
(S) (3:01) Time-Life AM1-04 AM Gold - 1968.

MAURICE WILLIAMS & THE ZODIACS
1960 STAY
(M) (1:34) Warner Special Products 27602 20 Party Classics. Classics.
(M) (1:38) Rhino 70621 Billboard's Top Rock & Roll Hits Of 1960.
(M) (1:38) Rhino 72004 Billboard's Top Rock & Roll Hits 1957-1961 Box Set.
(E) (1:33) Original Sound CDGO-8 Golden Oldies Volume. 8.
(M) (1:34) RCA 6408 O.S.T. Dirty Dancing.
(M) (1:33) DCC Compact Classics 033 Beachbeat Shaggin'.
(M) (1:38) Arista 8605 16 Original Doo-Wop Classics.
(M) (1:35) Relic 7004 Best Of.
(M) (1:35) Ripete 2392192 Beach Music Anthology Box Set.
(M) (1:35) Collectables 5061 History Of Rock Volume 1.
(M) (1:33) Ripete 2162 Anthology.
(M) (1:50) Ripete 2162 Anthology. (alternate take)
(M) (1:35) Rhino 71463 Doo Wop Box.
(M) (1:34) Ripete 0001 Coolin' Out/24 Carolina Classics Volume 1.
(M) (1:36) Relic 7059 Golden Era Of Doo-Wops: Herald Records.
(M) (1:38) Time-Life 2RNR-11 Rock 'N' Roll Era - 1960. (this song ran (1:32) on original pressings of this cd)
(M) (1:37) Time-Life RHD-15 Rhythm & Blues - 1960.
(M) (1:34) Collectables 2502 WCBS-FM History Of Rock - The 60's Part 3.
(M) (1:34) Collectables 4502 History Of Rock/The 60s Part Three.

(M) (1:36) Collectables 2603 WCBS-FM Jukebox Giants Vol. 1.
(M) (1:36) Collectables 5056 Harlem Holiday - N.Y. Rhythm & Blues Vol. 6.
(M) (1:35) Collectables 5021 Best Of.
(M) (1:32) Time-Life R10513 40 Lovin' Oldies.
(M) (1:32) JCI 3125 1960 - Only Rock 'N Roll - 1964.
(M) (1:34) Ripete 2148-RE Beach Beat Classics Volume III.
(M) (1:38) Time-Life R857-02 The Heart Of Rock 'n' Roll - 1960.
(M) (1:36) Collectables 5657 Spotlite On Herald Records Volume 2.
(M) (1:34) Collectables 2554 CBS-FM History Of Rock Volume 2.
(M) (1:32) JCI 3164 Eighteen Soulful Ballads.
(M) (1:35) Eclipse Music Group 64867 Rock 'n Roll Relix 1960-1961.
(M) (1:35) Eclipse Music Group 64872 Rock 'n Roll Relix 1960-1969.
(M) (1:33) K-Tel 3812 Doo Wop's Greatest Hits.
(M) (1:37) Time-Life R838-20 Solid Gold Soul 1960.

OTIS WILLIAMS and HIS CHARMS (see CHARMS)

ROGER WILLIAMS
1955 AUTUMN LEAVES
(S) (2:55) Curb 77403 All-Time Great Instrumental Hits Volume 1. *(rerecording)*
(S) (2:55) Curb 77267 Greatest Hits. *(rerecording)*
(E) (2:59) MCA 63 Greatest Hits.
(S) (2:55) MFSL 868 Collection. *(rerecording)*
(M) (2:52) MCA 10698 The Greatest Popular Pianist.
(M) (2:52) Time-Life HPD-09 Your Hit Parade 1955.
(S) (2:53) K-Tel 478 More 50's Jukebox Favorites. *(rerecording)*
(M) (2:52) MCA Special Products 20849 Piano Music Classics.
(M) (2:53) JCI 7010 Those Wonderful Years - Melodies Of Love.
(M) (2:52) K-Tel 3472 Those Wonderful Instrumentals Volume 2.
(M) (2:53) Time-Life R986-06 Instrumental Favorites.
(M) (2:52) Pair 1349 The Great Piano Hits.
(S) (2:55) Varese Sarabande 5908 The Roger Williams Collection. *(rerecording)*
1957 ALMOST PARADISE
(S) (2:30) MCA 63 Greatest Hits. *(rerecording)*
(M) (2:29) MCA 10698 The Greatest Popular Pianist.
(M) (2:29) Time-Life R986-06 Instrumental Favorites.
1957 TILL
(M) (2:58) MCA 10698 The Greatest Popular Pianist.
1958 NEAR YOU
(S) (2:44) MCA 63 Greatest Hits.
(M) (2:46) MCA 10698 The Greatest Popular Pianist.
(M) (2:46) Time-Life HPD-30 Your Hit Parade - 50's Instrumentals.
(M) (2:46) Time-Life R986-06 Instrumental Favorites.
1966 BORN FREE
(S) (2:15) Curb 77403 All-Time Great Instrumental Hits Volume 1. *(rerecording)*
(S) (2:15) Curb 77267 Greatest Hits. *(rerecording)*
(S) (2:16) MFSL 868 Collection. *(rerecording)*
(S) (2:21) MCA 10698 The Greatest Popular Pianist.
(S) (2:21) MCA Special Products 20849 Piano Music Classics.
(S) (2:20) Time-Life R986-06 Instrumental Favorites.
(S) (2:20) Rhino 72423 Billboard Top Movie Hits - 1960s.
(S) (2:21) K-Tel 3583 Those Wonderful Instrumentals Volume 3.
(S) (2:22) MCA Special Products 21035 Classic Rock & Roll Instrumental Hits, Volume 2.
(S) (2:21) MCA Special Products 21025 The Best Of Easy Listening.
(S) (2:17) Varese Sarabande 5908 The Roger Williams Collection. *(rerecording)*

VANESSA WILLIAMS
1989 DREAMIN'
(S) (5:26) Wing/Mercury 835694 The Right Stuff.

(S) (5:24) Rebound 314520370 Soul Classics - Quiet Storm/The 80's.
1991 RUNNING BACK TO YOU
(S) (4:39) Wing/Mercury 843522 The Comfort Zone.
1992 SAVE THE BEST FOR LAST
(S) (3:39) Foundation/RCA 66104 Hot #1 Hits.
(S) (3:38) Mercury 314525354 Women For Women. *(live)*
(S) (3:39) Mother 314516937 O.S.T. The Adventures Of Priscilla - Queen Of The Desert.
(S) (3:38) Wing/Mercury 843522 The Comfort Zone.
(S) (3:40) Rhino 72159 Black Entertainment Television - 15th Anniversary.
(S) (3:41) Rebound 314520439 Soul Classics - Best Of The 90's.
(S) (3:38) Polygram TV 314555610 The One And Only Love Album.
1992 JUST FOR TONIGHT
(S) (4:26) Wing/Mercury 843522 The Comfort Zone.
released as by VANESSA WILLIAMS & BRIAN McKNIGHT:
1993 LOVE IS
(S) (4:44) Giant 24465 Beverly Hills, 90210 - The Soundtrack.
(S) (4:44) Foundation/RCA 66563 Number 1 Hit Mix.
released as by VANESSA WILLIAMS:
1995 THE SWEETEST DAYS
(S) (3:30) Wing/Mercury 314526172 The Sweetest Days.
1995 COLORS OF THE WIND
(S) (4:16) Walt Disney 60874 O.S.T. Pocahontas.
(S) (4:16) EMI-Capitol Music Group 54555 Movie Luv.

WILLIAMS BROTHERS
1992 CAN'T CRY HARD ENOUGH
(S) (3:10) Warner Brothers 26503 The Williams Brothers.

BRUCE WILLIS
1987 RESPECT YOURSELF
(S) (3:49) Columbia 44382 Heart Of Soul.
(S) (3:50) Motown 314530557 Motown Year By Year - 1987.
(S) (3:50) Motown 6222 The Return Of Bruno.
(S) (3:51) Razor & Tie 2127 The Return Of Bruno.
(S) (3:49) Rebound 314520438 No. 1 Hits Of The 80's.
(S) (3:49) Polygram Special Markets 314520457 #1 Radio Hits Of The 80's.

CHUCK WILLIS
1957 C.C. RIDER
(M) (2:33) JCI 3202 Rockin' Fifties.
(M) (2:32) Atlantic 81295 Atlantic Rhythm & Blues Volume 3.
(M) (2:33) Atlantic 82305 Atlantic Rhythm And Blues 1947-1974 Box Set.
(M) (2:32) Time-Life 2RNR-01 Rock 'N' Roll Era - 1957.
(M) (2:30) Time-Life RHD-08 Rhythm & Blues - 1957.
(M) (2:28) Razor & Tie 2055 Stroll On.
(M) (2:31) Rhino 72961 Ultimate '50s R&B Smashes!
(M) (2:27) Time-Life R859-13 Living The Blues - Vocal Classics.
(M) (2:30) Time-Life R838-23 Solid Gold Soul 1957.
1958 BETTY AND DUPREE
(M) (2:24) Atlantic 81295 Atlantic Rhythm & Blues Volume 3.
(M) (2:24) Atlantic 82305 Atlantic Rhythm And Blues 1947-1974 Box Set.
(M) (2:24) Razor & Tie 2055 Stroll On.
1958 WHAT AM I LIVING FOR
(M) (2:25) Atlantic 81295 Atlantic Rhythm & Blues Volume 3.
(M) (2:25) Atlantic 82305 Atlantic Rhythm And Blues 1947-1974 Box Set.
(M) (2:25) Time-Life 2RNR-21 Rock 'N' Roll Era - 1958 Still Rockin'.
(M) (2:25) Time-Life RHD-16 Rhythm & Blues - 1958.
(S) (2:24) Razor & Tie 2055 Stroll On.
(M) (2:25) JCI 3165 #1 Radio Hits 1955 - Only Rock 'n Roll - 1959.
(S) (2:24) Hip-O 40028 The Glory Of Love - '50s Sweet & Soulful Love Songs.
(S) (2:24) Time-Life R857-16 The Heart Of Rock 'n' Roll The Late '50s.

    (M) (2:25)   Time-Life R838-22 Solid Gold Soul 1958.

1958 HANG UP MY ROCK AND ROLL SHOES

    (M) (2:18)   Atlantic 81295 Atlantic Rhythm & Blues Volume 3.

    (M) (2:18)   Atlantic 82305 Atlantic Rhythm And Blues 1947-1974 Box Set.

    (M) (2:18)   Time-Life R962-01 Rock 'N' Roll Classics 1957-1959.

    (M) (2:17)   Time-Life 2RNR-24 The Rock 'N' Roll Era - The 50's: Keep On Rockin'.

    (S) (2:16)   Razor & Tie 2055 Stroll On.

WILL TO POWER

1988 BABY I LOVE YOUR WAY/FREEBIRD MEDLEY

    (S) (4:06)   Foundation/WEA 26097 Super Sessions Volume Two.

    (S) (4:06)   Rhino 71643 Billboard Top Hits - 1988.

    (S) (4:07)   Scotti Brothers 75434 Romantic Duets.

    (S) (4:07)   Epic 40940 Will To Power.

    (S) (4:06)   Time-Life R988-10 Sounds Of The 80's: 1988.

    (S) (4:07)   Risky Business 66396 Oldies But 80's: Best Of The 80's.

1991 I'M NOT IN LOVE

    (S) (3:47)   Epic 46051 Journey Home.

    (S) (3:47)   K-Tel 3850 90s Now Volume 3.

    (S) (4:07)   Madacy Entertainment 6806 Best Of Love.

    (S) (4:08)   Time-Life R834-16 Body Talk - Sweet Nothings.

AL WILSON

1968 THE SNAKE

    (S) (3:24)   Ripete 0002 Coolin' Out/24 Carolina Classics Vol. 2.

1974 SHOW AND TELL

    (S) (3:26)   Rhino 70552 Soul Hits Of The 70's Volume 12.

    (S) (3:25)   Collectables 5070 History Of Rock Volume 10.

    (S) (3:26)   Original Sound 8865 Oldies But Goodies Vol. 15. *(this compact disc uses the "Waring - fds" noise reduction process)*

    (S) (3:26)   Original Sound 2222 Oldies But Goodies Volumes 3,5,11,14 and 15 Box Set. *(this box set uses the "Waring - fds" noise reduction process)*

    (S) (3:26)   Original Sound 2500 Oldies But Goodies Volumes 1-15 Box Set. *(this box set uses the "Waring - fds" noise reduction process)*

    (S) (3:25)   Original Sound CDGO-8 Golden Oldies Volume. 8.

    (S) (3:25)   Original Sound 8908 Best Love Songs Vol 3.

    (S) (3:25)   Original Sound 9327 Best Love Songs Vol. 3 & 4.

    (S) (3:25)   Original Sound 1236 Best Love Songs Box Set.

    (S) (3:26)   Original Sound 8881 Twenty-One #1 Hits. *(this compact disc uses the "Waring - fds" noise reduction process)*

    (S) (3:26)   Original Sound 9603 Best Of Oldies But Goodies Vol. 3.

    (S) (3:25)   Razor & Tie 22047 Sweet 70's Soul.

    (S) (3:26)   Time-Life SOD-07 Sounds Of The Seventies - 1974.

    (S) (3:26)   Ripete 0003 Coolin' Out/24 Carolina Classics Vol. 3.

    (S) (3:29)   LaserLight 12318 Chart Busters.

    (S) (3:28)   K-Tel 6013 70's Soul - Sexy Ballads.

    (S) (3:29)   Curb 77774 Hard To Find Hits Of Rock 'N' Roll Volume Two.

    (E) (3:26)   Total 1017 Show & Tell.

    (S) (3:28)   K-Tel 3518 Sweet Soul Music.

    (S) (3:26)   Madacy Entertainment 1974 Rock On 1974.

    (S) (3:27)   K-Tel 3625 Dynamite.

    (S) (3:27)   JCI 3173 1970 - Only Soul - 1974.

    (S) (3:26)   Priority 53129 Deep Soul Volume One.

    (S) (3:27)   Time-Life R103-18 Great Love Songs Of The '70s & '80s.

    (S) (3:26)   Time-Life AM1-21 AM Gold - 1974.

    (S) (3:26)   Time-Life R834-06 Body Talk - Only You.

    (S) (3:25)   Simitar 55542 The Number One's: Soul On Fire. *(poor stereo separation)*

    (S) (3:26)   Beast 53442 Original Players Of Love.

1974 LA LA PEACE SONG

    (E) (3:44)   Total 1017 Show & Tell.

    (E) (3:50)   Ichiban 2511 Love, Peace & Understanding.

1976 I'VE GOT A FEELING (WE'LL BE SEEING EACH OTHER AGAIN)

ANN WILSON

released as by MIKE RENO and ANN WILSON:

1984 ALMOST PARADISE...LOVE THEME FROM "FOOTLOOSE"

    (S) (3:48)   Columbia 39242 O.S.T. Footloose.

    (S) (3:49)   Priority 53681 80's Greatest Rock Hits - Agony & Ecstasy.

    (S) (3:38)   Madacy Entertainment 6806 Best Of Love.

released as by ANN WILSON and ROBIN ZANDER:

1989 SURRENDER TO ME

    (S) (4:07)   Capitol 91185 O.S.T. Tequila Sunrise.

BRIAN WILSON

1966 CAROLINE, NO

    (M) (2:16)   Capitol 46324 Made In U.S.A. *(45 version)*

    (M) (2:49)   Capitol 48421 Pet Sounds. *(LP version)*

    (M) (2:15)   Capitol 96796 Absolute Best Volume 2. *(45 version)*

    (M) (2:49)   Capitol 81294 Thirty Years Of The Beach Boys. *(LP version)*

    (S) (2:51)   Capitol 37662 The Pet Sounds Sessions. *(LP version)*

    (M) (1:50)   Capitol 37662 The Pet Sounds Sessions. *(vocal track)*

    (S) (4:16)   Capitol 37662 The Pet Sounds Sessions. *(several alternate takes strung together)*

    (S) (2:50)   Capitol 37662 The Pet Sounds Sessions. *(instrumental track)*

    (M) (2:51)   Capitol 37662 The Pet Sounds Sessions. *(LP version; found on the bonus disc titled "Pet Sounds" included with this box set)*

JACKIE WILSON

1957 REET PETITE (THE FINEST GIRL YOU EVER WANT TO MEET)

    (E) (2:42)   Columbia 40866 Reet Petite.

    (E) (2:42)   Epic 38623 Jackie Wilson Story.

    (M) (2:40)   Rhino 70775 Mr. Excitement!

    (M) (2:40)   Rhino 71559 Very Best Of.

    (M) (2:41)   Time-Life 2RNR-28 Rock 'N' Roll Era - The 50's Rave On.

    (M) (2:42)   MCA 11119 The Decca Rock 'N' Roll Collection.

    (M) (2:40)   RCA 66443 O.S.T. Corrina, Corrina.

    (M) (2:39)   Rhino 71806 The R&B Box: Thirty Years Of Rhythm & Blues.

    (M) (2:39)   Rhino 71850 Higher And Higher. *(noisy ending)*

1958 TO BE LOVED

    (E) (2:26)   Columbia 40866 Reet Petite.

    (E) (2:26)   Epic 38623 Jackie Wilson Story.

    (M) (2:27)   Rhino 70775 Mr. Excitement!

    (M) (2:27)   Rhino 71559 Very Best Of.

    (M) (2:27)   Motown 314530436 A Tribute To Berry Gordy.

1959 LONELY TEARDROPS

    (E) (2:39)   Columbia 40866 Reet Petite.

    (S) (2:30)   Rhino 70906 American Bandstand Greatest Hits Collection.

    (S) (2:30)   Rhino 70644 Billboard's Top R&B Hits Of 1958.

    (E) (2:39)   Epic 38623 Jackie Wilson Story. *(truncated fade)*

    (M) (2:41)   Rhino 70775 Mr. Excitement! *(truncated fade)*

    (S) (2:30)   Ripete 2392192 Beach Music Anthology Box Set.

    (M) (2:41)   Curb 77637 All Time Greatest Hits Of Rock 'N' Roll Volume 3.

    (M) (2:41)   Rhino 71559 Very Best Of. *(truncated fade)*

    (M) (2:40)   Time-Life 2RNR-20 Rock 'N' Roll Era - 1959 Still Rockin'.

    (M) (2:37)   Time-Life RHD-03 Rhythm & Blues - 1959.

    (M) (2:41)   Rhino 71850 Higher And Higher. *(truncated fade)*

    (M) (2:41)   Motown 314530436 A Tribute To Berry Gordy.

    (M) (2:41)   Brunswick 81009 The Brunswick Years Volume One.

(M) (2:41) Rebound 314520420 Soul Classics - Best Of The 60's.
(M) (2:37) Time-Life R838-21 Solid Gold Soul 1959.

1959 THAT'S WHY (I LOVE YOU SO)
(S) (2:00) Rhino 70645 Billboard's Top R&B Hits Of 1959.
(S) (2:03) Columbia 40866 Reet Petite.
(S) (2:03) Epic 38623 Jackie Wilson Story.
(S) (2:04) Rhino 70775 Mr. Excitement!
(S) (2:04) Rhino 71559 Very Best Of.
(S) (2:01) Time-Life RHD-03 Rhythm & Blues - 1959.
(S) (2:01) Time-Life R838-21 Solid Gold Soul 1959.

1959 I'LL BE SATISFIED
(S) (2:08) Columbia 40866 Reet Petite.
(E) (2:06) Epic 38623 Jackie Wilson Story.
(S) (2:09) Rhino 70775 Mr. Excitement!
(S) (2:09) Rhino 71559 Very Best Of.

1959 YOU BETTER KNOW IT
(S) (2:00) Columbia 40866 Reet Petite.
(S) (1:59) Epic 38623 Jackie Wilson Story. (truncated fade)
(S) (1:59) Rhino 70775 Mr. Excitement!

1960 TALK THAT TALK
(E) (2:13) Columbia 40866 Reet Petite.
(E) (2:13) Epic 38623 Jackie Wilson Story.
(S) (2:13) Rhino 70775 Mr. Excitement!
(S) (2:10) Time-Life 2RNR-49 Rock 'N' Roll Era - Lost Treasures II.

1960 NIGHT
(S) (2:45) Epic 38623 Jackie Wilson Story.
(S) (2:47) Rhino 70775 Mr. Excitement!
(S) (2:47) Rhino 71559 Very Best Of.
(S) (2:47) Rhino 71581 Billboard Top Pop Hits, 1960.

1960 DOGGIN' AROUND
(actual 45 time is (2:50) not (2:45) as stated on the record label)
(S) (2:48) Rhino 70646 Billboard's Top R&B Hits Of 1960.
(S) (2:49) Columbia 40866 Reet Petite.
(E) (2:50) Epic 38623 Jackie Wilson Story.
(S) (2:52) Rhino 70775 Mr. Excitement!
(S) (2:52) Rhino 71559 Very Best Of.
(S) (2:39) Time-Life 2RNR-48 Rock 'N' Roll Era - R&B Gems II. (faded :11 early)
(S) (2:43) Time-Life RHD-15 Rhythm & Blues - 1960. (faded :07 early)
(S) (2:52) Ripete 2220 Soul Patrol Vol. 2.
(S) (2:51) Brunswick 81009 The Brunswick Years Volume One.
(S) (2:48) Time-Life R857-14 The Heart Of Rock 'n' Roll 1960-1961 Take Two.
(S) (2:43) Time-Life R838-20 Solid Gold Soul 1960. (faded :07 early)

1960 (YOU WERE MADE FOR) ALL MY LOVE
(S) (2:03) Rhino 70775 Mr. Excitement!

1960 A WOMAN, A LOVER, A FRIEND
(S) (2:31) Epic 38623 Jackie Wilson Story.
(S) (2:34) Rhino 70775 Mr. Excitement!
(S) (2:34) Rhino 71559 Very Best Of.
(S) (2:30) Repeat/Relativity 1610 Tighten Up: #1 Soul Hits Of The 60's Volume 2.

1960 ALONE AT LAST
(S) (3:00) Rhino 70775 Mr. Excitement!
(S) (3:00) Rhino 71559 Very Best Of.
(S) (3:00) LaserLight 12321 Soulful Love.

1960 AM I THE MAN
(S) (2:31) Epic 38623 Jackie Wilson Story.
(S) (2:34) Rhino 70775 Mr. Excitement!
(S) (2:33) Rhino 71559 Very Best Of.

1961 MY EMPTY ARMS
(S) (2:49) Rhino 70775 Mr. Excitement!
(S) (2:49) Rhino 71559 Very Best Of.

1961 THE TEAR OF THE YEAR
(E) (2:35) Epic 38623 Jackie Wilson Story.
(S) (2:35) Rhino 70775 Mr. Excitement!

1961 PLEASE TELL ME WHY
(E) (1:58) Epic 38623 Jackie Wilson Story.
(S) (1:59) Rhino 70775 Mr. Excitement!

1961 I'M COMIN' ON BACK TO YOU
(E) (2:12) Epic 38623 Jackie Wilson Story.
(S) (2:20) Rhino 70775 Mr. Excitement!

1962 THE GREATEST HURT
(S) (3:09) Rhino 70775 Mr. Excitement!

1963 BABY WORKOUT
(S) (2:58) Rhino 70649 Billboard's Top R&B Hits Of 1963.
(S) (2:57) Columbia 40866 Reet Petite.
(S) (2:57) Epic 38623 Jackie Wilson Story.
(S) (3:00) Rhino 70775 Mr. Excitement!
(S) (3:00) Rhino 71559 Very Best Of.
(S) (2:52) Time-Life 2RNR-29 Rock 'N' Roll Era - The 60's Rave On.
(S) (2:52) Time-Life RHD-02 Rhythm & Blues - 1963. (first word partially truncated)
(S) (2:59) Rhino 71850 Higher And Higher.
(S) (2:52) Time-Life R838-14 Solid Gold Soul - 1963. (first word partially truncated)
(M) (2:59) Rhino 72815 Beg, Scream & Shout! The Big Ol' Box Of '60s Soul.
(S) (2:57) Repeat/Relativity 1611 A Brand New Bag: #1 Soul Hits Of The 60's Volume 3.

released as by JACKIE WILSON and LINDA HOPKINS:
1963 SHAKE A HAND
(S) (3:04) Rhino 70775 Mr. Excitement!
(S) (3:04) Rhino 71850 Higher And Higher.

released as by JACKIE WILSON:
1963 SHAKE! SHAKE! SHAKE!
(S) (2:06) Rhino 70775 Mr. Excitement!
(S) (2:06) Rhino 71850 Higher And Higher.

1966 WHISPERS (GETTIN' LOUDER)
(E) (2:16) Columbia 40866 Reet Petite.
(S) (2:16) Epic 38623 Jackie Wilson Story.
(S) (2:24) Rhino 70775 Mr. Excitement!
(S) (2:24) Ripete 0002 Coolin' Out/24 Carolina Classics Vol. 2.
(S) (2:24) Rhino 71559 Very Best Of.
(S) (2:24) Rhino 71850 Higher And Higher.

1967 (YOUR LOVE KEEPS LIFTING ME) HIGHER AND HIGHER
(E) (2:58) JCI 3100 Dance Sixties.
(S) (2:57) Rhino 70243 Greatest Movie Rock Hits.
(S) (2:56) Rhino 70653 Billboard's Top R&B Hits Of 1967.
(S) (2:56) Rhino 72006 Billboard's Top R&B Hits 1965-1969 Box Set.
(S) (2:56) Columbia 40866 Reet Petite.
(S) (2:55) Epic 38623 Jackie Wilson Story.
(S) (2:57) Rhino 70775 Mr. Excitement!
(S) (2:57) Rhino 71559 Very Best Of.
(S) (2:49) Time-Life RHD-10 Rhythm & Blues - 1967.
(M) (2:54) Time-Life 2CLR-05 Classic Rock - 1967.
(S) (2:57) Rhino 71850 Higher And Higher.
(S) (2:49) JCI 3126 1965 - Only Rock 'N Roll - 1969.
(S) (2:54) K-Tel 3130 60's Sound Explosion.
(S) (2:56) Hollywood 62032 O.S.T. Operation Dumbo Drop.
(S) (2:56) MCA 11329 Soul Train 25th Anniversary Box Set.
(S) (2:57) Brunswick 81009 The Brunswick Years Volume One.
(S) (2:56) MCA Special Products 20941 R&B Crossover Oldies Vol. 1.
(S) (2:49) Time-Life R838-02 Solid Gold Soul - 1967.
(S) (2:54) Repeat/Relativity 1609 Tell It Like It Is: #1 Soul Hits Of The 60's Volume 1.

1967 SINCE YOU SHOWED ME HOW TO BE HAPPY
(S) (2:48) Rhino 70775 Mr. Excitement!
(S) (2:47) Rhino 71850 Higher And Higher.

1968 I GET THE SWEETEST FEELING
(S) (2:54) Rhino 70775 Mr. Excitement!
(S) (2:52) Columbia 40866 Reet Petite.
(S) (2:55) K-Tel 3518 Sweet Soul Music.
(S) (2:53) Brunswick 81009 The Brunswick Years Volume One.

J. FRANK WILSON and THE CAVALIERS
1964 LAST KISS
(M) (2:25) Rhino 70625 Billboard's Top Rock & Roll Hits Of 1964.
(M) (2:25) Rhino 72007 Billboard's Top Rock & Roll Hits 1962-1966 Box Set.

J. FRANK WILSON and THE CAVALIERS *(Continued)*

- (M) (2:24) Rhino 70995 One Hit Wonders Of The 60's Volume 1.
- (E) (2:24) Original Sound 8859 Oldies But Goodies Vol. 9. *(this compact disc uses the "Waring - fds" noise reduction process)*
- (M) (2:23) Original Sound 8859r Oldies But Goodies Vol. 9. *(remastered edition)*
- (M) (2:23) Original Sound 2223 Oldies But Goodies Volumes 2,7,9,12 and 13 Box Set. *(Volumes 2, 7 and 12 of this box set use the "Waring - fds" noise reduction process)*
- (M) (2:23) Original Sound 2500 Oldies But Goodies Volumes 1-15 Box Set. *(most volumes in this box set use the "Waring - fds" noise reduction process)*
- (M) (2:25) Collectables 5062 History Of Rock Volume 2.
- (M) (2:24) Time-Life 2RNR-10 Rock 'N' Roll Era - 1964.
- (M) (2:24) Time-Life SUD-12 Superhits - The Mid 60's.
- (M) (2:24) Time-Life R962-05 History Of Rock 'N' Roll: The Teenage Years 1957-1964.
- (E) (2:23) Collectables 2500 WCBS-FM History Of Rock - The 60's Part 1.
- (E) (2:23) Collectables 4500 History Of Rock/The 60s Part One.
- (M) (2:24) Time-Life R102-17 Lost Treasures Of Rock 'N' Roll.
- (M) (2:24) DCC Compact Classics 078 Best Of Tragedy.
- (M) (2:24) Time-Life R857-09 The Heart Of Rock 'n' Roll 1964.
- (M) (2:24) Time-Life AM1-05 AM Gold - The Mid '60s.

MERI WILSON
1977 TELEPHONE MAN
- (S) (1:58) Rhino 71201 Super Hits Of The 70's Volume 21.
- (S) (1:57) Time-Life R830-02 The Dr. Demento Collection - The Late 70's.

NANCY WILSON
1964 (YOU DON'T KNOW) HOW GLAD I AM
- (S) (2:38) Capitol 91210 Best Of. *(alternate mix)*
- (S) (2:36) Time-Life HPD-32 Your Hit Parade - Into The 60's. *(alternate mix)*
- (S) (2:35) JCI 7022 Those Wonderful Years - It Must Be Him. *(alternate mix)*
1968 FACE IT GIRL, IT'S OVER
- (S) (3:08) Capitol 91210 Best Of.

WILSON PHILLIPS
1990 HOLD ON
- (S) (3:38) SBK 31181 Moments In Love. *(45 length)*
- (S) (4:23) SBK 93745 Wilson Phillips. *(LP length)*
- (S) (4:19) JCI 3132 1990 - Only Rock 'n Roll - 1994. *(LP length)*
- (S) (4:23) K-Tel 3847 90s Now Volume 1. *(LP length)*
1990 RELEASE ME
- (S) (3:49) Foundation/Capitol 96427 Hearts Of Gold: The Pop Collection. *(45 version)*
- (S) (4:53) SBK 93745 Wilson Phillips. *(LP version)*
- (S) (4:53) K-Tel 3848 90s Now Volume 2. *(LP version)*
1990 IMPULSIVE
- (S) (4:32) SBK 93745 Wilson Phillips. *(LP length)*
1991 YOU'RE IN LOVE
- (S) (4:49) Foundation/RCA 66104 Hot #1 Hits. *(LP version)*
- (S) (4:49) SBK 93745 Wilson Phillips. *(LP version)*
- (S) (4:46) Madacy Entertainment 6806 Best Of Love. *(LP version)*
- (S) (4:04) Time-Life R834-11 Body Talk - After Dark. *(45 version)*
1991 THE DREAM IS STILL ALIVE
- (S) (4:08) SBK 93745 Wilson Phillips.
1992 YOU WON'T SEE ME CRY
- (S) (3:50) SBK 98924 Shadows And Light.
1992 GIVE IT UP
- (S) (4:48) SBK 98924 Shadows And Light.

WILTON PLACE STREET BAND
1977 DISCO LUCY (I LOVE LUCY THEME)

JESSE WINCHESTER
1981 SAY WHAT
- (S) (3:07) Rhino 70085 Best Of.
- (S) (3:05) Time-Life R105-26 Our Songs: Singers & Songwriters Encore.

WIND
1969 MAKE BELIEVE

KAI WINDING
1963 MORE
- (S) (2:01) Rhino 70995 One Hit Wonders Of The 60's Volume 1.
- (S) (2:00) Time-Life HPD-34 Your Hit Parade - 60's Instrumentals.
- (S) (2:00) K-Tel 3091 Those Wonderful Instrumentals.
- (S) (2:00) Chronicles 314535875 Bachelor Pad Favorites.
- (S) (1:59) Collectors' Choice 5190 More Instrumental Gems Of The 60's.
- (S) (2:00) Time-Life R986-22 Instrumental Classics - Pop Classics.

WING AND A PRAYER FIFE & DRUM CORPS.
1976 BABY FACE

WINGER
1989 SEVENTEEN
- (S) (4:05) Atlantic 81867 Winger. *(LP version)*
- (S) (4:03) Rhino 72292 Heavy Metal Hits Of The 80's Volume 2. *(LP version)*
- (S) (4:04) Priority 50937 Best Of 80's Metal Volume Two: Bang Your Head. *(LP version)*
- (S) (4:03) Razor & Tie 89004 Monsters Of Rock. *(LP version)*
1989 HEADED FOR A HEARTBREAK
- (S) (4:57) JCI 4545 Masters Of Metal: Thunder 'N Spice. *(LP version but faded :14 early)*
- (S) (3:58) Time-Life R105-40 Rock Dreams. *(45 version)*
- (S) (5:11) Atlantic 81867 Winger. *(LP version)*
- (S) (3:57) Time-Life R968-18 Guitar Rock - The Heavy '80s. *(45 version)*
- (S) (3:57) JCI 3186 1985 - Only Love - 1989. *(45 version)*
- (S) (3:58) Rhino 72579 Feel Like Makin' Love - Romantic Power Ballads. *(45 version)*
1990 CAN'T GET ENOUGH
- (S) (4:19) Atlantic 82103 In The Heart Of The Young.
1990 MILES AWAY
- (S) (4:09) JCI 3135 14 Original Metal Ballads.
- (S) (4:09) Atlantic 82103 In The Heart Of The Young.
- (S) (4:10) K-Tel 3999 Glam Rock Vol. 2: The 80's And Beyond.
1991 EASY COME EASY GO
- (S) (4:02) Atlantic 82103 In The Heart Of The Young.
- (S) (4:00) Time-Life R968-25 Guitar Rock - The '90s.

PETE WINGFIELD
1975 EIGHTEEN WITH A BULLET
- (S) (3:27) Original Sound 1960 Art Laboe's Memories Of El Monte.
- (S) (3:27) Original Sound 4001 Art Laboe's 60 Killer Oldies.
- (S) (3:28) Island 90684 and 842901 The Island Story.
- (S) (3:29) Rhino 70762 Super Hits Of The 70's Volume 15.
- (S) (3:27) Time-Life SOD-33 Sounds Of The Seventies - AM Pop Classics II.

WINGS (see PAUL McCARTNEY)

WINSTONS
1969 COLOR HIM FATHER
- (S) (3:04) Rhino 70781 Soul Hits Of The 70's Volume 1.
- (S) (3:04) Rhino 72028 Soul Hits Of The 70's Volumes 1-5 Box Set.
- (S) (3:04) Ripete 2392192 Beach Music Anthology Box Set.
- (S) (3:04) Ripete 2392146 Beach Beat Classics Volume 1.
- (S) (3:04) Ripete 2146-RE Beach Beat Classics Vol. 1.

(M) (3:13) Thump 7060 Low Rider Oldies Volume 6. *(:07 longer than the 45 or LP)*

EDGAR WINTER GROUP
1973 FRANKENSTEIN
(S) (3:25) Rhino 70929 Super Hits Of The 70's Volume 9. *(45 version)*
(S) (3:25) Rhino 70634 Billboard's Top Rock & Roll Hits Of 1973. *(45 version)*
(S) (4:43) JCI 3302 Electric Seventies. *(LP version)*
(S) (4:44) Rhino 70895 Collection. *(LP version)*
(S) (4:43) Epic 31584 They Only Come Out At Night. *(LP version)*
(S) (4:44) Priority 7055 Heavy Hitters/70's Greatest Rock Hits Volume 11. *(LP version)*
(S) (4:42) Hollywood 61330 O.S.T. Encino Man. *(LP version)*
(S) (4:44) Priority 53680 Spring Break. *(LP version)*
(S) (4:42) Reprise 45485 O.S.T. Wayne's World 2. *(LP version)*
(S) (3:24) Rhino 71603 Rock Instrumental Classics Volume 3: The Seventies. *(45 version)*
(S) (3:24) Rhino 72035 Rock Instrumental Classics Vols. 1-5 Box Set. *(45 version)*
(S) (4:44) Rhino 71549 Let There Be Drums Vol. 3: The 70's. *(LP version)*
(S) (4:43) Razor & Tie 22502 Those Rocking 70's. *(LP version)*
(S) (4:43) Time-Life R968-05 Guitar Rock 1972-1973. *(LP version)*
(S) (3:24) Time-Life SOD-21 Sounds Of The Seventies - Rock 'N' Soul Seventies. *(45 version)*
(S) (4:44) Risky Business 66391 Ghastly Grooves. *(LP version)*
(S) (3:25) K-Tel 3625 Dynamite. *(45 version)*
(S) (4:43) Epic/Legacy 65020 Ultimate Rock 'n' Roll Collection. *(LP version)*
(S) (3:25) Eclipse Music Group 64893 Rock 'n Roll Relix 1972-1973. *(45 version)*
(S) (3:25) Eclipse Music Group 64897 Rock 'n Roll Relix 1970-1979. *(45 version)*
(S) (4:43) Hip-O 40039 Power Chords Volume 2. *(LP version)*
(S) (3:24) Time-Life R840-04 Sounds Of The Seventies: A Loss For Words. *(45 version)*
(S) (4:44) Priority 50991 The Best Of The 70's - Rock Chart Toppers. *(LP version)*
(S) (4:45) Rhino 72893 Hard Rock Cafe: Classic Rock. *(LP version)*
(S) (4:43) Hip-O 40013 Synth Me Up - 14 Classic Electronic Hits. *(LP version)*
(S) (4:43) K-Tel 4033 Ghasty Grooves. *(LP version)*
(S) (4:46) Simitar 55502 The Number One's: Classic Rock. *(LP version)*
(S) (4:43) Thump 6010 Easyriders Volume 1. *(LP version)*
(S) (4:43) Rebound 314520507 Class Reunion '73. *(LP version)*

1973 FREE RIDE
(S) (3:04) Rhino 70895 Collection. *(45 version)*
(S) (3:06) Priority 8662 Hard 'N Heavy/70's Greatest Rock Hits Volume 1. *(LP version)*
(S) (3:06) Epic 31584 They Only Come Out At Night. *(LP version)*
(S) (3:04) Time-Life SOD-14 Sounds Of The Seventies - 1973: Take Two. *(45 version)*
(S) (3:00) Time-Life R105-24 Guitar Rock Monsters. *(45 version)*
(S) (3:04) Varese Sarabande 5503 and 5504 and 5505 and 5506 and 5507 and 5508 and 5509 and 5513 and 5571 Arrow: All Rock & Roll Oldies Volume One. *(45 version)*
(S) (3:03) Risky Business 66662 Swingin' Singles/Greatest Hits Of The 70's. *(45 version)*
(S) (3:06) Medicine Label 24588 Even More Dazed And Confused. *(LP version)*
(S) (3:04) Time-Life R968-08 Guitar Rock - The Mid '70s. *(45 version)*
(S) (3:06) K-Tel 3996 Rockin' Down The Highway. *(LP version)*

released as by EDGAR WINTER:
1974 RIVER'S RISIN'
(S) (2:51) Rhino 70895 Collection. *(45 version)*
(S) (3:18) Epic 32461 Shock Treatment. *(LP version)*

HUGO WINTERHALTER/EDDIE HEYWOOD
1956 CANADIAN SUNSET
(M) (2:52) RCA 8467 Nipper's Greatest Hits Of The 50's Volume 2.
(M) (2:52) Time-Life HPD-27 Your Hit Parade - The Unforgettable 50's.
(E) (2:51) JCI 7010 Those Wonderful Years - Melodies Of Love.
(M) (2:51) K-Tel 3472 Those Wonderful Instrumentals Volume 2.
(M) (2:51) Time-Life R986-17 Instrumental Favorites - Around The World.

STEVE WINWOOD
1981 WHILE YOU SEE A CHANCE
(S) (5:13) Island 9576 and 842365 Arc Of A Diver. *(LP version)*
(S) (5:13) MFSL 579 Arc Of A Diver. *(LP version; gold disc)*
(S) (5:09) Island 25660 and 842364 Chronicles. *(LP version)*
(S) (5:09) Polydor 314515913 Classic Rock Box. *(LP version)*
(S) (5:13) Island 314516860 The Finer Things. *(LP version)*
(S) (5:12) Rebound 314520361 Class Reunion '81. *(LP version)*
(S) (4:05) Time-Life R988-18 Sounds Of The Eighties: The Early '80s Take Two. *(45 version)*
(S) (5:11) Simitar 55502 The Number One's: Classic Rock. *(LP version)*

1986 HIGHER LOVE
(S) (5:46) Island 314516860 The Finer Things. *(LP version)*
(S) (5:45) Island 25660 and 842364 Chronicles. *(LP version)*
(S) (5:47) Island 25448 and 830148 Back In The High Life. *(LP version)*
(S) (5:47) MFSL 611 Back In The High Life. *(gold disc)*
(S) (4:12) Time-Life R988-12 Sounds Of The 80's: 1985-1986. *(45 version)*
(S) (5:44) Time-Life R988-28 Sounds Of The Eighties: The Rolling Stone Collection 1986-1987. *(LP version)*
(S) (5:46) Rebound 314520372 The Roots Of Rock: Soft Rock. *(LP version)*

1986 FREEDOM OVERSPILL
(S) (4:14) Island 314516860 The Finer Things. *(45 version)*
(S) (5:33) Island 25448 and 830148 Back In The High Life. *(LP version)*
(S) (5:33) MFSL 611 Back In The High Life. *(gold disc; LP version)*

1987 THE FINER THINGS
(actual 45 time is (4:10) not (4:00) as stated on the record label)
(S) (4:10) Island 314516860 The Finer Things. *(45 version)*
(S) (5:47) Island 25448 and 830148 Back In The High Life. *(LP version)*
(S) (5:47) MFSL 611 Back In The High Life. *(gold disc; LP version)*
(S) (5:46) Time-Life R834-13 Body Talk - Just The Two Of Us. *(LP version)*

1987 BACK IN THE HIGHLIFE AGAIN
(actual 45 time is (4:18) not (4:09) as stated on the record label)
(S) (4:21) Island 314516860 The Finer Things. *(45 version)*
(S) (5:33) Island 25448 and 830148 Back In The High Life. *(LP version)*
(S) (5:33) MFSL 611 Back In The High Life. *(gold disc; LP version)*
(S) (5:33) Time-Life R834-04 Body Talk - Together Forever. *(LP version)*
(S) (4:21) Time-Life R13610 Gold And Platinum Box Set - The Ultimate Rock Collection. *(45 version)*

1987 VALERIE
(S) (4:05) Island 314516860 The Finer Things. *("Talking Back To The Night" vinyl LP version - not the hit version)*
(S) (4:06) Island 25660 and 842364 Chronicles. *(this is the "hit" version)*
(S) (4:05) Island 9777 and 842366 Talking Back To The Night. *("Talking Back To The Night" vinyl LP version - not the hit version)*

STEVE WINWOOD (Continued)

- (S) (4:05) MFSL 674 Talking Back To The Night. *(gold disc; "Talking Back To The Night" vinyl LP version - not the hit version)*
- (S) (4:06) Time-Life R988-19 Sounds Of The Eighties: The Late '80s. *(this is the "hit" version)*
- (S) (4:06) Time-Life R834-18 Body Talk - Romantic Moments. *(this is the "hit" version)*

1988 ROLL WITH IT
- (S) (4:26) Mercury 846043 O.S.T. Nuns On The Run. *(45 length)*
- (S) (5:18) Sandstone 33042 and 5008 Rock The First Volume 2. *(LP length)*
- (S) (4:28) Island 314516860 The Finer Things. *(45 length)*
- (S) (5:18) Virgin 90946 and 86069 Roll With It. *(LP length)*

1988 DON'T YOU KNOW WHAT THE NIGHT CAN DO?
- (S) (4:27) Island 314516860 The Finer Things. *(45 version)*
- (S) (6:53) Virgin 90946 and 86069 Roll With It. *(LP version)*
- (S) (4:28) Time-Life R834-11 Body Talk - After Dark. *(45 version)*

1989 HOLDING ON
- (S) (6:14) Virgin 90946 and 86069 Roll With It. *(LP version)*

1990 ONE AND ONLY MAN
- (S) (4:38) Island 314516860 The Finer Things. *(45 length)*
- (S) (4:58) Virgin 91405 and 86189 Refugees Of The Heart. *(LP length)*

BILL WITHERS
1971 AIN'T NO SUNSHINE
- (S) (2:03) Rhino 70786 Soul Hits Of The 70's Volume 6.
- (S) (2:03) Columbia 37199 Greatest Hits.
- (S) (2:02) Essex 7060 The Buddah Box.
- (S) (2:02) Time-Life SUD-16 Superhits - The Early 70's.
- (S) (2:03) Time-Life SOD-02 Sounds Of The Seventies - 1971.
- (S) (2:03) Columbia/Legacy 52924 Lean On Me: Best Of.
- (S) (2:03) Legacy/Epic 66912 Legacy's Rhythm & Soul Revue.
- (S) (2:03) JCI 3145 1970 - Only Love - 1974.
- (S) (2:02) Time-Life AM1-13 AM Gold - The Early '70s.
- (S) (2:03) Time-Life R834-09 Body Talk - Magic Moments.
- (S) (2:03) Rhino 72737 Billboard Top Soft Rock Hits - 1971.

1971 GRANDMA'S HANDS
- (S) (1:59) Columbia 37199 Greatest Hits.
- (S) (1:59) Columbia/Legacy 52924 Lean On Me: Best Of.

1972 LEAN ON ME
- (S) (3:46) Rhino 70660 Billboard's Top R&B Hits Of 1972. *(45 length)*
- (S) (3:54) Rhino 70788 Soul Hits Of The 70's Volume 8. *(:08 longer than the 45 and :22 shorter than the LP length)*
- (S) (4:16) Columbia 37199 Greatest Hits. *(LP length)*
- (S) (3:54) Rhino 71618 Soul Train Hall Of Fame/20th Anniversary. *(:08 longer than 45 and :22 shorter than LP length)*
- (S) (4:15) Essex 7060 The Buddah Box. *(LP length)*
- (S) (3:45) Time-Life RHD-20 Rhythm & Blues - 1972. *(45 length)*
- (S) (3:45) Time-Life SUD-20 Superhits - Early 70's Classics. *(45 length)*
- (S) (3:46) Time-Life SOD-03 Sounds Of The Seventies - 1972. *(45 length)*
- (S) (3:45) Time-Life R921-38 Get Together. *(45 length)*
- (S) (3:40) Ripete 2198 Soul Patrol. *(45 length faded :05 early)*
- (S) (4:16) Columbia/Legacy 52924 Lean On Me: Best Of. *(LP length)*
- (S) (3:45) Time-Life AM1-15 AM Gold - Early '70s Classics. *(45 length)*
- (S) (3:45) Time-Life R838-07 Solid Gold Soul - 1972. *(45 length)*
- (S) (4:16) Time-Life R834-01 Body Talk - Forever Yours. *(LP length)*
- (S) (4:15) K-Tel 3910 Fantastic Volume 1. *(LP length)*
- (S) (4:16) K-Tel 3912 Superstars Greatest Hits Volume 1. *(LP length)*
- (S) (4:15) Thump 4740 Old School Love Songs Volume 4. *(LP length)*

- (S) (3:45) Time-Life R814-04 Love Songs. *(45 length)*
- (S) (4:15) K-Tel 3987 70s Heavy Hitters: #1 Pop Hits. *(LP length)*

1972 USE ME
- (S) (3:44) Rhino 70789 Soul Hits Of The 70's Volume 9.
- (S) (3:40) Columbia 37199 Greatest Hits.
- (S) (3:43) Razor & Tie 22047 Sweet 70's Soul.
- (S) (3:44) Time-Life SOD-13 Sounds Of The Seventies - 1972: Take Two.
- (S) (3:46) Columbia/Legacy 52924 Lean On Me: Best Of.

1973 KISSING MY LOVE
- (S) (3:49) Columbia/Legacy 52924 Lean On Me: Best Of.

1978 LOVELY DAY
- (S) (4:10) Columbia 37199 Greatest Hits. *(LP length)*
- (S) (4:13) Columbia/Legacy 52924 Lean On Me: Best Of. *(LP length)*
- (S) (4:13) Time-Life R838-17 Solid Gold Soul 1978. *(LP length)*
- (S) (3:46) Simitar 55602 The Number One's: Silky Soul. *(45 length)*

released as by GROVER WASHINGTON JR. with BILL WITHERS:
1981 JUST THE TWO OF US
(actual 45 time is (3:56) not (3:40) as stated on the record label)
- (S) (7:23) Elektra 305 Grover Washington Jr. - Winelight. *(LP version)*
- (S) (7:19) Elektra 60415 Grover Washington Jr. - Anthology. *(LP version)*
- (S) (3:56) Columbia 37199 Bill Withers Greatest Hits. *(45 version)*
- (S) (3:57) Columbia/Legacy 52924 Bill Withers: Lean On Me/Best Of. *(45 version)*
- (S) (3:56) Rhino 71894 Radio Daze: Pop Hits Of The 80's Volume Five. *(45 version)*
- (S) (3:55) Rhino 71971 Video Soul - Best Soul Of The 80's Vol. 1. *(45 version)*
- (S) (3:29) Time-Life R138-18 Body Talk. *(45 version faded :27 early)*
- (S) (3:56) Rhino 72136 Billboard Hot R&B Hits 1981. *(45 version)*
- (S) (7:22) MCA 11431 Quiet Storms 2. *(LP version)*
- (S) (3:29) JCI 3170 #1 Radio Hits 1980 - Only Rock 'n Roll - 1984. *(45 version faded :27 early)*
- (S) (3:57) Time-Life R834-03 Body Talk - Moonlit Nights. *(45 version)*
- (S) (3:29) K-Tel 6257 The Greatest Love Songs - 16 Soft Rock Hits. *(45 version faded :27 early)*
- (S) (3:57) Time-Life R988-22 Sounds Of The Eighties 1980-1983. *(45 version)*

PETER WOLF
1984 LIGHTS OUT
- (S) (4:25) EMI 46046 Lights Out. *(LP version)*

1984 I NEED YOU TONIGHT
- (S) (3:40) EMI 46046 Lights Out.

1987 COME AS YOU ARE
- (S) (2:43) EMI 46563 Come As You Are.

BOBBY WOMACK
1972 THAT'S THE WAY I FEEL ABOUT CHA
- (S) (3:14) Rhino 70787 Soul Hits Of The 70's Volume 7. *(45 version)*
- (S) (3:11) Razor & Tie 2009 Lookin' For A Love (1968-1975). *(45 version)*
- (S) (3:34) EMI 27673 Midnight Mover/Bobby Womack Story. *(45 version but :22 longer)*
- (S) (5:07) Right Stuff 29141 Communication. *(LP version)*
- (S) (3:39) Priority 53130 Deep Soul Volume Three. *(45 version but :27 longer)*
- (S) (5:09) EMI 38310 Sex & Soul Volume One. *(LP version)*
- (S) (3:39) EMI 48403 Greatest Hits. *(45 version but :27 longer)*
- (S) (5:06) EMI 53965 The Soul Of: Stop On By. *(LP version)*

1973 HARRY HIPPIE
- (S) (3:50) Razor & Tie 2009 Lookin' For A Love (1968-1975).
- (S) (3:50) EMI 27673 Midnight Mover/Bobby Womack Story.

(S) (3:48) Right Stuff 29144 Understanding.
(S) (3:50) Ripete 2198 Soul Patrol.
(S) (3:52) EMI 48403 Greatest Hits.
(S) (3:49) EMI 53965 The Soul Of: Stop On By.

1973 NOBODY WANTS YOU WHEN YOU'RE DOWN AND OUT
(S) (2:57) Razor & Tie 2009 Lookin' For A Love (1968-1975).
(S) (2:56) EMI 27673 Midnight Mover/Bobby Womack Story.
(S) (2:56) Right Stuff 29142 Facts Of Life.
(S) (2:56) Rhino 72126 Soul Hits Of The 70's Vol. 16.
(S) (2:57) EMI 48403 Greatest Hits.
(S) (2:55) EMI 53965 The Soul Of: Stop On By.

1974 LOOKIN' FOR A LOVE
(S) (2:36) Rhino 70662 Billboard's Top R&B Hits Of 1974.
(S) (2:36) Rhino 70552 Soul Hits Of The 70's Volume 12.
(S) (2:37) Razor & Tie 2009 Lookin' For A Love (1968-1975).
(S) (2:37) EMI 27673 Midnight Mover/Bobby Womack Story.
(S) (2:35) Time-Life SOD-15 Sounds Of The Seventies - 1974: Take Two.
(S) (2:35) Right Stuff 29968 Lookin' For A Love Again.
(S) (2:37) EMI 48403 Greatest Hits.
(S) (2:35) EMI 53965 The Soul Of: Stop On By.
(S) (2:36) Time-Life R838-09 Solid Gold Soul - 1974.

STEVIE WONDER
released as by LITTLE STEVIE WONDER:
1963 FINGERTIPS (PART 2)
(actual LP time is (6:40) not (7:00) as stated on the record label)
(E) (3:10) Motown 6159 The Good-Feeling Music Of The Big Chill Generation Volume 1.
(E) (3:10) Rhino 70624 Billboard's Top Rock & Roll Hits Of 1963. *(found only on the original 1988 release of this cd)*
(E) (3:10) Rhino 72007 Billboard's Top Rock & Roll Hits 1962-1966 Box Set.
(E) (3:10) Motown 6159 The Good Feeling Music Of The Big Chill Generation Volume 1.
(E) (3:10) Motown 5449 A Collection Of 16 Big Hits Volume 2.
(E) (3:10) Motown 9017 and 5248 16 #1 Hits From The Early 60's.
(E) (3:09) Motown 9060 Motown's Biggest Pop Hits.
(E) (3:09) Motown 0282 Greatest Hits.
(M) (6:37) Motown 5131 The 12 Year Old Genius. *(LP version which is Parts 1 & 2)*
(M) (3:09) Motown 6312 Hitsville USA.
(M) (2:55) Motown 5219 Jazz Soul Of Little Stevie Wonder. *(original recording but not the hit version)*
(E) (3:10) Time-Life 2RNR-07 Rock 'N' Roll Era - 1963.
(E) (3:10) Polygram Special Markets 314520283 Motown Legends Volume 2.
(M) (3:08) Motown 314530419 Motown Classic Hits Vol. II.
(M) (3:08) Nick At Nite/Epic 67149 Dick Van Dyke's Dance Party.
(M) (3:10) Motown 314530647 O.S.T. Nothing But A Man.

1963 WORKOUT STEVIE, WORKOUT
(S) (2:38) Motown 0282 Greatest Hits.

released as by STEVIE WONDER:
1964 HEY HARMONICA MAN
(S) (2:36) Motown 5450 A Collection Of 16 Big Hits Volume 3.
(S) (2:36) Motown 0282 Greatest Hits.
(M) (2:31) Motown 314530421 Motown Classics Vol. IV.

1966 UPTIGHT (EVERYTHING'S ALRIGHT)
(S) (2:53) Motown 6160 The Good Feeling Music Of The Big Chill Generation Volume 2.
(S) (2:51) Motown 5453 A Collection Of 16 Big Hits Volume 6.
(S) (2:53) Motown 9018 and 5249 16 #1 Hits From The Late 60's.
(S) (2:52) Motown 9071 Motown Dance Party Volume 1. *(all selections on this cd are segued together)*
(S) (2:52) Motown 0282 Greatest Hits.
(S) (2:53) Motown 8025 and 8125 For Once In My Life/Uptight.
(S) (2:53) Motown 5183 Uptight.

(M) (2:52) Motown 6312 Hitsville USA.
(S) (2:53) Time-Life 2CLR-07 Classic Rock - 1966: The Beat Goes On.
(M) (2:51) Motown/Essex 374638527 Motown Legends - I Was Made To Love Her.
(S) (2:53) Polygram Special Markets 314520284 Motown Legends Volume 3.
(S) (2:52) Motown 314530522 Motown Year By Year - 1966.
(S) (2:53) Polydor 314529508 O.S.T. Mr. Holland's Opus.
(S) (2:52) Motown 314530767 Song Review - A Greatest Hits Collection. *(all songs on this cd are segued together)*

1966 NOTHING'S TOO GOOD FOR MY BABY
(S) (2:37) Motown 6144 and 9050 Love Songs: 20 Classic Hits.
(S) (2:42) Motown 0282 Greatest Hits. *(truncated fade)*
(S) (2:37) Motown 8025 and 8125 For Once In My Life/Uptight.
(S) (2:37) Motown 5183 Uptight.

1966 BLOWIN' IN THE WIND
(S) (3:44) Motown 6159 The Good-Feeling Music Of The Big Chill Generation Volume 1. *(LP version)*
(S) (3:44) Motown 6144 and 9050 Love Songs: 20 Classic Hits. *(LP version)*
(S) (3:03) Motown 0282 Greatest Hits. *(45 version)*
(S) (3:44) Motown 8025 and 8125 For Once In My Life/Uptight. *(LP version)*
(S) (3:43) Motown 5183 Uptight. *(LP version)*
(S) (3:44) Right Stuff 28373 Movin' On Up. *(LP version)*
(S) (3:44) Polygram Special Markets 314520283 Motown Legends Volume 2. *(LP version)*
(S) (3:43) Motown 314530522 Motown Year By Year - 1966. *(LP version)*

1966 A PLACE IN THE SUN
(S) (2:49) Motown 5454 A Collection Of 16 Big Hits Volume 7.
(S) (2:48) Motown 6144 and 9050 Love Songs: 20 Classic Hits.
(S) (2:50) Motown 0282 Greatest Hits.
(S) (2:51) Motown 8053 and 8153 I Was Made To Love Her/Down To Earth.
(S) (2:49) Motown 5166 Down To Earth.
(S) (2:48) Motown/Essex 374638527 Motown Legends - I Was Made To Love Her.

1967 TRAVLIN' MAN
(S) (2:44) Motown 5455 A Collection Of 16 Big Hits Vol. 8.
(S) (2:47) Motown 313 Greatest Hits Volume 2.

1967 I WAS MADE TO LOVE HER
(S) (2:34) Motown 6161 The Good-Feeling Music Of The Big Chill Generation Volume 3.
(S) (2:34) Motown 5456 A Collection Of 16 Big Hits Volume 9.
(S) (2:35) Motown 6177 Endless Love.
(S) (2:35) Motown 9018 and 5249 16 #1 Hits From The Late 60's.
(S) (2:34) Motown 6192 You Can't Hurry Love: All The Great Love Songs Of The Past 25 Years.
(S) (2:35) Motown 6144 and 9050 Love Songs: 20 Classic Hits.
(S) (2:34) Motown 0282 Greatest Hits.
(S) (2:36) Motown 5273 I Was Made To Love Her.
(S) (2:36) Motown 8053 and 8153 I Was Made To Love Her/Down To Earth.
(S) (2:35) Time-Life 2CLR-10 Classic Rock - 1967: The Beat Goes On.
(S) (2:34) Motown/Essex 374638527 Motown Legends - I Was Made To Love Her.
(S) (2:35) Polygram Special Markets 314520293 Motown Legends - Volume 5.
(S) (2:36) Capitol 35818 O.S.T. Dead Presidents Volume II.
(S) (2:35) Motown 314530767 Song Review - A Greatest Hits Collection. *(all songs on this cd are segued together)*
(M) (2:35) Rhino 72815 Beg, Scream & Shout! The Big Ol' Box Of '60s Soul.

1967 I'M WONDERING
(S) (2:51) Motown 5457 A Collection Of 16 Big Hits Volume 10.

STEVIE WONDER (Continued)

(S) (2:53) Motown 6144 and 9050 Love Songs: 20 Classic Hits.
(S) (2:52) Motown 0282 Greatest Hits.

1968 SHOO-BE-DOO-BE-DOO-DA-DAY
(S) (2:44) Motown 6159 The Good-Feeling Music Of The Big Chill Generation Volume 1.
(S) (2:44) Motown 6144 and 9050 Love Songs: 20 Classic Hits.
(S) (2:45) Motown 0313 Greatest Hits Volume 2.
(S) (2:44) Motown 8025 and 8125 For Once In My Life/Uptight.
(S) (2:44) Motown 9032 and 5234 For Once In My Life.
(S) (2:44) Polygram Special Markets 314520282 Motown Legends - Volume 1.

1968 YOU MET YOUR MATCH
(S) (2:36) Motown 0313 Greatest Hits Volume 2.
(S) (2:37) Motown 8025 and 8125 For Once In My Life/Uptight.
(S) (2:37) Motown 9032 and 5234 For Once In My Life.

1968 FOR ONCE IN MY LIFE
(S) (2:48) Motown 6159 The Good-Feeling Music Of The Big Chill Generation Volume 1. *(truncated fade)*
(S) (2:48) Motown 6137 20 Greatest Songs In Motown History.
(S) (2:48) Motown 6110 Motown Grammy R&B Performances Of The 60's & 70's.
(S) (2:48) Motown 6144 and 9050 Love Songs: 20 Classic Hits. *(truncated fade)*
(S) (2:46) Motown 0313 Greatest Hits Volume 2.
(S) (2:48) Motown 8025 and 8125 For Once In My Life/Uptight.
(S) (2:47) Motown 9032 and 5234 For Once In My Life.
(M) (2:49) Motown 6312 Hitsville USA.
(S) (2:48) Polygram Special Markets 314520282 Motown Legends - Volume 1.
(S) (2:47) Motown 314530507 Motown Year By Year 1968.

1969 MY CHERIE AMOUR
(S) (2:50) Motown 5324 and 9035 Top Ten With A Bullet: Motown Love Songs.
(S) (2:50) Motown 9098 Radio's #1 Hits.
(S) (2:50) Motown 6144 and 9050 Love Songs: 20 Classic Hits.
(S) (2:50) Motown 0313 Greatest Hits Volume 2.
(S) (2:52) Motown 9083 and 5179 My Cherie Amour.
(S) (2:52) Motown 8006 and 8106 My Cherie Amour/Signed, Sealed And Delivered.
(S) (2:49) Polygram Special Markets 314520030 Motown Legends - Love Songs.
(S) (2:51) Motown 314530525 Motown Year By Year - 1969.
(S) (2:51) Motown 314530767 Song Review - A Greatest Hits Collection. *(all songs on this cd are segued together)*
(S) (2:50) Rebound 314520420 Soul Classics - Best Of The 60's.
(S) (2:51) Motown 314530849 Motown 40 Forever.

1969 YESTER-ME, YESTER-YOU, YESTERDAY
(S) (3:03) Motown 6144 and 9050 Love Songs: 20 Classic Hits.
(S) (3:00) Motown 0313 Greatest Hits Volume 2.
(S) (3:05) Motown 9083 and 5179 My Cherie Amour.
(S) (3:04) Motown 8006 and 8106 My Cherie Amour/Signed, Sealed And Delivered.

1970 NEVER HAD A DREAM COME TRUE
(S) (3:10) Motown 6144 and 9050 Love Songs: 20 Classic Hits.
(S) (3:11) Motown 0313 Greatest Hits Volume 2.
(S) (3:12) Motown 8006 and 8106 My Cherie Amour/Signed, Sealed And Delivered. *(noisy fadeout)*
(S) (3:12) Motown 9029 and 5176 Signed, Sealed And Delivered. *(noisy fadeout)*

1970 SIGNED, SEALED, DELIVERED I'M YOURS
(S) (2:39) Motown 6110 Motown Grammy R&B Performances Of the 60's & 70's.
(S) (2:38) Motown 0937 20/20 Twenty No. 1 Hits From Twenty Years At Motown.
(S) (2:39) Motown 6144 and 9050 Love Songs: 20 Classic Hits.
(S) (2:37) Motown 0313 Greatest Hits Volume 2.
(S) (2:38) Motown 8006 and 8106 My Cherie Amour/Signed, Sealed And Delivered.
(S) (2:38) Motown 9029 and 5176 Signed, Sealed And Delivered.
(M) (2:46) Motown 6312 Hitsville USA.
(S) (2:38) MCA 11065 O.S.T. Crooklyn Volume II.
(S) (2:39) Motown 314530528 Motown Year By Year - 1970.
(S) (2:38) Columbia 67380 O.S.T. Now And Then.

(S) (2:37) Motown 314530767 Song Review - A Greatest Hits Collection. *(all songs on this cd are segued together)*
(S) (2:38) Rebound 314520447 Soul Classics - Best Of The 70's.

1970 HEAVEN HELP US ALL
(S) (3:12) Motown 6144 and 9050 Love Songs: 20 Classic Hits.
(S) (3:10) Motown 0313 Greatest Hits Volume 2.
(S) (3:12) Motown 8006 and 8106 My Cherie Amour/Signed, Sealed And Delivered.
(S) (3:12) Motown 9029 and 5176 Signed, Sealed And Delivered.

1971 WE CAN WORK IT OUT
(S) (3:16) Motown 6144 and 9050 Love Songs: 20 Classic Hits.
(S) (3:11) Motown 0313 Greatest Hits Volume 2.
(S) (3:17) Motown 8006 and 8106 My Cherie Amour/Signed, Sealed And Delivered.
(S) (3:17) Motown 9029 and 5176 Signed, Sealed And Delivered.
(S) (3:15) Razor & Tie 2031 Motown Sings The Blues.
(S) (3:17) Motown 314530410 Motown Meets The Beatles.

1971 IF YOU REALLY LOVE ME
(S) (2:55) Motown 9105 and 5410 Motown Memories Volume 2.
(S) (2:56) Motown 5324 and 9035 Top Ten With A Bullet: Motown Love Songs.
(S) (2:56) Motown 6144 and 9050 Love Songs: 20 Classic Hits.
(S) (2:56) Motown 0313 Greatest Hits Volume 2.
(S) (3:00) Motown 5247 Where I'm Coming From.
(S) (2:56) Polygram Special Markets 314520030 Motown Legends - Love Songs.
(S) (2:56) Rebound 314520364 Class Reunion '71.

1972 SUPERWOMAN (WHERE WERE YOU WHEN I NEEDED YOU)
(S) (7:58) Motown 6113 and 6002 Original Musiquarium Volumes 1 & 2. *(all selections on this cd are segued together; LP version)*
(S) (8:08) Motown 9076 and 0314 Music Of My Mind. *(LP version)*

1973 SUPERSTITION
(actual 45 time is (4:06) not (3:59) as stated on the record label)
(S) (4:26) Motown 6132 25 #1 Hits From 25 Years. *(LP length)*
(S) (4:24) MCA 10063 Original Television Soundtrack "The Sounds Of Murphy Brown". *(LP length)*
(S) (4:23) Motown 9072 Motown Dance Party Volume 2. *(all selections on this cd are segued together; LP length)*
(S) (4:24) Motown 0937 20/20 Twenty No. 1 Hits From Twenty Years At Motown. *(LP length)*
(S) (4:26) Motown 6113 and 6002 Original Musiquarium Volumes 1 & 2. *(all selections on this cd are segued together; LP length)*
(S) (4:25) Motown 6151 and 0319 Talking Book. *(tracks into next selection; LP length)*
(S) (4:12) Motown 6358 Hitsville USA Volume Two. *(:06 longer fade than the 45)*
(S) (4:22) Time-Life R102-34 The Rolling Stone Collection. *(LP length)*
(S) (4:12) Thump 9947 Cruizin' To Motown. *(:06 longer fade than the 45)*
(S) (4:12) MCA 11329 Soul Train 25th Anniversary Box Set. *(:06 longer fade than the 45)*
(S) (4:25) Capitol 37436 O.S.T. Stealing Beauty. *(LP length)*
(S) (3:58) Motown 314530767 Song Review - A Greatest Hits Collection. *(all songs on this cd are segued together; :08 shorter than the 45)*
(S) (4:24) TVT 8090 O.S.T. My Fellow Americans. *(LP length)*
(S) (3:59) Motown 314530849 Motown 40 Forever. *(:07 shorter than the 45)*

1973 YOU ARE THE SUNSHINE OF MY LIFE
(actual 45 and LP time is (3:00) not (2:45) as stated on the record label)
(S) (2:51) Motown 6132 25 #1 Hits From 25 Years. *(45 version)*
(S) (2:57) Motown 0937 20/20 Twenty No. 1 Hits From Twenty Years At Motown. *(LP version)*

(S) (2:50) Motown 6113 and 6002 Original Musiquarium Volumes 1 & 2. *(all selections on this cd are segued together; 45 version)*
(S) (2:58) Motown 6151 and 0319 Talking Book. *(LP version)*
(S) (2:52) Motown 314530510 Motown Year By Year 1973. *(45 version)*
(S) (2:54) Motown 314530767 Song Review - A Greatest Hits Collection. *(all songs on this cd are segued together; 45 version)*
(S) (2:52) Time-Life R814-04 Love Songs. *(45 version)*

1973 HIGHER GROUND
(S) (3:47) Motown 6113 and 6002 Original Musiquarium Volumes 1 & 2. *(all selections on this cd are segued together; LP version)*
(S) (3:42) Motown 6152 and 0326 Innervisions. *(all selections on this cd are segued together; LP version)*
(S) (3:42) MFSL 554 Innervisions. *(all selections on this cd are segued together; gold disc; LP version)*
(S) (3:07) Motown 314530767 Song Review - A Greatest Hits Collection. *(all songs on this cd are segued together; 45 version)*

1974 LIVING FOR THE CITY
(S) (7:24) Motown 6113 and 6002 Original Musiquarium Volumes 1 & 2. *(all selections on this cd are segued together; LP version)*
(S) (7:24) Motown 6152 and 0326 Innervisions. *(LP version; all selections on this cd are segued together)*
(S) (7:23) MFSL 554 Innervisions. *(all selections on this cd are segued together; LP version; gold disc)*
(S) (7:24) Right Stuff 29669 Movin' On Up Vol. 2. *(LP version)*
(S) (3:40) Motown 314530510 Motown Year By Year 1973. *(45 version)*
(S) (3:40) Motown 314530767 Song Review - A Greatest Hits Collection. *(all songs on this cd are segued together; 45 version)*
(S) (3:39) Time-Life R13610 Gold And Platinum Box Set - The Ultimate Rock Collection. *(45 version)*

1974 DON'T YOU WORRY 'BOUT A THING
(S) (4:45) Motown 6152 and 0326 Innervisions. *(LP version; all selections on this cd are segued together)*
(S) (4:44) MFSL 554 Innervisions. *(all selections on this cd are segued together; LP version; gold disc)*
(S) (4:45) Rebound 314520247 Class Reunion 1974. *(LP version)*

1974 YOU HAVEN'T DONE NOTHIN
(S) (3:29) Motown 6113 and 6002 Original Musiquarium Volumes 1 & 2. *(all selections on this cd are segued together)*
(S) (3:22) Motown 0332 Fulfillingness' First Finale. *(most selections on this cd are segued together)*

1975 BOOGIE ON REGGAE WOMAN
(actual 45 time is (4:10) not (4:05) as stated on the record label)
(S) (4:55) Motown 6113 and 6002 Original Musiquarium Volumes 1 & 2. *(all selections on this cd are segued together; LP version)*
(S) (4:57) Motown 0332 Fulfillingness' First Finale. *(LP version; most selections on this cd are segued together)*
(S) (4:06) Motown 314530767 Song Review - A Greatest Hits Collection. *(all songs on this cd are segued together; 45 version)*

1977 I WISH
(actual 45 time is (4:10) not (3:37) as stated on the record label)
(S) (4:13) Motown 6113 and 6002 Original Musiquarium Volumes 1 & 2. *(all selections on this cd are segued together)*
(S) (4:12) Motown 6115 and 0340 Songs In The Key Of Life. *(almost all selections on this cd are segued together)*
(S) (4:12) Motown 314530513 Motown Year By Year 1976.
(S) (4:10) Motown 314530572 Funkology Volume Two - Behind The Groove.
(S) (4:10) Motown 314530767 Song Review - A Greatest Hits Collection. *(all songs on this cd are segued together)*
(S) (4:12) Time-Life R838-16 Solid Gold Soul 1977.

1977 SIR DUKE
(S) (3:51) Motown 6113 and 6002 Original Musiquarium Volumes 1 & 2. *(all selections on this cd are segued together)*
(S) (3:52) Motown 6115 and 0340 Songs In The Key Of Life. *(almost all selections on this cd are segued together)*
(S) (3:52) Motown 6358 Hitsville USA Volume Two.
(S) (3:51) Motown 314530767 Song Review - A Greatest Hits Collection. *(all songs on this cd are segued together)*

1977 ANOTHER STAR
(S) (8:08) Motown 6115 and 0340 Songs In The Key Of Life. *(LP version; almost all selections on this cd are segued together)*

1978 AS
(S) (7:08) Motown 6115 and 0340 Songs In The Key Of Life. *(LP version; almost all selections on this cd are segued together)*

1979 SEND ONE YOUR LOVE
(S) (4:00) Motown 6113 and 6002 Original Musiquarium Volumes 1 & 2. *(all selections on this cd are segued together)*
(S) (4:01) Motown 6127 Journey Through The Secret Life Of Plants.
(S) (4:00) Motown 314530767 Song Review - A Greatest Hits Collection. *(all songs on this cd are segued together)*

1980 MASTER BLASTER (JAMMIN')
(S) (5:07) Motown 6113 and 6002 Original Musiquarium Volumes 1 & 2. *(all selections on this cd are segued together; LP length)*
(S) (5:07) Motown 6205 Hotter Than July. *(tracks into next selection; LP length)*
(S) (4:48) Motown 314530516 Motown Year By Year 1980. *(45 length)*
(S) (5:07) Time-Life R988-25 Sounds Of The Eighties: The Rolling Stone Collection 1980-1981. *(LP length)*
(S) (4:50) Rhino 72159 Black Entertainment Television - 15th Anniversary. *(45 length)*
(S) (4:49) Motown 314530767 Song Review - A Greatest Hits Collection. *(all songs on this cd are segued together; 45 length)*

1981 I AIN'T GONNA STAND FOR IT
(S) (4:38) Motown 6205 Hotter Than July. *(tracks into next selection)*
(S) (4:34) Motown 314530516 Motown Year By Year 1980.

1982 THAT GIRL
(S) (5:13) Motown 314530534 Motown Year By Year - 1982.
(S) (5:13) Motown 6113 and 6002 Original Musiquarium Volumes 1 & 2. *(all selections on this cd are segued together)*
(S) (5:14) Rhino 72159 Black Entertainment Television - 15th Anniversary.
(S) (5:12) Motown 314530767 Song Review - A Greatest Hits Collection. *(all songs on this cd are segued together)*

released as by PAUL McCARTNEY with STEVIE WONDER:
1982 EBONY AND IVORY
(S) (3:42) Capitol 46057 Paul McCartney - Tug Of War.
(S) (3:40) Capitol 48287 Paul McCartney - All The Best.
(S) (3:41) Chrysalis 21750 After The Hurricane - Songs For Montserrat.
(S) (3:40) Motown 314530767 Stevie Wonder: Song Review - A Greatest Hits Collection. *(all songs on this cd are segued together)*

released as by STEVIE WONDER:
1982 DO I DO
(S) (5:01) Motown 314530534 Motown Year By Year - 1982. *(45 version)*
(S) (10:28) Motown 6113 and 6002 Original Musiquarium Volumes 1 & 2. *(all selections on this cd are segued together; LP version)*
(S) (10:27) Motown 314530767 Song Review - A Greatest Hits Collection. *(all songs on this cd are segued together; LP version)*

STEVIE WONDER *(Continued)*

1984 I JUST CALLED TO SAY I LOVE YOU
- (S) (6:16) Motown 9043 O.S.T. The Woman In Red. *(LP version)*
- (S) (4:18) Original Sound 8909 Best Love Songs Vol. 4. *(45 version)*
- (S) (4:18) Original Sound 9322 Best Love Songs Vol. 3 & 4. *(45 version)*
- (S) (4:18) Original Sound 1236 Best Love Songs Box Set. *(45 version)*
- (S) (4:21) Rhino 71868 Academy Award Winning Songs. *(45 version)*
- (S) (4:22) Motown 6358 Hitsville USA Volume Two. *(45 version)*
- (S) (4:21) Rhino 72280 Academy Award Winning Songs Volume 5. *(45 version)*
- (S) (4:20) Motown 314530767 Song Review - A Greatest Hits Collection. *(all songs on this cd are segued; 45 version)*

1985 LOVE LIGHT IN FLIGHT
- (S) (6:54) Motown 9043 O.S.T. The Woman In Red. *(LP version)*

1985 PART-TIME LOVER
- (S) (3:42) Motown 314530519 Motown Year By Year 1985. *(45 length)*
- (S) (3:42) Motown 6358 Hitsville USA Volume Two. *(45 length)*
- (S) (4:12) Motown 6134 In Square Circle. *(LP length)*
- (S) (3:42) Rhino 72159 Black Entertainment Television - 15th Anniversary. *(45 length)*
- (S) (3:43) Motown 314530767 Song Review - A Greatest Hits Collection. *(all songs on this cd are segued together; 45 length)*

released as by DIONNE and FRIENDS: DIONNE WARWICK, ELTON JOHN, GLADYS KNIGHT and STEVIE WONDER:
1986 THAT'S WHAT FRIENDS ARE FOR
- (S) (4:15) Arista 8398 Dionne Warwick - Friends.
- (S) (4:15) Arista 8540 Dionne Warwick - Greatest Hits 1979 - 1990.

released as by STEVIE WONDER:
1986 GO HOME
- (S) (4:08) Motown 314530519 Motown Year By Year 1985. *(45 version)*
- (S) (5:17) Motown 6134 In Square Circle. *(LP version)*

1986 OVERJOYED
- (S) (3:42) Motown 6134 In Square Circle.
- (S) (3:41) Motown 314530767 Song Review - A Greatest Hits Collection. *(all songs on this cd are segued together)*

1987 SKELETONS
- (S) (5:24) EMI 91419 MTV, BET, VH-1 Power Players. *(LP version)*
- (S) (5:24) Motown 314530557 Motown Year By Year - 1987. *(LP version)*
- (S) (5:24) Motown 6248 Characters. *(LP version)*

WONDER WHO? (see also FOUR SEASONS)
1965 DON'T THINK TWICE
- (S) (2:57) Rhino 72998 Four Seasons 25th Anniversary Collection.
- (S) (2:57) Rhino 70248 Four Seasons Sing Hits Of Bacharach/David/Dylan.
- (S) (2:57) Rhino 71490 Four Seasons Anthology.
- (S) (2:57) Rhino 70594 Four Seasons Greatest Hits Volume 1.
- (S) (2:57) Curb 77712 Four Seasons New Gold Hits.

BRENTON WOOD
1967 THE OOGUM BOOGUM SONG
- (M) (2:27) Rhino 71461 Soul Hits, Vol. 3.
- (M) (2:24) Collectables 5069 History Of Rock Volume Nine.
- (E) (2:26) Original Sound 8857 Oldies But Goodies Vol. 7. *(this compact disc uses the "Waring - fds" noise reduction process)*
- (E) (2:26) Original Sound 2223 Oldies But Goodies Volumes 2,7,9,12 and 13 Box Set. *(this box set uses the "Waring - fds" noise reduction process)*

- (E) (2:26) Original Sound 2500 Oldies But Goodies Volumes 1-15 Box Set. *(this box set uses the "Waring - fds" noise reduction process)*
- (E) (2:25) Original Sound CDGO-6 Golden Oldies Volume. 6.
- (E) (2:31) Original Sound 9601 Best Of Oldies But Goodies Vol. 1.
- (M) (2:27) Rhino 75770 Soul Shots Volume 2.
- (M) (2:24) Time-Life 2CLR-28 Classic Rock - On The Soul Side II.
- (S) (2:31) Original Sound 8886 18 Best.
- (M) (2:27) Flashback 72659 '60s Soul: When A Man Loves A Woman.
- (M) (2:27) Flashback 72091 '60s Soul Hits Box Set.
- (M) (2:26) Rhino 72815 Beg, Scream & Shout! The Big Ol' Box Of '60s Soul.

1967 GIMME LITTLE SIGN
- (M) (2:21) Warner Special Products 27602 20 Party Classics. *(hum noticeable on the introduction)*
- (E) (2:19) Original Sound 8859 Oldies But Goodies Vol. 9. *(this compact disc uses the "Waring - fds" noise reduction process; hum noticeable on the introduction)*
- (S) (2:19) Original Sound 8859r Oldies But Goodies Vol. 9. *(remastered edition; hum noticeable on the introduction)*
- (S) (2:19) Original Sound 2223 Oldies But Goodies Volumes 2,7,9 and 13 Box Set. *(Volumes 2, 7 and 12 of this box set use the "Waring - fds" noise reduction process; hum noticeable on the introduction)*
- (S) (2:19) Original Sound 2500 Oldies But Goodies Volumes 1-15 Box Set. *(most volumes in this box set use the "Waring - fds" noise reduction process; hum noticeable on the introduction)*
- (E) (2:16) Original Sound CDGO-3 Golden Oldies Volume. 3. *(hum noticeable on the introduction)*
- (E) (2:16) Original Sound 8892 Dick Clark's 21 All-Time Hits Vol. 2. *(hum noticeable on the introduction)*
- (S) (2:19) Original Sound 9602 Best Of Oldies But Goodies Vol. 2.
- (M) (2:16) Rhino 75757 Soul Shots Volume 3. *(hum noticeable on the introduction)*
- (M) (2:19) JCI 3105 Soul Sixties. *(hum noticeable on the introduction)*
- (S) (2:19) Original Sound 8886 18 Best. *(hum noticeable on the introduction)*
- (M) (2:16) Collectables 5067 History Of Rock Volume 7. *(hum noticeable on the introduction)*
- (M) (2:16) Rhino 71459 Soul Hits, Volume 1. *(hum noticeable on the introduction)*
- (S) (2:15) Time-Life 2CLR-10 Classic Rock - 1967: The Beat Goes On. *(hum noticeable on the introduction)*
- (S) (2:15) Collectables 2504 WCBS-FM History Of Rock - The 60's Part 4. *(hum noticeable on the introduction)*
- (S) (2:15) Collectables 4504 History Of Rock/The 60s Part Four. *(hum noticeable on the introduction)*
- (S) (2:15) Ripete 0003 Coolin' Out/24 Carolina Classics Vol. 3. *(hum noticeable on the introduction)*
- (M) (2:15) K-Tel 3518 Sweet Soul Music. *(hum noticeable on the introduction)*
- (M) (2:16) Collectables 2554 CBS-FM History Of Rock Volume 2. *(hum noticeable on the introduction)*
- (S) (2:19) K-Tel 3269 Carolina Beach Music. *(hum noticeable on the introduction)*
- (M) (2:17) Time-Life 2CLR-31 Classic Rock - Totally Fantastic '60s. *(hum noticeable on the introduction)*
- (M) (2:16) Flashback 72657 '60s Soul: Try A Little Tenderness. *(hum noticeable on the introduction)*
- (M) (2:16) Flashback 72091 '60s Soul Hits Box Set. *(hum noticeable on the introduction)*

1967 BABY YOU GOT IT
- (E) (1:55) Original Sound 8886 18 Best.
- (M) (2:00) Rhino 72869 Brown Eyed Soul Vol. 2.
- (S) (1:52) Original Sound CDGO-5 Golden Oldies Volume. 5.

LAUREN WOOD
1979 PLEASE DON'T LEAVE
- (S) (3:54) Rhino 71890 Radio Daze: Pop Hits Of The 80's Volume One.

STEVIE WOODS
1981 STEAL THE NIGHT
1982 JUST CAN'T WIN 'EM ALL

SHEB WOOLEY
⚔1958 THE PURPLE PEOPLE EATER
    (M) (2:12) Rhino 71492 Elvira Presents Haunted Hits.
    (M) (2:11) Rhino 75768 Dr. Demento Presents.
  ✓(M) (2:12) Rhino 70743 Dr. Demento 20th Anniversary Collection.
    (M) (2:12) Rhino 70535 Halloween Hits.
    (M) (2:12) Mercury 832041 45's On CD Volume 1.
    (M) (2:12) DCC Compact Classics 050 Monster Rock 'n Roll Show.
    (M) (2:12) Time-Life 2RNR-37 Rock 'N' Roll Era - Weird, Wild & Wacky.
  ✓(S) (2:14) K-Tel 3037 Wacky Weirdos. *(rerecording)*
    (M) (2:11) Priority 53747 Wild & Crazy Tunes.
    (M) (2:12) Polygram Special Markets 314520258 No. 1 Hits Of The 50's.
    (M) (2:11) Music For Little People 42581 A Child's Celebration Of Rock 'N' Roll.
    (S) (2:14) K-Tel 3795 Music For Your Halloween Party. *(rerecording)*
    (S) (2:14) K-Tel 3795 Spooktacular Party Songs. *(rerecording)*
    (M) (2:14) Varese Sarabande 5882 They Came From Outer Space.

WORLD PARTY
1987 SHIP OF FOOLS (SAVE ME FROM TOMORROW)
    (S) (4:13) Geffen 24236 Greenpeace - Rainbow Warriors. *(faded :14 earlier than the 45 or LP)*
    (S) (4:27) Chrysalis 41552 and 21552 Private Revolution.

LINK WRAY & HIS RAY MEN
⌐1958 RUMBLE
    (M) (2:24) Rhino 70719 Legends Of Guitar - Rock; The 50's.
    (M) (2:24) Rhino 71601 Rock Instrumental Classics Volume 1: The Fifties.
    (M) (2:24) Rhino 72035 Rock Instrumental Classics Vols. 1-5 Box Set.
    (M) (2:19) Compose 9923 James Dean/Tribute To A Rebel. *(mastered from vinyl)*
    (M) (2:20) Time-Life 2RNR-21 Rock 'N' Roll Era - 1958 Still Rockin'. *(mastered from vinyl)*
    (M) (2:24) Time-Life R962-01 History Of Rock 'N' Roll: Rock 'N' Roll Classics 1957-1959.
    (E) (2:19) Era 840 Rock N' Roll Guitar Classics. *(mastered from vinyl)*
    (M) (2:24) K-Tel 3062 Rockin' Rebels.
    (M) (2:24) Varese Sarabande 5579 History Of Cadence Records Volume 2.
    (M) (2:24) Priority 50950 I Love Rock & Roll Volume 1: Hits Of The 50's.
    (M) (2:24) Right Stuff 53318 Hot Rod Rock Volume 3: Big Boss Instrumentals.
    (M) (2:24) K-Tel 4018 Forefathers Of Rock.
    (M) (2:24) I.D. 90072 Jenny McCarthy's Surfin' Safari.
⚔1959 RAW-HIDE
    (E) (2:04) CBS Special Products 37618 Rockabilly Stars Volume 1.
    (M) (2:05) Epic/Legacy 47904 Walkin' With Link.
    (M) (2:04) Rhino 71601 Rock Instrumental Classics Volume 1: The Fifties.
  ✓(M) (2:04) Rhino 72035 Rock Instrumental Classics Vols. 1-5 Box Set.
    (E) (2:04) Time-Life 2RNR-33 Rock 'N' Roll Era - The 50's Last Dance.
    (M) (2:05) Collectables 5454 Golden Classics.
    (M) (2:04) Nouveau 1060 O.S.T. This Boy's Life.
    (M) (2:04) K-Tel 3453 Rockin' Instrumentals.

WRECKX-N-EFFECT
1993 RUMP SHAKER
    (S) (5:10) MCA 10566 Hard Or Smooth.
    (S) (3:55) Robbins 75002 Strip Jointz - Hot Songs For Sexy Dancers.

BETTY WRIGHT
1968 GIRLS CAN'T DO WHAT THE GUYS DO
    (M) (2:03) Collectables 5118 Golden Classics. *(mastered from scratchy vinyl)*
    (S) (2:03) Rhino 71085 Best Of.
1972 CLEAN UP WOMAN
    (S) (2:44) Rhino 70787 Soul Hits Of The 70's Volume 7.
    (S) (2:43) Rhino 70659 Billboard's Top R&B Hits Of 1971.
    (S) (2:46) Atlantic 81299 Atlantic Rhythm & Blues Volume 7.
    (S) (2:45) Atlantic 82305 Atlantic Rhythm And Blues 1947-1974 Box Set.
    (S) (2:44) Rhino 71085 Best Of.
    (S) (2:45) Rhino 71210 70's Smash Hits Volume 6.
    (S) (2:43) Time-Life RHD-20 Rhythm & Blues - 1972.
    (S) (2:46) Time-Life SOD-13 Sounds Of The Seventies - 1972: Take Two.
    (M) (2:43) Collectables 5118 Golden Classics. *(mastered from scratchy vinyl)*
    (S) (2:43) Ripete 2198 Soul Patrol.
    (S) (2:44) Ichiban 2507 Cheatin': From A Woman's Point Of View.
    (S) (2:43) JCI 3191 1970 - Only Dance - 1974.
    (S) (2:44) TK/Hot Productions 33 Best Of T.K. Soul Singles.
    (S) (2:43) Time-Life R838-07 Solid Gold Soul - 1972.
    (S) (2:44) Flashback 72686 '70s Radio Hits Volume 6.
    (S) (2:43) TVT 4010 Rhythm Revue.

CHARLES WRIGHT and THE WATTS 103RD STREET BAND
released as by THE WATTS 103rd STREET BAND:
1969 DO YOUR THING
    (M) (2:54) JCI 3105 Soul Sixties. *(45 version)*
    (S) (3:28) Warner Brothers 45306 Express Yourself: Best Of. *(LP version)*
    (S) (3:28) Time-Life RHD-13 Rhythm & Blues - 1969. *(LP version)*
    (S) (3:28) Priority 53131 Deep Soul Volume Two. *(LP version)*
    (S) (3:28) Time-Life R838-04 Solid Gold Soul - 1969. *(LP version)*
    (S) (3:28) Capitol 93076 More Music From O.S.T. Boogie Nights. *(LP version)*

released as by CHARLES WRIGHT and THE WATTS 103rd STREET BAND:
1970 LOVE LAND
    (S) (3:03) Rhino 70782 Soul Hits Of The 70's Volume 2.
    (S) (3:03) Rhino 72028 Soul Hits Of The 70's Volumes 1-5 Box Set.
    (S) (3:03) Rhino 71205 70's Smash Hits Volume 1.
    (S) (3:04) Warner Brothers 45306 Express Yourself: Best Of.
    (S) (3:04) Thump 4710 Old School Love Songs.
    (S) (3:03) Flashback 72682 '70s Radio Hits Volume 2.
    (S) (3:03) Flashback 72090 '70s Radio Hits Box Set.
    (S) (3:04) Warner Brothers 46459 In The Jungle, Babe/Express Yourself.
1970 EXPRESS YOURSELF
    (S) (3:50) Rhino 70783 Soul Hits Of The 70's Volume 3.
    (S) (3:50) Rhino 72028 Soul Hits Of The 70's Volumes 1-5 Box Set.
    (S) (3:50) Rhino 71431 In Yo Face! History Of Funk Volume 1.
    (S) (3:50) Warner Brothers 45306 Express Yourself: Best Of.
    (S) (3:50) Time-Life RHD-18 Rhythm & Blues - 1970.
    (S) (3:50) Time-Life R838-05 Solid Gold Soul - 1970.
    (S) (3:50) Warner Brothers 46459 In The Jungle, Babe/Express Yourself.
    (S) (3:50) Chronicles 314555137 Funk Of The 70's.
    (S) (3:36) Thump 9960 Old School Funk II. *(faded :14 early)*

GARY WRIGHT
⚔1976 DREAM WEAVER
    (S) (4:15) Priority 8667 FM Hits/70's Greatest Rock Hits Volume 6. *(LP version)*
    (S) (3:24) Rhino 70671 Billboard Top Hits - 1976. *(:09 longer fade than the 45 version)*

GARY WRIGHT *(Continued)*

- (S) (3:39) Razor & Tie 4543 The '70s Preservation Society Presents: Easy '70s. *(:24 longer fade than the 45 version)*
- (S) (4:22) Reprise 26805 Music From The Motion Picture "Wayne's World". *(LP version)*
- (S) (4:15) Warner Brothers 2868 The Dream Weaver. *(LP version)*
- (S) (3:25) Rhino 71198 Super Hits Of The 70's Volume 18. *(:10 longer fade than the 45 version)*
- (S) (3:39) JCI 3307 Easy Seventies. *(:24 longer fade than the 45 version)*
- (S) (3:24) Rhino 71549 Let There Be Drums Vol. 3: The 70's. *(:09 longer fade than the 45 version)*
- (S) (3:40) Time-Life SOD-04 Sounds Of The Seventies - 1976. *(:25 longer fade than the 45 version)*
- (S) (3:39) Time-Life R138-18 Body Talk. *(:24 longer fade than the 45 version)*
- (S) (3:24) Time-Life AM1-23 AM Gold - 1976. *(:09 longer fade than the 45 version)*
- (S) (3:40) Time-Life R834-02 Body Talk - Just For You. *(:25 longer fade than the 45 version)*
- (S) (4:15) Angel 56344 O.S.T. The People Vs. Larry Flynt. *(LP version)*
- (S) (3:40) Simitar 55502 The Number One's: Classic Rock. *(:25 longer fade than the 45 version)*
- (S) (3:39) Thump 6010 Easyriders Volume 1. *(:24 longer fade than the 45 version)*

1976 LOVE IS ALIVE

- (S) (3:49) Warner Brothers 2868 The Dream Weaver. *(LP length)*

- (S) (3:24) Time-Life SOD-18 Sounds Of The Seventies - 1976: Take Two. *(45 length)*
- (S) (3:24) Madacy Entertainment 1976 Rock On 1976. *(45 length)*
- (S) (3:24) JCI 3169 #1 Radio Hits 1975 - Only Rock 'n Roll - 1979. *(45 length)*
- (S) (3:24) JCI 3192 18 Rock Classics Volume 2. *(45 length)*

1981 REALLY WANNA KNOW YOU

TAMMY WYNETTE

1969 STAND BY YOUR MAN

- (S) (2:37) Rhino 70689 Billboard's Top Country Hits Of 1968.
- (S) (2:38) Columbia 46032 Columbia Country Classics Volume 4.
- (S) (2:38) Epic 38312 Biggest Hits.
- (S) (2:38) Epic 26846 Greatest Hits.
- (S) (2:38) Epic 40625 Anniversary: 20 Years Of Hits.
- (S) (2:39) Epic 52741 25th Anniversary Collection.
- (S) (2:38) Time-Life CTD-06 Country USA - 1968.
- (S) (2:39) K-Tel 3085 Great Ladies Of Country.
- (S) (2:37) K-Tel 413 Country Music Classics Volume III.
- (S) (2:38) Time-Life R990-08 Tammy Wynette - Legendary Country Singers.
- (S) (2:39) Epic 67539 Super Hits.
- (S) (2:38) Nick At Nite/550 Music/Epic 67689 Stand By Your Man.
- (S) (2:37) K-Tel 3355 101 Greatest Country Hits Vol. One: Forever Country.
- (S) (2:37) Koch 7946 Stand By Your Man.
- (S) (2:39) Columbia 69083 Ladies Choice Super Hits.
- (S) (2:39) Time-Life R808-02 Classic Country 1965-1969.

XSCAPE

1993 JUST KICKIN' IT

- (S) (3:23) So So Def/Columbia 57107 Hummin' Comin' At 'Cha.

1994 UNDERSTANDING

- (S) (5:40) So So Def/Columbia 57107 Hummin' Comin' At 'Cha.

1995 FEELS SO GOOD

- (S) (3:31) So So Def/Columbia 67022 Off The Hook.

1995 WHO CAN I RUN TO

- (S) (3:35) So So Def/Columbia 67022 Off The Hook.
- (S) (3:35) EMI-Capitol Music Group 54548 Smooth Luv.

WEIRD AL YANKOVIC
1984 EAT IT
  (S) (3:17) Rhino 70743 Dr. Demento 20th Anniversary
            Collection.
  (S) (3:19) Scotti Bros. 5211 Greatest Hits.
  (S) (3:19) Rock 'N' Roll 44478 Greatest Hits.
  (S) (3:19) Scotti Bros. 75451 Al In The Box.
  (S) (3:17) Scotti Bros. 75421 The Food Album.
  (S) (3:19) Rock 'N' Roll 39221 In 3-D.
  (S) (3:19) Scotti Bros. 75207 In 3-D.
1992 SMELLS LIKE NIRVANA
  (S) (3:43) Rhino 72124 Dr. Demento 25th Anniversary
            Collection.
  (S) (3:42) Scotti Bros. 75456 Greatest Hits Volume II.
  (S) (3:42) Scotti Bros. 75256 Off The Deep End.
  (S) (3:42) Scotti Bros. 75451 Al In The Box.

GLENN YARBROUGH
1965 BABY THE RAIN MUST FALL
  (S) (2:19) RCA 8474 Nipper's Greatest Hits Of The 60's
            Volume 1.
  (S) (2:18) Time-Life R132-22 Treasury Of Folk Music
            Volume One.
  (S) (2:18) Folk Era 1708 Baby The Rain Must Fall.

YARBROUGH & PEOPLES
1981 DON'T STOP THE MUSIC
  (S) (7:54) Rhino 71754 and 72831 Phat Trax: The Best Of
            Old School Volume 3. *(LP version)*
  (S) (4:09) Priority 53786 Planet Funk Volume 3. *(45 version)*
  (S) (4:07) Rhino 72136 Billboard Hot R&B Hits 1981. *(45
            version)*
  (S) (4:09) JCI 3163 18 Disco Superhits. *(45 version)*
  (S) (7:45) Thump 4060 Old School Volume 6. *(LP version;
            all selections on this cd are segued together)*
  (S) (7:49) Mercury 314534848 Best Of. *(LP version)*
  (S) (7:20) Chronicles 314555140 Dance Funk. *(all
            selections on this cd are segued together)*
  (S) (4:08) JCI 3176 1980 - Only Soul - 1984. *(45 version)*

YARDBIRDS
1965 FOR YOUR LOVE
  (E) (2:27) Pair 1151 Best Of British Rock - The Yardbirds.
  (M) (2:28) Original Sound 8894 Dick Clark's 21 All-Time
            Hits Vol. 3.
  (M) (2:28) Rhino 70319 History Of British Rock Volume 1.
  (M) (2:28) Rhino 70319 History Of British Rock Box Set.
  (M) (2:28) Rhino 72008 History Of British Rock Volumes 1-
            4 Box Set.
  (M) (2:28) Sony Music Special Products 48655 Volume 1:
            Smokestack Lightning.
  (M) (2:28) Rhino 75895 Greatest Hits Volume 1.
  (M) (2:28) Polydor 835269 Crossroads.
  (M) (2:27) Rhino 71025 The Yardbirds/Rhino Special Editions.
  (M) (2:27) Time-Life 2CLR-01 Classic Rock - 1965.
  (M) (2:28) Time-Life R962-07 History Of Rock 'N' Roll: The
            British Invasion 1964-1966.
  (M) (2:27) JCI 3167 #1 Radio Hits 1965 - Only Rock 'n Roll - 1969.
  (M) (2:27) Flashback 72699 Heart Full Of Soul And Other Hits.
  (E) (2:36) Geffen 25218 O.S.T. Fear And Loathing In Las
            Vegas. *(time includes :12 of movie dialogue; all
            songs and the movie dialogue are segued together)*
1965 HEART FULL OF SOUL
  (E) (2:26) Pair 1151 Best Of British Rock - The Yardbirds.

  (M) (2:27) Rhino 70320 History Of British Rock Volume 2.
  (M) (2:27) Rhino 70319 History Of British Rock Box Set.
  (M) (2:27) Rhino 72008 History Of British Rock Volumes 1-
            4 Box Set.
  (M) (2:27) Original Sound 8895 Dick Clark's 21 All-Time
            Hits Vol. 4.
  (M) (2:27) Epic/Legacy 48661 Jeff Beck: Beckology.
  (M) (2:27) Sony Music Special Products 48655 Volume 1:
            Smokestack Lightning.
  (M) (2:27) Sony Music Special Products 48658 Volume 2:
            Blues, Backtracks And Shapes Of Things.
  (M) (2:27) Rhino 75895 Greatest Hits Volume 1.
  (M) (2:27) Rhino 71025 The Yardbirds/Rhino Special Editions.
  (M) (2:27) Time-Life 2CLR-01 Classic Rock - 1965.
  (M) (2:26) Time-Life OPCD-4521 Guitar Rock.
  (M) (2:27) Flashback 72699 Heart Full Of Soul And Other Hits.
1965 I'M A MAN
  (E) (2:34) Pair 1151 Best Of British Rock - The Yardbirds.
  (M) (2:36) Rhino 70321 History Of British Rock Volume 3.
  (M) (2:36) Rhino 70319 History Of British Rock Box Set.
  (M) (2:36) Rhino 72008 History Of British Rock Volumes 1-
            4 Box Set.
  (M) (2:35) Original Sound 8895 Dick Clark's 21 All-Time
            Hits Vol. 4.
  (M) (2:35) Warner Special Products 27607 Highs Of The 60's.
  (M) (2:35) Epic/Legacy 48661 Jeff Beck: Beckology.
  (M) (2:35) Sony Music Special Products 48655 Volume 1:
            Smokestack Lightning.
  (M) (2:36) Rhino 75895 Greatest Hits Volume 1.
  (M) (2:35) JCI 3107 British Sixties.
  (M) (2:36) Time-Life 2CLR-08 Classic Rock - 1965: The
            Beat Goes On.
1966 SHAPES OF THINGS
  (E) (2:23) Pair 1151 Best Of British Rock - The Yardbirds.
  (M) (2:35) Original Sound 8894 Dick Clark's 21 All-Time
            Hits Vol. 3. *(time includes :10 of studio talk)*
  (M) (2:25) Rhino 70322 History Of British Rock Volume 4.
  (M) (2:25) Rhino 70319 History Of British Rock Box Set.
  (M) (2:25) Rhino 72008 History Of British Rock Volumes 1-
            4 Box Set.
  (M) (2:23) JCI 3103 Electric Sixties.
  (M) (2:23) Epic/Legacy 48661 Jeff Beck: Beckology.
  (M) (2:24) Sony Music Special Products 48658 Volume 2:
            Blues, Backtracks And Shapes Of Things.
  (M) (2:35) Rhino 75895 Greatest Hits Volume 1. *(includes
            :10 of studio talk)*
  (M) (2:24) Rhino 71025 The Yardbirds/Rhino Special Editions.
  (M) (2:24) Time-Life 2CLR-02 Classic Rock - 1966.
  (M) (2:24) Risky Business 53919 Songs Of Peacemakers,
            Protesters And Potheads.
  (M) (2:24) Flashback 72699 Heart Full Of Soul And Other Hits.
1966 OVER UNDER SIDEWAYS DOWN
  (E) (2:20) Epic/Legacy 48661 Jeff Beck: Beckology.
  (M) (2:20) Time-Life 2CLR-07 Classic Rock - 1966: The
            Beat Goes On.
  (M) (2:20) Time-Life R968-09 Guitar Rock 1966-1967.
  (M) (2:20) Thump 6010 Easyriders Volume 1.
1967 HAPPENINGS TEN YEARS TIME AGO
  (M) (2:54) Epic/Legacy 48661 Jeff Beck: Beckology.
  (M) (2:54) Time-Life 2CLR-17 Classic Rock - Rock
            Renaissance.

TRISHA YEARWOOD
1997 HOW DO I LIVE
  (S) (4:01) MCA 70011 (Songbook) A Collection Of Hits.

YELLOW BALLOON
1967 YELLOW BALLOON
- (S) (2:16) Varese Sarabande 5803 Sunshine Days - Pop Classics Of The '60s Volume 3.
- (S) (2:15) Sundazed 11069 Yellow Balloon.

YES
1971 YOUR MOVE
(the LP version of this song is a medley of "I'VE SEEN ALL GOOD PEOPLE", "YOUR MOVE" and "ALL GOOD PEOPLE")
- (S) (6:52) Atlantic 81908 Classic Rock 1966-1988. *(LP version)*
- (S) (6:51) Atlantic 82306 Atlantic Rock & Roll Box Set. *(LP version)*
- (S) (7:09) Atlantic 100-2 Yessongs. *(live)*
- (S) (7:09) Atlantic 82682 Yessongs. *(remastered edition; live)*
- (S) (6:53) Atlantic 19131 Yes Album. *(LP version)*
- (S) (6:54) Atlantic 82665 Yes Album. *(remastered edition; LP version)*
- (S) (6:53) Atco 91644 Yes Years. *(LP version)*
- (S) (6:53) Atlantic 82517 Highlights/Very Best Of. *(LP version)*

1972 ROUNDABOUT
- (S) (8:32) Atlantic 100-2 Yessongs. *(live)*
- (S) (8:32) Atlantic 82682 Yessongs. *(remastered edition; live)*
- (S) (8:29) Atlantic 19132 Fragile. *(LP version)*
- (S) (8:30) Atlantic 82667 Fragile. *(remastered edition; LP version)*
- (S) (8:30) Atco 91644 Yes Years. *(LP version)*
- (S) (3:25) Time-Life R968-05 Guitar Rock 1972-1973. *(45 version)*
- (S) (3:25) Time-Life SOD-13 Sounds Of The Seventies - 1972: Take Two. *(45 version)*
- (S) (8:30) Atlantic 82517 Highlights/Very Best Of. *(LP version)*
- (S) (8:30) Atlantic 82524 Fragile. *(gold disc; LP version)*
- (S) (3:25) JCI 3140 18 Screamers From The 70's. *(45 version)*
- (S) (3:25) Time-Life R13610 Gold And Platinum Box Set - The Ultimate Rock Collection. *(45 version)*
- (S) (8:21) CMC International 86233 Superstar Hits. *(live)*
- (S) (3:26) Simitar 55502 The Number One's: Classic Rock. *(45 version)*
- (S) (8:30) Atlantic 83088 Atlantic Records: 50 Years - The Gold Anniversary Collection. *(LP version)*

1984 OWNER OF A LONELY HEART
(dj copies of this 45 ran (3:50) and (4:28); commercial copies were all (3:50))
- (S) (4:26) Atlantic 81908 Classic Rock 1966-1988. *(LP length)*
- (S) (7:47) JCI 3122 Lost Mixes. *(remixed)*
- (S) (3:48) Rhino 70679 Billboard Top Hits - 1984. *(45 length)*
- (S) (3:47) JCI 3127 1980 - Only Rock 'N Roll - 1984. *(45 length)*
- (S) (4:25) Atco 90125 90125. *(LP length)*
- (S) (4:26) Atlantic 82517 Highlights/Very Best Of. *(LP length)*
- (S) (3:47) Epic/Legacy 65020 Ultimate Rock 'n' Roll Collection. *(45 length)*
- (S) (4:25) Rebound 314520434 Classic Rock - 80's. *(LP length)*
- (S) (3:48) Time-Life R988-15 Sounds Of The Eighties: The Mid 80's. *(45 length)*
- (S) (4:25) Thump 6010 Easyriders Volume 1. *(LP length)*

1984 LEAVE IT
- (S) (4:12) Atco 90125 90125. *(LP version)*
- (S) (4:12) Atlantic 82517 Highlights/Very Best Of. *(LP version)*
- (S) (4:15) Rhino 72597 Billboard Top Album Rock Hits, 1984. *(LP version)*

1987 LOVE WILL FIND A WAY
(dj copies of this 45 ran (4:14) and (4:48); commercial copies were all (4:14))
- (S) (4:12) Time-Life R105-40 Rock Dreams. *(45 version)*
- (S) (4:48) Atco 90522 Big Generator. *(LP version)*

1988 RHYTHM OF LOVE
- (S) (4:46) Atco 90522 Big Generator.
- (S) (4:45) Atlantic 82517 Highlights/Very Best Of.
- (S) (4:43) JCI 3193 18 Rock Classics Volume 3.

BARRY YOUNG
1966 ONE HAS MY NAME (THE OTHER HAS MY HEART)

FARON YOUNG
1961 HELLO WALLS
- (S) (2:21) Rhino 70682 Billboard's Top Country Hits Of 1961.
- (M) (2:22) Curb 77343 60's Hits - Country Volume 1.
- (M) (2:22) Curb 77334 All-Time Greatest Hits.
- (M) (2:23) Capitol 95916 Golden Country Jukebox Favorites.
- (S) (2:21) Time-Life CTD-01 Country USA - 1961.
- (S) (2:21) K-Tel 320 Country Music Classics Volume II.
- (M) (2:23) JCI 3153 1960 - Only Country - 1964.
- (S) (2:14) K-Tel 3359 101 Greatest Country Hits Vol. Five: Country Memories. *(rerecording)*
- (M) (2:23) Angel 56344 O.S.T. The People Vs. Larry Flynt.
- (S) (2:21) Time-Life R808-01 Classic Country 1960-1964.

JOHN PAUL YOUNG
1978 LOVE IS IN THE AIR
- (S) (3:28) Rhino 71202 Super Hits Of The 70's Volume 22.
- (S) (3:25) Time-Life SOD-35 Sounds Of The Seventies - AM Nuggets.
- (S) (3:24) Madacy Entertainment 1978 Rock On 1978.
- (S) (3:28) Time-Life AM1-25 AM Gold - 1978.

KATHY YOUNG with THE INNOCENTS
1960 A THOUSAND STARS
- (M) (3:11) Collectables 5070 History Of Rock Volume 10.
- (E) (3:09) Original Sound 8855 Oldies But Goodies Vol. 5. *(this compact disc uses the "Waring - fds" noise reduction process; ambient background noise throughout the disc)*
- (E) (3:09) Original Sound 2222 Oldies But Goodies Volumes 3,5,11,14 and 15 Box Set. *(this box set uses the "Waring - fds" noise reduction process; ambient background noise throughout the song)*
- (E) (3:09) Original Sound 2500 Oldies But Goodies Volumes 1-15 Box Set. *(this box set uses the "Waring - fds" noise reduction process; ambient background noise throughout the song)*
- (E) (3:09) Original Sound 9603 Best Of Oldies But Goodies Vol. 3. *(ambient background noise throughout the song)*
- (M) (3:10) Time-Life 2RNR-11 Rock 'N' Roll Era - 1960.
- (M) (3:10) Collectables 2500 WCBS-FM History Of Rock - The 60's Part 1.
- (M) (3:10) Collectables 4500 History Of Rock/The 60s Part One.
- (M) (3:11) Rhino 71581 Billboard Top Pop Hits, 1960.
- (E) (3:13) Curb 77773 Hard To Find Hits Of Rock 'N' Roll Volume One.
- (M) (3:11) Eclipse Music Group 64867 Rock 'n Roll Relix 1960-1961.
- (M) (3:11) Eclipse Music Group 64872 Rock 'n Roll Relix 1960-1969.
- (M) (3:08) Collectors' Choice 5189 I Wish I Were A Princess - The Great Lost Female Teen Idols.

1961 HAPPY BIRTHDAY BLUES
- (M) (2:59) Time-Life 2RNR-46 Rock 'N' Roll Era - 60's Juke Box Memories.
- (M) (2:58) Collectors' Choice 5189 I Wish I Were A Princess - The Great Lost Female Teen Idols.
- (M) (2:59) Time-Life R857-19 The Heart Of Rock 'n' Roll 1960-1961 Take Three.

NEIL YOUNG
1970 ONLY LOVE CAN BREAK YOUR HEART
- (S) (3:07) Reprise 2283 After The Gold Rush.

1972 HEART OF GOLD
- (S) (3:06) Reprise 2277 Harvest.
- (S) (3:06) Reprise 2257 Decade.

1972 OLD MAN
- (S) (3:21) Reprise 2277 Harvest.
- (S) (3:21) Reprise 2257 Decade.

PAUL YOUNG
1984 COME BACK AND STAY
- (S) (3:34) Rhino 71975 New Wave Hits Of The 80's Vol. 12. *(45 length)*
- (S) (4:22) Columbia 48829 From Time To Time - The Singles Collection. *(LP length)*
- (S) (4:24) Columbia 38976 No Parlez. *(LP length)*
- (S) (4:20) Simitar 55562 The Number One's: Smooth Love. *(LP length)*

1985 EVERYTIME YOU GO AWAY
(actual 45 time is (4:14) not (4:10) as stated on the record label)
- (S) (4:16) T.J. Martell Foundation/Columbia 40315 Music For The Miracle. *(45 version)*
- (S) (4:26) Priority 53681 80's Greatest Rock Hits - Agony & Ecstasy. *(45 version but with a :12 longer fade)*
- (S) (4:26) Columbia 48829 From Time To Time - The Singles Collection. *(45 version but with a :12 longer fade)*
- (S) (5:23) Columbia 39957 The Secret Of Association. *(LP version)*
- (S) (4:27) Time-Life R988-02 Sounds Of The Eighties: 1985. *(45 version but with a :13 longer fade)*
- (S) (4:25) Time-Life R138-18 Body Talk. *(45 version but with a :11 longer fade)*
- (S) (4:25) JCI 3171 #1 Radio Hits 1985 - Only Rock 'n Roll - 1989. *(45 version but with a :11 longer fade)*
- (S) (4:24) Madacy Entertainment 6803 Power Of Love. *(45 version but with a :10 longer fade)*
- (S) (4:25) Time-Life R834-01 Body Talk - Forever Yours. *(45 version but with a :11 longer fade)*
- (S) (4:26) Hip-O 40047 The '80s Hit(s) Back 3. *(45 version but with a :12 longer fade)*
- (S) (4:26) Priority 50974 Premiere The Movie Magazine Presents The Greatest Soundtrack Love Songs. *(45 version but with a :12 longer fade)*
- (S) (4:26) K-Tel 3864 Slow Dancin'. *(45 version but with a :12 longer fade)*

1985 I'M GONNA TEAR YOUR PLAYHOUSE DOWN
- (S) (5:05) Columbia 39957 The Secret Of Association. *(LP version)*
- (S) (4:45) Columbia 48829 From Time To Time - The Singles Collection. *(45 version)*
- (S) (4:45) Simitar 55552 The Number One's: Eighties Rock. *(45 version)*

1990 OH GIRL
- (S) (3:31) Foundation/Capitol 96427 Hearts Of Gold: The Pop Collection.
- (S) (3:34) Columbia 48829 From Time To Time - The Singles Collection.
- (S) (3:33) Columbia 46755 Other Voices.
- (S) (3:34) Madacy Entertainment 6806 Best Of Love.
- (S) (3:31) Time-Life R834-13 Body Talk - Just The Two Of Us.

1992 WHAT BECOMES OF THE BROKEN HEARTED
- (S) (4:32) MCA 10461 O.S.T. Fried Green Tomatoes.

VICTOR YOUNG
1957 AROUND THE WORLD
- (S) (3:02) MCA 31134 Music From Around The World In 80 Days. *(soundtrack version)*
- (M) (2:35) Time-Life HPD-17 Your Hit Parade - 1957. *(45 version)*
- (S) (3:03) DCC Compact Classics 079 Music For A Bachelor's Den. *(soundtrack version)*

YOUNGBLOODS
1969 GET TOGETHER
(dj copies of this 45 ran (3:24) and (4:37); commercial copies were all (4:37))
- (S) (4:15) Polydor 837362 O.S.T. 1969. *(rerecording of this song by Jesse Colin Young, former lead singer of the Youngbloods)*

- (S) (4:37) Rhino 70630 Billboard's Top Rock & Roll Hits Of 1969.
- (S) (4:37) Rhino 72005 Billboard's Top Rock & Roll Hits 1968-1972 Box Set.
- (M) (4:38) Rhino 70536 San Francisco Nights.
- (S) (4:33) DCC Compact Classics 045 Golden Age Of Underground Radio.
- (S) (4:36) RCA 8475 Nipper's Greatest Hits Of The 60's Volume 2.
- (S) (4:36) RCA 3280 Best Of.
- (S) (4:36) Priority 53706 Singers/Songwriters/70's Greatest Rock Hits Volume 15.
- (M) (4:38) Rhino 71065 Summer Of Love Volume 1.
- (S) (4:36) Time-Life 2CLR-06 Classic Rock - 1969.
- (S) (4:36) Time-Life SUD-07 Superhits - 1969.
- (S) (4:36) Time-Life R103-33 Singers & Songwriters.
- (S) (4:38) Time-Life R921-38 Get Together.
- (S) (4:35) Epic 66329 O.S.T. Forrest Gump.
- (S) (4:35) K-Tel 3438 Best Of Folk Rock.
- (M) (4:37) RCA 66881 RCA's Greatest One-Hit Wonders.
- (S) (4:36) JCI 3160 18 Free & Easy Hits From The 60's.
- (S) (4:36) Priority 50951 I Love Rock & Roll Volume 2: Hits Of The 60's.
- (S) (4:37) Eclipse Music Group 64871 Rock 'n Roll Relix 1968-1969.
- (S) (4:37) Eclipse Music Group 64872 Rock 'n Roll Relix 1960-1969.
- (S) (4:36) Time-Life AM1-01 AM Gold - 1969.
- (S) (4:35) Time-Life R132-22 Treasury Of Folk Music Volume Two.
- (S) (3:21) Varese Sarabande 5846 On The Radio Volume One. *(dj 45 version)*
- (S) (5:41) Geffen 25218 O.S.T. Fear And Loathing In Las Vegas. *(time includes 1:05 of movie dialogue; all songs and the movie dialogue are segued together)*

YOUNG-HOLT UNLIMITED
1969 SOULFUL STRUT
- (S) (2:59) Rhino 71604 Rock Instrumental Classics Vol. 4: Soul.
- (S) (2:59) Rhino 72035 Rock Instrumental Classics Vols. 1-5 Box Set.
- (S) (2:52) Time-Life RHD-04 Rhythm & Blues - 1968.
- (S) (2:56) Time-Life 2CLR-11 Classic Rock - 1968: The Beat Goes On.
- (S) (2:58) Brunswick 81007 Best Of.
- (S) (2:58) Rhino 71939 Billboard Top Pop Hits, 1969.
- (S) (2:57) Brunswick 81009 The Brunswick Years Volume One.
- (S) (2:59) MCA Special Products 20902 Classic Rock & Roll Instrumental Hits, Volume 1.
- (S) (2:58) Hip-O 40008 Soulful Grooves - R&B Instrumental Classics Volume 2.
- (S) (2:58) Priority 50929 Rare Grooves Volume 2.
- (S) (2:52) Time-Life R838-03 Solid Gold Soul - 1968.

YOUNG MC
1989 BUST A MOVE
- (S) (4:23) JCI 2713 Bust It.
- (S) (4:23) Priority 7986 Bust A Rap.
- (S) (4:23) K-Tel 315 Rap's Biggest Hits.
- (S) (4:23) Sandstone 33043 and 5009 Rock The First Volume Three.
- (S) (4:23) Delicious Vinyl 91309 and 71814 Stone Cold Rhymin'.
- (S) (4:01) Thump 4530 Old School Rap Volume 3. *(all songs on this cd are segued together; alternate take)*
- (S) (4:23) Priority 50982 Rap's Greatest Hits Volume Two.
- (S) (4:23) Street Life 75510 West Coast Collection, Volume 1.
- (S) (4:22) Cold Front 6246 Classic Club Mix - R&B Grooves. *(all selections on this cd are segued together)*
- (S) (4:21) Cold Front 6255 Greatest Sports Rock And Jams Volume 2. *(all selections on this cd are segued together)*

1990 PRINCIPAL'S OFFICE
- (S) (4:14) Delicious Vinyl 91309 and 71814 Stone Cold Rhymin'.

YOUNG RASCALS (see RASCALS)

TIMI YURO
✗**1961 HURT**
    (S) (2:26)   EMI 80182 Best Of.
    (S) (2:26)   EMI 81128 Rock Is Dead But It Won't Lie Down.
    (S) (2:26)   Time-Life SUD-15 Superhits - The Early 60's.
    (S) (2:26)   Time-Life HPD-32 Your Hit Parade - Into The 60's.
    (E) (2:26)   Original Sound 8859 Oldies But Goodies Vol. 9. *(this compact disc uses the "Waring - fds" noise reduction process)*
    (S) (2:25)   Original Sound 8859r Oldies But Goodies Vol. 9. *(remastered edition)*
    (S) (2:25)   Original Sound 2223 Oldies But Goodies Volumes 2,7,9,12 and 13 Box Set. *(Volumes 2, 7 and 12 of this box set use the "Waring - fds" noise reduction process)*
    (S) (2:25)   Original Sound 2500 Oldies But Goodies Volumes 1-15 Box Set. *(most volumes in this box set use the "Waring - fds" noise reduction process)*
    (S) (2:25)   Risky Business 66388 The Big Hurt/Songs To Cry By.
    (S) (2:27)   Time-Life R857-03 The Heart Of Rock 'n' Roll - 1961.
    (S) (2:26)   MCA 11389 O.S.T. Casino.
    (S) (2:26)   Time-Life AM1-19 AM Gold - The Early '60s.
✗**1962 WHAT'S A MATTER BABY (IS IT HURTING YOU)**
    (S) (2:42)   EMI 80182 Best Of.
    (S) (2:43)   Era 5025 The Brill Building Sound.
    (S) (2:40)   Time-Life 2RNR-49 Rock 'N' Roll Era - Lost Treasures II.
✗**1963 MAKE THE WORLD GO AWAY**
    (S) (2:35)   EMI 80182 Best Of.

FLORIAN ZABACH
1956 WHEN THE WHITE LILACS BLOOM AGAIN

HELMUT ZACHARIAS and HIS MAGIC VIOLINS
1956 WHEN THE WHITE LILACS BLOOM AGAIN

JOHN ZACHERLE
1958 DINNER WITH DRAC (PART 1)

PIA ZADORA
1983 THE CLAPPING SONG

MICHAEL ZAGER BAND
1978 LET'S ALL CHANT
    (S) (7:00) Rebound 314520309 Disco Nights Vol. VII - D.J. Pix. *(12" single version)*
    (S) (6:59) Varese Sarabande 5787 Let's All Chant: The Michael Zager Collection. *(12" single version)*
    (S) (6:17) Chronicles 314553404 Non-Stop Disco Vol. 1. *(all songs on this cd are segued together)*
    (S) (4:28) Thump 4840 Flashback Disco. *(all selections on this cd are segued together)*

ZAGER & EVANS
1969 IN THE YEAR 2525 (EXORDIUM AND TERMINUS)
    (S) (3:15) RCA 8475 Nipper's Greatest Hits Of The 60's Volume 2.
    (S) (3:14) RCA 9902 Nipper's #1 Hits 1956-1986.
    (S) (3:12) Time-Life 2CLR-12 Classic Rock - 1969: The Beat Goes On.
    (S) (3:17) Rhino 71939 Billboard Top Pop Hits, 1969.
    (S) (3:13) RCA 66881 RCA's Greatest One-Hit Wonders.
    (S) (3:17) Time-Life 2CLR-31 Classic Rock - Totally Fantastic '60s.

ZAPP & ROGER
1994 SLOW AND EASY
    (S) (5:10) Reprise 45143 Zapp & Roger - All The Greatest Hits.

FRANK ZAPPA featuring MOON UNIT ZAPPA
1982 VALLEY GIRL
    (S) (3:47) Rhino 71698 New Wave Hits Of The 80's Vol. 5.

SI ZENTNER
1961 UP A LAZY RIVER
    (S) (2:04) Curb 77403 All-Time Great Instrumental Hits Volume 1.
    (S) (2:02) Collectors' Choice 003/4 Instrumental Gems Of The 60's.

WARREN ZEVON
1978 WEREWOLVES OF LONDON
    (S) (3:24) Sandstone 33001 Reelin' In The Years Volume 2.
    (S) (3:25) Asylum 60503 Best Of/A Quiet Normal Life.
    (S) (3:24) Asylum 118 Excitable Boy.
    (S) (3:24) Rhino 71201 Super Hits Of The 70's Volume 21.
    (S) (3:24) DCC Compact Classics 063 Rock Of The 70's Volume 2.
    (S) (3:23) Time-Life R102-34 The Rolling Stone Collection.
    (S) (3:27) Time-Life SOD-10 Sounds Of The Seventies - 1978.
    (S) (3:27) Time-Life R105-26 Our Songs: Singers & Songwriters Encore.

    (S) (3:24) Rhino 71777 Dr. Demento Presents: Spooky Tunes & Scary Melodies.
    (S) (3:23) Rhino 72179 Elvira Presents: Revenge Of The Monster Hits.
    (S) (3:23) K-Tel 3795 Music For Your Halloween Party.
    (S) (3:23) K-Tel 3795 Spooktacular Party Songs.
    (S) (3:25) Rhino 73510 I'll Sleep When I'm Dead (An Anthology).
    (S) (3:24) Eclipse Music Group 64896 Rock 'n Roll Relix 1978-1979.
    (S) (3:24) Eclipse Music Group 64897 Rock 'n Roll Relix 1970-1979.
    (S) (3:24) Rhino 72481 Haunted Hits.
    (S) (3:23) Rebound 314520492 Class Reunion '78.

ZHANE
1993 HEY MR. D.J.
    (M) (4:16) Epic 57634 Hey Mr. D.J. The 4th Compilation.
    (S) (6:36) Epic 57634 Hey Mr. D.J. The 4th Compilation. *(remix)*
    (S) (5:58) Tommy Boy 1097 MTV Party To Go Volume 5. *(remix; all tracks on this cd are segued together)*
    (M) (4:22) Flavor Unit/Epic 57110 and 53615 Roll Wit Tha Flava.
    (M) (4:10) Motown 6369 Pronounced Jah-Nay. *(introduction of :02 is stereo)*
    (M) (4:10) Rebound 314520439 Soul Classics - Best Of The 90's. *(introduction of :02 is stereo)*
1994 GROOVE THANG
    (S) (3:54) Motown 6369 Pronounced Jah-Nay. *(very narrow stereo separation)*
1994 SENDING MY LOVE
    (S) (3:41) Motown 6369 Pronounced Jah-Nay.
1994 SHAME
    (S) (4:13) Jive 41536 O.S.T. A Low Down Dirty Shame.
1997 REQUEST LINE
    (S) (3:54) Illtown/Motown 314530751 Saturday Night.

ZOMBIES
1964 SHE'S NOT THERE
    (M) (2:22) Rhino 70906 American Bandstand Greatest Hits Collection. *(45 version)*
    (S) (2:23) Original Sound 8894 Dick Clark's 21 All-Time Hits Vol. 3. *(LP version; with countoff)*
    (M) (2:22) Rhino 70319 History Of British Rock Volume 1. *(45 version)*
    (M) (2:22) Rhino 70319 History Of British Rock Box Set. *(45 version)*
    (M) (2:22) Rhino 72008 History Of British Rock Volumes 1-4 Box Set. *(45 version)*
    (M) (2:22) Rhino 70625 Billboard's Top Rock & Roll Hits Of 1964. *(45 version)*
    (M) (2:22) Rhino 72007 Billboard's Top Rock & Roll Hits 1962-1966 Box Set. *(45 version)*
    (M) (2:22) DCC Compact Classics 052 Greatest Hits. *(45 version)*
    (M) (2:22) Time-Life 2CLR-03 Classic Rock - 1964. *(45 version)*
    (M) (2:22) Time-Life SUD-09 Superhits - 1964. *(45 version)*
    (M) (2:22) Time-Life R962-07 History Of Rock 'N' Roll: The British Invasion 1964-1966. *(45 version)*
    (S) (2:21) Capitol 89098 O.S.T. Wild Palms. *(LP version)*
    (S) (2:21) Translux 57803 Greatest Hits - Greatest Recordings. *(LP version)*
    (M) (2:22) Eclipse Music Group 64869 Rock 'n Roll Relix 1964-1965. *(45 version)*

ZOMBIES *(Continued)*

(M) (2:22) Eclipse Music Group 64872 Rock 'n Roll Relix 1960-1969. *(45 version)*

(M) (2:22) Time-Life AM1-11 AM Gold - 1964. *(45 version)*

1965 TELL HER NO

(S) (2:04) Rhino 70320 History Of British Rock Volume 2.

(S) (2:04) Rhino 70319 History Of British Rock Box Set.

(S) (2:04) Rhino 72008 History Of British Rock Volumes 1-4 Box Set.

(S) (2:05) Original Sound 8895 Dick Clark's 21 All-Time Hits Vol. 4.

(S) (2:05) DCC Compact Classics 052 Greatest Hits.

(S) (2:04) Time-Life 2CLR-14 Classic Rock - 1965: Shakin' All Over.

(S) (2:04) Varese Sarabande 5503 and 5504 and 5505 and 5506 and 5507 and 5508 and 5509 and 5513 and 5571 Arrow: All Rock & Roll Oldies Volume One.

(S) (2:05) Translux 57803 Greatest Hits - Greatest Recordings.

(S) (2:05) Rebound 314520435 Classic Rock - 60's.

1969 TIME OF THE SEASON

(S) (3:31) Rhino 70630 Billboard's Top Rock & Roll Hits Of 1969.

(S) (3:31) Rhino 72005 Billboard's Top Rock & Roll Hits 1968-1972 Box Set.

(S) (3:30) Polydor 837362 O.S.T. 1969.

(S) (3:29) DCC Compact Classics 052 Zombies Greatest Hits.

(S) (3:31) Rhino 70186 Odessey And Oracle.

(S) (3:31) Time-Life 2CLR-06 Classic Rock - 1969.

(S) (3:31) Rebound 314520269 Class Reunion 1969.

(S) (3:31) Translux 57803 Greatest Hits - Greatest Recordings.

(S) (3:31) Priority 50951 I Love Rock & Roll Volume 2: Hits Of The 60's.

(S) (3:31) Eclipse Music Group 64871 Rock 'n Roll Relix 1968-1969.

(S) (3:31) Eclipse Music Group 64872 Rock 'n Roll Relix 1960-1969.

(S) (3:31) Big Beat 181 Odessey & Oracle.

(M) (3:29) Big Beat 181 Odessey & Oracle.

(M) (3:29) Big Beat 181 Odessey & Oracle. *(alternate mix)*

ZZ TOP

1974 LA GRANGE

(S) (3:50) Warner Brothers 3270 Tres Hombres. *(LP length; remixed)*

(S) (3:50) Warner Brothers 26846 Greatest Hits. *(LP length; remixed)*

(S) (3:50) Warner Brothers 25661 Z Z Top Sixpack. *(remixed; LP length)*

(S) (3:50) Warner Brothers 3273 Best Of. *(LP length)*

(S) (3:50) Time-Life R968-08 Guitar Rock - The Mid '70s. *(LP length)*

1975 TUSH

(S) (2:14) Warner Brothers 26846 Greatest Hits. *(remixed)*

(S) (2:14) Warner Brothers 3271 Fandango. *(remixed)*

(S) (2:14) Warner Brothers 25661 Z Z Top Sixpack. *(remixed)*

(S) (2:16) Warner Brothers 3273 Best Of.

(S) (2:14) Medicine Label 24533 O.S.T. Dazed And Confused.

(S) (2:14) Island 90017 and 422842715 O.S.T. An Officer And A Gentleman.

1980 I THANK YOU

(S) (3:23) Warner Brothers 3361 Deguello.

1983 GIMME ALL YOUR LOVIN

(S) (3:58) Warner Brothers 26846 Greatest Hits. *(LP version)*

(S) (3:59) Warner Brothers 23774 Eliminator. *(LP version)*

1984 LEGS

(S) (4:31) JCI 3122 Lost Mixes. *(remixed)*

(S) (4:30) Warner Brothers 26846 Greatest Hits. *(LP version)*

(S) (4:32) Warner Brothers 23774 Eliminator. *(LP version)*

(S) (3:35) Time-Life R988-01 Sounds Of The Eighties: The Rockin' Eighties. *(45 version)*

(S) (3:34) Time-Life R13610 Gold And Platinum Box Set - The Ultimate Rock Collection. *(45 version)*

(S) (3:34) Madacy Entertainment 6805 The Power Of Rock. *(45 version)*

1985 SLEEPING BAG

(S) (4:01) Warner Brothers 25342 Afterburner.

(S) (4:01) Warner Brothers 26846 Greatest Hits.

(S) (4:02) Time-Life R988-02 Sounds Of The Eighties: 1985.

1986 STAGES

(S) (3:31) Warner Brothers 25342 Afterburner.

1986 ROUGH BOY

(S) (4:48) Warner Brothers 25342 Afterburner. *(LP version)*

(S) (4:50) Warner Brothers 26846 Greatest Hits. *(LP version)*

1986 VELCRO FLY

(S) (3:28) Warner Brothers 25342 Afterburner.

Key to the Song Title Index

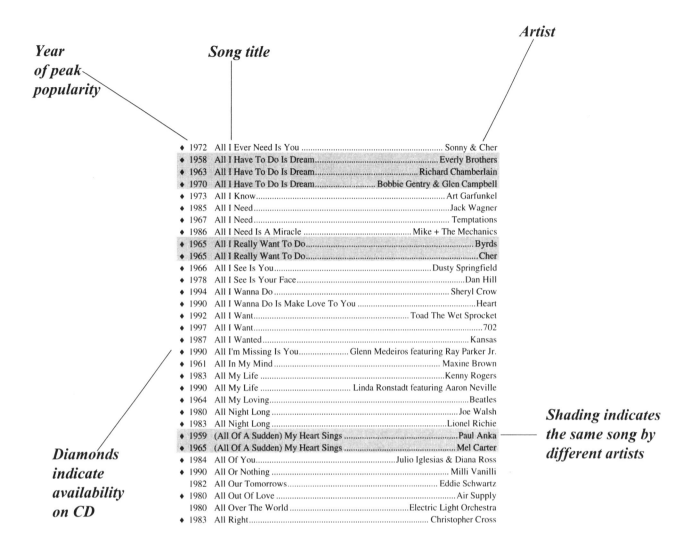

Year of peak popularity

Song title

Artist

♦ 1972	All I Ever Need Is You	Sonny & Cher
♦ 1958	All I Have To Do Is Dream	Everly Brothers
♦ 1963	All I Have To Do Is Dream	Richard Chamberlain
♦ 1970	All I Have To Do Is Dream	Bobbie Gentry & Glen Campbell
♦ 1973	All I Know	Art Garfunkel
♦ 1985	All I Need	Jack Wagner
♦ 1967	All I Need	Temptations
♦ 1986	All I Need Is A Miracle	Mike + The Mechanics
♦ 1965	All I Really Want To Do	Byrds
♦ 1965	All I Really Want To Do	Cher
♦ 1966	All I See Is You	Dusty Springfield
♦ 1978	All I See Is Your Face	Dan Hill
♦ 1994	All I Wanna Do	Sheryl Crow
♦ 1990	All I Wanna Do Is Make Love To You	Heart
♦ 1992	All I Want	Toad The Wet Sprocket
♦ 1997	All I Want	702
♦ 1987	All I Wanted	Kansas
♦ 1990	All I'm Missing Is You	Glenn Medeiros featuring Ray Parker Jr.
♦ 1961	All In My Mind	Maxine Brown
♦ 1983	All My Life	Kenny Rogers
♦ 1990	All My Life	Linda Ronstadt featuring Aaron Neville
♦ 1964	All My Loving	Beatles
♦ 1980	All Night Long	Joe Walsh
♦ 1983	All Night Long	Lionel Richie
♦ 1959	(All Of A Sudden) My Heart Sings	Paul Anka
♦ 1965	(All Of A Sudden) My Heart Sings	Mel Carter
♦ 1984	All Of You	Julio Iglesias & Diana Ross
♦ 1990	All Or Nothing	Milli Vanilli
1982	All Our Tomorrows	Eddie Schwartz
♦ 1980	All Out Of Love	Air Supply
1980	All Over The World	Electric Light Orchestra
♦ 1983	All Right	Christopher Cross

Diamonds indicate availability on CD

Shading indicates the same song by different artists

677

Song Title Index

- ♦ 1995 Any Man Of Mine .... Shania Twain
- ♦ 1994 Any Time, Any Place .... Janet Jackson
- ♦ 1964 Any Way You Want It .... Dave Clark Five
- ♦ 1980 Any Way You Want It .... Journey
- ♦ 1961 Anybody But Me .... Brenda Lee
- 1960 Anymore .... Teresa Brewer
- ♦ 1964 Anyone Who Had A Heart .... Dionne Warwick
- ♦ 1994 Anything .... SWV
- ♦ 1996 Anything 3T
- ♦ 1988 Anything For You .... Gloria Estefan And Miami Sound Machine
- ♦ 1990 Anything I Want .... Kevin Paige
- ♦ 1991 Anything Is Possible .... Debbie Gibson
- ♦ 1962 Anything That's Part Of You .... Elvis Presley
- ♦ 1976 Anytime (I'll Be There) .... Paul Anka
- ♦ 1994 Anytime You Need A Friend .... Mariah Carey
- ♦ 1956 Anyway You Want Me (That's How I Will Be) .... Elvis Presley
- ♦ 1961 Apache .... Jorgen Ingmann
- ♦ 1956 Ape Call .... Nervous Norvus
- ♦ 1971 Apeman .... Kinks
- 1960 Apple Green .... June Valli
- ♦ 1965 Apple Of My Eye .... Roy Head And The Traits
- ♦ 1967 Apples, Peaches, Pumpkin Pie .... Jay And The Techniques
- ♦ 1969 April Fools .... Dionne Warwick
- ♦ 1957 April Love .... Pat Boone
- ♦ 1969 Aquarius/Let The Sunshine In .... Fifth Dimension
- ♦ 1984 Are We Ourselves? .... Fixx
- ♦ 1969 Are You Happy .... Jerry Butler
- ♦ 1967 Are You Lonely For Me .... Freddie Scott
- ♦ 1960 Are You Lonesome Tonight .... Elvis Presley
- ♦ 1974 Are You Lonesome Tonight .... Donny Osmond
- ♦ 1973 Are You Man Enough .... Four Tops
- ♦ 1970 Are You Ready? .... Pacific Gas & Electric
- ♦ 1958 Are You Really Mine .... Jimmie Rodgers
- 1956 Are You Satisfied? .... Rusty Draper
- ♦ 1958 Are You Sincere .... Andy Williams
- ♦ 1966 Are You There (With Another Girl) .... Dionne Warwick
- ♦ 1977 Ariel .... Dean Friedman
- ♦ 1970 Arizona .... Mark Lindsay
- ♦ 1989 Armageddon It .... Def Leppard
- ♦ 1973 Armed And Extremely Dangerous .... First Choice
- 1956 Armen's Theme .... David Seville
- ♦ 1989 Arms Of Orion .... Prince With Sheena Easton
- ♦ 1991 Around The Way Girl .... L.L. Cool J
- ♦ 1957 Around The World .... Bing Crosby
- ♦ 1957 Around The World .... Mantovani
- ♦ 1957 Around The World .... Victor Young
- ♦ 1979 Arrow Through Me .... Wings
- ♦ 1981 Arthur's Theme (Best That You Can Do) .... Christopher Cross
- ♦ 1960 Artificial Flowers .... Bobby Darin
- ♦ 1978 As .... Stevie Wonder
- ♦ 1995 As I Lay Me Down .... Sophie B. Hawkins
- 1961 As If I Didn't Know .... Adam Wade
- ♦ 1989 As Long As You Follow .... Fleetwood Mac
- ♦ 1965 As Tears Go By .... Marianne Faithfull
- ♦ 1966 As Tears Go By .... Rolling Stones
- ♦ 1970 As The Years Go By .... Mashmakhan
- ♦ 1964 As Usual .... Brenda Lee
- ♦ 1987 As We Lay .... Shirley Murdock
- ♦ 1996 Ascension (Don't Ever Wonder) .... Maxwell
- ♦ 1980 Ashes By Now .... Rodney Crowell
- ♦ 1961 Asia Minor .... Kokomo
- ♦ 1964 Ask Me .... Elvis Presley
- 1956 Ask Me .... Nat King Cole
- ♦ 1972 Ask Me What You Want .... Millie Jackson
- ♦ 1995 Ask Of You .... Raphael Saadiq
- ♦ 1965 Ask The Lonely .... Four Tops
- ♦ 1961 Astronaut (Parts 1 & 2) .... Jose Jimenez
- ♦ 1961 At Last .... Etta James
- ♦ 1977 At Midnight (My Love Will Lift You Up) .... Rufus featuring Chaka Khan
- ♦ 1955 At My Front Door (Crazy Little Mama) .... Pat Boone
- ♦ 1955 At My Front Door .... El Dorados
- ♦ 1975 At Seventeen .... Janis Ian
- ♦ 1958 At The Hop .... Danny & The Juniors
- 1958 At The Hop .... Nick Todd
- ♦ 1966 At The Scene .... Dave Clark Five
- ♦ 1967 At The Zoo .... Simon & Garfunkel
- ♦ 1987 At This Moment .... Billy & The Beaters
- ♦ 1994 At Your Best (You Are Love) .... Aaliyah
- ♦ 1982 Athena .... Who
- ♦ 1981 Atlanta Lady (Something About Your Love) .... Marty Balin
- ♦ 1969 Atlantis .... Donovan
- ♦ 1997 Atliens .... Outkast
- ♦ 1966 Attack .... Toys
- ♦ 1975 Attitude Dancing .... Carly Simon
- ♦ 1973 Aubrey .... Bread
- ♦ 1956 Auctioneer .... Leroy Van Dyke
- ♦ 1984 Authority Song .... John Cougar Mellencamp
- ♦ 1975 Autobahn .... Kraftwerk
- ♦ 1984 Automatic .... Pointer Sisters
- 1983 Automatic Man .... Michael Sembello
- ♦ 1972 Automatically Sunshine .... Supremes
- ♦ 1955 Autumn Leaves .... Roger Williams
- ♦ 1968 Autumn Of My Life .... Bobby Goldsboro
- 1956 Autumn Waltz .... Tony Bennett
- ♦ 1997 Avenues .... Refugee Camp All Stars
- ♦ 1985 Axel F .... Harold Faltermeyer

B

- ♦ 1990 B.B.D. (I Thought It Was Me)? .... Bell Biv DeVoe
- ♦ 1979 Babe .... Styx
- ♦ 1995 Baby .... Brandy
- ♦ 1966 B-A-B-Y .... Carla Thomas
- ♦ 1991 Baby Baby .... Amy Grant
- ♦ 1992 Baby-Baby-Baby .... TLC
- ♦ 1969 Baby, Baby Don't Cry .... Smokey Robinson & The Miracles
- ♦ 1972 Baby Blue .... Badfinger
- ♦ 1961 Baby Blue .... Echoes
- ♦ 1988 Baby Can I Hold You .... Tracy Chapman
- ♦ 1968 Baby, Come Back .... Equals
- ♦ 1978 Baby Come Back .... Player
- ♦ 1974 Baby Come Close .... Smokey Robinson
- ♦ 1983 Baby, Come To Me .... Patti Austin With James Ingram
- ♦ 1956 Baby Doll .... Andy Williams
- ♦ 1989 Baby Don't Forget My Number .... Milli Vanilli
- ♦ 1972 Baby Don't Get Hooked On Me .... Mac Davis
- ♦ 1965 Baby Don't Go .... Sonny & Cher
- ♦ 1964 Baby Don't You Do It .... Marvin Gaye
- ♦ 1963 Baby Don't You Weep .... Garnet Mimms & The Enchanters
- ♦ 1962 Baby Face .... Bobby Darin
- 1976 Baby Face .... Wing And A Prayer Fife & Drum Corps.
- ♦ 1992 Baby Got Back .... Sir Mix-A-Lot
- ♦ 1978 Baby Hold On .... Eddie Money
- ♦ 1970 Baby Hold On .... Grass Roots
- 1984 Baby I Lied .... Deborah Allen
- ♦ 1964 Baby, I Love You .... Ronettes
- 1969 Baby, I Love You .... Andy Kim
- ♦ 1967 Baby I Love You .... Aretha Franklin
- ♦ 1976 Baby I Love Your Way .... Peter Frampton
- ♦ 1988 Baby I Love Your Way/Freebird Medley .... Will To Power
- ♦ 1994 Baby I Love Your Way .... Big Mountain
- ♦ 1964 Baby I Need Your Loving .... Four Tops
- ♦ 1967 Baby I Need Your Lovin' .... Johnny Rivers
- ♦ 1971 Baby I'm A Want You .... Bread
- ♦ 1979 Baby I'm Burnin' .... Dolly Parton
- ♦ 1969 Baby, I'm For Real .... Originals
- ♦ 1965 Baby, I'm Yours .... Barbara Lewis
- ♦ 1993 Baby I'm Yours .... Shai
- ♦ 1973 Baby I've Been Missing You .... Independents
- ♦ 1990 Baby, It's Tonight .... Jude Cole
- ♦ 1962 Baby It's You .... Shirelles
- ♦ 1969 Baby It's You .... Smith
- ♦ 1983 Baby Jane .... Rod Stewart
- ♦ 1971 Baby Let Me Kiss You .... King Floyd
- 1972 Baby Let Me Take You (In My Arms) .... Detroit Emeralds
- ♦ 1969 Baby Let's Wait .... Royal Guardsmen
- ♦ 1986 Baby Love .... Regina
- ♦ 1964 Baby Love .... Supremes
- 1982 Baby Makes Her Blue Jeans Talk .... Dr. Hook
- ♦ 1968 Baby, Now That I've Found You .... Foundations
- ♦ 1961 Baby Oh Baby .... Shells
- ♦ 1966 Baby Scratch My Back .... Slim Harpo

♦ 1966	Bus Stop	Hollies
♦ 1956	Bus Stop Song (A Paper Of Pins)	Four Lads
♦ 1989	Bust A Move	Young MC
♦ 1963	Bust Out	Busters
♦ 1963	Busted	Ray Charles
♦ 1979	Bustin' Loose (Part 1)	Chuck Brown & The Soul Searchers
♦ 1961	But I Do	Clarence Henry
♦ 1966	But It's Alright	J.J. Jackson
♦ 1969	But You Know I Love You	First Edition
♦ 1965	But You're Mine	Sonny & Cher
♦ 1997	Butta Love	Next
1975	Butter Boy	Fanny
1957	Butterfly	Charlie Gracie
♦ 1957	Butterfly	Andy Williams
1963	Butterfly Baby	Bobby Rydell
♦ 1997	Butterfly Kisses	Raybon Brothers
♦ 1958	Buzz Buzz Buzz	Hollywood Flames
♦ 1967	By The Time I Get To Phoenix	Glen Campbell
♦ 1993	By The Time This Night Is Over	Kenny G With Peabo Bryson
♦ 1965	Bye, Bye, Baby (Baby Goodbye)	Four Seasons
♦ 1957	Bye Bye Love	Everly Brothers

C

♦ 1987	C'est La Vie	Robbie Nevil
♦ 1955	C'est La Vie	Sarah Vaughan
♦ 1961	C'est Si Bon (It's So Good)	Conway Twitty
♦ 1968	Cab Driver	Mills Brothers
♦ 1962	Cajun Queen	Jimmy Dean
♦ 1961	Calcutta	Lawrence Welk And His Orchestra
♦ 1961	Calendar Girl	Neil Sedaka
♦ 1966	California Dreamin'	Mama's & Papa's
♦ 1965	California Girls	Beach Boys
♦ 1985	California Girls	David Lee Roth
♦ 1996	California Love	2Pac
♦ 1967	California Nights	Lesley Gore
♦ 1969	California Soul	Fifth Dimension
♦ 1964	California Sun	Rivieras
♦ 1989	Call It Love	Poco
♦ 1991	Call It Poison	Escape Club
♦ 1970	Call Me	Aretha Franklin
♦ 1980	Call Me	Blondie
♦ 1958	Call Me	Johnny Mathis
♦ 1966	Call Me	Chris Montez
♦ 1982	Call Me	Skyy
♦ 1997	Call Me	Le Click
♦ 1973	Call Me (Come Back Home)	Al Green
♦ 1968	Call Me Lightning	Who
♦ 1962	Call Me Mr. In-Between	Burl Ives
♦ 1963	Call On Me	Bobby Bland
♦ 1974	Call On Me	Chicago
♦ 1985	Call To The Heart	Giuffria
♦ 1986	Calling America	Electric Light Orchestra
♦ 1977	Calling Dr. Love	Kiss
♦ 1977	Calling Occupants Of Interplanetary Craft	Carpenters
♦ 1975	Calypso	John Denver
♦ 1969	Can I Change My Mind	Tyrone Davis
♦ 1963	Can I Get A Witness	Marvin Gaye
♦ 1971	Can I Get A Witness	Lee Michaels
♦ 1957	Can I Steal A Little Love	Frank Sinatra
♦ 1995	Can I Touch You....There?	Michael Bolton
♦ 1974	Can This Be Real	Natural Four
♦ 1978	Can We Still Be Friends	Todd Rundgren
♦ 1994	Can We Talk	Tevin Campbell
♦ 1994	Can You Feel The Love Tonight	Elton John
♦ 1956	Can You Find It In Your Heart	Tony Bennett
♦ 1978	Can You Fool	Glen Campbell
♦ 1964	Can Your Monkey Do The Dog	Rufus Thomas
♦ 1964	Can't Buy Me Love	Beatles
♦ 1995	Can't Cry Anymore	Sheryl Crow
♦ 1992	Can't Cry Hard Enough	Williams Brothers
♦ 1985	Can't Fight This Feeling	REO Speedwagon
♦ 1974	Can't Get Enough	Bad Company
♦ 1990	Can't Get Enough	Winger
♦ 1974	Can't Get Enough Of Your Love	Barry White
♦ 1993	Can't Get Enough Of Your Love	Taylor Dayne

♦ 1975	Can't Get It Out Of My Head	Electric Light Orchestra
♦ 1963	Can't Get Used To Losing You	Andy Williams
♦ 1962	Can't Help Falling In Love	Elvis Presley
♦ 1987	Can't Help Falling In Love	Corey Hart
♦ 1993	Can't Help Falling In Love	UB40
♦ 1992	Can't Let Go	Mariah Carey
♦ 1990	(Can't Live Without Your) Love And Affection	Nelson
♦ 1997	Can't Nobody Hold Me Down	Puff Daddy featuring Mase
1983	Can't Shake Loose	Agnetha Faltskog
♦ 1978	Can't Smile Without You	Barry Manilow
♦ 1988	Can't Stay Away From You	Gloria Estefan And Miami Sound Machine
♦ 1990	Can't Stop	After 7
♦ 1977	Can't Stop Dancin'	Captain & Tennille
♦ 1990	Can't Stop Fallin' Into Love	Cheap Trick
1970	Can't Stop Loving You	Tom Jones
♦ 1995	Can't Stop Lovin' You	Van Halen
♦ 1991	Can't Stop This Thing We Started	Bryan Adams
♦ 1967	Can't Take My Eyes Off You	Frankie Valli
♦ 1957	Can't Wait For Summer	Steve Lawrence
♦ 1987	Can't We Try	Dan Hill With Vonda Sheppard
♦ 1965	Can't You Hear My Heartbeat	Herman's Hermits
♦ 1995	Can't You See	Total featuring The Notorious B.I.G.
♦ 1964	Can't You See That She's Mine	Dave Clark Five
♦ 1987	Can'tcha Say (You Believe In Me)/Still In Love	Boston
♦ 1956	Canadian Sunset	Andy Williams
♦ 1956	Canadian Sunset	Hugo Winterhalter/Eddie Heywood
♦ 1970	Candida	Dawn
♦ 1988	Candle In The Wind	Elton John
1997	Candle In The Wind 1997	Elton John
♦ 1987	Candy	Cameo
♦ 1991	Candy	Iggy Pop With Kate Pierson
♦ 1963	Candy Girl	Four Seasons
♦ 1961	Candy Man	Roy Orbison
♦ 1972	Candy Man	Sammy Davis Jr. With The Mike Curb Congregation
♦ 1995	Candy Rain	Soul For Real
♦ 1970	Canned Ham	Norman Greenbaum
♦ 1958	Cannonball	Duane Eddy
♦ 1985	Cannonball	Supertramp
♦ 1994	Cantaloop (Flip Fantasia)	Us3
♦ 1986	Captain Of Her Heart	Double
♦ 1977	Car Wash	Rose Royce
♦ 1965	Cara Mia	Jay & The Americans
♦ 1965	Cara-Lin	Strangeloves
♦ 1974	Carefree Highway	Gordon Lightfoot
♦ 1985	Careless Whisper	Wham! featuring George Michael
1959	Caribbean	Mitchell Torok
♦ 1984	Caribbean Queen (No More Love On The Run)	Billy Ocean
♦ 1995	Carnival	Natalie Merchant
♦ 1958	Carol	Chuck Berry
♦ 1975	Carolina In The Pines	Michael Murphey
♦ 1966	Caroline, No	Brian Wilson
♦ 1968	Carpet Man	Fifth Dimension
♦ 1980	Carrie	Cliff Richard
♦ 1987	Carrie	Europe
♦ 1967	Carrie-Anne	Hollies
♦ 1969	Carry Me Back	Rascals
♦ 1977	Carry On Wayward Son	Kansas
♦ 1980	Cars	Gary Numan
♦ 1987	Casanova	Levert
♦ 1967	Casino Royale	Herb Alpert & The Tijuana Brass
♦ 1963	Cast Your Fate To The Wind	Vince Guaraldi Trio
♦ 1965	Cast Your Fate To The Wind	Sounds Orchestral
♦ 1981	Castles In The Air	Don McLean
1956	Casual Look	Six Teens
1967	Cat In The Window (The Bird In The Sky)	Petula Clark
♦ 1977	Cat Scratch Fever	Ted Nugent
♦ 1974	Cat's In The Cradle	Harry Chapin
♦ 1993	Cat's In The Cradle	Ugly Kid Joe
♦ 1958	Catch A Falling Star	Perry Como
♦ 1987	(Catch Me) I'm Falling	Pretty Poison
♦ 1965	Catch The Wind	Donovan
♦ 1965	Catch Us If You Can	Dave Clark Five
1962	Caterina	Perry Como
♦ 1960	Cathy's Clown	Everly Brothers
♦ 1987	Caught Up In The Rapture	Anita Baker
♦ 1982	Caught Up In You	38 Special
♦ 1987	Causing A Commotion	Madonna

685

♦	1995	Creep...TLC
♠	1967	Creeque Alley...................................Mama's & Papa's
♠	1971	Cried Like A Baby .... Bobby Sherman
♦	1997	Criminal.. Fiona Apple
♠	1969	Crimson And Clover ....Tommy James And The Shondells
♦	1982	Crimson And Clover ....Joan Jett & The Blackhearts
♠	1973	Crocodile Rock .... Elton John
	1963	Cross Fire! ....Orlons
♦	1987	Cross My Broken Heart ....Jets
♦	1959	Crossfire ....Johnny And The Hurricanes
♦	1992	Crossover ....EPMD
♦	1969	Crossroads ....Cream
♦	1968	Crosstown Traffic ....Jimi Hendrix Experience
♠	1962	Crowd...Roy Orbison
♦	1984	Cruel Summer...................................Bananarama
♦	1979	Cruel To Be Kind .... Nick Lowe
♦	1980	Cruisin'.....................................Smokey Robinson
♦	1990	Cruising For Bruising ....Basia
♦	1983	Crumblin' Down ....John Cougar Mellencamp
♦	1986	Crush On You ....Jets
♦	1985	Cry ....Godley & Creme
♠	1966	Cry ....Ronnie Dove
♦	1989	Cry ....Waterfront
♠	1963	Cry Baby.......................Garnet Mimms & The Enchanters
♦	1971	Cry Baby ....Janis Joplin
♠	1962	Cry Baby Cry ....Angels
♦	1991	Cry For Help ....Rick Astley
♦	1993	Cry For You..Jodeci
♠	1968	Cry Like A Baby ....Box Tops
♠	1956	Cry Me A River ....Julie London
♦	1970	Cry Me A River .... Joe Cocker
♦	1962	Cry To Me ....Solomon Burke
♦	1963	Cry To Me ....Betty Harris
♦	1993	Cryin' ....Aerosmith
♦	1989	Cryin' ....Vixen
♠	1961	Crying...Roy Orbison
♠	1966	Crying ....Jay & The Americans
♦	1981	Crying ....Don McLean
♦	1993	Crying Game ....Boy George
♠	1965	Crying In The Chapel ....Elvis Presley
♠	1962	Crying In The Rain ....Everly Brothers
♠	1966	Crying Time ....Ray Charles
♠	1969	Crystal Blue Persuasion ....Tommy James And The Shondells
♦	1989	Cuddly Toy (Feel For Me) .... Roachford
♦	1989	Cult Of Personality ....Living Colour
♦	1983	Cum On Feel The Noize .... Quiet Riot
♦	1996	Cumbersome ....Seven Mary Three
♠	1961	Cupid ....Sam Cooke
♠	1970	Cupid ....Johnny Nash
♠	1976	Cupid ....Tony Orlando & Dawn
♦	1980	Cupid/I've Loved You For A Long Time.................... Spinners
♦	1997	Cupid 112
♠	1964	Curious Mind (Um, Um, Um, Um, Um, Um)...........Major Lance
	1978	Curious Mind (Um, Um, Um, Um, Um, Um)...........Johnny Rivers
♦	1984	Curly Shuffle ....Jump 'N The Saddle
♠	1975	Cut The Cake ....Average White Band
♦	1983	Cuts Like A Knife ....Bryan Adams
♦	1997	C U When U Get There ....Coolio featuring 40 Thevz
♦	1968	Cycles ....Frank Sinatra

D

♠	1971	D.O.A. .... Bloodrock
♦	1968	D.W. Washburn ....Monkees
♦	1973	D'yer Mak'er ....Led Zeppelin
♦	1988	Da' Butt...E.U.
♦	1997	Da' Dip ....Freak Nasty
♠	1963	Da Doo Ron Ron ....Crystals
♠	1977	Da Doo Ron Ron ....Shaun Cassidy
♦	1973	Daddy Could Swear, I Declare.............. Gladys Knight & The Pips
♦	1972	Daddy Don't You Walk So Fast .... Wayne Newton
	1956	Daddy-O ....Bonnie Lou
♠	1956	Daddy-O ....Fontane Sisters
♠	1961	Daddy's Home ....Shep And The Limelites
♦	1973	Daddy's Home ....Jermaine Jackson
♦	1982	Daddy's Home ....Cliff Richard

	1969	Daddy's Little Man ..............................O.C. Smith
♦	1973	Daisy A Day ....Jud Strunk
♠	1975	Daisy Jane .... America
♦	1972	Daisy Mae ....Hamilton, Joe Frank & Reynolds
♠	1964	Daisy Petal Pickin'...............Jimmy Gilmer & The Fireballs
♦	1992	Damn I Wish I Was Your Lover ....Sophie B. Hawkins
♦	1979	Damned If I Do .... Alan Parsons Project
♠	1961	Dance By The Light Of The Moon .... Olympics
♠	1964	Dance Dance Dance...........................Beach Boys
♦	1978	Dance, Dance, Dance (Yowsah, Yowsah, Yowsah) .... Chic
♦	1978	Dance (Disco Heat) .... Sylvester
♦	1958	Dance Everyone Dance ....Betty Madigan
♦	1984	Dance Hall Days ....Wang Chung
♦	1988	Dance Little Sister (Part 1) ....Terence Trent D'Arby
♠	1961	Dance On Little Girl .... Paul Anka
	1961	(Dance The) Mess Around ....Chubby Checker
♦	1979	Dance The Night Away ....Van Halen
♠	1957	Dance To The Bop ....Gene Vincent And His Blue Caps
♦	1968	Dance To The Music ....Sly & The Family Stone
♦	1976	Dance Wit Me ....Rufus featuring Chaka Khan
♦	1959	Dance With Me ....Drifters
♦	1975	Dance With Me.......................................Orleans
♦	1978	Dance With Me ....Peter Brown
♦	1955	Dance With Me Henry (Wallflower)..................Georgia Gibbs
♠	1962	(Dance With The) Guitar Man...................Duane Eddy
♦	1975	Dancin' Fool ....Guess Who
	1979	Dancing In The City ....Marshall Hain
♦	1984	Dancing In The Dark .... Bruce Springsteen
♠	1973	Dancing In The Moonlight .... King Harvest
♦	1984	Dancing In The Sheets ....Shalamar
♠	1964	Dancing In The Street.................Martha & The Vandellas
♦	1982	Dancing In The Street................................Van Halen
♦	1985	Dancing In The Street................Mick Jagger/David Bowie
♦	1974	Dancing Machine ....Jackson Five
♦	1977	Dancin' Man ....Q
♦	1986	Dancing On The Ceiling ....Lionel Richie
	1962	Dancin' Party...............................Chubby Checker
♠	1977	Dancing Queen .... Abba
♦	1979	Dancin' Shoes ....Nigel Olsson
♠	1967	Dandelion...................................Rolling Stones
♠	1966	Dandy...................................Herman's Hermits
♠	1964	Dang Me .... Roger Miller
♦	1955	Danger! Heartbreak Ahead...................Jaye P. Morgan
♦	1986	Danger Zone .... Kenny Loggins
♦	1990	Dangerous...Roxette
♦	1966	Dangling Conversation ....Simon & Garfunkel
♦	1973	Daniel...Elton John
♦	1963	Danke Shoen ....Wayne Newton
♠	1959	Danny Boy ....Conway Twitty
♠	1973	Danny's Song .... Anne Murray
♦	1985	Dare Me ....Pointer Sisters
♦	1990	Dare To Fall In Love ....Brent Bourgeois
♦	1975	Dark Horse ....George Harrison
♦	1974	Dark Lady ....Cher
♠	1957	Dark Moon ....Bonnie Guitar
♦	1957	Dark Moon ....Gale Storm
♦	1968	Darlin' ....Beach Boys
♦	1967	Darling Be Home Soon......................Lovin' Spoonful
♠	1955	Darling Je Vous Aime Beaucoup ....Nat King Cole
♦	1970	Daughter Of Darkness ....Tom Jones
♠	1964	Dawn (Go Away) ....Four Seasons
♠	1965	Dawn Of Correction.............................Spokesmen
♠	1972	Day After Day.................................... Badfinger
♦	1972	Day By Day..Godspell
♦	1986	Day By Day .... Hooters
♦	1972	Day Dreaming .... Aretha Franklin
	1966	Day For Decision ....Johnny Sea
♦	1972	Day I Found Myself ....Honey Cone
♦	1987	Day-In-Day-Out ....David Bowie
♠	1969	Day Is Done ....Peter, Paul & Mary
	1958	Day The Rains Came ....Raymond Lefevre
♦	1958	Day The Rains Came .... Jane Morgan
♠	1966	Day Tripper ....Beatles
♦	1977	Daybreak ....Barry Manilow
♦	1974	Daybreak ....Nilsson
♠	1966	Daydream ....Lovin' Spoonful
♠	1967	Daydream Believer ....Monkees
♦	1980	Daydream Believer .... Anne Murray

1965	Do You Believe In Magic	Lovin' Spoonful
1978	Do You Believe In Magic	Shaun Cassidy
1992	Do You Believe In Us	Jon Secada
1976	Do You Feel Like We Do	Peter Frampton
1968	Do You Know The Way To San Jose	Dionne Warwick
1971	Do You Know What I Mean	Lee Michaels
1997	Do You Know What It Takes	Robyn
1997	Do You Like This	Rome
1962	Do You Love Me	Contours
1964	Do You Love Me	Dave Clark Five
1988	Do You Love Me	Contours
1980	Do You Love What You Feel	Rufus And Chaka
1983	Do You Really Want To Hurt Me	Culture Club
1990	Do You Remember?	Phil Collins
1970	Do You See My Love (For You Growing)	Jr. Walker & The All Stars
1995	Do You Sleep?	Lisa Loeb & Nine Stories
1994	Do You Wanna Get Funky	C + C Music Factory
1977	Do You Wanna Make Love	Peter McCann
1982	Do You Wanna Touch Me (Oh Yeah)	Joan Jett & The Blackhearts
1985	Do You Want Crying	Katrina And The Waves
1991	Do You Want Me	Salt-N-Pepa
1958	Do You Want To Dance?	Bobby Freeman
1965	Do You Want To Dance?	Beach Boys
1973	Do You Want To Dance?	Bette Midler
1964	Do You Want To Know A Secret	Beatles
1977	Do Your Dance (Part 1)	Rose Royce
1972	Do Your Thing	Isaac Hayes
1969	Do Your Thing	Watts 103rd Street Band
1989	Doctor	Doobie Brothers
1984	Doctor! Doctor!	Thompson Twins
1989	Dr. Feelgood	Motley Crue
1983	Dr. Heckyll & Mr. Jive	Men At Work
1972	Doctor My Eyes	Jackson Browne
1975	Doctor's Orders	Carol Douglas
1991	Does Anybody Really Fall In Love Anymore?	Kane Roberts
1971	Does Anybody Really Know What Time It Is?	Chicago
1983	Does It Make You Remember	Kim Carnes
1991	Does She Love That Man?	Breathe
1961	Does Your Chewing Gum Lose It's Flavor (On The Bedpost Overnight)	Lonnie Donegan And His Skiffle Group
1968	Does Your Mama Know About Me	Bobby Taylor & The Vancouvers
1979	Does Your Mother Know	Abba
1971	Doesn't Somebody Want To Be Wanted	Partridge Family
1979	Dog & Butterfly	Heart
1960	Doggin' Around	Jackie Wilson
1969	Doggone Right	Smokey Robinson & The Miracles
1996	Doin It	L.L. Cool J
1987	Doing It All For My Baby	Huey Lewis
1973	Doing It To Death	Fred Wesley & The JB's
1961	Doll House	Donnie Brooks
1955	Domani (Tomorrow)	Julius LaRosa
1963	Dominique	Singing Nun
1971	Domino	Van Morrison
1988	Domino Dancing	The Pet Shop Boys
1987	Dominoes	Robbie Nevil
1958	Don't	Elvis Presley
1984	Don't Answer Me	Alan Parsons Project
1980	Don't Ask Me Why	Billy Joel
1958	Don't Ask Me Why	Elvis Presley
1989	Don't Ask Me Why	Eurythmics
1966	Don't Be A Dropout	James Brown
1963	Don't Be Afraid Little Darlin'	Steve Lawrence
1955	Don't Be Angry	Nappy Brown
1955	Don't Be Angry	Crew-Cuts
1956	Don't Be Cruel	Elvis Presley
1960	Don't Be Cruel	Bill Black's Combo
1988	Don't Be Cruel	Cheap Trick
1988	Don't Be Cruel	Bobby Brown
1961	Don't Bet Money Honey	Linda Scott
1961	Don't Blame Me	Everly Brothers
1967	Don't Blame The Children	Sammy Davis Jr.
1962	Don't Break The Heart That Loves You	Connie Francis
1966	Don't Bring Me Down	Animals
1979	Don't Bring Me Down	Electric Light Orchestra
1975	Don't Call Us, We'll Call You	Sugarloaf/Jerry Corbetta
1974	Don't Change Horses (In The Middle Of A Stream)	Tower Of Power
1971	Don't Change On Me	Ray Charles
1989	Don't Close Your Eyes	Kix
1985	Don't Come Around Here No More	Tom Petty And The Heartbreakers
1960	Don't Come Knockin'	Fats Domino
1973	Don't Cross The River	America
1983	Don't Cry	Asia
1991	Don't Cry	Guns N' Roses
1996	Don't Cry	Seal
1970	Don't Cry Daddy	Elvis Presley
1997	Don't Cry For Me Argentina	Madonna
1979	Don't Cry Out Loud	Melissa Manchester
1987	Don't Disturb This Groove	System
1972	Don't Do It	Band
1980	Don't Do Me Like That	Tom Petty And The Heartbreakers
1987	Don't Dream It's Over	Crowded House
1972	Don't Ever Be Lonely (A Poor Little Fool Like Me)	Cornelius Brothers & Sister Rose
1964	Don't Ever Leave Me	Connie Francis
1979	Don't Ever Wanna Lose Ya	New England
1973	Don't Expect Me To Be Your Friend	Lobo
1980	Don't Fall In Love With A Dreamer	Kenny Rogers With Kim Carnes
1976	(Don't Fear) The Reaper	Blue Oyster Cult
1982	Don't Fight It	Kenny Loggins With Steve Perry
1957	Don't Forbid Me	Pat Boone
1965	Don't Forget I Still Love You	Bobbi Martin
1986	Don't Forget Me When I'm Gone	Glass Tiger
1983	Don't Forget To Dance	Kinks
1986	Don't Get Me Wrong	Pretenders
1969	Don't Give In To Him	Gary Puckett And The Union Gap
1981	Don't Give It Up	Robbie Patton
1968	Don't Give Up	Petula Clark
1977	Don't Give Up On Us	David Soul
1990	Don't Go Away Mad (Just Go Away)	Motley Crue
1976	Don't Go Breaking My Heart	Elton John And Kiki Dee
1958	Don't Go Home	Playmates
1962	Don't Go Near The Indians	Rex Allen
1967	Don't Go Out Into The Rain (You're Going To Melt)	Herman's Hermits
1960	Don't Go To Strangers	Etta Jones
1962	Don't Hang Up	Orlons
1979	Don't Hold Back	Chanson
1991	Don't Hold Back Your Love	Daryl Hall & John Oates
1977	Don't It Make My Brown Eyes Blue	Crystal Gayle
1965	Don't Just Stand There	Patty Duke
1971	Don't Knock My Love (Part 1)	Wilson Pickett
1989	Don't Know Much	Linda Ronstadt featuring Aaron Neville
1988	Don't Know What You Got (Till It's Gone)	Cinderella
1977	Don't Leave Me This Way	Thelma Houston
1958	Don't Let Go	Roy Hamilton
1980	Don't Let Go	Isaac Hayes
1984	Don't Let Go	Wang Chung
1997	Don't Let Go (Love)	En Vogue
1981	Don't Let Him Go	Reo Speedwagon
1982	Don't Let Him Know	Prism
1983	Don't Let It End	Styx
1973	Don't Let Me Be Lonely Tonight	James Taylor
1965	Don't Let Me Be Misunderstood	Animals
1978	Don't Let Me Be Misunderstood	Santa Esmeralda
1969	Don't Let Me Down	Beatles
1971	Don't Let The Green Grass Fool You	Wilson Pickett
1969	Don't Let The Joneses Get You Down	Temptations
1964	Don't Let The Rain Come Down (Crooked Little Man)	Serendipity Singers
1967	Don't Let The Rain Fall Down On Me	Critters
1964	Don't Let The Sun Catch You Crying	Gerry And The Pacemakers
1974	Don't Let The Sun Go Down On Me	Elton John
1992	Don't Let The Sun Go Down On Me	George Michael/Elton John
1978	Don't Look Back	Boston
1989	Don't Look Back	Fine Young Cannibals
1987	Don't Look Down - The Sequel	Go West
1985	Don't Lose My Number	Phil Collins
1963	Don't Make Me Over	Dionne Warwick
1989	Don't Make Me Over	Sybil
1987	Don't Make Me Wait For Love	Kenny G
1987	Don't Mean Nothing	Richard Marx
1965	Don't Mess Up A Good Thing	Fontella Bass & Bobby McClure
1966	Don't Mess With Bill	Marvelettes
1987	Don't Need A Gun	Billy Idol
1983	Don't Pay The Ferryman	Chris DeBurgh
1959	Don't Pity Me	Dion & The Belmonts

689

◆	1962	Don't Play That Song	Ben E. King
◆	1970	Don't Play That Song	Aretha Franklin
◆	1971	Don't Pull Your Love	Hamilton, Joe Frank & Reynolds
◆	1976	Don't Pull Your Love/Then You Can Tell Me Goodbye	Glen Campbell
◆	1989	Don't Rush Me	Taylor Dayne
◆	1980	Don't Say Goodnight (It's Time For Love) Parts 1 & 2	Isley Brothers
◆	1963	Don't Say Goodnight And Mean Goodbye	Shirelles
◆	1963	Don't Say Nothin' Bad (About My Baby)	Cookies
◆	1972	Don't Say You Don't Remember	Beverly Bremers
◆	1963	Don't Set Me Free	Ray Charles
◆	1988	Don't Shed A Tear	Paul Carrack
◆	1989	Don't Shut Me Out	Kevin Paige
◆	1967	Don't Sleep In The Subway	Petula Clark
◆	1981	Don't Stand So Close To Me	Police
◆	1977	Don't Stop	Fleetwood Mac
◆	1981	Don't Stop Believin'	Journey
◆	1976	Don't Stop Believin'	Olivia Newton-John
◆	1981	Don't Stop The Music	Yarbrough & Peoples
◆	1979	Don't Stop 'Til You Get Enough	Michael Jackson
◆	1976	Don't Take Away The Music	Tavares
◆	1995	Don't Take It Personal (Just One Of Dem Days)	Monica
◆	1968	Don't Take It So Hard	Paul Revere And The Raiders
◆	1994	Don't Take The Girl	Tim McGraw
◆	1959	Don't Take Your Guns To Town	Johnny Cash
◆	1975	Don't Take Your Love	Manhattans
◆	1982	Don't Talk To Strangers	Rick Springfield
◆	1975	Don't Tell Me Goodnight	Lobo
◆	1989	Don't Tell Me Lies	Breathe
◆	1963	Don't Think Twice, It's All Right	Peter, Paul & Mary
◆	1965	Don't Think Twice, It's All Right	Wonder Who?
◆	1960	Don't Throw Away All Those Teardrops	Frankie Avalon
◆	1964	Don't Throw Your Love Away	Searchers
◆	1969	Don't Touch Me	Bettye Swann
◆	1991	Don't Treat Me Bad	Firehouse
◆	1994	Don't Turn Around	Ace Of Base
◆	1993	Don't Walk Away	Jade
◆	1984	Don't Walk Away	Rick Springfield
◆	1997	Don't Wanna Be A Player	Joe
◆	1990	Don't Wanna Fall In Love	Jane Child
◆	1989	Don't Wanna Lose You	Gloria Estefan
◆	1991	Don't Want To Be A Fool	Luther Vandross
◆	1978	Don't Want To Live Without It	Pablo Cruise
◆	1981	Don't Want To Wait Anymore	Tubes
◆	1961	Don't Worry	Marty Robbins
◆	1964	Don't Worry Baby	Beach Boys
◆	1977	Don't Worry Baby	B.J. Thomas
◆	1988	Don't Worry Be Happy	Bobby McFerrin
◆	1971	(Don't Worry) If There's A Hell Below We're All Going To Go	Curtis Mayfield
◆	1967	Don't You Care	Buckinghams
◆	1985	Don't You (Forget About Me)	Simple Minds
◆	1983	Don't You Get So Mad	Jeffrey Osborne
◆	1958	Don't You Just Know It	Huey "Piano" Smith And The Clowns
◆	1959	Don't You Know	Della Reese
◆	1988	Don't You Know What The Night Can Do?	Steve Winwood
◆	1982	Don't You Want Me	Human League
◆	1987	Don't You Want Me	Jody Watley
◆	1974	Don't You Worry 'Bout A Thing	Stevie Wonder
◆	1979	Don't You Write Her Off	McGuinn Clark & Hillman
◆	1958	Doncha' Think It's Time	Elvis Presley
◆	1959	Donna	Ritchie Valens
◆	1963	Donna The Prima Donna	Dion
◆	1974	Doo Doo Doo Doo Doo (Heartbreaker)	Rolling Stones
	1964	Door Is Still Open To My Heart	Dean Martin
◆	1974	Doraville	Atlanta Rhythm Section
◆	1976	Dose Of Rock 'N' Roll	Ringo Starr
◆	1971	Double Barrel	Dave And Ansil Collins
◆	1981	Double Dutch Bus	Frankie Smith
◆	1971	Double Lovin'	Osmonds
◆	1966	Double Shot (Of My Baby's Love)	Swingin' Medallions
◆	1978	Double Vision	Foreigner
◆	1968	Down At Lulu's	Ohio Express
◆	1963	(Down At) Papa Joe's	Dixiebelles
◆	1989	Down Boys	Warrant
◆	1972	Down By The Lazy River	Osmonds
◆	1960	Down By The Station	Four Preps
◆	1965	Down In The Boondocks	Billy Joe Royal
◆	1996	Down Low (Nobody Has To Know)	R. Kelly
◆	1969	Down On The Corner	Creedence Clearwater Revival
◆	1963	Down The Aisle (Wedding Song)	Patti LaBelle & The Blue Belles
◆	1958	Down The Aisle Of Love	Quin-Tones
◆	1976	Down To The Line	Bachman-Turner Overdrive
◆	1983	Down Under	Men At Work
◆	1993	Down With The King	Run-D.M.C.
	1960	Down Yonder	Johnny And The Hurricanes
◆	1989	Downtown	One 2 Many
◆	1965	Downtown	Petula Clark
◆	1993	Downtown	SWV
◆	1988	Downtown Life	Daryl Hall & John Oates
◆	1990	Downtown Train	Rod Stewart
◆	1963	Drag City	Jan & Dean
◆	1971	Draggin' The Line	Tommy James
◆	1981	Draw Of The Cards	Kim Carnes
◆	1977	Draw The Line	Aerosmith
◆	1993	Dre Day	Dr. Dre
	1958	Dream	Betty Johnson
◆	1968	Dream A Little Dream Of Me	Mama Cass
◆	1995	Dream About You	Stevie B
◆	1962	Dream Baby (How Long Must I Dream)	Roy Orbison
◆	1971	Dream Baby (How Long Must I Dream)	Glen Campbell
◆	1984	Dream (Hold On To Your Dream)	Irene Cara
◆	1991	Dream Is Still Alive	Wilson Phillips
◆	1959	Dream Lover	Bobby Darin
◆	1975	Dream Merchant	New Birth
◆	1976	Dream On	Aerosmith
◆	1974	Dream On	Righteous Brothers
◆	1965	Dream On Little Dreamer	Perry Como
◆	1979	Dream Police	Cheap Trick
◆	1976	Dream Weaver	Gary Wright
◆	1977	Dreamboat Annie	Heart
◆	1980	Dreamer	Supertramp
◆	1960	Dreamin'	Johnny Burnette
◆	1989	Dreamin'	Vanessa Williams
◆	1979	Dreaming	Blondie
◆	1980	Dreaming	Cliff Richard
◆	1988	Dreaming	Orchestral Manoeuvres In The Dark
◆	1983	Dreamin' Is Easy	Steel Breeze
◆	1995	Dreaming Of You	Selena
◆	1993	Dreamlover	Mariah Carey
◆	1977	Dreams	Fleetwood Mac
◆	1994	Dreams	Gabrielle
◆	1986	Dreams	Van Halen
◆	1968	Dreams Of The Everyday Housewife	Glen Campbell
◆	1986	Dreamtime	Daryl Hall
◆	1962	Dreamy Eyes	Johnny Tillotson
◆	1973	Dreidel	Don McLean
◆	1985	Dress You Up	Madonna
◆	1989	Dressed For Success	Roxette
◆	1973	Drift Away	Dobie Gray
◆	1973	Drinking Wine Spo-Dee-O'Dee	Jerry Lee Lewis
◆	1963	Drip Drop	Dion
◆	1984	Drive	Cars
◆	1992	Drive	R.E.M.
◆	1979	Driver's Seat	Sniff 'n The Tears
◆	1980	Drivin' My Life Away	Eddie Rabbitt
◆	1977	Drivin' Wheel	Foghat
◆	1963	Drownin' My Sorrows	Connie Francis
◆	1972	Drowning In The Sea Of Love	Joe Simon
◆	1971	Drum	Bobby Sherman
◆	1962	Drums Are My Beat	Sandy Nelson
◆	1967	Dry Your Eyes	Brenda & The Tabulations
◆	1966	Duck	Jackie Lee
◆	1987	Dude (Looks Like A Lady)	Aerosmith
◆	1973	Dueling Banjos	Eric Weissberg & Steve Mandell
◆	1962	Duke Of Earl	Gene Chandler
◆	1966	Dum-De-Da	Bobby Vinton
◆	1961	Dum Dum	Brenda Lee
◆	1956	Dungaree Doll	Eddie Fisher
◆	1994	Dunkie Butt	12 Gauge
◆	1977	Dusic	Brick
◆	1978	Dust In The Wind	Kansas
	1960	Dutchman's Gold	Walter Brennan
◆	1984	Dynamite	Jermaine Jackson
◆	1975	Dynomite (Part 1)	Bazuka

E

♦	1974	Earache My Eye	Cheech & Chong
♦	1958	Early In The Morning	Buddy Holly
♦	1958	Early In The Morning	Rinky Dinks
♦	1982	Early In The Morning	Gap Band
♦	1988	Early In The Morning	Robert Palmer
♦	1970	Early In The Morning	Vanity Fare
♦	1955	Earth Angel	Crew-Cuts
	1955	Earth Angel	Gloria Mann
♦	1955	Earth Angel	Penguins
♦	1969	Earth Angel	Vogues
♦	1986	Earth Angel	New Edition
♦	1996	Earth, The Sun, The Rain	Color Me Badd
♦	1963	Easier Said Than Done	Essex
	1967	East West	Herman's Hermits
♦	1977	Easy	Commodores
♦	1991	Easy Come Easy Go	Winger
♦	1970	Easy Come, Easy Go	Bobby Sherman
♦	1972	Easy Livin'	Uriah Heep
♦	1985	Easy Lover	Philip Bailey With Phil Collins
♦	1971	Easy Loving	Freddie Hart
♦	1969	Easy To Be Hard	Three Dog Night
♦	1977	Easy To Love	Leo Sayer
♦	1984	Eat It	Weird Al Yankovic
♦	1964	Ebb Tide	Lenny Welch
♦	1966	Ebb Tide	Righteous Brothers
♦	1982	Ebony And Ivory	Paul McCartney With Stevie Wonder
♦	1978	Ebony Eyes	Bob Welch
♦	1961	Ebony Eyes	Everly Brothers
♦	1969	Echo Park	Keith Barbour
	1973	Ecstasy	Ohio Players
♦	1956	Eddie My Love	Chordettes
♦	1956	Eddie My Love	Fontane Sisters
♦	1956	Eddie My Love	Teen Queens
♦	1988	Edge Of A Broken Heart	Vixen
♦	1986	Edge Of Heaven	Wham!
♦	1982	Edge Of Seventeen	Stevie Nicks
♦	1977	Edge Of The Universe	Bee Gees
♦	1978	Ego	Elton John
♦	1965	Eight Days A Week	Beatles
♦	1988	853-5937	Squeeze
♦	1966	Eight Miles High	Byrds
♦	1982	867-5309/Jenny	Tommy Tutone
♦	1971	Eighteen	Alice Cooper
♦	1989	18 And Life	Skid Row
♦	1975	Eighteen With A Bullet	Pete Wingfield
♦	1963	18 Yellow Roses	Bobby Darin
♦	1970	El Condor Pasa	Simon & Garfunkel
♦	1960	El Paso	Marty Robbins
♦	1958	El Rancho Rock	Champs
♦	1963	El Watusi	Ray Barretto
♦	1966	Eleanor Rigby	Beatles
♦	1968	Eleanor Rigby	Ray Charles
♦	1969	Eleanor Rigby	Aretha Franklin
♦	1972	Elected	Alice Cooper
♦	1985	Election Day	Arcadia
♦	1983	Electric Avenue	Eddy Grant
♦	1988	Electric Blue	Icehouse
♦	1989	Electric Youth	Debbie Gibson
♦	1968	Elenore	Turtles
♦	1996	Elevators (Me & You)	Outkast
	1956	11th Hour Melody	Al Hibbler
♦	1969	Eli's Coming	Three Dog Night
♦	1966	Elusive Butterfly	Bob Lind
♦	1981	Elvira	Oak Ridge Boys
♦	1986	Emergency	Kool & The Gang
♦	1975	Emma	Hot Chocolate
♦	1975	Emotion	Helen Reddy
♦	1978	Emotion	Samantha Sang
♦	1986	Emotion In Motion	Ric Ocasek
♦	1980	Emotional Rescue	Rolling Stones
♦	1961	Emotions	Brenda Lee
♦	1991	Emotions	Mariah Carey
♦	1980	Empire Strikes Back	Meco
♦	1957	Empty Arms	Teresa Brewer
♦	1957	Empty Arms	Ivory Joe Hunter
♦	1982	Empty Garden (Hey Hey Johnnie)	Elton John
♦	1959	Enchanted	Platters
	1958	Enchanted Island	Four Lads
♦	1959	Enchanted Sea	Martin Denny
♦	1959	Enchanted Sea	Islanders
♦	1958	End	Earl Grant
♦	1968	End Of Our Road	Gladys Knight & The Pips
♦	1970	End Of Our Road	Marvin Gaye
♦	1989	End Of The Innocence	Don Henley
♦	1992	End Of The Road	Boyz II Men
♦	1963	End Of The World	Skeeter Davis
♦	1981	Endless Love	Diana Ross & Lionel Richie
♦	1994	Endless Love	Luther Vandross & Mariah Carey
♦	1987	Endless Nights	Eddie Money
♦	1958	Endless Sleep	Jody Reynolds
♦	1988	Endless Summer Nights	Richard Marx
♦	1959	Endlessly	Brook Benton
♦	1974	Energy Crisis '74	Dickie Goodman
♦	1965	Engine Engine #9	Roger Miller
♦	1970	Engine Number 9	Wilson Pickett
♦	1966	England Swings	Roger Miller
♦	1990	Enjoy The Silence	Depeche Mode
♦	1977	Enjoy Yourself	Jacksons
♦	1991	Enter Sandman	Metallica
♦	1975	Entertainer	Billy Joel
♦	1974	Entertainer	Marvin Hamlisch
♦	1965	Entertainer	Tony Clarke
♦	1990	Epic	Faith No More
♦	1967	Epistle To Dippy	Donovan
♦	1974	Eres Tu (Touch The Wind)	Mocedades
♦	1992	Erotica	Madonna
♦	1990	Escapade	Janet Jackson
♦	1979	Escape (The Pina Colada Song)	Rupert Holmes
♦	1971	Escape-Ism (Part 1)	James Brown
♦	1962	Eso Beso (That Kiss!)	Paul Anka
♦	1997	ESPN Presents The Jock Jam	Various Artists
♦	1989	Eternal Flame	Bangles
♦	1965	Eve Of Destruction	Barry McGuire
♦	1992	Even Better Than The Real Thing	U2
♦	1980	Even It Up	Heart
♦	1978	Even Now	Barry Manilow
♦	1983	Even Now	Bob Seger & The Silver Bullet Band
♦	1967	Even The Bad Times Are Good	Tremeloes
♦	1982	Even The Nights Are Better	Air Supply
♦	1978	An Everlasting Love	Andy Gibb
♦	1967	Everlasting Love	Robert Knight
♦	1974	Everlasting Love	Carl Carlton
♦	1981	Everlasting Love	Rex Smith/Rachel Sweet
♦	1995	Everlasting Love	Gloria Estefan
♦	1989	Everlasting Love	Howard Jones
♦	1961	Everlovin'	Rick Nelson
♦	1961	Every Beat Of My Heart	The Pips
♦	1961	Every Breath I Take	Gene Pitney
♦	1983	Every Breath You Take	Police
♦	1956	Every Day Of My Life	McGuire Sisters
	1972	Every Day Of My Life	Bobby Vinton
♦	1995	Every Day Of The Week	Jade
♦	1991	Every Heartbeat	Amy Grant
♦	1978	Every Kinda People	Robert Palmer
♦	1964	Every Little Bit Hurts	Brenda Holloway
♦	1987	Every Little Kiss	Bruce Hornsby
♦	1989	Every Little Step	Bobby Brown
♦	1995	Every Little Thing I Do	Soul For Real
♦	1981	Every Little Thing She Does Is Magic	Police
♦	1958	Every Night (I Pray)	Chantels
♦	1988	Every Rose Has Its Thorn	Poison
	1963	Every Step Of The Way	Johnny Mathis
	1985	Every Step Of The Way	John Waite
♦	1979	Every Time I Think Of You	Babys
♦	1978	(Every Time I Turn Around) Back In Love Again	L.T.D.
♦	1975	Every Time You Touch Me (I Get High)	Charlie Rich
♦	1979	Every Which Way But Loose	Eddie Rabbitt
♦	1981	Every Woman In The World	Air Supply
♦	1963	Everybody	Tommy Roe
♦	1978	Everybody Dance	Chic

◆ 1986 Everybody Dance .... Ta Mara & The Seen
◆ 1990 Everybody Everybody .... Black Box
◆ 1986 Everybody Have Fun Tonight .... Wang Chung
◆ 1993 Everybody Hurts ....R.E.M.
◆ 1970 Everybody Is A Star .... Sly & The Family Stone
◆ 1964 Everybody Knows (I Still Love You) ....Dave Clark Five
◆ 1959 Everybody Likes To Cha Cha Cha..................................... Sam Cooke
◆ 1965 Everybody Loves A Clown ....Gary Lewis And The Playboys
◆ 1958 Everybody Loves A Lover ....Doris Day
◆ 1963 Everybody Loves A Lover ....Shirelles
◆ 1962 Everybody Loves Me But You..Brenda Lee
◆ 1964 Everybody Loves Somebody ....Dean Martin
◆ 1978 Everybody Needs Love ....Stephen Bishop
◆ 1967 Everybody Needs Somebody To Love......................Wilson Pickett
◆ 1972 Everybody Plays The Fool ....Main Ingredient
◆ 1991 Everybody Plays The Fool ....Aaron Neville
◆ 1985 Everybody Wants To Rule The World....................Tears For Fears
◆ 1982 Everybody Wants You ....Billy Squier
◆ 1971 Everybody's Everything ....Santana
◆ 1992 Everybody's Free (To Feel Good) .... Rozalla
◆ 1970 Everybody's Got The Right To Love ....Supremes
1980 Everybody's Got To Learn Sometime ....Korgis
◆ 1970 Everybody's Out Of Town ....B.J. Thomas
◆ 1960 Everybody's Somebody's Fool ....Connie Francis
◆ 1969 Everybody's Talkin' ....Nilsson
◆ 1994 Everyday .... Phil Collins
◆ 1983 Everyday I Write The Book ....Elvis Costello
◆ 1997 Everyday Is A Winding Road .... Sheryl Crow
◆ 1969 Everyday People .... Sly & The Family Stone
◆ 1983 Everyday People....................................Joan Jett & The Blackhearts
◆ 1969 Everyday With You Girl ....Classics IV
◆ 1979 Every 1's A Winner .... Hot Chocolate
◆ 1965 Everyone's Gone To The Moon .... Jonathan King
◆ 1989 Everything .... Jody Watley
◆ 1997 Everything .... Mary J Blige
◆ 1992 Everything About You ....Ugly Kid Joe
◆ 1992 Everything Changes ....Kathy Troccoli
◆ 1991 (Everything I Do) I Do It For You .... Bryan Adams
◆ 1972 Everything I Own ....Bread
◆ 1986 Everything In My Heart .... Corey Hart
◆ 1970 Everything Is Beautiful .... Ray Stevens
◆ 1985 Everything She Wants ....Wham!
◆ 1968 Everything That Touches You .... Association
◆ 1988 Everything Your Heart Desires ....Daryl Hall & John Oates
◆ 1964 Everything's Alright ....Newbeats
◆ 1993 Everything's Gonna Be Alright ....Father M.C.
◆ 1970 Everything's Tuesday ....Chairmen Of The Board
◆ 1997 Everytime I Close My Eyes .... Babyface
◆ 1985 Everytime You Go Away .... Paul Young
◆ 1988 Everywhere .... Fleetwood Mac
◆ 1970 Evil Ways ....Santana
◆ 1976 Evil Woman .... Electric Light Orchestra
◆ 1970 Evil Woman Don't Play Your Games With Me........................ Crow
◆ 1995 Exhale (Shoop Shoop) ....Whitney Houston
◆ 1961 Exodus ....Ferrante & Teicher
◆ 1955 Experience Unnecessary .... Sarah Vaughan
◆ 1968 Explosion (In Your Soul) .... Soul Survivors
◆ 1975 Express ....B.T. Express
◆ 1970 Express Yourself ....Charles Wright And The Watts 103rd Street Band
◆ 1989 Express Yourself .... Madonna
◆ 1990 Expression ....Salt-N-Pepa
◆ 1967 Expressway To Your Heart .... Soul Survivors
◆ 1982 Eye In The Sky ....Alan Parsons Project
◆ 1982 Eye Of The Tiger.. Survivor
◆ 1968 Eyes Of A New York Woman .... B.J. Thomas
◆ 1984 Eyes Without A Face... Billy Idol

F

◆ 1978 FM (No Static At All) .... Steely Dan
◆ 1994 Fa All Y'all ....Da Brat
◆ 1966 Fa-Fa-Fa-Fa-Fa (Sad Song)..Otis Redding
1957 Fabulous ....Charlie Gracie
◆ 1956 Fabulous Character .... Sarah Vaughan
◆ 1968 Face It Girl, It's Over... Nancy Wilson

◆ 1986 Face The Face .... Pete Townshend
◆ 1987 Facts Of Love ....Jeff Lorber featuring Karyn White
◆ 1981 Fade Away .... Bruce Springsteen
◆ 1991 Fading Like A Flower (Every Time You Leave) .... Roxette
◆ 1990 Fairweather Friend ....Johnny Gill
◆ 1974 Fairytale...Pointer Sisters
◆ 1987 Faith ....George Michael
◆ 1993 Faithful .... Go West
◆ 1983 Faithfully ....Journey
◆ 1987 Fake .... Alexander O'Neal
◆ 1983 Fake Friends....................................Joan Jett & The Blackhearts
◆ 1967 Fakin' It .... Simon & Garfunkel
◆ 1994 Fall Down ....Toad The Wet Sprocket
◆ 1983 Fall In Love With Me ....Earth, Wind & Fire
1976 Fallen Angel...Frankie Valli
◆ 1988 Fallen Angel .... Poison
◆ 1957 Fallen Star .... Ferlin Husky
◆ 1957 Fallen Star ....Jimmy Newman
◆ 1957 Fallen Star .... Nick Noble
◆ 1958 Fallin' ....Connie Francis
◆ 1996 Falling ....Montell Jordan
◆ 1978 Falling ....LeBlanc And Carr
◆ 1963 Falling .... Roy Orbison
◆ 1975 Fallin' In Love.........................Hamilton, Joe Frank & Reynolds
◆ 1974 Fallin' In Love .... Souther, Hillman, Furay Band
◆ 1997 Falling In Love (Is Hard On The Knees)............................. Aerosmith
◆ 1987 Falling In Love (Uh-Oh).....................Miami Sound Machine
◆ 1975 Fame ....David Bowie
◆ 1980 Fame .... Irene Cara
◆ 1960 Fame And Fortune ....Elvis Presley
◆ 1971 Family Affair .... Sly & The Family Stone
◆ 1983 Family Man .... Daryl Hall & John Oates
◆ 1972 Family Of Man ....Three Dog Night
◆ 1970 Fancy .... Bobbie Gentry
◆ 1960 Fannie Mae.. Buster Brown
◆ 1976 Fanny (Be Tender With My Love)... Bee Gees
◆ 1994 Fantastic Voyage ....Coolio
◆ 1982 Fantasy .... Aldo Nova
◆ 1978 Fantasy...Earth, Wind & Fire
◆ 1995 Fantasy .... Mariah Carey
◆ 1994 Far Behind ....Candlebox
◆ 1983 Far From Over .... Frank Stallone
◆ 1984 Farewell My Summer Love .... Michael Jackson
◆ 1964 Farmer John ....Premiers
◆ 1987 Fascinated ....Company B
◆ 1957 Fascination... Dick Jacobs
◆ 1957 Fascination... Jane Morgan
◆ 1957 Fascination...Dinah Shore
◆ 1988 Fast Car .... Tracy Chapman
◆ 1996 Fastlove ....George Michael
◆ 1978 Fat Bottomed Girls ....Queen
◆ 1988 Father Figure ....George Michael
◆ 1986 Feel It Again .... Honeymoon Suite
◆ 1975 Feel Like Makin' Love .... Bad Company
◆ 1974 Feel Like Makin' Love .... Roberta Flack
◆ 1995 Feel Me Flow ....Naughty By Nature
◆ 1960 Feel So Fine .... Johnny Preston
◆ 1997 Feel So Good .... Mase
◆ 1972 Feeling Alright ....Joe Cocker
◆ 1973 Feelin' Stronger Every Day...Chicago
◆ 1975 Feelings ....Morris Albert
◆ 1990 Feels Good ....Tony! Toni! Tone!
◆ 1977 Feels Like The First Time .... Foreigner
◆ 1978 Feels So Good ....Chuck Mangione
◆ 1989 Feels So Good .... Van Halen
◆ 1995 Feels So Good ....Xscape
◆ 1996 Feels So Good (Show Me Your Love) ....Lina Santiago
◆ 1981 Feels So Right ....Alabama
◆ 1994 Feenin'...Jodeci
◆ 1976 Fernando .... Abba
◆ 1965 Ferry Across The Mersey ....Gerry And The Pacemakers
◆ 1956 Fever..Little Willie John
◆ 1958 Fever ....Peggy Lee
◆ 1965 Fever ....McCoys
◆ 1978 Ffun ....Con Funk Shun
1958 Fibbin' ....Patti Page
◆ 1993 Fields Of Gold ....Sting

G

695

♦ 1967	Gonna Give Her All The Love I've Got	Jimmy Ruffin
♦ 1991	Gonna Make You Sweat	C + C Music Factory
♦ 1960	Gonzo	James Booker
♦ 1969	Goo Goo Barabajagal (Love Is Hot)	Donovan With The Jeff Beck Group
♦ 1995	Good	Beter Than Ezra
♦ 1993	Good Enough	Bobby Brown
♦ 1992	Good For Me	Amy Grant
♦ 1979	Good Girls Don't	Knack
♦ 1958	Good Golly Miss Molly	Little Richard
♦ 1976	Good Hearted Woman	Waylon & Willie (Waylon Jennings & Willie Nelson)
♦ 1963	Good Life	Tony Bennett
♦ 1966	Good Lovin'	Young Rascals
♦ 1975	Good Lovin' Gone Bad	Bad Company
♦ 1962	Good Luck Charm	Elvis Presley
♦ 1973	Good Morning Heartache	Diana Ross
♦ 1969	Good Morning Starshine	Oliver
♦ 1964	Good News	Sam Cooke
♦ 1969	Good Old Rock 'N Roll	Cat Mother And The All Night News Boys
♦ 1992	Good Stuff	B-52's
♦ 1968	Good, The Bad And The Ugly	Hugo Montenegro
♦ 1989	Good Thing	Fine Young Cannibals
♦ 1967	Good Thing	Paul Revere And The Raiders
1961	Good Time Baby	Bobby Rydell
♦ 1972	Good Time Charlie's Got The Blues	Danny O'Keefe
♦ 1979	Good Times	Chic
♦ 1964	Good Times	Sam Cooke
♦ 1979	Good Timin'	Beach Boys
♦ 1960	Good Timin'	Jimmy Jones
♦ 1966	Good Vibrations	Beach Boys
♦ 1976	Good Vibrations	Todd Rundgren
♦ 1991	Good Vibrations	Marky Mark & The Funky Bunch featuring Loleatta Holloway
1969	Goodbye	Mary Hopkin
♦ 1986	Goodbye	Night Ranger
♦ 1959	Goodbye Baby	Jack Scott
♦ 1964	Goodbye Baby (Baby Goodbye)	Solomon Burke
♦ 1961	Goodbye Cruel World	James Darren
♦ 1978	Goodbye Girl	David Gates
♦ 1979	Goodbye, I Love You	Firefall
♦ 1986	Goodbye Is Forever	Arcadia
♦ 1959	Goodbye Jimmy, Goodbye	Kathy Linden
♦ 1968	Goodbye My Love	James Brown
♦ 1979	Goodbye Stranger	Supertramp
♦ 1972	Goodbye To Love	Carpenters
♦ 1973	Goodbye Yellow Brick Road	Elton John
♦ 1965	Goodnight	Roy Orbison
♦ 1957	Goodnight My Love	Jesse Belvin
♦ 1957	Goodnight My Love	McGuire Sisters
♦ 1963	Goodnight My Love	Fleetwoods
♦ 1969	Goodnight My Love	Paul Anka
♦ 1978	Goodnight Tonight	Wings
♦ 1957	Goody Goody	Frankie Lymon And The Teenagers
♦ 1968	Goody Goody Gumdrops	1910 Fruitgum Company
♦ 1983	Goody Two Shoes	Adam Ant
1985	Goonies 'R' Good Enough	Cyndi Lauper
♦ 1960	Got A Girl	Four Preps
♦ 1984	Got A Hold On Me	Christine McVie
1958	Got A Match?	Daddy-0's
1958	Got A Match?	Frank Gallop
♦ 1994	Got Me Waiting	Heavy D. & The Boyz
♦ 1988	Got My Mind Set On You	George Harrison
♦ 1979	Got To Be Real	Cheryl Lynn
♦ 1972	Got To Be There	Michael Jackson
♦ 1976	Got To Get You Into My Life	Beatles
♦ 1978	Got To Get You Into My Life	Earth, Wind & Fire
♦ 1965	Got To Get You Off My Mind	Solomon Burke
♦ 1977	Got To Give It Up (Part 1)	Marvin Gaye
♦ 1997	Gotham City	R. Kelly
♦ 1970	Gotta Get Back To You	Tommy James And The Shondells
♦ 1970	Gotta Hold On To This Feeling	Jr. Walker & The All Stars
♦ 1979	Gotta Serve Somebody	Bob Dylan
♦ 1959	Gotta Travel On	Billy Grammer
♦ 1956	Graduation Day	Four Freshmen
♦ 1956	Graduation Day	Rover Boys
♦ 1959	Graduation's Here	Fleetwoods
♦ 1971	Grandma's Hands	Bill Withers

♦ 1963	Grass Is Greener	Brenda Lee
♦ 1962	Gravy (For My Mashed Potatoes)	Dee Dee Sharp
♦ 1968	Grazing In The Grass	Hugh Masekela
♦ 1969	Grazing In The Grass	Friends Of Distinction
♦ 1978	Grease	Frankie Valli
♦ 1966	Great Airplane Strike	Paul Revere And The Raiders
♦ 1958	Great Balls Of Fire	Jerry Lee Lewis
♦ 1956	Great Pretender	Platters
♦ 1962	Greatest Hurt	Jackie Wilson
♦ 1977	Greatest Love Of All	George Benson
♦ 1986	Greatest Love Of All	Whitney Houston
♦ 1959	Green Chritma	Stan Freberg
♦ 1956	Green Door	Jim Lowe
♦ 1970	Green-Eyed Lady	Sugarloaf
♦ 1966	Green Grass	Gary Lewis And The Playboys
♦ 1963	Green, Green	New Christy Minstrels
♦ 1967	Green, Green Grass Of Home	Tom Jones
♦ 1968	Green Light	American Breed
♦ 1962	Green Onions	Booker T & The MG's
♦ 1969	Green River	Creedence Clearwater Revival
♦ 1968	Green Tambourine	Lemon Pipers
♦ 1963	Greenback Dollar	Kingston Trio
♦ 1960	Greenfields	Brothers Four
1957	Greensleeves	Beverly Sisters
♦ 1990	Groove Is In The Heart	Deee-Lite
♦ 1978	Groove Line	Heatwave
♦ 1971	Groove Me	King Floyd
♦ 1994	Groove Thang	Zhane
♦ 1967	Groovin'	Booker T & The MG's
♦ 1967	Groovin'	Young Rascals
♦ 1969	Groovy Grubworm	Harlow Wilcox And The Oakies
♦ 1966	Groovy Kind Of Love	Mindbenders
♦ 1988	Groovy Kind Of Love	Phil Collins
♦ 1970	Groovy Situation	Gene Chandler
♦ 1991	Groovy Train	Farm
♦ 1976	Grow Some Funk Of Your Own	Elton John
♦ 1966	Guantanamera	Sandpipers
♦ 1958	Guess Things Happen That Way	Johnny Cash
♦ 1959	Guess Who	Jesse Belvin
♦ 1981	Guilty	Barbra Streisand & Barry Gibb
♦ 1959	Guitar Boogie Shuffle	Virtues
♦ 1972	Guitar Man	Bread
♦ 1968	Guitar Man	Elvis Presley
♦ 1981	Guitar Man	Elvis Presley
♦ 1955	Gum Drop	Crew-Cuts
♦ 1982	Gypsy	Fleetwood Mac
♦ 1963	Gypsy Cried	Lou Christie
♦ 1973	Gypsy Man	War
♦ 1961	Gypsy Woman	Impressions
♦ 1970	Gypsy Woman	Brian Hyland
♦ 1991	Gypsy Woman (She's Homeless)	Crystal Waters
♦ 1971	Gypsys, Tramps & Thieves	Cher

H

♦ 1969	Hair	Cowsills
♦ 1966	Hair On My Chinny Chin Chin	Sam The Sham And The Pharaohs
♦ 1973	Hairy Hippie	Bobby Womack
♦ 1973	Half-Breed	Cher
♦ 1963	Half Heaven - Half Heartache	Gene Pitney
♦ 1979	Half The Way	Crystal Gayle
♦ 1961	Halfway To Paradise	Tony Orlando
♦ 1968	Halfway To Paradise	Bobby Vinton
♦ 1971	Hallelujah	Sweathog
♦ 1973	Hallelujah Day	Jackson Five
♦ 1970	Hand Me Down World	Guess Who
♦ 1983	Hand To Hold On To	John Cougar
♦ 1972	Handbags And Gladrags	Rod Stewart
♦ 1988	Hands To Heaven	Breathe
♦ 1960	Handy Man	Jimmy Jones
♦ 1964	Handy Man	Del Shannon
♦ 1977	Handy Man	James Taylor
♦ 1969	Hang 'Em High	Booker T & The MG's
♦ 1982	Hang Fire	Rolling Stones
♦ 1990	Hang In Long Enough	Phil Collins

699

I

♦ 1964	I Like It Like That	Miracles
♦ 1967	I Like The Way	Tommy James And The Shondells
♦ 1991	I Like The Way (Kissing Game)	Hi-Five
♦ 1974	I Like To Live The Love	B.B. King
♦ 1957	I Like Your Kind Of Love	Andy Williams
♦ 1989	I Live By The Groove	Paul Carrack
♦ 1988	I Live For Your Love	Natalie Cole
♦ 1995	I Live My Life For You	Firehouse
♦ 1974	I Love.	Tom T. Hall
♦ 1981	I Love A Rainy Night	Eddie Rabbitt
♦ 1961	I Love How You Love Me	Paris Sisters
♦ 1969	I Love How You Love Me	Bobby Vinton
♦ 1997	I Love Me Some Him	Toni Braxton
♦ 1976	I Love Music (Part 1)	O'Jays
♦ 1974	I Love My Friend	Charlie Rich
♦ 1982	I Love Rock 'N Roll	Joan Jett & The Blackhearts
♦ 1978	I Love The Nightlife (Disco 'Round)	Alicia Bridges
♦ 1960	I Love The Way You Love	Marv Johnson
1981	I Love You	Climax Blues Band
♦ 1978	I Love You	Donna Summer
♦ 1968	I Love You	People
♦ 1962	I Love You	Volumes
♦ 1996	I Love You Always Forever	Donna Lewis
♦ 1963	I Love You Because	Al Martino
1966	I Love You Drops	Vic Dana
♦ 1971	I Love You For All Seasons	Fuzz
♦ 1958	(I Love You) For Sentimental Reasons	Sam Cooke
♦ 1955	I Love You Madly	Four Coins
♦ 1964	I Love You More And More Every Day	Al Martino
♦ 1966	I Love You 1000 Times	Platters
♦ 1993	I Love You Period	Dan Baird
♦ 1962	I Love You The Way You Are	Bobby Vinton
♦ 1992	I Love Your Smile	Shanice
♦ 1981	I Loved 'Em Every One	T.G. Sheppard
♦ 1959	I Loves You, Porgy	Nina Simone
♦ 1981	I Made It Through The Rain	Barry Manilow
♦ 1967	I Make A Fool Of Myself	Frankie Valli
♦ 1958	I Met Him On A Sunday (Ronde-Ronde)	Shirelles
♦ 1997	I Miss My Homies	Master P featuring Pimp C And The Shocker
♦ 1994	I Miss You	Aaron Hall
♦ 1986	I Miss You	Klymaxx
♦ 1995	I Miss You	N II U
♦ 1959	I Miss You So	Paul Anka
♦ 1965	I Miss You So	Little Anthony And The Imperials
♦ 1981	I Missed Again	Phil Collins
♦ 1965	I Must Be Seeing Things	Gene Pitney
♦ 1979	I Need A Lover	John Cougar
♦ 1987	I Need Love	L.L. Cool J
1966	I Need Somebody	? & The Mysterians
♦ 1976	I Need To Be In Love	Carpenters
♦ 1972	I Need You	America
♦ 1982	I Need You	Paul Carrack
♦ 1984	I Need You Tonight	Peter Wolf
♦ 1959	I Need Your Love Tonight	Elvis Presley
♦ 1981	I Need Your Lovin'	Teena Marie
♦ 1962	I Need Your Loving	Don Gardner And Dee Dee Ford
♦ 1976	I Never Cry	Alice Cooper
♦ 1967	I Never Loved A Man (The Way I Love You)	Aretha Franklin
♦ 1995	I Never Seen A Man Cry	Scarface
♦ 1959	I Only Have Eyes For You	Flamingos
♦ 1975	I Only Have Eyes For You	Art Garfunkel
♦ 1956	I Only Know I Love You	Four Aces
♦ 1989	I Only Wanna Be With You	Samantha Fox
♦ 1964	I Only Want To Be With You	Dusty Springfield
♦ 1976	I Only Want To Be With You	Bay City Rollers
♦ 1971	I Play And Sing	Dawn
♦ 1980	I Pledge My Love	Peaches & Herb
♦ 1982	I Ran (So Far Away)	Flock Of Seagulls
♦ 1960	I Really Don't Want To Know	Tommy Edwards
♦ 1966	I Really Don't Want To Know	Ronnie Dove
♦ 1971	I Really Don't Want To Know	Elvis Presley
♦ 1961	I Really Love You	Stereos
♦ 1989	I Remember Holding You	Boys Club
♦ 1962	I Remember You	Frank Ifield
♦ 1990	I Remember You	Skid Row
♦ 1964	I Rise, I Fall	Johnny Tillotson
♦ 1974	I Saw A Man And He Danced With His Wife	Cher
♦ 1966	I Saw Her Again	Mama's & Papa's
♦ 1964	I Saw Her Standing There	Beatles
♦ 1988	I Saw Him Standing There	Tiffany
♦ 1963	I Saw Linda Yesterday	Dickey Lee
♦ 1991	I Saw Red	Warrant
♦ 1972	I Saw The Light	Todd Rundgren
♦ 1967	I Say A Little Prayer	Dionne Warwick
♦ 1968	I Say A Little Prayer	Aretha Franklin
♦ 1997	I Say A Little Prayer	Diana King
♦ 1967	I Second That Emotion	Smokey Robinson & The Miracles
♦ 1966	I See The Light	Five Americans
♦ 1974	I Shall Sing	Garfunkel
♦ 1974	I Shot The Sheriff	Eric Clapton
♦ 1997	I Shot The Sheriff	Warren G
♦ 1988	I Should Be So Lucky	Kylie Minogue
♦ 1962	I Sold My Heart To The Junkman	Blue-Belles
♦ 1970	I Stand Accused	Isaac Hayes
♦ 1969	I Started A Joke	Bee Gees
♦ 1988	I Still Believe	Brenda K. Starr
♦ 1984	I Still Can't Get Over Loving You	Ray Parker Jr.
♦ 1964	I Still Get Jealous	Louis Armstrong And The All Stars
♦ 1979	I Still Have Dreams	Richie Furay
♦ 1987	I Still Haven't Found What I'm Looking For	U2
♦ 1994	I Swear	All-4-One
♦ 1967	I Take It Back	Sandy Posey
♦ 1968	I Thank You	Sam & Dave
♦ 1980	I Thank You	ZZ Top
♦ 1970	I Think I Love You	Partridge Family
♦ 1986	I Think It's Love	Jermaine Jackson
♦ 1967	I Think We're Alone Now	Tommy James And The Shondells
♦ 1987	I Think We're Alone Now	Tiffany
♦ 1991	I Touch Myself	Divinyls
♦ 1969	I Turned You On	Isley Brothers
♦ 1961	I Understand (Just How You Feel)	G-Clefs
♦ 1959	I Waited Too Long	Lavern Baker
♦ 1956	I Walk The Line	Johnny Cash
♦ 1986	I Wanna Be A Cowboy	Boys Don't Cry
♦ 1963	I Wanna Be Around	Tony Bennett
♦ 1994	I Wanna Be Down	Brandy
♦ 1960	I Wanna Be Loved	Ricky Nelson
♦ 1990	I Wanna Be Rich	Calloway
♦ 1989	I Wanna Be The One	Stevie B
♦ 1997	I Wanna Be There	Blessid Union Of Souls
♦ 1972	I Wanna Be Where You Are	Michael Jackson
♦ 1973	I Wanna Be With You	Raspberries
♦ 1980	I Wanna Be Your Lover	Prince
♦ 1975	I Wanna Dance Wit' Choo (Doo Dat Dance) Part 1	Disco Tex & The Sex-O-Lettes
♦ 1987	I Wanna Dance With Somebody	Whitney Houston
♦ 1977	I Wanna Get Next To You	Rose Royce
♦ 1986	I Wanna Go Back	Eddie Money
♦ 1988	I Wanna Have Some Fun	Samantha Fox
♦ 1985	I Wanna Hear It From Your Lips	Eric Carmen
♦ 1975	I Wanna Learn A Love Song	Harry Chapin
♦ 1968	I Wanna Live	Glen Campbell
♦ 1964	I Wanna Love Him So Bad	Jelly Beans
♦ 1961	(I Wanna) Love My Life Away	Gene Pitney
♦ 1992	I Wanna Love You	Jade
♦ 1991	I Wanna Sex You Up	Color Me Badd
♦ 1967	(I Wanna) Testify	Parliaments
♦ 1969	(I Wanna) Testify	Johnnie Taylor
1961	I Wanna Thank You	Bobby Rydell
♦ 1984	I Want A New Drug	Huey Lewis
♦ 1965	I Want Candy	Strangeloves
♦ 1988	I Want Her	Keith Sweat
♦ 1975	I Want To Be Free	Ohio Players
♦ 1960	I Want To Be Wanted	Brenda Lee
♦ 1988	I Want To Be Your Man	Roger
♦ 1996	I Want To Come Over	Melissa Etheridge
♦ 1965	I Want To (Do Everything For You)	Joe Tex
♦ 1966	I Want To Go With You	Eddy Arnold
♦ 1964	I Want To Hold Your Hand	Beatles
♦ 1985	I Want To Know What Love Is	Foreigner
1963	I Want To Stay Here	Steve And Eydie (Steve Lawrence And Eydie Gorme)
♦ 1970	I Want To Take You Higher	Sly & The Family Stone
♦ 1970	I Want To Take You Higher	Ike & Tina Turner
♦ 1959	I Want To Walk You Home	Fats Domino

703

♦ 1959	I'm A Man	Fabian
♦ 1967	I'm A Man	Spencer Davis Group
♦ 1965	I'm A Man	Yardbirds
♦ 1968	I'm A Midnight Mover	Wilson Pickett
♦ 1966	(I'm A) Road Runner	Jr. Walker & The All Stars
♦ 1961	I'm A Telling You	Jerry Butler
♦ 1974	I'm A Train	Albert Hammond
♦ 1975	I'm A Woman	Maria Muldaur
1980	I'm Alive	Electric Light Orchestra
♦ 1983	I'm Alive	Neil Diamond
♦ 1980	I'm Almost Ready	Pure Prairie League
♦ 1980	I'm Alright (Theme From "Caddyshack")	Kenny Loggins
♦ 1957	I'm Available	Margie Rayburn
♦ 1962	I'm Blue (The Gong Gong Song)	Ikettes
♦ 1971	I'm Comin' Home	Tommy James
♦ 1974	I'm Coming Home	Spinners
♦ 1966	I'm Comin' Home, Cindy	Trini Lopez
♦ 1961	I'm Comin' On Back To You	Jackie Wilson
♦ 1980	I'm Coming Out	Diana Ross
♦ 1964	I'm Crying	Animals
♦ 1973	I'm Doin' Fine Now	New York City
♦ 1976	I'm Easy	Keith Carradine
♦ 1978	I'm Every Woman	Chaka Khan
♦ 1993	I'm Every Woman	Whitney Houston
♦ 1993	I'm Free	Jon Secada
♦ 1969	I'm Free	Who
♦ 1984	I'm Free (Heaven Helps The Man)	Kenny Loggins
♦ 1985	I'm Goin' Down	Bruce Springsteen
♦ 1995	I'm Goin' Down	Mary J. Blige
♦ 1959	I'm Gonna Be A Wheel Some Day	Fats Domino
♦ 1993	I'm Gonna Be (500 Miles)	Proclaimers
♦ 1964	I'm Gonna Be Strong	Gene Pitney
♦ 1963	I'm Gonna Be Warm This Winter	Connie Francis
♦ 1959	I'm Gonna Get Married	Lloyd Price
♦ 1961	I'm Gonna Knock On Your Door	Eddie Hodges
♦ 1973	I'm Gonna Love You Just A Little More Baby	Barry White
♦ 1968	I'm Gonna Make You Love Me	Madeline Bell
♦ 1969	I'm Gonna Make You Love Me	
	Diana Ross And The Supremes & The Temptations	
♦ 1969	I'm Gonna Make You Mine	Lou Christie
♦ 1957	I'm Gonna Sit Right Down And Write Myself A Letter	Billy Williams
1978	I'm Gonna Take Care Of Everything	Rubicon
♦ 1985	I'm Gonna Tear Your Playhouse Down	Paul Young
♦ 1980	I'm Happy That Love Has Found You	Jimmy Hall
♦ 1965	I'm Henry VIII I Am	Herman's Hermits
♦ 1961	I'm Hurtin'	Roy Orbison
♦ 1974	I'm In Love	Aretha Franklin
♦ 1956	I'm In Love Again	Fats Domino
♦ 1994	I'm In The Mood	Ce Ce Peniston
♦ 1961	I'm In The Mood For Love	Chimes
♦ 1977	I'm In You	Peter Frampton
♦ 1964	I'm Into Something Good	Herman's Hermits
♦ 1973	I'm Just A Singer (In A Rock And Roll Band)	Moody Blues
♦ 1971	I'm Leavin'	Elvis Presley
♦ 1963	I'm Leaving It Up To You	Dale & Grace
♦ 1974	I'm Leaving It Up To You	Donny And Marie Osmond
♦ 1969	I'm Living In Shame	Diana Ross And The Supremes
♦ 1973	I'm Never Gonna Be Alone Anymore	Cornelius Brothers & Sister Rose
♦ 1959	I'm Never Gonna Tell	Jimmie Rodgers
♦ 1960	I'm Not Afraid	Ricky Nelson
♦ 1978	I'm Not Gonna Let It Bother Me Tonight	Atlanta Rhythm Section
♦ 1975	I'm Not In Love	10cc
♦ 1991	I'm Not In Love	Will To Power
♦ 1975	I'm Not Lisa	Jessi Colter
♦ 1970	I'm Not My Brothers Keeper	Flaming Ember
♦ 1986	I'm Not The One	Cars
♦ 1966	(I'm Not Your) Steppin' Stone	Monkees
♦ 1975	I'm On Fire	5000 Volts
♦ 1985	I'm On Fire	Bruce Springsteen
♦ 1975	I'm On Fire	Dwight Twilley Band
♦ 1964	I'm On The Outside (Looking In)	Little Anthony And The Imperials
♦ 1959	I'm Ready	Fats Domino
♦ 1994	I'm Ready	Tevin Campbell
♦ 1966	I'm Ready For Love	Martha & The Vandellas
♦ 1982	I'm So Excited	Pointer Sisters
♦ 1984	I'm So Excited	Pointer Sisters
♦ 1993	I'm So Into You	SWV

♦ 1966	I'm So Lonesome I Could Cry	B.J. Thomas And The Triumphs
♦ 1964	I'm So Proud	Impressions
♦ 1960	I'm Sorry	Brenda Lee
♦ 1975	I'm Sorry	John Denver
♦ 1957	I'm Sorry	Platters
♦ 1958	I'm Sorry I Made You Cry	Connie Francis
♦ 1957	I'm Stickin' With You	Jimmy Bowen
♦ 1972	I'm Still In Love With You	Al Green
♦ 1997	I'm Still In Love With You	New Edition
♦ 1988	I'm Still Searching	Glass Tiger
♦ 1983	I'm Still Standing	Elton John
♦ 1972	I'm Stone In Love With You	Stylistics
♦ 1965	I'm Telling You Now	Freddie And The Dreamers
♦ 1989	I'm That Type Of Guy	L.L. Cool J
1962	(I'm The Girl On) Wolverton Mountain	Jo Ann Campbell
♦ 1974	I'm The Leader Of The Gang	Brownsville Station
♦ 1992	I'm The One You Need	Jody Watley
♦ 1994	I'm The Only One	Melissa Etheridge
♦ 1992	I'm Too Sexy	Right Said Fred
1957	I'm Waiting Just For You	Pat Boone
♦ 1957	I'm Walkin'	Fats Domino
♦ 1957	I'm Walkin'	Ricky Nelson
♦ 1967	I'm Wondering	Stevie Wonder
♦ 1990	I'm Your Baby Tonight	Whitney Houston
♦ 1977	I'm Your Boogie Man	KC And The Sunshine Band
♦ 1986	I'm Your Man	Wham!
♦ 1966	I'm Your Puppet	James & Bobby Purify
♦ 1965	I'm Yours	Elvis Presley
♦ 1969	I've Been Hurt	Bill Deal & The Rhondels
♦ 1987	I've Been In Love Before	Cutting Crew
♦ 1972	I've Been Lonely For So Long	Frederick Knight
♦ 1967	I've Been Lonely Too Long	Young Rascals
♦ 1965	I've Been Loving You Too Long (To Stop Now)	Otis Redding
♦ 1974	(I've Been) Searchin' So Long	Chicago
♦ 1991	I've Been Thinking About You	Londonbeat
1959	I've Come Of Age	Billy Storm
♦ 1981	I've Done Everything For You	Rick Springfield
♦ 1971	I've Found Someone Of My Own	Free Movement
1976	I've Got A Feeling (We'll Be Seeing Each Other Again)	Al Wilson
♦ 1992	I've Got A Lot To Learn About Love	Storm
♦ 1983	I've Got A Rock N' Roll Heart	Eric Clapton
♦ 1974	I've Got A Thing About You Baby	Elvis Presley
♦ 1965	I've Got A Tiger By The Tail	Buck Owens
♦ 1962	I've Got A Woman (Part 1)	Jimmy McGriff
1962	I've Got Bonnie	Bobby Rydell
♦ 1968	I've Got Dreams To Remember	Otis Redding
♦ 1977	I've Got Love On My Mind	Natalie Cole
♦ 1964	I've Got Sand In My Shoes	Drifters
♦ 1973	I've Got So Much To Give	Barry White
♦ 1974	I've Got The Music In Me	Kiki Dee
♦ 1966	I've Got To Be Somebody	Billy Joe Royal
♦ 1974	I've Got To Use My Imagination	Gladys Knight & The Pips
♦ 1966	I've Got You Under My Skin	Four Seasons
♦ 1969	I've Gotta Be Me	Sammy Davis Jr.
♦ 1968	I've Gotta Get A Message To You	Bee Gees
♦ 1978	I've Had Enough	Wings
♦ 1959	I've Had It	Bell Notes
♦ 1987	(I've Had) The Time Of My Life	Bill Medley And Jennifer Warnes
♦ 1970	I've Lost You	Elvis Presley
♦ 1982	I've Never Been To Me	Charlene
♦ 1967	I've Passed This Way Before	Jimmy Ruffin
♦ 1961	I've Told Every Little Star	Linda Scott
♦ 1990	Ice Ice Baby	Vanilla Ice
♦ 1991	Iesha	Another Bad Creation
♦ 1971	If	Bread
♦ 1993	If	Janet Jackson
♦ 1962	If A Man Answers	Bobby Darin
♦ 1962	If A Woman Answers (Hang Up The Phone)	Leroy Van Dyke
♦ 1983	If Anyone Falls	Stevie Nicks
♦ 1958	If Dreams Came True	Pat Boone
♦ 1978	If Ever I See You Again	Roberta Flack
♦ 1984	If Ever You're In My Arms Again	Peabo Bryson
♦ 1969	If I Can Dream	Elvis Presley
♦ 1978	If I Can't Have You	Yvonne Elliman
♦ 1968	If I Could Build My Whole World Around You	
	Marvin Gaye & Tammi Terrell	
♦ 1972	If I Could Reach You	Fifth Dimension

♦ 1966	Just Like A Woman	Bob Dylan
♦ 1989	Just Like Jesse James	Cher
♦ 1966	Just Like Me	Paul Revere And The Raiders
♦ 1988	Just Like Paradise	David Lee Roth
♦ 1964	(Just Like) Romeo & Juliet	Reflections
♦ 1980	(Just Like) Starting Over	John Lennon
♦ 1991	Just Like You	Robbie Nevil
♦ 1958	Just Married	Marty Robbins
♦ 1971	Just My Imagination (Running Away With Me)	Temptations
♦ 1981	Just Once	Quincy Jones featuring James Ingram
♦ 1965	Just Once In My Life	Righteous Brothers
♦ 1963	Just One Look	Doris Troy
♦ 1960	Just One Time	Don Gibson
♦ 1961	Just Out Of Reach (Of My Two Open Arms)	Solomon Burke
♦ 1977	Just Remember I Love You	Firefall
♦ 1971	Just Seven Numbers (Can Straighten Out My Life)	Four Tops
♦ 1992	Just Take My Heart	Mr. Big
♦ 1981	Just The Two Of Us	Grover Washington Jr. With Bill Withers
♦ 1991	Just The Way It Is Baby	Rembrandts
♦ 1978	Just The Way You Are	Billy Joel
♦ 1976	Just To Be Close To You	Commodores
♦ 1957	Just To Hold My Hand	Clyde McPhatter
♦ 1987	Just To See Her	Smokey Robinson
♦ 1975	Just Too Many People	Melissa Manchester
♦ 1956	Just Walking In The Rain	Johnnie Ray
♦ 1991	Just Want To Hold You	Jasmine Guy
♦ 1978	Just What I Needed	Cars
♦ 1979	Just When I Needed You Most	Randy Vanwarmer
♦ 1965	Just You	Sonny & Cher
♦ 1976	Just You And I	Melissa Manchester
♦ 1973	Just You 'N' Me	Chicago
♦ 1992	Justified And Ancient	KLF
♦ 1991	Justify My Love	Madonna

K

♦ 1971	K-Jee	Nite-Liters
♦ 1956	Ka-Ding-Dong	Diamonds
♦ 1956	Ka-Ding-Dong	G-Clefs
♦ 1956	Ka-Ding-Dong	Hilltoppers
♦ 1959	Kansas City	Wilbert Harrison
♦ 1964	Kansas City	Trini Lopez
♦ 1965	Kansas City Star	Roger Miller
♦ 1984	Karma Chameleon	Culture Club
1958	Kathy-O	Diamonds
♦ 1969	Keem-O-Sabe	Electric Indian
♦ 1957	Keep A Knockin'	Little Richard
♦ 1991	Keep Coming Back	Richard Marx
♦ 1983	(Keep Feeling) Fascination	Human League
♦ 1992	Keep It Comin'	Keith Sweat
♦ 1977	Keep It Comin' Love	KC And The Sunshine Band
♦ 1990	Keep It Together	Madonna
♦ 1979	Keep On Dancin'	Gary's Gang
♦ 1965	Keep On Dancing	Gentrys
♦ 1996	Keep On, Keepin' On	MC Lyte featuring Xscape
♦ 1968	Keep On Lovin' Me Honey	Marvin Gaye & Tammi Terrell
♦ 1981	Keep On Loving You	REO Speedwagon
♦ 1989	Keep On Movin'	Soul II Soul
♦ 1964	Keep On Pushing	Impressions
♦ 1974	Keep On Singing	Helen Reddy
♦ 1974	Keep On Smilin'	Wet Willie
♦ 1973	Keep On Truckin' (Part 1)	Eddie Kendricks
♦ 1992	Keep On Walkin'	Ce Ce Peniston
♦ 1965	Keep Searchin' (We'll Follow The Sun)	Del Shannon
♦ 1967	Keep The Ball Rollin'	Jay And The Techniques
♦ 1992	Keep The Faith	Bon Jovi
♦ 1982	Keep The Fire Burnin'	REO Speedwagon
♦ 1995	Keep Their Heads Ringin'	Dr. Dre
♦ 1993	Keep Ya Head Up	2Pac
♦ 1962	Keep Your Hands Off My Baby	Little Eva
♦ 1987	Keep Your Hands To Yourself	Georgia Satellites
♦ 1973	Keeper Of The Castle	Four Tops
♦ 1985	Keeping The Faith	Billy Joel

♦ 1970	Kentucky Rain	Elvis Presley
♦ 1967	Kentucky Woman	Neil Diamond
♦ 1968	Kentucky Woman	Deep Purple
♦ 1958	Kewpie Doll	Perry Como
♦ 1982	Key Largo	Bertie Higgins
♦ 1996	Key West Intermezzo (I Saw You First)	John Mellencamp
♦ 1966	Kicks	Paul Revere And The Raiders
♦ 1990	Kickstart My Heart	Motley Crue
♦ 1984	Kid's American	Matthew Wilder
♦ 1960	Kiddio	Brook Benton
♦ 1982	Kids In America	Kim Wilde
♦ 1963	Killer Joe	Rocky Fellers
♦ 1975	Killer Queen	Queen
♦ 1973	Killing Me Softly With His Song	Roberta Flack
♦ 1977	Killing Of Georgie (Part 1 & 2)	Rod Stewart
♦ 1981	Killin' Time	Fred Knoblock And Susan Anton
♦ 1967	Kind Of A Drag	Buckinghams
♦ 1963	Kind Of Boy You Can't Forget	Raindrops
♦ 1986	King For A Day	Thompson Twins
♦ 1972	King Heroin	James Brown
♦ 1977	King Is Gone	Ronnie McDowell
♦ 1983	King Of Pain	Police
♦ 1980	King Of The Hill	Rick Pinette And Oak
♦ 1965	King Of The Road	Roger Miller
♦ 1962	King Of The Whole Wide World	Elvis Presley
♦ 1990	King Of Wishful Thinking	Go West
♦ 1978	King Tut	Steve Martin And The Toot Uncommons
♦ 1974	Kings Of The Party	Brownsville Station
♦ 1986	Kiss	Prince And The Revolution
♦ 1988	Kiss	Art Of Noise featuring Tom Jones
♦ 1972	Kiss An Angel Good Mornin'	Charley Pride
♦ 1976	Kiss And Say Goodbye	Manhattans
♦ 1988	Kiss And Tell	Bryan Ferry
♦ 1965	Kiss Away	Ronnie Dove
♦ 1995	Kiss From A Rose	Seal
♦ 1987	Kiss Him Goodbye	Nylons
♦ 1988	Kiss Me Deadly	Lita Ford
♦ 1968	Kiss Me Goodbye	Petula Clark
♦ 1980	Kiss Me In The Rain	Barbra Streisand
♦ 1964	Kiss Me Quick	Elvis Presley
♦ 1964	Kiss Me Sailor	Diane Renay
♦ 1981	Kiss On My List	Daryl Hall & John Oates
♦ 1983	Kiss The Bride	Elton John
♦ 1991	Kiss Them For Me	Siouxsie And The Banshees
♦ 1990	Kiss This Thing Goodbye	Del Amitri
♦ 1978	Kiss You All Over	Exile
♦ 1989	Kisses On The Wind	Neneh Cherry
♦ 1957	Kisses Sweeter Than Wine	Jimmie Rodgers
♦ 1988	Kissing A Fool	George Michael
♦ 1964	Kissin' Cousins	Elvis Presley
♦ 1973	Kissing My Love	Bill Withers
♦ 1961	Kissin' On The Phone	Paul Anka
1959	Kissin' Time	Bobby Rydell
♦ 1996	Kissin' You	Total
♦ 1957	Knee Deep In The Blues	Guy Mitchell
♦ 1967	Knight In Rusty Armour	Peter And Gordon
♦ 1966	Knock On Wood	Eddie Floyd
♦ 1967	Knock On Wood	Otis & Carla (Otis Redding & Carla Thomas)
♦ 1979	Knock On Wood	Amii Stewart
♦ 1971	Knock Three Times	Dawn
♦ 1990	Knockin' Boots	Candyman
♦ 1993	Knockin' Da Boots	H-Town
♦ 1973	Knockin' On Heaven's Door	Bob Dylan
♦ 1977	Knowing Me, Knowing You	Abba
♦ 1955	Ko Ko Mo (I Love You So)	Perry Como
♦ 1955	Ko Ko Mo (I Love You So)	Crew-Cuts
♦ 1973	Kodachrome	Paul Simon
♦ 1988	Kokomo	The Beach Boys
♦ 1959	Kookie, Kookie (Lend Me Your Comb)	Edward Byrnes And Connie Stevens
♦ 1969	Kozmic Blues	Janis Joplin
♦ 1974	Kung Fu	Curtis Mayfield
♦ 1974	Kung Fu Fighting	Carl Douglas
♦ 1986	Kyrie	Mr. Mister

L

♦	1959	La Bamba	Ritchie Valens
♦	1987	La Bamba	Los Lobos
	1958	La Dee Dah	Billy & Lillie
♦	1958	La-Do-Dada	Dale Hawkins
♦	1974	La Grange	ZZ Top
♦	1987	La Isla Bonita	Madonna
♦	1970	La La La (If I Had You)	Bobby Sherman
♦	1968	La-La Means I Love You	Delfonics
♦	1974	La La Peace Song	Al Wilson
♦	1958	La Paloma	Billy Vaughn
♦	1979	Ladies Night	Kool & The Gang
♦	1996	Lady	D'Angelo
♦	1967	Lady	Jack Jones
♦	1980	Lady	Kenny Rogers
♦	1979	Lady	Little River Band
♦	1975	Lady	Styx
♦	1980	Lady	Whispers
♦	1967	Lady Bird	Nancy Sinatra & Lee Hazlewood
♦	1975	Lady Blue	Leon Russell
♦	1966	Lady Godiva	Peter And Gordon
♦	1987	Lady In Red	Chris DeBurgh
♦	1966	Lady Jane	Rolling Stones
♦	1978	Lady Love	Lou Rawls
♦	1983	Lady Love Me (One More Time)	George Benson
♦	1960	Lady Luck	Lloyd Price
♦	1968	Lady Madonna	Beatles
♦	1975	Lady Marmalade	LaBelle
♦	1968	Lady Willpower	Gary Puckett And The Union Gap
♦	1981	Lady (You Bring Me Up)	Commodores
♦	1968	Lalena	Donovan
♦	1965	Land Of 1000 Dances	Cannibal & The Headhunters
♦	1966	Land Of 1000 Dances	Wilson Pickett
♦	1987	Land Of Confusion	Genesis
♦	1966	Land Of Milk And Honey	Vogues
♦	1984	Language Of Love	Dan Fogelberg
	1961	Language Of Love	John D. Loudermilk
♦	1965	Last Chance To Turn Around	Gene Pitney
♦	1976	Last Child	Aerosmith
♦	1978	Last Dance	Donna Summer
♦	1960	Last Date	Floyd Cramer
♦	1960	Last Date	Lawrence Welk And His Orchestra
♦	1975	Last Farewell	Roger Whittaker
♦	1975	Last Game Of The Season (A Blind Man In The Bleachers)	David Geddes
♦	1964	Last Kiss	J. Frank Wilson And The Cavaliers
♦	1974	Last Kiss	Wednesday
♦	1989	Last Mile	Cinderella
♦	1961	Last Night	Mar-Keys
♦	1996	Last Night	AZ Yet
♦	1972	(Last Night) I Didn't Get To Sleep At All	Fifth Dimension
♦	1973	Last Song	Edward Bear
♦	1992	Last Song	Elton John
♦	1965	Last Time	Rolling Stones
♦	1974	Last Time I Saw Him	Diana Ross
♦	1966	Last Train To Clarksville	Monkees
♦	1980	Last Train To London	Electric Light Orchestra
♦	1967	Last Waltz	Engelbert Humperdinck
♦	1966	Last Word In Lonesome Is Me	Eddy Arnold
♦	1989	Last Worthless Evening	Don Henley
♦	1957	Lasting Love	Sal Mineo
♦	1980	Late In The Evening	Paul Simon
♦	1993	Lately	Jodeci
♦	1967	Laudy Miss Claudy	Buckinghams
♦	1965	Laugh At Me	Sonny
♦	1965	Laugh Laugh	Beau Brummels
♦	1969	Laughing	Guess Who
♦	1963	Laughing Boy	Mary Wells
♦	1975	Laughter In The Rain	Neil Sedaka
♦	1965	Laurie (Strange Things Happen)	Dickey Lee
♦	1959	Lavender-Blue	Sammy Turner
♦	1983	Lawyers In Love	Jackson Browne
♦	1970	Lay A Little Lovin' On Me	Robin McNamara
♦	1970	Lay Down (Candles In The Rain)	Melanie With The Edwin Hawkins Singers

♦	1978	Lay Down Sally	Eric Clapton
♦	1956	Lay Down Your Arms	Chordettes
♦	1969	Lay Lady Lay	Bob Dylan
♦	1989	Lay Your Hands On Me	Bon Jovi
♦	1985	Lay Your Hands On Me	Thompson Twins
♦	1994	(Lay Your Head On My) Pillow	Tony! Toni! Tone!
♦	1972	Layla	Derek And The Dominos
♦	1992	Layla	Eric Clapton
♦	1967	Lazy Day	Spanky And Our Gang
	1964	Lazy Elsie Molly	Chubby Checker
♦	1958	Lazy Mary	Lou Monte
♦	1961	Lazy River	Bobby Darin
♦	1958	Lazy Summer Night	Four Preps
♦	1978	Le Freak	Chic
♦	1979	Lead Me On	Maxine Nightingale
♦	1982	Leader Of The Band	Dan Fogelberg
♦	1965	Leader Of The Laundromat	Detergents
♦	1964	Leader Of The Pack	Shangri-Las
♦	1962	Leah	Roy Orbison
♦	1972	Lean On Me	Bill Withers
♦	1987	Lean On Me	Club Nouveau
♦	1966	Leaning On The Lamp Post	Herman's Hermits
♦	1955	Learnin' The Blues	Frank Sinatra
♦	1991	Learning To Fly	Tom Petty And The Heartbreakers
♦	1982	Leather And Lace	Stevie Nicks With Don Henley
♦	1989	Leave A Light On	Belinda Carlisle
♦	1984	Leave A Tender Moment Alone	Billy Joel
♦	1984	Leave It	Yes
♦	1974	Leave Me Alone (Ruby Red Dress)	Helen Reddy
♦	1973	Leaving Me	Independents
♦	1969	Leaving On A Jet Plane	Peter, Paul & Mary
♦	1958	Left Right Out Of Your Heart	Patti Page
♦	1997	Legend Of A Cowgirl	Imani Copolla
♦	1980	Legend Of Wooley Swamp	Charlie Daniels Band
♦	1984	Legs	ZZ Top
♦	1962	Lemon Tree	Peter, Paul & Mary
♦	1965	Lemon Tree	Trini Lopez
♦	1958	Leroy	Jack Scott
♦	1968	Les Bicyclettes De Belsize	Engelbert Humperdinck
♦	1968	Lesson	Vikki Carr
♦	1987	Lessons In Love	Level 42
♦	1969	Let A Man Come In And Do The Popcorn (Part 1)	James Brown
♦	1976	Let 'Em In	Wings
♦	1989	Let Go	Sharon Bryant
♦	1995	Let Her Cry	Hootie & The Blowfish
♦	1976	Let Her In	John Travolta
♦	1985	Let Him Go	Animotion
♦	1970	Let It Be	Beatles
♦	1960	Let It Be Me	Everly Brothers
♦	1964	Let It Be Me	Betty Everett & Jerry Butler
♦	1996	Let It Flow	Toni Braxton
♦	1997	Let It Go	Ray J
♦	1967	Let It Out (Let It All Hang Out)	Hombres
♦	1974	Let It Ride	Bachman-Turner Overdrive
♦	1976	Let It Shine	Olivia Newton-John
♦	1982	Let It Whip	Dazz Band
♦	1967	Let Love Come Between Us	James & Bobby Purify
♦	1969	Let Me	Paul Revere And The Raiders
♦	1965	Let Me Be	Turtles
♦	1980	Let Me Be The Clock	Smokey Robinson
♦	1995	Let Me Be The One	Blessid Union Of Souls
♦	1987	Let Me Be The One	Expose
♦	1974	Let Me Be There	Olivia Newton-John
♦	1980	Let Me Be Your Angel	Stacy Lattisaw
♦	1957	(Let Me Be Your) Teddy Bear	Elvis Presley
♦	1961	Let Me Belong To You	Brian Hyland
♦	1997	Let Me Clear My Throat	DJ Kool
♦	1970	Let Me Go To Him	Dionne Warwick
♦	1980	Let Me Go, Love	Nicolette Larson
♦	1955	Let Me Go Lover	Teresa Brewer With The Lancers
♦	1955	Let Me Go Lover	Joan Weber
♦	1973	Let Me In	Osmonds
♦	1962	Let Me In	Sensations
♦	1980	Let Me Love You Tonight	Pure Prairie League
♦	1993	Let Me Ride	Dr. Dre
♦	1973	Let Me Serenade You	Three Dog Night
♦	1982	Let Me Tickle Your Fancy	Jermaine Jackson

◆	1980	Let My Love Open The Door	Pete Townshend
◆	1991	Let The Beat Hit 'Em	Lisa Lisa And Cult Jam
◆	1958	Let The Bells Keep Ringing	Paul Anka
◆	1957	Let The Four Winds Blow	Roy Brown
◆	1961	Let The Four Winds Blow	Fats Domino
◆	1956	Let The Good Times Roll	Shirley & Lee
	1967	Let The Good Times Roll & Feel So Good	Bunny Sigler
◆	1960	Let The Little Girl Dance	Billy Bland
◆	1976	Let The Music Play	Barry White
◆	1984	Let The Music Play	Shannon
◆	1961	Let There Be Drums	Sandy Nelson
◆	1974	Let Your Hair Down	Temptations
◆	1976	Let Your Love Flow	Bellamy Brothers
◆	1971	Let Your Love Go	Bread
◆	1978	Let's All Chant	Michael Zager Band
◆	1962	Let's Dance	Chris Montez
◆	1983	Let's Dance	David Bowie
◆	1975	Let's Do It Again	Staple Singers
	1965	Let's Do The Freddie	Chubby Checker
◆	1967	Let's Fall In Love	Peaches & Herb
◆	1973	Let's Get It On	Marvin Gaye
◆	1974	Let's Get Married	Al Green
◆	1992	Let's Get Rocked	Def Leppard
◆	1980	Let's Get Serious	Jermaine Jackson
◆	1961	Let's Get Together	Hayley Mills
◆	1965	Let's Get Together	We Five
◆	1970	Let's Give Adam And Eve Another Chance	
			Gary Puckett And The Union Gap
◆	1979	Let's Go	Cars
◆	1987	Let's Go	Wang Chung
◆	1962	Let's Go	Routers
◆	1986	Let's Go All The Way	Sly Fox
◆	1984	Let's Go Crazy	Prince And The Revolution
◆	1983	Let's Go Dancin' (Ooh La, La, La)	Kool & The Gang
◆	1966	Let's Go Get Stoned	Ray Charles
◆	1960	Let's Go, Let's Go, Let's Go	Hank Ballard And The Midnighters
◆	1963	Let's Go Steady Again	Neil Sedaka
◆	1981	Let's Groove	Earth, Wind & Fire
◆	1965	Let's Hang On!	Four Seasons
◆	1982	Let's Hang On!	Barry Manilow
◆	1960	Let's Have A Party	Wanda Jackson
◆	1984	Let's Hear It For The Boy	Deniece Williams
◆	1963	Let's Kiss And Make Up	Bobby Vinton
	1963	Let's Limbo Some More	Chubby Checker
◆	1967	Let's Live For Today	Grass Roots
◆	1965	Let's Lock The Door (And Throw Away The Key)	Jay & The Americans
◆	1959	Let's Love	Johnny Mathis
◆	1996	Let's Make A Night To Remember	Bryan Adams
◆	1973	Let's Pretend	Raspberries
◆	1974	Let's Put It All Together	Stylistics
◆	1967	Let's Spend The Night Together	Rolling Stones
◆	1966	Let's Start All Over Again	Ronnie Dove
◆	1972	Let's Stay Together	Al Green
◆	1984	Let's Stay Together	Tina Turner
◆	1974	Let's Straighten It Out	Latimore
◆	1991	Let's Talk About Sex	Salt-N-Pepa
◆	1960	Let's Think About Living	Bob Luman
◆	1963	Let's Turkey Trot	Little Eva
	1961	Let's Twist Again	Chubby Checker
◆	1987	Let's Wait A While	Janet Jackson
◆	1987	Let's Work	Mick Jagger
◆	1970	Let's Work Together	Canned Heat
◆	1970	Let's Work Together (Part 1)	Wilbert Harrison
◆	1994	Letitgo	Prince
◆	1967	Letter	Box Tops
◆	1969	Letter	Arbors
◆	1970	Letter	Joe Cocker
◆	1964	Letter From Sherry	Dale Ward
◆	1962	Letter Full Of Tears	Gladys Knight & The Pips
◆	1958	Letter To An Angel	Jimmy Clanton
◆	1973	Letter To Myself	Chi-Lites
◆	1972	Levon	Elton John
◆	1971	Liar	Three Dog Night
◆	1965	Liar Liar	Castaways
◆	1989	Licence To Chill	Billy Ocean
◆	1968	Licking Stick - Licking Stick (Part 1)	James Brown
◆	1977	Lido Shuffle	Boz Scaggs
◆	1962	Lie To Me	Brook Benton
	1958	Liechtensteiner Polka	Will Glahe
◆	1991	Lies	EMF
◆	1990	Lies	En Vogue
◆	1986	Lies	Jonathan Butler
◆	1966	Lies	Knickerbockers
◆	1983	Lies	Thompson Twins
◆	1991	Life Goes On	Poison
◆	1986	Life In A Northern Town	Dream Academy
◆	1985	Life In One Day	Howard Jones
◆	1977	Life In The Fast Lane	Eagles
◆	1992	Life Is A Highway	Tom Cochrane
◆	1974	Life Is A Rock (But The Radio Rolled Me)	Reunion
◆	1981	Life Of Illusion	Joe Walsh
◆	1978	Life's Been Good	Joe Walsh
◆	1992	Lift Me Up	Howard Jones
◆	1967	Light My Fire	Doors
◆	1968	Light My Fire	Jose Feliciano
◆	1987	Light Of Day	The Barbusters
◆	1971	Light Sings	Fifth Dimension
◆	1966	Lightnin' Strikes	Lou Christie
◆	1967	Lightning's Girl	Nancy Sinatra
◆	1984	Lights Out	Peter Wolf
◆	1967	(The Lights Went Out In) Massachusetts	Bee Gees
◆	1966	Like A Baby	Len Barry
◆	1989	Like A Prayer	Madonna
◆	1986	Like A Rock	Bob Seger & The Silver Bullet Band
◆	1965	Like A Rolling Stone	Bob Dylan
	1978	Like A Sunday In Salem (The Amos & Andy Song)	Gene Cotton
◆	1985	Like A Virgin	Madonna
◆	1967	Like An Old Time Movie	Scott McKenzie
◆	1961	Like, Long Hair	Paul Revere And The Raiders
◆	1986	Like No Other Night	38 Special
◆	1960	Like Strangers	Everly Brothers
◆	1995	Like The Way I Do	Melissa Etheridge
◆	1995	Like This And Like That	Monica
◆	1968	Like To Get To Know You	Spanky And Our Gang
◆	1966	Lil' Red Riding Hood	Sam The Sham And The Pharaohs
◆	1991	Lily Was Here	David A. Stewart Introducing Candy Dulfer
◆	1962	Limbo Rock	Champs
◆	1962	Limbo Rock	Chubby Checker
◆	1963	Linda	Jan & Dean
◆	1955	Ling, Ting, Tong	Charms
◆	1994	Linger	Cranberries
◆	1961	Lion Sleeps Tonight	Tokens
◆	1972	Lion Sleeps Tonight	Robert John
◆	1957	Lips Of Wine	Andy Williams
	1956	Lipstick And Candy And Rubbersole Shoes	Julius LaRosa
◆	1959	Lipstick On Your Collar	Connie Francis
	1956	Lisbon Antigua	Mitch Miller
	1956	Lisbon Antigua	Nelson Riddle
◆	1966	Listen People	Herman's Hermits
◆	1972	Listen To The Music	Doobie Brothers
◆	1975	Listen To What The Man Said	Wings
◆	1989	Listen To Your Heart	Roxette
◆	1968	Little Arrows	Leapy Lee
	1963	Little Band Of Gold	James Gilreath
◆	1967	Little Bit Me, A Little Bit You	Monkees
◆	1976	Little Bit More	Dr. Hook
◆	1965	Little Bit Of Heaven	Ronnie Dove
◆	1986	Little Bit Of Love (Is All It Takes)	New Edition
◆	1961	Little Bit Of Soap	Jarmels
◆	1979	Little Bit Of Soap	Nigel Olsson
◆	1967	Little Bit O' Soul	Music Explosion
◆	1957	Little Bitty Pretty One	Bobby Day And The Satellites
◆	1957	Little Bitty Pretty One	Thurston Harris
◆	1962	Little Bitty Pretty One	Clyde McPhatter
◆	1972	Little Bitty Pretty One	Jackson Five
◆	1962	Little Bitty Tear	Burl Ives
◆	1962	Little Black Book	Jimmy Dean
◆	1958	Little Blue Man	Betty Johnson
◆	1961	Little Boy Sad	Johnny Burnette
◆	1985	Little By Little	Robert Plant
◆	1964	Little Children	Billy J. Kramer With The Dakotas
◆	1960	Little Coco Palm	Jerry Wallace
◆	1957	Little Darlin'	Diamonds
◆	1963	Little Deuce Coupe	Beach Boys

♦ 1987	Looking For A New Love	Jody Watley
♦ 1980	Lookin' For Love	Johnny Lee
♦ 1964	Looking For Love	Connie Francis
♦ 1976	Looking For Space	John Denver
♦ 1970	Lookin' Out My Back Door	Creedence Clearwater Revival
♦ 1993	Looking Through Patient Eyes	P.M. Dawn
♦ 1965	Looking Through The Eyes Of Love	Gene Pitney
♦ 1973	Looking Through The Eyes Of Love	Partridge Family
♦ 1972	Lookin' Through The Windows	Jackson Five
♦ 1977	Looks Like We Made It	Barry Manilow
♦ 1963	Loop De Loop	Johnny Thunder
♦ 1974	Lord's Prayer	Sister Janet Mead
♦ 1976	Lorelei	Styx
♦ 1994	Loser	Beck
♦ 1967	Loser (With A Broken Heart)	Gary Lewis And The Playboys
♦ 1991	Losing My Religion	R.E.M.
♦ 1963	Losing You	Brenda Lee
♦ 1980	Lost Her In The Sun	John Stewart
♦ 1987	Lost In Emotion	Lisa Lisa And Cult Jam
♦ 1980	Lost In Love	Air Supply
♦ 1985	Lost In Love	New Edition
♦ 1988	Lost In You	Rod Stewart
♦ 1989	Lost In Your Eyes	Debbie Gibson
♦ 1961	Lost Someone	James Brown
♦ 1977	Lost Without Your Love	Bread
♦ 1979	Lotta Love	Nicolette Larson
♦ 1957	Lotta Lovin'	Gene Vincent And His Blue Caps
♦ 1964	Louie Louie	Kingsmen
♦ 1966	Louie Louie	Sandpipers
♦ 1996	Loungin	L.L. Cool J
♦ 1990	Love And Emotion	Stevie B
♦ 1955	Love And Marriage	Frank Sinatra
♦ 1991	Love And Understanding	Cher
♦ 1991	Love At First Sight	Styx
♦ 1976	Love Ballad	L.T.D.
♦ 1979	Love Ballad	George Benson
♦ 1988	Love Bites	Def Leppard
♦ 1986	Love Bizarre	Sheila E.
♦ 1970	Love Bones	Johnnie Taylor
♦ 1967	Love Bug Leave My Heart Alone	Martha & The Vandellas
♦ 1962	Love Came To Me	Dion
♦ 1969	Love (Can Make You Happy)	Mercy
♦ 1993	Love Can Move Mountains	Celine Dion
♦ 1988	Love Changes (Everything)	Climie Fisher
♦ 1968	Love Child	Diana Ross And The Supremes
♦ 1990	Love Child	Sweet Sensation
♦ 1982	Love Come Down	Evelyn King
♦ 1979	Love Don't Live Here Anymore	Rose Royce
♦ 1974	Love Don't Love Nobody (Part 1)	Spinners
♦ 1993	Love Don't Love You	En Vogue
♦ 1967	Love Eyes	Nancy Sinatra
♦ 1976	Love Fire	Jigsaw
♦ 1997	Love Gets Me Every Time	Shania Twain
♦ 1970	Love Grows (Where My Rosemary Goes)	Edison Lighthouse
♦ 1976	Love Hangover	Diana Ross
♦ 1971	Love Her Madly	Doors
♦ 1976	Love Hurts	Nazareth
♦ 1973	Love I Lost (Part 1)	Harold Melvin And The Blue Notes
♦ 1967	Love I Saw In You Was Just A Mirage	Smokey Robinson & The Miracles
♦ 1989	Love In An Elevator	Aerosmith
♦ 1983	Love In Store	Fleetwood Mac
♦ 1982	Love In The First Degree	Alabama
♦ 1976	Love In The Shadows	Neil Sedaka
♦ 1989	Love In Your Eyes	Eddie Money
♦ 1990	Love Is	Alannah Myles
♦ 1993	Love Is	Vanessa Williams & Brian McKnight
♦ 1983	Love Is A Battlefield	Pat Benatar
♦ 1957	Love Is A Golden Ring	Frankie Laine
♦ 1966	Love Is A Hurtin' Thing	Lou Rawls
♦ 1955	Love Is A Many-Splendored Thing	Four Aces
♦ 1983	Love Is A Stranger	Eurythmics
♦ 1991	Love Is A Wonderful Thing	Michael Bolton
♦ 1976	Love Is Alive	Gary Wright
♦ 1968	Love Is All Around	Troggs
♦ 1958	Love Is All We Need	Tommy Edwards
♦ 1982	Love Is Alright Tonite	Rick Springfield
♦ 1968	Love Is Blue	Paul Mauriat

♦ 1986	Love Is Forever	Billy Ocean
♦ 1967	Love Is Here And Now You're Gone	Supremes
♦ 1982	Love Is In Control (Finger On The Trigger)	Donna Summer
♦ 1978	Love Is In The Air	John Paul Young
♦ 1968	(Love Is Like A) Baseball Game	Intruders
♦ 1982	Love Is Like A Rock	Donnie Iris
♦ 1966	Love Is Like An Itching In My Heart	Supremes
♦ 1978	Love Is Like Oxygen	Sweet
♦ 1992	Love Is On The Way	Saigon Kick
♦ 1957	Love Is Strange	Mickey And Sylvia
♦ 1967	Love Is Strange	Peaches & Herb
♦ 1979	Love Is The Answer	England Dan & John Ford Coley
♦ 1976	Love Is The Drug	Roxy Music
♦ 1986	Love Is The Seventh Wave	Sting
♦ 1956	(Love Is) The Tender Trap	Frank Sinatra
♦ 1978	(Love Is) Thicker Than Water	Andy Gibb
♦ 1973	Love Jones	Brighter Side Of Darkness
♦ 1970	Love Land	Charles Wright And The Watts 103rd Street Band
♦ 1962	Love Letters	Ketty Lester
♦ 1966	Love Letters	Elvis Presley
♦ 1957	Love Letters In The Sand	Pat Boone
♦ 1985	Love Light In Flight	Stevie Wonder
♦ 1975	L-O-V-E (Love)	Al Green
♦ 1956	Love, Love, Love	Clovers
♦ 1956	Love, Love, Love	Diamonds
♦ 1976	Love Machine (Part 1)	Miracles
♦ 1968	Love Makes A Woman	Barbara Acklin
♦ 1963	Love (Makes The World Go 'Round)	Paul Anka
♦ 1966	Love Makes The World Go Round	Deon Jackson
♦ 1991	Love Makes Things Happen	Pebbles
♦ 1956	Love Me	Elvis Presley
♦ 1977	Love Me	Yvonne Elliman
♦ 1992	Love Me All Up	Stacy Earl
♦ 1964	Love Me Do	Beatles
♦ 1974	Love Me For A Reason	Osmonds
♦ 1990	Love Me For Life	Stevie B
♦ 1957	Love Me Forever	Four Esquires
♦ 1957	Love Me Forever	Eydie Gorme
♦ 1955	Love Me Or Leave Me	Sammy Davis Jr.
♦ 1956	Love Me Tender	Elvis Presley
♦ 1962	Love Me Tender	Richard Chamberlain
♦ 1957	Love Me To Pieces	Jill Corey
♦ 1982	Love Me Tomorrow	Chicago
♦ 1969	Love Me Tonight	Tom Jones
♦ 1968	Love Me Two Times	Doors
♦ 1962	Love Me Warm And Tender	Paul Anka
♦ 1964	Love Me With All Your Heart	Ray Charles Singers
1971	Love Means (You Never Have To Say You're Sorry)	Sounds Of Sunshine
♦ 1991	Love Of A Lifetime	Firehouse
♦ 1963	Love Of My Man	Theola Kilgore
♦ 1991	Love On A Rooftop	Desmond Child
♦ 1970	Love On A Two-Way Street	Moments
♦ 1981	Love On A Two Way Street	Stacy Lattisaw
♦ 1981	Love On The Rocks	Neil Diamond
♦ 1976	Love Or Leave	Spinners
♦ 1970	Love Or Let Me Be Lonely	Friends Of Distinction
♦ 1978	Love Or Something Like It	Kenny Rogers
♦ 1988	Love Overboard	Gladys Knight
♦ 1986	Love Parade	Dream Academy
♦ 1982	Love Plus One	Haircut One Hundred
♦ 1959	Love Potion No. 9	Clovers
♦ 1965	Love Potion No. 9	Searchers
♦ 1987	Love Power	Dionne Warwick & Jeffrey Osborne
♦ 1968	Love Power	Sandpebbles
♦ 1976	Love Really Hurts Without You	Billy Ocean
♦ 1976	Love Rollercoaster	Ohio Players
♦ 1989	Love Shack	B-52's
♦ 1993	Love Shoulda Brought You Home	Toni Braxton
♦ 1994	Love Sneakin' Up On You	Bonnie Raitt
♦ 1963	Love So Fine	Chiffons
♦ 1976	Love So Right	Bee Gees
♦ 1984	Love Somebody	Rick Springfield
♦ 1974	Love Song	Anne Murray
♦ 1989	Love Song	Cure
♦ 1990	Love Song	Tesla
♦ 1980	Love Stinks	J. Geils Band
♦ 1990	Love Takes Time	Mariah Carey

M

♦	1983	Making Love Out Of Nothing At All	Air Supply
♦	1967	Making Memories	Frankie Laine
♦	1976	Making Our Dreams Come True	Cyndi Grecco
♦	1966	Mama	B.J. Thomas
♦	1960	Mama	Connie Francis
♦	1979	Mama Can't Buy You Love	Elton John
♦	1963	Mama Didn't Lie	Jan Bradley
♦	1956	Mama From The Train	Patti Page
♦	1992	Mama, I'm Coming Home	Ozzy Osbourne
♦	1970	Mama Liked The Roses	Elvis Presley
♦	1957	Mama Look At Bubu	Harry Belafonte
♦	1961	Mama Said	Shirelles
♦	1991	Mama Said Knock You Out	L.L. Cool J
	1962	Mama Sang A Song	Walter Brennan
	1962	Mama Sang A Song	Stan Kenton
	1956	Mama, Teach Me To Dance	Eydie Gorme
♦	1970	Mama Told Me (Not To Come)	Three Dog Night
♦	1982	Mama Used To Say	Junior
♦	1971	Mama's Pearl	Jackson Five
♦	1955	Mambo Rock	Bill Haley And His Comets
♦	1966	Mame	Herb Alpert & The Tijuana Brass
♦	1976	Mamma Mia	Abba
♦	1979	Man I'll Never Be	Boston
♦	1988	Man In The Mirror	Michael Jackson
♦	1993	Man On The Moon	R.E.M.
♦	1982	Man On Your Mind	Little River Band
♦	1986	Man Size Love	Klymaxx
♦	1962	(The Man Who Shot) Liberty Valance	Gene Pitney
♦	1968	Man Without Love	Engelbert Humperdinck
♦	1987	Mandolin Rain	Bruce Hornsby
♦	1975	Mandy	Barry Manilow
♦	1983	Maneater	Daryl Hall & John Oates
♦	1957	Mangos	Rosemary Clooney
	1959	Manhattan Spiritual	Reg Owen
♦	1983	Maniac	Michael Sembello
♦	1986	Manic Monday	Bangles
♦	1960	Many Tears Ago	Connie Francis
♦	1958	March From The River Kwai And Colonel Bogey	Mitch Miller
♦	1977	Margaritaville	Jimmy Buffett
♦	1963	Maria Elena	Los Indios Tabajaras
♦	1957	Marianne	Terry Gilkyson And The Easy Riders
♦	1957	Marianne	Hilltoppers
♦	1971	Marianne	Stephen Stills
♦	1965	Marie	Bachelors
♦	1961	(Marie's The Name) His Latest Flame	Elvis Presley
	1959	Marina	Willy Alberti
	1959	Marina	Rocco Granata
♦	1963	Marlena	Four Seasons
♦	1969	Marrakesh Express	Crosby, Stills & Nash
♦	1963	Martian Hop	Ran-Dells
	1962	Mary Ann Regrets	Burl Ives
♦	1972	Mary Had A Little Lamb	Wings
♦	1967	Mary In The Morning	Al Martino
♦	1994	Mary Jane's Last Dance	Tom Petty And The Heartbreakers
♦	1959	Mary Lou	Ronnie Hawkins & The Hawks
♦	1957	Mary's Boy Child	Harry Belafonte
♦	1987	Mary's Prayer	Danny Wilson
♦	1962	Mashed Potato Time	Dee Dee Sharp
♦	1980	Master Blaster (Jammin')	Stevie Wonder
♦	1968	Master Jack	Four Jacks And A Jill
♦	1973	Master Of Eyes (The Deepness Of Your Eyes)	Aretha Franklin
♦	1992	Masterpiece	Atlantic Starr
♦	1973	Masterpiece	Temptations
♦	1964	Matador	Major Lance
♦	1964	Matchbox	Beatles
♦	1985	Material Girl	Madonna
♦	1986	Matter Of Trust	Billy Joel
♦	1969	May I	Bill Deal & The Rhondels
♦	1965	May The Bird Of Paradise Fly Up Your Nose	"Little" Jimmy Dickens
♦	1959	May You Always	McGuire Sisters
♦	1958	Maybe	Chantels
♦	1970	Maybe	Three Degrees
♦	1958	Maybe Baby	Crickets
♦	1964	Maybe I Know	Lesley Gore
♦	1979	Maybe I'm A Fool	Eddie Money
♦	1977	Maybe I'm Amazed	Wings
♦	1971	Maybe Tomorrow	Jackson Five

♦	1955	Maybellene	Chuck Berry
♦	1964	Maybelline	Johnny Rivers
♦	1974	Me And Baby Brother	War
♦	1971	Me And Bobby McGee	Janis Joplin
♦	1972	Me And Julio Down By The Schoolyard	Paul Simon
♦	1972	Me And Mrs. Jones	Billy Paul
♦	1971	Me And My Arrow	Nilsson
♦	1971	Me And You And A Dog Named Boo	Lobo
♦	1989	Me Myself And I	De La Soul
♦	1989	Me So Horny	2 Live Crew
♦	1963	Mean Woman Blues	Roy Orbison
♦	1963	Mecca	Gene Pitney
♦	1969	Medicine Man (Part 1)	Buchanan Brothers
	1981	Medley	Stars On 45
♦	1987	Meet Me Halfway	Kenny Loggins
♦	1994	(Meet) The Flintstones	The BC-52's
♦	1966	Mellow Yellow	Donovan
♦	1955	Melody Of Love	David Carroll
♦	1955	Melody Of Love	Four Aces
♦	1955	Melody Of Love	Billy Vaughn
♦	1957	Melody Of Love	Ames Brothers
♦	1969	Memories	Elvis Presley
♦	1956	Memories Are Made Of This	Dean Martin
♦	1956	Memories Are Made Of This	Gale Storm
♦	1956	Memories Of You	Four Coins
♦	1983	Memory	Barry Manilow
♦	1997	Memory Remains	Metallica
♦	1963	Memphis	Lonnie Mack
♦	1964	Memphis	Johnny Rivers
♦	1967	Memphis Soul Stew	King Curtis
♦	1968	Men Are Gettin' Scarce	Joe Tex
♦	1966	Men In My Little Girl's Life	Mike Douglas
♦	1969	Mendocino	Sir Douglas Quintet
♦	1995	Mental Picture	Jon Secada
♦	1990	Mentirosa	Mellow Man Ace
♦	1988	Mercedes Boy	Pebbles
♦	1969	Mercy	Ohio Express
♦	1964	Mercy, Mercy	Don Covay & The Goodtimers
♦	1971	Mercy Mercy Me (The Ecology)	Marvin Gaye
♦	1991	Mercy Mercy Me (The Ecology)	Robert Palmer
♦	1967	Mercy, Mercy, Mercy	Cannonball Adderley
♦	1967	Mercy, Mercy, Mercy	Buckinghams
♦	1960	Mess Of Blues	Elvis Presley
♦	1966	Message To Michael	Dionne Warwick
♦	1985	Method Of Modern Love	Daryl Hall & John Oates
	1958	Mexican Hat Rock	Applejacks
♦	1961	Mexico	Bob Moore
♦	1985	"Miami Vice" Theme	Jan Hammer
♦	1961	Michael	Highwaymen
	1966	Michelle	David & Jonathan
♦	1982	Mickey	Toni Basil
♦	1963	Mickey's Monkey	Miracles
♦	1984	Middle Of The Road	Pretenders
♦	1974	Midnight At The Oasis	Maria Muldaur
♦	1987	Midnight Blue	Lou Gramm
♦	1975	Midnight Blue	Melissa Manchester
♦	1968	Midnight Confessions	Grass Roots
♦	1970	Midnight Cowboy	Ferrante & Teicher
♦	1962	Midnight In Moscow	Kenny Ball
♦	1964	Midnight Mary	Joey Powers
♦	1972	Midnight Rider	Joe Cocker And The Chris Stainton Band
♦	1974	Midnight Rider	Gregg Allman
♦	1980	Midnight Rocks	Al Stewart
♦	1960	Midnight Special	Paul Evans
♦	1965	Midnight Special	Johnny Rivers
♦	1959	Midnight Stroll	Revels
♦	1973	Midnight Train To Georgia	Gladys Knight & The Pips
♦	1979	Midnight Wind	John Stewart
♦	1971	Mighty Clouds Of Joy	B.J. Thomas
♦	1970	Mighty Joe	Shocking Blue
♦	1974	Mighty Love (Part 1)	Spinners
♦	1974	Mighty Mighty	Earth, Wind & Fire
♦	1968	Mighty Quinn (Quinn The Eskimo)	Manfred Mann
♦	1990	Miles Away	Winger
♦	1964	Miller's Cave	Bobby Bare
♦	1960	Million To One	Jimmy Charles
♦	1973	Million To One	Donny Osmond

◆	1973	Mind Games	John Lennon
◆	1992	Mind Playing Tricks On Me	Geto Boys
◆	1969	Mind, Body And Soul	Flaming Ember
	1983	Minimum Love	Mac McAnally
◆	1969	Minotaur	Dick Hyman & His Electric Eclectics
◆	1979	Minute By Minute	Doobie Brothers
◆	1990	Miracle	Jon Bon Jovi
◆	1991	Miracle	Whitney Houston
	1956	Miracle Of Love	Eileen Rodgers
◆	1975	Miracles	Jefferson Starship
◆	1983	Miracles	Stacy Lattisaw
◆	1967	Mirage	Tommy James And The Shondells
◆	1983	Mirror Man	Human League
◆	1982	Mirror, Mirror	Diana Ross
◆	1973	Misdemeanor	Foster Sylvers
◆	1995	Misery	Soul Asylum
◆	1995	Mishale	Andru Donalds
◆	1994	Misled	Celine Dion
◆	1985	Misled	Kool & The Gang
◆	1970	Miss America	Mark Lindsay
◆	1984	Miss Me Blind	Culture Club
◆	1981	Miss Sun	Boz Scaggs
◆	1978	Miss You	Rolling Stones
◆	1994	Miss You In A Heartbeat	Def Leppard
◆	1989	Miss You Like Crazy	Natalie Cole
◆	1989	Miss You Much	Janet Jackson
◆	1988	Missed Opportunity	Daryl Hall & John Oates
◆	1996	Missing	Everything But The Girl
◆	1982	Missing You	Dan Fogelberg
◆	1985	Missing You	Diana Ross
◆	1984	Missing You	John Waite
◆	1961	Missing You	Ray Peterson
◆	1996	Missing You	Brandy, Tamia, Glays Knight and Chaka Khan
◆	1992	Missing You Now	Michael Bolton
◆	1960	Mission Bell	Donnie Brooks
◆	1968	Mission-Impossible	Lalo Schifrin
◆	1996	Mission-Impossible	Adam Clayton & Larry Mullen
◆	1986	Missionary Man	Eurythmics
◆	1970	Mississippi	John Phillips
◆	1970	Mississippi Queen	Mountain
◆	1985	Mistake No. 3	Culture Club
	1972	Mister Can't You See	Buffy Sainte-Marie
◆	1981	Mister Sandman	Emmylou Harris
◆	1959	Misty	Johnny Mathis
◆	1963	Misty	Lloyd Price
◆	1966	Misty	Richard "Groove" Holmes
◆	1975	Misty	Ray Stevens
◆	1976	Misty Blue	Dorothy Moore
◆	1980	Misunderstanding	Genesis
◆	1989	Mixed Emotions	Rolling Stones
◆	1964	Mixed-Up, Shook-Up, Girl	Patty & The Emblems
◆	1997	Mmmbop	Hanson
◆	1994	Mmm Mmm Mmm Mmm	Crash Test Dummies
◆	1997	Mo Money Mo Problems	Notorious B.I.G. featuring Puff Daddy & Mase
◆	1963	Mockingbird	Inez Foxx
◆	1974	Mockingbird	Carly Simon And James Taylor
◆	1961	Model Girl	Johnny Maestro
	1984	Modern Day Delilah	Van Stephenson
◆	1981	Modern Girl	Sheena Easton
◆	1983	Modern Love	David Bowie
◆	1986	Modern Woman	Billy Joel
◆	1965	Mohair Sam	Charlie Rich
◆	1955	Moments To Remember	Four Lads
◆	1959	Mona Lisa	Carl Mann
◆	1959	Mona Lisa	Conway Twitty
◆	1966	Monday, Monday	Mama's & Papa's
◆	1973	Money	Pink Floyd
◆	1985	Money Changes Everything	Cyndi Lauper
◆	1992	Money Don't Matter 2 Night	Prince And The N.P.G.
◆	1985	Money For Nothing	Dire Straits
◆	1976	Money Honey	Bay City Rollers
◆	1991	Money Talks	AC/DC
◆	1960	Money (That's What I Want)	Barrett Strong
◆	1964	Money (That's What I Want)	Kingsmen
◆	1986	Money$ Too Tight (To Mention)	Simply Red
◆	1988	Monkey	George Michael
◆	1963	Monkey Time	Major Lance

◆	1970	Monster	Steppenwolf
◆	1962	Monster Mash	Bobby "Boris" Pickett And The Crypt-Kickers
◆	1973	Monster Mash	Bobby "Boris" Pickett And The Crypt-Kickers
◆	1962	Monster's Holiday	Bobby "Boris" Pickett And The Crypt-Kickers
◆	1970	Montego Bay	Bobby Bloom
◆	1968	Monterey	Eric Burdon & The Animals
◆	1968	Mony Mony	Tommy James And The Shondells
◆	1987	Mony Mony	Billy Idol
◆	1977	Moody Blue	Elvis Presley
◆	1961	Moody River	Pat Boone
◆	1969	Moody Woman	Jerry Butler
◆	1957	Moon-Light Swim	Tony Perkins
◆	1961	Moon River	Jerry Butler
◆	1961	Moon River	Henry Mancini
◆	1971	Moon Shadow	Cat Stevens
	1958	Moon Talk	Perry Como
◆	1969	Moonflight	Vik Venus
◆	1956	Moonglow And Theme From "Picnic"	George Cates
◆	1956	Moonglow And Theme From "Picnic"	McGuire Sisters
◆	1956	Moonglow And Theme From "Picnic"	Morris Stoloff
◆	1976	Moonlight Feels Right	Starbuck
◆	1957	Moonlight Gambler	Frankie Laine
	1956	Moonlight Love	Perry Como
◆	1987	Moonlighting (Theme)	Al Jarreau
◆	1956	More	Perry Como
◆	1963	More	Vic Dana
◆	1963	More	Kai Winding
◆	1993	More And More	Captain Hollywood Project
◆	1966	More I See You	Chris Montez
◆	1967	More Love	Smokey Robinson & The Miracles
◆	1980	More Love	Kim Carnes
◆	1961	More Money For You And Me	Four Preps
◆	1976	More, More, More (Part 1)	Andrea True Connection
◆	1976	More Than A Feeling	Boston
◆	1978	More Than A Woman	Tavares
◆	1991	More Than Ever	Nelson
◆	1980	More Than I Can Say	Leo Sayer
	1982	More Than Just The Two Of Us	Sneaker
◆	1997	More Than This	10,000 Maniacs
◆	1991	More Than Words	Extreme
◆	1990	More Than Words Can Say	Alias
◆	1989	More Than You Know	Martika
◆	1969	More Today Than Yesterday	Spiral Starecase
	1959	Morgen	Ivo Robic
		Moritat (see Mack The Knife)	
◆	1983	Mornin'	Jarreau
◆	1973	Morning After	Maureen McGovern
◆	1975	Mornin' Beautiful	Tony Orlando & Dawn
◆	1979	Morning Dance	Spyro Gyra
◆	1969	Morning Girl	Neon Philharmonic
◆	1972	Morning Has Broken	Cat Stevens
◆	1959	Morning Side Of The Mountain	Tommy Edwards
◆	1975	Morning Side Of The Mountain	Donny And Marie Osmond
◆	1981	Morning Train (Nine To Five)	Sheena Easton
◆	1973	Most Beautiful Girl	Charlie Rich
◆	1994	Most Beautiful Girl In The World	Prince
◆	1971	Most Of All	B.J. Thomas
◆	1962	Most People Get Married	Patti Page
◆	1971	Mother	John Lennon/Plastic Ono Band
◆	1972	Mother And Child Reunion	Paul Simon
◆	1961	Mother-In-Law	Ernie K-Doe
◆	1969	Mother Popcorn (You Got To Have A Mother For Me) (Part 1)	James Brown
◆	1966	Mothers Little Helper	Rolling Stones
◆	1986	Mothers Talk	Tears For Fears
◆	1972	Motorcycle Mama	Sailcat
◆	1987	Motortown	Kane Gang
◆	1991	Motown Song	Rod Stewart
◆	1991	Motownphilly	Boyz II Men
◆	1960	Mountain Of Love	Harold Dorman
◆	1964	Mountain Of Love	Johnny Rivers
◆	1986	Mountains	Prince And The Revolution
◆	1961	Mountain's High	Dick And DeeDee
◆	1996	Mouth	Merril Bainbridge
◆	1992	Move Any Mountain	Shamen
◆	1986	Move Away	Culture Club
◆	1969	Move Over	Steppenwolf

♦ 1990	Move This	Technotronic
♦ 1961	Movin'.	Bill Black's Combo
♦ 1976	Movin'.	Brass Construction
♦ 1975	Movin' On	Bad Company
♦ 1994	Moving On Up	M People
♦ 1978	Movin' Out (Anthony's Song)	Billy Joel
♦ 1963	Mr. Bass Man	Johnny Cymbal
♦ 1971	Mr. Big Stuff	Jean Knight
♦ 1959	Mr. Blue	Fleetwoods
♦ 1978	Mr. Blue Sky	Electric Light Orchestra
♦ 1971	Mr. Bojangles	Nitty Gritty Dirt Band
♦ 1968	Mr. Businessman	Ray Stevens
♦ 1960	Mr. Custer	Larry Verne
♦ 1966	Mr. Dieingly Sad	Critters
♦ 1975	Mr. Jaws	Dickie Goodman
♦ 1957	Mr. Lee	Bobbettes
♦ 1964	Mr. Lonely	Bobby Vinton
♦ 1960	Mr. Lucky	Henry Mancini
♦ 1983	Mr. Roboto	Styx
♦ 1966	Mr. Spaceman	Byrds
♦ 1958	Mr. Success	Frank Sinatra
♦ 1969	Mr. Sun, Mr. Moon	Paul Revere And The Raiders
♦ 1965	Mr. Tambourine Man	Byrds
♦ 1985	Mr. Telephone Man	New Edition
♦ 1994	Mr. Vain	Culture Beat
♦ 1993	Mr. Wendall	Arrested Development
♦ 1956	Mr. Wonderful	Sarah Vaughan
♦ 1965	Mrs. Brown You've Got A Lovely Daughter	Herman's Hermits
♦ 1968	Mrs. Robinson	Simon & Garfunkel
♦ 1969	Mrs. Robinson	Booker T & The MG's
♦ 1969	Muddy River	Johnny Rivers
♦ 1960	Mule Skinner Blues	Fendermen
♦ 1962	Multiplication	Bobby Darin
1982	Murphy's Law	Cheri
♦ 1982	Muscles	Diana Ross
1967	Museum	Herman's Hermits
♦ 1979	Music Box Dancer	Frank Mills
♦ 1967	Music To Watch Girls By	Bob Crewe Generation
♦ 1967	Music To Watch Girls By	Andy Williams
♦ 1976	Muskrat Love	Captain & Tennille
♦ 1975	Must Of Got Lost	J. Geils Band
♦ 1966	Must To Avoid	Herman's Hermits
♦ 1966	Mustang Sally	Wilson Pickett
♦ 1956	Mutual Admiration Society	Teresa Brewer
♦ 1978	My Angel Baby	Toby Beau
♦ 1965	My Baby	Temptations
♦ 1997	My Baby Daddy	B-Rock & The Bizz
♦ 1955	(My Baby Don't Love Me) No More	De John Sisters
♦ 1956	My Baby Left Me	Elvis Presley
♦ 1970	My Baby Loves Lovin'	White Plains
♦ 1966	My Baby Loves Me	Martha & The Vandellas
♦ 1968	My Baby Must Be A Magician	Marvelettes
♦ 1967	My Back Pages	Byrds
♦ 1956	My Blue Heaven	Fats Domino
♦ 1997	My Body	LSG
♦ 1964	My Bonnie	Beatles
♦ 1955	My Bonnie Lassie	Ames Brothers
♦ 1996	My Boo	Ghost Town DJ's
♦ 1962	My Boomerang Won't Come Back	Charlie Drake
♦ 1975	My Boy	Elvis Presley
♦ 1964	My Boy Lollipop	Millie Small
♦ 1963	My Boyfriend's Back	Angels
♦ 1989	My Brave Face	Paul McCartney
♦ 1958	My Bucket's Got A Hole In It	Ricky Nelson
♦ 1969	My Cherie Amour	Stevie Wonder
♦ 1963	My Coloring Book	Kitty Kallen
♦ 1963	My Coloring Book	Sandy Stewart
♦ 1967	My Cup Runneth Over	Ed Ames
♦ 1963	My Dad	Paul Petersen
♦ 1960	My Dearest Darling	Etta James
♦ 1972	My Ding-A-Ling	Chuck Berry
♦ 1957	My Dream	Platters
1970	My Elusive Dreams	Bobby Vinton
♦ 1961	My Empty Arms	Jackie Wilson
♦ 1984	My Ever Changing Moods	Style Council
♦ 1975	My Eyes Adored You	Frankie Valli
1977	My Fair Share	Seals & Crofts

♦ 1969	My Favorite Things	Herb Alpert & The Tijuana Brass
♦ 1982	My Girl	Donnie Iris
♦ 1965	My Girl	Temptations
♦ 1968	My Girl/Hey Girl	Bobby Vee
♦ 1988	My Girl	Suave
♦ 1974	My Girl Bill	Jim Stafford
1981	My Girl (Gone, Gone, Gone)	Chilliwack
♦ 1965	My Girl Has Gone	Miracles
♦ 1960	My Girl Josephine	Fats Domino
♦ 1967	My Girl Josephine	Jerry Jaye
♦ 1964	My Girl Sloopy	Vibrations
♦ 1964	My Guy	Mary Wells
♦ 1982	My Guy	Sister Sledge
♦ 1959	My Happiness	Connie Francis
♦ 1977	My Heart Belongs To Me	Barbra Streisand
♦ 1964	My Heart Belongs To Only You	Bobby Vinton
♦ 1991	My Heart Belongs To You	Russ Irwin
♦ 1989	My Heart Can't Tell You No	Rod Stewart
♦ 1960	My Heart Has A Mind Of Its Own	Connie Francis
♦ 1959	My Heart Is An Open Book	Carl Dobkins Jr.
♦ 1991	My Heart Is Failing Me	Riff
♦ 1957	My Heart Reminds Me	Kay Starr
♦ 1966	My Heart's Symphony	Gary Lewis And The Playboys
♦ 1960	My Home Town	Paul Anka
♦ 1986	My Hometown	Bruce Springsteen
♦ 1961	My Kind Of Girl	Matt Monro
♦ 1983	My Kind Of Lady	Supertramp
♦ 1990	My Kinda Girl	Babyface
♦ 1961	My Last Date (With You)	Skeeter Davis
♦ 1979	My Life	Billy Joel
♦ 1966	My Little Red Book	Love
♦ 1975	My Little Town	Simon & Garfunkel
♦ 1983	My Love	Lionel Richie
♦ 1973	My Love	Paul McCartney & Wings
♦ 1966	My Love	Petula Clark
♦ 1965	My Love, Forgive Me (Amore, Scusami)	Robert Goulet
♦ 1990	My Love Is A Fire	Donny Osmond
♦ 1995	My Love Is For Real	Paula Abdul
♦ 1997	My Love Is The Shhh!	Somethin' For The People
♦ 1992	My Lovin' (You're Never Gonna Get It)	En Vogue
1967	My Mammy	Happenings
♦ 1972	My Man, A Sweet Man	Millie Jackson
♦ 1973	My Maria	B.W. Stevenson
♦ 1970	My Marie	Engelbert Humperdinck
♦ 1959	My Melancholy Baby	Tommy Edwards
♦ 1974	My Melody Of Love	Bobby Vinton
♦ 1974	My Mistake (Was To Love You)	Diana Ross & Marvin Gaye
♦ 1973	My Music	Loggins And Messina
♦ 1991	My Name Is Not Susan	Whitney Houston
♦ 1992	My Name Is Prince	Prince And The N.P.G.
♦ 1984	My Oh My	Slade
♦ 1957	My One Sin	Four Coins
♦ 1959	My Own True Love	Jimmy Clanton
♦ 1962	My Own True Love	Duprees
1957	My Personal Possession	Nat King Cole
♦ 1969	My Pledge Of Love	Joe Jeffrey Group
♦ 1956	My Prayer	Platters
♦ 1988	My Prerogative	Bobby Brown
♦ 1979	My Sharona	Knack
♦ 1991	My Side Of The Bed	Susanna Hoffs
♦ 1957	My Special Angel	Bobby Helms
♦ 1968	My Special Angel	Vogues
♦ 1963	My Summer Love	Ruby And The Romantics
♦ 1974	My Sweet Lady	Cliff DeYoung
♦ 1977	My Sweet Lady	John Denver
♦ 1970	My Sweet Lord	George Harrison
♦ 1974	My Thang	James Brown
♦ 1965	My Town, My Guy And Me	Lesley Gore
♦ 1956	My Treasure	Hilltoppers
♦ 1963	My True Confession	Brook Benton
♦ 1958	My True Love	Jack Scott
♦ 1961	My True Story	Jive Five
♦ 1969	My Way	Frank Sinatra
♦ 1977	My Way	Elvis Presley
♦ 1969	My Whole World Ended (The Moment You Left Me)	David Ruffin
♦ 1963	My Whole World Is Falling Down	Brenda Lee
♦ 1959	My Wish Came True	Elvis Presley

◆	1970	My Woman, My Woman, My Wife	Marty Robbins
◆	1972	My World	Bee Gees
◆	1966	My World Is Empty Without You	Supremes
◆	1990	My, My, My	Johnny Gill
◆	1992	Mysterious Ways	U2
◆	1985	Mystery Lady	Billy Ocean
◆	1965	Mystic Eyes	Them

N

◆	1969	Na Na Hey Hey Kiss Him Goodbye	Steam
	1976	Nadia's Theme	Perry Botkin Jr.
◆	1964	Nadine (Is It You?)	Chuck Berry
◆	1961	"Nag"	Halos
◆	1997	Naked Eye	Luscious Jackson
◆	1996	Name	Goo Goo Dolls
◆	1965	Name Game	Shirley Ellis
◆	1978	Name Of The Game	Abba
◆	1967	Nashville Cats	Lovin' Spoonful
◆	1986	Nasty	Janet Jackson
◆	1971	Nathan Jones	Supremes
◆	1978	Native New Yorker	Odyssey
◆	1973	Natural High	Bloodstone
◆	1971	Natural Man	Lou Rawls
◆	1996	Natural One	Folk Implosion
◆	1967	Natural Woman (You Make Me Feel Like)	Aretha Franklin
◆	1968	Naturally Stoned	Avant-Garde
◆	1961	Nature Boy	Bobby Darin
◆	1988	Naughty Girls (Need Love Too)	Samantha Fox
◆	1955	Naughty Lady Of Shady Lane	Ames Brothers
◆	1985	Naughty, Naughty	John Parr
◆	1964	Navy Blue	Diane Renay
◆	1970	Neanderthal Man	Hotlegs
◆	1958	Near You	Roger Williams
	1974	Need To Be	Jim Weatherly
◆	1964	Need To Belong	Jerry Butler
◆	1958	Need You	Donnie Owens
◆	1988	Need You Tonight	Inxs
◆	1964	Needles And Pins	Searchers
◆	1986	Needles And Pins	Tom Petty And The Heartbreakers With Stevie Nicks
◆	1973	Neither One Of Us (Wants To Be The First To Say Goodbye) Gladys Knight & The Pips
◆	1967	Neon Rainbow	Box Tops
◆	1985	Neutron Dance	Pointer Sisters
◆	1985	Never	Heart
◆	1993	Never A Time	Genesis
◆	1986	Never As Good As The First Time	Sade
◆	1959	Never Be Anyone Else But You	Ricky Nelson
◆	1980	Never Be The Same	Christopher Cross
	1982	Never Been In Love	Randy Meisner
◆	1972	Never Been To Spain	Three Dog Night
◆	1971	Never Can Say Goodbye	Isaac Hayes
◆	1971	Never Can Say Goodbye	Jackson Five
◆	1975	Never Can Say Goodbye	Gloria Gaynor
◆	1971	Never Ending Song Of Love	Delaney & Bonnie & Friends
◆	1985	Never Ending Story	Limahl
◆	1968	Never Give You Up	Jerry Butler
◆	1976	Never Gonna Fall In Love Again	Eric Carmen
◆	1988	Never Gonna Give You Up	Rick Astley
◆	1991	Never Gonna Let You Down	Surface
◆	1983	Never Gonna Let You Go	Sergio Mendes
◆	1970	Never Had A Dream Come True	Stevie Wonder
◆	1994	Never Keeping Secrets	Babyface
◆	1988	Never Knew Love Like This	Alexander O'Neal featuring Cherrelle
◆	1980	Never Knew Love Like This Before	Stephanie Mills
	1996	Never Leave Me Alone	Nate Dogg featuring Snoop Doggy Dogg
◆	1975	Never Let Her Go	David Gates
◆	1987	Never Let Me Down	David Bowie
◆	1973	Never Let You Go	Bloodstone
◆	1994	Never Lie	Immature
◆	1997	Never Make A Promise	Dru Hill
◆	1967	Never My Love	Association
◆	1971	Never My Love	Fifth Dimension
◆	1974	Never My Love	Blue Swede
◆	1974	Never, Never Gonna Give You Up	Barry White

◆	1960	Never On Sunday	Don Costa
◆	1961	Never On Sunday	Chordettes
◆	1993	Never Should've Let You Go	Hi-Five
◆	1985	Never Surrender	Corey Hart
◆	1988	Never Tear Us Apart	Inxs
◆	1981	Never Too Much	Luther Vandross
	1956	Never Turn Back	Al Hibbler
◆	1995	New Age Girl	Deadeye Dick
◆	1985	New Attitude	Patti LaBelle
◆	1964	New Girl In School	Jan & Dean
◆	1977	New Kid In Town	Eagles
◆	1963	New Mexican Rose	Four Seasons
◆	1984	New Moon On Monday	Duran Duran
◆	1960	New Orleans	Gary U.S. Bonds
	1980	New Romance (It's A Mystery)	Spider
◆	1988	New Sensation	Inxs
◆	1984	New Song	Howard Jones
◆	1970	New World Coming	Mama Cass Elliot
◆	1982	New World Man	Rush
◆	1978	New York Groove	Ace Frehley
◆	1967	New York Mining Disaster 1941 (Have You Seen My Wife, Mr. Jones) Bee Gees
◆	1977	New York, You Got Me Dancing	Andrea True Connection
◆	1965	New York's A Lonely Town	Tradewinds
◆	1962	Next Door To An Angel	Neil Sedaka
◆	1967	Next Plane To London	Rose Garden
◆	1970	Next Step Is Love	Elvis Presley
◆	1986	Next Time I Fall	Peter Cetera With Amy Grant
	1982	Nice Girls	Eye To Eye
◆	1976	Nice 'N' Naasty	Salsoul Orchestra
◆	1972	Nice To Be With You	Gallery
◆	1990	Nicety	Michel'le
◆	1972	Nickel Song	Melanie
◆	1981	Nicole	Point Blank
◆	1960	Night	Jackie Wilson
◆	1974	Night Chicago Died	Paper Lace
◆	1978	Night Fever	Bee Gees
◆	1963	Night Has A Thousand Eyes	Bobby Vee
◆	1985	Night Is Still Young	Billy Joel
◆	1956	Night Lights	Nat King Cole
◆	1977	Night Moves	Bob Seger
◆	1986	Night Moves	Marilyn Martin
◆	1981	Night Owls	Little River Band
◆	1973	Night The Lights Went Out In Georgia	Vicki Lawrence
◆	1971	Night They Drove Old Dixie Down	Joan Baez
◆	1966	Night Time	Strangeloves
◆	1982	Night To Remember	Shalamar
◆	1962	Night Train	James Brown
◆	1984	Nightbird	Stevie Nicks With Sandy Stewart
◆	1988	Nightime	Pretty Poison
◆	1975	Nightingale	Carole King
◆	1988	Nightmare On My Street	D.J. Jazzy Jeff & The Fresh Prince
◆	1976	Nights Are Forever Without You	England Dan & John Ford Coley
◆	1972	Nights In White Satin	Moody Blues
◆	1991	Nights Like This	After 7
◆	1975	Nights On Broadway	Bee Gees
◆	1985	Nightshift	Commodores
◆	1967	Niki Hoeky	P.J. Proby
◆	1986	Nikita	Elton John
◆	1981	9 To 5	Dolly Parton
◆	1985	19	Paul Hardcasle
◆	1971	1900 Yesterday	Liz Damon's Orient Express
◆	1983	1999	Prince
◆	1996	1979	Smashing Pumpkins
◆	1966	19th Nervous Breakdown	Rolling Stones
	1966	96 Tears	? & The Mysterians
◆	1967	98.6	Keith
◆	1980	99	Toto
◆	1984	99 Luftballons	Nena
◆	1957	Ninety-Nine Ways	Tab Hunter
	1956	Ninety Nine Years (Dead Or Alive)	Guy Mitchell
◆	1988	Nite And Day	Al B. Sure!
◆	1964	Nitty Gritty	Shirley Ellis
◆	1969	Nitty Gritty	Gladys Knight & The Pips
◆	1965	No Arms Can Ever Hold You	Bachelors
◆	1958	No Chemise, Please	Gerry Granahan
◆	1996	No Diggity	Blackstreet featuring Dr. Dre

◆	1986	No Easy Way Out	Robert Tepper
◆	1960	No If's - No And's	Lloyd Price
◆	1985	No Lookin' Back	Michael McDonald
◆	1957	No Love (But Your Love)	Johnny Mathis
◆	1971	No Love At All	B.J. Thomas
◆	1970	No Matter What	Badfinger
◆	1966	No Matter What Shape (Your Stomach's In)	T-Bones
◆	1969	No Matter What Sign You Are	Diana Ross And The Supremes
◆	1967	No Milk Today	Herman's Hermits
◆	1993	No Mistakes	Patty Smyth
◆	1995	No More "I Love You's"	Annie Lennox
◆	1990	No More Lies	Michel'le
◆	1984	No More Lonely Nights	Paul McCartney
◆	1973	No More Mr. Nice Guy	Alice Cooper
◆	1989	No More Rhyme	Debbie Gibson
◆	1979	No More Tears (Enough Is Enough)	Barbra Streisand/Donna Summer
◆	1984	No More Words	Berlin
◆	1990	No Myth	Michael Penn
◆	1980	No Night So Long	Dionne Warwick
◆	1998	No, No, No	Destiny's Child
◆	1975	No No Song	Ringo Starr
◆	1956	No, Not Much!	Four Lads
◆	1969	No, Not Much	Vogues
◆	1963	No One	Ray Charles
	1958	No One But You	Ames Brothers
◆	1996	No One Else	Total
◆	1986	No One Is To Blame	Howard Jones
◆	1958	No One Knows	Dion & The Belmonts
◆	1972	No One To Depend On	Santana
◆	1993	No Ordinary Love	Sade
◆	1959	No Other Arms, No Other Lips	Chordettes
◆	1964	No Particular Place To Go	Chuck Berry
◆	1993	No Rain	Blind Melon
◆	1981	No Reply At All	Genesis
◆	1991	No Son Of Mine	Genesis
◆	1970	No Sugar Tonight	Guess Who
◆	1979	No Tell Lover	Chicago
◆	1970	No Time	Guess Who
◆	1997	No Time	Lil' Kim featuring Puff Daddy
◆	1983	No Time For Talk	Christopher Cross
◆	1984	No Way Out	Jefferson Starship
◆	1982	Nobody	Sylvia
◆	1996	Nobody	Keith Sweat featuring Athena Cage
◆	1968	Nobody But Me	Human Beinz
◆	1959	Nobody But You	Dee Clark
◆	1969	Nobody But You Babe	Clarence Reid
◆	1977	Nobody Does It Better	Carly Simon
◆	1964	Nobody I Know	Peter And Gordon
◆	1996	Nobody Knows	Tony Rich Project
◆	1982	Nobody Said It Was Easy	Le Roux
◆	1984	Nobody Told Me	John Lennon
◆	1973	Nobody Wants You When You're Down And Out	Bobby Womack
◆	1981	Nobody Wins	Elton John
◆	1987	Nobody's Fool	Cinderella
◆	1988	Nobody's Fool	Kenny Loggins
	1959	Nola	Billy Williams
◆	1958	Non Dimenticar (Don't Forget)	Nat King Cole
◆	1994	None Of Your Business	Salt-N-Pepa
◆	1962	Norman	Sue Thompson
◆	1960	North To Alaska	Johnny Horton
◆	1985	Not Enough Love In The World	Don Henley
◆	1992	Not Enough Time	Inxs
◆	1996	Not Gon' Cry	Mary J. Blige
◆	1988	Not Just Another Girl	Ivan Neville
	1963	Not Me	Orlons
◆	1960	Not One Minute More	Della Reese
◆	1965	Not The Lovin' Kind	Dino, Desi & Billy
◆	1992	Not The Only One	Bonnie Raitt
◆	1997	Not Tonight	Lil' Kim
◆	1986	Nothin' At All	Heart
◆	1992	Nothing Broken But My Heart	Celine Dion
◆	1988	Nothin' But A Good Time	Poison
◆	1969	Nothing But A Heartache	Flirtations
◆	1965	Nothing But Heartaches	Supremes
◆	1997	Nothin' But The Cavi Hit	Mack 10 & Tha Dogg Pound
◆	1962	Nothing Can Change This Love	Sam Cooke
◆	1965	Nothing Can Stop Me	Gene Chandler

◆	1990	Nothing Compares 2 U	Sinead O'Connor
◆	1992	Nothing Else Matters	Metallica
◆	1974	Nothing From Nothing	Billy Preston
◆	1993	Nothin' My Love Can't Fix	Joey Lawrence
◆	1972	Nothing To Hide	Tommy James
◆	1987	Nothing's Gonna Change My Love For You	Glenn Medeiros
◆	1987	Nothing's Gonna Stop Us Now	Starship
◆	1966	Nothing's Too Good For My Baby	Stevie Wonder
◆	1990	Notice Me	Nikki
◆	1986	Notorious	Duran Duran
◆	1987	Notorious	Loverboy
◆	1992	November Rain	Guns N' Roses
◆	1958	Now And For Always	George Hamilton IV
◆	1994	Now And Forever	Richard Marx
◆	1959	(Now And Then There's) A Fool Such As I	Elvis Presley
◆	1991	Now That We Found Love	Heavy D. & The Boyz
◆	1996	Nowhere To Go	Melissa Etheridge
◆	1966	Nowhere Man	Beatles
◆	1965	Nowhere To Run	Martha & The Vandellas
◆	1992	Nu Nu	Lidell Townsell
◆	1975	#9 Dream	John Lennon
◆	1962	Nut Rocker	B. Bumble & The Stingers
◆	1973	Nutbush City Limits	Ike & Tina Turner
◆	1993	Nuthin' But A "G" Thang	Dr. Dre
◆	1994	Nuttin' But Love	Heavy D. & The Boyz
◆	1956	Nuttin' For Christmas	Art Mooney

O

◆	1991	O.P.P.	Naughty By Nature
◆	1960	O Dio Mio	Annette
◆	1986	Object Of My Desire	Starpoint
◆	1994	Objects In The Rear View Mirror May Appear Closer Than They Are	Meatloaf
◆	1984	Obscene Phone Caller	Rockwell
◆	1985	Obsession	Animotion
◆	1967	Ode To Billie Joe	Bobbie Gentry
◆	1967	Ode To Billie Joe	King Curtis
◆	1980	Off The Wall	Michael Jackson
◆	1973	Oh Babe, What Would You Say?	Hurricane Smith
◆	1964	Oh Baby Don't You Weep (Part 1)	James Brown
◆	1958	Oh Boy!	The Crickets
◆	1959	Oh! Carol	Neil Sedaka
◆	1978	Oh! Darling	Robin Gibb
◆	1989	Oh Father	Madonna
◆	1985	Oh Girl	Boy Meets Girl
◆	1972	Oh Girl	Chi-Lites
◆	1990	Oh Girl	Paul Young
◆	1969	Oh Happy Day	Edwin Hawkins Singers
◆	1970	Oh Happy Day	Glen Campbell
◆	1966	Oh How Happy	Shades Of Blue
	1982	Oh Julie	Barry Manilow
◆	1958	Oh Julie	Crescendos
◆	1973	Oh La De Da	Staple Singers
◆	1958	Oh Lonesome Me	Don Gibson
◆	1970	Oh Me Oh My (I'm A Fool For You Baby)	Lulu
◆	1974	Oh My My	Ringo Starr
◆	1981	Oh No	Commodores
◆	1964	Oh No Not My Baby	Maxine Brown
◆	1958	Oh-Oh, I'm Falling In Love Again	Jimmie Rodgers
◆	1986	Oh, People	Patti LaBelle
◆	1964	Oh, Pretty Woman	Roy Orbison And The Candy Men
◆	1982	Oh, Pretty Woman	Van Halen
◆	1985	Oh Sheila	Ready For The World
◆	1984	Oh Sherrie	Steve Perry
◆	1974	Oh Very Young	Cat Stevens
◆	1979	Oh Well	Rockets
◆	1969	Oh, What A Night	Dells
◆	1978	Oh What A Night For Dancing	Barry White
◆	1970	Ohio	Crosby, Stills, Nash & Young
◆	1957	Old Cape Cod	Patti Page
◆	1975	Old Days	Chicago
◆	1980	Old-Fashion Love	Commodores
	1977	Old Fashioned Boy (You're The One)	Stallion
◆	1971	Old Fashioned Love Song	Three Dog Night

♦	1960	Old Lamplighter	Browns
♦	1960	Old MacDonald	Frank Sinatra
♦	1972	Old Man	Neil Young
♦	1996	Old Man & Me	Hootie & The Blowfish
♦	1985	Old Man Down The Road	John Fogerty
♦	1956	Old Philosopher	Eddie Lawrence
♦	1962	Old Rivers	Walter Brennan
♦	1981	Old Songs	Barry Manilow
♦	1979	Old Time Rock & Roll	Bob Seger & The Silver Bullet Band
	1961	Ole Buttermilk Sky	Bill Black's Combo
♦	1967	On A Carousel	Hollies
♦	1974	On A Night Like This	Bob Dylan
♦	1974	On And On	Gladys Knight & The Pips
♦	1977	On And On	Stephen Bishop
♦	1997	On & On	Erykah Badu
♦	1995	On Bended Knee	Boyz II Men
♦	1963	On Broadway	Drifters
♦	1978	On Broadway	George Benson
	1956	On London Bridge	Jo Stafford
♦	1986	On My Own	Patti LaBelle And Michael McDonald
♦	1997	On My Own	Peach Union
♦	1957	On My Word Of Honor	Platters
♦	1989	On Our Own	Bobby Brown
♦	1977	On The Border	Al Stewart
♦	1984	On The Dark Side	John Cafferty And The Beaver Brown Band
♦	1983	On The Loose	Saga
♦	1980	On The Radio	Donna Summer
♦	1961	On The Rebound	Floyd Cramer
♦	1968	On The Road Again	Canned Heat
♦	1980	On The Road Again	Willie Nelson
♦	1978	On The Shelf	Donny & Marie Osmond
♦	1956	On The Street Where You Live	Vic Damone
♦	1964	On The Street Where You Live	Andy Williams
♦	1982	On The Way To The Sky	Neil Diamond
♦	1990	On The Way Up	Elisa Fiorillo
♦	1983	On The Wings Of Love	Jeffrey Osborne
♦	1963	On Top Of Spaghetti	Tom Glazer And The Do-Re-Mi Children's Chorus
♦	1989	Once Bitten Twice Shy	Great White
♦	1961	Once In Awhile	Chimes
♦	1964	Once Upon A Time	Marvin Gaye & Mary Wells
♦	1961	Once Upon A Time	Rochell And The Candles
♦	1975	Once You Get Started	Rufus featuring Chaka Khan
	1972	Once You Understand	Think
♦	1989	One	Bee Gees
♦	1992	One	Elton John
♦	1989	One	Metallica
♦	1969	One	Three Dog Night
♦	1992	One	U2
♦	1991	One And Only	Chesney Hawkes
♦	1990	One And Only Man	Steve Winwood
♦	1971	One Bad Apple	Osmonds
♦	1963	One Broken Heart For Sale	Elvis Presley
♦	1974	One Chain Don't Make No Prison	Four Tops
♦	1965	One Dyin' And A Buryin'	Roger Miller
♦	1963	One Fine Day	Chiffons
♦	1980	One Fine Day	Carole King
♦	1971	One Fine Morning	Lighthouse
♦	1987	One For The Mockingbird	Cutting Crew
♦	1988	One Good Reason	Paul Carrack
♦	1988	One Good Woman	Peter Cetera
	1966	One Has My Name (The Other Has My Heart)	Barry Young
♦	1987	One Heartbeat	Smokey Robinson
♦	1974	One Hell Of A Woman	Mac Davis
♦	1986	One Hit (To The Body)	Rolling Stones
♦	1994	100% Pure Love	Crystal Waters
♦	1982	One Hundred Ways	Quincy Jones featuring James Ingram
♦	1997	One I Gave My Heart To	Aaliyah
♦	1987	One I Love	R.E.M.
♦	1957	One In A Million	Platters
♦	1984	One In A Million	Romantics
♦	1980	One In A Million You	Larry Graham
♦	1965	One Kiss For Old Times Sake	Ronnie Dove
♦	1993	One Last Cry	Brian McKnight
♦	1979	One Last Kiss	J. Geils Band
♦	1970	One Less Bell To Answer	Fifth Dimension
♦	1973	One Less Set Of Footsteps	Jim Croce
♦	1985	One Lonely Night	REO Speedwagon
♦	1976	One Love In My Lifetime	Diana Ross
♦	1970	One Man Band	Three Dog Night
♦	1973	One Man Band (Plays All Alone)	Ronnie Dyson
♦	1975	One Man Woman/One Woman Man	Paul Anka With Odia Coates
♦	1961	One Mint Julep	Ray Charles
♦	1988	One Moment In Time	Whitney Houston
♦	1972	One Monkey Don't Stop No Show (Part 1)	Honey Cone
♦	1995	One More Chance	Notorious B.I.G.
♦	1966	One More Heartache	Marvin Gaye
♦	1985	One More Night	Phil Collins
♦	1965	One More Time	Ray Charles Singers
♦	1997	One More Time	Real McCoy
♦	1988	One More Try	George Michael
♦	1991	One More Try	Timmy -T-
♦	1978	One Nation Under A Groove (Part 1)	Funkadelic
♦	1958	One Night	Elvis Presley
♦	1985	One Night In Bangkok	Murray Head
♦	1985	One Night Love Affair	Bryan Adams
♦	1973	One Of A Kind (Love Affair)	Spinners
	1985	One Of The Living	Tina Turner
♦	1975	One Of These Nights	Eagles
♦	1996	One Of Us	Joan Osborne
♦	1960	One Of Us (Will Weep Tonight)	Patti Page
♦	1983	One On One	Daryl Hall & John Oates
♦	1976	One Piece At A Time	Johnny Cash
♦	1981	One Step Closer	Doobie Brothers
♦	1986	One Step Closer To You	Gavin Christopher
♦	1988	One Step Up	Bruce Springsteen
♦	1958	One Summer Night	Danleers
♦	1961	One Summer Night	Diamonds
♦	1996	One Sweet Day	Mariah Carey & Boyz II Men
♦	1981	One That You Love	Air Supply
♦	1983	One Thing	Inxs
♦	1983	One Thing Leads To Another	Fixx
	1970	One Tin Soldier	Original Caste
♦	1971	One Tin Soldier	Coven
♦	1971	One Toke Over The Line	Brewer & Shipley
♦	1961	One Track Mind	Bobby Lewis
♦	1965	1-2-3	Len Barry
♦	1988	1-2-3	Gloria Estefan And Miami Sound Machine
♦	1996	1,2,3,4 (Sumpin' New)	Coolio
♦	1968	1,2,3 Red Light	1910 Fruitgum Company
♦	1979	One Way Or Another	Blondie
♦	1962	One Who Really Loves You	Mary Wells
♦	1993	One Woman	Jade
♦	1982	One You Love	Glenn Frey
♦	1980	Only A Lonely Heart Sees	Felix Cavaliere
♦	1963	Only In America	Jay & The Americans
♦	1987	Only In My Dreams	Debbie Gibson
♦	1962	Only Love Can Break A Heart	Gene Pitney
♦	1970	Only Love Can Break Your Heart	Neil Young
♦	1976	Only Love Is Real	Carole King
	1957	Only One Love	George Hamilton IV
♦	1959	Only Sixteen	Sam Cooke
♦	1976	Only Sixteen	Dr. Hook
♦	1978	Only The Good Die Young	Billy Joel
♦	1982	Only The Lonely	Motels
♦	1960	Only The Lonely (Know How I Feel)	Roy Orbison
♦	1969	Only The Strong Survive	Jerry Butler
♦	1985	Only The Young	Journey
♦	1982	Only Time Will Tell	Asia
♦	1991	Only Time Will Tell	Nelson
♦	1995	Only Wanna Be With You	Hootie & The Blowfish
♦	1984	Only When You Leave	Spandau Ballet
♦	1975	Only Women	Alice Cooper
♦	1975	Only Yesterday	Carpenters
♦	1955	Only You (And You Alone)	Platters
♦	1956	Only You (And You Alone)	Hilltoppers
♦	1959	Only You	Franck Pourcel
♦	1975	Only You	Ringo Starr
♦	1996	Only You	112
♦	1970	Only You Know And I Know	Dave Mason
♦	1971	Only You Know And I Know	Delaney & Bonnie
♦	1965	Oo Wee Baby, I Love You	Fred Hughes
♦	1992	Oochie Coochie	MC Brains
♦	1967	Oogum Boogum Song	Brenton Wood
♦	1997	Ooh Ah...Just A Little Bit	Gina G

♦ 1973	Ooh Baby	Gilbert O'Sullivan
♦ 1965	Ooh Baby Baby	Miracles
♦ 1979	Ooh Baby Baby	Linda Ronstadt
♦ 1970	O-O-H Child	Five Stairsteps
♦ 1993	O-O-H Child	Dino
♦ 1990	Ooh La La (I Can't Get Over You)	Perfect Gentlemen
♦ 1985	Ooh Ooh Song	Pat Benatar
♦ 1960	Ooh Poo Pah Doo (Part 2)	Jesse Hill
♦ 1990	Ooops Up	Snap
♦ 1982	Open Arms	Journey
1967	Open Letter To My Teenage Son	Victor Lundberg
♦ 1966	Open The Door To Your Heart	Darrell Banks
♦ 1987	Open Your Heart	Madonna
♦ 1975	Operator	Manhattan Transfer
♦ 1985	Operator	Midnight Star
♦ 1972	Operator (That's Not The Way It Feels)	Jim Croce
♦ 1986	Opportunities (Let's Make Lots Of Money)	Pet Shop Boys
♦ 1990	Opposites Attract	Paula Abdul
♦ 1966	Opus 17 (Don't You Worry 'Bout Me)	Four Seasons
♦ 1993	Ordinary World	Duran Duran
♦ 1989	Orinoco Flow (Sail Away)	Enya
♦ 1983	Other Guy	Little River Band
♦ 1967	Other Man's Grass Is Always Greener	Petula Clark
♦ 1990	Other Side	Aerosmith
♦ 1982	Other Woman	Ray Parker Jr.
♦ 1963	Our Day Will Come	Ruby And The Romantics
♦ 1975	Our Day Will Come	Frankie Valli
♦ 1970	Our House	Crosby, Stills, Nash & Young
♦ 1983	Our House	Madness
♦ 1981	Our Lips Are Sealed	Go Go's
♦ 1978	Our Love	Natalie Cole
♦ 1978	(Our Love) Don't Throw It All Away	Andy Gibb
♦ 1963	Our Winter Love	Bill Pursell
♦ 1967	Out & About	Tommy Boyce & Bobby Hart
♦ 1980	Out Here On My Own	Irene Cara
♦ 1970	Out In The Country	Three Dog Night
♦ 1964	Out Of Limits	Marketts
♦ 1986	Out Of Mind, Out Of Sight	Models
♦ 1963	Out Of My Mind	Johnny Tillotson
♦ 1964	Out Of Sight	James Brown
♦ 1956	Out Of Sight, Out Of Mind	Five Keys
♦ 1988	Out Of The Blue	Debbie Gibson
♦ 1967	Out Of The Blue	Tommy James And The Shondells
♦ 1973	Out Of The Question	Gilbert O'Sullivan
♦ 1984	Out Of Touch	Daryl Hall & John Oates
♦ 1982	Out Of Work	Gary U.S. Bonds
♦ 1972	Outa-Space	Billy Preston
♦ 1960	Outside My Window	Fleetwoods
♦ 1974	Outside Woman	Bloodstone
♦ 1965	Over And Over	Dave Clark Five
♦ 1976	Over My Head	Fleetwood Mac
♦ 1957	Over The Mountain (Across The Sea)	Johnnie & Joe
♦ 1963	Over The Mountain (Across The Sea)	Bobby Vinton
♦ 1960	Over The Rainbow	Demensions
♦ 1966	Over Under Sideways Down	Yardbirds
♦ 1968	Over You	Gary Puckett And The Union Gap
♦ 1986	Overjoyed	Stevie Wonder
♦ 1983	Overkill	Men At Work
♦ 1974	Overnight Sensation (Hit Record)	Raspberries
♦ 1970	Overture From Tommy (A Rock Opera)	Assembled Multitude
♦ 1984	Owner Of A Lonely Heart	Yes
♦ 1971	Oye Como Va	Santana

P

♦ 1964	P.S. I Love You	Beatles
♦ 1962	P.T. 109	Jimmy Dean
♦ 1983	P.Y.T. (Pretty Young Thing)	Michael Jackson
♦ 1982	Pac-Man Fever	Buckner & Garcia
♦ 1958	Padre	Toni Arden
♦ 1966	Paint It, Black	Rolling Stones
♦ 1973	Painted Ladies	Ian Thomas
♦ 1963	Painted, Tainted Rose	Al Martino
♦ 1962	Palisades Park	Freddy Cannon
1976	Paloma Blanca	George Baker Selection

♦ 1988	Pamela	Toto
♦ 1984	Panama	Van Halen
♦ 1966	Pandora's Golden Heebie Jeebies	Association
♦ 1986	Papa Don't Preach	Madonna
♦ 1974	Papa Don't Take No Mess (Part 1)	James Brown
♦ 1962	Papa-Oom-Mow-Mow	Rivingtons
♦ 1972	Papa Was A Rollin' Stone	Temptations
♦ 1967	Papa Was Too	Joe Tex
♦ 1965	Papa's Got A Brand New Bag (Part 1)	James Brown
♦ 1968	Papa's Got A Brand New Bag	Otis Redding
♦ 1967	Paper Cup	Fifth Dimension
♦ 1992	Paper Doll	P.M. Dawn
♦ 1987	Paper In Fire	John Cougar Mellencamp
1970	Paper Mache	Dionne Warwick
♦ 1960	Paper Roses	Anita Bryant
♦ 1973	Paper Roses	Marie Osmond
♦ 1965	Paper Tiger	Sue Thompson
♦ 1966	Paperback Writer	Beatles
♦ 1982	Paperlate	Genesis
♦ 1988	Paradise	Sade
♦ 1978	Paradise By The Dashboard Light	Meatloaf
♦ 1989	Paradise City	Guns N' Roses
♦ 1986	Paranoimia	Art Of Noise With Max Headroom
♦ 1988	Parents Just Don't Understand	D.J. Jazzy Jeff & The Fresh Prince
♦ 1975	Part Of The Plan	Dan Fogelberg
♦ 1963	Part Time Love	Little Johnny Taylor
♦ 1970	Part Time Love	Ann Peebles
♦ 1975	Part Time Love	Gladys Knight & The Pips
♦ 1978	Part-Time Love	Elton John
♦ 1985	Part-Time Lover	Stevie Wonder
♦ 1986	Party All The Time	Eddie Murphy
♦ 1957	Party Doll	Buddy Knox With The Rhythm Orchids
♦ 1957	Party Doll	Steve Lawrence
♦ 1962	Party Lights	Claudine Clark
♦ 1981	Party's Over (Hopelessly In Love)	Journey
♦ 1989	Partyman	Prince
♦ 1983	Pass The Dutchie	Musical Youth
♦ 1991	P.A.S.S.I.O.N.	Rythm Syndicate
♦ 1981	Passion	Rod Stewart
♦ 1967	Pata Pata	Miriam Makeba
♦ 1970	Patch It Up	Elvis Presley
♦ 1970	Patches	Clarence Carter
♦ 1962	Patches	Dickey Lee
♦ 1989	Patience	Guns N' Roses
♦ 1958	Patricia	Perez Prado
♦ 1962	Patti Ann	Johnny Crawford
♦ 1971	Pay To The Piper	Chairmen Of The Board
♦ 1967	Pay You Back With Interest	Hollies
♦ 1974	Payback (Part 1)	James Brown
♦ 1989	Peace In Our Time	Eddie Money
♦ 1977	Peace Of Mind	Boston
♦ 1967	Peace Of Mind	Paul Revere And The Raiders
♦ 1975	Peace Pipe	B.T. Express
♦ 1971	Peace Train	Cat Stevens
♦ 1970	Peace Will Come (According To Plan)	Melanie
♦ 1973	Peaceful	Helen Reddy
♦ 1973	Peaceful Easy Feeling	Eagles
♦ 1996	Peaches	Presidents Of The United States
♦ 1961	Peanut Butter	Marathons
♦ 1957	Peanuts	Little Joe & The Thrillers
♦ 1959	Peek-A-Boo	Cadillacs
♦ 1978	Peg	Steely Dan
♦ 1958	Peggy Sue	Buddy Holly
♦ 1964	Penetration	Pyramids
♦ 1960	Pennies From Heaven	Skyliners
♦ 1982	Penny For Your Thoughts	Tavares
♦ 1967	Penny Lane	Beatles
♦ 1984	Penny Lover	Lionel Richie
♦ 1964	People	Barbra Streisand
♦ 1985	People Are People	Depeche Mode
♦ 1991	People Are Still Having Sex	LaTour
♦ 1967	People Are Strange	Doors
♦ 1992	People Everyday	Arrested Development
♦ 1965	People Get Ready	Impressions
♦ 1968	People Got To Be Free	Rascals
♦ 1974	People Gotta Move	Gino Vannelli
♦ 1972	People Make The World Go Round	Stylistics

♦ 1979	People Of The South Wind	Kansas	♦ 1960	Please Help Me, I'm Falling	Hank Locklin
♦ 1964	People Say	Dixie Cups	♦ 1961	Please Love Me Forever	Cathy Jean & The Roommates
♦ 1961	"Pepe"	Duane Eddy	♦ 1967	Please Love Me Forever	Bobby Vinton
♦ 1963	Pepino The Italian Mouse	Lou Monte	♦ 1975	Please Mr. Please	Olivia Newton-John
♦ 1962	Peppermint Twist (Part 1)	Joey Dee & The Starliters	♦ 1961	Please Mr. Postman	Marvelettes
♦ 1962	Percolator (Twist)	Billy Joe & The Checkmates	♦ 1975	Please Mr. Postman	Carpenters
♦ 1985	Perfect Way	Scritti Politti	♦ 1959	Please Mr. Sun	Tommy Edwards
♦ 1988	Perfect World	Huey Lewis	♦ 1964	Please Please Me	Beatles
♦ 1960	Perfidia	Ventures	♦ 1968	Please Return Your Love To Me	Temptations
♦ 1990	Personal Jesus	Depeche Mode	♦ 1961	Please Stay	Drifters
♦ 1959	Personality	Lloyd Price	♦ 1966	Please Tell Me Why	Dave Clark Five
♦ 1982	Personally	Karla Bonoff	♦ 1961	Please Tell Me Why	Jackie Wilson
♦ 1959	Peter Gunn	Ray Anthony	♦ 1987	Pleasure Principle	Janet Jackson
♦ 1960	Peter Gunn	Duane Eddy	1957	Pledge Of Love	Dick Contino
♦ 1959	Petite Fleur (Little Flower)	Chris Barber's Jazz Band	1957	Pledge Of Love	Ken Copeland
1956	Petticoats Of Portugal	Dick Jacobs	1957	Pledge Of Love	Mitchell Torok
♦ 1975	Philadelphia Freedom	Elton John	♦ 1955	Pledging My Love	Johnny Ace
1958	Philadelphia, U.S.A.	Nu Tornados	♦ 1955	Pledging My Love	Teresa Brewer
♦ 1966	Phoenix Love Theme	Brass Ring	♦ 1996	Po Pimp	Do Or Die featuring Tung Twista
♦ 1983	Photograph	Def Leppard	♦ 1962	Pocketful Of Miracles	Frank Sinatra
♦ 1973	Photograph	Ringo Starr	♦ 1960	Poetry In Motion	Johnny Tillotson
♦ 1981	Physical	Olivia Newton-John	♦ 1975	Poetry Man	Phoebe Snow
♦ 1988	Piano In The Dark	Brenda Russell	♦ 1978	Point Of Know Return	Kansas
♦ 1974	Piano Man	Billy Joel	♦ 1987	Point Of No Return	Expose
♦ 1975	Pick Up The Pieces	Average White Band	♦ 1962	Point Of No Return	Gene McDaniels
♦ 1968	Pickin' Wild Mountain Berries	Peggy Scott & Jo Jo Benson	♦ 1986	Point Of No Return	Nu Shooz
♦ 1968	Pictures Of Matchstick Men	Status Quo	♦ 1989	Poison	Alice Cooper
♦ 1968	Piece Of My Heart	Big Brother And The Holding Company	♦ 1990	Poison	Bell Biv DeVoe
♦ 1991	Piece Of My Heart	Tara Kemp	♦ 1983	Poison Arrow	ABC
♦ 1973	Pieces Of April	Three Dog Night	♦ 1959	Poison Ivy	Coasters
1983	Pieces Of Ice	Diana Ross	♦ 1990	Policy Of Truth	Depeche Mode
♦ 1966	Pied Piper	Crispian St. Peters	♦ 1984	Politics Of Dancing	Re-Flex
♦ 1973	Pillow Talk	Sylvia	♦ 1969	Polk Salad Annie	Tony Joe White
♦ 1980	Pilot Of The Airwaves	Charlie Dore	♦ 1996	Pony	Ginuwine
♦ 1969	Pinball Wizard	Who	1961	Pony Time	Chubby Checker
1973	Pinball Wizard/See Me, Feel Me	New Seekers	♦ 1968	Poor Baby	Cowsills
♦ 1960	Pineapple Princess	Annette	♦ 1957	Poor Boy	Elvis Presley
♦ 1988	Pink Cadillac	Natalie Cole	♦ 1958	Poor Boy	Royaltones
♦ 1984	Pink Houses	John Cougar Mellencamp	♦ 1962	Poor Fool	Ike & Tina Turner
♦ 1964	Pink Panther Theme	Henry Mancini	♦ 1959	Poor Jenny	Everly Brothers
♦ 1959	Pink Shoe Laces	Dodie Stevens	♦ 1958	Poor Little Fool	Ricky Nelson
♦ 1963	Pipeline	Chantays	1963	Poor Little Rich Girl	Steve Lawrence
♦ 1966	Place In The Sun	Stevie Wonder	♦ 1957	Poor Man's Roses (Or A Rich Man's Gold)	Patti Page
♦ 1991	Place In This World	Michael W. Smith	♦ 1981	Poor Man's Son	Survivor
♦ 1994	Place Where You Belong	Shai	♦ 1956	Poor People Of Paris	Les Baxter
♦ 1959	Plain Jane	Bobby Darin	♦ 1956	Poor People Of Paris	Russ Morgan
♦ 1973	Plastic Man	Temptations	♦ 1956	Poor People Of Paris	Lawrence Welk And His Orchestra
♦ 1972	Play Me	Neil Diamond	♦ 1978	Poor Poor Pitiful Me	Linda Ronstadt
♦ 1955	Play Me Hearts And Flowers	Johnny Desmond	♦ 1966	Poor Side Of Town	Johnny Rivers
♦ 1974	Play Something Sweet (Brickyard Blues)	Three Dog Night	1982	Pop Goes The Movies (Part 1)	Meco
♦ 1976	Play That Funky Music	Wild Cherry	♦ 1991	Pop Goes The Weasel	3rd Bass
♦ 1991	Play That Funky Music	Vanilla Ice	♦ 1988	Pop Goes The World	Men Without Hats
♦ 1980	Play The Game	Queen	♦ 1985	Pop Life	Prince And The Revolution
♦ 1982	Play The Game Tonight	Kansas	♦ 1979	Pop Muzik	M
♦ 1994	Playaz Club	Rappin' 4-Tay	♦ 1962	Pop Pop Pop-Pie	Sherrys
♦ 1968	Playboy	Gene & Debbe	♦ 1989	Pop Singer	John Cougar Mellencamp
♦ 1962	Playboy	Marvelettes	♦ 1972	Pop That Thang	Isley Brothers
♦ 1995	Player's Anthem	Junior M.A.F.I.A.	♦ 1972	Popcorn	Hot Butter
♦ 1994	Player's Ball	Outkast	♦ 1969	Popcorn	James Brown
♦ 1991	Playground	Another Bad Creation	1962	Popeye (The Hitchhiker)	Chubby Checker
♦ 1973	Playground In My Mind	Clint Holmes	♦ 1966	Popsicle	Jan & Dean
♦ 1957	Playing For Keeps	Elvis Presley	♦ 1964	Popsicles And Icicles	Murmaids
1957	Plaything	Ted Newman	♦ 1956	Port Au Prince	Nelson Riddle
♦ 1957	Plaything	Nick Todd	1961	Portrait Of My Love	Steve Lawrence
♦ 1967	Pleasant Valley Sunday	Monkees	1967	Portrait Of My Love	Tokens
♦ 1978	Please Come Home For Christmas	Eagles	♦ 1965	Positively 4th Street	Bob Dylan
♦ 1974	Please Come To Boston	Dave Loggins	♦ 1990	Possession	Bad English
♦ 1962	Please Don't Ask About Barbara	Bobby Vee	♦ 1985	Possession Obsession	Daryl Hall & John Oates
♦ 1979	Please Don't Go	KC And The Sunshine Band	♦ 1988	Pour Some Sugar On Me	Def Leppard
♦ 1992	Please Don't Go	K.W.S.	♦ 1990	Power	Snap
♦ 1961	Please Don't Go	Ral Donner	♦ 1978	Power Of Gold	Dan Fogelberg/Tim Weisberg
♦ 1996	Please Don't Go	Immature	♦ 1994	Power Of Love	Celine Dion
♦ 1997	Please Don't Go	No Mercy	♦ 1985	Power Of Love	Huey Lewis
♦ 1988	Please Don't Go Girl	New Kids On The Block	♦ 1972	Power Of Love	Joe Simon
♦ 1979	Please Don't Leave	Lauren Wood	♦ 1988	Power Of Love	Laura Branigan
♦ 1963	Please Don't Talk To The Lifeguard	Diane Ray	♦ 1991	Power Of Love/Love Power	Luther Vandross
♦ 1993	Please Forgive Me	Bryan Adams	♦ 1971	Power To The People	John Lennon/Plastic Ono Band

♦	1991	Power Windows	Billy Falcon
♦	1994	Practice What You Preach	Barry White
♦	1990	Pray	M.C. Hammer
♦	1994	Prayer For The Dying	Seal
♦	1990	Praying For Time	George Michael
♦	1972	Precious And Few	Climax
♦	1979	Precious Love	Bob Welch
♦	1971	Precious Precious	Jackie Moore
♦	1981	Precious To Me	Phil Seymour
♦	1986	Press	Paul McCartney
♦	1982	Pressure	Billy Joel
♦	1957	Pretend You Don't See Her	Jerry Vale
♦	1967	Pretty Ballerina	Left Banke
♦	1960	Pretty Blue Eyes	Steve Lawrence
♦	1966	Pretty Flamingo	Manfred Mann
♦	1995	Pretty Girl	Jon B
♦	1980	Pretty Girls	Melissa Manchester
♦	1961	Pretty Little Angel Eyes	Curtis Lee
♦	1965	Pretty Little Baby	Marvin Gaye
♦	1964	Pretty Paper	Roy Orbison
♦	1990	Price Of Love	Bad English
♦	1963	Pride And Joy	Marvin Gaye
♦	1984	Pride (In The Name Of Love)	U2
♦	1984	Prime Time	Alan Parsons Project
♦	1959	Primrose Lane	Jerry Wallace
♦	1965	Princess In Rags	Gene Pitney
♦	1990	Principal's Office	Young MC
♦	1956	Priscilla	Eddie Cooley And The Dimples
♦	1989	Prisoner	Howard Jones
♦	1963	Prisoner Of Love	James Brown
♦	1978	Prisoner Of Your Love	Player
♦	1985	Private Dancer	Tina Turner
♦	1981	Private Eyes	Daryl Hall & John Oates
♦	1958	Problems	Everly Brothers
♦	1988	Promise	When In Rome
♦	1958	Promise Me, Love	Andy Williams
♦	1991	Promise Of A New Day	Paula Abdul
♦	1965	Promised Land	Chuck Berry
♦	1975	Promised Land	Elvis Presley
♦	1979	Promises	Eric Clapton
♦	1981	Promises In The Dark	Pat Benatar
♦	1968	Promises, Promises	Dionne Warwick
♦	1983	Promises, Promises	Naked Eyes
♦	1963	Proud	Johnny Crawford
♦	1969	Proud Mary	Creedence Clearwater Revival
♦	1971	Proud Mary	Ike & Tina Turner
♦	1975	Proud One	Osmonds
♦	1978	Prove It All Night	Bruce Springsteen
♦	1988	Prove Your Love	Taylor Dayne
♦	1970	Psychedelic Shack	Temptations
♦	1966	Psychotic Reaction	Count Five
♦	1967	Pucker Up Buttercup	Jr. Walker & The All Stars
♦	1963	Puff (The Magic Dragon)	Peter, Paul & Mary
♦	1990	Pump Up The Jam	Technotronic featuring Felly
♦	1988	Pump Up The Volume	M/A/R/R/S
♦	1994	Pumps And A Bump	Hammer
♦	1962	Punish Her	Bobby Vee
♦	1970	Puppet Man	Fifth Dimension
♦	1971	Puppet Man	Tom Jones
♦	1965	Puppet On A String	Elvis Presley
♦	1960	Puppy Love	Paul Anka
♦	1972	Puppy Love	Donny Osmond
♦	1964	Puppy Love	Barbara Lewis
♦	1990	Pure	Lightning Seeds
♦	1958	Purple People Eater	Sheb Wooley
♦	1984	Purple Rain	Prince And The Revolution
♦	1962	Push And Kick	Mark Valentino
♦	1988	Push It	Salt-N-Pepa
♦	1967	Pushin' Too Hard	Seeds
♦	1963	Pushover	Etta James
	1958	Pussy Cat	Ames Brothers
♦	1958	Put A Light In The Window	Four Lads
♦	1969	Put A Little Love In Your Heart	Jackie DeShannon
♦	1989	Put A Little Love In Your Heart	Annie Lennox & Al Green
	1958	Put A Ring On My Finger	Les Paul & Mary Ford
♦	1971	Put Your Hand In The Hand	Ocean
♦	1974	Put Your Hands Together	O'Jays

♦	1959	Put Your Head On My Shoulder	Paul Anka
♦	1989	Put Your Mouth On Me	Eddie Murphy
♦	1983	Puttin' On The Ritz	Taco

Q

♦	1993	Quality Time	Hi-Five
♦	1961	Quarter To Three	Gary U.S. Bonds
♦	1981	Queen Of Hearts	Juice Newton
♦	1983	Queen Of The Broken Hearts	Loverboy
♦	1958	Queen Of The Hop	Bobby Darin
♦	1965	Queen Of The House	Jody Miller
♦	1969	Quentin's Theme	Charles Randolph Grean Sounde
♦	1960	Question	Lloyd Price
♦	1970	Question	Moody Blues
♦	1968	Question Of Temperature	Balloon Farm
♦	1971	Questions 67 & 68	Chicago
♦	1968	Quick Joey Small (Run Joey Run)	Kasenetz-Katz Singing Orchestral Circus
♦	1964	Quicksand	Martha & The Vandellas
♦	1959	Quiet Village	Martin Denny
♦	1997	Quit Playing Games	Backstreet Boys
♦	1961	Quite A Party	Fireballs

R

♦	1965	Race Is On	Jack Jones
♦	1974	Radar Love	Golden Earring
♦	1984	Radio Ga Ga	Queen
♦	1989	Radio Romance	Tiffany
♦	1985	Radioactive	Firm
♦	1988	Rag Doll	Aerosmith
♦	1964	Rag Doll	Four Seasons
♦	1971	Rags To Riches	Elvis Presley
♦	1959	Ragtime Cowboy Joe	David Seville And The Chipmunks
♦	1966	Rain	Beatles
♦	1993	Rain	Madonna
♦	1986	Rain	Oran "Juice" Jones
♦	1971	Rain Dance	Guess Who
♦	1966	Rain On The Roof	Lovin' Spoonful
♦	1986	Rain On The Scarecrow	John Cougar Mellencamp
♦	1962	Rain Rain Go Away	Bobby Vinton
♦	1967	Rain, The Park & Other Things	Cowsills
♦	1957	Rainbow	Russ Hamilton
♦	1979	Rainbow Connection	Kermit
♦	1961	Raindrops	Dee Clark
♦	1970	Raindrops Keep Fallin' On My Head	B.J. Thomas
♦	1961	Rainin' In My Heart	Slim Harpo
♦	1966	Rains Came	Sir Douglas Quintet
♦	1975	Rainy Day People	Gordon Lightfoot
♦	1966	Rainy Day Women #12 & 35	Bob Dylan
♦	1971	Rainy Days And Mondays	Carpenters
♦	1970	Rainy Night In Georgia	Brook Benton
♦	1973	Raised On Rock	Elvis Presley
♦	1961	Ram-Bunk-Shush	Ventures
♦	1961	Rama Lama Ding Dong	Edsels
♦	1969	Ramblin' Gamblin' Man	Bob Seger System
♦	1973	Ramblin' Man	Allman Brothers Band
♦	1962	Ramblin' Rose	Nat King Cole
♦	1958	Ramrod	Duane Eddy
♦	1970	Rapper	Jaggerz
♦	1997	Rapper's Ball	E-40
♦	1980	Rapper's Delight	Sugarhill Gang
♦	1981	Rapture	Blondie
♦	1985	Raspberry Beret	Prince And The Revolution
♦	1957	Raunchy	Ernie Freeman
♦	1957	Raunchy	Bill Justis
♦	1957	Raunchy	Billy Vaughn
♦	1958	Rave On	Buddy Holly
♦	1959	Raw-Hide	Link Wray & His Ray Men
♦	1968	Ray Of Hope	Rascals
♦	1956	Razzle-Dazzle	Bill Haley And His Comets
♦	1970	Reach Out And Touch (Somebody's Hand)	Diana Ross
♦	1964	Reach Out For Me	Dionne Warwick

♦ 1966	Reach Out I'll Be There	Four Tops
♦ 1971	Reach Out I'll Be There	Diana Ross
♦ 1968	Reach Out Of The Darkness	Friend And Lover
♦ 1984	Read 'Em And Weep	Barry Manilow
♦ 1975	Ready	Cat Stevens
♦ 1990	Ready Or Not	After 7
♦ 1969	Ready Or Not Here I Come (Can't Hide From Love)	Delfonics
♦ 1956	Ready Teddy	Little Richard
♦ 1978	Ready To Take A Chance Again	Barry Manilow
♦ 1996	Real Love	Beatles
♦ 1991	Real Love	Bob Seger & The Silver Bullet Band
♦ 1980	Real Love	Doobie Brothers
♦ 1989	Real Love	Jody Watley
♦ 1992	Real Love	Mary J. Blige
♦ 1991	Real, Real, Real	Jesus Jones
♦ 1994	Really Doe	Ice Cube
1981	Really Wanna Know You	Gary Wright
♦ 1993	Reason To Believe	Rod Stewart
♦ 1958	Rebel-'Rouser	Duane Eddy
♦ 1984	Rebel Yell	Billy Idol
♦ 1993	Rebirth Of Slick (Cool Like Dat)	Digable Planets
♦ 1969	Reconsider Me	Johnny Adams
♦ 1966	Recovery	Fontella Bass
♦ 1995	Red Light Special	TLC
♦ 1984	Red Red Wine	UB40
♦ 1988	Red Red Wine	UB40
♦ 1959	Red River Rock	Johnny And The Hurricanes
1959	Red River Rose	Ames Brothers
♦ 1965	Red Roses For A Blue Lady	Vic Dana
♦ 1965	Red Roses For A Blue Lady	Bert Kaempfert
♦ 1965	Red Roses For A Blue Lady	Wayne Newton
♦ 1966	Red Rubber Ball	Cyrkle
♦ 1960	Red Sails In The Sunset	Platters
♦ 1965	Reelin' And Rockin'	Dave Clark Five
♦ 1973	Reelin' And Rockin'	Chuck Berry
♦ 1973	Reeling In The Years	Steely Dan
♦ 1957	Reet Petite (The Finest Girl You Ever Want To Meet)	Jackie Wilson
♦ 1967	Reflections	Diana Ross And The Supremes
♦ 1970	Reflections Of My Life	Marmalade
♦ 1984	Reflex	Duran Duran
♦ 1980	Refugee	Tom Petty And The Heartbreakers
♦ 1993	Regret	New Order
♦ 1994	Regulate	Warren G. & Nate Dogg
♦ 1985	Relax	Frankie Goes To Hollywood
♦ 1973	Relay	Who
♦ 1962	Release Me	Esther Phillips
♦ 1967	Release Me	Engelbert Humperdinck
♦ 1990	Release Me	Wilson Phillips
♦ 1964	Remember (Walkin' In The Sand)	Shangri-Las
♦ 1963	Remember Diana	Paul Anka
♦ 1971	Remember Me	Diana Ross
♦ 1964	Remember Me	Rita Pavone
1965	(Remember Me) I'm The One Who Loves You	Dean Martin
♦ 1977	(Remember The Days Of The) Old Schoolyard	Cat Stevens
♦ 1984	Remember The Nights	Motels
♦ 1992	Remember The Time	Michael Jackson
♦ 1963	Remember Then	Earls
♦ 1975	Remember What I Told You To Forget	Tavares
♦ 1959	Remember When	Platters
♦ 1957	Remember You're Mine	Pat Boone
♦ 1978	Reminiscing	Little River Band
♦ 1975	Rendezvous	Hudson Brothers
♦ 1996	Renee	Lost Boyz
♦ 1979	Renegade	Styx
♦ 1997	Request Line	Zhane
♦ 1965	Rescue Me	Fontella Bass
♦ 1991	Rescue Me	Madonna
♦ 1965	Respect	Otis Redding
♦ 1967	Respect	Aretha Franklin
♦ 1971	Respect Yourself	Staple Singers
♦ 1987	Respect Yourself	Bruce Willis
♦ 1966	Respectable	Outsiders
♦ 1992	Restless Heart	Peter Cetera
♦ 1971	Resurrection Shuffle	Ashton, Gardner & Dyke
♦ 1971	Resurrection Shuffle	Tom Jones
♦ 1997	Return Of The Mack	Mark Morrison
♦ 1967	Return Of The Red Baron	Royal Guardsmen
♦ 1994	Return To Innocence	Enigma
♦ 1958	Return To Me	Dean Martin
♦ 1962	Return To Sender	Elvis Presley
♦ 1979	Reunited	Peaches & Herb
♦ 1959	Reveille Rock	Johnny And The Hurricanes
♦ 1962	Revenge	Brook Benton
♦ 1963	Reverend Mr. Black	Kingston Trio
♦ 1968	Revolution	Beatles
♦ 1966	Rhapsody In The Rain	Lou Christie
♦ 1976	Rhiannon (Will You Ever Win)	Fleetwood Mac
♦ 1975	Rhinestone Cowboy	Glen Campbell
♦ 1964	Rhythm	Major Lance
♦ 1992	Rhythm Is A Dancer	Snap
♦ 1987	Rhythm Is Gonna Get You	Gloria Estefan And Miami Sound Machine
♦ 1989	Rhythm Nation	Janet Jackson
♦ 1988	Rhythm Of Love	Yes
♦ 1991	Rhythm Of My Heart	Rod Stewart
♦ 1995	Rhythm Of The Night	Corona
♦ 1985	Rhythm Of The Night	DeBarge
♦ 1963	Rhythm Of The Rain	Cascades
♦ 1977	Rich Girl	Daryl Hall & John Oates
♦ 1991	Rico Suave	Gerardo
1962	Ride!	Dee Dee Sharp
♦ 1965	Ride Away	Roy Orbison
♦ 1970	Ride Captain Ride	Blues Image
♦ 1975	Ride 'Em Cowboy	Paul Davis
♦ 1980	Ride Like The Wind	Christopher Cross
♦ 1964	Ride The Wild Surf	Jan & Dean
♦ 1991	Ride The Wind	Poison
♦ 1965	Ride Your Pony	Lee Dorsey
♦ 1971	Riders On The Storm	Doors
♦ 1976	Right Back Where We Started From	Maxine Nightingale
♦ 1984	Right By Your Side	Eurythmics
♦ 1978	Right Down The Line	Gerry Rafferty
♦ 1993	Right Here (Human Nature)	SWV
♦ 1991	Right Here, Right Now	Jesus Jones
♦ 1989	Right Here Waiting	Richard Marx
♦ 1993	Right Kind Of Love	Jeremy Jordan
♦ 1971	Right On The Tip Of My Tongue	Brenda & The Tabulations
♦ 1987	Right On Track	Breakfast Club
♦ 1961	Right Or Wrong	Wanda Jackson
♦ 1964	Right Or Wrong	Ronnie Dove
♦ 1973	Right Place Wrong Time	Dr. John
♦ 1987	Right Thing	Simply Red
♦ 1973	Right Thing To Do	Carly Simon
♦ 1977	Right Time Of The Night	Jennifer Warnes
♦ 1974	Rikki Don't Lose That Number	Steely Dan
♦ 1959	Ring-A-Ling-A-Lario	Jimmie Rodgers
♦ 1965	Ring Dang Doo	Sam The Sham And The Pharaohs
♦ 1979	Ring My Bell	Anita Ward
♦ 1991	Ring My Bell	D.J. Jazzy Jeff & The Fresh Prince
♦ 1963	Ring Of Fire	Johnny Cash
♦ 1972	Ring The Living Bell	Melanie
♦ 1964	Ringo	Lorne Greene
♦ 1971	Rings	Cymarron
♦ 1974	Rings	Lobo
♦ 1962	Rinky Dink	Dave "Baby" Cortez
♦ 1983	Rio	Duran Duran
♦ 1956	Rip It Up	Bill Haley And His Comets
♦ 1956	Rip It Up	Little Richard
♦ 1964	Rip Van Winkle	Devotions
♦ 1979	Rise	Herb Alpert
♦ 1971	River Deep - Mountain High	Supremes & Four Tops
♦ 1969	River Is Wide	Grass Roots
♦ 1993	River Of Dreams	Billy Joel
♦ 1978	Rivers Of Babylon	Boney M
♦ 1974	River's Risin'	Edgar Winter
♦ 1990	Roam	B-52's
♦ 1959	Robbin' The Cradle	Tony Bellus
♦ 1956	R-O-C-K	Bill Haley And His Comets
♦ 1956	Rock-A-Beatin' Boogie	Bill Haley And His Comets
♦ 1957	Rock-A-Billy	Guy Mitchell
♦ 1956	Rock-A-Bye Your Baby With A Dixie Melody	Jerry Lewis
1961	Rock-A-Bye Your Baby With A Dixie Melody	Aretha Franklin
♦ 1962	Rock-A-Hula Baby	Elvis Presley
♦ 1989	Rock And A Hard Place	Rolling Stones
♦ 1972	Rock And Roll (Part 2)	Gary Glitter

♦ 1976	Rock And Roll All Nite...Kiss
♦ 1981	Rock And Roll Dreams Come Through.....................Jim Steinman
♦ 1994	Rock And Roll Dreams Come Through.............................Meatloaf
♦ 1985	Rock And Roll Girls...John Fogerty
♦ 1974	Rock And Roll Heaven.............................Righteous Brothers
♦ 1974	Rock And Roll, Hoochie Koo ....Rick Derringer
♦ 1958	Rock And Roll Is Here To Stay ....Danny & The Juniors
♦ 1976	Rock And Roll Love Letter ....Bay City Rollers
♦ 1972	Rock And Roll Lullaby.............................B.J. Thomas
♦ 1957	Rock & Roll Music ....Chuck Berry
♦ 1976	Rock & Roll Music ....Beach Boys
♦ 1977	Rock And Roll Never Forgets ....Bob Seger
♦ 1956	Rock And Roll Waltz ....Kay Starr
♦ 1986	R.O.C.K. In The U.S.A. ....John Cougar Mellencamp
♦ 1956	Rock Island Line ....Lonnie Donegan And His Skiffle Group
♦ 1955	Rock Love ....Fontane Sisters
♦ 1969	Rock Me ....Steppenwolf
♦ 1986	Rock Me Amadeus ....Falco
♦ 1964	Rock Me Baby ....B.B. King
1972	Rock Me Baby.................................David Cassidy
♦ 1974	Rock Me Gently ....Andy Kim
♦ 1985	Rock Me Tonight (For Old Times Sake) ....Freddie Jackson
♦ 1984	Rock Me Tonite ....Billy Squier
♦ 1976	Rock 'N Me ....Steve Miller
♦ 1979	Rock 'N' Roll Fantasy ....Bad Company
♦ 1978	Rock 'N' Roll Fantasy ....Kinks
♦ 1975	Rock N' Roll (I Gave You The Best Years Of My Life) ....Mac Davis
♦ 1983	Rock 'N' Roll Is King ....ELO
♦ 1972	Rock 'N Roll Soul ....Grand Funk Railroad
♦ 1983	Rock Of Ages ....Def Leppard
♦ 1988	Rock Of Life ....Rick Springfield
♦ 1974	Rock On ....David Essex
♦ 1989	Rock On ....Michael Damian
♦ 1971	Rock Steady...Aretha Franklin
♦ 1987	Rock Steady.. Whispers
♦ 1974	Rock The Boat.................................Hues Corporation
♦ 1983	Rock The Casbah...Clash
♦ 1987	Rock The Night ....Europe
♦ 1982	Rock This Town ....Stray Cats
♦ 1989	Rock Wit'cha ....Bobby Brown
♦ 1980	Rock With You ....Michael Jackson
♦ 1984	Rock You Like A Hurricane ....Scorpions
♦ 1974	Rock Your Baby ....George McCrae
♦ 1957	Rock Your Little Baby To Sleep........Buddy Knox With The Rhythm Orchids
1959	Rocka-Conga ....Applejacks
♦ 1989	Rocket ....Def Leppard
♦ 1988	Rocket 2 U ....Jets
♦ 1972	Rocket Man ....Elton John
♦ 1975	Rockford Files ....Mike Post
1975	Rockin' All Over The World ....John Fogerty
♦ 1961	Rockin' Around The Christmas Tree......................Brenda Lee
♦ 1985	Rockin' At Midnight ....Honeydrippers
♦ 1975	Rockin' Chair ....Gwen McCrae
♦ 1960	Rockin' Good Way (To Mess Around And Fall In Love).................... Dinah Washington & Brook Benton
♦ 1960	Rockin' Little Angel ....Ray Smith
♦ 1973	Rockin' Pneumonia - Boogie Woogie Flu.......................Johnny Rivers
♦ 1958	Rockin' Robin...Bobby Day
♦ 1972	Rockin' Robin..................................Michael Jackson
♦ 1973	Rockin' Roll Baby ....Stylistics
♦ 1974	Rockin' Soul ....Hues Corporation
♦ 1975	Rocky...Austin Roberts
♦ 1973	Rocky Mountain High ....John Denver
♦ 1973	Rocky Mountain Way ....Joe Walsh
♦ 1979	Rolene...Moon Martin
♦ 1983	Roll Me Away ....Bob Seger & The Silver Bullet Band
♦ 1975	Roll On Down The Highway.................Bachman-Turner Overdrive
♦ 1956	Roll Over Beethoven...................................Chuck Berry
♦ 1964	Roll Over Beethoven.......................................Beatles
♦ 1995	Roll To Me ....Del Amitri
♦ 1988	Roll With It ....Steve Winwood
♦ 1979	Roller ....April Wine
♦ 1984	Romancing The Stone ....Eddy Grant
♦ 1991	Romantic ....Karyn White
♦ 1990	Romeo...Dino
♦ 1992	Romeo And Juliet.......................................Stacy Earl
♦ 1980	Romeo's Tune ....Steve Forbert

♦ 1989	Roni ....Bobby Brown
♦ 1964	Ronnie ....Four Seasons
♦ 1990	Room At The Top ....Adam Ant
♦ 1989	Room To Move ....Animotion
♦ 1989	Rooms On Fire ....Stevie Nicks
♦ 1982	Rosanna .... Toto
♦ 1980	Rose ....Bette Midler
♦ 1956	Rose And A Baby Ruth ....George Hamilton IV
♦ 1971	Rose Garden ....Lynn Anderson
♦ 1962	Roses Are Red (My Love) ....Bobby Vinton
♦ 1957	Rosie Lee ....Mello-Tones
♦ 1980	Rotation..Herb Alpert
♦ 1986	Rough Boy ....ZZ Top
♦ 1957	Round And Round ....Perry Como
♦ 1984	Round And Round ....Ratt
♦ 1991	Round And Round ....Tevin Campbell
♦ 1965	Round Every Corner ....Petula Clark
♦ 1972	Roundabout ....Yes
♦ 1982	Route 101 ....Herb Alpert
♦ 1962	Route 66 Theme ....Nelson Riddle
♦ 1979	Roxanne ....Police
♦ 1974	Rub It In ....Billy "Crash" Craddock
♦ 1990	Rub You The Right Way ....Johnny Gill
♦ 1961	Rubber Ball ....Bobby Vee
1970	Rubber Duckie...Ernie
♦ 1976	Rubberband Man ....Spinners
♦ 1970	Rubberneckin' ....Elvis Presley
♦ 1969	Ruben James ....Kenny Rogers And The First Edition
♦ 1960	Ruby ....Ray Charles
♦ 1962	Ruby Ann ....Marty Robbins
♦ 1963	Ruby Baby ....Dion
♦ 1969	Ruby, Don't Take Your Love To Town....................................Kenny Rogers And The First Edition
1960	Ruby Duby Du ....Tobin Mathews & Co.
♦ 1967	Ruby Tuesday ....Rolling Stones
♦ 1971	Ruby Tuesday ....Melanie
♦ 1956	Rudy's Rock ....Bill Haley And His Comets
♦ 1993	Ruffneck ....MC Lyte
♦ 1958	Rumble ....Link Wray & His Ray Men
♦ 1986	Rumbleseat ....John Cougar Mellencamp
♦ 1962	Rumors...Johnny Crawford
♦ 1986	Rumors...Timex Social Club
♦ 1993	Rump Shaker ....Wreckx-N-Effect
♦ 1995	Run Away ....Real McCoy
♦ 1969	Run Away Child, Running Wild ....Temptations
♦ 1965	Run, Baby Run (Back Into My Arms)...................Newbeats
1978	Run For Home ....Lindisfarne
♦ 1982	Run For The Roses ....Dan Fogelberg
♦ 1975	Run Joey Run ....David Geddes
♦ 1966	Run, Run, Look And See ....Brian Hyland
♦ 1972	Run Run Run ....Jo Jo Gunne
♦ 1984	Run Runaway ....Slade
♦ 1960	Run Samson Run ....Neil Sedaka
♦ 1970	Run Through The Jungle ....Creedence Clearwater Revival
♦ 1961	Run To Him ....Bobby Vee
♦ 1972	Run To Me ....Bee Gees
♦ 1985	Run To You ....Bryan Adams
♦ 1993	Run To You ....Whitney Houston
♦ 1995	Run-Around ....Blues Traveler
♦ 1960	Runaround ....Fleetwoods
♦ 1961	Runaround ....Regents
♦ 1961	Runaround Sue ....Dion
♦ 1978	Runaround Sue ....Leif Garrett
♦ 1984	Runaway ....Bon Jovi
♦ 1961	Runaway ....Del Shannon
♦ 1995	Runaway ....Janet Jackson
♦ 1978	Runaway ....Jefferson Starship
♦ 1993	Runaway Train ....Soul Asylum
1984	Runner.....................Manfred Mann's Earth Band
♦ 1972	Runnin' Away ....Sly & The Family Stone
♦ 1991	Running Back To You ....Vanessa Williams
♦ 1960	Running Bear ....Johnny Preston
♦ 1989	Runnin' Down A Dream ....Tom Petty
♦ 1978	Running On Empty ....Jackson Browne
♦ 1961	Running Scared ....Roy Orbison
♦ 1985	Running Up That Hill ....Kate Bush
♦ 1984	Running With The Night ....Lionel Richie

♦ 1964	She's Not There	Zombies
♦ 1977	She's Not There	Santana
♦ 1962	She's Not You	Elvis Presley
♦ 1980	She's Out Of My Life	Michael Jackson
♦ 1992	She's Playing Hard To Get	Hi-Five
♦ 1983	(She's) Sexy + 17	Stray Cats
♦ 1980	She's So Cold	Rolling Stones
1964	She's The One	Chartbusters
♦ 1962	Sheila	Tommy Roe
♦ 1991	Shelter Me	Cinderella
♦ 1964	Shelter Of Your Arms	Sammy Davis Jr.
♦ 1962	Sherry	Four Seasons
♦ 1955	Shifting Whispering Sands	Rusty Draper
♦ 1955	Shifting Whispering Sands	Billy Vaughn
♦ 1970	Shilo	Neil Diamond
♦ 1960	Shimmy Like Kate	Olympics
♦ 1960	Shimmy, Shimmy, Ko-Ko-Bop	Little Anthony And The Imperials
♦ 1994	Shine	Collective Soul
♦ 1979	Shine A Little Love	Electric Light Orchestra
♦ 1981	Shine On	L.T.D.
1984	Shine Shine	Barry Gibb
♦ 1974	Shinin' On	Grand Funk
♦ 1975	Shining Star	Earth, Wind & Fire
♦ 1980	Shining Star	Manhattans
♦ 1991	Shiny Happy People	R.E.M.
♦ 1987	Ship Of Fools (Save Me From Tomorrow)	World Party
♦ 1979	Ships	Barry Manilow
♦ 1957	Shish-Kebab	Ralph Marterie
♦ 1983	Shock The Monkey	Peter Gabriel
♦ 1975	Shoeshine Boy	Eddie Kendricks
♦ 1968	Shoo-Be-Doo-Be-Doo-Da-Day	Stevie Wonder
♦ 1993	Shoop	Salt-N-Pepa
♦ 1964	Shoop Shoop Song (It's In His Kiss)	Betty Everett
♦ 1991	Shoop Shoop Song (It's In His Kiss)	Cher
1968	Shoot 'Em Up Baby	Andy Kim
♦ 1961	Shop Around	Miracles
♦ 1976	Shop Around	Captain & Tennille
♦ 1995	Short Dick Man	20 Fingers
♦ 1957	Short Fat Fannie	Larry Williams
♦ 1978	Short People	Randy Newman
♦ 1958	Short Shorts	Royal Teens
♦ 1965	Shotgun	Jr. Walker & The All Stars
♦ 1982	Should I Do It	Pointer Sisters
♦ 1987	Should've Known Better	Richard Marx
♦ 1980	Should've Never Let You Go	Neil Sedaka And Dara Sedaka
♦ 1989	Shoulder To Cry On	Tommy Page
♦ 1985	Shout	Tears For Fears
♦ 1959	Shout (Part 1)	Isley Brothers
♦ 1962	Shout (Part 1)	Joey Dee & The Starliters
♦ 1976	Shout It Out Loud	Kiss
♦ 1962	Shout! Shout! (Knock Yourself Out)	Ernie Maresca
♦ 1974	Show And Tell	Al Wilson
♦ 1967	Show Me	Joe Tex
♦ 1984	Show Me	Pretenders
♦ 1993	Show Me Love	Robin S
♦ 1997	Show Me Love	Robyn
♦ 1976	Show Me The Way	Peter Frampton
♦ 1991	Show Me The Way	Styx
♦ 1974	Show Must Go On	Three Dog Night
♦ 1985	Show Some Respect	Tina Turner
♦ 1977	Show You The Way To Go	Jacksons
♦ 1989	Shower Me With Your Love	Surface
♦ 1976	Shower The People	James Taylor
♦ 1961	Shu Rah	Fats Domino
♦ 1963	Shut Down	Beach Boys
♦ 1963	Shutters And Boards	Jerry Wallace
♦ 1995	Shy Guy	Diana King
♦ 1958	Sick And Tired	Fats Domino
♦ 1974	Sideshow	Blue Magic
♦ 1964	Sidewalk Surfin'	Jan & Dean
♦ 1986	Sidewalk Talk	Jellybean
♦ 1994	Sign	Ace Of Base
♦ 1987	Sign 'O' The Times	Prince
♦ 1984	Sign Of Fire	Fixx
♦ 1966	Sign Of The Times	Petula Clark
♦ 1988	Sign Your Name	Terence Trent D'Arby

♦ 1970	Signed, Sealed, Delivered I'm Yours	Stevie Wonder
♦ 1977	Signed, Sealed, Delivered (I'm Yours)	Peter Frampton
♦ 1971	Signs	Five Man Electrical Band
♦ 1991	Signs	Tesla
♦ 1967	Silence Is Golden	Tremeloes
♦ 1991	Silent Lucidity	Queensryche
♦ 1992	Silent Prayer	Shanice featuring Johnny Gill
♦ 1986	Silent Running	Mike + The Mechanics
♦ 1988	Silhouette	Kenny G
♦ 1957	Silhouettes	Diamonds
♦ 1957	Silhouettes	Rays
♦ 1965	Silhouettes	Herman's Hermits
♦ 1976	Silly Love Songs	Wings
♦ 1970	Silver Bird	Mark Lindsay
♦ 1971	Silver Moon	Michael Nesmith & The First National Band
♦ 1962	Silver Threads And Golden Needles	Springfields
♦ 1968	Simon Says	1910 Fruitgum Company
♦ 1993	Simple Life	Elton John
♦ 1988	Simply Irresistible	Robert Palmer
♦ 1959	Since I Don't Have You	Skyliners
♦ 1981	Since I Don't Have You	Don McLean
♦ 1963	Since I Fell For You	Lenny Welch
♦ 1965	Since I Lost My Baby	Temptations
♦ 1956	Since I Met You Baby	Ivory Joe Hunter
♦ 1967	Since You Showed Me How To Be Happy	Jackie Wilson
♦ 1959	Since You've Been Gone	Clyde McPhatter
♦ 1987	Since You've Been Gone	Outfield
♦ 1955	Sincerely	McGuire Sisters
♦ 1955	Sincerely	Moonglows
♦ 1989	Sincerely Yours	Sweet Sensation
♦ 1973	Sing	Carpenters
♦ 1976	Sing A Song	Earth, Wind & Fire
♦ 1970	Sing A Song For Freedom	Frijid Pink
♦ 1958	Sing Boy Sing	Tommy Sands
♦ 1956	Singing The Blues	Guy Mitchell
♦ 1956	Singing The Blues	Marty Robbins
♦ 1967	Single Girl	Sandy Posey
♦ 1960	Sink The Bismarck	Johnny Horton
♦ 1977	Sir Duke	Stevie Wonder
♦ 1984	Sister Christian	Night Ranger
♦ 1975	Sister Golden Hair	America
♦ 1974	Sister Mary Elephant (Shudd-Up!)	Cheech & Chong
♦ 1985	Sisters Are Doin' It For Themselves	Eurythmics And Aretha Franklin
♦ 1967	Sit Down, I Think I Love You	Mojo Men
♦ 1971	Sit Yourself Down	Stephen Stills
♦ 1973	Sitting	Cat Stevens
♦ 1983	Sitting At The Wheel	Moody Blues
♦ 1957	Sittin' In The Balcony	Eddie Cochran
♦ 1957	Sittin' In The Balcony	Johnny Dee
♦ 1990	Sittin' In The Lap Of Luxury	Louie Louie
♦ 1965	Sitting In The Park	Billy Stewart
♦ 1968	(Sittin' On) The Dock Of The Bay	Otis Redding
♦ 1988	(Sittin' On) The Dock Of The Bay	Michael Bolton
♦ 1996	Sittin' On Top Of The World	Da Brat
♦ 1996	Sittin' Up In My Room	Brandy
♦ 1963	Six Days On The Road	Dave Dudley
♦ 1968	Six Man Band	Association
♦ 1959	Six Nights A Week	Crests
♦ 1967	Six O'Clock	Lovin' Spoonful
♦ 1966	634-5789 (Soulsville U.S.A.)	Wilson Pickett
♦ 1959	16 Candles	Crests
♦ 1960	Sixteen Reasons	Connie Stevens
♦ 1955	Sixteen Tons	Tennessee Ernie Ford
♦ 1982	'65 Love Affair	Paul Davis
♦ 1987	Skeletons	Stevie Wonder
♦ 1974	Skin Tight	Ohio Players
♦ 1968	Skinny Legs And All	Joe Tex
♦ 1958	Skinny Minnie	Bill Haley And His Comets
♦ 1968	Skip A Rope	Henson Cargill
♦ 1975	Sky High	Jigsaw
♦ 1968	Sky Pilot	Eric Burdon & The Animals
♦ 1993	Slam	Onyx
♦ 1964	Slaughter On Tenth Avenue	Ventures
♦ 1986	Sledgehammer	Peter Gabriel
♦ 1960	Sleep	Little Willie John
♦ 1959	Sleep Walk	Santo & Johnny

♦	1985	Sleeping Bag	ZZ Top
♦	1993	Sleeping Satellite	Tasmin Archer
♦	1977	Slide	Slave
♦	1968	Slip Away	Clarence Carter
♦	1978	Slip Slidin' Away	Paul Simon
♦	1975	Slippery When Wet	Commodores
♦	1972	Slippin' Into Darkness	War
♦	1983	Slipping Away	Dave Edmunds
♦	1966	Sloop John B	Beach Boys
♦	1994	Slow And Easy	Zapp & Roger
♦	1993	Slow And Sexy	Shabba Ranks featuring Johnny Gill
♦	1977	Slow Dancin' Don't Turn Me On	Addrisi Brothers
♦	1964	Slow Down	Beatles
♦	1981	Slow Hand	Pointer Sisters
♦	1992	Slow Motion	Color Me Badd
♦	1976	Slow Ride	Foghat
	1962	Slow Twistin'	Chubby Checker
♦	1956	Slow Walk	Sil Austin
♦	1956	Slow Walk	Bill Doggett
♦	1977	Slowdown	John Miles
♦	1970	Sly, Slick, And The Wicked	Lost Generation
♦	1971	Smackwater Jack	Carole King
♦	1972	Small Beginnings	Flash
	1962	Small Sad Sam	Phil McLean
♦	1986	Small Town	John Cougar Mellencamp
♦	1988	Small World	Huey Lewis
♦	1959	Small World	Johnny Mathis
♦	1992	Smells Like Nirvana	Weird Al Yankovic
♦	1992	Smells Like Teen Spirit	Nirvana
♦	1997	Smile	Scarface featuring 2Pac & Johnny P
♦	1969	Smile A Little Smile For Me	Flying Machine
♦	1983	Smile Has Left Your Eyes	Asia
♦	1972	Smilin'	Sly & The Family Stone
♦	1971	Smiling Faces Sometimes	Undisputed Truth
♦	1977	Smoke From A Distant Fire	Sanford/Townsend Band
♦	1959	Smoke Gets In Your Eyes	Platters
♦	1973	Smoke Gets In Your Eyes	Blue Haze
♦	1973	Smoke On The Water	Deep Purple
♦	1960	Smokie (Part 2)	Bill Black's Combo
♦	1987	Smoking Gun	Robert Cray Band
♦	1974	Smokin' In The Boys Room	Brownsville Station
♦	1985	Smokin' In The Boys Room	Motley Crue
♦	1997	Smokin' Me Out	Warren G featuring Ronald Isley
♦	1981	Smoky Mountain Rain	Ronnie Milsap
♦	1962	Smoky Places	Corsairs
♦	1989	Smooth Criminal	Michael Jackson
♦	1985	Smooth Operator	Sade
♦	1959	Smooth Operator	Sarah Vaughan
♦	1985	Smuggler's Blues	Glenn Frey
♦	1968	Snake	Al Wilson
♦	1962	Snap Your Fingers	Joe Henderson
♦	1969	Snatching It Back	Clarence Carter
♦	1967	Snoopy Vs. The Red Baron	Royal Guardsmen
♦	1967	Snoopy's Christmas	Royal Guardsmen
♦	1970	Snowbird	Anne Murray
♦	1989	So Alive	Love And Rockets
♦	1993	So Alone	Men At Large
♦	1984	So Bad	Paul McCartney
♦	1990	So Close	Daryl Hall & John Oates
♦	1983	So Close	Diana Ross
♦	1987	So Emotional	Whitney Houston
♦	1971	So Far Away	Carole King
♦	1986	So Far Away	Dire Straits
♦	1959	So Fine	Fiestas
♦	1979	So Good, So Right	Brenda Russell
	1969	So Good Together	Andy Kim
♦	1969	So I Can Love You	Emotions
♦	1985	So In Love	Orchestral Manoeuvres In The Dark
♦	1977	So Into You	Atlanta Rhythm Section
♦	1961	So Long Baby	Del Shannon
♦	1959	So Many Ways	Brook Benton
♦	1963	So Much In Love	Tymes
♦	1994	So Much In Love	All-4-One
♦	1957	So Rare	Jimmy Dorsey
♦	1960	So Sad (To Watch Good Love Go Bad)	Everly Brothers
♦	1962	So This Is Love	Castells
♦	1958	So Tough	Original Casuals

♦	1973	So Very Hard To Go	Tower Of Power
	1983	So Wrong	Patrick Simmons
♦	1974	So You Are A Star	Hudson Brothers
♦	1967	So You Want To Be A Rock 'N' Roll Star	Byrds
♦	1967	Society's Child	Janis Ian
♦	1967	Sock It To Me Baby!	Mitch Ryder And The Detroit Wheels
♦	1997	Sock It 2 Me	Missy "Misdemeanor" Elliott
	1956	Soft Summer Breeze	Diamonds
♦	1956	Soft Summer Breeze	Eddie Heywood
♦	1964	Softly, As I Leave You	Frank Sinatra
♦	1972	Softly Whispering I Love You	English Congregation
♦	1962	Soldier Boy	Shirelles
♦	1989	Soldier Of Love	Donny Osmond
♦	1985	Solid	Ashford & Simpson
♦	1975	Solitaire	Carpenters
♦	1961	Solitaire	Embers
♦	1983	Solitaire	Laura Branigan
♦	1970	Solitary Man	Neil Diamond
♦	1964	Some Day We're Gonna Love Again	Searchers
♦	1965	Some Enchanted Evening	Jay & The Americans
	1973	Some Guys Have All The Luck	Persuaders
♦	1984	Some Guys Have All The Luck	Rod Stewart
♦	1959	Some Kind-A-Earthquake	Duane Eddy
♦	1983	Some Kind Of Friend	Barry Manilow
♦	1988	Some Kind Of Lover	Jody Watley
♦	1961	Some Kind Of Wonderful	Drifters
♦	1975	Some Kind Of Wonderful	Grand Funk
♦	1985	Some Like It Hot	Power Station
♦	1985	Some Things Are Better Left Unsaid	Daryl Hall & John Oates
♦	1968	Some Things You Never Get Used To	Diana Ross And The Supremes
♦	1968	Some Velvet Morning	Nancy Sinatra & Lee Hazlewood
♦	1985	Somebody	Bryan Adams
♦	1967	Somebody To Love	Jefferson Airplane
♦	1977	Somebody To Love	Queen
♦	1993	Somebody To Love	George Michael And Queen
♦	1958	Somebody Touched Me	Buddy Knox With The Rhythm Orchids
♦	1956	Somebody Up There Likes Me	Perry Como
♦	1982	Somebody's Baby	Jackson Browne
♦	1970	Somebody's Been Sleeping	100 Proof Aged In Soul
♦	1981	Somebody's Knockin'	Terri Gibbs
♦	1986	Somebody's Out There	Triumph
♦	1984	Somebody's Watching Me	Rockwell
♦	1971	Somebody's Watching You	Little Sister
♦	1987	Someday	Glass Tiger
♦	1991	Someday	Mariah Carey
♦	1996	Someday	All-4-One
♦	1972	Someday Never Comes	Creedence Clearwater Revival
♦	1982	Someday, Someway	Marshall Crenshaw
♦	1969	Someday Soon	Judy Collins
♦	1969	Someday We'll Be Together	Diana Ross And The Supremes
♦	1959	Someone	Johnny Mathis
♦	1997	Someone	SWV featuring Puff Daddy
♦	1982	Someone Could Lose A Heart Tonight	Eddie Rabbitt
♦	1975	Someone Saved My Life Tonight	Elton John
♦	1980	Someone That I Used To Love	Natalie Cole
♦	1992	Someone To Hold	Trey Lorenz
♦	1995	Someone To Love	Jon B featuring Babyface
♦	1955	Someone You Love	Nat King Cole
♦	1969	Something	Beatles
♦	1997	Something About The Way You Look Tonight	Elton John
♦	1965	Something About You	Four Tops
♦	1986	Something About You	Level 42
♦	1975	Something Better To Do	Olivia Newton-John
♦	1995	Something 4 Da Honeyz	Montell Jordan
♦	1991	Something Got Me Started	Simply Red
♦	1990	Something Happened On The Way To Heaven	Phil Collins
♦	1976	Something He Can Feel	Aretha Franklin
♦	1991	Something In My Heart	Michel'le
♦	1969	Something In The Air	Thunderclap Newman
♦	1993	Something In Your Eyes	Bell Biv DeVoe
♦	1987	Something Real (Inside Me/Inside You)	Mr. Mister
♦	1987	Something So Strong	Crowded House
♦	1967	Somethin' Stupid	Nancy Sinatra & Frank Sinatra
♦	1990	Something To Believe In	Poison
♦	1991	Something To Talk About	Bonnie Raitt
♦	1970	Something's Burning	Kenny Rogers And The First Edition
♦	1993	Something's Goin' On	UNV

♦	1962	Something's Got A Hold On Me	Etta James
♦	1955	Something's Gotta Give	Sammy Davis Jr.
♦	1955	Something's Gotta Give	McGuire Sisters
♦	1972	Something's Wrong With Me	Austin Roberts
♦	1980	Sometimes A Fantasy	Billy Joel
♦	1992	Sometimes Love Just Ain't Enough	Patty Smyth
♦	1990	Sometimes She Cries	Warrant
♦	1978	Sometimes When We Touch	Dan Hill
♦	1966	Somewhere	Len Barry
	1964	Somewhere	Tymes
♦	1982	Somewhere Down The Road	Barry Manilow
♦	1976	Somewhere In The Night	Helen Reddy
♦	1979	Somewhere In The Night	Barry Manilow
♦	1965	Somewhere In Your Heart	Frank Sinatra
♦	1966	Somewhere My Love	Ray Conniff And The Singers
♦	1987	Somewhere Out There	Linda Ronstadt And James Ingram
♦	1966	Somewhere There's A Someone	Dean Martin
♦	1969	Son-Of-A Preacher Man	Dusty Springfield
♦	1968	Son Of Hickory Holler's Tramp	O.C. Smith
♦	1972	Son Of My Father	Giorgio
	1974	Son Of Sagittarius	Eddie Kendricks
♦	1998	Song For Mama	Boyz II Men
	1970	Song Of Joy	Miguel Rios
♦	1979	Song On The Radio	Al Stewart
♦	1972	Song Sung Blue	Neil Diamond
♦	1978	Songbird	Barbra Streisand
♦	1987	Songbird	Kenny G
♦	1970	Soolaimon (African Trilogy II)	Neil Diamond
♦	1996	Soon As I Get Home	Faith Evans
♦	1971	Sooner Or Later	Grass Roots
♦	1969	Sophisticated Cissy	Meters
♦	1976	Sophisticated Lady (She's A Different Lady)	Natalie Cole
♦	1959	Sorry (I Ran All The Way Home)	Impalas
♦	1977	Sorry Seems To Be The Hardest Word	Elton John
♦	1975	SOS	Abba
♦	1987	Soul City	Partland Brothers
♦	1969	Soul Deep	Box Tops
♦	1967	Soul Finger	Bar-Kays
♦	1985	Soul Kiss	Olivia Newton-John
♦	1968	Soul Limbo	Booker T & The MG's
♦	1973	Soul Makossa	Manu Dibango
♦	1967	Soul Man	Sam & Dave
♦	1979	Soul Man	Blues Brothers
♦	1971	Soul Power (Part 1)	James Brown
♦	1989	Soul Provider	Michael Bolton
♦	1968	Soul Serenade	Willie Mitchell
♦	1969	Soul Shake	Peggy Scott & Jo Jo Benson
♦	1973	Soul Song	Joe Stampley
♦	1993	Soul To Squeeze	Red Hot Chili Peppers
♦	1962	Soul Twist	King Curtis
♦	1969	Soulful Strut	Young-Holt Unlimited
♦	1983	Souls	Rick Springfield
♦	1967	Sound Of Love	Five Americans
♦	1991	Sound Of Your Voice	38 Special
♦	1966	Sounds Of Silence	Simon & Garfunkel
	1963	South Street	Orlons
♦	1975	South's Gonna Do It Again	Charlie Daniels Band
♦	1982	Southern Cross	Crosby, Stills & Nash
♦	1977	Southern Nights	Glen Campbell
♦	1964	Southtown U.S.A.	Dixiebelles
♦	1989	Sowing The Seeds Of Love	Tears For Fears
♦	1983	Space Age Love Song	Flock Of Seagulls
♦	1997	Space Jam	Quad City DJ's
♦	1973	Space Oddity	David Bowie
♦	1973	Space Race	Billy Preston
♦	1972	Spaceman	Nilsson
♦	1985	Spanish Eddie	Laura Branigan
♦	1966	Spanish Eyes	Al Martino
♦	1966	Spanish Flea	Herb Alpert & The Tijuana Brass
♦	1961	Spanish Harlem	Ben E. King
♦	1971	Spanish Harlem	Aretha Franklin
♦	1962	Spanish Lace	Gene McDaniels
♦	1972	Speak To The Sky	Rick Springfield
♦	1969	Special Delivery	1910 Fruitgum Company
♦	1980	Special Lady	Ray, Goodman & Brown
♦	1968	Special Occasion	Smokey Robinson & The Miracles
♦	1956	Speedo	Cadillacs
♦	1962	Speedy Gonzales	Pat Boone
♦	1991	Spend My Life	Slaughter
♦	1991	Spending My Time	Roxette
♦	1997	Spice Up Your Life	Spice Girls
♦	1974	Spiders & Snakes	Jim Stafford
	1986	Spies Like Us	Paul McCartney
♦	1970	Spill The Wine	Eric Burdon & War
♦	1971	Spill The Wine	Isley Brothers
♦	1994	Spin The Black Circle	Pearl Jam
♦	1969	Spinning Wheel	Blood, Sweat & Tears
♦	1966	Spinout	Elvis Presley
♦	1970	Spirit In The Dark	Aretha Franklin
♦	1970	Spirit In The Sky	Norman Greenbaum
♦	1975	Spirit Of The Boogie	Kool & The Gang
♦	1982	Spirits In The Material World	Police
♦	1958	Splish Splash	Bobby Darin
♦	1968	Spooky	Classics IV
♦	1979	Spooky	Atlanta Rhythm Section
♦	1966	Spread It On Thick	Gentrys
♦	1976	Springtime Mama	Henry Gross
♦	1988	Spy In The House Of Love	Was (Not Was)
♦	1976	Squeeze Box	Who
♦	1985	St. Elmo's Fire (Man In Motion)	John Parr
♦	1956	St. Therese Of The Roses	Billy Ward And His Dominoes
♦	1986	Stages	ZZ Top
♦	1959	Stagger Lee	Lloyd Price
♦	1967	Stagger Lee	Wilson Pickett
♦	1971	Stagger Lee	Tommy Roe
♦	1960	Stairway To Heaven	Neil Sedaka
♦	1989	Stand	R.E.M.
♦	1969	Stand!	Sly & The Family Stone
♦	1983	Stand Back	Stevie Nicks
♦	1961	Stand By Me	Ben E. King
♦	1967	Stand By Me	Spyder Turner
♦	1975	Stand By Me	John Lennon
♦	1980	Stand By Me	Mickey Gilley
♦	1986	Stand By Me	Ben E. King
♦	1969	Stand By Your Man	Tammy Wynette
♦	1970	Stand By Your Man	Candi Staton
♦	1976	Stand Tall	Burton Cummings
♦	1993	Stand Up (Kick Love Into Motion)	Def Leppard
♦	1974	Standing At The End Of The Line	Lobo
♦	1967	Standing In The Shadows Of Love	Four Tops
♦	1956	Standing On The Corner	Four Lads
♦	1974	Star	Stealers Wheel
♦	1974	Star Baby	Guess Who
♦	1957	Star Dust	Billy Ward And His Dominoes
♦	1964	Star Dust	Nino Tempo & April Stevens
♦	1977	Star Wars (Main Title)	London Symphony Orchestra
♦	1977	Star Wars Theme/Cantina Band	Meco
♦	1960	Starbright	Johnny Mathis
♦	1997	Staring At The Sun	U2
♦	1992	Stars	Simply Red
	1982	Stars On 45 III	Stars On 45
♦	1981	Start Me Up	Rolling Stones
♦	1957	Start Movin' (In My Direction)	Sal Mineo
♦	1972	Starting All Over Again	Mel And Tim
♦	1984	State Of Shock	Jacksons
♦	1985	State Of The Heart	Rick Springfield
♦	1991	State Of The World	Janet Jackson
♦	1994	Stay	Eternal
♦	1960	Stay	Maurice Williams & The Zodiacs
♦	1964	Stay	Four Seasons
♦	1978	Stay	Jackson Browne
♦	1992	Stay	Shakespear's Sister
♦	1971	Stay Awhile	Bells
♦	1964	Stay Awhile	Dusty Springfield
♦	1994	Stay (I Missed You)	Lisa Loeb & Nine Stories
♦	1968	Stay In My Corner	Dells
♦	1987	Stay The Night	Benjamin Orr
♦	1984	Stay The Night	Chicago
♦	1972	Stay With Me	Faces
♦	1984	Stay With Me Tonight	Jeffrey Osborne
♦	1978	Stayin' Alive	Bee Gees
♦	1961	Stayin' In	Bobby Vee
♦	1988	Staying Together	Debbie Gibson

♦	1964	Steal Away	Jimmy Hughes
♦	1970	Steal Away	Johnnie Taylor
♦	1980	Steal Away	Robbie Dupree
	1981	Steal The Night	Stevie Woods
♦	1993	Steam	Peter Gabriel
♦	1973	Steamroller Blues	Elvis Presley
♦	1990	Steamy Windows	Tina Turner
♦	1962	Steel Guitar And A Glass Of Wine	Paul Anka
♦	1996	Steelo	702
♦	1960	Step By Step	Crests
♦	1981	Step By Step	Eddie Rabbitt
♦	1973	Step By Step	Joe Simon
♦	1990	Step By Step	New Kids On The Block
♦	1997	Step By Step	Whitney Houston
♦	1967	Step Out Of Your Mind	American Breed
♦	1982	Steppin' Out	Joe Jackson
♦	1974	Steppin' Out (Gonna Boogie Tonight)	Tony Orlando & Dawn
♦	1964	Stewball	Peter, Paul & Mary
♦	1986	Stick Around	Julian Lennon
♦	1961	Stick Shift	Duals
♦	1971	Stick Up	Honey Cone
♦	1960	Sticks And Stones	Ray Charles
♦	1963	Still	Bill Anderson
♦	1979	Still	Commodores
♦	1982	Still In Saigon	Charlie Daniels Band
♦	1981	Still Right Here In My Heart	Pure Prairie League
♦	1976	Still The One	Orleans
♦	1978	Still The Same	Bob Seger & The Silver Bullet Band
♦	1982	Still They Ride	Journey
♦	1970	Still Water (Love)	Four Tops
♦	1973	Stir It Up	Johnny Nash
♦	1980	Stomp!	Brothers Johnson
♦	1982	Stone Cold	Rainbow
♦	1991	Stone Cold Gentleman	Ralph Tresvant
♦	1987	Stone Love	Kool & The Gang
♦	1970	Stoned Love	Supremes
♦	1973	Stoned Out Of My Mind	Chi-Lites
♦	1968	Stoned Soul Picnic	Fifth Dimension
♦	1971	Stones	Neil Diamond
♦	1971	Stoney End	Barbra Streisand
♦	1958	Stood Up	Ricky Nelson
♦	1974	Stop And Smell The Roses	Mac Davis
♦	1964	Stop And Think It Over	Dale & Grace
♦	1981	Stop Draggin' My Heart Around
			Stevie Nicks With Tom Petty And The Heartbreakers
♦	1965	Stop In The Name Of Love	Supremes
	1983	Stop In The Name Of Love	Hollies
♦	1971	Stop, Look, Listen (To Your Heart)	Stylistics
♦	1966	Stop Stop Stop	Hollies
	1971	Stop The War Now	Edwin Starr
♦	1962	Stop The Wedding	Etta James
♦	1987	Stop To Love	Luther Vandross
♦	1968	Stormy	Classics IV
♦	1979	Stormy	Santana
♦	1971	Story In Your Eyes	Moody Blues
♦	1958	Story Of My Life	Marty Robbins
♦	1959	Story Of My Love	Conway Twitty
♦	1961	Story Of My Love	Paul Anka
♦	1955	Story Untold	Crew-Cuts
♦	1981	Straight From The Heart	Allman Brothers Band
♦	1983	Straight From The Heart	Bryan Adams
♦	1968	Straight Life	Bobby Goldsboro
♦	1978	Straight On	Heart
♦	1974	Straight Shootin' Woman	Steppenwolf
♦	1991	Straight To Your Heart	Bad English
♦	1989	Straight Up	Paula Abdul
♦	1990	Stranded	Heart
♦	1956	Stranded In The Jungle	Cadets
♦	1956	Stranded In The Jungle	Jayhawks
♦	1988	Strange But True	Times Two
♦	1976	Strange Magic	Electric Light Orchestra
♦	1978	Strange Way	Firefall
♦	1983	Stranger In My House	Ronnie Milsap
♦	1965	Stranger In Town	Del Shannon
♦	1984	Stranger In Town	Toto
♦	1962	Stranger On The Shore	Mr. Acker Bilk
	1962	Stranger On The Shore	Andy Williams

♦	1966	Strangers In The Night	Frank Sinatra
♦	1967	Strawberry Fields Forever	Beatles
♦	1977	Strawberry Letter 23	Brothers Johnson
♦	1968	Strawberry Shortcake	Jay And The Techniques
♦	1983	Stray Cat Strut	Stray Cats
♦	1974	Streak	Ray Stevens
♦	1978	Street Corner Serenade	Wet Willie
♦	1997	Street Dreams	Nas
♦	1968	Street Fighting Man	Rolling Stones
♦	1979	Street Life	Crusaders
♦	1991	Street Of Dreams	Nia Peeples
♦	1976	Street Singin'	Lady Flash
♦	1994	Streets Of Philadelphia	Bruce Springsteen
♦	1991	Strike It Up	Black Box
♦	1960	String Along	Fabian
♦	1963	String Along	Rick Nelson
♦	1962	Stripper	David Rose
♦	1981	Stroke	Billy Squier
♦	1994	Stroke You Up	Changing Faces
♦	1958	Stroll	Diamonds
♦	1995	Strong Enough	Sheryl Crow
	1981	Stronger Than Before	Carole Bayer Sager
♦	1984	Strung Out	Steve Perry
♦	1984	Strut	Sheena Easton
♦	1975	Struttin'	Billy Preston
♦	1962	Stubborn Kind Of Fellow	Marvin Gaye
♦	1973	Stuck In The Middle With You	Stealers Wheel
♦	1960	Stuck On You	Elvis Presley
♦	1984	Stuck On You	Lionel Richie
♦	1986	Stuck With You	Huey Lewis
♦	1978	Stuff Like That	Quincy Jones
♦	1979	Stumblin' In	Suzi Quatro And Chris Norman
♦	1958	Stupid Cupid	Connie Francis
♦	1996	Stupid Girl	Garbage
♦	1972	Suavecito	Malo
♦	1965	Subterranean Homesick Blues	Bob Dylan
♦	1964	Such A Night	Elvis Presley
♦	1979	Such A Woman	Tycoon
♦	1965	(Such An) Easy Question	Elvis Presley
♦	1985	Suddenly	Billy Ocean
♦	1980	Suddenly	Olivia Newton-John And Cliff Richard
♦	1983	Suddenly Last Summer	Motels
♦	1955	Suddenly There's A Valley	Gogi Grant
♦	1955	Suddenly There's A Valley	Julius LaRosa
♦	1955	Suddenly There's A Valley	Jo Stafford
♦	1968	Suddenly You Love Me	Tremeloes
♦	1974	Sugar Baby Love	Rubettes
♦	1972	Sugar Daddy	Jackson Five
♦	1989	Sugar Daddy	Thompson Twins
♦	1984	Sugar Don't Bite	Sam Harris
♦	1965	Sugar Dumpling	Sam Cooke
♦	1987	Sugar Free	Wa Wa Nee
♦	1995	Sugar Hill	AZ
♦	1964	Sugar Lips	Al Hirt
♦	1958	Sugar Moon	Pat Boone
♦	1969	Sugar On Sunday	Clique
♦	1963	Sugar Shack	Jimmy Gilmer & The Fireballs
♦	1969	Sugar Sugar	Archies
♦	1970	Sugar Sugar	Wilson Pickett
♦	1967	Sugar Town	Nancy Sinatra
♦	1985	Sugar Walls	Sheena Easton
♦	1958	Sugartime	McGuire Sisters
♦	1990	Suicide Blonde	Inxs
♦	1969	Suite: Judy Blue Eyes	Crosby, Stills & Nash
♦	1963	Sukiyaki	Kyu Sakamoto
♦	1981	Sukiyaki	Taste Of Honey
♦	1995	Sukiyaki	4 P.M. (For Positive Music)
♦	1979	Sultans Of Swing	Dire Straits
♦	1976	Summer	War
♦	1972	Summer Breeze	Seals & Crofts
♦	1966	Summer In The City	Lovin' Spoonful
♦	1978	Summer Nights	John Travolta And Olivia Newton-John
♦	1965	Summer Nights	Marianne Faithfull
♦	1985	Summer Of '69	Bryan Adams
♦	1990	Summer Rain	Belinda Carlisle
♦	1968	Summer Rain	Johnny Rivers
♦	1966	Summer Samba (So Nice)	Walter Wanderly

♦ 1971	Summer Sand	Dawn
1960	Summer Set	Monty Kelly
♦ 1964	Summer Song	Chad & Jeremy
♦ 1973	Summer (The First Time)	Bobby Goldsboro
♦ 1966	Summer Wind	Frank Sinatra
♦ 1960	Summer's Gone	Paul Anka
♦ 1966	Summertime	Billy Stewart
♦ 1991	Summertime	D.J. Jazzy Jeff & The Fresh Prince
♦ 1958	Summertime Blues	Eddie Cochran
♦ 1968	Summertime Blues	Blue Cheer
♦ 1970	Summertime Blues	Who
♦ 1958	Summertime, Summertime	Jamies
♦ 1966	Sun Ain't Gonna Shine (Anymore)	Walker Brothers
♦ 1986	Sun Always Shines On TV	A-Ha
♦ 1985	Sun City	Artists United Against Apartheid
♦ 1965	Sunday And Me	Jay & The Americans
♦ 1967	Sunday For Tea	Peter And Gordon
♦ 1968	Sunday Mornin'	Spanky And Our Gang
1969	Sunday Mornin'	Oliver
♦ 1967	Sunday Will Never Be The Same	Spanky And Our Gang
♦ 1974	Sundown	Gordon Lightfoot
♦ 1977	Sunflower	Glen Campbell
♦ 1984	Sunglasses At Night	Corey Hart
♦ 1966	Sunny	Bobby Hebb
♦ 1966	Sunny Afternoon	Kinks
♦ 1997	Sunny Came Home	Shawn Colvin
♦ 1972	Sunny Days	Lighthouse
♦ 1976	Sunrise	Eric Carmen
♦ 1985	Sunset Grill	Don Henley
♦ 1989	Sunshine	Dino
♦ 1972	Sunshine	Jonathan Edwards
♦ 1967	Sunshine Girl	Parade
♦ 1965	Sunshine, Lollipops And Rainbows	Lesley Gore
♦ 1968	Sunshine Of Your Love	Cream
♦ 1974	Sunshine On My Shoulders	John Denver
♦ 1966	Sunshine Superman	Donovan
♦ 1970	Super Bad (Parts 1 & 2)	James Brown
♦ 1981	Super Freak (Part 1)	Rick James
♦ 1973	Superfly	Curtis Mayfield
♦ 1973	Superman	Donna Fargo
1979	Superman	Herbie Mann
♦ 1975	Supernatural Thing (Part 1)	Ben E. King
♦ 1988	Supersonic	J.J. Fad
♦ 1971	Superstar	Carpenters
♦ 1971	Superstar	Murray Head
1976	Superstar	Paul Davis
♦ 1971	Superstar (Remember How You Got Where You Are)	Temptations
♦ 1973	Superstition	Stevie Wonder
♦ 1988	Superstitious	Europe
♦ 1989	Superwoman	Karyn White
♦ 1972	Superwoman (Where Were You When I Needed You)	Stevie Wonder
♦ 1974	Sure As I'm Sittin' Here	Three Dog Night
♦ 1966	Sure Gonna Miss Her	Gary Lewis And The Playboys
♦ 1963	Surf City	Jan & Dean
♦ 1963	Surfer Girl	Beach Boys
♦ 1962	Surfer's Stomp	Marketts
♦ 1964	Surfin' Bird	Trashmen
♦ 1962	Surfin' Safari	Beach Boys
♦ 1963	Surfin' U.S.A.	Beach Boys
♦ 1974	Surfin' U.S.A.	Beach Boys
♦ 1977	Surfin' U.S.A.	Leif Garrett
♦ 1961	Surrender	Elvis Presley
♦ 1989	Surrender To Me	Ann Wilson And Robin Zander
♦ 1968	Susan	Buckinghams
♦ 1958	Susie Darlin'	Robin Luke
1962	Susie Darlin'	Tommy Roe
♦ 1964	Suspicion	Terry Stafford
♦ 1979	Suspicions	Eddie Rabbitt
♦ 1969	Suspicious Minds	Elvis Presley
♦ 1985	Sussudio	Phil Collins
♦ 1986	Suzanne	Journey
♦ 1957	Suzie-Q	Dale Hawkins
♦ 1968	Suzie Q (Part 1)	Creedence Clearwater Revival
♦ 1973	Swamp Witch	Jim Stafford
1960	Sway	Bobby Rydell
♦ 1977	Swayin' To The Music (Slow Dancin')	Johnny Rivers
♦ 1975	Swearin' To God	Frankie Valli

♦ 1993	Sweat (A La La La La Song)	Inner Circle
♦ 1955	Sweet And Gentle	Alan Dale
♦ 1955	Sweet And Gentle	Georgia Gibbs
♦ 1971	Sweet And Innocent	Donny Osmond
♦ 1981	Sweet Baby	Stanley Clarke/George Duke
♦ 1968	Sweet Blindness	Fifth Dimension
♦ 1969	Sweet Caroline (Good Times Never Seemed So Good)	Neil Diamond
♦ 1973	Sweet Charlie Babe	Jackie Moore
♦ 1969	Sweet Cherry Wine	Tommy James And The Shondells
♦ 1988	Sweet Child O' Mine	Guns N' Roses
♦ 1971	Sweet City Woman	Stampeders
♦ 1969	Sweet Cream Ladies, Forward March	Box Tops
♦ 1982	Sweet Dreams	Air Supply
♦ 1996	Sweet Dreams	La Bouche
♦ 1966	Sweet Dreams	Tommy McLain
♦ 1983	Sweet Dreams (Are Made Of This)	Eurythmics
♦ 1975	Sweet Emotion	Aerosmith
♦ 1986	Sweet Freedom	Michael McDonald
♦ 1971	Sweet Hitch-Hiker	Creedence Clearwater Revival
♦ 1974	Sweet Home Alabama	Lynyrd Skynyrd
♦ 1968	Sweet Inspiration	Sweet Inspirations
♦ 1978	Sweet Life	Paul Davis
♦ 1958	Sweet Little Sixteen	Chuck Berry
♦ 1986	Sweet Love	Anita Baker
♦ 1976	Sweet Love	Commodores
♦ 1971	Sweet Mary	Wadsworth Mansion
♦ 1960	Sweet Nothin's	Brenda Lee
♦ 1956	Sweet Old Fashioned Girl	Teresa Brewer
♦ 1966	Sweet Pea	Tommy Roe
♦ 1994	Sweet Potatoe Pie	Domino
♦ 1972	Sweet Seasons	Carole King
♦ 1987	Sweet Sixteen	Billy Idol
♦ 1967	Sweet Soul Music	Arthur Conley
♦ 1975	Sweet Sticky Thing	Ohio Players
♦ 1972	Sweet Surrender	Bread
♦ 1975	Sweet Surrender	John Denver
♦ 1968	(Sweet Sweet Baby) Since You've Been Gone	Aretha Franklin
♦ 1966	Sweet Talkin' Guy	Chiffons
♦ 1978	Sweet Talkin' Woman	Electric Light Orchestra
♦ 1976	Sweet Thing	Rufus featuring Chaka Khan
♦ 1993	Sweet Thing	Mary J. Blige
♦ 1982	Sweet Time	REO Speedwagon
♦ 1973	Sweet Understanding Love	Four Tops
1964	Sweet William	Millie Small
♦ 1966	Sweet Woman Like You	Joe Tex
♦ 1959	Sweeter Than You	Ricky Nelson
♦ 1995	Sweetest Days	Vanessa Williams
♦ 1986	Sweetest Taboo	Sade
♦ 1982	Sweetest Thing (I've Ever Known)	Juice Newton
♦ 1967	Sweetest Thing This Side Of Heaven	Chris Bartley
♦ 1981	Sweetheart	Franke & The Knockouts
♦ 1961	Sweets For My Sweet	Drifters
♦ 1984	Swept Away	Diana Ross
♦ 1990	Swing The Mood	Jive Bunny And The Mastermixers
♦ 1983	Swingin'	John Anderson
♦ 1963	Swinging On A Star	Big Dee Irwin
♦ 1962	Swingin' Safari	Billy Vaughn
1960	Swingin' School	Bobby Rydell
♦ 1958	Swingin' Shepherd Blues	Moe Koffman Quartette
1958	Swingin' Shepherd Blues	Johnny Pate Quintet
♦ 1978	Swingtown	Steve Miller Band
♦ 1961	Switch-A-Roo	Hank Ballard And The Midnighters
♦ 1972	Sylvia's Mother	Dr. Hook And The Medicine Show
♦ 1988	Symptoms Of True Love	Tracie Spencer
♦ 1983	Synchronicity II	Police

T

♦ 1992	T.L.C.	Linear
♦ 1960	T.L.C. Tender Love And Care	Jimmie Rodgers
♦ 1974	TSOP (The Sound Of Philadelphia)	MFSB featuring The Three Degrees
♦ 1960	Ta Ta	Clyde McPhatter
♦ 1982	Tainted Love	Soft Cell
♦ 1995	Take A Bow	Madonna
♦ 1978	Take A Chance On Me	Abba

731

♦ 1969	Take A Letter Maria	R.B. Greaves
♦ 1980	Take A Little Rhythm	Ali Thomson
♦ 1970	Take A Look Around	Smith
♦ 1972	Take A Look Around	Temptations
♦ 1959	Take A Message To Mary	Everly Brothers
♦ 1969	Take Care Of Your Homework	Johnnie Taylor
♦ 1961	Take Five	Dave Brubeck Quartet
1961	Take Good Care Of Her	Adam Wade
♦ 1974	Take Good Care Of Her	Elvis Presley
♦ 1961	Take Good Care Of My Baby	Bobby Vee
♦ 1968	Take Good Care Of My Baby	Bobby Vinton
♦ 1982	Take It Away	Paul McCartney
1986	Take It Easy	Andy Taylor
♦ 1972	Take It Easy	Eagles
♦ 1982	Take It Easy On Me	Little River Band
♦ 1976	Take It Like A Man	Bachman-Turner Overdrive
♦ 1981	Take It On The Run	REO Speedwagon
♦ 1976	Take It To The Limit	Eagles
♦ 1997	Take It To The Streets	Rampage featuring Billy Lawrence
♦ 1965	Take Me Back	Little Anthony And The Imperials
♦ 1982	Take Me Down	Alabama
♦ 1979	Take Me Home	Cher
♦ 1986	Take Me Home	Phil Collins
♦ 1971	Take Me Home, Country Roads	John Denver
♦ 1986	Take Me Home Tonight	Eddie Money
♦ 1975	Take Me In You Arms (Rock Me)	Doobie Brothers
♦ 1983	Take Me To Heart	Quarterflash
♦ 1979	Take Me To The River	Talking Heads
♦ 1985	Take Me With U	Prince And The Revolution
♦ 1986	Take My Breath Away	Berlin
♦ 1981	Take My Heart	Kool & The Gang
♦ 1982	Take Off	Bob & Doug McKenzie
♦ 1985	Take On Me	A-Ha
♦ 1979	Take The Long Way Home	Supertramp
♦ 1976	Take The Money And Run	Steve Miller
♦ 1963	Take These Chains From My Heart	Ray Charles
♦ 1992	Take This Heart	Richard Marx
♦ 1966	Take This Heart Of Mine	Marvin Gaye
♦ 1992	Take Time	Chris Walker
♦ 1968	Take Time To Know Her	Percy Sledge
♦ 1980	Take Your Time (Do It Right) Part 1	S.O.S. Band
♦ 1986	Taken In	Mike + The Mechanics
♦ 1974	Takin' Care Of Business	Bachman-Turner Overdrive
♦ 1976	Takin' It To The Streets	Doobie Brothers
♦ 1964	Talk Back Trembling Lips	Johnny Tillotson
♦ 1987	Talk Dirty To Me	Poison
♦ 1989	Talk It Over	Grayson Hugh
♦ 1966	Talk Talk	Music Machine
♦ 1960	Talk That Talk	Jackie Wilson
♦ 1987	Talk To Me	Chico DeBarge
♦ 1959	Talk To Me	Frank Sinatra
♦ 1986	Talk To Me	Stevie Nicks
1958	Talk To Me	Little Willie John
1963	Talk To Me	Sunny & The Sunglows
♦ 1964	Talking About My Baby	Impressions
♦ 1978	Talking In Your Sleep	Crystal Gayle
♦ 1984	Talking In Your Sleep	Romantics
♦ 1972	Talking Loud And Saying Nothing (Part 1)	James Brown
1957	Talkin' To The Blues	Jim Lowe
♦ 1988	Tall Cool One	Robert Plant
♦ 1959	Tall Cool One	Wailers
♦ 1959	Tall Paul	Annette
♦ 1959	Tallahassee Lassie	Freddy Cannon
♦ 1957	Tammy	Ames Brothers
♦ 1957	Tammy	Debbie Reynolds
♦ 1976	Tangerine	Salsoul Orchestra
♦ 1975	Tangled Up In Blue	Bob Dylan
1966	Tar And Cement	Verdelle Smith
♦ 1986	Tarzan Boy	Baltimora
♦ 1965	Taste Of Honey	Herb Alpert & The Tijuana Brass
1972	Taurus	Dennis Coffey And The Detroit Guitar Band
♦ 1972	Taxi	Harry Chapin
♦ 1958	Tea For Two Cha Cha Cha	Tommy Dorsey Orchestra Starring Warren Covington
♦ 1962	Teach Me Tonight	George Maharis
♦ 1970	Teach Your Children	Crosby, Stills, Nash & Young

♦ 1984	Teacher Teacher	38 Special
♦ 1958	Teacher, Teacher	Johnny Mathis
♦ 1961	Tear	Gene McDaniels
♦ 1960	Tear Drop	Santo & Johnny
♦ 1957	Tear Drops	Lee Andrews And The Hearts
♦ 1956	Tear Fell	Teresa Brewer
♦ 1961	Tear Of The Year	Jackie Wilson
♦ 1976	Tear The Roof Off The Sucker (Give Up The Funk)	Parliament
♦ 1984	Tears	John Waite
♦ 1964	Tears And Roses	Al Martino
♦ 1992	Tears In Heaven	Eric Clapton
♦ 1970	Tears Of A Clown	Smokey Robinson & The Miracles
♦ 1958	Tears On My Pillow	Little Anthony And The Imperials
1959	Teasin'	Quaker City Boys
♦ 1960	Teddy	Connie Francis
♦ 1976	Teddy Bear	Red Sovine
♦ 1973	Teddy Bear Song	Barbara Fairchild
♦ 1957	Teen-Age Crush	Tommy Sands
♦ 1962	Teen Age Idol	Rick Nelson
♦ 1956	Teen Age Prayer	Gloria Mann
♦ 1956	Teen Age Prayer	Gale Storm
♦ 1960	Teen Angel	Mark Dinning
♦ 1959	Teen Beat	Sandy Nelson
♦ 1964	Teen Beat '65	Sandy Nelson
♦ 1959	Teen Commandments	Paul Anka-George Hamilton IV-Johnny Nash
♦ 1959	Teenager In Love	Dion & The Belmonts
♦ 1957	Teenager's Romance	Ricky Nelson
♦ 1983	Telefone (Long Distance Love Affair)	Sheena Easton
♦ 1977	Telephone Line	Electric Light Orchestra
♦ 1977	Telephone Man	Meri Wilson
♦ 1983	Tell Her About It	Billy Joel
♦ 1974	Tell Her Love Has Felt The Need	Eddie Kendricks
♦ 1965	Tell Her No	Zombies
♦ 1983	Tell Her No	Juice Newton
♦ 1974	Tell Her She's Lovely	El Chicano
♦ 1963	Tell Him	Exciters
♦ 1959	Tell Him No	Travis & Bob
♦ 1970	Tell It All Brother	Kenny Rogers And The First Edition
♦ 1967	Tell It Like It Is	Aaron Neville
♦ 1981	Tell It Like It Is	Heart
♦ 1964	Tell It On The Mountain	Peter, Paul & Mary
♦ 1988	Tell It To My Heart	Taylor Dayne
♦ 1967	Tell It To The Rain	Four Seasons
♦ 1960	Tell Laura I Love Her	Ray Peterson
♦ 1968	Tell Mama	Etta James
♦ 1962	Tell Me	Dick And DeeDee
♦ 1995	Tell Me	Groove Theory
♦ 1996	Tell Me	Dru Hill
1974	Tell Me A Lie	Sami Jo
♦ 1990	Tell Me Something	Indecent Obsession
♦ 1974	Tell Me Something Good	Rufus
♦ 1967	Tell Me To My Face	Keith
♦ 1982	Tell Me Tomorrow (Part 1)	Smokey Robinson
♦ 1992	Tell Me What You Want Me To Do	Tevin Campbell
♦ 1995	Tell Me When	Human League
♦ 1961	Tell Me Why	Belmonts
♦ 1964	Tell Me Why	Bobby Vinton
♦ 1966	Tell Me Why	Elvis Presley
♦ 1990	Tell Me Why	Expose
♦ 1964	Tell Me (You're Coming Back)	Rolling Stones
♦ 1962	Telstar	Tornadoes
♦ 1991	Temptation	Corina
♦ 1961	Temptation	Everly Brothers
♦ 1971	Temptation Eyes	Grass Roots
♦ 1958	Ten Commandments Of Love	Moonglows
♦ 1965	10 Little Bottles	Johnny Bond
♦ 1984	10-9-8	Face To Face
♦ 1983	Tender Is The Night	Jackson Browne
♦ 1986	Tender Love	Force M.D.'s
♦ 1990	Tender Lover	Babyface
♦ 1985	Tender Years	John Cafferty & The Beaver Brown Band
♦ 1961	Tenderly	Bert Kaempfert
♦ 1985	Tenderness	General Public
♦ 1992	Tennessee	Arrested Development
♦ 1970	Tennessee Bird Walk	Jack Blanchard & Misty Morgan
1964	Tennessee Waltz	Sam Cooke

733

♦ 1984 Think Of Laura...Christopher Cross
♦ 1961 Think Twice...Brook Benton
♦ 1992 Thinkin' Back...Color Me Badd
♦ 1973 Thinking Of You.................................Loggins And Messina
♦ 1989 Thinking Of You...Sa-Fire
♦ 1997 Thinking Of You.................................Tony! Toni! Tone!
♦ 1994 Thinkin' Problem...David Ball
  1975 Third Rate Romance.................................Amazing Rhythm Aces
♦ 1980 Third Time Lucky (First Time I Was A Fool).................... Foghat
♦ 1997 Thirty-Three.................................Smashing Pumpkins
♦ 1995 This Ain't A Love Song.................................Bon Jovi
♦ 1960 This Bitter Earth.................................Dinah Washington
♦ 1986 This Could Be The Night.................................Loverboy
♦ 1994 This D.J..Warren G
♦ 1965 This Diamond Ring.................Gary Lewis And The Playboys
♦ 1966 This Door Swings Both Ways.................Herman's Hermits
♦ 1960 This Friendly World...Fabian
♦ 1969 This Girl Is A Woman Now.............Gary Puckett And The Union Gap
♦ 1969 This Girl's In Love With You.................Dionne Warwick
♦ 1968 This Guy's In Love With You.................Herb Alpert
  1974 This Heart.................................Gene Redding
♦ 1991 This House.................................Tracie Spencer
♦ 1995 This House Is Not A Home.................................Rembrandts
♦ 1959 This I Swear.................................Skyliners
♦ 1996 This Is For The Lover In You.................................Babyface
♦ 1995 This Is How We Do It.................................Montell Jordan
♦ 1980 This Is It.................................Kenny Loggins
♦ 1978 This Is Love.................................Paul Anka
♦ 1969 This Is My Country.................................Impressions
♦ 1967 This Is My Song.................................Petula Clark
♦ 1985 This Is Not America.................David Bowie/Pat Metheny Group
♦ 1990 This Is The Right Time.................................Lisa Stansfield
♦ 1987 This Is The Time.................................Billy Joel
♦ 1996 This Is Your Night.................................Amber
♦ 1965 This Little Bird.................................Marianne Faithfull
♦ 1995 This Little Game We Play.................Subway featuring 702
♦ 1963 This Little Girl.................................Dion
♦ 1981 This Little Girl.................................Gary U.S. Bonds
♦ 1958 This Little Girl Of Mine.................................Everly Brothers
♦ 1958 This Little Girl's Gone Rockin'.................................Ruth Brown
♦ 1960 This Magic Moment.................................Drifters
♦ 1969 This Magic Moment.................Jay & The Americans
♦ 1982 This Man Is Mine.................................Heart
♦ 1976 This Masquerade.................................George Benson
♦ 1979 This Night Won't Last Forever.................Michael Johnson
♦ 1966 This Old Heart Of Mine (Is Weak For You).................Isley Brothers
♦ 1990 This Old Heart Of Mine.................Rod Stewart With Ronald Isley
♦ 1989 This One's For The Children.................New Kids On The Block
♦ 1976 This One's For You.................................Barry Manilow
♦ 1959 This Should Go On Forever.................................Rod Bernard
♦ 1977 This Song.................................George Harrison
♦ 1983 This Time.................................Bryan Adams
♦ 1980 This Time.................................John Cougar
♦ 1961 This Time.................................Troy Shondell
♦ 1989 This Time I Know It's For Real.................................Donna Summer
♦ 1978 This Time I'm In It For Love.................................Player
♦ 1992 This Used To Be My Playground.................................Madonna
♦ 1975 This Will Be.................................Natalie Cole
♦ 1984 This Woman.................................Kenny Rogers
♦ 1972 This World.................................Staple Singers
♦ 1963 Those Lazy Hazy Crazy Days Of Summer.................Nat King Cole
♦ 1961 Those Oldies But Goodies (Remind Me Of You).................
  ....Little Caesar And The Romans
♦ 1968 Those Were The Days.................................Mary Hopkin
♦ 1965 Thou Shalt Not Steal.................................Dick And DeeDee
♦ 1992 Thought I'd Died And Gone To Heaven.................Bryan Adams
♦ 1956 Thousand Miles Away.................................Heartbeats
♦ 1960 Thousand Stars.................Kathy Young With The Innocents
♦ 1991 3 A.M. Eternal.................................KLF
♦ 1959 Three Bells.................................Browns
♦ 1993 Three Little Pigs.................................Green Jello
♦ 1960 Three Nights A Week.................................Fats Domino
♦ 1965 Three O'Clock In The Morning.................Bert Kaempfert
♦ 1974 Three Ring Circus.................................Blue Magic
  1959 Three Stars.................................Tommy Dee
♦ 1978 Three Times A Lady.................................Commodores

♦ 1980 Three Times In Love.................................Tommy James
♦ 1964 Three Window Coupe.................................Rip Chords
♦ 1970 Thrill Is Gone.................................B.B. King
♦ 1984 Thriller.................................Michael Jackson
♦ 1989 Through The Storm.................Aretha Franklin And Elton John
♦ 1982 Through The Years.................................Kenny Rogers
♦ 1986 Throwing It All Away.................................Genesis
♦ 1994 Thuggish Ruggish Bone.................Bone Thugs N Harmony
♦ 1972 Thunder And Lightning.................................Chi Coltrane
♦ 1977 Thunder In My Heart.................................Leo Sayer
♦ 1977 Thunder Island.................................Jay Ferguson
♦ 1966 Thunderball.................................Tom Jones
♦ 1990 Tic-Tac-Toe.................................Kyper
♦ 1965 Ticket To Ride.................................Beatles
♦ 1981 Tide Is High.................................Blondie
♦ 1973 Tie A Yellow Ribbon Round The Old Oak Tree.................
  ....Dawn featuring Tony Orlando
♦ 1963 Tie Me Kangaroo Down, Sport.................................Rolf Harris
♦ 1960 Ties That Bind.................................Brook Benton
♦ 1959 Tiger.................................Fabian
♦ 1972 Tight Rope.................................Leon Russell
♦ 1968 Tighten Up.................Archie Bell & The Drells
♦ 1970 Tighter, Tighter.................Alive And Kicking
♦ 1959 Tijuana Jail.................................Kingston Trio
♦ 1996 Til I Hear It From You.................................Gin Blossoms
♦ 1959 ('Til) I Kissed You.................................Everly Brothers
♦ 1985 'Til My Baby Comes Home.................Luther Vandross
♦ 1975 Til The World Ends.................................Three Dog Night
♦ 1995 'Til You Do Me Right.................................After 7
♦ 1957 Till.................................Roger Williams
♦ 1961 Till.................................Angels
♦ 1968 Till.................................Vogues
♦ 1971 Till.................................Tom Jones
  1962 Till Death Do Us Part.................................Bob Braun
♦ 1988 Till I Loved You.................Barbra Streisand And Don Johnson
♦ 1963 Till Then.................................Classics
  1959 Till There Was You.................................Anita Bryant
♦ 1981 Time.................................Alan Parsons Project
♦ 1996 Time.................Hootie & The Blowfish
♦ 1966 Time After Time.................................Chris Montez
♦ 1984 Time After Time.................................Cyndi Lauper
♦ 1993 Time And Chance.................................Color Me Badd
♦ 1988 Time And Tide.................................Basia
♦ 1983 Time (Clock Of The Heart).................................Culture Club
♦ 1990 Time For Letting Go.................................Jude Cole
♦ 1968 Time For Livin'.................................Association
  1974 Time For Livin'.................Sly & The Family Stone
♦ 1968 Time Has Come Today.................Chambers Brothers
♦ 1974 Time In A Bottle.................................Jim Croce
♦ 1964 Time Is On My Side.................................Rolling Stones
♦ 1969 Time Is Tight.................Booker T & The MG's
♦ 1981 Time Is Time.................................Andy Gibb
♦ 1991 Time, Love And Tenderness.................Michael Bolton
♦ 1969 Time Of The Season.................................Zombies
♦ 1981 Time Out Of Mind.................................Steely Dan
♦ 1978 Time Passages.................................Al Stewart
♦ 1973 Time To Get Down.................................O'Jays
♦ 1984 Time Will Reveal.................................DeBarge
♦ 1966 Time Won't Let Me.................................Outsiders
♦ 1976 Times Of Your Life.................................Paul Anka
♦ 1971 Timothy.................................Buoys
♦ 1974 Tin Man.................................America
♦ 1955 Tina Marie.................................Perry Como
♦ 1972 Tiny Dancer.................................Elton John
♦ 1966 Tip Of My Fingers.................................Eddy Arnold
♦ 1968 Tip-Toe Thru' The Tulips With Me.................................Tiny Tim
♦ 1971 Tired Of Being Alone.................................Al Green
♦ 1980 Tired Of Toein' The Line.................................Rocky Burnette
♦ 1965 Tired Of Waiting For You.................................Kinks
♦ 1962 To A Sleeping Beauty.................................Jimmy Dean
♦ 1984 To All The Girls I've Loved Before.................Julio Iglesias & Willie Nelson
♦ 1986 To Be A Lover.................................Billy Idol
♦ 1958 To Be Loved.................................Jackie Wilson
♦ 1992 To Be With You.................................Mr. Big
♦ 1960 To Each His Own.................................Platters
♦ 1968 To Give (The Reason I Live).................................Frankie Valli

♦ 1958	To Know Him, Is To Love Him	Teddy Bears
♦ 1965	To Know You Is To Love You	Peter And Gordon
♦ 1969	To Know You Is To Love You	Bobby Vinton
♦ 1973	To Know You Is To Love You	B.B. King
♦ 1985	To Live And Die In L.A.	Wang Chung
♦ 1967	To Love Somebody	Bee Gees
♦ 1993	To Love Somebody	Michael Bolton
♦ 1967	To Sir With Love	Lulu
♦ 1969	To Susan On The West Coast Waiting	Donovan
♦ 1957	To The Aisle	Five Satins
♦ 1975	To The Door Of The Sun (Alle Porte Del Sole)	Al Martino
♦ 1956	To The Ends Of The Earth	Nat King Cole
♦ 1997	To The Moon And Back	Savage Garden
1956	To You My Love	Nick Noble
♦ 1971	Toast And Marmalade For Tea	Tin Tin
♦ 1964	Tobacco Road	Nashville Teens
♦ 1964	Today	New Christy Minstrels
♦ 1963	(Today I Met) The Boy I'm Gonna Marry	Darlene Love
♦ 1976	Today's The Day	America
♦ 1961	Together	Connie Francis
♦ 1981	Together	Tierra
♦ 1966	Together Again	Ray Charles
♦ 1998	Together Again	Janet Jackson
♦ 1988	Together Forever	Rick Astley
♦ 1972	Together Let's Find Love	Fifth Dimension
♦ 1960	Togetherness	Frankie Avalon
♦ 1963	Tom Cat	Rooftop Singers
♦ 1958	Tom Dooley	Kingston Trio
♦ 1990	Tom's Diner	D.N.A. featuring Suzanne Vega
1959	Tomboy	Perry Como
♦ 1968	Tomorrow	Strawberry Alarm Clock
♦ 1986	Tomorrow Doesn't Matter Tonight	Starship
♦ 1988	Tomorrow People	Ziggy Marley
♦ 1961	Tonight	Ferrante & Teicher
♦ 1984	Tonight	Kool & The Gang
♦ 1990	Tonight	New Kids On The Block
♦ 1961	Tonight (Could Be The Night)	Velvets
♦ 1983	Tonight, I Celebrate My Love	Peabo Bryson/Roberta Flack
♦ 1961	Tonight I Fell In Love	Tokens
♦ 1982	Tonight I'm Yours (Don't Hurt Me)	Rod Stewart
♦ 1961	Tonight My Love, Tonight	Paul Anka
♦ 1986	Tonight She Comes	Cars
♦ 1996	Tonight, Tonight	Smashing Pumpkins
♦ 1987	Tonight, Tonight, Tonight	Genesis
♦ 1956	Tonight You Belong To Me	Patience & Prudence
♦ 1956	Tonight You Belong To Me	Lawrence Welk & The Lennon Sisters
♦ 1996	Tonight's Tha Night	Kris Kross
♦ 1960	Tonight's The Night	Shirelles
♦ 1965	Tonight's The Night	Solomon Burke
♦ 1976	Tonight's The Night (Gonna Be Alright)	Rod Stewart
♦ 1969	Too Busy Thinking About My Baby	Marvin Gaye
♦ 1992	Too Funky	George Michael
♦ 1997	Too Gone, Too Long	En Vogue
♦ 1996	Too Hot	Coolio
♦ 1980	Too Hot	Kool & The Gang
♦ 1978	Too Hot Ta Trot	Commodores
♦ 1985	Too Late For Goodbyes	Julian Lennon
♦ 1990	Too Late To Say Goodbye	Richard Marx
♦ 1972	Too Late To Turn Back Now	Cornelius Brothers & Sister Rose
♦ 1992	2 Legit 2 Quit	Hammer
♦ 1965	Too Many Fish In The Sea	Marvelettes
♦ 1967	Too Many Fish In The Sea & Three Little Fishes	Mitch Ryder And The Detroit Wheels
♦ 1965	Too Many Rivers	Brenda Lee
♦ 1991	Too Many Walls	Cathy Dennis
♦ 1957	Too Much	Elvis Presley
♦ 1978	Too Much Heaven	Bee Gees
♦ 1967	Too Much Of Nothing	Peter, Paul & Mary
♦ 1992	Too Much Passion	Smithereens
♦ 1968	Too Much Talk	Paul Revere And The Raiders
♦ 1960	Too Much Tequila	Champs
♦ 1981	Too Much Time On My Hands	Styx
♦ 1978	Too Much, Too Little, Too Late	Johnny Mathis/Deniece Williams
♦ 1983	Too Shy	Kajagoogoo
♦ 1981	Too Tight	Con Funk Shun
♦ 1969	Too Weak To Fight	Clarence Carter
♦ 1972	Too Young	Donny Osmond

1956	Too Young To Go Steady	Nat King Cole
♦ 1978	Took The Last Train	David Gates
♦ 1995	Tootsee Roll	69 Boyz
♦ 1973	Top Of The World	Carpenters
♦ 1991	Top Of The World	Van Halen
♦ 1958	Topsy II	Cozy Cole
♦ 1958	Torero	Renato Carosone
♦ 1958	Torero	Julius LaRosa
♦ 1977	Torn Between Two Lovers	Mary MacGregor
♦ 1959	Torquay	Fireballs
♦ 1984	Torture	Jacksons
♦ 1962	Torture	Kris Jensen
♦ 1961	Tossin' And Turnin'	Bobby Lewis
♦ 1983	Total Eclipse Of The Heart	Bonnie Tyler
♦ 1995	Total Eclipse Of The Heart	Nicki French
♦ 1974	Touch A Hand, Make A Friend	Staple Singers
♦ 1980	Touch And Go	Cars
♦ 1969	Touch Me	Doors
1974	Touch Me	Fancy
♦ 1991	Touch Me (All Night Long)	Cathy Dennis
♦ 1987	Touch Me (I Want Your Body)	Samantha Fox
♦ 1973	Touch Me In The Morning	Diana Ross
♦ 1996	Touch Me, Tease Me	Case featuring Foxy Brown
♦ 1981	Touch Me When We're Dancing	Carpenters
♦ 1996	Touch Myself	T-Boz
♦ 1987	Touch Of Grey	Grateful Dead
♦ 1985	Tough All Over	John Cafferty And The Beaver Brown Band
♦ 1961	Tower Of Strength	Gene McDaniels
♦ 1962	Town Without Pity	Gene Pitney
♦ 1989	Toy Soldiers	Martika
1956	Tra La La	Georgia Gibbs
♦ 1964	Tra La La La Suzy	Dean And Jean
♦ 1969	Traces	Classics IV
♦ 1965	Tracks Of My Tears	Miracles
♦ 1967	Tracks Of My Tears	Johnny Rivers
♦ 1976	Tracks Of My Tears	Linda Ronstadt
♦ 1969	Tracy	Cuff Links
♦ 1960	Tracy's Theme	Spencer Ross
♦ 1979	Tragedy	Bee Gees
♦ 1959	Tragedy	Thomas Wayne
♦ 1961	Tragedy	Fleetwoods
1985	Tragedy	John Hunter
♦ 1980	Train In Vain (Stand By Me)	Clash
♦ 1960	Train Of Love	Annette
♦ 1974	Train Of Thought	Cher
♦ 1979	Train, Train	Blackfoot
♦ 1966	Trains And Boats And Planes	Dionne Warwick
♦ 1967	Tramp	Otis & Carla (Otis Redding & Carla Thomas)
♦ 1975	Trampled Under Foot	Led Zeppelin
♦ 1956	Transfusion	Nervous Norvus
♦ 1961	Transistor Sister	Freddy Cannon
♦ 1971	Trapped By A Thing Called Love	Denise LaSalle
♦ 1970	Travelin' Band	Creedence Clearwater Revival
♦ 1961	Travelin' Man	Ricky Nelson
♦ 1967	Travlin' Man	Stevie Wonder
♦ 1956	Treasure Of Love	Clyde McPhatter
1958	Treasure Of Your Love	Eileen Rodgers
♦ 1971	Treat Her Like A Lady	Cornelius Brothers & Sister Rose
♦ 1965	Treat Her Right	Roy Head And The Traits
♦ 1957	Treat Me Nice	Elvis Presley
♦ 1981	Treat Me Right	Pat Benatar
♦ 1994	Tremor Christ	Pearl Jam
♦ 1996	Tres Delinquentes	Delinquent Habits
♦ 1961	Triangle	Janie Grant
♦ 1957	Tricky	Ralph Marterie
♦ 1972	Troglodyte (Cave Man)	Jimmy Castor Bunch
♦ 1975	T-R-O-U-B-L-E	Elvis Presley
♦ 1982	Trouble	Lindsey Buckingham
♦ 1988	Trouble	Nia Peeples
♦ 1960	Trouble In Paradise	Crests
♦ 1963	Trouble Is My Middle Name	Bobby Vinton
♦ 1973	Trouble Man	Marvin Gaye
♦ 1983	True	Spandau Ballet
♦ 1986	True Blue	Madonna
♦ 1990	True Blue Love	Lou Gramm
♦ 1986	True Colors	Cyndi Lauper
♦ 1988	True Faith	New Order

♦ 1969	True Grit	Glen Campbell
♦ 1956	True Love	Bing Crosby And Grace Kelly
1956	True Love	Jane Powell
♦ 1988	True Love	Glenn Frey
♦ 1963	True Love Never Runs Smooth	Gene Pitney
♦ 1965	True Love Ways	Peter And Gordon
♦ 1982	Truly	Lionel Richie
♦ 1998	Truly Madly Deeply	Savage Garden
1959	Trust In Me	Patti Page
♦ 1961	Trust In Me	Etta James
♦ 1991	Truth	Tami Show
♦ 1969	Try A Little Kindness	Glen Campbell
♦ 1967	Try A Little Tenderness	Otis Redding
♦ 1969	Try A Little Tenderness	Three Dog Night
♦ 1983	Try Again	Champaign
♦ 1964	Try It Baby	Marvin Gaye
♦ 1958	Try The Impossible	Lee Andrews And The Hearts
♦ 1966	Try Too Hard	Dave Clark Five
♦ 1976	Tryin' To Get The Feeling Again	Barry Manilow
♦ 1974	Trying To Hold On To My Woman	Lamont Dozier
♦ 1981	Tryin' To Live My Life Without You	Bob Seger
♦ 1977	Tryin' To Love Two	William Bell
♦ 1970	Trying To Make A Fool Of Me	Delfonics
♦ 1997	Tubthumping	Chumbawamba
♦ 1974	Tubular Bells	Mike Oldfield
♦ 1996	Tuckers Town	Hootie & The Blowfish
♦ 1959	Tucumcari	Jimmie Rodgers
♦ 1968	Tuesday Afternoon (Forever Afternoon)	Moody Blues
♦ 1962	Tuff	Ace Cannon
♦ 1986	Tuff Enough	Fabulous Thunderbirds
♦ 1980	Tulsa Time	Eric Clapton
♦ 1972	Tumbling Dice	Rolling Stones
♦ 1978	Tumbling Dice	Linda Ronstadt
♦ 1958	Tumbling Tumbleweeds	Billy Vaughn
♦ 1988	Tunnel Of Love	Bruce Springsteen
♦ 1964	Turn Around	Dick And DeeDee
♦ 1968	Turn Around, Look At Me	Vogues
♦ 1970	Turn Back The Hands Of Time	Tyrone Davis
♦ 1966	Turn Down Day	Cyrkle
♦ 1959	Turn Me Loose	Fabian
♦ 1981	Turn Me Loose	Loverboy
♦ 1962	Turn On Your Love Light	Bobby Bland
♦ 1976	Turn The Beat Around	Vicki Sue Robinson
♦ 1994	Turn The Beat Around	Gloria Estefan
♦ 1978	Turn To Stone	Electric Light Orchestra
♦ 1984	Turn To You	Go Go's
♦ 1965	Turn! Turn! Turn! (To Everything There Is A Season)	Byrds
♦ 1985	Turn Up The Radio	Autograph
♦ 1982	Turn Your Love Around	George Benson
♦ 1980	Turning Japanese	Vapors
♦ 1990	Turtle Power!	Partners In Kryme
1958	Turvy II	Cozy Cole
♦ 1975	Tush	ZZ Top
♦ 1979	Tusk	Fleetwood Mac
♦ 1956	Tutti Frutti	Pat Boone
♦ 1956	Tutti-Frutti	Little Richard
♦ 1955	Tweedlee Dee	Lavern Baker
♦ 1955	Tweedlee Dee	Georgia Gibbs
♦ 1957	Twelfth Of Never	Johnny Mathis
♦ 1973	Twelfth Of Never	Donny Osmond
♦ 1967	Twelve Thirty (Young Girls Are Coming To The Canyon)	Mama's & Papa's
♦ 1969	Twenty-Five Miles	Edwin Starr
♦ 1970	25 Or 6 To 4	Chicago
♦ 1963	Twenty Four Hours From Tulsa	Gene Pitney
1963	Twenty Miles	Chubby Checker
♦ 1964	20-75	Willie Mitchell
♦ 1958	26 Miles (Santa Catalina)	Four Preps
♦ 1981	Twilight	ELO
♦ 1958	Twilight Time	Platters
♦ 1988	Twilight World	Swing Out Sister
♦ 1983	Twilight Zone	Golden Earring
♦ 1980	Twilight Zone/Twilight Tone	Manhattan Transfer
♦ 1965	Twine Time	Alvin Cash & The Crawlers
♦ 1966	Twinkle Toes	Roy Orbison

♦ 1960	Twist	Hank Ballard And The Midnighters
1960	Twist	Chubby Checker
1962	Twist	Chubby Checker
♦ 1988	Twist (Yo, Twist!)	Fat Boys With Chubby Checker
♦ 1962	Twist And Shout	Isley Brothers
♦ 1964	Twist And Shout	Beatles
♦ 1986	Twist And Shout	Beatles
♦ 1996	Twisted	Keith Sweat
1962	Twist-Her	Bill Black's Combo
1963	Twist It Up	Chubby Checker
♦ 1984	Twist Of Fate	Olivia Newton-John
♦ 1962	Twist, Twist Senora	Gary U.S. Bonds
♦ 1962	Twistin' Matilda	Jimmy Soul
♦ 1962	Twistin' Postman	Marvelettes
♦ 1962	Twistin' The Night Away	Sam Cooke
♦ 1960	Twistin' U.S.A.	Danny & The Juniors
♦ 1959	Twixt Twelve And Twenty	Pat Boone
♦ 1997	2 Become 1	Spice Girls
♦ 1956	Two Different Worlds	Don Rondo
♦ 1971	Two Divided By Love	Grass Roots
♦ 1978	Two Doors Down	Dolly Parton
♦ 1963	Two Faces Have I	Lou Christie
♦ 1975	Two Fine People	Cat Stevens
♦ 1955	Two Hearts	Pat Boone
♦ 1989	Two Hearts	Phil Collins
♦ 1983	Two Less Lonely People In The World	Air Supply
♦ 1968	Two Little Kids	Peaches & Herb
♦ 1963	Two Lovers	Mary Wells
♦ 1988	Two Occasions	Deele
♦ 1962	Two Of A Kind	Sue Thompson
♦ 1986	Two Of Hearts	Stacey Q
♦ 1978	Two Out Of Three Ain't Bad	Meatloaf
♦ 1987	Two People	Tina Turner
♦ 1980	Two Places At The Same Time	Ray Parker Jr. & Raydio
♦ 1993	Two Princes	Spin Doctors
♦ 1984	Two Sides Of Love	Sammy Hagar
♦ 1993	Two Steps Behind	Def Leppard
♦ 1963	Two Tickets To Paradise	Brook Benton
♦ 1978	Two Tickets To Paradise	Eddie Money
♦ 1990	Two To Make It Right	Seduction
♦ 1986	Typical Male	Tina Turner

U

♦ 1994	U.N.I.T.Y.	Queen Latifah
♦ 1968	U.S. Male	Elvis Presley
♦ 1987	U Got The Look	Prince
♦ 1994	U Send Me Swingin'	Mint Condition
♦ 1994	U Will Know	B.M.U. (Black Men United)
♦ 1959	Uh! Oh! (Part 2)	Nutty Squirrels
♦ 1992	Uhh Ahh	Boyz II Men
♦ 1964	Um, Um, Um, Um, Um, Um	Major Lance
1978	Um, Um, Um, Um, Um, Um	Johnny Rivers
♦ 1991	Unbelievable	EMF
♦ 1994	Unbelievable	Notorious B.I.G.
♦ 1997	Un-Break My Heart	Toni Braxton
♦ 1962	Unchain My Heart	Ray Charles
♦ 1955	Unchained Melody	Les Baxter
♦ 1955	Unchained Melody	Roy Hamilton
♦ 1955	Unchained Melody	Al Hibbler
♦ 1965	Unchained Melody	Righteous Brothers
♦ 1990	Unchained Melody	Righteous Brothers
♦ 1971	Uncle Albert/Admiral Halsey	Paul & Linda McCartney
♦ 1982	Under Pressure	Queen & David Bowie
♦ 1964	Under The Boardwalk	Drifters
♦ 1992	Under The Bridge	Red Hot Chili Peppers
♦ 1988	Under The Milky Way	Church
♦ 1966	Under Your Spell Again	Johnny Rivers
♦ 1977	Undercover Angel	Alan O'Day
♦ 1983	Undercover Of The Night	Rolling Stones
♦ 1964	Understand Your Man	Johnny Cash
♦ 1984	Understanding	Bob Seger & The Silver Bullet Band
♦ 1994	Understanding	Xscape

V

W

♦ 1964	Walking In The Rain	Ronettes
♦ 1970	Walking In The Rain	Jay & The Americans
♦ 1972	Walkin' In The Rain With The One I Love	Love Unlimited
♦ 1967	Walkin' In The Sunshine	Roger Miller
♦ 1963	Walkin' Miracle	Essex
♦ 1966	Walkin' My Cat Named Dog	Norma Tanega
♦ 1984	Walking On A Thin Line	Huey Lewis
♦ 1992	Walking On Broken Glass	Annie Lennox
♦ 1985	Walking On Sunshine	Katrina And The Waves
1963	Walking Proud	Steve Lawrence
♦ 1963	Walking The Dog	Rufus Thomas
♦ 1960	Walking The Floor Over You	Pat Boone
♦ 1970	Walking Through The Country	Grass Roots
♦ 1960	Walking To New Orleans	Fats Domino
♦ 1980	Walks Like A Lady	Journey
♦ 1962	Wanderer	Dion
♦ 1980	Wanderer	Donna Summer
♦ 1997	Wannabe	Spice Girls
♦ 1983	Wanna Be Startin' Somethin'	Michael Jackson
♦ 1993	Wannagirl	Jeremy Jordan
♦ 1971	Want Ads	Honey Cone
♦ 1987	Wanted Dead Or Alive	Bon Jovi
♦ 1970	War	Edwin Starr
♦ 1986	War	Bruce Springsteen & The E Street Band
♦ 1984	War Song	Culture Club
♦ 1966	Warm And Tender Love	Percy Sledge
♦ 1992	Warm It Up	Kris Kross
♦ 1962	Warmed Over Kisses (Left Over Love)	Brian Hyland
♦ 1995	Warning	Notorious B.I.G.
♦ 1984	Warrior	Scandal featuring Patty Smyth
♦ 1990	Was It Nothing At All	Michael Damian
♦ 1963	Washington Square	Village Stompers
1981	Wasn't That A Party	Rovers
♦ 1975	Wasted Days And Wasted Nights	Freddy Fender
♦ 1982	Wasted On The Way	Crosby, Stills & Nash
♦ 1997	Watch Me Do My Thing	Immature
♦ 1967	Watch The Flowers Grow	Four Seasons
♦ 1971	Watching Scotty Grow	Bobby Goldsboro
♦ 1971	Watching The River Flow	Bob Dylan
♦ 1981	Watching The Wheels	John Lennon
♦ 1961	Water Boy	Don Shirley Trio
♦ 1995	Water Runs Dry	Boyz II Men
♦ 1995	Waterfalls	TLC
♦ 1974	Waterloo	Abba
♦ 1959	Waterloo	Stonewall Jackson
♦ 1963	Watermelon Man	Mongo Santamaria
♦ 1961	Watusi	Vibrations
♦ 1977	Way Down	Elvis Presley
♦ 1960	Way Down Yonder In New Orleans	Freddy Cannon
♦ 1983	Way He Makes Me Feel	Barbra Streisand
♦ 1992	Way I Feel About You	Karyn White
♦ 1978	Way I Feel Tonight	Bay City Rollers
♦ 1959	Way I Walk	Jack Scott
♦ 1975	Way I Want To Touch You	Captain & Tennille
♦ 1986	Way It Is	Bruce Hornsby
♦ 1969	Way It Used To Be	Engelbert Humperdinck
♦ 1972	Way Of Love	Cher
♦ 1994	Way She Loves Me	Richard Marx
♦ 1974	Way We Were	Barbra Streisand
♦ 1975	Way We Were/Try To Remember	Gladys Knight & The Pips
♦ 1964	Way You Do The Things You Do	Temptations
♦ 1978	Way You Do The Things You Do	Rita Coolidge
♦ 1985	Way You Do The Things You Do/My Girl .... Dary Hall/John Oates With David Ruffin And Eddie Kendrick
♦ 1990	Way You Do The Things You Do	UB40
♦ 1961	Way You Look Tonight	Lettermen
♦ 1989	Way You Love Me	Karyn White
♦ 1988	Way You Make Me Feel	Michael Jackson
♦ 1958	Ways Of A Woman In Love	Johnny Cash
♦ 1956	Wayward Wind	Gogi Grant
♦ 1967	(We Ain't Got) Nothin' Yet	Blues Magoos
♦ 1988	We All Sleep Alone	Cher
♦ 1979	We Are Family	Sister Sledge
♦ 1978	We Are The Champions	Queen
♦ 1985	We Are The World	U.S.A. For Africa
♦ 1984	We Are The Young	Dan Hartman
♦ 1984	We Belong	Pat Benatar

♦ 1958	We Belong Together	Robert & Johnny
♦ 1985	We Built This City	Starship
♦ 1968	We Can Fly	Cowsills
♦ 1966	We Can Work It Out	Beatles
♦ 1971	We Can Work It Out	Stevie Wonder
♦ 1990	We Can't Go Wrong	Cover Girls
♦ 1987	We Connect	Stacey Q
♦ 1989	We Didn't Start The Fire	Billy Joel
♦ 1986	We Don't Have To Take Our Clothes Off	Jermaine Stewart
♦ 1985	We Don't Need Another Hero	Tina Turner
♦ 1980	We Don't Talk Anymore	Cliff Richard
♦ 1992	We Got A Love Thang	Ce Ce Peniston
♦ 1996	We Got It	Immature
1959	We Got Love	Bobby Rydell
♦ 1982	We Got The Beat	Go Go's
♦ 1969	We Gotta All Get Together	Paul Revere And The Raiders
♦ 1965	We Gotta Get Out Of This Place	Animals
♦ 1971	We Gotta Get You A Woman	Runt
♦ 1977	We Just Disagree	Dave Mason
♦ 1980	We Live For Love	Pat Benatar
1964	We Love You Beatles	Carefrees
♦ 1973	We May Never Pass This Way (Again)	Seals & Crofts
♦ 1983	We Two	Little River Band
♦ 1991	We Want The Funk	Gerardo
♦ 1980	We Were Meant To Be Lovers	Photoglo
♦ 1987	We'll Be Together	Sting
♦ 1978	We'll Never Have To Say Goodbye Again	England Dan & John Ford Coley
♦ 1964	We'll Sing In The Sunshine	Gale Garnett
♦ 1968	We're A Winner	Impressions
♦ 1977	We're All Alone	Rita Coolidge
♦ 1990	We're All In The Same Gang	West Coast Rap All-Stars
♦ 1973	We're An American Band	Grand Funk
♦ 1965	We're Gonna Make It	Little Milton
♦ 1955	(We're Gonna) Rock Around The Clock	Bill Haley And His Comets
♦ 1974	(We're Gonna) Rock Around The Clock	Bill Haley And His Comets
♦ 1981	We're In This Love Together	Al Jarreau
♦ 1984	We're Not Gonna Take It	Twisted Sister
♦ 1998	We're Not Making Love No More	Dru Hill
♦ 1987	We're Ready	Boston
♦ 1972	We've Got To Get It On Again	Addrisi Brothers
♦ 1979	We've Got Tonite	Bob Seger & The Silver Bullet Band
♦ 1983	We've Got Tonite	Kenny Rogers And Sheena Easton
♦ 1970	We've Only Just Begun	Carpenters
♦ 1993	Weak	SWV
♦ 1958	Wear My Ring Around Your Neck	Elvis Presley
♦ 1967	Wear Your Love Like Heaven	Donovan
1959	Wedding	June Valli
♦ 1965	Wedding	Julie Rogers
♦ 1969	Wedding Bell Blues	Fifth Dimension
1971	Wedding Song (There Is Love)	Paul Stookey
♦ 1979	Weekend	Wet Willie
♦ 1977	Weekend In New England	Barry Manilow
♦ 1969	Weight	Aretha Franklin
♦ 1969	Weight	Diana Ross And The Supremes & The Temptations
♦ 1976	Welcome Back Kotter	John Sebastian
♦ 1962	Welcome Home Baby	Shirelles
♦ 1960	(Welcome) New Lovers	Pat Boone
♦ 1983	Welcome To Heartlight	Kenny Loggins
♦ 1986	Welcome To The Boomtown	David & David
♦ 1988	Welcome To The Jungle	Guns N' Roses
♦ 1961	Well, I Told You	Chantels
♦ 1966	Well Respected Man	Kinks
♦ 1978	Werewolves Of London	Warren Zevon
♦ 1986	West End Girls	Pet Shop Boys
♦ 1962	West Of The Wall	Miss Toni Fisher
♦ 1970	Westbound #9	Flaming Ember
♦ 1958	Western Movies	Olympics
♦ 1967	Western Union	Five Americans
♦ 1963	Wham!	Lonnie Mack
♦ 1976	Wham Bam Shang-A-Lang	Silver
♦ 1995	What	Notorious B.I.G.
♦ 1959	What A Diff'rence A Day Makes	Dinah Washington
♦ 1975	What A Diff'rence A Day Makes	Esther Phillips
♦ 1979	What A Fool Believes	Doobie Brothers
♦ 1963	What A Guy	Raindrops
♦ 1961	What A Party	Fats Domino
♦ 1961	What A Price	Fats Domino

738

◆ 1976	Wreck Of The Edmund Fitzgerald	Gordon Lightfoot
1957	Wringle, Wrangle	Bill Hayes
1957	Wringle Wrangle	Fess Parker
◆ 1961	Writing On The Wall	Adam Wade
◆ 1991	Written All Over Your Face	Rude Boys
1964	Wrong For Each Other	Andy Williams
◆ 1957	Wun'erful Wun'erful! (Parts 1 & 2)	Stan Freberg

X

◆ 1980	Xanadu	Olivia Newton-John/Electric Light Orchestra

Y

◆ 1979	Y.M.C.A.	Village People
◆ 1961	Ya Ya	Lee Dorsey
◆ 1984	Yah Mo B There	James Ingram With Michael McDonald
◆ 1963	Yakety Sax	Boots Randolph
◆ 1958	Yakety Yak	Coasters
◆ 1986	Yankee Rose	David Lee Roth
◆ 1988	Yeah, Yeah, Yeah	Judson Spence
◆ 1977	Year Of The Cat	Al Stewart
◆ 1980	Years	Wayne Newton
◆ 1965	Yeh, Yeh	Georgie Fame
◆ 1967	Yellow Balloon	Yellow Balloon
◆ 1961	Yellow Bird	Arthur Lyman Group
◆ 1970	Yellow River	Christie
1955	Yellow Rose Of Texas	Johnny Desmond
◆ 1955	Yellow Rose Of Texas	Stan Freberg
◆ 1955	Yellow Rose Of Texas	Mitch Miller
◆ 1966	Yellow Submarine	Beatles
◆ 1959	"Yep!"	Duane Eddy
◆ 1965	Yes, I'm Ready	Barbara Mason
◆ 1980	Yes, I'm Ready	Teri DeSario With K.C.
1957	Yes Tonight, Josephine	Johnnie Ray
◆ 1973	Yes We Can Can	Pointer Sisters
◆ 1968	Yester Love	Smokey Robinson & The Miracles
◆ 1969	Yester-Me, Yester-You, Yesterday	Stevie Wonder
◆ 1965	Yesterday	Beatles
◆ 1967	Yesterday	Ray Charles
◆ 1973	Yesterday Once More	Carpenters
◆ 1969	Yesterday, When I Was Young	Roy Clark
◆ 1968	Yesterday's Dreams	Four Tops
◆ 1964	Yesterday's Gone	Chad & Jeremy
◆ 1982	Yesterday's Songs	Neil Diamond
◆ 1971	Yo-Yo	Osmonds
1960	Yogi	Ivy Three
◆ 1958	You	Aquatones
◆ 1968	You	Marvin Gaye
◆ 1975	You	George Harrison
◆ 1978	You	Rita Coolidge
◆ 1996	You	Monifah
◆ 1974	You Ain't Seen Nothing Yet	Bachman-Turner Overdrive
◆ 1961	You Always Hurt The One You Love	Clarence Henry
◆ 1983	You And I	Eddie Rabbitt With Crystal Gayle
◆ 1978	You And I	Rick James
◆ 1977	You And Me	Alice Cooper
◆ 1974	You And Me Against The World	Helen Reddy
◆ 1983	You Are	Lionel Richie
◆ 1972	You Are Everything	Stylistics
◆ 1962	You Are Mine	Frankie Avalon
◆ 1958	You Are My Destiny	Paul Anka
◆ 1985	You Are My Lady	Freddie Jackson
1955	You Are My Love	Joni James
◆ 1976	You Are My Starship	Norman Connors
◆ 1962	You Are My Sunshine	Ray Charles
◆ 1995	You Are Not Alone	Michael Jackson
◆ 1975	You Are So Beautiful	Joe Cocker
◆ 1987	You Are The Girl	Cars
◆ 1961	You Are The Only One	Ricky Nelson
◆ 1973	You Are The Sunshine Of My Life	Stevie Wonder
◆ 1976	You Are The Woman	Firefall
◆ 1966	You Baby	Turtles

◆ 1986	You Be Illin'	Run-D.M.C.
◆ 1962	You Beat Me To The Punch	Mary Wells
◆ 1978	You Belong To Me	Carly Simon
◆ 1962	You Belong To Me	Duprees
◆ 1985	You Belong To The City	Glenn Frey
◆ 1959	You Better Know It	Jackie Wilson
◆ 1962	You Better Move On	Arthur Alexander
◆ 1966	You Better Run	Young Rascals
◆ 1967	You Better Sit Down Kids	Cher
◆ 1994	You Better Wait	Steve Perry
◆ 1981	You Better You Bet	Who
◆ 1997	You Bring Me Up	K-Ci & JoJo
◆ 1987	You Can Call Me Al	Paul Simon
◆ 1961	You Can Depend On Me	Brenda Lee
◆ 1982	You Can Do Magic	America
◆ 1961	You Can Have Her	Roy Hamilton
1974	You Can Have Her	Sam Neely
◆ 1958	You Can Make It If You Try	Gene Allison
◆ 1963	You Can Never Stop Me Loving You	Johnny Tillotson
◆ 1973	You Can't Always Get What You Want	Rolling Stones
◆ 1979	You Can't Change That	Raydio
◆ 1990	You Can't Deny It	Lisa Stansfield
◆ 1984	You Can't Get What You Want	Joe Jackson
◆ 1966	You Can't Hurry Love	Supremes
◆ 1983	You Can't Hurry Love	Phil Collins
◆ 1966	You Can't Roller Skate In A Buffalo Herd	Roger Miller
◆ 1956	You Can't Run Away From It	Four Aces
◆ 1961	You Can't Sit Down	Philip Upchurch Combo
◆ 1963	You Can't Sit Down	Dovells
◆ 1990	You Can't Touch This	M.C. Hammer
◆ 1978	You Can't Turn Me Off (In The Middle Of Turning Me On)	High Inergy
◆ 1958	You Cheated	Shields
◆ 1991	You Could Be Mine	Guns N' Roses
◆ 1972	You Could Have Been A Lady	April Wine
◆ 1982	You Could Have Been With Me	Sheena Easton
1981	You Could Take My Heart Away	Silver Condor
◆ 1979	You Decorated My Life	Kenny Rogers
◆ 1966	You Didn't Have To Be So Nice	Lovin' Spoonful
◆ 1978	You Don't Bring Me Flowers	Barbra & Neil (Barbra Streisand & Neil Diamond)
◆ 1963	You Don't Have To Be A Baby To Cry	Caravelles
◆ 1977	You Don't Have To Be A Star (To Be In My Show)	Marilyn McCoo & Billy Davis Jr.
◆ 1991	You Don't Have To Go Home Tonight	Triplets
◆ 1997	You Don't Have To Hurt No More	Mint Condition
◆ 1966	(You Don't Have To) Paint Me A Picture	Gary Lewis And The Playboys
◆ 1966	You Don't Have To Say You Love Me	Dusty Springfield
◆ 1970	You Don't Have To Say You Love Me	Elvis Presley
◆ 1988	You Don't Know	Scarlett & Black
◆ 1964	(You Don't Know) How Glad I Am	Nancy Wilson
◆ 1995	You Don't Know How It Feels	Tom Petty And The Heartbreakers
◆ 1956	You Don't Know Me	Jerry Vale
◆ 1962	You Don't Know Me	Ray Charles
◆ 1967	You Don't Know Me	Elvis Presley
◆ 1961	You Don't Know What You've Got (Until You Lose It)	Ral Donner
◆ 1972	You Don't Mess Around With Jim	Jim Croce
◆ 1957	You Don't Owe Me A Thing	Johnnie Ray
◆ 1964	You Don't Own Me	Lesley Gore
◆ 1982	You Don't Want Me Anymore	Steel Breeze
◆ 1982	You Dropped A Bomb On Me	Gap Band
◆ 1969	You Gave Me A Mountain	Frankie Laine
◆ 1985	You Give Good Love To Me	Whitney Houston
◆ 1986	You Give Love A Bad Name	Bon Jovi
◆ 1979	You Gonna Make Me Love Somebody Else	Jones Girls
◆ 1995	You Got It	Bonnie Raitt
◆ 1989	You Got It	Roy Orbison
◆ 1989	You Got It (The Right Stuff)	New Kids On The Block
◆ 1987	You Got It All	Jets
◆ 1983	You Got Lucky	Tom Petty And The Heartbreakers
◆ 1974	You Got The Love	Rufus featuring Chaka Khan
◆ 1967	You Got To Me	Neil Diamond
◆ 1960	You Got What It Takes	Marv Johnson
◆ 1967	You Got What It Takes	Dave Clark Five
◆ 1969	You Got Yours And I'll Get Mine	Delfonics
◆ 1995	You Gotta Be	Des'ree
◆ 1987	(You Gotta) Fight For Your Right (To Party!)	Beastie Boys

Z